The new 1988 edition provides fast access to the answers—

- What's happening in world affairs
- The latest scientific information
- The earth's vital statistics
- Special articles by experts
- More sports pages than any other almanac
- Plus history, religion, taxes, cities and states, calendars, celebrities, travel, and much more!

If you need to know, turn to

INFORMATION PLEASE!

Ordering Information Please Almanac by Mail

Information Please Almanac is available in bookstores everywhere. Copies of the *Almanac* may also be ordered directly by mail from the publisher.

To order, write to: Customer Service Department, Houghton Mifflin Publishing Company, Burlington, Massachusetts 01803. Readers may phone Customer Service, Toll-Free (800) 225-3362 for the latest price and shipping information. In Massachusetts, telephone 272-1500.

Other reference books published by Houghton Mifflin Company are: *The American Heritage Dictionary, Webster's II New Riverside University Dictionary, The Professional Secretary's Handbook, Roget's II: The New Thesaurus, Word Mysteries & Histories: From Quiche to Humble Pie, The American Heritage Larousse Spanish Dictionary, Contemporary Quotations,* and *Wall Street Words.*

INFORMATION PLEASE ALMANAC®

ATLAS & YEARBOOK

1988

41ST EDITION

HOUGHTON MIFFLIN COMPANY BOSTON

1988

Executive Editor
Otto Johnson
Associate Editor
Vera Dailey
Contributing Editors
Arthur Reed, Jr. (Current Events)
William E. Bruno (World Countries)
Dennis M. Lyons (Sports)
Staff
Editorial Assistants:
Bern Boyle, John McNamara, and Roy Murphy, III
Maps
Maps copyright © Hammond Incorporated.
Requests for map use should be sent to Hammond Incorporated, Maplewood, New Jersey 07040.

The Information Please Almanac invites comments and suggestions from readers. Because of the many letters received, however, it is not possible to respond personally to every correspondent. Nevertheless, all suggestions are most welcome, and the editors will consider them carefully. (Information Please Almanac does not rule on bets or wagers.)

ISBN (Hardcover): 0-395-44611-2
ISBN (Paperback): 0-395-44610-4
ISSN: 0073-7860

Previous editions of INFORMATION PLEASE were published in 1986, 1985, and 1984 by Houghton Mifflin Company, in 1982 by A&W Publishing Company, and in 1981, 1980, and 1979 by Simon & Schuster, in 1978 and 1977 by Information Please Publishing, Inc., and from 1947–1976 by Dan Golenpaul Associates.

Copies of Information Please Almanac may be ordered directly by mail from:
Customer Service Department
Houghton Mifflin Company
Burlington, Ma 01803
Phone toll-free, (800) 225-3362 for price and shipping information. In Massachusetts phone: 272-1500.

INFORMATION PLEASE ALMANAC®
Editorial Office
Houghton Mifflin Company
52 Vanderbilt Avenue
New York, N.Y. 10017

Printed in the United States of America

WP Pa BP Hbd 10 9 8 7 6 5 4 3 2 1

CONTENTS

SPECIAL FEATURE ARTICLES

Because we recognize the need to go beyond the traditional almanac compilation of data, this section offers readers a wealth of additional information about subjects not usually covered in other almanacs. Therefore, General Information has been organized as a mini-encyclopedia containing 500 illuminating entries listed in alphabetical order for quick reference.

Almost 50 pages of selected ideas and beliefs which people have held in different periods of human history that have influenced mankind. Whether these beliefs are true or false, meaningful or meaningless, they are worth serious study. This section will enable readers to gain a better understanding of the present through a better understanding of the past. Also see Religion, page 400.

TABLE OF CONTENTS

COMPREHENSIVE INDEX

A

B

C

D

H

M

N

O

Q

R

S

T

U

V

Special Features

Love, The Key to Happiness

By Dr. Joyce Brothers

Three essential elements for happiness are something to do, something to hope for, and someone to love. In our personal lives, it is necessary that we have the opportunity to love another person, or other people. To give to another unconditionally, with no strings attached, is the essence of love. We need to give love and we need to receive love from others. Love is what makes us feel good about ourselves. Love is the key to happiness. We must have others in our lives whom we can love and from whom we can receive love, but we must love ourselves first in order to give love to others. *Do I love myself? Am I secure enough to love others?*

Dr. Joyce Brothers says, "I don't think you can be happy without some love in your life."

Joyce Brothers, Ph.D., is probably America's best-known psychologist. She has frequently appeared on "most admired women" polls conducted by United Press International, Gallup, Roper, and Good Housekeeping *magazine. Joyce broadcasts daily on the NBC radio network's "Newsline"; her daily column appears in more than three hundred and fifty newspapers; and her books, including her latest,* What Every Woman Ought to Know about Love and Marriage, *have been translated into twenty-six languages.*

Joyce Brothers, Ph.D.

You must have some love in your life in order to be happy. It doesn't have to be love of man for woman. It can be love of God; it can be love of mankind. Happiness is not possible without love, although I think you can love and be very unhappy. You need to be able to give love to be happy. When you're not getting love, you're unhappy. Some studies have shown that babies die if they're not loved.

Relationships with people—friends, partners, those for whom we'd lay down our lives—can be used to promote happiness, but not if you seek happiness through them. The more you pursue happiness, the less likely it is that you're going to find it.

Self-worth or self-love is really a matter of degree. We have a continuum of "I hate myself" to "I love myself." If you love yourself too much, you're incapable of love. The thing that makes us fall in love is the differential between what we would like ourselves to be—our idealized image—and the image of ourselves as we think we are, which is more realistic. Dissatisfaction with the self makes us fall in love when we find somebody who we think has cured our problem. If that differential is so great that we can't bear ourselves, we're not capable of falling in love.

We've heard over and over, "You can't love somebody else unless you love yourself." What we're really saying is that we respect rather than love ourselves. When we feel comfortable with what we are doing in general, we feel respect for ourselves, If you demand of your love relationship that happiness pursue you because of it, you're going to destroy that love relationship. It only happens as a by-product of your giving and your getting. If you say, "I'm only going to give because I expect happiness and if I don't get happiness I'm not going to give," it never happens.

Think of two people with baskets by their side. One says, "Okay, I'm giving you this to put in your basket, so now you must give me something to put in my basket and we have to keep our baskets even." In that case happiness is not possible. However, if you sometimes give and sometimes receive, and in the long run the baskets balance out, then happiness is possible. When a relationship gets too far out of kilter, when you are on the giving end all the time, or you're on the receiving end all the time, there's no happiness. There is no happiness for the partner who is given too much, and no happiness for the partner who is giving too much. In any master/slave relationship there's resentment on both sides.

A healthy relationship is like a seesaw. One person isn't always dominant and the other person isn't always submissive. No person is totally independent except a hermit, and a hermit is grossly abnormal. So in any relationship, whether it's friendship, parent/child, or marriage, sometimes one is more dominant than the other, but it evens out in the end.

The link between sexuality and happiness is probably one of the weakest links. You would think that researchers would have conducted enormous numbers of studies of sex in happy marriages, but they never really got around to it until fairly recently. Most of the studies on sexuality and marriage have been done on couples who go to therapists because they have troubled marriages. They find in such populations impotence, frigidity, and premature ejaculation. Now there are studies on sex in a happy marriage, and lo and behold, they've found frigidity, impotence, and premature ejaculation and the same number of problems, the only difference being that the people love each other. It doesn't seem to matter all that much.

A great many priests and nuns who are happy and fulfilled have no sex life at all. Many, many widows and widowers who have loved their husbands and wives dearly have lost their partners. There is no sex in their lives, yet they are content. There are virgin boys and girls who are happy, too. It is possible for gay people to be just as happy as heterosexual people, but I don't think a sex life is necessary for happiness.

Secure people look for something complementary to themselves in their relationships. "You give me something that I am missing and makes my life more complete, and I will give you something you're missing that makes your life more complete." The old Greek myth said, "Once male and female were one and as a joke the gods divided them into two, and people have been wandering

---

the earth looking for their own lost opposite half." There isn't only one other half. Lots of people can make that other half, but it is the meshing that increases happiness. Insecure people are looking for security in their relationships, but you can't look for security in a relationship. Nobody can give you security. The insecure person holds on so tightly that the relationship is smothered. You have to be able to bring your half to the relationship, with the other person bringing his or her half to the relationship, to make it total. The insecure person brings only a quarter to the relationship and asks for three-quarters. The purpose of marriage is having someone who cares as much about your success, your happiness, your comfort, and your delight as he or she would care about his or her own.

In terms of what they say about their own happiness, the happiest of all people are married men, then single women, then married women; least happy of all are bachelors. No one really knows for sure why this is so, but many married men enjoy enormous comfort. Who wouldn't want a stereotypical wife? I'd love to come home after a hard day to somebody who makes supper, has my slippers out, and scratches my back. It's really nice to have someone else worry about getting the clothes back from the cleaners. Many married men have the comforts of home. Single women probably expect that life is going to be simply hell for them because they're single in an environment where people are married or paired off. They think their lives are going to be dreadful. They find out they're fulfilled, and very happy, so much better than they thought they would be. I guess that's why they're more satisfied. The women's movement has helped out in this area. A lot of women who should never marry have the option now of not marrying and not being embarrassed by the fact that they're not married.

Marriage, it appears, is good for men but not so hot for women. In marriages husbands really should do more than just help. They should take an equal share and an equal responsibility in making marriage work. Women do much more to keep their marriages together than men do. One area of conflict in relationships arises because we have trained our males not to communicate, to be silent about their emotions. In many cases men and women talk about two different things. So many problems can be resolved by the willingness to talk about them and work them through. Many men are reluctant to talk about things that matter to them. If communication opened up it would be a huge step forward.

Being able to take your partner for granted is a big plus in marriage. When we were young we went away to summer camp and it was fun. When we got home from camp it was different. The feeling was "I'm home, I can relax now." That's what a marriage should be. We go out into the world and do our best, and we have our problems and our triumphs. Marriage should be a situation in which, when we get home, we kick off our shoes, take off our girdles or ties, relax and say with a sigh of relief, "Home." If we have to start charming one another it isn't a relief. That is one of the reasons why the living-together relationship is decreasing in popularity. People are still performing. It's wonderful that the divorce rate is leveling off. People are discovering that you don't get divorced and live happily ever after. □

Thresholds of Change

By Lester R. Brown and Sandra Postel

Daily news events remind us that our relationship with the earth and its natural systems is changing, often in ways we do not understand. In May 1985, a British research team reported finding a sharp decline in the level of atmospheric ozone over Antarctica. Verified by other scientists, the discovery of this unanticipated "hole" in the earth's protective shield of ozone sent waves of concern throughout the international scientific community. . . .

In late July 1986, a team of scientists studying the effect of rising atmospheric levels of carbon dioxide (CO_2) and other "greenhouse gases" published evidence that the predicted global warming has begun. . . .

Sometime in mid-1986, world population reached 5 billion. Yet no celebrations were held in recognition of this demographic milestone. Indeed, many who reflected on it were left with a profound sense of unease about the mounting pressures on the earth's forests, soils, and other natural systems. With 3 billion young people entering their reproductive years over the next generation, these pressures are certain to intensify.

In October 1986, the U.S. National Academy of Sciences and the Smithsonian Institution convened a National Forum on Biodiversity in Washington, D.C. Addressed by nearly 100 prominent biologists, the conference sounded a clear note of urgency about the multiplying threats to species survival. Scientists warned of a forthcoming wave of mass extinction—one that would approach the magnitude of that which wiped out the dinosaurs and half of all other extant species some 65 million years ago. There is one important difference: Whereas the earlier cataclysm was of natural origin, the one now unfolding is driven by human activities.

* * *

Many thresholds have been breached inadvertently from advances in technology and growth in human numbers. Corporations manufacturing the family of chemicals known as chlorofluorocarbons, for example, surely did not intend for these compounds to deplete the ozone layer. Their goal was to produce efficient refrigerants, a practical propellant for aerosol spray cans, and a chemical agent used to make foam products.

* * *

Lester R. Brown is the President of Worldwatch Institute. Sandra Postel is a Senior Researcher with the organization. Worldwatch is an independent, nonprofit research organization that was established to inform policy makers and the general public about the interdependence of the world economy and its environmental support systems. This article was excerpted from a report of the same title with permission from *State of the World 1987*, copyright © 1987 by the Worldwatch Institute. The annual *State of The World* may be ordered from Worldwatch, 1776 Massachusetts Ave., N.W., Washington, D.C., $18.95 cloth, $9.95 paperback, prepaid, or through bookstores in the United States or directly from the publishers, W.W. Norton & Company, Inc., 500 Fifth Ave., New York, N.Y. 10110. A list of other publications is available from Worldwatch.

Other trends of the mid-eighties also call into question the viability of our path toward economic progress. World agriculture is producing surpluses, but for the wrong reasons. A portion of today's surplus is being produced only by diminishing the agricultural resource base—for example, by plowing highly erodible land and overdrafting underground water supplies.

* * *

Burgeoning populations in many urban areas are overtaxing local water sources, fuel supplies, and waste disposal capacities, crossing natural thresholds and translating directly into economic costs. Resource demands in numerous cities already exceed the limits of local supplies, whether it be water in Tucson and Mexico City, or firewood in Hyderabad. Especially in Third World areas experiencing unprecedented rates of urbanization, these imbalances will frustrate efforts to improve living standards.

* * *

Energy, Environment, and the Economy

When this century began, scarcely one life span ago, world population numbered 1.6 billion. Assuming an average per capita income of $400 per year (1986 dollars), the gross world product was $640 billion, just slightly more than France's 1986 national product of $550 billion. Over the next half-century, world population grew by nearly a billion, bringing the total to 2.5 billion. Modest progress in raising per capita income brought the gross world product to roughly $3 trillion in 1950.

Though impressive by historical standards, this growth was dwarfed by what followed. Between 1950 and 1986, human numbers doubled to 5 billion, expanding as much during these 36 years as during the preceding few million. Per capita income also roughly doubled, pushing the gross world product over $13 trillion. Within a generation, the global output of goods and services quadrupled. A variety of technological advances aided this expansion, but none compares with the growth in fossil fuel use. Between 1950 and 1986, world fossil fuel consumption also increased fourfold, paralleling the growth in the global economy.

Resource constraints on global economic expansion emerged from time to time throughout the century. But a combination of advancing technology and cheap energy repeatedly pushed them back. As opportunities for adding new cropland diminished, for example, energy was widely substituted for land in boosting food production. After mid-century, relatively little new land was brought under the plow in most regions, yet global crop output expanded even faster than before. World agriculture made a smooth transition from expanding cropland area to raising yields, and even picked up the pace of food production in doing so.

* * *

While the global economy has expanded continuously, the natural systems that support it unfortunately have not. Economist Herman Daly suggests that "as the economy grows beyond its present physical scale, it may increase costs faster than benefits and initiate an era of uneconomic growth which impoverishes rather than enriches." In essence, Daly points to an economic threshold with profound implications. As currently pursued, economic activity could be approaching a level where further growth in the gross world product costs more than it is worth.

The burning of fossil fuels literally fueled industrial expansion throughout the century and remains at the heart of many Third World development plans. Yet the buildup of atmospheric carbon dioxide attributable to that energy path threatens to make the earth far warmer than at any time in human history. The cost to farmers of adjusting to new temperature and rainfall regimes could deprive agriculture of the investment capital needed to expand output. And the costs of protecting populations in low-lying areas from a rise in sea level could divert vast amounts of capital away from other development goals.

The earth's forest cover is diminishing, most dramatically in the Third World as a result of land clearing, firewood gathering, and logging, but also in central Europe as a result of air pollution and acid deposition. Besides the direct losses forest damage causes to forest industries, serious environmental consequences are emerging, including increased rainfall runoff, accelerated soil erosion, and diminished water quality. Only time will reveal the complete tally of ecological costs, since the forest damage continues to spread.

World food production increased an impressive two-and-a-half times between 1950 and 1986, but this too has its costs. Four-fifths of this increase resulted from more intensive use of land, but between 1950 and 1976, the year growth in the cropland area ended, some 130 million hectares of grainland were added. Though small compared with growth in the demand for food, this addition exceeded that of earlier, equivalent periods when cropland expansion accounted for virtually all growth in output. In the headlong rush to meet the demand for food, many countries overexpanded their cropland base. Farmers plowed land that was steeply sloping, and hence vulnerable to water erosion, or so arid that it was easily eroded by wind. Besides contributing to price-depressing surpluses, such unsustainable production cannot be supported indefinitely. Several countries are already reducing the amount of land planted to crops.

The negative side effects of this century's twentyfold expansion of economic activity are now becoming inescapable. Whether through spreading forest damage, a changing climate, or eroding soils, the pursuit of short-term economic growth at the environment's expense will exact a price. As the natural systems that underpin economies deteriorate, actions that make good sense environmentally will begin to converge with those that make good sense economically. But that convergence may not occur before irreversible changes have unfolded.

* * *

Oil Depletion and Food Production

At mid-century, world agriculture crossed a major threshold in its efforts to feed a global population that had reached 2.5 billion. As population growth accelerated and the expansion of cropland slowed, farmers were forced for the first time to rely primarily on raising land productivity. The crossing of this population/cropland threshold started a rise in the oil intensity of world food production that has continued to date.

Notwithstanding pockets of modernized farms, the world's farmers were still largely self-sufficient in energy in 1950, relying on livestock wastes for fertilizer and draft animals for tillage power. Since then, however, the agricultural use of energy has multiplied sevenfold. Between 1950 and 1985, the farm tractor fleet quadrupled, world irrigated area tripled, and fertilizer use increased ninefold. Coal is used to fabricate the steel in tractors and natural gas is widely used to synthesize nitrogen fertilizer, but it is oil that provides most of the energy for modern farming.

* * *

The best available indicator of the energy intensity of food production is the amount of energy used to produce a ton of grain. Between 1950 and 1985, this more than doubled, rising from the equivalent of 0.44 barrels of oil to more than 1 barrel. The oil equivalent of energy used in farming in 1985 totaled 1.9 billion barrels, less than one tenth the world's petroleum output of 21 billion barrels.

* * *

As the twenty-first century approaches, two issues are of paramount concern in the oil/food relationship. One is the increase in competition among different oil-using sectors of the economy as total petroleum production diminishes. The second is the location of oil reserves.

By 1986, nearly half of all oil discovered had already been consumed. In North America, which produces nearly one-fourth of the world's grain, four-fifths of all the oil discovered to date has already been burned. Current proven U.S. reserves in the United States total 36 billion barrels, enough to supply U.S. needs for less than eight years at current rates of use. Without the jump of one-fifth in oil imports in 1986, the U.S. economy would be facing some difficult adjustments.

* * *

Agriculture cannot expand indefinitely its use of petroleum over the next several decades if oil production is declining. Ever expanding oil-based agriculture simply is not sustainable, and this underlines the need for food production technologies that are less energy-intensive. In addition, the prospect of higher energy prices suggests that the real cost of producing food is likely to rise. If it does, the affluent of the world will adjust by boosting the share of their incomes used to purchase food. But for those on the lower rungs of the global economic ladder, the only adjustments possible may be cuts in consumption of the sort seen in Africa since 1970 and in Latin America since 1981.

The Costs of Crossing Natural Limits

Natural thresholds are not merely of scientific interest; the consequences of crossing them can directly affect economies and people's livelihoods. Deforestation is driving up firewood prices in scores of Third World countries. Excessive soil erosion is contributing to reductions in per capita food production in many more. The economic costs of some approaching thresholds, such as CO_2-induced climate change, are only beginning to be assessed. Unfortunately, a lack of integrated research makes it difficult to detect linkages between the economy and its environmental underpinnings. As a result, many of the economic consequences of environmental deterioration are only realized after the fact.

* * *

Dozens of developing countries are feeling the economic effects of deforestation. Many that were once exporters of forest products have become importers as their woodlands have diminished while their demand for wood products has climbed. Deforestation has worsened flooding and the silting of reservoirs in some areas. . . .

The excessive erosion of soils—which, like forests, are a renewable resource if properly managed—imposes numerous economic costs. In four countries that contain roughly a quarter of Africa's population—Mozambique, Nigeria, Sudan, and Tanzania—crop yields in the mid-eighties were lower than in the early fifties, in part because of heavy topsoil losses. The extension of agriculture onto marginal land may also have contributed to this decline in cropland productivity, which among the four countries averaged some 17 percent over three decades. In agrarian economies, declining crop yields often translate into falling incomes and living standards.

* * *

Worldwide, the costs of adjusting to a greenhouse-gas induced warming of the earth may loom the largest. Agriculture, a highly climate-dependent sector, will face numerous adjustments. The existing pattern of world crop production evolved in response to particular climatic regimes that have been more or less stable over the last few centuries. The global warming will bring not only higher temperatures, but also changes in rainfall patterns. As a result, areas that do not now need irrigation and drainage systems may require them to sustain crop production. Water supplies could diminish in some regions, forcing farmers to take land out of irrigated production. . . .

One of the most feared consequences of the projected global warming is the rise in sea level that will result from both thermal expansion of the oceans and the melting of glaciers and polar ice caps. During this century, the ocean has been rising at just over one millimeter per year, or one centimeter per decade. A 1-degree Celsius increase in ocean temperature would raise sea level an estimated 60 centimeters, or roughly two feet.

* * *

Coastal areas are obviously most at risk from rising seas. Many major cities are close to sea level, including Shanghai, London, and New York. Low-lying, densely populated regions of Asia, including parts of Bangladesh and Indonesia and the deltas of the Indus, Mekong, and Chang Jiang (Yangtze) rivers, would be especially threatened.

* * *

Our New Responsibility

As we near the end of the twentieth century, we are entering uncharted territory. Localized changes in natural systems are now being overlaid with continental and global shifts, some of which may be irreversible. Everyday human activities—driving automobiles, generating electricity, and producing food—may collectively cause changes of geological proportions within a matter of decades.

* * *

A human population of 5 billion, expanding at 83 million per year, has combined with the power of industrial technologies to create unprecedented momentum toward human-induced environmental change. We have inadvertently set in motion grand ecological experiments involving the entire earth without yet having the means to systematically monitor the results.

* * *

We have crossed many natural thresholds in a short period of time. No one knows how the affected natural systems will respond, much less how changes in natural systems will in turn affect economic and political systems. We can be reasonably certain that deforestation will disrupt hydrologic cycles and that ozone depletion will induce more skin cancer. But beyond these first-order effects, scientists can provide little detail.

* * *

Matters of the global environment now warrant the kind of high-level attention and concern that the global economy receives. World leaders historically have cooperated to preserve economic stability, even to the point of completely overhauling the international monetary system at the 1944 conference in Bretton Woods. Summit meetings are held periodically to attempt to iron out international economic problems. Policymakers carefully track economic indicators to determine when adjustments—national or international—are required.

Similar efforts are needed to delineate the bounds of environmental stability, along with mechanisms for making prompt adjustments when these bounds draw near.

With so many natural systems becoming unstable within such a short period of time, discontinuous, surprising, and rapid changes may become commonplace. Resulting economic and political pressures could overwhelm the capacity of governments and individuals to adjust adequately. Societies faced with multiplying, self-generated stresses have two options: Initiate the needed reforms in population, energy, agricultural, and economic policies, or risk deterioration and decline. □

New Technologies

By Oxford Analytica

Western economies are beginning to feel a rising and long-term tide of applied science and technology advances. Modest assessment of its impact foresees significant effects in productivity and employment. More lyrical observers predict a cultural revolution, the groundwork for a renaissance of vitality in individual achievement and human fulfillment. Over the next decade the growing effects will be confined to new products, employment, productivity and technology-provoked optimism.

Lasers and fiber optics will have a continued economic impact by refining production processed in a very wide variety of applications and as components in telecommunications systems, information processing, and entertainment (videodisc and holography, including 3-D television). As capital goods for a relatively small market or as components of consumer goods, lasers are likely to continue their function of refining processes and improving products; thus, they will substitute for inferior goods rather than create many new products or new employment by the late 1980s. Fiber optics may generate considerable investment by enabling the creation of more efficient, larger-capacity communications networks.

Robotics and computer-controlled machines similarly hold potential for improved industrial productivity. Computer-aided design (CAD) and computer-aided manufacturing (CAM) will have a growing impact on production efficiency through the 1990s. Computer-controlled machines are substituting for conventional machine tools, and American technology superiority is well poised to increase U.S. share of world markets in these capital goods. The main impact, however, is likely to be on productivity and in displacing rather than creating jobs.

Likewise, the use of industrial robots will increase dramatically through the decade and will commensurately improve productivity and U.S. competitiveness. The rate of substitution will depend on alternative employment opportunities (some observers predict larger "replacement" industries in servicing and programming robots), the cost (unemployment compensation, social unrest) of additional unemployed workers, and union success in negating the gain in productivity from robots by demanding retraining or wage raises as work time diminishes. On the other hand, the use of robots by foreign industrial competitors, particularly Japan, may require that U.S. industry conform or seek protection with renewed urgency. The overall job-displacing effects of robots will not be dramatic in the next decade, though they will be significant in certain industries.

Finally, the use of computer-aided techniques of management (e.g., management information systems and computer-aided planning) will coordinate and enhance CAD and CAM to create CIM, *computer-integrated manufacturing.* These powerful tools will increase overall productivity, allow flexible production runs and greater control, and lower inventory levels. On the other hand, they will change the nature and organization of the workplace and influence levels of job satisfaction, stress, skills and productivity; CIM is not a panacea for problems in manufacturing. Applications are spreading, but aggregate use will be relatively limited through the 1980s. They will be first felt in metal-working industries in the northeast, central and mid-Atlantic states. The impact on the number and kinds of jobs will begin to be large in the 1990s and the long-term potential impact is enormous.

Solar energy increasingly seems likely to be cost effective in the 1990s for the direct production of electricity by photo-voltaic conversion. With large-scale production of conversion equipment, such methods will be competitive unless oil prices falter. Commercial use of solar cells is fairly imminent as large private investment, mainly by oil companies, reduces the lead times. The most promising new process uses amorphous or non-crystalline (and thus cheaper) silicon printed onto thin plastic film. Mass production (with cost per kilowatt hour as cheap as oil-fired or nuclear electricity) for a wide variety of uses could occur by 1990. If so, this first real alternative to conventional energy sources holds great potential for transforming the economy and perhaps even society. However, the economic impact even in the early 1990s is likely to be conventional in reducing or containing rises in energy costs, as elements of total costs of production. The substantial economic effects would occur in the later 1990s.

Of much greater economic significance for the next decade than the above new technologies are of course *biotechnology* and *micro-electronics.* These industries are widely expected to form, in this decade, the industrial foundation for the 1990s and beyond, when joined by new energy sources

The economic impact will steadily affect productivity and jobs.

Biotechnology is likely to bring dramatic changes over the next fifteen years to a wide range of products and processes in a number of industries. The use of single-cell protein, enzymes, and various bacteria will continue to be more widespread in foods, agriculture, fuel, effluents treatment, natural resource recovery, pharmaceuticals, chemicals, and medical applications. For instance, enzyme technology could generate an entirely new type of chemical industry utilizing moderate conditions of pH, temperature, and pressure to produce complex chemical and renewable feed stock from wastes; it is likely to be cost effective before 1990. Moreover, the less conventional techniques of microbial genetics, such as protoplast fusion, gene amplification, and recombinant DNA technology, are likely to have significant commercial impact in the coming decade. The bacterial synthesis of human insulin, human growth hormones, and interferon is nearly commercially viable.

Genetic engineering in agriculture, however, is not so likely to have large impact on the national economy before 1995. Commercial achievement is expected in accelerated photosynthesis, acid-tolerant crops, herbicide resistance, and grains that fix nitrogen directly from the atmosphere, but this research will not be complete for at least ten years. Before that, recombinant DNA technology may lead to improved crops, new crop types, and techniques to manipulate plants. Many industrial laboratories are shifting emphasis and many others have been established in the past two years to exploit the large biotechnology opportunities in agriculture. In this and in industrial micro-biology generally it is clear that the surface of potential application and economic effect has been merely scratched. Minor plant improvements will occur in the 1980s, but economic effects of major breakthroughs will wait for the later 1990s.

Micro-electronics will continue its revolution as the world's fastest-growing industry as computer power continues to grow and as micro-processors spread to virtually every electrical product, commercial or consumer. While the trend holds profound implications for medicine, transport, education, and household life, *the area of greatest economic impact in the next decade is likely to be telematics, the information economy.* This is the development of a wide range of micro-chip-based systems of information processing combined with communications and control technologies. The technology is based on distributed processing to meet local, regional, or central decision-making, and therefore on distributed access.

High-performance computing is expected to generate growing excitement over the next decade but limited effect on the national economy. Industry specialists expect supercomputers to hold potential for profound social and economic change in the long run. New ideas, techniques and ways of building computers aim at more powerful, faster processors and memory chips, and machines that function in entirely new ways in order to think and learn. Systems that use "parallel processing"—allowing many operations simultaneously—would enable artificial intelligence applications: distinguishing between fragrances; vision; reading, hearing and speaking natural language; and the ability to reason and make judgments. "Fifth generation" or "artificial intelligence" computers would be simple for an untrained person to operate and could solve a range of problems that are not readily handled by existing numerical computers.

The applications are wide and important. An immediate use might be in expert systems, programs which mimic problem-solving abilities of human experts by encapsulating human experience, like medical diagnoses or financial advice. Machine vision would aid robotic assembly and military uses to guide land vehicles and aircraft. Supercomputers would be capable of being mass-produced and general-purpose enough for use in a very broad market by 2000. They are expected to enter economic sectors and social activities that have been little affected, thus far, by computers.

Certainly computers have more potential to affect a wide range of activities than do most other technologies, such as electronic chips, communications, biotechnology or even automobiles. Understandably, there is severe international competition for supremacy. The U.S. is still judged the world leader, with Japan threatening to overtake and Europe and Russia lagging behind.

Dozens of American universities and corporations pursue research on "fifth generation" computers. The U.S. government has boosted funding, mainly for military uses. American industry efforts involve mainly a cooperative R&D effort called Microelectronics and Computer Technology Corporation, involving about twenty large corporations. Current abundance of funds is allowing researchers to pick up the pace of research. There is a major U.S. initiative to retain primacy in the marketplace for computers, and it has new urgency.

Japanese projects to extend the limits of computing power aim to overcome U.S. dominance in the field. With a consortium of companies and government laboratories guided by the Ministry of Trade and Industry, Japan expects to build the fastest computer by far by 1990 and one with advanced artificial intelligence capabilities by 1992. Commercial models should be available in the 1990s. Already Japanese companies have high-performance computers that appear comparable to U.S. machines. If the U.S. falls behind in development and application of high-performance computers, it is likely to lose supremacy in many areas of scientific research and technology, and suffer in economic and national security. In addition, supercomputer research could help Japan gain leadership in the multi-billion-dollar business and personal computer field, as well as in development and promotion of many new products.

Supercomputers, artificial intelligence and the race with Japan are unlikely to have much effect on the U.S. economy by 1995. In the long term these topics will hold wide impact on jobs and markets, as well as U.S. image. However, even before the actual effects, news about these topics will affect American life. They will introduce a new note of competitiveness, stress for high stakes in an area about which the U.S. has never had to worry. The National Academy of Sciences concluded that the U.S. is well positioned to retain its computing lead, that Japanese supercomputers are equal to but not greater than America's, and that there will be "a very closely run race in this area." The race for computer supremacy could determine which nation will dominate the world in economic, military and scientific fields in the next century. Certainly it threatens U.S. leadership position in computers, the field which, above all others, has come to symbolize the nation's technological pre-eminence.□

Election Reportage: From the Vacuous To the Vulnerable

By John Kenneth Galbraith

On occasion, reflecting my enjoyment in the exercise, I've written letters that never got sent. This one, as indicated, was to The New York Times. *It was much too long, and, alas, I didn't think it could be shortened.*
To the Editor of *The New York Times:* October 29, 1984.

It is reasonably well accepted that the media—newspapers, television, the radio—should inform the public on a wide range of subjects extending from politics to personal hygiene. The time has now come for the public to inform the media that their coverage of electoral campaigns is, not to put too fine a point on the matter, a national disgrace. The disgrace is not lessened by the evident fact that those involved have a high sense of professional accomplishment in their error. The matters I here address reflect some past personal experience in political campaigns, but I am principally impressed with how rapidly in recent elections things have become worse.

The first of two major faults is the concentration on political strategy and tactics as opposed to issues in nearly, if not quite all, reporting. In the Democratic primaries of 1984, only the most diligent or accidentally fortunate reader could have learned where the various candidates stood on economic policy, arms control, the military budget or, for that matter, abortion. Senator Gary Hart was thought solidly associated with new ideas, which, however, almost no one paused to identify; there was only brief mention of the position of the other candidates against the B-1 bomber, the MX or high interest rates. What the reader was given, instead, was enduring comment on the strategic details of each candidate's campaign: his reliance on personality as opposed to organization, his supply of money and what access that allowed him to buy more television commercials and, above all, his plans for the various primaries—where he would make a major or only a token effort; where he would stand or stand aside; what he expected the other candidates to do; how he would contend with their more pedestrian strategies. One had wonderful information on the candidate's itineraries and his reception at meetings, nothing or next to nothing on what he said there.

The reasons for this emphasis (or misemphasis) are not, I think, seriously in doubt. As compared with comment on issues, it is enormously economical of intellectual effort. Reporting a presidential campaign is hard enough work without having to resort to thought. Additionally, a huge supply of untaxing material is available from the campaign manager, a political figure who, out of greatly misplaced self-confidence, claims a penetrating knowledge of how campaigns are conducted and won and who manages thus to impress reporters until the day of final defeat, after which he or she is never heard from again. Of the near infinity of such political geniuses in the last fifty years only James A. Farley is remembered, and his achievement belonged, in fact, to Franklin D. Roosevelt; had he managed a Reubin Askew, Farley would also have been forgotten. The myth of strategic genius is, however, an appealing thing while it lasts; all reporters have an enhanced sense of their own perception in telling of it; and, as I have noted, the manager in question has a compelling, sometimes pathological, desire to communicate his own strategic wisdom to the people covering his candidate. This is not a case of the blind leading the blind; it is a powerful manifestation of the vacuous leading the vulnerable.

There is a deeper reason for this emphasis on alleged strategy as opposed to issues. It is a requirement of the modern, highly institutionalized press, television and radio that political reporting must be objective—which is to say it must be neutral. One cannot have a reporter passing judgment or seeming to pass judgment on a candidate's position on deficit spending, survival in a nuclear-armed world or silent prayer in the schools. But it is very difficult to report a candidate's views on these matters without allowing common sense or, more especially, absurdity to shine through. This is perhaps especially true of Ronald Reagan on the budget deficit and school prayer, but it is a general problem. So the reporter, when he gets to issues, runs the risk that editors will suddenly come alert, that questions will be asked in the sacred name of so-called objectivity. Far better and certainly far safer to stick with the candidate's thinking on by-passing Maine, ignoring the nonbinding preference vote in Vermont, coming down hard on downstate Illinois as the very heart of the American political scene.

The second electoral aberration of the modern media is, of course, the devotion to polling. This, also, is wholly undemanding intellectually. It is far, far easier to tell who is numerically ahead and who behind than to get into the tedious business of telling what is being said and how, in consequence, people are reacting. Polls have also a persuasive if spurious aspect of neutrality—spurious because

---

John Kenneth Galbraith is the Paul M. Warburg Professor of Economics Emeritus at Harvard University, a past president of the American Economic Association, and a former ambassador to India. He is a member for literature of the American Academy of Arts and Letters and is currently the president of the combined Academy and Institute of Arts and Letters. This article is from *A View from the Stands* by John Kenneth Galbraith.

they favor the frontrunner right up until the day when, in the frequent manner of such phenomena, they are proved to have been wrong. The polls also appeal in some deeply subjective way to the curious journalistic belief that there is some supreme value in being first with a story, even if it's not right. Why wait for the result of the election when at modest cost and a less than modest risk of error one can tell what it will be a few hours, days or weeks before!

This is very silly. Children are taught that they must wait until Christmas Day to learn the nature of their gifts. We are presumed to be adults; we can also wait. There is no point whatever in predicting with inaccuracy what, in a few hours or a few days, we will know for sure. And this is especially so when the polling—the general fascination with who is ahead, who is behind and who will win—has replaced solid reporting on what the election is really about.

Realization that grownup people can wait and may, in all reason, prefer to wait will not come easily. A few years ago I was invited by one of the networks to comment on the results on the morning after the election, itself very possibly a questionable exercise. The studio, which had been in service throughout the night, looked like the underground command post of the Eighth Air Force at High Wycombe after a particularly difficult operation. The excitement was still high; a gubernatorial race in Ohio was close and as yet undecided. I was asked tensely my view as to the probable outcome. I replied that I wouldn't dream of offering it; it was profoundly stupid to be so concerned; in a mere hour or so all would know for certain. Rarely have I had such an adverse reaction. My host's voice quavered in anger; I thought I saw tears in his eyes; clearly I had been subversive of everything for which he stood, including the way he made his living. Only with difficulty did I avoid expressing my regrets.

But I still stand firm. I plead for a deeply negative public response to the present preoccupation with electoral tactics and strategy. I propose that all who are questioned on their voting intentions or on how, on coming out of a polling booth, they have voted give, with all solemnity, a totally false reply. Let us hear instead about the issues; let us be informed when candidates seek to avoid them; and let all political strategists remain far back in the background of the campaign, where they belong. □

The Hundredth Congress

Composition of 99th and 100th Congresses

	99th Congress				100th Congress			
	Dem.	Rep.	Male	Female	Dem.	Rep.	Male	Female
Senate	47	53	98	2	54	46	98	2
House	253	182	411	24	258	177	411	24

The Senate

Senior Senator is listed first. The dates in the first column indicate period of service. The date given in parentheses after the Senator's name is year of birth. All terms are for six years and expire in January. Mailing address of Senators: The Senate, Washington, D.C. 20510.

ALABAMA
1979–91 Howell T. Heflin (D) (1921)
1987–93 Richard C. Shelby (D) (1934)
ALASKA
1968–91 Ted Stevens (R) (1923)
1981–93 Frank H. Murkowski (R) (1933)
ARIZONA
1977–89 Dennis DeConcini (D) (1937)
1987–93 John McCain (R) (1936)
ARKANSAS
1975–93 Dale Bumpers (D) (1925)
1979–91 David H. Pryor (D) (1934)
CALIFORNIA
1969–93 Alan Cranston (D) (1914)
1983–89 Pete Wilson (R) (1933)
COLORADO
1979–91 William L. Armstrong (R) (1937)
1983–93 Timothy E. Wirth (D) (1939)
CONNECTICUT
1971–89 Lowell P. Weicker, Jr. (R) (1931)
1981–93 Christopher J. Dodd (D) (1944)
DELAWARE
1971–89 William V. Roth (R) (1921)
1973–91 Joseph R. Biden, Jr. (D) (1942)
FLORIDA
1971–89 Lawton Chiles (D) (1930)
1987–93 Bob Graham (D) (1936)
GEORGIA
1972–91 Sam Nunn (D) (1938)
1987–93 Wyche Fowler, Jr. (D) (1940)
HAWAII
1963–87 Daniel K. Inouye (D) (1924)
1977–89 Spark M. Matsunaga (D) (1916)
IDAHO
1973–91 James A. McClure (R) (1924)
1981–93 Steven D. Symms (R) (1938)
ILLINOIS
1981–93 Alan J. Dixon (D) (1927)
1985–91 Paul Simon (D) (1928)
INDIANA
1977–89 Richard G. Lugar (R) (1932)
1981–93 Dan Quayle (R) (1947)
IOWA
1981–93 Charles E. Grassley (R) (1933)
1985–91 Tom Harkin (D) (1939)
KANSAS
1969–93 Robert J. Dole (R) (1923)
1978–91 Nancy Landon Kassebaum (R) (1932)

KENTUCKY
1975–93 Wendell H. Ford (D) (1924)
1985–91 Mitch McConnell (R) (1942)
LOUISIANA
1971–91 J. Bennett Johnson (D) (1932)
1987–93 John B. Breaux (D) (1944)
MAINE
1979–91 William S. Cohen (R) (1940)
1980–89 George J. Mitchell (D) (1933)
MARYLAND
1977–89 Paul S. Sarbanes (D) (1933)
1987–93 Barbara A. Mikulski (D) (1936)
MASSACHUSETTS
1962–89 Edward M. Kennedy (D) (1932)
1985–91 John F. Kerry (D) (1943)
MICHIGAN
1977–89 Donald W. Riegle, Jr. (D) (1938)
1979–91 Carl Levin (D) (1934)
MINNESOTA
1978–89 David F. Durenberger (R) (1934)
1979–91 Rudy Boschwitz (R) (1930)
MISSISSIPPI
1947–89 John C. Stennis (D) (1901)
1978–91 Thad Cochran (R) (1937)
MISSOURI
1977–89 John C. Danforth (R) (1936)
1987–91 Christopher S. (Kit) Bond (R) (1939)
MONTANA
1977–89 John Melcher (D) (1924)
1979–91 Max Baucus (D) (1941)
NEBRASKA
1979–91 J. James Exon (D) (1921)
1987–89 David Karnes (R) (1948)
NEVADA
1983–89 Chic Hecht (R) (1928)
1987–93 Harry M. Reid (D) (1939)
NEW HAMPSHIRE
1979–91 Gordon J. Humphrey (R) (1940)
1981–93 Warren B. Rudman (R) (1930)
NEW JERSEY
1979–91 Bill Bradley (D) (1943)
1983–89 Frank R. Lautenberg (D) (1924)
NEW MEXICO
1973–91 Pete V. Domenici (R) (1932)
1983–89 Jeff Bingaman (D) (1943)
NEW YORK
1977–89 Daniel P. Moynihan (D) (1927)
1981–93 Alfonse M. D'Amato (R) (1937)
NORTH CAROLINA
1973–91 Jesse Helms (R) (1921)
1987–93 Terry Sanford (D) (1917)
NORTH DAKOTA
1960–89 Quentin N. Burdick (D) (1908)
1987–93 Kent Conrad (D) (1948)
OHIO
1975–93 John H. Glenn, Jr. (D) (1921)
1976–89 Howard M. Metzenbaum (D) (1917)
OKLAHOMA
1979–91 David L. Boren (D) (1941)
1981–93 Don Nickles (R) (1948)
OREGON
1967–91 Mark O. Hatfield (R) (1922)
1969–93 Bob Packwood (R) (1932)
PENNSYLVANIA
1977–89 John Heinz (R) (1938)
1981–93 Arlen Specter (R) (1930)
RHODE ISLAND
1961–91 Claiborne Pell (D) (1918)
1977–89 John H. Chafee (R) (1922)
SOUTH CAROLINA
1956–91 Strom Thurmond (R) (1902)
1966–93 Ernest F. Hollings (D) (1922)
SOUTH DAKOTA
1979–91 Larry Pressler (R) (1942)
1987–93 Thomas A. Daschle (D) (1947)
TENNESSEE
1977–89 James R. Sasser (D) (1936)
1985–91 Albert Gore, Jr. (D) (1948)
TEXAS
1971–89 Lloyd M. Bentsen (D) (1921)
1985–91 Phil Gramm (R) (1942)
UTAH
1975–93 E. J. (Jake) Garn (R) (1932)
1977–89 Orrin G. Hatch (R) (1934)
VERMONT
1971–89 Robert T. Stafford (R) (1913)
1975–93 Patrick J. Leahy (D) (1940)
VIRGINIA
1971–91 John W. Warner (R) (1927)
1983–89 Paul S. Trible, Jr. (R) (1946)
WASHINGTON
1983–89 Daniel L. Evans (R) (1925)
1987–93 Brock Adams (D) (1927)
WEST VIRGINIA
1959–89 Robert C. Byrd (D) (1918)
1985–91 John D. (Jay) Rockefeller IV (D) (1937)
WISCONSIN
1957–89 William Proxmire (D) (1915)
1981–93 Robert W. Kasten, Jr. (R) (1942)
WYOMING
1977–89 Malcolm Wallop (R) (1933)
1979–91 Alan K. Simpson (R) (1931)

The House of Representatives

The numerals indicate the Congressional Districts of the states; the designation AL means At Large. All terms end January 1989. Mailing address of Representatives: House of Representatives, Washington, D.C. 20515

ALABAMA
(7 Representatives)
1. H.L. (Sonny) Callahan (R)
2. William L. Dickinson (R)
3. William Nichols (D)
4. Thomas Bevill (D)
5. Ronald G. Flippo (D)
6. Ben Erdreich (D)
7. Claude Harris (D)

ALASKA
(1 Representative)
AL Don Young (R)

ARIZONA
(5 Representatives)
1. John J. Rhodes III (R)
2. Morris K. Udall (D)
3. Bob Stump (R)
4. Jon Kyl (R)
5. Jim Kolbe (R)

ARKANSAS
(4 Representatives)
1. Bill Alexander (D)
2. Tommy F. Robinson (D)
3. John Paul Hammerschmidt (R)
4. Beryl Anthony, Jr. (D)

CALIFORNIA
(45 Representatives)
1. Douglas H. Bosco (D)
2. Wally Herger (R)
3. Robert T. Matsui (D)
4. Vic Fazio (D)
5. Nancy Pelosi (D)
6. Barbara Boxer (D)
7. George Miller (D)
8. Ronald V. Dellums (D)
9. Fortney H. (Pete) Stark (D)
10. Don Edwards (D)
11. Tom Lantos (D)
12. Ernest L. Konnyu (R)
13. Norman Y. Mineta (D)
14. Norman D. Shumway (R)
15. Tony Coelho (D)
16. Leon E. Panetta (D)
17. Charles Pashayan, Jr. (R)
18. Richard H. Lehman (D)
19. Robert J. Lagomarsino (R)
20. William M. Thomas (R)
21. Elton Gallegly (R)
22. Carlos J. Moorhead (R)
23. Anthony C. Beilenson (D)
24. Henry A. Waxman (D)
25. Edward R. Roybal (D)
26. Howard L. Berman (D)
27. Mel Levine (D)
28. Julian C. Dixon (D)
29. Augustus F. Hawkins (D)
30. Matthew G. Martinez (D)
31. Mervyn M. Dymally (D)
32. Glenn M. Anderson (D)
33. David Dreier (R)

34. Esteban Edward Torres (D)
35. Jerry Lewis (R)
36. George E. Brown, Jr. (D)
37. Al McCandless (R)
38. Robert K. Dornan (R)
39. William E. Dannemeyer (R)
40. Robert E. Badham (R)
41. William Lowery (R)
42. Dan Lungren (R)
43. Ron Packard (R)
44. James Bates (D)
45. Duncan L. Hunter (R)

COLORADO
(6 Representatives)
1. Patricia Schroeder (D)
2. David E. Skaggs (D)
3. Ben Nighthorse Campbell (D)
4. Hank Brown (R)
5. Joel Hefley (R)
6. Daniel L. Schaefer (R)

CONNECTICUT
(6 Representatives)
1. Barbara B. Kennelly (D)
2. Sam Gejdenson (D)
3. Bruce A. Morrison (D)
4. Christopher H. Shays (R)
5. John G. Rowland (R)
6. Nancy L. Johnson (R)

DELAWARE
(1 Representative)
AL Thomas R. Carper (D)

FLORIDA
(19 Representatives)
1. Earl D. Hutto (D)
2. William Grant (D)
3. Charles E. Bennett (D)
4. William V. Chappell, Jr. (D)
5. Bill McCollum (R)
6. Kenneth H. MacKay (D)
7. Sam Gibbons (D)
8. C.W. Bill Young (R)
9. Michael Bilirakis (R)
10. Andy Ireland (R)
11. Bill Nelson (D)
12. Tom Lewis (R)
13. Connie Mack (R)
14. Daniel A. Mica (D)
15. E. Clay Shaw, Jr. (R)
16. Larry Smith (D)
17. William Lehman (D)
18. Claude D. Pepper (D)
19. Dante B. Fascell (D)

GEORGIA
(10 Representatives)
1. Robert Lindsay Thomas (D)
2. Charles Hatcher (D)
3. Richard Ray (D)
4. Patrick Lynn Swindall (R)
5. John Lewis (D)
6. Newt Gingrich (R)
7. George (Buddy) Darden (D)
8. J. Roy Rowland (D)
9. Edgar L. Jenkins (D)
10. Doug Barnard, Jr. (D)

HAWAII
(2 Representatives)
1. Patricia Saiki (R)
2. Daniel K. Akaka (D)

IDAHO
(2 Representatives)
1. Larry E. Craig (R)
2. Richard H. Stallings (D)

ILLINOIS
(22 Representatives)
1. Charles A. Hayes (D)
2. Gus Savage (D)
3. Marty Russo (D)
4. Jack Davis (R)
5. William O. Lipinski (D)
6. Henry J. Hyde (R)
7. Cardiss Collins (D)
8. Dan Rostenkowski (D)
9. Sidney R. Yates (D)
10. John Edward Porter (R)
11. Frank Annunzio (D)
12. Philip M. Crane (R)
13. Harris W. Fawell (R)
14. J. Dennis Hastert (R)
15. Edward R. Madigan (R)
16. Lynn Martin (R)
17. Lane Evans (D)
18. Robert H. Michel (R)
19. Terry L. Bruce (D)
20. Richard Durbin (D)
21. Melvin Price (D)
22. Kenneth J. Gray (D)

INDIANA
(10 Representatives)
1. Peter Visclosky (D)
2. Philip R. Sharp (D)
3. John P. Hiler (R)
4. Daniel Coats (R)
5. Jim Jontz (D)
6. Daniel Burton (R)
7. John T. Meyers (R)
8. Frank McClosky (D)
9. Lee H. Hamilton (D)
10. Andrew Jacobs, Jr. (D)

IOWA
(6 Representatives)
1. Jim Leach (R)
2. Thomas J. Tauke (R)
3. Dave R. Nagle (D)
4. Neal Smith (D)
5. Jim Ross Lightfoot (R)
6. Fred Grandy (R)

KANSAS
(5 Representatives)
1. Pat Roberts (R)
2. James Slattery (D)
3. Jan Meyers (R)
4. Dan Glickman (D)
5. Bob Whittaker (R)

KENTUCKY
(7 Representatives)
1. Carroll Hubbard, Jr. (D)
2. William H. Natcher (D)
3. Romano L. Mazzoli (D)
4. Jim Bunning (R)
5. Harold Rogers (R)
6. Larry J. Hopkins (R)
7. Carl C. Perkins (D)

LOUISIANA
(8 Representatives)
1. Robert L. Livingston, Jr. (R)
2. Corrine C. (Lindy) Boggs (D)
3. W.J. (Billy) Tauzin (D)
4. Buddy Roemer (D)
5. Thomas J. Huckaby (D)
6. Richard Baker (R)
7. Jimmy Hayes (D)
8. Clyde Holloway (R)

MAINE
(2 Representatives)
1. Joseph E. Brennan (D)
2. Olympia J. Snowe (R)

MARYLAND
(8 Representatives)
1. Roy Dyson (D)
2. Helen Delich Bentley (R)
3. Benjamin L. Cardin (D)
4. Thomas McMillen (D)
5. Steny H. Hoyer (D)
6. Beverly B. Byron (D)
7. Kweisi Mfume (D)
8. Constance A. Morella (R)

MASSACHUSETTS
(11 Representatives)
1. Silvio O. Conte (R)
2. Edward P. Boland (D)
3. Joseph D. Early (D)
4. Barney Frank (D)
5. Chester G. Atkins (D)
6. Nicholas Mavroules (D)
7. Edward J. Markey (D)
8. Jospeh P. Kennedy II (D)
9. Joe Moakley (D)
10. Gerry E. Studds (D)
11. Brian J. Donnelly (D)

MICHIGAN
(18 Representatives)
1. John Conyers, Jr. (D)
2. Carl D. Pursell (R)
3. Howard Wolpe (D)
4. Fred Upton (R)
5. Paul B. Henry (R)
6. Bob Carr (D)
7. Dale E. Kildee (D)
8. Bob Traxler (D)
9. Guy Vander Jagt (R)
10. Bill Schuette (R)
11. Robert W. Davis (R)
12. David E. Bonior (D)
13. George W. Crockett, Jr. (D)
14. Dennis M. Hertel (D)
15. William D. Ford (D)
16. John D. Dingell (D)
17. Sander M. Levin (D)
18. William S. Broomfield (R)

MINNESOTA
(8 Representatives)
1. Timothy J. Penny (D)
2. Vin Weber (R)
3. Bill Frenzel (R)
4. Bruce F. Vento (D)
5. Martin Olav Sabo (D)
6. Gerry Sikorski (D)
7. Arlan Strangeland (R)
8. Colin C. Peterson (D)*
8. James L. Oberstar (D)

MISSISSIPPI
(5 Representatives)
1. Jamie L. Whitten (D)
2. Mike Espy (D)
3. G.V. (Sonny) Montgomery (D)
4. Wayne Dowdy (D)
5. Trent Lott (R)

MISSOURI
(9 Representatives)
1. William L. Clay (D)
2. Jack Buechner (R)
3. Richard A. Gephardt (D)
4. Ike Skelton (D)
5. Alan Wheat (D)
6. E. Thomas Coleman (R)
7. Gene Taylor (R)
8. William Emerson (R)
9. Harold L. Volkmer (D)

MONTANA
(2 Representatives)
1. Pat Williams (D)
2. Ron Marlenee (R)

NEBRASKA
(3 Representatives)
1. Douglas K. Bereuther (R)
2. Hal Daub (R)
3. Virginia Smith (R)

NEVADA
(2 Representatives)
1. James H. Bilbray (D)
2. Barbara F. Vucanovich (R)

NEW HAMPSHIRE
(2 Representatives)
1. Robert C. Smith (R)
2. Judd Gregg (R)

NEW JERSEY
(14 Representatives)
1. James J. Florio (D)
2. William J. Hughes (D)
3. James J. Howard (D)
4. Christopher H. Smith (R)
5. Marge Roukema (R)
6. Bernard J. Dwyer (D)
7. Matthew J. Rinaldo (R)
8. Robert A. Roe (D)
9. Robert G. Torricelli (D)
10. Peter W. Rodino, Jr. (D)
11. Dean A. Gallo (R)
12. Jim Courter (R)
13. H. James Saxton (R)
14. Frank J. Guarini (D)

NEW MEXICO
(3 Representatives)
1. Manuel Lujan, Jr. (R)
2. Joseph R. Skeen (R)
3. William Richardson (D)

NEW YORK
(34 Representatives)
1. George J. Hochbreuckner (D)
2. Thomas J. Downey (D)
3. Robert J. Mrazek (D)
4. Norman F. Lent (R)
5. Raymond J. McGrath (R)
6. Floyd H. Flake (D)
7. Gary L. Ackerman (D)
8. James H. Scheuer (D)
9. Thomas J. Manton (D)
10. Charles E. Schumer (D)
11. Edolphus Towns (D)
12. Major R. Owens (D)
13. Stephen J. Solarz (D)
14. Guy V. Molinari (R)
15. Bill Green (R)
16. Charles B. Rangel (D)
17. Ted Weiss (D)
18. Robert Garcia (D)
19. Mario Biaggi (D)
20. Joseph D. DioGuardi (R)
21. Hamilton Fish, Jr. (R)
22. Benjamin A. Gilman (R)
23. Samuel S. Stratton (D)
24. Gerald B.H. Solomon (R)
25. Sherwood Boehlert (R)
26. David O'B. Martin (R)
27. George C. Wortley (R)*
27. Rosemary S. Pooler (D)*
28. Matthew F. McHugh (D)
29. Frank Horton (R)
30. Louise M. Slaughter (D)
31. Jack F. Kemp (R)
32. John J. LaFalce (D)
33. Henry J. Nowak (D)
34. Amory Houghton, Jr. (R)

NORTH CAROLINA
(11 Representatives)
1. Walter B. Jones (D)
2. Tim Valentine (D)
3. Martin Lancaster (D)
4. David E. Price (D)
5. Stephen L. Neal (D)
6. Howard Coble (R)
6. Robin Britt (D)
7. Charlie Rose (D)
8. W.G. (Bill) Hefner (D)
9. J. Alex McMillan (R)
10. Cass Ballenger (R)
11. James McClure Clarke (D)

NORTH DAKOTA
(1 Representative)
AL Byron L. Dorgan (D)

OHIO
(21 Representatives)
1. Thomas A. Luken (D)
2. Willis D. Gradison, Jr. (R)
3. Tony P. Hall (D)
4. Michael G. Oxley (R)
5. Delbert L. Latta (R)
6. Bob McEwen (R)
7. Michael DeWine (R)
8. Donald E. (Buz) Lukens (R)
9. Marcy Kaptur (D)
10. Clarence E. Miller (R)
11. Dennis E. Eckart (D)
12. John R. Kasich (R)
13. Don J. Pease (D)
14. Tom Sawyer (D)
15. David L. Jackson (D)
16. Ralph Regula (R)
17. James A. Traficant, Jr. (D)
18. Douglas Applegate (D)
19. Edward F. Feighan (D)
20. Mary Rose Oakar (D)
21. Louis Stokes (D)

OKLAHOMA
(6 Representatives)
1. James M. Inhofe (R)
2. Mike Synar (D)
3. Wesley W. Watkins (D)
4. Dave McCurdy (D)
5. Mickey Edwards (R)
6. Glenn English (D)

OREGON
(5 Representatives)
1. Les AuCoin (D)
2. Robert F. Smith (R)
3. Ronald L. Wyden (D)
4. Peter A. De Fazio (D)
5. Denny Smith (R)

PENNSYLVANIA
(23 Representatives)
1. Thomas M. Foglietta (D)
2. William H. Gray III (D)
3. Robert A. Borski (D)
4. Joseph P. Kolter (D)
5. Richard T. Schulze (R)
6. Gus Yatron (D)
7. Curt Weldon (R)
8. Peter H. Kostmayer (D)
9. Bud Shuster (R)
10. Joseph M. McDade (R)
11. Paul E. Kanjorski (D)
12. John P. Murtha (D)
13. Lawrence Coughlin (R)
14. William J. Coyne (D)
15. Don Ritter (R)
16. Robert S. Walker (R)
17. George W. Gekas (R)
18. Doug Walgren (D)
19. William F. Goodling (R)
20. Joseph M. Gaydos (D)
21. Tom Ridge (R)
22. Austin J. Murphy (D)
23. William F. Clinger, Jr. (R)

RHODE ISLAND
(2 Representatives)
1. Fernand J. St. Germain (D)
2. Claudine J. Schneider (R)

SOUTH CAROLINA
(6 Representatives)
1. Arthur Ravenel, Jr. (R)
2. Floyd Spence (R)
3. Butler Derrick (D)
4. Elizabeth J. Patterson (D)
5. John M. Spratt, Jr. (D)
6. Robin Tallon (D)

SOUTH DAKOTA
(1 Representative)
AL Tim Johnson (D)

TENNESSEE
(9 Representatives)
1. James H. Quillen (R)
2. John J. Duncan (R)
3. Marilyn Lloyd (D)
4. James Cooper (D)
5. William H. Boner (D)
6. Bart Gordon (D)
7. Don Sundquist (R)
8. Ed Jones (D)
9. Harold E. Ford (D)

TEXAS
(27 Representatives)
1. Jim Chapman (D)
2. Charles Wilson (D)
3. Steven Bartlett (R)
4. Ralph M. Hall (D)
5. John Bryant (D)
6. Joe L. Barton (R)
7. Bill Archer (R)
8. Jack Fields (R)
9. Jack Brooks (D)
10. J.J. Pickle (D)
11. Marvin Leath (D)
12. Jim Wright (D)
13. Beau Boulter (R)
14. Mac Sweeney (R)
15. E. (Kika) de la Garza (D)
16. Ronald D. Coleman (D)
17. Charles W. Stenholm (D)
18. George T. (Mickey) Leland (D)
19. Larry Combest (R)
20. Henry B. Gonzalez (D)
21. Lamar Smith (R)
22. Thomas D. DeLay (R)
23. Albert G. Bustamante (D)
24. Martin Frost (D)
25. Michael A. Andrews (D)
26. Richard Armey (R)
27. Solomon P. Ortiz (D)

UTAH
(3 Representatives)
1. James V. Hansen (R)
2. Wayne Owens (D)
3. Howard C. Nielson (R)

VERMONT
(1 Representative)
AL James M. Jeffords (R)

VIRGINIA
(10 Representatives)
1. Herbert H. Batemateman (R)
2. Owen B. Pickett (D)
3. Thomas J. Bliley, Jr. (R)
4. Norman Sisisky (D)
5. Dan Daniel (D)
6. James R. Olin (D)
7. D. French Slaughter (R)
8. Stan Parris (R)
9. Frederick C. Boucher (D)
10. Frank R. Wolf (R)

WASHINGTON
(8 Representatives)
1. John R. Miller (R)
2. Al Swift (D)
3. Don L. Bonker (D)
4. Sid W. Morrison (R)
5. Thomas S. Foley (D)
6. Norman D. Dicks (D)
7. Mike Lowry (D)
8. Rodney Chandler (R)

WEST VIRGINIA
(4 Representatives)
1. Alan B. Mollohan (D)
2. Harley O. Staggers, Jr. (D)
3. Robert Wise (D)
4. Nick J. Rahall II (D)

WISCONSIN
(9 Representatives)
1. Les Aspin (D)
2. Robert W. Kastenmeier (D)

3. Steve Gunderson (R)
4. Gerald D. Kleczka (D)
5. James Moody (D)
6. Thomas E. Petri (R)
7. David P. Obey (D)
8. Toby Roth (R)
9. F. James Sensenbrenner, Jr. (R)

WYOMING
(1 Representative)
AL Dick Cheney (R)

Senate and House Standing Committees, 100th Congress

Committees of the Senate

Agriculture, Nutrition, and Forestry (17 members)
Chairman: Patrick J. Leahy (Vt.)
Ranking Rep.: Jesse Helms (N.C.)

Appropriations (29 members)
Chairman: John C. Stennis (Miss.)
Ranking Rep.: Mark O. Hatfield (Ore.)

Armed Services (20 members)
Chairman: Sam Nunn (Ga.)
Ranking Rep.: John Warner (Va.)

Banking, Housing, and Urban Affairs (18 members)
Chairman: William Proxmire (Wis.)
Ranking Rep.: E. J. (Jake) Garn (Utah)

Budget (22 members)
Chairman: Lawton Chiles (Fla.)
Ranking Rep.: Pete V. Domenici (N.M.)

Commerce, Science, and Transportation (20 members)
Chairman: Ernest F. Hollings (S.C.)
Ranking Rep.: John C. Danforth (Mo.)

Energy and Natural Resources (19 members)
Chairman: J. Bennett Johnston (La.)
Ranking Rep.: James A. McClure (Idaho)

Environment and Public Works (16 members)
Chairman: Quentin N. Burdick (N.D.)
Ranking Rep.: Robert T. Stafford (Vt.)

Finance (20 members)
Chairman: Lloyd M. Bentsen (Texas)
Ranking Rep.: Bob Packwood (Ore.)

Foreign Relations (19 members)
Chairman: Claiborne Pell (R.I.)
Ranking Rep.: Jesse Helms (N.C.)

Governmental Affairs (14 members)
Chairman: John Glenn (Ohio)
Ranking Rep.: William V. Roth, Jr. (Del.)

Judiciary (14 members)
Chairman: Joseph R. Biden, Jr. (Del)
Ranking Rep.: Strom Thurmond (S.C.)

Labor and Human Resources (16 members)
Chairman: Edward M. Kennedy (Mass.)
Ranking Rep.: Orrin G. Hatch (Utah)

Rules and Administration (16 members)
Chairman: Wendell H. Ford (Ky.)
Ranking Rep.: Mark O. Hatfield (Ore.)

Small Business (18 members)
Chairman: Dale Bumpers (Ark.)
Ranking Rep.: Lowell P. Weicker, Jr. (Conn.)

Veterans' Affairs (11 members)
Chairman: Alan Cranston (Calif.)
Ranking Rep: Frank H. Murkowski (Alas.)

Select and Special Committees

Aging (19 members)
Chairman: John Melcher (Mont.)
Ranking Rep.: John Heinz (Pa.)

Ethics (6 members)
Chairman: Howell T. Heflin (Ala.)
Ranking Rep.: Warren Rudman (N.H.)

Indian Affairs (8 members)
Chairman: Daniel K. Inouye (Hawaii)
Ranking Rep.: Daniel J. Evans (Wash.)

Intelligence (16 members)
Chairman: David L. Boren (Okla.)
Ranking Rep.: William S. Cohen (Me.)

Committees of the House

Agriculture (43 members)
Chairman: E. (Kika) de la Garza (Texas)
Ranking Rep.: Edward R. Madigan (Ill.)

Appropriations (57 members)
Chairman: Jamie L. Whitten (Miss.)
Ranking Rep.: Silvio O. Conte (Mass.)

Armed Services (52 members)
Chairman: Les Aspin (Wis.)
Ranking Rep.: William L. Dickinson (Ala.)

Banking, Finance, and Urban Affairs (51 members)
Chairman: Fernand J. St. Germain (R.I.)
Ranking Rep.: Chalmers P. Wylie (Ohio)

Budget (35 members)
Chairman: William H. Gray, 3rd (Pa.)
Ranking Rep.: Delbert L. Latta (Ohio)

District of Columbia (10 members)
Chairman: Ronald V. Dellums (Calif.)
Ranking Rep.: Stanford E. Parris (Va.)

Education and Labor (34 members)
Chairman: Augustus F. Hawkins (Calif.)
Ranking Rep.: James M. Jeffords (Vt.)

Energy and Commerce (42 members)
Chairman: John D. Dingell (Mich.)
Ranking Rep.: Norman Lent (N.Y.)

Foreign Affairs (45 members)
Chairman: Dante B. Fascell (Fla.)
Ranking Rep.: William S. Broomfield (Mich.)

Government Operations (39 members)
Chairman: Jack Brooks (Texas)
Ranking Rep.: Frank Horton (N.Y.)

House Administration (18 members)
Chairman: Frank Annunzio (Ill.)
Ranking Rep.: Bill Frenzel (Minn.)

Interior and Insular Affairs (41 members)
Chairman: Morris K. Udall (Ariz.)
Ranking Rep.: Don Young (Alas.)

Judiciary (35 members)
Chairman: Peter W. Rodino, Jr. (N.J.)
Ranking Rep.: Hamilton Fish, Jr. (N.Y.)

Merchant Marine and Fisheries (42 members)
Chairman: Walter B. Jones (N.C.)
Ranking Rep.: Robert W. Davis (Mich.)

Post Office and Civil Service (22 members)
Chairman: William D. Ford (Mich.)
Ranking Rep.: Gene Taylor (Miss.)

Public Works and Transportation (52 members)
Chairman: James J. Howard (N.J.)
Ranking Rep.: John P. Hammerschmidt (Ark.)

Rules (13 members)
Chairman: Claude Pepper (Fla.)
Ranking Rep.: James H. Quillen (Tenn.)

Science, Space, and Technology (45 members)
Chairman: Robert A. Roe (N.J.)
Ranking Rep.: Manuel Lujan, Jr. (N.M.)

Small Business (43 members)
Chairman: John J. LaFalce (N.Y.)
Ranking Rep.: Joseph M. McDade (Pa.)

Standards of Official Conduct (12 members)
Chairman: Julian C. Dixon (Calif.)
Ranking Rep.: Floyd D. Spence (S.C.)

Veterans' Affairs (34 members)
Chairman: G. V. (Sonny) Montgomery (Miss.)
Ranking Rep.: Gerald B. Solomon (N.Y.)

Ways and Means (36 members)
Chairman: Dan Rostenkowski (Ill.)
Ranking Rep.: John J. Duncan (Tenn.)

Select Committees

Aging (66 members)
Chairman: Edward Roybal (Calif.)
Ranking Rep.: Matthew J. Rinaldo (N.J.)
Children, Youth, and Families (31 members)
Chairman: George Miller (Calif.)
Ranking Rep.: Daniel Coats (Ind.)
Hunger (23 members)
Chairman: Mickey Leland (Texas)
Ranking Rep.: Marge Roukema (N.J.)
Intelligence (17 members)
Chairman: Louis Stokes (Ohio)
Ranking Rep.: Henry Hyde (Ill.)
Narcotics Abuse and Control (25 members)
Chairman: Charles B. Rangel (N.Y.)
Ranking Rep.: Benjamin Gilman II (N.Y.)

Speakers of the House of Representatives

Dates served	Congress	Name and state
1789–1791	1	Frederick A. C. Muhlenberg (Pa.)
1791–1793	2	Jonathan Trumbull (Conn.)
1793–1795	3	Frederick A. C. Muhlenberg (Pa.)
1795–1799	4–5	Jonathan Dayton (N.J.)[1]
1799–1801	6	Theodore Sedgwick (Mass.)
1801–1807	7–9	Nathaniel Macon (N.C.)
1807–1811	10–11	Joseph B. Varnum (Mass.)
1811–1814	12–13	Henry Clay (Ky.)[2]
1814–1815	13	Langdon Cheves (S.C.)
1815–1820	14–16	Henry Clay (Ky.)[3]
1820–1821	16	John W. Taylor (N.Y.)
1821–1823	17	Philip P. Barbour (Va.)
1823–1825	18	Henry Clay (Ky.)
1825–1827	19	John W. Taylor (N.Y.)
1827–1834	20–23	Andrew Stevenson (Va.)[4]
1834–1835	23	John Bell (Tenn.)
1835–1839	24–25	James K. Polk (Tenn.)
1839–1841	26	Robert M. T. Hunter (Va.)
1841–1843	27	John White (Ky.)
1843–1845	28	John W. Jones (Va.)
1845–1847	29	John W. Davis (Ind.)
1847–1849	30	Robert C. Winthrop (Mass.)
1849–1851	31	Howell Cobb (Ga.)
1851–1855	32–33	Linn Boyd (Ky.)
1855–1857	34	Nathaniel P. Banks (Mass.)
1857–1859	35	James L. Orr (S.C.)
1859–1861	36	Wm. Pennington (N.J.)
1861–1863	37	Galusha A. Grow (Pa.)
1863–1869	38–40	Schuyler Colfax (Ind.)
1869–1869	40	Theodore M. Pomeroy (N.Y.)[5]
1869–1875	41–43	James G. Blaine (Me.)
1875–1876	44	Michael C. Kerr (Ind.)[6]
1876–1881	44–46	Samuel J. Randall (Pa.)
1881–1883	47	J. Warren Keifer (Ohio)
1883–1889	48–50	John G. Carlisle (Ky.)
1889–1891	51	Thomas B. Reed (Me.)
1891–1895	52–53	Charles F. Crisp (Ga.)
1895–1899	54–55	Thomas B. Reed (Me.)
1899–1903	56–57	David B. Henderson (Iowa)
1903–1911	58–61	Joseph G. Cannon (Ill.)
1911–1919	62–65	Champ Clark (Mo.)
1919–1925	66–68	Frederick H. Gillett (Mass.)
1925–1931	69–71	Nicholas Longworth (Ohio)
1931–1933	72	John N. Garner (Tex.)
1933–1934	73	Henry T. Rainey (Ill.)[7]
1935–1936	74	Joseph W. Byrns (Tenn.)[8]
1936–1940	74–76	William B. Bankhead (Ala.)[9]
1940–1947	76–79	Sam Rayburn (Tex.)
1947–1949	80	Joseph W. Martin, Jr. (Mass.)
1949–1953	81–82	Sam Rayburn (Tex.)
1953–1955	83	Joseph W. Martin, Jr. (Mass.)
1955–1961	84–87	Sam Rayburn (Tex.)[10]
1962–1971	87–91	John W. McCormack (Mass.)[11]
1971–1977	92–94	Carl Albert (Okla.)[12]
1977–1987	95–99	Thomas P. O'Neill, Jr. (Mass.)[13]
1987–	100–	James C. Wright, Jr. (Tex.)

1. George Dent (Md.) was elected Speaker pro tempore for April 20 and May 28, 1798. 2. Resigned during second session of 13th Congress. 3. Resigned between first and second sessions of 16th Congress. 4. Resigned during first session of 23rd Congress. 5. Elected Speaker and served the day of adjournment. 6. Died between first and second sessions of 44th Congress. During first session, there were two Speakers pro tempore: Samuel S. Cox (N.Y.), appointed for Feb. 17, May 12, and June 19, 1876, and Milton Sayler (Ohio), appointed for June 4, 1876. 7. Died in 1934 after adjournment of second session of 73rd Congress. 8. Died during second session of 74th Congress. 9. Died during third session of 76th Congress. 10. Died between first and second sessions of 87th Congress. 11. Not a candidate in 1970 election. 12. Not a candidate in 1976 election. 13. Not a candidate in 1986 election. *Source: Congressional Directory.*

Floor Leaders of the Senate

Democratic	Republican
Gilbert M. Hitchcock, Neb. (Min. 1919–20)	Charles Curtis, Kan. (Maj. 1925–29)
Oscar W. Underwood, Ala. (Min. 1920–23)	James E. Watson, Ind. (Maj. 1929–33)
Joseph T. Robinson, Ark. (Min. 1923–33, Maj. 1933–37)	Charles L. McNary, Ore. (Min. 1933–44)
Alben W. Barkley, Ky. (Maj. 1937–46, Min. 1947–48)	Wallace H. White, Jr., Me. (Min. 1944–47, Maj. 1947–48)
Scott W. Lucas, Ill. (Maj. 1949–50)	Kenneth S. Wherry, Neb. (Min. 1949–51)
Ernest W. McFarland, Ariz. (Maj. 1951–52)	Styles Bridges, N. H. (Min. 1951–52)
Lyndon B. Johnson, Tex. (Min. 1953–54, Maj. 1955–60)	Robert A. Taft, Ohio (Maj. 1953)
Mike Mansfield, Mont. (Maj. 1961–77)	William F. Knowland, Calif. (Maj. 1953–54, Min. 1955–58)
Robert C. Byrd, W. Va. (Maj. 1977–81, Min. 1981–86, Maj. 1987 —)	Everett M. Dirksen, Ill. (Min. 1959–69)
	Hugh Scott, Pa. (Min. 1969–1977)
	Howard H. Baker, Jr., Tenn. (Min. 1977–81, Maj. 1981–84)
	Robert J. Dole, Kan. (Maj. 1985–86, Min. 1987–)

NOTE: Min. = Minority Leader; Maj. = Majority Leader. *Source:* United States Senate, Secretary for the Majority.

Presidential Election of 1984

Principal Candidates for President and Vice President
Republican: Ronald W. Reagan; George Bush
Democratic: Walter F. Mondale; Geraldine A. Ferraro

State	Total	*Reagan* Rep.	Percent	*Mondale* Dem.	Percent	Plurality	Electoral vote R	Electoral vote D
Alabama	1,441,713	872,849	60.5	551,899	38.2	320,950	9	—
Alaska	209,605	138,377	66.6	62,007	29.8	76,370	3	—
Arizona	1,025,897	681,416	66.4	333,854	32.5	347,562	7	—
Arkansas	884,406	534,774	60.4	338,646	38.2	196,128	6	—
California	9,505,423	5,467,009	57.5	3,922,519	41.2	1,544,490	47	—
Colorado	1,295,380	821,817	63.4	454,975	35.1	366,842	8	—
Connecticut	1,466,900	890,877	60.7	569,597	38.8	321,280	8	—
Delaware	254,572	152,190	59.7	101,656	39.9	50,534	3	—
D.C.	211,288	29,009	13.7	180,408	85.3	151,399	—	3
Florida	4,180,051	2,730,350	65.3	1,448,816	34.6	1,281,534	21	—
Georgia	1,776,120	1,068,722	60.1	706,628	39.7	362,094	12	—
Hawaii	335,846	185,050	55.1	147,154	43.8	37,896	4	—
Idaho	411,144	297,523	72.3	108,510	26.3	189,013	4	—
Illinois	4,819,088	2,707,103	56.1	2,086,499	43.3	620,604	24	—
Indiana	2,233,069	1,377,230	61.6	841,481	37.6	535,749	12	—
Iowa	1,319,805	703,088	53.2	605,620	45.8	97,468	8	—
Kansas	1,021,991	677,296	66.2	333,149	32.6	344,147	7	—
Kentucky	1,369,345	821,702	60.1	539,539	39.4	282,163	9	—
Louisiana	1,706,822	1,037,299	60.7	651,586	38.1	385,713	10	—
Maine	553,144	336,500	60.8	214,515	38.7	121,985	4	—
Maryland	1,675,873	879,918	52.5	787,935	47.0	91,983	10	—
Massachusetts	2,559,453	1,310,936	51.2	1,239,606	48.4	163,313	13	—
Michigan	3,801,658	2,251,571	67.7	1,529,638	31.8	721,933	20	
Minnesota	2,084,449	1,032,603	49.5	1,036,364	49.7	3,761	—	10
Mississippi	941,104	582,377	61.8	352,192	37.4	230,185	7	—
Missouri	2,122,783	1,274,188	60.0	848,583	39.9	425,605	11	—
Montana	384,377	232,450	60.4	146,742	38.1	85,708	4	—
Nebraska	652,090	460,054	70.5	187,866	28.8	272,188	5	—
Nevada	286,667	188,770	66.8	91,655	31.9	97,115	4	—
New Hampshire	389,066	267,051	68.6	120,395	30.9	146,656	4	—
New Jersey	3,217,862	1,933,630	60.0	1,261,323	39.2	672,307	16	—
New Mexico	514,370	307,101	59.7	201,769	39.2	105,332	5	—
New York[1]	6,806,810	3,664,763	53.8	3,119,609	45.8	545,154	36	—
North Carolina	2,175,361	1,346,481	61.9	824,287	37.8	522,194	13	—
North Dakota	308,971	200,336	64.8	104,429	33.8	95,907	3	—
Ohio	4,547,619	2,678,560	58.9	1,825,440	40.1	853,120	23	—
Oklahoma	1,255,676	861,530	68.6	385,080	30.6	476,450	8	—
Oregon	1,226,527	685,700	55.9	536,479	43.7	149,221	7	—
Pennsylvania	4,844,903	2,584,323	53.3	2,228,131	45.9	356,192	25	—
Rhode Island	410,492	212,080	51.6	197,106	48.0	14,974	4	—
South Carolina	968,529	615,539	63.5	344,459	35.5	271,080	8	—
South Dakota	317,867	200,267	63.0	116,113	36.5	84,154	3	—
Tennessee	1,711,994	990,212	57.8	711,714	41.5	278,498	11	—
Texas	5,397,571	3,433,428	63.6	1,949,276	36.1	1,484,152	29	—
Utah	629,656	469,105	74.5	155,369	24.6	313,736	5	—
Vermont	234,561	135,865	57.9	95,730	40.8	40,135	3	—
Virginia	2,146,635	1,337,078	62.2	796,250	37.0	540,828	12	—
Washington	1,883,910	1,051,670	55.8	807,352	42.8	244,318	10	—
West Virginia	735,742	405,483	55.1	328,125	44.6	77,358	6	—
Wisconsin	2,211,689	1,198,584	54.1	995,740	45.0	202,844	11	—
Wyoming	188,968	133,241	70.5	53,370	28.2	79,871	3	—
Total	**92,652,842**	**54,455,075**	**58.7**	**37,577,185**	**40.5**	**16,877,890**	**525**	**13**

1. Reagan figure is combined Republican and Conservative Party votes; Mondale figure is combined Democratic and Liberal Party votes. NATIONAL TOTALS OF OTHER CANDIDATES FOR PRESIDENT: David Bergland, Libertarian, 227,204; Lyndon H. LaRouche, Jr., Independent, 78,773; Sonia Johnson, Citizens, 71,976; Bob Richards, Populist 66,241; Dennis L. Serrette, Independent Alliance, 46,809; Gus Hall, Communist, 36,225; Mel Mason, Socialist Workers, 24,681; others and write-ins, 68,673. *Source: Federal Elections 84,* Federal Election Commission.

The Governors of the Fifty States

State	Governor	Current term[1]	State	Governor	Current term[1]
Ala.	Guy Hunt (R)	1987-91	Mont.	Tim Schwinden (D)	1985-89
Alaska	Steve Cowper (D)	1986-90[2]	Neb.	Kay A. Orr (R)	1987-91
Ariz.	Evan Mechan (R)	1987-91	Nev.	Richard H. Byran (D)	1987-91
Ark.	Bill Clinton (D)	1987-91	N.H.	John H. Sununu (R)	1985-87
Calif.	George Deukmejian (R)	1987-91	N.J.	Thomas H. Kean (R)	1986-90
Colo.	Roy Romer (D)	1987-91	N.M.	Garrey E. Carruthers (R)	1987-91
Conn.	William A. O'Neill (D)	1987-91	N.Y.	Mario M. Cuomo (D)	1987-91
Del.	Michael N. Castle (R)	1985-89	N.C.	James G. Martin (R)	1985-89
Fla.	Bob Martinez (R)	1987-91	N.D.	George Sinner (D)	1985-89
Ga.	Joe Frank Harris (D)	1987-91	Ohio	Richard F. Celeste (D)	1987-91
Hawaii	John Waikee (D)	1986-90[2]	Okla.	Henry Bellmon (R)	1987-91
Idaho	Cecil D. Andrus (D)	1987-91	Ore.	Neil Goldschmidt (R)	1987-91
Ill.	James R. Thompson (R)	1987-91	Pa.	Robert P. Casey (D)	1987-91
Ind.	Robert D. Orr (R)	1985-89	R.I.	Edward D. DiPrete (R)	1987-89
Iowa	Terry E. Branstad (R)	1987-91	S.C.	Carroll A. Campbell, Jr. (R)	1987-91
Kan.	Mike Hayden (R)	1987-91	S.D.	George Mickelson (R)	1987-91
Ky.	Martha Layne Collins (D)	1983-87[2]	Tenn.	Ned Ray McWherter (D)	1987-91
La.	Edwin W. Edwards (D)	1984-88[3]	Tex.	William Clements (R)	1987-91
Me.	John R. McKernan, Jr. (R)	1987-91	Utah	Norman H. Bangerter (R)	1985-89
Md.	William Donald Schaefer (D)	1987-91	Vt.	Madeline M. Kunin (D)	1987-89
Mass.	Michael S. Dukakis (D)	1987-91	Va.	Gerald L. Baliles (D)	1986-90
Mich.	James J. Blanchard (D)	1987-91	Wash.	Booth Gardner (D)	1985-89
Minn.	Rudy Perpich (D)	1987-91	W. Va.	Arch A. Moore, Jr. (R)	1985-89
Miss.	Bill Allain (D)	1984-88	Wis.	Tommy G. Thompson (R)	1987-91
Mo.	John Ashcroft (R)	1985-89	Wyo.	Mike Sullivan (D)	1987-91

1. Except where indicated, all terms begin in January. 2. December. 3. March.

Black Elected Officials

Year	U.S. and State Legislatures[1]	City and County Offices[2]	Law Enforcement[3]	Education[4]	Total
1970 (Feb.)	182	715	213	362	1,472
1973 (Apr.)	256	1,264	334	767	2,621
1974 (Apr.)	256	1,602	340	793	2,991
1975 (Apr.)	299	1,878	387	939	3,503
1976 (Apr.)	299	2,274	412	994	3,979
1977 (July)	316	2,497	447	1,051	4,311
1978 (July)	316	2,595	454	1,138	4,503
1979 (July)	315	2,647	486	1,136	4,584
1980 (July)	326	2,832	526	1,206	4,890
1981 (July)	343	2,863	549	1,259	5,014
1982 (July)	342	2,951	563	1,259	5,115
1983 (July)	366	3,197	607	1,369	5,559
1984 (Jan.)	396	3,259	636	1,363	5,654
1985 (Jan.)	407	3,517	661	1,431	6,016[5]
1986 (Jan.)	420	3,824	676	1,504	6,424[5]
1987 (Jan.)	440	3,966	728	1,547	6,681

1. Includes elected State administrators. 2. County commissioners and councilmen, mayors, vice mayors, aldermen, regional officials, and other. 3. Judges, magistrates, constables, marshals, sheriffs, justices of the peace, and other. 4. Members of State education agencies, college boards, school boards, and other. 5. Includes Black elected officials in the Virgin Islands. *Source:* Joint Center for Political Studies, Washington, D.C., *Black Elected Officials: A National Roster,* Copyright.

Annual Salaries of Federal Officials

President of the U.S.	$200,000[1]	Secretaries of the Army, Navy, Air Force	89,500
Vice President of the U.S.	115,000[2]	Senators and Representatives	89,500
Cabinet members	99,500	President Pro Tempore of Senate	89,500
Under secretaries of executive departments	82,500	Majority and Minority Leader of the Senate	89,500
Deputy Secretaries of State, Defense, Treasury	89,500	Majority and Minority Leader of the House	89,500
Deputy Attorney General	89,500	Speaker of the House	115,800
Under Secretary of Transportation	82,500	Chief Justice of the United States	115,000
		Associate Justices of the Supreme Court	110,000

1. Plus taxable $50,000 for expenses and a nontaxable sum (not to exceed $100,000 a year) for travel expenses. 2. Plus taxable $10,000 for expenses. NOTE: All salaries shown above are taxable. Data are as of 1987.

Prescription for Ailing Industries

By Peter Drucker

Q Professor Drucker, is American manufacturing in trouble?

If you talk of manufacturing employment, yes, manufacturing is in trouble. But if you talk of manufacturing production, no. Manufacturing production is growing. Except for wartimes, it has remained 22 percent of gross national product since 1920.

Nevertheless, manufacturing industries are no longer central. When you look at basic values today, they are not material goods. Our society has chosen that its values are health care, education and leisure. This is not the materialist society—1900 was the materialist society. Now, mind you, yes, the kids are buying things like crazy. But the real deprivation for the 28-year-old lawyer is when the boss says, "We have that big law case, and you better not go skiing this weekend."

Q Should we abandon smokestack industries that aren't competitive internationally?

When it comes to smokestack industry, ours is no worse off than any other. Steel has been a dying commodity since World War I. But I'm not saying we should abandon steel. The question of how to maintain enough steel capacity so that we have it in case of war is a very real problem. One of the reasons steel and other obsolete industries are in such trouble is that they don't face up to reality.

Q In what sense?

In terms of closing mills. The mills that lose the most money are the modernized ones. That's always true of an obsolete industry. In an old and dying industry in which demand drops, the worst thing to do is to modernize. You can pour capital in, and you can lay off people. But you have to keep on paying interest. It doesn't help you any that your costs of production are lower if the demand ain't there. You can fault steel managements for lots of things. But occasionally doing nothing is the right thing to do.

Q Many critics say Japanese managers are better than American managers. Are they correct?

No. There are some exceedingly well-managed Japanese firms, but the proportion is no greater than here. Most Japanese companies are managed differently—not better, differently. There are many things we can learn from them. But every Japanese management practice is of American origin, not Japanese. Only they practice it, and we just preach it. A real difference in the Japanese is that they work. Also, the Japanese do not go in for the unconscionable executive salaries we pay.

Q Why is high executive pay so bad?

Because it alienates the work force. Believe me, Lee Iacocca is a folk hero, but not to the Chrysler worker. He was a hero until he rightly refused to give wage increases but then he got an enormous bonus himself. The official reason given for high executive pay is that you have to have sufficient differentiation between ranks to make a promotion worthwhile. At GM, you now have about 52 levels of management. So in order to pay the foreman a decent salary, you have to pay the chairman that outrageous sum. Why don't they just eliminate two thirds of those levels of management? Probably the greatest weakness in our big corporations is that they have built enormous hierarchies of management.

Q Could you really cut out two thirds?

Yes, if you shift an organization and organize it around information needs, like in an orchestra. The bassoonist plays directly to the conductor, because both have the same score. I just got the book on 14 American companies that over several decades show nothing but superior results. They have one thing in common: The score is clear. The mission is clear. Believe me, the organization of the future will be one that will have far fewer managers and far more specialists with knowledge. We are on the verge of a change in the business organization—not just in America—from one that is hierarchical, because it depends on layers of people for communication, to one that is very lean and information-based. It basically looks like the symphony orchestra, not like the Army.

Q What will the future be in the knowledge-based society for the man or woman who toils in an auto plant today?

He or she won't be there. What is no longer possible is that a worker will make an upper-middle-class living except through knowledge.

Q It sounds as though we may have to make a very complex and difficult transition—

We have already had 10 years of tremendous transition. The most important phenomenon in this country is that during that time we have had no real unemployment, except in a few spots, and no real social upheaval. Here the U.S. has been undergoing an enormous industrial restructuring. We have moved several million people out of smokestack industries, and we are still operating at the lowest unemployment rate in the Western world. At less than 6 percent for adult men, U.S. unemployment is probably even lower than Japan's. For in Japan, the bulk of the unemployment is concealed. Japanese companies keep people on the payroll even if there is no work for them at all. And don't forget, we have made the biggest demographic change any country has ever made in terms of labor-force participation of women. It's an incredible achievement. What did we do right? I don't know. I don't understand it. □

Peter Drucker is a professor of social science at Claremont Graduate School and consults on corporate management worldwide. *The Frontiers of Management* is the latest of his more than 20 books.

Economic Preview of the Year 2000

The U.S. Department of Labor's Bureau of Labor Statistics' economic and employment projections to the year 2000 offer three alternative scenarios of the labor force, economic growth, and employment by industry and occupation. All three scenarios project substantial employment increases ranging from 15 million for the low scenario, 21 million for the moderate, and 26 million for the high growth one.

Moderate growth projection highlights:

The labor force will grow more slowly than in the past and will reach 139 million in 2000. The workforce will be older and made up of more women and minority workers than in the past.

Productivity growth will contribute more to economic growth than it has during the previous 14 years but the rate of economic growth will stay about the same.

Service-producing industries will add nearly 21 million jobs.

Employment in manufacturing will decline as manufacturing's share of total employment goes to 14 percent in 2000. Factory output is projected to hold steady.

Some industries will grow very rapidly, including most business services—especially computer and data processing and personnel supply.

Employment in broad occupational groups that require the most educational preparation will grow faster than average while those occupational groups requiring the least educational preparation are expected to grow slowly or decline.

Survey of Displaced Workers, 1981-1985

One of the harsh realities of economic change is the closing of plants or the severe cutbacks in their operations. The mass layoffs create instant pockets of unemployment, often made up of people with years of dedicated service and acquired skills and no place to apply them. The ability of these workers to readjust after plant closings or large cutbacks has been a subject of considerable interest to policymakers, labor leaders, and economic analysts.

In January 1986, the Employment and Training Administration sponsored a special supplement to the Current Population Survey designed to answer some of the questions about "displaced workers." The survey was almost identical to a study conducted in January 1984, which permitted additional insight into the problem. The principal findings of the survey include:

A total of 10.8 million workers 20 years of age and over lost jobs because of plant closings or employment cutbacks over the January 1981–January 1986 period. Those who had been at their jobs at least 3 years numbered about 5.1 million. This estimate was very similar to that obtained in the 1984 survey, which had covered the 1979-83 period.

While both surveys yielded about the same number of displaced workers with at least 3 years of tenure on the lost jobs, the reemployed proportion was much higher in 1986 than in 1984—67, compared with 60 percent.

Close to 18 percent of those displaced were unemployed when surveyed in January 1986. This was an improvement over 1984, when 26 percent of those displaced were looking for work.

The number of labor force exits among displaced workers was very close to the 14-percent level observed in 1984. More than 1 of every 3 older workers (over 55 years of age) left the labor force after losing their jobs. Of the 3.4 million workers who found work following the displacement, 2.7 million were working at full-time wage and salary jobs. More than half of those re-employed earned as much or more in their new jobs as in their lost jobs.

About 2 of 3 displaced workers were men.

The geographic distribution of displaced workers was again heavily concentrated in the East North Central States. More than 1.1 million workers there had lost jobs since 1981.

Following displacement, reemployment was more difficult for black and Hispanic workers. The percentage of those who were reemployed as of January 1986 was about 10 percentage points lower than the comparable level for whites.

Source: U.S. Department of Labor, Bureau of Labor Statistics, *Monthly Labor Review,* June 1987.

Consumer Price Indexes

(1967 = 100)

Year	Commodities	Services	Housing	All items	Percent change[1]
1940	40.6	43.6	52.4	42.0	1.0
1945	56.3	48.2	59.1	53.9	2.3
1950	78.8	58.7	72.8	72.1	1.0
1955	85.1	70.9	82.3	80.2	−0.4
1960	91.5	83.5	90.2	88.7	1.6
1965	95.7	92.2	94.9	94.5	1.7
1970	113.5	121.6	118.9	116.3	5.9
1975	158.4	166.6	166.8	161.2	8.9
1980	233.9	270.3	263.3	246.8	13.6
1981	253.6	305.7	293.5	272.4	10.4
1982	263.8	333.3	314.7	289.1	6.1
1983	271.5	344.9	322.0	298.4	3.2
1984	280.7	363.0	361.7	311.1	4.3
1985	286.7	381.5	382.0	322.2	3.6

1. Over previous year. *Source:* Department of Labor, Bureau of Labor Statistics.

Consumer Price Index for All Urban Consumers

(1967 = 100)

Group	Feb. 1987	Feb. 1986	Group	Feb. 1987	Feb. 1986
All items	334.4	327.5	Fuel oil, coal, bottled gas	503.2	591.2
Food	330.1	315.3	House operation[1]	253.5	249.0
Alcoholic beverages	243.2	238.3	House furnishings	203.2	199.7
Apparel and upkeep	208.4	204.1	Transportation	310.0	319.2
Men's and boys' apparel	199.9	196.8	Medical care	452.4	422.3
Women's and girls' apparel	167.8	163.4	Personal care	296.4	289.1
Footwear	211.0	207.9	Tobacco products	368.3	344.7
Housing, total	365.1	356.5	Entertainment	278.7	272.0
Rent	288.0	273.7	Personal and educational		
Gas and electricity	428.9	444.5	expenses	452.0	417.7

1. Combines house furnishings and operation. *Source:* Department of Labor, Bureau of Labor Statistics.

Consumer Price Index for Urban Wage Earners and Clerical Workers

(1967 = 100)

Effective January 1978, the Consumer Price Index was revised, with two indexes now being produced: A new index for All Urban Consumers covers 80% of the non-institutional population; the other index, the Consumer Price Index for Urban Wage Earners and Clerical Workers, covers about half of those included in the new index and is a major revision of the one that had been published for many years.

	1987[1]	1985	1980	1975	1970	1965	1960	1955	1950
All items	330.5	318.5	247.0	161.2	116.3	94.5	88.7	80.2	72.1
Food total	329.4	301.8	255.3	175.4	114.9	94.4	88.0	81.6	—
Apparel and upkeep	213.7	205.0	177.4	142.3	116.1	93.7	89.6	84.1	79.0
Housing total	358.8	343.3	263.2	166.8	118.9	94.9	90.2	82.3	72.8
Rent	287.3	263.7	191.3	137.3	110.1	96.9	91.7	84.3	70.4
Gas and electricity	427.0	451.6	301.2	169.6	107.3	99.4	98.6	87.5	81.2
Fuel oil, coal, bottled gas	501.4	622.0	557.2	253.3	110.1	94.6	89.2	82.3	72.7
House operation[2]	250.1	243.4	202.9	158.1	113.4	95.3	93.8	89.9	—
House furnishings	198.4	197.6	172.6	144.4	111.4	97.1	99.3	99.2	95.5
Transportation	310.8	321.6	250.5	150.6	112.7	95.9	89.6	77.4	68.2
Medical care	452.3	401.2	267.2	168.6	120.6	89.5	79.1	64.8	53.7
Personal care	293.9	279.6	212.7	150.7	113.2	95.2	90.1	77.9	68.3
Entertainment	274.4	260.1	203.7	144.4	113.4	95.9	87.3	76.7	74.4

1. March 1987. 2. Combines house furnishings and operation. *Source:* Department of Labor, Bureau of Labor Statistics.

Total Family Income

(figures in percent)

	White				Black and other races			
Income range	1985	1980	1970	1960	1985	1980	1970	1960
Families (thousands)[1]	54,991	52,710	46,535	41,123	8,567	7,599	5,413	4,333
Under $2,500	1.6	1.6	5.6	15.1	3.9	5.0	15.6	39.8
$2,500 to $7,499	5.7	8.6	25.8	52.9	16.3	22.5	41.4	48.9
$7,500 to $12,499	8.7	13.1	33.4	24.6	14.8	18.5	25.6	9.9
$12,500 to $14,999	4.9	6.8	11.5	3.3	5.9	7.4	6.5	0.9
$15,000 to $19,999	10.3	14.1	13.8	2.2	12.1	12.8	7.4	0.3
$20,000 to $24,999	10.4	14.2	4.9	0.9	9.4	10.6	2.1	0.3
$25,000 to $34,999	19.2	20.8	3.2	—	14.7	12.9	1.1	—
$35,000 to $49,999	19.7	13.6	1.2	1.1	13.2	7.6	0.3	—
$50,000 and over	19.6	7.2	0.6	—	9.7	2.8	0.1	—
Median income	$29,152	$21,904	$10,236	$5,835	$18,635	$13,843	$6,516	$3,230

1. As of March 1985. *Source:* Department of Commerce, Bureau of the Census.

Per Capita Personal Income

Year	Amount	Year	Amount	Year	Amount	Year	Amount	Year	Amount
1929	$705	1960	$2,219	1969	3,667	1975	5,851	1981	10,940
1935	474	1964	2,592	1970	3,893	1976	6,402	1982	11,470
1940	593	1965	2,773	1971	4,132	1977	7,043	1983	12,093
1945	1,223	1966	$2,987	1972	$4,493	1978	$7,729	1984	13,115
1950	1,501	1967	3,167	1973	4,980	1979	8,638	1985	13,867
1955	1,881	1968	3,433	1974	5,428	1980	9,910	1986[1]	14,461

1. Preliminary. *Source:* Department of Commerce, Bureau of Economic Analysis.

Median Weekly Earnings of Full-Time Workers by Occupation and Sex

	MEN		WOMEN		TOTAL	
Occupation	Number of workers (in thousands)	Median weekly earnings	Number of workers (in thousands)	Median weekly earnings	Number of workers (in thousands)	Median weekly earnings
Managerial and prof. specialty	11,566	$610	8,966	$424	20,532	$511
Executive, admin, and managerial	6,110	623	4,012	405	10,121	514
Professional specialty	5,456	599	4,955	445	10,411	508
Technical, sales, and admin. support	9,048	449	15,170	290	24,217	327
Technicians and related support	1,549	505	1,279	360	2,828	435
Sales occupations	4,396	454	2,910	243	7,306	354
Administrative support, incl. clerical	3,103	413	10,980	291	14,083	308
Service occupations	3,852	292	4,004	188	7,856	222
Private household	13	(1)	331	130	343	134
Protective service	1,366	410	131	313	1,496	403
Service, except private household and protective	2,474	244	3,543	191	6,016	209
Precision production, craft, and repair	10,141	423	923	276	11,064	412
Mechanics and repairers	3,567	422	153	409	3,720	422
Construction trades	3,495	406	30	(1)	3,526	405
Other precision production, craft, and repair	3,078	449	740	260	3,818	408
Operators, fabricators, and laborers	10,341	336	3,480	225	13,821	303
Machine operators, assemblers, and inspectors	4,143	356	2,764	220	6,907	295
Transportation and material moving occupations	3,473	375	204	296	3,677	369
Handlers, equipment cleaners, helpers, and laborers	2,724	275	512	236	3,237	269
Farming, forestry, and fishing	1,147	222	141	184	1,288	218

1. Data not shown where base is less than 100,000. NOTE: Figures are for the fourth quarter of 1986. *Source:* U.S. Department of Labor, Bureau of Labor Statistics, "Employment and Earnings," January 1987.

The Public Debt

	Gross debt			Gross debt	
Year	Amount (in millions)	Per capita	Year	Amount (in millions)	Per capita
1800 (Jan. 1)	$ 83	$ 15.87	1950	$256,087[2]	$1,688.30
1860 (June 30)	65	2.06	1955	272,807[2]	1,650.63
1865	2,678	75.01	1960	284,093[2]	1,572.31
1900	1,263	16.60	1965	313,819[2]	1,612.70
1920	24,299	228.23	1970	370,094[2]	1,807.09
1925	20,516	177.12	1975	533,189	2,496.90
1930	16,185	131.51	1980	907,701	3,969.55
1935	28,701	225.55	1984	1,572,266	6,626.57
1940	42,968	325.23	1985	1,823,103	7,598.51
1945	258,682	1,848.60	1986[1]	2,125,303	8,779.74

1. Preliminary, Sept. 30, 1986. 2. Adjusted to exclude issues to the international Monetary Fund and other international lending institutions to conform to the budget presentation. *Source:* Department of the Treasury, Financial Management Service.

Gross National Product or Expenditure

(in billions)

Item	1986	1985	1984	1983	1980	1970	1960	1950	1929
Gross national product	$4,206	$3,998	$3,774	$3,304	$2,626	$982	$506	$286	$103
GNP in constant (1972) dollars[1]	3,675	3,585	3,492	1,534	1,481	1,075	737	534	315
Personal consumption expenditures	2,763	2,601	2,423	2,155	1,673	619	325	192	77
Durable goods	388	359	331	279	212	85	43	31	9
Nondurable goods	933	905	872	801	676	265	151	98	38
Services	1,442	1,336	1,220	1,074	785	269	131	63	30
Gross private domestic investment	684	661	674	471	395	141	76	54	16
Residential structures	217	192	179	128	105	36	24	20	4
Nonresidential structures	460	458	428	129	109	38	18	9	5
Producers' durable equipment	317	303	280	226	190	64	30	18	6
Change in business inventories	7	11	67	−13	−6	4	4	7	2
Net export of goods and services	−104	−79	−59	−8	23	4	4	2	1
Government purchases	864	815	737	685	535	219	100	38	8
Federal	366	354	313	269	199	96	54	19	1
National defense	278	259	237	200	132	74	44	14	n.a.
Other	89	95	76	69	67	22	9	5	n.a.
State and local	498	461	424	415	336	123	47	20	7
Implicit price deflator[1]	115	112	108	215	177	91	69	54	33

1. For 1984, 1985, and 1986 GNP in constant (1982) dollars. NOTE: n.a. = not available. *Source:* Department of Commerce, Bureau of Economic Analysis.

Producer Price Indexes by Major Commodity Groups

(1967 - 100)

Commodity	1986	1985	1980	1975	1970	1965	1960
All commodities	299.8	308.7	268.8	174.9	110.4	96.6	94.9
Farm products	224.7	230.5	249.4	186.7	111.0	98.7	97.2
Processed foods	265.1	260.4	241.2	182.6	112.1	95.5	89.5
Textile products and apparel	211.1	210.4	183.5	137.9	107.1	99.8	99.5
Hides, skins, and leather products	296.7	286.1	248.9	148.5	110.3	94.3	90.8
Fuels and related products and power	483.5	633.6	574.0	245.1	106.2	95.5	96.1
Chemicals and allied products	299.7	303.2	260.3	181.3	102.2	99.0	101.8
Rubber and plastic products	246.1	245.9	217.4	150.2	108.3	95.9	103.1
Lumber and wood products	305.3	303.6	288.9	176.9	113.6	95.9	95.3
Pulp, paper, and allied products	335.3	327.2	249.2	170.4	108.2	96.2	98.1
Metals and metal products	311.3	314.9	286.4	185.6	116.6	96.4	92.4
Machinery and equipment	303.3	298.9	239.8	161.4	111.4	93.9	92.0
Furniture and household durables	223.9	221.6	187.7	139.7	107.5	96.9	99.0
Nonmetallic mineral products	352.0	347.8	283.0	174.0	112.9	97.5	97.2
Transportation equipment (Dec. 1968—100)	276.2	269.5	207.0	141.5	104.6	98.5	98.8
Miscellaneous products	n.a.	300.9	258.8	147.7	109.9	95.9	93.0

Source: Department of Commerce, Bureau of Economic Analysis.

Life Insurance in Force

(in millions of dollars)

As of Dec. 31	Ordinary	Group	Industrial	Credit	Total
1915	$16,650	$100	$4,279	—	$21,029
1930	78,756	9,801	17,693	73	106,413
1945	101,550	22,172	27,675	365	151,762
1950	149,071	47,793	33,415	3,844	234,168
1955	216,812	101,345	39,682	14,493	373,332
1960	341,881	175,903	39,563	29,101	586,448
1965	499,638	308,078	39,818	53,020	900,554
1970	734,730	551,357	38,644	77,392	1,402,123
1980	1,760,474	1,579,355	35,994	165,215	3,541,038
1984	2,887,574	2,392,358	30,104	189,951	5,499,987
1985	3,247,289	2,561,595	28,250	215,973	6,053,107
1986	3,658,203	2,801,049	27,168	233,859	6,720,279

Source: American Council of Life Insurance.

Farm Indexes

(1977 - 100)

Year	Prices paid by farmers[1]	Prices rec'd by farmers[2]	Ratio
1950	37	56	151
1955	40	51	128
1960	44	52	118
1965	49	54	115
1970	56	60	109
1975	90	101	113
1980	137	134	97
1984	160	142	86
1985	163	128	79
1986	160	123	77

1. Commodities, interest, and taxes and wage rates. 2. All crops and livestock. *Source:* Department of Agriculture, National Agricultural Statistics Service.

Consumer Credit

(installment credit outstanding; in billions of dollars, seasonally adjusted)

Holder	1986	1985	1984	1983	1982	1981	1980	1975
Commercial banks	261.6	240.8	209.2	169.3	149.1	146.0	145.6	83.0
Finance companies	136.5	120.1	96.1	86.2	77.0	73.1	63.8	32.7
Credit unions	77.9	75.1	66.5	53.1	46.9	45.6	43.7	25.5
Retailers[1]	40.6	39.2	37.1	34.2	29.4	28.5	26.1	16.7
Other[2]	61.2	59.9	44.7	33.5	24.8	21.1	18.5	9.2
Total	**577.8**	**535.1**	**453.6**	**376.3**	**327.2**	**314.3**	**297.7**	**167.7**

1. Excludes 30-day charge credit held by retailers, oil and gas companies, and travel and entertainment companies. 2. Includes mutual savings banks, savings and loan associations, and gasoline companies. *Source:* Federal Reserve Bulletin.

Estimated Annual Retail and Wholesale Sales by Kind of Business

(in millions of dollars)

Kind of business	1986	1985
Retail trade, total	1,454,411	1,379,621
Building materials, hardware, garden supply, and mobile home dealers	88,093	75,556
Automotive dealers	335,822	311,859
Furniture, home furnishings, and equipment stores	78,487	69,584
General merchandise group stores	155,262	149,592
Food stores	296,040	283,987
Gasoline service stations	86,618	101,266
Apparel and accessory stores	80,775	74,321
Eating and drinking places	144,966	133,457
Drug stores and proprietary stores	49,316	46,191
Liquor stores	19,792	19,491
Merchant wholesale trade, total	1,381,311	1,374,752
Total, (excluding farm-product raw materials)	1,302,116	1,281,500
Durable goods, total	664,108	630,312
Motor vehicles and automotive parts and supplies	145,216	132,391
Furniture and home furnishings	26,337	24,210
Lumber and other construction materials	51,435	46,193
Electrical goods	92,350	88,753
Hardware, plumbing, heating and supplies	43,618	41,623
Machinery, equipment, supplies	169,216	165,820
Scrap and waste materials	(s)	(s)
Nondurable goods, total	717,203	744,440
Total, (excluding farm-product raw materials)	638,008	651,188
Paper and paper products	40,521	36,798
Drugs, drug proprietaries, and druggists' sundries	27,576	25,095
Apparel, piece goods, and notions	(s)	40,701
Groceries and related products	234,748	217,085
Beer, wine, distilled alcoholic beverages	40,262	39,358
Miscellaneous nondurable goods	109,170	104,008
Tobacco and tobacco products	(s)	(s)

NOTE: (S) = does not meet publication standards. *Source:* Department of Commerce, Bureau of the Census.

Weekly Earnings of Full-Time Women Workers

Major occupation group	1986 weekly earnings	% Men's weekly earnings
Managerial and professional specialty	$414	68.1
Executive, administrative, and managerial	395	63.7
Professional specialty	428	71.4
Technical, sales, and administrative support	282	64.5
Technicians and related support	343	70.0
Sales occupations	239	53.4
Administrative support, including clerical	284	70.4
Service occupations	191	67.2
Precision production, craft, and repair	277	66.3
Operators, fabricators, and laborers	225	67.8
Machine operators, assemblers, and inspectors	223	63.0
Transportation and material moving	287	77.2
Handlers, equipment cleaners, helpers, and laborers	226	83.4
Farming, forestry, and fishing	187	85.0
Total; all occupations	**290**	**69.2**

1. Median usual weekly earnings. Half the workers earn more and half the workers usually earn less each week. *Source:* U.S. Department of Labor, Bureau of Labor Statistics.

Median Family Income

(in current dollars)

Year	Income	Percent change	Year	Income	Percent change
1960	$ 5,620	—	1981	22,388	6.5
1970	9,867	—	1982	23,433	4.7
1975	13,719	—	1983	24,580	4.9
1978	17,640	10.2	1984	25,948	5.1
1979	19,661	11.5	1985	27,144	5.0
1980	21,023	6.9	1986	28,236	4.0

Source: U.S. Department of Labor, Bureau of Labor Statistics, *Employment and Earnings.*

Expenditures for New Plant and Equipment[1]

(in billions of dollars)

Year	Manufacturing	Transportation[2]	Total nonmanufacturing	Total
1950	$7.73	$2.87	$18.08	$25.81
1955	12.50	3.10	24.58	37.08
1960	16.36	3.54	32.63	48.99
1965	25.41	5.66	45.39	70.79
1970	36.99	7.17	69.16	106.15
1975	53.66	9.95	108.95	162.60
1980	112.33	16.60	202.15	314.47
1981	126.54	15.84	222.72	349.26
1982	120.68	14.79	226.79	347.47
1983	116.20	13.97	227.15	343.35
1984	138.82	16.52	260.16	398.99
1985	153.48	18.02	278.46	431.94
1986	142.73	18.75	284.30	427.03

1. Data exclude agriculture. 2. Transportation is included in total nonmanufacturing. NOTE: This series was revised in February 1987. *Source:* Department of Commerce, Bureau of Economic Analysis.

New Housing Starts[1] and Mobile Homes Shipped

(in thousands)

Year	No. of units started	Year	No. of units started	Year	Mobile homes shipped
1900	189	1970	1,469	1965	217
1910	387	1975	1,171	1970	401
1920	247	1977	2,002	1975	213
1925	937	1978	2,036	1978	276
1930	330	1979	1,760	1979	277
1935	221	1980	1,313	1980	222
1940	603	1981	1,100	1981	241
1945	326	1982	1,072	1982	240
1950	1,952	1983	1,712	1983	296
1955	1,646	1984	1,756	1984	296
1960[1]	1,296	1985	1,745	1985	284
1965	1,510	1986	1,807	1986	244

1. Prior to 1960, starts limited to nonfarm housing; from 1960 on, figures include farm housing. *Sources:* Department of Commerce, Housing Construction Statistics, 1900–1965, and Construction Reports, Housing Starts, 1970–83, Manufactured Housing Institute, 1965–76; National Conference of States on Building Codes and Standards.

Shareholders in Public Corporations

Characteristic	1985	1983	1980	1975	1970	1965	1959
Individual shareholders (thousands)	47,040	42,360	30,200	25,270	30,850	20,120	12,490
Owners of shares listed on New York Stock Exchange (thousands)	25,263	26,029	23,804	17,950	18,290	12,430	8,510
Adult shareowner incidence in population	1 in 4	1 in 4	1 in 5	1 in 6	1 in 4	1 in 6	1 in 8
Median household income	$36,800	$33,200	$27,750	$19,000	$13,500	$9,500	$7,000
Adult shareowners with household income: under $10,000 (thousands)	2,151	1,460	1,742	3,420	8,170	10,080	9,340
$10,000 and over (thousands)	40,999	36,261	25,715	19,970	20,130	8,410	2,740
Adult female shareowners (thousands)	22,509	20,385	13,696	11,750	14,290	9,430	6,350
Adult male shareowners (thousands)	22,484	19,226	14,196	11,630	14,340	9,060	5,740
Median age	44	45	46	53	48	49	49

NOTE: Latest figures available. *Source:* New York Stock Exchange.

50 Most Active Stocks in 1986

Stock	Share volume	Stock	Share volume	Stock	Share volume
American Tel. & Tel. (1)	418,312,400	Morris (Philip) (50)	157,859,500	Coca-Cola Co.	128,407,400
Int'l Business Machines (2)	349,992,400	RJR Nabisco (36)[3]	157,126,900	Salomon Inc. (18)[4]	126,657,700
USX Corp.[1] (40)	329,088,700	Ford Motor (8)	156,021,300	Southern Co. (48)	126,509,100
Mobil Corp. (9)	211,675,800	Digital Equipment (29)	147,779,200	BankAmerica Corp. (41)	125,420,100
Eastman Kodak (37)	206,616,700	Commonwealth Edison (31)	147,537,900	Pacific Gas & Electric	122,293,700
Exxon Corp. (7)	190,052,300	Occidental Petroleum	146,899,600	AMR Corp. (21)	121,811,800
General Motors (12)	186,716,500	Chrysler Corp. (25)	146,594,200	Pan Am Corp. (16)	119,986,300
Navistar International[2]	184,789,300	K mart Corp. (47)	144,786,700	PepsiCo, Inc.	119,594,900
Goodyear Tire & Rubber	183,681,800	Chevron Corp.	143,664,400	Atlantic Richfield (15)	119,003,700
American Express (4)	179,049,700	ITT Corp. (17)	142,518,600	Middle South Utilities (14)	117,813,600
Phillips Petroleum (3)	178,742,300	Baxter Travenol (23)	141,077,000	Texas Utilities	115,740,700
Sears, Roebuck (19)	172,820,500	Johnson & Johnson (43)	140,158,500	Boeing Co. (46)	115,218,500
Union Carbide (28)	167,940,800	BellSouth Corp.	135,364,900	Motorola, Inc. (34)	114,536,100
Schlumberger Ltd. (24)	166,664,300	Western Air Lines	134,404,900	Sperry Corp. (27)	113,641,500
Texaco Inc. (13)	164,555,200	Hewlett-Packard (20)	133,768,600	Archer-Daniels-Midland	112,073,600
Merrill Lynch (11)	163,110,700	Dow Chemical (42)	133,292,400	Philadelphia Electric	111,598,800
General Electric (22)	161,236,200	Federal Nat'l Mortgage (30)	132,018,500		

NOTE: 1985 rank in parentheses, if among top 50. 1. Formerly United States Steel. 2. Formerly International Harvester. 3. Formerly Reynolds (R.J.) Industries. 4. Formerly Phibro-Salomon Inc. *Source:* New York Stock Exchange.

50 Companies With Largest Number of Stockholders

Company	Stockholders	Company	Stockholders
American Tel. & Tel.	2,782,000	Detroit Edison	218,000
General Motors	1,854,000	du Pont de Nemours	217,000
BellSouth Corp.	1,583,000	Ohio Edison	202,000
Bell Atlantic	1,406,000	Centerior Energy Corp.	200,000
NYNEX Corp.	1,285,000	Occidental Petroleum	193,000
American Information Tech.	1,250,000	USX Corp.[1]	191,000
Southwestern Bell	1,246,000	Dominion Resources	189,000
Pacific Telesis Group	1,109,000	Tenneco Inc.	187,000
US WEST	1,083,000	Atlantic Richfield	178,000
International Business Machines	793,000	Consolidated Edison	178,000
Exxon Corporation	740,000	Niagara Mohawk Power	175,000
General Electric	492,000	Eastman Kodak	174,000
GTE Corporation	424,000	Northeast Utilities	172,000
Bell Canada Enterprises	332,000	Union Electric	172,000
Sears, Roebuck	320,000	Amoco Corp.	165,000
Pacific Gas & Electric	298,000	Southern California Edison	158,000
Philadelphia Electric	295,000	Westinghouse Electric	150,000
Southern Company	287,000	Pennsylvania Power & Light	148,000
Texaco Inc.	278,000	BankAmerica Corp.	138,000
Ford Motor	266,000	Chrysler Corp.	135,000
American Electric Power	265,000	Middle South Utilities	132,000
Chevron Corp.	261,000	Consumers Power	130,000
Mobil Corp.	260,000	Long Island Lighting	130,000
Commonwealth Edison	254,000	Duquesne Light	125,000
Public Service Enterprises	218,000	Allied Signal	124,000

1. Formerly United States Steel. Note: As of Dec. 31, 1986. *Source:* New York Stock Exchange.

New York Stock Exchange Seat Sales for Cash, 1986

	Price				Price		
Month	High	Low	Number	Month	High	Low	Number
January	—	—	—	July	$505,000	—	1
February	—	—	—	August	—	—	—
March	$465,000	$460,000	2	September	480,000	$475,000	2
April	500,000	455,000	4	October	510,000	475,000	4
May	575,000	535,000	2	November	500,000	460,000	4
June	580,000	575,000	3	December	600,000	515,000	3

NOTE: In addition, there were four private seat sales, ranging from a high of $480,000 and a low of $410,000. *Source:* New York Stock Exchange.

Largest Businesses, 1986

(in thousands of dollars)

Source: FORTUNE 500 and SERVICE 500 © 1987 Time Inc. All rights reserved.

50 LARGEST INDUSTRIAL CORPORATIONS

	Sales	Assets
General Motors	$102,813,700	$72,593,000
Exxon	69,888,000	69,484,000
Ford Motor	62,715,800	37,933,000
International Business Machines	51,250,000	57,814,000
Mobil	44,866,000	39,412,000
General Electric	35,211,000	34,591,000
American Tel. & Tel.	34,087,000	38,883,000
Texaco	31,613,000	34,940,000
E.I. du Pont de Nemours	27,148,000	26,733,000
Chevron	24,351,000	34,583,000
Chrysler	22,513,500	14,463,200
Philip Morris	20,681,000	17,642,000
Amoco	18,281,000	23,706,000
RJR Nabisco	16,998,000	17,019,000
Shell Oil	16,833,000	26,214,000
Boeing	16,341,000	11,068,000
United Technologies	15,669,157	11,091,787
Procter & Gamble	15,439,000	13,055,000
Occidental Petroleum	15,344,100	17,466,777
Atlantic Richfield	14,585,802	21,603,543
Tenneco	14,558,000	18,021,000
USX	14,000,000	21,823,000
McDonnell Douglas	12,660,600	7,910,700
Rockwell International	12,295,700	7,703,400
Allied-Signal	11,794,000	11,268,000
Eastman Kodak	11,550,000	12,902,000
Dow Chemical	11,113,000	12,242,000
Westinghouse Electric	10,731,000	8,481,800
Goodyear Tire & Rubber	10,327,700	8,609,500
Lockheed	10,273,000	5,943,000
Phillips Petroleum	9,786,000	12,399,000
Xerox	9,377,000	10,608,000
Sun	9,376,000	11,684,000
PepsiCo	9,290,800	8,024,700

Standard Oil	9,219,000	15,955,000
General Dynamic	9,211,400	4,552,500
Kraft	8,742,200	4,749,300
Coca-Cola	8,668,556	8,373,438
Minnesota Mining & Manufacturing	8,602,000	7,348,000
Sara Lee	7,937,722	3,503,106
ITT	7,895,540	12,920,407
Union Carbide	7,828,000	7,571,000
Anheuser-Busch	7,677,200	5,833,800
Digital Equipment	7,590,357	7,173,326
Unocal	7,482,000	10,133,000
Unisys	7,432,400	9,408,800
Caterpillar	7,321,000	6,288,000
Raytheon	7,307,952	3,555,899
LTV	7,271,400	5,498,700
Georgia-Pacific	7,223,000	5,114,000

25 LARGEST RETAILING COMPANIES

	Sales	*Assets*
Sears Roebuck	$44,281,500	$65,994,600
K mart	24,246,000	10,578,000
Safeway Stores	20,311,480	7,443,877
Kroger	18,386,408	4,076,447
J.C. Penney	14,740,000	11,188,000
American Stores	14,021,484	3,590,174
Wal-Mart Stores	11,909,076	4,049,092
Southland	11,081,835	3,421,088
Federated Department Stores	10,512,425	5,687,738
May Department Stores	10,376,000	6,209,000
Dayton Hudson	9,773,800	5,282,000
Lucky Stores	8,775,871	1,551,671
Winn-Dixie Stores	8,225,244	1,355,354
Great Atlantic & Pacific Tea	6,615,422	1,663,760
F.W. Woolworth	6,501,000	2,850,000
Supermarkets General	5,560,130	1,173,053
Albertson's	5,379,643	1,264,656
Zayre	5,350,638	1,879,122
Marriott	5,266,500	4,579,300
Melville	5,262,364	1,998,782
Allied Stores	5,025,000	5,124,683
Montgomery Ward	4,383,000	3,827,000
McDonald's	4,143,508	5,968,507
Carter Hawley Hale Stores	4,089,794	2,161,876
Stop & Shop Cos.	4,033,843	1,154,519

10 LARGEST TRANSPORTATION COMPANIES

	Operating revenues	*Assets*
UAL	$9,196,233	$8,716,517
United Parcel Service of America	8,619,703	4,801,133
Burlington Northern	6,941,413	10,650,956
Union Pacific	6,688,000	10,863,000
CSX	6,345,000	12,661,000
AMR	6,018,175	7,527,969
Santa Fe Southern Pacific	5,801,600	11,601,800
Delta Air Lines	4,460,062	3,785,462
Texas Air	4,406,897	8,194,611
Norfolk Southern	4,076,407	9,752,445

10 LARGEST DIVERSIFIED FINANCIAL COMPANIES

	Assets	*Revenues*
Federal Nat'l Mortgage Ass'n	$100,406,000	$10,540,000
American Express	99,476,000	14,652,000
Salomon	78,164,000	6,789,000
Aetna Life & Casualty	66,829,900	20,482,900
Merrill Lynch	53,013,471	9,606,349
CIGNA	50,015,800	17,064,100
First Boston	48,618,206	1,309,765
Travelers Corp.	46,299,600	16,046,600
Morgan Stanley Group	29,190,361	2,463,484
Bear Stearns Cos.	26,939,440	1,188,951

10 LARGEST LIFE INSURANCE COMPANIES

	Assets	*Premium and annuity income*
Prudential of America	$103,317,115	$17,380,277
Metropolitan Life	81,581,350	12,148,965
Equitable Life Assurance	48,577,698	5,500,913
Aetna Life	42,957,155	10,506,887
New York Life	29,793,627	3,477,186
Teachers Insurance & Annuity	27,887,103	2,654,607
John Hancock Mutual Life	27,213,497	4,173,912
Travelers	27,210,137	4,023,926
Connecticut General Life	24,806,504	2,869,639
Northwestern Mutual Life	20,187,343	2,934,270

10 LARGEST COMMERCIAL BANKS

	Assets	*Deposits*
Citicorp	$196,124,000	$114,689,000
BankAmerica Corp.	104,189,000	82,205,000
Chase Manhattan Corp.	94,765,815	66,002,844
J.P. Morgan & Co.	76,039,000	42,960,000
Manufacturers Hanover Corp.	74,397,389	45,544,277
Security Pacific Corp.	62,606,000	38,408,000
Chemical New York Corp.	60,564,123	39,054,910
Bankers Trust New York Corp.	56,419,945	29,535,520
First Interstate Bancorp	55,421,736	39,457,006
Wells Fargo & Co.	44,577,100	32,992,800

10 LARGEST UTILITIES

	Assets	*Operating revenues*
GTE	$27,401,801	$15,111,528
BellSouth	26,218,100	11,444,100
NYNEX	21,804,600	11,341,500
Bell Atlantic	21,090,900	9,920,800
Pacific Gas & Electric	21,002,253	7,816,661
Pacific Telesis Group	20,320,500	8,977,300
Southwestern Bell	20,299,800	7,902,400
U S West	18,747,400	8,308,400
American Information Technologies	18,739,400	9,362,100
Southern	18,141,116	6,846,591

New Business Concerns and Business Failures

Formations and Failures	1985[1]	1984	1983	1982	1981	1980	1975	1970
Business formations								
Index, net formations (1967 = 100)	121.2	121.3	117.5	113.2	118.6	122.4	107.0	106.4
New Incorporations (1,000)	669	635	600	567	582	534	326	264
Failures, number (1,000)	57.0	52.0	31.3	24.9	16.8	11.7	11.4	10.7
Rate per 10,000 concerns	114	107	110	88	61	42	43	44

1. Preliminary. *Sources:* U.S. Bureau of Economic Analysis and Dun & Bradstreet Corporation.

50 Leading Stocks in Market Value

Stock	Market value (millions)	Listed shares (millions)
International Business Machines	$74,120	615.7
Exxon Corp.	63,898	906.3
General Electric	39,842	463.3
American Telephone & Telegraph	26,935	1,072.0
General Motors	21,115	319.9
du Pont de Nemours	20,256	240.4
Merck & Co.	18,809	151.8
BellSouth Corp.	18,533	320.9
Amoco Corp.	17,649	269.5
Morris (Philip)	17,372	239.6
Mobil Corp.	17,341	429.5
Eastman Kodak	17,127	248.7
Coca-Cola Co.	15,579	414.1
Chevron Corp.	15,523	342.1
Sears, Roebuck	15,108	381.3
Ford Motor	14,155	250.5
Minnesota Mining & Manufacturing	13,806	118.0
Bell Atlantic	13,583	199.7
Digital Equipment	13,510	129.0
Atlantic Richfield	13,095	217.4
NYNEX Corp.	13,073	202.7
Wal-Mart Stores	13,032	280.3
American Information Technologies (Ameritech)	12,997	98.1
American Home Products	12,986	168.9
Procter & Gamble	12,932	169.3
GTE Corp.	12,875	220.6
Johnson & Johnson	12,567	191.9
Dow Chemical	12,512	213.4
American Express	12,491	220.1
RJR Nabisco[1]	12,009	242.6
Bristol-Myers	11,734	142.0
Pacific Telesis	11,460	215.2
Southwestern Bell	11,182	99.6
Abbott Laboratories	11,145	243.6
Eli Lilly	10,768	146.0
Hewlett-Packard	10,697	257.0
U S WEST	10,483	193.2
Westinghouse Electric	10,311	182.9
American Int'l Group	10,142	165.9
Pfizer Inc.	10,065	165.0
Texaco Inc.	9,875	274.3
Royal Dutch Petroleum	9,713	101.7
Schlumberger Ltd.	9,594	303.4
Pacific Gas & Electric	8,808	363.2
McDonald's Corp.	8,442	138.1
Dun & Bradstreet Corp.	8,066	76.6
SmithKline Beckman	7,957	83.4
Kellogg Co.	7,954	153.7
Boeing Co.	7,937	155.2
Kraft, Inc.[2]	7,799	164.6
Total	**$788,962**	**12,962.2**

NOTE: As of Dec. 31, 1986. 1. Formerly Reynolds (R.J.) Industries. 2. Formerly Dart & Kraft. *Source:* New York Stock Exchange.

Per Capita Personal Income by States

State	1986[1]	1985	1984	1980
Alabama	$11,115	$10,670	$ 9,987	$ 7,465
Alaska	17,744	18,140	17,550	13,007
Arizona	13,220	12,771	11,822	8,854
Arkansas	10,773	10,471	9,734	7,113
California	16,778	16,070	14,471	11,021
Colorado	15,113	14,797	13,848	10,143
Connecticut	19,208	18,101	16,547	11,532
Delaware	15,010	14,269	13,692	10,059
D.C.	18,980	18,239	16,870	12,251
Florida	14,281	13,744	12,773	9,246
Georgia	13,224	12,546	11,548	8,021
Hawaii	14,691	13,845	13,028	10,129
Idaho	11,432	11,130	10,146	8,105
Illinois	15,420	14,736	13,705	10,454
Indiana	12,944	12,443	11,725	8,914
Iowa	13,222	12,603	12,123	9,226
Kansas	14,379	13,782	13,311	9,880
Kentucky	11,129	10,815	10,232	7,679
Louisiana	11,227	11,261	10,741	8,412
Maine	12,709	11,873	10,849	7,760
Maryland	16,588	15,862	14,443	10,394
Massachusetts	17,516	16,387	14,755	10,103
Michigan	14,064	13,608	12,621	9,801
Minnesota	14,737	14,092	13,212	9,673
Mississippi	9,552	9,182	8,684	6,573
Missouri	13,657	13,228	12,075	8,812
Montana	$11,904	$10,984	$10,607	$ 8,342
Nebraska	13,777	13,286	12,572	8,895
Nevada	15,074	14,479	13,298	10,848
New Hampshire	15,922	14,947	13,386	9,150
New Jersey	18,284	17,214	15,389	10,966
New Mexico	11,037	10,909	10,256	7,940
New York	17,118	16,083	14,341	10,179
North Carolina	12,245	11,605	10,852	7,780
North Dakota	12,284	12,052	12,290	8,642
Ohio	13,743	13,223	12,326	9,399
Oklahoma	12,368	12,215	11,629	9,018
Oregon	13,217	12,630	11,613	9,309
Pennsylvania	13,944	13,426	12,292	9,353
Rhode Island	14,670	13,926	12,860	9,227
South Carolina	11,096	10,626	10,111	7,392
South Dakota	11,850	11,159	10,904	7,800
Tennessee	11,831	11,230	10,400	7,711
Texas	13,523	13,467	12,575	9,439
Utah	10,743	10,491	9,715	7,671
Vermont	12,845	12,111	10,828	7,957
Virginia	15,374	14,553	13,291	9,413
Washington	14,498	13,882	12,755	10,256
West Virginia	10,530	10,190	9,708	7,764
Wisconsin	13,796	13,152	12,378	9,364
Wyoming	13,230	13,212	12,238	11,018
United States	**14,461**	**13,867**	**12,772**	**9,494**

1. Preliminary. *Source:* U.S. Department of Commerce, Bureau of Economic Analysis, *Survey of Current Business.*

National Labor Organizations With Membership Over 100,000

Members[1]	Union
974,000	Automobile, Aerospace and Agricultural Implement Workers of America, International Union, United
115,000	Bakery, Confectionary, and Tobacco Workers International Union
110,000	Boilermakers, Iron Ship Builders, Blacksmiths, Forgers and Helpers, International Brotherhood of
95,000	Bricklayers and Allied Craftsmen, International Union of
609,000	Carpenters and Joiners of America, United Brotherhood of
228,000	Clothing and Textile Workers Union, Amalgamated
524,000	Communications Workers of America
1,800,000	Education Association, National (Ind.)
200,000	Electrical, Radio and Machine Workers, International Union of
85,000	Electrical, Radio and Machine Workers of America, United (Ind.)
791,000	Electrical Workers, International Brotherhood of
142,000	Fire Fighters, International Association of
989,000	Food and Commercial Workers International Union, United
199,000	Government Employees, American Federation of
141,000	Graphic Communications Workers
327,000	Hotel and Restaurant Employees and Bartenders, International Union
140,000	Iron Workers
383,000	Laborers' International Union of North America
210,000	Ladies' Garment Workers' Union, International
186,000	Letter Carriers, National Association of
520,000	Machinists and Aerospace Workers, International Association of
230,000	Mine Workers of America, United (Ind.)
188,000	Nurses' Association; American (Ind.)
125,000	Office and Professional Employees International Union
108,000	Oil, Chemical and Atomic Workers International Union
350,000	Operating Engineers, International Union of
133,000	Painters and Allied Trades of the United States and Canada, International Brotherhood of
232,000	Paper Workers International Union, United
226,000	Plumbing and Pipe Fitting Industry of the United States and Canada, United Association of Journeymen and Apprentices of the
160,000[2]	Police, Fraternal Order of (Ind.)*
232,000	Postal Workers Union, American
102,000	Railway, Airline and Steamship Clerks, Freight Handlers, Express and Station Employees, Brotherhood of
106,000	Retail, Wholesale and Department Store Union
106,000	Rubber, Cork, Linoleum and Plastic Workers of America, United
688,000	Service Employees International Union
144,000[2]	Sheet Metal Workers' International Association
997,000	State, County and Municipal Employees of America, American Federation of
572,000	Steelworkers of America, United
470,000	Teachers, American Federation of
1,800,000	Teamsters, Chauffeurs, Warehousemen and Helpers of America, International Brotherhood of (Ind.)
160,000	Transit Union, Amalgamated
108,000	Transportation Union, United

1. Data are for 1986. 2. 1982. *Did not reply. NOTE: Figures are most recent available.

Work Stoppages Involving 1,000 Workers or More[1]

Year	Work stop-pages	Workers involved (thousands)	Man-days idle (thousands)	Year	Work stop-pages	Workers involved (thousands)	Man-days idle (thousands)
1950	424	1,698	30,390	1977	298	1,212	21,258
1955	363	2,055	21,180	1978	219	1,006	23,774
1960	222	896	13,260	1979	235	1,021	20,409
1965	268	999	15,140	1980	187	795	20,844
1970	381	2,468	52,761	1981	145	729	16,908
1972	250	975	16,764	1982	96	656	9,061
1973	317	1,400	16,260	1983	81	909	17,461
1974	424	1,796	31,809	1984	68	391	8,499
1975	235	965	17,563	1985	61	584	7,079
1976	231	1,519	23,962	1986	72	900	11,861

1. The number of stoppages and workers relate to stoppages that began in the year. Days of idleness include all stoppages in effect. Workers are counted more than once if they were involved in more than one stoppage during the year. *Source:* U.S. Department of Labor, Bureau of Labor Statistics, *Monthly Labor Review, August 1986.*

Corporate Profits

(in billions of dollars)

Item	1987[1]	1986	1985	1984	1983	1980	1975	1970
Domestic industries	222.0	208.5	190.8	200.1	167.2	161.9	107.6	62.4
Financial	32.7	29.3	21.0	19.2	29.6	26.9	11.8	12.1
Nonfinancial	189.3	179.2	169.7	180.9	137.6	134.9	95.8	50.2
Manufacturing	78.9	76.1	73.0	88.5	65.2	72.9	52.6	26.6
Wholesale and retail trade	55.6	49.8	49.7	50.7	33.4	23.6	21.3	9.5
Other	15.9	14.8	14.0	13.0	16.4	38.4	21.9	14.1
Rest of world	38.7	35.5	31.8	32.2	24.8	29.9	13.0	6.5
Total	**260.7**	**244.1**	**222.6**	**232.3**	**225.2**	**191.7**	**120.6**	**68.9**

1. Preliminary. *Source:* U.S. Bureau of Economic Analysis, *Survey of Current Business.*

Foreign Assistance

(in millions of dollars)

Calendar years	Non-military programs: Net new grants	Net new credits	Net other assistance	Military programs: Net grants	Net credits	Total net assistance
1945–1950	$18,413	$8,086	—	$ 1,525	—	$28,023
1951–55	10,459	550	$ 541	13,286	$ 7	24,842
1956–60	8,291	1,462	2,226	13,269	42	25,290
1961–65	9,384	5,538	576	8,295	−16	23,777
1966–70	8,808	9,238	−564	13,296	192	30,970
1971–75	12,939	5,479	−725	16,940	2,044	36,677
1976–80	14,268	10,919	−286	5,662	6,959	37,522
1981–1985	29,025	7,082	−2	9,297	10,836	56,238
1986	7,900	155	21	4,131	1,212	13,419
Total postwar period	**119,487**	**48,508**	**1,787**	**85,700**	**21,277**	**276,758**

1. Excludes investment in international nonmonetary financial institutions of $15,923 million. 2. Includes transactions after V-J Day (Sept. 2, 1945). NOTE: Detail may not add to total due to rounding. *Source:* Department of Commerce, Bureau of Economic Analysis.

The Federal Budget—Receipts and Outlays

(in billions of dollars)

Description	1988[1]	1987[1]	1986
RECEIPTS BY SOURCE			
Individual income taxes	392.8	364.0	349.0
Corporation income taxes	117.2	104.8	63.1
Social insurance taxes and contributions:	333.2	301.5	283.9
Employment taxes and contributions	307.4	273.2	255.1
Unemployment insurance	22.2	23.8	24.1
Other retirement contributions	3.5	4.4	4.7
Excise taxes	33.4	32.6	32.9
Estate and gift taxes	5.8	6.0	7.0
Customs duties	15.3	14.4	13.3
Miscellaneous receipts	18.9	19.1	19.9
Total budget receipts	**916.6**	**842.4**	**769.1**
OUTLAYS BY FUNCTION			
National defense	297.6	282.2	273.4
International affairs	15.2	14.6	14.2
General science, space, and technology	11.4	9.5	9.0
Energy	3.3	3.8	4.7
Natural resources and environment	14.2	13.9	13.6
Agriculture	26.3	31.1	31.4
Commerce and housing credit	2.5	9.3	4.4
Transportation	25.5	27.0	28.1
Community and regional development	5.5	6.2	7.2
Education, training, employment, and social services	28.4	29.8	30.6
Health	38.9	39.7	35.9
Social security and medicare	280.9	270.4	282.4
Income security	124.8	124.9	119.8
Veterans benefits and services	27.2	26.7	26.4
Administration of justice	9.2	8.3	6.6
General government	7.5	6.8	6.1
General purpose fiscal assistance	1.5	1.9	6.4
Net interest	139.0	137.5	136.0
Allowances	−0.8	—	—
Undistributed offsetting receipts	−45.4	−37.1	−33.0
Total outlays	**1,024.3**	**1,015.6**	**989.8**
Total budget deficit	**−107.7**	**−173.2**	**−220.7**

1. Estimated. NOTE: The fiscal year is from Oct. 1 to Sept. 30. *Source:* Executive Office of the President, Office of Management and Budget.

National Income by Type
(in billions of dollars)

Type of share	1986	1985	1984	1980	1975	1970	1965	1960	1950
National income	$3,386.4	$3,222.3	$3,039.3	$2,121.4	$1,215.0	$800.5	$564.3	$414.5	$241.1
Compensation of employees	2,498.0	2,368.2	2,221.3	1,596.5	931.1	603.9	393.8	294.2	154.6
Wages and salaries	2,073.5	1,965.8	1,835.2	1,343.6	805.9	542.0	358.9	270.8	146.8
Supplements to wages and salaries	424.5	402.4	386.2	252.9	125.2	61.9	35.0	23.4	7.8
Proprietors' income	278.8	254.4	233.7	130.6	87.0	66.9	57.3	46.2	37.5
Business and professional	252.7	225.2	201.6	107.2	63.5	50.0	42.4	34.2	24.0
Farm	26.1	29.2	32.1	23.4	23.5	16.9	14.8	12.0	13.5
Rental income of persons	15.0[1]	7.6[1]	10.8[1]	31.8	22.4	23.9	19.0	15.8	9.4
Corporate profits[1 2]	300.7	280.7	273.3	182.7	95.9	69.4	76.1	49.9	37.7
Net interest	294.0	311.4	300.2	179.8	78.6	36.4	18.2	8.4	2.0

1. Includes capital consumption adjustment. 2. Includes inventory valuation adjustment. *Source:* Department of Commerce, Bureau of Economic Analysis.

Persons in the Labor Force

Year	Labor force[1] Number (thousands)	Labor force[1] % working-age population	Percent of labor force in Farm occupation	Percent of labor force in Nonfarm occupation	Year	Labor force[1] Number (thousands)	Labor force[1] % working-age population	Percent of labor force in Farm occupation	Percent of labor force in Nonfarm occupation
1830	3,932	45.5	70.5	29.5	1910	37,371	52.2	31.0	69.0
1840	5,420	46.6	68.6	31.4	1920	42,434	51.3	27.0	73.0
1850	7,697	46.8	63.7	36.3	1930	48,830	49.5	21.4	78.6
1860	10,533	47.0	58.9	41.1	1940	52,789	52.2	17.4	82.6
1870	12,925	45.8	53.0	47.0	1950	60,054	53.5	11.6	88.4
1880	17,392	47.3	49.4	50.6	1960	69,877	55.3	6.0	94.0
1890	23,318	49.2	42.6	57.4	1970	82,049	58.2	3.1	96.9
1900	29,073	50.2	37.5	62.5	1980	106,085	62.0	2.2	97.8

1. For 1830 to 1930, the data relate to the population and gainful workers at ages 10 and over. For 1940 to 1960, the data relate to the population and labor force at ages 14 and over; for 1970 and 1980, the data relate to the population and labor force at age 16 and over. The farm and nonfarm percentages relate only to the experienced civilian labor force. For 1940 to 1980, the data include the Armed Forces. *Source:* Department of Commerce, Bureau of the Census.

Women in the Civilian Labor Force
(16 years of age and over; in thousands)

Labor force status	1986	1985	1984	1983	1982	1981
In the labor force:	52,413	51,050	49,709	48,503	47,755	46,696
16 to 19 years of age	3,824	3,767	3,810	3,868	4,056	4,211
20 years and over	48,589	47,283	45,900	44,636	43,699	42,485
Employed	48,706	47,259	45,915	44,047	43,256	43,000
16 to 19 years of age	3,149	3,105	3,122	3,043	3,170	3,411
20 years and over	45,557	44,154	42,793	41,004	40,086	39,590
Unemployed	3,707	3,791	3,794	4,457	4,499	3,696
16 to 19 years of age	675	661	687	825	886	800
20 years and over	3,032	3,129	3,107	3,632	3,613	2,895
Not in the labor force:	42,376	42,686	43,068	43,181	42,993	42,922
Women as percent of labor force	44.5	44.2	43.8	43.5	43.3	43.0
Total civilian noninstitutional population	94,789	93,736	92,778	91,684	90,748	89,618

Source: Department of Labor, Bureau of Labor Statistics, annual averages.

Employed Persons 16 Years and Over, by Race and Major Occupational Groups

(number in thousands)

Race and occupational group	1986 Number	1986 Percent distribution	1985 Number	1985 Percent distribution
WHITE				
Managerial and professional	24,134	25.2	23,561	25.1
Executive, administrative, & managerial	11,649	12.2	11,256	12.0
Professional	12,485	13.1	12,305	13.1
Technical, sales, & administrative support	30,497	31.9	29,553	31.5
Technicians & support	2,953	3.1	2,823	3.0
Sales occupations	12,168	12.7	11,669	12.4
Administrative support	15,377	16.1	15,061	16.1
Service occupations	11,685	12.2	11,432	12.2
Precision production, craft, and repair	12,083	12.6	12,107	12.9
Operators, fabricators, and laborers	14,107	14.7	13,951	14.9
Farming, forestry, fishing	3,154	3.3	3,132	3.3
Total	**95,660**	**100.0**	**93,736**	**100.0**
BLACK				
Managerial and professional	1,594	14.7	1,514	14.4
Executive, administrative, & managerial	658	6.1	649	6.2
Professional	936	8.7	865	8.2
Technical, sales, & administrative support	2,923	27.0	2,785	26.5
Technicians & support	277	2.6	291	2.8
Sales occupations	750	6.9	696	6.6
Administrative support	1,896	17.5	1,798	17.1
Service occupations	2,480	22.9	2,522	24.0
Precision production, craft, and repair	1,009	9.3	946	9.0
Operators, fabricators, and laborers	2,583	23.9	2,465	23.5
Farming, forestry, and fishing	224	2.1	269	2.6
Total	**10,814**	**100.0**	**10,501**	**100.0**

Source: Department of Labor, Bureau of Labor Statistics.

Mothers Participating in Labor Force

(figures in percentage)

Year	Mothers with children: Under 18 years	6 to 17 years	Under 6 years[1]
1950	21.6	32.8	13.6
1955	27.0	38.4	18.2
1965	35.0	45.7	25.3
1975	47.4	54.8	38.9
1979	54.5	61.6	45.4
1980	56.6	64.4	46.6
1981	58.1	65.5	48.9
1982	58.5	65.8	49.9
1983	58.9	66.3	50.5
1984	60.5	68.2	52.1
1985	62.1	69.9	53.5
1986	62.8	70.4	54.4

1. May also have older children. NOTE: For 1950 and 1955 data are for April; for 1965 and 1975–86, data are for March. *Source:* Department of Labor, Bureau of Labor Statistics.

Women in the Working Population

Year[1]	Number (thousands)	% Female population aged 10 and over[1]	% of Total working population aged 10 and over[1]
1900	5,319	18.8	18.3
1910	7,445	21.5	19.9
1920	8,637	21.4	20.4
1930	10,752	22.0	22.0
1940	12,845	25.4	24.3
1950	18,408	33.9	29.0
1960[2]	23,268	37.8	32.5
1970	31,580	43.4	37.2
1980	45,611	51.6	42.0
1984	49,855	53.7	43.3
1985	51,200	54.5	43.7
1986	52,568	55.4	44.0

1. For 1900–1930, data relate to population and gainful workers at ages 10 and over; for 1940, to ages 14 and over; beginning 1950, to population at ages 16 and over. 2. Beginning in 1960, figures include Alaska and Hawaii. *Sources:* Department of Commerce, Bureau of the Census, and Department of Labor, Bureau of Labor Statistics.

Persons Below the Poverty Level, 1960-1985

(in thousands)

Year	All persons	White	Black	Spanish origin[1]	Year	All persons	White	Black	Spanish origin[1]
1960	39,851	28,309	—	—	1976	24,975	16,713	7,595	2,783
1965	33,185	22,496	—	—	1977	24,720	16,416	7,726	2,700
1966	28,510	19,290	8,867	—	1978	24,497	16,259	7,625	2,607
1969	24,147	16,659	7,095	—	1979	26,072	17,214	8,050	2,921
1970	25,420	17,484	7,548	—	1980	29,272	19,699	8,579	3,491
1971	25,559	17,780	7,396	—	1981	31,822	21,553	9,173	3,713
1972	24,460	16,203	7,710	—	1982	34,398	23,517	9,697	4,301
1973	22,973	15,142	7,388	2,366	1983[2]	35,303	23,984	9,882	4,633
1974	23,370	15,736	7,182	2,575	1984	33,700	22,955	9,490	4,806
1975	25,877	17,770	7,545	2,991	1985	33,064	22,860	8,926	5,236

1. Persons of Spanish origin may be of any race. 2. Revised. *Source:* U.S. Department of Commerce, Bureau of the Census.

Manufacturing Industries—Gross Average Weekly Earnings and Hours Worked

Industry	1986		1985		1984		1980		1975		1970	
	Earnings	Hours worked	Earnings	Hours worked	Earnings	Hours worked	Earnings	Hours worked	Earnings	Hours worked	Earnings	Hours worked
All manufacturing	$396.01	40.7	$385.56	40.5	$370.78	40.7	$288.62	39.7	$189.51	39.4	$133.73	39.8
Durable goods	424.98	41.3	415.71	41.2	400.75	41.4	310.78	40.1	205.09	39.9	143.07	40.3
Primary metal industries	499.87	41.9	484.72	41.5	480.06	42.0	391.78	40.1	246.80	40.0	159.17	40.5
Iron and steel foundries	441.74	41.4	429.62	40.8	423.26	41.7	328.00	40.0	220.99	40.4	151.03	40.6
Nonferrous foundries	395.62	41.6	388.74	41.8	381.43	42.1	291.27	39.9	190.03	39.1	138.16	39.7
Fabricated metal products	407.63	41.3	398.96	41.3	385.74	41.3	300.98	40.4	201.60	40.0	143.67	40.7
Hardware, cutlery, hand tools	398.21	40.8	396.42	40.7	371.69	40.8	275.89	39.3	187.07	39.3	132.33	40.1
Other hardware	418.00	40.9	385.40	41.3	286.21	39.1	195.42	39.4	133.46	40.2		
Structural metal products	371.69	40.8	369.00	41.0	354.16	40.2	291.85	40.2	202.61	40.2	142.61	40.4
Electric and electronic equipment	396.47	41.0	384.48	40.6	364.90	41.0	276.21	39.8	180.91	39.5	130.54	39.8
Machinery, except electrical	439.30	41.6	427.04	41.5	416.91	41.9	328.00	41.0	219.22	40.9	154.95	41.1
Transportation equipment	545.26	42.4	542.72	42.7	522.02	43.0	379.61	40.6	242.61	40.3	163.22	40.3
Motor vehicles and equipment	577.30	42.7	584.64	43.5	562.93	44.5	394.00	40.0	262.68	40.6	170.07	40.3
Lumber and wood products	337.31	40.3	326.36	39.8	312.83	39.8	252.18	38.5	167.35	39.1	117.51	39.7
Furniture and fixtures	294.62	39.6	283.29	39.4	266.34	39.4	209.17	38.1	142.13	37.9	108.58	39.2
Nondurable goods	356.31	39.9	342.86	39.5	327.10	39.6	255.45	39.0	168.78	38.8	120.43	39.1
Textile mill products	286.34	41.2	266.39	39.7	261.06	40.6	203.31	40.1	133.28	39.2	97.76	39.9
Apparel and other textile products	213.23	36.7	208.00	36.3	200.75	36.7	161.42	35.4	111.97	35.1	84.37	35.3
Leather and leather products	217.71	36.9	217.09	37.3	205.25	36.2	169.09	36.7	120.80	37.4	92.63	37.2
Food and kindred products	349.60	40.0	341.60	40.0	328.94	39.3	271.95	39.7	184.17	40.3	127.98	40.5
Tobacco manufactures	480.15	37.6	448.26	37.2	414.77	37.0	294.89	38.1	171.38	38.0	110.00	37.8
Paper and allied products	482.36	43.3	466.34	43.1	437.68	42.7	330.85	42.2	207.58	41.6	144.14	41.9
Printing and publishing	378.86	38.0	365.31	37.7	353.78	38.0	279.36	37.1	198.32	37.0	147.78	37.7
Chemicals and allied products	502.74	42.0	484.78	41.9	456.46	41.8	344.45	41.5	219.63	40.9	153.50	41.6
Petroleum and allied products	620.10	43.7	603.72	43.0	584.64	44.0	422.18	41.8	267.07	41.6	182.76	42.7

Source: Department of Labor, Bureau of Labor Statistics.

Nonmanufacturing Industries—Gross Average Weekly Earnings and Hours Worked

Industry	1986 Earnings	1986 Hours worked	1985 Earnings	1985 Hours worked	1975 Earnings	1975 Hours worked	1970 Earnings	1970 Hours worked	1958 Earnings	1958 Hours worked
Bituminous coal and lignite mining	$630.04	40.9	$630.77	41.4	$284.53	39.2[2]	$186.41	40.8	$97.57	33.3
Metal mining	544.16	41.1	547.24	40.9	250.72	42.3	165.68	42.7	94.96	38.6
Nonmetallic minerals	465.03	44.5	451.68	44.5	213.09	43.4	155.11	44.7	88.33	43.3
Telephone communications	531.16	41.4	512.52	41.1	221.18	38.4	131.60	39.4	78.72	38.4
Radio and TV broadcasting	402.93	37.0	381.39	37.1	214.50	39.0	147.45	38.2	100.70	38.0
Electric, gas, and sanitary services	559.28	41.8	534.59	41.7	246.79	41.2	172.64	41.5	98.57	40.9
Local and suburban transportation	323.94	38.2	309.85	38.3	196.89	40.1	142.30	42.1	87.29	43.0
Wholesale trade	359.04	38.4	358.36	38.7	188.75	38.6	137.60	40.0	84.02	40.2
Retail trade	175.78	29.2	177.31	29.7	108.22	32.4	82.47	33.8	54.10	38.1
Hotels, tourist courts, motels	183.88	30.8	176.90	30.5	89.64	31.9	68.16	34.6	40.89	39.7
Laundries and dry cleaning plants	203.66	34.0	198.70	34.2	106.05	35.0	77.47	35.7	45.28	38.7
General building contracting	421.83	37.1	414.78	37.1	254.88	36.0	184.40	36.3	96.92	35.5

Source: Department of Labor, Bureau of Labor Statistics.

Median Income Comparisons of Year-Round Workers by Educational Attainment 1984

(persons 25 years and over)

Years of school completed	Median income: Women	Median income: Men	Income gap in dollars	Women's income as a percent of men's	Percent men's income exceeded women's
Elementary school:					
Less than 8 years	$9,828	$14,624	$4,796	67	49
8 years	10,848	16,812	5,964	65	55
High School:					
1 to 3 years	11,843	19,120	7,277	62	61
4 years	14,569	23,269	8,700	63	60
College:					
1 to 3 years	17,007	25,831	8,824	66	52
4 years or more	21,889	33,934	12,045	65	55

Source: Department of Commerce, Bureau of the Census. NOTE: Data are latest available.

Characteristics of Households With Female Householder, 1986

Characteristics	Number of households	Income bracket	Number of households
All female householders	27,420,000	3 persons	4,050,000
MARITAL STATUS		4 persons or more	3,757,000
Married, husband present	2,957,000	**RELATED CHILDREN UNDER 18**	
Married, husband absent	2,551,000	No related children	19,090,000
Widowed	9,699,000	1 or more related children	8,330,000
Divorced	6,430,000	**TOTAL HOUSEHOLD INCOME[2]**	
Single (never married)	5,782,000	Under $2,500	1,151,000
RACE AND SPANISH ORIGIN		$2,500 to $4,999	3,341,000
OF HOUSEHOLDER		$5,000 to $7,499	3,705,000
White	22,127,000	$7,500 to $9,999	2,585,000
Black	4,763,000	$10,000 to $14,999	4,035,000
Spanish origin[1]	1,696,000	$15,000 to $24,999	5,786,000
SIZE OF HOUSEHOLD		$25,000 to $49,000	5,329,000
1 person	12,893,000	$50,000 and over	1,488,000
2 persons	6,721,000	Median income	13,471
		Mean income	18,706

1. Persons of Spanish origin may be of any race. 2. As of March 1985. *Source:* Department of Commerce, Bureau of the Census.

Occupations of Employed Women

(16 years of age and over)

Occupations	Percent 1986[1]	1985[1]	1984[1]	1983[1]	1982[1]	1981[1]	1980[1]
Managerial and professional	23.7	23.4	22.5	21.9	21.7	20.9	20.4
Technical, sales, administrative support	45.6	45.5	45.6	45.8	45.7	45.9	46.0
Service occupations	18.3	18.5	18.7	18.9	19.0	18.8	18.9
Precision production, craft and repair	2.4	2.4	2.4	2.3	1.9	1.9	1.9
Operators, fabricators, laborers	8.9	9.1	9.6	9.7	10.3	11.1	11.4
Farming, forestry, fishing	1.1	1.2	1.2	1.3	1.4	1.3	1.4

1. Annual averages. NOTE: Details may not add up to totals because of rounding. *Source:* Department of Labor, Bureau of Labor Statistics.

Unemployment by Marital Status, Sex, and Race[1]

Marital status and race	Men: Number	Men: Unemployment rate	Women: Number	Women: Unemployment rate
White, 16 years and over	3,678,000	6.4	2,427,000	5.4
Married, spouse present	1,654,000	4.4	1,064,000	4.1
Widowed, divorced, or separated	463,000	8.5	537,000	6.5
Single (never married)	1,561,000	10.8	827,000	7.6
Black, 16 years and over	855,000	13.5	905,000	14.2
Married, spouse present	222,000	7.0	198,000	8.2
Widowed, divorced, or separated	98,000	10.6	199,000	11.4
Single (never married)	536,000	23.9	508,000	23.3
Total, 16 years and over	4,693,000	7.2	3,432,000	6.5
Married, spouse present	1,943,000	4.7	1,309,000	4.5
Widowed, divorced, or separated	579,000	8.9	759,000	7.4
Single (never married)	2,170,000	12.6	1,364,000	10.1

1. April, 1987. *Source:* U.S. Department of Labor, Bureau of Labor Statistics.

Earnings Distribution of Year-Round, Full-Time Workers, by Sex, 1985

(persons 15 years old and over as of March 1986)

Earnings group	Number: Women	Number: Men	Distribution (percent): Women	Distribution (percent): Men	Likelihood of a woman in each earnings group (percent)[1]
$2,999 or less	533,000	924,000	1.9	2.1	0.9
$3,000 to $4,999	401,000	422,000	1.5	0.9	1.7
$5,000 to $6,999	1,108,000	814,000	4.0	1.8	2.2
$7,000 to $9,999	3,218,000	2,233,000	11.8	5.0	2.4
$10,000 to $14,999	7,527,000	5,872,000	27.5	13.1	2.1
$15,000 to $19,999	5,926,000	6,621,000	21.6	14.7	1.5
$20,000 to $24,999	4,085,000	6,425,000	14.9	14.3	1.0
$25,000 to $49,999	4,297,000	17,489,000	15.7	32.9	0.4
$50,000 and over	287,000	4,141,000	1.0	9.2	0.1
Total	**27,383,000**	**44,943,000**	**100.0**	**100.0**	—

Figures obtained by dividing percentages for women by percentages for men. *Source:* Department of Commerce, Bureau of the Census.

Comparison of Median Earnings of Year-Round, Full-Time Workers 15 Years and Over, by Sex, 1960 to 1985

Year	Median earnings: Women	Median earnings: Men	Earnings gap in current dollars	Women's earnings as a percent of men's	Percent men's earnings exceeded women's	Earnings gap in constant 1985 dollars
1960	$3,257	$5,368	$2,111	60.7	64.8	$7,668
1965	3,828	6,388	2,560	60.0	66.9	8,728
1970	5,323	8,966	3,643	59.4	68.4	10,093
1975	7,504	12,758	5,254	58.8	70.0	10,501
1976	8,099	13,455	5,356	60.2	66.1	10,121
1978	9,350	15,730	6,380	59.4	68.2	10,521
1979	10,169	17,045	6,876	59.7	67.6	10,191
1980	11,197	18,612	7,415	60.2	66.2	9,680
1981	12,001	20,260	8,259	59.2	68.8	9,769
1982	13,014	21,077	8,063	61.7	62.0	8,986
1983	13,915	21,881	7,966	63.6	57.2	8,601
1984	14,780	23,218	8,438	63.7	57.1	8,739
1985	15,624	24,195	8,571	64.7	54.9	8,571

Source: Department of Commerce, Bureau of the Census.

Full- and Part-Time Status of the Civilian Labor Force: 1970 to 1986

(In thousands except percent)

ITEM	Full-Time 1986	Full-Time 1985	Full-Time 1980	Full-Time 1975	Full-Time 1970	Part-Time 1986	Part-Time 1985	Part-Time 1980	Part-Time 1975	Part-Time 1970
Civilian labor force	**97,237**	**99,178**	**91,295**	**80,117**	**71,069**	**20,598**	**16,283**	**15,644**	**13,659**	**11,703**
Percent of total	78.8	83.6	85.4	85.4	85.9	21.1	16.4	14.6	14.6	14.1
Employed	90,529	92,385	85,027	73,595	67,863	19,069	14,764	14,275	12,251	10,814
Unemployed	6,708	6,793	6,269	6,523	3,206	1,529	1,519	1,369	1,408	889
Percent[1]	6.9	6.8	6.9	8.1	4.5	7.4	9.3	8.8	10.3	7.6
Males, 20 yr. and over	56,825	57,129	53,571	48,895	44,962	4,495	3,148	2,883	2,601	2,259
Employed	53,317	53,650	50,405	45,640	43,460	4,252	2,912	2,697	2,378	2,122
Unemployed	3,508	3,479	3,167	3,255	1,502	243	236	186	223	137
Percent[1]	6.1	6.1	5.9	6.7	3.3	5.4	7.5	6.5	8.6	6.1
Females, 20 yr and over	37,280	38,116	32,722	26,359	22,226	11,309	9,167	8,383	7,052	6,074
Employed	34,812	35,580	30,588	24,148	21,149	10,744	8,574	7,904	6,578	5,803
Unemployed	2,468	2,536	2,135	2,210	1,077	565	593	480	474	271
Percent[1]	6.6	6.7	6.5	8.4	4.8	5.0	6.5	5.7	6.7	4.5
Persons, 16–19 yr	3,133	3,933	5,001	4,864	3,881	4,794	3,968	4,377	4,005	3,370
Employed	2,400	3,156	4,035	3,807	3,254	4,073	3,278	3,676	3,295	2,889
Unemployed	733	777	966	1,057	626	721	690	701	709	480
Percent[1]	23.4	19.8	19.3	21.7	16.1	15.0	17.4	16.0	17.7	14.3

1. Unemployment as percent of civilian labor force in specified group.

Advertising Expenditures by Medium

(in billions)

Medium	1986 Amt.	1986 % of total	1985 Amt.	1985 % of total	1980 Amt.	1980 % of total	1975 Amt.	1975 % of total	1970 Amt.	1970 % of total	1960 Amt.	1960 % of total
Newspapers	27.0	26.4	25.2	26.5	$14.8	27.7	$8.2	29.5	$5.7	29.2	$3.7	31.0
Magazines	5.3	5.2	5.2	5.4	3.1	5.9	1.5	5.2	1.3	6.6	0.9	7.9
Business Papers	2.4	2.3	2.4	2.5	1.7	3.1	0.9	3.3	0.7	3.8	0.6	5.1
Radio	6.9	6.8	6.5	6.9	3.7	6.9	2.0	7.1	1.3	6.7	0.7	5.8
Television	22.6	22.1	20.8	21.9	11.4	21.2	5.3	18.9	3.6	18.4	1.6	13.3
Direct mail	17.1	16.8	15.5	16.4	7.6	14.2	4.1	14.8	2.8	14.1	1.8	15.3
Outdoor	1.0	1.0	.9	1.0	0.6	1.1	0.3	1.2	0.2	1.2	0.2	1.7
Miscellaneous[1]	19.6	19.2	18.2	19.2	10.7	19.9	5.6	20.0	3.9	20.0	2.4	19.8
Total	**102.1**	**100.0**	**94.8**	**100.0**	**53.6**	**100.0**	**27.9**	**100.0**	**19.5**	**100.0**	**11.9**	**100.0**

1. Includes regional farm papers. *Sources:* McCann-Erickson, Inc., and *Advertising Age.*

Leading Advertising Agencies in World Billings

(in millions of dollars)

Agency	1986	1985
Young & Rubicam	$4,191.4	$3,575.3
Saatchi & Saatchi Compton Worldwide	3,320.0	3,033.1
Ted Bates Worldwide	3,261.8	3,106.9
BBDO Worldwide	3,259.0	2,894.7
Ogilvy & Mather Worldwide	3,154.6	2,752.1
J. Walter Thompson Co.	3,141.5	2,899.1
McCann-Erickson Worldwide	2,852.7	2,464.6
DDB Needham Worldwide	2,557.5	2,512.9
D'Arcy Masius Benton & Bowles	2,258.6	2,229.5
Foote, Cone & Belding Communications	2,154.5	1,900.7

Source: Reprinted with permission from the March 27, 1987, issue of *Advertising Age.* Copyright © 1987 by Crain Communications, Inc.

Unemployment Rate, 1986

Race and age	Women[1]	Men[1]
All races:	7.1	6.9
16 to 19 years	17.6	19.0
20 years and over	6.2	6.1
White	6.1	6.0
16 to 19 years	14.9	16.3
20 years and over	5.4	5.3
Minority races:	12.8	13.4
16 to 19 years	35.7	36.3
20 years and over	11.2	11.7

1. Annual averages. *Source:* Bureau of Labor Statistics, Department of Labor.

Unemployment Rate in the Civilian Labor Force

Year	Unemployment Rate	Year	Unemployment Rate
1920	5.2	1974	5.6
1922	6.7	1976	7.7
1924	5.0	1978	6.0
1926	1.8	1979	5.8
1928	4.2	1980	7.1
1930	8.7	1981	7.6
1932	23.6	1982	9.7
1934	21.7	1983	9.6
1936	16.9	1984	7.5
1938	19.0	1985	7.2
1940	14.6	1986	7.0
1942	4.7	Jan.	6.7
1944	1.2	Feb.	7.3
1946	3.9	March	7.2
1948	3.8	April	7.1
1950	5.3	May	7.2
1952	3.0	June	7.1
1954	5.5	July	7.0
1956	4.1	Aug.	6.8
1958	6.8	Sept.	7.0
1960	5.5	Oct.	6.9
1962	5.5	Nov.	6.9
1964	5.2	Dec.	6.7
1966	3.8	1987	
1968	3.6	Jan.	6.7
1970	4.9	Feb.	6.7
1972	5.6	March	6.6
		April	6.3

NOTE: Estimates prior to 1940 are based on sources other than direct enumeration. *Source:* Department of Labor, Bureau of Labor Statistics.

Employment and Unemployment

(in millions of persons)

Category	1987[2]	1986	1985	1980	1975	1970	1950	1945	1941	1932	1929
EMPLOYMENT STATUS[1]											
Civilian noninstitutional population	182.7	180.6	178.2	167.7	153.2	137.1	105.0	94.1	99.9	—	—
Civilian labor force	119.5	117.8	115.5	106.9	93.8	82.8	62.2	53.9	55.9	—	—
Civilian labor force participation rate	65.4	65.3	64.8	63.8	61.2	60.4	59.2	57.2	56.0	—	—
Employed	112.3	109.6	107.2	99.3	85.8	78.7	58.9	52.8	50.4	38.9	47.6
Employment-population ratio	61.4	60.7	60.1	59.2	56.1	57.4	56.1	56.1	50.4	—	—
Agriculture	3.2	3.2	3.2	3.4	3.4	3.5	7.2	8.6	9.1	10.2	10.5
Nonagricultural industries	109.1	106.4	104.0	95.9	82.4	75.2	51.8	44.2	41.3	28.8	37.2
Unemployed	7.3	8.2	8.3	7.6	7.9	4.1	3.3	1.0	5.6	12.1	1.6
Unemployment rate	6.1	7.0	7.2	7.1	8.5	4.9	5.3	1.9	9.9	23.6	3.2
Not in labor force	63.2	62.8	62.7	60.8	59.4	54.3	42.8	40.2	44.0	—	—
INDUSTRY											
Total nonagricultural employment	101.8	99.6	97.5	90.4	76.9	70.9	45.2	40.4	36.5	23.6	31.3
Goods-producing industries	24.8	24.7	24.9	25.7	22.6	23.6	18.5	17.5	16.0	8.6	13.3
Mining	0.7	0.8	0.9	1.0	0.8	0.6	0.9	0.8	1.0	0.7	1.1
Construction	5.0	4.9	4.7	4.3	3.5	3.6	2.4	1.1	1.8	1.0	1.5
Manufacturing: Durable goods	11.2	11.2	11.5	12.2	10.7	11.2	8.1	9.1	7.0	—	—
Nondurable goods	7.8	7.8	7.8	8.1	7.6	8.2	7.1	6.5	6.2	—	—
Services-producing industries	77.0	74.9	72.7	64.7	54.3	47.3	26.7	22.9	20.6	15.0	18.0
Transportation and public utilities	5.4	5.2	5.2	5.1	4.5	4.5	4.0	3.9	3.3	2.8	3.9
Trade, Wholesale	5.8	5.7	5.7	5.3	4.4	4.0	2.6	1.9	2.0	—	—
Retail	18.2	17.8	17.4	15.0	12.6	11.0	6.8	5.4	5.3	—	—
Finance, insurance, and real estate	6.6	6.3	6.0	5.2	4.2	3.6	1.9	1.5	1.5	1.3	1.5
Services	24.0	23.1	22.0	17.9	13.9	11.5	5.4	4.2	3.9	2.9	3.4
Federal government	2.9	2.9	2.9	2.9	2.7	2.7	1.9	2.8	1.3	0.6	0.5
State and local government	14.1	13.8	13.5	13.4	11.9	9.8	4.1	3.1	3.3	2.7	2.5

1. For 1929–45, figures on employment status relate to persons 14 years and over; beginning in 1950, 16 years and over.
2. As of June; seasonally adjusted; industry data are preliminary. NOTE: Figures may not add to totals because of rounding. *Source:* Department of Labor, Bureau of Labor Statistics.

Livestock on Farms (in thousands)

Type	1987	1986	1985	1980	1975	1970	1965	1960	1950	1945
Cattle[1]	102,031	105,468	109,749	111,242	132,028	112,369	109,000	96,236	77,963	85,573
Dairy cows[1]	10,547	11,177	10,805	10,758	11,220	13,303	16,981	19,527	23,853	27,770
Sheep[1]	10,328	9,983	10,443	12,699	14,515	20,423	25,127	33,170	29,826	39,609
Swine[2]	51,160	52,313	54,073	67,318	54,693	57,046	56,106	59,026	58,937	59,373
Chickens[2]	368,681	368,548	374,008	400,585	384,101	422,000	401,000	369,000	457,000	516,000
Turkeys[3]	n.a.	n.a.	3,159	3,749	3,014	6,715	6,100	5,633	5,124	7,082

1. As of Jan. 1. 2. As of Jan. 1 the previous year for 1945–60 and Dec. 1 for 1965–85. 3. Turkey breeder hens for 1975–85 as of Dec. 1 the previous year. *Source:* Department of Agriculture, Statistical Reporting Service, Economic Research Service.

Agricultural Output by States, 1986 Crops

State	Corn (1,000 bu)	Wheat (1,000 bu)	Cotton (1,000 ba[1])	Potatoes (1,000 cwt)	Tobacco (1,000 lb)	Cattle[2] (1,000 head)	Swine[3] (1,000 head)
Alabama	15,390	5,720	330.0	1,668	—	1,780	380
Alaska	—	—	—	—	—	9.2	1.0
Arizona	2,640	8,688	680.0	1,298	—	1,050	155
Arkansas	8,480	31,980	605.0	—	—	1,750	460
California	38,000	51,525	2,250.0	18,457	—	5,000	150
Colorado	99,400	96,430	—	20,296	—	2,850	190
Connecticut	—	—	—	225	3,124	100	7.0
Delaware	14,027	1,530	—	1,311	—	27	60
Florida	9,920	3,100	33.5	8,543	13,303	2,120	140
Georgia	42,340	15,400	200.0	—	67,815	1,700	1,100
Hawaii	—	—	—	—	—	209	50
Idaho	7,800	81,750	—	87,320	—	1,750	80
Illinois	1,404,000	36,080	—	783	—	2,470	5,000
Indiana	695,400	30,100	—	990	12,600	1,570	4,150
Iowa	1,626,750	1,680	—	332	—	4,950	12,600
Kansas	181,560	336,600	1.0	—	—	5,800	1,450
Kentucky	139,840	8,910	—	—	331,055	2,480	880
Loisiana	44,660	7,350	680.0	35	—	1,240	53
Maine	—	—	—	21,000	—	135	8.0
Maryland	42,340	6,815	—	272	24,300	370	190
Massachusetts	—	—	—	667	702	100	32
Michigan	257,250	30,600	—	11,190	—	1,410	1,250
Minnesota	707,600	103,666	—	15,293	—	3,400	4,260
Mississippi	13,500	6,200	1,200.0	—	—	1,430	210
Missouri	280,720	18,810	197.0	—	4,884	4,800	2,900
Montana	1,495	138,520	—	2,233	—	2,450	190
Nebraska	896,000	76,000	—	2,399	—	5,800	3,900
Nevada	—	1,720	—	2,800	—	610	14
New Hampshire	—	—	—	—	—	69	8.8
New Jersey	11,128	1,290	—	1,944	—	97	40
New Mexico	8,250	10,120	82.5	2,745	—	1,390	36
New York	64,350	7,595	—	7,780	—	1,970	128
North Carolina	93,840	14,260	110.0	2,264	444,380	1,100	2,360
North Dakota	49,290	289,820	—	21,600	—	2,000	275
Ohio	476,160	48,300	—	2,377	15,080	1,840	1,950
Oklahoma	5,220	150,800	240.0	—	—	5,200	220
Oregon	4,800	58,405	—	23,172	—	1,575	115
Pennsylvania	127,720	9,680	—	5,160	21,830	1,960	890
Rhode Island	—	—	—	416	—	7.0	4.8
South Carolina	21,160	7,500	87.0	—	75,480	635	430
South Dakota	233,700	108,660	—	2,340	—	3,600	1,520
Tennessee	56,980	10,725	400.0	234	92,734	2,500	770
Texas	148,960	120,000	2,542.0	3,591	—	13,600	510
Utah	2,250	9,750	—	1,760	—	790	25
Vermont	—	—	—	20	—	350	5.8
Virginia	21,600	6,970	1.6	1,112	73,649	1,840	360
Washington	20,400	116,850	—	60,180	—	1,460	50
West Virginia	6,300	396	—	—	2,848	520	37
Wisconsin	365,800	8,040	—	20,125	14,480	4,280	1,330
Wyoming	5,814	8,445	—	536	—	1,325	35
U.S. Total	**8,252,834**	**2,086,780**	**9,784.6**	**354,468**	**1,198,264**	**105,468**	**50,960**

1. 480-lb net-weight bales. 2. Number on farms as of Jan. 1, 1987. 3. Number on farms as of Dec. 1, 1986. *Source:* Department of Agriculture, Statistical Reporting Service.

Farm Income

(in millions of dollars)

Year	Cash receipts from marketings: Crops	Cash receipts from marketings: Livestock, livestock products	Government payments	Total cash income
1920	$6,644	$5,956	—	$12,600
1925	5,545	5,476	—	11,021
1930	3,868	5,187	—	9,055
1935	2,977	4,143	$573	7,693
1940	3,469	4,913	723	9,105
1945	9,655	12,008	742	22,405
1950	12,356	16,105	283	28,744
1955	13,523	15,967	229	29,719
1960	15,259	18,989	702	34,950
1965	17,479	21,886	2,463	41,828
1970	20,977	29,532	3,717	54,226
1975	45,813	43,087	807	89,707
1980	72,269	67,800	1,286	141,355
1981	72,465	69,151	1,932	143,548
1982	72,375	70,249	3,492	146,116
1983	67,007	69,453	9,295	145,755
1984	69,248	72,905	8,430	150,583
1985	72,702	69,401	7,704	149,807
1986	63,997	71,690	11,813	147,500

1. Includes value of PIK commodities. *Source:* Department of Agriculture, Economic Research Service. NOTE: Figures are latest available.

Per Capita Consumption of Principal Foods[1]

Foods	1985	1984	1983
Red meat[2]	144.4	143.7	143.9
Poultry	70.5	67.5	65.5
Fish and shellfish[3]	14.4	13.7	13.1
Eggs (no.)	255	261	261
Fluid milk and cream[4]	245.1	243.3	242.3
Cheese	22.4	21.6	20.6
Butter	4.9	4.9	4.9
Margarine	10.7	10.4	10.4
Total fats and oils	67.2	61.8	63.0
Selected fresh fruits	88.2	87.5	88.0
Selected processed fruits	34.7	33.5	36.3
Selected fresh vegetables	81.9	81.1	76.1
Potatoes, sweet potatoes[5]	84.0	77.6	76.9
Cane and beet sugar	62.8	66.7	70.2
Corn sweeteners	87.5	77.3	69.4
Flour and cereal products	154.7	148.7	148.0
Soft drinks (gal)	45.6	44.2	41.1
Coffee (gal)	25.9	26.3	25.6
Beer (gal)	23.4	24.9	25.2
Juices (gal)	7.3	6.4	7.2
Cocoa	3.6	3.5	3.1

1. As of July 1986. Except where noted, consumption is from commercial sources and is in terms of retail weight. 2. Skeletal meat; excludes edible offals. 3. Edible weight. 4. Includes milk and cream produced and consumed on farms. 5. Farm-weight equivalent of fresh and processed use.

Government Employment and Payrolls

Year and function	Employees (in thousands): Total	Federal[1]	State	Local	October payrolls (in millions): Total	Federal[1]	State	Local
1940	4,474	1,128	3,346 (State and Local)		$566	177	$389 (State and Local)	
1945	6,677	3,496	3,181 (State and Local)		1,059	591	468 (State and Local)	
1950	6,402	2,117	1,057	3,228	1,528	613	218	696
1955	7,432	2,378	1,199	3,855	2,265	846	326	1,093
1960	8,808	2,421	1,527	4,860	3,333	1,118	524	1,691
1965	10,589	2,588	2,028	5,973	4,884	1,484	849	2,551
1970	13,028	2,881	2,755	7,392	8,334	2,428	1,612	4,294
1972	13,759	2,795	2,957	8,007	9,950	2,710	1,937	5,303
1975	14,973	2,890	3,271	8,813	13,224	3,584	2,653	6,987
1976	15,012	2,843	3,343	8,826	13,924	3,565	2,894	7,465
1977	15,459	2,848	3,491	9,120	15,338	3,918	3,195	8,225
1978	15,628	2,885	3,539	9,204	16,483	4,344	3,483	8,656
1979	15,971	2,869	3,699	9,403	18,077	4,728	3,869	9,480
1980	16,213	2,898	3,753	9,562	19,935	5,205	4,285	10,445
1981	15,968	2,865	3,726	9,377	21,193	5,239	4,668	11,287
1982	15,841	2,848	3,744	9,249	23,173	5,959	5,022	12,192
1983	16,034	2,875	3,816	9,344	24,525	6,302	5,346	12,878
1984	16,436	2,942	3,898	9,595	26,904	7,137	5,815	13,952
1985, total	16,690	3,021	3,984	9,685	28,945	7,580	6,329	15,036
National defense and international relations	1,101	1,101	(2)	(2)	2,898	2,898	(2)	(2)
Postal service	754	754	(2)	(2)	1,741	1,741	(2)	(2)
Education	7,119	15	1,764	5,340	10,722	38	2,444	8,240
Instructional employees	4,002	n.a.	526	3,475	7,486	n.a.	1,096	6,390
Highways	552	4	252	296	922	14	460	448
Health and hospitals	1,653	263	678	712	2,774	640	1,091	1,043
Police protection	760	66	81	613	1,516	188	175	1,153
Local fire protection	317	(2)	(2)	317	554	(2)	(2)	554
Sewerage and sanitation	221	n.a.	1	220	358	n.a.	1	358
Parks and recreation	263	n.a.	33	230	293	n.a.	44	249
Natural resources	443	241	163	39	906	598	258	50
Financial administration	438	118	131	190	744	253	229	262
All other	3,069	459	881	1,728	5,517	1,210	1,628	2,679

1. Civilians only. 2. Not applicable. NOTE: n.a. = not available. *Source:* Department of Commerce, Bureau of the Census.

Receipts and Outlays of the Federal Government

(in millions of dollars)

From 1789 to 1842, the federal fiscal year ended Dec. 31; from 1844 to 1976, on June 30; and beginning 1977, on Sept. 30.

Receipts

Year	Customs (including tonnage tax)[1]	Internal revenue: Income and profits tax	Internal revenue: Other	Miscellaneous taxes and receipts	Total receipts	Net receipts[2]
1789–1791	$ 4	—	—	—	$ 4	$ 4
1800	9	—	$ –1	$ 1	11	11
1810	9	—	—	1	9	9
1820	15	—	—	3	18	18
1830	22	—	—	3	25	25
1840	14	—	—	6	20	20
1850	40	—	—	4	44	44
1860	53	—	—	3	56	56
1865	85	—	209	39	334	334
1870	195	—	185	32	411	411
1880	187	—	124	23	334	334
1890	230	—	143	31	403	403
1900	233	—	295	39	567	567
1910	334	—	290	52	675	675
1915	210	$ 80	335	72	698	683
1918	180	2,314	872	299	3,665	3,645
1929	602	2,331	607	493	4,033	3,862
1933	251	746	858	225	2,080	1,997
1939	319	2,189	2,972	188	5,668	4,979
1943	324	16,094	6,050	934	23,402	21,947
1944	431	34,655	7,030	3,325	45,441	43,563
1945	355	35,173	8,729	3,494	47,750	44,362
1950	423	28,263	11,186	1,439	41,311	36,422
1956[4]	705	56,639	20,564	389	78,297	74,547
1960	1,123	67,151	28,266	1,190	97,730	92,492
1965	1,478	79,792	39,996	1,598	122,863	116,833
1970	2,494	138,689	65,276	3,424	209,883	193,743
1975	3,782	202,146	108,371	6,711	321,010	280,997
1980	7,482	359,927	192,436	12,797	572,641	520,050
1983	9,060	411,410	251,491	15,620	687,581	600,563
1984	11,791	434,905	286,585	16,987	750,269	666,457
1985	12,079	474,074	311,092	18,576	815,821	733,996
1986	13,323	412,102	323,779	19,887	([5])	769,091

Outlays

Year	Department of Defense (Army, 1789–1950)	Department of the Navy	Interest on public debt	All other	Net outlays[3]	Surplus (+) or deficit (–)
1789–1791	$ 1	—	$ 2	$ 1	$ 4	—
1800	3	$ 3	3	1	11	—
1810	2	2	3	1	8	$ +1
1820	3	4	5	6	18	—
1830	5	3	2	5	15	+10
1840	7	6	—	11	24	–4
1850	9	8	4	18	40	+4
1860	16	12	3	32	63	–7
1865	1,031	123	77	66	1,298	–964
1870	58	22	129	101	310	+101
1880	38	14	96	120	268	+66
1890	45	22	36	215	318	+85
1900	135	56	40	290	521	+46
1910	190	123	21	359	694	–19
1915	202	142	23	379	746	–63
1918	4,870	1,279	190	6,339	12,677	–9,032
1929	426	365	678	1,658	3,127	+734
1933	435	349	689	3,125	4,598	–2,602
1939	695	673	941	6,533	8,841	–3,862
1943	42,526	20,888	1,808	14,146	79,368	–57,420

Year	Outlays: Department of Defense (Army, 1789–1950)	Department of the Navy	Interest on public debt	All other	Net outlays[3]	Surplus (+) or deficit (−)
1944	49,438	26,538	2,609	16,401	94,986	−51,423
1945	50,490	30,047	3,617	14,149	98,303	−53,941
1950	5,789	4,130	5,750	23,875	39,544	−3,122
1956[4]	35,693	—	6,787	27,981	70,460	+4,087
1960	43,969	—	9,180	39,075	92,223	+269
1965	47,179	—	11,346	59,904	118,430	−1,596
1970	78,360	—	19,304	98,924	196,588	−2,845
1975	87,471	—	32,665	205,969	326,105	−45,108
1980	136,138	—	74,860	368,013	579,011	−58,961
1983	207,939	—	128,813	459,165	795,917	−195,354
1984	223,877	—	153,838	464,085	841,800	−175,342
1985	244,054	—	178,945	513,810	936,809	−202,813
1986	273,369	—	135,284	581,136	989,789	−220,698

1. Beginning 1933, tonnage tax is included in "Other receipts." 2. Net receipts equal total receipts less (a) appropriations to federal old-age and survivors' insurance trust fund beginning fiscal year 1939 and (b) refunds of receipts beginning fiscal year 1933. 3. Includes Air Force 1950–65 (in millions): 1950—$3,521; 1956—$16,750; 1960—$19,065; 1965—$18,471. 4. Beginning 1956, computed on unified budget concepts; not strictly comparable with preceding figures. 5. Net receipts are now the total receipts. Public Law 99-177 moved two social security trust funds off-budget. *Source:* Department of the Treasury, Financial Management Service.

Contributions to International Organizations

(for fiscal year 1986 in millions of dollars)

Organization	Amount[1]
United Nations and Specialized Agencies	
United Nations	$164.90
Food and Agriculture Organization	36.76
International Atomic Energy Agency	19.08
International Civil Aviation Organization	6.94
International Labor Organization	30.51
International Telecommunication Union	3.30
World Health Organization	58.52
World Meteorological Organization	4.61
Others (8 Programs, less than $1 million)	2.03
Peacekeeping Forces	
United Nations Force in Cyprus	8.61
United Nations Disengagement Observer Force (UNDOF) and UNIFIL	28.14
Multinational Force and Observers	18.30
Inter-American Organizations	
Organization of American States	30.40
Inter-American Institute for Cooperation on Agriculture	9.22
Inter-American Tropical Tuna Commission	2.85
Pan American Health Organization	25.58
Others (4 Programs, less than $1 million)	.54
Regional Organizations	
NATO Civilian Headquarters (and MBFR)	18.32
Organization for Economic Cooperation and Development	20.40
Others (3 Programs, less than $1 million)	.88
Other International Organizations	
Customs Cooperation Council	1.41
General Agreement on Tariffs and Trade	3.87
International Institute for Cotton	2.65
Others (35 Programs, less than $1 million)	4.65
Special Voluntary Programs	
Consultative Group on International Agricultural Research	46.25
Intergovernmental Committee for Migration	6.01
International Atomic Energy Agency Technical Assistance Fund	10.37[2]
International Fund for Agricultural Development	28.71
OAS Special Development Assistance Fund	5.56
OAS Special Multilateral Fund (Education and Science)	6.09
OAS Special Projects Fund (Mar del Plata)	2.10
PAHO Special Health Promotion Funds	3.00
United Nations Children's Fund	50.50
United Nations Development Program	137.92
United Nations Environment Program	8.00
U.N./FAO World Food Program	135.10[3]
U.N. Fund for Drug Abuse Control	3.00
U.N. High Commissioner for Refugees Program:	
Regular Programs (5)	81.76
Special Programs (5)	20.17
United Nations Relief and Works Agency:	
Regular Program	67.00
West African Rice Development Association (WARDA)	2.28
WHO Special Programs	8.00
WMO Voluntary Cooperation Program	1.71
Others (10 Programs, less than $1 million)	3.33
Total U.S. Contributions	$1,129.33

1. Estimated. 2. Includes cash, commodities and services, $1.44 million for the Safeguards Program and $125,000 for the Nuclear Safety Program. 3. Includes commodities and services. No cash contribution made in fiscal year 1986. *Source:* Department of State.

Social Welfare Expenditures Under Public Programs

(in millions of dollars)

Year and source of funds	Social insurance	Public aid	Health and medical programs	Veterans' programs	Education	Housing	Other social welfare	All health and medical care[1]	Total social welfare	Total social welfare as: Percent of gross national product	Total social welfare as: Percent of total gov't outlays
FEDERAL											
1950	$2,103	$1,103	$604	$6,386	$157	$15	$174	$1,362	$10,541	4.0	26.2
1955	6,385	1,504	1,150	4,772	485	75	252	1,948	14,623	3.9	22.3
1960	14,307	2,117	1,737	5,367	868	144	417	2,918	24,957	5.0	28.1
1965	21,807	3,594	2,781	6,011	2,470	238	812	4,625	37,712	5.7	32.6
1970	45,246	9,649	4,775	8,952	5,876	582	2,259	16,600	77,337	8.1	40.1
1975	99,715	27,205	8,513	16,570	8,629	2,541	4,264	34,645	167,436	11.5	53.8
1980	191,162	48,666	12,886	21,254	13,452	6,608	8,786	68,989	303,276	11.5	53.2
1981	224,574	55,946	13,596	23,229	13,372	6,045	7,304	80,505	344,066	11.6	54.0
1982	250,551	52,485	14,598	24,463	11,917	7,176	6,500	90,776	367,691	12.0	52.5
1983	274,212	55,895	15,594	25,561	12,397	8,087	7,046	100,274	398,792	12.0	51.9
1984[2]	289,884	57,666	16,496	25,822	12,979	9,068	7,349	108,603	419,264	11.3	50.2
STATE AND LOCAL											
1950	2,844	1,393	1,460	480	6,518	([3])	274	1,704	12,967	4.9	59.2
1955	3,450	1,499	1,953	62	10,672	15	367	2,473	18,017	4.7	55.3
1960	4,999	1,984	2,727	112	16,758	33	723	3,478	27,337	5.5	60.1
1965	6,316	2,690	3,466	20	25,638	80	1,254	4,911	39,464	6.0	60.4
1970	9,446	6,839	5,132	127	44,970	120	1,886	8,791	68,519	7.1	64.0
1975	23,298	14,122	9,195	449	72,234	631	2,683	17,847	122,612	8.4	63.7
1980	38,592	23,133	14,771	212	107,597	601	4,813	31,309	189,720	7.2	66.5
1981	42,821	26,477	17,124	212	114,773	688	4,679	36,327	206,774	7.0	63.1
1982	52,481	28,367	19,195	245	121,957	778	5,154	40,738	228,178	7.4	62.6
1983	56,846	29,935	20,382	265	129,416	1,003	5,438	42,854	243,285	7.3	60.1
1984[2]	52,381	32,206	21,368	305	139,046	1,306	6,096	46,490	252,707	6.8	58.9
TOTAL											
1950	4,947	2,496	2,064	6,866	6,674	15	448	3,065	23,508	8.9	37.4
1955	9,835	3,003	3,103	4,834	11,157	89	619	4,421	32,640	8.6	32.7
1960	19,307	4,101	4,464	5,479	17,626	177	1,139	6,395	52,293	10.5	38.4
1965	28,123	6,283	6,246	6,031	28,108	318	2,066	9,535	77,175	11.7	42.2
1970	54,691	16,488	9,907	9,078	50,846	701	4,145	25,391	145,856	15.2	48.2
1975	123,013	41,326	17,708	17,019	80,863	3,172	6,947	52,492	290,047	20.0	57.4
1980	229,754	71,799	27,657	21,466	121,050	7,210	13,599	100,298	492,534	18.7	57.4
1981	267,395	82,424	30,720	23,441	128,145	6,734	11,983	116,832	550,841	18.6	56.9
1982	303,033	80,852	33,793	24,708	133,874	7,954	11,654	131,514	595,869	19.4	55.7
1983	331,058	85,830	35,976	25,826	141,813	9,090	12,484	143,128	642,077	19.3	54.5
1984[2]	342,264	89,871	37,864	26,127	152,025	10,374	13,445	155,092	671,972	18.2	52.8
PERCENT OF TOTAL, BY TYPE											
1950	21.0	10.6	8.8	29.2	28.4	0.1	1.9	13.0	100.0	([3])	([3])
1955	30.1	9.2	9.5	14.8	34.2	0.3	1.9	13.5	100.0	([3])	([3])
1960	36.9	7.8	8.5	10.5	33.7	0.3	2.2	12.2	100.0	([3])	([3])
1965	36.4	8.1	8.1	7.8	36.4	0.4	2.7	12.4	100.0	([3])	([3])
1970	37.5	11.3	6.7	6.2	34.9	0.5	3.0	17.2	100.0	([3])	([3])
1975	42.4	14.2	6.1	5.9	27.9	1.1	2.4	18.1	100.0	([3])	([3])
1980	46.6	14.6	5.6	4.4	24.6	1.5	2.8	20.4	100.0	([3])	([3])
1984[2]	50.9	13.4	5.6	3.9	22.6	1.5	2.0	23.1	100.0	([3])	([3])
FEDERAL PERCENT OF TOTAL											
1950	42.5	44.2	29.2	93.0	2.3	100.0	38.9	44.4	44.8	([3])	([3])
1955	64.9	50.1	37.1	98.7	4.3	83.7	40.7	44.1	44.8	([3])	([3])
1960	74.1	51.6	38.9	98.0	4.9	81.2	36.6	45.6	47.7	([3])	([3])
1965	77.5	57.2	44.5	99.7	8.8	74.9	39.3	48.5	48.9	([3])	([3])
1970	82.7	58.5	48.2	98.6	11.6	82.9	54.5	65.4	53.0	([3])	([3])
1975	81.1	65.8	48.1	97.4	10.7	80.1	61.4	66.0	57.7	([3])	([3])
1980	83.2	67.8	46.6	99.0	11.1	91.7	64.6	68.8	61.6	([3])	([3])
1984[2]	84.7	64.2	43.6	99.0	8.5	87.4	54.7	70.0	62.4	([3])	([3])

1. Combines health and medical programs with medical services provided in connection with social insurance, public aid, veterans, and other social welfare programs. 2. Preliminary. 3. Not applicable. NOTE: n.a. = not available. Figures are latest available. *Source:* Department of Health and Human Services. *Social Security Bulletin,* December 1984.

Domestic Freight Traffic by Major Carriers

(in millions of ton-miles)[1]

Year	Railroads Ton-miles	Railroads % of total	Inland waterways[2] Ton-miles	Inland waterways[2] % of total	Motor trucks Ton-miles	Motor trucks % of total	Oil pipelines Ton-miles	Oil pipelines % of total	Air carriers Ton-miles	Air carriers % of total
1940	379,201	61.3	118,057	19.1	62,043	10.0	59,277	9.6	14	—
1945	690,809	67.3	142,737	13.9	66,948	6.5	126,530	12.3	91	—
1950	596,940	56.2	163,344	15.4	172,860	16.3	129,175	12.1	318	—
1955	631,385	49.5	216,508	17.0	223,254	17.5	203,244	16.0	481	—
1960	579,130	44.1	220,253	16.8	285,483	21.7	228,626	17.4	778	—
1965	708,700	43.3	262,421	16.0	359,218	21.9	306,393	18.7	1,910	0.1
1970	771,168	39.8	318,560	16.4	412,000	21.3	431,000	22.3	3,274	0.2
1975	759,000	36.7	342,210	16.5	454,000	22.0	507,300	24.6	3,732	0.2
1979	927,000	35.7	431,000	16.6	628,000	24.2	605,000	23.3	4,439	0.2
1980	932,000	37.2	420,000	16.9	567,000	22.6	588,000	23.1	4,528	0.2
1981	926,000	37.5	423,000	17.1	565,000	22.9	553,000	22.4	4,657	0.2
1982	810,000	35.8	351,000	15.5	525,000	23.2	571,000	25.3	4,476	0.2
1983	841,000	36.0	359,000	15.4	575,000	24.6	556,000	23.8	5,870	0.3
1985	895,000	36.4	382,000	15.6	610,000	24.9	564,000	22.9	6,080	0.2
1986[3]	897,000	35.9	376,000	15.1	636,000	25.5	580,000	23.2	7,100	0.3

1. Mail and express included, except railroads for 1970. 2. Rivers, canals, and domestic traffic on Great Lakes. 3. Estimated. *Sources:* Interstate Commerce Commission; Dept. of Transportation; Association of American Railroads.

Tonnage Handled by Principal U.S. Ports

(Over 10 million tons annually; in thousands of tons)

Port	1985	1984	Port	1985	1984
New York	152,054	161,676	Newport News, Va.	19,169	15,552
New Orleans	146,678	154,220	Toledo Harbor, Ohio	18,400	20,836
Valdez Harbor, Alaska	99,624	92,047	Boston	17,269	19,888
Houston	90,669	96,777	Richmond, Calif.	17,178	16,341
Baton Rouge, La.	70,716	66,198	Seattle	16,230	20,327
Norfolk Harbor, Va.	47,181	44,897	Cincinnati	16,215	15,936
Tampa Harbor	46,905	46,517	Paulsboro, N.J.	16,101	18,197
Long Beach, Calif.	43,977	42,848	Tacoma Harbor, Wash.	15,795	17,383
Corpus Christi Ship Chnl., Tex.	42,682	44,081	Port Arthur, Tex.	15,755	16,430
Mobile, Ala.	37,749	35,718	Detroit	15,612	17,530
Baltimore Harbor	36,425	37,306	Cleveland	13,767	12,290
Los Angeles	36,374	31,242	Indiana, Ind.	13,549	14,568
Texas City, Tex.	33,441	30,656	Freeport, Tex.	12,918	15,122
Philadelphia	32,690	28,509	Port Everglades, Fla.	11,649	—
Duluth-Superior, Minn.	28,817	37,255	San Juan, P.R.	11,642	10,935
Pittsburgh	28,552	34,297	Jacksonville, Fla.	11,332	11,849
Marcus Hook, Pa.	27,418	26,110	Savannah, Ga.	11,327	11,245
Beaumont, Tex.	26,842	33,004	Memphis, Tenn.	10,375	12,717
St. Louis (Metropolitan)	26,620	26,976	Anacortes, Wash.	10,208	—
Lake Charles, La.	25,494	27,238	St. Paul	9,968	12,535
Chicago	22,574	23,813	Lorain Harbor, Ohio	9,426	—
Portland, Ore.	21,845	27,302	New Haven, Conn.	9,349	10,625
Pascagoula, Miss.	20,006	24,153	Conneaut Harbor, Ohio	9,148	12,660
Huntington, W. Va.	19,644	21,731	Charleston, S.C.	8,882	—

Source: Department of the Army, Corps of Engineers.

Annual Railroad Carloadings

Year	Total	Year	Total	Year	Total	Year	Total
1920	33,754,000	1945	41,918,000	1970	27,160,000	1981	21,612,000
1925	34,783,000	1950	38,903,000	1975	23,217,000	1982	18,498,000
1930	30,173,000	1955	37,636,000	1978	23,355,000	1983	18,815,000
1935	22,015,000	1960	30,441,000	1979	23,892,000	1984	20,257,000
1940	36,358,000	1965	29,248,000	1980	22,598,000	1985	19,418,000

Source: Association of American Railroads.

Estimated Motor Vehicle Registration, 1986

(in thousands; including publicly owned vehicles)

State	Autos[1]	Trucks and buses	Motor-cycles	Total
Alabama	2,417	1,044	58	3,519
Alaska	217	131	9	357
Arizona	1,662	691	84	2,437
Arkansas	939	496	30	1,465
California	15,384	4,319	677	20,380
Colorado	2,027	742	107	2,876
Connecticut	2,377	160	58	2,595
Delaware	383	102	11	496
Dist. of Col.	328	17	4	349
Florida	8,142	2,207	226	10,575
Georgia	3,375	1,311	115	4,801
Hawaii	589	83	18	690
Idaho	528	334	48	910
Illinois	6,137	1,648	221	8,006
Indiana	3,035	1,055	130	4,220
Iowa	1,988	776	274	3,038
Kansas	1,490	681	94	2,265
Kentucky	1,777	864	38	2,679
Louisiana	2,079	975	55	3,109
Maine	641	220	44	905
Maryland	2,771	588	63	3,422
Massachusetts	3,264	473	124	3,861
Michigan	5,762	1,425	214	7,401
Minnesota	2,744	804	175	3,723
Mississippi	1,375	435	25	1,835
Missouri	2,648	945	78	3,671
Montana	382	246	24	652
Nebraska	842	420	40	1,302
Nevada	502	194	18	714
New Hampshire	854	165	66	1,085
New Jersey	4,428	498	128	5,054
New Mexico	732	423	41	1,196
New York	8,185	1,188	253	9,626
North Carolina	3,314	1,222	67	4,603
North Dakota	376	273	29	678
Ohio	6,972	1,359	279	8,610
Oklahoma	1,915	1,000	105	3,020
Oregon	1,561	662	84	2,307
Pennsylvania	5,980	1,360	215	7,555
Rhode Island	517	98	27	642
South Carolina	1,715	561	39	2,315
South Dakota	429	248	35	712
Tennessee	3,070	844	105	4,019
Texas	8,606	4,006	273	12,885
Utah	733	372	52	1,157
Vermont	315	103	21	439
Virginia	3,838	625	84	4,547
Washington	2,652	1,115	136	3,903
West Virginia	860	379	32	1,271
Wisconsin	2,528	753	206	3,487
Wyoming	286	221	19	526
TOTAL	**135,671**	**40,861**	**5,358**	**181,890**

1. Includes taxicabs. NOTE: Figures are latest available. *Source:* Department of Transportation, Federal Highway Administration.

Passenger Car Production by Make

Companies and models	1986	1985	1980	1975	1970	1965
American Motors Corporation	49,503	109,919	164,725	323,704	276,127	346,367
Chrysler Corporation						
Plymouth	422,619	369,487	293,342	443,550	699,031	679,539
Dodge	506,370	482,388	263,169	354,482	405,699	547,531
Chrysler	791,210	414,193	82,440	102,940	158,614	224,061
Imperial	—	—	—	1,930	10,111	16,422
Total	**1,297,580**	**1,266,068**	**638,974**	**902,902**	**1,273,455**	**1,467,553**
Ford Motor Company						
Ford	1,221,871	1,098,627	929,627	1,301,414	1,647,918	2,164,902
Mercury	359,332	374,446	324,528	405,104	310,463	355,404
Lincoln	183,032	163,077	52,793	101,520	58,771	45,470
Total	**1,764,235**	**1,636,150**	**1,306,948**	**1,808,038**	**2,017,152**	**2,565,776**
General Motors Corporation						
Chevrolet	1,499,230	1,691,254	1,737,336	1,687,091	1,504,614	2,587,509
Pontiac	794,737	702,617	556,429	523,469	422,212	860,652
Oldsmobile	927,173	1,168,982	783,225	654,342	439,632	650,801
Buick	775,966	1,001,461	783,575	535,820	459,931	653,838
Cadillac	319,037	322,765	203,991	278,404	152,859	196,595
Total	**4,316,143**	**4,887,079**	**4,064,556**	**3,679,126**	**2,979,248**	**4,949,395**
Checker Motors Corporation	—	—	3,197	3,181	4,146	6,136
Volkswagen of America	84,397	96,458	197,106	—	—	—
Honda	238,159					
Nissan	65,117	145,337	—	—	—	—
Industry total	**7,828,783**	**8,184,821**	**6,375,506**	**6,716,951**	**6,550,128**	**9,335,227**

Source: Motor Vehicle Manufacturers Association of the United States.

Motor Vehicle Data

	1985	1980	1970	1960	1950
U.S. passenger cars and taxis registered (thousands)	132,108	121,724	89,280	61,671	40,339
Total mileage of U.S. passenger cars (millions)	1,298,199	1,111,950	901,000	588,083	363,613
Total fuel consumption of U.S. passenger cars (millions of gallons)	72,512	73,375	65,784	41,169	24,305
World registration of cars, trucks, and buses (thousands)	487,544	411,113	248,900	126,908	70,424
U.S. registration of cars, trucks, and buses (thousands)	171,691	155,890	108,407	73,858	49,162
U.S. share of world registration of cars, trucks, and buses	35.2%	37.9%	43.6%	58.2%	69.8%

Source: Motor Vehicle Manufacturers Association of the U.S.

Domestic Passenger Car Sales

Company and model	1986	1985	1984
American Motors	72,853	123,449	190,255
Total Renault	65,115	110,673	169,601
Alliance	48,874	71,494	100,366
Encore	16,241	39,179	69,235
Total AMC	7,738	12,776	20,654
Eagle	7,738	12,776	20,654
Chrysler Corp.	1,173,463	1,139,936	986,998
Total Plymouth	362,798	329,371	289,244
Horizon	111,092	84,500	78,298
Sundance	18,714	—	—
Turismo	46,368	52,817	47,109
Reliant	130,043	138,833	138,154
Caravelle	39,138	35,954	9,074
Plymouth	17,443	17,627	16,609
Total Chrysler	353,888	375,880	328,499
Laser	27,762	50,957	53,131
LeBaron GTS	66,985	71,018	2,494
LeBaron K	93,761	87,482	98,830
LeBaron J	831	—	—
Fifth Avenue	106,897	109,010	94,340
New Yorker	57,653	36,490	39,303
E-Class	—	20,923	40,265
Total Dodge	456,777	434,325	369,255
Omni	97,634	71,473	67,933
Shadow	20,140	—	—
Charger	50,196	57,171	51,940
Daytona	35,768	49,533	44,717
Aries	108,051	116,284	111,984
600 Coupe/400	—	3,012	18,953
Lancer	47,996	49,615	1,984
Diplomat	34,656	34,919	28,623
Dodge 600	62,336	55,330	42,843
Ford Motor	2,066,507	2,070,392	1,957,461
Ford Division	1,397,141	1,386,195	1,300,644
EXP	—	17,927	31,213
Escort	402,181	420,690	353,578
Mustang	167,699	157,821	138,296
Tempo	265,382	281,144	236,532
Taurus	263,450	4,056	—
Thunderbird	140,713	157,209	154,865
LTD	23,587	180,514	196,907
Crown Victoria	134,129	162,334	169,253
L-M Division	669,366	684,197	678,673
Total Mercury	491,182	519,059	527,198
Lynx	65,497	85,871	67,725
Topaz	67,499	73,098	73,454
Sable	98,593	2,430	—
Cougar	114,270	119,225	120,964
Capri	12,647	15,389	17,739
Marquis	10,180	87,844	103,722
Grand Marquis	123,096	135,202	143,594
Total Lincoln	177,584	165,138	151,475
Continental	20,629	27,679	31,110
Lincoln	133,175	117,606	90,869
Mark VII	23,780	19,853	29,496
General Motors	4,532,798	4,607,458	4,587,508
Buick Division	769,434	845,579	941,611
Skyhawk	72,384	85,639	121,858
Skylark	2,522	54,513	104,589
Somerset Regal	111,744	95,098	13,811
Century	240,747	234,508	217,042
Regal	78,340	112,590	182,185
LeSabre	132,406	115,212	164,314
Electra	107,999	99,185	84,414
Riviera	23,292	48,834	53,398
Cadillac Division	304,057	298,762	320,017
Cimarron	23,435	23,754	18,014
Seville	21,150	29,034	35,349
Cadillac	235,206	187,664	195,177
Eldorado	24,266	58,310	70,577
Chevrolet Division	1,558,476	1,600,200	1,565,143
Chevette	74,389	129,927	164,917
Nova	170,507	35,594	—
Cavalier	357,112	431,031	377,446
Citation	1,033	43,677	92,174
Camaro	163,204	199,985	202,172
Celebrity	408,946	363,619	322,198
Malibu	—	—	881
Corsica/Beretta	12,879	—	—
Monte Carlo	111,247	112,585	115,930
Chevrolet	226,132	245,826	258,902
Corvette	33,027	37,956	30,424
Oldsmobile Division	1,059,390	1,066,122	1,056,053
Firenza	34,113	49,580	62,456
Calais	116,018	122,810	14,881
Cutlass Ciera	329,930	333,585	242,209
Cutlass Supreme	191,937	217,504	302,087
Olds 88	261,260	188,129	258,297
Olds 98	109,370	122,421	100,419
Toronado	16,762	32,093	41,605
Pontiac Division	841,441	796,795	704,684
Fiero	68,340	90,303	93,485
1000	18,329	22,424	28,004
Sunbird	104,216	116,837	126,916
Phoenix	—	896	13,202
Firebird	94,241	100,610	101,414
Grand Am	205,254	121,273	16,751
6000	199,443	165,728	125,828
Bonneville/Grand Prix	41,588	52,972 [1]	65,387 [1]
Grand Prix	35,650	57,153	71,609
Parisienne/Bonn	74,380	69,049 [2]	62,084 [2]
Volkswagen	73,912	77,537	73,838
Honda	235,247	145,976	133,601
Nissan	52,602	39,794	—
Toyota	7,281	—	—
Domestic Total	8,214,663	8,204,547	7,951,517
Import Total	3,237,647	2,838,116	2,440,258
Industry Total	**11,452,310**	**11,042,658**	**10,391,775**

1. Bonneville only. 2. Parisienne only. *Source: Automotive News, Jan. 12, 1987.*

Domestic and Export Factory Sales of Motor Vehicles

(in thousands)

	From plants in United States								
	Passenger cars			Motor trucks and buses			Total motor vehicles		
Year	Total	Domestic	Exports	Total	Domestic	Exports	Total	Domestic	Exports
1965	9,306	9,101	205	1,752	1,616	136	11,058	10,717	341
1970	6,547	6,187	360	1,692	1,566	126	8,239	7,753	486
1975	6,713	6,073	640	2,272	2,003	269	8,985	8,076	909
1980	6,400	5,840	560	1,667	1,464	203	8,067	7,304	763
1982	5,049	4,696	353	1,906	1,779	127	6,955	6,475	480
1983	6,739	6,201	538	2,414	2,260	154	9,153	8,461	692
1984	7,621	7,030	591	3,075	2,884	191	10,696	9,914	782
1985	8,002	7,337	665	3,357	3,126	231	11,359	10,463	896
1986	7,516	6,869	647	3,393	3,130	263	10,909	9,999	910

Source: Motor Vehicle Manufacturers Association of the U.S.

Balance of International Payments

(in billions of dollars)

Item	1986	1985	1984	1980	1975	1970	1965	1960	1955
Exports of goods and services (excluding transfers under military grants)	$372.8	$358.5	$360.1	$344.7	$155.7	$65.7	$41.1	$28.9	$19.9
Merchandise, adjusted, excluding military	224.4	214.4	220.0	224.0	107.1	42.5	26.5	19.7	14.4
Transfers under U.S. military agency sales contracts	9.0	9.0	10.1	8.2	3.9	1.5	0.8	0.3	0.2
Receipts of income on U.S. investments abroad	88.2	90.0	86.2	75.9	25.4	11.8	7.4	4.6	2.6
Other services	51.1	45.0	43.9	36.5	19.3	9.9	6.4	4.3	2.7
Imports of goods and services	−498.5	−461.2	−454.4	−333.9	−132.6	−60.0	−32.8	−23.7	−17.8
Merchandise, adjusted, excluding military	−368.7	−339.0	−332.4	−249.3	−98.0	−39.9	−21.5	−14.8	−11.5
Direct defense expenditures	−12.6	−12.0	−12.0	−10.7	−4.8	4.9	−3.0	−3.1	−2.9
Payments of income on foreign assets in U.S.	−67.4	−65.0	−67.4	−43.2	−12.6	−5.5	−2.1	−1.2	−0.5
Other services	−49.9	−46.0	−42.5	−30.7	−17.2	−9.8	−6.2	−4.6	−2.8
Unilateral transfers, excluding military grants, net	−15.7	−15.0	−12.1	−7.0	−4.6	−3.3	−2.9	−2.3	−2.5
U.S. Government assets abroad, net	−96.0	−32.4	−24.0	−84.8	−3.5	−1.6	−1.6	−1.1	−0.3
U.S. private assets abroad, net	−94.4	−26.0	−15.0	−71.5	−35.4	−10.2	−5.3	−5.1	−1.3
U.S. assets abroad, official reserve, net	.3	−4.0	−3.1	−8.2	−0.6	2.5	1.2	2.1	0.2
Foreign assets in U.S., net	213.4	127.1	103.0	50.3	15.6	6.4	0.7	2.3	−1.4
Statistical discrepancy	24.0	23.0	27.3	29.6	5.5	−0.2	−0.5	−1.0	0.4
Balance on goods and services	−125.7	−103.0	−94.3	10.8	23.1	5.7	8.3	5.1	2.2
Balance on goods, services, and remittances	−129.6	−106.4	−98.0	8.4	21.3	4.1	7.2	4.5	1.6
Balance on current account	−141.4	−118.0	−106.4	3.7	18.4	2.4	5.4	2.8	−0.3

NOTE: — denotes debits. *Source:* Department of Commerce, Bureau of Economic Analysis.

Foreign Investors in U.S. Business Enterprises

	Number				Investment outlays (millions of dollars)			
	1986[1]	1985	1984	1983	1986[1]	1985	1984	1983
Investments, total	659	753	764	775	$31,472	$23,106	$15,197	$8,091
Acquisitions	338	390	315	299	25,467	20,083	11,836	4,848
Establishments	321	363	449	476	6,005	3,023	3,361	3,244
Investors, total	714	817	831	850	31,472	23,106	15,197	8,091
Foreign direct investors	316	320	434	460	6,309	4,225	4,181	2,528
U.S. affilates	398	497	397	390	25,164	18,881	11,016	5,564

1. Figures are preliminary. *Source:* U.S. Department of Commerce, *Survey of Current Business,* May 1987.

Imports of Leading Commodities
(value in millions of dollars)

Commodity	1986	1985
Food and live animals	$22,395	$20,292
Cattle, except for breeding	422	301
Meat and preparations	2,601	2,472
Dairy products and eggs	453	446
Fish	4,933	3,462
Grains and feed for animals	803	767
Vegetables and fruit	4,825	4,619
Sugar, cane or beet	717	1,001
Coffee	4,432	3,284
Cocoa beans	449	604
Tea	151	184
Beverages and tobacco	4,226	4,124
Alcoholic beverages	3,362	1,388
Tobacco, unmanufactured	626	571
Crude materials, inedible, except fuels	11,176	11,167
Hides and skins, except fur skins	67	76
Fur skins, undressed	147	175
Crude rubber	691	745
Wood—simply worked	3,268	3,195
Paper base stocks	1,657	1,572
Textile fibers and wastes	386	377
Industrial diamonds	130	139
Ores and metal scrap	2,362	2,564
Iron ore and concentrates	549	561
Nonferrous metal ores and concentrates	1,140	1,418
Precious metal ores and concentrates, except gold	267	240
Mineral fuels and related materials	39,838	55,843
Petroleum products	36,550	51,471
Natural gas	3,092	4,176
Animal and vegetable oils and fats	581	730
Chemicals	15,804	15,321
Organic chemicals	4,968	4,832
Inorganic chemicals	3,425	3,554
Medicinal and pharmaceutical products	1,267	1,108
Fertilizers, manufactured	953	1,049
Machinery and transport equipment	166,240	141,721
Machinery	90,101	77,717
Transport equipment	76,140	64,003
Automobiles, buses, trucks	56,275	47,009
Motor vehicle parts	12,245	10,568
Aircraft and parts	4,525	3,600
Misc. manufactured goods	60,079	51,684
Paper and manufactures	6,630	6,248
Glass, glassware, and pottery	2,699	2,406
Gem diamonds	3,476	3,020
Metals and manufactures	7,575	7,022
Iron and steel-mill products	9,559	10,614
Nonferrous metals	7,881	7,172
Precious metals, except gold	1,951	1,834
Textile yarn and thread	736	574
Clothing	18,554	16,056
Footwear	6,857	6,104
Scientific and contolling instruments	3,987	3,298
Printed matter	1,446	1,175
Clocks and watches	1,576	1,406
Baby carriages, toys, games and sporting goods	5,088	4,451
Artworks and antiques	2,123	2,216
Other transactions	15,042	11,245
Total	**387,082**	**$361,626**

Exports of Leading Commodities
(value in millions of dollars)

Commodity	1986	1985
Food and live animals	$17,303	$19,268
Meat and preparations	1,424	1,153
Dairy products and eggs	407	388
Grains and preparations	7,368	11,050
Wheat, including wheat flour	3,217	3,780
Rice	621	664
Corn	2,718	5,318
Vegetables and fruit	2,657	2,377
Feed for animals	2,622	1,890
Beverages and tobacco	2,920	2,958
Cigarettes	1,298	1,179
Tobacco	1,210	1,520
Crude materials, inedible, except fuels	17,324	16,939
Hides and skins, except fur skins	1,314	1,088
Soybeans	4,334	3,906
Synthetic rubber	649	583
Logs and lumber	2,240	2,036
Pulpwood and wood pulp	2,318	1,945
Raw cotton, excluding wastes	773	1,633
Ores and metal scrap	2,802	2,692
Mineral fuels and related materials	8,115	9,970
Coal	4,005	4,553
Petroleum and products	3,640	4,707
Animal and vegetable oils and fats	1,015	1,434
Soybean oil	260	439
Chemicals	22,766	21,758
Chemical elements and compounds	9,367	9,290
Medicines and pharmaceuticals	3,090	2,708
Fertilizers	1,935	2,160
Plastic materials and resins	4,301	3,777
Machinery and transport equipment	95,290	94,278
Machinery	60,397	59,488
Power generating machinery	9,165	9,271
Aircraft engines, parts	10,280	2,232
Automotive engines, parts	3,755	1,290
Agricultural machinery, including tractors, and parts	1,421	1,601
Office machines, computers	15,457	14,927
Metalworking machinery	1,467	1,249
Textile and leather machinery	554	498
Transport equipment	34,893	34,790
Motor vehicles and parts	18,575	19,364
Aircraft, spacecraft, accessories	15,106	14,373
Misc. manufactured goods	16,269	15,338
Tires and tubes	315	342
Paper and manufactures	2,602	2,328
Nonmetallic mineral manufactures	1,886	1,820
Metals and manufactures	5,281	5,958
Iron and steel-mill products	1,020	1,234
Nonferrous base metals	1,194	1,471
Other manufactures of metal	3,007	3,253
Textile yarns and fabrics	2,570	2,366
Clothing	899	754
Scientific instruments	6,732	6,505
Photographic supplies	1,418	1,313
Printed matter	1,342	1,279
Other transactions	11,010	10,970
Total	**217,304**	**$213,146**

Source: Department of Commerce, Bureau of the Census, Foreign Trade Division.

TAXES

History of the Income Tax in the United States

Source: Touche Ross & Co.

The nation had few taxes in its early history. From 1791 to 1802, the United States Government was supported by internal taxes on distilled spirits, carriages, refined sugar, tobacco and snuff, property sold at auction, corporate bonds, and slaves. The high cost of the War of 1812 brought about the nation's first sales taxes on gold, silverware, jewelry, and watches. In 1817, however, Congress did away with all internal taxes, relying on tariffs on imported goods to provide sufficient funds for running the Government.

In 1862, in order to support the Civil War effort, Congress enacted the nation's first income tax law. It was a forerunner of our modern income tax in that it was based on the principles of graduated, or progressive, taxation and of withholding income at the source. During the Civil War, a person earning from \$600 to \$10,000 per year paid tax at the rate of 3%. Those with incomes of more than \$10,000 paid taxes at a higher rate. Additional sales and excise taxes were added, and an "inheritance" tax also made its debut. In 1866, internal revenue collections reached their highest point in the nation's 90-year history—more than \$310 million, an amount not reached again until 1911.

The Act of 1862 established the office of Commissioner of Internal Revenue. The Commissioner was given the power to assess, levy, and collect taxes, and the right to enforce the tax laws through seizure of property and income and through prosecution. His powers and authority remain very much the same today.

In 1868, Congress again focused its taxation efforts on tobacco and distilled spirits and eliminated the income tax in 1872. It had a short-lived revival in 1894 and 1895. In the latter year, the U.S. Supreme Court decided that the income tax was unconstitutional because it was not apportioned among the states in conformity with the Constitution.

By 1913, with the 16th Amendment to the Constitution, the income tax had become a permanent fixture of the U.S. tax system. The amendment gave Congress legal authority to tax income and resulted in a revenue law that taxed incomes of both individuals and corporations. In fiscal year 1918 annual internal revenue collections for the first time passed the billion-dollar mark, rising to \$5. billion by 1920. With the advent of World War II employment increased, as did tax collections—to \$7.3 billion. The withholding tax on wages was introduced in 1943 and was instrumental in increasing the number of taxpayers to 60 million and tax collections to \$43 billion by 1945.

In 1981, Congress enacted the largest tax cut in U.S. history, approximately \$750 billion over six years. The tax reduction, however, was offset by two tax acts, in 1982 and 1984, which attempted to raise approximately \$265 billion.

On Oct. 22, 1986, President Reagan signed into law one of the most far-reaching reforms of the United States tax system since the adoption of the income tax. The Tax Reform Act of 1986, as it was called, attempted to be revenue neutral by increasing business taxes and correspondingly decreasing individual taxes by approximately \$120 billion over a five-year period.

Internal Revenue Service

The Internal Revenue Service (IRS), a bureau of the U.S. Treasury Department, is the federal agency charged with the administration of the tax laws passed by Congress. The IRS functions through a national office in Washington, 7 regional offices, 63 district offices, and 10 service centers.

Operations involving most taxpayers are carried out in the district offices and service centers. District offices are organized into Resources Management, Examination, Collection, Taxpayer Service, Employee Plans and Exempt Organizations, and Criminal Investigation. All tax returns are filed with the service centers, where the IRS computer operations are located.

IRS service centers are processing an ever increasing number of returns and documents. In 1986 the number of returns and supplemental documents processed totaled 188 million. This represented a 5.5% increase over 1985.

In prior years, all processing of documents was performed by hand. This process was time consuming and costly. In an attempt to improve the speed and efficiency of the manual processing procedure the IRS began testing an electronic return filing system beginning with the filing of 1985 returns. This filing system permits selected firms to transfer returns from their computers directly into the IRS system, thus bypassing the manual processing.

The pilot test for 1985 returns involved 5 tax firms. Collectively, they transferred 25,000 individual income tax forms. The two most significant results of the test were that refunds for the electronically filed returns were issued more quickly and the tax processing error rate was significantly lower when compared to paper returns.

This testing process was expanded for filing 1986 returns. The IRS's goal is to have the electronic filing system fully operational in the early 1990's.

Internal Revenue Service

	1986	1985	1984	1970	1960	1950
U.S. population (in thousands)	241,888	239,714	237,051	204,878	180,671	152,271
Number of IRS employees	95,880	92,254	87,635	68,098	50,199	55,551
Cost to govt. of collecting $100 in taxes	$0.49	$0.48	$0.48	$0.45	$0.40	$0.59
Tax per capita	$3,233.94	$3,098.99	$2,870.59	$955.31	$507.96	$255.84
Collections by principal sources (in thousands of dollars)						
Total IRS collections	$782,251,812	$742,871,541	$680,475,229	$195,722,096	$91,744,803	$38,957,132
Income and profits taxes						
Individual	416,568,384	396,659,558	362,891,679	103,651,585	44,945,711	17,153,308
Corporation	80,441,620	77,412,769	74,179,370	35,036,983	22,179,414	10,854,351
Employment taxes	244,374,767	225,214,568	199,210,028	37,449,188	11,158,589	2,644,575
Estate and gift taxes	7,194,956	6,579,703	6,176,667	3,680,076	1,626,348	706,227
Alcohol taxes	5,647,485	5,398,100	5,402,467	4,746,382	3,193,714	2,219,202
Tobacco taxes	4,607,845	4,483,193	4,663,610	2,094,212	1,931,504	1,328,464
Manufacturers' excise taxes	9,927,742	10,020,574	10,097,242	6,683,061	4,735,129	1,836,053
All other taxes	13,489,014	17,103,077	17,854,167	2,380,609	2,004,394	2,214,951

NOTE: For fiscal year ending September 30th.

Auditing Tax Returns

Most taxpayers' contacts with the IRS arise through the auditing of their tax returns. The Service has been empowered by Congress to inquire about all persons who may be liable for any tax and to obtain for review the books and/or records pertinent to those taxpayers' returns. A wide-ranging audit operation is carried out in the 63 district offices by some 14,500 field agents and 3,400 office auditors.

Selecting Returns for Audit

The primary method used by the IRS in selecting returns for audits is a computer program that measures the probability of tax error in each return. The data base (established by an in-depth audit of randomly selected returns in various income categories) consists of approximately 200–250 individual items of information taken from each return. These 200–250 variables individually or in combination are weighted as relative indicators of potential tax change. Returns are then scored according to the weights given the combinations of variables as they appear on each return. The higher the score, the greater the tax change potential. Other returns are selected for examination on the basis of claims for refund, multi-year audits, related return audits, and other audits initiated by the IRS as a result of informants' information, special compliance programs, and the information document matching program.

In 1986, the IRS recommended additional tax and penalties on 914,964 returns, totaling $19.3 billion.

The Appeals Process

The IRS attempts to resolve tax disputes through an administrative appeals system. Taxpayers who, after audit of their tax returns, disagree with a proposed change in their tax liabilities are entitled to an independent review of their cases. Taxpayers are able to seek an immediate, informal appeal with the Appeals Office. If, however, the dispute arises from a field audit and the amount in question exceeds $2,500, a taxpayer must submit a written protest. Alternatively, the taxpayer can wait for the examiner's report and then request consideration by the Appeals Office and file a protest if necessary. Taxpayers may represent themselves or be represented by an attorney, accountant, or any other advisor authorized to practice before the IRS. Taxpayers can forego their right to the above process and await receipt of a deficiency notice. At this juncture, taxpayers can either (1) not pay the deficiency and petition the Tax Court by a required deadline or (2) pay the deficiency and file a claim for refund with the District Director's office. If the claim is denied, a suit for refund may be brought either in the District Court or the Claims Court within a specified period.

Federal Individual Income Tax

The Federal individual income tax is levied on the world-wide income of U.S. citizens and resident aliens and on certain types of U.S. source income of non-residents. For a non-itemizer, "tax table income" is adjusted gross income (*see* below) less $1,900 for each personal exemption and the standard deduction (*see* below). If a taxpayer itemizes, tax table income is adjusted gross income minus total itemized deductions and personal exemptions. Previous law provided 15 tax brackets, with a top rate of 50 percent. For the 1987 tax year, there are only five tax brackets ranging from 11% to a maximum of 38 1/2%.

Who Must File a Return[1]

You must file a return if you are:	and your gross income is at least:
Single (legally separated, divorced, or married living apart from spouse with dependent child) and are under 65	$4,440

Single (legally separated, divorced, or married living apart from spouse with dependent child) and are 65 or older	$5,650
A person who can be claimed as a dependent on your parent's return, and who has taxable dividends, interest, or other unearned income	$500
Head of household under age 65	$4,440
Head of household over age 65	$7,050
Married, filing jointly, living together at end of year (or at date of death of spouse), and both are under 65	$7,560
Married, filing jointly, living together at end of year (or at date of death of spouse), and one is 65 or older	$9,400
Married, filing jointly, living together at end of year (or at date of death of spouse), and both are 65 or older	$10,000
Married, filing separate return, or married but not living together at end of year	$1,900
A person with income from sources within U.S. possessions	$1,900
Self-employed and your net earnings from self-employment were at least $400	
A person who received any advance earned income credit payments from their employer during the year	
A person who owes minimum tax, individual retirement arrangement tax, investment credit recapture tax or social security tax on unreported tips	

1. In 1987.

Adjusted Gross Income

Gross income consists of wages and salaries, unemployment compensation, tips and gratuities, interest, dividends, annuities, rents and royalties, up to 1/2 of Social Security Benefits if the recipient's income exceeds a base amount, and certain other types of income. Among the items excluded from gross income, and thus not subject to tax, are public assistance benefits and interest on exempt securities (mostly state and local bonds). Under the new law, both the 60 percent of net capital gains exclusion and the $100 ($200 on a joint return) eligible dividends received exclusion have been eliminated.

Adjusted gross income is determined by subtracting from gross income: alimony paid, penalties on early withdrawal of savings, reimbursed employee business expenses, payments to an I.R.A. (reduced proportionately based upon adjusted gross income levels if taxpayer is an active participant in an employer maintained retirement plan), payments to a Keogh retirement plan and self-employed health insurance payments (25% limit). Unreimbursed business expenses and job related moving expenses are now treated as itemized deductions (see below).

Itemized Deductions

Taxpayers may itemize deductions or take the standard deduction. The standard deduction replaces the zero bracket amount. The standard deduction amounts for 1987 are as follows: Married filing jointly and surviving spouses $3,760; Heads of household $2,540; Single $2,540; and Married filing separate returns $1,880. Tax payers who are age 65 or over or are blind have separate standard deduction amounts for the 1987 tax year. The 1987 standard deduction amounts are: married filing jointly and surviving spouses $5,000; heads of households $4,400; single tax payers $3,000; and married filing separate returns $2,500. In addition, a standard deduction of $750 for single taxpayers and $600 for a married taxpayer is provided if the taxpayer is over age 65 or blind.

In itemizing deductions, the following are major items that may be deducted in 1987: state and local income and property taxes, charitable contributions, employee moving expenses, medical expenses (exceeding 7.5% of adjusted gross income), casualty losses (only the amount over the $100 floor which exceeds 10% of adjusted gross income), interest payments (only 65% of personal interest payments are deductable) and miscellaneous deductions (deductible only to the extent by which cumulatively they exceed 2% of adjusted gross income).

Personal Exemptions

Personal exemptions are available to the taxpayer for himself, his spouse, and his dependents. The 1987 amount is $1,900 for each individual. Under the new law, no exemption is allowed a taxpayer who can be claimed as a dependent on another taxpayer's return. Additionally, the personal exemptions for taxpayers age 65 or over or blind have been eliminated.

Credits

Taxpayers can reduce their income tax liability by claiming the benefit of certain tax credits. Each dollar of tax credit offsets a dollar of tax liability. The following are a few of the available tax credits:

Certain lower-income households with dependent children may claim an Earned Income Credit of up to $800 on $5,714 of earned income. This maximum credit will be reduced if earned income or adjusted gross income exceeds $6,500, and the credit will be zero for families with incomes over $14,500.

A credit for Child and Dependent Care Expenses is available for amounts paid to care for a child or other dependent so that the taxpayer can work. The credit is between 20% and 30% (depending on adjusted gross income) of up to $2,400 of employment-related expenses for one qualifying child or dependent and up to $4,800 of expenses for two or more qualifying individuals.

The elderly and those under 65 who are retired under total disability may be entitled to a credit of up to $750 (if single) or $1,125 (if married and filing jointly). No credit is available if the taxpayer is single and has adjusted gross income of $17,500 or more, or $5,000 or more in nontaxable Social Security benefits. Similarly, the credit is unavailable to a married couple if their adjusted gross income exceeds $25,000 or if their nontaxable Social Security benefits equal or exceed $7,500.

Other tax credits available to taxpayers include the targeted jobs credit, and the foreign tax credit. The new law has eliminated the investment tax credit and the contibutions to candidates for public office credit.

Federal Income Tax Comparisons

Taxes at Selected Rate Brackets After Standard Deductions and Personal Exemptions[1]

Adjusted gross income	Single return listing no dependents				Joint return listing two dependents			
	1988	1987	1986[1]	1975	1988	1987	1986[1]	1975
$ 10,000	$ 758	$ 762	$ 863	$ 1,506	$ -700[2]	$-450[2]	$ 96	$ 829
20,000	2,258	2,262	2,788	4,153	1,080	1,176	1,625	2,860
30,000	4,694	4,901	5,509	8,018	2,580	2,676	3,548	5,804
40,000	7,494	8,300	8,908	12,765	4,080	4,259	6,125	9,668
50,000	10,389	11,800	12,873	18,360	6,549	7,059	9,310	14,260

1. For comparison purposes, tax rate schedules were used. 2. Refund based on earned income credit for families with dependent children.

Federal Corporation Taxes

Corporations are taxed under a graduated tax rate structure as shown in the charts below. For tax years beginning before July 1, 1987, the benefits of the lower rates are phased out for corporations with taxable income between $1,000,000 and $1,405,000 and totally eliminated for corporations with incomes equal to or in excess of $1,405,000. For tax years beginning on or after July 1, 1987, the benefits of the lower rates are phased out for corporations with taxable income between $100,000 and $235,000 and totally eliminated for corporations with income equal to or in excess of $235,000.

If the corporation qualifies, it may elect to be an S corporation. If it makes this election, the corporation will not (with certain exceptions) pay corporate tax on its income. Its income is instead passed through and taxed to its shareholders. There are several requirements a corporation must meet to qualify as an S corporation including having 35 or fewer shareholders, and having only one class of stock.

Tax Years Beginning Before July 1, 1987

Taxable income	Tax	Percent over excess
$0 to $25,000	$ 0	15% over $0
$25,000 to $50,000	$ 3,750	18% over $25,000
$50,000 to $75,000	$ 8,250	30% over $50,000
$75,000 to $100,000	$ 15,750	40% over $75,000
$100,000 and over	$ 25,750	46% over $100,000

Tax Years Beginning on or After July 1, 1987

Taxable income	Tax	Percent over excess
$0 to $50,000	$ 0	15% over $0
$50,000 to $75,000	$ 7,500	25% over $50,000
$75,000 and over	$ 13,750	34% over $75,000

State Corporation Income and Franchise Taxes

All states but Nevada, South Dakota, Texas, Washington, and Wyoming impose a tax on corporation net income. The majority of states impose the tax at flat rates ranging from 2.35% to 11.5%. Several states have adopted a graduated basis of rates for corporations.

Nearly all states follow the federal law in defining net income. However, many states provide for varying exclusions and adjustments.

A state is empowered to tax all of the net income of its domestic corporations. With regard to non-resident corporations, however, it may only tax the net income on business carried on within its boundaries. Corporations are, therefore, required to apportion their incomes among the states where they do business and pay a tax to each of these states. Nearly all states provide an apportionment to their domestic corporations, too, in order that they not be unduly burdened.

Several states tax unincorporated businesses separately.

Federal Estate and Gift Taxes

A Federal Estate Tax Return must be filed for the estate of every U.S. citizen or resident whose gross estate, if the decedent died in 1987, exceeds $600,000. An estate tax return must also be filed for the estate of a non-resident, if the value of his gross estate in the U.S. is more than $60,000 at the date of death. The estate tax return is due nine months after the date of death of the decedent, but a reasonable extension of time to file may be obtained for good reason. Tax due is to be paid when the return is filed. The executor of an estate with an interest in closely held business that comprises at least 35% of the adjusted gross estate may pay estate tax attributable to the business in from two to ten equal annual installments. In such a case, a 5-year extension for the payment of estate taxes may be exercised for that portion of the tax attributable to a closely held business.

Under the unified federal estate and gift tax structure, individuals who made taxable gifts during the calendar year are required to file a gift tax return by April 15 of the following year.

A unified credit of $192,800 (during 1987) is available to offset both estate and gift taxes. Any part of the credit used to offset gift taxes is not available to offset estate taxes. As a result, although they are still taxable as gifts, lifetime transfers no longer cushion the impact of progressive estate tax rates. Lifetime transfers and transfers made at death are cumulated for estate tax rate purposes. Gift taxes are computed by applying the uniform rate schedule to lifetime taxable transfers (after deducting the unified credit) and subtracting the taxes payable for prior taxable periods. In general, estate taxes are computed by applying the uniform rate schedule to cumulated transfers and subtracting the gift taxes paid. An appropriate adjustment is made for taxes on lifetime transfers—such as certain gifts within three years of death—in a decedent's estate.

Among the deductions allowed in computing the amount of the estate subject to tax are funeral expenditures, administrative costs, claims and bequests to religious, charitable, and fraternal organizations or government welfare agencies, and state inheritance taxes. For transfers made after 1981 during life or death, there is an unlimited marital deduction.

An annual gift tax exclusion is provided that permits tax-free gifts to each donee of $10,000 for each year. A husband and wife who agree to treat gifts to third persons as joint gifts can exclude up to $20, 000 a year to each donee. An unlimited exclusion for medical expenses and school tuition paid for the benefit of any donee is also available.

Federal Estate and Gift Taxes

Unified Rate Schedule, 1987[1]

If the net amount is:		Tentative tax is:		
From	To	Tax +	%	On excess over
$ 0	$ 10,000	$ 0	18	$ 0
10,001	20,000	1,800	20	10,000
20,001	40,000	3,800	22	20,000
40,001	60,000	8,200	24	40,000
60,001	80,000	13,000	26	60,000
80,001	100,000	18,200	28	80,000
100,001	150,000	23,800	30	100,000
150,001	250,000	38,800	32	150,000
250,001	500,000	70,800	34	250,000
500,001	750,000	155,800	37	500,000
750,001	1,000,000	248,300	39	750,000
1,000,001	1,250,000	345,800	41	1,000,000
1,250,001	1,500,000	448,300	43	1,250,000
1,500,001	2,000,000	555,800	45	1,500,000
2,000,001	2,500,000	780,800	49	2,000,000
2,500,001	3,000,000	1,025,800	53	2,500,000
3,000,001 and up	—	1,290,800	55	3,000,000

1. The estate and gift tax rates are combined in the single rate schedule effective for the estates of decedents dying, and for gifts made, after Dec. 31, 1976.

State General Sales and Use Taxes, July 1987[1]

State	Percent rate	State	Percent rate	State	Percent rate
Alabama	4	Kentucky	5	Ohio	5
Arizona	5	Louisiana	4	Oklahoma	4
Arkansas	4	Maine	5	Pennsylvania	6
California	4.75	Maryland	5	Rhode Island	6
Colorado	3	Massachusetts	5	South Carolina	5
Connecticut	7.5	Michigan	4	South Dakota	5
D.C.	6	Minnesota	6	Tennessee	5.5
Florida	5	Mississippi	6	Texas	5.25
Georgia	3	Missouri	4.225	Utah	5.09375
Hawaii	4	Nebraska	4	Vermont	4
Idaho	5	Nevada	5.75	Virginia	3.5
Illinois	5	New Jersey	6	Washington	6.5
Indiana	5	New Mexico	4.75	West Virginia	5
Iowa	4	New York	4	Wisconsin	5
Kansas	4	North Carolina	3	Wyoming	3
		North Dakota	5		

1. Local and county taxes, if any, are additional. NOTE: Alaska, Delaware, Montana, New Hampshire and Oregon have no statewide sales and use taxes. *Source: Information Please Almanac* questionnaires to the states, and Tax Foundation, Inc.

Sales Tax Rates in Selected Cities[1]

City	Percent rate	City	Percent rate	City	Percent rate
Amarillo, Tex.	1	Jefferson City, Mo.[2,4]	2	Richmond, Va.	1
Anaheim, Calif.[2]	1.25	Lincoln, Neb.	1.5	Roanoke, Va.	1
Austin, Tex.[4]	2	Los Angeles[4]	1.75	Sacramento, Calif.[2]	1.25
Baton Rouge, La.[3]	3	Lynchburg, Va.	1	St. Louis[4]	1.875
Berkeley, Calif.[2,4]	2.25	Minneapolis, Minn.	.5	San Antonio, Tex.[4]	1.5
Birmingham, Ala.[4]	3	Mobile, Ala.	3	San Diego, Calif.[2]	1.25
Boulder, Colo.[4]	2.75	Montgomery, Ala.[2]	4	San Francisco[2 4]	1.75
Chicago[4]	3	New Orleans[3]	5.0	Seattle[2,4]	2.0
Dallas[4]	2	New York[4]	4.25	Shreveport, La.[3]	3.5
Denver[4]	4.1	Nome, Alaska	4	Spokane, Wash.[4]	1.6
El Paso	1	Norfolk, Va.	1	Springfield, Ill.[2]	2.25
Fort Worth[4]	1.25	Oakland, Calif.[2,4]	2.25	Topeka, Kan.	1.0
Fresno, Calif.[4]	1.75	Oklahoma City	2	Troy, N.Y.[2]	3
Glendale, Calif.[4]	1.75	Omaha, Neb.	1.5	Tucson, Ariz.	2
Houston[4]	2	Pasadena, Calif.[4]	1.75	Tulsa, Okla.	3
Huntsville, Ala.	3	Phoenix, Ariz.[4]	1.7	Washington, D.C.	6
Ithaca, N.Y.[2]	3	Rapid City, S.D.	2	Yonkers, N.Y.[2,4]	1.7

1. Excludes state and county sales taxes unless otherwise indicated. 2. Combined city and county rate. 3. Includes Parish School Board tax. 4. Includes tax imposed for public transit or transportaion purposes. *Source:* Tax Foundation, Inc.

Income Tax Rates in Selected Cities

(Population exceeding 50,000)

City	Percent rate	Year begun	City	Percent rate	Year begun
Akron, Ohio	2	1962	Lakewood, Ohio	1.5	1968
Allentown, Pa.	1	1958	Lancaster, Pa	0.5	1959
Altoona, Pa.	1	1948	Lansing, Mich	1	1968
Baltimore	(1)	1966	Lexington, Ky.	2	1952
Bethlehem, Pa.	1	1957	Lima, Ohio	1.5	1959
Birmingham, Ala.	1	1970	Lorain, Ohio	1.5	1967
Canton, Ohio	2	1954	Louisville, Ky.	2.2	1948
Cincinnati	2	1954	Mansfield, Ohio	1.25	1966
Cleveland	2	1967	New York[2]	1.5–4.1	1966
Cleveland Heights, Ohio	2	1968	Owensboro, Ky.	1	1960
Columbus, Ohio	2	1947	Parma, Ohio	2	1967
Covington, Ky.	2.5	1956	Philadelphia	4.96	1939
Dayton, Ohio	2.25	1949	Pittsburgh	2.125	1954
Detroit	3	1965	Pontiac, Mich.	1	1968
District of Columbia[2]	6–10	1947	Reading, Pa.	1	1969
Elyria, Ohio	1.5	1969	Saginaw, Mich.	1	1965
Erie, Pa.	1	1948	St. Louis	1	1948
Euclid, Ohio	2	1967	Scranton, Pa.	2.2	1948
Flint, Mich.	1	1965	Springfield, Ohio	2.0	1948
Gadsden, Ala.	2	1956	Toledo, Ohio	2.25	1946
Grand Rapids, Mich.	1	1967	Warren, Ohio	1.5	1952
Hamilton, Ohio	1.75	1960	Wilkes-Barre, Pa.	2.5	1966
Harrisburg, Pa.	1	1966	Wilmington, Del.	1.25	1970
Kansas City, Mo.	1	1964	York, Pa.	1.0	1965
Kettering, Ohio	1.75	1968	Youngstown, Ohio	2	1948

1. Tax is 50% of state income tax. 2. Further reductions scheduled. NOTE: Rates are for residents only, except in Kentucky and Ohio cities, where non-resident rate is the same. *Source:* Tax Foundation, Inc.

Origin of The Dollar

"The almighty dollar" is actually mightier than one might think if omnipresence be considered a part of might, for the word *dollar* has been used to indicate several different coins. The German form of *dollar* is *Taler,* which is short for *Joachimstaler,* a silver coin minted in Joachimstal (now Jachymov in northwestern Czechoslovakia) in the sixteenth century. The North German and Dutch form of *taler* was *daler,* the form borrowed into English as *dollar.* From the sixteenth to the eighteenth century the English used *dollar* to refer to the Spanish coin also known as a *piece of eight* or *peso* that was a medium of exchange in Spain and the Spanish-American colonies. This Spanish coin was derived from the Dutch *daler.* Because the North American colonists were familiar with the Spanish coin, Thomas Jefferson proposed that the monetary unit of the newly independent United States be called a *dollar* and resemble the Spanish peso. His proposal was adopted in 1785. A coin similar to the Spanish and American dollar has also been the monetary unit of China, Arabia, and elsewhere.—*Source:* "Word Mysteries & Histories," © 1986 by Houghton Mifflin Company.

State and Local Taxes Paid by a Family of Four in Selected Large Cities, 1985

City	Total Taxes Paid by Gross Family Income Level			Percent of Income by Income Level		
	$15,000	$25,000	$35,000	$15,000	$25,000	$35,000
Albuquerque	1,014	1,786	2,578	6.8	7.1	7.4
Atlanta	1,142	2,155	3,198	7.6	8.6	9.1
Baltimore	1,673	2,874	3,933	11.2	11.5	11.2
Boston	1,071	1,984	2,976	7.1	7.9	8.5
Bridgeport	2,696	4,182	5,746	18.0	16.7	16.4
Burlington	1,167	1,995	2,793	7.8	8.0	8.0
Charleston, W.V.	1,013	1,694	2,387	6.8	6.8	6.8
Charlotte	1,069	1,913	2,706	7.1	7.7	7.7
Chicago	1,115	1,925	2,676	7.4	7.7	7.6
Cleveland	1,292	2,255	3,251	8.6	9.0	9.3
Columbia	1,101	2,062	2,923	7.3	8.2	8.4
Des Moines	1,180	2,223	3,202	7.9	8.9	9.1
Detroit	1,764	3,074	4,262	11.8	12.3	12.2
Honolulu	1,082	2,200	3,118	7.2	8.8	8.9
Indianapolis	1,464	2,343	3,214	9.8	9.4	9.2
Jackson, MS	1,037	1,731	2,428	6.9	6.9	6.9
Louisville	1,097	1,984	2,775	7.3	7.9	7.9
Milwaukee	1,695	2,902	4,107	11.3	11.6	11.7
Newark, NJ	2,662	4,261	5,962	17.7	17.0	17.0
New York City	1,372	2,456	3,690	9.1	9.8	10.5
Norfolk	1,044	1,846	2,585	7.0	7.4	7.4
Oklahoma City	996	1,692	2,513	6.6	6.8	7.2
Omaha	1,096	1,811	2,495	7.3	7.2	7.1
Philadelphia	1,953	3,086	4,230	13.0	12.3	12.1
Portland, ME	1,191	2,037	3,077	7.9	8.1	8.8
Portland, OR	1,425	2,767	3,957	9.5	11.1	11.3
Providence	1,924	3,167	4,379	12.8	12.7	12.5
Salt Lake City	1,264	2,267	3,115	8.4	9.1	8.9
Washington, DC	1,214	2,290	3,284	8.1	9.2	9.4
Wilmington	1,691	3,034	4,365	11.3	12.1	12.5
Median[1]	1,097	1,846	2,585	7.3	7.4	7.4

1. Median of all 51 cities *see* following table. For complete list of cities. NOTE: Data based on average family of four (one wage earner, wife or husband, and two school age children) owning their own home and living in a city where taxes apply. Comprises State and local sales, income, auto, and real estate taxes. *Source:* Government of the District of Columbia, Department of Finance and Revenue, *Tax Burdens in Washington, D.C. Compared With Those in The Largest City in Each of the 50 States, 1985.*

Residential Property Tax Rates by Rank in Selected Large Cities: 1985

City	Effective Tax Rate Per $100 — Rate	Assessment level (percent)	Nominal rate per $100	City	Effective Tax Rate Per $100 — Rate	Assessment level (percent)	Nominal rate per $100
Newark, NJ	5.46	45.8	11.93	Cleveland	2.08	35.0	5.94
Wilmington, DE	4.26	92.0	4.63	Sioux Falls	2.05	29.8	6.89
Bridgeport	4.21	63.8	6.60	Portland, ME	2.03	75.0	2.71
Detroit	4.16	50.0	8.32	Omaha	2.01	72.4	2.77
Indianapolis	3.32	33.3	9.96				
Milwaukee	3.22	99.3	3.24	Chicago	1.63	16.0	10.16
Providence	3.21	44.3	7.25	Jackson, MS	1.61	15.0	10.75
Des Moines	2.73	72.5	3.76	Boise City	1.50	98.7	1.52
				Fargo	1.47	4.5	32.58
Baltimore	2.70	43.5	6.21	New York City	1.37	15.0	9.10
Philadelphia	2.62	35.0	7.48	Louisville	1.30	92.0	1.41
Portland, OR	2.57	100.0	2.57	New Orleans	1.30	92.0	1.41
Manchester	2.38	30.0	7.93	Billings	1.26	3.7	34.09
Minneapolis	2.27	20.8	10.89	Charlotte	1.16	90.5	1.28

Norfolk	1.15	92.0	1.25	Wichita	.99	7.8	12.68
Columbia	1.15	4.0	28.65	Anchorage	.94	100.0	.94
Washington, DC	1.14	93.7	1.22	Little Rock	.92	20.0	4.61
Phoenix	1.09	10.0	10.89	Las Vegas	.85	35.0	2.44
Charleston, WV	1.07	62.0	1.73	Denver	.74	7.8	9.48
Salt Lake City	1.04	11.9	8.75	Birmingham	.70	10.0	6.95
St. Louis	1.04	19.0	5.48	Los Angeles	.65	61.2	1.06
Seattle	.99	93.8	1.06	Honolulu	.61	90.0	.68
				Casper	.58	8.0	7.22

Source: Government of the District of Columbia, Department of Finance and Revenue, *Tax Burdens in Washington, DC Compared With Those in The Largest City in Each of the 50 States, 1985.*

Labor Firsts in America

Source: U.S. Department of Labor.

The first . . .

Labor organization was formed by the Boston shoemakers and coopers guilds, which obtained a three-year charter (1648).

Women's labor organization was established by maidservants in New York City to protest abuses they suffered from their mistresses' husbands (1734).

National labor union that still exists today is the International Typographical Union (1850).

Union of federal employees was formed by New York City letter carriers (1863).

National federation of industrial unions was the Committee of Industrial Organization (1935).

State to create a permanent agency to mediate labor disputes was New York (1886).

Federal arbitration law was passed (1888).

President to act as mediator in a labor dispute was Theodore Roosevelt, who personally attempted to settle the anthracite coal strike (1902).

Arbitration Association, the American Society of Arbitration, Inc., was formed in New York City (1922).

Report on occupational health hazards was by B.W. M'Cready, who wrote "On the Influence of Trades Professions and Occupations in the United States in the Production of Diseases." (1837)

State to study occupational safety was Massachusetts (1850), which also passed the first legislation requiring factory safeguards (1877) and factory inspections (1879).

Federal agency to promote occupational safety was the Working Conditions Services, which sought to improve working conditions for defense workers during the war (1918).

Federal legislation setting safety and health standards for workers in general in the private sector was the Occupational Safety and Health Act, which is administered by the Department of Labor (1970).

Pension was established by the Plymouth Colony for disabled soldiers (1638).

Federal government pension was established to assist wounded and disabled Revolutionary soldiers (1776).

Private pension plan offered by a company was established by the American Express Company (1875).

Pension law to be declared constitutional was in Alaska. The law covered all residents over 65, who had lived in the state for 10 years (1915).

Federal regulation of pension plans resulted from the passage of the Employee Retirement Income Security Act (1974).

Legislation dealing with child labor was a Massachusetts Bay colony court order calling for town magistrates to investigate the possibility of "teaching the boys and girls in all towns the spinning of the yarn" (1640).

State law restricting child labor was in Massachusetts. It states that no child under the age of 15 shall work in "manufacturing establishments" unless the child attended school for at least three of the 12 months preceding any year of employment (1836).

Federal legislation to set a minimum age for child labor was the National Industrial Recovery Act, placing a 16 year minimum age for general work and 18 for hazardous jobs (1933).

Dispute that may be labeled a strike occurred in Jamestown, Va., as Polish workers protested against being denied the right to vote (1619).

Criminal prosecution of strikers came after a strike of cartmen in New York City (1677).

Use of militia to break up a strike took place in Paterson, N.J., when factory workers protested the changing of their dinner hour and eventually demanded a ten-hour day. Militia quelled the strikers, but the workers were successful in preventing the change of their dinner hour (1828).

Strike of national importance occurred when railroad workers on several eastern and midwestern lines struck to protest wage cuts (1877).

National general strike, and the first designated "May Day" strike, occurred when approximately 340,000 workers demonstrated for an eight-hour day in several cities (1886).

Massive strike by federal employees was by postal workers (1970).

Fixed wage rates were set by the governor of Virginia and the Council of London Company (1621).

States to have equal pay legislation for women were Michigan and Montana (1919).

Minimum wage of 25 cents per hour was established by the Fair Labor Standards Act (1938).

Anti-discrimination law against women was in Illinois (1872).

Federal equal pay legislation was the Equal Pay Act (1963).

Workers' compensation agreement was made between Captain William Kidd, the pirate, and his crew. "If any man should Loose a Leg or Arm in ye said service, he should six hundred pieces of Eight, or six able slaves." (1695).

Federal legislation for a 40-hour work week with time and a half pay for overtime was the Walsh-Healey Act, which applied to workers under government contracts (1936).

CAREER PLANNING KIT

Looking Ahead: Jobs and Education in the Future

An Interview with Marvin Cetron, Barbara Soriano, and Margaret Gayle

What jobs will be in the greatest demand in the 1990s?

Marvin Cetron: Let's take non-college professional jobs to start off with—jobs such as robot technician, laser technician, computer education design technician, housing rehabilitation technician, hazardous waste disposal technician, cat scan reader, geriatrics social worker, emergency medical technician, telemarketing, and holographic inspector. They're going to be basically service jobs, and 75 percent of high school graduates will not go to college. Therefore, what students need is a good service background, and that means that vocational education has to be improved significantly. Education is necessary, it's crucial, but it's not sufficient. We must have the students trained, and they'd better be computer literate. They're not going to be able to make it unless they know how to use computers.

Barbara Soriano: I think the main thing is that a great many jobs are going to be involved in information processing; so, the vocational education that we look at today isn't the entire picture. Students are going to have to have, as part of vocational education, a strong liberal arts orientation to be able to gather information and evaluate it.

Margaret Gayle: Process it.

Cetron: Gather it, analyze it, synthesize it, process it, store it. By the year 2000, 88 percent of the population will be involved in service industries. Half—44 percent—will be in information fields. Half of those people will be working at home or be able to work at home because of interactive cable.

What accounts for these changes? Between 1979 and 1984, for example, 90 percent of all medical advances took place—meaning that a doctor, researcher, or surgeon who hasn't read the literature only knows 10 percent of what's going on. If you take a look at materials for instrumentation, cars, houses, automobiles—90 percent of every single thing we have in materials research came out in the past 10 years. So the information component becomes extremely important, and, therefore, you've got to be able to communicate, write, read, analyze, and solve problems. Those are crucial things. We don't learn them all in math, physics, or chemistry; we learn them by communication.

We know where the jobs will be, but which will command the highest salaries?

Cetron: The highest salaries will be made by writers, painters, sculptors . . . people who work in the theater, sports people—those jobs that can't be computerized or automated will command the highest salaries. The higher salaries will be the ones I mentioned earlier—those in high technology, genetic engineering, biomedical technology, people working with artificial intelligence, fifth generation computers, and voice activated computers. The highest salaries will be for people who can do something unique in the arts that can't be computerized. However, they'd also better be trained at jobs, so that between acting jobs or painting or sculpting or writing, they can earn a basic living.

How has the pattern of schooling and work changed over the last decade? And, what accounts for this change?

Gayle: It really hasn't changed. This is part of the problem. It's like schooling has been out of sync with what's happening in the real world and, suddenly, the major education reports have just brought attention to all of this. However, the recommendations suggest that in order to fix schooling, we need to go back to something we quit doing, but that really isn't what the problem is.

Cetron: Students themselves have changed. They are much more conservative. Ever since 1982, they believe it's chic to make money again. It's cool to do well in school. They'll listen to somebody over 30 again.

* * *

I was thinking about the pattern of completing college or an advanced degree before entering the job market. If a recent college graduate asked your advice about whether to continue pursuing his or her lucrative business as a computer consultant or to pursue a graduate degree or Ph.D., what would you advise?

Cetron: Both. Take your graduate degree part time at night. I think the experience you're getting is very good. Maybe you want to take off the last semester or so and finish up your Ph.D. But I should say that you can work and go to school at night. If it takes a little longer, so much the better. You get dirt under your fingernails. That's the difference between education and training.

That's also why cooperative education programs are going to be crucial in the future. It's going to be even more important for the schools and businesses to work closer together.

Soriano: Many people still think about going to college and being prepared for life. What we are talking about here is that you get some initial training and initial education and expect to go back to school every 10 years to switch fields or enhance your current field. So, it's not crucial to get a degree under your belt to be prepared for a career.

Cetron: Every 10 years you're going to have to go back to school. It's going to be lifelong learning. The reason for lifelong learning is because things are moving so quickly. The half-life of an engineer is five years. In five years, 50 percent of what he's learned goes into the computer. In 10 years, 90 percent of what he's learned is on the computer. He's got to go back every 10 years and get retreaded. The same is true across the board in almost everything.

You're not going to get educated once, and with both spouses, an average of every five years one

---

Marvin Cetron is president of Forecasting International, Ltd. Barbara Soriano is a Washington-based consultant. Margaret Gayle is an associate director of vocational education with the North Carolina State Department of Public Instruction. All three are co-authors of *Schools of the Future—Education in the 21st Century,* a project sponsored in part by the AASA Foundation Fund.

spouse or the other will go back to school. By the way, in 50 percent of cases, both spouses were working in 1984. By 1990, the figure will be 65 percent and 75 percent by the year 2000.

* * *

Cetron: Another important change may create a different outcome, however. There'll be more job sharing. That is two people sharing one job and working shorter work hours. You are talking a 32-hour work week by 1990. You're talking a 20-hour work week by the year 2000. There'll be more production because robots and computers will be producing more for everybody, not dividing the pie differently. There won't be as Lester Thoreau says, a working class and a leisure class. Rather, there'll be one massive middle class, and I think that's important to bring out. The Electronic Industry Association and the Society of Manufacturers are all showing more middle class jobs. That's an important distinction here.

* * *

How will people who are very competitive adapt to a shorter work week and to working in groups?

Cetron: Overachievers may take two different jobs, not because they have to but because their metabolism is such that they are going to want to. And there are a lot of people like that.

Gayle: Some people may be unable to make the change to group processes or team efforts to get a job done. We do have a lot of those people, and it's going to be hard for them to make those changes and help produce things that are good for a group of people.

Soriano: That's why we're suggesting that computers be used in schools right from the beginning, not so much for the technology but for how the work world will be organized around the computer.

The computer seems to be providing opportunities for cooperative group effort because some people have the technical skills, others have the organizational skills, and still others have the creative skills necessary to do the job; and they are all dependent on each other to do it.

Cetron: And computers will have a multiplier effect on teaching, decreasing the student-leader ratio and increasing the effectiveness of the teacher. Teachers will be able to spend more time on problem analysis and synthesis.

Gayle: And you'll see an increase in learning with computers, just as the Educational Testing Service study of the Writing to Read program and other studies are beginning to show. □

Career Guidance Information

The *Occupational Outlook Handbook* published annually by the U.S. Department of Labor and sold by the Superintendent of Documents, U.S. Government Printing Office, Washington, D.C. 20402, is a good place to begin if you have questions about a particular job or want to compare job prospects in various fields. Telephone (202) 783-3238 for latest price information. The Handbook describes major industries, their growth potential, salaries, and working conditions. Most public libraries have this book.

Professional societies, trade associations, labor unions, business firms, and educational institutions publish a great deal of free or inexpensive career material. Many of these organizations are identified in the *Occupational Outlook Handbook*.

Another good starting point is the *Encyclopedia of Associations*, published by Gale Research Company, Book Tower, Detroit, Mich. 48226, available in most public libraries. This multi-volume, annual publication lists thousands of trade associations, professional societies, labor unions, and fraternal and patriotic organizations.

Additional Sources

Libraries, career centers, and guidance offices are important sources of career information. Thousands of books, brochures, magazines, and audiovisual materials are available on such subjects as occupations, careers, self-assessment, and job hunting.

Career and Counseling Information for Special Groups

Certain groups of jobseekers face special difficulties in obtaining suitable and satisfying employment. All too often, veterans, youth, handicapped persons, minorities, and women experience difficulty in the labor market.

Agencies that provide employment counseling as well as other kinds of assistance are identified in the *Directory of Counseling Services*, published by the American Association for Counseling and Development (AACD), 5999 Stevenson Ave., Alexandria, Va. 22304. A copy may well be available in your library or school career counseling center.

Several public and private agencies provide information, such as publications or referral services, on career planning and job hunting techniques that are geared toward special groups. The organizations listed below should be able to provide you with such information:

Handicapped: President's Committee on Employment of the Handicapped, 1111 20th St., N.W., Room 636, Washington, D.C. 20036. Phone: (202) 653-5044.

Job Opportunities for the Blind: Call 1-800-638-7518 for toll-free information for blind and deaf-blind.

Minorities: League of United Latin American Citizens, National Educational Service Centers, 400 First St., N.W., Suite 716, Washington, D.C. 20001. Phone: (202) 347-1652.

National Association for the Advancement of Colored People (NAACP), 186 Remsen St., Brooklyn, N.Y. 11201. Phone: (718) 858-0800.

Older Workers: National Association of Older Workers Employment Services, c/o National Council on Aging, 600 Maryland Ave., S.W., Washington, D.C. 20024. Phone: (202) 479-1200.

Veterans: Department of Veterans Benefits, Veterans Administration Central Office, 810 Vermont Ave., N.W., Washington, D.C. 20420. Phone: (202) 233-4000.

Women: U.S. Department of Labor, Women's Bureau, 200 Constitution Ave., N.W., Washington, D.C. 20210. Phone: (202) 523-6652.

Catalyst, 250 Park Ave. South, New York, N.Y. 10003. Phone: (212) 777-8900.

Wider Opportunities for Women, 1325 G St., N.W., Lower Level, Washington, D.C. 20005. Phone: (202) 638-3143. □

How To Write A Successful Résumé

Source: The Professional Secretary's Handbook, Copyright © 1984, Houghton Mifflin Company.

The Résumé

Your personal résumé should be thought of as a marketing tool for selling yourself to a prospective employer. Since you will have limited page space on which to present everything relevant about your work history, you should go back to the "who," "what," "where," "when," "why" formula and be concise and clear in your presentation and format. A lot of people out there are looking for jobs—all of them with résumés in one form or another. An employer may have to look through as many as 100 résumés of applicants for the same job before selecting the people to be interviewed. Therefore, your résumé must be eye-catching and brief so that a person scanning a page can immediately pick out your best assets and work experience.

If you have a career objective, you may want to state it on your résumé. There are two schools of thought on this subject, however. If you state your job objective, you may be limiting or categorizing yourself into a specific job market. There may be a job out there that can combine all of your skills with a title that does not even resemble your career objective. On the other hand, you may have determined in your research that you definitely want the particular type of job atmosphere associated with the title that you are seeking.

The Format

You may put identical information into several different formats and thereby present totally different images with each. The choice of formats will depend on the way you want to focus attention on your proficiencies.

Guidelines

The appearance of your résumé is almost as important as its content, for your resume is a reflection of your professionalism. As such, it should project a businesslike image. Here are a few general guidelines for résumé preparation that will help you:

(1) Paper should be 8 1/2" × 11" and white or off-white. If you are going to use colored paper, it should be conservative in tone or shade.

(2) Use a high-quality copying process such as offset printing or laser printing.

(3) Don't include personal information other than your name, address, and telephone number. Employers do not need to know your marital status, height, weight, sex, etc. Most of that can be determined at your interview.

(4) Use the active voice throughout and be careful not to change tenses in the body of the résumé.

(5) Try to keep the format pleasing to the eye. Avoid overuse of underlining and capitalization.

(6) Spell out names of organizations and agencies. Titles also should be spelled out.

(7) Proofread your résumé carefully. In fact, have someone else proofread it for you a final time before you have it printed. There is nothing more embarrassing than finding a mistake on your résumé after having given it to a prospective employer.

The Chronological Résumé

The chronological format is one of the most commonly used. It starts with your latest job experience and works backward. It is easy to follow and focuses on your career development. Since tasks for each position are detailed separately in the chronological format, try not to repeat elements of job descriptions. Only the inclusive years should be used to designate employment dates; there is no need to specify the months. If you want to highlight skills instead of chronological work history, you should not use this format.

The Functional Résumé

If you want to highlight your skills as opposed to the individual tasks for each position that you have held, you may want to use the functional résumé for your resume. This format details your skills under the specific function areas that you choose to highlight. A disadvantage to the use of this format is the possibility that your interviewer might want to relate your duties to each previously held job. However, this format may give you an opportunity to cover each position in more detail at your interview.

If you have had more than three or four jobs or if your experience looks scattered, this is an excellent format to use. Because the functional résumé focuses on your marketable skills rather than on your job history, it also can be used advantageously if you are worried that a prospective employer will be concerned with too many moves.

Where To Find Your Niche

The newspaper. This is probably the first place that people look when they are trying to get information on available jobs. Look through all the jobs. One suiting all of your qualifications might be listed in any section of the classifieds.

Be sure to keep a file on all of the ads that you have answered so that you do not answer the same ad twice, and also so that you remember what positions you have applied for.

Trade journals and speciality publications. If you are looking for a job in a specialized industry, you may want to check out the classifieds in professional trade journals. Your local library will have trade journals and speciality publications available for you to browse through.

Employment agencies. If you are going to use an employment agency to find a job, be sure to find one that specializes in the jobs that you are seeking. Agencies screen and test job candidates before sending them on interviews. Hence, an agency interview should be treated exactly like an interview with a prospective employer.

The Application Cover Letter

When you answer an ad through the mail, you should always send a descriptive cover letter with your résumé. The letter should be brief and formal while at the same time sparking the interest of the prospective employer. Try to give a reason why you should be interviewed for the advertised position. Never prepare a cover form letter for photocopying and submission to numerous firms. Such letters indicate that the sender is lazy and uninterested in taking the time to write personally to a prospective employer.

Résumé

PROFILE

Margaret E. Longford
321 State Street Apartment 39
City, US 98765
(800) 555-1212

Experience

November 1975 - December 1983	Allied College Publications, Inc. College Textbook Division/Science Associate Editor, Acquisitions
July 1969 - November 1975	Howe & Row Publishers, Inc. College Textbook Department Assistant Editor, Life Sciences
March 1967 - July 1969	LangData Incorporated College Division Editorial Assistant

Experience Summary

Sixteen years' experience in line editing of college science textbooks . Author acquisitions . Production & Scheduling . Cost estimation . Budgets . Contracts . Revisions . Manuscript Review . Liaison with Typesetters, Artists, Designers, and Printers . Public Relations & Marketing Support . Liaison with Sales Personnel

Education

1964 - 1967	MBA	Taft Graduate School of Business Management
1960 - 1964	BA (cum laude)	Hartfield College Major: Biology
1956 - 1960	diploma	Stonleigh School for Girls

Languages

French (fluent)
German (fluent)
Russian (scientific only)

Publications List

Available upon request

References

Available upon request

Helpful Hints for the Interview

Source: U.S. Department of Labor, Employment and Training Administration

A job interview is your showcase for merchandising your talents. During the interview an employer judges your qualifications, appearance, and general fitness for the job opening. It is your opportunity to convince the employer that you can make a real contribution.

Equally important, it gives you a chance to appraise the job, the employer, and the firm. It enables you to decide if the job meets your career needs and interests and whether the employer is of the type and caliber you want to work for.

Before each interview, though, you should assume that the job you are applying for is precisely the one you want—because it may be. To present your qualifications most advantageously, you will need to prepare in advance. You should have the needed papers ready and the necessary information about yourself firmly in mind; and you should know how to act at the interview to make it an effective device for selling your skills.

Preparing for the Interview

Assemble all the papers that you may need. The main item will be your background and work experience inventory. It contains all the facts and figures you could possibly be asked—either in filling in the job application form, or in the job interview. Don't forget to take copies of your résumé, even though you may have already submitted one. Take your social security card, recent school records, military separation papers, and union card, if you have one. If your work is the sort you can show in an interview (such as artwork, publications, or procedures), take along a few samples. Be careful not to leave your only copy of something, as it could get lost.

Additional Pointers

* Learn all you can about the company where you are going for an interview—its product or service, standing in the industry, number and kinds of jobs available, and hiring policies.

* Know what you have to offer—what education and training you have had, what work you have done, and what you can do.

* Know what kind of job you want and why you want to work for the firm where you are applying.

* Bring along the names, addresses, and business affiliations of three persons (not relatives) who are familiar with your work and character. If you are a recent graduate, you can list your teachers. Ask references for permission to use their names.

* As you are filling in the job application, be aware that it in itself offers an excellent opportunity to convince an employer that you are a valuable person to hire. It is not only a chance to describe your accomplishments, but it also shows how clearly you can think and write, and how well you can present important details.

* Learn the area salary scale for the type of work you are seeking. If you have the required skill and experience, don't hesitate to state your salary expectations in filling in the application blank. On the other hand, if for any reason you don't want to commit yourself then, simply write "Open" in the space for salary desired. If asked, say you prefer to wait until the job interview to discuss salary.

* Never take anyone with you to the interview.

* Allow as much uninterrupted time for the interview as may be required. (For example, do not park your car in a limited-time space.)

* Dress conservatively. Avoid either too formal or too casual dress.

You and the Interview

* Be pleasant and friendly but businesslike.

* Let the employer control the interview. Your answers should be frank and brief but complete, without rambling. Avoid dogmatic statements.

* Be flexible and willing but give the employer a clear idea of your job preferences.

* Stress your qualifications without exaggeration. The employer's questions or statements will indicate the type of person wanted. Use these clues in presenting your qualifications. For example, if you are being interviewed for an engineering position and the employer mentions that the job will require some customer contact work, use this clue to emphasize any work, experience, or courses you have had in this kind of skill.

* If you have not sent your resume in advance, present it, or your work records, references, personal data, work samples, or other materials to support your statements when the employer requests them.

* In discussing your previous jobs and work situations, avoid criticizing former employers or fellow workers.

* Don't discuss your personal, domestic, or financial problems unless you are specifically asked. Answer only what relates to the job.

* Don't be in a hurry to ask questions unless the employer invites them. But don't be afraid to ask what you need to know. If the employer offers you a job, be sure you understand exactly what your duties will be. Also find out what opportunities for advancement will be open. A definite understanding about the nature of your job will avoid future disappointment for either you or your employer.

* Be prepared to state the salary you want, but not until the employer has introduced the subject. Be realistic in discussing salary. But don't sell yourself short.

* If the employer does not definitely offer you a job or indicate when you will hear about it, ask when you may call to learn the decision.

* If the employer asks you to call or return for another interview, make a note of the time, date, and place.

* Thank the employer for the interview. If the firm cannot use you, ask about other employers who may need a person with your qualifications.

The College Labor Market

According to the Bureau of Labor Statistics, the keen competition that characterized the job market for college graduates in the 1970s and early 1980s is not expected to abate appreciably.

Not since the late 1960s has the supply of college graduates been in rough balance with the number of jobs requiring a college degree.

Information Please Almanac is not responsible and assumes no responsibility for any action undertaken by anyone utilizing the first aid procedures which follow.

The Heimlich Maneuver[1]

Food-Choking

What to look for: Victim cannot speak or breathe; turns blue; collapses.

To perform the Heimlich Maneuver when the victim is standing or sitting:

1. Stand behind the victim and wrap your arms around his waist.
2. Place the thumb side of your fist against the victim's abdomen, slightly above the navel and below the rib cage.
3. Grasp your fist with the other hand and press your fist into the victim's abdomen with a quick upward thrust. Repeat as often as necessary.
4. If the victim is sitting, stand behind the victim's chair and perform the maneuver in the same manner.
5. After the food is dislodged, have the victim seen by a doctor.

When the victim has collapsed and cannot be lifted:

1. Lay the victim on his back.
2. Face the victim and kneel astride his hips.
3. With one hand on top of the other, place the heel of your bottom hand on the abdomen slightly above the navel and below the rib cage.
4. Press into the victim's abdomen with a quick upward thrust. Repeat as often as necessary
5. Should the victim vomit, quickly place him on his side and wipe out his mouth to prevent aspiration (drawing of vomit into the throat).
6. After the food is dislodged, have the victim seen by a doctor.

NOTE: If you start to choke when alone and help is not available, an attempt should be made to self-administer this maneuver.

Burns[2]

First Degree: Signs/Symptoms—reddened skin. **Treatment**—Immerse quickly in cold water or apply ice until pain stops.

Second Degree: Signs/Symptoms—reddened skin, blisters. **Treatment**—(1) Cut away loose clothing. (2) Cover with several layers of cold moist dressings or, if limb is involved, immerse in cold water for relief of pain. (3) Treat for shock.

Third Degree: Signs/Symtoms—skin destroyed, tissues damaged, charring. **Treatment**—(1) Cut away loose clothing (do not remove clothing adhered to skin). (2) Cover with several layers of sterile, cold, moist dressings for relief of pain and to stop burning action. (3) Treat for shock.

Poisons[2]

Treatment—(1) Dilute by drinking large quantities of water. (2) Induce vomiting except when poison is corrosive or a petroleum product. (3) Call the poison control center or a doctor.

Shock[2]

Shock may accompany any serious injury: blood loss, breathing impairment, heart failure, burns. Shock can kill—treat as soon as possible and con-

The Heimlich Maneuver

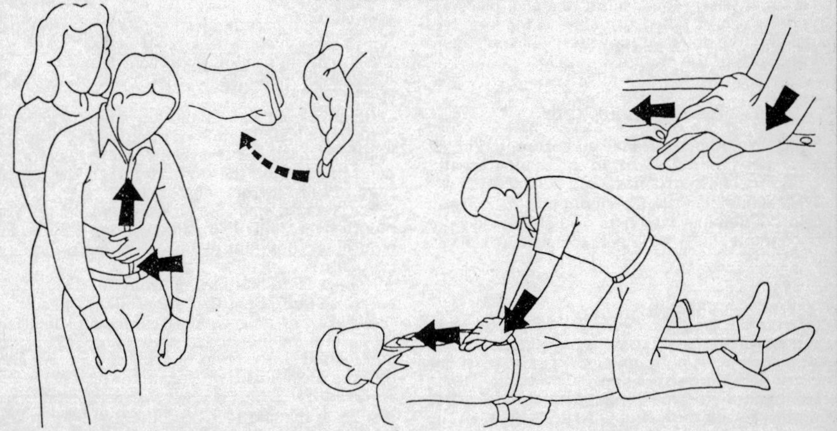

Courtesy of New York City Department of Health

tinue until medical aid is available.

Signs/Symptoms—(1) Shallow breathing. (2) Rapid and weak pulse. (3) Nausea, collapse, vomiting. (4) Shivering. (5) Pale, moist skin. (6) Mental confusion. (7) Drooping eyelids, dilated pupils.

Treatment—(1) Establish and maintain an open airway. (2) Control bleeding. (3) Keep victim lying down. Exception: Head and chest injuries, heart attack, stroke, sun stroke. If no spine injury, victim may be more comfortable and breathe better in a semi-reclining position. If in doubt, keep the victim flat. Elevate the feet unless injury would be aggravated. Maintain normal body temperature. Place blankets under and over victim.

Frostbite[2]

Most frequently frostbitten: toes, fingers, nose, and ears. It is caused by exposure to cold.

Signs/Symptoms—(1) Skin becomes pale or a grayish-yellow color. (2) Parts feel cold and numb. (3) Frozen parts feel doughy.

Treatment—(1) Until victim can be brought inside, he should be wrapped in woolen cloth and kept dry. (2) Do not rub, chafe, or manipulate frostbitten parts. (3) Bring victim indoors. (4) Place in warm water (102° to 105°) and make sure it remains warm. Test water by pouring on inner surface of your forearm. Never thaw if the victim has to go back out into the cold which may cause the affected area to be refrozen. (5) Do not use hot water bottles or a heat lamp, and do not place victim near a hot stove. (6) Do not allow victim to walk if feet are affected. (7) Once thawed, have victim gently exercise parts. (8) For serious frostbite, seek medical aid for thawing because pain will be intense and tissue damage extensive.

Heat Cramps[2]

Affects people who work or do strenous exercises in a hot environment. To prevent it, such people should drink large amounts of cool water and add a pinch of salt to each glass of water

Signs/Symptoms—(1) Painful muscle cramps in legs and abdomen. (2) Faintness. (3) Profuse perspiration.

Treatment—(1) Move victim to a cool place. (2) Give him sips of salted drinking water (one teaspoon of salt to one quart of water). (3) Apply manual pressure to the cramped muscle.

Heat Exhaustion[2]

Signs/Symptoms—(1) Pale and clammy skin. (2) Profuse perspiration. (3) Rapid and shallow breathing. (4) Weakness, dizziness, and headache.

Treatment—(1) Care for victim as if he were in shock. (2) Remove victim to a cool area, do not allow chilling. (3) If body gets too cold, cover victim.

Heat Stroke[2]

Signs/Symptoms—(1) Face is red and flushed. (2) Victim becomes rapidly unconscious. (3) Skin is hot and dry with no perspiration.

Treatment—(1) Lay victim down with head and shoulders raised. (2) Reduce the high body temperature as quickly as possible. (3) Apply cold applications to the body and head. (4) Use ice and fan if available. (5) Watch for signs of shock and treat accordingly. (6) Get medical aid as soon as possible.

Artificial Respiration[3]

(Mouth-to-Mouth Breathing—In Cases Like Drowning, Electric Shock or Smoke Inhalation.)

There is need for help in breathing when breathing movements stop or lips, tongue, and fingernails become blue. When in doubt, apply artificial respiration until you get medical help. No harm can result from its use and delay may cost the patient his life. Start immediately. Seconds count. Clear mouth and throat of any obstructions with your fingers.

For Adults: Place patient on back with face up.

Lift the chin and tilt the head back. If air passage is still closed, pull chin up by placing fingers behind the angles of the lower jaw and pushing forward.

Take deep breath, place you mouth over patient's mouth, making leak-proof seal.

Pinch patient's nostrils closed.

Blow into patient's mouth until you see his chest rise.

—OR—

Take deep breath, place your mouth over patient's nose, making leak-proof seal.

Seal patient's mouth with your hand.

Blow into patient's nose until you see his chest rise.

Remove your mouth and let patient exhale.

Repeat about 12 times a minute. (If the patient's stomach rises markedly, exert moderate hand pressure on the stomach just below the rib cage to keep it from inflating.)

For Infants and Small Children: Place your mouth over patient's mouth and nose. Blow into mouth and nose until you see patient's chest rise normally.

Repeat 20 to 30 times per minute. (Don't exaggerate the tilted position of an infant's head.)

NOTE: For emergency treatment of heart attack, cardiopulmonary resuscitation (CPR) is recommended. Instruction in CPR can be obtained through local health organizations or schools.

Sources: 1. New York City Department of Health. NOTE: Heimlich Maneuver, T.M. Pending. 2. *First Aid,* Mining Enforcement and Safety Administration, U.S. Department of the Interior. 3. *Health Emergency Chart,* Council on Family Health.

Facts You Should Know About AIDS

The Acquired Immune Deficiency Syndrome, or AIDS, was first reported in the United States in mid-1981. According to the Center for Disease Control, over 36,000 Americans have contracted AIDS and more than 21,000 have died from it. By 1991, according to the most conservative estimates, 270,000 people will have been stricken and 179,000 will have died. The CDC estimates that about 1.5 million Americans now carry the AIDS virus and that an average of 1 in 30 men between the ages of 20 and 50 are infected.

Worldwide, over 100 countries now report cases of AIDS to the World Health Organization in Geneva, for a global total of more than 50,000 cases. The WHO projects that 500,000 to 3 million people will develop AIDS by 1992.

AIDS is characterized by a defect in natural immunity against disease. People who have AIDS are vulnerable to serious illnesses which would not be a threat to anyone whose immune system was functioning normally. These illnesses are referred to as "opportunistic" infections or diseases: in AIDS patients the most common of these are Pneumocystis carinii pneumonia (PCP), a parasitic infection of the lungs; and a type of cancer known as Kaposi's sarcoma (KS). Other opportunistic infections include unusually severe infections with yeast, cytomegalovirus, herpes virus, and parasites such as Toxoplasma or Cryptosporidia. Milder infections with these organisms do not suggest immune deficiency.

AIDS is caused by a virus usually known as human immunodeficiency virus, or HIV. Symptoms of full-blown AIDS include a persistent cough, fever, and difficulty in breathing. Multiple purplish blotches and bumps on the skin may indicate Kaposi's sarcoma. The virus can also cause brain damage.

People infected with the virus can have a wide range of symptoms—from none to mild to severe. At least a fourth to a half of those infected will develop AIDS within four to ten years. Many experts think the percentage will be much higher.

AIDS is spread by sexual contact, needle sharing, or less commonly through transfused blood or its components. The risk of infection with the virus is increased by having multiple sexual partners, either homosexual or heterosexual, and sharing of needles among those using illicit drugs. The occurrence of the syndrome in hemophilia patients and persons receiving transfusions provides evidence for transmission through blood. It may be transmitted from infected mother to infant before, during, or shortly after birth (probably through breast milk).

Of the more than 36,000 U.S. cases, 65 percent have been homosexual or bisexual men, 25 percent intravenous drug users, 4 percent heterosexuals and 3 percent persons who received blood or blood products, a third of whom have been people with hemophilia or other blood disorders. How 3 percent more caught the disease hasn't been determined. There have been about 400 cases in children.

The need for education about AIDS reflects the medical consensus that a means of arresting the disease will come no sooner than five or 10 years. Just in the past year, scientists have discovered how AIDS infects brain cells and have identified genes that affect the AIDS virus. But efforts to devise a treatment or vaccine are complicated by the fact that AIDS is caused by two, perhaps three, similar viruses, and that the virus mutates frequently.

Even symptomatic relief has come from just one drug, azidothymidine or AZT. While not a cure, AZT stops the virus from reproducing. About 3,000 patients have received it since it was released for general use in September 1986. Most researchers believe that more than one drug will be necessary—one to suppress the AIDS virus, another to reconstitute the victim's damaged immune system. The cost of treatment can be very expensive—medical costs for a typical AIDS patient range from $50,000 to $150,000.

With no cure in sight, prudence could save thousands of people in the U.S. who have yet to be exposed to the virus. Their fate will depend less on science than on the ability of large numbers of human beings to change their behavior in the face of growing danger. Experts believe that couples who have had a totally monogamous relationship for the past decade are safe. A negative blood test would be near-certain evidence of safety.

People who should be tested for AIDS include gay men and intravenous drug users, their sex partners, and anyone who has had several sex partners, if their sexual history is unknown, during any one of the last five years. Anyone who tests positive should see a physician immediately for a medical evaluation. Persons testing positive should inform their sex partners and should use a condom during sex. They should not donate blood, body organs, other tissue or sperm, nor should they share toothbrushes, razors, or other implements that could become contaminated with blood.

Information about where to go for confidential testing for the presence of the AIDS virus is provided by local and state health departments. There is a National AIDS Hot Line: (800) 342-2437 for recorded information about AIDS, or (800) 433-0366 for specific questions. —*J.F.M.*

Can Insects Transmit AIDS?

At a July 1987 workshop sponsored by the Office of Technology Assessment, scientists addressed the public concern of AIDS being transmitted by blood-sucking insects such as mosquitoes or bedbugs. The experts found that there is no evidence to show that the disease is passed by insects.

The problem with an insect using its "needle-like" proboscis or mouthparts to infect a person with AIDS is in the volume of blood. These parts do not hold enough residual blood to transmit an infectious dose.

The scientists also found no evidence to suggest that an insect can reproduce and multiply the AIDS virus inside itself as in diseases such as malaria.

Dietary Guidelines for Americans

Source: FDA Consumer.

The "Dietary Guidelines for Americans" were made public in September 1985 by the U.S. Department of Agriculture and the Department of Health and Human Services. They are intended to provide healthy Americans with sensible, uncomplicated guidance on the kinds of foods they should be eating. Basically, their advice to Americans is: concentrate on eating a balanced and varied diet that provides the nutrients essential to good health, increase consumption of starch and fiber, but reduce fat, sugar, sodium, and alcohol.

The guidelines differ little from those announced by USDA and HHS in 1980. The advisory committee concluded that no recent nutrition research was persuasive enough to warrant any major changes. Not enough is known to describe an "ideal" diet for every individual because nutrition needs vary according to a person's sex, age, health, body size, and other factors. So the guidelines are aimed at those Americans who are in good health. They do not apply to people with diseases or conditions that affect nutritional needs.

More than 40 different nutrients—in the form of vitamins, minerals, amino acids (from proteins), essential fatty acids (from fats and oils), and calories from carbohydrates, fats, and proteins—are needed for good health. However, no one can be expected to keep track of all of them. Instead, most people generally can expect to satisfy their nutritional requirements by eating a variety of foods.

The guidelines do not suggest specific goals for such substances as fats and dietary fiber because of the need for more research. Instead, the guidelines state that "for the U.S. population as a whole, increasing starch and fiber in our diets and reducing calories (primarily from fats, sugars, and alcohol) is sensible. These suggestions are especially appropriate for people who have other risk factors for chronic diseases, such as a family history of obesity, premature heart disease, diabetes, high blood pressure, high blood cholesterol levels, or for those who use tobacco, particularly cigarette smokers."

Here are the guidelines and the rationale for each of them:

Eat a variety of foods

Most foods have more than one nutrient, but no single food provides all the essential nutrients. That is achieved by eating a balanced, varied diet that emphasizes the major food groups—fruits and vegetables; cereals and other foods made from grains; dairy products; and meats, fish, poultry, eggs, and dry beans and peas.

For example, dairy products such as milk are a source of protein, fats, sugar, vitamin A, riboflavin and other B vitamins, calcium, phosphorus, and other nutrients. But they provide little iron. Meat provides protein, several B vitamins, iron and zinc but little calcium. Vitamins A and C, folic acid, fiber, and various minerals are obtained from fruit and vegetables. Whole-grain and enriched breads, cereals, and other grain products provide B vitamins, iron, protein, and fiber.

Although there are some exceptions, a varied diet based on these food groups will satisfy the nutrient requirements of most healthy individuals without the need for supplements. "There are no known advantages and some potential harm in consuming excessive amounts of any nutrient," the guidelines stress. "Large dose supplements of any nutrient should be avoided. You will rarely need to take vitamin or mineral supplements if you eat a variety of foods."

However, there are some exceptions. Iron supplements often are needed by women in their childbearing years. Pregnant and breast-feeding women have an increased need for certain nutrients, notably iron, folic acid, vitamin A, and calcium. Infants also have special nutritional needs. Breast-feeding is recommended for the first three to six months because infants absorb nutrients from breast milk better than cow's milk. Breast milk also contains substances that provide immunity to some diseases until the infant's body is able to produce these substances itself.

After three to six months, babies can start taking solid foods. Prolonged breast- or bottle-feeding without solid foods or iron supplements can result in iron deficiency, the guidelines point out. Flavoring baby foods with salt and sugar is also discouraged.

Elderly people also have to be extra careful about getting enough of all the essential nutrients because many older people eat less. The guidelines stress meals based on the basic food groups and a reduction in the consumption of fats, oils, sugars, sweets, alcohol, and other foods that are high in calories but low in other nutrients. Some elderly men and women who take certain medications that affect nutrient intake also may require supplements. Such supplements, however, should be taken only under the guidance of a physician.

Maintain a Desirable Weight

Experts estimate that one-third or more of all adult Americans are overweight and that, at any given time, more than 20 million Americans are resorting to diets to shed excess weight. Obesity is a major health concern in the United States, for it increases the risk of such chronic diseases as high blood pressure, heart disease, stroke, and diabetes.

Although many Americans keep searching for easy paths to losing weight, most such efforts are doomed to failure, in the view of most nutrition experts. Losing weight and not regaining it, the guidelines suggest, means eating foods high in nutritional value but with fewer calories, getting more exercise, and shedding weight at a sensible, gradual rate, a pound or two each week.

The guidelines warn that diets of less than 800 calories a day can be hazardous and should be followed only under medical supervision. Severely restricted, low-calorie diets make it extremely difficult to obtain the nutrients essential to maintaining good health, and they can have adverse effects. The guidelines warned: "Some people have developed kidney stones, disturbing psychological changes, and other complications while following such diets. A few people have died suddenly and without warning."

Frequent use of laxatives, induced vomiting, and other extreme measures should not be used to lose weight, according to the guidelines. Such actions can cause imbalances that can lead to irregular heartbeats and even death.

The emphasis should be on keeping body weight

at a reasonable level for one's sex, age, and height.

Severe weight loss—below what is recommended—also is discouraged. Some people have suffered nutrient deficiencies, infertility, hair loss, skin changes, cold intolerance, severe constipation, psychiatric disturbances, and other complications from excessive weight losses. A doctor should be seen about any sudden, unexplained loss of weight.

Avoid Too Much Fat, Saturated Fat, and Cholesterol

The American diet generally is high in fat and cholesterol compared to some countries, and Americans tend to have high blood cholesterol levels. High blood cholesterol is one of the risk factors for heart attack. Nutritionists lack enough research data to make specific recommendations about how much fat and cholesterol the general public should eat, but the guidelines urge a sensible reduction in total fat—especially saturated fat—and cholesterol.

Among the suggested ways of doing this is to trim excess fat off meats and to eat lean meat, fish, poultry, and dry beans and peas as protein sources; use low-fat dairy products; eat moderate amounts of eggs and organ meats; limit intake of foods high in saturated fat, such as butter, cream, heavily hydrogenated fats, shortenings, and foods with palm and coconut oils; and broil or bake, rather than fry, foods.

The effect of diet on blood cholesterol levels varies among individuals. Some people—for reasons not completely understood—can eat foods high in saturated fat and cholesterol and maintain reasonable blood cholesterol levels, while others on low-fat, low-cholesterol diets still end up with high cholesterol levels. Heredity is believed to play a role. Acknowledging the controversy over what recommendations would be appropriate for the general public, the guidelines state that it would be "sensible" for Americans to reduce their daily consumption of fat. This is especially appropriate, the guidelines say, for individuals who have other cardiovascular risk factors, such as smoking or family histories of premature heart disease, high blood pressure, and diabetes. The guidelines do not suggest complete avoidance of any foods, because many foods that contain fat and cholesterol also provide high-quality protein and many essential vitamins and minerals.

Eat Foods With Adequate Starch and Fiber

The guidelines favor a moderate increase in consumption of fiber-containing foods. The American diet generally is low in fiber, yet there is evidence that fiber can help reduce chronic constipation, diverticular disease, and some types of "irritable bowel." Fruits, whole-grain breads and cereals, vegetables, dry beans and peas, and nuts are good sources of starch and fiber.

Carbohydrates and fat are major sources of energy (calories). If Americans cut back on fat consumption, energy needs can still be met from carbohydrates, especially the complex carbohydrates. "Carbohydrates are especially helpful in weight reduction diets, because, ounce for ounce, they contain about half as many calories as fats do," the guidelines said.

Simple carbohydrates like sugar provide calories but little other nutritional benefit. In contrast, complex carbohydrates—such as starch in bread and other grain products, beans, peas, nuts, seeds, fruits, and vegetables—contain other essential nutrients. Also, eating more foods with complex carbohydrates adds dietary fiber.

(Dietary fiber describes parts of plant foods that generally are not digestible by humans. Foods differ in the kinds of fiber they contain. Wheat bran has several kinds of fiber and has laxative properties but does not affect blood cholesterol levels. Other kinds of fiber have no laxative effects but seem to reduce blood cholesterol.)

Although in recent years there have been studies suggesting that the risk of colon cancer is greater among those with low-fiber diets, the guidelines state that more research is needed before definitive judgments can be made.

Avoid Too Much Sugar

It is not necessary to avoid eating simple sugars. It would, in fact, be difficult, because sugars are naturally present in many foods and are added to many processed products, usually in the form of sucrose, glucose, maltose, dextrose, lactose, fructose, corn sweeteners, honey and syrups. The major health concern with excess sugar consumption is tooth decay, especially when sugars (and starches, as well) are consumed between meals. The guidelines discourage eating sweets between meals. The guidelines also restate the age-old advice about proper dental hygiene, brushing after meals, drinking fluoridated water, and using fluoridated toothpastes and mouth rinses.

Avoid Too Much Sodium

Sodium is essential to the human body, but most Americans consume far more than they need, especially from table salt (which is 40 percent sodium). An intake of 1,100 to 3,300 milligrams a day is generally recommended. Salt is not the only source, for a wide variety of sodium compounds is used in many processed foods and beverages. The principal concern with high sodium consumption is for people with hypertension (high blood pressure) and those who may be susceptible to it.

If You Drink Alcoholic Beverages, Do So In Moderation

In urging moderate use of alcohol, the guidelines also support the national effort to discourage drinking and driving. From a nutritional standpoint, alcohol is high in calories but provides virtually no other nutritional benefit. The guidelines note that one or two standard-sized drinks daily appear to cause no harm in healthy adults.

Overweight people should be aware that alcohol adds calories. Heavy drinkers especially can suffer appetite loss, and this can lead to nutritional deficiencies and other health problems, such as cirrhosis of the liver and some types of cancer.

Pregnant women are advised by the National Institute of Alcohol Abuse and Alcoholism to refrain from drinking alcohol because excessive consumption may cause birth defects or other problems during pregnancy. The level of consumption at which risks to an unborn child occur has not been established, the guidelines declare. □

Fat, Cholesterol, and Your Health

For the U.S. population as a whole, it is sensible to reduce daily intake of total fat, saturated fat, and cholesterol. Why? High blood cholesterol levels increase the risk of heart disease and the blood cholesterol level of many Americans is undesirably high. Eating a diet high in fat—especially saturated fatty acids and cholesterol—causes elevated blood cholesterol levels in many people.

For many, high blood cholesterol levels can be reduced by eating diets lower in saturated fatty acids and cholesterol. However, some people can eat diets high in total fat, saturated fatty acids, and cholesterol and still maintain normal blood cholesterol. Others have high blood cholesterol levels even on lowfat, low-cholesterol diets.

For adults, blood cholesterol is considered to be high if it measures more than 200 to 240 milligrams of cholesterol per deciliter of blood, depending on age. Ask your doctor to check your blood cholesterol.

Fat and Cholesterol

Fat is the most concentrated source of food energy (calories). Each gram of fat supplies about 9 calories, compared with about 4 calories per gram of protein or carbohydrate and 7 calories per gram of alcohol. In addition to providing energy, fat aids in the absorption of certain vitamins. Some fats provide linoleic acid, an essential fatty acid which is needed by everyone in small amounts.

Butter, margarine, shortening, and oil are obvious sources of fat. Well-marbled meats, poultry skin, whole milk, cheese, ice cream, nuts, seeds, salad dressings, and some baked products also provide a lot of fat.

Cholesterol is a fat-like substance found in the body cells of humans and animals. Cholesterol is needed to form hormones, cell membranes, and other body substances. The body is able to make the cholesterol it needs for these functions. Cholesterol is not needed in the diet.

Cholesterol is present in all animal tissues—meat, poultry, and fish—in milk and milk products, and in egg yolks. Both the lean and fat of meats and the meat and skin of poultry contain cholesterol. Cholesterol is *not* found in foods of plant origin such as fruits, vegetables, grains, nuts, seeds, and dry beans and peas.

Fatty Acids are the basic chemical units in fat. They may be either "saturated," "monounsaturated," or "polyunsaturated." All dietary fats are made up of *mixtures* of these fatty acid types.

Saturated fatty acids are found in largest proportions in fats of animal origin. These include the fats in whole milk, cream, cheese, butter, meat, and poultry. Saturated fatty acids are also found in large amounts in some vegetable oils, including coconut and palm.

Monounsaturated fatty acids are found in fats of

Meat, Poultry, Fish

		Total fat (grams)	Saturated fatty acids (grams)	Cholesterol (milligrams)
Beef arm, roasted:				
Lean and fat	3 oz.	16	8	80
Lean only	3 oz.	6	3	77
Ground beef, cooked:				
Regular	3 oz. patty	17	7	77
Lean	3 oz. patty	15	6	80
Pork rib, roasted:				
Lean and fat	3 oz.	20	7	69
Lean only	3 oz.	12	4	67
Beef liver, fried	3 oz.	9	2	372
Chicken, light and dark meat, roasted:				
With skin	3 oz.	12	3	75
Without skin	3 oz.	6	2	76
Halibut fillets, broiled, with margarine	3 oz.	6	1	48
Tuna salad	1/2 cup	10	2	40
Crabs, hard-shell, steamed	2 med.	2	0	96
Dry beans, cooked	1/2 cup	1	trace	0
Peanut butter	2 tbsp.	16	2	0
Egg, large, cooked	1 yolk	6	2	274
	1 white	trace	0	0

Source: USDA, Human Nutrition Information Service.

Milk, Cheese, Yogurt

		Total fat (grams)	Saturated fatty acids (grams)	Cholesterol (milligrams)
Milk:				
Whole	1 cup	8	5	33
2% fat	1 cup	5	3	18
Skim	1 cup	1	trace	5
Buttermilk	1 cup	2	1	9
Yogurt:				
Lowfat plain	8 oz. carton	4	2	14
Lowfat fruit-flavored	8-oz. carton	2	2	10
Cottage cheese:				
Creamed	1 cup	9	6	31
Lowfat	1 cup	4	3	19
Cheese:				
Natural				
Cheddar	1 oz.	9	6	30
Mozzarella, part skim milk	1 oz.	5	3	15
Process				
American	1 oz.	9	6	27
Macaroni and cheese	3/4 cup	17	7	32
Vanilla ice cream	1/2 cup	7	4	30
Vanilla ice milk	1/2 cup	3	2	9

Source: USDA, Human Nutrition Information Service.

both plant and animal origin. Olive oil and peanut oil are the most common examples of fat with mostly monounsaturated fatty acids. Also, most margarines and hydrogenated vegetable shortenings tend to be high in monounsaturated fatty acids.

Polyunsaturated fatty acids are found in largest proportions in fats of plant origin. Sunflower, corn, soybean, cottonseed, and safflower oils are vegetable fats that usually contain a high proportion of polyunsaturated fatty acids. Some fish are also sources of polyunsaturated fatty acids.

NOTE: *All* fats, whether they contain mainly saturated fatty acids, monounsaturated fatty acids, or polyunsaturated fatty acids, provide the same number of calories. □

Fats and Sweets

		Total fat (grams)	Saturated fatty acids (grams)	Cholesterol (milligrams)
Butter	1 tbsp.	11	7	31
Margarine:				
Soft	1 tbsp.	11	2	0
Stick	1 tbsp.	11	2	0
Vegetable oil (corn)	1 tbsp.	14	2	0
Salad dressing:				
Mayonnaise	1 tbsp.	11	2	8
Mayonnaise-type	1 tbsp.	5	1	4
Italian, low-calorie	1 tbsp.	trace	trace	0
Italian	1 tbsp.	9	1	0
Cream:				
Sour	1 tbsp.	3	2	5
Light (table)	1 tbsp.	3	2	10
Nondairy, frozen	1 tbsp.	2	1	0
Cream cheese	1 oz. (2 tbsp.)	10	6	31
Cake, frosted, devil's food	1/12 8"-layer	11	5	50
Brownie	1 brownie	6	1	18
Pie, apple	1/6 pie	18	5	2

Source: USDA, Human Nutrition Information Service.

Cholesterol Labeling Proposed

The Food and Drug Administration has proposed a regulation on food labels that would offer millions of health conscious Americans more information on cholesterol. The proposal includes allowing manufacturers to have the option of using these terms on the labels of their products:

Cholesterol free—can be used if the cholesterol content is less than 2 milligrams in each serving.

Low cholesterol—would describe products with less than 20 milligrams of cholesterol in each serving.

Cholesterol reduced or **reduced in cholesterol**—would be permitted in products that have been reformulated so that the cholesterol content has been reduced at least 75 percent from the original product.

Manufacturers would have to state what the original cholesterol content was, along with that of the cholesterol-reduced version. For example, "Cholesterol reduced from 120 milligrams to 30 milligrams per serving."

For foods that have less cholesterol, but not 75% less, FDA's proposed regulation would allow such language as "less cholesterol" or "lowered cholesterol." Again, the cholesterol content of both the original and reformulated products would have to be stated.

If adopted, the regulation would not go into effect until FDA evaluates comments received from the public and makes any necessary changes. Also, the food industry would be allowed ample time to use up existing supplies of labels.

Facts on Sodium

What is sodium?

Sodium is a mineral that occurs naturally in some foods and is added to many foods and beverages. Most of the sodium in the American diet comes from table salt, which is 40% sodium and 60% chloride. One teaspoon of salt contains about 2,000 milligrams of sodium.

Why Is Sodium Important?

Sodium attracts water into the blood vessels and helps maintain normal blood volume and blood pressure. Sodium is also needed for the normal function of nerves and muscles.

How Much Sodium Do I Need?

Although some sodium is essential to your health, you need very little. The National Research Council of the National Academy of Sciences suggests that a "safe and adequate" range of sodium intake per day is about 1,100 to 3,300 milligrams for adults. This is well below the amount that most American adults consume.

Sodium in Processed Foods

Most of the sodium in processed foods is added to preserve and/or flavor them. Salt is the major source of sodium added to these foods. It is added to most canned and some frozen vegetables, smoked and cured meats, pickles, and sauerkraut. Salt is used in most cheeses, sauces, soups, salad dressings, and in many breakfast cereals. Sodium is also found in many other ingredients used in food processing. Examples of sodium-containing ingredients, and their uses in foods are: baking powder—leavening agent; baking soda—leavening agent; monosodium glutamate—flavor enhancer; sodium benzoate—preservative; sodium caseinate—thickener and binder; sodium citrate—buffer, used to control acidity in soft drinks and fruit drinks; sodium nitrate—curing agent in meat, provides color, prevents botulism (a food poisoning); sodium phosphate—emulsifier, stabilizer, buffer; sodium propionate—mold inhibitor; sodium saccharin—artificial sweetener.

About Condiments

Watch out for commercially prepared condiments, sauces, and seasonings when preparing and serving foods for you and your family. Many, like those that follow, are high in sodium: onion salt, celery salt, garlic salt, seasoned salt, meat tenderizer, bouillon, baking powder, baking soda, monosodium glutamate (msg), soy sauce, steak sauce, barbecue sauce, catsup, mustard, Worcestershire sauce, salad dressings, pickles, chili sauce, relish.

The link between salt and sodium may be a little hard to understand at first. If you remember that 1 teaspoon of salt provides 2,000 milligrams of sodium, however, you can estimate the amount of sodium that you add to foods during cooking and preparation, or even at the table.

Salt-Sodium Conversions

1/4 tsp. salt	= 500 mg sodium
1/2 tsp. salt	= 1,000 mg sodium
3/4 tsp. salt	= 1,500 mg sodium
1 tsp. salt	= 2,000 mg sodium

Sodium Content of Some Foods

This table shows the sodium content of some types of foods. The ranges are rough guides; individual food items may be higher or lower in sodium.

Foods	Approximate sodium content (in milligrams)
Breads, Cereals, and Grain Products	
Cooked cereal, pasta, rice (unsalted)	Less than 5 per 1/2 cup
Ready-to-eat cereal	100-360 per oz.
Bread, whole-grain or enriched	110-175 per slice
Biscuits and muffins	170-390 each
Vegetables	
Fresh or frozen vegetables (cooked without added salt)	Less than 70 per 1/2 cup
Vegetables, canned or frozen with sauce	140-460 per 1/2 cup
Fruit	
Fruits (fresh, frozen, or canned)	Less than 10 per 1/2 cup
Milk, Cheese, and Yogurt	
Milk and yogurt	120-160 per cup
Buttermilk (salt added)	260 per cup
Natural cheeses	110-450 per 1-1/2-oz. serving
Cottage cheese (regular and lowfat)	450 per 1/2 cup
Process cheese and cheese spreads	700-900 per 2-oz. serving
Meat, Poultry, and Fish	
Fresh meat, poultry, finfish	Less than 90 per 3-oz. serving
Cured ham, sausages, luncheon meat, frankfurters, canned meats	750-1,350 per 3-oz. serving
Fats and Dressings	
Oil	None
Vinegar	Less than 6 per tbsp.
Prepared salad dressings	80-250 per tbsp.
Unsalted butter or margarine	1 per tsp.
Salted butter or margarine	45 per tsp.
Salt pork, cooked	360 per oz.
Condiments	
Catsup, mustard, chili sauce, tartar sauce, steak sauce	125-275 per tbsp.
Soy sauce	1,000 per tbsp.
Salt	2,000 per tsp.
Snack and Convenience Foods	
Canned and dehydrated soups	630-1,300 per cup
Canned and frozen main dishes	800-1,400 per 8-oz. serving
Unsalted nuts and popcorn	Less than 5 per oz.
Salted nuts, potato chips, corn chips	150-300 per oz.
Deep-fried pork rind	750 per oz.

Source: FDA, Human Nutrition Information Service.

Some Major Points About The Table

Unprocessed grains are naturally low in sodium. Ready-to-eat cereals vary widely in sodium content.

Fresh, frozen, and canned fruits and fruit juices are low in sodium. Most canned vegetables, vegetable juices, and frozen vegetables with sauce are higher in sodium than fresh or frozen ones cooked without salt.

A serving of milk or yogurt is lower in sodium than most natural cheeses, which vary widely in their sodium content. Process cheeses, cheese foods, and cheese spreads contain more sodium than natural cheeses.

Most fresh meats, poultry, and fish are low in sodium. Canned poultry are higher. Most cured and processed meats such as hotdogs, sausage, and luncheon meats are even higher in sodium.

Most "convenience" foods are quite high in sodium. Frozen dinners and combination dishes, canned soups, and dehydrated mixes for soups, sauces, and salad dressings contain a lot of sodium. Condiments are also high in sodium.

Facts on Fiber

Dietary fiber is the parts of plants that humans can't digest.

There are several types of fiber, such as cellulose, pectin, lignin, and gums. Plants differ in the types and amounts of fiber they contain.

Different types of fiber function differently in the body. It is important to eat a variety of plant foods to benefit from effects of different kinds of fiber.

Some kinds of fiber have a laxative effect, producing softer, bulkier stools and more rapid movement of wastes through the intestine. Fiber is helpful in preventing and treating constipation and diverticular disease.

The possible benefits of dietary fiber for colon cancer, heart disease, diabetes, and obesity are being studied. Whether such benefits exist is not yet known.

It is not clear exactly how much and what types of fiber we need in our diets daily. However, for most Americans, a moderate increase in dietary fiber by eating more fiber-containing foods like those listed on this page is desirable.

There is no reason to take fiber supplements or to add fiber to foods that already contain it.

Some fiber foods are: whole-grain breads; whole-grain breakfast cereals; whole-wheat pasta; vegetables, especially with edible skins, stems, seeds; dry beans and peas; whole fruits, especially with edible skins or seeds; nuts and seeds.

High Fiber Food Sources

(4 grams or more per serving)

Food source	Serving
Breads and cereals	
All Bran*	1/3 cup-1 oz
Bran Buds*	1/3 cup-1 oz
Bran Chex	2/3 cup-1 oz
Corn bran	2/3 cup-1 oz
Cracklin' Bran	1/3 cup-1 oz
100% Bran*	1/2 cup-1 oz
Raisin Bran	3/4 cup-1 oz
Bran, unsweetened*	1/4 cup
Wheat germ, toasted, plain	1/4 cup-1 oz
Legumes (Cooked portions)	
Kidney beans	1/2 cup
Lima beans	1/2 cup
Navy beans	1/2 cup
Pinto beans	1/2 cup
White beans	1/2 cup
Fruits	
Blackberries	1/2 cup
Dried prunes	3

*Indicates foods that have 6 or more grams of fiber per serving. *Source:* National Cancer Institute.

What Are Whole Grains?

Whole grains are products that contain the entire grain, or all the grain that is edible. They include the bran and germ portions which contain most of the fiber, vitamins, and minerals, as well as the starchy endosperm.

Some examples are whole wheat, cracked wheat, bulgur, oatmeal, whole cornmeal, popcorn, brown rice, whole rye, and scotch barley.

Whole wheat doesn't have to mean bread or cereal. Try these: brown rice, corn tortillas, unbuttered popcorn, scotch barley—in soups, tabbouleh—a bulgar wheat salad, whole-wheat pasta.

Recognizing the *Real* Whole Wheat

All whole-wheat bread is brown, but not all brown bread is whole wheat.

By law, bread that is labeled "whole wheat" must be made from 100 percent whole-wheat flour. "Wheat bread" may be made from varying proportions of enriched white flour and whole-wheat flour. The type of flour present in the largest amount is listed first on the ingredient label. Sometimes a dark color is provided by caramel coloring, also listed on the label.

The milling of the wheat to produce white flour results in the loss of nutrients as the bran and germ are removed. Enrichment replaces four important nutrients: iron, thiamin, riboflavin, and niacin. But flours made from the whole grain contain more of other nutrients, such as folic acid, vitamin B_6, vitamin E, phosphorus, magnesium, and zinc, than enriched white flour.

You don't have to switch to whole-wheat bread to increase your intake of whole grains.

Many products on the market are made of a mixture of whole-grain flours and enriched flour. Try those listed below for variety in taste and texture, as well as a bonus of fiber and nutrients. Or, try substituting whole-grain flour for half the amount of white flour when you bake quick breads or cookies.

Bran muffins; cornbread, from whole, ground cornmeal; cracked wheat bread; graham crackers; oatmeal bread; pumpernickel bread; rye bread. □

Mixing Antacids and RX Drugs Can Spell Trouble

Although many consumers take antacids almost casually, these drugs are not as harmless as they may seem. For one thing, antacids can affect the way other drugs behave in the body. They can speed the absorption of some prescription drugs—possibly causing an overdose—and slow it for others, thus reducing their effectiveness.

Among the drugs absorbed faster are: salicylates (for example, aspirin); indomethacin and naproxen, both used to treat arthritis; pseudoephedrine, a nasal decongestant; sulfadiazine, an infection fighter, and levodopa, a mainstay of Parkinson's disease therapy.

In other cases, the effectiveness of prescription drugs such as the antibiotic tetracycline, the heart drug digoxin, and the tuberculosis drug isoniazid are delayed.

Check with your physician first, to be safe.

Alcohol Facts

About two-thirds of Americans 18 or older drink alcoholic beverages, and about three-quarters of students in the 10th and 12th grades also indulge. Long-term alcohol abuse lops 10 years or so off the lifespan and prematurely ages the brain by about the same.

One-half of the traffic deaths that occur on U.S. highways are alcohol related.

Toxic Effects of Water-Soluble Vitamins

By Carol Henderson

Every day millions of people participate in the daily ritual of vitamin gulping in hopes of a healthier self or a little extra "get up and go." While our vitamin supplement may be miniscule compared to our intake of other nutrients such as fat, protein and minerals, large quantities of vitamins, even those that are water-soluble, can be harmful or toxic.

Vitamins are essential to the normal functioning of our body and contribute to our general well-being, growth and energy. They consist of a mixed group of chemical compounds, constituents of food, that cannot be manufactured by the body. Essentially, vitamins act to energize and regulate our metabolism in order to keep us functioning at high performance, much like an automobile's spark plugs and engine.

There are two classes of vitamins: fat soluble and water-soluble. Water-soluble vitamins function as coenzymes (helpers) in energy, protein/amino acid and nucleic acid metabolism. Fat-soluble vitamins (A,D,E, and K) have more individualized functions, including the role of vitamin A in maintaining eyesight and the importance of vitamin D in maintaining calcium balance.

Vitamins in tablet or capsule form are primarily used as dietary supplements and as therapeutic agents. As dietary supplements, they serve to strengthen the diet when a person is unable to consume all the necessary foods, as in times of illness, severe emotional crisis or when experiencing allergies. Vitamins as therapeutic agents are generally prescribed by doctors after surgery, prolonged illness or any situation in which the food supply has been drastically reduced or the body has suffered extensive damage. Vitamins are normally prescribed in these instances in quantities from three to five times the Recommended Dietary Allowance. The RDA is an estimate of nutritional needs to ensure satisfactory growth of children and the prevention of nutrient depletion in adults. Generally, the literature seems to show that the toxic effects of vitamins start to appear at doses of about ten times the RDA.

Pursuit of Superhealth

The somewhat recent phenomenon of the pursuit of the superbody and superhealth has led to conflicting schools of thought on vitamin therapy, some of which advocate megavitamin therapy or megadosing. This school believes that the more vitamin pills one takes the healthier one will be. However, anything and everything ingested in excess is toxic, even water, and therefore it is important to know how much vitamin consumption is too much.

While a daily vitamin supplement adds nutrients to an unbalanced diet, supplements are unnecessary in well balanced diets of healthy individuals and may augment problems associated with megadosing. Megadosing is essentially the saturation of a cell with a vitamin, roughly 10 times the RDA, at which point the body must work to reduce the excess. In the case of water-soluble vitamins, specifically vitamin C, niacin and vitamin B_6, all of which have been shown to have toxic effects if ingested in excess, the body excretes the additional vitamin content through the urine. Problems begin when the body cannot eliminate the vitamin overdose fast enough.

The following is a description of vitamin C, niacin, and vitamin B_6; what they do for our bodies; their natural food sources; and their levels of toxicity.

Vitamin C

The recommended daily allowance for vitamin C for adults is 45 mg. At 450 mg the vitamin may begin to show toxic effects. Vitamin C is essential to the strength of body cells and blood vessels. It is important for healthy teeth and gums, helps in synthesis of procollagen essentially important to growth and development, aids in synthesis of neurotransmitters necessary for central nervous system function, aids in the body's absorption of iron and prevents scurvy. The best natural sources of vitamin C include citrus fruits, berries, green and leafy vegetables, tomatoes, cauliflower, and potatoes. Excessive intake may cause unpleasant side effects including occasional diarrhea, excess urination, kidney stones, skin rashes and more serious complications of reproductive failure, thrombosis, and possible damage to the insulin secreting beta-cells of the pancreas.

Niacin

The recommended daily allowance for niacin is 12 to 18 mg for adults. Toxic effects can be seen at approximately 150 mg. Niacin is necessary for a healthy nervous system and brain function, essential for synthesis of sex hormones, aids in promoting a healthy digestive system, prevents pellagra, increases circulation and reduces high blood pressure, and is essential to the process of converting food into energy. The best natural sources of niacin include eggs, whole grain cereal, liver, kidneys, meat, fish, and poultry. Toxic effects of niacin include burning and itching skin and excessive sweating and flushing.

Vitamin B_6

The recommended daily allowance of vitamin B_6 for adults is 1.6 to 2.0 mg. At 200 mg toxic effects may occur. Vitamin B_6 is essential for the production of antibodies and red blood cells. It helps assimilate protein and fat, aids in the prevention of nervous and skin disorders, aids in maintenance of blood glucose levels and helps provide immediate energy to muscle cells when needed. Vitamin B_6 can be found in wheat germ, liver, kidney, heart, cantaloupe, cabbage, milk, molasses and eggs. Serious toxic effects can include loss of sensation in hands and feet, loss of sensation of temperature, feeling of vibration, restlessness and vivid dreams.

The American Council on Science and Health recommends that consumers be aware of the potentially hazardous effects of some water-soluble vitamins and the toxic effects of ingesting excess fat-soluble vitamins. ACSH recommends the consumption of a well balanced diet and the use of vitamin supplements only upon the advice of a physician or dietician/nutritionist. □

Carol Henderson, M.P.H., M.S.W., is a freelance writer. Reprinted with permission from *ACSH News & Views*, a publication of the American Council on Science and Health, 1995 Broadway, New York, N.Y. 10023.

Recommended Daily Dietary Allowances[1]

Designed for the maintenance of good nutrition of practically all healthy persons in the U.S. (revised 1980)

						Fat-Soluble Vitamins			Water-Soluble Vitamins				
Persons	Age (years)	Wgt. (lbs)	Wgt. (kg)	Hgt. (in.)	Hgt. (cm)	Vitamin A μg R.E.[2]	Vitamin D (μg)[3]	Vitamin E (mgα T.E.)[4]	Ascorbic Acid (mg)	Folacin (μg)	Niacin[5] (mg)	Riboflavin (mg)	Thiamin (mg)
Infants	0.0–0.5	13	6	24	60	420	10	3	35	30	6	0.4	0.3
	0.5–1.0	20	9	28	71	400	10	4	35	45	8	0.6	0.5
Children	1–3	29	13	35	90	400	10	5	45	100	9	0.8	0.7
	4–6	44	20	44	112	500	10	6	45	200	11	1.0	0.9
	7–10	62	28	52	132	700	10	7	45	300	16	1.4	1.2
Males	11–14	99	45	62	157	1,000	10	8	50	400	18	1.6	1.4
	15–18	145	66	69	176	1,000	10	10	60	400	18	1.7	1.4
	19–22	154	70	70	177	1,000	7.5	10	60	400	19	1.7	
	23–50	154	70	70	178	1,000	5	10	60	400	18	1.6	1.4
	51+	154	70	70	178	1,000	5	10	60	400	16	1.4	1.2
Females	11–14	101	46	62	157	800	10	8	50	400	15	1.3	1.1
	15–18	120	55	64	163	800	10	8	60	400	14	1.3	1.1
	19–22	120	55	64	163	800	7.5	8	60	400	14	1.3	1.1
	23–50	120	55	64	163	800	5	8	60	400	13	1.2	1.0
	51+	120	55	64	163	800	5	8	60	400	13	1.2	1.0
Pregnant	—	—	—	—	—	+200	+5	+2	+20	+400	+2	+0.3	+0.4
Lactating	—	—	—	—	—	+400	+5	+3	+40	+100	+5	+0.5	+0.5

						Water-Soluble Vitamins		Minerals					
Persons	Age (years)	Wgt. (lbs)	Wgt. (kg)	Hgt. (in.)	Hgt. (cm)	Vitamin B_6 (mg)	Vitamin B_{12} (μg)	Calcium (mg)	Phosphorus (mg)	Iodine (μg)	Iron (mg)	Magnesium (mg)	Zinc (mg)
Infants	0.0–0.5	13	6	24	60	0.3	0.5[6]	360	240	40	10	50	3
	0.5–1.0	20	9	28	71	0.6	1.5	540	360	50	15	70	5
Children	1–3	29	13	35	90	0.9	2.0	800	800	70	15	150	10
	4–6	44	20	44	112	1.3	2.5	800	800	90	10	200	10
	7–10	62	28	52	132	1.6	3.0	800	800	120	10	250	10
Males	11–14	99	45	62	157	1.8	3.0	1,200	1,200	150	18	350	15
	15–18	145	66	69	176	2.0	3.0	1,200	1,200	150	18	400	15
	19–22	154	70	70	177	2.2	3.0	800	800	150	10	350	15
	23–50	154	70	70	178	2.2	3.0	800	800	150	10	350	15
	51+	154	70	70	178	2.2	3.0	800	800	150	10	350	15
Females	11–14	101	46	62	157	1.8	3.0	1,200	1,200	150	18	300	15
	15–18	120	55	64	163	2.0	3.0	1,200	1,200	150	18	300	15
	19–22	120	55	64	163	2.0	3.0	800	800	150	18	300	15
	23–50	120	55	64	163	3.0	3.0	800	150	150	18	300	15
	51+	120	55	64	163	2.0	3.0	800	800	150	10	300	15
Pregnant	—	—	—	—	—	+0.6	+1.0	+400	+400	+25	[7]	+150	+5
Lactating	—	—	—	—	—	+0.5	+1.0	+400	+400	+50	[7]	+150	+10

1. Allowances provide for individual variances among most normal persons living in the United States under usual environmental stresses. 2. Retinol equivalents. 1. Retinol equivalent = 1 μg retinol. 3. As cholecalciferol. 10 μg cholecalciferol = 400 I.U. vitamin D. 4. αtocopherol equivalents. 1 mg d-α-tocopherol = 1 α T.E. 5. 1 NE (niacin equivalent) is equal to 1 mg of niacin or 60 mg of dietary tryptophan. 6. The RDA for vitamin B12 in infants is based on average concentration of the vitamin in human milk. 7. Cannot be met by ordinary diets: use of supplemental iron is recommended. NOTE: mg—milligram; μg—microgram; IU—International Units; lbs—pounds; Wgt.—Weight; Hgt.—Height. *Source: Recommended Dietary Allowances,* Ninth Edition (1980), with the permission of the National Academy of Sciences, Washington, D.C. Most recent. A 1985 revision was not adapted.

Mean Heights and Weights and Recommended Energy Intake

Category	Age (years)	Weight (lb)	Weight (kg)	Height (in.)	Height (cm)	Energy needs (with range) (kcal)	Energy needs (MJ)
Infants	0.0–0.5	13	6	24	60	kg × 115 (95–145)	kg × .48
	0.5–1.0	20	9	28	71	kg × 105 (80–135)	kg × .44
Children	1-3	29	13	35	90	1300 (900–1800)	5.5
	4–6	44	20	44	112	1700 (1300–2300)	7.1
	7–10	62	28	52	132	2400 (1650–3300)	10.1
Males	11–14	99	45	62	157	2700 (2000–3700)	11.3
	15–18	145	66	69	176	2800 (2100–3900)	11.8
	19–22	154	70	70	177	2900 (2500–3300)	12.2
	23–50	154	70	70	178	2700 (2300–3100)	11.3
	51–75	154	70	70	178	2400 (2000–2800)	10.1
	76 +	154	70	70	178	2050 (1650–2450)	8.6
Females	11–14	101	46	62	157	2200 (1500–3000)	9.2
	15–18	120	55	64	163	2100 (1200–3000)	8.8
	19–22	120	55	64	163	2100 (1700–2500)	8.8
	23–50	120	55	64	163	2000 (1600–2400)	8.4
	51–75	120	55	64	163	1800 (1400–2200)	7.6
	76 +	120	55	64	163	1600 (1200–2000)	6.7
Pregnancy						+ 300	
Lactation						+ 500	

The energy allowances for the young adults are for men and women doing light work. The allowances for the two older age groups represent mean energy needs over these age spans, allowing for a 2% decrease in basal (resting) metabolic rate per decade and a reduction in activity of 200 kcal/day for men and women between 51 and 75 years, 500 kcal for men over 75 years, and 400 kcal for women over 75. The customary range of daily energy output is shown for adults in parentheses, and is based on a variation in energy needs of ± 400 kcal at any one age, emphasizing the wide range of energy intakes appropriate for any group of people. Energy allowances for children through age 18 are based on median energy intakes of children these ages followed in longitudinal growth studies. The values in parentheses are 10th and 90th percentile of energy intake, to indicate the range of energy consumption among children of these ages. NOTE: kg—kilogram; cm—centimeter; kcal—kilocalorie; MJ—megajoule. 1 kcal is equivalent to 4.18 kilojoules. 1 megajoule is equal to 1000 kilojoules. *Source: Recommended Dietary Allowances,* Ninth Edition (1980), with the permission of the National Academy of Sciences, Washington, D.C.

Desirable Weights[1]

Height[2]		Weight[3]			
		Men		Women	
in.	cm	lb	kg	lb	kg
58	147	— —	— —	102 (92–119)	46 (42–54)
60	152	— —	— —	107 (96–125)	49 (44–57)
62	158	123 (112–141)	56 (51–64)	113 (102–131)	51 (46–59)
64	163	130 (118–148)	59 (54–67)	120 (108–138)	55 (49–63)
66	168	136 (124–156)	62 (56–71)	128 (114–146)	58 (52–66)
68	173	145 (132–166)	66 (60–75)	136 (122–154)	62 (55–70)
70	178	154 (140–174)	70 (64–79)	144 (130–163)	65 (59–74)
72	183	162 (148–184)	74 (67–84)	152 (138–173)	69 (63–79)
74	188	171 (156–194)	78 (71–88)	— —	— —
76	193	181 (164–204)	82 (74–93)	— —	— —

1. Desirable weights for men and women of different heights, based on evidence from insurance statistics of weight in relation to longevity. According to the National Center for Health Statistics, the average American male adult is 70 in. tall (178 cm) and the average female is 64 in. tall (163 cm). Accordingly, the average desirable weights are 154 lb (70 kg) and 120 lb (55 kg) throughout adult life. 2. Without shoes. 3. Without clothes. Average weight ranges in parentheses. *Source: Recommended Dietary Allowances,* 9th Edition (1980), with permission of the National Academy of Sciences, Washington, D.C.

Sunbathing and Skin Cancer

Scientists agree that ultraviolet radiation from the sun is the leading cause of skin cancer, which is responsible for an estimated 6,500 to 7,500 deaths in the United States every year.

People can reduce the potential hazard from the sun by not exposing themselves to it unnecessarily for extended periods between 10 a.m. and 2 p.m. when most ultraviolet radiation is strongest.

HEADLINE HISTORY

In any broad overview of history, arbitrary compartmentalization of facts is self-defeating (and makes locating interrelated people, places, and things that much harder). Therefore, Headline History is designed as a "timeline"—a chronology that highlights both the march of time and interesting, sometimes surprising, juxtapositions.

Also see related sections of *Information Please,* particularly Inventions and Discoveries, Countries of the World, etc.

B.C.

Before Christ or Before Common Era (B.C.E.)

5 billion B.C. Planet Earth formed.
3 billion B.C. First signs of primeval life (bacteria and blue-green algae) appear in oceans.
600 million B.C. Earliest date to which fossils can be traced.
1.7 million B.C. First discernible hominids (*Australopithecus* and *Homo habilis*). Early hunters and food-gatherers.
500,000 B.C. *Homo erectus* (crude chopping tools).
70,000 B.C. Neanderthal man (use of fire and advanced tools).
35,000 B.C. Neanderthal man being replaced by later groups of *Homo sapiens* (i.e. Cro-Magnon man, etc.).
18,000 B.C. Cro-Magnons being replaced by later cultures.
15,000 B.C. Migrations across Bering Straits into the Americas.
10,000 B.C. Semi-permanent agricultural settlements in Old World.
10,000-4,000 B.C. Development of settlements into cities and development of skills such as the wheel, pottery and improved methods of cultivation in Mesopatamia and elsewhere.

Brontosaur

NOTE: For futher information on the geographic development in Earth's prehistory, read pages 369-370 in the Science section.

4500–3000 B.C. Sumerians in the Tigris and Euphrates valleys develop a city-state civilization; first phonetic writing (**c.3500 B.C.**). Egyptian agriculture develops. Western Europe is neolithic, without metals or written records. Earliest recorded date in Egyptian calendar (**4241 B.C.**). First year of Jewish calendar (**3760 B.C.**). Copper used by Egyptians and Sumerians.

Moses

3000–2000 B.C. Pharaonic rule begins in Egypt. Cheops, 4th dynasty (**2700–2675 B.C.**). The Great Sphinx of Giza. Earliest Egyptian mummies. Papyrus. Phoenician settlements on coast of what is now Syria and Lebanon. Semitic tribes settle in Assyria. Sargon, first Akkadian king, builds Mesopotamian empire. The Gilgamesh epic (**c.3000 B.C.**). Abraham leaves Ur (**c.2000 B.C.**). Systematic astronomy in Egypt, Babylon, India, China.
2000–1500 B.C. Hyksos invaders drive Egyptians from Lower Egypt (**17th century B.C.**). Amosis I frees Egypt from Hyksos (**c.1600 B.C.**). Assyrians rise to power—cities of Ashur and Nineveh. Twenty-four-character alphabet in Egypt. Israelites enslaved in Egypt. Cuneiform inscriptions used by Hittites. Peak of Minoan culture on Isle of Crete—earliest form of written Greek. Hammurabi, king of Babylon, develops oldest existing code of laws (**18th century B.C.**). In Britain, Stonehenge erected on some unknown astronomical rationale.
1500–1000 B.C. Ikhnaton develops monotheistic religion in Egypt (**c.1375 B.C.**). His successor, Tutankhamen, returns to earlier gods. Moses leads Israelites out of Egypt into Canaan—Ten Commandments. Greeks destroy Troy (**c.1193 B.C.**). End of Greek civilization in Mycenae with invasion of Dorians. Chinese civilization develops under Shang dynasty. Olmec civilization in Mexico—stone monuments; picture writing.
1000–900 B.C. Solomon succeeds King David, builds Jerusalem temple. After Solomon's death, kingdom divided into Israel and Judah. Hebrew elders begin to write Old Testament books of Bible. Phoenicians colonize Spain with settlement at Cadiz.
900–800 B.C. Phoenicians establish Carthage (**c.810 B.C.**). The *Iliad* and the *Odyssey,* perhaps composed by Greek poet Homer.
800–700 B.C. Prophets Amos, Hosea, Isaiah. First recorded Olympic games (**776 B.C.**). Legendary founding of Rome by Romulus (**753 B.C.**). Assyrian

Egyptian chariots (1500 B.C.)

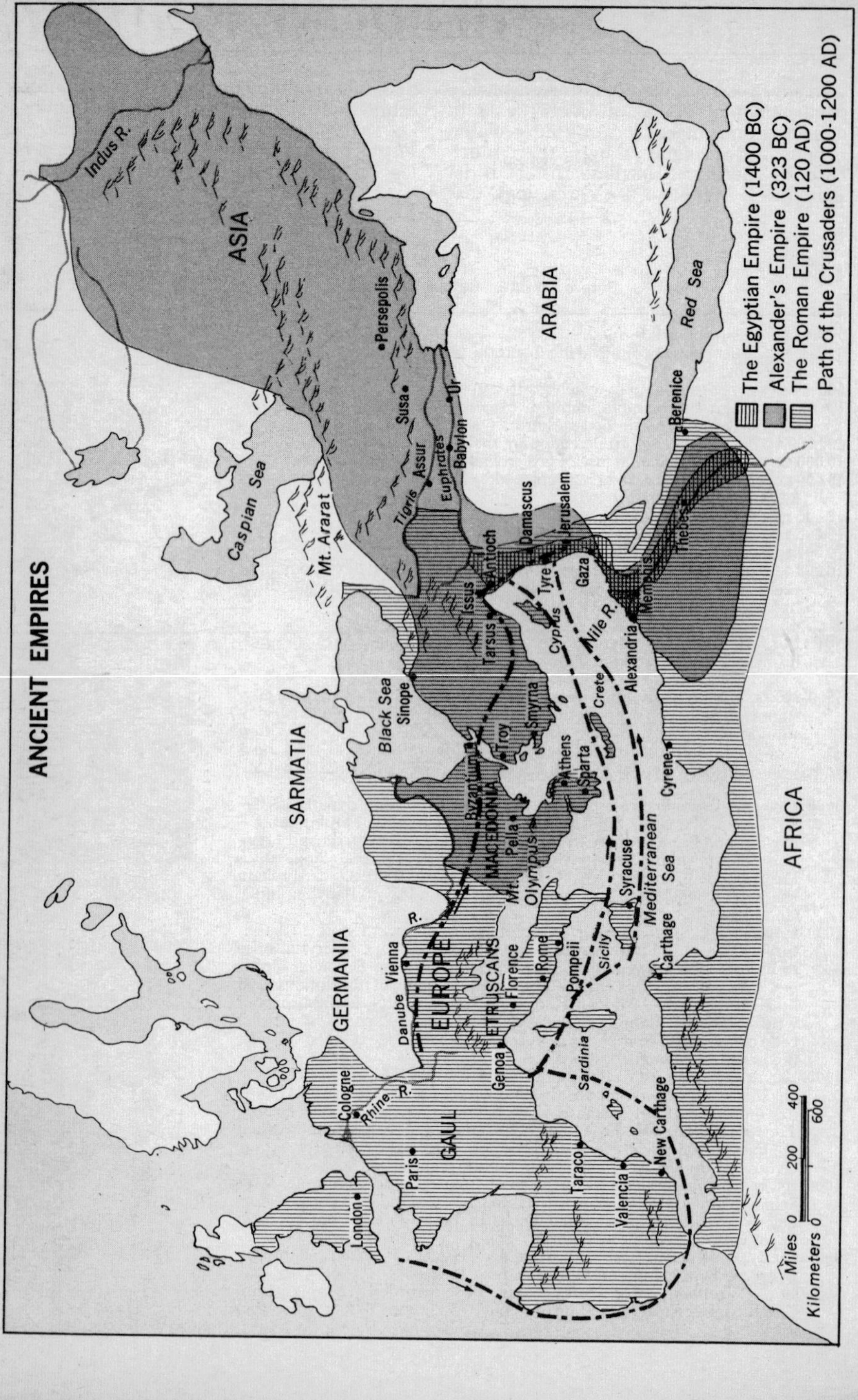
ANCIENT EMPIRES
The Egyptian Empire (1400 BC)
Alexander's Empire (323 BC)
The Roman Empire (120 AD)
Path of the Crusaders (1000-1200 AD)
Miles 0 200 400
Kilometers 0 600
ASIA
Indus R.
Persepolis
Susa
Ur
Babylon
Euphrates
Tigris
Assur
Caspian Sea
Mt. Ararat
ARABIA
Red Sea
Berenice
Thebes
Memphis
Damascus
Jerusalem
Antioch
Issus
Tarsus
Tyre
Gaza
Cyprus
Nile R.
Alexandria
Black Sea
Sinope
SARMATIA
Troy
Smyrna
Crete
Athens
Sparta
Cyrene
Byzantium
MACEDONIA
Pella
Mt. Olympus
Syracuse
Mediterranean Sea
AFRICA
GERMANIA
Vienna
Danube R.
EUROPE
ETRUSCANS
Florence
Rome
Pompeii
Sicily
Carthage
Genoa
Sardinia
New Carthage
Cologne
Rhine R.
GAUL
Paris
London
Taraco
Valencia

Some Ancient Civilizations

Name	Approximate dates	Location	Major cities
Akkadian	2350–2230 B.C.	Mesopotamia, parts of Syria, Asia Minor, Iran	Akkad, Ur, Erich
Assyrian	1800–889 B.C.	Mesopotamia, Syria	Assur, Nineveh, Calah
Babylonian	1728–1686 B.C. (old) 625–539 B.C. (new)	Mesopotamia, Syria, Palestine	Babylon
Cimmerian	750–500 B.C.	Caucasus, northern Asia Minor	—
Egyptian	2850–715 B.C.	Nile valley	Thebes, Memphis, Tanis
Etruscan	900–396 B.C.	Northern Italy	—
Greek	900–200 B.C.	Greece	Athens, Sparta, Thebes, Mycenae, Corinth
Hittite	1640–1200 B.C.	Asia Minor, Syria	Hattusas, Nesa
Lydian	700–547 B.C.	Western Asia Minor	Sardis, Miletus
Mede	835–550 B.C.	Iran	Media
Minoan	3000–1100 B.C.	Crete	Knossos
Persian	559-330 B.C.	Iran, Asia Minor, Syria	Persepolis, Pasargadae
Phoenician	1100–332 B.C.	Palestine (colonies: Gibraltar, Carthage Sardinia)	Tyre, Sidon, Byblos
Phrygian	1000–547 B.C.	Central Asia Minor	Gordion
Roman	500 B.C.–A.D. 300	Italy, Mediterranean region, Asia Minor, western Europe	Rome, Byzantium
Scythian	800–300 B.C.	Caucasus	—
Sumerian	3200–2360 B.C.	Mesopotamia	Ur, Nippur

king Sargon II conquers Hittites, Chaldeans, Samaria (end of Kingdom of Israel). Earliest written music. Chariots introduced into Italy by Etruscans.

700–600 B.C. End of Assyrian Empire (**616 B.C.**)—Nineveh destroyed by Chaldeans (Neo-Babylonians) and Medes (**612 B.C.**). Founding of Byzantium by Greeks (**c.660 B.C.**). Building of the Acropolis in Athens. Solon, Greek lawgiver (**640–560 B.C.**). Sappho of Lesbos, Greek poetess, Lao-Tse, Chinese philosopher and founder of Taoism (born **c.604 B.C.**).

600–500 B.C. Babylonian king Nebuchadnezzar builds empire, destroys Jerusalem (**586 B.C.**). Babylonian Captivity of the Jews (starting **587 B.C.**). Hanging Gardens of Babylon. Cyrus the Great of Persia creates great empire, conquers Babylon (**539 B.C.**), frees the Jews. Athenian democracy develops. Aeschylus, Greek dramatist (**525–465 B.C.**). Confucius (**551–479 B.C.**) develops philosophy-religion in China. Buddha (**563–483 B.C.**) founds Buddhism in India.

Confucius (551-479 B.C.)

500–400 B.C. Greeks defeat Persians: battles of Marathon (**490 B.C.**), Thermopylae (**480 B.C.**), Salamis (**480 B.C.**). Peloponnesian Wars between Athens and Sparta (**431–404 B.C.**)—Sparta victorious. Pericles comes to power in Athens (**462** B.C.). Flowering of Greek culture during the Age of Pericles (**450–400 B.C.**). Sophocles, Greek dramatist (**496–c.406 B.C.**). Hippocrates, Greek "Father of Medicine" (born **460 B.C.**). Xerxes I, king of Persia (rules **485–465 B.C.**).

400–300 B.C. Pentateuch—first five books of the Old Testament evolve in final form. Philip of Macedon assassinated (**336 B.C.**) after conquering Greece; succeeded by son, Alexander the Great (**356–323 B.C.**), who destroys Thebes (**335 B.C.**), conquers Tyre and Jerusalem (**332 B.C.**), occupies Babylon (**330 B.C.**), invades India, and dies in Babylon. His empire is divided among his generals; one of them, Seleucis I, establishes Middle East empire with capitals at Antioch (Syria) and Seleucia (in Iraq). Trial and execution of Greek philosopher Socrates (**399 B.C.**). Dialogues recorded by his student, Plato. Euclid's work on geometry (**323 B.C.**). Aristotle, Greek philosopher (**384–322 B.C.**). Demosthenes, Greek orator (**384–322 B.C.**). Praxiteles, Greek sculptor (**400–330 B.C.**).

Plato (427?-347 B.C.)

300–251 B.C. First Punic War (**264–241 B.C.**): Rome defeats the Carthaginians and begins its domination of the Mediterranean. Temple of the Sun at Teotihuacan, Mexico (**c.300 B.C.**). Invention of Mayan calendar in

Archimedes
(287-212 B.C.)

Yucatán—more exact than older calendars. First Roman gladiatorial games (**264 B.C.**). Archimedes, Greek mathematician (**287–212 B.C.**).

250–201 B.C. Second Punic War (**219–201 B.C.**): Hannibal, Carthaginian general (**246–142 B.C.**), crosses the Alps (**218 B.C.**), reaches gates of Rome (**211 B.C.**), retreats, and is defeated by Scipio Africanus at Zama (**202 B.C.**). Great Wall of China built (**c.215 B.C.**).

200–151 B.C. Romans defeat Seleucid King Antiochus III at Thermopylae (**191 B.C.**)—beginning of Roman world domination. Maccabean revolt against Seleucids (**167 B.C.**).

150–101 B.C. Third Punic War (**149–146 B.C.**): Rome destroys Carthage, killing 450,000 and enslaving the remaining 50,000 inhabitants. Roman armies conquer Macedonia, Greece, Anatolia, Balearic Islands, and southern France. Venus de Milo (**c.140 B.C.**). Cicero, Roman orator (**106–43 B.C.**).

100–51 B.C. Julius Caesar (**100–44 B.C.**) invades Britain (**55 B.C.**) and conquers Gaul (France) (**c.50 B.C.**). Spartacus leads slave revolt against Rome (**71 B.C.**). Romans conquer Seleucid empire. Roman general Pompey conquers Jerusalem (**63 B.C.**). Cleopatra on Egyptian throne (**51–31 B.C.**). Chinese develop use of paper (**c.100 B.C.**). Virgil, Roman poet (**70–19 B.C.**). Horace, Roman poet (**65–8 B.C.**).

50–1 B.C. Caesar crosses Rubicon to fight Pompey (**50 B.C.**). Herod made Roman governor of Judea (**47 B.C.**). Caesar murdered (**44 B.C.**). Caesar's nephew, Octavian, defeats Mark Antony and Cleopatra at Battle of Actium (**31 B.C.**), and establishes Roman empire as Emperor Augustus—rules **27 B.C.—A.D.** 14. Birth of Jesus Christ (variously given from **4 B.C.** to **A.D.** 7). Ovid, Roman poet (**43 B.C.—A.D. 18**).

A.D.

The Christian or Common Era (C.E.)

Jesus Christ
(4? B.C.-29? B.C.)

1–49 After Augustus, Tiberius becomes emperor (dies, **37**), succeeded by Caligula (assassinated, **41**), who is followed by Claudius. Crucifixion of Jesus (probably **30**). Han dynasty in China founded by Emperor Kuang Wu Ti. Buddhism introduced to China.

50–99 Claudius poisoned (**54**), succeeded by Nero (commits suicide, **68**). Missionary journeys of Paul the Apostle (**34–60**). Jews revolt against Rome; Jerusalem destroyed (**70**). Roman persecutions of Christians begin (**64**). Colosseum built in Rome (**71–80**). Trajan (rules **98–116**); Roman empire extends to Mesopotamia, Arabia, Balkans. First Gospels of St. Mark, St. John, St. Matthew.

100–149 Hadrian rules Rome (**117–138**); codifies Roman law, establishes postal system, builds wall between England and Scotland. Jews revolt under Bar Kokhba (**122–135**); final *Diaspora* (dispersion) of Jews begins.

150–199 Marcus Aurelius (rules Rome **161–180**). Oldest Mayan temples in Central America (**c.200**)., Mayan civilization develops writing, astronomy, mathematics.

200–249 Goths invade Asia Minor (**c.220**). Roman persecutions of Christians increase. Persian (Sassanid) empire re-established. End of Chinese Han dynasty.

250–299 Increasing invasions of the Roman empire by Franks and Goths. Buddhism spreads in China.

300–349 Constantine the Great (rules **312–337**) reunites eastern and western Roman empires, with new capital (Constantinople) on site of Byzantium (**330**); issues Edict of Milan legalizing Christianity (**313**); becomes a Christian on his deathbed (**337**). Council of Nicaea (**325**) defines orthodox Christian doctrine. First Gupta dynasty in India (**c.320**).

Mayan Bas-Reliefs

350–399 Huns (Mongols) invade Europe (**c.360**). Theodosius the Great (rules **392–395**)—last emperor of a united Roman empire. Roman empire permanently divided in **395**: western empire ruled from Rome; eastern empire ruled from Constantinople.

400–449 Western Roman empire disintegrates under weak emperors. Alaric, king of the Visigoths, sacks Rome (**410**). Attila, Hun chieftain, attacks Roman provinces (**433**). St. Patrick returns to Ireland (**432**). St. Augustine's *City of God* (**411**).

450–499 Vandals destroy Rome (**455**). Western Roman empire ends as Odoacer, German chieftain, overthrows last Roman emperor, Romulus Augustulus, and becomes king of Italy (**476**). Ostrogothic kingdom of Italy established by Theodoric the Great (**493**). Clovis, ruler of the Franks, is converted to Christianity (**496**). First schism between western and eastern churches (**484**). Peak of Mayan culture in Mexico (**c.460**).

500–549 Eastern and western churches reconciled (**519**). Justinian I, the

Great (483–565), becomes Byzantine emperor (527), issues his first code of civil laws (529), conquers North Africa, Italy, and part of Spain. Plague spreads through Europe (from 542). Arthur, semi-legendary king of the Britons (killed, c.537). Boëthius, Roman scholar (executed, 524).

550–599 Beginnings of European silk industry after Justinian's missionaries smuggle silkworms out of China (553). Mohammed, founder of Islam (570–632). Buddhism in Japan (c.560). St. Augustine of Canterbury brings Christianity to Britain (597). After killing about half the population, plague in Europe subsides (594).

600–649 Mohammed flees from Mecca to Medina (the *Hegira*); first year of the Muslim calendar (622). Muslim empire grows (634). Arabs conquer Jerusalem (637), destroy Alexandrian library (641), conquer Persians (641). Fatima, Mohammed's daughter (606–632).

Mohammed (570-632)

650–699 Arabs attack North Africa (670), destroy Carthage (697). Venerable Bede, English monk (672–735).

700–749 Arab empire extends from Lisbon to China (by 716). Charles Martel, Frankish leader, defeats Arabs at Tours/Poitiers, halting Arab advance in Europe (732). Charlemagne (742–814).

750–799 Caliph Harun al-Rashid rules Arab empire (786–809): the "golden age" of Arab culture. Vikings begin attacks on Britain (790), land in Ireland (795). Charlemagne becomes king of the Franks (771). City of Machu Picchu flourishes in Peru.

800–849 Charlemagne (Charles the Great) crowned first Holy Roman Emperor in Rome (800). Arabs conquer Crete, Sicily, and Sardinia (826–827). Charlemagne dies (814), succeeded by his son, Louis the Pious, who divides France among his sons (817).

850–899 Norsemen attack as far south as the Mediterranean but are repulsed (859), discover Iceland (861). Alfred the Great becomes king of Britain (871), defeats Danish invaders (878). Russian nation founded by Vikings under Prince Rurik, establishing capital at Novgorod (855–879).

900–949 Vikings discover Greenland (c.900). Arab Spain under Abd ar-Rahman III becomes center of learning (912–961).

950–999 Eric the Red establishes first Viking colony in Greenland (982). Mieczyslaw I becomes first ruler of Poland (960). Hugh Capet elected King of France in 987; Capetian dynasty to rule until 1328. Musical notation systematized (c.990). Vikings and Danes attack Britain (988–999). Holy Roman Empire founded by Otto I, King of Germany since 936, crowned by Pope John XII in 962.

11th century A.D.

c.1000 Hungary and Scandinavia converted to Christianity. Viking raider Leif Ericson discovers North America, calls it *Vinland*. Chinese invent gunpowder. *Beowulf*, Old English epic.

1009 Moslems destroy Holy Sepulchre in Jerusalem.

1013 Danes control England. Canute takes throne (1016), conquers Norway (1028), dies (1035); kingdom divided among his sons: Harold Harefoot (England), Sweyn (Norway), Hardecanute (Denmark).

1040 Macbeth murders Duncan, king of Scotland.

1053 Robert Guiscard, Norman invader, establishes kingdom in Italy, conquers Sicily (1072).

1054 Final separation between Eastern (Orthodox) and Western (Roman) churches.

1055 Seljuk Turks, Asian nomads, move west, capture Baghdad, Armenia (1064), Syria, and Palestine (1075).

1066 William of Normandy invades England, defeats last Saxon king, Harold II, at Battle of Hastings, crowned William I of England ("the Conqueror").

1073 Emergence of strong papacy when Gregory VII is elected. Conflict with English and French kings and German emperors will continue throughout medieval period.

1095 (*See* special material on "The Crusades.")

Viking Discovery of Greenland (c.900)

12th century A.D.

1150–67 Universities of Paris and Oxford founded in France and England.

1162 Thomas à Becket named Archbishop of Canterbury, murdered by Henry II's men (1170). Troubadours (wandering minstrels) glorify romantic concepts of feudalism.

1189 Richard I ("the Lionhearted") succeeds Henry II in England, killed in France (1199), succeeded by King John.

13th century A.D.

1211 Genghis Khan invades China, captures Peking (1214), conquers Persia (1218), invades Russia (1223), dies (1227).

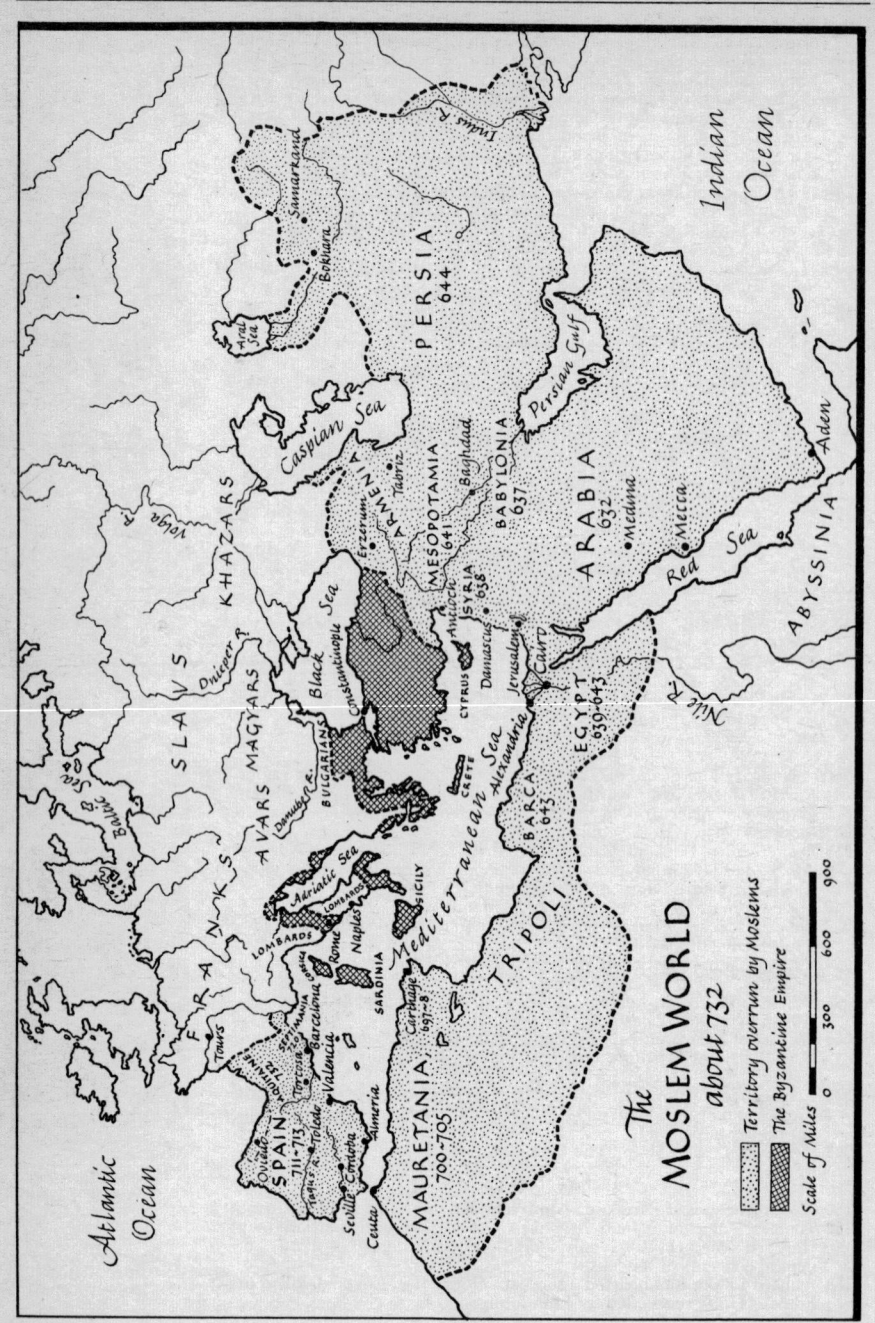

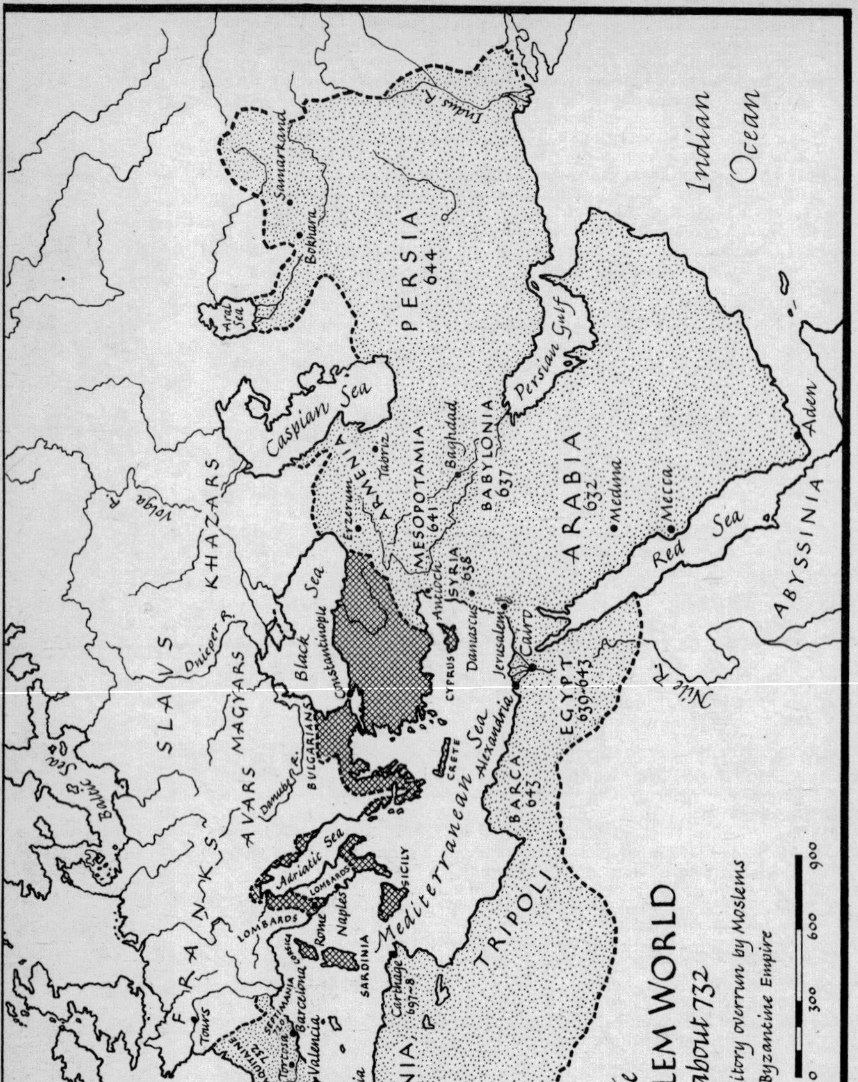
The MOSLEM WORLD about 732
Territory overrun by Moslems
The Byzantine Empire
Scale of Miles
0
300
600
900
Atlantic Ocean
Indian Ocean
Mediterranean Sea
Black Sea
Caspian Sea
Aral Sea
Red Sea
Persian Gulf
Adriatic Sea
Baltic Sea
SPAIN 711-713
AQUITAINE 732
SEPTIMANIA 720
MAURETANIA 700-705
TRIPOLI
BARCA 643
EGYPT 639-643
ARABIA 632
SYRIA 638
MESOPOTAMIA 641
BABYLONIA 637
ARMENIA
PERSIA 644
ABYSSINIA
FRANKS
LOMBARDS
AVARS
MAGYARS
SLAVS
KHAZARS
BULGARIANS
SARDINIA
CORSICA
SICILY
CRETE
CYPRUS
Oviedo
Toledo
Cordoba
Seville
Almeria
Valencia
Tortosa
Barcelona
Tours
Ceuta
Carthage 697-8
Rome
Naples
Constantinople
Alexandria
Cairo
Jerusalem
Damascus
Antioch
Erzerum
Tabriz
Baghdad
Medina
Mecca
Aden
Bokhara
Samarkand
Tagus R.
Danube R.
Dnieper R.
Volga R.
Nile R.
Indus R.

1215 King John forced by barons to sign Magna Carta at Runneymede, limiting royal power.

1233 The Inquisition begins as Pope Gregory IX assigns Dominicans responsibility for combatting heresy. Torture used (**1252**). Ferdinand and Isabella establish Spanish Inquisition (**1478**). Tourquemada, Grand Inquisitor, forces conversion or expulsion of Spanish Jews (**1492**). Forced conversion of Moors (**1499**). Inquisition in Portugal (**1531**). First Protestants burned at the stake in Spain (**1543**). Spanish Inquisition abolished (**1834**).

1241 Mongols defeat Germans in Silesia, invade Poland and Hungary, withdraw from Europe after Ughetai, Mongol leader, dies.

1251 Kublai Khan governs China, becomes ruler of Mongols (1259), establishes Yuan dynasty in China (1280), invades Burma (1287), dies (1294).

1271 Marco Polo of Venice travels to China, in court of Kublai Khan (1275–1292), returns to Genoa (1295) and writes *Travels*.

1295 English King Edward I summons the Model Parliament.

John Wycliffe (1320-1384)

14th century A.D.

1312–37 Mali Empire reaches its height in Africa under King Mansa Musa.

1337–1453 Hundred Years' War—English and French kings fight for control of France.

c.1325 The beginning of the Renaissance in Italy: writers Dante, Petrarch, Boccaccio; painter Giotto. Development of *No* drama in Japan. Aztecs establish capital on site of modern Mexico City. Peak of Moslem culture in Spain. Small cannon in use.

1347–1351 At least 25 million people die in Europe's "Black Death" (bubonic plague).

1368 Ming dynasty begins in China.

1376–82 John Wycliffe, pre-Reformation religious reformer and followers translate Latin Bible into English.

1378 The Great Schism (to 1417)—rival popes in Rome and Avignon, France, fight for control of Roman Catholic Church.

c.1387 Chaucer's *Canterbury Tales*.

Joan of Arc (1412-1431)

15th century A.D.

1415 Henry V defeats French at Agincourt. Jan Hus, Bohemian preacher and follower of Wycliffe, burned at stake in Constance as heretic.

1418–60 Portugal's Prince Henry the Navigator sponsors exploration of Africa's coast.

1428 Joan of Arc leads French against English, captured by Burgundians (1430) and turned over to the English, burned at the stake as a witch after ecclesiastical trial (1431).

1438 Inca rule in Peru.

1450 Florence becomes center of Renaissance arts and learning under the Medicis.

1453 Turks conquer Constantinople, end of the Byzantine empire. Hundred Years' War between France and England ends.

1455 The Wars of the Roses, civil wars between rival noble factions, begin in England (to 1485). Having invented printing with movable type at Mainz, Germany, Johann Gutenberg completes first Bible.

1462 Ivan the Great rules Russia until 1505 as first czar; ends payment of tribute to Mongols.

1492 Moors conquered in Spain by troops of Ferdinand and Isabella. Columbus discovers Caribbean islands, returns to Spain (1493). Second voyage to Dominica, Jamaica, Puerto Rico (1493–1496). Third voyage to Orinoco (1498). Fourth voyage to Honduras and Panama (1502–1504).

1497 Vasco da Gama sails around Africa and discovers sea route to India (1498). Establishes Portuguese colony in India (1502). John Cabot, employed by England, reaches and explores Canadian coast. Michelangelo's *Bacchus* sculpture.

Christopher Columbus (1451-1506)

THE CRUSADES (1096–1291)

In 1095 at Council of Clermont, Pope Urban II calls for war to rescue Holy Land from Moslem infidels. *First Crusade* (1096)—about 500,000 peasants led by Peter the Hermit prove so troublesome that Byzantine Emperor Alexius ships them to Asia Minor; only 25,000 survive return after massacre by Seljuk Turks. Followed by organized army, led by nobility, which reaches Constantinople (1097), conquers Jerusalem (1099), Acre (1104), establishes Latin Kingdom protected by Knights of St. John the Hospitaller (1100), and Knights Templar (1123). Seljuk Turks start series of counterattacks (1144). *Second Crusade* (1146) led by King Louis VIII of France and Emperor Conrad III. Crusaders perish in Asia Minor (1147).

Saladin controls Egypt (1171), unites Islam in Holy War *(Jihad)* against Christians, recaptures Jerusalem (1187). *Third Crusade* (1189) under kings of France, England, and Germany fails to reduce Saladin's power. *Fourth Crusade* (1200–1204)—French knights sack Greek Christian Constantinople, establish Latin empire in Byzantium. Greeks reestablish Orthodox faith (1262).

Children's Crusade (1212)—Only 1 of 30,000 French children and about 200 of 20,000 German children survive to return home. Other Crusades—against Egypt (1217), *Sixth* (1228), *Seventh* (1248), *Eighth* (1270). Mamelukes conquer Acre; end of the Crusades (1291).

Michelangelo Buonarreti
(1475-1564)

Martin Luther
(1483-1546)

Anthony Van Dyck
(1599-1641)

16th century A.D.

1501 First black slaves in America brought to Spanish colony of Santo Domingo.

c.1503 Leonardo da Vinci paints the *Mona Lisa.*

1506 St. Peter's Church started in Rome; designed and decorated by such artists and architects as Bramante, Michelangelo, da Vinci, Raphael, and Bernini before its completion in **1626**.

1509 Henry VIII ascends English throne. Michelangelo paints the ceiling of the Sistine Chapel.

1517 Turks conquer Egypt, control Arabia. Martin Luther posts his 95 theses denouncing church abuses on church door in Wittenberg—start of the Reformation in Germany.

1519 Ulrich Zwingli begins Reformation in Switzerland. Hernando Cortes conquers Mexico for Spain. Charles I of Spain is chosen Holy Roman Emperor Charles V. Portuguese explorer Fernando Magellan sets out to circumnavigate the globe.

1520 Luther excommunicated by Pope Leo X. Suleiman I ("the Magnificent") becomes Sultan of Turkey, invades Hungary (**1521**), Rhodes (**1522**), attacks Austria (**1529**), annexes Hungary (**1541**), Tripoli (**1551**), makes peace with Persia (**1553**), destroys Spanish fleet (**1560**), dies (**1566**). Magellan reaches the Pacific, is killed by Philippine natives (**1521**). One of his ships under Juan Sebastián del Cano continues around the world, reaches Spain (**1522**).

1524 Verrazano, sailing under the French flag, explores the New England coast and New York Bay.

1527 Troops of the Holy Roman Empire attack Rome, imprison Pope Clement VII—the end of the Italian Renaissance. Castiglione writes *The Courtier.* The Medici expelled from Florence.

1532 Pizarro marches from Panama to Peru, kills the Inca chieftain, Atahualpa, of Peru (**1533**). Machiavelli's *Prince* published posthumously.

1535 Reformation begins as Henry VIII makes himself head of English Church after being excommunicated by Pope. Sir Thomas More executed as traitor for refusal to acknowledge king's religious authority. Jacques Cartier sails up the St. Lawrence River, basis of French claims to Canada.

1536 Henry VIII executes second wife, Anne Boleyn. John Calvin establishes Presbyterian form of Protestantism in Switzerland, writes *Institutes of the Christian Religion.* Danish and Norwegian Reformations. Michelangelo's *Last Judgment.*

1541 John Knox leads Reformation in Scotland, establishes Presbyterian church (**1560**).

1543 Publication of *On the Revolution of Heavenly Bodies* by Polish scholar Nicolaus Copernicus—giving his theory that the earth revolves around the sun.

1545 Council of Trent to meet intermittently until **1563** to define Catholic dogma and doctrine, reiterate papal authority.

1547 Ivan IV ("the Terrible") crowned as Czar of Russia, begins conquest of Astrakhan and Kazan (**1552**), battles nobles (boyars) for power (**1564**), kills his son (**1580**), dies, and is succeeded by a son who gives power to Boris Godunov (**1584**).

1553 Roman Catholicism restored in England by Queen Mary I, who rules until **1558**. Religious radical Michael Servetus burned as heretic in Geneva by order of John Calvin.

1554 Benvenuto Cellini completes the bronze *Perseus.*

1556 Akbar the Great becomes Mogul emperor of India, conquers Afghanistan (**1581**), continues wars of conquest (until **1605**).

1558 Queen Elizabeth I ascends the throne (rules to **1603**). Restores Protestantism, establishes state Church of England (Anglicanism). Renaissance will reach height in England—Shakespeare, Marlowe, Spenser.

1561 Persecution of Huguenots in France stopped by Edict of Orleans. French religious wars begin again with massacre of Huguenots at Vassy. St. Bartholomew's Day Massacre—thousands of Huguenots murdered (**1572**). Amnesty granted (**1573**). Persecution continues periodically until Edict of Nantes (**1598**) gives Huguenots religious freedom (until **1685**).

1568 Protestant Netherlands revolts against Catholic Spain; independence will be acknowledged by Spain in **1648**. High point of Dutch Renaissance—painters Rubens, Van Dyck, Hals, and Rembrandt.

1570 Japan permits visits of foreign ships. Queen Elizabeth I excommunicated by Pope. Turks attack Cyprus and war on Venice. Turkish fleet defeated at Battle of Lepanto by Spanish and Italian fleets (**1571**). Peace of Constantinople (**1572**) ends Turkish attacks on Europe.

1580 Francis Drake returns to England after circumnavigating the globe. Knighted by Queen Elizabeth I (**1581**). Montaigne's *Essays* published.
1583 William of Orange rules The Netherlands; assassinated on orders of Philip II of Spain (**1584**).
1587 Mary, Queen of Scots, executed for treason by order of Queen Elizabeth I. Monteverdi's *First Book of Madrigals.*
1588 Defeat of the Spanish Armada by English. Henry, King of Navarre and Protestant leader, recognized as Henry IV, first Bourbon king of France. Converts to Roman Catholicism in **1593** in attempt to end religious wars.
1590 Henry IV enters Paris, wars on Spain (**1595**), marries Marie de Medici (**1600**), assassinated (**1610**). Spenser's *The Faerie Queen,* El Greco's *St. Jerome.* Galileo's experiments with falling objects.
1598 Boris Godunov becomes Russian Czar. Tycho Brahe describes his astronomical experiments.

Francis Bacon (1561-1626)

17th century A.D.

1600 Giordano Bruno burned as a heretic. Ieyasu rules Japan, moves capital to Edo (Tokyo). Shakespeare's *Hamlet* begins his most productive decade. English East India Company established to develop overseas trade.
1607 Jamestown, Virginia, established—first permanent English colony on American mainland.
1609 Samuel de Champlain establishes French colony of Quebec.
1611 Gustavus Adolphus elected King of Sweden. King James Version of the Bible published in England. Rubens paints his *Descent from the Cross.*
1614 John Napier discovers logarithms.
1618 Start of the Thirty Years' War (to **1648**)—Protestant revolt against Catholic oppression; Denmark, Sweden, and France will invade Germany in later phases of war. Kepler proposes his Third Law of planetary motion.
1620 Pilgrims, after three-month voyage in *Mayflower,* land at Plymouth Rock. Francis Bacon's *Novum Organum.*
1633 Inquisition forces Galileo to recant his belief in Copernican theory.
1642 English Civil War. Cavaliers, supporters of Charles I, against Roundheads, parliamentary forces. Oliver Cromwell defeats Royalists (**1646**). Parliament demands reforms. Charles I offers concessions, brought to trial (**1648**), beheaded (**1649**). Cromwell becomes Lord Protector (**1653**). Rembrandt paints his *Night Watch.*
1644 End of Ming Dynasty in China—Manchus come to power. Descartes' *Principles of Philosophy.* John Milton's *Areopagitica* on the freedom of the press.
1648 End of the Thirty Years' War. German population about half of what it was in **1618** because of war and pestilence.
1658 Cromwell dies; his son, Richard, resigns and Puritan government collapses.
1660 English Parliament calls for the restoration of the monarchy; invites Charles II to return from France.
1661 Charles II is crowned King of England. Louis XIV begins personal rule as absolute monarch; starts to build Versailles.

Giordano Bruno (1548-1600)

George Washington (1732-1779)

THE FOUNDING OF THE AMERICAN NATION

Colonization of America begins: Jamestown, Va. **(1607)**; Pilgrims in Plymouth **(1620)**; Massachusetts Bay Colony **(1630)** New Netherland founded by Dutch West India Company **(1623)**, captured by English **(1664)**. Delaware established by Swedish trading company **(1638)**, absorbed later by Penn family. Proprietorships by royal grants to Lord Baltimore (Maryland, **1632**); Captain John Mason (New Hampshire, **1635**); Sir William Berkeley and Sir George Carteret (New Jersey, **1663**); friends of Charles II (the Carolinas, **1663**); William Penn (Pennsylvania, **1682**); James Oglethorpe and others (Georgia, **1732**).

Increasing conflict between colonists and Britain on western frontier because of royal edict limiting western expansion **(1763)**, and regulation of colonial trade and increased taxation of colonies (Writs of Assistance allow search for illegal shipments, **1761**; Sugar Act, **1764**; Currency Act, **1764**; Stamp Act, **1765**; Quartering Act, **1765**; Duty Act, **1767**.) Boston Massacre **(1770)**. Lord North attempts conciliation **(1770)**. Boston Tea Party **(1773)**, followed by punitive measures passed by Parliament—the "Intolerable Acts."

First Continental Congress **(1774)** sends "Declaration of Rights and Grievances" to king, urges colonies to form Continental Association. Paul Revere's Ride and Lexington and Concord battle between Massachusetts minutemen and British **(1775)**.

Second Continental Congress **(1775)**, while sending "olive branch" to the king, begins to raise army, appoints Washington commander-in-chief, and seeks alliance with France. Some colonial legislatures urge their delegates to vote for independence. Declaration of Independence **(July 4, 1776)**.

Major Battles of the Revolutionary War: *Long Island:* Howe defeats Putnam's division of Washington's Army in Brooklyn Heights, but Americans escape across East River **(1776)**. *Trenton and Princeton:* Washington defeats Hessians at Trenton. British at Princeton, winters at Morristown **(1776–77)**. Howe winters in Philadelphia; Washington at Valley Forge **(1777–78)**. Burgoyne surrenders British army to General Gates at *Saratoga* **(1777)**.

France recognizes American independence **(1778)**. The War moves south: Savannah captured by British **(1778)**; Charleston occupied **(1780)**; Americans fight successful guerrilla actions under Marion, Pickens, and Sumter. In the West, George Rogers Clark attacks Forts Kaskaskia and Vincennes **(1778–1779)**, defeating British in the region. Cornwallis surrenders at *Yorktown,* Virginia **(Oct. 19, 1781)**. By **1782**, Britain is eager for peace because of conflicts with European nations. *Peace of Paris* **(1783)**: Britain recognizes American independence.

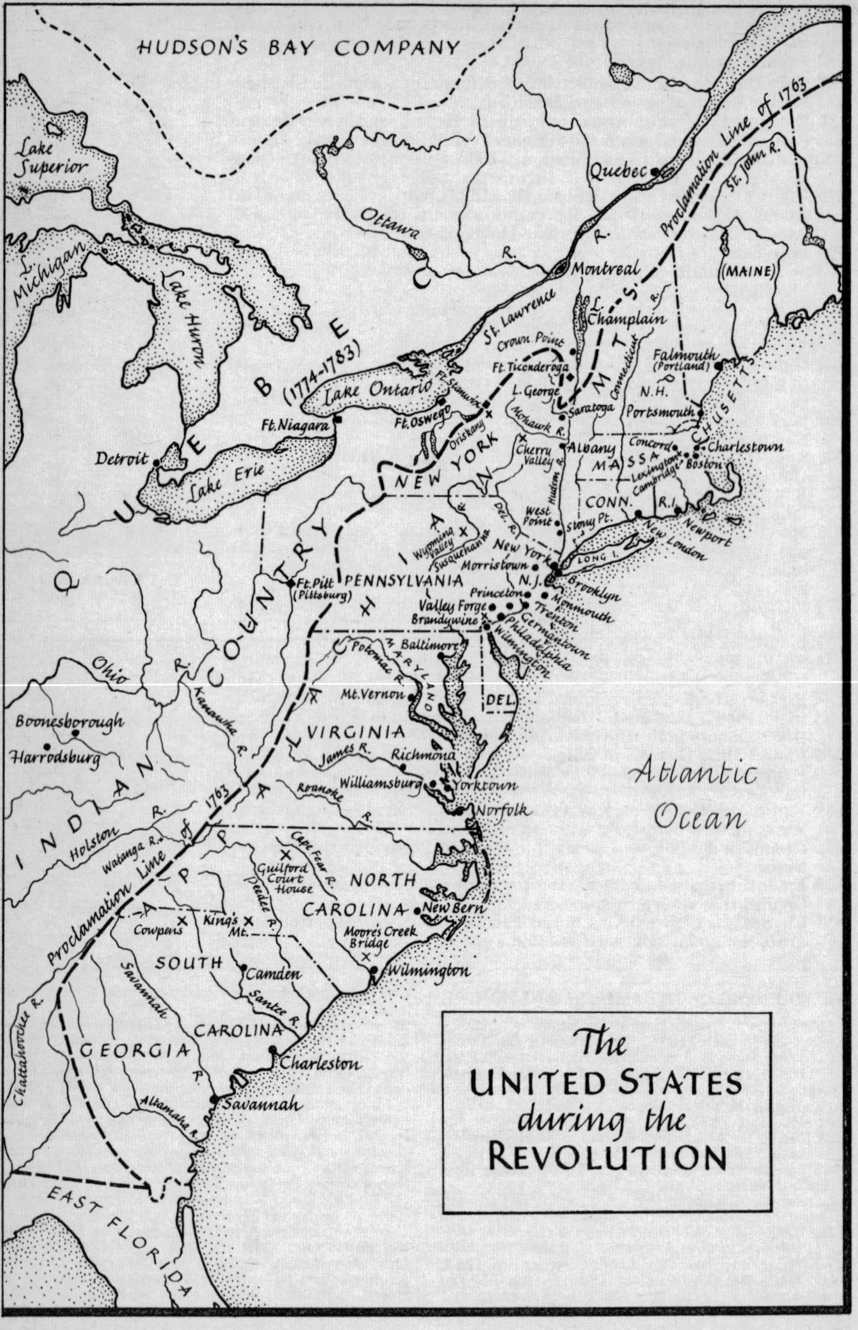

The UNITED STATES during the REVOLUTION

1664 British take New Amsterdam from the Dutch. English limit "Nonconformity" with re-established Anglican Church. Isaac Newton's experiments with gravity.
1665 Great Plague in London kills 75,000.
1666 Great Fire of London. Molière's *Misanthrope.*
1683 War of European powers against the Turks (to **1699**). Vienna withstands three-month Turkish siege; high point of Turkish advance in Europe.
1685 James II succeeds Charles II in England, calls for freedom of conscience (**1687**). Protestants fear restoration of Catholicism and demand "Glorious Revolution." William of Orange invited to England and James II escapes to France (**1688**). William III and his wife, Mary, crowned. In France, Edict of Nantes of **1598**, granting freedom of worship to Huguenots (French Protestants), is revoked by Louis XIV; thousands of Protestants flee.
1689 Peter the Great becomes Czar of Russia—attempts to westernize nation and build Russia as a military power. Defeats Charles XII of Sweden at Poltava (**1709**). Beginning of the French and Indian Wars (to **1763**), campaigns in America linked to a series of wars between France and England for domination of Europe.
1690 William III of England defeats former King James II and Irish rebels at Battle of the Boyne in Ireland. John Locke's *Human Understanding.*

John Locke (1632-1704)

18th century A.D.

1701 War of the Spanish Succession begins—the last of Louis XIV's wars for domination of the continent. The Peace of Utrecht (**1714**) will end the conflict and mark the rise of the British Empire. Called Queen Anne's War in America, it ends with the British taking New Foundland, Acadia, and Hudson's Bay Territory from France, and Gibraltar and Minorca from Spain.
1704 Deerfield (Conn.) Massacre of English colonists by French and Indians. Bach's first cantata. Jonathan Swift's *Tale of a Tub. Boston News Letter*—first newspaper in America.
1707 United Kingdom of Great Britain formed—England, Wales, and Scotland joined by parliamentary Act of Union.
1729 J. S. Bach's *St. Matthew Passion.* Isaac Newton's *Principia* translated from Latin into English.
1735 John Peter Zenger, New York editor, acquitted of libel in New York, establishing press freedom.
1740 Capt. Vitus Bering, Dane employed by Russia, discovers Alaska.
1746 British defeat Scots under Stuart Pretender Prince Charles at Culloden Moor. Last battle fought on British soil.
1751 Publication of the *Encyclopédie* begins in France, the "bible" of the Enlightenment.
1755 Samuel Johnson's *Dictionary* first published. Great earthquake in Lisbon, Portugal—over 60,000 die.
1756 Seven Years' War (French and Indian War in America) (to **1763**), in which Britain and Prussia defeat France, Spain, Austria, and Russia. France loses North American colonies; Spain cedes Florida to Britain in exchange for Cuba. In India, over 100 British prisoners die in "Black Hole of Calcutta."
1757 Beginning of British Empire in India as Robert Clive, British commander, defeats Nawab of Bengal at Plassey.
1759 British capture Quebec from French. Voltaire's *Candide.* Haydn's *Symphony No. 1.*
1762 Catherine II ("the Great") becomes Czarina of Russia. J. J. Rousseau's *Social Contract.* Mozart tours Europe as six-year-old prodigy.
1765 James Watt invents the steam engine.
1769 Sir William Arkwright patents a spinning machine—an early step in the Industrial Revolution.
1772 Joseph Priestley and Daniel Rutherford independently discover nitrogen. Partition of Poland—in **1772, 1793,** and **1795**, Austria, Prussia, and Russia divide land and people of Poland, end its independence.
1775 The American Revolution (*see* "The Founding of the American Nation"). Priestley discovers hydrochloric and sulfuric acids.
1776 Adam Smith's *Wealth of Nations.* Edward Gibbon's *Decline and Fall of the Roman Empire.* Thomas Paine's *Common Sense.* Fragonard's *Washerwoman.* Mozart's *Haffner Serenade.*
1778 Capt. James Cook discovers Hawaii. Franz Mesmer uses hypnotism.
1781 Immanuel Kant's *Critique of Pure Reason.* Herschel discovers Uranus.
1783 End of Revolutionary War (*see* special material on "The Founding of

Catherine II (1729-1796)

Napoleon Bonaparte (1769-1821)

Thomas Jefferson (1743-1826)

Alexander Hamilton (1755-1804)

the American Nation"). William Blake's poems. Beethoven's first printed works.

1784 Crimea annexed by Russia. John Wesley's *Deed of Declaration*, the basic work of Methodism.

1785 Russians settle Aleutian Islands.

1787 The Constitution of the United States signed. Lavoisier's work on chemical nomenclature. Mozart's *Don Giovanni.*

1788 French *Parlement* presents grievances to Louis XVI who agrees to convening of Estates-General in **1789**—not called since **1613.** Goethe's *Egmont.* Laplace's *Laws of the Planetary System.*

1789 French Revolution (*see* special material on the "French Revolution"). In U.S., George Washington elected President with all 69 votes of the Electoral College, takes oath of office in New York City. Vice President: John Adams. Secretary of State: Thomas Jefferson. Secretary of Treasury: Alexander Hamilton.

1790 H.M.S. *Bounty* mutineers settle on Pitcairn Island. Aloisio Galvani experiments on electrical stimulation of the muscles. Philadelphia temporary capital of U.S. as Congress votes to establish new capital on Potomac. U.S. population about 3,929,000, including 698,000 slaves. Lavoisier formulates *Table of 31 chemical elements.*

1791 U.S. Bill of Rights ratified. Boswell's *Life of Johnson.*

1794 Kosciusko's uprising in Poland quelled by the Russians. In U.S., Whiskey Rebellion in Pennsylvania as farmers object to liquor taxes. U.S. Navy and Post Office Department established.

1796 Napoleon Bonaparte, French general, defeats Austrians. In the U.S., Washington's Farewell Address (**Sept. 17**); John Adams elected President; Thomas Jefferson, Vice President. Edward Jenner introduces smallpox vaccination.

1798 Napoleon extends French conquests to Rome and Egypt.

1799 Napoleon leads coup that overthrows Directory, becomes First Consul—one of three who rule France.

19th century A.D.

1800 Napoleon conquers Italy, firmly establishes himself as First Consul in France. In the U.S., Federal Government moves to Washington. Robert Owen's social reforms in England. William Herschel discovers infrared rays. Alessandro Volta produces electricity.

1801 Austria makes temporary peace with France. United Kingdom of Great Britain and Ireland established with one monarch and one parliament; Catholics excluded from voting.

1803 U.S. negotiates Louisiana Purchase from France: For $15 million, U.S. doubles its domain, increasing its territory by 827,000 sq. mi. (2,144,500 sq km), from Mississippi River to Rockies and from Gulf of Mexico to British North America.

1804 Haiti declares independence from France; first black nation to gain freedom from European colonial rule. Napoleon proclaims himself emperor of France, systematizes French law under *Code Napoleon.* In the U.S., Alexander Hamilton is mortally wounded in duel with Aaron Burr. Lewis and Clark expedition begins exploration of what is now northwestern U.S.

1805 Lord Nelson defeats the French-Spanish fleets in the Battle of Trafalgar. Napoleon victorious over Austrian and Russian forces at the Battle of Austerlitz.

1807 Robert Fulton makes first successful steamboat trip on *Clermont* between New York City and Albany.

1808 French armies occupy Rome and Spain, extending Napoleon's empire. Britain begins aiding Spanish guerrillas against Napoleon in Peninsular War. In the U.S., Congress bars importation of slaves. Beethoven's *Fifth* and *Sixth Symphonies* performed.

1812 Napoleon's Grand Army invades Russia in June. Forced to retreat in winter, most of Napoleon's 600,000 men are lost. In the U.S., war with

FRENCH REVOLUTION (1789–1799)

Revolution begins when Third Estate (Commons) delegates swear not to disband until France has a constitution. Paris mob storms Bastille, symbol of royal power **(July 14, 1789).** National Assembly votes for Constitution, Declaration of the Rights of Man, a limited monarchy, and other reforms **(1789–90).** Legislative Assembly elected, Revolutionary Commune formed, and French Republic proclaimed **(1792).** War of the First Coalition—Austria, Prussia, Britain, Netherlands, and Spain fight to restore French nobility **(1792–97).** Start of series of wars between France and European powers that will last, almost without interruption, for 23 years. Louis XVI and Marie Antoinette executed. Committee of Public Safety begins Reign of Terror as political control measure. Interfactional rivalry leads to mass killings. Danton and Robespierre executed. Third French Constitution sets up Directory government **(1795).**

Britain declared over freedom of the seas for U.S. vessels. U.S.S. *Constitution* sinks British frigate. (*See* special material on the "War of 1812.")
1814 French defeated by allies (Britain, Austria, Russia, Prussia, Sweden, and Portugal) in War of Liberation. Napoleon exiled to Elba, off Italian coast. Bourbon King Louis XVIII takes French throne. George Stephenson builds first practical steam locomotive.
1815 Napoleon returns: "Hundred Days" begin. Napoleon defeated by Wellington at Waterloo, banished again to St. Helena in South Atlantic. Congress of Vienna: victorious allies change the map of Europe.
1817 Simón Bolívar establishes independent Venezuela, as Spain loses hold on South American countries. Bolívar named President of Colombia (**1819**). Peru, Guatemala, Panama, and Santo Domingo proclaim independence from Spain (**1821**).
1820 Missouri Compromise—Missouri admitted as slave state but slavery barred in rest of Louisiana Purchase north of 36°30′ N.
1822 Greeks proclaim a republic and independence from Turkey. Turks invade Greece. Russia declares war on Turkey (**1828**). Greece also aided by France and Britain. War ends and Turks recognize Greek independence (**1829**). Brazil becomes independent of Portugal. Schubert's *Eighth Symphony* ("The Unfinished").
1823 U.S. Monroe Doctrine warns European nations not to interfere in Western Hemisphere.
1824 Mexico becomes a republic, three years after declaring independence from Spain. Beethoven's *Ninth Symphony.*
1825 First passenger-carrying railroad in England.
1830 French invade Algeria. Louis Philippe becomes "Citizen King" as revolution forces Charles X to abdicate. Mormon church formed in U.S. by Joseph Smith.
1831 Polish revolt against Russia fails. Belgium separates from the Netherlands. In U.S., Nat Turner leads unsuccessful slave rebellion.
1833 Slavery abolished in British Empire.
1834 Charles Babbage invents "analytical engine," precursor of computer. McCormick patents reaper.
1836 Boer farmers start "Great Trek"—Natal, Transvaal, and Orange Free State founded in South Africa. Mexican army besieges Texans in Alamo. Entire garrison, including Davy Crockett and Jim Bowie, wiped out. Texans gain independence from Mexico after winning Battle of San Jacinto. Dicken's *Pickwick Papers.*
1837 Victoria becomes Queen of Great Britain. Mob kills Elijah P. Lovejoy, Illinois abolitionist publisher.
1839 First Opium War (to **1842**) between Britain and China, over importation of drug into China.
1840 Lower and Upper Canada united.
1841 U.S. President Harrison dies (**April 4**) one month after inauguration; John Tyler becomes first Vice President to succeed to Presidency.
1844 Democratic convention calls for annexation of Texas and acquisition of Oregon ("Fifty-four-forty-or-fight"). Five Chinese ports opened to U.S. ships. Samuel F. B. Morse patents telegraph.
1845 Congress adopts joint resolution for annexation of Texas.
1846 Failure of potato crop causes famine in Ireland. U.S. declares war on Mexico. California and New Mexico annexed by U.S. Brigham Young leads Mormons to Great Salt Lake. W.T. Morton uses ether as anesthetic. Sewing machine patented by Elias Howe.
1848 Revolt in Paris: Louis Philippe abdicates; Louis Napoleon elected President of French Republic. Revolutions in Vienna, Venice, Berlin, Milan, Rome, and Warsaw. Put down by royal troops in **1848–49.** U.S.-Mexico War ends; Mexico cedes claims to Texas, California, Arizona, New Mexico, Utah, Nevada. U.S. treaty with Britain sets Oregon Territory boundary at 49th parallel. Karl Marx and Friedrich Engels' *Communist Manifesto.*
1849 California gold rush begins.
1850 Henry Clay opens great debate on slavery, warns South against secession.
1851 Herman Melville's *Moby Dick.* Harriet Beecher Stowe's *Uncle Tom's Cabin.*
1852 South African Republic established. Louis Napoleon proclaims himself Napoleon III ("Second Empire").

Charles Dickens (1812-1870)

Henry Clay (1777-1852)

WAR OF 1812

British interference with American trade, impressment of American seamen, and "War Hawks" drive for western expansion lead to war. American attacks on Canada foiled; U.S. Commodore Perry wins battle of Lake Erie (**1813**). British capture and burn Washington (**1814**) but fail to take Fort McHenry at Baltimore. Andrew Jackson repulses assault on New Orleans after treaty of Ghent ends war (**1815**). War settles little but strengthens U.S. as independent nation.

Dred Scott
(1795?-1858)

Abraham Lincoln
(1809-1865)

Ulysses S. Grant
(1822-1885)

1853 Crimean War begins as Turkey declares war on Russia. Commodore Perry reaches Tokyo.

1854 Britain and France join Turkey in war on Russia. In U.S., Kansas-Nebraska Act permits local option on slavery; rioting and bloodshed. Japanese allow American trade. Antislavery men in Michigan form Republican Party. Tennyson's *Charge of the Light Brigade.* Thoreau's *Walden.*

1855 Armed clashes in Kansas between pro- and anti-slavery forces. Florence Nightingale nurses wounded in Crimea. Walt Whitman's *Leaves of Grass.*

1856 Flaubert's *Madame Bovary.*

1857 Supreme Court, in Dred Scott decision, rules that a slave is not a citizen. Financial crisis in Europe and U.S. Great Mutiny (Sepoy Rebellion) begins in India. India placed under crown rule as a result.

1858 Pro-slavery constitution rejected in Kansas. Abraham Lincoln makes strong antislavery speech in Springfield, Ill.: ". . . this Government cannot endure permanently half slave and half free." Lincoln-Douglas debates. First trans-Atlantic telegraph cable completed by Cyrus W. Field.

1859 John Brown raids Harpers Ferry; is captured and hanged. Work begins on Suez Canal. Unification of Italy starts under leadership of Count Cavour, Sardinian premier. Joined by France in war against Austria. Edward Fitzgerald's *Rubaiyat of Omar Khayyam.* Charles Darwin's *Origin of Species.* J. S. Mill's *On Liberty*

1861 U.S. Civil War begins as attempts at compromise fail (*see* special material on "The Civil War"). Congress creates Colorado, Dakota, and Nevada territories; adopts income tax; Lincoln inaugurated. Serfs emancipated in Russia. Pasteur's theory of germs. Independent Kingdom of Italy proclaimed under Sardinian King Victor Emmanuel II.

1863 French capture Mexico City; proclaim Archduke Maximilian of Austria emperor.

1865 Lincoln fatally shot at Ford's Theater by John Wilkes Booth. Vice President Johnson sworn as successor. Booth caught and dies of gunshot wounds; four conspirators are hanged. Joseph Lister begins antiseptic surgery. Gregor Mendel's Law of Heredity. Lewis Carroll's *Alice's Adventures in Wonderland.*

1866 Alfred Nobel invents dynamite (patented in Britain 1867). Seven Weeks' War: Austria defeated by Prussia and Italy.

1867 Austria-Hungary Dual Monarchy established. French leave Mexico; Maximilian executed. Dominion of Canada established. U.S. buys Alaska from Russia for $7,200,000. South African diamond field discovered. Volume I of Marx's *Das Kapital.* Strauss's *Blue Danube.*

1868 Revolution in Spain; Queen Isabella deposed, flees to France. In U.S., Fourteenth Amendment giving civil rights to blacks is ratified. Georgia under military government after legislature expels blacks.

1869 First U.S. transcontinental rail route completed. James Fisk and Jay Gould attempt to control gold market causes Black Friday panic. Suez Canal opened. Mendeleev's periodic table of elements.

1870 Franco-Prussian War (to 1871): Napoleon III capitulates at Sedan. Revolt in Paris; Third Republic proclaimed.

THE CIVIL WAR
(The War Between the States or the War of the Rebellion)

Apart from the matter of slavery, the Civil War arose out of both the economic and political rivalry between an agrarian South and an industrial North and the issue of the right of states to secede from the Union.

1861 After South Carolina secedes **(Dec. 20, 1860),** Mississippi, Florida, Alabama, Georgia, Louisiana, and Texas follow, forming the Confederate States of America, with Jefferson Davis as president **(Jan.-March).** War begins as Confederates fire on Fort Sumter **(April 12).** Lincoln calls for 75,000 volunteers. Southern ports blockaded by superior Union naval forces. Virginia, Arkansas, Tennessee, and North Carolina secede to complete 11-state Confederacy. Union army advancing on Richmond repulsed at first Battle of Bull Run **(July).**

1862 Edwin M. Stanton named Secretary of War **(Jan.).** Grant wins first important Union victory in West, at Fort Donelson; Nashville falls **(Feb.).** Ironclads, Union's *Monitor* and Confederate's *Virginia (Merrimac)* duel at Hampton Roads **(March).** New Orleans falls to Union fleet under Farragut; city occupied **(April).** Grant's army escapes defeat at Shiloh. Memphis falls as Union gunboats control upper Mississippi **(June).** Confederate general Robert E. Lee victorious at second Battle of Bull Run **(Aug.).** Union army under McClellan halts Lee's attack on Washington in the Battle of Antietam **(Sept.).** Lincoln removes McClellan for lack of aggressiveness. Burnside's drive on Richmond fails at Fredericksburg **(Dec.).** Union forces under Rosecrans chase Bragg through Tennessee; battle of Murfreesboro **(Oct.-Jan. 1863).**

1863 Lee defeats Hooker at Chancellorsville; "Stonewall" Jackson, Confederate general, dies **(May).** Confederate invasion of Pennsylvania stopped at Gettysburg by George Meade—Lee loses 20,000 men—the greatest battle of the War **(July).** It and the Union victory at Vicksburg mark the war's turning point. Union general George H. Thomas, the "Rock of Chickamauga," holds Bragg's forces on Georgia-Tennessee border **(Sept.).** Sherman, Hooker, and Thomas drive Bragg back to Georgia. Tennessee restored to the Union **(Nov.).**

1864 Ulysses S. Grant named commander-in-chief of Union forces **(March).** In the Wilderness campaign, Grant forces Lee's Army of Northern Virginia back toward Richmond **(May-June).** Sherman's Atlanta campaign and "march to the sea" **(May-Sept.).** Farragut's victory at Mobile Bay **(Aug.).** Hood's Confederate army defeated at Nashville. Sherman takes Savannah **(Dec.).**

1865 Sheridan defeats Confederates at Five Forks; Confederates evacuate Richmond **(April).** On **April 9,** Lee surrenders to Grant at Appomattox.

1871 France surrenders Alsace-Lorraine to Germany; war ends. German Empire proclaimed with Prussian King as Kaiser Wilhelm I. Fighting with Apaches begins in American West. Boss Tweed corruption exposed in New York. The Chicago Fire, with 250 deaths and $196-million damage. Stanley meets Livingston in Africa.

1872 Congress gives amnesty to most Confederates. Jules Verne's *Around the World in 80 Days.*

1873 Economic crisis in Europe. U.S. establishes gold standard.

1875 First Kentucky Derby.

1876 Sioux kill Gen. George A. Custer and 264 troopers at Little Big Horn River. Alexander Graham Bell patents the telephone.

1877 After Presidential election of **1876,** Electoral Commission gives disputed Electoral College votes to Rutherford B. Hayes despite Tilden's popular majority. Russo-Turkish war (ends in **1878** with power of Turkey in Europe broken). Reconstruction ends in the American South. Thomas Edison patents phonograph.

1878 Congress of Berlin revises Treaty of San Stefano ending Russo-Turkish War; makes extensive redivision of southeastern Europe. First commercial telephone exchange opened in New Haven, Conn.

1880 U.S.-China treaty allows U.S. to restrict immigration of Chinese labor.

1881 President Garfield fatally shot by assassin; Vice President Arthur succeeds him. Charles J. Guiteau convicted and executed (in **1882**).

1882 Terrorism in Ireland after land evictions. Britain invades and conquers Egypt. Germany, Austria, and Italy form Triple Alliance. In U.S., Congress adopts Chinese Exclusion Act. Rockefeller's Standard Oil Trust is first industrial monopoly. In Berlin, Robert Koch announces discovery of tuberculosis germ.

1883 Congress creates Civil Service Commission. Brooklyn Bridge and Metropolitan Opera House completed.

1885 British Gen. Charles G. "Chinese" Gordon killed at Khartoum in Egyptian Sudan.

1886 Bombing at Haymarket Square, Chicago, kills seven policemen and injures many others. Eight alleged anarchists accused—three imprisoned, one commits suicide, four hanged. (In **1893,** Illinois Governor Altgeld, critical of trial, pardons three survivors.) Statue of Liberty dedicated. Geronimo, Apache Indian chief, surrenders.

1887 Queen Victoria's Golden Jubilee. Sir Arthur Conan Doyle's first Sherlock Holmes story, "A Study in Scarlet."

1888 Historic March blizzard in Northeast U.S.—many perish, property damage exceeds $25 million. George Eastman's box camera (the Kodak). J.B. Dunlop invents pneumatic tire. Jack the Ripper murders in London.

1889 Second (Socialist) International founded in Paris. Indian Territory in Oklahoma opened to settlement. Thousands die in Johnstown, Pa., flood. Mark Twain's *A Connecticut Yankee in King Arthur's Court.*

1890 Congress votes Sherman Antitrust Act. Sitting Bull killed in Sioux uprising.

1892 Battle between steel strikers and Pinkerton guards at Homestead, Pa.; union defeated after militia intervenes. Silver mine strikers in Idaho fight non-union workers; U.S. troops dispatched. Diesel engine patented.

1894 Sino-Japanese War begins (ends in **1895** with China's defeat). In France, Capt. Alfred Dreyfus convicted on false treason charge (pardoned in **1906**). In U.S., Jacob S. Coxey of Ohio leads "Coxey's Army" of unemployed on Washington. Eugene V. Debs calls general strike of rail workers to support Pullman Company strikers; strike broken, Debs jailed for six months. Thomas A. Edison's kinetoscope given first public showing in New York City.

1895 X-rays discovered by German physicist, Wilhelm Roentgen.

1896 Supreme Court's *Plessy v. Ferguson* decision—"separate but equal" doctrine. Alfred Nobel's will establishes prizes for peace, science, and literature. Marconi receives first wireless patent in Britain. William Jennings Bryan delivers "Cross of Gold" speech at Democratic Convention

Geronimo (1829-1909)

Samuel Clemens (Mark Twain) (1835-1910)

Thomas A. Edison (1847-1931)

SPANISH-AMERICAN WAR (1898–1899)

War fires stoked by "jingo journalism" as American people support Cuban rebels against Spain. American business sees economic gain in Cuban trade and resources and American power zones in Latin America. Outstanding events: Submarine mine explodes U.S. battleship *Maine* in Havana Harbor **(Feb. 15)**; 260 killed; responsibility never fixed. Congress declares independence of Cuba **(April 19).** Spain declares war on U.S. **(Apr. 24);** Congress **(Apr. 25)** formally declares nation has been at war with Spain since Apr. 21. Commodore George Dewey wins seven-hour battle of Manila Bay **(May 1).** Spanish fleet destroyed off Santiago, Cuba **(July 3);** city surrenders **(July 17).** Treaty of Paris (ratified by Senate **1899**) ends war. U.S. given Guam and Puerto Rico and agrees to pay Spain $20 million for Philippines. Cuba independent of Spain; under U.S. military control for three years until **May 20, 1902.** Yellow fever is eradicated and political reforms achieved.

in Chicago. First modern Olympic games held in Athens, Greece.

1898 Chinese "Boxers," anti-foreign organization, established. They stage uprisings against Europeans in **1900**; U.S. and other Western troops relieve Peking legations. Spanish-American War (*see* special material on the "Spanish-American War"). Pierre and Marie Curie discover radium and polonium.

1899 Boer War (or South African War). Conflict between British and Boers (descendants of Dutch settlers of South Africa). Causes rooted in longstanding territorial disputes and in friction over political rights for English and other "uitlanders" following 1886 discovery of vast gold deposits in Transvaal. (British victorious as war ends in **1902**.) Casualties: 5,774 British dead, about 4,000 Boers. Union of South Africa established in **1908** as confederation of colonies; becomes British dominion in **1910**.

20th century A.D.

1900 Hurricane ravages Galveston, Tex.; 6,000 drown. Sigmund Freud's *The Interpretation of Dreams.*

Albert Einstein (1879-1955)

1901 Queen Victoria dies; succeeded by son, Edward VII. As President McKinley begins second term, he is shot fatally by anarchist Leon Czolgosz. Theodore Roosevelt sworn in as successor.

1902 Enrico Caruso's first gramophone recording.

1903 Wright brothers, Orville and Wilbur, fly first powered, controlled, heavier-than-air plane at Kitty Hawk, N.C. Henry Ford organizes Ford Motor Company.

1904 Russo-Japanese War—competition for Korea and Manchuria: In **1905**, Port Arthur surrenders to Japanese and Russia suffers other defeats; President Roosevelt mediates Treaty of Portsmouth, N.H., ending war with concessions for Japan. *Entente Cordiale:* Britain and France settle their international differences. General theory of radioactivity by Rutherford and Soddy. New York City subway opened.

1905 General strike in Russia; first workers' soviet set up in St. Petersburg. Sailors on battleship *Potemkin* mutiny; reforms including first Duma (parliament) established by Czar's "October Manifesto." Albert Einstein's special theory of relativity and other key theories in physics. Franz Lehar's *Merry Widow.*

1906 San Francisco earthquake and three-day fire; 500 dead. Roald Amundsen, Norwegian explorer, fixes magnetic North Pole.

1907 Second Hague Peace Conference, of 46 nations, adopts 10 conventions on rules of war. Financial panic of **1907** in U.S.

1908 Earthquake kills 150,000 in southern Italy and Sicily. U.S. Supreme Court, in Danbury Hatters' case, outlaws secondary union boycotts.

1909 North Pole reached by American explorers Robert E. Peary and Matthew Henson.

1910 Boy Scouts of America incorporated.

1911 First use of aircraft as offensive weapon in Turkish-Italian War. Italy defeats Turks and annexes Tripoli and Libya. Chinese Republic proclaimed after revolution overthrows Manchu dynasty. Sun Yat-sen named president. Mexican Revolution: Porfirio Diaz, president since 1877, replaced by Francisco Madero. Triangle Shirtwaist Company fire in New York; 145 killed. Richard Strauss's *Der Rosenkavalier.* Irving Berlin's *Alexander's Ragtime Band.* Amundsen reaches South Pole.

1912 Balkan Wars (**1912–13**) resulting from territorial disputes: Turkey defeated by alliance of Bulgaria, Serbia, Greece, and Montenegro; London peace treaty (**1913**) partitions most of European Turkey among the victors. In second war (**1913**), Bulgaria attacks Serbia and Greece and is defeated after Romania intervenes and Turks recapture Adrianople. *Titanic* sinks on maiden voyage; over 1,500 drown.

1913 Suffragettes demonstrate in London. Garment workers strike in New York and Boston; win pay raise and shorter hours. Sixteenth Amendment (income tax) and 17th (popular election of U.S. senators) adopted. Bill creating U.S. Federal Reserve System becomes law. Stravinsky's *The Rite of Spring.*

1914 World War I begins (*see* special material on "World War I"). Panama Canal officially opened. Congress sets up Federal Trade Commission, passes Clayton Antitrust Act. U.S. Marines occupy Veracruz, Mexico, intervening in civil war to protect American interests.

1915 U.S. protests German submarine actions and British blockade of Germany. U.S. banks lend $500 million to France and Britain. D. W. Griffith's film *Birth of a Nation.* Albert Einstein's *General Theory of Relativity.*

1916 Congress expands armed forces. Tom Mooney arrested for San Francisco bombing (pardoned in **1939**). Pershing fails in raid into Mexico in

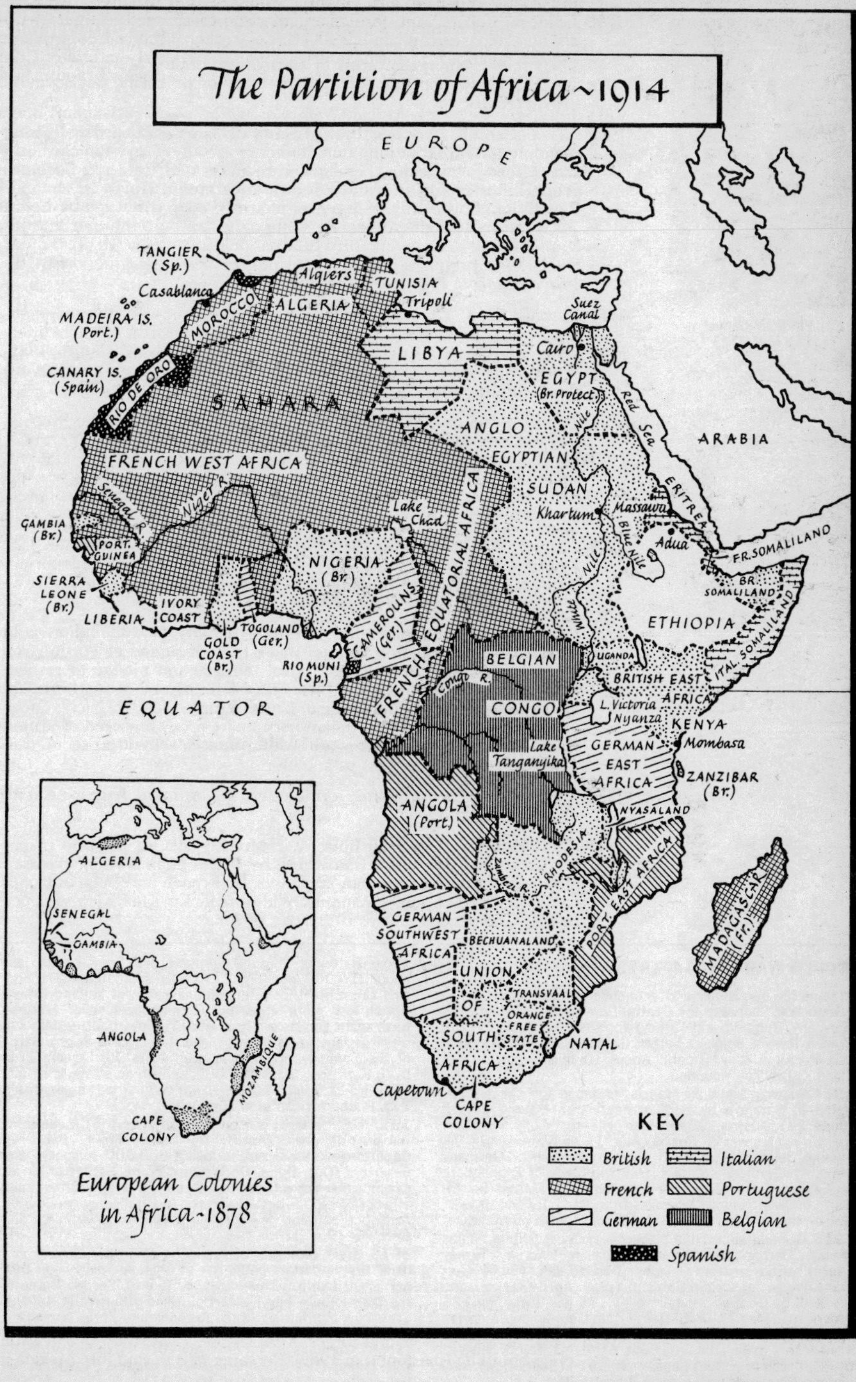
The Partition of Africa~1914
EUROPE
TANGIER (Sp.)
Casablanca
MADEIRA IS. (Port.)
CANARY IS. (Spain)
RIO DE ORO
MOROCCO
Algiers
ALGERIA
TUNISIA
Tripoli
LIBYA
SAHARA
FRENCH WEST AFRICA
Senegal R.
Niger R.
GAMBIA (Br.)
PORT. GUINEA
SIERRA LEONE (Br.)
LIBERIA
IVORY COAST
GOLD COAST (Br.)
TOGOLAND (Ger.)
NIGERIA (Br.)
Lake Chad
CAMEROUNS (Ger.)
FRENCH EQUATORIAL AFRICA
RIO MUNI (Sp.)
Suez Canal
Cairo
EGYPT (Br. Protect.)
Nile
Red Sea
ARABIA
ANGLO EGYPTIAN SUDAN
Khartum
Massawa
ERITREA
Adua
Blue Nile
White Nile
FR. SOMALILAND
BR. SOMALILAND
ITAL. SOMALILAND
ETHIOPIA
UGANDA
BRITISH EAST AFRICA
KENYA
L. Victoria Nyanza
Mombasa
BELGIAN CONGO
Congo R.
Lake Tanganyika
GERMAN EAST AFRICA
ZANZIBAR (Br.)
NYASALAND
EQUATOR
ANGOLA (Port.)
RHODESIA
Zambezi R.
PORT. EAST AFRICA
MADAGASCAR (Fr.)
GERMAN SOUTHWEST AFRICA
BECHUANALAND
UNION OF SOUTH AFRICA
TRANSVAAL
ORANGE FREE STATE
NATAL
Capetown
CAPE COLONY
KEY
British
Italian
French
Portuguese
German
Belgian
Spanish
ALGERIA
SENEGAL
GAMBIA
ANGOLA
MOZAMBIQUE
CAPE COLONY
European Colonies in Africa~1878

Vladimir Lenin (1870-1924)

quest of rebel Pancho Villa. U.S. buys Virgin Islands from Denmark for $25 million. President Wilson re-elected with "he kept us out of war" slogan. "Black Tom" explosion at munitions dock in Jersey City, N.J., $40,000,000 damages; traced to German saboteurs. Margaret Sanger opens first birth control clinic. Easter Rebellion in Ireland put down by British troops.

1917 First U.S. combat troops in France as U.S. declares war (**April 6**). Russian Revolution—climax of long unrest under czars. February Revolution—Czar forced to abdicate, liberal government created. Kerensky becomes prime minister and forms provisional government (**July**). In October Revolution, Bolsheviks seize power in armed coup d'état led by Lenin and Trotsky. Kerensky flees. Revolutionaries execute the czar and his family (**1918**). Reds set up Third International in Moscow (**1919**). Balfour Declaration promises Jewish homeland in Palestine. Sigmund Freud's *Introduction to Psychoanalysis.*

1918 Russian Civil War between Reds (Bolsheviks) and Whites (anti-Bolsheviks); Reds win in **1920.** Allied troops (U.S., British, French) intervene (**March**); leave in **1919.** Japanese hold Vladivostok until **1922.** World-wide influenza epidemic strikes; by **1920,** nearly 20 million are dead. In U.S. alone, 500,000 perish.

1919 Third International (Comintern) establishes Soviet control over international Communist movements. Paris peace conference. Versailles Treaty, incorporating Wilson's draft Covenant of League of Nations, signed by Allies and Germany; rejected by U.S. Senate. Congress formally ends war in **1921.** Eighteenth (Prohibition) Amendment adopted. Alcock and Brown make first trans-Atlantic non-stop flight.

1920 League of Nations holds first meeting at Geneva, Switzerland. U.S. Dept. of Justice "red hunt" nets thousands of radicals; aliens deported. Women's suffrage (19th) amendment ratified. First Agatha Christie mystery. Sinclair Lewis's *Main Street.*

1921 Reparations Commission fixes German liability at 132 billion gold marks. German inflation begins. Major treaties signed at Washington Disarmament Conference limit naval tonnage and pledge to respect territorial integrity of China. Irish Free State formed in southern Ireland as self-governing dominion of British Empire. In U.S., Nicola Sacco and Bartolomeo Vanzetti, Italian-born anarchists, convicted of armed robbery murder; case stirs world-wide protests; they are executed in **1927.**

1922 Mussolini marches on Rome; forms Fascist government. Irish Free State officially proclaimed.

1923 Adolf Hitler's "Beer Hall Putsch" in Munich fails; in **1924** he is sentenced to five years in prison where he writes *Mein Kampf;* released after eight months. Occupation of Ruhr by French and Belgian troops to enforce reparations payments. Widespread Ku Klux Klan violence in U.S. George Gershwin's *Rhapsody in Blue.*

WORLD WAR I (1914–1918)

Imperial, territorial, and economic rivalries lead to the "Great War" between the Central Powers (Austria-Hungary, Germany, Bulgaria, and Turkey) and the Allies (U.S., Britain, France, Russia, Belgium, Serbia, Greece, Romania, Montenegro, Portugal, Italy, Japan). About 10 million combatants killed, 20 million wounded.

1914 Austrian Archduke Francis Ferdinand and wife assassinated in Sarajevo by Serbian nationalist, Gavrilo Princip (**June 28**). Austria declares war on Serbia (**July 28**). Germany declares war on Russia (**Aug. 1**), on France (**Aug. 3**), invades Belgium (**Aug. 4**). Britain declares war on Germany (**Aug. 4**). Germans defeat Russians in Battle of Tannenberg on Eastern Front (**Aug.**). First Battle of the Marne (**Sept.**). German drive stopped 25 miles from Paris. By end of year, war on the Western Front is "positional" in the trenches.

1915 German submarine blockade of Great Britain begins (**Feb.**). Dardanelles Campaign—British land in Turkey (**April**), withdraw from Gallipoli (**Dec. to Jan. 1916**). Germans use gas at second Battle of Ypres (**April–May**). *Lusitania* sunk by German submarine—1,198 lost, including 128 Americans (**May 7**). On Eastern Front, German and Austrian "great offensive" conquers all of Poland and Lithuania; Russians lose 1 million men (by **Sept. 6**). "Great Fall Offensive" by Allies results in little change from 1914 (**Sept.–Oct.**). Britain and France declare war on Bulgaria (**Oct. 14**).

1916 Battle of Verdun—Germans and French each lose about 350,000 men (**Feb.**). Extended submarine warfare begins (**March**). British-German sea battle of Jutland (**May**); British lose more ships, but German fleet never ventures forth again. On Eastern front, the Brusilov offensive demoralizes Russians, costs them 1 million men (**June–Sept.**). Battle of the Somme—British lose over 400,000; French, 200, 000; Germans, about 450,000; all with no strategic results (**July–Nov.**). Romania declares war on Austria-Hungary (**Aug. 27**). Bucharest captured (**Dec.**).

1917 U.S. declares war on Germany (**April 6**). Submarine warfare at peak (**April**). On Italian Front, Battle of Caporetto—Italians retreat, losing 600,000 prisoners and deserters (**Oct.–Dec.**). On Western Front, Battles of Arras, Champagne, Ypres (third battle), etc. First large British tank attack (**Nov.**). U.S. declares war on Austria-Hungary (**Dec. 7**). Armistice between new Russian Bolshevik government and Germans (**Dec. 15**).

1918 Great offensive by Germans (**March–June**). Americans' first important battle role at Château-Thierry—as they and French stop German advance (**June**). Second Battle of the Marne (**July–Aug.**)—start of Allied offensive at Amiens, St. Mihiel, etc. Battles of the Argonne and Ypres panic German leadership (**Sept.–Oct.**). British offensive in Palestine (**Sept.**). Germans ask for armistice (**Oct. 4**). British armistice with Turkey (**Oct.**). German Kaiser abdicates (**Nov.**). Hostilities cease on Western Front (**Nov. 11**).

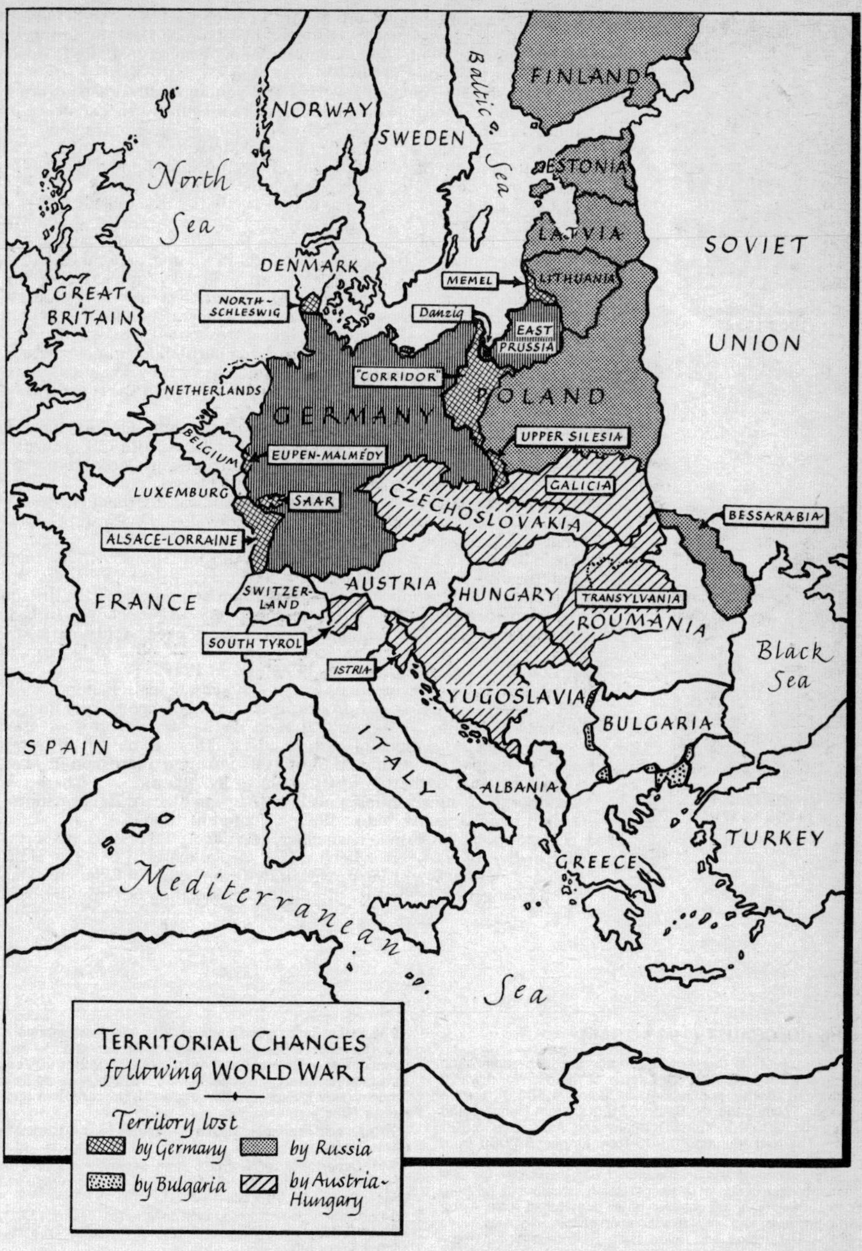

1924 Death of Lenin; Stalin wins power struggle, rules as Soviet dictator until death in **1953**. Italian Fascists murder Socialist leader Giacomo Matteotti. Interior Secretary Albert B. Fall and oilmen Harry Sinclair and Edward L. Doheny are charged with conspiracy and bribery in the Teapot Dome scandal, involving fraudulent leases of naval oil reserves. In **1931**, Fall is sentenced to year in prison; Doheny and Sinclair acquitted of

Charles A. Lindbergh
(1902-1974)

Amelia Earhart
(1898-1937)

bribery. Nathan Leopold and Richard Loeb convicted in "thrill killing" of Bobby Franks in Chicago; defended by Clarence Darrow; sentenced to life imprisonment. (Loeb killed by fellow convict in **1936**; Leopold paroled in **1958**, dies in **1971**.)

1925 Nellie Tayloe Ross elected governor of Wyoming; first woman governor elected in U.S. Locarno conferences seek to secure European peace by mutual guarantees. John T. Scopes convicted and fined for teaching evolution in a public school in Tennessee "Monkey Trial"; sentence set aside. John Logie Baird, Scottish inventor, transmits human features by television. Adolf Hitler publishes Volume I of *Mein Kampf*.

1926 General strike in Britain brings nation's activities to standstill. U.S. marines dispatched to Nicaragua during revolt; they remain until **1933**. Gertrude Ederle of U.S. is first woman to swim English Channel.

1927 German economy collapses. Socialists riot in Vienna; general strike follows acquittal of Nazis for political murder. Trotsky expelled from Russian Communist Party. Charles A. Lindbergh flies first successful solo non-stop flight from New York to Paris. Ruth Snyder and Judd Gray convicted of murder of Albert Snyder; they are executed at Sing Sing prison in **1928**. *The Jazz Singer*, with Al Jolson, first part-talking motion picture.

1928 Kellogg-Briand Pact, outlawing war, signed in Paris by 65 nations. Alexander Fleming discovers penicillin. Richard E. Byrd starts expedition to Antarctic; returns in **1930**.

1929 Trotsky expelled from U.S.S.R. Lateran Treaty establishes independent Vatican City. In U.S., stock market prices collapse, with U.S. securities losing $26 billion—first phase of Depression and world economic crisis. St. Valentine's Day gangland massacre in Chicago.

1930 Britain, U.S., Japan, France, and Italy sign naval disarmament treaty. Nazis gain in German elections. Cyclotron developed by Ernest O. Lawrence, U.S. physicist.

1931 Spain becomes a republic with overthrow of King Alfonso XIII. German industrialists finance 800,000-strong Nazi party. British parliament enacts statute of Westminster, legalizing dominion equality with Britain. Mukden Incident begins Japanese occupation of Manchuria. In U.S., Hoover proposes one-year moratorium of war debts. Harold C. Urey discovers heavy hydrogen. Gangster Al Capone sentenced to 11 years in prison for tax evasion (freed in **1939**; dies in **1947**).

1932 Nazis lead in German elections with 230 Reichstag seats. Famine in U.S. S.R. In U.S., Congress sets up Reconstruction Finance Corporation to stimulate economy. Veterans march on Washington—most leave after Senate rejects payment of cash bonuses; others removed by troops under Douglas MacArthur. U.S. protests Japanese aggression in Manchuria. Amelia Earhart is first woman to fly Atlantic solo. Charles A. Lindbergh's baby son kidnapped, killed. (Bruno Richard Hauptmann arrested in **1934**, convicted in **1935**, executed in **1936**.)

1933 Hitler appointed German chancellor, gets dictatorial powers. Reichstag fire in Berlin; Nazi terror begins. (*See* special material on "The Holocaust.") Germany and Japan withdraw from League of Nations. Giuseppe Zangara executed for attempted assassination of President-elect

THE HOLOCAUST (1933–1945)

"Holocaust" is the term describing the Nazi annihilation of about 6 million Jews (two thirds of the pre-World War II European Jewish population), including 4,500,000 from Russia, Poland, and the Baltic; 750,000 from Hungary and Romania; 290,000 from Germany and Austria; 105,000 from The Netherlands; 90,000 from France; 54,000 from Greece, etc.

The Holocaust was unique in its being *genocide*—the systematic destruction of a people solely because of religion, race, ethnicity, or nationality—on an unmatched scale. Along with the Jews, another 9 to 10 million people—Gypsies, Slavs (Poles, Ukrainians, and Belorussians)—were exterminated.

The only comparable act of genocide in modern times was launched in April 1915, when an estimated 600,000 Armenians were massacred by the Turks.

1933 Hitler named German Chancellor **(Jan.)**. Dachau, first concentration camp, established **(March)**. Boycotts against Jews begin **(April)**.

1935 Anti-Semitic Nuremberg Laws passed by Reichstag **(Sept.)**.

1937 Buchenwald concentration camp opens **(July)**.

1938 Extension of anti-Semitic laws to Austria after annexation **(March)**. *Kristallnacht* (Night of Broken Glass)—anti-Semitic riots in Germany and Austria **(Nov. 9)**. 26,000 Jews sent to concentration camps; Jewish children expelled from schools **(Nov.)**. Expropriation of Jewish property and businesses **(Dec.)**.

1940 As war continues, Nazi acts against Jews extended to German-conquered areas.

1941 Deportation of German Jews begins; massacres of Jews in Odessa and Kiev—68,000 killed **(Nov.)**; in Riga and Vilna—almost 60,000 killed **(Dec.)**.

1942 Unified Jewish resistance in ghettos begins **(Jan.)**. 300,000 Jews from Warsaw Ghetto deported to Treblinka death camp **(July)**.

1943 Warsaw Ghetto uprisings **(Jan.** and **April)**; Ghetto exterminated **(May)**.

1944 476,000 Hungarian Jews sent to Auschwitz **(May–June)**. D-day **(June 6)**. Soviet Army liberates Maidanek death camp **(July)**. Nazis try to hide evidence of death camps **(Nov.)**.

1945 Americans liberate Buchenwald, Bergen-Belsen camps **(April)**. Nuremberg War Crimes Trial **(Nov. 1945** to **Oct. 1946)**.

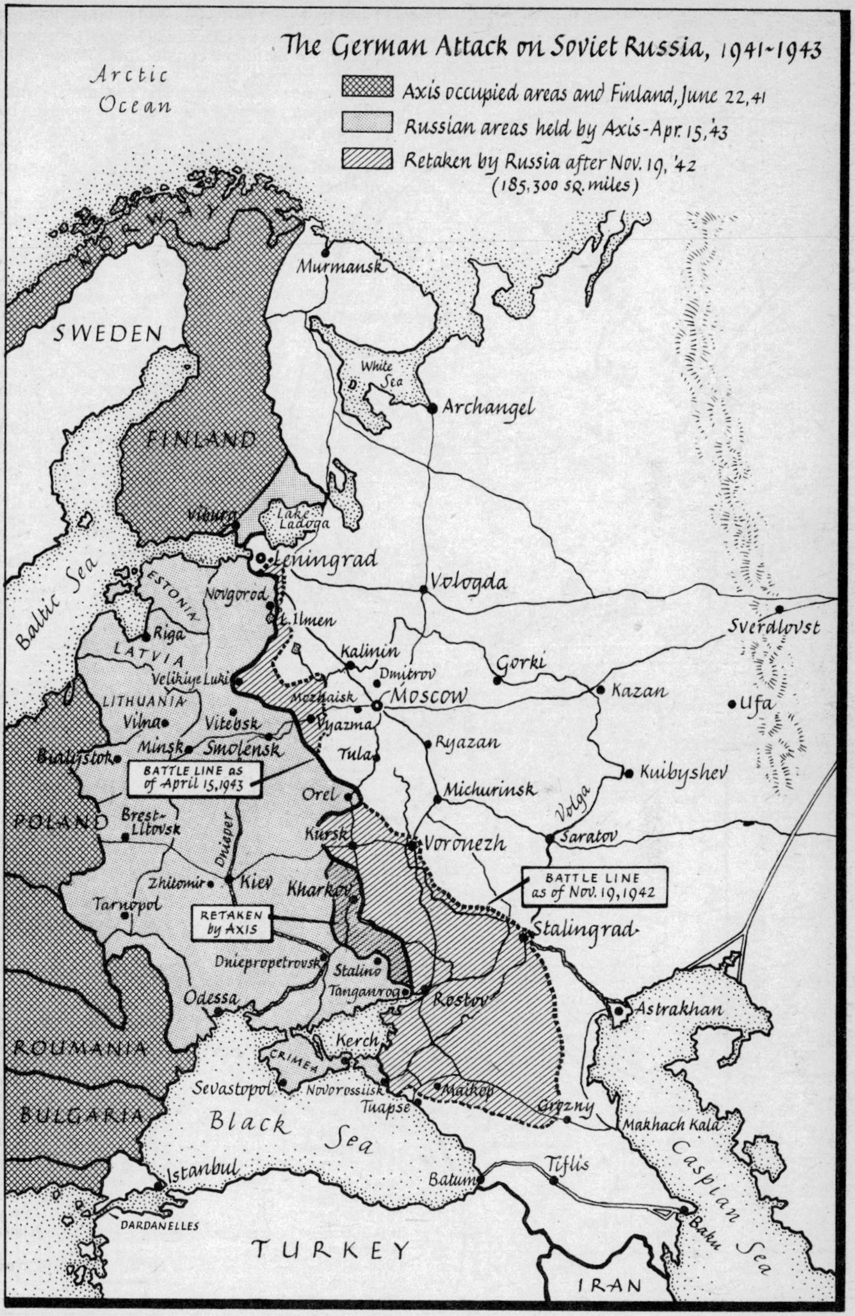
The German Attack on Soviet Russia, 1941-1943
Axis occupied areas and Finland, June 22, 41
Russian areas held by Axis-Apr. 15, '43
Retaken by Russia after Nov. 19, '42 (185,300 sq. miles)
Arctic Ocean
NORWAY
SWEDEN
FINLAND
Murmansk
White Sea
Archangel
Viburg
Lake Ladoga
Leningrad
Baltic Sea
ESTONIA
Novgorod
L. Ilmen
Vologda
Riga
LATVIA
Velikiye Luki
LITHUANIA
Vilna
Vitebsk
Minsk
Smolensk
Bialystok
Kalinin
Dmitrov
Mozhaisk
Moscow
Vyazma
Tula
Ryazan
Gorki
Kazan
Sverdlovsk
Ufa
Kuibyshev
BATTLE LINE as of April 15, 1943
POLAND
Brest-Litovsk
Orel
Michurinsk
Volga
Saratov
Kursk
Voronezh
Dnieper
Zhitomir
Kiev
Kharkov
Tarnopol
BATTLE LINE as of Nov. 19, 1942
RETAKEN by AXIS
Stalingrad
Dniepropetrovsk
Stalino
Taganrog
Rostov
Odessa
Astrakhan
ROUMANIA
Kerch
CRIMEA
Sevastopol
Novorossiisk
Maikop
Tuapse
Grozny
Makhach Kala
BULGARIA
Black Sea
Caspian Sea
Tiflis
Istanbul
Batum
Baku
DARDANELLES
TURKEY
IRAN

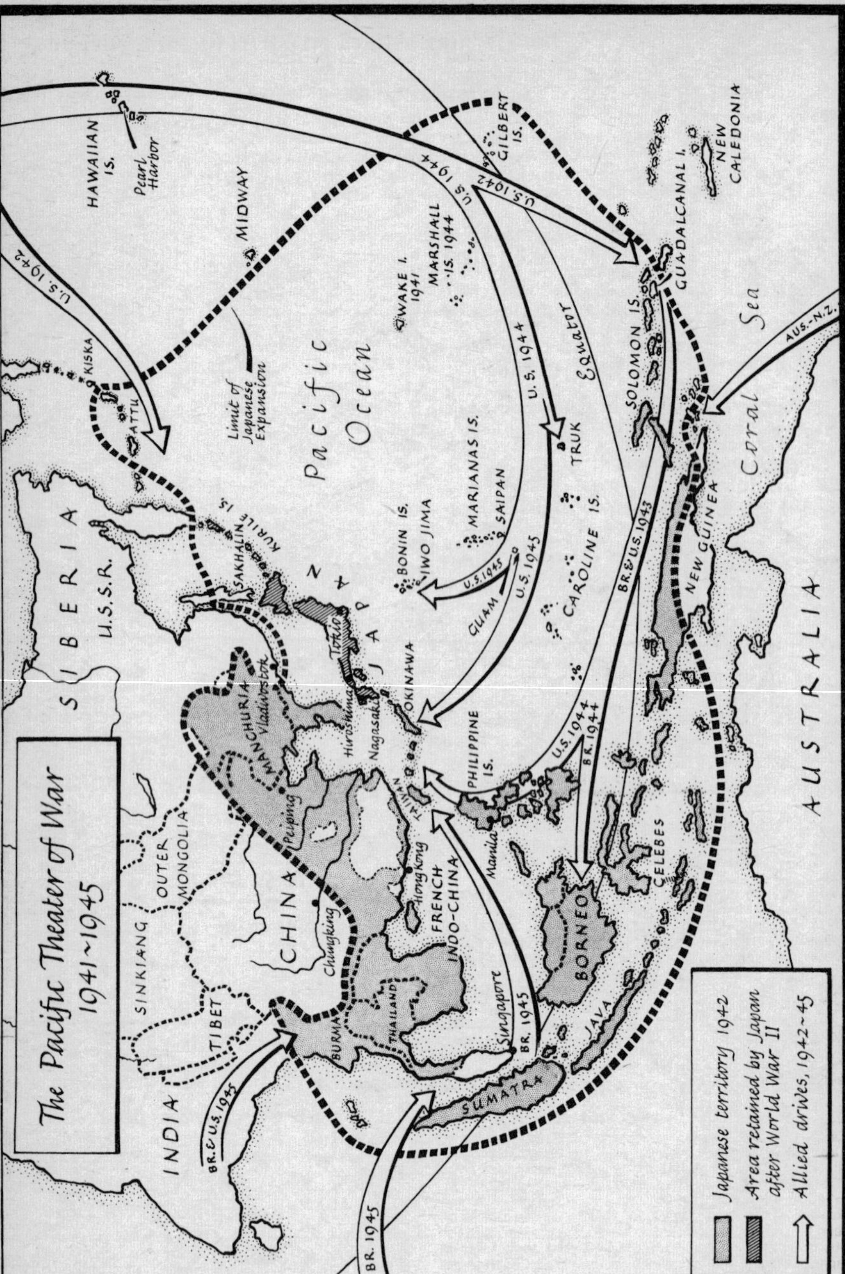
The Pacific Theater of War
1941~1945
SIBERIA
U.S.S.R.
MANCHURIA
Vladivostok
Peiping
OUTER MONGOLIA
SINKIANG
TIBET
INDIA
CHINA
Chungking
Hong Kong
FRENCH INDO-CHINA
BURMA
THAILAND
Singapore
SUMATRA
JAVA
BORNEO
CELEBES
Manila
PHILIPPINE IS.
TAIWAN
OKINAWA
Nagasaki
Hiroshima
Tokio
JAPAN
SAKHALIN
KURILE IS.
KISKA
ATTU
Limit of Japanese Expansion
Pacific Ocean
MIDWAY
HAWAIIAN IS.
Pearl Harbor
WAKE I. 1941
MARSHALL IS. 1944
GILBERT IS.
U.S. 1942
U.S. 1944
BONIN IS.
IWO JIMA
MARIANAS IS.
SAIPAN
GUAM
U.S. 1945
TRUK
CAROLINE IS.
Equator
SOLOMON IS.
GUADALCANAL I.
NEW CALEDONIA
Coral Sea
AUS.-N.Z.
NEW GUINEA
AUSTRALIA
BR. & U.S. 1943
U.S. 1944
BR. 1944
BR. 1945
BR. & U.S. 1945
Japanese territory 1942
Area retained by Japan after World War II
Allied drives, 1942–45

Roosevelt in which Chicago Mayor Cermak is fatally shot. Roosevelt inaugurated ("the only thing we have to fear is fear itself"); launches New Deal. Prohibition repealed. U.S.S.R. recognized by U.S.

1934 Chancellor Dollfuss of Austria assassinated by Nazis. Hitler becomes Führer. U.S.S.R. admitted to League of Nations. Dionne sisters, first quintuplets to survive beyond infancy, born in Canada.

1935 Saar incorporated into Germany after plebiscite. Nazis repudiate Versailles Treaty, introduce compulsory military service. Mussolini invades Ethiopia; League of Nations invokes sanctions. Roosevelt opens second phase of New Deal in U.S., calling for social security, better housing, equitable taxation, and farm assistance. Huey Long assassinated in Louisiana.

Adolf Hitler (1889-1945)

1936 Germans occupy Rhineland. Italy annexes Ethiopia. Rome-Berlin Axis proclaimed (Japan to join in **1940**). Trotsky exiled to Mexico. King George V dies; succeeded by son, Edward VIII, who soon abdicated to marry American-born divorcée, and is succeeded by brother, George VI. Spanish civil war begins. (Franco's fascist forces defeat Loyalist forces by **1939**, when Madrid falls.) War between China and Japan begins, to continue through World War II. Japan and Germany sign anti-Comintern pact; joined by Italy in **1937**.

1937 Hitler repudiates war guilt clause of Versailles Treaty; continues to build German power. Italy withdraws from League of Nations. U.S. gunboat *Panay* sunk by Japanese in Yangtze River. Japan invades China, conquers most of coastal area. Amelia Earhart lost somewhere in Pacific on round-the-world flight.

1938 Hitler marches into Austria; political and geographical union of Germany and Austria proclaimed. Munich Pact—Britain, France, and Italy agree to let Germany partition Czechoslovakia. Douglas "Wrong-Way" Corrigan flies from New York to Dublin.

1939 Germany occupies Bohemia and Moravia; renounces pacts with Poland and England and concludes 10-year non-aggression pact with U.S.S.R. Russo-Finnish War begins; Finns to lose one-tenth of territory in **1940** peace treaty. World War II begins (*see* special material on "World War II"). In U.S., Roosevelt submits $1,319-million defense budget, proclaims U.S. neutrality, and declares limited emergency. Einstein writes FDR about feasibility of atomic bomb. New York World's Fair opens.

1940 Trotsky assassinated in Mexico. Estonia, Latvia, and Lithuania annexed by U.S.S.R. U.S. trades 50 destroyers for leases on British bases in Western Hemisphere. Selective Service Act signed.

WORLD WAR II (1939–1945)

Axis powers (Germany, Italy, Japan, Hungary, Romania, Bulgaria) *vs.* Allies (U.S., Britain, France, U.S.S.R., Australia, Belgium, Brazil, Canada, China, Denmark, Greece, Netherlands, New Zealand, Norway, Poland, South Africa, Yugoslavia).

1939 Germany invades Poland and annexes Danzig; Britain and France give Hitler ultimatum **(Sept. 1)**, declare war **(Sept. 3)**. Disabled German pocket battleship *Admiral Graf Spee* blown up off Montevideo, Uruguay, on Hitler's orders **(Dec. 17)**. Limited activity ("Sitzkrieg") on Western Front.

1940 Nazis invade Netherlands, Belgium, and Luxembourg **(May 10)**. Chamberlain resigns as Prime Minister; Churchill takes over **(May 10)**. Germans cross French frontier **(May 12)** using air/tank/infantry "Blitzkrieg" tactics. Dunkerque evacuation—about 335,000 out of 400,000 Allied soldiers rescued from Belgium by British civilian and naval craft **(May 26–June 3)**. Italy declares war on France and Britain; invades France **(June 10)**. Germans enter Paris; city undefended **(June 14)**. France and Germany sign armistice at Compiègne **(June 22)**. Nazis bomb Coventry, England **(Nov. 14)**.

1941 Germans launch attacks in Balkans. Yugoslavia surrenders—General Mihajlovic continues guerrilla warfare; Tito leads left-wing guerrillas **(April 17)**. Nazi tanks enter Athens; remnants of British Army quit Greece **(April 27)**. Hitler attacks Russia **(June 22)**. Atlantic Charter—FDR and Churchill agree on war aims **(Aug. 14)**. Japanese attacks on Pearl Harbor, Philippines, Guam force U.S. into war; U.S. Pacific fleet crippled **(Dec. 7)**. U.S. and Britain declare war on Japan. Germany and Italy declare war on U.S.; Congress declares war on those countries **(Dec. 11)**.

1942 British surrender Singapore to Japanese **(Feb. 15)**. U.S. forces on Bataan peninsula in Philippines surrender **(April 9)**. U.S. and Filipino troops on Corregidor island in Manila Bay surrender to Japanese **(May 6)**. Village of Lidice in Czechoslovakia razed by Nazis **(June 10)**. U.S. and Britain land in French North Africa **(Nov. 8)**.

1943 Casablanca Conference—Churchill and FDR agree on unconditional surrender goal **(Jan. 14–24)**. German 6th Army surrenders at Stalingrad—turning point of war in Russia **(Feb. 1–2)**. Remnants of Nazis trapped on Cape Bon, ending war in Africa **(May 12)**. Mussolini deposed; Badoglio named premier **(July 25)**. Allied troops land on Italian mainland after conquest of Sicily **(Sept. 3)**. Italy surrenders **(Sept. 8)**. Nazis seize Rome **(Sept. 10)**. Cairo Conference: FDR, Churchill, Chiang Kai-shek pledge defeat of Japan, free Korea **(Nov. 22–26)**. Teheran Conference: FDR, Churchill, Stalin agree on invasion plans **(Nov. 28–Dec. 1)**.

1944 U.S. and British troops land at Anzio on west Italian coast and hold beachhead **(Jan. 22)**. U.S. and British troops enter Rome **(June 4)**. D-Day—Allies launch Normandy invasion **(June 6)**. Hitler wounded in bomb plot **(July 20)**. Paris liberated **(Aug. 25)**. Athens freed by Allies **(Oct. 13)**. Americans invade Philippines **(Oct. 20)**. Germans launch counter-offensive in Belgium—Battle of Bulge **(Dec. 16)**.

1945 Yalta Agreement signed by FDR, Churchill, Stalin—establishes basis for occupation of Germany, returns to Soviet Union lands taken by Germany and Japan; U.S.S.R. agrees to friendship pact with China **(Feb. 11)**. Mussolini killed at Lake Como **(April 28)**. Admiral Doenitz takes command in Germany; suicide of Hitler announced **(May 1)**. Berlin falls **(May 2)**. V-E Day—Germany signs unconditional surrender terms at Rheims **(May 7)**. Potsdam Conference—Truman, Churchill, Atlee (after **July 28**), Stalin establish council of foreign ministers to prepare peace treaties; plan German postwar government and reparations **(July 17–Aug. 2)**. A-bomb blasts Hiroshima **(Aug. 6)**. U.S.S.R. declares war on Japan **(Aug. 8)**. Nagasaki hit by A-bomb **(Aug. 9)**. Japan surrenders **(Aug. 14)**. V-J Day—Japanese sign surrender terms aboard battleship *Missouri* **(Sept. 2)**.

D-Day, June 6, 1944

Winston Churchill, Franklin D. Roosevelt, and Joseph V. Stalin at Yalta

Mao Zedong (1893-1976)

1941 Japanese surprise attack on U.S. fleet at Pearl Harbor brings U.S. into World War II. Manhattan Project (atomic bomb research) begins. Roosevelt enunciates "four freedoms," signs lend-lease act, declares national emergency, promises aid to U.S.S.R.

1942 Declaration of United Nations signed in Washington. Women's military services established. Enrico Fermi achieves nuclear chain reaction. Japanese and persons of Japanese ancestry moved inland from Pacific Coast. Coconut Grove nightclub fire in Boston kills 491.

1943 President freezes prices, salaries, and wages to prevent inflation. Income tax withholding introduced.

1944 G.I. Bill of Rights enacted. Bretton Woods Conference creates International Monetary Fund and World Bank. Dumbarton Oaks Conference—U.S., British Commonwealth, and U.S.S.R. propose establishment of United Nations.

1945 Yalta Conference (Roosevelt, Churchill, Stalin) plans final defeat of Germany (**Feb.**). Germany surrenders (**May 7**). San Francisco Conference establishes U.N. (**April–June**). FDR dies (April 12). Potsdam Conference (Truman, Churchill, Stalin) establishes basis of German reconstruction (**July–Aug**). Japan surrenders (**Sept. 2**).

1946 First meeting of U.N. General Assembly opens in London (**Jan. 10**). League of Nations dissolved (**April**). Italy abolishes monarchy (**June**). Verdict in Nuremberg war trial: 12 Nazi leaders (including 1 tried in absentia) sentenced to hang; 7 imprisoned; 3 acquitted (**Oct. 1**). Goering commits suicide a few hours before 10 other Nazis are executed (**Oct. 15**). Winston Churchill's "Iron Curtain" speech warns of Soviet expansion.

1947 Britain nationalizes coal mines (**Jan. 1**). Peace treaties for Italy, Romania, Bulgaria, Hungary, Finland signed in Paris (**Feb. 10**). Soviet Union rejects U.S. plan for U.N. atomic-energy control (**March 4**). Truman Doctrine proposed—the first significant U.S. attempt to "contain" communist expansion (**March 12**). Marshall Plan for European recovery proposed—a coordinated program to help European nations recover from ravages of war (**June**). (By **1951**, this "European Recovery Program" had cost $11 billion.) India and Pakistan gain independence from Britain (**Aug. 15**). Cominform (Communist Information Bureau) founded under Soviet auspices to rebuild contacts among European Communist parties, missing since dissolution of Comintern in **1943** (**Sept.**). (Yugoslav party expelled in **1948** and Cominform disbanded in **1956**.)

1948 Gandhi assassinated in New Delhi by Hindu fanatic (**Jan. 30**). Communists seize power in Czechoslovakia (**Feb. 23–25**). Burma and Ceylon granted independence by Britain. Organization of American States (OAS) Charter signed at Bogotá, Colombia (**April 30**). Nation of Israel proclaimed; British end Mandate at midnight; Arab armies attack (**May 14**). Berlin airlift begins (**June 21**); ends **May 12, 1949.** Stalin and Tito break (**June 28**). Independent Republic of Korea is proclaimed, following election supervised by U.N. (**Aug. 15**). Verdict in Japanese war trial: Tojo and six others sentenced to hang (hanged Dec. 23); 18 imprisoned (**Nov. 12**). United States of Indonesia established as Dutch and Indonesians settled conflict (**Dec. 27**). Alger Hiss, former U.S. State Department official, indicted on perjury charges after denying passing secret documents to communist spy ring. Convicted in second trial (**1950**) and sentenced to five-year prison term.

1949 Cease-fire in Palestine (**Jan. 7**). Truman proposes Point Four Program to help world's backward areas (**Jan. 20**). Israel signs armistice with Egypt (**Feb. 24**). Start of North Atlantic Treaty Organization (NATO)—treaty signed by 12 nations (**April 4**). German Federal Republic (West Germany) established (**Sept. 21**). Truman discloses Soviet Union has set off atomic explosion (**Sept. 23**). Communist People's Republic of China formally proclaimed by Chairman Mao Zedong. (**Oct. 1**).

1950 Truman orders development of hydrogen bomb (**Jan. 31**). Korean War (*see* special material on the "Korean War"). Assassination attempt on

KOREAN WAR (1950–1953)

1950 North Korean Communist forces invade South Korea (June 25). U.N. calls for cease-fire and asks U.N. members to assist South Korea (June 27). Truman orders U.S. forces into Korea (June 27). North Koreans capture Seoul (June 28). Gen. Douglas MacArthur designated commander of unified U.N. forces (July 8). Pusan Beachhead—U.N. forces counterattack and capture Seoul (Aug.–Sept.), capture Pyongyang, North Korean capital **(Oct.)**. Chinese Communists enter war **(Oct. 26)**, force U.N. retreat toward 39th parallel **(Dec.)**.

1951 Gen. Matthew B. Ridgeway replaces MacArthur after he threatens Chinese with massive retaliation **(April 11)**. Armistice negotiations **(July)** continue with interruptions until **June 1953.**

1953 Armistice signed **(June 26)**. Chinese troops withdraw from North Korea **(Oct. 26, 1958)**, but over 200 violations of armistice noted to **1959.**

President Truman by Puerto Rican nationalists (**Nov. 1**). Brink's robbery in Boston; almost $3 million stolen (**Jan. 17**).

1951 Six nations agree to Schuman Plan to pool European coal and steel (**March 19**)—in effect **Feb. 10, 1953.** Julius and Ethel Rosenberg sentenced to death for passing atomic secrets to Russians (**March**). Japanese peace treaty signed in San Francisco by 49 nations (**Sept. 8**). Color television introduced in U.S.

1952 George VI dies; his daughter becomes Elizabeth II (**Feb. 6**). NATO conference approves European army (**Feb.**). AEC announces "satisfactory" experiments in hydrogen-weapons research; eyewitnesses tell of blasts near Enewetak (**Nov.**).

1953 Gen. Dwight D. Eisenhower inaugurated President of United States (**Jan. 20**). Stalin dies (**March 5**). Malenkov becomes Soviet Premier; Beria, Minister of Interior; Molotov, Foreign Minister (**March 6**). Dag Hammarskjold begins term as U.N. Secretary-General (**April 10**). Edmund Hillary, of New Zealand, and Tenzing Norkay, of Nepal, reach top of Mt. Everest (**May 29**). East Berliners rise against Communist rule; quelled by tanks (**June 17**). Egypt becomes republic ruled by military junta (**June 18**). Julius and Ethel Rosenberg executed in Sing Sing prison (**June 19**). Korean armistice signed (**July 27**). Moscow announces explosion of hydrogen bomb (**Aug. 20**).

Jackie Robinson (1919-1972)

1954 First atomic submarine *Nautilus,* launched (**Jan. 21**). Five U.S. Congressmen shot on floor of House as Puerto Rican nationalists fire from spectators' gallery; all five recover (**March 1**). Army *vs.* McCarthy inquiry—Senate subcommittee report blames both sides (**Apr. 22–June 17**). Dien Bien Phu, French military outpost in Vietnam, falls to Vietminh army (**May 7**). (*see* special material on the "Vietnam War.") U.S. Supreme Court (in *Brown* v. *Board of Education of Topeka*) unanimously bans racial segregation in public schools (**May 17**). Eisenhower launches world atomic pool without Soviet Union (**Sept. 6**). Eight-nation Southeast Asia defense treaty (SEATO) signed at Manila (**Sept. 8**). West Germany is granted sovereignty, admitted to NATO and Western European Union (**Oct. 23**). Dr. Jonas Salk starts innoculating children against polio. Algerian War of Independence against France begins (**Nov.**); France struggles to maintain colonial rule until 1962 when it agrees to Algeria's independence.

1955 Nikolai A. Bulganin becomes Soviet Premier, replacing Malenkov (**Feb. 8**). Churchill resigns; Anthony Eden succeeds him (**April 6**). Federal Republic of West Germany becomes a sovereign state (**May 5**). Warsaw

VIETNAM WAR (1950–1975)

U.S., South Vietnam, and Allies versus North Vietnam and National Liberation Front (Viet Cong). Outstanding events:

1950 President Truman sends 35-man military advisory group to aid French fighting to maintain colonial power in Vietnam.

1954 After defeat of French at Dienbienphu, Geneva Agreements (**July**) provide for withdrawal of French and Vietminh to either side of demarcation zone (DMZ) pending reunification elections, which are never held. Presidents Eisenhower and Kennedy (from **1954** onward) send civilian advisors and, later, military personnel to train South Vietnamese.

1960 Communists from National Liberation Front in South.

1963 Ngo Dinh Diem, South Vietnam's premier, slain in coup (**Nov. 1**).

1961–1963 U.S. military advisors rise from 2,000 to 15,000.

1964 North Vietnamese torpedo boats reportedly attack U.S. destroyers in Gulf of Tonkin (**Aug. 2**). President Johnson orders retaliatory air strikes. Congress approves Gulf of Tonkin resolution (**Aug. 7**) authorizing President to take necessary steps to "maintain peace."

1965 U.S. planes begin combat missions over South Vietnam. In **June,** 23,000 American advisors committed to combat. By end of year over 184,000 U.S. troops in area.

1966 B-52s bomb DMZ, reportedly used by North Vietnam for entry into South (**July 31**).

1967 South Vietnam National Assembly approves election of Nguyen Van Thieu as President (**Oct. 21**).

1968 U.S. has almost 525,000 men in Vietnam. In Tet offensive (**Jan.–Feb.**), Viet Cong guerrillas attack Saigon, Hue, and some provincial capitals. President Johnson orders halt to U.S. bombardment of North Vietnam (**Oct. 31**). Saigon and N.L.F. join U.S. and North Vietnam in Paris peace talks.

1969 President Nixon announces Vietnam peace offer (**May 14**) —begins troop withdrawals (**June**). Viet Cong forms Provisional Revolutionary Government. U.S. Senate calls for curb on commitments (**June 25**). Ho Chi Minh, 79, North Vietnam president, dies (**Sept. 3**); collective leadership chosen. Some 6,000 U.S. troops pulled back from Thailand and 1,000 marines from Vietnam (announced **Sept. 30**). Massive demonstrations in U.S. protest or support war policies (**Oct. 15**).

1970 Nixon announces sending of troops to Cambodia (**April 30**). Last U.S. troops removed from Cambodia (**June 29**).

1971 Congress bars use of combat troops, but not air power, in Laos and Cambodia (**Jan. 1**). South Vietnamese troops, with U.S. air cover, fail in Laos thrust. Many American ground forces withdrawn from Vietnam combat. *New York Times* publishes Pentagon papers, classified material on expansion of war (**June**).

1972 Nixon responds to North Vietnamese drive across DMZ by ordering mining of North Vietnam ports and heavy bombing of Hanoi-Haiphong area (**April 1**). Nixon orders "Christmas bombing" of north to get North Vietnamese back to conference table (**Dec.**).

1973 President orders halt to offensive operations in North Vietnam (**Jan. 15**). Representatives of North and South Vietnam, U.S., and N.L.F. sign peace pacts in Paris, ending longest war in U.S. history (**Jan. 27**).

1974 Both sides accuse each other of frequent violations of cease-fire agreement.

1975 Full-scale warfare resumes. Communists victorious (**April 30**). South Vietnam Premier Nguyen Van Thieu resigns (**April 21**). American troops evacuated (**April 30**). More than 140,000 Vietnamese refugees leave by air and sea, many to settle in U.S. Provisional Revolutionary Government takes control (**June 6**).

1976 Election of National Assembly paves way for reunification of North and South.

Yuri A. Gagarin
(1934-1968)

Pact, east European mutual defense agreement, signed (**May 14**). Argentina ousts Perón (**Sept. 19**). President Eisenhower suffers coronary thrombosis in Denver (**Sept. 24**). Martin Luther King, Jr., leads black boycott of Montgomery, Ala., bus system (**Dec. 1**); desegregated service begun (**Dec. 21**). AFL and CIO become one organization—AFL-CIO (**Dec. 5**).

1956 Nikita Khrushchev, First Secretary of U.S.S.R. Communist Party, denounces Stalin's excesses (**Feb. 24**). First aerial H-bomb tested over Namu islet, Bikini Atoll—10 million tons TNT equivalent (**May 21**). Worker's uprising against Communist rule in Poznan, Poland, is crushed (**June 28–30**). Egypt takes control of Suez Canal (**July 26**). Israel launches attack on Egypt's Sinai peninsula and drives toward Suez Canal (**Oct. 29**). British and French invade Egypt at Port Said (**Nov. 5**). Cease-fire forced by U.S. pressure stops British, French, and Israeli advance (**Nov. 6**). Revolt starts in Hungary—Soviet troops and tanks crush anti-Communist rebellion (**Nov.**).

1957 Eisenhower Doctrine calls for aid to Mideast countries which resist armed aggression from Communist-controlled nations (**Jan. 5**). Eisenhower sends troops to Little Rock, Ark., to quell mob and protect school integration (**Sept. 24**). Russians launch *Sputnik I,* first earth-orbiting satellite—the Space Age begins (**Oct. 4**).

1958 Army's Jupiter-C rocket fires first U.S. earth satellite, *Explorer I,* into orbit (**Jan. 31**). Egypt and Syria merge into United Arab Republic (**Feb. 1**). European Economic Community (Common Market) established by Rome Treaty becomes effective **Jan. 1, 1958.** Khrushchev becomes Premier of Soviet Union as Bulganin resigns (**Mar. 27**). Gen. Charles de Gaulle becomes French premier (**June 1**), remaining in power until **1969.** New French constitution adopted (**Sept. 28**), de Gaulle elected president of 5th Republic (**Dec. 21**). Eisenhower orders U.S. Marines into Lebanon at request of President Chamoun, who fears overthrow (**July 15**).

1959 Cuban President Batista resigns and flees—Castro takes over (**Jan. 1**). Tibet's Dalai Lama escapes to India (**Mar. 31**). St. Lawrence Seaway opens, allowing ocean ships to reach Midwest (**April 25**).

1960 American U-2 spy plane, piloted by Francis Gary Powers, shot down over Russia (**May 1**). Khrushchev kills Paris summit conference because of U-2 (**May 16**). Powers sentenced to prison for 10 years (**Aug. 19**)—freed in **February 1962** in exchange for Soviet spy. Top Nazi murderer of Jews, Adolf Eichmann, captured by Israelis in Argentina (**May 23**)—executed in Israel in **1962.** Communist China and Soviet Union split in conflict over Communist ideology. Belgium starts to break up its African colonial empire, gives independence to Belgian Congo (Zaire) on **June 30.** Cuba begins confiscation of $770 million of U.S. property (**Aug. 7**).

1961 U.S. breaks diplomatic relations with Cuba (**Jan. 3**). John F. Kennedy inaugurated President of U.S. (**Jan. 20**). Kennedy proposes Alliance for Progress—10-year plan to raise Latin American living standards (**Mar. 13**). Moscow announces putting first man in orbit around earth, Maj. Yuri A. Gagarin (**April 12**). Cuba invaded at Bay of Pigs by an estimated 1,200 anti-Castro exiles aided by U.S.; invasion crushed (**April 17**). First U.S. spaceman, Navy Cmdr. Alan B. Shepard, Jr., rockets 116.5 miles up in 302-mile trip (**May 5**). Virgil Grissom becomes second American astronaut, making 118-mile-high, 303-mile-long rocket flight over Atlantic (**July 21**). Gherman Stepanovich Titov is launched in Soviet spaceship *Vostok II:* makes 17 1/2 orbits in 25 hours, covering 434,960 miles before landing safely (**Aug. 6**). East Germans erect Berlin Wall between East and West Berlin to halt flood of refugees (**Aug. 13**). U.S.S.R. fires 50-megaton hydrogen bomb, biggest explosion in history (**Oct. 29**).

1962 Lt. Col. John H. Glenn, Jr., is first American to orbit earth—three times in 4 hr 55 min (**Feb. 20**). Adolf Eichmann hanged in Israel for his part in Nazi extermination of six million Jews (**May 31**). France transfers sovereignty to new republic of Algeria (**July 3**). Cuban missile crisis—U.S. S.R. to build missile bases in Cuba; Kennedy orders Cuban blockade, lifts blockade after Russians back down (**Aug.–Nov.**). James H. Meredith, escorted by Federal marshals, registers in University of Mississippi (**Oct. 1**). Pope John XXIII opens Second Vatican Council (Oct. 11)—Council holds four sessions, finally closing Dec. 8, 1965. Cuba releases 1,113 prisoners of 1961 invasion attempt (**Dec. 24**).

1963 France and West Germany sign treaty of cooperation ending four centuries of conflict (**Jan. 22**). Pope John XXIII dies (**June 3**)—succeeded June 21 by Cardinal Montini, who becomes Paul VI. U.S. Supreme Court rules no locality may require recitation of Lord's Prayer or Bible verses in public schools (**June 17**). Civil rights rally held by 200,000 blacks and whites in Washington, D.C. (**Aug. 28**). Washington-to-Moscow "hot line" communications link opens, designed to reduce risk of accidental war (**Aug. 30**). President Kennedy shot and killed by sniper in Dallas, Tex. Lyndon B. Johnson becomes President same day (**Nov. 22**). Lee Harvey Oswald, accused assassin of President Kennedy, is shot and killed by Jack Ruby, Dallas nightclub owner (**Nov. 24**).

1964 U.S. Supreme Court rules that Congressional districts should be roughly equal in population (**Feb. 17**). Jack Ruby convicted of murder in slaying of Lee Harvey Oswald; sentenced to death by Dallas jury (**March 14**)—conviction reversed **Oct. 5, 1966**; Ruby dies **Jan. 3, 1967**, before second trial can be held. Three civil rights workers—Schwerner, Goodman, and Cheney—murdered in Mississippi (**June**). Twenty-one arrests result in trial and conviction of seven by Federal jury. President's Commission on the Assassination of President Kennedy issues Warren Report concluding that Lee Harvey Oswald acted alone.

John F. Kennedy (1917-1963)

1965 Rev. Dr. Martin Luther King, Jr., and more than 2,600 other blacks arrested in Selma, Ala., during three-day demonstrations against voter-registration rules (**Feb. 1**). Malcolm X, black-nationalist leader, shot to death at Harlem rally in New York City (**Feb. 21**). U.S. Marines land in Dominican Republic as fighting persists between rebels and Dominican army (**April 28**). Medicare, senior citizens' government medical assistance program, begins (**July 1**). Blacks riot for six days in Watts section of Los Angeles: 34 dead, over 1,000 injured, nearly 4,000 arrested, fire damage put at $175 million (**Aug. 11–16**). Power failure in Ontario plant blacks out parts of eight northeastern states of U.S. and two provinces of southeastern Canada (**Nov. 9**).

1966 Black teen-agers riot in Watts, Los Angeles; two men killed and at least 25 injured (**March 15**). Michael E. De Bakey implants artificial heart in human for first time at Houston hospital; plastic device functions and patient lives (**April 21**).

1967 Three Apollo astronauts—Col. Virgil I. Grissom, Col. Edward White II, and Lt. Cmdr. Roger B. Chaffee—killed in spacecraft fire during simulated launch (**Jan. 27**). Israeli and Arab forces battle; six-day war ends with Israel occupying Sinai Peninsula, Golan Heights, Gaza Strip, and east bank of Suez Canal (**June 5**). Red China announces explosion of its first hydrogen bomb (**June 17**). Racial violence in Detroit; 7,000 National Guardsmen aid police after night of rioting. Similar outbreaks occur in New York City's Spanish Harlem, Rochester, N.Y., Birmingham, Ala., and New Britain, Conn. (**July 23**). Thurgood Marshall sworn in as first black U.S. Supreme Court justice (**Oct. 2**). Dr. Christian N. Barnard and team of South African surgeons perform world's first successful human heart transplant (**Dec. 3**)—patient dies 18 days later.

Martin Luther King, Jr. (1929-1968)

1968 North Korea seizes U.S. Navy ship *Pueblo;* holds 83 on board as spies (**Jan. 23**). President Johnson announces he will not seek or accept presidential renomination (**March 31**). Martin Luther King, Jr., civil rights leader, is slain in Memphis (**April 4**)—James Earl Ray, indicted in murder, captured in London on **June 8**. In **1969** Ray pleads guilty and is sentenced to 99 years. Sen. Robert F. Kennedy is shot and critically wounded in Los Angeles hotel after winning California primary (**June 5**)—dies **June 6**. Sirhan B. Sirhan convicted **1969**. Czechoslovakia is invaded by Russians and Warsaw Pact forces to crush liberal regime (**Aug. 20**).

1969 Richard M. Nixon is inaugurated 37th President of the U.S. (**Jan. 20**). Apollo 11 astronauts—Neil A. Armstrong, Edwin E. Aldrin, Jr., and Michael Collins—take man's first walk on moon (**July 20**). Sen. Edward M. Kennedy pleads guilty to leaving scene of fatal accident at Chappaquiddick, Mass. (**July 18**) in which Mary Jo Kopechne was drowned—gets two-month suspended sentence (**July 25**).

1970 Biafra surrenders after 32-month fight for independence from Nigeria (**Jan. 12**). Rhodesia severs last tie with British Crown and declares itself a racially segregated republic (**March 1**). Four students at Kent State University in Ohio slain by National Guardsmen at demonstration protesting April 30 incursion into Cambodia (**May 4**). Senate repeals Gulf of Tonkin resolution (**June 24**).

1971 Supreme Court rules unanimously that busing of students may be ordered to achieve racial desegregation (**April 20**). Anti-war militants attempt to disrupt government business in Washington (**May 3**)—police and military units arrest as many as 12,000; most are later released. Twenty-sixth Amendment to U.S. Constitution lowers voting age to 18. U.N. seats Communist China and expels Nationalist China (**Oct. 25**).

1972 President Nixon makes unprecedented eight-day visit to Communist China (**Feb.**). Britain takes over direct rule of Northern Ireland in bid for peace (**March 24**). Gov. George C. Wallace of Alabama is shot by Arthur H. Bremer at Laurel, Md., political rally (**May 15**). Five men are apprehended by police in attempt to bug Democratic National Commit-

Viking I and II
(Launched 1975)

tee headquarters in Washington D.C.'s Watergate complex—start of the Watergate scandal (**June 17**). Supreme Court rules that death penalty is unconstitutional (**June 29**). Eleven Israeli athletes at Olympic Games in Munich are killed after eight members of an Arab terrorist group invade Olympic Village; five guerrillas and one policeman are also killed (**Sept. 5**).

1973 Great Britain, Ireland, and Denmark enter European Common Market (**Jan. 1**). Nixon, on national TV, accepts responsibility, but not blame, for Watergate; accepts resignations of advisers H. R. Haldeman and John D. Ehrlichman, fires John W. Dean III as counsel. (**April 30**). Greek military junta abolishes monarchy and proclaims republic (**June 1**). U.S. bombing of Cambodia ends, marking official halt to 12 years of combat activity in Southeast Asia (**Aug. 15**). Fourth and biggest Arab-Israeli War begins as Egyptian and Syrian forces attack Israel as Jews mark Yom Kippur, holiest day in their calendar. (**Oct. 6**). Spiro T. Agnew resigns as Vice President and then, in Federal Court in Baltimore, pleads no contest to charges of evasion of income taxes on $29,500 he received in 1967, while Governor of Maryland. He is fined $10,000 and put on three years' probation (**Oct. 10**). In the "Saturday Night Massacre," Nixon fires special Watergate prosecutor Archibald Cox and Deputy Attorney General William D. Ruckelshaus; Attorney General Elliot L. Richardson resigns (**Oct. 20**). Egypt and Israel sign U.S.-sponsored cease-fire accord (**Nov. 11**).

1974 Patricia Hearst, 19-year-old daughter of publisher Randolph Hearst, kidnapped by Symbionese Liberation Army. (**Feb. 5**). House Judiciary Committee adopts three articles of impeachment charging President Nixon with obstruction of justice, failure to uphold laws, and refusal to produce material subpoenaed by the committee (**July 30**). Richard M. Nixon announces he will resign the next day, the first President to do so (**Aug. 8**). Vice President Gerald R. Ford of Michigan is sworn in as 38th President of the U.S. (**Aug. 9**). Ford grants "full, free, and absolute pardon" to ex-President Nixon (**Sept. 8**).

1975 John N. Mitchell, H. R. Haldeman, John D. Ehrlichman, and Robert C. Mardian found guilty of Watergate cover-up. Mitchell, Haldeman, and Ehrlichman are sentenced on Feb. 21 to 30 months-8 years in jail and Mardian to 10 months-3 years (**Jan. 1**). American merchant ship *Mayaguez*, seized by Cambodian forces, is rescued in operation by U.S. Navy and Marines, 38 of whom are killed (**May 15**). *Apollo* and *Soyuz* spacecraft take off for U.S.-Soviet link-up in space (**July 15**). President Ford escapes assassination attempt in Sacramento, Calif., (**Sept. 5**). President Ford escapes second assassination attempt in 17 days. (**Sept. 22**).

Voyager I and II
(Launched 1977)

1976 Supreme Court rules that blacks and other minorities are entitled to retroactive job seniority (**March 24**). Ford signs Federal Election Campaign Act (**May 11**). Supreme Court rules that death penalty is not inherently cruel or unusual and is a constitutionally acceptable form of punishment (**July 3**). Nation celebrates Bicentennial (**July 4**). Israeli airborne commandos attack Uganda's Entebbe Airport and free 103 hostages held by pro-Palestinian hijackers of Air France plane; one Israeli and several Ugandan soldiers killed in raid (**July 4**). Mysterious disease that eventually claims 29 lives strikes American Legion convention in Philadelphia (**Aug. 4**). Jimmy Carter elected U.S. President (**Nov. 2**).

1977 First woman Episcopal priest ordained (**Jan. 1**). Scientists identify previously unknown bacterium as cause of mysterious "legionnaire's disease" (**Jan. 18**). Carter pardons Vietnam draft evaders (**Jan. 21**). Scientists report using bacteria in lab to make insulin (**May 23**). Supreme Court rules that states are not required to spend Medicaid funds on elective abortions (**June 20**). Deng Xiaoping, purged Chinese leader, restored to power as "Gang of Four" is expelled from Communist Party (**July 22**). Nuclear-proliferation pact, curbing spread of nuclear weapons, signed by 15 countries, including U.S. and U.S.S.R. (**Sept. 21**).

1978 President chooses Federal Appeals Court Judge William H. Webster as F.B.I. Director (**Jan. 19**). Rhodesia's Prime Minister Ian D. Smith and three black leaders agree on transfer to black majority rule (**Feb. 15**). Former Italian Premier Aldo Moro kidnapped by left-wing terrorists, who kill five bodyguards (**March 16**); he is found slain (**May 9**). U.S. Senate approves Panama Canal neutrality treaty (**March 16**); votes treaty to turn canal over to Panama by year 2000 (**April 18**). Californians in referendum approve Proposition 13 for nearly 60% slash in property tax revenues (**June 6**). Supreme Court, in Bakke case, bars quota systems in college admissions but affirms constitutionality of programs giving advantage to minorities (**June 28**). Pope Paul VI, dead at 80, mourned (**Aug. 6**); new Pope, John Paul I, 65, dies unexpectedly after 34 days in office (**Sept. 28**); succeeded by Karol Cardinal Wojtyla of Poland as John Paul II (**Oct. 16**). "Framework for Peace" in Middle East signed by

Egypt's President Anwar el-Sadat and Israel Premier Menachem Begin after 13-day conference at Camp David led by President Carter (**Sept. 17**).

1979 Oil spills pollute ocean waters in Atlantic and Gulf of Mexico (**Jan. 1, June 8, July 21**). Ohio agrees to pay $675,000 to families of dead and injured in Kent State University shootings (**Jan. 4**). Vietnam and Cambodian insurgents it backs announce fall of Phnom Penh, Cambodian capital, and collapse of Pol Pot regime (**Jan. 7**). Shah leaves Iran after year of turmoil (**Jan. 16**); revolutionary forces under Moslem leader, Ayatollah Ruhollah Khomeini take over (**Feb. 1** et seq.). Conservatives win British election; Margaret Thatcher new Prime Minister (**March 28**). Nuclear power plant accident at Three Mile Island, Pa., releases radioactivity (**March 28**). Carter and Brezhnev sign SALT II agreement (**June 14**). China signs three-year trade treaty with U.S. (**July 7**). Nicaraguan President Gen. Anastasio Somoza Debayle resigns and flees to Miami (**July 17**); Sandinists form government (**July 19**). Earl Mountbatten of Burma, 79, British World War II hero, and three others killed by blast on fishing boat off Irish coast (**Aug. 27**); two I.R.A. members accused (**Aug. 30**). Vietnamese start offensive against Pol Pot regime in Cambodia (**Sept. 25**). Park Chung Hee, 62, South Korea president for 18 years, assassinated by intelligence chief (**Oct. 26**). Iranian militants seize U.S. Embassy in Teheran and hold hostages (**Nov. 4**). Soviet invasion of Afghanistan stirs world protests (**Dec. 27**).

Margaret Thatcher (Oct. 13, 1925)

1980 Six U.S. Embassy aides escape from Iran with Canadian help (**Jan. 29**). F.B.I.'s two-year undercover operation "Abscam" (for Arab scam) implicates public officials (**Feb. 2**). U.S. breaks diplomatic ties with Iran (**April 7**). Eight U.S. servicemen are killed and five are injured as helicopter and cargo plane collide in abortive desert raid to rescue American hostages in Teheran (**April 25**). Cyrus R. Vance resigns as Secretary of State (**April 28**); Senator Edmund S. Muskie of Maine succeeds him (**April 29**). Supreme Court upholds limits on federal aid for abortions (**June 30**). Justices approve affirmative action for minority contractors in federal works program (**July 2**). Olympic games open in Moscow, boycotted by U.S. and other nations (**July 19**). Shah of Iran dies at 60 (**July 27**). Anastasio Somoza Debayle, ousted Nicaragua ruler, and two aides assassinated in Asunción, Paraguay capital (**Sept. 17**). Iraq troops hold 90 square miles of Iran after invasion (**Sept. 19**). Aleksei N. Kosygin, 79, ailing Soviet Prime Minister, resigns (**Oct. 23**). Ronald Reagan elected President in Republican sweep (**Nov. 4**). Three U.S. nuns and lay worker found slain in El Salvador (**Dec. 4**). John Lennon of Beatles shot dead in New York City (**Dec. 8**).

1981 U.S.-Iran agreement frees 52 hostages held in Teheran since Nov. 4, 1979 (**Jan. 18**); hostages welcomed back in U.S. (**Jan. 25**). Ronald Reagan takes oath as 40th President (**Jan. 20**). President Reagan wounded by gunman, with press secretary, and two law-enforcement officers (**March 30**). Hunger strikers die in Belfast prison protest (**May 5-July 13**). Pope John Paul II wounded by gunman (**May 14**). Israeli planes destroy Iraqi atomic reactor (**June 8**). Supreme Court rules, 4-4, that former President Nixon and three top aides may be required to pay monetary damages for unconstitutional wiretap of home telephone of former national security aide (**June 22**). Congress supports Reagan's $35.5-billion budget cuts designed to reverse government's expansion (**June 26-July 31**). Reagan nominates Judge Sandra Day O'Connor, 51, of Arizona as first woman on Supreme Court (**July 7**). More than 110 die in collapse of aerial walkways in lobby of Hyatt Regency Hotel in Kansas City; 188 injured (**July 18**). Millions around world view wedding of Prince Charles of Britain, 32, and Lady Diana Spencer, 20 (**July 29**). Air controllers strike, disrupting flights (**Aug. 3**). Government dismisses strikers (**Aug. 11**).

Ayatollah Ruhollah Khomeini (Feb. 9, 1902)

1982 *Philadelphia Bulletin* ceases publication (**Jan. 29**). British overcome Argentina in Falklands war (**April 2-June 15**). British Queen gives Canada its Constitution (**April 17**). Israel completes withdrawal from Sinai (**April 25**). Israel invades Lebanon in attack on P.L.O. (**June 4**). John W. Hinckley, Jr., found not guilty because of insanity in shooting of President Reagan (**June 21**). Princess of Wales gives birth to a boy (**June 21**). Alexander M. Haig, Jr., resigns as Secretary of State (**June 25**). Equal rights amendment fails ratification (**June 30**). Bomb blast kills Lebanon President-elect, Bashir Gemayel (**Sept. 14**). His brother, Amin Gemayel, is elected to succeed him (**Sept. 21**). Lebanese Christian Phalangists kill hundreds of people in two Palestinian refugee camps in West Beirut (**Sept. 15**). Princess Grace, 52, dies of injuries when car plunges off mountain road. Daughter Stephanie, 17, suffers serious injuries (**Sept. 14**). Polish Parliament outlaws Solidarity and all existing labor unions (**Oct. 8**). Leonid I. Brezhnev, Soviet leader, dies at 75 (**Nov. 10**). Yuri V. Andropov, 68, chosen as his successor (**Nov. 15**). Space shuttle *Columbia* lands at Ed-

Space Shuttle Columbia (Launched April 12, 1981)

Sally K. Ride
(May 26, 1951)

Sandra Day O'Connor
(March 26, 1930)

wards Air Force Base, Calif., after successful five-day inaugural trip (**Nov. 16**). Artificial heart implanted for first time in Dr. Barney B. Clark, 61, at University of Utah Medical Center in Salt Lake City (**Dec. 2**). Barney Clark dies (**March 23, 1983**).

1983 Pope John Paul II signs new Roman Catholic code incorporating changes brought about by Second Vatican Council (**Jan. 25**). Congressional commission charges internment of 120,000 Japanese citizens and resident aliens in World War II was a grave injustice (**Feb. 24**). Supreme Court votes 5-4 to uphold age bias law (**March 2**). EPA head, Anne McGill Burford, resigns in dispute over investigation of environmental agency (**March 9**). More than 200 are killed in Popauan, Colombia, earthquake (**March 31**). Thousands demonstrate in Europe to protest nuclear weapons on continent (**April 1**). Second space shuttle, *Challenger,* makes successful maiden voyage, which includes the first U.S. space walk in nine years (**April 4**). Lt. Cmdr. Albert Schaufelberger, 3rd, American military adviser in San Salvador, killed by four assassins (**May 25**). Death toll over 200 after a Nile steamer burns and sinks (**May 25**). Earthquake strikes northern Japan, killing almost 100 (**May 26**). U.S. Supreme Court declares many local abortion restrictions unconstitutional (**June 15**). Sally K. Ride, 32, first U.S. woman astronaut in space as a crew member aboard space shuttle *Challenger* (**June 18**). Supreme Court declares life prison sentence without possibility of parole unconstitutional (**June 28**). Ecuadorean jetliner crashes in mountains, killing 119 (**July 11**). Armenian terrorists explode bomb at Orly Airport, Paris, killing 6 and injuring 56 (**July 15**). Polish government lifts martial law (**July 22**). U.S. admits shielding former Nazi Gestapo chief, Klaus Barbie, 69, the "butcher of Lyons," wanted in France for war crimes (**Aug. 15**). Benigno S. Aquino, Jr., 50, political rival of Philippines President Marcos, slain in Manila (**Aug. 21**). South Korean Boeing 747 jetliner bound for Seoul apparently strays into Soviet airspace and is shot down by a Soviet SU-15 fighter after it had tracked the airliner for two hours; all 269 aboard are killed, including 61 Americans (**Aug. 30**). Terrorist explosion kills 237 U.S. Marines in Beirut (**Oct. 23**). U.S. and Caribbean Allies invade Grenada (**Oct. 25**). Rita Lavelle, former EPA official, guilty of perjury (**Dec. 1**). Lech Walesa's wife accepts his Nobel Peace Prize (**Dec. 10**). Hundreds die in Guinean earthquake (**Dec. 21**).

1984 Bell System broken up (**Jan. 1**). France gets first deliveries of Soviet natural gas (**Jan. 1**). Syria frees captured U.S. Navy pilot, Lieut. Robert C. Goodman, Jr. (**Jan. 3**). Woman in Australia is mother of first "test-tube" quadruplets (**Jan. 6**). Rita Lavelle sentenced for lying about EPA program to clean up hazardous waste (**Jan. 9**). U.S. and Vatican exchange diplomats after 116-year hiatus (**Jan. 10**). U.S. and China sign agreements on industrial cooperation and renew accords on science and technology (**Jan. 12**). George Orwell's *1984* becomes fastest-selling book in U.S. (**Jan. 18**). Reagan orders U.S. Marines withdrawn from Beirut international peacekeeping force (**Feb. 7**). Yuri V. Andropov dies at 69; Konstantin U. Chernenko, 72, named Soviet Union leader (**Feb. 9**). China and Soviet Union sign $1.2-billion trade agreement (**Feb. 10**). Italy and Vatican agree to end Roman Catholicism as state religion (**Feb. 18**). Supreme Court rules, 5-4, that a city can constitutionally use public funds for Christmas crèche (**March 5**). Four armed men seize $21.8 million in Rome, Italy's largest single theft (**March 24**). Reagan ends U.S. role in Beirut by relieving Sixth Fleet from peacekeeping force (**March 30**). First baby born from frozen embryo in Australia (**April 10**). Congress rebukes President Reagan on use of federal funds for mining Nicaraguan harbors (**April 10**). Space shuttle *Challenger* ends seven-day mission on which satellite was repaired in orbit (**April 13**). Gunman fires from Libyan Embassy into London crowd, killing British policewoman (**April 17**). Soviet Union withdraws from summer Olympic games in U.S., and other bloc nations follow (**May 7** et seq.). World Court rules against U.S. on mining of Nicaraguan harbors (**May 10**). Federal judge finds U.S. negligent in 1950 atomic tests (**May 10**). José Napoleón Duarte, moderate, elected president of El Salvador (**May 11**). Three hundred slain as Indian Army occupies Sikh Golden Temple in Amritsar (**June 6**). Summit conference of industrial nations pledges aid to debtor countries (**June 7**). Fire damages York Minster Cathedral in England (**July 9**). Nation's first compulsory seatbelt law enacted in New York (**July 11**). Thirty-ninth Democratic National Convention, in San Francisco, nominates Walter F. Mondale and Geraldine A. Ferraro (**July 16–19**). Thirty-third Republican National Convention, at Dallas, renominates President Reagan and Vice President Bush (**Aug. 20–25**). Russians successfully test cruise missiles (**Aug. 25**). Brian Mulroney and Conservative party win Canadian election in landslide (**Sept. 4**). British Prime Minister Margaret Thatcher nearly killed by I.R.A. assassination attempt (**Oct. 12**). Indian Prime Minister Indira Gandhi assassinated by two Sikh bodyguards; 1,000 killed in anti-Sikh riots; son Rajiv succeeds her (**Oct. 31**). President Reagan re-elected in landslide with 59% of vote (**Nov. 7**). Toxic gas leaks from Union Carbide plant in Bhopal, India, killing 2,000 and injuring 150,000 (**Dec. 3**). Bronze Age artifacts uncovered in 3,400-year-old shipwreck (**Dec. 4**).

Indira Gandhi (1917-1984)

1985 U.S. and Soviet Union reach compromise agreement on resuming negotiations on limiting and reducing nuclear arms and preventing arms race in space (**Jan. 8**). Two thousand refugee Ethiopian Jews perish in Sudan (**Jan. 18**). Ronald Reagan, 73, takes oath for second term as 40th President (**Jan. 20**). U.S. Court jury clears *Time* magazine of deliberate falsehood in libel suit brought by Ariel Sharon, Israeli leader (**Jan. 24**). New Zealand bars U.S. ship when Washington refuses to say whether she carries nuclear arms (**Feb. 4**). President Reagan calls on Congress for major budget reductions (**Feb. 4**); in State of Union message he stresses tax revision and economic growth (**Feb. 6**). Border of Gibraltar reopened under Spain-Britain agreement (**Feb. 5**). Four Polish security officials convicted in abduction and murder of Rev. Jerzy Popieluszko, pro-Solidarity activist (**Feb. 7**). Worldwide Conservative Rabbinical Assembly approves women in clergy (**Feb. 14**). Vietnamese drive Cambodian rebels from last of their bases (**Feb. 15**). General Westmoreland settles libel action against CBS (**Feb. 18**). Prime Minister Margaret Thatcher addresses Congress, endorsing Reagan's policies (**Feb. 20**). I.R.A. terrorists kill nine officers and civilians at Ulster police base (**Feb. 28**). Uruguay ends military rule after 12 years (**March 1**). Car bomb kills 62 in Beirut suburb; 200 wounded (**March 6**). Kidnapped U.S. drug agent and his pilot slain in Mexico (**March 6**). U.S.S.R. leader Chernenko dies at 73 and is replaced by Mikhail Gorbachev, 54 (**March 11**). Secretary of Labor Raymond J. Donovan, facing New York fraud trial, resigns; first sitting Cabinet member to be indicted (**March 15**). Civilian rule returns to Brazil after 12 years (**March 15**). World honors Bach on 300th birthday (**March 21**). A.H. Robins sets aside $615 million to settle claims over Dalkon Shield, contraceptive device (**April 2**). Tens of thousands mark 40th anniversary of liberation of Buchenwald death camp (**April 13**). Reagan target of wide attacks by Jewish leaders and others over visit to Bitburg Cemetery, West Germany, where SS troops are buried (**April 18** et seq. **May 5**). Philadelphia police firebomb home of MOVE, organization of armed blacks, and fire spreads to neighboring homes; 11 dead and 200 homeless (**May 13**). Thirty-eight killed in Brussels football riot (**May 29**). Two Shiite Moslem gunmen capture TWA airliner with 133 aboard, 104 of them Americans (**June 14**); 39 remaining hostages freed in Beirut (**June 30**). Supreme Court, 5-4, bars public school teachers from parochial schools (**July 1**). South Africa decrees state of emergency giving police and army near absolute power in black townships (**July 20**). President Reagan undergoes surgery for removal of intestinal polyp, found to be noncancerous (**July 13–15**). Arthur James Walker, 50, retired naval officer, convicted by federal judge of participating in Soviet spy ring (**Aug. 9**). Spy scandal flares up in West Germany as top counterintelligence officer defects to East Germany (**Aug. 23**). Pentagon scraps Sergeant York antiaircraft weapon after $1.8-billion outlay (**Aug. 27**). Thousands dead in Mexico earthquake (**Sept. 19**). French government shaken by scandal over sinking of antinuclear ship off New Zealand (**Sept. 22**). Israelis bomb P.L.O. headquarters in Tunis in retaliation for slaying of three Israelis in Cyprus (**Oct. 1**). P.L.O. terrorists hijack *Achille Lauro*, Italian cruise ship, with 80 passengers, plus crew (**Oct. 7**); American, Leon Klinghoffer, killed (**Oct. 8**). Italian government toppled by political crisis over hijacking of *Achille Lauro* (**Oct. 16**). John A. Walker and son, Michael I. Walker, 22, sentenced in Navy espionage case (**Oct. 28**). U.S. arrests Oregon guru, Bhagwan Shree Rayneesh, 53, from India, on immigration charges (**Oct. 28**). Largest crew ever flies space shuttle *Challenger* on international mission (**Oct. 30**). Forty dead in Middle Atlantic floods (**Nov. 6**). Volcano eruption leaves 25,000 dead and missing in Colombia (**Nov. 14**). Reagan and Gorbachev meet at summit (**Nov. 19**); agree to step up arms control talks and renew cultural contacts (**Nov. 21**). Terrorists seize Egyptian Boeing 737 airliner after takeoff from Athens (**Nov. 23**); 59 dead as Egyptian forces storm plane on Malta (**Nov. 24**). U.S. budget-balancing bill enacted (**Dec. 12**). Newfoundland plane crash kills 248 U.S. soldiers (**Dec. 12**). Terrorists kill 19 at Rome and Vienna airports (**Dec. 30**); President Reagan accuses Libya of aiding attackers.

Ronald W. Reagan (Feb. 6, 1911)

Mikhail S. Gorbachev (March 2, 1931)

1986 Spain and Portugal join Common Market (**Jan. 1**). President freezes Libyan assets in U.S. (**Jan. 8**). Supreme Court bars racial bias in trial jury selection (**Jan. 14**). Britain and France plan Channel tunnel (**Jan. 20**). *Voyager 2* spacecraft reports secrets of Uranus (**Jan. 26**). Space shuttle

Corazon C. Aquino
(Jan. 25, 1933)

Halley's comet
(April, 1986)

Challenger explodes after launch at Cape Canaveral, Fla., killing all seven aboard (**Jan. 28**); space agency reports solid-fuel booster rocket lost power before blast (**Jan. 31**). Sale of intrauterine contraceptive devices halted (**Jan. 31**). Reagan names 12-man panel for *Challenger* inquiry (**Feb. 3**). Haiti President Jean-Claude Duvalier flees to France (**Feb. 7**). F.B.I. presses investigation of death from tainted Tylenol capsule (**Feb. 14**); Johnson & Johnson withdraws capsules (**Feb. 17**). Supreme Court voids Indiana antipornography ordinance (**Feb. 24**); approves local curbs on sex films (**Feb. 25**). President Marcos flees Philippines after ruling 20 years, as newly elected Corazon Aquino succeeds him (**Feb. 26**). Prime Minister Olof Palme of Sweden shot dead (**Feb. 28**). Seven baseball players suspended over drug use (**Feb. 28**). Kurt Waldheim service as Nazi army officer revealed (**March 3**). Leo M. Frank, Georgia lynching victim, pardoned posthumously on killing charge (**March 11**). Worldwide Marcos fortune identified by Philippines (**March 13**). Rightist parties victorious in France (**March 16**). Union Carbide agrees to settlement with victims of Bhopal gas leak in India (**March 22**). U.S. forces clash with Libyans during Navy maneuvers in Gulf of Sidra (**March 24** et seq.). Thirty dead as police fire on crowds in South Africa (**March 26**). Two scientific teams report finding AIDS viruses (**March 26**). Bombs kill two in Berlin nightclub patronized by U.S. troops (**April 5**). Halley's Comet yields information on return visit (**April 10**). U.S. planes attack Libyan "terrorist centers" (**April 14**). Desmond Tutu elected Archbishop in South Africa (**April 14**). Three hostages slain in Lebanon in reprisal for bombing of Libya (**April 17**). British hostage slain in Beirut (**April 23**). Major nuclear accident at Soviet Union's Chernobyl power station alarms world (**April 28** et seq.). Bangladesh river ferry with 1,000 aboard capsizes (**May 26**). U.S. abandons arms limitation treaty (**May 27**). Senate debates go on television (**June 2**). Ex-Navy analyst, Jonathan Jay Pollard, 31, guilty as spy for Israel (**June 4**). Final report on shuttle blast inquiry faults management policies (**June 9**). Supreme Court reaffirms abortion rights (**June 11**). Millions of blacks strike in South Africa on anniversary of 1976 Soweto uprising (**June 16**). Richard W. Miller, 48, former F.B.I. agent, convicted as spy in Los Angeles (**June 19**). Lebanon kidnappers free two victims (**June 20**). Cocaine blamed in death of Len Bias, University of Maryland basketball star (**June 24**). House, in reversal, votes aid to contras fighting Nicaragua (**June 25**). Irish voters uphold legal ban on divorce (**June 27**). World Court rules U.S. broke international law in mining Nicaraguan waters (**June 27**). Nation rededicates Statue of Liberty (**July 3**). Supreme Court voids automatic provisions of budget-balancing law (**July 7**). Earthquakes rock California area (**July 8**). Terrorists bomb Paris police headquarters (**July 9**). U.S. troops join in Bolivian cocaine raids (**July 15**). Moslem captors release Lebanon hostage, Rev. Lawrence Martin Jenco (**July 26**). Jerry A. Whitworth, ex-Navy radioman, convicted as spy (**July 24**). U.S. court finds National Football League violated antitrust laws (**July 29**). Senate Judiciary Committee approves William H. Rehnquist to be Chief Justice of U.S. (**Aug. 14**). Mexican police torture U.S. narcotics agent (**Aug. 14**). House votes arms appropriations bill rejecting Administration's "star wars" policy (**Aug. 15**). Vatican strips Rev. Charles E. Curran, liberal theologian, of authority to teach theology at Catholic University (**Aug. 18**). Volcano gas from lake bottom kills 1,500 in Cameroon (**Aug. 25**). Three Lutheran church groups in U.S. set to merge (**Aug. 29**). Nicholas Daniloff, correspondent for *U.S. News & World Report*, detained in Moscow on espionage charges (**Aug. 30**); released and allowed to leave Soviet Union (**Sept. 29**); in apparent U.S.-Soviet agreement, Gennadi F. Zakharov, accused spy, allowed to leave U.S. (**Sept. 30**).

(For later events, *See* Current Events, pages 961–974).

PICTURE CREDITS. The following credits list the names of organizations and individuals who have contributed illustrations to HEADLINE HISTORY. The editors wish to thank all of them for their assistance. The credits are arranged alphabetically by picture source, then picture title and page number in HEADLINE HISTORY. **Credits:** British Information Services, **Margaret Thatcher**, p. 131; Dover Publications, Inc., *Treasury of Fantastic and Mythological Creatures,* **Mayan Bas-Reliefs**, p. 106; Embassy of The Philippines, **Corazon C. Aquino**, p. 134; John Fitzgerald Kennedy Library, Boston, **John F. Kennedy**, p. 129; Matthew Kalmenoff, **Brontosaur**, p. 103; NASA Photos, **Charles A. Lindbergh**, p. 122, **Voyager and Viking**, p.130, **Space Shuttle Columbia**, p. 131, **Sally K. Ride**, p. 132; Novosti Photos, **Vladimir Lenin**, p.120, **Yuri A. Gagarin**, p.128; **Mikhail S. Gorbachev**, p. 133; The Baseball Hall of Fame, **Jackie Robinson**, p. 127; The Library of Congress Picture Collection, **Christopher Columbus**, p. 109, **Dred Scott**, p. 116, **Geronimo**, p. 117, **Amelia Earhart**, p.122; The Permanent Mission of India to the U.N., **Indira Gandhi**, p.133; The Permanent Mission of the Islamic Republic of Iran to the U.N., **Ayatollah Ruhollah Khomeini**, p. 131; Republican National Committee, **Ronald W. Reagan**, p. 133; The Supreme Court Historical Society, **Sandra Day O'Connor**, p. 132; U.S. Army Photos, **D-Day, Yalta Conference**, p. 126; AP/Wide World Photos, Inc., **Albert Einstein**, p. 118, **Adolf Hitler**, 125, **Martin Luther King, Jr.**, p.129, **Halley's Comet**, p. 134; **Mao Zedong**, p. 126, Xinhua News Agency, United Nations Bureau. **MAP CREDITS:** Maps on pp. 108, 112, 119, 121, 123, and 124 from *An Encyclopedia of World History,* by William L. Langer, The Fifth Edition, Copyright 1940, 1948, 1952, and © 1967, 1972 by Houghton Mifflin Company. Reprinted by permission of Houghton Mifflin Company.

WORLD STATISTICS

Area and Population by Country

Mid-1987 Estimates

Country	Area[1]	Population
Afghanistan	249,999	14,200,000
Albania	11,100	3,100,000
Algeria	919,591	23,500,000
Angola	481,351	8,000,000
Antigua and Barbuda	171	100,000
Argentina	1,068,297	31,500,000
Australia	2,967,894	16,200,000
Austria	32,374	7,600,000
Bahamas	5,380	200,000
Bahrain	240	400,000
Bangladesh	55,598	107,100,000
Barbados	166	300,000
Belgium	11,749	9,900,000
Belize	8,867	200,000
Benin	43,483	4,300,000
Bhutan	18,147	1,500,000
Bolivia	424,162	6,500,000
Botswana	231,804	1,200,000
Brazil	3,286,472	141,500,000
Brunei	2,226	200,000
Bulgaria	42,823	9,000,000
Burkina Faso[2]	105,869	7,300,000
Burma	261,216	38,800,000
Burundi	10,747	5,000,000
Cambodia	69,898	6,500,000
Cameroon	183,568	10,300,000
Canada	3,851,790	25,900,000
Cape Verde	1,557	300,000
Central African Republic	240,534	2,700,000
Chad	495,753	4,600,000
Chile	292,257	12,400,000
China, People's Republic of	3,705,390	1,062,000,000
China, Republic of	13,885	19,600,000
Colombia	439,735	29,900,000
Comoros	694	400,000
Congo	132,046	2,100,000
Costa Rica	19,575	2,800,000
Cuba	42,803	10,300,000
Cyprus	3,572	700,000
Czechoslovakia	49,370	15,600,000
Denmark	16,629	5,100,000
Djibouti	8,494	300,000
Dominica	290	100,000
Dominican Republic	18,816	6,500,000
Ecuador	109,483	10,000,000
Egypt	386,660	51,900,000
El Salvador	8,124	5,300,000
Equatorial Guinea	10,830	300,000
Ethiopia	471,776	46,000,000
Fiji	7,055	700,000
Finland	130,119	4,900,000
France	211,207	55,600,000
Gabon	103,346	1,200,000
Gambia	4,361	800,000
Germany, East	41,826	16,700,000
Germany, West	95,976	61,000,000
Ghana	92,099	13,900,000
Greece	50,944	10,000,000
Grenada	133	100,000
Guatemala	42,042	8,400,000
Guinea	94,927	6,400,000
Guinea-Bissau	13,948	900,000
Guyana	83,000	800,000
Haiti	10,714	6,200,000
Honduras	43,277	4,700,000
Hungary	35,919	10,600,000
Iceland	39,768	200,000
India[3]	1,269,340	800,300,000
Indonesia	735,355	174,900,000
Iran	636,293	50,400,000
Iraq	167,924	17,000,000
Ireland	27,136	3,500,000
Israel	8,019	4,400,000
Italy	116,303	57,400,000
Ivory Coast	124,503	10,800,000
Jamaica	4,243	2,500,000
Japan	143,750	122,200,000
Jordan	37,737	3,700,000
Kenya	224,960	22,400,000
Korea, North	46,540	21,400,000
Korea, South	38,025	42,100,000
Kuwait	6,880	1,900,000
Laos	91,429	3,800,000
Lebanon	4,015	3,300,000
Lesotho	11,720	1,600,000
Liberia	43,000	2,400,000
Libya	679,359	3,800,000
Luxembourg	998	400,000
Madagascar	226,657	10,600,000
Malawi	45,747	7,400,000
Malaysia	127,316	16,100,000
Maldives	115	200,000
Mali	478,764	8,400,000
Malta	122	400,000
Mauritania	397,954	2,000,000
Mauritius	718	1,100,000
Mexico	761,601	81,900,000
Mongolia	604,247	2,000,000
Morocco	172,413	24,400,000
Mozambique	309,494	14,700,000
Nepal	54,362	17,800,000
Netherlands	14,405	14,600,000
New Zealand	103,736	3,300,000
Nicaragua	50,193	3,500,000
Niger	489,189	7,000,000
Nigeria	356,667	108,600,000
Norway	125,181	4,200,000
Oman	82,030	1,300,000
Pakistan[4]	310,403	104,600,000
Panama	29,761	2,300,000
Papua New Guinea	178,259	3,600,000
Paraguay	157,047	4,300,000
Peru	496,222	20,700,000
Philippines	115,830	61,500,000
Poland	120,725	37,800,000
Portugal	35,553	10,300,000
Qatar	4,247	300,000
Romania	91,699	22,900,000
Rwanda	10,169	6,800,000
St. Lucia	238	100,000
St. Vincent and the Grenadines	150	100,000
Saudi Arabia	829,996	14,800,000
Senegal	75,750	7,100,000
Sierra Leone	27,699	3,900,000
Singapore	224	2,600,000
Solomon Islands	10,983	300,000

Country	Area[1]	Population	Country	Area[1]	Population
Somalia	246,200	7,700,000	Uganda	91,134	15,900,000
South Africa	471,443	34,300,000	U.S.S.R.	8,649,496	284,000,000
Spain	194,896	39,000,000	United Arab Emirates	32,278	1,400,000
Sri Lanka	25,332	16,300,000	United Kingdom	94,525	56,800,000
Sudan	967,495	23,500,000	United States	3,615,105	243,800,000
Suriname	63,037	400,000	Uruguay	68,037	3,100,000
Swaziland	6,704	700,000	Vanuatu	5,700	200,000
Sweden	173,731	8,400,000	Venezuela	352,143	18,300,000
Switzerland	15,941	6,600,000	Vietnam	127,243	62,200,000
Syria	71,498	11,300,000	Western Samoa	1,097	200,000
Tanzania	364,898	23,500,000	Yemen, People's Democratic Republic of	128,559	2,400,000
Thailand	198,456	53,600,000			
Togo	21,927	3,200,000	Yemen Arab Republic	75,290	6,500,000
Tonga	270	105,000	Yugoslavia	98,766	23,400,000
Trinidad and Tobago	1,981	1,300,000	Zaire	905,563	31,800,000
Tunisia	63,170	7,600,000	Zambia	290,584	7,100,000
Turkey	301,381	51,400,000	Zimbabwe	150,803	9,400,000

1. Square miles. 2. Formerly Upper Volta. 3. Includes the Indian-held part of Jammu and Kashmir. 4. Excludes the Pakistani-held part of Jammu and Kashmir. *Source: 1987 World Population Data Sheet,* Population Reference Bureau, Inc., Washington, D.C.

Some Large Cities of the World

Census figures and population estimates in the following table are based on data reflecting different years. Some cities include metropolitan areas or contiguous suburbs, while others report only those residing within precise geographical or physical boundaries. Therefore, the ratings in this listing must be considered approximate.

City	Population	Year[1]	City	Population	Year[1]
Addis Ababa, Ethiopia	1,423,111	1984E	Chicago	2,992,472	1984E
Ahmedabad, India	2,548,057	1981E	Chittagong, Bangladesh	1,388,476[2]	1981C
Alexandria, Egypt	2,705,000	1983E	Chongqing (Chungking), China	3,890,000	1983E
Algiers	2,500,000	1982E	Cologne, West Germany	919,300	1985E
Amman, Jordon	800,000	1985E	Copenhagen	1,358,540	1985E
Amsterdam	679,100	1986E	Cordoba, Argentina	1,000,000	1983E
Ankara, Turkey	2,251,533	1985C	Cuenca, Ecuador	193,000	1986E
Antwerp, Belgium	488,425	1984C	Damascus, Syria	1,200,000	1981E
Athens	3,027,000	1981C	Delhi, India	5,729,283[2]	1981E
Auckland, New Zealand	894,000	1985E	Dhaka, Bangladesh	3,950,000	1984E
Baghdad, Iraq	3,500,000	1985E	Dnepropetrovsk, U.S.S.R.	1,153,000	1985C
Baku, U.S.S.R.	1,693,000	1985E	Donetsk, U.S.S.R.	1,073,000	1985C
Bandung, Indonesia	1,602,000	1983E	Dresden, East Germany	519,860	1984E
Bangalore, India	2,921,751[2]	1981E	Dublin	550,000	1982E
Bangkok	5,174,682	1984E	Düsseldorf, West Germany	563,000	1985E
Barcelona	1,765,905	1986E	Edinburgh, Scotland	444,700	1982E
Barranquilla, Colombia	896,649	1985E	Edmonton, Canada	657,057	1981C
Beirut, Lebanon	750,000	1981E	Essen, West Germany	625,705	1984E
Belfast, Northern Ireland	324,900	1982E	Florence, Italy	435,698	1984E
Belgrade, Yugoslavia	1,250,000	1982E	Frankfurt, West Germany	598,000	1985E
Belo Horizonte, Brazil	2,500,000	1980E	Fukuoka, Japan	1,172,000	1986E
Berlin[3]	3,033,900	1983E	Geneva	160,000	1987E
Bern, Switzerland	138,600	1987E	Genoa, Italy	738,099	1984E
Birmingham, England	1,017,300	1982E	Glasgow, Scotland	761,000	1982E
Bogotá, Colombia	3,982,941	1985E	Gorky, U.S.S.R.	1,399,000	1985C
Bombay	8,248,405	1981E	Guadalajara, Mexico	3,000,000	1980C
Brisbane, Australia	1,157,200	1985E	Guatemala City	1,250,000	1982E
Brussels	982,434	1984E	Guayaquil, Ecuador	1,509,100	1986E
Bucharest	1,961,189	1984E	The Hague	440,000	1986E
Budapest	2,100,000	1982E	Haifa, Israel	227,900	1983E
Buenos Aires	3,000,000	1983E	Hamburg, West Germany	1,585,900	1985E
Cairo	12,560,000	1987E	Harbin, China	3,730,000	1983E
Calcutta	9,194,018	1981E	Havana	1,992,600	1985E
Calgary, Canada	592,743[2]	1981C	Helsinki, Finland	484,471	1983E
Cali, Colombia	1,323,944	1985E	Ho Chi Minh City (Saigon), Vietnam	3,450,000	1979E
Canton, China	6,840,000	1983E	Hyderabad, India	2,545,836[2]	1981C
Cape Town, South Africa	1,000,000	1984E	Hyderabad, Pakistan	751,529[2]	1981C
Caracas, Venezuela	3,000,000[2]	1981E	Ibadan, Nigeria	1,060,000	1983E
Casablanca, Morocco	2,158,369[2]	1984E	Istanbul	5,494,916	1985C

City	Population	Year[1]
Jakarta, Indonesia	7,636,000	1983E
Jerusalem	431,800	1983E
Johannesburg, South Africa	1,700,000	1984E
Kanpur, India	1,639,064[2]	1981E
Karachi, Pakistan	5,180,562	1981C
Kharkov, U.S.S.R.	1,554,000	1985C
Kiev, U.S.S.R.	2,448,000	1985C
Kinshasa, Zaire	3,000,000	1982E
Kobe, Japan	1,481,000	1986E
Kuala Lumpur, Malaysia	1,000,000	1980E
Kuilbyshev, U.S.S.R.	1,257,000	1985C
Lagos, Nigeria	1,097,000	1983E
Lahore, Pakistan	2,952,700	1981C
La Paz, Bolivia	954,000	1983E
Lausanne, Switzerland	125,000	1987E
Leipzig, East Germany	554,595	1984E
Leningrad	4,867,000	1985C
Liege, Belgium	203,065	1984E
Lima	5,008,400	1985E
Lisbon	900,000	1982E
Liverpool, England	510,700	1982E
Lódz, Poland	849,427	1984E
London	6,765,100	1982E
Los Angeles	3,096,721	1984E
Lyons, France	410,455	1982E
Madras, India	4,289,347[2]	1981E
Madrid	3,217,461	1986E
Managua	682,111	1985E
Manchester, England	458,600	1982E
Manila	1,728,441	1984E
Marseilles, France	868,435	1983E
Mecca, Saudi Arabia	750,000	1980E
Medellin, Colombia	1,418,554	1985E
Melbourne	2,916,600	1985E
Mexico City	12,900,000	1980C
Milan, Italy	1,535,722	1984E
Minsk, U.S.S.R.	1,472,000	1984E
Monterrey, Mexico	2,700,000	1980C
Montevideo, Uruguay	1,325,000	1982E
Montreal	2,878,200	1985E
Moscow	8,642,000	1985C
Munich, West Germany	1,266,100	1985E
Nagoya, Japan	2,128,000	1986E
Nanjing (Nanking), China	4,560,000	1983E
Nantes, France	237,789	1983E
Naples, Italy	1,206,955	1984E
New York	7,164,742	1984E
Nice, France	331,165	1983E
Novosibirsk, U.S.S.R.	1,393,000	1985C
Odessa, U.S.S.R.	1,300,000	1985C
Osaka, Japan	2,642,000	1986E
Oslo	449,300	1985E
Ottawa	769,900	1985E
Palermo	716,149	1984E
Panama City, Panama	424,204	1984E
Paris	2,150,000	1983E
Peking (Beijing)	9,330,000	1983E
Port-au-Prince, Haiti	738,342	1984E
Porto Alegre, Brazil	1,275,483	1985E
Prague	1,193,500	1985E
Pusan, South Korea	3,500,000	1985E
Pyongyang, North Korea	1,500,000	1982E
Quebec	576,075	1981C
Quezon City, Philippines	1,326,035	1984E
Quito, Ecuador	1,093,300	1986E
Rangoon, Burma	2,250,000	1983E
Recife, Brazil	1,289,627	1985E
Rio de Janeiro	5,615,149	1985E
Riyadh, Saudi Arabia	1,250,000	1980E
Rome	2,826,733	1984E
Rosario, Argentina	950,000	1983E
Rotterdam	571,400	1986E
Salvador, Brazil	1,811,367	1985E
San José, Costa Rica	278,500	1984E
Santiago, Chile	4,231,500	1985E
Santo Domingo, Dominican Republic	1,410,000	1983E
São Paulo	12,600,000	1980C
Sapporo, Japan	1,562,000	1986E
Seoul, South Korea	9,600,000	1985E
Seville, Spain	763,949	1986E
Shanghai	11,940,000	1983E
Sheffield, England	545,800	1982E
Shenyang, China	5,210,000	1983E
Singapore, Singapore	2,558,000	1985E
Sofia, Bulgaria	1,094,000	1982E
Stockholm	1,409,000	1985E
Stuttgart, West Germany	561,200	1985E
Surabaja, Indonesia	2,289,000	1983E
Sverdlovsk, U.S.S.R.	1,300,000	1985C
Sydney	3,391,600	1985E
Taipei, Taiwan	2,449,702	1984E
Tashkent, U.S.S.R.	2,030,000	1985C
Tbilisi, U.S.S.R.	1,158,000	1985C
Teheran	6,037,656	1986E
Tel Aviv, Israel	330,400	1983E
Tianjin (Tientsin), China	7,850,000	1983E
Tokyo	8,386,000	1986E
Toronto	2,998,947[2]	1981C
Tripoli, Libya	587,400	1980E
Tunis, Tunisia	600,000	1981E
Turin, Italy	1,049,997	1984E
Valparaiso, Chile	266,900	1985E
Valencia, Spain	763,949	1986E
Vancouver, Canada	1,348,000	1985E
Venice	340,873	1984C
Vienna	1,550,000	1983E
Volgograd, U.S.S.R.	974,000	1985C
Warsaw	1,659,400	1986E
Washington, D.C.	622,823	1984E
Wellington, New Zealand	587,700	1985E
Winnipeg, Canada	584,842[2]	1981C
Yokohama, Japan	3,037,000	1986E
Zurich	351,500	1987E

1. E = estimated; C = census. 2. Figure is for metropolitan area and may include suburbs or some rural population. 3. West Berlin, 1,860,900; East Berlin, 1,173,000 1983E. NOTE: The population of many other cities will be found throughout the World History section under individual countries. *See* Table of Contents.

Our Divided World

Demographically our world is divided in two: the slowly growing portion and the rapidly growing part. The slow-growth portion includes North America, Western and Eastern Europe, including the U.S.S.R., and East Asia, including China. This part of the world contains 2.3 billion people, just under half of the world total and has an annual growth rate of 0.8 percent.

The rapid-growth segment includes Africa, the Middle East, the Indian subcontinent, Southeast Asia, and Latin America. It contains 2.6 billion people and has an annual growth rate of 2.5 percent per year, and adds 64 million people annually compared with 19 million in the slow-growth portion.

Expectation of Life by Age and Sex for Selected Countries

Country	Period	Average future lifetime in years at stated age											
		Males						Females					
		0	1	10	20	40	60	0	1	10	20	40	60
NORTH AMERICA													
United States[1]	1983	71.0	70.9	62.1	52.6	34.1	17.8	78.3	78.0	69.2	59.5	40.2	22.6
Canada	1980-82	71.9	71.7	62.9	53.4	34.7	18.0	78.9	78.6	69.8	60.0	40.7	22.8
Mexico	1975-80	61.9	65.3	58.7	49.4	32.4	17.6	66.3	69.2	62.6	53.2	35.4	19.2
Trinidad and Tobago	1980-85	66.9	67.3	59.0	49.4	31.1	15.8	71.6	71.6	63.2	53.4	34.5	18.4
CENTRAL AND SOUTH AMERICA													
Brazil	1980-85	60.9	—	—	—	—	—	66.0	—	—	—	—	—
Chile	1980-85	63.8	67.0	58.7	49.2	31.4	16.3	70.4	72.7	64.3	54.6	35.9	19.4
Costa Rica	1980-85	70.5	—	—	—	—	—	75.7	—	—	—	—	—
Ecuador[2]	1974-79	59.5	63.3	57.4	48.6	32.1	16.5	61.8	65.4	59.2	50.3	33.5	17.4
Guatemala	1980-85	56.8	—	—	—	—	—	61.3	—	—	—	—	—
Panama[3]	1980-85	69.2	70.2	62.4	53.0	35.0	18.5	72.8	73.6	65.7	56.2	37.6	20.3
Peru[4]	1980-85	56.8	—	—	—	—	—	60.5	—	—	—	—	—
Uruguay	1980-85	67.1	—	—	—	—	—	73.7	—	—	—	—	—
Venezuela	1975-80	64.8	67.1	59.3	50.0	32.4	16.9	70.7	72.5	64.7	55.0	36.4	19.7
EUROPE													
Austria	1984	70.1	70.0	61.2	51.7	33.2	17.0	77.2	77.0	68.2	58.4	39.1	21.1
Belgium	1979-82	70.0	70.0	61.3	51.6	33.0	16.3	76.8	76.6	67.9	58.1	38.8	20.9
Cyprus	1979-81	72.3	72.6	63.8	54.0	34.6	17.3	76.0	76.0	67.2	57.3	37.7	19.5
Czechoslovakia	1984	67.1	67.3	58.7	49.0	30.3	14.8	74.3	74.3	65.9	56.1	36.6	18.9
Denmark[5]	1983-84	71.5	71.2	62.4	52.7	33.9	17.2	77.5	77.1	68.2	58.4	39.1	21.6
Finland	1984	70.4	70.0	61.1	51.4	32.8	16.5	78.8	78.2	69.4	59.5	40.0	21.6
France	1980-82	70.4	70.2	61.5	51.9	33.5	17.4	78.4	78.0	69.3	59.5	40.3	22.3
Germany, East[6]	1984	69.6	69.4	60.7	51.1	32.4	15.9	75.4	75.1	66.4	56.5	37.2	19.3
Germany, West[6]	1982-84	70.8	70.6	61.9	52.3	33.5	16.8	77.5	77.2	68.4	58.6	39.2	21.2
Greece	1980-85	72.1	—	—	—	—	—	76.0	—	—	—	—	—
Hungary	1984	65.5	66.0	57.3	47.6	29.5	15.0	73.7	74.0	65.2	55.4	36.3	19.2
Ireland	1980-82	70.1	69.9	61.2	51.6	32.6	15.9	75.6	75.3	66.6	56.7	37.3	19.5
Italy	1977-79	70.6	70.9	62.2	52.6	33.6	17.0	77.2	77.3	68.5	58.7	39.2	21.1
Netherlands	1983-84	73.0	72.7	63.9	54.2	35.0	17.6	79.5	79.1	70.3	60.5	41.0	22.8
Norway	1982-83	72.7	72.3	63.6	54.0	35.0	18.0	79.5	79.1	70.3	60.5	40.9	22.6
Poland	1984	66.8	67.3	58.6	48.9	30.7	15.5	75.0	75.2	66.5	56.6	37.4	19.7
Portugal	1975	65.1	67.0	58.8	49.4	31.4	15.6	72.9	74.5	66.2	56.5	37.3	19.6
Spain	1975	70.4	70.9	62.3	52.6	33.8	17.1	76.2	76.5	67.8	58.0	38.6	20.6
Sweden	1984	73.8	73.4	64.5	54.7	35.8	18.5	79.9	79.3	70.4	60.6	41.1	22.8
Switzerland	1981-82	72.7	72.3	63.6	53.9	35.3	18.1	79.6	79.1	70.3	60.5	41.2	22.9
U.S.S.R.	1971-72	64.0	—	—	—	—	—	74.0	—	—	—	—	—
United Kingdom													
England and Wales	1982-84	71.6	71.4	62.6	52.9	33.8	16.7	77.6	77.3	68.5	58.6	39.1	21.3
Northern Ireland[1]	1983	69.2	69.3	60.6	50.9	32.1	15.6	75.6	75.4	66.6	56.8	37.4	19.1
Scotland	1982-84	69.8	69.7	61.0	51.3	32.3	15.7	75.9	75.6	66.8	56.9	37.5	20.2
Yugoslavia	1980-81	67.7	69.0	60.4	50.8	32.2	16.2	73.2	74.4	65.9	56.1	36.8	19.0
ASIA													
Bangladesh	1981	55.3	61.3	57.5	48.2	30.0	14.7	54.4	60.0	56.8	47.9	30.8	16.0
India	1980-85	55.6	—	—	—	—	—	55.2	—	—	—	—	—
Iran[4]	1980-85	55.7	60.7	53.8	45.1	29.1	14.5	55.0	60.1	54.3	49.9	30.4	15.3
Israel[7]	1984	73.1	73.0	64.3	54.6	35.6	18.4	76.6	76.6	67.9	58.0	38.5	20.4
Japan[8]	1984	74.5	74.0	65.3	55.6	36.5	19.2	80.2	79.6	70.8	60.9	41.5	23.0
Korea, South	1978-79	62.7	63.7	55.6	46.2	28.1	12.7	69.1	71.0	63.5	53.9	35.0	17.9
Pakistan	1980-85	51.0	—	—	—	—	—	49.0	—	—	—	—	—
Sri Lanka[4]	1981	67.8	69.0	61.0	51.6	33.2	17.7	71.7	72.7	64.7	55.4	37.0	19.6
Syria	1981	63.8	66.9	59.9	50.7	32.7	16.2	64.7	67.0	60.1	50.9	32.8	16.2
AFRICA													
Egypt[4]	1980-85	56.8	—	—	—	—	—	59.5	—	—	—	—	—
Kenya[4]	1980-85	51.2	—	—	—	—	—	54.7	—	—	—	—	—
South Africa[4]	1980-85	51.8	—	—	—	—	—	55.2	—	—	—	—	—
OCEANIA													
Australia[9]	1984	72.6	72.4	63.6	53.9	35.1	17.9	79.1	78.7	69.9	60.1	40.7	22.5
New Zealand	1984	71.2	71.1	62.5	52.9	34.2	17.3	77.7	77.4	68.6	58.8	39.5	21.8

1. Provisional. 2. Excluding nomadic Indian tribes. 3. Excluding tribal Indian population. 4. Estimates prepared by the Population Division of the United Nations. 5. Excluding data for Faeroe Islands and Greenland. 6. Including relevant data relating to Berlin. No separate data have been supplied. 7. Including data for East Jerusalem and Israeli residents in certain other territories under occupation by Israeli military forces since June 1967. 8. Japanese nationals in Japan only. 9. Excluding full-blooded aborigines. NOTE: Figures are latest available. *Source:* United Nations *Demographic Yearbook, 1985.*

Estimates of World Population by Regions

Year	North America[1]	Latin America[2]	Europe[3]	U.S.S.R.	Asia[4]	Africa	Oceania	World total
	Estimated population in millions							
1650	1	7	103	(5)	257	100	2	470
1750	1	10	144	(5)	437	100	2	694
1850	26	33	274	(5)	656	100	2	1,091
1900	81	63	423	(5)	857	141	6	1,571
1950	166	164	392	180	1,380	219	13	2,513
1960	199	215	425	214	1,683	275	16	3,027
1970	226	283	460	244	2,091	354	19	3,678
1980	252	365	484	266	2,618	472	23	4,478
1981	254	370	487	268	2,691	484	23	4,577
1982	257	381	487	270	2,720	501	23	4,640
1983	259	390	489	272	2,771	516	24	4,722
1984	262	398	491	275	2,785	532	24	4,766
1985	264	410	492	278	2,831	566	24	4,865
1986	267	419	493	280	2,876	583	25	4,942
1987	270	421	495	284	2,930	601	25	5,026

1. U.S. (including Alaska and Hawaii), Bermuda, Canada, Greenland, and St. Pierre and Miquelon. 2. Mexico, Central and South America, and Caribbean Islands. 3. Includes Russia 1650–1900. 4. Excludes Russia (U.S.S.R.). 5. Included in Europe. NOTE: From 1930 on European Turkey included in Asia not Europe. *Sources:* W.F. Willcox, 1650–1900; United Nations, 1930–79. United States Department of Commerce, Bureau of the Census, 1981, 1982, 1983, 1984; *1986* & *1987 World Population Data Sheet*, Population Reference Bureau, Inc., Washington, D.C.

Crude Birth and Death Rates for Selected Countries

(per 1,000 population)

Country	Birth rates 1985	1984	1983	1980	1975	Death rates 1985	1984	1983	1980	1975
Australia	15.7	15.1	15.8	15.3	16.9	7.5	7.1	7.3	7.4	7.9
Austria	11.4	11.7	11.9	12.0	12.5	11.9	11.6	12.3	12.2	12.8
Belgium	11.5	11.7	11.9	12.7	12.2	11.2	11.1	11.3	11.6	12.2
Canada	14.8	15.0	15.0	15.4	15.8	7.2	7.0	7.0	7.2	7.4
Cuba	18.0	16.6	16.7	14.1	n.a.	6.4	6.0	5.9	5.7	n.a.
Czechoslovakia	14.5	14.7	14.8	16.4	19.6	11.8	11.8	12.0	12.1	11.5
Denmark	10.6	10.1	9.9	11.2	14.2	11.4	11.2	11.2	10.9	10.1
El Salvador	n.a.	29.8	27.6	34.7	38.9	n.a.	6.0	6.3	7.9	7.9
Finland	12.8	13.3	13.8	13.1	13.9	9.8	9.2	9.3	9.3	9.3
France	13.9	13.8	13.7	14.8	14.1	10.1	9.8	10.2	10.2	10.6
Germany, East	13.7	13.7	14.0	14.6	10.8	13.5	13.3	13.3	14.2	14.3
Germany, West	9.6	9.5	9.7	10.0	9.7	11.5	11.3	11.7	11.6	12.1
Greece	11.7	12.8	13.6	15.4	15.7	9.4	8.9	9.1	9.1	8.9
Hong Kong	14.0	14.4	15.4	16.9	n.a.	4.6	4.8	5.0	5.1	n.a.
Hungary	12.2	11.7	11.9	13.9	18.4	13.9	13.7	13.9	13.6	12.4
Ireland	17.5	18.2	19.0	21.9	21.5	9.0	9.1	9.3	9.7	10.6
Israel	23.5	23.7	24.1	24.1	28.2	6.6	6.7	6.8	6.7	7.1
Italy	10.1	10.3	10.6	11.2	14.8	9.5	9.3	9.9	9.7	9.9
Japan	11.9	12.5	12.7	13.7	17.2	6.2	6.2	6.2	6.2	6.4
Luxembourg	11.2	11.5	11.5	11.5	11.2	11.8	11.2	11.3	11.5	12.2
Malta	14.2	14.8	15.0	16.0	18.3	7.4	7.9	8.3	8.8	8.8
Mauritius	18.8	19.7	20.7	27.0	25.1	6.8	6.6	6.6	7.2	8.1
Mexico	n.a.	n.a.	n.a.	35.3	37.5	n.a.	n.a.	n.a.	6.2	7.2
Netherlands	12.3	12.1	11.8	12.8	13.0	8.5	8.3	8.2	8.1	8.3
New Zealand	15.6	16.0	15.8	n.a.	18.4	8.4	7.9	8.1	n.a.	8.1
Norway	12.3	12.1	12.1	12.5	14.1	10.7	10.3	10.2	10.1	9.9
Panama	26.6	25.5	26.4	26.8	32.3	n.a.	n.a.	n.a.	n.a.	n.a.
Poland	18.2	18.9	19.7	19.5	18.9	10.3	9.9	9.5	9.8	8.7
Portugal	12.5	13.6	14.4	16.4	19.1	9.6	n.a	9.3	9.9	10.4
Singapore	16.6	16.4	16.2	17.3	17.8	5.2	5.2	5.3	5.2	5.1
Spain	n.a.	12.0	12.5	16.1	19.1	n.a.	7.6	7.8	7.7	8.2
Sweden	11.8	11.3	11.0	11.7	12.6	11.3	10.9	10.9	11.0	10.8
Switzerland	11.6	11.5	11.4	11.3	12.3	9.2	9.1	9.3	9.2	8.7
Tunisia	n.a.	n.a.	n.a.	35.2	36.6	n.a.	n.a.	n.a.	n.a.	n.a.
United Kingdom	13.3	12.9	13.0	13.5	12.5	11.8	11.4	11.9	11.8	11.9
United States	15.7	15.7	15.5	16.2	14.8	8.7	8.7	8.6	8.9	8.9
Yugoslavia	15.9	16.4	16.6	17.0	18.2	9.1	9.3	9.6	9.0	8.7

NOTE: n.a. = not available. *Source:* United Nations, *Monthly Bulletin of Statistics,* May 1987.

Cost of Living of United Nations Personnel in Selected Cities as Reflected by Index of Retail Prices, 1986

(New York City, December 1986 = 100)

City	Index	City	Index	City	Index
Abu Dhabi	87[1]	Dar es Salaam	56[1]	New Delhi	51
Addis Ababa	76[1]	Geneva	122	Panama City	84
Algiers	98[1]	Guatemala City	70	Paris	100
Amman	85	The Hague	89	Port-au-Prince	73
Ankara	50	Islamabad	50	Quito	61
Athens	77	Jakarta	70	Rabat	61
Baghdad	111[1]	Kabul	77	Rangoon	81
Bangkok	62	Katmandu	45	Rio de Janeiro	60
Beirut	41	Kingston	68	San Salvador	70
Belgrade	71	Kinshasa	72[1]	Santiago	54
Bogota	53	La Paz	83	Seoul	80
Bonn	108	Lagos	55[1]	Sofia	88
Brazzaville	77[1]	Lima	80	Sydney	66
Brussels	106	London	88	Tokyo	142
Budapest	49	Madrid	97	Tripoli	98[1]
Buenos Aires	87	Managua	59	Tunis	55
Cairo	80	Manila	63	Valetta	68
Caracas	35	Mexico City	43	Vienna	97
Colombo	50	Montevideo	63	Vientiane	75[1]
Copenhagen	99	Montreal	72	Warsaw	54
Dacca	52	Nairobi	60	Washington D.C.	93
Dakar	95	Nassau	107		

1. Calculated on the basis of cost of Government or subsidized housing which is normally lower than prevailing rentals. *Source:* United Nations, *Monthly Bulletin of Statistics, March 1987.*

Unemployment Figures for Selected Countries: 1981-1986

(In thousands except for percentages)

	1986		1985		1984		1983		1982		1981	
Country	No.	%	No.	%	No.	%	No.	%	No.	%	No.	%
Australia	609.9	8.1	601.6	8.3	642.1	9.0	697.0	10.0	494.9	7.2	393.9	5.8
Austria[1]	152.0	5.2	139.5	4.8	130.5	4.5	127.4	4.5	105.3	3.7	69.3	2.4
Belgium[1 2 8]	516.8	12.3	557.4	13.5	595.0	14.4	589.5	14.3	559.8	13.8	471.6	11.6
Canada	1,236.0	9.6	1,327.9	10.5	1,399.0	11.3	1,448.0	11.9	1,314.0	11.0	898.0	7.5
Chile	n.a.	n.a.	273.4	17.0	285.0	18.4	279.0	19.0	272.1	20.0	121.3	9.0
Cyprus[1]	n.a.	n.a.	8.3	3.3	8.0	3.3	7.8	3.3	6.4	2.8	5.9	2.6
Denmark	217.3	8.0	247.8	9.2	276.3	10.3	283.0	10.6	262.8	9.8	243.0	9.2
Finland[3]	140.0	5.4	163.2	6.3	158.0	6.2	156.0	6.1	149.0	5.9	127.0	5.1
Germany, West[1]	2,228.0	9.0	2,304.0	9.3	2,265.6	9.1	2,258.2	9.1	1,833.2	7.5	1,271.6	5.5
Hong-Kong	n.a.	n.a.	83.6	3.2	101.0	3.9	113.9	4.5	95.6	3.8	96.4	3.9
Ireland[4]	236.4	18.2	230.6	17.7	214.2	16.2	192.7	14.7	156.6	12.1	96.1	13.5
Israel[5]	n.a.	n.a.	97.0	6.7	85.0	5.9	63.0	4.5	68.4	5.0	68.4	5.0
Italy	2,611.0	n.a.	2,471.0	10.6	2,391.0	10.4	2,264.0	9.9	2,052.0	9.1	1,895.0	8.4
Japan	1,670.0	2.8	1,564.3	2.6	1,600.0	2.7	1,560.0	2.6	1,360.0	2.4	1,260.0	2.2
Korea	611.0	3.8	619.0	4.0	567.0	3.8	614.0	4.1	656.0	4.4	661.0	4.5
Netherlands[1 2]	710.7	12.0	761.0	15.6	822.4	17.6	800.6	17.1	541.7	12.6	385.3	9.1
Norway	40.0	1.9	51.0	2.5	61.0	3.0	67.0	3.3	52.0	2.6	40.0	2.0
Philippines[6]	n.a.	n.a.	1,316.0	6.1	1,231.0	6.1	850.0	4.1	1,084.0	5.5	1,008.0	5.4
Portugal	n.a.	n.a.	384.7	8.5	381.0	8.3	354.8	7.7	315.5	7.4	355.5	8.2
Puerto Rico[7]	n.a.	n.a.	211.0	21.8	198.0	20.7	220.0	23.4	208.0	22.8	184.0	19.9
Sweden	117.0	2.1	125.0	2.8	136.0	3.1	151.0	3.5	137.0	3.1	107.6	2.5
Switzerland[1 8]	25.7	0.8	30.3	1.0	35.2	1.1	26.3	0.9	13.2	0.4	6.0	0.2
United Kingdom[1 9]	3,289.1	11.9	3,271.2	13.5	3,159.8	13.1	3,104.7	12.9	3,119.0	13.1	2,733.8	11.1
United States	8,237.0	7.0	8,312.0	7.2	8,539.0	7.5	10,717.0	9.6	10,678.0	9.7	8,273.0	7.6
Yugoslavia[1]	1,086.7	13.9	1,040.0	13.8	974.8	13.3	910.3	12.8	862.5	12.4	808.6	11.9

1. Employment office statistics. All others labor force sample surveys unless otherwise indicated. 2. Scope of series revised as of 1983. 3. Scope of series revised as of 1983 and 1986. 4. Excluding agriculture, fishing and private domestic services. 5. Including persons who did not work in the country during the previous 12 months. 6. Average of less than 12 months. 7. Excluding people temporarily laid off. 8. Scope of series revised as of 1984. 9. Excluding persons temporarily laid off. Excluding adult students registered for vacation employment. NOTE: n.a.= not available. *Source:* United Nations, *Monthly Bulletin of Statistics, June 1987.*

Value of Exports and Imports

(in millions of U.S. dollars)

Country	Exports[1]	Imports[1]
Afghanistan	566[2]	999[2]
Algeria	11,886[3]	10,289[3]
Argentina	8,396[2]	3,814[2]
Australia	22,883[2]	23,450[2]
Austria	22,522	26,843
Bahamas	1,426[2]	2,420[2]
Bahrain	2,863[2]	3,159[2]
Bangladesh	927[2]	2,170[2]
Barbados	352[2]	607[2]
Belgium-Luxembourg	68,873	68,650
Benin	24[4]	464[4]
Bolivia	673[2]	765[2]
Brazil	25,639[2]	13,168[2]
Bulgaria	13,348[2]	13,656[2]
Burkina Faso	79[3]	207[3]
Burma	265	304
Burundi	233	206
Cameroon	605[2]	1,314[2]
Canada	86,725	81,099
Cape Verde	4[5]	68[5]
Central African Republic	88[2]	109[2]
Chile	3,823[2]	3,007[2]
Colombia	3,552[2]	4,131[2]
Congo	1,066[6]	806[6]
Costa Rica	1,026	1,130
Cuba	8,567[2]	8,593[2]
Cyprus	499	1,336
Czechoslovakia	20,456	20,950
Denmark	21,201	22,811
Dominican Republic	741[2]	1,378[2]
Ecuador	2,780[2]	1,674[2]
Egypt	3,714[2]	9,962[2]
El Salvador	679[2]	961[2]
Ethiopia	333[2]	996[2]
Fiji	236[2]	442[2]
Finland	16,340	15,325
France	119,435	128,836
Gabon	1,920[2]	976[2]
Gambia	43[2]	93[2]
Germany, East	24,189	22,100
Germany, West	242,411	189,484
Ghana	617[2]	731[2]
Greece	5,650	11,349
Guatemala	1,066[2]	1,175[2]
Guinea-Bissau	12[4]	50[4]
Guyana	189[6]	230[6]
Haiti	179[3]	472[3]
Honduras	746[3]	954[3]
Hungary	9,183	9,613
Iceland	1,096	1,116
India	8,510[2]	15,092[2]
Indonesia	14,805	10,718
Iran	20,247[6]	18,296[6]
Iraq	10,530[7]	7,903[7]
Ireland	13,161	12,610
Israel	6,080[2]	8,021[2]
Italy	97,835	99,937
Ivory Coast	2,939[2]	1,742[2]
Jamaica	564[2]	1,110[2]
Japan	209,153	126,408
Jordan	647	2,432
Kenya	1,200	1,613
Korea, South	35,710	32,742
Kuwait	10,751[3]	7,699[3]
Liberia	436[2]	284[2]
Libya	13,951[4]	7,175[4]
Madagascar	274[2]	402[2]
Malawi	243	252
Malaysia	13,917[4]	13,987[4]
Mali	192	438
Malta	497	887
Mauritania	374[2]	234[2]
Mauritius	441[2]	528[2]
Mexico	21,822[2]	14,015[2]
Morocco	2,165[2]	3,849[2]
Netherlands	80,744	75,580
New Zealand	5,944	6,135
Nicaragua	385[3]	826[3]
Nigeria	12,547[2]	8,855[2]
Norway	18,096	20,306
Oman	4,972[2]	3,153[2]
Pakistan	3,306	5,373
Panama	306[2]	1,391[2]
Papua-New Guinea	909[2]	873[2]
Paraguay	403[2]	719[2]
Peru	2,467	2,160
Philippines	4,842	5,394
Poland	11,913	11,114
Portugal	7,205	9,458
Qatar	3,297[6]	1,456[6]
Romania	10,735[3]	7,565[3]
Rwanda	118	352
Saudi Arabia	45,835[6]	39,206[6]
Senegal	547[2]	903[2]
Sierra Leone	112[2]	156[2]
Singapore	22,494	25,512
Solomon Islands	67	73
Somalia	91[2]	112[2]
Spain	27,158	35,022
Sri Lanka	1,180	1,829
Sudan	367[2]	757[2]
Suriname	356[3]	346[3]
Sweden	37,221	32,508
Switzerland	37,674	41,278
Syria	1,637[2]	3,967[2]
Tanzania	284[2]	1,026[2]
Thailand	7,119[2]	9,261[2]
Togo	197[3]	278[3]
Tonga	5[2]	41[2]
Trinidad	2,164	1,525[2]
Tunisia	1,760	2,888
Turkey	7,913[2]	11,394[2]
Uganda	345[5]	293[5]
U.S.S.R.	87,041[2]	82,748[2]
United Arab Emirates	17,257[4]	9,419[4]
U.K.	107,013	126,208
U.S.	217,304	387,081
Uruguay	854[2]	708[2]
Vanuatu	31[2]	71[2]
Venezuela	12,272[2]	7,559[2]
Western Samoa	11	48
Yemen, People's	27[3]	821[3]
Yemen Arab	27[6]	1,593[6]
Yugoslavia	10,297	11,749
Zaire	591[2]	997[2]
Zambia	539[2]	698[2]
Zimbabwe	1,053[2]	969[2]

1. 1986 unless otherwise indicated. 2. 1985. 3. 1984. 4. 1982. 5. 1980. 6. 1983. 7. 1981. *Source:* United Nations, *Monthly Bulletin of Statistics,* June 1987.

Energy, Petroleum, and Coal, by Country

	Energy consumed[1] (coal equiv.)				Electric energy production[2] (bil. kwh)		Crude petroleum production[3] (mil. metric tons)		Coal production[4] (mil. metric tons)	
	Total (mil. metric tons)		Per capita (kilograms)							
Country	1984	1980	1984	1980	1984	1980	1984	1980	1984	1980
Algeria	15.0	24.8	707	1,327	11.5	7.1	36.9	47.4	(Z)[6]	(Z)
Argentina	51.7	49.3	1,718	1,746	44.9	39.7	24.6	25.3	.5	.4
Australia[7]	95.1	91.2	6,128	6,195	112.9	96.1	20.6	18.9	104.2	72.5
Austria	30.0	30.5	4,007	4,058	41.8	42.0	1.2	1.5	(X)	—
Bahrain	5.5	4.4	13,242	12,651	2.1	1.7	2.0	2.4	n.a.	—
Bangladesh	5.2	3.8	53	44	4.3	2.7	(Z)	(Z)	(X)	(X)
Belgium	48.8	59.1	4,939	5,997	53.7	53.6	(X)	(X)	6.3	6.3
Brazil	87.1	92.5	656	763	175.7	139.5	23.1	9.1	7.5	5.2
Bulgaria	50.7	47.3	5,523	5,254	44.6	34.8	.3	.3[6]	.2	.3
Burma	3.0	2.2	78	62	1.7	1.3	1.6	1.6	(Z)	(Z)
Canada	247.3	254.2	9,773	10,547	438.0	377.5	70.6	70.4	32.1	20.2
Chile	10.9	11.4	920	1,025	13.5	11.8	1.9	1.6	1.2	1.0
China: Mainland	684.0	562.8	664	571	377.0	300.6	114.6	105.9	759.1	595.8
Taiwan[8]	41.2[18]	37.9	2,197[18]	2,127	47.5[18]	42.0	.1[18]	.2	2.2[18]	2.6
Colombia	24.1	23.8	857	923	27.8	22.9	8.6	6.5	6.1[6]	4.9
Cuba	14.6	13.6	1,467	1,394	12.3	9.9	.8	.3	(X)	(X)
Czechoslovakia	96.6	97.4	6,197	6,364	78.4	72.7	.1	.1	26.4[9]	28.3[9]
Denmark	23.2	26.9	4,521	5,254	22.4	27.1	2.3	.3	(X)	(X)
Ecuador	6.2	5.7	677	708	4.4	3.4	13.1	10.4	n.a.	(NA)
Egypt	29.3	20.1	641	488	22.9	18.9	41.2	29.4	(X)	(X)
Ethiopia	.7	.9	20	27	.8	.7	(X)	(X)	n.a.	(NA)
Finland	24.3	26.4	5,002	5,514	43.3[5]	38.7[5]	(X)	(X)	(X)	(X)
France[10]	213.7	237.3	3,923	4,409	306.8[5]	246.4[5]	2.1	1.2	18.3[9]	20.2[9]
Germany, East	126.6	121.8	7,600	7,276	110.1	98.8	(Z)	.1	(Z)	(Z)
Germany, West	340.6	359.4	5,564	5,829	376.6	368.8	4.1	4.6	84.9	94.5
Greece	22.2	20.1	2,243	2,088	24.8	22.7	1.3	(Z)	(X)	(X)
Hong Kong	9.7	7.3	1,761	1,448	17.9	12.6	n.a.	(NA)	(X)	(X)
Hungary	40.9	40.6	3,790	3,787	26.3	23.9	2.1	2.0	2.6[9]	3.1[9]
India	176.9	139.4	237	202	165.4	119.3	27.9	9.4	144.9	109.1
Indonesia	42.6	34.7	263	230	21.3	14.2	68.5	77.6	1.1	.3
Iran	58.2	45.7[15]	1,328	1,177[15]	37.2	22.4[15]	109.2	72.7[15]	.9[6]	.9[15]
Iraq	8.1	10.7	535	807	18.5	11.4	58.5[6]	130.1	n.a.	(NA)
Ireland	11.5	11.1	3,248	3,268	11.2	10.9	(X)	(X)	.1	.1
Israel	9.8	8.8	2,329	2,273	14.9	12.5	(Z)	(Z)	(X)	(X)
Italy[11]	176.2	174.9	3,105	3,112	179.5	185.7	2.2	1.8	(Z)	(Z)[6]
Japan	454.1	434.8	3,800	3,726	647.4	577.5	.4	.4	16.6	18.0
North Korea	52.7	48.5	2,685	2,713	45.0	35.0	(X)	(X)	38.0[6]	36.0[6]
South Korea	61.4	52.3	1,524	1,373	58.2	40.1	(X)	(X)	20.6	18.6
Kuwait[12]	11.5	6.9	6,727	5,019	14.2	9.4	58.9	84.1	n.a.	n.a.
Libya	13.1	7.3	3,772	2,456	7.3	4.8	52.8	88.3	(X)	(X)
Malaysia	13.3	12.2	875	882	13.7	10.2	21.7	13.2	(X)	(X)
Mexico	132.1	118.6	1,714	1,709	87.1[5]	67.0[5]	143.3	99.9	7.8[6]	7.0
Morocco	6.8	6.4	296	319	6.6	4.9	(Z)[6]	(Z)	.8[6]	.7
Netherlands	84.6	93.0	5,853	6,543	62.8	64.8	3.1	1.3	(Z)[6 17]	(Z)
New Zealand	12.6	10.0	3,866	3,152	26.5	22.0	.8	.3	2.3	2.0
Nigeria	21.2	11.0	231	136	8.8	7.2	67.5	104.2	(Z)[6]	.2
Norway[16]	27.2	26.3	6,570	6,423	106.1	84.1	35.0	24.6	.5	.3
Pakistan	21.3	16.6	215	191	21.9	15.3	.7	.5	1.9	1.5
Peru	12.3	12.0	640	693	11.8	9.8	9.1	9.6	.1[6]	.1[6]
Philippines	16.7	16.7	312	346	20.8	17.9	.6[6]	.5	1.1[6]	.3
Poland	167.3	176.8	4,494	4,935	134.8	121.9	.2	.3	191.6	193.1
Portugal	13.1	11.2	1,307	1,153	19.0	15.3	(X)	(X)	.2	.2
Romania	104.4	100.0	4,558	4,505	72.5	67.5	11.5	11.5	8.0[6]	8.1
Saudi Arabia[11]	39.4	25.3	3,640	2,745	31.2	18.9	229.0	495.9	n.a.	n.a.
South Africa[13]	94.5	90.2	2,606	2,751	122.4	90.4	(X)	(X)	140.6	116.6
Soviet Union	1,648.3	1,473.1	5,977	5,549	1,493.0	1,293.9	612.7	603.2	482.3	492.9
Spain	84.4	88.4	2,180	2,359	115.5	110.5	2.3	1.6	15.6[9]	13.1[9]
Sudan	1.6	1.5	77	82	1.0	1.0	(X)	(X)	n.a.	n.a.
Sweden	39.0	44.5	4,703	5,376	123.5	96.7	(Z)	(Z)	(Z)	(Z)
Switzerland[14]	23.7	23.3	3,733	3,636	48.1[5]	48.1[5]	(X)	(X)	(X)	(X)
Syria	9.2	7.3	902	835	6.8	3.8	9.5	8.3	(X)	(X)
Tanzania	.9	.8	42	44	.9	.7	(X)	(X)	(Z)[6]	(Z)
Thailand	20.9	17.3	414	372	22.0	15.1	.8	(Z)	(Z)	(Z)
Trinidad and Tobago	5.9	7.5	5,311	6,992	2.7	2.0	8.8	11.0	n.a.	n.a.

Country	Energy consumed[1] (coal equiv.) Total (mil. metric tons) 1984	Total 1980	Per capita (kilograms) 1984	Per capita 1980	Electric energy production[2] (bil. kwh) 1984	1980	Crude petroleum production[3] (mil. metric tons) 1984	1980	Coal production[4] (mil. metric tons) 1984	1980
Tunisia	4.7	4.1	671	639	3.6	2.8	5.5	5.6	(X)	(X)
Turkey	42.2	31.9	865	718	30.6	23.3	2.1	2.3	3.6	3.6
United Arab Emirates	9.6	16.8	7,678	17,188	6.6	6.3	56.1	82.8	n.a.	n.a.
United Kingdom	264.7	271.0	4,760	4,850	280.5	284.9	121.2	78.9	51.2[9]	130.1[9]
United States	2,257.1	2,364.5	9,577	10,386	2,472.0	2,354[6]	438.1	424.2	750.3	710.4
Venezuela	55.2	49.0	3,100	3,140	44.3	35.9	94.9	114.8	.1	(Z)
Vietnam	7.2	6.6	123	122	5.8	3.8	n.a.	n.a.	6.0[6]	5.2
Yugoslavia	57.2	48.0	2,484	2,152	72.3	59.4	4.0	4.2	.4	.4
Zaire	2.0	2.0	63	69	4.6	4.2	1.5[6]	1.0	.1[6]	.1
Zambia	2.2	2.3	339	403	10.1[5]	9.2	(X)	(X)	.5[6]	.6
World, total	**8,855.8**	**8,544.3**	**1,859**	**1,919**	**9,267.0**	**8,247**	**2,709.0**	**2,979**	**2,942.0**	**2,728**

— Represents zero. n.a.=not available. X=Not applicable. Z=Less than 50,000 metric tons. 1. Based on apparent consumption of coal, lignite, petroleum products, natural gas, and hydro, nuclear, and geothermal electricity. 2. Comprises production by utilities generating primarily for public use, and production by industrial establishments generating primarily for own use. Relates to production at generating centers, including station use and transmission losses. 3. Includes shale oil, but excludes natural gasoline. 4. Excludes lignite and brown coal, except as noted. 5. Net production, i.e. excluding station use. 6. United Nations Statistical Office estimate. 7. For year ending June 30 of year shown. 8. Source: U.S. Bureau of the Census. Data from Republic of China publications. 9. Includes slurries. 10. Includes Monaco. 11. Includes San Marino. 12. Includes share of production and consumption in the Neutral Zone. 13. Includes Botswana, Lesotho, Namibia, and Swaziland. 14. Includes Liechtenstein. 15. For the year ending March 20 of year shown. 16. Includes Svalbard and Jan Mayen Islands. 17. Includes patent fuel and hard coal briquettes. 18. 1983 data. *Source:* Except as noted, Statistical Office of the United Nations, New York, N.Y., *Energy Statistics Yearbook, 1983.* (copyright.) From: *Statistical Abstract of the United States 1987.*

Wheat, Rice, and Corn—Production by Country

(in thousands of metric tons)

Country	Wheat 1984	Wheat 1983	Wheat 1982	Rice 1984	Rice 1983	Rice 1982	Corn 1984	Corn 1983	Corn 1982
Afghanistan	2,850[2]	3,750[1]	2,862	466[2]	650[1]	473	800[2]	1,000[1]	800
Argentina	13,000[1]	11,700	15,130	476	277	437	9,500	8,840	9,600
Australia	18,580	21,780	8,879	635	522	854	210	95	212
Austria	1.501	1,415	1,236	n.a.	n.a.	n.a.	1,542	1,437	1,551
Bangladesh	1,200	1,095	967	21,500	21,700	21,322	1[2]	1[1]	1
Belgium[3]	1,330	1,084[2]	1,068	n.a.	n.a.	n.a.	39[2]	38[2]	36[1]
Brazil	1,830	2,273	1,849	9,023	7,760	9,716	21,174	18,756	21,865
Bulgaria	3,600[1]	3,600	4,913	74[1]	72	75	3,000[2]	3,101	3,418
Burma	191	183	124	14,500[2]	14,500[2]	14,758	360	301	206
Cambodia	n.a.	n.a.	n.a.	1,300[2]	1,700	1,400	75[2]	60[2]	46
Canada	21,199	26,914	26,790	n.a.	n.a.	n.a.	7,024	5,875	6,513
Chile	988	800[2]	650	165	107	131	721	512[1]	425
China: Mainland[2]	87,682	81,392	68,422	181,028	172,184	164,493	72,690	64,135	60,413
Colombia	76[1]	73[1]	69[1]	1,696	1,780	2,018	874[1]	867[1]	899
Cuba	n.a.	n.a.	n.a.	555	490	520	97[2]	96[2]	96[2]
Czechoslovakia	6,170	5,820[1]	4,606	n.a.	n.a.	n.a.	940	710[2]	941
Denmark	2,446	1,577	1,207	n.a.	n.a.	n.a.	n.a.	n.a.	n.a.
Ecuador	24[1]	23[1]	39	470[1]	222	384	300[1]	258[1]	324
Egypt	1,815	1,996	2,017	2,230[1]	2,440	2,441	3,600	3,510[1]	3,347
Ethiopia	675[2]	950[2]	917	n.a.	n.a.	n.a.	1,275[2]	1,600[2]	1,603
Finland	478	550	435	n.a.	n.a.	n.a.	n.a.	n.a.	n.a.
France	32,884	24,781	25,342	42	32	27	10,321	10,143	10,381
Germany, East	4,100[2]	3,470	2,739	n.a.	n.a.	n.a.	20[1]	1[1]	1
Germany, West	10,223	8,998	8,632	n.a.	n.a.	n.a.	1,026	934	1,054
Greece	2,646	2,026	2,983	91	78	83	1,992	1,622	1,448
Hungary	7,300[1]	4,800[2]	5,762	30[1]	40[2]	48	6,700[1]	7,600[2]	7,959
India	45,148	42,502	37,452	91,000[2]	90,000[2]	69,648	7,750[2]	7,300[2]	6,274
Indonesia	n.a.	n.a.	n.a.	37,500[1]	34,300	34,104	4,000[2]	4,000[1]	3,207
Iran	5,500[2]	6,669[2]	6,500[1]	1,230[2]	1,400[2]	1,400[2]	50[2]	55[2]	53[2]
Iraq	300[2]	1,000	965	95[2]	200[2]	163	25[2]	90[2]	28
Ireland	660	350[1]	400	n.a.	n.a.	n.a.	n.a.	n.a.	n.a.
Israel	130	335	147	n.a.	n.a.	n.a.	26	28	22
Italy	10,005	8,514	8,903	1,027	1,060	964	6,781	6,900	6,847

Japan	741	747	742	14,848	12,958	12,838	3[1]	2[1]	2
Korea, North[2]	600	500	450	5,400	5,200	5,000	2,580	2,500	2,330
Korea, South	17	112	66	7,970	7,608	7,308	133	101	117
Laos	n.a.	n.a.	n.a.	1,322	1,002	1,088	40[2]	39	35
Madagascar	([4])	([4])	([4])	2,132	2,147	1,967	141	115	113
Malaysia	n.a.	n.a.	n.a.	1,755	2,000	1,832	22	9[2]	8
Mexico	4,262	3,697	4,468	635	655	600	14,050	13,928	10,129
Nepal	634	657	526	2,760[2]	2,744	1,833	751	768	718
Netherlands	1,133	1,043	967	n.a.	n.a.	n.a.	2[2]	([4])	2[2]
New Zealand	294	280	321	n.a.	n.a.	n.a.	172	176[1]	214
Pakistan	11,053	12,414	11,304	5,009	5,210	5,167	1,100[2]	1,000[1]	1,005
Panama	n.a.	n.a.	n.a.	175[1]	169[2]	176	80[1]	68[1]	62
Peru	88	75	101	1,134	770	765	576	583	625
Philippines	n.a.	n.a.	n.a.	8,280[1]	8,150	7,731	3,400[2]	3,385	3,126
Poland	6,010	5,165	4,476	n.a.	n.a.	n.a.	57	64	68
Portugal	475	281	437	134	100[1]	143	530[1]	475[1]	464
Romania	7,900[1]	5,000[1]	6,460	75[1]	50	46	13,000[1]	10,500[2]	12,620
South Africa	2,150	1,770	2,420	3	3[2]	3[2]	4,440	3,910	8,359
Soviet Union[2]	76,000[2]	82,000	87,000	2,500[2]	2,500	2,500	13,000[2]	14,000	12,000
Spain	6,044	4,330	4,410	437	223	402	2,505	1,788	2,330
Sri Lanka	n.a.	n.a.	n.a.	2,270[1]	2,200	2,156	31[2]	25[2]	24[2]
Sweden	1,776	1,721	1,490	n.a.	n.a.	n.a.	n.a.	n.a.	n.a.
Switzerland	577	436	433	n.a.	n.a.	n.a.	143	136	173
Syria	1,051	1,612	1,556	([4])	([4])	([4])	40[2]	70[1]	50
Thailand	n.a.	n.a.	n.a.	19,200[2]	18,535	16,878	4,150	3,552	3,002
Turkey	17,235	16,400	17,542	280	325[2]	350	1,500	1,375[2]	1,360
United Kingdom	14,960	10,880	10,320	n.a.	n.a.	n.a.	1[2]	1[2]	1[2]
United States	70,638	66,010	76,538	6,216	4,523	6,967	194,475	106,781	212,338
Uruguay	450[2]	450[1]	316	340	332[1]	419	120[1]	103[1]	97
Venezuela	([4])	([4])	([4])	408	509	670	547	429	501
Vietnam	n.a.	n.a.	n.a.	15,416	14,500[2]	14,500	475[2]	420[2]	437
Yugoslavia	5,596	5,519	5,218	36	40	42	11,265[1]	10,688	11,126
World, total	521,682	498,182	486,423	469,959	449,827	423,464	449,255	344,103	451,080

1. Unofficial figure. 2. FAO estimate 3. Includes Luxembourg. 4. None or negligible. NOTES: Rice data cover rough and paddy. Data for each country pertain to the calendar year in which all or most of the crop was harvested. n.a.= not available. *Source: Food and Agriculture Organization of the United Nations, Rome, Italy. 1983 FAO Production Yearbook, vol. 37* (copyright). From: *Statistical Abstract of the United States 1987.*

Consumer Price Indexes for Selected Countries

(1967=100)

Country	Total Indexes[1]				Average annual percent change	Indexes for Selected Items, 1985			
	1985	1984	1983	1980	1980–1985	Food[1]	Clothing	Housing[2]	Transportation
Australia	440.2	412.4	396.7	295.5	8.3	423.0	415.8	497.2	(NA)
Austria	258.0	249.9	236.6	203.3	4.9	228.4	210.0	308.7	281.5
Canada	348.4	334.9	321.0	243.5	7.4	390.2	242.1	352.3	361.0
France	464.8	439.2	408.9	294.2	9.6	468.4	418.9	505.3	543.6
Germany, West	212.4	207.9	201.9	175.8	3.9	185.7	211.6	239.0	229.3
Italy	767.3	702.7	634.2	403.2	13.7	689.3	832.7	765.0	917.1
Japan	322.9	316.4	309.4	281.8	2.7	329.7	346.7	263.4	280.6
Netherlands	291.4	284.9	276.2	237.4	4.2	232.3	297.0	323.7	278.1
Sweden	416.2	387.5	358.8	270.6	9.0	487.8	262.1	472.0	(NA)
United Kingdom	599.5	565.1	538.3	423.6	7.2	615.0	332.5	642.6	612.2
United States	322.2	311.1	298.4	246.8	5.5	309.8	191.6	349.9	319.9

1. Includes other items not shown separately. 2. Restaurant meals, alcohol, and tobacco are included for some countries, excluded for others. 3. Includes shelter, utilities, and household furnishings and operations. However, actual coverage and measurements vary significantly from country to country. NOTE: n.a. = not available. *Source:* United States Department of Labor, Bureau of Labor Statistics.

India To Surpass China As Most Populous

China's one-child-per-family campaign, seen by Chinese leaders as being for this generation only, will succeed in its goal of holding the country's population to 1.2 billion in the year 2000. India, on the other hand, is unlikely to come anywhere near its goal of replacement level fertility by 2000. India's population, estimated at 785 million in 1986 and growing by 16 million a year, compared to 9 million in China, will overtake China's as the world's largest by 2020.

Meat—Production by Country

(in thousands of metric tons)

Country	1984, est.	1983	1980	Country	1984, est.	1983	1980
Argentina	2,919	2,764	3,267	Italy	2,455	2,382	2,305
Australia[1]	1,983	2,313	2,332	Japan	1,969	1,924	1,893
Belgium[2]	1,014	1,003	985	Mexico	1,318	1,269	1,145
Brazil	3,205	3,362	3,115	Netherlands	1,849	1,707	1,565
Canada	1,869	1,898	1,852	New Zealand[1]	1,175	1,298	1,091
China: Mainland	16,103	14,826	19,364	Pakistan	890	872	657
Czechoslovakia	1,232	1,189	1,210	Poland	1,917	2,026	2,397
Denmark	1,289	1,290	1,218	Romania	1,238	1,294	1,359
France	3,983	3,785	3,880	Soviet Union	13,885	13,608	12,609
Germany, East	1,638	1,575	1,612	Spain	1,691	1,682	1,545
Germany, West	4,828	4,694	4,800	United Kingdom	2,367	2,346	2,307
Hungary	1,317	1,231	1,065	United States	17,818	17,812	17,680
India	742	727	654	Yugoslavia	1,280	1,224	1,117
Iran	450	450	459	**World, total**	**110,348**	**108,216**	**110,222**

1. Year ending June 30 for Australia and September 30 for New Zealand. 2. includes Luxembourg. NOTE: Covers beef and veal (incl. buffalo meat), pork (incl. bacon and ham), and mutton and lamb (incl. goat meat). Refers to meat from animals slaughtered within the national boundaries irrespective of origin of animals, and relates to commercial and farm slaughter. In terms of carcass weight. Excludes lard, tallow, and edible offals. NOTE: Data are most recent available. *Source:* Office of the United Nations, New York, NY, *Statistical Yearbook.* (Copyright.) From: *Statistical Abstract of the United States 1987.*

Crude Steel Production and Consumption

Country	Production (mil. metric tons)			Consumption: Total (mil. metric tons)			Consumption: Per capita (kilograms)		
	1983	1982	1981	1984	1983	1982	1984	1983	1982
Argentina	2.8	2.8	2.4	2.7	3.6	2.4	88	120	84
Australia	5.4[4]	7.3[1]	8.0[1]	5.7	4.9	5.6	370	318	367
Austria	4.4	4.3	4.7	1.9	2.0	2.1	257	263	279
Bangladesh	z	n.a.	.1	.4	.3	.2	4	3	3
Belgium	10.3	9.9	12.3	3.6[2]	5.8	4.7[2]	353[2]	564[2]	461[2]
Brazil	8.2	7.7	8.4	9.3	7.9	10.7	70	61	85
Bulgaria	2.8	2.6	2.5	2.9	3.2	3.0	323	353	337
Canada	12.8	11.9	14.8	13.2	11.0	9.1	525	443	371
China: Mainland	40.1	37.2	35.6	57.9	51.7	42.1	55	50	41
Czechoslovakia	15.0	15.0	15.3	10.8	11.1	11.1	700	719	724
France	17.6	18.4	21.3	15.2	15.0	17.2	276	275	318
Germany, East	7.2	7.2	7.5	8.9	n.a.	9.5	536	n.a.	570
Germany, West	35.7	35.9	41.6	29.9	29.8	26.8	489	486	436
Greece	.9[3,5]	.8[3]	1.0[3]	1.5	2.0	1.5	149	207	150
India	10.1	10.9	10.7	12.7	12.1	13.6	17	16	18
Italy	21.8	24.2	25.0	20.9	18.2	20.4	366	319	360
Japan	97.2	99.5	101.7	68.3	59.6	63.7	569	500	538
Korea, North	3.5[3]	3.5[3]	3.5[3]	6.3	6.1	5.8	323	320	312
Korea, South	5.1	5.7	5.9	8.1	8.9	7.5	198	222	192
Mexico	6.7	6.9	7.4	8.7	7.5	8.5	113	100	117
Netherlands	2.9	3.0	4.3	4.3	3.4	3.7	295	237	259
Nigeria	.1[5]	.1	z	.6	.9	1.4	7	10	16
Poland	16.2	14.1	15.1	15.3	14.9	14.4	416	406	398
Romania	12.6	13.1	13.0	11.5	10.9	11.6	503	482	512
South Africa	7.0[5]	8.4	9.0	n.a.	4.6	5.6	n.a.	130	162
Soviet Union	152.5	147.2	148.4	n.a.	n.a.	n.a.	n.a.	n.a.	n.a.
Spain	13.3	13.4	12.9	6.6	9.3	9.0	170	244	237
Sweden	4.2[5]	3.9	3.8	3.7	3.5	3.5	439	419	423
Turkey	2.5	1.9	1.5[3]	5.1	4.2	3.3	105	88	70
United Kingdom	15.0	13.7	15.6	14.4[5]	14.1	14.2	255[5]	249	251
United States	76.8[4]	67.7[4]	109.6[4]	113.3	94.5	85.8	479	403	263
Venezuela	2.2[5]	2.3	1.8	2.9	2.6	3.4	173	158	213
Yugoslavia	2.0	2.0	2.3	5.0	5.3	5.2	217	231	231
World	**642.0**	**629.0**	**692.1**	**n.a.**	**n.a.**	**n.a.**	**n.a.**	**n.a.**	**n.a.**

1. Year ending June 30. 2. Luxembourg included with Belgium. 3. Data from U.S. Bureau of Mines. 4. Excludes steel for castings made in foundries operated by companies not producing ingots. 5. Estimated. n.a. = not available. Z less than 50,000 metric tons. NOTE: Production data cover both ingots and steel for castings and exclude wrought (puddled) iron. Consumption data represent apparent consumption (i.e. production plus imports minus exports) and do not take into account changes in stock. *Source:* Statistical Office of the United Nations, New York, NY, *Statistical Yearbook.* (Copyright.)

Urban Population and Energy and Land Use

Country	Urban Population (%)	Energy Consumption per Capita[1] (1984)	Land use (percent)		
			Cultivated	Pastureland	Forested
Afghanistan	16	2	12	46	3
Algeria	43	21	3	13	2
Angola	25	4	3	23	43
Argentina	84	50	13	52	22
Australia	86	180	6	57	14
Austria	55	117	18	24	38
Bahrain	81	388	3	6	0
Belgium	95	145	25	20	21
Bolivia	48	10	3	24	51
Brazil	71	19	9	19	66
Bulgaria	66	166	37	18	35
Burma	24	2	15	1	48
Burundi	5	Z	47	33	2
Cameroon	42	13	15	17	53
Canada	76	288	5	2	33
Chad	27	1	2	35	10
Chile	83	27	7	16	20
China	32	19	11	30	14
Colombia	65	25	5	26	44
Congo	48	3	2	29	62
Costa Rica	48	13	13	43	31
Cuba	71	43	29	22	17
Czechoslovakia	74	183	40	13	36
Denmark	84	133	61	5	11
Djibouti	74	8	0	9	0
Dominican Republic	52	14	30	43	
Ecuador	51	20	9	17	50
Egypt	46	19	2	0	0
El Salvador	43	5	34	29	6
Ethiopia	10	Z	11	37	23
Finland	60	146	7	0	69
France	73	114	34	23	27
Gabon	41	33	2	18	75
Germany, East	77	223	46	12	27
Germany, West	85	163	30	19	29
Ghana	31	2	12	14	36
Greece	70	66	30	40	20
Guatemala	39	6	17	12	39
Guinea	22	2	6	12	42
Haiti	26	2	33	18	2
Honduras	40	7	16	30	33
Hungary	56	112	57	13	18
India	25	7	51	4	21
Iran	51	39	9	27	11
Iraq	68	15	13	9	4
Ireland	56	96	14	69	5
Israel	90	69	21	39	6
Italy	72	90	41	16	21
Ivory Coast	43	6	12	9	24
Japan	76	111	13	2	68
Jordan	60	29	4	1	0
Kenya	16	3	4	6	6
Korea, South	65	44	22	1	66
Lebanon	80	25	29	1	8
Libya	76	111	1	8	0
Malaysia	32	26	13	0	62
Mali	18	1	2	24	7
Mauritius	42	8	58	4	31
Mexico	70	50	13	38	23
Morocco	43	9	19	28	12
Netherlands	89	172	23	31	8
New Zealand	84	113	2	52	39
Nicaragua	53	8	10	39	31
Nigeria	28	7	34	23	16
Norway	70	193	3	0	26
Pakistan	28	6	25	6	4
Panama	51	22	7	15	53

Country	Urban Population (%)	Energy Consumption per Capital[1] (1984)	Land use (percent) Cultivated	Pastureland	Forested
Paraguay	43	7	5	38	50
Peru	69	19	3	21	54
Philippines	40	9	38	4	40
Poland	60	133	47	13	28
Portugal	30	38	38	6	40
Qatar	86	637	0	5	0
Romania	53	134	45	19	27
Saudi Arabia	72	104	1	40	1
Senegal	36	5	27	29	30
Sierra Leone	28	2	25	31	29
Singapore	100	196	10	0	5
Somalia	34	4	2	45	14
Spain	91	65	41	21	31
Sri Lanka	22	4	34	7	36
Sweden	83	137	7	1	59
Switzerland	57	108	10	39	25
Syria	49	27	31	45	3
Tanzania	18	1	5	37	45
Thailand	17	12	38	1	30
Tunisia	53	20	29	18	3
Turkey	46	26	35	12	26
United Kingdom	90	138	29	48	9
United States	74	280	20	26	28
Uruguay	85	18	8	77	4
USSR	65	176	10	17	42
Venezuela	76	96	4	19	35
Vietnam	19	4	20	1	40
Yugoslavia	46	73	30	25	36
Zaire	34	2	3	4	75
Zimbabwe	24	13	7	12	61

1. Domestic production plus net imports, minus net stock increase, minus aircraft and marine bunkers of commercially traded fuels (bituminous coal, lignite, peat, directly burned oil shale, crude petroleum, and natural gas). Fuelwood, bagasse, charcoal, and solar energy are excluded. Gigajoules, equivalent to 0.163 "UN standard" barrels of oil. Z signifies an amount which rounds to zero. *Source:* Population Reference Bureau, Inc.

World's 20 Most Populous Countries: 1987 and 2100

1987 Rank	Country	Population	2100 Rank	Country	Population
1.	China	1,062,000,000	1.	India	1,631,800,000
2.	India	800,300,000	2.	China	1,571,400,000
3.	USSR	284,000,000	3.	Nigeria	508,800,000
4.	United States	243,800,000	4.	USSR	375,900,000
5.	Indonesia	174,900,000	5.	Indonesia	356,300,000
6.	Brazil	141,500,000	6.	Pakistan	315,800,000
7.	Japan	122,200,000	7.	United States	308,700,000
8.	Nigeria	108,600,000	8.	Bangladesh	297,100,000
9.	Bangladesh	107,100,000	9.	Brazil	293,200,000
10.	Pakistan	104,600,000	10.	Mexico	195,500,000
11.	Mexico	81,900,000	11.	Ethiopia	173,300,000
12.	Vietnam	62,200,000	12.	Vietnam	168,100,000
13.	Philippines	61,500,000	13.	Iran	163,800,000
14.	Germany, West	61,000,000	14.	Zaire	138,900,000
15.	Italy	57,400,000	15.	Japan	127,900,000
16.	United Kingdom	56,800,000	16.	Philippines	125,100,000
17.	France	55,600,000	17.	Tanzania	119,600,000
18.	Thailand	53,600,000	18.	Kenya	116,400,000
19.	Egypt	51,900,000	19.	Burma	111,700,000
20.	Turkey	51,400,000	20.	Egypt	110,500,000

From the *1987 World Population Data Sheet* of the Population Reference Bureau, Inc. *Original sources:* 1986, Population Reference Bureau; 2100, World Bank.

Countries of the World by Groupings

KEY

1—Member of the Organization of American States (OAS)
2—Member of the Organization of African Unity (OAU)
3—Member of the Organization of Petroleum Exporting Countries (OPEC)
4—Member of the North Atlantic Treaty Organization (NATO)
5—Member of the Association of Southeast Asian Nations (ASEAN)
6—African States associated with EEC (EAMA)
7—Member of the Arab League
8—Member of the Warsaw Pact
9—Member of the European Economic Community (EEC)
10—Member of the European Free Trade Association (EFTA)
11—Member of British Commonwealth of Nations
12—Member of the Economic Community of West African States (ECOWAS)
13—Member of the Organization for Economic Cooperation and Development (OECD)
14—Member of Inter-American Treaty of Reciprocal Assistance (Rio Pact)
15—Member of the Nonaligned Movement

NORTH AMERICA

Canada: 4, 11, 13
Mexico: 1, 14
United States: 1, 4, 13, 14

SOUTH AMERICA

Argentina: 1, 14, 15
Bolivia: 1, 14, 15
Brazil: 1, 14
Chile: 1, 14
Colombia: 1, 14
Ecuador: 1, 3, 14, 15
Guyana: 11, 15
Paraguay: 1, 14
Peru: 1, 14, 15
Seriname: 1, 15
Uruguay: 1, 14
Venezuela: 1, 3, 14

CENTRAL AMERICA

Belize: 11, 15
Costa Rica: 1, 14
El Salvador: 1, 14
Guatemala: 1, 14
Honduras: 1, 14
Nicaragua: 1, 14, 15
Panama: 1, 14, 15

CARIBBEAN REGION

Antigua and Barbuda: 11
Bahamas: 11
Barbados: 1, 11, 15
Cuba: 15
Dominica: 1, 11
Dominican Republic: 1, 14
Grenada: 1, 11, 15
Haiti: 1, 14
Jamaica: 1, 11, 15
St. Lucia: 1, 11, 15
St. Vincent and the Grenadines: 11
Trinidad and Tobago: 1, 11, 14, 15

EUROPE

Albania
Andorra
Austria: 10, 13
Belgium: 4, 9, 13
Bulgaria: 8
Cyprus: 9, 11
Czechoslovakia: 8
Denmark: 4, 9, 13
Finland: 10 (assoc. mem.), 13
France: 4, 9, 13
Germany, East: 8
Germany, West: 4, 9, 13
Greece: 4, 9, 13
Hungary: 8
Iceland: 4, 10, 13
Ireland: 9, 13
Italy: 4, 9, 13
Liechtenstein
Luxembourg: 4, 9, 13
Malta: 11, 15
Monaco
Netherlands: 4, 9, 13
Norway: 4, 10, 13
Poland: 8
Portugal: 4, 9, 10, 13
Romania: 8
San Marino
Spain: 4, 9, 13
Sweden: 10, 13
Switzerland, 10, 13
U.S.S.R.: 8
United Kingdom: 4, 9, 13
Vatican City State
Yugoslavia: 15

MIDDLE EAST

Bahrain: 7, 15
Iran: 3, 15
Iraq: 3, 7, 15
Israel: 15
Jordan: 7, 15
Kuwait: 3, 7, 15
Lebanon: 7, 15
Oman: 7, 15
Qatar: 3, 7, 15
Saudi Arabia: 3, 7, 15
Syria: 7, 15
Turkey: 4, 9 (assoc. mem.), 13
United Arab Emirates: 3, 7, 15
Yemen, People's Democratic Republic of: 7, 15
Yemen Arab Republic: 7, 15

FAR EAST

China, People's Republic of
China, Republic of
Japan: 13
Korea, North: 15
Korea, South
Mongolia
Philippines: 5

SOUTHEAST ASIA

Cambodia
Indonesia: 3, 5, 15
Laos: 15
Malaysia: 5, 11, 15
Singapore: 5, 11, 15
Thailand: 5
Vietnam: 15

SOUTH ASIA

Afghanistan: 15
Bangladesh: 11, 15
Bhutan: 15
Burma
India: 11, 15
Maldives: 15
Nepal: 15
Pakistan: 15
Sri Lanka: 11, 15

OCEANIA

Australia: 11, 13
Fiji: 11
Kiribati: 11
Nauru: 11
New Zealand: 11, 13
Papua New Guinea: 11
Solomon Islands: 11
Tonga: 11
Tuvalu
Vanuatu (New Hebrides)
Western Samoa: 11

AFRICA

Algeria: 2, 3, 7, 15
Angola: 2, 15
Benin: 2, 12, 15
Bophuthatswana
Botswana: 2, 11, 15
Burkina Faso 2, 6, 15
Burundi: 2, 15
Cameroon: 2, 6, 15
Cape Verde: 2, 15
Central African Republic: 2, 15
Chad: 2, 15
Comoro Islands: 2, 15
Congo: 2, 15
Djibouti: 2, 7, 15
Egypt: 2, 15
Equatorial Guinea: 2, 15
Ethiopia: 2, 15
Gabon: 2, 3, 15
Gambia: 2, 11, 12, 15
Ghana: 2, 11, 12, 15
Guinea: 2, 12, 15
Guinea-Bissau: 2, 15
Ivory Coast: 2, 12, 15
Kenya: 2, 11, 15
Lesotho: 2, 11, 15
Liberia: 2, 12, 15
Libya: 2, 3, 7, 15
Madagascar: 2, 15
Malawi: 6, 11, 15
Mali: 2, 12, 15
Mauritania: 2, 7, 15
Mauritius: 2, 11, 15
Morocco: 6, 7, 15
Mozambique: 2, 15
Niger: 6, 12, 15
Nigeria: 2, 3, 11, 12, 15
Rwanda: 2, 15
São Tomé and Príncipe: 2, 15
Senegal: 2, 6, 12, 15
Seychelles: 2, 15
Sierra Leone: 2, 11, 12, 15
Somalia: 2, 6, 7, 15
South Africa, Rep. of: 15
Sudan: 2, 7, 15
Swaziland: 2, 15
Tanzania: 2, 11, 15
Togo: 2, 6, 12, 15
Transkei
Tunisia: 2, 7, 15
Uganda: 2, 11, 15
Venda
Zaire: 2, 6, 15
Zambia: 2, 11, 15
Zimbabwe: 2, 11, 15

COUNTRIES OF THE WORLD

AFGHANISTAN

Democratic Republic of Afghanistan
President: Lt. Gen. Mohammed Najibullah (1986)
Premier: Sultan Ali Keshtmand (1981)
Area: 251,000 sq mi. (650,090 sq km)
Population (est. mid-1987): 14,200,000 (average annual growth rate: 2.6%)
Density per square mile: 61.35
Capital: Kabul
Largest cities (est. 1983): Kabul, 750,000; Kandahar, 225,000; Herat, 150,000
Monetary unit: Afghani
Languages: Pushtu and Dari Persian (both official)
Religion: Islam (Sunni, 74%; Shiite, 25%; other 1%)
National name: Jamhouri Democratike Afghanistan
Literacy rate: 12%
Economic summary: Gross national product (1985): $3.0 billion. Average annual growth rate (1976–79): 2.5%. Per capita income (1984): $160. Land used for agriculture: 12%; labor force: 68%; principal products: wheat, grains, cotton, fruits, nuts. Labor force in industry: 10%; major products: carpets and textiles. Natural resources: natural gas, oil, coal, copper, sulfur, lead, zinc, iron, salt, precious and semi-precious stones. Exports: fresh and dried fruits, natural gas, carpets. Imports: petroleum products and food supplies. Major trading partners: U.S.S.R., and Soviet bloc countries.

Geography. Afghanistan, approximately the size of Texas, lies wedged between the U.S.S.R., China, Pakistan, and Iran. The country is split east to west by the Hindu Kush mountain range, rising in the east to heights of 24,000 feet (7,315 m). With the exception of the southwest, most of the country is covered by high snow-capped mountains and is traversed by deep valleys.

Government. A Marxist "people's republic" was created by Noor Taraki's coup of April 27, 1978. In May 1986, Lt. Gen. Mohammed Najibullah, head of the secret police, became general secretary of the Central Committee of the People's Democratic Party of Afghanistan, replacing Babrak Karmal. Najibullah became President in Nov. 1986.

History. Darius I and Alexander the Great were the first conquerors to use Afghanistan as the gateway to India. Islamic conquerors arrived in the 7th century and Genghis Khan and Tamerlane followed in the 13th and 14th centuries.

In the 19th century, Afghanistan became a battleground in the rivalry of imperial Britain and Czarist Russia for the control of Central Asia. The Afghan Wars (1838–42 and 1878–81) fought against the British by Dost Mohammed and his son and grandson ended in defeat.

Afghanistan regained autonomy by the Anglo-Russian agreement of 1907 and full independence by the Treaty of Rawalpindi in 1919. Emir Amanullah founded the kingdom in 1926.

Taraki's attempts to create a Marxist state with Soviet aid brought armed resistance from conservative Muslim opposition.

Taraki was succeeded by Prime Minister Hafizullah Amin. Amin was replaced by Babrak Karmal, who had called for Soviet troops under a mutual defense treaty. Pakistan and other Moslem nations called for a U.N. Security Council session and charged that Amin had been executed on Dec. 27 by Soviet troops already present in Kabul. The Council's call for immediate withdrawal of Soviet troops was vetoed by the U.S.S.R. on Jan. 8, 1980.

The Soviet invasion was met with unanticipated fierce resistance from the Afghan population, resulting in a bloody, dirty and to an extent, secret war that still raged late in 1987. Soviet troops were estimated by Western sources in 1987 to number about 110,000 in Afghanistan, with another 40,000 backing them up just across the Soviet border. Pitted against the Soviets' bombers, helicopter gunships, heavy artillery and mechanized infantry were upward of 90,000 Afghan tribesmen who called themselves "mujahedeen," or "holy warriers." In the early fighting, many of the guerrillas were armed only with 19th-century flintlock rifles, but later they acquired more modern weapons, including rockets that they used to attack Soviet installations.

Soviet saturation bombing has demolished many villages in several regions of the country. The nation's population was reported to have shrunk by as much as one third, with at least four million having fled to Iran or Pakistan and up to one million killed in the war.

U.N.-sponsored talks showed signs of progress with the timetable for a Soviet withdrawal being the sole remaining obstacle.

ALBANIA

People's Socialist Republic of Albania
President of Presidium: Ramiz Alia (1982)
Premier: Adil Carcani (1982)
Area: 11,100 sq mi. (28,748 sq km)
Population (est. mid-1987): 3,100,000 (average annual growth rate: 2.0%)
Density per square mile: 270.3
Capital and largest city (est. 1983): Tirana, 200,000
Monetary unit: Lek
Language: Albanian
Religions: Historically Islam 70%; Greek Orthodox, 20%; Roman Catholic, 10%
National name: Republika Popullore Socialiste e Shqipërisë
Literacy rate 75%
Economic summary: Gross national product (1985 est.): $2.7 billion. Average annual growth rate (1970–78): 4.2%. Per capita income (1984 est.): $900. Land used for agriculture: 43%; labor force: 61%; principal products: wheat, corn, potatoes, sugar beets, cotton, tobacco. Labor force in industry: 18%; major products: textiles, timber, construction materials, fuels, semi-processed minerals. Exports: minerals, metals, fuels, foodstuffs, agricultural materials. Imports: machinery, equipment, and spare parts, minerals, metals, fuels, construction materials, foodstuffs. Major trading partner: Yugoslavia

Geography. Albania is situated on the eastern shore of the Adriatic Sea, with Yugoslavia to the north and east and Greece to the south. Slightly larger than Maryland, it is a mountainous country, mostly over 3,000 feet (914 m) above sea level, with a narrow, marshy coastal plain crossed by several rivers. The centers of population are contained in the interior mountain plateaus and basins.

Government. The last staunchly Stalinist Communist state, Albania is ruled by the Albanian Workers (Communist) Party, headed by a Politburo which hands down all policy decisions. President Ramiz Alia took over as First Secretary of the party and the Politburo upon the death in 1985 of Enver Hoxha, who wielded absolute power in the party posts for four decades.

History. Albania proclaimed its independence on Nov. 28, 1912, after a history of Roman, Byzantine, and Turkish domination.

Largely agricultural, Albania is one of the poorest countries in Europe. A battlefield in World War I, after the war it became a republic in which a conservative Moslem landlord, Ahmed Zogu, proclaimed himself President in 1925, and then proclaimed himself King Zog I in a monarchy in 1928. He ruled until Italy annexed Albania in 1939. Communist guerrillas under Enver Hoxha seized power in 1944, near the end of World War II.

His regime closed all of the nation's 2,169 churches and mosques in 1967 in a move to make Albania "the first atheist state in the world."

Hoxha died on April 11, 1985, at the age of 78. His successor as Communist party chief was Ramiz Alia, 59, who had been President since 1982.

ALGERIA

Democratic and Popular Republic of Algeria
President: Chadli Bendjedid (1979)
Prime Minister: Abdelhamid Brahimi (1984)
Area: 919,595 sq mi. (2,381,751 sq km)
Population (est. mid-1987): 23,500,000 (average annual growth rate: 3.2%)
Density per square mile: 25.6
Capital: Algiers
Largest cities (est. 1982): Algiers, 2,500,000; Oran, 600,000; Constantine, 500,000; Annaba, 300,000
Monetary unit: Dinar
Languages: Arabic (official), French
Religion: Islam (Sunni)
National name: République Algérienne Democratique et Populaire—El Djemhouria El Djazaïria Demokratia Echaabia
Literacy rate 46%
Economic summary: Gross national product (est. 1984): $51.9 billion. Annual growth rate (1984): 4.0%. Per capita income (1984): $2,430. Land used for agriculture: 3%; labor force: 19%; principal products: wheat, barley, oats, wine, fruits, olives, vegetables, livestock. Labor force in industry: 20%; major products: petroleum, gas, petrochemicals, fertilizers, iron and steel, textiles, transport equipment. Natural resources: petroleum, natural gas, iron ore, phosphates, lead, zinc, mercury. Exports: petroleum and gas. Imports: food, capital and consumer goods. Major trading partners: U.S., West Germany, France, Italy.

Geography. Nearly four times the size of Texas, Algeria is bordered on the west by Morocco and on the east by Tunisia and Libya. To the south are Mauritania, Mali, and Niger. Low plains cover small areas near the Mediterranean coast, with 68% of the country a plateau between 2,625 and 5,250 feet (800 and 1,600 m) above sea level. The highest point is Mount Tahat in the Sahara, which rises 9,850 feet (3,000 m).

Government. Algeria is governed by the President, whose term runs for 5 years. A new Constitution was approved on Nov. 19, 1976.

A National Popular Assembly of 281 members exercises legislative power, serving for a five-year term. The National Liberation Front, which led the struggle for independence from France, is the only legal party.

History. As ancient Numidia, Algeria became a Roman colony at the close of the Punic Wars (145 B.C.). Conquered by the Vandals about A.D. 440, it fell from a high state of civilization to virtual barbarism, from which it partly recovered after invasion by the Moslems about 650.

In 1492 the Moors and Jews, who had been expelled from Spain, settled in Algeria. Falling under Turkish control in 1518, Algiers served for three centuries as the headquarters of the Barbary pirates. The French took Algeria in 1830 and made it a part of France in 1848.

On July 5, 1962, Algeria was proclaimed independent. In October 1963, Ahmed Ben Bella was elected President. He began to nationalize foreign holdings and aroused opposition. He was overthrown in a military coup on June 19, 1965, by Col. Houari Boumediène, who suspended the Constitution and sought to restore financial stability.

Boumediène died in December 1978 after a long illness. Chadli Bendjedid, Secretary-General of the National Liberation Front, took the presidency in a smooth transition of power. On July 4, 1979, he released from house arrest former President Ahmed Ben Bella, who had been confined for 14 years since his overthrow.

Algeria, chosen by Iran to represent it in negotiations in November 1980 with the United States, was able to secure the eventual release of 52 Americans who had been held hostage in the U.S. Embassy in Teheran. The hostages were flown to Algiers on Jan. 20, 1981, and turned over to U.S. custody, ending 444 days in captivity.

ANDORRA

Principality of Andorra
Episcopal Co-Prince: Msgr. Joan Martí y Alanis, Bishop of Seo de Urgel, Spain
French Co-Prince: François Mitterrand, President of France (1981)
First Syndic: Francesc Cerqueda Pasquet (1982)
Area: 175 sq mi. (453 sq km)
Population (est. 1987): 48,000 (average annual growth rate: 1.1%)
Density per square mile: 274.3
Capital (est. 1983): Andorra la Vella, 15,000
Monetary units: French franc and Spanish peseta
Languages: Catalán (official); French, Spanish
Religion: Roman Catholic
National names: Les Vallées d'Andorre-Valls d'Andorra
Literacy rate 100%
Economic summary: Land used for agriculture: 4%; labor force: 20%; principal products: oats, barley, cattle, sheep. Labor force in industry: 80%; major products: tobacco products and electric power; tourism. Natural resources: water power, mineral water. Major trading partners: Spain and France.

Geography. Andorra lies high in the Pyrenees

Mountains on the French-Spanish border. The country is drained by the Valira River.

Government. A General Council of 28 members, elected for four years, chooses the First Syndic and Second Syndic. In 1976 the Andorran Democratic Party, the principality's first political party, was formed.

History. An autonomous and semi-independent co-principality, Andorra has been under the joint suzerainty of the French state and the Spanish bishops of Urgel since 1278.

ANGOLA

People's Republic of Angola
President: José Eduardo dos Santos (1979)
Area: 481,350 sq mi. (1,246,700 sq km)
Population (est. mid-1987): 8,000,000 (average annual growth rate: 2.5%)
Density per square mile: 16.6
Capital and largest city (est. 1983): Luanda, 525,000
Monetary unit: Kwanza
Languages: Bantu, Portuguese (official)
Religions: Roman Catholic, 69%; Protestant, 20%; Animist, 10%
Literacy rate: 20%
Economic summary: Gross national product (1982): $7.6 billion. Average annual growth rate (1981): 0.1%. Per capita income (1982): $1,030. Principal agricultural products: coffee, sisal, corn, cotton, sugar, tobacco, bananas. Major industrial products: oil, diamonds, processed fish, tobacco, textiles, cement, processed food and sugar. Natural resources: diamonds, gold, iron, oil. Exports: oil, coffee, diamonds, fish and fish products, iron ore, timber, corn. Imports: machinery and electrical equipment, bulk iron, steel and metals, textiles, clothing. Major trading partners: Brazil, U.S.S.R., Portugal, U.S.

Geography. Angola, more than three times the size of California, extends for more than 1,000 miles (1,609 km) along the South Atlantic in southwestern Africa. Zaire is to the north and east; Zambia to the east, and South-West Africa (Namibia) to the south. A plateau averaging 6,000 feet (1,829 m) above sea level rises abruptly from the coastal lowlands. Nearly all the land is desert or savanna, with hardwood forests in the northeast.

Government. A Marxist "people's republic" is the recognized government, but large areas in the east and south are held by the Union for the Total Independence of Angola (Unita), led by Jonas Savimbi. President José Eduardo dos Santos heads the only official party, the Popular Movement for the Liberation of Angola-Workers Party. The Popular Movement won out over Savimbi's group and a third element in an internal struggle after Portugal granted its former colony independence on Nov. 11, 1975. Elections promised at the time of independence have never taken place, and the government relies heavily on Soviet support and Cuban troops, while Savimbi receives aid from South Africa and the U.S.

History. Discovered by the Portuguese navigator Diego Cao in 1482, Angola became a link in trade with India and the Far East. Later it was a major source of slaves for Portugual's New World colony of Brazil. Development of the interior began after the Treaty of Berlin in 1885 fixed the colony's borders, and British and Portuguese investment pushed mining, railways, and agriculture.

Following World War II, independence movements began but were sternly suppressed by military force. The April revolution of 1974 brought about a reversal of Portugal's policy, and the next year President Francisco da Costa Gomes signed an agreement to grant independence to Angola. The plan called for election of a constituent assembly and a settlement of differences by the MPLA and the National Front for the Liberation of Angola (FNLA) and the National Union for the Total Independence of Angola (UNITA).

The Organization of African Unity, recognized the MPLA government led by Agostinho Neto on Feb. 11, 1976, and the People's Republic of Angola became the 47th member of the organization.

Although militarily victorious, Neto's regime had yet to consolidate its power in opposition strongholds in the east and south.

In March 1977 and May 1978, Zairean refugees in Angola invaded Zaire's Shaba Province, bringing charges by Zairean President Mobutu Sese Seko that the unsucessful invasions were Soviet-backed with Angolan help. Angola, the U.S.S.R., and Cuba denied complicity.

Neto died in Moscow of cancer on Sept. 10, 1979. The Planning Minister, José Eduardo dos Santos, was named President.

The South-West Africa People's Organization, or Swapo, the guerrillas fighting for the independence of the disputed territory south of Angola also known as Namibia, fought from bases in Angola and the South African armed forces also maintained troops there until early June 1985.

The South African troops left after Angola agreed to try to limit guerrilla activity in the Namibia border region and to patrol the area jointly with South African forces until the withdrawal was complete. However, after their departure, South African troops pursued Swapo guerrillas into Angola and killed 61 of them in late June of 1985.

In February 1986, President Reagan, following a repeal of an earlier ban on military aid to Joseph Savimbi's UNITA rebels, resumed military aid.

ANTIGUA AND BARBUDA

Sovereign: Queen Elizabeth II
Governor-General: Sir Wilfred E. Jacobs (1981)
Prime Minister: Vere Bird (1981)
Area: 170 sq mi. (442 sq km)
Population (est. mid-1987): 100,000 (average annual growth rate: 1%)
Density per square mile: 588.2
Capital and largest city (est. 1983): St. John's, 25,000
Monetary unit: East Caribbean dollar
Language: English
Religions: Anglican and Roman Catholic
Literacy rate: 88%
Member of Commonwealth of Nations
Economic summary: Gross national product (1986): $130 million. Average annual growth rate (1978–82): –5.2%. Per capita income (1983): $1,750. Land used for agriculture: 54%; principal product: cotton. Major industry: tourism. Exports: clothing, rum, lobsters. Imports: fuel, food, machinery. Major trading partners: U.K., U.S.

Geography. Antigua, the larger of the two main islands, is low-lying except for a range of hills in the south that rise to their highest point at Boggy Peak (1,330 ft; 405 m). Deforested and without major streams, the island is subject to droughts despite a mean annual rainfall of 44 inches. Barbuda is a coral island, well wooded.

Government. Executive power is held by the Cabinet, presided over by Prime Minister Vere C. Bird. A 17-member Parliament is elected by universal suffrage. The Antigua Labour Party, led by Prime Minister Bird, holds 16 seats and the remaining one is held by an independent member, Eric Burton, who has been appointed opposition leader.

History. Antigua was discovered by Christopher Columbus in 1493 and named for the Church of Santa Maria la Antigua in Seville. Colonized by Britain in 1632, it joined the West Indies Federation in 1958. With the breakup of the Federation, it became one of the West Indies Associated States in 1967, self-governing in internal affairs. Full independence was granted Nov. 1, 1981.

ARGENTINA

Argentine Republic
President: Rául Alfonsín (1983)
Area: 1,072,067 sq mi. (2,776,654 sq km)
Population (est. mid-1987): 31,500,000 (average annual growth rate: 1.6%)
Density per square mile: 29.3
Capital: Buenos Aires
Largest cities (est. 1983): Buenos Aires, 3,000,000; Córdoba, 1,000,000; Rosario, 950,000; La Plafa, 450,000; San Miguel de Tucumán, 400,000
Monetary unit: Austral
Language: Spanish
Religion: Predominantly Roman Catholic
National name: República Argentina
Literacy rate 94%
Economic summary: Gross national product (1984): $76.2 billion. Average annual growth rate (1970–79): 1.0%. Per capita income (1980): $2,390. Land used for agriculture: 57%; labor force: 19%; principal products: grains, oilseeds, livestock products. Labor force in industry: 25%; major products: processed foods, motor vehicles, consumer durables, textiles, chemicals. Natural resources: minerals, lead, zinc, tin, copper, iron, manganese, oil, uranium. Exports: meats, corn, wheat, wool, hides. Imports: machinery, fuel and lubricating oils, iron and steel. Major trading partners: U.S., Brazil, Italy, West Germany, Netherlands, Soviet Union.

Geography. With an area slightly less than one third of the United States and second in South America only to its eastern neighbor, Brazil, in size and population, Argentina is a plain, rising from the Atlantic to the Chilean border and the towering Andes peaks. Aconcagua (23,034 ft.; 7,021 m) is the highest peak in the world outside Asia. It is bordered also by Bolivia and Paraguay on the north, and by Uruguay on the east.

The northern area is the swampy and partly wooded Gran Chaco, bordering on Bolivia and Paraguay. South of that are the rolling, fertile pampas, rich for agriculture and grazing and supporting most of the population. Next southward is Patagonia, a region of cool, arid steppes with some wooded and fertile sections.

Government. Argentina is a federal union of 22 provinces, one national territory, and the Federal District. Under the Constitution of 1853 (restored by a Constituent National Convention in 1957), the President and Vice President are elected every six years by popular vote through an electoral college. The President appoints his Cabinet. The Vice President presides over the Senate but has no other powers. The Congress consists of two houses: a 46-member Senate and a 254-member Chamber of Deputies.

President Raúl Alfonsín's civilian government was inaugurated in December 1983. His Radical Union Party has 130 seats in the Chamber. The main opposition is the Peronist Movement for National Justice (103 seats).

History. Discovered in 1516 by Juan Díaz de Solis, Argentina developed slowly under Spanish colonial rule. Buenos Aires was settled in 1580; the cattle industry was thriving as early as 1600.

Invading British forces were expelled in 1806–07, and when Napoleon conquered Spain, the Argentinians set up their own government in the name of the Spanish King in 1810. On July 9, 1816, independence was formally declared.

As in World War I, Argentina proclaimed neutrality at the outbreak of World War II, but in the closing phase declared war on the Axis on March 27, 1945, and became a founding member of the United Nations. Juan D. Perón, an army colonel, emerged as the strongman of the postwar era, winning the Presidential elections of 1946 and 1951.

Opposition to Perón's increasing authoritarianism, led to a coup by the armed forces that sent Perón into exile in 1955. Argentina entered a long period of military dictatorships with brief intervals of constitutional government.

The former dictator returned to power in 1973 and his wife was elected Vice-President.

After Peron's death in 1974, his widow became the hemisphere's first woman chief of state, but was deposed in 1976 by a military junta.

In December 1981. Lt. Gen. Leopoldo Galtieri, commander of the army, was named president.

On April 2, 1982, Galtieri landed thousands of troops on the Falkland Islands on and reclaimed the Malvinas, their Spanish name, as national territory. By May 21, 5,000 British marines and paratroops landed from the British armada, and regained control of the islands.

Galtieri resigned three days after the surrender of the island garrison on June 14. Maj. Gen. Reynaldo Bignone, took office as President on July 1. Civilian rule was promised by early 1984 and on July 16 Bignone lifted the six-year ban on political parties.

In the presidential election of October 1983, Raúl Alfonsín, leader of the middle-class Radical Civic Union, handed the Peronist Party its first defeat since its founding.

Among the enormous problems facing Alfonsín after eight years of mismanagement under military rule was a $45-billion foreign debt, the developing world's third largest. In some circles, fears were voiced that the new civilian government might repudiate the debt, triggering a wholesale repudiation by debtor countries that could bring on a worldwide financial collapse. But after cliff-hanging negotiations with American, European, and Japanese banks representing the country's private creditors, the Alfonsín government agreed on June 29, 1984, to pay $350 million in overdue interest and was moving toward austerity measures.

With the arrears mounting at the rate of $150

million a month, the debt to foreign creditors mounted to $48 billion by mid-1985, and more than $1 billion was past due. On June 11, the Alfonsin government reached agreement with the International Monetary Fund on an austerity program designed to put Argentina into a position to pay its way internationally and keep current with its debt obligations. The agreement opened the door for up to $1.2 billion of new loans to Argentina. A key requirement of the pact was that inflation, which had been running at 1,010%, be brought down to 150% by April 1986.

Three days later, on June 14, President Alfonsin announced an "economy of war" to bring the inflation rate down. The program combined the creation of a new currency—the austral, meaning southern—to replace the peso, wage and price controls and a halt to the government's deficit spending. After a brief bank holiday, banks reopened and exchanged australs for pesos. To maintain the value of the new currency, the government promised to stop printing money to balance its budget. In April 1986, the austral was devalued to spur exports.

AUSTRALIA

Commonwealth of Australia
Sovereign: Queen Elizabeth II
Governor-General: Sir Ninian Stephen (1982)
Prime Minister: Robert J. L. Hawke (1983)
Area: 2,966,150 sq mi. (7,682,300 sq km)
Population (est. mid-1987): 16,200,000 (average annual growth rate: 0.8%)
Density per square mile: 5.5
Capital (est. 1984): Canberra, 264,400
Largest cities (est. 1985 for metropolitan area): Sydney, 3,391,600; Melbourne, 2,916,600; Brisbane, 1,157,200; Adelaide, 937,100; Perth, 1,001,000
Monetary unit: Australian dollar
Language: English
Religions: Roman Catholic, 28%; Anglican, 28%; Uniting Church (combined Methodist-Presbyterian), 14%
Literacy rate: 99%
Member of Commonwealth of Nations
Economic summary: Gross national product (1983): $166.2 billion. Average annual growth rate (1970–79): 1.4%. Per capita income (1980): $9,820. Land used for agriculture: 64%; labor force: 6% (1984); principal products: wool, meat, cereals, sugar, wine grapes, sheep, cattle, dairy products. Labor force in industry: 26% (1984); major products: machinery, motor vehicles, iron and steel, textiles, chemicals. Natural resources: gold, iron ore, bauxite, zinc, lead, tin, coal, oil, gas, copper, nickel, diamonds, uranium, timber. Exports: meat, wheat, metal ores, wool, coal. Imports: manufactured raw materials, capital equipment, consumer goods. Major trading partners: Japan, U.S., U.K., New Zealand, West Germany, Singapore, U.S.S.R.

Geography. The continent of Australia, with the island state of Tasmania, is approximately equal in area to the United States (excluding Alaska and Hawaii), and is nearly 50% larger than Europe (excluding the U.S.S.R.).

Mountain ranges run from north to south along the east coast, reaching their highest point in Mount Kosciusko (7,308 ft; 2,228 m). The western half of the continent is occupied by a desert plateau that rises into barren, rolling hills near the west coast. It includes the Great Victoria Desert to the south and the Great Sandy Desert to the north. The Great Barrier Reef, extending about 1,245 miles (2,000 km), lies along the northeast coast.

The island of Tasmania (26,178 sq mi.; 67,800 sq km) is off the southeastern coast.

Government. The Federal Parliament consists of a bicameral legislature. The House of Representatives has 148 members elected for three years by popular vote. The Senate has 76 members elected by popular vote for six years. One half of the Senate is elected every three years. Voting is compulsory at 18. Supreme federal judicial power is vested in the High Court of Australia in the Federal Courts, and in the State Courts invested by Parliament with Federal jurisdiction. The High Court consists of seven justices, appointed by the Governor-General in Council. Each of the states has its own judicial system.

The major political parties are the Australian Labor Party (82 seats in the House of Representatives), led by Prime Minister R.J.L. (Bob) Hawke; Liberal Party (45 seats) led by John Howard; National Party (21 seats), led by Ian M. Sinclair.

History. Dutch, Portuguese, and Spanish ships sighted Australia in the 17th century; the Dutch landed at the Gulf of Carpentaria in 1606. Australia was called New Holland, Botany Bay, and New South Wales until about 1820.

Captain James Cook, in 1770, claimed possession for Great Britain.

Free settlers established six colonies: New South Wales (1786), Tasmania (then Van Diemen's Land) (1825), Western Australia (1829), South Australia (1834), Victoria (1851), and Queensland (1859).

The six colonies became states and in 1901 federated into the Commonwealth of Australia with a Constitution that incorporated British parliamentary tradition and U.S. federal experience. Australia became known for liberal legislation: free compulsory education, protected trade unionism with industrial conciliation and arbitration, the "Australian" ballot facilitating selection, the secret ballot, women's suffrage, maternity allowances, and sickness and old age pensions.

In the election of 1983, Robert Hawke, head of the Labor Party, became Prime Minister. The Labor government was reelected in a Federal election in December 1984.

By mid-1982, however, world recession was slowing the resources boom. Low resource prices were an issue in the election of 1987 but Hawke was able secure re-election on a platform of diversifying the economy.

Australian External Territories

Norfolk Island (13 sq mi.; 36.3 sq km) was placed under Australian administration in 1914. Population in 1983 was about 1,800.

The Ashmore and Cartier Islands (.8 sq mi.), situated in the Indian Ocean off the northwest coast of Australia, came under Australian administration in 1934. In 1938 the islands were annexed to the Northern Territory. On the attainment of self-government by the Northern Territory in 1978, the islands which are uninhabited were retained as Commonwealth Territory.

The Australian Antarctic Territory (2,360,000 sq

mi.; 6,112,400 sq km), comprises all the islands and territories, other than Adélie Land, situated south of lat. 60° S and lying between long. 160° to 45° E. It came under Australian administration in 1936.

Heard Island and the McDonald Islands (158 sq mi.; 409.2 sq km), lying in the sub-Antarctic, were placed under Australian administration in 1947. The islands are uninhabited.

Christmas Island (52 sq mi.; 134.7 sq km) is situated in the Indian Ocean. It came under Australian administration in 1958. Population in 1985 was 2,278.

Coral Sea Islands (400,000 sq mi.; 1,036,000 sq km, but only a few sq mi. of land) became a territory of Australia in 1969. There is no permanent population on the islands.

AUSTRIA

Republic of Austria
President: Kurt Waldheim (1986)
Chancellor: Franz Vranitzky (1986)
Area: 32,375 sq mi. (83,851 sq km)
Population (est. mid-1987): 7,600,000 (average annual growth rate: 0.0%)
Density per square mile: 234.7
Capital: Vienna
Largest cities (est. 1983): Vienna, 1,550,000; Graz, 240,000; Linz, 200,000; Salzburg, 135,000; Innsbruck, 115,000; Klagenfurt, 85,000
Monetary unit: Schilling
Language: German
Religion: Roman Catholic, 89%
Literacy rate: 98%
National name: Republik Österreich
Economic summary: Gross national product (1984): $64.21 billion. Average annual growth rate (1984): 2.2%. Per capita income (1984): $8,500. Land used for agriculture: 20%; labor force: 18%; principal products: livestock, forest products, grains, sugar beets, potatoes. Labor force in industry: 49%; principal products: iron and steel, chemicals, machinery, paper and pulp. Natural resources: iron ore, petroleum, timber, magnesite, aluminum, coal, lignite, cement, copper. Exports: iron and steel products, timber, paper, textiles, electrotechnical machines, chemical products. Imports: machinery, chemicals, foodstuffs, textiles and clothing, petroleum. Major trading partners: West Germany, Italy, Switzerland, U.S., Eastern Europe.

Geography. Slightly smaller than Maine, Austria includes much of the mountainous territory of the eastern Alps (about 75% of the area). The country contains many snowfields, glaciers, and snow-capped peaks, the highest being the Grossglockner (12,530 ft; 3,819 m). The Danube is the principal river. Forests and woodlands cover about 40% of the land area.

Almost at the heart of Europe, Austria has as its neighbors Italy, Switzerland, West Germany, Czechoslovakia, Hungary, Yugoslavia, and Liechtenstein.

Government. Austria is a federal republic composed of nine provinces (Bundesländer), including Vienna. The President is elected by the people for a term of six years. The bicameral legislature consists of the Bundesrat, with 58 members chosen by the provincial assemblies, and the Nationalrat, with 183 members popularly elected for four years. Presidency of the Bundesrat revolves every six months, going to the provinces in alphabetical order.

The major political parties are the Social Democratic Party (80 of 183 seats in Nationalrat), led by Chancellor Franz Vranitzky; People's Party (77 seats); Freedom Party (18 seats); Greens (8 seats).

History. Settled in prehistoric times, the Central European land that is now Austria was overrun in pre-Roman times by various tribes, including the Celts. Charlemagne conquered the area in 788 and encouraged colonization and Christianity. In 1252, Ottokar, King of Bohemia, gained possession, only to lose the territories to Rudolf of Hapsburg in 1278. Thereafter, until World War I, Austria's history was largely that of its ruling house, the Hapsburgs.

Austria emerged from the Congress of Vienna in 1815 as the Continent's dominant power. The *Ausgleich* of 1867 provided for a dual sovereignty, the empire of Austria and the kingdom of Hungary, under Francis Joseph I, who ruled until his death on Nov. 21, 1916. He was succeeded by his grand-nephew, Charles I.

During World War I, Austria-Hungary was one of the Central Powers with Germany, Bulgaria, and Turkey, and the conflict left the country in political chaos and economic ruin. Austria, shorn of Hungary, was proclaimed a republic in 1918, and the monarchy was dissolved in 1919.

A parliamentary democracy was set up by the Constitution of Nov. 10, 1920. On March 12, 1938, German troops occupied the country, and Hitler proclaimed its *Anschluss* (union) with Germany, annexing it to the Third Reich.

After World War II, the U.S. and Britain declared the Austrians a "liberated" people. But the Russians prolonged the occupation. Finally Austria concluded a state treaty with the U.S.S.R. and the other occupying powers and regained its independence on May 15, 1955. The second Austrian republic, established Dec. 19, 1945, on the basis of the 1920 Constitution (amended in 1929), was declared by the federal parliament to be permanently neutral.

Vienna has since become a headquarters for several international organizations such as OPEC.

On June 8, 1986, former UN Secretary-General Kurt Waldheim was elected to the ceremonial office of President in a campaign marked by controversy over his alleged links to Nazi war-crimes in Yugoslavia.

BAHAMAS

Commonwealth of the Bahamas
Sovereign: Queen Elizabeth II
Governor-General: Sir Gerald Cash (1979)
Prime Minister: Lynden O. Pindling (1967)
Area: 5,380 sq mi. (13,939 sq km)
Population (est. mid-1987): 200,000 (average annual growth rate: 1.8%)
Density per square mile: 37.2
Capital and largest city (est. 1984 for metropolitan area): Nassau, 139,000
Monetary unit: Bahamian dollar
Language: English
Religions: Baptist, 29%; Anglican, 23%; Roman Catholic, 23%; Methodist, 7%

Literacy rate: 89%
Member of Commonwealth of Nations
Economic summary: Gross national product (1984): $1.8 billion. Average annual growth rate (1970–82): 4.1%. Per capita income (1984): $7,950. Principal agricultural products: fruits, vegetables. Major industrial products: fish, petroleum, pharmaceutical products; tourism. Natural resources: salt, aragonite. Exports: lobster, fish, pharmaceuticals, cement, rum. Imports: foodstuffs, manufactured goods, fuels. Major trading partners: U.S., U.K., Nigeria, Canada.

Geography. The Bahamas are an archipelago of about 700 islands and 2,400 uninhabited islets and cays lying 50 miles off the east coast of Florida. They extend from northwest to southeast for about 760 miles (1,223 km). Only 22 of the islands are inhabited; the most important is New Providence (80 sq mi.; 207 sq km), on which Nassau is situated. Other islands include Grand Bahama, Abaco, Eleuthera, Andros, Cat Island, San Salvador (or Watling's Island), Exuma, Long Island, Crooked Island, Acklins Island, Mayaguana, and Inagua.

The islands are mainly flat, few rising above 200 feet (61 m). There are no fresh water streams. There are several large brackish lakes on several islands including Inagua and New Providence.

Government. The Bahamas moved toward greater autonomy in 1968 after the overwhelming victory in general elections of the Progressive Liberal Party, led by Prime Minister Lynden O. Pindling. The black leader's party won 29 seats in the House of Assembly to only 7 for the predominantly white United Bahamians, who had controlled the islands for decades before Pindling became Premier in 1967.

With its new mandate from the 85%-black population, Pindling's government negotiated a new Constitution with Britain under which the colony became the Commonwealth of the Bahama Islands in 1969. On July 10, 1973, The Bahamas became an independent nation as the Commonwealth of the Bahamas.

In the 1987 election, Pindling's Progressive Liberal Party won 32 of 49 seats in Parliament; the Free National Movement, 15.

History. The islands were reached by Columbus in October 1492, and were a favorite pirate area in the early 18th century. The Bahamas were a crown colony from 1717 until they were granted internal self-government in 1964.

BAHRAIN

State of Bahrain
Emir: Sheik Isa ibn-Sulman al-Khalifa (1961)
Prime Minister: Sheik Khalifa bin Sulman al-Khalifa (1970)
Area: 254 sq mi. (659 sq km)
Population (est. mid-1987): 400,000 (average annual growth rate: 2.8%)
Density per square mile: 1,562.5
Capital (est. 1982): Manama, 150,000
Monetary unit: Bahrain dinar
Languages: Arabic (official), English, French
Religion: Islam
Literacy rate : 40%
Economic summary: Gross national product (1984): $4.3 billion. Average annual growth rate (1973–82): 10.7%. Per capita income (1984): $10,640. Land used for agriculture: 5%; labor force: 5%; principal products: eggs, vegetables, fruits. Labor force in industry: 90%; major products: oil, aluminum, fish. Natural resources: oil, fish. Exports: oil, aluminum, fish. Imports: machinery, oil-industry equipment, motor vehicles, foodstuffs. Major trading partners: Saudi Arabia, U.S., U.K., Japan, Italy.

Geography. Bahrain is an archipelago in the Persian Gulf off the coast of Saudi Arabia. The islands for the most part are level expanses of sand and rock.

Government. A new Constitution was approved in 1973. It created the first elected parliament in the country's history. Called the National Council, it consisted of 30 members elected by male citizens for four-year terms, plus up to 16 Cabinet ministers as ex-officio members. In August 1975, the Amir dissolved the National Council.

History. A sheikdom that passed from the Persians to the al-Khalifa family from Arabia in 1782, Bahrain became, by treaty, a British protectorate in 1820. It has become a major Middle Eastern oil center and, through use of oil revenues, is one of the most developed of the Persian Gulf sheikdoms. The Emir, Sheik Isa ibn-Sulman al-Khalifa, who succeeded to the post in 1961, is a member of the original ruling family. Bahrain announced its independence on Aug. 14, 1971.

BANGLADESH

People's Republic of Bangladesh
President: H. M. Ershad (1983)
Vice President: A.K.M. Nurul Islam (1986)
Area: 55,598 sq mi. (143,998 sq km)
Population (est. mid-1987): 107,100,000 (average annual growth rate: 2.7%)
Density per square mile: 1,926.3
Capital and largest city (est 1984): Dhaka, 3,950,000
Monetary unit: Taka
Principal languages: Bengali (official), English
Religions: Islam, 83%; Hindu, 16%
Literacy rate: 25%
Member of Commonwealth of Nations
Economic summary: Gross national product (1984): $14.7 billion. Average annual growth rate (1970–79): 0.8%. Per capita income (1985): $150. Land used for agriculture: 66%; labor force, 75%; principal products: rice, jute, tea, sugar, wheat. Labor force in industry, 11%; major products: jute goods, textiles, leather, sugar, fertilizer, paper, pharmaceuticals. Natural resources: natural gas. Exports: jute goods, jute, tea, leather. Imports: food grains, fuels, raw cotton, manufactured goods. Major trading partners: U.S., Japan, Singapore.

Geography. Bangladesh, on the northern coast of the Bay of Bengal, is surrounded by India, with a small common border with Burma in the southeast. It is approximately the size of Wisconsin. The country is low-lying riverine land traversed by the many branches and tributaries of the Ganges and Brahmaputra rivers. Elevations averages less than 600 feet (183 m) above sea level. Tropical monsoons and frequent floods and cyclones inflict heavy damage in the delta region.

Government. On Oct. 15, 1986, Ershad was elected President, in an election boycotted by the opposition, for a five-year term. Martial law ended in November. Parliamentary elections were held in May 1986, the major parties are: Jatiya Party (183 of 330 seats) led by President Ershad; Awami League (76 seats), led by Sheik Hasina Wazed.

History. The former East Pakistan was part of imperial British India until Britain withdrew in 1947. The two Pakistans were united by religion (Islam), but their peoples were separated by culture, physical features, and 1,000 miles of Indian territory. Bangladesh consists primarily of East Bengal (West Bengal is part of India and its people are primarily Hindu) plus the Sylhet district of the Indian state of Assam. For almost 25 years after independence from Britain, its history was as part of Pakistan (*see* Pakistan).

The East Pakistanis unsuccessfully sought greater autonomy from West Pakistan. The first general elections in Pakistani history, in December 1970, saw virtually all 171 seats of the region (out of 300 for both East and West Pakistan) go to Sheik Mujibur Rahman's Awami League.

Attempts to write an all-Pakistan Constitution to replace the military regime of Gen. Yahya Khan failed. Yahya put down a revolt in March 1971. An estimated one million Bengalis were killed in the fighting or later slaughtered. Ten million more took refuge in India.

In December 1971, India invaded East Pakistan, routed the West Pakistani occupation forces, and created Bangladesh. In February 1974, Pakistan agreed to recognize the independence of Bangladesh.

On Aug. 15, 1975, Mujibur, his wife, and several relatives were assassinated in a coup led by young Army officers. They installed Khondakar Mushtaque Ahmed, a founder of the Awami League, as President.

A military coup forced Ahmed from power Nov. 6, 1975, and Abu Sadat Mohammed Sayem became President and "chief martial law administrator." On April 21, 1977, Gen. Ziaur Rahman, Army Chief of Staff, became president following Sayem's resignation.

On May 30, 1981, Ziaur was killed by a group of army officers in an attempted coup. Vice President Abdus Sattar assumed power and was elected President Nov. 15. On March 24, 1982, Gen. Hossain Mohammad Ershad, army chief of staff, took control in a bloodless coup. Ershad assumed the office of President in 1983.

BARBADOS

Sovereign: Queen Elizabeth II
Governor-General: Sir Hugh Springer (1984)
Prime Minister: E.W. Barrow (1986)
Area: 166 sq. mi. (431 sq km)
Population (est. mid-1987): 300,000 (average annual growth rate: 0.9%)
Density per square mile: 1,807.2
Capital and largest city (est. 1982): Bridgetown, 8,000
Monetary unit: Barbados dollar
Language: English
Religions: Anglican, 70%; Methodist, 9%; Roman Catholic, 4%
Literacy rate: 99%
Member of Commonwealth of Nations
Economic summary: Gross national product (1985): $1, 121 million. Average annual growth rate (1970–79): 2.1%. Per capita income (1985): $4,430. Land used for agriculture: 60%; principal products: sugar cane, subsistence foods. Major industrial products: light manufactures, sugar milling, tourism. Exports: sugar and sugar cane byproducts, clothing. Imports: foodstuffs, machinery, manufactured goods. Major trading partners: U.S.; Caribbean nations, U.K., Canada.

Geography. An island in the Atlantic about 300 miles (483 km) north of Venezuela, Barbados is only 21 miles long (34 km) and 14 miles across (23 km) at its widest point. It is circled by fine beaches and narrow coastal plains. The highest point is Mount Hillaby (1,105 ft; 337 m) in the north central area.

Government. The Barbados legislature dates from 1627. It is bicameral, with a Senate of 21 appointed members and an Assembly of 27 elected members.

The major political parties are the Democratic Labor Party (24 seats in Assembly), led by Prime Minister Errol Barrow; Barbados Labor Party (3 seats), led by H. Bernard St. John.

History. Barbados, with a population 90% black, was settled by the British in 1627. It became a crown colony in 1885. It was a member of the Federation of the West Indies from 1958 to 1962. Britain granted the colony independence on Nov. 30, 1966, and it became a parliamentary democracy.

While retaining membership in the Commonwealth of Nations and economic ties with Britain, Barbados seeks broader economic and political relations with Western Hemisphere countries. Diplomatic ties with Cuba were established in 1972.

BELGIUM

Kingdom of Belgium
Sovereign: King Baudouin I (1951)
Premier: Wilfried Martens (1981)
Area: 11,781 sq mi. (30,513 sq km)
Population (est. mid-1987): 9,900,000 (average annual growth rate: 0.0%)
Density per square mile: 835.14
Capital: Brussels
Largest cities (est. 1984): Brussels, 982,434; Ghent, 235, 401; Charleroi, 213,041; Liège, 203,065; Antwerp, 488, 425; Bruges, 118,146
Monetary Unit: Belgian franc
Languages: Dutch, 57%; French, 32%; bilingual (Brussels), 10%; German, 0.7%.
Religion: Roman Catholic, 97%
National name: Royaume de Belgique—Koninkrijk van België
Literacy rate: 98%
Economic summary: Gross national product (1984): $76.3 billion. Annual growth rate (1984): 2.2%. Per capita income (1984): $7,801. Land used for agriculture: 46%; labor force: 25%; principal products: livestock, poultry, grain, sugar beets, flax, tobacco, potatoes, vegetables, fruits. Labor force in industry: 27%; major products: fabricated metal, iron and steel, coal, textiles, chemicals. Exports: iron and steel products, precious stones, textile products. Imports: nonelectrical machinery, motor vehicles, textiles, chemicals, fuels. Major trading partners: West Germany, France, Netherlands, U.K., U.S., Italy.

Geography. A neighbor of France, West Germany, the Netherlands, and Luxembourg, Belgium has about 40 miles of seacoast on the North Sea at the Strait of Dover. In area, it is approximately the size of Maryland. The northern third of the country is a plain extending eastward from the seacoast. North of the Sambre and Meuse Rivers is a low plateau; to the south lies the heavily wooded Ardennes plateau, attaining an elevation of about 2,300 feet (700 m).

The Schelde River, which rises in France and flows through Belgium, emptying into the Schelde estuaries, enables Antwerp to be an ocean port.

Government. Belgium, a parliamentary democracy under a constitutional monarch, consists of nine provinces. Its bicameral legislature has a Senate, with its 181 members elected for four years—106 by general election, 50 by provincial councillors and 25 by the Senate itself. The 212-member Chamber of Representatives is directly elected for four years by proportional representation. There is universal suffrage, and those who do not vote are fined.

Belgium joined the North Atlantic Alliance in 1949 and is a member of the European Community. NATO and the European Community have their headquarters in Brussels.

The sovereign, Baudouin I, was born Sept. 7, 1930, the son of King Leopold III and Queen Astrid. He became King on July 17, 1951, after the abdication of his father. He married Doña Fabiola de Mora y Aragón on Dec. 15, 1960. Since he has no children, his brother, Prince Albert, is heir to the throne.

The major political parties are the Flemish-speaking Social Christian Party (40 Senators, 49 Representatives); French-speaking Social Christian Party (16 Senators, 20 Representatives); Flemish-speaking Socialist Party (31 Senators, 32 Representatives); French-speaking Socialist Party (21 Senators, 35 Representatives); Flemish-speaking Liberal Party (23 Senators, 22 Representatives); Flemish People's Party (17 Senators, 26 Representatives); French-speaking Liberal Party (20 Senators, 24 Representatives).

History. Belgium occupies part of the Roman province of Belgica, named after the Belgae, a people of ancient Gaul. The area was conquered by Julius Caesar in 57–50 B.C., then was overrun by the Franks in the 5th century. It was part of Charlemagne's empire in the 8th century, then in the next century was absorbed into Lotharingia and later into the Duchy of Lower Lorraine. In the 12th century it was partitioned into the Duchies of Brabant and Luxembourg, the Bishopric of Liège, and the domain of the Count of Hainaut, which included Flanders.

In the 16th century, Belgium, with most of the area of the Low Countries, passed to the Duchy of Burgundy and was the marriage portion of Archduke Maximilian of Hapsburg and the inheritance of his grandson, Charles V, who incorporated it into his empire. Then, in 1555, they were united with Spain.

By the treaty of Utrecht in 1713, the country's sovereignty passed to Austria. During the wars that followed the French Revolution, Belgium was occupied and later annexed to France. But with the downfall of Napoleon, the Congress of Vienna in 1815 gave the country to the Netherlands. The Belgians revolted in 1830 and declared their independence.

Germany's invasion of Belgium in 1914 set off World War I. The Treaty of Versailles (1919) gave the areas of Eupen, Malmédy, and Moresnet to Belgium. Leopold III succeeded Albert, King during World War I, in 1934. In World War II, Belgium was overwhelmed by Nazi Germany, and Leopold III was made prisoner. When he attempted to return in 1950, Socialists and Liberals revolted. He abdicated July 16, 1951, and his son, Baudouin, became King the next day.

Despite the increasingly strong divisions between the French- and Flemish-speaking communities, a Christian Democrat-Liberal coalition that took office in December 1981 came close to setting a record for longevity among the 32 governments that had ruled Belgium since World War II. Headed by Prime Minister Wilfried Martens—the fifth government he had led since 1979—it survived several serious political challenges, including the implementation of an unpopular economic austerity program in 1983 and the deployment of NATO cruise missiles in March 1985. But a riot in a soccer stadium set off a chain of events that threatened its continued existence later that year.

Before the start of the European Soccer Cup final in Brussels on May 29, 1985, 38 people, mostly fans of the Juventus team of Italy, were killed when supporters of the British Liverpool team went on a rampage. Most of the deaths occurred when a stadium wall collapsed. A parliamentary inquiry primarily blamed the English fans for the violence but also faulted Interior Minister Charles Ferdinand Nothomb for security lapses. When he refused to resign, the French-speaking Liberals withdrew from Martens' coalition. Martens thereupon, on July 16, submitted the government's resignation to King Baudouin. The king, who plays a key mediating role during the country's frequent leadership crises, refused the resignation and the coalition remained in office until September, when early elections increased Martens' coalition majority.

BELIZE

Sovereign: Queen Elizabeth II
Governor-General: Dame Minita Gordon (1981)
Prime Minister: Manuel Esquivel (1984)
Area: 8,867 sq mi. (22,965 sq km)
Population (est. mid-1987): 200,000 (average annual growth rate: 2.7%)
Density per sq mi.: 22.6
Capital (est. 1985): Belmopan, 5,000
Largest city (est. 1985): Belize City, 47,000
Monetary unit: Belize dollar
Languages: English (official) and Spanish
Religions: Roman Catholic, 62%; Anglican, 12%; Methodist, 6%; Baha'i, 2.5%
Literacy rate: 93%
Member of Commonwealth of Nations
Economic summary: Gross national product (1984): $180 million. Average annual growth rate (1984): 1.3%. Per capita income (1983 est. $1,140). Land used for agriculture: 35%; labor force: 30%; principal products: sugar cane, citrus fruits, corn, molasses, rice, bananas, livestock. Labor force in industry: 20%; major products: timber, processed foods, furniture, rum, soap. Natural resource: timber. Exports: sugar, molasses, clothing, lumber, citrus fruits, fish. Imports: fuels, transportation equipment, foodstuffs, textiles, machinery. Major trading partners: U.S., U.K., Trinidad and Tobago, Canada.

Geography. Belize (formerly British Honduras) is situated on the Caribbean Sea south of Mexico and east and north of Guatemala. In area, it is about the size of New Hampshire. Most of the country is heavily forested with various hardwoods. Mangrove swamps and cays along the coast give way to hills and mountains in the interior. The highest point is Victoria Peak, 3,681 feet (11,220 m).

Government. Formerly the colony of British Honduras, Belize became a fully independent commonwealth on Sept. 21, 1981, after having been self-governing since 1964. Executive power is nominally wielded by Queen Elizabeth II through an appointed Governor-General but effective power is held by the Prime Minister, who is responsible to a 28-member parliament elected by universal suffrage. The major parties are the United Democratic Party (21 of 28 seats), led by Prime Minister Manuel Esquivel; and the People's United Party (7 seats), led by former Prime Minister George Price.

History. Once a part of the Mayan empire, the area was deserted until British timber cutters began exploiting valuable hardwoods in the 17th century. Efforts by Spain to dislodge British settlers, including a major naval attack in 1798, were defeated. The territory was formally named a British colony in 1862 but administered by the Governor of Jamaica until 1884.

Guatemala has long made claims to the territory and refused to recognize Britain's efforts to grant independence to Belize. Fear of Guatemala caused many inhabitants to oppose independence until a tentative agreement was reached between Britain, Belize, and Guatemala in March 1981 that would offer access to the Caribbean through Belizean territory for Guatemala. The agreement broke down, however, and 1,600 British troops remained to protect the new state after the flag-raising ceremony on Sept. 21, 1981.

BENIN

People's Republic of Benin
President: General Mathieu Kerekou (1972)
Area: 43,483 sq mi. (112,622 sq km)
Population (est. mid-1987): 4,300,000 (average annual growth rate: 3.0%)
Density per square mile: 98.9
Capital (est. 1984): Porto-Novo, 208,000
Largest city (est. 1982): Cotonou, 490,000
Monetary unit: Franc CFA
Ethnic groups: Fons and Adjas, Baribas, Yorubas, Mahis
Languages: French, African languages
Religions: Animist, 70%; Christian, 15%; Islam, 15%
National name: Republique Populaire du Benin
Literacy rate (1981): 20%
Economic summary: Gross national product (1984 est.): $974 million. Average annual growth rate (1970–79): 0.6%. Per capita income (1983): $270. Labor force in agriculture: 70%; principal products: oil palms, peanuts, cotton, coffee, tobacco, corn, rice, livestock, fish. Major industrial products: processed palm oil, palm kernel oil. Natural resources: low-grade iron ore, limestone, some offshore oil. Exports: palm and agricultural products. Imports: clothing, consumer goods, lumber, fuels, foodstuffs, machinery, transportation equipment. Major trading partners: France and other Western European countries.

Geography. This West African nation on the Gulf of Guinea, between Togo on the west and Nigeria on the east, is about the size of Tennessee. It is bounded also by Upper Volta and Niger on the north. The land consists of a narrow coastal strip that rises to a swampy, forested plateau and then to highlands in the north. A hot and humid climate blankets the entire country.

Government. The change in name from Dahomey to Benin was announced by President Mathieu Kerekou in November 1975. Benin commemorates an African kingdom that flourished in the 17th century. At the same time, Kerekou announced the formation of a political organization, the Party of the People's Revolution of Benin, to mark the first anniversary of his declaration of a "new society" guided by Marxist-Leninist principles.

History. One of the smallest and most densely populated states in Africa, Benin was annexed by the French in 1893. The area was incorporated into French West Africa in 1904. It became an autonomous republic within the French Community in 1958, and on Aug. 1, 1960, was granted its independence within the Community.

Gen. Christophe Soglo deposed the first president, Hubert Maga, in an army coup in 1963. He dismissed the civilian government in 1965, proclaiming himself chief of state. A group of young army officers seized power in December 1967, deposing Soglo. They promulgated a new Constitution in 1968.

In December 1969, Benin had its fifth coup of the decade, with the army again taking power. In May 1970, a three-man presidential commission was created to take over the government. The commission had a six-year term; each member serves as president for two years. Maga turned over power as scheduled to Justin Ahomadegbe in May 1972, but six months later yet another army coup ousted the triumvirate and installed Lt. Col. Mathieu Kerekou as President.

BHUTAN

Kingdom of Bhutan
Ruler: King Jigme Singye Wangchuk (1972)
Area: 18,000 sq mi. (46,620 sq km)
Population (est. mid-1987): 1,500,000 (average annual growth rate: 2.0%)
Density per square mile: 83.3
Capital (est. 1984): Thimphu, 30,000
Monetary unit: Ngultrum
Language: Dzongkha
Religions: Buddhist, 70%; Hindu, 25%; Islam, 5%
National name: Druk-yul
Literacy rate: 12%
Economic summary: Gross national product (est. 1984): $169 million. Average annual growth rate (1982/83): 1.4%. Per capita income (1984): $140. Labor force in agriculture: 95%; principal products: rice, barley, wheat, potatoes, fruit. Major industrial product: cement. Natural resources: timber, hydroelectric power. Exports: fruits and vegetables, timber, coal, cement. Imports: fuels, machinery, vehicles. Major trading partner: India.

Geography. Mountainous Bhutan, half the size of Indiana, is situated on the southeast slope of the Himalayas, bordered on the north and east by Tibet and on the south and west by India. The landscape consists of a succession of lofty and rugged mountains running generally from north to south and separated by deep valleys. In the north, towering peaks reach a height of 24,000 feet (7,315 m).

Government. Bhutan is a constitutional monarchy. The King rules with a Council of Ministers and a Royal Advisory Council. There is a National Assembly (Parliament), which meets semiannually, but no political parties.

History. British troops invaded the country in 1865 and negotiated an agreement under which Britain undertook to pay an annual allowance to Bhutan on condition of good behavior. A treaty with India in 1949 increased this subsidy and placed Bhutan's foreign affairs under Indian control.

In the 1960s, Bhutan undertook modernization, abolishing slavery and the caste system, emancipating women and enacting land reform. In 1985, Bhutan made its first diplomatic links with non-Asian countries.

BOLIVIA

Republic of Bolivia
President: Victor Paz Estenssoro (1985)
Area: 424,162 sq mi. (1,098,581 sq km)
Population (est. mid-1987): 6,500,000 (average annual growth rate, 2.6%) (Indian, 53%; mestizo, 32%; white, 15%)
Density per square mile: 15.3
Judicial capital (est. 1985): Sucre, 86,609
Administrative capital (est. 1985): La Paz, 992,592
Largest cities (est. 1985): Santa Cruz, 441,717; Cochabamba, 317,251; Oruro, 178,393
Monetary unit: Peso boliviano
Languages: Spanish, Quechua, Aymara
Religion: Roman Catholic, 94%; Baha'i, 3%
National name: República de Bolivia
Literacy rate est. 75%
Economic summary: Gross national product (est. 1985): \$4.0 billion. Average annual growth rate (1984): −4%. Per capita income (1985 est.): \$400. Labor force in agriculture: 47%; principal products: potatoes, corn, rice, sugar cane, bananas. Labor force in industry: 19%; major products: refined petroleum, processed foods, tin, textiles, clothing. Natural resources: petroleum, natural gas, tin, lead, zinc, copper, tungsten, bismuth, antimony, gold, sulfur, silver, iron ore. Exports: tin, lead, zinc, silver, antimony, coffee, sugar, cotton, natural gas. Imports: foodstuffs, chemicals, capital goods, pharmaceuticals, transport equipment. Major trading partners: U.S., Argentina, U.K., Brazil, Netherlands.

Geography. Landlocked Bolivia, equal in size to California and Texas combined, lies to the west of Brazil. Its other neighbors are Peru and Chile on the west and Argentina and Paraguay on the south.

The country is a low alluvial plain throughout 60% of its area toward the east, drained by the Amazon and Plata river systems. The western part, enclosed by two chains of the Andes, is a great plateau—the Altiplano, with an average altitude of 12,000 feet (3,658 m). More than 80% of the population lives on the plateau, which also contains La Paz. At an altitude of 11,910 feet (3,630 m), it is the highest capital city in the world.

Lake Titicaca, half the size of Lake Ontario, is one of the highest large lakes in the world, at an altitude of 12,507 feet (3,812 m). Islands in the lake hold ruins of the ancient Incas.

Government. President Victor Paz Estensoro was inaugurated on Aug. 7, 1985, after the Congress, at a raucous session, chose him over Hugo Banzer, the candidate who had received the most votes in a popular election on July 14. Banzer won 28.6% of the 1.7 million votes tallied and Paz won 26.4%. Under the Constitution, if no Presidential candidate receives 50% of the vote, Congress chooses between the top two vote-getters. Paz's National Revolutionary Movement won 60 of the 157 congressional seats in the 1985 election, against 52 for Banzer's Nationalist Democratic Action Party. Several smaller parties split the remainder.

History. Famous since Spanish colonial days for its mineral wealth, modern Bolivia was once a part of the ancient Incan Empire. After the Spaniards defeated the Incas in the 16th century, Bolivia's predominantly Indian population was reduced to slavery. The country won its independence in 1825 and was named after Simón Bolívar, the famed liberator.

Since 1825 Bolivia has had more than 60 revolutions, 70 Presidents, and 11 Constitutions.

Harassed by internal strife, Bolivia lost great slices of territory to three neighbor nations. Several thousand square miles and its outlet to the Pacific were taken by Chile after the War of the Pacific (1879–84). In 1903 a piece of Bolivia's Acre province, rich in rubber, was ceded to Brazil. And in 1938, after a war with Paraguay, Bolivia gave up claim to nearly 100,000 square miles of the Gran Chaco.

In 1965 a guerrilla movement mounted from Cuba and headed by Maj. Ernesto (Ché) Guevara began a revolutionary war. With the aid of U.S. military advisers, the Bolivian army, helped by the peasants, smashed the guerrilla movement, wounding and capturing Guevara on Oct. 8, 1967, and shooting him to death the next day.

Faltering steps toward restoration of civilian government were halted abruptly on July 17, 1980, when Gen. Luis Garcia Meza Tejada seized power. A series of military leaders followed before the military moved, in 1982, to return the government to civilian rule. Hernán Siles Zuazo was inaugurated President on Oct. 10, 1982.

Under Siles' left-of-center government, the country was regularly shut down by work stoppages, the bulk of Bolivia's natural resources—natural gas, gold, lithium, potassium and tungsten—were either sold on the black market or left in the ground, the country had the lowest per-capita income in South America, and inflation approached 3,000 percent. In 1985, the 73-year-old Siles decided he was unable to carry on and quit a year early.

No candidate won a majority in the elections in 1985 and Victor Paz Estensoro, 77, was picked by Congress to become President. During his administration, inflation continued to rise and the currency collapsed. Drastic economic measures were taken toward the end of the year, including a wage freeze and a cutback of government price subsidies, which lowered the inflation rate to about 55%.

BOPHUTHATSWANA

See South Africa

BOTSWANA

Republic of Botswana
President: Quett K. Masire (1980)
Area: 222,000 sq mi. (576,000 sq km)
Population (est. mid-1987): 1,200,000 (average annual growth rate: 3.4%)

Density per square mile: 4.95
Capital and largest city (est. 1984): Gaborone, 79,000
Monetary unit: Pula
Languages: English, Setswana
Religions: Christian, 48%; Animist, 49%
Member of Commonwealth of Nations
Literacy rate: 54%
Economic summary: Gross national product (1984): $940 million. Average annual growth rate (1970–79): 12.0%. Per capita income (1984): $900. Land used for agriculture: 1%; principal products: livestock, sorghum, corn, millet, cowpeas, beans. Major industrial products: diamonds, copper, nickel, salt, soda ash, potash, coal, frozen beef; tourism. Natural resources: diamonds, copper, nickel, salt, soda ash, potash, coal. Exports: diamonds, cattle, animal products, copper, nickel. Imports: foodstuffs, vehicles, textiles, petroleum products. Major trading partners: South Africa, U.K., U.S.

Geography. Twice the size of Arizona, Botswana is in south central Africa, bounded by South-West Africa, Zambia, Zimbabwe, and South Africa. Most of the country is near-desert, with the Kalahari occupying the western part of the country. The eastern part is hilly, with salt lakes in the north.

Government. The Botswana Constitution provides, in addition to the unicameral National Assembly, for a House of Chiefs, which has a voice on bills affecting tribal affairs. There is universal suffrage.

The major political parties are the Democratic Party (29 of 34 elective seats in 36-man Legislative Assembly), led by President Quett Masire; National Front (4 seats), led by Kenneth Koma; People's Party (1 seat), led by Kenneth Nkhwa.

History. Botswana is the land of the Batawana tribes, which, when threatened by the Boers in Transvaal, asked Britain in 1885 to establish a protectorate over the country, then known as Bechuanaland. In 1961, Britain granted a Constitution to the country. Self-government began in 1965, and on Sept. 30, 1966, the country became independent. Since 1975, it has been an associate member of the European Common Market.

BRAZIL

Federative Republic of Brazil
President: José Sarney (1985)
Area: 3,286,470 sq mi. (8,511,957 sq km)
Population (est. mid-1987): 141,500,000 (average annual growth rate, 2.1%) (approx.: white, 60%; mestizo, 26%; black, 11%)
Density per square mile: 43.0
Capital (1980 census): Brasília, 1,470,300
Largest cities (1980 census): São Paulo, 12,600,000; Rio de Janeiro, 9,000,000; Salvador, 1,800,000; Belo Horizonte, 2,500,000; Recife, 2,300,000; Porto Alegre, 2,200,000
Monetary unit: Cruzado
Language: Portuguese
Religion: Roman Catholic, 88%; Protestant, 6%
National name: República Federativa de Brasil
Literacy rate: 74%
Economic summary: Gross national product (1985): $321.4 billion. Average annual growth rate (est. 1985): 8.3%. Per capita income (1984): $1,610. Land used for agriculture; 4%; labor force: 27%; principal products: coffee, rice, beef, corn, milk, sugar cane, soybeans, cocoa. Labor force in industry: 24%; major products: steel, chemicals, petrochemicals, machinery, motor vehicles, cement, lumber. Natural resources: iron ore, manganese, bauxite, nickel, other industrial metals. Exports: coffee, iron ore, soybeans, sugar, beef, transport equipment, footwear. Imports: wheat, copper, aluminum, petroleum, machinery, chemicals, pharmaceuticals. Major trading partners: U.S., West Germany, Japan, Saudi Arabia.

Geography. Brazil covers nearly half of South America, extends 2,965 miles (4,772 km) north-south, 2,691 miles (4,331 km), east-west, and borders every nation on the continent except Chile and Ecuador. It is the fifth largest country in the world, ranking after the U.S.S.R., Canada, China, and the U.S.

More than a third of Brazil is drained by the Amazon and its more than 200 tributaries. The Amazon is navigable for ocean steamers to Iquitos, Peru, 2,300 miles (3,700 km) upstream. Southern Brazil is drained by the Plata system—the Paraguay, Uruguay, and Paraná Rivers. The most important stream entirely within Brazil is the Sao Francisco, navigable for 1,000 miles (1,903 km), but broken near its mouth by the 275-foot (84 m) Paulo Afonso Falls.

Government. Under the Constitution, Brazil is a union of 22 states, 4 territories, and 1 federal district. The President is elected for a six-year term by an electoral college made up of members of the National Congress. The National Congress is composed of two houses—the Senate, whose members serve eight-year terms, and the Chamber of Deputies, elected for four-year terms. Members of Congress are elected by equal, direct, compulsory, and secret suffrage under proportional representation.

The military took control in 1964, ousting the last elected civilian President and installing a series of military men (with the Congress ratifying the junta's choice). Election of a civilian President by the 686-member electoral college took place in January 1985.

Opposition Democratic Movement candidate Tancredo Neves was chosen overwhelmingly to head the first civilian government in 21 years, defeating the governing Democratic Social Party's candidate, Paulo Salim Maluf, by 480 votes to 180 votes, with 17 college delegates abstaining and nine absent. But Neves died of complications following intestinal surgery before taking office, and his Vice Presidential running mate, José Sarney, became President.

History. Brazil is the only Latin American nation deriving its language and culture from Portugal. Adm. Pedro Alvares Cabral claimed the territory for the Portuguese in 1500. He brought to Portugal a cargo of wood, pau-brasil, from which the land received its name. Portugal began colonization in 1532 and made the area a royal colony in 1549.

During the Napoleonic wars, King João VI, then Prince Regent, fled the country in 1807 in advance of the French armies and in 1808 set up his court in Rio de Janeiro. João was drawn home in 1820 by a revolution, leaving his son as Regent. When Portugal sought to reduce Brazil again to colonial status, the prince declared Brazil's independence on Sept. 7, 1822, and became Pedro I, Emperor of Brazil.

Harassed by his parliament, Pedro I abdicated in 1831 in favor of his five-year-old son, who became Emperor in 1840 as Pedro II. The son was a popular monarch, but discontent built up and, in 1889, following a military revolt, he had to abdicate. Although a republic was proclaimed, Brazil was under two military dictatorships during the next four years. A revolt permitted a gradual return to stability under civilian Presidents.

The President during World War I, Wenceslau Braz, cooperated with the Allies and declared war on Germany.

In World War II, Brazil cooperated with the Western Allies, welcoming Allied air bases, patrolling the South Atlantic, and joining the invasion of Italy after declaring war on the Axis.

Gen. João Baptista de Oliveira Figueiredo, became President in 1979 and pledged a return to democracy in 1985.

The electoral college's choice of Tancredo Neves on Jan. 15, 1985, as the first civilian President since 1964 brought a nationwide wave of optimism, but the 75-year-old President-elect was hospitalized and underwent a series of intestinal operations. The civilian government was inaugurated on schedule on March 15, but only Neves' Vice Presidential running mate, José Sarney, was sworn in, and he was widely distrusted because he had previously been a member of the governing military regime's political party. When Neves died on April 21, Sarney became President.

Congressional elections in Nov. 1986 gave pro-Sarney candidates a large majority.

Economically, Brazil's $93-billion foreign debt was the Third World's largest, and inflation reached a staggering 229% annual rate in 1984, almost double the 115% rate in 1983. But tough austerity measures imposed by the International Monetary Fund appeared to be taking hold and, by mid-1984, Brazilian economists said the country's recession had ended and Brazil was on the road to recovery.

In 1985 the GNP increased by 8.3% and in February 1986, President Sarney announced an across-the-board price and wage freeze that failed to stop a resurgence of inflation in early 1987.

BRUNEI

State of Brunei
Sultan: Sir Mudo Hassanal Bolkiah (1968)
Area: 2,226 sq mi. (5,765 sq km)
Population (est. mid-1987): 200,000 (average annual growth rate: 2.6%)
Density per square mile: 98
Capital and largest city (est. 1981): Bandar Seri Begawan, 64,000
Monetary unit: Brunei dollar
Ethnic groups: Malay, 65%; Chinese, 24%; other, 11%
Languages: Malay and English official; Chinese
Religions: Islam, 66%; Christian, 10%; Buddhist, 14%; other, 10%
Literacy rate: 45%
Member of Commonwealth of Nations
Economic summary: Gross national product (1983): $4.4 billion. Average annual growth rate (1970–79): 4.6%. Per capita income (1983): $21,140. Land used for agriculture: 3%; labor force: 5%; principle agricultural products: fruit, rice, pepper. Labor force in industry: 22%; major industrial products: crude petroleum, liquified natural gas. Natural resources: petroleum, natural gas. Exports: crude petroleum, liquified natural gas. Imports: machinery, transport equipment, manufactured goods, foodstuffs. Major trading partners: Japan, U.S., U.K., Singapore, South Korea.

Geography. About the size of Delaware, Brunei is an independent sultanate on the northwest coast of the island of Borneo in the South China Sea, wedged between the Malaysian states of Sabah and Sarawak. Three quarters of the thinly populated country is covered with tropical rain forest; there are rich oil and gas deposits.

Government. Sultan Hassanal Bolkiah is ruler of the state, a former British protectorate which became fully sovereign and independent on New Year's Day, 1984, presiding over a Privy Council and Council of Ministers appointed by himself. The Constitution provides for a three-tiered system of indirect elections, but the last elections were held in 1965. The only known opposition leader is in exile. In 1985, the Brunei National Democratic Party (BDNP) was formed. The sole political party, it supports an "Islamic monarchy."

History. Brunei (pronounced broon-eye) was a powerful state from the 16th to the 19th century, ruling over the northern part of Borneo and adjacent island chains. But it fell into decay and lost Sarawak in 1841, becoming a British protectorate in 1888 and a British dependency in 1905.

The Sultan regained control over internal affairs in 1959, but Britain retained responsibility for the state's defense and foreign affairs until the end of 1983, when the sultanate became fully independent.

Sultain Bolkiah was crowned in 1968 at the age of 22, succeeding his father, Sir Omar Ali Saifuddin, who had abdicated. During his reign, exploitation of the rich Seria oilfield has made the sultanate wealthy. The majority of the population lives in and around the capital, situated on the Brunei River nine miles from its mouth.

BULGARIA

People's Republic of Bulgaria
Chairman of the State Council: Todor Zhivkov (1971)
Prime Minister (Chairman of Council of Ministers): Georgy Atanasov (1986)
Area: 42,823 sq mi. (110,912 sq km)
Population (est. mid-1987): 9,000,000 (average annual growth rate: 0.1%)
Density per square mile: 210.2
Capital: Sofia
Largest cities (est. 1982): Sofia, 1,094,000; Plovdiv, 367,000; Varna, 295,000; Ruse, 179,000; Burgas, 175,000; Stara Zagora, 165,000
Monetary unit: Lev
Language: Bulgarian
Religions: Reliable figures not available
National name: Narodna Republika Bulgariya
Literacy rate: 95%
Economic summary: Gross national product (1984): $56.4 billion. Annual growth rate (1984): 3.1%. Per capita income (1984): $6,295. Labor force in agriculture: 23%; principal products: grains, tobacco, fruits, vegetables. Labor force in industry: 35%; major products: processed agricultural products, machinery, textiles, clothing. Natural resources: metals, minerals, lumber. Exports: machinery and transport equipment, fuels, minerals, raw materials, agricultural products. Imports: machinery and transportation equipment, fuels, raw materials, metals, agricultural raw materials. Major trading partners: U.S. S.R., Soviet bloc countries.

Geography. Two mountain ranges and two great valleys mark the topography of Bulgaria, a country the size of Tennessee. Situated on the Black Sea in the eastern part of the Balkan peninsula, it shares borders with Yugoslavia, Romania, Greece, and

Turkey. The Balkan belt crosses the center of the country, almost due east-west, rising to a height of 7,800 feet (2,377 m). The Rhodope range breaks off from the Balkans in the west, curves, and then straightens out to run nearly parallel along the southern border. Between the two ranges, is the valley of the Maritsa, Bulgaria's principal river. Between the Balkan range and the Danube, which forms most of the northern boundary with Romania, is the Danubian tableland.

Southern Dobruja, a fertile region of 2,900 square miles (7,511 sq km), below the Danube delta, is an area of low hills, fens, and sandy steppes.

Government. The present Constitution has been in effect since May 18, 1971. The National Assembly, consisting of 400 members elected for five-year terms, is the governing body. It elects the State Council and the Council of Ministers.

The Communist Party is led by the chairman of the State Council, Todor Zhivkov.

History. The first Bulgarians, a tribe of wild horsemen akin to the Huns, crossed the Danube from the north in A.D. 679 and subjugated the Slavic population of Moesia. They adopted a Slav dialect and Slavic customs and twice conquered most of the Balkan peninsula between 893 and 1280. After the Serbs subjected their kingdom in 1330, the Bulgars gradually fell prey to the Turks, and from 1396 to 1878 Bulgaria was a Turkish province. In 1878, Russia forced Turkey to give the country its independence; but the European powers, fearing that Bulgaria might become a Russian dependency, intervened. By the Treaty of Berlin in 1878, Bulgaria became autonomous under Turkish sovereignty.

In 1887, Prince Ferdinand of Saxe-Coburg-Gotha was elected ruler of Bulgaria; on Oct. 5, 1908, he declared the country independent and took the title of Tsar.

Bulgaria joined Germany in World War I and lost. On Oct. 3, 1918, Tsar Ferdinand abdicated in favor of his son, Tsar Boris III. Boris assumed dictatorial powers in 1934–35. When Hitler awarded Bulgaria southern Dobruja, taken from Romania in 1940, Boris joined the Nazis in war the next year and occupied parts of Yugoslavia and Greece. Later the Germans tried to force Boris to send his troops against the Russians. Boris resisted and died under mysterious circumstances on Aug. 28, 1943.

Simeon II, infant son of Boris, became nominal ruler under a regency. Russia declared war on Bulgaria on Sept. 5, 1944. An armistice was agreed to three days later, after Bulgaria had declared war on Germany. Russian troops streamed in the next day.

A Soviet-style people's republic was established in 1947. Since then, Bulgaria acquired the reputation of being the most slavishly loyal to Moscow of all the East European Communist countries. An Italian prosecutor's report in 1984 charged that Bulgaria, possibly with Soviet support, masterminded the 1981 attempt by Turkish gunman Mehmet Ali Agca to assassinate Pope John Paul II.

BURKINA FASO

President of National Council of the Revolution: Capt. Thomas Sankara (1983)
Area: 105,870 sq mi. (274,200 sq km)
Population (est. mid-1987): 7,300,000 (average annual growth rate, 2.8%)
Density per square mile: 69.0
Capital and largest city (est. 1985): Ouagadougou, 360,000
Monetary unit: Franc CFA
Ethnic groups: Mossis, Bobos, Lobis, Fulanis
Languages: French, African languages
Religions: Animist, 65%; Islam, 25%; Roman Catholic, 10%
National name: Burkina Faso
Literacy rate: 10%
Economic summary: Gross national product (1983): $1.2 billion. Average annual growth rate (1970–79): —1.2%. Per capita income (1984): $160. Labor force in agriculture: 90%; principal products: millet, sorghum, corn, rice, livestock, peanuts, sugar cane, cotton. Major industrial products: processed agricultural products, light industrial items, brick, brewed products. Natural resources: manganese, limestone, marble, gold, uranium, bauxite, copper. Exports: livestock, peanuts, cotton. Imports: textiles, food and consumer goods, transport equipment, machinery, fuels. Major trading partners: Ivory Coast, France, Ghana, Western European nations, Taiwan.

Geography. Slightly larger than Colorado, Burkina Faso, formerly known as Upper Volta, is a landlocked country in West Africa. Its neighbors are the Ivory Coast, Mali, Niger, Benin, Togo, and Ghana. The country consists of extensive plains, low hills, high savannas, and a desert area in the north.

Government. The former French colony has been governed by a series of military leaders since a coup in November 1980 overthrew the last elected president. All political parties were banned and the political process suspended following the coup.

History. The country, called Upper Volta by the French, consists chiefly of the lands of the Mossi Empire, where France established a protectorate over the Kingdom of Ouagadougou in 1897. Upper Volta became a separate colony in 1919, was partitioned among Niger, the Sudan, and the Ivory Coast in 1933 and was reconstituted in 1947. An autonomous republic within the French Community, it became independent on Aug. 5, 1960.

President Maurice Yameogo was deposed on Jan. 3, 1966, by a military coup led by Col. Sangoulé Lamizana, who dissolved the National Assembly and suspended the Constitution. A new Constitution was adopted later that year and a new Assembly was elected. However, dissension within the Volta Democratic Union, the major party, led to renewed military rule. Constitutional rule returned in 1978 with the election of an Assembly and a presidential vote in June in which Gen. Lamizana won by a narrow margin over three other candidates.

On Nov. 25, 1980, there was a bloodless coup which placed Gen. Lamizana under house arrest. Col. Sayé Zerbo took charge as the President of the Military Committee of Reform for National Progress. Maj. Jean-Baptiste Ouedraogo toppled Zerbo in another coup on Nov. 7, 1982. Captain Thomas Sankara, in turn, deposed Ouedraogo a year later. His government changed the country's name on Aug. 3, 1984, to Burkina Faso (the "land of upright men") to sever ties with its colonial past.

BURMA

Socialist Republic of the Union of Burma
President: U San Yu (1981)
Prime Minister: U Maung Maung Kha (1977)

Area: 261,789 sq mi. (678,036 sq km)
Population (est. mid-1987): 38,800,000 (average annual growth rate: 2.1%)
Density per square mile: 148.2
Capital: Rangoon
Largest cities (est. 1983): Rangoon, 2,250,000; **(est. 1977 for metropolitan area by U.N.):** Mandalay, 533,-000; Moulmein, 220,000; Bassein, 144,000; Pegu, 151,000
Monetary unit: Kyat
Language: Burmese
Religions: Buddhist, 87%; Christian, Islam
National name: Pyidaungsu Socialist Thammada Myanma Naingngandau
Literacy rate: 78%
Economic summary: Gross national product (1984): $6.6 billion. Average annual growth rate (1973–82): 6.0%. Per capita income (1984): $180. Labor force in agriculture: 66%; principal products: sugar cane, corn, rice, peanuts. Labor force in industry: 9%; major products: textiles, footwear, processed agricultural products, wood and wood products, refined petroleum. Natural resources: timber, nickel, cobalt, copper, gold, rubies, sapphires, jade. Exports: rice, teak. Imports: machinery, transportation and construction equipment, manufactured goods. Major trading partners: Singapore, West Germany, U.K., Japan, Indonesia.

Geography. Burma occupies the northwest portion of the Indochinese peninsula. India lies to the northwest and China to the northeast. Bangladesh, Laos, and Thailand are also neighbors. The Bay of Bengal touches the southwestern coast.

Slightly smaller than Texas, the country is divided into three natural regions: the Arakan Yoma, a long, narrow mountain range forming the barrier between Burma and India; the Shan Plateau in the east, extending southward into Tenasserim; and the Central Basin, running down to the flat fertile delta of the Irrawaddy in the south. This delta contains a network of intercommunicating canals and nine principal river mouths.

Government. On March 2, 1962, the government of U Nu was overthrown and replaced by a Revolutionary Council, which assumed all power in the state. Gen. U Ne Win, as chairman of the Revolutionary Council, became the chief executive.

A new Constitution was approved in 1973 and took effect Jan. 4, 1974. Under it, Burma is a Socialist Democratic Republic with a 475-seat unicameral legislature called the People's Congress. In 1972, Ne Win and his colleagues resigned their military titles and thereafter ruled as "civilians." In 1974, Ne Win dissolved the Revolutionary Council and became President under the new Constitution. He voluntarily relinquished the presidency on Nov. 9, 1981, and the leadership of the Burmese Socialist Program Party (BSPP), the only legal party, in 1986. U Sun Yu was elected President by the People's Congress and leads the BSPP.

History. In 1612, the British East India Company sent agents to Burma, but the Burmese long resisted efforts of British traders, and Dutch and Portuguese as well, to establish posts on the Bay of Bengal. By the Anglo-Burmese War in 1824–26 and two following wars, the British East India Company expanded to the whole of Burma by 1886. Burma was annexed to India. It became a separate colony in 1937.

During World War II, Burma was a key battleground; the 800-mile Burma Road was the Allies' vital supply line to China. The Japanese invaded the country in December 1941, and by May 1942 had occupied most of it, cutting the Burma Road. After one of the most difficult campaigns of the war, Allied forces liberated most of Burma prior to the Japanese surrender in August 1945.

Burma became independent on Jan. 4, 1948. In 1951 and 1952 the Socialists achieved power, and Burma became the first Asian country to introduce social legislation.

In 1968, after the government had made headway against the Communist and separatist rebels, the military regime adopted a policy of strict nonalignment and followed "the Burmese Way" to socialism. But the insurgents, reportedly numbering several thousand, continued active.

BURUNDI

Republic of Burundi
Head of Government: Col. Jean-Baptiste Bagaza (1976)
Area: 10,747 sq mi. (27,834 sq km)
Population (est. mid-1987): 5,000,000 (average annual growth rate: 2.9%)
Density per square mile: 465.2
Capital and largest city (1986): Bujumbura, 272,600
Monetary unit: Burundi franc
Languages: Kirundi (official), French
Religions: Roman Catholic, 78%; Protestant, 5%
National name: Republika Y'Uburundi
Literacy rate: 23%
Economic summary: Gross national product (1983): $1.05 billion. Average annual growth rate (1970–79): 1.5%. Per capita income (1983): $240. Principal agricultural products: coffee, tea, cotton, bananas, sorghum. Major industrial products: light consumer goods. Natural resources: nickel, kaolin, gold, unexploited copper and platinum deposits. Exports: coffee, tea, cotton. Imports: textiles, food, transport equipment, petroleum products. Major trading partners: U.S., Belgium, West Germany, France.

Geography. Wedged among Tanzania, Zaire, and Rwanda in east central Africa, Burundi occupies a high plateau divided by several deep valleys. It is equal in size to Maryland.

Government. Legislative and executive power is vested in the president.

Burundi's first Constitution, approved July 11, 1974, placed UPRONA (Unity and National Progress), the only political party, in control of national policy.

History. Burundi was once part of German East Africa. An integrated society developed among the Watusi, a tall, warlike people and nomad cattle raisers, and the Bahutu, a Bantu people, who were subject farmers. Belgium won a League of Nations mandate in 1923, and subsequently Burundi, with Rwanda, was transferred to the status of a United Nations trust territory.

In 1962, Burundi gained independence and became a kingdom under Mwami Mwambutsa IV. His son deposed him in 1966 to rule as Ntaré V.

Premier Micombero overthrew the Mwami, a

few months later, installing himself as president.

One of Africa's worst tribal wars, which became genocide, occurred in Burundi in April 1972, following the return of Ntare V. He was given a safe-conduct promise in writing by President Micombero but was "judged and immediately executed" by the Burundi leader. His return was apparently attended by an invasion of exiles of Burundi's Hutu tribe. Whether Hutus living in Burundi joined the invasion is unclear, but after it failed, the victorious Tutsis proceeded to massacre some 100,000 persons in six weeks, with possibly 100,000 more slain by summer.

On Nov. 1, 1976, a military coup led by Lt. Col. Jean-Baptiste Bagaza ousted Micombero, who was serving his second term. Bagaza assumed the presidency Nov. 3, suspended the Constitution, and announced that a 30-member Supreme Revolutionary Council would be the governing body.

Bagaza was elected head of the only legal political party in 1979 and re-elected to a second five-year term as party chieftain in 1984.

CAMBODIA

People's Republic of Kampuchea
President: Heng Samrin (1979)
Prime Minister: Hun Sen (1985)
Area: 69,884 sq mi. (181,000 sq km)
Population (est. mid-1987): 6,500,000 (average annual growth rate: 2.1%)
Density per square mile: 93.1
Capital and largest city (est. 1980 for metropolitan area): Phnom Penh, 500,000
Monetary unit: Riel
Ethnic groups: Khmer, 90%; Chinese, 5%; other minorities 5%
Languages: Khmer (official), French, Vietnamese, Chinese
Religion: Theravada Buddhist
Literacy rate: 48%
Economic summary: Gross national product (1971): $500 million. Principal agricultural products: rice, rubber, corn. Major industrial products: fish, wood and wood products, milled rice. Natural resources: timber, gemstones, iron ore, manganese, phosphate. Exports: natural rubber, rice, pepper, wood. Imports: foodstuffs, fuel, machinery. Major trading partners: China, North Korea, Vietnam, U.S.S.R.

Geography. Situated on the Indochinese peninsula, Cambodia is bordered by Thailand and Laos on the north and Vietnam on the east and south. The Gulf of Siam is off the western coast. The country, the size of Missouri, consists chiefly of a large alluvial plain ringed in by mountains and on the east by the Mekong River. The plain is centered on Lake Tonle Sap, which is a natural storage basin of the Mekong.

Government. A bloodless coup toppled Prince Sihanouk in 1970. It was led by Lon Nol and Prince Sisowath Sirik Matak, Sihanouk's cousin. Sihanouk moved to Peking to head a government-in-exile. On Oct. 9, 1970, Lon Nol proclaimed himself President.

The Lon Nol regime was overthrown in April 1975 by Pol Pot, a leader of the Communist Khmer Rouge forces, who instituted a xenophobic reign of terror. Pol Pot was in turn ousted on Jan. 8, 1979, by Heng Samrin, a dissident backed by strong Vietnamese forces.

History. Cambodia came under Khmer rule about A.D. 600. Under the Khmers, magnificent temples were built at Angkor. The Khmer kingdom once ruled over most of Southeast Asia, but attacks by the Thai and the Vietnamese almost annihilated the empire until the French joined Cambodia, Laos, and Vietnam into French Indochina.

Under Norodom Sihanouk, enthroned in 1941, and particularly under Japanese occupation during World War II, nationalism revived. After the ouster of the Japanese, the Cambodians sought independence, but the French returned in 1946, granting the country a Constitution in 1947 and independence within the French Union in 1949. Sihanouk won full military control during the French-Indochinese War in 1953. He abdicated in 1955 in favor of his parents, remaining head of the government, and when his father died in 1960, became chief of state without returning to the throne. In 1963, he sought a guarantee of Cambodia's neutrality from all parties to the Vietnam War.

On March 18, 1970, while Sihanouk was abroad trying to get North Vietnamese and the Vietcong out of border sanctuaries near Vietnam, anti-Vietnamese riots occurred, and Sihanouk was overthrown.

North Vietnamese and Vietcong units in border sanctuaries began moving deeper into Cambodia, threatening rapid overthrow of the new regime headed by Lon Nol. President Nixon sent South Vietnamese and U.S. troops across the border on April 30. U.S. ground forces, limited to 30-kilometer penetration, withdrew by June 30.

The Vietnam peace agreement of 1973 stipulated withdrawal of foreign forces from Cambodia, but fighting continued between Hanoi-backed insurgents and U.S.-supplied government troops. U.S. air support for the government forces was ended by Congress on Aug. 15, 1973.

Fighting continued and reached a quick climax early in 1975.

As government troops fell back in bitter fighting, Lon Nol fled by air April 1, leaving the government under the interim control of Premier Long Boret. On April 16, the government's capitulation ended the five-year war, but not the travails of war-ravaged Cambodia.

A new Constitution was proclaimed in December 1975, establishing a 250-member People's Assembly, a State Presidium headed by Pol Pot, and a Supreme Judicial Tribunal. Samphan replaced Sihanouk as head of state in April 1976, and the former monarch became a virtual prisoner until freed by Pol Pot in 1979.

In the next two years, from 2 million to 4 million Cambodians are estimated to have died under the brutality of the Pol Pot regime. Border clashes with Vietnam developed into a Vietnamese invasion and by the end of 1978 the Pol Pot government appeared to be collapsing.

Despite the capture of Phnom Penh on Jan. 8 by Heng Samrin, a dissident Khmer Rouge backed by Vietnamese troops, fighting continued in isolated areas. Retreating Pol Pot forces and refugees totaling 40,000 were driven into Thailand by May.

At a meeting in Kuala Lumpur, Malaysia, on June 22, 1982, Sihanouk formed an alliance with Son Sann, his former prime minister, and Khieu Samphan, Pol Pot's representative, to oppose the Heng Samrin regime installed in Phnom Pehn by the Vietnamese.

While Sihanouk remained in exile in North Korea, about 9,000 noncommunist troops loyal to him and another 15,000 under Son Sann joined about 35,000 communist Pol Pot forces fighting the 170,000 Vietnamese troops supporting the Heng Samrin government. According to Washington sources, the Central Intelligence Agency covertly aided the noncommunist resistance groups, funnelling assistance through Thailand. The Cambodian insurgents suffered a major defeat in March 1985 when Vietnamese forces overran their camps in Cambodia and forced them into Thailand. Resistance forces were able to switch to hit-and-run tactics and operate effectively inside the country.

CAMEROON

Republic of Cameroon
President: Paul Biya (1982)
Area: 183,569 sq mi. (475,442 sq km)
Population (est. mid-1987): 10,300,000 (average annual growth rate: 2.7%)
Density per square mile: 56.1
Capital: Yaoundé
Largest cities (est. 1985): Douala, 852,700; Yaoundé, 583,500
Monetary unit: Franc CFA
Languages: French and English (both official); Foulbé, Bamiléke, Ewondo, Donala, Mungaka, Bassa
Religions: Roman Catholic, 35%; Animist, 12%; Islam, 35%; Protestant, 18%
National name: République du Cameroun
Literacy rate: 55%
Economic summary: Gross national product (1984): $8.0 billion. Annual growth rate (1983): 5%. Per capita income (1984): $850. Land used for agriculture: 15%; labor force: 73%; principal products: coffee, cocoa, corn, peanuts. Labor force in industry: 5%. Major products: small manufacturing, consumer goods, aluminum. Natural resources: timber, some oil, bauxite. Exports: cocoa, coffee, timber, aluminum, petroleum. Imports: consumer goods, machinery, food, beverages, tobacco, fuel. Major trading partners: France, U.S., Western European nations.

Geography. Cameroon is a West African nation on the Gulf of Guinea, bordered by Nigeria, Chad, the Central African Republic, the Congo, Equatorial Guinea, and Gabon. It is nearly twice the size of Oregon.

The interior consists of a high plateau, rising to 4,500 feet (1,372 m), with the land descending to a lower, densely wooded plateau and then to swamps and plains along the coast. Mount Cameroon (13,350 ft.; 4,069 m), near the coast, is the highest elevation in the country. The main rivers are the Benue, Nyong, and Sanaga.

Government. After a 1972 plebiscite, a unitary nation was formed out of East and West Cameroon to replace the former Federal Republic. A Constitution was adopted, providing for election of a president every five years and of a 150-seat National Assembly, whose nominal five-year term can be extended or shortened by the president. The Cameroon National Union is the only political party.

History. The Republic of Cameroon is inhabited by Hamitic and Semitic peoples in the north, where Islam is the principal religion, and by Bantu peoples in the central and southern regions, where native animism prevails. The tribes were conquered by many invaders.

The land escaped colonial rule until 1884, when treaties with tribal chiefs brought the area under German domination. After World War I, the League of Nations gave the French a mandate over 80% of the area, and the British 20% adjacent to Nigeria. After World War II, when the country came under a U.N. trusteeship in 1946, self-government was granted, and the Cameroun People's Union emerged as the dominant party by campaigning for reunification of French and British Cameroon and for independence. Accused of being under Communist control, it waged a campaign of revolutionary terror from 1955 to 1958, when it was crushed. In British Cameroon, unification was pressed also by the leading party, the Kamerun National Democratic Party, led by John Foncha.

France set up Cameroun as an autonomous state in 1957, and the next year its legislative assembly voted for independence by 1960. In 1959 a fully autonomous government of Cameroun was formed under Ahmadou Ahidjo. Cameroun became an independent republic on Jan. 1, 1960, adopted a Constitution in a referendum in February, and chose a National Assembly in April. The Assembly elected Ahidjo president. A federal Constitution was approved in 1961, and the Federal Republic of Cameroon came into being in October, headed by Ahidjo and Foncha.

CANADA

Sovereign: Queen Elizabeth II
Governor General: Jeanne Sauvé (1984)
Prime Minister: Brian Mulroney (1984)
Area: 3,851,809 sq mi. (9,976,186 sq km)
Population (est. mid-1987): 25,900,000 (British, 44.6%; French, 28.7%; other European, 23%) (average annual growth rate: 0.8%)
Density per square mile: 6.7
Capital: Ottawa, Ont.
Largest cities (1981 census; metropolitan areas): Toronto, 2,998,947; Montreal, 2,828,349; Vancouver, 1,268,-183; Ottawa, 717,978; Edmonton, 657,057; Calgary, 592,743; Winnipeg, 584,842; Quebec, 576,075; Hamilton, 542,095; St. Catherines-Niagara, 304,353; Kitchener, 287,801; London, 283,668; Halifax, 277,727
Monetary Unit: Canadian dollar
Languages: English, French
Religions: Roman Catholic, 47.3%; Protestant, 41.2%; no religion, 7.4%; Eastern Orthodox, 1.5%; Jewish, 1.2%; other, 1.3%
Literacy rate: 98%
Economic Summary: Gross national product: (1985) $335 billion. Average annual growth rate (1986) 3.1%. Per capita income: (1985): $13,541. Land use for agriculture: 7%; labor force: 4%; Principal products; wheat, barley, oats, livestock. Labor force in industry: 18%. Major products; transportation equipment, petroleum, chemicals, wood products. Exports: wheat, petroleum, lumber and wood products, motor vehicles. Imports: electronic equipment, chemicals. Major trading partners: U.S., Japan, U.K., U.S.S.R., West Germany.

Geography. Covering most of the northern part of the North American continent and with an area larger than that of the United States, Canada has

Canadian Governors General and Prime Ministers Since 1867

Term of office	Governor General	Term	Prime Minister	Party
1867–1868	Viscount Monck[1]	1867–1873	Sir John A. MacDonald	Conservative
1869–1872	Baron Lisgar	1873–1878	Alexander Mackenzie	Liberal
1872–1878	Earl of Dufferin	1878–1891	Sir John A. MacDonald	Conservative
1878–1883	Marquess of Lorne	1891–1892	Sir John J. C. Abbott	Conservative
1883–1888	Marquess of Lansdowne	1892–1894	Sir John S. D. Thompson	Conservative
1888–1893	Baron Stanley of Preston	1894–1896	Sir Mackenzie Bowell	Conservative
1893–1898	Earl of Aberdeen	1896	Sir Charles Tupper	Conservative
1898–1904	Earl of Minto	1896–1911	Sir Wilfrid Laurier	Liberal
1904–1911	Earl Grey	1911–1917	Sir Robert L. Borden	Conservative
1911–1916	Duke of Connaught	1917–1920	Sir Robert L. Borden	Unionist
1916–1921	Duke of Devonshire	1920–1921	Arthur Meighen	Unionist
1921–1926	Baron Byng of Vinny	1921–1926	W. L. Mackenzie King	Liberal
1926–1931	Viscount Willingdon	1926	Arthur Meighen	Conservative
1931–1935	Earl of Bessborough	1926–1930	W. L. Mackenzie King	Liberal
1935–1940	Baron Tweedsmuir	1930–1935	Richard B. Bennett	Conservative
1940–1946	Earl of Athlone	1935–1948	W. L. Mackenzie King	Liberal
1946–1952	Viscount Alexander	1948–1957	Louis S. St. Laurent	Liberal
1952–1959	Vincent Massey	1957–1963	John G. Diefenbaker	Conservative
1959–1967	George P. Vanier	1963–1968	Lester B. Pearson	Liberal
1967–1973	Roland Michener	1968–1979	Pierre Elliott Trudeau	Liberal
1974–1979	Jules Léger	1979–1980	Charles Joseph Clark	Conservative
1979–1984	Edward R. Schreyer	1980–1984	Pierre Elliott Trudeau	Liberal
1984–	Jeanne Sauvé	1984–1984	John Turner	Liberal
		1984–	Brian Mulroney	Conservative

1. Became Governor General of British North America in 1861.

an extremely varied topography. In the east the mountainous maritime provinces have an irregular coast line on the Gulf of St. Lawrence and the Atlantic. The St. Lawrence plain, covering most of southern Quebec and Ontario, and the interior continental plain, covering southern Manitoba and Saskatchewan and most of Alberta, are the principal cultivable areas. They are separated by a forested plateau rising from lakes Superior and Huron.

Westward toward the Pacific, most of British Columbia, Yukon, and part of western Alberta are covered by parallel mountain ranges including the Rockies. The Pacific border of the coast range is ragged with fiords and channels. The highest point in Canada is Mount Logan (19,850 ft; 6,050 m), which is in the Yukon.

Canada has an abundance of large and small lakes. In addition to the Great Lakes on the U.S. border, there are 9 others that are more than 100 miles long (161 km) and 35 that are more than 50 miles long (80 km).

The two principal river systems are the Mackenzie and the St. Lawrence. The St. Lawrence, with its tributaries, is navigable for over 1,900 miles (3,058 km).

Government. Canada, a self-governing member of the Commonwealth of Nations, is a federation of 10 provinces (Alberta, British Columbia, Manitoba, New Brunswick, Newfoundland, Nova Scotia, Ontario, Prince Edward Island, Quebec, and Saskatchewan) and two territories (Northwest Territories and Yukon) whose powers were spelled out in the British North America Act of 1867. With the passing of the Constitution Act of 1981, the act and the Constitutional amending power were transferred from the British government to Canada so that the Canadian Constitution is now entirely in the hands of the Canadians.

Actually the Governor General acts only with the advice of the Canadian Prime Minister and the Cabinet, who also sit in the federal Parliament. The Parliament has two houses: a Senate of 104 members appointed for life, and a House of Commons of 282 members apportioned according to provincial population. Elections are held at least every five years or whenever the party in power is voted down in the House of Commons or considers it expedient to appeal to the people. The Prime Minister is the leader of the majority party in the House of Commons—or, if no single party holds a majority, the leader of the party able to command the support of a majority of members of the House. Laws must be passed by both houses of Parliament and signed by the Governor General in the Queen's name.

The 10 provincial governments are nominally headed by Lieutenant Governors appointed by the federal government, but the executive power in each actually is vested in a Cabinet headed by a Premier, who is leader of the majority party. The provincial legislatures are composed of one-house assemblies whose members are elected for four-year terms. They are known as Legislative Assemblies, except in Newfoundland, where it is the House of Assembly, and in Quebec, where it is the National Assembly.

The judicial system consists of a Supreme Court in Ottawa (established in 1875), with appellate jurisdiction, and a Supreme Court in each province, as well as county courts with limited jurisdiction in most of the provinces. The Governor General in Council appoints these judges.

The major political parties are the Progressive Conservative Party (209 of 282 seats in House of Commons), led by Prime Minister Brian Mulroney; Liberal Party (40 seats), led by John T. Turner; New Democratic Party (31 seats), led by Edward Broadbent, independents (2 seats).

History. The Norse explorer Leif Ericson probably reached the shores of Canada (Labrador or Nova Scotia) in A.D. 1000, but the history of the white

Population by Provinces and Territories

Province	1981 (Census)	1983 (June Estimate)
Alberta	2,237,724	2,352,300
British Columbia	2,744,467	2,825,000
Manitoba	1,026,241	1,046,300
New Brunswick	696,403	706,600
Newfoundland	567,681	576,200
Nova Scotia	847,442	859,300
Ontario	8,625,107	8,816,000
Prince Edward Island	122,506	123,900
Quebec	6,438,403	6,514,900
Saskatchewan	968,313	992,000
Northwest Territories	45,741	48,600
Yukon Territory	23,153	22,200
Total	**24,343,181**	**24,883,400**

Source: Statistics Canada.

man in the country actually began in 1497, when John Cabot, an Italian in the service of Henry VII of England, reached Newfoundland or Nova Scotia. Canada was taken for France in 1534 by Jacques Cartier. The actual settlement of New France, as it was then called, began in 1604 at Port Royal in what is now Nova Scotia; in 1608, Quebec was founded. France's colonization efforts were not very successful, but French explorers by the end of the 17th century had penetrated beyond the Great Lakes to the western prairies and south along the Mississippi to the Gulf of Mexico. Meanwhile, the English Hudson's Bay Company had been established in 1670. Because of the valuable fisheries and fur trade, a conflict developed between the French and English; in 1713, Newfoundland, Hudson Bay, and Nova Scotia (Acadia) were lost to England.

During the Seven Years' War (1756–63), England extended its conquest, and the British Maj. Gen. James Wolfe won his famous victory over Gen. Louis Montcalm outside Quebec on Sept. 13, 1759. The Treaty of Paris in 1763 gave England control.

At that time the population of Canada was almost entirely French, but in the next few decades, thousands of British colonists emigrated to Canada from the British Isles and from the American colonies. In 1849, the right of Canada to self-government was recognized. By the British North America Act of 1867, the Dominion of Canada was created through the confederation of Upper and Lower Canada, Nova Scotia, and New Brunswick. Prince Edward Island joined the Dominion in 1873.

In 1869 Canada purchased from the Hudson's Bay Company the vast middle west (Rupert's Land) from which the provinces of Manitoba (1870), Alberta, and Saskatchewan (1905) were later formed. In 1871, British Columbia joined the Dominion. The country was linked from coast to coast in 1885 by the Canadian Pacific Railway.

During the formative years between 1866 and 1896, the Conservative Party, led by Sir John A. MacDonald, governed the country, except during the years 1873–78. In 1896, the Liberal Party took over and, under Sir Wilfrid Laurier, an eminent French Canadian, ruled until 1911.

By the Statute of Westminster in 1931 the British Dominions, including Canada, were formally declared to be partner nations with Britain, "equal in status, in no way subordinate to each other," and bound together only by allegiance to a common Crown.

Newfoundland became Canada's 10th province on March 31, 1949, following a plebiscite. Canada includes two territories—the Yukon Territory, the area north of British Columbia and east of Alaska, and the Northwest Territories, including all of Canada north of 60° north latitude except Yukon and the northernmost sections of Quebec and Newfoundland. This area includes all of the Arctic north of the mainland, Norway having recognized Canadian sovereignty over the Svendrup Islands in the Arctic in 1931.

The Liberal Party, led by William Lyon Mackenzie King, dominated Canadian politics from 1921 until 1957, when it was succeeded by the Progressive Conservatives. The Liberals, under the leadership of Lester B. Pearson, returned to power in 1963. Pearson remained Prime Minister until 1968, when he retired and was replaced by a former law professor, Pierre Elliott Trudeau. Trudeau maintained Canada's defensive alliance with the United States, but began moving toward a more independent policy in world affairs.

Trudeau set about creating what he termed a "just society," stressing domestic reforms. His election was considered in part a response to the most serious problem confronting the country, the division between French- and English-speaking Canadians, which had led to a separatist movement in the predominantly French province of Quebec. Trudeau, himself a French Canadian, supported programs for bilingualism and an increased measure of provincial autonomy, although he would not tolerate the idea of separatism. In 1974, the provincial government voted to make French the official language of Quebec.

Conflicts over the law establishing French as the dominant language in Quebec, particularly in schooling, kept separatism as a national issue, but by-elections in 1977 produced easy victories for Trudeau's ruling Liberals in four Quebec seats in the national legislature, and polls showed a decline in separatist support both in the province and elsewhere in Canada.

Economic problems appeared to take precedence over politics in 1978, as the Sun Life Assurance Company of Canada, the nation's largest insurance firm, announced that it would move its headquarters from Montreal to Toronto. Many businesses had left the province earlier, but Sun Life was the first to cite the language law as the reason for its departure.

Despite Trudeau's removal of price and wage controls in 1978, continuing inflation and a high rate of unemployment caused him to delay elections until May 22, 1979, the first time since 1935 that a Canadian government had retained office for the allowable five-year term. The delay gave Trudeau no advantage—the Progressive Conservatives under Charles Joseph Clark defeated the Liberals everywhere except in Quebec, New Brunswick, and Newfoundland.

Clark took office as the head of Canada's fifth minority government in the last 20 years, needing the support of 26 New Democratic Party members and six Social Credit members to obtain an absolute majority in the 282-seat House.

Clark's government collapsed after only six months when a motion to defeat the Tory budget carried by 139-133 on Dec. 13, 1979. On the same day, the Quebec law making French the exclusive official language of the province—an issue which had been expected to provide Clark's first major internal test—was voided by the Canadian Supreme Court.

In national elections Feb. 18, 1980, the resurgent Liberals under Trudeau scored an unexpectedly big victory, winning 146 seats (147 when a vacancy was filled a month later), while the Conservatives fell from 136 to 103 and the New Democrats won 32 seats.

Resolving a dispute that had occupied Trudeau since the beginning of his tenure, Queen Elizabeth II, in Ottawa on April 17, 1982, signed the Constitution Act, cutting the last legal tie between Canada and Britain. Since 1867, the British North America Act required British Parliament approval for any Canadian constitutional change.

The new charter was approved by the federal House of Commons, 246–24, on Dec. 2, 1981, and by a 59–23 vote of the Senate six days later. The Constitution retains Queen Elizabeth as Queen of Canada and keeps Canada's membership in the Commonwealth.

Ending an era, Trudeau retired on June 30, 1984, after 16 years as prime minister, except for the nine-month interruption in 1979–80.

His successor as Liberal Party leader and Prime Minister, John N. Turner, called an early election for a new Parliament after polls showed the Liberals had made a big comeback from the last months of Trudeau's term, despite Canada's continuing recession and 11.2% unemployment, the highest in 40 years.

In the national election on Sept. 4, 1984, the Progressive Conservative Party scored an overwhelming victory, fundamentally changing the country's political landscape. The Conservatives, led by Brian Mulroney, a 45-year-old corporate lawyer, won the highest political majority in Canadian history. Mulroney was sworn in as Canada's 18th Prime Minister on Sept. 17.

Foreign issues have tended to be dominated by talks with the U.S. aimed at establishing a free-trade pact, an effort hindered by protectionist measures taken by the U.S. against Canadian products.

CAPE VERDE

Republic of Cape Verde
President: Aristides Pereira (1975)
Premier: Maj. Pedro Pires (1975)
Area: 1,557 sq mi. (4,033 sq km)
Population: (est. mid-1987): 300,000 (average annual growth rate: 2.6%)
Density per square mile: 192.7
Capital (est. 1982): Praia, 37,676
Largest city (est. 1982): Mindelo, 50,000
Monetary unit: Cape Verde escudo
Language: Portuguese
Religion: Roman Catholic, 98%
National name: República de Cabo Verde
Literacy rate: 37%
Economic summary: Gross national product (1983): $123 million. Average annual growth rate (1970–79): 4.8%. Per capita income (1983): $400. Principal agricultural products: bananas, corn, sugar cane, coconuts. Major industry: fishing, salt mining. Natural resources: salt, siliceous rock. Exports: fish and shellfish, bananas, salt. Imports: machinery, textiles, petroleum products. Major trading partners: Portugal, Netherlands, Algeria, neighboring African states.

Geography: Cape Verde, only slightly larger than Rhode Island, is an archipelago in the Atlantic 385 miles (620 km) west of Dakar, Senegal.

The islands are divided into two groups: Barlavento in the north, comprising Santo Antão (291 sq mi.; 754 sq km), Boa Vista (240 sq mi.; 622 sq km), São Nicolau (132 sq mi.; 342 sq km), São Vicente (88 sq mi.; 246 sq km), Sal (83 sq mi.; 298 sq km), and Santa Luzia (13 sq mi.; 34 sq km); and Sotavento in the south, consisting of São Tiago (383 sq mi.; 992 sq km), Fogo (184 sq mi.; 477 sq km), Maio (103 sq mi.; 267 sq km), and Brava (25 sq mi.; 65 sq km). The islands are mostly mountainous, with the land deeply scarred by erosion. There is an active volcano on Fogo.

Government. The islands became independent on July 5, 1975, under an agreement negotiated with Portugal in 1974. The 56-member National Assembly chose Aristides Pereira as President and Maj. Pedro Pires as Premier. All members of the Assembly belong to the African Party for the Independence of Portuguese Guinea and Cape Verde, then the only party that entered candidates in the election. It is committed to union with Guinea-Bissau, another former Portuguese colony.

History. Uninhabited upon their discovery in 1456, the Cape Verde islands became part of the Portuguese empire in 1495. A majority of their modern inhabitants are of mixed Portuguese and African ancestry. A coaling station developed during the 19th century on the island of São Vicente has grown in recent years to an oil and gasoline storage depot for ships and aircraft.

CENTRAL AFRICAN REPUBLIC

Head of Government: Gen. André Kolingba (1981)
Area: 241,313 sq mi. (625,000 sq km)
Population (est. mid-1987): 2,700,000 (average annual growth rate, 2.5%)
Density per square mile: 11.2
Capital and largest city (est. 1985): Bangui, 473,800
Monetary unit: Franc CFA
Ethnic groups: Mandja-Baya, Banda, Mbaka, Azande, Yakoma
Languages: French (official) and Sango
Religions: Protestant, 50%; Roman Catholic, 33%; Animist, 12%, Islam, 3%
National name: République Centrafricaine
Member of French Community
Literacy rate: 33%
Economic summary: Gross national product (1984): $680 million. Average annual growth rate (1970–79): 0.9%. Per capita income (1984): $270. Land used for agriculture: 15%; labor force: 88%; principal products: cotton, coffee, peanuts, food crops, livestock. Major industrial products: timber, textiles, soap, cigarettes, processed food. Natural resources: diamonds, timber. Exports: diamonds, cotton, timber, coffee. Imports: machinery and electrical equipment, petroleum products, textiles. Major trading partners: France, Japan, U.S., Belgium-Luxembourg, Zaire, West Germany.

Geography. Situated about 500 miles north (805 km) of the equator, the Central African Republic is a landlocked nation bordered by Cameroon, Chad, the Sudan, Zaire, and the Congo. Twice the size of New Mexico, it is covered by tropical forests in the south and semidesert land in the east. The Ubangi and Shari are the largest of many rivers.

Government. On Dec. 4, 1976, the Central African Republic became the Central African Empire. Marshal Jean-Bédel Bokassa, who had ruled the republic since he took power in a military coup Dec.

31, 1965, was declared Emperor Bokassa I. He was overthrown in a coup on Sept. 20, 1979. Former President David Dacko, returned to power and changed the country's name back to the Central African Republic. An army coup on Sept. 1, 1981, deposed Dacko and suspended the Constitution and all political parties. A Military Committee of National Redress was set up to run the country. A new constitution was enacted on Nov. 21, 1986 that extended Kolingba's term another six years and allowed for parliamentary elections in which the Centrafrican Democratic Assembly would be the only party.

History. As the colony of Ubangi-Shari, what is now the Central African Republic was united with Chad in 1905 and joined with Gabon and the Middle Congo in French Equatorial Africa in 1910. After World War II a rebellion in 1946 forced the French to grant self-government. In 1958 the territory voted to become an autonomous republic within the French Community, but on Aug. 13, 1960, President David Dacko proclaimed the republic's independence from France.

Dacko undertook to move the country into Peking's orbit, but was overthrown in a coup on Dec. 31, 1965, by the then Col. Jean-Bédel Bokassa, Army Chief of Staff. In August 1977, the U.S. State Department protested the Emperor's jailing of American and British newsmen.

Bokassa staged an elaborate coronation ceremony on the first anniversary of the Empire. The cost of the ceremony was one fourth of the annual foreign-exchange earnings of the country.

CHAD

Republic of Chad
President: Hissen Habré (1982)
Area: 495,752 sq mi. (1,284,000 sq km)
Population (est. mid-1987): 4,600,000 (average annual growth rate, 2.0%)
Density per square mile: 10.5
Capital and largest city (est. 1986): N'djamena, 511,700
Monetary unit: Franc CFA
Ethnic groups: Baguirmiens, Kanembous, Saras, Massas, Arabs, Toubous, Goranes
Languages: French and Arabic (official), many tribal languages
Religions: Islam, 44%; Christian, 33%; Animist, 23%
National name: République du Tchad
Literacy rate: about 20%
Economic summary: Gross national product (1984): $360 million. Average annual growth rate (1970–81): 0.6%. Per capita income (1985): $80. Land used for agriculture: 17%; labor force: 85%; principal products: cotton, cattle, sugar, subsistence crops. Labor force in industry: 4%; major products: livestock and livestock products, beer, food processing, textiles, cigarettes. Natural resources: petroleum, unexploited uranium, kaolin. Exports: cotton, livestock and animal products. Imports: food, motor vehicles and parts, petroleum products, machinery, cement, textiles. Major trading partners: France, Nigeria, and central African countries.

Geography. A landlocked country in north central Africa, Chad is about 85% the size of Alaska. Its neighbors are Niger, Libya, the Sudan, the Central African Republic, Cameroon, and Nigeria.

Lake Chad, from which the country gets its name, lies on the western border with Niger and Nigeria. In the north is a desert that runs into the Sahara.

Government. Hissen Habré became president of Chad on June 7, 1982, by overthrowing Goukouni Oueddei.

History. Chad was absorbed into the colony of French Equatorial Africa, as part of Ubangi-Shari, in 1910. France began the country's development after 1920, when it became a separate colony. In 1946, French Equatorial Africa was admitted to the French Union. By referendum in 1958 the Chad territory became an autonomous republic within the French Union.

An independence movement led by the first Premier and President, François (later Ngarta) Tombalbaye, achieved complete independence on Aug. 11, 1960.

Tombalbaye was killed in the 1975 coup and was succeeded by Gen. Félix Malloum, who faced a Libyan-financed rebel movement throughout his tenure in office. A ceasefire backed by Libya, Niger, and the Sudan early in 1978 failed to end the fighting, and French military aid was increased.

Nine rival groups meeting in Lagos, Nigeria, in March 1979 agreed to form a provisional government headed by Goukouni Oueddei, a former rebel leader. Fighting broke out again in Chad in March 1980, when Defense Minister Hissen Habré challenged Goukouni and seized the capital. By the year's end, Libyan troops supporting Goukouni recaptured N'djamena, and Libyan President Muammar el-Qaddafi, in January 1981, proposed a merger of Chad with Libya.

The Libyan merger proposal was rejected and Libyan troops withdrew from Chad but in 1983 poured back into the barren northern part of the country in support of Goukouni. France, in turn, sent troops into southern Chad in support of Habré.

A Qaddafi-Goukouni break in Nov. 1986 led to the defection of his troops. Government troops then launched an offensive in early 1987 that drove the Libyans out of most of the country.

CHILE

Republic of Chile
President: Gen. Augusto Pinochet (1973)
Area: 292,132 sq mi. (756,622 sq km)
Population (est. mid-1987): 12,400,000 (average annual growth rate: 1.6%)
Density per square mile: 42.4
Capital: Santiago
Largest cities (est. 1985): Santiago, 4,231,500; Valparaiso, 266,900; Concepción, 215,800; Antofagasta, 174,100
Monetary unit: Peso
Language: Spanish
Religion: Roman Catholic, 79%
National name: República de Chile
Literacy rate: 96%
Economic summary: Gross national product (1984): $17.5 billion. Average annual growth rate (1973–82): 0.8%. Per capita income (1983): $1,870. Land used for agriculture: 7%; labor force 16%; principal products: wheat, corn, sugar beets, vegetables, wine, livestock. Labor force in industry: 15%; major products: processed fish, transportation equipment, iron and steel, pulp, paper. Natural resources: copper, timber, iron ore, nitrates. Exports: copper, iron ore, paper and wood products, fruits. Imports: vehicles, petroleum, capital goods. Major trading partners: U.S., Japan, West Germany, Brazil, Argentina, Venezuela.

Geography. Situated south of Peru and west of Bolivia and Argentina, Chile fills a narrow 1,800-mile (2,897 km) strip between the Andes and the Pacific. Its area is nearly twice that of Montana.

One third of Chile is covered by the towering ranges of the Andes. In the north is the mineral-rich Atacama Desert, between the coastal mountains and the Andes. In the center is a 700-mile-long (1,127 km) valley, thickly populated, between the Andes and the coastal plateau. In the south, the Andes border on the ocean.

At the southern tip of Chile's mainland is Punta Arenas, the southernmost city in the world, and beyond that lies the Strait of Magellan and Tierra del Fuego, an island divided between Chile and Argentina. The southernmost point of South America is Cape Horn, a 1,390-foot (424-m) rock on Horn Island in the Wollaston group, which belongs to Chile.

The Juan Fernández Islands, in the South Pacific about 400 miles (644 km) west of the mainland, and Easter Island, about 2,000 miles (3,219 km) west, are Chilean possessions.

Government. The 1980 Constitution calls for a 1989 plebiscite to confirm a president who would serve until 1997, when open elections would be held. A Congress is to be elected in 1989.

Leftist parties were abolished immediately after the 1973 military coup that ousted President Salvador Allende Gossens. Other parties were placed "in recess," and on March 12, 1977, the government officially dissolved them.

History. Chile was originally under the control of the Incas in the north and the fierce Araucanian people in the south. In 1541, a Spaniard, Pedro de Valdivia, founded Santiago. Chile won its independence from Spain in 1818 under Bernardo O'Higgins and an Argentinian, José de San Martin. O'Higgins, dictator until 1823, laid the foundations of the modern state with a two-party system and a centralized government.

The dictator from 1830 to 1837, Diego Portales, fought a war with Peru in 1836–39 that expanded Chilean territory. The Conservatives were in power from 1831 to 1861. Then the Liberals, winning a share of power for the next 30 years, disestablished the church and limited presidential power. Chile fought the War of the Pacific with Peru and Bolivia from 1879 to 1883, winning Antofagasta, Bolivia's only outlet to the sea, and extensive areas from Peru. A revolt in 1890 led by Jorge Montt overthrew, in 1891, José Balmaceda and established a parliamentary dictatorship that existed until a new Constitution was adopted in 1925. Industrialization began before World War I and led to the formation of Marxist groups.

Juan Antonio Ríos, President during World War II, was originally pro-Nazi but in 1944 led his country into the war on the side of the U.S.

A small abortive army uprising in 1969 raised fear of military intervention to prevent a Marxist, Salvador Allende Gossens, from taking office after his election to the presidency on Sept. 4, 1970, with 36.3% of the vote in a three-way battle. Dr. Allende was the first President in a non-Communist country freely elected on a Marxist-Leninist program.

Allende quickly established relations with Cuba and the People's Republic of China and nationalized several American companies.

Allende's overthrow and death in an army assault on the presidential palace in September 1973 ended a 46-year era of constitutional government in Chile, which had boasted the longest such record in Latin America.

The takeover was led by a four-man junta headed by Army Chief of Staff Augusto Pinochet Ugarte, who assumed the office of President.

Committed to "exterminate Marxism," the junta embarked on a right-wing dictatorship. It suspended parliament, banned political activity, and broke relations with Cuba.

The Human Rights Commission of the Organization of American States charged the junta with "most grave violations" of basic liberties. In July, Chile denied entry to a U.N. investigatory panel. On June 9, 1978, the government reversed that policy to permit the U.N. Human Rights Commission to send an investigative mission to Chile.

In 1977, Pinochet, in a speech marking his fourth year in power, promised elections by 1985 if conditions warranted. Earlier, he had abolished DINA, the secret police, and decreed an amnesty for political prisoners, an action Amnesty International said might affect only 200–400 of some 1,500 political prisoners.

Pinochet was inaugurated on March 11, 1981, for an eight-year term as President. In July 1986, in the face of increasing protests, Pinochet announced that he might run for another eight-year term and spent much of 1986-87 making appearances around the country "campaigning."

CHINA

People's Republic of China
President: Li Xiannian (1983)
Premier: Zhao Ziyang (1980)
Area: 3,691,521 sq mi. (9,561,000 sq km)[1]
Population (est. mid-1987): 1,062,000,000 (average annual growth rate, 1.3%)
Density per square mile: 287.7
Capital: Beijing
Largest cities (est. 1983): Shanghai, 11,940,000; Beijing (Peking) 9,330,000; Tianjin (Tientsin) 7,850,000; Canton, 6,840,000; Wuhan, 5,940,000; Shenyang (Mukden), 5,210,000; Nanjing (Nanking), 4,560,000; Chongqing (Chungking), 3,890,000; Harbin; 3,730,000
Monetary unit: Yuan
Languages: Chinese, (Mandarin, Cantonese, and local dialects)
Religions: Non-religious, 59%; folk religions, 20%; atheist, 12%
National name: Zhonghua Renmin Gongheguo
Literacy rate: 76.5%
Economic summary: Gross national product (1985 est.); $343 billion. Average annual growth rate (1979–83): 8.2%. Per capita income (1985): $330. Land used for agriculture: 11%; labor force: 75%; principal products: rice, wheat, grains, cotton. Major industrial products: iron and steel, textiles, armaments, petroleum. Natural resources: coal, natural gas, limestone, marble. Exports: agricultural products, oil, minerals, metals, manufactured goods. Imports: grains, chemical fertilizer, steel, industrial raw materials, machinery and equipment. Major trading partners: Japan, Hong Kong, U.S., West Germany, Jordan, Australia, U.S.S.R., U.K., Italy.

1. Including Manchuria and Tibet.

Geography. China, which occupies the eastern part of Asia, is slightly larger in area than the U.S. Its coastline is roughly a semicircle. The greater part

Provinces and Regions of China

Name	Area (sq mi.)	Area (sq km)	Capital
Provinces			
Anhui (Anhwei)	54,015	139,900	Hefei (Hofei)
Fujian (Fukien)	47,529	123,100	Fuzhou (Fukien)
Gansu (Kansu)	137,104	355,100	Lanzhou (Lanchow)
Guangdong (Kwangtung)	89,344	231,400	Canton
Guizhou (Kweichow)	67,181	174,000	Guiyang (Kweiyang)
Hebei (Hopei)	81,479	211,030	Shijiazhuang (Shitikiachwang)
Heilongjiang (Heilungkiang)[1]	178,996	463,600	Harbin
Henan (Honan)	64,479	167,000	Zhengzhou (Chengchow)
Hubei (Hupeh)	72,394	187,500	Wuhan
Hunan	81,274	210,500	Changsha
Jiangsu (Kiangsu)	40,927	106,000	Nanjing (Nanking)
Jiangxi (Kiangsi)	63,629	164,800	Nanchang
Jilin (Kirin)[1]	72,201	187,000	Changchun
Liaoning[1]	53,301	138,050	Shenyang
Quinghai (Chinghai)	278,378	721,000	Xining (Sining)
Shaanxi (Shensi)	75,598	195,800	Xian (Sian)
Shandong (Shantung)	59,189	153,300	Jinan (Tsinan)
Shanxi (Shansi)	60,656	157,100	Taiyuan
Sichuan (Szechwan)	219,691	569,000	Chengdu (Chengtu)
Yunnan	168,417	436,200	Kunming
Zhejiang (Chekiang)	39,305	101,800	Hangzhou (Hangchow)
Autonomous Region			
Guangxi Zhuang (Kwangsi Chuang)	85,096	220,400	Nanning
Nei Monggol (Inner Mongolia)[1]	454,633	1,177,500	Hohhot (Huhehot)
Ningxia Hui	30,039	77,800	Yinchuan (Yinchwan)
Xinjiang Uygur (Sinkiang Uighur)[1]	635,829	1,646,800	Urumqi (Urumchi)
Xizang (Tibet)	471,660	1,221,600	Lhasa

1. Together constitute (with Taiwan) what has been traditionally known as Outer China, the remaining territory forming the historical China Proper. NOTE: Names are in Pinyin, with conventional spelling in parentheses.

of the country is mountainous, and only in the lower reaches of the Yellow and Yangtze Rivers are there extensive low plains.

The principal mountain ranges are the Tien Shan, to the northwest; the Kunlun chain, running south of the Taklimakan and Gobi Deserts; and the Trans-Himalaya, connecting the Kunlun with the borders of China and Tibet. Manchuria is largely an undulating plain connected with the north China plain by a narrow lowland corridor. Inner Mongolia contains the relatively fertile southern and eastern portions of the Gobi. The large island of Hainan (13,500 sq mi.; 34,380 sq km) lies off the southern coast.

Hydrographically, China proper consists of three great river systems. The northern part of the country is drained by the Yellow River (Huang Ho), 2,109 miles long (5,464 km) and mostly unnavigable. The central part is drained by the Chang Jiang (Yangtze Kiang), the third longest river in the world 2,432 miles (6,300 km). The Zhujiang (Si Kiang) in the south is 848 miles long (2,197 km) and navigable for a considerable distance. In addition, the Amur (1,144 sq mi.; 2,965 km) forms part of the northeastern boundary.

Government. With 2,978 deputies, elected for four-year terms by universal suffrage, the National People's Congress is the chief legislative organ. A State Council has the executive authority. The Congress elects the Premier and Deputy Premiers. All ministries are under the State Council, headed by the Premier.

The Communist Party controls the government.

History. By 2000 B.C.; the Chinese were living in the Huang Ho basin, and they had achieved an advanced stage of civilization by 1200 B.C. The great philosophers Lao-tse, Confucius Mo Ti, and Mencius lived during the Chou dynasty (1122–249 B.C.). The warring feudal states were first united under Emperor Ch'in Shih Huang Ti, during whose reign (246–210 B.C.) work was begun on the Great Wall. Under the Han dynasty (206 B.C.–A.D. 220), China prospered and traded with the West.

In the T'ang dynasty (618–907), often called the golden age of Chinese history, painting, sculpture, and poetry flourished, and printing made its earliest known appearance.

The Mings, last of the native rulers (1368–1644), overthrew the Mongol, or Yuan, dynasty (1280–1368) established by Kublai Khan. The Mings in turn were overthrown in 1644 by invaders from the north, the Manchus.

China closely restricted foreign activities, and by the end of the 18th century only Canton and the Portuguese port of Macao were open to European merchants. Following the Anglo-Chinese War of 1839–42, however, several treaty ports were opened, and Hong Kong was ceded to Britain. Treaties signed after further hostilities (1856–60) weakened Chinese sovereignty and removed foreigners from Chinese jurisdiction. The disastrous Chinese-Japanese War of 1894–95 was followed by a scramble for Chinese concessions by European powers, leading to the Boxer Rebellion (1900), suppressed by an international force.

The death of the Empress Dowager Tzu Hsi in 1908 and the accession of the infant Emperor Hsüan T'ung (Pu-Yi) were followed by a nationwide rebellion led by Dr. Sun Yat-sen, who became first President of the Provisional Chinese Republic in 1911. The Manchus abdicated on Feb. 12, 1912. Dr. Sun resigned in favor of Yuan Shih-k'ai, who suppressed the republicans but was forced by a serious rising in 1915–16 to abandon his intention of declaring himself Emperor. Yuan's death in June 1916 was followed by years of civil war between rival militarists and Dr. Sun's republicans.

Nationalist forces, led by Gen. Chiang Kai-shek and with the advice of Communist experts, soon occupied most of China, setting up a Kuomintang regime in 1928. Internal strife continued, however, and Chiang broke with the Communists.

An alleged explosion on the South Manchurian Railway on Sept. 18, 1931, brought invasion of Manchuria by Japanese forces, who installed the last Manchu Emperor, Henry Pu-Yi, as nominal ruler of the puppet state of "Manchukuo." Japanese efforts to take China's northern provinces in July 1937 were resisted by Chiang, who meanwhile had succeeded in uniting most of China behind him. Within two years, however, Japan seized most of the ports and railways. The Kuomintang government retreated first to Hankow and then to Chungking, while the Japanese set up a puppet government at Nanking headed by Wang Jingwei.

Japan's surrender in 1945 touched off civil war between Nationalist forces under Chiang and Communist forces led by Mao Zedong, the party chairman. Despite U. S. aid, the Chiang forces were overcome by the Maoists, backed by the Soviet bloc, and were expelled from the mainland. The Mao regime, established in Peking as the new capital, proclaimed the People's Republic of China on Oct. 1, 1949, with Zhou Enlai as Premier.

After the Korean War began in June 1950, China led the Communist bloc in supporting North Korea, and on Nov. 26, 1950, the Mao regime intervened openly.

In 1958, Mao undertook the "Great Leap Forward" campaign, which combined the establishment of rural communes with a crash program of village industrialization. These efforts also failed, causing Mao to lose influence to Liu Shaoqi, who became President in 1959, to Premier Zhou, and to Party Secretary Deng Xiaoping.

China exploded its first atomic (fission) bomb in 1964 and produced a fusion bomb in 1967.

Mao moved to Shanghai, and from that base he and his supporters waged what they called a Cultural Revolution. In the spring of 1966 the Mao group formed Red Guard units dominated by youths and students, closing the schools to free the students for agitation.

The Red Guards campaigned against "old ideas, old culture, old habits, and old customs." Often they were no more than uncontrolled mobs, and brutality was frequent. Early in 1967 efforts were made to restore control. The Red Guards were urged to return home. Schools started opening.

Persistent overtures by the Nixon Administration resulted in the dramatic announcement in July that Henry Kissinger, President Richard M. Nixon's national security adviser, had secretly visited Peking and reached agreement on a visit by the President to China.

The movement toward reconciliation, which signaled the end of the U.S. containment policy toward China, provided irresistible momentum for Chinese admission to the U.N. Despite U.S. opposition to expelling Taiwan (Nationalist China), the world body overwhelmingly ousted Chiang in seating Peking.

President Nixon went to Peking for a week early in 1972, meeting Mao as well as Zhou. The summit ended with a historic communiqué on February 28, in which both nations promised to work toward improved relations.

In 1973, the U.S. and China agreed to set up "liaison offices" in each other's capitals, which constituted de facto diplomatic relations. Full diplomatic relations were barred by China as long as the U.S. continued to recognize Nationalist China.

On Jan. 8, 1976, Zhou died. His successor, Vice Premier Deng Xiaoping was supplanted within a month by Hua Guofeng, former Minister of Public Security. Hua became permanent Premier in April. In October he was named successor to Mao as Chairman of the Communist Party.

After Mao died on Sept. 10, a campaign against his widow, Jiang Qing, and three of her "radical" colleagues began. The "Gang of Four" was denounced for having undermined the party, the government, and the economy.

Jiang was brought to trial in 1980 and sentenced on Jan. 25, 1981, to die within two years unless she showed repentance, in which case she would be imprisoned for life.

At the Central Committee meeting of 1977, Deng was reinstated as Deputy Premier, Chief of Staff of the Army, and member of the Central Committee of the Politburo.

At the same time, Jiang Qing, Wang Hongwen, Zhang Chunqiao, and Yao Wenyuan—the notorious "Gang of Four"—were removed from all official posts and banished from the party.

In May 1978, expulsion of ethnic Chinese by Vietnam produced an open rupture. Peking sided with Cambodia in the border fighting that flared between Vietnam and Cambodia, charging Hanoi with aggression.

On Aug. 12, 1978, China and Japan signed a treaty of peace and friendship. Peking and Washington then announced that they would open full diplomatic relations on Jan. 1, 1979. Over Congressional objections, the Carter Administration abrogated the Taiwan defense treaty. Deputy Premier Deng sealed the agreement with a visit to the United States that coincided with the opening of embassies in both capitals on March 1.

On Deng's return from the U.S. 200,000 to 300, 000 Chinese troops invaded Vietnam to avenge alleged violations of Chinese territory. The action was seen as a reaction to Vietnam's invasion of Cambodia.

The first People's Congress in five years confirmed Zhao Ziyang, an economic planner, as Premier replacing Hua Guofeng, who had held the post since 1976.

After the Central Committee meeting of June 27–29, 1981, Hu Yaobang, a Deng protégé, was elevated to the party chairmanship, replacing Hua Guofeng. Deng became chairman of the military commission of the central committee, giving him control over the army. The committee's 215 members concluded the session with a statement holding Mao Zedong responsible for the "grave blunder" of the Cultural Revolution.

On June 18, 1983, the Chinese Parliament elected Li Xiannian, an economics and financial specialist, as the first national president since 1969. Previously an outspoken critic of the United States, he was the official host when President Ronald Reagan visited China in April 1984.

Under Deng Xiaoping's leadership, meanwhile, China's Communist idealogy was almost totally reinterpreted and sweeping economic changes were set in motion in the early 1980s. The Chinese scrapped the personality cult that idolized Mao Zedong, muted Mao's old call for class struggle and exportation of the Communist revolution, and imported Western technology and management techniques to replace the Marxist tenets that retarded modernization. In the countryside, commune production brigades were disbanded in favor of family-style sharecropping. In the cities, small-scale private enterprise was encouraged.

Also under Deng's leadership, the Chinese Communists worked out an arrangement with Britain for the future of Hong Kong after 1997. The flag of China will be raised but the territory will retain its present social, economic and legal system.

The removal of Hu Yaobang as party chairman in January 1987 was a sign of a hard-line resurgence against Deng's economic policies.

CHINA (TAIWAN)

Republic of China
President: Chiang Ching-kuo (1978)
Premier: Yu Kuo-hwa
Area: 13,895 sq mi. (35,988 sq km)[1]
Population (est. mid-1987): 19,600,000 (average annual growth rate: 1.2%)
Density per square mile: 1,410.6
Capital: Taipei
Largest cities (est. 1984): Taipei, 2,449,702; Kaohsiung, 1,299,082; Taichung, 595,000; Tainan, 585,000; Chilung (Keelung), 350,000
Monetary unit: New Taiwan dollar
Languages: Chinese (Mandarin) and various dialects
Religions: Confucianist, Buddhist, Christian, Taoist
Literacy rate: about 89.7%
Economic summary: Gross national product (1985 est.): $60 billion. Real growth rate (1985): 4.7%. Per capita income (1983): $3,142. Land used for agriculture: 24%; labor force: 59%; principal products: rice, yams, sugar cane, bananas, pineapples, citrus fruits. Labor force in industry: 42%; major products: textiles, clothing, chemicals, processed foods, electronic equipment, cement, ships, plywood. Natural resources: timber, camphor. Exports: textiles, electrical machinery, plywood. Imports: machinery, basic metals, crude oil, chemicals. Major trading partners: U.S., Japan, Saudi Arabia.

1. Excluding Quemoy and Matsu.

Geography. The Republic of China today consists of the island of Taiwan, an island 100 miles (161 km) off the Asian mainland in the Pacific; two offshore islands, Quemoy and Matsu; and the nearby islets of the Pescadores chain. It is slightly larger than the combined areas of Massachusetts and Connecticut.

Taiwan is divided by a central mountain range that runs from north to south, rising sharply on the east coast and descending gradually to a broad western plain, where cultivation is concentrated.

Government. The President and the Vice President are elected by the National Assembly for a term of six years. There are five major governing bodies called Yuans: Executive, Legislative, Judicial, Control, and Examination. Taiwan's internal affairs are administered by the Taiwan Provincial Government under the supervision of the Provincial Assembly, which is popularly elected.

The majority and ruling party is the Kuomintang (KMT) (Nationalist Party) led by President Chiang Chingkuo. The main opposition party is the Democratic Progressive Party (DPP).

History. Taiwan was inhabited by aborigines of Malayan descent when Chinese from the areas now designated as Fukien and Kwangtung began settling it beginning in the 7th century, becoming the majority.

The Portuguese explored the area in 1590, naming it The Beautiful (Formosa). In 1624 the Dutch set up forts in the south, the Spanish in the North. The Dutch threw out the Spanish in 1641 and controlled the island until 1661, when the Chinese General Koxinga took it over, established an independent kingdom, and expelled the Dutch. The Manchus seized the island in 1683 and held it until 1895, when it passed to Japan after the first Sino-Japanese War. Japan developed and exploited it, and it was heavily bombed by American planes during World War II, after which it was restored to China.

After the defeat of its armies on the mainland, the Nationalist Government of Generalissimo Chiang Kai-shek retreated to Taiwan in December 1949. With only 15% of the population consisting of the 1949 immigrants, Chiang dominated the island, maintaining a 600,000-man army in the hope of eventually recovering the mainland. Japan renounced its claim to the island by the San Francisco Peace Treaty of 1951.

By stationing a fleet in the Strait of Formosa the U.S. prevented a mainland invasion in 1953.

The "China seat" in the U.N., which the Nationalists held with U.S. help for over two decades was lost in October 1971, when the People's Republic of China was admitted and Taiwan ousted by the world body.

Chiang died at 87 of a heart attack on April 5, 1975. His son, Chiang Ching-kuo, continued as Premier and dominant power in the Taipei regime. He assumed the presidency in 1978, and Sun Yunhsuan became Premier.

President Carter's announcement that the U.S. would recognize only the People's Republic of China after Jan. 1, 1979, and that the U.S. defense treaty with the Nationalists would end aroused protests in Taiwan and in the U.S. Congress. Against Carter's wishes, Congress, in a bill governing future relations with Taiwan, guaranteed U.S. action in the event of an attack on the island. The legislation also provided for the continuation of trade and other relations through an American Institute in Taipei, housed in the former American Embassy.

Although the U.S. had assured Taiwan of continuing arms aid, a communiqué on Aug. 17, 1982, signed by Washington and Peking and promising a gradual reduction of such aid, cast a shadow over Taiwan. The striking success of the DPP in legislative elections in December 1986 marked a slight loosening of the KMT's hold on power.

COLOMBIA

Republic of Colombia
President: Virgilio Barco Vargas (1986)
Area: 455,355 sq mi. (1,179,369 sq km)
Population (est. mid-1987): 29,900,000 (average annual growth rate, 2.1%) (mestizo, 68%; white, 20%; Indian, 7%; black, 5%)
Density per square mile: 65.7
Capital: Bogotá
Largest cities (est. 1985): Bogotá, 3,982,941; Medellín, 1,418,554; Cali, 1,323,944; Baranquilla, 896,649; Cartagena, 491,368; Bucaramanga, 896,649

Monetary unit: Peso
Language: Spanish
Religion: Roman Catholic
National name: República de Colombia
Literacy rate (1985): 81%
Economic summary: Gross national product (est. 1985): $29.0 billion. Average annual growth rate (1970–79): 3.7%. Per capita income (est. 1984): $1,430. Land used for agriculture: 5%; labor force: 29%; principal products: coffee, bananas, rice, corn, sugar cane, cotton, tobacco, sorghum. Labor force in industry: 13%; major products: textiles, processed food, beverages, chemicals, cement. Natural resources: petroleum, natural gas, coal, iron ore, nickel, gold, silver. Exports: coffee, fuel oil, cotton, bananas. Imports: machinery, electrical equipment, chemical products, metals and metal products, transportation equipment. Major trading partners: U.S., West Germany, Japan, Venezuela, Netherlands, Ecuador, Peru.

Geography. Colombia, in the northwestern part of South America, is the only country on that continent that borders on both the Atlantic and Pacific Oceans. It is nearly equal to the combined areas of California and Texas.

Through the western half of the country, three Andean ranges run north and south, merging into one at the Ecuadorean border. The eastern half is a low, jungle-covered plain, drained by spurs of the Amazon and Orinoco, inhabited mostly by isolated, tropical-forest Indian tribes. The fertile plateau and valley of the eastern range are the most densely populated parts of the country.

Government. Colombia's President, who appoints his own Cabinet, serves for a four-year term. The Senate, the upper house of Congress, has 114 members elected for four years by direct vote. The House of Representatives of 199 members is directly elected for four years.

The major political parties are the Liberal Party (100 of 199 seats in House), Conservative Party (82 seats), New Liberals (7 seats), Patriotic Union (10 seats).

History. Spaniards in 1510 founded Darien, the first permanent European settlement on the American mainland. In 1538 the Spaniards established the colony of New Granada, the area's name until 1861. After a 14-year struggle, in which Simón Bolívar's Venezuelan troops won the battle of Boyacá in Colombia on Aug. 7, 1819, independence was attained in 1824. Bolívar united Colombia, Venezuela, Panama, and Ecuador in the Republic of Greater Colombia (1819–30), but lost Venezuela and Ecuador to separatists. Bolívar's Vice President, Francisco de Paula Santander, founded the Liberal Party as the Federalists while Bolívar established the Conservatives as the Centralists.

Santander's presidency (1832–36) re-established order, but later periods of Liberal dominance (1849–57 and 1861–80), when the Liberals sought to disestablish the Roman Catholic Church, were marked by insurrection and even civil war. Rafael Nuñez, in a 15-year-presidency, restored the power of the central government and the church, which led in 1899 to a bloody civil war and the loss in 1903 of Panama over ratification of a lease to the U.S. of the Canal Zone. For 21 years, until 1930, the Conservatives held power as revolutionary pressures built up.

The Liberal administrations of Enrique Olaya Herrera and Alfonso López (1930–38) were marked by social reforms that failed to solve the country's problems, and in 1946, insurrection and banditry broke out, claiming hundreds of thousands of lives by 1958. Laureano Gómez (1950–53), the Army Chief of Staff, Gen. Gustavo Rojas Pinilla (1953–56), and a military junta (1956–57) sought to curb disorder by repression.

Julio César Turbay Ayala, Liberal Party candidate in 1978, won a narrow victory—approximately 140,000 of a total of nearly 2.5 million votes—over the Conservative Party candidate. The Liberals also retained control of both the Senate and House.

Government efforts to stamp out the Movement of April 19 (M-19), an urban guerrilla organization, intensified in 1981 with the capture of some of the leaders. In 1986 three of its founders were killed in separate gun battles. The Liberals won a solid majority in 1982, but a party split enabled Belisario Betancur Cuartas, the Conservative candidate, to win the presidency on May 31. After his inauguration, he ended the state of siege that had existed almost continuously for 34 years and renewed the general amnesty of 1981.

On May 25, the liberal Virgilio Barco Vargas was elected by a record-breaking margin.

COMOROS

Federal Islamic Republic of the Comoros
President: Ahmed Abdallah Abderemane (1978)
Area: 719 sq mi. (1,862 sq km)
Population (est. 1987): 400,000 (average annual growth rate: 3.3%)
Density per square mile: 652.3
Capital and largest city (est. 1980): Moroni (on Grande Comoro), 20,000
Monetary unit: Franc CFA
Languages: French, Arabic
Religions: Islam
National name: République Fédéral Islamique des Comores
Literacy rate (1981): 15%
Economic summary: Gross national product (1984 est.): $92 million. Annual growth rate (1984): 3.1%. Per capita income (1984 est.): $250. Principal agricultural products: perfume essences, copra, coconuts, cloves, vanilla, cinnamon, yams; major industrial products: perfume distillations. Exports: perfume essences, vanilla, copra, cloves. Imports: foodstuffs, fuels, chemicals, cotton textiles, cement. Major trading partners: France, Madagascar, Kenya, Pakistan, West Germany, Saudi Arabia.

Geography. The Comoros Islands—Grande Comoro, Anjouan, Mohéli, and Mayotte (which retains ties to France)—are an archipelago of volcanic origin in the Indian Ocean between Mozambique and Madagascar.

Government. A coup by foreign mercenaries on May 13, 1978, deposed President Ali Soilih, who had held power since 1975. A "political and military directorate" headed by Ahmed Abdallah Abderemane and Mohammed Ahmed governed until the adoption of a constitution on Oct. 1 ushered in a republic. With the resignation of Ahmed two days later, Abdallah became president.

History. Under French rule since 1886, the Comoros declared themselves independent July 6, 1975. However, Mayotte, with a Christian majority, voted against joining the other, mainly Islamic, islands, in the move to independence and remains French.

A month after independence, Justice Minister Ali Soilih staged a coup with the help of mercenaries, overthrowing the new nation's first president, Ahmed Abdallah. Soilih lowered the voting age to 14, destroyed all records and killed many Comorans. He was overthrown on May 13, 1978, when a small boatload of French mercenaries, some of whom had aided him three years earlier, seized government headquarters.

CONGO

People's Republic of the Congo
President: Col. Denis Sassou-Nguessou (1979)
Prime Minister: Ange Edouard Poungui (1984)
Area: 132,046 sq mi. (342,000 sq km)
Population (est. mid-1987): 2,100,000 (average annual growth rate, 3.4%)
Density per sq mile: 13.6
Capital and largest city (est. 1984): Brazzaville, 595,102
Monetary unit: Franc CFA
Ethnic groups: Kongo, Teke, Bukongui
Languages: French, Lingala, Kokongo
Religions: Animist, 48%; Christian, 47%; Muslim, 2%
National name: République Populaire du Congo
Literacy rate: 56%
Economic summary: Gross national product (1983): $2.18 billion. Annual growth rate (1984): 3.1%. Per capita income (1983): $1,320. Principal agricultural products: sugar cane, bananas, coffee, cocoa, peanuts. Labor force in industry: 20%; major products: refined oil, cigarettes, cement, beverages, milled sugar. Natural resources: wood, potash, petroleum, natural gas. Exports: oil, lumber, tobacco, veneer and plywood. Imports: machinery, transportation equipment, manufactured consumer goods, iron and steel, foodstuffs. Major trading partners: France, U.S., Italy, Spain, Brazil.

Geography. The Congo is situated in west Central Africa astride the Equator. It borders on Gabon, Cameroon, the Central African Republic, Zaire, and the Angola exclave of Cabinda, with a short stretch of coast on the South Atlantic. Its area is nearly three times that of Pennsylvania.

Most of the inland is tropical rain forest, drained by tributaries of the Zaire (Congo) River, which flows south along the eastern border with Zaire to Stanley Pool. The narrow coastal plain rises to highlands separated from the inland plateaus by the 200-mile-wide Niari River Valley, which gives passage to the coast.

Government. Since the coup of September 1968 the country has been governed by a military regime. The Congolese Labor Party is the only party.

History. The inhabitants of the former French Congo, mainly Bantu peoples with Pygmies in the north, were subjects of several kingdoms in earlier times.

The Frenchman Pierre Savorgnan de Brazza signed a treaty with Makoko, ruler of the Bateke people, in 1880, which established French control. The area, with Gabon and Ubangi-Shari, was constituted the colony of French Equatorial Africa in 1910. It joined Chad in supporting the Free French cause in World War II. The Congo proclaimed its independence without leaving the French Community in 1960.

Maj. Marien Ngouabi, head of the National Council of the Revolution, took power as president on Jan. 1, 1969. He was sworn in for a second five-year term in 1975. A visit to Moscow by Ngouabi in March ended with the signing of a Soviet-Congolese economic and technical aid pact.

A four-man commando squad assassinated Ngouabi in Brazzaville on March 18, 1977. Five days later the assassination of Émile Cardinal Biayenda, Archbishop of Brazzaville, was announced. Former President Alphonse Massamba-Débat, accused of plotting both deaths, was executed.

Col. Joachim Yhombi-Opango, Army Chief of Staff, assumed the presidency on April 4. In June, the new government agreed to resume diplomatic relations with the U.S., ending a 12-year rift. Yombhi-Opango resigned on Feb. 4, 1979, and was replaced by Col. Denis Sassou-Neguessou.

COSTA RICA

Republic of Costa Rica
President: Oscar Arias Sanchez (1986)
Area: 19,652 sq mi. (50,898 sq km)
Population (est. mid-1987): 2,800,000 (average annual growth rate, 2.7%)
Density per square mile: 142.5
Capital and largest city (est. 1984): San José, 278,500
Monetary unit: Colón
Language: Spanish
Religion: Roman Catholic
National name: República de Costa Rica
Literacy rate (1984): 93%
Economic summary: Gross national product (1983): $3.5 billion. Average annual growth rate (1981–83): 3.5%. Per capita income (1984): $1,400. Land used for agriculture: 13%; labor force: 27%; principal products: bananas, coffee, sugar cane, rice, corn, livestock. Labor force in industry: 21%; major products: processed foods, textiles and clothing, construction materials, fertilizer. Natural resource: timber. Exports: coffee, bananas, beef, sugar. Imports: manufactured products, machinery, chemicals, foodstuffs, fuels, fertilizer. Major trading partners: U.S., Central American countries, West Germany.

Geography. This Central American country lies between Nicaragua to the north and Panama to the south. Its area slightly exceeds that of Vermont and New Hampshire combined.

Most of Costa Rica is tableland, from 3,000 to 6,000 feet (914 to 1,829 m) above sea level. Cocos Island (10 sq mi.; 26 sq km), about 300 miles (483 km) off the Pacific Coast, is under Costa Rican sovereignty.

Government. Under the 1949 Constitution, the president and the one-house Legislative Assembly of 57 members are elected for terms of four years.

The army was abolished in 1949. There is a civil guard and a rural guard.

The major political parties are the National Liberation Party (29 of 57 seats in the Legislative Assembly), led by Guillermo Vargas; Unity Party (25 seats), led by Oscar Aguilar.

History. Costa Rica was inhabited by 25,000 Indians when Columbus discovered it and probably named it in 1502. Few of the Indians survived the Spanish conquest, which began in 1563. The region was administered as a Spanish province. Costa Rica achieved independence in 1821 but was absorbed for two years by Agustín de Iturbide in his Mexican Empire. It was established as a republic in 1848.

Except for the military dictatorship of Tomás Guardia from 1870 to 1882, Costa Rica has enjoyed one of the most democratic governments in Latin America.

Rodrigo Carazo Odio, leader of a four-party coalition called the Unity Party, won the presidency in February 1978. His tenure was marked by a disastrous decline in the economy, which forced postponement of foreign debt payments at the end of 1981. Luis Alberto Monge Álvarez, a former union organizer and cofounder of the National Liberation Party, swept to victory in the Feb. 7, 1982, national elections.

On Feb. 2, 1986, Oscar Arias Sanchez won the national elections on a neutralist platform, defeating Rafael Angel Calderon, who was a stronger supporter of U.S. policies in Central America. Arias initiated a policy of preventing contra usage of Costa Rican territory.

CUBA

Republic of Cuba
President: Fidel Castro Ruz (1976)
Area: 44,218 sq mi. (114,524 sq km)
Population (est. mid-1987): 10,300,000 (average annual growth rate, 1.2%)
Density per square mile: 232.9
Capital: Havana
Largest cities (est. 1985): Havana, 1,992,600; Santiago de Cuba, 356,000; Santa Clara, 176,900; Camagüey, 287,400; Holguin, 194,100
Monetary unit: Peso
Language: Spanish
Religion: Roman Catholic, 40%; non-religious, 49%; atheist, 6%
National name: República de Cuba
Literacy rate: 96%
Economic summary: Gross national product (est. 1983): $15.8 billion. Average annual growth rate (1984-85): 6.1%. Per capita income (1983): $1,590. Land used for agriculture: 29%; labor force: 22%; principal products: sugar, tobacco, coffee, rice, fruits. Labor force in industry: 21%; major products: refined oil products, textiles, chemicals, processed food, metals, light consumer products. Natural resources: metals, primarily nickel. Exports: sugar, nickel, shellfish, tobacco. Imports: capital goods, industrial raw materials, petroleum, foodstuffs. Major trading partners: U.S.S.R., other Communist bloc countries, Spain, Japan.

Geography. The largest island of the West Indies group (equal in area to Pennsylvania), Cuba is also the westernmost—just west of Hispaniola (Haiti and the Dominican Republic), and 90 miles (145 km) south of Key West, Fla., at the entrance to the Gulf of Mexico.

The island is mountainous in the southeast and south central area (Sierra Maestra). Elsewhere it is flat or rolling.

Government. Since 1976, elections have been held every five years to elect the National Assembly, which in turn elects the 31-member Council of States, its President, First Vice-President, five Vice-Presidents, and Secretary. Fidel Castro is President of the Council of State and of the government and First Secretary of the Communist Party of Cuba, the only political party.

History. Arawak Indians inhabiting Cuba when Columbus discovered the island in 1492 died off from diseases brought by sailors and settlers. By 1511, Spaniards under Diego Velásquez were founding settlements that served as bases for Spanish exploration. Cuba soon after served as an assembly point for treasure looted by the conquistadores, attracting French and English pirates.

Black slaves and free laborers were imported to work sugar and tobacco plantations, and waves of chiefly Spanish immigrants maintained a European character in the island's culture. Early slave rebellions and conflicts between colonials and Spanish rulers laid the foundation for an independence movement that turned into open warfare from 1867 to 1878. The poet, José Marti, in 1895 led the struggle that finally ended Spanish rule, thanks largely to U.S. intervention in 1898 after the sinking of the battleship *Maine* in Havana harbor.

A treaty in 1899 made Cuba an independent republic under U.S. protection. The U.S. occupation, which ended in 1902, suppressed yellow fever and brought large American investment. From 1906 to 1909, Washington invoked the Platt Amendment to the treaty, which gave it the right to intervene in order to suppress any revolt. U.S. troops came back in 1912 and again in 1917 to restore order. The Platt Amendment was abrogated in 1934.

Fulgencio Batista, an army sergeant, led a revolt in 1934 that overthrew the regime of President Gerado Machado.

Batista's Cuba was a police state. Corrupt officials took payoffs from American gamblers who operated casinos, demanded bribes from Cubans for various public services and enriched themselves with raids on the public treasury. Dissenters were murdered and their bodies dumped in gutters.

Fidel Castro Ruz, a hulking, bearded attorney in his 30s, landed in Cuba on Christmas Day 1956 with a band of 12 fellow revolutionaries, evaded Batista's soldiers, and set up headquarters in the jungled hills of the Sierra Maestra range. By 1958 his force had grown to about 2,000 guerrillas, for the most part young and middle class. Castro's brother, Raul, and Ernesto (Che) Guevara, an Argentine physician, were his top lieutenants. Businessmen and landowners who opposed the Batista regime gave financial support to the rebels. The United States, meanwhile, cut off arms shipments to Batista's army.

The beginning of the end for Batista came when the rebels routed 3,000 government troops and captured Santa Clara, capital of Las Villas province 150 miles from Havana, and a trainload of Batista reinforcements refused to get out of their railroad cars. On New Year's Day 1959, Batista flew to exile in the Dominican Republic and Castro took over the government. Crowds cheered the revolutionaries on their seven-day march to the capital.

The United States initially welcomed what looked like the prospect for a democratic Cuba, but a rude awakening came within a few months when Castro established military tribunals for political opponents, jailed hundreds, and began to veer leftward. Castro disavowed Cuba's 1952 military pact with the United States. He confiscated U.S. investments in banks and industries and seized large U.S.

landholdings, turning them first into collective farms and then into Soviet-type state farms. The United States broke relations with Cuba on Jan. 3, 1961. Castro thereupon forged an alliance with the Soviet Union.

From the ranks of the Cuban exiles who had fled to the United States, the Central Intelligence Agency recruited and trained an expeditionary force, numbering less than 2,000 men, to invade Cuba, with the expectation that the invasion would spark an uprising of the Cuban populace against Castro. The invasion was planned under the Eisenhower administration and President John F. Kennedy gave the go-ahead for it in the first months of his administration, but rejected a CIA proposal for U.S. planes to provide air support. The landing at the Bay of Pigs on April 17, 1961, was a fiasco. Not only did the invaders fail to receive any support from the populace, but Castro's tanks and artillery made short work of the small force.

A Soviet attempt to change the global power balance by installing in Cuba medium-range missiles—capable of striking targets in the United States with nuclear warheads—provoked a crisis between the superpowers in 1962 that had the potential of touching off World War III. After a visit to Moscow by Cuba's war minister, Raul Castro, work began secretly on the missile launching sites.

Denouncing the Soviets for "deliberate deception," President Kennedy on Oct. 22 announced that the U.S. navy would enforce a "quarantine" of shipping to Cuba and search Soviet bloc ships to prevent the missiles themselves from reaching the island. After six days of tough public statements on both sides and secret diplomacy, Soviet Premier Nikita Khrushchev on Oct. 28 ordered the missile sites dismantled, crated and shipped back to the Soviet Union, in return for a U.S. pledge not to attack Cuba. Limited diplomatic ties were re-established on Sept. 1, 1977.

Emigration increased dramatically after April 1, 1980, when Castro, irritated by the granting of asylum to would-be refugees by the Peruvian embassy in Havana, removed guards and allowed 10,000 Cubans to swarm into the embassy grounds.

As an airlift began taking the refugees to Costa Rica, Castro opened the port of Mariel to a "freedom flotilla" of ships and yachts from the United States, many of them owned or chartered by Cuban-Americans to bring out relatives. More than 125,000 Cubans poured out of Mariel in a mass exodus. It wasn't until after they had reached the United States that it was discovered that the regime had opened prisons and mental hospitals to permit criminals, homosexuals and others unwanted in Cuba to join the refugees.

For most of President Ronald Reagan's first term, U.S.-Cuban relations were frozen, with Secretary of State Alexander Haig calling Havana the "source" of troubles in Central America. But late in 1984, an agreement was reached between the two countries. Cuba would take back more than 2,700 Cubans who had come to the United States in the Mariel exodus but were not eligible to stay in the country under U.S. immigration law because of criminal or psychiatric disqualification. The United States, in exchange, would reinstitute regular immigration for Cubans to the United States. Castro cancelled it when the U.S. began the Radio Marti broadcasts in May 1985. The broadcasts are intended to bring a non-Communist view to the Cuban people.

As the first step in the accord, 23 Cuban aliens were moved from Atlanta Federal Penitentiary on Feb. 21, 1985, and put aboard a chartered airliner that flew them to Havana.

After a machinegun attack by leftist rebels in June 1985 killed 13 diners—including six Americans—at an outdoor cafe in El Salvador, President Reagan listed Cuba with Iran, Libya, North Korea and Nicaragua in what he called "a confederation of terrorist states".

In January 1987, the U.S. withdrew its chief of mission when Cuba excluded him from diplomatic functions.

CYPRUS

Republic of Cyprus
President: Spyros Kyprianou (1977)
Area: 3,572 sq mi (9,251 sq km)
Population (est. mid-1987): 700,000 (average annual growth rate: 1.3%) (Greek, 80%; Turkish, 18%)
Density per square mile: 196
Capital and largest city (est. 1982): Nicosia, 123,298
Monetary unit: Cyprus pound
Languages: Greek, Turkish, English
Religions: Greek Orthodox, 76%; Islam, 19%
National name: Kypriaki Dimokratia—Kibris Cumhuriyeti
Member of Commonwealth of Nations
Literacy rate (1981): 89%
Economic summary: Gross national product (1985): $3.7 billion. Average annual growth rate (1970–78): 1.4%. Per capita income (1983): $3,270. Land used for agriculture: 47%; labor force: 20%; principal products: vine products, citrus, potatoes, other vegetables. Labor force in industry: 30%; major products: beverages, footwear, clothing, cement, asbestos mining. Natural resources: copper, asbestos, gypsum, building stone, marble, clay, salt. Exports: clothing, machinery. Imports: manufactured goods, machinery and transportation equipment, petroleum products, foodstuffs. Major trading partners: U.K., Lebanon, Italy

Geography. The third largest island in the Mediterranean (one and one half times the size of Delaware), Cyprus lies off the southern coast of Turkey and the western shore of Syria. Most of the country consists of a wide plain lying between two mountain ranges that cross the island. The highest peak is Mount Olympus at 6,406 feet (1,953 m).

Government. Under the republic's Constitution, for the protection of the Turkish minority the vice president as well as three of the 10 Cabinet ministers must be from the Turkish community, while the House of Representatives is elected by each community separately, 70% Greek Cypriote and 30% Turkish Cypriote representatives.

The Greek and Turkish communities are self-governing in questions of religion, education, and culture. Other governmental matters are under the jurisdiction of the central government. Each community is entitled to a Communal Chamber.

The Greek Communal Chamber, which had 23 members, was abolished in 1965 and its function was absorbed by the Ministry of Education. The Turkish Communal Chamber, however, has continued to function.

The following is a breakdown of the 56 seats held by Greeks: Democratic Front of Spyros Kyprianou (16); AKEL Progressive Party of the Working People (15); Democratic Rally (19); Socialist Party of Dr. Vassos Lyssarides (6). The 24 Turkish members have not attended sessions of the House since 1964.

History. Cyprus was the site of early Phoenician and Greek colonies. For centuries its rule passed through many hands. It fell to the Turks in 1571, and a large Turkish colony settled on the island.

In World War I, on the outbreak of hostilities with Turkey, Britain annexed the island. It was declared a crown colony in 1925.

For centuries the Greek population, regarding Greece as its mother country, has sought self-determination and reunion with it *(enosis)*. The resulting quarrel with Turkey threatened NATO. Cyprus became an independent nation on Aug. 16, 1960, with Britain, Greece, and Turkey as guarantor powers.

Archbishop Makarios, president since 1959, was overthrown July 15, 1974, by a military coup led by the Cypriot National Guard. The new regime named Nikos Giorgiades Sampson as president and Bishop Gennadios as head of the Cypriot Church to replace Makarios. The rebels were led by rightist Greek officers who supported *enosis*.

Diplomacy failed to resolve the crisis. Turkey invaded Cyprus by sea and air July 20, 1974, asserting its right to protect the Turkish Cypriote minority.

Geneva talks involving Greece, Turkey, Britain, and the two Cypriote factions failed in mid-August, and the Turks subsequently gained control of 40% of the island. Greece made no armed response to the superior Turkish force, but bitterly suspended military participation in the NATO alliance.

The tension continued after Makarios returned to become President on Dec. 7, 1974. He offered self-government to the Turkish minority, but rejected any solution "involving transfer of populations and amounting to partition of Cyprus."

Turkish Cypriots proclaimed a separate state in the northern part of the island and proposed a "biregional federation."

Makarios died on Aug. 3, 1977, and Spyros Kyprianou was elected to serve the remaining five months of his term. Kyprianou, running unopposed, won a full five-year term in 1978. In February 1983, President Kyprianou was re-elected for another five-year term, polling 57% of the vote.

Kyprianou's victory in the legislative elections on December 8, 1985, was seen as a vote of support for his hard-line approach to reunification talks, which remained deadlocked.

CZECHOSLOVAKIA

Czechoslovak Socialist Republic
President: Gustav Husak (1975)
Premier: Lubomir Strougal (1970)
Area: 49,374 sq mi. (127,896 sq km)
Population (est. mid-1987): 15,600,000 (average annual growth rate: 0.3%) (Czech, 64%; Slovak, 30%)
Density per square mile: 316.0
Capital: Prague
Largest cities (est. 1985): Prague, 1,193,500; Bratislava, 417,100; Brno, 385,900; Ostrova, 327,800; Kosice, 222,200
Monetary unit: Koruna
Languages: Czech, Slovak, Hungarian
Religions: Roman Catholic, 67%; atheist, 20%; Czechoslovak Church, 4%
National name: Ceskoslovenská Socialistická Republika
Literacy rate (1981): 100%
Economic summary: Gross national product (1985); $166 billion. Average annual growth rate (1985); 3.3%. Per capita income (1985): $5,914. Labor force in agriculture: 16.8%; principal products: wheat, rye, oats, corn, barley, potatoes, sugar beets, hogs, cattle, horses. Labor force in industry: 51.4%; major products: iron and steel, machinery and equipment, cement, textiles, motor vehicles, armaments, chemicals, ceramics. Natural resources: coal/coke, timber, lignite, uranium, magnesite. Exports: machinery, fuels and raw materials, consumer goods. Imports: machinery, equipment, fuels, raw materials, food, consumer goods. Major trading partners: U.S.S.R. and Soviet bloc, West Germany, Austria

Geography. Czechoslovakia lies in central Europe, a neighbor of East and West Germany, Poland, the U.S.S.R., Hungary, and Austria. It is equal in size to New York State. The principal rivers—the Elbe, Danube, Oder, and Moldau—are vital commercially to this landlocked country, for both waterborne commerce and agriculture, which flourishes in fertile valleys irrigated by these rivers and their tributaries.

Government. Since 1969 the supreme organ of the state has been the Federal Assembly, which has two equal chambers: the Chamber of People, with 200 deputies, and the Chamber of Nations, with 150 deputies (75 from the Czech Socialist Republic and 75 from the Slovak Socialist Republic). The chief executive is the President, who is elected by the Federal Assembly for a five-year term. The Premier and his Cabinet are appointed by the President but are responsible to the Federal Assembly.

The major political parties are the Communist Party, led by General Secretary Gustav Husak in both republics; Socialist Party; People's Party in the Czech Socialist Republic; Slovak Freedom Party and Slovak Reconstruction Party in the Slovak Socialist Republic. Together with trade unions, youth organizations, and other organizations, they form the National Front.

History. Probably about the 5th century A.D., Slavic tribes from the Vistula basin settled in the region of modern Czechoslovakia. Slovakia came under Magyar domination. The Czechs founded the kingdom of Bohemia, the Premyslide dynasty, which ruled Bohemia and Moravia from the 10th to the 16th century. One of the Bohemian kings, Charles IV, Holy Roman Emperor, made Prague an imperial capital and a center of Latin scholarship. The Hussite movement founded by Jan Hus (1369?–1415) linked the Slavs to the Reformation and revived Czech nationalism, previously under German domination. A Hapsburg, Ferdinand I, ascended the throne in 1526. The Czechs rebelled in 1618. Defeated in 1620, they were ruled for the next 300 years as part of the Austrian Empire.

In World War I, Czech and Slovak patriots, notably Thomas G. Masaryk and Milan Stefanik, promoted Czech-Slovak independence from abroad while their followers fought against the Central Powers. On Oct. 28, 1918, Czechoslovakia proclaimed itself a republic. Shortly thereafter Masaryk was unanimously elected first President.

Hitler provoked the country's German minority in the Sudetenland to agitate for autonomy. At the Munich Conference on Sept. 30, 1938, France and the U.K., seeking to avoid World War II, agreed that the Nazis could take the Sudetenland. Dr. Eduard Beneš, who had succeeded Masaryk, resigned on Oct. 5, 1938, and fled to London. Czechoslovakia became a state within the German orbit and was known as Czecho-Slovakia. In March 1939, the Nazis occupied the country.

Soon after Czechoslovakia was liberated in World War II and the government returned in April 1945, it was obliged to cede Ruthenia to the U.S.S.R. In 1946, a Communist, Klement Gottwald, formed a six-party coalition Cabinet. Pressure from Moscow increased until Feb. 23–25, 1948, when the Communists seized complete control in a coup. Following constituent assembly elections in which the Communists and their allies were unopposed, a new Constitution was adopted.

The "people's democracy" was converted into a "socialist" state by a new Constitution adopted June 11, 1960.

After the death of Stalin and the relaxing of Soviet controls, Czechoslovakia witnessed a nationalist awakening. In 1968 conservative Stalinists were driven from power and replaced by more liberal, reform-minded Communists.

Soviet military maneuvers on Czechoslovak soil in May 1968 were followed in July by a meeting of the U.S.S.R. with Poland, Bulgaria, East Germany, and Hungary in Warsaw that demanded an accounting, which Prague refused. Czechoslovak-Soviet talks on Czechoslovak territory, at Cierna, in late July led to an accord. But the Russians charged that the Czechoslovaks had reneged on pledges to modify their policies, and on Aug. 20–21, troops of the five powers, estimated at 600,000, executed a lightning invasion and occupation.

Soviet secret police seized the top Czechoslovak leadership and detained it for several days in Moscow. But Soviet efforts to establish a puppet regime failed. President Ludvik Svoboda negotiated an accord providing for a gradual troop withdrawal in return for "normalization" of political policy.

Czechoslovakia signed a new friendship treaty with the U.S.S.R. that codified the "Brezhnev doctrine," under which Russia can invade any Eastern European socialist nation that threatens to leave the satellite camp.

One of the most vigorous of the Eastern European groups formed to support human rights in the wake of the 1975 Helsinki Conference on Security and Cooperation in Europe was the Czech "Charter 77," an association of 240 intellectuals who signed a New Year manifesto protesting the suppression of freedom. Detentions of the signers began immediately, and a second manifesto appeared on January 8 with 300 signatures condemning the official reaction to the first. On Jan. 28, the government offered to let five of the dissidents leave the country, but they refused.

Charter 77 adherents marked their first anniversary with a manifesto Jan. 1, 1978, calling for open debate on the observance of human rights in Czechoslovakia. Enough of the group remained in May 1981 for the government to jail 36 persons in the biggest roundup of dissidents since 1971, as part of the precautions against any show of sympathy for Polish workers. The Czech Communist Party was among the most severe of the Eastern European states in condemning what Husak called an attempted "counterrevolutionary coup" in Poland.

DENMARK

Kingdom of Denmark
Sovereign: Queen Margrethe II (1972)
Premier: Poul Schlüter (1982)
Area: 16,631 sq mi. (43,075 sq km)[1]
Population (est. mid-1987): 5,100,000 (average annual growth rate: –0.1%)
Density per square mile: 306.7
Capital: Copenhagen
Largest cities (est. 1985): Copenhagen, 1,358,540; Aarhus, 252,071; Odense, 171,468; Alborg, 154,750
Monetary unit: Krone
Language: Danish
Religion: Lutheran (established)
National name: Kongeriget Danmark
Literacy rate: 100%
Economic summary: Gross national product (1985): $72.2 billion. Average annual growth rate (1984–86): 3.9%. Per capita income (1984): $11,290. Labor force in agriculture: 6.3%; principal products: meat, dairy products, fish, grains. Labor force in industry: 27.6%; major products; industrial and construction equipment, electronics, chemicals, textiles. Natural resources: oil, zinc, lead, coal, molybdenum, cryolite, uranium. Exports: meat and dairy products, industrial machinery, textiles and clothing, chemical products, transportation equipment. Imports: industrial raw materials, fuel, machinery and equipment, transport equipment, petroleum, chemicals. Major trading partners: West Germany, Sweden, U.K., U.S.

1. Excluding Faeroe Islands and Greenland.

Geography. Smallest of the Scandinavian countries (half the size of Maine), Denmark occupies the Jutland peninsula, which extends north from Germany between the tips of Norway and Sweden. To the west is the North Sea and to the east the Baltic.

The country also consists of several Baltic islands; the two largest are Sjaelland, the site of Copenhagen, and Fyn. The narrow waters off the north coast are called the Skagerrak and those off the east, the Kattegat.

Government. Denmark has been a constitutional monarchy since 1849. Legislative power is held jointly by the Sovereign and parliament. The Constitution of 1953 provides for a unicameral parliament called the Folketing, consisting of 179 popularly elected members who serve for four years. The Cabinet is presided over by the Sovereign, who appoints the Prime Minister.

The Sovereign, Queen Margrethe II, was born April 16, 1940, and became Queen—the first in Denmark's history—Jan. 15, 1972, the day after her father, King Frederik IX, died at 72 in the 25th year of his reign. Margrethe was the eldest of his three daughters (by Princess Ingrid of Sweden). The nation's Constitution was amended in 1953 to permit her to succeed her father in the absence of a male heir to the throne. (Denmark was ruled six centuries ago by Margrethe I, but she was never crowned Queen since there was no female right of succession.)

The major political parties are the Social Democratic Party (56 seats in the Folketing), led by former Premier Anker Jørgensen; Conservative People's Party (42 seats), led by Premier Poul Schlüter; Socialist People's Party (21 seats), led by Gert Petersen; Liberal Party (22 seats), led by Henning Christophersen; Radical Liberal Party (10 seats); Center Democrats (8 seats); Progress Party (6 seats), Christian People's Party (5 seats); Leftwing Socialists (5 seats).

History. Denmark emerged with establishment of the Norwegian dynasty of the Ynglinger in Jutland at the end of the 8th century. Danish mariners played a major role in the raids of the Vikings, or

Norsemen, on Western Europe and particularly England. The country was Christianized by St. Ansgar and Harald Blaatand (Bluetooth)—the first Christian king—in the 10th century. Harald's son, Sweyn, conquered England in 1013. His son, Canute the Great, who reigned from 1014 to 1035, united Denmark, England, and Norway under his rule; the southern tip of Sweden was part of Denmark until the 17th century. On Canute's death, civil war tore the country until Waldemar I (1157–82) re-established Danish hegemony over the north.

In 1282, the nobles won the Great Charter, and Eric V was forced to share power with parliament and a Council of Nobles. Waldemar IV (1340–75) restored Danish power, checked only by the Hanseatic League of north German cities allied with ports from Holland to Poland. His daughter, Margrethe, in 1397 united under her rule Denmark, Norway, and Sweden. But Sweden later achieved autonomy and in 1523, under Gustavus I, independence.

Denmark supported Napoleon, for which it was punished at the Congress of Vienna in 1815 by the loss of Norway to Sweden. In 1864, Bismarck, together with the Austrians, made war on the little country as an initial step in the unification of Germany. Denmark was neutral in World War I.

In 1939, Denmark signed a 10-year pact with Hitler, but less than a year later it was invaded by the Nazis. King Christian X reluctantly cautioned his countrymen to accept the occupation, but there was widespread resistance against the Nazis. In 1944, Iceland declared its independence from Denmark, ending a union that had existed since 1380.

Liberated by British troops in May 1945, the country staged a fast recovery in both agriculture and manufacturing and was a leader in liberalizing trade. It joined the United Nations in 1945 and NATO in 1949.

The Social Democrats largely ran Denmark after the war but were ousted in 1973 in an election dominated by protests against high taxes. A minority government was formed by the Liberal Democrats, with their leader, Poul Hartling, as Premier. After losing a vote of confidence in January 1975, Hartling resigned and was succeeded by Anker Jørgensen, a Social Democrat who was Premier in 1972–73.

Disputes over economic policy led to elections in 1981 that led to Poul Schülter coming to power in early 1982.

Outlying Territories of Denmark

FAEROE ISLANDS

Status: Autonomous part of Denmark
Lagmand (President): Pauli Ellefsen (1981)
Area: 540 sq mi. (1,399 sq km)
Population (est. 1985): 46,000 (average annual growth rate: 1.0%)
Density per square mile: 79.9
Capital (est. 1982): Thorshavn, 12,750
Monetary unit: Faeroese krone
Literacy rate: 99%
Economic summary: Gross national product (1980): $440 million. Average annual growth rate (1970–79): 5.6 %. Per capita income (1980): $10,620. Principal agricultural products: sheep and cattle. Major industrial product: fish. Exports: fish and fish products. Imports: machinery and transport equipment, foodstuffs, petroleum and petroleum products. Major trading partners: Denmark, U.S., U.K., West Germany

This group of 21 islands, lying in the North Atlantic about 200 miles (322 km) northwest of the Shetland Islands, joined Denmark in 1386 and has since been part of the Danish kingdom. The islands were occupied by British troops during World War II, after the German occupation of Denmark.

The Faeroes have home rule under a bill enacted in 1948; they also have two representatives in the Danish Folketing.

GREENLAND

Status: Autonomous part of Denmark
Premier: Jonathan Motzfeldt (1983)
Area: 840,000 sq mi. (incl. 708,069 sq mi. covered by icecap) (2,175,600 sq km)
Population (est. 1985): 54,000 (average annual growth rate: 1.2%)
Capital (est. 1982): Godthaab, 10,000
Monetary unit: Krone
Literacy rate: 99%
Economic summary: Gross national product (1980): $430 million. Average annual growth rate (1970–79): 4.4%. Per capita income (1980): $8,290. Principal agricultural products: hay, sheep, garden produce. Major industries: mining, slaughtering, fishing, sealing. Natural resource: cryolite. Exports: fish and fish products, metalic ores and concentrates. Imports: petroleum and petroleum products, machinery and transport equipment, foodstuffs. Major trading partners: Denmark, U.S., Finland, West Germany, U.K.

Greenland, the world's largest island, was colonized in 985–86 by Eric the Red. Danish sovereignty, which covered only the west coast, was extended over the whole island in 1917. In 1941 the U.S. signed an agreement with the Danish minister in Washington, placing it under U.S. protection during World War II but maintaining Danish sovereignty. A definitive agreement for the joint defense of Greenland within the framework of NATO was signed in 1951. A large U.S. air base at Thule in the far north was completed in 1953.

Under 1953 amendments to the Danish Constitution, Greenland became part of Denmark, with two representatives in the Danish Folketing. On May 1, 1979, Greenland gained home rule, with its own local parliament (Landsting), replacing the Greenland Provincial Council.

In February 1982, Greenlanders voted to withdraw from the European Community, which they had joined as part of Denmark in 1973. Danish Premier Anker Jørgensen said he would support the request, but with reluctance.

Greenland is the world's only source of natural cryolite, important in making aluminum.

DJIBOUTI

Republic of Djibouti
President: Hassan Gouled Aptidon (1977)
Prime Minister: Gourad Hamadou Barkat (1978)
Area: 8,996 sq mi. (23,300 sq km)
Population (est. mid-1987): 300,000 (average annual growth rate: 2.5%)

Density per square mile: 33.3
Capital (est. 1980): Djibouti, 200,000
Monetary unit: Djibouti franc
Languages: Arabic, French, Afar, Somali, Issa
Religions: Islam, 94%; Christian, 6%
National name: Jumhouriyya Djibouti
Literacy rate: 20%
Economic summary: Gross national product (1984): $308 million. Average annual growth rate (1970–79): −4.9%. Per capita income (1984): $270. Principal agricultural products: goats, sheep, camels. Industries: port and maritime support, construction. Exports: hides, cattle, coffee (in transit from Ethiopia). Imports: machinery, transport equipment, foodstuffs. Major trading partners: France, Ethiopia, Japan, Belgium, U.K., Saudi Arabia, Yemen

Geography. Djibouti lies in northeastern Africa on the Gulf of Aden at the southern entrance to the Red Sea. It borders on Ethiopia and Somalia. The country, the size of Massachusetts, is mainly a stony desert, with scattered plateaus and highlands.

Government. On May 8, 1977, the population of the French Territory of the Afars and Issas voted by more than 98% for independence. Voters also approved a 65-member interim Constituent Assembly. France transferred sovereignty to the new nation of Djibouti on June 27. Later in the year it became a member of the Organization of African Unity and the Arab League. The People's Progress Assembly is the only legal political party.

History. The territory that is now Djibouti was acquired by France between 1843 and 1886 by treaties with the Somali sultans. Small, arid, and sparsely populated, Djibouti is important chiefly because of the capital city's port, the terminal of the Djibouti-Addis Ababa railway that carries 60% of Ethiopia's foreign trade.

Originally known as French Somaliland, the colony voted in 1958 and 1967 to remain under French rule. It was renamed the Territory of the Afars and Issas in 1967 and took the name of its capital city on attaining independence.

Somali rebels in Ethiopia's Ogaden Province cut the railway to Djibouti in June 1977 and there was fear that the new nation might be absorbed by Somalia. In July 1980, Djibouti granted base rights to United States ships and planes in exchange for undisclosed amounts of aid.

DOMINICA

Commonwealth of Dominica
President: Sir Clarence Seignoret (1985)
Prime Minister: Mary Eugenia Charles (1980)
Area: 290 sq mi. (751 sq km)
Population: (est. mid-1987): 100,000 (average annual growth rate: 1.7%)
Density per square mile: 344.8
Capital and largest city (est. 1981): Roseau, 20,000
Monetary unit: East Caribbean dollar
Languages: English and French patois
Religions: Roman Catholic, Anglican, Methodist
Member of Commonwealth of Nations
Literacy rate: 80%
Economic summary: Gross national product (1984): $80.0 million. Average annual growth rate (1981): 8%. Per capita income (1984): $940. Labor force in agriculture: 40%; principal products: bananas, citrus fruits, coconuts, cocoa. Major industries: agricultural processing; tourism. Exports: bananas, lime juice, cocoa, coconut oil. Imports: machinery and equipment, foodstuffs, manufactured goods, chemicals. Major trading partners: U.K., Caribbean countries, U.S.

Geography. Dominica is an island of the Lesser Antilles in the Caribbean south of Guadeloupe and north of Martinique.

Government. Dominica is a republic, with a president elected by the House of Assembly as head of state and a prime minister appointed by the president on the advice of the Assembly. The Freedom Party (16 of 21 seats in the Assembly) is led by Prime Minister Mary Eugenia Charles. The Opposition Democratic Labor Party holds three seats and the United Dominica Labor Party one.

History. Discovered by Columbus in 1493, Dominica was claimed by Britain and France until 1815, when Britain asserted sovereignty. Dominica, along with other Windward Isles, became a self-governing member of the West Indies Associated States in free association with Britain in 1967.

Full independence was granted on Nov. 3, 1978, and the first Prime Minister, Patrick R. John, declared a socialist course for the new republic.

Dissatisfaction over the slow pace of reconstruction after Hurricane David struck the island in September 1979 brought a landslide victory for the opposition Freedom Party in July 1980. The vote gave the prime ministership to Mary Eugenia Charles, a strong advocate of free enterprise. The Freedom Party won again in 1985 elections, giving Miss Charles a second five-year term as prime minister.

DOMINICAN REPUBLIC

President: Joaquin Balaguer (1986)
Area: 18,704 sq mi. (48,442 sq km)
Population (est. mid-1987): 6,500,000 (average annual growth rate: 2.5%) (approx.): mulatto, 75%; white, 15%; Negro, 10%
Density per square mile: 347.5
Capital: Santo Domingo
Largest cities (est. 1983): Santo Domingo, 1,410,000; Santiago de los Caballeros, 285,000
Monetary unit: Peso
Language: Spanish
Religion: Roman Catholic
National name: República Dominicana
Literacy rate: 68%
Economic summary: Gross national product (1984 est.): $11.0 billion. Average annual growth rate (1971–82): · 4.5%. Per capital income (1983): $1,371. Land used for agriculture: 14%; labor force: 47%; principal products: sugar cane, coffee, cocoa, tobacco, bananas. Labor force in industry: 20%; major products: processed sugar, textiles, nickel, silver, and gold mining. Natural resources: nickel, gold, silver. Exports: sugar, nickel, coffee, tobacco, cocoa. Imports: foodstuffs, petroleum, industrial raw materials, capital equipment. Major trading partners: U.S., Venezuela

Geography. The Dominican Republic in the West Indies, occupies the eastern two thirds of the island of Hispaniola, which it shares with Haiti. Its area equals that of Vermont and New Hampshire combined.

Crossed from northwest to southeast by a mountain range with elevations exceeding 10,000 feet (3,048 m), the country has fertile, well-watered land in the north and east, where nearly two thirds of the population lives. The southwest part is arid and has poor soil, except around Santo Domingo.

Government. The president is elected by direct vote every four years. Legislative powers rest with a Senate and a Chamber of Deputies, both elected by direct vote, also for four years. All citizens must vote when they reach 18 years of age, or even earlier if they are married.

The major political parties are the Dominican Revolutionary Party (48 of 120 seats), led by Jacobo Majluta; the Reformist Party (56 seats) led by President Joaquín Balaguer; Dominican Liberation Party, led by Juan Bosch (16 seats).

History. The Dominican Republic was discovered by Columbus in 1492. He named it La Española, and his son, Diego, was its first viceroy. The capital, Santo Domingo, founded in 1496, is the oldest European settlement in the Western Hemisphere. Spain ceded the colony to France in 1795, and Haitian blacks under Toussaint L'Ouverture conquered it in 1801.

In 1808 the people revolted and the next year captured Santo Domingo, setting up the first republic. Spain regained title to the colony in 1814. In 1821 the people overthrew Spanish rule, but in 1822 they were reconquered by the Haitians. They revolted again in 1844, threw out the Haitians, and established the Dominican Republic, headed by Pedro Santana. Uprisings and Haitian attacks led Santana to make the country a province of Spain from 1861 to 1865. The U.S. Senate refused to ratify a treaty of annexation. Disorder continued until the dictatorship of Ulíses Heureaux; in 1916, when disorder broke out again, the U.S. sent in a contingent of marines, who remained until 1934.

A sergeant in the Dominican army trained by the marines, Rafaél Leonides Trujillo Molina, overthrew Horacio Vásquez in 1930 and established a dictatorship that lasted until his assassination 31 years later.

A new Constitution was adopted in 1962, and the first free elections since 1924 put Juan Bosch, a leftist leader, in office. A planned program of reforms with U.S. support was cut off by a right-wing military coup that replaced Bosch with a civilian triumvirate.

Leftists rebelled April 24, 1965, and President Lyndon Johnson sent in marines and troops. After an OAS ceasefire request May 6, a compromise installed Hector Garcia-Godoy as provisional president. Joaquin Balaguer won in free elections in 1966 against Bosch, and a peacekeeping force of 9,000 U.S. troops and 2,000 from other countries withdrew. Balaguer restored political and economic stability.

Balaguer's longtime support for free elections faltered in May 1978, when the army suspended the counting of ballots as he trailed in a fourth-term bid. After a warning from President Jimmy Carter, however, Balaguer accepted the victory of Antonio Guzmán of the opposition Dominican Revolutionary Party.

Salvador Jorge Blanco of the Dominican Revolutionary Party was elected President on May 16, 1982, defeating Balaguer and Bosch. Austerity measures imposed by the International Monetary Fund, including sharply higher prices for food and gasoline, provoked rioting in the spring of 1984 that left more than 50 dead.

Saying he feared they would provoke "some kind of revolution," Blanco dragged his feet about putting into effect further IMF demands for higher prices and taxes and devaluation of the peso, and came within weeks of defaulting on several big loans.

The root of the economic difficulties was the country's dependence on earnings from exports of sugar, gold and silver, all of which were selling at depressed prices.

Balaguer was elected President in May 1986 and aimed economic policy at diversifying the economy. On April 30, 1987, Blanco asked for political asylum in Venezuela after charges of corruption during his term were levelled against him.

ECUADOR

Republic of Ecuador
President: León Febres Cordero (1984)
Area: 109,484 sq mi. (270,670 sq km)
Population (est. mid-1987): 10,000,000 (average annual growth rate: 2.8%)
Density per square mile: 91.3
Capital: Quito
Largest cities (est. 1986): Guayaquil, 1,509,100; Quito, 1,093,300; Cuenca, 193,000
Monetary unit: Sucre
Languages: Spanish, Quéchua, Jibaro
Religion: Roman Catholic, 92%
National name: República del Ecuador
Literacy rate: 84%
Economic summary: Gross national product (1985). $11.9 billion. Annual growth rate (1985) 3.8%. Per capita income (1985): $1,272. Land used for agriculture: 11%; labor force: 52%; principal products: bananas, cocoa, coffee, sugar cane, fruits, corn, potatoes, rice. Labor force in industry: 13%; major products: processed foods, textiles, fish, petroleum. Natural resources: petroleum, fish, silver, gold. Exports: petroleum, shrimp, bananas, coffee, cocoa, fish products. Imports: agricultural and industrial machinery, industrial raw materials, foodstuffs, chemical products, transportation and communication equipment. Major trading partners: U.S., Latin American and Western European countries, Japan.

Geography. Ecuador, equal in area to Nevada, is in the northwest part of South America fronting on the Pacific. To the north is Colombia and to the east and south is Peru. Two high and parallel ranges of the Andes, traversing the country from north to south, are topped by tall volcanic peaks. The highest is Chimborazo at 20,577 feet (6,272 m).

The Galápagos Islands (or Colón Archipelago) (3,029 sq mi.; 7,845 sq km) in the Pacific Ocean about 600 miles (966 km) west of the South American mainland, became part of Ecuador in 1832.

Government. A 1978 Constitution returned Ecuador to civilian government after eight years of military rule. The President is elected to a term of four years and a House of Representatives of 71 members is popularly elected for the same period.

History. The tribes in the northern highlands of Ecuador formed the Kingdom of Quito around A.D. 1000. It was absorbed, by conquest and marriage, into the Inca Empire. Pizarro conquered the land in 1532, and through the 17th century a thriving colony was built by exploitation of the Indians. The first revolt against Spain occurred in 1809. Ecuador then joined Venezuela, Colombia, and Panama in a confederacy known as Greater Colombia.

On the collapse of this union in 1830, Ecuador became independent. Subsequent history was one of revolts and dictatorships; it had 48 presidents during the first 131 years of the republic. Conservatives ruled until the Revolution of 1895 ushered in nearly a half century of Radical Liberal rule, during which the church was disestablished and freedom of worship, speech, and press was introduced.

A three-man military junta headed by Vice Adm. Alfredo Poveda, which had taken power in a 1976 coup, agreed to a free presidential election on July 16, 1978. Jaime Roldós Aguilera won the runoff on April 29, 1979, backed by a "center leftist" coalition, the Concentration of Popular Forces.

The 40-year-old President died in the crash of a small plane May 24, 1981. Vice President Osvaldo Hurtado Larrea became President. León Febres Cordero, leader of the National Reconstruction Front, narrowly won two rounds of voting in 1984 elections and was installed President in August. Combined opposition parties won a majority in the 71-member Congress large enough to block significant action, a majority increased in the June 1986 elections.

Problems with the military plagued Cordero in 1986-87, he faced two rebellions and was held hostage for one day by dissident soldiers.

EGYPT

Arab Republic of Egypt
President: Hosni Mubarak (1981)
Premier: Dr. Atef Sedki (1986)
Area: 386,900 sq. mi. (1,002,000 sq km)
Population (est. mid-1987): 51,900,000 (average annual growth rate: 2.6%)
Density per square mile: 134.1
Capital: Cairo
Largest cities (est. 1987): Cairo, 12,560,000; **(1976 census):** Alexandria, 2,317,705; Giza, 1,246,713; Shubra el Khema, 393,700; El Mahalla el Kubra, 292,853; Tanta, 284,636; Port Said, 262,620; Mansura, 257,866
Monetary unit: Egyptian pound
Language: Arabic
Religions: Islam, 93%; Christian (mostly Copt), 7%
Literacy rate: 50.6%
Economic summary: Gross national product (1983): $20.0 billion. Average annual growth rate (1982): 6%. Per capita income (1985): $500. Land used for agriculture: 3%; labor force: 36%; principal products: cotton, wheat, rice, corn. Labor force in industry: 13%; major products: textiles, processed foods, chemicals, fertilizer, petroleum and petroleum products. Natural resources: iron ore, phosphates, petroleum, gypsum. Exports: cotton, rice, petroleum, cement. Imports: foodstuffs, machinery, fertilizers, woods. Major trading partners: West Germany, Italy, France, U.S.

Geography. Egypt, at the northeast corner of Africa on the Mediterranean Sea, is bordered on the west by Libya, on the south by the Sudan, and on the east by the Red Sea and Israel. It is nearly one and one half times the size of Texas.

The historic Nile flows through the eastern third of the country. On either side of the Nile valley are desert plateaus, spotted with oases. In the north, toward the Mediterranean, plateaus are low, while south of Cairo they rise to a maximum of 1,015 feet (309 m) above sea level. At the head of the Red Sea is the Sinai Peninsula, between the Suez Canal and Israel.

Navigable throughout its course in Egypt, the Nile is used largely as a means of cheap transport for heavy goods. The principal port is Alexandria.

The Nile delta starts 100 miles (161 km) south of the Mediterranean and fans out to a sea front of 155 miles between the cities of Alexandria and Port Said. From Cairo north, the Nile branches into many streams, the principal ones being the Damietta and the Rosetta.

Except for a narrow belt along the Mediterranean, Egypt lies in an almost rainless area, in which high daytime temperatures fall quickly at night.

Government. Executive power is held by the President, who can appoint one or more Vice Presidents.

The National Democratic Party, led by President Hosni Mubarak, is the dominant political party. Elections on April 6, 1987 confirmed its huge majority (348 of 448 seats). There is also a three-party alliance, that includes Moslem fundamentalists, that forms the main opposition (60 seats). The New Wafd is the third largest party (35 seats).

History. Egyptian history dates back to about 4000 B.C., when the kingdoms of upper and lower Egypt, already highly civilized, were united. Egypt's "Golden Age" coincided with the 18th and 19th dynasties (16th to 13th centuries B.C.), during which the empire was established. Persia conquered Egypt in 525 B.C.; Alexander the Great subdued it in 332 B.C.; and then the dynasty of the Ptolemies ruled the land until 30 B.C., when Cleopatra, last of the line, committed suicide and Egypt became a Roman province. From 641 to 1517 the Arab caliphs ruled Egypt, and then the Turks took it for their Ottoman Empire.

Napoleon's armies occupied the country from 1798 to 1801. In 1805, Mohammed Ali, leader of a band of Albanian soldiers, became Pasha of Egypt. After completion of the Suez Canal in 1869, the French and British took increasing interest in Egypt.

British troops occupied Egypt in 1882, and British resident agents became its actual administrators, though it remained under nominal Turkish sovereignty. In 1914, this fiction was ended, and Egypt became a protectorate of Britain.

Egyptian nationalism forced Britain to declare Egypt an independent, sovereign state on Feb. 28, 1922, although the British reserved rights for the protection of the Suez Canal and the defense of Egypt. In 1936, by an Anglo-Egyptian treaty of alliance, all British troops and officials were to be withdrawn, except from the Suez Canal Zone. When World War II started, Egypt remained neutral. British imperial troops finally ended the Nazi threat to Suez in 1942 in the battle of El Alamein, west of Alexandria.

In 1951, Egypt abrogated the 1936 treaty and the 1899 Anglo-Egyptian condominium of the Sudan (*See* Sudan). Rioting and attacks on British troops in the Suez Canal Zone followed, reaching a climax in January 1952. The army, led by Gen. Mohammed Naguib, seized power on July 23, 1952. Three days later, King Farouk abdicated in favor of his infant son. The monarchy was abolished and a republic proclaimed on June 18, 1953, with Naguib holding the posts of Provisional President and Premier. He relinquished the latter in 1954 to Gamal Abdel Nasser, leader of the ruling military junta. Naguib was deposed seven months later and Nasser confirmed as President in a referendum on June 23, 1956.

Nasser's policies embroiled his country in continual conflict. In 1956, the U.S. and Britain withdrew their pledges of financial aid for the building of the Aswan High Dam. In reply, Nasser nationalized the Suez Canal and expelled British oil and embassy officials. Israel, barred from the Canal and exasperated by terrorist raids, invaded the Gaza Strip and the Sinai Peninsula. Britain and France, after demanding Egyptian evacuation of the Canal Zone, attacked Egypt on Oct. 31, 1956. Worldwide pressure forced Britain, France, and Israel to halt the hostilities. A U.N. emergency force occupied the Canal Zone, and all troops were evacuated in the spring of 1957.

On Feb. 1, 1958, Egypt and Syria formed the United Arab Republic, which was joined by Yemen in an association known as the United Arab States. However, Syria withdrew from the United Arab Republic in 1961 and Egypt dissolved its ties with Yemen in the United Arab States.

On June 5, 1967, Israel invaded the Sinai Peninsula, the East Bank of the Jordan River, and the zone around the Gulf of Aqaba. A U.N. ceasefire on June 10 saved the Arabs from complete rout.

Nasser declared the 1967 cease-fire void along the Canal in April 1969 and began a war of attrition. The U.S. peace plan of June 19, 1970, resulted in Egypt's agreement to reinstate the cease-fire for at least three months, (from August) and to accept Israel's existence within "recognized and secure" frontiers that might emerge from U.N.-mediated talks. In return, Israel accepted the principle of withdrawing from occupied territories.

Then, on Sept. 28, 1970, Nasser died, at 52, of a heart attack. The new President was Anwar el-Sadat, an associate of Nasser and a former newspaper editor.

The Aswan High Dam, whose financing by the U.S.S.R. was its first step into Egypt, was completed and dedicated in January 1971.

In July 1972, Sadat ordered the expulsion of Soviet "advisors and experts" from Egypt because the Russians had not provided the sophisticated weapons he felt were needed to retake territory lost to Israel in 1967.

The fourth Arab-Israeli war broke out Oct. 6, 1973, while Israelis were commemorating Yom Kippur, the Jewish high holy day. Egypt swept deep into the Sinai, while Syria strove to throw Israel off the Golan Heights.

A U.N.-sponsored truce was accepted on October 22. In January 1974, both sides agreed to a settlement negotiated by U.S. Secretary of State Henry A. Kissinger that gave Egypt a narrow strip along the entire Sinai bank of the Suez Canal. In June, President Nixon made the first visit by a U.S. President to Egypt and full diplomatic relations were established. The Suez Canal was cleared and reopened on June 5, 1975.

Kissinger pursued "shuttle diplomacy" between Cairo and Jerusalem to extend areas of agreement. Israel yielded on three points—the possession of the Mitla and Giddi passes in the Sinai and the Abu Rudeis oil field in the peninsula—and both sides committed themselves to annual renewal of the U.N. peacekeeping force in the Sinai.

In the most audacious act of his career, Sadat flew to Jerusalem at the invitation of Prime Minister Menachem Begin and pleaded before Israel's Knesset on Nov. 20, 1977, for a permanent peace settlement. The Arab world reacted with fury—only Morocco, Tunisia, Sudan, and Oman approved.

Egypt and Israel signed a formal peace treaty on March 26, 1979. The pact ended 30 years of war and established diplomatic and commercial relations.

Egyptian and Israeli officials met in the Sinai desert on April 26, 1979, to implement the peace treaty calling for the phased withdrawal of occupation forces from the peninsula. By mid-1980, two thirds of the Sinai was transferred, but progress here was not matched—the negotiation of Arab autonomy in the Gaza Strip and the West Bank.

Sadat halted further talks in August 1980 because of continued Israeli settlement of the West Bank. On October 6 1981, Sadat was assassinated by extremist Muslim soldiers at a parade in Cairo. Vice President Hosni Mubarak, a former Air Force chief of staff, was confirmed by the parliament as president the next day.

Although feared unrest in Egypt did not occur in the wake of the assassination, and Israel completed the return of the Sinai to Egyptian control on April 25, 1982, Mubarak was unable to revive the autonomy talks. Israel's invasion of Lebanon in June imposed a new strain on him, and brought a marked cooling in Egyptian-Israeli relations, but not a disavowal of the peace treaty.

During 1985, pressures by Moslem fundamentalists to implement Islamic law in Egypt increased. In response, the government began putting all mosques under control of the minister for religious endowments. In July, authorities arrested at least 45 fundamentalists including Sheik Hafez Salama, the fundamentalist cleric spearheading the campaign for immediate application of *sharia*, the Islamic legal code dating back 1,300 years.

In February 1986, a riot by the security forces had to be quelled by the army; an incident that underscored Mubarak's dependence on the army in the face of growing Islamic fundamentalism and increasing discontent with the failing economy.

Suez Canal. The Suez Canal, in Egyptian territory between the Arabian Desert and the Sinai Peninsula, is an artificial waterway about 100 miles (161 km) long between Port Said on the Mediterranean and Suez on the Red Sea. Construction work, directed by the French engineer Ferdinand de Lesseps, was begun April 25, 1859, and the Canal was opened Nov. 17, 1869. The cost was 432,807,882 francs. The concession was held by an Egyptian joint stock company, *Compagnie Universelle du Canal Maritime de Suez*, in which the British government held 353,504 out of a total of 800,000 shares. The concession was to expire Nov. 17, 1968, but the company was nationalized July 26, 1956, by unilateral action of the Egyptian government.

The Canal was closed in June 1967 after the Arab-Israeli conflict. With the help of the U.S. Navy, work was begun on clearing the Canal in 1974, after the cease-fire ending the Arab-Israeli war. It was reopened to traffic June 5, 1975.

EL SALVADOR

Republic of El Salvador
President: José Napoleón Duarte (1984)
Area: 8,260 sq mi. (21,393 sq km)
Population (est. mid-1987): 5,300,000 (average annual growth rate: 2.6%)
Density per square mile: 641.6
Capital: San Salvador
Largest cities (est. 1984): San Salvador, 455,300; Santa Ana, 135,200; Mejicanos, 89,000; San Miguel, 86,700
Monetary unit: Colón
Language: Spanish
Religion: Roman Catholic
National name: República de El Salvador
Literacy rate: 69%
Economic summary: Gross national product (1984): $3.82 billion. Average annual growth rate (1973–82): 0.6%. Per capita income (1984): $730. Land used for agriculture: 35%; labor force: 40%; principal products: coffee, cotton, corn, sugar, rice, sorghum. Labor force in industry: 16%; major products: processed foods, clothing and textiles, petroleum products. Natural resources: timber, balsam. Exports: coffee, cotton, sugar. Imports: machinery, automotive vehicles, petroleum, foodstuffs, fertilizer. Major trading partners: U.S., Guatemala, Japan, West Germany, Mexico, Costa Rica, Venezuela.

Geography. Situated on the Pacific coast of Central America, El Salvador has Guatemala to the west and Honduras to the north and east. It is the smallest of the Central American countries, its area equal to that of Massachusetts, and the only one without an Atlantic coastline.

Most of the country is a fertile volcanic plateau about 2,000 feet (607 m) high. There are some active volcanoes and many scenic crater lakes.

Government. A new Constitution enacted in 1983 vests executive power in a President elected for a nonrenewable, five-year term, and legislative power in a 60-member National Assembly elected by universal suffrage and proportional representation. Judicial power is vested in a Supreme Court, composed of a President and nine magistrates elected by the Assembly, and subordinate courts.

José Napoleón Duarte, a Christian Democrat regarded as a moderate, was elected President in 1984. In national legislative and municipal elections in 1985, Duarte's Christian Democratic Party won almost 54% of the vote and the majority it was seeking in the National Assembly, badly splintering the previously dominant rightist parties.

History. Pedro de Alvarado, a lieutenant of Cortés, conquered El Salvador in 1525. El Salvador, with the other countries of Central America, declared its independence from Spain on Sept. 15, 1821, and was part of a federation of Central American states until that union was dissolved in 1838. Its independent career for decades thereafter was marked by numerous revolutions and wars against other Central American republics.

On Oct. 15, 1979, a junta deposed the President, Gen. Carlos Humberto Romero, seeking to halt increasingly violent clashes between leftist and rightist forces.

On Dec. 4, 1980, three American nuns and an American lay worker were killed in an ambush near San Salvador, causing the Carter Administration to suspend all aid pending an investigation. The naming of José Napoleón Duarte, a moderate civilian, as head of the governing junta brought a resumption of U.S. aid.

Defying guerrilla threats, voters on March 28, 1982, elected a rightist majority to a constituent assembly that dismissed Duarte and replaced him with a centrist physician, Dr. Alvaro Alfredo Magaña. The rightist majority repealed the laws permitting expropriation of land, and critics charged that the land-reform program begun under Duarte was dead. Even though fighting continued, with reports of government violations of human rights, the Reagan Administration asked certification of El Salvador's eligibility for resumed foreign aid, and this was approved by Congress.

In an election closely monitored by American and other foreign observers, Duarte was elected President in May 1984.

Duarte's Christian Democratic Party scored an unexpected electoral triumph in national legislative and municipal elections held in March 1985, winning almost 54% of the vote and the majority it was seeking in the new National Assembly. The rightist parties that had been dominant in the previous Constituent Assembly demanded that the vote be nullified, but the army high command rejected their assertion the voting had been fraudulent. The army's refusal to support the rightists was interpreted as a turning point in El Salvador's struggle for political stability.

At the same time, U.S. officials said that while the rebels still were far from being defeated, there had been marked improvement in the effectiveness of government troops in the civil war against antigovernment guerrillas that has been waged mainly in the countryside. The rebels responded by initiating a campaign of urban terror; killing and kidnapping pro-government figures. In 1986, Duarte called for a new round of talks with the rebels. This was seen as an attempt to revive a popularity that was falling due to his perceived failure to improve the economy, implement promised social programs or end the war. These broke down in September.

EQUATORIAL GUINEA

Republic of Equatorial Guinea
Head of junta: Lieut. Col. Teodoro Obiang Nguema Mbasogo (1979)
Area: 10,830 sq mi. (28,051 sq km)
Population (est. mid-1987): 300,000 (average annual growth rate: 1.8%)
Density per square mile: 27.7
Capital and largest city (est. 1983): Malabo, 37,500
Monetary unit: Ekuele
Languages: Spanish, Fang, Bubi
Religions: Roman Catholic, Protestant, Animist
National name: Républica de Guinea Ecuatorial
Literacy rate: 55%
Economic summary: Gross national product (1983): $75 million. Per capita income (1985): $172. Land used for agriculture: 8%; labor force: 73%; principal products: cocoa, wood, coffee. Natural resource: wood. Exports: cocoa, wood, coffee. Imports: foodstuffs, textiles, machinery. Major trading partners: Spain, France, China, Netherlands, Italy

Geography. Equatorial Guinea, formerly Spanish Guinea, consists of Rio Muni (10,045 sq mi.; 26,117 sq km), on the western coast of Africa, and several islands in the Gulf of Guinea, the largest of which is Bioko (formerly Fernando Po) (785 sq mi.; 2,033 sq km). The other islands are Pagalu (formerly Annobón), Corisco, Elobey Grande, and Elobey Chico. The total area is twice that of Connecticut.

Government. The Constitution of 1973 was suspended after a coup on Aug. 3, 1979. A Supreme Military Council, headed by the president, exercises all power. Political parties are banned.

History. Fernando Po and Annobón came under Spanish control in 1778. From 1827 to 1844, with Spanish consent, Britain administered Fernando Po, but in the latter year Spain reclaimed the island. Río Muni was given to Spain in 1885 by the Treaty of Berlin.

Negotiations with Spain led to independence on Oct. 12, 1968.

In 1969, anti-Spanish incidents in Río Muni, including the tearing down of a Spanish flag by national troops, caused 5,000 Spanish residents to flee for their safety, and diplomatic relations between the two nations became strained. A month later, President Masie Nguema Biyogo Negue Ndong charged that a coup had been attempted against him. He seized dictatorial powers and arrested 80 opposition politicians and even several of his Cabinet ministers and the secretary of the National Assembly.

A coup on Aug. 3, 1979, deposed Masie, and a junta led by Lieut. Col. Teodoro Obiang Nguema Mbasogo took over the government. Obiang expelled Soviet technicians and reinstated cooperation with Spain.

ETHIOPIA

People's Democratic Republic of Ethiopia
Head of State: Mengistu Haile Mariam (1977)
Area: 472,432 sq mi. (1,223,600 sq km)
Population (est. mid-1987): 46,000,000 (average annual growth rate: 2.3%)
Density per square mile: 97.4
Capital: Addis Ababa
Largest cities (est. 1984): Addis Ababa, 1,423,111; Asmara, 275,385
Monetary unit: Birr
Languages: Amharic (official), Galligna, Tigrigna
Religions: Ethiopian Orthodox, 49%; Islam, 31%; Animist, 11%
Literacy rate: 15%
Economic summary: Gross national product (1985): $4.74 billion. Average annual growth rate (1973–82): 2.6%. Per capita income (1985): $110. Land used for agriculture: 13%; labor force: 77%; principal products: coffee, barley, wheat, corn, sugar cane, cotton, oilseeds, livestock. Labor force in industry: 10%; Major industrial products: cement, cotton textiles, refined sugar, processed foods, refined oil. Natural resources: potash, salt, gold, platinum. Exports: coffee, hides and skins, oilseeds. Imports: petroleum, foodstuffs. Major trading partners: Saudi Arabia, Japan, Italy, U.S., U.S.S.R., Djibouti.

Geography. Ethiopia is in east central Africa, bordered on the west by the Sudan, the east by Somalia and Djibouti, the south by Kenya, and the north by the Red Sea. It is nearly three times the size of California.

Over its main plateau land, Ethiopia has several high mountains, the highest of which is Ras Dashan at 15,158 feet (4,620 m). The Blue Nile, or Abbai, rises in the northwest and flows in a great semicircle east, south, and northwest before entering the Sudan. Its chief reservoir, Lake Tana, lies in the northwestern part of the plateau.

Government. On Feb. 22, 1987, a new constitution came into effect. It establishes a Communist civilian government with a national assembly, the Shengo, which will elect a president for a five-year term. Mengistu is expected to be elected. The Workers Party of Ethiopia is the only party.

History. Black Africa's oldest state, Ethiopia can trace 2,000 years of recorded history. Its now deposed royal line claimed descent from King Menelik I, traditionally believed to have been the son of the Queen of Sheba and King Solomon. The present nation is a consolidation of smaller kingdoms that owed feudal allegiance to the Ethiopian Emperor.

Hamitic peoples migrated to Ethiopia from Asia Minor in prehistoric times. Semitic traders from Arabia penetrated the region in the 7th century B.C. Its Red Sea ports were important to the Roman and Byzantine Empires. Coptic Christianity came to the country in A.D. 341, and a variant of that communion became Ethiopia's state religion.

Ancient Ethiopia reached its peak in the 5th century, then was isolated by the rise of Islam and weakened by feudal wars. Modern Ethiopia emerged under Emperor Menelik II, who established its independence by routing an Italian invasion in 1896. He expanded Ethiopia by conquest.

Disorders that followed Menelik's death brought his daughter to the throne in 1917, with his cousin, Tafari Makonnen, as Regent, heir presumptive, and strongman. When the Empress died in 1930, Tafari was crowned Emperor Haile Selassie I.

As Regent, Haile Selassie outlawed slavery. As Emperor, he worked for centralization of his diffuse realm, in which 70 languages are spoken, and for moderate reform. In 1931, he granted a Constitution, revised in 1955, that created a parliament with an appointed Senate and an elected Chamber of Deputies, and a system of courts. But basic power remained with the Emperor.

Bent on colonial empire, fascist Italy invaded Ethiopia on Oct. 3, 1935, forcing Haile Selassie into exile in May 1936. Ethiopia was annexed to Eritrea, then an Italian colony, and Italian Somaliland to form Italian East Africa, losing its independence for the first time in recorded history. In 1941, British troops routed the Italians, and Haile Selassie returned to Addis Ababa.

Deep discontent erupted in the fall of 1973. A long drought had caused famine that killed 100,000 peasants and drove thousands of others to cities, where food was scarce and inflation was rampant. Charges of mismanagement of drought relief sparked riots in Addis Ababa in 1974, and unpaid troops in Asmara, capital of Eritrea, mutinied to protest conditions.

In August 1974, the Armed Forces Committee nationalized Haile Selassie's palace and estates and directed him not to leave Addis Ababa. On Sept. 12, 1974, he was deposed after nearly 58 years as Regent and Emperor. The 82-year-old "Lion of Judah" was placed under guard. Parliament was dissolved and the Constitution suspended.

On Aug. 27, 1975, Haile Selassie died in a small apartment in his former Addis Ababa palace where he had been treated as a state prisoner. He was 83.

Lt. Col. Mengistu Haile Mariam was named head of state Feb. 2, 1977, to replace Brig. Gen. Teferi Benti, who was killed in a factional fight of the Dirgue after having ruled since 1974. The government was losing its fight to hold Eritrea and in the southeastern region of Ogaden, Somali guerrillas backed by Somali regular forces threatened the ancient city of Harar. In October, the U.S.S.R. announced it would end military aid to Somalia and henceforth back its new ally, Ethiopia. This, together with the intervention of Cuban troops in Ogaden, turned the tide for Mengistu. By March 1978, the badly beaten Somalis had retreated to their homeland. This brought an end to large-scale fighting with Somalia, but border skirmishing continued intermittently.

The Marxist government still had not quelled the Eritrean secessionists in the north by 1987. In addition, a secessionist struggle was going on in Tigre, the province adjoining Eritrea.

A Communist regime was formally proclaimed on Sept. 10, 1984, with Mengistu as party leader. After enduring years of drought, the country in 1986 was in the throes of the worst famine in more than a decade. The spring rains of 1987 marked an end to the famine.

FIJI

Sovereign: Queen Elizabeth II
Governor General: Ratu Sir Penaia K. Gamibu (1983)
Chairman of Council of Ministers: Lt. Col. Sitiveni Rabuka (1987)
Area: 7,078 sq mi. (18,333 sq km)
Population (est. mid-1987): 700,000 (average annual growth rate: 2.3%) (Indian, 49%; Fijian, 47%)
Density per square mile: 98.9
Capital (1985): Suva (on Viti Levu), 75,000
Monetary unit: Fijian dollar
Languages: Fijian, Hindustani, English
Religions: Christian, 50%; Hindu, 41%; Islam, 8%
Member of Commonwealth of Nations
Literacy rate (1981): 80%
Economic summary: Gross national product (1984): $1.25 billion. Average annual growth rate (1980–85): 2%. Per capita income (1984): $1,820. Rate of inflation (1984): 4.4%. Labor force in agriculture: 44%; principal products: sugar, copra, rice, ginger. Labor force in industry: 16%; major industrial products: refined sugar, gold, lumber. Natural resources: timber, fish, gold, silver. Exports: sugar, copra. Imports: foodstuffs, machinery, manufactured goods, fuels, chemicals. Major trading partners: U.K., Australia, Japan, New Zealand

Geography. Fiji consists of more than 500 islands in the southwestern Pacific Ocean about 1,960 miles (3,152 km) from Sydney, Australia. The two largest islands are Viti Levu (4,109 sq mi.; 10,642 sq km) and Vanua Levu (2,242 sq mi.; 5,807 sq km). The island of Rotuma (18 sq mi.; 47 sq km), about 400 miles (644 km) to the north, is a dependency of Fiji. Overall, Fiji is nearly as large as New Jersey.

The largest islands in the group are mountainous and volcanic, with the tallest peak being Mount Victoria (4,341 ft; 1,323 m) on Viti Levu. The islands in the south have dense forests on the windward side and grasslands on the leeward.

Government. An April 1987 election brought the newly formed Fijian Labor Party to power. Riots by ethnic Fijians against the Indian-dominated government sparked a coup by the Fijian-dominated army on May 14, 1987. The new government is structured to preserve Fijian control.

History. In 1874, an offer of cession by the Fijian chiefs was accepted, and Fiji was proclaimed a possession and dependency of the British Crown.

During World War II, the archipelago was an important air and naval station on the route from the U.S. and Hawaii to Australia and New Zealand.

Fiji became independent on Oct. 10, 1970. The next year it joined the five-island South Pacific Forum, which intends to become a permanent regional group to promote collective diplomacy of the newly independent members. The Forum also includes Western Samoa, Tonga, Nauru, and the self-governing segments of the Cook Islands.

FINLAND

Republic of Finland
President: Mauno H. Koivisto (1982)
Premier: Harri Holkeri (1987)
Area: 130,119 sq mi. (337,009 sq km)
Population (est. mid-1987): 4,900,000 (average annual growth rate: 0.3%) (Finnish, 93%; Swedish, 6%)
Density per square mile: 37.7
Capital: Helsinki
Largest cities (est. 1983): Helsinki, 484,471; Tampere, 167,344; Turku, 163,002
Monetary unit: Markka
Languages: Finnish, Swedish
Religions: Lutheran, 90%; Orthodox, 1%
National name: Suomen Tasavalta—Republiken Finland
Literacy rate: almost 100%
Economic summary: Gross national product (1985): $54.4 billion. Average annual growth rate (1976–85): 3.0%. Per capita income (1986): $10,870. Land used for agriculture: 8%; labor force: 9%; principal products: dairy products, cereals, sugar beets, potatoes. Labor force in industry: 39%; major products: metal manufactures, forestry and wood products, refined copper, ships. Natural resource: timber. Exports: timber, paper and pulp, ships, machinery, iron and steel, clothing, footwear. Imports: petroleum and petroleum products, chemicals, transportation equipment, machinery, textile yarns. Major trading partners: U.S.S.R., Sweden, West Germany, U.K., U.S..

Geography. Finland stretches 700 miles (1,127 km) from the Gulf of Finland on the south to Soviet Petsamo, north of the Arctic Circle. The U.S.S.R. extends along the entire eastern frontier. In area, Finland is three times the size of Ohio.

Off the southwest coast are the Aland Islands, controlling the entrance to the Gulf of Bothnia. Finland has more than 60,000 lakes. Of the few rivers, only the Oulu (Ulea) is navigable to any important extent.

The Swedish-populated Aland Islands (581 sq mi.; 1,505 sq km) have an autonomous status under a law passed in 1951.

Government. The president, chosen for six years by the popularly elected Electoral College of 301 members, appoints the Cabinet. The one-chamber Diet, the Eduskunta, consists of 200 members elected for four-year terms by proportional representation.

The major political parties are the Social Democratic Party (56 seats in the Eduskunta), led by Kalevi Sorsa; National Coalition Party led by Premier Harri Holkeri (53 seats); Center Party (40 seats); People's Democratic League (Communist)

(16 seats); Finnish Rural Party (9 seats); Swedish People's Party (13 seats); Christian League (5 seats). Premier Holkeri leads a coalition of National Coalition, Social Democratic, Swedish People's Party, and Finnish Rural Party members totaling 131 seats.

History. At the end of the 7th century, the Finns came to Finland from their Volga settlements, taking the country from the Lapps, who retreated northward. The Finns' repeated raids on the Scandinavian coast impelled Eric IX, the Swedish King, to conquer the country in 1157 and bring it into contact with Western Christendom. By 1809 the whole of Finland was conquered by Alexander I of Russia, who set up Finland as a Grand Duchy.

The first period of Russification (1809–1905) resulted in a lessening of the powers of the Finnish Diet. The Russian language was made official, and the Finnish military system was superseded by the Russian. The pace of Russification was intensified from 1908 to 1914. When Russian control was weakened as a consequence of the March Revolution of 1917, the Diet on July 20, 1917, proclaimed Finland's independence, which became complete on Dec. 6, 1917.

Finland rejected Soviet territorial demands, and the U.S.S.R. attacked on Nov. 30, 1939. The Finns made an amazing stand of three months and finally capitulated, ceding 16,000 square miles (41,440 sq km) to the U.S.S.R. Under German pressure, the Finns joined the Nazis against Russia in 1941, but were defeated again and ceded the Petsamo area to the U.S.S.R. In 1948, a 20-year treaty of friendship and mutual assistance was signed by the two nations and renewed for another 20 years in 1970.

After 25 years in office, President Urho K. Kekkonen resigned in October 1981 because of ill health. Premier Mauno Koivisto, leader of the Social Democratic Party, was elected President on Jan. 26, 1982, winning decisively over a conservative rival with support from Finnish Communists. On Feb. 17, Kalevi Sorsa, a Social Democrat, took office as Premier, heading the same center-left coalition Koivisto had led but elections on Mar. 16, 1987 brought the conservative National Coalition Party into the government.

FRANCE

French Republic
President: François Mitterrand (1981)
Premier: Jacques Chirac (1986)
Area: 211,208 sq mi. (547,026 sq km)
Population (est. mid-1987): 55,600,000 (average annual growth rate: 0.4%)
Density per square mile: 263.2
Capital: Paris
Largest cities (est. 1983): Paris, 2,150,000; **(1982 est.):** Marseilles, 868,435; Lyons, 410,455; Toulouse, 344, 917; Nice, 331,165; Nantes, 237,789; Strasbourg, 247, 068; Bordeaux, 201,965
Monetary unit: Franc
Religion (est.): Roman Catholic, 76%
National name: République Française
Literacy rate (1981): 97%
Economic summary: Gross national product (1983): $569 billion. Average annual growth rate (1972–83): 2.3%. Per capita income (1983): $10,400. Land used for agriculture, 60%; labor force: 8%; principal products: cereals, feed grains, livestock and dairy products, wine, fruits, vegetables. Labor force in industry: 30%; major products: chemicals, automobiles, processed foods, iron and steel, aircraft, textiles, clothing. Natural resources: coal, iron ore, bauxite, fish, forests. Exports: textiles and clothing, chemicals, machinery and transport equipment, agricultural products. Imports: machinery, crude petroleum, chemicals, agricultural products. Major trading partners: West Germany, Italy, U.S., Belgium-Luxembourg, U.K., Netherlands.

Geography. France (80% the size of Texas) is second in size to the U.S.S.R. among Europe's nations. In the Alps near the Italian and Swiss borders is Europe's highest point—Mont Blanc (15,781 ft; 4,810 m). The forest-covered Vosges Mountains are in the northeast, and the Pyrenees are along the Spanish border.

Except for extreme northern France, which is part of the Flanders plain, the country may be described as four river basins and a plateau. Three of the streams flow west—the Seine into the English Channel, the Loire into the Atlantic, and the Garonne into the Bay of Biscay. The Rhône flows south into the Mediterranean. For about 100 miles (161 km), the Rhine is France's eastern border.

West of the Rhône and northeast of the Garonne lies the central plateau, covering about 15% of France's area and rising to a maximum elevation of 6,188 feet (1,886 m). In the Mediterranean, about 115 miles (185 km) east-southeast of Nice, is Corsica (3,367 sq mi.; 8,721 sq km).

Government. The president is elected for seven years by universal suffrage. He appoints the premier, and the Cabinet is responsible to Parliament. The president has the right to dissolve the National Assembly or to ask Parliament for reconsideration of a law. The Parliament consists of two houses: the National Assembly and the Senate.

The major political parties are the Socialists (207 of 577 seats in the National Assembly), led by Pierre Joxe; Rally for the Republic (147 seats), led by Claude Labbe; Union for French Democracy (130 seats), led by Jean-Claude Gaudin; National Front (35 seats), led by Jean-Marie le Pen, and Communist (35 seats), led by Georges Marchais. The rest are unaffiliated.

History. The history of France, as distinct from ancient Gaul, begins with the Treaty of Verdun (843), dividing the territories corresponding roughly to France, Germany, and Italy among the three grandsons of Charlemagne. Julius Caesar had conquered part of Gaul in 57–52 B.C., and it remained Roman until Franks invaded it in the 5th century.

Charles the Bald, inheritor of *Francia Occidentalis,* founded the Carolingian dynasty, which ruled over a kingdom increasingly feudalized. By 987, the crown passed to Hugh Capet, a princeling who controlled only the Ile-de-France, the region surrounding Paris. For 350 years, an unbroken Capetian line added to its domain and consolidated royal authority until the accession in 1328 of Philip VI, first of the Valois line. France was then the most powerful nation in Europe, with a population of 15 million.

The missing pieces in Philip's domain were the French provinces still held by the Plantagenet kings of England, who also claimed the French crown. Beginning in 1338, the Hundred Years' War eventually settled the contest. English longbows defeated French armored knights at Crécy

Rulers of France

Name	Born	Ruled[1]
CAROLINGIAN DYNASTY		
Pepin the Short	c. 714	751–768
Charlemagne[2]	742	768–814
Louis I the Debonair[3]	778	814–840
Charles I the Bald[4]	823	840–877
Louis II the Stammerer	846	877–879
Louis III[5]	c. 863	879–882
Carloman[5]	?	879–884
Charles II the Fat[6]	839	884–887
Eudes (Odo), Count of Paris	?	888–898
Charles III the Simple[8]	879	893–923[9]
Robert I[10]	c. 865	922–923
Rudolf (Raoul), Duke of Burgundy	?	923–936
Louis IV d'Outremer	c. 921	936–954
Lothair	941	954–986
Louis V the Sluggard	c. 967	986–987
CAPETIAN DYNASTY		
Hugh Capet	c. 940	987–996
Robert II the Pious[11]	c. 970	996–1031
Henry I	1008	1031–1060
Philip I	1052	1060–1108
Louis VI the Fat	1081	1108–1137
Louis VII the Young	c.1121	1137–1180
Philip II (Philip Augustus)	1165	1180–1223
Louis VIII the Lion	1187	1223–1226
Louis IX (St. Louis)	1214	1226–1270
Philip III the Bold	1245	1270–1285
Philip IV the Fair	1268	1285–1314
Louis X the Quarreler	1289	1314–1316
John I[12]	1316	1316
Philip V the Tall	1294	1316–1322
Charles IV the Fair	1294	1322–1328
HOUSE OF VALOIS		
Philip VI	1293	1328–1350
John II the Good	1319	1350–1364
Charles V the Wise	1337	1364–1380
Charles VI the Well-Beloved	1368	1380–1422
Charles VII	1403	1422–1461
Louis XI	1423	1461–1483
Charles VIII	1470	1483–1498
Louis XII the Father of the People	1462	1498–1515
Francis I	1494	1515–1547
Henry II	1519	1547–1559
Francis II	1544	1559–1560
Charles IX	1550	1560–1574
Henry III	1551	1574–1589
HOUSE OF BOURBON		
Henry IV of Navarre	1553	1589–1610
Louis XIII	1601	1610–1643
Louis XIV the Great	1638	1643–1715
Louis XV the Well-Beloved	1710	1715–1774
Louis XVI	1754	1774–1792[13]
Louis XVII (Louis Charles de France)[14]	1785	1793–1795
FIRST REPUBLIC		
National Convention	—	1792–1795
Directory (Directoire)	—	1795–1799
CONSULATE		
Napoleon Bonaparte[15]	1769	1799–1804
FIRST EMPIRE		
Napoleon I	1769	1804–1815[16]
RESTORATION OF HOUSE OF BOURBON		
Louis XVIII le Désiré	1755	1814–1824
Charles X	1757	1824–1830[17]
BOURBON-ORLEANS LINE		
Louis Philippe ("Citizen King")	1773	1830–1848[18]
SECOND REPUBLIC		
Louis Napoleon[19]	1808	1848–1852
SECOND EMPIRE		
Napoleon III (Louis Napoleon)	1808	1852–1870[20]
THIRD REPUBLIC (PRESIDENTS)		
Louis Adolphe Thiers	1797	1871–1873
Marie E. P. M. de MacMahon	1808	1873–1879
François P. J. Grévy	1807	1879–1887
Sadi Carnot	1837	1887–1894
Jean Casimir-Périer	1847	1894–1895
François Félix Faure	1841	1895–1899
Émile Loubet	1838	1899–1906
Clement Armand Fallières	1841	1906–1913
Raymond Poincaré	1860	1913–1920
Paul E. L. Deschanel	1856	1920–1920
Alexandre Millerand	1859	1920–1924
Gaston Doumergue	1863	1924–1931
Paul Doumer	1857	1931–1932
Albert Lebrun	1871	1932–1940
VICHY GOVERNMENT (CHIEF OF STATE)		
Henri Philippe Pétain	1856	1940–1944
PROVISIONAL GOVERNMENT (PRESIDENTS)		
Charles de Gaulle	1890	1944–1946
Félix Gouin	1884	1946–1946
Georges Bidault	1899	1946–1947
FOURTH REPUBLIC (PRESIDENTS)		
Vincent Auriol	1884	1947–1954
René Coty	1882	1954–1959
FIFTH REPUBLIC (PRESIDENTS)		
Charles de Gaulle	1890	1959–1969
Georges Pompidou	1911	1969–1974
Valéry Giscard d'Estaing	1926	1974–1981
François Mitterrand	1916	1981–

1. For Kings and Emperors through the Second Empire, year of end of rule is also that of death, unless otherwise indicated. 2. Crowned Emperor of the West in 800. His brother, Carloman, ruled as King of the Eastern Franks from 768 until his death in 771. 3. Holy Roman Emperor 814–840. 4. Holy Roman Emperor 875–877 as Charles II. 5. Ruled jointly 879–882. 6. Holy Roman Emperor 881–887 as Charles III. 7. Died 888. 8. King 893–898 in opposition to Eudes. 9. Died 929. 10. Not counted in regular line of Kings of France by some authorities. Elected by nobles but killed in Battle of Soissons. 11. Sometimes called Robert I. 12. Posthumous son of Louis X; lived for only five days. 13. Executed 1793. 14. Titular King only. He died in prison according to official reports, but many pretenders appeared during the Bourbon restoration. 15. As First Consul, Napoleon held the power of government. In 1804, he became Emperor. 16. Abdicated first time June 1814. Re-entered Paris March 1815, after escape from Elba; Louis XVIII fled to Ghent. Abdicated second time June 1815. He named as his successor his son, Napoleon II, who was not acceptable to the Allies. He died 1821. 17. Died 1836. 18. Died 1850. 19. President; became Emperor in 1852. 20. Died 1873.

(1346) and the English also won the second landmark battle at Agincourt (1415), but the final victory went to the French at Castillon (1453).

Absolute monarchy reached its apogee in the reign of Louis XIV (1643–1715), the Sun King, whose brilliant court was the center of the Western world.

Revolution plunged France into a blood bath beginning in 1789 and ending with a new authoritarianism under Napoleon Bonaparte, who had successfully defended the infant republic from foreign attack and then made himself First Consul in 1799 and Emperor in 1804.

The Congress of Vienna (1815) sought to restore the pre-Napoleonic order in the person of Louis XVIII, but industrialization and the middle class, both fostered under Napoleon, built pressure for change, and a revolution in 1848 drove Louis Philippe, last of the Bourbons, into exile.

A second republic elected as its president Prince Louis Napoleon, a nephew of Napoleon I, who declared the Second Empire in 1852 and took the throne as Napoleon III. His opposition to the rising power of Prussia ignited the Franco-Prussian War (1870–71), ending in his defeat and abdication.

A new France emerged from World War I as the continent's dominant power. But four years of hostile occupation had reduced northeast France to ruins. The postwar Third Republic was plagued by political instability and economic chaos.

From 1919, French foreign policy aimed at keeping Germany weak through a system of alliances, but it failed to halt the rise of Adolf Hitler and the Nazi war machine. On May 10, 1940, mechanized Nazi troops attacked, and, as they approached Paris, Italy joined with Germany. The Germans marched into an undefended Paris and Marshal Henri Philippe Pétain signed an armistice June 22. France was split into an occupied north and an unoccupied south, the latter becoming a totalitarian state with Pétain as its chief.

Allied armies liberated France in August 1944. The French Committee of National Liberation, formed in Algiers in 1943, established a provisional government in Paris headed by Gen. Charles de Gaulle. The Fourth Republic was born Dec. 24, 1946.

The Empire became the French Union; the National Assembly was strengthened and the presidency weakened; and France joined the North Atlantic Treaty Organization. A war against communist insurgents in Indochina was abandoned after the defeat at Dien Bien Phu. A new rebellion in Algeria (*see* Algeria) threatened a military coup, and on June 1, 1958, the Assembly invited de Gaulle to return as premier with extraordinary powers. He drafted a new Constitution for a Fifth Republic, adopted Sept. 28, which strengthened the presidency and reduced legislative power. He was elected president Dec. 21.

De Gaulle took France out of the NATO military command in 1967 and expelled all foreign-controlled troops from the country. He later went on to attempt to achieve a long-cherished plan of regional reform. This, however, aroused wide opposition. He decided to stake his fate on a referendum. At the voting in April 1969, the electorate defeated the plan.

His successor Georges Pompidou continued the de Gaulle policies of seeking to expand France's influence in the Mideast and Africa, selling arms to South Africa (despite the U.N. embargo), to Libya, and to Greece, and in 1971 he endorsed British entry into the Common Market.

Pompidou died of cancer in April 1974 and the special election to choose a successor was won by Valéry Giscard d'Estaing.

Socialist François Mitterand's stunning victory in the May 10, 1981, Presidential election over the Gaullist alliance that had held power since 1958 was attributed to the challenger's skill in maintaining the Communists' support while holding them at arm's length and Giscard's failure to hold Gaullist support.

The victors immediately moved to carry out campaign pledges to nationalize major industries, halt nuclear testing, suspend nuclear power plant construction, and impose new taxes on the rich. On Feb. 11, 1982, the nationalization bills became law.

The Socialists' policies during Mitterand's first two years created a 12% inflation rate, a huge trade deficit, and devaluations of the franc. In early 1983, Mitterand, embarked on an austerity program to control inflation and reduce the trade deficit. He increased taxes and slashed government spending. A halt in economic growth, declining purchasing power for the average Frenchman, and an increase in unemployment to 10% followed. Mitterand sank lower and lower in the opinion polls.

In mid-1984, Mitterand moved toward the political center. He appointed a new Premier, Laurent Fabius who appointed a new Cabinet of all Socialists, ending the Socialist-Communist coalition. He proposed cuts that would reduce the French worker's income and social security taxes by 5 to 8%. Mitterand promised further tax cuts.

On March 16, 1986, a center-right coalition led by Jacques Chirac won a slim majority in legislative elections. Chirac became Premier initiating a period of "co-habitation" between him and the Socialist President, Mitterand, a cooperation marked by sparring over Chirac's plan to denationalize major industries and effect a harder line on security issues.

Overseas Departments and Territories of France

FRENCH GUIANA (including ININI)

Status: Overseas Department
Prefect: Jacques Dewatre (1986)
Area: 35,126 sq mi. (90,976 sq km)
Population (est. 1987): 78,336 (average annual growth rate: 2.9%)
Capital (est. 1982): Cayenne, 37,097
Monetary unit: Franc
Language: Creole
Religion: Roman Catholic
Literacy rate: 82%
Economic summary: Gross national product (1982): $210 million. Average annual growth rate (1970–79): 0.4%. Per capita income (1982): $3,230. Labor force in agriculture: 14%; principal agricultural products: rice, corn, manioc, cocoa, bananas, sugar cane. Labor force in industry: 12%; major industrial products: timber, rum, rosewood essence, gold mining. Natural resources: bauxite, timber, cinnabar, low-grade iron ore. Exports: shrimp, timber, rum, rosewood essence. Imports: food, consumer and producer goods, petroleum. Major trading partners: U.S., France, Martinique, Japan.

French Guiana, lying north of Brazil and east of

Suriname on the northeast coast of South America, was first settled in 1604. Penal settlements, embracing the area around the mouth of the Maroni River and the Iles du Salut (including Devil's Island), were founded in 1852; they have since been abolished.

During World War II, French Guiana at first adhered to the Vichy government, but the Free French took over in 1943. French Guiana accepted in 1958 the new Constitution of the French Fifth Republic and remained an Overseas Department of the French Republic.

FRENCH POLYNESIA

Status: Overseas Territory
High Commissioner: Bernard Gerard (1986)
Area: 1,544 sq mi. (4,000 sq km)
Population (est. mid-1987): 200,000 (average annual growth rate: 2.4%)
Monetary unit: Pacific financial community franc
Language: French
Religions: Protestant, 47%; Roman Catholic, 40%
Capital (est. 1983): Papeete (on Tahiti), 23,496
Economic summary: Gross national product (1983): $1.3 billion. Average annual growth rate (1970–78): 2.8%. Per capita income (1983): $7,620. Principal agricultural product: copra. Major industries: tourism, maintenance of French nuclear test base. Exports: coconut products, mother of pearl, vanilla. Imports: fuels, foodstuffs, equipment. Major trading partners: France, U.S.

The term French Polynesia is applied to the scattered French possessions in the South Pacific—Mangareva (Gambier), Makatea, the Marquesas Islands, Rapa, Rurutu, Rimatara, the Society Islands, the Tuamotu Archipelago, Tubuai, Raivavae, and the island of Clipperton—which were organized into a single colony in 1903. There are 120 islands, of which 25 are uninhabited.

The High Commissioner is assisted by a Council of Government and a popularly elected Territorial Assembly. The principal and most populous island—Tahiti, in the Society group—was claimed as French in 1768. In 1958, French Polynesia voted in favor of the new Constitution of the French Fifth Republic and remained an Overseas Territory of the French Republic. The natives are mostly Maoris.

The Pacific Nuclear Test Center on the atoll of Mururoa, 744 miles (1,200 km) from Tahiti, was completed in 1966.

GUADELOUPE

Status: Overseas Department
Prefect: Yves Bonnet (1986)
Area: 687 sq mi. (1,779 sq km)
Population (est. mid-1987): 300,000 (average annual growth rate: 1.3%)
Capital (est. 1983): Basse-Terre, 35,000
Largest city (est. 1982): Pointe-à-Pitre, 50,000
Monetary unit: Franc
Language: French, Creole patois
Religions: Roman Catholic
Literacy rate: over 70%
Economic summary: Gross national product (1982): $1.37 billion. Average annual growth rate (1970–79): 5.1%. Per capita income (1982): $4,170. Land used for agriculture: 22%; labor force: 11%; principal agricultural products: sugar cane, bananas, rum, tobacco. Major industries: construction, public works. Exports: sugar, fruits and vegetables, bananas. Imports: foodstuffs, clothing, consumer goods, petroleum. Major trading partner: France.

Guadeloupe, in the West Indies about 300 miles (483 km) southeast of Puerto Rico, was discovered by Columbus in 1493. It consists of the twin islands of Basse-Terre and Grande-Terre and five dependencies—Marie-Galante, Les Saintes, La Désirade, St. Barthélemy, and the northern half of St. Martin. The volcano Soufrière (4,813 ft; 1,467 m), also called La Grande Soufrière, is the highest point on Guadeloupe. Violent activity in 1976 and 1977 caused thousands to flee their homes.

French colonization began in 1635. In 1958, Guadeloupe voted in favor of the new Constitution of the French Fifth Republic and remained an Overseas Department of the French Republic.

MARTINIQUE

Status: Overseas Department
Prefect: Edouard LaCroix (1986)
Area: 431 sq mi. (1,116 sq km)
Population (est. mid-1987): 300,000 (average annual growth rate: 1.1%)
Capital (est. 1984): Fort-de-France, 97,814
Monetary unit: Franc
Languages: French, Creole patois
Religion: Roman Catholic
Literacy rate (1981): 70%
Economic summary: Gross national product (1983): $1.33 billion. Average annual growth rate (1970–79): 4.3%. Per capita income (1983): $4,040. Land used for agriculture: 18%; labor force: 30%; principal agricultural products: sugar cane, bananas, rum, pineapples. Labor force in industry: 5%; major industries: sugar, rum, refined oil, cement, tourism. Natural resource: fish. Exports: bananas, refined petroleum products, rum, sugar, pineapples. Imports: foodstuffs, clothing and other consumer goods, petroleum products. Major trading partners: France, U.S.

Martinique, lying in the Lesser Antilles about 300 miles (483 km) northeast of Venezuela, was probably discovered by Columbus in 1502 and was taken for France in 1635. Following the Franco-German armistice of 1940, it had a semiautonomous status until 1943, when authority was relinquished to the Free French. The area, administered by a Prefect assisted by an elected council, is represented in the French Parliament. In 1958, Martinique voted in favor of the new Constitution of the French Fifth Republic and remained an Overseas Department of the French Republic.

MAYOTTE

Status: Territorial collectivity
Prefect: Guy DuPuis (1986)
Area: 146 sq mi. (378 sq km)
Population (est. 1985): 47,246
Capital (est. 1985): Dzaoudzi, 5,675
Principal products: vanilla, essential oils, copra

The most populous of the Comoro Islands in the Indian Ocean, with a Christian majority, Mayotte voted in 1974 and 1976 against joining the other, predominantly Moslem islands, in declaring themselves independent. It continues to retain its ties to France.

NEW CALEDONIA AND DEPENDENCIES

Status: Overseas Territory
High Commissioner: Jacques Roynette (1982)
Area: 7,374 sq mi. (19,103 sq km)[1]
Population (est. mid-1986): 200,000 (average annual growth rate: 0.8%)
Capital (est. 1983): Nouméa, 60,112
Monetary unit: Pacific financial community franc
Languages: Melanesian and Polynesian dialects
Religion: Christian
Literacy rate: Not known
Economic summary: Gross national product (1983): $1.14 billion. Average annual growth rate (1970–78): −4.9%. Per capita income (1983): $7,820. Principal agricultural products: coffee, copra. Major industrial product: nickel. Natural resources: nickel, chromite, iron ore. Exports: nickel, chrome. Imports: mineral fuels, machinery, transport equipment, foodstuffs. Major trading partners: France, Japan, U.S., Australia.

1. Including dependencies.

New Caledonia (6,466 sq mi.; 16,747 sq km), about 1,070 miles (1,722 km) northeast of Sydney, Australia, was discovered by Capt. James Cook in 1774 and annexed by France in 1853. The government also administers the Isle of Pines, the Loyalty Islands (Uvéa, Lifu, and Maré), the Belep Islands, the Huon Island group, and the Chesterfield Islands.

The natives are Melanesians; about one third of the population is white and one fifth Indochinese and Javanese. The French National Assembly on July 31, 1984, voted a bill into law that granted internal autonomy to New Caledonia and opened the way to possible eventual independence. This touched off ethnic tensions and violence between the natives and the European settlers, with the natives demanding full independence and sovereignty while the settlers wanted to remain part of France. Between November 1984 and February 1985, more than 20 people were killed.

RÉUNION

Status: Overseas Department
Prefect: Michel Blangy (1984)
Area: 970 sq mi. (2,510 sq km)
Population (est. mid-1986): 500,000 (average annual growth rate, 1.8%)
Capital (est. 1982): Saint-Denis, 126,323
Monetary unit: Franc
Languages: French, Creole
Religion: Roman Catholic
Economic summary: Gross national product (1983): $2.06 billion. Average annual growth rate (1970–79): −0.9%. Principal agricultural products: sugar cane, vanilla, bananas, perfume plants. Major industrial products: rum, cigarettes, processed sugar. Exports: sugar, perfume essences, rum, molasses. Imports: manufactured goods, foodstuffs, beverages, machinery and transportation equipment, petroleum products. Major trading partners: France, Mauritius.

Discovered by Portuguese navigators in the 16th century, the island of Réunion, then uninhabited, was taken as a French possession in 1642. It is located about 450 miles (724 km) east of Madagascar, in the Indian Ocean. In 1958, Réunion approved the Constitution of the Fifth French Republic and remained an Overseas Department of the French Republic.

ST. PIERRE AND MIQUELON

Status: Overseas Territory
Prefect: Gerard Lefebvre (1984)
Area: 93 sq mi. (242 sq km)
Population (est. 1983): 6,000
Capital (est. 1981): Saint Pierre, 5,800
Economic summary: Major industries: fishing, canneries. Exports: petroleum products, cattle, fish. Major trading partners: Canada, France, U.S.

The sole remnant of the French colonial empire in North America, these islands were first occupied by the French in 1604. Their only importance arises from proximity to the Grand Banks, located 10 miles south of Newfoundland, making them the center of the French Atlantic cod fisheries. On July 19, 1976, the islands became an Overseas Department of the French Republic.

SOUTHERN AND ANTARCTIC LANDS

Status: Overseas Territory
Administrator: Claude Pieri
Area: 169,614 sq mi. (439,300 sq km)
Capital: Port-au-Français

This territory is uninhabited except for the personnel of scientific bases. It consists of Adélie Land (166,752 sq mi.; 431,888 sq km) on the Antarctic mainland and the following islands in the southern Indian Ocean: the Kerguelen and Crozet archipelagos and the islands of Saint-Paul and New Amsterdam.

WALLIS AND FUTUNA ISLANDS

Status: Overseas Territory
Administrator Superior: Michel Kuhnmunch (1984)
Area: 77 sq mi. (200 sq km)
Population (est. 1985): 12,391
Capital (1980): Wallis (on Uvea), 600

The two islands groups in the South Pacific between Fiji and Samoa were settled by French missionaries at the beginning of the 19th century. A protectorate was established in the 1880s. Following a referendum by the Polynesian inhabitants, the status was changed to that of an Overseas Territory in 1961.

GABON

Gabonese Republic

President: Omar Bongo (1967)
Premier: Léon Mébiame (1975)
Area: 103,346 sq mi. (267,667 sq km)
Population (est. mid-1987): 1,200,000 (average annual growth rate: 1.6%) (Fang, Mpongwe, Mbete, Punu)
Density per square mile: 11.6
Capital and largest city (est. 1983): Libreville, 257,000
Monetary unit: Franc CFA
Ethnic groups: Bateke, Obamba, Bakota, Shake, Pongwés, Adumas, Chiras, Punu, and Lumbu
Languages: French (official) and Bantu dialects
Religions: Roman Catholic, 63.8%, Protestant, 18.4%
National name: République Gabonaise
Member of French Community
Literacy rate: 65%
Economic summary: Gross national product (1984): $2.8

billion. Average annual growth rate (1970–79): 5.2%. Per capita income (1984): $2,470. Labor force in agriculture: 65%; principal products: sugar cane, wood, palm, rice, bananas, peanuts. Labor force in industry: 30%; major products: petroleum, natural gas, processed wood, manganese, uranium. Natural resources: wood, petroleum, iron ore, manganese, uranium. Exports: crude petroleum, wood and wood products, minerals. Imports: mining and road-building machinery, electrical equipment, foodstuffs, textiles, transport vehicles. Major trading partners: France, U.S., Brazil, U.K.

Geography. This West African land with the Atlantic as its western border is also bounded by Equatorial Guinea, Cameroon, and the Congo. Its area is slightly less than Kentucky's.

From mangrove swamps on the coast, the land becomes divided plateaus in the north and east and mountains in the north. Most of the country is covered by a dense tropical forest.

Government. The president is elected for a seven-year term. Legislative powers are exercised by a National Assembly, which is elected for a seven-year term. After his conversion to Islam in 1973, President Bongo changed his given name, Albert Bernard, to Omar. The Parti Démocratique Gabonais (all National Assembly seats) is led by President Bongo. He was re-elected without opposition in 1973 and in 1980.

History. Little is known of Gabon's history, even in oral tradition, but Pygmies are believed to be the original inhabitants. Now there are many tribal groups in the country, the largest being the Fang people who constitute a third of the population.

Gabon was first visited by the Portuguese navigator Diego Cam in the 15th century. In 1839, the French founded their first settlement on the left bank of the Gabon Estuary and gradually occupied the hinterland during the second half of the 19th century. It was organized as a French territory in 1888 and became an autonomous republic within the French Union after World War II and an independent republic on Aug. 17, 1960.

Immense resources in oil, uranium, manganese, and iron help give Gabon's inhabitants a per capita annual income of $2,470, one of the highest in black Africa. To speed exploitation of a billion-ton iron ore reserve in the Belinga-Mekambo region, the government began work in 1969 on a 350-mile railroad leading from the coast into the area. The project was initiated by President León Mba, who died in 1967, and has been continued by his hand-picked successor, Omar Bongo.

In 1974, Bongo negotiated 60% control of an iron-ore venture half-owned by the Bethlehem Steel Corp. In October of that year, he visited Peking and concluded an economic and technical agreement with China.

GAMBIA

Republic of the Gambia
President: Sir Dawda K. Jawara (1970)
Area: 4,093 sq mi. (10,600 sq km)
Population (est. mid-1987): 800,000 (average annual growth rate: 2.1%)
Density per square mile: 195.5
Capital and largest city (est. 1980): Banjul, 48,000
Monetary unit: Dalasi
Languages: Native tongues, English (official)
Religions: Islam, 85%, Christian, 2%, Animist, 11%
Member of Commonwealth of Nations
Literacy rate: 20%
Economic summary: Gross national product (1984): $180 million. Average annual growth rate (1970–79): 0.4%. Per capita income (1984): $250. Land used for agriculture: 16%; labor force: 76%; principal products: peanuts, rice, palm kernels. Major industrial products: processed peanuts. Natural resources: fish. Exports: peanuts and peanut products, fish. Imports: textiles, foodstuffs, tobacco, machinery, petroleum products. Major trading partners: Western European countries, China, U.K.

Geography. Situated on the Atlantic coast in westernmost Africa and surrounded on three sides by Senegal, Gambia is twice the size of Delaware. The Gambia River flows for 200 miles (322 km) through Gambia on its way to the Atlantic. The country, the smallest on the continent, averages only 20 miles (32 km) in width.

Government. The president's five-year term is linked to the 35-member unicameral House of Representatives, from which he appoints his Cabinet members and the vice president.

The major political party is the People's Progressive Party (27 seats in House of Representatives), led by President Jawara.

History. During the 17th century, Gambia was settled by various companies of English merchants. Slavery was the chief source of revenue until it was abolished in 1807. Gambia became a crown colony in 1843 and an independent nation within the Commonwealth of Nations on Feb. 18, 1965.

Full independence was approved in a 1970 referendum, and on April 24 of that year Gambia proclaimed itself a republic.

President Dawda K. Jawara won overwhelming re-election to his fifth term on May 5, 1982, in a vote that was also seen as an endorsement of his proposal for a confederation with Senegal.

GERMANY, EAST

German Democratic Republic
Chairman of Council of State: Erich Honecker (1976)
Chairman of Council of Ministers: Willi Stoph (1976)
Area: 41,767 sq mi. (108,177 sq km)[1]
Population (est. mid-1987): 16,700,000 (average annual growth rate: 0.0%)
Density per square mile: 154
Capital: Berlin (eastern sector)
Largest cities (est. 1984): East Berlin, 1,202,895; Leipzig, 554,595; Dresden, 519,860; Karl-Marx Stadt, 316,361; Magdeburg, 288,914; Halle, 235,858; Rostock, 242,729; Erfurt, 215,499
Monetary unit: Mark of the Deutsche Demokratische Republik
Language: German
Religions: Protestant, 53%; Roman Catholic, 8%
National name: Deutsche Demokratische Republik
Literacy rate: 99%
Economic summary: Gross national product (1984): $163.7 billion. Annual growth rate (1970–79): 2.0%. Per capita income (1984): $9,800. Land used for agriculture: 47%; labor force: 11%; principal products: grains, potatoes, sugar beets, meat and dairy products. Labor force in industry: 38%; major products: steel, chemicals, machinery, electrical and precision engineer-

ing products. Natural resources: brown coal, potash, bauxite. Exports: machinery and equipment, chemical products, textiles, clothing. Imports: raw materials, fuels, agricultural products, machinery and equipment. Major trading partners: U.S.S.R., Soviet bloc, West Germany.

1. Including East Berlin (156 square miles), which has been incorporated into the German Democratic Republic.

Geography. East Germany lies on the Baltic Sea with Poland to the east and Czechoslovakia to the south. The border with West Germany is roughly a line running south from Lübeck for about 250 miles. The main river is the Elbe, which flows from Dresden in the southeast to the North Sea in the northwest. The Oder and Neisse Rivers form the border with Poland. Most of the country, which is the size of Tennessee, is situated in the north German plain.

Government. The People's Chamber, composed of 500 deputies elected for five-year terms, chooses the chairman and Council of State and the chairman and Council of Ministers, which carries on executive functions.

The major political party is the Socialist Unity (Communist) Party, led by Secretary General Erich Honecker. Others are Christian Democratic Union, Liberal Democratic Party, Democratic Farmers' Party, National Democratic Party.

History. (For history before 1945, *see* Germany, West.) The area now occupied by East Germany, as well as adjacent areas in Eastern Europe, consists of Mecklenburg, Brandenburg, Lusatia, Saxony, and Thuringia. Soviet armies conquered the five territories by 1945. In the division of 1945 they were allotted to the U.S.S.R. Soviet forces created a State controlled by the secret police with a single party, the Socialist Unity (Communist) Party. The Russians appropriated East German plants to restore their war-ravaged industry.

When the Federal Republic of Germany was established in West Germany, the East German states adopted a more centralized constitution for the Democratic Republic of Germany, and it was put into effect on Oct. 7, 1949. The U.S.S.R. thereupon dissolved its occupation zone, but Soviet troops remained. The Western Allies declared that the East German Republic was a Soviet creation undertaken without self-determination and refused to recognize it. It was recognized only within the Soviet bloc.

Talks between the two German states on normalization began in 1970, with the East seeking recognition of its existence and the West wanting easing of pressure on Berlin, and rapprochement between the two Germanys accelerated with agreement on a variety of issues (for details, *see* Germany, West). By 1973, normal relations were established, and the two states entered the United Nations.

The 25-year diplomatic hiatus between East Germany and the U.S. ended Sept. 4, 1974, with the establishment of formal relations.

The East German government has repeatedly challenged the Western powers' right of access to Berlin, most recently at the time of President Carter's July 15, 1978, visit to West Berlin. Autobahn traffic between the city and West Germany was deliberately slowed and, as in a similar 1977 case, the U.S., U.K., and France protested to the U.S.S.R. and the East Germans that such action was illegal under the 1971 Four Power Agreement.

Chairman of the Council of State Erich Honecker gave strong backing to the Soviet Union's stern policy toward Poland as the workers' demand for democratic rights advanced in 1980 and 1981. On Oct. 28, 1980, he closed the border, which had been open between the two states for 10 years, permitting only certified relatives or invited friends to visit. Five million Poles had visited East Germany in the previous year, largely to find cheaper and more abundant consumer goods.

In February 1981, Honecker, in a surprise gesture, declared at his party's 16th Congress that German reunification might eventually be possible, something the Communist regime had ruled out 10 years earlier. He also eased border restrictions on exchanges with West Germany imposed a few months before, but in September 1984 was pressured by the Soviet Union into canceling a planned milestone visit to West Germany.

GERMANY, WEST

Federal Republic of Germany
President: Richard von Weizsäcker (1984)
Chancellor: Helmut Kohl (1982)
Area: 96,010 sq mi. (248,667 sq km)[1]
Population (est. mid-1987): 61,000,000, includes West Berlin. (average annual growth rate: −0.2%)
Density per square mile: 635.4
Capital (est. 1985): Bonn, 292,600
Largest cities (1985): Hamburg, 1,585,900; Munich, 1, 266,100; Cologne, 919,300; Essen, 622,000; Frankfurt, 598,000; Dortmund, 575,200; Dusseldorf, 563,000; Stuttgart, 561,200; Bremen, 528,900; Hannover, 510, 800
Monetary unit: Deutsche Mark
Language: German
Religions: Protestant, 47%; Roman Catholic, 44%
National name: Bundesrepublik Deutschland
Literacy rate: 99%
Economic summary: Gross national product (1984): $678.8 billion. Average annual growth rate (1984–86) 2.6%. Per capita income (1984): $11,100. Land used for agriculture: 33%; labor force: 5%; principal products: grains, potatoes, sugar beets. Labor force in industry: 43%; major products: steel, coal, cement, chemicals, machinery, ships, vehicles. Natural resources: timber, iron, lead. Exports: machines and machine tools, chemicals, motor vehicles, iron and steel products. Imports: manufactured and agricultural products, raw materials, fuels. Major trading partners: France, Netherlands, Belgium-Luxembourg, Italy, U.S., U.K.

1. Excluding West Berlin (184 square miles with 1984 population of 1,860,900).

Geography. The Federal Republic of Germany occupies the western half of the central European area historically regarded as German. This was the part of Germany occupied by the United States, Britain, and France after World War II, when the eastern half of prewar Germany was split roughly between a Soviet-occupied zone, which became the present German Democratic Republic, and an area annexed by Poland.

West Germany's neighbors are France, Belgium, Luxembourg, and the Netherlands on the west, Switzerland and Austria on the south, Czechoslova-

Rulers of Germany and Prussia

Name	Born	Ruled[1]
KINGS OF PRUSSIA		
Frederick I[2]	1657	1701–1713
Frederick William I	1688	1713–1740
Frederick II the Great	1712	1740–1786
Frederick William II	1744	1786–1797
Frederick William III	1770	1797–1840
Frederick William IV	1795	1840–1861
William I	1797	1861–1871[3]
EMPERORS OF GERMANY		
William I	1797	1871–1888
Frederick III	1831	1888–1888
William II	1859	1888–1918[4]
HEADS OF THE REICH		
Friedrich Ebert[5]	1871	1919–1925
Paul von Hindenburg[5]	1847	1925–1934
Adolf Hitler[6] [7]	1889	1934–1945
Karl Doenitz[6]	1891	1945–1945
GERMAN FEDERAL REPUBLIC (WEST) (PRESIDENTS)		
Theodor Heuss	1884	1949–1959[9]
Heinrich Luebke	1895	1959–1969[8]
Gustav Heinemann[10]	1899	1969–1974
Walter Scheel	1919	1974–1979
Karl Carstens	1914	1979–1984
Richard von Weizsäcker	1920	1984–
GERMAN DEMOCRATIC REPUBLIC (EAST)		
Wilhelm Pieck[5]	1876	1949–1960
Walter Ulbricht[11]	1893	1960–1973
Willi Stoph[12]	1914	1973–1976
Erich Honecker[12]	1912	1976–

1. Year of end of rule is also that of death, unless otherwise indicated. 2. Was Elector of Brandenburg (1688–1701) as Frederick III. 3. Became Emperor of Germany in 1871. 4. Died 1941. 5. President. 6. Führer. 7. Named Chancellor by President Hindenburg in 1933. 8. Died 1972. 9. Died 1963. 10. Died 1976. 11. Chairman of Council of State. Died 1973. 12. Chairman of Council of State.

kia and East Germany on the east, and Denmark on the north.

The northern plain, the central hill country, and the southern mountain district constitute the main physical divisions of West Germany, which is slightly smaller than Oregon. The Bavarian plateau in the southwest averages 1,600 feet (488 m) above sea level, but it reaches 9,721 feet (2,962 m) in the Zugspitze Mountains, the highest point in the country.

Important navigable rivers are the Danube, rising in the Black Forest and flowing east across Bavaria into Austria, and the Rhine, which rises in Switzerland and flows across the Netherlands in two channels to the North Sea and is navigable by ocean-going and coastal vessels as far as Cologne. The Elbe, which also empties into the North Sea, is navigable within Germany for smaller vessels. The Weser, flowing into the North Sea, and the Main and Mosel (Moselle), both tributaries of the Rhine, are also important.

Government. Under the Constitution of May 23, 1949, the Federal Republic was established as a parliamentary democracy. The Parliament consists of the Bundesrat, an upper chamber representing and appointed by the 10 Länder, or states (plus West Berlin), and the Bundestag, a lower house elected for four years by universal suffrage. Each house has non-voting representatives from West Berlin. The entire legislature elects the President of the Republic for a five-year term; the Bundestag alone chooses the Chancellor, or Prime Minister. Each of the Länder and West Berlin have a legislature popularly elected for a four-year or five-year term.

The major political parties are the Christian Democratic Union-Christian Social Union (223 of 498 seats in the Bundestag), led by Chancellor Helmut Kohl; Social Democratic Party (186 seats) led by Hans-Jochen Vogel; and the Free Democratic Party (46 seats), led by Martin Bange Mann; the Greens (42 seats). Kohl's government is a coalition with the Free Democrats.

History. Immediately before the Christian era, when the Roman Empire had pushed its frontier to the Rhine, what is now Germany was inhabited by several tribes believed to have migrated from Central Asia between the 6th and 4th centuries B.C. One of these tribes, the Franks, attained supremacy in western Europe under Charlemagne, who was crowned Holy Roman Emperor A.D. 800. By the Treaty of Verdun (843), Charlemagne's lands east of the Rhine were ceded to the German Prince Louis. Additional territory acquired by the Treaty of Mersen (870) gave Germany approximately the area it maintained throughout the Middle Ages. For several centuries after Otto the Great was crowned King in 936, the German rulers were also usually heads of the Holy Roman Empire.

Relations between state and church were changed by the Reformation, which began with Martin Luther's 95 theses, and came to a head in 1547, when Charles V scattered the forces of the Protestant League at Mühlberg. Freedom of worship was guaranteed by the Peace of Augsburg (1555), but a Counter Reformation took place later, and a dispute over the succession to the Bohemian throne brought on the Thirty Years' War (1618–48), which devastated Germany and left the empire divided into hundreds of small principalities virtually independent of the Emperor.

Meanwhile, Prussia was developing into a state of considerable strength. Frederick the Great (1740–86) reorganized the Prussian army and defeated Maria Theresa of Austria in a struggle over Silesia. After the defeat of Napoleon at Waterloo (1815), the struggle between Austria and Prussia for supremacy in Germany continued, reaching its climax in the defeat of Austria in the Seven Weeks' War (1866) and the formation of the Prussian-dominated North German Confederation (1867).

The architect of German unity was Otto von Bismarck, a conservative, monarchist, and militaristic Prussian Junker who had no use for "empty phrase-making and constitutions." From 1862 until his retirement in 1890 he dominated not only the German but also the entire European scene. He unified all Germany in a series of three wars against Denmark (1864), Austria (1866), and France (1870–71), which many historians believe were instigated and promoted by Bismarck in his zeal to build a nation through "blood and iron."

On Jan. 18, 1871, King Wilhelm I of Prussia was proclaimed German Emperor in the Hall of Mirrors at Versailles. The North German Confederation, created in 1867, was abolished, and the Second German Reich, consisting of the North and South German states, was born. With a powerful army, an efficient bureaucracy, and a loyal bourgeoisie, Chancellor Bismarck consolidated a powerful centralized state.

Wilhelm II dismissed Bismarck in 1890 and embarked upon a "New Course," stressing an intensified colonialism and a powerful navy. His chaotic foreign policy culminated in the diplomatic isolation of Germany and the disastrous defeat in World War I (1914–18).

The Second German Empire collapsed following the defeat of the German armies in 1918, the naval mutiny at Kiel, and the flight of the Kaiser to the Netherlands on November 10. The Social Democrats, led by Friedrich Ebert and Philipp Scheidemann, crushed the Communists and established a moderate republic with Ebert as President.

The Weimar Constitution of 1919 provided for a President to be elected for seven years by universal suffrage and a bicameral legislature, consisting of the Reichsrat, representing the states, and the Reichstag, representing the people. It contained a model Bill of Rights. It was weakened, however, by a provision that enabled the President to rule by decree.

President Ebert died Feb. 28, 1925, and on April 26, Field Marshal Paul von Hindenburg was elected president.

The mass of Germans regarded the Weimar Republic as a child of defeat, imposed upon a Germany whose legitimate aspirations to world leadership had been thwarted by a world conspiracy. Added to this were a crippling currency debacle, a tremendous burden of reparations, and acute economic distress.

Adolf Hitler, an Austrian war veteran and a fanatical nationalist, fanned discontent by promising a Greater Germany, abrogation of the Treaty of Versailles, restoration of Germany's lost colonies, and destruction of the Jews. When the Social Democrats and the Communists refused to combine against the Nazi threat, President Hindenburg made Hitler chancellor on Jan. 30, 1933.

With the death of Hindenburg on Aug. 2, 1934, Hitler repudiated the Treaty of Versailles and began full-scale rearmament. In 1935 he withdrew Germany from the League of Nations, and the next year he reoccupied the Rhineland and signed the anti-Comintern pact with Japan, at the same time strengthening relations with Italy. Austria was annexed in March 1938. By the Munich agreement in September 1938 he gained the Czech Sudetenland, and in violation of this agreement he completed the dismemberment of Czechoslovakia in March 1939. But his invasion of Poland on Sept. 1, 1939, precipitated World War II.

On May 8, 1945, Germany surrendered unconditionally to Allied and Soviet military commanders, and on June 5 the four-nation Allied Control Council became the *de facto* government of Germany.

(For details of World War II, *see* Headline History.)

At the Berlin (or Potsdam) Conference (July 17–Aug. 2, 1945) President Truman, Premier Stalin, and Prime Minister Clement Attlee of Britain set forth the guiding principles of the Allied Control Council. They were Germany's complete disarmament and demilitarization, destruction of its war potential, rigid control of industry, and decentralization of the political and economic structure. Pending final determination of territorial questions at a peace conference, the three victors agreed in principle to the ultimate transfer of the city of Königsberg (now Kaliningrad) and its adjacent area to the U.S.S.R. and to the administration by Poland of former German territories lying generally east of the Oder-Neisse Line.

For purposes of control Germany was divided in 1945 into four national occupation zones, each headed by a Military Governor.

The Western powers were unable to agree with the U.S.S.R. on any fundamental issue. Work of the Allied Control Council was hamstrung by repeated Soviet vetoes; and finally, on March 20, 1948, Russia walked out of the Council. Meanwhile, the U.S. and Britain had taken steps to merge their zones economically (Bizone); and on May 31, 1948, the U.S., Britain, France, and the Benelux countries agreed to set up a German state comprising the three Western Zones.

The U.S.S.R. reacted by clamping a blockade on all ground communications between the Western Zones and Berlin, an enclave in the Soviet Zone. The Western Allies countered by organizing a gigantic airlift to fly supplies into the beleaguered city, assigning 60,000 men to it. The U.S.S.R. was finally forced to lift the blockade on May 12, 1949.

The Federal Republic of Germany was proclaimed on May 23, 1949, with its capital at Bonn. In free elections, West German voters gave a majority in the Constituent Assembly to the Christian Democrats, with the Social Democrats largely making up the opposition. Konrad Adenauer became chancellor, and Theodor Heuss of the Free Democrats was elected first president.

Agreements in Paris in 1954 giving the Federal Republic full independence and complete sovereignty came into force on May 5, 1955. Under it, West Germany and Italy became members of the Brussels treaty organization created in 1948 and renamed the Western European Union. West Germany also became a member of NATO. In 1955 the U.S.S.R. recognized the Federal Republic. The Saar territory, under an agreement between France and West Germany, held a plebiscite and despite economic links to France voted to rejoin West Germany. It became a state of West Germany on Jan. 1, 1957.

In 1963, Chancellor Adenauer concluded a treaty of mutual cooperation and friendship with France and then retired. He was succeeded by his chief inner-party critic, Ludwig Erhard, who was followed in 1966 by Kurt Georg Kiesinger. He, in turn, was succeeded in 1969 by Willy Brandt, former mayor of West Berlin.

The division between West Germany and East Germany was intensified when the Communists erected the Berlin Wall in 1961. In 1968, the East German Communist leader, Walter Ulbricht, imposed restrictions on West German movements into West Berlin. The Soviet-bloc invasion of Czechoslovakia in August 1968 added to the tension.

A treaty with the U.S.S.R. was signed in Moscow in August 1970 in which force was renounced and respect for the "territorial integrity" of present European states declared.

Three months later, West Germany signed a similar treaty with Poland, renouncing force and setting Poland's western border as the Oder-Neisse Line. It subsequently resumed formal relations with Czechoslovakia in a pact that "voided" the Munich treaty that gave Nazi Germany the Sudetenland.

Both German states were admitted to the United Nations in 1973.

Brandt, winner of a Nobel Peace Prize for his foreign policies, was forced to resign in 1974 when an East German spy was discovered to be one of his top staff members. Succeeding him was a moderate Social Democrat, Helmut Schmidt.

Helmut Schmidt, Brandt's successor as chancellor, staunchly backed U.S. military strategy in Europe nevertheless, staking his political fate on the strategy of placing U.S. nuclear missiles in Germany unless the Soviet Union reduced its arsenal of intermediate missiles.

The chancellor also strongly opposed nuclear freeze proposals and won 2-1 support for his stand at the convention of Social Democrats in April. The Free Democrats then deserted the Socialists after losing ground in local elections and joined with the Christian Democrats to unseat Schmidt and install Helmut Kohl as chancellor in 1982.

Kohl's tenure has seen a dwindling of the nuclear freeze issue after the deployment of the U.S. missiles. U.S.-Soviet negotiations in 1987 had possibilities of removing medium- and short-range missiles from Europe. An economic upswing in 1986 led to Kohl's re-election.

BERLIN

Status: West Berlin: State of West Germany; East Berlin: capital of East Germany
Governing Mayor, West Berlin: Eberhard Diepgen (1984)
Mayor, East Berlin: Erhard Krack
Area: 340 square miles (West Berlin, 184; East Berlin, 156)
Population (est. 1983): 3,033,900 (West Berlin, 1,860,-900; East Berlin, 1,173,000)

Berlin, the capital of prewar Germany, lies entirely within the borders of East Germany. After the war, the city was occupied by the forces of the U.S., Britain, France, and the U.S.S.R. The three western sectors, now known as West Berlin, contain 55% of the area and two thirds of the population.

West Berlin is a state of the Federal Republic of Germany, but supreme authority remains in the hands of the three Western powers in accordance with postwar agreements. The government is composed of the governing mayor, the 11-member Senate (his Cabinet), and the House of Representatives, a popularly elected legislative body that elects the governing mayor and the Senate.

East Berlin is governed by a City Assembly elected by Communist Party members, and a Magistrate (City Council) chosen by the Assembly and headed by the mayor. In violation of the Four Power Agreements, the Soviet Sector has been incorporated into the German Democratic Republic and is now the capital of that country.

Major anti-Communist riots broke out in East Berlin in June 1953 and, since Aug. 13, 1961, the Soviet Sector has been virtually sealed off by a Communist-built wall, 26 1/2 miles (43 km) long, running through the city. It was built to stem the flood of refugees seeking freedom in the West, 200,000 having fled in 1961 before the wall was erected.

GHANA

Republic of Ghana
Chairman of Provisional National Defense Council: Flight Lt. Jerry Rawlings (1981)
Area: 92,100 sq mi. (238,537 sq km)
Population (est. mid-1987): 13,900,000 (average annual growth rate: 2.8%)
Density per square mile: 150.9
Capital: Accra
Largest cities (est. 1984): Accra, 859,600; Kumasi, 348,900; Tamale, 136,800
Monetary unit: Cedi
Languages: Native tongues (Twi, Fanti, Ga, Ewe, Dagbani); English
Religions: Christian, 63%; Animist, 21%; Islam, 16%
Literacy rate: 45% (in English)
Member of Commonwealth of Nations
Economic summary: Gross national product (1984): $4.73 billion. Average annual growth rate (1984–86): 5.4%. Per capita income (1984): $380. Land used for agriculture: 12%; labor force: 50%; principal products: cocoa, coconuts, cassava, yams, rice, rubber. Labor force in industry: 19%; major products: mining products, cocoa products, aluminum. Natural resources: gold, diamonds, bauxite, manganese, fish. Exports: cocoa beans and products, gold, timber, manganese ore. Imports: textiles and manufactured goods, food, fuels, transport equipment. Major trading partners: U.K., Western European countries, U.S., Nigeria, U.S.S.R.

Geography. A West African country bordering on the Gulf of Guinea, Ghana has the Ivory Coast to the west, Burkina Faso to the north, and Togo to the east. It compares in size to Oregon.

The coastal belt, extending about 270 miles (435 km), is sandy, marshy, and generally exposed. Behind it is a gradually widening grass strip. The forested plateau region to the north is broken by ridges and hills. The largest river is the Volta.

Government. Ghana returned to military rule after two years of constitutional government when Flight Lt. Jerry Rawlings, who led a coup in 1979 and stepped down voluntarily, seized power on Dec. 31, 1981. Rawlings heads a Provisional National Defense Council, which exercises all power.

History. Created an independent country on March 6, 1957, Ghana is the former British colony of the Gold Coast. The area was first seen by Portuguese traders in 1470. They were followed by the English (1553), the Dutch (1595), and the Swedes (1640). British rule over the Gold Coast began in 1820, but it was not until after quelling the severe resistance of the Ashanti in 1901 that it was firmly established. British Togoland, formerly a colony of Germany, was incorporated into Ghana by referendum in 1956. As the result of a plebiscite, Ghana became a republic on July 1, 1960.

Premier Kwame Nkrumah attempted to take leadership of the Pan-African Movement, holding the All-African People's Congress in his capital, Accra, in 1958 and organizing the Union of African States with Guinea and Mali in 1961. But he oriented his country toward the Soviet Union and China and built an autocratic rule over all aspects of Ghanaian life.

In February 1966, while Nkrumah was visiting Peking and Hanoi, he was deposed by a military coup led by Gen. Emmanuel K. Kotoka.

A series of military coups followed and on June 4, 1979, Flight Lieutenant Jerry

Rawlings overthrew Lt. Gen. Frederick Akuffo's military rule on June 4, 1979. Rawlings permitted the election of a civilian president to go ahead as scheduled the following month, and Hilla Limann, candidate of the People's National Party, took office. Charging the civilian government with corruption and repression, Rawlings staged another coup on Dec. 31, 1981. As chairman of the Provisional National Defense Council, Rawlings instituted an austerity program and reduced budget deficits.

On July 11, 1985, a relative of Rawlings, Michael Agbotui Soussoudis, 39, and Sharon M. Scranage, 29, who had been a low-level clerk in the Central Intelligence Agency station in the West African country, were arrested in the United States on espionage charges. Reagan Administration officials said the American woman had given Soussoudis, her Ghanian lover, information about the agency's operations in Ghana and that as a result, at least one CIA informant had been murdered and the CIA feared reprisals would be taken by the Rawlings government against as many as 10 others.

GREECE

Hellenic Republic
President: Christos Sartzetakis (1985)
Premier: Andreas Papandreou (1981)
Area: 50,961 sq mi. (131,990 sq km)
Population (est. mid-1987): 10,000,000 (average annual growth rate: 0.2%)
Density per square mile: 196.2
Capital: Athens
Largest cities (1981 census): Athens, 3,027,000; Salonika, 706,000; Patras, 150,000; Larissa, 102,000; Heraklion, 111,000
Monetary unit: Drachma
Language: Greek
Religion: Greek Orthodox
National name: Elliniki Dimokratia
Literacy rate: 95%
Economic summary: Gross national product (1984): $33.5 billion. Annual growth rate (1984): 2.9%. Per capita income (1984): $3,380. Land used for agriculture: 30%; labor force: 28%; principal products: grains, fruits, vegetables, olives, olive oil, tobacco, cotton, livestock, dairy products. Labor force in industry: 29%; major products: textiles, chemicals, food processing. Natural resources: bauxite, iron, forests. Exports: fruits, textiles, tobacco. Imports: machinery and automotive equipment, petroleum, consumer goods, chemicals, foodstuffs. Major trading partners: West Germany, Italy, France, Saudi Arabia, U.S.A.

Geography. Greece, on the Mediterranean Sea, is the southernmost country on the Balkan Peninsula in southern Europe. It is bordered on the north by Albania, Yugoslavia, and Bulgaria; on the west by the Ionian Sea; and on the east by the Aegean Sea and Turkey. It is slightly smaller than Alabama.

North central Greece, Epirus, and western Macedonia all are mountainous. The main chain of the Pindus Mountains rises to 9,000 feet (2,743 m) in places, separating Epirus from the plains of Thessaly. Mt. Olympus, rising to 9,570 feet (2,909 m) in the north near the Aegean Sea, is the highest point in the country. Greek Thrace is mostly a lowland region separated from European Turkey by the lower Evros River.

Among the many islands are the Ionian group off the west coast; the Cyclades group to the southeast; other islands in the eastern Aegean, including the Dodecanese Islands, Euboea, Lesbos, Samos, and Chios; and Crete, the fourth largest Mediterranean island.

Government. A referendum in December 1974, five months after the collapse of a military dictatorship, ended the Greek monarchy and established a republic. Ceremonial executive power is held by the president; the Premier heads the government and is responsible to a 300-member unicameral Parliament.

The major political parties are the Panhellenic Socialist Movement (156 of 300 seats in Parliament), led by Premier Andreas Papandreou; New Democracy Party (110 seats), led by Constantine Mitsotakis; Communist Party (10 seats), led by Harilaos Florakis; Democratic Renewal (11 seats), led by Constantine Stefanopoulos; and the Greek Left (EAR) (one seat), led by Leonidas Kyrkos.

History. Greece, with a recorded history going back to 766 B.C., reached the peak of its glory in the 5th century B.C., and by the middle of the 2nd century B.C., it had declined to the status of a Roman province. It remained within the Eastern Roman Empire until Constantinople fell to the Crusaders in 1204.

In 1453, the Turks took Constantinople, and by 1460 Greece was a Turkish province. The insurrection made famous by the poet Lord Byron broke out in 1821, and in 1827 Greece won independence with sovereignty guaranteed by Britain, France, and Russia.

The protecting powers chose Prince Otto of Bavaria as the first king of modern Greece in 1832 to reign over an area only slightly larger than the Peloponnese Peninsula. Chiefly under the next king, George I, chosen by the protecting powers in 1863, Greece acquired much of its present territory. During his 57-year reign, a period in which he encouraged parliamentary democracy, Thessaly, Epirus, Macedonia, Crete, and most of the Aegean islands were added from the disintegrating Turkish empire. An unsuccessful war against Turkey after World War I brought down the monarchy, to be replaced by a republic in 1923.

Two military dictatorships and a financial crisis brought George II back from exile, but only until 1941, when Italian and German invaders defeated tough Greek resistance. After British and Greek troops liberated the country in October 1944, Communist guerrillas staged a long campaign in which the government received U.S. aid under the Truman Doctrine, the predecessor of the Marshall Plan.

A military junta seized power in April 1967, sending young King Constantine II into exile December 14. Col. George Papadopoulos, as premier, converted the government to republican form in 1973 and as President ended martial law. He was moving to restore democracy when he was ousted in November of that year by his military colleagues. The regime of the "colonels," which had tortured its opponents and scoffed at human rights, resigned July 23, 1974, after having bungled an attempt to seize Cyprus.

Former Premier Karamanlis returned from exile to become premier of Greece's first civilian government since 1967.

On Jan. 1, 1981, Greece became the 10th member of the European Community. On Oct. 18, the first Socialist government in Greek history won power, and Andreas Papandreou became the new Premier.

The Socialists won parliamentary elections on June 1, 1985, by a comfortable margin, giving Papandreou a license to continue on the leftist course he had set four years previously. Later the same month, a TWA airliner was hijacked by Lebanese Shiite extremists as it left Athens, bringing the Greek government under sharp criticism for what international aviation authorities said was its failure to take adequate security measures at its airports.

GRENADA

State of Grenada
Sovereign: Queen Elizabeth II
Governor General: Paul Scoon (1978)
Prime Minister: Herbert A. Blaize (1984)
Area: 133 sq mi. (344 sq km)
Population (est. mid-1987): 100,000 (black, 84%; mixed, 11%) (average annual growth rate, 1.9%)
Density per square mile: 751.9
Capital and largest city (est. 1981): St. George's, 4,800
Monetary unit: East Caribbean dollar
Ethnic groups: Caribs and Indians
Language: English
Religions: Roman Catholic, 64%; Anglican, 21%
Member of Commonwealth of Nations
Literacy rate: 85%
Economic summary: Gross national product (1984): $80 million. Annual growth rate (1983): 2.6%. Per capita income (1984): $860. Land used for agriculture: 41%; labor force: 24%; principal products: spices, cocoa, bananas. Exports: nutmeg, cocoa beans, bananas, mace. Imports: foodstuffs, machinery, building materials. Major trading partners: U.K., West Indies countries, West Germany, U.S., Belgium

Geography. Grenada (the first "a" is pronounced as in "gray") is the most southerly of the Windward Islands, about 100 miles (161 km) from the South American coast. It is a volcanic island traversed by a mountain range, the highest peak of which is Mount St. Catherine (2,756 ft.; 840 m).

History. Grenada was discovered by Columbus in 1498. After more than 200 years of British rule, most recently as part of the West Indies Associated States, it became independent Feb. 7, 1974, with Eric M. Gairy as Prime Minister.

The government of Prime Minister Gairy was ousted March 13, 1979, by the New Jewel Movement of Maurice Bishop. Bishop, a protégé of Cuban President Fidel Castro, invited Cuban military advisers to Grenada and on June 20, 1980, called on Grenadians to join a "people's militia" to fight a "people's war" against imperialism.

Bishop was killed in a military coup on Oct. 19, 1983. At the request of five members of the Organization of Eastern Caribbean States, President Reagan ordered an invasion of Grenada on Oct. 25 involving over 1,900 U.S. troops and a small military force from Barbados, Dominica, Jamaica, St. Lucia, and St. Vincent. The troops met strong resistance from Cuban military personnel on the island. Reagan said he ordered the invasion to protect some 1,000 American citizens on the island, and to help restore democratic institutions in that country. A centrist coalition led by Herbert A. Blaize, a 66-year-old lawyer, won 14 of the 15 seats in Parliament in an election in December 1984, and Blaize became Prime Minister.

GUATEMALA

Republic of Guatemala
President: Marco Vinicio Cerezo Arévalo (1986)
Area: 42,042 sq mi. (108,889 sq km)
Population (est. mid-1987): 8,400,000 (average annual growth rate: 3.2%)
Density per square mile: 204.6
Capital and largest city (est. 1982): Guatemala City, 1, 250,000
Monetary unit: Quetzal
Languages: Spanish, Indian dialects
Religion: Roman Catholic, Protestant demoninations.
National name: República de Guatemala
Literacy rate (1983): 51%
Economic summary: Gross national product (1984): $9.11 billion. Average annual growth rate (1975–80) 5.7%. Per capita income (1984) $1,180. Land used for agriculture: 14%; labor force. 58%; principal products: corn, beans, coffee, cotton, cattle, sugar, bananas, essential oils, timber. Labor force in industry: 14%; principal products: prepared foods, textiles, construction materials, tires, pharmaceuticals. Natural resources: nickel, timber, shrimp. Exports: coffee, cotton, sugar, petroleum, bananas. Imports: manufactured products, machinery, transportation equipment, chemicals, fuels. Major trading partners: U.S., Central American nations, West Germany, Mexico.

Geography. The northernmost of the Central American nations, Guatemala is the size of Tennessee. Its neighbors are Mexico on the north, west, and east and Belize, Honduras, and El Salvador on the east. The country consists of two main regions—the cool highlands with the heaviest population and the tropical area along the Pacific and Caribbean coasts. The principal mountain range rises to the highest elevation in Central America and contains many volcanic peaks. Volcanic eruptions are frequent.

The Petén region in the north contains important resources and archaeological sites of the Mayan civilization.

Government. On December 8, 1985, Marco Vinicio Cerezo Arévalo, a left-of-center Christian Democrat, won in elections that were generally free from military interference. A 100-seat Congress was also elected.

Both the President and the Congress are elected for five-year terms and the President may not be re-elected.

History. Once the site of the ancient Mayan civilization, Guatemala, conquered by Spain in 1524, set itself up as a republic in 1839. From 1898 to 1920, the dictator Manuel Estrada Cabrera ran the country, and from 1931 to 1944, Gen. Jorge Ubico Castaneda was the strongman. In 1944 the National Assembly elected Gen. Federico Ponce president, but he was overthrown in October. In December, Dr. Juan José Arévalo was elected as the head of a leftist regime that continued to press its reform program. Jacobo Arbenz Guzmán, administration candidate with leftist leanings, won the 1950 elections.

Arbenz expropriated the large estates, including

plantations of the United Fruit Company. With covert U.S. backing, a revolt was led by Col. Carlos Castillo Armas, and Arbenz took refuge in Mexico. Castillo Armas became president but was assassinated in 1957. Constitutional government was restored in 1958, and Gen. Miguel Ydigoras Fuentes was elected president.

A wave of terrorism, by left and right, began in 1967, and in August 1968 U.S. Ambassador John Gordon Mein was killed when he resisted kidnappers. Fear of anarchy led to the election in 1970 of Army Chief of Staff Carlos Araña Osorio, who had put down a rural guerrilla movement at the cost of nearly 3,000 lives. Araña, surprisingly, pledged social reforms when he took office. Another military candidate, Gen. Kjell Laugerud, won the presidency in 1974 amid renewed political violence.

The administration of Gen. Romeo Lucas Garcia, elected president in 1978, ended in a coup by a three-man military junta on March 23, 1982. Lucas Garcia was charged by Amnesty International with responsibility for at least 5,000 political murders in a reign of brutality and corruption that brought a cutoff of U.S. military aid in 1978. Hopes for improvement under the junta faded when Gen. José Efraín Ríos Montt took sole power in June.

President Oscar Mejía Victores, another general, seized power from Rios Montt in an August 1983 coup and pledged to turn over power to an elected civilian President in 1985. A constituent assembly was elected on July 1, 1984, to write a new Constitution.

Government. Military government headed by President Lansana Conté, who promoted himself from colonel to brigadier general after a 1984 coup.

History. Previously part of French West Africa, Guinea achieved independence by rejecting the new French Constitution, and on Oct. 2, 1958, became an independent state with Sékou Touré as president. Touré led the country into being the first avowedly Marxist state in Africa. Diplomatic relations with France were suspended in 1965, with the Soviet Union replacing France as the country's chief source of economic and technical assistance.

In 1966, when a Ghanaian military coup deposed Kwame Nkrumah as President, Touré welcomed him to Guinea and declared him joint president and party leader. The titles proved to be only honorary.

Prosperity came in 1960 after the start of exploitation of bauxite deposits. Touré was re-elected to a seven-year term in 1974 and again in 1981.

After 26 years as President, Touré died in the United States in March 1984, following surgery. A week later, a military regime headed by Col. Lansana Conté took power with a promise not to shed any more blood after Touré's harsh rule. Conté became President and his co-conspirator in the coup, Col. Diara Traoré, became Prime Minister, but Conté later demoted Traoré to Education Minister. Traoré tried to seize power on July 4, 1985, while Conté was out of the country, but his attempted coup was crushed by troops loyal to Conté.

GUINEA

Republic of Guinea
President: Brig. Gen. Lansana Conté (1984)
Area: 94,925 sq mi. (245,857 sq km)
Population (est. mid-1987): 6,400,000 (average annual growth rate: 2.4%)
Density per square mile: 67.4
Capital and largest city (est. 1983): Conakry, 656,000
Monetary unit: Guinean franc
Languages: French (official), native tongues (Malinké, Susu, Fulani)
Religions: Islam, 69%; Animist, 30%
National name: République de Guinée
Literacy rate: 28%
Economic summary: Gross national product (1984): $1.81 billion. Annual growth rate (1984): 1.4%. Per capita income (1984): $290. Principal agricultural products: rice, cassava, millet, corn, coffee, bananas, pineapples. Major industrial products: bauxite, alumina, light manufactured and processed goods. Natural resources: bauxite, iron ore, diamonds, gold, water power. Exports: bauxite, alumina, pineapples, bananas, coffee. Imports: petroleum, machinery, transport equipment, foodstuffs, textiles. Major trading partners: U.S., France, W. Germany, U.K.

Geography. Guinea, in West Africa on the Atlantic, is also bordered by Guinea-Bissau, Senegal, Mali, the Ivory Coast, Liberia, and Sierra Leone. Slightly smaller than Oregon, the country consists of a coastal plain, a mountainous region, a savanna interior, and a forest area in the Guinea Highlands. The highest peak is Mount Nimba at about 6,000 feet (1,829 m).

GUINEA-BISSAU

Republic of Guinea-Bissau
President of the Council of State: João Bernardo Vieira (1980)
Area: 13,948 sq mi. (36,125 sq km)
Population (est. mid-1987): 900,000 (average annual growth rate: 2.0%)
Density per square mile: 64.5
Capital and largest city (est. 1980): Bissau, 110,000
Monetary unit: Guinea-Bissau peso
Language: Portugese
Religions: Animist, 65%; Islam, 30%; Christian, 5%
National name: Républica da Guiné-Bissau
Literacy rate: 9%
Economic summary: Gross national product (1984): $160 million. Annual growth rate (1983): –5.1%. Per capita income (1984): $190. Labor force in agriculture: 90%; principal products: palm oil, root crops, rice, coconuts, peanuts. Natural resources: potential bauxite deposits. Exports: peanuts, coconuts, shrimp, fish, wood. Imports: foodstuffs, manufactured goods, fuels, transportation equipment. Major trading partner: Portugal.

Geography. A neighbor of Senegal and Guinea in West Africa, on the Atlantic coast, Guinea-Bissau is about half the size of South Carolina.

The country is a low-lying coastal region of swamps, rain forests, and mangrove-covered wetlands, with about 25 islands off the coast. The Bijagos archipelago extends 30 miles (48 km) out to sea. Internal communications depend mainly on deep estuaries and meandering rivers, since there are no railroads. Bissau, the capital, is the main port.

Government. After the overthrow of Louis Cabral

in November 1980, the nine-member Council of the Revolution formed an interm government. In 1982, they formed a new government consisting of the President, 2 Vice-Presidents, 18 ministers and 10 state secretaries.

History. Guinea-Bissau was discovered in 1446 by the Portuguese Nuno Tristao, and colonists in the Cape Verde Islands obtained trading rights in the territory. In 1879 the connection with the Cape Verde Islands was broken. Early in the 1900s the Portuguese managed to pacify some tribesmen, although resistance to colonial rule remained.

The African Party for the Independence of Guinea-Bissau and Cape Verde was founded in 1956 and several years later began guerrilla warfare that grew increasingly effective. By 1974 the rebels controlled most of the countryside, where they formed a government that was soon recognized by scores of countries. The military coup in Portugal in April 1974 brightened the prospects for freedom, and in August the Lisbon government signed an agreement granting independence to the province as of Sept. 10. The new republic took the name Guinea-Bissau. Its government was immediately recognized by the United States.

In November 1980, Prémier João Bernardo Vieira headed a coup that deposed Luis Cabral, President since 1974. A Revolutionary Council assumed the powers of government, with Vieira as its head.

GUYANA

Cooperative Republic of Guyana
President: Desmond Hoyte (1985)
Area: 83,000 sq mi. (214,969 sq km)
Population (est. mid-1987): 800,000 (average annual growth rate: 2.0%) (East Indian, 51%; African, 30%; mixed 10%; Amerindian, 5%)
Density per square mile: 9.6
Capital and largest city (est. 1981): Georgetown, 200,000
Monetary unit: Guyana dollar
Languages: English (official), Hindi, Urdu, Creole
Religions: Hindu, 34%; Protestant, 18%; Islam, 9%; Roman Catholic, 18%; Anglican, 16%; Muslim, 9%
Member of Commonwealth of Nations
Literacy rate: 86%
Economic summary: Gross national product (1984): $470 million. Average annual growth rate (1982): −10%. Per capita income (1984): $600. Labor force in agriculture: 34%; principal products: sugar, rice. Labor force in industry: 22%; major products: bauxite, alumina. Natural resources: bauxite, gold, diamonds, hardwood timber, shrimp. Exports: sugar, bauxite, alumina, rice, timber. Imports: fuels, machinery. Major trading partners: U.K., U.S., Trinidad, Venezuela.

Geography. Guyana is situated on the northern coast of South America east of Venezuela, west of Suriname, and north of Brazil. The country consists of a low coastal area and the Guiana Highlands in the south. There is an extensive north-south network of rivers. Guyana is the size of Idaho.

Government. Guyana, formerly British Guiana, proclaimed itself a republic on Feb. 23, 1970, ending its tie with Britain while remaining in the Commonwealth.

Guyana has a unicameral legislature, the National Assembly, with 53 members directly elected for five-year terms and 12 elected by local councils. A 24-member Cabinet is headed by the President.

The major political parties are the People's National Congress (42 of 53 seats in National Assembly), led by President Desmond Hoyte; People's Progressive Party (8 seats), led by Dr. Cheddi B. Jagan.

History. British Guiana won internal self-government in 1952. The next year the People's Progressive Party, headed by Cheddi B. Jagan, an East Indian dentist, won the elections and Jagan became Prime Minister. British authorities deposed him for alleged Communist connections. A coalition ousted Jagan in 1964, installing a moderate Socialist, Forbes Burnham, a black, as Prime Minister. On May 26, 1966, the country became an independent member of the Commonwealth and resumed its traditional name, Guyana.

After ruling Guyana for 21 years, Burnham died on Aug. 6 1985, in a Guyana hospital after a throat operation. Desmond Hoyte, the country's Prime Minister succeeded him under the Guyanese constitution.

HAITI

Republic of Haiti
Council President: Lt. Gen. Henri Namphy (1986)
Area: 10,714 sq mi. (27,750 sq km)
Population (est. mid-1987): 6,200,000 (average annual growth rate: 2.3%)
Density per square mile: 578.7
Capital and largest city (est. 1980): Port-au-Prince, 790,000
Monetary unit: Gourde
Languages: French, Creole
Religion: Roman Catholic, 80%; Baptist, 10%
National name: République d'Haïti
Literacy rate: 23%
Economic summary: Gross national product (1984): $1.8 billion. Annual growth rate (1984): 2.0%. Per capita income (1983): $333. Land used for agriculture: 31%; labor force: 79%; principal products: coffee, sugar cane, corn, sorghum. Labor force in industry: 7%; major products: refined sugar, textiles, flour, cement, light assembly products. Natural resource: bauxite. Exports: coffee, light industrial products, sugar, cocoa, sisal. Imports: consumer goods, foodstuffs, industrial equipment, petroleum products. Major trading partner: U.S.

Geography. Haiti, in the West Indies, occupies the western third of the island of Hispaniola, which it shares with the Dominican Republic. About the size of Maryland, Haiti is two thirds mountainous, with the rest of the country marked by great valleys, extensive plateaus, and small plains. The most densely populated region is the Cul-de-Sac plain near Port-au-Prince.

Government. In the face of public protests that began November, 1985, and increased in intensity, Duvalier fled the country on February 7 to exile in France. The army chief of staff, Lt. Gen. Henri Namphy, established a governing council with himself as head.

A new constitution was voted in on March 29, 1987 and a new president will take power on February 7, 1988 after elections.

History. Discovered by Columbus, who landed at Môle Saint Nicolas on Dec. 6, 1492, Haiti in 1697 became a French possession known as Saint Domingue. An insurrection among a slave population of 500,000 in 1791 ended with a declaration of independence by Pierre-Dominique Toussaint l'Ouverture in 1801. Napoleon Bonaparte suppressed the independence movement, but it eventually triumphed in 1804 under Jean-Jacques Dessalines, who gave the new nation the aboriginal name Haiti.

Its prosperity dissipated in internal strife as well as disputes with neighboring Santo Domingo during a succession of 19th-century dictatorships, a bankrupt Haiti accepted a U.S. customs receivership from 1905 to 1941. Direct U.S. rule from 1915 to 1934 brought a measure of stability and a population growth that made Haiti the most densely populated nation in the hemisphere.

In 1949, after four years of democratic rule by President Dumarsais Estimé, dictatorship returned under Gen. Paul Magloire, who was succeeded by François Duvalier in 1957.

Duvalier established a dictatorship. Duvalier's son, Jean-Claude, or "Baby Doc," succeeded his father in 1971 as ruler of the poorest nation in the Western Hemisphere.

The ruling council that took power upon the exile of Duvalier has been plagued by protests against the inclusion of former Duvalier aides in the council and by the slow pace of reform.

HONDURAS

Republic of Honduras
President: José Azcona Hoyo (1986)
Area: 43,277 sq mi. (112,088 sq km)
Population (est. mid-1987): 4,700,000 (average annual growth rate: 3.1%) (60% mestizo)
Density per square mile: 108.6
Capital and largest city (1984): Tegucigalpa, 539,600
Monetary unit: Lempira
Languages: Spanish, some Indian dialects, English in Bay Islands Department
Religion: Roman Catholic
National name: República de Honduras
Literacy rate: 56%
Economic summary: Gross national product (1984): $2.9 billion. Growth rate (1984): 2.4%. Per capita income (1984): $815. Labor force in agriculture: 59%; principal products: bananas, coffee, corn, beans, cotton, sugar cane, tobacco. Labor force in industry: 14%; major products: processed agricultural products, textiles and clothing, wood products. Natural resources: timber, gold, silver, lead, zinc, antimony. Exports: bananas, coffee, lumber, meat, petroleum products, tobacco, sugar, shrimp and lobster. Imports: manufactured goods, machinery, transportation equipment, chemicals, petroleum. Major trading partners: U.S., Caribbean countries, West Germany, Venezuela, Japan, Spain, Netherlands.

Geography. Honduras, in the north central part of Central America, has a 400-mile (644-km) Caribbean coastline and a 40-mile (64-km) Pacific frontage. Its neighbors are Guatemala to the west, El Salvador to the south, and Nicaragua to the east. Honduras is slightly larger than Tennessee.

Generally mountainous, the country is marked by fertile plateaus, river valleys, and narrow coastal plains.

Government. José Azcona Hoyo was elected to succeed Roberto Suazo Córdova. He was inaugurated on January 27, 1986.

History. Columbus discovered Honduras on his last voyage in 1502. Honduras, with four other countries of Central America, declared its independence from Spain in 1821 and was part of a federation of Central American states until 1838. In that year it seceded from the federation and became a completely independent country.

U.S. Marines intervened in 1903 and 1923. In 1931, 1932, and 1937, major revolutions were crushed by force.

In July 1969, El Salvador invaded Honduras after Honduran landowners had deported several thousand Salvadorans. The fighting left 1,000 dead and tens of thousands homeless. By threatening economic sanctions and military intervention, the OAS induced El Salvador to withdraw.

Although parliamentary democracy returned with the election of Roberto Suazo Córdova as President in 1982 after a decade of military rule, Honduras faced severe economic problems and tensions along its border with Nicaragua. An estimated 12,000 "contra" rebels, waging a guerrilla war against the Sandinista regime in Nicaragua, used Honduras as a training and staging area. At the same time, the United States used Honduras as a site for military exercises and built bases to train both Honduran and Salvadoran troops. Honduras received $125 million in U.S. economic and military aid in 1984.

HUNGARY

Hungarian People's Republic
President: Pál Losonczi (1967)
Premier: Gyorgy Lazar (1975)
Area: 35,919 sq mi. (93,030 sq km)
Population (est. mid-1987): 10,600,000 (average annual growth rate: −0.2%)
Density per square mile: 295.1
Capital: Budapest
Largest cities (est. 1982): Budapest, 2,100,000; Miskolc, 225,000; Debrecen, 215,000; Szeged, 200,000; Pécs, 195,000; Györ, 150,000
Monetary unit: Forint
Language: Magyar
Religions: Roman Catholic, 54%; Protestant, 22%; atheist, 7%
National name: Magyar Népköztársaság
Literacy rate: 98%
Economic summary: Gross national product (1984): $77 billion. Annual growth rate (1984): 1.3%. Per capita income (1984): $7,200. Land used for agriculture: 57%; labor force: 21%; principal products: corn, wheat, potatoes, sugar beets, vegetables, wine grapes, fruits. Labor force in industry: 32%; major products: steel, chemicals, pharmaceuticals, textiles, transport equipment. Natural resources: some bauxite and iron. Exports: machinery and tools, industrial and consumer goods, raw materials. Imports: machinery, raw materials. Major trading partners: U.S.S.R., Warsaw Pact countries, West Germany, Yugoslavia, Austria, and Italy.

Geography. This central European country the size of Indiana is bordered by Austria to the west, Czechoslovakia to the north, the U.S.S.R. and Romania to the east, and Yugoslavia to the south.

Most of Hungary is a fertile, rolling plain lying east of the Danube River and drained by the Danube and Tisza rivers. In the extreme northwest is the Little Hungarian Plain. South of that area is Lake Balaton (250 sq mi.; 648 sq km).

Government. Hungary is a People's Republic with legislative power vested in the unicameral National Assembly, whose 352 members are elected directly for four-year terms. The supreme body of state power is the 21-member Presidential Council elected by the National Assembly. The supreme administrative body is the Council of Ministers, headed by the Premier.

The Hungarian Socialist Workers (Communist) Party, led by János Kádár, is the only political party.

History. About 2,000 years ago, Hungary was part of the Roman provinces of Pannonia and Dacia. In A.D. 896 it was invaded by the Magyars, who founded a kingdom. Christianity was accepted during the reign of Stephen I (St. Stephen) (997–1038).

The peak of Hungary's great period of medieval power came during the reign of Louis I the Great (1342–82), whose dominions touched the Baltic, Black, and Mediterranean seas.

War with the Turks broke out in 1389, and for more than 100 years the Turks advanced through the Balkans. When the Turks smashed a Hungarian army in 1526, western and northern Hungary accepted Hapsburg rule to escape Turkish occupation. Transylvania became independent under Hungarian princes. Intermittent war with the Turks was waged until a peace treaty was signed in 1699.

After the suppression of the 1848 revolt against Hapsburg rule, led by Louis Kossuth, the dual monarchy of Austria-Hungary was set up in 1867.

The dual monarchy was defeated with the other Central Powers in World War I. After a short-lived republic in 1918, the chaotic Communist rule of 1919 under Béla Kun ended with the Romanians occupying Budapest on Aug. 4, 1919. When the Romanians left, Adm. Nicholas Horthy entered the capital with a national army. The Treaty of Trianon of June 4, 1920, cost Hungary 68% of its land and 58% of its population. Meanwhile, the National Assembly had restored the legal continuity of the old monarchy; and, on March 1, 1920, Horthy was elected Regent.

Following the German invasion of Russia on June 22, 1941, Hungary joined the attack against the Soviet Union, but the war was not popular and Hungarian troops were almost entirely withdrawn from the eastern front by May 1943. German occupation troops set up a puppet government after Horthy's appeal for an armistice with advancing Soviet troops on Oct. 15, 1944, had resulted in his overthrow. The German regime soon fled the capital, however, and on December 23 a provisional government was formed in Soviet-occupied eastern Hungary. On Jan. 20, 1945, it signed an armistice in Moscow. Early the next year, the National Assembly approved a constitutional law abolishing the thousand-year-old monarchy and establishing a republic.

By the Treaty of Paris (1947), Hungary had to give up all territory it had acquired since 1937 and to pay $300 million reparations to the U.S.S.R., Czechoslovakia, and Yugoslavia. In 1948 the Communist Party, with the support of Soviet troops seized control. Hungary was proclaimed a People's Republic and one-party state in 1949. Industry was nationalized, the land collectivized into state farms, and the opposition terrorized by the secret police.

The terror, modeled after that of the U.S.S.R., reached its height with the trial of Jozsef Cardinal Mindszenty, Roman Catholic primate. He confessed to fantastic charges under duress of drugs or brainwashing and was sentenced to life imprisonment in 1949. Protests were voiced in all parts of the world.

On Oct. 23, 1956, anti-Communist revolution broke out in Budapest. To cope with it, the Communists set up a coalition government and called former Premier Imre Nagy back to head it. But he and most of his ministers were swept by the logic of events into the anti-Communist opposition, and he declared Hungary a neutral power, withdrawing from the Warsaw Treaty and appealing to the United Nations for help.

One of his ministers, János Kádár, established a counter-regime and asked the U.S.S.R. to send in military power. Soviet troops and tanks suppressed the revolution in bloody fighting after 190,000 people had fled the country and Mindszenty, freed from jail, had taken refuge in the U.S. Embassy.

Kádár was succeeded as Premier, but not party secretary, by Gyula Kallai in 1965. Continuing his program of national reconciliation, Kádár emptied prisons, reformed the secret police, and eased travel restrictions.

Hungary developed the reputation of being the freest East European state.

After 15 years' asylum in the U.S. Embassy, Mindszenty, under an agreement between the Vatican and the Hungarian regime, was allowed to travel into exile to Rome in 1971. In a move applauded by Kádár, Pope Paul VI removed Mindszenty from his honorary post as Primate of Hungary in 1974. The Cardinal died in Vienna in 1975.

Relations with the U.S. improved in 1972 when World War II debt claims between the two nations were settled. On Jan. 6, 1978, the U.S. returned to Hungary, over anti-Communist protests, the 977-year-old crown of St. Stephen, held at Fort Knox since World War II.

ICELAND

Republic of Iceland

President: Vigdis Finnbogadottir (1980)
Prime Minister: Steingrimur Hermannsson (1983)
Area: 39,709 sq mi. (102,846 sq km)
Population (est. mid-1987): 200,000 (average annual growth rate: 0.9%)
Density per square mile: 5.04
Capital and largest city (est. 1983): Reykjavik, 87,100
Monetary unit: New króna
Language: Icelandic
Religion: Evangelical Lutheran
National name: Lydveldid Island
Literacy rate: 99.9%
Economic summary: Gross national product (1984): $2.1 billion. Annual growth rate (1985): 1.5%. Per capita income (1984): $9,153. Labor force in agriculture: 9%; fishing and fish processing: 13.4%; principal agricultural products: livestock, hay, fodder, cheese. Labor force in

industry: 17%; major products: processed aluminum, fish. Natural resources: fish, diatomite, hydroelectric and geothermal power. Exports: fish, animal products, aluminum. Imports: petroleum products, machinery and transportation equipment, food, textiles. Major trading partners: U.S., U.S.S.R., Western European countries.

1. Including some offshore islands.

Geography. Iceland, an island about the size of Kentucky, lies in the north Atlantic Ocean east of Greenland and just touches the Arctic Circle. It is one of the most volcanic regions in the world.

Small fresh-water lakes are to be found throughout the island, and there are many natural phenomena, including hot springs, geysers, sulfur beds, canyons, waterfalls, and swift rivers. More than 13% of the area is covered by snowfields and glaciers, and most of the people live in the 7% of the island comprising fertile coastlands.

Government. The president is elected for four years by popular vote. Executive power resides in the prime minister and his Cabinet. The Althing (Parliament) is composed of 60 members in two houses. They elect 20 of themselves to constitute the Upper House, the remaining 40 representing the Lower House.

The major political parties are the Independence Party (18 of 60 seats in the Althing), led by Thorsteinn Palsson; Progressive Party (13 seats), led by Steingrimur Hermannsson; Social Democratic People's Party (10 seats), led by Jon B. Hannibalsson; People's Alliance (8 seats), led by Svavar Gestsson; Citizen's Party (7 seats), led by Albert Gudmundsson; Women's Alliance (6 seats).

History. Iceland was first settled shortly before 900, mainly by Norse. A Constitution drawn up about 930 created a form of democracy and provided for an Althing, or General Assembly.

In 1262–64, Iceland came under Norwegian rule and passed to ultimate Danish control through the formation of the Union of Kalmar in 1483. In 1874, Icelanders obtained their own Constitution. In 1918, Denmark recognized Iceland as a separate state with unlimited sovereignty but still nominally under the Danish king.

On June 17, 1944, after a popular referendum, the Althing proclaimed Iceland an independent republic.

The British occupied Iceland in 1940, immediately after the German invasion of Denmark. In 1942, the U.S. took over the burden of protection. Iceland refused to abandon its neutrality in World War II and thus forfeited charter membership in the United Nations, but it cooperated with the Allies throughout the conflict. Iceland joined the North Atlantic Treaty Organization in 1949.

Iceland unilaterally extended its territorial waters from 12 to 50 nautical miles in 1972, precipitating a running dispute with Britain known as the "cod war." Icelandic warships harassed British trawlers, which then received aid from British gunboats; some trawlers were shelled, and Icelandic and British warships collided in 1973. The World Court ruled in 1974 that the 50-mile limit could not be applied unilaterally, but Iceland rejected the ruling.

An agreement calling for registration of all British trawlers fishing within 200 miles of Iceland and a 24-hour time limit on incursions was finally reached in 1976.

INDIA

Republic of India
President: Ramaswamy Venkataraman (1987)
Prime Minister: Rajiv Gandhi (1984)
Area: 1,229,737 sq mi. (3,185,019 sq km)
Population (est. mid-1987): 800,300,000 (average annual growth rate: 2.1%)
Density per square mile: 650.8
Capital (1980 census): New Delhi, 619,417
Largest cities (1981 est.): Calcutta, 9,194,018; Greater Bombay, 8,243,405; Delhi, 5,729,283; Madras, 4,289,347; Bangalore, 2,921,751; Ahmedabad, 2,548,057; Kanpur, 1,639,064
Monetary unit: Rupee
Principal languages; Hindi (official), English (official), Bengali, Gujarati, Kashmiri, Malayalam, Marathi, Oriya, Punjabi, Tamil, Telugu, Urdu, Kannada, Assamese (all recognized by the Constitution)
Religions: Hindu, 83%; Islam, 11%; Christian, 3%; Sikh, 2%
National name: Bharat
Literacy rate: 36%
Member of Commonwealth of Nations
Economic summary: Gross national product (1984): $193 billion. Average annual growth rate (1983–84): 8.0%. Per capita income (1984): $240. Land used for agriculture: 57%; labor force: 63%; principal products: rice, wheat, oilseeds, cotton, tea. Major industrial products: jute, processed food, steel, machinery, transport machinery, cement. Natural resources: iron ore, coal, manganese, mica, bauxite, limestone. Exports: diamonds, iron goods, textiles and clothing, tea. Imports: machinery and transport equipment, petroleum, edible oils, fertilizers. Major trading partners: U.S., U.S.S.R., Japan, Saudi Arabia, U.K.

Geography. One third the area of the United States, the Republic of India occupies most of the subcontinent of India in south Asia. It borders on China in the northeast. Other neighbors are Pakistan on the west, Nepal and Bhutan on the north, and Burma and Bangladesh on the east.

The country contains a large part of the great Indo-Gangetic plain, which extends from the Bay of Bengal on the east to the Afghan frontier on the Arabian Sea on the west. This plain is the richest and most densely settled part of the subcontinent. Another distinct natural region is the Deccan, a plateau of 2,000 to 3,000 feet (610 to 914 m) in elevation, occupying the southern portion of the subcontinent.

Forming a part of the republic are several groups of islands—the Laccadives (14 islands) in the Arabian Sea and the Andamans (204 islands) and the Nicobars (19 islands) in the Bay of Bengal.

India's three great river systems, all rising in the Himalayas, have extensive deltas. The Ganges flows south and then east for 1,540 miles (2,478 km) across the northern plain to the Bay of Bengal; part of its delta, which begins 220 miles (354 km) from the sea, is within the republic. The Indus, starting in Tibet, flows northwest for several hundred miles in the Kashmir before turning southwest toward the Arabian Sea; it is important for irrigation in Pakistan. The Brahmaputra, also rising in Tibet, flows eastward, first through India and then south into Bangladesh and the Bay of Bengal.

Government. India is a federal republic. It is also a member of the Commonwealth of Nations, a status defined at the 1949 London Conference of Prime Ministers, by which India recognizes

Queen as head of the Commonwealth. Under the Constitution effective Jan. 26, 1950, India has a parliamentary type of government.

The constitutional head of the state is the President, who is elected every five years. He is advised by the Prime Minister and a Cabinet based on a majority of the bicameral Parliament, which consists of a Council of States (Rajya Sabha), representing the constituent units of the republic and a House of the People (Lok Sabha), elected every five years by universal suffrage.

The major political parties are Congress Party I (412 of 544 seats in the Lok Sabha), led by Prime Minister Rajiv Gandhi; Telegu Desam (30 seats); Communist (Marxist independent) Party (22 seats); Janata Party (13 seats); Communist (pro-Soviet) Party (6 seats).

History. The Aryans, or Hindus, who invaded India between 2400 and 1500 B.C. from the northwest found a land already well civilized. Buddhism was founded in the 6th century B.C. and spread through northern India.

In 1526, Moslem invaders founded the great Mogul empire, centered on Delhi, which lasted, at least in name, until 1857. Akbar the Great (1542–1605) strengthened this empire and became the ruler of a greater portion of India than had ever before acknowledged the suzerainty of one man. The long reign of his great-grandson, Aurangzeb (1658–1707), represents both the culmination of Mogul power and the beginning of its decay.

Vasco da Gama, the Portuguese explorer, visited India first in 1498, and for the next 100 years the Portuguese had a virtual monopoly on trade with the subcontinent. Meanwhile, the English founded the East India Company, which set up its first factory at Surat in 1612 and began expanding its influence, fighting the Indian rulers and the French, Dutch, and Portuguese traders simultaneously.

Bombay, taken from the Portuguese, became the seat of English rule in 1687. The defeat of French and Islamic armies by Lord Clive in the decade ending in 1760 laid the foundation of the British Empire in India. From then until 1858, when the administration of India was formally transferred to the British Crown following the Sepoy Mutiny of native troops in 1857, the East India Company suppressed native uprisings and extended British rule.

After World War I, in which the Indian states sent more than 6 million troops to fight beside the Allies, Indian nationalist unrest rose to new heights under the leadership of a little Hindu lawyer, Mohandas K. Gandhi, called Mahatma Gandhi. His tactics called for nonviolent revolts against British authority. He soon became the leading spirit of the All-India Congress Party, which was the spearhead of revolt. In 1919 the British gave added responsibility to Indian officials, and in 1935 India was given a federal form of government and a measure of self-rule.

In 1942, with the Japanese pressing hard on the eastern borders of India, the British War Cabinet tried and failed to reach a political settlement with nationalist leaders. The Congress Party took the position that the British must quit India. In 1942, fearing mass civil disobedience, the government of India carried out widespread arrests of Congress leaders, including Gandhi.

Gandhi was released in 1944 and negotiations for a settlement were resumed. Finally, in February 1947, the Labor government announced its determination to transfer power to "responsible Indian hands" by June 1948 even if a Constitution had not been worked out.

Lord Mountbatten as Viceroy, by June 1947, achieved agreement on the partitioning of India along religious lines and on the splitting of the provinces of Bengal and the Punjab, which the Moslems had claimed.

The Indian Independence Act, passed quickly by the British Parliament, received royal assent on July 18, 1947, and on August 15 the Indian Empire passed into history.

Jawaharlal Nehru, leader of the Congress Party, was made Prime Minister. Before an exchange of populations could be arranged, bloody riots occurred among the communal groups, and armed conflict broke out over rival claims to the princely state of Jammu and Kashmir. Peace was restored only with the greatest difficulty. In 1949 a Constitution, along the lines of the U.S. Constitution, was approved making India a sovereign republic. Under a federal structure the states were organized on linguistic lines.

The dominance of the Congress Party contributed to stability. In 1956 the republic absorbed the former French settlements. Five years later, it forcibly annexed the Portuguese enclaves of Goa, Damao, and Diu.

Nehru died in 1964. His successor, Lal Bahadur Shastri, died on Jan. 10, 1966. Nehru's daughter, Indira Gandhi, became Prime Minister, and she continued his policy of nonalignment.

In 1971 the Pakistani Army moved in to quash the independence movement in East Pakistan that was supported by clandestine aid from India, and some 10 million Bengali refugees poured across the border into India, creating social, economic, and health problems. After numerous border incidents, India invaded East Pakistan and in two weeks forced the surrender of the Pakistani army. East Pakistan was established as an independent state and renamed Bangladesh.

In the summer of 1975, the world's largest democracy veered suddenly toward authoritarianism when a judge in Allahabad, Mrs. Gandhi's home constituency, found her landslide victory in the 1971 elections invalid because civil servants had illegally aided her campaign. Amid demands for her resignation, Mrs. Gandhi decreed a state of emergency on June 26 and ordered mass arrests of her critics, including all opposition party leaders except the Communists.

In 1976, India and Pakistan formally renewed diplomatic relations.

Despite strong opposition to her repressive measures and particularly the resentment against compulsory birth control programs, Mrs. Gandhi in 1977 announced parliamentary elections for March. At the same time, she freed most political prisoners.

The landslide victory of Morarji R. Desai unseated Mrs. Gandhi and also defeated a bid for office by her son, Sanjay.

Mrs. Gandhi staged a spectacular comeback in the elections of January 1980.

In 1984, Mrs. Gandhi ordered the Indian Army to root out a band of Sikh holy men and gunmen who were using the holiest shrine of the Sikh religion, the Golden Temple in Amritsar, as a base for terrorist raids in a violent campaign for greater political autonomy in the strategic Punjab border state. As many as 1,000 people were reported killed in the June 5–6 battle, including Jarnall Singh Bhindranwale, the Khomeini-like militant leader, and 93 soldiers. The perceived sacrilege to the Golden Temple kindled outrage among many of India's 14 million Sikhs and brought a spasm of mutinies and desertions by Sikh officers and soldiers in the army.

On Oct. 31, 1984, Mrs. Gandhi was assassinated by two men identified by police as Sikh members of her bodyguard. The ruling Congress I Party chose her second son, Rajiv Gandhi, to succeed her as Prime Minister.

On July 24, Rajiv Gandhi and moderate Sikh leaders agreed on a package of steps to ease Sikh hostility toward the government and end the turmoil in the state of Punjab. A key element called for a change in the Punjab boundaries to increase the Sikh population within the state and give it greater political influence. Prime Minister Gandhi also yielded to demands for more lenient treatment of Sikhs arrested in riots over the last three years. Violence continued unabated with about 1,000 people being killed in 1986 and the first half of 1987 and Gandhi established direct rule on May 11, 1987, dissolving the local government.

Native States. Most of the 560-odd native states and subdivisions of pre-1947 India acceded to the new nation, and the central government pursued a vigorous policy of integration. This took three forms: merger into adjacent provinces, conversion into centrally administered areas, and grouping into unions of states. Finally, under a controversial reorganization plan effective Nov. 1, 1956, the unions of states were abolished and merged into adjacent states, and India became a union of 15 states and 8 centrally administered areas. A 16th state was added in 1962, and in 1966, the Punjab was partitioned into two states.

Resolution of the territorial dispute over Kashmir grew out of peace negotiations following the two-week India-Pakistan war of 1971. After sporadic skirmishing, an accord reached July 3, 1972, committed both powers to withdraw troops from a temporary cease-fire line after the border was fixed. Agreement on the border was reached Dec. 7, 1972.

In April 1975, the Indian Parliament voted to make the 300-year-old kingdom of Sikkim a full-fledged Indian state, and the annexation took effect May 16.

Situated in the Himalayas, Sikkim was a virtual dependency of Tibet until the early 19th century. Under an 1890 treaty between China and Great Britain, it became a British protectorate, and was made an Indian protectorate after Britain quit the subcontinent.

INDONESIA

Republic of Indonesia
President: Suharto (1969)[1]
Area: 735,268 sq mi. (1,904,344 sq km)[2]
Population (est. mid-1987): 174,900,000 (average annual growth rate: 2.1%)
Density per square mile: 237.8
Capital: Jakarta
Largest cities (est. 1983): Jakarta, 7,636,000; Surabaja, 2,289,000; Bandung, 1,602,000; Medan, 1,966,000; Semarang, 1,269,000
Monetary unit: Rupiah
Languages: Bahasa Indonesia (official), Dutch, English, and more than 60 regional languages
Religions: Islam, 88%; Christian, 9%; Hindu, Buddhist
National name: Republik Indonesia
Literacy rate: 64%
Economic summary: Gross national product (1985): $90.3 billion. Average annual growth rate (1980–84): 5.9%. Per capita income (1985 est.): $540. Land used for agriculture: 9%; labor force: 66%; principal products: rice, cassava, sugarcane, rubber, coffee. Labor force in industry: 9%; major products: textiles, food and beverages, light manufactures, cement, fertilizer. Natural resources: oil, timber, nickel, natural gas, tin, bauxite, copper. Exports: petroleum and liquid natural gas, timber, rubber, coffee, tin. Imports: rice, wheat, textiles, chemicals, iron and steel. Major trading partners: Japan, U.S., Singapore.

1. General Suharto served as Acting President of Indonesia from 1967 to 1969. 2. Includes West Irian (former Netherlands New Guinea), renamed Irian Jaya in March 1973 (159,355 sq mi.; 412,731 sq km), and former Portuguese Timor (5,763 sq mi.; 14,925 sq km), annexed in 1976.

Geography. Indonesia is part of the Malay archipelago in Southeast Asia with an area nearly three times that of Texas. It consists of the islands of Sumatra, Java, Madura, Borneo (except Sarawak in the north), the Celebes, the Moluccas, and about 30 smaller archipelagos, totaling 13,677 islands, of which about 6,000 are inhabited. Its neighbor to the north is Malaysia and to the east Papua New Guinea.

A backbone of mountain ranges extends throughout the main islands of the archipelago. Earthquakes are frequent, and there are many active volcanoes.

Government. The President is elected by the People's Consultative Assembly, whose 920 members include the functioning legislative arm, the 500-member House of Representatives. Meeting at least once every five years, the Assembly has broad policy functions. The House, 100 of whose members are appointed by the President, meets at least once annually. General Suharto was elected unopposed to a fourth five-year term in 1983.

The major political parties are Sekber Golkar, 299 of 500 contested seats in the House; Islamic United Development Party, 63 seats; Democratic Party, 38 seats.

History. Indonesia is inhabited by Malayan and Papuan peoples ranging from the more advanced Javanese and Balinese to the more primitive Dyaks of Borneo. Invasions from China and India contributed Chinese and Indian admixtures.

During the first few centuries of the Christian era, most of the islands came under the influence of Hindu priests and traders, who spread their culture and religion. Moslem invasions began in the 13th century, and most of the area was Moslem by the 15th. Portuguese traders arrived early in the 16th century but were ousted by the Dutch about 1595. After Napoleon subjugated the Netherlands homeland in 1811, the British seized the islands but returned them to the Dutch in 1816. In 1922 the islands were made an integral part of the Netherlands kingdom.

During World War II, Indonesia was under Japanese military occupation with nominal native self-government. When the Japanese surrendered to the Allies, President Sukarno and Mohammed Hatta, his Vice President, proclaimed Indonesian independence from the Dutch on Aug. 17, 1945. Allied troops—mostly British Indian troops—fought the nationalists until the arrival of Dutch troops. In November 1946, the Dutch and the Indonesians reached a draft agreement contemplating formation of a Netherlands-Indonesian Union, but differences in interpretation resulted in more fighting between Dutch and Indonesian forces.

On Nov. 2, 1949, Dutch and Indonesian leaders agreed upon the terms of union. The transfer of sovereignty took place at Amsterdam on Dec. 27, 1949. In February 1956 Indonesia abrogated the Union with the Netherlands and in August 1956 repudiated its debt to the Netherlands. In 1963, Netherlands New Guinea was transferred to Indonesia and renamed West Irian. In 1973 it became Irian Jaya.

Hatta and Sukarno, the co-fathers of Indonesian independence, split after it was achieved over Sukarno's concept of "guided democracy." Under Sukarno, the country's leading political figure for almost a half century, the Indonesian Communist Party gradually gained increasing influence.

After an attempted coup was put down by General Suharto, the army chief of staff, and officers loyal to him, thousands of Communist suspects were sought out and killed all over the country. Suharto took over the reins of government, gradually eased Sukarno out of office, and took full power in 1967. Under President Suharto, Indonesia has been strongly anticommunist. It also has been politically stable and has made progress in economic development.

Indonesia invaded the former Portuguese half of the island of Timor in 1975, and annexed the territory in 1976. On a visit to Jakarta in July 1984, Secretary of State George P. Shultz expressed concern about reports of human rights abuses being carried out by Indonesian forces in East Timor. More than 100,000 Timorese, a sixth of the mostly Catholic population, were reported to have died from famine, disease, and fighting since the annexation.

IRAN

Islamic Republic of Iran

President: Hojatolislam Sayed Ali Khamenei (1981)
Prime Minister: Mir Hussein Moussavi (1981)
Area: 636,293 sq mi. (1,648,000 sq km)
Population (est. mid-1987): 50,400,000 (average annual growth rate: 3.2%) (Iranian, Kurdish)
Density per square mile: 79.2
Capital: Teheran
Largest cities (est. 1986): Teheran, 6,037,658; Isfahan, 1,422,308; Mashed, 2,038,388; Tabriz, 1,566,932
Monetary unit: Rial
Languages: Farsi (Persian), Kurdish, Arabic
Religions: Shi'ite Moslem, 93%; Sunni Moslem, 5%
Literacy rate: 48%
Economic summary: Gross national product (1984): $80.4 billion. Per capita income (1982): $1,621. Land used for agriculture: 12%; Labor force: 33%; principal products: wheat, barley, rice, sugar beets, cotton, dates, raisins, sheep, goats. Labor force in industry: 21%; major products: crude and refined oil, textiles, cement, processed foods, steel and copper fabrication. Natural resources: oil, gas, iron, copper. Exports: petroleum. Imports: machinery, military supplies, foodstuffs, pharmaceuticals. Major trading partners: Japan, West Germany, U.K., Italy, U.S.S.R., Switzerland, Austria

Geography. Iran, a Middle Eastern country south of the Caspian Sea and north of the Persian Gulf, is three times the size of Arizona. It shares borders with Iraq, Turkey, the U.S.S.R., Afghanistan, and Pakistan.

In general, the country is a plateau averaging 4,000 feet (1,219 m) in elevation. There are also maritime lowlands along the Persian Gulf and the Caspian Sea. The Elburz Mountains in the north rise to 18,603 feet (5,670 m) at Mt. Damavend. From northwest to southeast, the country is crossed by a desert 800 miles (1,287 km) long.

Government. The Pahlavi dynasty was overthrown on Feb. 11, 1979, by followers of the Ayatollah Ruhollah Khomeini. After a referendum endorsed the establishment of a republic, Khomeini drafted a Constitution calling for a President to be popularly elected every four years, an appointed Prime Minister, and a unicameral National Consultative Assembly, popularly elected every four years.

Khomeini also instituted a Revolutionary Council to insure the adherence to Islamic principles in all phases of Iranian life. The Council formally handed over its powers to the Assembly after the organization of the legislature in July 1980, but continued to exercise power behind the scenes.

History. Oil-rich Iran was called Persia before 1935. Its key location blocks the lower land gate to Asia and also stands in the way of traditional Russian ambitions for access to the Indian Ocean. After periods of Assyrian, Median, and Achaemenidian rule, Persia became a powerful empire under Cyrus the Great, reaching from the Indus to the Nile at its zenith in 525 B.C. It fell to Alexander in 331–30 B.C. and to the Seleucids in 312–02 B.C., and a native Persian regime arose about 130 B.C. Another Persian regime arose about A.D. 224, but it fell to the Arabs in 637. In the 12th century, the Mongols took their turn ruling Persia, and in the early part of the 18th century, the Turks occupied the country.

An Anglo-Russian convention of 1907 divided Persia into two spheres of influence. British attempts to impose a protectorate over the entire country were defeated in 1919. Two years later, Gen. Reza Pahlavi seized the government and was elected hereditary Shah in 1925. Subsequently he did much to modernize the country and abolished all foreign extraterritorial rights.

Increased pro-Axis activity led to Anglo-Russian occupation of Iran in 1941 and deposition of the Shah in favor of his son, Mohammed Reza Pahlavi.

Ali Razmara became premier in 1950 and pledged to restore efficient and honest government, but he was assassinated after less than nine months in office and Mohammed Mossadegh took over. Mossadegh was ousted in August 1953, by Fazollah Zahedi, whom the Shah had named premier.

Opposition to the Shah spread, despite the imposition of martial law in September 1978, and massive demonstrations demanded the return of the exiled Ayatollah Ruhollah Khomeini. Riots and strikes continued despite the appointment of an opposition leader, Shahpur Bakhtiar, as premier on Dec. 29. The Shah and his family left Iran on Jan.

16, 1979, for a "vacation," leaving power in the hands of a regency council.

Khomeini returned on Feb. 1 to a nation in turmoil as military units loyal to the Shah continued to support Bakhtiar and clashed with revolutionaries. Khomeini appointed Mehdi Bazargan as premier of the provisional government and in two days of fighting, revolutionaries forced the military to capitulate on Feb. 11.

The new government began a program of nationalization of insurance companies, banks, and industries both locally and foreign-owned. Oil production fell amid the political confusion.

Khomeini, ignoring opposition, proceeded with his plans for revitalizing Islamic traditions. He urged women to return to the veil, or chador; banned alcohol and mixed bathing, and prohibited music from radio and television broadcasting, declaring it to be "no different from opium."

Revolutionary militants invaded the U.S. Embassy in Teheran on Nov. 4, 1979, seized staff members as hostages, and precipitated an international crisis.

Khomeini refused all appeals, even a unanimous vote by the U.N. Security Council demanding immediate release of the hostages.

Iranian hostility toward Washington was reinforced by the Carter administration's economic boycott and deportation order against Iranian students in the U.S., the break in diplomatic relations and ultimately an aborted U.S. raid in April aimed at rescuing the hostages.

Even the death of the deposed Shah Mohammed Reza Pahlavi on July 17 had no effect. As the first anniversary of the embassy seizure neared, Khomeini and his followers insisted on their original conditions: guarantee by the U.S. not to interfere in Iran's affairs, cancellation of U.S. damage claims against Iran, release of $8 billion in frozen Iranian assets, an apology, and the return of the assets held by the former imperial family.

These conditions were largely met in an agreement signed by Deputy Secretary of State Warren Christopher on Jan. 19 and the 52 American hostages were released the following day, ending 444 days in captivity.

From the release of the hostages onward, President Bani-Sadr and the conservative clerics of the dominant Islamic Republican Party clashed with growing frequency. He was stripped of his command of the armed forces by Khomeini on June 6 and ousted as President on June 22. On July 24, Prime Minister Mohammed Ali Rajai was elected overwhelmingly to the Presidency.

Rajai and Prime Minister Mohammed Javad Bahonar were killed on Aug. 30 by a bomb in Bahonar's office.

Hojatolislam Mohammed Ali Khamenei, a clergyman, leader of the Islamic Republican Party and spokesman for Khomeini, was elected President on Oct. 2, 1981.

The sporadic war with Iraq regained momentum in 1982, as Iran launched an offensive in March and regained much of the border area occupied by Iraq in late 1980. Khomeini rejected Iraqi bids for a truce, insisting that Iraq's President Saddam Hussein must leave office first.

Iran continued to be at war with Iraq well into 1986. Although Iraq expressed its willingness to cease fighting, Iran stated that it would not stop the war until Iraq agreed to make payment for war damages to Iran, and punish the Iraqi government leaders involved in the conflict. The fighting, spread into the Persian Gulf in 1984, with Iraq using French-made Exocet air-to-surface missiles to attack tankers loading at Iran's Kharg Island, and Iran striking back at tankers calling at Saudi Arabia and the smaller, oil-rich Arab Gulf states.

IRAQ

Republic of Iraq
President: Saddam Hussein (1979)
Area: 169,284 sq mi. (438,446 sq km)
Population (est. mid-1987): 17,000,000 (average annual growth rate: 3.3%) (Arab, 77%; Kurds, 19%)
Density per square mile: 100.4
Capital: Baghdad
Largest cities (est. 1985): Baghdad, 3,500,000; Basra, 616,700; Mosul, 570,926
Monetary unit: Iraqi dinar
Languages: Arabic and Kurdish
Religions: Islam, 96%; Christian, 4%
National name: Al Jumhouriya Al Iraqia
Literacy rate: about 50%
Economic summary: Gross national product (1984 est.): $27 billion. Average annual growth rate (1970–79): 9.3%. Per capita income (1981): $2,300. Land used for agriculture, 13%; labor force, 40%; principal products: livestock, wheat, barley, sugarcane, rice. Labor force in industry: 27%; major products: petroleum, cement, textiles. Natural resources: oil, natural gas, gypsum, sulfur. Exports: petroleum, foodstuffs. Imports: manufactured goods, food grains, machinery, chemicals, livestock. Major trading partners: France, Italy, Japan, West Germany, Brazil, U.K., U.S., Pakistan

Geography. Iraq, a triangle of mountains, desert, and fertile river valley, is bounded on the east by Iran, on the north by Turkey, the west by Syria and Jordan, and the south by Saudi Arabia and Kuwait. It is twice the size of Idaho.

The country has arid desertland west of the Euphrates, a broad central valley between the Euphrates and Tigris, and mountains in the northeast. The fertile lower valley is formed by the delta of the two rivers, which join about 120 miles (193 km) from the head of the Persian Gulf. The gulf coastline is 26 miles (42 km) long. The only port for seagoing vessels is Basra, which is on the Shatt-al-Arab River near the head of the Persian Gulf.

Government. Since the coup d'etat of July 1968, Iraq has been governed by the Arab Ba'ath Socialist Party through a Council of Command of the Revolution headed by the President. There is also a Council of Ministers headed by the President.

History. From earliest times Iraq was known as Mesopotamia—the land between the rivers—for it embraces a large part of the alluvial plains of the Tigris and Euphrates.

An advanced civilization existed by 4000 B.C. Sometime after 2000 B.C. the land became the center of the ancient Babylonian and Assyrian empires. It was conquered by Cyrus the Great of Persia in 538 B.C., and by Alexander in 331 B.C. After an Arab conquest in A.D. 637–40, Baghdad became capital of the ruling caliphate. The country was cruelly pillaged by the Mongols in 1258, and during the 16th, 17th, and 18th centuries was the object of repeated Turkish-Persian competition.

Nominal Turkish suzerainty imposed in 1638

was replaced by direct Turkish rule in 1831. In World War I, an Anglo-Indian force occupied most of the country, and Britain was given a mandate over the area in 1920. The British recognized Iraq as a kingdom in 1922 and terminated the mandate in 1932 when Iraq was admitted to the League of Nations. In World War II, Iraq generally adhered to its 1930 treaty of alliance with Britain, but in 1941, British troops were compelled to put down a pro-Axis revolt led by Premier Rashid Ali.

Iraq became a charter member of the Arab League in 1945, and Iraqi troops took part in the Arab invasion of Palestine in 1948.

Faisal II, born on May 2, 1935, succeeded his father, Ghazi I, who was killed in an automobile accident on April 4, 1939. Faisal and his uncle, Crown Prince Abdul-Ilah, were assassinated in August 1958 in a swift revolutionary coup that brought to power a military junta headed by Abdul Karem Kassim. Kassim, in turn, was overthrown and killed in a coup staged March 8, 1963, by the Ba'ath Socialist Party.

Abdel Salam Arif, a leader in the 1958 coup, staged another coup in November 1963, driving the Ba'ath members of the revolutionary council from power. He adopted a new constitution in 1964. In 1966, he, two Cabinet members, and other supporters died in a helicopter crash. His brother, Gen. Abdel Rahman Arif, assumed the presidency, crushed the opposition, and won an indefinite extension of his term in 1967. His regime was ousted in July 1968 by a junta led by Maj. Gen. Ahmed Hassan al-Bakr.

A long-standing dispute over control of the Shatt al-Arab waterway between Iraq and Iran broke into full-scale war on Sept. 20, 1980. Iraqi planes attacked Iranian airfields and the Abadan refinery, and Iraqi ground forces moved into Iran.

Despite the smaller size of its armed forces, Iraq took and held the initiative by seizing Abadan and Khurramshahr together with substantial Iranian territory by December and beating back Iranian counterattacks in January. Peace efforts by the Islamic nations, the nonaligned, and the United Nations failed as 1981 wore on and the war stagnated.

In 1982, the Iraqis fell back to their own country and dug themselves in behind sandbagged defensive fortifications. With massive firepower, they turned back wave after wave of attacking Iranian troops and revolutionary guards, many of them in their teens. From the beginning of the war in September 1980 to September 1984, foreign military analysts estimated that more than 100,000 Iranians and perhaps 50,000 Iraqis had been killed.

The Iraqis clearly wanted to end the war, but the Iranians refused. In March of 1985, Iraq apparently won the largest battle of the long war, crushing a major Iranian offensive in the southern marshes in a week of heavy fighting that killed an estimated 30,000 Iranians and perhaps 10,000 Iraqis.

In February 1986, Iranian forces gained on two fronts; on the Fao peninsula in the south and in the northern mountains, but the war continued a stalemate.

IRELAND

President: Patrick J. Hiliery (1976)
Taoiseach (Prime Minister): Charles J. Haughey (1987)
Area: 26,600 sq mi. (68,394 sq km)
Population (est. mid-1987): 3,500,000 (average annual growth rate, 0.8%)
Density per square mile: 131.6
Capital: Dublin
Largest cities (est. 1982): Dublin, 550,000; Cork, 140,000; Limerick, 60,000
Monetary unit: Irish pound (punt)
Languages: Irish, English
Religions: Roman Catholic, 94%; Protestant, 5%
National name: Eire
Literacy rate: 99%
Economic summary: Gross national product (1984): $16.0 billion. Average annual growth rate (1985–87): 0.2%; Per capita Income (1984): $4,440. Land used for agriculture, 70%; labor force in agriculture and fishing: 17%; principal products: cattle and dairy products, pigs, poultry and eggs, sheep and wool, horses, barley, sugar beets. Labor force in industry: 30%; major products: processed foods, metals and engineering, electronics, beverages and tobacco, chemicals. Natural resources: zinc, lead, natural gas, barite, copper, gypsum, limestone, dolomite, peat, silver. Exports: livestock, dairy products, machinery, chemicals, processed foods, manufactured goods, raw materials and minerals. Imports: grains, petroleum products, machinery, chemicals, textile yarn, cereals. Major trading partners: U.K., Western European countries, U.S., Canada.

Geography. Ireland is situated in the Atlantic Ocean and separated from Britain by the Irish Sea. Half the size of Arkansas, it occupies the entire island except for the six northern counties of Ulster.

Ireland resembles a basin—a central plain rimmed with mountains, except in the Dublin region. The mountains are low, with the highest peak, Carrantuohill in County Kerry, rising to 3,415 feet (1,041 m).

The principal river is the Shannon, which begins in the north central area, flows south and southwest for about 240 miles (386 km), and empties into the Atlantic.

Government. Ireland is a parliamentary democracy. The National Parliament (Oireachtas) consists of the president and two Houses, the House of Representatives (Dáil Éireann) and the Senate (Seanad Éireann), whose members serve for a maximum term of five years. The House of Representatives has 166 members elected by proportional representation; the Senate has 60 members of whom 11 are nominated by the prime minister, 6 by the universities and the remaining 43 from five vocational panels. The prime minister (Taoiseach), who is the head of government, is appointed by the president on the nomination of the House of Representatives, to which he is responsible.

The major political parties are Fianna Fáil (81 of 166 seats in the Dáil), led by Prime Minister Charles J. Haughey; Fine Gael (51 seats), led by Alan Dukes; Progressive Democrats (14 seats), led by Desmond O'Malley; Labor Party (12 seats), led by Dick Spring; Workers Party (4 seats) led by Thomas MacGiolla; Independents (3 seats). The Fianna Fáil party forms the government.

History. In the Stone and Bronze Ages, Ireland was inhabited by Picts in the north and a people called the Erainn in the south, the same stock, apparently, as in all the isles before the Anglo-Saxon invasion of Britain. About the fourth century B.C., tall, red-haired Celts arrived from Gaul or Galicia. They subdued and assimilated the inhabitants and established a Gaelic civilization.

By the beginning of the Christian Era, Ireland was divided into five kingdoms—Ulster, Connacht, Leinster, Meath, and Munster. St. Patrick introduced Christianity in 432 and the country developed into a center of Gaelic and Latin learning. Irish monasteries, the equivalent of universities, attracted intellectuals as well as the pious and sent out missionaries to many parts of Europe and, some believe, to North America.

Norse depredations along the coasts, starting in 795, ended in 1014 with Norse defeat at the Battle of Clontarf by forces under Brian Boru. In the 12th century, the Pope gave all Ireland to the English Crown as a papal fief. In 1171, Henry II of England was acknowledged "Lord of Ireland," but local sectional rule continued for centuries, and English control over the whole island was not reasonably absolute until the 17th century. By the Act of Union (1801), England and Ireland became the "United Kingdom of Great Britain and Ireland."

A steady decline in the Irish economy followed in the next decades. The population had reached 8.25 million when the great potato famine of 1846–48 took many lives and drove millions to emigrate to America. By 1921 it was down to 4.3 million.

In the meantime, anti-British agitation continued along with demands for Irish home rule. The advent of World War I delayed the institution of home rule and resulted in the Easter Rebellion in Dublin (April 24–29, 1916), in which Irish nationalists unsuccessfully attempted to throw off British rule. Guerrilla warfare against British forces followed proclamation of a republic by the rebels in 1919.

The Irish Free State was established as a dominion on Dec. 6, 1922, with the six northern counties as part of the United Kingdom. Ireland was neutral in World War II.

In 1948, Éamon de Valera, American-born leader of the Sinn Fein, who had won establishment of the Free State in 1921 in negotiations with Britain's David Lloyd George, was defeated by John A. Costello, who demanded final independence from Britain. The Republic of Ireland was proclaimed on April 18, 1949. It withdrew from the Commonwealth but in 1955 entered the United Nations. Since 1949 the prime concern of successive governments has been economic development.

Through the 1960s, two antagonistic currents dominated Irish politics. One sought to bind the wounds of the rebellion and civil war. The other was the effort of the outlawed extremist Irish Republican Army to bring Northern Ireland into the republic. Despite public sympathy for unification of Ireland, the Dublin government dealt rigorously with IRA guerrillas caught inside the republic's borders.

In the elections of June 11, 1981, Garret M. D. FitzGerald, leader of the Fine Gael, was elected Prime Minister by 81 to 78 with the support of 15 Labor Party members and one independent Socialist added to his own party's 65 members. Other independents abstained, among them Kieran Doherty, a prisoner in Northern Ireland's Maze Prison, who with another prisoner had won election to the Southern Parliament (the Republic's Constitution extends citizenship to anyone born in Northern Ireland). Doherty died after a hunger strike on Aug. 3, one of nine Maze prisoners to do so.

FitzGerald resigned Jan. 27, 1982, after his presentation of an austerity budget aroused the opposition of independents who had backed him previously. Former Prime Minister Haughey was sworn in on March 9 and presented a budget with nearly a $1 billion deficit, with additional public spending aimed at stimulating the lagging economy. FitzGerald was re-elected Prime Minister on Dec. 14, 1982 but was unable to solve the problem of unemployment and the elections of 1987 brought Haughey back into power on March 10.

ISRAEL

State of Israel
President: Chaim Herzog (1983)
Prime Minister: Yitzhak Shamir (1986)
Area: 7,992 sq mi. (20,699 sq km)
Population (est. mid-1987): 4,400,000[1] (average annual growth rate: 1.7%)
Density per square mile: 550.6
Capital: Jerusalem[2]
Largest cities (est. 1983): Jerusalem, 431,800[3]; Tel Aviv, 330,400; Haifa, 227,900; Holon, 133,900; Bat Yam, 129,700
Monetary unit: Shekel
Languages: Hebrew, Arabic, English
Religions: Jewish, 83%, Islam 13.1%, Christian 2.3%, Druze and others, 1.6%
National name: Medinat Yisra'el
Literacy rate: Jews 94%, non-Jews 83.2%
Economic summary: Gross national product (1985): $25.9 billion. Annual growth rate (1985): 2.0%. Per capita income (1984): $6,093. Land used for agriculture: 22%; labor force: 6%; principal products: citrus and other fruits, vegetables, beef, dairy and poultry products. Labor force in industry: 23%; major products: processed foods, cut diamonds, clothing and textiles, chemicals, metal products, transport and electrical equipment, plastics. Natural resources: sulfur, rock salt, phosphates, potash, bromine. Exports: polished diamonds, citrus and other fruits, clothing and textiles, processed foods, high technology products, computerized medical equipment, military hardware, fertilizer and chemical products. Imports: rough diamonds, chemicals, oil, machinery, iron and steel, cereals, textiles, vehicles, ships. Major trading partners: U.S., West Germany, U.K., Switzerland, France, Italy.

1. Excludes West Bank, Gaza Strip, East Jerusalem. 2. Not recognized by U.S. which recognizes Tel Aviv. 3. Includes East Jerusalem.

Geography. Israel, slightly smaller than Massachusetts, lies at the eastern end of the Mediterranean Sea. It is bordered by Egypt on the west, Syria and Jordan on the east, and Lebanon on the north.

Northern Israel is largely a plateau traversed from north to south by mountains and broken by great depressions, also running from north to south.

The maritime plain of Israel is remarkably fertile. The southern Negev region, which comprises almost half the total area, is largely a wide desert steppe area. The National Water Project irrigation scheme is now transforming it into fertile land. The Jordan, the only important river, flows from the north through Lake Hule (Waters of Merom) and Lake Kinneret (Sea of Galilee or Sea of Tiberias), finally entering the Dead Sea, 1,290 feet (393 m) below sea level. This "sea," which is actually a salt lake (394 sq mi.; 1,020 sq km), has no outlet, its water balance being maintained by evaporation.

Government. Israel, which does not have a written constitution, has a republican form of government headed by a president elected for a five-year term by the Knesset. He may serve no more than two terms. The Knesset has 120 members elected by universal suffrage under proportional representation for four years. The government is administered by the Cabinet, which is headed by the prime minister.

The Knesset decided in June 1950 that Israel would acquire a constitution gradually through the years by the enactment of fundamental laws. Israel grants automatic citizenship to every Jew who desires to settle within its borders, subject to control of the Knesset.

The major political parties are Labor Alignment (46 of 120 seats in the Knesset), led by Shimon Peres; Likud (41 seats), led by Prime Minister Yitzhak Shamir; Tehiya-Tzomet (5 seats); National Religious Party (5 seats); Democratic Front for Peace and Equality (Communist) (4 seats); Sephardi Torah Guardians (4 seats); Shinui (3 seats); Movement for Citizens Rights and Peace (4 seats); Yahad (3 seats); other parties (9 seats).

History. Palestine, cradle of two great religions and homeland of the modern state of Israel, was known to the ancient Hebrews as the "Land of Canaan." Palestine's name derives from the Philistines, a people who occupied the southern coastal part of the country in the 12th century B.C.

A Hebrew kingdom established in 1000 B.C. was later split into the kingdoms of Judah and Israel; they were subsequently invaded by Assyrians, Babylonians, Egyptians, Persians, Macedonians, Romans, and Byzantines. The Arabs took Palestine from the Byzantine Empire A.D. 634–40. With the exception of a Frankish Crusader kingdom from 1099 to 1187, Palestine remained under Moslem rule until the 20th century (Turkish rule from 1516), when British forces under Gen. Sir Edmund Allenby defeated the Turks and captured Jerusalem Dec. 9, 1917. The League of Nations granted Britain a mandate to govern Palestine, effective in 1923.

Jewish colonies—Jews from Russia established one as early as 1882—multiplied after Theodor Herzl's 1897 call for a Jewish state. The Zionist movement received official approval with the publication of a letter Nov. 2, 1917, from Arthur Balfour, British Foreign Secretary, to Lord Rothschild, a British Jewish leader. Balfour promised support for the establishment of a Jewish homeland in Palestine on the understanding that the civil and religious rights of non-Jewish Palestinians would be safeguarded.

A 1937 British proposal called for an Arab and a Jewish state separated by a mandated area incorporating Jerusalem and Nazareth. Arabs opposed this, demanding a single state with minority rights for Jews, and a 1939 British White Paper retreated, offering instead a single state with further Jewish immigration to be limited to 75,000. Although the White Paper satisfied neither side, further discussion ended on the outbreak of World War II, when the Jewish population stood at nearly 500,000, or 30% of the total. Illegal and legal immigration during the war brought the Jewish population to 678,000 in 1946, compared with 1,269,000 Arabs. Unable to reach a compromise, Britain turned the problem over to the United Nations in 1947, which on November 29 voted for partition—despite strong Arab opposition.

Britain did not help implement the U.N. decision and withdrew on expiration of its mandate May 14, 1948. Zionists had already seized control of areas designated as Jewish, and, on the day of British departure, the Jewish National Council proclaimed the State of Israel.

U.S. recognition came within hours. The next day, Jordanian and Egyptian forces invaded the new nation. At the cease-fire Jan. 7, 1949, Israel increased its original territory by 50%, taking western Galilee, a broad corridor through central Palestine to Jerusalem, and part of modern Jerusalem. (In April 1950, Jordan annexed areas of eastern and central Palestine that had been designated for an Arab state, together with the old city of Jerusalem).

Chaim Weizmann and David Ben-Gurion became Israel's first president and prime minister. The new government was admitted to the U.N. May 11, 1949.

The next clash with Arab neighbors came when Egypt nationalized the Suez Canal in 1956 and barred Israeli shipping. Coordinating with an Anglo-French force, Israeli troops seized the Gaza Strip and drove through the Sinai to the east bank of the Suez Canal, but withdrew under U.S. and U.N. pressure. In 1967, Israel threatened retaliation against Syrian border raids, and Syria asked Egyptian aid. Egypt demanded the removal of U.N. peace-keeping forces from Suez, staged a national mobilization, closed the Gulf of Aqaba, and moved troops into the Sinai. Starting with simultaneous air attacks against Syrian, Jordanian, and Egyptian air bases on June 5, Israel during a six-day war totally defeated its Arab enemies. Expanding its territory by 200%, Israel at the cease-fire held the Golan Heights, the West Bank of the Jordan River, the Old City, and all of the Sinai and the east bank of the Suez Canal.

Israel insisted that Jerusalem remain a unified city and that peace negotiations be conducted directly, something the Arab states had refused to do because it would constitute a recognition of their Jewish neighbor.

Egypt's President Gamal Abdel Nasser renounced the 1967 cease-fire in 1969 and began a "war of attrition" against Israel, firing Soviet artillery at Israeli forces on the east bank of the canal. Nasser died of a heart attack on Sept. 28, 1970, and was succeeded by Anwar el-Sadat.

In the face of Israeli reluctance even to discuss the return of occupied territories, the fourth Mideast war erupted Oct. 6, 1973, with a surprise Egyptian and Syrian assault on the Jewish high holy day of Yom Kippur. Initial Arab gains were reversed when a cease-fire took effect two weeks later, but Israel suffered heavy losses in manpower.

U.S. Secretary of State Henry A. Kissinger arranged a disengagement of forces on both the Egyptian and Syrian fronts. Geneva talks, aimed at a lasting peace, foundered, however, when Israel balked at inclusion of the Palestine Liberation Organization, a group increasingly active in terrorism directed against Israel.

A second-stage Sinai withdrawal signed by Israel and Egypt in September 1975 required Israel to give up the strategic Mitla and Gidi passes and to return the captured Abu Rudeis oil fields. Egypt guaranteed passage of Israeli cargoes through the reopened Suez Canal, and both sides renounced force in the settlement of disputes. Two hundred U.S. civilian technicians were stationed in a widened U.N. buffer zone to monitor and warn either side of truce violations.

A dramatic breakthrough in the tortuous history of Mideast peace efforts occurred Nov. 9, 1977, when Egypt's President Sadat declared his willingness to go anywhere to talk peace. Prime Minister Menachem Begin on Nov. 15 extended an invitation to the Egyptian leader to address the Knesset. Sadat's arrival in Israel four days later raised worldwide hopes. But optimism ebbed even before Begin was invited to Ismailia by Sadat, December 25–26.

An Israeli peace plan unveiled by Begin on his return, and approved by the Knesset, offered to end military administration in the West Bank and the Gaza Strip, with a degree of Arab self-rule but no relinquishment of sovereignty by Israel. Sadat severed talks on Jan. 18 and, despite U.S. condemnation, Begin approved new West Bank settlements by Israelis.

A PLO raid on Israel's coast on March 11, 1978, killed 30 civilians and provoked a full-scale invasion of southern Lebanon by Israel three days later to attack PLO bases. Israel withdrew three months later, turning over strongpoints to Lebanese Christian militia wherever possible rather than to a U.N. peacekeeping force installed in the area.

On March 14, 1979, after a visit by Carter, the Knesset approved a final peace treaty, and 12 days later Begin and Sadat signed the document, together with Carter, in a White House ceremony. Israel began its withdrawal from the Sinai on May 25 by handing over the coastal town of El Arish and the two countries opened their border on May 29.

One of the most difficult periods in Israel's history began with a confrontation with Syria over the placing by Syria of Soviet surface-to-air missiles in the Bekaa Valley of Lebanon in April 1981. President Reagan dispatched Philip C. Habib to prevent a clash. While Habib was seeking a settlement, Begin ordered a bombing raid against an Iraqi nuclear reactor on June 7, invoking the theory of preemptive self-defense because he said Iraq was planning to make nuclear weapons to attack Israel.

Although Israel withdrew its last settlers from the Sinai in April 1982 and agreed to a Sinai "peace patrol" composed of troops from four West European nations, the fragile peace engineered by Habib in Lebanon was shattered on June 9 by a massive Israeli assault on southern Lebanon. The attack was in retaliation for what Israel charged was a PLO attack that critically wounded the Israeli ambassador to London six days earlier.

Israeli armor swept through UNIFIL lines in southern Lebanon, destroyed PLO strongholds in Tyre and Sidon, and reached the suburbs of Beirut on June 10. As Israeli troops ringed Moslem East Beirut, where 5,000 PLO guerrillas were believed trapped, Habib sought to negotiate a safe exit for them. The Arab world loudly protested the entire action, estimated by Lebanon to have cost the lives of 10,000 civilians by mid-July.

A U.S.-mediated accord between Lebanon and Israel, signed on May 17, 1983, provided for Israeli withdrawal from Lebanon. Israeli withdrawal was conditioned on withdrawal of Syrian troops from the Bekaa Valley, however, and the Syrians refused to leave. Israel eventually withdrew its troops from the Beirut area, but kept them in southern Lebanon. Lebanon, under pressure from Syria, canceled the accord in March 1984.

Prime Minister Begin resigned on Sept. 15, 1983. On Oct. 10, Likud Party stalwart Yitzhak Shamir was elected Prime Minister.

After a close election, the two major parties worked out a carefully balanced power-sharing agreement and the Knesset, on Sept. 14, 1984 approved a national unity government including both the Labor Alignment and the Likud bloc. Under the terms, Labor leader Peres was to serve as Prime Minister for the first half of a 50-month term and Shamir, the Likud leader, was to be Deputy Prime Minister and Foreign Minister. For the second half of the term, the two men were to reverse roles.

By the anniversary of the invasion of Lebanon in June of 1985, Israel had withdrawn most—but not all—of its troops from the country. Israeli combat units left, but military advisers remained in a security zone along Israel's northern frontier. In addition to Israel's failure to meet its goals in Lebanon, several other developments during 1985 threatened the tenuous Labor-Likud coalition.

The Peres government decided in May to exchange 1,150 Palestinian prisoners—including terrorists—for three Israeli soldiers who had been held since the Lebanon war by the Popular Front for the Liberation of Palestine, and the subsequent pressure in June for Israel to release more than 700 detained Lebanese Shiites as demanded by Shiites who hijacked a TWA airliner and held 39 Americans hostage. Another development dividing Israelis was the verdict by a three-judge court on July 10 convicting three Jewish settlers of murder and 12 others of different violent crimes against Arabs.

In one hopeful development, the coalition government declared an economic emergency on July 1 and imposed sweeping austerity measures intended to break the country's 260% inflation. Key elements were an 18.8% devaluation of the shekel, price increases in such government-subsidized products as gasoline, dismissal of 9,000 government employees, government spending cuts and a wage and price freeze.

By the end of Peres' term in October 1986, the shekel had been revalued and stabilized and inflation was down to less than 20%.

Differences in the approach to take to peace talks started to strain the government in 1987.

ITALY

Italian Republic

President: Francesco Cossiga (1985)
Premier: Giovanni Goria (1987)
Area: 116,500 sq mi. (301,278 sq km)
Population (est. mid-1987): 57,400,000 (average annual growth rate: 0.1%)
Density per square mile: 492.7
Capital: Rome
Largest cities (1984): Rome, 2,826,733; Milan, 1,535,-722; Naples, 1,206,955; Turin, 1,049,997; Genoa, 738,099; Palermo, 716,149; Bologna, 442,307; Florence, 435,698; Catania, 377,707; Bari, 368,216.
Monetary unit: Lira
Language: Italian
Religion: Roman Catholic
National name: Repubblica Italiana
Literacy rate: 97%
Economic summary: Gross national product (1985): $408.1 billion. Average annual growth rate (1982–85): 1.1%. Per capita income (1985): $7,151. Land used for agriculture: 40%; labor force: 10%; principal products:

grapes, olives, citrus fruits, vegetables, wheat, corn. Labor force in industry: 30%; major products: machinery, autos, textiles, shoes, chemicals. Natural resources: fish, gas, marble. Exports: Engineering, chemicals, textiles, metals, shoes, food. Imports: engineering, chemicals, food, metals. Major trading partners: West Germany, France, United States, United Kingdom.

Geography. Italy is a long peninsula shaped like a boot bounded on the west by the Tyrrhenian Sea and on the east by the Adriatic. Slightly larger than Arizona, it has for neighbors France, Switzerland, Austria, and Yugoslavia.

Approximately 600 of Italy's 708 miles (1,139 km) of length are in the long peninsula that projects into the Mediterranean from the fertile basin of the Po River. The Apennine Mountains, branching off from the Alps between Nice and Genoa, form the peninsula's backbone, and rise to a maximum height of 9,560 feet (2,912 m) at the Gran Sasso d'Italia (Corno). The Alps form Italy's northern boundary.

Several islands form part of Italy. Sicily (9,926 sq mi.; 25,708 sq km) lies off the toe of the boot, across the Strait of Messina, with a steep and rockbound northern coast and gentler slopes to the sea in the west and south. Mount Etna, an active volcano, rises to 10,741 feet (3,274 m), and most of Sicily is more than 500 feet (3,274 m) in elevation. Sixty-two miles (100 km) southwest of Sicily lies Pantelleria (45 sq mi.; 117 sq km), and south of that are Lampedusa and Linosa. Sardinia (9,301 sq mi.; 24,090 sq km), which is just south of Corsica and about 125 miles (200 km) west of the mainland, is mountainous, stony, and unproductive.

Italy has many northern lakes, lying below the snow-covered peaks of the Alps. The largest are Garda (143 sq mi.; 370 sq km), Maggiore (83 sq mi.; 215 sq km), and Como (55 sq mi.; 142 sq km).

The Po, the principal river, flows from the Alps on Italy's western border and crosses the Lombard plain to the Adriatic.

Government. The president is elected for a term of seven years by Parliament in joint session with regional representatives. The president nominates the premier and, upon the premier's recommendations, the members of the Cabinet. Parliament is composed of two houses: a Senate with 315 elective members and a Chamber of Deputies of 630 members elected by the people for a five-year term.

The major political parties are: Christian Democratic Party (225 seats of 630 in Chamber of Deputies), led by Ciriaco De Mita; Communist Party (198 seats), led by Alessandro Natta; Socialist Party (73 seats), led by Premier Bettino Craxi; Italian Social Movement (42 seats), led by Giorgio Almirante; Republican Party (29 seats), led by Giovanni Spadolini; Social Democratic Party (23 seats), led by Franco Nicolazzi; Liberal Party (16 seats), led by Alfredo Biondi; Radical Party (11 seats), led by Giovanni Negri; Proletarian Democracy (7 seats), led by Mario Capanna; South Tyrol Popular Party (3 seats), led by Silvius Magnago; and other groups (3 seats).

History. Until A.D. 476, when the German Odoacer became head of the Roman Empire in the west, the history of Italy was largely the history of Rome. From A.D. 800 on, the Holy Roman Emperors, Popes, Normans, and Saracens all vied for control over various segments of the Italian peninsula. Numerous city states, such as Venice and Genoa, and many small principalities flourished in the late Middle Ages.

In 1713, after the War of the Spanish Succession, Milan, Naples, and Sardinia were handed over to Austria, which lost some of its Italian territories in 1735. After 1800, Italy was unified by Napoleon, who crowned himself King of Italy in 1805; but with the Congress of Vienna in 1815, Austria once again became the dominant power in Italy.

Austrian armies crushed Italian uprisings in 1820-1821, and 1831. In the 1830s Giuseppe Mazzini, brilliant liberal nationalist, organized the Risorgimento (Resurrection), which laid the foundation for Italian unity.

Disappointed Italian patriots looked to the House of Savoy for leadership. Count Camille di Cavour (1810–61), Premier of Sardinia in 1852 and the architect of a united Italy, joined England and France in the Crimean War (1853–56), and in 1859, helped France in a war against Austria, thereby obtaining Lombardy. By plebiscite in 1860, Modena, Parma, Tuscany, and the Romagna voted to join Sardinia. In 1860, Giuseppe Garibaldi conquered Sicily and Naples and turned them over to Sardinia. Victor Emmanuel II, King of Sardinia, was proclaimed King of Italy in 1861.

Allied with Germany and Austria-Hungary in the Triple Alliance of 1882, Italy declared its neutrality upon the outbreak of World War I on the ground that Germany had embarked upon an offensive war. In 1915, Italy entered the war on the side of the Allies.

Benito (Il Duce) Mussolini, a former Socialist, organized discontented Italians in 1919 into the Fascist Party to "rescue Italy from Bolshevism." He led his Black Shirts in a march on Rome and, on Oct. 28, 1922, became premier. He transformed Italy into a dictatorship, embarking on an expansionist foreign policy with the invasion and annexation of Ethiopia in 1935 and allying himself with Adolf Hitler in the Rome-Berlin Axis in 1936. He was executed by Partisans on April 28, 1945 at Dongo on Lake Como.

Following the overthrow of Mussolini's dictatorship and the armistice with the Allies (Sept. 3, 1943), Italy joined the war against Germany as a co-belligerent. King Victor Emmanuel III abdicated May 9, 1946, and left the country after having installed his son as King Humbert II. A plebiscite rejected monarchy, however, and on June 13, King Humbert followed his father into exile.

The peace treaty of Sept. 15, 1947, required Italian renunciation of all claims in Ethiopia and Greece and the cession of the Dodecanese to Greece and of five small Alpine areas to France. Much of the Istrian Peninsula, including Fiume and Pola, went to Yugoslavia.

The Trieste area west of the new Yugoslav territory was made a free territory (until 1954, when the city and a 90-square-mile zone were transferred to Italy and the rest to Yugoslavia).

Scandal brought the long reign of the Christian Democrats to an end when Italy's 40th premier since World War II, Arnaldo Forlani, was forced to resign in the wake of disclosure that many high-ranking Christian Democrats and civil servants belonged to a secret Masonic lodge known as "P-2."

When the Socialists deserted the coalition, Forlani was forced to resign on May 26, 1981, leaving to Giovanni Spadolini of the small Republican Party the task of forming a new government. He was succeeded by Amintore Fanfani, a Christian Democrat, the following year. Bettino Craxi, a Socialist, became Premier in 1983.

Craxi was forced to resign on June 27, 1986 following the loss of a key secret-ballot vote in Parliament.

After a month of political wrangling, Craxi was able to form a new government on condition that his term end in March 1987.

Disputes over who Craxi's successor would be led to general elections in June 1987 in which the Socialists and the Christian Democrats gained at the expense of the Communists and the smaller parties. Giovanni Goria, a Christian Democrat, became the new Premier.

IVORY COAST

Republic of Côte d'Ivoire
President: Félix Houphouët-Boigny (1960)
Area: 124,502 sq mi. (322,462 sq km)
Population (est. mid-1987): 10,800,000 (average annual growth rate: 3.0%)
Density per square mile: 84.3
Capital: Yamoussoukro[1]
Monetary unit: Franc CFA
Ethnic groups: Bete, Senufo, Baule, Anui
Languages: French and African languages (Diaula esp.)
Religions: folk beliefs, 44%; Christian, 32%; Islam, 24%
National name: République de la Côte d'Ivoire
Literacy rate: 35%
Economic summary: Gross national product (1983): $6.7 billion. Annual growth rate (1982): 1.8%. Per capita income (1983): $720. Labor force in agriculture: 79%; principal products: coffee, cocoa, timber, sugar, corn, cotton. Major industrial products: food, cement. Natural resources: diamonds, iron ore. Exports: coffee, cocoa, tropical woods. Imports: raw materials, consumer goods, fuels. Major trading partners: France, U.S., Western European countries, Nigeria.

1. Not recognized by U.S. which recognizes Abidjan.

Geography. The Ivory Coast, in western Africa on the Gulf of Guinea, is a little larger than New Mexico. Its neighbors are Liberia, Guinea, Mali, Burkina Faso, and Ghana.

The country consists of a coastal strip in the south, dense forests in the interior, and savannas in the north. Rainfall is heavy, especially along the coast.

Government. The government is headed by a President who is elected every five years by popular vote, together with a National Assembly of 175 members.

The Parti Démocratique de la Côte d'Ivoire, a member of the Rassemblement Démocratique Africain, is the only political party.

History. The Ivory Coast attracted both French and Portuguese merchants in the 15th century. French traders set up establishments early in the 19th century, and in 1842, the French obtained territorial concessions from local tribes, gradually extending their influence along the coast and inland. The area was organized as a territory in 1893, became an autonomous republic in the French Union after World War II, and achieved independence on Aug. 7, 1960.

The Ivory Coast formed a customs union in 1959 with Dahomey (Benin), Niger, and Burkina Faso. The country is one of the most prosperous and stable in West Africa.

JAMAICA

Sovereign: Queen Elizabeth II
Governor-General: Sir Florizel Glasspole (1973)
Prime Minister: Edward P. G. Seaga (1980)
Area: 4,411 sq mi. (11,424 sq km)
Population (est. mid-1987): 2,500,000 (average annual growth rate: 2.0%)
Density per square mile: 566.8
Capital and largest city (est. 1982): Kingston, 104,000
Monetary unit: Jamaican dollar
Language: English
Religions: Anglican, Baptist, Roman Catholic
Member of Commonwealth of Nations
Literacy rate: 76%
Economic summary: Gross national product (1984): $2.0 billion. Average annual growth rate (1985): –1.9%. Per capita income (1984): $1,090. Land used for agriculture: 25%; labor force: 33% (includes fishing and mining); principal products: sugar cane, citrus fruits, bananas, spices, coconuts, coffee, cocoa. Labor force in industry: 13%; major products: bauxite, textiles, processed foods, light manufactures. Natural resources: bauxite, gypsum. Exports: alumina, bauxite, sugar, clothing, citrus fruits, rum, cocoa. Imports: fuels, machinery, transport and electrical equipment, food, fertilizer. Major trading partners: U.S., U.K., Venezuela.

Geography. Jamaica is an island in the West Indies, 90 miles (145 km) south of Cuba and 100 miles (161 km) west of Haiti. It is a little smaller than Connecticut.

The island is made up of a plateau and the Blue Mountains, a group of volcanic hills, in the east. Blue Mountain (7,402 ft.; 2,256 m) is the tallest peak.

Government. The legislature is a 60-member House of Representatives elected by universal suffrage and an appointed Senate of 21 members. The Prime Minister is appointed by the Governor-General and must, in the Governor-General's opinion, be the person best able to command the confidence of a majority of the members of the House of Representatives.

The major political parties are the Jamaica Labor Party (all 60 seats in the House of Representatives), led by Prime Minister Edward P. G. Seaga; and the People's National Party (PNP) (no seats), led by former Prime Minister Michael Manley.

History. Jamaica was inhabited by Arawak Indians when Columbus discovered it in 1494 and named it St. Iago. It remained under Spanish rule until 1655, then became a British possession. The island prospered from wealth brought by buccaneers to their base, Port Royal, the capital, until the city disappeared in the sea in 1692 after an earthquake. The Arawaks died off from disease and exploitation, and slaves, mostly black, were imported to work sugar plantations. Abolition of the slave trade (1807), emancipation of the slaves (1833), and a gradual drop in sugar prices led to depressed economic conditions that resulted in an uprising in 1865.

The following year Jamaica's status was changed to that of a colony, and conditions improved considerably. Introduction of banana cultivation made the island less dependent on the sugar crop for its well-being. Overpopulation and problems inherited from the colonial era, such as illiteracy, produced chronic substantial unemployment, leading to much emigration to the Caribbean countries and to the U.S.

On May 5, 1953, Jamaica attained internal autonomy, and in 1958 it led in organizing the West Indies Federation. This effort at Caribbean unification failed. A nationalist labor leader, Sir Alexander Bustamente, led a campaign for withdrawal from the Federation. As the result of a popular referendum in 1961, Jamaica became independent on Aug. 6, 1962.

Michael Manley became Prime Minister in 1972 and initiated a socialist program and in 1977, the government bought 51% of the Kaiser and Reynolds bauxite operations.

The Labor Party defeated Manley's People's National Party in 1980 and its capitalist-oriented leader, Edward P.G. Seaga, became Prime Minister. He instituted measures to encourage private investment. Manley's party boycotted the next election in 1983, leading to a Labor Party sweep of all 60 seats in the House of Representatives.

Like other Caribbean countries, Jamaica was hard-hit by the 1981–82 recession. By 1984, austerity measures that Seaga instituted in the hope of bringing the economy back into balance included elimination of government subsidies. Devaluation of the Jamaican dollar made Jamaican products more competitive on the world market and Jamaica achieved record growth in tourism and agriculture. Manufacturing also grew. But at the same time, the cost of many foods went up 50% to 75% and thousands of Jamaicans fell deeper into poverty. An increase in fuel prices ignited rioting in January 1985 in which four were killed and 23 were injured.

The PNP decisively won local elections in mid-July, signaling a weakening in Seaga's position.

JAPAN

Emperor: Hirohito (1926)
Prime Minister: Yasuhiro Nakasone (1982)
Area: 143,574 sq mi. (371,857 sq km)
Population (est. mid-1987): 122,200,000 (average annual growth rate: 0.6%)
Density per square mile: 851.1
Capital: Tokyo
Largest cities (est. 1986): Tokyo, 8,386,000; Yokohama, 3,037,000; Osaka, 2,642,000; Nagoya, 2,128,000; Sapporo, 1,562,000; Kyoto, 1,481,000; Kobe, 1,481, 000; Fukuoka, 1,172,000; Kitakyusho, 1,053,000; Kawasaki, 1,104,000
Monetary unit: Yen
Language: Japanese
Religions: Shintoist, Buddhist
National name: Nippon
Literacy rate (1981): 99%
Economic summary: Gross national product (1984): $1,233 billion. Average annual growth rate (1980–84): 4.3%. Per capita income (1984): $10,200. Land used for agriculture, 13%; labor force, including fishing, 9%; principal products: rice, vegetables, fruits, sugar. Labor force in industry: 33%; major products: machinery and equipment, metals and metal products, textiles, autos, chemicals, electrical and electronic equipment. Natural resource: fish. Exports: machinery and equipment, automobiles, metals and metal products, textiles. Imports: fossil fuels, metal ore, raw materials, foodstuffs, machinery and equipment. Major trading partners: U.S., Saudi Arabia, Indonesia, UAE, China, Australia, Canada, South Korea

Geography. An archipelago extending more than 1,744 miles (2,790 km) from northeast to southwest in the Pacific, Japan is separated from the east coast of Asia by the Sea of Japan. It is approximately the size of Montana.

Japan's four main islands are Honshu, Hokkaido, Kyushu, and Shikoku. The Ryukyu chain to the southwest was U.S.-occupied and the Kuriles to the northeast are Russian-occupied. The surface of the main islands consists largely of mountains separated by narrow valleys. There are about 60 more or less active volcanoes, of which the best-known is Mount Aso. Mount Fuji, seen on postcards, is not active.

Government. Japan's Constitution, promulgated on Nov. 3, 1946, replaced the Meiji Constitution of 1889. The 1946 Constitution, sponsored by the U.S. during its occupation of Japan, brought fundamental changes to the Japanese political system, including the abandonment of the Emperor's divine rights. The Diet (Parliament) consists of a House of Representatives of 512 members, elected for four years, and a House of Councilors of 252 members, half of whom are elected every three years for six-year terms. Executive power is vested in the Cabinet, which is headed by a Prime Minister, nominated by the Diet from its members.

Emperor Hirohito, who was born April 29, 1901, succeeded his father, Yoshihito, on Dec. 25, 1926. He was married on Jan. 26, 1924, to Princess Nagako, born in 1903. They have two sons—Crown Prince Akihito (born Dec. 23, 1933) and Prince Hitachi (born Nov. 28, 1935)—and four daughters. Succession to the Japanese throne is in the male line only.

The major political parties are the Liberal Democratic Party (309 of 511 seats in the House of Representatives), led by Prime Minister Yasuhiro Nakasone; Socialist Party (87 seats), led by Takado Doi; Clean Government (Komeito) Party (57 seats), led by Yoshikatsu Takeiri; Communist Party (27 seats), led by Kenji Miyamoto; Democratic Socialist Party (28 seats), led by Riyosaku Sasaki.

History. A series of legends attributes creation of Japan to the sun goddess, from whom the later emperors were allegedly descended. The first of them was Jimmu Tenno, supposed to have ascended the throne in 660 B.C.

Recorded Japanese history begins with the first contact with China in the 5th century A.D. Japan was then divided into strong feudal states, all nominally under the Emperor, but with real power often held by a court minister or clan. In 1185, Yoritomo, chief of the Minamoto clan, was designated Shogun (Generalissimo) with the administration of the islands under his control. A dual government system—Shogun and Emperor—continued until 1867.

First contact with the West came about 1542, when a Portuguese ship off course arrived in Japanese waters. Portuguese, traders, Jesuit missionaries, and Spanish, Dutch, and English traders followed. Suspicious of Christianity and of Portuguese support of a local Japanese revolt, the shoguns prohibited all trade with foreign countries; only a Dutch trading post at Nagasaki was permitted. Western attempts to renew trading relations failed until 1853, when Commodore Matthew Perry sailed an American fleet into Tokyo Bay.

Japan now quickly made the transition from a medieval to a modern power. Feudalism was abolished and industrialization was speeded. An imperial army was established with conscription. The shogun system was abolished in 1868 by Emperor Meiji, and parliamentary government was established in 1889. After a brief war with China in 1894–95, Japan acquired Formosa (Taiwan), the Pescadores Islands, and part of southern Manchuria. China also recognized the independence of Korea (Chosen), which Japan later annexed (1910).

In 1904–05, Japan defeated Russia in the Russo-Japanese War, gaining the territory of southern Sakhalin (Karafuto) and Russia's port and rail rights in Manchuria. In World War I Japan seized Germany's Pacific islands and leased areas in China. The Treaty of Versailles then awarded it a mandate over the islands.

At the Washington Conference of 1921–22, Japan agreed to respect Chinese national integrity. The series of Japanese aggressions that was to lead to the nation's downfall began in 1931 with the invasion of Manchuria. The following year, Japan set up this area as a puppet state, "Manchukuo," under Emperor Henry Pu-Yi, last of China's Manchu dynasty. On Nov. 25, 1936, Japan joined the Axis by signing the anti-Comintern pact. The invasion of China came the next year and the Pearl Harbor attack on the U.S. on Dec. 7, 1941.

(For details of World War II (1939–45), *see* Headline History.)

Japan surrendered formally on Sept. 2, 1945, aboard the battleship *Missouri* in Tokyo Bay after atomic bombs had hit Hiroshima and Nagasaki. Southern Sakhalin and the Kurile Islands reverted to the U.S.S.R., and Formosa (Taiwan) and Manchuria to China. The Pacific islands remained under U.S. occupation. General of the Army Douglas MacArthur was appointed Supreme Commander for the Allied Powers on Aug. 14, 1945.

A new Japanese Constitution went into effect in 1947. In 1949, many of the responsibilities of government were returned to the Japanese. Full sovereignty was granted to Japan by the Japanese Peace Treaty in 1951.

The treaty took effect on April 28, 1952, when Japan returned to full status as a nation. It was admitted into the United Nations in 1958.

Following the visit of Prime Minister Eisaku Sato to Washington in 1969, the U.S. agreed to return Okinawa and other Ryukyu Islands to Japan in 1972, and both nations renewed the security treaty in 1970.

When President Nixon opened a dialogue with Peking in 1972, Prime Minister Kakuei Tanaka, who succeeded Sato in 1972, quickly established diplomatic relations with the mainland Chinese and severed ties with Formosa.

Masayoshi Ohira, Prime Minister since November 1978, died on June 12, 1980, and in national elections held June 22, the ruling Liberal Democrats reversed an eight-year decline in public support, winning a firm parliamentary majority. The party chose Zenko Suzuki, a little-known 66-year-old follower of Ohira, as the new Prime Minister.

Announcement on June 19, 1981 that Japan's gross national product grew at a rate of nearly 5% for the fiscal year ending March 31 brought new demands for increased imports of manufactured goods by Japan, which international trade experts charged was still creating barriers against trade despite repeated promises by Tokyo to relax such restrictions.

The same figure was agreed to by Japan for the following year, and for the first time, Japanese automobile exports declined for the 12-month period ending March 31, 1982. In an effort to remove non-tariff trade barriers, which U.S. businessmen held responsible for their inability to increase sales in Japan, the Suzuki government appointed a special ombudsman with authority to cut red tape.

Under continued U.S. prodding, Tokyo announced an increase in defense spending with the 1987 budget reaching the target figure of 1% of the gross national product.

Suzuki was defeated in 1982 by Yasuhiro Nakasone who is considered pro-Western and better relations with the United States have ensued.

Nakasone initiated policies aimed at making the Japanese economy less export-intensive. Despite some opposition to this and his pro-Western policies in general, his Liberal Democratic party won decisively in the elections of July 7, 1986 and he was granted another year beyond his four-year limit which would have expired in October 1986.

JORDAN

The Hashemite Kingdom of Jordan
Ruler: King Hussein I (1952)
Prime Minister: Zeid al-Rifa'i (1985)
Area: 37,297 sq mi. (96,599 sq km)[1]
Population (est. mid-1987): 3,700,000[1] (average annual growth rate: 3.7%)
Density per square mile: 99.2
Capital: Amman
Largest cities (est. 1985): Amman, 800,000; Zarka, 274,300; Irbid, 144,650
Monetary unit: Jordanian dinar
Languages: Arabic, English
Religions: Islam, 93%; Christian, 5%
National name: Al Mamlaka al Urduniya al Hashemiyah
Literacy rate: 75%
Economic summary: Gross national product (1985): $5.0 billion. Annual growth rate (1985): 4.2%. Per capita income (1985): $1,650. Land used for agriculture: 5%; labor force: 10%; principal products: barley, fruits, vegetables, olive oil. Labor force in industry: 21.5%; major products: phosphate, refined petroleum products, cement. Natural resources: phosphate, potash. Exports: foodstuffs, cement, phosphate. Imports: petroleum products, textiles, capital goods, motor vehicles, foodstuffs. Major trading partners: U.S., Japan, Saudi Arabia, Iraq.

1. Includes territory occupied by Israel in 1967 war.

Geography. The Middle East kingdom of Jordan is bordered on the west by Israel and the Dead Sea, on the north by Syria, on the east by Iraq, and on the south Saudi Arabia. It is comparable in size to Indiana.

Arid hills and mountains make up most of the country. The southern section of the Jordan River flows through the country.

Government. Jordan is a constitutional monarchy with a bicameral parliament. Its Chamber of Deputies of 60 members is elected for four years by the people, and the 30 members of the Senate are appointed by the King.

All political parties were banned in 1957.

History. In biblical times, the country that is now Jordan contained the lands of Edom, Moab, Ammon, and Bashan. In A.D. 106 it became part of the Roman province of Arabia and in 633–36 was conquered by the Arabs.

Taken from the Turks by the British in World War I, Jordan (formerly known as Transjordan) was separated from the Palestine mandate in 1920, and in 1921, placed under the rule of Abdullah ibn Hussein.

In 1923, Britain recognized Jordan's independence, subject to the mandate. In 1946, grateful for Jordan's loyalty in World War II, Britain abolished the mandate. That part of Palestine occupied by Jordanian troops was formally incorporated by action of the Jordanian Parliament in 1950.

King Abdullah was assassinated in 1951. His son Talal was deposed as mentally ill the next year. Talal's son Hussein, born Nov. 14, 1935, succeeded him.

From the beginning of his reign, Hussein had to steer a careful course between his powerful neighbor to the west, Israel, and rising Arab nationalism, frequently a direct threat to this throne. Riots erupted when he joined the Central Treaty Organization (the Baghdad Pact) in 1955, and he incurred further unpopularity when Britain, France, and Israel attacked the Suez Canal in 1956, forcing him to place his army under nominal command of the United Arab Republic of Egypt and Syria.

The 1961 breakup of the UAR eased Arab national pressure on Hussein, who was the first to recognize Syria after it reclaimed its independence. Jordan was swept into the 1967 Arab-Israeli war, however, and lost the old city of Jerusalem and all of its territory west of the Jordan river, the West Bank. Embittered Palestinian guerrilla forces virtually took over sections of Jordan in the aftermath of defeat, and open warfare broke out between the Palestinians and government forces in 1970.

Despite intervention of Syrian tanks, Hussein's Bedouin army defeated the Palestinians, suffering heavy casualties. A U.S. military alert and Israeli armor massed on the Golan Heights contributed psychological weight, but the Jordanians alone drove out the Syrians and invited the departure of 12,000 Iraqi troops who had been in the country since the 1967 war.

In October 1974, Hussein concurred in an Arab summit resolution calling for an independent Palestinian state and endorsing the Palestine Liberation Organization as the "sole legitimate representative of the Palestinian people." This apparent reversal of policy changed with the growing disillusion of Arab states with the P.L.O., however, and by 1977 Hussein referred again to the unity of people on both banks of the Jordan.

As Egypt and Israel neared final agreement on a peace treaty early in 1979, Hussein met with Yassir Arafat, the PLO leader, on March 17 and issued a joint statement of opposition. Although the U.S. pressed Jordan to break Arab ranks on the issue, Hussein elected to side with the great majority, cutting ties with Cairo and joining the boycott against Egypt.

In September 1980, Jordan declared itself with Iraq in its conflict with Iran and, despite threats from Syria, opened ports to war shipments for Iraq.

In April 1983, Jordan rejected the American-sponsored Palestine peace plan.

An attempt to enlist Arafat in a new peace process collapsed in early 1986. Hussein then began a rapproachment with President Assad of Syria.

KAMPUCHEA

See Cambodia

KENYA

Republic of Kenya
President: Daniel arap Moi (1978)
Area: 224,960 sq mi. (582,646 sq km)
Population (est. mid-1987): 22,400,000 (average annual growth rate: 3.9%)
Density per square mile: 100.0
Capital: Nairobi
Largest cities (est. 1985): Nairobi, 1,000,000; Mombasa, 700,000
Monetary unit: Kenyan shilling
Languages: Swahili (official), Bantu, Kikuyu, English
Religions: Protestant, 27%; Roman Catholic, 26%; Animist, 19%; Islam, 6%
Literacy rate: 59%
Member of Commonwealth of Nations
National name: Jamhuri ya Kenya
Economic summary: Gross national product (1984): $5.7 billion. Average annual growth rate (1973–82): 5.0%. Per capita income (1984): $290. Land used for agriculture: 20%; labor force in agriculture: 17%; principal products: coffee, sisal, tea, pyrethrum, cotton, livestock. Labor force in industry: 14%; major products: textiles, processed foods, consumer goods, refined oil. Natural resources: wildlife. Exports: coffee, tea, foodstuffs. Imports: machinery, transport equipment, crude oil, paper, iron and steel products. Major trading partners: Western European countries, Japan, U.S., Uganda, U.K. UAE, Saudi Arabia.

Geography. Kenya lies on the equator in east central Africa on the coast of the Indian Ocean. It is twice the size of Nevada. Kenya's neighbors are Tanzania, Uganda, the Sudan, Ethiopia, and Somalia.

In the north, the land is arid; the southwestern corner is in the fertile Lake Victoria Basin; and a length of the eastern depression of Great Rift Valley separates western highlands from those that rise from the lowland coastal strip. Large game reserves have been developed.

Government. Under its Constitution of 1963, amended in 1964, Kenya has a one-house National Assembly of 171 members, elected for five years by universal suffrage. Since 1969, the president has been chosen by a general election.

The Kenya African National Union, led by the president, is the only political party.

President Jomo Kenyatta died in his sleep on Aug. 22, 1978. Vice President Daniel arap Moi was elected to succeed him on Oct. 10.

History. Kenya, formerly a British colony and protectorate, was made a crown colony in 1920. The whites' domination of the rich plateau area, the White Highlands, long regarded by the Kikiyu people as their territory, was a factor leading to native terrorism, called the Mau Mau movement, in 1952. In 1954 the British began preparing the territory for African rule and independence. In 1961 Jomo Kenyatta was freed from banishment to become leader of the Kenya African National Union.

Internal self-government was granted in 1963; Kenya became independent on Dec. 12, 1963, with Kenyatta the first president. Kenya obtained economic and technical assistance from Communist China beginning in 1964 and later a World Bank loan.

KIRIBATI

Republic of Kiribati
Sovereign: Queen Elizabeth II
Governor General: Reginald J. Wallace (1980)
President: Ieremia Tabai (1979)
Area: 264 sq mi. (683 sq km)
Population (est. 1987): 62,000 (average annual growth rate: 1.6%)
Density per square mile: 234.8
Capital (est. 1974): Bairiki (on Tarawa Atoll), 17,100
Monetary unit: Australian dollar
Language: English
Religions: Roman Catholic, 50%; Protestant, 44%
Member of Commonwealth of Nations
Literacy rate: 20%
Economic summary: Gross national product (1983): $30 million. Per capita income (1984): $480. Principal agricultural products: copra, vegetables. Exports: fish, copra. Imports: foodstuffs, fuel, transportation equipment. Major trading partners: New Zealand, Australia, South Korea

Geography. Kiribati, formerly the Gilbert Islands, consists of three widely separated main groups of Southwest Pacific islands, the Gilberts on the equator, the Phoenix Islands to the east, and the Line Islands further east. Ocean Island, producer of phosphates, which constitute 99% of the new nation's annual income of $18 million, is also included in the two million square miles of ocean, which will give Kiribati an important fishery resource.

Government. The president holds executive power. The legislature consists of a House Assembly with 37 members.

History. A British protectorate since 1892, the Gilbert and Ellice Islands became a colony in 1915–16. The two island groups were separated in 1975 and given internal self-government.

Tarawa and others of the Gilbert group were occupied by Japan during World War II. Tarawa was the site of one of the bloodiest battles in U.S. Marine Corps history when Marines landed in November 1943 to dislodge the Japanese defenders.

Princess Anne, representing Queen Elizabeth II, presented the independence documents to the new government on July 12, 1979.

KOREA, NORTH

Democratic People's Republic of Korea
President: Marshal Kim Il Sung (1972)
Premier: Li Gunmo (1986)
Area: 46,768 sq mi. (121,129 sq km)
Population (est. mid-1987): 21,400,000 (average annual growth rate: 2.5%)
Density per square mile: 457.6
Capital and largest city (est. 1982): Pyongyang, 1,500,000
Monetary unit: Won
Language: Korean
Religions: atheist, 68%; traditional, 16%
National name: Choson Minjujuui Inmin Konghwaguk
Literacy rate: 95% (est.)
Economic summary: Gross national product (1984): $23.0 billion. Average annual growth rate (1970–79): 3.8%. Per capita income (1984): $1,170. Land used for agriculture: 19%; labor force, 44%; principal products: corn, rice, vegetables. Major industrial products: machines, electric power, chemicals, textiles, fertilizers, metallurgical products. Natural resources: coal, iron ore. Exports: minerals, chemical and metallurgical products. Imports: machinery and equipment, petroleum, foodstuffs, coking coal. Major trading partners: U.S.S.R., China, Japan.

Geography. Korea is a 600-mile (966 km) peninsula jutting from Manchuria and China (and a small portion of the U.S.S.R.) into the Sea of Japan and the Yellow Sea off eastern Asia. North Korea occupies an area slightly smaller than Pennsylvania north of the 38th parallel.

The country is almost completely covered by a series of north-south mountain ranges separated by narrow valleys. The Yalu River forms part of the northern border with Manchuria.

Government. The elected Supreme People's Assembly, as the chief organ of government, chooses a Presidium and a Cabinet. The Cabinet, which exercises executive authority, is subject to approval by the Assembly and the Presidium.

The Korean Workers (Communist) Party, led by President Kim Il Sung, is the only political party.

History. According to myth, Korea was founded in 2333 B.C. by Tangun. In the 17th century, it became a vassal of China and was isolated from all but Chinese influence and contact until 1876, when Japan forced Korea to negotiate a commercial treaty, opening the land to the U. S. and Europe. Japan achieved control as the result of its war with China (1894–95) and with Russia (1904–05) and annexed Korea in 1910. Japan developed the country but never won over the Korean nationalists.

After the Japanese surrender in 1945, the country was divided into two occupation zones, the U.S.S.R. north of and the U.S. south of the 38th parallel. When the cold war developed between the U.S. and U.S.S.R., trade between the zones was cut off. In 1948, the division between the zones was made permanent with the establishment of separate regimes in the north and south. By mid-1949, the U.S. and U.S.S.R. withdrew all troops. The Democratic People's Republic of Korea (North Korea) was established on May 1, 1948. The Communist Party, headed by Kim Il Sung, was established in power.

On June 25, 1950, the North Korean army launched a surprise attack on South Korea. On June 26, the U.N. Security Council condemned the invasion as aggression and ordered withdrawal of the invading forces. On June 27, President Harry S. Truman ordered air and naval units into action to enforce the U.N. order. The British government did the same, and soon a multinational U.N. command was set up to aid the South Koreans. The North Korean invaders took Seoul and pushed the South Koreans into the southeast corner of their country.

Gen. Douglas MacArthur, U.N. commander, made an amphibious landing at Inchon on September 15 behind the North Korean lines, which resulted in the complete rout of the North Korean army. The U.N. forces drove north across the 38th parallel, approaching the Yalu River. Then Communist China entered the war, forcing the U.N. forces into headlong retreat. Seoul was lost again, then regained; ultimately the war stabilized near the 38th parallel but dragged on for two years while the belligerents negotiated. An armistice was agreed to on July 27, 1953.

President Carter, visiting Seoul from June 29 to July 1, 1979, proposed that the U.S., North Korea, and South Korea meet "to promote dialogue and reduce tensions in the area," possibly leading to reunification of the two Koreas. Pyongyang's official party newspaper rejected the proposal, saying the North favors reunification talks but without the "alien interference" of the U.S.

Kim again rejected as a "foolish burlesque" an invitation on Jan. 12, 1981, by South Korea's military chief, Chun Doo Hwan, to hold reunification talks in Seoul. Kim refused again when Chun repeated the invitation on March 3 during his inauguration as President of the Southern republic.

KOREA, SOUTH

Republic of Korea
President: Chun Doo Hwan (1980)
Premier: Kim Chung Yul (1987)
Area: 38,031 sq mi. (98,500 sq km)
Population (est. mid-1987): 42,100,000 (average annual growth rate: 1.4%)
Density per square mile: 1,107.0
Capital: Seoul
Largest cities (est. 1985): Seoul, 9,600,000; Pusan, 3,500,000; Taegu, 2,000,000; Inchon, 1,300,000
Monetary unit: Won
Language: Korean
Religions: Buddhist, 37%; Protestant, 26%; Roman Catholic, 5%
National name: Taehan Min'guk
Literary rate: 93%
Economic summary: Gross national product (1986): $90.6 billion. Average annual growth rate (1976–85): 7.52%. Per capita income (1986): $2,180. Land used for agriculture: 21%; labor force, including fishing, 22.16%; principal products: rice, barley. Labor force in industry: 25.35%; major products: clothing and textiles, processed foods, chemical fertilizers, chemicals, plywood, steel, electronics equipment. Natural resources: iron and copper ore, tungsten, graphite, limestone, coal, gold, silver. Exports: Textiles, electric and electronics, ships, and steel. Imports: oil, grains, chemicals, machinery, electronics. Major trading partners: U.S., Japan.

Geography. Slightly larger than Indiana, South Korea lies below the 38th parallel on the Korean peninsula. It is mountainous in the east; in the west and south are many harbors on the mainland and offshore islands.

Government. A national referendum in October 1980 approved a new Constitution that provides for election of the President by an electoral college chosen by popular vote. The term of office is for seven years, limited to one term. A unicameral National Assembly has 276 members, 184 elected directly by popular vote, the remainder appointed in proportion to party strength in the selection.

Major parties are the Democratic Justice Party, (DJP), (148 of 276 National Assembly seats), led by President Chun Doo Hwan, and the opposition Party of Unification and Democracy (73 seats), led by Kim Dae Jung and Kim Yung Sam, with the remaining seats held by splinter parties and independents.

History. South Korea came into being in the aftermath of World War II as the result of a 1945 agreement making the 38th parallel the boundary between a northern zone occupied by the U.S.S.R. and a southern zone occupied by U.S. forces. (For details, *see* North Korea.)

Elections were held in the U.S. zone in 1948 for a national assembly, which adopted a republican Constitution and elected Syngman Rhee president. The new republic was proclaimed on August 15 and was recognized as the legal government of Korea by the U.N. on Dec. 12, 1948.

On June 25, 1950, South Korea was attacked by North Korean Communist forces. U.S. armed intervention was ordered on June 27 by President Harry S. Truman, and on the same day the U.N. invoked military sanctions against North Korea. Gen. Douglas MacArthur was named commander of the U.N. forces. U.S. and South Korean troops fought a heroic holding action but, by the first week of August, they had been forced back to a 4,000-square-mile beachhead in southeast Korea.

There they stood off superior North Korean forces until September 15, when a major U.N. amphibious attack was launched far behind the Communist lines at Inchon, port of Seoul. By September 30, U.N. forces were in complete control of South Korea. They then invaded North Korea and were nearing the Manchurian and Siberian borders when several hundred thousand Chinese Communist troops entered the conflict in late October. U.N. forces were then forced to retreat below the 38th parallel.

On May 24, 1951, U.N. forces recrossed the parallel and had made important new inroads into North Korea when truce negotiations began on July 10. An armistice was finally signed at Panmunjom on July 27, 1953, leaving a devastated Korea in need of large-scale rehabilitation.

The U.S. and South Korea signed a mutual-defense treaty on Oct. 1, 1953.

Rhee, president since 1948, resigned in 1960 in the face of rising disorders. PoSun Yun was elected to succeed him, but political instability continued. In 1961, Gen. Park Chung Hee took power and subsequently built up the country. The U.S. stepped up military aid, building up South Korea's armed forces to 600,000 men. The South Koreans sent 50,000 troops to Vietnam, at U.S. expense.

Park's assassination on Oct. 26, 1979, by Kim Jae Kyu, head of the Korean Central Intelligence Agency, brought a liberalizing trend as Choi Kyu Hah, the new President, freed imprisoned dissidents. The release of opposition leader Kim Dae Jung in February 1980 generated anti-government demonstrations that turned into riots by May. Choi resigned on Aug. 16. Chun Doo Wha, head of a military Special Committee for National Security Measures, was the sole candidate as the electoral college confirmed him as President on Aug. 27. On Sept. 17, Kim Dae Jung was sentenced to death by a military court on charges of high treason. Chun commuted the sentence on Jan. 23, 1981, and lifted martial law the next day.

Elected to a full seven-year term on Feb. 11, Chun had visited Washington on Feb. 2 to receive President Reagan's assurance that U.S. troops would remain in South Korea. General elections on March 25 gave the ruling Democratic Justice Party a majority of the National Assembly.

Debate over the Presidential succession in 1988 was the main dispute in 1986-87 with Chun wanting election by the electoral college and the opposition demanding a direct popular vote, charging that Chun could manipulate the college. On April 13, 1987, Chun declared a close on the debate but when, in June, he appointed Roh Toe Woo, the DJP chairman as his successor, violent protests broke out. Roh, and later, Chun, agreed that direct elections should be held.

KUWAIT

State of Kuwait
Emir: Sheik Jaber al-Ahmad al-Sabah (1977)
Prime Minister: Sheik Sa'ad Abdullah al-Salim (1978)
Area: 7,780 sq mi. (20,150 sq km)
Population (est. mid-1987): 1,900,000 (average annual growth rate: 3.2%)
Density per square mile: 244.2
Capital (est. 1980): Kuwait, 60,525
Largest city (est. 1980): Hawalli, 152,402
Monetary unit: Kuwaiti dinar
Languages: Arabic and English
Religions: Islam, 92%; Christian 6%
National name: Dawlat al Kuwayt
Literacy rate: about 71%
Economic summary: Gross national product (1983): $30.3 billion. Average annual growth rate (1973–82): 10.3%. Per capita income (1983): $18,180. Land used for agriculture: 1%. Labor force in industry: 22%; major products: crude and refined oil, fertilizer, chemicals, building materials, shrimp. Natural resources: petroleum, fish, shrimp. Exports: crude and refined petroleum, shrimp. Imports: foodstuffs, automobiles, building materials, machinery, textiles. Major trading partners: U.S., Japan, Italy, Singapore, Japan, Iraq.

Geography. Kuwait is situated northeast of Saudi Arabia at the northern end of the Persian Gulf, south of Iraq. It is slightly larger than Hawaii. The low-lying land is mainly sandy and barren.

Government. Sheik Jaber al-Ahmad al-Sabah rules as Emir of Kuwait and appoints the Prime Minister, who appoints his Cabinet (Council of Ministers). The National Assembly was suspended on July 3, 1986. There are no political parties in Kuwait.

History. Kuwait obtained British protection in 1897 when the Sheik feared that the Turks would take over the area. In 1961, Britain ended the protectorate, giving Kuwait independence, but agreed to give military aid on request. Iraq immediately threatened to occupy the area and Sheik Sabah al-Salem al-Sabah called in British troops in 1961. Soon afterward the Arab League sent in troops, replacing the British. The prize was oil.

Oil was discovered in the 1930s. Kuwait proved to have 20% of the world's known oil resources. It has been a major producer since 1946, the world's second largest oil exporter. The Sheik, who gets half the profits, devotes most of them to the education, welfare, and modernization of his kingdom. In 1966, Sheik Sabah designated a relative, Jaber al-Ahmad al-Sabah, as his successor.

By 1968, the sheikdom had established a model welfare state, and it sought to establish dominance among the sheikdoms and emirates of the Persian Gulf.

A worldwide decline in the price of oil reduced Kuwait's oil income from $18.4 billion in 1980 to only $9 billion in 1984. During the same period Kuwait's support for Iraq in its war with Iran sparked terrorist attacks in Kuwait by radical Shiite Moslem supporters of Iran's Ayatollah Khomeini. The risk of Iranian attack prompted Kuwait to obtain U.S. protection for its tankers in 1987.

In May 1985, a suicide bomber drove into the motorcade of Sheik Jaber al-Ahmad al-Sabah, the ruler. The Sheik escaped with minor cuts and bruises but five people, including the suicide bomber, were killed. In July, bombs exploded in two popular cafes, killing nine people and wounding 56.

LAOS

Lao People's Democratic Republic
President (acting): Phuomi Vongvichit (1986)
Premier: Kaysone Phomvihane (1975)
Area: 91,429 sq mi. (236,800 sq km)
Population (est. mid-1987): 3,800,000 (average annual growth rate: 2.5%)
Density per square mile: 41.6
Capital and largest city (est. 1980): Vientiane, 250,000
Monetary unit: Kip
Languages: Lao (official), French, English
Religions: Buddhist, 58%; tribal, 34%
Literacy rate: 28%
Economic summary: Gross national product: (1984): $765 million. Per capita income (1984): $220. Land used for agriculture, 49%; labor force, 75%; principal products: rice, corn, vegetables. Major industrial products: tin, timber, tobacco, textiles, electric power. Natural resources: tin, timber, hydroelectric power. Exports: electric power, forest products, tin concentrates, coffee. Imports: rice, foodstuffs, petroleum products, machinery, transport equipment. Major trading partners: Thailand, Singapore, China, Japan

Geography. A landlocked nation in Southeast Asia occupying the northwestern portion of the Indochinese peninsula, Laos is surrounded by China, Vietnam, Cambodia, Thailand, and Burma. It is twice the size of Pennsylvania.

Laos is a mountainous country, especially in the north, where peaks rise above 8,000 feet (2,438 m). Dense forests cover the northern and eastern areas. The Mekong River, which forms the boundary with Burma and Thailand, flows entirely through the country for 300 miles (483 km) of its course.

Government. Laos is a people's democratic republic with executive power in the hands of the premier. The monarchy was abolished Dec. 2, 1975, when the Pathet Lao ousted a coalition government and King Sisavang Vatthana abdicated. The King was appointed "Supreme Adviser" to the President, the former Prince Souphanouvong. Former Prince Souvanna Phouma, Premier since

1962, was made an "adviser" to the government. The Lao People's Revolutionary Party (Pathet Lao), led by Premier Kaysone Phomvihane, is the only political party.

History. Laos became a French protectorate in 1893, and the territory was incorporated into the union of Indochina. A strong nationalist movement developed during World War II, but France reestablished control in 1946 and made the King of Luang Prabang constitutional monarch of all Laos. France granted semiautonomy in 1949 and then, spurred by the Viet Minh rebellion in Vietnam, full independence within the French Union in 1950. In 1951, Prince Souphanouvong organized the Pathet Lao, a Communist independence movement, in North Vietnam. The Viet Minh in 1953 established the Pathet Lao in power at Samneua. Viet Minh and Pathet Lao forces invaded central Laos, and civil war resulted.

By the Geneva agreements of 1954 and an armistice of 1955, two northern provinces were given the Pathet Lao, the royal regime the rest. Full sovereignty was given the kingdom by the Paris agreements of Dec. 29, 1954. In 1957, Prince Souvanna Phouma, the royal Premier, and the Pathet Lao leader, Prince Souphanouvong, the Premier's half-brother, agreed to reestablishment of a unified government, with Pathet Lao participation and integration of Pathet Lao forces into the royal army. The agreement broke down in 1959, and armed conflict broke out again.

In 1960, the struggle became three-way as Gen. Phoumi Nosavan, controlling the bulk of the royal army, set up in the south a pro-Western revolutionary government headed by Prince Boun Gum. General Phoumi took Vientiane in December, driving Souvanna Phouma into exile in Cambodia. The Soviet bloc supported Souvanna Phouma. In 1961, a cease-fire was arranged and the three princes agreed to a coalition government headed by Souvanna Phouma.

But North Vietnam, the U.S. (in the form of Central Intelligence Agency personnel), and China remained active in Laos after the settlement. North Vietnam used a supply line (Ho Chi Minh trail) running down the mountain valleys of eastern Laos into Cambodia and South Vietnam, particularly after the U.S.-South Vietnamese incursion into Cambodia in 1970 stopped supplies via Cambodian seaports.

An agreement, reached in 1973 revived coalition government. The Communist Pathet Lao seized complete power in 1975, installing Souphanouvong as president and Kaysone Phomvihane as premier. Since then other parties and political groups have been moribund and most of their leaders have fled the country.

In July 1985, Laos agreed to help the United States search for U.S. servicemen missing since the Indochina war.

In 1985, border clashes between Laos and Thailand intensified, with over 120 skirmishes reported in 1984 and 1985.

LEBANON

Republic of Lebanon
President: Amin Gemayel (1982)
Premier (acting): Selim al-Hoss (1987)
Area: 4,015 sq mi. (10,400 sq km)
Population (est. mid-1987): 3,300,000 (average annual growth rate: 2.2%)
Density per square mile: 821.9
Capital: Beirut
Largest cities (est. 1981): Beirut, 750,000; Tripoli, 200,000
Monetary unit: Lebanese pound
Languages: Arabic (official), French, English
Religions: Christian and Islam
National name: Al-Joumhouriya al-Lubnaniya
Literacy rate: 75%
Economic summary: Gross national product (1983 est.): $5.0 billion. Per capita income: n.a. Land used for agriculture: 27%; labor force: 17%; principal products: fruits, wheat, corn, barley, potatoes, tobacco, olives, onions. Labor force in industry: 19%; major products: processed foods, textiles, cement, chemicals, refined oil. Exports: fruits, vegetables, textiles. Imports: metals, machinery, foodstuffs. Major trading partners: U.S., Western European and Arab countries.

Geography. Lebanon lies at the eastern end of the Mediterranean Sea north of Israel and west of Syria. It is four fifths the size of Connecticut.

The Lebanon Mountains, which parallel the coast on the west, cover most of the country, while on the eastern border is the Anti-Lebanon range. Between the two lies the Bekaa Valley, the principal agricultural area.

Government. Lebanon is governed by a President, elected by Parliament for a six-year term, and a Cabinet of Ministers appointed by the President but responsible to Parliament.

Parliament has 99 members elected for a four-year term by universal suffrage and chosen by proportional division of religious groups.

History. After World War I, France was given a League of Nations mandate over Lebanon and its neighbor Syria, which together had previously been a single political unit in the Ottoman Empire. France divided them in 1920 into separate colonial administrations, drawing a border that separated predominantly Moslem Syria from the kaleidoscope of religious communities in Lebanon in which Maronite Christians were then dominant. After 20 years of the French mandate regime, Lebanon's independence was proclaimed on Nov. 26, 1941, but full independence came in stages. Under an agreement between representatives of Lebanon and the French National Committee of Liberation, most of the powers exercised by France were transferred to the Lebanese government on Jan. 1, 1944. The evacuation of French troops was completed in 1946.

Civil war broke out in 1958, with Moslem factions led by Kamal Jumblat and Saeb Salam rising in insurrection against the Lebanese government headed by President Camille Chamoun, a Maronite Christian. At Chamoun's request, President Eisenhower on July 15 sent U.S. troops to reestablish the government's authority.

Clan warfare between various factions in Lebanon goes back centuries. The hodgepodge includes Maronite Christians, who since independence have dominated the government; Sunni Moslems, who have prospered in business and shared political power; the Druse, a secretive Islamic splinter group; and at the bottom of the heap until recently, Shiite Moslems.

A new—and bloodier—Lebanese civil war that broke out in 1975 resulted in the addition of still another ingredient in the brew—the Syrians. In the fighting between Lebanese factions, 40,000 Lebanese were estimated to have been killed and 100,000 wounded between March 1975 and November 1976. At that point, a Syrian-dominated Arab Deterrent Force intervened and brought large-scale fighting to a halt.

Palestinian guerrillas staging raids on Israel from Lebanese territory drew punitive Israeli raids on Lebanon, and two large-scale Israeli invasions. The first invasion, in retaliation for a PLO terrorist raid on Israel, began on March 14, 1979, and was limited in scope. Chief targets were PLO bases in southern Lebanon. The Israelis withdrew in June after the U.N. Security Council created a 6,000-man peacekeeping force for the area, called UNIFIL. As they departed, the Israelis turned their strongpoints over to a Christian militia that they had organized, instead of to the United Nations force.

The second Israeli invasion came on June 6, 1982, and this time it was a total one. It was in response to an assassination attempt by Palestinian terrorists on the Israeli ambassador in London.

A U.S. special envoy, Philip C. Habib, negotiated the dispersal of most of the PLO to other Arab nations and Israel pulled back some of its forces. The violence seemed to have come to an end when, on Sept. 14, Bashir Gemayel, the 34-year-old President-elect, was killed by a bomb that destroyed the headquarters of his Christian Phalangist Party.

The day after Gemayel's assassination, Israeli troops moved into west Beirut in force. On Sept. 17 it was revealed that Christian militiamen had massacred hundreds of Palestinians in two refugee camps. Israel denied responsibility although its troops had permitted the militiamen to enter the camps.

On Sept. 20, Amin Gemayel, older brother of Bashir Gemayel, was elected President by the parliament.

The massacre in the refugee camps prompted the return of a multinational peacekeeping force composed of U.S. Marines and British, French, and Italian soldiers. Their mandate was to support the central Lebanese government, but they soon found themselves drawn into the struggle for power between different Lebanese factions. During their stay in Lebanon, 260 U.S. Marines and about 60 French soldiers were killed, most of them in suicide bombings of the Marine and French Army compounds on Oct. 23, 1983. The multinational force left in the spring of 1984.

During 1984, Israeli troops remained in southern Lebanon and Syrian troops remained in the Bekaa Valley. By the third anniversary of the invasion, June 6, 1985, all Israeli troops had withdrawn except for several hundred "advisers" to a Christian militia trained and armed by the Israelis.

During 1985, the long-deprived Shiites shouldered aside the traditional urban upper class of Sunni oligarchs as the dominant Moslem faction in west Beirut. The more extremist Shiite factions such as Hizbullah (Party of God), inspired by Iran's Ayatollah Ruhollah Khomeini, wanted to establish an Iranian-style religious state in Lebanon and were virulently anti-Israel and anti-U.S. Fanatic youngsters recruited by Hizbullah drove explosive-laden cars in suicide missions against the Christian militia and its Israeli advisers in southern Lebanon and have conducted hit-and-run warfare since.

Events since the Israeli withdrawal have included Shiite-PLO fighting resulting from PLO attempts to reestablish its old power base in areas now held by Shiite militia.

In July 1986, Syrian observers took position in Beirut to monitor a peacekeeping agreement that involved a cease-fire and the closing of the militia offices. An earlier accord failed when the Christian militia leader, Elias Hobeika, was defeated by troops loyal to Gemayel, who opposed the agreement. The agreement broke down and fighting between Shiite and Druze militia in West Beirut became so intense that Syrian troops moved in force in February 1987, suppressing militia resistance.

LESOTHO

Kingdom of Lesotho

Sovereign: King Moshoeshoe II (1966)

Chairman, Military Council: Maj. Gen. Justin Lekhanya (1986)

Area: 11,720 sq mi. (30,355 sq km)

Population (est. mid-1987): 1,600,000 (average annual growth rate: 2.6%)

Density per square mile: 136.5

Capital and largest city (est. 1983): Maseru, 70,000

Monetary unit: Loti

Languages: English and Sesotho (official)

Religions: Roman Catholic, 44%; Lesotho Evangelical Church, 30%; Anglican, 12%

Member of Commonwealth of Nations

Literacy rate: 55%

Economic summary: Gross national product (1984): $790 million. Average annual growth rate (1973–82): 6.5%. Per capita income (1984): $520. Land used for agriculture: 15%; labor force: 87%; principal products: corn, wheat, sorghum, barley. Labor force in industry: 2%. Natural resources: diamonds. Exports: wool, mohair, wheat, cattle, diamonds, hides and skins. Imports: corn, building materials, clothing, vehicles, machinery. Major trading partner: South Africa.

Geography. Mountainous Lesotho, the size of Maryland, is surrounded by the Republic of South Africa in the east central part of that country except for short borders on the east and south with two discontinuous units of the Republic of Transkei. The Drakensberg Mountains in the east are Lesotho's principal chain. Elsewhere the region consists of rocky tableland.

Government. In January 1986, following an economic crisis caused by a South African blockade, the military overthrew Chief Johnathan and established a Military Council and a Council of Ministers that would exercise a policy less tolerant of anti-apartheid activists within its borders.

The King has also been given greater powers.

History. Lesotho (formerly Basutoland) was constituted a native state under British protection by a treaty signed with the native chief Moshesh in 1843. It was annexed to Cape Colony in 1871, but in 1884 it was restored to direct control by the Crown.

The colony of Basutoland became the independent nation of Lesotho on Oct. 4, 1966.

In the 1970 elections, Ntsu Mokhehle, head of the Basutoland Congress Party, claimed a victory, but Jonathan declared a state of emergency, suspended the Constitution, and arrested Mokhehle. The major issue in the election was relations with South Africa, with Jonathan for close ties to the surrounding white nation, while Mokhehle was for a more independent policy. Jonathan jailed 45 opposition politicians, declared the King had "technically abdicated" by siding with the opposition party, exiled him to the Netherlands, and named his Queen and her seven-year-old son as Regent.

The King returned after a compromise with Jonathan in which the new Constitution would name him head of state but forbid his participation in politics.

LIBERIA

Republic of Liberia
President: Gen. Samuel K. Doe (1980)
Area: 43,000 sq mi. (111,370 sq km)
Population (est. mid-1987): 2,400,000 (average annual growth rate: 3.2%)
Density per square mile: 55.8
Capital and largest city (est. 1984): Monrovia, 425,000
Monetary unit: Liberian dollar
Languages: English (official) and tribal dialects
Religions: Animist, 75%; Christian, 10%; Islam, 15%
Literacy rate: 35%
Economic summary: Gross national product (1984): $990 million. Average annual growth rate (1973–82): 2.5%. Per capita income (1984): $460. Land used for agriculture: 20%; labor force: 71%; principal products: rubber, rice, palm oil, cassava, coffee, cocoa. Labor force in industry: 5%; major products: iron ore, diamonds, processed rubber, processed food, construction materials. Natural resources: iron ore, rubber, timber, diamonds. Exports: iron ore, rubber, timber, diamonds. Imports: machinery, petroleum products, transport equipment, foodstuffs. Major trading partners: U.S., West Germany, Netherlands, Italy, Belgium.

Geography. Lying on the Atlantic in the southern part of West Africa, Liberia is bordered by Sierra Leone, Guinea, and the Ivory Coast. It is comparable in size to Tennessee.

Most of the country is a plateau covered by dense tropical forests, which thrive under an annual rainfall of about 160 inches a year.

Government. Since April 25, 1980, Liberia had been under military rule by the 17-member People's Redemptive Council, which suspended the Constitution after overthrowing the civilian government. On July 22, 1984, the Council was replaced with an interim, appointed National Assembly in a step toward return of civilian rule.

History. Liberia was founded in 1822 as a result of the efforts of the American Colonization Society to settle freed American slaves in West Africa. In 1847, it became the Free and Independent Republic of Liberia.

The government of Africa's first republic was modeled after that of the United States, and Joseph J. Roberts of Virginia was elected the first president. He laid the foundations of a modern state and initiated efforts, never too successful but pursued for more than a century, to bring the aboriginal inhabitants of the territory to the level of the emigrants. The English-speaking descendants of U.S. blacks, known as Americo-Liberians, were the intellectual and ruling class. The indigenous inhabitants, divided, constitute 99% of the population.

After 1920, considerable progress was made toward opening up the interior, a process that was spurred in 1951 by the establishment of a 43-mile (69-km) railroad to the Bomi Hills from Monrovia.

In July 1971, while serving his sixth term as president, William V. S. Tubman died following surgery and was succeeded by his long-time associate, Vice President William R. Tolbert, Jr.

Tolbert was ousted in a military coup carried out April 12, 1980, by army enlisted men led by Master Sgt. Samuel K. Doe. Tolbert and 27 other high officials were executed. Doe and his colleagues based their action on the grievances of "native" Liberians against corruption and misrule by the Americo-Liberians who had ruled the country since its founding.

In November 1985, an attempted coup against Doe following a disputed re-election, was bloodily put down and the coup leader, a former associate of Doe's, was executed.

LIBYA

Socialist People's Libyan Arab Jamahiriya
Head of State: Col. Muammar el-Qaddafi (1969)
Secretary-General of the General People's Committee: Muhammad al-Zarruq Rajah (1981)
Premier: Jadallah Azzuz et Talhi (1979)
Area: 679,536 sq mi. (1,759,998 sq km)
Population (est. mid-1987): 3,800,000 (average annual growth rate: 3.0%)
Density per square mile: 5.6
Capital: Tripoli
Largest cities (est. 1980): Tripoli, 587,400; Benghazi, 267,700
Monetary unit: Libyan dinar
Language: Arabic
Religion: Islam
National name: Al-Jumhuria al-Arabia al-Libya
Literacy rate: 50%
Economic summary: Gross national product (1983): $29.8 billion. Average annual growth rate (1970–79): –1.6%. Per capita income (1983): $8,220. Land used for agriculture: 6%; labor force: 17%; principal products: wheat, barley, olives, dates, citrus fruits, peanuts. Labor force in industry: 10%; major products: petroleum, processed foods, textiles, handicrafts. Natural resources: petroleum, natural gas. Export: petroleum. Imports: machinery, foodstuffs, manufactured goods. Major trading partners: Italy, West Germany, U.K., France, Spain.

Geography. Libya stretches along the northeastern coast of Africa between Tunisia and Algeria on the west and Egypt on the east; to the south are the Sudan, Chad, and Niger. It is one sixth larger than Alaska.

A greater part of the country lies within the Sahara. Along the Mediterranean coast and farther inland is arable plateau land.

Government. In a bloodless coup d'etat on Sept. 1, 1969, the military seized power in Libya. King Idris I, who had ruled since 1951, was deposed and the Libyan Arab Republic proclaimed. The official name was changed in 1977 to the Socialist People's Libyan Arab Jamahiriya. The Revolutionary Council that had governed since the coup was renamed the General Secretariat of the General People's Congress. The Arab Socialist Union Organization is the only political party.

History. Libya was a part of the Turkish dominions from the 16th century until 1911. Following the outbreak of hostilities between Italy and Turkey in that year, Italian troops occupied Tripoli; Italian sovereignty was recognized in 1912.

Libya was the scene of much desert fighting during World War II. After the fall of Tripoli on Jan. 23, 1943, it came under Allied administration. In 1949, the U.N. voted that Libya should become independent by 1952.

Discovery of oil in the Libyan Desert promised financial stability and funds for economic development.

The Reagan Administration, accusing Libya of supporting international terrorism, closed the Libyan embassy in Washington on May 6, 1981. After talks with Libyan officials in July, the U.S. concluded that no improvement in relations was possible, although U.S. oil companies remained active in Libya and 2,000 U.S. citizens continued to work there.

On Aug. 19, 1981, two U.S. Navy F-14's shot down two Soviet-made SU-22's of the Libyan air force that had attacked them in air space above the Gulf of Sidra, claimed by Libya but held to be international by the U.S. In December, Washington asserted that Libyan "hit squads" had been dispatched to the U.S. and security was drastically tightened around President Reagan and other officials. Reagan requested remaining American citizens to leave Libya and nearly all did by Dec. 15. When the Mobil Oil Company abandoned its operations in April 1982, only four U.S. firms were still in Libya, using Libyan or third-country personnel.

Qaddafi's troops also supported rebels in Chad but suffered major military reverses in 1987.

In December 1985, Qaddafi lauded as "heroic" a terrorist attack on Rome and Vienna airports that killed 20 people.

On March 24, 1986, U.S. and Libyan forces skirmished in the Gulf of Sidra, with two Libyan patrol boats being sunk.

On April 14, after a Libyan-backed attack on a West Berlin disco in which two people, including an American serviceman, were killed, Reagan ordered an air raid on Libyan military installations.

LIECHTENSTEIN

Principality of Liechtenstein
Ruler: Prince Franz Josef II (1938)
Prime Minister: Hans Brunhart (1978)
Area: 61 sq mi. (157 sq km)
Population (est. 1985): 28,000 (average annual growth rate: 1.8%)
Density per square mile: 459.0
Capital and largest city (est. 1985): Vaduz, 4,872
Monetary unit: Swiss franc
Language: German (Alemannish dialect)
Religions: Roman Catholic, 86%; Protestant, 9%
Literacy rate: 100%
Economic summary: Per capita income (1984 est.): $15,000. Labor force in agriculture: 3%; principal products: livestock, vegetables, corn, wheat, potatoes, grapes. Labor force in industry: 43%; major products: high-technology products, building equipment, food products, machinery, industrial goods. Natural resources: timber, hydroelectric power, salt. Exports: manufactured metal products, machines and instruments, chemical products. Imports: raw materials, machinery, processed foods and goods. Major trading partners: Switzerland and other Western European countries.

Geography. Tiny Liechtenstein, not quite as large as Washington, D.C., lies on the east bank of the Rhine River south of Lake Constance between Austria and Switzerland. It consists of low valley land and Alpine peaks. Falknis (8,401 ft; 2,561 m) and Naatkopf (8,432 ft; 2,570 m) are the tallest.

Government. The Constitution of 1921, amended in 1972, provides for a legislature, the Landtag, of 15 members elected by direct male suffrage.

Prince Hans Adam has been defacto ruler since 1984, when his father, Prince Franz Josef II, relinquished his responsibilities but not his title to the throne.

The major political parties are the Homeland Union (8 of 15 seats in the Landtag) and the Progressive Citizens Party (7 seats).

History. Founded in 1719, Liechtenstein was a member of the German Confederation from 1815 to 1866, when it became an independent principality. It abolished its army in 1868 and has managed to stay neutral and undamaged in all European wars since then. In a referendum on July 1, 1984, male voters granted women the right to vote, a victory for Prince Hans Adam.

LUXEMBOURG

Grand Duchy of Luxembourg
Ruler: Grand Duke Jean (1964)
Premier: Jacques Santer (1984)
Area: 999 sq mi. (2,586 sq km)
Population (est. mid-1987): 400,000 (Luxembourgian, French, German) (average annual growth rate: 0.0%)
Density per square mile: 400.4
Capital and largest city (est. 1982): Luxembourg, 80,000
Monetary unit: Luxembourg franc
Languages: Letzeburgesch, French, German
Religion: Mainly Roman Catholic
National name: Grand-Duché de Luxembourg
Literacy rate: 100%
Economic summary: Gross national product (1983): $4.7 billion. Average annual growth rate (1984): 4%. Per capita income (1983): $13,988. Land used for agriculture: 21%; labor force: 1%; principal products: livestock, dairy products, wine. Labor force in industry: 39%; major products: steel, plastics, synthetic fibers. Natural resource: Iron ore. Export: steel. Imports: machinery, chemicals, transport equipment. Major trading partners: European Common Market countries.

Geography. Luxembourg is a neighbor of Belgium on the west, West Germany on the east, and France on the south. The Ardennes Mountains extend from Belgium into the northern section of Luxembourg.

Government. Luxembourg's unicameral legislature, the Chamber of Deputies, consists of 59 members elected for five years.

The major political parties are the Christian Social Party (25 of 64 seats in Chamber of Deputies), led by Prime Minister Jacques Santer; Socialist-Labor (21 seats), led by Robert Krieps; Democratic Party (14 seats), led by Colette Flesch; Communist Party (2 seats); Green Party (2 seats).

History. Sigefroi, Count of Ardennes, an offspring of Charlemagne, was Luxembourg's first sovereign ruler. In 1060, the country came under the rule of the House of Luxembourg. From the 15th to the 18th century, Spain, France, and Austria held it in turn. The Congress of Vienna in 1815 made it a Grand Duchy and gave it to William I, King of the Netherlands. In 1839 the Treaty of London ceded the western part of Luxembourg to Belgium.

The eastern part, continuing in personal union with the Netherlands and a member of the German Confederation, became autonomous in 1848 and a neutral territory by decision of the London Conference of 1867, governed by its Grand Duke. Germany occupied the duchy in World Wars I and II. Allied troops liberated the enclave in 1944.

In 1961, Prince Jean, son and heir of Grand Duchess Charlotte, was made head of state, acting for his mother. She abdicated in 1964, and Prince Jean became Grand Duke. Grand Dutchess Charlotte died in 1985.

By a customs union between Belgium and Luxembourg, which came into force on May 1, 1922, to last for 50 years, customs frontiers between the two countries were abolished. On Jan. 1, 1948, a customs union with Belgium and the Netherlands (Benelux) came into existence. On Feb. 3, 1958, it became an economic union.

MADAGASCAR

Democratic Republic of Madagascar
President and Head of State: Didier Ratsiraka (1975)
Prime Minister: Lt. Col. Desiré Rakotoarijaona (1977)
Area: 230,035 sq mi. (595,791 sq km)
Population (est. mid-1987): 10,600,000 (average annual growth rate: 2.8%)
Density per square mile: 44.8
Capital and largest city (est. 1983): Antananarivo, 700,000
Monetary unit: Malagasy franc
Languages: Malagasy, French
Ethnic groups: Merina (or Hova), Betsimisaraka, Betsileo, Tsimihety, Antaisaka, Sakalava, Antandroy
Religions: Animist, 47%; Roman Catholic, 26%; Protestant, 23%; Islam, 2%
National name: Repoblika Demokratika Malagasy
Literacy rate: 53%
Economic summary: Gross national product (1983): $3 billion. Annual growth rate (1984): 1.6%. Per capita income (1983): $290. Land used for agriculture: 63%; labor force: 75%; principal products: rice, livestock, coffee, vanilla, sugar, cloves, cotton, sisal, peanuts, tobacco. Labor force in industry: 15%; major products: processed food, textiles, assembled automobiles, soap, mining products. Natural resources: graphite, chromium, ilmenite, tar sands, semiprecious stones. Exports: coffee, cloves, vanilla, chromium, graphite, cotton products. Imports: consumer goods, foodstuffs, crude petroleum, rice. Major trading partners: France, U.S.

Geography. Madagascar lies in the Indian Ocean off the southeast coast of Africa opposite Mozambique. The world's fourth-largest island, it is twice the size of Arizona. The country's low-lying coastal area gives way to a central plateau. The once densely wooded interior has largely been cut down.

Government. The Constitution of Dec. 30, 1975, approved by referendum following a military coup, provides for direct election by universal suffrage of a president for a seven-year term, a Supreme Council of the Revolution as a policy-making body, a unicameral People's National Assembly of 137 members (elected for five-year terms), and a military Committee for Development. The new constitution followed a period of martial rule that began with the suspension of the republic's original bicameral legislature in 1972.

History. The present population is of black and Malay stock, with perhaps some Polynesian, called Malagasy. The French took over a protectorate in 1885, and then in 1894–95 ended the monarchy, exiling Queen Rànavàlona III to Algiers. A colonial administration was set up, to which the Comoro Islands were attached in 1908, and other territories later. In World War II, the British occupied Madagascar, which retained ties to Vichy France.

An autonomous republic within the French Community since 1958, Madagascar became an independent member of the Community in 1960. In May 1973, an army coup led by Maj. Gen. Gabriel Ramanantsoa ousted Philibert Tsiranana, president since 1959.

With unemployment and inflation both high, Ramanantsoa resigned Feb. 5, 1975. His leftist-leaning successor, Interior Minister Richard Ratsimandrava, an Army lieutenant colonel, was killed six days later by a machine-gun ambush in Antananarivo, the capital.

On June 15, 1975, Comdr. Didier Ratsiraka was named President. He announced that he would follow a socialist course and, after nationalizing banks and insurance companies, declared all mineral resources nationalized.

MALAWI

Republic of Malawi
President: Hastings Kamuzu Banda (1966)
Area: 45,747 sq mi. (118,484 sq km)
Population (est. mid-1987): 7,400,000 (average annual growth rate: 3.2%)
Density per square mile: 161.8
Capital (est. 1984): Lilongwe, 172,100
Largest city (est. 1984): Blantyre, 333,800
Monetary unit: Kwacha
Languages: English (official) and Chichewa (National)
Religions: Christian, 57%; Animist, 19%; Islam, 16%
Member of Commonwealth of Nations
Literacy rate: 25%
Economic summary: Gross national product (1983): $1.4 billion. Average annual growth rate (1979–82): 2.5%. Per capita income (1982): $222. Average rate of inflation (1974–78): 10%. Land used for agriculture: 25%; labor force: 52%; principal products: tobacco, tea, sugar, corn, peanuts. Labor force in industry: 16%; major products: food, beverages, tobacco, textiles, footwear, cement. Natural resource: limestone. Exports: tobacco, sugar, tea. Imports: machinery, transport equipment, building and construction materials, fuel. Major trading partners: U.K., U.S., Zimbabwe, Netherlands, Japan, West Germany, South Africa.

Geography. Malawi is a landlocked country the size of Pennsylvania in southeastern Africa, surrounded by Mozambique, Zambia, and Tanzania. Lake Malawi, formerly Lake Nyasa, occupies most of the country's eastern border. The north-south Rift Valley is flanked by mountain ranges and high plateau areas.

Government. Under a Constitution that came into effect on July 6, 1966, the president is the sole head of state; there is neither a prime minister nor a vice president. The National Assembly has 107 members.

There is only one national party—the Malawi Congress Party led by President Hastings K. Banda.

History. The first European to make extensive explorations in the area was David Livingstone in the 1850s and 1860s. In 1884, Cecil Rhodes's British South African Company received a charter to develop the country. The company came into conflict with the Arab slavers in 1887–89. After Britain annexed the Nyasaland territory in 1891, making it a protectorate in 1892, Sir Harry Johnstone, the first high commissioner, using Royal Navy gunboats, wiped out the slavers.

Nyasaland became the independent nation of Malawi on July 6, 1964. Two years later, it became a republic within the Commonwealth of Nations.

Dr. Hastings K. Banda, Malawi's first Prime Minister, became its first President. He pledged to follow a policy of "discretionary nonalignment." Banda alienated much of Black Africa by maintaining good relations with South Africa. He argued that his landlocked country had to rely on South Africa for access to the sea and trade.

MALAYSIA

Paramount Ruler: Sultan Iskandar Alhaj D.K., Sultan of Johore (1984)
Prime Minister: Mahathir Bin Mohamed (1981)
Area: 128,328 sq mi. (332,370 sq km)
Population (est. mid-1987): 16,100,000 (average annual growth rate: 2.4%)
Density per square mile: 125.4
Capital: Kuala Lumpur
Largest cities (est. 1980 by U.N.): Kuala Lumpur, 1,000,000; George Town (Pinang), 300,000; Ipoh, 275,000
Monetary unit: Ringgit
Languages: Malay (official), Chinese, Tamil, English
Religions: Islam, (official), Buddhist, Hindu, Christian, Confucian, Taoist
Member of Commonwealth of Nations
Literacy rate: 75%
Economic summary: Gross national product (1984): $28.4 billion. Average annual growth rate (1973–82): 7.4%. Per capita income (1985): $1,976. Labor force: 12%; principal products: natural rubber, palm oil, tin, petroleum, rice, timber. Major industrial products: processed rubber, timber, and palm oil, tin, petroleum, light manufactures, electronics equipment. Natural resources: tin, oil, copper, timber. Exports: natural rubber, palm oil, tin, timber, petroleum. Imports: machinery, transport equipment, chemicals. Major trading partners: Japan, Singapore, U.S., Western European countries.

Geography. Malaysia is at the southern end of the Malay Peninsula in southeast Asia. The nation also includes Sabah and Sarawak on the island of Borneo to the southeast. Its area slightly exceeds that of New Mexico.

Most of Malaysia is covered by dense jungle and swamps, with a mountain range running the length of the peninsula. Extensive forests provide ebony, sandalwood, teak, and other woods.

Government. Malaysia is a sovereign constitutional monarchy within the Commonwealth of Nations. The Paramount Ruler is elected for a five-year term by the hereditary rulers of the states from among themselves. He is advised by the prime minister and his cabinet. There is a bicameral legislature. The Senate, whose role is comparable more to that of the British House of Lords than to the U.S. Senate, has 68 members, partly appointed by the Paramount Ruler to represent minority and special interests, and partly elected by the legislative assemblies of the various states.

The House of Representatives, is made up of 180 members, who are elected for five-year terms.

The major political parties are the National Front, a coalition of 10 parties (148 of 177 seats in the House of Representatives); Democratic Action Party (24 seats); Islamic Party (1 seat); Independents (4 seats).

History. Malaysia came into existence on Sept. 16, 1963, as a federation of Malaya, Singapore, Sabah (North Borneo), and Sarawak. In 1965, Singapore withdrew from the federation. Since 1966, the 11 states of former Malaya have been known as West Malaysia, and Sabah and Sarawak have been known as East Malaysia.

The Union of Malaya was established April 1, 1946, being formed from the Federated Malay States of Negri Sembilan, Pahang, Perak, and Selangor; the Unfederated Malay States of Johore, Kedah, Kelantan, Perlis, and Trengganu; and two of the Straits Settlements—Malacca and Penang. The Malay states had been brought under British administration during the late 19th and early 20th centuries.

It became the Federation of Malaya on Feb. 1, 1948, and the Federation attained full independence within the Commonwealth of Nations in 1957.

Sabah, constituting the extreme northern portion of the island of Borneo, was a British protectorate administered under charter by the British North Borneo Company from 1881 to 1946, when it assumed the status of a colony. It was occupied by Japanese troops from 1942 to 1945.

Sarawak extends along the northwestern coast of Borneo for about 500 miles (805 km). In 1841, part of the present territory was granted by the Sultan of Brunei to Sir James Brooke. Sarawak continued to be ruled by members of the Brooke family until the Japanese occupation.

From 1963, when Malaysia became independent, it was the target of guerrilla infiltration from Indonesia, but beat off invasion attempts. In 1966, when Sukarno fell and the Communist Party was liquidated in Indonesia, hostilities ended.

In the late 1960s, the country was torn by communal rioting directed against Chinese and Indians, who controlled a disproportionate share of the country's wealth. Beginning in 1968, the government moved to achieve greater economic balance through a rural development program.

Malaysia felt the impact of the "boat people" fleeing Vietnam early in 1978. Because the refugees were mostly ethnic Chinese, the government was apprehensive about any increase of a minority that previously had been the source of internal conflict in the country. In November, authorities banned landings and reversed the order only after several hundred refugees drowned when their fragile boats were towed offshore by Malaysian police.

MALDIVES

Republic of Maldives
President: Maumoon Abdul Gayoom (1978)
Area: 115 sq mi. (298 sq km)
Population (est. mid-1987): 200,000 (average annual growth rate: 3.8%)
Density per square mile: 1739.1
Capital and largest city (est. 1985): Malé, 46,344
Monetary unit: Maldivian rupee
Language: Divehi
Religion: Islam
Literacy rate: 36%
Economic summary: Gross national product (1983 est.): $56.0 million. Average annual growth rate (1970–79): –0.7%. Per capita income (est. 1983): $334. Principal agricultural products: coconuts, millet. Labor force in industry: 26%, major products: fish, processed coconuts. Natural resource: fish, coconuts. Export: fish, clothing, ambergris. Imports: rice, foodstuffs. Major trading partners: Japan, Sri Lanka, Singapore, U.S., Thailand

Geography. The Republic of Maldives is a group of atolls in the Indian Ocean about 417 miles (671 km) southwest of Sri Lanka. Its 1,300 coral islets stretch over an area of 35,200 square miles (90,000 sq km).

Government. The 9-member Cabinet is headed by the president. The Majlis (Parliament) is a unicameral legislature consisting of 48 members. Eight of these are appointed by the president. The others are elected for five-year terms, 2 from the capital island of Malé and 2 from each of the 19 administrative atolls.

There are no political parties in the Maldives.

History. The Maldives (formerly called the Maldive Islands) are inhabited by an Islamic seafaring people. Originally the islands were under the suzerainty of Ceylon. They came under British protection in 1887 and were a dependency of the then colony of Ceylon until 1948. The independence agreement with Britain was signed July 26, 1965.

For centuries a sultanate, the islands adopted a republican form of government in 1952, but the sultanate was restored in 1954. In 1968, however, as the result of a referendum, a republic was again established in the islands.

Ibrahim Nasir, president since 1968, was removed from office by the Majlis in November 1978 and replaced by Maumoon Abdul Cayoom. A national referendum confirmed the new leader.

MALI

Republic of Mali
President of the Republic: Gen. Moussa Traoré
Prime Minister: Mamadou Dembelé (1986)
Area: 478,819 sq mi. (1,240,142 sq km)
Population (est. mid-1987): 8,400,000 (average annual growth rate, 2.9%)
Density per square mile: 17.5
Capital and largest city (est. 1981): Bamako, 750,000
Monetary unit: Franc CFA
Ethnic groups: Bambara, Peul, Soninke, Malinke, Songhai, Dogon, Senoufo, Minianka, Berbers, and Moors
Languages: French (official), African languages
Religions: Islam, 90%; Animist, 9%; Christian, 1%
National name: République de Mali
Literacy rate: 10%
Economic summary: Gross national product (1983): $1.1 billion. Average annual growth rate (1973–82): 4.8%. Per capita income (1983): $150. Principal agricultural products: millet, sorghum, corn, rice, sugar, cotton, peanuts, livestock. Major industrial products: processed foods, textiles. Natural resources: bauxite, iron ore, maganese, phosphate, goats, salt, limestone, gold. Exports: livestock, peanuts, dried fish, cotton, skins. Imports: textiles, vehicles, petroleum products, machinery, sugar. Major trading partners: Western European countries, China.

Geography. Most of Mali, in West Africa, lies in the Sahara. A landlocked country four fifths the size of Alaska, it is bordered by Guinea, Senegal, Mauritania, Algeria, Niger, Burkina Faso, and the Ivory Coast.

The only fertile area is in the south, where the Niger and Senegal Rivers provide irrigation.

Government. The army overthrew the government on Nov. 19, 1968, and formed a provisional government. The Military Committee of National Liberation consists of 14 members and forms the decision-making body.

In late 1969 an attempted coup was foiled, and Lt. Moussa Traoré, president of the Military Committee took over as chief of state and later as head of government, ousting Capt. Yoro Diakité as Premier.

The Malian People's Democratic Union, established in 1976, is the only political party.

History. Subjugated by France by the end of the 19th century, this area became a colony in 1904 (named French Sudan in 1920) and in 1946 became part of the French Union. On June 20, 1960, it became independent and, under the name of Sudanese Republic, was federated with the Republic of Senegal in the Mali Federation. However, Senegal seceded from the Federation on Aug. 20, 1960, and the Sudanese Republic then changed its name to the Republic of Mali on September 22.

In the 1960s, Mali concentrated on economic development, continuing to accept aid from both Soviet bloc and Western nations, as well as international agencies. In the late 1960s, it began retreating from close ties with China. But a purge of conservative opponents brought greater power to President Modibo Keita, and in 1968 the influence of the Chinese and their Malian sympathizers increased. By a treaty signed in Peking in 1968, China agreed to help build a railroad from Mali to Guinea, providing Mali with vital access to the sea.

Mali, with Mauritania, the Ivory Coast, Senegal, Dahomey (Benin), Niger, and Burkina Faso signed a treaty establishing the Economic Community for West Africa.

A six-year sub-Sahara drought devastated Mali before disastrously heavy rains began in 1974. Emergency shipments from a dozen nations and international organizations helped alleviate a famine that affected 1.8 million Malians and killed thousands.

Mali and Burkina Faso fought a brief border war from December 25 to 29, 1985.

MALTA

Republic of Malta
President: Paul Xuereb (1987)
Prime Minister: Edward Fenech Adami (1987)
Area: 122 sq mi. (316 sq km)
Population (est. mid-1987): 400,000 (average annual growth rate: 0.8%)
Density per square mile: 3,278.7
Capital (est. 1982): Valetta, 15,000
Largest city (est. 1982): Sliema, 20,500
Monetary unit: Maltese lira
Languages: Maltese and English
Religion: Roman Catholic
National name: Repubblika Ta Malta
Member of Commonwealth of Nations, Council of Europe
Literacy rate: 83%
Economic summary: Gross national product (1985): $1.4 billion. Average annual growth rate (1973–82): 1.5%. Per capita income (1985): $4,057. Land used for agriculture, 45%; labor force: 6%; principal products: fodder crops, potatoes, onions, fruits and vegetables. Labor force in industry: 27%; major products: textiles, wine, beer, processed foods, plastics, electronic equipment. Natural resources: limestone, salt. Exports: textiles, yarns, manufactured goods, ships. Imports: manufactured goods, machinery, transport equipment. Major trading partners: West Germany, U.K., Italy.

Geography. The five Maltese islands—with a combined land area smaller than Philadelphia—are in the Mediterranean about 60 miles (97 km) south of the southeastern tip of Sicily.

Government. The government is headed by a Prime Minister, responsible to a 69-member House of Representatives elected by universal suffrage.

The major political parties are the Nationalists (35 of 69 seats in the House,) led by Prime Minister Edward Fenech Adami; Malta Labor Party (34 seats), led by Carmelo Mifsud Bonnici.

History. The strategic importance of Malta was recognized by the Phoenicians, who occupied it, as did in their turn the Greeks, Carthaginians, and Romans. The apostle Paul was shipwrecked there in A.D. 58.

The Knights of St. John (Malta), who obtained the three habitable Maltese islands of Malta, Gozo, and Comino from Charles V in 1530, reached their highest fame when they withstood an attack by superior Turkish forces in 1565.

Napoleon seized Malta in 1798, but the French forces were ousted by British troops the next year, and British rule was confirmed by the Treaty of Paris in 1814.

Malta was heavily attacked by German and Italian aircraft during World War II, but was never invaded by the Axis.

Malta became an independent nation on Sept. 21, 1964, and a republic Dec. 13, 1974, but remained in the British Commonwealth. The Governor-General, Sir Anthony Mamo, was sworn in as first president and Dom Mintoff became prime minister.

After 13 years in office, Mintoff resigned as Prime Minister on Dec. 22, 1984, giving way to chosen successor, Carmelo Mifsud Bonnici, who had been Senior Deputy Prime Minister. Fenech Adami's election ended 16 years of Labor rule.

MAURITANIA

Islamic Republic of Mauritania
Chief of State and Head of Government: Col. Maaouye Ould Sidi Ahmed Taya (1984)
Area: 397,953 sq mi. (1,030,700 sq km)
Population (est. mid-1987): 2,000,000 (average annual growth rate: 3.0%)
Density per square mile: 5.0
Capital and largest city (est. 1981): Nouakchott, 175,000
Monetary unit: Ouguyia
Ethnic groups: Moors; a black minority (Poulars, Soninkes, and Wolofs)
Languages: Arabic and French
Religion: Islam
National name: République Islamique de Mauritanie
Literacy rate: 17%
Economic summary: Gross national product (1983): $720 million. Average annual growth rate (1973–82): 3.0%. Per capita income (1983): $450. Principal agricultural products: livestock, millet, maize, wheat, dates, rice. Major industrial products: iron ore, processed fish. Natural resources: copper, iron ore, gypsum, fish. Exports: iron ore, fish, copper. Imports: foodstuffs, petroleum, capital goods. Major trading partners: France, Spain, U.S., U.K., Italy, Japan.

Geography. Mauritania, three times the size of Arizona, is situated in northwest Africa with about 350 miles (592 km) of coastline on the Atlantic Ocean. It is bordered by Morocco on the north, Algeria and Mali on the east, and Senegal on the south.

The country is mostly desert, with the exception of the fertile Senegal River valley in the south and grazing land in the north.

Government. An Army coup on July 10, 1978, deposed Moktar Ould Daddah, who had been President since Mauritania's independence in 1960. President Mohammed Khouna Ould Haldala, who seized power in the 1978 coup, was in turn deposed in a Dec. 12, 1984, coup by army chief of staff Maaouye Ould Sidi Ahmed Taya, who assumed the title of President.

History. Mauritania was first explored by the Portuguese. The French organized the area as a territory in 1904.

Mauritania became an independent nation on Nov. 28, 1960, and was admitted to the United Nations in 1961 over the strenuous opposition of Morocco, which claimed the territory. With Moors, Arabs, Berbers, and blacks frequently in conflict, the government in the late 1960s sought to make Arab culture dominant to unify the land.

Mauritania acquired administrative control of the southern part of the former Spanish Sahara when the colonial administration withdrew in 1975, under an agreement with Morocco and Spain. Mauritanian troops moved into the territory but encountered resistance from the Polisario Front, a Saharan independence movement backed by Algeria. The task of trying to pacify the area proved a heavy burden. Mauritania signed a peace agreement with the Polisario insurgents in August 1979, withdrew from the territory and renounced territorial claims.

Increased military spending and rising casulaties in Western Sahara contributed to the discontent that brought down the civilian government of Ould Daddah in 1978. A succession of military rulers has followed.

MAURITIUS

Sovereign: Queen Elizabeth II
Governor-General: Sir Veerasamy Ringadoo (1986)
Prime Minister: Aneerood Jugnauth (1982)
Area: 787 sq mi. (2,040 sq km)
Population (est. mid-1987): 1,100,000 (average annual growth rate: 1.2%) (Indian, 51%; Creole, 33%)
Density per square mile: 1,397.7
Capital and largest city (est. 1980): Port Louis, 155,000
Monetary unit: Mauritian rupee
Languages: English (official), French, Creole, Hindi, Urdu, Chinese
Religions: Hindu, 46%, Christian (mainly Roman Catholic), 33%; Islam, 16%
Member of Commonwealth of Nations
Literacy rate: 61%
Economic summary: Gross national product (1983): $1.25 billion. Average annual growth rate (1973–82): 3.9%. Per capita income (1983): $1,000. Land used for agriculture: 50%; labor force: 29%; principal products: sugar cane. Labor force in industry: 22%; major products: processed sugar and tea, molasses, rum, textiles. Natural resources: fish. Exports: sugar, tea, molasses. Imports: foodstuffs, manufactured goods. Major trading partners: Western European countries, U.S., U.K.

Geography. Mauritius is a mountainous island in the Indian Ocean east of Madagascar.

Government. Mauritius is a member of the British Commonwealth, with Queen Elizabeth II as head of state. She is represented by a governor-general, who chooses the prime minister from the unicameral Legislative Assembly. The Legislative Assembly has 70 members, 62 of whom are elected by direct suffrage. The remaining 8 are chosen from among the unsuccessful candidates.

The major parties are the governing Alliance Party coalition, composed of the Mouvement Socialiste Mauricien, the Parti Mauricien Social Democrate, the Labor Party, and the Organisation du Peuple Rodriguais (48 of 70 seats in the Legislative Assembly, led by Prime Minister Aneerood Jugnauth, and the opposition Mouvement Militant Mauricien, led by Paul Berenger.

History. Mauritius was seized from France by British troops in 1810 and ceded to Britain by the Treaty of Paris in 1814. Until 1903, Mauritius and the Seychelles were administered as a single colony. The colony of Mauritius became an independent nation on March 12, 1968.

The nation has an Indian majority, descendants of laborers imported from India to work the sugar plantations after the abolition of slavery in 1834. The native blacks speak French and are Roman Catholics.

The Labor Party government of Sir Seewoosagur Ramgoolam, who had ruled Mauritius since independence, was toppled in a 1982 election by the Movement Militant Mauricien, which had campaigned for recovery of Diego Garcia island, separated from Mauritius during the colonial period and leased by Britain to the United States for a naval base. But an Alliance Party coalition, including the Labor Party, regained power at the end of 1983 and brought back Ramgoolam as Prime Minister. He was succeeded by Aneerood Jugnauth of his party in 1982.

MEXICO

United Mexican States
President: Miguel de la Madrid Hurtado (1982)
Area: 761,600 sq mi. (1,972,547 sq km)
Population (est. mid-1987): 81,900,000 (average annual growth rate: 2.5%) (60% mestizo; 30% Indian)
Density per square mile: 107.5
Capital: Mexico City
Largest cities (1980 census): Mexico City, 12,900,000; Guadalajara, 3,000,000; Monterrey, 2,700,000; Ciudad Juarez, 1,120,000; Puebla de Zaragoza, 1,100,000; Leon, 1,000,000
Monetary unit: Peso
Languages: Spanish, Indian languages
Religion: Roman Catholic, 93%
Official name: Estados Unidos Mexicanos
Literacy rate: 81%
Economic summary: Gross national product (1983): $168 billion. Annual growth rate (1983): –5.3%. Per capita income (1983): $2,240. Land used for agriculture, 12%; labor force: 26%; principal products: corn, cotton, sugar cane, fruits. Labor force in industry: 17%; major products: processed foods, chemicals, basic metals and metal products, petroleum. Natural resources: petroleum, silver, copper, gold, lead, zinc, natural gas, timber. Exports: cotton, sugar, shrimp, cattle and meat, petroleum. Imports: machinery, equipment, industrial vehicles, intermediate goods. Major trading partners: U.S., Japan, Western European countries.

Geography. The United States' neighbor to the south, Mexico is about one fifth its size. Baja California in the west, an 800-mile (1,287-km) peninsula, forms the Gulf of California. In the east are the Gulf of Mexico and the Bay of Campeche, which is formed by Mexico's other peninsula, the Yucatán.

The center of Mexico is a great, high plateau, open to the north, with mountain chains on east and west and with ocean-front lowlands lying outside of them.

Government. The President, who is popularly elected for six years and is ineligible to succeed himself, governs with a Cabinet of secretaries. Congress has two houses—a 400-member Chamber of Deputies, elected for three years, and a 64-member Senate, elected for six years.

Each of the 31 states has considerable autonomy, with a popularly elected governor, a legislature, and a local judiciary. The President of Mexico appoints the mayor of the Federal District.

The major parties are the Partido Revolucionario Institucional (all 64 seats in the Senate and 289 of 400 seats in the Chamber of Deputies); Partido Acción Nacional (38 of 400 seats in Chamber); Unified Socialist Party (12 seats); and other parties.

History. At least two civilized races—the Mayas and later the Toltecs—preceded the wealthy Aztec empire, conquered in 1519–21 by the Spanish under Hernando Cortés. Spain ruled for the next 300 years until 1810 (the date was Sept. 16 and is now celebrated as Independence Day), when the Mexicans first revolted. They continued the struggle and finally won independence in 1821.

From 1821 to 1877, there were two emperors, several dictators, and enough presidents and provisional executives to make a new government on the average of every nine months. Mexico lost Texas (1836), and after defeat in the war with the

U.S. (1846–48) it lost the area comprising the present states of California, Nevada, and Utah, most of Arizona and New Mexico, and parts of Wyoming and Colorado.

In 1855, the Indian patriot Benito Juárez began a series of liberal reforms, including the disestablishment of the Catholic Church, which had acquired vast property. A subsequent civil war was interrupted by the French invasion of Mexico (1861), the crowning of Maximilian of Austria as Emperor (1864), and then his overthrow and execution by forces under Juárez, who again became President in 1867.

The years after the fall of the dictator Porfirio Diaz (1877–80 and 1884–1911) were marked by bloody political-military strife and trouble with the U.S., culminating in the punitive expedition into northern Mexico (1916–17) in unsuccessful pursuit of the revolutionary Pancho Villa. Since a brief period of civil war in 1920, Mexico has enjoyed a period of gradual agricultural, political, and social reforms. Relations with the U.S. were again disturbed in 1938 when all foreign oil wells were expropriated. Agreement on compensation was finally reached in 1941.

The last year of José López Portillo's presidency was shadowed by economic problems caused by falling oil prices.

Miguel de la Madrid Hurtado, candidate of the ruling Partido Revolucionario Institucional, won the July 4 election for a six-year term.

During 1983 and 1984, Mexico suffered its worst financial crisis in 50 years, leading to critically high unemployment and an inability to pay its foreign debt. The collapse of oil prices in 1986 cut into Mexico's export earnings and worsened the situation.

In an election held on July 7, 1985, the ruling Institutional Party declared it had won all seven contested governorships and an overwhelming majority in the national Chamber of Deputies. Accusations of vote fraud by the ruling party intensified after state elections in 1986 in which it claimed a victory amidst reports of election irregularities such as ballot stuffing.

Mexican-American relations were strained when, on May 13, 1986, U.S. officials told the Senate that high officials in the Mexican government were involved in drug trafficking. Mexico angrily denied the charges.

MONACO

Principality of Monaco
Ruler: Prince Rainier III (1949)
Minister of State: Jean Ausseil (1986)
Area: 0.73 sq mi. (465 acres)
Population (est. 1987): 28,000 (average annual growth rate: 1.2%)
Density per square mile: 38,356.2
Capital: Monaco-Ville
Monetary unit: French franc
Languages: French, Monégasque, Italian
Religion: Roman Catholic
National name: Principauté de Monaco
Literacy rate: 99%

Geography. Monaco is a tiny, hilly wedge driven into the French Mediterranean coast nine miles east of Nice.

Government. Prince Albert of Monaco gave the principality a Constitution in 1911, creating a National Council of 18 members popularly elected for five years. The head of government is the Minister of State.

Prince Rainier III, born May 31, 1923, succeeded his grandfather, Louis II, on the latter's death, May 9, 1949. Rainier was married April 18, 1956, to Grace Kelly, U.S. actress. A daughter, Princess Caroline Louise Marguerite, was born on Jan. 23, 1957 (married to Philippe Junot June 28, 1978 and divorced in 1980; married to Stefano Casiraghi Dec. 29, 1983, and gave birth to a son, Andrea Albert, June 9, 1984); a son, Prince Albert Louis Pierre, on March 14, 1958; and Princess Stéphanie Marie Elisabeth, on Feb. 1, 1965. Princess Grace died Sept. 14, 1982, of injuries received the day before when the car she was driving went off the road near Monte Carlo. She was 52. Her daughter Stéphanie suffered neck injuries.

The special significance attached to the birth of descendants to Prince Rainier stems from a clause in the Treaty of July 17, 1919, between France and Monaco stipulating that in the event of vacancy of the Crown, the Monégasque territory would become an autonomous state under a French protectorate.

The National and Democratic Union (all 18 seats in National Council), led by Auguste Medecin, is the only political party.

History. The Phoenicians, and after them the Greeks, had a temple on the Monacan headland honoring Hercules. From *Monoikos*, the Greek surname for this mythological strong man, the principality took its name. After being independent for 800 years, Monaco was annexed to France in 1793 and was placed under Sardinia's protection in 1815. In 1861, it went under French guardianship but continued to be independent.

By a treaty in 1918, France stipulated that the French government be given a veto over the succession to the throne.

Monaco is a little land of pleasure with a tourist business that runs as high as 1.5 million visitors a year. It had popular gaming tables as early as 1856. Five years later, a 50-year concession to operate the games was granted to François Blanc, of Bad Homburg. This concession passed into the hand of a private company in 1898.

Monaco's practice of providing a tax shelter for French businessmen resulted in a dispute between the countries. When Rainier refused to end the practice, France retaliated with a customs tax. In 1967, Rainier took control of the Société des Bains de Mer, operator of the famous Monte Carlo gambling casino, in a program to increase hotel and convention space. He paid $8 million to Greek shipping magnate Aristotle Onassis for his shares.

MONGOLIA

Mongolian People's Republic
Chairman of Presidium of the Great People's Khural (President): Jambyn Batmunkh (1984)
Chairman of Council of Ministers (Premier): Dumagiin Sodnom (1984)
Area: 604,250 sq mi. (1,565,000 sq km)
Population (est. mid-1987): 2,000,000 (average annual growth rate: 2.6%)
Density per square mile: 3.3

Capital and largest city (est. 1985): Ulan Bator, 488,200
Monetary unit: Tugrik
Language: Mongolian
Religion: Lamaistic Buddhism
National name: Bugd Nairamdakh Mongol Ard Uls
Literacy rate: about 90%
Economic summary: Gross national product (1984): $1.8 billion. Average annual growth rate (1970–81): 3.1%. Per capita income: (1984): $1,000 Principal agricultural products: livestock, wheat, oats, barley. Major industrial products: animal products, building materials, minerals. Natural resources: coal, copper, molybdenum. Exports: livestock, animal products, nonferrous metals. Imports: machinery and equipment, clothing, petroleum. Major trading partners: U.S.S.R. and Soviet bloc countries.

Geography. Mongolia lies in eastern Asia between Soviet Siberia on the north and China on the south. It is slightly larger than Alaska.

The productive regions of Mongolia—a tableland ranging from 3,000 to 5,000 feet (914 to 1,524 m) in elevation—are in the north, which is well drained by numerous rivers, including the Hovd, Onon, Selenga, and Tula.

Much of the Gobi Desert falls within Mongolia.

Government. The Mongolian People's Republic is a socialist state. The highest organ of state power is the Great People's Khural (Parliament), which is elected for a term of four years and is convened once a year. The Great People's Khural elects the Presidium, which consists of a chairman, two vice chairmen, a secretary, and six members. The Council of Ministers is set up by the Great People's Khural and consists of a chairman, vice chairmen, and ministers.

The Mongolian People's Revolutionary Party, led by President Jambyn Batmunkh, is the only political party.

History. The Mongolian People's Republic, formerly known as Outer Mongolia, is a Soviet satellite. It contains the original homeland of the historic Mongols, whose power reached its zenith during the 13th century under Kublai Khan. The area accepted Manchu rule in 1689, but after the Chinese Revolution of 1911 and the fall of the Manchus in 1912, the northern Mongol princes expelled the Chinese officials and declared independence under the Khutukhtu, or "Living Buddha."

In 1921, Soviet troops entered the country and facilitated the establishment of a republic by Mongolian revolutionaries in 1924 after the death of the last Living Buddha. China, meanwhile, continued to claim Outer Mongolia but was unable to back the claim with any strength. Under the 1945 Chinese-Russian Treaty, China agreed to give up Outer Mongolia, which, after a plebiscite, became a nominally independent country.

Allied with the U.S.S.R. in its dispute with China, Mongolia has mobilized troops along its borders since 1968 when the two powers became involved in border clashes on the Kazakh-Sinkiang frontier to the west and on the Amur and Ussuri Rivers. A 20-year treaty of friendship and cooperation, signed in 1966, entitled Mongolia to call upon the U.S.S.R. for military aid in the event of invasion.

MOROCCO

Kingdom of Morocco
Ruler: King Hassan II (1961)
Prime Minister: Azzedine Laraki (1986)
Area: 177,116 sq mi. (458,730 sq km)
Population (est. mid-1987): 24,400,000 (average annual growth rate: 2.5%)
Density per square mile: 137.8
Capital: Rabat
Largest cities (1984): Casablanca, 2,158,369; Rabat, 556,000; Fez, 548,206; Marrakech, 482,603
Monetary unit: Dirham
Languages: Arabic, French, Spanish
Religions: Islam
National name: al-Mamlaka al-Maghrebia
Literacy rate: 28%
Economic summary: Gross national product (1985): $17.5 billion. Average annual growth rate (est. 1984): 2.0%. Per capita income (1983): $750. Land used for agriculture; 19%; labor force: 50%; products: barley, wheat, citrus fruits, vegetables, wool. Labor force in industry, 15%; major products: textiles, fish, chemicals. Natural resources: phosphates, lead, manganese, fisheries. Exports: phosphates, citrus fruits, vegetables, canned fruits and vegetables, canned fish, carpets. Imports: capital goods, fuels, foodstuffs, iron and steel. Major trading partners: France, West Germany, Italy, Saudi Arabia.

Geography. Morocco, about one tenth larger than California, is just south of Spain across the Strait of Gibraltar and looks out on the Atlantic from the northwest shoulder of Africa. Algeria is to the east and Mauritania to the south.

On the Atlantic coast there is a fertile plain. The Mediterranean coast is mountainous. The Atlas Mountains, running northeastward from the south to the Algerian frontier, average 11,000 feet (3,353 m) in elevation.

Government. The King, after suspending the 1962 Constitution and dissolving Parliament in 1965, promulgated a new Constitution in 1972. He continued to rule by decree until June 3, 1977, when the first free elections since 1962 took place. The 306-member Chamber of Deputies has 204 elected seats, with the balance chosen by local councils and groups.

A coalition of independents loyal to the King and three right-of-center parties, the Constitutional Union Party (83 seats), the National Rally of Independents (61 seats), and the National Democratic Party (24 seats), constitute the government. Opposition parties include the Popular Movement (47 seats) and Isviglol (41 seats).

History. Morocco was once the home of the Berbers, who helped the Arabs invade Spain in A.D. 711 and then revolted against them and gradually won control of large areas of Spain for a time after 739.

The country was ruled successively by various native dynasties and maintained regular commercial relations with Europe, even during the 17th and 18th centuries when it was the headquarters of the famous Salé pirates. In the 19th century, there were frequent clashes with the French and Spanish. Finally, in 1904, France and Spain divided Morocco into zones of French and Spanish influence, and these were established as protectorates in 1912.

Meanwhile, Morocco had become the object of big-power rivalry, which almost led to a European war in 1905 when Germany attempted to gain a foothold in the rich mineral country. By terms of the Algeciras Conference (1906), Morocco was internationalized economically, and France's privileges were limited.

The Tangier Statute, concluded by Britain, France, and Spain in 1923, created an international zone at the port of Tangier, permanently neutralized and demilitarized. In World War II, Spain occupied the zone, ostensibly to ensure order, but was forced to withdraw in 1945.

Sultan Mohammed V was deposed by the French in 1953 and replaced by his uncle, but nationalist agitation forced his return in 1955. On his death on Feb. 26, 1961, his son, Hassan, became King.

France and Spain recognized the independence and sovereignty of Morocco in 1956. Later the same year, the Tangier international zone was abolished.

In 1975, tens of thousands of Moroccans crossed the border into Spanish Sahara to back their government's contention that the northern part of the territory was historically part of Morocco. At the same time, Mauritania occupied the southern half of the territory in defiance of Spanish threats to resist such a takeover. Abandoning its commitment to self-determination for the territory, Spain withdrew, and only Algeria protested.

When Mauritania signed a peace treaty with the Algerian-backed Polisario Front in August 1979, Morocco occupied and assumed administrative control of the southern part of the Western Sahara, in addition to the northern part it already occupied. Under pressure from other African leaders, Hassan agreed in mid-1981 to a cease-fire with a referendum under international supervision to decide the fate of the Sahara territory, but the referendum was never carried out.

King Hassan, startled the Reagan Administration in mid-August 1984 by signing a treaty of union with Col. Muammar el-Qaddafi, the Libyan leader.

The Moroccans described the treaty as the culmination of a process in which Libya had withdrawn its support for the Polisario in the Western Sahara, and Morocco had agreed to refrain from sending troops to help the French in Chad.

King Hassan became the second Arab leader to meet with an Israeli leader when, on July 21, 1986, Israeli Prime Minister Shimon Peres came to Morocco. Libyan criticism of the meeting led to King Hassan's abrogation of the treaty with Libya.

MOZAMBIQUE

People's Republic of Mozambique
President: Joaquim Chissano (1986)
Area: 303,073 sq mi. (799,380 sq. km.)
Population (est. mid-1987): 14,700,000 (average annual growth rate: 2.6%)
Density per square mile: 48.5
Capital and largest city (est. mid-1986): Maputo, 882,800
Monetary unit: Metical
Languages: Portuguese (official), Bantu languages
Religions: Animist, 48%; Christian, 17%; Islam, 17%
National name: República Popular de Moçambique
Literacy rate: 27%
Economic summary: Gross national product (1983): $2.0 billion. Average annual growth rate (1970–79): –5.3%. Per capita income (1983): $150. Principal agricultural products: cotton, cashew nuts, sugar, tea, copra, peanuts. Labor force in industry: 6%; major products: processed foods, petroleum products, beverages, textiles, tobacco. Natural resources: bauxite, coal, iron ore, fluorite, tantalite, timber. Exports: cashew nuts, cotton, sugar, petroleum products, tea, copra, prawns, citrus, textiles. Imports: machinery and electrical equipment, cotton textiles, vehicles, petroleum, iron and steel. Major trading partners: Portugal, South Africa, U.S., U.K., West Germany, U.S.S.R., Zimbabwe.

Geography. Mozambique stretches for 1,535 miles (2,470 km) along Africa's southeast coast. It is nearly twice the size of California. Tanzania is to the north; Malawi, Zambia, and Zimbabwe to the west; and South Africa and Swaziland to the south.

The country is generally a low-lying plateau broken up by 25 sizable rivers that flow into the Indian Ocean. The largest is the Zambezi; which provides access to central Africa. The principal ports are Maputo and Beira, which is the port for Zimbabwe.

Government. After having been under Portuguese colonial rule for 470 years, Mozambique became independent on June 25, 1975. It is a Marxist state. The first President, Samora Moises Machel, headed the National Front for the Liberation of Mozambique (FRELIMO) in its 10-year guerrilla war for independence. He died in a plane crash on Oct. 19, 1986 and was succeeded by his Foreign Minister, Joaquim Chissano.

History. Mozambique was discovered by Vasco da Gama in 1498, although the Arabs had penetrated into the area as early as the 10th century. It was first colonized in 1505, and by 1510, the Portuguese had control of all the former Arab sultanates on the east African coast.

FRELIMO was organized in 1963. Guerrilla activity had become so extensive by 1973 that Portugal was forced to dispatch 40,000 troops to fight the rebels. A cease-fire was signed in September 1974, when Portugal agreed to grant Mozambique independence.

On Jan. 25, 1985, Mozambique's celebration of a decade of independence from Portugal was not a happy one. The Marxist government was locked in a five-year-old, stalemated, paralyzing war with anti-government guerrillas, known as the MNR, backed by the white minority government in South Africa. At the same time, like those in much of eastern Africa, the peasants who make up most of the population suffered from the consequences of four years of drought, with thousands reported starving.

NAMIBIA

See South Africa

NAURU

Republic of Nauru
President and Head Chief: Hammer DeRoburt (1968)
Area: 8.2 sq mi. (21 sq km)
Population (est. 1987): 8,000 (average annual growth rate: 1.3%)
Density per square mile: 975.6
Capital: Yaren
Monetary unit: Australian dollar
Languages: Nauruan and English
Religions: Protestant, 58%; Roman Catholic, 24%;

Confucian and Taoist, 8%
Special relationship within the Commonwealth of Nations
Literacy rate: 99%
Economic summary: Gross national product (1984): over $160 million. Per capita income (1981): $21,400. Major industrial products: phosphates. Natural resources: phosphates. Exports: phosphates. Imports: foodstuffs, fuel. Major trading partners: Australia, New Zealand, U.K., Japan.

Geography. Nauru (pronounced NAH oo roo) is an island in the Pacific just south of the equator, about 2,500 miles (4,023 km) southwest of Honolulu.

Government. Legislative power is invested in a popularly elected 18-member Parliament, which elects the President from among its members. Executive power rests with the President, who is assisted by a five-member Cabinet.

History. Nauru was annexed by Germany in 1888. It was placed under joint Australian, New Zealand, and British mandate after World War I, and in 1947 it became a U.N. trusteeship administered by the same three powers. On Jan. 31, 1968, Nauru became an independent republic.

NEPAL

Kingdom of Nepal
Ruler: King Birendra Bir Bikram Shah Dev (1972)
Prime Minister: Marich Man Singh Shrestha (1986)
Area: 54,463 sq mi. (141,059 sq km)
Population (est. mid-1987): 17,800,000 (average annual growth rate: 2.5%)
Density per square mile: 326.8
Capital and largest city (est. 1980): Katmandu, 400,000
Monetary unit: Nepalese rupee
Languages: Nepali (official), Newari, Bhutia
Religions: Hindu, 90%; Buddhist, 5%; Islam, 3%
Literacy rate: 23%
Economic summary: Gross national product (1983): $2.7 billion. Average annual growth rate (1973–82): 3.0%. Per capita income (1983): $170. Labor force in agriculture: 93%; principal products: rice, maize, wheat, millet, jute, sugar cane, oilseed, potatoes. Labor force in industry: 2%; major products: sugar, lumber, jute, hydroelectric power, cement. Natural resources: water, timber, hydroelectric potential. Exports: rice and food products, and timber. Imports: textiles, manufactured goods, construction materials, fuel. Major trading partners: India, Japan.

Geography. A landlocked country the size of Arkansas, lying between India and the Tibetan Autonomous Region of China, Nepal contains Mount Everest (29,028 ft.; 8,848 m), the tallest mountain in the world. Along its southern border, Nepal has a strip of level land that is partly forested, partly cultivated. North of that is the slope of the main section of the Himalayan range, including Everest and many other peaks higher than 20,000 feet (6,096 m).

Government. A new Constitution promulgated by King Mahendra in 1962 provided for a unicameral legislature called the National Panchayat. All political parties were banned in 1960.

History. The Kingdom of Nepal was unified in 1768 by King Prithwi Narayan Shah. A commercial treaty was signed with Britain in 1792, and in 1816, after more than a year's hostilities, the Nepalese agreed to allow British residents to live in Katmandu, the capital. In 1923, Britain recognized the absolute independence of Nepal. Between 1846 and 1951, the country was ruled by the Rana family, which always held the office of prime minister. In 1951, however, the King took over all power and proclaimed a constitutional monarchy.

Mahendra Bir Bikram Shah became King in 1955. Nepal and China settled their differences in 1956, and thereafter Nepal accepted economic aid from the Chinese. The U.S. and the U.S.S.R. also provide aid.

After Mahendra, who had ruled since 1955, died of a heart attack in 1972, Prince Birendra, at 26, succeeded to the throne.

In the first election in 22 years, on May 2, 1980, voters approved the continued autocratic rule by the King with the advice of a partyless Parliament. The King, however, permitted the election of a new legislature, in May 1986, to which the Prime Minister and Cabinet are responsible.

THE NETHERLANDS

Kingdom of the Netherlands
Sovereign: Queen Beatrix (1980)
Premier: Ruud Lubbers (1982)
Area: 16,041 sq. mi. (41,548 sq. km.)
Population (est. mid-1987): 14,600,000 (average annual growth rate: 0.4%)
Density per square mile: 910.2
Capital: Amsterdam; seat of government: The Hague
Largest cities (est. 1986): Amsterdam, 679,100; Rotterdam, 571,400; 's-Gravenhage, 444,000; Utrecht, 229,900; Eindhoven, 190,800
Monetary unit: Guilder
Language: Dutch
Religions: Roman Catholic, 36%; Dutch Reformed, 19%; unaffiliated, 27%
National name: Koninkrijk der Nederlanden
Literacy rate: 99%
Economic summary: Gross national product (1984): $123.8 billion. Annual growth rate (1984): 1.7%. Per capita income (1983): $8,492. Land used for agriculture: 59%; labor force, 10%; principal products: wheat, barley, sugar beets, potatoes, meat and dairy products. Labor force in industry: 30%; major products: metal fabrication, textiles, chemicals, electronic equipment. Exports: foodstuffs, machinery, natural gas, chemicals, petroleum products, textiles. Imports: machinery, crude petroleum, chemicals, textiles, mineral ores. Major trading partners: West Germany, Belgium, France, U.K.

Geography. The Netherlands, on the coast of the North Sea, has West Germany to the east and Belgium to the south. It is twice the size of New Jersey.

Part of the great plain of north and west Europe, the Netherlands has maximum dimensions of 190 by 160 miles (360 by 257 km) and is low and flat except in Limburg in the southeast, where some hills rise to 300 feet (92 m). About half the country's area is below sea level, making the famous Dutch dikes a requisite to the use of much land. Reclamation of land from the sea through dikes has continued through recent times.

All drainage reaches the North Sea, and the principal rivers—Rhine, Maas (Meuse), and Schelde—

have their sources outside the country. The Rhine is the most heavily used waterway in Europe.

Government. The Netherlands and its former colony of the Netherlands Antilles form the Kingdom of the Netherlands.

The Netherlands is a constitutional monarchy with a bicameral Parliament. The Upper Chamber has 75 members elected for six years by representative bodies of the provinces, half of the members retiring every three years. The Lower Chamber has 150 members elected by universal suffrage for four years. The two Chambers have the right of investigation and interpellation; the Lower Chamber can initiate legislation and amend bills.

The Sovereign, Queen Beatrix Wilhelmina Armgard, born Jan. 31, 1938, was married on March 11, 1966, to Claus von Amsberg, a former West German diplomat. The marriage drew public criticism because of the bridegroom's service in the German army during World War II. In 1967, Beatrix gave birth to a son, Willem-Alexander Claus George Ferdinand, the first male heir to the throne since 1884. She also has two other sons, Johan Friso Bernhard Christian David, born in 1968, and Constantijn Christof Frederik Aschwin, born the next year.

Premier Ruud Lubber heads a coalition of Christian Democrats (54 of 150 seats in the Lower Chamber), and Liberals (27 seats). Other major parties are the opposition Labor Party (52 seats), and Democrats '66 (9 seats).

History. Julius Caesar found the low-lying Netherlands inhabited by Germanic tribes—the Nervii, Frisii, and Batavi. The Batavi on the Roman frontier did not submit to Rome's rule until 13 B.C., and then only as allies.

A part of Charlemagne's empire in the 8th and 9th centuries A.D., the area later passed into the hands of Burgundy and the Austrian Hapsburgs, and finally in the 16th century came under Spanish rule.

When Philip II of Spain suppressed political liberties and the growing Protestant movement in the Netherlands, a revolt led by William of Orange broke out in 1568. Under the Union if Utrecht (1579), the seven northern provinces became the Republic of the United Netherlands.

The Dutch East India Company was established in 1602, and by the end of the 17th century Holland was one of the great sea and colonial powers of Europe.

The nation's independence was not completely established until after the Thirty Years' War (1618–48), after which the country's rise as a commercial and maritime power began. In 1814, all the provinces of Holland and Belgium were merged into one kingdom, but in 1830 the southern provinces broke away to form the Kingdom of Belgium. A liberal Constitution was adopted by the Netherlands in 1848.

In spite of its neutrality in World War II, the Netherlands was invaded by the Nazis in May 1940, and the East Indies were later taken by the Japanese. The nation was liberated in May 1945. In 1948, after a reign of 50 years, Queen Wilhelmina resigned and was succeeded by her daughter Juliana.

In 1949, after a four-year war, the Netherlands granted independence to the East Indies, which became the Republic of Indonesia. In 1963, it turned over the western half of New Guinea to the new nation, ending 300 years of Dutch presence in Asia. Attainment of independence by Suriname on Nov. 25, 1975, left the Dutch Antilles as the Netherlands' only overseas territory.

Prime Minister Van Agt lost his narrow majority in elections on May 26, 1981, in which the major issue was the deployment of U.S. cruise missiles on Dutch soil. Public opposition to the missiles forced the Netherlands, along with Belgium, to reverse its position in 1982 despite the Prime Minister's personal support for the NATO decision to deploy the new weapons in Western Europe. Van Agt lost his centrist coalition in May 1982 in a dispute over economic policy, and was succeeded by Ruud Lubber as Premier. Lubber announced on November 1, 1985 to accept the deployment of the U.S. missiles.

Netherlands Autonomous Country

NETHERLANDS ANTILLES

Status: Part of the Kingdom of the Netherlands
Governor: Prof. R. A. Romer (1986)
Premier: Domenico F. Martina
Area: 383 sq mi. (993 sq km)
Population (est. mid-1987): 200,000 (average annual growth rate: 1.4%)
Capital (est. 1978): Willemstad, 152,000
Literacy rate: 95%
Economic summary: Gross national product (1983): $131.6 billion. Average annual growth rate (1970–79): 0.9%. Per capita income: $9,140. Principal agricultural products: pigs, goats. Major industries: oil refining, tourism. Natural resource: phosphate. Export: petroleum. Import: petroleum. Major trading partners: U.S., Venezuela.

Geography. The Netherlands Antilles comprise two groups of Caribbean islands 500 miles (805 km) apart: one, about 40 miles (64 km) off the Venezuelan coast, consists of Curaçao (173 sq mi.; 448 sq km), Bonaire (95 sq mi.; 246 sq km), and Aruba (69 sq mi.; 179 sq km); the other, lying to the northeast, consists of three small islands with a total area of 34 square miles (88 sq km). Aruba was given separate status within the kingdom effective Jan. 1, 1986. The Dutch acquired Curaçao from Spain in 1643.

Government. There is a constitutional government formed by the Governor and Cabinet and an elected Legislative Council. The area has complete autonomy in domestic affairs.

NEW ZEALAND

Sovereign: Queen Elizabeth II
Governor-General: Sir Paul Reeves (1985)
Prime Minister: David R. Lange (1984)
Area: 103,884 sq mi. (269,062 sq km) (excluding dependencies)
Population (est. mid-1987): 3,300,000 (average annual growth rate: 0.8%) (European, 87%; Maori, 9%)
Density per square mile: 31.8
Capital: Wellington (587,700)
Largest cities (est. 1985): Auckland, 894,000; Wellington, 587,700; Christchurch, 289,400; Hamilton, 103,800; Dunedin, 104,600
Monetary unit: New Zealand dollar

Languages: English, Maori
Religions: Church of England, 26%; Presbyterian, 17%; Roman Catholic, 14%
Member of Commonwealth of Nations
Literacy rate: 98%
Economic summary: Gross domestic product (1985): $18.9 billion. Average annual growth rate (1975–85): 2.0%. Per capita income (1983): $7,410. Labor force in agriculture: 10%; principal products: wool, meat, dairy products, livestock. Labor force in industry: 27%; major products: processed foods, textiles, machinery, transport equipment, wood and paper products. Natural resources: forests, coal, gold. Exports: meat, dairy products, wool. Imports: machinery, minerals, chemicals, consumer goods. Major trading partners: Japan, Australia, U.K., U.S.

Geography. New Zealand, about 1,250 miles (2,012 km) east of Australia, consists of two main islands and a number of smaller, outlying islands so scattered that they range from the tropical to the antarctic. The country is the size of Colorado.

New Zealand's two main components are North Island and South Island, separated by Cook Strait, which varies from 16 to 190 miles (26 to 396 km) in width. North Island (44,281 sq mi.; 114,688 sq km) is 515 miles (829 km) long and volcanic in its south-central part. It contains many hot springs and beautiful geysers. South Island (58,093 sq mi.; 150,461 sq km) has the Southern Alps along its west coast, with Mount Cook (12,349 ft; 3,764 m) the highest point.

The largest of the outlying islands are the Auckland Islands (234 sq mi.; 606 sq km), Campbell Island (44 sq mi.; 114 sq km), the Antipodes Islands (24 sq mi.; 62 sq km), and the Kermadec Islands (13 sq mi.; 34 sq km).

Government. New Zealand was granted self-government in 1852, a full parliamentary system and ministries in 1856, and dominion status in 1907. The Queen is represented by a Governor-General, and the Cabinet is responsible to a unicameral Parliament of 95 members, who are elected by popular vote for three years.

The major political parties are the Labor Party (56 of 95 seats in the House of Representatives), led by Prime Minister David R. Lange; the National Party (37 seats), led by James Bolger; and the Social Party (2 seats).

History. New Zealand was discovered and named in 1642 by Abel Tasman, a Dutch navigator. Captain James Cook explored the islands in 1769. In 1840, Britain formally annexed them.

From the first, the country has been in the forefront in instituting social welfare legislation. It adopted old age pensions (1898); a national child welfare program (1907); social security for the aged, widows, and orphans, along with family benefit payments; minimum wages; a 40-hour week and unemployment and health insurance (1938); and socialized medicine (1941).

The New Zealand Labor Party, headed by David Lange, swept Sir Robert Muldoon's conservative National Party from power in a parliamentary election on July 14, 1984. Lange's campaign promise to ban American nuclear-powered and nuclear-armed naval vessels from New Zealand waters provoked a crisis in the 33-year-old Anzus alliance of the United States, Australia and New Zealand. After New Zealand refused to let a U.S. warship make a port call on the ground it might be carrying nuclear weapons, Secretary of State George P. Shultz on July 17, 1985, accused New Zealand of undermining the U.S. nuclear deterrent and weakening its own security.

Cook Islands and Overseas Territories

The Cook Islands (93 sq mi.; 241 sq km) were placed under New Zealand administration in 1901. They achieved self-governing status in association with New Zealand in 1965. Population in 1978 was about 19,600. The seat of government is on Rarotonga Island.

The island's chief exports are citrus juice, clothing, canned fruit, and pineapple juice. Nearly all of the trade is with New Zealand.

Niue (100 sq mi.; 259 sq km) was formerly administered as part of the Cook Islands. It was placed under separate New Zealand administration in 1901 and achieved self-governing status in association with New Zealand in 1974. The capital is Alofi. Population in 1980 was about 3,300.

Niue exports passion fruit, copra, plaited ware, honey, and limes. Its principal trading partner is New Zealand.

The Ross Dependency (160,000 sq mi.; 414,400 sq km), an Antarctic region, was placed under New Zealand administration in 1923.

Tokelau (4 sq mi.; 10 sq km) was formerly administered as part of the Gilbert and Ellice Islands colony. It was placed under New Zealand administration in 1925. Its population is about 1,600.

NICARAGUA

Republic of Nicaragua
President: Daniel Ortega (1985)
Area: 50,180 sq mi. (130,000 sq km)
Population (est. mid-1987): 3,500,000 (average annual growth rate: 3.4%) (mestizo, 70%; white, 17%; black, 9%; Indian, 4%)
Density per square mile: 69.7
Capital and largest city (est. 1985): Managua, 682,111
Monetary unit: Cordoba
Language: Spanish
Religion: Roman Catholic, 91%
National name: República de Nicaragua
Literacy rate: 87%
Economic summary: Gross national product (1984): $2.4 billion. Average annual growth rate (1985–86): –2%. Per capita income (1983): $850. Land used for agriculture: 7%; labor force: 43%; principal products: cotton, coffee, sugar cane, rice, corn, beans, cattle. Labor force in industry: 15%; major products: processed foods, chemicals, metal products, clothing and textiles. Natural resources: timber, fisheries. Exports: coffee, chemical products, meat, sugar. Imports: machinery, chemicals and pharmaceuticals, transport equipment, clothing, petroleum. Major trading partners: Mexico, West Germany, Japan, France, Cuba, Costa Rica, Guatemala

Geography. Largest but most sparsely populated of the Central American nations, Nicaragua borders on Honduras to the north and Costa Rica to the south. It is slightly larger than New York State.

Nicaragua is mountainous in the west, with fertile valleys. A plateau slopes eastward toward the Caribbean.

Two big lakes—Nicaragua, about 100 miles long (161 km), and Managua, about 38 miles long (61 km)—are connected by the Tipitapa River. The Pacific coast is volcanic and very fertile. The Caribbean coast, swampy and indented, is aptly called the "Mosquito Coast."

Government. After an election on Nov. 4, 1984, Daniel Ortega began a six-year term as President on Jan. 10, 1985. The major political parties are the Sandinista National Liberation Front (61 of 96 members of the National Assembly), led by President Ortega; the Democratic Conservative Party (14 seats); Independent Liberal Party (9 seats); Popular Social Christian Party (6 seats) and three small Marxist-Leninist groups with two seats each.

History. Nicaragua, which established independence in 1838, was first visited by the Spaniards in 1522. The chief of the country's leading Indian tribe at that time was called Nicaragua, from whom the nation derived its name. A U.S. naval force intervened in 1909 after two American citizens had been executed, and a few U.S. Marines were kept in the country from 1912 to 1925. The Bryan-Chamorro Treaty of 1916 (terminated in 1970) gave the U.S. an option on a canal route through Nicaragua, and naval bases. Disorder after the 1924 elections brought in the marines again.

A guerrilla leader, Gen. César Augusto Sandino, began fighting the occupation force in 1927. He fought the U.S. troops until their withdrawal in 1933. They trained Gen. Anastasio (Tacho) Somoza García to head a National Guard. In 1934, Somoza assassinated Sandino and overthrew the Liberal President Juan Batista Sacassa, establishing a military dictatorship with himself as president. He spurred the economic development of the country, meanwhile enriching his family through estates in the countryside and investments in air and shipping lines. On his assassination in 1956, he was succeeded by his son Luis, who alternated with trusted family friends in the presidency until his death in 1967. Another son, Maj. Gen. Anastasio Somoza Debayle, became President in 1967.

Sandinista guerrillas, leftists who took their name from Gen. Sandino, launched an offensive in May 1979.

After seven weeks of fighting, Somoza fled the country on July 17, 1979. The Sandinistas assumed power on July 19, promising to maintain a mixed economy, a non-aligned foreign policy, and a pluralist political system. However, the prominence of Cuban President Fidel Castro at the celebration of the first anniversary of the revolution and a delay of more than five years in holding elections increased debate over the true political color of the Sandinistas.

On Jan. 23, 1981, the Reagan Administration suspended U.S. aid, charging that Nicaragua, with the aid of Cuba and the Soviet Union, was supplying arms to rebels in El Salvador. The Sandinistas denied the charges. Later that year, Nicaraguan guerrillas known as "contras," or counterrevolutionaries, began a war to overthrow the Sandinistas.

The long-promised elections were held as scheduled on Nov. 4, 1984, with Daniel Ortega Saavedra, the Sandinista junta coordinator, winning 63% of the votes cast for President. President Reagan dismissed the voting as a Soviet-style sham election. He began a six-year term on Jan. 10, 1985, with Castro attending the inauguration.

Meanwhile, the war between the Sandinistas and the U.S.-backed contras continued. Ortega said the war "could be interminable" because the Reagan Administration seemed determined to continue its support of the rebels.

On Feb. 21, 1985, President Reagan denounced the Sandinista regime and said his objective was to "remove it in the sense of its present structure." On May 1, Reagan ordered an embargo on U.S. trade with Nicaragua, telling Congress that the policies and actions of the Sandinistas constituted a threat to U.S. security.

In October 1985, Nicaragua suspended civil liberties and in June 1986, Congress voted $100 million in aid, military and non-military, to the contras. Nicaragua condemned the action and used it as a pretext to close down *La Prensa*, the sole opposition newspaper.

The war intensified in 1986-87 with the resupplied contras establishing themselves inside the country while negotiations sponsored by the Contadora (neutral Latin American) nations and a peace plan sponsored by the Costa Rican president, Arias, foundered.

NIGER

Republic of Niger

Chief of State: Gen. Seyni Kountché (1974)
Area: 489,206 sq mi. (1,267,044 sq km)
Population (est. mid-1987): 7,000,000 (average annual growth rate: 2.9%)
Density per square mile: 11.5
Capital and largest city (est. 1983): Niamey, 399,100
Monetary unit: Franc CFA
Ethnic groups: Hausa, 54%; Djerma and Songhai, 24%; Peul, 11%
Languages: French (official); Hausa, Songhai; Arabic
Religions: Islam, 90%; Animist and Christian, 10%
National name: République du Niger
Literacy rate: 10%
Economic summary: Gross national product (1983): $1.5 billion. Average annual growth rate (1973–82): 6.1%. Per capita income (1983): $300. Land used for agriculture: 3%; labor force: 90%; principal products: peanuts, cotton, livestock, millet, sorghum, bananas, rice. Major industrial products: uranium, cement, bricks, light industrial products. Natural resources: uranium. Exports: uranium, peanuts, livestock, hides, skins. Imports: fuels, machinery, transport equipment, foodstuffs, consumer goods. Major trading partners: France, Nigeria, Japan, Algeria, Libya

Geography. Niger, in West Africa's Sahara region, is four fifths the size of Alaska. It is surrounded by Mali, Algeria, Libya, Chad, Nigeria, Benin, and Burkina Faso.

The Niger River in the southwest flows through the country's only fertile area. Elsewhere the land is semiarid.

Government. After a military coup on April 15, 1974, Gen. Seyni Kountché suspended the Constitution and instituted rule by decree. Previously, the President was elected by direct universal suffrage for a five-year term and a National House of Assembly of 50 members was elected for the same term.

The Parti Progressiste Nigérien-Rassemblement Démocratique Africain, the only political party, was dissolved in 1974.

History. Niger was incorporated into French West Africa in 1896. There were frequent rebellions, but when order was restored in 1922, the French made the area a colony. In 1958, the voters approved the French Constitution and voted to make the territory an autonomous republic within the French Community. The republic adopted a Constitution in 1959 and the next year withdrew from the Community, proclaiming its independence.

The 1974 army coup ousted President Hamani Diori, who had held office since 1960. He was charged with having mishandled relief for the terrible drought that had devastated Niger and five neighboring sub-Saharan nations for several years. An estimated 2 million people were starving in Niger, but 200,000 tons of imported food, half U.S.-supplied, substantially ended famine conditions by the year's end. The new President, Lt. Col. Seyni Kountché, Chief of Staff of the army, installed a 12-man military government. A predominantly civilian government was formed by Kountché in 1976.

NIGERIA

Federal Republic of Nigeria
President: Maj. Gen. Ibrahim Babangida (1985)
Area: 356,700 sq mi. (923,853 sq km)
Population (est. mid-1987): 108,600,000 (average annual growth rate: 2.8%)
Density per square mile: 304.6
Capital: Abuja
Largest cities (est. 1983): Lagos, 1,097,000; Ibadan, 1,060,000; Ogbomosho, 527,400; Kano, 487,100
Monetary unit: Naira
Languages: English (official) and native tongues
Religions: Islam, 47%; Christian, 34%; Animist, 18%
Member of Commonwealth of Nations
Literacy rate: 25-30%
Economic summary: Gross national product (1984): $74.1 billion. Average annual growth rate (1970–79): 5.3%. Per capita income (1984): $790. Land used for agriculture: 13%; labor force: 55%; principal products: peanuts, cotton, cocoa, grains, fish, yams, cassava, livestock. Labor force in industry: 10%; major products: crude oil, natural gas, coal, tin, processed rubber, cotton, petroleum, hides, textiles, cement, chemicals. Natural resources: petroleum, tin, columbite, iron ore, coal, limestone, timber. Exports: oil, cocoa, palm products, rubber, timber, tin. Imports: machinery and transport equipment, manufactured goods, chemicals. Major trading partners: U.K., Western European countries, U.S.

Geography. Nigeria, one third larger than Texas and black Africa's most populous nation, is situated on the Gulf of Guinea in West Africa. Its neighbors are Benin, Niger, Cameroon, and Chad.

The lower course of the Niger River flows south through the western part of the country into the Gulf of Guinea. Swamps and mangrove forests border the southern coast; inland are hardwood forests.

Government. After 12 years of military rule, a new Constitution re-established democratic government in 1979, but it lasted less than four years. The military again took over from the democratically elected civilian government on Dec. 31, 1983. The arms of the military government include a Supreme Military Council and a National Council of State. The various ministers make up the Federal Executive Council. There are state military governors.

History. Between 1879 and 1914, private colonial developments by the British, with reorganizations of the Crown's interest in the region, resulted in the formation of Nigeria as it exists today. During World War I, native troops of the West African frontier force joined with French forces to defeat the German garrison in the Cameroons.

Nigeria became independent on Oct. 1, 1960.

Organized as a loose federation of self-governing states, the independent nation faced an overwhelming task of unifying a country with 250 ethnic and linguistic groups.

Rioting broke out again in 1966, the military commander was seized, and Col. Yakubu Gowon took power. Also in that year, the Moslem Hausas in the north massacred the predominantly Christian Ibos in the east, many of whom had been driven from the north. Thousands of Ibos took refuge in the Eastern Region. The military government there asked Ibos to return to the region and, in May 1967, the assembly voted to secede from the federation and set up the Republic of Biafra. Civil war broke out.

In January 1970, after 31 months of civil war, Biafra surrendered to the federal government.

Gowon's nine-year rule was ended in 1975 by a bloodless coup that made Army Brigadier Muritala Rufai Mohammed the new chief of state. Mohammed was assassinated the next year 1976 by a group of seven young officers, who failed to seize control of the government.

The return of civilian leadership was established with the election of Alhaji Shehu Shagari, as president in 1979.

A coup on December 31, 1983, restored military rule. The military regime headed by Maj. Gen. Mohammed Buhari was overthrown in a bloodless coup on Aug. 27, 1985, led by Maj. Gen. Ibrahim Babangida, who proclaimed himself president.

NORWAY

Kingdom of Norway
Sovereign: King Olav V (1957)
Prime Minister: Gro Harlem Bruntland (1986)
Area: 125,056 sq mi. (323,895 sq km)
Population (est. mid-1987): 4,200,000 (average annual growth rate: 0.2%)
Density per square mile: 33.6
Capital: Oslo
Largest cities (est. 1985): Oslo, 449,300; Bergen, 207,900; Trondheim, 134,400; Stavanger, 95,100
Monetary unit: Krone
Language: Norwegian
Religion: Evangelical Lutheran (state), 88%
National name: Kongeriket Norge
Literacy rate: 100%
Economic summary: Gross national product (1984): $54.8 billion. Average annual growth rate (1978–83): 2.8%. Per capita income (1984): $13,333. Land used for agriculture: 3%; labor force, including fishing: 7%; principal products: dairy products, livestock, grain, potatoes, furs, wool. Labor force in industry: 26%; major products: oil and gas, fish, pulp and paper, ships, aluminum, iron, steel, nickel, fertilizers, transportation equipment, hydroelectric power, petrochemicals. Natural resources: fish, timber, hydroelectric power, ores, oil, gas. Exports: oil, natural gas, fish products,

chemicals, pulp and paper, aluminum. reports: machinery, motor vehicles, foodstuffs, iron and steel, textiles and clothing. Major trading partners: U.K., Sweden, West Germany, U.S., Denmark, Netherlands.

Geography. Norway is situated in the western part of the Scandinavian peninsula. It extends about 1,100 miles (1,770 km) from the North Sea along the Norwegian Sea to more than 300 miles (483 km) above the Arctic Circle, the farthest north of any European country. It is slightly larger than New Mexico. Sweden borders on most of the eastern frontier, with Finland and the U.S.S.R. in the northeast.

Nearly 70% of Norway is uninhabitable and covered by mountains, glaciers, moors, and rivers. The hundreds of deep fiords that cut into the coastline give Norway an overall oceanfront of more than 12,000 miles (19,312 km). Nearly 50,000 islands off the coast form a breakwater and make a safe coastal shipping channel.

Government. Norway is a constitutional hereditary monarchy. Executive power is vested in the King together with a Cabinet, or Council of State, consisting of a Prime Minister and at least seven other members. The Storting, or Parliament, is composed of 157 members elected by the people under proportional representation. The Storting discusses and votes on political and financial questions, but divides itself into two sections (Lagting and Odelsting) to discuss and pass on legislative matters. The King cannot dissolve the Storting before the expiration of its term.

The sovereign is Olav V, born July 2, 1903, only son of Haakon VII and Princess Maud (1869–1938), third daughter of Edward VII of England. He succeeded to the throne on the death of his father Sept. 20, 1957. He married Princess Märtha of Sweden (1901–1954) on March 21, 1929. Their children are Princess Ragnhild Alexandra (born 1930), Princess Astrid (born 1932), and Crown Prince Harald (born 1937). In 1968, the Crown Prince married Sonja Haraldsen, a commoner.

The major political parties are the Labor Party (71 of 157 seats in the Storting), led by Prime Minister Gro Harlem Brundtland; Conservative Party (50 seats), led by Jan P. Syse; Christian Democratic Party (16 seats), led by Harald Synnes; Center Party (12 seats), led by Johan Buttedal; Socialist Left Party (6 seats), led by Hanna Kvanmo; and Party of Progress (2 seats), led by Carl I. Hagen.

History. Norwegians, like the Danes and Swedes, are of Teutonic origin. The Norsemen, also known as Vikings, ravaged the coasts of northwestern Europe from the 8th to the 11th century.

In 1815, Norway fell under the control of Sweden. The union of Norway, inhabited by fishermen, sailors, merchants, and peasants, and Sweden, an aristocratic country of large estates and tenant farmers, was not a happy one, but it lasted for nearly a century. In 1905, the Norwegian Parliament arranged a peaceful separation and invited a Danish prince to the Norwegian throne—King Haakon VII. A treaty with Sweden provided that all disputes be settled by arbitration and that no fortifications be erected on the common frontier.

When World War I broke out, Norway joined with Sweden and Denmark in a decision to remain neutral and to cooperate in the joint interest of the three countries. In World War II, Norway was invaded by the Germans on April 9, 1940. It resisted for two months before the Nazis took over complete control. King Haakon and his government fled to London, where they established a government-in-exile. Maj. Vidkun Quisling, whose name is now synonymous with traitor or fifth columnist, was the most notorious Norwegian collaborator with the Nazis. He was executed by the Norwegians on Oct. 24, 1945.

Despite severe losses in the war, Norway recovered quickly. The country led the world in social experimentation. A neighbor of the U.S.S.R., Norway sought to retain good relations with the Soviet Union without losing its identity with the West. It entered the North Atlantic Treaty Organization in 1949.

Verification of U.S. and Soviet oil strikes in separated areas of Norway's sector of the North Sea bottom led the Storting in 1975 to impose stiff tax and royalty rates on concession holders. Following discovery of a North Sea field expected to produce 900,000 barrels a day by 1984, Parliament in 1976 approved establishment of a national refining and distributing company to market petroleum products at home and abroad.

Dependencies of Norway

Svalbard (24,208 sq mi.; 62,700 sq km), in the Arctic Ocean about 360 miles north of Norway, consists of the Spitsbergen group and several smaller islands, including Bear Island, Hope Island, King Charles Land, and White Island (or Gillis Land). It came under Norwegian administration in 1925. The population in 1985 was 3,480 of which 1,227 were Norwegians.

Bouvet Island (23 sq mi.; 60 sq km), in the South Atlantic about 1,600 miles south-southwest of the Cape of Good Hope, came under Norwegian administration in 1928.

Jan Mayen Island (147 sq mi.; 380 sq km), in the Arctic Ocean between Norway and Greenland, came under Norwegian administration in 1929.

Peter I Island (96 sq mi.; 249 sq km), lying off Antarctica in the Bellinghausen Sea, came under Norwegian administration in 1931.

Queen Maud Land, a section of Antarctica, came under Norwegian administration in 1939.

OMAN

Sultanate of Oman
Sultan: Qabus Bin Said (1970)
Area: 105,000 sq mi. (271,950 sq km)[1]
Population (est. mid-1987): 1,300,000 (average annual growth rate: 3.3%)
Density per square mile: 12.4
Capital and largest city (est. 1981): Muscat, 70,000
Monetary unit: Omani rial
Language: Arabic
Religion: Islam, 86%
National name: Saltonat Uman
Literacy rate: 20%
Economic summary: Gross national product (1984): $7.7 billion. Average annual growth rate (1973–82): 10.4%. Per capita income (1984): $6,300. Principal agricultural products: dates, bananas, cereal, livestock.

Major industries: petroleum drilling, fishing, construction. Natural resources: oil, marble, copper, limestone. Exports: oil. Imports: machinery and transport equipment, food, mineral fuels. Major trading partners: U.K., U.S., China, Japan, UAE, Singapore

1. Excluding the Kuria Muria Islands.

Geography. Oman is a 1,000-mile-long (1,700-km) coastal plain at the southeastern tip of the Arabian peninsula lying on the Arabian Sea and the Gulf of Oman. The interior is a plateau. The country is the size of Kansas.

Government. The Sultan of Oman (formerly called Muscat and Oman), an absolute monarch, is assisted by a council of ministers, six specialized councils, a consultative council and personal advisers.

There are no political parties.

History. Although Oman is an independent state under the rule of the Sultan, it has been under British protection since the early 19th century.

Muscat, the capital of the geographical area known as Oman, was occupied by the Portuguese from 1508 to 1648. Then it fell to Persian princes and later was regained by the Sultan.

The Kuria Muria Islands, formerly part of Aden, were given to Oman by the British in 1967.

In a palace coup on July 23, 1970, the Sultan, Sa'id bin Taimur, who had ruled since 1932, was overthrown by his son, who promised to establish a modern government and use new-found wealth to aid the people of this very isolated state.

PAKISTAN

Islamic Republic of Pakistan
President: Gen. Mohammad Zia ul-Haq (1977)
Prime Minister: Mohammad Khan Junejo (1985)
Area: 310,400 sq mi. (803,936 sq km)[1]
Population (est. mid-1987): 104,600,000 (average annual growth rate: 2.9%)
Density per square mile: 328.3
Capital (1981 census): Islamabad, 201,000
Largest cities (1981 census for metropolitan area): Karachi, 5,208,100; Lahore, 2,952,700; Faisalabad, (Lyallpur) 1,920,000; Rawalpindi, 920,000; Hyderabad, 795,000
Monetary unit: Pakistan rupee
Principal languages: Urdu (national), English (official), Punjabi, Sindhi, Pashtu, and Baluchi
Religions: Islam, 97%; Hindu, Christian, Buddhist, Parsi
Literacy rate: 26%
Economic summary: Gross national product (1985): $31.0 billion. Annual growth rate (1985): 8.4%. Per capita income (1985): $300. Land used for agriculture: 24%; labor force: 52%; principal products: wheat, rice, cotton. Labor force in industry: 21%; major products: cotton textiles, processed foods, tobacco, chemicals, natural gas. Natural resources: natural gas, limited petroleum, iron ore. Exports: raw and manufactured cotton, rice, carpets, leather, fish. Imports: food grains, edible oil, crude oil, machinery, chemicals, transport equipment. Major trading partners: U.S., U.K., West Germany, Saudi Arabia, Japan, China, UAE.

1. Excluding Kashmir and Jammu. 2. Does not include about 3 million refugees from Afghanistan.

Geography. Pakistan is situated in the western part of the Indian subcontinent, with Afghanistan and Iran on the west, India on the east, and the Arabian Sea on the south.

Nearly twice the size of California, Pakistan consists of towering mountains, including the Hindu Kush in the west, a desert area in the east, the Punjab plains in the north, and an expanse of alluvial plains. The 1,000-mile-long (1,609 km) Indus River flows through the country from the Kashmir to the Arabian Sea.

Government. On July 5, 1977, Gen. Mohammad Zia ul-Haq, Army Chief of Staff, ousted the civilian government of Prime Minister Zulfikar Ali Bhutto. Zia declared himself Chief Administrator of Martial Law as head of a four-man council. The national and state assemblies were dissolved and all political parties banned, while the Chief Justices of the four states replaced the governors. Elections for new national and provincial assemblies were held in February 1985 and the new Parliament and Prime Minister took office on March 23.

History. Pakistan was one of the two original successor states to British India. For almost 25 years following independence in 1947, it consisted of two separate regions East and West Pakistan, but now comprises only the western sector. It consists of Sind, Baluchistan, the former North-West Frontier Province, western Punjab, the princely state of Bahawalpur, and several other smaller native states.

The British became the dominant power in the region in 1797 following Lord Clive's military victory, but rebellious tribes kept the northwest in turmoil. In the northeast, the formation of the Moslem League in 1906 estranged the Moslems from the Hindus. In 1930, the league, led by Mohammed Ali Jinnah, demanded creation of a Moslem state wherever Moslems were in the majority. He supported Britain during the war. Afterward, the league received almost a unanimous Moslem vote in 1946 and Britain agreed to the formation of Pakistan as a separate dominion.

Pakistan was proclaimed a republic March 23, 1956. Iskander Mirza, then Governor General, was elected Provisional President and H. S. Suhrawardy became the first non-Moslem League Prime Minister.

The election of 1970 set the stage for civil war when Sheik Muuibur told East Pakistanis to stop paying taxes to the central government. West Pakistan troops moved in and fighting began. The independent state of Bangladesh, or Bengali nation, was proclaimed March 26, 1971.

The intervention of Indian troops protected the new state and brought President Yahya Kahn down. Bhutto took over and accepted Bangladesh as an independent entity.

Diplomatically, 1976 saw the resumption of formal relations between India and Pakistan.

Pakistan's first elections under civilian rule took place in March 1977 and provoked bitter opposition protest when Bhutto's party was declared to have won 155 of the 200 elected seats in the 216-member National Assembly. A rising tide of violent protest and political deadlock led to a military takeover on July 5. Gen. Mohammed Zia ul-Haq became Chief Martial Law Administrator.

Bhutto was tried and convicted for the 1974 murder of a political opponent, and despite worldwide protests was executed on April 4, 1979, touching off riots by his supporters. Zia declared himself President on Sept. 16, 1978, a month after Fazel Elahi Chaudhry left office upon the completion of his 5-year term.

A measure of representative government was restored with the election of a new National Assembly in February 1985, although leaders of opposition parties were banned from the election and it was unclear what powers Zia would yield to the legislature.

On December 30, 1985, Zia ended martial law. This was tempered by his stated intent to remain in office until 1990. In April 1986, Benazir Bhutto, daughter of Zulfikar Bhutto, returned from exile. She organized demonstrations but had lost much support by the end of the year.

PANAMA

Republic of Panama
President: Eric Arturo Delvalle (1985)
Area: 29,761 sq mi. (77,082 sq km)
Population (est. mid-1987): 2,300,000 (average annual growth rate: 2.2%) (mestizo, 70%; black, 12%; white, 12%; Indian, 6%)
Density per square mile: 73.9
Capital and largest city (est. 1980): Panama City, 400,-000
Monetary unit: Balboa
Language: Spanish (official)
Religions: Roman Catholic, 89%; Islam, 5%; Protestant, 5%
National name: República de Panamá
Literacy rate: 90%
Economic summary: Gross national product (1984): $4.2 billion. Annual growth rate (1984): –1.0%. Per capita income (1984): $1,970. Land used for agriculture: 24%; labor force: 29%; principal products: bananas, corn, sugar, rice, cattle. Labor force in industry: 16%; major industrial products: refined petroleum, sugar. Natural resources: copper (unexploited). Exports: bananas, refined petroleum, sugar, shrimp. Imports: crude oil, crude petroleum, chemicals, food. Major trading partners: U.S., West Germany, Mexico, Venezuela.

Geography. The southernmost of the Central American nations, Panama is south of Costa Rica and north of Colombia. The Panama Canal bisects the isthmus at its narrowest and lowest point, allowing passage from the Caribbean Sea to the Pacific Ocean.

Panama is slightly smaller than South Carolina. It is marked by a chain of volcanic mountains in the west, moderate hills in the interior, and a low range on the east coast. There are extensive forests in the fertile Caribbean area.

Government. In 1972, a new Constitution was approved by a new 505-seat National Assembly of Community Representatives (corregidores), which was created in the first election in five years. The Charter provides for indirect election of the President by the Assembly for a six-year term.

History. Visited by Columbus in 1502 on his fourth voyage and explored by Balboa in 1513, Panama was the principal transshipment point for Spanish treasure and supplies to and from South and Central America in colonial days. In 1821, when Central America revolted against Spain, Panama joined Colombia, which already had declared its independence. For the next 82 years, Panama attempted unsuccessfully to break away from Colombia. After U. S. proposals for canal rights over the narrow isthmus had been rejected by Colombia, Panama proclaimed its independence with U.S. backing in 1903.

For canal rights in perpetuity, the U.S. paid Panama $10 million and agreed to pay $250,000 each year, increased to $430,000 after devaluation of the U.S. dollar in 1933 and was further increased under a revised treaty signed in 1955. In exchange, the U.S. got the Canal Zone—a 10-mile-wide strip across the isthmus—and a considerable degree of influence in Panama's affairs.

Panama and the U.S. agreed in 1974 to negotiate the eventual reversion of the canal to Panama, despite strongly expressed opposition in the U.S. Congress. The texts of two treaties—one governing the transfer of the canal and the other guaranteeing its neutrality after transfer—were negotiated by August 1977 and were signed by Pres. Omar Torrijos Herara and President Carter in Washington on September 7. A Panamanian referendum approved the treaties by more than two thirds on October 23, but further changes were insisted upon by the U.S. Senate.

The principal change was a reservation specifying that despite the neutrality treaty's specification that only Panama shall maintain forces in its territory after transfer of the canal Dec. 31, 1999, the U.S. should have the right to use military force to keep the canal operating if it should become obstructed. After lengthy debate, the Senate approved the treaties in March-April, 1978. On June 16, Carter and Torrijos exchanged instruments of ratification in Panama City.

The basic treaty provides an increase from the present $2.3 million a year in royalties to $10 million a year during the transition period, with an additional annual payment of $10 million if it can be obtained from tolls. It also requires the use of more Panamanians as canal employees in the interim and pledges the U.S. not to pursue the development of another canal without the agreement of Panama.

Nicolas Ardito Barletta, Panama's first directly elected President in 16 years, was inaugurated on Oct. 11, 1984, for a five-year term. He lacked the necessary support to solve the country's economic crisis and resigned September 28, 1985. He was replaced by Vice President Eric Arturo Delvalle, a member of the Republican Party.

In June, 1986, reports surfaced that the behind-the-scenes strongman, Gen. Manuel Noriega, was involved in drug trafficking and the murder of an opposition leader. In 1987, Noriega was accused by his ex-Chief of Staff of assassinating Torrijos. He denied the charges.

Panama Canal. First conceived by the Spaniards in 1524, when King Charles V of Spain ordered a survey of a waterway across the Isthmus, a construction concession was granted by the Colombian government in 1878 to St. Lucien N. B. Wyse, representing a French company. Two years later, the French Canal Company, inspired by Ferdinand de Lesseps, began construction of what was to have been a sea-level canal. The effort ended in bankruptcy nine years later and the United States ultimately paid the French $40 million for their rights and assets.

The U.S. project, built on territory controlled by the United States, and calling for the creation of an interior lake connected to both oceans by locks, got under way in 1904. Completed in 1914, the Canal is 40.27 miles long and lifts ships 85 feet above sea level through a series of three locks on the Pacific and Atlantic sides. Enlarged in later years, each lock now measures 1,000 feet in length, 110 feet in width, and 40 feet in depth of water.

PAPUA NEW GUINEA

Sovereign: Queen Elizabeth II
Governor General: Sir Kingsford Díbela (1983)
Prime Minister: Paias Wingti (1985)
Area: 178,704 sq mi. (462,840 sq km)
Population (est. mid-1987): 3,600,000 (average annual growth rate: 2.4%)
Density per square mile: 20.1
Capital and largest city (est. 1985): Port Moresby, 200,000
Monetary unit: Kina
Languages: English, Melanesian pidgin, and 717 distinct native languages
Religions: Protestant, 64%; Roman Catholic, 33%
Member of Commonwealth of Nations
Literacy rate: 32%
Economic summary: Gross national product (1984): $2.0 billion. Average annual growth rate (1973–82): 1.4%. Per capita income (1984): $850. Labor force in agriculture, including fishing: 77%; principal products: sweet potatoes, coffee, copra, palm oil, cocoa, tea, coconuts, cattle. Major industrial products: clothing, light fabricated metal products, furniture. Natural resources: copper, gold, silver, timber, tuna. Exports: copper, coffee and cocoa beans, copra, timber. Imports: food, machinery, transport equipment, fuels. Major trading partners: Australia, U.K., Japan, West Germany, Singapore.

Geography. Papua New Guinea occupies the eastern half of the island of New Guinea, just north of Australia, and many outlying islands. The Indonesian province of Irian Jaya is to the west. To the north and east are the islands of Manus, New Britain, New Ireland, and Bougainville, all part of Papua New Guinea.

Papua New Guinea is about one tenth larger than California. Its mountainous interior has only recently been explored. The high-plateau climate is temperate, in contrast to the tropical climate of the coastal plains. Two major rivers, the Sepik and the Fly, are navigable for shallow-draft vessels.

Government. Papua New Guinea attained independence Sept. 16, 1975, ending a United Nations trusteeship under the administration of Australia. Parliamentary democracy was established by a Constitution that invests power in a 109-member national legislature.

The Pangu Party, People's Progress Party, National Party, and United Party are the largest of half a dozen political parties.

History. The eastern half of New Guinea was first visited by Spanish and Portuguese explorers in the 16th century, but a permanent European presence was not established until 1884, when Germany declared a protectorate over the northern coast and Britain took similar action in the south. Both nations formally annexed their protectorates and, in 1901, Britain transferred its rights to a newly independent Australia. Australian troops invaded German New Guinea in World War I and retained control under a League of Nations mandate that eventually became a United Nations trusteeship, incorporating a territorial government in the southern region, known as Papua.

Australia granted limited home rule in 1951 and, in 1964, organized elections for the first House of Assembly. Autonomy in internal affairs came nine years later.

PARAGUAY

Republic of Paraguay
President: Gen. Alfredo Stroessner (1954)
Area: 157,047 sq mi. (406,752 sq km)
Population (est. mid-1987): 4,300,000 (average annual growth rate: 2.9%) (mestizo, 91%; white, 2%; Indian, 3%)
Density per square mile: 27.4
Capital and largest city (est. 1980): Asunción, 530,000
Monetary unit: Guaraní
Languages: Spanish (official), Guaraní
Religion: Roman Catholic (official)
National name: República del Paraguay
Literacy rate: 84%
Economic summary: Gross national product (1984): $4.12 billion. Average annual growth rate (1982–83): −1.5%. Per capita income (1984): $1,260. Labor force in agriculture: 44%; principal products: soybeans, cotton, hides, sweet potatoes, tobacco, corn, rice, sugar cane. Labor force in industry: 19%; major products: packed meats, crushed oilseeds, beverages, textiles, light consumer goods, cement. Natural resource: timber. Exports: cotton, soybeans, meat products, tobacco, timber, coffee, hides. Imports: fuels and lubricants, machinery and motors, motor vehicles, beverages, tobacco, foodstuffs. Major trading partners: Argentina, Brazil, West Germany, U.S., Netherlands, Algeria

Geography. California-size Paraguay is surrounded by Brazil, Bolivia, and Argentina in south central South America. Eastern Paraguay, between the Paraná and Paraguay Rivers, is upland country with the thickest population settled on the grassy slope that inclines toward the Paraguay River. The greater part of the Chaco region to the west is covered with marshes, lagoons, dense forests, and jungles.

Government. The President is elected by popular vote for five years. The legislature is bicameral, consisting of a Senate of 30 members and a Chamber of Representatives of 60 members. There is also a Council of State, whose members are nominated by the government.

The governing Partido Colorado was further strengthened in 1977 when the Partido Liberal Unido, a merger of the Partido Liberal Radical and Partido Liberal, was declared illegal.

History. In 1526 and again in 1529, Sebastian Cabot explored Paraguay when he sailed up the Paraná and Paraguay Rivers. From 1608 until their expulsion from the Spanish dominions in 1767, the Jesuits maintained an extensive establishment in the south and east of Paraguay. In 1811, Paraguay revolted against Spanish rule and became a nominal republic under two Consuls.

Actually, Paraguay was governed by three dictators during the first 60 years of independence. The third, Francisco López, waged war against Brazil and Argentina in 1865–70, a conflict in which the male population was almost wiped out. A new Constitution in 1870, designed to prevent dictatorships and internal strife, failed to do so, and not until 1912 did a period of comparative economic and political stability begin.

After World War II, politics became particularly unstable.

Stroessner ruled under a state of siege until 1965, when the dictatorship was relaxed and exiles returned. The Constitution was revised in 1967 to permit Stroessner to be re-elected, and every five years since, he has been re-elected.

Although oil exploration begun by U.S. companies in the Chaco boreal in 1974 has been fruitless, Paraguay found prosperity in another form of energy when construction started in 1978 on the Itaipu Dam on the Parana River as a joint Paraguayan-Brazilian project. The largest hydroelectric development in the world when completed in 1988, Itaipu will generate 12.6 megawatts of electricity, surpassing the U.S. Grand Coulee Dam.

The Stroessner regime was criticized by the U.S. State Department during the Carter administration as a violator of human rights, but unlike Argentina and Uruguay, Paraguay did not suffer cuts in U.S. military aid. The criticism is credited with having reduced the number of political prisoners to a "few hundred."

The government was forced to devalue the guarani as a condition for IMF help for the ailing economy.

PERU

Republic of Peru
President: Alan Garcia Pérez (1985)
Premier: vacant
Area: 496,222 sq mi. (1,285,216 sq km)
Population (mid-1987): 20,700,000 (average annual growth rate: 2.5%) (white and mestizo, 52%; Indian, 46%)
Density per square mile: 41.7
Capital: Lima
Largest cities (est. 1985): Lima, 5,169,000; Arequipa, 531,800; Callao, 515,200; Trujillo, 438,700; Chiclayo, 347,700
Monetary unit: Inti
Languages: Spanish and Quéchua
Religion: Roman Catholic
National name: República del Perú
Literacy rate: est. 72%
Economic summary: Gross national product (1984): $17.9 billion. Average annual growth rate (1973–82): 2.0%. Per capita income (1984): $980. Land used for agriculture: 2%; labor force: 40%; principal products: corn, sugar, cotton, coffee, wool. Labor force in industry: 15%; major products: processed minerals, fish meal, refined petroleum, textiles. Natural resources: minerals and metals, fish, petroleum, timber. Exports: copper, fish products, cotton, sugar, coffee, lead, silver, zinc, wool, iron ore. Imports: machinery, foodstuffs, chemicals, pharmaceuticals. Major trading partners: U.S., Japan, Western European, and Latin American countries.

Geography. Peru, in western South America, extends for nearly 1,500 miles (2,414 km) along the Pacific Ocean. Colombia and Ecuador are to the north, Brazil and Bolivia to the east, and Chile to the south.

Five sixths the size of Alaska, Peru is divided by the Andes Mountains into three sharply differentiated zones. To the west is the coastline, much of it arid, extending 50 to 100 miles (80 to 160 km) inland. The mountain area, with peaks over 20,000 feet (6,096 m), lofty plateaus, and deep valleys, lies centrally. Beyond the mountains to the east is the heavily forested slope leading to the Amazonian plains.

Government. The President, elected by universal suffrage for a five-year term, holds executive power. A Senate of 60 members and a Chamber of Deputies of 180 members, both elected for five-year terms, share legislative power.

The American Popular Revolutionary Alliance, led by President Alan Garcia Pérez, won control of both houses in 1985 elections. The next largest voting bloc was the United Left, made up of six Marxist parties. Other parties include the Democratic Convergence Party and the Popular Action Party.

History. Peru was once part of the great Incan empire and later the major vice-royalty of Spanish South America. It was conquered in 1531–33 by Francisco Pizarro. On July 28, 1821, Peru proclaimed its independence, but the Spanish were not finally defeated until 1824. For a hundred years thereafter, revolutions were frequent, and a new war was fought with Spain in 1864–66.

Peru emerged from 20 years of dictatorship in 1945 with the inauguration of President José Luis Bustamente y Rivero after the first free election in many decades. But he served for only three years and was succeeded in turn by Gen. Manual A. Odria, Manuel Prado y Ugarteche, and Fernando Belaúnde Terry. On Oct. 3, 1968, Belaúnde was overthrown by Gen. Juan Velasco Alvarado.

In 1975, Velasco was replaced in a bloodless coup by his Premier, Gen. Francisco Morales Bermudez, who promised to restore civilian government. In elections held on May 18, 1980, Belaunde Terry, the last previous civilian President and the candidate of the conservative parties that have traditionally ruled Peru, was elected President again. By the end of his five-year term in 1985, the country was in the midst of acute economic and social crisis.

But Peru's fragile democracy survived this period of stress and when he left office in 1985 Belaunde Terry was the first elected President to turn over power to a constitutionally elected successor since 1945. Alan Garcia Pérez, a 36-year-old Social Democrat, was inaugurated President on July 28, 1985. In his inaugural address, he said Peru would limit payments on its foreign debt to no more than 10% of its export earnings, instead of the terms demanded by the International Monetary Fund.

The savage war with the Sendero Luminoso guerrillas, a Maoist group, continued unabated.

THE PHILIPPINES

Republic of the Philippines
President: Corazon C. Aquino (1986)
Vice President: Salvador H. Laurel (1986)
Area: 115,830 sq mi. (300,000 sq km)
Population (est. mid-1987): 61,500,000 (average annual growth rate: 2.8%)
Density per square mile: 531.0
Capital: Manila
Largest cities (est. 1981): Manila, 1,750,000[1]; Quezon City, 1,175,000; Davao, 625,000; Cebu, 500,000
Monetary unit: Peso
Languages: Philipino, English, Spanish; dialects: Cebuano, Ilocano

Religions: Roman Catholic, 85%; Islam, 4%; Aglipayan (Independent Philippine Christian), 4%; Protestant, 3%
National name: Republika ng Pilipinas
Literacy rate: 88%
Economic summary: Gross national product (1985): $32 billion. Growth rate (1986): 1.6%. Per capita income (1985): $594. Land used for agriculture: 37%; labor force: 50%; principal products: rice, corn, coconuts, sugar cane, bananas, tobacco. Labor force in industry: 12%; major products: processed agricultural products, textiles, chemicals and chemical products. Natural resources: forests, metallic and non-metallic minerals. Exports: coconut products, sugar, logs and lumber, copper concentrates, bananas, garments, nickel. Imports: petroleum, industrial equipment, wheat. Major trading partners: U.S., Japan.

1. Metropolitan area population is 7,500,000.

Geography. The Philippine Islands are an archipelago of over 7,000 islands lying about 500 miles (805 km) off the southeast coast of Asia. The overall land area is comparable to that of Arizona. The northernmost island, Y'Ami, is 65 miles (105 km) from Taiwan, while the southernmost, Saluag, is 40 miles (64 km) east of Borneo.

Only about 7% of the islands are larger than one square mile, and only one third have names. The largest are Luzon in the north (40,420 sq mi.; 104,687 sq km), Mindanao in the south (36,537 sq mi.; 94,631 sq km), Samar (5,124 sq mi.; 13,271 sq km).

The islands are of volcanic origin, with the larger ones crossed by mountain ranges. The highest peak is Mount Apo (9,690 ft; 2,954 m) on Mindanao.

Government. On February 2, 1987, the Filipino people voted for a new Constitution that established a 24-seat Senate and a 250-seat House of Representatives and gave President Aquino a six-year term. It limits the powers of the President, who can't be re-elected.

History. Fernando Magellan, the Portuguese navigator in the service of Spain, discovered the Philippines in 1521. Twenty-one years later, a Spanish exploration party named the group of islands in honor of Prince Philip, later Philip II of Spain. Spain retained possession of the islands for the next 350 years.

The Philippines were ceded to the U.S. in 1899 by the Treaty of Paris after the Spanish-American War. Meanwhile, the Filipinos, led by Emilio Aguinaldo, had declared their independence. They continued guerrilla warfare against U.S. troops until the capture of Aguinaldo in 1901. By 1902, peace was established except among the Moros.

The first U.S. civilian Governor-General was William Howard Taft (1901–04). The Jones Law (1916) provided for the establishment of a Philippine Legislature composed of an elective Senate and House of Representatives. The Tydings-McDuffie Act (1934) provided for a transitional period until 1946, at which time the Philippines would become completely independent.

Under a Constitution approved by the people of the Philippines in 1935, the Commonwealth of the Philippines came into being, with Manuel Quezon y Molina as president.

On Dec. 8, 1941, the Philippines were invaded by Japanese troops. Following the fall of Bataan and Corregidor, Quezon established a government-in-exile, which he headed until his death in 1944. He was succeeded by Vice President Sergio Osmeña.

U.S. forces led by Gen. Douglas MacArthur reinvaded the Philippines in October 1944 and, after the liberation of Manila in February 1945, Osmeña re-established the government.

The Philippines achieved full independence on July 4, 1946. Manual A. Roxas y Acuña was elected first president. Subsequent presidents have been Elpidio Quirino (1948–53), Ramón Magsaysay (1953–57). Carlos P. García (1957–61), Diosdado Macapagal (1961–65), Ferdinand E. Marcos (1965–86).

Marcos, who had freed the last of the national leaders still in detention, former Senator Benigno S. Aquino, Jr., in 1980 and permitted him to go to the United States, ended eight years of martial law on January 17, 1981.

Despite having been warned by First Lady Imelda Marcos that he risked being killed if he came back, opposition leader Aquino returned to the Philippines from self-exile on Aug. 21, 1983. He was shot to death as he was being escorted from his plane by military police at Manila International Airport. The government contended the assassin was a small-time hoodlum allegedly hired by communists, who was in turn shot dead by Filipino troops, but there was widespread suspicion that the Marcos government was involved in the murder.

The assassination sparked huge anti-government rallies and violent clashes between demonstrators and police, which continued intermittently through most of 1984, and helped the fragmented opposition parties score substantial gains in the May 14, 1984, elections for a National Assembly with greater power than a previous interim parliament.

On Jan. 23, 1985, one of Marcos' closest associates, Gen. Fabian C. Ver, the armed forces chief of staff, and 25 others were charged with the 1983 assassination of Aquino. Their trial dragged on through most of the year, with defense attorneys charging the evidence against Ver and the other defendants was fabricated.

In an attempt to re-secure American support, Marcos set Presidential elections for Feb. 7, 1986. After Ver's acquittal, and with the support of the Catholic church, Corazon Aquino, widow of Benigno Aquino, declared her candidacy. Marcos was declared the winner but the vote was widely considered to be rigged and anti-Marcos protests continued. The defection of Defense Minister Juan Enrile and Lt. Gen. Fidel Ramos signaled an end of military support for Marcos, who fled into exile in the U.S. on Feb. 25, 1986.

The Aquino government survived coup attempts by Marcos supporters and one, in November, by Enrile. Legislative elections on May 11, 1987, gave pro-Aquino candidates a large majority.

The growth of the Communist insurgency in the Philippines remains a matter of increasing concern, both in Manila and Washington.

POLAND

Polish People's Republic
President of the Council of State: Gen. Wojciech Jaruzelski (1985)
Premier: Zbigniew Messner (1985)
Area: 120,727 sq mi. (312,683 sq km)
Population (est. mid-1987): 37,800,000 (average annual growth rate: 0.8%)
Density per square mile: 313.1

Capital: Warsaw
Largest cities (est. 1986): Warsaw, 1,659,400; Lodz, 847,900; Krakow, 740,100; Wroclaw, 637,200; Poznan, 575,100; Gdansk, 464,600; Szczecin, 392,300
Monetary unit: Zloty
Language: Polish
Religions: Roman Catholic.
National name: Polska Rzeczpospolita Ludowa
Literacy rate: 98%
Economic summary: Gross national product (1984): $143.0 billion. Average annual growth rate (1984): 3.4%. Per capita income (1984): $3,890. Labor force in agriculture: 30%; principal products: grains, sugar beets, potatoes, hogs and other livestock. Labor force in industry: 29%; major products: iron and steel, chemicals, textiles, processed foods, transport equipment. Natural resources: coal, sulfur, copper, natural gas. Exports: coal, machinery and equipment, chemicals, industrial products. Imports: machinery and equipment, fuels, raw materials, agricultural and food products. Major trading partners: Communist bloc countries, U.K., Italy, U.S., West Germany, France.

Geography. Poland, a country the size of New Mexico in north central Europe, borders on East Germany to the west, Czechoslovakia to the south, and the U.S.S.R. to the east. In the north is the Baltic Sea.

Most of the country is a plain with no natural boundaries except the Carpathian Mountains in the south and the Oder and Neisse Rivers in the east. Other major rivers, which are important to commerce, are the Vistula, Warta, and Bug.

Government. The 1952 Constitution describes Poland as a people's republic. The supreme organ of state authority is the Sejm (Parliament), which is composed of 460 members elected for four years.

The major political parties are the Polish United Workers' (Communist) Party (245 of 460 seats in the Sejm), led by First Secretary Wojciech Jaruzelski; United Peasant Party (106 seats), led by Stefan Malinowski; Democratic Party (35 seats), led by Edward Kowalczyk; non-party members and Catholic organizations (74 seats).

History. Little is known about Polish history before the 11th century, when King Boleslaus I (the Brave) ruled over Bohemia, Saxony, and Moravia. Meanwhile, the Teutonic knights of Prussia conquered part of Poland and barred the latter's access to the Baltic. The knights were defeated by Wladislaus II at Tannenberg in 1410 and became Polish vassals, and Poland regained a Baltic shoreline. Poland reached the peak of power between the 14th and 16th centuries, scoring military successes against the Russians and Turks. In 1683, John III (John Sobieski) turned back the Turkish tide at Vienna.

An elective monarchy failed to produce strong central authority, and Prussia, and Austria were able to carry out a first partition of the country in 1772, a second in 1792, and a third in 1795. For more than a century thereafter, there was no Polish state, but the Poles never ceased their efforts to regain their independence.

Poland was formally reconstituted in November 1918, with Marshal Josef Pilsudski as Chief of State. In 1919, Ignace Paderewski, the famous pianist and patriot, became the first premier. In 1926, Pilsudski seized complete power in a coup and ruled dictatorially until his death on May 12, 1935, when he was succeeded by Marshal Edward Smigly-Rydz.

Despite a 10-year nonaggression pact signed in 1934, Hitler attacked Poland on Sept. 1, 1939. Russian troops invaded from the east on September 17, and on September 28 a German-Russian agreement divided Poland between Russia and Germany. Wladyslaw Raczkiewicz formed a government-in-exile in France, which moved to London after France's defeat in 1940.

All of Poland was occupied by Germany after the Nazi attack on the U.S.S.R. in June 1941.

The legal Polish government soon fell out with the Russians, and, in 1944, a Communist-dominated Polish Committee of National Liberation received Soviet recognition. Moving to Lublin after that city's liberation, it proclaimed itself the Provisional Government of Poland. Some former members of the Polish government in London joined with the Lublin government to form the Polish Government of National Unity, which Britain and the U.S. recognized.

On Aug. 2, 1945, in Berlin, President Harry S. Truman, Joseph Stalin and Prime Minister Clement Attlee of Britain established a new *de facto* western frontier for Poland along the Oder and Neisse Rivers. (The border was finally agreed to by West Germany in a nonagression pact signed Dec. 7, 1970.) On Aug. 16, 1945, the U.S.S.R. and Poland signed a treaty delimiting the Soviet-Polish frontier. Under these agreements, Poland was shifted westward. In the east it lost 69,860 square miles (180,934 sq km) with 10,772,000 inhabitants; in the west it gained (subject to final peace-conference approval) 38,986 square miles (100,973 sq km) with a prewar population of 8,621,000.

A New Constitution in 1952 made Poland a "people's democracy" of the Soviet type. In 1955, Poland, which had joined the Council for Economic Mutual Assistance in 1949, became a member of the Warsaw Treaty Organization, and its foreign policy became identical with that of the U.S.S.R. The government undertook persecution of the Roman Catholic Church as a remaining source of opposition and in 1953 arrested the primate, Stefan Cardinal Wyszynski. But in June 1956, worker and student riots in Poznan forced reconsideration of the repression.

Wladyslaw Gomulka was elected leader of the United Workers (Communist) Party in 1956. He denounced the Stalinist terror, ousted many Stalinists, relieved Rokossovsky, freed Wyszynski, and improved relations with the church. Most collective farms were dissolved, and the press became freer.

A strike that began in shipyards and spread to other industries in August 1980 produced a stunning victory for workers when the economically hard-pressed government accepted for the first time in a Marxist state the right of workers to organize in independent unions.

Led by Solidarity, a free union founded by Lech Walesa, workers launched a drive for liberty and improved conditions. A national strike for a five-day week in January 1981 led to the dismissal of Premier Pinkowski and the naming of the fourth Premier in less than a year, Gen. Wojciech Jaruzelski.

Antistrike legislation was approved on Dec. 2 and martial law declared on Dec. 13, when Walesa and other Solidarity leaders were arrested. Ten days later, President Reagan ordered sanctions against the Polish government, stopping food shipments and cutting commercial air traffic. The sanctions were lifted in early 1987.

Despite demands for declaring Poland in default, Congress in February authorized payment of $3.5 million in interest charges to U.S. banks that had given loans to Poland for food purchases.

Martial law was formally ended in 1984 but the government retained emergency powers. On July 21, 1984, the Parliament marked the 40th anniversary of Communist rule in Poland by enacting an amnesty bill authorizing the release of 652 political prisoners—virtually all except for those charged with high treason, espionage, and sabotage—and 35,000 common criminals. On September 10, 1986, the government freed all 225 remaining political prisoners.

The abduction and murder in October 1984 of a pro-Solidarity, Roman Catholic priest, the Rev. Jerzy Popieluszko, jolted the government as no other event had since the start of the Solidarity movement in 1980. After a 25-day trial before a five-judge tribunal, four state security policemen were convicted on Feb. 7, 1985, and sentenced to prison terms of 14 to 25 years for the murder. During the trial, the prosecution sought to show that the four had acted on their own, without the involvement of higher-ups.

PORTUGAL

Republic of Portugal
President: Mario Soares (1986)
Prime Minister: Anibal Cavaco Silva (1987)
Area: 34,340 sq mi. (88,941 sq km)
Population (est. mid-1987): 10,300,000 (average annual growth rate: 0.3%)
Density per square mile: 299.9
Capital: Lisbon
Largest cities (est. 1982): Lisbon, 900,000; Opporto, 400,000
Monetary unit: Escudo
Language: Portuguese
Religion: Roman Catholic
National name: República Portuguesa
Literacy rate: 80%
Economic summary: Gross national product (1984): $19.2 billion. Average annual growth rate (1984): −1.7%. Per capita income (1983): $2,247. Land used for agriculture: 39%; labor force: 23%; principal products: grains, potatoes, olives, wine grapes. Labor force in industry: 35%; major products: textiles, footwear, wood pulp, paper, cork, metal products, refined oil, chemicals, canned fish, wine. Natural resources: fish, cork, tungsten ore. Exports: cotton, textiles, cork and cork products, canned fish, wine, timber and timber products, resin. Imports: petroleum, cotton, industrial machinery, iron and steel, chemicals. Major trading partners: Western European countries, U.S.

Geography. Portugal occupies the western part of the Iberian Peninsula, bordering on the Atlantic Ocean to the west and Spain to the north and east. It is slightly smaller than Indiana.

The country is crossed by many small rivers, and also by three large ones that rise in Spain, flow into the Atlantic, and divide the country into three geographic areas. The Minho (Miño in Spain) River, part of the northern boundary, cuts through a mountainous area that extends south to the vicinity of the Douro (Duero) River. South of the Douro, the mountains slope to the plains about the Tajo (Tejo) River. The remaining division is the southern one of Alentejo.

The Azores, stretching over 340 miles (547 km) in the Atlantic, consist of nine islands divided into three groups, with a total area of 902 square miles (2,335 sq km). The nearest continental land is Cape da Roca, Portugal, about 900 miles (1,448 km) to the east. The Azores are an important station on Atlantic air routes, and Britain and the U.S. established air bases there during World War II.

Madeira, consisting of two inhabited islands, Madeira and Porto Santo, and two groups of uninhabited islands, lies in the Atlantic about 535 miles (861 km) southwest of Lisbon. The Madeiras are 307 square miles (796 sq km) in area.

Government. The Constitution of 1976, revised in 1982, provides for popular election of a President for a five-year term and for a legislature, the Assembly of the Republic, for four years.

The major political parties are the Social Democratic Party (147 of 250 seats in the Assembly), led by Prime Minister Cavaco Silva; the Socialists (58 seats) led by Vitor Constâncio; the Democratic Renewal Party, led by Antonio Eanes; The United People's Alliance, Álvaro Cunhal and the Democratic and Social Centre led by Francisco Lucas Pires.

History. Portugal was a part of Spain until it won its independence in the middle of the 12th century. King John I (1385–1433) unified his country at the expense of the Castilians and the Moors of Morocco. The expansion of Portugal was brilliantly coordinated by John's son, Prince Henry the Navigator. In 1488, Bartolomew Diaz reached the Cape of Good Hope, proving that the Far East was accessible by sea. In 1498, Vasco da Gama reached the west coast of India. By the middle of the 16th century, the Portuguese Empire was in West and East Africa, Brazil, Persia, Indochina, and Malaya.

In 1581, Philip II of Spain invaded Portugal and held it for 60 years, precipitating a catastrophic decline of Portuguese commerce. Courageous and shrewd explorers, the Portuguese proved to be inefficient and corrupt colonizers. By the time the Portuguese dynasty was restored in 1640, Dutch, English, and French competitors began to seize the lion's share of the world's colonies and commerce. Portugal retained Angola and Mozambique in Africa, and Brazil (until 1822).

The corrupt King Carlos, who ascended the throne in 1889, made Joao Franco the Premier with dictatorial power in 1906. In 1908, Carlos and his heir were shot dead on the streets of Lisbon. The new King, Manoel II, was driven from the throne in the Revolution of 1910 and Portugal became a French-style republic.

Traditionally friendly to Britain, Portugal fought in World War I on the Allied side in Africa as well as on the Western Front. Weak postwar governments and a revolution in 1926 brought Antonio Oliveira Salazar to power. He kept Portugal neutral in World War II but gave the Allies naval and air bases after 1943.

Portugal lost the tiny remnants of its Indian empire—Goa, Daman, and Diu—to Indian military occupation in 1961, the year an insurrection broke out in Angola. For the next 13 years, Salazar, who died in 1970, and his successor, Marcello Caetano, fought independence movements amid growing world criticism. Leftists in the armed forces, weary of a losing battle, launched a successful revolution on April 25, 1974.

In 1980, President General Antonia Ramalho

Eanes won a second four-year term with 57% of the popular vote.

In late-1985, a PSP-PSD split ended the Soares coalition government. Cavaco Silva, an advocate of free-market economics, was the Social Decmocratic candidate. His party emerged with a pluraity, unseating the Socialists.

In July 1987, the governing Social Democratic Party was swept back into office with 51.1% of the popular vote, giving Portugal its first majority Government since democracy was restored in 1974.

Portuguese Overseas Territory

After the April 1974 revolution, the military junta moved to grant independence to the territories, beginning with Portuguese Guinea in September 1974, which became the Republic of Guinea-Bissau.

Mozambique and Angola followed, leaving only Portuguese Timor and Macao of the former empire. Despite Lisbon's objections, Indonesia annexed Timor.

MACAO

Status: Territory
Governor: Adm. Vasco Almeida Costa (1981)
Area: 6 sq mi. (15.5 sq km)
Population (est. 1987): 400,000 (average annual growth rate: 1.7%)
Capital (1970 census): Macao, 241,413
Monetary unit: Patacá
Literacy rate (1981): 99% (excluding Chinese)
Economic summary: Gross national product (1980): $550 million. Annual average growth rate (1970–79): 15%. Land used for agriculture: 10%; labor force: 5%; principal products: rice and vegetables; Labor force in industry: 30%; major products: textiles, fireworks, fish products. Exports: textiles and clothing, manufactured goods, foodstuffs. Imports: consumer goods, foodstuffs. Major trading partners: Hong Kong, China, U.S., West Germany, France.

Macao comprises the peninsula of Macao and the two small islands of Taipa and Colôane on the South China coast, about 35 miles (53 km) from Hong Kong. Established by the Portuguese in 1557, it is the oldest European outpost in the China trade, but Portugal's sovereign rights to the port were not recognized by China until 1887. The port has been eclipsed in importance by Hong Kong, but it is still a busy distribution center and also has an important fishing industry. Portugal will return Macao to China in 1999.

QATAR

State of Qatar
Ruler: Sheikh Khalifa bin Hamad al-Thani (1972)
Area: 4,000 sq mi. (11,437 sq km)
Population (est. mid-1987): 300,000 (average annual growth rate: 3.0%)
Density per square mile: 75.0
Capital (est. 1981): Doha, 190,000
Monetary unit: Qatari riyal
Language: Arabic
Religion: Islam
Literacy rate: 40%
Economic summary: Gross national product (1983): $7.6 billion. Average annual growth rate (1970–79): −1.2%. Per capita income (1983): $27,000. Major industrial product: oil. Natural resources: oil, gas. Export: oil. Major trading partners: U.K., U.S., France, Japan, West Germany.

Geography. Qatar occupies a small peninsula that extends into the Persian Gulf from the east side of the Arabian Peninsula. Saudi Arabia is to the west and the United Arab Emirates to the south. The country is mainly barren.

Government. Qatar, one of the Arabian Gulf states, lies between Bahrain and United Arab Emirates. For a long time, it was under Turkish protection, but in 1916, the sultan accepted British protection. After the discovery of oil in the 1940s and its exploitation in the 1950s and 1960s, political unrest spread to the sheikhdoms. Qatar declared its independence in 1971. The next year the current Sheikh, Khalifa bin Hamad al-Thani, ousted his cousin in a bloodless coup.

ROMANIA

Socialist Republic of Romania
President: Nicolae Ceausescu (1974)
Premier: Constantin Dascalescu (1982)
Area: 91,700 sq mi. (237,500 sq km)
Population (est. mid-1987): 22,900,000 (Romanian, 87.1%, Hungarian 7.7%, Germans, 1.5%) (average annual growth rate: 0.5%)
Density per square mile: 249.72
Capital: Bucharest
Largest cities (est. 1986): Bucharest, 1,975,808; Brasov, 346,640; Timisoara, 318,955; Constanta, 323,236; Cluj-Napoca, 309,843; Iasi, 314,456; Galati, 292,805
Monetary unit: Leu
Languages: Romanian, Hungarian, Serbian, German, Turkish
Religions: Romanian Orthodox, 80%; Greek Orthodox, 10%
National name: Republica Socialista România
Literacy rate: 99%
Economic summary: Gross national product (1984): $117.6 billion. Average annual growth rate (1984): 4.3%. Per capita income (1984): $5,200. Land used for agriculture: 63%; labor force: 29%; principal products: corn, wheat, beets, potatoes. Labor force in industry: 38%; major products: steel, cement, metal production and processing, chemicals, food processing, textiles. Natural resources: oil, timber, natural gas, coal. Exports: machinery, minerals and metals, foodstuffs, lumber, fuel, manufactures. Imports: machinery, iron ore, coke and coking coal, minerals. Major trading partners: U.S.S.R., East Germany, West Germany, Iran, Egypt, U.S.A.

Geography. A country in southeastern Europe slightly smaller than Oregon, Romania is bordered on the west by Hungary and Yugoslavia, on the north and east by the U.S.S.R., on the east by the Black Sea, and on the south by Bulgaria.

The Carpathian Mountains divide Romania's upper half from north to south and connect near the center of the country with the Transylvanian Alps, running east and west.

North and west of these ranges lies the Transylvanian plateau, and to the south and east are the plains of Moldavia and Walachia. In its last 190 miles (306 km), the Danube River flows through Romania only. It enters the Black Sea in northern Dobruja, just south of the border with the Soviet Union.

Government. The supreme body of state power and the sole legislative body is the Grand National Assembly, with 465 members elected for five-year terms. It elects a State Council, which provides for the continuity of state power and settles problems between sessions of the Assembly. The supreme executive and administrative body is the Council of Ministers elected by the Assembly.

The Communist Partry, led by Secretary General Nicolae Ceausescu, is the only political party.

History. Most of Romania was the Roman province of Dacia from about A.D. 100 to 271. From the 6th to the 12th century, wave after wave of barbarian conquerors—Vlachs, Bulgars, and others—passed over the area. By the 16th century, the main Romanian principalities of Moldavia and Walachia had become satellites within the Ottoman Empire, although they retained much independence. After the Russo-Turkish War of 1828–29, they became Russian protectorates. The nation became a kingdom in 1881 after the Congress of Berlin.

King Ferdinand ascended the throne in 1914. At the start of World War I, Romania proclaimed its neutrality, but later joined the Allied side and in 1916 declared war on the Central Powers. The armistice of Nov. 11, 1918, gave Romania vast territories from Russia and the Austro-Hungarian Empire.

The gains of World War I, making Romania the largest Balkan state, included Bessarabia, Transylvania, and Bukovina. The Banat, a Hungarian area, was divided with Yugoslavia.

In 1925, Crown Prince Carol renounced his rights to the throne, and when King Ferdinand died in 1927, Carol's son, Michael (Mihai) became King under a regency. However, Carol returned from exile in 1930, was crowned King Carol II, and gradually became a powerful political force in the country. In 1938, he abolished the democratic Constitution of 1923.

In 1940, the country was reorganized along Fascist lines, and the Fascist Iron Guard became the nucleus of the new totalitarian party. On June 27, the Soviet Union occupied Bessarabia and northern Bukovina. By the Axis-dictated Vienna Award of 1940, two fifths of Transylvania went to Hungary, after which Carol dissolved Parliament and granted the new premier, Ion Antonescu, full power. He abdicated and again went into exile.

Romania subsequently signed the Axis Pact on Nov. 23, 1940, and the following June joined in Germany's attack on the Soviet Union, reoccupying Bessarabia. Following the invasion of Romania by the Red Army in August 1944, King Michael led a coup that ousted the Antonescu government. An armistice with the Soviet Union was signed in Moscow on Sept. 12, 1944.

A Communist-dominated government bloc won elections in 1946, Michael abdicated on Dec. 30, 1947, and Romania became a "people's republic." In 1955, Romania joined the Warsaw Treaty Organization and the United Nations. A decade later, with the adoption of a new Constitution emphasizing national autonomy, and especially after Nicolae Ceausescu came to power in 1967, Bucharest became an increasingly dissident voice in the Soviet bloc.

Despite his liberal international record, at home Ceausescu has harshly suppressed dissidents calling for freedom of expression in the wake of the Helsinki agreements.

RWANDA

Republic of Rwanda
President: Maj. Gen. Juvénal Habyarimana (1973)
Area: 10,169 sq mi. (26,338 sq km)
Population (est. mid-1987): 6,800,000 (average annual growth rate: 3.7%)
Density per square mile: 668.7
Capital and largest city (est. 1981): Kigali, 155,000
Monetary unit: Rwanda franc
Languages: Kinyarwanda and French
Religions: Roman Catholic, 56%; Protestant, 12%; Islam, 9%; Animist, 23%
National name: Repubulika y'u Rwanda
Literacy rate: 49%
Economic summary: Gross national product (1984): $1.61 billion. Average annual growth rate (1984 est.): 2.9%. Per capita income (1983): $270. Land used for agriculture: 41%; labor force: 88%; principal products: coffee, tea, bananas, yams, beans. Labor force in industry: less than 5%; major products: processed foods, light consumer goods, minerals. Natural resources: cassiterite, wolfram. Exports: coffee, tea, tungsten, tin. Imports: textiles, foodstuffs, machinery, and equipment. Major trading partners: Belgium, West Germany, Kenya, Japan, France.

Geography. Rwanda, in east central Africa, is surrounded by Zaire, Uganda, Tanzania, and Burundi. It is slightly smaller than Maryland.

Steep mountains and deep valleys cover most of the country. Lake Kivu in the northwest, at an altitude of 4,829 feet (1,472 m) is the highest lake in Africa. Extending north of it are the Virunga Mountains, which include Volcan Karisimbi (14,187 ft.; 4,324 m), Rwanda's highest point.

Government. Grégoire Kayibanda was President from 1962 until he was overthrown in a bloodless coup on July 5, 1973, by the military led by Gen. Juvénal Habyarimana.

In a plebiscite in December 1978, Habyarimana was elected to a five-year term as president and a new constitution adopted that provides for an elected Assembly and a single official party, the National Revolutionary Development Movement.

History. Rwanda, which was part of German East Africa, was first visited by European explorers in 1854. During World War I, it was occupied in 1916 by Belgian troops. After the war, it became a Belgian League of Nations mandate, along with Burundi, under the name of Ruanda-Urundi. The mandate was made a U.N. trust territory in 1946. Until the Belgian Congo achieved independence in 1960, Ruanda-Urundi was administered as part of that colony.

Ruanda became the independent nation of Rwanda on July 1, 1962.

ST. KITTS AND NEVIS

Federation of St. Kitts and Nevis
Sovereign: Queen Elizabeth II
Governor General: Sir Clement Athelston Arrindell (1985)
Prime Minister: Kennedy Alphonse Simmonds (1980)
Area: St. Christopher (Kitts) 65 sq mi. (169 sq km); Nevis 35 sq mi. (93 sq km)
Total population (est. mid-1987): 50,000 (average annual growth rate: 1.6%)
Capital: Basseterre (on St. Kitts), 14,725

Largest town on Nevis: Charlestown, 1,771
Monetary unit: East Caribbean dollar
Economic summary: Gross national product (1984): $60 million. Per capita income: $1,360. Principal agricultural products: sugar, cotton. Major industries: sugar processing, salt extraction. Exports: sugar, molasses. Imports: foodstuffs, manufactured goods. Major trading partners: U.S., U.K., Trinidad.

St. Christopher-Nevis, now St. Kitts and Nevis, was formerly part of the West Indies Associated States which were established in 1967 and consisted of Antigua and St. Kitts-Nevis-Anguilla of the Leeward Islands, and Dominica, Grenada, St. Lucia, and St. Vincent of the Windward Islands. Statehood for St. Vincent was held up until 1969 because of local political uncertainties. (Grenada, became independent in 1974, Dominica in 1978, St. Lucia and St. Vincent in 1979, and Antigua (known as Antigua and Barbuda) in 1981.) Anguilla's association with St. Christopher-Nevis ended in 1980. St. Kitts and Nevis remains a British dependency.

Two members of the Leeward group—the British Virgin Islands and Montserrat—did not become Associated States.

St. Christopher-Nevis, now St. Kitts and Nevis, became independent on September 19, 1983.

ST. LUCIA

Sovereign: Queen Elizabeth II
Governor-General: Sir Allen Lewis (1982)
Prime Minister: John Compton (1975)
Area: 238 sq mi. (616 sq km)
Population (est. mid-1987): 100,000 (average annual growth rate: 2.5%)
Density per square mile: 420.2
Capital (est. 1972): Castries, 45,000
Monetary unit: East Caribbean dollar
Languages: English and patois
Religions: Roman Catholic, 91%; Anglican, 3%; Seventh-day Adventist, 2%
Member of Commonwealth of Nations
Literacy rate: 80%
Economic summary: Gross national product (1983): $177.6 million. Average annual growth rate (est. 1982): 3.1%. Per capita income (1980): $1,200. Labor force in agriculture: 44%; principal products: bananas, coconuts, sugar, cocoa, spices. Major industrial products: processed limes. Exports: bananas, clothing. Imports: foodstuffs, machinery and equipment, fertilizers, petroleum products. Major trading partners: U.K., U.S., Caribbean countries.

Geography. One of the Windward Isles of the Eastern Caribbean, St. Lucia lies just south of Martinique. It is of volcanic origin. A chain of wooded mountains runs from north to south, and from them flow many streams into fertile valleys.

Government. A Governor-General represents the sovereign, Queen Elizabeth II. A Prime Minister is head of government, chosen by a 17-member House of Assembly elected by universal suffrage for a maximum term of five years.

History. Discovered by Spain in 1503 and ruled by Spain and then France, St. Lucia became a British territory in 1803. With other Windward Isles, St. Lucia was granted home rule in 1967 as one of the West Indies Associated States. On Feb. 22, 1979, St. Lucia achieved full independence in ceremonies boycotted by the opposition St. Lucia Labor Party, which had advocated a referendum before cutting ties with Britain.

Unrest and a strike by civil servants forced Prime Minister John Compton to hold elections in July, in which his United Workers Party lost its majority for the first time in 15 years.

A Labor Party government was ousted in turn by Compton and his followers, who won 14 of 17 seats in elections in May 1982. Labor seats fell from 12 to 2, with one seat won by the Progressive Labor Party.

Formerly dependent on a single crop, bananas, St. Lucia has sought to lower its chronic unemployment and payments deficit. The government provided tax incentives to a U.S. corporation, Amerada Hess, to facilitate location of a $150-million oil refinery and transshipment terminal on the island.

ST. VINCENT AND THE GRENADINES

Sovereign: Queen Elizabeth II
Governor-General: Sir Joseph Lambert Eustace (1986)
Prime Minister: James Mitchell (1984)
Area: 150 sq mi. (389 sq km)
Population (est. mid-1987): 100,000 (average annual growth rate: 2.0%)
Density per square mile: 666.7
Capital and largest city (est. 1981): Kingstown, 30,000
Monetary unit: East Caribbean dollar
Language: English
Religions: Anglican, 47%; Methodist, 28%; Roman Catholic, 13%
Member of Commonwealth of Nations
Literacy rate: 85%
Economic summary: Gross national product (1984): $100 million. Average annual growth rate: 3%. Per capita income (1984): $920. Land used for agriculture: 50%; labor force: 29%; principal products: bananas, arrowroot, coconuts. Major industry: food processing. Exports: bananas, arrowroot, copra. Imports: foodstuffs, machinery and equipment, chemicals, fuels, clothing. Major trading partners: U.K., U.S., Canada, Caribbean nations.

Geography. St. Vincent, chief island of the chain, is 18 miles (29 km) long and 11 miles (18 km) wide. One of the Windward Islands in the Lesser Antilles, it is 100 miles (161 km) west of Barbados. The island is mountainous and well forested. The Grenadines, a chain of nearly 600 islets with a total area of only 17 square miles (27 sq km), extend for 60 miles (96 km) from northeast to southwest between St. Vincent and Grenada, southernmost of the Windwards.

St. Vincent is dominated by the volcano La Soufrière, part of a volcanic range running north and south, which rises to 4,048 feet (1,234 m). The volcano erupted over a 10-day period in April 1979, causing the evacuation of the northern two thirds of the island. (There is also a volcano of the same name on Basse-Terre, Guadeloupe, which became violently active in 1976 and 1977.)

Government. A Governor-General represents the sovereign, Queen Elizabeth II. A Prime Minister, elected by a 13-member unicameral legislature, holds executive power. Major political parties are the New Democrats (9 of the 13 seats), led by

Prime Minister James Mitchell; and the Labor Party (4 seats), led by Vincent Beache.

History. Discovered by Columbus in 1498, and alternately claimed by Britain and France, St. Vincent became a British colony by the Treaty of Paris in 1783. The islands won home rule in 1969 as part of the West Indies Associated States and achieved full independence Oct. 26, 1979. Prime Minister Milton Cato's government quelled a brief rebellion Dec. 8, 1979 attributed to economic problems following the eruption of La Soufrière in April, 1979. Unlike a 1902 eruption which killed 2,000, there was no loss of life but widespread losses to agriculture.

SAN MARINO

Most Serene Republic of San Marino
Co-Regents: Two selected every six months by Grand and General Council
Area: 23.6 sq mi. (62 sq km)
Population (est. 1985): 23,000 (mostly Italian) (average annual growth rate: 1.6%)
Density per square mile: 974.6
Capital and largest city (est. 1982 for metropolitan area): San Marino, 4,500
Monetary unit: Italian lira
Language: Italian
Religion: Roman Catholic
National name: Repubblica di San Marino
Literacy rate: 98%
Economic summary: Land used for agriculture: 74%; principal products: wheat and other grains, grapes, fruits, vegetables. Major industrial products: textiles, paper, leather, cement and other building materials. Exports: building stone, lime, chestnuts, wheat, hides, baked goods. Imports: manufactured consumer goods. Major trading partner: Italy.

Geography: One tenth the size of New York City, San Marino is surrounded by Italy. It is situated in the Apennines, a little inland from the Adriatic Sea near Rimini.

Government. The country is governed by two co-regents. Executive power is exercised by ten ministers. In 1959, the Grand Council granted women the vote.

The major political parties are the Christian Democratic Party (26 of 60 seats in the Grand and General Council); Communist Party (15 seats); Socialist Party (9 seats); United Socialist Party (8 seats); Democratic Socialist Party (1 seat); and Republican Party (1 seat). The government is a Christian Democratic-Communist coalition.

History. According to tradition, San Marino was founded about A.D. 350 and had good luck for centuries in staying out of the many wars and feuds on the Italian peninsula. It is the oldest republic in the world.

A person born in San Marino remains a citizen and can vote no matter where he lives.

SÃO TOMÉ AND PRÍNCIPE

Democratic Republic of São Tomé and Principe
President: Manuel Pinto da Costa (1975)
Area: 372 sq mi. (1001 sq km)
Population (est. mid-1987): 100,000 (average annual growth rate: 2.7%)
Density per square mile: 268.8
Capital and largest city (est. 1984): São Tomé, 34,997
Monetary unit: Dobra
Language: Portuguese
Religions: Roman Catholic, Evangelical Protestant, Seventh-Day Adventist
Literacy rate: 54%
Economic summary: Gross national product (1985): $80 million. Average annual growth rate (1982–85): 1.4%. Per capita income (1984): $330. Principal agricultural products: cocoa, copra, coconuts, palm oil, coffee, bananas. Major industrial products: timber, copra. Exports: cocoa, coffee, copra, palm oil. Imports: foodstuffs, textiles, machinery, electrical equipment, fuels, lubricants. Major trading partners: Netherlands, Portugal, East Germany, Rep. China, Angola, France.

Geography. The tiny volcanic islands of São Tomé and Príncipe lie in the Gulf of Guinea about 150 miles (240 km) off West Africa. São Tomé (about 330 sq mi.; 859 sq km) is covered by a dense mountainous jungle, out of which have been carved large plantations. Príncipe (about 40 sq. mi.; 142 sq km) consists of jagged mountains. Other islands in the republic are Pedras Tinhosas and Rolas.

Government. The Constitution grants supreme power to a People's Assembly composed of members elected for four years. The Assembly chooses the President of the republic from candidates named by the Movement for the Liberation of São Tomé and Príncipe, the only legal party.

History. São Tomé and Príncipe were discovered, by Portuguese navigators in 1471 and settled by the end of the century. Intensive cultivation by slave labor made the islands a major producer of sugar during the 17th century but output declined until the introduction of coffee and cacao in the 19th century brought new prosperity. The island of São Tomé was the world's largest producer of cacao in 1908 and the crop is still the most important. An exile liberation movement was formed in 1953 after Portuguese landowners quelled labor riots by killing several hundred African workers.

The Portuguese revolution of 1974 brought the end of the overseas empire and the new Lisbon government transferred power to the liberation movement on July 12, 1975. Most of the 4,000 Portuguese inhabitants departed during the transition period.

SAUDI ARABIA

Kingdom of Saudi Arabia
Ruler and Prime Minister: King Fahd bin 'Abdulaziz (1982)
Area: 865,000 sq mi. (2,250,070 sq km)
Population (est. mid-1987): 14,800,000 (average annual growth rate: 3.1%)
Density per square mile: 17.1
Capital: Riyadh
Largest cities (est. 1980): Riyadh, 1,250,000; Jeddah, 1,000,000; Mecca, 750,000
Monetary unit: Riyal
Language: Arabic
Religion: Islam
National name: Al-Mamlaka al-'Arabiya as-Sa'udiya
Literacy rate: 52%

Economic summary: Gross national product (1984): $116 billion. Average annual non-oil growth rate: 5%. Per capita income (1984): $10,750. Labor force in agriculture: 30%; principal products: dates, grains, livestock. Labor force in industry: 29%; major products: petroleum, cement, plastic products, steel. Natural resource: oil. Exports: petroleum and petroleum products. Imports: manufactured goods, transport equipment, construction materials, processed food. Major trading partners: U.S., Western European countries, Japan, West Germany.

Geography. Saudi Arabia occupies most of the Arabian Peninsula, with the Red Sea and the Gulf of Aqaba to the west, the Arabian Gulf to the east. Neighboring countries are Jordan, Iraq, Kuwait, Qatar, the United Arab Emirates, the Sultanate of Oman, the Yemen Arab Republic, and the People's Democratic Republic of Yemen.

A narrow coastal plain on the Red Sea rims a mountain range that spans the length of the western coastline. These mountains gradually rise in elevation from north to south. East of these mountains is a massive plateau which slopes gently downward toward the Arabian Gulf. Part of this plateau is covered by the world's largest sand desert, the Rub Al-Khali, or Empty Quarter. Saudi Arabia's oil region lies primarily along the Arabian Gulf.

Government. Saudi Arabia is a monarchy based on the Sharia (Islamic law), as revealed in the Koran (the holy book) and the Hadith (teachings and sayings of the prophet Mohammed). A Council of Ministers was formed in 1953, which acts as a Cabinet under the leadership of the King. There are 21 Ministries.

Royal and ministerial decrees account for most of the promulgated legislation, treaties, and conventions. There are no political parties.

History. Mohammed united the Arabs in the 7th century, and his followers, led by the caliphs, founded a great empire, with its capital at Medina. Later, the caliphate capital was transferred to Damascus and then Baghdad, but Arabia retained its importance because of the holy cities of Mecca and Medina. In the 16th and 17th centuries, the Turks established at least nominal rule over much of Arabia, and in the middle of the 18th century, it was divided into separate principalities.

The Kingdom of Saudi Arabia is almost entirely the creation of King Ibn Saud (1882–1953). A descendant of earlier Wahabi rulers, he seized Riyadh, the capital of Nejd, in 1901 and set himself up as leader of the Arab nationalist movement. By 1906 he had established Wahabi dominance in Nejd. He conquered Hejaz in 1924–25, consolidating it and Nejd into a dual kingdom in 1926. In 1932, Hejaz and Nejd became a single kingdom, which was officially named Saudi Arabia. A year later the region of Asir was incorporated into the kingdom.

Oil was discovered in 1936, and commercial production began during World War II. Saudi Arabia was neutral until nearly the end of the war, but it was permitted to be a charter member of the United Nations. The country joined the Arab League in 1945 and took part in the 1948–49 war against Israel.

On Ibn Saud's death in 1953, his eldest son, Saud, began an 11-year reign marked by an increasing hostility toward the radical Arabism of Egypt's Gamal Abdel Nasser. In 1964, the ailing Saud was deposed and replaced by the Premier, Crown Prince Faisal, who gave vocal support but no military help to Egypt in the 1967 Mideast war.

Faisal's assassination by a deranged kinsman in 1975 shook the Middle East, but failed to alter his kingdom's course. His successor was his brother, Prince Khalid. Khalid gave influential support to Egypt during negotiations on Israeli withdrawal from the Sinai desert.

King Khalid died of a heart attack June 13, 1982, and was succeeded by his half-brother, Prince Fahd bin 'Abdulaziz, 60, who had exercised the real power throughout Khalid's reign. King Fahd, a pro-Western modernist, chose his 58-year-old half-brother, Abdullah, as Crown Prince.

Saudi Arabia and the smaller, oil-rich Arab states on the Persian Gulf, fearful that they might become Ayatollah Ruhollah Khomeini's next targets if Iran conquered Iraq, made large financial contributions to the Iraqi war effort. They began being dragged into the conflict themselves in the spring of 1984, when Iraq and Iran extended their ground war to attacks on Gulf shipping. First, Iraq attacked tankers loading at Iran's Kharg Island terminal with air-to-ground missiles, then Iran struck back at tankers calling at Saudi Arabia and other Arab countries.

President Reagan ordered the sale, at the end of May, of 400 Stinger antiaircraft missiles to Saudi Arabia. Shortly afterward, Saudi fighter planes shot down two Iranian planes as they approached a foreign tanker over the Gulf. The Saudis were directed to the targets by a U.S. Air Force AWAC plane.

At the same time, cheating by other members of the Organization of Petroleum Exporting Countries, competition from nonmember oil producers, and conservation efforts by consuming nations combined to drive down the world price of oil. Saudi Arabia has one-third of all known oil reserves, but falling demand and rising production outside OPEC combined to reduce its oil revenues from $120 billion in 1980 to $43 billion in 1984 to less the $25 billion in 1985, threatening the country with domestic unrest and undermining its influence in the Gulf area. Oil prices plunged to $9 a barrel in 1986, partly due to a Saudi-initiated price war but later rebounded when the Saudis drove prices back up.

SENEGAL

Republic of Senegal
President: Abdou Diouf (1981)
Area: 75,954 sq mi. (196,722 sq km)
Population (est. mid-1987): 7,100,000 (average annual growth rate: 2.8%)
Density per square mile: 90.8
Capital and largest city (est. 1982): Dakar, 975,000
Monetary unit: Franc CFA
Ethnic groups: Wolofs, Sereres, Peuls, Tukulers, and others
Languages: French (official); Wolof, Serer, other ethnic dialects
Religions: Islam, 91%; Christian, 6%
National name: République du Sénegal
Literacy rate: 10%
Economic summary: Gross national product (1983): $2.5 billion. Average annual growth rate (1986): 4.5%. Per capita income (1983): $400. Land used for agriculture: 27%; labor force: 70%; principal products: peanuts,

millet, corn, rice, sorghum. Labor force in industry: 8%; major products: peanut oil, fertilizer, cement, processed food and fish. Natural resources: fish, phosphate. Exports: peanuts, phosphate rock, canned fish. Imports: foodstuffs, consumer goods, machinery, transport equipment. Major trading partners: France, Western European countries, African neighbors.

Geography. The capital of Senegal, Dakar, is the westernmost point in Africa. The country, slighty smaller than South Dakota, surrounds The Gambia on three sides and is bordered on the north by Mauritania, on the east by Mali, and on the south by Guinea and Guinea-Bissau.

Senegal is mainly a low-lying country, with a semidesert area in the north and northeast and forests in the southwest. The largest rivers include the Senegal in the north and the Casamance in the south tropical climate region.

Government. There is a National Assembly of 120 members, elected every five years. There is universal suffrage and a constitutional guarantee of equality before the law.

The major political party is the Socialist Party, led by President Abdou Diouf. Legal opposition was reconstituted in 1974 with formation of the Senegalese Democratic Party, headed by Abdoulaye Wade, which urged reduction in French and Western influences. Other opposition parties include the Rassemblement National Démocratique and the Democratic League (Communist). Among the other 14 parties are: the Democratic League, the National Democratic Union, the Republican Party, the Party of Independence and Labor.

History. The Portuguese had some stations on the banks of the Senegal River in the 15th century, and the first French settlement was made at Saint-Louis about 1650. The British took parts of Senegal at various times, but the French gained possession in 1840 and organized the Sudan as a territory in 1904. In 1946, together with other parts of French West Africa, Senegal became part of the French Union. On June 20, 1960, it became an independent republic federated with the Sudanese Republic inthe Mali Federation, from which it withdrew two months later.

In 1973, Senegal joined with six other states to create the West African Economic Community.

Senegal exists in a confederation with The Gambia.

SEYCHELLES

Republic of Seychelles
President: France-Albert René (1977)
Area: 175 sq mi. (453 sq km)
Population (est. mid-1987): 100,000 (average annual growth rate: 1.9%)
Density per square mile: 571.4
Capital: Victoria, 24,000
Monetary unit: Seychelles rupee
Languages: Creole (official), English, French
Religions: Roman Catholic, 90%; Anglican, 8%
Member of Commonwealth of Nations, United Nations, Nonaligned Movement
Literacy rate: 65%
Economic summary: Gross national product (1984): $145 million. Average annual growth rate: −0.2%. Per capita income (1984): $2,240. Land used for agriculture: 37%; labor force: 18%; principal products: vanilla, copra, cinnamon. Labor force in industry: 55%; major products: processed copra and vanilla, coconut oil. Exports: cinnamon, vanilla, copra. Imports: food, tobacco, manufactured goods, machinery, petroleum products, textiles, transport equipment. Major trading partners: U.K., Bahrain, Japan, Pakistan.

Geography. Seychelles consists of an archipelago of about 100 islands in the Indian Ocean northeast of Madagascar. The principal islands are Mahé (55 sq mi.; 142 sq km), Praslin (15 sq mi.; 38 sq km), and La Digue (4 sq mi.; 10 sq km). The Aldabra, Farquhar, and Desroches groups are included in the territory of the republic.

Government. Seized from France by Britain in 1810, the Seychelles Islands remained a colony until June 29, 1976. The state is an independent republic within the Commonwealth.

On June 5, 1977, Prime Minister Albert René ousted the islands' first President, James Mancham, suspending the Constitution and the 25-member National Assembly. Mancham, whose "lavish spending" and flamboyance were cited by René in seizing power, charged that Soviet influence was at work. The new president denied this and, while more left than his predecessor, pledged to keep the Seychelles in the nonaligned group of countries.

An unsuccessful attempted coup against René attracted international attention when a group of 50 South African mercenaries posing as rugby players attacked the Victoria airport on Nov. 25, 1981. They caused extensive damage before they hijacked an Air India plane and returned to South Africa, where all but five were freed. Only after widespread international protest did the Pretoria government, which denied any responsibility for the attack, reverse the decision and order all the mercenaries tried as hijackers.

SIERRA LEONE

Republic of Sierra Leone
President: Maj. Gen. Joseph Saidu Momoh (1985)
Area: 27,925 sq mi. (72,326 sq km)
Population (est. mid-1987): 3,900,000 (average annual growth rate: 1.8%)
Density per square mile: 139.7
Capital and largest city (est. 1985): Freetown, 500,000
Monetary unit: Leone
Languages: English (official), Mende, Temne, Creole
Religions: Animist, 52%; Islam, 40%; Christian, 9%
Member of Commonwealth of Nations, United Nations
Literacy rate: 25%
Economic summary: Gross national product (1985): $1 billion. Average annual growth rate (1983–84): 0.5%. Per capita income (1983): $380. Land used for agriculture: 25%; labor force: 75%; principal products: coffee, cocoa, ginger, rice. Labor force in industry: 22%; major products: diamonds, bauxite, rutile, beverages, cigarettes, construction goods. Natural resources: diamonds, bauxite, iron ore, rutile. Exports: diamonds, iron ore, palm kernels, cocoa, coffee. Imports: food, petroleum products, chemicals, machinery. Major trading partners: U.K., U.S., Western European countries, Japan.

Geography. Sierra Leone, on the Atlantic Ocean in West Africa, is half the size of Illinois. Guinea, in the north and east, and Liberia, in the south, are its neighbors.

Mangrove swamps lie along the coast, with wooded hills and a plateau in the interior. The eastern region is mountainous.

Government. Sierra Leone became an independent nation on April 27, 1961, and declared itself a republic on April 19, 1971.

Sierra Leone became a one party state under the aegis of the All People's Congress Party in April 1978.

History. The coastal area of Sierra Leone was ceded to English settlers in 1788 as a home for blacks discharged from the British armed forces and also for runaway slaves who had found asylum in London. The British protectorate over the hinterland was proclaimed in 1896.

After elections in 1967, the British Governor-General replaced Sir Albert Margai, head of SLPP, which had held power since independence, with Dr. Stevens, head of APC, as prime minister. The Army took over the government; then another coup in April 1968 restored civilian rule and put the military leaders in jail.

A coup attempt early in 1971 by the army commander was apparently foiled by loyal army officers, but the then Prime Minister Stevens called in troops of neighboring Guinea's army, under a 1970 mutual defense pact, to guard his residence. After perfunctorily blaming the U.S. for the coup attempt, Stevens switched Governors-General, changed the Constitution, and ended up with a republic, of which he was first president. He was accused of taking "sweeping dictatorial powers," but was re-elected in 1978. Dr. Stevens' picked successor, Major-General Joseph Saidu Momoh was elected unopposed on Oct. 1, 1985.

SINGAPORE

Republic of Singapore
Prime Minister: Lee Kuan Yew (1959)
Area: 240 sq mi. (621.7 sq km)
Population (est. mid-1987): 2,600,000 (average annual growth rate: 1.1%) (Chinese, 76%; Malay, 15%; Indian, 7%)
Density per square mile: 10,924.4
Capital (est. 1983): Singapore, 2,500,000
Monetary unit: Singapore dollar
Languages: Malay, Chinese (Mandarin), Tamil, English
Religions: Islam, Christian, Buddhist, Hindu, Taoist
Member of Commonwealth of Nations
Literacy rate: 85%
Economic summary: Gross national product (1984): $18.4 billion. Annual growth rate (1986): 1.9%. Per capita income (1984): $7,270. Land used for agriculture: 7.6%; labor force; 1%; principal products: poultry, hogs, vegetables, fruits. Labor force in industry: 29.4%; major industries: petroleum refining, oil exploration, ship repair, rubber processing, electronics and other light industry. Exports: petroleum products, rubber, manufactured goods. Imports: capital equipment, manufactured goods, petroleum. Major trading partners: U.S., Japan, Malaysia, Hong Kong, Saudi Arabia, West Germany, China, Thailand.

Geography. The Republic of Singapore consists of the main island of Singapore, off the southern tip of the Malay Peninsula between the South China Sea and the Indian Ocean, and 54 nearby islands.

There are extensive mangrove swamps extending inland from the coast, which is broken by many inlets.

Government. There is a Cabinet, headed by the Prime Minister, and a Parliament of 79 members elected by universal suffrage.

The People's Action Party, led by Prime Minister Lee Kuan Yew, is the ruling political party in Parliament, holding all but two seats.

History. Singapore, founded in 1819 by Sir Stamford Raffles, became a separate crown colony of Britain in 1946, when the former colony of the Straits Settlements was dissolved. The other two settlements—Penang and Malacca—were transferred to the Union of Malaya, and the small island of Labuan was transferred to North Borneo. The Cocos (or Keeling) Islands were transferred to Australia in 1955 and Christmas Island in 1958.

Singapore attained full internal self-government in 1959. On Sept. 16, 1963, it joined Malaya, Sabah (North Borneo), and Sarawak in the Federation of Malaysia. It withdrew from the Federation on Aug. 9, 1965, and proclaimed itself a republic the next month.

SOLOMON ISLANDS

Sovereign: Queen Elizabeth II
Governor-General: Sir Baddeley Devesi (1978)
Prime Minister: Ezekiel Alebua (1986)
Area: 11,500 sq mi. (29,785 sq km)
Population (est. mid-1987): 300,000 (average annual growth rate: 3.6%)
Density per square mile: 26.1
Capital and largest city (est. 1981): Honiara (on Guadalcanal), 21,000
Monetary unit: Solomon Islands dollar
Languages: English, Melanesian dialects
Religions: Anglican, 34%; Roman Catholic, 19%; South Seas Evangelical, 25%; other Protestant, 15%
Member of British Commonwealth
Literacy rate: 60%
Economic summary: Gross national product (1983): $160. million. Average annual growth rate (1970–79): 2.3%. Per capita income (1983): $637. Principal agricultural products: copra, palm oil, rice, cocoa, yams, pigs. Major industrial products: processed fish, timber, jute, soap, canned meat, handicrafts. Natural resources: fish, timber. Exports: fish, timber, copra, palm oil. Imports: machinery and transport equipment, foodstuffs, fuel, manufactured goods. Major trading partners: Japan, Australia, U.K.

Geography. Lying east of New Guinea, this island nation consists of the southern islands of the Solomon group: Guadalcanal, Malaita, Santa Isabel, San Cristóbal, Choiseul, New Georgia, and numerous smaller islands.

Government. After 85 years of British rule, the Solomons achieved independence July 7, 1978. The Crown is represented by a Governor-General and legislative power is vested in a unicameral legislature of 38 members, led by the Prime Minister.

History. Discovered in 1567 by Alvaro de Mendana, the Solomons were not visited again for about 200 years. In 1886, Great Britain and Germany divided the islands between them. In 1914, Australian forces took over the German islands and the Solomons became an Australian mandate in

1920. In World War II, most of the islands were occupied by the Japanese. American forces landed on Guadalcanal on Aug. 7, 1942. The islands were the scene of several important U.S. naval and military victories. They are still largely undeveloped, with only 60 miles of paved road and fewer than 2,500 motor vehicles.

SOMALIA

Somali Democratic Republic
President: Maj. Gen. Mohamed Siad Barre (1969)
Area: 246,199 sq mi. (637,655 sq km)
Population (est. mid-1987): 7,700,000 (average annual growth rate: 2.5%)
Density per square mile: 31.3
Capital and largest city (est. 1982): Mogadishu, 700,000
Monetary unit: Somali shilling
Language: Somali and Arabic (official), Arabic, English, Italian
Religion: Islam
National name: Al Jumhouriya As-Somalya Dimocradia
Literacy rate: 60%
Economic summary: Gross national product (1983): $1.25 billion. Average annual growth rate: 4.7%. Per capita income (1983): $228. Labor force in agriculture: 30%; principal products: livestock, bananas, sorghum, cereals, sugar cane, maize. Labor force in industry: 3%; major products: flour, meat, fish, canned fruit juices. Natural resources: timber. Exports: livestock, skins and hides, bananas. Imports: textiles, construction materials and equipment, machinery, manufactured goods, transport equipment. Major trading partners: Arab countries, Italy, U.S.

Geography. Somalia, situated in the Horn of Africa, lies along the Gulf of Aden and the Indian Ocean. It is bounded by Djibouti in the northwest, Ethiopia in the west, and Kenya in the southwest. In area it is slightly smaller than Texas.

Generally arid and barren, Somalia has two chief rivers, the Shebelle and the Juba.

Government. Maj. Gen. Mohamed Siad Barre took power on Oct. 21, 1969, in a coup that established a Supreme Revolutionary Council as the governing body, replacing a parliamentary government. On July 1, 1976, Barre dissolved the Council, naming its members to the Somali Socialist Party, organized that day as the nation's only legal political party. In December 1979, a 171-member People's Assembly was elected under a new Constitution adopted in August. The Assembly confirmed Barre as President for a six-year term. He was re-elected in 1986.

History. From the 7th to the 10th century, Arab and Persian trading posts were established along the coast of present-day Somalia. Nomadic tribes occupied the interior, occasionally pushing into Ethiopian territory. In the 16th century, Turkish rule extended to the northern coast and the Sultans of Zanzibar gained control in the south.

After British occupation of Aden in 1839, the Somali coast became its source of food. The French established a coaling station in 1862 at the site of Djibouti and the Italians planted a settlement in Eritrea. Egypt, which for a time-claimed Turkish rights in the area, was succeeded by Britain. By 1920, a British protectorate and an Italian protectorate occupied what is now Somalia. The British ruled the entire area after 1941, with Italy returning in 1950 to serve as United Nations trustee for its former territory.

In mid-1960, Britain and Italy granted independence to their respective sectors, enabling the two to join as the Republic of Somalia on July 1. Somalia broke diplomatic relations with Britain in 1963 when the British granted the Somali-populated Northern Frontier District of Kenya to the Republic of Kenya.

On Oct. 15, 1969, President Abdi Rashid Ali Shermarke was assassinated and the army seized power, dissolving the legislature and arresting all government leaders. Maj. Gen. Mohamed Siad Barre, as President of a renamed Somali Democratic Republic, leaned heavily toward the U.S.S.R.

In 1977, Somalia openly backed rebels in the westernmost area of Ethiopia, the Ogaden desert, which had been seized by Ethiopia at the turn of the century.

Somalia acknowledged defeat in an eight-month war against the Ethiopians, having lost much of it's 32,000-man army and most of its tanks and planes. In March 1978, the U.S. agreed to supply $7 million in food over six months, in addition to $6 million in emergency food relief provided in December. The U.S. refused to consider weapons sales, however, unless Somalia gave up all claims to northern Kenya, the Ogaden, and the Republic of Djibouti, all once claimed as "Greater Somalia." Barre refused to do this.

A U.S. announcement on Jan. 9, 1980, that bases for U.S. ships and planes in the Indian Ocean would be sought in Somalia, Oman, and Kenya, brought a request from Somalia for $1 billion worth of modern arms and an equal amount of economic aid. In August, an agreement was signed giving the U.S. use of military bases in Somalia in return for $25 million in military aid in 1981 and more in subsequent years.

SOUTH AFRICA

Republic of South Africa
President: Pieter W. Botha (1984)
Area: 437,876 sq mi. (1,134,100 sq km)
Population (est. mid-1987): 34,300,000 (average annual growth rate: 2.3%) (black, 68%; white, 18%; colored [mixed], 11%; Asian, 3%)
Density per square mile: 75.8[1]
Administrative capital: Pretoria
Legislative capital: Cape Town
Judicial capital: Bloemfontein
Largest cities (est. 1984): Johannesburg, 1,700,000; Cape Town, 1,000,000; Durban, 1,000,000; Pretoria, 700,-000; Port Elizabeth, 600,000; Bloemfontein, 200,000.
Monetary unit: Rand
Languages: English, Afrikaans, 9 Bantu languages
Religions (1984): Dutch Reformed, 40%; Anglican, 11%; Roman Catholic, 8%; other Christian, 25%
National name: Repubilek van Suid-Afrika
Literacy rate: 99% (whites), 50% (Africans)
Economic summary: Gross national product (1983): $77 billion. Average annual growth rate (1983): −3%. Per capita income (1983): $2,500. Labor force in agriculture: 53%; principal products: corn, wool, wheat, sugar cane, tobacco, citrus fruits. Labor force in industry: 17%; major products: assembled automobiles, machinery, textiles, iron and steel, chemicals, fertilizer, fish. Natural resources: gold, diamonds, platinum, uranium, coal, iron ore, asbestos, manganese. Exports: gold, wool, diamonds, corn, uranium, sugar, fruits, hides and skins, asbestos, fish

products. Imports: motor vehicles, machinery, metals, petroleum products, chemicals, textiles. Major trading partners: U.S., West Germany, Japan, U.K.

1. Excluding South-West Africa (Namibia).

Geography. South Africa, on the continent's southern tip, is washed by the Atlantic Ocean on the west and by the Indian Ocean on the south and east. Its neighbors are South-West Africa (Namibia) in the northwest, Zimbabwe and Botswana in the north, and Mozambique and Swaziland in the northeast. The kingdom of Lesotho forms an enclave within the southeastern part of South Africa. Bophuthatswana, Transkei, Ciskei, and Venda are independent states within South Africa, which occupies an area nearly three times that of California.

The country has a high interior plateau, or veld, nearly half of which averages 4,000 feet (1,219 m) in elevation.

There are no important mountain ranges, although the Great Escarpment, separating the veld from the coastal plain, rises to over 11,000 feet (3,350 m) in the Drakensberg Mountains in the east. The principal river is the Orange, rising in Lesotho and flowing westward for 1,300 miles (2,092 km) to the Atlantic.

The southernmost point of Africa is Cape Agulhas, located in Cape Province about 100 miles (161 km) southeast of the Cape of Good Hope.

Government. A new Constitution in 1984 created a new office of Executive State President, with potentially authoritarian powers. Pieter W. Botha, Prime Minister since 1978, was sworn in as President on Sept. 14, 1984.

The new Constitution brought Indian and mixed-race people into a racially divided Parliament made up of three separate chambers for different racial groups. It continued to exclude blacks, who make up 68% of the population. It provides for selection of the President by an Electoral College made up of representatives from the three chambers, with the white chamber controlling the election. The major parties in the white chamber are the Nationalist Party (133 seats out of 178) led by President Pieter Botha; Conservative Party (23 seats) led by Andries Treunicht and the Progressive Liberals (20 seats) led by Colin Eglin. It empowers him to veto legislation, declare war, summon Parliament, and dismiss it.

Ten "Bantustans," or black homelands, have unicameral legislatures elected by black voters.

History. The Dutch East India Company landed the first settlers on the Cape of Good Hope in 1652, launching a colony that by the end of the 18th century numbered only about 15,000. Known as Boers or Afrikaners, speaking a Dutch dialect known as Afrikaans, the settlers as early as 1795 tried to establish an independent republic.

After occupying the Cape Colony in that year, Britain took permanent possession in 1814 at the end of the Napoleonic wars, bringing in 5,000 settlers. Anglicization of government and the freeing of slaves in 1833 drove about 12,000 Afrikaners to make the "great trek" north and east into African tribal territory, where they established the republics of the Transvaal and the Orange Free State.

The discovery of diamonds in 1867 and gold nine years later brought an influx of "outlanders" into the republics and spurred Cecil Rhodes to plot annexation. Rhodes's scheme of sparking an "outlander" rebellion to which an armed party under Leander Starr Jameson would ride to the rescue misfired in 1895, forcing Rhodes to resign as prime minister of the Cape colony. What British expansionists called the "inevitable" war with the Boers eventually broke out on Oct. 11, 1899.

The defeat of the Boers in 1902 led in 1910 to the Union of South Africa, composed of four provinces, the two former republics and the old Cape and Natal colonies. Louis Botha, a Boer, became the first Prime Minister.

Jan Christiaan Smuts brought the nation into World War II on the Allied side against Nationalist opposition, and South Africa became a charter member of the United Nations in 1945, but refused to sign the Universal Declaration of Human Rights. Apartheid—racial separation—dominated domestic politics as the Nationalists gained power and imposed greater restrictions on Bantus, Coloreds, and Asians.

Afrikaner hostility to Britain triumphed in 1961 with the declaration on May 31 of the Republic of South Africa and the severing of ties with the Commonwealth. Nationalist Prime Minister H. F. Verwoerd's government in 1963 asserted the power to restrict freedom of those who opposed rigid racial laws. Three years later, amid increasing racial tension and criticism from the outside world, Verwoerd was assassinated. His Nationalist successor, Balthazar J. Vorster, launched a campaign of conciliation toward conservative black African states, offering development loans and trade concessions.

A scandal led to Vorster's resignation on June 4, 1978. Pieter W. Botha succeeded him as Prime Minister, and became President on Sept. 14, 1984, after a new Constitution was promulgated substituting a strong Presidency for the previous parliamentary form of government.

South Africa's policy of apartheid—or racial separation—excluded the country's black majority from participation in the country's government and kept blacks at the bottom rung of the economic ladder. Protests against apartheid by militant blacks, beginning in the latter half of 1984, led to a state of emergency being declared twice, the first on July 20, 1985, covered 36 cities and towns and gave the police powers to make arrests without warrants and to detain people indefinitely. The second, declared on June 12, 1986, covered the whole nation. It gave the police a similar extension of powers and banned "subversive" press reports. Several thousand activists were detained.

Elections on May 7, 1987 increased the power of Botha's Nationalist party while enabling the far-right Conservative Party to replace the liberal Progressives as the official opposition. The results of the whites-only vote indicated a strong conservative reaction against Botha's policy of limited reform.

BOPHUTHATSWANA

Republic of Bophuthatswana
President: Kgosi Lucas Mangope (1977)
Area: 15,573 sq mi. (40,333 sq km)
Population (est. 1987): 1,736,000 (average annual growth rate: 2.8%)
Density per square mile: 111.5
Capital: Mmabatho
Largest city (est. 1987): Mabopane, 100,570
Monetary unit: South African rand
Languages: Setswana, English, Afrikaans
Religions: Methodist, Lutheran, Anglican, Bantu Christian, Dutch Reformed, Roman Catholic, A.M.E.

Geography. Bophuthatswana consists of seven discontinuous areas within the boundaries of South Africa, most of them share a common border with Botswana.

Government. The republic has a 108-member Legislative Assembly, three quarters of whom are elected and the others appointed. President Mangope's Democratic Party is the majority party.

History. Bophuthatswana was given independence by South Africa on Dec. 6, 1977, following Transkei as the second "homeland" to be established by Pretoria. The new state and Transkei are recognized only by South Africa and each other.

Mangope, as chief minister in the pre-independence period, sought linkage of the six units into a consolidated area, but was unable to achieve his objective. A second issue, the citizenship of Tswanas in South Africa who wished to remain South African nationals, was settled by enabling them to have citizenship in South African homelands not yet independent.

About two thirds of the population of Bophuthatswana live permanently or as migrants in white areas of South Africa.

Economy. Bophuthatswana is richer than many other South African homelands, as it has more than half of the republic's platinum deposits. All foreign trade is included with South Africa's, and it is economically dependent at present on that country.

CISKEI

Republic of Ciskei
President: Chief Lennox Leslie Wongama Sebe (1981)
Area: 3,282 sq mi. (8,500 sq km)
Population (est. 1982): 675,000
Density per square mile: 205.7
Capital (est. 1980): Zwelitsha, 30,750
Largest city (est. 1981): Mdantsane, 159,000
Monetary unit: South African rand
Languages: Xhosa (official) and English
Religions: Methodist, Lutheran, Anglican, and Bantu Christian

Geography. Ciskei is surrounded by South Africa on three sides, with the Indian Ocean on the south. From a subtropical coastal strip, the land rises through grasslands to the mountainous escarpment that edges the South African interior plateau.

Government. Legislative power is vested in a National Assembly with 22 elected seats. Thirty-three hereditary chiefs complete the membership of the Assembly. The President holds executive power. South Africa's State President retains the power to legislate by proclamation and has veto power over the budget. The Ciskei National Independence Party holds all elective seats in the Assembly.

History. Oral tradition ascribes the origin of the Cape Nguni peoples to the central lakes area of Africa. They arrived in what is now Ciskei in the mid-17th century. White settlers from the Cape Colony first entered the territory a century later, but the Dutch East India Colony sought unsuccessfully to discourage white penetration. Nine wars between whites and the inhabitants, by now known as Xhosas, occurred between 1779 and 1878.

A Ciskeian territorial authority was established in 1961, with 84 chiefs and an executive council exercising limited self-government. In 1972, 20 elected members were added to the legislative assembly and a chief minister and six cabinet members elected by the assembly to function as an executive.

A proposed Constitution was approved by referendum on Oct. 30, 1980, and independence ceremonies held on Dec. 4. No government outside South Africa recognized the new state.

Economy. A subsistence agricultural economy has been superseded by commuter and migratory labor, which accounted for 64% of national income in 1977. There is some light industry and a potential for exploitation of limestone and other minerals.

SOUTH-WEST AFRICA (NAMIBIA)

Status: Mandate
Area: 318,261 sq mi. (824,296 sq km)
Population (est. 1987): 1,300,000 (average annual growth rate: 3.3%)
Density per square mile: 3.6
Administrator-General: Louis Pienaar (1986)
Capital (est. 1980): Windhoek, 85,000
Summer capital (est. 1980): Swakopmund, 17,500
Monetary unit: South African rand
National name: Suidwes-Afrika/Namibië; South-West Africa/Namibia
Literacy rate: 100% whites/28% non-whites
Economic summary: Gross national product (1983): $1.5 billion. Average annual growth rate (1970–85); –0.3%. Land used for agriculture: 30%; labor force: 60%; principal products: corn, millet, sorghum, livestock. Labor force in industry: 4%; major products: canned meat, dairy products, tanned leather, textiles, clothing. Natural resources: diamonds, copper, lead, zinc, uranium, fish. Exports: diamonds, copper, lead, zinc, beef cattle, karakul pelts. Imports: construction materials, fertilizer, grain, foodstuffs. Major trading partner: South Africa.

Geography. The mandate, bounded on the north by Angola and Zambia and on the east by Botswana and South Africa, was discovered by the Portuguese explorer Diaz in the late 15th century. It is for the most part a portion of the high plateau of southern Africa with a general elevation of from 3,000 to 4,000 feet.

History. The territory became a German colony in 1884 but was taken by South African forces in 1915, becoming a South African mandate by the terms of the Treaty of Versailles.

South Africa's application for incorporation of the territory was rejected by the U.N. General Assembly in 1946 and South Africa was invited to prepare a trusteeship agreement instead. By a law passed in 1949, however, the territory was brought into much closer association with South Africa—including representation in its Parliament.

In 1969, South Africa extended its laws to the mandate over the objection of the U.N., particularly its black African members. When South Africa refused to withdraw them, the Security Council condemned it.

Under a 1974 Security Council resolution, South Africa was required to begin the transfer of power to the Namibians by May 30, 1975, or face U.N. action, but 10 days before the deadline Prime Minister Balthazar J. Vorster rejected U.N. supervision. He said, however, that his government was prepared to negotiate Namibian independence, but not with the South-West African People's Organization, the principal black separatist group. Meanwhile, the all-white legislature of South-West Africa eased several laws on apartheid in public places.

Despite international opposition, the Turnhalle Conference in Windhoek drafted a constitution to organize an interim government based on racial divisions, a proposal overwhelmingly endorsed by white voters in the territory in 1977. At the urging of ambassadors of the five Western members of the Security Council—the U.S., Britain, France, West Germany, and Canada—South Africa on June 11 announced rejection of the Turnhalle constitution and acceptance of the Western proposal to include the South-West Africa People's Organization (SWAPO) in negotiations.

Although negotiations continued between South Africa, the western powers, neighboring black African states, and internal political groups, there was still no agreement on a final independence plan. A new round of talks aimed at resolving the 18-year-old conflict ended in a stalemate on July 25, 1984. Dr. Willie van Niekerk, South Africa's Administrator-General in the territory, met in the remote Cape Verde Islands with leaders of the insurgents, including SWAPO leader Sam Nujoma, to "explore the possibilities of bringing about a cessation of violent and armed activities in South-West Africa." South Africa said the insurgents' "inflexible attitude" made it impossible to reach an agreement on a cease-fire.

As policemen wielding riot sticks charged demonstrators in a black, South-West Africa township, South Africa handed over limited powers to a new, multiracial administration in the former German colony on June 17, 1985. Installation of the new government ended South Africa's direct rule, but South Africa retained an effective veto over the new government's decisions along with responsibility for the territory's defense and foreign policy, and South Africa's efforts to quell the insurgents seeking independence continued.

TRANSKEI

Republic of Transkei
President: Chief Tutor N. Ndaware (1986)
Prime Minister: Paramount Chief George Matanzima (1979)
Area: 15,831 sq mi. (41,002 sq km)
Population (est. 1982): 2,400,000 (growth rate: 2.2%)
Density per square mile: 151.6
Capital (est. 1980): Umtala, 40,000
Monetary unit: South African rand
Languages: English, Xhosa, Southern Sotho
Religions: Christian, 66%; tribal, 24%
Economic summary: Gross domestic product: $150 million. Per capita income: $86. Principal agricultural products: tea, corn, sorghum, dry beans. Major industrial products: timber, textiles. Natural resource: timber. Exports: timber, tea, sacks. Imports: foodstuffs, machines, equipment. Major trading partner: South Africa.

Geography. Transkei occupies three discontinuous enclaves within southeast South Africa that add up to twice the size of Massachusetts. It has a 270-mile (435 km) coastline on the Indian Ocean. A port is being developed at Port St. Johns. The capital, Umtala, is connected by rail to the South African port of East London, 100 miles (161 km) to the southwest.

Government. Transkei was granted independence by South Africa as of Oct. 26, 1976. A constitution called for organization of a parliament composed of 77 chiefs and 75 elected members, with a ceremonial president and executive power in the hands of a prime minister.

The Organization of African States and the chairman of the United Nations Special Committee Against Apartheid denounced the new state as a sham and urged governments not to recognize it.

History. British rule was established over the Transkei region between 1866 and 1894, and the Transkeian Territories were formed in 1903. Under the Native Land Act of 1913, the Territories were reserved for black occupation. In 1963, Transkei was given internal self-government and a legislature that elected Paramount Chief Kaiser Matanzima as Chief Minister, a post he retained in elections in 1968 and 1973.

Economy. Some 60% of Transkei is cultivated, producing corn, wheat, beans, and sorghum. Grazing is important. Some light industry has been established.

VENDA

Republic of Venda
President: Chief Patrick R. Mphephu (1979)
Area: 2,510 sq mi. (6,500 sq km)
Population (est. 1982): 400,000 (average annual growth rate: 2.4%)
Density per square mile: 214.5
Capital: Thohoyandou
Largest town (est. 1980): Makearela, 2,500
Monetary unit: South African rand
Languages: Venda, English, Afrikaans
Religions: Christian, tribal
Economic summary: Gross domestic product: $156 million. Per capita income: $312. Principal agricultural products: meat, tea, fruit, sisal, corn. Major industrial products: timber, graphite, magnetite.

Geography. Venda is composed of two noncontiguous territories in northeast South Africa with a total area of about half that of Connecticut. It is mountainous but fertile, well-watered land, with a climate ranging from tropical to subtropical.

Government. The third of South Africa's homelands to be granted independence, Venda became a separate republic on Sept. 13, 1979, unrecognized by any government other than South Africa and its sister homelands, Transkei and Bophuthatswana. The President is popularly elected. An 84-seat legislature is half elected, half appointed.

History. The first European reached Venda in 1816, but the isolation of the area prevented its involvement in the wars of the 19th century between blacks and whites and with other tribes. Venda came under South African administration after the Boer War in 1902. Limited home rule was granted in 1962. Chief Patrick R. Mphephu, leader of one of the 27 tribes that historically made up the Venda nation, became Chief Minister of the interim government in 1973 and President upon independence in 1979.

SOVIET UNION

Union of Soviet Socialist Republics
Chairman of Presidium (President): Andrei A. Gromyko (1985)
Chairman of Council of Ministers (Premier): Nikolai I. Ryzhkov (1985)
Area: 8,649,489 sq mi. (22,402,200 sq km)
Population (est. mid-1987): 284,000,000 (average annual growth rate: 0.9%) (Russian, 52%; Ukrainian, 17%; Uzbek, 5%; Byelorussian, 4%; Kazak, 3%; Tatar, 2%)
Density per square mile: 32.4
Capital: Moscow
Largest cities (est. 1984): Moscow, 8,537,000; Leningrad, 4,827,000; Kiev, 2,409,000; Tashkent, 1,986,000; Baku, 1,661,000; Kharvov, 1,536,000; Minsk, 1,442,000; Gorky, 1,392,000; Novosibirsk, 1,384,000; Sverdlovsk, 1,286,000; Kuibyshev, 1,251,000; Dnepropetrovsk, 1,140,000; Tbilisi, 1,140,000; Odessa, 1,097,000; Erevan, 1,095,000; Omsk, 1,080,000; Chelyabinsk, 1,077,000; Donetsk, 1,055,000
Monetary unit: Ruble
Languages: *See* Population, above
Religions: Russian Orthodox (predominant), Islam, Roman Catholic, Jewish, Lutheran, atheist
National name: Soyuz Sovyetskikh Sotsialisticheskikh Respublik
Literacy rate: 99%
Economic summary: Gross national product (1985): $2,062 billion. Average annual growth rate (1976–83): 2.2%. Per capita income (1985): $7,896. Land used for agriculture: 10%; labor force: 19%; principal products: wheat, rye, corn, oats, potatoes, sugar beets, cotton and flax, cattle, pigs, sheep. Labor force in industry: 42%; major products: ferrous and nonferrous metals, fuels andpower, building materials, chemicals, machinery. Natural resources: fossil fuels, water power, timber, manganese, lead, zinc, nickel, mercury, potash, phosphate. Exports: petroleum and petroleum products, natural gas, machinery and equipment, manufactured goods. Imports: grain, machinery and equipment, foodstuffs, raw materials, consumer manufactures. Major trading partners: Soviet bloc, Western industrialized countries.

Geography. The U.S.S.R. is the largest unbroken political unit in the world, occupying more than one seventh of the land surface of the globe. The greater part of its territory is a vast plain stretching from eastern Europe to the Pacific Ocean. This plain, relieved only occasionally by low mountain ranges (notably the Urais), consists of three zones running east and west: the frozen marshy tundra of the Arctic; the more temperate forest belt; and the steppes or prairies to the south, which in southern Soviet Asia become sandy deserts.

The topography is more varied in the south, particularly in the Caucasus between the Caspian and Black Seas, and in the Tien-Pamir mountain system bordering Afghanistan, Sinkiang, and Mongolia. Mountains (Stanovoi and Kolyma) and great rivers (Amur, Yenisei, Lena) also break up the sweep of the plain in Siberia.

In the west, the major rivers are the Volga, Dnieper, Don, Kama, and Southern Bug.

Government. Legislative authority is vested in the Supreme Soviet of the U.S.S.R., which consists of two chambers—the Soviet of the Union, with 767 members, and the Soviet of Nationalities, with 750 members. All members of the Supreme Soviet are elected for five years by the people.

A Presidium is elected by the Supreme Soviet to deal with state matters when the latter is not in session. It consists of a chairman, first vice chairman, 15 vice chairmen (one for each union republic), 21 members, and a secretary. The chairman of the Presidium is sometimes referred to as the President.

Executive authority rests with the Council of Ministers. It is appointed by the Supreme Soviet and includes a chairman, a first vice chairman, and various vice chairmen, chairmen of state committees, ministers, etc. The chairman of the Council of Ministers is often referred to as the Premier.

Judicial authority is vested in the Supreme Court of the U.S.S.R. It consists of a chairman, vice chairman, members, and people's assessors, who are elected by the Supreme Soviet for five years.

Each of the 15 union republics and the 20 autonomous republics has a Supreme Soviet (with a Presidium), a Council of Ministers, and a Supreme Court. Each of the eight autonomous regions has a Soviet of People's Deputies.

The Communist Party of the Soviet Union is the only party. It is the basic power in the country and has a membership of 18,500,000.

The supreme organ of the party is the Party Congress, which meets at least once in five years. It elects a Central Committee, consisting of 320 members and 151 candidate members, to carry on party work between sessions of the Congress.

Within the Central Committee is a Political Bureau (Politburo), which was called the Presidium from 1952 to 1966. It functions between sessions of the Central Committee. Also within the Central Committee is the Secretariat. The present General Secretary of the Central Committee, Mikhail S. Gorbachev, has served since March 10, 1985.

History. Tradition says the Viking Rurik came to Russia in A.D. 862 and founded the first Russian dynasty in Novgorod. The various tribes were united by the spread of Christianity in the 10th and 11th centuries; Vladimir "the Saint" was converted in 988. During the 11th century, the grand dukes of Kiev held such centralizing power as existed. In 1240, Kiev was destroyed by the Mongols, and the Russian territory was split into numerous smaller dukedoms, early dukes of Moscow extended their dominions through their office of tribute collector for the Mongols.

In the late 15th century, Duke Ivan III acquired

Republics of the U.S.S.R.

Republic and capital	Area sq mi.	Population est. 1981 (thousands)
Russian S.F.S.R. (Moscow)	6,593,391	139,150
Ukraine (Kiev)	233,089	50,130
Kazakhstan (Alma-Ata)	1,064,092	15,050
Byelorussia (Minsk)	80,154	9,660
Uzbekistan (Tashkent)	158,069	16,160
Georgia (Tbiksi)	26,872	5,070
Azerbaijan (Baku)	33,475	6,205
Lithuania[1] (Vilnius)	25,174	3,445
Moldavia (Kishinev)	13,012	4,000
Latvia[1] (Riga)	24,595	2,540
Kirghizia (Frunze)	76,641	3,655
Tadzhikistan (Duschambe)	55,019	4,010
Armenia (Erevan)	11,506	3,120
Turkmenistan (Ashkhabad)	188,417	2,900
Estonia[1] (Tallin)	17,413	1,485

1. Soviet jurisdiction not recognized by the United States.

Rulers of Russia Since 1533

Name	Born	Ruled[1]
Ivan IV the Terrible	1530	1533–1584
Theodore I	1557	1584–1598
Boris Godunov	c.1551	1598–1605
Theodore II	1589	1605–1605
Demetrius I[2]	?	1605–1606
Basil IV Shuiski	?	1606–1610[3]
"Time of Troubles"	—	1610–1613
Michael Romanov	1596	1613–1645
Alexis I	1629	1645–1676
Theodore III	1656	1676–1682
Ivan V[4]	1666	1682–1689[5]
Peter I the Great[4]	1672	1682–1725
Catherine I	c.1684	1725–1727
Peter II	1715	1727–1730
Anna	1693	1730–1740
Ivan VI	1740	1740–1741[6]
Elizabeth	1709	1741–1762
Peter III	1728	1762–1762
Catherine II the Great	1729	1762–1796
Paul I	1754	1796–1801
Alexander I	1777	1801–1825
Nicholas I	1796	1825–1855
Alexander II	1818	1855–1881
Alexander III	1845	1881–1894
Nicholas II	1868	1894–1917[7]
PROVISIONAL GOVERNMENT (PREMIERS)		
Prince Georgi Lvov	1861	1917–1917
Alexander Kerensky	1881	1917–1917
POLITICAL LEADERS		
N. Lenin	1870	1917–1924
Aleksei Rykov	1881	1924–1930
Vyacheslav Molotov	1890	1930–1941
Joseph Stalin[8]	1879	1941–1953
Georgi M. Malenkov	1902	1953–1955
Nikolai A. Bulganin	1895	1955–1958
Nikita S. Khrushchev	1894	1958–1964
Leonid I. Brezhnev	1906	1964–1982
Yuri V. Andropov	1914	1982–1984
Konstantin U. Chernenko	1912	1984–1985
Mikhail S. Gorbachev	1931	1985–

1. For Tsars through Nicholas II, year of end of rule is also that of death, unless otherwise indicated. 2. Also known as Pseudo-Demetrius. 3. Died 1612. 4. Ruled jointly until 1689, when Ivan was deposed. 5. Died 1696. 6. Died 1764. 7. Killed 1918. 8. General Secretary of Communist Party, 1924–53.

Novgorod and Tver and threw off the Mongol yoke. Ivan IV, the Terrible (1533–84), first Muscovite Tsar, is considered to have founded the Russian state. He crushed the power of rival princes and boyars (great landowners), but Russia remained largely medieval until the reign of Peter the Great (1689–1725), grandson of the first Romanov Tsar, Michael (1613–45). Peter made extensive reforms aimed at westernization and, through his defeat of Charles XII of Sweden at the Battle of Poltava in 1709, he extended Russia's boundaries to the west.

Catherine the Great (1762–96) continued Peter's westernization program and also expanded Russian territory, acquiring the Crimea and part of Poland. During the reign of Alexander I (1801–25), Napoleon's attempt to subdue Russia was defeated (1812–13), and new territory was gained, including Finland (1809) and Bessarabia (1812). Alexander originated the Holy Alliance, which for a time crushed Europe's rising liberal movement.

Alexander II (1855–81) pushed Russia's borders to the Pacific and into central Asia. Serfdom was abolished in 1861, but heavy restrictions were imposed on the emancipated class. Revolutionary strikes following Russia's defeat in the war with Japan forced Nicholas II (1894–1917) to grant a representative national body (Duma), elected by narrowly limited suffrage. It met for the first time in 1906, little influencing Nicholas in his reactionary course.

World War I demonstrated tsarist corruption and inefficiency and only patriotism held the poorly equipped army together for a time. Disorders broke out in Petrograd (now Leningrad) in March 1917, and defection of the Petrograd garrison launched the revolution. Nicholas II was forced to abdicate on March 15, 1917, and he and his family were killed by revolutionists on July 16, 1918.

A provisional government under the successive premierships of Prince Lvov and a moderate, Alexander Kerensky, lost ground to the radical, or Bolshevik, wing of the Socialist Democratic Labor Party. On Nov. 7, 1917, the Bolshevik revolution, engineered by N. Lenin[1] and Leon Trotsky, overthrew the Kerensky government and authority was vested in a Council of People's Commissars, with Lenin as Premier.

The humiliating Treaty of Brest-Litovsk (March 3, 1918) concluded the war with Germany, but civil war and foreign intervention delayed Communist control of all Russia until 1920. A brief war with Poland in 1920 resulted in Russian defeat.

The Union of Soviet Socialist Republics was established as a federation on Dec. 30, 1922.

The death of Lenin on Jan. 21, 1924, precipitated an intraparty struggle between Joseph Stalin, General Secretary of the party, and Trotsky, who favored swifter socialization at home and fomentation of revolution abroad. Trotsky was dismissed as Commissar of War in 1925 and banished from the Soviet Union in 1929. He was murdered in Mexico City on Aug. 21, 1940, by a political agent.

Stalin further consolidated his power by a series of purges in the late 1930s, liquidating prominent party leaders and military officers. Stalin assumed the premiership May 6, 1941.

Soviet foreign policy, at first friendly toward Germany and antagonistic toward Britain and France and then, after Hitler's rise to power in 1933, becoming anti-Fascist and pro-League of Nations, took an abrupt turn on Aug. 24, 1939, with the signing of a nonaggression pact with Nazi Germany. The next month, Moscow joined in the German attack on Poland, seizing territory later incorporated into the Ukrainian and Byelorussian S.S.R.'s. The war with Finland, 1939–40, added territory to the Karelian S.S.R. set up March 31, 1940; the annexation of Bessarabia and Bukovina from

1. N. Lenin was the pseudonym taken by Vladimir Ilich Ulyanov. It is sometimes given as Nikolai Lenin or V.

Romania became part of the new Moldavian S.S.R. on Aug. 2, 1940; and the annexation of the Baltic republics of Estonia, Latvia, and Lithuania in June 1940 (still unrecognized by the U.S.) created the 14th, 15th, and 16th Soviet Republics. (The number of so-called "Union" republics was reduced to 15 in 1956 when the Karelian S.S.R. became one of the 20 Autonomous Soviet Socialist Republics based on ethnic groups.)

The Soviet-German collaboration ended abruptly with a lightning attack by Hitler on June 22, 1941, which seized 500,000 square miles of Russian territory before Soviet defenses, aided by U.S. and British arms, could halt it. The Soviet resurgence at Stalingrad from November 1942 to February 1943 marked the turning point in a long battle, ending in the final offensive of January 1945.

Then, after denouncing a 1941 nonaggression pact with Japan in April 1945, when Allied forces were nearing victory in the Pacific, the Soviet Union declared war on Japan on Aug. 8, 1945, and quickly occupied Manchuria, Karafuto, and the Kurile islands.

The U.S.S.R. built a cordon of Communist states running from Poland in the north to Albania and Bulgaria in the south, including East Germany, Czechoslovakia, Hungary, and Romania, composed of the territories Soviet troops occupied at the war's end. With its Eastern front solidified, the Soviet Union launched a political offensive against the non-Communist West, moving first to block the Western access to Berlin. The Western powers countered with an airlift, completed unification of West Germany, and organized the defense of Western Europe in the North Atlantic Treaty Organization.

Stalin died on March 6, 1953, and was succeeded the next day by G. M. Malenkov as Premier. His chief rivals for power—Lavrenti P. Beria (chief of the secret police), Nikolai A. Bulganin, and Lazar M. Kaganovich—were named first deputies. Beria was purged in July and executed on Dec. 23, 1953.

The new power in the Kremlin was Nikita S. Khrushchev, First Secretary of the party.

Khrushchev formalized the Eastern European system into a Council for Mutual Economic Assistance (Comecon) and a Warsaw Pact Treaty Organization as a counterweight to NATO.

In its technological race with the U.S., the Soviet Union exploded a hydrogen bomb in 1953, developed an intercontinental ballistic missile by 1957, sent the first satellite into space (Sputnik I) in 1957, and put Yuri Gagarin in the first orbital flight around the earth in 1961.

Khrushchev's downfall stemmed from his decision to place Soviet nuclear missiles in Cuba and then, when challenged by the U.S., backing down and removing the weapons. He was also blamed for the ideological break with China after 1963.

Khrushchev was forced into retirement on Oct. 15, 1964, and was replaced by Leonid I. Brezhnev as First Secretary of the Party and Aleksei N. Kosygin as Premier.

President Nixon visited the U.S.S.R. for summit talks in May 1972, concluding agreements on strategic-arms limitation and a declaration of principles on future U.S.-Soviet relations.

Presidents Gerald R. Ford and Brezhnev met in Vladivostok in November 1974 and reached tentative agreements to be incorporated into a treaty at the Geneva SALT talks in 1975. They proposed a ceiling of 2,400 ICBM's for each side, of which no more than 1,320 could have MIRV's.

President Carter, actively pursuing both human rights and disarmament, joined with the Soviet Union in September 1977 to declare that the SALT I accord, which would have expired Oct. 1 without further action, be maintained in effect while the two sides sought a new agreement (SALT II).

Brezhnev's 1977 election to the presidency followed publication of a new Constitution supplanting the one adopted in 1936. It specified the dominance of the Communist Party, previously unstated.

Carter and the ailing Brezhnev signed the SALT II treaty in Vienna on June 18, 1979, setting ceilings on each nation's arsenal of intercontinental ballistic missiles. Doubts about Senate ratification grew, and became a certainty on Dec. 27, when Soviet troops invaded Afghanistan. Despite protests from the Moslem and Western worlds, Moscow insisted that Afghan President Hafizullah Amin had asked for aid in quelling a rebellion.

In the face of evidence that Amin had been liquidated by Soviet advisers before the troops arrived, the Soviet Union vetoed a Security Council resolution on Jan. 7, 1980, that called for a withdrawal. Carter ordered a freeze on grain exports and high-technology equipment.

On Jan. 20, Carter called for a world boycott of the Summer Olympic Games scheduled for Moscow. The boycott, less than complete, nevertheless marred the first Olympics to be held in Moscow as the United States, Canada, Japan, and to a partial extent all the western allies except France and Italy shunned the event.

The Soviet Union maintained a stony defense in the face of criticism from Western Europe and the U.S., and a summit meeting of 37 Islamic nations that unanimously condemned the "imperialist invasion" of Afghanistan.

Despite the tension between Moscow and Washington, Strategic Arms Reduction Talks (START) began in Geneva between U.S. and Soviet delegations in mid-1982. Negotiations on intermediate missile reduction also continued in Geneva.

On November 10, 1982, Soviet radio and television announced the death of Leonid Brezhnev. Yuri V. Andropov, who formerly headed the K.G.B., was chosen to succeed Brezhnev as General Secretary. By mid-June 1983, Andropov had assumed all of Brezhnev's three titles.

The Soviet Union broke off both the START talks and the parallel negotiations on European-based missiles in November 1983 in protest against the deployment of medium-range U.S. missiles in Western Europe.

After months of illness, Andropov died in February 1984. Konstantin U. Chernenko, a 72-year-old party stalwart who had been close to Brezhnev, succeeded him as General Secretary and, by mid-April, had also assumed the title of President. In the months following Chernenko's assumption of power, the Kremlin took on a hostile mood toward the West of a kind rarely seen since the height of the cold war 30 years before. Led by Moscow, all the Soviet bloc countries except Romania boycotted the 1984 Summer Olympic Games in Los Angeles—tit-for-tat for the U.S.-led boycott of the 1980 Moscow Games, in the view of most observers.

After 13 months in office, Chernenko died on March 10, 1985. He had been ill much of the time and left only a minor imprint on Soviet history.

Chosen to succeed him as Soviet leader was Mikhail S. Gorbachev, at 54 the youngest man to take charge of the Soviet Union since Stalin. Under Gorbachev, the Soviet Union began its long-awaited shift to a new generation of leadership. Unlike his immediate predecessors, Gorbachev did not also assume the title of President but wielded power from the post of party General Secretary. In a surprise move, Gorbachev elevated Andrei Gromyko, 75, for 28 years the Soviet Union's stony-faced Foreign Minister, to the largely ceremonial post of President. He installed a younger man with no experience in foreign affairs, Eduard Shevardnadze, 57, as Foreign Minister.

A new round of U.S. Soviet arms reduction negotiations began in Geneva in March 1985, this time involving three types of weapons systems—strategic, or long-range, missiles and bombers; medium-range systems in Europe, and space-based systems. In the new talks, the two sides differed sharply on how to approach the three-part negotiations, with the United States putting the focus on cuts in land-based weapons while the Soviet Union made curbing space weapons its first priority.

After months of quiet negotiations, Reagan and Gorbachev agreed to meet in Geneva on Nov. 19-20,1985—the 11th postwar meeting between the leaders of the two superpowers. Expectations for concrete results were low because the Geneva arms talks appeared to be at an impasse, with both sides repeating old slogans. But after a meeting in Helsinki, Finland, with the new Soviet Foreign Minister, Shevardnadze, Secretary of State George Shultz said that if the session turned out well, the two leaders might hold a rotating series of meetings in each other's capitals.

In advance of the summit, the Soviet Union announced that it would halt nuclear testing from Aug. 6.

The Soviet Union took much criticism in early 1986 over the April 24 meltdown at the Chernobyl nuclear plant and its reluctance to give out any information on the accident.

In October 1986, a potential agreement on strategic weapons reduction broke down over Soviet insistence that SDI be terminated as the price of such an agreement, but by mid-1987 the superpowers were close to an accord eliminating medium-range missiles in Europe.

In June 1987, Gorbachev obtained the support of the Central Committee for proposals that would loosen some government controls over the economy.

SPAIN

Kingdom of Spain
Ruler: King Juan Carlos I (1975)
Prime Minister: Felipe González Márquez (1982)
Area: 194,885 sq mi. (504,750 km)[1]
Population (est. mid-1987): 39,000,000 (average annual growth rate: 0.5%) (Spanish, Basque, Catalan, Galician)
Density per square mile: 200.1
Capital: Madrid
Largest cities (est. 1986): Madrid, 3,217,461; Barcelona, 1,765,905; Valencia, 763,949; Seville, 763,949
Monetary unit: Peseta
Languages: Spanish, Basque, Catalan, Galician
Religion: Roman Catholic
National name: Reino de España
Literacy rate: 97%
Economic summary: Gross national product (1984): $160.4 billion. Average annual growth rate (1984): 2.2%. Per capita income (1983): $4,760. Land used for agriculture: 41%; labor force: 17%; principal products: cereals, vegetables, citrus fruits, wine, olives and olive oil, livestock. Labor force in industry: 35%; major products: processed foods, textiles, footwear, petro-chemicals, steel, automobiles, ships. Natural resources: coal, lignite, water power, uranium, mercury, pyrites, fluorospar, gypsum, iron ore, zinc, lead, tungsten, copper. Exports: fresh fruits, iron and steel products, textiles, footwear, automobiles, fruits and vegetables. Imports: machinery and transportation equipment, chemicals, fuels, automobiles, iron, steel. Major trading partners: Western European nations, U.S., Middle Eastern countries.

1. Including the Balearic and Canary Islands.

Geography. Spain occupies 85% of the Iberian Peninsula in southwestern Europe, which it shares with Portugal; France is to the northeast, separated by the Pyrenees. The Bay of Biscay lies to the north, the Atlantic Ocean to the west, and the Mediterranean Sea to the south and east: Africa is less than 10 miles (16 km) south at the Strait of Gibraltar.

A broad central plateau slopes to the south and east, crossed by a series of mountain ranges and river valleys.

Principal rivers are the Ebro in the northeast, the Tajo in the central region, and the Guadalquivir in the south.

Off Spain's east coast in the Mediterranean are the Balearic Islands (1,936 sq mi.; 5,014 sq km), the largest of which is Majorca. Sixty miles (97 km) west of Africa are the Canary Islands (2,808 sq mi.; 7,273 sq km).

Government. King Juan Carlos I (born Jan. 5, 1938) succeeded Generalissimo Francisco Franco Bahamonde as Chief of State Nov. 27, 1975.

The Cortes, or Parliament, consists of a Chamber of Deputies of 350 members and a Senate of 208, all elected by universal suffrage. The new Cortes, replacing one that was largely appointed or elected by special constituencies, was organized under a constitution adopted by referendum Dec. 6, 1978.

The major political parties are the Spanish Socialist Workers Party (184 of 350 seats in the Chamber of Deputies, 124 of 208 elected Senate seats), led by Prime Minister Felipe González Márquez; Popular Coalition (105 seats in Chamber, 63 in Senate), led by Antonio Hernandez Mancha; United Left (7 seats in Chamber, none in Senate), led by Gerardo Iglesias; Social and Democratic Center (19 seats in Chamber, 3 in Senate), led by Adolfo Suárez; Convergencia i Unió (Catalonian Party) (18 seats in Chamber, 8 in Senate); Basque Nationalist Party (6 seats in Chamber, 7 in Senate).

History. Spain, originally inhabited by Celts, Iberians and Basques, became a part of the Roman Empire in 206 B.C., when it was conquered by Scipio Africanus. In A.D. 412, the barbarian Visigothic leader Ataulf crossed the Pyrenees and ruled Spain, first in the name of the Roman emperor and then independently. In 711, the Moslems under Tariq entered Spain from Africa and within a few years completed the subjugation of the country. In

732, the Franks, led by Charles Martel, defeated the Moslems near Poitiers, thus preventing the further expansion of Islam in southern Europe. Internal dissension of Spanish Islam invited a steady Christian conquest from the north.

Aragon and Castile were the most important Spanish states from the 12th to the 15th century, consolidated by the marriage of Ferdinand II and Isabella I in 1469. The last Moslem stronghold, Granada, was captured in 1492. Roman Catholicism was established as the official state religion and the Jews (1492) and the Moslems (1502) expelled.

In the era of exploration, discovery, and colonization, Spain amassed tremendous wealth and a vast colonial empire through the conquest of Peru by Pizarro (1532–33) and of Mexico by Cortés (1519–21). The Spanish Hapsburg monarchy became for a time the most powerful in the world.

In 1588, Philip II sent his Invincible Armada to invade England, but its destruction cost Spain its supremacy on the seas and paved the way for England's colonization of America. Spain then sank rapidly to the status of a second-rate power and never again played a major role in European politics. Its colonial empire in the Americas and the Philippines vanished in wars and revolutions during the 18th and 19th centuries.

In World War I, Spain maintained a position of neutrality. In 1923, Gen. Miguel Primo de Rivera became dictator. In 1930, King Alfonso XIII revoked the dictatorship, but a strong antimonarchist and republican movement led to his leaving Spain in 1931. The new Constitution declared Spain a workers' republic, broke up the large estates, separated church and state, and secularized the schools. The elections held in 1936 returned a strong Popular Front majority, with Manuel Azaña as President.

On July 18, 1936, a conservative army officer in Morocco, Francisco Franco Bahamonde, led a mutiny against the government. The civil war that followed lasted three years and cost the lives of nearly a million people. Franco was aided by Fascist Italy and Nazi Germany, while Soviet Russia helped the Loyalist side. Several hundred leftist Americans served in the Abraham Lincoln Battalion on the side of the republic. The war ended when Franco took Madrid on March 28, 1939.

Franco became head of the state, national chief of the Falange Party (the governing party), and Premier and Caudillo (leader). In a referendum in 1947, the Spanish people approved a Franco-drafted succession law declaring Spain a monarchy again. Franco, however, continued as Chief of State.

In 1969, Franco and the Cortes designated Prince Juan Carlos Alfonso Victor María de Borbón (who married Princess Sophia of Greece on May 14, 1962) to become King of Spain when the provisional government headed by Franco came to an end. He is the grandson of Alfonso XIII and the son of Don Juan, pretender to the throne.

Franco died of a heart attack on Nov. 20, 1975, after more than a year of ill health, and Juan Carlos was proclaimed King seven days later.

Over strong rightist opposition, the government legalized the Communist Party in advance of the 1977 elections. Premier Adolfo Suaraz Gonzalez's Union of the Democratic Center, a coalition of a dozen centrist and rightist parties, claimed 34.3% of the popular vote in the election.

Under pressure from Catalonian and Basque nationalists, Suárez granted home rule to these regions in 1979, but centrists backed by him did poorly in the 1980 elections for local assemblies in the two areas. Economic problems persisted, along with new incidents of terrorism, and Suárez resigned on Jan. 29, 1981 and was succeded by Leopoldo Calvo Sotelo.

With the overwhelming election of Prime Minister Felipe González Márquez and his Spanish Socialist Workers Party in the Oct. 20, 1982, parliamentary elections, the Franco past was finally buried. The thrust of Gonzalez, a pragmatic moderate, was to modernize rather than radicalize Spain. As promised, the Socialists did not carry out widespread nationalization of private industry, but did seek to nationalize the high-tension power grid.

A treaty admitting Spain, along with Portugal, to the European Economic Community was to take effect on Jan. 1, 1986. Later that year, in June, Spain voted to remain in NATO, but outside of its military command and Gonzalez's Socialists retained their majority in national elections.

SRI LANKA

Democratic Socialist Republic of Sri Lanka
President: J. R. Jayewardene (1978)
Prime Minister: Ranasinghe Premadasa (1978)
Area: 25,332 sq mi. (65,610 sq km)
Population (est. mid-1987): 16,300,000 (average annual growth rate: 1.8%)
Density per square mile: 602.0
Capital: Sri Jayewardenepura Kotte (Colombo)
Largest cities (est. 1983): Colombo, 623,000; Dehiwela, 181,000; Jaffna, 128,000
Monetary unit: Sri Lanka rupee
Languages: Sinhala, Tamil, English
Religions: Buddhist, 69%; Hindu, 15%; Islam, 8%; Christian, 8%
Member of Commonwealth of Nations
Literacy rate: 87%
Economic summary: Gross national product (1984): $5.66 billion. Average annual growth rate (1985): 5.1%. Per capita income (1984): $320. Land used for agriculture: 25%; labor force: 53%; principal products: tea, coconuts, rubber, rice, spices. Labor force in industry: 15%; major products: consumer goods, textiles, chemicals, paper and paper products. Natural resources: limestone, graphite, gems. Exports: tea, rubber, petroleum products. Imports: petroleum, machinery, transport equipment, sugar. Major trading partners: Saudi Arabia, Iraq, U.S., U.K., Japan.

Geography. An island in the Indian Ocean off the southeast tip of India, Sri Lanka is about half the size of Alabama. Most of the land is flat and rolling; mountains in the south central region rise to over 8,000 feet (2,438 m).

Government. After 24 years as a British dominion, Ceylon became an independent republic and reverted to the traditional name Sri Lanka (resplendent island) on May 22, 1972. A new Constitution was adopted, replacing that of 1948.

The new Constitution set up the National State Assembly, a 168-member unicameral legislature that serves for six years unless dissolved earlier.

The major political parties are the United National Party (140 of 168 seats in the National Assembly), led by President J.R. Jayewardene: Tamil United Liberation Front (18 seats); Sri Lanka Freedom Party (8 seats), led by Anura Bandaranaike. A split in the Freedom Party has resulted in the formation of the Sri Lanka Mahajaua Party (SLMP).

History. Following Portuguese and Dutch rule, Ceylon became an English crown colony in 1798. The British developed coffee, tea, and rubber plantations and granted six Constitutions between 1798 and 1924. The Constitution of 1931 gave a large measure of self-government.

Ceylon became a self-governing dominion of the Commonwealth of Nations in 1948.

Presidential elections were held in December 1982, and won by J.R. Jayewardene.

Tension between the Tamil minority and the Sinhalese majority continued to build and erupted in bloody violence in 1983 that has grown worse since. There are about 2.6 million Tamils in Sri Lanka, while the Sinhalese make up about three-quarters of the 16-million population. Tamil extremists are fighting for a separate nation.

During 1985, bombings, killings and arrests spread through the northern and eastern regions of the island nation, and the Tamil problem began to undermine economic development. President Jayewardene announced extraordinary measures to combat the separatists, but at the same time sent representatives to the Himalayan kingdom of Bhutan for talks with Tamil representatives.

Negotiations broke down in late 1986. A string of Tamil atrocities in early 1987 brought on a government offensive in May-June against guerilla base areas. Although it was largely successful, the increased intensity of the civil war dimmed hopes for a settlement.

SUDAN

Republic of the Sudan
Prime Minister: Sadig el-Mahdi (1986)
Area: 967,491 sq mi. (2,505,802 sq km)
Population (est. mid-1987): 23,500,000 (average annual growth rate: 2.8%)
Density per square mile: 24.3
Capital: Khartoum
Largest cities (est. 1981): Khartoum, 1,250,000; Omdurman, 350,000; Port Sudan, 250,000
Monetary unit: Sudanese pound
Languages: Arabic, English, tribal dialects
Religions: Islam, 73%; Animist, 18%; Christian, 9%
National name: Jamhuryat es-Sudan
Literacy rate: 20%
Economic summary: Gross national product (1984): $7.31 billion. Average annual growth rate (1970–79): 1.5%. Per capita income (1984): $320. Land used for agriculture: 3%; labor force: 78%; principal products: cotton, peanuts, sesame seeds, gum arabic, sorghum, wheat sugar cane. Labor force in industry: 10%; major products: cement, textiles, pharmaceuticals, shoes, processed foods. Natural resources: some iron ore, copper, chrome, industrial metals. Exports: cotton, peanuts, gum arabic, livestock. Imports: textiles, petroleum products, vehicles, tea, wheat. Major trading partners: U.K., West Germany, Italy, India, China, France, Japan.

Geography. The Sudan, in northeast Africa, is the largest country on the continent, measuring about one fourth the size of the United States. Its neighbors are Chad and the Central African Republic on the west, Egypt and Libya on the north, Ethiopia on the east, and Kenya, Uganda, and Zaire on the south. The Red Sea washes about 500 miles of the eastern coast.

The country extends from north to south about 1,200 miles (1,931 km) and west to east about 1,000 miles (1,609 km). The northern region is a continuation of the Libyan Desert. The southern region is fertile, abundantly watered, and, in places, heavily forested. It is traversed from north to south by the Nile, all of whose great tributaries are partly or entirely within its borders.

Government. A multi-party democracy was established. The centrist Umma party formed a coalition government after the elections of April 4, 1986.

History. The early history of the Sudan (known as the Anglo-Egyptian Sudan between 1898 and 1955) is linked with that of Nubia, where a powerful local kingdom was formed in Roman times with its capital at Dongola. After conversion to Christianity in the 6th century, it joined with Ethiopia and resisted Mohammedanization until the 14th century. Thereafter the area was broken up into many small states until 1820–22, when it was conquered by Mohammed Ali, Pasha of Egypt. Egyptian forces were evacuated during the Mahdist revolt (1881–98), but the Sudan was reconquered by the Anglo-Egyptian expeditions of 1896–98, and in 1899 became an Anglo-Egyptian condominium, which was reaffirmed by the Anglo-Egyptian treaty of 1936.

Egypt and Britain agreed in 1953 to grant self-government to the Sudan under an appointed Governor-General. An all-Sudanese Parliament was elected in November-December 1953, and an all-Sudanese government was formed. In December 1955, the Parliament declared the independence of the Sudan, which, with the approval of Britain and Egypt, was proclaimed on Jan. 1, 1956.

In October 1969, Maj. Gen. Gaafar Mohamed Nimeiri, the president of the Council for the Revolution, took over as prime minister. He was elected the nation's first president in 1971 by a reported 98.6% of the vote in a national referendum.

In 1976, a third attempted coup against Nimeiri left 1,000 rebels and loyal troops dead after a fierce battle in Khartoum. Nimeiri accused President Muammar el Qaddafi of Libya of having instigated the attempt and broke relations with Libya.

On April 6, 1985, while out of the country on visits to the United States and Egypt, Nimeiry lost power on April 6, 1985, in the same way he gained it 16 years previously—by a military coup. The new military regime that took over was headed by Nimeiry's Defense Minister, Gen. Abdel Rahman Siwar el-Dahab.

Among the problems that the new government faced were a debilitating civil war with rebels in the south of the country, other sectarian and tribal conflicts, enormous economic problems, and coping with both the continuing arrival of starving refugees from neighboring, famine-stricken Ethiopia, and the famine that affected more than four million Sudanese.

SURINAME

Republic of Suriname
President: L. F. Ramdat Misier (1982)
Prime Minister: Pretaapnarian Radhakishun (1986)
Area: 63,251 sq mi. (163,820 sq km)
Population (est. mid-1987): 400,000 (average annual

growth rate: 2.1%) (Hindi, 37%; Creole, 31%; Indonesian, 15%; Bush Negro, 10%)
Density per square mile: 6.3
Capital and largest city (est. 1982): Paramaribo, 100,000
Monetary unit: Suriname guilder
Languages: Dutch, Surinamese (lingua franca)
Religions: Protestant, Roman Catholic, Hindu, Islam
Literacy rate: 80%
Economic summary: Gross national product (1984): $1.35 billion. Average annual growth rate (1979–83): 8%. Per capita income (1984): $3,550. Land used for agriculture: 0.3%; labor force: 29%; principal products: rice, citrus fruits, sugar, coffee. Labor force in industry: 15%; major products: aluminum, alumina, processed foods, lumber, bricks, cigarettes. Natural resources: bauxite, iron ore, timber, fish, shrimp. Exports: bauxite, alumina, aluminum, rice, shrimp, lumber and wood products. Imports: capital equipment, petroleum, iron and steel, cotton, flour, meat, dairy products. Major trading partners: U.S., Western European countries.

Geography. Suriname lies on the northeast coast of South America, with Guyana to the west, French Guiana to the east, and Brazil to the south. It is about one tenth larger than Michigan. The principal rivers are the Corantijn on the Guyana border, the Marowijne in the east, and the Suriname, on which the capital city of Paramaribo is situated. The Tumuc-Humac Mountains are on the border with Brazil.

Government. Suriname, formerly known as Dutch Guiana, became an independent republic on Nov. 25, 1975. The first prime minister, Henck A. E. Arron, was ousted by a 16-man military junta on Feb. 25, 1980, and replaced by Dr. Henk R. Chin A Sen. In 1982, L.F. Ramdat Misier replaced Sen as president.

Lt. Col. Desi Bouterse, who led the 1980 coup, retains *de facto* power.

History. England established the first European settlement on the Suriname River in 1650 but transferred sovereignty to the Dutch in 1667 in the Treaty of Breda, by which the British acquired New York. Colonization was confined to a narrow coastal strip, and until the abolition of slavery in 1863, African slaves furnished the labor for the plantation economy. After 1870, laborers were imported from British India and the Dutch East Indies.

In 1948, the colony was integrated into the Kingdom of the Netherlands and two years later was granted full home rule in other than foreign affairs and defense. After race rioting over unemployment and inflation, the Netherlands offered complete independence in 1973. Henck A. E. Arron, leader of a coalition of Creole (Surinamese of African descent) parties, advocated independence, while Jaggernath Lachmon, leader of the Surinamese of East Indian descent, urged delay.

Arron retained power in the first post-independence elections in 1977. He had promised early elections when Army sergeants and a lieutenant staged a coup on Feb. 25 and installed a civilian, Dr. Henk R. Chin A Sen, as Prime Minister. A subsequent military intervention made Chin A Sen president, abolishing the legislature and instituting a military government.

In mid-1986, Ronnie Brunswijk, a former army private, began a rebellion aimed at ending Bouterse's rule. Fighting in eastern Suriname has intensified since.

SWAZILAND

Kingdom of Swaziland
Ruler: King Mswati III (1986)
Prime Minister: Sotsha Dlamini (1986)
Area: 6,704 sq mi. (17,363 sq km)
Population (est. mid-1987): 700,000 (average annual growth rate: 3.1%)
Density per square mile: 104.4
Capital and largest city (est. 1985): Mbabane, 45,000
Monetary unit: Lilangeni
Languages: English and Swazi (official)
Religions: Christian, 77%; Animist, 27%
Member of Commonwealth of Nations
Literacy rate (1985): 68%
Economic summary: Gross national product (1984): $478 million. Average annual growth rate (1979–82): 1.7%. Per capita income (1983): $900. Land used for agriculture: 8%; labor force: 32%; principal products: corn, livestock, sugar cane, citrus fruits, cotton, rice, pineapples. Labor force in industry: 25%; major products: milled sugar, ginned cotton, processed meat and wood. Natural resources: asbestos, diamonds. Exports: sugar, wood products, iron ore, asbestos, citrus fruits, cotton. Imports: motor vehicles, fuels and lubricants, foodstuffs, chemicals. Major trading partners: South Africa, U.K., U.S.

Geography. Swaziland, 85% the size of New Jersey, is surrounded by South Africa and Mozambique. The country consists of a high veld in the west and a series of plateaus descending from 6,000 feet (1,829 m) to a low veld of 1,500 feet (457 m).

Government. In 1967, a new Constitution established King Sobhuza II as head of state and provided for an Assembly of 24 members elected by universal suffrage, together with a Senate of 12 members—half appointed by the Assembly and half by the King. In 1973, the King renounced the Constitution, suspended political parties, and took total power for himself. In 1977, he replaced the Parliament with an assembly of tribal leaders. The Parliament reconvened in 1979.

History. Bantu peoples migrated southwest to the area of Mozambique in the 16th century. A number of clans broke away from the main body in the 18th century and settled in Swaziland. In the 19th century they organized as a tribe, partly because they were in constant conflict with the Zulu. Their ruler, Mswazi, applied to the British in the 1840s for help against the Zulu. The British and the Transvaal governments guaranteed the independence of Swaziland in 1881.

South Africa held Swaziland as a protectorate from 1894 to 1899, but after the Boer War, in 1902, Swaziland was transferred to British administration. The Paramount Chief was recognized as the native authority in 1941.

In 1963, the territory was constituted a protectorate, and on Sept. 6, 1968, it became the independent nation of Swaziland.

King Sobhuza died in August 1982, the world's longest-reigning monarch.

SWEDEN

Kingdom of Sweden
Sovereign: King Carl XVI Gustaf (1973)
Prime Minister: Ingvar Carlsson (1986)
Area: 173,800 sq mi. (449,964 sq km)

Population (est. mid-1987): 8,400,000 (average annual growth rate: 0.1%)
Density per square mile: 48.3
Capital: Stockholm
Largest cities (est. 1985): Stockholm, 1,409,000; Göteborg, 696,000; Malmö, 454,000; Uppsala, 150,000
Monetary unit: Krona
Language: Swedish
Religion: Swedish Lutheran, 95%
National name: Konungariket Sverige
Literacy rate: 99%
Economic summary: Gross national product (1985): $95 billion. Average annual growth rate (1970–1984): 2.2%. Per capita income (1984): $11,363. Principal agricultural products: dairy products, grains, sugar beets, potatoes, wood. Labor force in industry: 31%; major products: machinery, instruments, metal products, automobiles. Natural resources: forests, iron ore, hydroelectric power, unmined uranium. Exports: machinery, motor vehicles, wood pulp, paper products, iron and steel products. Imports: machinery, petroleum, yarns, foodstuffs, iron and steel, chemicals. Major trading partners: Norway, West Germany, U.K., Denmark, Finland, U.S.

Geography. Sweden occupies the eastern part of the Scandinavian peninsula, with Norway to the west, Finland and the Gulf of Bothnia to the east, and Denmark and the Baltic Sea in the south. It is one tenth larger than California.

The country slopes eastward and southward from the Kjólen Mountains along the Norwegian border, where the peak elevation is Kebnekaise at 6,965 feet (2,123 m) in Lapland. In the north are mountains and many lakes. To the south and east are central lowlands and south of them are fertile areas of forest, valley, and plain.

Along Sweden's rocky coast, chopped up by bays and inlets, are many islands, the largest of which are Gotland and Oland.

Government. Sweden is a constitutional monarchy. Under the 1975 Constitution, the Riksdag is the sole governing body. The prime minister is the political chief executive.

In 1967, agreement was reached on part of a new Constitution after 13 years of work. It provided for a single-house Riksdag of 350 members (later amended to 349 seats) to replace the 104-year old bicameral Riksdag. The members are popularly elected for three years. Ninety-two present members of the Riksdag are women.

The King, Carl XVI Gustaf, was born April 30, 1946, and succeeded to the throne Sept. 19, 1973, on the death at 90 of his grandfather, Gustaf VI Adolf. Carl Gustaf was married on June 19, 1976, to Silvia Sommerlath, a West German commoner. They have three children: Princess Victoria, born July 14, 1977; Prince Carl Philip, born May 13, 1979; and Princess Madeleine, born June 10, 1982. Under the new Act of Succession, effective Jan. 1, 1980, the first child of the reigning monarch, regardless of sex, is heir to the throne.

The major political parties are the Social Democratic Party (159 seats in the Riksdag), led by Prime Minister Ingvar Carlsson; Conservative Party (76 seats), led by Carl Bildt; Center Party (44 seats), led by Karin Söder; Liberal Party (51 seats), led by Bengt Westerberg; Communist Party (19 seats), led by Lars Werner.

History. The earliest historical mention of Sweden is found in Tacitus' *Germania*, where reference is made to the powerful king and strong fleet of the Suiones. Toward the end of the 10th century, Olaf Sköttkonung established a Christian stronghold in Sweden. Around 1400, an attempt was made to unite the northern nations into one kingdom, but this led to bitter strife between the Danes and the Swedes.

In 1520, the Danish King, Christian II, conquered Sweden and in the "Stockholm Bloodbath" put leading Swedish personalities to death. Gustavus Vasa (1523–60) broke away from Denmark and fashioned the modern Swedish state.

Sweden played a leading role in the second phase (1630–35) of the Thirty Years' War (1618–48). By the Treaty of Westphalia (1648), Sweden obtained western Pomerania and some neighboring territory on the Baltic. In 1700, a coalition of Russia, Poland, and Denmark united against Sweden and by the Peace of Nystad (1721) forced it to relinquish Livonia, Ingria, Estonia, and parts of Finland.

Sweden emerged from the Napoleonic Wars with the acquisition of Norway from Denmark and with a new royal dynasty stemming from Marshal Jean Bernadotte of France, who became King Charles XIV (1818–44). The artificial union between Sweden and Norway led to an uneasy relationship, and the union was finally dissolved in 1905.

Sweden maintained a position of neutrality in both World Wars.

An elaborate structure of welfare legislation, imitated by many larger nations, began with the establishment of old-age pensions in 1911. Economic prosperity based on its neutralist policy enabled Sweden, together with Norway, to pioneer in public health, housing, and job security programs.

Forty-four years of Socialist government were ended in 1976 with the election of a conservative coalition headed by Thorbjörn Fälldin, a 50-year-old sheep farmer.

Fälldin resigned on Oct. 5, 1978, when his conservative parties partners demanded less restrictions on nuclear power, and his successor, Ola Ullsten, resigned a year later after failing to achieve a consensus on the issue. Returned to office by his coalition partners, Fälldin said he would follow the course directed by a national referendum. On March 23, 1980, voters backed the development of 12 nuclear plants and use of them for at least 25 years to supply 40% of national energy needs while the search for alternative sources continued.

Olof Palme and the Socialists were returned to power in the election of 1982.

In February 1986, Palme was killed by an unknown assailant. His death shocked the world.

SWITZERLAND

Swiss Confederation
President: Pierre Aubert (1987)
Vice President: Otto Stich (1987)
Area: 15,941 sq mi. (41,288 sq km)
Population (est. mid-1987): 6,600,000 (average annual growth rate: 0.2%) (Swiss, 85%; Italian, 8%; German, 2%; Spanish, 2%; French, 1%—figures by place of birth)
Density per square mile: 414.0
Capital: Bern
Largest cities (est. 1987): Zurich, 351,500; Basel, 174,600; Geneva, 160,000; Bern, 138,600; Lausanne, 125,000

Monetary unit: Swiss franc
Languages: German, 65%; French, 18%; Italian, 10%; Romansch, 1%
Religions: Roman Catholic, 48%; Protestant, 44%
National name: Schweiz/Suisse/Svizzera/Svizra
Literacy rate: 99.5%
Economic summary: Gross national product (1984): $96.1 billion. Average annual growth rate (1970–79): 0.2%. Per capita income (1984): $14,300. Land used for agriculture: 26%; labor force: 7%; principal products: cheese and other dairy products, livestock, fruits, grains, wine. Labor force in industry: 38%; major products: watches and clocks, precision instruments, machinery, chemicals, pharmaceuticals, textiles, generators, turbines. Natural resources: water power, timber, salt. Exports: electrical machinery, chemicals, precision instruments, textiles, foodstuffs, textile yarns, dyestuffs, chemicals. Imports: transport equipment, metals and metal products, foodstuffs, chemicals, textile yarns. Major trading partners: West Germany, France, U.S., Italy, U.K.

Geography. Switzerland, in central Europe, is the land of the Alps. Its tallest peak is the Dufourspitze at 15,203 feet (4,634 m) on the Swiss side of the Italian border, one of 10 summits of the Monte Rose massif in the Pennine Alps. The tallest peak in all of the Alps, Mont Blanc (15,771 ft; 4,807 m), is actually in France.

Most of Switzerland comprises a mountainous plateau bordered by the great bulk of the Alps on the south and by the Jura Mountains on the northwest. About one fourth of the total area is covered by mountains and glaciers.

The country's largest lakes—Geneva, Constance (Bodensee), and Maggiore—straddle the French, German-Austrian, and Italian borders, respectively.

The Rhine, navigable from Basel to the North Sea, is the principal inland waterway. Other rivers are the Aare and the Rhône.

Switzerland, twice the size of New Jersey, is surrounded by France, West Germany, Austria, Liechtenstein, and Italy.

Government. The Swiss Confederation consists of 23 sovereign cantons, of which three are divided into six half-cantons. Federal authority is vested in a bicameral legislature. The Ständerat, or State Council, consists of 46 members, two from each canton. The lower house, the Nationalrat, or National Council, has 200 deputies, elected for four-year terms.

Executive authority rests with the Bundesrat, or Federal Council, consisting of seven members chosen by parliament. The parliament elects the President, who serves for one year and is succeeded by the Vice President. The federal government regulates foreign policy, railroads, postal service, and the national mint. Each canton reserves for itself important local powers.

A constitutional amendment adopted in 1971 by referendum gave women the vote in federal elections and the right to hold federal office. An equal rights amendment was passed in a national referendum June 14, 1981, barring discrimination against women under canton as well as federal law.

The major political parties are the Social Democratic Party (47 of 200 seats in National Council); Radical Democratic Party (54 seats); Christian-Democratic Party (42 seats); People's Party (23 seats). These four parties constitute the ruling coalition.

History. Called Helvetia in ancient times, Switzerland in the Middle Ages was a league of cantons of the Holy Roman Empire. Fashioned around the nucleus of three German forest districts of Schwyz, Uri, and Unterwalden, the Swiss Confederation slowly added new cantons. In 1648 the Treaty of Westphalia gave Switzerland its independence from the Holy Roman Empire.

French revolutionary troops occupied the country in 1798 and named it the Helvetic Republic, but Napoleon in 1803 restored its federal government. By 1815, the French- and Italian-speaking peoples of Switzerland had been granted political equality.

In 1815, the Congress of Vienna guaranteed the neutrality and recognized the independence of Switzerland. In the revolutionary period of 1847, the Catholic cantons seceded and organized a separate union called the *Sonderbund.* In 1848 the new Swiss Constitution established a union modeled upon that of the U.S. The Federal Constitution of 1874 established a strong central government while maintaining large powers of control in each canton.

National unity and political conservatism grew as the country prospered from its neutrality. Its banking system became the world's leading repository for international accounts. Strict neutrality was its policy in World Wars I and II. Geneva was the seat of the League of Nations (later the European headquarters of the United Nations) and of a number of international organizations.

In 1971, the Swiss Supreme Court ruled that Swiss banks must show U.S. tax officials records of U.S. citizens suspected of tax fraud, thus significantly modifying a 1934 law that had seemed to forbid any bank disclosures.

SYRIA

Syrian Arab Republic
President: Hafez al-Assad (1971)
Premier: Abdel Raouf al-Kasm (1980)
Area: 71,498 sq mi. (185,180 sq km)
Population (est. mid-1987): 11,300,000 (average annual growth rate: 3.8%)
Density per square mile: 158.0
Capital: Damascus
Largest cities (est. 1984): Damascus, 1,200,000; Aleppo, 1,100,000; Homs, 400,000; Hama, 190,000; Latakia, 222,000
Monetary unit: Syrian pound
Language: Arabic
Religions: Islam, 90%; Christian, 10%
National name: Al-Jamhouriya al Arabiya As-Souriya
Literacy rate: 50%
Economic summary: Gross national product (1984): $18.5 billion. Average annual growth rate (1983): 3%. Per capita income (1984): $1,870. Land used for agriculture: 76%; labor force: 29%; principal products: fruits, wheat, sugar beets, sheep, goats. Labor force in industry: 29%; major products: textiles, cement, petroleum, processed food. Natural resources: chrome, manganese, asphalt, iron ore, rock salt, phosphate, oil, natural gas. Exports: petroleum, textiles, tobacco, fruits and vegetables, cotton. Imports: machinery and metal products, textiles, fuels, foodstuffs. Major trading partners: Italy, Romania, U.S.S.R., U.S., Iran, Libya, France, West Germany.

Geography. Slightly larger than North Dakota,

Syria lies at the eastern end of the Mediterranean Sea. It is bordered by Lebanon and Israel on the west, Turkey on the north, Iraq on the east, and Jordan on the south.

Coastal Syria is a narrow plain, in back of which is a range of coastal mountains, and still farther inland a steppe area. In the east is the Syrian Desert, and in the south is the Jebel Druze Range. The highest point in Syria is Mount Hermon (9,232 ft; 2,814 m) on the Lebanese border.

Government. Syria's first permanent Constitution was approved in 1973, replacing a provisional charter that had been in force for 10 years. It provided for an elected People's Council as the legislature.

In the first election in 10 years, in 1973, the Ba'ath Arab Socialist Party of President Hafez al-Assad, running on a unified National Progressive ticket with the Communist and Socialist parties, won 70% of the vote and a commensurate proportion of the seats in the People's Assembly. In 1977 and 1981 elections, the ruling Ba'athists won by similar margins.

History. Ancient Syria was conquered by Egypt about 1500 B.C., and after that by Hebrews, Assyrians, Chaldeans, Persians, and Greeks. From 64 B.C. until the Arab conquest in A.D. 636, it was part of the Roman Empire except during brief periods. The Arabs made it a trade center for their extensive empire, but it suffered severely from the Mongol invasion in 1260 and fell to the Ottoman Turks in 1516. Syria remained a Turkish province until World War I.

A secret Anglo-French pact of 1916 put Syria in the French zone of influence. The League of Nations gave France a mandate over Syria after World War I, but the French were forced to put down several nationalist uprisings. In 1930, France recognized Syria as an independent republic, but still subject to the mandate. After nationalist demonstrations in 1939, the French High Commissioner suspended the Syrian Constitution. In 1941, British and Free French forces invaded Syria to eliminate Vichy control. During the rest of World War II, Syria was an Allied base.

Again in 1945, nationalist demonstrations broke into actual fighting, and British troops had to restore order. Syrian forces met a series of reverses while participating in the Arab invasion of Palestine in 1948. In 1958, Egypt and Syria formed the United Arab Republic, with Gamal Abdel Nasser of Egypt as President. However, Syria became independent again on Sept. 29, 1961, following a revolution.

In the war of 1967, Israel quickly vanquished the Syrian army. Before acceding to the U.N. ceasefire, the Israeli forces took over control of the fortified Golan Heights commanding the Sea of Galilee.

Syria joined Egypt in attacking Israel in October 1973 in the fourth Arab-Israeli war, but was pushed back from initial successes on the Golan Heights to end up losing more land. However, in the settlement worked out by U.S. Secretary of State Henry A. Kissinger in 1974, the Syrians recovered all the territory lost in 1973 and a token amount of territory, including the deserted town of Quneitra, lost in 1967.

Syrian troops, in Lebanon since 1976 as part of an Arab peacekeeping force whose other members subsequently departed, intervened increasingly during 1980 and 1981 on the side of Moslem Lebanese in their clashes with Christian militants supported by Israel. When Israeli jets shot down Syrian helicopters operating in Lebanon in April 1981, Syria moved Soviet-built surface-to-air (SAM 6) missiles into Lebanon's Bekaa Valley. Israel demanded that the missiles be removed because they violated a 1976 understanding between the governments. The demand, backed up by bombing raids, prompted the Reagan Administration to send veteran diplomat Philip C. Habib as a special envoy to avert a new conflict between the nations.

Habib's carefully engineered cease-fire was shattered by a new Israeli invasion in June 1982, when Israeli aircraft bombed Bekaa Valley missile sites, claiming to destroy all of them along with 25 Syrian planes that had sought to defend the sites. On the ground, Syrian army units were driven back by Israeli armor along the Lebanese coast. The Syrians, who were equipped with Soviet weapons, were outfought everywhere by U.S.-equipped Israelis.

Nevertheless, while the Israelis overran most of the rest of Lebanon, the Syrians retained their positions in the Bekaa Valley. Over the next three years, as the Israelis gradually withdrew their forces, the Syrians remained. As the various Lebanese factions fought each other, the Syrians became the dominant force in the country, both militarily and politically.

The extent of Syrian influence in Lebanaon was demonstrated dramatically after Lebanese Shiite extremists hijacked a TWA airliner from Athens to Beirut on June 14, 1985. President al-Assad played the key role in delicate, many-sided negotiations that obtained the release of the 39 American hostages from the plane 17 days later.

TANZANIA

United Republic of Tanzania
President: Ali Hassan Mwinyi (1985)
Prime Minister: Joseph Warioba (1985)
Area: 364,900 sq mi. (945,087 sq km)[1]
Population (est. mid-1987): 23,500,000 (average annual growth rate: 3.5%)
Density per square mile: 64.4
Capital and largest city (est. 1980): Dar es Salaam, 900,-000
Monetary unit: Tanzanian shilling
Languages: Swahili, Arabic, English
Religions: Christian, 40%; Islam, 30%; Animist, 30%
Member of Commonwealth of Nations
Literacy rate: 79%
Economic summary: Gross national product (1984): $4.2 billion. Average annual growth rate (1984): 0.6%. Per capita income (1984): $210. Land used for agriculture: 45%; labor force: 90%; Principal products: coconuts, maize, rice, wheat, cotton, coffee, sisal, cashew nuts, pyrethrum, cloves. Major industrial products: textiles, light manufactures, refined oil, processed agricultural products, diamonds, cement, fertilizer. Natural resources: hydroelectric potential, unexploited iron and coal. Exports: coffee, cotton, sisal, diamonds, cloves, cashew nuts. Imports: manufactured goods, textiles, machinery and transport equipment, crude oil, foodstuffs. Major trading partners: U.K., China, India, Hong Kong, Uganda, U.S., Japan.

1. Including Zanzibar.

Geography. Tanzania is in East Africa on the Indian Ocean. To the north are Uganda and Kenya; to the west, Burundi, Rwanda, and Zaire; and to the south, Mozambique, Zambia, and Malawi. Its area is three times that of New Mexico.

Tanzania contains three of Africa's best-known lakes—Victoria in the north, Tanganyika in the west, and Nyasa in the south. Mount Kilimanjaro in the north, 19,340 feet (5,895 m), is the highest point on the continent.

Government. Under the republican form of government, Tanzania has a President elected by universal suffrage who appoints the Cabinet ministers. The 218-member National Assembly is composed of 96 elected members from the mainland, 10 members appointed by the President (from both Tanganyika and Zanzibar), 35 national members (elected by the National Assembly after nomination by various national institutions), 32 members of the Zanzibar Revolutionary Council, 20 other Zanzibar members appointed by the President in agreement with the President of Zanzibar, and up to 20 other Zanzibar members appointed by the President in agreement with the first Vice President, who represents Zanzibar.

The Tanganyika African National Union, the only authorized party on the mainland, and the Afro-Shirazi Party, the only party in Zanzibar and Pemba, merged in 1977 as the Revolutionary Party (Chama Cha Mapinduzi) and elected Julius K. Nyerere as its head.

History. Arab traders first began to colonize the area in A.D. 700. Portuguese explorers reached the coastal regions in 1500 and held some control until the 17th century, when the Sultan of Oman took power. With what are now Burundi and Rwanda, Tanganyika became the colony of German East Africa in 1885. After World War I, it was administered by Britain under a League of Nations mandate and later as a U.N. trust territory.

Although not mentioned in old histories until the 12th century, Zanzibar was believed always to have had connections with southern Arabia. The Portuguese made it one of their tributaries in 1503 and later established a trading post, but they were driven out by Arabs from Oman in 1698. Zanzibar was declared independent of Oman in 1861 and, in 1890, it became a British protectorate.

Tanganyika became independent on Dec. 9, 1961; Zanzibar, on Dec. 10, 1963. On April 26, 1964, the two nations merged into the United Republic of Tanganyika and Zanzibar. The name was changed to Tanzania six months later.

An invasion by Ugandan troops in November 1978 was followed by a counterattack in January 1979, in which 5,000 Tanzanian troops were joined by 3,000 Ugandan exiles opposed to President Idi Amin. Within a month, full-scale war developed.

Nyerere kept troops in Uganda in open support of former Ugandan President Milton Obote, despite protests from opposition groups, until the national elections in December 1980. Although Obote asked that the Tanzanians remain after his victory in order to control guerrilla resistance, Nyerere ordered their withdrawal in May 1981, citing the $1-million-a-month drain on his precarious finances.

In November 1985, Nyerere stepped down as President. Ali Hassan Myinyi, his Vice-President, succeeded him. Nyerere remained chariman of the party.

THAILAND

Kingdom of Thailand
Ruler: King Bhumibol Adulyadej (1946)
Prime Minister: Gen. Prem Tinsulanonda (1980)
Area: 198,455 sq mi. (514,000 sq km)
Population (est. mid-1987): 53,600,000 (average annual growth rate: 2.1%) (incl. 2.5 million of Chinese descent born in Thailand)
Density per square mile: 270.1
Capital and largest city (est. 1984): Bangkok, 5,174,682
Monetary unit: Baht
Languages: Thai (Siamese), Chinese, English
Religions: Buddhist, 95%; Islam, 4%
National name: Prathet Thai
Literacy rate (1985): 85.5%
Economic summary: Gross national product (1984): $52.4 billion. Average annual growth rate (1981–86): approx. 4%. Per capita income (1984): $1,030. Land used for agriculture: 38%; labor force; 68%; principal products: rice, rubber, corn, tapioca, sugar, coconuts. Labor force in industry: 10%; major products: processed food, textiles, wood, cement, tin, tungsten. Natural resources: fish, natural gas, forests, fluorite, tin, tungsten. Exports: rice, tapioca, sugar, rubber, tin, textiles. Imports: machinery and transport equipment, fertilizer, crude oil, fuels and lubricants, base metals, chemicals. Major trading partners: Japan, U.S., Singapore, Malaysia, Netherlands, U.K., Hong Kong.

Geography. Thailand occupies the western half of the Indochinese peninsula and the northern two thirds of the Malay peninsula in southeast Asia. Its neighbors are Burma on the north and west, Laos on the north and northeast, Cambodia on the east, and Malaysia on the south. Thailand is about the size of France.

Most of the population is supported in the fertile central alluvial plain, which is drained by the Chao Phnaya River and its tributaries.

Government. King Bhumibol Adulyadej, who was born Dec. 5, 1927, second son of Prince Mahidol of Songkhla, succeeded to the throne on June 9, 1946, when his brother, King Ananda Mahidol, died of a gunshot wound. He was married on April 28, 1950, to Queen Sirikit; their son, Vajiralongkorn, born July 28, 1952, is the Crown Prince.

After three years of civilian government ended with a military coup on Oct. 6, 1976, Thailand reverted to military rule. Political parties, banned after the coup, gained limited freedom in 1980. The same year, the National Assembly elected Gen. Prem Tinsulanonda as prime minister. General elections on April 18, 1983, and July 27, 1986 resulted in Prem continuing as prime minister over a coalition government.

History. The Thais first began moving down into their present homeland from the Asian continent in the 6th century A.D. and by the end of the 13th century ruled most of the western portion. During the next 400 years, the Thais fought sporadically with the Cambodians and the Burmese. The British obtained recognition of paramount interest in Thailand in 1824, and in 1896 an Anglo-French accord guaranteed the independence of Thailand.

A coup in 1932 changed the absolute monarchy into a representative government with universal suffrage. After five hours of token resistance on Dec. 8, 1941, Thailand yielded to Japanese occupation and became one of the springboards in World War II for the Japanese campaign against Malaya.

After the fall of its pro-Japanese puppet government in July 1944, Thailand pursued a policy of passive resistance against the Japanese, and after the Japanese surrender, Thailand repudiated the declaration of war it had been forced to make against Britain and the U.S. in 1942.

Thailand's major problem in the late 1960s was suppressing guerrilla action by Communist invaders in the north.

Although Thailand had received $2 billion in U.S. economic and military aid since 1950 and had sent troops (paid by the U.S.) to Vietnam while permitting U.S. bomber bases on its territory, the collapse of South Vietnam and Cambodia in the spring of 1975 brought rapid changes in the country's diplomatic posture.

At the Thai government's insistence, the U.S. agreed to withdraw all 23,000 U.S. military personnel remaining in Thailand by March 1976. Diplomatic relations with China were established in 1975. Meanwhile, overtures toward an accommodation with the new regime in South Vietnam were initiated.

Refugees from Laos, Cambodia, and Vietnam flooded into Thailand in 1978 and 1979, and despite efforts by the United States and other Western countries to resettle them, a total of 130,000 Laotian and Vietnamese refugees were living in camps along the Cambodian border in mid-1980. A drive by Vietnamese occupation forces on western Cambodian areas loyal to the Pol Pot government, culminating in invasions of Thai territory in late June, drove an estimated 100,000 Cambodians across the line as refugees, adding to the 200,000 of their countrymen already in Thailand. The total of 430,000 were being fed by United Nations and church relief organizations but the Thai government complained of the burden of their presence.

The Vietnamese incursions, notwithstanding Hanoi's claim that the troops were only seeking guerrillas hidden in the refugee camps, prompted a Thai appeal to Washington for military aid. In July, 35 reconditioned tanks and other weapons were flown to Thailand, and the Carter administration pledged its help in the event of a larger attack. Border incursions are still a problem.

On April 3, 1981, a military coup against the Prem government failed. Another coup attempt on Sept. 9, 1985, was crushed by loyal troops after 10 hours of fighting in Bangkok. Four persons were killed and about 60 wounded.

TOGO

Republic of Togo
President: Gen. Gnassingbé Eyadema (1967)
Area: 21,925 sq mi. (56,785 sq km)
Population (est. mid-1987): 3,200,000 (average annual growth rate: 3.1%)
Density per square mile: 136.8
Capital and largest city (est. 1982): Lomé, 285,000
Monetary unit: Franc CFA
Languages: Ewé, Mona (south), Kabyé, Cotocoli (north), French (official), and many dialects
Religions: Animist, 46%; Christian, 37%; Islam, 17%
National name: République Togolaise
Member of Commonwealth of Nations
Literacy rate: 18%
Economic summary: Gross national product (1985): $950 million. Average annual growth rate (1982): 3.2%. Per capita income (1982): $340. Land used for agriculture: 26%; labor force: 78%; principal products: yams, manioc, millet, sorghum, cocoa, coffee, peanuts. Labor force in industry: 22%; major products: phosphate, textiles. Natural resources: marble, manganese, phosphate, limestone. Exports: phosphate, cocoa, coffee. Imports: consumer goods, fuels, machinery, foodstuffs. Major trading partners: France, U.K., Japan, Netherlands.

Geography. Togo, twice the size of Maryland, is on the south coast of West Africa bordering on Ghana to the west, Burkina Faso to the north and Benin to the east.

The Gulf of Guinea coastline, only 32 miles long (51 km), is low and sandy. The only port is at Lomé. The Togo hills traverse the central section.

Government. The government of Nicolas Grunitzky was overthrown in a bloodless coup on Jan. 13, 1967, led by Lt. Col. Etienne Eyadema (now Gen. Gnassingbé Eyadema). A National Reconciliation Committee was set up to rule the country. In April, however, Eyadema dissolved the Committee and took over as President. In December 1979, a 67-member National Assembly was voted in by national referendum. The Assembly of the Togolese People is the only political party.

History. Freed slaves from Brazil were the first traders to settle in Togo. Established as a German colony (Togoland) in 1884, the area was split between the British and the French as League of Nations mandates after World War I and subsequently administered as U. N. trusteeships. The British portion voted for incorporation with Ghana.

Togo became independent on April 27, 1960. Sylvanus Olympio, its first President, was assassinated in 1963 and succeeded by Nicolas Grunitzky.

TONGA

Kingdom of Tonga
Sovereign: King Taufa'ahau Tupou IV (1965)
Prime Minister: Prince Fatafehi Tu'ipelehake (1965)
Area: 290 sq mi. (751 sq km)
Population (est. 1987): 107,000 (average annual growth rate: 1.9%)
Density per square mile: 369.0
Capital (est. 1983): Nuku'alofa, 21,000
Monetary unit: Pa'anga
Languages: Tongan, English
Religions: Free Wesleyan, 47%; Roman Catholic, 16%; Free Church of Tonga, 14%; Mormon, 9%; Church of Tonga, 9%
Member of Commonwealth of Nations
Literacy rate: 95%
Economic summary: Gross national product (1984): $65 million. Average annual growth rate (1970–78): 1.2%. Per capita income (1984): $580. Land used for agriculture: 80%; labor force: 75%; principal products: yams, taro, papaya, pineapples, coconuts, bananas, copra. Major industrial products: copra, desiccated coconut. Natural resources: fish, timber. Exports: copra, coconut products, bananas. Imports: manufactures, foodstuffs, machinery, petroleum. Major trading partners: New Zealand, Australia, U.S., U.K.

Geography. Situated east of the Fiji Islands in the South Pacific, Tonga (also called the Friendly Islands) consists of some 150 islands, of which 36 are inhabited.

Most of the islands contain active volcanic craters; others are coral atolls.

Government. Tonga is a constitutional monarchy. Executive authority is vested in the Sovereign, a Privy Council, and a Cabinet headed by the Prime Minister. Legislative authority is vested in the Legislative Assembly.

History. The present dynasty of Tonga was founded in 1831 by Taufa'ahau Tupou, who took the name George I. He consolidated the kingdom by conquest and in 1875 granted a Constitution.

In 1900, his great-grandson, George II, signed a treaty of friendship with Britain, and the country became a British protected state. The treaty was revised in 1959.

Queen Salote Tupou reigned from 1918 to 1964 and was succeeded by her son, who became King Taufa'ahau Tupou IV.

Tonga became independent on June 4, 1970.

TRANSKEI

See South Africa

TRINIDAD AND TOBAGO

Republic of Trinidad and Tobago
President: Noor Hassanali (1987)
Prime Minister: A.N.R. Robinson (1986)
Area: 1,980 sq mi. (5,128 sq km)
Population (est. mid-1987): 1,300,000 (average annual growth rate: 2.0%) (black, 43%; East Indian, 40%; mixed, 14%)
Density per square mile: 656.6
Capital and largest city (est. 1981): Port-of-Spain, 125,000
Monetary unit: Trinidad and Tobago dollar
Languages: English (official); Hindi
Religions: Christian, 64%; Hindu, 25%; Islam, 6%
Member of Commonwealth of Nations
Literacy rate: 95%
Economic summary: Gross national product (1986): $7.2 billion. Average annual growth rate (1984): −7.4%. Per capita income (1985): $6,900. Land used for agriculture: 26%; labor force: 9%; principal products: sugar cane, cocoa, coffee, citrus. Labor force in industry: 33%; major products: petroleum, processed food, cement; tourism. Natural resources: petroleum. Exports: petroleum, ammonia, fertilizer. Imports: chemicals, foodstuffs, machinery and equipment. Major trading partners: U.S., CARICOM, EEC.

Geography. Trinidad and Tobago lies in the Caribbean Sea off the northeast coast of Venezuela. The area of the two islands is slightly less than that of Delaware.

Trinidad, the larger, is mainly flat and rolling, with mountains in the north that reach a height of 3,085 feet (940 m) at Mount Aripo. Tobago is heavily forested with hardwood trees.

Government. The legislature consists of a 24-member Senate and a 36-member House of Representatives.

The political parties are the National Alliance for Reconstruction, led by Prime Minister A.N.R. Robinson (33 seats in the House of Representatives); People's National Movement (3 seats).

History. Trinidad was discovered by Columbus in 1498 and remained in Spanish possession, despite raids by other European nations, until it capitulated to the British in 1797 during a war between Britain and Spain.

Trinidad was ceded to Britain in 1802, and in 1899 it was united with Tobago as a colony. From 1958 to 1962, Trinidad and Tobago was a part of the West Indies Federation, and on Aug, 31, 1962, it became independent.

On Aug. 1, 1976, Trinidad and Tobago cut its ties with Britain and became a republic, remaining within the Commonwealth and recognizing Queen Elizabeth II only as head of that organization.

TUNISIA

Republic of Tunisia
President: Habib Bourguiba (1957)
Prime Minister: Rachid Sfar (1986)
Area: 63,379 sq mi. (164,152 sq km)
Population (est. mid-1987); 7,600,000 (average annual growth rate: 2.5%)
Density per square mile: 119.9
Capital and largest city (est. 1981): Tunis, 600,000
Monetary unit: Tunisian dinar
Languages: Arabic, French
Religions: Islam: 99.4%
National name: Al-Joumhouria Attunisia
Literacy rate: 64%
Economic summary: Gross national product (1985): $9.3 billion. Average annual growth rate (1980–83): 4%. Per capita income (1986): $1,100. Land used for agriculture: 28%; labor force: 40%; principal products: wheat, olives, citrus fruits, grapes, dates. Labor force in industry: 21%; major products: crude oil, olive oil, textiles, and leather, chemical fertilizers, petroleum. Natural resources: oil, phosphates, iron ore, lead, zinc. Exports: petroleum, phosphates, textiles. Imports: machinery and equipment, consumer goods, foodstuffs. Major trading partners: France, West Germany, Italy, Greece, U.S.

Geography. Tunisia, at the northernmost bulge of Africa, thrusts out toward Sicily to mark the division between the eastern and western Mediterranean Sea. Twice the size of South Carolina, it is bordered on the west by Algeria and by Libya on the south.

Coastal plains on the east rise to a north-south escarpment which slopes gently to the west. Saharan in the south, Tunisia is more mountainous in the north, where the Atlas range continues from Algeria.

Government. Executive power is vested by the Constitution in the president, elected for five years and eligible for re-election to two additional terms. Legislative power is vested in a National Assembly elected by universal suffrage.

In 1975, the National Assembly amended the Constitution to make Habib Bourguiba president for life. At 71, Bourguiba was re-elected to a fourth five-year term when he ran unopposed in 1974. There are four political parties, the Socialist Destourian, led by Bourguiba, the Social Democratic Movement, the Popular Unity Movement and the Communist Party.

History. Tunisia was settled by the Phoenicians and Carthaginians in ancient times. Except for an interval of Vandal conquest in A.D. 439–533, it was part of the Roman Empire until the Arab conquest of 648–69. It was ruled by various Arab and Berber dynasties until the Turks took it in 1570–74. French troops occupied the country in 1881, and the Bey signed a treaty acknowledging a French protectorate.

Nationalist agitation forced France to grant internal autonomy to Tunisia in 1955 and to recognize Tunisian independence and sovereignty in 1956. The Constituent Assembly deposed the Bey on July 25, 1957, declared Tunisia a republic, and elected Habib Bourguiba as president.

Bourguiba maintained a pro-Western foreign policy that earned him enemies. Tunisia refused to break relations with the U.S. during the Israeli-Arab war in June 1967.

Tunisia ended its traditionally neutral role in the Arab world when it joined with the majority of Arab League members to condemn Egypt for concluding a peace treaty with Israel. The Tunisian capital was offered as the temporary headquarters of the League, following the expulsion of Egypt.

In 1985, Israeli jets bombed the PLO headquarters near Tunis in response to the murder of three Israelis by terrorists. U.S. support for the raid strained U.S.-Tunisian relations.

Developments in 1986-87 were characterized by a consolidation of power by the 84-year-old Bourguiba and his failure to arrange for a successor.

TURKEY

Republic of Turkey
President: Kenan Evren (1982)
Prime Minister: Turgut Özal (1983)
Area: 300,947 sq mi. (incl. 9,121 in Europe) (779,452 sq km)
Population (est. mid-1987): 51,400,000 (average annual growth rate: 2.8%)
Density per square mile: 170.9
Capital: Ankara
Largest cities (1985 census): Istanbul, 5,858,558; Ankara, 3,462,880; Izmir, 2,316,843; Adana, 1,757,102; Bursa, 1,327,762; Gaziantep, 953,859
Monetary unit: Turkish Lira
Language: Turkish
Religion: Islam (Sunni)
National name: Türkiye Cumhuriyeti
Literacy rate: 80%
Economic summary: Gross national product (1985): $52 billion. Average annual growth rate (1985): 4.0%. Per capita income (est. 1985): $1,250. Land used for agriculture: 35%; labor force: 60%; principal products: cotton, tobacco, cereals, sugar beets, fruits, nuts. Labor force in industry: 16%; major products: textiles, processed foods, steel, petroleum. Natural resources: coal, chromite, copper, boron, oil. Exports: cotton, tobacco, fruits, nuts, livestock products, textiles. Imports: crude oil, machinery, transport equipment, metals, mineral fuels, fertilizer, chemicals. Major trading partners: Iran, West Germany, Iraq, France, Italy, U.S.S.R., U.S.

Geography. Turkey is at the northeastern end of the Mediterranean Sea in southeast Europe and southwest Asia. To the north is the Black Sea and to the west the Aegean Sea. Its neighbors are Greece and Bulgaria to the west, the U.S.S.R. to the north, Iran to the east, and Syria and Iraq to the south. Overall, it is a little larger than Texas.

The Dardanelles, the Sea of Marmara, and the Bosporus divide the country.

Turkey in Europe comprises an area about equal to the state of Massachusetts. It is hilly country drained by the Maritsa River and its tributaries.

Turkey in Asia, or Anatolia, about the size of Texas, is roughly a rectangle in shape with its short sides on the east and west. Its center is a treeless plateau rimmed by mountains.

Government. The President is elected by the Grand National Assembly for a seven-year term and is not eligible for re-election.

In a military coup on Sept. 12, 1980, led by Gen. Kenan Evren, the Chief of General Staff, Premier Süleyman Demirel was ousted, the Grand National Assembly dissolved and the Constitution suspended. Demirel, former Premier Bülent Ecevit, and some 100 legislators and political figures were detained, but later released. Martial law was declared and all political parties were dissolved.

Following the adoption of a new Constitution in 1982, parliamentary elections were held in 1983. Prime Minister Turgut Özal's Motherland Party came to power with a 211-seat majority in the 400-seat Grand National Assembly. Other parties include Süleyman Demirel's True Party, the Free Democratic Party, and the Populists.

History. The Ottoman Turks first appeared in the early 13th century in Anatolia, subjugating Turkish and Mongol bands pressing against the eastern borders of Byzantium. They gradually spread through the Near East and Balkans, capturing Constantinople in 1453 and storming the gates of Vienna two centuries later. At its height, the Ottoman Empire stretched from the Persian Gulf to western Algeria.

Defeat of the Turkish navy at Lepanto by the Holy League in 1571 and failure of the siege of Vienna heralded the decline of Turkish power. By the 18th century, Russia was seeking to establish itself as the protector of Christians in Turkey's Balkan territories. Russian ambitions were checked by Britain and France in the Crimean War (1854–56), but the Russo-Turkish War (1877–78) gave Bulgaria virtual independence and Romania and Serbia liberation from their nominal allegiance to the Sultan.

Turkish weakness stimulated a revolt of young liberals known as the Young Turks in 1909. They forced Sultan Abdul Hamid to grant a constitution and install a liberal government. Reforms were no barrier to further defeats, however, in a war with Italy (1911–12) and the Balkan Wars (1912–13). Under the influence of German military advisors, Turkey signed a secret alliance with Germany on Aug. 2, 1914, that led to a declaration of war by the Allied powers and the ultimate humiliation of the occupation of Turkish territory by Greek and other Allied troops.

In 1919, the new Nationalist movement, headed by Mustafa Kemal, was organized to resist the Allied occupation and, in 1920, a National Assembly elected him President of both the Assembly and the government. Under his leadership, the Greeks were driven out of Smyrna, and other Allied forces were withdrawn.

The present Turkish boundaries (with the exception of Alexandretta, ceded to Turkey by France in 1939) were fixed by the Treaty of Lausanne (1923) and later negotiations. The caliphate and sultanate were separated, and the sultanate was abolished in 1922. On Oct. 29, 1923, Turkey formally became a republic, with Mustafa Kemal, who took the name Kemal Atatürk, as its first President.

The caliphate was abolished in 1924, and Atatürk proceeded to carry out an extensive program of reform, modernization, and industrialization.

Gen. Ismet Inönü was elected to succeed Atatürk in 1938 and was re-elected in 1939, 1943, and 1946. Defeated in 1950, he was succeeded by Celâl Bayar. In 1939, a mutual assistance pact was concluded with Britain and France. Neutral during most of World War II Turkey, on Feb. 23, 1945, declared war on Germany and Japan, but took no active part in the conflict.

Turkey became a full member of NATO in 1952.

Turkey invaded Cyprus by sea and air July 20, 1974, following the failure of diplomatic efforts to resolve the crisis caused by the ouster of Archbishop Makarios.

Talks in Geneva involving Greece, Turkey, Britain, and Greek Cypriot and Turkish Cypriot leaders brokers down in mid-August. Turkey unilaterally announced a cease-fire August 16, after having gained control of 40% of the island. Turkish Cypriots established their own state in the north on Feb. 13, 1975.

U.S.-Turkish relations, excellent for a generation, were seriously damaged when Congress voted to end arms sales to Turkey in 1975 because arms the U.S. had supplied for mutual defense had been used in the invasion of Cyprus.

In July 1975, after a 30-day warning, Turkey took over control of all the U.S. installations except the big joint defense base at Incirlik, which it reserved for "NATO tasks alone."

The establishment of military government in September 1980 stopped the slide toward anarchy and brought some improvement in the economy. The military regime was criticized, however, for suppression of human rights.

A Constituent Assembly, consisting of the six-member National Security Council and members appointed by them, drafted a new Constitution that was approved by an overwhelming (91.5%) majority of the voters in a Nov. 6, 1982, referendum. Prime Minister Turgut Özal's Motherland Party came to power in parliamentary elections held in late 1983.

TUVALU

Sovereign: Queen Elizabeth II
Governor-General: Tupua Leupena (1986)
Prime Minister: Tomasi Puapua (1981)
Area: 10 sq mi. (26 sq km)
Population (est. 1985): 8,000 (average annual growth rate: 1.7%)
Density per square mile: 700.0
Capital and largest city (est. 1981): Funafuti, 2,500
Monetary unit: Australian dollar
Languages: Tuvaluan, English
Member of the Commonwealth of Nations
Literacy rate: 50%
Economic summary: Gross national product (1984): $4 million. Per capita Income (1984): $450. Principal agricultural products: copra and coconuts. Export: copra. Imports: food and fuels. Major trading partners: Australia, U.K., Fiji, New Zealand

Geography. Formerly the Ellice Islands, Tuvalu consists of nine small islands scattered over 500,000 square miles of the western Pacific, just south of the equator.

Government. Official executive power is vested in a Governor-General, representing the Queen, who is appointed by her on the recommendation of the Tuvalu government. Actual executive power lies with a Prime Minister, who is responsible to a House of Assembly composed of eight elected members.

History. The Ellice Islands became a British protectorate in 1892 and were annexed by Britain in 1915–16 as part of the Gilbert and Ellice Islands Colony. The Ellice Islands were separated in 1975, given home rule, and renamed Tuvalu. Full independence was granted on Sept. 30, 1978.

UGANDA

Republic of Uganda
President: Yoweri Museveni (1986)
Prime Minister: Dr. Samson Kiseka (1985)
Area: 91,343 sq mi. (236,880 sq km)
Population (est. mid-1987): 15,900,000 (average annual growth rate: 3.4%)
Density per square mile: 174.1
Capital and largest city (est. 1980): Kampala, 458,000
Monetary unit: Ugandan shilling
Languages: English (official), Swahili, Luganda, Ateso, Luo
Religions: Christian, 63%; Islam, 6%
Member of Commonwealth of Nations
Literacy rate: 52%
Economic summary: Gross national product (1984): $6.2 billion. Average annual growth rate (1983): 5.0%. Per capita income (1984): $434. Land used for agriculture: 21%; labor force: 90%; principal products: coffee, tea, cotton, sugar, bananas, corn. Labor force in industry: 3%; major products: processed agricultural products, copper, cement, shoes, fertilizer, sheet iron, beverages. Natural resources: copper, sugar, skins and hides. Exports: coffee, cotton. Imports: petroleum products, machinery, transport equipment, metals, food. Major trading partners: U.S., U.K., Kenya, West Germany.

Geography. Uganda, twice the size of Pennsylvania, is in east Africa. It is bordered on the west by Zaire, on the north by the Sudan, on the east by Kenya, and on the south by Tanzania and Rwanda.

The country, which lies across the Equator, is divided into three main areas—swampy lowlands, a fertile plateau with wooded hills, and a desert region. Lake Victoria forms part of the southern border.

Government. The country has been run by the National Reistance Council since January 1986.

History. Uganda was first visited by European explorers as well as Arab traders in 1844. An Anglo-German agreement of 1890 declared it to be in the British sphere of influence in Africa, and the Imperial British East Africa Company was chartered to develop the area. The company did not prosper financially, and in 1894 a British protectorate was proclaimed.

Uganda became independent on Oct. 9, 1962.

Sir Edward Mutesa was elected the first President and Milton Obote the first Prime Minister of the newly independent country. With the help of a young army officer, Col. Idi Amin, Prime Minister Obote seized control of the government from President Mutesa four years later.

On Jan. 25, 1971, Col. Amin deposed President Obote. Obote went into exile in Tanzania. Amin expelled Asian residents and launched a reign of terror against Ugandan opponents, torturing and killing tens of thousands. In 1976, he had himself proclaimed President for Life. In 1977, Amnesty International estimated that 300,000 may have died under his rule, including church leaders and recalcitrant cabinet ministers.

After Amin held military exercises on the Tanzanian border, angering Tanzania's President Julius Nyerere, a combined force of Tanzanian troops and Ugandan exiles loyal to former President Obote invaded Uganda and chased Amin into exile.

After a series of interim administrations, President Obote led his People's Congress Party to victory in 1980 elections that opponents charged were rigged.

Obote continued Amin's human rights abuses. The U.S. reported in August 1984 that the abuses—"among the most grave in the world"—included large-scale massacres.

On July, 27, 1985, army troops staged a coup taking over the government. Obote fled into exile. The military regime installed Gen. Tito Okello as chief of state.

The National Resistance Army (NRA), an anti-Obote group led by Yoweri Musevni, kept fighting after being excluded from the new regime. They seized Kampala on January 29, 1986, and Musevni was declared President.

UNION OF SOVIET SOCIALIST REPUBLICS

See Soviet Union

UNITED ARAB EMIRATES

President: Sheikh Zayed Bin Sultan Al-Nahayan (1971)
Prime Minister: Sheik Rashid Bin Said al-Maktoum (1979)
Area: 32,000 sq mi. (82,880 sq km)
Population (est. mid-1987): 1,400,000 (Arab, 42%; South Asian, 50%) (average annual growth rate: 2.6%)
Density per square mile: 43.8
Capital and largest city (est. 1981): Abu Dhabi, 225,000
Monetary unit: Dirham
Language: Arabic
Religion: Islam
Literacy rate: 56%
Economic summary: Gross national product (1983): $25.7 billion. Average annual growth rate (1973–82): 11.5%. Per capita income (1985): $22,710. Land used for agriculture: 8%; labor force: 5%; principal products: vegetables, dates, tobacco, fruit. Labor force in industry: 36%; major products: fish, light manufactures, petroleum, construction materials. Natural resources: oil. Exports: petroleum, dates, fish. Imports: consumer goods, food. Major trading partners: U.K., Japan, U.S., France.

Geography. The United Arab Emirates, in the eastern part of the Arabian Peninsula, extends along part of the Gulf of Oman and the southern coast of the Persian Gulf. The nation is the size of Maine. Its neighbors are Saudi Arabia in the west and south, Qatar in the north, and Oman in the east. Most of the land is barren and sandy.

Government. The United Arab Emirates was formed in 1971 by seven emirates known as the Trucial States—Abu Dhabi (the largest), Dubai, Sharjah, Ajman, Fujairah, Ras al Khaimah and Umm al-Qaiwain.

The loose federation allows joint policies in foreign relations, defense, and development, with each member state keeping its internal local system of government headed by its own ruler. A 40-member legislature consists of eight seats each for Abu Dhabi and Dubai, six seats each for Ras al Khaimah and Sharjah, and four each for the others. It is a member of the Arab League.

History. Originally the area was inhabited by a seafaring people who were converted to Islam in the seventh century. Later, a dissident sect, the Carmathians, established a powerful sheikdom, and its army conquered Mecca. After the sheikdom disintegrated, its people became pirates.

Threatening the sultanate of Muscat and Oman early in the 19th century, the pirates provoked the intervention of the British, who in 1820 enforced a partial truce and in 1853 a permanent truce. Thus what had been called the Pirate Coast was renamed the Trucial Coast.

UNITED KINGDOM

United Kingdom of Great Britain and Northern Ireland

Sovereign: Queen Elizabeth II (1952)
Prime Minister: Margaret Thatcher (1979)
Area: 94,247 sq mi. (244,100 sq km)
Population (est. mid-1987): 56,800,000 (average annual growth rate: 0.2%) (English, Scottish, Welsh, Northern Irish)
Density per square mile: 602.7
Capital: London, England
Largest cities (est. mid-1982): Greater London, 6,765,-100; Birmingham, 1,017,300; Glasgow, 761,000; Leeds, 716,100; Sheffield, 545,800; Liverpool, 510,700; Bradford 464,700; Manchester, 458,600; Edinburgh, 444,700; Bristol, 399,600
Monetary unit: Pound sterling (£)
Languages: English, Welsh, Gaelic
Religions: Church of England (established church); Church of Wales (disestablished); Church of Scotland (established church—Presbyterian); Church of Ireland (disestablished); Roman Catholic; Methodist; Congregational; Baptist; Jewish
Literacy rate: 99.5%
Economic summary: Gross national product (1985): $443.2 billion. Average annual growth rate (1984): 2.0%. Per capita income (1985): $7,860. Land used for agriculture: 29%, principal products: cereals, livestock, and livestock products. Major industrial products: steel, heavy engineering and metal manufactures, textiles, motor vehicles and aircraft, electronics, chemicals. Natural resources: coal, oil, gas. Exports: machinery, transport equipment, chemicals, petroleum. Imports: foodstuffs, petroleum, machinery, chemicals, crude materials. Major trading partners: Western European nations, U.S., West Germany, France.

Geography. The United Kingdom, consisting of England, Wales, Scotland, and Northern Ireland, is twice the size of New York State. England, in the southeast part of the British Isles, is separated from Scotland on the north by the granite Cheviot Hills; from them the Pennine chain of uplands extends south through the center of England, reaching its highest point in the Lake District in the northwest. To the west along the border of Wales—a land of steep hills and valleys—are the Cambrian Moun-

Area and Population of United Kingdom

Subdivision	Area sq mi	Area sq km	Population (est. mid-1983)
England and Wales	58,381	151,207	49,600,000
Scotland	30,414	78,772	5,200,000
Northern Ireland	5,452	14,121	1,600,000
Total	**94,247**	**244,100**	**56,400,000**

tains, while the Cotswolds, a range of hills in Gloucestershire, extend into the surrounding shires.

The remainder of England is plain land, though not necessarily flat, with the rocky sand-topped moors in the southwest, the rolling downs in the south and southeast, and the reclaimed marshes of the low-lying fens in the east central districts.

Scotland is divided into three physical regions—the Highlands, the Central Lowlands, containing two-thirds of the population, and the Southern Uplands. The western Highland coast is intersected throughout by long, narrow sea-lochs, or fiords. Scotland also includes the Outer and Inner Hebrides and other islands off the west coast and the Orkney and Shetland Islands off the north coast.

Wales is generally hilly; the Snowdon range in the northern part culminates in Mount Snowdon (3,560 ft, 1,085 m), highest in both England and Wales.

Important rivers flowing into the North Sea are the Thames, Humber, Tees, and Tyne. In the west are the Severn and Wye, which empty into the Bristol Channel and are navigable, as are the Mersey and Ribble.

Government. The United Kingdom is a constitutional monarchy, with a Queen and a Parliament that has two houses: the House of Lords with about 830 hereditary peers, 26 spiritual peers, about 270 life peers and peeresses, and 9 law-lords, who are hereditary, or life, peers, and the House of Commons, which has 650 popularly elected members. Supreme legislative power is vested in Parliament, which sits for five years unless sooner dissolved.

The executive power of the Crown is exercised by the Cabinet, headed by the Prime Minister. The latter, normally the head of the party commanding a majority in the House of Commons, is appointed by the Sovereign, with whose consent he or she in turn appoints the rest of the Cabinet. All ministers must be members of one or the other house of Parliament; they are individually and collectively responsible to the Crown and Parliament. The Cabinet proposes bills and arranges the business of Parliament, but it depends entirely on the votes in the House of Commons. The Lords cannot hold up "money" bills, but they can delay other bills for a maximum of one year.

By the Act of Union (1707), the Scottish Parliament was assimilated with that of England, and Scotland is now represented in Commons by 71 members. The Secretary of State for Scotland, a member of the Cabinet, is responsible for the administration of Scottish affairs.

The major political parties are the Conservative Party (375 of the 650 seats in the House of Commons), led by Prime Minister Margaret Thatcher; Labour Party (229 seats), led by Neil Kinnock; Social Democrats (5 seats), led by David Owen; Liberal Party (17 seats), led by David Steel; Ulster Unionists and other Northern Irish parties (17 seats); Scottish Nationalist Party (3 seats); Social Democratic and Labour Party (3 seats). The Speaker does not normally vote.

Ruler. Queen Elizabeth II, born April 21, 1926, elder daughter of King George VI and Queen Elizabeth, succeeded to the throne on the death of her father on Feb. 6, 1952; married Nov. 20, 1947, to Prince Philip, Duke of Edinburgh, born June 10, 1921; their children are Prince Charles[1] (heir presumptive), born Nov. 14, 1948; Princess Anne, born Aug. 15, 1950; Prince Andrew, born Feb. 19, 1960; and Prince Edward, born March 10, 1964. The Queen's sister is Princess Margaret, born Aug. 21, 1930. Prince William Arthur Philip Louis, son of the Prince and Princess of Wales and second in line to the throne, was born June 21, 1982. A second son, Prince Henry Charles Albert David, was born Sept. 15, 1984, and is third in line.

History. Roman invasions of the 1st century B.C. brought Britain into contact with the Continent. When the Roman legions withdrew in the 5th century A.D., Britain fell easy prey to the invading hordes of Angles, Saxons, and Jutes from Scandinavia and the Low Countries. Seven large kingdoms were established, and the original Britons were forced into Wales and Scotland. It was not until the 10th century that the country finally became united under the kings of Wessex. Following the death of Edward the Confessor (1066), a dispute about the succession arose, and William, Duke of Normandy, invaded England, defeating the Saxon King, Harold II, at the Battle of Hastings (1066). The Norman conquest introduced Norman law and feudalism.

The reign of Henry II (1154–89), first of the Plantagenets, saw an increasing centralization of royal power at the expense of the nobles, but in 1215 John (1199–1216) was forced to sign the Magna Carta, which awarded the people, especially the nobles, certain basic rights. Edward I (1272–1307) continued the conquest of Ireland, reduced Wales to subjection and made some gains in Scotland. In 1314, however, English forces led by Edward II were ousted from Scotland after the Battle of Bannockburn. The late 13th and early 14th centuries saw the development of a separate House of Commons with tax-raising powers.

Edward III's claim to the throne of France led to the Hundred Years' War (1338–1453) and the loss of almost all the large English territory in France. In England, the great poverty and discontent caused by the war were intensified by the Black Death, a plague that reduced the population by about one third. The Wars of the Roses (1455–85), a struggle for the throne between the House of York and the House of Lancaster, ended in the victory of Henry Tudor (Henry VII) at Bosworth Field (1485).

During the reign of Henry VIII (1509–47), the Church in England asserted its independence from the Roman Catholic Church. Under Edward VI and Mary, the two extremes of religious fanaticism

1. The title Prince of Wales, which is not inherited, was conferred on Prince Charles by his mother on July 26, 1958. The investiture ceremony took place on July 1, 1969. The previous Prince of Wales was Prince Edward Albert, who held the title from 1911 to 1936 before he became Edward VIII.

Rulers of England and Great Britain

Name	Born	Ruled[1]
SAXONS[2]		
Egbert[3]	c.775	828–839
Ethelwulf	?	839–858
Ethelbald	?	858–860
Ethelbert	?	860–866
Ethelred I	?	866–871
Alfred the Great	849	871–899
Edward the Elder	c.870	899–924
Athelstan	895	924–939
Edmund I the Deed-doer	921	939–946
Edred	c.925	946–955
Edwy the Fair	c.943	955–959
Edgar the Peaceful	943	959–975
Edward the Martyr	c.962	975–979
Ethelred II the Unready	968	979–1016
Edmund II Ironside	c.993	1016–1016
DANES		
Canute	995	1016–1035
Harold I Harefoot	c.1016	1035–1040
Hardecanute	c.1018	1040–1042
SAXONS		
Edward the Confessor	c.1004	1042–1066
Harold II	c.1020	1066–1066
HOUSE OF NORMANDY		
William I the Conqueror	1027	1066–1087
William II Rufus	c.1056	1087–1100
Henry I Beauclerc	1068	1100–1135
Stephen of Boulogne	c.1100	1135–1154
HOUSE OF PLANTAGENET		
Henry II	1133	1154–1189
Richard I Coeur de Lion	1157	1189–1199
John Lackland	1167	1199–1216
Henry III	1207	1216–1272
Edward I Longshanks	1239	1272–1307
Edward II	1284	1307–1327
Edward III	1312	1327–1377
Richard II	1367	1377–1399[4]
HOUSE OF LANCASTER		
Henry IV Bolingbroke	1367	1399–1413
Henry V	1387	1413–1422
Henry VI	1421	1422–1461[5]
HOUSE OF YORK		
Edward IV	1442	1461–1483[5]
Edward V	1470	1483–1483
Richard III	1452	1483–1485
HOUSE OF TUDOR		
Henry VII	1457	1485–1509
Henry VIII	1491	1509–1547
Edward VI	1537	1547–1553
Jane (Lady Jane Grey)[6]	1537	1553–1553
Mary I ("Bloody Mary")	1516	1553–1558
Elizabeth I	1533	1558–1603
HOUSE OF STUART		
James I[7]	1566	1603–1625
Charles I	1600	1625–1649
COMMONWEALTH		
Council of State	—	1649–1653
Oliver Cromwell[8]	1599	1653–1658
Richard Cromwell[8]	1626	1658–1659[9]
RESTORATION OF HOUSE OF STUART		
Charles II	1630	1660–1685
James II	1633	1685–1688[10]
William III[11]	1650	1689–1702
Mary II[11]	1662	1689–1694
Anne	1665	1702–1714
HOUSE OF HANOVER		
George I	1660	1714–1727
George II	1683	1727–1760
George III	1738	1760–1820
George IV	1762	1820–1830
William IV	1765	1830–1837
Victoria	1819	1837–1901
HOUSE OF SAXE-COBURG[12]		
Edward VII	1841	1901–1910
HOUSE OF WINDSOR[12]		
George V	1865	1910–1936
Edward VIII	1894	1936–1936[13]
George VI	1895	1936–1952
Elizabeth II	1926	1952–

1. Year of end of rule is also that of death, unless otherwise indicated. 2. Dates for Saxon kings are still subject of controversy. 3. Became King of West Saxons in 802; considered (from 828) first King of all England. 4. Died 1400. 5. Henry VI reigned again briefly 1470–71. 6. Nominal Queen for 9 days; not counted as Queen by some authorities. She was beheaded in 1554. 7. Ruled in Scotland as James VI (1567–1625). 8. Lord Protector. 9. Died 1712. 10. Died 1701. 11. Joint rulers (1689–1694). 12. Name changed from Saxe-Coburg to Windsor in 1917. 13. Was known after his abdication as the Duke of Windsor, died 1972.

were reached, and it remained for Henry's daughter, Elizabeth I (1558-1603), to set up the Church of England on a moderate basis. In 1588, the Spanish Armada, a fleet sent out by Catholic King Philip II of Spain, was defeated by the English and destroyed during a storm. During Elizabeth's reign, England became a world power.

Elizabeth's heir was a Stuart—James VI of Scotland—who joined the two crowns as James I (1603–25). The Stuart kings incurred large debts and were forced either to depend on Parliament for taxes or to raise money by illegal means. In 1642, war broke out between Charles I and a large segment of the Parliament; Charles was defeated and executed in 1649, and the monarchy was then abolished. After the death in 1658 of Oliver Cromwell, the Lord Protector, the Puritan Commonwealth fell to pieces and Charles II was placed on the throne in 1660. The struggle between the King and Parliament continued, but Charles II knew when to compromise. His brother, James II (1685–88), possessed none of his ability and was ousted by the Revolution of 1688, which confirmed the primacy of Parliament. James's daughter, Mary, and her husband, William of Orange, were now the rulers.

Queen Anne's reign (1702–14) was marked by the Duke of Marlborough's victories over France at Blenheim, Oudenarde, and Malplaquet in the War of the Spanish Succession. England and Scot-

British Prime Ministers Since 1770

Name	Term	Name	Term
Lord North (Tory)	1770–1782	Marquis of Salisbury (Conservative)	1886–1892
Marquis of Rockingham (Whig)	1782–1782	William E. Gladstone (Liberal)	1892–1894
Earl of Shelburne (Whig)	1782–1783	Earl of Rosebery (Liberal)	1894–1895
Duke of Portland (Coalition)	1783–1783	Marquis of Salisbury (Conservative)	1895–1902
William Pitt, the Younger (Tory)	1783–1801	Earl Balfour (Conservative)	1902–1905
Henry Addington (Tory)	1801–1804	Sir H. Campbell-Bannerman (Liberal)	1905–1908
William Pitt, the Younger (Tory)	1804–1806	Herbert H. Asquith (Liberal)	1908–1915
Baron Grenville (Whig)	1806–1807	Herbert H. Asquith (Coalition)	1915–1916
Duke of Portland (Tory)	1807–1809	David Lloyd George (Coalition)	1916–1922
Spencer Perceval (Tory)	1809–1812	Andrew Bonar Law (Conservative)	1922–1923
Earl of Liverpool (Tory)	1812–1827	Stanley Baldwin (Conservative)	1923–1924
George Canning (Tory)	1827–1827	James Ramsay MacDonald (Labor)	1924–1924
Viscount Goderich (Tory)	1827–1828	Stanley Baldwin (Conservative)	1924–1929
Duke of Wellington (Tory)	1828–1830	James Ramsay MacDonald (Labor)	1929–1931
Earl Grey (Whig)	1830–1834	James Ramsay MacDonald (Coalition)	1931–1935
Viscount Melbourne (Whig)	1834–1834	Stanley Baldwin (Coalition)	1935–1937
Sir Robert Peel (Tory)	1834–1835	Neville Chamberlain (Coalition)	1937–1940
Viscount Melbourne (Whig)	1835–1841	Winston Churchill (Coalition)	1940–1945
Sir Robert Peel (Tory)	1841–1846	Clement R. Attlee (Labor)	1945–1951
Earl Russell (Whig)	1846–1852	Sir Winston Churchill (Conservative)	1951–1955
Earl of Derby (Tory)	1852–1852	Sir Anthony Eden (Conservative)	1955–1957
Earl of Aberdeen (Coalition)	1852–1855	Harold Macmillan (Conservative)	1957–1963
Viscount Palmerston (Liberal)	1855–1858	Sir Alec Frederick Douglas-Home (Conservative)	1963–1964
Earl of Derby (Conservative)	1858–1859	Harold Wilson (Labor)	1964–1970
Viscount Palmerston (Liberal)	1859–1865	Edward Heath (Conservative)	1970–1974
Earl Russell (Liberal)	1865–1866	Harold Wilson (Labor)	1974–1976
Earl of Derby (Conservative)	1866–1868	James Callaghan (Labor)	1976–1979
Benjamin Disraeli (Conservative)	1868–1868	Margaret Thatcher (Conservative)	1979–
William E. Gladstone (Liberal)	1868–1874		
Benjamin Disraeli (Conservative)	1874–1880		
William E. Gladstone (Liberal)	1880–1885		
Marquis of Salisbury (Conservative)	1885–1886		
William E. Gladstone (Liberal)	1886–1886		

land meanwhile were joined by the Act of Union (1707). Upon the death of Anne, the distant claims of the elector of Hanover were recognized, and he became King of Great Britain and Ireland as George I.

The unwillingness of the Hanoverian kings to rule resulted in the formation by the royal ministers of a Cabinet, headed by a Prime Minister, which directed all public business. Abroad, the constant wars with France expanded the British Empire all over the globe, particularly in North America and India. This imperial growth was checked by the revolt of the American colonies (1775–81).

Struggles with France broke out again in 1793 and, during the Napoleonic Wars, which ended at Waterloo in (1815).

The Victorian era, named after Queen Victoria (1837–1901), saw the growth of a democratic system of government that had begun with the Reform Bill of 1832. The two important wars in Victoria's reign were the Crimean War against Russia (1853–56) and the Boer War (1899–1902), the latter enormously extending Britain's influence in Africa.

Increasing uneasiness at home and abroad marked the reign of Edward VII (1901–10). Within four years after the accession of George V in 1910, Britain entered World War I when Germany invaded Belgium. The nation was led by coalition Cabinets, headed first by Herbert Asquith and then, starting in 1916, by the Welsh statesman David Lloyd George. Postwar labor unrest culminated in the general strike of 1926.

King Edward VIII succeeded to the throne on Jan. 20, 1936, at his father's death, but abdicated on Dec. 11, 1936 (in order to marry an American divorcee, Wallis Warfield Simpson) in favor of his brother, who became George VI.

The efforts of Prime Minister Neville Chamberlain to stem the rising threat of Nazism in Germany failed with the German invasion of Poland on Sept. 1, 1939, which was followed by Britain's entry into World War II on September 3. Allied reverses in the spring of 1940 led to Chamberlain's resignation and the formation of another coalition war Cabinet by the Conservative leader, Winston Churchill, who led Britain through most of World War II. Churchill resigned shortly after V-E Day, May 7, 1945, but then formed a "caretaker" government that remained in office until after the parliamentary elections in July, which the Labor Party won overwhelmingly. The government formed by Clement R. Attlee began a moderate socialist program.

For details of World War II (1939–45), *see* Headline History.

In 1951, Churchill again became Prime Minister at the head of a Conservative government. George VI died Feb. 6, 1952, and was succeeded by his daughter Elizabeth II.

Churchill stepped down in 1955 in favor of Sir Anthony Eden, who resigned on grounds of ill health in 1957, and was succeeded by Harold Macmillan and Sir Alec Douglas-Home. In 1964, Harold Wilson led the Labor Party to victory.

A lagging economy brought the Conservatives

back to power in 1970. Prime Minister Edward Heath won Britain's admission to the European Community.

Margaret Thatcher became Britain's first woman Prime Minister as the Conservatives won 339 seats on May 3, 1979.

An Argentine invasion of the Falkland Islands on April 2, 1982, involved Britain in a war 8,000 miles from the home islands. Although Argentina had long claimed the Falklands, known as the Malvinas in Spanish, negotiations were in progress until a month before the invasion. The Thatcher government responded to the invasion with a 40-ship task force, which sailed from Portsmouth on April 5. U.S. efforts to settle the dispute failed and United Nations efforts collapsed as the Argentine military government ignored Security Council resolutions calling for a withdrawal of its forces.

When more than 11,000 Argentine troops on the Falklands surrendered on June 14, 1982, Mrs. Thatcher declared her intention to garrison the islands indefinitely, together with a naval presence.

The military victory bolstered Conservative fortunes at least temporarily, but economic problems continued for the government. Unemployment had risen to a record 2.91 million by mid-June.

In the general election of June 9, 1983, Prime Minister Thatcher and her Conservative party won a landslide victory over the Laborites and other opponents. The Tories seized 58-seats in the House of Commons, giving the Labor party its worst defeat since 1922.

Although there were continuing economic problems and foreign policy disputes, an upswing in the economy in 1986-87 led Thatcher to call elections for June 11 in which she won a near-unprecedented third consecutive term.

NORTHERN IRELAND

Status: Part of United Kingdom
Secretary of State: James Prior (1981)
Area: 5,452 sq mi. (14,121 sq km)
Population (est. mid-1987): 1,567,000
Density per square mile: 279.7
Capital and largest city (est. mid-1982): Belfast, 324,900
Monetary unit: British pound sterling
Languages: English, Gaelic
Religions: Roman Catholic, 35%; Presbyterian, 29%; Church of Ireland, 24%; Methodist, 5%

Geography. Northern Ireland comprises the counties of Antrim, Armagh, Down, Fermanagh, Londonderry, and Tyrone, which make up predominantly Protestant Ulster and form the northern part of the island of Ireland, westernmost of the British Isles. It is slightly larger than Connecticut.

Government. Northern Ireland is an integral part of the United Kingdom (it has 12 representatives in the British House of Commons), but under the terms of the government of Ireland Act in 1920, it had a semiautonomous government. But in 1972, after three years of internal strife which resulted in over 400 dead and thousands injured, Britain suspended the Ulster parliament. The Ulster counties became governed directly from London after an attempt to return certain powers to an elected Assembly in Belfast.

The Northern Ireland Assembly was dissolved in 1975 and a Constitutional Convention was elected to write a Constitution acceptable to Protestants and Catholics. The convention failed to reach agreement and closed down the next year.

The major political parties are the United Ulster Unionist Coalition (Protestant) (46 of 78 delegates to the Constitutional Convention); Social Democratic Labor Party (Catholic) (17 delegates); Alliance Party (8 delegates); New Unionist Party of Northern Ireland (Protestant) (5 delegates).

History. Ulster was part of Catholic Ireland until the reign of Elizabeth I (1558–1603) when, after crushing three Irish rebellions, the crown confiscated lands in Ireland and settled in Ulster the Scot Presbyterians who became rooted there. Another rebellion in 1641–51, crushed as brutally by Oliver Cromwell, resulted in the settlement of Anglican Englishmen in Ulster. Subsequent political policy favoring Protestants and disadvantaging Catholics encouraged further settlement in Northern Ireland.

But the North did not separate from the South until William Gladstone presented in 1886 his proposal for home rule in Ireland as a means of settling the Irish Question. The Protestants in the North, although they had grievances like the Catholics in the South, feared domination by the Catholic majority. Industry, moreover, was concentrated in the north and dependent on the British market.

When World War I began, civil war threatened between the regions. Northern Ireland, however, did not become a political entity until the six counties accepted the Home Rule Bill of 1920. This set up a semiautonomous Parliament in Belfast and a Crown-appointed Governor advised by a Cabinet of the Prime Minister and eight ministers, as well as a 12-member representation in the House of Commons in London.

As the Republic of Ireland gained its sovereignty, relations improved between North and South, although the Irish Republican Army, outlawed in recent years, continued the struggle to end the partition of Ireland. In 1966–69, communal rioting and street fighting between Protestants and Catholics occurred in Londonderry, fomented by extremist nationalist Protestants, who feared the Catholics might attain a local majority, and by Catholics demonstrating for civil rights.

Rioting, terrorism, and sniping killed more than 2,200 people from 1969 through 1984 and the religious communities, Catholic and Protestant, became hostile armed camps. British troops were brought in to separate them but themselves became a target of Catholics.

In 1973, a new British charter created a 78-member Assembly elected by proportional representation that gave more weight to Catholic strength. It created a Province Executive with committee chairmen of the Assembly heading all government departments except law enforcement, which remained under London's control. Assembly elections in 1973 produced a majority for the new Constitution that included Catholic assemblymen.

Ulster's leaders agreed in 1973 to create an 11-member Executive Body with six seats assigned to Unionists (Protestants) and four to members of Catholic parties. Unionist leader Brian Faulkner headed the Executive. Also agreed to was a Council of Ireland, with 14 seats evenly divided between Dublin and Belfast, which could act only by unanimous vote.

Although the Council lacked real authority, its creation sparked a general strike by Protestant extremists in 1974. The two-week strike caused Faulkner's resignation from the Executive and resumption of direct rule from London.

In April 1974, London instituted a new program that responded to some Catholic grievances, but assigned more British troops to cut off movement of arms and munitions to Ulster's violence-racked cities.

Violence continued unabated, with new heights reached early in 1976 when the Brtish government announced the end of special privileges for political prisoners in Northern Ireland. British Prime Minister James Callaghan visited Belfast in July and pledged that Ulster would remain part of the United Kingdom unless a clear majority wished to separate.

In October 1977, the 1976 Nobel Prize for Peace was awarded to Mairead Corrigan and Betty Williams for their campaign for peace in Northern Ireland. Intermittent violence continued, however, and on Aug. 27, 1979, an I.R.A. bomb killed Earl Mountbatten as he was sailing off southern Ireland.

New talks aimed at a restoration of home rule in Northern Ireland began and quickly ended in January 1980. In May, Mrs. Thatcher met with the new Prime Minister of the Irish Republic, Charles Haughey, but she insisted that the future of Ulster must be decided only by its people and the British Parliament. Haughey declared that an internal solution "cannot and will not succeed."

Civil disturbances reached new heights in the summer of 1981 as Irish nationalist prisoners went on hunger strikes in Maze Prison to attain their demands for "political" status.

Ten nationalists died before the strike ended in August as families of fasters asked that they be fed.

On November 15, 1985, Mrs. Thatcher signed an agreement with Irish Prime Minister Garrett Fitzgerald giving Ireland a consultative role in the affairs of Northern Ireland. It was met with intense disapproval by the Ulster Unionists.

Dependencies of the United Kingdom

ANGUILLA

Status: Dependency
Governor: A.T. Baille (1985)
Area: 35 sq mi. (91 sq km)
Population (1986): 7,000
Monetary unit: East Caribbean dollar
Literacy: 80%

Anguilla was originally part of the West Indies Associated States as a component of St. Kitts-Nevis-Anguilla.

In 1967, Anguilla declared its independence from the St. Kitts-Nevis-Anguilla federation. Britain however, did not recognize this action. In February 1969, Anguilla voted to cut all ties with Britain and become an independent republic. In March, Britain landed troops on the island and, on March 30, a truce was signed. In July 1971, Anguilla became a dependency of Britain and two months later Britain ordered the withdrawal of all its troops.

A new Constitution for Anguilla, effective in February 1976, provides for separate administration and a government of elected representatives. The Associated State of St. Kitts-Nevis-Anguilla ended Dec. 19, 1980.

BERMUDA

Status: Self-governing dependency
Governor: Viscount Dunrossil (1983)
Premier: John Swan (1982)
Area: 20 sq mi. (52 sq km)
Population (est. 1986): 58,000 (average annual growth rate: 0.5%)
Capital (est. 1985): Hamilton, 1,700
Monetary unit: Bermuda dollar
Literacy rate: 98%
Economic summary: Gross national product (1982): $810 million. Average annual growth rate (1982): 4.4%. Per capita income (1981): $12,910. Land used for agriculture: 8%; labor force: 1%; principal products: bananas, vegetables, citrus fruits, dairy products. Labor force in industry: 6.2%; major products: structural concrete, paints, perfumes, furniture. Natural resource: limestone. Exports: semi-tropical produce, light manufactures. Imports: foodstuffs, fuel, machinery. Major trading partners: U.S., U.K., Canada.

Bermuda is an archipelago of about 360 small islands, 580 miles (934 km) east of North Carolina. The largest is (Great) Bermuda, or Long Island. Discovered by Juan de Bermúdez, a shipwrecked Spaniard, early in the 16th century, the islands were settled in 1612 by an offshoot of the Virginia Company and became a crown colony in 1684.

In 1940, sites on the islands were leased for 99 years to the U.S. for air and navy bases. Bermuda is also the headquarters of the West Indies and Atlantic squadron of the Royal Navy.

In 1968, Bermuda was granted a new Constitution, its first Prime Minister, and autonomy, except for foreign relations, defense, and internal security. The predominantly white United Bermuda Party has retained power in four elections against the opposition—the black-led Progressive Laborites—although Bermuda's population is 60% black. Serious rioting occurred in December 1977 after two blacks were hanged for a series of murders, including the 1973 assassination of the Governor, Sir Richard Sharples, and British troops were summoned to restore order.

BRITISH ANTARCTIC TERRITORY

Status: Dependency
High Commissioner: Gordon Wesley Jewkes
Area: 500,000 sq mi. (1,395,000 sq km)
Population (1986): no permanent residents

The British Antarctic Territory consists of the South Shetland Islands, South Orkney Islands, and Nearby Graham Land on the Antarctic continent, largely uninhabited. They are dependencies of the British crown colony of the Falkland Islands but received a separate administration in 1962, being governed by a British-appointed High Commissioner who is Governor of the Falklands.

BRITISH INDIAN OCEAN TERRITORY

Status: Dependency
Commissioner: W. Marsden
Administrator: T.C.S. Stitt
Administrative headquarters: Victoria, Seychelles
Area: 85 sq mi, (220 sq km)

This dependency, consisting of the Chagos Archipelago and other small island groups, was formed in 1965 by agreement with Mauritius and the Seychelles. There is no permanent civilian population in the territory.

BRITISH VIRGIN ISLANDS

Status: Dependency
Governor: D. R. Barwick
Area: 59 sq mi. (153 sq km)
Population (est. 1986): 12,000
Capital (est. 1975): Road Town (on Tortola): 3,500
Monetary unit: U.S. dollar

Some 36 islands in the Caribbean Sea northeast of Puerto Rico and west of the Leeward Islands, the British Virgin Islands are economically interdependent with the U.S. Virgin Islands to the south. They were formerly part of the administration of the Leeward Islands. They received a separate administration in 1956 as a crown colony. In 1967 a new Constitution was promulgated that provided for a ministerial system of government headed by the Governor. The principal islands are Tortola, Virgin Gorda, Anegada and Jost Van Dyke.

CAYMAN ISLANDS

Status: Dependency
Governor: G. P. Lloyd
Area: 100 sq mi. (259 sq km)
Population (est. 1986): 23,000
Capital (est. 1980): Georgetown (on Grand Cayman), 7,600
Monetary unit: Cayman Islands dollar

This dependency consists of three islands—Grand Cayman (76 sq mi; 197 sq km), Cayman Brac (22 sq mi; 57 sq km), and Little Cayman (20 sq mi; 52 sq km)—situated about 180 miles (290 km) northwest of Jamaica. They were dependencies of Jamaica until 1959, when they became a unit territory within the Federation of the West Indies. In 1962, upon the dissolution of the Federation, the Cayman Islands became a British dependency.

The islands' chief export is turtle products.

CHANNEL ISLANDS

Status: Crown dependencies
Lieutenant Governor of Jersey: Adm. Sir William Pillar (1985)
Lieutenant Governor of Guernsey: Sir Alexander Boswell
Area: 75 sq mi. (194 sq km)
Population (est. 1986): 134,000
Capital of Jersey: St. Helier
Capital of Guernsey: St. Peter Port
Monetary units: Guernsey pound; Jersey pound

This group of islands, lying in the English Channel off the northwest coast of France, is the only portion of the Duchy of Normandy belonging to the English Crown, to which it has been attached since the conquest of 1066. It was the only British possession occupied by Germany during World War II.

For purposes of government, the islands are divided into the Bailiwick of Jersey (45 sq mi.; 117 sq km) and the Bailiwick of Guernsey (30 sq mi.; 78 sq km), including Alderney (3 sq mi.; 7.8 sq km); Sark (2 sq mi.; 5.2 sq km), Herm, Jethou, etc. The islands are administered according to their own laws and customs by local governments. Acts of Parliament in London are not binding on the islands unless they are specifically mentioned. The Queen is represented in each Bailiwick by a Lieutenant Governor.

FALKLAND ISLANDS AND DEPENDENCIES

Status: Dependency
Civil Commissioner: Gordon Wesley Jewkes
Area: 4,700 sq mi. (12,173 sq km)
Population est. (1986): 2,000
Capital (est. 1978): Stanley (on East Falkland), 1,100
Monetary unit: Falkland Island pound

This sparsely inhabited dependency consists of a group of islands in the South Atlantic, about 250 miles (402 km) east of the South American mainland. The largest islands are East Falkland and West Falkland. Dependencies are South Georgia Island (1,450 sq mi.; 3,756 sq km), the South Sandwich Islands, and other islets. Three former dependencies—Graham Land, the South Shetland Islands, and the South Orkney Islands—were established as a new British dependency, the British Antarctic Territory, in 1962.

The chief industry is sheep raising and, apart from the production of wool, hides and skins, and tallow, there are no known resources. The whaling industry is carried on from South Georgia Island.

The chief export is wool.

GIBRALTAR

Status: Self-governing dependency
Governor: Sir Peter Terry
Chief Minister: Sir Joshua Hassan
Area: 2.25 sq mi. (5.8 sq km)
Population (est. 1986): 29,000
Monetary unit: Gibraltar pound
Literacy rate: Negligible
Economic summary: Gross national product (1980): $150 million. Average annual growth rate (1970–79): 4.6%. Exports: re-exports of tobacco, petroleum, wine. Imports: manufactured goods, fuels, foodstuffs. Major trading partners: U.K., Morocco, Portugal, Netherlands.

Gibraltar, at the south end of the Iberian Peninsula, is a rocky promonotory commanding the western entrance to the Mediterranean. Aside from its strategic importance, it is also a free port, naval base, and coaling station. It was captured by the Arabs crossing from Africa into Spain in A.D. 711. In the 15th century, it passed to the Moorish ruler of Granada and later became Spanish. It was captured by an Anglo-Dutch force in 1704 during the War of the Spanish Succession and passed to Great Britain by the Treaty of Utrecht in 1713. Most of the inhabitants of Gibraltar are of Spanish, Italian, and Maltese descent.

Spanish efforts to recover Gibraltar culminated in a referendum in 1967 in which the residents voted overwhelmingly to retain their link with Britain. Spain sealed Gibraltar's land border in 1969 and did not open communications until April 1980, after the two governments had agreed to solve their dispute in keeping with a United Nations resolution calling for restoration of the "Rock" to Spain.

HONG KONG

Status: Dependency
Governor: Sir David Wilson
Area: 398 sq mi. (1,031 sq km)
Population (est. mid-1987): 5,600,000 (average annual growth rate: 0.9%)
Density per square mile: 14,321.6
Capital (1976 census): Victoria (Hong Kong Island), 501,-700
Monetary unit: Hong Kong dollar
Literacy rate: 75%
Economic summary: Gross national product (1980): $21.5 billion. Average annual growth rate (1970–79): 6.5%. Per capita income (1980): $4,210. Land used for agriculture: 14%. labor force, 3%; principal products: vegetables, rice, dairy products. Labor force in industry: 45%; major industrial products: textiles, clothing, toys, transistor radios, watches, electronic components. Exports: clothing, textiles, toys, watches, transistor radios, electronic components. Imports: raw materials, consumer goods, food. Major trading partners: U.S., U.K., Japan, West Germany, China.

The crown colony of Hong Kong comprises the island of Hong Kong (32 sq mi.; 83 sq km), Stonecutters' Island, Kowloon Peninsula, and the New Territories on the adjoining mainland. The island of Hong Kong, located at the mouth of the Pearl River about 90 miles (145 km) southeast of Canton, was ceded to the Britain in 1841.

Stonecutters' Island and Kowloon were annexed in 1860, and the New Territories, which are mainly agricultural lands, were leased from China in 1898 for 99 years. Hong Kong was attacked by Japanese troops Dec. 7, 1941, and surrendered the following Christmas. It remained under Japanese occupation until August 1945.

After two years of painstaking negotiation, authorities of Britain and the People's Republic of China agreed in 1984 that Hong Kong would return to Chinese sovereignty on June 30, 1997, when Britain's lease on the New Territories expires. They also agreed that the vibrant capitalist enclave on China's coast would retain its status as a free port and its social, economic, and legal system as a special administrative region of China. Current laws will remain basically unchanged.

Under a unique "One Country, Two Systems" arrangement, the Chinese government promised that Hong Kong's lifestyle would remain unchanged for 50 years, and that freedoms of speech, press, assembly, association, travel, right to strike and religious belief would be guaranteed by law.

Hong Kong will continue to have its own finances and issue its own travel documents, and Peking will not levy taxes.

ISLE OF MAN

Status: Self-Governing Crown Dependency
Lieutenant Governor: Maj. Gen. Laurence A.W. New
Area: 227 sq mi. (588 sq km)
Population (est. 1986): 65,000
Capital (est. 1976): Douglas, 20,300
Monetary unit: Isle of Man pound

Situated in the Irish Sea, equidistant from Scotland, Ireland, and England, the Isle of Man is administered according to its own laws by a government composed of the Lieutenant Governor, a Legislative Council, and a House of Keys, one of the most ancient legislative assemblies in the world.

The chief exports are beef and lamb, fish, and livestock.

LEEWARD ISLANDS

See British Virgin Islands; Montserrat

MONTSERRAT

Status: Dependency
Governor: A. C. Watson (1985)
Area: 40 sq mi. (104 sq km)
Population (est. 1986): 12,000
Capital (est. 1982): Plymouth, 3,500
Monetary unit: East Caribbean dollar

The island of Montserrat is in the Lesser Antilles of the West Indies. Until 1956, it was a division of the Leeward Islands. It did not join the West Indies Associated States established in 1967.

The chief exports are cattle, potatoes, cotton, lint, recapped tires, mangoes, tomatoes.

PITCAIRN ISLAND

Status: Dependency
Governor: B. Young
Island Magistrate: Ivan Christian
Area: 1.75 sq mi. (4.5 sq km)
Population (est. 1986): 55
Capital: Adamstown

Pitcairn Island, in the South Pacific about midway between Australia and South America, consists of the island of Pitcairn and the three uninhabited islands of Henderson, Duicie, and Oeno. The island of Pitcairn was settled in 1790 by British mutineers from the ship *Bounty,* commanded by Capt. William Bligh. It was annexed as a British colony in 1838. Overpopulation forced removal of the settlement to Norfolk Island in 1856, but about 40 persons soon returned.

The colony is governed by a 10-member Council presided over by the Island Magistrate, who is elected for a three-year term.

ST. HELENA

Status: Dependency
Governor: F. E. Baker (1985)
Area: 47 sq mi. (122 sq km)
Population (est. 1986): 9,000
Capital (est. 1982): Jamestown, 1,500
Monetary unit: Pound sterling

St. Helena is a volcanic island in the South Atlantic about 1,100 miles (1,770 km) from the west coast of Africa. It is famous as the place of exile of Napoleon (1815–21).

It was taken for England in 1659 by the East India Company and was brought under the direct government of the Crown in 1834.

St. Helena has two dependencies: Ascension (34 sq mi.; 88 sq km), an island about 700 miles (1,127 km) northwest of St. Helena; and Tristan da Cunha (40 sq mi.; 104 sq km), a group of six islands about 1,500 miles (2,414 km) south-southwest of St. Helena.

TURKS AND CAICOS ISLANDS

Status: Dependency
Governor: Christopher Turner
Area: 193 sq mi. (500 sq km)
Population (est. 1986): 16,000
Capital (est. 1982): Grand Turk, 3,150
Monetary unit: U.S. dollar

These two groups of islands are situated at the southeast end of the Bahamas. The principal islands in the Turks group are Grand Turk and Salt Cay; the principal ones in the Caicos group are South Caicos, East Caicos, Middle (or Grand) Caicos, North Caicos, Providenciales, and West Caicos.

The Turks and Caicos Islands were dependencies of Jamaica until 1959, when they became a unit territory within the Federation of the West Indies. In 1962, when Jamaica became independent, the Turks and Caicos became a British crown colony. The present Constitution has been in force since 1969.

Chief exports in 1974 were crayfish (73%) and conch (25%).

VIRGIN ISLANDS

See British Virgin Islands

UNITED STATES

The United States of America
President: Ronald Reagan (1981)
Area: 3,540,939 sq mi. (9,171,032 sq km)
Population (est. mid-1987): 243,800,000 (average annual growth rate: 0.7%)
Density per square mile: 68.85
Capital (1984 est.): Washington, D.C., 622,823
Largest cities (1984 est.): New York, 7,164,742; Los Angeles, 3,096,721; Chicago, 2,992,472; Houston, 1,-705,697; Philadelphia, 1,646,713; Detroit, 1,088,973
Monetary unit: Dollar
Language: English
Religions: Protestant (73.5 million members); Roman Catholic (50.5 million members); Jewish (5.9 million members)
Literacy rate: 95.5%
Economic summary: Gross national product (1986): $4,-206.1 billion; per capita income (1986): $14,461. Labor force in agriculture: 2.7%; principal products: corn, wheat, barley, oats, sugar, potatoes, soybeans, fruits, beef, veal, pork. Labor force in non-agricultural occupations: 97.3%. Major industrial products: petroleum products, fertilizers, cement, pig iron and steel, plastics and resins, newsprint, motor vehicles, machinery, natural gas, electricity. Natural resources: coal, oil, water power, copper, gold, silver, minerals, timber. Exports: machinery, chemicals, aircrafts, military equipment, cereals, motor vehicles, grains. Imports: crude and partly refined petroleum, machinery, automobiles. Major trading partners: Canada, Japan, United Kingdom, West Germany, Mexico, Saudi Arabia.

Government. The president is elected for a four-year term and may be re-elected only once. In 1987, the bicameral Congress consisted of the 100-member Senate (54 Democrats, 46 Republicans) and the 435-member House of Representatives (261 Democrats, 174 Republicans) which is elected every two years. The minimum voting age is 18.

URUGUAY

Oriental Republic of Uruguay
President: Julio Maria Sanguinetti (1985)
Area: 72,172 sq mi. (186,926 sq km)
Population (est. mid-1987): 3,100,000 (average annual growth rate: 0.8%)
Density per square mile: 42.95
Capital and largest city (est. 1982): Montevideo, 1,325,-000
Monetary unit: Peso
Language: Spanish
Religion: Roman Catholic, 60%
National name: Republica Oriental del Uruguay
Literacy rate: 94%
Economic summary: Gross national product (1984): $5.9 billion. Average annual growth rate (1983): −4.7%. Per capita income (1983): $2,491. Land used for agriculture: 85%; labor force: 12%; principal products: livestock, grains. Labor force in industry: 29%; major products: processed meats, wool and hides, textiles, shoes, handbags and leather wearing apparel, cement, refined petroleum. Natural resources: hydroelectric power potential. Exports: meat, hides, wool, textiles. Imports: crude petroleum, transportation equipment, chemicals, machinery, metals. Major trading partners: U.S., Brazil, Argentina, Nigeria.

Geography. Uruguay, on the east coast of South America south of Brazil and east of Argentina, is comparable in size to the State of Washington.

The country consists of a low, rolling plain in the south and a low plateau in the north. It has a 120-mile (193 km) Atlantic shore line, a 235-mile (378 km) frontage on the Rio de la Plata, and 270 miles (435 km) on the Uruguay River, its western boundary.

Government. After elections in November 1984, Julio Maria Sanguinetti was inaugurated as President on March 1, 1985, ending 12 years of military rule. Under the Constitution, Presidents serve a single five-year term. The bicameral Congress, dissolved by the military in 1973, also was restored in 1985. The three political parties are President Sanguinetti's Colorado Party; the Blanco Party, led by Wilson Ferreira Aldunato; and the left-leaning Broad Front.

History. Juan Díaz de Solis, a Spaniard, discovered Uruguay in 1516, but the Portuguese were first to settle it when they founded Colonia in 1680. After a long struggle, Spain wrested the country from Portugal in 1778. Uruguay revolted against Spain in 1811, only to be conquered in 1817 by the Portuguese from Brazil. Independence was reasserted with Argentine help in 1825, and the republic was set up in 1828.

Independence, however, did not restore order, and a revolt in 1836 touched off nearly 50 years of factional strife, with occasional armed intervention from Argentina and Brazil.

Uruguay, made prosperous by meat and wool exports, founded a welfare state early in the 20th century. A decline began in the 1950s as successive governments struggled to maintain a large bureaucracy and costly social benefits. Economic stagnation and political frustration followed.

A military coup ousted the civilian government in 1973. The military dictatorship that followed used fear and terror to demobilize the population, taking thousands of political prisoners, probably the highest proportion of citizens jailed for political reasons anywhere in the world.

Under the generals, the country's worst economic crisis in decades produced 66% inflation, 30% unemployment and a foreign debt of $5 billion. Per capita income sank to $1,100.

After ruling for 12 years, the military regime permitted election of a civilian government in November 1984 and relinquished rule in March 1985.

VANUATU

Republic of Vanuatu
President: Ati George Sokomanu (1980)
Prime Minister: Fr. Walter Lini (1980)
Area: 5,700 sq mi. (14,763 sq km)
Population (est. mid-1987): 200,000 (average annual growth rate: 3.3%)
Density per square mile: 17.5
Capital (est. 1982): Port Vila, 17,500
Monetary unit: Vatu
Religions: Presbyterian, 47%; Roman Catholic, 15%; Anglican, 15%; other Christian, 10%; Animist, 9%
Literacy rate: 10-20%
Economic Summary: Gross national product (1982): $63 million. Per Capita Income (1982): $530. Average annual growth rate (1970–78): 1.9%. Principal agricultural products: copra, cocoa, coffee, livestock. Exports: copra, cocoa, coffee, frozen fish. Imports: food. Major trading partners: France, New Zealand, Japan, Australia, Netherlands.

Geography. Formerly known as the New Hebrides, Vanuatu is an archipelago of some 80 islands lying between New Caledonia and Fiji in the South Pacific. Largest of the islands is Espiritu Santo (875 sq mi.; 2,266 sq km); others are Efate, Malekula, Malo, Pentecost, and Tanna. The population is largely Melanesian of mixed blood.

Government. The constitution by which Vanuatu achieved independence on July 30, 1980, vests executive authority in a President, elected by an electoral college for a five-year term. A unicameral legislature of 39 members exercises legislative power. The Vanuaaku party, led by Prime Minister Walter Lini, holds 24 seats.

History. The islands were discovered by Pedro Fernandes de Queiros of Portugal in 1606 and were charted and named by the British navigator James Cook in 1774. Conflicting British and French interests were resolved by a joint naval commission that administered the islands from 1887. A condominium government was established in 1906.

The islands' plantation economy, based on imported Vietnamese labor, was prosperous until the 1920s, when markets for its products declined. The New Hebrides escaped Japanese occupation in World War II and the French population was among the first to support the Gaullist Free French movement.

A brief rebellion by French settlers and plantation workers on Espiritu Santo led by Jimmy Stevens in May 1980 threatened the scheduled independence of the islands. Britain sent a company of Royal Marines and France a contingent of 50 policemen to quell the revolt, which the new government said was financed by the Phoenix Foundation, a right-wing U.S. group. With the British and French forces replaced by soldiers from Papua New Guinea, independence ceremonies took place on July 30. The next month it was reported that Stevens had been arrested and the revolt quelled.

VATICAN CITY STATE

Ruler: Pope John Paul II (1978)
Area: 0.17 sq mi. (0.44 sq km)
Population (est. 1985): 1,000 (Italian, 85%; Swiss and others, 15%)
Density per square mile: 5,882.4
Monetary unit: Lira
Languages: Latin and Italian
Religion: Roman Catholic
National name: Stato della Città del Vaticano

Geography. The Vatican City State is situated on the Vatican hill, on the right bank of the Tiber River, within the commune of Rome.

Government. The Pope has full legal, executive, and judicial powers. Executive power over the area is in the hands of a Commission of Cardinals appointed by the Pope. The College of Cardinals is the Pope's chief advisory body, and upon his death the cardinals elect his successor for life. The cardinals themselves are created for life by the Pope.

In the Vatican the central administration of the Roman Catholic Church throughout the world is carried on by 11 congregations, three tribunals, three main secretariats, and numerous councils, committees, and commissions. In its diplomatic relations, the Holy See is represented by the Papal Secretary of State.

History. The Vatican City State, sovereign and independent, is the survivor of the papal states that in 1859 comprised an area of some 17,000 square miles (44,030 sq km). During the struggle for Italian unification, from 1860 to 1870, most of this area became part of Italy.

By an Italian law of May 13, 1871, the temporal power of the Pope was abrogated, and the territory of the Papacy was confined to the Vatican and Lateran palaces and the villa of Castel Gandolfo. The Popes consistently refused to recognize this arrangement and, by the Lateran Treaty of Feb. 11, 1929, between the Vatican and the Kingdom of Italy, the exclusive dominion and sovereign jurisdiction of the Holy See over the city of the Vatican was again recognized, thus restoring the Pope's temporal authority over the area.

The first session of Ecumenical Council Vatican II was opened by John XXIII on Oct. 11, 1962, to plan and set policies for the modernization of the Roman Catholic Church. Pope Paul VI continued the Council, opening the second session on Sept. 29, 1963.

On Aug. 26, 1978, Cardinal Albino Luciani was chosen by the College of Cardinals to succeed Paul VI, who had died of a heart attack on Aug. 6. The new Pope, who took the name John Paul I, was born on Oct. 17, 1912, at Forno di Canale in Italy.

(For a listing of all the Popes, *see* the Index.)

Only 34 days after his election, John Paul I died of a heart attack, ending the shortest reign in 373 years. On Oct. 16, Cardinal Karol Wojtyla, 58, was chosen Pope and took the name John Paul II.

A visit to the Irish Republic and to the United States in September and October 1979, followed by a 12-nation African tour in May 1980 and a visit in July to Brazil, the most populous Catholic nation, further established John Paul's image as a "people's" Pope. On May 13, 1981, a Turkish terrorist shot the Pope in St. Peter's Square, the first assassination attempt against the Pontiff in modern times. Mehmet Ali Agca was sentenced on July 22 to life imprisonment by an Italian Court.

The Pontiff traveled to Britain and Argentina in 1982. He also made another visit to Poland.

On June 3, 1985, the Vatican and Italy ratified a new church-state treaty, known as a concordat, replacing the Lateran Pact of 1929. The new accord affirmed the independence of Vatican City but ended a number of privileges the Catholic Church had in Italy, including its status as the state religion. The treaty ended Rome's status as a "sacred city."

VENEZUELA

Republic of Venezuela
President: Jaime Lusinchi (1984)
Area: 352,143 sq mi. (912,050 sq km)
Population (est. mid-1987): 18,300,000 (average annual growth rate: 2.7%) (mestizo, 67%; white, 21%; black, 10%; Indian, 2%)
Density per square mile: 51.97
Capital: Caracas
Largest cities (est. 1981 for metropolitan area): Caracas, 3,000,000; Maracaibo, 890,000; Valencia, 616,000; Barquisimento, 498,000
Monetary unit: Bolivar
Language: Spanish
Religion: Roman Catholic
National name: Republica de Venezuela
Literacy rate: 85.6%
Economic summary: Gross national product (1983): $70.8 billion. Average annual growth rate (1982): −1.7%. Per capita income (1983): $4,110. Land used for agriculture, 4%; labor force, 16%; principal products: rice, coffee, corn, sugar, bananas, dairy and meat products. Labor force in industry, 23%; principal products: refined petroleum products, iron and steel, paper products, cement, textiles, transport equipment. Natural resources: petroleum, natural gas, iron ore, hydroelectric power. Exports: petroleum, iron ore. Imports: industrial machinery and equipment, manufactures, chemicals, foodstuffs. Major trading partners: U.S., Canada, Japan, Netherland Antilles.

Geography. Venezuela, a third larger than Texas, occupies most of the northern coast of South America on the Caribbean Sea. It is bordered by Colombia to the west, Guyana to the east, and Brazil to the south.

Mountain systems break Venezuela into four distinct areas: (1) the Maracaibo lowlands; (2) the mountainous region in the north and northwest; (3) the Orinoco basin, with the llanos (vast grass-covered plains) on its northern border and great forest areas in the south and southeast; (4) the Guiana Highlands, south of the Orinoco, accounting for nearly half the national territory. About 80% of Venezuela is drained by the Orinoco and its tributaries.

Government. Venezuela is a federal republic consisting of 20 states, the Federal District, two territories and 72 islands in the Caribbean. There is a bicameral Congress, the 52 members of the Senate and the 213 members of the Chamber of Deputies being elected by popular vote to five-year terms. The President is also elected for five years. He must be a Venezuelan by birth and over 30 years old. He is not eligible for re-election until 10 years after the end of his term.

The major political parties are the Democratic Action Party, with 23 of 52 Senate seats and 83 of 213 seats in the Chamber of Deputies; Social Christian Party, with 22 Senate seats and 83 Chamber seats, People's Electoral Movement, Democratic Republican Union.

History. Columbus discovered Venezuela on his third voyage in 1498. A subsequent Spanish explorer gave the country its name, meaning "Little Venice." There were no important settlements until Caracas was founded in 1567. Simón Bolívar, who led the liberation of much of the continent from Spain, was born in Caracas in 1783. With Bolívar taking part, Venezuela was one of the first South American colonies to revolt against Spain, in 1810, but it was not until 1821 that independence was won. Federated at first with Colombia and Ecuador, the country set up a republic in 1830 and then sank for many decades into a condition of revolt, dictatorship, and corruption.

From 1908 to 1935, Gen. Juan Vicente Gómez ruled tyrannically, picking satellites to alternate with him in the presidential palace. Thereafter, there was a struggle between democratic forces and those backing a return to strong-man rule. Dr. Rómulo Betancourt and the liberal Acción Democrática Party won a majority of seats in a constituent assembly to draft a new Constitution in 1946. A well-known writer, Rómulo Gallegos, candidate of Betancourt's party, easily won the presidential election of 1947. But, the army ousted Gallegos the next year and instituted a military junta.

The country overthrew the dictatorship in 1958 and thereafter enjoyed democratic government. Rafael Caldera Rodríguez, President from 1969 to 1974, legalized the Communist Party and established diplomatic relations with Moscow. In 1974, President Carlos Andrés Perez took office.

In 1976, Venezuela nationalized 21 oil companies, mostly subsidiaries of U.S. firms, offering compensation of $1.28 billion. Oil income in that year was $9.9 billion, and although production decreased 2.2%, revenue remained at the same level in 1977 because of higher prices, largely financing an ambitious social welfare program.

Despite difficulties at home, Pérez continued to play an active foreign role in extending economic aid to Latin neighbors, in backing the human-rights policy of President Carter, and in supporting Carter's return of the Panama Canal to Panama.

Opposition Christian Democrats capitalized on Pérez's domestic problems to elect Luis Herrera Campíns President in Venezuela's fifth consecutive free election, on Dec. 3, 1978.

Herrera Campins at first supported U.S. policy in Central America, lining up behind the government of El Salva but he later shifted toward a "political solution" that would include the insurgents. In March 1982, he assailed Reagan's policy as "interventionist."

When the Falklands war broke out, Venezuela became one of the most vigorous advocates of the Argentine cause and one of the sharpest critics of the U.S. decision to back Britain.

Jaime Lusinchi of the Democratic Action party won the country's sixth consecutive free election, on Dec. 4, 1983, and was inaugurated President in March 1984. In 1985, he reached a debt-rescheduling agreement with Venezuela's creditors for its $21-billion debt.

VIETNAM

Socialist Republic of Vietnam
President: Vo Chi Cong (1987)
Premier: Pham Hung (1987)
Area: 127,246 sq mi. (329,566 sq km)
Population (est. mid-1987): 62,200,000 (average annual growth rate: 2.6%)
Density per square mile: 488.82
Capital: Hanoi
Largest cities (est. 1979): Ho Chi Minh City (Saigon),[1] 3,450,000; Hanoi, 2,600,000; Haiphong, 1,280,000; (est. 1973); Da Nang, 492,200; Nha Trang, 216,200; Qui Nho'n, 213,750; Hué 209,000
Monetary unit: Dong
Language: Vietnamese
Religions: Buddhist, Roman Catholic, Islam, Taoist, Confucian, Animist
National name: Công Hòa Xa Hôi Chú Nghia Viêt Nam
Literacy rate: 78%
Economic summary: Gross national product (1983): $9.8 billion. Per capita income (1983): $170. Land used for agriculture: 23%; labor force: 70%; principal products: rice, rubber, fruits and vegetables, corn, sugar cane, fish. Labor force in industry, 5%; major products: processed foods, textiles, cement, chemical fertilizers, glass, tires. Natural resources: forests, coal. Exports: agricultural products, coal, handicrafts. Imports: petroleum, steel products, railroad equipment, chemicals, medicines, raw cotton, fertilizer, grain. Major trading partners: U.S.S.R., Singapore, Japan, India, Hong Kong.

1. Includes suburb of Cholon.

Geography. Vietnam occupies the eastern and southern part of the Indochinese peninsula in Southeast Asia, with the South China Sea along its entire coast. China is to the north and Laos and Cambodia to the west. Long and narrow on a north-south axis, Vietnam is about twice the size of Arizona.

The Mekong River delta lies in the south and the Red River delta in the north. Heavily forested mountain and plateau regions make up most of the country.

Government. Less than a year after the capitulation of the former Republic of Vietnam (South Vietnam) on April 30, 1975, a joint National Assembly convened with 249 deputies representing the North and 243 representing the South. The Assembly set July 2, 1976, as the official reunification date. Hanoi became the capital, with North Vietnamese President Ton Duc Thang becoming President of the new Socialist Republic of Vietnam and North Vietnamese Premier Pham Van Dong becoming its head of government. By 1981, the National Assembly had increased to 496 members. Truong Chinh succeeded Thang in 1981.

Dang Cong san Vietnam (Communist Party), led by General Secretary Nguyen Von Linh, is the ruling political party. There are also the Socialist Party and the Democratic Party.

History. The Vietnamese are descendants of Mongoloid nomads from China and migrants from Indonesia. They recognized Chinese suzerainty until the 15th century, an era of nationalistic expansion, when Cambodians were pushed out of the southern area of what is now Vietnam.

A century later, the Portuguese were the first Europeans to enter the area. France established its influence early in the 19th century and within 80 years conquered the three regions into which the country was then divided—Cochin-China in the south, Annam in the center, and Tonkin in the north.

France first unified Vietnam in 1887, when a single governor-generalship was created, followed by the first physical links between north and south—a rail and road system. Even at the beginning of World War II, however, there were internal differences among the three regions.

Japan took over military bases in Vietnam in 1940 and a pro-Vichy French administration remained until 1945. A veteran Communist leader, Ho Chi Minh, organized an independence movement known as the Vietminh to exploit a confused situation. At the end of the war, Ho's followers seized Hanoi and declared a short-lived republic, which ended with the arrival of French forces in 1946.

Paris proposed a unified government within the French Union under the former Annamite emperor, Bao Dai. Cochin-China and Annam accepted the proposal, and Bao Dai was proclaimed emperor of all Vietnam in 1949. Ho and the Vietminh withheld support, and the revolution in China gave them the outside help needed for a war of resistance against French and Vietnamese troops armed largely by the U.S.

A bitter defeat at Dien Bien Phu in northwest Vietnam on May 5, 1954, broke the French military campaign and brought the division of Vietnam at the conference of Geneva that year.

In the new South, Ngo Dinh Diem, Premier under Bao Dai, deposed the monarch in 1955 and established a republic with himself as President. Diem used strong U.S. backing to create an authoritarian regime that suppressed all opposition but could not eradicate the Northern-supplied Communist Viet Cong.

Skirmishing grew into a full-scale war, with escalating U.S. involvement. A military coup, U.S.-inspired in the view of many, ousted Diem Nov. 1, 1963, and a kaleidoscope of military governments followed. The most savage fighting of the war occurred in early 1968, during the Tet holidays.

Although the Viet Cong failed to overthrow the Saigon government, U.S. public reaction to the apparently endless war forced a limitation of U.S. troops to 550,000 and a new emphasis on shifting the burden of further combat to the South Vietnamese. Ho Chi Minh's death on Sept. 3, 1969, brought a quadrumvirate to replace him but no flagging in Northern will to fight.

U.S. bombing and invasion of Cambodia in the summer of 1970—an effort to destroy Viet Cong bases in the neighboring state—marked the end of major U.S. participation in the fighting. Most American ground troops were withdrawn from combat by mid-1971 as heavy bombing of the Ho Chi Minh trail from North Vietnam appeared to cut the supply of men and matériel to the South.

Secret negotiations for peace by Secretary of State Henry A. Kissinger with North Vietnamese officials during 1972 after heavy bombing of Hanoi and Haiphong brought the two sides near agreement in October. When the Northerners demanded the removal of the South's President Nguyen Van Thieu as their price, President Nixon ordered the "Christmas bombing" of the North. The conference resumed and a peace settlement was signed in Paris on Jan. 27, 1973. It called for release of all U.S. prisoners, withdrawal of U.S. forces, limitation of both sides' forces inside South

Vietnam, and a commitment to peaceful reunification.

Despite Chinese and Soviet endorsement, the agreement foundered. U.S. bombing of Communist-held areas in Cambodia was halted by Congress in August 1973, and in the following year Communist action in South Vietnam increased.

An armored attack across the 17th parallel in January 1975 panicked the South Vietnamese army and brought the invasion within 40 miles of Saigon by April 9. Thieu resigned on April 21 and fled, to be replaced by Vice President Tran Van Huong, who quit a week later, turning over the office to Gen. Duong Van Minh. "Big Minh" surrendered Saigon on April 30, ending a war that took 1.3 million Vietnamese and 56,000 American lives, at the cost of $141 billion in U.S. aid.

On May 3, 1977, the U.S. and Vietnam opened negotiations in Paris to normalize relations. One of the first results was the withdrawal of U.S. opposition to Vietnamese membership in the United Nations, formalized in the Security Council on July 20. Two major issues remained to be settled, however: the return of the bodies of some 2,500 U.S. servicemen missing in the war and the claim by Hanoi that former President Nixon had promised reconstruction aid under the 1973 agreement. Negotiations failed to resolve these issues.

The new year also brought an intensification of border clashes between Vietnam and Cambodia and accusations by China that Chinese residents of Vietnam were being subjected to persecution. Peking cut off all aid and withdrew 800 technicians.

By June, 133,000 ethnic Chinese were reported to have fled Vietnam, and a year later as many as 500,000 of the 1.8 million Vietnamese of Chinese ancestry were believed to have escaped.

Hanoi was undoubtedly preoccupied with a continuing war in Cambodia, where 60,000 Vietnamese troops were aiding the Heng Samrin regime in suppressing the last forces of the pro-Chinese Pol Pot regime. In early 1979, Vietnam was conducting a two-front war, defending its northern border against a Chinese invasion and at the same time supporting its army in Cambodia.

Despite Hanoi's claims of total victory, resistance in Cambodia continued through 1984. Vietnam's second conflict, on its border with China, also flared sporadically.

The Hanoi government agreed in July 1984 to resume technical talks with U.S. officials on the possible whereabouts of the 2,490 Americans still listed as missing, most of them believed dead. In August 1985, the North Vietnamese turned over to an American team 26 numbered crates described as containing the remains of 26 U.S. servicemen.

Economic troubles continued, with the government seeking to reschedule its $1.4-billion foreign hard-currency debt, owed mainly to Japan and the International Monetary Fund. The exodus of the Vietnamese boat people also continued, despite a growing tendency by passing ships not to help the Vietnamese fleeing their country by boat.

Starting in 1984, the Vietnamese government began cracking down on Buddhist and Christian groups in the south, detaining clergymen and establishing government-controlled religious organizations.

(For a Vietnam War chronology, see Headline History, page 127.)

WESTERN SAMOA

Independent State of Western Samoa
Head of State: Malietoa Tanumafili II (1962)
Prime Minister: Va'ai Kolone (1986)
Area: 1,093 sq mi. (2,831 sq km)
Population (est. mid-1987): 200,000 (average annual growth rate: 2.4%)
Density per square mile: 183
Capital and largest city (1980): Apia, 33,400
Monetary unit: Tala
Languages: Samoan and English
Religions: Congregational, 50%; Roman Catholic, 22%; Methodist, 16%
National name: Samoa i Sísífo
Member of Commonwealth of Nations
Literacy rate: 90%
Economic summary: Gross national product (1978): $130 million. Per capita income (1978): $770. Land used for agriculture: 50%; labor force: 50%; principal products: copra, cocoa, bananas, timber. Labor force in industry: 10%; major products: timber, light industrial products. Natural resource: timber. Exports: copra, cocoa, bananas, timber. Imports: food, manufactured goods, machinery. Major trading partners: New Zealand, Australia, U.S., Fiji, Japan

Geography. Western Samoa, the size of Rhode Island, is in the South Pacific Ocean about 2,200 miles (3,540 km) south of Hawaii midway to Sydney, Australia, and about 800 miles (1,287 km) northeast of Fiji. The larger islands in the Samoan chain are mountainous and of volcanic origin. There is little level land except in the coastal areas, where most cultivation takes place.

Government. Western Samoa has a 47-member Legislature, consisting mainly of the titleholders (chiefs) of family groups, with two members elected by universal suffrage to represent those not belonging to such groups. When the present Head of State dies, successors will be elected by the Legislature for five-year terms.

History. The Samoan islands were discovered in the 18th century and visited by Dutch and French traders. Toward the end of the 19th century, conflicting interests of the U.S., Britain, and Germany resulted in a treaty signed in 1899. It recognized the paramount interests of the U.S. in those islands east of 171° west longitude (American Samoa) and Germany's interests in the other islands (Western Samoa); the British withdrew in return for recognition of their rights in Tonga and the Solomons.

New Zealand occupied Western Samoa in 1914, and was granted a League of Nations mandate. In 1947, the islands became a U.N. trust territory administered by New Zealand.

Western Samoa became independent on Jan. 1, 1962.

YEMEN

People's Democratic Republic of Yemen
President: Haider Abubaker Al-Attas (1986)
Area: 111,000 sq mi. (287,490 sq km)[1]
Population (est. mid-1987): 2,400,000 (average annual growth rate: 3.0%)
Density per square mile: 21.62[1]
National capital and largest city (est. 1981): Aden, 365,000
Administrative capital: Aden
Monetary unit: Yemen dinar

Language: Arabic
Religion: Islam (Sunni)
National name: Jumhurijah al-Yemen al Dimuqratiyah al Sha'abijah
Literacy rate: 38.9%
Economic summary: Gross national product (1983): $1, 130 million. Average annual growth rate (1973–78): 12.7%. Per capita income (1983): $510. Land used for agriculture: 0.6%; labor force: 45%; principal products: sorghum, millet, wheat, cotton, goats. Labor force in industry: 14%; major products: refined oil products, salt, fish meal, cloth. Natural resource: fish. Exports: petroleum products, textiles, cotton. Imports: crude oil, foodstuffs, manufactured goods. Major trading partners: U.K., Japan, Yemen Arab Republic, India, Italy, UAE.

1. Excluding Perim and Kamaran islands.

Geography. Formerly known as Southern Yemen, the People's Democratic Republic of Yemen extends along the southern part of the Arabian Peninsula on the Gulf of Aden and the Indian Ocean. It is comparable in size to Nevada. The Yemen Arab Republic is to the northwest, Saudi Arabia to the north, and Oman to the east.

A 700-mile (1,130-km) narrow coastal plain gives way to a mountainous region and then a plateau area.

Government. On June 22, 1969, President Qahtan Mohammed al Shaabi resigned and was replaced by a five-man Presidential Council.

A Constitution published in 1970 changed the state's name from Southern Yemen and established a 111-seat legislature, the People's Supreme Council of which al-Attas is chairman, and thus head of state. The only legal political party is the Yemeni Socialist Party.

History. The People's Republic of Southern Yemen was established Nov. 30, 1967, when Britain granted independence to the Federation of South Arabia. This Federation consisted of the state (once the colony) of Aden and 16 of the 20 states of the Protectorate of South Arabia (once the Aden Protectorate). The four states of the Protectorate that did not join the Federation later became part of Southern Yemen.

Salim Robea Ali, chairman of the Presidential Council since its establishment in 1969, was ousted and executed June 26, 1978, two days after the assassination of President Ahmed Hussein al-Ghashmi of the Yemen Arab Republic. Premier Ali Nasir Muhammad al-Husani assumed the added duty of Council head.

Abdul Fattah Ismail was elected President by the Supreme Council on Dec. 27, 1978 and reversed Robea's movement toward reconciliation with the Yemen Arab Republic and an accommodation with Saudi Arabia. His sudden resignation on April 21, 1980, was reported to have stemmed from the new Soviet desire to win friends in the Yemen Arab Republic and Saudi Arabia.

In December 1985, a purge of Ismail's hardline faction led to a brief civil war in which Ismail was killed but al-Husani was overthrown by Haider al-Attas, an Ismail ally.

YEMEN ARAB REPUBLIC

President: Col. Ali Abdullah Saleh (1978)
Premier: Abdulaziz Abdulghani (1983)
Area: 75,290 sq mi. (195,000 sq km)
Population (est. mid-1987): 6,500,000 (average annual growth rate: 3.4%)
Density per square mile: 86.33
Capital and largest city (est. 1986): San'a', 427,185
Monetary unit: Rial
Language: Arabic
Religion: Islam
National name: Al Jamhuriya al Arabiya Yamaniya
Literacy rate: 15% (est.)
Economic summary: Gross national product (1984): $3.94 billion. Per capita income (1984): $620. Land used for agriculture: 20%; labor force: 74%; principal products: wheat, sorghum, cattle, sheep, cotton, fruits. Major industrial products: consumer goods, construction materials. Natural resources: traces of copper, sulfur, coal, quartz. Exports: cotton, coffee, hides and skins. Imports: textiles and other manufactured consumer goods, petroleum and petroleum products, sugar, grain, flour. Major trading partners: France, Yemen (Aden), Japan, Saudi Arabia, Italy.

Geography. The Yemen Arab Republic, also known as North Yemen, occupies the southwestern tip of the Arabian Peninsula, with its western coast on the Red Sea opposite Ethiopia. Its neighbors are Saudi Arabia to the north and east and the People's Democratic Republic of Yemen to the south. Its area is slightly less than that of South Dakota.

A north-south coastal plain 20–50 miles wide (32–80 km) lies in the west; eastward, there are the interior highlands, which attain a height of 12,000 feet (3,660 m), and the expanse of the Rub 'al-Khali Desert.

Government. The country's first permanent Constitution was submitted to the National Assembly in 1971. It provided for a 179-member legislature, the Consultative Council, 20 of whose members would be chosen by the President and the rest elected every four years. A five-man executive Presidential Council was to be chosen by the Consultative Council.

In 1974, the army ousted the government in a bloodless coup and suspended the Constitution and its various legislative bodies.

History. The history of Yemen dates back to the Minaean kingdom (1200–650 B.C.). It accepted Islam in A.D. 628, and in the 10th century came under the control of the Rassite dynasty of the Zaidi sect. The Turks occupied the area from 1538 to 1630 and from 1849 to 1918. The sovereign status of Yemen was confirmed by treaties signed with Saudi Arabia and Britain in 1934.

Yemen joined the Arab League in 1945 and established diplomatic relations with the U.S. in 1946.

In 1962, a military revolt of elements favoring President Gamal Abdel Nasser of Egypt broke out. A ruling junta proclaimed a republic, and Yemen became an international battleground, with Egypt and the U.S.S.R. supporting the revolutionaries, and King Saud of Saudi Arabia and King Hussein of Jordan the royalists. The civil war continued until the war between the Arab states and Israel broke out in June 1967. Nasser had to pull out many of his troops and agree to a cease-fire and withdrawal of foreign forces. The war finally ended with the defeat of the royalists in mid-1969.

In 1977, Col. Ibrahim al-Hamidi was assassinated after three years as head of government and was succeeded by Lt. Col. Ahmed Hussein al-Ghashmi as head of the Presidential Council. On June 24, 1978, al-Ghashmi was killed by a bomb as he received the credentials of a new ambassador from the People's Democratic Republic of Yemen. The People's Council elected Col. Ali Abdullah Saleh as President on July 17.

In 1984, the Hunt Oil Co. of Dallas discovered oil in North Yemen, the first time it has been found in the desolate Arab state, one of the world's poorest nations. Construction of a pipeline began in 1986 and exports are expected to begin in 1988.

YUGOSLAVIA

Socialist Federal Republic of Yugoslavia
President: Lazar Mojsov (1987)
President of Federal Executive Council (Premier): Branko Mikulic (1986)
Area: 98,766 sq mi. (255,804 sq km)
Population (est. mid-1987): 23,400,000 (average annual growth rate: 0.7%) (Serbian, 36%; Croatian, 20%; Moslem, 9%; Slovene, 8%; Albanian, 8%; Macedonian, 6%, Montenegrin, 3%)
Density per square mile: 236.92
Capital: Belgrade
Largest cities (est. 1982): Belgrade, 1,250,000; Zagreb, 765,000; Skopje, 505,000; Sarajevo, 450,000; Ljubljana, 255,000; Split, 200,000
Monetary unit: Dinar
Languages: Serbo-Croatian, Slovene, Macedonian (all official)
Religions: Greek Orthodox, 41%; Roman Catholic, 32%; Islam, 12%
National name: Socijalisticka Federativna Republika Jugoslavija
Literacy rate: 85%
Economic summary: Gross national product (1984): $128 billion. Average annual growth rate (1984): 1.7%. Per capita income (1984): $5,600. Land used for agriculture: 33%; labor force: 29%; principal products: corn, wheat, tobacco, sugar beets. Labor force in industry: 28%; major products: wood, processed food, nonferrous metals, machinery, textiles. Natural resources: timber, copper, iron, lead, zinc, bauxite. Exports: leather goods, textiles, machinery. Imports: machinery, chemicals, iron, and steel. Major trading partners: U.S.S.R., West Germany, Italy, U.S., Czechoslovakia.

Geography. Yugoslavia fronts on the eastern coast of the Adriatic Sea opposite Italy. Its neighbors are Austria, Italy, and Hungary to the north, Romania and Bulgaria to the east, and Greece and Albania to the south. It is slightly larger than Wyoming.

About half of Yugoslavia is mountainous. In the north, the Dinaric Alps rise abruptly from the sea and progress eastward as a barren limestone plateau called the Karst. Montenegro is a jumbled mass of mountains, containing also some grassy slopes and fertile river valleys. Southern Serbia, too, is mountainous. A rich plain in the north and northeast, drained by the Danube, is the most fertile area of the country.

Government. Yugoslavia is a federal republic composed of six socialist republics—Serbia (which includes the provinces of Vojvodina and Kosovo), Croatia, Slovenia, Bosnia-Herzegovina, Macedonia, and Montenegro. Actual administration is carried on by the Federal Executive Council and its secretaries.

The League of Communists and the Socialist Alliance of the Working People are the major political parties.

History. Yugoslavia was formed Dec. 4, 1918, from the patchwork of Balkan states and territories where World War I began with the assassination of Archduke Ferdinand of Austria at Sarajevo on June 28, 1914. The new Kingdom of Serbs, Croats, and Slovenes included the former kingdoms of Serbia and Montenegro; Bosnia-Herzegovina, previously administered jointly by Austria and Hungary; Croatia-Slavonia, a semi-autonomous region of Hungary, and Dalmatia, formerly administered by Austria. King Peter I of Serbia became the first monarch, his son acting as Regent until his accession as Alexander I on Aug. 16, 1921.

Croatian demands for a federal state forced Alexander to assume dictatorial powers in 1929 and to change the country's name to Yugoslavia. Serbian dominance continued despite his efforts, amid the resentment of other regions. A Macedonian associated with Croatian dissidents assassinated Alexander in Marseilles, France, on Oct. 9, 1934, and his cousin, Prince Paul, became Regent for the King's son, Prince Peter.

Paul's pro-Axis policy brought Yugoslavia to sign the Axis Pact on March 25, 1941, and opponents overthrew the government two days later. On April 6 the Nazis occupied the country, and the young King and his government fled. Two guerrilla armies—the Chetniks under Draza Mihajlovic supporting the monarchy and the Partisans under Tito (Josip Broz) leaning toward the U.S.S.R.—fought the Nazis for the duration of the war. In 1943, Tito established an Executive National Committee of Liberation to function as a provisional government.

Tito won the election held in the fall of 1945, as monarchists boycotted the vote. A new Assembly abolished the monarchy and proclaimed the Federal People's Republic of Yugoslavia, with Tito as Prime Minister.

Ruthlessly eliminating opposition, the Tito government executed Mihajlovic in 1946. With Soviet aid, Tito annexed the greater part of Italian Istria under the 1947 peace treaty with Italy but failed in his claim to the key port of Trieste. Zone B of the former free territory of Trieste went to Yugoslavia in 1954.

Tito broke with the Soviet bloc in 1948 and Yugoslavia has since followed a middle road, combining orthodox Communist control of politics and general overall economic policy with a varying degree of freedom in the arts, travel, and individual enterprise. Tito, who became President in 1953 and President for life under a revised Constitution adopted in 1963, has played a major part in the creation of a "non-aligned" group of states, the so-called "third world."

The Marshal supported his one-time Soviet mentors in their quarrel with Communist China, but even though he imprisoned the writer Mihajlo Mihajlov and other dissenters at home, he criticized Soviet repression of Czecholovakia in 1968.

Tito's death on May 4, 1980, three days before his 88th birthday, removed from the scene the last World War II leader. A rotating presidency designed to avoid internal dissension was put into effect immediately, and the feared clash of Yugoslavia's multiple nationalities and regions appeared to have been averted. A collective presidency, rotated annually among the six republics and two autonomous provinces of the federal republic, continued to govern according to a constitutional change made in 1974.

In March 1981, the Albanian minority, which

forms 80 per cent of the population of the autonomous province of Kosovo, backed Albanian students demonstrating against conditions at the university. By April, the demonstrations had swelled to riots in which 11 were killed as 100,000 people demanded the status of a separate republic, which would enable Kosovo to secede from the Yugoslav federation. Unrest still continues.

ZAIRE

Republic of Zaire
President: Mobutu Sese Seko (1965)
Prime Minister: Kengo Wa Dondo (1982)
Area: 905,365 sq mi. (2,344,885 sq km)
Population (est. mid-1987): 31,800,000 (average annual growth rate: 3.1%)
Density per square mile: 35.12
Capital: Kinshasa
Largest cities (est. 1982): Kinshasa, 3,000,000; Kananga, 800,000; Lubumbashi, 525,000; Mbuji-Maji, 425,000
Monetary unit: Zaire
Languages: French; Bantu dialects, mainly Swahili, Lingala, Ishiluba, and Kikongo
Religions: Roman Catholic 48%, Protestant 29%, Islam 10%
Ethnic groups: Bantu, Sudanese, Nilotics, Pygmies, Hamites
National name: République du Zaïre
Literacy rate: 40% male, 15% female
Economic summary: Gross national product (1983): $5.1 billion. Average annual growth rate: 3.0%. Per capita income (1983): $160. Land used for agriculture: 3%; labor force: 70%, principal products: coffee, palm oil, rubber, sugar, cotton, cocoa, bananas, plantains, vegetables, fruits. Major industrial products: processed and unprocessed minerals. Natural resources: copper, cobalt, zinc, industrial diamonds, manganese, tin, gold, silver, bauxite, iron, coal, 13% of world hydroelectric potential. Exports: copper, cobalt, diamonds, petroleum, coffee. Imports: consumer goods, foodstuffs, mining and other machinery, transport equipment. Major trading partners: Belgium, France, U.S.

Geography. Zaire is situated in west central Africa and is bordered by the Congo, the Central African Republic, the Sudan, Uganda, Rwanda, Burundi, Tanzania, Zambia, Angola, and the Atlantic Ocean. It is one quarter the size of the U.S.

The principal rivers are the Ubangi and Bomu in the north and the Zaire (Congo) in the west, which flows into the Atlantic. The entire length of Lake Tanganyika lies along the eastern border with Tanzania and Burundi.

Government. Under the Constitution approved by referendum in 1967 and amended in 1974, the third Constitution since 1960, the president and a unicameral Legislature are elected by universal suffrage for five-year terms.

In 1971, the government proclaimed that the Democratic Republic of the Congo would be known as the Republic of Zaire, since the Congo River's name had been changed to the Zaire. In addition, President Joseph D. Mobutu took the name Mobutu Sese Seko and Katanga Province became Shaba.

There is only one political party: the Popular Movement of the Revolution, led by President Mobutu.

History. Formerly the Belgian Congo, this territory was inhabited by ancient Negrito peoples (Pygmies), who were pushed into the mountains by Bantu and Nilotic invaders. The American correspondent Henry M. Stanley navigated the Congo River in 1877 and opened the interior to exploration. Commissioned by King Leopold II of the Belgians, Stanley made treaties with native chiefs that enabled the King to obtain personal title to the territory at the Berlin Conference of 1885.

Criticism of forced labor under royal exploitation prompted Belgium to take over administration of the Congo, which remained a colony until agitation for independence forced Brussels to grant freedom on June 30, 1960. Moise Tshombe, Premier of the then Katanga Province seceded from the new republic on July 11, and another mining province, South Kasai, followed. Belgium sent paratroopers to quell the civil war, and with President Joseph Kasavubu and Premier Patrice Lumumba of the national government in conflict, the United Nations flew in a peacekeeping force.

Kasavubu staged an army coup in 1960 and handed Lumumba over to the Katangan forces. A U.N. investigating commission found that Lumumba had been killed by a Belgian mercenary in the presence of Tshombe. Dag Hammarskjold, U.N. Secretary-General, died in a plane crash en route to a peace conference with Tshombe on Sept. 17, 1961.

U.N. Secretary-General U Thant submitted a national reconciliation plan in 1962 that Tshombe rejected. Tshombe's troops fired on the U.N. force in December, and in the ensuing conflict Tshombe capitulated on Jan. 14, 1963. The peacekeeping force withdrew, and, in a complete about-face, Kasavubu named Tshombe Premier to fight a spreading rebellion. Tshombe used foreign mercenaries and, with the help of Belgian paratroops airlifted by U.S. planes, defeated the most serious opposition, a Communist-backed regime in the northeast.

Kasavubu abruptly dismissed Tshombe in 1965 and was himself ousted by Gen. Joseph-Desiré Mobutu, Army Chief of Staff. The new President nationalized the Union Minière, the Belgian copper mining enterprise that had been a dominant force in the Congo since colonial days. The plane carrying the exiled Tshombe was hijacked in 1967 and he was held prisoner in Algeria until his death from a heart attack was announced June 29, 1969.

Mobutu eliminated opposition to win election in 1970 to a term of seven years, which was renewed in a 1977 election. He invited U.S., South African, and Japanese investment to replace Belgian interests. In 1975, he nationalized much of the economy, barred religious instruction in schools, and decreed the adoption of African names.

On March 8, 1977, invaders from Angola calling themselves the Congolese National Liberation Front pushed into Shaba and threatened the important mining center of Kolwezi. France and Belgium responded to Mobutu's pleas for help with weapons, but the U.S. gave only nonmilitary supplies.

In April, France flew 1,500 Moroccan troops to Shaba to defeat the invaders, who were, Mobutu charged, Soviet-inspired, and Cuban-led. U.S. intelligence sources, however, confirmed Soviet and Cuban denials of any participation and identified the rebels as former Katanga gendarmes who had fled to Angola after their 1963 defeat.

On May 15, 1978, a new assault from Angola resulted in the capture of Kolwezi and the death of 100 whites and 300 blacks. In this second invasion,

France and Belgium intervened directly as 1,000 Foreign Legion paratroopers repelled the Katangese and 1,750 Belgian soldiers helped evacuate 2,000 Europeans. The U.S. supplied 18 air transports for both the troop movement and the evacuation. This time President Carter himself backed Mobutu's renewed assertions of Soviet-Cuban participation.

In 1984 and 1985, Zaire and Angola signed bilateral agreements aimed at improved relations, including an agreement not to support rebels in each other's country.

ZAMBIA

Republic of Zambia
President: Kenneth D. Kaunda (1964)
Prime Minister: Kebby Musokotwane (1985)
Area: 290,586 sq mi. (752,618 sq km)
Population (est. mid-1987): 7,100,000 (average annual growth rate: 3.5%)
Density per square mile: 24.4
Capital: Lusaka
Largest cities (est. 1982): Lusaka, 650,000; Kitwe, 345,000; Ndola, 325,000; Chingola, 195,000
Monetary unit: Kwacha
Languages: English and local dialects
Religions: Animist, Roman Catholic, Protestant.
Member of Commonwealth of Nations
Literacy rate: 55.5%
Economic summary: Gross national product (1984): $2.6 billion. Average annual growth rate (1981): –1.85%. Per capita income (1984): $397. Land used for agriculture: 5%; labor force: 9%; principal products: corn, tobacco, fruits, sugar cane. Labor force in industry: 15%; major products: copper, cobalt, chemicals, zinc, fertilizers. Natural resources: copper, zinc, lead, cobalt, coal. Exports: copper, zinc, lead, cobalt, tobacco. Imports: manufactured goods, machinery and transport equipment, foodstuffs. Major trading partners: U.K., Japan, South Africa, U.S., W. Germany.

Geography. Zambia, a landlocked country in south central Africa, is about one tenth larger than Texas. It is surrounded by Angola, Zaire, Tanzania, Malawi, Mozambique, Zimbabwe, Botswana, and SouthWest Africa (Namibia). The country is mostly a plateau that rises to 8,000 feet (2,434 m) in the east.

Government. Zambia (formerly Northern Rhodesia) is governed by a president, elected by universal suffrage, and a Legislative Assembly, consisting of 125 members elected by universal suffrage and up to 10 additional members nominated by the president.

In 1972, the Assembly passed a law making the ruling United National Independence Party, led by President Kenneth D. Kaunda, the only legal political party.

History. Empire builder Cecil Rhodes obtained mining concessions in 1889 from King Lewanika of the Barotse and sent settlers to the area soon thereafter. It was ruled by the British South Africa Company, which he established, until 1924, when the British government took over the administration.

From 1953 to 1964, Northern Rhodesia was federated with Southern Rhodesia and Nyasaland in the Federation of Rhodesia and Nyasaland. On Oct. 24, 1964, Northern Rhodesia became the independent nation of Zambia.

Kenneth Kaunda, the first president, kept Zambia within the Commonwealth of Nations. The country's economy, dependent on copper exports, was threatened when Rhodesia declared its independence from British rule in 1965 and defied U.N. sanctions, which Zambia supported, an action that deprived Zambia of its trade route through Rhodesia. The U.S., Britain, and Canada organized an airlift in 1966 to ship gasoline into Zambia. In 1967, Britain agreed to finance new trade routes for Zambia.

Kaunda visited China in 1967, and China later agreed to finance a 1,000-mile railroad from the copper fields to Dar es Salaam in Tanzania. A pipeline was opened in 1968 from Ndola in Zambia's copper belt to the Indian Ocean at Dar es Salaam, ending the three-year oil drought.

In 1969, Kaunda announced the nationalization of the foreign copper-mining industry, with Zambia to take 51% (over $1 billion, estimated), and an agreement was reached with the companies on payment. He then announced a similar takeover of foreign oil producers.

Zambia suffered heavy damage from bombing raids by the former Rhodesian air force on Zimbabwean guerrilla bases and on its transportation links. These actions, combined with falling prices for copper and cobalt, forced Kaunda to declare a state of economic austerity in January 1981.

A strike by copper-belt workers, in 1981, directed partly against cuts in consumer subsidies and partly at UNIP, the regime's single party, brought a quick victory for the workers after they shut down production. In February, Kaunda installed a new Prime Minister and a new party chief, both more acceptable to the powerful copper-belt unions, and in April, UNIP readmitted union leaders who had been expelled at the time of the strike.

ZIMBABWE

Republic of Zimbabwe
President: Rev. Canaan Banana (1980)
Prime Minister: Robert Mugabe (1980)
Area: 150,699 sq mi. (390,308 sq km)
Population (est. mid-1987): 9,400,000 (average annual growth rate: 3.5%) (black, 98%; white, 2%)
Density per square mile: 62.38
Capital: Harare (Salisbury)
Largest cities (est. 1983 for metropolitan area): Harare, 681,000; Bulawayo, 429,000
Monetary unit: Zimbabwean dollar
Languages: English (official), Ndebele, Shona
Religions: Christian, 25%; Animist 24%; Syncretic 50%
Literacy rate: 30% (blacks), 99% (whites)
Economic summary: Gross national product (1982): $6.6 billion. Average annual growth rate (1980–81): 12%. Per capita income (1982): $870. Land used for agriculture: 6%; labor force: 35%; principal agricultural products: tobacco, corn, sugar, cotton, livestock. Labor force in industry: 25%; major products: steel, textiles, chemicals, vehicles, gold, copper. Natural resources: gold, copper, chrome, nickel, tin, asbestos. Exports: gold, tobacco, asbestos, copper, meat, chrome, nickel, corn, sugar. Imports: machinery, petroleum products, transport equipment. Major trading partners: South Africa, UK

Geography. Zimbabwe, a landlocked country in south central Africa, is slightly smaller than California. It is bordered by Botswana on the west, Zambia on the north, Mozambique on the east, and South Africa on the south.

A high veld up to 6,000 feet (1,829 m) crosses the country from northeast to southwest. This is flanked by a somewhat lower veld that contains ranching country. Tropical forests that yield hardwoods lie in the southeast.

In the north, on the border with Zambia, is the 175-mile-long (128-m) Kariba Lake, formed by the Kariba Dam across the Zambezi River. It is the site of one of the world's largest hydroelectric projects.

Government. Executive power rests with the 26-member Cabinet, headed by the Prime Minister. The President, elected by a majority of the House of Assembly, exercises formal executive powers. The legislature is composed of a 100-member House of Assembly, 80 of whom are elected by black voters and 20 by whites, and a 40-member Senate. Black House members elect 14 Senators and whites elect 10. Ten tribal chiefs—five from Mashonaland and five from Matabeleland—are elected by their peers and six appointed by the President complete the Senate membership.

Major political parties are the Zimbabwe African National Union (66 seats in the House of Assembly), led by Prime Minister Robert Mugabe; Zimbabwe African People's Union (14 seats), led by Joshua Nkomo. The Conservative Alliance, led by former Prime Minister Ian Smith, holds 14 of the 20 seats reserved for whites.

History. Zimbabwe was colonized by Cecil Rhodes's British South Africa Company at the end of the 19th century. In 1923, European settlers voted to become the self-governing British colony of Southern Rhodesia rather than merge with the Union of South Africa. After a brief federation with Northern Rhodesia and Nyasaland in the post-World War II period, Southern Rhodesia chose to remain a colony when its two partners voted for independence in 1963.

On Nov. 11, 1965, the white-minority government of Rhodesia unilaterally declared its independence from Britain.

In 1967, the U.N. imposed mandatory sactions against Rhodesia. The country moved slowly toward meeting the demands of black Africans. The white-minority regime of Prime Minister Ian Smith withstood British pressure, economic sanctions, guerrilla attacks, and a right-wing assault.

On March 1, 1970, Rhodesia formally proclaimed itself a republic, and within the month nine nations, including the U.S., closed their consulates there.

Heightened guerrilla war and a withdrawal of South African military aid—particularly helicopters—marked the beginning of the collapse of Smith's 11 years of resistance in the spring of 1976. Under pressure from South Africa, Smith agreed with the U.S. that majority rule should come within two years.

In the fall, Smith met with black nationalist leaders in Geneva. The meeting broke up six weeks later when the Rhodesian Premier insisted that whites must retain control of the police and armed forces during the transition to majority rule. A British proposal called for Britons to take over these powers.

Divisions between Rhodesian blacks—Bishop Abel Muzorewa of the African National Congress and Ndabaningi Sithole as moderates versus Robert Mugabe and Joshua Nkomo of the Patriotic Front as advocates of guerrilla force—sharpened in 1977 and no agreement was reached. In July, with white residents leaving in increasing numbers and the economy showing the strain of war, Smith rejected outside mediation and called for general elections in order to work out an "internal solution" of the transfer of power.

On March 3, 1978, Smith, Muzorewa, Sithole, and Chief Jeremiah Chirau signed an agreement to transfer power to the black majority by Dec. 31, 1978. They constituted themselves an Executive Council, with chairmanship rotating but Smith retaining the title of Prime Minister. Blacks were named to each cabinet ministry, serving as co-ministers with the whites already holding these posts. African nations and the Patriotic Front leaders immediately denounced the action, but Western governments were more reserved, although none granted recognition to the new regime.

White voters ratified a new constitution on Jan. 30, 1979, enfranchising all blacks, establishing a black majority Senate and Assembly, and changing the country's name to Zimbabwe Rhodesia. A general election on April 24 gave Muzorewa's party 67.3% of the vote.

Muzorewa agreed to negotiate with Mugabe and Nkomo in British-sponsored talks beginning Sept. 9. By December, all parties accepted a new draft constitution, a cease-fire, and a period of British administration pending a general election.

In voting completed on Feb. 29, 1980, Mugabe's ZANU-Patriotic Front party won 57 of the 80 Assembly seats reserved for blacks. Nkomo's ZAPU-Patriotic Front party won 20 seats and Muzorewa's United African National Council only three. In an earlier vote on Feb. 14, the Rhodesian Front won all 20 seats reserved for whites in the Assembly.

At a ceremony on April 18, Prince Charles of Britain handed to President-elect Rev. Canaan Banana the symbols of independence. Mugabe, a Marxist, had already pledged his support for continuation of the existing free-market economy.

On April 18, 1980, Britain formally recognized the independence of Zimbabwe.

In January 1981, Mugabe dismissed Nkomo as Home Minister and his onetime rival left the government in protest. At the same time, the Prime Minister discharged Edgar Z. Tekere, Manpower and Planning Minister, who had been tried and acquitted of the murder of a white farmer.

Mugabe survived both tests and scored an unprecedented triumph when, in response to his appeal for economic aid, Western nations pledged $1.8 billion for the next three years.

The 1985 harvest was good in Zimbabwe and the country could feed itself. But political turmoil and civil strife continued. In what Western analysts viewed as a free and fair election, President Mugabe's African National Union increased its sizeable majority in the House of Assembly but Mugabe was frustrated because it did not win the 70 seats he sought to cement one-party rule. After the election, Mugabe cracked down on Nkomo's ZAPU-Patriotic Front party.

Pressure on ZAPU has alternated with efforts to bring about a ZANU-ZAPU union as part of Mugabe's plans for one-party rule.

(For late reports, see Current Events of 1986-1987)

UNITED NATIONS

The 159 Members of the United Nations

Country	Joined U.N.[1]
Afghanistan	1946
Albania	1955
Algeria	1962
Angola	1976
Antigua and Barbuda	1981
Argentina	1945
Australia	1945
Austria	1955
Bahamas	1973
Bahrain	1971
Bangladesh	1974
Barbados	1966
Belgium	1945
Belize	1981
Benin	1960
Bhutan	1971
Bolivia	1945
Botswana	1966
Brazil	1945
Brunei	1984
Bulgaria	1955
Burkina Faso	1960
Burma	1948
Burundi	1962
Byelorussian S.S.R.	1945
Cambodia	1955
Cameroon	1960
Canada	1945
Cape Verde	1975
Central African Republic	1960
Chad	1960
Chile	1945
China[2]	1945
Colombia	1945
Comoros	1975
Congo	1960
Costa Rica	1945
Cuba	1945
Cyprus	1960
Czechoslovakia	1945
Denmark	1945
Djibouti	1977
Dominica	1978
Dominican Republic	1945
Ecuador	1945
Egypt	1945
El Salvador	1945
Equatorial Guinea	1968
Ethiopia	1945
Fiji	1970
Finland	1955
France	1945
Gabon	1960
Gambia	1965
Germany, East	1973
Germany, West	1973
Ghana	1957
Greece	1945
Grenada	1974
Guatemala	1945
Guinea	1958
Guinea-Bissau	1974
Guyana	1966
Haiti	1945
Honduras	1945
Hungary	1955
Iceland	1946
India	1945
Indonesia	1950
Iran	1945
Iraq	1945
Ireland	1955
Israel	1949
Italy	1955
Ivory Coast	1960
Jamaica	1962
Japan	1956
Jordan	1955
Kenya	1963
Kuwait	1963
Laos	1955
Lebanon	1945
Lesotho	1966
Liberia	1945
Libya	1955
Luxembourg	1945
Madagascar	1960
Malawi	1964
Malaysia	1957
Maldives	1965
Mali	1960
Malta	1964
Mauritania	1961
Mauritius	1968
Mexico	1945
Mongolia	1961
Morocco	1956
Mozambique	1975
Nepal	1955
Netherlands	1945
New Zealand	1945
Nicaragua	1945
Niger	1960
Nigeria	1960
Norway	1945
Oman	1971
Pakistan	1947
Panama	1945
Papua New Guinea	1975
Paraguay	1945
Peru	1945
Philippines	1945
Poland	1945
Portugal	1955
Qatar	1971
Romania	1955
Rwanda	1962
St. Kitts and Nevis	1983
St. Lucia	1979
St. Vincent and the Grenadines	1980
São Tomé and Príncipe	1975
Saudi Arabia	1945
Senegal	1960
Seychelles	1976
Sierra Leone	1961
Singapore	1965
Solomon Islands	1978
Somalia	1960
South Africa	1945
Spain	1955
Sri Lanka	1955
Sudan	1956
Suriname	1975
Swaziland	1968
Sweden	1946
Syria	1945
Tanzania	1961
Thailand	1946
Togo	1960
Trinidad and Tobago	1962
Tunisia	1956
Turkey	1945
Uganda	1962
Ukrainian S.S.R.	1945
U.S.S.R.	1945
United Arab Emirates	1971
United Kingdom	1945
United States	1945
Uruguay	1945
Vanuatu	1981
Venezuela	1945
Vietnam	1977
Western Samoa	1976
Yemen Arab Republic	1947
Yemen, People's Dem. Republic of	1967
Yugoslavia	1945
Zaire	1960
Zambia	1964
Zimbabwe	1980

1. The U.N. officially came into existence on Oct. 24, 1945. 2. On Oct. 25, 1971, the U.N. voted membership to the People's Republic of China, which replaced the Republic of China (Taiwan) in the world body.

Six Official Languages Used by U.N.

There are six official working languages recognized by the United Nations. They are Chinese, English, French, Russian, and Spanish, which have been in use since the world body was organized, and Arabic, which was added by the General Assembly in 1973 and by the Security Council in 1982.

Member Countries' Assessments to U.N. Budget, 1987

Country	Total	Country	Total	Country	Total
Afghanistan	$72,454	Gambia	72,454	Panama	144,906
Albania	72,454	Germany, East	9,636,338	Papua New Guinea	72,454
Algeria	1,014,351	Germany, West	59,846,735	Paraguay	144,906
Angola	72,454	Ghana	72,454	Peru	507,176
Antigua and Barbuda	72,454	Greece	3,187,962	Philippines	724,537
Argentina	4,492,128	Grenada	72,454	Poland	4,637,035
Australia	12,027,310	Guatemala	144,906	Portugal	1,304,166
Austria	5,361,572	Guinea	72,454	Qatar	289,813
Bahamas	72,454	Guinea-Bissau	72,454	Romania	1,376,620
Bahrain	144,906	Guyana	72,454	Rwanda	72,454
Bangladesh	144,906	Haiti	72,454	Saint Kitts and Nevis	72,454
Barbados	72,454	Honduras	72,454	St. Lucia	72,454
Belgium	8,549,533	Hungary	1,593,981	St. Vincent and the Grenadines	72,454
Belize	72,454	Iceland	217,360	São Tomé and Príncipe	72,454
Benin	200,826	India	2,535,879	Saudi Arabia	7,028,006
Bhutan	72,454	Indonesia	1,014,351	Senegal	72,454
Bolivia	72,454	Iran	4,564,582	Seychelles	72,454
Botswana	72,454	Iraq	869,444	Sierra Leone	72,454
Brazil	10,143,514	Ireland	1,304,166	Singapore	724,537
Brunei Darussalam	289,813	Israel	1,593,981	Solomon Islands	72,454
Bulgaria	1,159,259	Italy	27,459,942	Somalia	72,454
Burkina Faso	72,454	Jamaica	144,906	South Africa	3,187,962
Burma	72,454	Japan	78,539,783	Spain	14,708,096
Burundi	72,454	Jordan	72,454	Sri Lanka	72,454
Byelorussian SSR	2,463,425	Kenya	72,454	Sudan	72,454
Cambodia	72,454	Kuwait	2,101,157	Suriname	72,454
Cameroon	72,454	Laos	72,454	Swaziland	72,454
Canada	22,184,754	Lebanon	72,454	Sweden	9,056,709
Cape Verde	72,454	Lesotho	72,454	Syria	289,813
Central African Republic	72,454	Liberia	72,454	Tanzania	72,454
Chad	72,454	Libya	1,883,796	Thailand	652,083
Chile	507,176	Luxembourg	362,270	Togo	72,454
China	5,723,840	Madagascar	72,454	Trinidad and Tobago	289,813
Colombia	941,897	Malawi	72,454	Tunisia	217,360
Comoros	72,454	Malaysia	724,537	Turkey	2,465,021
Congo	72,454	Maldives	72,454	Uganda	72,454
Costa Rica	144,906	Mali	72,454	Ukrainian SSR	9,274,070
Cote D'Ivoire	144,906	Malta	72,454	U.S.S.R.	73,902,748
Cuba	652,083	Mauritania	72,454	United Arab Emirates	1,304,166
Cyprus	144,906	Mauritius	72,454	United Kingdom	35,212,486
Czechoslovakia	5,071,757	Mexico	6,448,352	United States	212,875,525
Denmark	5,216,665	Mongolia	72,454	Uruguay	289,813
Djibouti	72,454	Morocco	362,270	Vanuatu	72,454
Dominica	72,454	Mozambique	72,454	Venezuela	4,347,220
Dominican Republic	217,360	Nepal	72,454	Vietnam	72,454
Ecuador	217,360	Netherlands	12,606,939	Western Samoa	72,454
Egypt	507,176	New Zealand	1,738,889	Yemen Arab Republic	72,454
El Salvador	72,454	Nicaragua	72,454	Yemen, People's Dem. Republic of	72,454
Equatorial Guinea	72,454	Niger	72,454	Yugoslavia	3,332,869
Ethiopia	72,454	Nigeria	1,376,620	Zaire	72,454
Fiji	72,454	Norway	3,912,499	Zambia	72,454
Finland	3,622,684	Oman	144,906	Zimbabwe	144,906
France	46,152,990	Pakistan	434,722	**TOTAL**	**756,293,609**
Gabon	217,360				

United Nations Headquarters

The first regular session of the General Assembly held at Central Hall, Westminster, London, voted that interim headquarters of the Organization should be located in New York. From London the U.N. moved to Hunter College in the Bronx. In August 1946, an interim headquarters was set up at Lake Success on Long Island. The New York City building at Flushing Meadows, site of the 1939 World's Fair, was converted for the use of the General Assembly. The search for a permanent home ended in December 1946, when the General Assembly accepted an offer from John D. Rockefeller, Jr., of $8,500,000[1] for the purchase of the present Headquarters site—an 18-acre tract in Manhattan, alongside the East River. The U.S. Government lent the U.N. $65,000,000 interest free, which is being repaid in annual installments.

Architectural plans drawn up by an international Board of Design were approved by the Assembly, and construction began in September 1948. By mid-1950, the 39-story Secretariat Building was ready for occupancy, and in the spring of 1951 "United Nations, New York" became the Organization's permanent address.

1. This amount paid for two-thirds of the land; New York City gave one-third.

Preamble of the United Nations Charter

The Charter of the United Nations was adopted at the San Francisco Conference of 1945. The complete text may be obtained by writing to the United Nations Sales Section, United Nations, New York, N.Y. 10017, and enclosing $1.

We the peoples of the United Nations determined to save succeeding generations from the scourge of war, which twice in our lifetime has brought untold sorrow to mankind, and

To reaffirm faith in fundamental human rights, in the dignity and worth of the human person, in the equal rights of men and women and of nations large and small, and

To establish conditions under which justice and respect for the obligations arising from treaties and other sources of international law can be maintained, and

To promote social progress and better standards of life in larger freedom, and for these ends

To practice tolerance and live together in peace with one another as good neighbors, and

To unite our strength to maintain international peace and security, and

To insure, by the acceptance of principles and the institution of methods, that armed force shall not be used, save in the common interest, and

To employ international machinery for the promotion of the economic and social advancement of all peoples, have resolved to combine our efforts to accomplish these aims.

Accordingly, our respective Governments, through representatives assembled in the city of San Francisco, who have exhibited their full powers found to be in good and due form, have agreed to the present Charter of the United Nations and do hereby establish an international organization to be known as the United Nations.

Principal Organs of the United Nations

Secretariat

This is the directorate on U.N. operations, apart from political decisions. All members contribute to its upkeep. Its staff of over 6,000 specialists is recruited from member nations on the basis of as wide a geographical distribution as possible. The staff works under the Secretary-General, whom it assists and advises.

Secretaries-General

Javier Pérez de Cuéllar, Peru, Jan. 1, 1982.
Kurt Waldheim, Austria, Jan. 1, 1972, to Dec. 31, 1981.
U Thant, Burma, Nov. 3, 1961, to Dec. 31, 1971.
Dag Hammarskjöld, Sweden, April 11, 1953, to Sept. 17, 1961.
Trygve Lie, Norway, Feb. 1, 1946, to April 10, 1953.

General Assembly

The General Assembly is the world's forum for discussing matters affecting world peace and security, and for making recommendations concerning them. It has no power of its own to enforce decisions.

The Assembly is composed of the 51 original member nations and those admitted since, a total of 159. Each nation has one vote. On important questions including international peace and security, a two-thirds majority of those present and voting is required. Decisions on other questions are made by a simple majority.

The Assembly's agenda can be as broad as the Charter. It can make recommendations to member nations, the Security Council, or both. Emphasis is given on questions relating to international peace and security brought before it by any member, the Security Council, or nonmembers.

The Assembly also maintains a broad program of international cooperation in economic, social, cultural, educational, and health fields, and for assisting in human rights and freedoms.

Among other duties, the Assembly has functions relating to the trusteeship system, and considers and approves the U.N. Budget. Every member contributes to operating expenses according to its means.

Security Council

The Security Council is the primary instrument for establishing and maintaining international peace. Its main purpose is to prevent war by settling disputes between nations.

Under the Charter, the Council is permitted to dispatch a U.N. force to stop aggression. All member nations undertake to make available armed forces, assistance, and facilities to maintain international peace and security.

Any member may bring a dispute before the Security Council or the General Assembly. Any nonmember may do so if it accepts the charter obligations of pacific settlement.

The Security Council has 15 members. There are five permanent members: the United States, the Soviet Union, Britain, France, and China; and 10 temporary members elected by the General Assembly for two-year terms, from five different regions of the world.

Voting on procedural matters requires a nine-vote majority to carry. However, on questions of substance, the vote of each of the five permanent members is required.

Current temporary members are (term expires Dec. 31, 1987): Bulgaria, Congo, Ghana, United Arab Emirates, Venezuela; (term expires Dec. 31, 1988): Argentina, Germany, West, Italy, Japan, and Zambia.

Economic and Social Council

This council is composed of 54 members elected by the General Assembly to 3-year terms. It works closely with the General Assembly as a link with groups formed within the U.N. to help peoples in such fields as education, health, and human rights. It insures that there is no overlapping and sets up commissions to deal with economic conditions and collect facts and figures on conditions over the world. It issues studies and reports and may make recommendations to the Assembly and specialized agencies.

Functional Commissions

Statistical Commission; Population Commission; Commission for Social Development; Commission on Human Rights; Commission on the Status of Women; Commission on Narcotic Drugs.

Regional Commissions

Economic Commission for Europe (ECE); Economic and Social Commission for Asia and the Pacific (ESCAP); Economic Commission for Latin America and the Caribbean (ECLAC); Economic Commission for Africa (ECA); Economic and Social Commission for Western Asia (ESCWA).

Trusteeship Council

This council supervises territories administered by various nations and placed under an international trusteeship system by the United Nations. Each nation is charged with developing the self-government of the territory and preserving and advancing the cultural, political, economic, and other forms of welfare of the people.

The Trusteeship Council is currently composed of 5 members: 1 member—the United States—that administers a trust territory, and 4 members—China, France, the Soviet Union, and the United Kingdom—that are permanent members of the Security Council but do not administer trust territories.

The following countries ceased to be administering members because of the independence of territories they had administered: Italy and France in 1960, Belgium in 1962, New Zealand and the United Kingdom in 1968 and Australia in 1975. France and the U.K. became nonadministering members.

As of December 1985, there was only one trust territory: the Trust Territory of the Pacific Islands (administered by the United States).

International Court of Justice

The International Court of Justice sits at The Hague, the Netherlands. Its 15-judge bench was established to hear disputes among states, which must agree to accept its verdicts. Its judges, charged with administering justice under international law, deal with cases ranging from disputes over territory to those concerning rights of passage.

Following are the members of the Court and the years in which their terms expire:

President: Nagendra Singh, India (1991)
Vice President: Keba Mbaye, Senegal V.P. 1988 (1991)
Jose Sette Camara, Brazil (1988)
Nikolai Tarasov, U.S.S.R. (1988)
Roberto Ago, Italy (1988)
Stephen Schwebel, U.S. (1988)
Mohammed Bedjaoui, Algeria (1988)
Jose Maria Ruda, Argentina (1991)
Robert Y. Jennings, United Kingdom (1991)
Taslim Olawale Elias, Nigeria (1994)
Jens Evensen, Norway (1994)
Ni Zhengyu, China (1994)
Manfred Lachs, Poland (1994)
Shigeru Oda, Japan (1994)

Agencies of the United Nations

INTL. ATOMIC ENERGY AGENCY (IAEA)

Established: Statute for IAEA, approved on Oct. 26, 1956, at a conference held at U.N. Headquarters, New York, came into force on July 29, 1957. The Agency is under the aegis of the U.N., but unlike the following, it is not a specialized agency.

Purpose: To promote the peaceful uses of atomic energy; to ensure that assistance provided by it or at its request or under its supervision or control is not used in such a way as to further any military purpose.

Headquarters: Vienna International Center, P.O. Box 100, A-1400 Vienna, Austria

FOOD AND AGRICULTURE ORGANIZATION OF THE UNITED NATIONS (FAO)

Established: October 16, 1945, when constitution became effective.

Purpose: To raise nutrition levels and living standards; to secure improvements in production and distribution of food and agricultural products.

Headquarters: Via delle Terme di Caracalla, 00100, Rome, Italy.

GENERAL AGREEMENT ON TARIFFS AND TRADE (GATT)

Established: Jan. 1, 1948.

Purpose: An International Trade Organization (ITO) was originally planned. Although this agency has not materialized, some of its objectives have been embodied in an international commercial treaty, the General Agreement on Tariffs and Trade. Its purpose is to sponsor trade negotiations.

Headquarters: Centre William Rappard, 154 Rue de Lausanne, 1211, Geneva 21, Switzerland.

INTERNATIONAL BANK FOR RECONSTRUCTION AND DEVELOPMENT (IBRD) (WORLD BANK)

Established: December 27, 1945, when Articles of Agreement drawn up at Bretton Woods Conference in July 1944 came into force. Began operations on June 25, 1946.

Purpose: To assist in reconstruction and development of economies of members by facilitating capital investment and by making loans to governments and furnishing technical advice.

Headquarters: 1818 H St., N.W., Washington, D.C. 20433.

INTL. CIVIL AVIATION ORGANIZATION (ICAO)

Established: April 4, 1947, after working as a provisional organization since June 1945.

Purpose: To study problems of international civil aviation; to establish international standards and regulations; to promote safety measures, uniform regulations for operation, simpler procedures at international borders, and the use of new technical methods and equipment. It has evolved standards for meteorological services, traffic control, communications, radio beacons and ranges, search and rescue organization, and other facilities. It has brought about much simplification of customs, immigration, and public health regulations as they apply to international air transport. It drafts international air law conventions, and is concerned with economic aspects of air travel.

Headquarters: International Aviation Square, 1000 Sherbrooke St. West, Montreal, Quebec, H3A 2R2, Canada.

INTL. DEVELOPMENT ASSOCIATION (IDA)

Established: Sept. 24, 1960. An affiliate of the World Bank, IDA has the same officers and staff as the Bank.

Purpose: To further economic development of its members by providing finance on terms which bear less heavily on balance of payments of members than those of conventional loans.

Headquarters: 1818 H St., N.W., Washington, D.C. 20433.

INTERNATIONAL FINANCE CORPORATION (IFC)

Established: Charter of IFC came into force on July 20, 1956. Although IFC is affiliated with the World Bank, it is a separate legal entity, and its funds are entirely separate from those of the Bank. However, membership in the Corporation is open only to Bank members.

Purpose: To further economic development by encouraging the growth of productive private enterprise in its member countries, particularly in the less developed areas; to invest in productive private enterprises in association with private investors, without government guarantee of repayment where sufficient private capital is not available on reasonable terms; to serve as a clearing house to bring together investment opportunities, private capital (both foreign and domestic), and experienced management.

Headquarters: 1818 H St., N.W., Washington, D.C. 20433.

INTERNATIONAL FUND FOR AGRICULTURAL DEVELOPMENT (IFAD)

Established: June 18, 1976. Began operations in December 1977.

Purpose: To mobilize additional funds for agricultural and rural development in developing countries through projects and programs directly benefiting the poorest rural populations.

Headquarters: 107 Via del Serafico, 00142, Rome, Italy.

INTERNATIONAL LABOR ORGANIZATION (ILO)

Established: April 11, 1919, when constitution was adopted as Part XIII of Treaty of Versailles. Became specialized agency of U.N. in 1946.

Purpose: To contribute to establishment of lasting peace by promoting social justice; to improve labor conditions and living standards through international action; to promote economic and social stability. The U.S. withdrew from the ILO in 1977 and resumed membership in 1980.

Headquarters: 4, route des Morillons, CH-1211 Geneva 22, Switzerland.

INTERNATIONAL MARITIME ORGANIZATION (IMO)

Established: March 17, 1958.

Purpose: To give advisory and consultative help to promote international cooperation in maritime navigation and to encourage the highest standards of safety and navigation. Its aim is to bring about a uniform system of measuring ship tonnage; systems now vary widely in different parts of the world. Other activities include cooperation with other U.N. agencies on matters affecting the maritime field.

Headquarters: 4 Albert Embankment, London SE 1 7SR England.

INTERNATIONAL MONETARY FUND (IMF)

Established: Dec. 27, 1945, when Articles of Agreement drawn up at Bretton Woods Conference in July 1944 came into force. Fund began operations on March 1, 1947.

Purpose: To promote international monetary cooperation and expansion of international trade; to promote exchange stability; to assist in establishment of multilateral system of payments in respect of currency transactions between members.

Headquarters: 700 19th St., N.W., Washington, D.C. 20431.

INTERNATIONAL TELECOMMUNICATION UNION (ITU)

Established: 1865. Became specialized agency of U.N. in 1947.

Purpose: To extend technical assistance to help members keep up with present day telecommunication needs; to standardize communications equipment and procedures; to lower costs. It also works for orderly sharing of radio frequencies and makes studies and recommendations to benefit its members.

Headquarters: Place des Nations, 1211 Geneva 20, Switzerland.

UNITED NATIONS EDUCATIONAL, SCIENTIFIC, AND CULTURAL ORGANIZATION (UNESCO)

Established: Nov. 4, 1946, when twentieth signatory to constitution deposited instrument of acceptance with government of U.K.

Purpose: To promote collaboration among nations through education, science, and culture in order to further justice, rule of law, and human rights and freedoms without distinction of race, sex, language, or religion.

Headquarters: UNESCO House. Place de Fontenoy, 7e, Paris, France.

UNITED NATIONS INDUSTRIAL DEVELOPMENT ORGANIZATION (UNIDO)

Established: Nov. 17, 1966. Became specialized agency of the U.N. in 1985.

Purpose: To promote and accelerate the industrialization of the developing countries.

Headquarters: UNIDO, Vienna International Centre, P.O. Box 300, A-1400 Vienna, Austria.

UNIVERSAL POSTAL UNION (UPU)

Established: Oct. 9, 1874. Became specialized agency of U.N. in 1947.

Purpose: To facilitate reciprocal exchange of correspondence by uniform procedures by all UPU members; to help governments modernize and speed up mailing procedures.

Headquarters: Weltpostrasse 4, Berne, Switzerland.

WORLD HEALTH ORGANIZATION (WHO)

Established: April 7, 1948, when 26 members of the U.N. had accepted its constitution, adopted July 22, 1946, by the International Health Conference in New York City.

Purpose: To aid attainment by all people of highest possible level of health.

Headquarters: 20 Avenue Appia, 1211 Geneva 27, Switzerland.

WORLD INTELLECTUAL PROPERTY ORGANIZATION (WIPO)

Established: April 26, 1970, when its Convention came into force. Originated as International Bureau of Paris Union (1883) and Berne Union (1886), later succeeded by United International Bureau for the Protection of Intellectual Property (BIRPI). Became a specialized agency of the U.N. in December 1974.

Purpose: To promote legal protection of intellectual property, including artistic and scientific works, artistic performances, sound recordings, broadcasts, inventions, trademarks, industrial designs, and commercial names.

Headquarters: 34 Chemin des Colombettes, 1211 Geneva 20, Switzerland.

WORLD METEOROLOGICAL ORGANIZATION (WMO)

Established: March 23, 1950, succeeding the International Meteorological Organization, a nongovernmental organization founded in 1878.

Purpose: To promote international exchange of weather reports and maximum standardization of observations; to help developing countries establish weather services for their own economic needs; to fill gaps in observation stations; to promote meterological investigations affecting jet aircraft, satellites, energy resources, etc.

Headquarters: 41 Avenue Giuseppe Motta, Geneva, Switzerland.

MEDIA

Leading Magazines: United States and Canada

Magazine	Circulation[1]
American Health—Fitness of Body and Mind	795,236
Better Homes and Gardens	8,091,751
Bon Appetit	1,341,047
Business Week (North America)	788,205
Car and Driver	905,492
Changing Times, The Kiplinger Magazine	1,379,781
Chatelaine	1,089,496
Consumers Digest	901,670
Cosmopolitan	2,873,071
Country Living	1,619,121
Creative Ideas for Living	778,191
Discover	1,328,534
Ebony	1,703,019
Essence	800,064
Family Circle	6,261,519
The Family Handyman	1,201,581
Field & Stream	2,007,479
Glamour	2,386,150
Globe	1,600,963
Golf (Incorporating Golfing)	850,893
Golf Digest	1,239,045
Good Food	952,134
Good Housekeeping	5,221,575
Gourmet	817,782
Health	1,016,410
Home	808,917
Home Mechanix	1,201,584
Hot Rod	794,996
House Beautiful	837,938
Jet	831,543
Ladies' Home Journal	5,020,551
Life	1,718,726
McCall's	5,186,393
Mademoiselle	1,297,938
Money	1,862,106
Nation's Business	862,410
National Enquirer	4,381,242
National Examiner	1,066,066
National Geographic	10,764,998
New Woman	1,234,726
Newsweek	3,101,152
Omni	857,614
1,001 Home Ideas	1,540,428
Outdoor Life	1,520,915
Parents Magazine	1,721,816
Penthouse	2,379,333
People Weekly	3,038,363
Playboy	3,477,324
Popular Mechanics	1,634,930
Popular Photography	838,844
Popular Science	1,843,067
Prevention	2,820,748
Psychology Today	901,771
Reader's Digest	16,609,847
Reader's Digest (Canadian English Edition)	1,345,184
Redbook	4,009,450
Rodale's Organic Gardening	1,212,151
Rolling Stone	1,109,812
Self	1,090,027
Sesame Street Magazine	1,156,119
Seventeen	1,853,314
Smithsonian	2,310,970
Soap Opera Digest	849,385
Southern Living	2,263,922
Sport	932,084
Sports Illustrated	2,895,116
Star	3,706,131
Sunset, The Magazine of Western Living	1,442,478
'Teen	1,181,862
Time	4,720,159
Travel & Leisure	1,118,132
Traveler	847,749
True Story	1,405,087
TV Guide (USA)	16,800,441
TV Guide (Canada)	820,634
U.S. News & World Report	2,287,016
US	1,021,288
Vogue	1,281,597
Weekly World News	1,016,555
Weight Watchers Magazine	902,525
Woman's Day	5,743,842
The Workbasket	1,779,463
Workbench	887,180
Working Woman	775,512
Yankee	1,018,245
YM	808,168

1. Average total paid circulation for the six-month period ending December 31, 1986. The table lists magazines with combined newsstand and subscription circulation of over 750,000. *Source:* Audit Bureau of Circulations. Publishers' Statements for six-month period ending December 31, 1986.

Major U.S. Daily Newspapers[1]

City and newspaper	Net paid circulation: Morning[2]	All-Day[2]	Evening[2]	Sunday
Akron, Ohio: *Beacon Journal*	—		153,581	227,462
Albany, N.Y.: *Times-Union* (M & S); *Knickerbocker News* (E)	87,446		28,927 [3]	175,532
Albuquerque, N.M.: *Journal* (M & S); *Tribune* (E)	111,331 [4]		42,283 [4]	147,993 [4]
Allentown, Pa.: *Call* (M & S)	134,156		—	176,970
Amarillo, Tex.: *News* (M); *Globe-Times* (E); *News-Globe* (S)	44,147		26,033 [3]	77,078
Asbury Park, N.J.: *Press*	—		139,954	205,007
Atlanta: *Constitution* (M); *Journal* (E); *Journal and Constitution* (S)	264,812 [3]		188,617 [3]	645,916

City and newspaper	Net paid circulation			
	Morning[2]	All-Day[2]	Evening[2]	Sunday
Atlantic City, N.J.: *Press*	77,534		—	87,382
Augusta, Ga.: *Chronicle* (M); *Herald* (E); *Chronicle—Herald* (S)	63,536[3]		17,249[3]	85,996
Austin, Tex.: *American-Statesman*	—	166,980[3]	—	204,816
Bakersfield, Calif.: *Californian*	81,831[4]		—	87,937[4]
Baltimore: *Sun*	223,334[3]		187,304[3]	489,771
Bangor, Me.: *News*	77,795[3]		—	93,674[5]
Baton Rouge, La.: *Advocate* (M & S); *State-Times* (E)	83,676		33,188	140,895
Bergen County (Hackensack), N.J.: *Record* (E); *Sunday Record*	—		159,151[3,4]	231,030[3,4]
Beaumont, Tex.: *Enterprise*	68,918		—	80,184
Binghamton, N.Y.: *Press & Sun-Bulletin* (M & S)	65,738		—	87,930
Birmingham, Ala.: *Post-Herald* (M); *News* (E & S)	62,318[3]		171,281[3]	218,509
Boston: *Globe*	500,106[3]		—	798,118
Herald	355,494[3]		—	265,548
Christian Science Monitor	186,195[3]		—	—
Bridgeport, Conn: *Telegram* (M); *Post* (E); *Sunday Post*	18,498[3,4]		61,028[3,4]	91,443[4]
Buffalo, N.Y.: *News*	—	321,301[3]	—	375,897
Camden, N.J.: *Courier-Post*	—		99,419[3]	98,497
Canton, Ohio: *Repository*	—		56,398[4]	75,273[4]
Cedar Rapids, Iowa: *Gazette*	71,123		—	81,475
Charleston, S.C.: *News & Courier* (M); *Evening Post; News & Courier Post* (S)	73,427[3]		37,390[3]	120,131
Charleston, W. Va.: *Gazette* (M); *Daily Mail* (E); *Gazette-Mail* (S)	55,151		53,268	108,686
Charlotte, N.C.: *Observer*	218,501		—	275,180
Chattanooga, Tenn.: *Times* (M); *News-Free Press* (E & S)	47,855[3]		57,320[3]	112,545
Chicago: *Tribune*	758,464[3]		—	1,126,293
Sun-Times	612,600[3]		—	633,051
Daily Herald (M); *Sunday Herald*	73,323		—	71,701
Cincinnati: *Enquirer* (M & S); *Post* (E)	191,645		115,718	323,390
Cleveland: *Plain Dealer*	454,954[3]		—	562,813
Colorado Springs, Colo.: *Gazette Telegraph*	87,550[3]		24,854[3]	122,523
Columbia, S.C.: *State* (M & S); *Record* (E)	118,080		29,484	152,643
Columbus, Ohio: *Dispatch*	255,976		—	383,806
Corpus Christi, Tex.: *Caller* (M); *Times* (E); *Caller-Times* (S)	60,940[3,4]		21,509[3,4]	90,857[4]
Dallas: *News*	n.a.		—	n.a.
Times Herald	—	n.a.	—	n.a.
Wall Street Journal (Southwest edition)	218,819[3]		—	—
Davenport, Iowa: *Quad City Times*	—	58,278	—	83,121
Dayton, Ohio: *Journal Herald* (M); *News* (E & S)		196,417[3]		228,680
Daytona Beach, Fla.: *News-Journal*	82,935		—	100,278
Denver: *Post*	229,731		—	415,250
Rocky Mountain News	345,778		—	379,984
Des Moines, Iowa: *Register*	216,677		—	364,405
Detroit: *News*		678,399[3]		839,319
Free Press	639,720[3]		—	724,342
Duluth, Minn.: *News-Tribune & Herald*	62,190		—	82,928
Erie, Pa.: *News* (M); *Times* (E); *Times-News* (S)	28,467[3]		42,039[3]	103,185
El Paso, Tex.: *Times* (M & S); *Herald-Post* (E)	59,273[4]		31,178[4]	94,266[4]
Evansville, Ind.: *Courier* (M); *Press* (E); *Courier & Press* (S)	63,219		38,556	116,339
Fayetteville, N.C.: *Times* (M); *Observer* (E); *Observer-Times* (S)	26,644[3,4]		47,014[3,4]	76,197[4]
Flint, Mich.: *Journal*	—		112,161[3]	123,792
Fort Lauderdale, Fla.: *Sun-Sentinel* (M); *News* (E); *News & Sun-Sentinel* (S)	176,093[3]		66,622[3]	308,052
Fort Myers, Fla.: *News-Press*	83,487		—	106,497
Fort Wayne, Ind.: *Journal-Gazette* (M & S); *News-Sentinel* (E)	60,248[4]		56,579[4]	133,922[4]
Fort Worth: *Star-Telegram*	131,923[3]		129,929[3]	315,644
Fresno, Calif.: *Bee*	139,888[4]		—	166,899[4]
Gary, Ind.: *Post-Tribune*	74,185		—	88,578
Grand Rapids, Mich.: *Press*	—		136,511	182,388
Green Bay, Wis.: *Press-Gazette*	—		55,533	76,966
Greensboro, N.C.: *News & Record*	112,292		—	127,748
Greensburg, Pa.: *Tribune-Review*	51,857		—	80,591
Greenville, S.C.: *News* (M); *Piedmont* (E); *News & Piedmont* (S)	87,020[3]		25,394[3]	126,553
Harrisburg, Pa.: *Patriot* (M); *Evening News*; *Sunday Patriot-News*	51,973[3]		53,235[3]	169,718
Hartford, Conn.: *Courant*	221,962		—	309,329

City and newspaper	Net paid circulation Morning[2]	All-Day[2]	Evening[2]	Sunday
Honolulu: *Advertiser* (M); *Star-Bulletin* (E); *Star-Bulletin & Advertiser* (S)	91,916		99,963	203,277
Houston: *Chronicle*	—	n.a.	—	n.a.
Post	n.a.		n.a.	n.a.
Indianapolis: *Star* (M & S); *News* (E)	227,225[4]		119,720[4]	401,776[4]
Jackson, Miss.: *Clarion-Ledger* (M); *News* (E); *Clarion Ledger-News* (S)	69,079[3]		30,398[3]	117,055
Jacksonville, Fla.: *Florida Times-Union* (M); *Journal* (E); *Times-Union & Journal* (S)	160,405[3]		41,340[3]	228,584
Kalamazoo, Mich.: *Gazette*	—		62,956	76,493
Kansas City, Mo.: *Times* (M); *Star* (E & S)	273,750		216,765[3]	411,029
Knoxville, Tenn.: *Journal* (E); *News-Sentinel* (M & S)	100,452		44,093	166,218
Lakeland, Fla.: *Ledger*	79,023[4]		—	96,990[4]
Lancaster, Pa.: *Intelligencer-Journal* (M); *New Era* (E); *News* (S)	43,745[4]		56,930[4]	100,398[4]
Lansing, Mich.: *State-Journal*	64,786		—	84,886
Las Vegas, Nev.: *Review-Journal*	—	114,269[3]	—	135,407
Sun	60,274[3]			60,487
Lexington, Ky.: *Herald-Leader*	116,720		—	144,022
Lincoln, Neb.: *Star* (M); *Journal* (E); *Journal & Star* (S)	36,610		43,781	79,647
Little Rock, Ark.: *Gazette*	136,814		—	185,311
Democrat	82,156		—	158,011
Long Beach, Calif.: *Press-Telegram*	124,506[3]		4,966[3]	141,646
Long Island (Melville), N.Y.: *Newsday*	—		624,291[3]	680,618
Los Angeles: *Times*	1,117,952[3]		—	1,397,192
Herald-Examiner	240,232[3]		—	200,377
News	153,084[3]		—	168,217
Louisville, Ky.: *Courier-Journal* (M & S); *Times* (E)	166,152[5]	246,957[3,6]	110,444[5]	325,764
Lubbock, Tex.: *Avalanche-Journal* (M & S); *Journal* (E)	59,685[3]		12,535[3]	76,497
Macon, Ga.: *Telegraph and News*	72,601		—	96,957
Madison, Wis.: *State Journal* (M & S); *Capital Times* (E)	78,568[3]		28,126[3]	147,589
Melbourne, Fla.: *Today*	69,721		—	93,687
Memphis, Tenn.: *Commercial Appeal*	225,016		—	298,003
Miami, Fla.: *Herald* (M & S); *News* (E)	437,233		56,590	546,980
Middletown, N.Y.: *Times Herald-Record* (M); *Sunday Record* (S)	81,638		—	94,062
Milwaukee: *Sentinel* (M); *Journal* (E & S)	192,638[3]		289,254[3]	516,890
Minneapolis: *Star & Tribune*	382,832		—	625,504
Mobile, Ala.: *Register* (M); *Press* (E); *Press-Register* (S)	54,421[3,4]		47,031[3,4]	107,620[4]
Modesto, Calif.: *Bee*	75,675[4]		—	81,592[4]
Montgomery, Ala. *Advertiser* (M); *Journal* (E); *Journal & Advertiser* (S)	50,682[3]		18,122[3]	84,316
Naperville, Ill.: *Wall Street Journal* (Midwest edition)	560,983[3]		—	—
Nashville, Tenn.: *Tennessean* (M & S); *Banner* (E)	122,589		67,408	259,705
New Haven, Conn.: *Journal-Courier* (M); *Register* (E & S)	35,753[3]		85,133	139,262
New Orleans: *Times-Picayune*	—	276,248[3,4]	—	348,577[4]
New York: *News*	1,278,118[3]		—	1,631,688
Times	1,056,924[3]		—	1,645,060
Post	—	740,123[3]	—	550,390[7]
Wall Street Journal (Eastern edition)	820,501[3]		—	—
National edition	2,026,276[3]		—	—
Women's Wear Daily	n.a.		—	—
Newark, N.J.: *Star-Ledger*	461,080[3,4]		—	681,802[4]
Newport News—Hampton, Va.: *Press* (M & S); *Times Herald* (E)	69,529[3,4]		36,229[3,4]	116,542[4]
Norfolk-Portsmouth-Virginia Beach-Chesapeake, Va.: *Virginian-Pilot* (M); *Ledger-Star* (E); *Virginian-Pilot/Ledger-Star* (S)	143,093[3,4]		79,043[3,4]	227,274[4]
Oakland, Calif.: *Tribune* (M & S)	150,482[3]		—	152,287
Oklahoma City: *Oklahoman* (M & S)	239,024[3]		—	334,615
Omaha, Neb.: *World-Herald*	120,062[3]		101,991[3]	290,197
Orange County (Santa Ana), Calif.: *Register*	—	314,300[3]	—	360,404
Orlando, Fla.: *Sentinel*	—	258,915[3]	—	340,588
Palo Alto, Calif.: *Wall Street Journal* (Western edition)	425,973[3]		—	—
Peninsula Times Tribune	—		51,931	55,880
Pensacola, Fla.: *News-Journal*	60,592[4]		—	75,944[4]
Peoria, Ill.: *Journal Star*	—	98,318	—	113,943
Philadelphia: *Inquirer* (M & S); *Daily News* (E)	494,844[3]		249,925[3]	989,250
Phoenix, Ariz.: *Republic* (M & S); *Gazette* (E)	343,723[4]		111,253[4]	539,323[4]

City and newspaper	Net paid circulation Morning[2]	All-Day[2]	Evening[2]	Sunday
Pittsburgh: *Post-Gazette, Sun-Telegraph* (M); *Press* (E & S)	170,242[3]		232,887[3]	564,987
Pontiac, Mich.: *Press*	—		71,335[3]	79,639
Portland, Me.: *Press-Herald* (M); *Express* (E)	59,008		26,163	—
Maine Sunday Telegram	—		—	134,216
Portland, Ore.: *Oregonian*	—	327,251[3]	—	406,895
Providence, R.I.: *Journal* (M & S); *Bulletin* (E)	93,578[3]		110,180[3]	260,404
Quincy, Mass.: *Patriot-Ledger*	—		90,518[3,4]	97,142[4,7]
Raleigh, N.C.: *News & Observer* (M & S); *Times* (E)	139,432[4]		33,546[4]	182,891[4]
Reading, Pa.: *Times* (M); *Eagle* (E & S)	45,835		35,675	115,173
Richmond, Va.: *Times-Dispatch* (M & S); *News-Leader* (E)	141,544		109,103	245,741
Riverside, Calif.: *Press-Enterprise* (M & S)	138,856		—	145,063
Roanoke, Va.: *Times & World-News*	79,747[3]		43,992[3]	127,579
Rochester, N.Y.: *Democrat & Chronicle* (M & S); *Times-Union* (E)	124,993[3]		97,644[3]	258,494
Rockford, Ill.: *Register Star*	69,909		—	87,850
Sacramento, Calif.: *Bee*	245,377		—	289,083
Union	90,888		—	89,561
St. Louis: *Post-Dispatch*	357,314[3]		—	548,955
St. Paul: *Pioneer Press & Dispatch*	—	188,448[3]	—	247,492
St. Petersburg, Fla.: *Times*	314,696		—	406,331
Salt Lake City, Utah: *Tribune* (M & S);	112,625		—	142,644
Deseret News (E & S)	—		63,204	69,954
San Antonio: *Express News*	—	178,812[3]	—	249,397
Light	—	142,407	—	217,006
San Bernardino, Calif.: *Sun*	82,573		—	88,328
San Diego, Calif.: *Union* (M & S); *Tribune* (E)	252,686[4]		123,087[4]	415,588[4]
San Francisco: *Chronicle* (M); *Examiner* (E); *Examiner & Chronicle* (S)	557,934[3]		142,335[3]	708,035
San Gabriel Valley, Calif.: *Tribune* (M); *Tribune-News* (S)	61,695		—	81,904
San Jose, Calif.: *Mercury-News*	—	268,711	—	315,577
Santa Rosa, Calif.: *Press Democrat*	79,389		—	87,995
Sarasota, Fla.: *Herald-Tribune* (M & S)	125,307[4]		—	152,425[4]
Savannah, Ga.: *News* (M & S); *Press* (E)	55,931		20,133	75,338
Seattle: *Post-Intelligencer* (M); *Times* (E); combined (S)	203,726[3]		231,207[3]	500,781
Shreveport, La.: *Times* (M & S); *Journal* (E)	75,506[4]		21,985[4]	109,897[4]
South Bend-Mishawaka, Ind.: *Tribune*	—		92,132	123,560
Spokane, Wash.: *Spokesman-Review* (M & S); *Daily Chronicle* (E)	86,321[3]		34,671[3]	134,189
Springfield, Ill.: *State Journal-Register*	—	68,339	—	76,160
Springfield, Mass.: *Union* (M); *News* (E); *Republican* (S)	67,218		63,575	158,943
Springfield, Mo.: *News* (M); *Leader & Press* (E); *News & Leader* (S)	36,306[3,4,8]		21,602[4,8]	97,443[4]
News-Leader	60,313[4,9]		—	—
Staten Island, N.Y.: *Advance* (E&S)	—		77,654	88,328
Syracuse, N.Y.: *Post-Standard* (M); *Herald-Journal* (E); *Herald-American* (S)	84,393		99,981	228,413
Tacoma, Wash.: *News-Tribune*	—		110,184	122,948
Tampa, Fla.: *Tribune* (M); *Tribune & Times* (S)	248,415[4]		—	337,514[4]
Toledo, Ohio: *Blade*	—		158,047	220,696
Topeka, Kan.: *Capital-Journal*	67,677		—	77,496
Trenton, N.J.: *Times* (M&S)	65,474		—	84,117
Trentonian (M&S)	68,532[3]		—	65,582
Tucson, Ariz.: *Daily Star* (M & S); *Citizen* (E)	87,571[4]		60,496[4]	168,657[4]
Tulsa, Okla.: *World* (M & S); *Tribune* (E)	127,857[4]		72,106[4]	232,837[4]
Walnut Creek, Calif.: *Contra Costa Times*	85,812		—	92,282
Washington, D.C.: *Post*	796,659[3]		—	1,112,802
Times	104,890[3]		—	—
USA Today	1,311,792[3]		—	—
West Palm Beach, Fla.: *Post* (M & S), *Times* (E)	130,033[3]		19,032[3]	193,958
Wichita, Kan.: *Eagle-Beacon*	128,865		—	193,502
Wilmington, Del.: *News* (M); *Journal* (E); *Sunday News Journal*	67,384[3,4]		50,869[3,4]	132,374[4]
Winston-Salem, N.C.: *Journal*	91,571		—	102,800
Worcester, Mass.: *Telegram* (M & S); *Gazette* (E)	55,616[4]		79,109[4]	128,112[4]
Youngstown, Ohio: *Vindicator*	—		93,929[4]	144,353[4]

1. Listing is of cities in which any one edition of a newspaper exceeds an average net paid circulation of 75,000; newspapers of smaller circulation in those cities are also included. 2. Unless otherwise indicated, figures are average Monday-through-Saturday circulation for six-month period ending March 31, 1987. 3. Average Monday-through-Friday circulation. 4. Three-month average for period ending March 31, 1987. 5. Oct. 1, 1986 to Feb. 14, 1987. 6. Feb. 15, 1987 to March 31, 1987. 7. Saturday edition. 8. Dec. 29, 1986 to March 22, 1987. 9. March 23, 1987 to March 28, 1987. n.a. = not available.

English Language Daily and Sunday U.S. Newspapers

(number of newspapers as of Feb. 1, 1987; circulation as reported for Sept. 30, 1986)

State	Morning papers and circulation		Evening papers and circulation		Total M and E and circulation		Sunday papers and circulation	
Alabama	16	303,589	12	454,719	28	758,308	20	762,910
Alaska	2	59,790	6	70,894	8	130,684	4	141,142
Arizona	6	422,041	13	252,626	19	674,667	11	713,974
Arkansas[1]	9	304,500	24	199,817	32	504,317	16	534,797
California[1]	45	4,413,955	75	1,807,157	117	6,221,112	61	6,150,134
Colorado	8	731,693	19	209,727	27	941,420	10	1,117,226
Connecticut	11	500,231	15	395,587	24	895,818	11	816,116
Delaware	2	91,704	1	51,821	3	143,525	2	161,850
District of Columbia	3	2,311,254	0	0	3	2,311,254	1	1,079,109
Florida[1]	28	2,362,407	22	525,622	49	2,888,029	33	3,328,952
Georgia	11	540,437	25	558,161	36	1,098,598	16	1,183,820
Hawaii	2	93,078	4	143,541	6	236,619	6	249,604
Idaho	4	104,559	8	100,854	12	205,413	8	216,735
Illinois[1]	16	1,829,989	56	821,610	70	2,651,599	24	2,698,652
Indiana	12	585,298	62	960,452	74	1,545,750	20	1,285,650
Iowa[1]	11	441,276	27	311,681	37	752,957	11	751,110
Kansas[1]	7	263,942	40	281,488	46	545,430	18	497,677
Kentucky	5	328,169	20	383,097	25	711,266	13	655,091
Louisiana[1]	12	471,407	16	320,224	27	791,631	21	897,885
Maine	5	222,671	4	68,597	9	291,268	2	178,376
Maryland	8	387,197	7	301,010	15	688,207	4	570,050
Massachusetts	7	1,231,409	39	902,349	46	2,133,758	11	1,727,222
Michigan[1]	12	1,107,090	41	1,441,968	52	2,549,058	15	2,468,261
Minnesota	10	612,619	16	304,745	25	917,364	12	1,046,463
Mississippi	6	176,481	17	225,220	23	401,701	12	333,771
Missouri	11	742,369	37	510,320	48	1,252,689	19	1,248,820
Montana	5	141,898	6	49,920	11	191,818	7	189,679
Nebraska	4	186,671	15	285,447	19	472,118	7	435,151
Nevada[1]	4	182,000	4	71,059	7	253,059	4	303,993
New Hampshire	1	68,838	8	146,377	9	215,215	4	139,251
New Jersey	10	855,640	16	858,331	26	1,713,971	17	1,846,068
New Mexico	4	138,693	16	163,230	20	301,923	13	272,306
New York[1]	24	5,594,086	51	2,112,674	73	7,706,760	33	5,746,958
North Carolina	11	749,707	43	676,944	54	1,426,651	29	1,327,612
North Dakota[1]	4	79,171	7	109,002	10	188,173	6	173,108
Ohio[1]	10	1,117,680	78	1,710,528	87	2,828,208	31	2,774,113
Oklahoma	9	443,077	42	352,445	51	795,522	43	902,368
Oregon[1]	5	297,836	16	356,489	20	654,325	10	646,632
Pennsylvania[1]	32	1,682,202	60	1,638,374	91	3,320,576	23	2,906,609
Rhode Island	1	94,220	6	209,041	7	303,261	3	302,369
South Carolina	9	454,056	9	185,056	18	639,112	11	630,627
South Dakota	4	70,742	8	94,694	12	165,436	4	128,953
Tennessee[1]	9	573,714	20	405,077	28	978,791	15	1,049,601
Texas[1]	36	2,191,077	78	1,435,446	109	3,626,523	96	4,333,492
Utah	1	112,817	5	174,243	6	287,060	6	326,123
Vermont	4	90,871	4	32,198	8	123,069	3	90,490
Virginia	15	632,960	23	554,141	36	1,187,101	15	939,077
Washington[1]	7	425,276	20	720,210	26	1,145,486	14	1,127,723
West Virginia	9	242,725	14	203,185	23	445,910	10	397,643
Wisconsin	6	307,606	29	882,880	35	1,190,486	13	1,043,694
Wyoming	6	68,407	4	30,633	10	99,040	4	75,481
Total	**499**	**37,441,125**	**1,188**	**25,060,911**	**1,657**	**62,502,036**	**802**	**58,924,518**
Total U.S., Sept. 30, 1985	482	36,361,561	1,220	26,404,671	1,676	62,766,232	798	58,825,978
Total U.S., Sept. 30, 1984	458	35,424,418	1,257	27,657,322	1,688	63,081,740	783	57,573,979
Total U.S., Sept. 30, 1983	446	33,842,142	1,284	28,802,461	1,701	62,644,603	722	56,747,436
Total U.S., Sept. 30, 1982	434	33,174,087	1,310	29,313,090	1,711	62,487,177	768	56,260,764
Total U.S., Sept. 30, 1981	408	30,552,316	1,352	30,878,429	1,730	61,430,745	755	55,180,004
Total U.S., Sept. 30, 1980	387	29,414,036	1,388	32,787,804	1,745	62,201,840	736	54,676,173
Total U.S., Sept. 30, 1979	382	28,574,879	1,405	33,648,161	1,763	62,223,040	720	54,379,923
Total U.S., Sept. 30, 1978	355	27,656,739	1,419	34,333,258	1,756	61,989,997	696	53,990,033
Total U.S., Sept. 30, 1977	352	26,742,318	1,435	34,752,822	1,753	61,495,140	668	52,429,234
Total U.S., Sept. 30, 1976	346	25,858,386	1,435	35,118,625	1,762	60,977,011	650	51,565,334

1. "All-day" newspapers are listed in morning and evening columns but only once in the total, and their circulations are divided between morning and evening figures. Adjustments have been made in state and U.S. total figures. *Source: Editor and Publisher International Yearbook, 1987.*

See **the Entertainment and Culture section for additional Media information.**

MILITARY

The Evolving Medal of Honor

By Virginia Thomas

The Army Medal of Honor. U.S. Army photo

First cast during the Civil War, the Medal of Honor has been awarded to 3,394 individuals who performed outstanding acts of resourcefulness and courage at the risk of their lives. It has come to symbolize "the bravest of the brave." But at its inception in 1861, it was intended not so much to award deeds of valor but to boost the flagging spirits of a demoralized navy.

Union spirits were lagging when Lt. Col. Edward D. Townsend proposed the creation of a meritorious service award that could be given to enlisted men as well as officers. The precedent for a military medal had been set when Gen. George Washington was honored for his effort against the British in 1776. Having no U.S. mint, the medal was cast in Paris.

Later, Washington established the formal system for rewarding American fighting men and initiated the Purple Heart in 1782. But only three Purple Hearts were given and the award fell into disuse until 1932. In 1847, Congress honored heroism in the Mexican War by giving 539 men additional pay of two dollars per month and a certificate. But without an actual medal, the honor received little public recognition.

At first, Col. Townsend met opposition to his idea. The U.S. Constitution prohibits granting any title of nobility, and the Army thought his proposal sounded too much like European privilege. But the Navy supported it. Navy Secretary Gideon Welles felt that a visible form of recognition such as a medal might ". . . further promote the efficiency of the Navy." On 21 December 1861, President Lincoln signed into law a resolution that appropriated $1,000 to design and make the medal.

Neither the Navy nor the U.S. mint had any experience in medal design. Welles rejected five different models before he approved an inverted, five-pointed star attached by an anchor to a red, white, and blue ribbon. At the center of the star were two figures: a male holding serpents with forked tongues striking at a female wearing a helmet bearing an eagle. Minerva, the Roman goddess of wisdom and the arts, was the female representing America and the engraving was called "Minerva Repulsing Discord." Thirty-four stars—the number of states in the Union at the time—encircled the figures. The Navy ordered 175 medals, which cost $1.85 each to produce.

Meanwhile, the Army reconsidered its cool reception to the medal. On 12 July 1862, a resolution was signed into law calling for a medal to honor "such noncommissioned officers and privates as shall most distinguish themselves by their gallantry in action. . . ." The medal was also "Minerva Repulsing Discord," but it was attached to the ribbon by a spread-winged eagle standing on crossed cannons and cannonballs. The medal cost slightly more than the Navy's—two dollars each—and the Army ordered 2,000.

But since its inception, both the design of the Medal of Honor and the standards for awarding it have evolved. By the early 1900s, imitations of the Medal of Honor were widespread and the Army wanted a new design. In 1904, it adopted an inverted five-point star with a profile of Minerva, encircled by a green enameled laurel wreath. The Army eagle sat atop a bar inscribed with "Valor." A blue ribbon with 13 stars (representing the 13 original colonies) replaced the red, white, and blue ribbon. In 1918, Congress made it illegal to duplicate military medals.

Meanwhile, the Navy had awarded many Medals of Honor for peacetime service and wanted a new design for outstanding service in combat. It became a Maltese cross with the American eagle surrounded by four anchors. This medal was used mainly during World War I, and in 1942, the Navy returned to its original Medal of Honor. It hung on a blue silk ribbon with 13 stars.

Until 1963, bravery in the Air Corps was awarded with the Army's Medal of Honor. Vietnam fliers were the first to receive the Air Force's own distinctive Medal of Honor. It is an inverted five-pointed star encircled with a green enameled laurel wreath, and bears the head of the Statue of Liberty in its center.

Virginia Thomas is a news correspondent with the Boulder, Colorado-based National News Service, covering events in Guatemala, Nicaragua, and El Salvador.

Medal of Honor winners still in active duty wear a five-starred blue ribbon on the left breast of their uniform in the highest position. Civilians who won the Medal during their military service wear a starred rosette on the lapel.

Just as imitations of the Medal once proliferated, so did exaggerated claims of bravery. Men often recommended themselves for the highest award, and many times the secretary of war took the man's word and gave him the Medal. All of the crewmen of the USS *Maine* were awarded, as were the 29 honor guardsmen who accompanied President Lincoln's body to Illinois. Over 500 Medals of Honor were awarded from 1891 to 1897 for Civil War acts.

Finally, the Medal of Honor Legion urged Secretary of War Russell Alger to set higher standards for bestowal of the Medal. Thereafter, Alger declared that a deed must demonstrate "most distinguished gallantry in action" based on "incontestable proof." Later it was required that official reports accompany the request along with testimony of eyewitnesses.

To correct past indiscretions, President Wilson signed a law in 1916 creating an "Army and Navy Medal of Honor Roll" for those who had "been awarded a Medal of Honor for having distinguished himself conspicuously by gallantry or intrepidity, at the risk of his life, above and beyond the call of duty." With that, the Army reviewed its 2,625 Medal of Honor winners and removed 911. It became illegal for those expunged to wear their Medals.

But Dr. Mary Walker vowed to wear hers every day if she wanted to. The only woman to receive the medal, Dr. Walker was a field surgeon in men's trousers on the Union's front lines during the Civil War. As a civilian, however, she was ineligible for the Medal under the new rules.

Dr. Walker finally died from a fall on the Capitol steps when she was seeking reinstatment of her Medal. Nearly 60 years after her death, her Medal was restored and she is now listed as the sole female recipient of the Medal of Honor.

Today, the time limit between the action and the awarding of the medal is three years for the Army and Air Force and five years for the Navy and Marines. And the review process is complex. A commander's recommendation must pass the awards board of the respective service, the service secretary, the secretary of defense, and the president. At any point, the award may be denied.

On February 24, 1981, retired Master Sergeant Roy Benavidez received the Medal of Honor from President Reagan. Sgt. Benavidez was the last living Vietnam veteran to receive the Medal. AP/Wide World Photos.

Medal of Honor recipients often return to civilian life and may rarely speak of the honor with which they have been bestowed. Others live in the public eye, their actions scrutinized.

Medal of Honor winners Alvin York, Eddie Rickenbacker, Audie Murphy and Jimmy Doolittle became the subjects of numerous books and motion pictures. Shortcomings that would be overlooked in ordinary men are magnified by their reputations as war heroes. "It's a lot harder to wear than it is to earn," said one recipient. □

Medal of Honor Recipients[1]

	Total	Army	Navy	Marines	Air Force	Coast Guard
Civil War	1,520	1,196	307	17	—	—
Indian Wars (1861–98)	423	423			—	—
Korean Expedition (1871)	15	—	9	6	—	—
Spanish-American War	109	30	64	15	—	—
Philippines/Samoa (1899–1913)	91	70	12	9	—	—
Boxer Rebellion (1900)	59	4	22	33	—	—
Dominican Republic (1904)	3	—	—	3	—	—
Nicaragua (1911)	2	—	—	2	—	—
Mexico (Veracruz) (1914)	55	—	46	9	—	—
Haiti (1915)	6	—	—	6	—	—
Misc. (1865–1920)	166	1	161	4	—	—
World War I	123	95	21	7	—	—
Haitian Action (1919–20)	2	—	—	2	—	—
Misc. (1920–1940)	18	2	15	1	—	—
World War II	433	294	57	81	—	1
Korean War	131	78	7	42	4	—
Vietnam War	238	155	14	57	12	—
Total	**3,394***	**2,348**	**735**	**294**	**16**	**1**

1. Total number of actual medals awarded is 3,412. This includes nine awarded to Unknown Soldiers, and some soldiers received more than one medal. *Source:* The Congressional Medal of Honor Society, New York, N.Y.

Offensive Nuclear Missiles—U.S. and U.S.S.R.

(Deployed as of early 1987)

United States

Land-based (ICBMs)[1]	No. silos deployed	Max. No. warheads	Max. range[8] (km)
Titan 2	4	1	12,000
Minuteman 2	450	1	12,500
Minuteman 3	540	3	14,000
Peacekeeper (MX)[3]	0[6]	10	14,000
Total:	**994**		
Sea-based (SLBMs)[2]			
Poseidon C-3	619[7]	10	4,000
Trident 1 (C-4)	570[7]	8	7,400
Total:	**1,189**		

Soviet Union

Land-based (ICBMs)[1]	No. silos deployed	Max. No. warheads[4]	Max. range[8] (km)
SS-11	440	3	13,000
SS-13	60	1	9,400
SS-16	—[5]	1	9,000
SS-17	150	4	10,000
SS-18	308	10	11,000
SS-19	360	6	10,000
SS-X-24[3]	0	10	10,000
SS-25	100	1	10,500
Total:	**1,418**		
Sea-based (SLBMs)[2]			
SS-N-5	39	1	1,400
SS-N-6	272	2	3,000
SS-N-8	292	1	9,100
SS-N-17	12	3	3,900
SS-N-18	224	7	8,000
SS-N-20	80	9	8,300
SS-NX-23	48	10	8,300
Total:	**967**		

1. ICBM: Intercontental Ballistic Missile 2. SLBM: Submarine-Launched Ballistic Missile 3. In development 4. Number of warheads varies within different models of same type 5. Nearing deployment 6. Twenty-two are scheduled to become operational by mid-1987. 7. Authorized for 1987. 8. One kilometer = .6214 miles. *Source:* U.S. Department of Defense.

Defense Budget by Major Categories

(In billions of dollars)

Major Missions and Programs	1986 actual	1987 estimate	1988 estimate	1989 estimate	1990 estimate
Strategic forces[1]	24.2	21.5	23.7	27.7	32.9
General purpose forces	116.2	117.2	118.8	126.8	135.6
Intelligence and communications	26.4	28.2	30.2	31.5	33.5
Airlift and sealift	7.6	7.2	6.0	6.6	7.1
Guard and reserve	15.6	16.0	17.5	18.6	19.5
Research and development[2]	25.7	28.0	35.1	36.5	35.8
Central supply and maintenance	24.4	23.1	26.0	27.0	29.7
Training, medical, and other general personnel activities	33.6	36.3	38.8	41.0	42.0
Administration and associated activities	7.1	6.7	6.3	6.7	6.9
Support of other nations	0.5	0.7	0.9	0.9	0.9
Total	**281.4**	**284.9**	**303.3**	**323.3**	**343.9**

1. Excludes strategic systems development included in the research and development category. 2. Excludes research and development in other program areas on systems approved for production.

The Battle of Tokyo

The change in the American bombing campaign against Tokyo to incendiary bombs instead of explosive bombs produced horrifyingly effective results. On March 9, 1945, 279 American B 29s—each carrying 6–8 tons of incendiaries—devastated Tokyo. A quarter of the total area of the city, nearly 16 square miles, was burnt out, and over 267,000 buildings were destroyed. Civilian casualties totaled approximately 185,000, while American attackers lost only 14 aircraft. In the next ten days the United States dropped nearly 10,000 tons of incendiaries, devastating not only Tokyo but the cities of Osaka, Kobe, and Nagoya as well.

For three months early in 1945 the use of explosive bombs had had disappointing results, but civilian morale declined badly after the Tokyo fire-raid. Over 8 1/2 million people fled into the countryside, causing war production to practically cease. More than 600 major war factories were destroyed by bombing.

The incendiary bombing campaign brought home to Japan's people that surrender had become unavoidable. The atomic bombs in August merely confirmed what everyone, except for military fanatics, had already come to realize.

North Atlantic Treaty Organization (NATO)

Set up April 4, 1949, under a regional defense treaty for the North Atlantic area stating that "an armed attack against one . . . shall be considered an attack against . . . all" and that participating nations will take necessary joint counteraction under the United Nations Charter, including the use of armed force. The founding members were the U.S., Canada, Iceland, Norway, Great Britain, the Netherlands, Denmark, Belgium, Luxembourg, Portugal, France, and Italy. Greece, Turkey, and West Germany were added later. Spain formally became the 16th member on May 30, 1982. NATO marked the first time that the United States pledged to go to war to support allies before the outbreak of hostilities. The member nations are represented on the governing NATO Council. Its organization comprises their top foreign, economic, defense, and financial ministers. Its major military commands are SACEUR for Europe and SACLANT for the Atlantic Ocean area.

France and Spain do not participate in NATO's integrated military structure. In an invasion of Western Europe, France and Spain would defend their sovereignty with their own forces.

Warsaw Pact

Signed May 14, 1955, by Albania, Bulgaria, Czechoslovakia, East Germany, Hungary, Poland, Romania, and the U.S.S.R. Albania, barred from meetings in 1962, withdrew in 1968 after ideological differences. The pact is the Communist equivalent of NATO, providing that an attack on one shall be regarded as an attack on all.

Comparing NATO and Warsaw Pact Forces

Many factors contribute to the capability to deter or defend against aggression. These include political and social stability, geography, economic strength, human resources, industrial and technological resources, as well as military capabilities. The military forces possessed by each side are clearly important but are not the only elements in this equation, and in comparing each side's military forces it is important to avoid over-simplification. A complete assessment of the global balance of power would have to take into account forces other than those that are available to NATO and the Warsaw Pact. Even if consideration was to be restricted to NATO and the Warsaw Pact capabilities only, a full assessment would have to take into account not just the conventional forces deployed by each side in Europe but also certain worldwide deployments by a number of NATO countries as well as by the Soviet Union. For instance, both the United States and the Soviet Union maintain substantial forces in Asia and the Pacific.

In addition to quantifiable force differences there are also other elements important to an understanding of the balance. These include, for example, differences in military strategy and structure, political organization and cohesion, the qualitative aspect of forces and the availability of timely reinforcements. Other important considerations are the amount of ammunition, fuel, and other stocks possessed by each side, the quality of their equipment, the quality of their civil and military infrastructure, their organization, their personnel, their leadership and morale, as well as each side's economic, industrial, and technological ability to sustain a military conflict.

Geographic and economic dissimilarities between NATO and the Warsaw Pact directly affect the roles and missions of their armed forces. For example, the Warsaw Pact is one geographic entity in contrast to NATO, which is separated by oceans, seas, and in some regions, particularly in the south, by the territory of nations which are not members of the Alliance. This allows the Warsaw Pact to transfer land and air forces and support between different areas via internal and generally secure lines of communications. It also contributes to enabling the Warsaw Pact to select the time and place in which to concentrate its forces.

NATO, on the other hand, must transfer resources along lengthy and vulnerable air and sea routes to and around Europe. The most powerful partner in NATO, the United States, is separated from its European allies by an ocean 3,728 miles (6,000 km) wide. Moreover, NATO nations, to a far greater extent than those of the Warsaw Pact, depend on shipping for vital economic purposes. Thus, unlike the Warsaw Pact, NATO has a fundamental dependence on shipping during peace and war. This fact requires markedly different missions for Warsaw Pact naval forces on the one hand and NATO naval forces on the other. Additionally, NATO lacks geographical depth in Europe between the possible areas of conflict and the coasts, so rendering its rear areas, headquarters and supplies more vulnerable to enemy attack and more difficult to defend.

The Warsaw Pact nations have a standing force of some 6 million personnel of which some 4 million face NATO in Europe. By comparison, the standing forces of the NATO nations total 4.5 million personnel, of which nearly 2.6 million are stationed in Europe.

Military Pensions

The Military Reform Act of 1986 changed pensions for anyone entering the armed forces after August 1, 1986. Under the old law, those who retired after 20 years of service received a pension equal to half of their base pay in the three highest-paid years. The pension increased 2.5 percent of base pay for each additional year of service up to 30 years when it stopped at 75 percent of base pay.

Under the new law, those who retire after 20 years (and usually go on to a new career) will receive 40 percent of base pay for the three highest years. It rises to 75 percent after 30 years of service.

The bill also provides for annual cost-of-living increases.

Early retirement pensions would be adjusted up to a base of 50 percent at age 62, with a 1 percent penalty added after the cost-of-living adjustment for each year of service less than 30 years.

Highest Ranking Officers in the Armed Forces

ARMY[1]
Generals: Carl E. Vuono, Chief of Staff; Maxwell R. Thurman, Vice Chief of Staff; Bernard W. Rogers, Supreme Allied Commander, Europe; James J. Lindsay, Glenn K. Otis, William J. Livsey, John R. Galvin, Fred K. Mahaffey; Jack N. Merritt; Joseph T. Palastra, Jr.

AIR FORCE
Generals: Robert W. Bazley, Charles L. Donnelly, Jr., Jack I. Gregory, Robert T. Herres, Earl T. O'Loughlin, Robert H. Reed, Thomas C. Richards, Lawrence A. Skantze, Larry D. Welch, Duane H. Cassidy, John T. Chain, Jr., John L. Piotrowski, Robert D. Russ.

NAVY
Admirals: Carlisle A. H. Trost, Chief of Naval Operations; William J. Crowe, Jr., Chairman of the Joint Chiefs of Staff; Kinnaird R. McKee; Ronald J. Hays; Lee Baggett, Jr., James A. Lyons, Jr., Frank B. Kelso, II, James B. Busey.

MARINE CORPS
Generals: Alfred M. Gray, Commandant of the Marine Corps; George B. Crist, Commander in Chief, U.S. Central Command; Thomas R. Morgan, Assistant Commandant of the Marine Corps.
Lieutenant Generals: D'Wayne Gray, Alfred M. Gray, Jr., Keith A. Smith, Ernest C. Cheatham, Jr., Joseph J. Went, John Phillips, Frank E. Petersen, Clyde D. Dean.

COAST GUARD
Admiral: Adm. Paul A. Yost, Jr., Commandant.
Vice Admirals: James C. Irwin, Vice Commandant; Donald C. Thompson, Commander Atlantic Area; John D. Costello, Commander, Pacific Area.

1. On March 15, 1978, George Washington, the commander of the Continental Army in the American Revolution and our first President, was promoted posthumously to the newly-created rank of General of the Armies of the United States. Congress authorized this title to make it clear that Washington is the Army's senior general. *Source:* Department of Defense.

History of the Armed Services

Source: Department of Defense.

U.S. Army

On June 14, 1775, the Continental Congress "adopted" the New England Armies—a mixed force of volunteers besieging the British in Boston—appointing a committee to draft "Rules and regulations for the government of the Army" and voting to raise 10 rifle companies as a reinforcement. The next day, it appointed Washington commander-in-chief of the "Continental forces to be raised for the defense of liberty," and he took command at Boston on July 3, 1775. The Continental Army that fought the Revolution was our first national military organization, and hence the Army is the senior service. After the war, the army was radically reduced but enough survived to form a small Regular Army of about 700 men under the Constitution, a nucleus for expansion in the 1790s to successfully meet threats from the Indians and from France. From these humble beginnings, the U.S. Army has developed, normally expanding rapidly by absorbing citizen soldiers in wartime and contracting just as rapidly after each war.

U.S. Navy

The antecedents of the U.S. Navy go back to September 1775, when Gen. Washington commissioned 7 schooners and brigantines to prey on British supply vessels bound for the Colonies or Canada. On Oct. 13, 1775, a resolve of the Continental Congress called for the purchase of 2 vessels for the purpose of intercepting enemy transports. With its passage a Naval Committee of 7 men was formed, and they rapidly obtained passage of legislation calling for procurement of additional vessels. The Continental Navy was supplemented by privateers and ships operated as state navies, but soon after the British surrender it was disestablished.

In 1794, because of dissatisfaction with the payment of tribute to the Barbary pirates, Congress authorized construction of 6 frigates. The first, *United States,* was launched May 10, 1797, but the Navy still remained under the control of the Secretary of War until April 1798, when the Navy Department was created under the Secretary of the Navy with Cabinet rank.

U.S. Air Force

Until creation of the National Military Establishment in September 1947, which united the services under one department, military aviation was a part of the U.S. Army. In the Army, aeronautical operations came under the Signal Corps from 1907 to 1918, when the Army Air Service was established. In 1926, the Army Air Corps came into being and remained until 1941, when the Army Air Forces succeeded it as the Army's air arm. On Sept. 18, 1947, the U.S. Air Force was established as an independent military service under the National Military Establishment. At that time, the name "Army Air Forces" was abolished.

U.S. Coast Guard

Our country's oldest continuous seagoing service, the U.S. Coast Guard, traces its history back to 1790, when the first Congress authorized the construction of ten vessels for the collection of revenue. Known first as the Revenue Marine, and later as the Revenue Cutter Service, the Coast Guard received its present name in 1915 under an act of Congress combining the Revenue Cutter Service with the Life-Saving Service. In 1939, the Lighthouse Service was also consolidated with this unit. The Bureau of Marine Inspection and Navigation was transferred temporarily to the Coast Guard in 1942, permanently in 1946. Through its antecedents, the Coast Guard is one of the oldest organizations under the federal government and, until the Navy Department was established in 1798, served as the only U.S. armed force afloat. In times of peace, it operates under the Department of Transportation, serving as the nation's primary agency for promoting marine safety and enforcing federal maritime laws. In times of war, or on direction of the President, it is attached to the Navy Department.

U.S. Marine Corps

Founded in 1775 and observing its official birthday on Nov. 10, the U.S. Marine Corps was developed to serve on land, on sea, and in the air.

Marines have fought in every U.S. war. From an initial two battalions in the Revolution, the Corps reached a peak strength of six divisions and five aircraft wings in World War II. Its present strength is three active divisions and aircraft wings and a Reserve division/aircraft wing team. In 1947, the National Security Act set Marine Corps strength at not less than three divisions and three aircraft wings.

Service Academies

U.S. Military Academy

Source: U.S. Military Academy.

Established in 1802 by an act of Congress, the U.S. Military Academy is located on the west bank of the Hudson River some 50 miles north of New York City. To gain admission a candidate must first secure a nomination from an authorized source. These sources, and the number of cadetships allocated to each, are:

Congressional

Representatives	5 each
Senators	5 each
Other: Vice Presidential	5
District of Columbia	5
Puerto Rico	6
Am. Samoa, Guam, Virgin Is.	1 each

Military-Service-Connected Nominations (Each Class)

Presidential	100
Enlisted members of Army	85
Enlisted members of Army Reserve/ National Guard	85
Sons and daughters of deceased and disabled veterans (approximately)	10
Honor military, naval schools and ROTC	20
Sons and daughters of persons awarded the Medal of Honor	(unlimited)

Any number of applicants can meet the requirements for a *nomination* in these categories. *Appointments* (offers of admission), however, can only be made to the number of applicants shown above.

Candidates may be nominated for vacancies during the year preceding the day of admission, which occurs in early July. The best time to apply is during the junior year in high school.

Candidates must be citizens of the U.S., be unmarried, be at least 17 but not yet 22 years old on July 1 of the year admitted, have a secondary-school education or its equivalent, and be able to meet the academic, medical, and physical aptitude requirements. Academic qualification is determined by an analysis of entire scholastic record, and performance on either the American College Testing (ACT) Assessment Program Test or the College Entrance Examination Board Scholastic Aptitude Test (SAT). Entrance requirements and procedures for appointment are described in the Admissions Bulletin, available without charge from Admissions, U.S. Military Academy, West Point, N.Y. 10996-1797.

Cadets are members of the Regular Army. As such they receive full scholarships and annual salaries from which they pay for their uniforms, textbooks, and incidental expenses. Upon successful completion of the four-year course, the graduate receives the degree of Bachelor of Science and is commissioned a second lieutenant in the Regular Army with a requirement to serve as an officer for a minimum of five years.

U.S. Naval Academy

Source: U.S. Naval Academy.

The Naval School, established in 1845 at Fort Severn, Annapolis, Md., was renamed the U.S. Naval Academy in 1850. A four-year course was adopted a year later.

The Superintendent is a rear admiral. A civilian academic dean heads the academic program. A captain heads the 4,500-man Brigade of Midshipmen and military, professional, and physical training. The faculty is half military and half civilian.

Graduates are awarded the Bachelor of Science or Bachelor of Science in Engineering and are commissioned as officers in the U.S. Navy or Marine Corps.

Applicants *must* obtain a nomination from an official source in order to be considered by the Naval Academy for an appointment. The principle sources are: U.S. Senators, Representatives, the Vice President, the Mayor of Washington, D. C., and the Resident Commissioner of Puerto Rico, who may each have 5 midshipmen at the Academy at any one time. Ten candidates may be nominated for each vacancy. Well over half of the more than 1,300 appointments as midshipmen made annually originate from these sources.

The President appoints the 65 best-qualified sons and daughters of deceased or disabled veterans, or sons and daughters of prisoners of war or servicemen missing in action, and the 100 best-qualified sons and daughters of officers and enlisted men in the regular Armed Services. He also appoints sons and daughters of Medal of Honor holders.

The Secretary of the Navy awards 170 (85 + 85) appointments to regular and reserve personnel of the Navy or Marine Corps; 150 to congressional alternate nominees, all on a competitive, best-qualified basis; and 20 outstanding graduates of NROTC or Honor Naval and Military Schools. He may also make additional appointments each year, to bring the Brigade up to authorized strength, from among qualified congressional and competitive nominees, again on a best-qualified basis. Three fourths of these additional appointments must, by law, be congressional nominees.

There are also limited numbers of appointments available from the Philippines, Canal Zone, Virgin Islands, Guam, American Samoa, and the American republics.

To have basic eligibility for admission, candidates must be citizens of the U.S., of good moral character, at least 17 and not more than 22 years of age on July 1 of their entering year, in the top 40% of their high school class, and unmarried.

In order to be considered for admission, a candidate must obtain a nomination from one of the sources of appointments listed above. The Admissions Board at the Naval Academy examines the candidate's school record, College Board or ACT scores, recommendations from school officials, extracurricular activities, and evidence from other sources concerning his or her character, leadership potential, academic preparation, and physical fitness. Qualification for admission is based on all of the above factors.

Tuition, board, lodging, and medical and dental care are provided. Midshipmen receive over $460 a month for books, uniforms, and personal needs.

For a catalogue or answers to specific questions, write: Superintendent, U.S. Naval Academy, (Attention: Candidate Guidance), Annapolis, Md. 21402-5018.

U.S. Air Force Academy

Source: U.S. Air Force Academy.

The bill establishing the Air Force Academy was signed by President Eisenhower on April 1, 1954. The first class of 306 cadets was sworn in on July 11, 1955, at Lowry Air Force Base, Denver, the Academy's temporary location. The Cadet Wing moved into the Academy's permanent home north of Colorado Springs, Colorado, in 1958.

Cadets receive four years of academic, military, and physical education to prepare them for leadership as officers in the Air Force. The Academy is authorized a total of 4,546 cadets. Each new class averages 1,400. The candidates for the Academy must be at least 17 but less than 22 on July 1 of the year for which they enter the Academy, must be a United States citizen, never married, and be able to meet the mental and physical requirements. A candidate is required to take the following examinations and tests: (1) the Service Academies' Qualifying Medical Examination; (2) either the American College Testing (ACT) Assessment Program test or the College Entrance Examination Board Scholastic Aptitude Test (SAT); and (3) a Physical Aptitude Examination.

Each new cadet must deposit $1,000 at the time of admission to the Academy, otherwise cadets receive their entire education at government expense and, in addition, are paid $480 per month base pay. From this sum, they pay for their uniforms, textbooks, tailoring, laundry, entertainment tickets, etc. Upon completion of the four-year course, leading to a Bachelor of Science degree, a cadet who meets the qualifications is commissioned a second lieutenant in the regular U.S. Air Force. About 70 percent enter pilot or navigator training. For details on admissions, write: Director of Cadet Admissions (RRS), HQ USAF Academy, Colorado Springs, CO 80840-5651.

U.S. Coast Guard Academy

Source: U.S. Coast Guard Academy.

The U.S. Coast Guard Academy, New London, Conn., was founded on July 31, 1876, to serve as the "School of Instruction" for the Revenue Cutter Service, predecessor to the Coast Guard.

The J.C. Dobbin, a converted schooner, housed the first Coast Guard Academy, and was succeeded in 1878 by the barque Chase, a ship built for cadet training. First winter quarters were in a sail loft at New Bedford, Mass. The school was moved in 1900 to Curtis Bay, Md., to provide a more technical education, and in 1910 was moved back to New England to Fort Trumbull, New London, Conn. In 1932 the Academy moved to its present location in New London.

The Academy today offers a four-year curriculum for the professional and academic training of cadets, which leads to a Bachelor of Science degree and a commission as ensign in the Coast Guard.

Cadets receive appointment through nationwide competition, which includes either the December administration of the College Entrance Examination Board tests, or the American College Testing (ACT) Program tests. Applications must be submitted to the Coast Guard not later than December 15 and to the College Entrance Examination Board, 30 days prior to the tests.

Women were admitted to the Coast Guard Academy for the first time during 1976 as members of the Class of 1980. Candidates must be between 17 and 22 years of age, physically sound, and unmarried. They must agree to remain unmarried until graduation and to serve at least five years on active duty. Cadets receive one-half of an Ensign's base pay per year to cover their uniform and incidental expenses and are furnished their rations and quarters. Applications may be made to Director of Admissions, U.S. Coast Guard Academy, New London, Conn. 06320.

U.S. Merchant Marine Academy

Source: U.S. Merchant Marine Academy.

The U.S. Merchant Marine Academy, situated at Kings Point, N.Y., on the north shore of Long Island, was dedicated Sept. 30, 1943. It is maintained by the Department of Transportation under direction of the Maritime Administration.

The Academy has a complement of approximately 880 men and women representing every state, D.C., the Canal Zone, Puerto Rico, Guam, American Samoa, and the Virgin Islands. It is also authorized to admit up to 12 candidates from the Western Hemisphere and 30 other foreign students at any one time.

Candidates are nominated by Senators and members of the House of Representatives. Nominations to the Academy are governed by a state and territory quota system based on population and the results of the College Entrance Examination Board tests.

A candidate must be a citizen not less than 17 and not yet 22 years of age by July 1 of the year in which admission is sought. Fifteen high school credits, including 3 units in mathematics (from algebra, geometry and/or trigonometry), 1 unit in science (physics or chemistry) and 3 in English are required.

The course is four years and includes one year of practical training aboard a merchant ship. Study includes marine engineering, navigation, satellite navigation and communications, electricity, ship construction, naval science and tactics, economics, business, languages, history, etc.

Upon completion of the course of study, a graduate receives a Bachelor of Science degree, a license as a merchant marine deck or engineering officer, and a commission as an Ensign in the Naval Reserve.

The National Guard

Source: Departments of the Army and the Air Force, National Guard Bureau.

The National Guard of the U.S. originated in 1636 with the Old North, South and East Regiments of the Colonial Militia in Massachusetts Bay Colony. It is the oldest military force in the country. Guardmembers have served this country at home and overseas in every major conflict in which the U.S. has been involved.

As of February 1987, the Army National Guard totaled about 449,741 individuals making it the 11th largest Army in the world. The Air National Guard is made up of 114,232 members and represents the 5th largest Air Force in the world.

In peacetime, the National Guard is commanded by the governors of the respective states/territories and may be called to state active duty by the governor to assist in state emergencies, disasters, and civil disturbances. During a war or national emergency, the National Guard may be called to active duty by the President or Congress. The National Guard serves as the primary source of augmentation for the Army and the Air Force.

Budget requests for fiscal year 1988 were $5.2 billion for the Army National Guard and $3.1 billion for the Air National Guard. Additional money is appropriated directly for the National Guard by the states. Substantial support is also provided by state, county, and municipal governments in land, police and fire protection, maintenance of roads, and the provision of direct county and municipal fiscal support to local units.

The Army National Guard is made up of 4,347 units/subunits located in 2,680 communities throughout the 50 states, Puerto Rico, Guam, the Virgin Islands and the District of Columbia.

The Army National Guard provides 46% of the total Army's combat capability and approximately 20 percent of its support units. The Army Guard consists of 10 combat divisions, 14 separate combat brigades, 4 divisional roundout brigades, 4 armored cavalry regiments, 2 special forces groups, 1 infantry scout group (arctic reconnaissance) and 17 major command headquarters units.

Army National Guard forces are vital to the nation's first-line of defense. For example, the 48th Infantry Brigade in the Georgia National Guard is a round out brigade for the active Army's 24th Infantry Division. Under the round out concept, Army Guard units work and train with the active Army combat divisions of which they would become part upon mobilization. Integral to the "total force policy," programs for increasing readiness are continually being improved.

The Air National Guard has 91 flying units and 542 mission support units which, upon mobilization, would be gained by one of six major commands of the USAF. The gaining major commands are Tactical Air Command (TAC), Strategic Air Command (SAC), Military Airlift Command (MAC), Air Force Communications Command (AFCC), Pacific Air Forces (PACAF), and Alaskan Air Command (AAC).

The Air National Guard is a vital contributor to the total force mission. The U.S. Air Force relies on the Air Guard for 78% of its fighter interceptor force, 54% of its tactical reconnaissance force, 40% of tactical airlift, 35% of tactical air support, 25% of fighters and 17% of its air refueling capability.

In the mission support areas the Air Guard contributes 65% of Air Force combat communications units, 65% of tactical air control, 55% of engineering and installation capability and 40% of base services.

The National Guard is administered by the National Guard Bureau, a joint Army and Air Force office in the Pentagon. Chief of the Bureau is Lt. Gen. Herbert R. Temple, Jr., of California.

The National Guard offers its young men and women a broad spectrum of educational opportunities. These not only include skill training associated with their military assignment, but in many instances embrace civilian occupations as well. The list of skills is not limited to those that are equipment oriented but includes management, medical, and other career fields. Some of these educational opportunities may even be pursued in civilian institutions, specifically that of the Clinical Specialist, which is compatible with a Licensed Practical Nurse or Licensed Vocational Nurse.

Participation in the military education system by National Guard personnel is not limited to initial entry skill-level training. There are opportunities available to become a qualified aviator, improve managerial and leadership abilities through attending courses designed for middle managers, and, finally, there are the courses offered at the prestigious Senior Service Colleges that address the needs of personnel at the executive level and positions of greater responsibilities.

If openings exist, men and women between the ages of 17 and 35 may enlist for a period of six years followed by a two-year inactive reserve period during which they are subject to recall, should the need arise. In certain circumstances the period of active participation may be less than six years. Upon enlistment, they serve a minimum of 12 weeks on active duty, training with the U.S. Army or the U.S. Air Force, depending upon which branch of the National Guard they choose. The remainder of their term of enlistment is spent in part-time training with their Guard unit.

A woman between the ages of 17 and 35 who has no previous military experience may also enlist in the National Guard for a period of six years. Women in the Army National Guard will receive basic training at either Fort McClellan, Ala., Fort Dix, N.J., or Fort Jackson, S.C.; women in the Air National Guard train at Lackland Air Force Base, Tex. Advanced training takes place at appropriate training centers.

Guard members receive a full day's pay of their military rank for each unit training assembly attended. Additionally, they receive a day's pay of their military rank for each day of their 15 days of annual training, plus any other days on active duty for training at military schools or special assignments. All such training counts toward retirement eligibility at age 60 with 20 or more years of qualifying service.

Nuclear Weapons Yield

The most widely used standard for measuring the power of nuclear weapons is "yield," expressed as the quantity of TNT that would produce the same energy release. The first atomic bomb exploded at Hiroshima had a yield of 13 to 15 kilotons, or the explosive power of 13 to 15,000 tons of TNT.

Veterans' Benefits

Although benefits of various kinds date back to Colonial days, veterans of World War I were the first to receive disability compensation, allotments for dependents, life insurance, medical care, and vocational rehabilitation. In 1940, these benefits were slowly broadened.

The following benefits available to veterans require certain minimum periods of active duty during qualifying periods of service and, except for service personnel, are applicable only to those whose discharges are not dishonorable.

For information or assistance in applying for veterans benefits, write, call, or visit a V.A. Regional Office. Consult your local telephone directory under United States Government, Veterans Administration, for the address and telephone number. Toll-free telephone service is available in all 50 States. Former POW's may call a toll-free number (800-821-8139) in Washington, D.C.

Unemployment allowances. Every effort is being made to secure employment for Vietnam veterans. Unemployment benefits are administered by the U.S. Department of Labor.

Loans. GI loans are made for a variety of purposes, such as: to buy or build a home; to purchase a manufactured home with or without a lot; and to refinance a home presently owned and occupied by the veteran. The VA will guarantee the lender against loss up to 60% of a home loan with a maximum of $27,500. On mobile home loans, the amount of the guaranty is 50% of the loan with a maximum of $20,000. The interest rate may not exceed the maximum rate set by the VA and in effect when the loan is made.

Compensation and rehabilitation benefits. These are available to those having some service-connected illness or disability.

Disability compensation. The VA pays from $69 to $1,355 per month, and for specific conditions up to $3,869 per month, plus allowances for dependents, where the disability is rated 30% or more.

Vocational Rehabilitation. The VA provides professional counseling, training and other assistance to help compensably service-disabled veterans who have an employment handicap to achieve maximum independence in daily living and, to the extent possible, to obtain and maintain suitable employment. Generally, a veteran may receive up to 48 months of this assistance during the 12 years from the date he or she is notified of entitlement to VA compensation. All the expenses of a veteran's rehabilitation program are paid by the VA. In addition, the veteran receives a subsistence allowance which varies based on the rate of training and number of dependents. For example, a single veteran training full time would receive $310 monthly.

Vocational Training for VA Pension Recipients. Veterans who are awarded pension during the period from February 1, 1985, through January 31, 1989, may participate in a program of vocational training essentially identical to that provided in the VA's vocational rehabilitation program. Participants do not receive any direct payments, such as subsistence allowance, while in training.

Medical and dental care. This includes care in VA and, in certain instances, in non-VA, or other federal hospitals. It also covers outpatient treatment at a VA field facility or, in some cases, by an approved private physician or dentist. Full domiciliary care is also provided where necessary. Nursing home care may be provided at certain VA medical facilities or in approved community nursing homes. Hospital and other medical care may also be provided for the spouse and child dependents of a veteran who is permanently and totally disabled due to a service-connected disability; or for survivors of a veteran who dies from a service-connected disability; or for survivors of a veteran who at the time of death had a total disability, permanent in nature, resulting from a service-connected disability. These latter benefits are usually provided in nonfederal facilities. Eligibility criteria for these benefits vary and certain veterans must agree to make a copayment for the care they receive from the VA. Veterans and/or their dependents or survivors should always apply in advance. Contact the nearest VA medical facility.

Readjustment Counseling. The VA provides readjustment counseling to veterans of the Vietnam Era in need of assistance in resolving post-war readjustment problems in the areas of employment, family, education, and personal readjustment including post-traumatic stress disorder. Services are provided at community-based Vet Centers and at VA Medical Centers in certain locations. Services include individual family and group counseling, employment and educational counseling, and assistance in obtaining referrals to various governmental and nongovernmental agencies with an interest in assisting Vietnam Era veterans. All Vietnam Era veterans are eligible for services except those with a type of discharge which may limit eligibility for VA services. Certain types of discharges are subject to special adjudication to determine eligibility. Contact the nearest Vet Center or VA facility to determine location of Vet Center.

Dependents' educational assistance. The VA pays $376 a month for up to 45 months of schooling to sons and daughters of veterans who died of service-connected causes or who were permanently and totally disabled from service-connected causes or died while permanently and totally disabled or who are missing in action, captured in the line of duty, or forcibly detained or interned in line of duty by a foreign power for more than 90 days. Students must usually be between 18 and 26.

Spouses of veterans whose deaths are adjudged to be service-connected, and spouses of veterans who are permanently and totally disabled due to service-connected causes or who are prisoners of war or are missing in action are also eligible for this educational benefit.

Veterans readjustment education. Veterans who served on active duty for at least 181 days after Jan. 31, 1955, but before Jan. 1, 1977, may receive monthly educational assistance under the GI Bill for post-Korean conflict veterans, varying from $376 for single full-time students to $510 for veterans with two dependents, plus $32 for each additional dependent. Veterans and servicepersons who initially entered the military on or after Jan. 1, 1977, and before July 1, 1985, may receive educational assistance under a contributory plan. Individuals contribute $25 to $100 from military pay, up to a maximum of $2,700. This amount is matched by the Federal Government on a 2 for 1 basis. Participants, while on active duty, may make a lump sum contribution. Participants receive monthly payments for the number of months they contributed, or for 36 months, whichever is less. No initial enrollments are permitted after March 31, 1987.

Veterans Educational Assistance Act of 1984. This Act established a program of education benefits for individuals entering military service from July 1, 1985, through June 30, 1988. Servicepersons entering active duty during that period will have their basic pay reduced by $100 a month for the first 12 months of their service, unless they specifically elect not to participate in the program. Servicepersons eligible for post-Korean GI Bill benefits as of December 31, 1989, and who serve 3 years in active duty service after July 1, 1985, are also eligible for the new program, but will not have their basic pay reduced. Servicepersons who, after December 31, 1976, received commissions as officers from service academies or scholarship senior ROTC programs are not eligible for this program.

Active duty for three years (two years, if the initial obligated period of active duty is less than three years), or two years active duty plus four years in the Selected Reserve or National Guard will entitle an individual to $300 a month basic benefits. There is also a targeted, discretionary kicker of up to an additional $400 available. A supplemental benefit of up to an additional $300 with a targeted, discretionary kicker of up to $300 more is also available.

An educational entitlement program is also available for members of the Selected Reserve. Eligibility applies to individuals who, from July 1, 1985, through June 30, 1988, enlist, re-enlist, or extend an enlistment for a six-year period. Benefits may be paid to eligible members of the Selected Reserve who complete their initial period of active duty training and complete 180 days of service in the Selected Reserve. Full-time payments are $140 a month for 36 months.

Veterans' Benefits Improvement Act of 1984. Veterans awarded a VA pension during the period February 1, 1985, through January 31, 1989, for whom vocational training is reasonably feasible may be provided training expenses and special services and equipment toward a definite vocational goal. Veterans who participate in this special vocational training program and subsequently lose entitlement to pension for excessive work or training income may continue to receive VA health care and retain priority for treatment for 3 years after the date pension is terminated.

Veterans awarded 100 percent disability compensation based upon unemployability during the period February 1, 1985, through January 31, 1989, for whom a vocational goal is feasible are required to participate in a rehabilitation program. Necessary training expenses, special equipment, etc., toward a definite job objective are paid for, plus a monthly allowance up to $310, with increased amounts for dependents, in addition to compensation. In addition, all veterans granted an unemployability rating before February 1, 1985, the start of the special program period, may receive special assistance in securing employment under the Vocational Rehabilitation Program. Any veteran with an unemployability rating who secures gainful employment during the special program period will be protected from reduction until such veteran has worked continuously for 12 months.

Pensions. Pension benefits are payable for wartime veterans totally disabled from non-service-connected causes. These benefits are based on need. Surviving spouses and orphans of wartime veterans have the same eligibility status.

Insurance. The VA life insurance programs have approximately 7.4 million policyholders with total coverage of about $209.6 billion. Detailed information on NSLI (National Service Life Insurance), USGLI (United States Government Life Insurance), and VMLI (Veterans Mortgage Life Insurance) may be obtained at any VA Office. Informa-

Insignia and Ranks of the Armed Forces

Army, Air Force, and Marines

Insignia	Rank
Five silver stars	General of the Army, AF
Four silver stars	General
Three silver stars	Lieutenant General
Two silver stars	Major General
One silver star	Brigadier General
Silver eagle	Colonel
Silver oak leaf	Lieutenant Colonel
Gold oak leaf	Major
Two silver bars	Captain
One silver bar	First Lieutenant
One gold bar	Second Lieutenant
Silver bar with 4 enamel bands[3]	Chief Warrant Officer (W-4)
Silver bar with 3 enamel bands[3]	Chief Warrant Officer (W-3)
Silver bar with 2 enamel bands[3]	Chief Warrant Officer (W-2)
Silver bar with 1 enamel band[3]	Warrant Officer (W-1)

Navy and Coast Guard

Insignia	Rank	Stripes[1]
Five silver stars	Fleet Admiral	1—4—0
Four silver stars	Admiral	1—3—0
Three silver stars	Vice Admiral	1—2—0
Two silver stars	Rear Admiral[2]	1—1—0
One silver star	Rear Admiral 0-7[2]	1—0—0
Silver eagle	Captain	0—4—0
Silver oak leaf	Commander	0—3—0
Gold oak leaf	Lt. Commander	0—2—1
Two silver bars	Lieutenant	0—2—0
One silver bar	Lieutenant (jg)	0—1—1
One gold bar	Ensign	0—1—0
Silver bar with 3 enamel bands[3]	Chief Warrant Officer (W-4)	0—1—0[4]
Silver bar with 2 enamel bands[3]	Chief Warrant Officer (W-3)	0—1—0[5]
Gold bar with 3 enamel bands[3]	Chief Warrant Officer (W-2)	0—1—0[6]
Gold bar with 2 enamel bands[3]		

1. Of gold embroidery; first figure is number of 2-in. stripes, second is number of 1/2-inch strips, third is number of 1/4-in. stripes. 2. The Navy and the Coast Guard changed the rank of Commodore to Rear Admiral (lower half), a 0–7 grade, in Fiscal Year 1986. The 0–8 grade will be designated Rear Admiral (upper half). 3. Navy and Marine Corps use same size insignia as Army when worn on shoulder straps, but miniature size on shirt collars. Enamel bands are black for Army, scarlet for Marines, medium blue for Air Force, and blue for Navy and Coast Guard. 4. One break. 5. Two breaks. 6. Three breaks.

tion regarding SGLI (Servicemen's Group Life Insurance) and VGLI (Veterans Group Life Insurance) may be obtained from the Office of Servicemen's Group Life Insurance, 213 Washington St., Newark, N.J. 07102

Burial benefits. Burial is provided in any VA national cemetery with available grave space to any deceased veteran of wartime or peacetime service, other than for training, who was discharged under conditions other than dishonorable. Laws of the Congress extend eligibility for burial in a national cemetery to the veteran's spouse, widow, widower, minor children, and under certain conditions, unmarried adult children.

Headstone or marker. A government headstone or marker is furnished for any deceased veteran of wartime or peacetime service, other than for training, who was discharged under conditions other than dishonorable and is interred in a national, state veterans', or private cemetery. VA also will furnish markers to veterans' eligible dependents interred in a national or state veterans' cemetery.

Budget Outlays for National Defense Functions

(In Billions)

Item	1986	1985	1984	1983	1982	1981	1980	1975	1970
Defense Dept., military	265.6	245.4	220.8	204.4	180.7	153.8	131.0	85.9	80.2
Military personnel	71.5	67.8	64.2	60.9	55.2	47.9	40.9	32.2	29.0
Percent of military	26.9	27.6	29.1	30.0	30.5	31.1	31.2	37.5	36.2
Operation, maintenance	75.2	72.3	67.4	64.9	59.7	51.9	44.8	26.3	21.6
Procurement	76.5	70.4	61.9	53.6	43.3	35.2	29.0	16.0	21.6
Research and development	32.3	27.1	23.1	20.6	17.7	15.3	13.1	8.9	7.2
Military construction	5.0	4.3	3.7	3.5	2.9	2.5	2.5	1.5	1.2
Family housing	2.8	2.6	2.4	2.1	2.0	1.7	1.7	1.1	.6
Other[1]	1.4	.8	−1.8	1.2	.1	.6	1.0	.1	1.0
Atomic energy activities[2]	7.4	7.1	6.1	5.2	4.3	3.4	2.9	1.5	1.4
Defense-related activities[3]	.3	.3	.5	.3	.3	.3	.1	.8	.1
Total	**273.4**	**252.7**	**227.4**	**209.9**	**185.3**	**157.5**	**134.0**	**86.5**	**81.7**

1. Revolving and management funds, trust funds, special foreign currency program, allowances, and offsetting receipts. 2. Defense activities only. 3. Includes civil defense activities. *Source:* Office of Management and Budget.

Average Military Strength[1]

(in thousands)

Year	Army	Air Force	Navy	Marine Corps	Total
1941	755	[2]	218	44	1,017
1942	1,992	[2]	416	89	2,498
1943	5,224	[2]	1,206	232	6,662
1944	7,507	[2]	2,386	398	10,290
1945	8,131	[2]	3,205	473	11,809
1950	632	415	412	80	1,539
1951	1,090	584	566	153	2,394
1952	1,597	899	789	219	3,504
1953	1,536	971	809	237	3,554
1954	1,477	939	767	242	3,425
1955	1,311	958	692	217	3,178
1960	871	828	617	173	2,489
1965	966	844	669	190	2,668
1970	1,432	834	732	295	3,293
1971	1,238	763	656	234	2,891
1972	955	749	604	202	2,510
1973	839	706	580	198	2,323
1975	779	628	545	193	2,145
1977	779	577	527	190	2,073
1978	777	570	530	191	2,068
1979	765	565	527	188	2,045
1980	762	561	525	185	2,033
1983	778	581	547	192	2,098
1984	781	597	566	196	2,140
1985	781	602	571	198	2,151
1986	781	608	581	199	2,169

1. Data represent averages of month-end strengths. 2. Air Force data prior to June 30, 1948 included with Army data. NOTE: Detail may not add to totals due to rounding. *Source:* Department of Defense.

U.S. Military Actions Other Than Declared Wars

Hawaii (1893): U.S. Marines, ordered to land by U.S. Minister John L. Stevens, aided the revolutionary Committee of Safety in overthrowing the native government. Stevens then proclaimed Hawaii a U.S. protectorate. Annexation, resisted by the Democratic administration in Washington, was not formally accomplished until 1898.

China (1900): Boxers (a group of Chinese revolutionists) occupied Peking and laid siege to foreign legations. U.S. troops joined an international expedition which relieved the city.

Panama (1903): After Colombia had rejected a proposed agreement for relinquishing sovereignty over the Panama Canal Zone, revolution broke out, aided by promoters of the Panama Canal Co. Two U.S. warships were standing by to protect American privileges. The U.S. recognized the Republic of Panama on November 6.

Dominican Republic (1904): When the Dominican Republic failed to meet debts owed to the U.S. and foreign creditors, President Theodore Roosevelt declared the U.S. intention of exercising "international police power" in the Western Hemisphere whenever necessary. The U.S. accordingly administered customs and managed debt payments of the Dominican Republic from 1905 to 1907.

Nicaragua (1911): The possibility of foreign control over Nicaragua's canal route led to U.S. intervention and agreement. The U.S. landed Marines in Nicaragua (Aug. 14, 1912) to protect American interests there. A small detachment remained until 1933.

Mexico (1914): Mexican dictator Victoriano Huerta, opposed by President Woodrow Wilson, had the support of European governments. An incident involving unarmed U.S. sailors in Tampico led to the landing of U.S. forces on Mexican soil. Veracruz was bombarded by the Navy to prevent the landing of munitions from a German vessel. At the point of war, both powers agreed to mediation by Argentina, Brazil, and Chile. Huerta abdicated, and Venustiano Carranza succeeded to the presidency.

Haiti (1915): U.S. Marines imposed a military occupation. Haiti signed a treaty making it a virtual protectorate of the U.S. until troops were withdrawn in 1934.

Mexico (1916): Raids by Pancho Villa cost American lives on both sides of the border. President Carranza consented to a punitive expedition led by Gen. John J. Pershing, but antagonism grew in Mexico. Wilson withdrew the U.S. force when war with Germany became imminent.

Dominican Republic (1916): Renewed intervention in the Dominican Republic with internal administration by U.S. naval officers lasted until 1924.

Korea (1950): In this undeclared war, which terminated with the July 27, 1953, truce at Panmunjom and the establishment of a neutral nations' supervisory commission, the U.S. and 15 member-nations of the U.N. came to the aid of the Republic of South Korea, whose 38th-parallel border was crossed by the invading Russian Communist-controlled North Koreans, who were later joined by the Chinese Communists.

Lebanon (1958 and 1983): Fearful of the newly formed U.A.R. abetting the rebels of his politically and economically torn country, President Camille Chamoun appealed to the U.S. for military assistance. U.S. troops landed in Beirut in mid-July and left before the end of the year, after internal and external quiet were restored. In September 1983, President Reagan ordered Marines to join an international peacekeeping force in Beirut. On October 23, 241 were killed in the terrorist bombing of the Marine compound. On February 7, 1984, Reagan ordered the Marine contingent withdrawn. He ended the U.S. role in Beirut on March 30 by releasing the Sixth Fleet from the international force.

Dominican Republic (1965): On April 28, when a political coup-turned-civil war endangered the lives of American nationals, President Lyndon B. Johnson rushed 400 marines into Santo Domingo, the beginning of an eventual U.S. peak-commitment of 30,000 troops, constituting the preponderant military strength of the OAS-created Inter-American Peace Force, and 6,500 troops, including 5,000 Americans, remained until after the peaceful inauguration of President Joaquín Balaguer on July 1, 1966, and the entire force left the country on September 20.

Vietnam: This longest war in U.S. history began with economic and technical assistance after 1954 Geneva accords ending the Indochinese War. By 1964 it had escalated into a major conflict.

This involvement spanning the administrations of five Presidents led to domestic discontent in the late 1960s. By April 1969, U.S. troop strength reached a peak of 543,400. Peace negotiations began in Paris in 1968 but proved fruitless. Finally, on Jan. 27, 1973, a peace accord was signed in Paris by the U.S., North and South Vietnam, and the Vietcong. Within 60 days, U.S. POWs were returned, and the U.S. withdrew all military forces from South Vietnam.

Grenada (1983): A left-wing military coup resulted in the intervention of a 1,900-man United States contingent, supported by token forces from Caribbean allies, which engaged an 800-man Cuban Force and secured the island within a few days. The American combat force was brought home two months later although a small non-combat unit was left behind to assist in peacekeeping functions.

U.S. Casualties in Major Wars

War	Branch of service	Numbers engaged	Battle deaths	Other deaths	Total deaths	Wounds not mortal	Total casualties[1]
Revolutionary War 1775 to 1783	Army	n.a.	4,044	n.a.	n.a.	6,004	n.a.
	Navy	n.a.	342	n.a.	n.a.	114	n.a.
	Marines	n.a.	49	n.a.	n.a.	70	n.a.
	Total	**n.a.**	**4,435**	**n.a.**	**n.a.**	**6,188**	**n.a.**
War of 1812 1812 to 1815	Army	n.a.	1,950	n.a.	n.a.	4,000	n.a.
	Navy	n.a.	265	n.a.	n.a.	439	n.a.
	Marines	n.a.	45	n.a.	n.a.	66	n.a.
	Total	**286,730**	**2,260**	**n.a.**	**n.a.**	**4,505**	**n.a.**
Mexican War 1846 to 1848	Army	n.a.	1,721	11,550	13,271	4,102	17,373
	Navy	n.a.	1	n.a.	n.a.	3	n.a.
	Marines	n.a.	11	n.a.	n.a.	47	n.a.
	Total	**78,718**	**1,733**	**n.a.**	**n.a.**	**4,152**	**n.a.**
Civil War[2] 1861 to 1865	Army	2,128,948	138,154	221,374	359,528	280,040	639,568
	Navy	84,415	2,112	2,411	4,523	1,710	6,233
	Marines		148	312	460	131	591
	Total	**2,213,363**	**140,414**	**224,097**	**364,511**	**281,881**	**646,392**
Spanish-American War 1898	Army	280,564	369	2,061	2,430	1,594	4,024
	Navy	22,875	10	0	10	47	57
	Marines	3,321	6	0	6	21	27
	Total	**306,760**	**385**	2,061	**2,446**	**1,662**	**4,108**
World War I 1917 to 1918	Army	4,057,101	50,510	55,868	106,378	193,663	300,041
	Navy	599,051	431	6,856	7,287	819	8,106
	Marines	78,839	2,461	390	2,851	9,520	12,371
	Total	**4,734,991**	**53,402**	**63,114**	**116,516**	**204,002**	**320,518**
World War II 1941 to 1946	Army[3]	11,260,000	234,874	83,400	318,274	565,861	884,135
	Navy	4,183,466	36,950	25,664	62,614	37,778	100,392
	Marines	669,100	19,733	4,778	24,511	67,207	91,718
	Total	**16,112,566**	**291,557**	**113,842**	**405,399**	**670,846**	**1,076,245**
Korean War 1950 to 1953	Army	2,834,000	27,704	9,429	37,133	77,596	114,729
	Navy	1,177,000	458	4,043	4,501	1,576	6,077
	Marines	424,000	4,267	1,261	5,528	23,744	29,272
	Air Force	1,285,000	1,200	5,884	7,084	368	7,452
	Total	**5,720,000**	**33,629**	**20,617**	**54,246**	**103,284**	**157,530**
War in Southeast Asia[4]	Army	4,386,000	30,904	7,270	38,174	96,802	134,976
	Navy[5]	1,842,000	1,634	916	2,552	4,178	6,730
	Marines	794,000	13,079	1,750	14,829	51,392	66,221
	Air Force	1,740,000	1,765	815	2,580	931	3,511
	Total	**8,744,000**	**47,382**	**10,753**	**58,135**	**153,303**	**211,438**

1. Excludes captured or interned and missing in action who were subsequently returned to military control. 2. Union forces only. Totals should probably be somewhat larger as data or disposition of prisoners are far from complete. Final Confederate deaths, based on incomplete returns, were 133,821, to which should be added 26,000–31,000 personnel who died in Union prisons. 3. Army data include Air Force. 4. As of Nov. 11, 1986. 5. Includes a small number of Coast Guard of which 5 were battle deaths. NOTE: All data are subject to revision. For wars before World War I, information represents best data from available records. However, due to incomplete records and possible difference in usage of terminology, reporting systems, etc., figures should be considered estimates. n.a. = not available. *Source:* Department of Defense.

The Kamikazes in World War II

During the 13th century, a great typhoon off the coast of Japan nearly destroyed the ships of an invading Mongol army. This seeming intervention by Providence was considered a "Divine Wind" or Kamikaze by the Japanese people.

In late 1944, the United States was in the process of recapturing the Philippine Islands from Japan. In a desperate act to prevent it, Japanese military leaders authorized the formation of a Special Attack Force whose mission was to destroy American aircraft carriers. Each member of this special unit had volunteered to sacrifice his life by diving a bomb-laden plane into the deck of a U.S. flattop.

The suicide fliers were called the Kamikaze, named after the Divine Wind that had saved their country from invasion in the past.

By the end of the war, over 1,200 Kamikaze pilots had sunk 34 U.S. ships and damaged 288 others. There was never a shortage of volunteers for the suicide missions, only a shortage of planes and fuel for them to make their desperate attacks in.

Casualties in World War I

Country	Total mobilized forces	Killed or died[1]	Wounded	Prisoners or missing	Total casualties
Austria-Hungary	7,800,000	1,200,000	3,620,000	2,200,000	7,020,000
Belgium	267,000	13,716	44,686	34,659	93,061
British Empire[2]	8,904,467	908,371	2,090,212	191,652	3,190,235
Bulgaria	1,200,000	87,500	152,390	27,029	266,919
France[2]	8,410,000	1,357,800	4,266,000	537,000	6,160,800
Germany	11,000,000	1,773,700	4,216,058	1,152,800	7,142,558
Greece	230,000	5,000	21,000	1,000	27,000
Italy	5,615,000	650,000	947,000	600,000	2,197,000
Japan	800,000	300	907	3	1,210
Montenegro	50,000	3,000	10,000	7,000	20,000
Portugal	100,000	7,222	13,751	12,318	33,291
Romania	750,000	335,706	120,000	80,000	535,706
Russia	12,000,000	1,700,000	4,950,000	2,500,000	9,150,000
Serbia	707,343	45,000	133,148	152,958	331,106
Turkey	2,850,000	325,000	400,000	250,000	975,000
United States	4,734,991	116,516	204,002	—	320,518

1. Includes deaths from all causes. 2. Official figures. NOTE: For additional U.S. figures, *see* the table on U.S. Casualties in Major Wars in this section.

Casualties in World War II

Country	Men in war	Battle deaths	Wounded
Australia	1,000,000	26,976	180,864
Austria	800,000	280,000	350,117
Belgium	625,000	8,460	55,513[1]
Brazil[2]	40,334	943	4,222
Bulgaria	339,760	6,671	21,878
Canada	1,076,343[7]	32,714[7]	53,145
China[3]	17,250,521	1,324,516	1,762,006
Czechoslovakia	—	6,683[4]	8,017
Denmark	—	4,339	—
Finland	500,000	79,047	50,000
France	—	201,568	400,000
Germany	20,000,000	3,250,000[4]	7,250,000
Greece	—	17,024	47,290
Hungary	—	147,435	89,313
India	2,393,891	32,121	64,354
Italy	3,100,000	149,496[4]	66,716
Japan	9,700,000	1,270,000	140,000
Netherlands	280,000	6,500	2,860
New Zealand	194,000	11,625[4]	17,000
Norway	75,000	2,000	—
Poland	—	664,000	530,000
Romania	650,000[5]	350,000[6]	—
South Africa	410,056	2,473	—
U.S.S.R.	—	6,115,000[4]	14,012,000
United Kingdom	5,896,000	357,116[4]	369,267
United States	16,112,566	291,557	670,846
Yugoslavia	3,741,000	305,000	425,000

1. Civilians only. 2. Army and Navy figures. 3. Figures cover period July 7, 1937–Sept. 2, 1945, and concern only Chinese regular troops. They do not include casualties suffered by guerrillas and local military corps. 4. Deaths from all causes. 5. Against Soviet Russia; 385,847 against Nazi Germany. 6. Against Soviet Russia; 169,822 against Nazi Germany. 7. National Defense Ctr., Canadian Forces Hq., Director of History. NOTE: The figures in this table are unofficial estimates obtained from various sources.

The Fire-Bombing of Dresden

Early in 1945 Allied forces obliterated the greater part of one of the most beautiful cities in Europe, killing at least 35,000 people and perhaps 135,000.

The fire-bombing of Dresden was launched by the British Royal Air Force with 800 aircraft in the night of February 13–14 and continued by the U.S. 8th Air Force with 400 aircraft in daylight on February 14, with 200 on February 15, with 400 again on March 2, and, finally, with 572 on April 17. The raids allegedly were intended to promote the Soviet advance by destroying a center of communications important to the German defense of the Eastern Front, but, in fact, they did nothing to help the Red Army militarily and may have been motivated as retribution for the German bombing of Coventry earlier in the war.

History of Arms Control Agreements

League of Nations

The League was established in 1920 by the peace treaties ending World War I and dissolved in 1946 after the U.N. had come into being. It was designed to promote peace and social progress.

The League functioned in a period when most of today's countries were still under colonial rule and thus ineligible for membership in an organization composed of sovereign states.

India was an original member of the League because it had attended the peace conferences and signed the treaties as a separate unit of the British Empire. Iraq was admitted in 1932 as an independent country even though it was still dependent on the United Kingdom in foreign affairs. Nor did all the major powers all participate fully in League activities.

The United States did not choose to become a member, and when the U.S.S.R. joined in 1934, Brazil, Germany, and Japan had already withdrawn.

Treaty for a Partial Nuclear Test Ban

Agreement, effective Oct. 10, 1963, signed in Moscow Aug. 8, 1963, by the U.S., U.K., and the U.S.S.R. Although over 100 nations have since signed, France and China have not. The treaty banned nuclear testing in the atmosphere, in outer space, or under water. The signatories can withdraw under certain conditions.

The Nuclear Nonproliferation Treaty (NPT)

The agreement pledged to limit the spread of nuclear arms. Under its terms, nations party to the treaty that did not possess nuclear weapons when the treaty was concluded may not acquire them in the future. While the treaty affirms the right to develop nuclear energy for peaceful purposes, the non-nuclear weapons states must accept inspection by the International Atomic Energy Agency (IAEA) to insure that nuclear materials are not diverted from peaceful to military uses.

The treaty was adopted in 1958 and 130 states are party to it, including all NATO and Warsaw Pact countries. The treaty calls for a review conference to take place every five years. The last conference was held in Geneva in August 1985.

Strategic Arms Limitation Talks (SALT I)

Two agreements limiting American and Soviet nuclear weapons were signed in Moscow in 1972 after three years of negotiations. One was a five-year interim pact limiting some offensive strategic weapons and the number of launchers for intercontinental ballistic missiles carrying nuclear warheads. The other, a treaty of indefinite duration, restricted antiballistic or defensive missiles to 200 on each side. (That number was reduced to 100 in a 1974 amendment.) The agreements were signed by President Richard M. Nixon and Leonid I. Brezhnev, the Soviet Communist Party leader. The two countries continued to observe the limits in the strategic arms pact long after the theoretical expiration date.

(SALT II)

A treaty resulting from the second round of strategic arms limitation talks was signed in Vienna on June 18, 1979, by President Carter and Soviet leader Leonid Brezhnev. It was sent to the U.S. Senate for ratification, but ran into sharp opposition. Following the Soviet invasion of Afghanistan in December 1979, Carter delayed ratification efforts indefinitely. However, both the United States and the Soviet Union continued to abide by the major provisions while accusing each other of violating some of the fine print. The pact, which was to run to 1985, set equal overall ceilings on major categories of strategic nuclear weapons. Specific ceilings for each side included 2,400 (2,250 after 1981) ICBM launchers, submarine-launched ballistic missiles and long-range heavy bombers. Before his election in 1980, President Reagan described the Salt II treaty as "fatally flawed." But when it was due to expire in 1985, Reagan said he would go "the extra mile" in pursuit of arms control by continuing to abide by the unratified agreement at least until the end of the year.

The Baruch Plan for Atomic Controls

The horror of the wartime atom bomb and its potential as a cheap and widely available weapon aroused universal concern for methods of taming atomic energy to save civilization. In 1946 the United States adopted as its official policy a report drawn up by State Department consultants and presented formally by Bernard M. Baruch, the statesman, U.S. representative on a newly formed United Nations Atomic Energy Commission. This "Baruch plan" distinguished between "dangerous" activities—production of fissionable material for atomic bombs—and peaceful development of atomic energy, the different processes involved making this distinction possible. Thus, the Baruch plan sought the creation of an Atomic Development Authority by the United Nations with complete control over production of dangerous materials, including control of all uranium and thorium mines and of plants producing fissionable materials. The plan called for rigid international inspection and swift punishment of violators, with no veto over atomic weapons questions.

The Soviet U.N. delegate, Andrei A. Gromyko, however, rejected the Baruch proposal and instead demanded a treaty to outlaw atomic bombs, destruction of all atomic bombs within three months from its signing, and with each nation to supervise its own policing. This, of course, was viewed as reflecting the Soviet Union's own concern for its international position since it then had no bombs of its own.

The details of those early discussions and the potentials for the peaceful use of atomic energy were set forth by William L. Laurence, the famed Pulitzer-Prize-winning science writer of *The New York Times*, in the 1947 edition of *Information Please Almanac.*

Have You Won a Vacation?

By the Council of Better Business Bureaus, Inc.

How Do Vacation Certificates Work?

Timeshare resorts, travel clubs, automobile dealers, and even solar energy companies may notify you by mail or telephone that "You have been selected for an island vacation that includes free airfare and accommodations" or that you can "Join our travel club and get a 'free' vacation." Maybe you filled out an entry form for a vacation sweepstakes or other prize giveaway at a store, fair, trade show, or other local event. Some companies may advertise "free" vacations as a bonus for buying products or services.

To receive the vacation certificate, you may be required to make a purchase or attend a sales presentation, often at a timeshare resort, membership campground, or other land sales promotion. In addition, there may be other conditions for acceptance, such as age or income requirements, or attendance with your spouse. You might also have to bring the notice you received from the company, and proof of your identity.

Vacation certificate offers vary. Some certificates include lodging in a hotel or timeshare resort for a certain number of days and nights in the United States or out of the country. Other offers include "free" airfare or a cruise, or give you one "free" ticket with the purchase of the second. Some certificates include discount or "free" coupons for restaurants, tours, or attractions in the resort area.

You are usually required to fill out the vacation certificate with information such as your three choices of when you wish to take the vacation. You return it to the company 30 to 60 days before you wish to use the vacation offer.

Companies may require a non-refundable processing and handling fee, or a refundable deposit from $50 to $100 to reserve the vacation time request. Vacation certificates requiring a refundable deposit usually state that the deposit will be returned upon your arrival at the place of lodging or after you have used the vacation. Companies usually advise that written confirmation will be sent when the deposit is received.

Businesses often provide vacation certificates in large quantities believing that the attraction of a "free" vacation will draw customers to their sales site. The goal of the business is to sell a specific product or service. Although many people receive these offers, one promoter stated that very few will actually use the vacation certificate. For this reason, they can afford to promote the vacation certificate to many people.

According to one timeshare resort operator, the offer of "free" lodging is used to introduce a new timeshare resort to potential buyers. Another company stated that in offering the "free" vacation to its customers, it sold products and created goodwill.

Why Does the Airfare or Other Costs Seem So Low?

In many cases, if a low fare for transportation or low hotel rates are offered, the company makes up its loss in another area. In other words, you don't get something for nothing. For example, one marketing company offered low airfare to a resort island with hotel bookings made through the company. However, the marketing company did not state that it was on a space-available basis or that hotel rates were $40 a day higher than the average hotel, and you had to stay at least seven nights.

BBB Customer Experience

A survey of local Better Business Bureaus across the country showed that there have been consumer complaints about vacation certificate offers. Some consumers complained they did not receive the offered vacation certificate. Others complained the offer was misrepresented. For example, some participants stated that they received incomplete information regarding airfare costs and couldn't get airfare reservations or requested vacation times. One consumer claimed that the offer described over the phone was different from written information given after the sales presentation. Some consumers stated that other eligibility requirements were added to those conditions listed in promotional literature.

State Regulations

At least one state (Florida) requires companies such as timeshare resorts that offer lodging promotions to file certain information with the state's attorney general. In Maryland, timeshare promoters must register with the state's real estate commission. Also, Maryland residents receiving a "free" gift or prize promotion do not have to listen to a sales presentation or buy any product/service. Texas and New York state laws require, among other things, that the odds of winning and the approximate retail value of the prizes be given in a company promotion.

Many states have actively sought to protect consumers against misrepresentations made by some vacation certificate promoters. For example, the Arizona Attorney General took legal action against one vacation certificate promoter who did not disclose all the limitations of the vacation offer. Although buyers had been told that extra fees would be charged for the peak season, they weren't told that 80% of the year was considered the peak season. The California Attorney General filed a complaint against a travel club company that called consumers and asked them for a major credit card number to validate a complimentary vacation. However, the company charged fees on the consumers' credit card accounts without their permission.

Consumers should contact their state's attorney general and find out if companies offering vacation certificates are required to register their offers with the state. □

U.S. Passport and Customs Information

Source: Department of State, Bureau of Consular Affairs and Department of the Treasury, Customs Service.

With a few exceptions, a passport is required for all U.S. citizens to depart and enter the United States and to enter most foreign countries. A valid U.S. passport is the best documentation of U.S. citizenship available. Persons who travel to a country where a U.S. passport is not required should be in possession of documentary evidence of their U.S. citizenship and identity to facilitate reentry into the United States. Travelers should check passport and visa requirements with consular officials of the countries to be visited well in advance of their departure date.

Application for a passport may be made at a passport agency; to a clerk of any Federal court or State court of record; or a judge or clerk of any probate court accepting applications; or at a post office selected to accept passport applications. Passport agencies are located in Boston, Chicago, Honolulu, Houston, Los Angeles, Miami, New Orleans, New York, Philadelphia, San Francisco, Seattle, Stamford, Conn., and Washington, D.C.

All persons are required to obtain individual passports in their own names. Neither spouses nor children may be included in each others' passports. Any applicant who is 13 years of age or older must appear in person before the clerk or agent executing the application. For children under the age of 13, a parent or legal guardian may execute an application for them.

First time passport applicants must apply in person. Applicants must present evidence of citizenship (e.g., a certified copy of birth certificate), personal identification (e.g., a valid driver's license), two identical photographs taken within six months (2 × 2 inches, with the image size measured from the bottom of the chin to the top of the head [including hair] not less than 1 inch nor more than 1 3/8 inches on a plain white or off-white background, vending machine photographs not acceptable), plus a completed passport application (DSP-11). If you claim citizenship by naturalization, a Certificate of Naturalization is also required. A fee of $35 plus a $7 execution fee is charged for adults 18 years and older for a passport valid for ten years from the date of issue. The fee for minor children under 18 years of age is $20 for a five-year passport plus $7 for the execution of the application.

You may apply for a passport by mail if you have been the bearer of a passport issued within 12 years prior to the date of a new application, are able to submit your most recent U.S. passport with your new application, and your previous passport was not issued before your 16th birthday. If you are eligible to apply by mail, include your previous passport, a completed and signed DSP-82 "Application for Passport by Mail," new photographs, and the passport fee of $35. The $7 execution fee is not required when applying by mail.

Passports may be presented for amendment to show a married name or legal change of name or to correct descriptive data. Any alterations to the passport by the bearer *other than* in the spaces provided for change of address and next of kin data are forbidden.

Loss, theft or destruction of a passport should be reported to Passport Services, Washington, D.C. 20524 immediately, or if overseas, to the nearest U.S. embassy or consulate. Your passport is a valuable citizenship and identity document. It should be carefully safeguarded. Its loss could cause you unnecessary travel complications as well as significant expense. It is advisable to photocopy the data page of your passport and keep it in a place separate from your passport to facilitate the issuance of a replacement passport should one be necessary.

Customs

United States residents must declare all articles acquired abroad and in their possession at the time of their return. In addition, articles acquired in the U.S. Virgin Islands, American Samoa, or Guam and not accompanying you must be declared at the time of your return. The wearing or use of an article acquired abroad does *not* exempt it from duty. Customs declaration forms are distributed on vessels and planes, and should be prepared in advance of arrival for presentation to the customs inspectors.

If you have not exceeded the duty-free exemption allowed, you may make an oral declaration to the customs inspector. A written declaration is necessary when (1) total fair retail value of articles exceeds $1,400 ($400 tax-free exemption plus $1,000 dutiable at a flat 10% rate) (keep your sales slips); (2) over 1 liter of liquor, 200 cigarettes, or 100 cigars are included; (3) items are not intended for your personal or household use, or articles brought home for another person; and (4) when a customs duty or internal revenue tax is collectible on any article in your possession.

An exception to the above are regulations applicable to articles purchased in the U.S. Virgin Islands, American Samoa, or Guam where you may receive a customs exemption of $800. Not more than $400 of this exemption may be applied to merchandise obtained elsewhere than in these islands. Five liters of alcoholic beverages and 1000 cigarettes may be included provided not more than one liter and 200 cigarettes were acquired elsewhere than in these islands. Articles acquired in and sent from these islands to the United States may be claimed under your duty-free personal exemption if properly declared at the time of your return.

Articles accompanying you, in excess of your personal exemption, up to $1000 will be assessed at a flat rate of duty of 10% based on fair retail value in country of acquisition. (If articles were acquired in the insular possessions, the flat rate of duty is 5% and these goods may accompany you or be shipped home.) These articles must be for your personal use or for use as gifts and not for sale. This provision may be used every 30 days, excluding the day of your last arrival. Any items which have a "free" duty rate will be excluded before duty is calculated.

Other exemptions include in part: automobiles, boats, planes, or other vehicles taken abroad for noncommercial use. Foreign-made personal articles (e.g., watches, cameras, etc.) taken abroad should be registered with Customs before departure. Gifts of not more than $50 can be shipped back to the United States tax and duty free ($100 if mailed from the Virgin Islands, American Samoa, or Guam). Household effects and tools of trade which you take out of the United States are duty ree at time of return.

Prohibited and restricted articles include in part: bsinthe, narcotics and dangerous drugs, obscene rticles and publications, seditious and treasonable naterials, hazardous articles (e.g., fireworks, dangerous toys, toxic and poisonous substances, and witchblade knives), biological materials of public ealth or veterinary importance, fruit, vegetables nd plants, meats, poultry and products thereof, irds, monkeys, and turtles.

If you understate the value of an article you de-lare, or if you otherwise misrepresent an article n your declaration, you may have to pay a penalty n addition to payment of duty. Under certain cir-umstances, the article could be seized and for-eited if the penalty is not paid.

If you fail to declare an article acquired abroad, ot only is the article subject to seizure and forfei-ure, but you will be liable for a personal penalty n an amount equal to the value of the article in the United States. In addition, you may also be liable to criminal prosecution.

If you carry more than $10,000 into or out of the United States in currency (either United States or foreign money), negotiable instruments in bearer form, or travelers checks, a report must be filed with United States Customs at the time you arrive or depart with such amounts.

As U.S. restrictions on travel to Cuba, North Korea, Vietnam, and Cambodia have been eased, the Office of Foreign Assets Control (FAC) issued a general license, effective March 21, 1977, which allows visitors to those countries to purchase a maximum of $100 worth of goods. This amount is based on retail value in the country where acquired. These articles must be for personal use—not for resale—and must accompany the traveler on his entry into the U.S. This allowance may be used only once every 6 months.

Consular Assistance Abroad

Source: U.S. Department of State.

U.S. consular officers are located at U.S. Embassies and consulates in most countries abroad. Consular officers can advise you of any adverse conditions in the places you are visiting and can help you in emergencies. If you plan more than a short stay in one place or if you are in an area experiencing civil unrest or some natural disaster, it is advisable to register with the nearest U.S. Embassy or consulate. This will make it easier should someone at home need to locate you urgently or in the unlikely event that you need to be evacuated due to an emergency. It will also facilitate the issuance of a new passport should yours be lost or stolen.

Should you find yourself in any legal difficulty, contact a consular officer immediately. Consular officers cannot serve as attorneys or give legal advice but they can provide lists of local attorneys and help you find legal representation. Consular officers cannot get you out of jail. However, if you are arrested, ask permission to notify a consular official—it is your right. American consular officials will visit you, advise you of your rights under local laws, ensure that you aren't held under inhumane conditions, and contact your family and friends for you if you desire. They can transfer money, and will try to get relief for you, including food and clothing in countries where this is a problem. If you become destitute overseas, consular officers can help you get in touch with your family, friends, bank, or employer and inform them how to wire funds to you.

Travel Advisories

Source: U.S. Department of State.

The Department of State tries to alert American travelers to adverse conditions abroad—including violence—through the travel advisory program. In consultation with our embassies and consulates overseas, and various bureaus of the Department of State, the Office of Overseas Citizens Services in the Bureau of Consular Affairs issues travel advisories about conditions in specific countries. Advisories generally do not pertain to isolated international terrorist incidents since these can occur anywhere and at any time. The majority of these advisories deal with short-term or temporary difficulties which Americans may encounter when they go abroad. Some mention conditions of political or civil unrest which could pose a threat to personal safety.

There are only a few advisories in effect which advise avoiding all travel to a particular country because of a high incidence of terrorism within the region or because a long-term problem exists. Most of the security-related advisories do not recommend against travel to an entire country but suggest avoiding specific areas within a country where unrest is endemic.

Ask about current travel advisories for specific countries at any of the 13 regional U.S. passport agencies and at U.S. Embassies and consulates abroad. Travel advisories are also widely disseminated to interested organizations, travel associations, and airlines.

Avoiding Motion Sickness

(*Source:* American Council on Science and Health)

The Food and Drug Administration suggests the following:

(1) Place yourself where there is the least motion: on deck and amidships on a ship, in the front seat of a car, and over the wing of a plane.

(2) When traveling in a vehicle where seat belts are not necessary, lie on your back, in a semireclined position, and keep your head as still as possible. In an automobile, do this only to the extent possible without removing your seat belt. Safety must take priority over motion sickness.

(3) Don't watch the waves or fast-moving scenery.

(4) Avoid food and tobacco odors.

(5) Don't overindulge in food or alcohol the night before a trip.

When buying over-the-counter remedies for motion sickness, read the labels carefully. Some are unsuitable for children. All are unsuitable if you have certain medical problems or if you're the one who will be driving or piloting the vehicle in question (they cause drowsiness). If you must take other medications, consult your doctor before using motion sickness remedies; some drugs should not be mixed because they magnify or antagonize each other's effects.

State and City Tourism Offices

The following is a selected list of state, tourism offices. Where a toll-free 800 number is available, it is given. However, the numbers are subject to change.

ALABAMA
Bureau of Tourism & Travel
532 S. Perry St.
Montgomery, AL 36104
205-261-4169 or
1-800-ALABAMA (out of state)
1-800-392-8096 (in state)

ALASKA
Alaska Division of Tourism
P.O. Box E
Juneau, AK 99811
907-465-2010

ARIZONA
Arizona Office of Tourism
Suite 180
1480 E. Bethany Home Rd.
Phoenix, AZ 85014
602-255-3618

ARKANSAS
Arkansas Department of Parks and Tourism
1 Capitol Mall
Little Rock, AR 72201
501-371-7777 or
1-800-482-8999 or
1-800-643-8383
(Out of state)

CALIFORNIA
California Office of Tourism
Department of Commerce
1121 L Street
Suite 103
Sacramento, CA 95814
916-322-2881

COLORADO
Colorado Tourism Board
1625 Broadway, Suite 1700
Denver, CO 80202
303-592-5410

CONNECTICUT
Tourism Promotion Service
Connecticut Department of Economic Development
210 Washington St.
Hartford, CT 06106
203-566-3948 or
1-800-842-7492 (Connecticut)
1-800-243-1685 (Maine through Virginia)

DELAWARE
Delaware Tourism Office
Delaware Development Office
99 Kings Highway
P.O. Box 1401
Dover, DE 19903
302-736-4271 or
1-800-441-8846

DISTRICT OF COLUMBIA
Washington Convention and Visitors Association
Suite 250
1575 Eye Street, NW
Washington, D.C. 20005
202-789-7000

FLORIDA
Department of Commerce Visitors Inquiry
126 Van Buren St.
Tallahassee, FL 32301
904-487-1462

GEORGIA
Tourist Division
P.O. Box 1776
Atlanta, GA 30301
404-656-3590 or
1-800-VISIT-GA

HAWAII
Hawaii Visitors Bureau
2270 Kalakaua Ave., Suite 801
Honolulu, HI 96815
808-923-1811

IDAHO
Department of Commerce
Statehouse, Rm. 108
Boise, ID 83720
208-334-2470 or
1-800-635-7820
(Out of state)

ILLINOIS
Illinois Department of Commerce and Community Affairs, Office of Tourism
620 East Adams Street
Springfield, IL 62701
217-782-7139

INDIANA
Indiana Dept. of Commerce
Tourism Division
1 North Capitol, Suite 700
Indianapolis, IN 46204
317-232-8860

IOWA
Iowa Department of Economic Development
Tourism/Film Office
200 East Grand Avenue
Des Moines, IA 50309
515-281-3100

KANSAS
Travel & Tourism Development Division
Department of Commerce
400 W. 8th St., 5th Floor
Topeka, KS 66603
913-296-2009

KENTUCKY
Department of Travel Development
Capital Plaza Tower
Frankfort, KY 40601
502-564-4930 or
1-800-225-TRIP
(Continental United States and provinces of Ontario and Quebec, Canada)

LOUISIANA
Office of Tourism
P.O. Box 94291
Baton Rouge, LA 70804-9291
504-925-3860 or
1-800-33GUMBO

MAINE
Maine Publicity Bureau
97 Winthrop St., P.O. Box 2300
Hallowell, ME 04347-2300
207-289-2423

MARYLAND
Office of Tourist Development
45 Calvert Street
Annapolis, MD 21401
301-974-3517

MASSACHUSETTS
Dept. of Food & Agriculture
Bureau of Markets
100 Cambridge St.
Boston, MA 02202
617-727-3018

MICHIGAN
Travel Bureau
Department of Commerce
P.O. Box 30226
Lansing, MI 48909
517-373-1195 or 1-800-5432-YES
or for latest recorded information on special seasonal activities, 1-800-292-5404 (in state) or 1-800-248-5708

MINNESOTA
Minnesota Office of Tourism
375 Jackson St.
250 Skyway Level
Farm Credit Services Bldg.
St. Paul, MN 55101
612-296-5029 or
1-800-328-1461

MISSISSIPPI
Division of Tourism
Department of Economic Development
P.O. Box 849
Jackson, MS 39205
601-359-3414 or
1-800-647-2290

Average Daily Temperatures (°F) in Tourist Cities

Location	January High	January Low	April High	April Low	July High	July Low	October High	October Low
U.S. CITIES								
(See Weather and Climate Section)								
CANADA								
Ottawa	21	3	51	31	81	58	54	37
Quebec	18	2	45	29	76	57	51	37
Toronto	30	16	50	34	79	59	56	40
Vancouver	41	32	58	40	74	54	57	44
MEXICO								
Acapulco	85	70	87	71	89	75	88	74
Mexico City	66	42	78	52	74	54	70	50
OVERSEAS								
Australia (Sydney)	78	65	71	58	60	46	71	56
Austria (Vienna)	34	26	57	41	75	59	55	44
Bahamas (Nassau)	77	65	81	69	88	75	85	73
Bermuda (Hamilton)	68	58	71	59	85	73	79	69
Brazil (Rio de Janeiro)	84	73	80	69	75	63	77	66
Denmark (Copenhagen)	36	29	50	37	72	55	53	42
Egypt (Cairo)	65	47	83	57	96	70	86	65
France (Paris)	42	32	60	41	76	55	59	44
Germany (Berlin)	35	26	55	38	74	55	55	41
Greece (Athens)	54	42	67	52	90	72	74	60
Hong Kong	64	56	75	67	87	78	81	73
India (Calcutta)	80	55	97	76	90	79	89	74
Italy (Rome)	54	39	68	46	88	64	73	53
Israel (Jerusalem)	55	41	73	50	87	63	81	59
Japan (Tokyo)	47	29	63	46	83	70	69	55
Nigeria (Lagos)	88	74	89	77	83	74	85	74
Netherlands (Amsterdam)	40	34	52	43	69	59	56	48
Puerto Rico (San Juan)	81	67	84	69	87	74	87	73
South Africa (Cape Town)	78	60	72	53	63	45	70	52
Spain (Madrid)	47	33	64	44	87	62	66	48
United Kingdom (London)	44	35	56	40	73	55	58	44
United Kingdom (Edinburgh)	43	35	50	39	65	52	53	44
U.S.S.R. (Moscow)	21	9	47	31	76	55	46	34
Venezuela (Caracas)	75	56	81	60	78	61	79	61
Yugoslavia (Belgrade)	37	27	64	45	84	61	65	47

MISSOURI
Missouri Division of Tourism
Truman State Office Bldg.
301 W. High St.
P.O. Box 1055
Jefferson City, MO 65102
314-751-4133

MONTANA
Travel Promotion
Department of Commerce
1424 9th Ave.
Helena, MT 59620
406-444-2654 or
1-800-548-3390

NEBRASKA
Dept. of Economic Development
Division of Travel and Tourism
301 Centennial Mall South
P.O. Box 94666
Lincoln, NE 68509
402-471-3796 or
1-800-742-7595 or
1-800-228-4307 (out of state)

NEVADA
Commission on Tourism
Capitol Complex
Carson City, NV 89710
1-800-237-0774

NEW HAMPSHIRE
Office of Vacation Travel
P.O. Box 856
Concord, NH 03301
603-271-2666
or for recorded weekly events, ski conditions, foliage reports
1-800-258-3608

NEW JERSEY
Division of Travel and Tourism
CN-826
Trenton, NJ 08625
609-292-2470

NEW MEXICO
Economic Development and Tourism Department
Tourism and Travel Division
Joseph Montoya Bldg.
1100 St. Francis Dr.
Santa Fe, NM 87502
505-827-0291 or
1-800-545-2040

NEW YORK
Division of Tourism
1 Commerce Plaza
Albany, NY 12245
Toll free from all continental states, Puerto Rico, and the Virgin Islands
1-800-225-5697 or
518-474-4116

NORTH CAROLINA
Travel and Tourism Division
Department of Commerce
430 North Salisbury St.
Raleigh, NC 27611
919-733-4171 or 1-800-VISIT NC

NORTH DAKOTA
North Dakota Tourism Promotion
Liberty Memorial Building
Capitol Grounds
Bismarck, ND 58505
701-224-2525 or
1-800-437-2077 (out of state)

OHIO
Ohio Division of Travel and Tourism
P.O. Box 1001
Columbus, OH 43266-0101
614-466-8844 (Business Office)
1-800-BUCKEYE (National Toll-Free Travel Hotline)

OKLAHOMA
Oklahoma Tourism and Recreation Dept.
Literature Distribution Center
215 NE 28th Street
Oklahoma City, OK 73105
405-521-2409 (in Oklahoma & states not mentioned below)
1-800-652-6552 (in AR, CO, KS, MO, NM, and TX except area code 512)

OREGON
Tourism Division
Oregon Economic Development
595 Cottage St., NE
Salem, OR 97310
503-378-3451 or
1-800-547-7842 (Out of state)

PENNSYLVANIA
Bureau of Travel Development
416 Forum Building
Harrisburg, PA 17120
717-787-5453 (Business Office)
1-800-VISIT PA, ext. 275 (Consumer Information)

RHODE ISLAND
Rhode Island Tourism Division
7 Jackson Walkway
Providence, RI 02903
401-277-2601 or
1-800-556-2484 (For residents from Maine to Virginia/West Virginia and Northern Ohio)

SOUTH CAROLINA
South Carolina Division of Tourism
Box 71
Columbia, SC 29202
803-253-6318

SOUTH DAKOTA
Department of Tourism
Capitol Lake Plaza
711 Wells
Pierre, South Dakota 57501
605-773-3301 or
1-800-843-1930

TENNESSEE
Department of Tourist Development
P.O. Box 23170
Nashville, TN 37202
615-741-2158

TEXAS
Travel Information Services
State Highway Department
P.O. Box 5064
Austin, TX 78763-5064
512-463-8586

UTAH
Utah Travel Council
Council Hall, Capitol Hill
Salt Lake City, UT 84114
801-533-5681

VERMONT
Agency of Development and Community Affairs
Travel Division
134 State St.
Montpelier, VT 05602
802-828-3236

VIRGINIA
Virginia Division of Tourism
202 North Ninth Street
Suite 500
Richmond, VA 23219
804-786-4484

WASHINGTON
Washington State Dept. of Trade and Economic Development
101 General Administration Bldg.
AX-13
Olympia, WA 98504
206-753-5630

WASHINGTON, D.C.
See District of Columbia

WEST VIRGINIA
Dept. of Commerce
State Capitol Complex
Charleston, WV 25305
304-348-2286 or
1-800-CALL-WVA

WISCONSIN
Department of Business Development
Division of Tourism Development
Box 7606
Madison, WI 53707
Toll free in WI and neighbor states 1-800-escapes
others: 608-266-2161

WYOMING
Wyoming Travel Commission
I-25 at College Drive
Cheyenne, WY 82002-0660
307-777-7777 or
1-800-225-5996

U.S. Embassy Addresses

Key Officers of Foreign Service Posts provides names of key officers and addresses for all U.S. Embassies and consulates abroad. This publication is updated three times a year. The single copy purchase price is $4.25. To obtain a copy, write to the Superintendent of Documents, U.S. Government Printing Office, Washington, D.C. 20402.

Additional Information

The booklet, *Your Trip Abroad*, contains some valuable information on loss and theft of a passport as well as other travel tips. To obtain a copy, write to the Superintendent of Documents, U.S. Government Printing Office, Washington, D.C. 20402. The single copy price is $1.

Country Information Notices provide advice on travel to specific areas of the world. Notices include topics such as currency and customs regulations, entry requirements, dual nationality, import and export controls, vaccination requirements, and drug warnings. Single copies of the following publications are free by sending a stamped, self-addressed envelope to Bureau of Consular Affairs, Public Affairs Staff, Room 5807, Department of State, Washington, D.C. 20520.

Foreign Currency Exchange

The Deak-Perera Group, the largest private organization specializing in foreign money exchange, has offices in some airports. It is generally advisable for an American traveling to a foreign destination to have a small amount of the foreign currency on hand on arrival. Currency can usually be exchanged at foreign entry points.

Road Mileages Between U.S. Cities[1]

Cities	Birmingham	Boston	Buffalo	Chicago	Cleveland	Dallas	Denver
Birmingham, Ala.	—	1,194	947	657	734	653	1,318
Boston, Mass.	1,194	—	457	983	639	1,815	1,991
Buffalo, N.Y.	947	457	—	536	192	1,387	1,561
Chicago, Ill.	657	983	536	—	344	931	1,050
Cleveland, Ohio	734	639	192	344	—	1,205	1,369
Dallas, Tex.	653	1,815	1,387	931	1,205	—	801
Denver, Colo	1,318	1,991	1,561	1,050	1,369	801	—
Detroit, Mich.	754	702	252	279	175	1,167	1,301
El Paso, Tex.	1,278	2,358	1,928	1,439	1,746	625	652
Houston, Tex.	692	1,886	1,532	1,092	1,358	242	1,032
Indianapolis, Ind.	492	940	510	189	318	877	1,051
Kansas City, Mo.	703	1,427	997	503	815	508	616
Los Angeles, Calif.	2,078	3,036	2,606	2,112	2,424	1,425	1,174
Louisville, Ky.	378	996	571	305	379	865	1,135
Memphis, Tenn.	249	1,345	965	546	773	470	1,069
Miami, Fla.	777	1,539	1,445	1,390	1,325	1,332	2,094
Minneapolis, Minn.	1,067	1,402	955	411	763	969	867
New Orleans, La.	347	1,541	1,294	947	1,102	504	1,305
New York, N.Y.	983	213	436	840	514	1,604	1,780
Omaha, Neb.	907	1,458	1,011	493	819	661	559
Philadelphia, Pa.	894	304	383	758	432	1,515	1,698
Phoenix, Ariz.	1,680	2,664	2,234	1,729	2,052	1,027	836
Pittsburgh, Pa.	792	597	219	457	131	1,237	1,411
St. Louis, Mo.	508	1,179	749	293	567	638	871
Salt Lake City, Utah	1,805	2,425	1,978	1,458	1,786	1,239	512
San Francisco, Calif.	2,385	3,179	2,732	2,212	2,540	1,765	1,266
Seattle, Wash.	2,612	3,043	2,596	2,052	2,404	2,122	1,373
Washington, D.C.	751	440	386	695	369	1,372	1,635

Cities	Detroit	El Paso	Houston	Indianapolis	Kansas City	Los Angeles	Louisville
Birmingham, Ala.	754	1,278	692	492	703	2,078	378
Boston, Mass.	702	2,358	1,886	940	1,427	3,036	996
Buffalo, N.Y.	252	1,928	1,532	510	997	2,606	571
Chicago, Ill.	279	1,439	1,092	189	503	2,112	305
Cleveland, Ohio	175	1,746	1,358	318	815	2,424	379
Dallas, Tex.	1,167	625	242	877	508	1,425	865
Denver, Colo.	1,310	652	1,032	1,051	616	1,174	1,135
Detroit, Mich.	—	1,696	1,312	290	760	2,369	378
El Paso, Tex.	1,696	—	756	1,418	936	800	1,443
Houston, Tex.	1,312	756	—	1,022	750	1,556	981
Indianapolis, Ind.	290	1,418	1,022	—	487	2,096	114
Kansas City, Mo.	760	936	750	487	—	1,609	519
Los Angeles, Calif.	2,369	800	1,556	2,096	1,609	—	2,128
Louisville, Ky.	378	1,443	981	114	519	2,128	—
Memphis, Tenn.	756	1,095	586	466	454	1,847	396
Miami, Fla.	1,409	1,957	1,237	1,225	1,479	2,757	1,111
Minneapolis, Minn.	698	1,353	1,211	600	466	2,041	716
New Orleans, La.	1,101	1,121	365	839	839	1,921	725
New York, N.Y.	671	2,147	1,675	729	1,216	2,825	785
Omaha, Neb.	754	1,015	903	590	204	1,733	704
Philadelphia, Pa.	589	2,065	1,586	647	1,134	2,743	703
Phoenix, Ariz.	1,986	402	1,158	1,713	1,226	398	1,749
Pittsburgh, Pa.	288	1,778	1,395	360	847	2,456	416
St. Louis, Mo.	529	1,179	799	239	255	1,864	264
Salt Lake City, Utah	1,721	877	1,465	1,545	1,128	728	1,647
San Francisco, Calif.	2,475	1,202	1,958	2,299	1,882	403	2,401
Seattle, Wash.	2,339	1,760	2,348	2,241	1,909	1,150	2,355
Washington, D.C.	526	1,997	1,443	565	1,071	2,680	601

1. These figures represent estimates and are subject to change.

Road Mileages Between U.S. Cities

Cities	Memphis	Miami	Minne-apolis	New Orleans	New York	Omaha	Phila-delphia
Birmingham, Ala.	249	777	1,067	347	983	907	894
Boston, Mass.	1,345	1,539	1,402	1,541	213	1,458	304
Buffalo, N.Y.	965	1,445	955	1,294	436	1,011	383
Chicago, Ill.	546	1,390	411	947	840	493	758
Cleveland, Ohio	773	1,325	763	1,102	514	819	432
Dallas, Tex.	470	1,332	969	504	1,604	661	1,515
Denver, Colo.	1,069	2,094	867	1,305	1,780	559	1,698
Detroit, Mich.	756	1,409	698	1,101	671	754	589
El Paso, Tex.	1,095	1,957	1,353	1,121	2,147	1,015	2,065
Houston, Tex.	586	1,237	1,211	365	1,675	903	1,586
Indianapolis, Ind.	466	1,225	600	839	729	590	647
Kansas City, Mo.	454	1,479	466	839	1,216	204	1,134
Los Angeles, Calif.	1,847	2,757	2,041	1,921	2,825	1,733	2,743
Louisville, Ky.	396	1,111	716	725	785	704	703
Memphis, Tenn.	—	1,025	854	401	1,134	658	1,045
Miami, Fla.	1,025	—	1,801	892	1,328	1,683	1,239
Minneapolis, Minn.	854	1,801	—	1,255	1,259	373	1,177
New Orleans, La.	401	892	1,255	—	1,330	1,043	1,241
New York, N.Y.	1,134	1,328	1,259	1,330	—	1,315	93
Omaha, Neb.	658	1,683	373	1,043	1,315	—	1,233
Philadelphia, Pa.	1,045	1,239	1,177	1,241	93	1,233	—
Phoenix, Ariz.	1,464	2,359	1,644	1,523	2,442	1,305	2,360
Pittsburgh, Pa.	810	1,250	876	1,118	386	932	304
St. Louis, Mo.	295	1,241	559	696	968	459	886
Salt Lake City, Utah	1,556	2,571	1,243	1,743	2,282	967	2,200
San Francisco, Calif.	2,151	3,097	1,997	2,269	3,036	1,721	2,954
Seattle, Wash.	2,363	3,389	1,641	2,606	2,900	1,705	2,818
Washington, D.C.	902	1,101	1,114	1,098	229	1,170	140

Cities	Phoenix	Pitts-burgh	St. Louis	Salt Lake City	San Francisco	Seattle	Wash-ington
Birmingham, Ala.	1,680	792	508	1,805	2,385	2,612	751
Boston, Mass.	2,664	597	1,179	2,425	3,179	3,043	440
Buffalo, N.Y.	2,234	219	749	1,978	2,732	2,596	386
Chicago, Ill.	1,729	457	293	1,458	2,212	2,052	695
Cleveland, Ohio	2,052	131	567	1,786	2,540	2,404	369
Dallas, Tex.	1,027	1,237	638	1,239	1,765	2,122	1,372
Denver, Colo.	836	1,411	871	512	1,266	1,373	1,635
Detroit, Mich.	1,986	288	529	1,721	2,475	2,339	526
El Paso, Tex.	402	1,778	1,179	877	1,202	1,760	1,997
Houston, Tex.	1,158	1,395	799	1,465	1,958	2,348	1,443
Indianapolis, Ind.	1,713	360	239	1,545	2,299	2,241	565
Kansas City, Mo.	1,226	847	255	1,128	1,882	1,909	1,071
Los Angeles, Calif.	398	2,456	1,864	728	403	1,150	2,680
Louisville, Ky.	1,749	416	264	1,647	2,401	2,355	601
Memphis, Tenn.	1,464	810	295	1,556	2,151	2,363	902
Miami, Fla.	2,359	1,250	1,241	2,571	3,097	3,389	1,101
Minneapolis, Minn.	1,644	876	559	1,243	1,997	1,641	1,114
New Orleans, La.	1,523	1,118	696	1,743	2,269	2,626	1,098
New York, N.Y.	2,442	386	968	2,282	3,036	2,900	229
Omaha, Neb.	1,305	932	459	967	1,721	1,705	1,178
Philadelphia, Pa.	2,360	304	886	2,200	2,954	2,818	140
Phoenix, Ariz.	—	2,073	1,485	651	800	1,482	2,278
Pittsburgh, Pa.	2,073	—	599	1,899	2,653	2,517	241
St. Louis, Mo.	1,485	599	—	1,383	2,137	2,164	836
Salt Lake City, Utah	651	1,899	1,383	—	754	883	2,110
San Francisco, Calif.	800	2,653	2,137	754	—	817	2,864
Seattle, Wash.	1,482	2,517	2,164	883	817	—	2,755
Washington, D.C.	2,278	241	836	2,110	2,864	2,755	—

Air Distances Between U.S. Cities in Statute Miles

Cities	Birmingham	Boston	Buffalo	Chicago	Cleveland	Dallas	Denver
Birmingham, Ala.	—	1,052	776	578	618	581	1,095
Boston, Mass.	1,052	—	400	851	551	1,551	1,769
Buffalo, N. Y.	776	400	—	454	173	1,198	1,370
Chicago, Ill.	578	851	454	—	308	803	920
Cleveland, Ohio	618	551	173	308	—	1,025	1,227
Dallas, Tex.	581	1,551	1,198	803	1,025	—	663
Denver, Colo.	1,095	1,769	1,370	920	1,227	663	—
Detroit, Mich.	641	613	216	238	90	999	1,156
El Paso, Tex.	1,152	2,072	1,692	1,252	1,525	572	557
Houston, Tex.	567	1,605	1,286	940	1,114	225	879
Indianapolis, Ind.	433	807	435	165	263	763	1,000
Kansas City, Mo.	579	1,251	861	414	700	451	558
Los Angeles, Calif.	1,802	2,596	2,198	1,745	2,049	1,240	831
Louisville, Ky.	331	826	483	269	311	726	1,038
Memphis, Tenn.	217	1,137	803	482	630	420	879
Miami, Fla.	665	1,255	1,181	1,188	1,087	1,111	1,726
Minneapolis, Minn.	862	1,123	731	355	630	862	700
New Orleans, La.	312	1,359	1,086	833	924	443	1,082
New York, N. Y.	864	188	292	713	405	1,374	1,631
Omaha, Neb.	732	1,282	883	432	739	586	488
Philadelphia, Pa.	783	271	279	666	360	1,299	1,579
Phoenix, Ariz.	1,456	2,300	1,906	1,453	1,749	887	586
Pittsburgh, Pa.	608	483	178	410	115	1,070	1,320
St. Louis, Mo.	400	1,038	662	262	492	547	796
Salt Lake City, Utah	1,466	2,099	1,699	1,260	1,568	999	371
San Francisco, Calif.	2,013	2,699	2,300	1,858	2,166	1,483	949
Seattle, Wash.	2,082	2,493	2,117	1,737	2,026	1,681	1,021
Washington, D.C.	661	393	292	597	306	1,185	1,494

Cities	Detroit	El Paso	Houston	Indianapolis	Kansas City	Los Angeles	Louisville
Birmingham, Ala.	641	1,152	567	433	579	1,802	331
Boston, Mass.	613	2,072	1,605	807	1,251	2,596	826
Buffalo, N. Y.	216	1,692	1,286	435	861	2,198	483
Chicago, Ill.	238	1,252	940	165	414	1,745	269
Cleveland, Ohio	90	1,525	1,114	263	700	2,049	311
Dallas, Tex.	999	572	225	763	451	1,240	726
Denver, Colo.	1,156	557	879	1,000	558	831	1,038
Detroit, Mich.	—	1,479	1,105	240	645	1,983	316
El Paso, Tex.	1,479	—	676	1,264	839	701	1,254
Houston, Tex.	1,105	676	—	865	644	1,374	803
Indianapolis, Ind.	240	1,264	865	—	453	1,809	107
Kansas City, Mo.	645	839	644	453	—	1,356	480
Los Angeles, Calif.	1,983	701	1,374	1,809	1,356	—	1,829
Louisville, Ky.	316	1,254	803	107	480	1,829	—
Memphis, Tenn.	623	976	484	384	369	1,603	320
Miami, Fla.	1,152	1,643	968	1,024	1,241	2,339	919
Minneapolis, Minn.	543	1,157	1,056	511	413	1,524	605
New Orleans, La.	939	983	318	712	680	1,673	623
New York, N. Y.	482	1,905	1,420	646	1,097	2,451	652
Omaha, Neb.	669	878	794	525	166	1,315	580
Philadelphia, Pa.	443	1,836	1,341	585	1,038	2,394	582
Phoenix, Ariz.	1,690	346	1,017	1,499	1,049	357	1,508
Pittsburgh, Pa.	205	1,590	1,137	330	781	2,136	344
St. Louis, Mo.	455	1,034	679	231	238	1,589	242
Salt Lake City, Utah	1,492	689	1,200	1,356	925	579	1,402
San Francisco, Calif.	2,091	995	1,645	1,949	1,506	347	1,986
Seattle, Wash.	1,938	1,376	1,891	1,872	1,506	959	1,943
Washington, D.C.	396	1,728	1,220	494	945	2,300	476

Source: National Geodetic Survey.

Air Distances Between U.S. Cities in Statute Miles

Cities	Memphis	Miami	Minneapolis	New Orleans	New York	Omaha	Philadelphia
Birmingham, Ala.	217	665	862	312	864	732	783
Boston, Mass.	1,137	1,255	1,123	1,359	188	1,282	271
Buffalo, N. Y.	803	1,181	731	1,086	292	883	279
Chicago, Ill.	482	1,188	355	833	713	432	666
Cleveland, Ohio	630	1,087	630	924	405	739	360
Dallas, Tex.	420	1,111	862	443	1,374	586	1,299
Denver, Colo.	879	1,726	700	1,082	1,631	488	1,579
Detroit, Mich.	623	1,152	543	939	482	669	443
El Paso, Tex.	976	1,643	1,157	983	1,905	878	1,836
Houston, Tex.	484	968	1,056	318	1,420	794	1,341
Indianapolis, Ind.	384	1,024	511	712	646	525	585
Kansas City, Mo.	369	1,241	413	680	1,097	166	1,038
Los Angeles, Calif.	1,603	2,339	1,524	1,673	2,451	1,315	2,394
Louisville, Ky.	320	919	605	623	652	580	582
Memphis, Tenn.	—	872	699	358	957	529	881
Miami, Fla.	872	—	1,511	669	1,092	1,397	1,019
Minneapolis, Minn.	699	1,511	—	1,051	1,018	290	985
New Orleans, La.	358	669	1,051	—	1,171	847	1,089
New York, N. Y.	957	1,092	1,018	1,171	—	1,144	83
Omaha, Neb.	529	1,397	290	847	1,144	—	1,094
Philadelphia, Pa.	881	1,019	985	1,089	83	1,094	—
Phoenix, Ariz.	1,263	1,982	1,280	1,316	2,145	1,036	2,083
Pittsburgh, Pa.	660	1,010	743	919	317	836	259
St. Louis, Mo.	240	1,061	466	598	875	354	811
Salt Lake City, Utah	1,250	2,089	987	1,434	1,972	833	1,925
San Francisco, Calif.	1,802	2,594	1,584	1,926	2,571	1,429	2,523
Seattle, Wash.	1,867	2,734	1,395	2,101	2,408	1,369	2,380
Washington, D.C.	765	923	934	966	205	1,014	123

Cities	Phoenix	Pittsburgh	St. Louis	Salt Lake City	San Francisco	Seattle	Washington
Birmingham, Ala.	1,456	608	400	1,466	2,013	2,082	661
Boston, Mass.	2,300	483	1,038	2,099	2,699	2,493	393
Buffalo, N. Y.	1,906	178	662	1,699	2,300	2,117	292
Chicago, Ill.	1,453	410	262	1,260	1,858	1,737	597
Cleveland, Ohio	1,749	115	492	1,568	2,166	2,026	306
Dallas, Tex.	887	1,070	547	999	1,483	1,681	1,185
Denver, Colo.	586	1,320	796	371	949	1,021	1,494
Detroit, Mich.	1,690	205	455	1,492	2,091	1,938	396
El Paso, Tex.	346	1,590	1,034	689	995	1,376	1,728
Houston, Tex.	1,017	1,137	679	1,200	1,645	1,891	1,220
Indianapolis, Ind.	1,499	330	231	1,356	1,949	1,872	494
Kansas City, Mo.	1,049	781	238	925	1,506	1,506	945
Los Angeles, Calif.	357	2,136	1,589	579	347	959	2,300
Louisville, Ky.	1,508	344	242	1,402	1,986	1,943	476
Memphis, Tenn.	1,263	660	240	1,250	1,802	1,867	765
Miami, Fla.	1,982	1,010	1,061	2,089	2,594	2,734	923
Minneapolis, Minn.	1,280	743	466	987	1,584	1,395	934
New Orleans, La.	1,316	919	598	1,434	1,926	2,101	966
New York, N. Y.	2,145	317	875	1,972	2,571	2,408	205
Omaha, Neb.	1,036	836	354	833	1,429	1,369	1,014
Philadelphia, Pa.	2,083	259	811	1,925	2,523	2,380	123
Phoenix, Ariz.	—	1,828	1,272	504	653	1,114	1,983
Pittsburgh, Pa.	1,828	—	559	1,668	2,264	2,138	192
St. Louis, Mo.	1,272	559	—	1,162	1,744	1,724	712
Salt Lake City, Utah	504	1,668	1,162	—	600	701	1,848
San Francisco, Calif.	653	2,264	1,744	600	—	678	2,442
Seattle, Wash.	1,114	2,138	1,724	701	678	—	2,329
Washington, D.C.	1,983	192	712	1,848	2,442	2,329	—

Source: National Geodetic Survey.

Air Distances Between World Cities in Statute Miles

Cities	Berlin	Buenos Aires	Cairo	Calcutta	Cape Town	Caracas	Chicago
Berlin	—	7,402	1,795	4,368	5,981	5,247	4,405
Buenos Aires	7,402	—	7,345	10,265	4,269	3,168	5,598
Cairo	1,795	7,345	—	3,539	4,500	6,338	6,129
Calcutta	4,368	10,265	3,539	—	6,024	9,605	7,980
Cape Town, South Africa	5,981	4,269	4,500	6,024	—	6,365	8,494
Caracas, Venezuela	5,247	3,168	6,338	9,605	6,365	—	2,501
Chicago	4,405	5,598	6,129	7,980	8,494	2,501	—
Hong Kong	5,440	11,472	5,061	1,648	7,375	10,167	7,793
Honolulu, Hawaii	7,309	7,561	8,838	7,047	11,534	6,013	4,250
Istanbul	1,078	7,611	768	3,638	5,154	6,048	5,477
Lisbon	1,436	5,956	2,363	5,638	5,325	4,041	3,990
London	579	6,916	2,181	4,947	6,012	4,660	3,950
Los Angeles	5,724	6,170	7,520	8,090	9,992	3,632	1,745
Manila	6,132	11,051	5,704	2,203	7,486	10,620	8,143
Mexico City	6,047	4,592	7,688	9,492	8,517	2,232	1,691
Montreal	3,729	5,615	5,414	7,607	7,931	2,449	744
Moscow	1,004	8,376	1,803	3,321	6,300	6,173	4,974
New York	3,965	5,297	5,602	7,918	7,764	2,132	713
Paris	545	6,870	1,995	4,883	5,807	4,736	4,134
Rio de Janeiro	6,220	1,200	6,146	9,377	3,773	2,810	5,296
Rome	734	6,929	1,320	4,482	5,249	5,196	4,808
San Francisco	5,661	6,467	7,364	7,814	10,247	3,904	1,858
Shanghai, China	5,218	12,201	5,183	2,117	8,061	9,501	7,061
Stockholm	504	7,808	2,111	4,195	6,444	5,420	4,278
Sydney, Australia	10,006	7,330	8,952	5,685	6,843	9,513	9,272
Tokyo	5,540	11,408	5,935	3,194	9,156	8,799	6,299
Warsaw	320	7,662	1,630	4,048	5,958	5,517	4,667
Washington, D.C.	4,169	5,218	5,800	8,084	7,901	2,059	597

Cities	Hong Kong	Honolulu	Istanbul	Lisbon	London	Los Angeles	Manila
Berlin	5,440	7,309	1,078	1,436	579	5,724	6,132
Buenos Aires	11,472	7,561	7,611	5,956	6,916	6,170	11,051
Cairo	5,061	8,838	768	2,363	2,181	7,520	5,704
Calcutta	1,648	7,047	3,638	5,638	4,947	8,090	2,203
Cape Town, South Africa	7,375	11,534	5,154	5,325	6,012	9,992	7,486
Caracas, Venezuela	10,167	6,013	6,048	4,041	4,660	3,632	10,620
Chicago	7,793	4,250	5,477	3,990	3,950	1,745	8,143
Hong Kong	—	5,549	4,984	6,853	5,982	7,195	693
Honolulu, Hawaii	5,549	—	8,109	7,820	7,228	2,574	5,299
Istanbul	4,984	8,109	—	2,012	1,552	6,783	5,664
Lisbon	6,853	7,820	2,012	—	985	5,621	7,546
London	5,982	7,228	1,552	985	—	5,382	6,672
Los Angeles, Calif.	7,195	2,574	6,783	5,621	5,382	—	7,261
Manila	693	5,299	5,664	7,546	6,672	7,261	—
Mexico City	8,782	3,779	7,110	5,390	5,550	1,589	8,835
Montreal	7,729	4,910	4,789	3,246	3,282	2,427	8,186
Moscow	4,439	7,037	1,091	2,427	1,555	6,003	5,131
New York	8,054	4,964	4,975	3,364	3,458	2,451	8,498
Paris	5,985	7,438	1,400	904	213	5,588	6,677
Rio de Janeiro	11,021	8,285	6,389	4,796	5,766	6,331	11,259
Rome	5,768	8,022	843	1,161	887	6,732	6,457
San Francisco	6,897	2,393	6,703	5,666	5,357	347	6,967
Shanghai, China	764	4,941	4,962	6,654	5,715	6,438	1,150
Stockholm	5,113	6,862	1,348	1,856	890	5,454	5,797
Sydney, Australia	4,584	4,943	9,294	11,302	10,564	7,530	3,944
Tokyo	1,794	3,853	5,560	6,915	5,940	5,433	1,866
Warsaw	5,144	7,355	863	1,715	899	5,922	5,837
Washington, D.C.	8,147	4,519	5,215	3,562	3,663	2,300	8,562

Source: Encyclopaedia Britannica.

Air Distances Between World Cities in Statute Miles

Cities	Mexico City	Montreal	Moscow	New York	Paris	Rio de Janeiro	Rome
Berlin	6,047	3,729	1,004	3,965	545	6,220	734
Buenos Aires	4,592	5,615	8,376	5,297	6,870	1,200	6,929
Cairo	7,688	5,414	1,803	5,602	1,995	6,146	1,320
Calcutta	9,492	7,607	3,321	7,918	4,883	9,377	4,482
Cape Town, South Africa	8,517	7,931	6,300	7,764	5,807	3,773	5,249
Caracas, Venezuela	2,232	2,449	6,173	2,132	4,736	2,810	5,196
Chicago	1,691	744	4,974	713	4,134	5,296	4,808
Hong Kong	8,782	7,729	4,439	8,054	5,985	11,021	5,768
Honolulu	3,779	4,910	7,037	4,964	7,438	8,285	8,022
Istanbul	7,110	4,789	1,091	4,975	1,400	6,389	843
Lisbon	5,390	3,246	2,427	3,364	904	4,796	1,161
London	5,550	3,282	1,555	3,458	213	5,766	887
Los Angeles	1,589	2,427	6,003	2,451	5,588	6,331	6,732
Manila	8,835	8,186	5,131	8,498	6,677	11,259	6,457
Mexico City	—	2,318	6,663	2,094	5,716	4,771	6,366
Montreal	2,318	—	4,386	320	3,422	5,097	4,080
Moscow	6,663	4,386	—	4,665	1,544	7,175	1,474
New York	2,094	320	4,665	—	3,624	4,817	4,281
Paris	5,716	3,422	1,544	3,624	—	5,699	697
Rio de Janeiro	4,771	5,097	7,175	4,817	5,699	—	5,684
Rome	6,366	4,080	1,474	4,281	697	5,684	—
San Francisco	1,887	2,539	5,871	2,571	5,558	6,621	6,240
Shanghai, China	8,022	7,053	4,235	7,371	5,754	11,336	5,677
Stockholm	5,959	3,667	762	3,924	958	6,651	1,234
Sydney, Australia	8,052	9,954	9,012	9,933	10,544	8,306	10,136
Tokyo	7,021	6,383	4,647	6,740	6,034	11,533	6,135
Warsaw	6,365	4,009	715	4,344	849	6,467	817
Washington, D.C.	1,887	488	4,858	205	3,829	4,796	4,434

Cities	San Francisco	Shanghai	Stockholm	Sydney	Tokyo	Warsaw	Wash-ington
Berlin	5,661	5,218	504	10,006	5,540	320	4,169
Buenos Aires	6,467	12,201	7,808	7,330	11,408	7,662	5,218
Cairo	7,364	5,183	2,111	8,952	5,935	1,630	5,800
Calcutta	7,814	2,117	4,195	5,685	3,194	4,048	8,084
Cape Town, South Africa	10,247	8,061	6,444	6,843	9,156	5,958	7,901
Caracas, Venezuela	3,904	9,501	5,420	9,513	8,799	5,517	2,059
Chicago	1,858	7,061	4,278	9,272	6,299	4,667	597
Hong Kong	6,897	764	5,113	4,584	1,794	5,144	8,147
Honolulu	2,393	4,941	6,862	4,943	3,853	7,355	4,519
Istanbul	6,703	4,962	1,348	9,294	5,560	863	5,215
Lisbon	5,666	6,654	1,856	11,302	6,915	1,715	3,562
London	5,357	5,715	890	10,564	5,940	899	3,663
Los Angeles	347	6,438	5,454	7,530	5,433	5,922	2,300
Manila	6,967	1,150	5,797	3,944	1,866	5,837	8,562
Mexico City	1,887	8,022	5,959	8,052	7,021	6,365	1,887
Montreal	2,539	7,053	3,667	9,954	6,383	4,009	488
Moscow	5,871	4,235	762	9,012	4,647	715	4,858
New York	2,571	7,371	3,924	9,933	6,740	4,344	205
Paris	5,558	5,754	958	10,544	6,034	849	3,829
Rio de Janeiro	6,621	11,336	6,651	8,306	11,533	6,467	4,796
Rome	6,240	5,677	1,234	10,136	6,135	817	4,434
San Francisco	—	6,140	5,361	7,416	5,135	5,841	2,442
Shanghai, China	6,140	—	4,825	4,899	1,097	4,951	7,448
Stockholm	5,361	4,825	—	9,696	5,051	501	4,123
Sydney, Australia	7,416	4,899	9,696	—	4,866	9,696	9,758
Tokyo	5,135	1,097	5,051	4,866	—	5,249	6,772
Warsaw	5,841	4,951	501	9,696	5,249	—	4,457
Washington, D.C.	2,442	7,448	4,123	9,758	6,772	4,457	—

Source: Encyclopaedia Britannica.

CALENDAR & HOLIDAYS

1988

JANUARY

S	M	T	W	T	F	S
—	—	—	—	—	1	2
3	4	5	6	7	8	9
10	11	12	13	14	15	16
17	18	19	20	21	22	23
24	25	26	27	28	29	30
31						

1—New Year's Day
6—Epiphany
15—Martin Luther King's Birthday

FEBRUARY

S	M	T	W	T	F	S
—	1	2	3	4	5	6
7	8	9	10	11	12	13
14	15	16	17	18	19	20
21	22	23	24	25	26	27
28	29					

2—Ground-hog Day
12—Lincoln's Birthday
14—St. Valentine's Day
15—Washington's Birthday
17—Ash Wednesday

MARCH

S	M	T	W	T	F	S
—	—	1	2	3	4	5
6	7	8	9	10	11	12
13	14	15	16	17	18	19
20	21	22	23	24	25	26
27	28	29	30	31		

3—Purim
17—St. Patrick's Day
27—Palm Sunday

APRIL

S	M	T	W	T	F	S
—	—	—	—	—	1	2
3	4	5	6	7	8	9
10	11	12	13	14	15	16
17	18	19	20	21	22	23
24	25	26	27	28	29	30

1—Good Friday
2—1st Day of Passover
3—Easter
18—1st Day of Ramadan
24—Daylight Savings Time begins

MAY

S	M	T	W	T	F	S
1	2	3	4	5	6	7
8	9	10	11	12	13	14
15	16	17	18	19	20	21
22	23	24	25	26	27	28
29	30	31				

8—Mother's Day
12—Ascension Day
22—Pentecost
22—1st Day of Shavuot
30—Memorial Day

JUNE

S	M	T	W	T	F	S
—	—	—	1	2	3	4
5	6	7	8	9	10	11
12	13	14	15	16	17	18
19	20	21	22	23	24	25
26	27	28	29	30		

14—Flag Day
19—Father's Day

JULY

S	M	T	W	T	F	S
—	—	—	—	—	1	2
3	4	5	6	7	8	9
10	11	12	13	14	15	16
17	18	19	20	21	22	23
24	25	26	27	28	29	30
31						

1—Canada Day
4—Independence Day

AUGUST

S	M	T	W	T	F	S
—	1	2	3	4	5	6
7	8	9	10	11	12	13
14	15	16	17	18	19	20
21	22	23	24	25	26	27
28	29	30	31			

SEPTEMBER

S	M	T	W	T	F	S
—	—	—	—	1	2	3
4	5	6	7	8	9	10
11	12	13	14	15	16	17
18	19	20	21	22	23	24
25	26	27	28	29	30	

5—Labor Day
12—1st Day of Rosh Hashana
21—Yom Kippur
26—1st Day of Sukkot

OCTOBER

S	M	T	W	T	F	S
—	—	—	—	—	—	1
2	3	4	5	6	7	8
9	10	11	12	13	14	15
16	17	18	19	20	21	22
23	24	25	26	27	28	29
30	31					

10—Thanksgiving Day (Canada)
12—Columbus Day
30—Daylight Savings Time ends
31—Halloween

NOVEMBER

S	M	T	W	T	F	S
—	—	1	2	3	4	5
6	7	8	9	10	11	12
13	14	15	16	17	18	19
20	21	22	23	24	25	26
27	28	29	30			

1—All Saint's Day
8—Election Day
11—Veteran's Day
24—Thanksgiving Day
27—1st Sunday of Advent

DECEMBER

S	M	T	W	T	F	S
—	—	—	—	1	2	3
4	5	6	7	8	9	10
11	12	13	14	15	16	17
18	19	20	21	22	23	24
25	26	27	28	29	30	31

4—1st Day of Hanukkah
25—Christmas

Seasons for the Northern Hemisphere, 1988

Eastern Standard Time

March 20, 4:39 a.m., sun enters sign of Aries; spring begins

June 20, 10:57 p.m., sun enters sign of Cancer; summer begins

Sept. 22, 2:29 p.m., sun enters sign of Libra; fall begins

Dec. 21, 10:28 a.m., sun enters sign of Capricorn; winter begins

1987

JANUARY

S	M	T	W	T	F	S
—	—	—	—	1	2	3
4	5	6	7	8	9	10
11	12	13	14	15	16	17
18	19	20	21	22	23	24
25	26	27	28	29	30	31

FEBRUARY

S	M	T	W	T	F	S
1	2	3	4	5	6	7
8	9	10	11	12	13	14
15	16	17	18	19	20	21
22	23	24	25	26	27	28

MARCH

S	M	T	W	T	F	S
1	2	3	4	5	6	7
8	9	10	11	12	13	14
15	16	17	18	19	20	21
22	23	24	25	26	27	28
29	30	31				

APRIL

S	M	T	W	T	F	S
—	—	—	1	2	3	4
5	6	7	8	9	10	11
12	13	14	15	16	17	18
19	20	21	22	23	24	25
26	27	28	29	30		

MAY

S	M	T	W	T	F	S
—	—	—	—	—	1	2
3	4	5	6	7	8	9
10	11	12	13	14	15	16
17	18	19	20	21	22	23
24	25	26	27	28	29	30
31						

JUNE

S	M	T	W	T	F	S
—	1	2	3	4	5	6
7	8	9	10	11	12	13
14	15	16	17	18	19	20
21	22	23	24	25	26	27
28	29	30				

JULY

S	M	T	W	T	F	S
—	—	—	1	2	3	4
5	6	7	8	9	10	11
12	13	14	15	16	17	18
19	20	21	22	23	24	25
26	27	28	29	30	31	

AUGUST

S	M	T	W	T	F	S
—	—	—	—	—	—	1
2	3	4	5	6	7	8
9	10	11	12	13	14	15
16	17	18	19	20	21	22
23	24	25	26	27	28	29
30	31					

SEPTEMBER

S	M	T	W	T	F	S
—	—	1	2	3	4	5
6	7	8	9	10	11	12
13	14	15	16	17	18	19
20	21	22	23	24	25	26
27	28	29	30			

OCTOBER

S	M	T	W	T	F	S
—	—	—	—	1	2	3
4	5	6	7	8	9	10
11	12	13	14	15	16	17
18	19	20	21	22	23	24
25	26	27	28	29	30	31

NOVEMBER

S	M	T	W	T	F	S
1	2	3	4	5	6	7
8	9	10	11	12	13	14
15	16	17	18	19	20	21
22	23	24	25	26	27	28
29	30					

DECEMBER

S	M	T	W	T	F	S
—	—	1	2	3	4	5
6	7	8	9	10	11	12
13	14	15	16	17	18	19
20	21	22	23	24	25	26
27	28	29	30	31		

1989

JANUARY

S	M	T	W	T	F	S
1	2	3	4	5	6	7
8	9	10	11	12	13	14
15	16	17	18	19	20	21
22	23	24	25	26	27	28
29	30	31				

FEBRUARY

S	M	T	W	T	F	S
—	—	—	1	2	3	4
5	6	7	8	9	10	11
12	13	14	15	16	17	18
19	20	21	22	23	24	25
26	27	28				

MARCH

S	M	T	W	T	F	S
—	—	—	1	2	3	4
5	6	7	8	9	10	11
12	13	14	15	16	17	18
19	20	21	22	23	24	25
26	27	28	29	30	31	

APRIL

S	M	T	W	T	F	S
—	—	—	—	—	—	1
2	3	4	5	6	7	8
9	10	11	12	13	14	15
16	17	18	19	20	21	22
23	24	25	26	27	28	29
30						

MAY

S	M	T	W	T	F	S
—	1	2	3	4	5	6
7	8	9	10	11	12	13
14	15	16	17	18	19	20
21	22	23	24	25	26	27
28	29	30	31			

JUNE

S	M	T	W	T	F	S
—	—	—	—	1	2	3
4	5	6	7	8	9	10
11	12	13	14	15	16	17
18	19	20	21	22	23	24
25	26	27	28	29	30	

JULY

S	M	T	W	T	F	S
—	—	—	—	—	—	1
2	3	4	5	6	7	8
9	10	11	12	13	14	15
16	17	18	19	20	21	22
23	24	25	26	27	28	29
30	31					

AUGUST

S	M	T	W	T	F	S
—	—	1	2	3	4	5
6	7	8	9	10	11	12
13	14	15	16	17	18	19
20	21	22	23	24	25	26
27	28	29	30	31		

SEPTEMBER

S	M	T	W	T	F	S
—	—	—	—	—	1	2
3	4	5	6	7	8	9
10	11	12	13	14	15	16
17	18	19	20	21	22	23
24	25	26	27	28	29	30

OCTOBER

S	M	T	W	T	F	S
1	2	3	4	5	6	7
8	9	10	11	12	13	14
15	16	17	18	19	20	21
22	23	24	25	26	27	28
29	30	31				

NOVEMBER

S	M	T	W	T	F	S
—	—	—	1	2	3	4
5	6	7	8	9	10	11
12	13	14	15	16	17	18
19	20	21	22	23	24	25
26	27	28	29	30		

DECEMBER

S	M	T	W	T	F	S
—	—	—	—	—	1	2
3	4	5	6	7	8	9
10	11	12	13	14	15	16
17	18	19	20	21	22	23
24	25	26	27	28	29	30
31						

Pre-Columbian Calendar Systems

The Mayans and the Aztecs both used two calendars—a sacred or ceremonial calendar of 260 days and a 365-day secular calendar that was divided into 18 months of 20 days each. An additional five days were added to complete the 365-day year.

The Mayans were able to approximate the true length of the tropical year with a greater accuracy than does the Gregorian calendar year we now use. The tropical year is 365.2422 days. The Mayans determined it to be 365.2420 days, whereas the Gregorian calendar year is 365.2425.

Very little is known about the Inca calendar. Because the Incas did not have a written language, early reports about their calendar cannot be verified.

PERPETUAL CALENDAR

1800 .. 4	1844 .. 9	1888 .. 8	1932 . 13	1976 . 12	2020 . 11
1801 .. 5	1845 .. 4	1889 .. 3	1933 .. 1	1977 .. 7	2021 .. 6
1802 .. 6	1846 .. 5	1890 .. 4	1934 .. 2	1978 .. 1	2022 .. 7
1803 .. 7	1847 .. 6	1891 .. 5	1935 .. 3	1979 .. 2	2023 .. 1
1804 .. 8	1848 . 14	1892 . 13	1936 . 11	1980 . 10	2024 .. 9
1805 .. 3	1849 .. 2	1893 .. 1	1937 .. 6	1981 .. 5	2025 .. 4
1806 .. 4	1850 .. 3	1894 .. 2	1938 .. 7	1982 .. 6	2026 .. 5
1807 .. 5	1851 .. 4	1895 .. 3	1939 .. 1	1983 .. 7	2027 .. 6
1808 . 13	1852 . 12	1896 . 11	1940 .. 9	1984 .. 8	2028 . 14
1809 .. 1	1853 .. 7	1897 .. 6	1941 .. 4	1985 .. 3	2029 .. 2
1810 .. 2	1854 .. 1	1898 .. 7	1942 .. 5	1986 .. 4	2030 .. 3
1811 .. 3	1855 .. 2	1899 .. 1	1943 .. 6	1987 .. 5	2031 .. 4
1812 . 11	1856 . 10	1900 .. 2	1944 . 14	1988 . 13	2032 . 12
1813 .. 6	1857 .. 5	1901 .. 3	1945 .. 2	1989 .. 1	2033 .. 7
1814 .. 7	1858 .. 6	1902 .. 4	1946 .. 3	1990 .. 2	2034 .. 1
1815 .. 1	1859 .. 7	1903 .. 5	1947 .. 4	1991 .. 3	2035 .. 2
1816 .. 9	1860 .. 8	1904 . 13	1948 . 12	1992 . 11	2036 . 10
1817 .. 4	1861 .. 3	1905 .. 1	1949 .. 7	1993 .. 6	2037 .. 5
1818 .. 5	1862 .. 4	1906 .. 2	1950 .. 1	1994 .. 7	2038 .. 6
1819 .. 6	1863 .. 5	1907 .. 3	1951 .. 2	1995 .. 1	2039 .. 7
1820 . 14	1864 . 13	1908 . 11	1952 . 10	1996 .. 9	2040 .. 8
1821 .. 2	1865 .. 1	1909 .. 6	1953 .. 5	1997 .. 4	2041 .. 3
1822 .. 3	1866 .. 2	1910 .. 7	1954 .. 6	1998 .. 5	2042 .. 4
1823 .. 4	1867 .. 3	1911 .. 1	1955 .. 7	1999 .. 6	2043 .. 5
1824 . 12	1868 . 11	1912 .. 9	1956 .. 8	2000 . 14	2044 . 13
1825 .. 7	1869 .. 6	1913 .. 4	1957 .. 3	2001 .. 2	2045 .. 1
1826 .. 1	1870 .. 7	1914 .. 5	1958 .. 4	2002 .. 3	2046 .. 2
1827 .. 2	1871 .. 1	1915 .. 6	1959 .. 5	2003 .. 4	2047 .. 3
1828 . 10	1872 .. 9	1916 . 14	1960 . 13	2004 . 12	2048 . 11
1829 .. 5	1873 .. 4	1917 .. 2	1961 .. 1	2005 .. 7	2049 .. 6
1830 .. 6	1874 .. 5	1918 .. 3	1962 .. 2	2006 .. 1	2050 .. 7
1831 .. 7	1875 .. 6	1919 .. 4	1963 .. 3	2007 .. 2	2051 .. 1
1832 .. 8	1876 . 14	1920 . 12	1964 . 11	2008 . 10	2052 .. 9
1833 .. 3	1877 .. 2	1921 .. 7	1965 .. 6	2009 .. 5	2053 .. 4
1834 .. 4	1878 .. 3	1922 .. 1	1966 .. 7	2010 .. 6	2054 .. 5
1835 .. 5	1879 .. 4	1923 .. 2	1967 .. 1	2011 .. 7	2055 .. 6
1836 . 13	1880 . 12	1924 . 10	1968 .. 9	2012 .. 8	2056 . 14
1837 .. 1	1881 .. 7	1925 .. 5	1969 .. 4	2013 .. 3	2057 .. 2
1838 .. 2	1882 .. 1	1926 .. 6	1970 .. 5	2014 .. 4	2058 .. 3
1839 .. 3	1883 .. 2	1927 .. 7	1971 .. 6	2015 .. 5	2059 .. 4
1840 . 11	1884 . 10	1928 .. 8	1972 . 14	2016 . 13	2060 . 12
1841 .. 6	1885 .. 5	1929 .. 3	1973 .. 2	2017 .. 1	2061 .. 7
1842 .. 7	1886 .. 6	1930 .. 4	1974 .. 3	2018 .. 2	2062 .. 1
1843 .. 1	1887 .. 7	1931 .. 5	1975 .. 4	2019 .. 3	2063 .. 2

DIRECTIONS: The number given with each year in the key above is number of calendar to use for that year

1

JANUARY

S	M	T	W	T	F	S
1	2	3	4	5	6	7
8	9	10	11	12	13	14
15	16	17	18	19	20	21
22	23	24	25	26	27	28
29	30	31				

FEBRUARY

S	M	T	W	T	F	S
			1	2	3	4
5	6	7	8	9	10	11
12	13	14	15	16	17	18
19	20	21	22	23	24	25
26	27	28				

MARCH

S	M	T	W	T	F	S
			1	2	3	4
5	6	7	8	9	10	11
12	13	14	15	16	17	18
19	20	21	22	23	24	25
26	27	28	29	30	31	

APRIL

S	M	T	W	T	F	S
						1
2	3	4	5	6	7	8
9	10	11	12	13	14	15
16	17	18	19	20	21	22
23	24	25	26	27	28	29
30						

MAY

S	M	T	W	T	F	S
	1	2	3	4	5	6
7	8	9	10	11	12	13
14	15	16	17	18	19	20
21	22	23	24	25	26	27
28	29	30	31			

JUNE

S	M	T	W	T	F	S
				1	2	3
4	5	6	7	8	9	10
11	12	13	14	15	16	17
18	19	20	21	22	23	24
25	26	27	28	29	30	

JULY

S	M	T	W	T	F	S
						1
2	3	4	5	6	7	8
9	10	11	12	13	14	15
16	17	18	19	20	21	22
23	24	25	26	27	28	29
30	31					

AUGUST

S	M	T	W	T	F	S
		1	2	3	4	5
6	7	8	9	10	11	12
13	14	15	16	17	18	19
20	21	22	23	24	25	26
27	28	29	30	31		

SEPTEMBER

S	M	T	W	T	F	S
					1	2
3	4	5	6	7	8	9
10	11	12	13	14	15	16
17	18	19	20	21	22	23
24	25	26	27	28	29	30

OCTOBER

S	M	T	W	T	F	S
1	2	3	4	5	6	7
8	9	10	11	12	13	14
15	16	17	18	19	20	21
22	23	24	25	26	27	28
29	30	31				

NOVEMBER

S	M	T	W	T	F	S
			1	2	3	4
5	6	7	8	9	10	11
12	13	14	15	16	17	18
19	20	21	22	23	24	25
26	27	28	29	30		

DECEMBER

S	M	T	W	T	F	S
					1	2
3	4	5	6	7	8	9
10	11	12	13	14	15	16
17	18	19	20	21	22	23
24	25	26	27	28	29	30
31						

2

JANUARY

S	M	T	W	T	F	S
	1	2	3	4	5	6
7	8	9	10	11	12	13
14	15	16	17	18	19	20
21	22	23	24	25	26	27
28	29	30	31			

FEBRUARY

S	M	T	W	T	F	S
				1	2	3
4	5	6	7	8	9	10
11	12	13	14	15	16	17
18	19	20	21	22	23	24
25	26	27	28			

MARCH

S	M	T	W	T	F	S
				1	2	3
4	5	6	7	8	9	10
11	12	13	14	15	16	17
18	19	20	21	22	23	24
25	26	27	28	29	30	31

APRIL

S	M	T	W	T	F	S
1	2	3	4	5	6	7
8	9	10	11	12	13	14
15	16	17	18	19	20	21
22	23	24	25	26	27	28
29	30					

MAY

S	M	T	W	T	F	S
		1	2	3	4	5
6	7	8	9	10	11	12
13	14	15	16	17	18	19
20	21	22	23	24	25	26
27	28	29	30	31		

JUNE

S	M	T	W	T	F	S
					1	2
3	4	5	6	7	8	9
10	11	12	13	14	15	16
17	18	19	20	21	22	23
24	25	26	27	28	29	30

JULY

S	M	T	W	T	F	S
1	2	3	4	5	6	7
8	9	10	11	12	13	14
15	16	17	18	19	20	21
22	23	24	25	26	27	28
29	30	31				

AUGUST

S	M	T	W	T	F	S
			1	2	3	4
5	6	7	8	9	10	11
12	13	14	15	16	17	18
19	20	21	22	23	24	25
26	27	28	29	30	31	

SEPTEMBER

S	M	T	W	T	F	S
						1
2	3	4	5	6	7	8
9	10	11	12	13	14	15
16	17	18	19	20	21	22
23	24	25	26	27	28	29
30						

OCTOBER

S	M	T	W	T	F	S
	1	2	3	4	5	6
7	8	9	10	11	12	13
14	15	16	17	18	19	20
21	22	23	24	25	26	27
28	29	30	31			

NOVEMBER

S	M	T	W	T	F	S
				1	2	3
4	5	6	7	8	9	10
11	12	13	14	15	16	17
18	19	20	21	22	23	24
25	26	27	28	29	30	

DECEMBER

S	M	T	W	T	F	S
						1
2	3	4	5	6	7	8
9	10	11	12	13	14	15
16	17	18	19	20	21	22
23	24	25	26	27	28	29
30	31					

3

JANUARY

S	M	T	W	T	F	S
		1	2	3	4	5
6	7	8	9	10	11	12
13	14	15	16	17	18	19
20	21	22	23	24	25	26
27	28	29	30	31		

FEBRUARY

S	M	T	W	T	F	S
					1	2
3	4	5	6	7	8	9
10	11	12	13	14	15	16
17	18	19	20	21	22	23
24	25	26	27	28		

MARCH

S	M	T	W	T	F	S
					1	2
3	4	5	6	7	8	9
10	11	12	13	14	15	16
17	18	19	20	21	22	23
24	25	26	27	28	29	30
31						

APRIL

S	M	T	W	T	F	S
	1	2	3	4	5	6
7	8	9	10	11	12	13
14	15	16	17	18	19	20
21	22	23	24	25	26	27
28	29	30				

MAY

S	M	T	W	T	F	S
			1	2	3	4
5	6	7	8	9	10	11
12	13	14	15	16	17	18
19	20	21	22	23	24	25
26	27	28	29	30	31	

JUNE

S	M	T	W	T	F	S
						1
2	3	4	5	6	7	8
9	10	11	12	13	14	15
16	17	18	19	20	21	22
23	24	25	26	27	28	29
30						

JULY

S	M	T	W	T	F	S
	1	2	3	4	5	6
7	8	9	10	11	12	13
14	15	16	17	18	19	20
21	22	23	24	25	26	27
28	29	30	31			

AUGUST

S	M	T	W	T	F	S
				1	2	3
4	5	6	7	8	9	10
11	12	13	14	15	16	17
18	19	20	21	22	23	24
25	26	27	28	29	30	31

SEPTEMBER

S	M	T	W	T	F	S
1	2	3	4	5	6	7
8	9	10	11	12	13	14
15	16	17	18	19	20	21
22	23	24	25	26	27	28
29	30					

OCTOBER

S	M	T	W	T	F	S
		1	2	3	4	5
6	7	8	9	10	11	12
13	14	15	16	17	18	19
20	21	22	23	24	25	26
27	28	29	30	31		

NOVEMBER

S	M	T	W	T	F	S
					1	2
3	4	5	6	7	8	9
10	11	12	13	14	15	16
17	18	19	20	21	22	23
24	25	26	27	28	29	30

DECEMBER

S	M	T	W	T	F	S
1	2	3	4	5	6	7
8	9	10	11	12	13	14
15	16	17	18	19	20	21
22	23	24	25	26	27	28
29	30	31				

4

JANUARY

S	M	T	W	T	F	S
			1	2	3	4
5	6	7	8	9	10	11
12	13	14	15	16	17	18
19	20	21	22	23	24	25
26	27	28	29	30	31	

FEBRUARY

S	M	T	W	T	F	S
						1
2	3	4	5	6	7	8
9	10	11	12	13	14	15
16	17	18	19	20	21	22
23	24	25	26	27	28	

MARCH

S	M	T	W	T	F	S
						1
2	3	4	5	6	7	8
9	10	11	12	13	14	15
16	17	18	19	20	21	22
23	24	25	26	27	28	29
30	31					

APRIL

S	M	T	W	T	F	S
		1	2	3	4	5
6	7	8	9	10	11	12
13	14	15	16	17	18	19
20	21	22	23	24	25	26
27	28	29	30			

MAY

S	M	T	W	T	F	S
				1	2	3
4	5	6	7	8	9	10
11	12	13	14	15	16	17
18	19	20	21	22	23	24
25	26	27	28	29	30	31

JUNE

S	M	T	W	T	F	S
1	2	3	4	5	6	7
8	9	10	11	12	13	14
15	16	17	18	19	20	21
22	23	24	25	26	27	28
29	30					

JULY

S	M	T	W	T	F	S
		1	2	3	4	5
6	7	8	9	10	11	12
13	14	15	16	17	18	19
20	21	22	23	24	25	26
27	28	29	30	31		

AUGUST

S	M	T	W	T	F	S
					1	2
3	4	5	6	7	8	9
10	11	12	13	14	15	16
17	18	19	20	21	22	23
24	25	26	27	28	29	30
31						

SEPTEMBER

S	M	T	W	T	F	S
	1	2	3	4	5	6
7	8	9	10	11	12	13
14	15	16	17	18	19	20
21	22	23	24	25	26	27
28	29	30				

OCTOBER

S	M	T	W	T	F	S
			1	2	3	4
5	6	7	8	9	10	11
12	13	14	15	16	17	18
19	20	21	22	23	24	25
26	27	28	29	30	31	

NOVEMBER

S	M	T	W	T	F	S
						1
2	3	4	5	6	7	8
9	10	11	12	13	14	15
16	17	18	19	20	21	22
23	24	25	26	27	28	29
30						

DECEMBER

S	M	T	W	T	F	S
	1	2	3	4	5	6
7	8	9	10	11	12	13
14	15	16	17	18	19	20
21	22	23	24	25	26	27
28	29	30	31			

5

JANUARY

S	M	T	W	T	F	S
				1	2	3
4	5	6	7	8	9	10
11	12	13	14	15	16	17
18	19	20	21	22	23	24
25	26	27	28	29	30	31

FEBRUARY

S	M	T	W	T	F	S
1	2	3	4	5	6	7
8	9	10	11	12	13	14
15	16	17	18	19	20	21
22	23	24	25	26	27	28

MARCH

S	M	T	W	T	F	S
1	2	3	4	5	6	7
8	9	10	11	12	13	14
15	16	17	18	19	20	21
22	23	24	25	26	27	28
29	30	31				

APRIL

S	M	T	W	T	F	S
			1	2	3	4
5	6	7	8	9	10	11
12	13	14	15	16	17	18
19	20	21	22	23	24	25
26	27	28	29	30		

MAY

S	M	T	W	T	F	S
					1	2
3	4	5	6	7	8	9
10	11	12	13	14	15	16
17	18	19	20	21	22	23
24	25	26	27	28	29	30
31						

JUNE

S	M	T	W	T	F	S
	1	2	3	4	5	6
7	8	9	10	11	12	13
14	15	16	17	18	19	20
21	22	23	24	25	26	27
28	29	30				

JULY

S	M	T	W	T	F	S
			1	2	3	4
5	6	7	8	9	10	11
12	13	14	15	16	17	18
19	20	21	22	23	24	25
26	27	28	29	30	31	

AUGUST

S	M	T	W	T	F	S
						1
2	3	4	5	6	7	8
9	10	11	12	13	14	15
16	17	18	19	20	21	22
23	24	25	26	27	28	29
30	31					

SEPTEMBER

S	M	T	W	T	F	S
		1	2	3	4	5
6	7	8	9	10	11	12
13	14	15	16	17	18	19
20	21	22	23	24	25	26
27	28	29	30			

OCTOBER

S	M	T	W	T	F	S
				1	2	3
4	5	6	7	8	9	10
11	12	13	14	15	16	17
18	19	20	21	22	23	24
25	26	27	28	29	30	31

NOVEMBER

S	M	T	W	T	F	S
1	2	3	4	5	6	7
8	9	10	11	12	13	14
15	16	17	18	19	20	21
22	23	24	25	26	27	28
29	30					

DECEMBER

S	M	T	W	T	F	S
		1	2	3	4	5
6	7	8	9	10	11	12
13	14	15	16	17	18	19
20	21	22	23	24	25	26
27	28	29	30	31		

6

JANUARY

S	M	T	W	T	F	S
					1	2
3	4	5	6	7	8	9
10	11	12	13	14	15	16
17	18	19	20	21	22	23
24	25	26	27	28	29	30
31						

FEBRUARY

S	M	T	W	T	F	S
	1	2	3	4	5	6
7	8	9	10	11	12	13
14	15	16	17	18	19	20
21	22	23	24	25	26	27
28						

MARCH

S	M	T	W	T	F	S
	1	2	3	4	5	6
7	8	9	10	11	12	13
14	15	16	17	18	19	20
21	22	23	24	25	26	27
28	29	30	31			

APRIL

S	M	T	W	T	F	S
				1	2	3
4	5	6	7	8	9	10
11	12	13	14	15	16	17
18	19	20	21	22	23	24
25	26	27	28	29	30	

MAY

S	M	T	W	T	F	S
						1
2	3	4	5	6	7	8
9	10	11	12	13	14	15
16	17	18	19	20	21	22
23	24	25	26	27	28	29
30	31					

JUNE

S	M	T	W	T	F	S
		1	2	3	4	5
6	7	8	9	10	11	12
13	14	15	16	17	18	19
20	21	22	23	24	25	26
27	28	29	30			

JULY

S	M	T	W	T	F	S
				1	2	3
4	5	6	7	8	9	10
11	12	13	14	15	16	17
18	19	20	21	22	23	24
25	26	27	28	29	30	31

AUGUST

S	M	T	W	T	F	S
1	2	3	4	5	6	7
8	9	10	11	12	13	14
15	16	17	18	19	20	21
22	23	24	25	26	27	28
29	30	31				

SEPTEMBER

S	M	T	W	T	F	S
			1	2	3	4
5	6	7	8	9	10	11
12	13	14	15	16	17	18
19	20	21	22	23	24	25
26	27	28	29	30		

OCTOBER

S	M	T	W	T	F	S
					1	2
3	4	5	6	7	8	9
10	11	12	13	14	15	16
17	18	19	20	21	22	23
24	25	26	27	28	29	30
31						

NOVEMBER

S	M	T	W	T	F	S
	1	2	3	4	5	6
7	8	9	10	11	12	13
14	15	16	17	18	19	20
21	22	23	24	25	26	27
28	29	30				

DECEMBER

S	M	T	W	T	F	S
			1	2	3	4
5	6	7	8	9	10	11
12	13	14	15	16	17	18
19	20	21	22	23	24	25
26	27	28	29	30	31	

7

JANUARY

S	M	T	W	T	F	S
						1
2	3	4	5	6	7	8
9	10	11	12	13	14	15
16	17	18	19	20	21	22
23	24	25	26	27	28	29
30	31					

FEBRUARY

S	M	T	W	T	F	S
		1	2	3	4	5
6	7	8	9	10	11	12
13	14	15	16	17	18	19
20	21	22	23	24	25	26
27	28					

MARCH

S	M	T	W	T	F	S
		1	2	3	4	5
6	7	8	9	10	11	12
13	14	15	16	17	18	19
20	21	22	23	24	25	26
27	28	29	30	31		

APRIL

S	M	T	W	T	F	S
					1	2
3	4	5	6	7	8	9
10	11	12	13	14	15	16
17	18	19	20	21	22	23
24	25	26	27	28	29	30

MAY

S	M	T	W	T	F	S
1	2	3	4	5	6	7
8	9	10	11	12	13	14
15	16	17	18	19	20	21
22	23	24	25	26	27	28
29	30	31				

JUNE

S	M	T	W	T	F	S
			1	2	3	4
5	6	7	8	9	10	11
12	13	14	15	16	17	18
19	20	21	22	23	24	25
26	27	28	29	30		

JULY

S	M	T	W	T	F	S
					1	2
3	4	5	6	7	8	9
10	11	12	13	14	15	16
17	18	19	20	21	22	23
24	25	26	27	28	29	30
31						

AUGUST

S	M	T	W	T	F	S
	1	2	3	4	5	6
7	8	9	10	11	12	13
14	15	16	17	18	19	20
21	22	23	24	25	26	27
28	29	30	31			

SEPTEMBER

S	M	T	W	T	F	S
				1	2	3
4	5	6	7	8	9	10
11	12	13	14	15	16	17
18	19	20	21	22	23	24
25	26	27	28	29	30	

OCTOBER

S	M	T	W	T	F	S
						1
2	3	4	5	6	7	8
9	10	11	12	13	14	15
16	17	18	19	20	21	22
23	24	25	26	27	28	29
30	31					

NOVEMBER

S	M	T	W	T	F	S
		1	2	3	4	5
6	7	8	9	10	11	12
13	14	15	16	17	18	19
20	21	22	23	24	25	26
27	28	29	30			

DECEMBER

S	M	T	W	T	F	S
				1	2	3
4	5	6	7	8	9	10
11	12	13	14	15	16	17
18	19	20	21	22	23	24
25	26	27	28	29	30	31

8

JANUARY

S	M	T	W	T	F	S
1	2	3	4	5	6	7
8	9	10	11	12	13	14
15	16	17	18	19	20	21
22	23	24	25	26	27	28
29	30	31				

FEBRUARY

S	M	T	W	T	F	S
			1	2	3	4
5	6	7	8	9	10	11
12	13	14	15	16	17	18
19	20	21	22	23	24	25
26	27	28	29			

MARCH

S	M	T	W	T	F	S
				1	2	3
4	5	6	7	8	9	10
11	12	13	14	15	16	17
18	19	20	21	22	23	24
25	26	27	28	29	30	31

APRIL

S	M	T	W	T	F	S
1	2	3	4	5	6	7
8	9	10	11	12	13	14
15	16	17	18	19	20	21
22	23	24	25	26	27	28
29	30					

MAY

S	M	T	W	T	F	S
		1	2	3	4	5
6	7	8	9	10	11	12
13	14	15	16	17	18	19
20	21	22	23	24	25	26
27	28	29	30	31		

JUNE

S	M	T	W	T	F	S
					1	2
3	4	5	6	7	8	9
10	11	12	13	14	15	16
17	18	19	20	21	22	23
24	25	26	27	28	29	30

JULY

S	M	T	W	T	F	S
1	2	3	4	5	6	7
8	9	10	11	12	13	14
15	16	17	18	19	20	21
22	23	24	25	26	27	28
29	30	31				

AUGUST

S	M	T	W	T	F	S
			1	2	3	4
5	6	7	8	9	10	11
12	13	14	15	16	17	18
19	20	21	22	23	24	25
26	27	28	29	30	31	

SEPTEMBER

S	M	T	W	T	F	S
						1
2	3	4	5	6	7	8
9	10	11	12	13	14	15
16	17	18	19	20	21	22
23	24	25	26	27	28	29
30						

OCTOBER

S	M	T	W	T	F	S
	1	2	3	4	5	6
7	8	9	10	11	12	13
14	15	16	17	18	19	20
21	22	23	24	25	26	27
28	29	30	31			

NOVEMBER

S	M	T	W	T	F	S
				1	2	3
4	5	6	7	8	9	10
11	12	13	14	15	16	17
18	19	20	21	22	23	24
25	26	27	28	29	30	

DECEMBER

S	M	T	W	T	F	S
						1
2	3	4	5	6	7	8
9	10	11	12	13	14	15
16	17	18	19	20	21	22
23	24	25	26	27	28	29
30	31					

9

JANUARY

S	M	T	W	T	F	S
	1	2	3	4	5	6
7	8	9	10	11	12	13
14	15	16	17	18	19	20
21	22	23	24	25	26	27
28	29	30	31			

FEBRUARY

S	M	T	W	T	F	S
				1	2	3
4	5	6	7	8	9	10
11	12	13	14	15	16	17
18	19	20	21	22	23	24
25	26	27	28	29		

MARCH

S	M	T	W	T	F	S
					1	2
3	4	5	6	7	8	9
10	11	12	13	14	15	16
17	18	19	20	21	22	23
24	25	26	27	28	29	30
31						

APRIL

S	M	T	W	T	F	S
	1	2	3	4	5	6
7	8	9	10	11	12	13
14	15	16	17	18	19	20
21	22	23	24	25	26	27
28	29	30				

MAY

S	M	T	W	T	F	S
			1	2	3	4
5	6	7	8	9	10	11
12	13	14	15	16	17	18
19	20	21	22	23	24	25
26	27	28	29	30	31	

JUNE

S	M	T	W	T	F	S
						1
2	3	4	5	6	7	8
9	10	11	12	13	14	15
16	17	18	19	20	21	22
23	24	25	26	27	28	29
30						

JULY

S	M	T	W	T	F	S
	1	2	3	4	5	6
7	8	9	10	11	12	13
14	15	16	17	18	19	20
21	22	23	24	25	26	27
28	29	30	31			

AUGUST

S	M	T	W	T	F	S
				1	2	3
4	5	6	7	8	9	10
11	12	13	14	15	16	17
18	19	20	21	22	23	24
25	26	27	28	29	30	31

SEPTEMBER

S	M	T	W	T	F	S
1	2	3	4	5	6	7
8	9	10	11	12	13	14
15	16	17	18	19	20	21
22	23	24	25	26	27	28
29	30					

OCTOBER

S	M	T	W	T	F	S
		1	2	3	4	5
6	7	8	9	10	11	12
13	14	15	16	17	18	19
20	21	22	23	24	25	26
27	28	29	30	31		

NOVEMBER

S	M	T	W	T	F	S
					1	2
3	4	5	6	7	8	9
10	11	12	13	14	15	16
17	18	19	20	21	22	23
24	25	26	27	28	29	30

DECEMBER

S	M	T	W	T	F	S
1	2	3	4	5	6	7
8	9	10	11	12	13	14
15	16	17	18	19	20	21
22	23	24	25	26	27	28
29	30	31				

10

JANUARY

S	M	T	W	T	F	S
		1	2	3	4	5
6	7	8	9	10	11	12
13	14	15	16	17	18	19
20	21	22	23	24	25	26
27	28	29	30	31		

FEBRUARY

S	M	T	W	T	F	S
					1	2
3	4	5	6	7	8	9
10	11	12	13	14	15	16
17	18	19	20	21	22	23
24	25	26	27	28	29	

MARCH

S	M	T	W	T	F	S
						1
2	3	4	5	6	7	8
9	10	11	12	13	14	15
16	17	18	19	20	21	22
23	24	25	26	27	28	29
30	31					

APRIL

S	M	T	W	T	F	S
		1	2	3	4	5
6	7	8	9	10	11	12
13	14	15	16	17	18	19
20	21	22	23	24	25	26
27	28	29	30			

MAY

S	M	T	W	T	F	S
				1	2	3
4	5	6	7	8	9	10
11	12	13	14	15	16	17
18	19	20	21	22	23	24
25	26	27	28	29	30	31

JUNE

S	M	T	W	T	F	S
1	2	3	4	5	6	7
8	9	10	11	12	13	14
15	16	17	18	19	20	21
22	23	24	25	26	27	28
29	30					

JULY

S	M	T	W	T	F	S
		1	2	3	4	5
6	7	8	9	10	11	12
13	14	15	16	17	18	19
20	21	22	23	24	25	26
27	28	29	30	31		

AUGUST

S	M	T	W	T	F	S
					1	2
3	4	5	6	7	8	9
10	11	12	13	14	15	16
17	18	19	20	21	22	23
24	25	26	27	28	29	30
31						

SEPTEMBER

S	M	T	W	T	F	S
	1	2	3	4	5	6
7	8	9	10	11	12	13
14	15	16	17	18	19	20
21	22	23	24	25	26	27
28	29	30				

OCTOBER

S	M	T	W	T	F	S
			1	2	3	4
5	6	7	8	9	10	11
12	13	14	15	16	17	18
19	20	21	22	23	24	25
26	27	28	29	30	31	

NOVEMBER

S	M	T	W	T	F	S
						1
2	3	4	5	6	7	8
9	10	11	12	13	14	15
16	17	18	19	20	21	22
23	24	25	26	27	28	29
30						

DECEMBER

S	M	T	W	T	F	S
	1	2	3	4	5	6
7	8	9	10	11	12	13
14	15	16	17	18	19	20
21	22	23	24	25	26	27
28	29	30	31			

11

JANUARY

S	M	T	W	T	F	S
			1	2	3	4
5	6	7	8	9	10	11
12	13	14	15	16	17	18
19	20	21	22	23	24	25
26	27	28	29	30	31	

FEBRUARY

S	M	T	W	T	F	S
						1
2	3	4	5	6	7	8
9	10	11	12	13	14	15
16	17	18	19	20	21	22
23	24	25	26	27	28	29

MARCH

S	M	T	W	T	F	S
1	2	3	4	5	6	7
8	9	10	11	12	13	14
15	16	17	18	19	20	21
22	23	24	25	26	27	28
29	30	31				

APRIL

S	M	T	W	T	F	S
			1	2	3	4
5	6	7	8	9	10	11
12	13	14	15	16	17	18
19	20	21	22	23	24	25
26	27	28	29	30		

MAY

S	M	T	W	T	F	S
					1	2
3	4	5	6	7	8	9
10	11	12	13	14	15	16
17	18	19	20	21	22	23
24	25	26	27	28	29	30
31						

JUNE

S	M	T	W	T	F	S
	1	2	3	4	5	6
7	8	9	10	11	12	13
14	15	16	17	18	19	20
21	22	23	24	25	26	27
28	29	30				

JULY

S	M	T	W	T	F	S
			1	2	3	4
5	6	7	8	9	10	11
12	13	14	15	16	17	18
19	20	21	22	23	24	25
26	27	28	29	30	31	

AUGUST

S	M	T	W	T	F	S
						1
2	3	4	5	6	7	8
9	10	11	12	13	14	15
16	17	18	19	20	21	22
23	24	25	26	27	28	29
30	31					

SEPTEMBER

S	M	T	W	T	F	S
		1	2	3	4	5
6	7	8	9	10	11	12
13	14	15	16	17	18	19
20	21	22	23	24	25	26
27	28	29	30			

OCTOBER

S	M	T	W	T	F	S
				1	2	3
4	5	6	7	8	9	10
11	12	13	14	15	16	17
18	19	20	21	22	23	24
25	26	27	28	29	30	31

NOVEMBER

S	M	T	W	T	F	S
1	2	3	4	5	6	7
8	9	10	11	12	13	14
15	16	17	18	19	20	21
22	23	24	25	26	27	28
29	30					

DECEMBER

S	M	T	W	T	F	S
		1	2	3	4	5
6	7	8	9	10	11	12
13	14	15	16	17	18	19
20	21	22	23	24	25	26
27	28	29	30	31		

12

JANUARY

S	M	T	W	T	F	S
				1	2	3
4	5	6	7	8	9	10
11	12	13	14	15	16	17
18	19	20	21	22	23	24
25	26	27	28	29	30	31

FEBRUARY

S	M	T	W	T	F	S
1	2	3	4	5	6	7
8	9	10	11	12	13	14
15	16	17	18	19	20	21
22	23	24	25	26	27	28
29						

MARCH

S	M	T	W	T	F	S
	1	2	3	4	5	6
7	8	9	10	11	12	13
14	15	16	17	18	19	20
21	22	23	24	25	26	27
28	29	30	31			

APRIL

S	M	T	W	T	F	S
				1	2	3
4	5	6	7	8	9	10
11	12	13	14	15	16	17
18	19	20	21	22	23	24
25	26	27	28	29	30	

MAY

S	M	T	W	T	F	S
						1
2	3	4	5	6	7	8
9	10	11	12	13	14	15
16	17	18	19	20	21	22
23	24	25	26	27	28	29
30	31					

JUNE

S	M	T	W	T	F	S
		1	2	3	4	5
6	7	8	9	10	11	12
13	14	15	16	17	18	19
20	21	22	23	24	25	26
27	28	29	30			

JULY

S	M	T	W	T	F	S
				1	2	3
4	5	6	7	8	9	10
11	12	13	14	15	16	17
18	19	20	21	22	23	24
25	26	27	28	29	30	31

AUGUST

S	M	T	W	T	F	S
1	2	3	4	5	6	7
8	9	10	11	12	13	14
15	16	17	18	19	20	21
22	23	24	25	26	27	28
29	30	31				

SEPTEMBER

S	M	T	W	T	F	S
			1	2	3	4
5	6	7	8	9	10	11
12	13	14	15	16	17	18
19	20	21	22	23	24	25
26	27	28	29	30		

OCTOBER

S	M	T	W	T	F	S
					1	2
3	4	5	6	7	8	9
10	11	12	13	14	15	16
17	18	19	20	21	22	23
24	25	26	27	28	29	30
31						

NOVEMBER

S	M	T	W	T	F	S
	1	2	3	4	5	6
7	8	9	10	11	12	13
14	15	16	17	18	19	20
21	22	23	24	25	26	27
28	29	30				

DECEMBER

S	M	T	W	T	F	S
			1	2	3	4
5	6	7	8	9	10	11
12	13	14	15	16	17	18
19	20	21	22	23	24	25
26	27	28	29	30	31	

13

JANUARY

S	M	T	W	T	F	S
					1	2
3	4	5	6	7	8	9
10	11	12	13	14	15	16
17	18	19	20	21	22	23
24	25	26	27	28	29	30
31						

FEBRUARY

S	M	T	W	T	F	S
	1	2	3	4	5	6
7	8	9	10	11	12	13
14	15	16	17	18	19	20
21	22	23	24	25	26	27
28	29					

MARCH

S	M	T	W	T	F	S
		1	2	3	4	5
6	7	8	9	10	11	12
13	14	15	16	17	18	19
20	21	22	23	24	25	26
27	28	29	30	31		

APRIL

S	M	T	W	T	F	S
					1	2
3	4	5	6	7	8	9
10	11	12	13	14	15	16
17	18	19	20	21	22	23
24	25	26	27	28	29	30

MAY

S	M	T	W	T	F	S
1	2	3	4	5	6	7
8	9	10	11	12	13	14
15	16	17	18	19	20	21
22	23	24	25	26	27	28
29	30	31				

JUNE

S	M	T	W	T	F	S
			1	2	3	4
5	6	7	8	9	10	11
12	13	14	15	16	17	18
19	20	21	22	23	24	25
26	27	28	29	30		

JULY

S	M	T	W	T	F	S
					1	2
3	4	5	6	7	8	9
10	11	12	13	14	15	16
17	18	19	20	21	22	23
24	25	26	27	28	29	30
31						

AUGUST

S	M	T	W	T	F	S
	1	2	3	4	5	6
7	8	9	10	11	12	13
14	15	16	17	18	19	20
21	22	23	24	25	26	27
28	29	30	31			

SEPTEMBER

S	M	T	W	T	F	S
				1	2	3
4	5	6	7	8	9	10
11	12	13	14	15	16	17
18	19	20	21	22	23	24
25	26	27	28	29	30	

OCTOBER

S	M	T	W	T	F	S
						1
2	3	4	5	6	7	8
9	10	11	12	13	14	15
16	17	18	19	20	21	22
23	24	25	26	27	28	29
30	31					

NOVEMBER

S	M	T	W	T	F	S
		1	2	3	4	5
6	7	8	9	10	11	12
13	14	15	16	17	18	19
20	21	22	23	24	25	26
27	28	29	30			

DECEMBER

S	M	T	W	T	F	S
				1	2	3
4	5	6	7	8	9	10
11	12	13	14	15	16	17
18	19	20	21	22	23	24
25	26	27	28	29	30	31

14

JANUARY

S	M	T	W	T	F	S
						1
2	3	4	5	6	7	8
9	10	11	12	13	14	15
16	17	18	19	20	21	22
23	24	25	26	27	28	29
30	31					

FEBRUARY

S	M	T	W	T	F	S
		1	2	3	4	5
6	7	8	9	10	11	12
13	14	15	16	17	18	19
20	21	22	23	24	25	26
27	28	29				

MARCH

S	M	T	W	T	F	S
			1	2	3	4
5	6	7	8	9	10	11
12	13	14	15	16	17	18
19	20	21	22	23	24	25
26	27	28	29	30	31	

APRIL

S	M	T	W	T	F	S
						1
2	3	4	5	6	7	8
9	10	11	12	13	14	15
16	17	18	19	20	21	22
23	24	25	26	27	28	29
30						

MAY

S	M	T	W	T	F	S
	1	2	3	4	5	6
7	8	9	10	11	12	13
14	15	16	17	18	19	20
21	22	23	24	25	26	27
28	29	30	31			

JUNE

S	M	T	W	T	F	S
				1	2	3
4	5	6	7	8	9	10
11	12	13	14	15	16	17
18	19	20	21	22	23	24
25	26	27	28	29	30	

JULY

S	M	T	W	T	F	S
						1
2	3	4	5	6	7	8
9	10	11	12	13	14	15
16	17	18	19	20	21	22
23	24	25	26	27	28	29
30	31					

AUGUST

S	M	T	W	T	F	S
		1	2	3	4	5
6	7	8	9	10	11	12
13	14	15	16	17	18	19
20	21	22	23	24	25	26
27	28	29	30	31		

SEPTEMBER

S	M	T	W	T	F	S
					1	2
3	4	5	6	7	8	9
10	11	12	13	14	15	16
17	18	19	20	21	22	23
24	25	26	27	28	29	30

OCTOBER

S	M	T	W	T	F	S
1	2	3	4	5	6	7
8	9	10	11	12	13	14
15	16	17	18	19	20	21
22	23	24	25	26	27	28
29	30	31				

NOVEMBER

S	M	T	W	T	F	S
			1	2	3	4
5	6	7	8	9	10	11
12	13	14	15	16	17	18
19	20	21	22	23	24	25
26	27	28	29	30		

DECEMBER

S	M	T	W	T	F	S
					1	2
3	4	5	6	7	8	9
10	11	12	13	14	15	16
17	18	19	20	21	22	23
24	25	26	27	28	29	30
31						

The Calendar

History of the Calendar

The purpose of a calendar is to reckon time in advance, to show how many days have to elapse until a certain event takes place—the harvest, a religious festival, or whatever. The earliest calendars, naturally, were crude, and they must have been strongly influenced by the geographical location of the people who made them. In the Scandinavian countries, for example, where the seasons are pronounced, the concept of the year was determined by the seasons, specifically by the end of winter. The Norsemen, before becoming Christians, are said to have had a calendar consisting of ten months of 30 days each.

But in warmer countries, where the seasons are less pronounced, the Moon became the basic unit for time reckoning; an old Jewish book actually makes the statement that "the Moon was created for the counting of the days." All the oldest calendars of which we have reliable information were lunar calendars, based on the time interval from one new moon to the next—a so-called "lunation." But even in a warm climate there are annual events that pay no attention to the phases of the Moon. In some areas it was a rainy season; in Egypt it was the annual flooding of the Nile. It was, therefore, necessary to regulate daily life and religious festivals by lunations, but to take care of the annual event in some other manner.

The calendar of the Assyrians was based on the phases of the Moon. The month began with the first appearance of the lunar crescent, and since this can best be observed in the evening, the day began with sunset. They knew that a lunation was 29 1/2 days long, so their lunar year had a duration of 354 days, falling eleven days short of the solar year.[1] After three years such a lunar calendar would be off by 33 days, or more than one lunation. We know that the Assyrians added an extra month from time to time, but we do not know whether they had developed a special rule for doing so or whether the priests proclaimed the necessity for an extra month from observation. If they made every third year a year of 13 lunations, their three-year period would cover 1,091 1/2 days (using their value of 29 1/2 days for one lunation), or just about four days too short. In one century this mistake would add up to 133 days by their reckoning (in reality closer to 134 days), requiring four extra lunations per century.

We now know that an eight-year period, consisting of five years with 12 months and three years with 13 months would lead to a difference of only 20 days per century, but we do not know whether such a calendar was actually used.

The best approximation that was possible in antiquity was a 19-year period, with seven of these 19 years having 13 months. This means that the period contained 235 months. This, still using the old value for a lunation, made a total of 6,932 1/2 days, while 19 solar years added up to 6,939.7 days, a difference of just one week per period and about five weeks per century. Even the 19-year period required constant adjustment, but it was the period that became the basis of the religious calendar of the Jews. The Arabs used the same calendar at first, but Mohammed forbade shifting from 12 months to 13 months, so that the Islamic religious calendar, even today, has a lunar year of 354 days. As a result the Islamic religious festivals run through all the seasons of the year three times per century.

The Egyptians had a traditional calendar with 12 months of 30 days each. At one time they added five extra days at the end of every year. These turned into a five-day festival because it was thought to be unlucky to work during that time.

When Rome emerged as a world power, the difficulties of making a calendar were well known, but the Romans complicated their lives because of their superstition that even numbers were unlucky. Hence their months were 29 or 31 days long, with the exception of February, which had 28 days. However, four months of 31 days, seven months of 29 days, and one month of 28 days added up to only 355 days. Therefore, the Romans invented an extra month called Mercedonius of 22 or 23 days. It was added every second year.

Even with Mercedonius, the Roman calendar was so far off that Caesar, advised by the astronomer Sosigenes, ordered a sweeping reform in 45 B.C. One year, made 445 days long by imperial decree, brought the calendar back in step with the seasons. Then the solar year (with the value of 365 days and 6 hours) was made the basis of the calendar. The months were 30 or 31 days in length, and to take care of the six hours, every fourth year was made a 366-day year. Moreover, Caesar decreed, the year began with the first of January, not with the vernal equinox in late March.

This was the Julian calendar, named after Julius Caesar. It is still the calendar of the Eastern Orthodox churches.

However, the year is 11 1/2 minutes shorter than the figure written into Caesar's calendar by Sosigenes, and after a number of centuries, even 11 1/2 minutes add up. *See* table.

While Caesar could decree that the vernal equinox should not be used as the first day of the new year, the vernal equinox is still a fact of Nature that could not be disregarded. One of the first (as far as we know) to become alarmed about this was Roger Bacon. He sent a memorandum to Pope Clement IV, who apparently was not impressed. But Pope Sixtus IV (reigned 1471 to 1484) decided that another reform was needed and called the German astronomer Regiomontanus to Rome to advise him. Regiomontanus arrived in 1475, but one year later he died in an epidemic, one of the recurrent outbreaks of the plague. The Pope himself survived, but his reform plans died with Regiomontanus.

Less than a hundred years later, in 1545, the Council of Trent authorized the then Pope, Gregory XIII, to reform the calendar once more. Most of the mathematical and astronomical work was done by Father Christopher Clavius, S.J. The immediate correction, advised by Father Clavius and ordered by Pope Gregory XIII, was that Thursday, Oct. 4, 1582, was to be the last day of the Julian calendar. The next day was Friday, with the date of October 15. For long-range accuracy, a formula suggested by the Vatican librarian Aloysius Giglio (latinized into Lilius) was adopted: every fourth year is a leap year *unless* it is a century year like 1700 or 1800. Century years can be leap years *only* when they are divisible by 400 (e.g., 1600).

1. The correct figures are: lunation: 29 d, 12 h, 44 min, 2.8 sec (29.530585 d); solar year: 365 d, 5 h, 48 min, 46 sec (365.242216 d); 12 lunations: 354 d, 8 h, 48 min, 34 sec (354.3671 d).

Drift of the Vernal Equinox in the Julian Calendar

Date	Julian year	Date	Julian year	Date	Julian year
March 21	325 A.D.	March 17	837 A.D.	March 13	1349 A.D.
March 20	453 A.D.	March 16	965 A.D.	March 12	1477 A.D.
March 19	581 A.D.	March 15	1093 A.D.	March 11	1605 A.D.
March 18	709 A.D.	March 14	1221 A.D.		

This rule eliminates three leap years in four centuries, making the calendar sufficiently correct for all ordinary purposes.

Unfortunately, all the Protestant princes in 1582 chose to ignore the papal bull; they continued with the Julian calendar. It was not until 1698 that the German professor Erhard Weigel persuaded the Protestant rulers of Germany and of the Netherlands to change to the new calendar. In England the shift took place in 1752, and in Russia it needed the revolution to introduce the Gregorian calendar in 1918.

The average year of the Gregorian calendar, in spite of the leap year rule, is about 26 seconds longer than the earth's orbital period. But this discrepancy will need 3,323 years to build up to a single day.

Modern proposals for calendar reform do not aim at a "better" calendar, but at one that is more convenient to use, especially for commercial purposes. A 365-day year cannot be divided into equal halves or quarters; the number of days per month is haphazard; the months begin or end in the middle of a week; a holiday fixed by date (e.g., the Fourth of July) will wander through a week; a holiday fixed in another manner (e.g., Easter) can fall on thirty-five possible dates. The Gregorian calendar, admittedly, keeps the calendar dates in reasonable unison with astronomical events, but it still is full of minor annoyances. Moreover, you need a calendar every year to look up dates; an ideal calendar should be one that you can memorize for one year and that is valid for all other years, too.

In 1834 an Italian priest, Marco Mastrofini, suggested taking one day out of every year. It would be made a holiday and *not* be given the name of a weekday. That would make every year begin with January 1 as a Sunday. The leap-year day would be treated the same way, so that in leap years there would be two unnamed holidays at the end of the year.

About a decade later the philosopher Auguste Comte also suggested a 364-day calendar with an extra day, which he called Year Day.

Since then there have been other unsuccessful attempts at calendar reform.

Time and Calendar

The two natural cycles on which time measurements are based are the year and the day. The year is defined as the time required for the Earth to complete one revolution around the Sun, while the day is the time required for the Earth to complete one turn upon its axis. Unfortunately the Earth needs 365 days plus about six hours to go around the Sun once, so that the year does not consist of so and so many days; the fractional day has to be taken care of by an extra day every fourth year.

But because the Earth, while turning upon its axis, also moves around the Sun there are two kinds of days. A day may be defined as the interval between the highest point of the Sun in the sky on two successive days. This, averaged out over the year, produces the customary 24-hour day. But one might also define a day as the time interval between the moments when a certain point in the sky, say a conveniently located star, is directly overhead. This is called:

Sidereal time. Astronomers use a point which they call the "vernal equinox" for the actual determination. Such a sidereal day is somewhat shorter than the "solar day," namely by about 3 minutes and 56 seconds of so-called "mean solar time."

Apparent solar time is the time based directly on the Sun's position in the sky. In ordinary life the day runs from midnight to midnight. It begins when the Sun is invisible by being 12 hours from its zenith. Astronomers use the so-called "Julian Day," which runs from noon to noon; the concept was invented by the astronomer Joseph Scaliger, who named it after his father Julius. To avoid the problems caused by leap-year days and so forth, Scaliger picked a conveniently remote date in the past and suggested just counting days without regard to weeks, months, and years. The Julian Day 2,446,795.5 is Jan. 1, 1987. The reason for having the Julian Day run from noon to noon is the practical one that astronomical observations usually extend across the midnight hour, which would require a change in date (or in the Julian Day number) if the astronomical day, like the civil day, ran from midnight to midnight.

Mean solar time, rather than apparent solar time, is what is actually used most of the time. The mean solar time is based on the position of a fictitious "mean sun." The reason why this fictitious sun has to be introduced is the following: the Earth turns on its axis regularly; it needs the same number of seconds regardless of the season. But the movement of the Earth around the Sun is not regular because the Earth's orbit is an ellipse. This has the result (as explained in the section The Seasons) that the Earth moves faster in January and slower in July. Though it is the Earth that changes velocity, it looks to us as if the Sun did. In January, when the Earth moves faster, the *apparent* movement of the Sun looks faster. The "mean sun" of time measurements, then, is a sun that moves regularly all year round; the real Sun will be either ahead of or behind the "mean sun." The difference between the real Sun and the fictitious mean sun is called the *equation of time.*

When the real Sun is west of the mean sun we have the "sun fast" condition, with the real Sun crossing the meridian ahead of the mean sun. The opposite is the "sun slow" situation when the real Sun crosses the meridian after the mean sun. Of course, what is observed is the real Sun. The equation of time is needed to establish mean solar time, kept by the reference clocks.

But if all clocks were actually set by mean solar time we would be plagued by a welter of time differences that would be "correct" but a major nuisance. A clock on Long Island, correctly showing mean solar time for its location (this would be *local*

The Names of the Days

Latin	Saxon	English	French	Italian	Spanish	German
Dies Solis	Sun's Day	Sunday	Dimanche	domenica	domingo	Sonntag
Dies Lunae	Moon's Day	Monday	Lundi	lunedi	lunes	Montag
Dies Martis	Tiw's Day	Tuesday	Mardi	martedi	martes	Dienstag
Dies Mercurii	Woden's Day	Wednesday	Mercredi	mercoledi	miércoles	Mittwoch
Dies Jovis	Thor's Day	Thursday	Jeudi	giovedi	jueves	Donnerstag
Dies Veneris	Frigg's Day	Friday	Vendredi	venedri	viernes	Freitag
Dies Saturni	Seterne's Day	Saturday	Samedi	sabato	sábado	Sonnabend

NOTE: The Romans gave one day of the week to each planet known, the Sun and Moon being considered planets in this connection. The Saxon names are a kind of translation of the Roman names: Tiw was substituted for Mars, Woden (Wotan) for Mercury, Thor for Jupiter (Jove), Frigg for Venus, and Seterne for Saturn. The English names are adapted Saxon. The Spanish and Italian names, which are normally not capitalized, and the French are derived from the Latin. The German names follow the Saxon pattern with two exceptions: Wednesday is Mittwoch (Middle of the Week), and Saturday is Sonnabend (Sunday's Eve).

civil time), would be slightly ahead of a clock in Newark, N.J. The Newark clock would be slightly ahead of a clock in Trenton, N.J., which, in turn, would be ahead of a clock in Philadelphia. This condition actually prevailed in the past until 1883, when *standard time* was introduced. Standard time is the correct mean solar time for a designated meridian, and this time is used for a certain area to the east and west of this meridian. In the U.S. four meridians have been designated to supply standard times; they are 75°, 90°, 105°, and 120° west of Greenwich. The 75° meridian determines Eastern Standard Time. It happens to run through Camden, N.J., where standard time, therefore, is also mean solar time and local civil time. The 90° meridian (which happens to pass through the western part of Memphis, Tenn.) determines Central Standard Time, the 105° meridian (passing through Denver) determines Mountain Standard Time, and the 120° meridian (which runs through Lake Tahoe) determines Pacific Standard Time.

Canada, extending over more territory from west to east, adds one time zone on either side: Atlantic Standard Time (based on 60° west of Greenwich) for New Brunswick, Nova Scotia, and Quebec, and Yukon Standard Time (determined by the 135° meridian) for its extreme West. Alaska, extending still farther to the west, adds two more time zones, Alaska Standard Time (determined by the 150° meridian that passes through Anchorage) and Nome Standard Time, based on the 165° meridian just east of Nome.

In general the Earth is divided into 24 such time zones, which run one hour apart. For practical purposes the time zones sometimes show indentations, and there are a few "subzones" that differ from the neighboring zone by only half an hour, e.g., Newfoundland.

The date line. While the time zones are based on the natural event of the Sun crossing the meridian, the date must be an arbitrary decision. The meridians are traditionally counted from the meridian of the observatory of Greenwich in England, which is called the zero meridian. The logical place for changing the date is 12 hours, or 180° from Greenwich. Fortunately, the 180th meridian runs mostly through the open Pacific. The date line makes a zigzag in the north to incorporate the eastern tip of Siberia into the Siberian time system and then another one to incorporate a number of islands into the Alaska time system. In the south there is a similar zigzag for the purpose of tying a number of British-owned islands to the New Zealand time system. Otherwise the date line is the same as 180° from Greenwich. At points to the east of the date line the calendar is one day earlier than at points to the west of it. A traveller going eastward across the date line from one island to another would not have to re-set his watch because he would stay inside the time zone (provided he does so where the date line does *not* coincide with the 180° meridian), but it would be the same time of the previous day.

The Seasons

The seasons are caused by the tilt of the Earth's axis (23.4°) and not by the fact that the Earth's orbit around the Sun is an ellipse. The average distance of the Earth from the Sun is 93 million miles; the difference between aphelion (farthest away) and perihelion (closest to the Sun) is 3 million miles, so that perihelion is about 91.4 million miles from the Sun. The Earth goes through the perihelion point a few days after New Year, just when the northern hemisphere has winter. Aphelion is passed during the first days in July. This by itself shows that the

The Names of the Months

January: named after Janus, protector of the gateway to heaven
February: named after Februalia, a time period when sacrifices were made to atone for sins
March: named after Mars, the god of war, presumably signifying that the campaigns interrupted by the winter could be resumed
April: from *aperire,* Latin for "to open" (buds)
May: named after Maia, the goddess of growth of plants
June: from *juvenis,* Latin for "youth"
July: named after Julius Caesar
August: named after Augustus, the first Roman Emperor
September: from *septem,* Latin for "seven"
October: from *octo,* Latin for "eight"
November: from *novem,* Latin for "nine"
December: from *decem,* Latin for "ten"

NOTE: The earliest Latin calendar was a 10-month one; thus September was the seventh month, October, the eighth, etc. July was originally called Quintilis, as the fifth month; August was originally called Sextilis, as the sixth month.

distance from the Sun is not important within these limits. What is important is that when the Earth passes through perihelion, the northern end of the Earth's axis happens to tilt away from the Sun, so that the areas beyond the Tropic of Cancer receive only slanting rays from a Sun low in the sky.

The tilt of the Earth's axis is responsible for four lines you find on every globe. When, say, the North Pole is tilted away from the Sun as much as possible, the farthest points in the North which can still be reached by the Sun's rays are 23 1/2° from the pole. This is the Arctic Circle. The Antarctic Circle is the corresponding limit 23.4° from the South Pole; the Sun's rays cannot reach beyond this point when we have mid-summer in the North.

When the Sun is vertically above the equator, the day is of equal length all over the Earth. This happens twice a year, and these are the "equinoxes" in March and in September. After having been over the equator in March, the Sun will seem to move northward. The northernmost point where the Sun can be straight overhead is 23.4° north of the equator. This is the Tropic of Cancer; the Sun can never be vertically overhead to the north of this line. Similarly the Sun cannot be vertically overhead to the south of a line 23.4° south of the equator—the Tropic of Capricorn.

This explains the climatic zones. In the belt (the Greek word *zone* means "belt") between the Tropic of Cancer and the Tropic of Capricorn, the Sun can be straight overhead; this is the tropical zone. The two zones where the Sun cannot be overhead but will be above the horizon every day of the year are the two temperate zones; the two areas where the Sun will not rise at all for varying lengths of time are the two polar areas, Arctic and Antarctic.

Holidays

Religious and Secular, 1988

Since 1971, by federal law, Washington's Birthday, Memorial Day, Columbus Day, and Veterans' Day have been celebrated on Mondays to create three-day weekends for federal employees. Many states now observe these holidays on the same Mondays. The dates given for the holidays listed below are the traditional ones.

New Year's Day, Friday, Jan. 1. A legal holiday in all states and the District of Columbia, New Year's Day has its origin in Roman Times, when sacrifices were offered to Janus, the two-faced Roman deity who looked back on the past and forward to the future.

Epiphany, Wednesday, Jan. 6. Falls the twelfth day after Christmas and commemorates the manifestation of Jesus as the Son of God, as represented by the adoration of the Magi, the baptism of Jesus, and the miracle of the wine at the marriage feast at Cana. Epiphany originally marked the beginning of the carnival season preceding Lent, and the evening (sometimes the eve) is known as Twelfth Night.

Martin Luther King, Jr.'s Birthday, Friday, Jan. 15. Honors the late civil rights leader. Became a legal public holiday in 1986.

Ground-hog Day, Tuesday, Feb. 2. Legend has it that if the ground-hog sees his shadow, he'll return to his hole, and winter will last another six weeks.

Lincoln's Birthday, Friday, Feb. 12. A legal holiday in many states, this day was first formally observed in Washington, D.C., in 1866, when both houses of Congress gathered for a memorial address in tribute to the assassinated President.

St. Valentine's Day, Sunday, Feb. 14. This day is the festival of two third-century martyrs, both named St. Valentine. It is not known why this day is associated with lovers. It may derive from an old pagan festival about this time of year, or it may have been inspired by the belief that birds mate on this day.

Shrove Tuesday, Feb. 16. Falls the day before Ash Wednesday and marks the end of the carnival season, which once began on Epiphany but is now usually celebrated the last three days before Lent. In France, the day is known as Mardi Gras (Fat Tuesday), and Mardi Gras celebrations are also held in several American cities, particularly in New Orleans. The day is sometimes called Pancake Tuesday by the English because fats, which were prohibited during Lent, had to be used up.

Ash Wednesday, Feb. 17. The first day of the Lenten season, which lasts 40 days. Having its origin sometime before A.D. 1000, it is a day of public penance and is marked in the Roman Catholic Church by the burning of the palms blessed on the previous year's Palm Sunday. With his thumb, the priest then marks a cross upon the forehead of each worshipper. The Anglican Church and a few Protestant groups in the United States also observe the day, but generally without the use of ashes.

Washington's Birthday, Monday, Feb. 22. The birthday of George Washington is celebrated as a legal holiday in every state of the Union, the District of Columbia, and all territories. The observance began in 1796.

Purim (Feast of Lots), Thursday, March 3. A day of joy and feasting celebrating deliverance of the Jews from a massacre planned by the Persian Minister Haman. The Jewish Queen Esther interceded with her husband, King Ahasuerus, to spare the life of her uncle, Mordecai, and Haman was hanged on the same gallows he had built for Mordecai. The holiday is marked by the reading of the Book of Esther (megillah), and by the exchange of gifts, donations to the poor, and the presentation of Purim plays.

St. Patrick's Day, Thursday, March 17. St. Patrick, patron saint of Ireland, has been honored in America since the first days of the nation. There are many dinners and meetings but perhaps the most notable part of the observance is the annual St. Patrick's Day parade on Fifth Avenue in New York City.

Palm Sunday, March 27. Is observed the Sunday before Easter to commemorate the entry of Jesus into Jerusalem. The procession and the ceremonies introducing the benediction of palms probably had their origin in Jerusalem.

Good Friday, April 1. This day commemorates the Crucifixion, which is retold during services from the Gospel according to St. John. A feature in Roman Catholic churches is the Liturgy of the Passion; there is no Consecration, the Host having been consecrated the previous day. The eating of hot cross buns on this day is said to have started in England.

Easter Sunday, April 3. Observed in all Christian churches, Easter commemorates the Resurrection of Jesus. It is celebrated on the first Sunday after the full moon which occurs on or next after March 21 and is therefore celebrated between March 22 and April 25 inclusive. This date was fixed by the Council of Nicaea in A.D. 325. The Orthodox Church celebrates Easter on April 19, 1987.

First Day of Passover (Pesach), Saturday, April 2. The Feast of the Passover, also called the Feast of Unleavened Bread, commemorates the escape of the Jews from Egypt. As the Jews fled they ate unleavened bread, and from that time the Jews have allowed no leavening in the houses during Passover, bread being replaced by matzoh.

Mother's Day, Sunday, May 8. Observed the second Sunday in May, as proposed by Anna Jarvis of Philadelphia in 1907.

Ascension Day, Thursday, May 12. Took place in the presence of His apostles 40 days after the Resurrection of Jesus. It is traditionally held to have occurred on Mount Olivet in Bethany.

Pentecost (Whitsunday), May 22. This day commemorates the descent of the Holy Ghost upon the apostles 50 days after the Resurrection. The sermon by the Apostle Peter, which led to the baptism of 3,000 who professed belief, originated the ceremonies that have since been followed. "Whitsunday" is believed to have come from "white Sunday" when, among the English, white robes were worn by those baptized on the day.

First Day of Shavuot (Hebrew Pentecost), Sunday, May 22. This festival, sometimes called the Feast of Weeks, or of Harvest, or of the First Fruits, falls 50 days after Passover and originally celebrated the end of the seven-week grain harvesting season. In later tradition, it also celebrated the giving of the Law to Moses on Mount Sinai.

Memorial Day, Monday, May 30. Also known as Decoration Day, Memorial Day is a legal holiday in most of the states and in the territories, and is also observed by the armed forces. In 1868, Gen. John A. Logan, Commander in Chief of the Grand Army of the Republic, issued an order designating the day as one in which the graves of soldiers would be decorated. The holiday was originally devoted to honoring the memory of those who fell in the Civil War, but is now also dedicated to the memory of all war dead.

Flag Day, Tuesday, June 14. This day commemorates the adoption by the Continental Congress on June 14, 1777, of the Stars and Stripes as the U.S. flag. Although it is a legal holiday only in Pennsylvania, President Truman, on Aug. 3, 1949, signed a bill requesting the President to call for its observance each year by proclamation.

Father's Day, Sunday, June 19. Observed the third Sunday in June. First celebrated June 19, 1910.

Independence Day, Monday, July 4. The day of the adoption of the Declaration of Independence in 1776, celebrated in all states and territories. The observance began the next year in Philadelphia.

Labor Day, Monday, Sept. 5. Observed the first Monday in September in all states and territories, Labor Day was first celebrated in New York in 1882 under the sponsorship of the Central Labor Union, following the suggestion of Peter J. McGuire, of the Knights of Labor, that the day be set aside in honor of labor.

First Day of Rosh Hashana (Jewish New Year), Monday, Sept. 12. This day marks the beginning of the Jewish year 5749 and opens the Ten Days of Penitence closing with Yom Kippur.

Yom Kippur (Day of Atonement), Wednesday, Sept. 21. This day marks the end of the Ten Days of Penitence that began with Rosh Hashana. It is described in *Leviticus* as a "Sabbath of rest," and synagogue services begin the preceding sundown, resume the following morning, and continue to sundown.

First Day of Sukkot (Feast of Tabernacles) Monday, Sept. 26. This festival, also known as the Feast of the Ingathering, originally celebrated the fruit harvest, and the name comes from the booths or tabernacles in which the Jews lived during the harvest, although one tradition traces it to the shelters used by the Jews in their wandering through the wilderness. During the festival many Jews build small huts in their back yards or on the roofs of their houses.

Simhat Torah (Rejoicing of the Law), Tuesday, Oct. 4. This joyous holiday falls on the eighth day of Sukkot. It marks the end of the year's reading of the Torah (Five Books of Moses) in the synagogue every Saturday and the beginning of the new cycle of reading.

Columbus Day, Wednesday, Oct. 12. A legal holiday in many states, commemorating the discovery of America by Columbus in 1492. Quite likely the first celebration of Columbus Day was that organized in 1792 by the Society of St. Tammany, or Columbian Order, more widely known as Tammany Hall.

United Nations Day, Monday, Oct. 24. Marking the founding of the United Nations.

Halloween, Monday, Oct. 31. Eve of All Saints' Day, formerly called All Hallows and Hallowmass. Halloween is traditionally associated in some countries with old customs such as bonfires, masquerading, and the telling of ghost stories. These are old Celtic practices marking the beginning of winter.

All Saints' Day, Tuesday, Nov. 1. A Roman Catholic and Anglican holiday celebrating all saints, known and unknown.

Election Day, (legal holiday in certain states), Tuesday, Nov. 8. Since 1845, by Act of Congress, the first Tuesday after the first Monday in November is the date for choosing Presidential electors. State elections are also generally held on this day.

Veterans Day, Friday, Nov. 11. Armistice Day was established in 1926 to commemorate the signing in 1918 of the Armistice ending World War I. On June 1, 1954, the name was changed to Veterans Day to honor all men and women who have served America in its armed forces.

Thanksgiving, Thursday, Nov. 24. Observed nationally on the fourth Thursday in November by Act of Congress (1941), the first such national proclamation having been issued by President Lincoln in 1863, on the urging of Mrs. Sarah J. Hale, editor of *Godey's Lady's Book.* Most Americans believe that the holiday dates back to the day of thanks ordered by Governor Bradford of Plymouth Colony in New England in 1621, but scholars point out that days of thanks stem from ancient times.

First Sunday of Advent, Nov. 27. Advent is the season in which the faithful must prepare themselves for the advent of the Saviour on Christmas. The four Sundays before Christmas are marked by special church services.

First Day of Hanukkah (Festival of Lights), Sunday, Dec. 4. This festival was instituted by Judas Maccabaeus in 165 B.C. to celebrate the purification of the Temple of Jerusalem, which had been desecrated three years earlier by Antiochus Epiphanes, who set up a pagan altar and offered sacrifices to Zeus Olympius. In Jewish homes, a light is lighted on each night of the eight-day festival.

Christmas (Feast of the Nativity), Sunday, Dec. 25. The most widely celebrated holiday of the Christian year, Christmas is observed as the anniversary of the birth of Jesus. Christmas customs are centuries old. The mistletoe, for example, comes from the Druids, who, in hanging the mistletoe, hoped for peace and good fortune. Use of such plants as holly comes from the ancient belief that such plants blossomed at Christmas. Comparatively recent is the Christmas tree, first set up in Germany in the 17th century, and the use of candles on trees developed from the belief that candles appeared by miracle on the trees at Christmas. Colonial Manhattan Islanders introduced the name Santa Claus, a corruption of the Dutch name for the 4th-century Asia Minor St. Nicholas.

State Observances

January 6, Three Kings' Day: Puerto Rico.
January 8, Battle of New Orleans Day: Louisiana.
January 11, De Hostos' Birthday: Puerto Rico.
January 19, Robert E. Lee's Birthday: Arkansas, Florida, Kentucky, Louisiana, South Carolina, **(third Monday)** Alabama, Mississippi.
January 19, Confederate Heroes Day: Texas.
January (third Monday): Lee-Jackson-King Day: Virginia.
January 30, F.D.Roosevelt's Birthday: Kentucky.
February 15, Susan B. Anthony's Birthday: Florida, Minnesota.
March (first Tuesday), Town Meeting Day: Vermont.
March 2, Texas Independence Day: Texas.
March (first Monday), Casimir Pulaski's Birthday: Illinois.
March 17, Evacuation Day: Massachusetts (in Suffolk County).
March 20 (First Day of Spring), Youth Day: Oklahoma.
March 22, Abolition Day: Puerto Rico.
March 25, Maryland Day: Maryland.
March 26, Prince Jonah Kuhio Kalanianaole Day: Hawaii.
March (last Monday), Seward's Day: Alaska.
April 2, Pascua Florida Day: Florida
April 13, Thomas Jefferson's Birthday: Alabama, Oklahoma.
April 16, De Diego's Birthday: Puerto Rico.
April (third Monday), Patriots' Day: Maine, Massachusetts.
April 21, San Jacinto Day: Texas.
April 22, Arbor Day: Nebraska.
April 22, Oklahoma Day: Oklahoma.
April 26, Confederate Memorial Day: Florida, Georgia.
April (fourth Monday), Fast Day: New Hampshire.
April (last Monday), Confederate Memorial Day: Alabama, Mississippi.
May 1, Bird Day: Oklahoma.
May 8, Truman Day: Missouri.
May 11, Minnesota Day: Minnesota.
May 20, Mecklenburg Independence Day: North Carolina.
June (first Monday), Jefferson Davis's Birthday: Alabama, Mississippi.
June 3, Jefferson Davis's Birthday: Florida, South Carolina.
June 3, Confederate Memorial Day: Kentucky, Louisiana.
June 9, Senior Citizens Day: Oklahoma.
June 11, King Kamehameha I Day: Hawaii.
June 15, Separation Day: Delaware.
June 17, Bunker Hill Day: Massachusetts (in Suffolk County).
June 19, Emancipation Day: Texas.
June 20, West Virginia Day: West Virginia.
July 17, Muñoz Rivera's Birthday: Puerto Rico.
July 24, Pioneer Day: Utah.
July 25, Constitution Day: Puerto Rico.
July 27, Barbosa's Birthday: Puerto Rico.
August (first Sunday), American Family Day: Arizona.
August (first Monday), Colorado Day: Colorado.
August (second Monday), Victory Day: Rhode Island.
August 16, Bennington Battle Day: Vermont.
August (third Friday), Admission Day: Hawaii.
August 27, Lyndon B. Johnson's Birthday: Texas.
August 30, Huey P. Long Day: Louisiana.
September 9, Admission Day: California.
September 12, Defenders' Day: Maryland.
September 16, Cherokee Strip Day: Oklahoma.
September (first Saturday after full moon), Indian Day: Oklahoma.
October 10, Leif Erickson Day: Minnesota.
October 10, Oklahoma Historical Day: Oklahoma.
October 18, Alaska Day: Alaska.
October 31, Nevada Day: Nevada.
November 4, Will Rogers Day: Oklahoma.
November (week of the 16th), Oklahoma Heritage Week: Oklahoma.
November 19, Discovery Day: Puerto Rico.
December 7, Delaware Day: Delaware.

Movable Holidays, 1988–1993

CHRISTIAN AND SECULAR

Year	Ash Wednesday	Easter	Pentecost	Labor Day	Election Day	Thanksgiving	1st Sun. Advent
1988	Feb. 17	April 3	May 22	Sept. 5	Nov. 8	Nov. 24	Nov. 27
1989	Feb. 8	March 26	May 14	Sept. 4	Nov. 7	Nov. 23	Dec. 3
1990	Feb. 28	April 15	June 3	Sept. 3	Nov. 6	Nov. 22	Dec. 2
1991	Feb. 13	March 31	May 19	Sept. 2	Nov. 5	Nov. 28	Dec. 1
1992	March 4	April 19	June 7	Sept. 7	Nov. 3	Nov. 26	Nov. 29
1993	Feb. 24	April 11	May 30	Sept. 6	Nov. 2	Nov. 25	Nov. 28

Shrove Tuesday: 1 day before Ash Wednesday
Palm Sunday: 7 days before Easter
Maundy Thursday: 3 days before Easter
Good Friday: 2 days before Easter
Holy Saturday: 1 day before Easter
Ascension Day: 10 days before Pentecost
Trinity Sunday: 7 days after Pentecost
Corpus Christi: 11 days after Pentecost

NOTE: Easter is celebrated on April 10, 1988, by the Orthodox Church.

JEWISH

Year	Purim[1]	1st day Passover[2]	1st day Shavuot[3]	1st day Rosh Hashana[4]	Yom Kippur[5]	1st day Sukkot[6]	Simhat Torah[7]	1st day Hanukkah[8]
1988	March 3	April 2	May 22	Sept. 12	Sept. 21	Sept. 26	Oct. 4	Dec. 4
1989	March 21	April 20	June 9	Sept. 30	Oct. 9	Oct. 14	Oct. 22	Dec. 23
1990	March 11	April 10	May 30	Sept. 20	Sept. 29	Oct. 4	Oct. 12	Dec. 12
1991	Feb. 28	March 30	May 19	Sept. 9	Sept. 18	Sept. 23	Oct. 1	Dec. 2
1992	March 14	April 18	June 7	Sept. 28	Oct. 7	Oct. 12	Oct. 20	Dec. 20
1993	March 7	April 6	May 26	Sept. 16	Sept. 25	Sept. 30	Oct. 8	Dec. 9

1. Feast of Lots. 2. Feast of Unleavened Bread. 3. Hebrew Pentecost; or Feast of Weeks, or of Harvest, or of First Fruits. 4. Jewish New Year. 5. Day of Atonement. 6. Feast of Tabernacles, or of the Ingathering. 7. Rejoicing of the Law. 8. Festival of Lights.

Length of Jewish holidays (O=Orthodox, C=Conservative, R=Reform):

Passover: O & C, 8 days (holy days: first 2 and last 2); R, 7 days (holy days: first and last)
Shavuot: O & C, 2 days; R, 1 day
Rosh Hashana: O & C, 2 days; R, 1 day.
Yom Kippur: All groups, 1 day
Sukkot: All groups, 7 days (holy days: O & C, first 2; R, first only) O & C observe two additional days: Shemini Atseret (Eighth Day of the Feast) and Simhat Torah. R observes Shemini Atseret but not Simhat Torah
Hanukkah: All groups, 8 days

NOTE: All holidays begin at sundown on the evening before the date given.

Chinese Calendar

The Chinese lunar year is divided into 12 months of 29 or 30 days. The calendar is adjusted to the length of the solar year by the addition of extra months at regular intervals.

The years are arranged in major cycles of 60 years. Each successive year is named after one of 12 animals. These 12-year cycles are continuously repeated. The Chinese New Year is celebrated at the first new moon after the sun enters Aquarius—sometime between Jan. 21 and Feb. 19.

Rat	Ox	Tiger	Cat (Rabbit)	Dragon	Snake	Horse	Sheep (Goat)	Monkey	Rooster	Dog	Pig
1864	1865	1866	1867	1868	1869	1870	1871	1872	1873	1874	1875
1876	1877	1878	1879	1880	1881	1882	1883	1884	1885	1886	1887
1888	1889	1890	1891	1892	1893	1894	1895	1896	1897	1898	1899
1900	1901	1902	1903	1904	1905	1906	1907	1908	1909	1910	1911
1912	1913	1914	1915	1916	1917	1918	1919	1920	1921	1922	1923
1924	1925	1926	1927	1928	1929	1930	1931	1932	1933	1934	1935
1936	1937	1938	1939	1940	1941	1942	1943	1944	1945	1946	1947
1948	1949	1950	1951	1952	1953	1954	1955	1956	1957	1958	1959
1960	1961	1962	1963	1964	1965	1966	1967	1968	1969	1970	1971
1972	1973	1974	1975	1976	1977	1978	1979	1980	1981	1982	1983
1984	1985	1986	1987	1988	1989	1990	1991	1992	1993	1994	1995

National Holidays Around the World, 1988

Afghanistan	April 27	Ghana	March 6	Peru	July 28
Albania	Nov. 29	Greece	March 25	Philippines	June 12
Algeria	Nov. 1	Grenada	Feb. 7	Poland	July 22
Angola	Nov. 11	Guatemala	Sept. 15	Portugal	June 10
Antigua and Barbuda	Nov. 1	Guinea	Oct. 2	Qatar	Sept. 3
Argentina	May 25	Guinea-Bissau	Sept. 24	Romania	Aug. 23
Australia	Jan. 26	Guyana	Feb. 23	Rwanda	July 1
Austria	Oct. 26	Haiti	Jan. 1	St. Kitts and Nevis	Sept. 19
Bahamas	July 10	Honduras	Sept. 15	St. Lucia	Feb. 22
Bahrain	Dec. 16	Hungary	April 4	St. Vincent and the Grenadines	Oct. 27
Bangladesh	March 26	Iceland	June 17	Sao Tomé and Príncipe	July 12
Barbados	Nov. 30	India	Jan. 26	Saudi Arabia	Sept. 23
Belgium	July 21	Indonesia	Aug. 17	Senegal	April 4
Belize	Sept. 21	Iran	Feb. 11	Seychelles	June 5
Benin	Nov. 30	Iraq	July 17	Sierra Leone	April 27
Bhutan	Dec. 17	Ireland	March 17	Singapore	Aug. 9
Bolivia	Aug. 6	Israel	April 21[1]	Solomon Islands	July 7
Botswana	Sept. 30	Italy	June 2	Somalia	Oct. 21
Brazil	Sept. 7	Ivory Coast	Dec. 7	South Africa	May 31
Brunei	Feb. 23	Jamaica	Aug. 1[2]	Spain	Oct. 12
Bulgaria	Sept. 9	Japan	April 29	Sri Lanka	Feb. 4
Burkina Faso	Aug. 4	Jordan	May 25	Sudan	Jan. 1
Burma	Jan. 4	Kenya	Dec. 12	Suriname	Nov. 25
Burundi	July 1	Kuwait	Feb. 25	Swaziland	Sept. 6
Cambodia	April 17	Laos	Dec. 2	Sweden	June 6
Cameroon	May 20	Lebanon	Nov. 22	Switzerland	Aug. 1
Canada	July 1	Lesotho	Oct. 4	Syria	April 17
Cape Verde	Sept. 12	Liberia	July 26	Tanzania	April 26
Central African Republic	Dec. 1	Libya	Sept. 1	Thailand	Dec. 5
Chad	June 7	Luxembourg	June 23	Togo	April 27
Chile	Sept. 18	Madagascar	June 26	Trinidad and Tobago	Aug. 31
China	Oct. 1	Malawi	July 6	Tunisia	June 1
Colombia	July 20	Malaysia	Aug. 31	Turkey	Oct. 29
Comoros	July 6	Maldives	July 26	Uganda	Oct. 9
Congo	Aug. 15	Mali	Sept. 22	U.S.S.R.	Nov. 7
Costa Rica	Sept. 15	Malta	March 31	United Arab Emirates	Dec. 2
Cuba	Jan. 1	Mauritania	Nov. 28	United Kingdom	June 11[3]
Cyprus	Oct. 1	Mauritius	March 12	United States	July 4
Czechoslovakia	May 9	Mexico	Sept. 16	Uruguay	Aug. 25
Denmark	April 16	Mongolia	July 11	Vanuatu	July 30
Djibouti	June 27	Morocco	March 3	Venezuela	July 5
Dominica	Nov. 3	Mozambique	June 25	Viet Nam	Sept. 2
Dominican Republic	Feb. 27	Nepal	Dec. 28	Western Samoa	June 1
Ecuador	Aug. 10	Netherlands	April 30	Yemen, People's Dem. Republic of	Oct. 14
Egypt	July 23	New Zealand	Feb. 6	Yemen Arab Republic	Sept. 26
El Salvador	Sept. 15	Nicaragua	Sept. 15	Yugoslavia	Nov. 29
Equatorial Guinea	Oct. 12	Niger	Dec. 18	Zaire	June 30
Ethiopia	Sept. 12	Nigeria	Oct. 1	Zambia	Oct. 24
Fiji	Oct. 10	Norway	May 17	Zimbabwe	April 18
Finland	Dec. 6	Oman	Nov. 18		
France	July 14	Pakistan	March 23		
Gabon	Aug. 17	Panama	Nov. 3		
Gambia	Feb. 18	Papua New Guinea	Sept. 16		
Germany, East	Oct. 7	Paraguay	May 14		

1. Changes yearly according to Hebrew calendar. 2. Celebrated on first Monday in August. 3. Celebrated the second Saturday in June. *Source:* United Nations.

The Basic Unit of the World Calendar

Days	First month					Second month					Third month				
Sunday	1	8	15	22	29	—	5	12	19	26	—	3	10	17	24
Monday	2	9	16	23	30	—	6	13	20	27	—	4	11	18	25
Tuesday	3	10	17	24	31	—	7	14	21	28	—	5	12	19	26
Wednesday	4	11	18	25	—	1	8	15	22	29	—	6	13	20	27
Thursday	5	12	19	26	—	2	9	16	23	30	—	7	14	21	28
Friday	6	13	20	27	—	3	10	17	24	—	1	8	15	22	29
Saturday	7	14	21	28	—	4	11	18	25	—	2	9	16	23	30

Signals From The Sky

By Carl Sagan

In the outskirts of the solar system, in the cold and dark beyond Pluto where the Sun is only a bright star, there is a plucky little spacecraft from Earth, outward bound. Pioneer 10's main mission, to make a preliminary reconnaissance of Jupiter and Saturn, was brilliantly fulfilled long ago. But its instruments are still measuring the ghostly touch of the solar wind and the weak interplanetary magnetic field, and it regularly transmits this information to its controllers on the distant planet Earth.

How does the information get back? Pioneer 10 has a radio transmitter aboard and an antenna, but the total communications power it can draw is only about one watt. A coded message containing the data flutters across the intervening distance, crossing the orbits of all the planets from Pluto to Mars, and then is collected by three large NASA radio telescopes on Earth—one in the Mojave Desert near Barstow, Calif.; one outside Madrid; and one in Australia. As the Earth turns, one of these three instruments can always "see" Pioneer 10.

It's hard to realize how feeble the signal is. A typical received power is less than a millionth of a quadrillionth of a watt—much too little to turn on a penlight or a transistor radio, not enough even to warm a microbe.

Out there, far beyond Pluto and Pioneer 10, lie the stars. If we were close to them, we would see not only yellow suns like our own but also red dwarfs and blue supergiants; double suns in physical contact, with star-stuff flowing between them; places with five or six suns in the sky; stars as small as cities and stars as big as the entire inner solar system—a magnificent diversity of hundreds of billions of suns that make up our Milky Way Galaxy.

A range of new findings (PARADE, Jan. 22, 1984) now suggests that around many of these stars—perhaps even most of them—are planetary systems, forming or formed, that something like the retinue of planets which accompanies our star is a cosmic commonplace. We also know that the chemical steps that, 4 billion years ago, led to the origin of life on Earth require only the most general chemical conditions and should have occurred on countless other worlds (PARADE, Dec. 2, 1984). Indeed, we find organic molecules on the surfaces and in the atmospheres of the worlds in the outer solar system, on the comets and even floating in the near-vacuum between the stars. And we know, too, that most of those other stars are as old or older than the Sun and Earth.

Thus, there seems to be a vast arena in space and time for the evolution of life in the Milky Way. But we can't be sure. Maybe it's easy to make the molecules of life, but the origin and early evolution of life have impediments that we can barely glimpse. Or maybe life gets going on billions of worlds, but the development of intelligence and technical civilization is highly improbable. Or maybe many civilizations like our own arise regularly and promptly self-destruct. Alternatively, life, intelligence and technical civilizations may fill the Galaxy. The truth is we don't really know.

How can we find out? It is not yet within our powers to visit nearby planetary systems. We have four spacecraft leaving the solar system—Pioneers 10 and 11 and Voyagers 1 and 2—and they are the fastest spacecraft ever launched by the human species. But even if they were headed toward the nearest star, which they aren't, they would take tens of thousands of years to get there.

We are not that patient. We'd like to know in our own lifetimes. And the reception of those astonishingly weak signals from Pioneer 10 reminds us of another method. Instead of the one-watt emitted power of Pioneer 10, imagine a transmitting station with a power output of a few million watts, roughly that of the largest radar transmitters now available on Earth. Or imagine another civilization with considerably greater powers. So the transmitter could be on some planet halfway across the Galaxy, and radio telescopes on Earth could detect its signal. Then, if the beings on another world are beaming us a message, we have the means to detect it.

The first really dedicated and technically modern search is now taking place at the Harvard-Smithsonian Oak Ridge Observatory in Harvard, Mass., supported by the Pasadena-based Planetary Society. (The fact that so sophisticated a search could be paid for by a private-membership organization—with help from moviemaker Steven Spielberg—indicates the disparity between what our technology permits and what we have had the courage to attempt.) Under the leadership of Harvard Physics Professor Paul Horowitz, this enterprise is called Project META, for Megachannel Extraterrestrial Assay. It systematically scans the northern skies at more than 8 million separate radio frequencies or channels, each very narrow—only about 0.05 hertz wide. This is thousands of times more channels than any previous detection system, but it is still small compared to the number of narrow radio bands in the spectrum. So Horowitz has centered his search around the so-called "magic frequencies," where, due to simple laws of physics, the extraterrestrials might guess we would look—for example, the frequency where hydrogen, the most abundant atom in the Galaxy, likes to emit and absorb radio waves.

META is exquisitely automated and knows how to reject spurious signals due to radio transmissions here on Earth or in Earth orbit. Thus far, it has not detected anything really suspicious. But only a small fraction of even the known magic frequencies have been examined so far. The search goes on.

Astronomer Carl Sagan of Cornell University is president of The Planetary Society, a nonprofit organization devoted to planetary exploration and the search for extraterrestrial life. His pioneering study of extraterrestrial intelligence, with Soviet astronomer I.S. Shklovskii, is widely considered a classic.

A much bigger, and still more sensitive, radio search is tooling up. For many years a dedicated band of scientists—led by Bernard M. Oliver, a recent winner of the National Medal of Science—has argued that the radio telescopes of NASA's deep-space tracking network, only intermittently used by such probes as Pioneer 10, ought to be mated with the most sophisticated available detectors to search for signals from space. After years of dealing with daunting technological problems, bureaucratic indifference and worse, Oliver's NASA team is now ready. It has designed a system that by some measures is billions of times more comprehensive even than Project META. It would be able to scan 10 million to 100 million separate 1-hertz radio channels, filling almost the entire radio spectrum accessible from the Earth and breaking loose from the constraint of having to guess what frequencies the extraterrestrials might be broadcasting at.

We are so ignorant about where to look that it would be foolish to spend all our time merely examining nearby Sun-like stars. Maybe intelligent life tends to spring up on planets huddling close to the more abundant cool, red dwarf stars. Maybe there are beings signaling us from neutron stars, or from massive engineering constructions in the vicinity of the black hole thought to exist at the center of our Galaxy. Maybe it is more effective to listen for very advanced civilizations signaling us from distant galaxies than from less advanced civilizations around stars within our Galaxy. Every now and then, a new astronomical finding is made that makes you want to point a radio telescope somewhere you never thought of before.

There are, for example, two otherwise unremarkable orange stars with the prosaic designations GC 20393 and GC 20394. They are about 110 light-years away. Dr. Wulff Heintz of Swarthmore College has recently determined the distance and velocity of these stars through our Milky Way Galaxy and has found that they are moving much faster than the galactic escape velocity. This not only means that they are on trajectories that will eventually leave our Galaxy but also suggests that they have arrived in our Galaxy from outside, perhaps entering the Milky Way somewhere in the direction of the bright star Vega.

Could these two stars be intergalactic emissaries, sent with a retinue of inhabited planets by some unimaginably more advanced civilization in a distant galaxy? The stars are warm enough and long-lived enough: an ambassador solar system and a spare.

The idea is, of course, only a casual speculation and should not be blamed on Heintz. Earlier, there would have been no reason to single out these stars for special attention. A targeted radio search would have missed them. But an all-sky survey would pick up any strong transmissions from GC 20393 and 20394 and any other exotic radio sources.

Clearly, what is needed is not only a detailed search of nearby Sun-like stars but also, like META, a systematic search of the entire sky. This is just what the NASA program proposes to do. It will use the 34-meter telescopes at the three NASA deep-space tracking stations for a survey of the entire sky, both in the northern and southern hemispheres, and proposes to use other telescopes for a specific, targeted search of all stars like the Sun out to 80 or 100 light-years.

The NASA project, as yet nameless, will soon be ready to order the special detectors and signal-recognition computers. If all goes well, the project could be "on the air" by 1990 or '91. Its total cost, for a 10-year search program, is roughly the same as a few months of nuclear-weapons testing by the United States. It is hard to imagine a more exciting research program, or one with a greater potential for broadening our understanding of the universe and ourselves. If the money is allocated, and if all goes well, it is just possible that we will receive a message from the stars by the turn of the Millennium. □

Astronomical Terms

Planet is the term used for a body in orbit around the Sun. Its origin is Greek; even in antiquity it was known that a number of "stars" did not stay in the same relative positions to the others. There were five such restless "stars" known—Mercury, Venus, Mars, Jupiter, and Saturn—and the Greeks referred to them as *planetes*, a word which means "wanderers." That the earth is one of the planets was realized later. The additional planets were discovered after the invention of the telescope.

Satellite (or *moon*) is the term for a body in orbit around a planet. As long as our own Moon was the only moon known, there was no need for a general term for the moons of planets. But when Galileo Galilei discovered the four main moons of the planet Jupiter, Johannes Kepler (in a letter to Galileo) suggested "satellite" (from the Latin *satelles*, which means attendant) as a general term for such bodies. The word is used interchangeably with "moons": astronomers speak and write about the moons of Neptune, Saturn, etc. A satellite may be any size.

Orbit is the term for the path traveled by a body in space. It comes from the Latin *orbis*, which means circle, circuit, etc., and *orbita*, which means a rut or a wheel track. Theoretically, four mathematical figures are possible orbits: two are open (hyperbola and parabola) and two are closed (ellipse and circle), but in reality all closed orbits are ellipses. These ellipses can be nearly circular, as are the orbits of most planets, or very elongated, as are the orbits of most comets. In these orbits, the Sun is in one focal point of the ellipse, and the other focal point is empty. In the orbits of satellites, the planet stands in one focal point of the orbit. The *primary* of an orbit is the body in the focal point. For planets, the point of the orbit closest to the Sun is the *perihelion*, and the point farthest from the Sun is the *aphelion*. For orbits around the Earth, the corresponding terms are *perigee* and *apogee;* for orbits around other planets, corresponding terms are coined when necessary.

Two heavenly bodies are in *inferior* or *superior conjunction* when they have the same Right Ascension, or are in the same meridian; that is, when one is due north or south of the other. If the bodies appear near each other as seen from the Earth, they will rise and set at the same time. They are in *opposition* when they are opposite each other in the heavens: when one rises as the other is setting. *Greatest elongation* is the greatest apparent angular distance from the Sun, when a planet is most favorably suited for observation. Mercury can be seen with the naked eye only at about this time. An *occultation* of a planet or star is an eclipse of it by some other body, usually the Moon.

Stars are the basic units of population in the universe. Our Sun is the nearest star. Stars are very large (our Sun has a diameter of 865,400 miles—a comparatively small star). Stars are composed of intensely hot gasses, deriving their energy from nuclear reactions going on in their interiors.

Galaxies are immense systems containing billions of stars. All that you can see in the sky (with a very few exceptions) belongs to our galaxy—a system of roughly 100 billion stars. The few exceptions are other galaxies. Our own galaxy, the rim of which we see as the "Milky Way," is about 100, 000 light-years in diameter and about 10,000 light-years in thickness. Its shape is roughly that of a thick lens; more precisely it is a "spiral nebula," a term first used for other galaxies when they were discovered and before it was realized that these were separate and distant galaxies. The spiral galaxy nearest to ours is in the constellation Andromeda. It is somewhat larger than our own galaxy and is visible to the naked eye.

Recent developments in radio astronomy have revealed additional celestial objects that are still incompletely understood.

Quasars ("quasi-stellar" objects), originally thought to be peculiar stars in our own galaxy, are now believed to be the most remote objects in the Universe. Spectral studies of quasars indicate that some are 9 billion light years away and moving away from us at the incredible rate of 150,000 miles per second. Quasars emit tremendous amounts of light and microwave radiation. Although they appear to be far smaller than ordinary galaxies, some quasars emit as much as 100 times more energy. Some astronomers believe that quasars are the cores of violently exploding galaxies.

Pulsars are believed to be rapidly spinning neutron stars, so crushed by their own gravity that a million tons of their matter would hardly fill a thimble. Pulsars are so named because they emit bursts of radio energy at regular intervals. Some have pulse rates as rapid as 10 per second.

A *black hole* is the theoretical end-product of the total gravitational collapse of a massive star or group of stars. Crushed even smaller than an incredibly dense neutron star, such a body may become so dense that not even light can escape its gravitational field. It has been suggested that black holes may be detectable in proximity to normal stars when they draw matter away from their visible neighbors. Strong sources of X-rays in our galaxy and beyond may also indicate the presence of black holes. One possible black hole now being studied is the invisible companion to a supergiant star in the constellation Cygnus.

Origin of the Universe

Evidence uncovered in recent years tends to confirm that the universe began its existence about 15 billion years ago as a dense, hot globule of gas expanding rapidly outward. At that time, the universe contained nothing but hydrogen and a small amount of helium. There were no stars and no planets. The first stars probably began to condense out of the primordial hydrogen when the universe was about 100 million years old and continued to form as the universe aged. The Sun arose in this way 4.6 billion years ago. Many stars came into being before the Sun was formed; many others formed after the Sun appeared. This process continues, and through telescopes we can now see stars forming out of compressed pockets of hydrogen in outer space.

Birth and Death of a Star

When a star begins to form as a dense cloud of gas, the individual hydrogen atoms fall toward the center of the cloud under the force of the star's gravity. As they fall, they pick up speed, and their energy increases. The increase in energy heats the gas. When this process has continued for some millions of years, the temperature reaches about 20 million degrees Fahrenheit. At this temperature, the hydrogen within the star ignites and burns in a continuing series of nuclear reactions in which all the elements in the universe are manufactured from hydrogen and helium. The onset of these reactions marks the birth of a star. When a star begins to exhaust its hydrogen supply, its life nears an end. The first sign of old age is a swelling and reddening of its outer regions. Such an aging, swollen star is called a red giant. The Sun, a middle-aged star, will probably swell to a red giant in 5 billion years, vaporizing the earth and any creatures that may be left on its surface. When all its fuel has been exhausted, a star cannot generate sufficient pressure at its center to balance the crushing force of gravity. The star collapses under the force of its own

Astronomical Constants

Light-year (distance traveled by light in one year)	5,880,000,000,000 mi.
Parsec (parallax of one second, for stellar distances)	3.259 light-yrs.
Velocity of light	186,281.7 mi./sec.
Astronomical unit (A.U.), or mean distance earth-to-sun	ca. 93,000,000 mi.[1]
Mean distance, earth to moon	238,860 mi.
General precession	50".26
Obliquity of the ecliptic	23° 27'8".26–0".4684(t–1900)[2]
Equatorial radius of the earth	3963.34 statute mi.
Polar radius of the earth	3949.99 statute mi.
Earth's mean radius	3958.89 statute mi.
Oblateness of the earth	1/297
Equatorial horizontal parallax of the moon	57' 2".70
Earth's mean velocity in orbit	18.5 mi./sec.
Sidereal year	365d.2564
Tropical year	365d.2422
Sidereal month	27d.3217
Synodic month	29d.5306
Mean sidereal day	23h56m4s.091 of mean solar time
Mean solar day	24h3m56s.555 of sidereal time

1. Actual mean distance derived from radar bounces: 92,935,700 mi. The value of 92,897,400 mi. (based on parallax of 8".80) is used in calculations. 2. *t* refers to the year in question, for example, 1988.

The Brightest Stars

Star	Constellation	Mag.	Dist. (l.-y.)	Star	Constellation	Mag.	Dist. (l.-y.)
Sirius	Canis Major	−1.6	8	Antares	Scorpius	1.2	170
Canopus	Carina	−0.9	650	Fomalhaut	Piscis Austrinus	1.3	27
Alpha Centauri	Centaurus	+0.1	4	Deneb	Cygnus	1.3	465
Vega[1]	Lyra	0.1	23	Regulus	Leo	1.3	70
Capella	Auriga	0.2	42	Beta Crucis	Crux	1.5	465
Arcturus	Boötes	0.2	32	Eta Carinae	Carina	1–7	—
Rigel	Orion	0.3	545	Alpha-one Crucis	Crux	1.6	150
Procyon	Canis Minor	0.5	10	Castor	Gemini	1.6	44
Achernar	Eridanus	0.6	70	Gamma Crucis	Crux	1.6	—
Beta Centari	Centaurus	0.9	130	Epsilon Canis Majoris	Canis Major	1.6	325
Altair	Aquila	0.9	18	Epsilon Ursae Majoris	Ursa Major	1.7	50
Betelgeuse	Orion	0.9	600	Bellatrix	Orion	1.7	215
Aldebaran	Taurus	1.1	54	Lambda Scorpii	Scorpius	1.7	205
Spica	Virgo	1.2	190	Epsilon Carinae	Carina	1.7	325
Pollux	Gemini	1.2	31	Mira	Cetus	2–10	250

1. In 1984, the discovery of a possible planetary system around Vega was reported.

weight; if it is a small star, it collapses gently and remains collapsed. Such a collapsed star, at its life's end, is called a white dwarf. The Sun will probably end its life in this way. A different fate awaits a large star. Its final collapse generates a violent explosion, blowing the innards of the star out into space. There, the materials of the exploded star mix with the primeval hydrogen of the universe. Later in the history of the galaxy, other stars are formed out of this mixture. The Sun is one of these stars. It contains the debris of countless other stars that exploded before the Sun was born.

Formation of the Solar System

The Sun, like other stars, seems to have been formed 4.6 billion years ago from a cloud of hydrogen mixed with small amounts of other substances that had been manufactured in the bodies of other stars before the Sun was born. This was the parent cloud of the solar system. The dense hot gas at the center of the cloud gave rise to the Sun; the outer regions of the cloud—cooler and less dense—gave birth to the planets.

Our solar system consists of one star (the Sun), nine planets and all their moons, several thousand minor planets called asteroids or planetoids, and an equally large number of comets.

The Sun

All the stars, including our Sun, are gigantic balls of superheated gas, kept hot by atomic reactions in their centers. In our Sun, this atomic reaction is hydrogen fusion: four hydrogen atoms are combined to form one helium atom. The temperature at the core of our Sun must be 20 million degrees centigrade, the surface temperature is around 6,000 degrees centigrade, or about 11,000 degrees Fahrenheit. The diameter of the sun is 865,400 miles, and its surface area is approximately 12,000 times that of the Earth. Compared with other stars, our Sun is just a bit below average in size and temperature. Its fuel supply (hydrogen) is estimated to last for another 5 billion years.

Our Sun is not motionless in space; in fact it has two proper motions. One is a seemingly straight-line motion in the direction of the constellation Hercules at the rate of about 12 miles per second. But since the Sun is a part of the Milky Way system and since the whole system rotates slowly around its own center, the Sun also moves at the rate of 175 miles per second as part of the rotating Milky Way system.

In addition to this motion, the Sun rotates on its axis. Observing the motion of sun spots (darkish areas which look like enormous whirling storms) and solar flares, which are usually associated with sun spots, has shown that the rotational period of our Sun is just short of 25 days. But this figure is valid for the Sun's equator only; the sections near the Sun's poles seem to have a rotational period of 34 days. Naturally, since the Sun generates its own heat and light, there is no temperature difference between poles and equator.

What we call the Sun's "surface" is technically known as the photosphere. Since the whole Sun is a ball of very hot gas, there is really no such thing as a surface; it is a question of visual impression. The next layer outside the photosphere is known as the chromosphere, which extends several thousand miles beyond the photosphere. It is in steady motion, and often enormous prominences can be seen to burst from it, extending as much as 100,000 miles into space. Outside the chromosphere is the corona. The corona consists of very tenuous gases (essentially hydrogen) and makes a magnificent sight when the Sun is eclipsed.

The Moon

Mercury and Venus do not have any moons. Therefore, the Earth is the planet nearest the Sun to be orbited by a moon.

The next planet farther out, Mars, has two very small moons. Jupiter has four major moons and twelve minor ones. Saturn, the ringed planet, has fifteen known moons, of which one (Titan) is larger than the planet Mercury. Uranus has five known moons (four of them large) as well as rings, while Neptune has one large and one small moon. Pluto has one moon, discovered in 1978. Some astronomers still consider Pluto to be a "runaway moon" of Neptune.

Our own Moon, with a diameter of 2,160 miles, is one of the larger moons in our solar system and is especially large when compared with the planet that it orbits. In fact, the common center of gravity of the Earth-Moon system is only about 1,000 miles below the Earth's surface. The closest our Moon can come to us (its perigee) is 221,463 miles; the

Data for Sun, Moon, and Planets

	Mean distance from Sun in millions of miles	Period of revolution around the Sun	Eccentricity of orbit	Inclination to ecliptic ° ′	Diameter (miles)	Period of rotation on axis	Inclination of equator to orbit plane °	Surface gravity (earth = 1)	Density $H_2O = 1$	Number of satellites	Mean velocity in orbit (mi./sec.)	Max. stellar mag.
Sun	—	—	—	—	865,400	24d.64[2]	7.2	28	1.4	0	—	−26.7
Moon	—	(27d.322)[1]	0.05	5 8	2,160	27d.322	6.7	0.16	3.3	0	0.63	−12.6
Mercury	36.00	87d.969	0.21	7 0	3,100	58.66d	7	0.28	3.8	0	30	−1.2
Venus	67.27	224d.701	0.01	3 24	7,700	243.2d	—	0.85	5.1	0	22	−4.4
Earth	93.00	365d.256	0.02	0 0	7,927[3]	23h 56m	23.4	1.00	5.5	1	18.5	—
Mars	141.71	1y.881	0.09	1 51	4,200	24h 37m	25.2	0.38	4.0	2	15	−2.8
Jupiter	483.88	11y.862	0.05	1 18	88,700[3]	9h 50m[2]	3.1	2.6	1.3	16	8	−2.5
Saturn	887.14	29y.458	0.06	2 29	75,100[3]	16h 39m[2]	26.8	1.2	0.7	21+	6	−0.4
Uranus	1783.98	84y.013	0.05	0 46	32,000	16.8h	97	1.1	1.3	15	4	+5.7
Neptune	2795.46	164y.794	0.01	1 46	27,700	17h 50m	29	1.4	2.2	2	3	+7.8
Pluto	3675.27	248y.430	0.25	17 9	1,500(?)	6d 8h(?)	—	—	>1.0	1	<3	+14

1. Period of revolution around the earth. 2. Voyager 1 and 2 data. 3. The equatorial diameters of the earth, Jupiter, and Saturn are given; polar diameters are: earth 7,900.0 mi., Jupiter 82,789 mi., Saturn 67,170 mi. OTHER DATA ON THE EARTH: Equatorial circumference, 24,902.4 mi.; total area, 196,949,970 sq. mi.; mass, 6.6 sextillion tons; mean diameter, 7,917.8 mi.

farthest it can go away (its apogee) is 252,710 miles. The period of rotation of our Moon is equal to its period of revolution around the Earth. Hence from Earth we can see only one hemisphere of the Moon. Both periods are 27 days, 7 hours, 43 minutes and 11.47 seconds. But while the rotation of the Moon is constant, its velocity in its orbit is not, since it moves more slowly in apogee than in perigee. Consequently, some portions near the rim which are not normally visible will appear briefly. This phenomenon is called "libration," and by taking advantage of the librations, astronomers have succeeded in mapping approximately 59% of the lunar surface. The other 41% can never be seen from the earth but has been mapped by American and Russian Moon-orbiting spacecraft.

Though the Moon goes around the Earth in the time mentioned, the interval from new Moon to new Moon is 29 days, 12 hours, 44 minutes and 2.78 seconds. This delay of nearly two days is due to the fact that the Earth is moving around the Sun, so that the Moon needs two extra days to reach a spot in its orbit where no part is illuminated by the Sun, as seen from Earth.

If the plane of the Earth's orbit around the Sun (the ecliptic) and the plane of the Moon's orbit around the Earth were the same, the Moon would be eclipsed by the Earth every time it is full, and the Sun would be eclipsed by the Moon every time the Moon is "new" (it would be better to call it the "black Moon" when it is in this position). But because the two orbits do not coincide, the Moon's shadow normally misses the Earth and the Earth's shadow misses the Moon. The inclination of the two orbital planes to each other is 5 degrees. The tides are, of course, caused by the Moon with the help of the Sun, but in the open ocean they are surprisingly low, amounting to about one yard. The very high tides which can be observed near the shore in some places are due to funnelling effects of the shorelines. At new Moon and at full Moon the tides raised by the Moon are reinforced by the Sun; these are the "spring tides." If the Sun's tidal power acts at right angles to that of the Moon (quarter moons) we get the low "neap tides."

Our Planet Earth

The Earth, circling the Sun at an average distance of 93 million miles, is the fifth largest planet and the third from the Sun. It orbits the Sun at a speed of 67,000 miles per hour, making one revolution in 365 days, 5 hours, 48 minutes, and 45.51 seconds. The Earth completes one rotation on its axis every 23 hours, 56 minutes, and 4.09 seconds. Actually a bit pear-shaped rather than a true sphere, the Earth has a diameter of 7,927 miles at the Equator and a few miles less at the poles. It has an estimated mass of about 6.6 sextillion tons, with an average density of 5.52 grams per cubic centimeter. The Earth's surface area encompasses 196,949,970 square miles of which about three-fourths is water.

Origin of the Earth. The Earth, along with the other planets, is believed to have been born 4.5 billion years ago as a solidified cloud of dust and gases left over from the creation of the Sun. For perhaps 500 million years, the interior of the Earth stayed solid and relatively cool, perhaps 2000° F. The main ingredients, according to the best available evidence, were iron and silicates, with small amounts of other elements, some of them radioactive. As millions of years passed, energy released by radioactive decay—mostly of uranium, thorium, and potassium—gradually heated the Earth, melting some of its consituents. The iron melted before the silicates, and, being heavier, sank toward the center. This forced upward the silicates that it found there. After many years, the iron reached the center, almost 4,000 miles deep, and began to accumulate. No eyes were around at that time to view the turmoil which must have taken place on the face of the Earth—gigantic heaves and bubbling of the surface, exploding volcanoes, and flowing lava covering everything in sight. Finally, the iron in the center accumulated as the core. Around it, a thin but fairly stable crust of solid rock formed as the Earth cooled. Depressions in the crust were natural basins in which water, rising from the interior of the planet through volcanoes and fissures, collected to form the oceans. Slowly the Earth acquired its present appearance.

The Earth Today. As a result of radioactive heating over millions of years, the Earth's molten *core* is probably fairly hot today, around 11,000° F. By comparison, lead melts at around 800° F. Most of the Earth's 2,100-mile-thick core is liquid, but there is evidence that the center of the core is solid. The liquid outer portion, about 95% of the core, is constantly in motion, causing the Earth to have a magnetic field that makes compass needles point north and south. The details are not known, but the latest evidence suggests that planets which have a magnetic field probably have a solid core or a partially liquid one.

Outside the core is the Earth's *mantle,* 1,800 miles thick, and extending nearly to the surface. The mantle is composed of heavy silicate rock, similar to that brought up by volcanic eruptions. It is somewhere between liquid and solid, slightly yielding, and therefore contributing to an active, moving Earth. Most of the Earth's radioactive material is in the thin *crust* which covers the mantle, but some is in the mantle and continues to give off heat. The crust's thickness ranges from 5 to 25 miles.

Continental Drift. A great deal of recent evidence confirms the long-disputed theory that the continents of the Earth, made mostly of relatively light granite, float in the slightly yielding mantle, like logs in a pond. For many years it had been noticed that if North and South America could be pushed toward western and southern Europe and western Africa, they would fit like pieces in a jigsaw puzzle. Today, there is little question—the continents have drifted widely and continue to do so.

In 10 million years, the world as we know it may be unrecognizable, with California drifting out to sea, Florida joining South America, and Africa moving farther away from Europe and Asia.

The Earth's Atmosphere. The thin blanket of atmosphere that envelops the Earth extends several hundred miles into space. From sea level—the very bottom of the ocean of air—to a height of about 60 miles, the air in the atmosphere is made up of the same gases in the same ratio: about 78% nitrogen, 21% oxygen, and the remaining 1% being a mixture of argon, carbon dioxide, and tiny amounts of neon, helium, krypton, xenon, and other gases. The atmosphere becomes less dense with increasing altitude: more than three-fourths of the Earth's huge envelope is concentrated in the first 5 to 10 miles above the surface. At sea level, a cubic foot of the atmosphere weighs about an ounce and a quarter. The entire atmosphere weighs 5,700,000,000,000,000 tons, and the force with which gravity holds it in place causes it to exert a pressure of nearly 15 pounds per square inch. Going out from the Earth's surface, the atmosphere is divided into five regions. The regions, and the heights to which they extend, are: *Troposphere,* 0 to 7 miles (at middle latitudes); *stratosphere,* 7 to 30 miles; *mesosphere,* 30 to 50 miles; *thermosphere,* 50 to 400 miles; and *exosphere,* above 400 miles. The boundaries between each of the regions are known respectively as the *tropopause, stratopause, mesopause,* and *thermopause.* Alternate terms often used for the layers above the troposhere are *ozonosphere* (for stratosphere) and *ionosphere* for the remaining upper layers.

The Seasons. Seasons are caused by the 23.4 degree tilt of the Earth's axis, which alternately turns the North and South Poles toward the Sun. Times when the Sun's apparent path crosses the Equator are known as *equinoxes.* Times when the Sun's apparent path is at the greatest distance from the Equator are known as *solstices.* The lengths of the days are most extreme at each solstice. If the Earth's axis were perpendicular to the plane of the Earth's orbit around the Sun, there would be no seasons, and the days always would be equal in length. Since the Earth's axis is at an angle, the Sun strikes the Earth directly at the Equator only twice a year: in March (vernal equinox) and September (autumnal equinox). In the Northern Hemisphere, spring begins at the vernal equinox, summer at the summer solstice, fall at the autumnal equinox, and winter at the winter solstice. The situation is reversed in the Southern Hemisphere.

Mercury

Mercury is the planet nearest the Sun. Appropriately named for the wing-footed Roman messenger of the gods, Mercury whizzes around the Sun at a speed of 30 miles per second, completeing one circuit in 88 days. The planet rotates on its axis over a period of nearly 59 days. Daytime on cratered Mercury is hot, about 800 degrees F., although at night the temperature may fall to room temperature. Mercury has no moons, but it does have a trace of atmosphere and a weak magnetic field, according to findings of Mariner 10. Until this spacecraft flew by Mercury in 1974 and 1975, very little was known about the planet, primarily because of its short angular distance from the Sun as seen from Earth, which puts it too close to the Sun to be easily observed.

• Mercury is a naked eye object at morning or evening twilight when it is at greatest elongation.

Venus

Although Venus is Earth's nearest neighbor, little is known about this planet because it is permanently covered by thick clouds. In 1962, Soviet and American space probes, coupled with Earth-based radar and infrared spectroscopy, began slowly unraveling some of the mystery surrounding Venus. According to the latest results, Venus' atmosphere is about 96% carbon dioxide, exerting a pressure at the surface 90.5 times greater than Earth's. Walking on Venus would be as difficult as walking a half-mile beneath the ocean. Because of the thick blanket of carbon dioxide, a "greenhouse effect" exists on Venus: Venus intercepts twice as much of the Sun's light as does the Earth. The light enters freely through carbon dioxide gas and is changed to heat radiation in molecular collisions. But carbon dioxide prevents the heat from escaping. Consequently, the temperature of the surface of Venus is over 800 degrees F., hot enough to melt lead. The atmosphere appears to have five distinct layers and to flash almost continuously with lightning. Radar bounced off the planet recently revealed what appear to be large craters and an immense, 900-mile-long canyon. Venus rotates in retrograde motion for a reason not yet known.

In March 1982, the Soviet *Venera 13* and *14* landing craft made the first actual test samples of the Venusian surface by x-ray fluorescence spectroscopy which gave an element-by-element analysis. The terrestrial samples revealed a terrain of basaltic uplands and lowlands.

• Venus is the brightest of all the planets and is often visible in the morning or evening, when it is frequently referred to as the Morning Star or Evening Star. At its brightest, it can sometimes be seen with the naked eye in full daylight, if one knows where to look.

Mars

Mars, on the other side of the Earth from Venus, is Venus' direct opposite in terms of physical properties. Its atmosphere is cold, thin, and transparent, and readily permits observation of the planet's features. We know more about Mars than any other planet except Earth. Mars is a forbidding, rugged planet with huge volcanoes and deep chasms. The largest volcano, Olympus Mons rises 78,000 feet above the surface, higher than Mount Everest. The plains of Mars are pockmarked by the hits of thousands of meteors over the years. Most of our information about Mars comes from the Mariner 9 spacecraft, which orbited the planet in 1971. Mariner 9, photographing 100% of the planet, uncovered spectacular geological formations, including a Martian Grand Canyon that dwarfs the one on Earth. The spacecraft's cameras also recorded what appeared to be dried riverbeds, suggesting the onetime presence of water on the planet. The latter idea gives encouragement to scientists looking for life on Mars, for where there is water, there may be life. However, by 1979, no evidence of life has been found. Temperatures near the equator range from −17 degrees F. in the daytime to −130 degrees F. at night. Mars rotates upon its axis in nearly the same period as Earth—24 hours, 37 minutes—so that a Mars day is almost identical to an Earth day. Mars takes 687 days to make one trip around the Sun. Because of its eccentric orbit Mars' distance from the Sun can vary by about 36 million miles. Its distance from Earth can vary by as much as 200 million miles. The atmosphere of Mars is much thinner than Earth's; atmospheric pressure is about 1% that of our planet. Its gravity is one-third of Earth's. Major constituents are carbon dioxide and nitrogen. Water vapor and oxygen are minor constituents. Mars' polar caps, composed mostly of carbon dioxide, recede and advance according to the Martian seasons. Mars was named for the Roman god of war, because when seen from Earth its distinct red color reminded the ancient people of blood. We know now that the reddish hue reflects the oxidized (rusted) iron in the surface material. The landing of two robot Viking spacecraft on the surface of Mars in 1976 provided more information about Mars in a few months than in all the time that has gone before.

Jupiter

Jupiter, with an equatorial diameter of 88,000 miles, is the largest of a group of planets which differ markedly from the terrestrial planets. The others in the group are Saturn, Uranus, and Neptune. All are large, with very dense atmospheres, and indeed may be giant balls of gas without any perceptible surfaces. They all whirl rapidly around their axes, but more slowly around the Sun, resulting in short days and long years. They have many moons. Majestic Jupiter, named for the king of the Roman gods, rotates so fast that it is greatly flattened at the poles. According to Pioneers 10 and 11, which flew past Jupiter in 1974 and 1975, this planet is a whirling ball of liquid hydrogen with perhaps an Earth-sized iron core. Other atmospheric constituents are helium, methane, and ammonia. Its clouds are probably ammonia ice crystals, becoming ammonia droplets deeper towards the "surface." Temperatures range from perhaps minus 300 degrees F. at the tops of the cloud decks to 100,000 degrees F. or more deep down at the center. The pressure at the center of the planet is estimated to be a crushing 10 million pounds per square inch. The Great Red Spot, a 13,000-mile-wide storm that may have been raging for thousands of years, was found by Voyagers 1 and 2 in 1979 to be cooler at the top than the surrounding clouds, indicating that the Red Spot may tower high above them. Jupiter has 16 satellites. The four largest moons, called Galilean moons, are Europa, Ganymede, Io, and Callisto. *Voyagers 1 and 2* found them to be very different from each other in terms of surface relief, volcanic activity, and other characteristics.

• Even when nearest the Earth, Jupiter is still almost 400 million miles away. But because of its size, it may rival Venus in brilliance when near. Jupiter's four large moons may be seen through field glasses, moving rapidly around Jupiter and changing their position from night to night.

Saturn

Saturn, the second largest planet in the solar system, is the least dense. It would float in an ocean if there were one big enough to hold it. Aside from its rings, Saturn is very similar to Jupiter except that it is probably colder, being twice as far from the Sun. Recent radar observations of Saturn's rings indicate that they are no more than 10 miles thick, and probably composed of chunks of rock and ice averaging a meter in size. Saturn's ring system begins about 7000 miles from the planet's disk, and extends out to about 35,000 miles. Recent observations have shown Saturn to have between 21 and 23 moons, more than any other planet. The two *Voyager* probes that examined Jupiter in 1979 flew by Saturn in 1980 and 1981.

• Saturn is the last of the planets visible to the naked eye. Saturn is never an object of overwhelming brilliance, but it looks like a bright star. The rings can be seen with a small telescope.

Uranus

Uranus is the seventh planet from the sun, twice as far out as Saturn. The axis of Uranus is tilted at 97 degrees, so it goes around the Sun nearly lying on its side. In 1977, American astronomers made the startling discovery that Uranus has rings, like Saturn.

The first *Voyager* to Uranus took extensive readings of the planet in January 1986. The information received drastically altered perceptions of the planet. Readings of the atmosphere confirmed previous theories that under the cloud layer a hot ocean of superheated water exists. The pressure caused by the thick atmosphere keeps the water, with a temperature that reaches thousands of degrees, from boiling away and the heat keeps the pressure from solidifying the water. This discovery suggested that Uranus differs in composition from Jupiter and Saturn and that the planet may have formed from a coalescence of comets, as comets and the atmosphere and ocean of Uranus are similarly constituted. Other discoveries about the planetary atmosphere were that the pole facing the sun was no hotter than the pole facing away from the sun and that four large methane clouds in the atmosphere were being blown around the planet in the same direction as the planet's rotation, exactly opposite the way in which they should have blown, according to calculations made based on observed conditions.

Another observation was that the planet's magnetic field is 60 degrees out of sync with the poles of the planet. Explanations for this unique feature included the possibility that Uranus may be experiencing a shift of north and south magnetic poles or that the churning of the ocean or of the molten core of the planet has generated this peculiar field. There is, however, insuffcent information for any definite conclusions to be drawn.

Voyager 2 also expanded the body of information pertaining to the rings and moons of Uranus. A tenth ring was discovered and the rings were discovered to be formed not of fine particles of ice and dust like Saturn but of chunky objects of rock and large ice "boulders".

In addition to the new ring, ten new moons, smaller in diameter and closer to the planet than the five known moons—Oberon, Titania, Umbriel, Ariel, and Miranda—were discovered.

The *Voyager* craft took the first close-up pictures of Uranus's five largest moons, with surprising results. The pictures of Oberon showed surprising activity going on underneath its icy surface. Titania and Ariel were seen to have large rift-valleys scarring the surface, evidence of some sort of eruption of frozen water from within their surfaces. The surface of Umbriel proved to be inexplicably darker than the other moons with no signs of recent crustal activity. Miranda was the biggest surprise with an unparalled variety of terrain features that caused scientists to label it as a "bizarre hybrid."

Uranus can—on rare occasions—become bright enough to be seen with the naked eye, if one knows exactly where to look; normally, a good set of field glasses or a small portable telescope is required.

Neptune

Little is known about the distant giant planet of Neptune, although it is believed to be similar to Jupiter and Saturn. Located 2.8 billion miles from the Sun, it must be a grim, frozen world. Neptune has two known moons. The larger moon, Triton, is, along with Jupiter's Ganymede and Callisto, and Saturn's Titan, one of the four largest moons in the solar system. More information about Neptune should be forthcoming when *Voyager 2* passes by the planet in August 1989.

Although Neptune can occasionally be seen with the naked eye, an aid, usually field glasses or small telescopes, is required.

Pluto

Pluto, the outermost and smallest planet in the solar system, looks more like a terrestrial planet than a gaseous planet. But so little is known about it, that it is difficult to classify. Appropriately named for the Roman god of the underworld, it must be frozen, dark, and dead.

In 1978, light curve studies gave evidence of a moon revolving around Pluto with the same period as Pluto's rotation. Therefore, it stays over the same point on Pluto's surface. In addition, it keeps the same face toward the planet. The discovery of this moon of 500–600 miles in diameter reduces the previously estimated diameter of Pluto to little more than 1,500 miles, making the pair more like a double planet than any other in the solar system. Previously, the Earth-Moon system held this distinction. The density of Pluto is slightly greater than that of water.

Pluto was predicted by calculation when Percival Lowell noticed irregularities in the orbits of Uranus and Neptune. Clyde Tombaugh discovered the planet in 1930, precisely where Lowell predicted it would be. The name Pluto was chosen because the first two letters represent the initials of Percival Lowell.

- Pluto has the most eccentric orbit in the solar system, bringing it at times closer to the Sun than Neptune. Pluto is now approaching the perihelion of its orbit, and for the rest of this century will be closer to the Sun than Neptune. Even then, it can be seen only with a large telescope.

The Asteroids

Between the orbits of Mars and Jupiter are an estimated 30,000 pieces of rocky debris, known collectively as the asteroids, or planetoids. The first and, incidentally, the largest was discovered during the New Year's night of 1801 by the Italian astronomer Father Piazzi, and its orbit was calculated by the German mathematician Karl Friedrich Gauss. (Gauss invented a new method of calculating orbits on that occasion.) A German amateur astronomer, the physician Olbers, discovered the second asteroid. The number now known, catalogued, and named is around 1,600; the estimated total is about 20 times that figure. A few asteroids do not move in orbits beyond the orbit of Mars, but in orbits which cross the orbit of Mars. The first of them was named Eros because of this peculiar orbit. It had become the rule to bestow female names on the asteroids, but when it was found that Eros crossed the orbit of a major planet, it received a male name. Since then around two dozen orbit-crossers have been discovered, and they are often referred to as the "male asteroids." A few of them—Albert, Adonis, Apollo, Amor, and Icarus—cross the orbit of the Earth, and two of them may come closer than our Moon; but the crossing is like a bridge crossing a highway, not like two highways intersecting. Hence there is very little danger of collision from these bodies. They are all small, three to five miles in diameter, and therefore very difficult objects to identify, even when quite close. Some scientists believe the asteroids represent the remains of an exploded planet.

Comets

Comets, according to the noted astronomer, Fred L. Whipple, are enormous "snowballs" of frozen gases (mostly carbon dioxide, methane, and water vapor) and contain very little solid material. The whole behavior of comets can then be explained as the behavior of frozen gas being heated by the Sun. When the comet Kohoutek made its first appearance to man in 1973, its behavior seemed to confirm this Whipple theory of the make-up of comets.

Since comets appear in the sky without any warning, people in classical times and especially during the Middle Ages believed that they had a special meaning, which, of course, was bad. Since a natural catastrophe of some sort of a military conflict occurs every year, it was quite simple to blame the comet that happened to be visible. But even in the past, there were some people who used logical reasoning. When, in Roman times, a comet was blamed for the loss of a battle and hence was called a "bad omen," a Roman writer observed that the victors in the battle probably did not think so.

Up until the middle of the sixteenth century, comets were believed to be phenomena of the upper atmosphere; they were usually "explained" as "burning vapors" which had risen from "distant swamps." That nobody had ever actually seen burning vapors rise from a swamp did not matter.

But a large comet which appeared in 1577 was carefully observed by Tycho Brahe, a Danish astronomer who is often, and with the best of reasons, called "eccentric" but who insisted on precise measurements for everything. It was Tycho Brahe's accumulation of literally thousands of precise measurements which later enable his younger collaborator, Johannes Kepler, to discover the laws of planetary motion. Measuring the motion of the comet of 1577, Tycho Brahe could show that it had been far beyond the atmosphere, even though he could not give figures for the distance. Tycho Brahe's work proved that comets were astronomical and not meteorological phenomena.

In 1682, the second Astronomer Royal of Great Britain, Dr. Edmond Halley, checked the orbit of a bright comet that was in the sky then and compared it with earlier comet orbits which were known in part. Halley found that the comet of 1682 was the third to move through what appeared to be the same orbit. And the three appearances were roughly 76 years apart. Halley concluded that this was the same comet, moving around the Sun in a closed orbit, like the planets. He predicted that it would reappear in 1758 or 1759. Halley himself died in 1742, but a large comet appeared sixteen years after his death as predicted and was immediately referred to as "Halley's comet."

In the Spring of 1973, the discovery of comet Kohoutek, apparently headed for a close-Christmastime rendezvous with the Sun, created worldwide excitement. The comet was a visual disappointment, but turned out to be a treasure trove of information on these little-understood celestial objects. Given an unprecedented advance notice of nine months on the advent of the fiery object, scientists were able to study the comet in visible, ultraviolet and infrared light; with optical telescopes, radio telescopes, and radar. They observed it from the ground, from high-flying aircraft, with instruments aboard unmanned satellites, with sounding rockets, and telescopes and cameras on the Earth-orbiting Skylab space station.

Halley's Comet appeared again in 1986, sparking a worldwide effort to study it up close. Five satellites in all took readings from the comet at various distances. Two Soviet craft, *Vega 1* and *Vega 2*, went in close to provide detailed pictures of the comet, including the first of the comet's core. The European Space Agency's craft, *Giotto*, entered the comet itself, coming to within 450 miles of the comet's center and successfully passing through its tail. In addition, two Japanese craft, the *Suisei* and the *Sakigake*, passed at a longer distance in order to analyze the cloud and tail of the comet and the effect of solar radiation upon it. The United States declined to launch a similar mission, citing budgetary constraints imposed by the shuttle program. A space telescope was to study Halley's Comet but was destroyed in the *Challenger* disaster.

The information gained included measurements of the size of the nucleus, an idea of its configuration and the rate of its rotation. The gas and dust of the comet were analyzed as was the material of the tail. This information is considered important because comets are believed to be debris from the formation of the solar system and to have changed little since then.

Astronomers refer to comets as "periodic" or as "non-periodic" comets, but the latter term does not mean that these comets have no period; it merely means that their period is not known. The actual periods of comets run from 3.3 years (the shortest known) to many thousands of years. Their orbits are elliptical, like those of the planets, but they are very eccentric, long and narrow ellipses. Only comet Schwassmann-Wachmann has an orbit which has such a low eccentricity (for a cometary orbit) that it could be the orbit of a minor planet.

When a comet, coming from deep space, approaches the Sun, it is at first indistinguishable from a minor planet. Somewhere between the orbits of Mars and Jupiter its outline becomes fuzzy; it is said to develop a "coma" (the word used here is the Latin word *coma*, which means "hair," not the phonetically identical Greek word which means "deep sleep"). Then, near the orbit of Mars, the comet develops its tail, which at first trails behind. This grows steadily as the comet comes closer and closer to the Sun. As it rounds the Sun (as first noticed by Girolamo Fracastoro) the tail always points away from the Sun so that the comet, when moving away from the Sun, points its tail ahead like the landing lights of an airplane.

The reason for this behavior is that the tail is pushed in these directions by the radiation pressure of the Sun. It sometimes happens that a comet loses its tail at perihelion; it then grows another one. Although the tail is clearly visible against the black of the sky, it is very tenuous. It has been said that if the tail of Halley's comet could be compressed to the density of iron, it would fit into a small suitcase.

Although very low in mass, comets are among the largest members of the solar system. The nucleus of a comet may be up to 10,000 miles in diameter; its coma between 10,000 and 50,000 miles in diameter; and its tail as long as 28 million miles.

Meteors and Meteorites

The term "meteor" for what is usually called a "shooting star" bears an unfortunate resemblance to the term "meteorology," the science of weather and weather forecasting. This resemblance is due to an ancient misunderstanding which wrongly considered meteors an atmospheric phenomenon. Actually, the streak of light in the sky that scientists call a meteor is essentially an astronomical phenomenon: the entry of a small piece of cosmic matter into our atmosphere.

The distinction between "meteors" and "fireballs" (formerly also called "bolides") is merely one of convenience; a fireball is an unusually bright meteor. Incidentally, it also means that a fireball is larger than a faint meteor.

Bodies which enter our atmosphere become visible when they are about 60 miles above the ground. The fact that they grow hot enough to emit light is not due to the "friction" of the atmosphere, as one can often read. The phenomenon responsible for the heating is one of compression. Unconfined air cannot move faster than the speed of sound. Since the entering meteorite moves with 30 to 60 times the speed of sound, the air simply can-

The 88 Recognized Constellations

In astronomical works, the Latin names of the constellations are used. The letter N or S following the Latin name indicates whether the constellation is located to the north or south of the Zodiac. The letter Z indicates that the constellation is within the Zodiac.

Latin name	Letter	English version
Andromeda	N	Andromeda
Antlia	S	Airpump
Apus	S	Bird of Paradise
Aquarius	Z	Water Bearer
Aquila	N	Eagle
Ara	S	Altar
Aries	Z	Ram
Auriga	N	Charioteer
Boötes	N	Herdsmen
Caelum	S	Sculptor's Tool
Camelopardalis	N	Giraffe
Cancer	Z	Crab
Canes Venatici	N	Hunting Dogs
Canis Major	S	Great Dog
Canis Minor	S	Little Dog
Capricornus	Z	Goat (or Sea-Goat)
Carina	S	Keel (of Argo)[1]
Cassiopeia	N	Cassiopeia
Centaurus	S	Centaur
Cepheus	N	Cepheus
Cetus	S	Whale
Chameleon	S	Chameleon
Circinus	S	Compasses
Columba	S	Dove
Coma Berenices	N	Berenice's Hair
Corona Australis	S	Southern Crown
Corona Borealis	N	Northern Crown
Corvus	S	Crow (Raven)
Crater	S	Cup
Crux	S	Southern Cross
Cygnus	N	Swan

Latin name	Letter	English version
Delphinus	N	Dolphin
Dorado	S	Swordfish (Goldfish)
Draco	N	Dragon
Equuleus	N	Filly
Eridanus	S	Eridanus (river)
Fornax	S	Furnace
Gemini	Z	Twins
Grus	S	Crane
Hercules	N	Hercules
Horologium	S	Clock
Hydra	N	Sea Serpent
Hydrus	S	Water Snake
Indus	S	Indian
Lacerta	N	Lizard
Leo	Z	Lion
Leo Minor	N	Little Lion
Lepus	S	Hare
Libra	Z	Scales
Lupus	S	Wolf
Lynx	N	Lynx
Lyra	N	Lyre (Harp)
Mensa	S	Table (mountain)
Microscopium	S	Microscope
Monoceros	S	Unicorn
Musca	S	Southern Fly
Norma	S	Rule (straightedge)
Octans	S	Octant
Ophiuchus	N	Serpent-Bearer
Orion	S	Orion

Latin name	Letter	English version
Pavo	S	Peacock
Pegasus	N	Pegasus
Perseus	N	Perseus
Phoenix	S	Phoenix
Pictor	S	Painter (or his Easel)
Pisces	Z	Fishes
Piscis Austrinus	S	Southern Fish
Puppis	S	Poop (of Argo)[1]
Pyxis	S	Mariner's Compass
Reticulum	S	Net
Sagitta	N	Arrow
Sagittarius	Z	Archer
Scorpius	Z	Scorpion
Sculptor	S	Sculptor
Scutum	N	Shield
Serpens	N	Serpent
Sextans	S	Sextant
Taurus	Z	Bull
Telescopium	S	Telescope
Triangulum	N	Triangle
Triangulum Australe	S	Southern Triangle
Tucana	S	Toucan
Ursa Major	N	Big Dipper
Ursa Minor	N	Little Dipper
Vela	S	Sail (of Argo)[1]
Virgo	Z	Virgin
Volans	S	Flying Fish
Vulpecula	N	Fox

1. The original constellation Argo Navis (the Ship Argo) has been divided into Carina, Puppis, and Vela. Normally the brightest star in each constellation is designated by alpha, the first letter of the Greek alphabet, the second brightest by beta, the second letter of the Greek alphabet, and so forth. But the Greek letters run through Carina, Puppis, and Vela as if it were still one constellation.

not get out of the way. Therefore, it is compressed like the air in the cylinder of a Diesel engine and is heated by compression. This heat—or part of it—is transferred to the moving body. The details of this process are now fairly well understood as a result of re-entry tests with ballistic-missile nose cones.

The average weight of a body producing a faint "shooting star" is only a small fraction of an ounce. Even a bright fireball may not weigh more than 2 or 3 pounds. Naturally, the smaller bodies are worn to dust by the passage through the atmosphere; only rather large ones reach the ground. Those that are found are called meteorites. (The "meteor," to repeat, is the term for the light streak in the sky.)

The largest meteorite known is still imbedded in the ground near Grootfontein in SW Africa and is estimated to weight 70 tons. The second largest known is the 34-ton Anighito (on exhibit in the Hayden Planetarium, New York), which was found by Admiral Peary at Cape York in Greenland. The largest meteorite found in the United States is the Willamette meteorite (found in Oregon, weight ca. 15 tons), but large portions of this meteorite weathered away before it was found. Its weight as it struck the ground may have been 20 tons.

All these are iron meteorites (an iron meteorite normally contains about 7% nickel), which form one class of meteorites. The other class consists of the stony meteorites, and between them there are the so-called "stony irons." The so-called "tektites" consist of glass similar to our volcanic glass obsidian, and because of the similarity, there is doubt in a number of cases whether the glass is of terrestrial or of extra-terrestrial origin.

Though no meteorite larger than the Grootfontein is actually known, we do know that the Earth has, on occasion, been struck by much larger bodies. Evidence for such hits are the meteorite craters, of which an especially good example is located near the Cañon Diablo in Arizona. Another meteor crater in the United States is a rather old crater near Odessa, Texas. A large number of others are known, especially in eastern Canada; and for many "probables," meteoric origin has now been proved.

The meteor showers are caused by multitudes of very small bodies travelling in swarms. The Earth travels in its orbit through these swarms like a car driving through falling snow. The point from which the meteors seem to emanate is called the *radiant* and is named for the constellation in that area. The Perseid meteor shower in August is the most spectacular of the year, boasting at peak roughly 60 meteors per hour under good atmospheric conditions. The presence of a bright moon diminishes the number of visible meteors.

The Constellations

Constellations are groupings of stars which form patterns that can be easily recognized and remembered, for example, Orion and the Big Dipper. Actually, the stars of the majority of all constellations do not "belong together." Usually they are at greatly varying distances from the Earth and just happen to lie more or less in the same line of sight as seen from our solar system. But in a few cases the stars of a constellation are actually associated; most of the bright stars of the Big Dipper travel together and form what astronomers call an open cluster.

If you observe a planet, say Mars, for one complete revolution, you will see that it passes successively through twelve constellations. All planets (except Pluto at certain times) can be observed only in these twelve constellations, which form the so-called Zodiac, and the Sun also moves through the Zodiacal signs, though the Sun's apparent movement is actually caused by the movement of the Earth.

Although the constellations are due mainly to the optical accident of line of sight and have no real significance, astronomers have retained them as reference areas. It is much easier to speak of a star in Orion than to give its geometrical position in the sky. During the Astronomical Congress of 1928, it was decided to recognize 88 constellations. A description of their agreed-upon boundaries was published at Cambridge, England, in 1930, under the title *Atlas Céleste.*

The Auroras

The "northern lights" *(Aurora borealis)* as well as the "southern lights" *(Aurora australis)* are upper-atmosphere phenomena of astronomical origin. The auroras center around the magnetic (not the geographical) poles of the Earth, which explains why, in the Western Hemisphere, they have been seen as far to the south as New Orleans and Florida while the equivalent latitude in the Eastern Hemisphere never sees an aurora. The northern magnetic pole happens to be in the Western Hemisphere.

The lower limit of an aurora is at about 50 miles. Upper limits have been estimated to be as high as 400 miles. Since about 1880, a connection between the auroras on Earth and the sun spots has been suspected and has gradually come to be accepted. It was said that the sun spots probably eject "particles" (later the word *electrons* was substituted) which on striking the Earth's atmosphere, cause the auroras. But this explanation suffered from certain difficulties. Sometimes a very large sun spot group on the Sun, with individual spots bigger than the Earth itself, would not cause an aurora. Moreover, even if a sun spot caused an aurora, the time that passed between the appearance of the one and the occurrence of the other was highly unpredictable.

This problem of the time lag is, in all probability, solved by the discovery of the Van Allen layer by artificial satellite *Explorer I.* The Van Allen layer is a double layer of charged sub-atomic particles around the Earth. The inner layer, with its center some 1,500 miles from the ground, reaches from about 40° N. to about 40° S. and does not touch the atmosphere. The outer layer, much larger and with its center several thousand miles from the ground, does touch the atmosphere in the vicinity of the magnetic poles.

It seems probable that the "leakage" of electrons from the outer Van Allen layer causes the auroras. A new burst of electrons from the Sun seems to be caught in the outer layer first. Under the assumption that all electrons are first caught in the outer layer, the time lag can be understood. There has to be an "overflow" from the outer layer to produce an aurora.

The Atmosphere

Astronomically speaking, the presence of our atmosphere is deplorable. Though reasonably transparent to visible light, the atmosphere may absorb as much as 60% of the visible and near-visible light. It is opaque to most other wave-lengths, except certain fairly short radio waves. In addition to absorbing much light, our atmosphere bends light rays entering at a slant (for a given observer) so that the true position of a star close to the horizon is not what it seems to be. One effect is that we see the Sun above the horizon before it actually is. And the unsteady movement of the atmosphere causes the "twinkling" of the stars, which may be romantic but is a nuisance when it comes to observing.

The composition of our atmosphere near the ground is 78% nitrogen and 21% oxygen, the remaining 1% consisting of other gases, most of it argon. The composition stays the same to an altitude of at least 70 miles (except that higher up two impurities, carbon dioxide and water vapor, are missing), but the pressure drops very fast. At 18, 000 feet, half of the total mass of the atmosphere is below, and at 100,000 feet, 99% of the mass of the atmosphere is below. The upper limit of the atmosphere is usually given as 120 miles; no definitive figure is possible, since there is no boundary line between the incredibly attenuated gases 120 miles up and space.

Astronomical Telescopes

Optical telescopes used in astronomy are of two basic kinds: refracting and reflecting. In the *refractor telescope,* a lens is used to collect light from a distant object and bring it to a focus. A second lens, the eyepiece, then magnifies the image which may be examined visually or photographed directly. The *reflector telescope* uses a concave mirror instead of a lens, which reflects the light rays back toward the upper end of the telescope where they are magnified and observed or photographed. Most large optical telescopes now being built are reflectors.

Radio telescopes are used to study radio waves coming from outside the Earth's atmosphere. The waves are gathered by an antenna or "dish," which is a parabolic reflecting surface made of metal or finely meshed wire. Radio signals have been received from the Sun, Moon, and planets, and from the center of our galaxy and other galaxies. Radio signals are the means by which the distant and mysterious quasars and pulsars were recently discovered.

The Hubble Space Telescope

Because of the *Challenger* disaster, the $1-billion Hubble Space Telescope will not be sent aloft until November 1988. It is the most powerful optical telescope ever constructed and, with its 94.5-in. (2.4-m) mirror, is able to detect celestial phenomena seven times more distant (up to 14 billion light years) than can land-based telescopes.

Conversion of Universal Time (U. T.) to Civil Time

U.T.	E.D.T.[1]	E.S.T.[2]	C.S.T.[3]	M.S.T.[4]	P.S.T.[5]	U.T.	E.D.T.[1]	E.S.T.[2]	C.S.T.[3]	M.S.T.[4]	P.S.T.[5]
00	*8P	*7P	*6P	*5P	*4P	**12**	8A	7A	6A	5A	4A
01	*9P	*8P	*7P	*6P	*5P	**13**	9A	8A	7A	6A	5A
02	*10P	*9P	*8P	*7P	*6P	**14**	10A	9A	8A	7A	6A
03	*11P	*10P	*9P	*8P	*7P	**15**	11A	10A	9A	8A	7A
04	M	*11P	*10P	*9P	*8P	**16**	N	11A	10A	9A	8A
05	1A	M	*11P	*10P	*9P	**17**	1P	N	11A	10A	9A
06	2A	1A	M	*11P	*10P	**18**	2P	1P	N	11A	10A
07	3A	2A	1A	M	*11P	**19**	3P	2P	1P	N	11A
08	4A	3A	2A	1A	M	**20**	4P	3P	2P	1P	N
09	5A	4A	3A	2A	1A	**21**	5P	4P	3P	2P	1P
10	6A	5A	4A	3A	2A	**22**	6P	5P	4P	3P	2P
11	7A	6A	5A	4A	3A	**23**	7P	6P	5P	4P	3P

1. Eastern Daylight Time. 2. Eastern Standard Time, same as Central Daylight Time. 3. Central Standard Time, same as Mountain Daylight Time. 4. Mountain Standard Time, same as Pacific Daylight Time. 5. Pacific Standard Time. NOTES: *denotes previous day. N = noon. M = midnight.

Eclipses of the Sun and the Moon, 1988

March 3. Partial eclipse of the Moon. The umbral phase lasts less than 14 minutes, and is visible in Asia, central and eastern Europe, northeast Africa, Wilkes Land of Antarctica, Australia, New Zealand, Alaska and Hawaii, the Arctic regions, the Indian Ocean, and the west half of the Pacific Ocean.

March 17-18. Total eclipse of the Sun. Totality crosses Indonesia and the southern Philippines with a path 109 miles (175 km) wide and the sun about 65° in altitude, and then continues into the Pacific. Maximum totality is 3 minutes 46 seconds. Partial phases visible in eastern Asia, Indonesia, Micronesia, northwestern Australia, and western Hawaiian Islands.

August 27. Partial eclipse of the Moon. The beginning of the umbral phase visible on the east coast of Asia, most of Antarctica, Australia, New Zealand, the eastern half of South America, Central America, North America except east of Hudson Bay, and the Pacific Ocean; the end visible in eastern Asia, most of Antarctica, Australia, New Zealand, northern Central America, central and western North America, and the Pacific Ocean.

September 11. Annular eclipse of the Sun. Annularity begins in Somalia, crosses the Indian Ocean, and passes south of Australia. Partial phases visible in eastern Africa, southern Asia, Indonesia, Australia, and New Zealand.

Sources: U.S. Naval Observatory and from "A Field Guide to the Stars and Planets," Second Edition, Revised.

Phenomena, 1988

Configurations of Sun, Moon, and Planets

NOTE: The hour listings are in Universal Time. For conversion to United States time zones, see conversion table above.

JANUARY

d	h	
4	00	Earth at perihelion
4	02	FULL MOON
7	06	Moon at apogee
12	07	LAST QUARTER
12	12	Spica 0° 4 N of Moon
15	16	Mars 5° N of Moon
15	23	Antares 0° 3 N of Moon
17	04	Saturn 6° N of Moon
17	06	Uranus 5° N of Moon
17	21	Neptune 6° N of Moon
19	05	NEW MOON
19	21	Moon at perigee
20	09	Mercury 2° N of Moon
21	19	Venus 0° 07 N of Moon
21	22	Mars 5° N of Antares
22	06	Vesta at opposition
25	02	Jupiter 4° S of Moon
25	22	FIRST QUARTER
26	17	Mercury greatest elong. E (19°)

FEBRUARY

1	10	Ceres in conjunction with Sun
1	15	Vesta 0° 2 S of Moon
1	16	Mercury stationary
2	21	FULL MOON
3	10	Moon at apogee
8	19	Spica 0° 7 N of Moon
10	23	LAST QUARTER
11	04	Mercury in inferior conjunction
12	08	Antares 0° 5 N of Moon
13	01	Saturn 1° 3 N of Uranus
13	09	Mars 5° N of Moon
13	19	Saturn 6° N of Moon
13	19	Uranus 5° N of Moon
14	09	Neptune 6° N of Moon
17	10	Moon at perigee
17	16	NEW MOON
18	23	Pluto stationary
20	17	Venus 1° 9 S of Moon
21	18	Jupiter 4° S of Moon
22	21	Mars 0° 01 N of Uranus
23	04	Mercury stationary
23	13	Mars 1° 3 S of Saturn
24	12	FIRST QUARTER
28	12	Vesta 0° 2 N of Moon

MARCH

1	12	Moon at apogee
3	16	FULL MOON (Penumbral Eclipse)
6	20	Venus 2° N of Jupiter
7	01	Spica 0° 7 N of Moon
7	22	Mars 1° 4 S of Neptune
8	06	Mercury greatest elong. W (27°)
10	10	Vesta stationary
10	15	Antares 0° 6 N of Moon
11	11	LAST QUARTER
12	04	Uranus 5° N of Moon
12	06	Saturn 6° N of Moon
12	19	Neptune 6° N of Moon
13	00	Mars 5° N of Moon
16	05	Mercury 0° 5 N of Moon
16	20	Moon at perigee
18	02	NEW MOON (Eclipse)
20	10	Equinox
20	14	Jupiter 5° S of Moon
21	12	Venus 2° S of Moon
25	05	FIRST QUARTER
26	20	Vesta 0° N of Moon
29	00	Moon at apogee

APRIL

2	09	FULL MOON
3	07	Spica 0° 7 N of Moon
3	08	Venus greatest elong. E (46°)
4	19	Uranus stationary
6	20	Antares 0° 5 N of Moon
8	10	Uranus 5° N of Moon
8	13	Saturn 6° N of Moon
9	01	Neptune 6° N of Moon
9	19	LAST QUARTER

10 15 Mars 3° N of Moon
11 02 Saturn stationary
11 12 Neptune stationary
13 23 Moon at perigee
15 14 Venus 10° N of Aldebaran
16 12 NEW MOON
20 00 Venus 1° 0 S of Moon
20 15 Mercury in superior conjunction
23 15 Vesta 0° 9 N of Moon
23 23 FIRST QUARTER
25 19 Moon at apogee
30 14 Spica 0° 7 N of Moon

MAY

1 09 Pluto at opposition
2 00 FULL MOON
2 21 Jupiter in conjunction with Sun
4 02 Antares 0° 4 N of Moon
5 15 Uranus 5° N of Moon
5 17 Saturn 6° N of Moon
6 07 Neptune 6° N of Moon
6 20 Venus greatest brilliancy
9 01 LAST QUARTER
9 06 Mars 0° 8 N of Moon
10 22 Moon at perigee
11 06 Mercury 8° N of Aldebaran
15 22 NEW MOON
17 17 Mercury 3° S of Moon
18 13 Venus 1° 2 S of Moon
19 02 Mercury greatest elong. E (22°)
22 13 Venus stationary
23 12 Juno in conjunction with Sun
23 14 Moon at apogee
23 17 FIRST QUARTER
27 23 Spica 0° 8 N of Moon
29 12 Pallas stationary
31 10 Antares 0° 4 N of Moon
31 11 FULL MOON

JUNE

1 01 Mercury stationary
1 21 Uranus 5° N of Moon
1 22 Saturn 6° N of Moon
2 12 Neptune 6° N of Moon
5 00 Moon at perigee
6 20 Mars 2° S of Moon
7 06 LAST QUARTER
12 03 Jupiter 6° S of Moon
13 00 Venus in inferior conjunction
13 04 Mercury in inferior conjunction
14 09 NEW MOON
19 18 Regulus 1° 2 S of Moon
20 04 Uranus at opposition
20 08 Moon at apogee
20 09 Saturn at opposition
21 04 Solstice
22 10 FIRST QUARTER
24 08 Spica 1° 1 N of Moon
24 23 Mercury stationary
27 02 Saturn 1° 3 N of Uranus
27 19 Antares 0° 4 N of Moon
29 04 Saturn 6° N of Moon
29 04 Uranus 5° N of Moon
29 20 FULL MOON
29 20 Neptune 6° N of Moon
30 10 Neptune at opposition

JULY

2 06 Moon at perigee
4 08 Venus stationary
5 07 Mars 5° S of Moon
6 00 Earth at aphelion
6 12 LAST QUARTER
6 16 Mercury greatest elong. W (21°)
9 19 Jupiter 6° S of Moon
11 01 Venus 10° S of Moon
12 04 Mercury 7° S of Moon
13 22 NEW MOON
17 01 Regulus 1° 0 S of Moon
18 00 Moon at apogee
19 18 Venus greatest brilliancy
22 02 FIRST QUARTER
25 05 Antares 0° 6 N of Moon
25 18 Pluto stationary
26 11 Saturn 6° N of Moon
26 12 Uranus 5° N of Moon
27 05 Neptune 6° N of Moon
29 03 FULL MOON
30 08 Moon at perigee

AUGUST

1 12 Ceres stationary
2 11 Mars 8° S of Moon
2 16 Pallas at opposition
3 04 Mercury in superior conjunction
4 18 LAST QUARTER
6 08 Jupiter 6° S of Moon
8 12 Venus 9° S of Moon
12 13 NEW MOON
14 12 Moon at apogee
20 16 FIRST QUARTER
21 14 Antares 0° 7 N of Moon
22 12 Venus greatest elong. W (46°)
22 19 Saturn 6° N of Moon
22 21 Uranus 5° N of Moon
23 14 Neptune 6° N of Moon
26 23 Mars stationary
27 11 FULL MOON (Eclipse)
27 17 Moon at perigee
30 03 Mars 9° S of Moon
30 11 Saturn stationary

SEPTEMBER

2 08 Venus 9° S of Pollux
2 20 Jupiter 6° S of Moon
3 04 LAST QUARTER
5 10 Uranus stationary
6 23 Venus 6° S of Moon
9 13 Regulus 1° 0 S of Moon
10 15 Moon at apogee
11 05 NEW MOON (Eclipse)
13 16 Mercury 0° 6 N of Moon
15 22 Mercury greatest elong. E (27°)
17 04 Ceres at opposition
17 21 Antares 0° 7 N of Moon
18 17 Neptune stationary
19 03 FIRST QUARTER
19 03 Saturn 6° N of Moon
19 05 Uranus 5° N of Moon
19 22 Neptune 6° N of Moon
20 16 Pallas stationary
21 04 Mercury 1° 3 S of Spica
22 03 Mars closest approach
22 19 Equinox
24 16 Jupiter stationary
25 04 Moon at perigee
25 19 FULL MOON
26 04 Mars 7° S of Moon
28 04 Mars at opposition
28 21 Mercury stationary
30 05 Jupiter 6° S of Moon

OCTOBER

2 11 Vesta in conjunction with Sun
2 17 LAST QUARTER
4 08 Venus 0° 2 S of Regulus
5 18 Mercury 1° 2 S of Spica
6 20 Regulus 1° 0 S of Moon
7 03 Venus 0° 6 S of Moon
7 20 Moon at apogee
10 22 NEW MOON
11 07 Mercury in inferior conjunction
15 02 Antares 0° 6 N of Moon
16 12 Saturn 6° N of Moon
16 12 Uranus 5° N of Moon
17 05 Neptune 6° N of Moon
18 02 Saturn 1° 1 N of Uranus
18 13 FIRST QUARTER
19 16 Mercury stationary
23 04 Mars 5° S of Moon
23 12 Moon at perigee
25 05 FULL MOON
26 21 Mercury greatest elong. W (18°)
27 12 Jupiter 6° S of Moon
30 14 Mars stationary

NOVEMBER

1 07 Mercury 4° N of Spica
1 10 LAST QUARTER
3 03 Regulus 0° 8 S of Moon
4 11 Moon at apogee
4 17 Pluto in conjunction with Sun
6 15 Venus 5° N of Moon
9 14 NEW MOON
11 08 Antares 0° 5 N of Moon
12 18 Ceres stationary
12 19 Uranus 5° N of Moon
12 21 Saturn 6° N of Moon
13 11 Neptune 5° N of Moon
16 22 FIRST QUARTER
17 04 Venus 4° N of Spica
19 16 Mars 3° S of Moon
20 10 Moon at perigee
23 03 Jupiter at opposition
23 16 FULL MOON
23 17 Jupiter 6° S of Moon
30 11 Regulus 0° 5 S of Moon

DECEMBER

1 07 LAST QUARTER
1 09 Mercury in superior conjunction
2 06 Moon at apogee
7 00 Venus 7° N of Moon
9 06 NEW MOON
10 20 Neptune 5° N of Moon
16 04 Moon at perigee
16 06 FIRST QUARTER
17 16 Mars 3° S of Moon
20 09 Mercury 3° S of Neptune
20 20 Jupiter 6° S of Moon
21 15 Solstice
22 20 Uranus in conjunction with Sun
23 05 FULL MOON
24 18 Venus 6° N of Antares
26 12 Saturn in conjunction with Sun
27 20 Regulus 0° 2 S of Moon
30 04 Moon at apogee
31 05 LAST QUARTER
31 09 Neptune in conjunction with Sun

AVIATION

Famous Firsts in Aviation

1782 First balloon flight. Jacques and Joseph Montgolfier of Annonay, France, sent up a small smoke-filled balloon about mid-November.

1783 First hydrogen-filled balloon flight. Jacques A. C. Charles, Paris physicist, supervised construction by A. J. and M. N. Robert of a 13-ft diameter balloon that was filled with hydrogen. It got up to about 3,000 ft and traveled about 16 mi. in a 45-min flight (Aug. 27).

First human balloon flights. A Frenchman, Jean Pilâtre de Rozier made the first captive-balloon ascension (Oct. 15). With the Marquis d'Arlandes, Pilâtre de Rozier made the first free flight, reaching a peak altitude of about 500 ft, and traveling about 5 1/2 mi. in 20 min (Nov. 21).

1784 First powered balloon. Gen. Jean Baptiste Marie Meusnier developed the first propeller-driven and elliptically-shaped balloon—the crew cranking three propellers on a common shaft to give the craft a speed of about 3 mph.

First woman to fly. Mme. Thible, a French opera singer (June 4).

1793 First balloon flight in America. Jean Pierre Blanchard, a French pilot, made it from Philadelphia to near Woodbury, Gloucester County, N.J., in a little over 45 min (Jan. 9).

1794 First military use of the balloon. Jean Marie Coutelle, using a balloon built for the French Army, made two 4-hr observation ascents. The military purpose of the ascents seems to have been to damage the enemy's morale.

1797 First parachute jump. André-Jacques Garnerin dropped from about 6,500 ft over Monceau Park in Paris in a 23-ft diameter parachute made of white canvas with a basket attached (Oct. 22).

1843 First air transport company. In London, William S. Henson and John Stringfellow filed articles of incorporation for the Aerial Transit Company (March 24). It failed.

1852 First dirigible. Henri Giffard, a French engineer, flew in a controllable (more or less) steam-engine powered balloon, 144 ft long and 39 ft in diameter, inflated with 88,000 cu ft of coal gas. It reached 6.7 mph on a flight from Paris to Trappe (Sept. 24).

1860 First aerial photographers. Samuel Archer King and William Black made two photos of Boston, still in existence.

1872 First gas-engine powered dirigible. Paul Haenlein, a German engineer, flew in a semi-rigid-frame dirigible, powered by a 4-cylinder internal-combustion engine running on coal gas drawn from the supporting bag.

1873 First transatlantic attempt. *The New York Daily Graphic* sponsored the attempt with a 400, 000 cu ft balloon carrying a lifeboat. A rip in the bag during inflation brought collapse of the balloon and the project.

1897 First successful metal dirigible. An all-metal dirigible, designed by David Schwarz, a Hungarian, took off from Berlin's Tempelhof Field and, powered by a 16-hp Daimler engine, got several miles before leaking gas caused it to crash (Nov. 13).

1900 First Zeppelin flight. Germany's Count Ferdinand von Zeppelin flew the first of his long series of rigid-frame airships. It attained a speed of 18 mi. per h and got 3 1/2 mi. before its steering gear failed (July 2).

1903 First successful heavier-than-air machine flight. Aviation was really born on the sand dunes at Kitty Hawk, N.C., when Orville Wright crawled to his prone position between the wings of the biplane he and his brother Wilbur had built, opened the throttle of their homemade 12-hp engine and took to the air. He covered 120 ft in 12 sec. Later that day, in one of four flights, Wilbur stayed up 59 sec and covered 852 ft (Dec. 17).

1904 First airplane maneuvers. Orville Wright made the first turn with an airplane (Sept. 15); 5 days later his brother Wilbur made the first complete circle.

1905 First airplane flight over half an hour. Orville Wright kept his craft up 33 min 17 sec (Oct. 4).

1906 First European airplane flight. Alberto Santos-Dumont, a Brazilian, flew a heavier-than-air machine at Bagatelle Field, Paris (Sept. 13).

1908 First airplane fatality. Lt. Thomas E. Selfridge, U.S. Army Signal Corps, was in a group of officers evaluating the Wright plane at Fort Myer, Va. He was up about 75 ft with Orville Wright when the propeller hit a bracing wire and was broken, throwing the plane out of control, killing Selfridge and seriously injuring Wright (Sept. 17).

1909 First cross-Channel flight. Louis Blériot flew in a 25-hp Blériot VI monoplane from Les Baraques near Calais, France, and landed near Dover Castle, England, in a 26.61-mi. (38-km) 37-min flight across the English Channel (July 25).

1910 First licensed woman pilot. Baroness Raymonde de la Roche of France, who learned to fly in 1909, received ticket No. 36 on March 8.

First flight from shipboard. Lt. Eugene Ely, USN, took a Curtiss plane off from the deck of cruiser *Birmingham* at Hampton Roads, Va., and flew to Norfolk (Nov. 14). The following January, he reversed the process, flying from Camp Selfridge to the deck of the armored cruiser *Pennsylvania* in San Francisco Bay (Jan. 18).

1911 First U.S. woman pilot. Harriet Quimby, a magazine writer, who got ticket No. 37.

1912 First woman's cross-Channel flight. Harriet Quimby flew from Dover, England, across the English Channel, and landed at Hardelot, France (25 mi. south of Calais) in a Blériot monoplane loaned to her by Louis Blériot (April 16). She was later killed in a flying accident over Dorchester Bay during a Harvard-Boston aviation meet on July 1, 1912.

1913 **First multi-engined aircraft.** Built and flown by Igor Ivan Sikorsky while still in his native Russia.

1914 **First aerial combat.** In August, Allied and German pilots and observers started shooting at each other with pistols and rifles—with negligible results.

1915 **First air raids on England.** German Zeppelins started dropping bombs on four English communities (Jan. 19).

1918 **First U.S. air squadron.** The U.S. Army Air Corps made its first independent raids over enemy lines, in DH-4 planes (British-designed) powered with 400-hp American-designed Liberty engines (April 8).

First regular airmail service. Operated for the Post Office Department by the Army, the first regular service was inaugurated with one round trip a day (except Sunday) between Washington, D.C., and New York City (May 15).

1919 **First transatlantic flight.** The NC-4, one of four Curtiss flying boats commanded by Lt. Comdr. Albert C. Read, reached Lisbon, Portugal, (May 27) after hops from Trepassy Bay, Newfoundland, to Horta, Azores (May 16–17), to Ponta Delgada (May 20). The Liberty-powered craft was piloted by Walter Hinton.

First nonstop transatlantic flight. Capt. John Alcock and Lt. Arthur Whitten Brown, British World War I flyers, made the 1,900 mi. from St. John's, Newfoundland, to Clifden, Ireland, in 16 h 12 min in a Vickers-Vimy bomber with two 350-hp Rolls-Royce engines (June 15–16).

First lighter-than-air transatlantic flight. The British dirigible R-34, commanded by Maj. George H. Scott, left Firth of Forth, Scotland, (July 2) and touched down at Mineola, L.I., 108 h later. The eastbound trip was made in 75 h (completed July 13).

First scheduled London-Paris passenger service (using airplanes). Aircraft Travel and Transport inaugurated London-Paris service (Aug. 25). Later the company started the first trans-channel mail service on the same route (Nov. 10).

1921 **First naval vessel sunk by aircraft.** Two battleships being scrapped by treaty were sunk by bombs dropped from Army planes in demonstration put on by Brig. Gen. William S. Mitchell (July 21).

First helium balloon. The C-7, non-rigid Navy dirigible was first to use non-inflammable helium as lifting gas, making a flight from Hampton Roads, Va., to Washington, D.C. (Dec. 1).

1922 **First member of Caterpillar Club.** Lt. (later Maj. Gen.) Harold Harris bailed out of a crippled plane he was testing at McCook Field, Dayton, Ohio (Oct. 20), and became the first man to join the Caterpillar Club—those whose lives have been saved by parachute.

1923 **First nonstop transcontinental flight.** Lts. John A. Macready and Oakley Kelly flew a single-engine Fokker T-2 nonstop from New York to San Diego, a distance of just over 2,500 mi. in 26 h 50 min (May 2–3).

First autogyro flight. Juan de la Cierva, a brilliant Spanish mathematician, made the first successful flight in a rotary wing aircraft in Madrid (June 9).

1924 **First round-the-world flight.** Four Douglas Cruiser biplanes of the U.S. Army Air Corps took off from Seattle under command of Maj. Frederick Martin (April 6). 175 days later, two of the planes (Lt. Lowell Smith's and Lt. Erik Nelson's) landed in Seattle after a circuitous route—one source saying 26,345 mi., another saying 27,553 mi.

1926 **First polar flight.** Then-Lt. Cmdr. Richard E. Byrd, acting as navigator, and Floyd Bennett as pilot, flew a trimotor Fokker from Kings Bay, Spitsbergen, over the North Pole and back in 15 1/2 h (May 8–9).

1927 **First solo transatlantic flight.** Charles Augustus Lindbergh lifted his Wright-powered Ryan monoplane, *Spirit of St. Louis,* from Roosevelt Field, L.I., to stay aloft 33 h 39 min and travel 3,600 mi. to Le Bourget Field outside Paris (May 20–21).

First transatlantic passenger. Charles A. Levine was piloted by Clarence D. Chamberlin from Roosevelt Field, L.I., to Eisleben, Germany, in a Wright-powered Bellanca (June 4–5).

1928 **First east-west transatlantic crossing.** Baron Guenther von Huenefeld, piloted by German Capt. Hermann Koehl and Irish Capt. James Fitzmaurice, left Dublin for New York City (April 12) in a single-engine all-metal Junkers monoplane. Some 37 h later, they crashed on Greely Island, Labrador. Rescued.

First U.S.-Australia flight. Sir Charles Kingsford-Smith and Capt. Charles T. P. Ulm, Australians, and two American navigators, Harry W. Lyon and James Warner, crossed the Pacific from Oakland to Brisbane. They went via Hawaii and the Fiji Islands in a trimotor Fokker (May 31–June 8).

First transarctic flight. Sir Hubert Wilkins, an Australian explorer and Carl Ben Eielson, who served as pilot, flew from Point Barrow, Alaska, to Spitsbergen (mid-April).

1929 **First of the endurance records.** With Air Corps Maj. Carl Spaatz in command and Capt. Ira Eaker as chief pilot, an Army Fokker, aided by refueling in the air, remained aloft 150 h 40 min at Los Angeles (Jan. 1–7).

First blind flight. James H. Doolittle proved the feasibility of instrument-guided flying when he took off and landed entirely on instruments (Sept. 24).

First rocket-engine flight. Fritz von Opel, a German auto maker, stayed aloft in his small rocket-powered craft for 75 sec, covering nearly 2 mi. (Sept. 30).

First South Pole flight. Comdr. Richard E. Byrd, with Bernt Balchen as pilot, Harold I. June, radio operator, and Capt. A. C. McKinley, photographer, flew a trimotor Fokker from the Bay of Whales, Little America, over the South Pole and back (Nov. 28–29).

1930 **First Paris–New York nonstop flight.** Dieudonné Coste and Maurice Bellonte, French pilots, flew a Hispano-powered Breguet biplane from Le Bourget Field to Valley Stream, L.I., in 37 h 18 min. (Sept. 2–3).

1931 **First flight into the stratosphere.** Auguste Piccard, a Swiss physicist, and Charles Knipfer ascended in a balloon from Augsburg, Germany, and reached a height of 51,793 ft in a 17-h flight that terminated on a glacier near Innsbruck, Austria (May 27).

First nonstop transpacific flight. Hugh Herndon and Clyde Pangborn took off from Sabishiro Beach, Japan, dropped their landing gear, and flew 4,860 mi. to near Wenatchee, Wash., in 41 h 13 min. (Oct. 4–5).

1932 **First woman's transatlantic solo.** Amelia Earhart, flying a Pratt & Whitney Wasp-powered Lockheed Vega, flew alone from Harbor Grace, Newfoundland, to Ireland in approximately 15 h (May 20–21).

First westbound transatlantic solo. James A. Mollison, a British pilot, took a de Havilland Puss Moth from Portmarnock, Ireland, to Pennfield, N.B. (Aug. 18).

First woman airline pilot. Ruth Rowland Nichols, first woman to hold three international records at the same time—speed, distance, altitude—was employed by N.Y.-New England Airways.

1933 **First round-the-world solo.** Wiley Post took a Lockheed Vega, *Winnie Mae,* 15,596 mi. around the world in 7 d 18 h 49 1/2 min (July 15–22).

1937 **First successful helicopter.** Hanna Reitsch, a German pilot, flew Dr. Heinrich Focke's FW-61 in free, fully controlled flight at Bremen (July 4).

1939 **First turbojet flight.** Just before their invasion of Poland, the Germans flew a Heinkel He-178 plane powered by a Heinkel S3B turbojet (Aug. 27).

1942 **First American jet plane flight.** Robert Stanley, chief pilot for Bell Aircraft Corp., flew the Bell XP-59 *Airacomet* at Muroc Army Base, Calif. (Oct. 1).

1947 **First piloted supersonic flight in an airplane.** Capt. Charles E. Yeager, U.S. Air Force, flew the X-1 rocket-powered research plane built by Bell Aircraft Corp., faster than the speed of sound at Muroc Air Force Base, California (Oct. 14).

1949 **First round-the-world nonstop flight.** Capt. James Gallagher and USAF crew of 13 flew a Boeing B-50A Superfortress around the world nonstop from Ft. Worth, returning to same point: 23,452 mi. in 94 h 1 min, with 4 aerial refuelings enroute (Feb. 27–March 2).

1950 **First nonstop transatlantic jet flight.** Col. David C. Schilling (USAF) flew 3,300 mi. from England to Limestone, Maine, in 10 h 1 min (Sept. 22).

1951 **First solo across North Pole.** Charles F. Blair, Jr., flew a converted P-51 (May 29).

1952 **First jetliner service.** De Havilland Comet flight inaugurated by BOAC between London and Johannesburg, South Africa (May 2). Flight, including stops, took 23 h 38 min.

First transatlantic helicopter flight. Capt. Vincent H. McGovern and 1st Lt. Harold W. Moore piloted 2 Sikorsky H-19s from Westover, Mass., to Prestwick, Scotland (3,410 mi.). Trip was made in 5 steps, with flying time of 42 h 25 min (July 15–31).

First transatlantic round trip in same day. British Canberra twin-jet bomber flew from Aldergrove, Northern Ireland, to Gander, Newfoundland, and back in 7 h 59 min flying time (Aug. 26).

1955 **First transcontinental round trip in same day.** Lt. John M. Conroy piloted F-86 Sabrejet across U.S. (Los Angeles–New York) and back—5,085 mi.—in 11 h 33 min 27 sec (May 21).

1957 **First round-the-world, nonstop jet plane flight.** Maj. Gen. Archie J. Old, Jr., USAF, led a flight of 3 Boeing B-52 bombers, powered with 8 10, 000-lb. thrust Pratt & Whitney Aircraft J57 engines around the world in 45 h 19 min; distance 24,325 mi.; average speed 525 mph. (Completed Jan. 18.)

1958 **First transatlantic jet passenger service.** BOAC, New York to London (Oct. 4). Pan American started daily service, N.Y. to Paris (Oct. 26).

First domestic jet passenger service. National Airlines inaugurated service between New York and Miami (Dec. 10).

1976 **First regularly-scheduled commercial supersonic transport (SST) flights begin.** Air France and British Airways inaugurate service (January 21). Air France flies the Paris-Rio de Janeiro route; B.A., the London-Bahrain. Both airlines begin SST service to Washington, D.C. (May 24).

1977 **First successful man-powered aircraft.** Paul MacCready, an aeronautical engineer from Pasadena, Calif., was awarded the Kremer Prize for creating the world's first successful man-powered aircraft. The *Gossamer Condor* was flown by Bryan Allen over the required 3-mile course on Aug. 23.

1978 **First successful transatlantic balloon flight.** Three Albuquerque, N.M., men, Ben Abruzzo, Larry Newman, and Maxie Anderson, completed the crossing (Aug. 16. Landed, Aug. 17) in their hot air balloon, *Double Eagle II.*

1979 **First man-powered aircraft to fly across the English Channel.** The Kremer Prize for the Channel crossing was won by Bryan Allen who flew the *Gossamer Albatross* from Folkestone, England to Cap Gris-Nez, France, in 2 h 55 min (June 12).

1980 **First successful balloon flight over the North Pole.** Sidney Conn and his wife Eleanor, in hot-air balloon *Joy of Sound* (April 11).

First nonstop transcontinental balloon flight, and also record for longest overland voyage in a balloon. Maxie Anderson and his son, Kris, completed four-day flight from Fort Baker, Calif., to successful landing outside Matane, Quebec, on May 12 in their helium-filled balloon, *Kitty Hawk.*

First long-distance solar-powered flight. Janice Brown, 98-lb former teacher, flew tiny experimental solar-powered aircraft, *Solar Challenger* six miles in 22-min near Marana, Ariz. (Dec. 3). The craft was powered by a 2.75-hp engine.

First solar-powered aircraft to fly across the English Channel. Stephen R. Ptacek flew the 210-lb *Solar Challenger* at the average speed of 30 mph from Cormeilles-en-Vexin near Paris to the Royal Manston Air Force Base on England's southeastern coast in 5 h 30 min (July 7).

1984 **First solo transatlantic balloon flight.** Joe W. Kittinger landed Sept. 18 near Savona, Italy, in his helium-filled balloon *Rosie O'Grady's Balloon of Peace* after a flight of 3,535 miles from Caribou, Me.

1987 **First nonstop flight around the world without refueling.** From Edwards AFB, Calif., Dick Rutan and Jeana Yeager flew in *Voyager* around the world (24,986.727 mi.), returning to Edwards in 216 h 3 min 44 s (Dec. 14–23).

Official World Airplane Records

(Current and previous record holders given)

Source: National Aeronautic Association.

Speed Over Measured Straightaway Course

Speed (mph)	Date	Type plane	Pilot	Place
2,070.101	May 1, 1965	Lockheed YF-12A Jet	Col. R. L. Stephens (USAF)	Edwards AFB, Calif.
2,193.16	July 28, 1976	Lockheed SR-71A	Capt. Eldon W. Joersz (USAF)	Beale AFB, Calif.

Fastest U.S. continental: Capt. Robert G. Sowers (USAF)—Convair B-58 "Hustler"—from Los Angeles, Calif., to Kennedy International Airport, N.Y.—2,458.58 statute miles—2 h 0 min 58.71 sec—average speed, 1,214.65 mph—March 5, 1962.

Speed Over A Closed Circuit

Speed (mph)	Date	Type plane	Pilot	Place
2,092	July 27,1976	Lockheed SR-71A	Maj. Adolphus H. Bledsoe, Jr. (USAF)	Beale, AFB, Calif.

Distance, Straight Line

Distance (mi.)	Date	Crew	From	To
11,235.60	Sept. 29–Oct. 1, 1946	Comdr. Thomas D. Davies, Comdrs. Eugene P. Rankin, Walter S. Reid, Lt. Comdr. Ray A. Tabeling (USN)	Perth, Australia	Columbus, Ohio
12,532.28	Jan. 11, 1962	Maj. Clyde P. Evely (USAF)	Kadena, Okinawa	Madrid

Longest light airplane (3,858–6,614 lb) distance: Maximillian A. Conrad—U.S. Piper Comanche 250, Lycoming 0-540-AIAS (250 hp), from Casablanca, Morocco, to Los Angeles, 7,668.48 mi.—June 2–4, 1959.

Distance, Closed Circuit

Distance (mi.)	Date	Crew	Place
11,593.68[1]	July 10–15, 1986	Dick Rutan & Jeana Yeager (U.S.)	California

1. First nonstop flight around the world without refueling, from Edwards Air Force Base, Calif., and return, Rick Rutan and Jeana Yeager, Dec. 14-23, 1987, 24,986.727-mi. distance, 216 h 3 min 44 s, official speed 115.65 mph (unoffical record, subject to approval by Federation Aeronautique Internationale (FAI), headquarters, Paris.

Altitude

Height (ft)	Date	Crew	Place
103,389[1]	Nov. 14, 1959	Capt. Joe B. Jordan (USAF)	Edwards AFB, Calif.
314,750[2]	July 17, 1962	Maj. Robert M. White (USAF)	Edwards AFB, Calif.
118,898	July 25, 1973	Alexander Fedotov (U.S.S.R.)	U.S.S.R.
85,069[3]	July 28, 1976	Capt. Robert C. Helt (USAF)	Beale, AFB, Calif.
123,524	Aug. 31, 1977	Alexander Fedotov (U.S.S.R.)	U.S.S.R.

1. Jet-propelled aircraft. 2. X-15-1-rocket plane. 3. In horizontal flight, SR-71.

The First Manned Helicopter Flights

Professor Charles Richet made a successful ascent of about two feet in a tethered aircraft with four biplane rotors at Douai, France, on September 19, 1907. The helicopter, designed by Louis and Jacques Breguet, was named the *Gyroplane.*

Paul Cornu, another French aviator, made a six-foot-high, 20-second free flight in a tandem-rotor helicopter that he built at Lisieux on November 13, 1907.

The World's Fastest Aircraft

The Lockheed SR-71 A/B "Blackbird," produced since January 1966, is still the world's fastest and highest flying production aircraft built. In July 1976, flown by three different USAF crews, the SR-71 set an absolute world speed record of 2,193.167 mph over a 15/25 km straight course, a speed of 2,092. 294 mph around a 1,000-km closed circuit, and a sustained altitude record of 85,069 ft in horizontal flight. Another SR-71A flew from New York to London, England, in 1 hr 54 min 56.4 sec in September 1974 at an average speed of 1,806.987 mph.

The Blackbird is unarmed and has a crew of two seated in tandem. The dimensions are: span 55 ft 7 in.; length 107 ft 5 in.; and height 18 ft 6 in. Its estimated maximum speed at 78,750 ft is over Mach 3, and its operational ceiling is above 80,000 ft. In a reconnaissance mission, the SR-71 can cover up to a 100,000-sq-mi. area in one hour. The aircraft is assigned to the 9th Strategic Reconnaissance Wing, Beale AFB, California. USAF Photo.

World's 50 Busiest Airports in 1987

Airport	Passengers[1]	Airport	Passengers[1]
1. O'Hare International: Chicago	53,338,056	26. Intercontinental: Houston	13,996,015
2. Hartsfield Atlanta International: Atlanta	45,191,480	27. Tacoma International: Seattle	13,642,666
3. International: Los Angeles	41,417,867	28. Sky Harbor Airport: Phoenix	13,274,015
4. International: Dallas/Ft. Worth	39,945,326	29. International: Philadelphia	12,780,306
5. Stapleton International: Denver	34,685,944	30. International: Orlando	12,495,346
6. Heathrow Airport: London	31,315,300	31. McCarran International: Las Vegas	12,303,400
7. International: Newark	29,433,046	32. Fiumicino Airport: Rome	12,241,145
8. International: San Francisco	28,607,363	33. Charlotte/Douglas International	11,987,339
9. Kennedy International: New York	27,223,733	34. Benito Juarez Airport: Mexico City	11,310,871
10. Tokyo International (Haneda): Japan	27,217,761	35. Stockholm-Arlanda Airport	10,599,000
11. La Guardia: New York	22,188,871	36. Kingsford Smith Airport: Australia	10,114,958
12. International: Miami	21,947,368	37. Salt Lake City International	9,990,986
13. International: Boston-Logan	21,862,718	38. Copenhagen Airport	9,971,012
14. International: Lambert-St. Louis	20,352,383	39. Athens Airport	9,599,651
15. Frankfurt-Main: West Germany	19,802,229	40. Zurich Airport	9,250,967
16. Orly Airport: Paris	18,543,670	41. International: Tampa	9,198,139
17. International: Honolulu	18,235,154	42. International: San Diego	9,084,438
18. Osaka International: Japan	17,694,649	43. Dulles International: Washington, D.C.	8,962,346
19. Detroit: (Wayne County)	17,604,583	44. Changi Airport: Singapore	8,912,233
20. International: Toronto	17,136,147	45. Memphis International Airport	8,725,359
21. International: Minneapolis-St. Paul	17,073,605	46. International: Baltimore	8,670,506
22. Gatwick Airport: London	16,309,300	47. Dusseldorf Airport	8,493,402
23. International: Pittsburgh	15,989,507	48. Vancouver International Airport	8,385,000
24. Charles De Gaulle: Paris	14,427,026	49. International: Kansas City	8,309,567
25. National Airport: Washington, D.C.	14,307,980	50. Amsterdam Airport Schiphol	8,207,969

1. Enplaned, deplaned, and transfer, in millions. *Source:* Airport Operators Council International, June 1987.

Selected U.S. Military Aircraft

Abbreviations: GA—Garrett AiResearch; All—Detroit Diesel Allison Div. of General Motors; Con—Continental; GD—General Dynamics; GE—General Electric; Lyc—Lycoming; RI—Rockwell International; P&W—Pratt & Whitney; PWC—Pratt & Whitney Aircraft of Canada, Ltd; Wr—Curtiss Wright; kt—knots.

Type	Manufacturer	Popular name	Power plant	Crew	Wing-span, ft/in.	Length, ft/in.	Height, ft/in.	Gross weight, lb	Speed, mph
ATTACK									
A-7D/K	LTV Corp.	Corsair II	1 All TF41-A-1	1	38/9	46/1	16/0	42,000	698
A-10A	Fairchild	Thunderbolt II	2 GE TF34-GE-100	1	57/5	53/4	14/8	50,000	439
A-37B	Cessna	Dragonfly	2 GE J85-GE-17A	1	35/8	29/3	8/9	14,000	507
BOMBERS									
B-52G	Boeing	Stratofortress	8 P&W J57-P-43W	6	185/0	160/11	40/8	488,000	595
B-52H	Boeing	Stratofortress	8 P&W TF33-P-3	6	185/0	—	40/8	488,000	595
FB-111A	GD/Ft. Worth	—	2 P&W TF30-P-7	2	70/0[3]	73/6	17/1	100,000	Mach 2+
B-1B	RI/N.Amer./Boeing Mil Airplane/GE Eaton Ail Div.	—	4GE F101-GE 102	4-6	136[5]	147/0	34/0	477,000	—[6]
FIGHTERS									
F-4D/E	McDonnell Douglas	Phantom II	2 GEJ79-GE-17A	2	38/7	63/0	16/5	61,795	Mach 2.0
F-15A/B/C/D	McDonnell Douglas	Eagle	2 P&W F100-PW-100	1/2	42/10	63/9	18/6	68,000	Mach 2.5
F-5E/F	Northrop	Tiger II	2 J85-GE-21B	1/2	26.8	47/2	13/2	24,722	Mach 1.6
F-16A/B/C/D	GD	Fighting Falcon	1 P&W F100-PW-200 /GE F-110-GE-100	1	32.10	49.6	16/8	35,400	Mach 2
F-106A	GD/Convair	Delta Dart	1 P&W J75-P-17	1/2	38/3	70/8	20/3	42,000	Mach 2.0
F-111A/E	GD	—	2 P&W TF30-P-3/100(F)	2	63/0[4]	73/6	17/1	100,000	Mach 2.5
RECONNAISSANCE									
RF-4C	McDonnell Douglas	Phantom II	2 GE J79-GE-17	2	38/7	63/0	16/5	61,795	Mach 2.0
SR-71	Lockheed	Blackbird	2 P&W T11D-20B	2	55/7	107/5	18/6	170,000	Mach 3+
U-2/TR-1	Lockheed	—	1 P &W J75-P-13B	1	103/0	63/0	16/0	40,000	430 +
OBSERVATION									
OV-10A[1]	RI	Bronco	2 T76-G-416/417	2	40/0	41/7	15/2	14,444	281
OA-37B	Cessna	Dragonfly	2GE J85-GE-17A	2	35/11	28/3	8/11	14,000	507
EARLY WARNING COMMAND, CONTROL AND COMMUNICATIONS									
E-3A	Boeing	Sentry (AWACS)	4 P&W TF33-P-100/A	20	145/9	152/11	41.9	325,000	530
E-4A/B	Boeing	—	4 GE CF6-50E2	5	195/7	231/4	63/5	800,000	—
CARGO/TRANSPORT									
C-5A	Lockheed/Georgia	Galaxy	4 GE TF39-GE-1C	5	222/8	247/8	65/0	769,000	571
C-9A	McDonnell Douglas	Nightingale	2 P&W JT8D-9	3-8	93/5	119/3	27/6	108,000	565
C-12A[2]	Beech		2 PWC PT6A-38	2	54/6	43/9	15	12,500	299 kt
C-130E/H	Lockheed/Georgia	Hercules	4 All T56-A-7/-15(H)	5	132/7	97/9	38/3	175,000	374
C-140A	Lockheed/Georgia	Jetstar	4 P&W J60-P-5A	5	54/5	60/5	20/5	40,920	550
C-141A	Lockheed/Georgia	Starlifter	4 P&W TF33-P-7	5	159/11	168/3	39/3	343,000	566
KC-10A	McDonnell Douglas	Extender	3 GE CF6-50C2	4	164.4	181/7	58.1	590,000	528
KC-135A	Boeing	Stratotanker	4 P&W J57-P-59W	4-5	130/10	136/3	38/4	297,000	585
C-137C[7]	Boeing	—	4 P&W JT3D-3	4	145/9	152/11	42/5	322,000	627
TRAINERS									
T-33A	Lockheed	Shooting Star	1 All J33-A-35	2	38/10	37/9	11/4	15,100	543
T-37B	Cessna	Tweet	2 CON J69-T-25	2	33/9	29/3	9/2	6,600	425
T-38A/B	Northrop	Talon	2 GE J85GE5	2	25/3	46/4	12/10	12,093	Mach 1.2
T-41C	Cessna	Mescalero	1 CON 10-360-D	2	35/10	26/11	8/9	2,300	139
T-43A	Boeing	—	2 P&W JT8D-9	2	93/0	100/0	37/0	115,500	Mach .7

1. Air Force/Marines. 2. Air Force/Army. 3. Wing extended; 34 ft fully swept. 4. Wing extended; 31.11 ft fully swept. 5. Wing extended; 78.2-1/2 ft fully swept. 6. High Subsonic, supersonic at altitude. 7. The President's plane, "Air Force One" is a C-137C. *Source:* Department of the Air Force. NOTE: Aircraft dimensions have been rounded to the nearest inch.

U.S. Airlines Transport Planes, 1987

Manufacturer	Type/Series	Number of passengers	Cruise speed	Range	Wingspan, ft	Length, ft
4-ENGINE JET						
Boeing	707-120B	100–181	615	6,325	142.4	145.1
Boeing	707-320B	145	615	5,750	145.8	152.9
Boeing	747-SP	331	564	6,730	195.7	184.8
Boeing	747 PAX	452	557	6,500	195.7	231.9
Boeing	747 PAX/FRT	238	600	5,500	195.7	231.9
British Aerospace	146-100	88	460	1,450	86.4	85.9
British Aerospace	146-200	100	460	1,450	86.4	93.8
McDonnell Douglas	DC8-30,-40,-50	116/176	544	7,010	142.2	150.3
McDonnell Douglas	DC8-60,-70	259	580	7,150	142.2	187.4
McDonnell Douglas	DC8 PAX/FRT	180/259	600	3,700	142.2	187.4
4-ENGINE TURBOPROP						
Canadair	CL44	Cargo	300	3,500	142.3	136.9
Canadair	CL44	178	300	3,500	142.3	136.9
DeHavilland	DHC7	50	275	850	93.0	80.0
Lockheed	L188	66/104	405	2,750	99.0	104.5
Lockheed	L382	Cargo	380	2,750	99.0	104.5
4-ENGINE PISTON						
DeHavilland	Heron	14/17	195	750	71.5	46.5
Douglas	DC6	90/100	300	3,070	117.5	106.5
Douglas	DC4	44/60	230	2,750	117.6	94.0
3-ENGINE JET						
Boeing	727 All Series	70/131	622	3,000	108.0	133.1
Boeing	727 PAX/FRT	96	600	3,000	108.0	133.1
Boeing	727-200	145	622	2,400	108.0	153.1
Boeing	727F	Cargo	620	1,400	108.0	153.1
Lockheed	L1011	250/400	615	3,450	155.2	177.5
Lockheed	L1011	266/330	580	5,998	155.2	164.2
McDonnell Douglas	DC10-10	250/380	608	6,350	155.2	182.2
McDonnell Douglas	DC10-30	250/380	615	6,350	165.3	181.6
McDonnell Douglas	DC10-40	250/350	615	6,350	165.3	182.3
2-ENGINE JET						
Airbus Industries	A300/310	220-345	460	2000	147.1	175.9
Boeing	737-100	105	577	1,300	93.0	94.0
Boeing	737-200	115/130	573	1,800	92.0	100.1
Boeing	737-200	115/130	577	2,300	93.0	100.1
Boeing	737-300	149	577	2,300	93.0	100.1
Boeing	757	178/224	494	2,440	124.5	155.2
Boeing	767	211/290	550	3,200	156.1	159.1
Fokker	F28	85	523	1,055	82.2	96.2
Gulfstream American	1159	19	445	4,060	77.10	83.1
British Aerospace	BAC111	74/79	550	1,430	88.5	93.5
McDonnell Douglas	DC9-10,-20	90	593	2,200	93.2	104.4
McDonnell Douglas	DC9-30,-40	125	593	2,700	93.2	125.5
McDonnell Douglas	DC9-30/40	139	593	2,550	93.2	133.2
McDonnell Douglas	DC9-80	137/172	576	3,060	107.9	147.9
2-ENGINE TURBOPROP						
Beechcraft	B-99	15	280	1,150	45.8	44.5
Beech	1900	19	256	791	54.5	57.8
British Aerospace	Jetstream	14/18	250	1,440	52.0	47.0
British Aerospace	748	48	244	2,760	98.5	67.0
CASA	C-212	22/28	230	1,400	62.5	45.9
Convair	CV-580	50	350	1,100	105.2	79.1
DeHavilland	DHC-6	20	209	745	65.0	51.8
DeHavilland	DHC-8	35-40	230	1420	85.	73.
Dornier	DO228	15	231	1,460	55.8	54.4
Embraer	EMB110	19	212	900	50.1	49.1
Fairchild	F-27	40/56	265	1,450	95.1	82.1
Fairchild Hiller	FH-227	44/52	294	1,520	95.1	83.1
Fokker	FK F27	40/56	265	1,450	95.1	82.1
Fairchild Swrngn	SA226	19	294	2,139	46.2	59.2
Fairchild Swrngn	SA227	21	302	2,139	46.2	59.2
Gulfstream Aerospace	GAG159	18/37	345	2,300	78.3	75.3

Manufacturer	Type/Series	Number of passengers	Cruise speed	Range	Wingspan, ft	Length, ft
Nihon	YS-11	60	292	1,980	105.0	86.2
Nord	ND262	27	240	500	71.9	63.2
Nord	ND STC 262	25	240	500	74.1	63.2
Piper	PA31T3	6	210	925	40.8	34.5
SAAB/Fairchild	SF340A	36/39	260	2400	147	175
Short Bro-Harland	SH SD3	30	218	1,137	94.7	58.0
SNIAS	SNATR42	46	267	980	80.7	74.5
3-ENGINE PISTON						
Britten-Norman	MK3	18	154	820	53.0	48.2
2-ENGINE PISTON						
Beechcraft	BE18	7-9	236	1,515	49.7	35.2
Beechcraft	B-58	4-6	195	1150	37.8	29.8
Britten-Norman	BN2	10	180	425	49.0	35.7
Cessna	310	4–6	210	600	32.0	37.0
Cessna	402	6–10	239	550	36.0	40.0
Cessna	404	6–11	200	1,500	40.0	46.3
Convair	440	50	270	1,100	105.3	79.1
Curtis Wright	CW46					
Douglas	DC3	21	207	1,330	95.0	64.5
Grumman	G21	10	160	825	49.0	38.2
Grumman	G73	10	180	1,245	66.6	48.2
Piper	PA23	6	206	1,519	37.2	31.1
Piper	PA31	6	210	925	40.8	34.5
Piper	PA34	6	220	1,036	39.0	28.5
Piper	PA44	4	190	1,000	38.5	27.5

NOTE: Aircraft performance statistics represented here are to be considered only as "typical" of an aircraft type. Due to the various series (models) of individual aircraft types and the engine options available, it is not feasible to show all the various combinations of performance statistics. Data show the most used manufacturers type and model aircraft used by air carriers and commercial operators as of April 1985. *Source:* Federal Aviation Administration.

Helicopter Records

Source: National Aeronautic Association.

Distance in Straight Line
International: 2,213.04 mi.; 3,561.55 km.
Robert G. Ferry (U.S.) in Hughes YOH-6A helicopter powered by Allison T-63-A-5 engine; from Culver City, Calif., to Ormond Beach, Fla., April 6–7, 1966.

Distance, Closed Circuit
International: 1,739.96 mi.; 2,800.20 km.
Jack Schweibold (U.S.) in Hughes YOH-6A helicopter powered by Allison T-62-A-5 engine; Edwards Air Force Base, Calif., March 26, 1966.

Altitude
International: 40,820 ft; 12,442 m.
Jean Boulet (France) in Alouette SA 315-001 "Lama" powered by Artouste IIIB 735 KW engine; Istres, France, June 21, 1972.

Speed Over a 15/25-Km Course
International: 228.91 mph; 368.4 kph.
Gourguen Karapetyan (U.S.S.R.) in A-10 helicopter powered by 2 TB-3-117 engines; Podmoskovnoye, U.S.S.R., Sept. 21, 1978.

Altitude in Horizontal Flight
International: 36,122 ft; 11,010 m.
CWO James K. Church, (U.S.) in Sikorsky CH-54B helicopter powered by 2 P&W JFTD-12 engines; Stratford, CT., Nov. 4, 1971.

Speed Over a 3-Km Course
216,839 mph; 348.971 kph.
Byron Graham (U.S.) at Windsor Locks, CT, Dec. 14, 1970 in Sikorsky S-67 Helicopter powered by 2 GE T-58 turbine engines.

Speed Around the World
35.40 mph; 56.97 kph.
H. Ross Perot, Jr., pilot; J.W. Coburn, co-pilot (U.S.) in Bell 206 L-II Long Ranger, powered by one Allison 250-C28B of 435 hp. Elapsed time: 29 days 3 h 8 min 13 sec, Sept. 1–30, 1982.

Speed for 100 Km (Closed Circuit)
International: 211.35 mph; 340.15 kph.
Boris Galitsky (U.S.S.R.) in MI-6 helicopter powered by 2 TB-2BM turbine engines; Podmoskovnoye, U.S.S.R., Aug. 26, 1964.

Speed for 500 Km (Closed Circuit)
International: 214.84 mph; 345.74 kph.
Thomas Doyle (U.S.) in Sikorsky S-76 helicopter powered by 2 Allison 250-C-30 engines; West Palm Beach, Fla., Feb. 8, 1982.

Speed for 1,000 Km (Closed Circuit)
International: 200.48 mph; 322.646 kph.
Galina Rastorgoueva (U.S.S.R.) in A-10 helicopter powered by 2 TV2 117A engines; Aug. 13, 1975.

Speed for 2,000 Km (Closed Circuit)
International: 146.09 mph; 235.19 kph.
Inna Kopets (U.S.S.R.) in MI-8 helicopter; Sept. 14, 1967.

Active Pilot Certificates Held[1]

(as of January 1)

Year	Total	Airline transport	Commercial	Private
1970	720,028	31,442	176,585	299,491
1975	733,728	41,002	192,425	305,848
1980	814,667	63,652	182,097	343,276
1985	722,376	79,192	155,929	320,086
1986	709,118	87,186	147,798	305,736

1. Includes other pilot categories—helicopter, glider and lighter-than-air (18,125), and students (150,273). *Source:* Department of Transportation, Federal Aviation Administration.

Return To Jupiter

By Gary L. Bennett

"On the seventh day of January in this present year 1610, at the first hour of night, when I was viewing the heavenly bodies with a spyglass, Jupiter presented itself to me; and because I had prepared a very excellent instrument for myself, I perceived . . . that beside the planet there were three starlets, small indeed, but very bright."

Galileo Galilei

The Galileo spacecraft will allow scientists to study, at close range and for almost two years, the largest planet in the solar system. NASA/JPL illustration.

A lot has happened in the years since Galileo documented the first observations of Jupiter's moons in his crude telescope. Technology has progressed to the point where, within the next three years, a spacecraft will be sent to Jupiter to explore and investigate that planet on a scale that has never before been attempted. The mission, appropriately named for Galileo, is designed to make the first long-term study of the giant planet and its retinue of satellites.

In November 1989, if all goes according to current plans, a Space Shuttle will roar into space carrying the Galileo spacecraft on the first leg of its six-year journey to Jupiter. Sometime after the Shuttle achieves orbit, the astronauts will gently eject the spacecraft with its attached Inertial Upper Stage (IUS) booster. The Shuttle will then maneuver out of the way and wait.

About an hour later the IUS's computer will sequentially fire its two stages, thrusting Galileo away from Earth with a peak force of about 276,000 newtons. (A newton is the amount of force required to give a mass of 1 kilogram an acceleration of one meter per second each second.) When the two stages have completed their burns and separated, Galileo will be traveling along a trajectory that will include three planetary flybys (sometimes referred to as the "cruiser" mission) designed to send Galileo to Jupiter with a minimum of propellant.

In February 1990, after three months in space, Galileo will sail past Venus at a distance of about 19,400 kilometers (12,055 miles) to gain more speed for the next phase of its journey. Eight days later the spacecraft will reach its closest approach to the Sun, a little over 106 million kilometers (62, 140,000 miles).

After coming round the Sun, Galileo will fly by Earth at an altitude of about 3,600 kilometers (2, 237 miles) in December 1990 on a trajectory that will lead (temporarily) inside Earth's orbit, and then round the Sun again. About a year later Galileo's thrusters will add approximately 100 meters per second (328 ft/sec) to the speed of the spacecraft. This deep-space maneuver will help set up Galileo's trajectory for the earliest encounter with Jupiter.

In December 1992 Galileo will make its second and final pass by Earth. At that time it will be moving at about 14.1 kilometers per second (8.70 mi./sec) and will pass only 300 kilometers (186.4 miles) above the surface of Earth.

The cumulative effect of this series of complicated maneuvers, known as the Venus-Earth-Earth Gravity Assist ("VEEGA"), will be to sling Galileo outward along a curving trajectory to intercept Jupiter in November 1995. However, the Galileo scientists and mission planners will also take advantage of the VEEGA trajectory to search for "investigations of opportunity," such as taking measurements around Venus and around any asteroids near the spacecraft's path.

This long, tortured journey will be well worth it. Because Jupiter still contains primordial material from the solar nebula, it is the best cosmological laboratory in the solar system and might hold the key to the origins of our planetary system.

The Spacecraft's Unique Design

Described as the most complex spacecraft flown by NASA since the Viking Mars probes, Galileo consists of two elements: a planetary orbiter and an atmospheric entry probe. The orbiter is designed for a twenty-two month primary orbital mission; the probe will make the first direct samplings of Jupiter's atmosphere.

Galileo also marks a major advance in spacecraft technology because it will be the first dual-spin planetary spacecraft: part of the spacecraft will be spinning at 3 revolutions per minute (the "spun"

Gary L. Bennett is the Deputy Director of the Division of Special Applications at the U.S. Department of Energy. For over ten years he has been working on space propulsion and power systems including both the Ulysses and Galileo missions. Reprinted with permission from *Astronomy*, January 1987, copyright © 1987 by Kalmbach Publishing Company.

section, in the jargon of spacecraft engineers), while the other part will not spin (the "despun" section). The spun section will provide the scanning motion (similar to the Pioneer spacecraft) necessary for the five particle and field sensors to make measurements in all directions. The despun section will provide the inertially stable platform (like the Mariner, Viking, and Voyager probes) for the camera and other remote sensing instruments.

Included among the orbiter's nine scientific instruments is an 800-line by 800-element charge-coupled device (CCD). The CCD is over one hundred times as sensitive as the TV vidicom tubes used by *Voyagers 1* and *2*. Fantastic resolution, in some cases on the order of meters, is expected from the Galileo images.

Other instruments include:

- a near-infrared mapping spectrometer, which will provide infrared images and measure the reflected sunlight and heat emission from Jupiter's atmosphere and satellites;
- an ultraviolet spectrometer for analyzing the atmosphere of Jupiter and its satellites;
- a photopolarimeter radiometer for measuring the temperatures of Jupiter's atmosphere and of the satellite's surfaces;
- a magnetometer for measuring the strength and changes in the Jovian magnetic field as well as searching for magnetic fields associated with the satellites;
- plasma and plasma-wave instruments to study the properties of the plasmas around Jupiter;
- an energetic-particle detector for measuring the composition, distribution, and energy spectra of high-energy particles (ions, electrons, and protons);
- a dust detection instrument for measuring the size, speed, and charge of dust particles near Jupiter and its satellites.

Radio equipment will make additional measurements of Jupiter's atmosphere as well as Jovian and solar gravitational fields and extra-solar gravitational radiation.

All instruments will be calibrated and the solar wind will be sampled during the Earth-to-Jupiter cruise phase.

The Probe's Descent to Jupiter

The atmospheric probe, located in the despun section of Galileo, consists of two major elements: a deceleration module and a descent module. The deceleration module includes the heat shields that are designed to protect the scientific instruments during the fastest atmospheric entry of any manmade craft. Almost two-thirds of the shield material will burn off during atmospheric entry.

The descent module contains six instruments designed to study the Jovian atmosphere. These include an atmospheric instrument to provide information on the temperature, density, and pressure within Jupiter's atmosphere; a neutral mass spectrometer for measuring the composition of atmospheric gases; and a helium-abundance interferometer to determine the ratio of hydrogen to helium. Still other instruments will study cloud particles, atmospheric lightning, and energetic particles.

The probe has been extensively tested to ensure that it will survive the high atmospheric entry temperatures (up to 40 kilowatts per square centimeter, which is nearly seven times as much thermal power emitted by each square centimeter of the surface of the Sun!), and the high-entry deceleration (perhaps up to 345 g for a worst-case entry).

Three days after releasing the probe the orbiter will fire its 400-newton engine for the first time to place it on a trajectory to fly over the probe as it descends into the Jovian atmosphere.

In November 1995 the Galileo probe and orbiter will arrive at Jupiter. The orbiter will shoot past volcanic Io at a distance of 1,000 kilometers (621.4 miles)—twenty times closer than the closest Voyager approach. The gravity of Io will slow the orbiter.

Four hours later the probe will tear into the Jovian atmosphere 450 kilometers (279.6 miles) above the cloud deck, just north of the equator. Its entry speed will be about 48 kilometers per second (30 mi./sec). Fortunately the probe will be entering the atmosphere in the same direction as the planet rotates, which reduces the entry speed and lessens the amount of frictional heat on the shield. Still, heating will be considerable: during the first twenty seconds the temperature of the gas layer around the probe is expected to reach 8,300° Celsius (14,972° F). Nearly two minutes later, after the strongest deceleration has passed, the descent module will be drifting down into the Jovian atmosphere under a Dacron parachute.

As it descends, the probe will make its atmopheric measurements and transmit the data to the orbiter. The orbiter in turn will relay the data to Earth in real time. Roughly one hour after entry the probe will be below the cloud deck, but rising pressures and temperatures will combine with a degraded radio link to cause a major loss of data. Although this will be the end of the primary data transmission, the orbiter, as programmed, will "listen" to the probe for another fifteen minutes for any information it might still be able to relay.

Immediately after the probe mission the orbiter will fire its engine for almost an hour to put it into the first of eleven orbits about Jupiter. For the next twenty-two months the orbiter will carry out its primary orbital mission, making close passes by Europa, Ganymede, and Callisto, and add immeasurably to our understanding of the Jovian system. (Galileo is scheduled to fly by Io only once due to the intense radiation belts in Jupiter's inner satellite system. Additional flybys would be dependent on the condition of the spacecraft.)

The amount of science we can expect from the Galileo mission will make our return trip to Jupiter well worth the effort, not to mention establishing more "firsts" for the space program to rally around. As mission design managers O'Neil and Mitchell stated: "Project Galileo stands at the threshold ready to revitalize the U.S. Solar System Exploration Program. The major obstacles that caused the many delays in Project Galileo have been overcome. . . . Galileo will be the first mission in history to send a probe into an outer planet atmosphere, and the first to place a spacecraft in orbit about an outer planet." □

Unmanned Planetary and Lunar Programs

Lunar Orbiter. Series of spacecraft designed to orbit the Moon, taking pictures and obtaining data in support of the subsequent manned Apollo landings. The U.S. launched five *Lunar Orbiters* between Aug. 10, 1966 and Aug. 2, 1967.

Mariner. Designation for a series of spacecraft designed to fly past or orbit the planets, particularly Mercury, Venus, and Mars. *Mariners* provided the early information on Venus and Mars. *Mariner 9,* orbiting Mars in 1971, returned the most startling photographs of that planet to date, and helped pave the way for a *Viking* landing in 1976. *Mariner 10* explored Venus and Mercury in 1973 and was the first probe to use a planet's gravity to whip it toward another.

Pioneer. Designation for the United States' first series of sophisticated interplanetary spacecraft. *Pioneers 10* and *11* reached Jupiter in 1973 and 1974 and continued on to explore Saturn and the other outer planets. *Pioneer 11,* renamed *Pioneer Saturn,* examined the Saturn system in September 1979. Significant discoveries were the finding of a small new moon and a narrow new ring. In 1986, *Pioneer 10* was the first man-made object to escape the solar system. *Pioneer Venus 1* and *2* reached Venus in 1978 and provided detailed information about that planet's surface and atmosphere.

Ranger. NASA's earliest moon exploration program. Spacecraft were designed for a crash landing on the Moon, taking pictures and returning scientific data up to the moment of impact. Provided the first closeup views of the lunar surface. The *Rangers* provided more than 17,000 closeup pictures, giving us more information about the Moon in a few years than in all the time that had gone before.

Surveyor. Series of unmanned spacecraft designed to land gently on the Moon and provide information on the surface in preparation for the manned lunar landings. Their legs were instrumented to return data on the surface hardness of the Moon. *Surveyor* dispelled the fear that Apollo spacecraft might sink several feet or more into the lunar dust.

Viking. Designation for two spacecraft designed to conduct detailed scientific examination of the planet Mars, including a search for life. *Viking 1* landed on July 20, 1976; *Viking 2,* Sept. 3, 1976. More was learned about the Red Planet in a few short months than in all the time that had gone before. But the question of life on Mars remains unresolved.

Voyager. Designation for two spacecraft designed to explore Jupiter and the other outer planets. *Voyager 1* and *Voyager 2* passed Jupiter in 1979 and sent back startling color TV images of that planet and its moons. They took a total of about 33,000 pictures. *Voyager 1* passed Saturn November 1980. *Voyager 2* passed Saturn August 1981 and Uranus January 1986. It should pass Neptune in 1989.

Notable Unmanned Lunar and Interplanetary Probes

Spacecraft	Launch date	Destination	Remarks
Pioneer 3 (U.S.)	Dec. 6, 1958	Moon	Max. alt.: 66,654 mi. Discovered outer Van Allen layer.
Lunik 1 (U.S.S.R.)	Sept. 12, 1959	Moon	Landed in area of Mare Serenitatis.
Mariner 2 (U.S.)	Aug. 27, 1962	Venus	Venus probe. Successful mid-course correction. Passed 21,648 mi. from Venus Dec. 14, 1962. Reported 800° F. surface temp. Contact lost Jan. 3, 1963 at 54 million mi.
Ranger 7 (U.S.)	July 28, 1964	Moon	Impacted near Crater Guericke 68.5 h after launch. Sent 4,316 pictures during last 15 min of flight as close as 1,000 ft above lunar surface.
Mariner 4 (U.S.)	Nov. 28, 1964	Mars	After mid-course correction, passed behind Mars July 14, 1965, taking 22 pictures from about 6,000 mi.
Zond 3 (U.S.S.R.)	July 18, 1965	Moon	Sent close-ups of 3 million sq mi. of Moon. Now in solar orbit.
Luna 9 (U.S.S.R.)	Jan. 31, 1966	Moon	3,428 lb. Instrument capsule of 220 lb soft-landed Feb. 3, 1966. Sent back about 30 pictures.
Surveyor 1 (U.S.)	May 30, 1966	Moon	Landed June 2, 1966. Sent almost 10,400 pictures, a number after surviving the 14-day lunar night.
Lunar Orbiter 1 (U.S.)	Aug. 10, 1966	Moon	Orbited Moon Aug. 14. 21 pictures sent.
Surveyor 3 (U.S.)	April 17, 1967	Moon	Soft-landed 65 h after launch on Oceanus Procellarum. Scooped and tested lunar soil.
Venera 4 (U.S.S.R.)	June 12, 1967	Venus	Arrived Oct. 17. Instrument capsule sent temperature and chemical data.
Surveyor 5 (U.S.)	Sept. 8, 1967	Moon	Landed near lunar equator Sept. 10. Radiological analysis of lunar soil. Mechanical claw for digging soil.
Surveyor 7 (U.S.)	Jan. 6, 1968	Moon	Landed near Crater Tycho Jan. 10. Soil analysis. Sent 3,343 pictures.
Pioneer 9 (U.S.)	Nov. 8, 1968	Sun Orbit	Achieved orbit. Six experiments returned solar radiation data.
Venera 5 (U.S.S.R.)	Jan. 5, 1969	Venus	Landed May 16, 1969. Returned atmospheric data.
Mariner 6 (U.S.)	Feb. 24, 1969	Mars	Came within 2000 mi. of Mars July 31, 1969. Sent back data & TV pictures.
Venera 7 (U.S.S.R.)	Aug. 17, 1970	Venus	Reached Venus Dec. 15, 1970. Sent data, apparently from surface, for 58 min.
Luna 16 (U.S.S.R.)	Sept. 12, 1970	Moon	Soft-landed Sept. 20, scooped up rock, returned to Earth Sept. 24.
Luna 17 (U.S.S.R.)	Nov. 10, 1970	Moon	Soft-landed on Sea of Rains Nov. 17. Lunokhod 1, self-propelled vehicle, used for first time. Sent TV photos, made soil analysis, etc.
Mariner 9 (U.S.)	May 30, 1971	Mars	First craft to orbit Mars, Nov. 13. 7,300 pictures, 1st closeups of Mars' moon. Transmission ended Oct. 27, 1972.
Luna 19 (U.S.S.R.)	Sept. 28, 1971	Moon	Orbited Moon, making measurements & taking photos. Soft-landed Feb. 21 in Sea of Fertility. Returned Feb. 25 with rock samples.

Spacecraft	Launch date	Destination	Remarks
Pioneer 10 (U.S.)	March 3, 1972	Jupiter	620-million-mile flight path through asteroid belt passed Jupiter Dec. 3, 1973, to give man first closeup of planet. In 1986, it became first man-made object to escape solar system.
Luna 21 (U.S.S.R.)	Jan. 8, 1973	Moon	Soft-landed Jan. 16. Lunokhod 2 (moon-car) scooped up soil samples, returned them to Earth Jan. 27.
Mars 4 (U.S.S.R.)	July 21, 1973	Mars	Arrived Feb. 1974, briefly sending back photos
Mariner 10 (U.S.)	Nov. 3, 1973	Venus, Mercury	Passed Venus Feb. 5, 1974. Arrived Mercury March 29, 1974, for man's first closeup look at planet. First time gravity of one planet (Venus) used to whip spacecraft toward another (Mercury).
Venera 9 (U.S.S.R.)	June 8, 1975	Venus	Soft-landed Oct. 25, 1976. Photographed surface of planet.
Viking 1 (U.S.)	Aug. 20, 1975	Mars	Carrying life-detection labs. Landed July 20, 1976, for detailed scientific research, including pictures. Designed to work for only 90 days, it operated for almost 6 1/2 years before it went silent in November 1982.
Viking 2 (U.S.)	Sept. 9, 1975	Mars	Like Viking 1. Landed Sept. 3, 1976. Functioned 3 1/2 years.
Luna 24 (U.S.S.R.)	Aug. 9, 1976	Moon	Soft-landed Aug. 18, 1976. Returned soil samples Aug. 22, 1976.
Voyager 1 (U.S.)	Sept. 5, 1977	Jupiter, Saturn, Uranus	Fly-by mission. Reached Jupiter in March 1979; passed Saturn Nov. 1980; passed Uranus 1986.
Voyager 2 (U.S.)	Sept. 20, 1977	Jupiter, Saturn, Uranus	Like Voyager 1. Encountered Jupiter in July 1979; flew by Saturn Aug. 1981; passed Uranus January 1986; to pass Neptune 1989.
Pioneer Venus 1 (U.S.)	May 20, 1978	Venus	Arrived Dec. 4 and orbited Venus, photographing surface and atmosphere.
Pioneer Venus 2 (U.S.)	Aug. 8, 1978	Venus	Four-part multi-probe, landed Dec. 9.
Venera 11 (U.S.S.R.)	Sept. 9, 1978	Venus	Soft-landed Dec. 25, 1978. Transmitted data for 95 minutes.
Venera 13 (U.S.S.R.)	Oct. 30, 1981	Venus	Landed March 1, 1982. Took first X-ray fluorescence analysis of the planet's surface. Transmitted data 2 hours 7 minutes.
VEGA 1 (U.S.S.R.)	Deployed on Venus, June 10, 1985	Encounter with Halley's comet	In flyby over Venus while enroute to encounter with Halley's Comet, VEGA 1 and 2 dropped scientific capsules onto Venus to study atmosphere and surface material. Encountered Halley's Comet on March 6 and March 9, 1986. Took TV pictures, and studied comet's dust particles.
VEGA 2 (U.S.S.R.)	Deployed on Venus, June 14, 1985		
Suisei (Japan)	Encountered Hally's Comet March 8, 1986	Halley's Comet	Spacecraft made fly-by of comet and studied atmosphere with ultraviolet camera. Observed rotation nucleus.
Sakigake (Japan)	Encountered Halley's Comet March 10, 1986	Halley's Comet	Spacecraft made fly-by to study solar wind and magnetic fields. Detected plasma waves.
Giotto (ESA)	Encountered Halley's Comet March 13, 1986	Halley's Comet	European Space Agency spacecraft made closest approach to comet. Studied atmosphere and magnetic fields. Sent back best pictures of nucleus.

Notable Manned Space Flights

Designation and country	Date	Astronauts	Flight time (h/min)	Remarks
Vostok 1(U.S.S.R.)	April 12, 1961	Yuri A. Gagarin	1/48	First manned orbital flight
MR III (U.S.)	May 5, 1961	Alan B. Shepard, Jr.	0/15	Range 486 km (302 mi.), peak 187 km (116.5 mi.); capsule recovered. First American in space.
Vostok 2 (U.S.S.R.)	Aug. 6–7, 1961	Gherman S. Titov	25/18	First long-duration flight
MA VI (U.S.)	Feb. 20, 1962	John H. Glenn, Jr.	4/55	First American in orbit
MA IX (U.S.)	May 15–16, 1963	L. Gordon Cooper, Jr.	34/20	Longest Mercury flight
Vostok 6 (U.S.S.R.)	June 16–19, 1963	Valentina V. Tereshkova	70/50	First orbital flight by female cosmonaut
Voskhod 1 (U.S.S.R.)	Oct. 12, 1964	Vladimir M. Komarov; Konstantin P. Feoktistov; Boris G. Yegorov	24/17	First 3-man orbital flight; also first flight without space suits
Voskhod 2 (U.S.S.R.)	March 18, 1965	Alexei A. Leonov; Pavel I. Belyayev	26/2	First "space walk" (by Leonov), 10 min
GT III (U.S.)	March 23, 1965	Virgil I. Grissom; John W. Young	4/53	First manned test of Gemini spacecraft
GT IV (U.S.)	June 3–7, 1965	James A. McDivitt; Edward H. White, 2d	97/48	First American "space walk" (by White), lasting slightly over 20 min
Apollo 7 (U.S.)	Oct. 11–22, 1968	Walter M. Schirra, Jr.; Donn F. Eisele; R. Walter Cunningham	260/9	First manned test of Apollo command module; first live TV transmissions from orbit

Designation and country	Date	Astronauts	Flight time (h/min)	Remarks
Soyuz 3 (U.S.S.R.)	Oct. 26-30, 1968	Georgi T. Bergeovoi	94/51	First manned rendezvous and possible docking by Soviet cosmonaut
Apollo 8 (U.S.)	Dec. 21-27, 1968	Frank Borman; James A. Lovell, Jr.; William A. Anders	147/00	First spacecraft in circumlunar orbit; TV transmissions from this orbit
Apollo 9 (U.S.)	Mar. 3-13, 1969	James A. McDivitt; David R. Scott; Russell L. Schweikart	241/1	First manned flight of Lunar Module
Apollo 10 (U.S.)	May 18-26, 1969	Thomas P. Stafford; Eugene A. Cernan; John W. Young	192/3	First descent to within 9 miles of moon's surface by manned craft
Apollo 11 (U.S.)	July 16–24, 1969	Neil A. Armstrong; Edwin E. Aldrin, Jr.; Michael Collins	195/18	First manned landing and EVA on Moon; soil and rock samples collected; experiments left on lunar surface
Soyuz 6 (U.S.S.R.)	Oct. 11–16, 1969	Gorgiy Shonin; Valriy Kabasov	118/42	Three spacecraft and seven men put into earth orbit simultaneously for first time
Apollo 12 (U.S.)	Nov. 14–24, 1969	Charles Conrad, Jr.; Richard F. Gordon, Jr.; Alan Bean	244/36	Manned lunar landing mission; investigated Surveyor 3 spacecraft; collected lunar samples. EVA time: 15 h 30 min
Soyuz 9 (U.S.S.R.)	June 1–17, 1970	Andreiyan Nikolayez; Vitaly Sevastianov	424/59	Mission to test man's ability to withstand long periods of weightlessness
Apollo 13 (U.S.)	April 11–17, 1970	James A. Lovell, Jr.; Fred W. Haise, Jr.; John L. Swigert, Jr.	142/54	Third manned lunar landing attempt; aborted due to pressure loss in liquid oxygen in service module and failure of fuel cells
Apollo 14 (U.S.)	Jan. 31–Feb. 9, 1971	Alan B. Shepard; Stuart A. Roosa; Edgar D. Mitchell	216/42	Third manned lunar landing: returned largest amount of lunar material
Soyuz 11 (U.S.S.R.)	June 6–30, 1971	Georgiy Tomofeyevich Dobrovolskiy; Vladislav Nikolayevich Volkov; Viktor Ivanovich Patsyev	569/40	Linked up with first space station, Salyut 1. Astronauts died just before re-entry due to loss of pressurization in spacecraft
Apollo 15 (U.S.)	July 26–Aug. 7, 1971	David R. Scott; James B. Irwin; Alfred M. Worden	295/12	Fourth manned lunar landing; first use of Lunar Rover propelled by Scott and Irwin; first live pictures of LM lift-off from Moon; exploration time: 18 hours
Apollo 16 (U.S.)	April 16–27, 1972	John W. Young; Thomas K. Mattingly; Charles M. Duke, Jr.	265/51	Fifth manned lunar landing; second use of Lunar Rover Vehicle, propelled by Young and Duke. Total exploration time on the Moon was 20 h 14 min, setting new record. Mattingly's in-flight "walk in space" was 1 h 23 min. Approximately 213 lb of lunar rock returned
Apollo 17 (U.S.)	Dec. 7-19, 1972	Eugene A. Cernan; Ronald E. Evans; Harrison H. Schmitt	301/51	Sixth and last manned lunar landing; third to carry lunar rover. Cernan and Schmitt, during three EVA's, completed total of 22 h 05 min 3 sec. USS Ticonderoga recovered crew and about 250 lbs of lunar samples
Skylab SL-2 (U.S.)	May 25-June 22, 1973	Charles Conrad, Jr.; Josep P. Kerwin; Paul J. Weitz	672/50	First manned Skylab launch. Established Skylab Orbital Assembly and conducted scientific and medical experiments
Skylab SL-3 (U.S.)	July 28-Sept. 25, 1973	Alan L. Bean, Jr.; Jack R. Lousma; Owen K. Garriott	1427/9	Second manned Skylab launch. New crew remained in space for 59 days, continuing scientific and medical experiments and earth observations from orbit
Skylab SL-4 (U.S.)	Nov. 16, 1973-Feb. 8, 1974	Gerald Carr; Edward Gibson; William Pogue	2017/16	Third manned Skylab launch; obtained medical data on crew for use in extending the duration of manned space flight; crews "walked in space" 4 times, totaling 44 h 40 min. Longest space mission yet—84 d 1 h 16 min. Splashdown in Pacific, Feb. 9, 1974
Apollo/Soyuz Test Project (U.S. and U.S.S.R.)	July 15–24, 1975 (U.S.)	U.S.: Brig. Gen. Thomas P. Stafford, Vance D. Brand, Donald K. Slayton	216/05	World's first international manned rendezvous and docking in space; aimed at developing a space rescue capability
	July 15–21, 1975 (U.S.S.R)	U.S.S.R.: Col. A. A. Leonov, V. N. Kubasov	223/35	Apollo and Soyuz docked and crewmen exchanged visits on July 17, 1975. Mission duration for Soyuz: 142 h 31 min. For Apollo: 217 h, 28 min.
Columbia (U.S.)	April 12–14, 1981	Capt. Robert L. Crippen; John W. Young	54/20	Maiden voyage of *Space Shuttle,* the first spacecraft designed specifically for re-use up to 100 times
Salyut 7 (U.S.S.R.)	Feb. 8, 1984—Oct. 2, 1985	Leonid Zizim; Vladimir Solovyov; Oleg Atkov	237 days	Record Russian endurance flight in orbiting space station

1. Approximate time. NOTE: The letters MR stand for Mercury (capsule) and Redstone (rocket); MA, for Mercury and Atlas (rocket); GT, for Gemini (capsule) and Titan-II (rocket). The first astronaut listed in the Gemini and Apollo flights is the command pilot. The Mercury capsules had names: MR-III was *Freedom 7,* MR-IV was *Liberty Bell 7,* MA-VI was *Friendship 7,* MA-VII was *Aurora 7,* MA-VIII was *Sigma 7,* and MA-IX was *Faith 7.* The figure 7 referred to the fact that the first group of U.S. astronauts numbered seven men. Only one Gemini capsule had a name: GT-III was called *Molly Brown* (after the Broadway musical *The Unsinkable Molly Brown*); thereafter the practice of naming the capsules was discontinued.

Konstantin E. Tsiolkovsky

Konstantin Eduardovich Tsiolkovsky, a deaf, provincial schoolteacher, is the acknowledged founder of theoretical cosmonautics. He pioneered the development of rocket and space research in the Soviet Union. Tsiolkovsky made many contributions to early space flight literature, and his classic article on astronautics, "The Investigation of Universal Space by Means of Reactive Devices" was published in 1903, the same year the Wright brothers made their famous flight. He also built the first wind tunnel in Russia for the testing of aerodynamic designs.

Konstantin E. Tsiolkovsky was born on September 17, 1857, in Izhevskoye, Ryazan Province, and died on September 19, 1935, at the age of ninety-eight. During his lifetime, details of his research were essentially unknown outside the Soviet Union. Photo reproduced by Novosti Press Agency.

Robert H. Goddard

Robert Hutchings Goddard is generally acknowledged to be the father of modern rocketry. He began his study of rockets in 1909 and he received a basic patent for a rocket apparatus as early as 1914. While a physics professor at Clark University, he conducted experimental and theoretical research on rocket devices. Goddard launched the world's first liquid-fuel rocket from a farm near Auburn, Mass., on March 16, 1926. In 1935, he became the first person to fire a liquid-fuel rocket faster than the speed of sound. Goddard was a brilliant inventor and he developed many rocket devices including the first automatic rocket steering mechanism.

Robert H. Goddard was born on Oct. 5, 1882, in Worcester, Mass., and he died on Aug. 10, 1945, at the age of sixty-three. Photo by AP/Wide World Photos, Inc.

U.S. Manned Space Flight Projects

Mercury. *Project Mercury,* America's first manned space program, was designed to further knowledge about man's capabilities in space. *Mercury 3* put the first American, Alan B. Shepard, into space. *Mercury 9,* with astronaut Gordon L. Cooper, was the longest flight.

Gemini. *Gemini* was an extension of *Project Mercury,* to determine the effects of prolonged space flight on man—two weeks or longer. "Walks in space" provided invaluable information for astronauts' later walks on the Moon. The *Gemini* spacecraft, twice as large as the *Mercury* capsule, accommodated two astronauts.

Apollo. *Apollo* was the designation for the United States' effort to land a man on the Moon and return him safely to Earth. The goal was successfully accomplished with *Apollo 11* on July 20, 1969, culminating eight years of rehearsal and centuries of dreaming. Astronauts Neil A. Armstrong and Col. Edwin E. Aldrin, Jr., scooped up and brought back the first lunar rocks ever seen on Earth—about 47 pounds. Six *Apollo* flights followed, ending with *Apollo 17* in December, 1972. The last three *Apollos* carried mechanized vehicles called lunar rovers for wide-ranging surface exploration of the Moon by astronauts. The rendezvous and docking of an *Apollo* spacecraft with a Russian *Soyuz* craft in Earth orbit on July 18, 1975, closed out the *Apollo* program.

Skylab. America's first Earth-orbiting space station. *Project Skylab* was designed to demonstrate that men can work and live in space for prolonged periods without ill effects. Originally the spent third stage of a Saturn 5 moon rocket, *Skylab* measured 118 feet from stem to stern, and carried the most varied assortment of experimental equipment ever assembled in a single spacecraft. Three three-man crews visited the space stations, spending more than 740 hours observing the Sun and bringing home more than 175,000 solar pictures. These were the first recordings of solar activity above

The Soviet Union's New Space Station

The Soviet space station *Mir (Peace)* was launched on Feb. 20, 1986. It is 43 ft long (13.10 m), has a diameter of 13.7 ft (4.14 m), and weighs 46,300 lb. Its two solar panels span about 100 ft (30 m). The Soviet Union has placed seven space stations in orbit since 1971. Two of them, the *Mir* and *Saylut 7* are in orbit now. The *Mir* is equipped with six docking ports so it can be docked simultaneously with six spacecraft, including passenger, cargo, and research ships. Novosti Photo.

Earth's obscuring atmosphere. *Skylab* also evaluated systems designed to gather information on Earth's resources and environmental conditions. *Skylab* biomedical findings indicated that man adapts well to space for at least a period of three months, provided he has a proper diet and adequately programmed exercise, sleep, work, and recreation periods. *Skylab* orbited Earth at a distance of about 300 miles. Five years after the last *Skylab* mission, the 77-ton space station's orbit began to deteriorate faster than expected, owing to unexpectedly high sunspot activity. On July 11, 1979, the parts of *Skylab* that did not burn up in the atmosphere came crashing down on parts of Australia and the Indian Ocean. No one was hurt.

Space Shuttle. The *Space Shuttle* is a manned space transportation system developed by NASA to reduce the cost of using space for commercial, scientific, and defense needs. The *Shuttle* is a manned rocket which, after depositing its payload in space, can be flown back to Earth like a conventional airplane and be available for re-use. Although most of its cargoes will be unmanned, the *Shuttle* can serve as an inhabited Earth-orbiting laboratory for up to 30 days. The *Space Shuttle Columbia* was successfully launched on April 12, 1981. It made five flights (the first four were test runs), the last completed on November 16, 1982. The second shuttle, *Challenger*, made its maiden flight on April 4, 1983. In April 1984, crew members of the *Challenger* captured, repaired, and returned the Solar Max satellite to orbit, making it the first time a disabled satellite had been repaired in space. The third shuttle, *Discovery*, made its first flight on August 30, 1984. The fourth space shuttle, *Atlantis*, made its maiden flight on Oct. 3, 1985. A tragedy occurred on Jan. 28, 1986, when the shuttle *Challenger* exploded, killing the crew of seven 73 seconds after takeoff. It was the world's worst space flight disaster. The next shuttle flight is not expected to occur before June 1988.

Soviet Manned Space Flight Programs

Vostok. The Soviets' first manned capsule, roughly spherical, used to place the first six cosmonauts in Earth orbit (1961–65).

Voskhod. Adaptation of the *Vostok* capsule to accommodate two and three cosmonauts. *Voskhod 1* orbited three persons, and *Voskhod 2* orbited two persons performing the world's first manned extravehicular activity.

Soyuz. Late-model manned spacecraft with provisions for three cosmonauts and a "working compartment" accessible through a hatch. Soyuz is the Russian word for "union". Since 1973, all *Soyuz* spacecraft have carried two cosmonauts. *Soyuz 19*, launched July 15, 1975, docked with the American *Apollo* spacecraft.

Salyut. Earth-orbiting space station intended for prolonged occupancy and re-visitation by cosmonauts. They are usually launched by Soviet Proton rockets. *Salyut 1* was launched April 19, 1971. *Salyut 2*, launched April 3, 1973, malfunctioned in orbit and was never occupied. *Salyut 3* was launched June 25, 1974. *Salyut 4* was launched Dec. 26, 1974. *Salyut 5* was launched June 22, 1976. *Salyut 6* was launched on Sept. 29, 1977. *Salyut 7* was launched on April 19, 1982 and is still in orbit. A record breaking Russian endurance flight was set (Feb. 8, 1984-Oct. 2, 1985) when Soviet astronauts spent 237 days in orbit aboard *Salyut-7*. On Feb. 20, 1986, a new Soviet space station *Mir* was launched into orbit.

The Soviet Mars Exploration Program

By Pat Jones

Soviet space scientist Dr. Valery Barsukov, director of the Vernadsky Institute for Geochemistry and Analytical Chemistry, outlined his nation's ambitious 10–15 year program of unmanned Mars exploration at the 18th Lunar and Planetary Science Conference held in Houston in March 1987.

The Soviet Mars exploration program will commence with the launch of two spacecraft in 1988 to study Mars and its moon Phobos—the only launches in the program that have already received official approval. While one spacecraft will study the evolution of Martian geology, atmosphere, and climate, the Phobos craft will deposit two small landers on the satellite's surface. One lander will be a long-stay experimental package to study the chemistry of the soil and variations in the orbit of Phobos around Mars. The second will be a "hopper" that "jumps like a frog," to study surface chemistry at a number of scattered locations.

Barsukov said that this two-spacecraft mission would mark "the beginning of a big new program," and emphasized that "[scientific] problems cannot be resolved by one launch or one mission. It needs a progressive program."

The second step in the Soviets' exploration of Mars will be to send a very large satellite there in 1992. This will carry two surface penetrators, balloons, and possibly a small Mars rover vehicle. The components of the scientific package to be carried are still under discussion, but the 440–550 pound payload will include a device for thermal mapping of the surface and a television camera capable of producing high resolution (10 meter) images, comparable to the French SPOT satellite's photography of Earth.

Radar and spectral analysis equipment will study Martian weather and the chemical composition of the surface. One of the surface penetrators will be attached to a double-shell balloon with helium in the inner skin and carbon dioxide in the outer skin. The balloon will respond to the Sun's daytime heating of Mars and fly over the surface by day at an altitude of no more than six kilometers (3.7 miles), taking high resolution images. Then, as the atmosphere cools, the balloon will "land in the evening, and rest overnight," says Barsukov. During the evening rest, the balloon's penetrator will sample the chemical composition of the soil at the landing site. Barsukov anticipates that the balloon will cover up to 5,000 km (3,100 miles) of the surface of Mars and take samples at ten landing sites in ten different "rise and rest" cycles.

The Soviets are also designing a small Mars rover. The heavy lift rockets expected to be available to the Soviets soon may allow room on the 1992 mission for a small experimental rover. Barsukov admitted good-naturedly that inclusion of the rover was perhaps more of a scientist's dream than a likelihood at the present time, but said "It is better to design than to dream."

Pat Jones is an expert in interpretation of shuttle earth observation photography and a writer and broadcaster on the U.S. space program and space science. Reprinted with permission from SPACE WORLD, May 1987, published in cooperation with the National Space Society, published by Palmer Publications, Inc.,

Whether the 1992 mission includes a rover or not, Barsukov was confident that the Soviets would be ready to launch a very large Mars rover during the launch window in 1994. This mission would use two robot "moles" to penetrate 20–30 meters (66–98 feet) into the Martian soil. One "mole" would carry instruments for chemical analysis of the soil while the second would search for signs of life on Mars. Soviet scientists are looking at the possibility of drilling and sampling at different stations along the route and then studying the materials gathered using several instruments onboard the Mars rover.

The multi-mission exploration program would culminate in a sample return mission in 1996. French scientists are already involved in planning discussions with the Soviets for the 1996 flight. Barsukov reported that the European Space Agency has expressed interest in the Soviet Mars program, and said "There is the possibility to make a large international project. I personally would be disappointed if American scientists [did] not participate in this project." He added that "this will be a suitable celebration of the end of the twentieth century."

American space scientists, faced with many years of delay resulting from budget cuts and the grounding of the Shuttle fleet, were genuinely, though somewhat painfully, amused when Barsukov said the complexity of the project and delays for formal approval could result in a two-year slip to 1998 for the sample return mission.

When asked "does the USSR expect to follow the sample return mission with a manned mission?" Barsukov said, "I will be optimistic, but it is difficult to answer this question." He reminded the audience that a round-trip mission to Mars would take 2.5 years and that we have accumulated very little information on the response of the human body to long-term exposure to both weightlessness and cosmic ray bombardment.

Many of the scientists present were aware of the current debate within NASA on the long-term human response to weightlessness. While engineers working on preliminary designs for a manned Mars vehicle are relying on the medical profession to provide solutions to counter the negative effects of prolonged weightlessness, physicians stress that some form of artificial gravity will have to be incorporated in the designs. Barsukov took the pragmatic approach: "When cosmonauts can fly in Earth orbit for three years, then let's decide whether to fly to Mars or not." □

The Mars Observer

A NASA mission is underway to launch an unmanned spacecraft to Mars in 1992. The craft will be launched from a NASA space shuttle.

After a one-year cruise, the spacecraft will arrive at and begin orbiting Mars. The scientific mission will last for one Martian year, or nearly two years. This will allow the spacecraft to study how Mars' atmosphere and surface change throughout the planet's seasons.

Other objectives are to determine the global elemental and mineralogical character of the planet's surface and establish the nature of the magnetic field.

SCIENCE

Danger: We're Losing Our Shield of Life

There was no life on land before the ozone layer formed—and now we're destroying it

By Isaac Asimov

Every oxygen molecule is made up of two oxygen atoms. Ozone is "oxygen and a half," for every ozone molecule is made up of *three* oxygen atoms.

It takes energy to force that third oxygen atom into the combination, and, once the ozone molecule is formed, it is easy for ozone to lose that extra atom per molecule and break down into ordinary oxygen again. In the presence of superfluous energy, as in the neighborhood of electrical-generating machinery, ozone is formed. It doesn't build up to a high concentration because it tends to break down as quickly as it is formed. This is fortunate, for ozone is poisonous.

Where ozone is chiefly formed is in the higher reaches of the atmosphere, about 15 miles above the Earth.

It isn't really much of a layer, since the air is very thin up there, but it is important—extremely important.

You see, ozone is opaque to ultraviolet light. The ultraviolet portion of sunlight is stopped by the ozone layer and very little of it gets through, while the longer waves of ordinary light penetrate easily.

This means that when we bask in sunlight, the damaging energetic waves of ultraviolet have been mostly filtered out. What's left is still enough to tan our skins (or burn them, if we are fair), but, by and large, we can walk in the sun with reasonable impunity.

On the primordial Earth, there was no oxygen in the atmosphere. It was only the gradual action of the tiny green plants of the ocean, as they evolved, that formed oxygen, which eventually allowed an ozone layer to be formed.

It may be that it was not till 400 million years ago that enough oxygen had collected to make it possible to produce a thick enough ozone layer in the upper atmosphere to shield the Earth. A layer of water absorbed ultraviolet and protected sea life, but energetic ultraviolet bathing the bare land would break down the complex chemicals of living things, and keep it sterile. Life could not invade the land, therefore, till the ozone layer had appeared.

But what if something now appears in the upper atmosphere that would help break down ozone molecules? The present equilibrium would fail, and the ozone layer would get thinner till it disappeared.

In the early 1970s, two scientists at the University of California at Irvine suggested that "chlorofluorocarbons" might represent such a danger. These "CFCs" don't burn, aren't poisonous, are absolutely safe to use. After World War II, these chemicals were increasingly used in refrigerators, automobile air conditioners and spray cans.

Eventually, all CFCs leak out of wherever they are and enter the atmosphere. More than 10 million tons have already leaked into the air and more is added every day. In the atmosphere, they stay, drifting upward steadily toward the ozone layer.

Once above that layer, the energetic ultraviolet of sunlight is strong enough to break up the CFC molecules and liberate a gas called chlorine. Chlorine, in turn, tends to decompose ozone into oxygen, and to thin the ozone layer.

When this was first pointed out, the U.S., in the interest of preserving the ozone layer, banned the use of CFCs in spray cans, and other gases were used instead. However, CFCs are still used in spray cans in many other countries. Furthermore, there are no good substitutes to replace CFCs in some appliances.

There were those who argued that the CFCs would not have any serious effect on the ozone layer, but it is possible that they have now been proven wrong.

In 1985, it was discovered that a thin spot, or hole, had appeared in the ozone layer over Antarctica in the autumn. Once the data, past as well as present, were studied closely, it seemed that the hole has been appearing there for many years and has been getting progressively larger. The amount of ozone in the Antarctic atmosphere may have decreased to half of what it was about 15 years ago. If the same trend occurred globally, the ozone layer could become perilously thin.

This *will* be dangerous. As it is, the ultraviolet radiation that reaches us, despite the ozone layer, is instrumental in producing skin cancer. As more and more ultraviolet penetrates and reaches us, that will increase, especially among those with fair skin. Over the next 80 years or so, there may well be up to 40 million cases of skin cancer among Americans alone, and 800,000 deaths. There would also be increases in cataracts.

If danger to the skin were all, we might just stay indoors as much as possible and carry sunshades out-of-doors—but it isn't all.

What about other land life?

Higher plants and animals have hair, feathers, scales, cuticles, skin, bark and so on to protect themselves. Microscopic life-forms in the soil and in the uppermost layers of the sea are not so protected, however. They would find sunshine becoming as deadly as it had been before the ozone layer formed 400 million years ago. And if these microorganisms are killed, this will surely seriously affect higher organisms that depend upon them ecologically. In short, it may be that the very fabric of life will be disrupted.

What do we do? Amid all the dangers of overpopulation, of pollution, of drugs, of terrorism, of nuclear war, we must now add our concern for the ozone layer. It is to the ozone layer that leaders in science and government are now increasingly turning their attention. □

Isaac Asimov is a celebrated educator and the author of 350-plus books.

Table of Geological Periods

It is now generally assumed that planets are formed by the accretion of gas and dust in a cosmic cloud, but there is no way of estimating the length of this process. Our earth acquired its present size, more or less, between 4,000 and 5,000 million years ago. Life on earth originated about 2,000 million years ago, but there are no good fossil remains from periods earlier than the Cambrian, which began about 550 million years ago. The largely unknown past before the Cambrian Period is referred to as the Pre-Cambrian and is subdivided into the Lower (or older) and Upper (or younger) Pre-Cambrian—also called the Archaeozoic and Proterozoic Eras.

The known geological history of the earth since the beginning of the Cambrian Period is subdivided into three "eras," each of which comprises a number of "periods." They, in turn, are subdivided into "subperiods." In a subperiod, a certain section may be especially well known because of rich fossil finds. Such a section is called a "formation," and it is usually identified by a place name.

Paleozoic Era

This era began 550 million years ago and lasted for 355 million years. The name was compounded from Greek *palaios* (old) and *zoön* (animal).

Period	Duration[1]	Subperiods	Events
Cambrian (from *Cambria*, Latin name for Wales)	70	Lower Cambrian Middle Cambrian Upper Cambrian	Invertebrate sea life of many types, proliferating during this and the following period
Ordovician (from Latin *Ordovices*, people of early Britain)	85	Lower Ordovician Upper Odovician	
Silurian (from Latin *Silures*, people of early Wales)	40	Lower Silurian Upper Silurian	First known fishes; gigantic sea scorpions
Devonian (from Devonshire in England)	50	Lower Devonian Upper Devonian	Proliferation of fishes and other forms of sea life, land still largely lifeless
Carboniferous (from Latin *carbo* = coal + *fero* = to bear)	85	Lower or Mississippian Upper of Pennsylvanian	Period of maximum coal formation in swampy forests; early insects and first known amphibians
Permian (from district of Perm in Russia)	25	Lower Permian Upper Permian	Early reptiles and mammals; earliest form of turtles

Mesozoic Era

This era began 195 million years ago and lasted for 135 million years. The name was compounded from Greek *mesos* (middle) and *zoön* (animal). Popular name: Age of Reptiles.

Period	Duration[1]	Subperiods	Events
Triassic (from *trias* = triad)	35	Lower or Buntsandstein (from German *bunt* = colorful + *Sandstein* = sandstone) Middle or Muschelkalk (from German *Muschel* = clam + *Kalk* = limestone) Upper or Keuper (old miners' term)	Early saurians
Jurassic (from Jura Mountains)	35	Lower or Black Jurassic, or Lias (from French *liais* = hard stone) Middle or Brown Jurassic, or Dogger (old provincial English for ironstone) Upper or White Jurassic, or Malm (Middle English for sand)	Many sea-going reptiles; early large dinosaurs; somewhat later, flying reptiles (pterosaurs), earliest known birds
Cretaceous (from Latin *creta* = chalk)	65	Lower Cretaceous Upper Cretaceous	Maximum development of dinosaurs; birds proliferating; oppossum-like mammals

Cenozoic Era

This era began 60 million years ago and includes the geological present. The name was compounded from Greek *kainos* (new) and *zoön* (animal). Popular name: Age of Mammals.

Period	Duration[1]	Subperiods	Events
Tertiary (originally thought to be the third of only three periods)	c. 60	Paleocene (from Greek *palaios* = old + *kainos* = new)	First mammals other than marsupials
		Eocene (from Greek *eos* = dawn + *kainos* = new)	Formation of amber; rich insect fauna; early bats
		Oligocene (from Greek *oligos* = few + *kainos* = new)	Steady increase of large mammals
		Miocene (from Greek *meios* = less + *kainos* = new)	
		Pliocene (from Greek *pleios* = more + *kainos* = new)	Mammals closely resembling present types; protohumans
Pleistocene (from Greek *pleistos* = most + *kainos* = new) (popular name: Ice Age)	1	Four major glaciations, named Günz, Mindel, Riss, and Würm, originally the names of rivers. Last glaciation ended 10,000 to 15,000 years ago	Various forms of early man
Holocene (from Greek *holos* = entire + *kainos* = new)		The present	The last 3,000 years are called "history"

1. In millions of years.

Chemical Elements

Element	Symbol	Atomic no.	Atomic weight	Specific gravity	Melting point °C	Boiling point °C	Number of isotopes[1]	Discoverer	Year
Actinium	Ac	89	227[2]	10.07[2]	1050	3200 ±300	11	Debierne	1899
Aluminum	Al	13	26.9815	2.6989	660.37	2467	8	Wöhler	1827
Americium	Am	95	243[6]	13.67	994 ±4	2607	13[3]	Seaborg et al.	1944
Antimony	Sb	51	121.75	6.691	630.74	1750	29	Early historic times	—
Argon	Ar	18	39.948	1.7837[4]	−189.2	−185.7	8	Rayleigh and Ramsay	1894
Arsenic (gray)	As	33	74.9216	5.73	817 (28 atm.)	613[5]	14	Albertus Magnus	1250?
Astatine	At	85	~210	—	302	337	21	Corson et al.	1940
Barium	Ba	56	137.34	3.5	725	1640	25	Davy	1808
Berkelium	Bk	97	247[6]	14.00[7]	—	—	8[3]	Seaborg et al.	1949
Beryllium	Be	4	9.01218	1.848	1278 ±5	2970 (5 mm.)	6	Vauquelin	1798
Bismuth	Bi	83	208.9806	9.747	271.3	1560 ±5	19	Geoffroy	1753
Boron	B	5	10.81	2.37[8]	2300	2550[5]	6	Gay-Lussac and Thénard; Davy	1808
Bromine	Br	35	79.904	3.12[4]	−7.2	58.78	19	Balard	1826
Cadmium	Cd	48	112.40	8.65	320.9	765	22	Stromeyer	1817
Calcium	Ca	20	40.08	1.55	839 ±2	1484	14	Davy	1808
Californium	Cf	98	251[6]	—	—	—	12[3]	Seaborg et al.	1950
Carbon	C	6	12.011	1.8–3.5[9]	~3550	4827	7	Prehistoric	—
Cerium	Ce	58	140.12	6.771	798 ±3	3257	19	Berzelius and Hisinger; Klaproth	1803
Cesium	Cs	55	132.9055	1.873	28.40	678.4	22	Bunsen and Kirchhoff	1860
Chlorine	Cl	17	35.453	1.56[4]	−100.98	−34.6	11	Scheele	1774
Chromium	Cr	24	51.996	7.18–7.20	1857 ±20	2672	9	Vauquelin	1797
Cobalt	Co	27	58.9332	8.9	1495	2870	14	Brandt	c.1735
Copper	Cu	29	63.546	8.96	1083.4±0.2	2567	11	Prehistoric	—
Curium	Cm	96	247[6]	13.51[2]	1340 ±40	—	13[3]	Seaborg et al.	1944
Dysprosium	Dy	66	162.50	8.540	1409	2335	21	Boisbaudran	1886
Einsteinium	Es	99	254[6]	—	—	—	12[3]	Ghiorso et al	1952
Erbium	Er	68	167.26	9.045	1522	2510	16	Mosander	1843
Europium	Eu	63	151.96	5.283	822 ±5	1597	21	Demarcay	1896
Fermium	Fm	100	257[6]	—	—	—	10[3]	Ghiorso et al	1953
Fluorine	F	9	18.9984	1.108[4]	−219.62	−188.14	6	Moissan	1886
Francium	Fr	87	223[6]	—	27[2]	677[2]	21	Perey	1939
Gadolinium	Gd	64	157.25	7.898	1311 ±1	3233	17	Marignac	1880
Gallium	Ga	31	69.72	5.904	29.78	2403	14	Boisbaudran	1875
Germanium	Ge	32	72.59	5.323	937.4	2830	17	Winkler	1886
Gold	Au	79	196.9665	19.32	1064.43	2807	21	Prehistoric	—
Hafnium	Hf	72	178.49	13.31	2227 ±20	4602	17	Coster and von Hevesy	1923
Helium	He	2	4.00260	0.1785[4]	−272.2 (26 atm.)	−268.934	5	Janssen	1868
Holmium	Ho	67	164.9303	8.781	1470	2720	29	Delafontaine and Soret	1878
Hydrogen	H	1	1.0080	0.070[4]	−259.14	−252.87	3	Cavendish	1766

Element	Symbol	Atomic no.	Atomic weight	Specific gravity	Melting point °C	Boiling point °C	Number of isotopes[1]	Discoverer	Year
Indium	In	49	114.82	7.31	156.61	2080	34	Reich and Richter	1863
Iodine	I	53	126.9045	4.93	113.5	184.35	24	Courtois	1811
Iridium	Ir	77	192.22	22.42	2410	4130	25	Tennant	1803
Iron	Fe	26	55.847	7.894	1535	2750	10	Prehistoric	—
Krypton	Kr	36	83.80	3.733[4]	−156.6	−152.30±0.10	23	Ramsay and Travers	1898
Lanthanum	La	57	138.9055	6.166	920±5	3454	19	Mosander	1839
Lawrencium	Lr	103	257[6]	—	—	—	20[3]	Ghiorso et al.	1961
Lead	Pb	82	207.2	11.35	327.502	1740	29	Prehistoric	—
Lithium	Li	3	6.941	0.534	180.54	1347	5	Arfvedson	1817
Lutetium	Lu	71	174.97	9.835	1656±5	3315	22	Urbain	1907
Magnesium	Mg	12	24.305	1.738	648.8±0.5	1090	8	Black	1755
Manganese	Mn	25	54.9380	7.21–7.44[10]	1244±3	1962	11	Gahn, Scheele, and Bergman	1774
Mendelevium	Md	101	256[6]	—	—	—	3[3]	Ghiorso et al.	1955
Mercury	Hg	80	200.59	13.546	−38.87	356.58	26	Prehistoric	—
Molybdenum	Mo	42	95.94	10.22	2617	4612	20	Scheele	1778
Neodymium	Nd	60	144.24	6.80 & 7.004[10]	1010	3127	16	von Welsbach	1885
Neon	Ne	10	20.179	0.89990 (g/1 0°C/1 atm)	−248.67	−246.048	8	Ramsay and Travers	1898
Neptunium	Np	93	237.0482	20.25	640±1	3902	15[3]	McMillan and Abelson	1940
Nickel	Ni	28	58.71	8.902	1453	2732	11	Cronstedt	1751
Niobium (Columbium)	Nb	41	92.9064	8.57	2468±10	4742	24	Hatchett	1801
Nitrogen	N	7	14.0067	0.808[4]	−209.86	−195.8	8	Rutherford	1772
Nobelium	No	102	254[6]	—	—	—	7[3]	Ghiorso et al.	1957
Osmium	Os	76	190.2	22.57	3045±30	5027±100	19	Tennant	1803
Oxygen	O	8	15.9994	1.14[4]	−218.4	−182.962	8	Priestley	1774
Palladium	Pd	46	106.4	12.02	1552	3140	21	Wollaston	1803
Phosphorus	P	15	30.9738	1.82 (white)	44.1	280	7	Brand	1669
Platinum	Pt	78	195.09	21.45	1772	3827±100	32	Ulloa	1735
Plutonium	Pu	94	244[6]	19.84	641	3232	16[3]	Seaborg et al.	1940
Polonium	Po	84	210[6]	9.32	254	962	34	Curie	1898
Potassium	K	19	39.102	0.862	63.65	774	10	Davy	1807
Praseodymium	Pr	59	140.9077	6.772	931±4	3212	15	von Welsbach	1885
Promethium	Pm	61	145[6]	—	≈1080	2460?	14	Marinsky et al.	1945
Protactinium	Pa	91	231.0359	15.37[2]	<1600	—	14	Hahn and Meitner	1917
Radium	Ra	88	226.0254	5.0?	700	1140	15	P. and M. Curie	1898
Radon	Rn	86	222[6]	4.4[4]	−71	−61.8	20	Dorn	1900
Rhenium	Re	75	186.2	21.02	3180	5627[7]	21	Noddack, Berg, and Tacke	1925
Rhodium	Rh	45	102.9055	12.41	1966±3	3727±100	20	Wollaston	1803
Rubidium	Rb	37	85.4678	1.532	38.89	688	20	Bunsen and Kirchoff	1861
Ruthenium	Ru	44	101.07	12.44	2310	3900	16	Klaus	1844
Samarium	Sm	62	150.4	7.536	1072±5	1778	17	Boisbaudran	1879
Scandium	Sc	21	44.9559	2.989	1539	2832	15	Nilson	1879
Selenium	Se	34	78.96	4.79 (gray)	217	684.9±1	20	Berzelius	1817
Silicon	Si	14	28.086	2.33	1410	2355	8	Berzelius	1824
Silver	Ag	47	107.868	10.50	961.93	2212	27	Prehistoric	—
Sodium	Na	11	22.9898	0.971	97.81±0.03	882.9	7	Davy	1807
Strontium	Sr	38	87.62	2.54	769	1384	18	Davy	1808
Sulfur	S	16	32.06	2.07[11]	112.8	444.674	10	Prehistoric	—
Tantalum	Ta	73	180.9479	16.654	2996	5425±100	19	Ekeberg	1801
Technetium	Tc	43	98.9062	11.50[2]	2172	4877	23	Perrier and Segrè	1937
Tellurium	Te	52	127.60	6.24	449.5±0.3	989.8±3.8	29	von Reichenstein	1782
Terbium	Tb	65	158.9254	8.234	1360±4	3041	24	Mosander	1843
Thallium	Tl	81	204.37	11.85	303.5	1457±10	28	Crookes	1861
Thorium	Th	90	232.0381	11.72	1750	4790	12	Berzelius	1828
Thulium	Tm	69	168.9342	9.314	1545±15	1727	18	Cleve	1879
Tin	Sn	50	118.69	7.31 (white)	231.9681	2270	28	Prehistoric	—
Titanium	Ti	22	47.90	4.55	1660±10	3287	9	Gregor	1791
Tungsten (Wolfram)	W	74	183.85	19.3	3410±20	5660	22	J. and F. d'Elhuyar	1783
Uranium	U	92	238.029	–18.95	1132.3±0.8	3818	15	Peligot	1841
Vanadium	V	23	50.9414	6.11	1890±10	3380	9	del Rio	1801
Xenon	Xe	54	131.30	3.52[4]	−111.9	−107.1±3	31	Ramsay and Travers	1898
Ytterbium	Yb	70	173.04	6.972	824±5	1193	16	Marignac	1878
Yttrium	Y	39	88.9059	4.457	1523±8	3337	21	Gadolin	1794
Zinc	Zn	30	65.38	7.133	419.58	907	15	Prehistoric	—
Zirconium	Zr	40	91.22	6.506[2]	1852±2	4377	20	Klaproth	1789

Elements No. 104, 105, and 106—See NOTE at end of footnotes.

1. Isotopes are different forms of the same element having the same atomic number but different atomic weights. 2. Calculated figure. 3. Artificially produced. 4. Liquid. 5. Sublimation point. 6. Mass number of the isotope of longest known life. 7. Estimated. 8. Amorphous. 9. Depending on whether amorphous, graphite or diamond. 10. Depending on allotropic form. 11. Rhombic. —Is approximately. < Is less than. NOTE: There is a dispute between groups at the Lawrence Berkeley Laboratory of the University of California and at the Dubna Laboratory in the Soviet Union concerning the discovery of elements 104, 105, and 106. The Lawrence Berkeley Laboratory claims that 104 and 105 were discovered in 1969 and 1970, respectively, by Ghiorso et al. and has suggested the names Rutherfordium and Hahnium. The U.S. laboratory claims also that Ghiorso et al. discovered element 106 in 1974. No name has yet been suggested for this element. Names will not be official until the controversy is resolved and they have been approved by the International Union of Pure and Applied Chemistry.

Scientific Inventions, Discoveries, and Theories

Most inventions are the results of the discoveries, theories, experiments, and improvements of many people. This list tries to suggest the development of certain particularly important ideas. In some instances, it tries to connect the fundamental theory with the ultimate practical invention.

Abacus: *See* Calculating machine
Adding machine: *See* Calculating machine; Computer
Adrenaline: (isolation of) John Jacob Abel, U.S., 1897
Air brake: George Westinghouse, U.S., 1868
Air conditioning: Willis Carrier, U.S., 1911
Airplane: (first powered, sustained, controlled flight) Orville and Wilbur Wright, U.S., 1903. *See also* Jet propulsion, aircraft
Airship: (non-rigid) Henri Giffard, France, 1852; (rigid) Ferdinand von Zeppelin, Germany, 1900
Aluminum manufacture: (by electrolytic action) Charles M. Hall, U.S., 1866
Anesthetic: (first use of anesthetic—ether—on man) Crawford W. Long, U.S., 1842
Antibiotics: (first demonstration of antibiotic effect) Louis Pasteur, Jules-François Joubert, France, 1887; (penicillin, first modern antibiotic) Alexander Fleming, England, 1928
Antiseptic: (surgery) Joseph Lister, England, 1867
Antitoxin, diphtheria: Emil von Behring, Germany, 1890
Atomic theory: (ancient) Leucippus, Democritus, Greece, c.500 B.C.; Lucretius, Rome, c.100 B.C.; (modern) John Dalton, England, 1808
Automobile: (first with internal combustion engine, 250 rpm) Karl Benz, Germany, 1885; (first with practical high-speed internal combustion engine, 900 rpm) Gottlieb Daimler, Germany, 1885; (first true automobile, not carriage with motor) René Panhard, Emile Lavassor, France, 1891; (carburetor, spray) Charles E. Duryea, U.S., 1892
Bacteria: Anton van Leeuwenhoek, The Netherlands, 1683
Bakelite: *See* Plastics
Balloon, hot-air: Joseph and Jacques Montgolfier, France, 1783
Ball-point pen: *See* Pen
Barometer: Evangelista Torricelli, Italy, 1643
Bicycle: Karl D. von Sauerbronn, Germany, 1816; (first modern model) James Starley, England, 1884
Bifocal lens: *See* Lens, bifocal
Blood, circulation of: William Harvey, England, 1628
Braille: Louis Braille, France, 1829
Bullet: (conical) Claude Minié, France, 1849
Calculating machine: (Abacus) China, c.190; (logarithms: made multiplying easier and thus calculators practical) John Napier, Scotland, 1614; (slide rule) William Oughtred, England, 1632; (digital calculator) Blaise Pascal, 1642; (multiplication machine) Gottfried Leibnitz, Germany, 1671; (important 19th-century contributors to modern machine) Frank S. Baldwin, Jay R. Monroe, Dorr E. Felt, W. T. Ohdner, William Burroughs, all U.S.; ("analytical engine" design, included concepts of programming, taping) Charles Babbage, England, 1835. *See also* Computer
Camera: (hand-held) George Eastman, U.S., 1888; (Polaroid Land) Edwin Land, U.S., 1948. *See also* Photography
Carburetor: *See* Automobile
Celanese: *See* Fibers, man-made
Celluloid: *See* Plastics
Classification of plants and animals: (by genera and species) Carolus Linnaeus, Sweden, 1737–53
Clock, pendulum: Christian Huygens, The Netherlands, 1656
Combustion: (nature of) Antoine Lavoisier, France, 1777
Computer: (differential analyzer, mechanically operated) Vannevar Bush, U.S., 1928; (Mark I, first information-processing digital computer) Howard Aiken, U.S., 1944; (ENIAC, Electronic Numerical Integrator and Calculator, first all-electronic) J. Presper Eckert, John W. Mauchly, U.S., 1946; (stored-program concept) John von Neumann, U.S., 1947
Conditioned reflex: Ivan Pavlov, Russia, c.1910
Converter, Bessemer: William Kelly, U.S., 1851
Cosmetics: Egypt, c.4000 B.C.
Cotton gin: Eli Whitney, U.S., 1793
Crossbow: China, c.300 B.C.
Cyclotron: Ernest O. Lawrence, U.S., 1931
Deuterium: (heavy hydrogen) Harold Urey, U.S., 1931
DNA: (deoxyribonucleic acid) Friedrich Meischer, Germany, 1869; (determination of double-helical structure) F. H. Crick, England, James D. Watson, U.S., 1953
Dynamite: Alfred Nobel, Sweden, 1867
Electric generator (dynamo): (laboratory model) Michael Faraday, England, 1832; Joseph Henry, U.S., c.1832; (hand-driven model) Hippolyte Pixii, France, 1833; (alternating-current generator) Nikola Tesla, U.S., 1892
Electric lamp: (arc lamp) Sir Humphrey Davy, England, 1801; (fluorescent lamp) A. E. Becquerel, France, 1867; (incandescent lamp) Sir Joseph Swann, England, Thomas A. Edison, U.S., contemporaneously, 1870s; (carbon arc street lamp) Charles F. Brush, U.S., 1879; (first widely marketed incandescent lamp) Thomas A. Edison, U.S., 1879; (mercury vapor lamp) Peter Cooper Hewitt, U.S., 1903; (neon lamp) Georges Claude, France, 1911; (tungsten filament) Irving Langmuir, U.S., 1915
Electric motor: *See* Motor
Electromagnet: William Sturgeon, England, 1823
Electron: Sir Joseph J. Thompson, England, 1897
Elevator, passenger: (safety device permitting use by passengers) Elisha G. Otis, U.S., 1852; (elevator utilizing safety device) 1857
$E = mc^2$: (equivalence of mass and energy) Albert Einstein, Switzerland, 1907
Engine, internal combustion: No single inventor. Fundamental theory established by Sadi Carnot, France, 1824; (two-stroke) Étienne Lenoir, France, 1860; (ideal operating cycle for four-stroke) Alphonse Beau de Rochet, France, 1862; (operating four-stroke) Nikolaus Otto, Germany, 1876; (diesel) Rudolf Diesel, Germany, 1892; (rotary) Felix Wankel, Germany, 1956. *See also* Automobile
Engine, steam: *See* Steam engine
Evolution: (by natural selection) Charles Darwin, England, 1859
Falling bodies, law of: Galileo Galilei, Italy, 1590
Fermentation: (micro-organisms as cause of) Louis Pasteur, France, c.1860
Fibers, man-made: (nitrocellulose fibers treated to change flammable nitrocellulose to harmless cel-

lulose, precursor of rayon) Sir Joseph Swann, England, 1883; (rayon) Count Hilaire de Chardonnet, France, 1889; (Celanese) Henry and Camille Dreyfuss, U.S., England, 1921; (research on polyesters and polyamides, basis for modern man-made fibers) U.S., England, Germany, 1930s; (nylon) Wallace H. Carothers, U.S., 1935

Fountain pen: *See* Pen

Geometry, elements of: Euclid, Alexandria, Egypt, c.300 B.C.

Gravitation, law of: Sir Isaac Newton, England, c. 1665 (published 1687)

Gunpowder: China, c.700

Gyrocompass: Elmer A. Sperry, U.S., 1905

Gyroscope: Léon Foucault, France, 1852

Helicopter: Igor Sikorsky, U.S., 1939

Helium first observed on sun: Sir Joseph Lockyer, England, 1868

Heredity, laws of: Gregor Mendel, Austria, 1865

Induction, electric: Joseph Henry, U.S., 1828

Insulin: Sir Frederick G. Banting, J. J. R. MacLeod, Canada, 1922

Intelligence testing: Alfred Binet, Theodore Simon, France, 1905

Isotopes: (concept of) Frederick Soddy, England, 1912; (stable isotopes) J. J. Thompson, England, 1913; (existence demonstrated by mass spectrography) Francis W. Ashton, 1919

Jet propulsion, aircraft: Sir Frank Whittle, England, 1930

Laser: (theoretical work on) Charles H. Townes, Arthur L. Schawlow, U.S., N. Basov, A. Prokhorov, U.S.S.R., 1958; (first working model) T. H. Maiman, U.S., 1960

Lens, bifocal: Benjamin Franklin, U.S., c.1760

Light, nature of: (wave theory) Christian Huygens, Denmark, 1678; (electromagnetic theory) James Clerk Maxwell, England, 1873

Light, speed of: (theory that light has finite velocity) Olaus Roemer, Denmark, 1675

Lightning rod: Benjamin Franklin, U.S., 1752

Linotype: *See* Printing

Lithography: *See* Printing

Locomotive: (steam-powered) Richard Trevithick, England, 1804; (first practical, due to multiple-fire-tube boiler) George Stephenson, England, 1829; (largest steam-powered) Union Pacific's "Big Boy," U.S., 1941

Logarithms: *See* Calculating machine

Loom: (horizontal, two-beamed) Egypt, c.4400 B.C.; (Jacquard drawloom, pattern controlled by punch cards) Jacques de Vaucanson, France, 1745, Joseph-Marie Jacquard, 1801; (flying shuttle) John Kay, England, 1733; (power-driven loom) Edmund Cartwright, England, 1785

Machine gun: James Puckle, England, 1718; Richard J. Gatling, U.S., 1861

Match: (phosphorus) François Derosne, France, 1816; (friction) Charles Sauria, France, 1831; (safety) J. E. Lundstrom, Sweden, 1855

Mendelian law: *See* Heredity

Microscope: (compound) Zacharias Janssen, The Netherlands, 1590; (electron) Vladimir Zworykin et al., U.S., Canada, Germany, 1932–1939

Motion pictures: Thomas A. Edison, U.S., 1893

Motion pictures, sound: Product of various inventions. First picture with synchronized musical score: *Don Juan,* 1926; with spoken dialogue: *The Jazz Singer,* 1927; both Warner Bros.

Motor, electric: Michael Faraday, England, 1822; (alternating-current) Nikola Tesla, U.S., 1892

Motor, gasoline: *See* Engine, internal combustion

Motorcycle: (motor tricycle) Edward Butler, England, 1884; (gasoline-engine motorcycle) Gottieb Daimier, Germany, 1885

Neptunium: (first transuranic element, synthesis of) Edward M. McMillan, Philip H. Abelson, U.S., 1940

Neutron: James Chadwick, England, 1932

Neutron-induced radiation: Enrico Fermi et al., Italy, 1934

Nitroglycerin: Ascanio Sobrero, Italy, 1846

Nuclear fission: Otto Hahn, Fritz Strassmann, Germany, 1938

Nuclear reactor: Enrico Fermi et al., U.S., 1942

Nylon: *See* Fibers, man-made

Ohm's law: (relationship between strength of electric current, electromotive force, and circuit resistance) Georg S. Ohm, Germany, 1827

Ozone: Christian Schönbein, Germany, 1839

Paper: China, c.100 B.C.

Parachute: Louis S. Lenormand, France, 1783

Pen: (fountain) Lewis E. Waterman, U.S., 1884; (ball-point, for marking on rough surfaces) John H. Loud, U.S., 1888; (ball-point, for handwriting) Lazlo Biro, Argentina, 1944

Penicillin: *See* Antibiotics

Periodic law: (that properties of elements are functions of their atomic weights) Dmitri Mendeleev, Russia, 1869

Periodic table: (arrangement of chemical elements based on periodic law) Dmitri Mendeleev, Russia, 1869

Phonograph: Thomas A. Edison, U.S., 1877

Photography: (first paper negative, first photograph, on metal) Joseph Nicéphore Niepce, France, 1816–1827; (discovery of fixative powers of hyposulfite of soda) Sir John Herschel, England, 1819; (first direct positive image on silver plate, the daguerreotype) Louis Daguerre, based on work with Niepce, France, 1839; (first paper negative from which a number of positive prints could be made) William Talbot, England, 1841. Work of these four men, taken together, forms basis for all modern photography. (First color images) Alexandre Becquerel, Claude Niepce de Saint-Victor, France, 1848–60; (commercial color film with three emulsion layers, Kodachrome) U.S., 1935. *See also* Camera

Plastics: (first material, nitrocellulose softened by vegetable oil, camphor, precursor to Celluloid) Alexander Parkes, England, 1855; (Celluloid, involving recognition of vital effect of camphor) John W. Hyatt, U.S., 1869; (Bakelite, first completely synthetic plastic) Leo H. Baekeland, U.S., 1910; (theoretical background of macromolecules and process of polymerization on which modern plastics industry rests) Hermann Staudinger, Germany, 1922. *See also* Fibers, man-made

Plow, forked: Mesopotamia, before 3000 B.C.

Plutonium, synthesis of: Glenn T. Seaborg, Edwin M. McMillan, Arthur C. Wahl, Joseph W. Kennedy, U.S., 1941

Polaroid Land camera: *See* Camera

Polio, vaccine against: (vaccine made from dead virus strains) Jonas E. Salk, U.S., 1954; (vaccine made from live virus strains) Albert Sabin, U.S., 1960

Positron: Carl D. Anderson, U.S., 1932

Pressure cooker: (early version) Denis Papin, France, 1679

Printing: (block) Japan, c.700; (movable type) Korea, c.1400; Johann Gutenberg, Germany, c. 1450 (lithography, offset) Aloys Senefelder, Germany, 1796; (rotary press) Richard Hoe, U.S., 1844; (linotype) Ottman Mergenthaler, U.S. 1884

Programming, information: *See* Calculating machine

Propeller, screw: Sir Francis P. Smith, England, 1836; John Ericsson, England, worked independently of and simultaneously with Smith, 1837

Proton: Ernest Rutherford, England, 1919

Psychoanalysis: Sigmund Freud, Austria, c.1904

Quantum theory: Max Planck, Germany, 1901

Rabies immunization: Louis Pasteur, France, 1885

Radar: (limited to one-mile range) Christian Hulsmeyer, Germany, 1904; (pulse modulation, used for measuring height of ionosphere) Gregory Breit, Merle Tuve, U.S., 1925; (first practical radar—radio detection and ranging) Sir Robert Watson-Watt, England, 1934–35

Radio: (electromagnetism, theory of) James Clerk Maxwell, England, 1873; (spark coil, generator of electromagnetic waves) Heinrich Hertz, Germany, 1886; (first practical system of wireless telegraphy) Guglielmo Marconi, Italy, 1895; (vacuum electron tube, basis for radio telephony) Sir John Fleming, England, 1904; (triode amplifying tube) Lee de Forest, U.S., 1906; (regenerative circuit, allowing long-distance sound reception) Edwin H. Armstrong, U.S., 1912; (frequency modulation—FM) Edwin H. Armstrong, U.S., 1933

Radioactivity: (X-rays) Wilhelm K. Roentgen, Germany, 1895; (radioactivity of uranium) Henri Becquerel, France, 1896; (radioactive elements, radium and polonium in uranium ore) Marie Sklodowska-Curie, Pierre Curie, France, 1898; (classification of alpha and beta particle radiation) Pierre Curie, France, 1900; (gamma radiation) Paul-Ulrich Villard, France, 1900; (carbon dating) Willard F. Libby et al., U.S., 1955

Rayon: *See* Fibers, man-made

Reaper: Cyrus McCormick, U.S., 1834

Relativity: (special and general theories of) Albert Einstein, Switzerland, Germany, U.S., 1905–53

Revolver: Samuel Colt, U.S., 1835

Rifle: (muzzle-loaded) Italy, Germany, c.1475; (breech-loaded) England, France, Germany, U.S., c.1866; (bolt-action) Paul von Mauser, Germany, 1889; (automatic) John Browning, U.S., 1918

Roller bearing: (wooden for cartwheel) Germany or France, c.100 B.C.

Rubber: (vulcanization process) Charles Goodyear, U.S., 1839

Safety match: *See* Match

Solar system, universe: (sun-centered universe) Nicolaus Copernicus, Warsaw, 1543; (establishment of planetary orbits as elliptical) Johannes Kepler, Germany, 1609; (infinity of universe) Giordano Bruno, Italian monk, 1584

Spectrum: (heterogeneity of light) Sir Isaac Newton, England, 1665–66

Spermatozoa: Anton van Leeuwenhoek, The Netherlands, 1683

Spinning: (spinning wheel) India, introduced to Europe in Middle Ages; (Saxony wheel, continuous spinning of wool or cotton yarn) England, c.1500–1600; (spinning jenny) James Hargreaves, England, 1764; (spinning frame) Sir Richard Arkwright, England, 1769; (spinning mule, completed mechanization of spinning, permitting production of yarn to keep up with demands of modern looms) Samuel Crompton, England, 1779

Steam engine: (first commercial version based on principles of French physicist Denis Papin) Thomas Savery, England, 1639; (atmospheric steam engine) Thomas Newcomen, England, 1705; (steam engine for pumping water from collieries) Savery, Newcomen, 1725; (modern condensing, doubleacting) James Watt, England, 1782

Steam engine, railroad: *See* Locomotive

Steamship: Claude de Jouffroy d'Abbans, France, 1783; James Rumsey, U.S., 1787; John Fitch, U.S., 1790. All preceded Robert Fulton, U.S., 1807, credited with launching first commercially successful steamship

Sulfa drugs: (parent compound, para-aminobenzenesulfanomide) Paul Gelmo, Austria, 1908; (antibacterial activity) Gerhard Domagk, Germany, 1935

Syphilis, test for: *See* Wassermann test

Tank, military: Sir Ernest Swinton, England, 1914

Telegraph: Samuel F. B. Morse, U.S., 1837

Telephone: Alexander Graham Bell, U.S., 1876

Telescope: Hans Lippershey, The Netherlands, 1608

Television: (mechanical disk-scanning method) successfully demonstrated by J. L. Baird, England, C. F. Jenkins, U.S., 1926; (electronic scanning method) Vladimir K. Zworykin, U.S., 1928; (color, all-electronic) Zworykin, 1925; (color, mechanical disk) Baird, 1928; (color, compatible with black and white) George Valensi, France, 1938; (color, sequential rotating filter) Peter Goldmark, U.S., first introduced, 1951; (color, compatible with black and white) commercially introduced in U.S., National Television Systems Committee, 1953

Thermometer: (open-column) Galileo Galilei, c. 1593; (clinical) Santorio Santorio, Padua, c. 1615; (mercury, also Fahrenheit scale) Gabriel D. Fahrenheit, Germany, 1714; (centigrade scale) Anders Celsius, Sweden, 1742; (absolute-temperature, or Kelvin, scale) William Thompson, Lord Kelvin, England, 1848

Tire, pneumatic: Robert W. Thompson, England, 1845; (bicycle tire) John B. Dunlop, Northern Ireland, 1888

Toilet, flush: Product of Minoan civilization, Crete, c.2000 B.C. Alleged invention by "Thomas Crapper" is untrue.

Tractor: Benjamin Holt, U.S., 1900

Transformer, electric: William Stanley, U.S., 1885

Transistor: John Bardeen, William Shockley, Walter Brattain, U.S., 1948

Uncertainty principle: (that position and velocity of an object cannot both be measured exactly, at the same time) Werner Heisenberg, Germany, 1927

Vaccination: Edward Jenner, England, 1796

Vacuum tube: *See* Radio

Van Allen (radiation) Belt: (around the earth) James Van Allen, U.S., 1958

Vitamins: (hypothesis of disease deficiency) Sir F. G. Hopkins, Casimir Funk, England, 1912; (vitamin A) Elmer V. McCollum, M. Davis, U.S., 1912–14; (vitamin B) Elmer V. McCollum, U.S., 1915–16; (thiamin, B_1) Casimir Funk, England, 1912; (riboflavin, B_2) D. T. Smith, E. G. Hendrick, U.S., 1926; (niacin) Conrad Elvehjem, U.S., 1937; (B_6) Paul Gyorgy, U.S., 1934; (vitamin C) C. A. Hoist, T. Froelich, Norway, 1912; (vitamin D) Elmer V. McCollum, U.S., 1922; (folic acid) Lucy Wills, England, 1933

Wassermann test: (for syphilis) August von Wassermann, Germany, 1906

Weaving, cloth: *See* Loom

Wheel: (cart, solid wood) Mesopotamia, c.3800–3600 B.C.

Windmill: Persia, c.600

X-ray: *See* Radioactivity

Xerography: Chester Carlson, U.S., 1938

Zero: India, c.600; (absolute zero, cessation of all molecular energy) William Thompson, Lord Kelvin, England, 1848

WEIGHTS & MEASURES

Measures and Weights

Source: Department of Commerce, National Bureau of Standards.

The International System (Metric)

The International System of Units is a modernized version of the metric system, established by international agreement, i.e. provides a logical and interconnected framework for all measurements in science, industry, and commerce. The system is built on a foundation of seven basic units, and all other units are derived from them. (Use of metric weights and measures was legalized in the United States in 1866, and our customary units of weights and measures are defined in terms of the meter and kilogram.)

Length. Meter. The meter is defined as 1,650,763.73 wavelengths in vacuum of the orange-red line of the spectrum of krypton-86.

Time. Second. The second is defined as the duration of 9,192,631,770 cycles of the radiation associated with a specified transition of the cesium 133 atom.

Mass. Kilogram. The standard for the kilogram is a cylinder of platinum-iridium alloy kept by the International Bureau of Weights and Measures at Paris. A duplicate at the National Bureau of Standards serves as the mass standard for the United States. The kilogram is the only base unit still defined by a physical object.

Temperature. Kelvin. The kelvin is defined as the fraction 1/273.16 of the thermodynamic temperature of the triple point of water; that is, the point at which water forms an interface of solid, liquid and vapor. This is defined as 0.01° C on the Centigrade or Celsius scale and 32.02° F on the Fahrenheit scale. The temperature 0° K is called "absolute zero."

Electric Current. Ampere. The ampere is defined as that current that, if maintained in each of two long parallel wires separated by one meter in free space, would produce a force between the two wires (due to their magnetic fields) of 2×10^{-7} newton for each meter of length. (A newton is the unit of force which when applied to one kilogram mass would experience an acceleration of one meter per second per second.)

Luminous Intensity. Candela. The candela is defined as the luminous intensity of 1/600,000 of a square meter of a cavity at the temperature of freezing platinum (2,042K).

Amount of Substance. Mole. The mole is the amount of substance of a system that contains as many elementary entities as there are atoms in 0.012 kilogram of carbon-12.

Tables of Metric Weights and Measures

LINEAR MEASURE

10 millimeters (mm) =	1 centimeter (cm)
10 centimeters =	1 decimeter (dm) = 100 millimeters
10 decimeters =	1 meter (m) = 1,000 millimeters
10 meters =	1 dekameter (dam)
10 dekameters =	1 hectometer (hm) = 100 meters
10 hectometers =	1 kilometer (km) = 1,000 meters

AREA MEASURE

100 square millimeters (mm^2) =	1 sq centimeter (cm^2)
10,000 square centimeters =	1 sq meter (m^2) = 1,000,000 sq millimeters
100 square meters =	1 are (a)
100 ares =	1 hectare (ha) = 10,000 sq meters
100 hectares =	1 sq kilometer (km^2) = 1,000,000 sq meters

VOLUME MEASURE

10 milliliters (ml) =	1 centiliter (cl)
10 centiliters =	1 deciliter (dl) = 100 milliliters
10 deciliters =	1 liter (1) = 1,000 milliliters
10 liters =	1 dekaliter (dal)
10 dekaliters =	1 hectoliter (hl) = 100 liters
10 hectoliters =	1 kiloliter (kl) = 1,000 liters

CUBIC MEASURE

1,000 cubic millimeters (mm^3) =	1 cu centimeter (cm^3)
1,000 cubic centimeters =	1 cu decimeter (dm^3) = 1,000,000 cu millimeters
1,000 cubic decimeters =	1 cu meter (m^3) = 1 stere = 1,000,000 cu centimeters = 1,000,000,000 cu millimeters

WEIGHT

10 milligrams (mg) =	1 centigram (cg)
10 centigrams =	1 decigram (dg) = 100 milligrams
10 decigrams =	1 gram (g) = 1,000 milligrams
10 grams =	1 dekagram (dag)
10 dekagrams =	1 hectogram (hg) = 100 grams
10 hectograms =	1 kilogram (kg) = 1,000 grams
1,000 kilograms =	1 metric ton (t)

Tables of Customary U.S. Weights and Measures

LINEAR MEASURE

12 inches (in.) =	1 foot (ft)
3 feet =	1 yard (yd)
5 1/2 yards =	1 rod (rd), pole, or perch (16 1/2 ft)
40 rods =	1 furlong (fur) = 220 yds = 660 ft
8 furlongs =	1 statute mile (mi.) = 1,760 yds = 5,280 ft
3 land miles =	1 league
5,280 feet =	1 statute or land mile
6,076.11549 feet =	1 international nautical mile

AREA MEASURE

144 square inches =	1 sq ft
9 square feet =	1 sq yd = 1,296 sq in.
30 1/4 square yards =	1 sq rd = 272 1/4 sq ft
160 square rods =	1 acre = 4,840 sq yds = 43,560 sq ft
640 acres =	1 sq mi.
1 mile square =	1 section (of land)
6 miles square =	1 township = 36 sections = 36 sq mi.

CUBIC MEASURE

1,728 cubic inches =	1 cu ft
27 cubic feet =	1 cu yd

LIQUID MEASURE

When necessary to distinguish the liquid pint or quart from the dry pint or quart, the word "liquid" or the abbreviation "liq" should be used in combination with the name or abbreviation of the liquid unit.

4 gills (gi) =	1 pint (pt) (= 28.875 cu in.)
2 pints =	1 quart (qt) (= 57.75 cu in.)
4 quarts =	1 gallon (gal) (= 231 cu in.) = 8 pts = 32 gills

APOTHECARIES' FLUID MEASURE

60 minims (min.) =	1 fluid dram (fl dr) (= 0.2256 cu in.)
8 fluid drams =	1 fluid ounce (fl oz) (= 1.8047 cu in.)
16 fluid ounces =	1 pt (= 28.875 cu in.) = 128 fl drs
2 pints =	1 qt (= 57.75 cu in.) = 32 fl oz = 256 fl drs
4 quarts =	1 gal (= 231 cu in.) = 128 fl oz = 1,024 fl drs

DRY MEASURE

When necessary to distinguish the dry pint or quart from the liquid pint or quart; the word "dry" should be used in combination with the name or abbreviation of the dry unit.

2 pints =	1 qt (=67.2006 cu in.)
8 quarts =	1 peck (pk) (=537.605 cu in.) = 16 pts
4 pecks =	1 bushel (bu) (= 2,150.42 cu in.) = 32 qts

AVOIRDUPOIS WEIGHT

When necessary to distinguish the avoirdupois dram from the apothecaries dram, or to distinguish the avoirdupois dram or ounce from the fluid dram or ounce, or to distinguish the avoirdupois ounce or pound from the troy or apothecaries ounce or pound, the word "avoirdupois" or the abbreviation "avdp" should be used in combination with the name or abbreviation of the avoirdupois unit.

(The "grain" is the same in avoirdupois, troy, and apothecaries weights.)

27 11/32 grains =	1 dram (dr)
16 drams =	1 oz = 437 1/2 grains
16 ounces =	1 lb = 256 drams = 7,000 grains
100 pounds =	1 hundredweight (cwt)[1]
20 hundredweights =	1 ton (tn) = 2,000 lbs[1]

In "gross" or "long" measure, the following values are recognized:

112 pounds =	1 gross or long cwt[1]
20 gross or long hundredweights =	1 gross or long ton = 2,240 lbs[1]

1. When the terms "hundredweight" and "ton" are used unmodified, they are commonly understood to mean the 100-pound hundredweight and the 2,000-pound ton, respectively; these units may be designated "net" or "short" when necessary to distinguish them from the corresponding units in gross or long measure.

UNITS OF CIRCULAR MEASURE

Second (″) =	—
Minute (′) =	60 seconds
Degree (°) =	60 minutes
Right angle =	90 degrees
Straight angle =	180 degrees
Circle =	360 degrees

TROY WEIGHT

24 grains =	1 pennyweight (dwt)
20 pennyweights =	1 ounce troy (oz t) = 480 grains
12 ounces troy =	1 pound troy (lb t) = 240 pennyweights = 5,760 grains

APOTHECARIES' WEIGHT

20 grains =	1 scruple (s ap)
3 scruples =	1 dram apothecaries' (dr ap) = 60 grains
8 drams apothecaries =	1 ounce apothecaries' (oz ap) = 24 scruples = 480 grains
12 ounces apothecaries =	1 pound apothecaries' (lb ap) = 96 drams apothecaries' = 288 scruples = 5,760 grains

GUNTER'S OR SURVEYOR'S CHAIN MEASURE

7.92 inches =	1 link (li)
100 links =	1 chain (ch) = 4 rods = 66 ft
80 chains =	1 statute mile = 320 rods = 5,280 ft

Metric and U.S. Equivalents

1 angstrom[1] (light wave measurement)	0.1 millimicron 0.000 1 micron 0.000 000 1 millimeter 0.000 000 004 inch
1 cable's length	120 fathoms 720 feet 219.456 meters
1 centimeter	0.3937 inch
1 chain (Gunter's or surveyor's)	66 feet 20.1168 meters
1 decimeter	3.937 inches
1 dekameter	32.808 feet
1 fathom	6 feet 1.8288 meters
1 foot	0.3048 meter
1 furlong	10 chains (surveyor's) 660 feet 220 yards 1/8 statute mile 201.168 meters

1 inch	2.54 centimeters
1 kilometer	0.621 mile
1 league (land)	3 statute miles 4.828 kilometers
1 link (Gunter's or surveyor's)	7.92 inches 0.201 168 meter
1 meter	39.37 inches 1.094 yards
1 micron	0.001 millimeter 0.000 039 37 inch
1 mil	0.001 inch 0.025 4 millimeter
1 mile (statute or land)	5,280 feet 1.609 kilometers
1 mile (nautical international)	1.852 kilometers 1.151 statute miles 0.999 U.S. nautical miles
1 millimeter	0.03937 inch
1 millimicron (mμ)	0.001 micron 0.000 000 039 37 inch
1 nanometer	0.001 micrometer or 0.000 000 039 37 inch
1 point (typography)	0.013 837 inch 1/72 inch (approximately) 0.351 millimeter
1 rod, pole, or perch	16 1/2 feet 5.0292 meters
1 yard	0.9144 meter

AREAS OR SURFACES

1 acre	43,560 square feet 4,840 square yards 0.405 hectare
1 are	119.599 square yards 0.025 acre
1 hectare	2.471 acres
1 square centimeter	0.155 square inch
1 square decimeter	15.5 square inches
1 square foot	929.030 square centimeters
1 square inch	6.4516 square centimeters
1 square kilometer	0.386 square mile 247.105 acres
1 square meter	1.196 square yards 10.764 square feet
1 square mile	258.999 hectares
1 square millimeter	0.002 square inch
1 square rod, square pole or square perch	25.293 square meters
1 square yard	0.836 square meters

CAPACITIES OR VOLUMES

1 barrel, liquid	31 to 42 gallons[2]
1 barrel, standard for fruits, vegetables, and other dry commodities except cranberries	7,056 cubic inches 105 dry quarts 3.281 bushels, struck measure
1 barrel, standard, cranberry	5.286 cubic inches 86 45/64 dry quarts 2.709 bushels, struck measure
1 bushel (U.S.) struck measure	2,150.42 cubic inches 35.238 liters
1 bushel, heaped (U.S.)	2,747.715 cubic inches 1.278 bushels, struck measure[3]
1 cord (firewood)	128 cubic feet
1 cubic centimeter	0.061 cubic inch
1 cubic decimeter	61.024 cubic inches
1 cubic foot	7.481 gallons 28.316 cubic decimeters
1 cubic inch	0.554 fluid ounce 4.433 fluid drams 16.387 cubic centimeters
1 cubic meter	1.308 cubic yards
1 cubic yard	0.765 cubic meter
1 cup, measuring	8 fluid ounces 1/2 liquid pint
1 dram, fluid or liquid (U.S.)	1/8 fluid ounces 0.226 cubic inch 3.697 milliliters 1.041 British fluid drachms
1 dekaliter	2.642 gallons 1.135 pecks
1 gallon (U.S.)	231 cubic inches 3.785 liters 0.833 British gallon 128 U.S. fluid ounces
1 gallon (British Imperial)	277.42 cubic inches 1.201 U.S. gallons 4.546 liters 160 British fluid ounces
1 gill	7.219 cubic inches 4 fluid ounces 0.118 liter
1 hectoliter	26.418 gallons 2.838 bushels
1 liter	1.057 liquid quarts 0.908 dry quart 61.024 cubic inches
1 milliliter	0.271 fluid dram 16.231 minims 0.061 cubic inch
1 ounce, fluid or liquid (U.S.)	1.805 cubic inch 29.574 milliliters 1.041 British fluid ounces

1 peck	8.810 liters
1 pint, dry	33.600 cubic inches 0.551 liter
1 pint, liquid	28.875 cubic inches 0.473 liter
1 quart, dry (U.S.)	67.201 cubic inches 1.101 liters 0.969 British quart
1 quart, liquid (U.S.)	57.75 cubic inches 0.946 liter 0.833 British quart
1 quart (British)	69.354 cubic inches 1.032 U.S. dry quarts 1.201 U.S. liquid quarts
1 tablespoon, measuring	3 teaspoons 4 fluid drams 1/2 fluid ounce
1 teaspoon, measuring	1/3 tablespoon 1 1/3 fluid drams
1 assay ton[4]	29.167 grams
1 carat	200 milligrams 3.086 grains
1 dram, apothecaries'	60 grains 3.888 grams
1 dram, avoirdupois	27 11/32 (=27.344) grains 1.772 grams
1 grain	64.798 91 milligrams
1 gram	15.432 grains 0.035 ounce, avoirdupois
1 hundredweight, gross or long[5]	112 pounds 50.802 kilograms
1 hundredweight, net or short	100 pounds 45.359 kilograms
1 kilogram	2.205 pounds
1 microgram [μg (the Greek letter mu in combination with the letter g)]	0.000 001 gram
1 milligram	0.015 grain
1 ounce, avoirdupois	437.5 grains 0.911 troy or apothecaries ounce 28.350 grams
1 ounce, troy or apothecaries	480 grains 1.097 avoirdupois ounces 31.103 grams
1 pennyweight	1.555 grams
1 point	0.01 carat 2 milligrams
1 pound, avoirdupois	7,000 grains 1.215 troy or apothecaries pounds 453.592 37 grams
1 pound, troy or apothecaries	5,760 grains 0.823 avoirdupois pound 373.242 grams
1 ton, gross or long[5]	2,240 pounds 1.12 net tons 1.016 metric tons
1 ton, metric	2,204.623 pounds 0.984 gross ton 1.102 net tons
1 ton, net or short	2,000 pounds 0.893 gross ton 0.907 metric ton

1. The angstrom is basically defined as 10^{-10} meter. 2. There is a variety of "barrels" established by law or usage. For example, federal taxes on fermented liquors are based on a barrel of 31 gallons; many state laws fix the "barrel for liquids" at 31 1/2 gallons; one state fixes a 36-gallon barrel for cistern measurement; federal law recognizes a 40-gallon barrel for "proof spirits"; by custom, 42 gallons comprise a barrel of crude oil or petroleum products for statistical purposes, and this equivalent is recognized "for liquids" by four states. 3. Frequently recognized as 1 1/4 bushels, struck measure. 4. Used in assaying. The assay ton bears the same relation to the milligram that a ton of 2,000 pounds avoirdupois bears to the ounce troy; hence the weight in milligrams of precious metal obtained from one assay ton of ore gives directly the number of troy ounces to the net ton. 5. The gross or long ton and hundredweight are used commercially in the United States to only a limited extent, usually in restricted industrial fields. These units are the same as the British "ton" and "hundredweight."

Miscellaneous Units of Measure

Acre: An area of 43,560 square feet. Originally, the area a yoke of oxen could plow in one day.

Agate: Originally a measurement of type size (5 1/2 points). Now equal to 1/14 inch. Used in printing for measuring column length.

Ampere: Unit of electric current. A potential difference of one volt across a resistance of one ohm produces a current of one ampere.

Astronomical Unit (A.U.): 93,000,000 miles, the average distance of the earth from the sun. Used in astronomy.

Bale: A large bundle of goods. In the U.S., the approximate weight of a bale of cotton is 500 pounds. The weight varies in other countries.

Board Foot (fbm): 144 cubic inches (12 in. × 12 in. × 1 in.). Used for lumber.

Bolt: 40 yards. Used for measuring cloth.

Btu: British thermal unit. Amount of heat needed to increase the temperature of one pound of water by one degree Fahrenheit (252 calories).

Carat (c): 200 milligrams or 3.086 grains troy.

Originally the weight of a seed of the carob tree in the Mediterranean region. Used for weighing precious stones. *See also* Karat.

Chain (ch): a chain 66 feet or one-tenth of a furlong in length, divided into 100 parts called links. One mile is equal to 80 chains. Used in surveying and sometimes called Gunter's or surveyor's chain.

Cubit: 18 inches or 45.72 cm. Derived from distance between elbow and tip of middle finger.

Decibel: Unit of relative loudness. One decibel is the smallest amount of change detectable by the human ear.

Ell, English: 1 1/4 yards or 1/32 bolt. Used for measuring cloth.

Freight Ton (also called Measurement Ton): 40 cubic feet of merchandise. Used for cargo freight.

Great Gross: 12 gross or 1728.

Gross: 12 dozen or 144.

Hand: 4 inches or 10.16 cm. Derived from the width of the hand. Used for measuring the height of horses at withers.

Hertz: Modern unit for measurement of electromagnetic wave frequencies (equivalent to "cycles per second").

Hogshead (hhd): 2 liquid barrels or 14,653 cubic inches.

Horsepower: The power needed to lift 33,000 pounds a distance of one foot in one minute (about 1 1/2 times the power an average horse can exert). Used for measuring power of steam engines, etc.

Karat (kt): A measure of the purity of gold, indicating how many parts out of 24 are pure. For example, 18 karat gold is 3/4 pure. Sometimes spelled *carat.*

Knot: Not a distance, but the rate of speed of one nautical mile per hour. Used for measuring speed of ships.

League: Rather indefinite and varying measure, but usually estimated at 3 miles in English-speaking countries.

Light-Year: 5,880,000,000,000 miles, the distance light travels in a year at the rate of 186,281.7 miles per second. (If an astronomical unit were represented by one inch, a light-year would be represented by about one mile.) Used for measurements in interstellar space.

Magnum: Two-quart bottle. Used for measuring wine, etc.

Ohm: Unit of electrical resistance. A circuit in which a potential difference of one volt produces a current of one ampere has a resistance of one ohm.

Parsec: Approximately 3.26 light-years of 19.2 trillion miles. Term is combination of first syllables of *par*allax and *sec*ond, and distance is that of imaginary star when lines drawn from it to both earth and sun form a maximum angle or parallax of one second (1/3600 degree). Used for measuring interstellar distances.

Pi (π): 3.14159265+. The ratio of the circumference of a circle to its diameter. For practical purposes, the value is used to four decimal places: 3.1416.

Pica: 1/6 inch or 12 points. Used in printing for measuring column width, etc.

Pipe: 2 hogsheads. Used for measuring wine and other liquids.

Point: .013837 (approximately 1/72) inch or 1/12 pica. Used in printing for measuring type size.

Quintal: 100,000 grams or 220.46 pounds avoirdupois.

Quire: Used for measuring paper. Sometimes 24 sheets but more often 25. There are 20 quires in a ream.

Ream: Used for measuring paper. Sometimes 480 sheets, but more often 500 sheets.

Roentgen: Dosage unit of radiation exposure produced by X-rays.

Score: 20 units.

Sound, Speed of: Usually placed at 1,088 ft per second at 32° F at sea level. It varies at other temperatures and in different media.

Span: 9 inches or 22.86 cm. Derived from the distance between the end of the thumb and the end of the little finger when both are outstretched.

Square: 100 square feet. Used in building.

Stone: Legally 14 pounds avoirdupois in Great Britain.

Therm: 100,000 Btu's.

Township: U. S. land measurement of almost 36 square miles. The south border is 6 miles long. The east and west borders, also 6 miles long, follow the meridians, making the north border slightly less than 6 miles long. Used in surveying.

Tun: 252 gallons, but often larger. Used for measuring wine and other liquids.

Watt: Unit of power. The power used by a current of one ampere across a potential difference of one volt equals one watt.

Kelvin Scale

Absolute zero, −273.16° on the Celsius (Centigrade) scale, is 0° Kelvin. Thus, degrees Kelvin are equivalent to degrees Celsius plus 273.16. The freezing point of water, 0° C. and 32° F., is 273.16° K. The conversion formula is $K^\circ = C^\circ + 273.16$.

Conversion of Miles to Kilometers and Kilometers to Miles

Miles	Kilometers	Miles	Kilometers	Miles	Kilometers	Kilometers	Miles	Kilometers	Miles	Kilometers	Miles
1	1.6	8	12.8	60	96.5	1	0.6	8	4.9	60	37.2
2	3.2	9	14.4	70	112.6	2	1.2	9	5.5	70	43.4
3	4.8	10	16.0	80	128.7	3	1.8	10	6.2	80	49.7
4	6.4	20	32.1	90	144.8	4	2.4	20	12.4	90	55.9
5	8.0	30	48.2	100	160.9	5	3.1	30	18.6	100	62.1
6	9.6	40	64.3	1,000	1609	6	3.7	40	24.8	1,000	621
7	11.2	50	80.4			7	4.3	50	31.0		

Bolts and Screws: Conversion from Fractions of an Inch to Millimeters

Inch	mm	Inch	mm	Inch	mm	Inch	mm
1/64	0.40	17/64	6.75	33/64	13.10	49/64	19.45
1/32	0/79	9/32	7.14	17/32	13.50	25/32	19.84
3/64	1.19	19/64	7.54	35/64	13.90	51/64	20.24
1/16	1.59	5/16	7.94	9/16	14.29	13/16	20.64
5/64	1.98	21/64	8.33	37/64	14.69	53/64	21.03
3/32	2.38	11/32	8.73	19/32	15.08	27/32	21.43
7/64	2.78	23/64	9.13	39/64	15.48	55/64	21.83
1/8	3.18	3/8	9.53	5/8	15.88	7/8	22.23
9/64	3.57	25/64	9.92	41/64	16.27	57/64	22.62
5/32	3.97	13/32	10.32	21/32	16.67	29/32	23.02
11/64	4.37	27/64	10.72	43/64	17.06	59/64	23.42
3/16	4.76	7/16	11.11	11/64	17.46	15/16	23.81
13/64	5.16	29/64	11.51	45/64	17.86	61/64	24.21
7/32	5.56	15/32	11.91	23/32	18.26	31/32	24.61
15/64	5.95	31/64	12.30	47/64	18.65	63/64	25.00
1/4	6.35	1/2	12.70	3/4	19.05	1	25.40

U.S.—Metric Cooking Conversions

U.S. customary system				Metric			
Capacity		Weight		Capacity		Weight	
1/5 teaspoon	1 milliliter	1 fluid oz	30 milliliters	1 milliliter	1/5 teaspoon	1 gram	.035 ounce
1 teaspoon	5 ml		28 grams	5 ml	1 teaspoon	100 grams	3.5 ounces
1 tablespoon	15 ml	1 pound	454 grams	15 ml	1 tablespoon	500 grams	1.10 pounds
1/5 cup	50 ml			34 ml	1 fluid oz	1 kilogram	2.205 pounds
1 cup	240 ml						35 oz
2 cups (1 pint)	470 ml			100 ml	3.4 fluid oz		
4 cups (1 quart)	.95 liter			240 ml	1 cup		
4 quarts (1 gal.)	3.8 liters			1 liter	34 fluid oz		
					4.2 cups		
					2.1 pints		
					1.06 quarts		
					0.26 gallon		

Cooking Measurement Equivalents

16 tablespoons = 1 cup
12 tablespoons = 3/4 cup
10 tablespoons + 2 teaspoons = 2/3 cup
8 tablespoons = 1/2 cup
6 tablespoons = 3/8 cup
5 tablespoons + 1 teaspoon = 1/3 cup
4 tablespoons = 1/4 cup
2 tablespoons = 1/8 cup
2 tablespoons + 2 teaspoons = 1/6 cup
1 tablespoon = 1/16 cup
2 cups = 1 pint
2 pints = 1 quart
3 teaspoons = 1 tablespoon
48 teaspoons = 1 cup

Prefixes and Multiples

Prefix	Symbol	Equivalent	Multiple/ submultiple	Prefix	Symbol	Equivalent	Multiple/ submultiple
atto	a	quintillionth part	10^{-18}	deci	d	tenth part	10^{-1}
femto	f	quadrillionth part	10^{-15}	deka	da	tenfold	10
pico	p	trillionth part	10^{-12}	hecto	h	hundredfold	10^{2}
nano	n	billionth part	10^{-9}	kilo	k	thousandfold	10^{3}
micro	μ	millionth part	10^{-6}	mega	M	millionfold	10^{6}
milli	m	thousandth part	10^{-3}	giga	G	billionfold	10^{9}
centi	c	hundredth part	10^{-2}	tera	T	trillionfold	10^{12}

Common Formulas

Circumference

Circle: $C=\pi d$, in which π is 3.1416 and d the diameter.

Area

Triangle: $A=\frac{ab}{2}$, in which a is the base and b the height.

Square: $A=a^2$, in which a is one of the sides.

Rectangle: $A=ab$, in which a is the base and b the height.

Trapezoid: $A=\frac{h(a+b)}{2}$, in which h is the height, a the longer parallel side, and b the shorter.

Regular pentagon: $A=1.720a^2$, in which a is one of the sides.

Regular hexagon: $A=2.598a^2$, in which a is one of the sides.

Regular octagon: $A=4.828a^2$, in which a is one of the sides.

Circle: $A=\pi r^2$, in which π is 3.1416 and r the radius.

Volume

Cube: $V=a^3$, in which a is one of the edges.

Rectangular prism: $V=abc$, in which a is the length, b the width, and c the depth.

Pyramid: $V=\frac{Ah}{3}$, in which A is the area of the base and h the height.

Cylinder: $V=\pi r^2 h$, in which π is 3.1416, r the radius of the base, and h the height.

Cone: $V=\frac{\pi r^2 h}{3}$, in which π is 3.1416, r the radius of the base, and h the height.

Sphere: $V=\frac{4\pi r^3}{3}$, in which π is 3.1416 and r the radius.

Miscellaneous

Distance in feet traveled by falling body: $d=16t^2$, in which t is the time in seconds.

Speed of sound in feet per second through any given temperature of air: $V=\frac{1087\sqrt{273+t}}{16.52}$, in which t is the temperature Centigrade.

Cost in cents of operation of electrical device: $C=\frac{Wtc}{1000}$, in which W is the number of watts, t the time in hours, and c the cost in cents per kilowatt-hour.

Conversion of matter into energy (Einstein's Theorem): $E=mc^2$, in which E is the energy in ergs, m the mass of the matter in grams, and c the speed of light in centimeters per second. ($c^2=9.10^{20}$).

Decimal Equivalents of Common Fractions

1/2	.5000	1/10	.1000	2/7	.2857	3/11	.2727	5/9	.5556	7/11	.6364
1/3	.3333	1/11	.0909	2/9	.2222	4/5	.8000	5/11	.4545	7/12	.5833
1/4	.2500	1/12	.0833	2/11	.1818	4/7	.5714	5/12	.4167	8/9	.8889
1/5	.2000	1/16	.0625	3/4	.7500	4/9	.4444	6/7	.8571	8/11	.7273
1/6	.1667	1/32	.0313	3/5	.6000	4/11	.3636	6/11	.5455	9/10	.9000
1/7	.1429	1/64	.0156	3/7	.4286	5/6	.8333	7/8	.8750	9/11	.8182
1/8	.1250	2/3	.6667	3/8	.3750	5/7	.7143	7/9	.7778	10/11	.9091
1/9	.1111	2/5	.4000	3/10	.3000	5/8	.6250	7/10	.7000	11/12	.9167

Conversion Factors

To change	To	Multiply by
acres	hectares	.4047
acres	square feet	43,560
acres	square miles	.001562
atmospheres	cms. of mercury	76
BTU	horsepower-hour	.0003931
BTU	kilowatt-hour	.0002928
BTU/hour	watts	.2931
bushels	cubic inches	2150.4
bushels (U.S.)	hectoliters	.3524
centimeters	inches	.3937
centimeters	feet	.03281
circumference	radians	6.283
cubic feet	cubic meters	.0283
cubic meters	cubic feet	35.3145
cubic meters	cubic yards	1.3079
cubic yards	cubic meters	.7646
degrees	radians	.01745
dynes	grams	.00102
fathoms	feet	6.0
feet	meters	.3048
feet	miles (nautical)	.0001645
feet	miles (statute)	.0001894
feet/second	miles/hour	.6818
furlongs	feet	660.0
furlongs	miles	.125
gallons (U.S.)	liters	3.7853
grains	grams	.0648
grams	grains	15.4324
grams	ounces avdp	.0353
grams	pounds	.002205
hectares	acres	2.4710
hectoliters	bushels (U.S.)	2.8378
horsepower	watts	745.7
hours	days	.04167
inches	millimeters	25.4000
inches	centimeters	2.5400
kilograms	pounds avdp or t	2.2046
kilometers	miles	.6214
kilowatts	horsepower	1.341
knots	nautical miles/hour	1.0
knots	statute miles/hour	1.151
liters	gallons (U.S.)	.2642
liters	pecks	.1135

To change	To	Multiply by
liters	pints (dry)	1.8162
liters	pints (liquid)	2.1134
liters	quarts (dry)	.9081
liters	quarts (liquid)	1.0567
meters	feet	3.2808
meters	miles	.0006214
meters	yards	1.0936
metric tons	tons (long)	.9842
metric tons	tons (short)	1.1023
miles	kilometers	1.6093
miles	feet	5280
miles (nautical)	miles (statute)	1.1516
miles (statute)	miles (nautical)	.8684
miles/hour	feet/minute	88
millimeters	inches	.0394
ounces avdp.	grams	28.3495
ounces	pounds	.0625
ounces (troy)	ounces (avdp)	1.09714
pecks	liters	8.8096
pints (dry)	liters	.5506
pints (liquid)	liters	.4732
pounds ap or t	kilograms	.3782
pounds avdp	kilograms	.4536
pounds	ounces	16
quarts (dry)	liters	1.1012
quarts (liquid)	liters	.9463
radians	degrees	57.30
rods	meters	5.029
rods	feet	16.5
square feet	square meters	.0929
square kilometers	square miles	.3861
square meters	square feet	10.7639
square meters	square yards	1.1960
square miles	square kilometers	2.5900
square yards	square meters	.8361
tons (long)	metric tons	1.016
tons (short)	metric tons	.9072
tons (long)	pounds	2240
tons (short)	pounds	2000
watts	Btu/hour	3.4129
watts	horsepower	.001341
yards	meters	.9144
yards	miles	.0005682

Fahrenheit and Celsius (Centigrade) Scales

Zero on the Fahrenheit scale represents the temperature produced by the mixing of equal weights of snow and common salt.

	F	C
Boiling point of water	212°	100°
Freezing point of water	32°	0°
Absolute zero	−459.6°	−273.1°

Absolute zero is theoretically the lowest possible temperature, the point at which all molecular motion would cease.

To convert Fahrenheit to Celsius (Centigrade), subtract 32 and multiply by 5/9.

To convert Celsius (Centigrade) to Fahrenheit, multiply by 9/5 and add 32.

° Centigrade	° Fahrenheit	° Centigrade	° Fahrenheit
−273.1	−459.6	30	86
−250	−418	35	95
−200	−328	40	104
−150	−238	45	113
−100	−148	50	122
−50	−58	55	131
−40	−40	60	140
−30	−22	65	149
−20	−4	70	158
−10	14	75	167
0	32	80	176
5	41	85	185
10	50	90	194
15	59	95	203
20	68	**100**	**212**
25	77		

Roman Numerals

Roman numerals are expressed by letters of the alphabet and are rarely used today except for formality or variety.

There are three basic principles for reading Roman numerals:

1. A letter repeated once or twice repeats its value that many times. (XXX=30, CC=200, etc.).

2. One or more letters placed after another letter of greater value increases the greater value by the amount of the smaller. (VI=6, LXX=70, MCC=1200, etc.).

3. A letter placed before another letter of greater value decreases the greater value by the amount of the smaller. (IV=4, XC=90, CM=900, etc.).

Letter	Value	Letter	Value	Letter	Value	Letter	Value	Letter	Value
I	1	VII	7	XXX	30	LXXX	80	$\overline{V}$	5,000
II	2	VIII	8	XL	40	XC	90	$\overline{X}$	10,000
III	3	IX	9	L	50	C	100	$\overline{L}$	50,000
IV	4	X	10	LX	60	D	500	$\overline{C}$	100,000
V	5	XX	20	LXX	70	M	1,000	$\overline{D}$	500,000
VI	6							$\overline{M}$	1,000,000

Mean and Median

The mean, also called the average, of a series of quantities is obtained by finding the sum of the quantities and dividing it by the number of quantities. In the series 1,3,5,18,19,20,25, the mean or average is 13—i.e., 91 divided by 7.

The median of a series is that point which so divides it that half the quantities are on one side, half on the other. In the above series, the median is 18.

The median often better expresses the common-run, since it is not, as is the mean, affected by an excessively high or low figure. In the series 1,3,4, 7,55, the median of 4 is a truer expression of the common-run than is the mean of 14.

Prime Numbers Between 1 and 1,000

1	2	3	5	7	11	13	17	19	23
29	31	37	41	43	47	53	59	61	67
71	73	79	83	89	97	101	103	107	109
113	127	131	137	139	149	151	157	163	167
173	179	181	191	193	197	199	211	223	227
229	233	239	241	251	257	263	269	271	277
281	283	293	307	311	313	317	331	337	347
349	353	359	367	373	379	383	389	397	401
409	419	421	431	433	439	443	449	457	461
463	467	479	487	491	499	503	509	521	523
541	547	557	563	569	571	577	587	593	599
601	607	613	617	619	631	641	643	647	653
659	661	673	677	683	691	701	709	719	727
733	739	743	751	757	761	769	773	787	797
809	811	821	823	827	829	839	853	857	859
863	877	881	883	887	907	911	919	929	937
941	947	953	967	971	977	983	991	997	(1009)

Definitions of Gold Terminology

The term "fineness" defines a gold content in parts per thousand. For example, a gold nugget containing 885 parts of pure gold, 100 parts of silver, and 15 parts of copper would be considered 885-fine.

The word "karat" indicates the proportion of solid gold in an alloy based on a total of 24 parts. Thus, 14-karat (14K) gold indicates a composition of 14 parts of gold and 10 parts of other metals.

The term "gold-filled" is used to describe articles of jewelry made of base metal which are covered on one or more surfaces with a layer of gold alloy. No article having a gold alloy portion of less than one twentieth by weight may be marked "gold-filled." Articles may be marked "rolled gold plate" provided the proportional fraction and fineness designations are also shown.

Electroplated jewelry items carrying at least 7 millionths of an inch of gold on significant surfaces may be labeled "electroplate." Plate thicknesses less than this may be marked "gold flashed" or "gold washed."

Portraits and Designs of U.S. Paper Currency[1]

Currency	Portrait	Design on back	Currency	Portrait	Design on back
$1	Washington	ONE between obverse and reverse of Great Seal of U.S.	$50	Grant	U.S. Capitol
$2[2]	Jefferson	Monticello	$100	Franklin	Independence Hall
$2[3]	Jefferson	"The Signing of the Declaration of Independence"	$500	McKinley	Ornate FIVE HUNDRED
$5	Lincoln	Lincoln Memorial	$1,000	Cleveland	Ornate ONE THOUSAND
$10	Hamilton	U.S. Treasury Building	$5,000	Madison	Ornate FIVE THOUSAND
$20	Jackson	White House	$10,000	Chase	Ornate TEN THOUSAND
			$100,000[4]	Wilson	Ornate ONE HUNDRED THOUSAND

1. Denominations of $500 and higher were discontinued in 1969. 2. Discontinued in 1966. 3. New issue, April 13, 1976. 4. For use only in transactions between Federal Reserve System and Treasury Department.

ENERGY

Atomic Energy

Just as the Space Age is said to have started with the orbiting of Sputnik I, the Atomic Age is said to have started with the explosion of a test bomb on July 16, 1945, near Alamogordo, N.M., at 5:30 A.M. local time. The bomb was placed on top of a steel tower, and observers were stationed in bunkers 10,000 yards away. The explosion vaporized the steel tower, produced a mushroom cloud rising to 40,000 feet, and melted the desert sand into glass for distances up to 800 yards from the tower.

The first operational use of an atom bomb took place only three weeks later, when a uranium bomb was exploded over Hiroshima, Japan, on Aug. 6, 1945. The bomb, cylindrical in shape, 10 feet long with a diameter of 2 feet 4 inches, weighed about 9,000 pounds. Its explosive force was equal to 20,000 tons of TNT, hence the term "20-kiloton bomb." Three days later another atomic bomb, this time of plutonium, was exploded over Nagasaki.

Of course, the Atomic Age did not begin with the explosion of the test bomb at Alamogordo, just as the Space Age did not begin with the orbiting of the first artificial satellite. In both cases these visible feats were just experiments that proved the theory that had been built up patiently over decades.

At the turn of the century, scientists began to wonder whether the atoms of the chemical elements might not be composed of smaller particles. This was actually a contradiction in terms, because the Greek word *atomos*, from which the word *atom* was derived, meant "indivisible." But there were some indications of particles smaller than an atom—the electrons. In 1907,* Albert Einstein suggested that matter might just be "condensed energy" and gave the conversion formula $E = mc^2$, in which E represents the energy, m the mass, and c the velocity of light. If this formula was correct, a small piece of matter should represent enormous amounts of energy.

Fission and Fusion

Atomic energy can be released in two ways. One is the *fission* of elements with very heavy atoms, such as uranium and plutonium, which will split when struck by a neutron, a sub-atomic particle.

*Einstein's famous formula was first published on May 14, 1907. His special theory of relativity was published in 1905.

Largest Nuclear Power Plants in the United States

(over a million kilowatts)

Location	Operating utility	Capacity (kilowatts)	Year operative
Wintersburg, AZ (Unit 1)	Arizona Public Service	1,200,000	1985
Wintersburg, AZ (Unit 2)	Arizona Public Service	1,200,000	1986
Cowans Ford Dam, NC (Unit 2)	Duke Power Company	1,180,000	1984
Cowans Ford Dam, NC (Unit 1)	Duke Power Company	1,180,000	1981
Burlington, Kan.	Kansas Gas & Electric	1,150,000	1985
Daisy, Tenn. (Unit 1)	Tennessee Valley Authority	1,148,000	1980
Daisy, Tenn. (Unit 2)	Tennessee Valley Authority	1,148,000	1982
Lake Wylie, S.C.(Unit 1)	Duke Power	1,145,000	1985
Lake Wylie, S.C. (Unit 2)	Duke Power	1,145,000	1986
Prescott, Ore. (Unit 1)	Portland General Electric Co.	1,130,000	1976
Byron, Ill. (Unit 1)	Commonwealth Edison	1,120,000	1985
Fulton, Mo.	Union Electric Co.	1,120,000	1984
Taft, La.	Louisiana Power & Light	1,100,000	1985
Richland, WA. (Unit 2)	Washington Public Power	1,100,000	1984
San Clemente, CA (Unit 3)	Southern Cal Edison Co.	1,100,000	1984
San Clemente, Calif. (Unit 2)	Southern Cal. Edison Co.	1,100,000	1983
Bridgman, Mich. (Unit 2)	Indiana & Michigan Electric Co.	1,100,000	1978
Salem, N.J. (Unit 2)	Public Service Electric & Gas, N.J.	1,100,000	1981
Salem, N.J. (Unit 1)	Public Service Electric & Gas, N.J.	1,090,000	1977
Diablo Canyon, Calif.	Pacific Gas & Electric	1,080,000	1985
Seneca Ill. (Unit 2)	Commonwealth Edison Co.	1,078,000	1984
Seneca, Ill. (Unit 1)	Commonwealth Edison Co.	1,078,000	1984
Decatur, Ala. (Unit 1)	Tennessee Valley Authority	1,065,000	1974
Decatur, Ala. (Unit 2)	Tennessee Valley Authority	1,065,000	1975
Decatur, Ala. (Unit 3)	Tennessee Valley Authority	1,065,000	1977
Peach Bottom, Pa. (Unit 2)	Philadelphia Electric Co.	1,065,000	1974
Peach Bottom, Pa. (Unit 3)	Philadelphia Electric Co.	1,065,000	1974
Bridgman, Mich. (Unit 1)	Indiana & Michigan Electric Co.	1,054,000	1975
Berwick, Pa. (Unit 1)	Pennsylvania Power & Light	1,050,000	1983
Zion, Ill. (Unit 1)	Commonwealth Edison Co.	1,040,000	1973
Zion, Ill. (Unit 2)	Commonwealth Edison Co.	1,040,000	1974

Source: Nuclear Regulatory Commission.

The splitting of the heavy atom releases more neutrons, which are then available to split other atoms—the so-called chain reaction. The other way of obtaining atomic energy is *fusion;* four light atoms (hydrogen) are fused together into the next heavier element (helium). The fusion reaction requires enormous heat and very high pressures. These pressures, coupled with very high temperatures, can most easily be produced by exploding a fission bomb.

From about 1910 to 1930, most physicists believed that the release of atomic energy, if it could be done, would be of no practical value. They asserted that causing the release would require more energy than could be obtained. Most astronomers, on the other hand, were convinced that atomic energy was released in the sun and the other stars, because there was no other way to account for the energy the stars radiated into space. Trying to account for the energy radiated by the stars led to theoretical papers predicting what we now call the fusion reaction. At the time (1930), atomic fission was still unknown; it was discovered first by Enrico Fermi in 1934. But nobody yet knew that the sudden bursts of energy observed in the experiments were due to the fission of the uranium-235 atom. This was established (by way of calculation) by Dr. Lise Meitner. Once it was known what happened, the way to a premeditated release of atomic energy was clear.

But nobody could be quite certain whether the release would take the form of an explosion or whether it would be slow enough to be used to generate power. American scientists proceeded under the assumption that the release would be sudden and violent (and the Alamogordo test proved them right), while Professor Heisenberg in Germany thought the slow release to be more likely, which is the reason why the Germans did not start a large-scale atomic energy project.

Atoms for Peace

The *peaceful* Atomic Age can be said to have been born in 1954, when the original U.S. Atomic Energy Act was amended to release many so-called "secrets" of nuclear energy so that nuclear power plants could be built and radioactive isotopes be used in medicine. The next year, the first International Conference on the Peaceful Uses of the Atom was convened at Geneva, bringing together scientists from all over the world to discuss what hitherto had been considered to be secret.

Actually there was little that was really secret about nuclear energy. When the results of the 1938 experiments were brought to the United States, scientists from different parts of the world openly stated that the possibility of atomic bombs was inherent in the scientific findings.

Once the veil of "secrecy" had been dispelled by revision of the Atomic Energy Act and the Geneva meeting, construction of plants to produce electricity by controlled fission of uranium atoms got under way in the United States and several other industrialized nations. Electric power was first produced as a result of nuclear fission in December 1951 at the National Reactor Testing Station in Idaho. When a reactor was connected to a generator, the nuclear power plant produced enough electricity for about 50 homes.

Major Energy Developments, 1986

Source: Energy Information Administration

Decline in World Oil Prices

World oil prices, after having trended downward since 1982, plummeted in 1986. Several factors contributed to the unprecedented decline in crude oil prices. Throughout the 1980's, higher oil prices stimulated new sources of production, even as the effects of conservation, fuel switching, and increased efficiency inhibited demand. In 1986, excess petroleum production became acute as OPEC sought to regain market share at almost any price. World crude oil production rose to 55.5 million barrels per day, with most of the gain due to a 1.7-million-barrel-per-day increase in Saudi Arabian production. The resulting oil glut, coupled with restrained demand and the continued use of netback pricing agreements, drove prices down during the first half of the year; uncertainty in world oil markets prolonged the slump.

Plunging petroleum prices brought the price of natural gas down with them. Estimated data indicate that the average U.S. wellhead price of all categories of natural gas fell from $2.51 per thousand cubic feet in 1985 to $1.87 in 1986. Primarily due to the existence of long-term contracts, U.S. coal prices proved sturdier. The average price of all coal delivered to electric utilities declined only 3% from $34.53 per short ton in 1985 to $33.45 in 1986.

Exploration and Production

U.S. energy production fell 0.8% in 1986 to 64 quadrillion Btu. and production declines in the petroleum and natural gas industry were responsible for the entire decrease. Production of crude oil (including lease condensate) fell 3% to 18 quadrillion Btu (8.7 million barrels per day).

Natural gas (dry) and natural gas liquids production fell to less than 19 quadrillion Btu (17 trillion cubic feet), down almost 3% from the year before.

The collapse in oil prices led to drastic cutbacks in petroleum exploration. The average number of seismic crews fell 47% to 201, the average number of rotary rigs in use fell 51% to 964, and completions of exploratory wells fell 45% to less than seven thousand.

In contrast, the domestic refinery industry benefited from the change in international energy markets, and in particular from netback pricing agreements that guaranteed refining margins. In 1986, the refinery utilization rate was 83%, much improved from the 78% rate in 1985.

As production of petroleum and natural gas declined, production of all other major energy sources increased, although only slightly.

Net generation of electricity rose less than 1% in 1986, while sales increased by about 3% compared with 1985, but total generation of 2.5 trillion kilowatthours set a record. Coal continued to fuel most of the generation, but as the price of oil fell, oil-fired generation increased at the expense of both coal and natural gas. The 1986 increase in oil-fired generation reversed a seven-year decline.

Nuclear-based generation reached an all-time

high in 1986 of 414 billion kilowatthours, and provided nearly 17% of total U.S. generation. The effects of the meltdown of the nuclear reactor at Chernobyl in the Soviet Union were not immediately apparent in non-Communist energy markets, where total nuclear-based generation rose to 1.4 trillion kilowatthours. The United States remained the world's largest producer of nuclear-based generation, accounting for 31% of the non-Communist countries' total, but the U.S. share continued to decline as West European generation increased at a faster rate.

Response to Lower Prices

Because total energy consumption* in 1986 was essentially unchanged from 1985 while gross national product (GNP) increased, the energy intensity of the economy declined for the 10th consecutive year, as service trades accounted for a greater share of domestic GNP. Per capita energy consumption declined for the second consecutive year.

*Total (gross) energy consumption includes energy consumed to produce, process, and transport energy.

Reliance on Petroleum Imports

As low oil prices depressed domestic oil produc tion and stimulated petroleum consumption, whil stocks also increased over the course of the yea petroleum net imports rose from 4.3 million bar rels per day in 1985 to 5.3 million barrels per da in 1986. In addition, coal net exports declined eigh percent. The changes in the oil and coal trade mor than offset the 21% decline in net imports of natu ral gas that occurred as imports from Mexico an Algeria fell to zero. As a result, energy net import were up 28% in 1986; the value of energy net im ports (excluding electricity) declined, however from $45 billion to $32 billion.

Crude oil net imports accounted for almost all o the increase in petroleum net imports; product ne imports were essentially unchanged. Venezuela Canada, and Saudi Arabia were the major source of U.S. petroleum imports.

U.S. reliance on foreign sources of oil increase markedly in 1986. As a percent of U.S. petroleun products supplied (consumption), petroleum ne imports from all countries rose to 33%, up fron 27% in 1985. Net imports from OPEC equalec 17% of U.S. petroleum products supplied in 1986

Production of Crude Petroleum by Countries

(in thousands of 42-gallon barrels)

Area and country	Est. 1987[1]	1986[1]	Est. percent change
Western Hemisphere	5,766,270	5,990,380	−3.7
Argentina	141,255	163,155	−13.4
Bolivia	6,570	7,300	−10.0
Brazil	208,415	210,605	−1.0
Canada	538,375	528,520	1.9
Chile	10,950	12,045	−9.1
Colombia	132,130	76,285	73.2
Ecuador	98,915	109,135	−9.4
Guatemala	1,460	1,460	—
Mexico	914,690	848,990	7.7
Peru	63,875	64,605	−1.1
Trinidad and Tobago	60,225	60,590	−0.6
United States	3,041,910	3,339,385	−8.9
Venezuela	547,500	568,305	−3.7
Western Europe	1,504,530	1,473,140	2.1
Austria	8,030	8,395	−4.3
Denmark	29,565	25,915	14.1
France	21,170	22,265	−4.9
West Germany	27,375	30,295	−9.6
Greece	9,125	10,220	−10.7
Italy	18,250	16,790	8.7
Netherlands	34,675	26,645	30.1
Norway	388,360	311,710	24.6
Spain	12,045	14,600	−17.5
Turkey	17,520	14,600	20.0
United Kingdom	938,415	991,705	−5.4
Middle East	4,044,565	4,294,955	−5.8
Bahrain	15,330	16,060	−4.5
Iran	733,650	707,005	3.8
Iraq	614,295	647,875	−5.2
Israel	365	365	—
Kuwait	356,240	382,155	−6.8
Neutral Zone[2]	166,805	103,295	61.5
Oman	195,640	182,500	7.2
Qatar	87,600	128,845	−32.0
Saudi Arabia	1,387,000	1,567,675	−11.5

Area and country	Est. 1987[1]	1986[1]	Est. percent change
Syria	80,300	67,525	18.9
United Arab Emirates	407,340	491,655	−17.1
Asia-Pacific	1,125,660	1,198,295	−6.1
Australia	208,050	217,905	−4.5
Brunei	56,940	62,050	−8.2
Burma	10,950	10,950	—
India	226,300	229,585	−1.4
Indonesia	407,340	455,520	−10.6
Japan	4,380	4,745	−7.7
Malaysia	170,820	175,565	−2.7
New Zealand	10,220	10,220	—
Pakistan	14,600	14,965	−2.4
Philippines	2,190	2,555	−14.3
Taiwan	1,460	730	100.0
Thailand	12,410	13,505	−8.1
Africa	1,689,585	1,697,250	−0.5
Algeria	231,775	220,095	5.3
Angola/Cabinda[3]	110,230	102,200	7.9
Cameroon	65,700	65,700	—
Congo	41,975	41,975	—
Egypt	326,310	299,665	8.9
Gabon	55,480	58,400	−5.0
Ghana	0	365	−100.0
Ivory Coast	7,300	7,300	—
Libya	355,875	375,585	−5.2
Morocco	0	365	−100.0
Nigeria	446,760	472,675	−5.5
Tunisia	36,500	41,245	−11.5
Zaire	11,680	11,680	—
Communist bloc	5,652,025	5,470,620	3.3
China	981,850	911,040	7.8
Romania	78,475	82,490	−4.9
U.S.S.R.	4,516,145	4,394,235	2.8
Other communist	75,555	82,855	−8.8
World total	**19,782,635**	**20,124,640**	−1.7

1. Based on Jan.–Feb. average. 2. Shared by Kuwait and Saudi Arabia. 3. An enclave in West Africa on Atlantic coast between the Congo and Angola.

Crude Oil Imports and Petroleum Products by Country of Origin, 1975–1986

(thousand barrels per day)

Year	Organization of Petroleum Exporting Countries (OPEC)						Canada	Mexico	United Kingdom	Virgin Is./ Puerto Rico
	Saudi Arabia	Vene-zuela	Indo-nesia	Algeria	Nigeria	Total OPEC[1]				
1975	715	702	390	282	762	3,601	846	71	14	496
1978	1,144	645	573	649	919	5,751	467	318	180	522
1979	1,356	690	420	636	1,080	5,637	538	439	202	523
1980	1,261	481	348	488	857	4,300	455	533	176	476
1981	1,129	406	366	311	620	3,323	447	522	375	389
1982	552	412	248	170	514	2,146	482	685	456	366
1983	337	422	338	240	302	1,862	547	826	382	322
1984	325	548	343	323	216	2,049	630	748	402	336
1985	168	605	314	187	293	1,830	770	816	310	275
1986[2]	681	772	309	266	420	2,768	790	694	351	265

1. Excludes petroleum imported into the U.S. indirectly from OPEC countries, primarily from Caribbean and West European refining areas, as petroleum products which were refined from crude oil produced in OPEC countries. 2. Preliminary. NOTE: Data include imports for Strategic Petroleum Reserve, which began in 1977. Sum of components may not equal total due to independent rounding. *Source:* 1975—U.S. Dept. of the Interior, Bureau of Mines; 1976 through 1986—U.S. Dept. of Energy, Energy Information Administration.

Exports of Crude Oil and Petroleum Products by Country of Destination, 1975–1986

(Thousand Barrels per Day)

Year	Canada	Japan	Mexico	Nether-lands	Belgium[1]	Italy	United Kingdom	France	Brazil	Virgin Is./ Puerto Rico
1975	22	27	42	23	9	10	7	6	6	12
1978	108	26	27	18	15	10	7	9	8	86
1979	100	34	21	28	19	15	7	13	7	170
1980	108	32	28	23	20	14	7	11	4	220
1981	89	38	26	42	12	22	5	15	1	221
1982	85	68	53	85	17	32	14	24	8	211
1983	76	104	24	49	22	35	8	23	2	144
1984	83	92	35	37	21	39	14	18	1	152
1985	74	108	61	44	26	30	14	11	3	161
1986[2]	82	106	56	58	30	39	8	11	2	110

1. Including Luxembourg. 2. Preliminary. NOTE: Sum of components may not equal total due to independent rounding. *Source:* 1975—Bureau of Mines, Mineral Industry Surveys, *Petroleum Statement, Annual.* • 1976 through 1980—Energy Information Administration, Energy Data Reports, *Petroleum Statement, Annual.* • 1981 through 1986—Energy Information Administration, *Petroleum Supply Annual.* • 1985—Energy Information Administration, *Petroleum Supply Monthly.*

U.S. Motor Vehicle Fuel Consumption and Related Data

(1985 estimate)

Type of vehicle	Total travel (million vehicle miles)	Number of registered vehicles	Average miles traveled per vehicle	Fuel consumed (thousand gallons)	Average fuel consumption per vehicle (gallons)	Average miles per gallon
All passenger vehicles	1,317,130	138,146,095	9,534	73,982,076	536	17.80
Total personal passenger vehicles	1,310,199	137,552,568	9,525	72,752,403	529	18.01
Cars	1,298,199	132,108,164	9,827	72,512,403	549	17.90
Motorcycles	12,000	5,444,404	2,204	240,000	44	50.00
All buses	6,931	593,527	11,678	1,229,673	2,072	5.64
All cargo vehicles	457,632	38,989,042	11,737	47,376,323	1,215	9.66
Single unit trucks	378,230	37,674,841	10,039	32,602,340	865	11.60
Combinations	79,402	1,314,201	60,418	14,773,983	11,242	5.37
All motor vehicles	**1,774,762**	**177,135,137**	**10,019**	**121,358,399**	**685**	**14.62**

Source: Department of Transportation, Federal Highway Administration.

WRITER'S GUIDE

A Concise Guide to Style

This section discusses and illustrates the basic conventions of American capitalization, punctuation, and italicization.

Capitalization

Capitalize the following: **1.** the first word of a sentence: Some spiders are poisonous; others are not. Are you my new neighbor?

2. the first word of a direct quotation, except when the quotation is split: Joyce asked, "Do you think that the lecture was interesting?" "No," I responded, "it was very boring." Tom Paine said, "The sublime and the ridiculous are often so nearly related that it is difficult to class them separately."

3. the first word of each line in a poem in traditional verse: Half a league, half a league,/Half a league onward,/All in the valley of Death/Rode the six hundred.—Alfred, Lord Tennyson

4. the names of people, of organizations and their members, of councils and congresses, and of historical periods and events: Marie Curie, Benevolent and Protective Order of Elks, an Elk, Protestant Episcopal Church, an Episcopalian, the Democratic Party, a Democrat, the Nuclear Regulatory Commission, the U.S. Senate, the Middle Ages, World War I, the Battle of Britain.

5. the names of places and geographic divisions, districts, regions, and locales: Richmond, Vermont, Argentina, Seventh Avenue, London Bridge, Arctic Circle, Eastern Hemisphere, Continental Divide, Middle East, Far North, Gulf States, East Coast, the North, the South Shore.

Do not capitalize words indicating compass points unless a specific region is referred to: Turn north onto Interstate 91.

6. the names of rivers, lakes, mountains, and oceans: Ohio River, Lake Como, Rocky Mountains, Atlantic Ocean.

7. the names of ships, aircraft, satellites, and space vehicles: U.S.S. *Arizona, Spirit of St. Louis,* the spy satellite Ferret-D, Voyager II, the space shuttle Challenger.

8. the names of nationalities, races, tribes, and languages: Spanish, Maori, Bantu, Russian.

9. words derived from proper names, except in their extended senses: the Byzantine Empire. *But:* byzantine office politics.

10. words indicating family relationships when used with a person's name as a title: Aunt Toni and Uncle Jack. *But:* my aunt and uncle, Toni and Jack Walker.

11. a title (i.e., civil, judicial, military, royal and noble, religious, and honorary) when preceding a name: Justice Marshall, General Jackson, Mayor Daley, Queen Victoria, Lord Mountbatten, Pope John Paul II, Professor Jacobson, Senator Byrd.

12. all references to the President and Vice President of the United States: The President has entered the hall. The Vice President presides over the Senate.

13. all key words in titles of literary, dramatic, artistic, and musical works: the novel *The Old Man and the Sea,* the short story "Notes from Underground," an article entitled "On Passive Verbs," James Dickey's poem "In the Tree House at Night," the play *Cat on a Hot Tin Roof,* Van Gogh's *Wheat Field and Cypress Trees,* Beethoven's *Emperor Concerto.*

14. *the* in the title of a newspaper if it is a part of the title: *The Wall Street Journal. But:* the New York *Daily News.*

15. the first word in the salutation and in the complimentary close of a letter: My dear Carol, Yours sincerely.

16. epithets and substitutes for the names of people and places: Old Hickory, Old Blood and Guts, The Oval Office, the Windy City.

17. words used in personifications: When is not Death at watch/Within those secret waters?/What wants he but to catch/Earth's heedless sons and daughters?—Edmund Blunden

18. the pronoun *I:* I told them that I had heard the news.

19. names for the Deity and sacred works: God, the Almighty, Jesus, Allah, the Supreme Being, the Bible, the Koran, the Talmud.

20. days of the week, months of the year, holidays, and holy days: Tuesday, May, Independence Day, Passover, Ramadan, Christmas.

21. the names of specific courts: The Supreme Court of the United States, the Massachusetts Appeals Court, the United States Court of Appeals for the First Circuit.

22. the names of treaties, accords, pacts, laws, and specific amendments: Panama Canal Treaty, Treaty of Paris, Geneva Accords, Warsaw Pact countries, Sherman Antitrust Law, Labor Management Relations Act, took the Fifth Amendment.

23. registered trademarks and service marks: Day-Glo, Comsat.

24. the names of geologic eras, periods, epochs, and strata and the names of prehistoric divisions: Paleozoic Era, Precambrian, Pleistocene, Age of Reptiles, Bronze Age, Stone Age.

25. the names of constellations, planets, and stars: Milky Way, Southern Crown, Saturn, Jupiter, Uranus, Polaris.

26. genus but not species names in binomial nomenclature: *Rana pipiens.*

27. New Latin names of classes, families, and all groups higher than genera in botanical and zoological nomenclature: Nematoda.

But do not capitalize derivatives from such names: nematodes.

28. many abbreviations and acronyms: Dec., Tues., Lt. Gen., M.F.A., UNESCO, MIRV.

Italicization

Use italics to:

1. indicate titles of books, plays, and epic poems:

War and Peace, The Importance of Being Earnest, Paradise Lost.

2. indicate titles of magazines and newspapers: *New York* magazine, *The Wall Street Journal*, the New York *Daily News.*

3. set off the titles of motion pictures and radio and television programs: *Star Wars, All Things Considered, Masterpiece Theater.*

4. indicate titles of major musical compositions: Handel's *Messiah*, Adam's *Giselle.*

5. set off the names of paintings and sculpture: *Mona Lisa, Pietà.*

6. indicate words, letters, or numbers that are referred to: The word *hiss* is onomatopoeic. *Can't* means *won't* in your lexicon. You form your *n*'s like *u*'s. A *6* looks like an inverted *9.*

7. indicate foreign words and phrases not yet assimilated into English: *C'est la vie* was the response to my complaint.

8. indicate the names of plaintiff and defendant in legal citations: *Roe* v. *Doe.*

9. emphasize a word or phrase: When you appear on the national news, you are *somebody.*

Use this device sparingly.

10. distinguish New Latin names of genera, species, subspecies, and varieties in botanical and zoological nomenclature: *Homo sapiens.*

11. set off the names of ships and aircraft but not space vehicles: U.S.S. *Arizona, Spirit of St. Louis,* Voyager II, the space shuttle Challenger, the spy satellite Ferret-D.

Punctuation

Apostrophe. 1. indicates the possessive case of singular and plural nouns, indefinite pronouns, and surnames combined with designations such as *Jr., Sr.,* and *II:* my sister's husband, my three sisters' husbands, anyone's guess, They answer each other's phones, John Smith, Jr.'s car.

2. indicates joint possession when used with the last of two or more nouns in a series: Doe and Roe's report.

3. indicates individual possession or authorship when used with each of two or more nouns in a series: Smith's, Roe's, and Doe's reports.

4. indicates the plurals of words, letters, and figures used as such: 60's and 70's; *x*'s, *y*'s, and *z*'s.

5. indicates omission of letters in contractions: aren't, that's, o'clock.

6. indicates omission of figures in dates: the class of '63.

Brackets. 1. enclose words or passages in quoted matter to indicate insertion of material written by someone other than the author: A tough but nervous, tenacious but restless race [the Yankees]; materially ambitious, yet prone to introspection. . . .—Samuel Eliot Morison

2. enclose material inserted within matter already in parentheses: (Vancouver [B.C.] January 1, 19—).

Colon. 1. introduces words, phrases, or clauses that explain, amplify, or summarize what has gone before: Suddenly I realized where we were: Rome.

There are two cardinal sins from which all the others spring: impatience and laziness.—Franz Kafka

2. introduces a long quotation: In his original draft of the *Declaration of Independence,* Jefferson wrote: "We hold these truths to be sacred and undeniable; that all men are created equal and independent, that from that equal creation they derive rights inherent and inalienable. . . ."

3. introduces a list: We need the following items: pens, paper, pencils, blotters, and erasers.

4. separates chapter and verse numbers in Biblical references: James 1:4.

5. separates city from publisher in footnotes and bibliographies: Chicago: Riverside Press, 1983.

6. separates hour and minute(s) in time designations: 9:30 a.m., a 9:30 meeting.

7. follows the salutation in a business letter: Gentlemen:

Comma. 1. separates the clauses of a compound sentence connected by a coordinating conjunction: A difference exists between the musical works of Handel and Haydn, and it is a difference worth noting.

The comma may be omitted in short compound sentences: I heard what you said and I am furious. I got out of the car and I walked and walked.

2. separates *and* or *or* from the final item in a series of three or more: Red, yellow, and blue may be mixed to produce all colors.

3. separates two or more adjectives modifying the same noun if *and* could be used between them without altering the meaning: a solid, heavy gait. *But:* a polished mahogany dresser.

4. sets off nonrestrictive clauses or phrases (i.e., those that if eliminated would not affect the meaning of the sentences): The burglar, who had entered through the patio, went straight to the silver chest.

The comma should not be used when a clause is restrictive (i.e., essential to the meaning of the sentence): The burglar who had entered through the patio went straight to the silver chest; the other burglar searched for the wall safe.

5. sets off words or phrases in apposition to a noun or noun phrase: Plato, the famous Greek philosopher, was a student of Socrates.

The comma should not be used if such words or phrases precede the noun: The Greek philosopher Plato was a student of Socrates.

6. sets off transitional words and short expressions that require a pause in reading or speaking: Unfortunately, my friend was not well traveled. Did you, after all, find what you were looking for? I live with my family, of course.

7. sets off words used to introduce a sentence: No, I haven't been to Paris. Well, what do you think we should do now?

8. sets off a subordinate clause or a long phrase that precedes a principal clause: By the time we found the restaurant, we were starved. Of all the illustrations in the book, the most striking are those of the tapestries.

9. sets off short quotations and sayings: The candidate said, "Actions speak louder than words." "Talking of axes," said the Duchess, "chop off her head!"—Lewis Carroll

10. indicates omission of a word or words: To err is human; to forgive, divine.

11. sets off the year from the month in full dates: Nicholas II of Russia was shot on July 16, 1918.

But note that when only the month and the year are used, no comma appears: Nicholas II of Russia was shot in July 1918.

12. sets off city and state in geographic names: Atlanta, Georgia, is the transportation center of the South. 34 Beach Drive, Bedford, VA 24523.

13. separates series of four or more figures into thousands, millions, etc.: 67,000; 200,000.

14. sets off words used in direct address: I tell you, folks, all politics is applesauce.—Will Rogers Thank you for your expert assistance, Dolores.

15. Separates a tag question from the rest of a sentence: You forgot your keys again, didn't you?

16. sets off sentence elements that could be misunderstood if the comma were not used: Some time after, the actual date for the project was set.

17. follows the salutation in a personal letter and the complimentary close in a business or personal letter: Dear Jessica, Sincerely yours.

18. sets off titles and degrees from surnames and from the rest of a sentence: Walter T. Prescott, Jr.; Gregory A. Rossi, S.J.; Susan P. Green, M.D., presented the case.

Dash. 1. indicates a sudden break or abrupt change in continuity: "If—if you'll just let me explain—" the student stammered. And the problem—if there really is one—can then be solved.

2. sets apart an explanatory, a defining, or an emphatic phrase: Foods rich in protein—meat, fish, and eggs—should be eaten on a daily basis.

More important than winning the election, is governing the nation. That is the test of a political party—the acid, final test.—Adlai E. Stevenson

3. sets apart parenthetical matter: Wolsey, for all his faults—and he had many—was a great statesman, a man of natural dignity with a generous temperament. . . .—Jasper Ridley

4. marks an unfinished sentence: "But if my bus is late—" he began.

5. sets off a summarizing phrase or clause: The vital measure of a newspaper is not its size but its spirit—that is its responsibility to report the news fully, accurately, and fairly.—Arthur H. Sulzberger

6. sets off the name of an author or source, as at the end of a quotation: A poet can survive everything but a misprint.—Oscar Wilde

Ellipses. 1. indicate, by three spaced points, omission of words or sentences within quoted matter: Equipped by education to rule in the nineteenth century, . . . he lived and reigned in Russia in the twentieth century.—Robert K. Massie

2. indicate, by four spaced points, omission of words at the end of a sentence: The timidity of bureaucrats when it comes to dealing with . . . abuses is easy to explain. . . .—*New York*

3. indicate, when extended the length of a line, omission of one or more lines of poetry:

Roll on, thou deep and dark blue
  ocean—roll!
. . . .
Man marks the earth with ruin—his
  control
Stops with the shore.—Lord Byron

4. are sometimes used as a device, as for example, in advertising copy:

To help you Move and Grow
  with the Rigors of
Business in the 1980's . . .
  and Beyond.—*Journal of Business Strategy*

Exclamation Point. 1. terminates an emphatic or exclamatory sentence: Go home at once! You've got to be kidding!

2. terminates an emphatic interjection: Encore!

Hyphen. 1. indicates that part of a word of more than one syllable has been carried over from one line to the next:

During the revolution, the nation was
beset with problems—looting, fighting, and famine.

2. joins the elements of some compounds: great-grandparent, attorney-at-law, ne'er-do-well.

3. joins the elements of compound modifiers preceding nouns: high-school students, a fire-and-brimstone lecture, a two-hour meeting.

4. indicates that two or more compounds share a single base: four- and six-volume sets, eight- and nine-year olds.

5. separates the prefix and root in some combinations; check the Dictionary when in doubt about the spelling: anti-Nazi, re-elect, co-author, re-form/reform, re-cover/recover, re-creation/-recreation.

6. substitutes for the word *to* between typewritten inclusive words or figures: pp. 145-155, the Boston-New York air shuttle.

7. punctuates written-out compound numbers from 21 through 99: forty-six years of age, a person who is forty-six, two hundred fifty-nine dollars.

Parentheses. 1. enclose material that is not essential to a sentence and that if not included would not alter its meaning: After a few minutes (some say less) the blaze was extinguished.

2. often enclose letters or figures to indicate subdivisions of a series: A movement in sonata form consists of the following elements: (1) the exposition, (2) the development, and (3) the recapitulation.

3. enclose figures following and confirming written-out numbers, especially in legal and business documents: The fee for my services will be two thousand dollars ($2,000.00).

4. enclose an abbreviation for a term following the written-out term, when used for the first time in a text: The patient is suffering from acquired immune deficiency syndrome (AIDS).

Period. 1. terminates a complete declarative or mild imperative sentence: There could be no turning back as war's dark shadow settled irrevocably across the continent of Europe.—W. Bruce Lincoln. Return all the books when you can. Would you kindly affix your signature here.

2. terminates sentence fragments: Gray clouds—and what looks like a veil of rain falling behind the East German headland. A pair of ducks. A tired or dying swan, head buried in its back feathers, sits on the sand a few feet from the water's edge.—Anthony Bailey

3. follows some abbreviations: Dec., Rev., St., Blvd., pp., Co.

Question Mark. 1. punctuates a direct question: Have you seen the new play yet? Who goes there? *But:* I wonder who said "Nothing is easy in war." I asked if they planned to leave.

2. indicates uncertainty: Ferdinand Magellan (1480?-1521), Plato (427?-347 B.C.).

Quotation Marks. 1. Double quotation marks enclose direct quotations: "What was Paris like in the Twenties?" our daughter asked. "Ladies and Gentlemen," the Chief Usher said, "the President of the United States." Robert Louis Stevenson said that "it is better to be a fool than to be dead." When advised not to become a lawyer because the profession was already overcrowded, Daniel Webster replied, "There is always room at the top."

2. Double quotation marks enclose words or phrases to clarify their meaning or use or to indicate that they are being used in a special way: This was the border of what we often call "the West" or "the Free World." "The Windy City" is a name for Chicago.

3. Double quotation marks set off the translation of a foreign word or phrase: *die Grenze,* "the border."

4. Double quotation marks set off the titles of series of books, of articles or chapters in publications, of essays, of short stories and poems, of individual radio and television programs, and of songs and short musical pieces: "The Horizon Concise History" series; an article entitled "On Reflexive

Verbs in English"; Chapter Nine, "The Prince and the Peasant"; Pushkin's "The Queen of Spades"; Tennyson's "Ode on the Death of the Duke of Wellington"; "The Bob Hope Special"; Schubert's "Death and the Maiden."

5. Single quotation marks enclose quotations within quotations: The blurb for the piece proclaimed, "Two years ago at Geneva, South Vietnam was virtually sold down the river to the Communists. Today the spunky little . . . country is back on its own feet, thanks to 'a mandarin in a sharkskin suit who's upsetting the Red timetable.' "—Frances FitzGerald

Put commas and periods inside quotation marks; put semicolons and colons outside. Other punctuation, such as exclamation points and question marks, should be put inside the closing quotation marks only if part of the matter quoted.

Semicolon. **1.** separates the clauses of a compound sentence having no coordinating conjunction: Do not let us speak of darker days; let us rather speak of sterner days.—Winston Churchill

2. separates the clauses of a compound sentence in which the clauses contain internal punctuation, even when the clauses are joined by conjunctions: Skis in hand, we trudged to the lodge, stowed our lunches, and donned our boots; and the rest of our party waited for us at the lifts.

3. separates elements of a series in which items already contain commas: Among those at the diplomatic reception were the Secretary of State; the daughter of the Ambassador to the Court of St. James's, formerly of London; and two United Nations delegates.

4. separates clauses of a compound sentence joined by a conjunctive adverb, such as *however*, *nonetheless*, or *hence:* We insisted upon a hearing; however, the Grievance Committee refused.

5. may be used instead of a comma to signal longer pauses for dramatic effect: But I want you to know that when I cross the river my last conscious thought will be of the Corps; and the Corps; and the Corps.—General Douglas MacArthur

Virgule. **1.** separates successive divisions in an extended date: fiscal year 1983/84.

2. represents *per:* 35 km/hr, 1,800 ft/sec.

3. means *or* between the words *and* and *or:* Take water skis and/or fishing equipment when you visit the beach this summer.

4. separates two or more lines of poetry that are quoted and run in on successive lines of a text: The student actress had a memory lapse when she came to the lines "Double, double, toil and trouble/Fire burn and cauldron bubble/Eye of newt and toe of frog/Wool of bat and tongue of dog" and had to leave the stage in embarrassment.

Forms of Address[1]

Source: Webster's II New Riverside University Dictionary.

Academics

Dean, college or university. *Address:* Dean ______ ______. *Salutation:* Dear Dean ______.

President. *Address:* President ______ ______. *Salutation:* Dear President ______.

Professor, college or university. *Address:* Professor ______ ______. *Salutation:* Dear Professor ______.

Clerical and Religious Orders

Abbot. *Address:* The Right Reverend ______ ______ O.S.B. Abbot of ______. *Salutation:* Right Reverend Abbot or Dear Father Abbot.

Archbishop, Eastern Orthodox. *Address:* The Most Reverend Joseph, Archbishop of ______. *Salutation:* Your Eminence.

Archbishop, Roman Catholic. The Most Reverend ______ ______, Archbishop of ______. *Salutation:* Your Excellency.

Archdeacon, Episcopal. *Address:* The Venerable ______ ______, Archdeacon of ______. *Salutation:* Venerable Sir or Dear Archdeacon ______.

Bishop, Episcopal. *Address:* The Right Reverend ______ ______, Bishop of ______. *Salutation:* Right Reverend Sir or Dear Bishop ______.

Bishop, other Protestant. *Address:* The Reverend ______ ______. *Salutation:* Dear Bishop ______.

Bishop, Roman Catholic. *Address:* The Most Reverend ______ ______, Bishop of ______. *Salutation:* Your Excellency or Dear Bishop ______.

Brotherhood, Roman Catholic. *Address:* Brother ______ ______, C.F.C. *Salutation:* Dear Brother or Dear Brother Joseph.

Brotherhood, superior of. *Address:* Brother Joseph C.F.C. Superior. *Salutation:* Dear Brother Joseph.

Cardinal. *Address:* His Eminence Joseph Cardinal Stone. *Salutation:* Your Eminence.

Clergyman/woman, Protestant. *Address:* The Reverend ______ ______ or The Reverend ______ ______, D.D. *Salutation:* Dear Mr./Ms. ______ or Dear Dr. ______.

Dean of a cathedral, Episcopal. *Address:* The Very Reverend ______ ______, Dean of ______. *Salutation:* Dear Dean ______.

Monsignor. *Address:* The Right Reverend Monsignor ______ ______. *Salutation:* Dear Monsignor.

Patriarch, Greek Orthodox. *Address:* His All Holiness Patriarch Joseph. *Salutation:* Your All Holiness.

Patriarch, Russian Orthodox. *Address:* His Holiness the Patriarch of ______. *Salutation:* Your Holiness.

Pope. *Address:* His Holiness The Pope. *Salutation:* Your Holiness or Most Holy Father.

Priest, Roman Catholic. *Address:* The Reverend ______ ______, S.J. *Salutation:* Dear Reverend Father or Dear Father.

Rabbi, man or woman. *Address:* Rabbi ______ ______ or ______ ______ D.D.. *Salutation:* Dear Rabbi ______ or Dear Dr. ______.

Sisterhood, Roman Catholic. *Address:* Sister ______ ______, C.S.J. *Salutation:* Dear Sister or Dear Sister ______.

Sisterhood, superior of. *Address:* The Reverend Mother Superior, S.C. *Salutation:* Reverend Mother.

Diplomats

Ambassador, U.S. *Address:* The Honorable ______ ______ The Ambassador of the United States. *Salutation:* Sir/Madam or Dear Mr./Madam Ambassador.

Ambassador to the U.S. *Address:* His/Her Excellency ______ ______, The Ambassador of ______. *Salutation:* Excellency or Dear Mr./Madam Ambassador.

Chargé d'Affaires, U.S. *Address:* The Honorable ______ ______, United States Chargé d'Affaires. *Salutation:* Dear Mr./Ms. ______.

Consul, U.S. *Address:* ______ ______, Esq., United

States Consul. *Salutation:* Dear Mr./Ms. ______.

Minister, U.S. or to U.S. *Address:* The Honorable ______ ______, The Minister of ______. *Salutation:* Sir/Madam or Dear Mr./Madame Minister.

Secretary General, United Nations. *Address:* His/Her Excellency ______ ______, Secretary General of the United Nations. *Salutation:* Dear Mr./Madam/Madame Secretary General.

United Nations Representative (Foreign). *Address:* His/Her Excellency ______ ______ Representative of ______ to the United Nations. *Salutation:* Excellency or My dear Mr./Madame ______.

United Nations Representative (U.S.) *Address:* The Honorable ______ ______, United States Representative to the United Nations. *Salutation:* Sir/Madam or Dear Mr./Ms. ______.

Government Officials

Assemblyman. *Address:* The Honorable ______ ______. *Salutation:* Dear Mr./Ms. ______.

Associate Justice, U.S. Supreme Court. *Address:* Mr./Madam Justice ______. *Salutation:* Dear Mr./Madam Justice or Sir/Madam.

Attorney General, U.S. *Address:* The Honorable ______ ______, Attorney General of the United States. *Salutation:* Dear Mr./Madam or Attorney General.

Cabinet member: *Address:* The Honorable ______ ______, Secretary of ______. *Salutation:* Sir/Madam or Dear Mr./Madam Secretary.

Chief Justice, U.S. Supreme Court. *Address:* The Chief Justice of the United States. *Salutation:* Dear Mr. Chief Justice.

Commissioner (federal, state, local). *Address:* The Honorable ______ ______. *Salutation:* Dear Mr./Ms. ______.

Governor. *Address:* The Honorable ______ ______, Governor of ______. *Salutation:* Dear Governor ______.

Judge, Federal: *Address:* The Honorable ______ ______, Judge of the United States District Court for the ______, District of ______. *Salutation:* Sir/Madam or Dear Judge ______.

Judge, state or local. *Address:* The Honorable ______ ______, Judge of the Court of ______. *Salutation:* Dear Judge ______.

Lieutenant Governor. *Address:* The Honorable ______ ______, Lieutenant Governor of ______. *Salutation:* Dear Mr./Ms. ______.

Mayor. *Address:* The Honorable ______ ______, Mayor of ______. *Salutation:* Dear Mayor ______.

President, U.S. *Address:* The President. *Salutation:* Dear Mr. President.

President, U.S., former. *Address:* The Honorable ______ ______. *Salutation:* Dear Mr. ______.

Representative, state. *Address:* The Honorable ______ ______. *Salutation:* Dear Mr./Ms. ______.

Representative, U.S. *Address:* The Honorable ______ ______, United States House of Representatives. *Salutation:* Dear Mr./Ms. ______.

Senator, state. *Address:* The Honorable ______ ______, The State Senate, State Capitol. *Salutation:* Dear Senator ______.

Senator, U.S. *Address:* The Honorable ______ ______, United States Senate. *Salutation:* Dear Senator ______.

Speaker, U.S. House of Representatives. *Address:* The Honorable ______ ______, Speaker of the House of Representatives. *Salutation:* Dear Mr./Madam Speaker.

Vice President, U.S. *Address:* The Vice President of the United States. *Salutation:* Sir or Dear Mr. Vice President.

Military and Naval Officers

Rank. *Address:* Full rank, USN (or USCG, USAF, USA, USMC). *Salutation:* Dear (full rank) ______.

Professions

Attorney. *Address:* Mr./Ms. ______ ______, Attorney at law or ______ ______, Esq. *Salutation:* Dear Mr./Ms. ______.

Dentist. *Address:* ______ ______, D.D.S. *Salutation:* Dear Dr. ______.

Physician. *Address:* ______ ______, M.D. *Salutation:* Dear Dr. ______.

Veterinarian. *Address:* ______ ______, D.V.M. *Salutation:* Dear Dr. ______.

1. Forms of address do not always follow set guidelines; the type of salutation is often determined by the relationship between correspondents or by the purpose and content of the letter. However, a general style applies to most occasions. In highly formal salutations, when the addressee is a woman, "Madam" should be substituted for "Sir." When the salutation is informal, "Ms.," "Miss," or "Mrs." should be substituted for "Mr." If a woman addressee has previously indicated a preference for a particular form of address, that form should be used.

Foreign Words and Phrases

(The English meanings given are not necessarily literal translations.)

Source: Webster's II New Riverside University Dictionary. Copyright © 1984 Houghton Mifflin Company.

à bientôt [Fr.]: goodbye; I'll see you later
à bon marché [Fr.]: at a bargain price
ab ovo [Lat.]: from the very beginning
à compte [Fr.]: on account
à deux [Fr.]: of or involving two individuals
ad infinitum [Lat.]: to infinity
ad valorem [Lat.]: according to the value
advocatus diaboli [Lat.]: devil's advocate
aide-toi, le ciel t'aidera [Fr.]: heaven helps those who help themselves—La Fontaine
à la bonne heure [Fr.]: at a good time; splendid; all right
aloha oe [Hawaiian]: love to you; greetings; farewell
amende honorable [Fr.]: public apology; just restitution
amicus curiae [Lat.]: friend of the court
amor vincit omnia [Lat.]: love conquers all—Virgil
ancien regime [Fr.]: the old order
à peu près [Fr.]: almost; approximately
a priori [Lat.]: from the former
arrivederci [Ital.]: goodbye
ars est celare artem [Lat.]: (true) art is to conceal art
ars gratia artis [Lat.]: art for art's sake
ars longa, vita brevis [Lat.]: art is long, life short
au contraire [Fr.]: on the contrary
au courant [Fr.]: up-to-date
au fait [Fr.]: well-informed
auf Wiedersehen [G.]: goodbye
autres temps, autres moeurs [Fr.]: other times, other customs
à votre santé [Fr.]: to your health
ben trovato [Ital.]: ingenious
bête noir [Fr.]: one particularly disliked

bona fide [Lat.]: in good faith; genuine
bon appétit [Fr.]: good appetite
bon mot [Fr.]: a clever saying
bon vivant [Fr.]: an epicure
carpe diem [Lat.]: enjoy today
carte blanche [Fr.]: unrestricted power to act on one's own
causa sine qua non [Lat.]: indispensable condition or cause
cause célèbre [Fr.]: a highly controversial issue
caveat emptor [Lat.]: let the buyer beware
chacun à son goût [Fr.]: everyone to his own taste
circa [Lat.]: in approximately
comme ci comme ça [Fr.]: so-so
corpus delicti [Lat.]: the material evidence of the fact that a crime has been committed
coup de grâce [Fr.]: finishing blow
cri de coeur [Fr.]: heartfelt appeal
cum grano salis [Lat.]: with a grain of salt
d'accord [Fr.]: agreed
danke (schön) [G.]: thank you (very much)
de bonne grâce [Fr.]: with good grace
de facto [Lat.]: in reality or fact
de gustibus non est disputandum [Lat.]: there is no arguing in matters of taste
Deo gratias [Lat.]: thanks be to God
Deo volente [Lat.]: God willing
de profundis [Lat.]: from the depths
dernier cri [Fr.]: the newest fashion
deus ex machina [Lat.]: a contrived device to resolve a situation
dolce far niente [Ital.]: pleasant idleness
dramatis personae [Lat.]: characters in a play
ecce homo [Lat.]: behold the man
éminence grise [Fr.]: gray eminence; power behind the throne
en bloc [Fr.]: wholesale; as one
enfin [Fr.]: in conclusion
en masse [Fr.]: all together
en passant [Fr.]: in passing
en rapport [Fr.]: in sympathy or accord; in touch
entre nous [Fr.]: between ourselves; confidentially
ex animo [Lat.]: from the heart
ex gratia [Lat.]: as a favor
ex more [Lat.]: according to custom
experto credite [Lat.]: believe one who knows from experience
fait accompli [Fr.]: an accomplished fact, presumably irreversible
faute de mieux [Fr.]: for lack of anything better
faux pas [Fr.]: a social blunder
feux d'artifice [Fr.]: fireworks; dazzling display, as of wit
fiat justitia, ruat caelum [Lat.]: let justice be done even if the heavens fall
flagrante delicto [Lat.]: in the very act
folie de grandeur [Fr.]: delusion of grandeur
force de frappe [Fr.]: strike force—used esp. of nuclear forces
frisson [Fr.]: thrill; shudder
Gesundheit [G]: good health
gnōthi seauton [Gr.]: know thyself
gracias [Sp.]: thank you
grande dame [Fr.]: great lady
guten Tag [G]: good day; hello
habeas corpus [Lat.]: writ to bring a person before a court or judge
hasta la vista [Sp.]: see you later
haut monde [Fr.]: high society; the fashionable world
hoi polloi [Gk.]: the common people
honi soit qui mal y pense [Fr.]: shame to him who thinks evil of it—motto of the Order of the Garter
hors concours [Fr.]: out of the running
ich dien [G.]: I serve—motto of the Prince of Wales
inshallah [Ar.]: if Allah wills it; God willing
in vino veritas [Lat.]: in wine there is truth
ipso facto [Lat.]: by the fact itself
je ne sais quoi [Fr.]: I know not what; an elusive quality
jeu de mots [Fr.]: play on words
jeu d'esprit [Fr.]: play of wit
jeunesse dorée [Fr.]: gilded youth
Kinder, Kirche, Küche [G.]: children, church, kitchen
laissez faire [Fr.]: noninterference
l'art pour l'art [Fr.]: art for art's sake
le coeur a ses raisons que la raison ne connaît point [Fr.]: the heart has its reasons that reason knows nothing of—Pascal
l'état c'est moi [Fr.]: I am the state—Attributed to Louis XIV
mano a mano [Sp.]: hand in hand; together
mauvais goût [Fr.]: bad taste
mea culpa [Lat.]: I am to blame
meden agan [Gk.]: nothing in excess
mens sana in corpore sano [Lat.]: a healthy mind in a healthy body—Juvenal
mirabile dictu [Lat.]: wonderful to relate
modus operandi [Lat.]: a method of operating
n'est-ce pas? [Fr.]: isn't that so?
nicht wahr? [G.]: isn't that so?
n'importe [Fr.]: no matter
nom de plume [Fr.]: pen name
non compos mentis [Lat.]: not of sound mind
non sequitur [Lat.]: it does not follow
omnia vincit amor [Lat.]: love conquers all—Virgil
O tempora! O mores! [Lat.]: O times! O morals!; what corrupt times we live in!—Cicero
per annum [Lat.]: by the year
per capita [Lat.]: per unit of population
per diem [Lat.]: by the day
persona non grata [Lat.]: unacceptable or unwelcome person
peu à peu [Fr.]: little by little
pièce d'occasion [Fr.]: musical or literary work composed for a special occasion
plus ça change, plus c'est le même chose [Fr.]: the more things change, the more they remain the same
post mortem [Lat.]: after death
prêt-à-porter [Fr.]: ready to wear
pro bono publico [Lat.]: for the public good
pro patria [Lat.]: for one's country
que será será [Sp.]: what will be will be
quid pro quo [Lat.]: something for something; an equal exchange
repondez s'il vous plaît [Fr.]: please reply— Used on invitation cards (abbr. R.S.V.P.)
requiescat in pace [Lat.]: rest in peace
salto mortale [Ital.]: deadly leap
salud [Sp.]: health; to your health
sans peur et sans reproche [Fr.]: without fear and above reproach; chivalrous
sans-souci [Fr.]: carefree pleasure
savoir faire [Fr.]: the ability to say and do the correct thing
se non è vero, è ben trovato [Ital.]: even if it isn't true, it's a wonderful invention
shalom [Heb.]: peace, used as a greeting
sic transit gloria mundi [Lat.]: thus passes away the glory of the world
s'il vous plaît [Fr.]: if you please
sine die [Lat.]: with no day set for a future meeting; indefinitely
sine qua non [Lat.]: indispensable
status (in) quo [Lat.]: the existing condition
sui generis [Lat.]: unique; individual
tant pis [Fr.]: so much the worse
tempus fugit [Lat.]: time flies
terra incognita [Lat.]: unknown territory
ton [Fr.]: fashionable society
tout de suite [Fr.]: immediately; all at once
tout le monde [Fr.]: everybody; everyone of importance
uomo universale [Ital.]: universal man; one of broad education and ability
utile dulci [Lat.]: the useful with the pleasurable—Horace
veni, vidi, vici [Lat.]: I came, I saw,

I conquered—attributed to Julius Caesar
vis-à-vis [Fr.]: face to face
vive la différence [Fr.]: long live the difference (between the sexes)
wie geht's? [G.]: how are things?
wunderbar [G.]: wonderful
Wunderkind [G.]: child prodigy

Clichés and Redundant Expressions

(*Source: Webster's II New Riverside Dictionary,* Office Edition, Houghton Mifflin Company 1984.)

Clichés

Webster's II defines the word cliché as "A hackneyed expression or idea." Since most clichés express rather clear meanings, the writer will have to determine whether it is a shade of meaning that is hard to convey by fresher wording. If the process of substitution is too difficult, use of some of the phrases that follow may be advisable. But few on the following list are truly indispensable.

acid test
add insult to injury
all in a day's work
all over but the shouting
all work and no play
apple of one's eye
armed to the teeth
as luck would have it
at a loss for words
at one fell swoop
axe to grind
bag and baggage
bark up the wrong tree
beat a dead horse
beat a hasty retreat
beat around the bush
best foot forward
best-laid plans
bigger (*or* larger) than life
bite off more than one can chew
bolt from the blue
bone of contention
breathe a sigh of relief
bright and early
bring home the bacon
budding genius
bull in a china shop
burning question
burn the midnight oil
busy as a bee
by leaps and bounds
calm before the storm
can't see the forest for the trees
caught red-handed
checkered career
chip off the old block
cool as a cucumber
crying need
cut a long story short
dead giveaway
diamond in the rough
discreet silence
down in the dumps (*or* mouth)
down one's alley
drastic action
draw the line
ear to the ground
easier said than done
eat one's hat (*or* words)
eloquent silence
epic struggle
face the music
fall on deaf ears
far cry
fast and loose
fat's in the fire
feather in one's cap
few and far between
fill the bill
first and foremost
fit as a fiddle
flash in the pan
flesh and blood
food for thought
foot in one's mouth
free as a bird (*or* the air)
fresh as a daisy
generous to a fault
gentle as a lamb
get down to brass tacks
get one's back (*or* dander) up
gift of gab
gild the lily
goes without saying
grain of salt
grind to a halt
hale and hearty
handwriting on the wall
hard row to hoe
haul (*or* rake) over the coals
head over heels
heave a sigh of relief
high and dry
high as a kite
hit the nail on the head
hit the spot
hook, line, and sinker
hook or crook
hue and cry
hungry as a bear (*or* lion)
in no uncertain terms
in on the ground floor
in the final (*or* last) analysis
in the long run
in the nick of time
in the twinkling of an eye
in this day and age
irons in the fire
jig is up
just deserts
keep one's chin up
labor of love
land-office business
last but not least
last straw
lean over backward
leaps and bounds
leave in the lurch
leave no stone unturned
lend a helping hand
let one's hair down
let the cat out of the bag
let well enough alone
like a house afire (*or* on fire)
lock, stock and barrel
mad as a hornet (or wet hen)
mad dash
make a long story short
make ends meet
matter of life and death
meet one's Waterloo
method in one's madness
milk of human kindness
mince words
month of Sundays
moot question (*or* point)
more than meets the eye
more the merrier
motley crew
naked truth
necessary evil
needle in a haystack
neither here nor there
never a dull moment
never rains but it pours
nip in the bud
none the worse for wear
no sooner said than done
nothing new under the sun
once in a blue moon
on cloud nine
opportunity knocks
other side of the coin
out of the frying pan and into the fire
own worst enemy
paint the town red
part and parcel
penny for one's thoughts
perfect gentleman
pet peeve
pick and choose
pillar of society
play it by ear
point with pride
poor but honest
powers that be
pretty as a picture
pretty kettle of fish
pretty penny
psychological moment
quick as a flash
quiet as a mouse
rack one's brains
rain cats and dogs
raise Cain
read the riot act
red-letter day
reliable source
ring true
ripe old age
rub one the wrong way
sadder but wiser
save for a rainy day
seal one's fate (*or* doom)

second to none
sell like hot cakes
separate the men from the boys
shot in the arm
show one's hand
sick and tired
sigh of relief
sight for sore eyes
six of one and (a) half dozen of the other
skeleton in one's closet
small world
smell a rat
sour grapes
sow one's wild oats
stick out like a sore thumb
stick to one's guns
stiff upper lip
stir up a hornet's nest
straight from the shoulder
straight and narrow
straw in the wind
straw that broke the camel's back
strong as an ox
stubborn as a mule
sweat of one's brow
take a dim view of
take the bull by the horns
talk through one's hat
this day and age
this point in time
throw caution to the winds
throw in the towel
throw the book at
time immemorial
time of one's life
tip the scales
tired as a dog
tit for tat
too funny for words
too little, too late
too numerous to mention
trials and tribulations
true blue
turn over a new leaf
uncharted seas
untimely end
up the creek without a paddle
vanish into thin air
view with alarm
wash one's hands of
wear and tear
wear two hats
wee (small) hours
when all is said and done
wide-open spaces
wise as an owl
without further ado
wolf in sheep's clothing
word to the wise
worse for wear

Redundant Expressions

Redundancy— the needless repetition of ideas— is one of the principal obstacles to writing clear, precise prose. The elements repeated in the phrases and in the brief definitions are italicized. To eliminate redundancy, delete the italic elements in the phrases.

***old* antique:** (= an object having special value because of its *age,* esp. a work of art or handicraft more than 100 years *old*)
ascend *upward*: (= to go or move *upward*)
assemble *together*: (= to bring or gather *together*)
***pointed* barb:** (= a sharp *point* projecting in reverse direction to the main point of a weapon or tool)
***first* beginning:** (= the *first* part)
big *in size*: (= of considerable *size*)
bisect *in two*: (= to cut *into two* equal parts)
blend *together*: (= to combine, mix, or go well *together*)
capitol *building*: (= a *building* in which a legislative body meets)
coalesce *together*: (= to grow or come *together* so as to form a whole)
collaborate *together* or *jointly*: (= to work *together,* esp. in a joint effort)
***fellow* colleague:** (= a *fellow* member of a profession, staff, or academic faculty)
congregate *together*: (= to bring or come *together* in a crowd)
connect *together*: (= to join or fasten *together*)
consensus *of opinion*: (= collective *opinion*)
courthouse *building*: (= a *building* in which judicial courts or county government offices are housed)
***habitual* custom:** (= a *habitual* practice)
descend *downward*: (= to move, slope, extend, or incline *downward*)
endorse (a check) *on the back*: (= to write one's signature *on the back of,* e.g., a check)
erupt *violently*: (= to emerge *violently* or to become *violently* active)
explode *violently*: (= to burst *violently* from internal pressure)
***real* fact:** (= something with *real,* demonstrable existence)
***passing* fad:** (= a *passing* fashion)
few *in number*: (= amounting to or made up of a *small number*)
founder *and sink*: (= to *sink* beneath the water)
***basic* fundamental:** (= a *basic* or essential part)
fuse *together*: (= to mix *together* by or as if by melting)
gather *together*: (= to come *together* or cause to come *together*)
***free* gift:** (= something bestowed voluntarily and *without compensation*)
***past* history:** (= a narrative of *past* events; something that took place *in the past*)
hoist *up*: (= to raise or to haul *up* with or as if with a mechanical device)
***current* or *present* incumbent:** (= one *currently* holding an office)
***new* innovation:** (= something *new* or unusual)
join *together*: (= to bring or put *together* so as to make continuous or form a unit
knots *per hour*: (= a unit of speed, one nautical mile *per hour,* approx. 1.15 statute miles *per hour*)
large *in size*: (= greater than average *in size*)
merge *together*: (= to blend or cause to blend *together* gradually)
***necessary* need:** (= something *necessary* or wanted)
***universal* panacea:** (= a remedy for *all* diseases, evils, or difficulties)
***continue to* persist:** (= to *continue* in existence)
***individual* person:** (= an *individual* human being)
***chief* or *leading* or *main* protagonist:** (= the *leading* character in a Greek drama or other literary form; a *leading* or *principal* figure)
***original* prototype:** (= an *original* type, form, or instance that is a model on which later stages are based or judged)
protrude *out*: (= to push or thrust *outward*)
recall *back*: (= to summon *back* to awareness; to bring *back*)
recoil *back*: (= to kick or spring *back;* to shrink *back* in fear or loathing; to fall *back*)
recur *again* or *repeatedly*: (= to occur *again* or *repeatedly*)
***temporary* reprieve:** (= *temporary* relief, as from danger or pain)
short *in length* or *height*: (= having very little *length* or *height*)
small *in size*: (= characterized by relatively little *size* or slight *dimensions*)
***completely* unanimous:** (= being in *complete* harmony, accord, or agreement)

Business Letter Styles

The Block Letter

Houghton Mifflin Company

Two Park Street, Boston, Massachusetts 02108
(617) 725-5000 Cable HOUGHTON

Reference Division

January 4, 19--

Mr. Peter C. Cunningham
Vice-president, Operations
CCC Chemicals, Ltd.
321 Park Avenue
City, US 98765

Dear Mr. Cunningham:

Subject: Block Letter Style

This is the Block Letter--a format featuring elements aligned with the left margin. The date is typed from two to six (or more) lines below the letterhead, depending on the length of the message. The inside address may be typed from two to four lines below the date line, also depending on message length. Double spacing is used between the inside address and the salutation. A subject line, if used, appears two lines below the salutation and two lines above the first message line. Had an attention line been used here, it would have been positioned two lines below the last line of the inside address and two lines above the salutation.

The paragraphs are single-spaced internally with double spacing separating them from each other. Displayed matter such as enumerations and long quotations are indented by six character spaces. Units within enumerations and any quoted matter are single-spaced internally with double spacing setting them off from the rest of the text.

The heading for a continuation sheet begins six lines from the top edge of the page. The heading is blocked flush with the left margin:

Page 2
Mr. Peter C. Cunningham
January 4, 19--

Skip two lines from the last line of the message to the complimentary close. Allow at least four blank lines for the written signature. Block the typed signature and corporate title under the complimentary close. Insert ancillary notations such as the typist's initials two spaces below the last line of the signature block.

Sincerely yours,

John M. Swanson

John M. Swanson
Executive Vice-president

JMS:ahs

Enclosures: 4

Atlanta / Dallas / Geneva, Illinois / Hopewell, New Jersey / Palo Alto / London

Source: The Professional Secretary's Handbook, Copyright ©, Houghton Mifflin Company.

Business Letter Styles

The Modified Block Letter

Houghton Mifflin Company

Two Park Street, Boston, Massachusetts 02108
(617) 725-5000 Cable HOUGHTON

Reference Division

January 14, 19--

CERTIFIED MAIL
CONFIDENTIAL

Sarah H. O'Day, Esq.
O'Day, Ryan & Sweeney
One Court Street
City, US 98765

Dear Ms. O'Day:

SUBJECT: MODIFIED BLOCK LETTER

This is the Modified Block Letter, the features of which are similar to those of the Block Letter with the exception of the positioning of the date line, the complimentary close, and the typewritten signature block. The positioning of the date line determines the placement of the complimentary close and the signature block, both of which must be vertically aligned with the date. The date itself may be centered on the page, placed about five spaces to the right of center as shown here, or set flush with the right margin. Any one of these positions is acceptable.

The subject line, typed here in capital letters, is set flush left. Had an attention line been used it too would have been positioned flush with the left margin. Note that the special mailing and handling notations appear flush left, two lines above the first line of the inside address.

The continuation sheet heading, unlike that of the Simplified and Block Letters, is spread across the top of the page, at least six vertical lines beneath the top edge:

Ms. O'Day - 2 - January 14, 19--

Notice the centered page number enclosed by spaced hyphens. Another way of styling the page number is to enclose it with hyphens set tight to the number. Either style is entirely acceptable.

The complimentary close--aligned with the date--appears two lines below the last message line. At least four blank lines have been allowed for the written signature. The typed signature block is then aligned with the complimentary close.

Ancillary notations such as typist's initials, enclosure notations, and lists of copy recipients are placed two lines below the signature block, flush with the left margin.

Very truly yours,

Kathleen N. Lear

Kathleen N. Lear
Permissions Editor

KNL:ahs

Atlanta Dallas Geneva, Illinois Hopewell, New Jersey Palo Alto London

Source: The Professional Secretary's Handbook, Copyright ©, Houghton Mifflin Company.

WHERE TO FIND OUT MORE

Reference Books And Other Sources

This cannot be a record of all the thousands of available sources of information. Nevertheless, these selected references will enable the reader to locate additional facts about many subjects covered in the *Information Please Almanac.* The editors have chosen sources that they believe will be helpful to the general reader.

General References

Encyclopedias are a unique category, since they attempt to cover most subjects quite thoroughly. The most valuable multivolume encyclopedias are the **Encyclopaedia Britannica** and the **Encyclopedia Americana.** Useful one-volume encyclopedias are the **New Columbia Encyclopedia** and the **Random House Encyclopedia.**

Dictionaries and similar "word books" are also unique: **The American Heritage Dictionary, Second College Edition,** containing 200,000 definitions and specialized usage guidance; **The American Heritage Illustrated Encyclopedic Dictionary,** containing 180,000 entries, 275 boxed encyclopedic features, and 175 colored maps of the world; **Webster's Third New International Dictionary, Unabridged; Webster's II New Riverside University Dictionary,** containing 200,000 definitions plus hundreds of word history paragraphs; and the multivolume **Oxford English Dictionary,** providing definitions in historical order. **Roget's II The New Thesaurus,** containing thousands of synonyms grouped according to meaning, assists writers in choosing just the right word. The quick reference set—**The Word Book II** (over 40,000 words spelled and divided), **The Right Word II** (a concise thesaurus), and **The Written Word II** (a concise guide to writing, style, and usage)—are based on **The American Heritage Dictionary** and are intended for the busy reader needing information fast. Two excellent books of quotations are **Bartlett's Familiar Quotations** and **The Oxford Dictionary of Quotations.**

There are a number of useful atlases: the **New York Times Atlas of the World,** a number of historical atlases (Penguin Books), **Oxford Economic Atlas of the World, Rand McNally Cosmopolitan World Atlas: New Census Edition,** and **Atlas of the Historical Geography of the United States** (Greenwood). Many contemporary road atlases of the United States and foreign countries are also available.

A source of information on virtually all subjects is the United States Government Printing Office (GPO). For information, write: Superintendent of Documents, Washington, D.C. 20402.

For help on any subject, consult: **Subject Guide to Books in Print, The New York Times Index,** and the **Reader's Guide to Periodical Literature** in your library.

Specific References

Airplanes, A Field Guide to (Houghton Mifflin)
Almanac, Places Rated (Rand McNally)
America Votes (Congressional Quarterly, Inc.)
American Indian, Reference Encyclopedia of the (B. Klein Publications)
American Revolution, The (American Heritage)
Anatomy, Gray's (Saunders)
Antiques and Collectibles Price List, the Kovels' (Crown)
Architecture, Encyclopedia of World (VanNostrand Reinhold)
Art, History of (Prentice-Hall)
Art, Oxford Companion to (Oxford University Press)
Art, Who's Who in American (R.R. Bowker)
Art Directory, American (R.R. Bowker)
Art Terms, Dictionary of: Architecture, Sculpture, Painting & the Graphic Arts (Sterling)
Associations, Encyclopedia of (Gale Research Co.)
Authors, 1000–1900, European (H.W. Wilson)
Authors, Twentieth Century (H.W. Wilson)
Automobile Facts and Figures (Kallman)
Automobile Year Book of Models (Motorbooks International)
Ballets, Balanchine's Complete Stories of the Great (Doubleday)
Banking and Finance, Encyclopedia of (Bankers Publishing Co.)
Baseball Encyclopedia (Macmillan)
(Baseball) **World Series Record Book** (Sporting News)
Biographical Dictionary, Chambers (Cambridge University Press)
Biography Yearbook, Current (H.W. Wilson)
Birds, Field Guide to the, Peterson Field Guide Series (Houghton Mifflin)
Black Americans, Who's Who Among (Who's Who Among Black Americans, Inc.)
Book Review Digest, 1905– (H.W. Wilson)
Catholic Encyclopedia, New (Publishers Guild)
Chemistry, Encyclopedia of (VanNostrand Rinehold)
Chemistry, Lange's Handbook of, 13th Edition (McGraw Hill)
Christian Church, Oxford Dictionary of the (Oxford University Press)
Churches, Yearbook of American and Canadian (Abingdon Press)
Citizens Band: Radio Rules and Regulations (AMECO)
College Cost Book, 1986-87, The (The College Board)
Communist Affairs, Yearbook on International (Hoover Institution Press)
Composers, Great 1300–1900 (H.W. Wilson)
Composers Since 1900 (H.W. Wilson)
Computer Science and Technology, Encyclopedia of (Dekker)
(Computer software) **Yellow Book: A Parent's Guide to Teacher Tested Educational Software** (NEA Computer Services Staff)
Computer Terms, Encyclopedia of (Barron)
Condo and Co-op Information Book, Complete (Houghton Mifflin)
Congressional Quarterly Almanac (Congressional Quarterly, Inc.)
Consumer Reports (Consumers Union)
Costume, The Dictionary of (Scribners)
Drama, Crowell's Handbook of Classical (T.Y. Crowell)

Drama, 20th Century, England, Ireland, the United States (Random House)
Ecology Information and Organizations, Guide to (H.W. Wilson)
Energy Factbook (McGraw-Hill)
Environmental Science (Saunders College Publishing)
Europa Year Book (Gale Research Co.)
Fact Books, The Rand McNally (Rand)
Facts, Famous First (H.W. Wilson)
Facts on File (Facts on File, Inc.)
Film: A Reference Guide (Greenwood)
(Film) **Guide to Movies on Video-cassette** (Consumers Reports)
(Finance) **Touche Ross Guide to Personal Financial Management** (Prentice-Hall)
Fishing: An Encyclopedic Guide (Dutton)
Food and Drink, Dictionary of American (Ticknor & Fields)
Football Made Easy (Jonathan David)
Games, Book of (Jazz Press)
Gardening, Encyclopedia of (Houghton Mifflin)
Gardening for Food and Fun (U.S. Department of Agriculture, Government Printing Office)
Geography, Dictionary of (Penguin Books)
Government Manual, U.S. (U.S. Office of the Federal Register, Government Printing Office)
History, Album of American (Scribner's)
History, Dictionary of American (Rowman)
History, Documents of American (Prentice-Hall)
History, Encyclopedia of Latin-American (Greenwood)
History, Encyclopedia of World (Houghton Mifflin)
Hockey, the Illustrated History: An Official Publication of the National Hockey League (Doubleday)
Infomania, The Guide to Essential Electronic Services (Houghton Mifflin Company)
Islam, Dictionary of (Orient Book Distributors)
Jazz in the Seventies, Encyclopedia of (Horizon)
Jewish Concepts, Encyclopedia of (Hebrew Publishers)
Legal Word Book, The (Houghton Mifflin)
Libraries, World Guide to (K. G. Saur)
Library Directory, American (R.R. Bowker)
Literary Market Place (R. R. Bowker)
Literature, Oxford Companion to American (Oxford University Press)
Literature, Oxford Companion to Classical (Oxford University Press)
Literature, Oxford Companion to English (Oxford University Press)
(Literature) **Reader's Adviser: A Layman's Guide to Literature** (R.R. Bowker)
Literature, Reader's Encyclopedia of American (T.Y. Crowell)
Medical Encyclopedia, Home (Fawcett)
Medical & Health Sciences Word Book, The (Houghton Mifflin)
Museums of the World (K.G. Saur)
Music and Musicians, Handbook of American (Da Capo)
Music, Concise Oxford Dictionary of (Oxford University Press)
Music, Harvard Dictionary of (Harvard University Press)
Musical Terms, Dictionary of (Gordon Press)
Mystery Writers, Twentieth Century Crime and (St. Martin's Press)
Mythology (Little, Brown and Co.)
National Park Guide (Rand McNally)
New Nations: A Student Handbook (Shoe String)
Numismatics (Oxford University Press)
Occupational Outlook Handbook (U.S. Bureau of Labor Statistics, Government Printing Office)
Operas, New Milton Cross Complete Stories of the Great (Doubleday)
Pain, Coping With Chronic (Sister Kenney Institute)
Physicians' Desk Reference (Medical Economics Company)
Physics, Handbook of, 2nd Edition (McGraw Hill)
Pocket Data Book, U.S.A. (U.S. Department of Commerce, Bureau of the Census, Government Printing Office)
Poetry, Granger's Index to (Columbia University Press)
Politics, Almanac of American (Barone & Co.)
Politics, Who's Who in American (R.R. Bowker)
Pop/Rock, Dictionary of American (Schirmer Books)
Religions, The Facts on File Dictionary of (Facts on File)
Robert's Rules of Order Revised (Morrow & Co.)
Sailboats, A Field Guide to (Houghton Mifflin)
Science, American Men and Women of (R.R. Bowker)
Science and Technology, Asimov's Biographical Encyclopedia of (Doubleday)
Scientific Encyclopedia, VanNostrand's (VanNostrand Reinhold)
Secondary Schools, Guide to Independent 1986-87 (Peterson's Guides)
Secretary's Handbook, The Professional (Houghton Mifflin)
Shakespeare, The Riverside (Houghton Mifflin)
Stagecraft for Nonprofessionals (University of Wisconsin Press)
Stamp Collection As a Hobby (Sterling)
Stars and Planets, Field Guide to the (Houghton Mifflin)
States, Book of (Council of State Governments)
Statesman's Year-Book (St. Martin's)
Theater, Oxford Companion to the (Oxford University Press)
Theater, Who's Who in the (Gale Research Co.)
(Travel) **The Birnbaum Guides** (Houghton Mifflin)
United Nations, Demographic Yearbook (Unipub)
United Nations, Statistical Yearbook of the (Unipub)
United States, Historical Statistics of the (U.S. Department of Commerce, Bureau of the Census, Government Printing Office)
United States, Statistical Abstract of the (U.S. Department of Commerce, Bureau of the Census, Government Printing Office)
Washington Information Directory (Congressional Quarterly, Inc.)
Weather Book, The American (Houghton Mifflin)
Who's Who in America (Marquis)
Wines, Dictionary of American (Morrow)
Women, Notable American (Harvard University Press)
World War I (American Heritage)
World War II (American Heritage)
Writer's Market (Writers Digest)
Zip Code and Post Office Directory, National (U.S. Postal Service, Government Printing Office)

See the full range of publications of Dun & Bradstreet and Standard & Poor's for corporate financial and stockholder information.

For detailed information on American colleges and universities, see the many publications of the **American Council on Education.**

Also see many other specialized **Who's Who** volumes not listed here for biographies of famous people in many fields.

RELIGION

Major Religions of the World

Judaism

The determining factors of Judaism are: descendance from Israel, the *Torah*, and Tradition.

The name Israel (Jacob, a patriarch) also signifies his descendants as a people. During the 15th–13th centuries B.C., Israelite tribes, coming from South and East, gradually settled in Palestine, then inhabited by Canaanites. They were held together by Moses, who gave them religious unity in the worship of *Jahweh*, the God who had chosen Israel to be his people.

Under Judges, the 12 tribes at first formed an amphictyonic covenant. Saul established kingship (circa 1050 B.C.), and under David, his successor (1000–960 B.C.), the State of Israel comprised all of Palestine with Jerusalem as religio-political center. A golden era followed under Solomon (965–926 B.C.), who built *Jahweh* a temple.

After Solomon's death, the kingdom separated into Israel in the North and Judah in the South. A period of conflicts ensued, which ended with the conquest of Israel by Assyria in 722 B.C. The Babylonians defeated Judah in 586 B.C., destroying Jerusalem and its temple, and deporting many to Babylon.

The era of the kings is significant also in that the great prophets worked in that time, emphasizing faith in *Jahweh* as both God of Israel and God of the universe, and stressing social justice.

When the Persians permitted the Jews to return from exile (539 B.C.), temple and cult were restored in Jerusalem. The Persian rulers were succeeded by the Seleucides. The Maccabaean revolt against these Hellenistic kings gave independence to the Jews in 128 B.C., which lasted till the Romans occupied the country.

Important groups that exerted influence during these times were the Sadducees, priests in the temple in Jerusalem; the Pharisees, teachers of the Law in the synagogues; Essenes, a religious order (from whom Dead Sea Scrolls, discovered in 1947, came); Apocalyptists, who were expecting the heavenly Messiah; and Zealots, who were prepared to fight for national independence.

When the latter turned against Rome in A.D. 66, Roman armies under Titus suppressed the revolt,

Estimated Membership of the Principal Religions of the World

Statistics of the world's religions are only very rough approximations. Aside from Christianity, few religions, if any, attempt to keep statistical records; and even Protestants and Catholics employ different methods of counting members. All persons of whatever age who have received baptism in the Catholic Church are counted as members, while in most Protestant Churches only those who "join" the church are numbered. The compiling of statistics is further complicated by the fact that in China one may be at the same time a Confucian, a Taoist, and a Buddhist. In Japan, one may be both a Buddhist and a Shintoist.

Religion	North America[1]	South America	Europe[2]	Asia	Africa	Oceania[3]	World
Total Christians	231,539,720	388,863,450	517,612,800	200,568,910	259,544,680	21,143,000	1,619,272,560
Roman Catholics	88,144,650	365,973,680	258,792,110	81,768,040	98,557,180	7,310,180	900,545,840
Protestants	96,293,800	13,417,650	88,382,650	51,920,810	69,087,120	7,449,790	326,551,820
Orthodox	5,948,530	421,240	124,071,350	3,275,450	24,129,950	506,130	158,352,650
Anglicans	7,760,000	1,191,100	33,076,870	613,760	21,496,950	5,463,380	69,602,060
Other Christians	33,392,740	7,859,780	13,289,820	62,990,850	46,273,480	413,520	164,220,190
Muslims	2,675,720	625,180	40,536,360	559,222,950	237,067,660	93,520	840,221,390
Nonreligious	19,310,020	12,751,380	131,770,570	637,770,890	1,433,850	2,859,170	805,895,880
Hindus	764,200	636,340	586,840	644,228,100	1,395,390	284,080	647,894,950
Buddhists	193,440	496,980	559,310	306,135,570	13,850	16,880	307,416,030
Atheists	1,029,120	2,388,410	77,715,300	138,666,370	234,470	507,920	220,541,590
Chinese folk religionists	116,160	68,460	50,450	202,491,510	10,220	19,170	202,755,970
New religionists	1,025,050	357,830	33,670	108,067,100	12,080	4,910	109,500,640
Tribal religionists	65,210	1,168,160	50	25,988,510	70,170,270	84,730	97,476,930
Jews	8,050,100	976,230	4,697,440	3,895,760	276,390	85,540	17,981,460
Sikhs	8,660	5,950	212,290	15,898,370	29,110	6,530	16,160,910
Shamanists	290	500	300,050	12,840,530	1,100	290	13,142,760
Confucians	1,020	500	1,190	5,637,090	550	290	5,640,640
Baha'is	300,110	543,460	71,990	2,272,460	1,319,350	56,540	4,563,910
Shintoists	710	990	490	3,424,160	50	590	3,426,990
Jains	2,040	1,980	9,890	3,305,080	49,980	980	3,369,950
Other religionists	685,050	6,725,010	301,140	274,250	63,400	23,270	8,072,120
Total	**265,766,620**	**415,610,810**	**774,459,830**	**2,870,687,610**	**571,622,400**	**25,187,410**	**4,923,334,680**

1. Includes Central America and West Indies. 2. Includes the U.S.S.R. and other countries with established Marxist ideology where continuing religious adherence is difficult to estimate. 3. Includes Australia and New Zealand, as well as islands of the South Pacific. *Source: Britiannica Book of the Year, 1987.*

destroying Jerusalem and its temple in A.D. 70. The Jews were scattered in the *diaspora* (Dispersion), subject to oppressions until the Age of the Enlightenment (18th century) brought their emancipation, although persecutions did not end entirely.

The fall of the Jerusalem temple was an important event in the religious life of the Jews, which now developed around *Torah* (Law) and synagogue. Around A.D. 100 the Sacred Scriptures were codified. Synagogue worship became central, with readings from *Torah* and prophets. Most important prayers are the *Shema* (Hear) and the Prayer of the 18 Benedictions.

Religious life is guided by the commandments contained in the *Torah:* circumcision and *Sabbath,* as well as other ethical and ceremonial commandments.

The *Talmud,* based on the *Mishnah* and its interpretations, took shape over many centuries in the Babylonian and Palestinian Schools. It was a strong binding force of Judaism in the Dispersion.

In the 12th century, Maimonides formulated his "13 Articles of Faith," which carried great authority. Fundamental in this creed are: belief in God and his oneness *(Sherma),* belief in the changeless *Torah,* in the words of Moses and the prophets, belief in reward and punishment, the coming of the Messiah, and the resurrection of the dead.

Judaism is divided into theological schools, the main divisions of which are Orthodox, Conservative, and Reform.

Christianity

Christianity is founded upon Jesus Christ, to whose life the New Testament writings testify. Jesus, a Jew, was born in about 7 B.C. and assumed his public life, after his 30th year, in Galilee. The Gospels tell of many extraordinary deeds that accompanied his ministry. He proclaimed the Kingdom of God, a future reality that is at the same time already present. Nationalistic-Jewish expectations of the Messiah he rejected. Rather, he referred to himself as the "Son of Man," the Christ, who has power to forgive sins now and who shall also come as Judge at the end of time. Jesus set forth the religio-ethical demands for participation in the Kingdom of God as change of heart and love of God and neighbor.

At the Last Supper he signified his death as a sacrifice, which would inaugurate the New Covenant, by which many would be saved. Circa A.D. 30 he died on a cross in Jerusalem. The early Church carried on Jesus' proclamation, the apostle Paul emphasizing his death and resurrection.

The person of Jesus is fundamental to the Christian faith since it is believed that in his life, death, and resurrection, God's revelation became historically tangible. He is seen as the turning point in history, and man's relationship to God as determined by his attitude to Jesus.

Historically Christianity thus arose out of Judaism, claiming fulfillment of the promises of the Old Testament in Jesus. The early Church designated itself as "the true Israel," which expected the speedy return of Jesus. The mother church was at Jerusalem, but churches were soon founded in many other places. The apostle Paul was instrumental in founding and extending a Gentile Christianity that was free from Jewish legalism.

The new religion spread rapidly throughout the eastern and western parts of the Roman Empire. In coming to terms with other religious movements within the Empire, Christianity began to take definite shape as an organization in its doctrine, liturgy, and ministry circa A.D. 200. In the 4th century the Catholic Church had taken root in countries stretching from Spain in the West to Persia and India in the East. Christians had been repeatedly subject to persecution by the Roman state, but finally gained tolerance under Constantine the Great (A.D. 313). Since that time, the Church became favored under his successors and in 380 the Emperor Theodosius proclaimed Christianity the State religion. Paganism was suppressed and public life was gradually molded in accordance with Christian ethical demands.

It was in these years also that the Church was able to achieve a certain unity of doctrine. Due to differences of interpretation of basic doctrines concerning Christ, which threatened to divide the Catholic Church, a standard Christian Creed was formulated by bishops at successive Ecumenical Councils, the first of which was held in A.D. 325 (Nicaea). The chief doctrines formulated concerned the doctrine of the Trinity, i.e., that there is one God in three persons: Father, Son, and Holy Spirit (Constantinople, A.D. 381); and the nature of Christ as both divine and human (Chalcedon, A.D. 541).

Through differences and rivalry between East and West the unity of the Church was broken by schism in 1054. In 1517 a separation occurred in the Western Church with the Reformation. From the major Protestant denominations [Lutheran, Presbyterian, Anglican (Episcopalian)], many Free Churches separated themselves in an age of individualism.

In the 20th century, however, the direction is toward unity. The Ecumenical Movement led to the formation of the World Council of Churches in 1948 (Amsterdam), which has since been joined by many Protestant and Orthodox Churches.

Through its missionary activity Christianity has spread to most parts of the globe.

Eastern Orthodoxy

Eastern Orthodoxy comprises the faith and practice of Churches stemming from ancient Churches in the Eastern part of the Roman Empire. The term covers Orthodox Churches in communion with the See of Constantinople, Uniate Churches in communion with Rome, and Nestorian and Monophysite Churches.

The Orthodox, Catholic, Apostolic Church is the direct descendant of the Byzantine State Church and consists of a series of independent national

U. S. Church Membership

Religious group	Members
Protestant bodies and others	79,095,746
Roman Catholics	52,654,908
Jewish congregations[1]	5,834,635
Eastern churches	4,025,698
Old Catholic, Polish National Catholic, Armenian churches	1,024,330
Buddhist Churches of America	100,000
Miscellaneous	191,046
Total[2]	**142,926,363**

1. Includes Orthodox, Conservative, and Reform. 2. As reported in the *1987 Yearbook* from statistics furnished by 218 religious bodies in the United States.

churches that are united by Doctrine, Liturgy, and Hierarchical organization (deacons and priests, who may either be married or be monks before ordination, and bishops, who must be celibates). The heads of these Churches are patriarchs or metropolitans; the Patriarch of Constantinople is only "first among equals." Rivalry between the Pope of Rome and the Patriarch of Constantinople, aided by differences and misunderstandings that existed for centuries between the Eastern and Western parts of the Empire, led to a schism in 1054. Repeated attempts at reunion have failed in past centuries. The mutual excommunication pronounced in that year was lifted in 1965, however, and because of greater interaction in theology between Orthodox Churches and those in the West, a climate of better understanding has been created in the 20th century. First contacts were with Anglicans and Old Catholics. Orthodox Churches belong to the World Council of Churches.

The Eastern Orthodox Churches recognize only the canons of the seven Ecumenical Councils (325–787) as binding for faith and they reject doctrines that have been added in the West.

The central worship service is called the Liturgy, which is understood as representation of God's acts of salvation. Its center is the celebration of the Eucharist, or Lord's Supper.

In their worship *icons* (sacred pictures) are used that have a sacramental meaning as representation. The Mother of Christ, angels, and saints are highly venerated.

The number of sacraments in the Orthodox Church is the same as in the Western Catholic Church.

Orthodox Churches are found in the Balkans and the Soviet Union also, since the 20th century, in Western Europe and other parts of the world, particularly in America.

Eastern Orthodoxy also includes the Uniate Churches that recognize the authority of the Pope but keep their own traditional liturgies and those Churches dating back to the 5th century that emanicipated themselves from the Byzantine State Church: the Nestorian Church in the Near East and India with approximately half a million members and the Monophysite Churches with some 17 million members (Coptic, Ethiopian, Syrian, Armenian, and the Mar Thoma Church in India).

Roman Catholicism

Roman Catholicism comprises the belief and practice of the Roman Catholic Church. The Church stands under the authority of the Bishop of Rome, the Pope, and is ruled by him and bishops who are held to be, through ordination, successors of Peter and the Apostles, respectively. Fundamental to the structure of the Church is the juridical aspect: doctrine and sacraments are bound to the power of jurisdiction and consecration of the hierarchy. The Pope, as the head of the hierarchy of archbishops, bishops, priests, and deacons, has full ecclesiastical power, granted him by Christ, through Peter. As successor to Peter, he is the Vicar of Christ. The powers that others in the hierarchy possess are delegated.

Roman Catholics believe their Church to be the one, holy, catholic, and apostolic Church, possessing all the properties of the one, true Church of Christ.

The faith of the Church is understood to be identical with that taught by Christ and his Apostles and contained in Bible and Tradition, i.e. the original deposit of faith, to which nothing new may be added. New definitions of doctrines, such as the Immaculate Conception of Mary (1854) and the bodily Assumption of Mary (1950), have been declared by Popes, however, in accordance with the principle of development (implicit-explicit doctrine).

At Vatican Council I (1870) the Pope was proclaimed "endowed with infallibility, *ex cathedra*, i.e., when exercising the office of Pastor and Teacher of all Christians."

The center of Roman Catholic worship is the celebration of the Mass, the Eucharist, which is the commemoration of Christ's sacrificial death and of his resurrection. Other sacraments are Baptism, Confirmation, Confession, Matrimony, Ordination, and Extreme Unction, seven in all. The Virgin Mary and saints, and their relics, are highly venerated and prayers are made to them to intercede with God, in whose presence they are believed to dwell.

The Roman Catholic Church is the largest Christian organization in the world, found in most countries. Some 8 million belong to the Uniate rites, the vast majority to the Latin rite.

Since Vatican Council II (1962–65), and the effort to "update" the Church, many interesting changes and developments have been taking place.

Protestantism

Protestantism comprises the Christian churches that separated from Rome during the Reformation in the 16th century, initiated by an Augustinian monk, Martin Luther. "Protestant" was originally applied to followers of Luther, who protested at the Diet of Spires (1529) against the decree which prohibited all further ecclesiastical reforms. Subsequently, Protestantism came to mean rejection of attempts to tie God's revelation to earthly institutions, and a return to the Gospel and the Word of God as sole authority in matters of faith and practice. Central in the biblical message is the justification of the sinner by faith alone. The Church is understood as a fellowship and the priesthood of all believers stressed.

The Augsburg Confession (1530) was the principal statement of Lutheran faith and practice. It became a model for other Confessions of Faith, which in their turn had decisive influence on Church polity. Major Protestant denominations are the Lutheran, Reformed (Calvinist), Presbyterian, and Anglican (Episcopal). Smaller ones are the Mennonite, Schwenkfeldians, and Unitarians. In Great Britain and America there are the Congregationalists, Baptists, Quakers, Methodists, and other free church types of communities. (In regarding themselves as being faithful to original biblical Christianity, these Churches differ from such religious bodies as Unitarians, Mormons, Jehovah's Witnesses, and Christian Scientists, who either teach new doctrines or reject old ones.)

Since the latter part of the 19th century, national councils of churches have been established in many countries, e.g. the Federal Council of Churches of Christ in America in 1908. Denominations across countries joined in federations and world alliances, beginning with the Anglican Lambeth Conference in 1867.

Protestant missionary activity, particularly strong in the last century, resulted in the founding of many younger churches in Asia and Africa. The Ecumenical Movement, which originated with Protestant missions, aims at unity among Christians and churches.

Islam

Islam is the religion founded in Arabia by Mohammed between 610 and 632. Its more than 600 million adherents are found in countries stretching from Morocco in the West to Indonesia in the East.

Mohammed was born in A.D. 570 at Mecca and belonged to the Quraysh tribe, which was active in caravan trade. At the age of 25 he joined the caravan trade from Mecca to Syria in the employment of a rich widow, Khadiji, whom he married. Critical of the idolatry of the inhabitants of Mecca, he began to lead a contemplative life in the deserts. There he received a series of revelations. Encouraged by Khadiji, he gradually became convinced that he was given a God-appointed task to devote himself to the reform of religion and society. Idolatry was to be abandoned.

The *Hegira (Hijra)* (migration) of Mohammed from Mecca, where he was not honored, to Medina, where he was well received, occurred in 622 and marks the beginning of the Muslim era. In 630 he marched on Mecca and conquered it. He died at Medina in 632. His grave there has since been a place of pilgrimage.

Mohammed's followers, called Moslems, revered him as the prophet of *Allah* (God), beside whom there is no other God. Although he had no close knowledge of Judaism and Christianity, he considered himself succeeding and completing them as the seal of the Prophets. Sources of the Islamic faith are the *Qur'an,* regarded as the uncreated, eternal Word of God, and Tradition *(hadith)* regarding sayings and deeds of the prophet.

Islam means surrender to the will of *Allah.* He is the all-powerful, whose will is supreme and determines man's fate. Good deeds will be rewarded at the Last Judgment in paradise and evil deeds will be punished in hell.

The Five Pillars, primary duties, of Islam are: witness; confessing the oneness of God and of Mohammed, his prophet; prayer, to be performed five times a day; almsgiving to the poor and the mosque (house of worship); fasting during daylight hours in the month of Ramadan; and pilgrimage to Mecca at least once in the Moslem's lifetime.

Islam, upholding the law of brotherhood, succeeded in uniting an Arab world that had disintegrated into tribes and castes. Disagreements concerning the succession of the prophet caused a great division in Islam between *Sunnis* and *Shias.* Among these, other sects arose *(Wahhabi).* Doctrinal issues also led to the rise of different schools of thought in theology. Nevertheless, since Arab armies turned against Syria and Palestine in 635, Islam has expanded successfully under Mohammed's successors. Its rapid conquests in Asia and Africa are unsurpassed in history. Turning against Europe, Moslems conquered Spain in 713. In 1453 Constantinople fell into their hands and in 1529 Moslem armies besieged Vienna. Since then, Islam has lost its foothold in Europe.

In modern times it has made great gains in Africa.

Hinduism

In India alone there are more than 300 million adherents of Hinduism. In contrast to other religions, it has no founder. Considered the oldest religion in the world, it dates back, perhaps, to prehistoric times.

Hinduism is hard to define, there being no common creed, no one doctrine to bind Hindus together. Intellectually there is complete freedom of belief, and one can be monotheist, polytheist, or atheist. What matters is the social system: a Hindu is one born into a caste.

As a religion, Hinduism is founded on the sacred scriptures, written in Sanskrit and called the *Vedas* (*Veda*-knowledge). There are four Vedic books, among which the *Rig Veda* is the most important. It speaks of many gods and also deals with questions concerning the universe and creation. The dates of these works are unknown (1000 B.C.?).

The *Upanishads* (dated 1000–300 B.C.), commentaries on the Vedic texts, have philosophical speculations on the origin of the universe, the nature of deity, of *atman* (the human soul), and its relationship to *Brahman* (the universal soul).

Brahman is the principle and source of the universe who can be indicated only by negatives. As the divine intelligence, he is the ground of the visible world, a presence that pervades all beings. Thus the many Hindu deities came to be understood as manifestations of the one *Brahman* from whom everything proceeds and to whom everything ultimately returns. The religio-social system of Hinduism is based on the concept of reincarnation and transmigration in which all living beings, from plants below to gods above, are caught in a cosmic system that is an everlasting cycle of becoming and perishing.

Life is determined by the law of *karma,* according to which rebirth is dependent on moral behavior in a previous phase of existence. The doctrine of transmigration thus provides a rationale for the caste system. In this view, life on earth is regarded as transient *(maya)* and a burden. The goal of existence is liberation from the cycle of rebirth and redeath and entrance into the indescribable state of what in Buddhism is called *nirvana* (extinction of passion).

Further important sacred writings are the Epics *(puranas),* which contain legendary stories about gods and men. They are the *Mahabharata* (composed between 200 B.C. and A.D. 200) and the *Ramayana.* The former includes the *Bhagavad-Gita* (Song of the Lord), its most famous part, that tells of devotion to *Krishna* (Lord), who appears as an *avatar* (incarnation) of the god *Vishnu,* and of the duty of obeying caste rules. The work begins with a praise of the *yoga* (discipline) system.

The practice of Hinduism consists of rites and ceremonies, performed within the framework of the caste system and centering on the main socio-religious occasions of birth, marriage, and death. There are many Hindu temples, which are dwelling places of the deities and to which people bring offerings. There are also places of pilgrimages, the chief one being Benares on the Ganges, most sacred among the rivers in India.

In modern times work has been done to reform and revive Hinduism. One of the outstanding reformers was Ramakrishna (1836–86), who inspired many followers, one of whom founded the Ramakrishna mission, which seeks to convert others to its religion. The mission is active both in India and in other countries.

Buddhism

Founded in the 6th century B.C. in northern India by Gautama Buddha, who was born in southern Nepal as son to a king. His birth is surrounded by many legends, but Western scholars agree that he lived from 563 to 483 B.C. Warned by a sage that his son would become an ascetic or a universal monarch, the king confined him to his home. He was able to escape and began the life of a homeless wanderer in search of peace, passing through many disappointments until he finally came to the Tree of Enlightenment, under which he lived in meditation till enlightenment came to him and he became a Buddha (enlightened one).

Now he understood the origin of suffering, summarized in the *Four Noble Truths,* which constitutes the foundation of Buddhism. The Four are the truth of suffering, which all living beings must endure; of the origin of suffering, which is craving and which leads to rebirth; that it can be destroyed; and of the way that leads to cessation of pain, i.e., the *Noble Eightfold Way,* which is the rule of practical Buddhism: right views, right intention, right speech, right action, right livelihood, right effort, right concentration, and right ecstasy.

Nirvana is the goal of all existence, the state of complete redemption, into which the redeemed enters. Buddha's insight can free every man from the law of reincarnation through complete emptying of the self.

The nucleus of Buddha's church or association was originally formed by monks and lay-brothers, whose houses gradually became monasteries used as places for religious instruction. The worship service consisted of a sermon, expounding of Scripture, meditation, and confession. At a later stage pilgrimages to the holy places associated with the Buddha came into being, as well as veneration of relics.

In the 3rd century B.C., King Ashoka made Buddhism the State religion of India but, as centuries passed, it gradually fell into decay through splits, persecutions, and the hostile Brahmans. Buddhism spread to countries outside India, however.

At the beginning of the Christian era, there occurred a split that gave rise to two main types: *Hinayana* (Little Vehicle), or southern Buddhism, and *Mahayana* (Great Vehicle), or northern Buddhism. The former type, more individualistic, survived in Ceylon and southern Asia. *Hinayana* retained more closely the original teachings of the Buddha, which did not know of a personal god or soul. *Mahayana,* more social, polytheistic, and developing a pluralistic pompous cult, was strong in the Himalayas, Tibet, Mongolia, China, Korea, and Japan.

In the present century, Buddhism has found believers also in the West and Buddhist associations have been established in Europe and the U.S.

Confucianism

Confucius (K'ung Fu-tzu), born in the state of Lu (northern China), lived from 551 to 479 B.C. Tradition, exaggerating the importance of Confucius in life, has depicted him as a great statesman but, in fact, he seems to have been a private teacher. Anthologies of ancient Chinese classics, along with his own Analects *(Lun Yu),* became the basis of Confucianism. These Analects were transmitted as a collection of his sayings as recorded by his students, with whom he discussed ethical and social problems. They developed into men of high moral standing, who served the State as administrators.

In his teachings, Confucius emphasized the importance of an old Chinese concept *(li),* which has the connotation of proper conduct. There is some disagreement as to the religious ideas of Confucius, but he held high the concepts handed down from centuries before him. Thus he believed in Heaven *(T'ien)* and sacrificed to his ancestors. Ancestor worship he indeed encouraged as an expression of filial piety, which he considered the loftiest of virtues.

Piety to Confucius was the foundation of the family as well as the State. The family is the nucleus of the State, and the "five relations," between king and subject, father and son, man and wife, older and younger brother, and friend and friend, are determined by the virtues of love of fellow men, righteousness, and respect.

An extension of ancestor worship may be seen in the worship of Confucius, which became official in the 2nd century B.C. when the emperor, in recognition of Confucius' teachings as supporting the imperial rule, offered sacrifices at his tomb.

Mencius (Meng Tse), who lived around 400 B.C., did much to propagate and elaborate Confucianism in its concern with ordering society. Thus, for two millennia, Confucius' doctrine of State, with its emphasis on ethics and social morality, rooted in ancient Chinese tradition and developed and continued by his disciples, has been standard in China and the Far East.

With the revolution of 1911 in China, however, students, burning Confucius in effigy, called for the removal of "the old curiosity shop."

Shintoism

Shinto, the Chinese term for the Japanese *Kami no Michi,* i.e., the Way of the Gods, comprises the religious ideas and cult indigenous to Japan. *Kami,* or gods, considered divine forces of nature that are worshipped, may reside in rivers, trees, rocks, mountains, certain animals, or, particularly, in the sun and moon. The worship of ancestors, heroes, and deceased emperors was incorporated later.

After Buddhism had come from Korea, Japan's native religion at first resisted it. Then there followed a period of compromise and amalgamation with Buddhist beliefs and ceremonies, resulting, since the 9th century A.D., in a syncretistic religion, a Twofold Shinto. Buddhist deities came to be regarded as manifestations of Japanese deities and Buddhist priests took over most of the Shinto shrines.

In modern times Shinto regained independence from Buddhism. Under the reign of the Emperor Meiji (1868–1912) it became the official State religion, in which loyalty to the emperor was emphasized. The line of succession of emperors is traced back to the first Emperor Jimmu (660 B.C.) and beyond him to the Sun-goddess *Amaterasuomikami.*

The centers of worship are the shrines and temples in which the deities are believed to dwell and believers approach them through *torii* (gateways). Most important among the shrines is the imperial shrine of the Sun-goddess at Ise, where state ceremonies were once held in June and December. The *Yasukuni* shrine of the war dead in Tokyo is also well known.

Acts of worship consist of prayers, clapping of hands, acts of purification, and offerings. On feast days processions and performances of music and dancing take place and priests read prayers before the gods in the shrines, asking for good harvest, the well-being of people and emperor, etc. In Japanese homes there is a god-shelf, a small wooden shrine that contains the tablets bearing the names of ancestors. Offerings are made and candles lit before it.

After World War II the Allied Command ordered the disestablishment of State Shinto. To be distinguished from State Shinto is Sect Shinto, consisting of 13 recognized sects. These have arisen in modern times. Most important among them is *Tenrikyo* in Tenri City (Nara), in which healing by faith plays a central role.

Taoism

Taoism, a religion of China, was, according to tradition, founded by Lao Tse, a Chinese philosopher, long considered one of the prominent religious leaders from the 6th century B.C.

Data about him are for the most part legendary, however, and the *Tao Te Ching* (the classic of the Way and of its Power), traditionally ascribed to him, is now believed by many scholars to have originated in the 3rd century B.C. The book is composed in short chapters, written in aphoristic rhymes. Central are the word *Tao,* which means way or path and, in a deeper sense, signifies the principle that underlies the reality of this world and manifests itself in nature and in the lives of men, and the word *Te* (power).

The virtuous man draws power from being absorbed in *Tao,* the ultimate reality within an ever-changing world. By non-action and keeping away from human striving it is possible for man to live in harmony with the principles that underlie and govern the universe. *Tao* cannot be comprehended by reason and knowledge, but only by inward quiet.

Besides the *Tao Te Ching,* dating from approximately the same period, there are two Taoist works, written by Chuang Tse and Lieh Tse.

Theoretical Taoism of this classical philosophical movement of the 4th and 3rd centuries B.C. in China differed from popular Taoism, into which it gradually degenerated. The standard of theoretical Taoism was maintained in the classics, of course, and among the upper classes it continued to be alive until modern times.

Religious Taoism is a form of religion dealing with deities and spirits, magic and soothsaying. In the 2nd century A.D. it was organized with temples, cult, priests, and monasteries and was able to hold its own in the competition with Buddhism that came up at the same time.

After the 7th century A.D., however, Taoist religion further declined. Split into numerous sects, which often operate like secret societies, it has become a syncretistic folk religion in which some of the old deities and saints live on.

Roman Catholic Pontiffs

St. Peter, of Bethsaida in Galilee, Prince of the Apostles, was the first Pope. He lived first in Antioch and then in Rome for 25 years. In AD 64 or 67, he was martyred. St. Linus became the second Pope.

Name	Birthplace	Reigned From	Reigned To
St. Linus	Tuscia	67	76
St. Anacletus (Cletus)	Rome	76	88
St. Clement	Rome	88	97
St. Evaristus	Greece	97	105
St. Alexander I	Rome	105	115
St. Sixtus I	Rome	115	125
St. Telesphorus	Greece	125	136
St. Hyginus	Greece	136	140
St. Pius I	Aquileia	140	155
St. Anicetus	Syria	155	166
St. Soter	Campania	166	175
St. Eleutherius	Epirus	175	189
St. Victor I	Africa	189	199
St. Zephyrinus	Rome	199	217
St. Callistus I	Rome	217	222
St. Urban I	Rome	222	230
St. Pontian	Rome	230	235
St. Anterus	Greece	235	236
St. Fabian	Rome	236	250
St. Cornelius	Rome	251	253
St. Lucius I	Rome	253	254
St. Stephen I	Rome	254	257
St. Sixtus II	Greece	257	258
St. Dionysius	Unknown	259	268
St. Felix I	Rome	269	274
St. Eutychian	Luni	275	283
St. Caius	Dalmatia	283	296
St. Marcellinus	Rome	296	304
St. Marcellus I	Rome	308	309
St. Eusebius	Greece	309[1]	309[1]
St. Meltiades	Africa	311	314
St. Sylvester I	Rome	314	335
St. Marcus	Rome	336	336
St. Julius I	Rome	337	352
Liberius	Rome	352	366
St. Damasus I	Spain	366	384
St. Siricius	Rome	384	399
St. Anastasius I	Rome	399	401
St. Innocent I	Albano	401	417
St. Zozimus	Greece	417	418
St. Boniface I	Rome	418	422
St. Celestine I	Campania	422	432
St. Sixtus III	Rome	432	440
St. Leo I (the Great)	Tuscany	440	461
St. Hilary	Sardinia	461	468
St. Simplicius	Tivoli	468	483
St. Felix III (II)[2]	Rome	483	492
St. Gelasius I	Africa	492	496
Anastasius II	Rome	496	498
St. Symmachus	Sardinia	498	514
St. Hormisdas	Frosinone	514	523
St. John I	Tuscany	523	526
St. Felix IV (III)	Samnium	526	530
Boniface II	Rome	530	532
John II	Rome	533	535
St. Agapitus I	Rome	535	536
St. Silverius	Campania	536	537
Vigilius	Rome	537	555
Pelagius I	Rome	556	561
John III	Rome	561	574
Benedict I	Rome	575	579
Pelagius II	Rome	579	590
St. Gregory I (the Great)	Rome	590	604
Sabinianus	Tuscany	604	606
Boniface III	Rome	607	607
St. Boniface IV	Marsi	608	615
St. Deusdedit (Adeodatus I)	Rome	615	618
Boniface V	Naples	619	625
Honorius I	Campania	625	638
Severinus	Rome	640	640
John IV	Dalmatia	640	642
Theodore I	Greece	642	649
St. Martin I	Todi	649	655
St. Eugene I[3]	Rome	654	657

Name	Birthplace	Reigned From	Reigned To
St. Vitalian	Segni	657	672
Adeodatus II	Rome	672	676
Donus	Rome	676	678
St. Agatho	Sicily	678	681
St. Leo II	Sicily	682	683
St. Benedict II	Rome	684	685
John V	Syria	685	686
Conon	Unknown	686	687
St. Sergius I	Syria	687	701
John VI	Greece	701	705
John VII	Greece	705	707
Sisinnius	Syria	708	708
Constantine	Syria	708	715
St. Gregory II	Rome	715	731
St. Gregory III	Syria	731	741
St. Zachary	Greece	741	752
Stephen II (III)[4]	Rome	752	757
St. Paul I	Rome	757	767
Stephen III (IV)	Sicily	768	772
Adrian I	Rome	772	795
St. Leo III	Rome	795	816
Stephen IV (V)	Rome	816	817
St. Paschal I	Rome	817	824
Eugene II	Rome	824	827
Valentine	Rome	827	827
Gregory IV	Rome	827	844
Sergius II	Rome	844	847
St. Leo IV	Rome	847	855
Benedict III	Rome	855	858
St. Nicholas I (the Great)	Rome	858	867
Adrian II	Rome	867	872
John VIII	Rome	872	882
Marinus I	Gallese	882	884
St. Adrian III	Rome	884	885
Stephen V (VI)	Rome	885	891
Formosus	Portus	891	896
Boniface VI	Rome	896	896
Stephen VI (VII)	Rome	896	897
Romanus	Gallese	897	897
Theodore II	Rome	897	897
John IX	Tivoli	898	900
Benedict IV	Rome	900	903
Leo V	Ardea	903	903
Sergius III	Rome	904	911
Anastasius III	Rome	911	913
Landus	Sabina	913	914
John X	Tossignano	914	928
Leo VI	Rome	928	928
Stephen VII (VIII)	Rome	928	931
John XI	Rome	931	935
Leo VII	Rome	936	939
Stephen VIII (IX)	Rome	939	942
Marinus II	Rome	942	946
Agapitus II	Rome	946	955
John XII	Tusculum	955	964
Leo VIII[5]	Rome	963	965
Benedict V[5]	Rome	964	966
John XIII	Rome	965	972
Benedict VI	Rome	973	974
Benedict VII	Rome	974	983
John XIV	Pavia	983	984
John XV	Rome	985	996
Gregory V	Saxony	996	999
Sylvester II	Auvergne	999	1003
John XVII	Rome	1003	1003
John XVIII	Rome	1004	1009
Sergius IV	Rome	1009	1012
Benedict VIII	Tusculum	1012	1024
John XIX	Tusculum	1024	1032
Benedict IX[6]	Tusculum	1032	1044
Sylvester III	Rome	1045	1045

Name	Birthplace	Reigned From	Reigned To
Benedict IX (2nd time)	—	1045	1045
Gregory VI	Rome	1045	1046
Clement II	Saxony	1046	1047
Benedict IX (3rd time)	—	1047	1048
Damasus II	Bavaria	1048	1048
St. Leo IX	Alsace	1049	1054
Victor II	Germany	1055	1057
Stephen IX (X)	Lorraine	1057	1058
Nicholas II	Burgundy	1059	1061
Alexander II	Milan	1061	1073
St. Gregory VII	Tuscany	1073	1085
Bl. Victor III	Benevento	1086	1087
Bl. Urban II	France	1088	1099
Paschal II	Ravenna	1099	1118
Gelasius II	Gaeta	1118	1119
Callistus II	Burgundy	1119	1124
Honorius II	Flagnano	1124	1130
Innocent II	Rome	1130	1143
Celestine II	Città di Castello	1143	1144
Lucius II	Bologna	1144	1145
Bl. Eugene III	Pisa	1145	1153
Anastasius IV	Rome	1153	1154
Adrian IV	England	1154	1159
Alexander III	Siena	1159	1181
Lucius III	Lucca	1181	1185
Urban III	Milan	1185	1187
Gregory VIII	Benevento	1187	1187
Clement III	Rome	1187	1191
Celestine III	Rome	1191	1198
Innocent III	Anagni	1198	1216
Honorius III	Rome	1216	1227
Gregory IX	Anagni	1227	1241
Celestine IV	Milan	1241	1241
Innocent IV	Genoa	1243	1254
Alexander IV	Anagni	1254	1261
Urban IV	Troyes	1261	1264
Clement IV	France	1265	1268
Bl. Gregory X	Piacenza	1271	1276
Bl. Innocent V	Savoy	1276	1276
Adrian V	Genoa	1276	1276
John XXI[7]	Portugal	1276	1277
Nicholas III	Rome	1277	1280
Martin IV[3]	France	1281	1285
Honorius IV	Rome	1285	1287
Nicholas IV	Ascoli	1288	1292
St. Celestine V	Isernia	1294	1294
Boniface VIII	Anagni	1294	1303
Bl. Benedict XI	Treviso	1303	1304
Clement V	France	1305	1314
John XXII	Cahors	1316	1334
Benedict XII	France	1334	1342
Clement VI	France	1342	1352
Innocent VI	France	1352	1362
Bl. Urban V	France	1362	1370
Gregory XI	France	1370	1378
Urban VI	Naples	1378	1389
Boniface IX	Naples	1389	1404
Innocent VII	Sulmona	1404	1406
Gregory XII	Venice	1406	1415
Martin V	Rome	1417	1431
Eugene IV	Venice	1431	1447
Nicholas V	Sarzana	1447	1455
Callistus III	Jativa	1455	1458
Pius II	Siena	1458	1464
Paul II	Venice	1464	1471
Sixtus IV	Savona	1471	1484
Innocent VIII	Genoa	1484	1492
Alexander VI	Jativa	1492	1503

Name	Birthplace	Reigned From	To	Name	Birthplace	Reigned From	To
Pius III	Siena	1503	1503	Bl. Innocent XI	Como	1676	1689
Július II	Savona	1503	1513	Alexander VIII	Venice	1689	1691
Leo X	Florence	1513	1521	Innocent XII	Spinazzola	1691	1700
Adrian VI	Utrecht	1522	1523	Clement XI	Urbino	1700	1721
Clement VII	Florence	1523	1534	Innocent XIII	Rome	1721	1724
Paul III	Rome	1534	1549	Benedict XIII	Gravina	1724	1730
Julius III	Rome	1550	1555	Clement XII	Florence	1730	1740
Marcellus II	Montepulciano	1555	1555	Benedict XIV	Bologna	1740	1758
Paul IV	Naples	1555	1559	Clement XIII	Venice	1758	1769
Pius IV	Milan	1559	1565	Clement XIV	Rimini	1769	1774
St. Pius V	Bosco	1566	1572	Pius VI	Cesena	1775	1799
Gregory XIII	Bologna	1572	1585	Pius VII	Cesena	1800	1823
Sixtus V	Grottammare	1585	1590	Leo XII	Genga	1823	1829
Urban VII	Rome	1590	1590	Pius VIII	Cingoli	1829	1830
Gregory XIV	Cremona	1590	1591	Gregory XVI	Belluno	1831	1846
Innocent IX	Bologna	1591	1591	Pius IX	Senegallia	1846	1878
Clement VIII	Florence	1592	1605	Leo XIII	Carpineto	1878	1903
Leo XI	Florence	1605	1605	St. Pius X	Riese	1903	1914
Paul V	Rome	1605	1621	Benedict XV	Genoa	1914	1922
Gregory XV	Bologna	1621	1623	Pius XI	Desio	1922	1939
Urban VIII	Florence	1623	1644	Pius XII	Rome	1939	1958
Innocent X	Rome	1644	1655	John XXIII	Sotto il Monte	1958	1963
Alexander VII	Siena	1655	1667	Paul VI	Concesio	1963	1978
Clement IX	Pistoia	1667	1669	John Paul I	Forno di Canale	1978	1978
Clement X	Rome	1670	1676	John Paul II	Wadowice, Poland	1978	

1. Or 310. 2. He should be called Felix II, and his successors of the same name should be numbered accordingly. The discrepancy was caused by the erroneous insertion in some lists of the name of St. Felix of Rome, Martyr. 3. He was elected during the exile of St. Martin I, who endorsed him as Pope. 4. After St. Zachary died, a Roman priest named Stephen was elected but died before his consecration as Bishop of Rome. His name is not included in all lists for this reason. In view of this historical confusion, the *National Catholic Almanac* lists the true Stephen II as Stephen II (III), the true Stephen III as Stephen III (IV), etc. 5. Confusion exists concerning the legitimacy of claims. If the deposition of John was invalid, Leo was an antipope until after the end of Benedict's reign. If the deposition of John was valid, Leo was the legitimate Pope and Benedict an antipope. 6. If the triple removal of Benedict IX was not valid, Sylvester III, Gregory VI, and Clement II were antipopes. 7. Elimination was made of the name of John XX in an effort to rectify the numerical designation of Popes named John. The error dates back to the time of John XV. 8. The names of Marinus I and Marinus II were construed as Martin. In view of these two pontificates and the earlier reign of St. Martin I, this pontiff was called Martin IV. *Source: National Catholic Almanac,* from *Annuarto Pontificio.*

Books of the Bible

OLD TESTAMENT—STANDARD VERSIONS

Genesis
Exodus
Leviticus
Numbers
Deuteronomy
Joshua
Judges
Ruth
I Samuel
II Samuel
I Kings
II Kings
I Chronicles
II Chronicles
Ezra
Nehemiah
Esther
Job
Psalms
Proverbs
Ecclesiastes
Song of Solomon
Isaiah
Jeremiah
Lamentations
Ezekiel
Daniel
Hosea
Joel
Amos
Obadiah
Jonah
Micah
Nahum
Habakkuk
Zephaniah
Haggai
Zechariah
Malachi

NEW TESTAMENT—STANDARD VERSIONS

Matthew
Mark
Luke
John
Acts
Romans
Corinthians
Galatians
Ephesians
Philippians
Colossians
Thessalonians
Timothy
Titus
Philemon
Hebrews
James
Peter
John
Jude
Revelation

OLD TESTAMENT—DOUAY VERSION[1]

Genesis
Exodus
Leviticus
Numbers
Deuteronomy
Josue
Judges
Ruth
I Kings
II Kings
III Kings
IV Kings
I Paralipomenon
II Paralipomenon
I Esdras
II Esdras
Tobias
Judith
Esther
Job
Psalms
Proverbs
Ecclesiastes
Canticle of Canticles
Wisdom
Ecclesiasticus
Isaias
Jeremias
Lamentations
Baruch
Ezechiel
Daniel
Osee
Joel
Amos
Abdias
Jonas
Micheas
Nahum
Habacuc
Sophonias
Aggeus
Zacharias
Malachias
I Machabees
II Machabees

1. In the Douay Version of the Bible, the books of the New Testament are the same as those of the Authorized (King James) Version, except that the Revelation of St. John is called the Apocalypse of St. John in the Douay Version.

IDEAS AND BELIEFS

Introduction

THIS section explains many of the ideas and beliefs which people have held at different periods in history. Beliefs may be true or false, meaningful or totally meaningless, regardless of the degree of conviction with which they are held. Since man has been moved to action so often by his beliefs they are worth serious study. The section throws a vivid light on human history.

Man has always felt a deep need for emotional security, a sense of "belonging." This need has found expression in the framing of innumerable religious systems, nearly all of which have been concerned with man's relation to a divine ruling power. In the past, people have been accustomed to think of their own religion as true and of all others as false. Latterly we have come to realize that in man's religious strivings there is common ground, for our need in the world today is a morality whereby human beings may live together in harmony.

There is also to be found in man an irresistible curiosity which demands an explanation of the world in which he finds himself. This urge to make the world intelligible takes him into the realm of science where the unknown is the constant challenge. Science is a creative process, always in the making, since the scientist's conjectures are constantly being submitted to severe critical tests.

A

Acupuncture, a quasi-medical system originating in China and based on the supposedly therapeutic effects of implanting fine gold needles in the spinal cord and other specific parts of the body. The site of needle implantation is decided according to traditional texts. The apparent lack of any logical relationship between the implantation sites and any known physiological or anatomical systems within the body has caused acupuncture to be held in low regard by Western medicine. Indeed it is certainly true that acupuncture and other similar practices tend to flourish in parts of the world where orthodox medicine has made little progress or where doctors and trained staff are scarce.

Recent years however have seen a curious and unexpected revival of interest in acupuncture in Europe and America, prompted in large part by the considerable press publicity which has surrounded a number of major surgical operations performed without anesthesia upon human patients and which have been witnessed by sceptical Western specialists. Considerable controversy still surrounds acupuncture and is likely to continue for many years—possibly because it is hard to envisage a theory to explain its effects which is consistent with orthodox medicine. No doubt the immensely powerful effects of suggestion and hypnosis need to be taken into account. Some recent discoveries on the psychology and physiology of pain which show that severe wound pain may be alleviated by electrical stimulation of the nerve endings in the site of the wound may also have some relevance. It is tempting to take the line that acupuncture is based on some "forgotten" or "hidden" medical system and to assume that it is only because Western scientists are blinkered and hidebound that it is not being incorporated in a big way into European and American hospitals. But there are always two sides to an argument; whereas the first reports from Western specialists visiting China were filled with grudging acceptance and genuine puzzlement, more recent visitors have brought back a subtly different story. One of the world's leading experts on pain, for example, who has himself witnessed acupuncture-based surgery, reports four significant findings: (1) contrary to earlier reports, patients *are* sedated, sometimes heavily so, before surgery; (2) those patients who do go for surgery using acupuncture are only chosen after a fairly rigorous selection procedure to see whether they have complete faith in the method; (3) acupuncture does not appear to work with children; and (4) its use appears to be on the decline in the major hospitals in China. Despite this rather sceptical analysis, it is clear that the full story about acupuncture, its nature and its practical value has not yet been told.

Adlerian Psychology. In 1911 the Viennese psychoanalyst Alfred Adler (1870–1937) together with his colleague Carl Gustav Jung broke with their friend Sigmund Freud over disputes concerning the latter's theoretic approach to psychoanalysis. Jung and Adler were themselves shortly also to part company, each to set up and develop his own "school" of psychoanalysis. Adler's system of psychotherapy is based on the idea, not of sex as a driving force as in the case of Freud, but on the concept of "compensation" or a drive for power in an attempt to overcome the "inferiority complex" which he held to be universal in human beings. The child naturally feels inferior to adults, but bullying, making him feel insignificant or guilty or contemptible, even spoiling, which makes him feel important within the family but relatively unimportant outside, increases this feeling. Or the child may have physical defects: he may be small or underweight, have to wear glasses, become lame, be constantly ill, or stupid at school. In these ways he develops a sense of inferiority which for the rest of his life he develops a technique to overcome.

This may be done in several ways: he may try to become capable in the very respects in which he feels incompetent—hence many great orators have originally had speech defects; many painters poor eyesight; many musicians have been partially deaf; like Nietzsche, the weakling, he may write about the superman, or like Sandow, the strong man, be born with poor health.

On the other hand he may overdo his attempt and overcompensate. Hence we have the bully who is really a coward, the small man who is self-assertive to an objectionable degree (Hitler, Napoleon, Stalin, and Mussolini were all small men) or the foreigner who like three of these men wanted to be the hero of his adopted country—Hitler the Austrian, Napoleon the Italian, Stalin the Georgian.

But what about the man who can do none of these things, who continues to fail to compensate? He, says Adler, becomes a neurotic because neurosis is an excuse which means "I could have done so-and-so but . . ." It is the unconscious flight into illness—the desire to be ill. Adler's treatment involves disclosing these subterfuges we play on ourselves so that we can deal with the real situation in a more realistic way. Adlerian psychoanalysis still attracts supporters, but its golden days were when the founder was at the head of the movement in the U.S.A., when his views were considered to provide a more "acceptable" theory of the mind than the enormously controversial theories of Freud with their strong sexual orientation.

Adventists, a group of American religious sects, the most familiar being the Seventh-Day Adventist Church, which observes Saturday as the true Sabbath. With more than a million members throughout the world, it shares with other Adventists a belief in the imminent second coming of Christ (a doctrine fairly widespread in the U.S.A. during the early decades of the 19th cent. when the end of the world was predicted by William Miller for 1843, then for 1844). Modern Adventists content themselves with the conviction that the "signs" of the Advent are multiplying, the "blessed event" which will solve the world's ills. Believers will be saved, but the sects differ as to whether the unjust will be tortured in hell, annihilated, or merely remain asleep eternally.

Agnosticism. *See* **God and Man.**

Albigenses, also known as Cathari. French heretical sect (named after the town of Albi in Provence) which appeared in the 11th cent. to challenge the Catholic Church on the way true Christians should lead their lives. They followed a life of extreme asceticism in contrast to the local clergy and their faith was adopted by the mass of the population, especially in Toulouse. Condemned as heretics by Pope Innocent III, the sect was exterminated in the savage Albigensian Crusade (1208–29), initially led by Simon de Montfort. (In his thoroughness, de Montfort also succeeded in destroying the high culture of the Troubadours.)

Alchemy, ancient art associated with magic and astrology in which modern chemistry has its roots. The earliest mention of alchemy comes from ancient Egypt but its later practitioners attributed its origins to such varied sources as the fallen angels of the Bible, to Moses and Aaron, but most commonly to Hermes Trismegistus, often identified with the Egyptian god Thoth, whose knowledge of the divine art was handed down only to the sons of kings (cf, the phrase "hermetically sealed"). Its main object was the transmutation of metals. Egyptian speculation concerning this reached its height during the 6th cent. in the Alexandrian period. Brought to Western Europe by the Moslems, one of its most famous Arab exponents was Jabir (*c.* 760–*c.* 815), known to the Latins as Geber, who had a laboratory at Kufa on the Tigris. One school of early Greek philosophy held that there was ultimately only one elemental matter of which everything was composed. Such men as Albertus Magnus (1206–80) and Roger Bacon (1214–94) assumed that, by removing impurities, this *materia prima* could be obtained. Although Bacon's ideas were in many ways ahead of his time, he firmly believed in the philosopher's stone, which could turn base metals into gold, and in an elixir of life which would give eternal youth. Modern science has, of course, shown in its researches into radioactivity, the possibility of transmutation of certain elements, but this phenomenon has little bearing on either the methods of the alchemist or the mysteries with which he surrounded them. In line with the current considerable revival of interest in the occult, alchemy appears to be staging a comeback, at least as a literary if not an experimental topic.

Anabaptists. *See* **Baptists.**

Analytical Psychology, the name given by Carl Gustav Jung (1875–1961) of Zürich to his system of psychology, which, like Adler's (*see* **Adlerian Psychology**), took its origin from Freud's psychoanalysis from which both diverged in 1911. Briefly, Jung differed from Freud: (1) in believing that the latter had laid too much emphasis on the sexual drive as the basic one in man and replacing it with the concept of *libido* or life energy of which sex forms a part; (2) in his theory of types: men are either extrovert or introvert (*i.e.* their interest is turned primarily outwards to the world or inwards to the self), and they apprehend experience in four main ways, one or other of which is predominant in any given individual—sensing, feeling, thinking, or intuiting; (3) in his belief that the individual's unconscious mind contains not only repressed materials which, as Freud maintained, were too unpleasant to be allowed into awareness, but also faculties which had not been allowed to develop—*e.g.,* the emotional side of the too rational man, the feminine side of the too masculine one; (4) in the importance he attaches to the existence of a collective unconscious at a still deeper level which contains traces of ancient ways of thought which mankind has inherited over the centuries. These are the *archetypes* and include primitive notions of magic, spirits and witches, birth and death, gods, virgin mothers, resurrection, etc. In the treatment of the neuroses Jung believed in the importance of *(a)* the present situation which the patient refuses to face; *(b)* the bringing together of conscious and unconscious and integrating them.

In the 1940s and '50s interest in Jung's ideas waned, at least in academic circles, as the emphasis among experimental psychologists shifted closer and closer to the "hard" scientific line. This was also true in the field of psychoanalysis where the Jungian as opposed to the Freudian point of view became progressively less popular. At the present time this trend is beginning to reverse, and while Jung's offbeat views on astrology, telepathy, etc., are still unfashionable, a reappraisal of the significance of his views on the nature of the unconscious is taking place and many psychologists feel that his contribution to our understanding of the nature of human mental processes has been greatly underrated. *See also* **Psychoanalysis.**

Anarchism, a political philosophy which holds, in the words of the American anarchist Josiah Warren (1798–1874), an early follower of Robert Owen, that "every man should be his own government, his own law, his own church." The idea that governmental interference or even the mere existence of authority is inherently bad is as old as Zeno, the Greek Stoic philosopher, who believed that compulsion perverts the normal nature of man. William Godwin's *Enquiry Concerning Political Justice* (1793) was the first systematic exposition of the doctrine. Godwin (father-in-law of Shelley) claimed that man is by nature sociable, cooperative, rational, and good when given the choice to act freely; that under such conditions men will form voluntary groups to work in complete social harmony. Such groups or communities would be based on equality of income, no state control, and no property: this state of affairs would be brought about by rational discussion and persuasion rather than by revolution.

The French economist Proudhon (1809–65) was the first to bring anarchism to the status of a mass movement. In his book *What is Property?* he stated bluntly that "property is theft" and "governments are the scourge of God". He urged the formation of cooperative credit banks where money could be had without interest and goods would be exchanged at cost value at a rate representing the hours of work needed to produce each commodity. Like Godwin, he disapproved of violence but, unlike Marx, disapproved of trade unions as representing organized groups.

In communistic anarchism these ideas were combined with a revolutionary philosophy, primarily by the Russians Michael Bakunin (1814–76) and Peter Kropotkin (1842–1921) who favored training workers in the technique of "direct action" to overthrow the state by all possible means, including political assassination. In 1868 anarchists joined the First International which broke up a few years later after a bitter struggle between Bakuninists and Marxists. Subsequently small anarchist groups murdered such political figures as Tsar Alexander II of Russia, King Humbert of Italy, Presidents Carnot of France and McKinley of America, and the Empress Elizabeth of Austria.

Anarchism and communism differ in three main ways: (1) anarchism forms no political party, rejects all relationship with established authority, and regards democratic reform as a setback; (2) communism is against capitalism, anarchism against the state as such; (3) both have the final goal of a classless society, but anarchism rejects the idea of an intermediate period of socialist state control accepted by communism. Philosophical anarchists, such as the American writer Henry David Thoreau (1817–62), were primarily individualists who believed in a return to nature, the nonpayment of taxes, and passive resistance to state control; in these respects Thoreau strongly influenced Gandhi as did the Christian anarchist Tolstoy.

Anarchism has traditionally been criticized as being impractical—*e.g.,* in a non-authoritarian society, who is going to look after the sewers or clean the streets?—and there is a good deal of force to this argument. In fact anarchistic ideas became progressively less fashionable in the first half of this century. A curious and probably significant revival of interest has taken place in the past decade, however, probably because of a growing sense of disillusion, particularly on the part of young people, with the progress of orthodox political systems. *See also* **Syndicalism.**

Animism. To early man and in primitive societies the distinction between animate and inanimate objects was not always obvious—it is not enough to say that living things move and nonliving things do not, for leaves blow about in the wind and streams flow down a hillside. In the religions of early societies, therefore, we find a tendency to believe that life exists in all objects from rocks and pools to seas and mountains. This belief is technically known as *animatism,* which differs from *animism,* a somewhat more sophisticated view which holds that natural objects have no life in themselves but may be the abode of dead people, spirits, or gods who occasionally give them the appearance of life. The classic example of this, of course, is the assumption that an erupting volcano is an expression of anger on the part of the god who resides in it. Such beliefs may seem absurd today, but it is worth realizing that we are not entirely free of them ourselves when we ascribe "personalities" of a limited kind to motor cars, boats, dolls, or models which incur our pleasure or anger depending upon how well they "behave".

Anthropomorphism, the attribution of human form, thoughts or motives to non-human entities or life forms from gods to animals. At one end this can be summed up in the once widespread image of God as a "white-bearded old gentleman sitting on a cloud." At the other end is the very common tendency to invest domestic animals and pets with man-like wishes and personalities. At both extremes the belief could be seriously misleading. Firstly, it could be very unwise to assume that God, if he exists, necessarily thinks as humans do and has human interests at heart. Secondly, we shall learn very little about animal behavior if we look upon them as mere extensions of our own personality, and we do them less than justice if we see them simply as human beings of diminutive intelligence.

Anthroposophy, a school of religious and philosophical thought based on the work of the German educationist and mystic Rudolf Steiner (1861–1925). Steiner was originally an adherent of Madame Blavatsky's theosophical movement (*cf* Theosophy) but in 1913 broke away to form his own splinter group, the Anthroposophical Society, following ideological disputes over the alleged "divinity" of the Indian boy Krishnamurtl. Steiner was much influenced by the German poet and scientist, Goethe, and believed that an appreciation and love for art was one of the keys to spiritual development. One of the first tasks of his new movement was the construction of a vast temple of arts and sciences, known as the Goetheanum, to act as the headquarters of the society. This structure, which was of striking and revolutionary architectural style, was unfortunately burnt down in 1922 to be replaced by an even more imaginative one which today is one of the most interesting buildings of its kind in the world. Anthroposophy, which ceased to expand greatly following its founder's death, is nevertheless well-established in various parts of the world with specialized, and often very well equipped, schools and clinics which propagate the educational and therapeutic theories of the movement. These, which include the allegedly beneficial powers of music, colored lights, etc., have made little impact on modern educational ideas, but the schools have acquired a reputation for success in the training of mentally handicapped children, though one suspects that these successes are due to the patience and tolerance exercised in these establishments rather than to the curative value of color or music "therapy" itself. Despite its apparent eccentricities, anthroposophy has made its mark on art and architecture, the outstanding modern painter Kandinsky, for example, being particularly influenced by Steiner's ideas and teachings.

Anticlericalism, resentment of priestly powers and privileges, traceable in England to Wyclif's insistence in the 14th cent. on the right of all men to have access to the Scriptures. The translation of the Bible into the common tongue was a great landmark in the history of the Bible and the English language. Wyclif's principles were condemned by the Roman Church of his time but were readily accepted during the Reformation. Tudor anticlericalism arose from motives ranging from a greedy desire to plunder the riches of the Church to a genuine dislike of the powers of the priesthood whose spiritual courts still had the right to decide on points of doctrine or morals in an age when the layman felt he was well able to decide for himself. In innumerable ways the Church was permitted to extort money from the laity. It is generally agreed, says Trevelyan, that the final submission of church to state in England was motivated quite as much by anticlericalism as by Protestantism. The rise of the Reformed churches in England satisfied the people generally and anticlericalism never became the fixed principle of permanent parties as happened in France and Italy from the time of Voltaire onwards.

Antisemitism, a term first applied about the middle of the last century to those who were anti-Jewish in their outlook. Although this attitude was prevalent for religious reasons throughout the Middle Ages, modern antisemitism differed *(a)* in being largely motivated by economic or political conditions, and *(b)* in being doctrinaire with a pseudoscientific rationale presented by such men as Gobineau (1816–82) and Houston Stewart Chamberlain (1855–1927), and later by the Nazi and Fascist "philosophers". Beginning in Russia and Hungary with the pogroms of 1882 it gradually spread south and westwards where, in France, the Dreyfus case provided an unsavory example in 1894. Thousands of Jews from Eastern Europe fled to Britain and America during this period; for in these countries antisemitism has rarely been more than a personal eccentricity. During the last war the murder of six million Jews by the Nazis and their accomplices led to a further exodus to various parts of the world and finally to the creation of the state of Israel.

The individual Jew-hater makes unconscious use of the psychological processes of projection and displacement: his greed or sexual guilt is projected on to the Jew (or Negro or Catholic) because he cannot bear to accept them as his own emotions, and his sense of failure in life is blamed on his chosen scapegoat rather than on his own inadequacy.

But there are social causes too and politicians in some lands are well versed in the technique of blaming unsatisfactory conditions (which they themselves may have in part produced) upon minority groups and persuading others to do the same. Historically, the Jew is ideally suited for this role of scapegoat: (1) in the Middle Ages when usury was forbidden to Christians but not to Jews, the latter often became moneylenders incurring the opprobrium generally associated with this trade (*e.g.,* to the simple-minded Russian peasant the Jew often represented, not only the "Christ-killer", but also the moneylender or small shopkeeper to whom he owed money); (2) many trades being closed to Jews, it was natural that they concentrated in others, thus arousing suspicions of "influence" (*i.e.* Jews are felt to occupy a place in certain trades and professions which far exceeds their numerical proportion to the population as a whole); (3) even with the ending of ghetto life, Jews often occupy *en masse* some parts of cities rather than others and this may lead to resentment on the part of the original inhabitants who begin to feel themselves dispossessed; (4) Jews tend to form a closed society and incur the suspicions attached to all closed societies within which social contacts are largely limited to members; marriage outside the group is forbidden or strongly disapproved of, and the preservation, among the orthodox, of cultural and religious barriers tends to isolate them from their fellow citizens. Discrimination, hateful as it is, does not come from one side only and it is such barriers as these that help to maintain an old and cruel folly. *See* **Zionism.**

Aquarius, one of the twelve "signs of the Zodiac". This has recently achieved special significance in the mythology of our time because of the pronouncements of astrologers that the world is shifting out of the 2000-years-old cycle of the Age of Pisces, the fish, into that of Aquarius the water-carrier. The exact date of the transition is a matter of astrological controversy, but the consensus is that it began in 1960 and will be completed sometime in the 24th century. The Aquarian Age is predicted to be one of peace and harmony, replacing the era of strife which, ironically, has marked the dominance of the Christian symbol of the fish. Such speculations are totally without scientific backing and are mentioned here only to draw attention to the grip which astrological and other mythical concepts still have on human thinking. One of the first spaceships to carry man to the moon, for example, was named Aquarius by its crew. *See also* **Astrology.**

Arianism, formed the subject of the first great controversy within the Christian Church over the doctrine of Arius of Alexandria (d. 336) who denied the divinity of Christ. The doctrine, although at first influential, was condemned at the Council of Nicaea (325), called by the Emperor Constantine, at which Arius was opposed by Athanasius, also of Alexandria, who maintained the now orthodox view that the Son is of one substance with the Father. Arius was banished but the heresy persisted until the 7th cent., especially among the barbarians, the Goths, Vandals and Lombards. Disbelief in the divinity of Christ has formed part of the doctrine of many minor sects since, notably in **Unitarianism** *(q.v.).*

Assassins, a sect of Moslem Shi'ites, founded by the Persian Hasan i Sabbath (*c.* 1090), which for more than two centuries established a rule of terror all over Persia and Syria. The coming of the Mongols in 1256 destroyed them in Persia and the Syrian branch suffered a similar fate at the hands of the then Mamluk sultan of Egypt, *c.* 1270. It was a secret order, ruled over by a grand master, under whom the members were strictly organized into classes, according to the degree of initiation into the secrets of the order. The devotees, belonging to one of the lower groups, carried out the actual assassinations under strict laws of obedience, and total ignorance of the objects and ritual of the society. It is believed that the latter were given ecstatic visions under the influence of hashish, whence the term *hashshashin,* which became corrupted to "assassin".

Associationism. In psychology, the Associationist school of the 19th cent. accepted the association of ideas as the fundamental principle in mental life. It was represented in Britain by the two Mills and Herbert Spencer, in Germany by J. F. Herbart (1776–1841). To these, mental activity was nothing but the association of "ideas" conceived of as units of both thought and feeling—the emotion of anger or the perception of a chair were both "ideas"—and apart from them the self did not exist. Personality was simply a series of these units coming and going, adding to or cancelling each other out, in accordance with rigid and mechanistic scientific laws.

Astrology was once the best available theory for explaining the course of human life and bears much the same historical relationship to astronomy as alchemy does to chemistry. Originally it was divided into the two branches of Natural Astrology which dealt with the movements of the heavenly bodies and their calculations, and Judicial Astrology which studied the alleged influence of the stars and the planets on human life and fate. It was the former that developed into modern astronomy; the latter was, and remains, a primitive myth.

Astrology owes most to the early Babylonians (or Chaldeans) who, being largely nomadic in an environment which permitted an unobstructed view of the sky, readily accepted the idea that divine energy is manifested in the movements of the sun and planets. Gradually this concept became enlarged and the relative positions of the planets both in relation to each other and to the fixed stars became important together with the idea of omens—that, if a particular event occurred while the planets were in a particular position, the recurrence of that position heralded a recurrence of the same sort of event. Soon the planets became associated with almost every aspect of human life. They were bound up with the emotions, with parts of the body, so that astrology played quite a large part in medicine up to late medieval times. Not only was the position of the planet to be considered but also the particular sign of the zodiac (or house of heaven) it was occupying, and it was believed possible to foretell the destiny of an individual by calculating which star was in the ascendant (*i.e.* the sign of the zodiac nearest the eastern horizon and the star which arose at that precise moment) at the time of his birth. Astrology was popular among the Egyptians, the Romans (whose authorities found the Chaldean astrologers a nuisance and expelled them from time to time), and during the Middle Ages when astrologers were often highly respected.

Despite the apparent absurdity of astrological beliefs—for example, how could the pattern of light from stars billions of miles away possibly influence the temperament of single individuals on earth—a substantial number of intelligent and well-educated people take its study in all seriousness. The most interesting "convert" was the psychologist and philosopher, Carl Jung, who conducted a complex experiment in which he compared the "birth signs" of happily married and divorced couples and claimed to find that those most favorably matched in astrological terms were also those more likely to have permanent wedded bliss. Jung's findings were subsequently shown to have been based on a simple statistical fallacy, which did not prevent the brilliant but eccentric psychologist from offering them up as evidence in support of his own theory of "synchronicity" *(q.v.),* an involved and vaguely metaphysical notion which suggests that events in the universe may be significantly related in a "non-causal" fashion. To add fuel to the controversy however, the French mathematician, Michel Gauquelin, has recently offered up fresh data which apparently supports the general astrological view. In a carefully controlled study he noticed statistically significant correspondences between certain astrological signs and the professions of a large number of Frenchmen whose birth time and date were accurately recorded. Gauquelin claims to have repeated his study on a second large sample of his fellow countrymen, though he has been unable to use English people as the exact times of birth are not recorded on their birth certificates! This apparent shot in the arm for astrology is still a matter of great scientific controversy, though Gauquelin's work has been given support from the distinguished British psychologist. H. J. Eysenck, who has pronounced his statistical data to to be incontrovertible. Both scientists, however, carefully refrain from discussing the implications of these curious findings, and the controversy will no doubt increase rather than decrease in the near future.

Atheism. *See* **God and Man.**

Atlantis, a mythical continent supposed to have lain somewhere between Europe and America and a center of advanced civilization before it was inundated by some great natural catastrophe in pre-Christian times. There is little, if any, serious historical or archaeological evidence for its existence, but the legend of the Golden Land destroyed when the waters of the Atlantic closed over it has remarkable staying power and is believed by large numbers of people. Plato wrote convincingly about the wonders of Atlantis in his dialogues *Timaeus* and *Critias,* while other writers have suggested that the biblical story of the Flood is based on fragmentary accounts of the Atlantean deluge. The lost continent is also of occult significance, largely as the result of the writings of W. Scott-Elliott whose book, *The Story of Atlantis* (recently republished by the Theosophical Society), alleged that by clairvoyance he had been able to contact the spirits of Atlanteans who had been destroyed because of their addiction to black magic. There even exists in Britain today a minor but ardent religious group, the "Atlanteans", who hold that Atlantis still exists today, but on a different metaphysical plane, and that it is possible to communicate with it via individuals with supposedly mediumistic powers (*see* **Spiritualism**). Members of the Atlanteans meet regularly to hear "trance addresses" by one of the high priests of Atlantis, Helio-Arconaphus. Such beliefs are essentially harmless and merely reflect the great variety of religious attitudes which human beings enjoy.

Atomism. In philosophy, the atomists were a group of early Greek thinkers, the most important of whom were Leucippus (fl. *c.* 440 B.C.) and his younger contemporary Democritus (*c.* 460–370 B.C.). Prior to these men, although it had been agreed that matter must be composed of tiny ultimate particles and that change must be due to the manner in which these mingled or separated from each other, it was supposed that there existed different types of particle for each material—*e.g.* for flesh, wood, hair, bone. The atomists taught that atoms were all made of a single substance and differed only in the connections (pictured as hooks, grooves, points, etc.) which enabled them to join each other in characteristic ways. Theirs was the first move towards modern atomic theory and a predecessor of the modern concept of chemical linkages.

Authoritarianism, a dictatorial form of government as contrasted with a democratic one based on popular sovereignty. Its alleged advantages are the avoidance of the delays and inefficiency said to be characteristic of the latter.

Automatism, the production of material, written or spoken in "automatic" fashion—*i.e.,* apparently not under the conscious or volitional control of the individual. This psychologically perplexing phenomenon has occurred from time to time throughout the history of literature and art, and while it has occasionally produced work of great merit (much of William Blake's poetry, Coleridge's "Kubla Khan", etc.) the bulk of it is indifferent and often simply rubbish. Spiritualists claim that the work is produced under the direct guidances of the spirit world, and their argument has attracted considerable attention through the compositions of the pianist Rosemary Brown who, with little or no academic background in musical theory, has produced a number of "original" piano pieces allegedly composed by Beethoven, Mozart, etc., from the astral plane. While few music critics doubt Mrs. Brown's honesty and integrity, most consider her work to be clever pastiche and barely comparable in quality to the masterworks of the dead composers. Nevertheless automatism wants some explaining, and most psychologists today defer judgment, taking the view that it serves to remind us of the fund of material which lies in the unconscious mind, and which is prone to pop up from time to time without warning. Rather similar is the case of Matthew Manning, a young English student who produced clever and artistically intriguing drawings and sketches, allegedly guided by the hands of famous dead artists.

B

Baconian Method, the use of the inductive (as opposed to the deductive or Aristotelian) method of reasoning as proposed by Francis Bacon in the 17th cent. and J. S. Mill in the 19th cent. Deduction argues from supposedly certain first principles (such as the existence of God or Descartes's "I think, therefore I am") what the nature of the universe and its laws *must* be, whereas the only means of obtaining true knowledge of the universe, in Bacon's view, was by the amassing of facts and observations so that when enough were obtained the certain truth would be known in the same way that a child's numbered dots in a playbook joined together by a pencilled line create a picture. However, this is not the way science progresses in practice. Bacon underrated the importance of hypothesis and theory and overrated the reliability of the senses. In discussing the scientific tradition, Sir Karl Popper in his book, *Conjecture and Refutations,* says: "The most important function of observation and reasoning, and even of intuition and imagination, is to help us in the critical examination of those bold conjectures which are the means by which we probe into the unknown." Two of the greatest men who clearly saw that there was no such thing as an inductive procedure were Galileo and Einstein.

Bahá'i Faith, a faith which teaches the unity of all religions and the unity of mankind. It arose in Iran from the teachings of the Bab (Mirza Ali Mohammed, 1820–50) and the Bahá'u'lláh (Mirza Husain Ali, 1817–92), thought to be manifestations of God, who in his essence is unknowable. Emphasis is laid on service to others. It has communities in many states and is surprisingly strong in England with a substantial following among university students. Its aims—universal peace, love, fellowship, sexual equality, etc.—are so laudable that it is hard to disagree with anything in the movement. Since the ruling Ayatollah Khomeini's fundamentalist Islamic regime came to power in Iran in 1979 members of the faith have been persecuted and a number of women who refused to recant were executed in 1983. The movement is now guided and administered by an elected order, "The Universal House of Justice".

Baptists, a Christian denomination whose distinctive doctrines are that members can only be received by baptism "upon the confession of their faith and sins" and that "baptism is no wise appertaineth to infants." Baptism is therefore by total immersion of adults. Modern Baptists base their doctrines upon the teaching of the Apostles and some hold that the Albigenses *(q.v.)* maintained the true belief through what they regarded as the corruption of the Roman Church in medieval times. On the other hand any connection with the Anabaptist movement during the Reformation is rejected and the beginning of the modern Church is traced to John Smyth, a minister of the Church of England who in Amsterdam came under the influence of the Arminians *(q.v.)* and Mennonites. Smyth died in 1612 when the first Baptist church in England was built at Newgate. This, the "General" Baptist Church, rejected Calvinistic beliefs and held the Arminian doctrine of redemption open to all, but some years later a split occurred with the formation of the "Particular" Baptist Church which was Calvinist in doctrine. In 1891 the two bodies were united in the Baptist Union and today the sect is spread throughout the world, notably in the United States.

The Anabaptist movements of Germany, Switzerland, and Holland also practiced adult baptism in addition to a primitive communism and demanded social reforms. Persecuted by both Catholics and Protestants, their leader, Thomas Münzer, and many others were burned at the stake (1525). However, this sect was noted for its violence under a religious guise, and its taking over of the state of Münster in 1533 was characterized by wild licentiousness, since, as Antinomians, they believed that the "elect" could do no wrong. A revival begun by Menno Simons (d. 1561), a Dutch religious reformer, led to the formation of the Mennonite sect which, while rejecting infant baptism, gave up the objectionable features of the Anabaptists. This reformed sect still exists as small agricultural groups in the original strongholds of the movement and in the United States.

Beat Generation, a term first used by the American

writer Jack Kerouac (d. 1969), author of *The Town and the City* and *On the Road,* to define various groups spread across the face of the country, but notably in New York and San Francisco, who, belonging to the post-war generation, represented a complex of attitudes. Briefly, these were: rejection of the values of the past and lack of conviction in the possibility of a future for humanity—hence an acceptance of nothing but the immediate present in terms of experience and sensations; rebellion against organized authority, not out of any political conviction (as in the case of anarchism), but rather from lack of any interest or desire to control events, nature, or people; contempt for the "Square"—the orthodox individual who, stuck firmly in his rut, "plays it safe" and remains confident of the rightness and decency of his moral values.

The Beat Generation of the 1940s and '50s gave way to the Love generation or Flower people, with their flowers, beads, and cowbells. Their social philosophy was the same—living in the present, unconventionally, seeking personal freedom, believing drugs to be essential, claiming to be acting against the rat race, dissociating themselves from politics, taking a superficial interest in the religions of the East, borrowing much of their language, music, and ideas on dress from the American hippy, yet believing in the creation of a new and gentler society based on different forms and values.

Both the Beat and Love generations were forerunners in America of an increasing and certainly welcome social awareness on the part of American students. This led in turn to the "campus revolutions" which were disruptive in their early stages but were also influential as part of the wave of public protest against the American involvement in Vietnam.

Behaviorism, a school of psychology founded in 1914 by J. B. Watson (1878–1958), an animal psychologist at Johns Hopkins University, Baltimore. Its main tenet was that the method of introspection and the study of mental states were unscientific and should be replaced by the study of behavior. When animals or human beings were exposed to specific stimuli and their responses objectively recorded, or when the development of a child, as seen in its changing behavior, was noted, these alone were methods which were truly scientific. Watson contributed an important idea to psychology and did a great deal towards ridding it of the largely philosophical speculations of the past. But he also went to absurd extremes, as in his view that thought is nothing but subvocal speech, consisting of almost imperceptible movements of the tongue, throat, and larynx (*i.e.,* when we think, we are really talking to ourselves), and his further opinion that heredity is, except in grossly abnormal cases, of no importance. He claimed that by "conditioning", the ordinary individual could be made into any desired type, regardless of his or her inheritance.

The work of Ivan Pavlov had begun about 1901, but was unknown in America until about ten years later, and it was through another Russian, Vladimir Bekhterev, that the concept of "conditioning" was introduced into the country. Bekhterev's book *Objective Psychology,* describing his new science of "reflexology", was translated in 1913 and played a great part in the development of Behaviorist ideas. The conditioned reflex became central to Watson's theory of learning and habit, formation (*e.g.,* he showed that a year-old child, at first unafraid of white rats, became afraid of them when they came to be associated with a loud noise behind the head). Finally all behavior, including abnormal behavior, came to be explained in terms of conditioned responses; these were built up by association on the infant's three innate emotions of fear, rage, and love, of which the original stimuli were, for the first, loud noises and the fear of falling; for the second, interference with freedom of movement; and for the third, patting and stroking.

Because of its considerable theoretical simplicity and its implicit suggestion that human behavior could be easily described (and even modified or controlled), Pavlovian psychology appeared very attractive to the Communist regime in Russia, and before long it became the "official" dogma in universities and research laboratories. Whereas in America and Western Europe its severe limitations became gradually apparent, in Russia these were ignored or disguised for ideological reasons with the inevitable outcome that Soviet psychology failed to evolve and, at one stage, seemed to be no more than a pallid offshoot of physiology. The recent liberalization which has been taking place throughout Soviet society has led to a considerable broadening of scientific horizons and Pavlovian ideas are no longer looked upon with such unquestioning reverence. In non-Communist countries simple Watsonian behaviorism has evolved into more sophisticated studies of animal learning, largely pioneered by the Harvard psychologist, Skinner. These techniques, which have shown that animals, from monkeys to rats, may be taught to solve a remarkable range of physical problems (such as pressing complex sequences of buttons or levers to escape from a cage) have themselves turned out to be rather disappointing in terms of advancing our general understanding of the workings of the human and animal brain. There is a growing feeling among psychologists that the real keys to the understanding of mankind will only be found through the study of man himself, and not his simpler animal cousins. *See also* **Gestalt Psychology**

Benthamism. *See* **Utilitarianism.**

Bolshevism, an alternative name for **Communism** *(q.v.),* usually used in the West in a derogatory sense. When the Russian Social Democratic Party at a conference held in London in 1903 split over the issue of radicalism or moderation, it was the radical faction headed by Lenin (who subsequently led the 1917 Revolution and became first Head of State of the Soviet Union) which polled the majority of votes. The Russian for majority is *bolshinstro* and for minority *menshinstro;* hence the radicals became known as Bolsheviki and the moderates as Mensheviki, anglicized as Bolsheviks and Mensheviks. *See* **Communism, Marxism.**

Bushido, the traditional code of honour of the Samurai or Japanese military caste corresponding to the European concept of knighthood and chivalry from which it took its separate origin in the 12th cent. Even today it is a potent influence among the upper classes, being based on the principles of simplicity, honesty, courage, and justice which together form a man's idea of personal honour.

C

Cabala, originally a collection of Jewish doctrines about the nature of the Universe, supposedly handed down by Moses to the Rabbis, which evolved into a kind of mystical interpretation of the Old Testament. Students of the history of religious belief have found its origins to be in fact extremely obscure, and some aspects appear to have been lifted from ancient Egyptian sources. Skilled Cabalists hold that the system contains a key to biblical interpretation based on the numerical values of the words and letters of the Scriptures which reveal hidden depths of meaning behind the allegorical Old Testament stories.

Calvinism, the branch of Protestantism founded basically (although preceded by Zwingli and others) by Jean Chauvin (1509–64), who was born in Noyon in Picardy. John Calvin, as he is usually called, from the Latin form of his name, Calvinius, provided in his *Institutions of the Christian Religion* the first logical definition and justification of Protestantism, thus becoming the intellectual leader of the Reformation as the older Martin Luther was its emotional instigator. The distinctive doctrine of Calvinism is its dogma of predestination which states that God has unalterably destined some souls to salvation to whom "efficacious grace and the gift of perseverance" is granted and others to eternal damnation. Calvinism, as defined in the Westminster Confession, is established in the Reformed or Presbyterian churches of France, Holland, Scotland, etc., as contrasted with the Lutheran churches, and its harsh but logical beliefs inspired the French Huguenots, the Dutch in their fight against Spanish Catholic domination, and the English Puritans. The rule set up under Calvin's influence in Geneva was marred by the burning at the stake of the anatomist Servetus for the heresy of "pantheism", or, as we should say, Unitarianism.

Perhaps its greatest single influence outside the Church was the result of Calvinist belief that to labor industriously was one of God's commands. This changed the medieval notions of the blessedness of poverty and the wickedness of usury, proclaimed that men should shun luxury and be thrifty, yet implied that financial success was a mark of God's favor. In this way it was related to the rise of capitalism either as cause or effect. Max Weber, the German sociologist, believed that Calvinism was a powerful incentive to, or even cause of, the rise of **capitalism** *(q.v.):* Marx, Sombart, and in England, Tawney, have asserted the reverse view—that Calvinism was a result of developing capitalism, being its ideological justification.

Capitalism is an economic system under which the means of production and distribution are owned by a relatively small section of society which runs them at its own discretion for private profit. There exists, on the other hand, a propertyless class of those who exist by the sale of their labor power. Capitalism arose towards the end of the 18th cent. in England where the early factory owners working with small-scale units naturally approved of free enterprise and free trade. But free enterprise has no necessary connection with capitalism; by the beginning of this century monopolies were developing and state protection against foreign competition was demanded. Capitalism is opposed by those who believe in socialism, first, for the moral reasons that it leads to economic inequality and the exploitation of labour and the consuming public, and that public welfare rather than private profit should motivate the economic system; secondly, for the practical reason that capitalism leads to recurrent economic crises. The recent world economic crisis has led to great hopes on the part of Marxists and Communists that capitalism is now involved in its final death throes. It is worth commenting however, that the European war of the 1940s, the great depression of the 30s, the first world war and the Russian Revolution were also, in their turn, confidently held up by Communists as heralding capitalism's imminent collapse.

Cartomancy, the art of fortunes or predicting the future by playing cards or by the Tarot pack. The elegant Tarot cards number 78 in all and are probably medieval in origin. They are rich in symbolism and include trump cards depicting the devil, the pope, death, the moon, the wheel of fortune, etc., and are an interesting part of our cultural mythology. There is no evidence whatsoever that they can be used in any objective way to divine the future, and professional fortune tellers and clairvoyants who use them almost certainly rely on a little native, basic psychology to achieve their results.

Characterology, the attempt made over many centuries to classify people into personality types on the basis of physical or psychological characteristics. The first attempt was made by Hippocrates in the 5th cent. B.C. who classified temperaments into the *sanguine* (or optimistic), the *melancholic,* the *choleric* (or aggressive), and the *phlegmatic* (or placid); these were supposed to result from the predominance of the following "humors" in the body: red blood, black bile, yellow bile, or phlegm respectively. Theophrastus, a pupil of Aristotle, described, with examples, thirty extreme types of personality (*e.g.* the talkative, the boorish, the miserly, etc.); these were basically literary and imaginative but about the same time "physiognomy" arose which attempted to interpret character from the face. Physiognomy became of importance again during the Renaissance and there are still those today who believe in it in spite of the fact that, broadly speaking, there is no connection whatever between facial features and personality (i.e. although it may be possible to tell from the features that a man is an idiot or some extreme abnormal type and some idea of character may be obtained from an individual's characteristic facial expressions, it is not possible to tell (as Johann Lavater, the best-known physiognomist of the late 18th cent. believed) from the shape of the nose, height of the brow, or dominance of the lower jaw, whether anyone is weak, intellectual or determined). The contention of the 19th cent. Italian criminologist Cesare Lombroso that criminals show typical facial characteristics—prominent cheekbones and jaw, slanting eyes, receding brow, large ears of a particular shape—was disproved by Karl Pearson early this century when he found that 3,000 criminals showed no significant differences of features, carefully measured from a similar number of students at Oxford and Cambridge.

It has, however, been noted that people in general tend to be intellectual or emotional, inward- or outward-looking, and this observation is reflected in the classification of the Scottish psychologist, Alexander Bain (d. 1903), into intellectual, artistic, and practical; Nietzsche's Apollonian and

Dionysian types; William James's "tender" and "toughminded"; and C. G. Jung's introvert and extrovert. Careful experiments have shown that these are not clear-cut and that most individuals fall in between the extremes.

Some connection has been found between temperament and body-build. The German psychiatrist Ernst Kretschmer (b. 1888) showed that manic-depressive patients and normal people who are extroverted and tend to alternate in mood (as do manic-depressives to an exaggerated degree) were usually short and stout or thick-set in build; schizophrenics and normal people, who both show shyness, serious or introverted reactions, were usually tall and slender. The former of "pyknic" body-build are "cyclothyme" in temperament, the latter with "schizothyme" temperament are of two bodily types—the tall and thin or "asthenic" and the muscularly well-proportioned or "athletic". The American Sheldon has confirmed these observations on the whole and gone into further details. According to him the basic body types are: (1) *endomorphic* (rounded build), corresponding to Kretschmer's pyknic, normally associated with the *viscerotonic* temperament (relaxed, sociable); (2) *mesomorphic* (squarish, athletic build), normally associated with the *somatotonic* temperament (energetic, assertive); and (3) *ectomorphic* (linear build) normally associated with the *cerebrotonic* temperament (anxious, submissive, restless). Glandular and metabolic factors have considerable effect on human personality and also, to some extent, on physique. It is not too surprising, therefore, to find an association between body build (or "somatotype" as Sheldon termed it) and general mood. However, Sheldon's original clear-cut and oversimplified categories of body-type are no longer looked upon as reliable indicators of personality.

Chauvinism, a term applied to any excessive devotion to cause, particularly a patriotic or military one. The word is derived from Nicholas Chauvin whose excessive devotion to Napoleon made him a laughing-stock.

Chirognomy, the attempt to read character from the lines in the hand (as contrasted with chiromancy or palmistry, in which an attempt is made to tell the future in the same way) is an ancient practice which, like astrology *(q.v.)* has no discernible scientific basis but a very considerable popular following. As with astrology, where it is hard to see what kind of link could exist between the constellations and human behavior, so it is equally hard to see how the configuration of lines on the hand could be paralleled by psychological attributes. This argument might be thought of as irrelevant if palmistry, etc. actually had predictive power, but the plain fact is that when put to a scientific test, practitioners of these arts turn out to show no abilities beyond those with which a normally perceptive individual is equipped.

Christadelphians, a religious denomination formed in the U.S.A. in the late 1840s by John Thomas, an Englishman from London. They claim to represent the simple apostolic faith of the 1st cent., and, in common with many other sects, hold that they alone interpret the Scriptures truly. They believe that Christ will return soon to set up the Kingdom of God with Jerusalem as its capital. In social life Christadelphians keep to themselves and hold aloof from organizational activities, though they do take an interest in political events if only from the point of view of their belief in biblical prophecy.

Christian Science, a religious denomination founded by Mary Baker Eddy (1821–1910), an American lady who sought to organize a church which would reinstate primitive Christianity and its lost element of healing. The sacred books of the movement are the Bible and *Science and Health with Key to the Scriptures* (1891), a revision of *Science and Health,* first published by Mrs. Eddy in 1875. Its main tenets (quoting from an official Christian Science source) are "that nothing is real save God and His spiritual creation, including man in His image and likeness; that man's essential nature is spiritual and wholly good; that matter, evil, disease and sickness are unreal—illusions existing only through ignorance of God. Therefore Christian Scientists renounce for themselves medicine, surgery and drugs and rely on healing through prayer."

The name of the movement seems misleading since it has nothing to do with any of the natural sciences of which Mrs. Eddy had no first-hand knowledge. In using the word, Mrs. Eddy meant that the teaching and acts of Jesus were rooted in unchanging divine law. Mrs. Eddy was at first interested in Spiritualism and afterwards, having been a patient of a faith-healer named Quimby, claimed to have been divinely healed.

There is a good deal of controversy about the efficacy of the Christian Science methods. In principle believers argue that if one has total, unquestioning faith in the healing power of Christ, then all sickness will be revealed as illusion and vanish. The trouble of course is that total faith is almost impossible to achieve, and hence even Christian Scientists inevitably fall ill and die. This makes the Church's argument irrefutable, but there is some evidence that the argument is convincing fewer individuals than it once did. On the other hand the growth of interest in "divine healing" within the more orthodox churches had led to a softening of barriers between Mrs. Eddy's splinter group and the hard-core Christian religions. Christian Science may well fade away after handing over to orthodoxy its single key concept.

Church of England. There is some evidence of possible continuity with the Christianity of Roman Britain, but in the main the Church derives from the fusion of the ancient Celtic church with the missionary church of St. Augustine, who founded the See of Canterbury in A.D. 597. To archbishop Theodore in 673 is ascribed its organization in dioceses with settled boundaries, and in parishes. St. Augustine's church was in communion with Rome from the first, but the Church of England was not brought within papal jurisdiction until after the Norman conquest, and was at no time under the complete domination of Rome. It remains the Catholic Church of England without break of continuity, but during the Reformation the royal supremacy was accepted and that of the pope repudiated. Its traditional forms of worship are embodied in the Book of Common Prayer, but the Alternative Service Book of 1980 is now widely used. In 1978, Easter communicants numbered 1,736,000.

The Anglican Communion comprises the churches in all parts of the world which are in communion with the Church of England (In the U.S. it is the Episcopal Church). All the bishops of the Anglican Communion meet every ten years in the Lambeth Conference (first held in 1867), over which the Archbishop of Canterbury by custom presides as *primus inter pares.* At the 1968 Conference observers and laymen were admitted for the first time. The last Conference was held in 1978. The next will meet in 1988.

Clairvoyance. *See* **Telepathy.**

Communism, ideally refers to the type of society in which all property belongs to the community and social life is based on the principle "from each according to his ability, to each according to his needs." There would be public ownership of all enterprises and all goods would be free. Since no such society as yet exists, the word in practice refers to the attempt to achieve such a society by initially overthrowing the capitalist system and establishing a dictatorship of the proletariat (Marx identified the dictatorship with a democratic constitution). Communists believe that their first task is the establishment of socialism under which there remain class distinctions, private property to some extent, and differences between manual and brain workers. The state is regulated on the basis "from each according to his ability, to each according to his work". Lenin applied Marx's analysis to the new conditions which had arisen in 20th-cent. capitalist society. Marxism-Leninism develops continuously with practice since failure to apply its basic principles to changed circumstances and times would result in errors of dogmatism. Mao Tse-tung worked out the techniques of revolutionary action appropriate to China; Che Guevara the guerrilla tactics appropriate to the peasants of Latin America. His counsel "It is not necessary to wait until conditions for making revolution exist; the insurrection can create them", was the opposite of Mao Tse-tung's "Engage in no battle you are not sure of winning", and Lenin's "Never play with insurrection". Two fundamental principles of communism are (1) peaceful coexistence between countries of different social systems, and (2) the class struggle between oppressed and oppressing classes and between oppressed and oppressor nations. Maoism, for example, holds that it is a mistake to lay one-sided stress on peaceful transition towards socialism otherwise the revolutionary will of the proletariat becomes passive and unprepared politically and organizationally for the tasks ahead.

In Russia the civil war developed *after* the revolution; in China the communists fought their civil war *before* they seized power: the Yugoslav partisans won their own guerrilla war *during* their stand against the fascist powers—differences which had important political consequences. Russia suffered three decades of isolationism and totalitarian suppression ("an isolated and besieged fortress") before the death of Stalin. Then came a marked, if zigzagging shift towards "liberalization." Mao Tsetung held to the orthodox Leninist view about capitalism and communism, regarded détente as a dangerous illusion, and compromise and "revisionism" as a fatal error. The ideological dispute between these two great communist powers which lasted from the '60s to the '80s is ending with the improvement in inter-party relations and today a movement towards détente is taking place. Communist parties in some countries, *e.g.,* Italy, are taking the democratic road to socialism and believe that a communist government should be installed by the ballot box. *See also,* **Marxism, Trotskyism.**

Congregationalists, the oldest sect of Nonconformists who hold that each church should be independent of external ecclesiastical authority. They took their origin from the Brownists of Elizabeth's days. Robert Browne (*c.* 1550–*c.* 1633), an Anglican clergyman, who had come to reject bishops, was forced with his followers to seek refuge, first in Holland and then in Scotland where he was imprisoned by the Kirk. In later life he changed his views and is disowned by Congregationalists because of his reversion to Anglicanism. His former views were spread by Henry Barrow and John Greenwood who, under an Act passed in 1592 "for the punishment of persons obstinately refusing to come to church" (and largely designed for the suppression of this sect), were hanged at Tyburn. They had preached *(a)* that the only head of the church is Jesus Christ; *(b)* that, contrary to Elizabethan doctrine, the church had no relationship to the state; *(c)* that the only statute-book was the Bible whereas the Articles of Religion and Book of Common Prayer were mere Acts of Parliament; *(d)* that each congregation of believers was independent and had the power of choosing its own ministers. The body fled once more to Holland and were among the Pilgrims who set sail in the *Mayflower* for America in 1620 while those who remained were joined by Puritans fleeing from Charles I. They became free once more to live in England under the Commonwealth only to be repressed again under Charles II. Finally full liberty of worship was granted under William III. In 1833 the Congregational Union of England and Wales was formed which had no legislative power. It had issued a Declaration of Faith by which no minister was bound; he was responsible to his own church and to nobody else. The sect is widespread both in Britain and the U.S.A. where it is held in special honor because of its connection with the Pilgrim Fathers. In 1972 the Congregational Church in England and Wales and the Presbyterian Church of England decided to unite to form the United Reformed Church. The majority of members who did not join comprise the Congregational Federation.

Coptic Church, the sect of Egyptian Christians who, holding "Monophysite" opinions (*i.e.,* refusing to grant the two natures, God and Man, of Christ), were declared heretical by the Council of Chalcedon in 451. They practice circumcision and have dietary laws. Their language is a direct descendant of ancient Egyptian. Like the Armenians, they are regarded as an heretical branch of Eastern Christianity. Their religious head is the patriarch of Alexandria.

Cynics, a school of philosophy founded in the time of Alexander the Great by Diogenes. Choosing to live like a dog by rejecting all conventions of religion, manners, or decency, and allegedly living in a tub, Diogenes unwittingly brought on his school the title "Cynic", meaning not "cynical", as the word is understood today, but "canine". His teacher, Antisthenes, who had been a disciple of Socrates, decided, after the latter's death, that all philosophy was useless quibbling and man's sole aim should be simple goodness. He believed in a return to nature, despised luxury, wanted no government, no private property, and associated with working men and slaves. Far from being cynics in the modern sense, Diogenes and Antisthenes were virtuous anarchists rather like old Tolstoy (except that in the practice of their beliefs they were more consistent).

D

Deism. *See* **God and Man.**

Demonism, Demons, and the Devil. Demons are ethereal beings of various degrees of significance and power which are believed to be implicated in men's good, but especially evil, fortune. They are common to most cultures. From the anthropological point of view the demon arose as a widespread concept in the following ways: (1) as a psychological projection into the outer world of man's own good or evil emotions and thoughts; (2) as a survival of primitive animism *(q.v.),* thus spirits are believed to haunt places, trees, stones, and other natural objects; (3) when by warlike invasion the gods of the vanquished become the devils of the conquerors (as when the Jews occupied Canaan); (4) as a primitive belief that spirits of the dead continue after death to hover near their former habitation, and not always entirely welcome to the living; (5) the conception of a supreme source of evil (the Devil or Satan) which took shape among the Jews during their sojourn in Babylon under the influence of Zoroastrianism *(q.v.),* a religion in which the struggle between the two spirits, Good and Evil, reached its height in the imagination of the ancient world. The Satan of the Old Testament was first regarded as one of God's servants (in the Book of Job he goes up and down the earth to see whether God's commands are obeyed), but when the Jews returned from their captivity he had become identified with Ahriman, the spirit of evil, who was in continual conflict with Ahursa Mazda, the spirit of good. As Dr. Margaret Murray has pointed out, the primitive mind ascribed both good and evil to one power alone; the division into God and the Devil, priest and witch, belongs to a higher stage of civilization. The worship of evil itself, or of its personification in Satan, is a curious practice which seems to have developed hand-in-hand with Christianity and to have received steady support from a small but measurable minority. Many of the ceremonies involved in Satanism or in the so-called Black Mass appear to have been no more than opportunities for sexual excesses of one kind or another—such indulgences being traditionally barred to devout Christians. The alleged power of sex as a form of magic was propagated by the talented but rather mad poet, Aleister Crowley (1875–1947), who scandalized pre-war Europe with his very well-publicized dabblings into Satanism. The self-styled "wickedest man in the world", Crowley was a pathetic rather than shocking figure and died a drug addict. He can hardly be said to have significantly advanced the cause of Demonology, though it has to be admitted that he tried very hard.

Determinism and Free Will. The question of whether man is, or is not, free to mold his own destiny is one which has exercised the minds of philosophers since Greek mythology conceived of the Fates as weaving a web of destiny from which no man can free himself. Socrates emphasized that man could through knowledge influence his destiny while ignorance made him the plaything of fate; Plato went further in pointing out that man can, and does, defeat the purposes of the universe and its divine Creator. It is our duty to live a good life, but we can live a foolish and wicked one if we chose. Aristotle wrote "Virtue is a disposition or habit involving deliberate purpose or choice". If this were not so morality would be a sham.

The Problem for Theology. The last of the great philosophers of Antiquity and one of the great influences in molding Catholic theology was Plotinus (*c.* 204–70). Soul, he taught, is free, but once enmeshed in the body loses its freedom in the life of sense. Nevertheless, man is free to turn away from sensuality and towards God who is perfect freedom; for even when incarnated in matter the soul does not entirely lose the ability to rescue itself. This conception was carried over into the beliefs of the early Christian Apologists because it appeared to be in line with the teaching of Jesus that He had come to save man from sin. Sin implies guilt, and guilt implies the freedom to act otherwise; furthermore an all-good God cannot be responsible for the sin in the world which must be man's responsibility and this again implies freedom. Pelagius (*c.* 355–*c.* 425), a Welsh priest, not only believed in free will but questioning the doctrine of original sin, said that when men act righteously it is through their own moral effort, and God rewards them for their virtues in heaven. This belief became fairly widespread and was declared a heresy by the Church, being attacked notably by St. Augustine (354–430), a contemporary of Pelagius, who believed in predestination—that, since the sin of Adam, God had chosen who in all future history would be saved and who damned. This represents one tradition in Christianity: the determinism which leads to Calvinism *(q.v.).* St. Thomas Aquinas (1227–74), the greatest figure of scholasticism and one of the principal saints in the Roman Catholic Church, compromised between the two positions in the sense that, believing man to be free, he yet held that Adam's sin was transmitted to all mankind and only divine grace can bring salvation. But even when God wishes to bestow this salvation, the human will must cooperate. God foresees that some will not accept the offer of grace and predestines them to eternal punishment.

The Problem for Philosophy. With the Renaissance, thinkers began to free themselves from the domination of the Church and so study the world objectively and freely without preconceptions. But the more man turned to science, the more he discovered that the world was ruled by apparently inexorable laws and, since the scientist must believe that every event has a cause, he was led back to determinism. Man as part of the universe was subject to law too and all that existed was a vast machine. Francis Bacon (1561–1626) separated the fields of religion and science but left man subject completely to the will of God. Thomas Hobbes (1588–1679) was a rigid determinist and materialist although, having had trouble with the Church in France whence, as a royalist, he had fled, he took care to announce that the Christian God is the Prime Mover.

Modern philosophy begins with René Descartes (1596–1650), a Frenchman who tried to reconcile the mechanical scientific universe of his time with the spiritual need for freedom. He did this by separating completely mind and body; the former, he said, is free, the latter completely determined. But, by admitting that the will can produce states of body, he was left with the problem of how this could happen—a problem which the so-called Occasionists solved to their own satisfaction by stating that the will is free and God so arranges the universe that what a person wills happens. Baruch Spinoza (1632–77), a Dutch Jew whose independence of thought had led to his excommunication from the Amsterdam Synagogue in 1656, was a complete determinist. He asserted that God and Nature are one, everything that happens is a manifestation of God's inscrutable nature, and it is logically impossible that things could be other than they are. Thus both Hobbes and Spinoza were determinists for entirely opposed reasons. The former as a materialist, the latter because he believed in the absolute perfection and universality of God. Yet the great religious mystic and mathematician Blaise Pascal (1623–62) held that, no matter what reason and cold logic may indicate we *know* from direct religious experience that we are free. John Calvin (1509–64) and Martin Luther (1483–1546) were both determinists. *See* **Calvinism.**

To the more practical British philosophers, John Locke (1632–1704) and David Hume (1711–76), free will was related to personality. Locke believed that God had implanted in each individual certain desires and these determine the will; the desires are already there, but we use our will to satisfy them. Hume argued that a man's behavior is the necessary result of his character and if he had a different character he would act otherwise. Accordingly, when a man's actions arise from his own nature and desires he is free. He is not free when external events compel him to act otherwise (*e.g.,* if he strikes another because his own nature is such he is free as he is not if he is compelled to do so against his desire). Leibnitz (1646–1716), although as a German metaphysical philosopher holding very different general views, said much the same thing—that choice is simply selecting the desire that is strongest. But most of the 18th cent. thinkers after Voltaire, with the great exceptions of Rousseau and the later German philosophers Kant, Fichte, Schopenhauer, and Hegel, who were initially influenced by him, accepted determinism. Rousseau (1712–78) began to stem the tide by his declaration that man is a free soul striving to remain free and only prevented from being so by society and the cold science which stifles his feeling heart. Once again the will became important as Kant (1724–1804) asserted that belief in freedom is a moral necessity although it cannot be proved by reason; the moral nature of man shows that there is a "transcendental" world beyond the senses where freedom applies. Fichte and Schelling found freedom in the Absolute ego or God, of whom each individual was part and thus also free. Hegel (1770–1831) saw the whole universe as evolving towards self-awareness and freedom in man although this could only be fully realized in a society that makes for freedom. Even God himself only attains full consciousness and self-realization through the minds of such individuals as are free. This is the goal of the dialectical process. (*See* **Dialectical Materialism.**)

The Scientist's View. For the scientist the law of cause and effect is a useful hypothesis since, by and large, it is necessary for him to assume that all events are caused. Nevertheless the modern tendency is to think in terms of statistical probability rather than relentless mechanistic causality, and, although the free will problem does not concern the scientist as such, it is clear that freedom and determinism (assuming the terms to have any meaning at all) are not necessarily opposed. In sociology, for example, we *know* that certain actions will produce certain results upon the behavior of people in general, *e.g.,* that raising the bank rate will discourage business expansion. But this does not mean that Mr. Brown who decides in the circumstances not to add a new wing to his factory is not using his free will. Even in the case of atoms, as Dr. Bronowski has pointed out, the observed results of allowing gas under pressure in a cylinder to rush out occur because most of the atoms are "obeying" the scientific "law" relating to such situations. But this does not mean that some atoms are not busy rushing across the stream or even against it—they are, but the general tendency is outwards and that is what we note. Lastly, the modern philosophical school of Logical Analysis would probably ask, not whether Freewill or Determinism is the true belief, but whether the question has any meaning. For what scientific experiment could we set up to prove one or the other true? The reader will note that some of the philosophers mentioned above are using the words to mean quite different concepts.

Dialectical Materialism, the combination of Hegel's dialectic method with a materialist philosophy produced by Karl Marx (1818–83) and his friend Friedrich Engels (1820–95). It is the philosophical basis of **Marxism** *(q.v.)* and **Communism** *(q.v.)* "Dialectic" to the ancient Greek philosophers meant a kind of dialogue or conversation, as used particularly by Socrates, in which philosophical disputes were resolved by a series of successive contradictions: a thesis is put forward and the opposing side holds its contradiction or antithesis until in the course of argument a synthesis is reached in which the conflicting ideas are resolved.

From Thesis through Antithesis to Synthesis. Hegel in the 19th century put forward the view that this process applies to the course of nature and history as they strive towards the perfect state. But to him, as to the Greeks, the conflict was in the field of ideas. The "universal reason" behind events works through the ideas held by a particular society until they are challenged by those of another which supersedes them and in turn, usually by war, becomes the agent of universal reason until the arrival of a new challenger. Hegel therefore regarded war as an instrument of progress and his Prussian compatriots found no difficulty in identifying their own state as the new agent of progress by universal conquest. Feuerbach, Lassalle, and other early socialists were impressed by some of Hegel's ideas: *e.g.,* that societies evolved (with the assumption that finally their own ideal society would be achieved) and that truth, morals, and concepts were relative so that a type of society that was "good" at one time was not necessarily so at another. But Marx and Engels in effect turned Hegel upside-down, accepted his dialectic but rejected his belief that ideas were the motive force. On the contrary, they said, ideas are determined by social and economic change as a result of materialistic forces. (*See* **Calvinism,** where it is pointed out that the Marxist view is not that Calvin changed men's economic ideas but rather that a developing capitalism unconsciously changed his.) The historical materialism of Marxism purports to show that the inexorable dialectic determines that feudalism is displaced by capitalism and capitalism by creating a proletariat (its antithesis) inevitably leads to socialism and a classless society. The state, as a tool of the dominant class, withers away. Dialectical materialism is applied in all spheres. As a philosophy there is little to be said for it save that it has shown us the close dependence of man's thoughts upon current material and social conditions. But as a battle cry or a rationalization of Marxism it wields immense power over the minds of men. *See* **Marxism.**

Dianetics. *See* **Scientology.**

Doukhobors, a religious sect of Russian origin, founded by a Prussian sergeant at Kharkov in the middle of the 18th century, and now mainly settled in Canada. Like many other sects they belong to that type of Christianity which seeks direct communication with God and such bodies tend to have certain traits in common, such as belief in the "inner light", opposition to war and authority in general, and often ecstasies which show themselves in physical ways such as shaking, speaking in strange tongues (glossolalia), and other forms of what to the unbeliever seem mass hysteria. Liturgy, ritual, or ceremony is non-existent. The Doukhobors were persecuted in Tsarist Russia, but in 1898 Tolstoy used his influence to have them removed to Canada where the government granted them uninhabited land in what is now Saskatchewan and seven or eight thousand settled down in peace which they enjoyed for many years. Recently, however, their practices have caused difficulties once more; for even the most tolerant government which is prepared to accept pacifism, total dependence on communally-owned agriculture, refusal to engage in commerce, non-payment of taxes, rejection of the marriage ceremony and separation "when love ceases", finds it difficult to tolerate, as civilization advances ever closer to Doukhobor communities, their proneness to "put off these troublesome disguises which we wear"—*i.e.,* to walk about naked in the communities of their more orthodox neighbors. What the future of the Doukhobors in their various sects (for even they have their differences) will be it is impossible to say, but it is difficult to believe that these simple people can long resist the pressure of modern civilization.

Dowsing. *See* **Radiesthesia.**

Druidism, the religion of Celtic Britain and Gaul of which Druids were the priesthood. They were finally wiped out by the Roman general Suetonius Paulinus about A.D. 58 in their last stronghold, the island of Anglesey. There are two sources of our present beliefs in Druidism: (1) the brief and factual records of the Romans, notably Pliny and Julius Caesar, which tell us that they worshipped in sacred oak groves and presumably practiced a religion doing reverence to the powers of nature which must have had its roots in early stone age times and had many cruel rites, *e.g.,* human sacrifice; (2) the beliefs put forward by William Stukeley, an amateur antiquarian who from 1718 did valuable work by his studies of the stone circles at Stonehenge and Avebury. However, influenced by the Romantic movement, he later put forward the most extravagant theories which unfortunately are those popularly accepted by those without archaeological knowledge today. Stonehenge and Avebury were depicted as the temples of the "white-haired Druid bard sublime" and an attempt was made to tie up Druidism with early Christianity, above all with the concept of the Trinity. In fact, these circles have no connection with the Druids. They may have made ceremonial use of them but recent evidence suggests that the megalithic stones at Stonehenge belong to a Bronze Age culture (2100–1600 B.C.). Nor have Druidism and Christianity any relationship. Almost nothing is known of the religion. Yet such were its romantic associations that, even today, one hears of "Druidic" ceremonies practiced at the appropriate time of year on Primrose Hill in the heart of London (though whether seriously or with tongue in cheek, one does not know). In Wales the name Druid survives as the title for the semi-religious leaders of the annual festivals of Celtic poetry, drama, and music known as Eisteddfods. Lingering, but now tenuous, druidic connections are to be found in all Celtic parts including Cornwall and Brittany where Eisteddfods are also held.

Dualism, any philosophical or theological theory which implies that the universe has a double nature, notably Plato's distinction between appearance and reality, soul and body, ideas and material objects, reason and the evidence of the senses, which infers that behind the world as we perceive it there lies an "ideal" world which is more "real" than that of mere appearance. In religions such as Zoroastrianism or the Gnostic and Manichaeism heresies, it was believed that the universe was ruled by good and evil "principles"—in effect that there was a good god and a bad one. In psychology, dualism refers to the philosophical theories which believe mind and body to be separate entities. The opposite of dualism is monism which asserts the essential unity of the substance of the universe.

An essential problem in the dualistic view lies in the question as to how and where the two separate and distinct properties of the universe interact. Where, for example, does the "mind" actually mesh with the physical mechanics of the brain and body—where does the ghost sit in his machine? Descartes decided that mind and body must interact somewhere and he selected the pineal gland (an apparently functionless part of the brain) as the spot. But this did nothing to explain how two *totally different* aspects of nature can possibly influence each other, and today most philosophers and psychologists reject dualistic views of life and personality as posing more problems than they solve. *See also* **Psychology, Occam's Razor.**

E

Education. Education was no great problem to primitive man, but as societies became more complex people began to ask themselves such questions as: *What* should young people be taught? *How* should they be taught? Should the aim of their education be to bring out their individual qualities or rather to make them good servants of the state?

The first teachers were priests who knew most about the traditions, customs, and lore of their societies and thus the first schools were in religious meeting places. This was notably true of the Jews who learned from the rabbis in the synagogue.

The Greeks. We begin, as always, with the Greeks whose city-states, based on slavery, educated men (not women) for the sort of life described in Plato's *Dialogues*—the leisured life of gentlemen arguing the problems of the universe at their banquets or in the market-place. This made it necessary to learn debate and oratory (or rhetoric) especially for those who proposed to take up politics. The Sophist philosophy taught the need to build up convincing arguments in a persuasive manner, to learn the rules of logic and master the laws and customs of the Athenians, and to know the literature of the past so that illustrations might be drawn from it. These strolling philosophers who taught for a fee were individualists showing the student how to advance himself at all costs within his community.

Socrates had a more ethical approach, believing that education was good in itself, made a man happier and a better citizen, and emphasized his position as a member of a group. His method of teaching, the dialectic or "Socratic" method, involved argument and discussion rather than overwhelming others by rhetoric and is briefly mentioned under **Dialectical Materialism** *(q.v.)*. Today this method is increasingly used in adult education where a lecture is followed by a period of discussion in which both lecturer and audience participate; for psychologists have shown that people accept ideas more readily when conviction arises through their own arguments than when they are passively thrust down their throats.

Socrates' pupil Plato produced in his book *The Republic* one of the first comprehensive systems of education and vocational selection. Believing that essentially men have very different and unequal abilities he considered that in an idealistic or utopian society they should be put into social classes corresponding to these differences, and suggested the following method: (1) For the first 18 years of a boy's life he should be taught gymnastics and sports, playing and singing music, reading and writing, a knowledge of literature, and if he passed this course sent on to the next stage; those who failed were to become tradesmen and merchants. (2) From 18–20 those successful in the first course were to be given two years of cadet training, the ones thought incapable of further education being placed in the military class as soldiers. (3) The remainder, who were to become the leaders of society, proceeded with advanced studies in philosophy, mathematics, science, and art. Such education was to be a state concern, state supported and controlled, selecting men and training them for service in the state according to their abilities.

Plato's pupil Aristotle even suggested that the state should determine shortly after birth which children should be allowed to live and destroy the physically or mentally handicapped; that marriage should be state-controlled to ensure desirable offspring. However, in their time the leisured and individualistic Sophists held the field and few accepted the educational views of Plato or his pupil.

Rome. The Romans were not philosophers and most of their culture came from Greece. Administration was their chief aptitude and Quintilian (A.D. *c.* 35–*c.* 95) based his higher education on the earlier classical tuition in public speaking, but he is important for emphasizing the training of character and for his humanistic approach to the method of teaching that caused his *Institutio oratoria* to be influential for centuries later—indeed one might almost say up to the time of the great Dr. Arnold of Rugby. Education, he believed, should begin early but one must "take care that the child not old enough to love his studies does not come to hate them" by premature forcing; studies must be made pleasant and interesting and students encouraged by praise rather than discouraged when they sometimes fail; play is to be approved of as a sign of a lively disposition and because gloomy, depressed children are not likely to be good students; corporal punishment should never be used because "it is an insult as you will realize if you imagine it yourself". The world became interested not in *what* he taught but *how* he taught it: he was the pioneer of humanistic education and character-training from Vittorino d. Feltre (1378–1446) of Mantua, through Milton and Pope who commended his works to the modern educationists who have studied their pupils as well as their books.

The Middle Ages: The Religious View. With the development of Christianity education once more became a religious problem. The earliest converts had to be taught Christian doctrine and were given instruction in "catechumenal" schools before admission to the group, but as the religion came increasingly into contact with other religions or heresies a more serious training was necessary, and from these newer "catechetical" schools, where the method used was the catechism (*i.e.,* question and answer as known to all Presbyterian children today), the Apologists arose among whom were Clement of Alexandria and the great Origen. From this time education became an instrument of the church and in 529 the Emperor Justinian ordered all pagan schools to be closed.

As typical of the best in medieval education while the lamp of civilization burned low during the Dark Ages, after the fall of Roman power, and survived only in the monasteries, we may mention St. Benedict (*c.* 480–*c.* 547) of Monte Cassino. There, in southern Italy, a rule was established which became a part of monastic life in general. Monastic schools were originally intended for the training of would-be monks, but later others were admitted who simply wanted some education; thus two types of schools developed: one for the *interni* and the other for *externi* or external pupils. Originally studies were merely reading in order to study the Bible, writing to copy the sacred books, and sufficient calculation to be able to work out the advent of holy days or festivals. But by the end of the 6th century the "seven liberal arts" (grammar, rhetoric, dialectic, arithmetic, geometry, music, and astronomy) were added.

The Renaissance. The close of the Middle Ages saw the development of two types of secular school. One came with the rise of the new merchant class and the skilled trader whose "guilds" or early trade unions established schools to train young men for their trades but ultimately gave rise to burgher or town schools; the other was the court school founded and supported by the wealthy rulers of the Italian cities—Vittorio da Feltre (mentioned above) presided over the most famous at Mantua.

These Renaissance developments are paralleled in northern Europe by the Protestant reformers who, having with Martin Luther held that everyone should know how to read his Bible in order to interpret it in his own way, were logically committed to popular education, compulsory and universal. In theory this was intended for biblical study, but writing, arithmetic, and other elementary subjects were taught and Luther said that, even if heaven and hell did not exist, education was important. Universal education is a Protestant conception.

Views of Philosophers. From this period onwards people were free to put forward any ideas about education, foolish or otherwise, and to create their own types of school. Of English philosophers who theorized about, but did not practice, education we may mention the rationalist Francis Bacon (1561–1626) who saw learning as the dissipation of all prejudices and the collection of concrete facts; the materialist and totalitarian Hobbes (1588–1679) who, as a royalist, believed that the right to determine the kind of education fit for his subjects is one of the absolute rights of the sovereign power or ruler; the gentlemanly Locke (1632–1704) whose ideal was a sound mind in a sound body to be attained by hard physical exercise, wide experience of the world, and enough knowledge to meet the requirements of the pupil's environment. The end result would be one able to get on with his fellows, pious but wise in the ways of the world, independent and able to look after himself, informed but reticent about his knowledge. Classics and religious study were not to be carried to excess, since Locke held that these subjects had been overrated in the past. Locke's pupil was the well-to-do, civilized young man of the 17th century who knew how to behave in society.

Jean-Jacques Rousseau (1712–78), a forerunner of the Romantic movement *(q.v.),* which despised society and its institutions, put emotion at a higher level than reason. His book *Emile* describes the education of a boy which is natural and spontaneous. Society, he holds, warps the growing mind and therefore the child should be protected from its influences until his development in accordance with his own nature is so complete that he cannot be harmed by it. During the first 4 years the body should be developed by physical training; from 5 to 12 the child would live in a state of nature such that he could develop his powers of observation and his senses; from 13, books would be used and intellectual training introduced, although only in line with the child's own interests, and he would be given instruction only as he came to ask for it. Moral training and contact with his fellows to learn the principles of sympathy, kindness, and helpfulness to mankind would be given between 15 and 20. Girls, however, should be educated to serve men in a spirit of modesty and restraint. His own five children he deposited in a foundling hospital.

Summary. Broadly speaking, then, there have been four main attitudes to education: (1) religious, with a view to a life beyond death; (2) state-controlled education, with a view to uniform subservience to authority; (3) "gentlemanly" education, with a view to social graces and easy congress in company; (4) the "child-centered" education, which attempts to follow the pupil's inner nature. It is unnecessary to mention the ordinary method of attempting to instill facts without any considerable degree of cooperation between pupil and teacher in order that the former may, with or without interest, follow some occupation in adult life; for this the philosophers did not consider. Today there remain the two fundamental principles: education for the advantage of the state and its ideology or education for individual development and freedom.

Four educationists of the modern period who have influenced us in the direction of freedom were Johann Pestalozzi of Switzerland (1746–1827) who, by trying to understand children, taught the "natural, progressive, and harmonious development of all the powers and capacities of the human being"; Friedrich Froebel (1782–1852) of Germany, the founder of the Kindergarten who, like Pestalozzi, was influenced by Rousseau but realized the need to combine complete personal development with social adjustment; Maria Montessori (1869–1952) whose free methods have revolutionized infant teaching; John Dewey (1859–1952) who held that the best interests of the group are served when the individual develops his own particular talents and nature.

Eleatics, the philosophers of Elea in ancient Greece who, at the time when Heraclitus (*c.* 535–475 B.C.) was teaching that change is all that exists and nothing is permanent, were asserting that change is an illusion. Of the three leaders of this school, Xenophanes asserted that the universe was a solid immovable mass forever the same; Parmenides explained away change as an inconceivable process, its appearance being due to the fact that what we see is unreal; and Zeno (the best-known today) illustrated the same thesis with his famous argument of the arrow which, at any given moment of its flight, must be where it is since it cannot be where it is not. But if it is where it is, it cannot move, this is based, of course, on the delusion that motion is discontinuous. The Eleatics were contemporaries of Socrates.

Empiricism. While not a single school of philosophy, empiricism is an approach to knowledge which holds that if a man wants to know what the universe is like the only correct way to do so is to go and look for himself, to collect facts which come to him through his senses. It is, in essence, the method of science as contrasted with rationalism *(q.v.)* which in philosophy implies that thinking or reasoning without necessarily referring to external observations can arrive at truth. Empiricism is typically an English attitude, for among the greatest empirical philosophers were John Locke, George Berkeley, and David Hume. *See* Rationalism.

Epicureanism. The two great schools of the Hellenistic period (*i.e.* the late Greek period beginning with the empire of Alexander the Great) were the Stoics and Epicureans, the former founded by Zeno of Citium (not to be confused with Zeno the Eleatic) *(q.v.),* the latter by Epicurus, born in Samos in 342 B.C. Both schools settled in Athens, where Epicurus taught that "pleasure is the beginning and end of a happy life." However, he was no sensualist and emphasized the importance of moderation in all things because excesses would lead to pain instead of pleasure and the best of all pleasures were mental ones. Pleasures could be active or passive but the former contain an element of pain since they are the process of satisfying desire not yet satiated. The latter involving the absence of desire are the more pleasant. In fact, Epicurus in his personal life was more stoical than many Stoics and wrote "when I live on bread and water I spit on luxurious pleasures." He disapproved of sexual enjoyment and thought friendship one of the highest of all joys. A materialist who accepted the atomic theory of Democritus, he was not a determinist, and if he did not disbelieve in the gods he regarded religion and the fear of death as the two primary sources of unhappiness.

Epiphenomenalism. *See* **Mind and Matter.**

Erastianism, the theory that the state has the right to decide the religion of its members, wrongly attributed to Erastus of Switzerland (1524–83) who was believed to have held this doctrine. The term has usually been made use of in a derogatory sense—*e.g.,* by the Scottish churches which held that the "call" of the congregation was the only way to elect ministers at a time when, about the turn of the 17th and 18th century, they felt that

Episcopalianism was being foisted on them. "Episcopalianism" (*i.e.* Anglicanism) with its state church, ecclesiastical hierarchy, and system of livings presented by patrons was to them "Erastian" in addition to its other "unscriptural practices."

Essenes, a Jewish sect which, during the oppressive rule of Herod (d. 4 B.C.), set up monastic communities in the region of the Dead Sea. They refused to be bound by the scriptural interpretations of the Pharisees and adhered rigorously to the letter of Holy Writ, although with additions of their own which cause them by orthodox Jews today to be regarded as a break-away from Judaism. Among their practices and beliefs were purification through baptism, renunciation of sexual pleasures, scrupulous cleanliness, strict observance of the Mosaic law, communal possession, asceticism. Akin in spirit, although not necessarily identical with them, were the writers of Apocalyptic literature preaching that the evils of the present would shortly be terminated by a new supernatural order heralded by a Messiah who would reign over a restored Israel. The casting out of demons and spiritual healing formed part of these general beliefs which were in the air at that time. The sect has an importance far beyond its size or what has been known about it in the past since the discovery from 1947 onwards of the Dead Sea Scrolls of the Qumran community occupying a monastery in the same area as the Essenes and holding the same type of belief. These scrolls with their references to a "Teacher of Righteousness" preceding the Messiah have obvious relevance to the sources of early Christianity and have given rise to speculations as to whether Jesus might have been influenced by views which, like His own, were unacceptable to orthodox Jews but in line with those of the Dead Sea communities. They seem to show that early Christianity was not a sudden development but a gradual one which had its predecessors.

Eugenics, a 19th century movement largely instigated by the British scientist and mathematician, Sir Francis Galton. Galton argued that many of the most satisfactory attributes of mankind—intelligence, physical strength, resistance to disease, etc.—were genetically determined and thus handed down in the normal process of inheritance. From this he reasoned that selective mating of physically "superior" individuals, and its converse, the controlled limitation on the breeding of criminals or the insane, would lead inevitably to a progressive improvement in the overall standards of the human race. In their simplest form these proposals are incontestable, though they do of course introduce marked restrictions on the choice of the individual for marriage and procreation. Worse yet is the way in which the argument can be misapplied or elaborated—as it was in Nazi Germany—to include the sterilization of alcoholics, confirmed criminals and even epileptics. Nevertheless there remains the feeling that there are some aspects of eugenics which intuitively at any rate make good sense and of course the widespread application of birth control is itself an enactment of eugenic principles.

Evangelicalism, the belief of those Protestant sects which hold that the essence of the Gospel consists in the doctrine of salvation by faith in the atoning death of Christ and not by good works or the sacraments; that worship should be "free" rather than liturgical through established forms; that ritual is unacceptable and superstitious. Evangelicals are Low Churchmen.

Evangelism, the preaching of the Gospel, emphasising the necessity for a new birth or conversion. The evangelistic fervor of John Wesley and George Whitefield (*see* Methodism) aroused the great missionary spirit of the late 18th and 19th century. George Fox, founder of the Society of Friends *(q.v.),* was also an evangelist. Evangelists can be Low, High, or Middle Churchmen.

Existentialism, a highly subjective philosophy which many people connect with such names as Jean-Paul Sartre (1905–80) or Albert Camus (1913–60) and assume to be a post-war movement associated with disillusion and a sordid view of life. However, existentialism stems from Sören Kierkegaard (1813–55), the Danish "religious writer"—his own description of himself—in such works as *Either/Or, Fear and Trembling,* and *Concluding Unscientific Postscript.* Between the two wars translations of Kierkegaard into German influenced Martin Heidegger's great work *Being and Time* and the other great existentialist Karl Jaspers; it has strongly influenced modern Protestant theology notably in Karl Barth, Reinhold Niebuhr, and Paul Tillich and beyond that field the French philosopher Gabriel Marcel, the Spanish writer Unamuno in his well-known *The Tragic Sense of Life,* and Martin Buber of Israel in his *I and Thou.* We have it on Heidegger's authority that "Sartre is no philosopher" even if it is to his works that modern existentialists often turn.

Existentialism is extremely difficult for the non-metaphysically-minded to understand. It deals, not with the nature of the universe of what are ordinarily thought of as philosophical problems but describes an attitude to life or God held by the individual. Briefly, its main essentials are: (1) it distinguishes between *essence, i.e.,* that aspect of an entity which can be observed and known—and its *existence*—the fact of its having a place in a changing and dangerous world which is what really matters; (2) existence being basic, each self-aware individual can grasp his own existence on reflection in his own immediate experience of himself and his situation as a free being in the world; what he finds is not merely a knowing self but a self that fears, hopes, believes, wills, and is aware of its need to find a purpose, plan, and destiny in life; (3) but we cannot grasp our existence by thought alone; thus the fact "all men must die" relates to the essence of man but it is necessary to be involved, to draw the conclusion as a person that "I too must die" and experience its impact on our own individual existence; (4) because of the preceding, it is necessary to abandon our attitude of objectivity and theoretical detachment when faced by the problems relating to the ultimate purpose of our own life and the basis of our own conduct; life remains closed to those who take no part in it because it can have no significance; (5) it follows that the existentialist cannot be rationalist in his outlook for this is merely an escape into thought from the serious problems of existence; none of the important aspects of life—failure, evil, sin, folly—nor (in the view of Kierkegaard) even the existence of God or the truth of Christianity—can be proved by reason. "God does not exist; He is eternal," was how he expressed it; (6) life is short and limited in space and time, therefore it is foolish to discuss in a leisurely fashion matters of life and death as if there were all eternity to argue them in. It is necessary to make a leap into the unknown, *e.g.,* accepting Christ (in the case of the Christian existentialist) by faith in the sense of giving and risking the self utterly. This means complete commitment, not a dependence on arguments as to whether certain historical events did, or did not, happen.

To summarize: existentialism of whatever type seems to the outsider to be an attitude to life concerning itself with the individual's ultimate problems (mine, not yours); to be anti-rationalist and anti-idealist (in the sense of being, as it seems to the believer, practical)—in effect it seems to say "life is too short to fool about with argument, you must dive in and become committed" to something. Sartre who called himself an "atheist existentialist" was apparently committed to the belief that "hell is other people," but for most critics the main argument against existentialist philosophy is that it often rests on a highly specialized personal experience and, as such, is incommunicable.

Existential Psychology, a new if rather diffuse movement in modern psychology with no specific founder but with a number of figures who have, perhaps against their will, acquired leader status. One of the key figures is the British psychiatrist, R. D. Laing, whose radical views on psychotherapy are counted as being heretical by the vast majority of his medical colleagues. Laing holds that many so-called neurotic and psychotic conditions are essentially not "abnormal" and merely represent extreme strategies by which an individual may adjust to environmental and personal stress. Instead of attempting to suppress or eliminate the psychosis in the traditional manner, one should lead the patient through it thus allowing the individual's "unconscious plan" for his own adjustment to be fulfilled.

Exorcism, the removal or ejection of an evil spirit by a ritual or prayer. It is easy to forget that the concept of insanity as representing a disorder of the brain, analogous to physical sickness of the body, is fairly recent in origin. Barely two centuries ago it was considered to be appropriate treatment to put lunatics into chains and beat them daily in the hope that the malevolent beings inhabiting them might be persuaded to depart. Tragically, many of the symptoms of severe forms of mental disorder induce such an apparent change in the personality of the individual as to suggest that an alien individual has indeed taken over their body, and this belief is still common in many parts of the world. Most religious systems have developed some ritual or set of rituals for expelling these demons, and while, not surprisingly, the practice of exorcism by the clergy has declined dramatically in the past century, it is still brought into play now and again in such circumstances as alleged hauntings, poltergeist phenomena, etc. From a scientific point of view, exorcism must be counted as a superstitious rite, but its suggestive power in cases of hysteria, and perhaps even more serious mental illnesses, cannot be completely ruled out. General interest in the topic has been stimulated in part by the resurgence of the practice of Black Magic and witchcraft, largely in the form of experimental dabbling by young people, who no doubt become disillusioned when it fails to live up to its promise. Testimony to the pulling-power of this remnant of our superstitious past is the fact that a sensational and terrifying novel, *The Exorcist,* which its author claimed was based on fact, topped the best-seller lists in 1972, and the even more horrific movie-version became one of the most successful (in box office terms) films of all time. The Church of England, incidentally, takes anything but a dismissive line on the matter, and in fact employs a number of ordained priests as "licensed exorcists". These services are apparently much in demand.

F

Fabian Society. In 1848 (the year of *The Communist Manifesto* by Marx and Engels) Europe was in revolt. In most countries the workers and intellectuals started bloody revolutions against the feudal ruling classes which were no less violently suppressed; hence on the continent socialism took on a Marxist tinge which to some extent it still retains. But at the same time England was undergoing a slow but nonviolent transition in her political and industrial life which led the workers in general to look forward to progress through evolution. Marxism never became an important movement in England even though it took its origin there. There were many reasons for this: the agitation of the Chartists *(q.v.);* the writings of Mill, Ruskin, and Carlyle; the reforms of Robert Owen; the religious movement led by the Wesleys; the cooperative societies; the Christian socialists. Furthermore legislation stimulated by these bodies had led to an extension of the franchise to include a considerable number of wage-earners, remedial measures to correct some of the worst abuses of the factory system, recognition of the trade unions, etc.

This was the background against which the Fabian Society was founded in 1884 with the conviction that social change could be brought about by gradual parliamentary means. (The name is derived from Quintus Fabius Maximus, the Roman general nicknamed "Cunctator," the delayer, who achieved his successes in defending Rome against Hannibal by refusing to give direct battle.) It was a movement of brilliant intellectuals, chief among whom were Sidney and Beatrice Webb, H. G. Wells, G. B. Shaw, Graham Wallas, Sidney Olivier, and Edward Pease. The Society itself was basically a research institution which furnished the intellectual information for social reform and supported all contributing to the gradual attainment by parliamentary means of socialism.

The Webbs's analysis of society emphasized that individualist enterprise in capitalism was a hang-over from early days and was bound to defeat itself since socialism is the inevitable accompaniment of modern industrialism; the necessary result of popular government is control of their economic system by the people themselves. Utopian schemes had been doomed to failure because they were based on the fallacy that society is static and that islands of utopias could be formed in the midst of an unchanging and antagonistic environment. On the contrary, it was pointed out, society develops: "The new becomes old, often before it is consciously regarded as new." Social reorganization cannot usefully be hastened by violent means but only through methods consonant with this natural historical progression—gradual, peaceful, and democratic. The Fabians were convinced that men are rational enough to accept in their common interest developments which can be demonstrated as necessary; thus public opinion will come to see that socialization of the land and industries is essential in the same way that they came to accept the already-existing acts in respect of housing, insurance, medical care, and conditions of work.

The Society collaborated first in the formation of the Independent Labour Party and then with the more moderate Labour Party and the trade unions and Cooperative movement. But in general it disapproved of independent trade union action since change should come from the government and take political form. The class war of Marx was rejected and so too was the idea of the exclusive role of the working class—reform must come from the enlightened cooperation of all classes—not from their opposition.

Faith Healing, the belief and practice of curing physical and mental ills by faith in some supernatural power, either allegedly latent in the individual (as with Christian Science) or drawn in some way from God. It is a characteristic of faith healing that it is supposed to be publicly demonstrable—*i.e.,* a "healer" will hold public meetings and invite sick people to come up to be cured on the platform. In the emotionally charged atmosphere which the healer generates, it is not unusual for people to show immediate and striking improvement in their illness, but the almost invariable rule is for relapses to occur within days or hours after the event. When remission is more permanent, the illness is generally hysterical in origin and will often return to the individual in some other form. Spiritualists claim that the healing in such cases is done not by "faith" but by direct intervention of the spirits of doctors, etc., who have died and passed on to another world. Perhaps the world's most famous faith healer in recent years was Harry Edwards (d. 1976), who had literally millions of letters from all parts of the world asking for the healing attention of his spirit guides. Many doctors, while remaining immensely sceptical about the origins and extent of this kind of therapy, are inclined to admit that it might have benefits when the sickness is mildly hysterical in origin. The real danger, of course, comes when patients seek unorthodox therapy before consulting their doctor.

Fascism. From the end of medieval times with the opening up of the world, the liberation of the mind and the release of business enterprise, a new spirit arose in Europe exemplified in such movements as the Renaissance, the Reformation, the struggle for democracy, the rise of capitalism, and the Industrial Revolution. With these movements there developed a certain tradition, which, in spite of hindrances and disagreement or failures, was universally held by both right- and left-wing parties however strongly they might fail to agree on the best means of attaining what was felt to be a universal ideal. The hard core of this tradition involved: belief in reason and the possibility of human progress; the essential sanctity and dignity of human life; tolerance of widely different religious and political views; reliance on popular government and the responsibility of the rulers to the ruled; freedom of thought and criticism; the necessity of universal education; impartial justice and the rule of law; the desirability of universal peace. Fascism was the negation of every aspect of this tradition and took pride in being so. Emotion took the place of reason, the "immutable, beneficial, and fruitful inequality of classes" and the right of a self-constituted élite to rule them replaced universal suffrage because absolute authority "quick, sure, unanimous" led to action rather than talk. Contrary opinions are not allowed and justice is in the service of the state; war is desirable to advance the power of the state; and racial inequality made a dogma. Those who belong to the "wrong" religion, political party, or race are outside the law.

The attacks on liberalism and exaltation of the state derive largely from Hegel and his German followers; the mystical irrationalism from such 19th century philosophers as Schopenhauer, Nietzsche, and Bergson; from Sorel (*see* **Syndicalism**) came the idea of the "myth", and an image which would have the power to arouse the emotions of the masses and from Sorel also the rationale of violence and justification of force. But these philosophical justifications of fascism do not explain why it arose at all and why it arose where it did—in Italy, Germany, and Spain. These countries had one thing in common—disillusionment. Germany had lost the 1914–18 war, Italy had been on the winning side but was resentful about her small gains. Spain had sunk to the level of a third-rate power, and people were becoming increasingly restive under the reactionary powers of the Catholic Church, the landed aristocracy, and the army. In Marxist theory, fascism is the last fling of the ruling class and the bourgeoisie in their attempt to hold down the workers.

Italian Fascism. The corporate state set up by Benito Mussolini in Italy claimed to be neither capitalist nor socialist, and after its inception in 1922 the Fascist Party became the only recognized one. Its members wore black shirts, were organized in military formations, used the Roman greeting of the outstretched arm, and adopted as their slogan "Mussolini is always right". Membership of the Party was not allowed to exceed a number thought to be suited to the optimum size of a governing class and new candidates were drawn, after strict examinations, from the youth organizations. The Blackshirts, a Fascist militia, existed separately from the army and were ruled by Fascist headquarters.

At the head of government was Mussolini, "Il Duce" himself, a cabinet of fourteen ministers selected by him and approved by the King to supervise the various functions of government, and the Grand Council or directorate of the Fascist Party, all the members of which were chosen by the Duce. Parliament, which was not allowed to initiate legislation but only to approve decrees from above, consisted of a Senate with life membership and a Chamber of Fasel and Corporations composed of nominated members of the Party, the National Council of Corporations, and selected representatives of the employers' and employees' confederations. Private enterprise was encouraged and protected but rigidly controlled; strikes were forbidden, but a Charter of Labour enforced the collaboration of workers and employers whose disputes were settled in labor courts presided over by the Party. All decisions relating to industry were government-controlled (*e.g.,* wages, prices, conditions of employment and dismissal, the expansion or limitation of production), and some industries such as mining, shipping, and armaments were largely state-owned.

Italian Fascism served as a model in other countries, notably for the German National Socialist Party, in Spain and Japan, and most European nations between the wars had their small fascist parties, the British version led by Sir Oswald Mosley being known as the British Union which relied on "strong-arm tactics", marches and violence. The Public Order Act of 1936 was passed to deal with it. Although fascism in all countries has certain recognizable characteristics, it would be wrong to think of it as an international movement taking fixed forms and with a clearly thought-out rationale as in the case of communism. While there have been minor revivals of interest in Fascism in Italy—presumably as a counter move against the considerable inroads being made by the Communist Party in that country—fascism's final remaining bastion in Europe—Spain—began to crumble with the death of its dictator, General Franco, in 1975. *See* **Nazism.**

Fatalism. *See* **Determinism.**

Fetichism, originally a practice of the natives of West Africa and elsewhere of attributing magical properties to an object which was used as an amulet, for putting spells on others, or regarded as possessing dangerous powers. In psychology the term refers to a sexual perversion in which objects such as shoes, brassières, hair, etc., arouse sexual excitement.

Feudalism. The feudal system took its origins from Saxon times and broadly speaking lasted until the end of the 13th cent. It was a military and political organization based on land tenure, for, of course, society throughout this period was based almost entirely on agriculture. The activities of men divided them into three classes or estates. The First Estate was the clergy, responsible for man's spiritual needs; the Second was the nobility, including kings and emperor as well as the lesser nobles; the Third was composed of all those who had to do with the economic and mainly agricultural life of Europe. The praying men, the fighting men and administrators, and the toilers were all held to be dependent on each other in a web of mutual responsibilities.

The theory of feudalism, although it by no means always worked out in practice, was as follows: the earth was God's and therefore no man owned land in the modern sense of the word. God had given the Pope spiritual charge of men, and secular power over them to the emperor from whom kings held their kingdoms, and in turn the dukes and counts received the land over which they held sway from the king. Members of the second estate held their lands on the condition of fulfilling certain obligations to their overlord and to the people living under them, so when a noble received a fief or piece of land he became the vassal of the man who bestowed it. To him he owed military service for a specified period of the year, attendance at court, and giving his lord counsel. He undertook to ransom his lord when he fell into enemy hands and to contribute to his daughter's dowry and at the knighting of his son. In return the lord offered his vassal protection and justice, received the vassal's sons into his household and educated them for knighthood.

The system was complicated by the fact that large fiefs might be subdivided and abbots often governed church lands held in fief from nobles. The serf or toiling man dwelt on the land of a feudal noble or churchman where he rendered service by tilling the soil or carrying out his craft for his manorial lord in return for protection, justice, and the security of his life and land. He was given a share in the common lands or pastures from which he provided for his own needs. In the modern sense he was not free (although at a later stage he could buy his freedom) since he was attached to the soil and could not leave without the lord's permission. On the other hand he could neither be deprived of his land nor lose his livelihood. Feudal tenures were abolished in England by statute in 1660, although they had for long been inoperative. In Japan a feudal system existed up to 1871, in Russia until 1917, and many relics of it still linger on (*e.g.* the *mezzadria* system of land tenure in parts of Italy).

Flying Saucers. In June 1947 an American private pilot, Kenneth Arnold, saw a series of wingless objects flying through the air at a speed which he estimated at thousands of miles an hour. He later told the press that the objects "flew as a saucer would if you skipped it across the water," and the phrase "flying saucers" was erroneously born. What Arnold actually saw has never been satisfactorily explained—it was probably a flight of jet fighters reflecting the sun's rays in a way that made them appear as discs—but since that date literally hundreds of thousands of people all over the world have reported the sighting of strange objects in the sky, coming in a bewildering range of shapes and sizes. Initially the American Air Force launched an official enquiry—Project Bluebook—to attempt to solve the mystery of these "unidentified flying objects" or "U.F.O.s," which finally folded in 1969 after concluding that the bulk of the sightings were probably misinterpretations of natural phenomena and that there was no evidence for the commonly held view that earth was being visited by spacecraft from some other planetary system. A rather similar conclusion was arrived at by the famous University of Colorado project—the Condon Committee—which published its findings in 1968. Despite this clear-cut official attitude, belief in the existence of flying saucers and their origin as alien space vehicles is exceedingly widespread and is held very strongly by people in all walks of life. In 1959 this striking social phenomenon attracted the attention of the psychologist C. G. Jung. He noticed that the press were inclined to report statements that saucers existed when made by prominent people and not publish contrary statements made by equally prominent people. He concluded that flying saucers were in some way welcome phenomena and in his brilliant little book. *Flying Saucers—A Modern Myth,* he hypothesized that the U.F.O.s were the modern equivalent of "signs in the skies." It was Jung's contention that the saucers were looked upon as the harbingers of advanced alien civilizations who had come to save the world from its descent into nuclear catastrophe—archangels in modern dress in fact.

Whatever the validity of this imaginative view of U.F.O.s, it is undeniably true that they exercise a great fascination for millions of people, some of whom invest them with definite religious significance. The best example of the open incorporation of flying saucers into a religious belief system is to be found in the Aetherius Society, an international organization with headquarters in Los Angeles but founded by a former London clerk, George King. Mr. King, who claims to be the mediumistic link between earth and the largely benevolent beings from outer space, regularly relays messages—notably from a Venusian known as Aetherius—to enthusiastic congregations at religious meetings. The sect, which is entirely sincere and dedicated in its beliefs, also makes pilgrimages to the tops of various mountains which have been "spiritually charged" with the aid of the spacebeings in their flying saucers.

Odd though such ideas may seem to most people, they can be readily understood within the context of the very marked decline in orthodox religious belief which we have seen in the past two decades. To an increasing number of people, many of whom feel a desperate need for spiritual guidance and enlightenment, the concepts of the traditionally Western religions seem somehow unsatisfactory. Many therefore turn to cults and splinter groups which use ideas and terminology which to them seem more at home in the twentieth century than those that sprung to life thousands of years ago. To members of the Aetherius Society, for example, the idea that Jesus Christ lives on Venus and rides around in a flying saucer is neither blasphemous nor ludicrous. As long as empty churches testify to the growing, if perhaps only temporary loss of contact between orthodox religions and the man-in-the-street, then one can expect such offbeat ideas as the cults surrounding flying saucers, and the science-fiction-like cult of Scientology *(q.v.)* to expand and flourish.

Freemasonry, a widespread, influential secret organization of English origin. Although it can be traced back to the Middle Ages when itinerant working masons in England and Scotland were organized in lodges with secret signs for the recognition of fellow-members, modern freemasonry first arose in England in the early decades of the 18th century. The first Grand Lodge was founded in London in 1716 and Freemasons' Hall was opened in 1776. With its clubs for discussion and social enjoyment (women were excluded) it met a need and became a well-known feature of English life. The movement quickly spread abroad to places which had direct trade links with England. The graded lodge structure, the social prestige conferred by membership, the symbolism, ritual and ceremony, and the emphasis on mutual help have had a lasting appeal. Interest in the occult had more appeal on the Continent than in England. Until a decade or so ago, membership conferred definite business and social advantages, particularly in small communities where the leading middle-class figures were generally members. Recently this advantage has markedly declined and freemason lodges nowadays tend to be little more than worthy charitable organizations. Fear of secret societies has given freemasonry many opponents; it was condemned by the Roman Catholic Church, banned by fascist dictators, and denounced by the Comintern. A statement from the congregation for the doctrine of the faith in 1981 reminded Catholics that under Article 2335 of the Code of Canon Law they are forbidden under pain of excommunication from joining masonic or similar associations.

Freudian theory. *See* **Psychoanalysis.**

Friends, The Society of. *See* **Quakers.**

Fundamentalism is a term covering a number of religious movements which adhere with the utmost rigidity to orthodox tenets; for example the Old Testament statement that the earth was created by God in six days and six nights would be held to be factual rather than allegorical or symbolic. Although the holding of rigid beliefs in the literal truth of the Bible might seem to be frequently contrary to modern scientific findings, the fundamentalists at least do not have the problems of compromise and interpretation to face, and to some people this is no doubt a great attraction. A factor influencing the present troubles in Northern Ireland is the narrow and intolerant form of fundamentalism represented by the extreme brand of Presbyterianism practiced there.

G

Gestalt Psychology. In the latter half of the 19th cent. it became evident to psychologists that in principle there was no good reason why "mental" events should not be just as measurable and manageable as "physical" ones. Intensive studies of learning, memory, perception, and so on were therefore undertaken and the beginnings of an empirical science of psychology were underway. In the early part of the 20th cent. the experiments of Pavlov (*see* **Behaviorism**) and his co-workers suggested that the behavior of an animal, or even men, might ultimately be reduced to a descriptive account of the activities of nervous reflex loops—the so-called conditioned reflexes. With the publication of Watson's important book on Behaviorism in 1914 it looked as though the transfer of psychological studies from the field of philosophy to that of science could now take place. Actually the over-simplified picture of cerebral and mental pictures which Behaviorism offered was rather comparable to the billiard ball view of the universe so fashionable in Victorian science. Just as Behaviorism implied that there was a fundamental building block (the conditioned reflex) from which all mental events could be constructed, so Victorian physics assumed that the entire universe could be described in terms of a vast collection of atoms pushing each other around like billiard balls. The development of nuclear physics was to shatter the latter dream and at the same time a challenge to the naïve "reflex psychology" came from the Gestalt experimental school.

The founders of this school were Max Wertheimer, Kurt Koffka and Wolfgang Köhler, three young psychologists who in 1912 were conducting experiments—notably in vision—which seemed to expose the inadequacies of the behaviorist position. The Pavlov-Watson view, as we have said, implied that complex sensory events were no more than a numerical sum of individual nervous impulses. Wertheimer's group proposed that certain facts of perceptual experiences (ruled out of court as subjective and therefore unreliable by Watson) implied that the whole *(Gestalt)* was something more than simply the sum of its parts. For example, the presentation of a number of photographs, each slightly different, in rapid series gives rise to cinematographic motion. In basic terms, the eye has received a number of discrete, "still" photographs, and yet "motion" is perceived. What, they asked, was the sensory input corresponding to this motion? Some processes within the brain clearly *added* something to the total input as defined in behaviorist terms. An obvious alternative—in a different sense modality—is that of the arrangement of musical notes. A cluster of notes played one way might be called a tune; played backwards they may form another tune, or may be meaningless. Yet in all cases the constituent parts are the same, and yet their relationship to one another is evidently vital. Once again the whole is something more than the simple sum of the parts.

The implications of all this appeared to be that the brain was equipped with the capacity to organize sensory input in certain well-defined ways, and that far from being misleading and scientifically unjustifiable, human subjective studies of visual experience might reveal the very principles of organization which the brain employs. Take a field of dots, more or less randomly distributed; inspection of the field will soon reveal certain patterns or clusters standing out—the constellations in the night sky are a good illustration. There are many other examples, and Wertheimer and his colleagues in a famous series of experiments made some effort to catalogue them and reduce them to a finite number of "Laws of Perceptual Organization" which are still much quoted today.

Ghosts, belief in ghosts is one of the most common features of supernatural and mystical philosophy. At its roots it is based on the assumption that Man is essentially an individual created of two separate and distinct substances, mind and body. Most religious systems hold to this dualistic view (*see* **Dualism**), arguing that whereas the body is transient and destructible, the mind or spirit is permanent and survives the death of its physical host. The discarnate spirit is normally assumed to progress to some other realm ("Heaven," "Nirvana," "The Spirit World," etc.) whereupon it loses contact with the mortal world. Occasionally, however, for one reason or another, the spirits may not progress and may become trapped and unable to escape the material world. Traditionally this is supposed to occur when the death of the individual is precipitated by some great tragedy—murder, suicide, etc.—when the site of the tragedy is supposed to be haunted by the earthbound spirit. Although the library of the Society for Psychical Research is crammed with supposedly authentic accounts of hauntings of this kind, scientific interest in ghosts has been waning rapidly in recent years. At one time, in particular in the latter part of the 19th cent., with the upsurge of scientific interest in Spiritualism *(q.v.)*, there were even attempts to call up ghosts in the laboratory. These led to spectacular opportunities for fraud on the part of Spiritualist mediums and the like, but in the long run added little to the cause of science. As we have said, belief in ghosts is largely dependent upon a parallel belief that the mind or soul of man is something essentially separate from the body. With the decline in belief of this notion (it is now almost totally dismissed by most scientists and philosophers) has come an inevitable decline in belief in ghosts.

Gnosticism. Among the many heresies of early Christianity, especially during its first two centuries, was a group which came under the heading of Gnosticism. This was a system or set of systems which attempted to combine Christian beliefs with others derived from Oriental and Greek sources, especially those which were of a mystical and metaphysical nature, such as the doctrines of Plato and Pythagoras. There were many Gnostic sects, the most celebrated being the Alexandrian school of Valentius (fl. *c.* 136–*c.* 160). "Gnosis" was understood not as meaning "knowledge" or "understanding" as we understand these words, but "revelation." As in other mystical religions, the ultimate object was individual salvation; sacraments took the most varied forms. Many who professed themselves Christians accepted Gnostic doctrines and even orthodox Christianity contains some elements of Gnostic mysticism. It was left to the bishops and theologians to decide at what point Gnosticism ceased to be orthodox and a difficult task this proved to be. Two of the greatest, Clement of Alexandria and his pupil Origen, unwittingly slipped into heresy when they tried to show that such men as Socrates and Plato, who were in quest of truth, were Christian in intention, and by their lives and works had prepared the way for Christ. Thus they contradicted Church doctrine which specifically said *Extra ecclesiam nulla salus*—outside the Church there is no salvation.

God and Man. The idea of gods came before the idea of God and even earlier in the evolution of religious thought there existed belief in spirits (*see* **Animism**). It was only as a result of a long period of development that the notion of a universal "God" arose, a development particularly well documented in the Old Testament. Here we are concerned only with the views of philosophers, the views of specific religious bodies being given under the appropriate headings. First, however, some definitions.

Atheism is the positive disbelief in the existence of a God. **Agnosticism** (a term coined by T. H. Huxley, the 19th cent. biologist and contemporary of Darwin) signifies that one cannot know whether God exists or not. **Deism** is the acceptance of the existence of God, not through revelation, but as a hypothesis required by reason. **Theism** also accepts the existence of God, but, unlike Deism, does not reject the evidence of revelation (*e.g.,* in the Bible or in the lives of the saints). **Pantheism** is the identification of God with all that exists (*i.e.,* with the whole universe). **Monotheism** is the belief in one God, **polytheism** the belief in many (*see also* **Dualism**).

Early Greek Views. Among the early Greek philosophers, Thales (*c.* 624–565 B.C.) of Miletus, in Asia Minor, Anaximander (611–547 B.C.), his pupil, and Anaximenes (b. *c.* 570 B.C.), another Miletan, were men of scientific curiosity and their speculations about the origin of the universe were untouched by religious thought. They founded the scientific tradition of critical discussion. Heraclitus of Ephesus (*c.* 540–475 B.C.), was concerned with the problem of change. How does a thing change and yet remain itself? For him all things are flames—processes. "Everything is in flux, and nothing is at rest." Empedocles of Agrigentum in Sicily (*c.* 500–*c.* 430 B.C.) introduced the idea of opposition and affinity. All matter is composed of the so-called four elements—*earth, water, air,* and *fire*—which are in opposition or alliance with each other. All these were materialist philosophers who sought to explain the working of the universe without recourse to the gods.

Socrates, Plato, and Aristotle. Socrates (470–899 B.C.) was primarily concerned with ethical matters and conduct rather than the nature of the universe. For him goodness and virtue come from knowledge. He obeyed an "inner voice" and suffered death rather than give up his philosophy. He believed in the persistence of life after death and was essentially a monotheist. Plato (427–347 B.C.) was chiefly concerned with the nature of reality and thought in terms of absolute truths which were unchanging, logical, and mathematical. (*See* **Mind and Matter.**) Aristotle (384–322 B.C.) took his views of matter not from Democritus (atomic view) but from Empedocles (doctrine of four elements), a view which came to fit in well with orthodox medieval theology. Matter is conceived of as potentially alive and striving to attain its particular form, being moved by divine spirit or mind *(nous)*. (An acorn, for example, is matter which contains the form "oak-tree" towards which it strives.) Thus there is a whole series from the simplest level of matter to the perfect living individual. But there must be a supreme source of all movement upon which the whole of Nature depends, a Being that Aristotle describes as the "Unmoved Mover", the ultimate cause of all becoming in the universe. This Being is pure intelligence, a philosopher's God, not a personal one. Unlike Plato, Aristotle did not believe in survival after death, holding that the divine, that is the immortal element in man, is mind.

Among the later Greek thinkers the Epicureans were polytheists whose gods, however, were denied supernatural powers. The Stoics built up a materialist theory of the universe, based on the Aristotelian model. To them God was an all-pervading force, related to the world as the soul is related to the body, but they conceived of it as material. They developed the mystical side of Plato's idealism and were much attracted by the astrology coming from Babylonia. They were pantheists. The Sceptics were agnostics.

From Pagan to Christian Thought. Philo, "the Jew of Alexandria," who was about 20 years older than Jesus, tried to show that the Jewish scriptures were in line with the best in Greek thought. He introduced the *Logos* as a bridge between the two systems. Philo's God is remote from the world, above and beyond all thought and being, and as His perfection does not permit direct contact with matter the divine *Logos* acts as intermediary between God and man. Plotinus (204–70), a Roman, and the founder of Neoplatonism, was the last of the great pagan philosophers. Like Philo, he believed that God had created the world indirectly through emanations—beings coming from Him but not of Him. The world needs God but God does not need the world. Creation is a fall from God, especially the human soul when enmeshed in the body and the world of the senses, yet (*see* **Determinism**) man has the ability to free himself from sense domination and turn towards God. Neoplatonism was the final stage of Greek thought drawing inspiration from the mystical side of Plato's idealism and its ethics from Stoicism.

Christianity: The Fathers and the Schoolmen. It was mainly through St. Augustine (354–430), Bishop of Hippo in North Africa, that certain of the doctrines of Neoplatonism found their way into Christianity. Augustine also emphasized the concept of God as all good, all wise, all knowing, transcendent, the Creator of the universe out of nothing. But, he added, since God knows everything, everything is determined by Him forever. This is the doctrine of predestination and its subsequent history is discussed under **Determinism.**

In the early centuries of Christianity, as we have seen, some found it difficult to reconcile God's perfection with His creation of the universe and introduced the concept of the *Logos* which many identified with Christ. Further, it came to be held that a power of divine origin permeated the universe, namely the Holy Spirit or Holy Ghost. Some theory had to be worked out to explain the relationships of these three entities whence arose the conception of the Trinity. God is One; but He is also Three: Father, Son (the *Logos* or Christ), and Holy Ghost.

This doctrine was argued by the Apologists and the Modalists. The former maintained that the *Logos* and the Holy Spirit were emanations from God and that Jesus was the *Logos* in the form of a man. The Modalists held that all three Persons of the Trinity were God in three forms or modes; the *Logos* is God creating, the Holy Spirit God reasoning, and God is God being. This led to a long discussion as to whether the *Logos* was an emanation from God or God in another form: was the *Logos* of like *nature* with God or of the same *substance?* This was resolved at the Council of Nicaea (325) when Athanasius formulated the orthodox doctrine against Arius *(q.v.):* that the one God is a Trinity of the same substance, three Persons of the same nature—Father, Son, and Holy Ghost.

St. Thomas Aquinas (1227–74), influenced greatly by Aristotle's doctrines, set the pattern for all subsequent Catholic belief even to the present time. He produced rational arguments for God's existence: *e.g.,* Aristotle's argument that, since movement exists, there must be a prime mover, the Unmoved Mover or God; further, we can see that things in the universe are related in a scale from the less to the more complex, from the less to the more perfect, and this leads us to suppose that at the peak there must be a Being with absolute perfection. God is the first and final cause of the universe, absolutely perfect, the Creator of everything out of nothing. He reveals Himself in his Creation and rules the universe through His perfect will. How Aquinas dealt with the problem of predestination is told under **Determinism.**

Break with Medieval Thought. Renaissance thinkers, free to think for themselves, doubted the validity of the arguments of the Schoolmen but most were unwilling to give up the idea of God (nor would it have been safe to do so). Mystics (*see* **Mysticism**) or near-mystics such as Nicholas of Cusa (*c.* 1401–64) and Jacob Boehme (1575–1624) taught that God was not to be found by reason but was a fact of the immediate intuition of the mystical experience, Giordano Bruno held that God was immanent in the infinite universe. He is the unity of all opposites, a unity without opposites, which the human mind cannot grasp. Bruno was burned at the stake in 1600 at the instigation of the Inquisition (a body which, so we are told, never caused pain to anyone since it was the civil power, not the Inquisition, that carried out the unpleasant sentences) for his heresy.

Francis Bacon, who died in 1626, separated, as was the tendency of that time, science from religion. The latter he divided into the two categories of natural and revealed theology. The former, through the study of nature, may give convincing proof of the existence of a God but nothing more. Of revealed theology he said: "We must quit the small vessel of human reason . . . as we are obliged to obey the divine law, though our will murmurs against it, so we are obliged to believe in the word of God, though our reason is shocked at it." Hobbes (d. 1679) was a complete materialist and one feels that his obeisance to the notion was politic rather than from conviction. However, he does mention God as starting the universe in motion; infers that God is corporeal but denies that His nature can be known.

From Descartes Onwards. Descartes (1596–1650) separated mind and body as different entities but believed that the existence of God could be deduced by the fact that the idea of him existed in the mind. Whatever God puts into man, including his ideas, must be real. God is self-caused, omniscient, omnipotent, eternal, all goodness and truth. But Descartes neglected to explain how mind separate from body can influence body, or God separate from the world can influence matter.

Spinoza (1632–77) declared that all existence is embraced in one substance—God, the all-in-all. He was a pantheist and as such was rejected by his Jewish brethren. But Spinoza's God has neither personality nor consciousness, intelligence nor purpose, although all things follow in strict law from His nature. All the thoughts of everyone in the world, make up God's thoughts.

Bishop Berkeley (1685–1753) took the view that things exist only when they are perceived, and this naturally implies that a tree, for example, ceases to exist when nobody is looking at it. This problem was solved to his own satisfaction by assuming that God, seeing everything, prevented objects from disappearing when we were not present. The world is a creation of God but it is a spiritual or mental world, not a material one.

Hume (1711–76), who was a sceptic, held that human reason cannot demonstrate the existence of God and all past arguments to show that it could were fallacious. Yet we must believe in God since the basis of all hope, morality, and society is based upon the belief. Kant (1724–1804) held a theory similar to that of Hume. We cannot know by reason that God exists, nor can we prove on the basis of argument anything about God. But we can form an idea of the whole of the universe, the one Absolute Whole, and personify it. We need the idea of God on which to base our moral life, although this idea of God is transcendent, *i.e.,* goes beyond experience.

William James (1842–1910), the American philosopher (*see* **Pragmatism**), held much the same view: God cannot be proved to exist, but we have a will to believe which must be satisfied, and the idea works in practice. Hegel (1770–1831) thought of God as a developing process, beginning with "the Absolute" or First Cause and finding its highest expression in man's mind, or reason. It is in man that God most clearly becomes aware of Himself. Finally Comte (1798–1857), the positivist, held that religion belongs to a more primitive state of society and, like many modern philosophers, turned the problem over to believers as being none of the business of science.

Golden Dawn, Order of, a strange but intellectually influential secret society founded in 1887 by three former Rosicrucians *(q.v.).* The Society, which was but one of the large number of occult organizations which flourished in the latter half of the 19th cent., was particularly interesting because it attracted so many scholarly eccentrics to its ranks. These included the poet W. B. Yeats, the actress Florence Farr, the writers Arthur Machen and Algernon Blackwood and the poetess Dion Fortune. A member with a less savory reputation was the notorious Aleister Crowley who was ultimately expelled from the order for practising Black Magic. Essentially the movement, like others of its kind, professed to offer important secrets of occult knowledge, and taught its followers the basic principles of White, as opposed to Black Magic. Mainly harmless in their aims and activities, societies such as this served largely as pastimes for individuals of intellectual and academic standing who found the concepts and rituals of the Established Church too dull for their inquisitive minds. Most members of the Order of the Golden Dawn, either became disillusioned when the white magic, which they had so arduously studied, failed to provide any genuine supernatural results and gave up in disgust, or broke away to form their own rival groups. Though these often had equally glamorous names and rituals, they tended to be no more successful and themselves vanished into the mists of obscurity. Today so-called White Magic has become fashionable with many young people, no doubt as the result of the almost total collapse of the authority of orthodox religion, but it is noticeable that such interest is generally to be found among the less well-educated and intelligent. White Magic had its intellectual heyday in the 19th century and it is unlikely ever to attract such sustained academic interest again.

Good and Evil.

Early Philosophers' Views. The early Greek philosophers were chiefly concerned with the laws of the universe, consequently it was common belief that knowledge of these laws, and living according to them, constituted the supreme good. Heraclitus, for example, who taught that all things carried with them their opposites, held that good and evil were like two notes in a harmony, necessary to each other. "It is the opposite which is good for us". Democritus, like Epicurus *(q.v.),* held that the main goal of life is happiness, but happiness in moderation. The good man is not merely the one who *does* good but who always *wants* to do so: "You can tell the good man not by his deeds alone but by his desires." Such goodness brings happiness, the ultimate goal. On the other hand, many of the wandering Sophist teachers taught that good was merely social convention, that there are no absolute principles of right and wrong, that each man should live according to his desires and make his own moral code. To Socrates knowledge was the highest good because doing wrong is the result of ignorance: "no man is voluntarily bad." Plato and Aristotle, differing in many other respects, drew attention to the fact that man is composed of three parts: his desires and appetites, his will, and his reason. A man whose reason rules his will and appetites is not only a good but a happy man; for happiness is not an aim in itself but a by-product of the good life. Aristotle, however, emphasized the goal of self-realization, and thought that if the goal of life is (as Plato had said) a rational attitude towards the feelings and desires, it needs to be further defined. Aristotle defined it as the "Golden Mean"—the good man is one who does not go to extremes but balances one extreme against another. Thus courage is a mean between cowardice and foolhardiness. The later philosophers Philo and Plotinus held that evil was in the very nature of the body and its senses. Goodness could only be achieved by giving up the life of the senses and, freed from the domination of the body, turning to God, the source of goodness.

Christian Views. St. Augustine taught that everything in the universe is good. Even those things which appear evil are good in that they fit with the harmony of the universe like shadows in a painting. Man should turn his back on the pleasures of the world and turn to the love of God. Peter Abelard (1079–1142) made the more sophisticated distinction when he suggested that the wrongness of an act lies not in the act itself, but in the intention of the doer: "God considers not what is done but in what spirit it is done; and the merit or praise of the agent lies not in the deed but in the intention." If we do what we believe to be right, we may err, but we do not sin. The only sinful man is he who deliberately sets out to do what he knows to be wrong. St. Thomas Aquinas agreed with Aristotle in that he believed the highest good to be realization of self as God has ordained, and he also agreed with Abelard that intention is important. Even a good act is not good unless the doer intended it to have good consequences. Intention will not make a bad act good, but it is the only thing that will make a good act genuinely good.

In general, Christianity has had difficulties in solving the problem of the existence of evil; for even when one accepts that the evil men do is somehow tied up with the body, it is still difficult to answer the question: how could an all-good God create evil? This is answered in one of two ways: *(a)* that Adam was given free will and chose to sin (an answer which still does not explain how sin could exist anywhere in the universe of a God who created everything); *(b)* by denying the reality of evil as some Christians have chosen to do (*e.g.,* Christian Science *q.v.*). The Eastern religions, on the other hand (*see* **Zoroastrianism**), solved the problem in a more realistic way by a dualism which denied that their gods were the creators of the whole universe and allowed the existence of at least two gods, one good and one evil. In Christianity there is, of course, a Devil, but it is not explained from where his evil nature came.

Later Philosophic Views. Hobbes equated good with pleasure, evil with pain. They are relative to the individual man in the sense that "one man's meat is another man's poison." Descartes believed that the power to distinguish between good and evil given by God to man is not complete, so that man does evil through ignorance. We act with insufficient knowledge and on inadequate evidence. Locke, believing that at birth the mind is a blank slate, held that men get their opinions of right and wrong from their parents. By and large, happiness is good and pain is evil. But men do not always agree over what is pleasurable and what not. Hence laws exist and these fall into three categories: (1) the divine law; (2) civil laws; (3) matters of opinion or reputation which are enforced by the fact that men do not like to incur the disapproval of their friends. We learn by experience that evil brings pain and good acts bring pleasure and, basically, one is good because not to be so would bring discomfort.

Kant (*see* **God and Man**) found moral beliefs to be inherent in man whether or not they can be proved by reason. There is a categorical imperative which makes us realize the validity of two universal laws: (1) "always act in such a way that the maxim determining your conduct might well become a universal law; act so that you can will that everybody shall follow the principle of your action; (2) "always act so as to treat humanity, whether in thine own person or in that of another, in every case as an end and never as a means."

Schopenhauer (1788–1860) was influenced by Buddhism and saw the will as a blind, impelling striving, and desire as the cause of all suffering. The remedy is to regard sympathy and pity as the basis of all morality and to deny one's individual will. This is made easier if we realise that everyone is part of the Universal Will and therefore the one against whom we are struggling is part of the same whole as ourselves.

John Stuart Mill and Jeremy Bentham were both representatives of the Utilitarian school, believing that good is the greatest good (happiness) of the greatest number (*see* **Utilitarianism**). Lastly, there is the view held mostly by political thinkers that good is what is good for the state or society in general.

Graphology, the study of the analysis of human handwriting. There are two approaches to this topic and it is important to separate them clearly. The first involves the attempt on the part of an expert to decide from looking at a signature *(a)* to whom it belongs, and *(b)* whether or not it is forgery. This art is a legitimate, though tricky area of study, and graphologists have been called in as expert witnesses in courts of law. The second approach involves attempts to detect such tenuous variables as character from a study of an individual's handwriting, and the facts here are altogether less clear. Psychologists find it difficult enough to assess character or personality in a face-to-face interview and even when they are equipped with a range of special tests. The general opinion here would seem to be that some slight information might be revealed by a careful study of handwriting, but that the overall effect would be too unreliable for this kind of graphology to be of practical value.

Gurdjieff, Russian-Greek mystic who set up an occult commune near Paris in the 1930s, to which were attracted a host of the intellectual and literary avant-garde of the time. His teachings, which are immensely obscure, are presented in allegorical form in a lengthy philosophical novel, *All and Everything,* which has the peculiar sub-title "Beelzebub's Tales to his Grandson." Opinions as to the merits of Gurdjieff's ideas are strikingly varied: some commentators hold that he was one of the century's leading philosophers, others that he was a brazen confidence trickster with a vivid personality and the gift of making trivial observations sound pregnant with meaning. The truth probably lies somewhere in between the two extremes and, despite the fact that a number of highly intelligent individuals still espouse his cause two decades after his death, most people continue to find his books largely unreadable and his philosophy muddled and pretentious.

H

Homoeopathy, a branch of fringe medicine whose motto *Similia Similibus Curantur* (like cures like) sums up its controversial approach to therapy. In essence the homoeopathists claim that a disease can be treated by administering quite minute doses of a substance which produce symptoms (in the healthy person) similar to those induced by the disease itself. The founder and popularizer of this unusual approach to medicine was the German Samuel Hahnemann who was born in 1775, a friend of the physician Mesmer who propagated hypnotherapy. Hahnemann lived to see his ideas spread across the civilized world and despite the grave theoretical difficulties implicit in the question of how the very minute dosages actually achieve any result at all, it remained a respectable approach of medicine until the latter half of the last century. Even today a number of qualified doctors still employ homeopathic ideas within the framework of the national health service, and the late King George V was treated by the eminent homoeopathist, Sir John Weir, but it seems nevertheless to be in slow but steady decline. This is probably due not to any revealed deficiences in homoeopathy itself, but rather to the extraordinary advances which have been made in orthodox medicine in the last few decades.

Humanism, the term applied to (1) a system of education based on the Greek and Latin classics; and (2) the vigorous attitudes that accompanied the end of the Middle Ages and were represented at different periods by the Renaissance, the Reformation, the Industrial Revolution, and the struggle for democracy. These include: release from ecclesiastical authority, the liberation of the intellect, faith in progress, the belief that man himself can improve his own conditions without supernatural help and, indeed has a duty to do so. "Man is the measure of all things" is the keynote of humanism. The humanist has faith in man's intellectual and spiritual resources not only to bring knowledge and understanding of the world but to solve the moral problems of how to use that knowledge. That man should show respect to man irrespective of class, race or creed is fundamental to the humanist attitude to life. Among the fundamental moral principles he would count those of freedom, justice, tolerance and happiness.

I

I Ching, the Chinese "Book of Changes" which is supposed to provide a practical demonstration of the truths of ancient Chinese philosophy. The method consists of casting forty-nine sticks into two random heaps, or more simply, of tossing three coins to see if there is a preponderance of heads or tails. The coins are cast six times whereupon the head-tail sequence achieved is referred to a coded series of phrases in the book, which are supposed to relate in some way to the question held in the mind when the sticks or coins are being cast. The phrases are without exception vague, and platitudinous remarks such as "Evil people do not further the perseverance of the superior man," etc., abound. Consequently it is not difficult to read into such amorphous stuff a suitable "interpretation" or answer to one's unspoken question. The I Ching might well be looked upon as an entertaining parlor game, but it is currently a great fad in Europe and America and is taken with great seriousness by an astonishing number of people.

Idealism, in a philosophical sense, the belief that there is no matter in the universe, that all that exists is mind or spirit. *See* **Mind and Matter** and **Realism.**

Illuminati, a secret society founded in 1776 by Adam Weishaupt, a Bavarian professor of canon law at Ingolstadt, in an attempt to combat superstition and ignorance by founding an association for rational enlightenment and the regeneration of the world. "He tried to give the social ideals of the Enlightenment realization by conspiratorial means" (J. M. Roberts, *The Mythology of the Secret Societies,* 1972). Under conditions of secrecy it sought to penetrate and control the Masonic lodges for subversive purposes. Among its members were Goethe and Schiller. The order spread to Austria, Italy and Hungary but was condemned by the Roman Catholic Church and dissolved in 1785 by the Bavarian government.

Immortality. The belief in a life after death has been widely held since the earliest times. It has certainly not been universal, nor has it always taken a form which everyone would find satisfying. In the early stages of human history or prehistory everything contained a spirit (*see* **Animism**) and it is obvious from the objects left in early graves that the dead were expected to exist in some form after death. The experience of dreams, too, seemed to suggest to the unsophisticated that there was a part of man which could leave his body and wander elsewhere during sleep. In order to save space, it will be helpful to classify the various types of belief which have existed in philosophical thought regarding this problem: (1) There is the idea that, although *something* survives bodily death, it is not necessarily eternal. Thus most primitive peoples were prepared to believe that man's spirit haunted the place around his grave and that food and drink should be set out for it, but that this spirit did not go on forever and gradually faded away. (2) The ancient Greeks and Hebrews believed for the most part that the souls of the dead went to a place of shades there to pine for the world of men. Their whining ghosts spent eternity in a dark, uninviting region in misery and remorse. (3) Other people, and there were many more of these, believed in the transmigration of souls with the former life of the individual determining whether his next life would be at a higher or lower level. Sometimes this process seems to have been thought of as simply going on and on, by others (*e.g.,* in Hinduism and Buddhism) as terminating in either non-sentience or union with God but in any case in annihilation of the self as self. Believers in this theory were the Greek philosophers Pythagoras, Empedocles, Plato (who believed that soul comes from God and strives to return to God, according to his own rather confused notions of the deity. If it fails to free itself completely from the body it will sink lower and lower from one body to another.) Plotinus held similar views to Plato, and many other religious sects in addition to those mentioned have believed in transmigration. (4) The belief of Plato and Aristotle that if souls continue to exist after death there is no reason why they should not have existed before birth (this in part is covered by (3), but some have pointed out that eternity does not mean "from now on," but the whole of the time before and after "now"—nobody, however, so far as one knows, held that *individual* souls so exist. (5) The theory that the soul does not exist at all and therefore immortality is meaningless: this was held by Anaximenes in early Greek times; by Leucippus, Democritus, and the other Greek atomists; by the Epicureans from the Greek Epicurus to the Roman Lucretius; by the British Hobbes and Hume; by Comte of France; and William James and John Dewey of America. (6) The thesis, held notably by Locke and Kant, that although we cannot prove the reality of soul and immortality by pure reason, belief in them should be held for moral ends. (For the orthodox Christian view *see* **God and Man, Determinism and Free-will.**) From this summary we can see that many philosophies and religions (with the important exceptions of Islam and Christianity) without denying a future life do deny the permanence of the individual soul in anything resembling its earthly form (*see* **Spiritualism, Psychic Research**).

J

Jainism. The Jains are a small Indian sect, largely in commerce and finance, numbering about 2 million. Their movement founded by Vardhamana, called Mahavira (the great hero), in the 6th cent. B.C. arose rather earlier than Buddhism in revolt against the ritualism and impersonality of **Hinduism** *(q.v.).* It rejects the authority of the early Hindu Vedas and does away with many of the Hindu deities whose place is largely taken by Jainism's twenty-four immortal saints; it despises caste distinctions and modifies the two great

Hindu doctrines of *karma* and transmigration. Jain philosophy is based on *ahimsa,* the sacredness of all life, regarding even plants as the brethren of mankind, and refusing to kill even the smallest insect.

Jehovah's Witnesses, a religious body who consider themselves to be the present-day representatives of a religious movement which has existed since Abel "offered unto God a more excellent sacrifice than Cain, by which he obtained witness that he was righteous." Abel was the first "witness," and amongst others were Enoch, Noah, Abraham, Moses, Jeremiah, and John the Baptist. Pre-eminent among witnesses, of course, was Jesus Christ who is described in the Book of Revelation as "the faithful and true witness." Thus they see themselves as "the Lord's organization," in the long line of those who through the ages have preserved on earth the true and pure worship of God or, as the Witnesses prefer to call Him, "Jehovah-God."

So far as other people are aware, the movement was founded by Charles Taze Russell (Pastor Russell) of Allegany, Pittsburgh, in 1881 under the name, adopted in 1896, of the Watch Tower Bible and Tract Society, which has continued as the controlling organization of Jehovah's Witnesses. Its magazine, *The Watch Tower Announcing Jehovah's Kingdom,* first published in 1879, and other publications are distributed by the zealous members who carry out the house-to-house canvassing. The movement has a strong leadership.

Their teaching centers upon the early establishment of God's new world on earth, preceded by the second coming of Christ. Witnesses believe this has already happened and that Armageddon "will come as soon as the Witness is completed." The millenial period will give sinners a second chance of salvation and "millions now living will never die" (the title of one of their pamphlets).

The dead will progressively be raised to the new earth until all the vacant places left after Armageddon are filled. There is, however, some doubt about the "goatish souls" who have made themselves unpleasant to the Witnesses, those who have accepted (or permitted to be accepted) a blood-transfusion contrary to the Scriptures, and others who have committed grave sins.

Every belief held by the movement, it is asserted, can be upheld, chapter and verse, by reference to the Scriptures. Witnesses regard the doctrine of the Trinity as devised by Satan. In both wars Witnesses have been in trouble for their refusal to take part in war, and it is only fair to add that six thousand suffered for the same reason in German concentration camps.

Jensenism, name given to the minority group of psychologists and educationalists who, in general, support the view of the American professor, Arthur Jensen. The latter's studies of individual variation in learning and of the genetic factor in mental ability has led him to argue that heredity is more crucial in determining intellectual ability than environment. By implication this has put him and his colleagues at the center of a divisive "race and intelligence" controversy which has acquired some political overtones. In 1978 Professor H. J. Eysenck was physically assaulted by students at a university lecture because he was reputed to be supporting the Jensenist position.

L

Lamaism, the religion of Tibet. Its beliefs and worship derive from the Mahayana form of Buddhism which was introduced into Tibet in 749. The emphasis laid by its founder on the necessity for self-discipline and conversion through meditation and the study of philosophy deteriorated into formal monasticism and ritualism. The Dalai Lama, as the reincarnated Buddha, was both king and high priest, a sort of pope and emperor rolled into one. Under him was a hierarchy of officials in which the lowest order was that of the monks who became as numerous as one man in every six or seven of the population. The main work carried out by this vast church-state was the collection of taxes to maintain the monasteries and other religious offices. Second in power to the Dalai Lama was the Panchen or Tashi Lama believed to be a reincarnation of Amitabha, another Buddha. The last Dalai Lama fled to India in 1959 when the Chinese entered his country. For a brief period following his departure, the Panchen Lama surprised the Western world by publicly welcoming the Communist invasion, but he later renounced the regime and the suppression of Lamaism in Tibet continued unchecked.

Logical Positivism, a school of philosophy founded in Vienna in the 1920s by a group known as "the Vienna circle". Their work was based on that of Ernst Mach, but dates in essentials as far back as Hume. Of the leaders of the group, Schlick was murdered by a student; Wittgenstein came to Britain, and Carnap went to America following the entry of the Nazis. Briefly the philosophy differs from all others in that, while most people have believed that a statement might be *(a)* true, or *(b)* false, logical positivists consider there to be a third category; a statement may be meaningless. There are only two types of statement which can be said to have meaning: (1) those which are tautological, *i.e.,* those in which the statement is merely a definition of the subject, such as "a triangle is a three-sided plane figure" ("triangle" and "three-sided plane figure" are the same thing); and (2) those which can be tested by sense experience. This definition of meaningfulness excludes a great deal of what has previously been thought to be the field of philosophy; in particular it excludes the possibility of metaphysics. Thus the question as to whether there is a God or whether free will exists is strictly meaningless for it is neither a tautological statement nor can it be tested by sense experience.

Luddites, a group of peasants and working men who deliberately destroyed spinning and farm machinery in England in the early part of the century, fearing that such devices would destroy their livelihood. Their name was taken from the eccentric Ned Lud who had done the same in a less organized way two or three decades earlier. The Luddites' worst fears were of course not realized, for far from putting human beings out of work the Industrial Revolution created jobs for a vastly increased population. Luddism, dormant for over a century, is beginning to appear again, if in muted form. Public anxiety about the rapid growth in computer technology is manifesting itself in the form of such groups as the Society for the Abolition of Data Processing Machines, which while not of course dedicated to the physical destruction of computers, urge for social and even governmental checks on the development of such things as "data banks." These are vast computer memory stores listing comprehensive records concerning all the people living in a city or country and able to cross-reference them in a way that has never previously been possible. The arguments for and against such data banks and other developments in computer technology are beyond the scope of this section, but the rise of this 20th-century Luddism is of considerable historical and social significance.

Lycanthropy, the belief that men may, by the exercise of magical powers or because of some inherited affliction, occasionally transform into wolves. The so-called werewolf is an important feature of mid-European folklore and much the same can be said of the were-tigers and were-bears of Africa and the Far East. There is, needless to say, no such thing as a genuine werewolf known to biology, but it is not hard to see how legends of their existence could arise. There are a number of mental illnesses in which men may deliberately or unconsciously mimic the actions of animals and there are a number of endocrinological disorders which may cause gross changes in the features of the individuals, including the excessive growth of hair. In times when the physiological bases of such afflictions were not properly understood, sufferers from such complaints could easily be persuaded, either by themselves or others, that they were in fact wolfmen. Once the mythology of lycanthropy is established in a society, then of course it will be used by unscrupulous individuals for their own ends—for example revenge killings by people dressed as animals—thus helping to perpetuate the legend.

M

Magic, a form of belief originating in very early days and based on the primitive's inability to distinguish between similarity and identity. The simplest example would perhaps be the fertility rites in which it is believed that a ceremony involving sexual relations between men and women will bring about fertility in the harvest. Or the idea that sticking pins in an image of an individual will bring about harm or even death to the real person. Magic is regarded by some as a form of early science in that man in his efforts to control Nature had recourse to magical practices when the only methods he knew had failed to bring the desired results. It filled a gap. By others magic is regarded as an elementary stage in the evolution of religion. It can be said to have served a purpose there too. Yet magic differs from religion, however closely at times it may come to be related with it in this important respect: religion depends upon a power *outside and beyond* human beings, whereas magic depends upon nothing but the casting of a spell or the performance of a ceremony—the result follows automatically.

The idea that "like produces like" is at the roots of imitative magic, and it is interesting to note that in some languages (*e.g.,* Hebrew and Arabic) there is no word for "resembles" or "similar to." Hence one says "All thy garments are myrrh" instead of "are *like* myrrh." It follows that an event can be compelled by imitating it. One engages in swinging, not for pleasure, but to produce a wind as the swing does; ball games are played to get rainy weather because the black ball represents dark rainclouds; other ball games, in which one attempts to catch the ball in a cup or hit it with a stick, represent the sexual act (as some gentlemen at Lords (cricket grounds, London) may be distressed to hear) and bring about fertility; in medicine until a few centuries ago herbs were chosen to cure a disease because in some respects their leaves or other parts looked like the part of the body affected (*e.g.,* the common wildflower still known as "eyebright" was used in bathing the eyes because the flower looks like a tiny eye). *See* **Witchcraft, Demonism.**

Malthusianism, the theory about population growth put forward by the Rev. Thomas Malthus (1766–1834) in *An Essay on Population* (1798). His three main propositions were (1) "Population is necessarily limited by means of subsistence." (2) "Population invariably increases where means of subsistence increase unless prevented by some very powerful and obvious checks." (3) "These checks, and the checks which repress the superior power of population, and keep its effects on a level with the means of subsistence, are all resolvable into moral restraint, vice and misery." In other words, no matter how great the food supply may become, human reproductive power will always adjust itself so that food will always be scarce in relation to population; the only means to deal with this is by "moral restraint" (*i.e.,* chastity or not marrying), "vice" (*i.e.,* birth-control methods), or misery (*i.e.,* starvation). More specifically, Malthus claimed that while food increases by arithmetical progression, population increases by geometrical progression. It is true that these gloomy predictions did not take place in Malthus's time largely owing to the opening up of new areas of land outside Europe, the development of new techniques in agriculture, the growth of international trade to poorer areas, the increased knowledge of birth-control, and developments in medical science which reduced the misery he had predicted. Furthermore, we now know that as a society becomes industrialized its birth-rate tends to fall. Growth in the world's population has increased from about 465 million in 1650 to over 4,500 million in 1982.

Manichaeism, an Asiatic religion which developed from Zoroastrianism *(q.v.)* and shows the influence of Buddhism *(q.v.)* and Gnosticism *(q.v.),* being founded by Mani, a Persian who was born in Babylonia, *c.* 216 A.D. Mani presented himself to Shapur I as the founder of a new religion which was to be to Babylonia what Buddhism was to India or Christianity to the West. His aspiration was to convert the East and he himself made no attempt to interfere directly with Christianity although he represented himself as the Paraclete (the Holy Ghost or "Comforter") and, like Jesus, had twelve disciples. His success in Persia aroused the fury of the Zoroastrian priests who objected to his reforming zeal towards their religion and in 276 Mani was taken prisoner and crucified.

Of Mani's complicated system little can be said here, save that it is based on the struggle of two eternal conflicting principles. God and matter, or light and darkness. Although its founder had no intention of interfering with the West, after his death his followers soon spread the religion from Persia and Mesopotamia to India and China. (Manichaeism flourished in China until the 11th cent.) It reached as far as Spain and Gaul and influenced many of the bishops in Alexandria and in Carthage where for a time St. Augustine accepted Manichaeism. Soon the toleration accorded it under Constantine ended and it was treated as a heresy and violently suppressed. Yet it later influenced many heresies, and even had some influence on orthodox Catholicism which had a genius for picking up elements in other religions which had been shown to appeal to worshippers provided they did not conflict unduly with fundamental beliefs.

Marxism. The sociological theories founded by Karl Marx and Friedrich Engels on which modern communist thought is based. Marx and Engels lived in a period of unrestrained capitalism when exploitation and misery were the lot of the industrial working classes, and it was their humanitarianism and concern for social justice which inspired their work. Marx wrote his *Communist Manifesto* in Brussels in 1848 and in his great work. *Das Kapital* (1867), he worked out a new theory of society. Marx showed that all social systems are economically motivated and change as a result of technical and economic changes in methods of production. The driving force of social change Marx found to be in the struggle which the oppressed classes wage to secure a better future. Thus in his celebrated theory of historical materialism he interpreted history in terms of economics and explained the evolution of society in terms of class struggle. (*See* **Dialectical Materialism.**) "In the social production of their means of existence," he wrote, "men enter into definite and unavoidable relations which are independent of their will. These productive relationships correspond to the particular stage in the development of their material productive forces." Marx's theory of historical materialism implies that history is propelled by class struggle with communism and the classless society as the final stage when man will have emancipated himself from the productive process. Marx was the first to put socialism on a rational and scientific basis, and he foretold that socialism would inevitably replace capitalism. His prophecy, however, came to realization not in the advanced countries as he had envisaged but in backward Russia and China. *See also* **Communism.**

Mesmerism, a rapidly vanishing name to denote the practice of hypnosis, which owes its popularity, though not its discovery, to the Austrian physician, Anton Mesmer (1733–1815). Mesmer's contribution was the realization that a large number of what we would today call psychosomatic or hysterical conditions could be cured (or at least temporarily alleviated) by one or another form of suggestion. Mesmer himself relied on the idea of what he called "animal magnetism," a supposedly potent therapeutic force emanating from the living body which could be controlled by the trained individual. Mesmer used wands and impressive gadgetry to dispense the marvellous force and he effected a remarkable number of cures of complaints, hitherto looked upon as incurable or totally mysterious in origin—the most typical of these being hysterical blindness, paralysis or deafness, nervous skin conditions, and so on. Hypnosis, which is a valid if very poorly understood psychological phenomenon even today, would probably have been developed much further had not efficient general anaesthetics such as ether, nitrous oxide, etc., been discovered, thus greatly diminishing its role as a pain reliever in surgery. Mesmer, who was three parts charlatan, never really troubled to think deeply about the cause of his undoubted success. The first man to treat hysteria as a formal class of illness and who made a scientific attempt to treat it with hypnosis was Ambrose Liébeault (1823–1904). He and his colleague Hippolyte Bernheim (1840–1919) believed: *(a)* that hysteria was produced by suggestion, and particularly by autosuggestion on the part of the patient, and *(b)* that suggestion was a normal trait found in varying degrees in everyone. These conclusions are true, but as Freud showed later are far from being the whole truth.

Messianism. Most varieties of religious belief rely on the assumption that the deity is a supernatural being either permeating the universe or dwelling in some other sphere, and normally inaccessible to man. Where divine intervention is necessary, the deity is traditionally believed to nominate a human being—in the case of Christianity, for example, Jesus is believed to be the actual son of God. Messianic cults introduce a novel variant on the traditional theme. In these a human being is held to be God himself. He may either nominate himself for this role, relying on his own personality or native talent to acquire the necessary following, or for one reason or another large numbers of people may alight on one individual and declare him the Messiah. While it might seem that beliefs of this kind would be confined to earlier epochs in man's recorded history, this is in fact not the case. In the past century, and even within recent decades, a number of individuals have been held by groups to be actually divine. Among these were the Dutchman Lourens van Voorthuizen, a former fisherman who declared himself to be God in 1950 and got large numbers to accept his claim; the Anglican priest Henry James Prince, who did much the same thing in 1850; and of course the famous Negro George Baker, who convinced hundreds of thousands of other Negroes that he was "Father Divine." To simple people the idea that God is to be found on earth and that one may even be personally introduced to him, is an obviously attractive one. The trouble is that all self-styled gods to this present date have sooner or later seriously disappointed their supporters by performing that most human of acts—dying.

Metapsychology. Not to be confused with parapsychology *(q.v.)*. The branch or off-shoot of psychology which goes beyond empirical and experimental studies to consider such philosophical matters as the nature of mind, the reality of free will and the mind/body problem. It was originally used by Freud as a blanket descriptive term denoting all mental processes, but this usage is now obsolete.

Methodism, the religious movement founded by John Wesley in 1738, at a time when the Anglican Church was in one of its periodic phases of spiritual torpor, with the simple aim of spreading "scriptural holiness" throughout the land. Up to that time Wesley had been a High Churchman but on a visit to Georgia in the United States he was much impressed by the group known as Moravians *(q.v.)*, and on his return to England was introduced by his brother Charles, who had already become an adherent, to Peter Böhler, a Moravian minister in England. Passing through a period of spiritual commotion following the meeting, he first saw the light at a small service in Aldersgate in May 1738 "where one was reading Luther's preface to the Epistle to the Romans" and from this time forth all Wesley's energies were devoted to the single object of saving souls.

Soon Whitefield, a follower with Calvinist views, was preaching throughout the country and Charles

Wesley was composing his well-known hymns; John's abilities at this time were taken up in organizing the movement described as "People called Methodists." They were to be arranged in "societies" which were united into "circuits" under a minister, the circuits into "districts" and all knit together into a single body under a conference of ministers which has met annually since 1744. Local lay preachers were also employed and to maintain interest the ministers were moved from circuit to circuit each year.

The class-meeting was the unit of the organization where members met regularly under a chosen leader to tell their "experiences" upon which they were often subjected to severe cross-examination.

Methodism, especially after Wesley's death in 1791, began, like other movements, to develop schisms. These were the long-standing differences which the Baptist movement *(q.v.)* had shown too between Arminian and Calvinist sections—*i.e.,* between those who did and those who did not accept the doctrine of predestination. In the case of the Methodists, this led to a complete break in 1811. Then there were differences associated with the status of the laity, or the relationship of the movement with the Anglican Church. The "Methodist New Connection" of 1797 differed only in giving the laity equal representation with the ministers but the more important break of the Primitive Methodists in 1810 gave still more power to the laity and reintroduced the "camp-meeting" type of service. Finally in 1932, at a conference in the Albert Hall in London, the Wesleyan Methodists, the Primitive Methodists, and the United Methodists became one Church, the Methodist Church.

Mind and Matter.

Early Greek Views: Idealism and Dualism. Primitive peoples could see that there is a distinction between those things which move and do things by themselves and others, such as stones, which do not. Following the early state of **Animism** *(q.v.),* in which spirits were believed to have their abode in everything, they began to differentiate between matter or substance and a force which seems to move it and shape it into objects and things. Thus to the Greek Parmenides (fl. *c.* 475 B.C.), who was a philosopher of pure reason, thought or mind was the creator of what we observe and in some way not quite clear to himself it seemed that mind was the cause of everything. This is perhaps the first expression of the movement known as Idealism which says, in effect, that the whole universe is mental—a creation either of our own minds or the mind of God. But from Anaxagorus (488–428 B.C.) we have the clearer statement that mind or *nous* causes all movement but is distinct from the substance it moves. He does not, however, think in terms of individual minds but rather of a kind of generalized mind throughout the universe which can be used as an explanation of anything which cannot be explained otherwise. This is the position known as Dualism *(q.v.)* which holds that both mind and matter exist and interact but are separate entities.

Most people in practice are dualists since, rightly or wrongly, mind and body are thought of as two different things: it is the "common-sense" (although not necessarily the true) point of view. Plato in a much more complex way was also a dualist although he held that the world of matter we observe is in some sense not the genuine world. The real world is the world of ideas and the tree we see is not real but simply matter upon which mind or soul has imprinted the idea of a tree. Everything that exists has its corresponding form in the world of ideas and imprints its pattern upon matter. Mind has always existed and, having become entangled with matter, is constantly seeking to free itself and return to God.

Plato's pupil Aristotle had a much more scientific outlook and held that, although it was mind which gave matter its form, mind is not *outside* matter, as Plato had thought, but *inside* it as its formative principle. Therefore there could be no mind without matter and no matter without mind; for even the lowest forms of matter have some degree of mind which increases in quantity and quality as we move up the scale to more complex things.

So far, nobody had explained how two such different substances as matter and mind could influence each other in any way, and this remains, in spite of attempts to be mentioned later, a basic problem in philosophy.

Two later ideas, one of them rather foolish and the other simply refusing to answer the question, are typified by the Stoics and some members of the Sceptic school. The first is that only matter exists and what we call mind is merely matter of a finer texture, a view which as an explanation is unlikely to satisfy anyone; the other, that of some Sceptics, is that we can know nothing except the fleeting images or thoughts that flicker through our consciousness. Of either mind or matter we know nothing.

Renaissance Attitude. Christian doctrines have already been dealt with (*see* **God and Man, Determinism and Free-will**), and the past and future of the soul is dealt with under **Immortality.** Nor need we mention the Renaissance philosophers who were really much more concerned about how to use mind than about its nature. When they did consider the subject they usually dealt with it, as did Francis Bacon, by separating the sphere of science from that of religion and giving the orthodox view of the latter because there were still good reasons for not wishing to annoy the Church.

17th-cent. Views: Hobbes, Descartes, Guelincx, Spinoza, Locke, Berkeley. Thomas Hobbes in the 17th cent. was really one of the first to attempt a modern explanation of mind and matter even if his attempt was crude. As a materialist he held that all that exists is matter and hence our thoughts, ideas, images, and actions are really a form of motion taking place within the brain and nerves. This is the materialist theory which states that mind does not exist.

Thus there are three basic theories of the nature of mind and body: idealism, dualism, and materialism, and we may accept any one of the three. But, if we accept dualism, we shall have to explain precisely the relationship between body and mind. In some of his later writings Hobbes seems to suggest that mental processes are the effects of motion rather than motion itself; *i.e.,* they exist, but only as a result of physical processes just as a flame does on a candle. This theory of the relationship is known as *epiphenomenalism.*

Descartes, the great French contemporary of Hobbes, was a dualist who believed that mind and matter both exist and are entirely different entities; therefore he had to ask himself how, for example, the desire to walk leads to the physical motion of walking. His unsatisfactory answer was that, although animals are pure automatons, man is different in that he has a soul which resides in the pineal gland (a tiny structure in the brain which today we know to be a relic of evolution with no present function whatever). In this gland the mind comes in contact with the "vital spirits" of the body and thus there is interaction between the two. This theory is known as *interactionism,* and since we do not accept its basis in the function of the pineal gland, we are simply left with the notion of interaction but without the explanation of how it takes place.

One of Descartes's successors, Arnold Guelinex, produced the even more improbable theory of *psychophysical parallelism* sometimes known as the theory of the "two clocks". Imagine you have two clocks, each keeping perfect time, then supposing you saw one and heard the other, every time one points to the hour the other will strike, giving the impression that the first event causes the second, although in fact they are quite unrelated. So it is with the body and mind in Guelinex's view, each is "wound up" by God in the beginning in such a way as to keep time with the other so that when I have the desire to walk, purely unrelated physical events in my legs cause them to move at the same time. A variety of this theory is *occasionism,* which says that whenever something happens in the physical world, God affects us so that we *think* we are being affected by the happening.

The trouble about all these theories is *(a)* that they really explain nothing, and *(b)* that they give us a very peculiar view of God as a celestial showman treating us as puppets when it would surely have been easier to create a world in which mind and matter simply interacted by their very nature. Spinoza, too, believed in a sort of psychophysical parallelism in that he did not think that mind and body interacted. But since in his theory everything is God, mind and matter are simply two sides of the same penny.

John Locke, another contemporary, thought of the mind as a blank slate upon which the world writes in the form of sensations, for we have no innate or inborn ideas and mind and matter do interact although he does not tell us how. All we know are sensations—*i.e.,* sense impressions. Bishop Berkeley carried this idea to its logical conclusion: if we know nothing but sensations, we have no reason to suppose that matter exists at all. He was, therefore, an idealist.

18th cent. Views: Hume, Kant. David Hume went further still and pointed out that, if all we know are sensations, we cannot prove the existence of matter but we cannot prove the existence of mind either. All we can ever know is that ideas, impressions, thoughts, follow each other. We do not even experience a self or personality because every time we look into our "minds" all we really experience are thoughts and impressions. Hume was quick to point out that this was not the same as saying that the self did not exist; it only proved that we cannot know that it does.

Kant made it clear that, although there is a world outside ourselves, we can never know what it is really like. The mind receives impressions and forms them into patterns which conform not to the thing-in-itself but to the nature of mind. Space and time, for example, are not realities but only the form into which our mind fits its sensations. In other words our mind shapes impressions which are no more like the thing in itself than the map of a battlefield with pins showing the position of various army groups at any given moment is like the battlefield. This, of course, is true. From physics and physiology we know that the sounds we hear are "really" waves in the air, the sights we see "really" electromagnetic waves. What guarantee do we have that the source is "really" like the impression received in our brain? Kant was the leader of the great German Idealist movement of the 18th cent. which in effect said: "why bother about matter when all we can ever know is mental?"

19th and 20th cent. Views. The Englishman Bradley, and the Frenchman Henri Bergson in the 19th and early 20th cent. both held in one form or another the belief that mind in some way creates matter and were, therefore, idealists, whereas Comte, the positivist *(q.v.),* and the Americans William James and John Dewey, held that mind is a form of behavior. Certain acts (*e.g.,* reflexes) are "mindless" because they are deliberate; others which are intended may be described for the sake of convenience as "minded" (*i.e.,* purposeful). But like the majority of modern psychologists—insofar as they take any interest in the subject—they regarded mind as a process going on in the living body. Is there any reason, many now ask, why we should think of mind as being any different in nature from digestion? Both are processes going on in the body, the one in the brain the other in the stomach and intestines. Why should we regard them as "things"?

Mithraism, a sun-religion which originated in Persia with the worship of the mythical Mithra, the god of light and of truth. It was for two centuries one of early Christianity's most formidable rivals, particularly in the West since the more philosophical Hellenic Christianity of the East had little to fear from it. (Arnold Toynbee has described Mithraism as "a pre-Zoroastrian Iranian paganism—in a Hellenic dress"; Manichaeism as "Zoroastrianism—in a Christian dress".) Mithraism was a mystery-faith with secret rites known only to devotees. It appealed to the soldiers of the Roman Army which explains its spread to the farthest limits of the Roman empire and its decline as the Romans retreated. The religion resembled Zoroastrianism *(q.v.)* in that it laid stress on the constant struggle between good and evil and there are a number of parallels with Christianity. *e.g.,* a miraculous birth, death, and a glorious resurrection, a belief in heaven and hell and the immortality of the soul, a last judgment. Both religions held Sunday as the holy day of the week, celebrated 25 December (date of the pagan winter solstice festival) as the birthday of the founder; both celebrated Easter, and in their ceremonies made use of bell, holy water, and the candle. Mithraism reached its height about 275 A.D. and afterwards declined both for the reason given above and, perhaps, because it excluded women, was emotional rather than philosophical, and had no general organization to direct its course. Yet even today, from the Euphrates to the Tyne, traces of the religion remain and antiquarians are familiar with the image of the sun-god and the inscription *Deo Soli Mithrae, Invicto, Seculari* (dedicated to the sun-god of Mithra, the unconquered). Mithraism enjoyed a brief revival of popular interest in the mid-1950s when workers excavating the foundations of the skyscraper, Bucklersbury House in the City of London, found the well-preserved remains of a Roman Mithraic temple. A campaign to save the temple as a national monument resulted in its now being on open display on a site in front of the skyscraper.

Monasticism. When in the 4th cent. A.D. Constantine

in effect united state and church there were naturally many who hastened to become Christians for the worldly benefits they expected it to bring in view of the new situation. But there were others who, in their efforts to escape from wordly involvement, went into the deserts of North Africa and Syria to live as hermits and so in these regions there grew up large communities of monks whose lives of renunciation made a considerable impression on the Christian world. They were men of all types but the two main groups were those who preferred to live alone and those who preferred a community life. Among the first must be included St. Anthony, the earliest of the hermits, who was born in Egypt *c.* 250 and who lived alone in a hut near his home for fifteen years and then in the desert for a further twenty. As his fame spread Anthony came forth to teach and advocate a life of extreme austerity, until by the end of his life the Thebaid (the desert around Thebes) was full of hermits following his example. (Not unnaturally, he was constantly assailed by lustful visions which he thoughtfully attributed to Satan.) In the Syrian desert St. Simeon Stylites and others were stimulated to even greater austerities and Simeon himself spent many years on the top of a pillar in a space so small that it was only possible to sit or stand. With some of these men it is obvious that ascetic discipline had become perverted into an unpleasant form of exhibitionism.

The first monastery was founded by Pachomius of Egypt *c.* 315 and here the monks had a common life with communal meals, worship, and work mainly of an agricultural type. In the Eastern part of the Empire St. Basil (*c.* 360) tried to check the growth of the extreme and spectacular practices of the hermits by organizing monasteries in which the ascetic disciplines of fasting, meditation, and prayer, would be balanced by useful and healthy activities. His monasteries had orphanages and schools for boys—not only those who were intended for a monkish life. But the Eastern Church in general continued to favor the hermitic life and ascetic extremes. Originally a spontaneous movement, the monastic life was introduced to the West by St. Athanasius in 339 who obtained its recognition from the Church of Rome and St. Augustine introduced it into North Africa beyond Egypt. The movement was promoted also by St. Jerome, St. Martin of Tours, who introduced it into France, and St. Patrick into Ireland. The monastery of Iona was founded by St. Colomba in 566. But it must be remembered that the Celtic Church had a life of its own which owed more to the Egyptian tradition than to Rome. Unlike the more elaborate monasteries of the Continent those of the early Celtic Church were often little more than a cluster of stone beehive huts, an oratory, and a stone cross. It had its own religious ceremonies and its own art (notably its beautifully carved crosses and the illuminated manuscripts such as the Lindisfarne Gospel (*c.* 700) and the Irish Book of Kells dating from about the same time). The Scottish St. Ninian played a major part in introducing Egyptian texts and art to Britain where, mixed with Byzantine influences and the art of the Vikings, it produced a typical culture of its own. Strangely enough, it was the relatively primitive Celts who played almost as large a part in preserving civilization in Europe during the Dark Ages as the Italians have since. It was St. Columbanus (*c.* 540–615) who founded the great monasteries of Annegray, Luxeuil, and Fontaine in the Vosges country, St. Gall in Switzerland, and Bobbio in the Apennines. So, too, it was the Anglo-Saxon Alcuin (*c.* 735–804) who was called from York by Charlemagne to set up a system of education throughout his empire; the most famous of the monastic schools he founded was at Tours. Among those influenced by him was the philosopher John Scotus Erigena.

Meanwhile from the south, as the disintegrating Roman empire became increasingly corrupt, St. Benedict of Nursia (*c.* 480–*c.* 543) fled the pleasures of Rome to lead a hermit's life near Subiaco. Here he founded some small monasteries, but *c.* 520 made a new settlement, the great monastery of Monte Cassino in southern Italy, where he established a "Rule" for the government of monks. This included both study and work and emphasized that education was necessary for the continuance of Christianity. As his influence spread his Rule was adopted by other monasteries, and schools became part of monastic life. It is not possible to describe the many different orders of monks and nuns formed since, nor the mendicant orders of friars (*e.g.,* Franciscans, Dominicans, Carmelites, Augustinians). Outside the Roman Catholic Church, both Eastern Orthodox and Anglican Christians owe much to the monastic movement. Monasticism, of course, is not peculiar to Christianity and forms a major aspect of Buddhism, especially in the form of Lamaism in Tibet *(q.v.).*

Monophysitism, a heresy of the 5th cent. which grew out of a reaction against Nestorianism *(q.v.).* The majority of Egyptian Christians were Monophysites (Mono-physite = one nature)—*i.e.* they declared Christ's human and divine nature to be one and the same. This view was condemned at the Council of Chalcedon (A.D. 451) which pronounced that Jesus Christ, true God and true man, has two natures, at once perfectly distinct and inseparably joined in one person and partaking of the one divine substance. However, many continued to hold Monophysite opinions, including the Coptic Church *(q.v.),* declaring the Council to be unoecumenical (*i.e.* not holding the views of the true and universal Christian Church).

Mormons, or **Latter-day Saints,** one of the very numerous American religious sects; founded in 1830 by Joseph Smith, the son of a Vermont farmer, who, as a youth, had been influenced by a local religious revival though confused by the conflicting beliefs of the various denominations. He said that while praying for guidance he had been confronted by two heavenly messengers who forbade him to join any existing church but prepare to become the prophet of a new one. Soon, in a series of visions, he was told of a revelation written on golden plates concealed in a nearby hillside. These he unearthed in 1827 and with the help of "Urim and Thummin" translated the "reformed Egyptian" characters into English. Described as the *Book of Mormon,* this was published in 1830 and at the same time a little church of those few who accepted his testimony was founded in Fayette, N.Y. In addition the first of Joseph Smith's "miracles"—the casting out of a devil—was performed. The *Book of Mormon* purports to be a record of early American history and religion, the American Indians being identified as the ten Lost Tribes of Israel, whose fate has never failed to attract the attention of those who prefer myth to fact (cf. British Israelites). Jesus Christ is alleged to have appeared in America after His ascension. Yet Smith's eloquence was able to influence quite educated people, including Sidney Rigdon with whom he went into business for a time. *Doctrine and Covenants* is the title of another book dealing with the revelations Smith claimed to have received. Soon the sect was in trouble with the community both because its members insisted on describing themselves as the Chosen People and others as Gentiles and because they took part in politics, voting as Smith ordered them to. Smith was constantly in trouble with the police. Therefore they were turned out from one city after another until they found themselves a dwelling-place at Nauvoo, Illinois, on the Mississippi.

That would probably have been the end of the story had not Smith been murdered in 1844 and thereby made to appear a martyr, and had there not appeared Brigham Young, a quite extraordinary leader, who stamped out warring factions and drove out the recalcitrant. While persecutions continued Brigham Young announced that it had been revealed that he must lead the faithful to Salt Lake, then outside the area of the United States. There followed the famous trek of more than a thousand miles across desert country in which he led the way, reaching his journey's end in the forbidding valley of the Great Salt Lake on 24 July 1847. By 1851 30,000 Mormons had reached the Promised Land. Here they held their own in a hostile environment and under the practical genius of their leader carried through a vast irrigation scheme and built Salt Lake City which still serves as the headquarters of their sect. In 1850 their pioneer settlement was made Utah Territory, and in 1896 incorporated in the Union. The church was strictly ruled by its leader who also looked after affairs of state for thirty years until his death in 1877.

Polygamy, although opposed by some Mormons, and only sanctioned by Brigham Young when Salt Lake City had been built, is the best-known of Mormon doctrines. It brought the sect into much disrepute and was renounced in 1880. Mormons are millenarians, believing that some time Christ will appear and rule for a thousand years.

Members of the Church of Jesus Christ of Latter-day Saints now number over three million in congregations throughout the world.

The Reorganized Church of Jesus Christ of Latter-day Saints with its headquarters at Independence, Missouri, has been separate and distinct since 1852.

Mysticism, a religious attitude which concerns itself with direct relationship with God, "reality" as contrasted with appearance or the "ultimate" in one form or another. All the higher religions have had their mystics who have not always been regarded without suspicion by their more orthodox members, and, as Bertrand Russell points out, there has been a remarkable unity of opinion among mystics which almost transcends their religious differences. Thus, characteristic of the mystical experience in general, have been the following features; (1) a belief in insight as opposed to analytical knowledge which is accompanied in the actual experience by the sense of a mystery unveiled, a hidden wisdom become certain beyond the possibility of doubt: this is often preceded by a period of utter hopelessness and isolation described as "the dark night of the soul"; (2) a belief in unity and a refusal to admit opposition or division anywhere; this sometimes appears in the form of what seem to be contradictory statements: "the way up and the way down is one and the same" (Heraclitus). There is no distinction between subject and object, the act of perception and the thing perceived; (3) a denial of the reality of time, since if all is one the distinction of past and future must be illusory; (4) a denial of the reality of evil (which does not maintain, *e.g.,* that cruelty is good but that it does not exist in the world of reality as opposed to the world of phantoms from which we are liberated by the insight of the vision). Among the great mystics have been Meister Eckhart and Jakob Boehme, the German religious mystics of the 13th and 16th cent. respectively, Acharya Sankara of India, and St. Theresa and St. John of the Cross of Spain. Mystical movements within the great religions have been: the Zen *(q.v.)* movement within Buddhism; Taoism in China; the Cabalists and Hasidim in Judaism; the Sufis within Islam; some of the Quakers within Christianity.

Mystery Religions. *See* **Orphism.**

N

Natural Law, the specifically Roman Catholic doctrine that there is a natural moral law, irrespective of time and place, which man can know through his own reason. Originally a product of early rational philosophy, the Christian form of the doctrine is basically due to St. Thomas Aquinas who defined natural law in relation to eternal law, holding that the eternal law is God's reason which governs the relations of all things in the universe to each other. The natural law is that part of the eternal law which relates to man's behavior. Catholic natural law assumes that the human reason is capable of deriving ultimate rules for right behavior, since there are in man and his institutions certain stable structures produced by God's reason which man's reason can know to be correct and true. Thus, the basis of marriage, property, the state, and the contents of justice are held to be available to man's natural reason. The rules of positive morality and civil law are held to be valid only insofar as they conform to the natural law, which man is not only capable of knowing but also of obeying.

Protestant theologians criticize this notion. Thus Karl Barth and many others hold that sinful and fallen man cannot have any direct knowledge of God or His reason or will without the aid of revelation. Another theologian, Reinhold Niebuhr, points out that the principles of the doctrines are too inflexible and that although they are the product of a particular time and circumstance, they are regarded as if they were absolute and eternal. In fact, as most social scientists would also agree, there is no law which can be regarded as "natural" for all men at all times. Nor does it seem sensible to suppose that all or even many men possess either the reason to discern natural law or the ability to obey it; whether or not we accept man's free will (and all Protestant sects do not), we know as a fact of science that people are not always fully responsible for their actions and some not at all.

Nazism, the term commonly used for the political and social ideology of the German National Socialist Party inspired and led by Hitler. The term *Nazi* was an abbreviation of Nazional-socialistische Deutsche Arbeiterpartei. Those in the Federal Republic today sympathetic to National Socialist aims are known as neo-Nazis. *See* **Fascism.**

Neoplatonism. *See* **Determinism and Free Will** and **God and Man.**

Nestorian Heresy. The 5th cent. of the Christian Church saw a battle of personalities and opinions waged with fanatical fury between St. Cyril, the patriarch of Alexandria, and Nestorius, patriarch of Constantinople. Nestorius maintained that Mary should not be called the mother of God, as she was only the mother of the human and not of the divine nature of Jesus. This view was contradicted by Cyril (one of the most unpleasant saints who ever lived) who held the orthodox view. In addition to his utter destruction of Nestorius by stealthy and unremitting animosity Cyril was also responsible for the lynching of Hypatia, a distinguished mathematician and saintly woman, head of the Neoplatonist school at Alexandria. She was dragged from her chariot, stripped naked, butchered and torn to pieces in the church, and her remains burned. As if this were not enough Cyril took pains to stir up pogroms against the very large Jewish colony of Alexandria. At the Council of Ephesus (A.D. 431) the Western Bishops quickly decided for Cyril. This Council (reinforced by the Council of Chalcedon in 451) clarified orthodox Catholic doctrine (*see* **Monophysitism**). Nestorius became a heretic, was banished to Antioch where he had a short respite of peace, but later, and in spite of his weakness and age, was dragged about from one place to another on the borders of Egypt. We are assured that his tongue was eaten by worms in punishment for the wicked words he had spoken, but later the Nestorian church flourished in Syria and Persia under the protection of the rulers of Persia and missions were sent to India and China.

Nihilism, the name commonly given to the earliest Russian form of revolutionary anarchism. It originated in the early years of Tsar Alexander II (1818–81), the liberator of the serfs, who, during his attempts to bring about a constitutional monarchy, was killed by a bomb. The term "nihilist", however, was first used in 1862 by Turgenev in his novel *Fathers and Children. See* **Anarchism.**

Nominalism. Early medieval thinkers were divided into two schools, those who regarded "universals" or abstract concepts as mere names without any corresponding realities (Nominalists), and those who held the opposite doctrine **(Realism)** that general concepts have an existence independent of individual things. The relation between universals and particulars was a subject of philosophical dispute all through the Middle Ages.

The first person to hold the nominalist doctrine was probably Roscelin or Roscellinus in the late 11th cent., but very little is known of him and none of his works remains except for a single letter to Peter Abelard who was his pupil. Roscelin was born in France, accused twice of heresy but recanted and fled to England where he attacked the views of Anselm, according to whom Roscelin used the phrase that universals were a *flatus voci* or breath of the voice. The most important nominalist was the Englishman William of Occam in the 13th cent. who, once and for all, separated the two schools by saying in effect that science is about things (the nominalist view) whereas logic, philosophy, and religion are about terms or concepts (the Platonic tradition). Both are justified, but we must distinguish between them. The proposition "man is a species" is not a proposition of logic or philosophy but a scientific statement since we cannot say whether it is true or false without knowing about man. If we fail to realize that words are conventional signs and that it is important to decide whether or not they have a meaning and refer to something, then we shall fall into logical fallacies of the type: "Man is a species, Socrates is a man, therefore Socrates is a species." This, in effect, is the beginning of the modern philosophy of logical analysis which, to oversimplify, tells us that a statement is not just true or untrue, it may also be meaningless. Therefore, in all the philosophical problems we have discussed elsewhere there is the third possibility that the problem we are discussing has no meaning because the words refer to nothing and we must ask ourselves before going any further "what do we mean by God", and has the word "free will" any definite meaning?

O

Occam's Razor, the philosophical maxim by which William of Occam, the 14th cent. Franciscan has become best-known. This states in the form which is most familiar: "Entities are not to be multiplied without necessity" and as such does not appear in his works. He did, however, say something much to the same effect: "It is vain to do with more what can be done with fewer." In other words, if everything in some science can be interpreted without assuming this or that hypothetical entity, there is no ground for assuming it. This is Bertrand Russell's version and he adds: "I have myself found this a most fruitful principle in logical analysis."

Occultism. *see,* **Alchemy, Astrology,** and **Theosophy.**

Orgonomy, a pseudo-psychological theory advanced by the German psychiatrist Wilhelm Reich (1897–1957), a pupil of Freud, who was expelled from Germany for attacking the Nazis and who started life afresh in the U.S.A. like so many of his colleagues. Moving quickly away from orthodox psychoanalytic theories, Reich became increasingly obsessed with the view that all living things were permeated with a unique force or energy which he termed "orgone" and which he believed could be photographed and measured with a geiger counter. The key to the successful flow of orgone throughout the body was sexual intercourse and the resulting orgasm (hence "orgone"). Reich achieved a substantial following for his increasingly bizarre views and when he was sentenced to two-years' imprisonment in 1956 for alleged medical malpractice a "civil rights" controversy developed which has not died down to this date. His unfortunate and rather tragic death in prison has fanned the emotional issues and granted him the important role of martyr to his cause. There is currently a strong revival of interest in Reich and orgonomy, partly in tune with the general occult revival. A recent witty, but not totally unsympathetic film about his work "W R—Mysteries of the Organism" has drawn the attention of a large new audience to his teachings.

Orphism. The Greeks in general thought very little of their gods, regarding them as similar human beings with human failings and virtues although on a larger scale. But there was another aspect of Greek religion which was passionate, ecstatic, and secret, dealing with the worship of various figures among whom were Bacchus or Dionysus, Orpheus, and Demeter and Persephone of the Eleusinian Mysteries. Dionysus (or Bacchus) was originally a god from Thrace where the people were primitive farmers naturally interested in fertility cults. Dionysus was the god of fertility who only later came to be associated with wine and the divine madness it produces. He assumed the form of a man or a bull and his worship by the time it arrived in Greece became associated with women (as was the case in most of the Mystery Religions) who spent nights on the hills dancing and possibly drinking wine in order to stimulate ecstasy; an unpleasant aspect of the cult was the tearing to pieces of wild animals whose flesh was eaten raw. Although the cult was disapproved of by the orthodox and, needless to say, by husbands, it existed for a long time.

This primitive and savage religion in time was modified by that attributed to Orpheus whose cult was more spiritualized, ascetic, and substituted mental for physical intoxication. Orpheus may have been a real person or a legendary hero and he, too, is supposed to have come from Thrace, but his name indicates that he, or the movement associated with him, came from Crete and originally from Egypt, which seems to have been the source of many of its doctrines. Crete, it must be remembered, was the island through which Egypt influenced Greece in other respects. Orpheus is said to have been a reformer who was torn to pieces by the Maenad worshippers of Dionysus. The Orphics believed in the transmigration of souls and that the soul after death might obtain either eternal bliss or temporary or permanent torment according to its way of life upon earth. They held ceremonies of purification and the more orthodox abstained from animal food except on special occasions when it was eaten ritually. Man is partly earthly, partly heavenly, and a good life increases the heavenly part so that, in the end, he may become one with Bacchus and be called a "Bacchus".

The religion had an elaborate theology. As the Bacchic rites were reformed by Orpheus, so the Orphic rites were reformed by Pythagoras (*c.* 582 –*c.* 507 B.C.) who introduced the mystical element into Greek philosophy, which reached its heights in Plato. Other elements entered Greek life from Orphism. One of these was feminism which was notably lacking in Greek civilization outside the Mystery Religions. The other was the drama which arose from the rites of Dionysus. The mysteries of Eleusis formed the most sacred part of the Athenian state religion, and it is clear that they had to do with fertility rites also, for they were in honour of Demeter and Persephone and all the myths speak of them as being associated with the supply of corn to the country. Without being provocative, it is accepted by most anthropologists and many theologians that Christianity, just as it accepted elements of Gnossticism and Mithraism, accepted elements from the Mystery Religions as they in turn must have done from earlier cults. The miraculous birth, the death and resurrection the sacramental feast of bread and wine, symbolizing the eating of the flesh and drinking of the blood of the god, all these are common elements in early religions and not just in one. None of this means that what we are told about Jesus is not true, but it surely does mean: *(a)* that Christianity was not a sudden development; *(b)* that the early Church absorbed many of the elements of other religions; *(c)* that perhaps Jesus Himself made use of certain symbols which He knew had a timeless significance for man and invested them with new meaning.

P

Pantheism. *See* **God and Man.**

Papal Infallibility. The basis of papal infallibility is *(a)* that every question of morals and faith is not dealt with in the Bible so it is necessary that there should be a sure court of appeal in case of doubt, and this was provided by Christ when he established the Church as His Teaching Authority upon earth; *(b)* ultimately this idea of the teaching function of the Church shapes the idea of papal infallibility which asserts that the Pope, when speaking officially on matters of faith or morals, is protected by God against the possibility of error. The doctrine was proclaimed in July 1870.

Infallibility is a strictly limited gift which does not mean that the Pope has extraordinary intelligence, that God helps him to find the answer to every conceivable question, or that Catholics have to accept the Pope's views on politics. He can make mistakes or fall into sin, his scientific or historical opinions may be quite wrong, he may write books that are full of errors. Only in two limited spheres is he infallible and in these only when he speaks officially as the supreme teacher and lawgiver of the Church, defining a doctrine that must be accepted by all its members. When, after studying a problem of faith or morals as carefully as possible, and with all available help from expert consultants, he emerges with the Church's answer—on these occasions it is not strictly an answer, it is *the* answer.

Historically speaking, the Roman Catholic Church of the early 19th century was at its lowest ebb of power. Pope Pius IX, in fear of Italian nationalism, revealed his reactionary attitude by the feverish declaration of new dogmas, the canonization of new saints, the denunciation of all modern ideals in the Syllabus of Errors, and the unqualified defence of his temporal power against the threat of Garibaldi. It is not too much to say that everything regarded as important by freedom-loving and democratic people was opposed by the papacy at that time. In 1870, after a long and sordid struggle, the Vatican Council, convened by Pius IX, pronounced the definition of his infallibility. Döllinger, a German priest and famous historian of the Church, was excommunicated because, like many others, he refused to accept the new dogma. It is difficult not to doubt that there was some connection between the pronouncement of the Pope's infallibility and his simultaneous loss of temporal power.

After the humanism of the Second Vatican Council (1962–5) Pope Paul's encyclical *Hummanae Vitae* (1968), condemning birth control, came as a great disappointment to the many people (including theologians, priests, and laymen) who had expected there would be a change in the Church's teaching. The Church's moral guidance on this controversial issue, however, does not involve the doctrine of infallibility. (The Roman Catholic Church teaches that papal pronouncements are infallible only when they are specifically defined as such.) That there is unlikely to be any immediate softening of the Church's line on infallibility was made clear in July 1973 when the Vatican's Sacred Congregation for the Doctrine of the Faith published a document strongly reaffirming papal infallibility. The document also reminded Catholics of their obligation to accept the Catholic Church's unique claims to authenticity.

Parapsychology, the name given to the study of psychical research *(q.v.)* as an academic discipline, and chosen to denote the topic's supposed status as a branch of psychology. The impetus behind parapsychology came from the psychologist William MacDougall who persuaded Duke University in North Carolina to found a department of parapsychology under J. B. Rhine. Throughout the 1930s and '40s the work of Rhine and his colleagues, who claimed to have produced scientific evidence for the existence of ESP, attracted worldwide attention. Increasing reservations about the interpretation of Rhine's results and an apparent lack of any readily repeatable experiments, however, gradually eroded scientific confidence in the topic. The academic status of parapsychology is at the present time exceedingly uncertain. Rhine retired from university life in 1965 and the world-famous parapsychology laboratory at Duke University was closed. On the other hand the American Association for the Advancement of Science recently admitted the Parapsychology Association (the leading organization for professional parapsychologists) as an affiliated member society. An American government body, the National Institute of Mental Health, has also officially supported some medical research into alleged telepathic dreams, the first "official" grant support of this kind. In Britain a poll of readers in the weekly journal, *New Scientist,* revealed a very high interest in the subject matter of parapsychology, and active research is currently going on at the Dept. of Psychology at Cambridge. Stories of intensive parapsychological research in Soviet Russia are however without foundation and are not supported by Western parapsychologists who have visited Russia.

Parsees. *See* **Zoroastrianism.**

Pavlovian theory. *See* **Behaviorism.**

Pentecostalism, a religious movement within the Protestant churches, holding the belief that an essential feature of true Christianity is a vigorous and profound spiritual or mystical experience which occurs after, and seemingly reinforces the initial conversion. The origins of modern Pentecostalism appear to lie in the occasion on 1 January 1901 when a member of a Bible College in Topeka, Kansas, one Agnes N. Ozman, spontaneously began to speak in an apparently unknown language at one of the college's religious meetings. This "speaking in tongues" was assumed to be evidence of her conversion and "spirit baptism", and became a feature of most Pentecostal meetings in due course. The movement spread rapidly across America, particularly in rural communities, and also was a strong feature of Welsh religious life in the early part of the century. Pentecostal services are enthusiastic and rousing with a strong emphasis on music and participation on the part of the congregation. Pentecostalism is evangelistic in nature and seems to be gaining in strength at the present time, at the expense of more orthodox and staid versions of Christianity. The fiery character Aimee Semple McPherson was one of its most prominent evangelists.

Phrenology, a psychological "school" founded in 1800 by two Germans, Franz Josef Gall and Johann Gaspar Spurzheim. Gall was an anatomist who believed there to be some correspondence between mental faculties and the shape of the head. He tested these ideas in prisons and mental hospitals and began to lecture on his findings, arousing a great deal of interest throughout both Europe and America, where his doctrines were widely accepted. Phrenology became fashionable, and people would go to "have their bumps read" as later men and women of fashion have gone to be psychoanalyzed. Roughly speaking, Gall divided the mind into thirty-seven faculties such as destructiveness, suavity, self-esteem, conscientiousness, and so on, and claimed that each of these was located in a definite area of the brain. He further claimed that the areas in the brain corresponded to "bumps" on the skull which could be read by the expert, thus giving a complete account of the character of the subject. In fact, *(a)* no such faculties are located in the brain anywhere, for this is simply not the way the brain works; *(b)* the faculties described by Gall are not pure traits which cannot be further analysed and are based on a long outdated psychology; *(c)* the shape of the brain bears no specific relationship to the shape of the skull. Phrenology is a pseudo-science; there is no truth in it whatever. But, even so, like astrology, it still has its practitioners.

Physiocrats. A French school of economic thought during the 18th cent., known at the time as *Les Economistes* but in later years named physiocrats by Du Pont de Nemours, a member of the School. Other members were Quesnay, Mirabeau, and the great financier Turgot. The physiocrats held the view, common to the 18th cent., and deriving ultimately from Rousseau, of the goodness and bounty of nature and the goodness of man "as he came from the bosom of nature". The aim of governments, therefore, should be to conform to nature; and so long as men do not interfere with each other's liberty and do not combine among themselves, governments should leave them free to find their own salvation. Criminals, madmen, and monopolists should be eliminated. Otherwise the duty of government is *laissez-faire, laissez passer.* From this follows the doctrine of free trade between nations on grounds of both justice and economy; for the greater the competition the more will each one strive to economize the cost of his labour to the general advantage. Adam Smith, although not sharing their confidence in human nature, learned much from the physiocrats, eliminated their errors, and greatly developed their teaching.

Physiognomy. *See* **Characterology.**

Plymouth Brethren, a religious sect founded by John Nelson Darby, a minister of the Protestant Church of Ireland, and Edward Cronin a former Roman Catholic, in 1827. Both were dissatisfied with the lack of spirituality in their own and other churches and joined together in small meetings in Dublin every Sunday for "the breaking of bread". Soon the movement began to spread through Darby's travels and writings and he finally settled in Plymouth, giving the popular name to the "Brethren". Beginning as a movement open to all who felt the need to "keep the unity of the Spirit", it soon exercized the right to exclude all who had unorthodox views and split up into smaller groups. Among these the main ones were the "Exclusives", the Kellyites, the Newtonites, and "Bethesda" whose main differences were over problems of church government or prophetical powers. Some of these are further split among themselves. Readers of *Father and Son* by Sir Edmund Gosse, which describes life with his father, the eminent naturalist Philip Gosse, who belonged to the Brethren, will recall how this basically kind, honest, and learned man was led through their teachings to acts of unkindness (*e.g.,* in refusing to allow his son and other members of his household to celebrate Christmas and throwing out the small tokens they had secretly bought), and lack of scientific rigor (*e.g.,* in refusing for religious reasons alone to accept Darwinism when all his evidence pointed towards it).

Today, the majority of Brethren belong to the "Open Brethren" assemblies and, unlike the "Exclusives" hold that the Lord's Supper (a commemorative act of "breaking the bread" observed once a week) is for all Christians who care to join them. Baptism is required and Brethren believe in the personal premillennial second coming of Christ.

Poltergeist, allegedly a noisy type of spirit which specializes in throwing things about, making loud thumpings and bangings, and occasionally bringing in "apports", *i.e.,* objects from elsewhere. Most so-called poltergeist activities are plain frauds, but the others are almost invariably associated with the presence in the house of someone (often, but not always a child) who is suffering from an adolescent malaise or an epileptic condition. The inference is that those activities which are not simply fraudulent are either due to some unknown influence exuded by such mentally disturbed people, or that they are actually carried out by ordinary physical means by such people when in an hysterical state—*i.e.,* unconsciously. The second hypothesis is much the more probable. *See* **Psychic Research.**

Polytheism. *See* **God and Man.**

Positivism, also known as the **Religion of Humanity,** was founded by Auguste Comte (1798–1857), a famous mathematician and philosopher born in Montpellier, France. His views up to the end of the century attracted many and it would have been impossible throughout that time to read a book on philosophy or sociology that did not mention them, but today his significance is purely of historical interest. In his *Cours de Philosophie Positive* (1830) he put forward the thesis that mankind had seen three great stages in human thought: (1) the theological, during which man seeks for supernatural causes to explain nature and invents gods and devils; (2) the metaphysical, through which he thinks in terms of philosophical and metaphysical abstractions; (3) the last positive or scientific stage when he will proceed by experimental and objective observation to reach in time "positive truth".

Broadly speaking, there is little to complain of in this analysis; for there does seem to have been some sort of general direction along these lines. However, Comte was not satisfied with having reached this point and felt that his system demanded a religion and, of course, one that was "scientific". This religion was to be the worship of Humanity in place of the personal Deity of earlier times, and for it he supplied not only a Positive Catechism but a treatise on Sociology in which he declared himself the High Priest of the cult. Since, as it stood, the religion was likely to appear somewhat abstract to many, Comte drew up a list of historical characters whom he regarded as worthy of the same sort of adoration as Catholics accord to their saints. The new Church attracted few members, even among those who had a high regard for Comte's scientific work, and its only significant adherents were a small group of Oxford scholars and some in his own country. Frederic Harrison was the best-known English adherent and throughout his life continued to preach Comtist doctrines in London to diminishing audiences.

Pragmatism, a typically American school of philosophy which comes under the heading of what Bertrand Russell describes as a "practical" as opposed to a "theoretical" philosophy. Whereas the latter, to which most of the great philosophical systems belong, seeks disinterested knowledge for its own sake, the former *(a)* regards action as the supreme good, *(b)* considers happiness an effect and knowledge a mere instrument of successful activity.

The originator of pragmatism is usually considered to have been the psychologist William James (1842–1910) although he himself attributed its basic principles to his life-long friend, the American philosopher, Charles Sanders Peirce (1839–1914). The other famous pragmatist is John Dewey, best-known in Europe for his works on education (for although American text-books on philosophy express opinions to the contrary, few educated people in Europe have taken the slightest interest in pragmatism and generally regard it as an eccentricity peculiar to Americans). James in his book *The Will to Believe* (1896) points out that we are often compelled to take a decision where no adequate theoretical grounds for a decision exist; for even to do nothing is to decide. Thus in religion we have a right to adopt a believing attitude although not intellectually fully convinced. We should believe truth and shun error, but the failing of the sceptical philosopher is that he adheres only to the latter rule and thus fails to believe various truths which a less cautious man will accept. If believing truth and avoiding error are equally important, then it is a good idea when we are presented with an alternative to believe one of the possibilities at will, since we then have an even chance of being right, whereas we have none if we suspend judgment. The function of philosophy, according to James, is to find out what difference it makes to the individual if a particular philosophy or world-system is true: "An idea is 'true' so long as to believe it is profitable to our lives" and, he adds, the truth is only the expedient in our way of thinking . . . in the long run and on the whole of course". Thus "if the hypothesis of God works satisfactorily in the widest sense of the word, it is true". Bertrand Russell's reply to this assertion is: "I have always found that the hypothesis of Santa Claus 'works satisfactorily in the widest sense of the word'; therefore 'Santa Claus exists' is true, although Santa Claus does not exist." Russell adds that James's concept of truth simply omits as unimportant the question whether God really *is* in His heaven; if He is a useful hypothesis that is enough. "God the Architect of the Cosmos is forgotten; all that is remembered is belief in God, and its effects upon the creatures inhabiting our petty planet. No wonder the Pope condemned the pragmatic defence of religion."

Predestination. *See* **Calvinism.**

Presbyterianism, a system of ecclesiastical government of the Protestant churches which look back to John Calvin as their Reformation leader. The ministry consists of presbyters who are all of equal rank. Its doctrinal standards are contained in the *Westminster Confession of Faith* (1647) which is, in general, accepted by English, Scottish, and American Presbyterians as the most thorough and logical statement in existence of the Calvinist creed.

The Presbyterian tradition includes uncompromizing stress upon the Word of God contained in the Scriptures of the Old and New Testaments as the supreme rule of faith and life, and upon the value of a highly trained ministry, which has given the Church of Scotland a high reputation for scholarship and has in turn influenced the standard of education in Scotland. The unity of the Church is guaranteed by providing for democratic representation in a hierarchy of courts (unlike the Anglican Church, which is a hierarchy of persons). The local kirk session consists of the minister and popularly elected elders (laymen). Ministers, elected by their flocks, are ordained by presbyters (ministers already ordained). Above the kirk session is the court of the presbytery which has jurisdiction over a specified area; above that the court of synod which rules over many presbyteries; and finally the General Assembly which is the Supreme Court of the Church with both judicial and legislative powers, and over which the Moderator of the General Assembly presides. The function of the elders is to help the minister in the work and government of the kirk. The episcopacy set up by James VI and I, and maintained by Charles I was brought to an end by the Glasgow Assembly (1638), but General Assemblies were abolished by Oliver Cromwell and at the Restoration Charles II re-established episcopacy. The Covenanters who resisted were hunted down, imprisoned, transported, or executed over a period of nearly thirty years before William of Orange came to the throne and Presbyterianism was re-established (1690). Today Presbyterians no less than other Christian communities are looking at Christianity as a common world religion in the sense that the principles which unite them are greater than those which divide them. A small but significant step in the direction of international Christian unity was made in 1972 when the Presbyterian and Congregationalist Churches in England were merged to form the United Reformed Church. *See* **Calvinism.**

Psychic Research is a general term for the various approaches to the scientific investigation of the paranormal, in particular supposed extrasensory powers of the mind, but also manifestations such as ghosts, poltergeists, spiritualistic phenomena, etc. In recent years the word parapsychology has also come into use, particularly for the investigation of ESP in a laboratory setting, but it is really part of psychic research as the subject's fascinating history reveals.

For all recorded history, and no doubt very much earlier, man has been puzzled at his apparent ability to perceive features of the universe without the use of the normal senses—mind-to-mind contact, dreams about the future which come true, etc. He has also been intrigued by the notion that in addition to the natural world of people and things, there exists in parallel, a *supernatural* world of ghosts, spirits and other similar strange manifestations. Belief in such oddities has been tremendously widespread and still forms one of the major casual conversational topics raised when people see each other socially today. Of course, until the 19th cent. or thereabouts such phenomena, while bizarre, unpredictable and possibly frightening, were not at odds with man's view of himself and his world as revealed through basic religious beliefs. Man was supposed to be in essence a supernatural being with eternal life, and the world was seen as the happy hunting ground of dynamic evil forces which could intervene directly in the lives of humans. The rise of material science in the 19th cent. however began to shake the orthodox religious framework, and as a result in due course scientists began to question the basis of all supernatural powers and manifestations, putting forward the reasonable argument: "if such things *are* real then they should be demonstrable in scientific terms—just as all other aspects of the universe are."

Once having advanced this argument, the next step was to carry it to its conclusion and set about the systematic investigation of the phenomena to see whether they *did* conform in any way to the immensely successful framework of 19th cent. science, and from this step psychic research was born. In fact one can date its origins rather precisely—to 1882 when a group of scholars formed the Society for Psychical Research in London—an organization which still exists today. The first experiments in this slightly eccentric field of science were haphazard and tended to be confined to spiritualistic phenomena such as table tapping, mediumistic messages, ectoplasmic manifestations, etc., which were having a great wave of popularity among the general public at the time. In fact what one might term as the first phase of psychic research—it has gone through three phases in its history—was really heavily tied up with Spiritualism. Before ridiculing it for this, it is only fair to point out that many of the most eminent figures of the time—the great physicists Sir Oliver Lodge and Sir William Crookes, Alfred Russell Wallace, co-discoverer with Darwin of the theory of evolution by natural selection, the brilliant author and creator of Sherlock Holmes, Sir Arthur Conan Doyle, and many others—became convinced Spiritualists as the result of their early experiments. Nevertheless, despite the ardent support of such intellectual giants, medium after medium was in due course detected in fraud sometimes of the most blatant kind—and the majority of scientists gradually became more critical and less likely to be taken in by even the subtlest of trickery. As a result, interest slowly shifted from the séance room to a different realm, and as it did so the first phase of psychic research drew to a close.

The second phase was, broadly speaking, the era of the ghost hunter. With the idea of spirits materializing in laboratories seeming intrinsically less and less credible, scientists began to study what struck them at the time to be basically more "plausible" matters—haunted houses, poltergeist phenomena and so on. For some reason the idea of a house dominated by a psychic presence as the result of some tragic history seemed (at the turn of the century) *somehow* scientifically and philosophically more acceptable than did the old Spiritualist notions about direct communication with the spirit world. The key figure in the "ghost hunting" era was Mr. Harry Price, an amateur magician who became the scourge of fraudulent mediums, but who staked his name and credibility on the authenticity of the alleged poltergeist phenomena at Borley Rectory in Suffolk, which became world famous through his book, *The Most Haunted House in England.* The ancient rectory's catalogue of ghosts and marvels allegedly witnessed by numerous "reliable witnesses" seemed irrefutable. Unfortunately investigations by the Society for Psychical Research some years after Price's death now make it seem certain that Price was responsible for faking some of the Borley phenomena himself, and with these disclosures scientifically "respectable" ghost hunting took a nasty tumble. Thus, with an increasingly critical attitude developing among scientists, haunted houses and poltergeists gradually began to shift out of favor to usher in the third phase of psychic research.

The date of the commencement of this phase can be identified as 1927 when the Parapsychology Laboratory at Duke University in North Carolina was formed by Dr. J. B. Rhine. Here the emphasis was on laboratory studies along the traditional lines of experimental psychology; spirit forms and poltergeists were ignored in favor of the routine testing of literally thousands of people for telepathy, precognition (the ability to see into the future), etc., almost always involving card tests which could be rigidly controlled and the results statistically analysed. By the 1940s Rhine was claiming irrefutable evidence of telepathy achieved by these means, but once again critical forces began to gather and it was pointed out that results obtained in Rhine's laboratory rarely seemed to be replicable in other scientists' laboratories in different parts of the world. In fact the failure of ESP experiments of this kind to be easily repeatable has turned out to be crucial and has led to a growing scepticism on the part of uncommitted scientists who now question whether psychic research and parapsychology have really advanced our understanding of the world of the paranormal in any way. At the present time the topic is in a highly controversial phase.

Although Rhine's university parapsychology laboratory closed with his retirement in 1965 research in the field has continued ever since, especially with the work of Dr. Helmut Schmidt who has made important contributions. In recent years a new Chair and research laboratory has been introduced at the University of Utrecht in the Netherlands.

To sum up the topic one could say that in a curious way, while the third phase of psychic research is now drawing to a close, the evidence suggests that a fourth phase is appearing, and that this may well feature a return to the study of the more sensational and dramatic phenomena reminiscent of the Victorian séance room. If this is so, a century after its foundation the wheel will have turned full circle and psychic research will be back where it started, without in the opinion of most scientists, having solved any of the basic questions which it had set out to answer. *See* **Parapsychology, Poltergeist, Telepathy, Spiritualism.**

Psychoanalysis, an approach to the study of human personality involving the rigorous probing, with the assistance of a specially trained practitioner, of an individual's personal problems, motives, goals and attitudes to life in general. Often, and quite understandably, confused with psychology (of which it is merely a part), psychoanalysis has an interesting historical background and has attracted the interest of philosophers, scientists and medical experts since it emerged as a radical and controversial form of mental therapy at the turn of the century. The traditionally accepted founder is the great Austrian Sigmund Freud, but he never failed to acknowledge the impetus that had been given to his own ideas by his talented friend, the physiologist Joseph Breuer, who for most of his working life had been interested in the curious phenomena associated with hypnosis. Breuer had successfully cured the hysterical paralysis of a young woman patient and had noticed that under hypnosis the girl seemed to be recalling emotional experiences, hitherto forgotten, which bore some relationship to the symptoms of her illness. Developing this with other patients Breuer then found that the mere recalling and discussing of the emotional events under hypnosis seemed to produce a dramatic alleviation of the symptoms—a phenomenon which came to be known as *catharsis.* Breuer also noticed another curious side-effect, that his women patients fell embarrassingly and violently in love with him, and he gradually dropped the practice of "mental catharsis", possibly feeling that it was a bit too dangerous to handle. This left the field clear for Freud, whose brilliant mind began to search beyond the therapeutic aspects of the topic to see what light might be thrown on the nature of human personality and psychological mechanisms in general. The most important question concerned the "forgotten" emotional material which turned up, apparently out of the blue, during the hypnotic session. Freud rightly saw that this posed problems for the current theories of memory, for how could something once forgotten *(a)* continue to have an effect on the individual without his being aware of it, and (b) ultimately be brought back to conscious memory again. It must be remembered that at this time memory was considered to be a fairly simple process—information was stored in the brain and was gradually eroded or destroyed with the passage of time and the decay of brain cells. Once lost, it was believed, memories were gone for ever, or at best only partially and inaccurately reproducible. Furthermore, human beings were supposed to be rational (if frequently wilful) creatures who never did anything without thinking about it (if only briefly) beforehand and without being well aware of their reasons for so doing. It was within this framework that Freud had his great insight, one which many people believe to be one of the most important ideas given to mankind. This was simply the realization that the human mind was not a simple entity controlling the brain and body more or less at will, but a complex system made up of a number of integrated parts with at least two major subdivisions—the conscious and the unconscious. The former concerned itself with the normal round of human behavior, including the larger part of rational thought, conversation, etc., and large areas of memory. The latter was principally devoted to the automatic control of bodily functions, such as respiration, cardiac activity, various types of emotional behavior not subject to much conscious modification and a large storehouse of relevant "memories" again not normally accessible to the conscious mind. Occasionally, Freud proposed, an exceedingly unpleasant emotional or otherwise painful event might be so troublesome if held in the conscious mind's store, that it would get shoved down into the unconscious or "repressed" where it would cease to trouble the individual in his normal life. The advantages of this mechanism are obvious, but they also brought with them hazards. With certain kinds of memory, particularly those involving psychological rather than physical pain—as for example a severe sexual conflict or marital problem—repression might be used as a device to save the individual from facing his problem in the "real" world, where he might be able ultimately to solve it, by merely hiding it away in the unconscious and thus pretending it did not exist. Unfortunately, Freud believed, conflicts of this kind were not snuffed out when consigned to the basements of the mind, but rather tended to smolder on, affecting the individual in various ways which he could not understand. Repressed marital conflicts might give rise to impotence, for example, or even to homosexual behavior. Guilt at improper social actions similarly repressed might provoke nervous ties, local paralysis, etc. etc. Following this line of reasoning, Freud argued that if the unwisely repressed material could be dredged up and the individual forced to face the crisis instead of denying it, then dramatic alleviations of symptoms and full recovery should follow.

To the great psychologist and his growing band of followers the stage seemed to be set for a dramatic breakthrough not only in mental therapy but also in a general understanding of the nature of human personality. To his pleasure—for various reasons he was never too happy about hypnosis—Freud discovered that with due patience, skill and guidance an individual could be led to resurrect the material repressed in his unconscious mind in the normal, as opposed to the hypnotic state. This technique, involving long sessions consisting of intimate discussions between patient and therapist became known as psychoanalysis, and it has steadily evolved from its experimental beginnings in the medical schools and universities of Vienna to being a major system of psychotherapy with a worldwide following and important theoretical connotations. Psychoanalysis, as practiced today, consists of a number of meetings between doctor and patient in which the latter is slowly taught to approach and enter the *territory* of his subconscious mind, and examine the strange and "forgotten" material within. A successful analysis, it is claimed, gives the individual greater insight into his own personality and a fuller understanding of the potent unconscious forces which are at work within him and in part dictating his goals.

Freud's initial ideas were of course tentative, and meant to be so. He was however a didactic and forceful personality himself, unwilling to compromise on many points which became controversial as the technique and practice of psychoanalysis developed. The outcome was that some of his early followers, notably the equally brilliant Carl Jung and Alfred Adler, broke away to found their own "schools" or versions of psychoanalysis, with varying degrees of success. Today, psychoanalysis is coming under increasingly critical scrutiny, and its claims are being treated with a good deal of reservation. Notable antagonists include the English psychologist Professor H. J. Eysenck who points out that there is little if any solid experimental data indicating that psychoanalysis is a valid method of treating or curing mental illness. Analysists respond by saying that their system is closer to an art than a craft and not amenable to routine scientific experiment. The controversy will no doubt continue for some time to come, but whatever its validity as therapy, the basic ideas behind psychoanalysis—notably the reality and power of the unconscious mind—are beyond question and have given human beings definite and major insights into the greatest enigma of all—the workings of the human mind.

Psychometry, the supposed talent or faculty of divining something about the history and previous owners of an object by holding it in the hand. A common feature of modern Spiritualistic practice, and to a certain extent synonymous with clairvoyance, psychometry is based on an ancient magical assumption that objects somehow take on traces or "memories" of their surroundings which are detectable by specially sensitive individuals. Controlled scientific tests on people claiming to have this power have however proved totally negative. *See also* **Psychic Research.**

Pyramidology, a curious belief that the dimensions of the Great Pyramid at Giza, if studied carefully, reveal principles of fundamental historical and religious significance. The perpetrator of this was a Victorian publisher, John Taylor, who discovered that if you divide the height of the pyramid into twice the side of its base you get a number very similar to *pi*—a number of considerable mathematical importance. Later discoveries in the same vein include the finding that the base of the pyramid (when divided by the width of a single casing stone) equals exactly 365—number of days in the year. Many books have been written on the interpretation of the dimensions of the pyramid, none of which has any scientific or archaeological validity. Pyramidology is simply a classic example of the well-known fact that hunting through even a random array of numbers will turn up sequences which appear to be "significant"—always provided that one carefully selects the numbers one wants and turns a blind eye to those that one doesn't! A peculiar variant of pyramidology has recently arisen through the publication of a claim that razor blades kept beneath a cardboard model of a pyramid never lose their cutting edge! Scientific tests have shown that this is not so, but the belief persists—implicit testimony to the mystical power of certain common emblems and symbols.

Pyrrhonism, a sceptical philosophy which doubts everything.

Q

Quakers, a religious body founded in England in the 17th cent. by George Fox (1624–91). The essence of their faith is that every individual who believes has the power of direct communication with God who will guide him into the ways of truth. This power comes from the "inner light" of his own heart, the light of Christ, Quakers meet for worship avoiding all ritual, without ordained ministers or prepared sermons; there is complete silence until someone is moved by the Holy Spirit to utter his message.

In the early days Quakers gave vent to violent outbursts and disturbed church services. Friends had the habit of preaching at anyone who happened to be nearby, their denunciation of "steeple-houses" and references to the "inner light," their addressing everyone as "thee" and "thou," their refusal to go beyond "yea" and "nay" in making an assertion and refusing to go further in taking an oath, must have played some part in bringing about the savage persecutions they were forced to endure. Many emigrated to Pennsylvania, founded by William Penn in 1682, and missionaries were sent to many parts of the world. The former violence gave way to gentleness. Friends not only refused to take part in war but even refused to resist personal violence. They took the lead in abolishing slavery, worked for prison reform and better education. As we know them today Quakers are quiet, sincere, undemonstrative people, given to a somewhat serious turn of mind. The former peculiarities of custom and dress have been dropped and interpretation of the Scriptures is more liberal. Although Quakers refuse to take part in warfare, they are always ready to help the victims of war, by organizing relief, helping refugees in distress, or sending their ambulance units into the heat of battle.

Quietism, a doctrine of extreme asceticism and contemplative devotion, embodied in the works of Michael Molinos, a 17th century Spanish priest, and condemned by Rome. It taught that the chief duty of man is to be occupied in the continual contemplation of God, so as to become totally independent of outward circumstances and the influence of the senses. Quietists taught that when this stage of perfection is reached the soul has no further need for prayer and other external devotional practices. Similar doctrines have been taught in the Moslem and Hindu religions. *See* **Yoga.**

R

Radiesthesia, the detection, either by some "psychic" faculty or with special equipment, of radiations alleged to be given off by all living things and natural substances such as water, oil, metal, etc. The word radiesthesia is in fact a fancy modern name for the ancient practice of "dowsing," whereby an individual is supposed to be able to detect the presence of hidden underground water by following the movements of a hazel twig held in his hands. Dowsers, or water diviners, as they are sometimes called, claim also to be able to detect the presence of minerals and, hard though it may seem to believe, have actually been hired by major oil companies to prospect for desert wells—though without any notable success. The theory of dowsing is that all things give off a unique radiation signal which the trained individual (via his twig, pendulum, or whatever) can "tune in" to, a theory which, while not backed up by any data known to orthodox sciences, is at least not too fantastically far-fetched. It is when radiesthesists claim to be able to detect the presence of oil, water, or precious metals by holding their pendulum *over a map* of the territory and declare that it is not necessary for them to visit the area in person to find the required spot that the topic moves from the remotely possible to the absurdly improbable. Some practitioners of this art state that they are able to perform even more marvellous feats such as determining the sex of chickens while still in the egg, or diagnosing illness by studying the movements of a pendulum held over a blood sample from the sick individual. Such claims when put to simple scientific test have almost invariably turned out as fiascos. Yet belief in dowsing, water-divining, and the like is still very widespread.

There is an important link between radiesthesia and the pseudo-science of *radionics,* which holds that the twig or pendulum can be superseded by complicated equipment built vaguely according to electronic principles. A typical radionic device consists of a box covered with knobs, dials, etc., by which the practitioner "tunes in" to the "vibration" given off by an object, such as a blood spot, a piece of hair, or even a signature. By the proper interpretation of the readings from the equipment the illness, or even the mental state, of the individual whose blood, hair, or signature is being tested, may be ascertained. The originator of radionics seems to have been a Dr. Albert Abrams who engaged in medical practice using radionic devices in America in the 1920s and '30s. The principal exponent in this country was the late George de la Warr who manufactured radionic boxes for diagnosis and treatment of illnesses, and even a "camera" which he believed to be capable of photographing thought. In a sensational court case in 1960 a woman who had purchased one of the diagnostic devices sued de la Warr for fraud. After a long trial the case was dismissed, the Judge commenting that while he had no good evidence that the device worked as claimed, he felt that de la Warr seriously believed in its validity and thus was not guilty of fraud or misrepresentation.

Ranters, a fanatical antinomian (the doctrine that Christians are not bound to keep the law of God) and pantheistic sect in Commonwealth England. The name was also applied to the Primitive Methodists because of their noisy preaching.

Rationalism is defined as "the treating of reason as the ultimate authority in religion and the rejection of doctrines not consonant with reason." In practice, rationalism had a double significance: (1) the doctrine was defined above, and (2) a 19th cent. movement which was given to what was then known as "free-thought," "secularism," or agnosticism—*i.e.,* it was in the positive sense anti-religious and was represented by various bodies such as the Secular Society, the National Secular Society, and the Rationalist Press Association (founded in 1899).

In the first sense, which implies a particular philosophical attitude to the universe and life, rationalism is not easy to pin down although, at first sight, it would appear that nothing could be simpler. Does it mean the use of pure reason and logic or does it mean, on the other hand, the use of what is generally called the "scientific method" based on a critical attitude to existing beliefs? If we are thinking in terms of the use of pure reason and logic then the Roman Catholic Church throughout most of its history has maintained, not that the whole truth about religion can be discovered by reason, but as St. Thomas Aquinas held, the basis of religion—*e.g.* the existence of God—can be rationally demonstrated. Nobody could have made more use of logic than the schoolmen of the Middle Ages, yet not many people today would accept their conclusions, nor would many non-Catholics accept St. Thomas's proofs of the existence of God even when they themselves are religious. The arguments of a First Cause or Prime Mover or the argument from Design on the whole leave us unmoved, partly because they do not lead up to the idea of a *personal God,* partly because we rightly distrust logic and pure reason divorced from facts and know that, if we begin from the wrong assumptions or premises, we can arrive at some very strange answers. If the existence of a Deity can be proved by reason, then one can also by the use of reason come to the conclusions, or rather paradoxes, such as the following: God is by definition all good, all knowing, all powerful—yet evil exists (because if it does not exist then it cannot be wrong to say "there is no God"). But if evil exists, then it must do so either because of God (in which case He is not all good) or in spite of God (in which case He is not all powerful).

Arguments of this sort do not appeal to the modern mind for two historical reasons: (1) many of us have been brought up in the Protestant tradition which—at least in one of its aspects—insists that we must believe in God by faith rather than by logic and in its extreme form insists on God as revealed by the "inner light"; (2) our increasing trust in the scientific method of observation, experiment and argument. Thus, no matter what Aristotle or St. Thomas may say about a Prime Mover or a First Cause, we remain unconvinced since at least one scientific theory suggests that the universe did not have a beginning and if scientific investigation proved this to be so, then we should be entirely indifferent to what formal logic had to say.

The secularist and rationalist movements of the 19th cent. were anti-religious—and quite rightly so—because at that time there were serious disabilities imposed even in Britain by the Established Church on atheism or agnosticism and freedom of thought. They are of little significance now because very little is left, largely thanks to their efforts, of these disabilities.

Finally, although most people are likely to accept the scientific method as the main means of discovering truth, there are other factors which equally make us doubt the value of "pure" logic and reason unaided by observation. The first of these is the influence of Freud which shows that much of our reasoning is mere rationalizing—*e.g.*, we are more likely to become atheists because we hated our father than because we can prove that there is no God. The second is the influence of a movement in philosophy which, in the form of logical positivism or logical analysis, makes us doubt whether metaphysical systems have any meaning at all. Today, instead of asking ourselves whether Plato was right or wrong, we are much more likely to ask whether he did anything but make for the most part meaningless noises. Religion is in a sense much safer today than it ever was in the 19th cent. when it made foolish statements over matters of science that could be *proved* wrong; now we tend to see it as an emotional attitude to the universe or God (a "feeling of being at home in the universe," as William James put it; which can no more be proved or disproved than being in love.

Realism is a word which has so many meanings, and such contradictory ones, in various spheres, that it is difficult to define. We shall limit ourselves to its significance in philosophy. In philosophy, "realism" has two different meanings, diametrically opposed. (1) The most usual meaning is the one we should least expect from the everyday sense of the word—*i.e.*, it refers to all those philosophies from Plato onwards which maintained that the world of appearance is illusory and that ideas, forms, or universals are the only true realities, belonging to the world beyond matter and appearance—the world of God or mind. In early medieval times St. Thomas Aquinas was the chief exponent of this doctrine which was held by the scholastics as opposed to the Nominalists *(q.v.)*. (2) In its modern everyday meaning "realism" is the belief that the universe is real and not a creation of mind, that there is a reality that causes the appearance, the "thing-in-itself" as Kant described it. Material things may not really be what they appear to be (*e.g.* a noise is not the "bang" we experience but a series of shock-waves passing through the atmosphere), yet, for all that, we can be sure that matter exists and it is very possible (some might add) that mind does not.

Reformation, the great religious movement of the 16th century, which resulted in the establishment of Protestantism. John Wyclif (d. 1384), John Hus (d. 1415) and others had sounded the warning note, and when later on Luther took up the cause in Germany, and Zwingli in Switzerland, adherents soon became numerous. The wholesale vending of indulgences by the papal agents had incensed the people, and when Luther denounced these things he spoke to willing ears. After much controversy, the reformers boldly prepounded the principles of the new doctrine, and the struggle for religious supremacy grew bitter. They claimed justification (salvation) by faith, and the use as well as the authority of the Scriptures, rejecting the doctrine of transubstantiation, the adoration of the Virgin and Saints, and the headship of the Pope. Luther was excommunicated. But the Reformation principles spread and ultimately a great part of Germany, as well as Switzerland, the Low Countries, Scandinavia, England, and Scotland were won over to the new faith. In England Henry VIII readily espoused the cause of the Reformation, his own personal quarrel with the Pope acting as an incentive. Under Mary there was a brief and sanguinary reaction, but Elizabeth gave completeness to the work which her father had initiated. *See* **Calvinism, Presbyterianism, Baptists, Methodism.**

Renaissance is defined in the *Oxford English Dictionary* as: "The revival of art and letters, under the influence of classical models, which began in Italy in the 14th century." It is a term which must be used with care for the following reasons: (1) Although it was first used in the form *rinascita* (rebirth) by Vasari in 1550 and people living at that time certainly were aware that something new was happening, the word had no wide currency until used by the Swiss historian Jacob Burchardt in his classic *The Civilization of the Renaissance in Italy* (1860). (2) The term as used today refers not only to art in its widest sense but to a total change in man's outlook on life which extended into philosophical, scientific, economic, and technical fields. (3) Spreading from Italy there were Renaissance movements in France, Spain, Germany, and northern Europe, all widely different with varying delays in time. As the historian Edith Sichel says: "Out of the Italian Renaissance there issued a new-born art; out of the Northern Renaissance there came forth a new-born religion. There came forth also a great school of poetry, and a drama the greatest that the world had seen since the days of Greece. The religion was the offspring of Germany and the poetry that of England."

The real cause of the Renaissance was not the fall of Constantinople, the invention of printing, or the discovery of America, though these were phases in the process; it was, quite simply, money. The birth of a new merchant class gave rise to individualist attitudes in economic affairs which prepared the way for individualism and humanism. The new wealthy class in time became patrons of the arts whereas previously the Church had been the sole patron and controller. Thus the artist became more free to express himself, more respected, and being more well-to-do could afford to ignore the Church and even, in time, the views of his patrons.

It is true that art continued to serve to a considerable extent the purposes of faith, but it was judged from the standpoint of art. Medieval art was meant to elevate and teach man: Renaissance art to delight his senses and enrich his life. From this free and questing spirit acquired from economic individualism came the rise of modern science and technology; here Italy learned much from the Arab scholars who had translated and commented upon the philosophical, medical, and mathematical texts of antiquity, while denying themselves any interest in Greek art and literature. Arabic-Latin versions of Aristotle were in use well into the 16th cent. The Byzantine culture, though it had preserved the Greek tradition and gave supremacy to Plato, had made no move forward. But the Greek scholars who fled to Italy after the fall of Constantinople brought with them an immense cargo of classical manuscripts. The recovery of these Greek masterpieces, their translation into the vernaculars, and the invention of printing, made possible a completer understanding of the Greek spirit. It was the bringing together of the two heritages, Greek science, and Greek literature, that gave birth to a new vision. But it was not only Aristotle and Plato who were being studied but Ovid, Catullus, Horace, Pliny and Lucretius. What interested Renaissance man was the humanism of the Latin writers, their attitude to science, their scepticism.

The period *c.* 1400–1500 is known as the **Early Renaissance.** During this time such painters as Masaccio, Uccello, Piero della Francesca, Botticelli, and Giovanni Bellini were laying the foundations of drawing and painting for all subsequent periods including our own. They concerned themselves with such problems as anatomy, composition, perspective, and representation of space, creating in effect a grammar or textbook of visual expression. The term **High Renaissance** is reserved for a very brief period when a pure, balanced, classical harmony was achieved and artists were in complete control of the techniques learned earlier. The High Renaissance lasted only from *c.* 1500 to 1527 (the date of the sack of Rome), yet that interval included the earlier works of Michelangelo, most of Leonardo's, and all the Roman works of Raphael.

Romantic Movement or Romanticism is the name given not so much to an individual way of thinking but to the gradual but radical transformation of basic human values that occurred in the Western world round about the latter part of the 18th cent. It was a great breakthrough in European consciousness and arose through the writings of certain men living during the half-century or more following, say, 1760. It arose then because both time and place were propitious for the birth of these new ideas. There was a revolution in basic values—in art, morals, politics, religion, etc. The new view was of a world transcending the old one, infinitely larger and more varied.

To understand the Romantic movement it is necessary first to take note of the climate of thought preceding the great change; then to account for its beginning in Germany where it did during the latter part of the 18th century, and finally to appraise the writings of those men whose ideas fermented the new awakening. Briefly, the shift was away from French classicism and from belief in the all-pervasive power of human reason (the Enlightenment) towards the unfettered freedom that the new consciousness was able to engender. What mattered was to live a passionate and vigorous life, to dedicate oneself to an ideal, no matter what the cost (*e.g.,* Byron).

The ideas of the Enlightenment (*e.g.,* Fontenelle, Voltaire, Montesquieu) had been attacked by the Germans Hamann and Herder and by the ideas of the English philosopher Hume, but Kant, Schiller, and Fichte, Goethe's novel *Wilhelm Meister,* and the French Revolution all had profound effects on the aesthetic, moral, social, and political thought of the time. Friedrich Schlegel (1772–1829) said: "There is in man a terrible unsatisfied desire to soar into infinity; a feverish longing to break through the narrow bonds of individuality." Romanticism undermined the notion that in matters of value there are objective criteria which operate between men. Henceforth there was to be a resurgence of the human spirit, deep and profound, that is still going on.

Rosicrucians, an ancient mystical society founded in the 16th cent. by Christian Rosenkreuz which attempted to forge a theoretical link between the great Egyptian religions and the Church of Rome, drawing rituals and philosophy from both camps. The Society did not long survive the death of its founder (he managed to reach the age of 106 incidentally) but has been revived in succeeding centuries by a series of rivalling factions. Perhaps the most famous of these is the Rosicrucian Order (A.M.O.R.C) which has become well-known in the Western world as a result of its heavy advertising in the popular press. Founded by the American H. Spencer Lewis, this offers a simple and good-natured doctrine preaching the Brotherhood of Man, the reincarnation of the soul and the immense latent potential of the human mind. As with many American-based organizations of this kind, the boundary between business and religion is hard to define. It is probably best summed up as a modern secret society which serves an important function in the lives of many people of mystical inclinations.

S

Salvation Army. The religious movement which in 1878 became known by this name arose from the Christian Mission meetings which the Rev. William Booth and his devoted wife had held in the East End of London for the previous thirteen years. Its primary aim was, and still is, to preach the gospel of Jesus Christ to men and women untouched by ordinary religious efforts. The founder devoted his life to the salvation of the submerged classes whose conditions at that time were unspeakably dreadful. Originally his aim had been to convert people and then send them on to the churches, but he soon found that few religious bodies would accept these "low-class" men and women. So it was that social work became part of their effort. Practical help like the provision of soup kitchens, accompanied spiritual ministration. Soon, in the interests of more effective "warfare" against social evils, a military form of organization, with uniforms, brass bands, and religious songs, was introduced. Its magazine *The War Cry* gave as its aim "to carry the Blood of Christ and the Fire of the Holy Ghost into every part of the world.'

General Booth saw with blinding clarity that conversion must be accompanied by an improvement of external conditions. Various books had earlier described the terrible conditions of the slums, but in 1890 he produced a monumental survey entitled *In Darkest England and The Way Out.* From that time forward the Army was accepted and its facilities made use of by the authorities. Today the Army's spiritual and social activities have spread to countries all over the world; every one, no matter what class, color, or creed he belongs to is a "brother for whom Christ died."

Sceptics. From Thales of Miletus (*c.* 624–565 B.C.) to the Stoics in the 4th cent. B.C. philosophers had been trying to explain the nature of the universe; each one produced a different theory and each could, apparently, prove that he was right. This diversity of views convinced the Sceptic school founded by Pyrrho (*c.* 360–270 B.C.) that man is unable to know the real nature of the world or how it came into being. In place of a futile search for what must be forever unknowable, the Sceptics recommended that men should be practical, follow custom, and accept the evidence of their senses.

Schoolmen. From the time of Augustine to the middle of the 9th cent. philosophy, like science, was dead or merely a repetition of what had gone before. But about that time there arose a new interest in the subject, although (since by then Western Europe was entirely under the authority of the Catholic Church) the main form it took was an attempt to justify Church teaching in the light of Greek philosophy. Those who made this attempt to reconcile Christian beliefs with the best in Plato and Aristotle were known as "schoolmen" and the philosophies which they developed were known as "scholasticism." Among the most famous schoolmen must be counted John Scotus Erigena (*c.* 800 –*c.* 877), born in Ireland and probably the earliest; St. Anselm, archbishop of Canterbury (1033–1109); the great Peter Abelard whose school was in Paris (1079–1142); Bernard of Chartres, his contemporary; and the best-known of all, St. Thomas Aquinas of Naples (1225–74), who was given the name of the "Angelic Doctor."

The philosophies of these men are discussed under various headings **(God and Man, Determinism and Free Will),** but being severely limited by the Church their doctrines differed from each other much less than those of later philosophical schools. However, one of the great arguments was between the orthodox Realists *(q.v.)* and the Nominalists *(q.v.)* and a second was between the Thomists (or followers of St. Thomas Aquinas) and the Scotists (followers of John Duns Scotus—not to be confused with John Scotus Erigena). The two latter schools were known as the Ancients, while the followers of William of Occam, the Nominalist, were known as the Terminalists. All became reconciled in 1482 in face of the threat from humanism of which the great exponent was Erasmus of Rotterdam (1466–1536).

Scientology, an unusual quasi-philosophical system started by the American science-fiction writer L. Ron Hubbard, which claims to be able to effect dramatic improvement in the mental and physical well-being of its adherents. Originally developed in the United States as "Dianetics, the modern science of mental health," it was hailed in Hubbard's first book to be "a milestone for Man comparable to his discovery of fire and superior to his inventions of the wheel and the arch." Such extravagant statements exemplify the literature of the movement, which in the late 1950s began to expand in England when its founder came to live in East Grinstead. Followers of Dianetics and Scientology advance within the cult through a series of levels or grades, most reached by undertaking courses of training and tuition, payment for which may amount to hundreds and, in total, even thousands of pounds. These courses consist largely of mental exercises known as "processing" and "auditing" (now called "pastoral counselling" since more emphasis has recently been laid on the religious aspect). One of the principal goals of a Scientologist is the attainment of the state known as "Clear" (roughly speaking, one "cleared" of certain mental and physical handicaps) when it is believed he (she) will be a literally superior being, equipped with a higher intelligence and a greater command over the pattern of his (her) own life. The Scientologists' claims that their movement is a genuine religion have generally been met with resistance from establishment bodies. In 1967 the Home Office announced that its centers would no longer be recognized as educational establishments and foreigners arriving for its courses would not be granted student status. In 1980 the Home Office lifted this ban. The international headquarters have been moved from East Grinstead to Los Angeles.

Shakers, members of a revivalist group, styled by themselves "The United Society of Believers in Christ's Second Appearing," who seceded from Quakerism in 1747 though adhering to many of the Quaker tenets. The community was joined in 1758 by Ann Lee, a young convert from Manchester, who had "revelations" that she was the female Christ; "Mother Ann" was accepted as their leader. Under the influence of her prophetic visions she set out with nine followers for "Immanuel's land" in America and the community settled near Albany, capital of New York state. They were known as the "Shakers" in ridicule because they were given to involuntary movements in moments of religious ecstasy. Central to their faith was the belief in the dual role of God through the male and female Christ: the male principle came to earth in Jesus; the female principle, in "Mother Ann." The sexes were equal and women preached as often as men at their meetings which sometimes included sacred dances—nevertheless the two sexes, even in dancing, kept apart. Their communistic way of living brought them economic prosperity, the Shakers becoming known as good agriculturists and craftsmen, noted for their furniture and textiles. After 1860, however, the movement began to decline and few, if any, are active today.

Shamans, the medicine men found in all primitive societies who used their magical arts to work cures, and protect the group from evil influences. The *shaman* was a man apart and wore special garments to show his authority. Shamanism with its magical practices, incantations, trances, exhausting dances, and self-torture is practiced even today by tribes that have survived in a primitive state of culture.

Shiites or Shia, a heretical Moslem sect in Persia, opposed by the orthodox Sunnites. The dispute, which came almost immediately after the death of the Prophet and led to bitter feuding, had little to do with matters of doctrine as such but with the succession. After Mohammed's death, there were three possible claimants: Ali, the husband of his daughter Fatima, and two others, one of whom gave up his claim in favor of the other, Omar. The orthodox selected Omar, who was shortly assassinated, and the same happened to his successor as Ali was passed over again. The Shiites are those who maintain that Ali was the true vicar of the Prophet, and that the three orthodox predecessors were usurpers.

Sikhism. The Sikh community of the Punjab, which has played a significant part in the history of modern India, came into being during a period of religious revival in India in the 15th and 16th cent. It was originally founded as a religious sect by Guru (teacher) Nanak (1469–1538) who emphasized the fundamental truth of all religions, and whose mission was to put an end to religious conflict. He condemned the formalism both of Hinduism and Islam, preaching the gospel of universal toleration, and the unity of the Godhead, whether He be called Allah, Vishnu, or God. His ideas were welcomed by the great Mogul Emperor Akbar (1542–1605). Thus a succession of Gurus were able to live in peace after Nanak's death; they established the great Sikh center at Amritsar, compiled the sacred writings known as the *Adi Granth,* and improved their organization as a sect. But the peace did not last long, for an emperor arose who was a fanatical Moslem, in face of whom the last Guru, Govind Singh (1666–1708), whose father was put to death for refusal to embrace Islam, had to make himself a warrior and instil into the Sikhs a more aggressive spirit. A number of ceremonies were instituted by Govind Singh; admission to the fraternity was by special rite; caste distinctions were abolished; hair was worn long; the word singh, meaning lion, was added to the original name. They were able to organize themselves into 12 *misls* or confederacies but divisions appeared with the disappearance of a common enemy and it was not until the rise of Ranjit Singh (1780–1839) that a single powerful Sikh kingdom was established, its influence only being checked by the English, with whom a treaty of friendship was made. After the death of Ranjit Singh two Anglo-Sikh wars followed, in 1845–46, and 1848–49, which resulted in British annexation of the Punjab and the end of Sikh independence. In the two world wars the Sikhs proved among the most loyal of Britain's Indian subjects. The partitioning of the continent of India in 1947 into two states, one predominantly Hindu and the other predominantly Moslem, presented a considerable problem in the Punjab, which was divided in such a way as to leave 2 million Sikhs in Pakistan, and a considerable number of Moslems in the Indian Punjab. Although numbering less than 2 per cent. of the population (*c.* 8 million) the Sikhs are a continuing factor in Indian political life. In 1966 the Punjab was divided on a linguistic basis—Punjabi-speaking Punjab and Hindi-speaking Hariana.

Spiritualism is a religion which requires to be distinguished from psychical research *(q.v.)* which is a scientific attempt carried on by both believers and non-believers to investigate psychic phenomena including those not necessarily connected with "spirits"—*e.g.,* telepathy or clairvoyance and precognition. As a religion (although for that matter the whole of history is filled with attempts to get in touch with the "spirit world") Spiritualism begins with the American Andrew Jackson Davis who in 1847 published *Nature's Divine Revelations,* a book which is still widely read. In this Davis states that on the death of the physical body, the human spirit remains alive and moves on to one or another of a considerable range of worlds or "spheres" where it commences yet another stage of existence. Since the spirit has not died, but exists with full (and possibly even expanded) consciousness, there should be no reason, Davis argues, why it should not make its presence known to the beings it has temporarily left behind on earth. In 1847, the year of the publication of Davis's book, two young girls, Margaret and Kate Fox, living in a farmhouse at Hydesville, New York, began apparently to act as unwitting mediums for attempts at such between-worlds communication. The girls were the focus for strange rappings and bangs which it was alleged defied normal explanation and which spelt out, in the form of a simple alphabetical code, messages from the spirits of "the dead." The Fox sisters were later to confess that they had produced the raps by trickery, but by that time the fashion had spread across the world and before long "mediums" in all lands were issuing spirit communications (often in much more spectacular form). In the late 19th cent. Spiritualism went into a phase of great expansion and for various reasons attracted the attention of many scientists. Among these were Sir William Crookes, Sir Oliver Lodge, Professor Charles Richet, Alfred Russell Wallace, to say nothing of the brilliant and shrewd creator of Sherlock Holmes, Sir Arthur Conan Doyle. Today many people find it astonishing that people of such brilliance should find the phenomena of the séance room of more than passing interest, but the commitment of the Victorian scientists is understandable if we realize that Spiritualists, after all, claim to do no more than demonstrate as fact what all Christians are called on to believe—that the human personality survives bodily death. Furthermore, at the time of the late 19th cent. peak of Spiritualism, much less was known about human psychology and about the great limitations of sensory perception in typical séance conditions, when lights are dimmed or extinguished and an emotionally charged atmosphere generated. Today the most striking phenomena of the séance room—the alleged materialization of spirit people and the production of such half-spiritual, half-physical substances as ectoplasm—are rarely if ever produced at Spiritualist meetings. Some say that the most probable explanation for this is that too many fraudulent mediums have been caught out and publicly exposed for the profession to be worth the risks. The movement today, which still has a large and often articulate following, now concentrates on the less controversial areas of "mental mediumship," clairvoyance and the like, or on the very widespread practice of "spirit healing." Where people are not deliberately deluded by bogus mediums acting for monetary reward (a practice which largely died out with the "death" of ectoplasm) Spiritualism probably has an important role to play in the life of many people whose happiness has been removed by the death of a much loved relative or spouse. It does not deserve the violent attacks that are often made on it by orthodox clergy who allege that Spiritualists are communicating not with the souls of the departed but with the devil or his emissaries.

Stoics, the followers of Zeno, a Greek philosopher in the 4th century B.C., who received their name from the fact that they were taught in the Stoa Poikile or Painted Porch of Athens. They believed that since the world is the creation of divine wisdom and is governed by divine law, it is man's duty to accept his fate. Zeno conceived virtue to be the highest good and condemned the passions. (*See* **God and Man, Determinism and Free Will** for a more detailed account of their beliefs.)

Swedenborgianism. The Church of the New Jerusalem, based on the writings of Emanuel Swedenborg (1688–1772), was founded by his followers eleven years after his death. The New Church is regarded by its members not as a sect but as a new dispensation bearing the same relationship to Christianity as Christianity does to Judaism.

Synchronicity, an attempt by the psychologist, Carl Gustav Jung, to explain the apparently significant relationship between certain events in the physical universe which seem to have no obvious "causal" link. This rather involved concept is easily understood if one realizes that almost all scientific and philosophical beliefs are based on the notion that the continuous process of change which is taking place in ourselves and in the universe around us is dependent upon a principle known as causality. We can express this another way by saying that an object moves because it has been pushed or pulled by another. We see because light strikes the retina and signals pass up the nervous system to the brain. A stone falls to the ground because the earth's gravity is pulling it towards its center, etc., etc. For all practical purposes every event can be looked upon as being "caused" by some other prior event and this is obviously one of the most important principles of the operation of the universe. Jung, however, felt that there is a sufficiently large body of evidence to suggest that events may be linked in a significant (*i.e.*, nonchance) way without there being any true causal relationship between them. The classic example he held to be the supposed predictive power of astrology by which there appears to be a relationship between the stellar configurations and the personality and life-pattern of individuals on earth. Jung was scientist enough to realize that there could be no causal connection between the aspect of the stars and the lives of people billions of miles from them, yet felt the evidence for astrology was strong enough to demand an alternative noncausal explanation. The trouble with synchronicity, which has not made much impact on the world of physics or of psychology, is that it is not really an explanation at all but merely a convenient word to describe some puzzling correspondences. The real question, of course, is whether there really are events occurring which are significantly but not *causally* linked, and most scientists today would hold that there were probably not. Still it was typical of the bold and imaginative mind of Jung to tackle head-on one of the principal mysteries of existence and come up with a hypothesis to attempt to meet it.

Syndicalism, a form of socialist doctrine which aims at the ownership and control of all industries by the workers, contrasted with the more conventional type of socialism which advocates ownership and control by the state. Since syndicalists have preferred to improve the conditions of the workers by direct action, *e.g.,* strikes and working to rule, rather than through the usual parliamentary procedures, they have been closely related to anarchists *(q.v.)* and are sometimes described as anarcho-syndicalists. Under syndicalism there would be no state; for the state would be replaced by a federation of units based on functional economic organization rather than on geographical representation. The movement had bodies in the United Kingdom, where guild socialism *(q.v.)* was strongly influenced by its doctrines, in France, Germany, Italy, Spain, Argentina, and Mexico, but these gradually declined after the first world war losing many members to the communists. Fascism *(q.v.)* was also strongly influenced by the revolutionary syndicalism of Georges Sorel in making use of his concept of the "myth of the general strike" as an emotional image or ideal goal to spur on the workers; with Mussolini the "myth" became that of the state. Mussolini was also influenced by Sorel's doctrine of violence and the justification of force. Syndicalism had a certain influence in the Labour Party in its early days, but was crushed by men like Ernest Bevin who began to fear that by involving the workers in direct responsibility for their industries, it would put them at a disadvantage when bargaining for wages.

T

Telepathy and Clairvoyance. Telepathy is the alleged communication between one mind and another other than through the ordinary sense channels. Clairvoyance is the supposed faculty of "seeing" objects or events which, by reason of space and time or other causes, are not discernible through the ordinary sense of vision. Such claims have been made from time immemorial but it was not until this century that the phenomena were investigated scientifically. The first studies were undertaken by the Society for Psychical Research, which was founded in 1882 with Professor Henry Sidgwick as its first president. Since then it has carried out a scholarly programme of research without—in accordance with its constitution—coming to any corporate conclusions. In America the center of this research was the Parapsychology Laboratory at Duke University (*see* **Parapsychology**) where at one time it was claimed clear scientific evidence for extra-sensory perception (ESP) had been obtained. These claims have been treated with great reservation by the majority of scientists but despite the belief that the study of ESP was going into eclipse, there remains a small but measurable residue of interest in scientific research in this area. It would be odd if some scientists were not interested in ESP because of the enormous weight of anecdotal evidence which has built up over centuries to support it. The weakness of the scientific as opposed to the casual evidence is however exemplified by the failure of ESP researchers to produce a reliable "repeatable" experiment.

Theism. *See* **God and Man.**

Theosophy (Sanskrit *Brahma Vidya* = divine wisdom), a system of thought that draws on the mystical teachings of those who assert the spiritual nature of the universe, and the divine nature of man. It insists that man is capable of intuitive insight into the nature of God. The way to wisdom, or self-knowledge, is through the practice of **Yoga** *(q.v.).* Theosophy has close connections with Indian thought through Vedic, Buddhist, and Brahmanist literature. The modern Theosophical Society was founded by Mme H. P. Blavatsky and others in 1875, and popularized by Mrs. Annie Besant.

Transcendental Meditation, popularized in the West by the Maharishi Mahesh Yogi, who achieved sensational worldwide publicity by his "conversion" of the Beatles a few years ago. This is a simple meditational system which it is claimed is an aid to relaxation and the reduction of psychological and physical stress. It is reported that the technique can be taught in under five minutes provided that someone trained by the Maharishi is the teacher. The pupil or would-be meditator is given a mantra—a meaningless word which acts as a focal point for the imagination—letting his thoughts flow freely while sitting in a comfortable position. Extraordinary claims are made on behalf of the system. As with most cults, religious and occult systems, there is an initial psychological benefit to anyone who becomes deeply involved. Nevertheless, apart from this simple "participation-effect", there is some evidence that the body's autonomic functions (heart rate, respiratory cycle, brain waves, etc.) can be modified by certain individuals including yogis. Whether it is ultimately beneficial to be able to modify these autonomic functions or not is another matter. The latest evidence from laboratory studies in fact shows that subjects in the most relaxed phase of TM are in fact in a (quite normal) stage of light sleep. The TM movement in Britain is based at Mentmore Towers in Buckinghamshire.

Transmigration of Souls. *See* **Immortality.**

Transubstantiation, the conversion in the Eucharist of the bread and wine into the body and blood of Christ—a doctrine of the Roman Catholic Church.

Trotskyism, a form of communism supporting the views of Leon Trotsky, the assumed name of Lev Bronstein (1879–1940) who, in 1924, was ousted from power by Stalin and later exiled and assassinated in Mexico. Trotsky held that excessive Russian nationalism was incompatible with genuine international communism and that Stalin was concentrating on the economic development of the Soviet Union to an extent which could only lead to a bureaucratic state with a purely nationalist outlook. After the Hungarian uprising in 1956, which was ruthlessly suppressed by the Soviet Armed Forces, a wave of resignations from Western Communist parties took place, many of the dissidents joining the Trotskyist movement.

U

Ufology, cultish interest in the study of strange and unexplained aerial phenomena (unidentified flying objects, hence UFOs). *See* **Flying Saucers.**

Unitarianism has no special doctrines, although clearly, as the name indicates, belief is in the single personality of God, *i.e.,* anti-trinitarian. This general statement, however, can be interpreted with varying degrees of subtlety. Thus Unitarian belief may range from a sort of Arianism which accepts that, although Christ was not of divine nature, divine powers had been delegated to him by the Father, to the simple belief that Christ was a man like anyone else, and his goodness was of the same nature as that of many other great and good men. Indeed, today many Unitarians deny belief in a personal God and interpret their religion in purely moral terms, putting their faith in the value of love and the brotherhood of man. The Toleration Act (1689) excluded Unitarians but from 1813 they were legally tolerated in England. Nevertheless attempts were made to turn them out of their chapels on the ground that the preachers did not hold the views of the original founders of the endowments. But this ended with the Dissenting Chapels Act of 1845. In America no such difficulties existed, and in the Boston of the 19th cent. many of the great literary figures were openly Unitarian in both belief and name: *e.g.,* Emerson, Longfellow, Lowell, and Oliver Wendell Holmes.

Utilitarianism, a school of moral philosophy of which the main proponents were J. S. Mill (1806–73) and Jeremy Bentham (1748–1832). Bentham based his ethical theory upon the utilitarian principle that the greatest happiness of the greatest number is the criterion of morality. What is good is pleasure or happiness; what is bad is pain. If we act on this basis of self-interest (pursuing what we believe to be our own happiness), then what we do will automatically be for the general good. The serious failing of this thesis is (1) that it makes no distinction between the quality of one pleasure and another, and (2) that Bentham failed to see that the law might not be framed and administered by men as benevolent as himself. J. S. Mill accepted Bentham's position in general but seeing its failings emphasized (1) that self-interest was an inadequate basis for utilitarianism and suggested that we should take as the real criterion of good the social consequences of the act; (2) that some pleasures rank higher than others and held that those of the intellect are superior to those of the senses. Not only is the social factor emphasized, but emphasis is also placed on the nature of the act.

Utopias. The name "utopia" is taken from a Greek word meaning "nowhere" and was first used in 1516 by Sir Thomas More (1478–1535) as the title of his book referring to a mythical island in the south Pacific where he sited his ideal society. Since then it has been used of any ideal or fanciful society, and here a few will be mentioned. (The reader may recall that Samuel Butler's 19th century novel, describing an imaginary society in New Zealand where criminals were treated and the sick punished, was entitled *Erewhon* which is the word "nowhere" in reverse.) It should be noted that not all utopias were entirely fanciful—*e.g.,* Robert Owen's and Françis Fourier's beliefs, although found to be impractical, were, in fact, tried out.

Sir Thomas More. More wrote at a time when the rise of the wool-growing trade had resulted in farming land being turned over to pasture and there was a great wave of unemployment and a rise in crime among the dispossessed. More began to think in terms of the medieval ideal of small co-operative communities in which class interests and personal gain played a decreasing part, a society which would have the welfare of the people at heart both from the physical and intellectual points of view. His utopia was one in which there was no private property, because the desire for acquisition and private possessions lay at the root of human misery. There was, therefore, only common ownership of land and resources. Each class of worker was equipped to carry out its proper function in the economic scheme and each was fairly rewarded for its share in production so that there was neither wealth nor poverty to inspire conflict. Nobody was allowed to idle, until the time came for him to retire when he became free to enjoy whatever cultural pleasures he wished, but since the system was devoid of the waste associated with competition, the working day would be only six hours. There was to be compulsory schooling and free medical care for everybody, full religious toleration, complete equality of the sexes, and a modern system of dealing with crime which was free from vindictiveness and cruelty. Government was to be simple and direct by democratically elected officials whose powers would be strictly limited and the public expenditure kept under close scrutiny. It will be seen that More was far in advance of his age, and to most democratically minded people in advance of an earlier utopia, Plato's *Republic,* which is described under the heading of Education.

James Harrington. James Harrington published his book *The Commonwealth of Oceana* in 1656 and offered it to Oliver Cromwell for his consideration but without tangible results. Better than any other man of his time Harrington understood the nature of the economic revolution which was then taking place, and, like More, saw the private ownership of land as the main cause of conflict. He put forward the theory that the control of property, particularly in the shape of land, determines the character of the political structure of the state; if property were universally distributed among the people the sentiment for its protection would naturally result in a republican form of government. The Commonwealth of Oceana was a society "of laws and not of men"—*i.e.,* it was to be legally based and structured so as to be independent of the good or ill will of any individuals controlling it. Thus there must be a written constitution, a two-house legislature, frequent elections with a secret ballot, and separation of powers between legislature and executive—all today familiar features of parliamentary democracy, but unique in his time.

Saint-Simon. The utopias of the late 18th and 19th century come, of course, into the period of the Industrial Revolution and of laissez-faire capitalism. Individual enterprise and complete freedom of competition formed the outlook of the ruling class. Naturally the utopias of this period tended to have a strongly socialist tinge since such theories are obviously produced by those who are not satisfied with existing conditions. Saint-Simon's *New Christianity* (1825) is one such, and by many, Claude Henri, Comte de Saint-Simon (1760–1825) is regarded as the founder of French socialism. His book urged a dedication of society to the principle of human brotherhood and a community which would be led by men of science motivated by wholly spiritual aims. Production property was to be nationalized (or "socialized" as he describes the process) and employed to serve the public good rather than private gain; the worker was to produce according to his capacity and to be rewarded on the basis of individual merit; the principle of inheritance was to be abolished since it denied the principle of reward for accomplishment on which the society was to be founded. Saint-Simon's proposals were not directed towards the poorer classes alone, but to the conscience and intellect of all. He was deeply impressed with the productive power of the new machines and his scheme was, first and foremost, intended as a method of directing that power to the betterment of humanity as a whole.

Fourier. François Marie Charles Fourier (1772–1837), although by conviction a philosophical anarchist who held that human beings are naturally good if allowed to follow their natural desires, was the originator of what, on the face of it, one would suppose to be the most regimented of the utopias. It consisted of a system of "phalanxes" or cooperative communities each composed of a group of workers and technicians assured of a minimum income and sharing the surplus on an equitable basis. Agriculture was to be the chief occupation of each phalanx and industrial employment planned and so carefully assigned that work would become pleasant and creative rather than burdensome. One of his ideas was that necessary work should receive the highest pay, useful work the next, and pleasant work the least pay. The land was to be scientifically cultivated and natural resources carefully conserved. Most of the members' property was to be privately owned, but the ownership of each phalanx was to be widely diffused among members by the sale of shares. Such "parasitic and unproductive" occupations as stockbroker, soldier, economist, middleman and philosopher would be eliminated and the education of children carried out along vocational lines to train them for their future employment.

The strange thing was that Fourier's suggestions appealed to many in both Europe and the United States and such men (admittedly no economic or technical experts) as Emerson, Thoreau, James Russell Lowell, and Nathaniel Hawthorne strongly supported them. An American Fourier colony known as Brook Farm was established and carried on for eight years when it was dissolved after a serious fire had destroyed most of its property.

Robert Owen. Robert Owen (1771–1858), a wealthy textile manufacturer and philanthropist, established communities founded on a kind of utopian socialism in Lanarkshire, Hampshire, and in America. Of his New Lanark community an American observer wrote: "There is not, I apprehend, to be found in any part of the world, a manufacturing community in which so much order, good government, tranquillity, and rational happiness prevail." The workers in Lanark were given better housing and education for their children, and it was administered as a cooperative self-supporting community in Scotland. Later in life Owen returned to sponsoring legislation that would remove some of the worst evils of industrial life in those days: reduction of the working day to twelve hours, prohibition of labor for children under the age of ten, public schools for elementary education, and so on. But he lived to see few of his reforms adopted. He also promoted the creation of cooperative societies, the formation of trade unions, labor banks, and exchanges, the workers' educational movement, and even an Anglo-American federation. There can be no doubt that, if he saw little result himself, he left the imprint of his convictions to benefit future communities who may not even know his name.

V

Vitalism, the philosophical doctrine that the behavior of the living organism is, at least in part, due to a vital principle which cannot possibly be explained wholly in terms of physics and chemistry. This belief was held by the rationalist thinker C. E. M. Joad (1891–1953) and is implicit in Henri Bergson's (1859–1941) theory of creative evolution. It was maintained by Bergson that evolution, like the work of an artist, is creative and therefore unpredictable; that a vague need exists beforehand within the animal or plant before the means of satisfying the need develops. Thus we might assume that sightless animals developed the need to become aware of objects before they were in physical contact with them and that this ultimately led to the origins of organs of sight. Earlier this century a form of vitalism described as "emergent evolution" was put forward. This theory maintains that when two or more simple entities come together there may arise a new property which none of them previously possessed. Today biologists would say that it is the *arrangement* of atoms that counts, different arrangements exhibiting different properties, and that biological organization is an essentially dynamic affair, involving the lapse of time.

W

Witchcraft. There are various interpretations and definitions of witchcraft from that of Pennethorne Hughes who states that "witchcraft, as it emerges into European history and literature, represents the old paleolithic fertility cult, plus the magical idea, plus various parodies of contemporary religions" to that of the fanatical Father Montague Summers who says that Spiritualism and witchcraft are the same thing. A leading authority on witchcraft, however, the late Dr. Margaret Murray, distinguishes between Operative Witchcraft (which is really Magic *(q.v.)* and Ritual Witchcraft which, she says, "embraces the religious beliefs and ritual of the people known in late medieval times as 'witches.' " That there were such people we know from history and we know, too, that many of them—the great majority of them women—were tortured or executed or both. Many innocent people perished, especially after the promulgation of the bull *Summis desiderantes* by Pope Innocent VIII in 1484. Himself "a man of scandalous life," according to a Catholic historian, he wrote to "his dear sons," the German professors of theology, Johann Sprenger and Heinrich Kraemer, "witches are hindering men from performing the sexual act and women from conceiving . . ." and delegated them as Inquisitors "of these heretical pravities." In 1494 they codified in the *Malleus Maleficarum* (Hammer of Witches) the ecclesiastical rules for detecting acts of witchcraft. Dr. Murray points out that there have ordinarily been two theories about witchcraft: (1) that there were such things as witches, that they possessed supernatural powers and that the evidence given at their trials was substantially correct; (2) that the witches were simply poor silly creatures who either deluded themselves into believing that they had certain powers or, more frequently, were tortured into admitting things that they did not do. She herself accepts a third theory: that there were such beings as witches, that they really did what they admitted to doing, but that they did not possess supernatural powers. They were in fact believers in the old religion of pre-Christian times and the Church took centuries to root them out. That there existed "covens" of witches who carried out peculiar rites Dr. Murray has no doubt whatever. The first to show that witchcraft was a superstition and that the majority of so-called witches were people suffering from mental illness was the physician Johann Weyer of Cleves (1515–88). His views were denounced by the Catholic Church. Few people realize how deeply the notion of witchcraft is implanted in our minds and how seriously its power is still taken. For example, the Witchcraft Act was not repealed in England until the 1950s. Furthermore, as recently as 1944, when the allied armies were invading Europe, the Spiritualist medium Mrs. Helen Duncan was charged with witchcraft and actually sent to prison—a prosecution which brought forth caustic comments from the then prime minister, Winston Churchill. *See also* **Demonism.**

Y

Yoga, a Hindu discipline which teaches a technique for freeing the mind from attachment to the senses, so that once freed the soul may become fused with the universal spirit (*atman* or Brahman), which is its natural goal. This is the sole function of the psychological and physical exercises which the Yogi undertakes, although few ever reach the final stage of *Samadhi* or union with Brahman which is said to take place in eight levels of attainment. These are: (1) *Yama,* which involves the extinction of desire and egotism and their replacement by charity and unselfishness; (2) *Niyama,* during which certain rules of conduct must be adopted, such as cleanliness, the pursuit of devotional studies, and the carrying out of rituals of purification; (3) *Asana,* or the attainment of correct posture and the reduction to a minimum of all bodily movement (the usual posture of the concentrating Yogi is the "lotus position" familiar from pictures); (4) *Pranayama,* the right control of the life-force or breath in which there are two stages at which the practitioner hopes to arrive, the first being complete absorption in the act of breathing which empties the mind of any other thought, the second being the ability almost to cease to breathe which allegedly enables him to achieve marvellous feats of endurance; (5) *Pratyahara* or abstraction which means the mind's complete withdrawal from the world of sense; (6) *Dharana* in which an attempt is made to think of one thing only which finally becomes a repetition of the sacred syllable OM; (7) *dhyana,* meditation, which finally leads to (8) *Samadhi* the trance state which is a sign of the complete unity of soul with reality.

Yoga is very old, and when the sage Patanjali (*c.* 300 B.C.) composed the book containing these instructions, the *Yoga Sutras,* he was probably collecting from many ancient traditions. Some of the claims made by Yogis seem, to the Western mind, frankly incredible; but in the West and especially in recent years Yoga methods have been used at the lower levels in order to gain improved self-control, better posture, and improved health. Whether it achieves these ends is another matter, but the genuine Yogi regards this as a perversion of the nature and purpose of the discipline.

Z

Zen Buddhism, a Buddhist sect which is believed to have arisen in 6th cent. China but has flourished chiefly in Japan; for some reason it has of recent years begun to attract attention in the West thanks to the voluminous writings of Dr. D. T. Suzuki and the less numerous but doubtless much-read books of Mr. Christmas Humphreys. But the fact that these writings exist does not explain their being read, nor why of all possible Eastern sects this particular one should be chosen in our times. What is Zen's attraction and why should anyone take the trouble to read about something (the word "something" is used for reasons that will become evident) that is not a religion, has no doctrine, knows no God and no afterlife, no good and no evil, and possesses no scriptures but has to be taught by parables which seem to be purposely meaningless? One of the heroes of Zen is the fierce-looking Indian monk Boddhidharma (fl. *c.* 516–34) who brought Buddhism to China, of whom it is recounted that when the Emperor asked him how much merit he had acquired by supporting the new creed, the monk shouted at him: "None whatever!" The emperor then wished to know what was the sacred doctrine of the creed and again the monk shouted: "It is empty—there is nothing sacred!" Dr. Suzuki, having affirmed that there is no God in Zen, goes on to state that this does not mean that Zen denies the existence of God because "neither denial nor affirmation concerns Zen." The most concrete statement he is prepared to make is that the basic idea of Zen is to come in touch with the inner workings of our being, and to do this in the most direct way possible without resorting to anything external or superadded. Therefore anything that has the semblance of an external authority is rejected by Zen. Absolute faith is placed in a man's own inner being. Apparently the intention is that, so far from indulging in inward meditations or such practices as the Yogi uses, the student must learn to act spontaneously, without thinking, and without self-consciousness or hesitation. This is the main purpose of the *koan*, the logically insoluble riddle which the pupil must try to solve. One such is the question put by master to pupil: "A girl is walking down the street, is she the younger or the older sister?" The correct answer, it seems, is to say nothing but put on a mincing gait, to *become* the girl, thus showing that what matters is the experience of being and not its verbal description. Another *koan:* "What is the Buddha?" "Three pounds of flax" is attributed to T'ungshan in the 9th cent. and a later authority's comment is that "none can excel it as regards its irrationality which cuts off all passages to speculation." Zen, in effect, teaches the uselessness of trying to use words to discuss the Absolute.

Zen came to Japan in the 13th cent., more than five centuries after Confucianism or the orthodox forms of Buddhism, and immediately gained acceptance while becoming typically Japanese in the process. One of the reasons why it appealed must have been that its spontaneity and insistence on action without thought, its emphasis on the uselessness of mere words, and such categories as logical opposites, had an inevitable attraction for a people given to seriousness, formality, and logic to a degree which was almost stifling. Zen must have been to the Japanese what nonsense rhymes and nonsense books, like those of Edward Lear and Lewis Carroll, were to the English intellectuals. Lear's limericks, like some of the *koans,* end up with a line which, just at the time when one expects a point to be made, has no particular point at all, and *Alice in Wonderland* is the perfect example of a world, not without logic, but with a crazy logic of its own which has no relationship with that of everyday life. Therefore Zen began to impregnate every aspect of life in Japan, and one of the results of its emphasis on spontaneous action rather than reason was its acceptance by the Samurai, the ferocious warrior class, in such activities as swordsmanship, archery, Japanese wrestling, and later Judo and the Kamikaze dive-bombers. But much of Japanese art, especially landscape gardening and flower-arrangement, was influenced similarly, and Zen is even used in Japanese psychiatry. The very strict life of the Zen monks is based largely on doing things, learning through experience; the periods of meditation in the Zendo hall are punctuated by sharp slaps on the face administered by the abbot to those who are unsatisfactory pupils. Dr. Suzuki denies that Zen is nihilistic, but it is probably its appearance of nihilism and its appeal to the irrational and spontaneous which attracts the Western world at a time when to many the world seems without meaning and life over-regimented. However, it has influenced such various aspects of Western life as philosophy (Heidegger), psychiatry (Erich Fromm and Hubert Benoit), writing (Aldous Huxley), and painting (Die Zen Gruppe in Germany).

Zionism, a belief in the need to establish an autonomous Jewish home in Palestine which, in its modern form, began with Theodor Herzl (1860–1904), a Hungarian journalist working in Vienna. Although Herzl was a more or less assimilated Jew, he was forced by the Dreyfus case and the pogroms in Eastern Europe to conclude that there was no real safety for the Jewish people until they had a state of their own. The Jews, of course, had always in a religious sense thought of Palestine as a spiritual homeland and prayed "next year in Jerusalem," but the religious had thought of this in a philosophical way as affirming old loyalties, not as recommending the formation of an actual state. Therefore Herzl was opposed both by many of the religious Jews and, at the other extreme, by those who felt themselves to be assimilated and in many cases without religious faith. Even after the Balfour Declaration of 1917, there was not a considerable flow of Jews to Palestine, which at that time was populated mainly by Arabs. But the persecutions of Hitler changed all this and, after bitter struggles, the Jewish state was proclaimed in 1948. Today Zionism is supported by the vast majority of the Jewish communities everywhere (although strongly disapproved of in the Soviet Union as "Western imperialism") and Zionism is now an active international force concerned with protecting the welfare and extending the influence of Israel.

Zoroastrianism, at one time one of the great world religions, competing in the 2nd cent. A.D. on almost equal terms from its Persian home with Hellenism and the Roman Imperial Government. Under the Achaemenidae (*c.* 550–330 B.C.) Zoroastrianism was the state religion of Persia. Alexander's conquest in 331 B.C. brought disruption but the religion flourished again under the Sassanian dynasty (A.D. *c.* 226–640). With the advance of the Mohammedan Arabs in the 7th cent. Zoroastrianism finally gave way to Islam. A number of devotees fled to India there to become the Parsees. In Persia itself a few scattered societies remain.

The name Zoroaster is the Greek rendering of Zarathustra, the prophet who came to purify the ancient religion of Persia. It is thought that he lived at the beginning of the 6th cent. B.C. He never claimed for himself divine powers but was given them by his followers. The basis of Zoroastrianism is the age-long war between good and evil, Ahura Mazda heading the good spirits and Ahriman the evil ones. Morality is very important since by doing right the worshipper is supporting Ahura Mazda against Ahriman, and the evil-doers will be punished in the last days when Ahura Mazda wins his inevitable victory.

The sacred book of this religion is the *Avesta.* If Zoroastrianism has little authority today, it had a very considerable influence in the past. Its doctrines penetrated into Judaism *(q.v.)* and, through Gnosticism, Christianity. The worship of Mithra by the Romans was an impure version of Zoroastrianism. Manichaeism *(q.v.)* was a Zoroastrian heresy and the Albigensianism of medieval times was the last relic of a belief which had impressed itself deeply in the minds of men.

World Geography

Explorations and Discoveries

(All years are A.D. unless B.C. is specified.)

Country or place	Event	Explorer or discoverer	Date
AFRICA			
Sierra Leone	Visited	Hanno, Carthaginian seaman	c. 520 B.C.
Congo River	Mouth discovered	Diogo Cão, Portuguese	c. 1484
Cape of Good Hope	Rounded	Bartolomeu Diaz, Portuguese	1488
Gambia River	Explored	Mungo Park, Scottish explorer	1795
Sahara	Crossed	Dixon Denham and Hugh Clapperton, English explorers	1822–23
Zambezi River	Discovered	David Livingstone, Scottish explorer	1851
Sudan	Explored	Heinrich Barth, German explorer	1852–55
Victoria Falls	Discovered	Livingstone	1855
Lake Tanganyika	Discovered	Richard Burton and John Speke, British explorers	1858
Congo River	Traced	Sir Henry M. Stanley, British explorer	1877
ASIA			
Punjab (India)	Visited	Alexander the Great	327 B.C.
China	Visited	Marco Polo, Italian traveler	c. 1272
Tibet	Visited	Odoric of Pordenone, Italian monk	c. 1325
Southern China	Explored	Niccolò dei Conti, Venetian traveler	c. 1440
India	Visited (Cape route)	Vasco da Gama, Portuguese navigator	1498
Japan	Visited	St. Francis Xavier of Spain	1549
Arabia	Explored	Carsten Niebuhr, German explorer	1762
China	Explored	Ferdinand Richthofen, German scientist	1868
Mongolia	Explored	Nikolai M. Przhevalsky, Russian explorer	1870–73
Central Asia	Explored	Sven Hedin, Swedish scientist	1890–1908
EUROPE			
Shetland Islands	Visited	Pytheas of Massilia (Marseille)	c. 325 B.C.
North Cape	Rounded	Ottar, Norwegian explorer	c. 870
Iceland	Colonized	Norwegian noblemen	c. 890–900
NORTH AMERICA			
Greenland	Colonized	Eric the Red, Norwegian	c. 985
Labrador; Nova Scotia (?)	Discovered	Leif Ericson, Norse explorer	1000
West Indies	Discovered	Christopher Columbus, Italian	1492
North America	Coast discovered	Giovanni Caboto (John Cabot), for British	1497
Pacific Ocean	Discovered	Vasco Núñez de Balboa, Spanish explorer	1513
Florida	Explored	Ponce de León, Spanish explorer	1513
Mexico	Conquered	Hernando Cortés, Spanish adventurer	1519–21
St. Lawrence River	Discovered	Jacques Cartier, French navigator	1534
Southwest U. S.	Explored	Francisco Coronado, Spanish explorer	1540–42
Colorado River	Discovered	Hernando de Alarcón, Spanish explorer	1540
Mississippi River	Discovered	Hernando de Soto, Spanish explorer	1541
Frobisher Bay	Discovered	Martin Frobisher, English seaman	1576

Country or place	Event	Explorer or discoverer	Date
Maine Coast	Explored	Samuel de Champlain, French explorer	1604
Jamestown, Va.	Settled	John Smith, English colonist	1607
Hudson River	Explored	Henry Hudson, English navigator	1609
Hudson Bay (Canada)	Discovered	Henry Hudson	1610
Baffin Bay	Discovered	William Baffin, English navigator	1616
Lake Michigan	Navigated	Jean Nicolet, French explorer	1634
Arkansas River	Discovered	Jacques Marquette and Louis Jolliet, French explorers	1673
Mississippi River	Explored	Sieur de La Salle, French explorer	1682
Bering Strait	Discovered	Vitus Bering, Danish explorer	1728
Alaska	Discovered	Vitus Bering	1741
Mackenzie River (Canada)	Discovered	Sir Alexander Mackenzie, Scottish-Canadian explorer	1789
Northwest U. S.	Explored	Meriwether Lewis and William Clark	1804–06
Northeast Passage (Arctic Ocean)	Navigated	Nils Nordenskjöld, Swedish explorer	1879
Greenland	Explored	Robert Peary, American explorer	1892
Northwest Passage	Navigated	Roald Amundsen, Norwegian explorer	1906
SOUTH AMERICA			
Continent	Visited	Columbus, Italian	1498
Brazil	Discovered	Pedro Alvarez Cabral, Portuguese	1500
Peru	Conquered	Francisco Pizarro, Spanish explorer	1532–33
Amazon River	Explored	Francisco Orellana, Spanish explorer	1541
Cape Horn	Discovered	Willem C. Schouten, Dutch navigator	1615
OCEANIA			
Papua New Guinea	Visited	Jorge de Menezes, Portuguese explorer	1526
Australia	Visited	Abel Janszoon Tasman, Dutch navigator	1642
Tasmania	Discovered		
Australia	Explored	John McDouall Stuart, English explorer	1828
Australia	Explored	Robert Burke and William Wills, Australian explorers	1861
New Zealand	Sighted (and named)	Abel Janszoon Tasman	1642
New Zealand	Visited	James Cook, English navigator	1769
ARCTIC, ANTARCTIC, AND MISCELLANEOUS			
Ocean exploration	Expedition	Magellan's ships circled globe	1519–22
Galápagos Islands	Visited	Diego de Rivadeneira, Spanish captain	1535
Spitsbergen	Visited	Willem Barents, Dutch navigator	1596
Antarctic Circle	Crossed	James Cook, English navigator	1773
Antarctica	Discovered	Nathaniel Palmer, U. S. whaler (archipelago) and Fabian Gottlieb von Bellingshausen, Russian admiral (mainland)	1820–21
Antarctica	Explored	Charles Wilkes, American explorer	1840
North Pole	Reached	Robert E. Peary, American explorer	1909
South Pole	Reached	Roald Amundsen, Norwegian explorer	1911

The Continents

A continent is defined as a large unbroken land mass completely surrounded by water, although in some cases continents are (or were in part) connected by land bridges.

The hypothesis first suggested late in the 19th century was that the continents consist of lighter rocks that rest on heavier crustal material in about the same manner that icebergs float on water. That the rocks forming the continents are lighter than the material below them and under the ocean bottoms is now established. As a consequence of this fact, Alfred Wegener (for the first time in 1912) suggested that the continents are slowly moving, at a rate of about one yard per century, so that their relative positions are not rigidly fixed. Many geologists that were originally skeptical have come to accept this theory of Continental Drift.

When describing a continent, it is important to remember that there is a fundamental difference between a deep ocean, like the Atlantic, and shallow seas, like the Baltic and most of the North Sea, which are merely flooded portions of a continent. Another and entirely different point to remember is that political considerations have often overridden geographical facts when it came to naming continents.

Geographically speaking, Europe, including the British Isles, is a large western peninsula of the continent of Asia; and many geographers, when referring to Europe and Asia, speak of the Eurasian Continent. But traditionally, Europe is counted as a separate continent, with the Ural and the Caucasus mountains forming the line of demarcation between Europe and Asia.

To the south of Europe, Asia has an odd-shaped peninsula jutting westward, which has a large number of political subdivisions. The northern section is taken up by Turkey; to the south of Turkey there are Syria, Iraq, Israel, Jordan, Saudi Arabia, and a number of smaller Arab countries. All this is part of Asia. Traditionally, the island of Cyprus in the Mediterranean is also considered to be part of Asia, while the island of Crete is counted as European.

The large islands of Java, Borneo, and Sumatra and the smaller islands near them are counted as part of "tropical Asia," while New Guinea is counted as related to Australia. In the case of the Americas, the problem arises as to whether they should be considered one or two continents. There are good arguments on both sides, but since there is now a land bridge between North and South America (in the past it was often flooded) and since no part of the sea east of the land bridge is deep ocean, it is more logical to consider the Americas as one continent.

Politically, based mainly on history, the Americas are divided into North America (from the Arctic to the Mexican border), Central America (from Mexico to Panama, with the Caribbean islands), and South America. Greenland is considered a section of North America, while Iceland is traditionally counted as a European island because of its political ties with the Scandinavian countries.

The island groups in the Pacific are often called "Oceania," but this name does *not* imply that scientists consider them the remains of a continent.

Volcanoes of the World

About 500 volcanoes have had recorded eruptions within historical times. Almost two thirds of these are in the Northern Hemisphere. Most volcanoes occur at the boundaries of the earth's crustal plates, such as the famous "Ring of Fire" that surrounds the Pacific Ocean plate. Of the world's active volcanoes, about 60% are along the perimeter of the Pacific, about 17% on mid-oceanic islands, about 14% in an arc along the south of the Indonesian islands, and about 9% in the Mediterranean area, Africa, and Asia Minor. Many of the world's volcanoes are submarine and have unrecorded eruptions.

Pacific "Ring of Fire"

NORTHWEST

Japan: At least 33 active vents.

Aso (5,223 ft; 1,592 m), on Kyushu, has one of the largest craters in the world.

Asama (over 8,300 ft; 2,530 m), on Honshu, is continuously active; violent eruption in 1783.

Azuma (nearly 7,700 ft; 2,347 m), on Honshu, erupted in 1900.

Chokai (7,300 ft; 2,225 m), on Honshu, erupted in 1974 after having been quiescent since 1861.

Fujiyama (Fujisan) (12,385 ft; 3,775 m), on Honshu, southwest of Tokyo. Symmetrical in outline, snow-covered. Regarded as a sacred mountain.

On-take (3,668 ft; 1,118 m), on peninsula of Kyushu. Strong smoke emissions and explosions began November 1973 and continued through 1974.

U.S.S.R.: Kamchatka peninsula, 14–18 active volcanoes. Klyuchevskaya (Kluchev) (15,500 ft; 4,724 m) reported active in 1974.

Kurile Islands: At least 13 active volcanoes and several submarine outbreaks.

SOUTHWEST

New Zealand: Mount Tarawera (3,645 ft; 1,112 m), on North Island, had a severe eruption in 1886 that destroyed the famous Pink and White sinter terraces of Rotomahana, a hot lake.

Ngauruhoe (7,515 ft; 2,291 m), on North Island, emits steam and vapor constantly. Erupted 1974.

Papua New Guinea: Karkar Island (4,920 ft; 1,500 m). Mild eruptions 1974.

Philippine Islands: About 100 eruptive centers; Hibok Hibok, on Camiguin, erupted September 1950 and again in December 1951, when about 750 were reported killed or missing; eruptions continued during 1952–53.

Taal (4,752 ft; 1,448 m), on Luzon. Major eruption in 1965 killed 190; erupted again, 1968.

Volcano Islands: Mount Suribachi (546 ft; 166 m), on Iwo Jima. A sulfurous steaming volcano. Raising of U.S. flag over Mount Suribachi was one of the dramatic episodes of World War II.

NORTHEAST

Alaska: Mount Wrangell (14,163 ft; 4,317 m) and Mount Katmai (about 6,700 ft; 2,042 m). On June 6, 1912, a violent eruption (Nova Rupta) of Mount Katmai occurred, during which the "Valley of Ten Thousand Smokes" was formed.

Aleutian Islands: There are 32 active vents known and numerous inactive cones. Akutan Island (over 4,000 ft; 1,220 m) erupted in 1974, with ash and debris rising over 300 ft.

Great Sitkin (5,741 ft; 1,750 m). Explosive activity February–September 1974, accompanied by earthquake originating at volcano that registered 2.3 on Richter scale.

Augustine Island: Augustine volcano (4,000 ft; 1,220 m) erupted March 27, 1986. It last erupted in 1976.

California, Oregon, Washington: Lassen Peak (10,453 ft; 3,186 m) in California is one of two observed active volcanoes in the U.S. outside Alaska and Hawaii. The last period of activity was 1914–17. Mt. St. Helens (9,677 ft; 2,950 m) in the Cascade Range of southwest Washington became active on March 27, 1980, and erupted on May 18 after being inactive since 1857. From April 15 through May 1, 1986, weak activity began for the first time in two years. Other mountains of volcanic origin include Mount Shasta (California), Mount Hood (Oregon), Mount Mazama (Oregon)—the mountain containing Crater Lake, Mount Rainier (Washington), and Mount Baker (Washington), which has been steaming since October 1975, but gives no sign of an impending eruption.

SOUTHEAST

Chile and Argentina: About 25 active or potentially active.

Colombia: Huila (nearly 18,900 ft; 5,760 m), a vapor-emitting volcano, and Tolima (nearly 18,500 ft; 5,640 m). Eruption of Puracé (15,600 ft; 4,755 m) in 1949 killed 17 people. Nevado del Ruiz (16, 200 ft; 4,938 m.), erupted Nov. 13, 1985, sending torrential floods of mud and water engulfing the town of Armero and killing more than 22,000 people.

Ecuador: Cayambe (nearly 19,000 ft; 5,791 m). Almost on the equator.

Cotopaxi (19,344 ft; 5,896 m). Perhaps highest active volcano in the world. Possesses a beautifully formed cone.

Reventador (11,434 ft; 3,485 m). Observed in active state in late 1973.

El Salvador: Izalco ("beacon of Central America") (7,830 ft; 2,387 m) first appeared in 1770 and is still growing (erupted in 1950, 1956; last erupted in October–November 1966). San Salvador (6,187 ft; 1,886 m) had a violent eruption in 1923. Conchagua (about 4100 ft; 1,250 m) erupted with considerable damage early in 1947.

Guatemala: Santa Maria Quezaltenango (12,361 ft; 3,768 m). Frequent activity between 1902–08 and 1922–28 after centuries of quiescence. Most dangerously active vent of Central America. Other volcanoes include Tajumulco (13,814 ft; 4,211 m) and Atitlán (11,633 ft; 3,546 m).

Mexico: Boquerón ("Big Mouth"), on San Benedicto, about 250 mi. south of Lower California. Newest volcano in Western Hemisphere, discovered September 1952.

Colima (about 14,000 ft; 4,270 m), in group that has had frequent eruptions.

Orizaba (Citlaltépetl) (18,701 ft; 5,700 m).

Parícutin (7,450 ft; 2,270 m). First appeared in February 1943. In less than a week, a cone over 140 ft high developed with a crater one quarter mile in circumference. Cone grew more than 1,500 ft (457 m) in 1943. Erupted 1952.

Popocatépetl (17,887 ft; 5,452 m). Large, deep, bell-shaped crater. Not entirely extinct; steam still escapes.

El Chinchonal (7,300 ft; 1,005.6 m) about 15 miles from Pichucalco. Long inactive, it erupted in March 1982.

Nicaragua: Volcanoes include Telica, Coseguina, and Momotombo. Between Momotombo on the west shore of Lake Managua and Coseguina overlooking the Gulf of Fonseca, there is a string of more than 20 cones, many still active. One of these, Cerro Negro, erupted in July 1947, with considerable damage and loss of life, and again in 1971.

Concepción (5,100 ft; 1,555 m). Ash eruptions 1973–74.

Mid-oceanic Islands

Canary Islands: Pico de Teide (12,192 ft; 3,716 m), on Tenerife.

Cape Verde Islands: Fogo (nearly 9,300 ft; 2,835 m). Severe eruption in 1857; quiescent until 1951.

Caribbean: La Soufrière (4,813 ft; 1,467 m), on Basse-Terre, Guadeloupe. Also called La Grande Soufrière. Violent activity in July–August 1976 caused evacuation of 73,000 people; renewed activity in April 1977 again caused thousands to flee their homes.

La Soufrière (4,048 ft; 1,234 m), on St. Vincent. Major eruption in 1902 killed over 1,000 people. Eruptions over 10-day period in April 1979 caused evacuation of northern two thirds of island.

Comoros: One volcano, Karthala (nearly 8,000 ft; 2,440 m), is visible for over 100 miles. Last erupted in 1904.

Hawaii: Mauna Loa ("Long Mountain") (13,680 ft; 4,170 m), on Hawaii, discharges from its high side vents more lava than any other volcano. Largest volcanic mountain in the world in cubic content. Area of crater is 3.7 sq mi. Violent eruption in June 1950, with lava pouring 25 miles into the ocean. Last major eruption in March 1984.

Mauna Kea (13,796 ft; 4,205 m), on Hawaii. Highest mountain in state.

Kilauea (4,090 ft; 1,247 m) is a vent in the side of Mauna Loa, but its eruptions are apparently independent. One of the most spectacular and active craters. Crater has an area of 4.14 sq mi. Earthquake in July 1975 caused major eruption. Eruptions began in September 1977 and reached a height of 980 ft (300 m). Activity ended Oct. 1. Became active again in January 1983, exploding in earnest in March 1983 forming the volcanic cone Pu'u O which has erupted periodically ever since. In July 1986, lava began flowing from a new place in Kilauea's East Rift Zone.

Iceland: At least 25 volcanoes active in historical times. Very similar to Hawaiian volcanoes. Askja (over 4,700 ft; 1,433 m) is the largest.

Lesser Antilles (West Indian Islands): Mount Pelée (over 4,500 ft; 1,370 m), northwestern Martinique. Eruption in 1902 destroyed town of St. Pierre and killed approximately 40,000 people.

Réunion Island (east of Madagascar): Piton de la Fournaise (Le Volcan) (8,610 ft; 2,624 m). Large lava flows. Last erupted in 1972.

Samoan archipelago: Savai'i Island had an eruption in 1905 that caused considerable damage. Niuafoo (Tin Can), in the Tonga Islands, has a crater that extends 6,000 feet below and 600 feet above water.

Indonesia

Sumatra: Ninety volcanoes have been discovered; 12 are now active. The most famous, Krakatau, is a small volcanic island in the Sunda Strait. Numerous volcanic discharges occurred in 1883. One extremely violent explosion caused the disappearance of the highest peak and the northern part of the island. Fine dust was carried around the world in the upper atmosphere. Over 36,000 persons lost their lives in resultant tidal waves that were felt as far away as Cape Horn. Active in 1972.

Mediterranean Area

Italy: Mount Etna (10,902 ft; 3,323 m), eastern Sicily. Two new craters formed in eruptions of February–March 1947. Worst eruption in 50 years occurred November 1950–January 1951. Erupted again in 1974, 1975, 1977, 1978, 1979, and 1983.

Stromboli (about 3,000 ft; 914 m), Lipari Islands (north of Sicily). Called "Lighthouse of the Mediterranean." Reported active in 1971.

Mount Vesuvius (4,200 ft; 1,280 m), southeast of Naples. Only active volcano on European mainland. Pompeii buried by an eruption, A.D. 79.

Antarctica

The discovery of two small active volcanoes in 1982 brings to five the total number known on Antarctica. The new ones, 30 miles apart, are on the Weddell Sea side of the Antarctic Peninsula. The largest, Mount Erebus (13,000 ft; 3,962 m), rises from McMurdo Sound. Mount Melbourne (9,000 ft; 2,743 m) is in Victoria Land. The fifth, off the northern tip of the Antartic Peninsula, is a crater known as Deception Island.

Principal Types of Volcanoes

(*Source:* U.S. Dept. of Interior, Geological Survey.)

The word "volcano" comes from the little island of Vulcano in the Mediterranean Sea off Sicily. Centuries ago, the people living in this area believed that Vulcano was the chimney of the forge of Vulcan—the blacksmith of the Roman gods. They thought that the hot lava fragments and clouds of dust erupting from Vulcano came from Vulcan's forge. Today, we know that volcanic eruptions are not supernatural but can be studied and interpreted by scientists.

Geologists generally group volcanoes into four main kinds—cinder cones, composite volcanoes, shield volcanoes, and lava domes.

Cinder Cones

Cinder cones are the simplest type of volcano. They are built from particles and blobs of congealed lava ejected from a single vent. As the gas-charged lava is blown violently into the air, it breaks into small fragments that solidify and fall as cinders around the vent to form a circular or oval cone. Most cinder cones have a bowl-shaped crater at the summit and rarely rise more than a thousand feet or so above their surroundings. Cinder cones are numerous in western North America as well as throughout other volcanic terrains of the world.

Composite Volcanoes

Some of the Earth's grandest mountains are composite volcanoes—sometimes called *stratovolcanoes.* They are typically steep-sided, symmetrical cones of large dimension built of alternating layers of lava flows, volcanic ash, cinders, blocks, and bombs and may rise as much as 8,000 feet above their bases. Some of the most conspicuous and beautiful mountains in the world are composite volcanoes, including Mount Fuji in Japan, Mount Cotopaxi in Ecuador, Mount Shasta in California, Mount Hood in Oregon, and Mount St. Helens and Mount Rainier in Washington.

Most composite volcanoes have a crater at the summit which contains a central vent or a clustered group of vents. Lavas either flow through breaks in the crater wall or issue from fissures on the flanks of the cone. Lava, solidified within the fissures, forms *dikes* that act as ribs which greatly strengthen the cone.

The essential feature of a composite volcano is a conduit system through which magma from a reservoir deep in the Earth's crust rises to the surface. The volcano is built up by the accumulation of material erupted through the conduit and increases in size as lava, cinders, ash, etc., are added to its slopes.

Shield Volcanoes

Shield volcanoes, the third type of volcano, are built almost entirely of fluid lava flows. Flow after flow pours out in all directions from a central summit vent, or group of vents, building a broad, gently sloping cone of flat, domical shape, with a profile much like that of a warrior's shield. They are built up slowly by the accretion of thousands of flows of highly fluid basaltic (from *basalt,* a hard, dense dark volcanic rock) lava that spread widely over great distances, and then cool as thin, gently dipping sheets. Lavas also commonly erupt from vents along fractures (rift zones) that develop on the flanks of the cone. Some of the largest volcanoes in the world are shield volcanoes. In northern California and Oregon, many shield volcanoes have diameters of 3 or 4 miles and heights of 1,500 to 2,000 feet. The Hawaiian Islands are composed of linear chains of these volcanoes, including Kilauea and Mauna Loa on the island of Hawaii.

In some shield-volcano eruptions, basaltic lava pours out quietly from long fissures instead of central vents and floods the surrounding countryside with lava flow upon lava flow, forming broad plateaus. Lava plateaus of this type can be seen in Iceland, southeastern Washington, eastern Oregon, and southern Idaho.

Lava Domes

Volcanic or lava domes are formed by relatively small, bulbous masses of lava too viscous to flow any great distance; consequently, on extrusion, the lava piles over and around its vent. A dome grows largely by expansion from within. As it grows its outer surface cools and hardens, then shatters, spilling loose fragments down its sides. Some domes form craggy knobs or spines over the volcanic vent, whereas others form short, steep-sided lava flows known as "coulees." Volcanic domes commonly occur within the craters or on the flanks of large composite volcanoes. The nearly circular Novarupta Dome that formed during the 1912 eruption of Katmai Volcano, Alaska, measures 800 feet across and 200 feet high. The internal structure of this dome—defined by layering of lava fanning upward and outward from the center—indicates that it grew largely by expansion from within. Mount Pelée in Martinique, West Indies, and Lassen Peak and Mono domes in California, are examples of lava domes.

Submarine Volcanoes

Submarine volcanoes and volcanic vents are common features on certain zones of the ocean floor. Some are active at the present time and, in shallow water, disclose their presence by blasting steam and rock-debris high above the surface of the sea. Many others lie at such great depths that the tremendous weight of the water above them results in high, confining pressure and prevents the formation and release of steam and gases. Even very large, deepwater eruptions may not disturb the ocean floor.

The famous black sand beaches of Hawaii were created virtually instantaneously by the violent interaction between hot lava and sea water.

The Pacific Ocean "Ring of Fire"

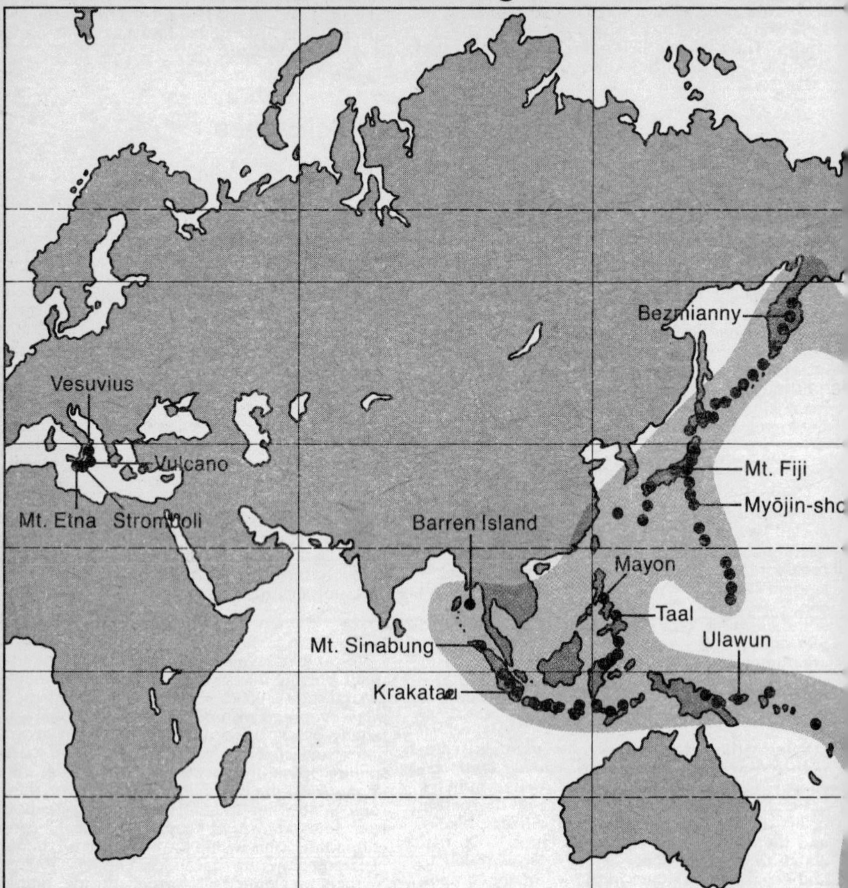

Volcanic Activity in the Solar System

(*Source:* U.S. Dept. of Interior, Geological Survey.)

From the 1976-1979 *Viking* mission, scientists have been able to study the volcanoes on Mars, and their studies are very revealing when compared with those of volcanoes on Earth. For example, Martian and Hawaiian volcanoes have gently sloping flanks, large multiple-collapse pits at their centers, and appear to be built of fluid lavas that have left their numerous flow features on their flanks. The most obvious difference between the two is size. The Martian shields are enormous. They can grow to over 17 miles in height and more than 350 miles across, in contrast to a maximum height of about 6 miles and width of 74 miles for the Hawaiian shields.

Source: U.S. Department of the Interior, U.S. Geological Survey.

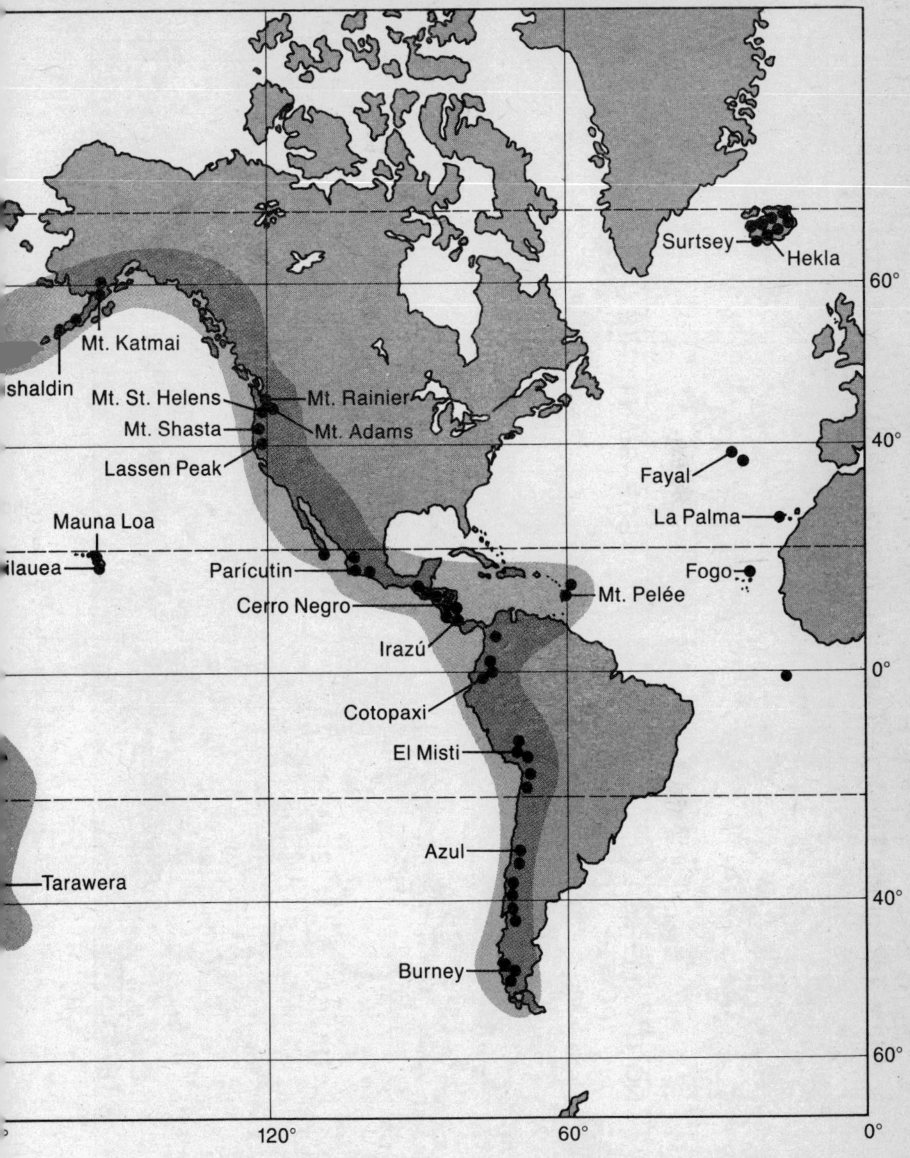

Earth's Volcanic Origin

In July 1979, *Voyager-2* spacecraft images taken of Io, a moon of Jupiter, captured volcanoes in the actual process of eruption. The volcanic plumes photographed rose to some 60 to 100 miles above the surface of the moon. Thus active volcanism is taking place, at present, on at least one planetary body in addition to our Earth.

More than 80 percent of the Earth's surface—above and below sea level—is of volcanic origin. Gaseous emissions from volcanic vents over hundreds of millions of years formed the Earth's earliest oceans and atmosphere. Over geologic eons, countless volcanic eruptions have produced mountains, plateaus, and plains which erosion and weathering have transformed into fertile soils.

Plate-Tectonics Theory—The Lithosphere Plates of the Earth

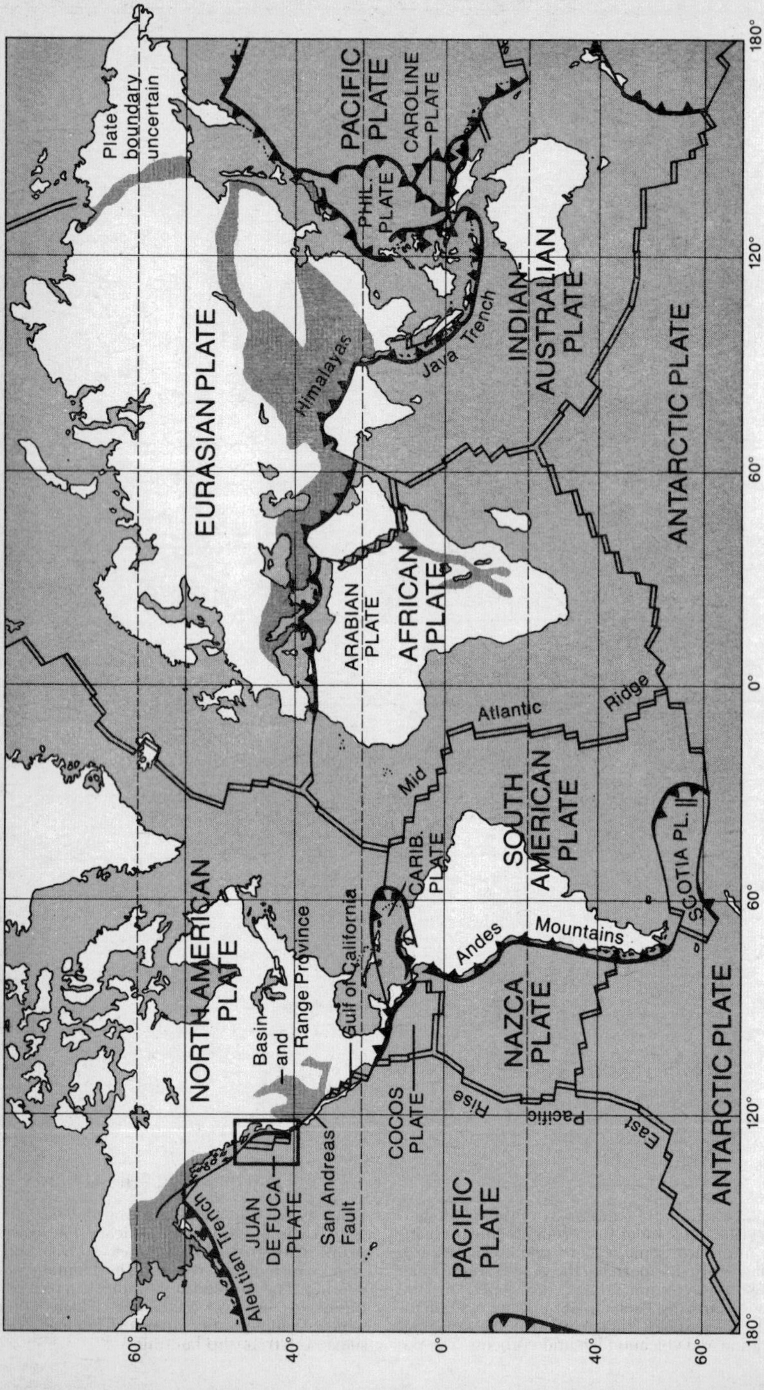

Source: U.S. Department of the Interior, U.S. Geological Survey.

World Population, Land Areas, and Elevations

Area	Estimated population, mid-1986	Approximate Land area sq mi.	Percent of total land area	Population density per sq mi.	Elevation, feet Highest	Elevation, feet Lowest
WORLD	5,026,000,000	58,433,000	100.0	95.9[1]	Mt. Everest, Asia, 29,028	Dead Sea, Asia, 1,290 below sea level
ASIA, incl. Philippines, Indonesia, and European and Asiatic Turkey; excl. Asiatic U.S.S.R.	2,930,000,000	10,644,000	18.2	275.3	Mt. Everest, Tibet-Nepal, 29,028	Dead Sea, Israel-Jordan, 1,290 below sea level
AFRICA	601,000,000	11,707,000	20.0	51.3	Mt. Kilimanjaro, Tanzania, 19,340	Lake Assal, Djibouti, 571 below sea level
NORTH AMERICA, including Hawaii, Central America, and Caribbean region	411,000,000	9,360,000	16.0	43.9	Mt. McKinley; Alaska, 20,320	Death Valley, Calif., 282 below sea level
SOUTH AMERICA	279,000,000	6,883,000	11.8	40.3	Mt. Aconcagua, Arg.-Chile, 23,034	Valdes Peninsula, 131 below sea level
ANTARCTICA	—	6,000,000	10.3	—	Vinson Massif, Sentinel Range, 16,863	Sea level
EUROPE, incl. Iceland; excl. European U.S.S.R. and European Turkey	495,000,000	1,905,000	3.3	259.8	Mont Blanc, France, 15,781	Sea level
OCEANIA, incl. Australia, New Zealand, Melanesia, Micronesia, and Polynesia[2]	25,000,000	3,284,000	5.6	7.6	Mauna Kea, Hawaii, 13,796	Lake Eyre, Australia, 38 below sea level
U.S.S.R., both European and Asiatic	284,000,000	8,647,000	14.8	32.8	Communism Peak, Pamir, 24,547	Caspian Sea, 96 below sea level

1. In computing density per square mile, the area of Antarctica is omitted. 2. Although Hawaii is geographically part of Oceania, its population is included in the population figure for North America. *Source:* Population Reference Bureau, Inc.

Plate-Tectonics Theory

(*Source:* U.S. Dept. of the Interior, Geological Survey.)

According to the generally accepted "plate-tectonics" theory, scientists believe that the Earth's surface is broken into a number of shifting slabs or plates, which average about 50 miles in thickness. These plates move relative to one another above a hotter, deeper, more mobile zone at average rates as great as a few inches per year. Most of the world's active volcanoes are located along or near the boundaries between shifting plates and are called "plate-boundary" volcanoes. However, some active volcanoes are not associated with plate boundaries, and many of these so-called "intra-plate" volcanoes form roughly linear chains in the interior of some oceanic plates. The Hawaiian Islands provide perhaps the best example of an "intra-plate" volcanic chain, developed by the northwest-moving Pacific plate passing over an inferred "hot spot" that initiates the magma-generation and volcano-formation process. The peripheral areas of the Pacific Ocean Basin, containing the boundaries of several plates, are dotted by many active volcanoes that form the so-called "Ring of Fire." The "Ring" provides excellent examples of "plate-boundary" volcanoes, including Mount St. Helens.

The accompanying figure on page 464 shows the boundaries of lithosphere plates that are active at present. The double lines indicate zones of spreading from which plates are moving apart. The lines with barbs show zones of underthrusting (subduction), where one plate is sliding beneath another. The barbs on the lines indicate the overriding plate. The single line defines a strike-slip fault along which plates are sliding horizontally past one another. The stippled areas indicate a part of a continent, exclusive of that along a plate boundary, which is undergoing active extensional, compressional, or strike-slip faulting.

The Severity of an Earthquake

(Source: U.S. Dept. of the Interior, Geological Survey.)

The Richter Magnitude Scale

The Richter magnitude scale was developed in 1935 by Charles F. Richter of the California Institute of Technology as a mathematical device to compare the size of earthquakes. The magnitude of an earthquake is determined from the logarithm of the amplitude of waves recorded by seismographs. Adjustments are included in the magnitude formula to compensate for the variation in the distance between the various seismographs and the epicenter of the earthquakes. On the Richter Scale, magnitude is expressed in whole numbers and decimal fractions. For example, a magnitude of 5.3 might be computed for a moderate earthquake, and a strong earthquake might be rated as magnitude 6.3.

Because of the logarithmic basis of the scale, each whole-number increase in magnitude represents a tenfold increase in measured amplitude; as an estimate of energy, each whole number step in the magnitude scale corresponds to the release of about 31 times more energy than the amount associated with the preceding whole number value.

Earthquakes with magnitudes of about 2.0 or less are usually called microearthquakes; they are not commonly felt by people and are generally recorded only on local seismographs. Events with magnitudes of about 4.5 or greater—there are several thousand such shocks annually—are strong enough to be recorded by sensitive seismographs all over the world.

Great earthquakes, such as the 1906 Good Friday earthquake in San Francisco, have magnitudes of 8.0 or higher. On the average, one earthquake of such size occurs somewhere in the world each year. Although the Richter Scale has no upper limit, the largest known shocks have had magnitudes in the 8.8 to 8.9 range.

The Richter Scale is not used to express damage. An earthquake in a densely populated area which results in many deaths and considerable damage may have the same magnitude as a shock in a remote area that does nothing more than frighten the wildlife. Large-magnitude earthquakes that occur beneath the oceans may not even be felt by humans.

The Modified Mercalli Intensity Scale

The effect of an earthquake on the Earth's surface is called the intensity. The intensity scale consists of a series of certain key responses such as people awakening, movement of furniture, damage to chimneys, and finally—total destruction. Although numerous *intensity scales* have been developed over the last several hundred years to evaluate the effects of earthquakes, the one currently used in the United States is the Modified Mercalli (MM) Intensity Scale. It was developed in 1931 by the American seismologists Harry Wood and Frank Neumann. This scale, composed of 12 increasing levels of intensity that range from imperceptible shaking to catastrophic destruction, is designated by Roman numerals. It does not have a mathematical basis; instead it is an arbitrary ranking based on observed effects.

The Modified Mercalli Intensity value assigned to a specific site after an earthquake has a more meaningful measure of severity to the nonscientist than the magnitude because intensity refers to the effects actually experienced at that place. After the occurrence of widely-felt earthquakes, the Geological Survey mails questionnaires to postmasters in the disturbed area requesting the information so that intensity values can be assigned. The results of this postal canvass and information furnished by other sources are used to assign an intensity value, and to compile isoseismal maps that show the extent of various levels of intensity within the felt area. The maximum observed intensity generally occurs near the epicenter.

The *lower* numbers of the intensity scale generally deal with the manner in which the earthquake is felt by people. The *higher* numbers of the scale are based on observed structural damage. Structural engineers usually contribute information for assigning intensity values of VIII or above.

The Mexico City earthquake on September 19, 1985, was assigned an intensity of IX on the Mercalli Scale.

The following is an abbreviated description of the 12 levels of Modified Mercalli intensity.

I. Not felt except by a very few under especially favorable conditions.

II. Felt only by a few persons at rest, especially on upper floors of buildings. Delicately suspended objects may swing.

III. Felt quite noticeably by persons indoors, especially on upper floors of buildings. Many people do not recognize it as an earthquake. Standing motor cars may rock slightly. Vibration similar to the passing of a truck. Duration estimated.

IV. Felt indoors by many, outdoors by few during the day. At night, some awakened. Dishes, windows, doors disturbed; walls make cracking sound. Sensation like heavy truck striking building. Standing motor cars rocked noticeably.

V. Felt by nearly everyone; many awakened. Some dishes, windows broken. Unstable objects overturned. Pendulum clocks may stop.

VI. Felt by all, many frightened. Some heavy furniture moved; a few instances of fallen plaster. Damage slight.

VII. Damage negligible in buildings of good design and construction; slight to moderate in well-built ordinary structures; considerable damage in poorly built or badly designed structures; some chimneys broken.

VIII. Damage slight in specially designed structures; considerable damage in ordinary substantial buildings with partial collapse. Damage great in poorly built structures. Fall of chimneys, factory stacks, columns, monuments, walls. Heavy furniture overturned.

IX. Damage considerable in specially designed structures; well-designed frame structures thrown out of plumb. Damage great in substantial buildings, with partial collapse. Buildings shifted off foundations.

X. Some well-built wooden structures destroyed; most masonry and frame structures destroyed with foundations. Rails bent.

XI. Few, if any (masonry) structures remain standing. Bridges destroyed. Rails bent greatly.

XII. Damage total. Lines of sight and level are distorted. Objects thrown into the air.

Longitude and Latitude of World Cities

(and time corresponding to 12:00 noon, eastern standard time)

City	Long. °	Long. ′		Lat. °	Lat. ′		Time
Aberdeen, Scotland	2	9	w	57	9	n	5:00 p.m.
Adelaide, Australia	138	36	e	34	55	s	2:30 a.m.[1]
Algiers	3	0	e	36	50	n	6:00 p.m.
Amsterdam	4	53	e	52	22	n	6:00 p.m.
Ankara, Turkey	32	55	e	39	55	n	7:00 p.m.
Asunción, Paraguay	57	40	w	25	15	s	1:00 p.m.
Athens	23	43	e	37	58	n	7:00 p.m.
Auckland, New Zealand	174	45	e	36	52	s	5:00 a.m.[1]
Bangkok, Thailand	100	30	e	13	45	n	midnight[1]
Barcelona	2	9	e	41	23	n	6:00 p.m.
Belém, Brazil	48	29	w	1	28	s	2:00 p.m.
Belfast, Northern Ireland	5	56	w	54	37	n	5:00 p.m.
Belgrade, Yugoslavia	20	32	e	44	52	n	6:00 p.m.
Berlin	13	25	e	52	30	n	6:00 p.m.
Birmingham, England	1	55	w	52	25	n	5:00 p.m.
Bogotá, Colombia	74	15	w	4	32	n	12:00 noon
Bombay	72	48	e	19	0	n	10:30 p.m.
Bordeaux, France	0	31	w	44	50	n	6:00 p.m.
Bremen, W. Germany	8	49	e	53	5	n	6:00 p.m.
Brisbane, Australia	153	8	e	27	29	s	3:00 a.m.[1]
Bristol, England	2	35	w	51	28	n	5:00 p.m.
Brussels	4	22	e	50	52	n	6:00 p.m.
Bucharest	26	7	e	44	25	n	7:00 p.m.
Budapest	19	5	e	47	30	n	6:00 p.m.
Buenos Aires	58	22	w	34	35	s	2:00 p.m.
Cairo	31	21	e	30	2	n	7:00 p.m.
Calcutta	88	24	e	22	34	n	10:30 p.m.
Canton, China	113	15	e	23	7	n	1:00 a.m.[1]
Cape Town, South Africa	18	22	e	33	55	s	7:00 p.m.
Caracas, Venezuela	67	2	w	10	28	n	1:00 p.m.
Cayenne, French Guiana	52	18	w	4	49	n	1:00 p.m.
Chihuahua, Mexico	106	5	w	28	37	n	11:00 a.m.
Chongqing, China	106	34	e	29	46	n	1:00 a.m.[1]
Copenhagen	12	34	e	55	40	n	6:00 p.m.
Córdoba, Argentina	64	10	w	31	28	s	2:00 p.m.
Dakar, Senegal	17	28	w	14	40	n	5:00 p.m.
Darwin, Australia	130	51	e	12	28	s	2:30 a.m.[1]
Djibouti	43	3	e	11	30	n	8:00 p.m.
Dublin	6	15	w	53	20	n	5:00 p.m.
Durban, South Africa	30	53	e	29	53	s	7:00 p.m.
Edinburgh, Scotland	3	10	w	55	55	n	5:00 p.m.
Frankfurt	8	41	e	50	7	n	6:00 p.m.
Georgetown, Guyana	58	15	w	6	45	n	1:15 p.m.
Glasgow, Scotland	4	15	w	55	50	n	5:00 p.m.
Guatemala City, Guatemala	90	31	w	14	37	n	11:00 a.m.
Guayaquil, Ecuador	79	56	w	2	10	s	12:00 noon
Hamburg	10	2	e	53	33	n	6:00 p.m.
Hammerfest, Norway	23	38	e	70	38	n	6:00 p.m.
Havana	82	23	w	23	8	n	12:00 noon
Helsinki, Finland	25	0	e	60	10	n	7:00 p.m.
Hobart, Tasmania	147	19	e	42	52	s	3:00 a.m.[1]
Iquique, Chile	70	7	w	20	10	s	1:00 p.m.
Irkutsk, U.S.S.R.	104	20	e	52	30	n	1:00 a.m.
Jakarta, Indonesia	106	48	e	6	16	s	0:30 a.m.[1]
Johannesburg, South Africa	28	4	e	26	12	s	7:00 p.m.
Kingston, Jamaica	76	49	w	17	59	n	12:00 noon
Kinshasa, Zaire	15	17	e	4	18	s	6:00 p.m.
La Paz, Bolivia	68	22	w	16	27	s	1:00 p.m.
Leeds, England	1	30	w	53	45	n	5:00 p.m.
Leningrad	30	18	e	59	56	n	8:00 p.m.
Lima, Peru	77	2	w	12	0	s	12:00 noon
Lisbon	9	9	w	38	44	n	5:00 p.m.
Liverpool, England	3	0	w	53	25	n	5:00 p.m.
London	0	5	w	51	32	n	5:00 p.m.
Lyons, France	4	50	e	45	45	n	6:00 p.m.
Madrid	3	42	w	40	26	n	6:00 p.m.
Manchester, England	2	15	w	53	30	n	5:00 p.m.
Manila	120	57	e	14	35	n	1:00 a.m.[1]
Marseilles, France	5	20	e	43	20	n	6:00 p.m.
Mazatlán, Mexico	106	25	w	23	12	n	10:00 a.m.
Mecca, Saudi Arabia	39	45	e	21	29	n	8:00 p.m.
Melbourne	144	58	e	37	47	s	3:00 a.m.[1]
Mexico City	99	7	w	19	26	n	11:00 a.m.
Milan, Italy	9	10	e	45	27	n	6:00 p.m.
Montevideo, Uruguay	56	10	w	34	53	s	2:00 p.m.
Moscow	37	36	e	55	45	n	8:00 p.m.
Munich, Germany	11	35	e	48	8	n	6:00 p.m.
Nagasaki, Japan	129	57	e	32	48	n	2:00 a.m.[1]
Nagoya, Japan	136	56	e	35	7	n	2:00 a.m.[1]
Nairobi, Kenya	36	55	e	1	25	s	8:00 p.m.
Nanjing (Nanking), China	118	53	e	32	3	n	1:00 a.m.[1]
Naples, Italy	14	15	e	40	50	n	6:00 p.m.
Newcastle-on-Tyne, Eng.	1	37	w	54	58	n	5:00 p.m.
Odessa, U.S.S.R.	30	48	e	46	27	n	8:00 p.m.
Osaka, Japan	135	30	e	34	32	n	2:00 a.m.[1]
Oslo	10	42	e	59	57	n	6:00 p.m.
Panama City, Panama	79	32	w	8	58	n	12:00 noon
Paramaribo, Surinam	55	15	w	5	45	n	1:30 p.m.
Paris	2	20	e	48	48	n	6:00 p.m.
Peking	116	25	e	39	55	n	1:00 a.m.[1]
Perth, Australia	115	52	e	31	57	s	1:00 a.m.[1]
Plymouth, England	4	5	w	50	25	n	5:00 p.m.
Port Moresby, Papua New Guinea	147	8	e	9	25	s	3:00 a.m.[1]
Prague	14	26	e	50	5	n	6:00 p.m.
Rangoon, Burma	96	0	e	16	50	n	11:30 p.m.
Reykjavik, Iceland	21	58	w	64	4	n	4:00 p.m.
Rio de Janeiro	43	12	w	22	57	s	2:00 p.m.
Rome	12	27	e	41	54	n	6:00 p.m.
Salvador, Brazil	38	27	w	12	56	s	2:00 p.m.
Santiago, Chile	70	45	w	33	28	s	1:00 p.m.
Sao Paulo, Brazil	46	31	w	23	31	s	2:00 p.m.
Shanghai, China	121	28	e	31	10	n	1:00 a.m.[1]
Singapore	103	55	e	1	14	n	0:30 a.m.[1]
Sofia, Bulgaria	23	20	e	42	40	n	7:00 p.m.
Stockholm	18	3	e	59	17	n	6:00 p.m.
Sydney, Australia	151	0	e	34	0	s	3:00 a.m.[1]
Tananarive, Madagascar	47	33	e	18	50	s	8:00 p.m.
Teheran, Iran	51	45	e	35	45	n	8:30 p.m.
Tokyo	139	45	e	35	40	n	2:00 a.m.[1]
Tripoli, Libya	13	12	e	32	57	n	7:00 p.m.
Venice	12	20	e	45	26	n	6:00 p.m.
Veracruz, Mexico	96	10	w	19	10	n	11:00 a.m.
Vienna	16	20	e	48	14	n	6:00 p.m.
Vladivostok, U.S.S.R.	132	0	e	43	10	n	3:00 a.m.[1]
Warsaw	21	0	e	52	14	n	6:00 p.m.
Wellington, New Zealand	174	47	e	41	17	s	5:00 a.m.[1]
Zürich	8	31	e	47	21	n	6:00 p.m.

1. On the following day.

Highest Mountain Peaks of the World

(For U.S. peaks, see Index)

Mountain peak	Range	Location	Height feet	Height meters
Everest[1]	Himalayas	Nepal-Tibet	29,028	8,848
Godwin Austen (K-2)	Karakoram	Kashmir	28,250	8,610
Kanchenjunga	Himalayas	Nepal-Sikkim	28,208	8,598
Lhotse	Himalayas	Nepal-Tibet	27,890	8,501
Makalu	Himalayas	Tibet-Nepal	27,790	8,470
Dhaulagiri I	Himalayas	Nepal	26,810	8,172
Manaslu	Himalayas	Nepal	26,760	8,156
Cho Oyu	Himalayas	Nepal	26,750	8,153
Nanga Parbat	Himalayas	Kashmir	26,660	8,126
Annapurna I	Himalayas	Nepal	26,504	8,078
Gasherbrum I	Karakoram	Kashmir	26,470	8,068
Broad Peak	Karakoram	Kashmir	26,400	8,047
Gasherbrum II	Karakoram	Kashmir	26,360	8,033
Gosainthan	Himalayas	Tibet	26,291	8,013
Gasherbrum III	Karakoram	Kashmir	26,090	7,952
Annapurna II	Himalayas	Nepal	26,041	7,937
Gasherbrum IV	Karakoram	India	26,000	7,925
Kangbachen	Himalayas	Nepal	25,925	7,902
Gyachung Kang	Himalayas	Nepal	25,910	7,897
Himal Chuli	Himalayas	Nepal	25,895	7,893
Disteghil Sar	Karakoram	Kashmir	25,868	7,885
Nuptse	Himalayas	Nepal	25,850	7,829
Kunyang Kish	Karakoram	Kashmir	25,760	7,852
Dakum (Peak 29)	Himalayas	Nepal	25,760	7,852
Masherbrum	Karakoram	Kashmir	25,660	7,821
Nanda Devi	Himalayas	India	25,645	7,817
Chomolonzo	Himalayas	Nepal-Tibet	25,640	7,815
Rakaposhi	Karakoram	Kashmir	25,550	7,788
Batura	Karakoram	Kashmir	25,540	7,785
Kanjut Sar	Karakoram	Kashmir	25,460	7,760
Kamet	Himalayas	India-Tibet	25,447	7,756
Namche Barwa	Himalayas	Tibet	25,445	7,756
Dhaulagiri II	Himalayas	Nepal	25,427	7,750
Saltoro Kangri	Karakoram	India	25,400	7,742
Gurla Mandhata	Himalayas	Tibet	25,355	7,728
Ulugh Muztagh	Kunlun	Tibet	25,341	7,724
Trivor	Karakoram	Kashmir	25,330	7,721
Jannu	Himalayas	Nepal	25,294	7,710
Tirich Mir	Hindu Kush	Pakistan	25,230	7,690
Saser Kangri	Karakoram	India	25,170	7,672
Makalu II	Himalayas	Nepal	25,130	7,660
Chogolisa	Karakoram	India	25,110	7,654
Dhaulagiri IV	Himalayas	Nepal	25,064	7,639
Fang	Himalayas	Nepal	25,013	7,624
Kula Kangri	Himalayas	Bhutan	24,783	7,554
Changtse	Himalayas	Tibet	24,780	7,553
Muztagh Ata	Muztagh Ata	China	24,757	7,546
Skyang Kangri	Himalayas	Kashmir	24,750	7,544
Communism Peak	Pamir	U.S.S.R.	24,590	7,495
Victory Peak	Pamir	U.S.S.R.	24,406	7,439
Sia Kangri	Himalayas	Kashmir	24,340	7,419
Chamlang	Himalayas	Nepal	24,012	7,319
Alung Gangri	Himalayas	Tibet	23,999	7,315
Chomo Lhari	Himalayas	Tibet-Bhutan	23,996	7,314
Muztagh (K-5)	Kunlun	China	23,891	7,282
Amne Machin	Kunlun	China	23,490	7,160
Gaurisankar	Himalayas	Népal-Tibet	23,440	7,145
Lenin Peak	Pamir	U.S.S.R.	23,405	7,134
Korzhenevski Peak	Pamir	U.S.S.R.	23,310	7,105
Kangto	Himalayas	Tibet	23,260	7,090
Dunagiri	Himalayas	India	23,184	7,066
Pauhunri	Himalayas	India-Tibet	23,180	7,065
Aconcagua	Andes	Argentina-Chile	23,034	7,021
Revolution Peak	Pamir	U.S.S.R.	22,880	6,974
Kangchenjhan	Himalayas	India	22,700	6,919
Siniolchu	Himalayas	India	22,620	6,895

Mountain peak	Range	Location	Height feet	meters
Ojos des Salado	Andes	Argentina-Chile	22,588	6,885
Bonete	Andes	Argentina-Chile	22,546	6,872
Simvuo	Himalayas	India	22,346	6,811
Tup	Andes	Argentina	22,309	6,800
Kungpu	Himalayas	Bhutan	22,300	6,797
Falso-Azufre	Andes	Argentina-Chile	22,277	6,790
Moscow Peak	Pamir	U.S.S.R.	22,260	6,785
Veladero	Andes	Argentina	22,244	6,780
Pissis	Andes	Argentina	22,241	6,779
Mercedario	Andes	Argentina-Chile	22,211	6,770
Huascarán	Andes	Peru	22,198	6,766
Tocorpuri	Andes	Bolivia-Chile	22,162	6,755
Karl Marx Peak	Pamir	U.S.S.R.	22,067	6,726
Llullaillaco	Andes	Argentina-Chile	22,057	6,723
Libertador	Andes	Argentina	22,047	6,720
Kailas	Himalayas	Tibet	22,027	6,714
Lingtren	Himalayas	Nepal-Tibet	21,972	6,697
Incahuasi	Andes	Argentina-Chile	21,719	6,620
Carnicero	Andes	Peru	21,689	6,611
Kurumda	Pamir	U.S.S.R.	21,686	6,610
Garmo Peak	Pamir	U.S.S.R.	21,637	6,595
Sajama	Andes	Bolivia	21,555	6,570
Ancohuma	Andes	Bolivia	21,490	6,550
El Muerto	Andes	Argentina-Chile	21,456	6,540
Nacimiento	Andes	Argentina	21,302	6,493
Illimani	Andes	Bolivia	21,184	6,457
Antofalla	Andes	Argentina-Chile	21,129	6,440
Coropuña	Andes	Peru	21,079	6,425
Cuzco (Ausangate)	Andes	Peru	20,995	6,399
Toro	Andes	Argentina-Chile	20,932	6,380
Parinacota	Andes	Bolivia-Chile	20,768	6,330
Chimboraso	Andes	Ecuador	20,702	6,310
Salcantay	Andes	Peru	20,575	6,271
General Manuel Belgrano	Andes	Argentina	20,505	6,250
Chañi	Andes	Argentina	20,341	6,200
Caca Aca	Andes	Bolivia	20,328	6,196
McKinley	Alaska	Alaska	20,320	6,194
Vudor Peak	Pamir	U.S.S.R.	20,118	6,132
Condoriri	Andes	Bolivia	20,095	6,125
Solimana	Andes	Peru	20,069	6,117
Nevada	Andes	Argentina	20,023	6,103

1. The U. S. Air Force Planning Charts list the height of Mt. Everest as 29,141 ft.

Oceans and Seas

Name	Area sq mi.	sq km	Average depth feet	meters	Greatest known depth feet	meters	Place greatest known depth
Pacific Ocean	64,000,000	165,760,000	13,215	4,028	35,820	10,918	Mindanao Deep
Atlantic Ocean	31,815,000	82,400,000	12,880	3,926	30,246	9,219	Puerto Rico Trough
Indian Ocean	25,300,000	65,526,700	13,002	3,963	24,460	7,455	Sunda Trench
Arctic Ocean	5,440,200	14,090,000	3,953	1,205	18,456	5,625	77° 45′ N; 175° W
Mediterranean Sea[1]	1,145,100	2,965,800	4,688	1,429	15,197	4,632	Off Cape Matapan, Greece
Caribbean Sea	1,049,500	2,718,200	8,685	2,647	22,788	6,946	Off Cayman Islands
South China Sea	895,400	2,319,000	5,419	1,652	16,456	5,016	West of Luzon
Bering Sea	884,900	2,291,900	5,075	1,547	15,659	4,773	Off Buldir Island
Gulf of Mexico	615,000	1,592,800	4,874	1,486	12,425	3,787	Sigsbee Deep
Okhotsk Sea	613,800	1,589,700	2,749	838	12,001	3,658	146° 10′ E; 46° 50′ N
East China Sea	482,300	1,249,200	617	188	9,126	2,782	25° 16′ N; 125° E
Hudson Bay	475,800	1,232,300	420	128	600	183	Near entrance
Japan Sea	389,100	1,007,800	4,429	1,350	12,276	3,742	Central Basin
Andaman Sea	308,100	797,700	2,854	870	12,392	3,777	Off Car Nicobar Island
North Sea	222,100	575,200	308	94	2,165	660	Skagerrak
Red Sea	169,100	438,000	1,611	491	7,254	2,211	Off Port Sudan
Baltic Sea	163,000	422,200	180	55	1,380	421	Off Gotland

1. Includes Black Sea and Sea of Azov. NOTE: For Caspian Sea, *see* Large Lakes of World elsewhere in this section.

World's Greatest Man-Made Lakes[1]

Name of dam	Location	Millions of cubic meters	Thousands of acre-feet	Year completed
Owen Falls	Uganda	204,800	166,000	1954
Kariba	Zimbabwe	181,592	147,218	1959
Bratsk	U.S.S.R.	169,270	137,220	1964
High Aswan (Sadd-el-Aali)	Egypt	168,000	136,200	1970
Akosombo	Ghana	148,000	120,000	1965
Daniel Johnson	Canada	141,852	115,000	1968
Guri (Raul Leoni)	Venezuela	136,000	110,256	1986
Krasnoyarsk	U.S.S.R.	73,300	59,425	1967
Bennett W.A.C.	Canada	70,309	57,006	1967
Zeya	U.S.S.R.	68,400	55,452	1978
Cabora Bassa	Mozambique	63,000	51,075	1974
LaGrande 2	Canada	61,720	50,037	1982
LaGrande 3	Canada	60,020	48,659	1982
Ust'—Ilimsk	U.S.S.R.	59,300	48,075	1980
Volga—V.I. Lenin	U.S.S.R.	58,000	47,020	1955
Caniapiscau	Canada	53,790	43,608	1981
Pati (Chapetón)	Argentina	53,700	43,535	UC
Upper Wainganga	India	50,700	41,103	UC
Sáo Felix	Brazil	50,600	41,022	UC
Bukhtarma	U.S.S.R.	49,740	40,325	1960
Atatürk (Karababa)	Turkey	48,700	39,482	UC
Cerros Colorados	Argentina	48,000	38,914	1973
Irkutsk	U.S.S.R.	46,000	37,290	1956
Tucurui	Brazil	36,375	29,489	1984
Vilyuy	U.S.S.R.	35,900	29,104	1967
Sanmenxia	China	35,400	28,700	1960
Hoover	Nevada/Arizona	35,154	28,500	1936
Sobridinho	Brazil	34,200	27,726	1981
Glen Canyon	Arizona	33,304	27,000	1964
Jenpeg	Canada	31,790	25,772	1975

1. Formed by construction of dams. NOTE: UC = under construction, *Source:* Department of the Interior, Bureau of Reclamation and *International Water Power and Dam Construction.*

Large Lakes of the World

Name and location	Area		Length		Maximum depth	
	sq mi.	sq km	mi.	km	feet	meters
Caspian Sea, U.S.S.R.-Iran[1]	152,239	394,299	745	1,199	3,104	946
Superior, U.S.-Canada	31,820	82,414	383	616	1,333	406
Victoria, Tanzania—Uganda	26,828	69,485	200	322	270	82
Aral, U.S.S.R.	25,659	66,457	266	428	223	68
Huron, U.S.-Canada	23,010	59,596	247	397	750	229
Michigan, U.S.	22,400	58,016	321	517	923	281
Tanganyika, Tanzania-Zaire	12,700	32,893	420	676	4,708	1,435
Baikal, U.S.S.R.	12,162	31,500	395	636	5,712	1,741
Great Bear, Canada	12,000	31,080	232	373	270	82
Nyasa, Malawi-Mozambique-Tanzania	11,600	30,044	360	579	2,316	706
Great Slave, Canada	11,170	28,930	298	480	2,015	614
Chad,[2] Chad-Niger-Nigeria	9,946	25,760	—	—	23	7
Erie, U.S.-Canada	9,930	25,719	241	388	210	64
Winnipeg, Canada	9,094	23,553	264	425	204	62
Ontario, U.S.-Canada	7,520	19,477	193	311	778	237
Balkash, U.S.S.R.	7,115	18,428	376	605	87	27
Ladoga, U.S.S.R.	7,000	18,130	124	200	738	225
Onega, U.S.S.R.	3,819	9,891	154	248	361	110
Titicaca, Bolivia-Peru	3,141	8,135	110	177	1,214	370
Nicaragua, Nicaragua	3,089	8,001	110	177	230	70
Athabaska, Canada	3,058	7,920	208	335	407	124
Rudolf, Kenya	2,473	6,405	154	248	—	—
Reindeer, Canada	2,444	6,330	152	245	—	—
Eyre, South Australia	2,400[3]	6,216	130	209	varies	varies
Issyk-Kul, U.S.S.R.	2,394	6,200	113	182	2,297	700
Urmia,[2] Iran	2,317	6,001	81	130	49	15
Torrens, South Australia	2,200	5,698	130	209	—	—
Vänern, Sweden	2,141	5,545	87	140	322	98

Name and location	Area		Length		Maximum depth	
	sq mi.	sq km	mi.	km	feet	meters
Winnipegosis, Canada	2,086	5,403	152	245	59	18
Mobutu Sese Seko, Uganda	2,046	5,299	100	161	180	55
Nettilling, Baffin Island, Canada	1,950	5,051	70	113	—	—
Nipigon, Canada	1,870	4,843	72	116	—	—
Manitoba, Canada	1,817	4,706	140	225	22	7
Great Salt, U.S.	1,800	4,662	75	121	15/25	5/8
Kioga, Uganda	1,700	4,403	50	80	about 30	9
Koko-Nor, China	1,630	4,222	66	106	—	—

1. The Caspian Sea is called "sea" because the Romans, finding it salty, named it *Mare Caspium.* Many geographers, however, consider it a lake because it is land-locked. 2. Figures represent high-water data. 3. Varies with the rainfall of the wet season. It has been reported to dry up almost completely on occasion.

Principal Rivers of the World

(For other U.S. rivers, see Index)

River	Source	Outflow	Approx. length	
			miles	km
Nile	Tributaries of Lake Victoria, Africa	Mediterranean Sea	4,180	6,690
Amazon	Glacier-fed lakes, Peru	Atlantic Ocean	3,912	6,296
Mississippi-Missouri-Red Rock	Source of Red Rock, Montana	Gulf of Mexico	3,880	6,240
Yangtze Kiang	Tibetan plateau, China	China Sea	3,602	5,797
Ob	Altai Mts., U.S.S.R.	Gulf of Ob	3,459	5,567
Yellow (Huang Ho)	Eastern part of Kunlan Mts., west China	Gulf of Chihli	2,900	4,667
Yenisei	Tannu-Ola Mts., western Tuva, U.S.S.R.	Arctic Ocean	2,800	4,506
Paraná	Confluence of Paranaiba and Grande rivers	Rio de la Plata	2,795	4,498
Irtish	Altai Mts., U.S.S.R.	Ob River	2,758	4,438
Congo	Confluence of Lualaba and Luapula rivers, Zaire	Atlantic Ocean	2,716	4,371
Amur	Confluence of Shilka (U.S.S.R.) and Argun (Manchuria) rivers	Tatar Strait	2,704	4,352
Lena	Baikal Mts., U.S.S.R.	Arctic Ocean	2,652	4,268
Mackenzie	Head of Finlay River, British Columbia, Canada	Beaufort Sea (Arctic Ocean)	2,635	4,241
Niger	Guinea	Gulf of Guinea	2,600	4,184
Mekong	Tibetan highlands	South China Sea	2,500	4,023
Mississippi	Lake Itasca, Minnesota	Gulf of Mexico	2,348	3,779
Missouri	Confluence of Jefferson, Gallatin, and Madison rivers, Montana	Mississippi River	2,315	3,726
Volga	Valdai plateau, U.S.S.R.	Caspian Sea	2,291	3,687
Madeira	Confluence of Beni and Maumoré rivers, Bolivia-Brazil boundary	Amazon River	2,012	3,238
Purus	Peruvian Andes	Amazon River	1,993	3,207
São Francisco	Southwest Minas Gerais, Brazil	Atlantic Ocean	1,987	3,198
Yukon	Junction of Lewes and Pelly rivers, Yukon Territory, Canada	Bering Sea	1,979	3,185
St. Lawrence	Lake Ontario	Gulf of St. Lawrence	1,900	3,058
Rio Grande	San Juan Mts., Colorado	Gulf of Mexico	1,885	3,034
Brahmaputra	Himalayas	Ganges River	1,800	2,897
Indus	Himalayas	Arabian Sea	1,800	2,897
Danube	Black Forest, W. Germany	Black Sea	1,766	2,842

River	Source	Outflow	Approx. length miles	km
Euphrates	Confluence of Murat Nehri and Kara Su rivers, Turkey	Shatt-al-Arab	1,739	2,799
Darling	Central part of Eastern Highlands, Australia	Murray River	1,702	2,739
Zambezi	11°21'S, 24°22'E, Zambia	Mozambique Channel	1,700	2,736
Tocantins	Goiás, Brazil	Pará River	1,677	2,699
Murray	Australian Alps, New South Wales	Indian Ocean	1,609	2,589
Nelson	Head of Bow River, western Alberta, Canada	Hudson Bay	1,600	2,575
Paraguay	Mato Grosso, Brazil	Paraná River	1,584	2,549
Ural	Southern Ural Mts., U.S.S.R.	Caspian Sea	1,574	2,533
Ganges	Himalayas	Bay of Bengal	1,557	2,506
Amu Darya (Oxus)	Nicholas Range, Pamir Mts., U.S.S.R.	Aral Sea	1,500	2,414
Japurá	Andes, Colombia	Amazon River	1,500	2,414
Salween	Tibet, south of Kunlun Mts.	Gulf of Martaban	1,500	2,414
Arkansas	Central Colorado	Mississippi River	1,459	2,348
Colorado	Grand County, Colorado	Gulf of California	1,450	2,333
Dnieper	Valdai Hills, U.S.S.R.	Black Sea	1,419	2,284
Ohio-Allegheny	Potter County, Pennsylvania	Mississippi River	1,306	2,102
Irrawaddy	Confluence of Nmai and Mali rivers, northeast Burma	Bay of Bengal	1,300	2,092
Orange	Lesotho	Atlantic Ocean	1,300	2,092
Orinoco	Serra Parima Mts., Venezuela	Atlantic Ocean	1,281	2,062
Pilcomayo	Andes Mts., Bolivia	Paraguay River	1,242	1,999
Xi Jiang (Si Kiang)	Eastern Yunnan Province, China	China Sea	1,236	1,989
Columbia	Columbia Lake, British Columbia, Canada	Pacific Ocean	1,232	1,983
Don	Tula, R.S.F.S.R., U.S.S.R.	Sea of Azov	1,223	1,968
Sungari	China-North Korea boundary	Amur River	1,215	1,955
Saskatchewan	Canadian Rocky Mts.	Lake Winnipeg	1,205	1,939
Peace	Stikine Mts., British Columbia, Canada	Great Slave River	1,195	1,923
Tigris	Taurus Mts., Turkey	Shatt-al-Arab	1,180	1,899

Highest Waterfalls of the World

Waterfall	Location	River	Height feet	meters
Angel	Venezuela	Tributary of Caroni	3,281	1,000
Tugela	Natal, South Africa	Tugela	3,000	914
Cuquenán	Venezuela	Cuquenán	2,000	610
Sutherland	South Island, N.Z.	Arthur	1,904	580
Takkakaw	British Columbia	Tributary of Yoho	1,650	503
Ribbon (Yosemite)	California	Creek flowing into Yosemite	1,612	491
Upper Yosemite	California	Yosemite Creek, tributary of Merced	1,430	436
Gavarnie	Southwest France	Gave de Pau	1,384	422
Vettisfoss	Norway	Mörkedola	1,200	366
Widows' Tears (Yosemite)	California	Tributary of Merced	1,170	357
Staubbach	Switzerland	Staubbach (Lauterbrunnen Valley)	984	300

Waterfall	Location	River	Height feet	Height meters
Middle Cascade (Yosemite)	California	Yosemite Creek, tributary of Merced	909	277
King Edward VIII	Guyana	Courantyne	850	259
Gersoppa	India	Sharavati	829	253
Kaieteur	Guyana	Potaro	822	251
Skykje	Norway	In Skykjedal (valley of Inner Hardinger Fjord)	820	250
Kalambo	Tanzania-Zambia	—	720	219
Fairy (Mount Rainier Park)	Washington	Stevens Creek	700	213
Trummelbach	Switzerland	Trummelbach (Lauterbrunnen Valley)	700	213
Aniene (Teverone)	Italy	Tiber	680	207
Cascata delle Marmore	Italy	Velino, tributary of Nera	650	198
Maradalsfos	Norway	Stream flowing into Ejkisdalsvand (lake)	643	196
Feather	California	Fall River	640	195
Maletsunyane	Lesotho	Maletsunyane	630	192
Bridalveil (Yosemite)	California	Yosemite Creek	620	189
Multnomah	Oregon	Multnomah Creek, tributary of Columbia	620	189
Vøringsfos	Norway	Bjoreia	597	182
Nevada (Yosemite)	California	Merced	594	181
Skjeggedal	Norway	Tysso	525	160
Marina	Guyana	Tributary of Kuribrong, tributary of Potaro	500	152
Tequendama	Colombia	Funza, tributary of Magdalena	425	130
King George's	Cape of Good Hope, South Africa	Orange	400	122
Illilouette (Yosemite)	California	Illilouette Creek, tributary of Merced	370	113
Victoria	Rhodesia-Zambia boundary	Zambezi	355	108
Handöl	Sweden	Handöl Creek	345	105
Lower Yosemite	California	Yosemite	320	98
Comet (Mount Rainier Park)	Washington	Van Trump Creek	320	98
Vernal (Yosemite)	California	Merced	317	97
Virginia	Northwest Territories, Canada	South Nahanni, tributary of Mackenzie	315	96
Lower Yellowstone	Wyoming	Yellowstone	310	94

NOTE: Niagara Falls (New York-Ontario), though of great volume, has parallel drops of only 158 and 167 feet.

Large Islands of the World

Island	Location and status	Area sq mi.	Area sq km
Greenland	North Atlantic (Danish)	839,999	2,175,597
New Guinea	Southwest Pacific (Irian Jaya, Indonesian, west part; Papua New Guinea, east part)	316,615	820,033
Borneo	West mid-Pacific (Indonesian, south part; British protectorate, and Malaysian, north part)	286,914	743,107
Madagascar	Indian Ocean (Malagasy Republic)	226,657	587,042
Baffin	North Atlantic (Canadian)	183,810	476,068
Sumatra	Northeast Indian Ocean (Indonesian)	182,859	473,605
Honshu	Sea of Japan-Pacific (Japanese)	88,925	230,316
Great Britain	Off coast of NW Europe (England, Scotland, and Wales)	88,758	229,883
Ellesmere	Arctic Ocean (Canadian)	82,119	212,688
Victoria	Arctic Ocean (Canadian)	81,930	212,199
Celebes	West mid-Pacific (Indonesian)	72,986	189,034
South Island	South Pacific (New Zealand)	58,093	150,461
Java	Indian Ocean (Indonesian)	48,990	126,884
North Island	South Pacific (New Zealand)	44,281	114,688

Island	Location and status	Area sq mi.	Area sq km
Cuba	Caribbean Sea (republic)	44,218	114,525
Newfoundland	North Atlantic (Canadian)	42,734	110,681
Luzon	West mid-Pacific (Philippines)	40,420	104,688
Iceland	North Atlantic (republic)	39,768	102,999
Mindanao	West mid-Pacific (Philippines)	36,537	94,631
Ireland	West of Great Britain (republic, south part; United Kingdom, north part)	32,597	84,426
Hokkaido	Sea of Japan—Pacific (Japanese)	30,372	78,663
Hispaniola	Caribbean Sea (Dominican Republic, east part; Haiti, west part)	29,355	76,029
Tasmania	South of Australia (Australian)	26,215	67,897
Sri Lanka (Ceylon)	Indian Ocean (republic)	25,332	65,610
Sakhalin (Karafuto)	North of Japan (U.S.S.R.)	24,560	63,610
Banks	Arctic Ocean (Canadian)	23,230	60,166
Devon	Arctic Ocean (Canadian)	20,861	54,030
Tierra del Fuego	Southern tip of South America (Argentinian, east part; Chilean, west part)	18,605	48,187
Kyushu	Sea of Japan—Pacific (Japanese)	16,223	42,018
Melville	Arctic Ocean (Canadian)	16,141	41,805
Axel Heiberg	Arctic Ocean (Canadian)	15,779	40,868
Southampton	Hudson Bay (Canadian)	15,700	40,663

Principal Deserts of the World

Desert	Location	Approximate size	Approx. elevation, ft
Atacama	North Chile	400 mi. long	7,000–13,500
Black Rock	Northwest Nevada	About 1,000 sq mi.	2,000–8,500
Colorado	Southeast California from San Gorgonio Pass to Gulf of California	200 mi. long and a maximum width of 50 mi.	Few feet above to 250 below sea level
Dasht-e-Kavir	Southeast of Caspian Sea, Iran	—	2,000
Dasht-e-Lūt	Northeast of Kerman, Iran	—	1,000
Gobi (Shamo)	Covers most of Mongolia	500,000 sq mi.	3,000–5,000
Great Arabian	Most of Arabia	1,500 mi. long	—
An Nafud (Red Desert)	South of Jauf	400 mi. by avg of 140 mi.	3,000
Dahna	Northeast of Nejd	400 mi. by 30 mi.	—
Rub' al-Khali	South portion of Nejd	Over 200,000 sq. mi.	—
Syrian (Al-Hamad)	North of lat. 30° N	—	1,850
Great Australian	Western portion of Australia	About one half the continent	600–1,000
Great Salt Lake	West of Great Salt Lake to Nevada—Utah boundary	About 110 mi. by 50 mi.	4,500
Kalahari	South Africa—South-West Africa	About 120,000 sq mi.	Over 3,000
Kara Kum (Desert of Kiva)	Southwest Turkmen, U.S.S.R.	115,000 sq mi.	—
Kyzyl Kum	Uzbek and Kazakh, U.S.S.R.	Over 100,000 sq. mi.	160 near Lake Aral to 2,000 in southeast
Libyan	Libya, Egypt, Sudan	Over 500,000 sq mi.	—
Mojave	North of Colorado Desert and south of Death Valley, southeast California	15,000 sq mi.	2,000
Nubian	From Red Sea to great west bend of the Nile, Sudan	—	2,500
Painted Desert	Northeast Arizona	Over 7,000 sq mi.	High plateau, 5,000
Sahara	North Africa to about lat. 15° N and from Red Sea to Atlantic Ocean	3,200 mi. greatest length along lat. 20° N; area over 3,500,000 sq mi.	440 below sea level to 11,000 above; avg elevation, 1,400–1,600
Takla Makan	South central Sinkiang, China	Over 100,000 sq mi.	—
Thar (Indian)	Pakistan-India	Nearly 100,000 sq mi.	Over 1,000

Interesting Caves and Caverns of the World

Aggtelek. In village of same name, northern Hungary. Large stalactitic cavern about 5 miles long.

Altamira Cave. Near Santander, Spain. Contains animal paintings (Old Stone Age art) on roof and walls.

Antiparos. On island of same name in the Grecian Archipelago. Some stalactites are 20 ft long. Brilliant colors and fantastic shapes.

Blue Grotto. On island of Capri, Italy. Cavern hollowed out in limestone by constant wave action. Now half filled with water because of sinking coast. Name derived from unusual blue light permeating the cave. Source of light is a submerged opening, light passing through the water.

Carlsbad Caverns. Southeast New Mexico. Largest underground labyrinth yet discovered. Three levels: 754, 900, and 1,320 ft below the surface.

Fingal's Cave. On island of Staffa off coast of western Scotland. Penetrates about 200 ft inland. Contains basaltic columns almost 40 ft high.

Ice Cave. Near Dobsina, Czechoslovakia. Noted for its beautiful crystal effects.

Jenolan Caves. In Blue Mountain plateau, New South Wales, Australia. Beautiful stalactitic formations.

Kent's Cavern. Near Torquay, England. Source of much information on Paleolithic man.

Luray Cavern. Near Luray, Va. Has large stalactitic and stalagmitic columns of many colors.

Mammoth Cave. Limestone cavern in central Kentucky. Cave area is about 10 miles in diameter but has at least 150 miles of irregular subterranean passageways at various levels. Temperature remains fairly constant at 54° F.

Peak Cavern or Devil's Hole. Derbyshire, England. About 2,250 ft into a mountain. Lowest part is about 600 ft below the surface.

Postojna (Postumia) Grotto. Near Postumia in Julian Alps, about 25 miles northeast of Trieste. Stalactitic cavern, largest in Europe. Piuca (Pivka) River flows through part of it. Caves have numerous beautiful stalactites.

Singing Cave. Iceland. A lava cave; name derived from echoes of people singing in it.

Wind Cave. In Black Hills of South Dakota. Limestone caverns with stalactites and stalagmites almost entirely missing. Variety of crystal formations called "boxwork."

Wyandotte Cave. In Crawford County, southern Indiana. A limestone cavern with five levels of passages; one of the largest in North America. "Monumental Mountain," approximately 135 ft high, is believed to be one of the world's largest underground "mountains."

U.S. Geography

Miscellaneous Data for the United States

Source: Department of the Interior, U.S. Geological Survey.

Highest point: Mount McKinley, Alaska	20,320 ft (6,198 m)
Lowest point: Death Valley, Calif.	282 ft (86 m) below sea level
Approximate mean altitude	2,500 ft (763 m)
Points farthest apart (50 states):	
Log Point, Elliot Key, Fla., and Kure Island, Hawaii	5,852 mi. (9,418 km)
Geographic center (50 states):	
In Butte County, S.D. (west of Castle Rock)	44° 58′ N. lat. 103° 46′ W. long.
Geographic center (48 conterminous states):	
In Smith County, Kan. (near Lebanon)	39° 50′ N. lat. 98° 35′ W. long.
Boundaries:	
Between Alaska and Canada	1,538 mi. (2,475 km)
Between the 48 conterminous states and Canada (incl. Great Lakes)	3,987 mi. (6,416 km)
Between the United States and Mexico	1,933 mi. (3,111 km)

Extreme Points of the United States (50 States)

Extreme point	Latitude	Longitude	Distance[1] mi.	Distance[1] km
Northernmost point: Point Barrow, Alaska	71°23′ N	156°29′ W	2,502	4,027
Easternmost point: West Quoddy Head, Me.	44°49′ N	66°57′ W	1,785	2,873
Southernmost point: Ka Lae (South Cape), Hawaii	18°56′ N	155°41′ W	3,456	5,562
Westernmost point: Cape Wrangell, Alaska (Attu Island)	52°55′ N	172°27′ E	3,620	5,826

1. From geographic center of United States (incl. Alaska and Hawaii), west of Castle Rock, S.D., 44°58′ N. lat., 103°46′ W long.

Highest, Lowest, and Mean Altitudes in the United States

State	Altitude, ft[1]	Highest point	Altitude, ft	Lowest point	Altitude, ft
Alabama	500	Cheaha Mountain	2,407	Gulf of Mexico	Sea level
Alaska	1,900	Mount McKinley	20,320	Pacific Ocean	Sea level
Arizona	4,100	Humphreys Peak	12,633	Colorado River	70
Arkansas	650	Magazine Mountain	2,753	Ouachita River	55
California	2,900	Mount Whitney	14,494	Death Valley	282[2]
Colorado	6,800	Mount Elbert	14,433	Arkansas River	3,350
Connecticut	500	Mount Frissell, on south slope	2,380	Long Island Sound	Sea level
Delaware	60	On Ebright Road	442	Atlantic Ocean	Sea level
D.C.	150	Tenleytown, northwest part	410	Potomac River	1
Florida	100	Sec. 30, T6N, R20W[3]	345	Atlantic Ocean	Sea level
Georgia	600	Brasstown Bald	4,784	Atlantic Ocean	Sea level
Hawaii	3,030	Mauna Kea	13,796	Pacific Ocean	Sea level
Idaho	5,000	Borah Peak	12,662	Snake River	710
Illinois	600	Charles Mound	1,235	Mississippi River	279
Indiana	700	Franklin Township, Wayne County	1,257	Ohio River	320
Iowa	1,100	Sec. 29, T100N, R41W[4]	1,670	Mississippi River	480
Kansas	2,000	Mount Sunflower	4,039	Verdigris River	680
Kentucky	750	Black Mountain	4,145	Mississippi River	257
Louisiana	100	Driskill Mountain	535	New Orleans	5[2]
Maine	600	Mount Katahdin	5,268	Atlantic Ocean	Sea level
Maryland	350	Backbone Mountain	3,360	Atlantic Ocean	Sea level
Massachusetts	500	Mount Greylock	3,491	Atlantic Ocean	Sea level
Michigan	900	Mount Arvon	1,979	Lake Erie	572
Minnesota	1,200	Eagle Mountain	2,301	Lake Superior	602
Mississippi	300	Woodall Mountain	806	Gulf of Mexico	Sea level
Missouri	800	Taum Sauk Mountain	1,772	St. Francis River	230
Montana	3,400	Granite Peak	12,799	Kootenai River	1,800
Nebraska	2,600	Johnson Township, Kimball County	5,426	Southeast corner of state	840
Nevada	5,500	Boundary Peak	13,143	Colorado River	470
New Hampshire	1,000	Mount Washington	6,288	Atlantic Ocean	Sea level
New Jersey	250	High Point	1,803	Atlantic Ocean	Sea level
New Mexico	5,700	Wheeler Peak	13,161	Red Bluff Reservoir	2,817
New York	1,000	Mount Marcy	5,344	Atlantic Ocean	Sea level
North Carolina	700	Mount Mitchell	6,684	Atlantic Ocean	Sea level
North Dakota	1,900	White Butte	3,506	Red River	750
Ohio	850	Campbell Hill	1,550	Ohio River	433
Oklahoma	1,300	Black Mesa	4,973	Little River	287
Oregon	3,300	Mount Hood	11,239	Pacific Ocean	Sea level
Pennsylvania	1,100	Mount Davis	3,213	Delaware River	Sea level
Rhode Island	200	Jerimoth Hill	812	Atlantic Ocean	Sea level
South Carolina	350	Sassafras Mountain	3,560	Atlantic Ocean	Sea level
South Dakota	2,200	Harney Peak	7,242	Big Stone Lake	962
Tennessee	900	Clingmans Dome	6,643	Mississippi River	182
Texas	1,700	Guadalupe Peak	8,749	Gulf of Mexico	Sea level
Utah	6,100	Kings Peak	13,528	Beaverdam Creek	2,000
Vermont	1,000	Mount Mansfield	4,393	Lake Champlain	95
Virginia	950	Mount Rogers	5,729	Atlantic Ocean	Sea level
Washington	1,700	Mount Rainier	14,410	Pacific Ocean	Sea level
West Virginia	1,500	Spruce Knob	4,863	Potomac River	240
Wisconsin	1,050	Timms Hill	1,951	Lake Michigan	581
Wyoming	6,700	Gannett Peak	13,804	Belle Fourche River	3,100
United States	2,500	Mount McKinley (Alaska)	20,320	Death Valley (California)	282[2]

1. Approximate mean altitude. 2. Below sea level. 3. Walton County. 4. Osceola County. *Source:* Department of the Interior, U.S. Geological Survey.

The Continental Divide

The Continental Divide is a ridge of high ground which runs irregularly north and south through the Rocky Mountains and separates eastward-flowing from westward-flowing streams. The waters which flow eastward empty into the Atlantic Ocean, chiefly by way of the Gulf of Mexico; those which flow westward empty into the Pacific.

Mason and Dixon's Line

Mason and Dixon's Line (often called the Mason-Dixon Line) is the boundary between Pennsylvania and Maryland, running at a north latitude of 39°43′19.11″. The greater part of it was surveyed from 1763–67 by Charles Mason and Jeremiah Dixon, English astronomers who had been appointed to settle a dispute between the colonies. As the line was partly the boundary between the free and the slave states, it has come to signify the division between the North and the South.

Longitude and Latitude of U.S. and Canadian Cities

(and time corresponding to 12:00 noon, eastern standard time)

City	Long. w °	Long. w '	Lat. n °	Lat. n '	Time
Albany, N.Y.	73	45	42	40	12:00 noon
Amarillo, Tex.	101	50	35	11	11:00 a.m.
Anchorage, Alaska	149	54	61	13	7:00 a.m.
Atlanta	84	23	33	45	12:00 noon
Atlantic City, N.J.	74	25	39	22	12:00 noon
Austin, Nev.	117	4	39	29	9:00 a.m.
Baker, Ore.	117	50	44	47	9:00 a.m.
Baltimore	76	38	39	18	12:00 noon
Bangor, Me.	68	47	44	48	12:00 noon
Birmingham, Ala.	86	50	33	30	11:00 a.m.
Bismarck, N.D.	100	47	46	48	11:00 a.m.
Boise, Idaho	116	13	43	36	10:00 a.m.
Boston	71	5	42	21	12:00 noon
Buffalo, N.Y.	78	50	42	55	12:00 noon
Calgary, Alberta	114	1	51	1	10:00 a.m.
Carlsbad, N.M.	104	15	32	26	10:00 a.m.
Charleston, S.C.	79	56	32	47	12:00 noon
Charleston, W.Va.	81	38	38	21	12:00 noon
Charlotte, N.C.	80	50	35	14	12:00 noon
Cheyenne, Wyo.	104	52	41	9	10:00 a.m.
Chicago	87	37	41	50	11:00 a.m.
Cincinnati	84	30	39	8	12:00 noon
Cleveland	81	37	41	28	12:00 noon
Columbia, S.C.	81	2	34	0	12:00 noon
Columbus, Ohio	83	1	40	0	12:00 noon
Dallas	96	46	32	46	11:00 a.m.
Denver	105	0	39	45	10:00 a.m.
Des Moines, Iowa	93	37	41	35	11:00 a.m.
Detroit	83	3	42	20	12:00 noon
Dubuque, Iowa	90	40	42	31	11:00 a.m.
Duluth, Minn.	92	5	46	49	11:00 a.m.
Eastport, Me.	67	0	44	54	12:00 noon
El Centro, Calif.	115	33	32	38	9:00 a.m.
El Paso	106	29	31	46	10:00 a.m.
Eugene, Ore.	123	5	44	3	9:00 a.m.
Fargo, N.D.	96	48	46	52	11:00 a.m.
Flagstaff, Ariz.	111	41	35	13	10:00 a.m.
Fresno, Calif.	119	48	36	44	9:00 a.m.
Garden City, Kan.	100	53	37	58	10:00 a.m.
Grand Junction, Colo.	108	33	39	5	10:00 a.m.
Grand Rapids, Mich.	85	40	42	58	12:00 noon
Havre, Mont.	109	43	48	33	10:00 a.m.
Helena, Mont.	112	2	46	35	10:00 a.m.
Honolulu	157	50	21	18	7:00 a.m.
Hoquiam, Wash.	123	54	46	59	9:00 a.m.
Hot Springs, Ark.	93	3	34	31	11:00 a.m.
Idaho Falls, Idaho	112	1	43	30	10:00 a.m.
Indianapolis	86	10	39	46	12:00 noon
Jackson, Miss.	90	12	32	20	11:00 a.m.
Jacksonville, Fla.	81	40	30	22	12:00 noon
Juneau, Alaska	134	24	58	18	9:00 a.m.
Kansas City, Mo.	94	35	39	6	11:00 a.m.
Key West, Fla.	81	48	24	33	12:00 noon
Kingston, Ont.	76	30	44	15	12:00 noon
Klamath Falls, Ore.	121	44	42	10	9:00 a.m.
Knoxville, Tenn.	83	56	35	57	12:00 noon
Lander, Wyo.	108	40	42	50	10:00 a.m.
Las Vegas, Nev.	115	12	36	10	9:00 a.m.
Lewiston, Idaho	117	2	46	24	9:00 a.m.
Lincoln, Neb.	96	40	40	50	11:00 a.m.
London, Ont.	81	34	43	2	12:00 noon
Los Angeles	118	15	34	3	9:00 a.m.
Louisville, Ky.	85	46	38	15	12:00 noon
Manchester, N.H.	71	30	43	0	12:00 noon
Memphis, Tenn	90	3	35	9	11:00 a.m.
Miami, Fla.	80	12	25	46	12:00 noon
Milwaukee	87	55	43	2	11:00 a.m.
Minneapolis	93	14	44	59	11:00 a.m.
Mobile, Ala.	88	3	30	42	11:00 a.m.
Montgomery, Ala.	86	18	32	21	11:00 a.m.
Montpelier, Vt.	72	32	44	15	12:00 noon
Montreal, Que.	73	35	45	30	12:00 noon
Moose Jaw, Sask.	105	31	50	37	10:00 a.m.
Nashville, Tenn.	86	47	36	10	11:00 a.m.
Needles, Calif.	114	36	34	50	9:00 a.m.
Nelson, B.C.	117	17	49	30	9:00 a.m.
New Haven, Conn.	72	55	41	19	12:00 noon
New Orleans	90	4	29	57	11:00 a.m.
New York	73	58	40	47	12:00 noon
Nogales, Ariz.	110	56	31	21	10:00 a.m.
Nome, Alaska	165	30	64	25	6:00 a.m.
North Platte, Neb.	100	46	41	8	11:00 a.m.
Oklahoma City	97	28	35	26	11:00 a.m.
Ottawa, Ont.	75	43	45	24	12:00 noon
Philadelphia	75	10	39	57	12:00 noon
Phoenix, Ariz.	112	4	33	29	10:00 a.m.
Pierre, S.D.	100	21	44	22	11:00 a.m.
Pittsburgh	79	57	40	27	12:00 noon
Port Arthur, Ont.	89	17	48	30	12:00 noon
Portland, Me.	70	15	43	40	12:00 noon
Portland, Ore.	122	41	45	31	9:00 a.m.
Providence, R.I.	71	24	41	50	12:00 noon
Quebec, Que.	71	11	46	49	12:00 noon
Raleigh, N.C.	78	39	35	46	12:00 noon
Reno, Nev.	119	49	39	30	9:00 a.m.
Richfield, Utah	112	5	38	46	10:00 a.m.
Richmond, Va.	77	29	37	33	12:00 noon
Roanoke, Va.	79	57	37	17	12:00 noon
Sacramento, Calif.	121	30	38	35	9:00 a.m.
St. John, N.B.	66	10	45	18	1:00 p.m.
St. Louis	90	12	38	35	11:00 a.m.
Salmon, Idaho	113	54	45	11	10:00 a.m.
Salt Lake City, Utah	111	54	40	46	10:00 a.m.
San Antonio	98	33	29	23	11:00 a.m.
San Diego, Calif.	117	10	32	42	9:00 a.m.
San Francisco	122	26	37	47	9:00 a.m.
San Juan, P.R.	66	10	18	30	1:00 p.m.
Santa Fe, N.M.	105	57	35	41	10:00 a.m.
Sault Ste. Marie, Mich.	84	21	46	30	11:00 a.m.
Savannah, Ga.	81	5	32	5	12:00 noon
Scranton, Pa.	75	39	41	24	12:00 noon
Seattle	122	20	47	37	9:00 a.m.
Shreveport, La.	93	42	32	28	11:00 a.m.
Sioux Falls, S.D.	96	44	43	33	11:00 a.m.
Sitka, Alaska	135	15	57	10	9:00 a.m.
Spokane, Wash.	117	26	47	40	9:00 a.m.
Springfield, Ill.	89	38	39	48	11:00 a.m.
Springfield, Mass.	72	34	42	6	12:00 noon
Springfield, Mo.	93	17	37	13	11:00 a.m.
Syracuse, N.Y.	76	8	43	2	12:00 noon
Tampa, Fla.	82	27	27	57	12:00 noon
Toronto, Ont.	79	24	43	40	12:00 noon
Trinidad, Colo.	104	30	37	10	10:00 a.m.
Victoria, B.C.	123	21	48	25	9:00 a.m.
Watertown, N.Y.	75	55	43	58	12:00 noon
Wichita, Kan.	97	17	37	43	11:00 a.m.
Wilmington, N.C.	77	57	34	14	12:00 noon
Winnipeg, Man.	97	7	49	54	11:00 a.m.

Named Summits in the U.S. Over 14,000 Feet Above Sea Level

Name	State	Height	Name	State	Height	Name	State	Height
Mt. McKinley	Alaska	20,320	Mt. Antero	Colo.	14,269	Windom Peak	Colo.	14,087
Mt. St. Elias	Alaska	18,008	Torreys Peak	Colo.	14,267	Mt. Russell	Calif.	14,086
Mt. Foraker	Alaska	17,400	Castle Peak	Colo.	14,265	Mt. Eolus	Colo.	14,084
Mt. Bona	Alaska	16,421	Quandary Peak	Colo.	14,265	Mt. Columbia	Colo.	14,073
Mt. Blackburn	Alaska	16,390	Mt. Evans	Colo.	14,264	Mt. Augusta	Alaska	14,070
Mt. Sanford	Alaska	16,237	Longs Peak	Colo.	14,255	Missouri Mtn.	Colo.	14,067
South Buttress	Alaska	15,885	Mt. Wilson	Colo.	14,246	Humboldt Peak	Colo.	14,064
Mt. Vancouver	Alaska	15,700	White Mtn. Peak	Calif.	14,246	Mt. Bierstadt	Colo.	14,060
Mt. Churchill	Alaska	15,638	North Palisade	Calif.	14,242	Sunlight Peak	Colo.	14,059
Mt. Fairweather	Alaska	15,300	Shavano Peak	Colo.	14,229	Split Mtn.	Calif.	14,058
Mt. Hubbard	Alaska	15,015	Crestone Needle	Colo.	14,197	Handies Peak	Colo.	14,048
Mt. Bear	Alaska	14,831	Mt. Belford	Colo.	14,197	Culebra Peak	Colo.	14,047
East Buttress	Alaska	14,730	Mt. Princeton	Colo.	14,197	Mt. Lindsey	Colo.	14,042
Mt. Hunter	Alaska	14,573	Mt. Yale	Colo.	14,196	Middle Palisade	Calif.	14,040
Mt. Alverstone	Alaska	14,565	Mt. Bross	Colo.	14,172	Little Bear Peak	Colo.	14,037
Browne Tower	Alaska	14,530	Kit Carson Mtn.	Colo.	14,165	Mt. Sherman	Colo.	14,036
Mt. Whitney	Calif.	14,494	Mt. Wrangell	Alaska	14,163	Redcloud Peak	Colo.	14,034
Mt. Elbert	Colo.	14,433	Mt. Shasta	Calif.	14,162	Mt. Langley	Calif.	14,027
Mt. Massive	Colo.	14,421	Mt. Sill	Calif.	14,162	Mt. Tyndall	Calif.	14,018
Mt. Harvard	Colo.	14,420	El Diente Peak	Colo.	14,159	Pyramid Peak	Colo.	14,018
Mt. Rainier	Wash.	14,410	Maroon Peak	Colo.	14,156	Wilson Peak	Colo.	14,017
Mt. Williamson	Calif.	14,375	Tabeguache Mtn.	Colo.	14,155	Mt. Muir	Calif.	14,015
Blanca Peak	Colo.	14,345	Mt. Oxford	Colo.	14,153	Wetterhorn Peak	Colo.	14,015
La Plata Peak	Colo.	14,336	Mt. Sneffels	Colo.	14,150	No. Maroon Pk.	Colo.	14,014
Uncompahgre Pk.	Colo.	14,309	Mt. Democrat	Colo.	14,148	San Luis Peak	Colo.	14,014
Crestone Peak	Colo.	14,294	Capitol Peak	Colo.	14,130	Huron Peak	Colo.	14,005
Mt. Lincoln	Colo.	14,286	Pikes Peak	Colo.	14,110	Mt. of the Holy Cross	Colo.	14,005
Grays Peak	Colo.	14,270	Snowmass Mtn.	Colo.	14,092	Sunshine Peak	Colo.	14,001

Source: Department of the Interior, U.S. Geological Survey.

Rivers of the United States

(350 or more miles long)

Alabama-Coosa (600 mi.; 966 km): From junction of Oostanula and Etowah R. in Georgia to Mobile R.
Altamaha-Ocmulgee (392 mi.; 631 km): From junction of Yellow R. and South R., Newton Co. in Georgia to Atlantic Ocean.
Apalachicola-Chattahoochee (524 mi.; 843 km): From Towns Co. in Georgia to Gulf of Mexico in Florida.
Arkansas (1,459 mi.; 2,348 km): From Lake Co. in Colorado to Mississippi R. in Arkansas.
Brazos (923 mi.; 1,490 km): From junction of Salt Fork and Double Mountain Fork in Texas to Gulf of Mexico.
Canadian (906 mi.; 1,458 km): From Las Animas Co. in Colorado to Arkansas R. in Oklahoma.
Cimarron (600 mi.; 966 km): From Colfax Co. in New Mexico to Arkansas R. in Oklahoma.
Clark Fork-Pend Oreille (505 mi.; 813 km): From Silver Bow Co. in Montana to Columbia R. in British Columbia.
Colorado (1,450 mi.; 2,333 km): From Rocky Mountain National Park in Colorado to Gulf of California in Mexico.
Colorado (862 mi.; 1,387 km): From Dawson Co. in Texas to Matagorda Bay.
Columbia (1,243 mi.; 2,000 km): From Columbia Lake in British Columbia to Pacific Ocean (entering between Oregon and Washington).
Colville (350 mi.; 563 km): From Brooks Range in Alaska to Beaufort Sea.
Connecticut (407 mi.; 655 km): From Third Connecticut Lake in New Hampshire to Long Island Sound in Connecticut.
Cumberland (720 mi.; 1,159 km): From junction of Poor and Clover Forks in Harlan Co. in Kentucky to Ohio R.
Delaware (390 mi.; 628 km): From Schoharie Co. in New York to Liston Point, Delaware Bay.
Gila (630 mi.; 1,014 km): From Catron Co. in New Mexico to Colorado R. in Arizona.
Green (360 mi.; 579 km): From Lincoln Co. in Kentucky to Ohio R. in Kentucky.
Green (730 mi.; 1,175 km): From Sublette Co. in Wyoming to Colorado R. in Utah.
Illinois (420 mi.; 676 km): From St. Joseph Co. in Indiana to Mississippi R. at Grafton in Illinois.
James (sometimes called *Dakota*) (710 mi.; 1,143 km): From Wells Co. in North Dakota to Missouri R. in South Dakota.
Kanawha-New (352 mi.; 566 km): From junction of North and South Forks of New R. in North Carolina, through Virginia and West Virginia (New River becoming Kanawha River), to Ohio River.
Koyukuk (470 mi.; 756 km): From Brooks Range in Alaska to Yukon R.
Kuskokwim (724 mi.; 1,165 km): From Alaska Range in Alaska to Kuskokwim Bay.
Licking (350 mi.; 563 km): From Magoffin Co. in Kentucky to Ohio R. at Cincinnati in Ohio.
Little Missouri (560 mi.; 901 km): From Crook Co. in Wyoming to Missouri R. in North Dakota.
Milk (625 mi.; 1,006 km): From junction of forks in Alberta Province to Missouri R.
Mississippi (2,348 mi.; 3,779 km): From Lake Itasca in Minnesota to mouth of Southwest Pass in La.
Mississippi-Missouri-Red Rock (3,710 mi.; 5,970

Coastline of the United States

State	General coastline[1]	Tidal shoreline[2]	State	General coastline[1]	Tidal shoreline[2]
	Lengths, statute miles			Lengths, statute miles	
Atlantic Coast:			Gulf Coast:		
Maine	228	3,478	Florida (Gulf)	770	5,095
New Hampshire	13	131	Alabama	53	607
Massachusetts	192	1,519	Mississippi	44	359
Rhode Island	40	384	Louisiana	397	7,721
Connecticut	—	618	Texas	367	3,359
New York	127	1,850	Total Gulf coast	1,631	17,141
New Jersey	130	1,792	Pacific Coast:		
Pennsylvania	—	89	California	840	3,427
Delaware	28	381	Oregon	296	1,410
Maryland	31	3,190	Washington	157	3,026
Virginia	112	3,315	Hawaii	750	1,052
North Carolina	301	3,375	Alaska (Pacific)	5,580	31,383
South Carolina	187	2,876	Total Pacific coast	7,623	40,298
Georgia	100	2,344	Arctic Coast:		
Florida (Atlantic)	580	3,331	Alaska (Arctic)	1,060	2,521
Total Atlantic coast	2,069	28,673	Total Arctic coast	1,060	2,521
			States Total	**12,383**	**88,633**

1. Figures are lengths of general outline of seacoast. Measurements made with unit measure of 30 minutes of latitude on charts as near scale of 1:1,200,000 as possible. Coastline of bays and sounds is included to point where they narrow to width of unit measure, and distance across at such point is included. 2. Figures obtained in 1939–40 with recording instrument on largest-scale maps and charts then available. Shoreline of outer coast, offshore islands, sounds, bays, rivers, and creeks is included to head of tidewater, or to point where tidal waters narrow to width of 100 feet. *Source:* Department of Commerce, National Oceanic and Atmospheric Administration, National Ocean Service.

km): From source of Red Rock R. in Montana to mouth of Southwest Pass in Louisiana.

Missouri (2,315 mi.; 3,726 km): From junction of Jefferson R., Gallatin R., and Madison R. in Montana to Mississippi R. near St. Louis.

Missouri-Red Rock (2,540 mi.; 4,090 km): From source of Red Rock R. in Montana to Mississippi R. near St. Louis.

Mobile-Alabama-Coosa (645 mi.; 1,040 km): From junction of Etowah R. and Oostanula R. in Georgia to Mobile Bay.

Neosho (460 mi.; 740 km): From Morris Co. in Kansas to Arkansas R. in Oklahoma.

Niobrara (431 mi.; 694 km): From Niobrara Co. in Wyoming to Missouri R. in Nebraska.

Noatak (350 mi.; 563 km): From Brooks Range in Alaska to Kotzebue Sound.

North Canadian (800 mi.; 1,290 km): From Union Co. in New Mexico to Canadian R. in Oklahoma.

North Platte (618 mi.; 995 km): From Jackson Co. in Colorado to junction with So. Platte R. in Nebraska to form Platte R.

Ohio (981 mi.; 1,579 km): From junction of Allegheny R. and Monongahela R. at Pittsburgh to Mississippi R. between Illinois and Kentucky.

Ohio-Allegheny (1,306 mi.; 2,102 km): From Potter Co. in Pennsylvania to Mississippi R. at Cairo in Illinois.

Osage (500 mi.; 805 km): From east-central Kansas to Missouri R. near Jefferson City in Missouri.

Ouachita (605 mi.; 974 km): From Polk Co. in Arkansas to Red R. in Louisiana.

Pearl (411 mi.; 661 km): From Neshoba County in Mississippi to Gulf of Mexico (Mississippi-Louisiana).

Pecos (926 mi.; 1,490 km): From Mora Co. in New Mexico to Rio Grande in Texas.

Pee Dee-Yadkin (435 mi.; 700 km): From Watauga Co. in North Carolina to Winyah Bay in South Carolina.

Pend Oreille (490 mi.; 789 km): Near Butte in Montana to Columbia R. on Washington-Canada border.

Porcupine (569 mi.; 916 km): From Yukon Territory, Canada, to Yukon R. in Alaska.

Potomac (383 mi.; 616 km): From Garrett Co. in Md. to Chesapeake Bay at Point Lookout in Md.

Powder (375 mi.; 603 km): From junction of forks in Johnson Co. in Wyoming to Yellowstone R. in Montana.

Red (1,290 mi.; 2,080 km): From source of Tierra Blanca Creek in Curry County, New Mexico to Mississippi R. in Louisiana.

Red (officially called *Red River of the North*) (545 mi.; 877 km): From junction of Otter Tail R. and Bois de Sioux R. in Minnesota to Lake Winnipeg in Manitoba.

Republican (445 mi.; 716 km): From junction of North Fork and Arikaree R. in Nebraska to junction with Smoky Hill R. in Kansas to form the Kansas R.

Rio Grande (1,760 mi.; 2,840 km): From San Juan Co. in Colorado to Gulf of Mexico.

Roanoke (380 mi.; 612 km): From junction of forks in Montgomery Co. in Virginia to Albemarle Sound in North Carolina.

Sabine (380 mi.; 612 km): From junction of forks in Hunt Co. in Texas to Sabine Lake between Texas and Louisiana.

Sacramento (377 mi.; 607 km): From Siskiyou Co. in California to Suisun Bay.

Saint Francis (425 mi.; 684 km): From Iron Co. in Missouri to Mississippi R. in Arkansas.

Salmon (420 mi.; 676 km): From Custer Co. in Idaho to Snake R.

San Joaquin (350 mi.; 563 km): From junction of forks in Madera Co. in California to Suisun Bay.

San Juan (360 mi.; 579 km): From Archuleta Co. in Colorado to Colorado R. in Utah.

Santee-Wateree-Catawba (538 mi.; 866 km): From McDowell Co. in North Carolina to Atlantic Ocean in South Carolina.

Smoky Hill (540 mi.; 869 km): From Cheyenne Co. in Colorado to junction with Republican R. in Kansas to form Kansas R.
Snake (1,038 mi.; 1,670 km): From Ocean Plateau in Wyoming to Columbia R. in Washington.
South Platte (424 mi.; 682 km): From Park Co. in Colorado to junction with North Platte R. in Nebraska to form Platte R.
Susquehanna (444 mi.; 715 km): From Otsego Lake in New York to Chesapeake Bay in Maryland.
Tanana (659 mi.; 1,060 km): From Wrangell Mts. in Yukon Territory, Canada, to Yukon R. in Alaska.
Tennessee (652 mi.; 1,049 km): From junction of Holston R. and French Broad R. in Tennessee to Ohio R. in Kentucky.
Tennessee-French Broad (870 mi.; 1,400 km): From Bland Co. in Virginia to Ohio R. at Paducah in Kentucky.
Tombigbee (525 mi.; 845 km): From junction of forks in Itawamba Co. in Mississippi to Mobile R. in Alabama.
Trinity (360 mi.; 579 km): From junction of forks in Dallas Co. in Texas to Galveston Bay.
Wabash (529 mi.; 851 km): From Darke Co. in Ohio to Ohio R. between Illinois and Indiana.
Washita (500 mi.; 805 km): From Hemphill Co. in Texas to Red R. in Oklahoma.
White (720 mi.; 1,159 km): From Madison Co. in Arkansas to Mississippi R.
Wisconsin (430 mi.; 692 km): From Vilas Co. in Wisconsin to Mississippi R.
Yellowstone (692 mi.; 1,110 km): From Park Co. in Wyoming to Missouri R. in North Dakota.
Yukon (1,979 mi.; 3,185 km): From junction of Lewes R. and Pelly R. in Yukon Territory, Canada, to Bering Sea in Alaska.

Geysers in The United States

Geysers are natural hot springs that intermittently eject a column of water and steam into the air. They exist in many parts of the volcanic regions of the world such as Japan and South America but their greatest development is in Iceland, New Zealand, and Yellowstone National Park.

There are 120 named geysers in Yellowstone National Park, Wyoming, and perhaps half that number unnamed. Most of the geysers and the 4,000 or more hot springs are located in the western portion of the park. The most important are the following:

Norris Geyser Basin has 24 or more active geysers; the number varies. There are scores of steam vents and hot springs. *Valentine* is highest, erupting 50-75 ft at intervals varying from 18 hr to 3 days or more. *Minuté* erupts 15-20 ft high, several hours apart. Others include *Steamboat, Fearless, Veteran, Vixen, Corporal, Whirligig, Little Whirligig,* and *Pinwheel.*

Lower Geyser Basin has at least 18 active geysers. *Fountain* throws water 50-75 ft in all directions at unpredictable intervals. *Clepsydra* erupts violently from four vents up to 30 ft. *Great Fountain* plays every 8 to 15 hr in spurts from 30 to 90 ft high.

Midway Geyser Basin has vast steaming terraces of red, orange, pink and other colors; there are pools and springs, including the beautiful *Grand Prismatic Spring. Excelsior* crater discharges boiling water into Firehole River at the rate of 6 cu ft per second.

Giant erupts up to 200 ft at intervals of 2 1/2 days to 3 mo; eruptions last about 1 1/2 hr. *Daisy* sends water up to 75 ft but is irregular and frequently inactive.

Old Faithful sends up a column varying from 116 to 175 ft at intervals of about 65 min, varying from 33 to 90 min. Eruptions last about 4 min, during which time about 12,000 gal are discharged.

Giantess seldom erupts, but during its active periods sends up streams 150-200 ft.

Lion Group: *Lion* plays up to 60 ft every 2-4 days when active; *Little Cub* up to 10 ft every 1-2 hr. *Big Cub* and *Lioness* seldom erupt.

Castle usually erupts twice daily to a height of 75 ft.

Mammoth Hot Springs: There are no geysers in this area. The formation is travertine. Sides of a hill are steps and terraces over which flow the steaming waters of hot springs laden with minerals. Each step is tinted by algae to many shades of orange, pink, yellow, brown, green, and blue. Terraces are white where no water flows.

How To Order Special Topographic Maps

Source: Maps of the Future, a selection from *The Futurist,* a publication of the World Future Society.

The National Cartographic Information Center (NCIC) is the best central source of information about U.S. maps and charts, aerial photographs and space images, land use data, and other cartographic data. NCIC provides a direct inquiry and ordering service for aerial photographs and space images from the EROS Data Center; provides information and accepts orders for advance material from topographic mapping and map separates held by the Topographic Division of USGS; and refers orders for Geological Survey maps to the Branch of Distribution Offices. NCIC also sells reproductions of out-of-print USGS topographic maps.

For more information, contact: National Cartographic Information Center, U.S. Geological Survey National Center, STOP 507, Reston, Va. 22092 (Telephone: 703-860-6045).

To order topographic maps of areas east of the Mississippi River (including Minnesota, Puerto Rico, and the Virgin Islands), contact Branch of Distribution, U.S. Geological Survey, 1200 South Eads St., Arlington, Va. 22202 (Telephone: 703-557-2751). For areas west of the Mississippi River (including Alaska, Hawaii, Louisiana, Guam, and American Samoa), contact Branch of Distribution, U.S. Geological Survey, Box 25286, STOP 306, Denver Federal Center (Building 41), Denver, Col. 80225 (Telephone: 303-234-3832). Photos are available for the cost of reproduction. A large lithographic copy of a satellite image mosaic of the conterminous United States is available from the Arlington Branch for $1.25.

If you would like to obtain an aerial photo showing your own house, these are available for many parts of the United States. Simply write to NCIC, identifying the location as specifically as possible (give latitude and longitude or enclose a map with your area marked). NCIC will let you know if any photos are available, and, if so, will send you an order form and price list.

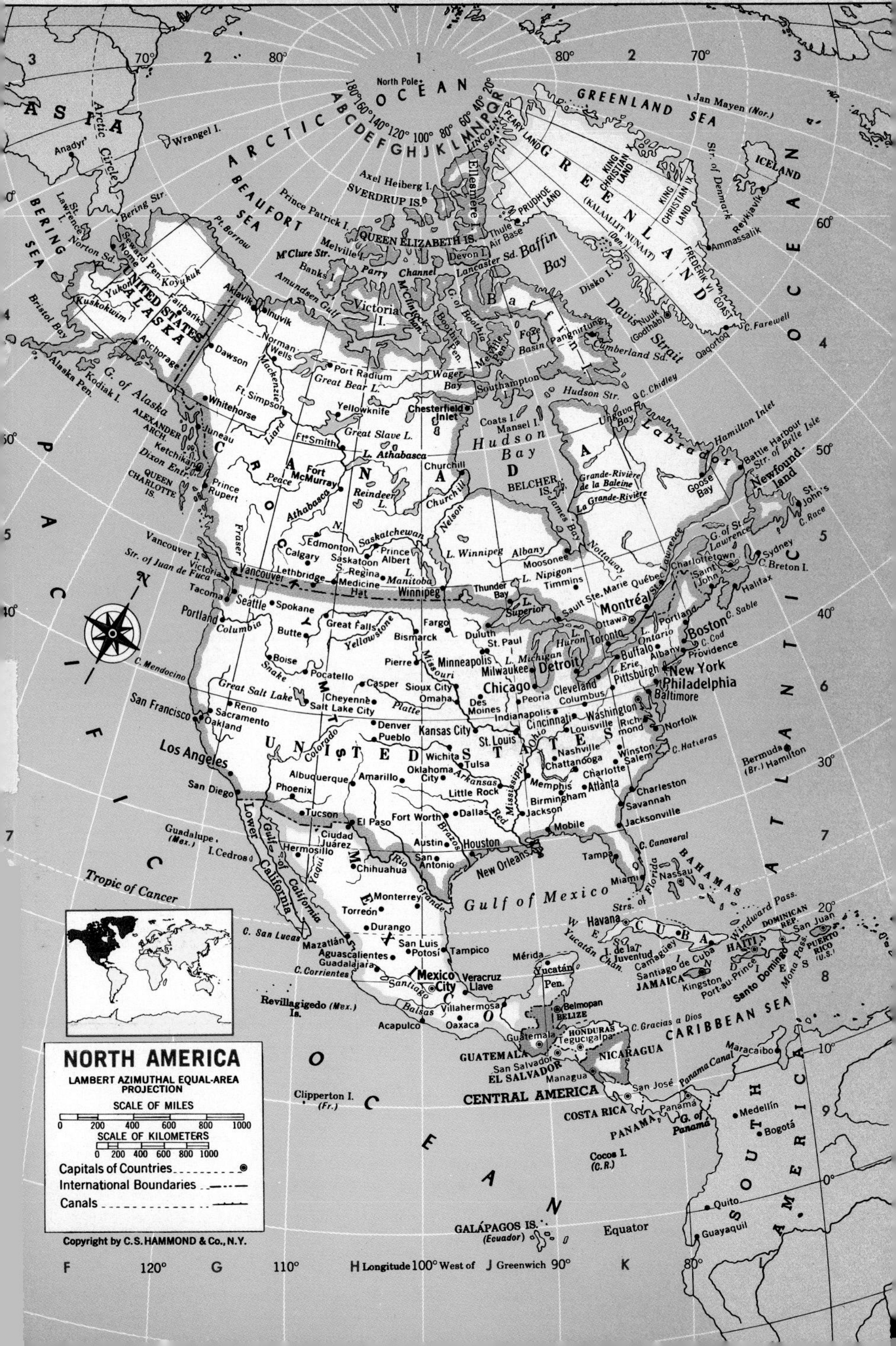
NORTH AMERICA
LAMBERT AZIMUTHAL EQUAL-AREA PROJECTION
SCALE OF MILES
0 200 400 600 800 1000
SCALE OF KILOMETERS
0 200 400 600 800 1000
Capitals of Countries
International Boundaries
Canals
Copyright by C.S.HAMMOND & Co., N.Y.
F 120° G 110° H Longitude 100° West of J Greenwich 90° K
North Pole
ARCTIC OCEAN
GREENLAND SEA
GREENLAND (KALAALLIT NUNAAT) (Den.)
BEAUFORT SEA
BERING SEA
ASIA
Arctic Circle
Baffin Bay
Baffin I.
Hudson Bay
Davis Strait
Labrador
Newfoundland
CANADA
UNITED STATES
ALASKA
MEXICO
CENTRAL AMERICA
GUATEMALA
EL SALVADOR
HONDURAS
NICARAGUA
COSTA RICA
PANAMA
BELIZE
CUBA
JAMAICA
HAITI
DOMINICAN REP.
PUERTO RICO (U.S.)
BAHAMAS
Gulf of Mexico
CARIBBEAN SEA
PACIFIC OCEAN
ATLANTIC OCEAN
SOUTH AMERICA
Tropic of Cancer
Equator
GALÁPAGOS IS. (Ecuador)
Clipperton I. (Fr.)
Cocos I. (C.R.)
Bermuda (Br.) Hamilton
ICELAND
Reykjavík
Jan Mayen (Nor.)
Anchorage
Whitehorse
Yellowknife
Edmonton
Calgary
Vancouver
Seattle
Portland
San Francisco
Los Angeles
San Diego
Winnipeg
Chicago
Detroit
Toronto
Montréal
Ottawa
Québec
Boston
New York
Philadelphia
Washington
Denver
Kansas City
St. Louis
Houston
Dallas
New Orleans
Atlanta
Miami
Havana
Mexico City
Monterrey
Guadalajara
Guatemala
San Salvador
Tegucigalpa
Managua
San José
Panamá
Kingston
Port-au-Prince
Santo Domingo
San Juan
Bogotá
Medellín
Quito
Guayaquil
Maracaibo

PACIFIC OCEAN
CANADA
ROCKY MOUNTAINS
Vancouver Island
Str. of Juan de Fuca
C. Flattery
Vancouver
Victoria
Bellingham
Everett
Seattle
Tacoma
Olympia
Bremerton
Aberdeen
Hoquiam
Centralia
Port Angeles
OLYMPIC NAT'L. PARK
WASHINGTON
Spokane
Wenatchee
Yakima
Richland
Walla Walla
Mt. Rainier 14,410 ft. (4392 m.)
Longview
Vancouver
Portland
Salem
Corvallis
Albany
Eugene
Oregon City
The Dalles
Pendleton
La Grande
Baker
Bend
Coos Bay
C. Blanco
OREGON
Grants Pass
Medford
Klamath Falls
Upper Klamath L.
Harney L.
Malheur L.
Summer L.
L. Abert
Eureka
C. Mendocino
Yreka
Mt. Shasta 14,162 ft. (4317 m.)
Redding
Pt. Arena
Clear L.
Santa Rosa
Marysville
Napa
Vallejo
Berkeley
Golden Gate
San Francisco
Oakland
Palo Alto
Fremont
San Jose
Santa Cruz
Monterey Bay
Monterey
Sacramento
Stockton
Modesto
Reno
Carson City
L. Tahoe
Sparks
Grass Valley
YOSEMITE NAT'L. PARK
Mono L.
Fresno
Visalia
Tulare L.
Bakersfield
San Luis Obispo
Pt. Conception
Santa Barbara
Los Angeles
Glendale
Pasadena
Pomona
San Bernardino
Riverside
Palm Springs
Torrance
Long Beach
Anaheim
Santa Ana
SANTA BARBARA IS.
San Diego
El Centro
Brawley
Salton Sea
Tijuana
Mt. Whitney 14,494 ft. (4418 m.)
Owens L.
Death Valley
CALIFORNIA
SIERRA NEVADA
NEVADA
Winnemucca
Winnemucca L.
Humboldt
Carson Sink
Austin
Walker L.
Tonopah
Goldfield
Elko
Ely
Las Vegas
L. Mead
Lower California
Gulf of California
MEXICO
Nelson
Lewiston
Moscow
Coeur d'Alene
Salmon
Caldwell
Nampa
Boise
IDAHO
Borah Pk. 12,662 ft. (3859 m.)
Arco
Idaho Falls
American Falls Res.
Twin Falls
Pocatello
Montpelier
Calgary
Lethbridge
Medicine Hat
Swift Current
Saskatoon
Moose Jaw
Regina
Weyburn
Brandon
Quill Lakes
L. Winnipegosis
Canora
Last Mountain L.
GLACIER NAT'L. PARK
Kalispell
Flathead L.
Missoula
Anaconda
Helena
Butte
Great Falls
Havre
MONTANA
Bozeman
Livingston
Billings
Miles City
Fort Peck Lake
YELLOWSTONE NAT'L. PARK
Yellowstone L.
Jackson L.
Gannett Pk. 13,804 ft. (4207 m.)
Lander
WYOMING
Sheridan
Casper
Pathfinder Res.
Rawlins
Seminoe Res.
Rock Springs
Green River
Evanston
Granger
Laramie
Cheyenne
Logan
Brigham City
Ogden
Great Salt Lake
Salt Lake City
Tooele
Murray
Provo
Utah L.
UTAH
Price
Sevier L.
Cedar City
St. George
Lake Powell
GRAND CANYON NAT'L. PARK
Grand Canyon
Flagstaff
Prescott
L. Havasu
Lake Havasu City
Needles
ARIZONA
Phoenix
Mesa
Globe
Roosevelt Res.
San Carlos L.
Casa Grande
Tucson
Yuma
Nogales
Bisbee
Douglas
Heroica Nogales
Fort Collins
Loveland
Longmont
Boulder
Greeley
Sterling
Denver
Aurora
Lakewood
Grand Junction
Mt. Elbert 14,433 ft. (4399 m.)
Leadville
COLORADO
Pikes Peak 14,110 ft. (4301 m.)
Colorado Springs
Cripple Creek
Pueblo
Mt. Wilson 14,246 ft. (4342 m.)
Durango
La Junta
Blanca Pk. 14,317 ft. (4364 m.)
Trinidad
Farmington
Raton
Wheeler Peak 13,161 ft. (4011 m.)
Los Alamos
Santa Fe
Las Vegas
Gallup
Albuquerque
Conchas Res.
Tucumcari
NEW MEXICO
Socorro
Clovis
Portales
Elephant Butte Res.
Alamogordo
Roswell
Artesia
Silver City
L. McMillan
Las Cruces
Hobbs
Carlsbad
El Paso
Ciudad Juárez
Williston
Minot
Devils Lake
NORTH DAKOTA
Lake Sakakawea
Mandan
Dickinson
Bismarck
Jamestown
Lake Oahe
Aberdeen
Lead
Rapid City
Black Hills
Pierre
SOUTH DAKOTA
L. Francis Case
Hot Springs
Scottsbluff
NEBRASKA
North Platte
Grand Island
Kearney
KANSAS
Garden City
Dodge City
Hutchinson
Oklahoma
Borger
Amarillo
Pampa
Lubbock
Wichita Falls
Lawton
Sweetwater
Big Spring
Abilene
Midland
Odessa
San Angelo
TEXAS
Amistad Res.
Del Rio
Piedras Negras
San Antonio
Nuevo Laredo
Laredo
Falcon Res.
ARCTIC OCEAN
U.S.S.R.
Barrow
Colville R.
Brooks Range
Point Hope
Kotzebue
Bering Str.
Wales
Nome
Provideniya
St. Lawrence I.
Norton Sd.
Unalakleet
Ft. Yukon
Fairbanks
Tanana
Eagle
Dawson
Inuvik
Ft. McPherson
Arctic Circle
ALASKA
Mt. McKinley 20,320 ft. (6194 m.)
Alaska Range
McGrath
Hooper Bay
St. Matthew I.
Bethel
Anchorage
Palmer
Cordova
Seward
Nunivak I.
Dillingham
Iliamna L.
Bristol Bay
Pribilof Is.
Alaska Pen.
Kodiak
Unimak I.
Unalaska
Aleutian Is.
Mt. St. Elias 18,008 ft. (5489 m.)
Whitehorse
Skagway
Yakutat
Juneau
Gulf of Alaska
Chichagof I.
Sitka
Petersburg
Ketchikan
Attu I.
Kiska I.
Amchitka I.
Atka
Same scale as Alaska map
Longitude West of Greenwich 156°
BERING SEA
International Date Line
HAWAII
PACIFIC OCEAN
Kauai
Kilauea
Kapaa
Lihue
Kekaha
Koloa
Niihau
Oahu
Kahuku
Wahiawa
Waipahu
Kailua
Pearl Harbor
Honolulu
Molokai
Lanai
Lanai City
Kahoolawe
Maui
Hawaii
Mauna Kea 13,796 ft. (4205 m.)
Mauna Loa 13,677 ft. (4169 m.)
Hilo
Kailua
Pahala
Naalehu
Midway Is. (U. S.)
Pearl & Hermes Reef
Lisianski I.
Laysan I.
Maro Reef
Gardner Pinnacles
French Frigate Shoals
Necker I.
Nihoa
Tropic of Cancer
Longitude West of Greenwich

UNITED STATES
POLYCONIC PROJECTION
SCALE OF MILES
0 50 100 200 300 400
SCALE OF KILOMETERS
0 100 200 300 400
Capitals of Countries
State Capitals
International Boundaries
Railroads
© Copyright HAMMOND INCORPORATED, Maplewood, N. J.
Longitude 95° West of H Greenwich 90° J 85° K 80° L 75°
CANADA
ATLANTIC
OCEAN
GULF OF MEXICO
BAHAMAS
CUBA
MINNESOTA
WISCONSIN
MICHIGAN
IOWA
ILLINOIS
INDIANA
OHIO
PENNSYLVANIA
NEW YORK
MAINE
VT.
N.H.
MASS.
CONN.
RHODE ISLAND
NEW JERSEY
DEL.
MD.
WEST VIRGINIA
VIRGINIA
KENTUCKY
MISSOURI
ARKANSAS
TENNESSEE
NORTH CAROLINA
SOUTH CAROLINA
GEORGIA
ALABAMA
MISSISSIPPI
LOUISIANA
FLORIDA
Lake Superior
L. Michigan
L. Huron
Lake Erie
Lake Ontario
James Bay
Tropic of Cancer
Havana
Nassau
Washington D.C.
Ottawa
Montréal
Québec
Toronto
New York
Philadelphia
Boston
Chicago
Detroit
Atlanta
Miami
New Orleans

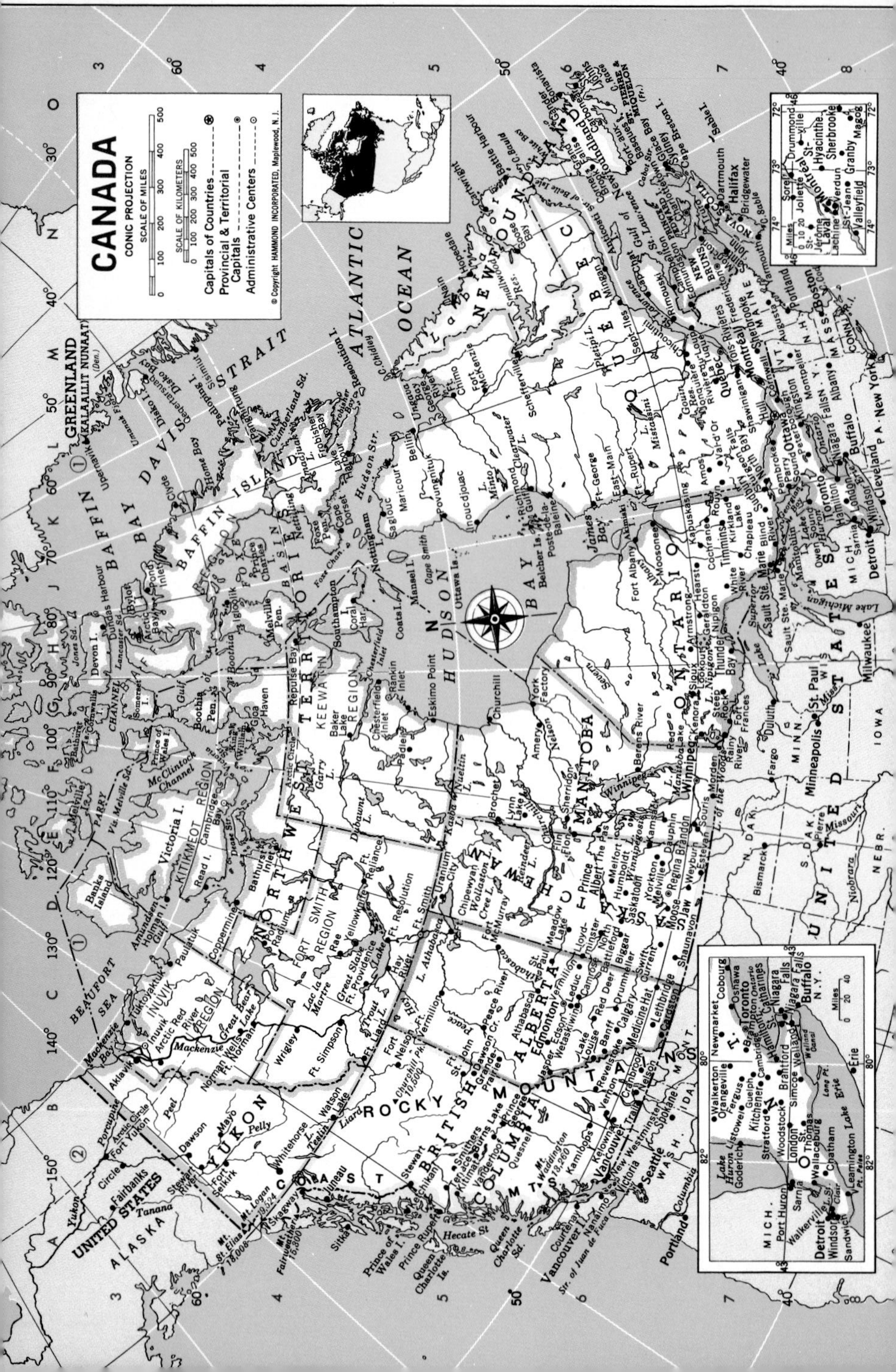
CANADA
CONIC PROJECTION
SCALE OF MILES
0 100 200 300 400 500
SCALE OF KILOMETERS
0 100 200 300 400 500
Capitals of Countries
Provincial & Territorial Capitals
Administrative Centers
© Copyright HAMMOND INCORPORATED, Maplewood, N. J.
ATLANTIC OCEAN
HUDSON BAY
BAFFIN BAY
DAVIS STRAIT
BEAUFORT SEA
GREENLAND (KALAALLIT NUNAAT) (Den.)
NORTHWEST TERRITORIES
YUKON
BRITISH COLUMBIA
ALBERTA
SASKATCHEWAN
MANITOBA
ONTARIO
QUEBEC
NEWFOUNDLAND
NEW BRUNSWICK
NOVA SCOTIA
PRINCE EDWARD I.
ALASKA
UNITED STATES
ROCKY MOUNTAINS
COAST MTS.
Ottawa
Toronto
Montréal
Québec
Winnipeg
Regina
Edmonton
Victoria
Vancouver
Halifax
Whitehorse
Yellowknife
St. John's
Fredericton
Charlottetown
ST. PIERRE & MIQUELON (Fr.)

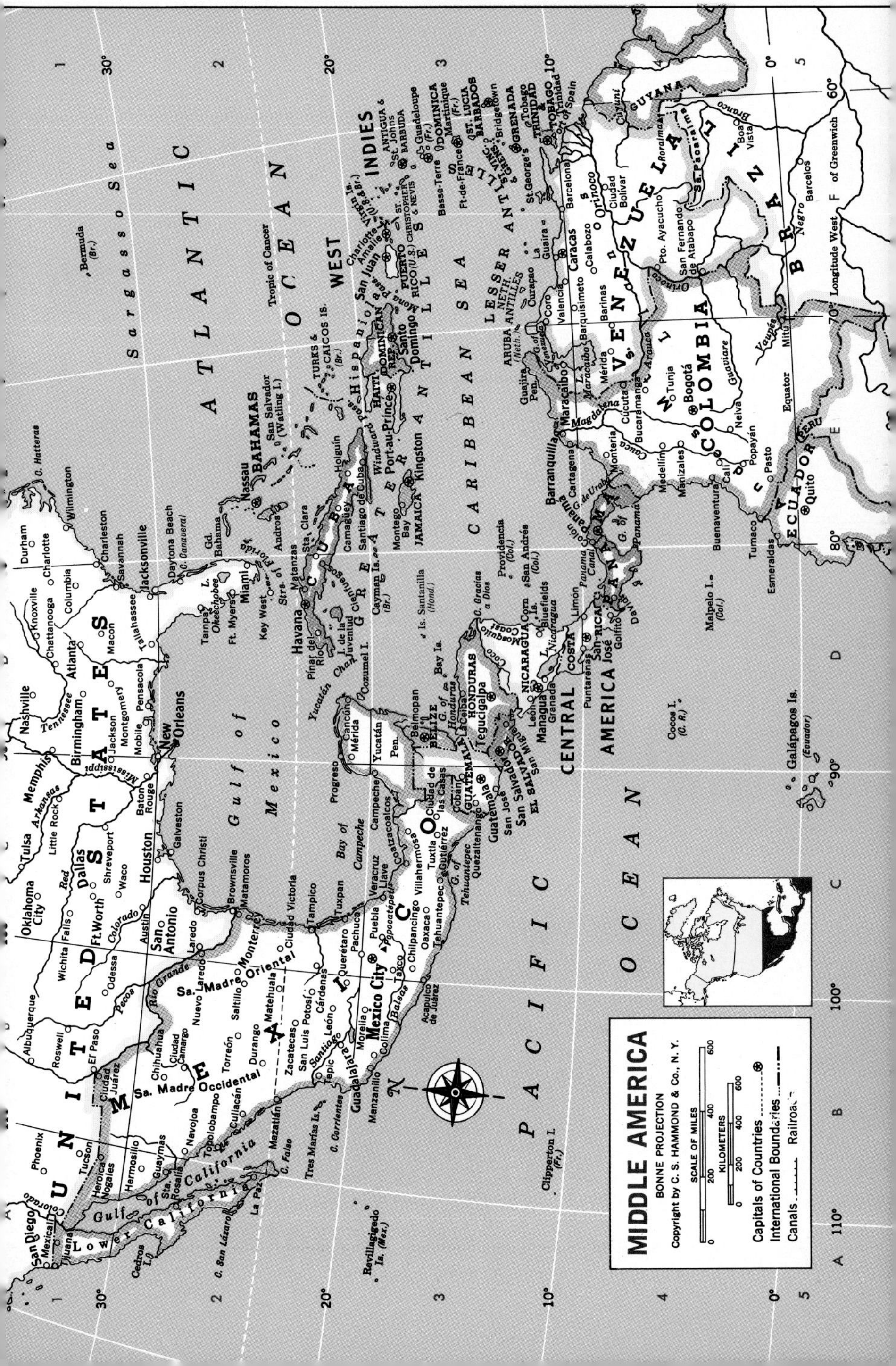
MIDDLE AMERICA
BONNE PROJECTION
Copyright by C. S. HAMMOND & Co., N. Y.
SCALE OF MILES
0 200 400 600
KILOMETERS
0 200 400 600
Capitals of Countries
International Boundaries
Canals
Railroads
UNITED STATES
MEXICO
CENTRAL AMERICA
WEST INDIES
GREATER ANTILLES
LESSER ANTILLES
ATLANTIC OCEAN
PACIFIC OCEAN
Sargasso Sea
Gulf of Mexico
CARIBBEAN SEA
Gulf of California
Lower California
Bay of Campeche
G. of Tehuantepec
G. of Honduras
G. of Panamá
G. de Urabá
Tropic of Cancer
Equator
Longitude West of Greenwich
BAHAMAS
CUBA
HAITI
DOMINICAN REP.
JAMAICA
PUERTO RICO (U.S.)
TURKS & CAICOS IS. (Br.)
Hispaniola
BELIZE
GUATEMALA
HONDURAS
EL SALVADOR
NICARAGUA
COSTA RICA
PANAMA
COLOMBIA
VENEZUELA
ECUADOR
PERU
BRAZIL
GUYANA
ARUBA (Neth.)
NETH. ANTILLES
ANTIGUA & BARBUDA
ST. CHRISTOPHER & NEVIS
DOMINICA
ST. LUCIA
BARBADOS
ST. VINCENT & THE GRENADINES
GRENADA
TRINIDAD & TOBAGO
Bermuda (Br.)
Guadeloupe (Fr.)
Martinique (Fr.)
Virgin Is. (U.S. & Br.)
Cayman Is. (Br.)
Is. Santanilla (Hond.)
Providencia (Col.)
San Andrés (Col.)
Malpelo I. (Col.)
Cocos I. (C. R.)
Galápagos Is. (Ecuador)
Clipperton I. (Fr.)
Revillagigedo Is. (Mex.)
Tres Marías Is.
Cedros I.
C. San Lázaro
C. Falso
C. Corrientes
C. Hatteras
C. Canaveral
C. Gracias a Dios
Mosquito Coast
Sa. Madre Occidental
Sa. Madre Oriental
Yucatán Pen.
Guajira Pen.
Yucatán Chan.
Windward Pass.
Mona Pass.
Strs. of Florida
L. Okeechobee
L. Nicaragua
L. Maracaibo
Panama Canal
Rio Grande
Colorado
Pecos
Red
Arkansas
Mississippi
Tennessee
Balsas
Santiago
Magdalena
Cauca
Orinoco
Meta
Guaviare
Vaupés
Negro
Branco
Roraima
Sa. Pacaraima
Cuyuni
Arauca
Popocatépetl
San Diego
Mexicali
Tijuana
Phoenix
Tucson
Heroica Nogales
Hermosillo
Guaymas
Sta. Rosalía
La Paz
Albuquerque
Roswell
El Paso
Ciudad Juárez
Chihuahua
Ciudad Camargo
Torreón
Durango
Culiacán
Topolobampo
Navojoa
Mazatlán
Oklahoma City
Tulsa
Wichita Falls
Ft. Worth
Dallas
Odessa
Waco
Shreveport
Little Rock
Memphis
Nashville
Birmingham
Jackson
Atlanta
Montgomery
Mobile
Pensacola
Baton Rouge
New Orleans
Houston
Galveston
Austin
San Antonio
Corpus Christi
Laredo
Nuevo Laredo
Brownsville
Matamoros
Monterrey
Saltillo
Matehuala
Zacatecas
San Luis Potosí
Cárdenas
Ciudad Victoria
Tampico
Tuxpan
León
Querétaro
Pachuca
Guadalajara
Tepic
Morelia
Colima
Manzanillo
Mexico City
Puebla
Veracruz Llave
Taxco
Chilpancingo
Acapulco de Juárez
Oaxaca
Tehuantepec
Tuxtla Gutiérrez
Villahermosa
Coatzacoalcos
Campeche
Progreso
Mérida
Cancún
Cozumel I.
Ciudad de las Casas
Quezaltenango
Cobán
Guatemala
Belmopan
Bay Is.
La Ceiba
Tegucigalpa
San Miguel
San Salvador
San José
Managua
León
Granada
Bluefields
Corn Is.
Puntarenas
Limón
Golfito
David
Colón
Panamá
Knoxville
Chattanooga
Columbia
Charlotte
Durham
Wilmington
Charleston
Savannah
Macon
Tallahassee
Jacksonville
Daytona Beach
Tampa
Ft. Myers
Miami
Key West
Gd. Bahama
Nassau
Andros
San Salvador (Watling I.)
Havana
Matanzas
Pinar del Río
I. de la Juventud
Sta. Clara
Camagüey
Holguín
Santiago de Cuba
Montego Bay
Kingston
Port-au-Prince
Santo Domingo
San Juan
Charlotte Amalie
St. Johns
Basse-Terre
Ft.-de-France
Bridgetown
St. George's
Port of Spain
Tobago
Trinidad
Curaçao
La Guaira
Barranquilla
Cartagena
Montería
Medellín
Manizales
Cúcuta
Bucaramanga
Tunja
Bogotá
Neiva
Cali
Popayán
Pasto
Buenaventura
Tumaco
Esmeraldas
Quito
Mitú
Maracaibo
Coro
Valencia
Caracas
Barquisimeto
Mérida
Barinas
Calabozo
Barcelona
Ciudad Bolívar
San Fernando de Atabapo
Pto. Ayacucho
Boa Vista
Barcelos
30° 20° 10° 0°
110° 100° 90° 80° 70° 60°
A B C D E F
1 2 3 4 5

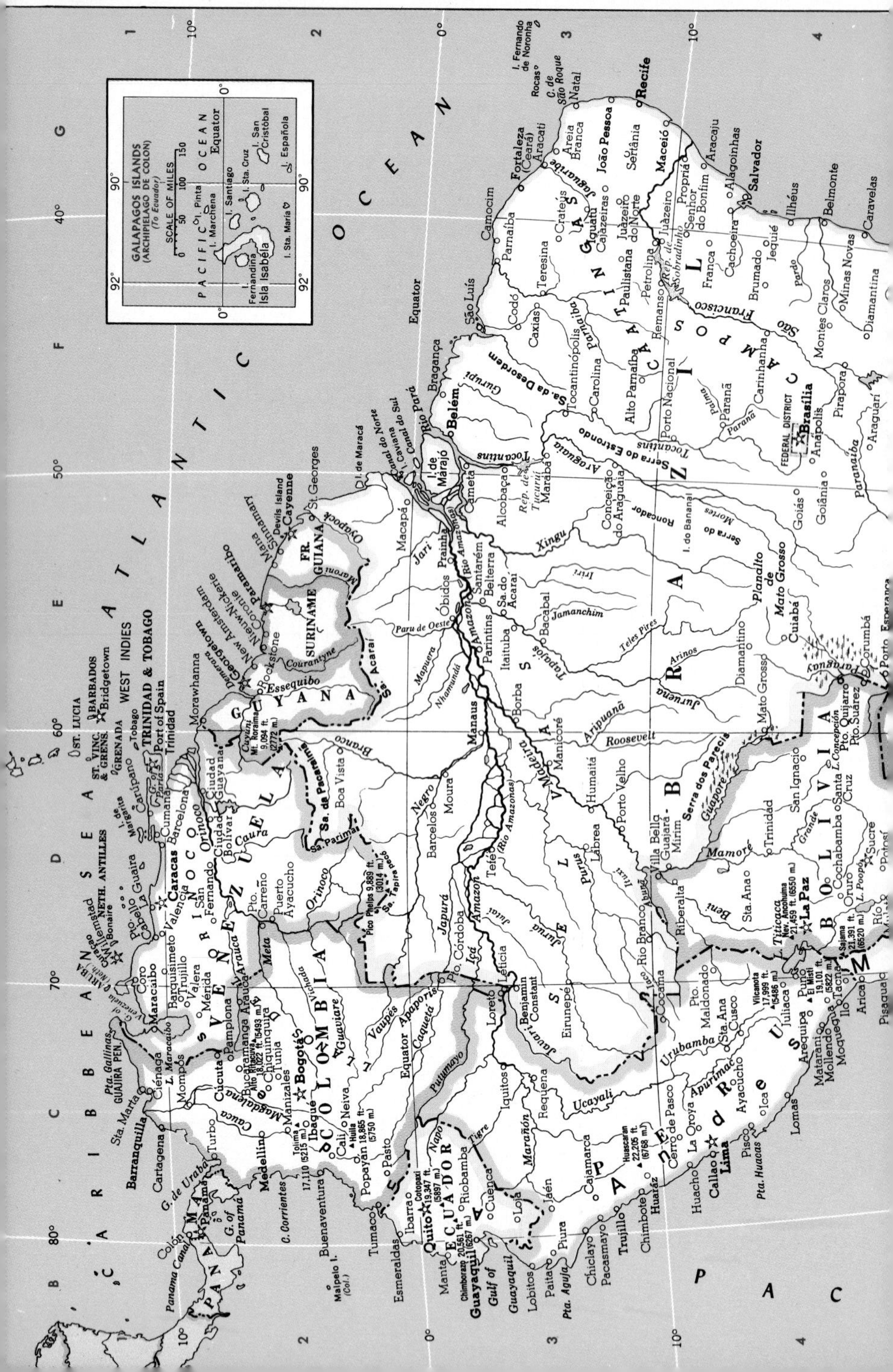

GALAPAGOS ISLANDS
(ARCHIPIELAGO DE COLON)
(To Ecuador)
SCALE OF MILES
PACIFIC OCEAN
Equator
Isla Isabela
I. Fernandina
I. Santiago
I. Sta. Cruz
I. San Cristóbal
I. Española
I. Sta. María
I. Pinta
I. Marchena
CARIBBEAN SEA
ATLANTIC OCEAN
PACIFIC
WEST INDIES
NETH. ANTILLES
ARUBA
Bonaire
Willemstad
ST. LUCIA
BARBADOS
Bridgetown
ST. VINC. & GRENS.
GRENADA
TRINIDAD & TOBAGO
Port of Spain
Tobago
Trinidad
VENEZUELA
Caracas
Maracaibo
L. Maracaibo
Orinoco
Ciudad Bolívar
Ciudad Guayana
Mt. Roraima 9,094 ft. (2772 m.)
Sa. Parima
Sa. de Pacaraima
GUYANA
Georgetown
New Amsterdam
Essequibo
SURINAME
Paramaribo
FR. GUIANA
Cayenne
Devils Island
St. Georges
COLOMBIA
Bogotá
Medellín
Cali
Barranquilla
Cartagena
Sta. Marta
Magdalena
Cauca
Pta. Gallinas
GUAJIRA PEN.
Malpelo I. (Col.)
PANAMA
Panamá
Colón
Panama Canal
G. of Panama
G. de Urabá
ECUADOR
Quito
Guayaquil
Gulf of Guayaquil
Cotopaxi 19,347 ft. (5897 m.)
Chimborazo 20,561 ft. (6267 m.)
Equator
PERU
Lima
Callao
Huascarán 22,205 ft. (6768 m.)
Iquitos
Cusco
Arequipa
Ucayali
Marañón
Amazon
BOLIVIA
La Paz
L. Titicaca
Sucre
Cochabamba
BRAZIL
Brasília
FEDERAL DISTRICT
Manaus
Belém
I. de Marajó
Rio Pará
Santarém
Xingu
Tapajós
Madeira
Purus
Juruá
Negro
Branco
Tocantins
Araguaia
São Luís
Fortaleza
Natal
Recife
João Pessoa
Maceió
Aracaju
Salvador
Teresina
São Francisco
Planalto de Mato Grosso
Cuiabá
Serra dos Parecis
Serra do Estrondo
Sa. da Desordem
Serra do Roncador
I. Fernando de Noronha
C. de São Roque
Rocas
Equator

SOUTH AMERICA
LAMBERT AZIMUTHAL EQUAL-AREA PROJECTION
SCALE OF MILES
0 100 200 400 600
SCALE OF KILOMETERS
0 100 200 400 600
Capitals of Countries
International Boundaries
Canals
Copyright by C. S. HAMMOND & CO., N.Y.
Longitude 60° West of Greenwich
Tropic of Capricorn
ATLANTIC OCEAN
PACIFIC OCEAN
PARAGUAY
URUGUAY
ARGENTINA
CHILE
FALKLAND ISLANDS
(IS. MALVINAS)
(Br.-claimed by Arg.)
Stanley
East Falkland
West Falkland
JUAN FERNÁNDEZ IS.
(Chile)
I. Robinson Crusoe
I. Alejandro Selkirk
I. San Félix
I. San Ambrosio
Asunción
Montevideo
BUENOS AIRES
Santiago
SÃO PAULO
RIO DE JANEIRO
Valparaíso
Córdoba
Rosario
Santa Fe
La Plata
Mar del Plata
Bahía Blanca
Porto Alegre
Curitiba
Florianópolis
Santos
Niterói
Río de la Plata
Tierra del Fuego
Cape Horn
(Cabo de Hornos)
I. de los Estados
(Staten I.)
Strait of Magellan
Punta Arenas
Ushuaia
ARCHIPIÉLAGO de los CHONOS
Isla de Chiloé
PEN. TAITAO
G. de Penas
Golfo San Jorge
Golfo San Matías
Pen. Valdés
Cerro Aconcagua 22,831 ft. (6959 m.)
Vol. Llullaillaco 22,057 ft. (6723 m.)
Nev. Ojos del Salado 22,572 ft. (6880 m.)
Maipo 17,464 ft. (5323 m.)
Antofagasta
Taltal
Chañaral
Caldera
Copiapó
Huasco
Vallenar
La Serena
Coquimbo
Ovalle
Los Vilos
Viña del Mar
Constitución
Talcahuano
Concepción
Arauco
Temuco
Villarrica
Valdivia
Pto. Montt
Ancud
Castro
Talca
Chillán
Mendoza
San Juan
San Luis
San Rafael
Tucumán
Salta
Jujuy
Santiago del Estero
Catamarca
La Rioja
Corrientes
Resistencia
Formosa
Posadas
Encarnación
Concordia
Paraná
Paysandú
Salto
Rivera
Mercedes
Florida
Rocha
Pelotas
Rio Grande
L. dos Patos
L. Mirim
Neuquén
Zapala
San Carlos de Bariloche
Puerto Madryn
Rawson
Trelew
Viedma
Comodoro Rivadavia
Puerto Deseado
San Julián
Santa Cruz
Río Gallegos
Lago Argentino
Paraná
Uruguay
Pilcomayo
Bermejo
Salado
Colorado
Negro
Chubut
Deseado
Chico
Iguaçu Falls
Itaipu Res.
Mar Chiquita
Pôrto Alegre
Londrina
Sorocaba
Campinas
Petrópolis
Angra dos Reis
Cabo Frio
C. de São Tomé
I. de Santa Catarina
Joinville
Paranaguá

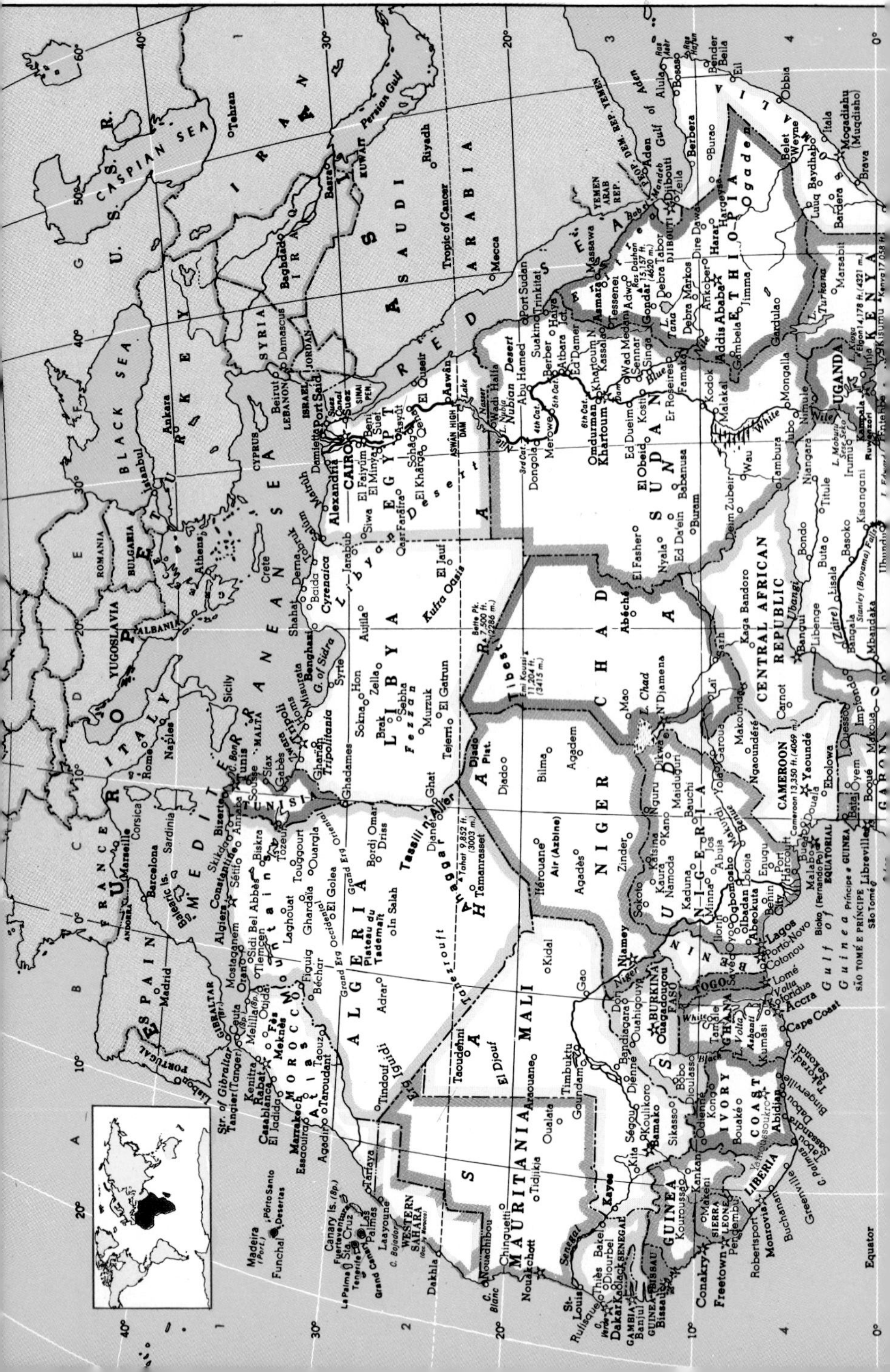
FRANCE
SPAIN
PORTUGAL
ANDORRA
ITALY
YUGOSLAVIA
ALBANIA
ROMANIA
BULGARIA
TURKEY
CYPRUS
SYRIA
LEBANON
ISRAEL
JORDAN
IRAQ
IRAN
KUWAIT
SAUDI ARABIA
YEMEN ARAB REP.
P.D.R. YEMEN
U.S.S.R.
BLACK SEA
CASPIAN SEA
MEDITERRANEAN SEA
RED SEA
Persian Gulf
Gulf of Aden
Tropic of Cancer
Equator
MOROCCO
ALGERIA
TUNISIA
LIBYA
EGYPT
SUDAN
CHAD
NIGER
MALI
MAURITANIA
WESTERN SAHARA
SENEGAL
GAMBIA
GUINEA-BISSAU
GUINEA
SIERRA LEONE
LIBERIA
IVORY COAST
GHANA
TOGO
BENIN
BURKINA FASO
NIGERIA
CAMEROON
CENTRAL AFRICAN REPUBLIC
EQUATORIAL GUINEA
SÃO TOMÉ E PRÍNCIPE
GABON
ETHIOPIA
DJIBOUTI
SOMALIA
KENYA
UGANDA
ZAIRE
SAHARA
Libyan Desert
Nubian Desert
Atlas Mts.
Ahaggar Mts.
Tibesti Mts.
Gulf of Guinea
Gulf of Sidra
Canary Is. (Sp.)
Madeira (Port.)
Balearic Is.
Corsica
Sardinia
Sicily
MALTA
Crete
Madrid
Lisbon
Barcelona
Marseille
Rome
Naples
Athens
Istanbul
Ankara
Beirut
Damascus
Baghdad
Tehran
Riyadh
Mecca
Cairo
Alexandria
Port Said
Suez
Aswân
Khartoum
Omdurman
Addis Ababa
Djibouti
Aden
Mogadishu
Kampala
Algiers
Tunis
Tripoli
Benghazi
Rabat
Casablanca
Marrakech
Dakar
Nouakchott
Bamako
Niamey
Ouagadougou
Conakry
Freetown
Monrovia
Abidjan
Accra
Lomé
Porto-Novo
Lagos
Yaoundé
Bangui
N'Djamena
Libreville
Malabo
Timbuktu
Lake Chad
L. Nasser
L. Tana
L. Turkana
L. Mobutu Sese Seko
Nile
Niger
Ubangi
Tahat 9,852 ft. (3003 m.)
Emi Koussi 11,204 ft. (3415 m.)
Ras Dashan 15,157 ft. (4620 m.)
Cameroon 13,350 ft. (4069 m.)
Mt. Elgon 14,178 ft. (4321 m.)

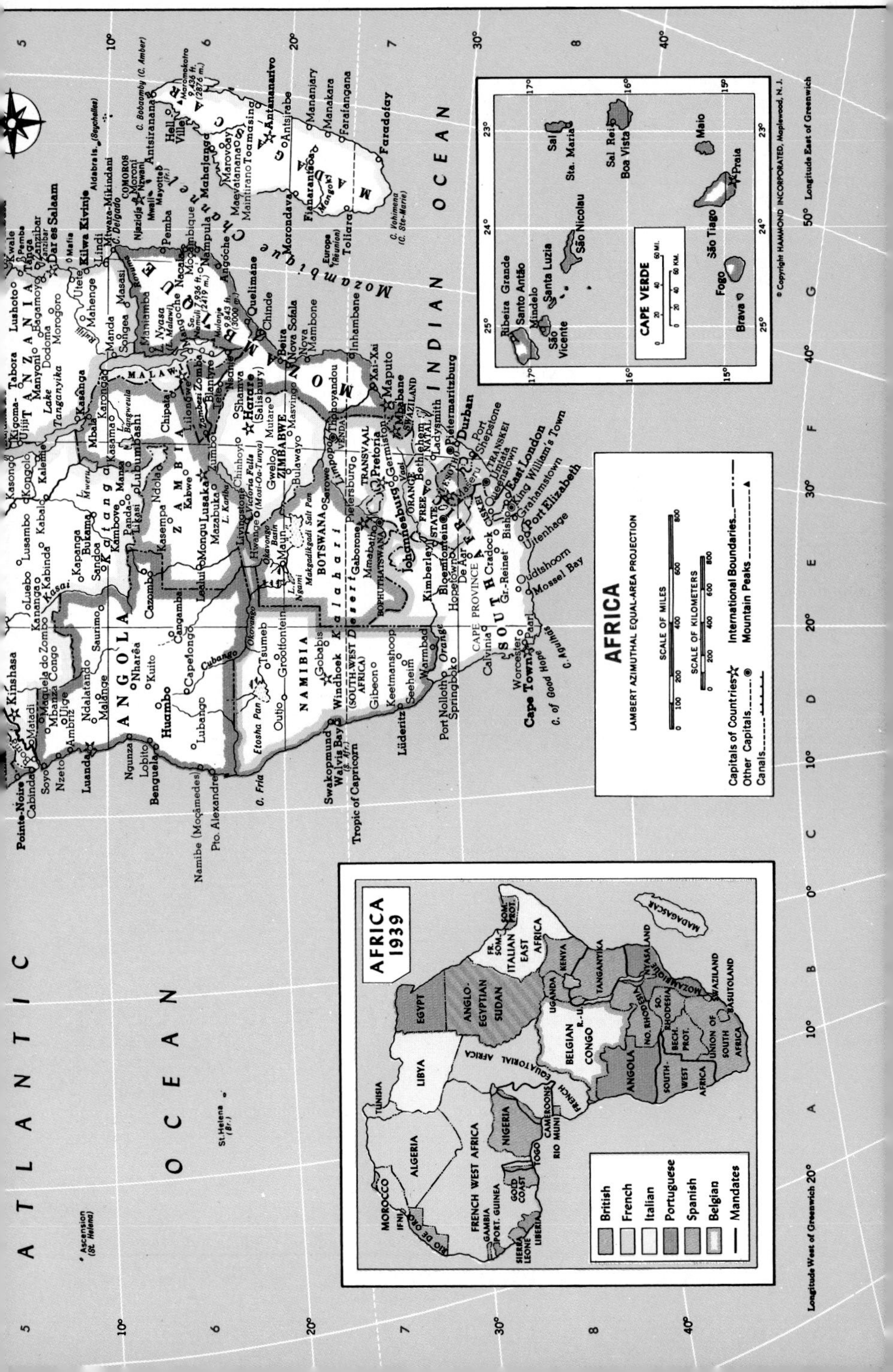
AFRICA
LAMBERT AZIMUTHAL EQUAL-AREA PROJECTION
SCALE OF MILES
0 100 200 400 600 800
SCALE OF KILOMETERS
0 200 400 600 800
Capitals of Countries
Other Capitals
Canals
International Boundaries
Mountain Peaks
AFRICA 1939
British
French
Italian
Portuguese
Spanish
Belgian
Mandates
CAPE VERDE
ATLANTIC OCEAN
INDIAN OCEAN
Mozambique Channel
ANGOLA
NAMIBIA
BOTSWANA
ZAMBIA
ZIMBABWE
MOZAMBIQUE
MALAWI
TANZANIA
MADAGASCAR
SOUTH AFRICA
Longitude West of Greenwich 20°
Longitude East of Greenwich
© Copyright HAMMOND INCORPORATED, Maplewood, N. J.

A
B
C
D
E
F
40°
30°
20°
10°
0°
70°
60°
50°
2
3
4
5
Jan Mayen
(Nor.)
NORWEGIAN SEA
Arctic Circle
Húnaflói
Horn
Breidhafjördhur
Reykjavik
ICELAND
Akureyri
Fontur
Seydhisfjördhur
Hornafjördhur
Hekla
ATLANTIC OCEAN
Faeroe Is.
(Den.)
Tórshavn
Shetland Is.
Lerwick
Orkney Is.
Kirkwall
Pentland Firth
Rockall
(U.K.)
Hebrides
The Minch
Moray Firth
Inverness
Aberdeen
SCOTLAND
BRITISH ISLES
UNITED KINGDOM
Glasgow
Edinburgh
Dundee
NO. IRELAND
Donegal Bay
North Chan.
IRELAND
Belfast
Dundalk
Galway
Limerick
(Luimneach)
Dublin
Waterford
Cork
Cobh
C. Clear
Isle of Man
IRISH SEA
Manchester
Liverpool
Leeds
Newcastle upon Tyne
Carlisle
Hull
Sheffield
The Wash
WALES
St. George's Chan.
Swansea
Birmingham
ENGLAND
Cardiff
LONDON
Bristol
Plymouth
Southampton
Portsmouth
Land's End
English Channel
NORTH SEA
Trondheimsfjorden
Namsos
Kristiansund
Ålesund
Trondheim
Sognefjorden
Bergen
Hardangerfjorden
Haugesund
Stavanger
Lillehammer
Oslo
Drammen
Fredrikstad
Larvik
Arendal
Lindesnes
Kristiansand
Skagerrak
Halden
NORWAY
Vesterålen
Lofoten
Vestfjorden
Östersund
Sundsvall
Söderhamn
Falun
Uppsala
Karlstad
Västerås
Vänern
Örebro
Göteborg
Vättern
Borås
Jönköping
Linköping
SWEDEN
Ålborg
Kattegat
DENMARK
Århus
Esbjerg
Copenhagen
Odense
Hälsingborg
Lund
Malmö
Karlskrona
Flensburg
Bornholm
BALTIC
Helgoland
Frisian Is.
Kiel
Lübeck
Stralsund
Rostock
Amsterdam
The Hague
NETHERLANDS
Utrecht
Rotterdam
Antwerp
Münster
Bremen
Hamburg
Weser
Elbe
Hannover
EAST BERLIN
Szczecin
(Stettin)
Kołobrzeg
Brunswick
Magdeburg
GERMANY
Oder
Essen
Dortmund
Düsseldorf
Cologne
Ghent
Calais
Brussels
BELGIUM
Liège
Aachen
Bonn
Kassel
Halle
Leipzig
Erfurt
Dresden
Wrocław
Plauen
Karl-Marx-Stadt
Lille
Amiens
LUX.
Mainz
Wiesbaden
Frankfurt
Mannheim
Prague
(Praha)
Saarbrücken
Rhine
Nuremberg
Karlsruhe
Plzeň
Regensburg
Stuttgart
Danube
Augsburg
Olomouc
Brno
CZECHOSLOVAKIA
Ostrava
Boulogne
Cherbourg
Le Havre
Channel Is.
(Br.)
Ushant I.
Brest
Rouen
Seine
Marne
Reims
Versailles
PARIS
Rennes
Belle Isle
Angers
Orléans
Nancy
Strasbourg
St-Nazaire
Loire
Nantes
Tours
Mulhouse
Freiburg
Munich
Linz
VIENNA
(Wien)
Bratislava
Bay of Biscay
La Rochelle
I. d'Oléron
FRANCE
Dijon
Basel
Zürich
L. of Constance
LIECHTENSTEIN
Innsbruck
Salzburg
AUSTRIA
Bern
SWITZERLAND
Lausanne
L. Geneva
Geneva
Mt. Blanc
Limoges
Vichy
Clermont-Ferrand
Lyon
St-Étienne
Bordeaux
Dordogne
Garonne
Grenoble
Rhône
Bolzano
Trento
Venice
(Venezia)
Ljubljana
Graz
HUNGARY
Balaton
Pécs
Sopron
Maribor
Zagreb
Trieste
Rijeka
Milan
Brescia
Verona
Padua
Turin
(Torino)
Montauban
Nîmes
Toulouse
Montpellier
G. of Lions
Toulon
Marseille
Nice
MONACO
Genoa
La Spezia
Parma
Modena
Ferrara
Bologna
Florence
(Firenze)
SAN MARINO
Ancona
Leghorn
(Livorno)
Siena
Perugia
Tiber
ADRIATIC SEA
Banja Luka
Zadar
Split
Sarajevo
YUGOSLAVIA
Corsica
(Corse)
Elba
Ajaccio
ROME
VATICAN CITY
ITALY
Foggia
Bari
Vesuvius
Naples
(Napoli)
Taranto
G. of Taranto
Brindisi
Sassari
Olbia
Sardinia
(Sardegna)
Iglesias
Cagliari
TYRRHENIAN SEA
Catanzaro
IONIAN SEA
Palermo
Messina
Reggio di Calabria
Etna
Sicily
(Sicilia)
Catania
Syracuse
Pantelleria
MALTA
Valletta
El Ferrol
La Coruña
C. Finisterre
Oviedo
Gijón
Santander
San Sebastián
Biarritz
Bayonne
Pyrénées
ANDORRA
Vigo
Miño
León
Bilbao
Burgos
Ebro
Porto
(Oporto)
Braga
Valladolid
Douro
Coimbra
Salamanca
(Duero)
Saragossa
PORTUGAL
Sa. de Guadarrama
MADRID
Lisbon
(Lisboa)
Tejo
Tagus
(Tajo)
Toledo
SPAIN
Setúbal
Guadiana
Évora
Badajoz
Barcelona
Tarragona
C. St. Vincent
Sierra Morena
Albacete
Valencia
Balearic Is.
Palma
Majorca
Minorca
Ibiza
Córdoba
Guadalquivir
Murcia
Lorca
Alicante
Cartagena
G. of Cádiz
Cádiz
Seville
Jerez
Granada
Sa. Nevada
Str. of Gibraltar
GIBRALTAR
(Br.)
Málaga
Almería
Tangier
Ceuta
(Sp.)
MEDITERRANEAN SEA
Kenitra
Rabat
Casablanca
Melilla
(Sp.)
Oran
Algiers
Skikda
Bizerte
C. Bon
Tunis
Sousse
Fès (Fez)
Meknès
MOROCCO
Marrakech
Constantine
Annaba
ALGERIA
TUNISIA
Biskra
Longitude West
of Greenwich
Longitude East
of Greenwich

EUROPE
LAMBERT AZIMUTHAL EQUAL AREA PROJECTION
SCALE OF MILES
0 100 200 300 400 500
SCALE OF KILOMETERS
0 100 200 300 400 500
Capitals of Countries
International Boundaries
Canals
Copyright by C.S. HAMMOND & CO., N.Y.
BARENTS SEA
UNION OF SOVIET SOCIALIST REPUBLICS
RUSSIAN SOVIET FEDERATED SOCIALIST REPUBLIC
BLACK SEA
CASPIAN SEA
TURKEY
ROMANIA
BULGARIA
MOSCOW (Moskva)
LENINGRAD
Kiev
Helsinki
Bucharest
Sofia
ISTANBUL
Ankara
Athens
Tbilisi
Baku
Volgograd (Stalingrad)
White Sea
Sea of Azov
Caucasus
IRAN
SYRIA
CYPRUS

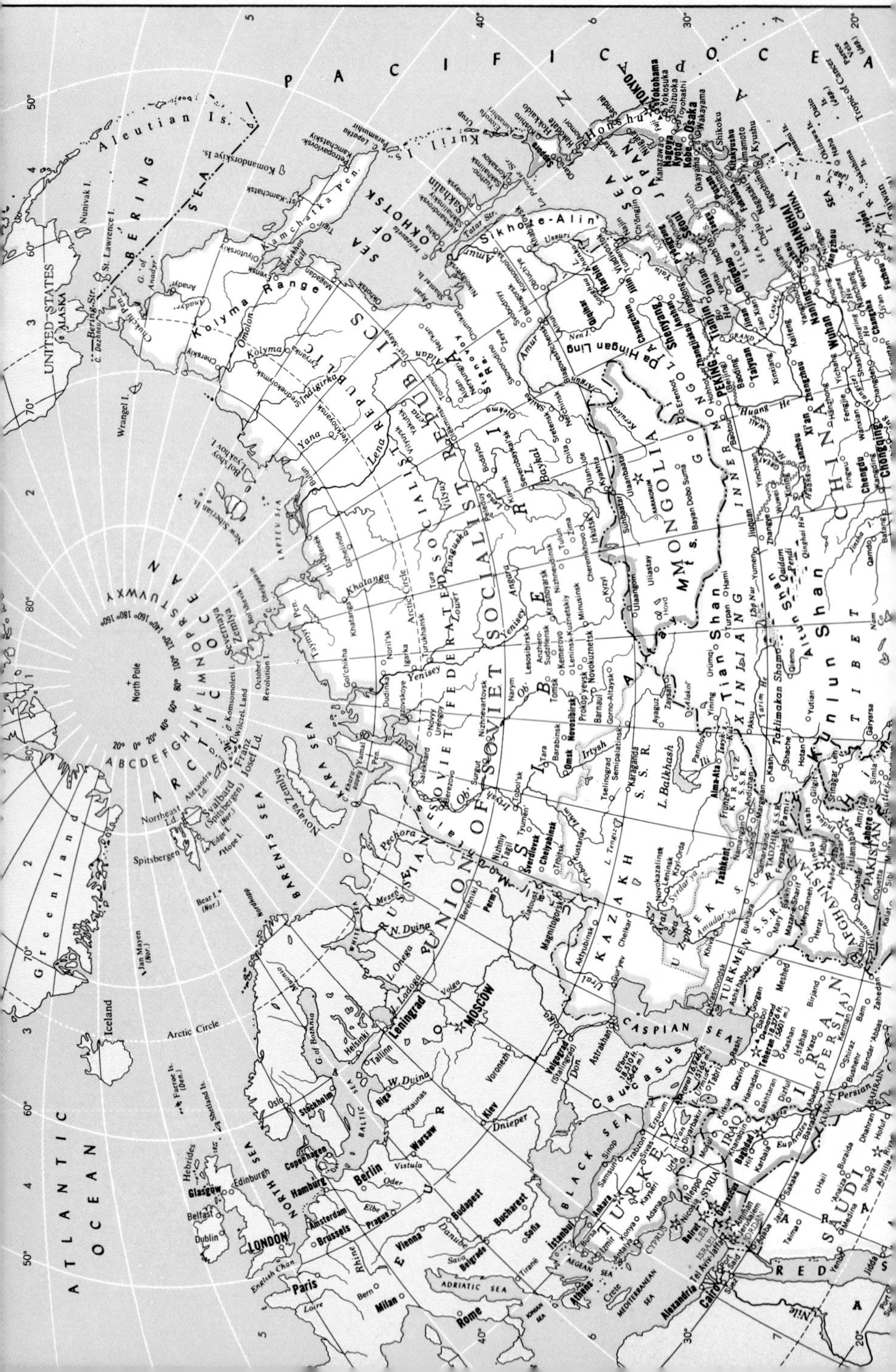
PACIFIC OCEAN
ARCTIC OCEAN
ATLANTIC OCEAN
North Pole
UNION OF SOVIET SOCIALIST REPUBLICS
RUSSIAN SOVIET FEDERATED SOCIALIST REPUBLIC
MONGOLIA
CHINA
TIBET
INNER MONGOLIA
XINJIANG
JAPAN
KAZAKH S.S.R.
UZBEK S.S.R.
TURKMEN S.S.R.
KIRGIZ S.S.R.
TADZHIK S.S.R.
AFGHANISTAN
PAKISTAN
IRAN (PERSIA)
IRAQ
SYRIA
TURKEY
SAUDI ARABIA
UNITED STATES
ALASKA
Greenland
Iceland
BERING SEA
SEA OF OKHOTSK
SEA OF JAPAN
BARENTS SEA
KARA SEA
LAPTEV SEA
NORTH SEA
BALTIC SEA
BLACK SEA
CASPIAN SEA
MEDITERRANEAN SEA
RED SEA
ADRIATIC SEA
Aleutian Is.
Kuril Is.
Kamchatka Pen.
Sakhalin
Novaya Zemlya
Severnaya Zemlya
Franz Josef Ld.
Svalbard (Spitsbergen)
New Siberian Is.
Wrangel I.
Kolyma Range
Sikhote-Alin'
Da Hingan Ling
Altay
Tian Shan
Kunlun Shan
Caucasus
Ural Mts.
Arctic Circle
Lena
Yenisey
Ob'
Irtysh
Amur
Volga
Dnieper
Danube
L. Baykal
L. Balkhash
Aral Sea
MOSCOW
Leningrad
Kiev
Warsaw
Berlin
Stockholm
Helsinki
Oslo
Copenhagen
Hamburg
Amsterdam
Brussels
LONDON
Paris
Prague
Vienna
Budapest
Bucharest
Sofia
Belgrade
Rome
Milan
Athens
Istanbul
Ankara
Cairo
Alexandria
Baghdad
Damascus
Tehran
Tashkent
Alma-Ata
Novosibirsk
Omsk
Sverdlovsk
Chelyabinsk
Irkutsk
Ulaanbaatar
Vladivostok
Khabarovsk
PEKING (Beijing)
Tianjin
Shenyang
SHANGHAI
Nanjing
Wuhan
Chongqing
Xi'an
Lanzhou
Seoul
Pyongyang
TOKYO
Yokohama
Nagoya
Kyoto
Osaka
Kobe
Sapporo
Lahore
Tropic of Cancer

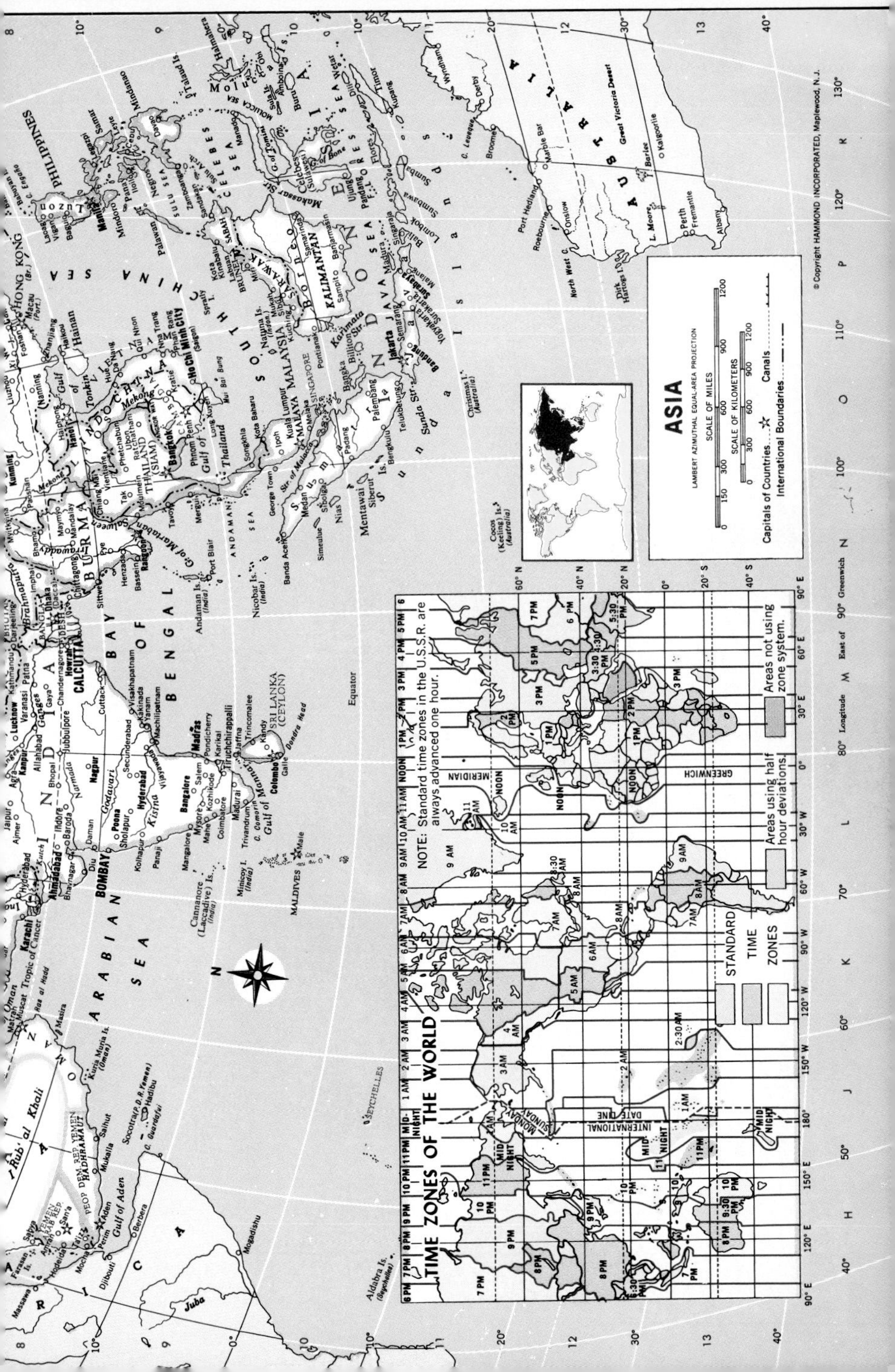
ASIA
LAMBERT AZIMUTHAL EQUAL-AREA PROJECTION
SCALE OF MILES
0 150 300 600 900 1200
SCALE OF KILOMETERS
0 300 600 900 1200
Capitals of Countries
International Boundaries
Canals
TIME ZONES OF THE WORLD
NOTE: Standard time zones in the U.S.S.R. are always advanced one hour.
STANDARD TIME ZONES
Areas using half hour deviations.
Areas not using zone system.
GREENWICH MERIDIAN
INTERNATIONAL DATE LINE
MONDAY
SUNDAY
ARABIAN SEA
BAY OF BENGAL
SOUTH CHINA SEA
INDIA
BURMA
THAILAND (SIAM)
INDOCHINA
PHILIPPINES
INDONESIA
MALAYSIA
AUSTRALIA
SRI LANKA (CEYLON)
Equator
Tropic of Cancer
Longitude East of Greenwich
© Copyright HAMMOND INCORPORATED, Maplewood, N.J.

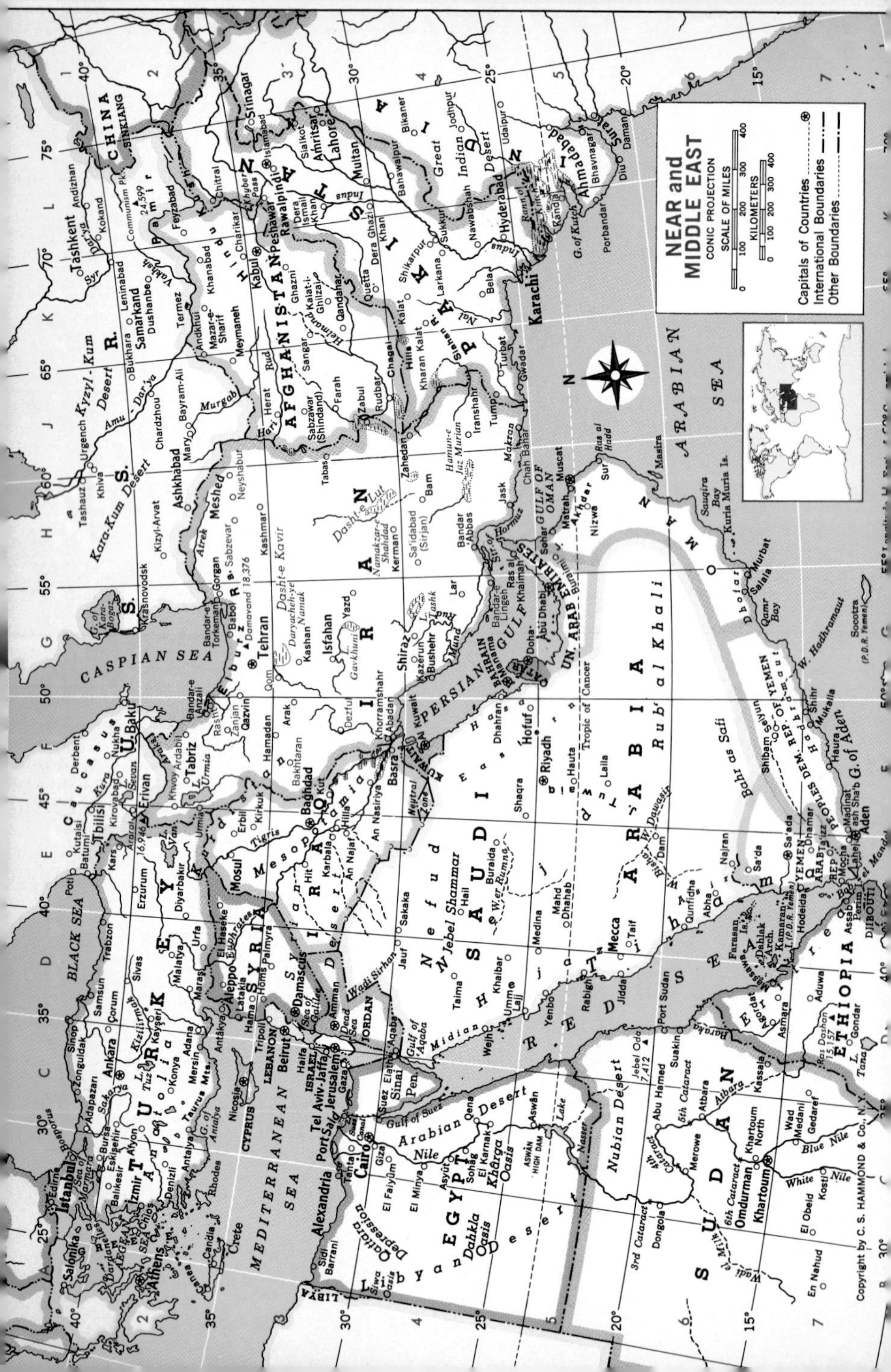
NEAR and MIDDLE EAST
CONIC PROJECTION
SCALE OF MILES
0 100 200 300 400
KILOMETERS
0 100 200 300 400
Capitals of Countries
International Boundaries
Other Boundaries
Copyright by C. S. HAMMOND & Co., N.Y.
BLACK SEA
CASPIAN SEA
MEDITERRANEAN SEA
RED SEA
ARABIAN SEA
PERSIAN GULF
GULF OF OMAN
G. of Aden
TURKEY
SYRIA
LEBANON
ISRAEL
JORDAN
IRAQ
IRAN
KUWAIT
BAHRAIN
QATAR
UN. ARAB EMIRATES
SAUDI ARABIA
OMAN
YEMEN
PEOPLES DEM. REP. OF YEMEN
AFGHANISTAN
PAKISTAN
INDIA
CHINA
SINKIANG
U.S.S.R.
EGYPT
SUDAN
ETHIOPIA
CYPRUS
LIBYA
DJIBOUTI
Istanbul
Ankara
Izmir
Athens
Nicosia
Beirut
Damascus
Amman
Jerusalem
Tel Aviv-Jaffa
Baghdad
Basra
Tehran
Isfahan
Shiraz
Kabul
Karachi
Riyadh
Mecca
Medina
Jidda
Aden
Muscat
Cairo
Alexandria
Port Said
Khartoum
Omdurman
Tashkent
Samarkand
Dushanbe
Baku
Tbilisi
Erivan
Rawalpindi
Lahore
Tropic of Cancer
Rub' al Khali
Nubian Desert
Libyan Desert
Arabian Desert

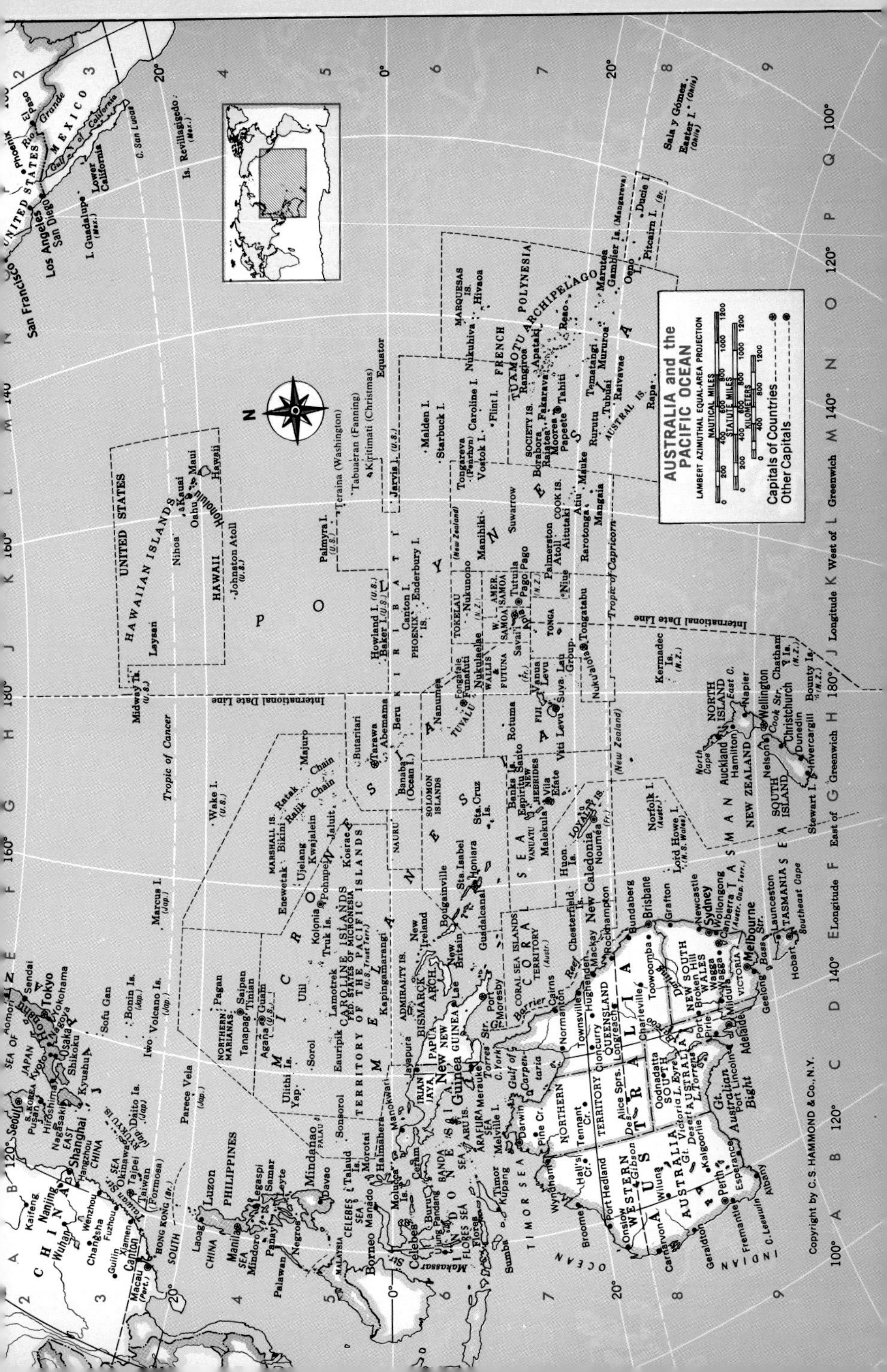
AUSTRALIA and the PACIFIC OCEAN
LAMBERT AZIMUTHAL EQUAL-AREA PROJECTION
NAUTICAL MILES
STATUTE MILES
KILOMETERS
Capitals of Countries
Other Capitals
Copyright by C.S. HAMMOND & Co., N.Y.
International Date Line
Tropic of Cancer
Tropic of Capricorn
Equator
Longitude East of Greenwich
Longitude West of Greenwich
AUSTRALIA
NEW ZEALAND
MICRONESIA
MELANESIA
POLYNESIA
HAWAIIAN ISLANDS
FRENCH POLYNESIA
CORAL SEA
TASMAN SEA
TIMOR SEA
ARAFURA SEA
INDONESIA
PHILIPPINES
JAPAN
CHINA
UNITED STATES
MEXICO
INDIAN OCEAN

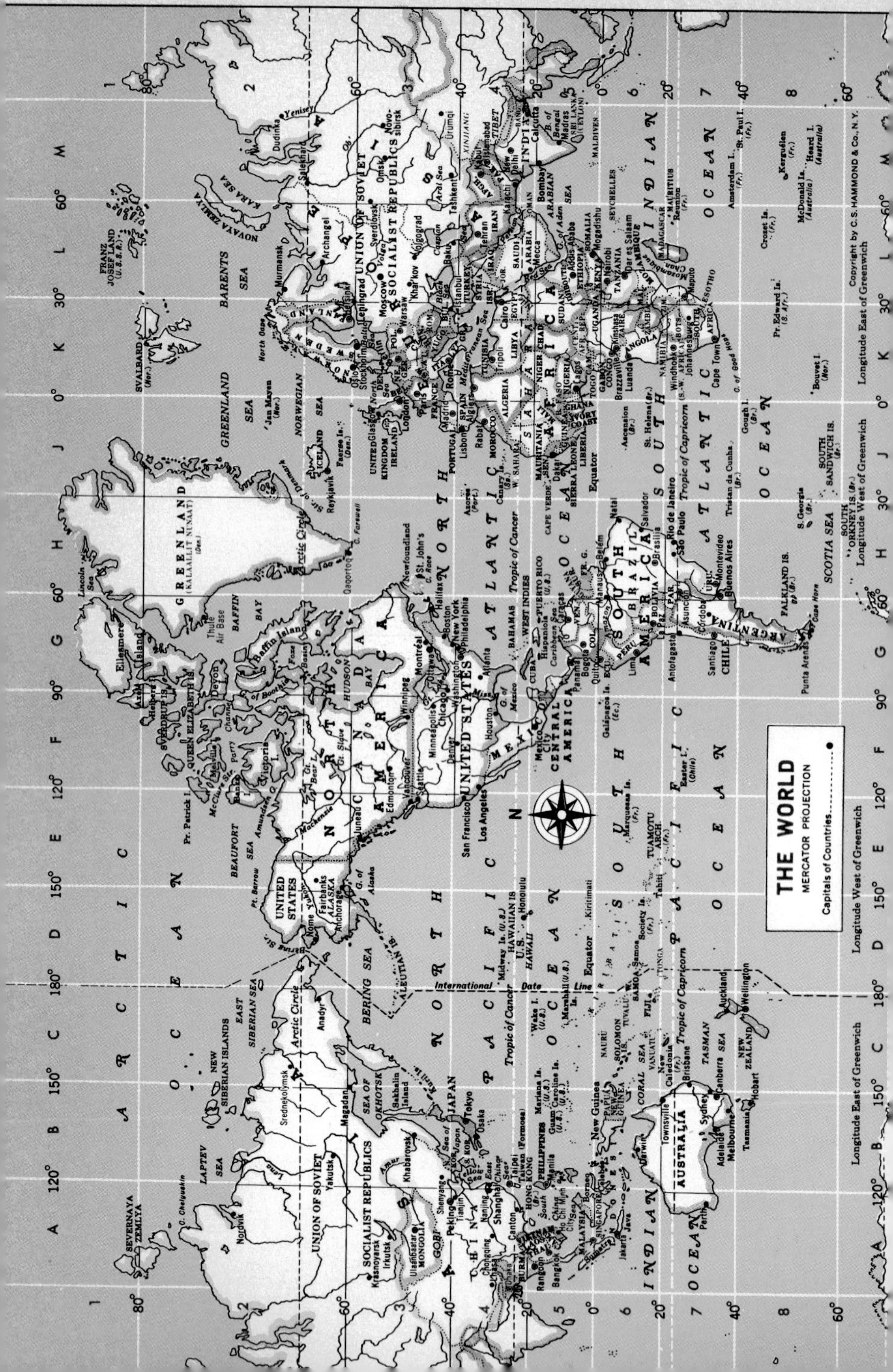
THE WORLD
MERCATOR PROJECTION
Capitals of Countries
Copyright by C.S. HAMMOND & Co., N.Y.
Longitude West of Greenwich
Longitude East of Greenwich
ARCTIC OCEAN
NORTH PACIFIC OCEAN
SOUTH PACIFIC OCEAN
NORTH ATLANTIC OCEAN
SOUTH ATLANTIC OCEAN
INDIAN OCEAN
NORTH AMERICA
SOUTH AMERICA
AFRICA
AUSTRALIA
UNION OF SOVIET SOCIALIST REPUBLICS
International Date Line
Tropic of Cancer
Tropic of Capricorn
Arctic Circle
Equator

Where Clean Water Act Funds Would Go

The Clean Water Act would allocate construction grants and funds through 1994. The annual allotment of Federal funds from fiscal year 1988 to fiscal year 1990 are shown in millions of dollars. Allocations from 1991-1994 would be determined later.

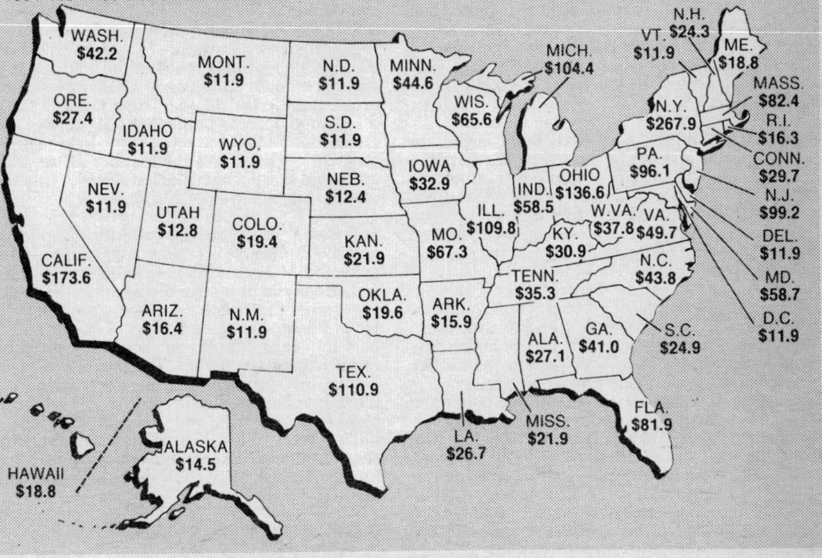

1987 Environmental Quality Index

Source: Copyright 1987 by the National Wildlife Federation.

Reprinted from the February-March issue of *National Wildlife Magazine.*

National Wildlife's annual Environmental Quality Index is a subjective analysis of the state of the nation's natural resources. The information included in each section is based on personal interviews, news reports, and the most recent scientific studies. The judgments on resource trends represent the collective thinking of the editors and the National Wildlife Federation staff, based on consultation with government experts, private specialists, and academic researchers.

Wildlife: Same. There were signs that the federal government was finally getting serious about attacking the sources of toxic threats to wildlife. The bald eagle already has benefited from efforts to detoxify wildlife habitat. It received a further boost when the U.S. Department of Interior announced it would phase out the use of lead shot for waterfowl hunting by 1991. In the last two decades, at least 124 bald eagles have died after eating lead-contaminated prey, and currently, more than two million waterfowl fall victim to lead poisoning each year. The chemical threat to birds was further relieved in 1986, when for the first time, the Environmental Protection Agency restricted the use of two pesticides solely on the basis of their harmful effect on wildlife. However, the continuing nationwide loss of habitat (wetlands) remains a threat to waterfowl. The U.S. Department of Agriculture proposed regulations that would significantly weaken the impact of "swampbuster" provisions of the 1985 Farm Act—a law that denies federal subsidies to farmers who drain wetlands for conversion to crops.

Air: Same. America has made significant progress in improving the quality of its air in recent years. But after more than a decade of steady decreases under the Clean Air Act, the levels of sulfur dioxide, nitrogen oxides, and particulates have begun to edge upward. EPA officials cautioned that it is too early to know if the latest increases represent a trend, but the figures added a note of urgency to efforts by environmentalists to clamp tighter control on sulfur and nitrogen emissions. They are also the air pollutants identified in scientific studies as the key precursors to acid rain. Efforts to control them got a significant boost in 1986 when, for the first time, President Reagan finally acknowledged that action on acid rain is necessary. Another air pollutant, ozone, has declined nationally about 10 percent between 1983 and 1984 but EPA Administrator Lee M. Thomas announced that more than a third of the 84 metropolitan areas being monitored will fail to meet the law's 1988 deadline for reducing ozone pollution to a "safe" level. A new source of concern is the level of toxic pollutants inside homes.

Water: Same. While there have been major improvements as a result of the Clean Water Act—Lake Erie and the Charles River are examples—"nonpoint" pollution continues to be a major problem. Nearly one out of every four miles of U.S. rivers and one out of every five lakes are being spoiled or threatened by pollutants cascading from farms, mines, and urban areas. The nation's inability to effectively control surface water pollution has exacted a heavy toll. According to U.S. and Canadian researchers, 37 million people who live around the Great Lakes generally have 20 percent higher levels of toxic chemicals in their bodies than other North Americans. Equally alarming is the growing knowledge of what years of unwitting abuse have done to groundwater supplies that provide drinking water for one out of every two U.S. families. Congress took an important step in 1986 toward controlling groundwater pollution by revising the 12-year-old Safe Drinking Water Act. In another action Congress voted a five-year, nine-billion-dollar extension of the Superfund program for cleaning up toxic dump sites.

Energy: Same. Although oil prices declined sharply in 1986, U.S. energy consumption failed to increase. The reason: the conservation measures implemented in the last decade are now so woven into the fabric of American life that they are not easily removed. However, the National Academy of Science warned that declines in government support for energy conservation research could prevent future gains. Meanwhile disputes over the use of federal lands simmer anew. The Interior Department agreed to hand over 82,000 acres of prime grazing and recreation land to an oil consortium for a token $2.50 per acre. Environmentalists also battled against abusive mining practices. In a suit filed against the federal Office of Surface Mining, NWF charged that hundreds of coal mines are spoiling streams with acid discharges because the government had failed to enforce strip-mining regulations.

Forests: Same. These are troubled times for the rich forests of the Northwest and South. Having depleted valuable virgin forests on western private land, forest product companies are fighting to harvest portions of the three million acres of "old growth" that remains on public forests. Clear-cut stands of "old growth" trees require centuries to regain their former stature. That is one reason the industry increasingly relies on the South where favorable climate and geography allow foresters to grow genetically refined "supertrees" that produce wood in record time. But last summer (1986) a study found that the rate of growth in many species had declined and the number of tree deaths increased sharply over the last decade. One factor may be air pollution.

Soil: Same. The nation took a historic step forward in the fight against erosion in 1986 as the U.S. Department of Agriculture began implementing key provisions of a new farm bill which authorized the government to create a "conservation reserve" by paying farmers for each acre of highly erodible land they take out of crop production and replant to soil-saving vegetation. The law also contains a "sodbuster" provision that penalizes farmers who plow and plant fragile grasslands without approved plans to control wind and water erosion. Forty-one million acres of highly erodible farmland (10 percent of the nation's total cropland) are responsible for nearly half of the soil erosion in the United States.

Quality of Life: Same. Throughout 1986 there were sobering signs that the nation's environmental problems were striking closer to home, threatening the quality of life of many Americans who had always believed that "it can't happen here." In a cross-section survey of some 1,300 readers of *National Wildlife*, 91 percent of the respondents said they would rather pay higher taxes than have the federal government reduce budget deficits by cutting back on important pollution clean-up programs. Readers ranked concerns as: drinking water contamination, leaking hazardous waste sites, toxic gases in the air, acid rain, air pollution from automobiles, water pollution from farm and city runoff, nuclear energy, and indoor air pollution, in that order. Readers ranked the threat posed by indoor air pollution last, perhaps reflecting the continued lack of information on this dangerous problem.

Some Endangered and Threatened Species of the World[1]

Common name	Scientific name	Range
MAMMALS		
Bear, brown	*Ursus arctos pruinosus*	China (Tibet)
Bear, brown or grizzly[2]	*Ursus arctos horribilis*	Canada, Western U.S.
Cat, leopard	*Felis bengalensis bengalensis*	Eastern Asia
Cat, tiger	*Felis tigrinus*	Costa Rica to northern Argentina
Cheetah	*Acinonyx jubatus*	Africa to India
Chimpanzee[2]	*Pan troglodytes*	Western and Central Africa
Chinchilla	*Chinchilla brevicaudata boliviana*	Bolivia
Deer, Columbian white-tailed	*Odocoileus virginianus leucurus*	U.S. (Ore., Wash.)

Common name	Scientific name	Range
Deer, marsh	*Blastocerus dichotomus*	Argentina, Uruguay, Bolivia Paraguay, Brazil
Deer, musk	*Moschus moschiferus moschiferus*	Central and East Asia
Elephant, Asian	*Elephas maximus*	Southcentral and Southeast Asia
Gazelle, Clark's (Dibatag)	*Ammodorcas clarkei*	Somalia, Ethiopia
Gazelle, slender-horned (Rhim)	*Gazella leptoceros*	Sudan, Algeria, Egypt, Libya
Gorilla	*Gorilla gorilla*	Central and western Africa
Ibex, Walia	*Capra walie*	Ethiopia
Jaguar	*Panthera onca*	Central and South America, and U.S. (Texas, N.M., Ariz.)
Kangaroo, red[2]	*Macropus (=Megaleia) rufus*	Australia
Leopard	*Panthera pardus*	Africa and Asia
Leopard, snow	*Panthera uncia*	Central Asia
Lion, Asiatic	*Panthera leo persica*	Turkey to India
Mandrill	*Papio sphinx*	Equatorial West Africa
Monkey, black howler[2]	*Alouatta pigra*	Mexico, Guatemala, Belize
Ocelot	*Felis pardalis*	Central and South America, Ariz., Texas
Orangutan	*Pongo pygmaeus*	Borneo, Sumatra
Otter, southern sea[2]	*Enhydra lutris nereis*	West coast U.S. (Wash., Ore., Calif.), south to Mexico (Baja Calif.)
Panther, Florida	*Felis concolor coryi*	U.S. (La. and Ark., east to S.C. and Fla.)
Prairie dog, Utah[2]	*Cynomys parvidens*	U.S. (Utah)
Pronghorn, Sonoran	*Antilocapra americana sonoriensis*	U.S. (Ariz.), Mexico
Rat, Morro Bay kangaroo	*Dipodomys heermanni morroensis*	U.S. (Calif.)
Rhinoceros, great Indian	*Rhinoceros unicornis*	India, Nepal
Sloth, Brazilian three-toed	*Bradypus torquatus*	Brazil
Tiger	*Panthera tigris*	Temperate and tropical Asia
Whale, humpback	*Megaptera novaeangliae*	Oceanic
Wolf, gray	*Canis lupus*	U.S. (48 conterminous other than Minn.[2]), Mexico
Zebra, mountain	*Equus zebra zebra*	South Africa
BIRDS		
Albatross, short-tailed	*Diomedea albatrus*	North Pacific Ocean: Japan, U.S.S.R U.S. (Alas., Calif., Hawaii, Ore., Wash.)
Condor, Andean	*Vultur gryphus*	Colombia to Chile and Argentina
Eagle, bald	*Haliaeetus leucocephalus*	Conterminous U.S. (except Wash., Ore., Minn., Wis., Mich.[2])
Falcon, Eurasian peregrine	*Falco peregrinus peregrinus*	Europe, Eurasia south to Africa and Mideast
Parakeet, paradise (=beautiful)	*Psephotus pulcherrimus*	Australia
Pelican, brown	*Pelecanus occidentalis*	U.S. (Carolinas, Texas, Calif.), West Indies, Central and South America, coastal
Penguin, Galápagos	*Spheniscus mendiculus*	Ecuador (Galápagos Islands)
Stork, oriental white	*Ciconia ciconia boyciana*	China, Japan, Korea, U.S.S.R.
REPTILES		
Crocodile, American	*Crocodylus acutus*	U.S. (Fla.), Mexico, South America, Central America, Caribbean
Iguana, Anegada ground	*Cyclura pinguis*	West Indies, British Virgin Is. (Anegada Is.)
Python, Indian	*Python molurus molurus*	Sri Lanka, India
Snake, Atlantic salt marsh[2]	*Nerodia fasciata taeniata*	U.S. (Fla.)
AMPHIBIANS		
Frog, Israel painted	*Discoglossus nigriventer*	Israel
Toad, African viviparous	*Nectophrynoides* spp.	Tanzania, Guinea, Ivory Coast, Cameroon, Liberia, Ethiopia
FISH		
Catfish, giant	*Pangasianodon gigas*	Thailand
Trout, greenback cutthroat[2]	*Salmo clarki stomias*	U.S. (Colo.)

1. Due to space limitations, does not include all mammals, birds, reptiles, amphibians, and fish or any clams, crustaceans, snails, insects, and plants. 2. Threatened. *Source:* Department of the Interior, Fish and Wildlife Service.

Water Supply of the World[1]

The Antarctic Icecap is the largest supply of fresh water, nearly 2 percent of the world's total of fresh and salt water. As can be seen from the table below, the amount of water in our atmosphere is over ten times as large as the water in all the rivers taken together. The fresh water actually available for human use in lakes and rivers and the accessible ground water amounts to only about one third of one percent of the world's total water supply.

	Surface area (square miles)	Volume (cubic miles)	Percentage of total
Salt Water			
The oceans	139,500,000	317,000,000	97.2
Inland seas and saline lakes	270,000	25,000	0.008
Fresh Water			
Freshwater lakes	330,000	30,000	0.009
All rivers (average level)	—	300	0.0001
Antarctic Icecap	6,000,000	6,300,000	1.9
Arctic Icecap and glaciers	900,000	680,000	0.21
Water in the atmosphere	197,000,000	3,100	0.001
Ground water within half a mile from surface	—	1,000,000	0.31
Deep-lying ground water	—	1,000,000	0.31
Total (rounded)	—	**326,000,000**	**100.00**

1. All figures are estimated. *Source:* Department of the Interior, Geological Survey.

Speed of Animals

Most of the following measurements are for maximum speeds over approximate quarter-mile distances. Exceptions—which are included to give a wide range of animals—are the lion and elephant, whose speeds were clocked in the act of charging; the whippet, which was timed over a 200-yard course; the cheetah over a 100-yard distance; man for a 15-yard segment of a 100-yard run; and the black mamba, six-lined race runner, spider, giant tortoise, three-toed sloth, and garden snail, which were measured over various small distances.

Animal	Speed mph	Animal	Speed mph	Animal	Speed mph
Cheetah	70	Mongolian wild ass	40	Man	27.89
Pronghorn antelope	61	Greyhound	39.35	Elephant	25
Wildebeest	50	Whippet	35.5	Black mamba snake	20
Lion	50	Rabbit (domestic)	35	Six-lined race runner	18
Thomson's gazelle	50	Mule deer	35	Squirrel	12
Quarter horse	47.5	Jackal	35	Pig (domestic)	11
Elk	45	Reindeer	32	Chicken	9
Cape hunting dog	45	Giraffe	32	Spider (Tegenearia atrica)	1.17
Coyote	43	White-tailed deer	30	Giant Tortoise	0.17
Gray fox	42	Wart hog	30	Three-toed sloth	0.15
Hyena	40	Grizzly bear	30	Garden snail	0.03
Zebra	40	Cat (domestic)	30		

Source: Natural History Magazine, March 1974, copyright 1974. The American Museum of Natural History; and James Doherty, Curator of Mammals, N.Y. Zoological Society.

Animal Group Terminology

Source: James Doherty, Curator of Mammals, N.Y. Zoological Society, and *Information Please* data.

ants: colony
bears: sleuth, sloth
bees: grist, hive, swarm
birds: flight, volery
cattle: drove
cats: clutter, clowder
chicks: brood, clutch
clams: bed
cranes: sedge, seige
crows: murder
doves: dule
ducks: brace, team
elephants: herd
elks: gang
finches: charm
fish: school, shoal, draught
foxes: leash, skulk
geese: flock, gaggle, skein
gnats: cloud, horde
goats: trip
gorillas: band
hares: down, husk
hawks: cast
hens: brood
hogs: drift
horses: pair, team
hounds: cry, mute, pack
kangaroos: troop
kittens: kindle, litter
larks: exaltation
lions: pride
locusts: plague
magpies: tidings
mules: span
nightingales: watch
oxen: yoke
oysters: bed
parrots: company
partridges: covey
peacocks: muster, ostentation
pheasants: nest, bouquet
pigs: litter
ponies: string
quail: bevy, covey
rabbits: nest
seals: pod
sheep: drove, flock
sparrows: host
storks: mustering
swans: bevy, wedge
swine: sounder
toads: knot
turkeys: rafter
turtles: bale
vipers: nest
whales: gam, pod
wolves: pack, route
woodcocks: fall

Animal Names: Male, Female, and Young

Animal	Male	Female	Young	Animal	Male	Female	Young	Animal	Male	Female	Young
Ass	Jack	Jenny	Foal	Duck	Drake	Duck	Duckling	Sheep	Ram	Ewe	Lamb
Bear	Boar	Sow	Cub	Elephant	Bull	Cow	Calf	Swan	Cob	Pen	Cygnet
Cat	Tom	Queen	Kitten	Fox	Dog	Vixen	Cub	Swine	Boar	Sow	Piglet
Cattle	Bull	Cow	Calf	Goose	Gander	Goose	Gosling	Tiger	Tiger	Tigress	Cub
Chicken	Rooster	Hen	Chick	Horse	Stallion	Mare	Foal	Whale	Bull	Cow	Calf
Deer	Buck	Doe	Fawn	Lion	Lion	Lioness	Cub	Wolf	Dog	Bitch	Pup
Dog	Dog	Bitch	Pup	Rabbit	Buck	Doe	Bunny				

Source: James Doherty, Curator of Mammals, N.Y. Zoological Society.

Gestation, Incubation, and Longevity of Certain Animals

Animal	Gestation or incubation, in days & (average)	Longevity, in years & (record exceptions)	Animal	Gestation or incubation, in days & (average)	Longevity, in years & (record exceptions)
Ass	365	18-20 (63)	Horse	329-345 (336)	20-25 (50+)
Bear	180-240 [1]	15-30 (47)	Kangaroo	32-39 [1]	4-6 (23)
Cat	52-69 (63)	10-12 (26+)	Lion	105-113 (108)	10 (29)
Chicken	22	7-8 (14)	Man	253-303	([2])
Cow	c. 280	9-12 (39)	Monkey	139-270 [1]	12-15[1](29)
Deer	197-300 [1]	10-15 (26)	Mouse	19-31 [1]	1-3 (4)
Dog	53-71 (63)	10-12 (24)	Parakeet (Budgerigar)	17-20 (18)	8 (12+)
Duck	21-35[1](28)	10 (15)	Pig	101-130 (115)	10 (22)
Elephant	510-730 (624) [1]	30-40 (71)	Pigeon	11-19	10-12 (39)
Fox	51-63 [1]	8-10 (14)	Rabbit	30-35 (31)	6-8 (15)
Goat	136-160 (151)	12 (17)	Rat	21	3 (5)
Groundhog	31-32	4-9	Sheep	144-152 (151) [1]	12 (16)
Guinea pig	58-75 (68)	3 (6)	Squirrel	44	8-9 (15)
Hamster, golden	15-17	2 (8)	Whale	365-547 [1]	—
Hippopotamus	220-255 (240)	30 (49+)	Wolf	60-63	10-12 (16)

1. Depending on kind. 2. For life expectancy charts, *see* Index. *Source:* James Doherty, Curator of Mammals, N.Y. Zoological Society.

Zoological Gardens

North America abounds in zoos from Canada to Mexico. The Metro Toronto Zoo, opened in 1974, is one of the largest in the world. Its six pavilions simulate the animals' natural habitats. So does the Calgary Zoo which also has a children's zoo. Mexico City's Chapultepec Park includes a large zoo featuring one of the few pairs of pandas outside of Red China, and a children's zoo.

The first zoological garden in the United States was established in Philadelphia in 1874. Since that time nearly every large city in the country has acquired a zoo. Among the largest are San Diego's on the West Coast; Chicago's Brookfield Zoo and those of St. Louis and Kansas City in the Middle West; New Orleans' Audubon Park and Zoological Garden in the South; and in the East the New York Zoological Society's park in the Bronx. The National Zoological Park in Washington, D.C., in a beautiful setting of hills, woods, and streams, was established in 1890 by an act of Congress. The major U.S. zoos now have created large natural-habitat areas for their collections.

In Europe, zoological gardens have long been popular public institutions. The modern concept of zoo keeping may be dated from 1752 with the founding of the Imperial Menagerie at the Schönbrunn Palace in Vienna. It was opened to the public in 1765 and is still in operation. In 1793 the zoological collection of the Jardin des Plantes was established in Paris in the Bois de Boulogne. At Antwerp the Royal Zoological Society founded a large menagerie in 1843. Now its aviary is noted for the principle of lighted and darkened spaces for confining the birds. Germany's famous Tiergarten zoo, in West Berlin, was founded in 1841 and officially opened in 1844. East Berlin has founded its own zoo.

In the British Isles, the Zoological Society of London established its collection in Regent's Park in 1828. It was also responsible for the establishment of the prototype of the open-range zoo, Whipsnade Park, in 1932. Edinburgh's zoo is famous for its collection of penguins, the largest colony in captivity.

Zoos and Aquariums

Source: The facilities listed are members of, and accredited by, the American Association of Zoological Parks and Aquariums to ensure that they are maintaining professional standards.

Abilene Zoological Gardens, Texas
Alaska Zoo, Anchorage
Alexandria Zoological Park, La.
Arizona-Sonora Desert Museum, Tucson
Audubon Park and Zoological Garden, New Orleans
John Ball Zoological Gardens, Grand Rapids, Mich.

Baltimore Zoo, Md.
Belle Isle Zoo and Aquarium, Detroit
Binder Park Zoo, Battle Creek, Mich.
Birmingham Zoo, Ala.
Blank Park Zoo of Des Moines, Iowa
Brandywine Zoo, Wilmington, Del.
Brookgreen Gardens, Murrells Inlet, S.C.
Buffalo Zoological Gardens, N.Y.
Busch Gardens, Tampa, Fla.
Caldwell Zoo, Texas
Calgary Zoo, Alberta, Canada
Central Florida Zoological Park, Lake Monroe, Fla.
Central Texas Zoo, Waco, Texas
Cheyenne Mountain Zoological Park, Colorado Springs
Chicago Zoological Park, Brookfield, Ill.
Cincinnati Zoo, Ohio
Cleveland Metroparks Zoo, Ohio
Columbus Zoological Gardens, Ohio
Dallas Aquarium, Texas
Dallas Zoo, Texas
Denver Zoological Gardens, Colo.
Detroit Zoological Park, Mich.
Dickerson Park Zoo, Springfield, Mo.
Discovery Island, Buena Vista, Fla.
Henry Doorly Zoo, Omaha, Neb.
El Paso Zoological Park, Texas
Emporia Zoo, Kan.
Erie Zoo, Pa.
Florida Cypress Gardens, Inc., Fla.
Fort Wayne Children's Zoo, Ind.
Fort Worth Zoological Park, Texas
Fossil Rim Wildlife Ranch, Fort Worth, Texas
Fresno Zoo, Calif.
Glen Oak Zoo, Ill.
Greater Baton Rouge Zoo, La.
Hogle Zoological Gardens, Salt Lake City, Utah
Honolulu Zoo, Hawaii
Houston Zoological Gardens, Texas
Indianapolis Zoo, Ind.
International Crane Foundation, Baraboo, Wis.
Kansas City Zoological Gardens, Mo.
Knoxville Zoological Park, Tenn.
Lake Superior Zoological Gardens, Duluth, Minn.
Lincoln Park Zoological Gardens, Chicago
Little Rock Zoological Gardens, Ark.
Living Desert, The, Palm Desert, Calif.
Los Angeles Zoo, Calif.
Louisville Zoological Garden, Ky.
Marine World Africa USA, Redwood City, Calif.
Memphis Zoological Gardens and Aquarium, Tenn.
Mesker Park Zoo, Evansville, Ind.
Metropolitan Toronto Zoo, Canada
Miami Metrozoo, Fla.
Miller Park Zoo, Bloomington, Ill.
Milwaukee County Zoological Gardens, Wis.
Minnesota Zoological Garden, Apple Valley, Minn.
Monkey Jungle, Inc., Miami, Fla.
Monterey Bay Aquarium, Calif.
Mystic Marinelife Aquarium, Mystic, Conn.
National Aquarium in Baltimore, Md.
National Zoological Park, Washington, D.C.
New England Aquarium, Boston
New York Aquarium, Brooklyn, N.Y.
New York Zoological Park, Bronx, N.Y.
North Carolina Zoological Park, Asheboro, N.C.
Northwest Trek Wildlife Park, Eatonville, Wash.
Oglebay's Good Children's Zoo, Wheeling, W.Va.
Oklahoma City Zoological Park, Okla.
Parrot Jungle, Inc., Miami, Fla.
Clyde Peeling's Reptiland Ltd., Williamsport, Pa.
Philadelphia Zoological Garden, Pa.
Phoenix Zoo, Ariz.
Pittsburgh Aviary, Pa.
Pittsburgh Zoo, Pa.
Point Defiance Zoo and Aquarium, Tacoma, Wash.
Gladys Porter Zoo, Brownsville, Texas
Potter Park Zoo, Lansing, Mich.
Racine Zoological Gardens, Wis.
Reid Park Zoo, Tucson, Ariz.
Lee Richardson Zoo, Garden City, Kan.
Rio Grande Zoological Park, Albuquerque, N.M.
Riverbanks Zoological Park, Columbia, S.C.
Henson Robinson Zoo, Springfield, Ill.
Sacramento Zoo, Calif.
St. Louis Zoological Park, Mo.
St. Paul's Como Zoo, Minn.
Salisbury Zoological Park, Md.
San Antonio Zoological Gardens and Aquarium, Texas
San Diego Wild Animal Park, Calif.
San Diego Zoo, Calif.
San Francisco Zoological Gardens, Calif.
Santa Ana Zoo, Calif.
Santa Barbara Zoological Gardens, Calif.
Sante Fe Teaching Zoo, Fla.
Sea Life Park, Waimanalo, Hawaii
Sea World of California, San Diego
Sea World of Florida, Orlando
Sea World of Ohio, Aurora
The Seattle Aquarium, Wash.
Sedgwick County Zoo, Wichita, Kan.
Seneca Park Zoo, Rochester, N.Y.
John G. Shedd Aquarium, Chicago
Toledo Zoological Gardens, Ohio
Topeka Zoological Park, Kan.
Ellen Trout Zoo, Lufkin, Texas
Tulsa Zoological Park, Okla.
Van Saun Park Zoo, Paramus, N.J.
Vancouver Public Aquarium, British Columbia
Henry Vilas Park Zoo, Madison, Wis.
Virginia Zoological Park, Norfolk, Va.
Waikiki Aquarium, Hawaii
Washington Park Zoo, Portland, Ore.
Wild Animal Park, Kings Island, Ohio
Wildlife Safari, Inc. Winston, Ore.
Roger Williams Park Zoo, Providence, R.I.
Woodland Park Zoological Gardens, Seattle
ZOOAMERICA North American Wildlife Park, Hershey, Pa.

The National Park System

Source: Department of the Interior, National Park Service.

The National Park System of the United States is administered by the National Park Service, a bureau of the Department of the Interior. Started with the establishment of Yellowstone National Park in 1872, the system includes not only the most extraordinary and spectacular scenic exhibits in the United States but also a large number of sites distinguished either for their historic or prehistoric importance or scientific interest, or for their superior recreational assets. The number and extent of the various types of areas that make up the system follow.

Type of area	Number	Total acreage[1]	Type of area	Number	Total acreage[1]
International Historic Site	1	35	National Battlefield Site	1	1
National Parks	49	47,158,418	National Historic Parks	26	150,865
National Monuments	76	4,722,093	National Scenic Trails	3	154,157
National Preserves	12	21,960,219	National Recreation Areas	17	3,686,385
National Lakeshores	4	224,973	National Parkways	4	163,230
National Seashores	10	597,030	National Scenic Rivers & Riverways[4]	12	553,873
National Historic Sites	62	17,941	Other Parks[2]	11	32,129
National Memorials	23	7,949	National Capital Parks[3]	1	6,469
National Military Parks	9	34,014	White House	1	18
National Battlefield Parks	3	8,169	National Mall	1	146
National Battlefields	11	12,722	Affiliated Areas*	32	51,340
			Total	337	79,566,952

1. Acreage as of December 31, 1986. 2. Parks without national designation. 3. Comprised of 346 units within the District of Columbia, Maryland, and Virginia. 4. National Park System Units and components of the Wild & Scenic Rivers System. *Not included in 337 total.

National Parks

Name, location, and year authorized	Acreage	Outstanding characteristics
Acadia (Maine), 1919	41,231.00	Rugged seashore on Mt. Desert Island and adjacent mainland
Arches (Utah), 1971	73,378.98	Unusual stone arches, windows, pedestals caused by erosion
Badlands (S.D.), 1978	243,302.33	Arid land of fossils, prairie, bison, deer, bighorn, antelope
Big Bend (Tex.), 1935	735,416.00	Mountains and desert bordering the Rio Grande
Biscayne (Fla.), 1980	173,039.00	Aquatic, coral reef park south of Miami was a national monument, 1968–80
Bryce Canyon (Utah), 1924	35,835.08	Area of grotesque eroded rocks brilliantly colored
Canyonlands (Utah), 1964	337,570.43	Colorful wilderness with impressive red-rock canyons, spires, arches
Capitol Reef (Utah), 1971	241,904.26	Highly colored sedimentary rock formations in high, narrow gorges
Carlsbad Caverns (N.M.), 1930	46,755.33	The world's largest known caves
Channel Islands (Calif.) 1980	249,353.77	Area is rich in marine mammals, sea birds, endangered species and archeology
Crater Lake (Ore.), 1902	183,227.00	Deep blue lake in heart of inactive volcano
Denali (Alaska), 1917	4,700,000.00	Mt. McKinley National Park was renamed and enlarged by Act of Dec. 2, 1980. Contains Mt. McKinley, N. America's highest mountain (20,320 ft)
Everglades (Fla.), 1934	1,398,937.00	Subtropical area with abundant bird and animal life
Gates of the Arctic (Alaska), 1980	7,500,000.00	Diverse north central wilderness contains part of Brooks Range
Glacier (Mont.), 1910	1,013,572.00	Rocky Mountain scenery with many glaciers and lakes
Glacier Bay (Alaska), 1980	3,225,198.00	Park was a national monument (1925–1980) popular for wildlife, whale-watching, glacier-calving, and scenery
Grand Canyon (Ariz.), 1919	1,218,375.24	Mile-deep gorge, 4 to 18 miles wide, 217 miles long
Grand Teton (Wyo.), 1929	310,521.00	Picturesque range of high mountain peaks
Great Basin (Nev.), 1986	78,800.00	Exceptional scenic, biologic, and geologic attractions
Great Smoky Mts. (N.C.-Tenn), 1926	520,269.44	Highest mountain range east of Black Hills; luxuriant plant life
Guadalupe Mountains (Tex.), 1966	76,293.06	Contains highest point in Texas: Guadalupe Peak (8,751 ft)
Haleakala (Hawaii), 1960	28,655.25	World-famous 10,023-ft. Haleakala volcano (dormant)
Hawaii Volcanoes (Hawaii), 1916	229,177.03	Spectacular volcanic area; luxuriant vegetation at lower levels
Hot Springs (Ark.), 1921	5,839.00	47 mineral hot springs said to have therapeutic value
Isle Royale (Mich.), 1931	571.790.11	Largest wilderness island in Lake Superior; moose, wolves, lakes
Katmai (Alaska), 1980	3,716,000.00	Expansion may assure brown bear's preservation. Park was national monument 1918–80; is known for fishing, 1912 eruption, bears
Kenai Fjords (Alaska), 1980	670,000.00	Mountain goats, marine mammals, birdlife are features at this seacoast park near Seward
Kings Canyon (Calif.), 1940	461,901.00	Huge canyons; high mountains; giant sequoias
Kobuk Valley (Alaska), 1980	1,750,000.00	Native culture and anthropology center around the broad Kobuk River in northwest Alaska
Lake Clark (Alaska), 1980	2,874,000.00	Park provides scenic and wilderness recreation across Cook Inlet from Anchorage
Lassen Volcanic (Calif.), 1916	106,372.36	Exhibits of impressive volcanic phenomena
Mammoth Cave (Ky.), 1926	52,420.00	Vast limestone labyrinth with underground river
Mesa Verde (Colo.), 1906	52,085.14	Best-preserved prehistoric cliff dwellings in United States
Mount Rainier (Wash.), 1899	235,404.00	Single-peak glacial system; dense forests, flowered meadows

Name, location, and year authorized	Acreage	Outstanding characteristics
North Cascades (Wash.), 1968	504,780.94	Roadless Alpine landscape; jagged peaks; mountain lakes; glaciers
Olympic (Wash.), 1938	914,816.00	Finest Pacific Northwest rain forest; scenic mountain park
Petrified Forest (Ariz.), 1962	93,533.00	Extensive natural exhibit of petrified wood
Redwood (Calif.), 1968	110,178.00	Coastal redwood forests; contains world's tallest known tree (369.2 ft)
Rocky Mountain (Colo.), 1915	265,192.86	Section of the Rocky Mountains; 107 named peaks over 10,000 ft
Sequoia (Calif.), 1890	402,482.00	Giant sequoias; magnificent High Sierra scenery, including Mt. Whitney
Shenandoah (Va.), 1926	195,347.00	Tree-covered mountains; scenic Skyline Drive
Theodore Roosevelt (N.D.), 1978	70,416.39	Scenic valley of Little Missouri River; T.R. Ranch; Wildlife
Virgin Islands (U.S. V.I.), 1956	14,695.85	Beaches; lush hills; prehistoric Carib Indian relics
Voyageurs (Minn.), 1971	215,059.00	Wildlife, canoeing, fishing, and hiking
Wind Cave (S.D.), 1903	28,292.08	Limestone caverns in Black Hills; buffalo herd
Wrangell-St. Elias (Alaska), 1980	8,945,000.00	Largest Park System area has abundant wildlife, second highest peak in U.S. (Mt. St. Elias); adjoins Canadian park
Yellowstone (Wyo.-Mont.-Idaho), 1872	2,219,785.00	World's greatest geyser area; abundant falls, wildlife, and canyons
Yosemite (Calif.), 1890	761,170.00	Mountains; inspiring gorges and waterfalls; giant sequoias
Zion (Utah), 1919	146,598.00	Multicolored gorge in heart of southern Utah desert

NATIONAL HISTORICAL PARKS

Name and location	*Total acreage*
Appomattox Court House (Va.)	1,325.08
Boston (Mass.)	41.03
Chaco Culture (N.M.)	33,974.00
Chesapeake and Ohio Canal (Md.-W.Va.-D.C.).	20,781.00
Colonial (Va.)	9,327.00
Cumberland Gap (Ky.-Tenn.-Va.)	20,274.00
George Rogers Clark (Ind.)	24.30
Harpers Ferry (W.Va.-Md.)	2,238.37
Independence (Pa.)	44.85
Jean Lafitte (La.)	20,000.00
Kalaupapa (Hawaii)	10,902.10
Klondike Goldrush (Alaska)	13,272.38
Kaioko-Honokohau (Hawaii)	1,160.91
Lowell (Mass.)	137.08
Lyndon B. Johnson (Tex.)	1,571.00
Minute Man (Mass.)	749.00
Morristown (N.J.)	1,671.00
Nez Perce (Idaho)	2,108.89
Puuhonua o Honaunau (Hawaii)	181,80
San Antonio Missions (Tex.)	477.41
San Juan Island (Wash.)	1,751.99
Saratoga (N.Y.)	3,389.00
Sitka (Alaska)	106.83
Valley Forge (Pa.)	3,468.00
War in the Pacific (Guam)	1,960.00
Women's Rights (N.Y.)	5.00

NATIONAL MONUMENTS

Name and location	*Total acreage*
Agate Fossil Beds (Neb.)	3,055.22
Alibates Flint Quarries (Tex.)	1,370.97
Aniakchak (Alaska)	137,176.00
Aztec Ruins (N.M.)	27.14
Bandelier (N.M.)	36,916.89
Black Canyon (Colo.)	20,766.00
Booker T. Washington (Va.)	223.92
Buck Island Reef (U.S. V.I.)	880.00
Cabrillo (Calif.)	143.94
Canyon de Chelly (Ariz.)	83,840.00
Cape Krusenstern (Alaska)	659,807.00
Capulin Mountain (N.M.)	775.38
Casa Grande (Ariz.)	472.50
Castillo de San Marcos (Fla.)	20.48
Castle Clinton (N.Y.)	1.00
Cedar Breaks (Utah)	6,154.60
Chiricahua (Ariz.)	11,985.00
Colorado (Colo.)	20,453.95
Congaree Swamp (S.C.)	15,138.25
Craters of the Moon (Idaho)	53,545.05
Custer Battlefield (Mont.)	765.34
Death Valley (Calif.-Nev.)	2,067,627.68
Devils Postpile (Calif.)	798.46
Devils Tower (Wyo.)	1,346.91
Dinosaur (Utah-Colo.)	211,142.00
Effigy Mounds (Iowa)	1,481.00
El Morro (N.M.)	1,278.72
Florissant Fossil Beds (Colo.)	5,998.09
Fort Frederica (Ga.)	216.00
Fort Jefferson (Fla.)	64,700.00
Fort Matanzas (Fla.)	228.00
Fort McHenry (Md.)	43.26
Fort Pulaski (Ga.)	5,623.10
Fort Stanwix (N.Y.)	15.52
Fort Sumter (S.C.)	158.00
Fort Union (N.M.)	720.60
Fossil Butte (Wyo.)	8,198.00
George Washington Birthplace (Va.)	538.23
George Washington Carver (Mo.)	210.00
Gila Cliff Dwellings (N.M.)	533.13
Grand Portage (Minn.)	709.97
Great Sand Dunes (Colo.)	38,662.18
Hohokam Pima (Ariz.)	1,690.00
Homestead (Neb.)	194.57
Hovenweep (Utah-Colo.)	785.43
Jewel Cave (S.D.)	1,273.51
John Day Fossil Beds (Ore.)	14,014.00
Joshua Tree (Calif.)	559,959.50
Lava Beds (Calif.)	46,559.87
Montezuma Castle (Ariz.)	857.69
Mound City Group (Ohio)	270.00
Muir Woods (Calif.)	553.55
Natural Bridges (Utah)	7,636.00
Navajo (Ariz.)	360.00
Ocmulgee (Ga.)	683.48
Oregon Caves (Ore.)	487.98
Organ Pipe Cactus (Ariz.)	330,688.86
Pecos (N.M.)	364.80
Pinnacles (Calif.)	16,265.00
Pipe Spring (Ariz.)	40.00
Pipestone (Minn.)	281.78
Rainbow Bridge (Utah)	160.00
Russell Cave (Ala.)	310.45
Saguaro (Ariz.)	83,573.88
St. Croix Island (Me.)	35.39

Name and location	Total acreage
Salinas (N.M.)	1,017.00
Scotts Bluff (Neb.)	2,997.08
Statue of Liberty (N.Y.-N.J.)	58.38
Sunset Crater (Ariz.)	3,040.00
Timpanogos Cave (Utah)	250.00
Tonto (Ariz.)	1,120.00
Tumacacori (Ariz.)	16.52
Tuzigoot (Ariz.)	801.00
Walnut Canyon (Ariz.)	2,249.46
White Sands (N.M.)	143,733.00
Wupatki (Ariz.)	35,253.24
Yucca House (Colo.)	10.00

NATIONAL PRESERVES

Aniakchak (Alaska)	465,603.00
Bering Land Bridge (Alaska)	2,784,760.00
Big Cypress (Fla.)	570,000.00
Big Thicket (Tex.)	85,774.00
Denali (Alaska)	1,330,000.00
Gates of the Arctic (Alaska)	940,000.00
Glacier Bay (Alaska)	55,000.00
Katmai (Alaska)	374,000.00
Lake Clark (Alaska)	1,171,000.00
Noatak (Alaska)	6,560,000.00
Wrangell-St. Elias (Alaska)	4,255,000.00
Yukon-Charley (Alaska)	2,520,000.00

NATIONAL MILITARY PARKS

Chickamauga and Chattanooga (Ga.-Tenn.)	8,102.54
Fredericksburg and Spotsylvania (Va.)	5,908.64
Gettysburg (Pa.)	3,865.00
Guilford Courthouse (N.C.)	220.25
Horseshoe Bend (Ala.)	2,040.00
Kings Mountain (S.C.)	3,945.29
Pea Ridge (Ark.)	4,300.35
Shiloh (Tenn.)	3,837.50
Vicksburg (Miss.)	1,620.00

NATIONAL BATTLEFIELDS

Antietam (Md.)	3,244.00
Big Hole (Mont.)	655.61
Cowpens (S.C.)	841.56
Fort Donelson (Tenn.)	536.66
Fort Necessity (Pa.)	902.80
Monocacy (Md.)	1,647.00
Moores Creek (N.C.)	86.52
Petersburg (Va.)	2,735.00
Stones River (Tenn.)	330.86
Tupelo (Miss.)	1.00
Wilson's Creek (Mo.)	1,749.91

NATIONAL BATTLEFIELD PARKS

Kennesaw Mountain (Ga.)	2,884.38
Manassas (Va.)	4,513.29
Richmond (Va.)	771.41

NATIONAL BATTLEFIELD SITE

Brices Crossroads (Miss.)	1.00

NATIONAL HISTORIC SITES

Abraham Lincoln Birthplace (Ky.)	116.50
Adams (Mass.)	10.00
Allegheny Portage Railroad (Pa.)	1,134.91
Andersonville (Ga.)	475.72
Andrew Johnson (Tenn.)	16.68
Bent's Old Fort (Colo.)	800.00
Carl Sandburg Home (N.C.)	263.52
Christiansted (V.I.)	27.15
Clara Barton (Md.)	8.59
Edgar Allan Poe (Pa.)	1.00
Edison (N.J.)	21.25
Eisenhower (Pa.)	690.46
Eleanor Roosevelt (N.Y.)	180.50
Eugene O'Neill (Calif.)	13.00

Name and location	Total acreage
Ford's Theatre (Lincoln Museum) (D.C.)	0.29
Fort Bowie (Ariz.)	1,000.00
Fort Davis (Tex.)	460.00
Fort Laramie (Wyo.)	832.45
Fort Larned (Kan.)	718.39
Fort Point (Calif.)	29.00
Fort Raleigh (N.C.)	157.27
Fort Scott (Kan.)	16.69
Fort Smith (Ark.-Okla.)	743.00
Fort Union Trading Post (N.D.-Mont.)	434.00
Fort Vancouver (Wash.)	208.89
Frederick Law Olmsted (Mass.)	2.00
Friendship Hill (Pa.)	674.56
Golden Spike (Utah)	2,735.28
Grant-Kohrs Ranch (Mont.)	1,498.82
Hampton (Md.)	59.44
Harry S Truman (Mo.)	0.78
Herbert Hoover (Iowa)	186.80
Home of F. D. Roosevelt (N.Y.)	290.00
Hopewell Furnace (Pa.)	848.06
Hubbell Trading Post (Ariz.)	160.09
James A. Garfield (Ohio)	7.82
Jefferson National Expansion Memorial (Mo.)	191.00
John F. Kennedy (Mass.)	0.09
John Muir (Calif.)	8.90
Knife River Indian Villages (N.D.)	1,293.35
Lincoln Home (Ill.)	12.28
Longfellow (Mass.)	1.98
Maggie L. Walker (Va.)	1.29
Martin Luther King, Jr. (Ga.)	23.16
Martin Van Buren (N.Y.)	39.58
Ninety Six (S.C.)	989.14
Palo Alto Battlefield (Tex.)	50.00
Puukohola Heiau (Hawaii)	80.00
Sagamore Hill (N.Y.)	83.00
Saint-Gaudens (N.H.)	148.33
Salem Maritime (Mass.)	9.10
San Juan (P.R.)	75.00
Saugus Iron Works (Mass.)	8.51
Sewall-Belmont House (D.C.)	0.35
Springfield Armory (Mass.)	54.93
Theodore Roosevelt Birthplace (N.Y.)	0.11
Theodore Roosevelt Inaugural (N.Y.)	1.03
Thomas Stone (Md.)	328.25
Tuskegee Institute (Ala.)	74.39
Vanderbilt Mansion (N.Y.)	211.65
Whitman Mission (Wash.)	98.15
William Howard Taft (Ohio)	3.07

NATIONAL MEMORIALS

Arkansas Post (Ark.)	389.18
Arlington House, the Robert E. Lee Memorial (Va.)	27.91
Chamizal (Tex.)	54.90
Coronado (Ariz.)	4,750.00
Desoto (Fla.)	26.84
Federal Hall (N.Y.)	0.45
Fort Caroline (Fla.)	138.39
Fort Clatsop (Ore.)	125.20
General Grant (N.Y.)	0.76
Hamilton Grange (N.Y.)	0.71
John F. Kennedy Center for Performing Arts (D.C.)	17.50
Johnstown Flood (Pa.)	163.47
Lincoln Boyhood (Ind.)	200.00
Lincoln Memorial (D.C.)	110.00
Lyndon Baines Johnson Memorial Grove on the Potomac (D.C.)	17.00
Mount Rushmore (S.D.)	1,278.45
Roger Williams (R.I.)	4.56
Thaddeus Kosciuszko (Pa.)	0.02
Theodore Roosevelt Island (D.C.)	88.50
Thomas Jefferson Memorial (D.C.)	18.36

Name and location	*Total acreage*
USS Arizona Memorial (Hawaii)	0.00
Washington Monument (D.C.)	106.01
Wright Brothers (N.C.)	431.40

NATIONAL CEMETERIES[1]

Antietam (Md.)	11.36
Battleground (D.C.)	1.03
Fort Donelson (Tenn.)	15.34
Fredericksburg (Va.)	12.00
Gettysburg (Pa.)	20.58
Poplar Grove (Va.)	8.72
Shiloh (Tenn.)	10.05
Stones River (Tenn.)	20.09
Vicksburg (Miss.)	116.28
Yorktown (Va.)	2.91

NATIONAL SEASHORES

Assateague Island (Md.-Va.)	39,630.93
Canaveral (Fla.)	57,627.07
Cape Cod (Mass.)	43,526.00
Cape Hatteras (N.C.)	30,319.43
Cape Lookout (N.C.)	28,414.74
Cumberland Island (Ga.)	36,415.00
Fire Island (N.Y.)	19,578.55
Gulf Islands (Fla.-Miss.)	139,775.46
Padre Island (Tex.)	130,696.83
Point Reyes (Calif.)	71,046.07

NATIONAL PARKWAYS

Blue Ridge (Va.-N.C.)	82,117.37
George Washington Memorial (Va.-Md.)	7,146.00
John D. Rockefeller, Jr., Memorial (Wyo.)	23,777.22
Natchez Trace (Miss.-Tenn.-Ala.)	50,189.33

NATIONAL LAKESHORES

Apostle Islands (Wis.)	68,085.00
Indiana Dunes (Ind.)	12,857.00
Pictured Rocks (Mich)	72,898.86
Sleeping Bear Dunes (Mich.)	71,132.00

NATIONAL SCENIC RIVERS AND RIVERWAYS

Alagnak Wild River (Alaska)	24,038.00
Big South Fork National River & Recreation Area (Ky.-Tenn.)	122,960.00
Buffalo (Ark.)	94,221.08
Delaware (N.Y.-N.J.-Pa.)	1,973.33
Lower St. Croix (Minn.-Wis.)	9,365.00
Missouri National Recreational River (Neb.)	59.00
New River Gorge (W. Va.)	62,024.00
Obed Wild & Scenic River (Tenn.)	5,101.00
Ozark (Mo.)	80,698.00
Rio Grande Wild & Scenic (Tex.)	9,600.00
St. Croix (Minn.-Wis.)	68,793.28
Upper Delaware (N.Y., N.J.-Pa.)	75,000.00

NATIONAL CAPITAL PARKS

National Capital Parks (D.C.-Va.-Md.)	6,465.85

WHITE HOUSE

White House (D.C.)	18.07

OTHER PARKS

Catoctin Mountain (Md.)	5,770.22
Constitution Gardens, (D.C.)	52.00
Fort Washington Park (Md.)	341.00
Frederick Douglass Home (D.C.)	8.08
Greenbelt Park (Md.)	1,175.99
Perry's Victory and International Peace Memorial (Ohio)	25.38
Piscataway (Md.)	4,263.00
Prince William Forest (Va.)	18,571.55

1. The National Cemeteries are not independent areas of the National Park System; each is part of a military park, battlefield, etc., except Battleground. Their acreage is kept separately. Arlington National Cemetery is under the Department of the Army. *See* Index.

Name and location	*Total acreage*
Rock Creek Park (D.C.)	1,754.37
Vietnam Veterans Memorial (D.C.)	2.00
Wolf Trap Farm Park for the Performing Arts (Va.)	130.28

NATIONAL RECREATION AREAS

Amistad (Tex.)	57,292.00
Bighorn Canyon (Wyo.-Mont.)	120,296.00
Chattahoochee River (Ga.)	9,200.00
Chickasaw (Okla.)	9,522.00
Coulee Dam (Wash.)	100,390.00
Curecanti (Colo.)	42,114.47
Cuyahoga Valley (Ohio)	32,460.19
Delaware Water Gap (Pa.-N.J.)	66,192.00
Gateway (N.Y.-N.J.)	26,310.93
Glen Canyon (Ariz.-Utah)	1,236,880.00
Golden Gate (Calif.)	73,117.00
Lake Chelan (Wash.)	61,890.07
Lake Mead (Ariz.-Nev.)	1,495,666.00
Lake Meredith (Tex.)	44,977.63
Ross Lake (Wash.)	117,574.09
Santa Monica Mountains (Calif.)	150,000.00
Whiskeytown-Shasta-Trinity (Calif.)	42,503.43

NATIONAL SCENIC TRAIL

Appalachian (Maine, N.H., Vt., Mass., Conn., N.Y., N.J., Pa., Md., W.Va., Va., N.C., Tenn., Ga.)	143,162.00
Natchez Trace (Ga.-Ala.-Tenn.)	10,995.00
Potomac Heritage (D.C.-Md.-Va.-Pa.)	n.a[3]

NATIONAL MALL

National Mall (D.C.)	146.35

AFFILIATED AREAS

(National Historic Sites unless otherwise noted.)

Afro-American History and Culture (Ohio)	0.00
American Memorial Park (N. Mariana Is.)	0.00
Benjamin Franklin (Pa.)[1]	0.00
Boston African American (Mass.)	0.00
Chicago Portage (Ill.)	91.20
Chimney Rock (Neb.)	83.36
David Berger (Ohio)[1]	0.00
Ebey's Landing (Wash.)	8,000.00
Father Marquette (Mich.)	52.00
Gloria Dei Church (Pa.)	3.71
Green Springs Historic District (Va.)	5,491.00
Historic Camden (S.C.)	0.00
Ice Age Scenic Trail (Wisc.)	0.00
Ice Age (Wis.)[2]	32,500.00
Iditarod National Historic Trail (Alaska)	0.00
International Peace Garden (N.D.)	2,330.30
Jamestown (Va.)	20.63
Lewis & Clark Natl. Historic Trail (Ill., Mo., Kan., Neb., Iowa, Idaho, S.D., N.D., Mont., Ore., Wash.)	0.00
M. McLeod Bethune Council House (D.C.)	0.00
McLoughlin House (Ore.)	0.63
Mormon Pioneer Natl. Historic Trail (Ill., Iowa, Neb., Wyo., Utah)	0.00
North Country Nat'l Scenic Trail (N.Y., Pa., Ohio, Mich., Wis., Minn., N.D.)	0.00
Old Post Office Tower (D.C.)	0.00
Oregon Natl. Historic Trail (Mo., Kan., Neb., Wyo., Idaho, Ore., Wash.)	0.00
Overmountain Victory Trail (Mo. to Ore.)	0.00
Pennsylvania Avenue (D.C.)	0.00
Pinelands Natl. Reserve (N.J.)	0.00
Red Hill Patrick Henry (Va.)[1]	0.00
Roosevelt-Campobello International Park (Canada)	2,721.50
St. Paul's Church (N.Y.)	6.12
Steamtown National Historic Site (Pa.)	40.00
Touro Synagogue (R.I.)	0.23

1. National Memorial. 2. National Scientific Reserve. 3. Undetermined.

GENERAL INFORMATION

NOTE: All conversions from metric to customary U.S. measurement systems were provided by *Information Please Almanac* for the convenience of U.S. readers.

A

Abacus, a device for making arithmetical calculations, consisting of parallel bars on which are strung movable colored beads. The earliest form of this instrument was used in Mesopotamia about 3000 B.C., and its use spread westward throughout the Graeco-Roman world and eastward to China. An efficient form of the abacus is still used today in parts of Asia.

Aberration, in astronomy, is the apparent displacement of a star due to the speed of the observer with the earth (*see* **Parallax**). In optics (i) spherical aberration is when there is blurring of the image and fringes of color at its edges, due to failure of lens to bring light to a single focus; (ii) chromatic aberration is due to the refractive index of glass being different for light of different colors. For instance, violet light is bent more than red.

Abiogenesis, or spontaneous generation; the origination of living from non-living matter. The term is applied to such discredited ideas as that frogs could be generated spontaneously by the action of sunlight on mud, or maggots arise spontaneously in dead meat without any eggs from which the maggots hatch being present. Spallanzani (1729–1799) upset the hypothesis of spontaneous generation; Pasteur dealt it a death blow.

Aborigines, a term first applied to an ancient mythical people of central Italy, derives from the Latin *ab origine* = from the beginning. It now signifies the original inhabitants of any country, in particular the aboriginal tribes of Australia. In contrast to their highly complex social and religious customs, the material culture of Australian aboriginals is very low and ill adapted to stand up to contact with European civilization. Originally estimated at 300, 000, their number has dropped in the last 200 years to some 80,000. They have no legal title to their ancient tribal lands, unlike the native people of the USA, Canada, and New Zealand.

Absolute Temperature, Absolute Zero. This is a refined notion requiring some study of thermodynamics for its full understanding. For setting up an absolute temperature scale one must first assign a numerical value to one fixed temperature. For this, the triple point of water has been chosen, *i.e.,* the temperature at which solid, liquid, and gaseous water are all in equilibrium. The triple point is defined to be 273·16 K where K is read for kelvin (after Lord Kelvin). This temperature is 0·01° C on the Celsius scale *(q.v.)* and is thus very close to the melting point of ice. Suppose the pressure and volume of a mass of gas are measured (i) at the triple point of water, giving $(pV)_{tr}$ as the product of the pressure and volume; and (ii) at any unknown temperature TK, giving (pV) as the product. Then the absolute temperature, TK, is defined by

$$T\,K = 273{\cdot}16\frac{(pV)}{(pV)_{tr}}$$

It is to be understood that the gas pressure is very low. The nature of the gas is immaterial. More subtly, it can be shown that the temperature so defined is identical with that derived in a rather abstract way in the science of thermodynamics. The absolute scale is therefore also called the thermodynamic scale. Absolute temperatures can be obtained from Celsius temperatures by adding 273·15; thus the absolute temperature of melting ice is 273·15 K. Conversely, absolute zero is a temperature 273·15 K below the temperature of melting ice, *i.e.,* −273·15° C. Theory shows that absolute zero is unattainable, but it has been approached to within about 1 millionth of a degree. Within ten or so degrees of absolute zero, matter develops some remarkable properties. *See* **Cryogenics, Superconductor, Helium.**

Acetic Acid, an organic acid produced when ordinary (ethyl) alcohol is fermented by the organism called *Acetobacter aceti.* The same oxidation process yields vinegar: this is a weak and crude solution of acetic acid obtained by trickling dilute alcoholic liquor over beechwood shavings at 35° C (95° F). The souring of wine is due to the same process. Acetic acid is used as a food preservative and flavouring material, and in the manufacture of cellulose acetate and white lead.

Acid Rain is the name given to rain, snow, or sleet contaminated with acid substances so that its acidity is greater than the limit expected by normal concentrations of carbon dioxide dissolving in the rain to give carbonic acid (*pH* 5.5–5.6). The *pH* of acid rain therefore is less than about 5.5. The increased acidity is caused by larger concentrations of a number of contaminants, principally the strong acids, nitric and sulfuric, which arise from industrial effluents containing oxides of nitrogen and sulfur. The European emission of sulfur dioxide doubled between 1940 and 1980. In some European and North American areas such contamination can give a rain *pH* as low as 3 (which is 100 times more acid than *pH* 5). The acid rain can mark fruit and leaves, and adversely affect soil but its main effect is on the aquatic ecosystems especially in regions which cannot naturally buffer acidic inputs such as those with thin soils and granite rocks. It is likely that the disappearance of fish from many Scandinavian lakes has been the result of pollution by acid rain.

Acids, substances having a tendency to lose a positive ion (a proton). This general definition overcomes difficulties of earlier views which merely described their properties and asserted that they are chemically opposite to bases. As a whole acids contain ionizable hydrogen, replaceable by a metal, to form a salt. Inorganic acids are compounds of non-metals or metalloids, *e.g.,* sulfuric phosphoric acid. Carboxylic acids contain the group –COOH.

Actinides, the fourteen metallic elements from thorium (no. 90) to lawrencium (no. 103). All known isotopes of these elements are radioactive and those with atomic number greater than 92 (uranium) have been produced only in significant quantities artificially. Plutonium (no. 94) is obtained from uranium during the course of nuclear reactor operation and the higher transuranic elements can be made from it by the successive capture of neutrons or nuclei of light atoms. The availability of only minute quantities of short-lived isotopes makes the determination of the physical and chemical properties of the higher actinides very difficult. Claims for the discovery of new elements can therefore be controversial and since the discoverers can name the elements their naming is also controversial. There were three different reports for Nobelium (no. 102). Lawrentium (no. 103) is called Jolistium by Russian authors. Element no. 104 was reported in 1964 by a Russian group and called Kurchatovium but is called Rutherfordium (Rf) in the West. Element no. 105 has been named Hahnium (Hn).

Aerodynamics, the science of gases (especially air) in motion, particularly in relation to aircraft (aeronautics). The idea of imitating the birds by the use of wings is of ancient origin. Leonardo da Vinci first carried out experiments in a scientific manner. The invention of the balloon in 1783 and the researches of scientists and engineers in the 19th cent. ultimately led to the development of the airplane.

Aerolites, the name given to the class of meteorites composed chiefly of heavy silicates. The other two main classes are *siderolites* (nickel iron and silicates) and *siderites* (nickel iron).

Agave, the American aloe or Century Plant which sometimes does not attain to flowering maturity under sixty or seventy years, and then dies. The flower spray may reach a height of 6m (20 ft) and in its development the rush of sap is so great that the Mexicans collect for brewing the strong spirit called mescal. 1,000 liters (264 gal) of sap can be obtained from a single plant. Some species of agave yield sisal used for making cord and rope.

Air Glow is the general name given to a large number of relatively weak optical emissions from the earth's upper atmosphere in the height range 70 to 400 km; 44 to 249 mi (approx.). It is distinct from the aurora polaris *(q.v.)* which is usually much brighter and normally only observable at high latitudes. Air glow is produced by a combination of photochemical reactions in the upper atmosphere, excitation by photoelectrons, or by solar ultra-violet light. In the latter case it is more correctly called "dayglow." These emissions occur in the ultra-violet and infra-red spectral regions as well as in visible light.

Alabaster, a soft crystalline form of sulphate of lime, or granulated gypsum, easily worked for statuary and other ornamental articles, and capable of being highly polished. Volterra, in Tuscany, yields the finest; that in highest ancient repute came from Alabastron in Egypt, near to the modern Antinoë.

Alcohols. A class of organic compounds of general formula R-OH, where R is an aliphatic radical. "Alcohol" is the name used for ethyl alcohol (ethanol); this is produced by distilling fermented liquors, and synthetically from ethylene, a product of petroleum cracking. Industrially ethyl alcohol is used in the manufacture of chloroform, ether, perfumes, etc. Diluted with wood alcohol or other denaturants ethyl alcohol is called "methylated spirits"; the denaturants are varied according to the industrial purposes for which it is required, the methylated spirits then being largely exempt from duty. Wood alcohol (methyl alcohol or methanol) can be obtained by distilling wood or synthetically from water gas.

Aldehyde, the generic term for a class of chemical compounds of general formula R-CHO, where R is an organic radical. Except for formaldehyde, which is a gas, aldehydes are volatile liquids. They are produced by oxidation of primary alcohols. Most important aldehyde is formaldehyde (methanol) used in making the plastics described as formaldehyde resins. Formalin (formaldehyde solution in water) is much used for preserving zoological specimens.

Aldine Editions are the beautiful books printed in Venice by the Renaissance printer Aldo Pio Manuzio and his family between 1490 and 1597. Italics were first introduced in these books.

Algebra, a branch of mathematics in which symbols are used in place of numbers. Sir Isaac Newton styled it the "universal arithmetic". The Chinese were able to solve the quadratic equation before the Christian era but it was Al-Khowarizmi, an Arab mathematician of the early 9th century, who introduced algebra to Europe.

Alkali, the general name given to a number of chemicals which are bases *(q.v.).* The term should be limited to the hydroxides of metals in the first and second group of the periodic table and of ammonia, *e.g.,* NaOH, KOH. They are used commercially in the manufacture of paper, glass, soap, and artificial silk. The word comes from the Arabic *al-kali* meaning calcined wood ashes. Alkalis are extremely soluble in water and neutralise acids to form salts and water.

Alkaloids, a large group of natural products which contain nitrogen; they are usually basic. Isolated from plants and animals, they include some hormones, vitamins, and drugs. Examples are nicotine, adrenalin, and cocaine. Many alkaloids are made synthetically for medicinal use, *e.g.,* morphine, quinine. Their function in plants is not well understood.

Allotropy. Depending on the temperature, pressure or method of preparation, an element may exist in one of several forms, each having different physical properties (crystal structure, electrical conductivity, melting point, etc.). This is known as allotropy and the different forms of the element are called allotropes. Many elements exhibit allotropy, *e.g.,* sulfur, phosphorus, oxygen, tin and carbon, the most well-known allotropes of carbon being diamond and graphite.

Alloys are combinations of metals made for their valuable special properties, *e.g.,* durability, strength, lightness, magnetism, rust-resistance, etc. Some well-known ones are brass (zinc + copper), coinage bronze (copper + zinc + tin), steels (iron + carbon + various other materials), soft solder (tin + lead), dental fillings (mercury + various ingredients).

Alluvium, river transported deposits of sand, mud and gravel which accumulate to form distinctive features such as levées, flood plains and deltas. The frequent renewal of alluvium by flooding causes riverine lands to be some of the most fertile. In Asia alluvial lands support high densities of population, *e.g.,* The Hwang-ho plains and the Ganges delta.

Almond, the fruit of the *Amygdalus communis* originally indigenous to Persia, Asia Minor and N. Africa, now cultivated in Italy, Spain, France, the USA and Australia. It yields both bitter and sweet oil. Bitter almond oil is obtained by macerating and distilling the ripe seeds; it is used for flavoring and scenting purposes, its fragrant odor being due to the presence of benzaldehyde and hydrogen cyanide. When the seeds are pressed sweet almond oil results: this is used in perfumery, and also as a lubricant for very delicate machinery.

Alpha Particle, *or* **alpha-ray,** fast-moving helium nucleus ejected by some radioactive atoms, *e.g.,* polonium. It is a combination of 2 neutrons and 2 protons.

Alphabet (so called from the first two letters of the Greek alphabet—alpha, beta) is the term applied to the collection of letters from which the words of a language are made up. It grew out of the knowledge that all words can be expressed by a limited number of sounds arranged in various combinations. The Phoenicians were the first to make use of an alphabetic script derived from an earlier Semitic alphabet (earliest known inscriptions *c.* 1500–950 B.C.) from which all other alphabets have sprung. The stages in the development of the alphabet were mnemonic (memory aids), pictorial (actual pictures), ideographic (symbols), and lastly phonetic. All the ideographic systems died out, with the exception of that of the Chinese.

Altimeter, an instrument used in aircraft to estimate altitude; its usual essential feature is an aneroid barometer which registers the decrease of pressure with height. Roughly 1 millibar corresponds to 9 m (30 ft). To read an aircraft altimeter correct for its destination, the zero setting must be adjusted for difference of ground height and difference of surface pressure, especially when pressure is falling or when flying towards low pressure.

Alum is a compound salt used in various industrial processes, especially dyeing, its constituents being the sulfate of one univalent metal or radical (*e.g.,* potassium, sodium, ammonium, rubidium, caesium, silver, thallium) and the sulfate of a tervalent metal (*e.g.,* aluminum, iron, chromium, manganese), and water of crystallisation.

Alumina is the oxide of aluminum. Very valuable as a refractory material. The ruby is almost 100 percent alumina; so also are the emerald, oriental amethyst, etc. An hydrated aluminum oxide is bauxite, chief ore of aluminum from which the metal is extracted electrolytically.

Aluminum, element no. 13, symbol Al, is a light metal which conducts electricity well. Its specific gravity at 20° C (68° F) is 2·705. Melting point of aluminium is 660.2° C (1220.4° F). It is made commercially by electrolyzing bauxite dissolved in cryolite (double fluoride of aluminum and sodium). Aluminium alloys because of their strength and lightness are being increasingly used for construction purposes.

Amalgam is the term applied to any alloy of which mercury forms a part.

Amber, a brittle resinous substance; in origin, fossilised resin. Obtained mostly from the Baltic coasts, and used for ornaments, pipe mouthpieces, etc.

Amblyopsis, a species of fish, practically sightless, and with inoperative organs of hearing and feeling, that inhabit the Mammoth Cave of Kentucky. A remarkable illustration of the failure of senses not brought into use.

Amethyst, the violet variety of quartz, used as a precious stone, containing traces of manganese, titanium and iron. The finest colored specimens come from Brazil and the Urals.

Amino acids, organic compounds containing an amine group and a carboxylic acid group. They are the "building bricks" of proteins *(q.v.).*

Ammeter, an instrument for measuring the current flowing in an electric circuit. A contraction of ampere-meter.

Ammonia, a colorless gaseous compound comprising three atoms of hydrogen to one of nitrogen. Formerly it was made by heating the horns and hoofs of deer, acquiring the name of spirits of hartshorn. The ammonia of commerce is now procured by coal decomposition in the course of gas-making and by direct synthesis. In the very important Haber process of ammonia production by fixation of atmospheric nitrogen, the nitrogen is made to combine with hydrogen and the ammonia so prepared is converted into nitric acid, ammonium nitrate or ammonium sulfate. The Haber process made Germany self-sufficient in nitrates in the first world war, and was afterwards exploited all over the world.

Ammonites, extinct animals related to the Nautilus. The enambered shell is coiled, usually in a plane spiral, and they are confined to Mesozoic rocks.

Ammonium, the basic radical of ammonium salts, Composed of one atom of nitrogen and four of hydrogen, it behaves chemically like an ion of a monovalent alkali metal. Ammonium chloride is known as "sal ammoniac". "Sal volatile" is ammonium carbonate.

Amorphous, a term used to indicate the absence of crystalline form in any body or substance.

Anemometer, an instrument for measuring the strength of the wind. In the most widely used pattern the rotation, about a vertical axis, of a group of hemispherical or conical cups gives a measure of the total flow of air past the cups, various registering devices being employed. The Dines anemograph provides a continuous record of the variation in both velocity and direction; changes of pressure produced in a horizontal tube, kept pointing into the wind by a vane, cause a float, to which a pen is attached, to rise and fall in sympathy with the gusts and lulls. The recently devised hot-wire anemometer, depending upon the change of electrical resistance experienced by a heated wire when cooled, enables very gentle air currents to be investigated.

Aneroid is the kind of barometer which does not depend upon atmospheric support of a mercury (or other liquid) column. It consists of a metallic box, partially exhausted of air, with a corrugated lid which moves with atmospheric changes. A lever system magnifies the lid movements about 200 times and atmospheric pressure is read from a dial. The construction of the vacuum chamber provides automatic compensation for temperature changes. An aneroid barometer is the basic component of an altimeter.

Aniline, a simple aromatic compound ($C_6H_5NH_2$) related to benzene and ammonia. It is obtained from coal-tar. The name recalls the fact that it was first prepared by distilling indigo (*anil* is Portuguese for indigo). In 1856 W. H. Perkin (1838–1907) discovered the first aniline or coal-tar dye, mauve, and thus founded the modern dyestuff industry.

Anise, an umbelliferous plant *(Pimpinella anisum)* found in Egypt and the Levant, and valued for its fruit, aniseed, possessing certain medicinal properties and yielding an aromatic, volatile oil, Also used in cooking. The anise of the Bible is *Anethum graveolens, i.e.,* dill.

Ant. There are about 6,000 species of ants, which belong to the same order (Hymenoptera) as the bees, wasps and ichneumon flies. They are social in habit, living in communities of varying size and development. There are three basic castes in ants—the females or *queens,* the *males,* and the *workers* (the last-named being neuter), although specialized forms of workers are sometimes found, *e.g.,* the *soldiers* of the harvesting ants. In the communities of those species of ants which evolved most recently there is a highly complex social life and well-developed division of labor. Some species of these ants make slaves of other species, stealing the cocoons before the adult forms emerge. Many ants "milk" green-flies, which they protect for their honey-like secretion, and most ants' nests contain many "guests", such as beetles and silver fish. Some ants harvest grains of corn, and others, from S. America, live on fungi which they cultivate in underground "mushroom beds".

Antarctic Exploration. In earlier centuries it was thought that a great continent must exist in the southern hemisphere, around the South Pole, to balance the known land masses in the north. Its supposed extent was greatly reduced in the 18th century, particularly when Capt. Cook sailed for the first time south of the Antarctic Circle and reached the edge of the icepack. A portion of the ice-covered continent—the coast of Graham Land—was first sighted by Lieut. Edward Bransfield in 1820. Explorers of several other nations sighted portions of the coast-line in other quarters, but the first extensive exploration was made by Capt. James Clarke Ross, who with the *Erebus* and *Terror* penetrated into the Ross Sea in 1841, and discovered the great Ross Ice Barrier in 78° South lat. Interest in the Antarctic did not revive until after 1890, when an international scheme of research was drawn up. A Norwegian, C. E. Borchgrevink, in 1898–1900, was the first to winter in the Antarctic and to travel on the ice barrier. The British share in this work was carried out by Capt. R. F. Scott's expedition in the *Discovery,* 1901–4. Scott's party sledged across the barrier to 82° 17′ South, then a record "farthest south". A little later, Ernest Shackleton beat this by travelling to within 160 km of the South Pole. The Scottish polar explorer William Spiers Bruce led the Scottish national Antarctic Expedition of 1902 in the *Scotia* and discovered Coats Land and founded a meteorological observatory on the South Orkneys. In 1910 Scott organized his second expedition in *Terra Nova,* and became engaged against his will in a "race for the Pole" when, after his departure, the Norwegian Arctic explorer, Roald Amundsen, suddenly announced that he was sailing for the Antarctic. Amundsen set up his base at the eastern end of the Barrier, and, relying on dog teams for hauling his sledges, reached the Pole on 14 December 1911. Meanwhile Scott and his party, their start delayed by adverse weather, were marching southwards, man-hauling their sledges, for Scott was against the use of dogs. After an arduous journey they reached the Pole one month after Amundsen. The return was a struggle against the weather and increasing weakness, probably due to scurvy, until at last they perished within a few kilometers of their base. After the first world war the development of the whaling industry greatly stimulated further exploration. Outstanding expeditions included that of Admiral R. E. Byrd, 1929, when he flew over the South Pole; the British Graham Land expedition, 1934, which carried out the first extensive mapping of any part of the Antarctic continent; and the US Navy's Antarctic Expedition of 1940, when the whole continent was circumnavigated and great areas photographed from the air. In recent years valuable work has been done by the first International expedition, the Norwegian-British-Swedish Expedition to Queen Maud Land, and by the French in Adélie Land. The Falkland Island Dependencies Survey, set up during the war, has continued the scientific exploration of Graham Land. The Antarctic was the scene of high adventure during the International Geophysical Year (1957–58), when scientists from many countries participated in the explorations. The Commonwealth Trans-Antarctic Expedition set out from opposite sides of the continent and met at the South Pole, the UK party, led by Sir Vivian Fuchs, from the Falklands, and Sir Edmund Hillary and his party from New Zealand. The UK party accomplished the first crossing of the White Continent in 99 days. Their scientific work included the marking of seismic and complementary gravimetric studies at frequent intervals along the 3,510 km (2,200 mi) traverse. Since the Antarctic is becoming important for many reasons, in weather forecasting, in the whaling industry, and as a possible centre for world air routes, the tempo of exploration and research will become even faster in the future.

Anthracite is a black coal with a brilliant luster. It contains 92 per cent and over of carbon and burns slowly, without smoke or flame.

Anthropoid, meaning "resembling man", a suborder of the primate mammals including man and also the gibbon, chimpanzee, orangutan, and gorilla.

Anticyclone, a region where barometric pressure is greater than that of its surroundings. Such a system is distinguished on weather charts by a pattern of isobars, usually circular or oval-shaped, enclosing the center of high pressure where the air is calm. In the remaining areas light or moderately strong winds blow spirally outwards in a clockwise direction in the Northern Hemisphere (and in the reverse direction in the Southern Hemisphere), in accordance with Buvs Ballot's law (an observer with back to wind in Northern Hemisphere has lower pressure to left; in Southern to right). Over the British Isles anticyclonic weather is generally quiet and settled, being fair, warm, and sunny in summer and either very cold and often foggy or overcast and gloomy in winter. These systems move slowly and sometimes remain practically stationary for days at a time, that over Siberia being particularly well defined. Extensive belts of almost permanent anticyclones occur in latitudes 30° N and 30° S.

Antimony. Metal element, no. 51, symbol Sb. In group 5 of the periodic table. Exists in various forms, the stable form being a grey metal with a layer structure. The other forms are nonconductors. On being burned, it gives off dense fumes of oxide of antimony. By itself it is not of special utility; but as an alloy for hardening other metals, it is much used. As an alloy with lead for type-metal, and with tin and copper or zinc for Britannia-metal, it is of great value. Most important antimony ore is stibnite (antimony sulfide).

Anti-proton, the "negative proton", an atomic particle created in high energy collisions of nuclear particles. Its existence was confirmed in Oct. 1955.

Aphids, green-flies or plant lice, a numerous species

of destructive insects living on young shoots and foliage, some on roots. Reproduction is by parthenogenesis (virgin birth).

Apocrypha (hidden writings), the books which were included in the Septuagint (Greek) and Vulgate (Latin) versions of the Old Testament but excluded from the sacred canon at the Reformation by the Protestants on the grounds that they were not originally written in Hebrew nor regarded as genuine by the Jews. The books include: 1 and 2 Esdras, Tobit, Judith, additions to Esther, Wisdom of Solomon, Ecclesiasticus, Baruch, Song of the Three Holy Children, History of Susannah, Bel and the Dragon, Prayer of Manasses, 1 and 2 Maccabees. The term is usually applied to the additions to the Old Testament, but there are also numerous Christian writings of the same character. *The New English Bible,* which contains the Apocrypha, was published in 1970.

Appian Way, the oldest and finest of the Roman roads originally laid by Appius Claudius (312 B.C.) from Rome to Capua and then to Brundisium (Brindisi).

Arabian Nights Entertainment *or* **Book of a Thousand and One Nights,** a collection of fascinating tales of the Orient, of mixed Indian, Persian, Arabic, and Egyptian origination, and first made known in Europe by Antoine Galland's French translation (1704–17) from Arabian texts. The "master" tale tells how the princess Shahrazad so beguiles the king through the telling of the tales over one thousand and one nights that her life was spared. English translators include E. W. Lane (1840), Sir Richard Burton (1885–8), John Payne (1882–4).

Arabic Numerals. The modern system of numbering, 0, 1, 2, 3, 4, 5, 6, 7, 8, 9, in which the digits depend on their position for their value is called the Arabic numerical notation. The method is, in fact, of Indian origin. By the 9th cent. Hindu science was available in Arabic, and the Persian mathematician Al-Kwarizimi (*c.* 830) in his *Arithmetic* used the so-called "Arabic" system of numbering. Gradually the method spread to Europe, taking the place of the Roman system which was useless for calculation. The West is indebted to the Arabs for the zero symbol, the lack of which had been a serious drawback to Greek mathematics. It made the invention of decimal fractions possible.

Aramaic Languages, the Semitic dialects current in Mesopotamia and the regions extending southwest from the Euphrates to Palestine from about the 12th century B.C. until after the rise of Islam, when Aramaic was superseded by Arabic. Both Aramaic and Greek were spoken in Palestine during the time of Christ.

Archaeopteryx, a fossil bird providing a connecting link between reptiles and birds. It had feathers, jaws with teeth, no bill, reptilian bones and skull, a long tail, and it probably used its fore-limbs for gliding flight. The first specimen, found in 1861, in the Solenhofen limestone of Bavaria, is in London's Natural History Museum.

Archimedes' Principle. When a body is weighed in air and then in any fluid, the apparent loss in weight is equal to the weight of fluid displaced. This scientific fact was noted by the Syracusan philosopher Archimedes (287–212 B.C.) and is frequently used as a basis for density measurements.

Architecture, the art and science of building. The provision of shelter for mankind by the orderly arrangement of materials in a manner which expresses man's attitude to living. The forms which buildings take are the outcome of the function for which they are to be used, of the architect's aesthetic sensibility and the structural method adopted. Until the last hundred years structural methods were limited to timber frames, and columns, lintels, load-bearing walls, arches, vaults, and domes in brick or stone. From these few basic elements have evolved the great variety of historic styles of building to be found throughout the world. To give but one example, the Greeks created those systems of decorated columns and beams, known as the Orders, which were adapted by the Romans, revived decoratively rather than structurally during the Renaissance and are still used in debased form on the more presumptuous type of modern building. In recent years, however, architecture has taken on a new meaning. Once confined to the rich, in the form of Church, State or Commerce, it is now, with the coming of democracy, recognized as an essential social service for all. This, and the development of new structural techniques and materials (steel, aluminium, sheet glass, reinforced concrete, plastics and plywoods, to name a few), have made the interest in historic styles, the mainstay of the older architect, of secondary importance. Modern architecture is the creation of buildings with the highest possible standards of functional performance in terms of efficient planning and structure, good artificial and natural lighting, adequate heating or cooling, and proper acoustic conditions consistent with the price the client can afford to pay. At the same time the architect's task is to design a structure and the spaces the structure delimits, internally and externally which are aesthetically stimulating and satisfying, and well related to the land and buildings around.

Arctic Exploration. Modern exploration of the Arctic begins in the 16th century when men sought to reach the East Indies by sailing through the Arctic to the Pacific Ocean. The Northeast Passage, via the shores of northern Asia, was the first attempted. In 1553 and 1554 the English navigators Sir Richard Chancellor and Stephen Burrough sailed into the White Sea, but were prevented by storms and ice from advancing farther eastwards. The project was later revived by the Dutch; Barents in 1594 discovered Spitsbergen, but also failed to get beyond Novaya Zemlya. It was not, in fact, until 1879 that the Swede, A. E. Nordenskjöld, in the *Vega,* succeeded in reaching the Pacific. The attempts to find a North-west Passage were more numerous and determined. In 1585 John Davis penetrated Davis Strait and coasted along Baffin Island. Hopes ran high when Henry Hudson discovered Hudson Bay in 1610, but a practicable passage continued to elude explorers. The problem was to find a navigable route through the maze of channels in the short summer season, and to avoid being frozen in with supplies exhausted. After the Napoleonic Wars the Admiralty sent out many naval expeditions which culminated in Sir John Franklin's expedition with the *Erebus* and *Terror* in 1845. The ships were beset by ice in Victoria Channel and, after Franklin's death, were abandoned by their crews, who perished from scurvy and starvation on their march southwards. To ascertain their fate, several further expeditions were despatched, and the crew of the *Investigator,* commanded by R. J. M'Clure, sailing eastwards from Bering Strait, were the first to make the Passage, though in doing so they were obliged to abandon their ship. It was thirty years before the Norwegian, Roald Amundsen, succeeded in sailing the *Gjoa* from the east to west.

In the meantime, the North Pole had become the goal of explorers. Nansen, in 1893, put the *Fram* into the ice-pack to drift across the Polar basin, and himself made an unsuccessful attempt on the Pole across the pack. This was eventually achieved by the American explorer Robert E. Peary, who after several expeditions in the North Greenland region, sledged to the Pole with Eskimo companions in 1909. The next phase was the employment of airships and aeroplanes in Arctic exploration. In 1926 Admiral Byrd made the first flight over the Pole, and in the same year Amundsen and Lincoln Ellsworth flew the airship *Norge* from Spitsbergen to Point Barrow Alaska. Two years later, the *Italia,* commanded by the Italian, Nobile, was wrecked on a return flight from the Pole, and Amundsen lost his life in an attempt to rescue the survivors. With modern developments in aircraft and navigation, flights over the Polar basin are almost a routine matter. The first voyage under the North Pole was made in August 1958 by the American nuclear-powered submarine *Nautilus.*

Arenaceous Rocks, the rocks composed of grains of sand, chiefly sandstones; quartz is the most abundant mineral in these rocks.

Argillaceous Rocks are a sedimentary group, including the shales and clays.

Argon, chemical element no. 18, symbol A. This was the first of the inert gases to be isolated from air by Rayleigh and Ramsay in 1894. Argon is used for filling gas-filled metal filament electric lamps. In gas discharge tube it gives a blue glow.

Arithmetic Progression, a sequence of numbers in which the successor of each number is obtained by adding or subtracting a fixed number, for example 2, 5, 8, 11, . . . or 100, 95, 90, 85. . . .

Armillary Sphere, an early form of astronomical apparatus with a number of circles representing equator, meridian, ecliptic, etc. Used by Hipparchus and Ptolemy and up to the time of Tycho Brahe for determining the position of the stars.

Arsenic, a metalloid element, no. 33, symbol As in group 5 of the periodic table usually met with as a constituent of other minerals, sometimes by itself. Its compounds are very poisonous. Lead arsenate is a powerful insecticide used for spraying fruit trees. The more stable allotropic form (grey) has a layer structure, and conducts electricity.

Artesian Wells take their name from Artois in France, where the first wells of this kind were constructed in 1126. They are to be found only when a water-bearing bed is sandwiched between two impervious beds. When a boring is made to the lower part of the bed, the pressure of water is sufficient to cause the water to overflow at the surface. Artesian wells were known to ancient Egypt and China, and have existed in the Sahara since the earliest times. The fountains in Trafalgar Square were once fed by artesian wells sunk through the London clay into the chalk about 250 m (820 ft)

Aryans, nomadic peoples who made their way in successive waves from the Eurasian steppes to the Indus and the Nile during the first half of the 2nd millennium B.C. They crossed the Hindu Kush into N.W. India and settled in the valleys of the Indus and Ganges, where an earlier Indus civilisation had flourished, *c.* 3240–2750 B.C. Their religious ideas are reflected in the Veda (oldest Hindu scriptures, written down many centuries later in Vedic, parent language of Sanskrit). Those who made their way to Syria and Egypt founded the Hyksos empire (*c.* 1720–1550 B.C.). The Aryans introduced the horse-drawn chariot and spoke a language from which the great Indo-European family of languages is derived, with one group in India and Iran, and another in Europe. Because of the misuse of the term by the Nazis, Aryan is now referred to as proto-Indo-European.

Ash, a familiar deciduous tree of the genus *Fraxinus,* of over 60 species, native to North temperate regions. The ash held an important place in Norse mythology, as it was supposed to support the heavens with its roots in Hell. The species native to Britain, and to Europe, is *F. excelsior,* a tall tree with compound leaves, greenish flowers, winged seeds, and black buds in winter. It is a valuable timber tree, tough and elastic, and largely used for wheels and handles. The rowan, or mountain ash, *Sorbus aucuparia,* with similar leaves and orange berries, belongs to a different family. *F. pendula* or weeping ash is a strain which makes an ideal natural summer house.

Astrolabe, a medieval scientific instrument for taking altitudes, observing the sun by day and the stars by night, and used for telling the time and finding the latitude. Used by the ancient Greeks, later by the Arabs and Persians, and introduced into Europe by way of Spain in the 14th cent. Chaucer is said to have sent his son Lois, a ten-year-old student at Oxford, an astrolabe with a treatise on its use in 1391.

Astronomy. The Pythagoreans believed the stars and planets moved with uniform circular velocity in crystalline spheres, centered round the earth (the "harmony of the spheres"). Hipparchus (190–120 B.C.) made the first star catalogue, discovered the precession of the equinoxes and introduced the idea of epicyclic motion. His planetary system, in the form it was presented by Ptolemy 200 years later, held until the Renaissance when Copernicus revived the heretical view first put forward by Aristarchus of Samos (310–230 B.C.) that the sun and not the earth was at the center. Galileo, accurate observer and experimenter, went beyond Copernicus; helped by the contributions of Tycho Brahe, Giordano Bruno, Kepler and others, he was able to overthrow the Ptolemaic system of the heavenly spheres and Aristotelian philosophy and pave the way for Newton and modern astronomy. To Galileo we owe the conception of acceleration; to Newton the theory of universal gravitation; they showed that the same laws govern both celestial and terrestrial physics. Three landmarks in more recent times were the discovery of Uranus by Herschel in 1781 which extended the solar system as then recognized; the estimation by Hubble in 1924 of the distance of Andromeda, which showed that our Galaxy was just one of many; and Einstein's theory of relativity which improved on Newton's theory of the solar system by bringing gravitation into the domain of space-time. Today radio-telescopes and space probes are advancing astronomical knowledge and making it possible to explore regions beyond the scope of optical telescopes.

Athanasian Creed, one of the three ancient creeds of the Christian Church, often referred to as the *Quicunque Vult,* is a statement of the doctrine of the Trinity and the Incarnation, and though named after St. Athanasius, it is thought to be the work of St. Ambrose (339–97).

Atmospherics are electrical impulses which are believed to originate in atmospheric electrical discharges such as lightning. They give rise to crashing background noises in the loudspeakers of radio sets, interfering with reception at distances of up to 6,400 km (3,970 mi) from the center of the disturbance. The location of atmospherics with the aid of radio direction-finding methods gives warning of the approach of thunderstorms.

Atomic Pile, an apparatus containing a fissionable element and a moderator, such as heavy water or graphite, in which a self-sustaining fission process proceeds at a controllable rate. The first atomic pile, constructed on a squash court at Chicago, was operated for the first time on 2 December 1942, under the direction of Enrico Fermi. The pile contained 12,400 lb (5,580 kg) of uranium.

Aurora Polaris. This wonderful phenomenon of the night sky is a common sight at high northern and southern latitudes, where it is called the aurora borealis and the aurora australis, respectively. It is visible less often at temperate latitudes, and only rarely in the tropics. The auroral ovals, or zones of maximum frequency of aurora, surround both of the earth's geomagnetic poles, and the northern auroral oval includes the northern parts of Scandinavia, Canada, and Alaska. The aurora is the visible manifestation of complex plasma processes occurring within the earth's magnetosphere (*q.v.*), whereby streams of high-energy electrons and protons (mainly) are accelerated and dumped via the earth's magnetic field lines into the upper atmosphere. This mechanism produces the light emission of the aurora. The brightest aurora, which may also extend to lower latitudes, occurs during geomagnetic storms, which are complex and large-scale plasma instabilities within the magnetosphere triggered by fluctuations in the solar wind (*q.v.*)—usually ascribed to "M" regions on the sun associated with coronal holes, flares, and active sunspot groups. Auroral displays may take several forms—a faint glow, a diffuse ribbon of light crossing the heavens, great folded waving curtains or draperies, or the entire sky may be flooded with a rapidly varying brilliant panoply of light. Specially instrumented spacecraft which can directly explore the magnetosphere and high-latitude ionosphere have provided a great deal of our knowledge about this fascinating and complex phenomenon. The aurora is a kind of light essentially different from that of the rainbow which is a partly subjective phenomenon. Each beholder sees his own rainbow, whose light is sunlight refracted and reflected by many raindrops. The raindrops that produce his rainbow depend on his position as well as on the direction of the sun. The aurora, on the contrary, is a light as objective as that of a candle, though produced differently. It is a self-luminescence of the air in particular regions of the atmosphere that lie far above the clouds.

Average is a single number designed to give a typical example of a set of numbers, *e.g.,* a cricketer's batting average for a season gives an idea of his typical score. There are several kinds of average and their uses are studied in the science of statistics. A statement that "so and so is the average value" can be misleading if one does not know which average is meant. Three common averages are: the arithmetic average (or mean), the mode, and the median. The arithmetic average of n numbers is found by adding them together and dividing by n; this is a very common method of averaging. The mode of n numbers is the most frequently occurring number. The median is the middle number, *i.e.,* the number which is smaller than just as many of the other numbers as it exceeds. Of the numbers 1, 2, 2, 2, 2, 3, 4, 5, 6, 8, 9, the arithmetic means is 4, the mode is 2, the median is 3.

Avogadro's Hypothesis. This is a fundamental concept of chemistry. Equal volumes of all gases under the same conditions of temperature and pressure contain the same number of molecules. This law was instrumental in assigning the formula of molecules. The hypothesis was put forward in 1811, but was not generally accepted until 1860.

B

Bacteriophage (Phage), literally "bacteria eater", *i.e.,* a virus which specifically infects bacteria. In common with viruses which attack animal or plant cells, isolated phages are inert, and can only reproduce by making use of the chemical apparatus of a more sophisticated host cell (in this case a bacterium). However phages may be of two types, virulent or temperate. Virulent phages completely disrupt the normal functioning of the infected bacterium and adapt its reproductive mechanism to produce more phage. This eventually kills the bacterium and the newly assembled phages are released. Temperate phages on the other hand may enter into a remarkable symbiotic relationship with the bacterium, known as lysogeny. The phage genetic material is incorporated into that of the bacterium and is reproduced each time the still functioning bacterium subsequently divides. Furthermore the bacterium is immune from attack by potentially virulent phages of the same type. When such lysogenic bacteria die, phage particles may again be released. Phages carried in lysogenic bacteria are in a state known as prophage and it is often difficult to obtain pure, prophage-free strains of bacteria. Because of their relatively simple structure, phages have been extensively used in research on genetics and molecular biology.

Baleen *or* "whalebone" the name given to a series of horny plates growing from the roof of the mouth in those whales classified as Whalebone or Baleen Whales *(Mystacoceti).* There are 300–400 or so plates on each side, and their inner edges are frayed, the whole system constituting a filter for collecting minute organisms used for food. The Baleen Whales include the Right-Whales, the Pacific Grey-Whale and the Rorquals.

Ballet is a combination of four arts; dancing, music, painting, and drama, each of which is ideally of equal importance. The movement of the individual dancers and the "orchestration" of the whole group is in the hands of the choreographer. The dancer's training follows certain basic rules but save in classical ballet there is considerable freedom of movement. Ballet as we know it today developed professionally at the Court of King Louis XIV of France, though it owes its origins to Italy and in the earliest times to Greece and Rome. Its movements were made up from the dances of courtiers, country folk and tumblers. Technique grew more complex as costume became modified, the body gaining complete freedom with the invention of tights. A succession of great dancers—French, Italian and latterly Russian left their imprint on the art. Contemporary ballet reflects the aesthetics of the Russian, Sergei Diaghilev.

Balloon, the modern balloon consists of a bag of plastic material inflated with a gas lighter than air. The first ascent by man in a hot-air ballon was made on 21 November 1783, and in a hydrogen balloon on December 1, 1783. The most famous of the early scientific flights by manned balloons were those of the Englishmen Coxwell and Glaisher, in 1862, when a height of 11 km (6.8 miles) was reached. The first aerial crossing of the English Channel by Blanchard and Jeffries was made on January 7, 1785. Piccard's ascent to 16 km (9.9 miles) in 1931 marked the conquest of the stratosphere. Four years later the American balloon *Explorer 11*, inflated with nearly 112,000 m³ of helium, carried a team of scientists with their floating laboratory to an altitude of 23 km (14.3 miles). In 1957 a pressurized balloon carrying an American doctor rose 31 km (19.3 miles) above the Earth. Meteorologists send their instruments up in balloons to collect data about the upper atmosphere, and of recent years physicists have learned much about cosmic radiation from the study of photographic plates sent to the upper regions in balloons.

Balsam, a big genus (140 species) of flowering plants. Many species are cultivated for their showy flowers, *e.g., Impatiens noli-me-tangere,* the yellow balsam or "touch-me-not", so called because the fruit explodes when touched, slinging out the seeds. Balsam fir is a conifer *(Abies balsamea)* from which Canada balsam gum is obtained.

Bamboo, a genus of strong grasses, some species growing to over 36 m (118 ft.) in height; much used by oriental peoples for all kinds of purposes. The young shoots of some species are tender and esculent.

Barbary Ape, a large monkey belonging to the genus *Macoca.* It is the only monkey living in relative freedom in Europe, a small colony being found on the Rock of Gibraltar. It has no tail.

Barium, metal element, no. 56, symbol Ba. In group 2 of the periodic table. The metal is soft and easily cut. It occurs as the sulfate and carbonate in nature. It was first prepared by Sir Humphry Davy in 1808, as an amalgam, by electrolysis of barium chloride. The pure metal was not isolated until 1901.

Barometer is an instrument for measuring atmospheric pressure, invented at Florence by Torricelli, pupil of Galileo, in 1644. The standard method consists of balancing the air column against a column of mercury, used on account of its high density. The mercury is contained in a long glass tube, closed at one end, and inverted in a cistern also containing mercury. The height of the mercury column, supporting the air column, is taken as the pressure at the time, and can be read off very accurately by means of a vernier scale. Present-day tendency is to express the readings in units of pressure instead of length, the millibar being adopted (1 mb = 1,000 dynes per sq. cm.; 1,000 mb = of mercury approx.). The standard instrument is correct for pressures at 0° C (32° F) in Lat. 45°, so that corrections have to be applied for temperatures and latitudes other than these. Also a correction has to be made for reducing the pressure to mean sea level.

Baryons, the group of heavier subatomic particles which includes the proton, neutron, lambda and omega-minus particles (and their corresponding anti-particles, called anti-baryons). Baryons interact by means of all the known forces of nature (strong, weak, electromagnetic and gravitational). However, in any closed system the total baryon number (*i.e.,* the number of baryons minus the number of anti-baryons) is constant. This means that the proton, being the lightest known baryon, must be stable against spontaneous decay. Unlike the lighter leptons *(q.v.),* baryons are now thought to have internal structure reflecting the fact that they are composed of quarks.

Basalt Rocks are fine-grained, dark coloured, of igneous origin and occur either as lava flows as in Mull and Staffa, or as intrusive sheets, like the Edinburgh Castle Rock and Salisbury Crags. One of the most noted examples of columnar basalt is that of the Giant's Causeway in Ireland.

Base, a substance having a tendency to accept a proton (H^+). This is a wide definition and covers unconventional types of compounds. In aqueous solution bases dissolve with formation of hydroxyl ions, and will neutralise an acid to form a salt. In non-aqueous solvents, like liquid ammonia or hydrogen fluoride, compounds classically regarded as salts can be bases, *e.g.,* sodium fluoride is a base in hydrogen fluoride solution.

Bas-Relief ("low relief"), a term used in sculpture to denote a class of sculptures the figures of which are only slightly raised from the surface of the stone or clay upon which the design is wrought.

Bauhaus, a German institution for the training of architects, artists and industrial designers founded in 1919 at Weimar by Walter Gropius, (d. 1969). It was closed by Hitler in 1933 and re-opened at Chicago. The Bauhaus doctrine held that there should be no separation between architecture and the fine and applied arts; that art, science and technology should cooperate to create "the compositely inseparable work of art, the great building". Thus it was an organization with a social purpose. The original institution, at the instigation of Gropius, included on its teaching staff not only architects and technicians but also such noted artists as Paul Klee and Wassily Kandinsky.

Bauxite, the chief ore of aluminum. Chemically it is aluminum oxide. Aluminum metal is made industrially by electrolyzing purified bauxite dissolved in fused cryolite. Chief producing areas; Jamaica, Australia, Surinam, USSR, Guyana, France, Greece, Guinea, USA, Hungary, Yugoslavia.

Bears belong to the Ursidae family of the Carnivora. They are plantigrade mammals, walking (like man) on the soles of their feet. Found in most parts of the world except Australia. The common Brown Bear was once spread over the whole of Europe: it became extinct in England about the 11th century; 2·2·5 m (6·5·8 ft) in length, and stands 1 m (3 ft) or more at the shoulder. The Grizzly Bear of N. America is larger, and the coat is shorter and greyer. The Polar Bear is remarkable in having a white coat all the year round; it spends much time in water, and unlike other bears is entirely carnivorous.

Beeswax, the secretion of the bee, used for the formation of the cells or honey comb of the hive; when melted it is what is commercially known as yellow wax, white wax being made by bleaching. Being impervious to water, it acts as a good resistant and is an article of much utility.

Beetles (Coleoptera) constitute one of the biggest orders of insects, numbering over 200,000 species. There are two pairs of wings; the hind pair are used for flight, while the front pair are hardened to form a pair of protective covers (clytra). Some beetles have lost the power of flight and then the elytra are joined together.

Bell, Book and Candle. To curse by "bell, book, and candle" was a form of excommunication in the Roman Church ending with the words: "Close the book, quench the candle, ring the bell".

Beryl, a mineral, of which the emerald is a grass-green variety. Composed of beryllium and aluminum silicates. The pure mineral is colorless; the color of most beryl comes from traces of impurities, notably iron and chromium. Otherwise it is yellowish, greenish-yellow, or blue, and is found in veins which traverse granite or gneiss, or embedded in granite, and sometimes in alluvial soil formed from such rocks.

Beryllium. Metallic element, no. 4, symbol Be. Very similar to aluminum, it is stronger than steel and only one-quarter its weight. It is not very abundant, its main source is the mineral, beryl. Copper containing 2 percent beryllium is used for making springs. Because of its special properties the metal is used as a component in spacecraft, missiles and nuclear reactors. This accounts for its recent development on a technical scale. The metal powder is toxic.

Binary Notation, for numbers, is a way of representing numbers using only two digits, 0 and 1. Electronic digital computers handle numbers in this form and many people these days are having to learn it. Many school children find it both easy and fascinating as did the great philosopher and mathematician Leibniz. The ordinary, or decimal numbers, 0, 1, 2, 3, 4, 5, 6, 7, 8, 9, 10 are written in binary notation as follows: 0, 1, 10, 11, 100, 101, 110, 111, 1000, 1001, 1010. The reader might divine the rules from this. The point is you "carry 1", *i.e.,* move the digit 1 a place to the left, when you reach 2. In decimal notation you move 1 a place left when you reach 10. In other words, instead of columns for units, tens, hundreds, thousands, etc., the columns are for units, twos, fours, eights, etc. In binary notation: "$1 + 1 = 0$ with 1 to carry". Since every digit in binary notation is either 0 or 1 it requires one bit of information to specify a binary digit.

Biological Clock. All living organisms undergo cyclical changes in activity of some sort. These are linked to the changes in their environment which are produced by the alternation of night and day, the phases of the moon and the tides, and the cycle of the seasons. These cycles of activity frequently persist if the organism is put into a constant environment in which there appear to be no external clues as to what time or what season it is. A squirrel, for example, wakes up at about the same time each evening even when it is put into constant darkness. It is usual to refer to these activity patterns as being driven by a biological clock inside the organism. But very little is known about how these biological clocks work.

Biological Warfare, is the use for warlike purposes of bacteria, viruses, fungi, or other biological agents. These can be used to spread distress, incapacity, disease or death among the enemy's people or livestock. One of the strange uses to which mankind puts its science is to make naturally infective organisms even more virulent for military use. This sort of research can be done in many countries; it is much cheaper and easier to hide than nuclear weapons development. Secret attack by biological agents is supposed to be easy and it may affect the populations without damaging buildings or bridges. In 1975 the Biological Weapons Convention, 1972, signed by Britain, the United States and Russia, came into force outlawing germ warfare. Any nation suspecting violation may lodge a complaint with the UN Security Council.

Bismuth, metallic element, no. 83, symbol Bi, in group 5 of the periodic table. Like antimony, the stable form is a grey, brittle, layer structure; electrical conductor. It is readily fusible, melting at 264° C (507° F) and boiling at about 1420° C (2590° F). Wood's metal, an alloy with one of the lowest melting points (under 65° C (150° F), so that a spoon made of it will melt when placed in a cup of hot tea), contains four parts bismuth, two parts lead, one part tin, one part cadmium.

Bit, formerly the word often referred to the metal piece in the mouth of a bridled horse, now more likely to be a technical expression in the mouth of a computer expert. A bit is a unit of information; it is the information that can be conveyed by indicating which of two possibilities obtains. Any object that can be either of two states can therefore store one bit of information. In a technical device, the two states could be the presence or the absence of a magnetic field, or of an electric voltage. Since all numbers can be represented in the binary system (*see* **Binary Notation**) by a row of digits which are *either* 0 *or* 1, it takes one bit of information to specify a binary digit. Bit is short for binary digit.

Bivalves, shell-fish whose shell consists of two hinged valves, lying one on each side of the body, such as mussels, oysters and cockles.

Black Death, the plague which swept across Europe in the years 1348–50, beginning in the ports of Italy, brought in by merchant ships from Black Sea ports. It was the worst scourge man has ever known; at least a quarter of the European population was wiped out in the first epidemic of 1348. It reached England in the winter of that year. The disease was transmitted to man by fleas from black rats, though this was not known at the time, the specific organism being *Bacillus pestis.* The disease continued to ravage Europe in recurrent outbreaks up to the late 17th cent. The epidemic which raged in England in 1665 wiped out whole villages and one-tenth of London's population of 460,000. Samuel Pepys wrote a grim account of it in his *Diary.*

Boa, a term applied to a family of snakes of large size, some attaining a length of 9 m. They are not poisonous, but kill their prey by crushing—constriction—hence the name "boa constrictor". They occur both in the Old World and the New, but are more abundant in the latter. Most Boas retain the eggs within the body until young are fully developed, whereas the Pythons almost all lay leather-shelled eggs.

Bode's Law, a numerical relationship formulated by Bode in 1772 (though pointed out earlier by J. D. Titius of Wittenberg), which states that the relative mean distances of the planets from the sun are found by adding 4 to each of the terms 0, 3, 6, 12, 24, 48, 96, and dividing each number by 10. The gap between Mars and Jupiter caused Bode to predict the existence of a planet there, which was later confirmed by the discovery of Ceres and other minor planets. The law breaks down however, for Neptune and Pluto.

Boiling-point is the temperature at which a liquid boils. At that point the pressure of the vapor is equal to the pressure of the atmosphere. Under increased pressure the b.p. rises and under less pressure, as on the top of a mountain, it is lower. At standard atmospheric pressure (760 mm of mercury) the b.p. of water is 100° C (212° F); alcohol 784° C (173.1° F; ether 35.6° C (96.1° F).

Borax (Sodium Pyroborate) is a white, soluble, crystalline salt. It is widely and diversely used, *e.g.,* as a mild antiseptic, in glazing pottery, in soldering, in the making of pyrex glass, as a cleansing agent and sometimes as a food preservative. Borax occurs naturally in the salt lakes of Tibet, where it is called tincal, in California (Borax Lake, Death Valley), and elsewhere.

Boron. A metalloid element, no. 5, symbol B. There are two forms, one crystalline, the other amorphous. It is not very abundant in nature but occurs in concentrated deposits. It is best known in boric acid, which is used as a mild antiseptic (called boracic acid) and borax *(q.v.).* Boron compounds are essential to some plants, *e.g.,* beans. Used in the preparation of various special-purpose alloys, such as impact resistant steel. Compounds of boron and hydrogen are used as rocket fuels.

Brass, an exceedingly useful alloy of copper and zinc. Much brass is about two-thirds copper but different proportions give different properties. It is harder than copper and easily worked. Brass in the Bible (Matt. x, 9) probably refers to bronze.

Breeder Reactor, a kind of nuclear reactor which besides producing energy by the fission process also produces ("breeds") more nuclear fuel at the same time. A typical reaction is: a neutron induces fission of a U-235 nucleus which breaks up into two medium-sized nuclei and some neutrons; one of the latter then enters a U-238 nucleus turning it into U-239 which then decays radioactively *via* neptunium into plutonium which is useful fuel. There are technical problems in breeder reactors which have delayed their practical use but the "breeding" principle is so valuable that experiments have gone on for many years in, *e.g.,* Scotland and Idaho, and breeder reactors will no doubt increase in importance the more the supply of natural nuclear fuel appears to become depleted.

Bromine. A non-metal element, no. 35, symbol Br. member of the halogen family *(q.v.).* It is a red, evil-smelling liquid (Greek *bromos,* a stink). It is an abundant element. In the USA bromide is extracted from sea-water on a large scale. It unites readily with many other elements, the products being termed bromides. Its derivatives with organic compounds are used in synthetic chemistry. Bromoform is a liquid resembling chloroform. Bromides are used in medicine to calm excitement.

Bronze is primarily an alloy of copper and tin, and was one of the earliest alloys known, the Bronze Age (began c. 4,000 B.C. in Middle East) in the evolution of tool-using man coming before the Iron Age (*c.* 2,000 B.C.) Some modern bronzes contain zinc or lead also, and a trace of phosphorus is present in "Phosphor-bronze".

Bubble Chamber. An instrument used by physicists to reveal the tracks of fast fundamental particles (*e.g.,* those produced in large accelerating machines) in a form suitable for photography; closely related to the Wilson cloud chamber, but the particles leave trails of small bubbles in a superheated liquid (often liquid hydrogen) instead of droplets of liquid in a supersaturated gas; invented in 1952 by the American physicist, Dr. D. Glaser, Nobel Prizeman, 1960, and developed by Prof. L. W. Alvarez, Univ. of California, Nobel Prizeman, 1968.

Byzantine Art developed in the eastern part of the Roman empire after Constantine founded the city of Constantinople (A.D. 330). It has many sources—Greek, Syrian, Egyptian and Islamic—and reached its zenith in the reign of Justinian (527–65). The major art form was ecclesiastical architecture, the basic plan of which was Roman—either basilican (symmetrical about an axis) or centralized (symmetrical about a point). Arched construction was developed, and the dome became the most typical feature, although, unlike the Roman dome which was placed on a round apartment, the Byzantine dome was placed on a square one on independent pendentives. Frequently small domes were clustered round a large one as in the case of the great church of Santa Sophia (537), the climax of Byzantine architecture. Usually the churches were small and include those of SS. Sergius and Bacchus, Sta. Irene (in Constantinople), S. Vitale in Ravenna, and the much later and larger St. Mark's in Venice. Byzantine art also took the form of miniatures, enamels, jewels, and textiles, but mosaics, frescos, and icons *(q.v.)* are its greatest treasures.

C

Cactus, a family of flowering plants numbering about a thousand species adapted to living in very dry situations. The stem is usually fleshy, being composed of succulent tissue, remarkably retentive of water; commonly equipped with sharp thorns which deter animals from eating them. The roots are generally very long, tapping soil water over a large area; a "prickly pear" cactus may have roots covering a circular area 7 m (23 ft.) or more in diameter. The leaves are commonly insignificant or absent, and the stem takes over the photosynthetic leaf function and becomes accordingly flattened to expose greater area to sunlight and air. In some kinds of cactus *(e.g., Echinocactus)* the stem is shaped almost like a sea-urchin.

Cadmium. A metallic element, no. 48, symbol Cd, chemically similar to zinc and mercury. Used in alloys to lower the melting point, as in Wood's metal with bismuth and tin. Alloyed with copper to make electric cables. Like zinc, it is a protective metal and is used in electroplating. The cadmium-vapor lamp gives a characteristic frequency used in measuring wavelength.

Caesium, also spelt **Cesium,** is an alkali metal element, no. 55, symbol Cs, in first group of the periodic table. It resembles rubidium and potassium and was discovered by Bunsen and Kirchoff in 1860. It was the first element whose existence was discovered spectroscopically. The caesium atom consists of a heavy nucleus surrounded by 55 electrons, 54 of which are arranged in stable orbits, and one of which, known as the valency electron, is in a less stable orbit surrounding them. Used in the construction of photo-electric cells and as an accurate time standard (atomic clock).

Calcium, a silvery-white metallic element, no. 20, symbol Ca. It melts at 810°C (1490°F) and is very reactive. It was discovered by Sir Humphry Davy in 1808, but not until 1898 was it obtained pure, by Moissan. Does not occur as metal in nature, but calcium compounds make up a large part of the earth's crust. Most important calcium sources are marble, limestone, chalk (all three are, chemically, calcium carbonate); dolomite, which is the double carbonate of calcium and magnesium; gypsum, a hydrated calcium sulfate; calcium phosphate and calcium fluoride. Igneous rocks contain much calcium silicate. Calcium compounds are essential to plants and are used in fertilizers. Animals require calcium and phosphorus for bone and teeth formation; deficiency is treated by administration of calcium phosphate. Strontium is chemically similar to calcium, and the radioactive strontium 90 from atomic "fall-out" is therefore easily assimilated by the body.

Carbon, a non-metallic chemical element no. 6, symbol C, which occurs in crystalline form as diamonds and graphite; amorphous forms of carbon include charcoal and soot, while coke consists mainly of elementary carbon. The biochemistry of plants and animals largely hinges upon carbon compounds. The study of carbon compounds is called Organic Chemistry. **Carbon 14.** A radioactive isotope of carbon, with a half-life *c.* 6,000 years, used in following the path of compounds and their assimilation in the body. Also used in determination of the age of carbon-containing materials such as trees, fossils and very old documents.

Carbon dioxide. Commonest of the oxides of carbon. It is formed when carbon and its compounds are burnt with abundant supply of air, and when carbon compounds are oxidized in the respiration process of animals. The atmosphere contains carbon dioxide to the extent of about 325 ppm and is increasing by about 1 ppm per year, principally because of the burning of fossil fuels and possibly because of deforestation which not only leaves more oxidisible material but lowers the amount of carbon dioxide removed by photosynthesis.

Carbon monoxide is a colorless gas with no taste or smell. It is formed when coal and coke are burnt with a restricted supply of air; the blue flame to be seen in a coke brazier, for instance, is the flame of carbon monoxide. This gas is very poisonous, forming with the haemoglobin of the blood a compound which is useless for respiration and cherry red in color, which gives a visible sympton of poisoning by carbon monoxide. With nickel it forms a volatile compound, called nickel carbonyl, and this reaction is the basis of the Mond process for extracting nickel.

Cardinal Virtues, according to Plato these were justice, prudence, temperance, fortitude—*natural* virtues as distinct from the *theological* virtues of the Roman Catholic Church, faith, hope, charity. The phrase "seven cardinal virtues", combining the two, figures in mediaeval literature. *See* **Sins, Seven Deadly.**

Cat, the general name for all members of the class *Felidae* of the carnivorous order, from the lion down to the domestic cat. The latter is believed to be descended from the European and African wild cats. Egypt is credited with having been the first country in which the cat was domesticated.

Ceramics, are substances in which a combination of one or more metals with oxygen confers special and valuable properties. These include hardness, and resistance to heat and chemicals. Ceramic comes from the Greek word for pottery, and pottery materials of mud and clay were probably the first man-made ceramics. Nowadays the range is enormous and growing; apart from all the pottery materials, there are firebricks, gems, glasses, concretes, nuclear reactor fuel elements, special materials for electronic devices, colored pigments, electrical insulators, abrasives, and many other things. The scientific study of ceramics is part of materials science. The need to design ceramic objects has inspired great art, and the production of ceramics has become a major industry.

Cerium, a scarce metallic element, no. 58, symbol Ce, discovered by Berzelius in 1803. A mixture of cerium and thorium nitrates is used in the manufacture of gas mantles, which owe their incandescent property to the deposit of cerium and thorium oxide with which they are coated.

Chalcedony, a mixture of crystalline silica and amorphous hydrated silica, *i.e.,* of quartz and opal. It has a waxy lustre, and is much used by jewellers for necklaces, bracelets, etc. Commonly it is white or creamy. Its bright orange-red variety is called carnelian; its brown variety, sard. Chrysoprase, plasma, bloodstone are varieties which are respectively pale apple-green, dark leek-green, green with red spots.

Chemical Warfare. This term is usually restricted to mean the use in war of anti-personnel gases, aerosols and smokes, although explosives, napalm, herbicides and defoliants are also chemical agents that are used in war. Antipersonnel chemical weapons may be classified as *(a)* vesicants (agents which produce skin blisters, *e.g.,* mustard gas); *(b)* lacrimators (*e.g.,* the original tear gas, CN, and its British-developed successor CS now preferred for riot control); *(c)* sternutators (sneeze and vomiting agents, usually arsenic compounds, *e.g.,* Adamsite DM); *(d)* nerve gases (extremely lethal agents which incapacitate the nervous system, *e.g.,* the G-agents developed during the second world war and the more powerful **V**-agents developed subsequently); *(e)* lung irritants *e.g.,* phosgene and chlorine). Most of these chemicals can be lethal at sufficiently high concentrations and for this reason it is doubtful whether there exists the "humane" chemical agent which instantly incapacitates but leaves no long-term side effects.

The first occasion when poison gas was used on a large scale was in the first world war; more than 100,000 fatalities resulted from the use of principally chlorine, phosgene and mustard gas. Worldwide revulsion at the hideous effects of chemical weapons and their potential as indiscriminate weapons of mass destruction resulted in the Geneva Protocol of 1925 which prohibited the use of both chemical and bacteriological weapons. It has now been ratified by over 90 nations including all the major powers (although Japan and America are only recent signatories). The Protocol has been generally well observed although notable violations have been by the Italians in Abyssinia (1935–6), the Japanese in China during the second world war and the Americans in South East Asia in the 1960s. It has however failed to prevent the continual development and stock-piling of lethal chemical agents by many nations, although recently there have been moves towards chemical weapons disarmament. *See also* **Biological Warfare.**

Chestnut, the fruit of trees of the genus *Castanea,* members of the family *Fagaceae.* C. *sativa* is the sweet or Spanish chestnut, C. *dentata* the American chestnut and C. *crenata* the Japanese chestnut. The nut is edible. The wood is used in carpentry and fencing.

Chivalry an international brotherhood of knights formed primarily during the 13th century to fight against the infidels in the Crusades. For the French the major battle was against the Moslems in the Holy Land and North Africa, the Spaniards fought the same enemy in their own country, and the Germans were concerned with the heathen of Baltic lands, but Chaucer's "very perfect gentle knight" had fought in all these areas. One did not easily become a knight who had to be of noble birth and then pass through a period of probation, beginning as a boy page in the castle of some great lord, serving his elders and betters humbly while he was taught good manners, singing, playing musical instruments, and the composition of verse. Probably he learned Latin, but he certainly learned French, which was the international language of knights as Latin was of scholars. At fourteen he became a squire and learned to fight with sword, battle-axe and lance, and to endure conditions of hard living while carrying out his duties of waiting on his lord, looking after his horses, and in time accompanying him in battle. Only if he showed himself suitable was he finally knighted by a stroke of the hand or sword on the shoulder from the king or lord. Knighthood was an international order and had its special code of behavior; to honor one's sworn word, to protect the weak, to respect women, and defend the Faith. To some extent it had a civilizing effect on the conduct of war (*e.g.* knights of opposing sides might slaughter each other in battle but feast together after), but, since war was regarded as the supreme form of sport, it cannot be said to have contributed to peace.

Chlorine, a gaseous element, no. 17, symbol Cl, of the halogen family, first isolated in 1774 by Scheele by the action of manganese dioxide in hydrochloric acid. It unites easily with many other elements, the compounds resulting being termed chlorides. The gaseous element is greenish-yellow, with a pungent odour. It is a suffocating gas, injuring the lungs at a concentration as low as 1 part in 50,000, and was used during the first world war as a poison gas. Has a powerful bleaching action, usually being used in form of bleaching powder, made by combining lime and chlorine. Also a valuable disinfectant; used, for instance, in rendering water of swimming baths sterile.

Christmas means "mass of Christ" from the old English *Cristes maesse,* which is celebrated by the Western church on 25 December. The actual day on which Christ was born is not known and there is some uncertainty about the year, 25 December as the day of Nativity was not generally observed until the 5th century A.D., though, as the winter solstice, it had long been observed as a pagan festival of *sol invictus* (unconquered sun). The first Christmas card dates from about 1843 and the Christmas tree, of pagan origin, was introduced into England from Germany where it had been a tradition since the Middle Ages. Santa Claus is a corruption of Santa Nikolaus (St. Nicholas) patron saint of children, whose feast day properly falls on 6 December.

Chromium, a very hard, bluish-white metal element, no. 24, symbol Cr, melting at very high temperature (above 1,900° C (3,450° F). Its chief ore is chromite or chrome iron-ore (ferrous chromite). "Ferrochrome" is produced by heating chromite and anthracite in an electric furnace, and chrome steels are prepared by adding the pre-calculated amount of ferrochrome to melted steel. Best known chrome steel is stainless steel first made by Brearley in 1912 and since then developed greatly at Sheffield. A typical formula is 18 percent, chromium, 8 percent, nickel, 74 percent, iron. Equally important are Stellite alloys, containing chromium, cobalt, tungsten (or molybdenum), which have made possible modern high-speed cutting tools. Dies used in manufacture of plastics are commonly of chrome steel. The elementary metal finds little use alone except in chromium-plating for motor cars, etc.

Chromosomes, the structures contained within the nucleus of every animal and plant cell by which genetic information is transmitted. The chromosome number in somatic (body) cells is constant for each species of plant and animal, *e.g.,* man (46), cat (38), mouse (40) honey bee (16), fruit fly *Drosophila* (8), potato (48). Chromosomes are long molecules composed of deoxyribonucleoproteins (*i.e.,* proteins and DNA). Human chromosomes have been the subject of much recent research since it has been found that certain disorders are associated with chromosomal aberration, e.g., in Mongolism an extra chromosome is present. *See also* **Genes.**

Clouds are formed by the cooling of moist air, the type depending on the way the air cools and the height at which condensation occurs. There are three main classes: (1) high cloud (about 6,100 m; 20,013 ft)—cirrus (delicate and fibrous) cirrostratus (thin white veil), and cirrocumulus (delicately rippled) consisting of ice crystals; (2) medium cloud (above 2,100 m; 6,890 ft)—altostratus (dense, greyish veil) and altocumulus (broken flattened cloudlets)—chiefly water particles, often supercooled; (3) low cloud (from near ground to 2,100 m)—cumulus (fair weather, broken, dome-topped), cumulominbus (heavy, towering to great heights), stratocumulus (layer of globular masses or rolls), stratus (like fog but off the ground), nimbostratus (low, rainy cloud). The highest clouds of all, and the rarest, are the noctiluccent, seen only on summer nights in high latitudes. They form at about 80 km (50 mi) above the earth and consist of ice-coated dust from meteors.

Coat of Arms, in heraldry, a device containing a family's armorial bearings. In medieval times an actual coat upon which such device was embroidered.

Cobalt, element no. 24, symbol Cr, a white metal melting at 1,490° C (2714° F). Two main ores are *cobalt glance* (in which the element is combined with arsenic and sulphur) and *smaltite* (cobalt arsenide). The principal sources are Ontario and Zaïre. Various cobalt alloys are important, *e.g.,* stellite, ferrocobalt and carboloy. Its monoxide is an important coloring medium, and is used for coloring glass and porcelain blue.

Coca, a S. American shrub, *Erythroxylon coca,* also cultivated in Java. The leaves yield cocaine, classified as a dangerous drug. When the natives chew the leaves they are enabled to withstand hunger and fatigue, as cocaine acts both as a mental stimulant and as an anaesthetic on the mucous lining of the stomach.

Composite Materials, or more simply composites, are materials which derive useful properties by combining the virtues of two or more components. Combining clay with straw to make tougher bricks is an ancient example in which fibers (straw) are embedded in a matrix or body (the clay). A modern example is fiberglass in which glass fibers are embedded in a plastic matrix. Nature also uses composites as in bamboo in which a lignin matrix binds together the fibers of cellulose to make a light strong structure. Composites may contain flakes or particles embedded in the matrix instead of fibers—it depends on the application. Although the idea is not new composite technology has made rapid strides in the last few decades guided by scientific insight into the nature of solids and the origin of their strengths and weaknesses. The motivation had been that scientifically designed composites offer materials with exceptional strength/weight ratio, desirable magnetic properties and other technological advantages which meet the extreme demands of a variety of industries. For example, composite aluminum containing boron fibers or resin containing graphite fibers can have strength/weight ratios over twice that of high strength solid aluminum. Composites of many kinds are now widespread in industrial use and are attracting much research and development.

Computer, a technical device for accepting an input of information, processing this information according to some prescribed program of operations and supplying an output of processed information. Many types of operation can be performed on many types of information and computers are now indispensable in science, business, warfare, government and other activities. Early thinkers in this field were Pascal (17th century), Babbage (19th century) and Turing (1930s), but electronic computers as we know them appeared during the second world war and the first commercial machine was on sale in 1950. Computers are millions of times faster than human beings at computing; and the introduction of computers into an organization does more than just speed up the calculations, it tends to transform the whole nature of the organization. The possibilities for future developments seem enormous. Analog computers and digital computers are two different kinds stemming from the difference between *measuring* and *counting*. Analog types handle data that is repeated by physical quantities of continuously variable size such as voltages or lengths. These quantities can be made to vary like the quantities in a problem which the computer is set to solve; the problem is thus solved by analogy. A slide rule is a rudimentary analog computer in which numbers are represented by lengths of rule. Digital computers handle actual numbers expressed in digits and the quantities in the problem are represented by discrete numbers. These can all be expressed in binary form and thus stored or handled in bits. *See* **Bit, Binary Notation.**

Continental Drift. The hypothesis of drifting continents is due to F. B. Taylor, an American geologist who published his theory in 1908, and to the Austrian meteorologist Alfred Wegener in 1910. The latter was impressed by the matching coasts of South America, and Africa, which seemed to him to fit together like the pieces of a jigsaw puzzle. Since then many other people have taken up and developed the idea. According to Wegener, at one time there were two primary super-continents. Laurasia and Gondwanaland. The one in the northern hemisphere consisted of North America, Europe, and the northern part of Asia. Its southern counterpart included Antarctica, Australia, India, Africa and South America. These super-continents broke up, and their various bits moved apart. In particular, the southern hemisphere continents drifted radially northwards away from the south pole, and the two Americas shifted westwards from Europe and Africa. What would have been the leading edges of the land masses on this hypothesis, are now heavily buckled up into mountain belts, such as the Cordillera and the Alpine-Himalayan chain. The resistance afforded to drifting by the strong ocean floors may well have been the cause of such structures. Despite the wealth of geological facts which have a bearing on the problem of continental drift, none of these has been able to decide the issue in a conclusive manner. Further studies of rock magnetism *(q.v.)* and of fossil climates should ultimately establish the concept of continental drift on a firm basis.

Copper, one of the most familiar of metals, element no. 29, symbol Cu, used in ancient times as an alloy with tin in producing bronze, and preceding iron as an industrial material. Copper ores are most abundant in the USA, Chile, Canada, Zambia and Zaïre. All copper compounds are poisonous.

Coral, an order of small marine animals closely related to the sea-anemone, but differing from it in their ability to develop a limy skeleton. They multiply sexually and by budding. The structure of the coral secretions assumes a variety of forms, fan-like, tree-like, mushroom shape, and so forth. Red coral (the skeleton of *Corallium rubrum*) is mainly obtained from the Mediterranean. The coral reefs of the Pacific and Indian Oceans are often many miles in extent. Living corals occur only in warm seas at about 23° C (73° F).

Corona *or* **Solar Corona,** the outer atmosphere of the sun. This glows by virtue of light emitted by the sun and scattered by electrons and dust particles at various heights in the sun's atmosphere and also by light emitted from ionised atoms in the corona itself. Corona light is much fainter than the bright disc of the sun and is invisible against the normal blue of the sky. During total solar eclipses, the corona can be seen by the human eye as a faint glow extending irregularly outwards a few solar diameters from the sun. The sun's atmosphere extends much further than this but is invisible to the eye at large distances from the sun. The corona gases are thought to be very hot (millions of degrees) and in complex violent motion; the gross structure of the corona is connected with the sunspot cycle.

Crusades were military expeditions undertaken by some of the Christian nations of Europe with the object of ensuring the safety of pilgrims visiting the Holy Sepulchre and to retain in Christian hands the Holy Places. For two centuries nine crusades were undertaken: First, 1095–99, under Godfrey of Bouillon, which succeeded in capturing Jerusalem; Second, 1147–49, led by Louis VII of France, a dismal failure, which ended with the fall of Jerusalem; Third, 1180–92, in which Richard I of England took part, making a truce with Saladin; Fourth, 1202–4, led by French and Flemish nobles, a shameful expedition, resulting in the founding of a Latin empire in Constantinople; Fifth, 1217–21, led by John of Brienne; Sixth, 1228–29, under the Emperor Frederick II; Seventh, 1248–54, under St. Louis of France; Eighth, 1270, under the same leadership, but cut short by his death on an ill-judged expedition to Tunis; Ninth, 1271–72, led by Prince Edward of England, which accomplished nothing. Millions of lives and an enormous amount of treasure were sacrificed in these enterprises and Jerusalem remained in the possession of the "infidels". The chief material beneficiaries were the Italian maritime cities; the chief spiritual beneficiary was the Pope; but in literature and the arts both Europe and the Levant benefited enormously from the bringing together of the different cultures.

Cryogenics (Greek roots: productive of cold) is the science dealing with the production of very low temperatures and the study of their physical and technological consequences. "Very low" is often taken to mean below about −150° C (−300° F). The growth of cryogenics (essentially a 20th-cent. science) is connected with the discovery of how to liquefy all gases including even helium which resisted liquefaction until 1908. Scientifically, cryogenics is important partly because special phenomena (*e.g.*, superconductivity appear at lower temperatures and partly because more can be learned about ordinary properties by studying them in the absence of heat. Technologically, cryogenics is becoming more and more significant, for example, liquefied gases are rocket propellants, superconductors make valuable magnets, tissue-freezing techniques (using very cold liquids) have been introduced into surgery. *See* **Absolute Temperature.**

Cuneiform, (Latin = *wedge-shaped*), an ancient method of writing by impressing wedge-like strokes into tablets of damp clay which when dried and hardened formed a permanent script, form writing developed from its original pictographic form into a phonetic writing and can be traced back to the non-Semitic Sumerians of ancient Mesopotamia, the earliest civilization known to us. It passed to the Semitic Accadians of Babylonia in the 3rd millennium B.C. who adapted it to their own language. Decipherment by Sir Henry Rawlinson, 1835.

D

Dactylopterus, a fish of the gurnard family, with wing-like pectoral fins; sometimes known as the flying fish, though that appellation is more generally given to *Exocaetus exiliens.*

Daguerreotype, the first practical photographic process, invented in Paris by M. Daguerre during the years 1824–39. The light-sensitive plate was prepared by bringing iodine in contact with a plate of silver. After exposure a positive image came by development of the plate in mercury vapour. Even for open-air scenes the first daguerreotypes involved exposure of 5–10 minutes. The picture came in one copy and the process was therefore of limited use. The wet collodion process (1851) rendered the technique obsolete.

Dead Sea Scrolls, a group of ancient Jewish documents, consisting of scrolls and fragments which have been recovered since 1947 in the vicinity of Qumran near the Dead Sea and which represent one of the most important finds ever made in the field of biblical archaeology and Christian origins. The scrolls written in Hebrew or Aramaic, were found in caves, the first by chance by an Arab shepherd in 1947. These consisted of biblical texts older by a thousand years than the earliest Hebrew manuscript of the Old Testament (A.D. 895). Many fragments have since been discovered, comprising the whole of the Old Testament with the exception of Esther. In addition there are commentaries and other non-biblical writings, including one called "The War of the Sons of Light with the Sons of Darkness". The writing on the scrolls indicates that they were written over a period of two centuries, the greater proportion before the birth of Christ. A nearby ruin is believed to have been the home of a religious sect called the Essenes, to whom the scrolls belonged. By the aid of the latest scientific techniques, including radiocarbon tests, the age of the scrolls is being accurately determined. An account of the scrolls and their implications is given in Edmund Wilson's *The Dead Sea Scrolls: 1947–1969.*

Deciduous Trees are such as shed their leaves at certain seasons as distinguished from evergreens or permanent foliaged trees or shrubs.

Deserts, vast, barren, stone or sandy wastes where there is almost no rainfall and little or no vegetation. These regions are found in the interior of the continents Africa, Asia and America between 20° and 30° north and south of the equator. Europe is the only continent without deserts. The most famous are the Sahara, the largest in the world, the Gobi desert of central Asia, the Kalahari desert of southwest Africa and the great Australian desert. The marginal extension of deserts (desertification) is a topic of considerable debate. The increasing size of deserts is thought to result from either climate change or the interference by man.

Deuterium or "heavy hydrogen". The second isotope of hydrogen; the third is called tritium. Deuterium atoms have in their nuclei a neutron as well as a proton; tritium nuclei have two neutrons and one proton. In ordinary hydrogen gas about one out of every 5,000 atoms is a deuterium atom. Deuterium was discovered in 1932 by Professor Harold Urey. The oxide of deuterium corresponding to water is called "heavy water". The nucleus of the deuterium atom is called a deuteron. An anti-deuteron consisting of anti-proton and anti-neutron was produced at Brookhaven in 1965, the first compound anti-nucleus ever to be produced.

Diamond, a mineral, one of the two crystalline forms of the element carbon (the other is graphite), the hardest known substance, used as a gem and in industry. India was the first country to mine diamonds (the Koh-i-noor, which means "mountain of light", known since 1304, came from Golconda near Hyderabad and came into British possession when the Punjab was annexed in 1849). The celebrated diamond mines of South Africa were discovered in the 1870s. Other important diamond producing countries are Zaïre, USSR, Congo, Ghana, Sierra Leone, Namibia, Angola, Tanzania. The world's biggest diamond is the 3,106-carat Cullinan, discovered near Pretoria, South Africa, in 1905. Diamonds can be made artificially by subjecting carbon to very high temperatures and pressures; many industrial diamonds are made this way. Antwerp is the main diamond centre of the world, London the main marketing centre, Amsterdam the main diamond cutting centre.

Diatoms. One-celled algae, comon in fresh and salt water. Distinctive feature is the siliceous wall which is in two halves, one fitting over the other like the lid of a box. These walls are often very finely and beautifully sculptured. The diatoms constitute a class of the plant kingdom known as the Bacillariophyta. *Diatom ooze* is a deep-sea deposit made up of diatom shells. *Diatomite* or *diatomaceous earth* is the mineral form that such diatom oozes assume (sometimes known as kieselguhr which mixed with nitroglycerine yields dynamite).

Dinosaur, the name given to a group of extinct reptiles of the Mesozoic period, some of which were of immense size—much larger than crocodiles. *See* **Diplodocus.**

Diplodocus, one of the best known of the extinct mammoth dinosaurs. Fossil remains have been discovered in the Jurassic rocks of the United States. Some reached a length of over 24 m.

Diptych was a folding two-leaved tablet of wood, ivory, or metal, with polished inner surfaces, utilised for writing with the style by the ancient Greeks and Romans. The same term was applied to the tablets on which the names of the persons to be commemorated were inscribed in the early Church. In art any pair of pictures hinged together is styled a diptych, a set of three, a triptych.

DNA (Deoxyribonucleic acid), a polymer molecule in the form of a double-strand helix containing many thousands of sub-units. Contains the genetic information coded in sequences of sub units called bases. The Nobel Prize for medicine was awarded in 1962 for the discovery of the structure of DNA: that for 1968 for interpreting the genetic code and its function in protein synthesis. *See* **Nucleic Acids.**

Doldrums, a nautical term applied to those areas of the Atlantic and Pacific within a few degrees of the Equator towards which the trade winds blow and where the weather is calm, hot and sultry. Pressure is low and the air often rises to produce heavy tropical rainfall and squalls, rendering navigation difficult.

E

Ebony, a name applied to various hard black woods, the best of which are grown in Mauritius and Sri Lanka. There are also Indian and American varieties. Only the inner portions, the heartwood, of the trees are of the necessary hardness and blackness. Ebony is largely used in ornamental cabinet work, for piano keys, canes, etc.

Edda, the name given to two important collections of early Icelandic literature—*the Elder or Poetic Edda,* poems handed down from the 9th and 10th cent., probably Norwegian in origin, and the *Younger* or *Prose Edda* of Snorri Sturluson compiled about 1230. They treat of mythical and religious legends of an early Scandinavian civilisation.

Electron Microscope. A microscope in which beams of electrons are focused by magnetic lenses in a manner analogous to the focusing of light beams in the ordinary optical microscope. Modern electron microscopes have very high resolving power and can magnify up to 1,500,000 times, making it possible to explore the cell and the virus. A development of the electron microscope is the scanning electron microscope (stereoscan), developed at Cambridge, which can examine an essentially thick object, giving a very large depth of focus.

Elementary Particle, one of the basic constituents of the material universe. The idea that matter consists of tiny particles goes back to classical times but the modern concept of the atom grew out of the chemistry and physics of the 19th cent. With the discovery of the electron in 1897 and the rise of nuclear physics in the 20th cent., the chemical atom was understood to be a structure built of even more fundamental particles—the electron, the proton and the neutron. In the last few decades, many more particles have been discovered, especially in the study of cosmic rays and by the use of large accelerating machines like those at CERN (Geneva) and Brookhaven National Laboratory (Long Island, New York). Among the later discoveries are the neutrino, the positron, the antiproton, the muon, the pion. These differ in electric charge and mass and other intrinsic properties and many have only a very short lifetime before they change into something else. Whether there is a small number of really elementary particles out of which all the others can be constructed is an unanswered question at the frontier of contemporary physics.

Elements. In chemistry, substances which cannot be separated into two or more simpler chemical substances. 91 elements are found naturally on the earth, some are observed spectroscopically in the stars and planets, and a further fourteen have been made artificially. Between them these elements can appear in some 1,200 different isotopes, of which 317 occur in Nature. (There are 274 stable isotopes among 81 stable elements.)

Emerald. The rich green variety of beryl (beryllium aluminum silicate). The color is due to the presence of chromium oxide.

Equator, the imaginary great circle of the earth, every point of which is 90 degrees from the earth's poles, and dividing the northern from the southern hemisphere. It is from this circle that the latitude of places north and south is reckoned. The celestial equator is the circle in which the plane of the earth's equator meets the celestial sphere (the imaginary sphere, in which the observer is at the centre, used for representing the apparent positions of the heavenly bodies).

Erbium, belongs to the group of rare-earth metals discovered by Mosander in 1842. Element no. 68, symbol Er.

Ether, in chemistry, is a volatile inflammable liquid composed of carbon, hydrogen and oxygen. It is a valuable anesthetic obtained by heating alcohol with sulfuric acid. In physics, in the 19th century, all space was supposed to be filled with a substance called ether, the chief property of which was to carry light waves, *i.e.,* light was supposed to be waves in this all-pervading medium known as the ether. Speculation and experiment concerned with the ether were very fruitful in advancing physics. Ultimately the attempts by Michelson and Morley to detect the motion of the earth through the ether were unsuccessful in this respect but profoundly successful in stimulating the theory of relativity. The ether concept has now been abandoned.

Etruscans, people believed to have come from Asia Minor who colonised Italy about 900 B.C., settled in what is now Tuscany and part of Umbria, reached the height of their civilization about 500 B.C., and were ultimately absorbed by the Romans. They were skilled technicians in bronze, silver and goldwork, and excelled in the art of granular decoration.

Eucalyptus. This genus includes 300 species of evergreen, leathery-leaved trees native to Australia. The oils yielded by different species vary a great deal in their scent and other properties and are chiefly used in pharmacy and perfumery; about 30 species produce oils suitable for medicinal purposes. Various species produce timber.

F

Fallout. Radioactive material produced by nuclear explosions which may cause bodily and genetic damage. (1) *Local fallout,* due to the return to earth of larger particles, occurs locally, and within a few hours after the explosion; (2) *Tropospheric fallout,* due to particles which remain in the troposphere and come down within a month or so, possibly all over the world, but within the altitude in which the explosion occurred; (3) *Stratospheric fallout,* which comes from fragments taken up into the stratosphere and then deposited, in the course of many years, uniformly all over the globe. The two radioactive materials which have given rise to the greatest concern for the health of the individual are strontium-90 and iodine-131. Both these materials are liable to become concentrated in certain parts of the human body, strontium-90 in bone and iodine-131 in the thyroid gland. Radiation exposure may produce genetic effects, that is effects which may show up in succeeding generations. An extensive survey was carried out by scientists of the US Atomic Energy Commission on the islands of Bikini atoll, site of some 23 nuclear tests, 1946–58. Their records, published in 1969, revealed that the intensity of radioactivity underneath the point of explosion was still exceedingly high. Most of the radiation remaining was due to the radioactive isotope caesium-137. The variation in intensity from one place to another seemed to be correlated with the variations of vegetation: where there was little vegetation weathering had been rapid. (The nuclear test ban treaty, 1963, applies to all nuclear tests except those held underground.)

Fault, a term designating a breakage coupled with displacement of geological strata.

Ferrites are compounds containing iron, oxygen, and one or two of a certain range of other possible metallic elements. Ferrites have recently become very important technically, because, unlike ordinary magnetic materials, they combine strong magnetism with electrical insulating properties. Ferrite-rod aerials are now common in portable radios, and ferrite devices are used in radar.

Fission, Nuclear. A nuclear reaction in which the nucleus of an atom (*e.g.,* uranium 235, plutonium) captures a neutron, and the unstable nucleus so produced breaks into two nearly equal fragments and throws out several neutrons as well. In biology the term fission is applied to reproduction by fragmentation of a single-cell organism, as in amoeba.

Fleas. Fleas are small parasitic insects belonging to the order *Aphaniptera* (so called because these creatures have no wings). They obtain their food by sucking blood from their host. They are laterally compressed, which immediately distinguishes them from lice. The human flea *(Pulex irritans)* is able to jump vertically a distance of over 18 cm.

Fluorine, chemical element, no. 9, member of the halogen family, symbol F, it is found in combination with calcium in fluorspar, and occurs in minute quantities in certain other minerals. Discovered by Scheele in 1771, it was first obtained by Moissan in 1886. A pale yellow gas, it is very reactive and combines with most elements except oxygen. Its acid, hydrogen fluoride, etches glass, the fluorine combining with the silicon to form volatile silicon fluoride. Organic fluorine compounds have found use as very stable polymers which resist a wide variety of chemical actions.

Fluorspar, a mineral; chemically calcium fluoride. Can be colorless, green or yellow, but is most common purple. Blue fluorspar under the name of Derbyshire "blue John" has been used for ornamental purposes.

Frankincense is of two kinds, one being used as incense in certain religious services and obtained from olibanum, an Eastern shrub, the other is a resinous exudation derived from firs and pines, and largely used in pharmacy.

Fresco, a painting executed upon plaster walls or ceilings, a technique which has remained unchanged since it was practised by the great Renaissance artists.

Frost occurs when the temperature falls to, or below, 0° C (32° F), which is freezing point. Hoar frost is applied to the needles or feather-like crystals of the ice deposited on the ground, in the same manner as dew. Glazed frost is the clear icy coating which may be formed as a result of rain falling on objects whose temperatures are below the freezing point. These layers of ice, often rendering roads impassable for traffic, damaging overhead power and communication systems and endangering aircraft, can also be caused by condensation from warm, damp winds coming into contact with very cold air and freezing surfaces.

Functionalism, in architecture, a movement originated by Le Corbusier, Swiss-born French architect and town-planner, who applied the austere principles of the Purist movement in painting to his own art. From about 1924 he designed in concrete, steel and glass, buildings in which every part had a significance in terms of function on the theory that objects created to carry out their particular function to perfection cannot help being beautiful. "A house is a machine for living in." The style was in vogue between the two wars, and although its severity became somewhat modified, it is still the basis of most modern architecture.

Futurism, an Italian school of art and literature initiated by Marinetti, an Italian writer and mountebank friend of Mussolini at a later period. Its origin took the form of a manifesto published in Paris in 1909 in which Marinetti glorified violence, war and the machine age. In its aggression it favored the growth of fascism. One of the distinctive features of Futurist art was the use of the principle of "simultaneity" in which the same figure (*e.g.,* a woman descending a flight of stairs) is represented in successive positions like film "stills" superimposed on each other. In spite of two further manifestoes it was not until 1911 that the first examples of Futurist painting and sculpture appeared by the artists Severini, Balla and Boccioni. Apart from the principle of simultaneity, Futurism derived from Cubist and Post-impressionist techniques. The movement faded out early in the first world war.

G

Gallium, metallic element, no. 31, symbol Ga. related to aluminum, but which can be cut with a knife. It was discovered spectroscopically by L. de Boisbaudran in 1875. Long before Mendeleyev had predicted that an element with its properties would be found to fill the then existing gap in the Periodic Table; this gap came immediately below aluminium, so he suggested the name "eka aluminium" for it.

Gargoyle, a projecting spout for carrying off water from the roof gutter of a building. Gargoyles are found only in old structures, modern waterpipe systems having rendered them unnecessary. In Gothic architecture they were turned to architectural account and made to take all kinds of grotesque forms—grinning goblins, hideous monsters, dragons and so forth.

Garnet, a group of minerals; chemically they are orthosilicates of the metals calcium, magnesium, titanium, iron, aluminium. Garnets can be colored yellow, brown, black, green or red; the blood-red garnet is an important gemstone.

Gas is an elastic fluid substance, the molecules of which are in constant rapid motion, and exerting pressure. The technique whereby gases are liquefied depends on increasing pressure and diminishing temperature. Each gas has a critical point; unless the temperature is brought down to this point no amount of pressure will bring about liquefaction. Last gas to be liquefied was helium (1908) which boils at 209° C (408° F)

Genes, the elementary units of heredity. They exist as highly differentiated regions arranged along the length of the chromosomes which the nuclei of cells carry. A chromosome may carry hundreds or even thousands of genes, each with its own particular structure and specific properties. The position of a particular gene on a chromosome is called its locus. The material of the gene is DNA *(q.v.).*

Genetic Code. The elucidation of the structure of DNA *(q.v.)* for which Crick, Wilkins and Watson were jointly awarded the 1962 Nobel Prize for medicine, revealed the code or chemical dictionary out of which messages serving as blueprints for living structures can be made.

Genetic Engineering is the name given to the introduction of human choice and design criteria into the construction and combination of genes. This refers not to breeding by selection, a traditional process, but to the biochemical alteration of the actual DNA in cells so as to produce novel self-reproducing organisms. Such manipulations became possible when techniques were recently discovered for severing and rejoining DNA molecules and inserting sections into them. Many people regard this development as fraught with enormous significance. Like nuclear power, it can lead to good, to evil, and to accidental hazards, not all of which can be foreseen. Thus when biologists realised they could create new lifeforms, *e.g.,* bacteria, with novel genes, they appreciated that, as well as medically beneficial strains, new virulent forms might by accident be produced and escape into the world. Ultimately, not imminently, men may be able to design the genes of higher animals and even of man himself and thus consciously influence biological evolution. Many scientists have been brought by these possibilities up against an old problem: is science going too far too fast?

Geneva Convention, an agreement made by the European Powers at Geneva in 1864, establishing humane regulations regarding the treatment of the sick and wounded in war and the status of those who minister to them. All persons, hospitals, hospital ships are required to display the Geneva cross—a red cross on a white ground. A second conference held at Geneva in 1868 drew up a supplementary agreement. An important result of this Convention was the establishment of the Red Cross Society in 1870.

Geothermal Energy. Some of the heavy elements within the earth's crust are radioactive and this gives rise to a temperature rise towards the centre of the earth. The practical exploitation of this geothermal energy comes about when there are hot springs or geysers. It is believed that these are caused by rainwater slowly percolating down to the hot rocks and blowing out as steam. The homes of people living in Reykjavik are heated by geothermal steam and there are a number of small power stations in various parts of the world. Although the costs in the few cases where geothermal power has actually been exploited are remarkably low, the expense of drilling, etc., required when attempting to exploit the heat in the rocks where surface manifestations do not occur, is likely to limit the use of this source of power.

Germanium. A grey, hard, brittle chemical element, no. 32, symbol Ge, chemically related to silicon and tin. Discovered by Winkler in 1886. Its richest ore is germanite containing 6% of the metal. Coal is also a relatively rich source. Since 1948 it has assumed great importance as a semi-conducting material for making transistors. Because of this it has been so intensively studied that more is known about its physical properties than about those of any other element.

Glaciers form in the higher Alpine ranges, and are immense consolidated masses of snow, which are gradually impelled by their force down the mountain-sides until they reach a point where the temperature causes them to melt, and they run off in streams. From such glaciers the five great rivers, the Rhine, the Po, the Rhône, the Inn and the Adige, have their source. The longest of the Swiss glaciers is the Gross Aletsch, which sometimes extends over 16 km. Some of the glaciers of the Himalayas are four times as long. The Muir in Alaska is of enormous magnitude, and that of Justeldals Brae in Norway is the largest in Europe.

Gladiators were professional athletes and combatants in ancient Rome, contesting with each other or with wild beasts. At first they were drawn from the slave and prisoner classes exclusively, but so much were the successful gladiators held in esteem that men came to make a profession of athletics, and gladiatorial training schools were established. When a gladiator was vanquished without being killed in combat, it was left with the spectators to decide his fate, death being voted by holding the hands out with the thumb turned inward, and life by putting forth the hands with the thumb extended. Gladiatorial shows were the chief public displays in Rome from the 3rd to the 4th century A.D.

Glass is an amorphous, man-made substance, fluid when hot, solid, though fragile, when cooled. It is made of sand mixed with an alkaline flux, usually soda or potash. While hot, glass can be formed into almost any shape by molding, blowing or, since the early 19th century, by machine pressing. Unrefined glass normally has a greenish tinge, due to the iron content of most sands, but it is transparent or at least translucent. To make truly colorless glass is a difficult and expensive process, and such glass resembling the natural mineral, rock crystal, is given the name crystal. Glass can be tinted by the addition of various metallic oxides, cobalt producing blue, manganese mauve, etc. Because it is at once solid and transparent, glass is the perfect material for windows for which it has been used since Roman times. And since it can be made cheaply and is easy to clean, it has been used for containers in homes, shops and pharmacies, again since Roman days. Glass can also be made into things of beauty, by the use of colored glass and by cutting, engraving, painting and gilding. The earliest vessels of glass so far found come from Egypt and date back to *c.* 1500 B.C. With the invention of glass-blowing in the 1st century A.D., the use of glass spread throughout the Roman empire. Many varieties were made, including superb art glass like the Portland vase. The Arabs were great glassmakers from the 7th to 15th century. During the Renaissance the Venetians created luxurious art glass, rich in color and often manipulated into fantastic forms. Bohemia's 17th-century glass is wonderfully engraved with pictures and cut into glittering facets. During the 1670s in England George Ravenscroft invented a new, heavy, water-clear crystal, with an addition of lead as the magic ingredient, and English lead glass is still the basis for all modern crystals.

Gneiss, a metamorphic rock usually containing quartz, felspar and mica. It is banded, the light-coloured minerals being concentrated apart from the dark minerals.

Gold. Metallic element, no. 79, symbol Au (Latin *Aurum*) related to silver and copper, the coinage metals. The greatest amount of gold is obtained by treating gold-bearing quartz by the cyanide process. The gold is dissolved out by cyanide solution, which is then run into long boxes filled with zinc shavings when the gold is precipitated as a black slime. This is melted with an oxidizing agent which removes the zinc.

Golden Number, the number of any year in the metonic cycle of 19 years, deriving its name from the fact that in the old calendars it was always printed in gold. It is found by adding 1 to the number of the year A.D. and dividing by 19, the remainder being the Golden Number; or, if no remainder, the Golden Number is 19. The only use to which the Golden Number is put now is in making ecclesiastical calculations for determining movable feasts.

Gothic, the predominant style of architecture in northern Europe from 12th–15th century. Its most striking characteristic is the extensive use of the pointed arch, but this is really a mere external reflection of the important structural invention of the 12th century, that of the rib vault, whereby the whole pressure of the stone vaulting is supported on slim ribs which cross each other at a rising center. On the outside of the building, the pressure from the vaults is caught up and supported by flying buttresses. A complete Gothic construction gives a marvellous effect of airy lightness, also of something striving upwards, towards the heavens, and this is further accentuated when the churches are crowned by lofty towers and spires. The vital structural elements of Gothic architecture were first put into use in the abbey church of St. Denis in Paris *c.* 1140. The style was further developed in a glorious sequence of cathedrals in northern France: Notre Dame in Paris, Rheims, Amiens, Beauvais and others. When, as in Chartres, the windows are filled with stained glass of glowing colours and the doorways flanked with magnificently carved life-size figures of saints and apostles, the whole effect is one of unsurpassed solemnity and grandeur. From France the style spread to other lands in each of which it developed its own characteristics; thus the English churches tended to have massive towers and delicate spires and, as at Salisbury, were often set in open grounds surrounded by lawns; Flemish and Dutch churches were sometimes built of brick as were those in north Germany and Scandinavia; in Spain the Flamboyant style was followed. The main Gothic cathedral in Italy, that of Milan, although begun in 1386 was not completed until the early 19th century. Late English Gothic is seen, for example, at King's College Chapel, Cambridge, Henry's Chapel at Westminster and St. George's Chapel at Windsor (all *c.* 1500). Gothic is also found in secular buildings, *e.g.,* Little Wenham Hall in Suffolk, the castle at Ghent, the town halls of Louvain and Middelburg and the streets of Gothic houses in Bruges still in use today. Virtually Gothic as a style (excluding the "Gothic revival" of 19th century England) ended at the close of the 15th century. Gothic art is best seen in the illuminated manuscripts of the 13th and 14th century and in the church sculpture. Its characteristic is a complete departure from the cool, perfectionist realism of classical times with distortion to produce emotional effects. The human figures are not ideal forms but recognizable as people we might meet in the street: yet there was also the element of wild imagination, intricate design and a wealth of feeling which might be grotesque, humorous, macabre, or even obscene. Gothic style also found expression in the decorative arts, retaining its architectural character even in small-scale works like caskets, chalices and the like in metalwork and ivory.

Gravitation. One of the four, possibly five, types of force known to physics. The others are electromagnetic, nuclear (two types) and color forces. Gravitational forces are an attraction that one piece of matter has for another; they dominate astronomical phenomena, but inside the atom they are negligible compared with the other types of force. Einstein's General Theory of Relativity is the only theory at present extant which attempts to interpret gravitational forces in terms of more fundamental concepts.

Gresham's Law states that if money, *i.e.,* money with the higher intrinsic value, and bad money are in circulation together, the bad money will tend to drive out the good money from circulation. For instance, the good money is more likely to be melted down or demanded in payment by foreign creditors.

Gunpowder, also called "black powder", the oldest of explosive mixtures, consists of saltpeter, sulfur and charcoal, intimately mixed, the proportions being varied for different intended uses.

Gypsum, a whitish mineral consisting of hydrated sulfate of calcium. The finest gypsum is alabaster. When heated gypsum is converted into the powder called Plaster of Paris; the water it loses can be taken up when the plaster is wetted, and the reconversion of Plaster of Paris into gypsum accounts for the way in which the former sets hard. The name "Plaster of Paris" came from the location of important gypsum quarries in the Montmartre district of Paris. It was found after the flood disasters of January 1953 that gypsum could undo the effect of sea-water. By spreading it for the rain to wash into the soil, thousands of acres of farmland in Holland and Britain were made productive again.

Gyroscope is a symmetrical rapidly rotating object, typically wheel-like, which because of its mass and rotation possesses a lot of the dynamical property known as angular momentum. Basic dynamical laws tell us that angular momentum is conserved and a consequence of this is that the axis of rotation tends to stay pointing in the same direction. Disturbing influences make a gyroscope's motion complicated but the general effect of the presence of a gyroscope attached to any body is to help to stabilise the body's motion. This is made use of in reducing the rocking of ships and in compasses and control systems in aircraft, torpedoes and missiles.

H

Haematite, ferric oxide, one of the principal iron ores, containing about 70% of the metal. It is usually found in kidney-shaped masses, and is specular, red or brown, in thin fragments but greyish in bulk.

Haemoglobin, the pigment containing iron which gives red blood corpuscles their color. It is a respiratory pigment, having the property of picking up oxygen when the blood passes through the lungs to produce the compound known as oxyhaemoglobin. In other parts of the body the oxyhaemoglobin breaks down, liberating oxygen, which is used in the oxidation process (respiration) that the body tissues carry on.

Hafnium, a metallic element, no. 72, symbol Hf, discovered by Coster and Hevesy in 1922 and important in the atomic-energy field. It occurs in most zirconium minerals to the extent of about 5 percent.

Halogens, the group name for the four non-metallic elements fluorine, chlorine, bromine and iodine. The term "halogen" means "salt-producer".

Harmonic Motion, regular periodic motion of the kind exemplified by a ball bobbing up and down at the end of a spring, and by the piston in a steam engine. It may be simple (simple harmonic motion) or composed of two or more simple harmonic motions. In simple harmonic motion the acceleration is proportional to the distance of the moving body from its original rest position.

Heat, after prolonged controversy over whether or not heat is a "substance" (formerly called "caloric"), it was established in the 19th century that heat is a form of energy; it is in fact the combined kinetic and potential energy of the atoms of which a body is composed. Heat can be turned into other forms of energy, *e.g.,* a red hot body loses heat by radiating it in the form of electromagnetic waves ("radiant heat"—chiefly infra-red rays). Heat may also be transferred from one place to another by conduction and, in fluids, by convection. All three processes occur when a glowing fire heats a room. A unit quantity of heat is the calorie, which is the amount of heat sufficient to raise the temperature of 1 g of water by 1° C. In general, adding heat to a body raises its temperature. The number of calories required per gram of material to raise the temperature 1° C is called the *specific heat* of the material. However, adding heat may not raise the temperature—but may instead cause a change of state, *e.g.*, from solid to liquid (melting) or liquid to gas (evaporation). The amount of heat required to melt 1 gram of a solid is called the latent heat of melting. Similarly, there is a latent heat of evaporation. Strictly speaking, the specific and latent heats of a substance depend on how much its pressure and volume are allowed to vary during the measurements. Water has a high specific heat, and this makes the oceans a vast heat reservoir, a factor of great meteorological significance. The science of heat is called thermodynamics, and is of great importance in physics and chemistry.

Helium, a gaseous element, no. 2, symbol He, first discovered by means of the spectroscope in the sun's atmosphere. This discovery, made in 1868 by the astronomer Sir Norman Lockyer, was followed in 1895 by Sir William Ramsay's proof that the element existed on earth. He found it in the uranium ore, elevite. Later it was established that helium is formed by the radioactive decay of many elements which emit *a*-particles (nuclei of helium atoms) and is contained in all radioactive minerals. The largest source of helium is natural gas, the richest in helium being the gas from certain wells in Utah, USA. Next to hydrogen, helium is the lightest gas known, has a lifting power equal to 92% of hydrogen and the advantage that it is inert and non-inflammable. It is used for inflating airships. Ordinary air contains 1 part in 200,000 of helium. It was the last gaseous element to be liquefied, this being achieved by Onnes in 1908 in Leyden. Liquid helium has many remarkable properties only imperfectly understood. As well as being scientifically fascinating it is indispensable in cryogenics *(q.v.)* as a medium for cooling other substances to temperatures near absolute zero. Hydrogen fusion in the "H bomb" produces helium.

Hellenic Art. The art of ancient Greece may be roughly divided into three periods: the prehistoric period (*c.* 1500–1000 B.C.) of the bronze age Mycenaeans; the archaic period (*c.* 600–500 B.C.); and the classical period (*c.* 500–300 B.C.). Of the first period centered on Mycenae in Peloponnesus but extending to the coasts of Asia and the city of Troy we can mention only the massive stone gateways and the shaft graves of Mycenae, where the archaeologist Schllemann discovered painted vases, gold cups, bronze swords and ornaments of what had once been a great, if primitive, civilization. During the archaic period sculpture was the principal form of art expression. The magnificent male and female figures are reminiscent of Egyptian art, but are distinctive in liveliness of facial expression. The vase-paintings of this period became more elaborate, depicting scenes from mythology or ceremonial events. Typical of classical Greek art is the representation of the beautiful and healthy human body deliberately posed and often carrying out heroic or athletic acts. The vast majority of these statues are known to us only through Roman copies. The *Hermes* of Praxiteles (born *c.* 385 B.C.) is possibly the only existing statue which can be assigned with any degree of certainty to an individual artist. Almost the whole of the Greek genius in architecture was expended on temples which are all basically similar in design—a rectangle with a low-pitched gabled roof resting on side walls. The three orders Doric, Corinthian and Ionic mainly referred to the type of column used, but naturally the whole building was influenced thereby. Some of the main buildings are on the Acropolis, a hill outside Athens, on which stand the Parthenon (from the outer frieze of which the Elgin marbles, now mostly in the British Museum, were taken), the Erechtheum, famous for its Porch of Maidens, and the gateway known as the Propylaca with its broad flight of marble steps. Apart from that on vases, no Greek painting has come down to us, although Greek painters existed and were noted in their time. All we have are copies in mosaic and fresco made by the Romans, at Naples and Pompeii. Of Greek literature in prose, verse and the drama little can be said here. To the early period (*i.e.*, the archaic age) belong Homer's *Iliad* and *Odyssey*. Hesiod's long poem *Work and Days* and Sappho's love poems, and Pindar's Odes. The period of Pericles in the 5th cent. B.C. produced more great literature than any comparable period in history: the philosophical writings of Plato and Aristotle, the tragedies of Aeschylus, Euripides and Sophocles, the comedies of Aristophanes—all these are still part of the European tradition, and together with Greek architecture played a major part in the Renaissance.

Hellenistic Art, the age of the period of Greek civilization which began with the conquests of Alexander the Great (356–323 B.C.) and lasted until his former empire (which encompassed most of the Middle East and part of North Africa) was conquered by the Romans in 146 B.C. Culturally it was an important period because it spread Greek culture far beyond its original boundaries—even as far as the north of India, and its centers spread from Athens to the cities of Alexandria in Egypt, Antioch in Syria and Pergamum in Asia Minor. But equally Eastern culture spread to the West: democracy was replaced by absolute monarchy, cosmopolitanism took the place of the Greek tendency to believe that all who were not Greeks were barbarians, and mystical philosophies took the place of Greek rationalism. This was a sensuous, secular, pleasure-loving, rootless society, and these tendencies were reflected in its art. Hellenistic sculpture was sensual, effeminate and violently emotional, depicting individuals and not always noble or beautiful ones. (Classical Greek sculpture was idealistic, showed types rather than individuals and appealed to the intellect rather than the emotions.) Some of the best examples came from the school at Pergamum and later from the island of Rhodes, and the titles themselves speak of their nature: *The Dying Gaul, Gaul Slaying his Wife and Himself* and the famous *Laocoön* (representing Laocoön and his two sons being crushed by two enormous serpents). All these date from about 240 to 50 B.C.—for the culture did not immediately end with the Roman conquest. The enormous frieze of the altar of the temple in Pergamum depicts a battle between gods and giants with tremendous realism and brutal violence far removed from the serene art of classical times. Portrait sculpture is typical of Hellenistic art, where it may almost be said to have been invented, since such ventures in the past had been idealistic rather than realistic. The great Hellenistic cities were geometrically planned and fine public buildings made their appearance in which the slender and graceful Ionic of the ornate Corinthian columns took the place of the more austere and heavy classical ones. Alexandria was celebrated for its vast libraries and was the center of a brilliant intellectual life (the Septuagint or Greek translation of the Bible was prepared here). Here too worked the mathematicians Euclid and Archimedes, the physicians Erasistratus and Herophilus, and the geographer Pytheas. But Hellenistic literature was a pale reflection of the glories of the past and we mention only the comedies of Menander and the pastoral verse of Theocritus of Syracuse.

Hickory, several species of American tree of the walnut family, remarkable for its very hard, solid, heavy white wood, and bearing an edible, four-lobed nut.

Hieroglyphics are the earliest form of pictured symbolic expression, and are supposed to have been introduced by the ancient Egyptians. They consist of rude depictions of animals, plants, signs and objects, and in their later examples express, in abridged form, ideas and records from which significant historical information has been gleaned. The deciphering of Egyptian hieroglyphics long formed an ardent study, but gradually the key to the riddle was discovered, and most of the ancient records can now be understood. Besides the Egyptian there are also Hittite, Minoan and Mayan hieroglyphic scripts.

Hittites, an ancient race (often mentioned in the Old Testament) who inhabited Cappadocia (region of Eastern Asia Minor) from the third to the first millennium B.C. Excavations have revealed that they attained a high level of civilization round about 1350 B.C. The Hittites were rivals of Egypt, disputing with the Pharaohs the mastery of the Middle East. They were the first to smelt iron successfully.

Holly, a hardy evergreen shrub, largely grown in England. Its bright dark green prickly curved leaves and clusters of red berries are familiar in all parts of the country, and used as house decoration between Christmas Eve and Twelfth Night, probably a relic from Roman and Teutonic customs. Its wood is white and hard, valued for carved work, while its bark yields a gummy substance which is converted into birdlime.

Hologram, a photographic record, taken under special optical conditions, of light reflected from a scene or object. The hologram is typically a piece of film. However it is nothing like a photographic negative of the ordinary kind; for one thing it will show an unintelligible pattern of light and dark patches. Nevertheless if it is illuminated (again under special optical conditions) the light coming through it will form a *three dimensional* image of the original object. Another radical difference between a hologram and an ordinary film is that if the hologram is cut up, each fragment can be used to construct the entire image. Holography, as a method of recording and reproducing photographic information, was conceived by Gabor in 1947 but was only fully realised in practice after the invention of the laser *(q.v.),* which made available powerful sources of coherent light. The use of laser light is one of the "special conditions" referred to above. Technical applications are being explored in many laboratories. Gabor received the 1971 Nobel prize for his discovery and invention.

Horizon, the limit of vision, the apparent line where sea and sky, or land and sky meet. This is termed the visible horizon. An ordinary person at the height of 1.5 m (5 ft.) can see for 4.8 km (3 mi.), at 6 m (20 ft.) can see 9.6 km (6 mi.), at 15 m (49 ft.) can see 14.8 km (9.2 mi.), and at 305 m (1000 ft.) can see 67.5 km (42 mi.). The figures are approximate.

Hornblende, the commonest member of the amphibole group of minerals, a silicate of calcium, magnesium, iron and aluminum, of a dark green color. It is a constituent of numerous rocks, including diorite, syenite and hornblende schist.

Hospitallers, Knights, were of the order of St. John of Jerusalem, at first devoted to the aid of the sick, but afterwards military monks, who became prominent figures in the Crusades of the 12th century. They adopted the Benedictine black habit with the eight-pointed cross worn by the modern St. John's Ambulance Brigade. In 1309 they took Rhodes, but were expelled by the Ottomans in 1522. In 1530 the emperor Charles V gave them the island of Malta, which as Knights of Malta, they held until 1798, when they were dislodged by Napoleon. The Knights still survive as a sovereign order, with headquarters in Rome. *See* **Templars**

Hydrocarbons are compounds of carbon and hydrogen. They include the *paraffins,* which are saturated compounds (*e.g.,* methane); the ethylene, acetylene and other series which are unsaturated; compounds with ring structures, *e.g.,* benzene, naphthalene and anthracene. Petroleum is composed almost entirely of hydrocarbons.

Hydrochloric Acid, a solution of hydrogen chloride gas in water, and resulting in considerable quantities as a by-product of the soda-ash or salt-cake manufacture. Its solution forms the common hydrochloric or muriatic acid of commerce. It is present to the extent of nearly half a per cent, in the digestive juice secreted by the stomach.

Hydrocyanic Acid, cyanide of hydrogen or prussic acid; very poisonous, and of the odor of bitter almonds. It is formed by the action of acids on sodium or potassium cyanide. Used to kill wasps (and in the gas chamber in the USA). It is a very important chemical on account of the reactions of its derivatives in many synthetic fluids. Discovered by Scheele in 1789.

Hydrogen, symbol H, the simplest element, atomic number of 1, colorless, and the lightest of all substances. Cavendish in 1766 was the first to recognize that it was an element. It is 14·4 times as light as air, and is found in a free state in volcanic regions. It can be obtained by the action of metals on acids, and forms an explosive mixture with air, burning with oxygen to form water. Commercially it is used to produce the very hot flame of the oxy-hydrogen blowpipe for cutting metals; to fill balloons and airships; to harden certain oils and render them suitable for margarine- and soap-production. The gas can be liquefied, and the presence of the isotope deuterium was detected by Urey in 1931 in the residue of the evaporated liquid. The third isotope, tritium, is very rare. *See also* **Deuterium, Tritium.**

Hydroponics, or soilless growth, is the craft and science of growing plants in liquid nutrients instead of soil. Originally a laboratory technique, hydroponics has become since the 1930s a practical method of vegetable, fruit and flower production on both small and large scale. Basically, the growing plants have their roots in troughs of nutrient solution, either in or out of doors. Advantages include: much higher crop yields; the close control of weeds and diseases; quicker growth; and, very important, the possibilities of growing food in places where ordinary agriculture would be impracticable, *e.g.,* deserts and stony land, city roofs, in houses and in remote situations like Antarctic stations. Hydroponics is widely practised and contributes usefully to agriculture and horticulture in many countries, including the USA, Britain, India and France. Its value in spaceships and planetary colonies has often been pointed out by technological prophets.

I

Ibis, belongs to a family of birds related to the stork. The sacred ibis of ancient Egypt is now extinct in Egypt but is found in the lakes and swamps of the Sudan near the Upper Nile. It has white and black plumage and a long curved beak. Other species are found elsewhere, the Glossy Ibis (black plumage glossed with purple and green) occasionally visiting England.

Ice Ages. Periods during which the continents were partly or largely covered by ice-sheets and glaciers. The present-day ice-sheets of Greenland and Antarctica are relics of the most recent ice age (one of the eight major ones during the past 700, 000 years), which began in the Pleistocene and ended about 10,000 years ago. During this last great glaciation ice sheets covered the northern part of Europe, Asia and North America. There is strong evidence that periodic changes in the earth's orbit around the sun caused the ice ages. The earth is now in one of its warm periods though there are signs that a moderate cooling trend has begun.

Ichthyosaurus was a gigantic marine reptile of the Mesozoic age. The fossils are mostly found in the lias formation. Some were over 9 m (29.5 ft).

Igneous Rocks are such as have been molten under conditions of great heat at some stage in their history: *e.g.,* granite, basalt.

Iguanodon, a genus of extinct dinosaurs, whose fossils are found in the Jurassic and Cretaceous rocks. Iguanodons were 4.5–7.6 m (15–25 ft) long, and walked on their hind legs, the front legs being small and adapted for grasping the branches of trees on the leaves of which they fed.

Iliad, the great epic poem of ancient Greece attributed to Homer (*c.* 700 B.C.). It consists of ancient folk tale and saga, welded into an artistic unity, having as plot the carrying off of Helen by Paris to Troy and the subsequent siege of Troy.

Indium, a scarce lead-colored metallic element, no. 49, symbol In, found in zinc blende in Saxony and certain other ores. Discovered in 1863 by Reich and Richter. It is an important material in the manufacture of transistors.

Industrial Revolution. The name, first given by Engels in 1844, to describe the radical changes that took place in Britain during *c.* 1730–1850 to transform a mainly agricultural country into one predominantly industrial. It began with the mechanization of the textile industry (Hargreave's spinning jenny, 1764, Arkwright's water-frame, 1769, Crompton's mule, 1770, and Watt's steam-engine, 1785), with subsequent major developments in mining, transport and industrial organization. It was based on Britain's rich mineral resources, particularly coal and iron ore. With the use of the steam-engine as power, industry became concentrated round the coalfields and the great new industrial towns developed—Birmingham, Manchester, Newcastle and Glasgow. Britain became supreme in constructional ironwork (Telford, George and Robert Stephenson). Canals, bridges, railways and ships were built, and great advances were made in the practical application of scientific principles. Aided by colonial exploitation Britain became the most prosperous country in the world. The new industrial capitalists began to replace the country squires as ruling class. But the great accumulation of wealth at one pole of society was matched at the other by poverty and misery, for child labor, long working hours, low wages and slums were features of the industrial revolution in its infancy. As with all great technological developments, the industrial revolution produced related changes in all fields of social life—in politics, art, religion, literature and morals, and with the rise of democracy, social reforms.

Infra-red Rays *or* **Radiation.** This is the range of rays which come between the visible red rays and the ultra-short Hertzian radiation. The wavelengths involved range between 0·75 micron ($0{\cdot}75 \times 10^{-6}$m) and 100 micron (1 millimeter). Infra-red rays penetrate haze; hence landscapes obscured by haze or cloud can be photographed using plates sensitive to infra-red. Many substances strongly absorb these rays and thereby become hot; this happens in toasting bread. Many industries use infra-red lamps for drying paints and lacquers. Very important to chemists, as a tool in the investigation of the structure of compounds, since various groups of elements absorb infra-red radiation at a characteristic frequency. Infra-red astronomy has developed in recent years.

Insects. This huge class of invertebrate animals includes about 100,000 species. Insects are ubiquitous except in the sea, only a very few species being adapted to marine existence. Characteristic features are: the body is divided into three parts, head, thorax and abdomen: the head carries a pair of antennae, the thorax three pairs of legs and usually two pairs of wings. The most primitive insects constituting the sub-class *Apterygota* are wingless. The other sub-class, *Pterygota,* is divided into the *Exopterygota (Hemimetabola),* which have a simple metamorphosis, *e.g.,* cockroach, and the *Endopterygota (Holometabola),* with a complex metamorphosis, *e.g.,* butterfly, bee. Although many are parasitic on man, animals and plants, innumerable animals and some plants use them as food, and many flowering plants are dependent on a variety of insects for pollination leading to the development of seeds and fruits.

Instruments, Musical. Musical instruments may be classified in a number of ways, but in general they fall into one of the three main classes, String, Wind and Percussion, according to how the sound in produced. **Stringed Instruments** are those which produce the sound by the vibration of a string: *(a)* by plucking, as in Harp, Lyre, Psaltery, Zither, Lute, Guitar, Balalaika, Ukelele, Harpsichord; *(b)* by friction (bowed), as in Crwth, Rebec, Viol, Violin, Marine Trumpet, Hurdy-Gurdy; *(c)* by striking (hammered), as in Dulcimer, Pianoforte, Clavichord; *(d)* by wind (blown), as in the Aeolian Harp. **Wind Instruments** are those in which the air in the instruments is set in vibration: *(a)* by blowing into a tube (flue-voiced), as in Recorder, Pandean Pipe,

Flute, Organ; *(b)* by means of reeds (reed-voiced), as in Oboe, Clarinet, Saxophone, Bagpipe, Cor Anglais, Bassoon, Organ reed-stops; *(c)* those in which the sound is produced by the vibration of the player's lips against the mouthpiece (lip-voiced), as in Bugle, Horn, Trumpet, Tuba, Trombone, Saxhorn, Flügelhorn, Cornet. In a modern orchestra these are known as the *Brass:* instruments of the flute, oboe and clarinet families as the *Woodwinds.* Then there are the **Percussion Instruments,** which include the Drums, Cymbals, Tambourines, Castenets.

Insulin is a hormone which controls the supply of sugar from the blood to muscles. The breakdown of sugar provides energy. In diabetes there is a lack of insulin, causing a build-up of blood sugar which can be released by the injection of insulin. It is secreted by the islet tissue of the pancreas, from which it was isolated in 1922 by Banting and Best. Dr. F. Sanger of Cambridge won the 1958 Nobel Prize in Chemistry for isolating and identifying its amino acid components. Prof. Dorothy Hodgkin and her team at the Dept. of Molecular Biophysics at Oxford succeeded in determining the structure of insulin, a task which would not have been possible without the electronic computer. In 1980 insulin became the first product of genetic engineering techniques to reach clinical trials.

Intelligence. Intelligence has been variously defined as the innate potential of a person to learn and understand; to make appropriate judgments; to see the relationships between things; to profit from experience; or to meet adequately new problems and conditions in life. There are many lines of evidence to show that intellectual capacity is closely related to heredity and influenced by environmental factors. The idea of intelligence testing was first devised by the French psychologist Binet at the beginning of this century. He was asked by the French government to invent a test which would weed out backward children in state schools, and thus save public money and avoid holding back the work of the class by teaching children who were incapable of learning at a given standard. Briefly, a series of problems are given to a large number of children and it is thus found out which series can be solved by the average child of a given age-group; if a child of 7 can only pass the tests suitable to the average child of 6, then his mental age is 6. The intelligence quotient or I.Q. is discovered by dividing his mental age by his chronological age and multiplying by 100. A gifted child can usually be spotted at an early age. Although I.Q. tests are the standard method of estimating intelligence, they are not universally accepted as a criterion; a teacher's general judgment may be the best assessment. High intelligence may be inherited, but fail to develop to the full because facilities for education are not available. Recent research suggests that the growth of the brain may be permanently affected by under-nutrition at the time of its fastest growth (the last weeks before birth, and, to a lesser extent, the first weeks after birth). At this vulnerable period even quite minor deprivation can affect the rate and ultimate extent of growth of the brain. This has significance not only for the severely under-nourished babies in the poor parts of the world, but for babies of low birth weight in our own communities.

Interferon, identified in 1957 as a defense protein produced in animal cells, is also produced in human immune systems. Its use as a possible anti-cancer agent as well as for other complaints has been limited by extraction problems. Modern production is likely to be by genetic engineering. In 1980 the amino acid sequence was determined for the 150 residues in human interferon.

Iodine, a non-metal element, no. 53, symbol I, member of the halogen family *(q.v.),* a substance formerly exclusively obtained from the ribbon-wrack seaweeds. These were burnt and the ashes (kelp) extracted with water. After concentrating the iodides, these were distilled with manganese dioxide and sulfuric acid to yield iodine vapor which was condensed in stoneware bottles. Nearly all iodine now in use is derived from the iodine salt present in Chile saltpeter (natural sodium nitrate). Iodine is used in photography, as an antiseptic solution in alcohol or potassium iodide (tincture of iodine), and in medicine. Discovered by Courtois in 1812.

Ions, electrically charged atoms, or groups of atoms. Atoms of the metals lose electrons to become positively charged ions, *e.g.,* the sodium ion (Na^+) has one electron less than the atom. The non-metal ions are negatively charged, *e.g.,* the chloride ion (Cl^-) has one electron more than the atom. Similarly, a group like the sulfate ion (SO_4^{2-}) has more electrons than the constituent atoms. Thus, the hydrogen atom without its electron is a hydrogen ion or *proton* and the helium atom without its two electrons is a helium ion or *alpha-particle.* When an electric force is applied to certain solutions, the ions into which molecules of the dissolved substance are broken up are attracted to the oppositely charged electrodes, their movements constituting an electric current through the solution. In the same way gases, including air, conduct electricity by virtue of free ions. Combustion, radioactivity and ultra-violet and cosmic radiations produce ionisation.

Iridium, a white and very hard metallic element, no. 77, symbol Ir, discovered by Tennant in 1804. It occurs naturally as an alloy with platinum or osmium; tips for fountain-pen nibs have been made from the former native alloy. The former standard meter was composed of platinum-iridium alloy as are parts of scientific apparatus and surgical tools that must be non-corrodible.

Iron is a metallic element, no. 53, symbol Fe (Latin *ferrum*), occurring widely in nature in such ores as haematite, loadstone (magnetic iron oxide), spathic ore and iron pyrites. It is extracted by a process known as smelting, with coke and limestone in a furnace. Its many uses are familiar, the most important being in the manufacture of cast- and wrought-iron products and of steels, which are alloys mainly of iron with added carbon and various metals. Iron rust is formed by the action of oxygen and water, and is a coating of iron oxide.

Isotopes. When one talks of an element, say, uranium or lead, the name of the element is a generic name for a collection of uranium species and lead species. The different species are called isotopes. For any particular element, the number and arrangement of electrons around the nucleus are the same in all the isotopes, so all the isotopes have the same chemical properties. Soddy has described isotopes as "elements, the atoms of which have similar outsides but different insides". For example, in the nucleus of the uranium isotopes, U 235, U 238 and U 239, there are respectively 143, 146 and 147 neutrons, but all have 92 protons. The isotopes have different atomic weights, in this instance respectively 235, 238 and 239. But all have the same chemical properties.

J

Jacobins, a French revolutionary club or party, formed in 1789, and accustomed to meet at a Jacobin convent, hence the name. It became a controlling force in the Revolution, especially in the movement which led to the Terror. Robespierre was its chief spokesman.

Jade, an exquisite kind of hardstone, ranging in color from a whitish green to a deep mauvish brown. It can be translucent or opaque and sometimes it is veined. Jade is the common name for two minerals—the rarer *jadeite* (found in Burma, Tibet and China), a sodium-aluminum-silicate, and *nephrite* (found in New Zealand, China, Turkestan and Siberia), a calcium-magnesium silicate. The presence of small quantities of other chemicals accounts for the wide range of shades. In China jade has for centuries been looked upon with great veneration, magical powers have been ascribed to it, and it has been fashioned into ritual objects, also into miniature sculptures of animals or even whole landscapes, charming to look at and incredibly skillfully made. The Chinese word for jade is *yü*, used as a symbol for all that is noble, beautiful and pure.

Janissaries, an élite band of Ottoman foot soldiers who acted as the Sultan's bodyguard. They were conscripts, raised by the "tribute of children" from conquered Christian countries, mainly Serbia and Albania. First recruited under Murad I (14th century). They were not allowed to marry. They gained great power under the Ottoman Empire. In 1826 the Sultan Mahmud II had them massacred.

Jasper, a precious stone of the chalcedony variety, opaque, and colored red, brown, yellow and sometimes green. It was greatly esteemed by the ancients, the Bible having numerous allusions to it.

Jelly-fish. The jelly-fishes, which have gelatinous, translucent bodies fringed at the margin with delicate tentacles, constitute the coelenterate order *Seyphozoa*. The mouth, with a squarish opening, is seen on the underside, and there are four horseshoe-shaped sex organs.

Jet Stream, a meteorological term coined in 1946 to describe the relatively narrow belt of strong winds (160–320 km/h; 99–199 mph) at levels in the atmosphere from 5–11 km (3–7 mi). These winds are important in forecasting weather, and can be a valuable aid to aircraft. From the ground, where there may be little wind, the jet stream can sometimes be seen as high cirrus cloud moving across the sky at high speed.

K

Kinetic Energy, the energy possessed by a particle or body in virtue of its motion. If the motion is destroyed, *e.g.*, by the impact of the body with an obstacle, the kinetic energy vanishes, being turned into some other form of energy such as heat and sound. If the body has mass m and speed v its kinetic energy (leaving out corrections due to relativity) is $1/2mv^2$.

Koto, a musical instrument in general use in Japan consisting of a series of 13 silken strings stretched across a curved wooden surface, and played with the fingers. Each string is 1.5 m (69 in.) long, and has a separate bridge so fixed as to give the vibration necessary for the note it has to produce. It is a sort of horizontal harp, and in the hands of an expert player is capable of giving forth excellent music.

Krypton, one of the rare gas elements, no. 36, symbol Kr, occurring in the air to the extent of 1 part in 20 million. It was discovered in 1898 by Ramsay and Travers. It is used in gas-filled electric lamps.

L

Labradorite, a felspar rich in calcium and of a pearly lustre on cleavage, found in masses in igneous rocks, the best samples of which come from Labrador.

Labyrinth, *or* **Maze,** a combination of roads and passages so constructed as to render it difficult for anyone ignorant of the clue to trace the way to the central part. The Egyptian labyrinth near Lake Moeris had 3,000 rooms, half of them subterranean and the remainder above ground. The labyrinth in Crete, according to Greek myth, was built by Daedalus to house the Minotaur. There was one at Lemnos, renowned for its stalactite columns; and another at Clusium constructed by Porsenna, King of Etruria, about 520 B.C. The labyrinth in which Fair Rosamond was concealed was at Woodstock. Hampton Court maze dates from the 16th cent.

Labyrinthodonts, gigantic fossil amphibians which get their name from the curious labyrinthine structure of their teeth, probably an evolutionary link between fishes and reptiles. They occur in the Carboniferous, Permian and Triassic formations, and remains have been found in Britain and other parts of Europe. Their heads were long, and their footprints, by which they were discovered, closely resemble the prints of the human hand.

Lake Dwelling, the name given to certain prehistoric habitations which were thought to have stood on platforms over lakes, like villages in certain Pacific islands. Recent excavations at the Lake of Burgäschi in Switzerland show that the prehistoric Swiss pile dwellings probably stood on the shores of lakes, not on platforms over the water. Also found at Mere and Glastonbury, Somerset.

Lamellibranchs (Pelecypods), the class of aquatic, bi-valve mollusks to which the oysters, cockles, mussels, clams and scallops belong. In these animals the body, which is compressed laterally, is enclosed in two hinged shells held together by muscular action. The gills are thin plates hence the name "lamellibranchs".

Lapis Lazuli, an azure-blue mineral, being a silicate of aluminum and sodium. The pigment ultramarine is made by grinding it, though artificial ultramarine has largely superseded it. The mineral (also called *lazurite*) has been used as a gemstone since ancient times.

Laser. A remarkable kind of light source that was discovered in 1960. With the laser it is possible to probe the behavior of matter under the influence of enormous energy densities, range and survey vast distances to microscopic accuracy and send millions of telephone and television messages between any two points that can see each other with telescopes. Laser light, in contrast to natural light, is coherent and can be expressed as a regular progression of waves carrying energy along a particular path. Thus the essential difference is that laser light is an orderly sort of wave motion in contrast to ordinary light which is inherently unsteady and therefore an inefficient carrier of information in time. The name *maser,* which is the microwave parent of the laser, derives from the expression "microwave amplification by the stimulated emission of radiation". Upon application to light wavelengths the microwave part of the name lost its meaning and the term maser became generally descriptive of any device in which stimulated emission dominates.

Laser Fusion is a method by which it has been proposed that thermonuclear reactions may be controlled and exploited as a source of energy. The idea is to irradiate a millimeter-sized pellet of a mixture of frozen deuterium and tritium with a short ($\sim 10^{-9}$ s) but very intense pulse of energy in the form of laser light. This has the effect of both compressing the pellet by a factor of at least a thousand and heating it to about 10^{8}° C. Under these conditions, thermonuclear reactions (principally $^{2}D + {}^{2}T \rightarrow {}^{4}He + {}^{1}n$) proceed sufficiently fast that a net output of energy is obtained before the pellet explosively separates. Formidable technical problems need to be solved before laser fusion can become a practical proposition. These include the development of efficient high-powered lasers and the design of a suitable reactor that can withstand up to 100 micro-hydrogen bomb explosions per second. It is still not clear whether this method of controlling nuclear fusion is more practical than the more conventional approach involving the magnetic confinement of plasmas.

Latent Heat is the quantity of heat required to convert 1 gram of a substance from one form into another. For example, when a solid changes into a liquid or a liquid into a gas, the addition of heat to bring about the change produces no rise in temperature, the energy being absorbed in the form of latent heat. An equal amount is released when the process is reversed. The latent heat of fusion of ice is about 79·6 calories per gram, that of the vaporization of water about 539 calories per gram.

Lateran Councils were the religious conventions held in the Lateran basilica at Rome for deciding important questions of Church doctrine. The most brilliant was that of 1215 which pronounced in favor of a Crusade.

Laterite refers to any tropical soil or soil horizon rich in hydrated ferric and aluminum oxides which harden when exposed to the atmosphere. It is difficult to cultivate and is commonly used for bricks and road metal. Laterite buildings have been known to withstand the weathering for many centuries and a number of fine examples are found in India and S.E. Asia.

Latitude of a point on the earth's surface is its angular distance from the equator, measured on the surface of the earth in degrees, minutes and seconds. Thus the equator is 0° Lat. and the poles 90° Lat. (N. or S.). First determined by Hipparchus of Nicaea about 160 B.C. Latitude introduces zones of climate, *e.g.,* tropical rain, subtropical steppe and desert, temperate rain and polar.

Lead, a soft malleable metallic element, no. 82, symbol Pb (Latin *plumbum*), occurring in numerous ores, which are easily smelted. Its most important source is the mineral galena which consists chiefly of lead sulfide; rarely is it found free. Lead is largely used in plumbing on account of its pliability, and in nuclear reactors as a shield against radiation because of its very high density. As an alloy element it combines in the formation of type metal, stereo metal, shot metal, pewter and many other compounds. Oxides of lead are used in some types of glass and in the manufacture of paints (red lead). All lead compounds are poisonous. Leading producers of lead are the United States (Missouri), Australia (Broken Hill) and the Soviet Union.

Leather was made in ancient Egypt, Greece and Rome, and has through succeeding centuries played an important part in the service of man. It consists of the dressed hides or skins of animals after the process of tanning has been gone through. Untanned skins are known as pelts. Leather is classed either according to the skins from which it is made or the system of preparation employed. The best-known kinds are morocco, kid, Russian, chamois, Cordovan, grained, patent, russet, tan, calf, Hungarian.

Lemur, almost the most primitive member of the primate order of mammals (to which man, apes and monkeys also belong). They are noted for having strong pliant toes enabling them to use their feet as hands, and also well-developed thumbs on the hands. They have long squirrel-like tails, fox-shaped heads and large staring eyes. True lemurs are confined to the Malagasy Rep.; closely related are the "bush-babies" of S. Africa.

Lenses, pieces of transparent material designed to focus an image of an illuminated object. Usually of glass, but plastic lenses are common, and quartz, etc. are used for special purposes. The surfaces of the simplest lenses are parts of spheres. Lenses which are thickest, or thinnest, at the center are called convex and concave respectively. Lenses of complex shape are often used in microscopes, etc. Electron lenses are arrangements of electric or magnetic fields which focus beams of electrons, *e.g.,* on to T.V. screens.

Lepidoptera, the order of insects with scaly wings and bodies, to which the 90,000 butterflies and moths belong.

Leptons. A group of particles which include electrons, neutrinos and muons. All are much lighter than protons or any baryons *(q.v.).*

Libretto (It. booklet), the literary text of an opera or oratorio. Usually the composer and the librettist collaborate in the writing of an opera, but several composers (*e.g.,* Wagner) wrote their own librettos. Boito, librettist to Verdi for *Otello* and *Falstaff,* himself composed two operas *Mefistofele* and *Nerone.* Most famous of Italian opera librettists was the poet and dramatist Metastasio (1698–1782). His librettos were set to music by many composers, including Gluck, Handel, Mozart, Rossini.

Lichens. In every lichen, two plants are associated, one being an alga and the other a fungus. The fungus derives its food from the alga; probably the alga gains too from the association, being protected against desiccation by the fungus (an example of symbiosis). Lichens are the first plants to colonize bare rocks.

Light, a particular kind of electromagnetic disturbance capable of travelling through space, and some kinds of matter, and of affecting our eyes to cause vision. Its finite speed was first demonstrated by O. Römer, using observations of the eclipses of Jupiter's satellites in 1675. In 1860 Maxwell showed that light waves are electromagnetic. Since Einstein's theory of relativity (1905) it has been generally realized that the speed of light is a fundamental natural constant. Visible light with wavelengths between about 4 and 7 $\times$ 10^{-5} cm is only a small part of the electromagnetic spectrum. The speed of light in vacuum is about 2 997925 $\times$ 10^8 m/s.

Lightning, the flash of a discharge of electricity between two clouds, or between a cloud and the earth, when the strength of the electric fields becomes so great as to break down the resistance of the intervening air. With "forked" lightning the actual path, often branched, is visible, while with "sheet" lightning the flash is hidden by the clouds which themselves are illuminated. "Ball" lightning or fireballs is the name given to the luminous balls which have been seen floating in the air during a thunderstorm. The Boys camera has provided much information regarding the sequence of events in a lightning discharge. It is found that a flash consists of a number of separate strokes, usually four or five, and that the discharge of electricity to earth begins with a faintly luminous "leader" moving downwards and branching at intervals. As the ground is approached a much brighter luminosity travels back along the conducting channels, lighting up with several branches. The multiple strokes which follow in fractions of a second have the same "return" nature and are rarely branched. Lightning flashes to earth damage structures, cause loss of life and endanger overhead power systems, often interrupting electricity supply. Such storms generally affect radio transmissions and present hazards to aircraft. Thunderclouds may develop energy far exceeding the capacity of our largest power generating stations.

Limestones, sedimentary rocks composed wholly or largely of calcium carbonate and formed by two main processes, (1) organic (skeletal remains of organisms), *e.g.,* chalk and (2) chemical (precipitation of calcium carbonate), *e.g.,* oolite. Marble is limestone that will polish after cutting.

Liquid Crystals form a special class of substance and are true liquids in that they flow easily and can be poured. However, unlike ordinary liquids, liquid crystals have their molecules arranged with geometrical regularity in one or two dimensions, so that they have a certain internal structure similar to that of solid crystals. They are fairly complicated chemicals with somewhat elongated molecules. Liquid crystals are of interest to biologists as well as to chemists and physicists, and not just because they account for the iridescence of beetles. Some body fluids are in fact liquid crystals. There are also technological applications because of their unique electrical and optical properties. They are receiving increasing attention for these reasons.

Lithium, a soft metallic element, no. 3, symbol Li, similar to sodium. It is very reactive and is stored under paraffin oil. It is the lightest metal element.

Lizard, the name given to a diversified order of reptiles, of which there are about 1,600 species. Included among the lizards are the geckos, chameleons, glass snakes, skinks and blind worms.

Loadstone *or* **Lodestone,** an oxide of iron, found chiefly in Sweden and Norway. Its scientific name is magnetite. It has the power of attracting pieces of iron and served as the first magnets used in compasses. One of the class of nonmetallic magnetic materials nowadays known as "ferrites" *(q.v.).*

Locust, insects of the grasshopper family, but much more powerful. They are inhabitants of hot countries, and often make their appearance in untold millions, like clouds, devastating all the vegetation that comes within their course. The locust-tree *(Ceratonia siligua)* is supposed to have furnished food to St. John the Baptist in the wilderness, and its "beans" have accordingly been styled "St. John's Bread".

Longitude of a point on the earth's surface is the angle which the meridian through the poles and that point makes with some standard meridian. The meridian through Greenwich is usually accepted as the standard meridian and the longitude is measured east or west of that line. As the earth revolves through 360° in 24 h, 15° longitude represent 1 hour's difference in apparent time.

LSD (d-lysergic acid diethylamide). This hallucinogenic drug has achieved wide notoriety because of its use by certain people to give themselves abnormal mental experiences. Doctors have frequently warned against the dangers of its use. It is active in extremely small quantities and a dose as small as a fifty-millionth part of a gram can cause marked disturbances of the mental function in man. LSD has been used in the study of mental disease because it produces symptoms very similar to mental disorders such as schizophrenia.

Lutecium, element (no.71) of the rare-earth metal group discovered in 1907 by Urbain. Symbol Lu.

M

Mach Number. Unit of flight speed. The ratio of speed of flight to speed of sound under same conditions of pressure and density. Speed of sound at sea-level is 762 mile/h (1,226 km/h), so flight speed of 381 mile/h (613 km/h) is equivalent to a Mach Number of 1/2. At supersonic speeds the Mach Number is greater than 1; subsonic speeds, less than 1.

Macromolecules are very large molecules about 10, 000 times or more as heavy as ordinary small molecules like hydrogen. Most are built up from a large number of simple sub-units, *i.e.,* are polymers. The term macromolecule is often used in biology, *e.g.,* starch and cellulose are biological macromolecules, both built from glucose sub-units. Other important ones are proteins and nucleic acids. The properties of macromolecules depend on the sub-units of which they are composed.

Maelstrom, a great whirlpool. The most famous is that off the coast of Norway, between the islands of Moskenës and Mosken, of the Lofoten group the power of which has been much exaggerated.

Magellan, Clouds of, the name given to a pair of small galaxies, satellite systems of our own galaxy, visible only from the southern hemisphere. On account of their relative nearness to the earth (186, 000 light-years), they are receiving much attention from astronomers.

Magenta, a blue-red aniline dye discovered in 1859 by Sir W. H. Perkin, and named after the great battle of that year between the French and Austrians.

Magma, molten rock material rich in volatile constituents prior to its eruption at the surface. With the loss of volatiles it becomes lava.

Magnesium, a metallic element, no. 12, symbol Mg, first isolated in 1808 by Sir Humphry Davy, who prepared it by electrolyzing the chloride. Its chief ores are magnesite and dolomite. Industrially it is obtained by electrolysis. Many important light alloys contain magnesium. The metal burns with a very bright light, and for this reason it is used in photographers' flash bulbs and also in firework manufacture.

Magnetic Storms. These are the effects of magnetospheric storms observed world wide at ground level as fluctuations of as much as 5% in the earth's magnetic field. The largest effects are observed at high latitudes, in the auroral ovals, and are due to electric currents flowing in the ionosphere and between the ionosphere and the magnetosphere. There may be concurrent disruption of radio communications.

Magnetism, originally the name given to the quality of attraction for iron possessed by lodestone *(q.v.)*. Now known to be a phenomenon inseparably connected with electricity. Strong magnetic attraction is possessed by a comparatively small class of substances; iron, nickel and cobalt are the most common elements, but there are several less well known, *e.g.,* gadolinium. Many alloys have valuable magnetic properties which make possible numberless technical devices. New magnetic substances are always being developed (*see* **Ferrites**). The earth acts like a huge magnet with its axis inclined at about 11° to the axis of rotation, the magnetic poles being on the Boothia Peninsula (North Canada) and South Victoria Land (Antarctica). The magnetic field at the surface consists of the regular field of a magnetized sphere with an irregular field superimposed upon it. Variation in the magnetic forces occurs from place to place and from time to time, and maps showing the distribution over the globe of points of the same declination (*i.e.,* the angle which the magnetic meridian makes with the geographical one) are of the utmost importance in navigation. Little is known regarding the origin of the main (regular) field of the earth, but it is believed that the irregularities are due to the presence of intense electric currents in the upper atmosphere and local magnetization of rock strata. In 1967 the discovery was claimed of isolated magnetic poles, *i.e.,* north and south magnetic poles existing separately, just as positive and negative electrical charges exist separately. If this is confirmed it will probably rank as one of the most important experimental results of the 20th century, because of its significance for the theory of electromagnetism and fundamental particles. Magnetic field strengths are measured in gauss (e.g.s.) or tesla (S.I.) units.

Magnetosphere. The magnetic field of the earth prevents the plasma of the solar wind from directly impinging on the earth's upper atmosphere and ionosphere. The cavity thus maintained within the solar wind is known as the magnetosphere. The tenuous plasma within this cavity is partly of solar and partly of terrestrial origin, from the solar wind and the ionosphere respectively. These plasmas are subject to large perturbations, known as magnetospheric storms, triggered by fluctuations within the solar wind. These storms generate intense auroral displays, magnetic field fluctuations at ground level, and often major disturbances of the upper atmosphere and ionosphere which may result in disruption of radio communications. The inner parts of the magnetosphere contain the Van Allen radiation belts *(q.v.)*. On the sunward side the magnetosphere extends to between 12 and 20 earth radii. However, on the side of the earth away from the sun it extends, like a comet tail, for many millions of km. Jupiter's large magnetic field produces a large magnetosphere, one of the largest features in our planetary system being as large as the sun itself.

Magnitude in astronomy is a measure of the apparent brightness of a star, which is inversely proportional to the square of its distance. A low number indicates a bright star, and a high one a faint star. The *absolute magnitude* is a measure of *real* brightness, *i.e.,* the brightness a star would have at a standard distance away of 10 parsecs (32·6 light years). The distance can be calculated if the apparent and absolute magnitudes are known.

Mammoth, extinct elephants of gigantic size. In 1799 the first perfectly preserved specimen was found in Siberia in a block of ice. It was in prehistoric times an inhabitant of Britain and other parts of Europe, as well as of Asia and America.

Manatee, an aquatic mammal of the sea cow (Sirenia) order of mammals, averaging when full grown from 3–3.6 m (10–12 ft) in length, with shovel-shaped tail, and forelimbs and nails which almost give the appearance of arms and hands. Gentle and trusting they are under threat from man. Protected in Florida. In spite of their ungainly aspect, they are believed to have given rise to the legend of mermaids.

Mandarin, the name given to a powerful Chinese official, civil or military, under the old regime, whose rank was shown by the wearing of a button on the cap. Mandarin is the major language of N. China.

Manganese, a metallic element, no. 25, symbol Mn, discovered by Scheele, 1774. It is silver-white, not very hard (it forms a hard alloy with carbon), brittle, and tarnishes when exposed to air. Its chief ore is pyrolusite (manganese dioxide). Steels containing manganese are very tough, used for making machine parts.

Manna, a tree of the ash genus, *Fraxinus ornus,* growing in the South of Europe and in the East and exuding a sweet substance which is gathered, boiled and eaten.

Mantis. Large insects belonging to the same order as the locusts and grasshoppers. The manner in which the forelegs are held, as though in suppliance, has gained for these insects the common name of "praying mantis". They are distributed throughout the warmer countries of the world.

Maple, trees native to the northern hemisphere. There are over 100 species. The sycamore is the best-known species growing in Britain. The sugar maple abounds in Canada and the eastern parts of the United States. The sugar is tapped by boring holes in the tree in February and March, and the juice that escapes is collected and evaporated. The maple-leaf is the Canadian national emblem.

Marble is limestone in its hardest and most crystalline form. There are many varieties—33 were used in the building of the Paris Opera House—but white is the purest and rarest. White marble was used by the ancient Greeks for their temples and statues. Among the famous marbles of Italy are the Carrara and Siena marbles, which were used by Renaissance sculptors. Devonshire and Derbyshire yield some beautiful marbles and Connemara furnishes a serpentine-marble.

Marionettes are puppets moved by strings. They originated in the *Fantoccini* of the 15th century which had such a vogue in Italy and elsewhere on the Continent. The English *Punch and Judy* is a version of Punchinello.

Marseillaise, the French national hymn, written and composed by Rouget de L'Isle, a French engineer officer, who was inspired to write it in 1792 to encourage the Strasburg conscripts. It immediately became popular, and received its name from the fact that it was sung by the Marseillaise troops while marching into Paris.

Marsupials, members of the order of pouched mammals. Except for the opossums of America, all marsupials occur in Australasia, and include the kangaroos, wallabies and wombats.

Mastodon, an extinct order of quadruped closely resembling the elephant in structure, but is larger.

Megalith, a prehistoric monument, consisting of a large single stone or a group of such stones, in a circle as at Stonehenge or in burial chambers as at New Grange, Ireland. Megalithic monuments have been constructed by different peoples in different parts of the world since the third millennium B.C.

Mercator's Projection, a method of indicating meridians and parallels of latitudes on maps, introduced by Mercator in the 16th century, and still universally used in navigators' charts.

Mercury *or* **Quicksilver,** element no. 80, symbol Hg (Latin *hydrargyrum*) is one of the oldest-known metals, whose chief ore is the sulfide, cinnabar, found in certain parts of Spain, China, Japan and South America. It is liquid at ordinary temperature and is used in the construction of barometers and thermometers. Alloys of mercury are called amalgams. It is also of great value in medicine. The metal is used in the mercury-vapor (or "sunlight") lamp, since the vapor gives a bright yellow-white glow in an electric discharge.

Meridian, an imaginary circle extending through the North and South Poles and any given place. When the sun is at its midday height at any place it is "on the meridian"; hence the terms ante-meridian (a.m.) and post-meridian (p.m.).

Mesons (from Greek *meso*—middle), a family of unstable particles of mass between that of an electron and that of a proton. Some are positive, some negative, some neutral. No stable meson is known, the longest-lived particle having a lifetime of only two-millionths of a second. The first of these particles was discovered in cosmic radiation in 1937 and called the mu-meson or *muon.* In 1947 a heavier type was discovered called the pi-meson or *pion* which behaved like the meson predicted on theoretical grounds by Yukawa in 1935. The pion is connected with the theory of nuclear forces.

Metamorphic Rocks are such geological deposits as have undergone alterations of structure and mineral reorganization. The most active agents in producing these metamorphic changes are heat, water and pressure.

Methane. The simplest hydrocarbon, compounded of one carbon atom and four hydrogen atoms. This gas occurs over marshes and swamps, where it is liberated in the decay of vegetable matter. It is the main constituent of natural gas, and also occurs in coal-mines, where it is called "fire-damp" because of the explosive character of its mixture with air. Formerly this natural gas was removed from the coal seams and ran to waste; now in many countries (including Britain) it is being used for commercial purposes.

Microbe, a term proposed by Sédillot in 1878 to denote any microscopic organism, vegetable or animal, or found on the borderland between the two great natural kingdoms. The term is commonly used, but not by scientists.

Middle Ages (*c.* A.D. 400–1500), usually considered to be the period between the decline and fall of the Western Roman Empire and the fall of Constantinople to the Turks. The period covers *(a)* an earlier part ending with the 12th century (sometimes called the Dark Ages) when science was dead, when theology was the main preoccupation, and when the language of the learned West was Latin; and *(b)* a later age of Arabian influence when alchemy and astrology (at that time indistinguishable from astronomy) were central interests, technology was advancing, and Greek learning was transmitted by Arab scholars. Characteristic features of the mediaeval scene were monasticism the Crusades *(q.v.),* Gothic art *(q.v.),* feudalism, and the supremacy of Islam in the field of learning. The period came to an end with the general decline of Christendom and the ushering in of the Renaissance. The term "Middle Ages" was coined by the 17th-century German historian Christoph Keller.

Millennium, a period of a thousand years. The term is specifically used of the period of a thousand years during which, according to Rev. xx. 1–5, Christ will reign in person on earth. The Millenarians are a sect that interprets the "Millennium" as beginning with the commencement of the 6001st year from the Creation, which, according to Archbishop Ussher (1581–1650), was in 4004 B.C.

Minnesingers were minstrel poets of Germany who, during the 12th and 13th centuries, composed and sang verses of heroism and love. They were of knightly rank, the counterpart of the French troubadours.

Minstrels were originally specially appointed instrumentalists and singers—pipers, harpers and gleemen—engaged by barons and manorial lords to amuse their tenants. Later, minstrels assumed nomadic habits, made their way into the houses of the great and were generally welcome. By Elizabeth's time, however, they were too numerous, and were classed as "rogues and vagabonds", along with actors.

Mirage, an optical illusion caused by unequal temperatures in different layers of the atmosphere near the earth's surface. These temperature variations alter the refracting power of the air and cause light rays to be curved, making the air act as a huge distorting lens. This can happen at sea, in deserts and elsewhere and various types of mirage are known. A common kind in deserts curves light from the sky so that it appears to come from the ground, deceiving the observer into thinking that the sky is reflected in a lake of water. Inverted images of hills, trees, etc. also look as if reflected in the non-existent lake.

Mistletoe, a parasitic evergreen with white berries used as a decoration at Christmas-time. The familiar mistletoe of Europe is the *Viscum album,* which grows on the boughs of lime, willow, apple, poplar, maple, ash, hawthorn but seldom on oak-trees. It was sacred to the Druids, and in Norse mythology it was a mistletoe dart that killed the god Baldur.

Mitosis, cell division whereby each daughter cell receives the same number of chromosomes as the parent cell. When the gametes (sex cells) are formed a special type of division occurs (meiosis) in which the number of chromosomes is halved.

Moabite Stone, a stone of the 9th century B.C. containing the earliest known inscription in Phoenician characters, and discovered in the highlands of Moab in 1868. It is now in the Louvre, Paris. It records the campaign between Moab and Israel (*c.* 850 B.C.), an account of which is given in the Old Testament (2 Kings 3:27).

Mohole Project, a scheme to bore through the earth's crust to take samples of the mantle rocks beneath. Drilling trials, led by an American team of geophysicists, began in 1961 near the island of Guadalupe off the Mexican coast in the Pacific. The project, however, was cancelled in 1966 on account of the escalating cost. Russian geophysicists started on a similar experiment, boring through land rocks where the digging is much deeper and higher temperatures are met with. The name "Anti-Cosmos" was given to the project. The boundary between the earth's crustal and mantle rocks is known as the Mohorovicic Discontinuity, or, more simply, as the Moho. The technology of deep sea drilling came from this project.

Molecule. A group of atoms held together by chemical forces.

Molybdenum, element no. 42, symbol Mo, a fairly hard white metal with properties resembling those of chromium. Its commonest ore is the sulfide, molybdenite. The chief use of the metals is in the manufacture of alloy steels.

Monitor, a family of lizards most resembling dragons. There are about 30 species widely distributed over the tropical parts of Asia, Australia and Africa.

Monsoons, regular persistent winds which blow at certain seasons in middle latitudes, mainly in South and East Asia. Their occurrence is related to the great changes of pressure which take place between summer and winter over the land mass. In India the south-west monsoon (June–October) is moisture-laden from its long passage over the sea and in the higher regions, especially, there is heavy rainfall. Sudden reversal of the wind results in the cold north-east monsoon (October–March) which is dry on account of the shelter afforded by the mountain ranges to the north. Frequently the term "monsoon" is applied to denote the associated rainfall without reference to the actual winds.

Moths, of the insect order, *Lepidoptera,* differing from butterflies which have clubbed antennae, in having feathery, sometimes thin, pointed antennae, rarely clubbed. Most are nocturnal, and the pupae are usually brown and enclosed in a cocoon unlike those of the butterfly, which are usually naked. *See also* **Lepidoptera.**

Motion, Laws of. According to Newton: (1) A body continues in its state of rest or uniform motion in a straight line except in so far as it is compelled by external forces to change that state. (2) Rate of change of momentum is proportional to the applied force, and takes place in the direction in which the force acts. (3) To every action there is an equal and opposite reaction. These laws are the basis of almost all engineering and everyday mechanics. Corrections to them have been made by relativity and the quantum theory.

Myrrh, a resinous substance obtained from a tree of the natural order *Amyridaceae,* growing plentifully in Ethiopia and Arabia. Its use for embalming, medical and aromatic purposes may be traced back to the most remote times.

N

Nadir, one of the two poles of the horizon, the other being the zenith. The nadir is the pole vertically below the observer's feet.

Narcotic, a medical dictionary definition is that a narcotic is a drug that produces stupor; complete insanity or sleep. In terms of drug addiction, a narcotic has been defined as altering and distorting the user's perception of himself and of the external world, being taken primarily for that purpose.

Nationalization is the taking over by the State of the ownership and operation of an industry or service—*e.g.,* coal-mining, railway, transport, gas and electricity. Where this is done without revolution, compensation is usually paid to the previous owners at what is regarded as a fair market price; the compensation is sometimes paid in cash, but more often in fixed-interest-bearing bonds issued either by the State or by the administration of the nationalized service, which is usually a publicly appointed Board or Corporation acting, with greater or lesser autonomy, under the direction of a Minister responsible to Parliament. In some cases the State becomes a partner with private investors in the ownership of a particular enterprise, *e.g.,* oil companies, such as the former Anglo-Iranian and some recent French examples. Nationalization is usually brought about by a separate Act of Parliament relating to each industry or service taken over. These Acts, in Great Britain, include provision for joint consultation at all levels between the administering boards and the workers employed and their Trade Unions. When, as in the Soviet Union, nationalization occurs as an outcome of social revolution no compensation is paid to the dispossessed owners.

Neanderthal, the name of the valley lying between Düsseldorf and Wuppertal, where in a limestone cave a now famous skull of a very early species of prehistoric man was discovered in 1856. Fossils of Neanderthal man have been found over a wide area, and from archaeological evidence he began to disappear from Europe during the last Ice Age, about 40,000 B.C.

Nekton, term used to differentiate actively swimming aquatic organisms (*e.g.,* fishes) from the "drifters" or plankton.

Neodymium, element no. 60, symbol Nd, belonging to the rare earth metal group. Discovered by Welsbach, 1885.

Neptunium, element no. 93, symbol Np, one of the four new elements discovered during the progress of the atomic bomb project in the second world war, Neptunium is formed when a neutron enters nucleus of Uranium 238, and it decays radioactively to yield plutonium.

Neutrino, a neutral particle which carries energy and spin and although possessing little or no mass plays an important part in the interaction of other fundamental particles. The discovery that there are in fact two distinct neutrinos, each with its counterpart, was discovered in 1962 as a result of an experiment made with the 30,000 million-electronvolt proton accelerator at Brookhaven.

Neutron, a neutral particle present in all atomic nuclei except the hydrogen nucleus which is a single proton. In the development of nuclear science and technology the neutron has played a most important role and neutrons produce the radioisotopes now widely used in medicine, agriculture and industry. Neutrons and protons are termed nucleons.

Neutron Bomb, a thermonuclear fusion weapon which produces increased lethal radiation while the destructive blast and fallout are significantly less than for a fission weapon of equivalent yield; it kills organic life while sparing property, except within a small radius. In 1978 President Carter reserved his decision on production; in 1981 the new Reagan administration decided to go ahead and stockpile the weapon.

Nickel, silver-colored metallic element, no. 28, symbol Ni, fairly soft though harder than iron. Chief source of the metal is the nickel sulfide in iron-copper pyrites deposits in Ontario. Chief uses are: in electroplating, in coins, as an element in alloy steels. A novel method of making pure nickel (by treating the metal with carbon monoxide and heating the resulting liquid, nickel carbonyl) was developed in 1890 by Mond. This discovery led to many technical advances in industrial chemistry, one of which is the production of catalysts.

Niobium is a metal element, no. 41, symbol Nb, related to vanadium. Technical development has been slow because of its rare occurrence, although niobium is now used in ferrous alloys to increase resistance to corrosion and produce steel which can be used at high temperatures.

Nitrogen, a non-combustible gaseous element, no. 7, symbol N, devoid of taste or smell, and constituting nearly four-fifths of the atmospheric air. Nitrogen compounds are essential to plants and animals, and are used in fertilizers.

Nitro-Glycerine, an explosive yellow fluid produced by mixing small quantities of glycerine with a combination of one part of nitric acid and two parts of sulfuric acid. By itself it is a dangerously explosive substance to handle. In 1867, Nobel produced dynamite, a safe explosive made by absorbing nitro-glycerine in kieselguhr.

Nucleic Acids. Living matter is built up of cells each of which has a nucleus surrounded by cytoplasm. Cell nuclei are composed chiefly of substances called nucleoproteins, which consist of a protein attached to a nucleic acid (this original name is still used, although nucleic acids are found in the cytoplasm as well as the nucleus). Nucleic acids are complex organic structures made up of chains of compounds called nucleotides. Nucleotide molecules have a sugar group attached to a nitrogenous base and a phosphate group. Only two sugar groups are found in the nucleotides, ribose, giving rise to ribonucleic acids (RNAs, found mainly in the cytoplasm) and deoxyribose, which forms deoxyribonucleic acids (DNAs, found mainly in cell nuclei). Seven different nitrogenous bases have been isolated, so that a number of different nucleotides are possible. A repeating, regular pattern of nucleotides is linked by the phosphate groups, forming nucleic acids. The functions of nucleic acids are of fundamental importance. They are concerned in the process of transmission of inherited qualities in reproduction and in building up body proteins.

Nylon, a generic term for any long-chain synthetic polymeric amide which has recurring amide groups as an integral part of the main polymer chain, and which is capable of being formed into a filament in which the structural elements are orientated in the direction of the axis. The first nylon of commercial interest was made in 1935, and the world's first nylon factory—in the United States—began production in 1940.

O

Odyssey, Homer's epic setting forth the incidents of the wanderings of Odysseus on his way back to Ithaca after the Siege of Troy.

Ohm's Law, propounded by G. S. Ohm in 1826, is expressed in the equation: electromotive force (in volts) = current (in amperes) × resistance (in ohms). The ohm is the unit of electrical resistance in the metre-kilogram-second system.

Onyx *or* **Sardonyx,** a variety of chalcedony built up of different-colored layers, which are parallel and straight (not curved as in agate).

Opal, a mineral consisting of hydrous silica, occurring in numerous varieties and colors. Opals have been prized as gems since at least 400 B.C. but the secret of their unique internal "fire" or opalescence has only recently been learned. It is a result of the diffraction of light by a regular array of tiny silica spheres, about 100 nm in diameter, of which gem opals are now known to be composed. Opal miners are called gougers. Chief source—the Andanooka and Coober Pedy fields of South Australia.

Opium was known to the ancients, and used by them as a medicine. It is obtained from the poppy *(Papaver somniferum),* the unripe "head" or seed capsule of that flower yielding a juice which when dried becomes the opium of commerce. The poppy is cultivated in India, Iran, Turkey, Macedonia and China for the sake of this juice, which yields various alkaloids, such as morphine, narcotine, codeine, etc. These days the drug is rarely used medicinally.

Optics, the branch of physics which investigates the nature and properties of light and the phenomena of colour. Burning lenses were known to the ancient Greeks and Ptolemy wrote a treatise on optics A.D. 150. Lenses as visual aids were known in ancient China but eyeglasses were not in use until the 13th century. Spectacles were in more general use after the invention of printing in the 15th century. The camera obscura was invented in the 16th century and the telescope and microscope at the beginning of the 17th century.

Orchestra, a group of instruments and instrumentalists whose playing is under the direction of a conductor. The composition of a typical symphony orchestra is as follows: STRINGS: 1st Violin (16), 2nd Violin (16), Viola (12), Violoncello (12), Double Bass (8). WOODWIND: Flute (3–4), Piccolo (1), Oboe (3), Cor Anglais (1), Bass Oboe (1), Clarinet (3), Bass Clarinet (1), Bassoon (3), Contra-bassoon (1). BRASS: Horn (6), Trumpet (5), Trombone (3–4), Tuba (2). PERCUSSION: Timpani (3–6), Side Drum (1), Bass Drum (1), Cymbals (1), Harp (2).

Organ is a musical wind instrument of ancient origin whose tones are produced by the vibrations of air in pipes of varying length. Basically, an organ consists of a number of pipes grouped in rows or ranks according to their special tone-character. The air is fed by bellows or, in modern organs, by a rotary fan electrically driven. Each rank is controlled by a slider, and the knob that controls the slider is called a stop. The organist pulls out the stops to give the tones he wants, the other pipes being kept out of action by the slider. When a particular note on the keyboard is depressed the player may hear, by pulling out the appropriate stop, not only the normal pitch but the note in several octaves. A stop of which the notes are of normal pitch is called an 8-foot stop, a 16-foot stop would give an octave lower, a 4-foot stop an octave higher and a 2-foot stop two octaves higher. The hand keyboard is called a manual, and the foot keyboard the pedal board. The basic tone of an organ is its diapason tone, and is normally of 8-foot length and pitch. Most large organs have four manual keyboards and one pedal board. The most important manual is the great organ which comprises the majority of basic stops. The next in importance is the swell organ, so called because the pipes are enclosed in a box fitted with movable shutters operated by a swell-pedal. The effect provides a controlled crescendo or diminuendo. The tone of a typical English swell has a reedy character. The third manual controls the choir organ—a collection of stops suitable for vocal accompaniment. The fourth manual controls the solo organ—a group of stops which, singly or in combination, may provide a solo melody which the remainder of the organ accompanies. The pedal keyboard controls most of the bass stops. In some very large organs there is a fifth manual controlling the echo organ. This is a small group of stops usually set high in the roof of the building to give the effect of distant music. Most church organs have two or three manuals. Modern cinema organs may have some normal stops but rely chiefly on a number of effects unknown to the straight organ.

Orion, a famous constellation of the heavens, comprising nearly a hundred stars, all visible to the naked eye. It contains three stars of the second magnitude in a line, and these are called "Orion's Belt".

Osmium, a very hard, bluish-white metallic element, no. 76, symbol Os, of the platinum group and one of the heaviest of known metals. It is obtained from certain sands of South America, California, Australia and Russia. The alloy of osmium and iridium (osmiridium) provides tips for gold fountain-pen nibs.

Osmosis, the process by which absorption of liquids through semi-permeable membranes takes place. A solution exerts osmotic pressure (O.P.) or suction in proportion to concentration but also depending on kind of dissolved substance. The roots of the higher plants are covered with fine root-hairs, within the cell-walls of which the sap is normally of a higher concentration than the dissolved matter in the surrounding soil. The root-hairs, therefore, draw into themselves these weaker salt-solutions. (The explanation of water and salt exchanges is complicated by the selective ability of some cells (*e.g.,* roots) to accept or reject particular dissolved substances along with the water. The absorption of salts by a plant is selective, each plant selecting through the semi-permeable membranes of its root-hairs those substances which are most suited to itself.)

Oxygen is the most abundant of all terrestrial elements, no. 8, symbol O. In combination, this gaseous element forms about 46% of the earth's crust; one-fifth of the atmosphere; eight-ninths by weight of all water. Discovered independently by Scheele (*c.* 1773) and Priestley (1774). It is colorless, tasteless and odorless, and forms the chief life-supporting element of animal and vegetable life.

Ozone, a modified form of oxygen, containing three atoms of oxygen per molecule instead of two. It is prepared by passing oxygen through a silent electric discharge. When present in air to the extent of 1 part in 4 million parts of air it kills bacteria, and has been used for this purpose in ventilating systems, *e.g.,* that of underground railways. It is present in extremely small quantities in the lower atmosphere but is comparatively plentiful at heights between 12 and 50 km. As ozone absorbs ultraviolet light of certain wavelengths spectroscopic methods, involving the analysis of sunlight, are chiefly used in ozone determination.

P

Palladium, a scarce metallic element, no. 46, symbol Pd, similar to platinum, with which it is usually found. It is an expensive metal, with desirable properties as a catalyst in reactions involving hydrogen, since it has a remarkable capacity for absorbing this gas; for example, coal gas and air will inflame in the presence of palladium at room temperature. It forms a silver-white alloy with gold, and this is used in some kinds of jewellery. It is used in expensive watches to make non-magnetic springs.

Paper has been known in one form or another from very early times. The papyrus reeds of the Nile swamps served the ancient Egyptians for sheets upon which to inscribe their records. The Chinese and Japanese, centuries later, were using something more akin to modern paper in substance, an Asiatic paper-mulberry, yielding a smooth fibrous material, being utilized. With the spread of learning in Western Europe the necessity of a readier medium made itself felt and paper began to be manufactured from pulped rags and other substances. The first known English paper-mill was Sele mill near Stevenage, built about 1490, which produced the paper for an edition of Chaucer in 1498. Other mills were set up under Elizabeth, using linen and cotton as raw material. Other papermaking staples were later introduced, such as surat, esparto grass and wood-pulp. The chief raw material in the world paper industry is wood-pulp, the main exporters being the timber-growing countries of Canada, Sweden and Finland. Canada is the world's chief producer of newsprint and supplies a large proportion of US requirements.

Papyrus, the earliest known paper made in Egypt at a very remote period from a large species of reed, *Cyperus papyrus.* This plant is to be found all over tropical Africa, especially in the "sudd" region of the White Nile.

Parallax, the change in direction of a body caused by a change in position of the observer. If the parallax is measured (in degrees of angle) and the distance between the two observation points is known the distance of the observed body can be calculated. The distance of heavenly bodies has been found this way. The first stellar distances were so obtained in 1838 by Henderson, Struve and Bessel. Stellar distances are so great that even when the two observations are made at opposite points of the earth's orbit round the sun, the parallax is always less than 1·0″ of arc.

Parchment, made chiefly from the skins of animals,

usually of goats and sheep, was employed in olden times before printing was invented and superseded papyrus as writing material. Vegetable parchment, invented by W. E. Gaine in 1853, though not equal in strength and durability to skin parchment, is about five times stronger than ordinary paper. Vellum is parchment made from the skins of young calves or lambs.

Pearl is produced by certain shelled mollusks, chiefly the oyster. The inner surface of the shells of the pearl oyster yield "mother-of-pearl", and distinct pearls are believed to be morbid secretions, caused by some external irritation. Many fine pearls are found in the actual body of the oyster. The Persian Gulf, Sri Lanka, the north-west coast of Western Australia, many Pacific islands and the Gulf of Mexico are among the most productive pearl-fishing grounds. In ancient times Britain was renowned for its pearl fisheries, the pearls being obtained from a species of freshwater mussel. Western Australia has produced a 40-grain pearl, the finest the world has seen. The largest pearl ever found was the "Beresford-Hope Pearl", which weighed 1,800 grains, over six times as much as the oyster that produced it.

Perfumes are essences or odors obtained from floral and other substances. The chief flower perfumes are those obtained from rose, jasmine, orange flower, violet and acacia. Heliotrope perfume is largely obtained from vanilla and almonds. Among the aromatic herbs which yield attractive perfumes are the rosemary, thyme, geranium, lavender, etc., while orange peel, citron peel, musk, sandalwood, patchouli and other vegetable products are largely drawn upon. In recent times chemistry has been called into play in aid of the perfumer, and many of the popular perfumes of today are chemically prepared in simulation of the scents of the flowers or other natural substances the names of which they bear.

***pH* Value.** Introduced in 1909 by the Danish chemist Sorensen to indicate hydrogen-ion concentration on the basis of electrical conductivity and a view of ionisation since discarded; is now taken as a logarithmic scale of acidity or alkalinity of aqueous solutions: acidity 0–7, neutrality at 7–0, alkalinity 7–14. The *pH* of blood is about 7–6 (faintly alkaline).

Phalanx, a name applied by the ancient Greeks to a body of pike-men drawn up in close array, with overlapping shields, and eight, ten or more rows deep. The Macedonians stood sixteen rows deep. As many as 500 men could be in the front row.

Phosphorus is a non-metal element, no. 15, symbol P. Most familiar as a waxy, yellow solid which is spontaneously inflammable in air. It has chemical similarities to arsenic, like which it is very poisonous. It was discovered by Brandt in urine in 1669. It is found in most animal and vegetable tissues. It is an essential element of all plants and of the bones of animals. In combination with various metals it forms different phosphates, which are largely utilised as manures. The chief commercial use of phosphorus is in the preparation of matches.

Photon. When light behaves like a stream of discrete particles and not like waves, the particles are called photons.

Pitchblende *or* **Uraninite,** a relatively scarce mineral. It is nearly all uranium oxide, but lead, thorium, etc., are also present. Pitchblende from Joachimstal in Czechoslovakia was the material in which radium was discovered by the Curies. Other major sources are the Great Lakes region of Canada and Zaïre.

Plasma Physics is the physics of wholly ionized gases, *i.e.,* gases in which the atoms initially present have lost practically the whole of the electrons that usually surround their nuclei, so that the gas consists of a mixture of two components, positively charged ions and negatively charged electrons. The physical properties of a *plasma* are very different from those of an unionized gas. In particular, a plasma has a high electrical conductivity and can carry large currents.

Plastics, a broad term covering those substances which become plastic when subjected to increased temperatures or pressures. The Plastics Industry is based on synthetic organic examples of this group. There are two classes of plastics: the *thermoplastic,* which become plastic every time they are heated (*e.g.* cellulosic plastics) and *thermosetting,* which undergo chemical change when heated, so that once set they cannot be rendered plastic again (*e.g.,* Bakelite). Plastics are composed of longchained molecules, *e.g.,* polyethylene.

Platinum, a metallic element, no. 78, symbol Pt. It is a scarce white metal generally allied with iridium, osmium, ruthenium and palladium. It can only be melted in an oxyhydrogen or electric furnace, but can be rolled out into a film-like sheet, or drawn out to the finest wire; being resistant to acids it is termed a noble metal.

Pleiades, famous cluster of stars in the constellation of Taurus. Of the seven principal stars in the group, one is rather faint, and many myths have sprung up about this "lost Pleiad".

Plutonium, a chemical element, no. 94, symbol Pu, capable of nuclear fission in the same way as Uranium 235. Not until after it had been synthesised in atomic piles during the second world war was it shown to occur in infinitesimally small traces in nature. Its synthesis in the atomic pile depends on the capture by Uranium 238 nuclei of neutrons; immediate product of this reaction is the element neptunium, but this undergoes rapid radioactive disintegration to plutonium.

Pogrom. Russian word meaning "destruction". First used to describe the Czarist attacks on the Jews in 1881 in Russia. In 1938 Hitler ordered a general pogrom in Germany: all synagogues were destroyed and nearly all Jewish shops and homes, Jewish hospitals and children's homes suffered. During the subsequent war Jews of central Europe were systematically exterminated in cold blood by the Nazis.

Pole-Star is of the second magnitude, and the last in the tail of the Little Bear constellation. Being near the North pole of the heavens—never more than about one degree from due north—it always remains visible in the Northern hemisphere; hence its use as a guide to seamen.

Polonium, a radioactive element, no. 84, symbol Po. discovered by Madame Curie in 1898, and named after her native land of Poland.

Porcelain. The word is thought to be derived from the Italian *porcellana,* indicating the texture of a piglet. The majority of porcelain made on the continent was of "hard-paste", or true porcelain, similar to that discovered by the Chinese as early as the T'ang Dynasty (A.D. 618 907). It was composed of *kaolin* (china-clay) and *petuntse* (china-stone) which when fired in a kiln at a temperature of *c.* 1300° C (2370° F) became an extremely hard and translucent material. The recipe of "hard-paste" porcelain remained a secret of the Chinese until 1709, when it was re-discovered in

Europe by Johann Böttger of the Meissen factory (popularly known as Dresden). Aided by disloyal Meissen workmen, factories were later established at Vienna, Venice and in many parts of Germany. Plymouth and Bristol were the only English factories to produce this type of porcelain, from 1768 to 1781. Elsewhere, both in England and France, the material manufactured was known as "soft-paste" or artificial porcelain which was made by blending varying white-firing clays with the ingredients of glass. The French factory of Sèvres began to make some hard-paste porcelain by 1768 and by the 19th century such porcelain was the only type being made throughout the whole of the continent. In England Josiah Spode is credited with the introduction of "bone-china" about 1794. This hybrid-paste was quickly adopted by many other factories and today remains the most popular type of English porcelain.

Porphyry, a form of crystalline rock of many varieties that in ancient Egypt was quarried and used for the decorative portions of buildings and vessels. The term is applied generally to the eruptive rocks in which large well-formed crystals of one mineral are set in a matrix of other minerals.

Positron, the "positive electron", an atomic particle having the same mass but an electric charge equal but opposite to that of an electron. It was discovered in 1932.

Potassium, a metal, no. 19, symbol K (German, *Kalium*). It is similar to sodium, reacting violently with water. It was discovered by Sir Humphry Davy in 1807, and is now generally obtained by the electrolysis of fused potassium hydroxide or chloride/fluoride mixture. Its principal minerals are caranallite and kainite, and it is relatively common in rocks, accounting for about 2 1/2% of the earth's crust. An essential element for healthy plant growth; the ashes of plants are relatively rich in potassium.

Proteins are the main chemical substances of living matter; they are a part of every living cell and are found in all animals and plants. All proteins are basically constructed of carbon hydrogen, oxygen and nitrogen, and some contain sulfur, phosphorus (nucleoproteins) and iron (haemoglobin). Proteins are built up of very long chains of amino-acids connected by amide linkages (the synthetic polymers such as "nylon" and casein plastics (from milk) are built up of the same linkages). The structure of protein molecules allows a variety of function. Enzymes, which bring about chemical reactions in living cells, are proteins having specific properties.

Proton, a basic constituent of the atomic nucleus, positively charged, having a mass about 1836 times that of the electron. It is a positive hydrogen ion.

Prout's hypothesis. The English chemist William Prout (1785–1850) advanced the idea that all atoms are made of hydrogen, and their weights are exact multiples of the weight of a hydrogen atom. With the modification that neutrons as well as protons occur in the nucleus, Prout's belief, though rejected for many years, has been substantially vindicated.

Psalms, Book of, for many years attributed to David, but present-day scholars are of opinion that the psalms were written by a series of authors at different times and for different purposes, and that few, if any, were written by David. The Holy Scriptures contain 150.

Q

Quartz is a common and usually colorless mineral, occurring both crystallized and massive. In the first form it is in hexagonal prisms, terminating in pyramids. When pure its specific gravity is 2.66. It is one of the constituents of granite, gneiss, etc. Among the quartz varieties are *rock crystal* (colorless), *smoky quartz* (yellow or brown), *amethyst* (purple), *rose quartz* (pink) and *milky quartz* (white). Quartz veins in metamorphic rocks may yield rich deposits of gold Mining for gold in the rock is termed quartz-mining.

R

Radar. The basic principle of radar is very similar to that of sight. We switch on a light in the dark, and we *see* an object because the light waves are reflected from it and return to our eye, which is able to detect them. Similarly, the radar station *sees* an object because the invisible radio waves sent out from the transmitter are reflected from it and return to the receiver, which is able to detect them. Thus radar is the use of radio signals that man broadcasts.

The utilization of radio waves for the detection of reflecting surfaces began with the classical experiment of the late Sir Edward Appleton in 1925, which he conducted in order to demonstrate the existence of the Heaviside layer in the upper atmosphere. During the course of the last war developments took place which tremendously improved the methods and instruments used. As in the case of so many of the inventions primarily developed for the purpose of waging war, many useful applications have been found for radar in times of peace, and, in particular, it has proved of great service as an aid to aerial and marine navigation, and in meteorology and astronomy. Radar astronomy investigates the solar system with the echoes of signals sent out from the Earth.

Radiation, energy emitted in the form of a beam of rays or waves, *e.g.,* acoustic (sound) radiation from a loudspeaker, radiant heat from a fire, β-radiation from a radioactive substance. The radiation of electromagnetic waves from a body depends on its temperature, the amount of energy radiated per second being proportional to the fourth power of the absolute temperature. The hotter the body, the shorter the wavelengths of the radiation; thus the color of a glowing body depends on its temperature. Of paramount importance to us is radiation from the sun. Amongst other radiations, the sun sends ultra-violet, visible and infra-red (heat) waves. The principal gases of the atmosphere are transparent to practically all of the solar and sky radiation and also that which the earth re-transmits to space. Carbon dioxide and water vapor, however, strongly absorb certain types, the latter, as clouds, playing an important rôle in regulating the temperature of the globe. The cooling of the ground on a clear night is a result of the outgoing long-wave radiation exceeding that coming down from the sky; at sunrise cooling ceases as the incoming radiation becomes sufficient to compensate for the loss of heat.

Radioactivity is the spontaneous transformation of atomic nuclei, accompanied by the emission of ionising radiations. It was discovered in 1896 by Becquerel, who noticed that salts containing uranium sent off radiations which, like X-rays, can blacken a photographic plate. Two years later Marie and Pierre Curie discovered several new chemical elements which possessed the same property, but many times more intense than uranium: the most important of these was radium. Shortly afterwards it was established, mainly by Rutherford, that three types of radiations called α-, β- and χ-rays, are emitted from radioactive substances. It was also Rutherford who, jointly with Soddy, deduced that the emission of the radiations is associated with the spontaneous disintegration of atoms which result in the transformation of one radioactive substance into another. A series of such transformations ends when a stable element is produced. All of the heavy radioactive elements can be arranged in three radioactive series, called, the uranium, thorium and actinium series. Initially, radioactivity was thought to be a property confined only to a few elements occurring in nature. In 1934, however, Irene and Frederick Joliot-Curie discovered that ordinary elements can be transformed into radioactive forms by subjecting them to bombardment with α-particles. Following this, it was found that beams of other fast particles produced in accelerators can also render ordinary substances radioactive. Nowadays it is known that radioactivity is a general property of matter; any chemical element can be produced in one or more radioactive forms, or isotopes.

Radiocarbon Dating is a method of dating the origin of organic materials or objects by observing their radioactivity. It is of great importance to archaeology because it enables prehistoric dates back to about 50,000 B.C. to be established for animal and vegetable remains. It works because cosmic rays entering the atmosphere create neutrons which convert nitrogen in the air to radioactive carbon. This forms radioactive carbon dioxide and gets incorporated into animals and vegetables throughout the world along with ordinary carbon dioxide in a definite ratio, approximately 1 radio carbon atom to 0.8×10^{13} ordinary carbon atoms. When the tissue dies it stops interchanging its carbon with the atmosphere, *e.g.*, by breathing, and the radioactive carbon in it gradually turns into nitrogen emitting a β-particle. The radiocarbon content decreases by about 1% in 88 years. By measuring the proportion of radioactive carbon left in, say, dead wood, and comparing it with living wood, the age of the dead sample can be calculated. This needs careful laboratory experiments. It is now believed that the proportion of radioactive carbon in the atmosphere varied from time to time in the past because changes in the earth's magnetic field affected the cosmic rays. This has to be allowed for in calculating the radiocarbon date. One use of radiocarbon dating has been to trace the spread of agriculture through the world from its origin in the Near East *c.* 7000 B.C.

Radium, a radioactive metallic element, no. 88, symbol Ra, discovered by Marie and Pierre Curie in 1898. Atomic weight 226. Radiotherapy (use of X-rays from radium) is used in the treatment of cancer.

Redwood *or* **Sequoia.** This genus of coniferous tree comprises two species of Redwoods occuring in N.W. America. Specimens of one species, the Giant Redwood, reach a height of over 90 m (295 ft.) and a thickness of 11 m (36 ft.) The age of the largest, the General Sherman tree, is put at 3,500 years.

Refraction. The change of direction which light rays undergo when passing from one medium to another. The phenomenon is due to the fact that in different media light (and other forms of radiation) has different speeds.

Refractory, a substance capable of standing high temperatures and therefore useful for making furnaces and allied apparatus. Some insulating refractories are fire-clay, alumina, porcelain, carborundum, graphite and silica. Some refractory metals are platinum, molybdenum, tungsten, tantalum and the alloys nichrome, chromel, alumel.

Rhodium, a metallic element, no. 45, symbol Rh, discovered by Wollaston in 1804. It is found in platinum ores in small amounts, generally less than 2 per cent. With platinum it gives a very hard and durable alloy. It is also used, instead of silver, in putting the reflecting layer on a mirror.

Rock Magnetism. The study of naturally occurring magnetism in rocks is a subject which has gained considerable importance in recent years. There are two principal reasons for this. One is that this so-called "fossillized magnetism" may be able to tell us more about the past history of the earth's magnetic field. The other is that after many years of heated dispute between geologists rock magnetism promises to settle once and for all the controversy as to whether or not the continents have changed their relative positions in past times (continental drift theory *(q.v.)*). This branch of geophysical research, in addition to its academic interest, may well have important economic consequences. It might, for instance, become possible to locate mineral deposits once accumulated under special conditions at certain latitudes but now drifted to other places. Salt and similar deposits formed by the continuous evaporation of solutions in hot countries are one example; oil may well be another. There has been a *steady* change in rock magnetization direction with geological time. It is now known with some accuracy that the most recent reversal took place 700,000 years ago. It has been found that the older the rock, the farther removed is its fossil magnetization from the present field.

Romanesque Architecture, prevailed throughout Europe from the mid-10th to the 13th century and implies an art which developed from that of the Romans. Notable in Romanesque style were the rounded arch and masonry vaulting. Romanesque led to the graceful and more complex Gothic *(q.v.)*. The Italians never regarded Gothic highly and Romanesque churches, generally based on the basilican plan (oblong with double colonnades and a semi-circular apse at the end), continued to be built there until the beginning of the 15th century. Some of the best examples can be seen at Pisa (11th century), Florence (San Miniato, 1013), Lucca (12th century) and Milan (the 12th century San Ambrogio, most famous of all). In Germany Romanesque architure flourished longer than in France or England; the most famous churches are in the valley of the Rhine, at Cologne (completely destroyed during the second world war), Mainz and Speyer. In France Romanesque churches are found in Burgundy, Provence and Normandy.

Rosetta Stone, discovered in 1799 by the French at Rosetta in Egypt, and deposited in the British Museum. It is a piece of black basalt about 91 cm (36 in.) long, and contains a decree of the Egyptian priests of Ptolemy V Epiphanes (205–181 B.C.) in (1) hieroglyphics, (2) demotic and (3) Greek characters. It was the three different inscriptions on the same stone that enabled hieroglyphic writing to be deciphered.

Rubber, substance obtained from the milky juice (latex) exuded by certain tropical trees and shrubs after tapping. Demand spread so rapidly in the 19th century that plantations were established wherever the tree would grow. Seeds of the Para rubber tree *(Hevea brasiliensis)* native to the Amazon basin were obtained by Kew, the young plants shipped to Ceylon and it was from these cultivated trees that the vast plantations of Malaysia and Indonesia developed. Recent years have seen great advances in the production of synthetic rubber.

Rubidium, a metallic element, no. 37, symbol Rb, most closely resembling potassium. It is silver-white and very soft, and was discovered in 1861 by Bunsen and Kirchhoff, using the spectroscope. It is rare, occurring in small amounts in the mica called lepidolite and in potash salts of the Stassfurt deposits in Germany.

Ruby is a deep red variety of Corundum (aluminum oxide); one of the most valued of precious stones. Burma yields some of the finest, and rubies of inferior color are found in Thailand, Sri Lanka, South Africa and Brazil.

Runes, certain characters of an alphabet found in inscriptions in the Germanic languages, found cut into buildings and implements of stone or wood in many parts of northern Europe, including Britain. The runic alphabet originally had 24 letters. Scholars agree that some of the runes derive from Greek and others from Latin.

Ruthenium, a greyish-white metallic element, no. 44, symbol Ru, discovered by Claus in 1845. It is harder and more brittle than platinum, in whose ores it occurs.

Rutile, mineral titanium dioxide. It is found in many igneous rocks, and in gneisses and schists. Its commonest colour is reddish-brown.

S

Saccharin, a white crystalline solid manufactured from toluene, 550 times as sweet as cane sugar. It is used as a sweetening agent; as a substitute for sugar when sugar is forbidden, as in certain diseases, or when there is a shortage. It has no value as a food.

St. Elmo's Fire, a glowing brush-like discharge of electricity which takes place from sharp-pointed objects on mountains or the masts of ships exposed to the intense electric fields of thunderclouds.

Sanskrit is the language of ancient India, spoken by the Brahmins, and existing in early Oriental literature. It was the language of literature and government and is now confined to temples and places of learning. Its relationship to the modern Indian languages is rather like that of Latin and Greek to modern European languages.

Sapphire, a valuable deep blue variety of Corundum (aluminum oxide) found mostly in India, Sri Lanka and Northern Italy. Synthetic sapphire is often used for gramophone styli.

Scandium, a metallic element, no. 21, symbol Sc. It was discovered in 1879 by Nilson, and occurs in small quantities in certain rarer minerals such as wolframite.

Schist, the geological name of certain metamorphic rocks composed for the most part of mineral with thin plate-like crystals (*e.g.,* mica) so that the layers of a schist are closely parallel. Quartz occurs in schists, and where it preponderates the term "quartz schist" is applied.

Scythians, nomadic conquerors and skilled horsemen of ancient times (9th–3rd century B.C.) who inhabited much of Southern Europe and Asiatic Russia.

Sea Anemones *or* **Actinaria,** an order of marine animals of the coelenterate class *Antozia.* They form a large and varied group of about 1,100 species and occur in many beautiful colors, flower-like in form.

Sea Cucumbers *or* **Holothurians.** These animals constitute the class of echinoderms called *Holothuroidea.* They are elongated and wormlike, with a ring of about twenty tentacles round the mouth. There are about 500 species.

Sea Elephant *or* **Elephant Seal,** a curious genus of seal, the males of which possess a proboscis of *c.* 30 cm (11.8 in.) in length that suggests an elephant's trunk. They are found on the coast of California and in certain parts of the Southern Ocean; their blubber has a commercial value.

Sea Gravimeter, an instrument to determine the density of the earth's crust beneath the oceans of the world. Designed by Dr. A. Graf of Munich and Dr. J. Lamar Worzel of Columbia University, it can detect changes of one-millionth of the value of gravity at the earth's surface and was used in the oceanographical research programe of the IGY.

Sea Horse, sea-fish *(Hippocampus),* very numerous in the tropics and comprising some twenty species. Their bodies are ringed and they have prehensile tails. Their heads are horse-shaped, and they swim in a vertical position.

Sea Urchin, species forming the class *Echinoidae.* The body is globular and covered with spines which may be used for both defence and locomotion. The main organs of locomotion are, however, the tube feet, as in starfishes. Much has been learnt of recent years by marine biologists from experiments with the purple sea urchin *Arbacia.*

Selenium, a non-metallic element, no. 34, symbol Se; related to sulfur. It is a dark red color, and solid, found associated with sulfur, iron, pyrites, etc., though only in small quantities. It is a semiconductor *(q.v.)* and its special electrical properties have led to its use in photoelectric cells and rectifiers. Selenium is widely used in the chemical industry as a catalyst in producing aromatic hydrocarbons from less useful hydrocarbons. Also used in making some types of glass.

Semiconductors, substances with numerous special and useful electrical properties a few of which are:

(i) they conduct electricity much better than do insulators, but much less well than metals (hence their name);

(ii) their power to conduct depends strongly on their temperatures—which makes them useful for temperature sensitive devices;

(iii) they are sensitive to light—hence their use in photoelectric cells and solar batteries;

(iv) when in contact with metals, or with other suitable semiconductors, they form a boundary layer which conducts electricity much better one way than the other—this is the basis of many rectifiers some of which, called crystal diodes, are an important component in radios and electronic devices;

(v) their electrical properties can be greatly influenced by putting in minute amounts of impurity, this enables semiconductor devices, especially transistors, to be made with carefully selected properties.

Semiconductors were known to Faraday, but the semiconductor age really arrived with the invention of the transistor in 1947. The ubiquitous transistor is only one of very many semiconductor devices which perform a variety of functions in technical apparatus of all kinds. Semiconductors used in technology are usually small crystals, frequently of germanium or silicon, and their robustness and small power consumption often make them superior to other devices, such as thermionic valves, which they often replace. Other semiconducting materials are cadmium sulfide, selenium lead telluride, indium antimonide.

Serpentine, a mineral: chemically a hydrous silicate of magnesium. Green serpentine is used as an ornament stone. Fibrous serpentine is called asbestos.

Silicon, an important non-metallic element, no. 14, symbol Si, it is related to carbon. Next to oxygen, it is the most abundant constituent of the earth's crust (27% by weight). It occurs in many rocks, and its oxide occurs in many forms (*e.g.* quartz, sand, flint, agate, chalcedony, opal, etc.). Principally used as a semiconducting material for making transistors and similar devices. The circuitry of the computer is etched on a chip of silicon.

Silk, the name given to a soft glossy fabric manufactured from the fine thread produced by the silkworm. It was known to, and highly prized by the ancients, being at one time paid for, weight for weight, with gold. The manufacture of silk was carried on in Sicily in the 12th century, later spreading to Italy, Spain and France, where Lyons has been the great center of production from 1450 to this day. It was not manufactured in England before 1604; but when certain French refugees established themselves at Spitalfields in 1688, the industry was developed and became of importance. In the 18th century the Lombes of Derby achieved great success in this industry. Japan, China, Italy, Korea and the Soviet Union are the chief silk-producing countries.

Silkworm, the larva of a species of moth, *Bombux mori.* It is native to China, and has been cultivated with success in India, Iran, Turkey and Italy. The silkworm of commerce feeds on mulberry leaves and produces a cocoon of silk varying in color from white to orange. The cocoon is the silken habitation constructed by the worm for its entrance upon the pupal condition, and to obtain the silk the pupa is killed by immersing in hot water.

Silver, a white precious metallic element, no. 47, symbol Ag (Latin *argentum*) found in a free state, also in certain combinations, and in a variety of ores. The chief silver-producing regions are the Andes and Cordilleras. Peru, Bolivia and Mexico have yielded vast supplies of the metal since the 16th century, and Colorado and Nevada in the United States have also been very prolific in silver yield.

Sins, The Seven Deadly or Capital sins are pride, avarice, lust, anger, gluttony, envy, sloth.

Sirius, the dog-star, so called because of its situation in the mouth of the Dog (Canis Major): it is the brightest star in the sky, and is also one of the nearest to us.

Snake. The snakes constitute the important reptilian order *Ophidia.* Snakes have a scaly, cylindrical, limbless body, lidless eyes, forked tongue, and the upper and lower jaws joined by an elastic ligament. All snakes have teeth used for seizing prey, and the poisonous varieties are furnished with poison fangs in the upper jaw. These fangs are hollow modified teeth and the venom passes into them from a special gland situated behind the angle of the mouth. Some 2,500 species of snakes are known, divided into 13 families. There are 3 British species—the grass-snake, smooth-snake, and adder.

Sodium, a metallic element, no. 11, symbol Na (Latin *Natrium*), first obtained by Sir Humphry Davy in 1807 from caustic soda by means of the electric battery. Its chloride is *common salt;* the deposits of salt (*e.g.,* in Cheshire and at Stassfurt) have come into existence through the drying up of inland seas. Salt occurs in sea-water to the extent of about 3 percent; the Dead Sea contains about 22 percent. The blood of animals is maintained at a level of about 0–6% sodium chloride. That there is sodium in the sun's atmosphere was confirmed in 1859 by Kirchhoff from his spectroscopic observations. Liquid sodium metal has properties which make it suitable as a coolant in some nuclear reactors; a technique of handling this very reactive liquid has had to be developed.

Solar Wind, a continuous stream of electrically charged particles blowing outwards from the sun, supplemented from time to time by intense outbursts from particular regions of the sun's surface. These streams of protons and electrons on encountering the earth's magnetic field distort it and cause magnetic storms *(q.v.)* and aurorae *(q.v.).*

Southern Cross, popular name of *Crux,* a constellation of the Southern hemisphere, consisting of four bright stars in the form of a Latin cross. It has been called the pole-star of the south and is indispensable to seafarers.

Specific Gravity, defined as the ratio of the mass of a particular volume of a substance to the mass of an equal volume of water at 4° C (39° F).

Spectroscopy. Newton's arrangement with the prism was the first spectroscope; its function was to separate out the color components of a source of light. Two hundred years elapsed before this apparatus was developed into a precise scientific instrument, capable of measuring both the wavelength and intensity of each color component. In this form it is called a spectrometer. All atoms and molecules have well defined characteristic spectra which can be uesd to recognize them. In order to produce emission spectra it is necessary to energize the material under investigation by some means, such as by heating in a flame. The resulting radiation then consists largely of sharp bright lines, characteristic of the material. Absorption spectra are produced by interposing the experimental material between a white light source and the spectrometer. Then dark lines are seen, corresponding to absorptions of energy, in exactly the same places as the bright lines are observed in the emission spectra. Spectroscopic techniques have now been developed to such an extent that accurate measurements of wavelength and intensity are possible not only in the visible region, but over almost the whole of the electromagnetic spectrum. Two of the most useful types for the chemist are infrared spectroscopy which reveals absorption characteristic of the type of chemical bonds because of their different bond vibration frequencies and nuclear magnetic resonance spectroscopy which operates in the radiofrequency region. It reveals the structure environments of atoms containing particular nuclei. Not only does spectroscopy play an important role in probing the structure of matter, but it can be applied in the field of astronomy. The use of radio wave spectroscopy has led to the discovery of several new types of stellar object, and this data is now producing a complete reappraisal of our understanding of the universe.

Stalactites are deposits of calcium carbonate formed on the roofs and sides of limestone caves, and in tunnels, under bridges, and other places where the carbonic acid of rain-water percolates through and partly dissolves the limestone, resulting in the growth of icicle-like forms that often assume groupings. The water that drops from these may deposit further calcium carbonate, which accumulates and hardens into sharp mounds or hillocks called stalagmites.

Steel, an alloy of iron and carbon, with varying proportions of other minerals. The famous blades of Damascus and steels of Toledo were made by the cementation and crucible method. The metal produced by the "Bessemer process" *(q.v.)* is of the highest value for structural purposes, rails, etc. In recent years the technique known as continuous casting has been developed which bypasses some major steps in the conventional process of steelmaking.

Steroids. A class of structurally related compounds, based on a system of condensed rings of carbon and hydrogen, which are widely distributed in animals and plants. Included in the steroid family are sterols, found in all animal cells, vitamin D, sex hormones, bile acids and cortisone, a drug used in the treatment of rheumatic fever.

Stoma (pl. **stomata**), microscopic pores on the surfaces of leaves through which gaseous exchanges take place and water is lost. It has been estimated that a single maize plant bears 200 million stomata, usually closed at night.

Stonehenge, a remarkable collection of Bronze Age monuments on Salisbury Plain. The site which contains ditches, earthwork-banks and megaliths (large stones) has long been recognised for its architectural innovations (the trilithon or freestanding arch and the circle of dressed and lintelled stone blocks) and for its astronomical, numerical and geometrical properties. The building and rebuilding, according to modern archaeological research, lasted from about 2100 to 1600 B.C.

Strontium. This silver-white metallic element, no. 38, was discovered by Hope and Klaproth in 1793, and isolated by Sir Humphry Davy in 1808. The chief strontium minerals are celestite (sulfate) and strontianite (carbonate). Compounds of strontium give a brilliant color to fireworks and signal flares. Radioactive isotopes of strontium (strontium-90) are formed as fission products in nuclear explosions and tend to collect in bone on account of the chemical similarity of strontium and calcium *(q.v.)*. This hazard is a cause of great alarm. *See* **Fallout.**

Sublimation, when a solid substance is heated and turns into vapor without passing through the liquid stage and then condenses as a solid on a cold surface, it is said to "sublime" and the process is called "sublimation". Iodine behaves in this way, and sublimation is used as a method of purifying it.

Sulfur, element no. 16, is a brittle, crystalline solid, symbol S, abounding in the vicinity of volcanoes. It is yellow in color. It occurs in combination with other elements, as sulfates and sulfides, and allied with oxygen, hydrogen, chlorine, etc., is of great commercial utility. Used in its pure state it constitutes the inflammable element in gunpowder; it is also used for matches and for making sulfuric acid.

Sulfuric Acid, a compound of great commercial importance, used in a variety of manufactures, and composed of sulfur, oxygen and hydrogen. Extremely corrosive, and is present in acid rain *(q.v.)*.

Superconductor, a metal in a state in which its electrical resistance has entirely vanished so that electric currents can flow indefinitely without generating heat or decreasing in strength. The superconducting state of metals was first discovered in mercury by Onnes in Leiden in 1911. There are many magnetic and thermal properties associated with superconductivity and the phenomenon as a whole has proved to be of great scientific interest: it resisted explanation till about 1957. In the meantime many metals and alloys were found to show the property but only at very low temperatures—below *c.* −260° C (−500° F). There is a growing number of practical applications, *e.g.*, coils of superconducting wire (kept very cold by liquid helium) can be made to carry enough electric current to produce strong magnetic fields. Such fields are very constant and do not require the large supply of electrical power that ordinary electromagnets need.

Supersonic Speed, a speed greater than the speed of sound (in air at sea-level sound waves travel at about 1223 km/h; 759.97 mph). When a body travels at a speed which is greater than the speed at which disturbances themselves can travel, a mechanism exists for the generation of waves of enhanced intensity. Thus aircraft traveling at supersonic speeds produce shock waves in the air somewhat analogous to the bow waves of fast-moving ships. These shock waves are regions of intensely disturbed air which produce the sonic boom effect so distressing to people living near supersonic routes. *Supersonic* is not to be confused with *ultrasonic (q.v.)*.

Symbiosis. When two organisms live together and both derive mutual benefit from the association, the partnership is known as symbiosis. An example is the symbiosis of an alga and a fungus in lichens; another is the ordinary pea plant and the bacteria which live in the nodules on the pea's roots.

Synapse is the point of association between one nerve cell and another. The nervous impulse traveling along one nerve has to be transmitted to the next across a minute gap. This is the synaptic gap. The mode of transmission is chemical though it was at first thought to be electrical. The impulse arriving at the synapse releases a chemical transmitter which diffuses across the gap and stimulates an impulse in the adjacent nerve cell.

T

Tantalum, a scarce bluish metallic element, no. 73, symbol Ta, discovered by Ekeburg in 1802. Chemically related to vanadium and niobium, it is usually associated with the latter in nature. For several purposes it can be used in place of platinum, and it finds application in the making of surgical instruments. Tantalum is very hard, and resistant to acids (other than hydrofluoric acid); it is used in alloys.

Telescope, an optical instrument for viewing objects at a distance, "the astronomer's intelligencer". Lippershey is credited with construction of the first in 1608; Galileo constructed several from 1609 and Newton was the first to construct a reflecting telescope. The ordinary telescope consists of an object-glass and an eye-lens, with two intermediates to bring the object into an erect position. A lens brings it near to us, and the magnifier enlarges it for inspection. A refracting telescope gathers the rays together near the eyepiece and is necessarily limited as to size, but the reflecting telescope collects the rays on a larger mirror, and these are thrown back to the eyepiece. The world's largest reflectors are at Mount Pastukhov, Caucasus (6 m; 19.7 ft), Mount Palomar, California (200 in), Mount Wilson, California (100 in), the McDonald Observatory at Mount Locke, Texas (82 in), and the Victoria B.C. Observatory (183 cm; 72.05 in). The *Hale* 200 in telescope at Mount Palomar has revealed objects never before photographed; it is able to probe space and photograph remote galaxies out to a limiting distance of 2,000 million light years. The *Schmidt* telescope at Mount Palomar has been used to make a huge photographic map of the universe. The 98 in *Isaac Newton* telescope has been moved from the Royal Observatory at Herstmonceux, Sussex, to La Palma, Canary Is. The giant steerable radio telescope built by Manchester University at Jodrell Bank, Cheshire, has a 250 ft reflector. The largest single radio dish in the world is the non-steerable 300 m (984.25 in.) instrument at Arecibo in Puerto Rico. Another instrument of radio astronomy is the interferometer which consists of spaced aerials. The biggest of these is in New Mexico, the array consisting of 27 steerable parabolic dishes 82 ft in diameter. Recently the technique of linking radio telescopes on different continents has been developed for fine observation.

Tellurium, a relatively scarce element, no. 52, symbol Te, discovered in 1782 by von Reichenstein. Chemically it behaves rather like sulfur; its salts are known as tellurides. It occurs chiefly combined with metals in ores of gold, silver, copper and lead. It is a semiconductor, and some of its compounds (also semiconductors) are coming into use in technical devices.

Templars were soldier knights organized in the 12th century for the purpose of protecting pilgrims in their journeyings to and from Jerusalem, and obtained their name from having had granted to them by Baldwin II a temple for their accommodation. At first they were nonmilitary, and wore neither crests nor helmets, but a long wide mantle and a red cross on the left shoulder. They were established in England about 1180. During the crusades they rendered valuable service, showing great bravery and devotion. In the 12th century they founded numerous religious houses in various parts of Europe and became possessed of considerable wealth. It was this that caused their downfall. Kings and Popes alike grew jealous of their influence, and they were subjected to much persecution, and Pope Clement V abolished the Order in 1312. Edward II in 1308 seized all the property of the English Templars. The English possessions of the Order were transferred to the Hospitallers of St. John, afterwards called the Knights of Malta.

Terbium, an element, no. 65, symbol Tb, discovered in 1842 by Mosander, belonging to the group of rare-earth metals.

Teredo, the scientific name of the ship-worm, a peculiar bivalve mollusk, which lodges itself when young on the bottoms of wooden ships and bores its way inwards, causing much injury.

Termites, also known as *White Ants,* though they are not related to the true ants and are placed in an entirely different insect order *(Isoptera).* They abound in the tropics and also occur in temperate countries, though only two species are common in Europe. There is no British species. They live in colonies and their nests take the form of mounds of earth and wood, cemented together with saliva, and up to 6 m; 19.69 ft). in height. Five separate castes are recognised, three of them being capable of reproduction, and the other two are sterile.

Thallium, a blue-grey metallic element, no. 81, symbol Tl, discovered by Crookes in 1861. It is obtained from the flue dust resulting from the burning of pyrites for sulfuric acid manufacture.

Thorium, a scarce, dark grey, metal element, no. 90, symbol Th, discovered by Berzelius in 1828. All substances containing thorium are radioactive. Chief source of thorium is monazite sand, big deposits of which occur in Travancore (India), Brazil and the USA. Considered important as a potential source of atomic energy since the discovery that it can be transmuted into U^{233}, which is capable of fission like U^{235}.

Tides, the periodical rise and fall of the waters of the ocean and its arms, are due to the gravitational effect of the moon and sun. Newton was the first to give a general explanation of the phenomenon of the tides. He supposed the ocean to cover the whole earth and to assume at each instant a figure of equilibrium, under the combined gravitational influence of earth, sun and moon, thus making and controlling the tides. At most places there are two tides a day, and the times of high- and low-water vary according to the positions of the sun and moon relative to the earth. When earth, moon and sun are in line (at full moon and new moon) the gravitational pull is greatest and we get "spring" tides. When sun and moon are at right angles (first and third quarters of the moon's phases) we get the smaller "neap" tides.

Tin is a white, metal element, no. 50, symbol Sn (Latin *Stannum*), whose commonest ore is cassiterite (tin oxide), which occurs in Malaya, Indonesia, Bolivia, Zaïre, Nigeria and Cornwall. It protects iron from rusting, and the tin coating on tinplate is applied by dipping the thin steel sheet in molten tin or by electrolysis. Tin alloys of importance include solder, bronze, pewter and Britannia metal.

Titanium, a scarce metallic element, no. 22, symbol Ti, difficult to extract from ores, found in association with oxygen in rutile, anatase and brookite, as well as with certain magnetic iron ores. It combines with nitrogen at a high temperature. Discovered by the Rev. William Gregor in 1791. Titanium alloys, being very resistant to stress and corrosion, and combining strength with lightness, and finding wide application not only in marine and chemical engineering but in the building of aircraft, rockets, and the nuclear-energy field. Titanium dioxide is now widely used in making paints.

TNT (Trinitrotoluene). A high explosive formed by the action of a mixture of nitric and sulfuric acids on toluene. Not highly sensitive to shock, it can be used in shells without danger, and is exploded by a time, or detonator, fuse. Apart from wartime applications, it is used in blasting in quarries and mines.

Topaz, a transparent mineral gem, being a silicate and fluoride of aluminum and generally found in granite rocks. Its color is yellow, but it also occurs in pink and blue shades. The best kinds come from Brazil.

Trade Winds form part of the circulation of air round the great permanent anticyclones of the tropics and blow inwards from north-east (Northern Hemisphere) and south-east (Southern Hemisphere) towards the equatorial region of low pressure. Atlantic trades are more regular than those of the Pacific. The belts may extend over 2,400 km; 1,491 mi) of latitude and, together with the Doldrums, move north and south in sympathy with the seasonal changes in the sun's declination, the average annual range being about 5 degrees of latitude.

Tree Rings as Natural Calendar. The approximate relationship between radiocarbon dating *(q.v.)* and true calendar age for the past 7,000 years has been established from measurements on tree-rings. Because one tree-ring is formed annually and its thickness is characteristic of the climatic conditions during its growth, it is possible, by comparing distinctive groups of rings, to date a series of trees. By using the long-lived Bristle Cone pines, tree-rings dating back to 500 B.C. have been obtained. It has been found that the radiocarbon age around, say, 3000 B.C. is too young by *c.* 600 years and because of short-term fluctuations near, say, 2000 B.C., a particular radiocarbon age can correspond to more than one true calendar age. These corrections are far less than those proved necessary after the publication of the first radiocarbon dates. Tree-rings (based on the measurement of deuterium in wood) can also show the pattern of temperature fluctuations over hundreds of years and thus make it possible to trace climatic changes before written records began. The term for tree-ring dating is dendrochronology.

Trilobites, extinct marine arthropods, most abundant in the Cambrian and Ordovician systems. Their appearance may be roughly described as resembling that of a woodlouse, and like that animal the trilobites were capable of rolling their bodies up into a ball.

Trireme, an ancient vessel with three rows of oars of great effectuality in early naval warfare. Mentioned by Thucydides. It was a long, narrow vessel propelled by 170 rowers. The Romans copied it from the Greeks.

Tritium, a radioactive isotope of hydrogen which has three times the weight of the ordinary hydrogen atom. It is produced by bombarding an isotope of lithium with neutrons and has a half-life of 121 years, decaying with the emission of β-particles (electrons).

Troubadours, lyric poets who flourished from the 12th to the end of the 13th century, chiefly in Provence and the north of Italy. They were often knightly amateurs, and cultivated a lyrical poetry intricate in metre and rhyme and usually of a romantic amatory strain, written in the *langue d'oc.* They did much to cultivate the romantic sentiment in days when society was somewhat barbaric and helped considerably in the formation of those unwritten codes of honor which served to mitigate the rudeness of medieval days.

Tsunami, a seismic sea wave originating from any one of several submarine geological phenomena such as volcanic explosions, landslides of earth movements. Tsunamis are extremely long wavelength waves which travel in the open ocean at speeds up to 640 km/h (398 mph). In deep water their height is only barely perceptible, but on reaching shallow coastal water they may attain heights of up to 30 m (98 ft) and can cause devastation to low-lying areas. The Pacific Ocean, whose rim is a seismically active area, is particularly susceptible to tsunamis. Following the damage caused by a tsunami which struck the volcanic islands of Hawaii on 1 April 1946, an early-warning system has been in operation. Tsunamis are often incorrectly referred to as tidal waves.

Tuatara *or* **Sphenodon,** a reptile of great antiquity, the sole surviving species of the *Rhynchocephalia,* found in New Zealand. It has a rudimentary third eye on the top of the head; this is called the pineal eye and corresponds to tissue which in mammals forms the pineal gland.

Tundra, the vast treeless plains lying in northern N. America and northern USSR where long severe winters and permanently frozen subsoils (permafrost) have resulted in specially adapted plant communities. The summer thaw and impervious permafrost cause waterlogging of lowland areas and marsh plants occur on these sites. In summer the ground cover of lichens and mosses with some flowering plants is distinctive. Stunted willows and birches occur in certain sites.

Tungsten, a hard, brittle metallic element, no. 74, symbol W (it was formerly called wolfram), silver to grey in color. Its chief ores are wolframite (iron and manganese tungstate) and scheelite (calcium tungstate). Tungsten is alloyed in steel for the manufacture of cutting tools; also in the nonferrous alloy stellite. Electric lamp filaments are made from tungsten. Tungsten carbide is one of the hardest substances known and is used for tipping tools.

Turquoise, formerly called Turkey-Stone, is a blue or greenish-blue precious stone, the earliest and best specimens of which came from Persia. It is composed of a phosphate of aluminum, with small proportions of copper and iron. India, Tibet, and Silesia yield turquoises, and a variety is found in New Mexico and Nevada. It derives its name from the fact that the first specimens were imported through Turkey.

U

Ultrasonics, sound waves of frequency so high as to be inaudible to humans, *i.e.,* above 15,000 Hz (Hz is SI unit for cycle per sec.). Ultrasonic waves are commonly produced by causing a solid object to vibrate with a suitable high frequency and to impart its vibrations to the air or other fluid. The object may be a quartz or other crystal in which vibrations are excited electrically, or a nickel component which is magnetically energised. There are numerous technical applications, *e.g.* submarine echo soundings, flaw detection in castings, drilling glass and ceramics, emulsification. Ultrasonic waves are an important tool of research in physics. Bats produce very loud sounds when they are flying, but at ultrasonic frequencies (20,000 to 150,000 Hz), so that we cannot ourselves hear them.

Ultra-Violet Rays. These are invisible electromagnetic rays whose wavelengths are less than 3900 A. (Angstrom = one hundred-millionth of a centimetre.) The sun's radiation is rich in ultra-violet light, but much of it never reaches the earth, being absorbed by molecules of atmospheric gases (in particular, ozone) as well as by soot and smoke particles. One beneficial effect of ultra-violet light on human beings is that it brings about synthesis of vitamin-I) from certain fatty substances (called sterols) in the skin. The wavelengths which effect this vitamin synthesis also cause sun tan and sun burn. Ultra-violet lamps (which are mercury-vapor discharge lamps) are also used for sterilising the air inside buildings, their rays being lethal to bacteria. Many substances fluoresce under ultra-violet light; for instance, zinc silicate glows green, while cadmium borate throws out red light. This phenomenon is applied practically in fluorescent lamps, the light of requisite hue being secured by judicious mixture of the fluorescent materials which coat the lamp.

Uranium, a metallic element, no. 92, symbol U, discovered by Klaproth in 1789 in pitchblende. It is a white metal which tarnishes readily in air. Great developments have followed the discovery that the nucleus of the uranium isotope U^{235} undergoes fission, and uranium minerals have become very important since it was found that atomic energy could be released controllably by taking advantage of fission. Before atomic energy work began to take the major part of the world's output of uranium minerals, the chief users of uranium compounds were the ceramics and textile industries.

Ursa Major and **Ursa Minor** ("Greater Bear" and "Lesser Bear"), two celebrated constellations, each of seven stars, in the northern celestial hemisphere, familiar since ancient times. Ursa Major has also been called "the Plough", "Charles's (Charlemagne's) Wain" or "the Wagon". The "Pointers" in this group of bright stars point to the brightest star in Ursa Minor, the Pole Star. Called the Big Dipper and the Little Dipper in the USA.

V

Valency. A term used by chemists is describe the combining ability of an element with respect to hydrogen. Thus oxygen, which forms water, H_2O, with hydrogen is said to have a valency of two, nitrogen (forms ammonia, NH_3) three, and carbon (forms methane, CH_4) four. Chlorine forms hydrogen chloride, HCl, and is said to be monovalent. This empirical approach cannot account for valency in such compounds as carbon monoxide, CO, which appears to require both elements to have the same valency. With the discovery of the electron it was realised that the concept of valency and chemical bonds is intimately concerned with the electronic structure of atoms, and theories have been advanced to explain why the same element can have different valencies in different compounds. Iron, for example, can have a valency of two ($FeCl_2$, ferrous chloride) or three ($FeCl_3$, ferric chloride).

Vanadium, a scarce metallic element, no. 23, symbol V, whose chief ores are carnotite and patronite. Some iron ores contain it. Most of the vanadium commercially produced finds its way into vanadium steels, which are used for tools and parts of vehicles, being hard, tough and very resistant to shocks. The oxide is used as a catalyst in industry, especially in making sulfuric acid.

Van Allen Belts. One of the most remarkable discoveries made during the IGY, 1957–58, was that the earth is surrounded by a great belt of radiation. Evidence came from *Sputnik II* (which carried the dog Laika) and from the American satellites, *Explorers I* and *III*. The American scientist, J. A. van Allen, was able to explain the puzzling data collected from these satellites. Subsequent observations with deep space-probes showed that there are in fact two zones of high intensity particle radiation surrounding the earth, one concentrated at a distance of about 1,600 km (994 mi), the other at about 24,000 km (14,913 mi). A close relation exists between the shapes of the zones and the earth's magnetic field. Recent evidence suggests that Jupiter also is surrounded by a dense belt of trapped high-energy particles.

Venus Fly-trap, a well-known insectivorous plant *(Dionaea muscipula)* occurring in Carolina in damp mossy places. It is related to the Sundew. The leaf is the organ that catches the insects. The leaf blade is in two halves, hinged along the centre line. Each half bears three sensitive hairs called "trigger hairs". When an insect touches a trigger, the two halves of the leaf clap together, trapping the insect between them, when it is digested by a secretion (digestive enzymes) from the leaf, which afterwards absorbs the soluble products.

Vitamins, name of a group of organic substances found in relatively minute amounts in certain foodstuffs, essential for growth and the maintenance of normal bodily structure and function. The Hungarian biochemist Szent-Györgyi, who first isolated vitamin C or ascorbic acid, defined the vitamin as "a substance that makes you ill if you don't eat it!"

W

Walrus, a very large marine mammal, related to the seals having in the upper jaw two large curved tusks, which average in length from 38 to 60 cm (15 to 24 in). It lives on bi-valve mollusks, and inhabits the Arctic seas. An adult walrus can exceed 4 m (13 ft) in length and weigh over a ton.

Water is the simplest compound of hydrogen and oxygen. It is formed when an electric spark is passed through a mixture of the gases, and is a product of combustion of all hydrogen-containing compounds, *e.g.,* petrol, coal, coal gas and wood. Water is essential to living matter, and is the medium which carries food to animals and plants. Salts in hard water may be removed by distillation of the water or by a process known as ion-exchange (water softening). Pure water freezes at 0° C (32° F) and boils at 100° C (212° F) and is used as a standard of temperature on this scale. It has a maximum density at 4° C (39° F). Heating water above 100° C (212° F) converts it into steam, which is used under pressure to convert heat energy into useful work, as in electrical power stations and steam engines. Water gas is a mixture mainly of carbon monoxide and hydrogen formed by blowing steam and oxygen through red-hot coke: it is used as a fuel. Water is one of the very few compounds which freezes from the surface down rather than from the bulk of the liquid up.

This property has important consequences on the preservation of life in rivers and lakes when they are frozen.

Whale, a completely aquatic mammal; the fore-limbs are modified to form fin-like paddles and there is virtually no external trace of the hind-limbs. There are two major groups of whales—the *Toothed Whales,* including the Sperm-whale (Cachalot), Dolphin, Killer-whales and Porpoises; and the *Whalebone Whales.* In the latter a series of whalebone plates grow down from the roof of the mouth, and, being frayed at their edges into a hairy fringe, together constitute a filtering mechanism. The animal takes in sea water containing minute organisms on which it feeds; the mouth is then closed and the tongue raised when the water is forced out through the filter, on which is left the food. As the tongue is lowered, the whalebone plates straighten up, flicking the food on to the tongue, which transfers it to the gut. Most whale oil is obtained from the thick layer of fat under the skin (blubber), but in the Sperm-whale there is a large reserve of oil in the head. One of the major users of sperm oil is the leather industry. Ambergris used in perfumery comes from the intestine of whales. The number of whales that may be killed in a season is limited by International Convention. The three main whaling nations are Japan, Norway and the Soviet Union.

Willow, a water-side-loving tree of the genus *Salix,* to which the osiers belong. The best cricket-bat blades are made from a white willow, *S. alba* var. *caerulea,* a fine tree with bluish-green leaves, mostly found in Essex. Willow is also used for polo balls. Weeping willow, *S. babylonica,* is native to China and is the willow seen on Old China willow-pattern plates.

Wind, air set in motion by special atmospheric conditions, is of various degrees, from a slight rustling breeze to a hurricane. Winds are *constant,* as in trade winds or anti-trade winds; *periodic,* as in monsoons and other wind-visitations occurring according to influences of season; *cyclonic* and *anticyclonic,* when their motion is spiral: *whirlwinds, hurricanes,* and *tornados,* when high temperature and great density induce extreme agitation. Ordinarily, a wind is named from the point of the compass from which it blows, or it may be expressed in degrees from true north. The *sirocco,* the *mistral,* and the *simoom* are local forms of winds of great velocity. A *blizzard* is a biting blast of icy temperature.

X

Xenon a rare gaseous element, no.54, symbol Xe, occurring in minute quantities in the atmosphere, discovered by Sir William Ramsay and M. W. Travers in 1898.

X-Rays were discovered in 1895 by Professor Röntgen, of Wurzburg, while experimenting with a Crookes vacuum tube, when a photographic plate enclosed in a dark box was noticed to have become fogged. X-rays are now commonly used to examine the internal structure of many opaque objects. In medicine, industry and for security, examination may be conducted without physical invasion. X-rays may also be used to probe the structure of matter, for example the atomic structure of crystals. The discovery in the 1960s that cosmic objects emitted intense X-rays has led to many important new astronomical phenomena being discovered.

Xylem, the woody tissue of higher plants whose function is to conduct water and mineral salts upwards, and to provide mechanical support.

Y

Yak, a curious, long-haired ox, found in Tibet used as a beast of burden, and also kept for milk and meat.

Ytterbium, a chemical, no.70, symbol Yb, element discovered by Urbain in 1907; one of the group of rare earth metals.

Yttrium, a chemical element, no.39, symbol Y, discovered by Mosander in 1842. It is found in a few rare minerals such as gadolinite, xenotine, fergusonite and euxenite. One of the group of rare earth metals.

Z

Zero, the cipher signifying nothing originally came from China. The West is indebted to the Arabs for it, who themselves obtained it from India and passed it to European mathematicians towards the end of the Middle Ages. The zero has also been found in Babylonian cuneiform. The Greeks had no such symbol, which hindered the development of their mathematics. The use of zero led to the invention of decimal fractions and to the later developments in astronomy, physics and chemistry. For absolute zero on the temperature scale *see* **Absolute Temperature.**

Zinc, a familiar metallic element, no.30, symbol Zn, known to the ancients, and used by them in the making of brass. It occurs as the sulfide carbonate, etc. The ores of zinc are crushed, roasted and reduced with coal. In combination with copper it constitutes the familiar alloy called brass, and zinc itself is much used for roofing and other protective purposes. Zinc ores are mined in Canada, the USA, Mexico, Poland, Australia, Russia, Italy, Spain and many other parts of the world. Zinc smelting is carried on in most industrial countries, including Great Britain.

Zirconium, metallic element, no.40, symbol Zr, was discovered by Klaproth in the sand of the rivers of Sri Lanka in 1789. The crystalline metal is white, soft and ductile; in its amorphous condition it is a blue-black powder. Zirconium is used in atomic reactors as containers for fuel elements, since it does not absorb neutrons.

Zodiacal Light, a faint cone of light occasionally seen stretching along the zodiac from the western horizon after evening twilight or the eastern horizon before morning twilight. It is believed to be due to the scattering of the sun's light by dust particles in orbit round the sun and extending beyond the earth. Recent observations at the high altitudes station at Chacaltaya in the Andes suggest that the dust is travelling round the sun in regular planetary orbits.

Zonda, a warm moist wind in Argentina of great velocity blowing from the north or northwest, and, like the Sirocco in Southern Europe, causes much discomfort. It happens when a depression is moving across the pampas, bringing with it a mass of air from the humid tropics. It is followed by a refreshing wind from the south east.

CROSSWORD PUZZLE GUIDE

First Aid to Crossword Puzzlers

We cannot begin to list all the odd words you will meet with in your daily and Sunday crossword puzzles, for such words run into many thousands. But we have tried to include those that turn up most frequently, as well as many others that should be of help to you when you are unable to go any further.

Also, we do not guarantee that the definitions in your puzzle will be exactly the same as ours, although we have checked every word with a standard dictionary and have followed its definition.

In nearly every case, we have used as the key word the principal noun of the definition, rather than any adjective, adjective phrase, or noun used as an adjective. And, to simplify your searching, we have grouped the words according to the number of spaces you have to fill.

For a list of Foreign Phrases, *see* Index. For Rulers of England and Great Britain, France, Germany and Prussia, and Russia, *see* Countries of the World.

Words of Two Letters

Ambary, DA
And (French, Latin), ET
Article (Arabic), AL
  (French), LA, LE, UN
  (Spanish), EL, LA, UN
At the (French), AU
  (Spanish), AL
Behold, LO
Bird: Hawaiian, OO
Birthplace: Abraham's, UR
Bone, OS
Buddha, FO
Butterfly: Peacock, IO
Champagne, AY
Chaos, NU
Chief: Burmese, BO
Coin: Roman, AS
  Siamese, AT
Concerning, RE
Dialect: Chinese, WU
Double (Egy. relig.), KA
Drama: Japanese, NO
Egg (comb. form), OO
Esker, OS
Eye (Scotch), EE
Factor: Amplification, MU
Fifty (Greek), NU
Fish: Carplike, ID
Force, OD
Forty (Greek), MU
From (French, Latin, Spanish), DE
  (Latin prefix), AB
From the (French), DU
God: Babylonian, EA, ZU
  Egyptian sun, RA
  Hindu unknown, KA
  Semitic, EL
Goddess: Babylonian, AI
  Greek earth, GE
Gold (heraldry), OR
Gulf: Arctic, OB
Heart (Egy. relig.), AB
Indian: South American, GE
King: Of Bashan, OG
Language: Artificial, RO
  Assamese, AO
Lava: Hawaiian, AA
Letter: Greek, MU, NU, PI, XI
  Hebrew, HE, PE
Lily: Palm, TI
Measure: Annamese, LY
  Chinese, HO, HU, KO, LI, MU, PU, TO, TU
  Japanese, GO, JO, MO, RI, SE, TO
  Metric land, AR
  Netherlands, EL
  Portuguese, PE
  Siamese, WA
  Swedish, AM
  Type, EM, EN
Monk: Buddhist, BO
Month: Jewish, AB
Mouth, OS
Mulberry: Indian, AL
Native: Burmese, WA
Note: Of Scale, DO, FA, MI, LA, RE, TI
Of (French, Latin, Spanish), DE
Of the (French), DU
One (Scotch), AE
Pagoda: Chinese, TA
Plant: East Indian fiber, DA
Ridge: Sandy, AS, OS
River: Russian, OB
Sloth: Three-toed, AI
Soul (Egy. relig.), BA
Sound: Hindu mystic, OM
Suffix: Comparative, ER
The. *See* Article
To the: French, AU
  Spanish, AL
Tree: Buddhist sacred, BO
Tribe: Assamese, AO
Type: Jumbled, PI
Weight: Annamese, TA
  Chinese, LI
  Danish, ES
  Japanese, MO
  Roman, AS
Whirlwind: Faeroe Is., OE
Yes (German), JA
  (Italian, Spanish), SI
  (Russian), DA

Words of Three Letters

Adherent: IST
Again, BIS
Age, ERA
Antelope: African, GNU, KOB
Apricot: Japanese, UME
Article (German), DAS, DEM, DEN, DER, DES, DIE, EIN
  (French), LES, UNE
  (Spanish), LAS, LOS, UNA
Banana: Polynesian, FEI
Barge, HOY
Bass: African, IYO
Beak, NEB, NIB
Beard: Grain, AWN
Beetle: June, DOR
Being, ENS
Berry: Hawthorn, HAW
Beverage: Hawaiian, AVA
Bird: Australian, EMU
  Crowlike, JAY
  Extinct, MOA
  Fabulous, ROC
  Frigate, IWA
  Parson, POE, TUE, TUI
  Sea, AUK
Blackbird, ANI, ANO
Born, NEE
Bronze: Roman, AES
Bugle: Yellow, IVA
By way of, VIA
Canton: Swiss, URI
Cap: Turkish, FEZ
Catnip, NEP
Character: In "Faerie Queene," UNA
Coin: Afghan, PUL
  Albanian, LEK
  British Guiana, BIT
  Bulgarian, LEV, LEW
  French, ECU, SOU
  Indian, PIE
  Japanese, SEN, YEN
  Korean, WON
  Lithuanian, LIT
  Macao, Timor, AVO
  Palestinian, MIL
  Persian, PUL
  Peruvian, SOL
  Rumanian, BAN, LEU, LEY
  Scandinavian, ORE
  Siamese, ATT
  See also Money of account
Collection: Facts, ANA
Commune: Belgian, ANS, ATH
  Netherlands, EDE, EPE
Community: Russian, MIR
Constellation: Southern, ARA
Contraction: Poetic, EEN, EER, OER
Covering: Apex of roof, EPI
Crab: Fiddler, UCA
Crag: Rocky, TOR
Cry: Crow, rook, raven, CAW
Cup: Wine, AMA
Cymbal, Oriental, TAL, ZEL

Disease: Silkworm, UJI
Division: Danish territorial, AMT
  Geologic, EON
Doctrine, ISM
Dowry, DOT
Dry (French), SEC
Dynasty: Chinese, CHI, HAN, SUI, WEI, YIN
Eagle: Sea, ERN
Earth (comb. form), GEO
Egg: Louse, NIT
Eggs: Fish, ROE
Emmet, ANT
Enzyme, ASE
Equal (comb. form), ISO
Extension: building, ELL
Far (comb. form), TEL
Farewell, AVE
Fiber: Palm, TAL
Finial, EPI
Fish: Carplike, IDE
  Pikelike, GAR
Flatfish, DAB
Fleur-de-lis, LIS, LYS
Food: Hawaiian, POI
Formerly, NEE
Friend (French), AMI
Game: Card, LOO
Garment: Camel-hair, ABA
Gateway, DAR
Gazelle: Tibetan, GOA
Genus: Ducks, AIX
  Grasses, POA
  Grasses (maize), ZEA
  Herbs or shrubs, IVA
  Lizards, UTA
  Rodents (incl. house mice), MUS
  Ruminants (incl. cattle), BOS
  Swine, SUS
Gibbon: Malay, LAR
God: Assyrian, SIN
  Babylonian, ABU, ANU, BEL, HEA, SIN, UTU
  Irish sea, LER
  Phrygian, MEN
  Polynesian, ORO
Goddess: Babylonian, AYA
  Etruscan, UNI
  Hindu, SRI, UMA, VAC
  Teutonic, RAN
Governor: Algerian, DEY
  Turkish, BEY
Grampus, ORC
Grape, UVA
Grass: Meadow, POA
Gypsy, ROM
Hail, AVE
Hare: Female, DOE
Hawthorn, HAW
Hay: Spread for drying, TED
Herb: Japanese, UDO
  Perennial, PIA
  Used for blue dye, WAD
Herd: Whales, GAM, POD
Hero: Spanish, CID
High (music), ALT
Honey (pharm.), MEL
Humorist: American, ADE
I (Latin), EGO
I love (Latin), AMO
Indian: Algonquian, FOX, SAC, WEA
  Chimakuan, HOH
  Keresan, SIA
  Mayan, MAM
  Shoshonean, UTE
  Siouan, KAW, OTO
  South American, ITE, ONA, URO, URU, YAO
  Tierra del Fuego, ONA
  Wakashan, AHT
Ingot, PIG
Inlet: Narrow, RIA
Island: Cyclades, IOS
  Dodecanese, COS, KOS
  (French), ILE
  River, AIT
Jackdaw, DAW
John (Gaelic), IAN
Keelbill, ANI, ANO
Kiln, OST
King: British legendary LUD
Kobold, NIS
Lace: To make, TAT
Lamprey, EEL
Language: Artificial, IDO
  Bantu, ILA
  Siamese, LAO, TAI
Leaf: Palm, OLA, OLE
Leaving, ORT
Left: Cause to turn, HAW
Letter: Greek, CHI, ETA, PHI, PSI, RHO, TAU
  Hebrew, MEM, NUN, SIN, TAV, VAU
Lettuce, COS
Life (comb. form), BIO
Lily: Palm, TOI
Lizard, EFT
Louse: Young, NIT
Love (Anglo-Irish), GRA
Lute: Oriental, TAR
Macaw: Bralizian, ARA
Marble, TAW
Match: Shooting (French), TIR
Meadow, LEA
Measure: Abyssinian, TAT
  Algerian, PIK
  Annamese, GON, MAU, NGU, VUO, SAO, TAO, TAT
  Arabian, DEN, SAA
  Belgian, VAT
  Bulgarian, OKA, OKE
  Chinese, FEN, TOU, YIN
  Cloth, ELL
  Cyprus, OKA, OKE, PIK
  Czech, LAN, SAH
  Danish, FOD, MIL, POT
  Dominican Republic, ONA
  Dutch, old, AAM
  East Indian, KIT
  Egyptian, APT, HEN, PIK, ROB
  Electric, MHO, OHM
  Energy, ERG
  English, PIN
  Estonian, TUN
  French, POT
  German, AAM
  Greek, PIK
  Hebrew, CAB, HIN, KOR, LOG
  Hungarian, AKO
  Icelandic, FET
  Indian, GAZ, GUZ, JOW, KOS
  Japanese, BOO, CHO, KEN, RIN, SHO, SUN, TAN
  Malabar, ADY
  Metric land, ARE
  Netherlands, KAN, KOP, MUD, VAT, ZAK
  Norwegian, FOT, POT
  Persian, GAZ, GUZ, MOU, ZAR, ZER
  Polish, CAL
  Rangoon, DHA, LAN
  Roman, PES, URN
  Russian, FUT, LOF
  Scotch, COP
  Siamese, KEN, NIU, RAI, SAT, SEN, SOK, WAH, YOT
  Somaliland, TOP
  Spanish, PIE
  Straits Settlements, PAU, TUN
  Swedish, ALN, FOT, MIL, REF, TUM
  Swiss, POT
  Tunisian, SAA
  Turkish, OKA, OKE, PIK
  Wire, MIL
  Württemberg, IMI
  Yarn, LEA
  Yugoslavian, OKA, RIF
Milk, LAC
Milkfish, AWA
Moccasin, PAC
Money: Yap stone, FEI
Money of Account: Anglo-Saxon, ORA, ORE
  French, SOU
  Indian, LAC
  Japanese, RIN
  Oman, GAJ
  Virgin Islands, BIT
  See also Coin
Monkey: Capuchin, SAI
Morsel, ORT
Mother: Peer Gynt's, ASE
Mountain: Asia Minor, IDA
Mulberry: Indian, AAL, ACH, AWL
Muttonbird: New Zealand, OII
Nahoor, SNA
Native: Mindanao, ATA
Neckpiece, BOA
Newt, EFT
No (Scotch), NAE
Note: Guido's highest, ELA
  Of scale, SOL
Nursemaid: Oriental, AMA, IYA
Ocher: Yellow, SIL
One (Scotch), YIN
Ornament: Pagoda, TEE
Oven: Polynesian, UMU
Ox: Tibetan, YAK
Pagoda: Chinese, TAA
Parrot: Hawk, HIA
  New Zealand, KEA
Part: Footlike, PES
Particle: Electrified, ION
Pasha, DEY
Pass: Mountain, COL
Paste: Rice, AME
Pea: Indian split, DAL
Peasant: Philippine, TAO
Penpoint, NEB, NIB
Piece out, EKE
Pigeon, NUN
Pine: Textile screw, ARA
Pistol (slang), GAT
Pit: Baking, IMU
Plant: Pepper, AVA
Play: By Capek, RUR
Poem: Old French, DIT
Porgy: Japanese, TAI
Priest: Biblical high, ELI
Prince Ethiopian, RAS
Pseudonym: Dickens', BOZ
Queen: Fairy, MAB
Quince: Bengal, BEL
Record: Ship's, LOG
Refuse: Flax (Scotch), PAB, POB
Resin, LAC
Resort, SPA
Revolver (slang), GAT
Right: Cause to turn, GEE
River: Scotch or English, DEE
  (Spanish), RIO
  Swiss, AAR
Room: Harem, ODA
Rootstock: Fern, ROI
Rose (Persian), GUL
Ruff: Female, REE
Rule: Indian, RAJ
Sailor, GOB, TAR
Saint: Female (abbr.), STE
  Mohammedan, PIR
Salt, SAL
Sash: Japanese, OBI
Scrap, ORT
Seed: Poppy, MAW
  Small, PIP
Self, EGO
Serpent: Vedic sky, AHI
Sesame, TIL
Sheep: Female, EWE
  Indian, SHA
  Male, RAM
Sheepfold (Scotch), REE
Shelter, LEE
Shield, ECU
Shooting match (French), TIR
Shrew: European, ERD
Shrub: Evergreen, YEW
Silkworm, ERI

Snake, ASP, BOA
Soak, RET
Son-in-law: Mohammed's, ALI
Sorrel: Wood, OCA
Spade: Long, narrow, LOY
Spirit: Malignant, KER
Spot: Playing-card, PIP
Spread for drying, TED
Spring: Mineral, SPA
Sprite: Water, NIX
Statesman: Japanese, ITO
Stern: Toward, AFT
Stomach: Bird's, MAW
Street (French), RUE
Summer (French), ETE
Sun, SOL
Swamp, BOG, FEN
Swan: Male, COB
Tea: Chinese, CHA
Temple: Shinto, SHA
The. *See* Article
Thing (law), RES
Title: Etruscan, LAR
  Monk's, FRA
  Portuguese, DOM
  Spanish, DON
  Turkish, AGA, BEY
Tool: Cutting, ADZ, AXE
  Mining, GAD
  Piercing, AWL
Tree: Candlenut, AMA
  Central American, EBO
  East Indian, SAJ, SAL
  Evergreen, YEW
  Hawaiian, KOA, KOU
  Indian, BEL, DAR
  Linden, LIN
  New Zealand, AKE
  Philippine, DAO, TUA, TUI
  Rubber, ULE
  South American, APA
Tribe: New Zealand, ATI
Turmeric, REA
Twice, BIS
Twin: Siamese, ENG
Uncle (dialect), EAM, EME
Veil: Chalice, AER, AIR
Vessel: Wine, AMA
Vestment: Ecclesiastical, ALB
Vetch: Bitter, ERS
Victorfish, AKU
Vine: New Zealand, AKA
  Philippine, IYO
Wallaba, APA
Wapiti, ELK
Water (French), EAU
Waterfall, LIN
Watering place: Prussian, EMS
Weave: Designating plain, UNI
Weight: Annamese, CAN
  Bulgarian, OKA, OKE
  Burmese, MOO, VIS
  Chinese, FEN, HAO, KIN, SSU, TAN, YIN
  Cyprus, OKA, OKE
  Danish, LOD, ORT, VOG
  East Indian, TJI
  Egyptian, KAT, OKA, OKE
  English, for wool, TOD
  German, LOT
  Greek, MNA, OKA, OKE
  Indian, SER
  Japanese, FUN, KIN, RIN, SHI
  Korean, KON
  Malacca, KIP
  Mongolian, LAN
  Netherlands, ONS
  Norwegian, LOD
  Polish, LUT
  Rangoon, PAI
  Roman, BES
  Russian, LOT
  Siamese, BAT, HAP, PAI
  Swedish, ASS, ORT
  Turkish, OKA, OKE
  Yugoslavian, OKA, OKE
Whales: Herd, GAM, POD
Wildebeest, GNU
Wing, ALA
Witticism, MOT
Wolframite, CAL
Worm: African, LOA
Wreath: Hawaiian, LEI
Yale, ELI
Yam: Hawaiian, HOI
Yes (French), OUI
Young: Bring forth, EAN
Z (letter), ZED

Words of Four Letters

Aborigine: Borneo, DYAK
Agave, ALOE
Animal: Footless, APOD
Ant: White, ANAI, ANAY
Antelope: African, ASSE, BISA, GUIB, KOBA, KUDU, ORYX, POKU, PUKU, TOPI, TORA
Apoplexy: Plant, ESCA
Apple, POME
Apricot, ANSU
Ardor, ELAN
Armadillo, APAR, PEBA, PEVA, TATU
Ascetic: Mohammedan, SUFI
Association: Chinese, TONG
Astronomer: Persian, OMAR
Avatar: Of Vishnu, RAMA
Axillary, ALAR
Band: Horizontal (heraldry), FESS
Barracuda, SPET
Bark: Mulberry, TAPA
Base: Column, DADO
Bearing (heraldry), ORLE
Beer: Russian, KVAS
Beige, ECRU
Being, ESSE
Beverage: Japanese rice, SAKE
Bird: Asian, MINA, MYNA
  Egyptian sacred, IBIS
  Extinct, DODO, MAMO
  Flightless, KIWI
  Gull-like, TERN
  Hawaiian, IIWI, MAMO
  Parson, KOKO
  Unfledged, EYAS
Birds: As class, AVES
Black, EBON
  (French), NOIR
Blackbird: European, MERL
Boat: Flat-bottomed, DORY
Bone: Forearm, ULNA
Bones, OSSA
Box, Japanese, INRO
Bravo (rare), EUGE
Buffalo: Indian wild, ARNA
Bull (Spanish), TORO
Burden, ONUS
Cabbage: Sliced, SLAW
Caliph: Mohammedan, OMAR
Canoe: Malay, PRAU, PROA
Cap: Military, KEPI
Cape, NESS
Capital: Ancient Irish, TARA
Case: Article, ETUI
Cat: Wild, BALU, EYRA
Chalcedony, SARD
Chamber: Indian ceremonial, KIVA
Channel: Brain, ITER
Cheese: Dutch, EDAM
Chest: Sepulchral stone, CIST
Chieftain: Arab, EMIR
Church: Part of, APSE, NAVE
  (Scotch), KIRK
Claim (law), LIEN
Cluster: Flower, CYME
Coin: Chinese, TAEL, YUAN
  German, MARK
  Indian, ANNA
  Iranian, RIAL
  Italian, LIRA
  Moroccan, OKIA
  Siamese, BAHT
  South American, PESO
  Spanish, DURO, PESO
  Turkish, PARA
Commune: Belgian, AATH
Composition: Musical, OPUS
Compound: Chemical, DIOL
Constellation: Southern, PAVO
Council: Russian, DUMA
Counsel, REDE
Covering: Seed, ARIL
Cross: Egyptian, ANKH
Cry: Bacchanalian, EVOE
Cup (Scotch), TASS
Cupbearer, SAKI
Dagger, DIRK
  Malay, KRIS
Dam: River, WEIR
Dash, ELAN
Date: Roman, IDES
Dawn: Pertaining to, EOAN
Dean: English, INGE
Decay: In fruit, BLET
Deer: Sambar, MAHA
Disease: Skin, ACNE
Disk: Solar, ATEN
Dog: Hunting, ALAN
Drink: Hindu intoxicating, SOMA
Duck, SMEE, SMEW, TEAL
Dynasty: Chinese, CHEN, CHIN, CHOU, CHOW, HSIA, MING, SUNG, TANG, TSIN
  Mongol, YUAN
Eagle: Biblical, GIER
  Sea, ERNE
Egyptian: Christian, COPT
Ear: Pertaining to, OTIC
Entrance: Mine, ADIT
Esau, EDOM
Escutcheon: Voided, ORLE
Eskers, OSAR
Evergreen: New Zealand, TAWA
Fairy: Persian, PERI
Family: Italian, ESTE
Far (comb. form), TELE
Farewell, VALE
Father (French), PERE
Fennel: Philippine, ANIS
Fever: Malarial, AGUE
Fiber: East Indian, JUTE
Firn, NEVE
Fish: Carplike, DACE
  Hawaiian, ULUA
  Herringlike, SHAD
  Mackerellike, CERO
  Marine, HAKE
  Sea, LING, MERO, OPAH
  Spiny-finned, GOBY
Food: Tropical, TARO
Foot: Metric, IAMB
Formerly, ERST
Founder: Of Carthage, DIDO
France: Southern, MIDI
Furze, ULEX
Gaelic, ERSE
Gaiter, SPAT
Game: Card, FARO, SKAT
Garlic: European wild, MOLY
Garment: Hindu, SARI
  Roman, TOGA
Gazelle, CORA

Gem, JADE, ONYX, OPAL, RUBY
Genus: Amphibians (incl. frogs), RANA
Amphibians (incl. tree toads), HYLA
Antelopes, ORYX
Auks, ALCA, URIA
Bees, APIS
Birds (American ostriches), RHEA
Birds (cranes), CRUS
Birds (magpies), PICA
Birds (peacocks), PAVO
Cetaceans, INIA
Ducks (incl. mallards), ANAS
Fishes (burbots), LOTA
Fishes (incl. bowfins), AMIA
Geese (snow geese), CHEN
Gulls, XEMA
Herbs, ARUM, GEUM
Insects (water scorpions), NEPA
Lilies, ALOE
Mammals (mankind), HOMO
Orchids, DISA
Owls, ASIO, BUBO, OTUS
Palms, NIPA
Sea birds, SULA
Sheep, OVIS
Shrubs, Eurasian, ULEX
Shrubs (hollies), ILEX
Shrubs (incl. Virginia Willow), ITEA
Shrubs, tropical, EVEA
Snakes (sand snakes), ERYX
Swans, OLOR
Trees, chocolate, COLA
Trees (ebony family), MABA
Trees (incl. maples), ACER
Trees (olives), OLEA
Trees, tropical, EVEA
Turtles, EMYS
Goat: Wild, IBEX, KRAS, TAHR, TAIR, THAR
God: Assyrian, ASUR
Babylonian, ADAD, ADDU, ENKI, ENZU, IRRA, NABU, NEBO, UTUG
Celtic, LLEU, LLEW
Hindu, AGNI, CIVA, DEVA, DEWA, KAMA, RAMA, SIVA, VAYU
Phrygian, ATYS
Semitic, BAAL
Teutonic, HLER
Goddess: Babylonian, ERUA, GULA
Hawaiian, PELE
Hindu, DEVI, KALI, SHRI, VACH
Gooseberry: Hawaiian, POHA
Gourd, PEPO
Grafted (heraldry), ENTE
Grandfather (obsolete), AIEL
Grandparents: Pertaining to, AVAL
Grass: Hawaiian, HILO
Gray (French), GRIS
Green (heraldry), VERT
Groom: Indian, SYCE
Half (prefix), DEMI, HEMI, SEMI
Hamlet, DORP
Hammer-head: Part of, PEEN
Handle, ANSA
Harp: Japanese, KOTO
Hartebeest, ASSE, TORA
Hautboy, OBOE
Hawk: Taken from nest (falconry), EYAS
Hearing (law), OYER
Heater: For liquids, ETNA
Herb: Aromatic, ANET, DILL
Fabulous, MOLY
Perennial, GEUM, SEGO
Pot, WORT
Used for blue dye, WADE, WOAD
Hill: Flat-topped, MESA
Sand, DENE, DUNE
Hoarfrost, RIME
Hog: Immature female, GILT
Holly, ILEX
House: Cow, BYRE
(Spanish), CASA
Ice: Floating, FLOE
Image, ICON, IKON
Incarnation: Of Vishnu, RAMA
Indian: Algonquian, CREE, SAUK
Central American, MAYA
Iroquoian, ERIE
Mexican, CORA
Peruvian, CANA, INCA, MORO
Shoshonean, HOPI
Siouan, OTOE
Southwestern, HOPI, PIMA, YUMA, ZUNI
Insect: Immature, PUPA
Instrument: Stringed, LUTE, LYRE
Ireland, EIRE, ERIN
Jacket: English, ETON
Jail (British), GAOL
Jar, OLLA
Judge: Mohammedan, CADI
Juniper: European, CADE
Kiln, OAST, OVEN
King: British legendary, LUDD, NUDD
Kiss, BUSS
Knife: Philippine, BOLO
Koran: Section of, SURA
Laborer: Spanish American, PEON
Lake: Mountain, TARN
(Scotch), LOCH
Lamp: Miner's, DAVY
Landing place: Indian, GHAT
Language: Buddhist, PALI
Japanese, AINU
Latvian, LETT
Layer: Of iris, UVEA
Leaf: Palm, OLAY, OLLA
Legislature: Ukrainian, RADA
Lemur, LORI
Leopard, PARD
Let it stand, STET
Letter: Greek, BETA, IOTA, ZETA
Hebrew, AYIN, BETH, CAPH, KOPH, RESH, SHIN, TETH, YODH
Papal, BULL
Lily, ALOE
Literature: Hindu sacred, VEDA
Lizard, GILA
Monitor, URAN
Loquat, BIWA
Magistrate: Genoese or Venetian, DOGE
Man (Latin), HOMO
Mark: Omission, DELE
armoset: South American, MICO
Meadow: Fertile, VEGA
Measure: Electric, VOLT, WATT
Force, DYNE
Hebrew, OMER
Printing, PICA
Spanish or Portuguese, VARA
Swiss land, IMMI
Medley, OLIO
Merganser, SMEW
Milk (French), LAIT
Molding, GULA
Curved, OGEE
Mongoose: Crab-eating, URVA
Monk: Tibetan, LAMA
Monkey: African, MONA, WAAG
Ceylonese, MAHA
Cochin-China, DOUC
South American, SAKI, TITI
Monkshood, ATIS
Month: Jewish, ADAR, ELUL, IYAR
Mother (French), MERE
Mountain: Thessaly, OSSA
Mouse: Meadow, VOLE
Mythology: Norse, EDDA
Nail (French), CLOU
Native: Philippine, MORO
Nest: Of pheasants, NIDE
Network, RETE
No (German), NEIN
Noble: Mohammedan, AMIR
Notice: Death, OBIT
Novel: By Zola, NANA
Nursemaid: Oriental AMAH, AYAH, EYAH
Nut: Philippine, PILI
Oak: Holm, ILEX
Oil (comb. form), OLEO
Ostrich: American, RHEA
Oven, KILN, OAST
Owl: Barn, LULU
Ox: Celebes wild, ANOE
Extinct wild, URUS
Palm, ATAP, NIPA, SAGO
Parliament, DIET
Parrot: New Zealand, KAKA
Pass: Indian mountain, GHAT
Passage: Closing (music), CODA
Peach: Clingstone, PAVY
Peasant: Indian, RYOT
Old English, CARL
Pepper: Australasian, KAVA
Perfume, ATAR
Persia, IRAN
Person: Extraordinary, ONER
Pickerel or pike, ESOX
Pitcher, EWER
Plant: Aromatic, NARD
Century, ALOE
Indigo, ANIL
Pepper, KAVA
Platform: Raised, DAIS
Plum: Wild, SLOE
Pods: Vegetable, OKRA, OKRO
Poem: Epic, EPOS
Poet: Persian, OMAR
Roman, OVID
Poison, BANE
Arrow, INEE
Porkfish, SISI
Portico: Greek, STOA
Premium, AGIO
Priest: Mohammedan, IMAM
Prima donna, DIVA
Prong: Fork, TINE
Pseudonym: Lamb's, ELIA
Queen: Carthaginian, DIDO
Hindu, RANI
Rabbit, CONY
Race: Of Japan, AINU
Rail: Ducklike, COOT
North American, SORA
Redshank, CLEE
Refuse: After pressing, MARC
Regiment: Turkish, ALAI
Reliquary, ARCA
Resort: Italian, LIDO
Ridges: Sandy, ASAR, OSAR
River: German, ELBE, ODER
Italian, ADDA
Siberian, LENA
Road: Roman, ITER
Rockfish: California, RENA
Rodent: Mouselike, VOLE
South American, PACA
Rootstock, TARO
Salamander, NEWT
Salmon: Silver, COHO
Young, PARR
Same (Greek), HOMO
(Latin), IDEM
Sauce: Fish, ALEC
School: English, ETON
Seaweed, AGAR, ALGA, KELP
Secular, LAIC
Sediment, SILT
Seed: Dill, ANET
Of vetch, TARE
Serf, ILOT
Sesame, TEEL
Settlement: Eskimo, ETAH
Shark: Atlantic, GATA
European, TOPE
Sheep: Wild, UDAD
Sheltered, ALEE
Shield, EGIS
Ship: Jason's, ARGO
Left side of, PORT
Two-masted, BRIG
Shrine: Buddhist, TOPE
Shrub: New Zealand, TUTU
Sign: Magic, RUNE
Silkworm, ERIA
Skin: Beaver, PLEW

Skink: Egyptian, ADDA
Slave, ESNE
Sloth: Two-toed, UNAU
Smooth, LENE
Snow: Glacial, NEVE
Soapstone, TALC
Society: African secret, EGBO, PORO
Son: Of Seth, ENOS
Song (German), LIED
 Unaccompanied, GLEE
Sound: Lung, RALE
Sour, ACID
Sow: Young, GILT
Spike: Brad-shaped, BROB
Spirit: Buddhist evil, MARA
Stake: Poker, ANTE
Star: Temporary, NOVA
Starch: East Indian, SAGO
Stone: Precious, OPAL
Strap: Bridle, REIN
Strewn (heraldry), SEME
Sweetsop, ATES, ATTA
Sword: Fencing, EPEE, FOIL
Tambourine: African, TAAR
Tapir: Brazilian, ANTA
Tax, CESS
Tea: South American, MATE
Therefore (Latin), ERGO
Thing: Extraordinary, ONER
Three (dice, cards, etc.), TREY
Thrush: Hawaiian, OMAO
Tide, NEAP
Tipster: Racing, TOUT
Tissue, TELA
Title: Etruscan, LARS
 Hindu, BABU
 Indian, RAJA
 Mohammedan, EMIR, IMAM
 Persian, BABA
 Spanish, DONA
 Turkish, AGHA, BABA
Toad: Largest-known, AGUA
 Tree, HYLA
Tool: Cutting, ADZE
Track: Deer, SLOT
Tract: Sandy, DENE
Tree: Apple, SORB
 Central American, EBOE
 East Indian, TEAK
 Eucalyptus, YATE
 Guiana and Trinidad, MORA
 Javanese, UPAS
 Linden, LIME, LINN, TEIL, TILL
 Sandarac, ARAR
 Sassafras, AGUE
 Tamarisk salt, ATLE
Tribe: Moro, SULU
Trout, CHAR
Urchin: Street, ARAB
Vessel: Arab, DHOW
Vestment: Ecclesiastical, COPE
Vetch, TARE
Vine: East Indian, SOMA
Violinist: Famous, AUER
Vortex, EDDY
Wampum, PEAG
Wapiti, STAG
Waste: Allowance for, TRET
Watchman: Indian, MINA
Water (Spanish), AGUA
Waterfall, LINN
Wavy (heraldry), ONDE, UNDE
Wax, CERE
 Chinese, PELA
Weed: Biblical, TARE
Weight: Ancient, MINA
 Danish (pl.), ESER
 East Asian, TAEL
 Greek, MINA
 Siamese, BAHT
Well done (rare), EUGE
Whale, CETE
 Killer, ORCA
 White, HUSE, HUSO
Whirlpool, EDDY
Wife: Of Geraint, ENID
Willow: Virginia, ITEA
Wine, PORT
Winged, ALAR
 (Heraldry), AILE
Wings, ALAE
Withered, SERE
Without (French), SANS
Wool: To comb, CARD
Work, OPUS
Wrong: Civil, TORT
Young: Bring forth, YEAN

Words of Five Letters

Abode of dead: Babylonian, ARALU
Aborigine: Borneo DAYAK
Aftersong, EPODE
Aloe, AGAVE
Animal: Footless, APODE
Ant, EMMET
Antelope: African, ADDAX, BEISA, CAAMA, ELAND, GUIBA,
 ORIBI, TIANG
 Goat, GORAL, SEROW
 Indian, SASIN
 Siberian, SAIGA
Arch: Pointed, OGIVE
Armadillo, APARA, POYOU, TATOU
Arrowroot, ARARU
Artery: Trunk, AORTA
Association: Russian, ARTEL
 Secret, CABAL
Author: English, READE
Automaton, GOLEM, ROBOT
Award: Motion-picture, OSCAR
Basket: Fishing, CREEL
Beer: Russian, KVASS
Bible: Mohammedan, KORAN
Bird: Asian, MINAH, MYNAH
 Indian, SHAMA
 Larklike, PIPIT
 Loonlike, GREBE
 Oscine, VIREO
 South American, AGAMI
 Swimming, GREBE
Black: (French), NOIRE
 (Heraldry), SABLE
Blackbird: European, MERLE, OUSEL, OUZEL
Block: Glacial, SERAC
Blue (heraldry), AZURE
Boat: Eskimo, BIDAR, UMIAK
Bobwhite, COLIN, QUAIL
Bone (comb. form), OSTEO
 Leg, TIBIA
 Thigh, FEMUR
Broom: Twig, BESOM
Brother (French), FRERE
 Moses, AARON
Canoe: Eskimo, BIDAR, KAYAK
Cape: Papal, FANON, ORALE
Caravansary, SERAI
Card: Old playing, TAROT
Caterpillar: New Zealand, AWETO
Catkin, AMENT
Cavity: Stone, GEODE
Cephalopod, SQUID
Cetacean, WHALE
Chariot, ESSED
Cheek: Pertaining to, MALAR
Chieftain: Arab, EMEER
Child (Scotch), BAIRN
Cigar, CLARO
Coating: Seed, TESTA
Cockatoo: Palm, ARARA
Coin: Costa Rican, COLON
 Danish, KRONE
 Ecuadorian, SUCRE
 English, GROAT, PENCE
 French, FRANC
 German, KRONE, TALER
 Hungarian, PENGO
 Icelandic, KRONA
 Indian, RUPEE
 Iraqi, DINAR
 Norwegian, KRONE
 Polish, ZLOTY
 Russian, COPEC, KOPEK, RUBLE
 Swedish, KRONA
 Turkish, ASPER
 Yugoslav, DINAR
Collar: Papal, FANON, ORALE
 Roman, RABAT
Commune: Italian, TREIA
Composition: Choral, MOTET
Compound: Chemical, ESTER
Conceal (law), ELOIN
Council: Ecclesiastical, SYNOD
Court: Anglo-Saxon, GEMOT
 Inner, PATIO
Crest: Mountain, ARETE
Crown: Papal, TIARA
Cuttlefish, SEPIA
Date: Roman, NONES
Decree: Mohammedan, IRADE
 Russian, UKASE
Deposit: Loam, LOESS
Desert: Gobi, SHAMO

Devilfish, MANTA
Disease: Cereals, ERGOT
Disk, PATEN
Dog: Wild, DHOLE, DINGO
Dormouse, LEROT
Drum, TABOR
Duck: Sea, EIDER
Dynasty: Chinese, CHING, LIANG, SHANG
Earthquake, SEISM
Eel, ELVER, MORAY
Ermine: European, STOAT
Ether: Crystalline, APIOL
Fabric: Velvetlike, PANNE
Fabulist, AESOP
Family: Italian, CENCI
Fiber: West Indian, SISAL
Fig: Smyrna, ELEME, ELEMI
Figure: Of speech, TROPE
Finch: European, SERIN
Fish: American small, KILLY
Flower: Garden, ASTER
Friend (Spanish), AMIGO
Fruit: Tropical, MANGO
Fungus: Rye, ERGOT
Furze, GORSE
Gateway, TORAN, TORII
Gem, AGATE, BERYL, PEARL, TOPAZ
Genus: Barnacles, LEPAS
  Bears, URSUS
  Birds (loons), GAVIA
  Birds (nuthatches), SITTA
  Cats, FELIS
  Dogs, CANIS
  Fishes (chiros), ELOPS
  Fishes (perch), PERCA
  Geese, ANSER
  Grasses, STIPA
  Grasses (incl. oats), AVENA
  Gulls, LARUS
  Hares, rabbits, LEPUS
  Hawks, BUTEO
  Herbs, old world, INULA
  Herbs, trailing or climbing, APIOS
  Herbs, tropical, TACCA, URENA
  Horses, EQUUS
  Insects (olive flies), DACUS
  Lice, plant, APHIS
  Lichens, USNEA
  Lizards, AGAMA
  Moles, TALPA
  Mollusks, OLIVA
  Monkeys, CEBUS
  Palms, ARECA
  Pigeons, GOURA
  Plants (amaryllis family), AGAVE
  Ruminants (goats), CAPRA
  Shrubs, Asiatic, SABIA
  Shrubs (heath), ERICA
  Shrubs (incl. raspberry), RUBUS
  Shrubs, tropical, IXORA, TREMA, URENA
  Ticks, ARGAS
  Trees (of elm family), TREMA, ULMUS
  Trees, tropical, IXORA, TREMA
Goat: Bezoar, PASAN
God: Assyrian, ASHIR, ASHUR, ASSUR
  Babylonian, DAGAN, SIRIS
  Gaelic, DAGDA
  Hindu, BHAGA, INDRA, SHIVA
  Japanese, EBISU
  Philistine, DAGON
  Phrygian, ATTIS
  Teutonic, AEGIR, GYMIR
  Welsh, DYLAN
Goddess: Babylonian, ISTAR, NANAI
  Hindu, DURGA, GAURI, SHREE
Group: Of six, HEXAD
Grove: Sacred to Diana, NEMUS
Growing out, ENATE
Guitar: Hindu, SITAR
Gull: PEWEE, PEWIT
Hartebeest, CAAMA
Headdress: Jewish or Persian, TIARA
  Liturgical, MITER, MITRE
Heath, ERICA
Herb: Grasslike marsh, SEDGE
Heron, EGRET
Hog: Young, SHOAT, SHOTE
Image, EIKON
Indian: Cariban, ARARA
  Iroquoian, HURON
  Mexican, AZTEC, OPATA, OTOMI
  Muskhogean, CREEK
  Siouan, OSAGE, TETON
  Spanish American, ARARA, CARIB
Inflorescence: Racemose, AMENT
Insect: Immature, LARVA
Intrigue, CABAL
Iris: Yellow, SEDGE
Juniper, GORSE, RETEM
Kidneys: Pertaining to, RENAL
King: British legendary, LLUDD
Kite: European, GLEDE
Kobold, NISSE
Land: Cultivated, ARADA, ARADO
Landholder (Scotch), LAIRD, THANE
Language: Dravidian, TAMIL
Lariat, LASSO, REATA
Laughing, RIANT
Lawgiver: Athenian, DRACO, SOLON
Leaf: Calyx, SEPAL
  Fern, FROND
Lemur, LORIS
Letter: English, AITCH
  Greek, ALPHA, DELTA, GAMMA, KAPPA, OMEGA, SIGMA, THETA
  Hebrew, ALEPH, CHETH, GIMEL, SADHE, ZAYIN
Lichen, USNEA
Lighthouse, PHARE
Lizard: Old World, AGAMA
Loincloth, DHOTI
Louse: Plant, APHID
Macaw: Brazilian, ARARA
Mahogany: Philippine, ALMON
Mammal: Badgerlike, RATEL
  Civetlike, GENET
  Giraffelike, OKAPI
  Raccoonlike, COATI
Man (French), HOMME
Marble, AGATE
Mark: Insertion, CARET
Market place: Greek, AGORA
Marsupial: Australian, KOALA
Measure: Electric, FARAD, HENRY
  Energy, JOULE
  Metric, LITER, STERE
  Printing, AGATE
  Russian, VERST
Mixture: Smelting, MATTE
Mohicans: Last of, UNCAS
Molding: Convex, OVOLO, TORUS
Mole, TALPA
Monkey: African, PATAS
  Capuchin, SAJOU
  Howling, ARABA
Monkshood, ATEES
Month: Jewish, NISAN, SIVAN, TEBET
Museum (French), MUSEE
Musketeer, ATHOS
Native: Aleutian, ALEUT
  New Zealand, MAORI
Neckpiece: Ecclesiastical, AMICE
Nerve (comb. form), NEURO
Nest: Eagle's or hawk's, AERIE
  Insect's, NIDUS
Net: Fishing, SEINE
Newsstand, KIOSK
Nitrogen, AZOTE
Noble: Mohammedan, AMEER
Nodule: Stone, GEODE
Nostrils, NARES
Notched irregularly, EROSE
Nymph: Mohammedan, HOURI
Official: Roman, EDILE
Oleoresin, ELEMI
Opening: Mouthlike, STOMA
Oration: Funeral, ELOGE
Ostiole, STOMA
Page: Left-hand, VERSO
  Right-hand, RECTO
Palm, ARECA, BETEL
Park: Colorado, ESTES
Perfume, ATTAR

Philosopher: Greek, PLATO
Pillar: Stone, STELA, STELE
Pinnacle: Glacial, SERAC
Plain, LLANO
Plant: Century, AGAVE
Climbing, LIANA
Dwarf, CUMIN
East Asian perennial, RAMIE
Medicinal, SENNA
Mustard family, CRESS
Plate: Communion, PATEN
Poem: Lyric, EPODE
Point: Lowest, NADIR
Poplar, ABELE, ALAMO, ASPEN
Porridge: Spanish American, ATOLE
Post: Stair, NEWEL
Priest: Mohammedan, IMAUM
Protozoan, AMEBA
Queen: (French), REINE
Hindu, RANEE
Rabbit, CONEY
Rail, CRAKE
Red (heraldry), GULES
Religion: Moslem, ISLAM
Resin, ELEMI
Revoke (law), ADEEM
Rich man, MIDAS, NABOB
Ridge: Sandy, ESKAR, ESKER
River: French, LOIRE, SEINE
Rockfish: California, REINA
Rootstock: Fragrant, ORRIS
Ruff: Female, REEVE
Sack: Pack, KYACK
Salt: Ethereal, ESTER
Saltpeter, NITER, NITRE
Salutation: Eastern, SALAM
Sandpiper: Old World, TEREK
Scented, OLENT
School: Fish, SHOAL
French public, LYCEE
Scriptures: Mohammedan, KORAN
Seaweeds, ALGAE
Seed: Aromatic, ANISE
Seraglio, HAREM, SERAI
Serf, HELOT
Sheep: Wild, AUDAD
Sheeplike, OVINE
Shield, AEGIS
Shoe: Wooden, SABOT
Shoots: Pickled bamboo, ACHAR
Shot: Billiard, CAROM, MASSE
Shrine: Buddhist, STUPA
Shrub: Burning bush, WAHOO
Ornamental evergreen, TOYON
Used in tanning, SUMAC
Silk: Watered, MOIRE
Sister (French), SOEUR
(Latin), SOROR
Six: Group of, HEXAD
Skeleton: Marine, CORAL
Slave, HELOT
Snake, ABOMA, ADDER, COBRA, RACER
Soldier: French, POILU
Indian, SEPOY
Sour, ACERB
Spirit: Air, ARIEL
Staff: Shepherd's, CROOK
Starwort, ASTER
Steel (German), STAHL
Stockade: Russian, ETAPE
Stop (nautical), AVAST
Storehouse, ETAPE
Subway: Parisian, METRO
Tapestry, ARRAS
Tea: Paraguayan, YERBA
Temple: Hawaiian, HEIAU
Terminal: Positive, ANODE
Theater: Greek, ODEON, ODEUM
Then (French), ALORS
Thread: Surgical, SETON
Thrush: Wilson's, VEERY
Title: Hindu, BABOO
Indian, RAJAH, SAHEB, SAHIB
Mohammedan, EMEER, IMAUM
Tree: Buddhist sacred, PIPAL
East Indian cotton, SIMAL
Hickory, PECAN
Light-wooded, BALSA
Malayan, TERAP
Mediterranean, CAROB
Mexican, ABETO
Mexican pine, OCOTE
New Zealand, MAIRE
Philippine, ALMON
Rain, SAMAN
South American, UMBRA
Tamarack, LARCH
Tamarisk salt, ATLEE
West Indian, ACANA
Trout, CHARR
Troy, ILION, ILIUM
Twin: Siamese, CHANG
Vestment: Ecclesiastical, STOLE
Violin: Famous, AMATI, STRAD
Volcano: Mud, SALSE
Wampum, PEAGE
War cry: Greek, ALALA
Wavy (heraldry), UNDEE
Weight: Jewish, GERAH
Wen, TALPA
Wheat, SPELT
Wheel: Persian water, NORIA
Whitefish, CISCO
Willow, OSIER
Window: Bay, ORIEL
Wine, MEDOC, RHINE, TINTA, TOKAY
Winged, ALATE
Woman (French), FEMME
Year: Excess of solar over lunar, EPACT
Zoroastrian, PARSI

Words of Six or More Letters

Agave, MAGUEY
Alkaloid: Crystalline, ESERIN, ESERINE
Alligator, CAYMAN
Amphibole, EDENITE, URALITE
Ant: White, TERMITE
Antelope: African, DIKDIK, DUIKER, GEMSBOK, IMPALA, KOODOO
European, CHAMOIS
Indian, NILGAI, NILGAU, NILGHAI, NILGHAU
Ape: Asian or East Indian, GIBBON
Appendage: Leaf, STIPEL, STIPULE
Armadillo, PELUDO, TATOUAY
Arrowroot, ARARAO
Ascetic: Jewish, ESSENE
Ass: Asian wild, ONAGER
Avatar: Of Vishnu, KRISHNA
Babylonian, ELAMITE
Badge: Shoulder, EPAULET
Baldness, ALOPECIA
Barracuda, SENNET
Bark: Aromatic, SINTOC
Bearlike, URSINE
Beetle, ELATER
Bible: Zoroastrian, AVESTA
Bird: Sea, PETREL
South American, SERIEMA
Wading, AVOCET, AVOSET
Bone: Leg, FIBULA
Branched, RAMATE
Brother (Latin), FRATER
Bunting: European, ORTOLAN
Call: Trumpet, SENNET
Canoe: Eskimo, BAIDAR, OOMIAK
Caravansary, IMARET
Cat: Asian or African, CHEETAH
Leopardlike, OCELOT
Cenobite: Jewish, ESSENE
Centerpiece: Table, EPERGNE

Cetacean, DOLPHIN, PORPOISE
Chariot, ESSEDA, ESSEDE
Chief: Seminole, OSCEOLA
Claim: Release as (law), REMISE
Clock: Water, CLEPSYDRA
Cloud, CUMULUS, NIMBUS
Coach: French hackney, FIACRE
Coin: Czech, KORUNA
  Ethiopian, TALARI
  Finnish, MARKKA
  German, THALER
  Greek, DRACHMA
  Haitian, GOURDE
  Honduran, LEMPIRA
  Hungarian, FORINT
  Indo-Chinese, PIASTER
  Netherlands, GUILDER
  Panamanian, BALBOA
  Paraguayan, GUARANI
  Portuguese, ESCUDO
  Russian, COPECK, KOPECK, ROUBLE
  Spanish, PESETA
  Venezuelan, BOLIVAR
Communion: Last holy, VIATICUM
Conceal (law), ELOIGN
Confection, PRALINE
Construction: Sentence, SYNTAX
Convexity: Shaft of column, ENTASIS
Court: Anglo-Saxon, GEMOTE
Cow: Sea, DUGONG, MANATEE
Cylindrical, TERETE
Dagger, STILETTO
  Malay, CREESE, KREESE
Date: Roman, CALENDS, KALENDS
Deer, CARIBOU, WAPITI
Disease: Plant, ERINOSE
Doorkeeper, OSTIARY
Dragonflies: Order of, ODANATA
Drink: Of gods, NECTAR
Drum: TABOUR
  Moorish, ATABAL, ATTABAL
Duck: Fish-eating, MERGANSER
  Sea, SCOTER
Dynasty: Chinese, MANCHU
Eel, CONGER
Edit, REDACT
Envelope: Flower, PERIANTH
Eskimo, AMERIND
Ether: Crystalline, APIOLE
Excuse (law), ESSOIN
Eyespots, OCELLI
Fabric, ESTAMENE, ESTAMIN, ETAMINE
Falcon: European, KESTREL
Figure: Used as column, CARYATID, TELAMON
Fine: For punishment, AMERCE
Fish: Asian fresh-water, GOURAMI
  Pikelike, BARRACUDA
Five: Group of, PENTAD
Fly: African, TSETSE
Foot: Metric, ANAPEST, IAMBUS
Foxlike, VULPINE
Frying pan, SPIDER
Fur, KARAKUL
Galley: Greek or Roman, BIREME, TRIREME
Game: Card, ECARTE
Garment: Greek, CHLAMYS
Gateway, GOPURA, TORANA
Genus: Birds (ravens, crows), CORVUS
  Eels, CONGER
  Fishes, ANABAS
  Foxes, VULPES
  Herbs, ANEMONE
  Insects, CICADA
  Lemurs, GALAGO
  Mints (incl. catnip), NEPETA
  Mollusks, ANOMIA, ASTARTE, TEREDO
  Mollusks (incl. oysters), OSTREA
  Monkeys (spider monkeys), ATELES
  Thrushes (incl. robins), TURDUS
  Trees (of elm family), CELTIS
  Trees (inc. dogwood), CORNUS
  Trees, tropical American, SAPOTA
  Wrens, NANNUS
Gibbon, SIAMANG, WOUWOU
Gland: Salivary, RACEMOSE
Goat: Bezoar, PASANG
Goatlike, CAPRINE
God: Assyrian, ASHSHUR, ASSHUR
  Babylonian, BABBAR, MARDUK, MERODACH, NANNAR, NERGAL, SHAMASH
  Hindu, BRAHMA, KRISHNA, VISHNU
  Tahitian, TAAROA
Goddess: Babylonian, ISHTAR
  Hindu, CHANDI, HAIMAVATI, LAKSHMI, PARVATI, SARASVATI, SARASWATI
Government, POLITY
Governor: Persian, SATRAP
Grandson (Scotch), NEPOTE
Group: Of five, PENTAD
  Of nine, ENNEAD
  Of seven, HEPTAD
Hare: in first year, LEVERET
Harpsichord, SPINET
Herb: Alpine, EDELWEISS
  Chinese, GINSENG
  South African, FREESIA
Hermit, EREMITE
Hero: Legendary, PALADIN
Heron, BITTERN
Horselike, EQUINE
Hound: Short-legged, BEAGLE
House (French), MAISON
Idiot, CRETIN
Implement: Stone, NEOLITH
Incarnation: Hindu, AVATAR
Indian, APACHE, COMANCHE, PAIUTE, SENECA
Inn: Turkish, IMARET
Insects: Order of, DIPTERA
Instrument: Japanese banjolike, SAMISEN
  Musical, CLAVIER, SPINET
Interstice, AREOLA
Ironwood, COLIMA
Juniper: Old Testament, RAETAM
Kettledrum, ATABAL
King: Fairy, OBERON
Kneecap, PATELLA
Knife, MACHETE
Langur: Sumatran, SIMPAI
Legislature: Spanish, CORTES
Lemur: African, GALAGO
  Madagascar, AYEAYE
Letter: Greek, EPSILON, LAMBDA, OMICRON, UPSILON
  Hebrew, DALETH, LAMEDH, SAMEKH
Lighthouse, PHAROS
Lizard, IGUANA
Llama, ALPACA
Lockjaw, TETANUS
Locust, CICADA, CICALA
Macaw: Brazilian, MARACAN
Maid: Of Astolat, ELAINE
Mammal: Madagascar, TENDRAC, TENREC
Man (Spanish), HOMBRE
Marmoset: South American, TAMARIN
Marsupial, BANDICOOT, WOMBAT
Massacre, POGROM
Mayor: Spanish, ALCALDE
Measure: Electric, AMPERE, COULOMB, KILOWATT
Medicine: Quack, NOSTRUM
Member: Religious order, CENOBITE
Molasses, TREACLE
Monkey: African, GRIVET, NISNAS
  Asian, LANGUR
  Philippine, MACHIN
  South American, PINCHE, SAIMIRI, SAMIRI, SAPAJOU
Monster, CHIMERA, GORGON
  (Comb. form), TERATO
  Cretan, MINOTAUR
Month: Jewish, HESHVAN, KISLEV, SHEBAT, TAMMUZ, TISHRI, VEADAR
Mountain: Asia Minor, ARARAT
Mulct, AMERCE
Musketeer, ARAMIS, PORTHOS
Nearsighted, MYOPIC
Net, TRAMMEL
New York City, GOTHAM
Nine: Group of, ENNEAD
Nobleman: Spanish, GRANDEE
Official: Roman, AEDILE
Onyx: Mexican, TECALI
Order: Dragonflies, ODANATA
  Insects, DIPTERA
Organ: Plant, PISTIL

Ornament: Shoulder, EPAULET
Overcoat: Military, CAPOTE
Ox: Wild, BANTENG
Oxidation: Bronze or copper, PATINA
Paralysis: Incomplete, PARESIS
Pear: Alligator, AVOCADO
Persimmon: Mexican, CHAPOTE
Pipe: Peace, CALUMET
Plaid (Scotch), TARTAN
Plain, PAMPAS, STEPPE, TUNDRA
Plant: Buttercup family, ANEMONE
  Century, MAGUEY
  On rocks, LICHEN
Plowing: Fit for, ARABLE
Poem: Heroic, EPOPEE
  Six-lined, SESTET
Point: Highest, ZENITH
Potion: Love, PHILTER, PHILTRE
Protozoan, AMOEBA
Punish, AMERCE
Purple (heraldry), PURPURE
Queen: Fairy, TITANIA
Race: Skiing, SLALOM
Rat, BANDICOOT, LEMMING
Retort, RIPOST, RIPOSTE
Ring: Harness, TERRET
  Little, ANNULET
Rodent: Jumping, JERBOA
  Spanish American, AGOUTI, AGOUTY
Sailor: East Indian, LASCAR
Salmon: Young, GRILSE
Salutation: Eastern, SALAAM
Sandpiper, PLOVER
Sandy, ARENOSE
Sapodilla, SAPOTA, SAPOTE
Saw: Surgical, TREPAN
Seven: Group of, HEPTAD
Sexes: Common to both, EPICENE
Shawl: Mexican, SERAPE
Sheathing: Flower, SPATHE
Sheep: Wild, AOUDAD, ARGALI
Shipworm, TEREDO
Shoes: Mercury's winged, TALARIA
Shortening: Syllable, SYSTOLE
Shrub, SPIRAEA
Sickle-shaped, FALCATE
Silver (heraldry), ARGENT
Snake, ANACONDA
Speech: Loss of, APHASIA
Spiral, HELICAL
Staff: Bishop's, CROSIER, CROZIER
Stalk: Plant, PETIOLE
State: Swiss, CANTON
Studio, ATELIER
Swan: Young, CYGNET
Swimming, NATANT
Sword-shaped, ENSATE
Terminal: Negative, CATHODE
Third (music), TIERCE
Thrust: Fencing, RIPOST, RIPOSTE
Tile: Pertaining to, TEGULAR
Tomb: Empty, CENOTAPH
Tooth (comb. form), ODONTO
Tower: Mohammedan, MINARET
Tree: African timber, BAOBAB
  Black gum, TUPELO
  East Indian, MARGOSA
  Locust, ACACIA
  Malayan, SINTOC
  Marmalade, SAPOTE
Urn: Tea, SAMOVAR
Vehicle, LANDAU, TROIKA
Verbose, PROLIX
Viceroy: Egyptian, KHEDIVE
Vulture: American, CONDOR
Warehouse (French), ENTREPOT
Whale: White, BELUGA
Whirlpool, VORTEX
Will: Addition to, CODICIL
  Having left, TESTATE
Wind, CHINOOK, MONSOON, SIMOOM, SIMOON, SIROCCO
Window: In roof, DORMER
Wine, BARBERA, BURGUNDY, CABERNET, CHABLIS, CHIANTI, CLARET, MUSCATEL, RIESLING, SAUTERNE, SHERRY, ZINFANDEL
Wolfish, LUPINE
Woman: Boisterous, TERMAGANT
Woolly, LANATE
Workshop, ATELIER
Zoroastrian, PARSEE

Old-Testament Names

(We do not pretend that this list is all-inclusive. We include only those names which in our opinion one meets most often in crossword puzzles.)

Aaron: First high priest of Jews; son of Amram; brother of Miriam and Moses; father of Abihu, Eleazer, Ithamar, and Nadab.

Abel: Son of Adam; slain by Cain.

Abigail: Wife of Nabal; later, wife of David.

Abihu: Son of Aaron.

Abimelech: King of Gerar.

Abner: Commander of army of Saul and Ishbosheth; slain by Joab.

Abraham (or Abram): Patriarch; forefather of the Jews; son of Terah; husband of Sarah; father of Isaac and Ishmael.

Absalom: Son of David and Maacah; revolted against David; slain by Joab.

Achish: King of Gath; gave refuge to David.

Achsa (or Achsah): Daughter of Caleb; wife of Othniel.

Adah: Wife of Lamech.

Adam: First man; husband of Eve; father of Cain, Abel, and Seth.

Adonijah: Son of David and Haggith.

Agag: King of Amalek; spared by Saul; slain by Samuel.

Ahasuerus: King of Persia; husband of Vashti and, later, Esther; sometimes identified with Xerxes the Great.

Ahijah: Prophet; foretold accession of Jeroboam.

Ahinoam: Wife of David.

Amasa: Commander of army of David; slain by Joab.

Amnon: Son of David and Ahinoam; ravished Tamar; slain by Absalom.

Amram: Husband of Jochebed; father of Aaron, Miriam and Moses.

Asenath: Wife of Joseph.

Asher: Son of Jacob and Zilpah.

Balaam: Prophet; rebuked by his donkey for cursing God.

Barak: Jewish captain; associated with Deborah.

Baruch: Secretary to Jeremiah.

Bathsheba: Wife of Uriah; later, wife of David.

Belshazzar: Crown prince of Babylon.

Benaiah: Warrior of David; proclaimed Solomon King.

Ben-Hadad: Name of several kings of Damascus.

Benjamin: Son of Jacob and Rachel.

Bezaleel: Chief architect of tabernacle.

Bilbah: Servant of Rachel; mistress of Jacob.

Bildad: Comforter of Job.

Boaz: Husband of Ruth; father of Obed.

Cain: Son of Adam and Eve; slayer of Abel; father of Enoch.

Cainan: Son of Enos.

Caleb: Spy sent out by Moses to visit Canaan; father of Achsa.

Canaan: Son of Ham.

Chilion: Son of Elimelech; husband of Orpah.

Cush: Son of Ham; father of Nimrod.

Dan: Son of Jacob and Bilhah.

Daniel: Prophet; saved from lions by God.

Deborah: Hebrew prophetess; helped Israelites conquer Canaanites.

Delilah: Mistress and betrayer of Samson.

Elam: Son of Shem.

Eleazar: Son of Aaron; succeeded him as high priest.

Eli: High priest and judge; teacher of Samuel; father of Hophni and Phinehas.

Eliakim: Chief minister of Hezekiah.

Eliezer: Servant of Abraham.

Elihu: Comforter of Job.

Elijah (or Elias): Prophet; went to heaven in chariot of fire.

Elimelech: Husband of Naomi; father of Chilion and Mahlon.

Eliphaz: Comforter of Job.

Elisha (or Eliseus): Prophet; successor of Elijah.

Elkanah: Husband of Hannah; father of Samuel.

Enoch: Son of Cain.

Enoch: Father of Methuselah.

Enos: Son of Seth; father of Cainan.

Ephraim: Son of Joseph.

Esau: Son of Isaac and Rebecca; sold his birthright to his brother Jacob.

Esther: Jewish wife of Ahasuerus; saved Jews from Haman's plotting.

Eve: First woman; created from rib of Adam.

Ezra (or Esdras): Hebrew scribe and priest.

Gad: Son of Jacob and Zilpah.

Gehazi: Servant of Elisha.

Gideon: Israelite hero; defeated Midianites.

Goliath: Philistine giant; slain by David.

Hagar: Handmaid of Sarah; concubine of Abraham; mother of Ishmael.

Haggith: Mother of Adonijah.

Ham: Son of Noah; father of Cush, Mizraim, Phut, and Canaan.

Haman: Chief minister of Ahasuerus; hanged on gallows prepared for Mordecai.

Hannah: Wife of Elkanah; mother of Samuel.

Hanun: King of Ammonites.

Haran: Brother of Abraham; father of Lot.

Hazael: King of Damascus.

Hephzi-Bah: Wife of Hezekiah; mother of Mannaseh.

Hiram: King of Tyre.

Holofernes: General of Nebuchadnezzar; slain by Judith.

Hophni: Son of Eli.

Isaac: Hebrew patriarch; son of Abraham and Sarah; half brother of Ishmael; husband of Rebecca; father of Esau and Jacob.

Ishmael: Son of Abraham and Hagar; half brother of Isaac.

Issachar: Son of Jacob and Leah.

Ithamar: Son of Aaron.

Jabal: Son of Lamech and Adah.

Jabin: King of Hazor.

Jacob: Hebrew patriarch, founder of Israel; son of Isaac and Rebecca; husband of Leah and Rachel; father of Asher, Benjamin, Dan, Gad, Issachar, Joseph, Judah, Levi, Naphtali, Reuben, Simeon, and Zebulun.

Jael: Slayer of Sisera.

Japheth: Son of Noah.

Jehoiada: High priest; husband of Jehoshabeath; revolted against Athaliah and made Joash King of Judah.

Jehoshabeath (or Jehosheba): Daughter of Jehoram of Judah; wife of Jehoiada.

Jephthah: Judge in Israel; sacrificed his only daughter because of vow.

Jesse: Son of Obed; father of David.

Jethro: Midianite priest; father of Zipporah.

Jezebel: Phoenician princess; wife of Ahab; mother of Ahaziah, Athaliah, and Jehoram.

Joab: Commander in chief under David; slayer of Abner, Absalom, and Amasa.

Job: Patriarch; underwent many afflictions; comforted by Bildad, Elihu, Eliphaz and Zophar.

Jochebed: Wife of Amram.

Jonah: Prophet; cast into sea and swallowed by great fish.

Jonathan: Son of Saul; friend of David.

Joseph: Son of Jacob and Rachel; sold into slavery by his brothers; husband of Asenath; father of Ephraim and Manassah.

Joshua: Successor of Moses; son of Nun.

Jubal: Son of Lamech and Adah.

Judah: Son of Jacob and Leah.

Judith: Slayer of Holofernes.

Kish: Father of Saul.

Laban: Father of Leah and Rachel.

Lamech: Son of Methuselah; father of Noah.

Lamech: Husband of Adah and Zillah; father of Jabal, Jubal, and Tubal-Cain.

Leah: Daughter of Laban; wife of Jacob.

Levi: Son of Jacob and Leah.

Lot: Son of Haran; escaped destruction of Sodom.

Maacah: Mother of Absalom and Tamar.

Mahlon: Son of Elimelech; first husband of Ruth.

Manasseh: Son of Joseph.

Melchizedek: King of Salem.

Methuselah: Patriarch; son of Enoch; father of Lamech.

Michal: Daughter of Saul; wife of David.

Miriam: Prophetess; daughter of Amram; sister of Aaron and Moses.

Mizraim: Son of Ham.

Mordecai: Uncle of Esther; with her aid, saved Jews from Haman's plotting.

Moses: Prophet and lawgiver; son of Amram; brother of Aaron and Miriam; husband of Zipporah.

Naaman: Syrian captain; cured of leprosy by Elisha.

Nabal: Husband of Abigail.

Naboth: Owner of vineyard; stoned to death because he would not sell it to Ahab.

Nadab: Son of Aaron.

Nahor: Father of Terah.

Naomi: Wife of Elimelech; mother-in-law of Ruth.

Naphtali: Son of Jacob and Bilhah.

Nathan: Prophet; reproved David for causing Uriah's death.

Nebuchadnezzar (or Nebuchadrezzar): King of Babylon; destroyer of Jerusalem.

Nehemiah: Jewish leader; empowered by Artaxerxes to rebuild Jerusalem.

Nimrod: Mighty hunter; son of Cush.

Noah: Patriarch; Son of Lamech; escaped Deluge by building Ark; father of Ham, Japheth and Shem.

Nun (or Non): Father of Joshua.

Obed: Son of Boaz; father of Jesse.

Og: King of Bashan.

Orpah: Wife of Chilion.

Othniel: Kenezite; judge of Israel; husband of Achsa.

Phinehas: Son of Eleazer.

Phinehas: Son of Eli.

Phut (or Put): Son of Ham.

Potiphar: Egyptian official; bought Joseph.

Rachel: Wife of Jacob.

Rebecca (or Rebekah): Wife of Isaac.

Reuben: Son of Jacob and Leah.

Ruth: Wife of Mahlon, later of Boaz; daughter-in-law of Naomi.

Samson: Judge of Israel; famed for strength; betrayed by Delilah.

Samuel: Hebrew judge and prophet; son of Elkanah.

Sarah (or Sara, Sarai): Wife of Abraham.

Sennacherib: King of Assyria.

Seth: Son of Adam; father of Enos.

Shem: Son of Noah; father of Elam.

Simeon: Son of Jacob and Leah.

Sisera: Canaanite captain; slain by Jael.

Tamar: Daughter of David and Maachah; ravished by Amnon.

Terah: Son of Nahor; father of Abraham.

Tubal-Cain: Son of Lamech and Zillah.

Uriah: Husband of Bathsheba; sent to death in battle by David.

Vashti: Wife of Ahasuerus; set aside by him.

Zadok: High priest during David's reign.

Zebulun (or Zabulon): Son of Jacob and Leah.

Zillah: Wife of Lamech.

Zilpah: Servant of Leah; mistress of Jacob.

Zipporah: Daughter of Jethro; wife of Moses.

Zophar: Comforter of Job.

Kings of Judah and Israel

Kings Before Division of Kingdom

Saul: First King of Israel; son of Kish; father of Ish-Bosheth, Jonathan and Michal.

Ish-Bosheth (or Eshbaal): King of Israel; son of Saul.

David: King of Judah; later of Israel; son of Jesse; husband of Abigail, Ahinoam, Bathsheba, Michal, etc.; father of Absalom, Adonijah, Amnon, Solomon, Tamar, etc.

Solomon: King of Israel and Judah; son of David; father of Rehoboam.

Rehoboam: Son of Solomon; during his reign the kingdom was divided into Judah and Israel.

Kings of Judah (Southern Kingdom)

Rehoboam: First King.

Abijah (or Abijam or Abia): Son of Rehoboam.

Asa: Probably son of Abijah.

Jehoshaphat: Son of Asa.

Jehoram (or Joram): Son of Jehoshaphat; husband of Athaliah.

Ahaziah: Son of Jehoram and Athaliah.

Athaliah: Daughter of King Ahab of Israel and Jezebel; wife of Jehoram.

Joash (or Jehoash): Son of Ahaziah.

Amaziah: Son of Joash.

Uzziah (or Azariah): Son of Amaziah.

Jotham: Regent, later King; son of Uzziah.

Ahaz: Son of Jotham.

Hezekiah: Son of Ahaz; husband of Hephzi-Bah.

Manasseh: Son of Hezekiah and Hephzi-Bah.

Amon: Son of Manasseh.

Josiah (or Josias): Son of Amon.

Jehoahaz (or Joahaz): Son of Josiah.

Jehoiachin: Son of Jehoiakim.

Jehoiakim: Son of Josiah.

Zedekiah: Son of Josiah; kingdom overthrown by Babylonians under Nebuchadnezzar.

Kings of Israel (Northern Kingdom)

Jeroboam I: Led secession of Israel.

Nadab: Son of Jeroboam I.

Baasha: Overthrew Nadab.

Elah: Son of Baasha.

Zimri: Overthrew Elah.

Omri: Overthrew Zimri.

Ahab: Son of Omri; husband of Jezebel.

Ahaziah: Son of Ahab.

Jehoram (or Joram): Son of Ahab.

Jehu: Overthrew Jehoram.

Jehoahaz (or Joahaz): Son of Jehu.

Jehoash (or Joash): Son of Jehoahaz.

Jeroboam II: Son of Jehoash.

Zechariah: Son of Jeroboam II.

Shallum: Overthrew Zechariah.

Menahem: Overthrew Shallum.

Pekahiah: Son of Menahem.

Pekah: Overthrew Pekahiah.

Hoshea: Overthrew Pekah; kingdom overthrown by Assyrians under Sargon II.

Prophets

Major.—Isaiah, Jeremiah, Ezekiel, Daniel.

Minor.—Hosea, Obadiah, Nahum, Haggai, Joel, Jonah, Habakkuk, Zechariah, Amos, Micah, Zephaniah, Malachi.

Greek and Roman Mythology

(Most of the Greek deities were adopted by the Romans, although in many cases there was a change of name. In the list below, information is given under the Greek name; the name in parentheses is the Latin equivalent. However, all Latin names are listed with cross references to the Greek ones. In addition, there are several deities which were exclusively Roman.)

Acheron: *See* Rivers.

Achilles: Greek warrior; slew Hector at Troy; slain by Paris, who wounded him in his vulnerable heel.

Actaeon: Hunter; surprised Artemis bathing; changed by her to stag and killed by his dogs.

Admetus: King of Thessaly; his wife, Alcestis, offered to die in his place.

Adonis: Beautiful youth loved by Aphrodite.

Aeacus: One of three judges of dead in Hades; son of Zeus.

Aeëtes: King of Colchis; father of Medea; keeper of Golden Fleece.

Aegeus: Father of Theseus; believing Theseus killed in Crete, he drowned himself, Aegean Sea named for him.

Aegisthus: Son of Thyestes; slew Atreus; with Clytemnestra, his paramour, slew Agamemnon; slain by Orestes.

Aegyptus: Brother of Danaus; his sons, except Lynceus, slain by Danaides.

Aeneas: Trojan; son of Anchises and Aphrodite; after fall of Troy, led his followers eventually to Italy; loved and deserted Dido.

Aeolus: *See* Winds.

Aesculapius: *See* Asclepius.

Aeson: King of Ioclus; father of Jason; overthrown by his brother Pelias; restored to youth by Medea.

Aether: Personification of sky.

Aethra: Mother of Theseus.

Agamemnon: King of Mycenae; son of Atreus; brother of Menelaus; leader of Greeks against Troy; slain on his return home by Clytemnestra and Aegisthus.

Agiaia: *See* Graces.

Ajax: Greek warrior; killed himself at Troy because Achilles' armor was awarded to Odysseus.

Alcestis: Wife of Admetus; offered to die in his place but saved from death by Hercules.

Alcmene: Wife of Amphitryon; mother by Zeus of Hercules.

Alcyone: *See* Pleiades.

Alecto: *See* Furies.

Alectryon: Youth changed by Ares into cock.

Althaea: Wife of Oeneus; mother of Meleager.

Amazons: Female warriors in Asia Minor; supported Troy against Greeks.

Amor: *See* Eros.

Amphion: Musician; husband of Niobe; charmed stones to build fortifications for Thebes.

Amphitrite: Sea goddess; wife of Poseidon.

Amphitryon: Husband of Alcmene.

Anchises: Father of Aeneas.

Ancile: Sacred shield that fell from heavens; palladium of Rome.

Andraemon: Husband of Dryope.

Andromache: Wife of Hector.

Andromeda: Daughter of Cepheus; chained to cliff for monster to devour; rescued by Perseus.

Anteia: Wife of Proetus; tried to induce Bellerophon to elope with her.

Anteros: God who avenged unrequited love.

Antigone: Daughter of Oedipus; accompanied him to Colonus; performed burial rite for Polynices and hanged herself.

Antinoüs: Leader of suitors of Penelope; slain by Odysseus.

Aphrodite (Venus): Goddess of love and beauty; daughter

of Zeus; mother of Eros.

Apollo: God of beauty, poetry, music; later identified with Helios as Phoebus Apollo; son of Zeus and Leto.

Aquilo: *See* Winds.

Arachne: Maiden who challenged Athena to weaving contest; changed to spider.

Ares (Mars): God of war; son of Zeus and Hera.

Argo: Ship in which Jason and followers sailed to Colchis for Golden Fleece.

Argus: Monster with hundred eyes; slain by Hermes; his eyes placed by Hera into peacock's tail.

Ariadne: Daughter of Minos; aided Theseus in slaying Minotaur; deserted by him on island of Naxos and married to Dionysus.

Arion: Musician; thrown overboard by pirates but saved by dolphin.

Artemis (Diana): Goddess of moon; huntress; twin sister of Apollo.

Asclepius (Aesculapius): Mortal son of Apollo; slain by Zeus for raising dead; later deified as god of medicine. Also known as Asklepios.

Astarte: Phoenician goddess of love; variously identified with Aphrodite, Selene, and Artemis.

Astraea: Goddess of Justice; daughter of Zeus and Themis.

Atalanta: Princess who challenged her suitors to a foot race; Hippomenes won race and married her.

Athena (Minerva): Goddess of wisdom; known poetically as Pallas Athene; sprang fully armed from head of Zeus.

Atlas: Titan; held world on his shoulders as punishment for warring against Zeus; son of Iapetus.

Atreus: King of Mycenae; father of Menelaus and Agamemnon; brother of Thyestes, three of whose sons he slew and served to him at banquet; slain by Aegisthus.

Atropos: *See* Fates.

Aurora: *See* Eos.

Auster: *See* Winds.

Avernus: Infernal regions; name derived from small vaporous lake near Vesuvius which was fabled to kill birds and vegetation.

Bacchus: *See* Dionysus.

Bellerophon: Corinthian hero; killed Chimera with aid of Pegasus; tried to reach Olympus on Pegasus and was thrown to his death.

Bellona: Roman goddess of war.

Boreas: *See* Winds.

Briareus: Monster of hundred hands; son of Uranus and Gaea.

Briseis: Captive maiden given to Achilles; taken by Agamemnon in exchange for loss of Chryseis, which caused Achilles to cease fighting, until death of Patroclus.

Cadmus: Brother of Europa; planter of dragon seeds from which first Thebans sprang.

Calliope: *See* Muses.

Calypso: Sea nymph; kept Odysseus on her island Ogygia for seven years.

Cassandra: Daughter of Priam; prophetess who was never believed; slain with Agamemnon.

Castor: *See* Dioscuri.

Celaeno: *See* Pleiades.

Centaurs: Beings half man and half horse; lived in mountains of Thessaly.

Cephalus: Hunter; accidentally killed his wife Procris with his spear.

Cepheus: King of Ethiopia; father of Andromeda.

Cerberus: Three-headed dog guarding entrance to Hades.

Ceres: *See* Demeter.

Chaos: Formless void; personified as first of gods.

Charon: Boatman on Styx who carried souls of dead to Hades; son of Erebus.

Charybdis: Female monster; personification of whirlpool.

Chimera: Female monster with head of lion, body of goat, tail of serpent; killed by Bellerophon.

Chiron: Most famous of centaurs.

Chronos: Personification of time.

Chryseis: Captive maiden given to Agamemnon; his refusal to accept ransom from her father Chryses caused Apollo to send plague on Greeks besieging Troy.

Circe: Sorceress; daughter of Helios; changed Odysseus' men into swine.

Clio: *See* Muses.

Clotho: *See* Fates.

Clytemnestra: Wife of Agamemnon, whom she slew with aid of her paramour, Aegisthus; slain by her son Orestes.

Cocytus: *See* Rivers.

Creon: Father of Jocasta; forbade burial of Polynices; ordered burial alive of Antigone.

Creüsa: Princess of Corinth, for whom Jason deserted Medea; slain by Medea, who sent her poisoned robe; also known as Glaüke.

Creusa: Wife of Aeneas; died fleeing Troy.

Cronus (Saturn): Titan; god of harvests; son of Uranus and Gaea; dethroned by his son Zeus.

Cupid: *See* Eros.

Cybele: Anatolian nature goddess; adopted by Greeks and identified with Rhea.

Cyclopes: Race of one-eyed giants (singular: Cyclops).

Daedalus: Athenian artificer; father of Icarus; builder of Labyrinth in Crete; devised wings attached with wax for him and Icarus to escape Crete.

Danae: Princess of Argos; mother of Perseus by Zeus, who appeared to her in form of golden shower.

Danaïdes: Daughters of Danaüs; at his command, all except Hypermnestra slew their husbands, the sons of Aegyptus.

Danaüs: Brother of Aegyptus; father of Danaïdes; slain by Lynceus.

Daphne: Nymph; pursued by Apollo; changed to laurel tree.

Decuma: *See* Fates.

Deino: *See* Graeae.

Demeter (Ceres): Goddess of agriculture; mother of Persephone.

Diana: *See* Artemis.

Dido: Founder and queen of Carthage; stabbed herself when deserted by Aeneas.

Diomedes: Greek hero; with Odysseus, entered Troy and carried off Palladium, sacred statue of Athena.

Diomedes: Owner of man-eating horses, which Hercules, as ninth labor, carried off.

Dione: Titan goddess; mother by Zeus of Aphrodite.

Dionysus (Bacchus): God of wine; son of Zeus and Semele.

Dioscuri: Twins Castor and Pollux; sons of Leda by Zeus.

Dis: *See* Hades.

Dryads: Wood nymphs.

Dryope: Maiden changed to Hamadryad.

Echo: Nymph who fell hopelessly in love with Narcissus; faded away except for her voice.

Electra: Daughter of Agamemnon and Clytemnestra; sister of Orestes; urged Orestes to slay Clytemnestra and Aegisthus.

Electra: *See* Pleiades.

Elysium: Abode of blessed dead.

Endymion: Mortal loved by Selene.

Enyo: *See* Graeae.

Eos (Aurora): Goddess of dawn.

Epimetheus: Brother of Prometheus; husband of Pandora.

Erato: *See* Muses.

Erebus: Spirit of darkness; son of Chaos.

Erinyes: *See* Furies.

Eris: Goddess of discord.

Eros (Amor or Cupid): God of love; son of Aphrodite.

Eteocles: Son of Oedipus, whom he succeeded to rule alternately with Polynices; refused to give up throne at end of year; he and Polynices slew each other.

Eumenides: *See* Furies.

Euphrosyne: *See* Graces.

Europa: Mortal loved by Zeus, who, in form of white bull, carried her off to Crete.

Eurus: *See* Winds.

Euryale: *See* Gorgons.

Eurydice: Nymph; wife of Orpheus.

Eurystheus: King of Argos; imposed twelve labors on Hercules.

Euterpe: *See* Muses.

Fates: Goddesses of destiny; Clotho (Spinner of thread of life), Lachesis (Determiner of length), and Atropos (Cutter of thread); also called Moirae. Identified by Romans with their goddesses of fate; Nona, Decuma, and Morta; called Parcae.

Fauns: Roman deities of woods and groves.

Faunus: *See* Pan.

Favonius: *See* Winds.

Flora: Roman goddess of flowers.

Fortuna: Roman goddess of fortune.

Furies: Avenging spirits; Alecto, Megaera, and Tisiphone; known also as Erinyes or Eumenides.

Gaea: Goddess of earth; daughter of Chaos; mother of Titans; known also as Ge, Gea, Gaia, etc.

Galatea: Statue of maiden carved from ivory by Pygmalion; given life by Aphrodite.

Galatea: Sea nymph; loved by Polyphemus.

Ganymede: Beautiful boy; successor to Hebe as cupbearer of gods.

Glaucus: Mortal who became sea divinity by eating magic grass.

Glauke: *See* Creüsa.

Golden Fleece: Fleece from ram that flew Phrixos to Colchis; Aeëtes placed it under guard of dragon; carried off by Jason.

Gorgons: Female monsters; Euryale, Medusa, and Stheno; had snakes for hair; their glances turned mortals to stone. *See* Medusa.

Graces: Beautiful goddesses: Aglaia (Brilliance), Euphrosyne (Joy), and Thalia (Bloom); daughters of Zeus.

Graeae: Sentinels for Gorgons; Deino, Enyo, and Pephredo; had one eye among them, which passed from one to another.

Hades (Dis): Name sometimes given Pluto; also, abode of dead, ruled by Pluto.

Haemon: Son of Creon; promised husband of Antigone; killed himself in her tomb.

Hamadryads: Tree nymphs.

Harpies: Monsters with heads of women and bodies of birds.

Hebe (Juventas): Goddess of youth; cupbearer of gods before Ganymede; daughter of Zeus and Hera.

Hecate: Goddess of sorcery and witchcraft.

Hector: Son of Priam; slayer of Patroclus; slain by Achilles.

Hecuba: Wife of Priam.

Helen: Fairest woman in world; daughter of Zeus and Leda; wife of Menelaus; carried to Troy by Paris, causing Trojan War.

Heliades: Daughters of Helios; mourned for Phaëthon and were changed to poplar trees.

Helios (Sol): God of sun; later identified with Apollo.

Helle: Sister of Phrixos; fell from ram of Golden Fleece; water where she fell named Hellespont.

Hephaestus (Vulcan): God of fire; celestial blacksmith; son of Zeus and Hera; husband of Aphrodite.

Hera (Juno): Queen of heaven; wife of Zeus.

Hercules: Hero and strong man; son of Zeus and Alcmene; performed twelve labors or deeds to be free from bondage under Eurystheus; after death, his mortal share was destroyed, and he became immortal. Also known as Herakles or Heracles. Labors: (1) killing Nemean lion; (2) killing Lernaean Hydra; (3) capturing Erymanthian boar; (4) capturing Cerynean hind; (5) killing man-eating Stymphalian birds; (6) procuring girdle of Hippolyte; (7) cleaning Augean stables; (8) capturing Cretan bull; (9) capturing man-eating horses of Diomedes; (10) capturing cattle of Geryon; (11) procuring golden apples of Hesperides; (12) bringing Cerberus up from Hades.

Hermes (Mercury): God of physicians and thieves; messenger of gods; son of Zeus and Maia.

Hero: Priestess of Aphrodite; Leander swam Hellespont nightly to see her; drowned herself at his death.

Hesperus: Evening star.

Hestia (Vesta): Goddess of hearth; sister of Zeus.

Hippolyte: Queen of Amazons; wife of Theseus.

Hippolytus: Son of Theseus and Hippolyte; falsely accused by Phaedra of trying to kidnap her; slain by Poseidon at request of Theseus.

Hippomenes: Husband of Atalanta, whom he beat in race by dropping golden apples, which she stopped to pick up.

Hyacinthus: Beautiful youth accidentally killed by Apollo, who caused flower to spring up from his blood.

Hydra: Nine-headed monster in marsh of Lerna; slain by Hercules.

Hygeia: Personification of health.

Hyman: God of marriage.

Hyperion: Titan; early sun god; father of Helios.

Hypermnestra: Daughter of Danaüs; refused to kill her husband Lynceus.

Hypnos (Somnus): God of sleep.

Iapetus: Titan; father of Atlas, Epimetheus, and Prometheus.

Icarus: Son of Daedalus; flew too near sun with wax-attached wings and fell into sea and was drowned.

Io: Mortal maiden loved by Zeus; changed by Hera into heifer.

Iobates: King of Lycia; sent Bellerophon to slay Chimera.

Iphigenia: Daughter of Agamemnon; offered as sacrifice to Artemis at Aulis; carried by Artemis to Tauris where she became priestess; escaped from there with Orestes.

Iris: Goddess of rainbow; messenger of Zeus and Hera.

Ismene: Daughter of Oedipus; sister of Antigone.

Iulus: Son of Aeneas.

Ixion: King of Lapithae; for making love to Hera he was bound to endlessly revolving wheel in Tartarus.

Janus: Roman god of gates and doors; represented with two opposite faces.

Jason: Son of Aeson; to gain throne of Ioclus from Pelias, went to Colchis and brought back Golden Fleece; married Medea; deserted her for Creüsa.

Jocasta: Wife of Laius; mother of Oedipus; unwittingly became wife of Oedipus; hanged herself when relationship was discovered.

Juno: *See* Hera.

Jupiter: *See* Zeus.

Juventas: *See* Hebe.

Lachesis: *See* Fates.

Laius: Father of Oedipus, by whom he was slain.

Laocoön: Priest of Apollo at Troy; warned against bringing wooden horse into Troy; destroyed with his two sons by serpents sent by Athena.

Lares: Roman ancestral spirits protecting descendants and homes.

Lavinia: Wife of Aeneas after defeat of Turnus.

Leander: Swam Hellespont nightly to see Hero; drowned in storm.

Leda: Mortal loved by Zeus in form of Swan; mother of Helen, Clytemnestra, Dioscuri.

Lethe: *See* Rivers.

Leto (Latona): Mother by Zeus of Artemis and Apollo.

Lucina: Roman goddess of childbirth; identified with Juno.

Lynceus: Son of Aegyptus; husband of Hypermnestra; slew Danaüs.

Maia: Daughter of Atlas; mother of Hermes.

Maia: *See* Pleiades.

Manes: Souls of dead Romans, particularly of ancestors.

Mars: *See* Ares.

Marsyas: Shepherd; challenged Apollo to music contest and lost; flayed alive by Apollo.

Medea: Sorceress; daughter of Aeëtes; helped Jason obtain Golden Fleece; when deserted by him for Creüsa, killed her children and Creüsa.

Medusa: Gorgon; slain by Perseus, who cut off her head.

Megaera: *See* Furies.

Meleager: Son of Althaea; his life would last as long as brand burning at his birth; Althaea quenched and saved it but destroyed it when Meleager slew his uncles.

Melpomene: *See* Muses.

Memnon: Ethiopian king; made immortal by Zeus; son of Tithonus and Eos.

Menelaus: King of Sparta; son of Atreus; brother of Agamemnon; husband of Helen.

Mercury: *See* Hermes.

Merope: *See* Pleiades.

Mezentius: Cruel Etruscan king; ally of Turnus against Aeneas; slain by Aeneas.

Midas: King of Phrygia; given gift of turning to gold all he touched.

Minerva: *See* Athena.

Minos: King of Crete; after death, one of three judges of dead in Hades; son of Zeus and Europa.

Minotaur: Monster, half man and half beast, kept in Labyrinth in Crete; slain by Theseus.

Mnemosyne: Goddess of memory; mother by Zeus of Muses.

Moirae: *See* Fates.

Momus: God of ridicule.

Morpheus: God of dreams.

Mors: *See* Thanatos.

Morta: *See* Fates.

Muses: Goddesses presiding over arts and sciences: Calliope (epic poetry), Clio (history), Erato (lyric and love poetry), Euterpe (music), Melpomene (tragedy), Polymnia or Polyhymnia (sacred poetry), Terpsichore (choral dance and song), Thalia (comedy and bucolic poetry), Urania (astronomy); daughters of Zeus and Mnemosyne.

Naiads: Nymphs of waters, streams, and fountains.

Napaeae: Wood nymphs.

Narcissus: Beautiful youth loved by Echo; in punishment for not returning her love, he was made to fall in love with his image reflected in pool; pined away and became flower.

Nemesis: Goddess of retribution.

Neoptolemus: Son of Achilles; slew Priam; also known as Pyrrhus.

Neptune: *See* Poseidon.

Nereids: Sea nymphs; attendants on Poseidon.

Nestor: King of Pylos; noted for wise counsel in expedition against Troy.

Nike: Goddess of victory.

Niobe: Daughter of Tantalus; wife of Amphion; her children slain by Apollo and Artemis; changed to stone but continued to weep her loss.

Nona: *See* Fates.

Notus: *See* Winds.

Nox: *See* Nyx.

Nymphs: Beautiful maidens; inferior deities of nature.

Nyx (Nox): Goddess of night.

Oceanids: Ocean nymphs; daughters of Oceanus.

Oceanus: Eldest of Titans; god of waters.

Odysseus (Ulysses): King of Ithaca; husband of Penelope; wandered ten years after fall of Troy before arriving home.

Oedipus: King of Thebes; son of Laius and Jocasta; unwittingly murdered Laius and married Jocasta; tore his eyes out when relationship was discovered.

Oenone: Nymph of Mount Ida; wife of Paris, who abandoned her; refused to cure him when he was poisoned by arrow of Philoctetes at Troy.

Ops: *See* Rhea.

Oreads: Mountain nymphs.

Orestes: Son of Agamemnon and Clytemnestra; brother of Electra; slew Clytemnestra and Aegisthus; pursued by Furies until his purification by Apollo.

Orion: Hunter; slain by Artemis and made heavenly constellation.

Orpheus: Famed musician; son of Apollo and Muse Calliope; husband of Eurydice.

Pales: Roman goddess of shepherds and herdsmen.

Palinurus: Aeneas' pilot; fell overboard in his sleep and was drowned.

Pan (Faunus): God of woods and fields; part goat; son of Hermes.

Pandora: Opener of box containing human ills; mortal wife of Epimetheus.

Parcae: *See* Fates.

Paris: Son of Priam; gave apple of discord to Aphrodite, for which she enabled him to carry off Helen; slew Achilles at Troy; slain by Philoctetes.

Patroclus: Great friend of Achilles; wore Achilles' armor and was slain by Hector.

Pegasus: Winged horse that sprang from Medusa's body at her death; ridden by Bellerophon when he slew Chimera.

Pelias: King of Iolcus; seized throne from his brother Aeson; sent Jason for Golden Fleece; slain unwittingly by his daughters at instigation of Medea.

Pelops: Son of Tantalus; his father cooked and served him to gods; restored to life; Peloponnesus named for him.

Penates: Roman household gods.

Penelope: Wife of Odysseus; waited faithfully for him for ten years while putting off numerous suitors.

Pephredo: *See* Graeae.

Periphetes: Giant; son of Hephaestus; slain by Theseus.

Persephone (Proserpine): Queen of infernal regions; daughter of Zeus and Demeter; wife of Pluto.

Perseus: Son of Zeus and Danaë; slew Medusa; rescued Andromeda from monster and married her.

Phaedra: Daughter of Minos; wife of Theseus; caused the death of her stepson, Hippolytus.

Phaethon: Son of Helios; drove his father's sun chariot and was struck down by Zeus before he set world on fire.

Philoctetes: Greek warrior who possessed Hercules' bow and arrows; slew Paris at Troy with poisoned arrow.

Phineus: Betrothed of Andromeda; tried to slay Perseus but turned to stone by Medusa's head.

Phlegethon: *See* Rivers.

Phosphor: Morning star.

Phrixos: Brother of Helle; carried by ram of Golden Fleece to Colchis.

Pirithous: Son of Ixion; friend of Theseus; tried to carry off Persephone from Hades; bound to enchanted rock by Pluto.

Pleiades: Alcyone, Celaeno, Electra, Maia, Merope, Sterope or Asterope, Taygeta; seven daughters of Atlas; transformed into heavenly constellation, of which six stars are visible (Merope is said to have hidden in shame for loving a mortal).

Pluto (Dis): God of Hades; brother of Zeus.

Plutus: God of wealth.

Pollux: *See* Dioscuri.

Polymnia: *See* Muses.

Polynices: Son of Oedipus; he and his brother Eteocles killed each other; burial rite, forbidden by Creon, performed by his sister Antigone.

Polyphemus: Cyclops; devoured six of Odysseus' men; blinded by Odysseus.

Polyxena: Daughter of Priam; betrothed to Achilles, whom Paris slew at their betrothal; sacrificed to shade of Achilles.

Pomona: Roman goddess of fruits.

Pontus: Sea god; son of Gaea.

Poseidon (Neptune): God of sea; brother of Zeus.

Priam: King of Troy; husband of Hecuba; ransomed Hector's body from Achilles; slain by Neoptolemus.

Priapus: God of regeneration.

Procris: Wife of Cephalus, who accidentally slew her.

Procrustes: Giant; stretched or cut off legs of victims to make them fit iron bed; slain by Theseus.

Proetus: Husband of Anteia; sent Bellerophon to Iobates to be put to death.

Prometheus: Titan; stole fire from heaven for man. Zeus punished him by chaining him to rock in Caucasus where vultures devoured his liver daily.

Proteus: Sea god; assumed various shapes when called on to prophesy.

Psyche: Beloved of Eros; punished by jealous Aphrodite; made immortal and united with Eros.

Pygmalion: King of Cyprus; carved ivory statue of maiden which Aphrodite gave life as Galatea.

Pyramus: Babylonian youth; made love to Thisbe through hole in wall; thinking Thisbe slain by lion, killed himself.

Pyrrhus: *See* Neoptolemus.

Python: Serpent born from slime left by Deluge; slain by Apollo.

Quirinus: Roman war god.

Remus: Brother of Romulus; slain by him.

Rhadamanthus: One of three judges of dead in Hades; son of Zeus and Europa.

Rhea (Ops): Daughter of Uranus and Gaea; wife of Cronus; mother of Zeus; identified with Cybele.

Rivers of Underworld: Acheron (woe), Cocytus (wailing), Lethe (forgetfulness), Phlegethon (fire), Styx (across which souls of dead were ferried by Charon).

Romulus: Founder of Rome; he and Remus suckled in infancy by she-wolf; slew Remus; deified by Romans.

Sarpedon: King of Lycia; son of Zeus and Europa; slain by Patroclus at Troy.

Saturn: *See* Cronus.

Satyrs: Hoofed demigods of woods and fields; companions of Dionysus.

Sciron: Robber; forced strangers to wash his feet, then hurled them into sea where tortoise devoured them; slain by Theseus.

Scylla: Female monster inhabiting rock opposite Charybdis; menaced passing sailors.

Selene: Goddess of moon.

Semele: Daughter of Cadmus; mother by Zeus of Dionysus; demanded Zeus appear before her in all his splendor and was destroyed by his lightnings.

Sibyis: Various prophetesses; most famous, Cumaean sibyl, accompanied Aeneas into Hades.

Sileni: Minor woodland deities similar to satyrs (singular: silenus). Sometimes Silenus refers to eldest of satyrs, son of Hermes or of Pan.

Silvanus: Roman god of woods and fields.

Sinis: Giant; bent pines, by which he hurled victims against side of mountain; slain by Theseus.

Sirens: Minor deities who lured sailors to destruction with their singing.

Sisyphus: King of Corinth; condemned in Tartarus to roll huge stone to top of hill; it always rolled back down again.

Sol: *See* Helios.

Somnus: *See* Hypnos.

Sphinx: Monster of Thebes; killed those who could not answer her riddle; slain by Oedipus. Name also refers to other monsters having body of lion, wings, and head and bust of woman.

Sterope: *See* Pleiades.

Stheno: *See* Gorgons.

Styx: *See* Rivers.

Symplegades: Clashing rocks at entrance to Black Sea; Argo passed through, causing them to become forever fixed.

Syrinx: Nymph pursued by Pan; changed to reeds, from which he made his pipes.

Tantalus: Cruel king; father of Pelops and Niobe; condemned in Tartarus to stand chin-deep in lake surrounded by fruit branches; as he tried to eat or drink, water or fruit always receded.

Tartarus: Underworld below Hades; often refers to Hades.

Taygeta: *See* Pleiades.

Telemachus: Son of Odysseus; made unsuccessful journey to find his father.

Tellus: Roman goddess of earth.

Terminus: Roman god of boundaries and landmarks.

Terpsichore: *See* Muses.

Terra: Roman earth goddess.

Thalia: *See* Graces; Muses.

Thanatos (Mors): God of death.

Themis: Titan goddess of laws of physical phenomena; daughter of Uranus; mother of Prometheus.

Theseus: Son of Aegeus; slew Minotaur; married and deserted Ariadne; later married Phaedra.

Thisbe: Beloved of Pyramus; killed herself at his death.

Thyestes: Brother of Atreus; Atreus killed three of his sons and served them to him at banquet.

Tiresias: Blind soothsayer of Thebes.

Tisiphone: *See* Furies.

Titans: Early gods from which Olympian gods were derived; children of Uranus and Gaea.

Tithonus: Mortal loved by Eos; changed into grasshopper.

Triton: Demigod of sea; son of Poseidon.

Turnus: King of Rutuli in Italy; betrothed to Lavinia; slain by Aeneas.

Ulysses: *See* Odysseus.

Urania: *See* Muses.

Uranus: Personification of Heaven; husband of Gaea; father of Titans; dethroned by his son Cronus.

Venus: *See* Aphrodite.

Vertumnus: Roman god of fruits and vegetables; husband of Pomona.

Vesta: *See* Hestia.

Vulcan: *See* Hephaestus.

Winds: Aeolus (keeper of winds), Boreas (Aquilo) (north wind), Eurus (east wind), Notus (Auster) (south wind), Zephyrus (Favonius) (west wind).

Zephyrus: *See* Winds.

Zeus (Jupiter): Chief of Olympian gods; son of Cronus and Rhea; husband of Hera.

Norse Mythology

Aesir: Chief gods of Asgard.

Andvari: Dwarf; robbed of gold and magic ring by Loki.

Angerbotha (Angrbotha): Giantess; mother by Loki of Fenrir, Hel, and Midgard serpent.

Asgard (Asgarth): Abode of gods.

Ask (Aske, Askr): First man; created by Odin, Hoenir, and Lothur.

Asynjur: Goddesses of Asgard.

Atli: Second husband of Gudrun; invited Gunnar and Hogni to his court, where they were slain; slain by Gudrun.

Audhumia (Audhumbla): Cow that nourished Ymir, created Buri by licking ice cliff.

Balder (Baldr, Baldur): God of light, spring, peace, joy; son of Odin; slain by Hoth at instigation of Loki.

Bifrost: Rainbow bridge connecting Midgard and Asgard.

Bragi (Brage): God of poetry; husband of Ithunn.

Branstock: Great oak in hall of Volsungs; into it, Odin thrust Gram, which only Sigmund could draw forth.

Brynhild: Valkyrie; wakened from magic sleep by Sigurd; married Gunnar; instigated death of Sigurd; killed herself and was burned on pyre beside Sigurd.

Bur (Bor): Son of Buri; father of Odin, Hoenir, and Lothur.

Buri (Bori): Progenitor of gods; father of Bur; created by Audhumla.

Embla: First woman; created by Odin, Hoenir, and Lothur.

Fafnir: Son of Rodmar, whom he slew for gold in Otter's skin; in form of dragon, guarded gold; slain by Sigurd.

Fenrir: Wolf; offspring of Loki; swallows Odin at Ragnarok and is slain by Vitharr.

Forseti: Son of Balder.

Frey (Freyr): God of fertility and crops; son of Njorth; originally one of Vanir.

Freya (Freyja): Goddess of love and beauty; sister of Frey; originally one of Vanir.

Frigg (Frigga): Goddess of sky; wife of Odin.

Garm: Watchdog of Hel; slays, and is slain by, Tyr at Ragnarok.

Gimle: Home of blessed after Ragnarok.

Giuki: King of Nibelungs; father of Gunnar, Hogni, Guttorm, and Gudrun.

Glathsehim (Gladsheim): Hall of gods in Asgard.

Gram (meaning "Angry"): Sigmund's sword; rewelded by Regin; used by Sigurd to slay Fafnir.

Greyfell: Sigmund's horse; descended from Sleipnir.

Grimhild: Mother of Gudrun; administered magic potion to Sigurd which made him forget Brynhild.

Gudrun: Daughter of Giuki; wife of Sigurd; later wife of Atli and Jonakr.

Gunnar: Son of Giuki; in his semblance Sigurd won Brynhild for him; slain at hall of Atli.

Guttorm: Son of Giuki; slew Sigurd at Brynhild's request.

Heimdall (Heimdallr): Guardian of Asgard.

Hel: Goddess of dead and queen of underworld; daughter of Loki.

Hiordis: Wife of Sigmund; mother of Sigurd.

Hoenir: One of creators of Ask and Embla; son of Bur.

Hogni: Son of Giuki; slain at hall of Atli.

Hoth (Hoder, Hodur): Blind god of night and darkness; slayer of Balder at instigation of Loki.

Ithunn (Ithun, Iduna): Keeper of golden apples of youth; wife of Bragi.

Jonakr: Third husband of Gudrun.

Jormunrek: Slayer of Swanhild; slain by sons of Gudrun.

Jotunnheim (Jotunheim): Abode of giants.

Lif and Lifthrasir: First man and woman after Ragnarok.

Loki: God of evil and mischief; instigator of Balder's death.

Lothur (Lodur): One of creators of Ask and Embla.

Midgard (Midgarth): Abode of mankind; the earth.

Midgard Serpent: Sea monster; offspring of Loki; slays, and is slain by, Thor at Ragnarok.

Mimir: Giant; guardian of well in Jotunnheim at root of Yggdrasill; knower of past and future.

Mjollnir: Magic hammer of Thor.

Nagifar: Ship to be used by giants in attacking Asgard at

Ragnarok; built from nails of dead men.

Nanna: Wife of Balder.

Nibelungs: Dwellers in northern kingdom ruled by Giuki.

Niflheim (Nifelheim): Outer region of cold and darkness; abode of Hel.

Njorth: Father of Frey and Freya; originally one of Vanir.

Norns: Demigoddesses of fate: Urth (Urdur) (Past), Verthandi (Verdandi) (Present), Skuld (Future).

Odin (Othin): Head of Aesir; creator of world with Vili and Ve; equivalent to Woden (Wodan, Wotan) in Teutonic mythology.

Otter: Son of Rodmar; slain by Loki; his skin filled with gold hoard of Andvari to appease Rodmar.

Ragnarok: Final destruction of present world in battle between gods and giants; some minor gods will survive, and Lif and Lifthrasir will repeople world.

Regin: Blacksmith; son of Rodmar; foster-father of Sigurd.

Rerir: King of Huns; son of Sigi.

Rodmar: Father of Regin, Otter, and Fafnir; demanded Otter's skin be filled with gold; slain by Fafnir, who stole gold.

Sif: Wife of Thor.

Siggeir: King of Goths; husband of Signy; he and his sons slew Volsung and his sons, except Sigmund; slain by Sigmund and Sinflotli.

Sigi: King of Huns; son of Odin.

Sigmund: Son of Volsung; brother of Signy, who bore him Sinflotli; husband of Hiordis, who bore him Sigurd.

Signy: Daughter of Volsung; sister of Sigmund; wife of Siggeir; mother by Sigmund of Sinflotli.

Sigurd: Son of Sigmund and Hiordis; wakened Brynhild from magic sleep; married Gudrun; slain by Guttorm at instigation of Brynhild.

Sigyn: Wife of Loki.

Sinflotli: Son of Sigmund and Signy.

Skuld: *See* Norns.

Sleipnir (Sleipner): Eight-legged horse of Odin.

Surt (Surtr): Fire demon; slays Frey at Ragnarok.

Svartalfaheim: Abode of dwarfs.

Swanhild: Daughter of Sigurd and Gudrun; slain by Jormunrek.

Thor: God of thunder; oldest son of Odin; equivalent to Germanic deity Donar.

Tyr: God of war; son of Odin; equivalent to Tiu in Teutonic mythology.

Ull (Ullr): Son of Sif; stepson of Thor.

Urth: *See* Norns.

Valhalla (Valhall): Great hall in Asgard where Odin received souls of heroes killed in battle.

Vali: Odin's son: Ragnarok survivor.

Valkyries: Virgins, messengers of Odin, who selected heroes to die in battle and took them to Valhalla; generally considered as nine in number.

Vanir: Early race of gods; three survivors, Njorth, Frey, and Freya, are associated with Aesir.

Ve: Brother of Odin; one of creators of world.

Verthandi: *See* Norns.

Vili: Brother of Odin; one of creators of world.

Vingolf: Abode of goddesses in Asgard.

Vitharr (Vithar): Son of Odin; survivor of Ragnarok.

Volsung: Descendant of Odin, and father of Signy, Sigmund; his descendants were called Volsungs.

Yggdrasill: Giant ash tree springing from body of Ymir and supporting universe; its roots extended to Asgard, Jotunnheim, and Niffheim.

Ymir (Ymer): Primeval frost giant killed by Odin, Vili, and Ve; world created from his body; also, from his body sprang Yggdrasill.

Egyptian Mythology

Aaru: Abode of the blessed dead.

Amen (Amon, Ammdn): One of chief Theban deities; united with sun god under form of Amen-Ra.

Amenti: Region of dead where souls were judged by Osiris.

Anubis: Guide of souls to Amenti; son of Osiris; jackal-headed.

Apis: Sacred bull, an embodiment of Ptah; identified with Osiris as Osiris-Apis or Serapis.

Geb (Keb, Seb): Earth god; father of Osiris; represented with goose on head.

Hathor (Athor): Goddess of love and mirth; cow-headed.

Horus: God of day; son of Osiris and Isis; hawk-headed.

Isis: Goddess of motherhood and fertility; sister and wife of Osiris.

Khepera: God of morning sun.

Khnemu (Khnum, Chnuphis, Chnemu, Chnum): Ram-headed god.

Khonsu (Khensu, Khuns): Son of Amen and Mut.

Mentu (Ment): Solar deity, sometimes considered god of war; falcon-headed.

Min (Khem, Chem): Principle of physical life.

Mut (Maut): Wife of Amen.

Nephthys: Goddess of the dead; sister and wife of Set.

Nu: Chaos from which world was created, personified as a god.

Nut: Goddess of heavens; consort of Geb.

Osiris: God of underworld and judge of dead; son of Geb and Nut.

Ptah (Phtha): Chief deity of Memphis.

Ra: God of the Sun, the supreme god; son of Nut; Pharaohs claimed descent from him; represented as lion, cat, or falcon.

Serapis: God uniting attributes of Osiris and Apis.

Set (Seth): God of darkness or evil; brother and enemy of Osiris.

Shu: Solar deity; son of Ra and Hathor.

Tem (Atmu, Atum, Tum): Solar deity.

Thoth (Dhouti): God of wisdom and magic; scribe of gods; ibis-headed.

Modern Wedding Anniversary Gift List

Anniversary	Gift	Anniversary	Gift	Anniversary	Gift
1st	Clocks	10th	Diamond jewelry	19th	Bronze
2nd	China	11th	Fashion jewelry and accessories	20th	Platinum
3rd	Crystal, glass			25th	Sterling Silver Jubilee
4th	Electrical Appliances	12th	Pearls or colored gems	30th	Diamond
5th	Silverware	13th	Textiles, furs	35th	Jade
6th	Wood	14th	Gold jewelry	40th	Ruby
7th	Desk sets, pen and pencil sets	15th	Watches	45th	Sapphire
		16th	Silver holloware	50th	Golden Jubilee
8th	Linens, laces	17th	Furniture	55th	Emerald
9th	Leather	18th	Porcelain	60th	Diamond Jubilee

Source: Jewelry Industry Council.

Your Credit Options

By Consumer Federation of America

Should I Borrow?

Can I Afford a Loan? Before borrowing, ask whether you can meet all essential expenses and still afford monthly loan payments. You can make this calculation in two ways: One is to add up all basic monthly expenses and subtract this total from your take-home pay. If the difference will not cover a monthly payment and still leave funds for other expenses, you cannot afford the loan.

An even more reliable method is to ask yourself what you plan to give up in order to make monthly loan payments. If you currently save a portion of your income greater than the monthly payment, then you can use these savings to pay off the loan. But if you do not, you will have to forego spending on entertainment, new appliances, or perhaps even on necessities. Are you prepared to make this trade-off?

One rule of thumb financial advisers suggest is to limit consumer debt to 15% of the income that remains after taxes and housing expenses. This means it is *not* wise for the American family, with an after-tax annual income of $20,000 and housing expenses of $6,000, to owe more than $2,100 in installment and credit card debt.

What Kind of Loan Should I Seek?

There are two types of credit—installment loans and the open-end credit provided by a credit card. Because the former carry a lower interest rate, they are the least expensive credit option when the loan is repaid over a period of many months, or years. But because credit cards usually provide a "float period" when no interest is charged, they represent the cheapest way to make credit purchases that are paid off in a month or two. Also, once one has a credit card, it is always easier to use than taking out an installment loan. An alternative to a credit card is a charge card, which requires full payment of the balance due each month, but does not impose a finance charge.

In seeking an installment loan, most consumers think first of borrowing from a bank or finance company. There are, however, other credit sources, some of which are less expensive.

Inexpensive Loans. Parents or family members are often the source of the least expensive loans. They may charge you only the interest they would have earned on the money—as little as the 5% earned on a passbook account. Such loans, however, can complicate family relationships.

Also relatively inexpensive is money borrowed on financial assets that are held by the lending institution; for example, a certificate of deposit purchased from a bank or the cash value of a whole life insurance policy. The interest rate on these types of loans typically ranges from 8% to 12%, but remember that your assets are tied up until the loan is repaid.

Medium-Priced Loans. Medium-priced loans can often be obtained from commercial banks and credit unions. New car loans, for example, may cost 11% to 15%, used car loans and home improvement loans slightly more.

There are several advantages in borrowing from credit unions. These institutions effectively provide free credit life insurance. Generally they are sympathetic to borrowers with legitimate payment problems. And they sometimes pay dividends to all their depositors at the end of the year. Unfortunately, membership in most credit unions is restricted to members of a group—trade union, employees of a firm, church or community.

Expensive Loans. The most expensive loans are available from finance companies, retailers, and banks through credit cards.

Finance companies often lend to those who cannot obtain credit from banks or credit unions. Typically the interest rate ranges from 15% to 30%. If you are denied credit by a bank or credit union, you should question your ability to afford the higher rate of a loan company.

Borrowing from car dealers, appliance stores, department stores, and other retailers is also relatively expensive. Interest rates are usually similar to those charged by finance companies, frequently 20% or more.

Banks lend funds not only through installment loans, but also through cash advances on MasterCard or VISA cards. Interest is charged on these advances at rates ranging from 14% to 24%. Most banks charge 18% to 20%.

There is, however, one type of loan from finance companies that is currently less expensive than most other credit. These are loans, often at a rate under 10%, available from the finance companies of major auto manufacturers—General Motors Acceptance Corporation, Ford Motor Credit, and others. Yet, keep in mind that a car dealer offering you such a rate may be less willing to discount the price of the car or throw in free options.

From What Specific Lender Should I Borrow?

After deciding what kind of institution to borrow from, it is important to shop around for the cheapest loan. This should be done by calling several lenders to ask about rates. Make sure you tell the lender the size of the loan, the size of the down payment, the length of the loan, and the product financed. A good indicator of price is not the monthly payment, but the annual percentage rate (APR), which takes into consideration nearly all charges. But ask whether there are any fees that are not included in the APR. At least on car loans, banks and finance companies are increasingly charging loan origination fees. □

Excerpted, with permission, from a pamphlet entitled "Your Credit Options" written by Stephen Brobeck, executive director of Consumer Federation of America, 1424 16th Street, N.W., Washington, D.C. 20036.

Home Equity Loans

Reprinted with permission, Department of Consumer Affairs, The City of New York.

Is the home in which you live your sole major asset? Using your house as collateral for a loan poses some risk, as failure to meet your obligations may result in foreclosure. This is particularly true with home equity loans.

What is a home equity loan?

A home equity loan is a form of refinancing identical to a second mortgage, except that it establishes a revolving line of credit. During the first phase of your loan, which typically lasts five to ten years, you may withdraw funds up to the limit of your line of credit as you desire. You are also allowed to borrow again any payments you may make on the balance owed. During the second phase of your loan, you cannot make further withdrawals; most banks then give you up to twenty years to pay back the loan.

Why can home equity loans be especially risky?

While other mortgages have fixed or maximum interest rates, home equity loans are offered with rates that may increase or decrease without limit. The rate offered to consumers is pegged to the "prime" rate. The prime rate fluctuates at the discretion of banks; currently it is 8%,[1] but it was over 20% just six years ago.

If your monthly payments only included interest during the first phase, they will increase or "balloon" significantly once you begin paying the balance owed. Therefore, in addition to facing unpredictable interest rates, you may experience a sharp jump in monthly payments when the second phase of your loan begins.

How can I get the best deal on a home equity loan?

Seek out a bank that offers a home equity loan with a maximum "cap" on the interest rate. If you cannot find one, consider taking out a second mortgage with a fixed or capped rate. The initial rate may be higher but you will be protected against unforeseen rate increases and "balloon" payments that might otherwise put your home at risk.

Before committing yourself to a home equity loan, ask your banker for a "worst-case" scenario of your monthly payments during the second phase of your loan. Some banks require a single lump-sum payment that may force you to refinance.

Compare the percent above the prime rate that will apply for the entire life of the loan; a loan set at 1.5% above the prime rate is cheaper than one set at 1.75% above. Take introductory discounts into consideration only if you plan to pay off the loan quickly.

Ask if there are any monthly service charges or transaction fees, and compare these among different lenders. Also, get estimates of all origination fees and closing costs; these can amount to well over $1,000.

If you own a co-op or condominium, double-check all terms; some banks offer less favorable terms for home equity loans on co-ops and condominiums. Some banks also offer less favorable terms to non-customers and even to customers who do not maintain preferred accounts.

Ask a tax advisor about your potential deductions. The amount of your loan depends on the assessed value of your house, but the deductibility of your interest payments depends in part on what you originally paid for your home. If the value of your house has increased substantially, not all of your interest payments may be deductible.

How can I make the best use of my loan?

Write down a spending plan for the entire period of your loan. If your bank only requires interest to be paid during the first phase of your loan, ask your banker to set up a schedule of monthly payments that also includes principle; there is no penalty for prepaying. This will reduce your obligations during the second phase of your loan, and will thereby reduce the risk of foreclosure. Your plan should also take into account tax deductions for your interest payments.

Establish a contingency plan for paying off the loan more rapidly in case interest rates rise substantially.

Plan to use the equity in your home to increase household assets through sound investments, or to enhance the value of household members in the work force through education or job training.

Never borrow for non-investments like cars and vacations. This is an ill-considered use of household assets, and it may leave you with a pile of debt and no equity in your home.

Similarly, avoid paying other debts, like credit card debts, with your home equity loan. Your other debts are not secured by your house, whereas you will risk foreclosure if you fail to meet the obligations of your home equity loan.

1. May 1987

Unsolicited Mail Merchandise

Most of us have received things in the mail at some time or other that we never ordered. The law says, quite simply, unordered merchandise is yours to keep. You may legally consider it a gift, and you cannot be forced to pay for it or return it.

There are only two kinds of merchandise that legally can be sent to you through the mail without your consent. They are: Free samples clearly labeled as such; and goods mailed by charities seeking contributions, such as key rings or other small items. You can keep these items, and it is illegal for any seller to try to force you to return anything you did not order.

There are many ways to send things besides the U.S. Postal Service. United Parcel Service (UPS) is one of them. If you get something that you did not order by a private delivery company you must do two things before you can keep the item: (1) You must tell the sender that you received merchandise that you did not order, preferably in writing so you can prove it if you are billed, and (2) you must give the sender a reasonable amount of time, such as 30 days, to pick up the merchandise at the *sender's* expense. Tell the sender what you will do with the merchandise if it is not picked up—keep it, toss it out, etc. *Source:* AARP and Federal Trade Commission.

How to Write a Complaint Letter

A Few Basic Tips

Source: Office of Special Advisor to the President for Consumer Affairs and the Consumer Information Center, Pueblo, CO 81009.

- Include your name, address, and home and work phone numbers.
- Type your letter if possible. If it is handwritten, make sure it is neat and easy to read.
- Make your letter brief and to the point. Include all important facts about your purchase, including the date and place where you made the purchase and any information you can give about the product or service such as serial or model numbers or specific type of service.
- State exactly what you want done about the problem and how long you are willing to wait to get it resolved. Be reasonable.
- Include all documents regarding your problem. Be sure to send COPIES, not originals.
- Avoid writing an angry, sarcastic, or threatening letter. The person reading your letter probably was not responsible for your problem, but may be very helpful in resolving it.
- Keep a copy of the letter for your records.

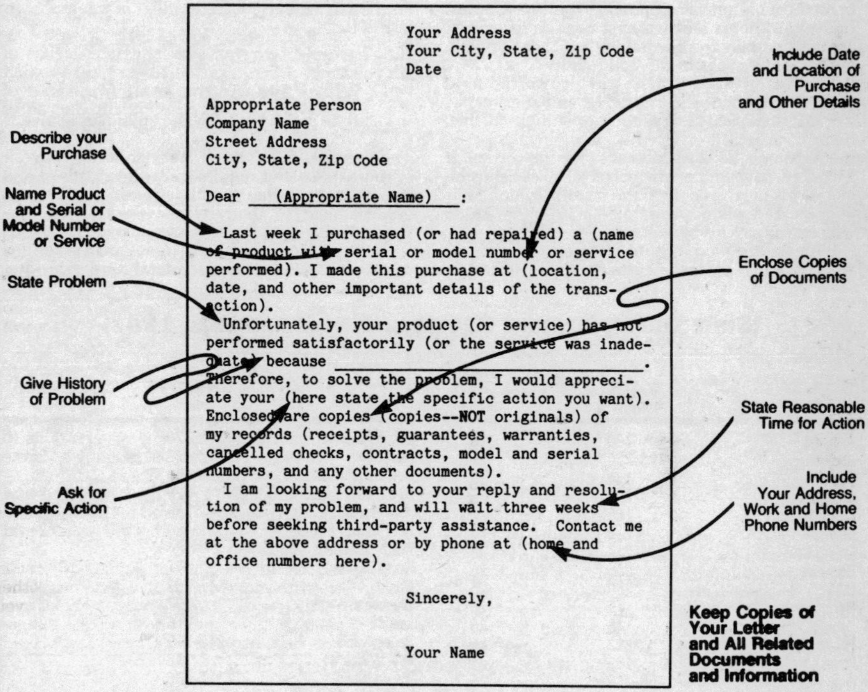

Your Address
Your City, State, Zip Code
Date

Appropriate Person
Company Name
Street Address
City, State, Zip Code

Dear (Appropriate Name) :

Last week I purchased (or had repaired) a (name of product with serial or model number or service performed). I made this purchase at (location, date, and other important details of the transaction).

Unfortunately, your product (or service) has not performed satisfactorily (or the service was inadequate) because ________________________. Therefore, to solve the problem, I would appreciate your (here state the specific action you want). Enclosed are copies (copies--NOT originals) of my records (receipts, guarantees, warranties, cancelled checks, contracts, model and serial numbers, and any other documents).

I am looking forward to your reply and resolution of my problem, and will wait three weeks before seeking third-party assistance. Contact me at the above address or by phone at (home and office numbers here).

Sincerely,

Your Name

Free Facts For Consumers

The Federal Trade Commission enforces a number of federal laws involving consumer credit for which free publications are available. Starred items (*) are also available in Spanish. If you would like additional information, ask for the following FTC fact sheets:

• Credit Billing Blues • Credit and Charge Card Fraud • Door-to-Door Sales • Equal Credit Opportunity* • Fair Credit Billing* • Fair Debt Collection* • FTC "Best Sellers' List" • Shopping By Mail • Should You Join a Buying Club? • Utility Credit • Women and Credit Histories • Work-At-Home Schemes

To order these free publications, write to Public Reference, Federal Trade Commission, Washington, D.C. 20580.

Although the Commission cannot solve individual problems for consumers, it can act when it sees a pattern of possible law violations develop. If you have a complaint that may involve a violation of consumer protection law, write to Correspondence Branch, Federal Trade Commission, Washington, D.C. 20580.

Unemployment Insurance

Unemployment insurance is managed jointly by the states and the federal government. Most states began paying benefits in 1938 and 1939.

Under What Conditions Can the Worker Collect?

The laws vary from state to state. In general, a waiting period of one week is required after a claim is filed before collecting unemployment insurance; the worker must be able to work, must not have quit without good cause or have been discharged for misconduct; he must not be involved in a labor dispute; above all, he must be ready and willing to work. He may be disqualified if he refuses, without good cause, to accept a job which is suitable for him in terms of his qualifications and experience, unless the wages, hours and working conditions offered are substantially less favorable than those prevailing for similar jobs in the community.

The unemployed worker must go to the local state employment security office and register for work. If that office has a suitable opening available, he must accept it or lose his unemployment payments, unless he has good cause for the refusal. If a worker moves out of his own state, he can still collect at his new residence; the state in which he is now located will act as agent for the other state, which will pay his benefits.

Benefits are paid only to unemployed workers who have had at least a certain amount of recent past employment or earnings in a job covered by the state law. The amount of employment or earnings, and the period used to measure them, vary from state to state, but the intent of the various laws is to limit benefits to workers whose recent records indicate that they are members of the labor force. The amount of benefits an unemployed worker may receive for any week is also determined by application to his past wages of a formula specified in the law. The general objective is to provide a weekly benefit which is about half the worker's customary weekly wages, up to a maximum set by the law (see table). In a majority of states, the total benefits a worker may receive in a 12-month period is limited to a fraction of his total wages in a prior 12-month period, as well as to a stated number of weeks. Thus, not all workers in a state are entitled to benefits for the number of weeks shown in the table.

Who Pays for the Insurance?

The total cost is borne by the employer in all but a few states. Each state has a sliding scale of rates. The standard rate is set at 5.4% of taxable payroll in most states. But employers with records of less unemployment (that is, with fewer unemployment benefits paid to their former workers) are rewarded with rates lower than the standard 5.4%.

During periods of high unemployment on either a state or national level, federal-state extended

State Unemployment Compensation Maximums, 1987

State	Weekly benefit[1]	Maximum duration, weeks	State	Weekly benefit[1]	Maximum duration, weeks
Alabama	120	26	Nebraska	126	26
Alaska	188–260	26	Nevada	171	26
Arizona	135	26	New Hampshire	150	26
Arkansas	196	26	New Jersey	228	26
California	166	26	New Mexico	158	26
Colorado	213	26	New York	180	26
Connecticut	204–254	26	North Carolina	184	26
Delaware	205	26	North Dakota	197	26
D. C.	250	26	Ohio	147–233	26
Florida	175	26	Oklahoma	197	26
Georgia	145	26	Oregon	216	26
Hawaii	212	26	Pennsylvania	241–249	26
Idaho	185	26	Puerto Rico	95	20
Illinois	168–219	26	Rhode Island	191–236	26
Indiana	96–161	26	South Carolina	125	26
Iowa	162–199	26	South Dakota	129	26
Kansas	197	26	Tennessee	130	26
Kentucky	140	26	Texas	203	26
Louisiana	205	26	Utah	197	26
Maine	152–228	26	Vermont	154	26
Maryland	195	26	Virgin Islands	167	26
Massachusetts	220–330	30	Virginia	138	26
Michigan	197	26	Washington	197	30
Minnesota	239	26	West Virginia	225	26
Mississippi	130	26	Wisconsin	196	26
Missouri	130	26	Wyoming	198	26
Montana	179	26			

1. Maximum amounts. When two amounts are shown, higher includes dependents' allowances. *Source:* Department of Labor, Employment and Training Administration.

benefits are available to workers who have exhausted their regular benefits. An unemployed worker may receive benefits equal to the weekly benefit he received under the state program for one half the weeks of his basic entitlement to benefits up to a maximum (including regular benefits) of 39 weeks.

Federal Programs

Amendments to the Social Security Act provided unemployment insurance for Federal civilian employees (1954) and for ex-servicemen (1958). Benefits under these programs are paid by state employment security agencies as agents of the federal government under agreements with the Secretary of Labor. Eligibility for benefits and the amount of benefits paid are determined according to the terms and conditions of the applicable state unemployment insurance law. Thus, federal civilian employees and ex-servicemen are subject to the same eligibility, disqualification, and benefit payment provisions as are claimants for benefits under the state unemployment insurance system.

Copyrights

Source: Library of Congress, Copyright Office.

The copyright law (Title 17 of the United States Code) was amended by the enactment of a statute for its general revision, Public Law 94–553 (90 Stat. 2541), which was signed by the President on October 19, 1976. The new law superseded the copyright act of 1909, as amended, which remained effective until the new enactment took effect on January 1, 1978.

Under the new law, all copyrightable works, whether published or unpublished, are subject to a single system of statutory protection which gives a copyright owner the exclusive right to reproduce the copyrighted work in copies or phonorecords and distribute them to the public by sale, rental, lease, or lending. Among the other rights given to the owner of a copyright are the exclusive rights to prepare derivative works based upon the copyrighted work, to perform the work publicly if it be literary, musical, dramatic, choreographic, a pantomime, motion picture, or other audiovisual work, and in the case of literary, musical, dramatic, and choreographic works, pantomimes, and pictorial, graphic, or sculptural works, including the individual images of a motion picture or other audiovisual work, to display the copyrighted work publicly. All of these rights are subject to certain exceptions, including the principle of "fair use" which the new statute specifically recognizes.

Special provisions are included which permit compulsory licensing for the recording of musical compositions, noncommercial transmissions by public broadcasters of published musical and graphic works, performances of copyrighted music by jukeboxes, and the secondary transmission of copyrighted works on cable television systems.

Copyright protection under the new law extends to original works of authorship fixed in any tangible medium of expression, now known or later developed, from which they can be perceived, reproduced, or otherwise communicated, either directly or with the aid of a machine or device. Works of authorship include books, periodicals and other literary works, musical compositions with accompanying lyrics, dramas and dramatico-musical compositions, pantomimes and choreographic works, motion pictures and other audiovisual works, and sound recordings.

As a mandatory condition of copyright protection under the law in effect before 1978, all published copies of a work were required to bear a copyright notice. The 1976 Act provides for a notice on published copies, but omission or errors will not immediately result in forfeiture of the copyright, and can be corrected within certain time limits. Innocent infringers misled by the omission or error will be shielded from liability.

Registration in the Copyright Office is not a condition of copyright protection but will be a prerequisite to bringing an action in a court of law for infringement. With certain exceptions, the remedies of statutory damages and attorney's fees will not be available for infringements occurring before registration. Copies or phonorecords published in the United States with notice of copyright are required to be deposited for the collections of the Library of Congress, not as a condition of copyright protection, but under provisions of the law subjecting the copyright owner to certain penalties for failure to deposit after a demand by the Register of Copyrights. Registration is permissive, but may be made either at the time the depository requirements are satisfied or at any other time during the subsistence of the copyright.

For works already under statutory protection, the new law retains the present term of copyright of 28 years from first publication (or from registration in some cases), renewable by certain persons for a second period of protection, but it increases the length of the second period to 47 years. Copyrights in their first term on January 1, 1978, must still be renewed during the last (28th) year of the original copyright term to receive the maximum statutory term of 75 years (a first term of 28 years plus a renewal term of 47 years).

Copyrights in their second term on January 1, 1978, are automatically extended up to a maximum of 75 years, without the need for further renewal. Unpublished works that are already in existence on January 1, 1978, but are not protected by statutory copyright and have not yet gone into the public domain, will generally obtain automatic Federal copyright protection for the author's life, plus an additional 50 years after the author's death, but in any event, for a minimal term of 25 years (that is, until December 31, 2002), and if the work is published before that date, then for an additional term of 25 years, through the end of 2027.

For works created on or after January 1, 1978, the new law provides a term lasting for the author's life, plus an additional 50 years after the author's death. For works made for hire, and for anonymous and pseudonymous works (unless the author's identity is revealed in Copyright Office records), the new term will be 75 years from publication or 100 years from creation, whichever is shorter. The new law provides that all terms of copyright will run through the end of the calendar year in which they would otherwise expire. This will not only affect the duration of copyrights, but also the time-limits for renewal registrations.

Works already in the public domain cannot be protected under the new law. The 1976 Act provides no procedure for restoring protection to works in which copyright has been lost for any reason. In general, works published before January 1, 1913, are not under copyright protection in the United States, at least insofar as any version published before that date is concerned.

The new law requires that all visually perceptible copies published in the United States or elsewhere bear a notice of copyright affixed in such manner and location as to give reasonable notice of the claim of copyright. The notice consists of the symbol © (the letter C in a circle), the word "Copyright," or the abbreviation "Copr.," and the year of first publication of the work, and the name of the owner of copyright in the work. EXAMPLE: © *1988 John Doe.*

The notice of copyright prescribed for sound recordings consists of the symbol ℗ (the letter P in a circle), the year of first publication of the sound recording, and the name of the owner of copyright in the sound recording, placed on the surface of the phonorecord, or on the phonorecord label or container, in such manner and location as to give reasonable notice of the claim of copyright EXAMPLE: ℗ *1988 Doe Records, Inc.*

A work by a U.S. citizen may obtain copyright protection in all countries that are members of the Universal Copyright Convention (UCC), provided the copyright notice appearing on all copies from the date of first publication includes the symbol ©, together with the name of the copyright owner and the year date of publication. EXAMPLE: © *John Doe 1988.*

Further information and application forms may be obtained free of charge upon request from the Copyright Office, Library of Congress, Washington, D.C. 20559.

Patents

Source: Department of Commerce, Patent and Trademark Office.

A patent, in the most general sense, is a document issued by a government, conferring some special right or privilege. The term is now restricted mainly to patents for inventions; occasionally, land patents.

The grant of a patent for an invention gives the inventor the privilege, for a limited period of time, of excluding others from making, using, or selling a certain article. However, it does not give him the right to make, use, or sell his own invention if it is an improvement on some unexpired patent whose claims are infringed thereby.

In the U.S., the law provides that a patent may be granted, for a term of 17 years, to any person who has invented or discovered any new and useful art, machine, manufacture, or composition of matter, as well as any new and useful improvements thereof. A patent may also be granted to a person who has invented or discovered and asexually reproduced a new and distinct variety of plant (other than a tuber-propagated one) or has invented a new, original and ornamental design for an article of manufacture.

A patent is granted only upon a regularly filed application, complete in all respects; upon payment of the fees; and upon determination that the disclosure is complete and that the invention is new, useful, and, in view of the prior art, unobvious to one skilled in the art. The disclosure must be of such nature as to enable others to reproduce the invention.

A complete application, which must be addressed to the Commissioner of Patents and Trademarks, Washington, D.C. 20231, consists of a specification with one or more claims; oath or declaration; drawing (whenever the nature of the case admits of it); and a basic filing fee of $170.00[1] The filing fee is not returned to the applicant if the patent is refused. If the patent is allowed, another fee of $280.00[1] is required before the patent is issued. The fee for design patent application is $70.00[1]; the issue fee is $100.00[1]. Maintenance fees are required on utility patents at stipulated intervals.

Applications are ordinarily considered in the order in which they are received. Patents are not granted for printed matter, for methods of doing business, or for devices for which claims contrary to natural laws are made. Applications for a perpetual-motion machine have been made from time to time, but until a working model is presented that actually fulfills the claim, no patent will be issued.

1. Fees quoted are for small entities. Fees are double for corporations.

Additional Consumer Sources

Consult the following special sections of *Information Please Almanac* for specific consumer information

Trademarks

Source: Department of Commerce, Patent and Trademark Office.

A trademark may be defined as a word, letter, device, or symbol, as well as some combination of these, which is used in connection with merchandise and which points distinctly to the origin of the goods.

Certificates of registration of trademarks are issued under the seal of the Patent and Trademark Office and may be registered by the owner if he is engaged in interstate or foreign commerce, since any Federal jurisdiction over trademarks arises under the commerce clause of the Constitution. Trademarks may be registered by foreign owners who comply with our law, as well as by citizens of foreign countries with which the U.S. has treaties relating to trademarks. American citizens may register trademarks in foreign countries by complying with the laws of those countries. The right to registration and protection of trademarks in many foreign countries is guaranteed by treaties.

General jurisdiction in trademark cases involving Federal Registrations is given to Federal courts. Adverse decisions of examiners on applications for registration are appealable to the Trademark Trial and Appeal Board, whose affirmances, and decisions in *inter partes* proceedings, are subject to court review. Before adopting a trademark, a person should make a search of prior marks to avoid infringing unwittingly upon them.

The duration of a trademark registration is 20 years, but it may be renewed indefinitely for 20-year periods, provided the trademark is still in use at the time of expiration.

The application fee is $200.

Beware of Illegal Patent Services

It is illegal under patent law (35 USC 33) for anyone to hold himself out as qualified to prepare and prosecute patent applications unless he is registered with the Patent Office. Also, Patent Office regulations forbid registered practitioners advertising for patent business. Some inventors, unaware of this, enter into binding contracts with persons and firms which advertise their assistance in making patent searches, preparing drawings, specifications, and patent applications, only to discover much later that their applications require the services of fully qualified agents or attorneys.

Birthstones

Month	Stone	Month	Stone
January	Garnet	July	Ruby or Star Ruby
February	Amethyst	August	Peridot or Sardonyx
March	Aquamarine or Bloodstone	September	Sapphire or Star Sapphire
April	Diamond	October	Opal or Tourmaline
May	Emerald	November	Topaz
June	Pearl or Alexandrite	December	Turquoise or Zircon

Source: Jewelry Industry Council.

Shopping By Phone

The Fair Credit Billing Act provides certain protections for people who pay for phone orders by credit card.

If you prefer the ease of buying by phone, you assume the responsibility if merchandise is not delivered or is delivered late. However, the FCBA contains a billing-error resolution procedure that applies to disputes over billing errors on periodic statements, including charges for goods or services that you did not accept and that were not delivered as agreed. By following the provisions of this federal law, you may withhold payment on the disputed portion of your credit card bill until the dispute is resolved.

To be protected under the law, you must send a separate written billing error notice to the creditor 60 days after the first bill containing the error was mailed to you. The creditor must acknowledge your billing error notice in writing within 30 days after it is received, unless the creditor has resolved the problem within that period. You are still required to pay any part of the bill that is not disputed, including finance charges.

Disputes concerning the quality of goods and services are not necessarily billing errors, so the billing-error procedure may not apply. If you purchased unsatisfactory goods or services with a credit card, the FCBA allows you to withhold payment from the credit card issuer up to the amount of credit withstanding for the disputed transaction and any finance or other charges on that amount. No special time limitation applies to this protection.

To take advantage of this protection regarding the quality of goods you first must have made a good faith attempt to resolve the dispute with the seller. However, you are not required to use any special procedure or form of correspondence in asking the seller to resolve your problem. In addition, in most cases, you must have bought the item in your home state or within 100 miles of your current billing address, and the amount charged must have been more than $50. These dollar and distance limitations do not apply if the seller also is the card issuer or if there is a special business relationship between the seller and the card issuer.

You might consider placing your order by phone but sending payment by mail, thus giving your telephone order the further protection of the Mail Order Rule, under which companies are required to ship your order within the time promised in their advertisement.

Directory of Federal Information Centers

If you have questions about any service or agency in the Federal Government, you may want to call the Federal Information Center (FIC) nearest you for a free call or minimum long-distance charge. FICs are prepared to help consumers find needed information or locate the right agency for help with problems. NOTE: Telephone numbers are subject to change.

Alabama
Birmingham (205) 322-8591
Mobile (205) 438-1421

Alaska
Anchorage (907) 271-3650

Arizona
Phoenix (602) 261-3313

Arkansas
Little Rock (501) 378-6177

California
Los Angeles (213) 894-3800
Sacramento (916) 551-2380
San Diego (619) 293-6030
San Francisco (415) 556-6600
Santa Ana (714) 836-2386

Colorado
Colorado Springs (303) 471-9491
Denver (303) 844-6575
Pueblo (303) 544-9523

Connecticut
Hartford (203) 527-2617
New Haven (203) 624-4720

Florida
Ft. Lauderdale (305) 522-8531
Jacksonville (904) 354-4756
Miami (305) 356-4155
Orlando (305) 422-1800
St. Petersburg (813) 893-3495
Tampa (813) 893-3495
West Palm Beach (305) 833-7566

Georgia
Atlanta (404) 331-6891

Hawaii
Honolulu (808) 546-8620

Illinois
Chicago (312) 353-4242

Indiana
Gary (219) 883-4110
Indianapolis (317) 269-7373

Iowa
From any Iowa location
800-532-1556 (toll free)

Kansas
From any Kansas location
800-432-2934 (toll free)

Kentucky
Louisville (502) 582-6261

Louisiana
New Orleans (504) 589-6696

Maryland
Baltimore (301) 962-4980

Massachusetts
Boston (617) 565-8121

Michigan
Detroit (313) 226-7016
Grand Rapids (616) 451-2628

Minnesota
Minneapolis (612) 349-5333

Missouri
St. Louis (314) 425-4106
From other Missouri locations
800-392-7711 (toll free)

Nebraska
Omaha (402) 221-3353
From other Nebraska locations
800-642-8383 (toll free)

New Jersey
Newark (201) 645-3600
Trenton (609) 396-4400

New Mexico
Albuquerque (505) 766-3091

New York
Albany (518) 463-4421
Buffalo (716) 846-4010
New York (212) 264-4464
Rochester (716) 546-5075
Syracuse (315) 476-8545

North Carolina
Charlotte (704) 376-3600

Ohio
Akron (216) 375-5638
Cincinnati (513) 684-2801
Cleveland (216) 522-4040
Columbus (614) 221-1014
Dayton (513) 223-7377
Toledo (419) 241-3223

Oklahoma
Oklahoma City (405) 231-4868
Tulsa (918) 584-4193

Oregon
Portland (503) 221-2222

Pennsylvania
Philadelphia (215) 597-7042
Pittsburgh (412) 644-3456

Rhode Island
Providence (401) 331-5565

Tennessee
Chattanooga (615) 265-8231
Memphis (901) 521-3285
Nashville (615) 242-5056

Texas
Austin (512) 472-5494
Dallas (214) 767-8585
Fort Worth (817) 334-3624
Houston (713) 229-2552
San Antonio (512) 224-4471

Utah
Salt Lake City (801) 524-5353

Virginia
Norfolk (804) 441-3101
Richmond (804) 643-4928
Roanoke (703) 982-8591

Washington
Seattle (206) 442-0570
Tacoma (206) 383-5230

Wisconsin
Milwaukee (414) 271-2273

Shopping for a Bank Credit Card

According to the "Bank Credit Card Observer," a monthly consumer newsletter published by New World Decisions, Inc., 120 Wood Avenue South, Iselin, N.J. 08830, you should ask the following questions when shopping for a bank credit card:

Are there any minimum transaction fees (service charges) for purchases and/or cash advances?

Is there a grace period for cash advances?

What is the annual fee?

Are free credit cards issued to customers who have certain kinds of accounts at the bank?

Is a fee charged for exceeding the credit limit?

Is there a fee for late payments?

Too many customers may assume they need a relationship with banks in their own states to qualify for a bank credit card, but in fact they can apply for cards through the mail from other states. Applicants should shop widely for such cards before making their selection.

TOLL-FREE NUMBERS

There are thousands of toll-free numbers available to consumers. However, very few of them can be used in all states. Most toll-free numbers are for local use only and are listed in your telephone directory.

The following is a selection of "800" numbers known to *Information Please Almanac* that can be used by readers throughout the United States.

AIDS
AIDS Hotline
U.S. Public Health Service
1-800-342-2437
Hours: 24 hours, 7 days

A recording provides the latest information to the public about Acquired Immune Deficiency Syndrome (AIDS).

ALZHEIMER'S DISEASE
Alzheimer's Disease and Related Disorders Association, Inc.
1-800-621-0379
1-800-572-6037 (Illinois)
Hours: 24 hours, 7 days

Information and referral service. Provides support for patients and their families, aids research efforts, etc.

AUTOMOBILE
Auto Safety Hotline
National Highway Traffic Safety Administration
202-366-0123 (Washington, D.C.)
1-800-424-9393 (Elsewhere)
Hours: 8:00–4:00, EST Mon.–Fri.
Answering service after hours.

Handles complaints on safety-related defects, and receives reports of vehicle safety problems. Provides information and in some cases literature on: •motor vehicle safety recalls •car seats •automobile equipment •tires •motor homes •drunk driving •gas mileage

BANKING
Federal Deposit Insurance Corporation
202-898-3536 (Washington, D.C.)
1-800-424-5488 (Elsewhere)
Hours: 9:00–4:00, EST Mon.–Fri.

Provides general banking information on consumer banking laws. Will refer consumer to proper regulatory agency that supervises institution complaint is being filed against.

Federal Home Loan Bank Board
202-377-6988 (Washington, D.C.)
1-800-424-5405 (Elsewhere)
Hours: 24-hour recording

Provides information on federal adjustable mortgage rates.

BOATING SAFETY HOTLINE
U.S. Coast Guard
1-800-368-5647
1-202-267-0972 (Washington, D.C.)
Hours: 8:00—4:00 EST Mon.-Fri.

Provides information on boats and associated equipment involved in safety defect (recall) campaigns for past five model years. Takes complaints about possible safety defects. Cannot resolve non-safety problems between consumer and manufacturer and cannot recommend or endorse specific boats or products.

BLIND
National Federation of the Blind
1-800-638-7518, 8-5 EST, Mon.-Fri.
1-301-659-9314 (Maryland)

Provides job information. Concerned about the rights of the blind.

CHEMICALS
Chemical Referral Center
1-800-262-8200
1-202-887-1315, collect (Alaska)
In Washington, D.C. call locally.
Hours: 8:00-9:00, EST, Mon.-Fri.

Answers questions regarding the toxicity of chemicals and how to dispose of toxic chemicals. A Chemical Manufacturers Association referral service giving information: Name and phone number of manufacturer's safety liaison.

CHILD ABUSE
Parents Anonymous
1-800-352-0386 (California)
1-800-421-0353 (Elsewhere)
Hours: 8:30–5:00 Mon.–Fri., PST
Has a 24-hour hotline.

COCAINE ABUSE
National Cocaine Hotline
1-800-COCAINE
Hours: 24 hours—7days

Provides information on cocaine and help for cocaine abusers and drug-related problems.

CIVIL RIGHTS HOTLINE
Office of Civil Rights
1-800-368-1019
Hours: 9:00—8:00, EST Mon.-Fri. Answering machine after 8:00 p.m., including weekends.

Accepts complaints regarding discrimination on the basis of race, color, national origin, handicap, or age occurring in Health and Human Services programs, i.e. in admission to hospitals, nursing homes, day care centers, or federally funded state health care assistance.

DEPARTMENT OF DEFENSE
1-800-424-9098 (Washington, D.C.)
223-5080 (Autovon Line)
693-5080 (FTS)
Hours: 8:00–5:00, EST

Operated for citizens to report suspected cases of fraud and waste involving the Department of Defense. The anonymity of callers will be respected.

DRUG ABUSE
National Institute on Drug Abuse Prevention Branch
1-800-638-2045
Hours: 8:00—5:00, EST Mon.-Fri.

Gives technical assistance service to individuals, schools, and organizations planning prevention programs for youth and their communities. NOTE: Does not accept crisis calls or provide medical information.

ELECTIONS
Federal Election Commission
Clearinghouse on Election Administration
1-800-424-9530
202-376-3120 (Wash. D.C., Alaska, and Hawaii)
Hours: 8:30—5:00, EST Mon.-Fri.

Provides information on Federal elections.

ENERGY
Conservation and Renewable Energy Inquiry and Referral Service
1-800-462-4983 (Pennsylvania)
1-800-233-3071 (Alaska and Hawaii)
1-800-523-2929 (Elsewhere)
Hours: 9:00–5:00, EST Mon.–Fri.

Provides non-technical information on solar, wind, and other energy heating and cooling technologies, energy conservation, and alcohol fuels.

ENVIRONMENT
Hazardous Waste
RCRA Superfund Hotline
Environmental Protection Agency
202-382-3000 (Washington, D.C.)
1-800-424-9346 (Elsewhere)
Hours: 8:30–4:30, EST Mon.–Fri.

Provides information and interpretation of federal hazardous waste regulations. Will provide referrals regarding other hazardous waste matters.

Pesticide Hotline
National Pesticide Telecommunications Network
1-800-858-7378
Hours: 24 hours—7 days

Provides information on health hazards of pesticides. Will refer callers to human and animal poison control centers in their states if necessary.

GAY-LESBIAN HOTLINE
National Gay/Lesbian Crisisline (NGLC)
1-800-221-7044
1-212-529-1604 (New York, Alaska and Hawaii)
Hours: 3:00—9:00 p.m., EST, Mon.-Fri.

Gives assistance to victims of anti-gay/lesbian violence and law enforcement agencies. Offers phone crisis-counseling and referrals, community mobilization, and incident documentation. Provides AIDS information and referrals. The NGLC is an all-purpose, gay-lesbian crisis line.

HANDICAPPED
Library of Congress
202-287-5100 (Washington, D.C.)
1-800-424-8567 (Elsewhere)
Hours: 8:00–4:30, EST Mon.–Fri.
Answering service after hours.

Provides information on programs and books for the blind and physically handicapped.

HEALTH CARE
Cancer Information Service
National Cancer Institute
National Institutes of Health
Department of Health & Human Services
808-524-1234 (Hawaii) (neighboring islands call collect)
1-800-638-6070 (Alaska)
1-800-422-6237 (National Cancer Institute)
1-800-4-Cancer (Elsewhere)
Hours: 9:00–5:00, EST Mon.–Fri.

Provides information on cancer, prevention, treatment and ongoing research; fills requests for pamphlets and other literature on cancer.

National Health Information Center
Department of Health & Human Services
202-429-9091 (Washington, D.C., Virginia, Alaska, and Hawaii)
1-800-336-4797 (Elsewhere)
Hours: 9:00–5:00 EST Mon.–Fri.

Provides referrals to sources of information on health-related issues.

Second Surgical Opinion Hotline for Non-Emergency Surgery
Sponsored by Health Care Financing Administration
Department of Health and Human Services
1-800-638-6833
1-800-492-6603 (Maryland)
Hours: 8:00—12:00, EST 7 days

Callers will be given a free referral to an agency that maintains listing of physicians in their area who will give a second opinion before an operation is performed.

HOUSING
Fair Housing Discrimination Hotline
Fair Housing and Equal Opportunity
Department of Housing and Urban Development
202-426-3500 (Washington, D.C.)
1-800-424-8590 (Elsewhere)
Hours: 8:00–8:00p.m., EST, Mon.–Fri.
Answering service after hours.

Receives housing discrimination complaints due to race, color, religion, sex or national origin.

HOUSEHOLD APPLIANCES
Major Appliance Consumer Action Panel (MACAP)
1-800-621-0477
1-312-984-5858 (Illinois)
Hours: 8:30—4:30, CST Mon.-Fri.

An independent mediation group that offers to help users of major household appliances resolve complaints if they have been unsuccessful in getting satisfaction from the manufacturer. The Panel's recommendations are not binding to either party.

INSURANCE
Federal Crime Insurance
Federal Emergency Management Administration
301-251-1660 (Maryland)
1-800-638-8780 (Elsewhere)
Hours: 8:30–5:00, EST Mon.–Fri.
Answering service after hours.

Provides information on federal crime insurance for both homes and businesses.

National Flood Insurance
301-731-5300 (Washington, D.C. area)
1-800-492-6605 (Maryland)
1-800-638-6831 (Alaska, Hawaii, Puerto Rico, Virgin Islands, Guam)
1-800-638-6620 (Elsewhere)
Hours: 8:00–8:00, EST Mon.–Fri.

Provides information on community participation in the flood program (emergency or regular). If the community does not have a program, it is not eligible for government-subsidized insurance relief. Complaints are referred to the proper office within the agency.

NUCLEAR TESTING HEALTH RESEARCH
Nuclear Test Personnel Review (NTPR)
Defense Nuclear Agency
1-800-336-3068
703-285-5610 (Alaska, Hawaii, Puerto Rico, and Virginia. Call collect if necessary)
Hours: 8:30—5:00, EST Mon.-Fri. Recorded message after hours.

Concerned with the health status of Department of Defense personnel, military, and civilians who participated in atmospheric nuclear tests in Nevada or the Pacific Ocean and those who participated in the U.S. post-war occupation of Hiroshima and Nagasaki, Japan. Seeks to make personal contact with those individuals involved.

ORGAN DONOR INFORMATION
The Living Bank
1-800-528-2971
1-713-528-2971 (TX call)
Hours: 8:00—5:00, CST Mon.-Fri. Has 24 hour answering service.

The Living Bank International is a nonprofit service organization dedicated to helping those who, after death, wish to donate part or all of their bodies for transplantation, therapy, medical research, or anatomical studies. It provides information and donor registration material. NOTE: The Bank does not receive donated organs and bodies and is not a storage facility for them.

The American Liver Foundation
1-800-223-0179
Hours: 8:30-4:30, EST, Mon.-Fri.
201-857-2626 (New Jersey)
Hours: 24 hour recording

Answers questions and keeps list of liver transplant centers.

PRODUCT SAFETY
Consumer Product Safety Commission
1-800-638-2772
Hours: 8:30–5:00, EST Mon.–Fri.

Provides information on the safety of consumer products. Receives reports of product-related deaths, illnesses, and injuries. Products are not rated or recommended.

RUNAWAYS
1-800-231-6946 (U.S.A. except Texas)
1-800-392-3352 (Texas)
Hours: 24 hours—7 days

Helps runaways by referring them to shelters, clinics, local hotlines. Will relay messages from parents to the runaway.

SOCIAL SECURITY AND MEDICARE FRAUD
Inspector General Hotline
Department of Health and Human Services
1-800-368-5779
Hours: 8:30—5:00, EST Mon.-Fri.

Takes calls on fraud in Social Security payments or abuse, Medicaid and Medicare fraud and other HHS programs. Recording machine after hours.

VIETNAM VETERANS
Vietnam Veterans of America
1-800-424-7275 (answering machine)
202-332-2700 (Washington, D.C.)
Hours: 9:00—5:30, EST Mon.-Fri.

Answering machine takes messages for information and help. Provides information on Agent Orange. Will answer questions on direct line.

Your Right to Federal Records

The Freedom of Informaction Act (FOIA) guarantees any person the right, enforceable in court, to look at all Federal agency records except for those exempted in the Act. FOIA applies only to records of the executive branch of the Federal Government, not to those of the Congress or the Federal courts. It also does not apply to records of any State or local government or any private entity.

The Act contains one very important provision concerning privacy—Exemption 6. It may protect you from others seeking information about you, but may block you if you seek information about others. FOIA Exemption 6 permits an agency to withold information about individuals if disclosing it would be a "clearly unwarranted invasion of personal privacy." This includes, for example, most of the information in medical and personnel files.

The Privacy Act gives citizens the right to see files about themselves and the right to sue the Government for permitting others to see their files without their knowledge and permission. You may order a copy of the Privacy Act, Public Law 93-579, from the Superintendent of Documents, U.S. Government Printing Office, for $2.50. Please specify stock number 022-003-90866-8.

You can purchase a booklet, "A Citizen's Guide on How To Use the Freedom of Information Act and the Privacy Act in Requesting Government Documents," for $1.75. from the Superintendent of Documents, U.S. Government Printing Office, Washington, D.C. 20402. Please specify stock number 052-071-00540-4.

U.S. Telephone Area Codes and Time Zones

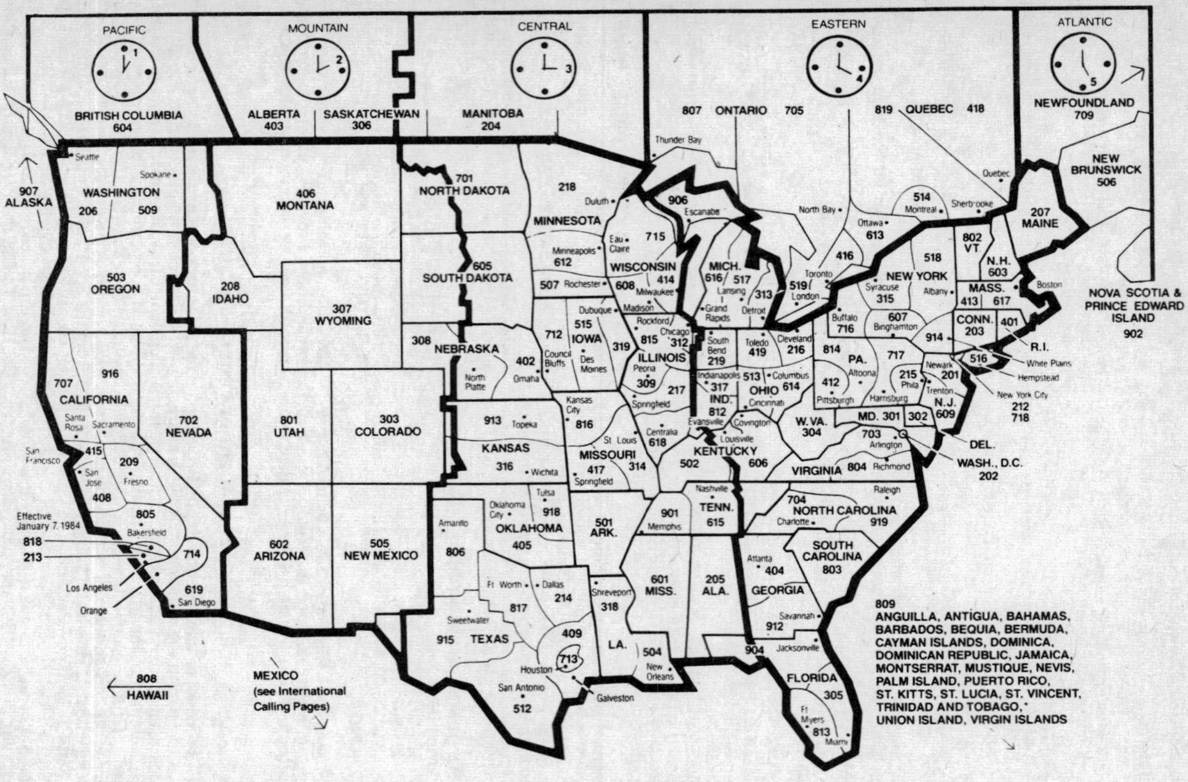

International Dialing: Codes and Time Differences for Many Countries

Source: The Professional Secretary's Handbook, Copyright ©, Houghton Mifflin Company.

To Determine the time in the countries listed below, add the number of hours shown under your own time zone to your local time (or subtract, if preceded by a minus sign). Time differences are based on Standard Time, observed in the U.S. (in most states) from the last Sunday in October until the first Sunday in April. This may vary in some countries. Several countries have more than one time zone. The time differences for these countries are based in the following cities: Sydney, Australia; Rio de Janeiro, Brazil; Jakarta, Indonesia; Kuala Lumpur, Malaysia; and Moscow, U.S.S.R.

Country Codes		City Codes	Time Difference U.S. Time Zones			
			EST	CST	MST	PST
Andorra	33	All Points 078	6	7	8	9
Argentina	54	Buenos Aires 1, Cordoba 51, Rosario 41	2	3	4	5
Australia	61	Canberra 62, Melbourne 3, Sydney 2	16	17	18	19
Austria	43	Graz 316, Linz 732, Vienna 222	6	7	8	9
Bahrain	973	*	8	9	10	11
Belgium	32	Antwerp 31, Brussels 2, Ghent 91, Liege 41	6	7	8	9
Belize	501	Belize City*, Belmopan 08, Corozal Town 04	−1	0	1	2
Bolivia	591	Cochabamba 42, La Paz 2, Santa Cruz 33	1	2	3	4
Brazil	55	Belo Horizonte 31, Brasilia 61, Sao Paulo 11	2	3	4	5
Chile	56	Concepcion 42, Santiago 2, Valparaiso 31	2	3	4	5
Colombia	57	Bogota*, Cali 3, Medellin 4	0	1	2	3
Costa Rica	506	*	−1	0	1	2
Cyprus	357	Limassol 51, Nicosia 21, Paphos 61	7	8	9	10
Denmark	45	Aarhus 6, Copenhagen 1 or 2, Odense 9	6	7	8	9
East Germany	37	Berlin 2, Dresden 51, Leipzig 41	6	7	8	9
Ecuador	593	Ambato 2, Cuenca 4, Guayaquil 4, Quito 2	0	1	2	3
El Salvador	503	*	−1	0	1	2
Fiji	679	*	17	18	19	20
Finland	358	Helsinki 0, Tampere 31, Turku-Abo 21	7	8	9	10
France	33	Bordeaux 56, Lille 20, Lyon 7, Marseille 91, Nice 93, Paris 1, Strasbourg 88, Toulouse 61	6	7	8	9
Great Britain	44	Belfast 232, Birmingham 21, Cardiff 222, Edinburgh 31, Glasgow 41, Leeds 532, Liverpool 51, London 1, Sheffield 742	5	6	7	8
Greece	30	Athens 1, Iraklion 81, Kavala 51, Larissa 41, Patrai 61, Piraeus 1, Thessaloniki 31, Volos 421	7	8	9	10
Guadeloupe	596	*	1	2	3	4
Guatemala	502	Guatemala City 2, Quezaltenango*	−1	0	1	2
Guyana	592	Bartica 05, Georgetown 02	2	3	4	5
Haiti	509	Cap Hatien 3, Gonaive 2, Port Au Prince 1	0	1	2	3
Honduras	504	*	−1	0	1	2
Hong Kong	852	Hong Kong 5, Kowloon 3, Sha Tin 0	13	14	15	16
Indonesia	62	Jakarta 21, Medan 61, Semarang 24	12	13	14	15
Iran	98	Esfahan 31, Mashad 51, Tabriz 41, Teheran 21	8½	9½	10½	11½
Iraq	964	Baghdad 1, Basra 40, Hilla 30, Mosul 60	8	9	10	11
Ireland	353	Cork 21, Dublin 1, Galway 91, Limerick 61	5	6	7	8
Israel	972	Haifa , Jerusalem 2, Ramat Gan 3, Tel Aviv 3	7	8	9	10

Country Codes		City Codes	Time Difference U.S. Time Zones			
			EST	CST	MST	PST
Italy	39	Bari 80, Bologna 51, Florence 55, Genoa 10, Milan 2, Naples 81, Palermo 91, Rome 6, Turin 11	6	7	8	9
Ivory Coast	225	*	5	6	7	8
Japan	81	Kitakyushu 93, Kobe 78, Kyoto 75, Nagoya 52, Osaka 6, Sapporo 11, Tokyo 3, Yokohama 45	14	15	16	17
Kenya	254	Mombasa 11, Nairobi 2, Nakuru 37	8	9	10	11
Kuwait	965	*	8	9	10	11
Liberia	231	*	5	6	7	8
Libya	218	Benghazi 61, Misuratha 51, Tripoli 21	7	8	9	10
Liechtenstein	41	All points 75	6	7	8	9
Luxembourg	352	*	6	7	8	9
Malaysia	60	Ipoh 5, Kelang 3, Kuala Lumpur 3	12½	13½	14½	15½
Martinique	596	*	1	2	3	4
Monaco	33	All points 93	6	7	8	9
Netherlands	31	Amsterdam 20, Rotterdam 10	6	7	8	9
Netherlands Antilles	599	Aruba 8, Curacoa 9	1	2	3	4
New Zealand	64	Auckland 9, Wellington 4	18	19	20	21
Nicaragua	505	Chinandega 341, Leon 31, Managua 2	−1	0	1	2
Nigeria	234	Ibadan 22, Kano 64, Lagos 1	6	7	8	9
Norway	47	Bergen 5, Oslo 2, Trondheim 75	6	7	8	9
Panama	507	*	0	1	2	3
Papua New Guinea	675	*	15	16	17	18
Paraguay	595	Asuncion 21, Concepcion 31	2	3	4	5
Peru	51	Arequipa 54, Callao 14, Lima 14, Trujillo 44	0	1	2	3
Philippines	63	Cebu 32, Davao 35, Iloilo 33, Manila 2	13	14	15	16
Portugal	351	Coimbra 39, Lisbon 19, Porto 29	5	6	7	8
Qatar	974	*	8	9	10	11
Rumania	40	Bucharest 0, Cluj 51, Constanta 16	7	8	9	10
San Marino	39	All points 541	6	7	8	9
Saudi Arabia	966	Jeddah 2, Mecca 2, Riyadh 1	8	9	10	11
Senegal	221	*	5	6	7	8
Singapore	65	*	12½	13½	14½	15½
South Africa	27	Cape Town 21, Johannesburg 11	7	8	9	10
South Korea	82	Pusan 51, Seoul 2, Taegu 53	14	15	16	17
Soviet Union	7	Kiev 044, Leningrad 812, Minsk 017, Moscow 095, Tallinn 0142	8	9	10	11
Spain	34	Barcelona 3, Madrid 1, Seville 54, Valencia 6	6	7	8	9
Sri Lanka	94	Colombo 1, Kandy 8, Moratuwa 72	10½	11½	12½	13½
Surinam	597	*	1½	2½	3½	4½
Sweden	46	Goteborg 31, Malmo 40, Stockholm 8	6	7	8	9
Switzerland	41	Basel 61, Berne 31, Geneva 22, St. Moritz 82, Zurich 1	6	7	8	9
Tahiti	689	*	−5	−4	−3	−2
Taiwan	886	Kaohsiung 7, Tainan 62, Taipei 2	13	14	15	16
Thailand	66	Bangkok 2	12	13	14	15
Tunisia	216	Menzel Bourguiba 2, Tunis 1	6	7	8	9
Turkey	90	Adana 711, Ankara 41, Istanbul 11, Izmir 51	7	8	9	10
United Arab Emirates	971	Abu Dhabi 2, Ajman 6	9	10	11	12
Uruguay	598	Canelones 332, Mercedes 532, Montevideo 2	2	3	4	5
Vatican City	39	All points 6	6	7	8	9
Venezuela	58	Caracas 2, Maracaibo 61, Valencia 41	1	2	3	4
West Germany	49	Berlin 30, Bonn 228, Essen 201, Frankfurt 611, Hamburg 40, Munich 89	6	7	8	9
Yugoslavia	38	Belgrade 11, Skoplje 91, Zagreb 41	6	7	8	9

For city codes not listed dial "0" (operator). *City Codes not required.

POSTAL REGULATIONS

Domestic Mail Service

(New postage rates are expected to go into effect sometime in 1988.) Check with your Post Office.

First Class

First-class consists of letters and written and sealed matter. The rate is 22¢ for the first oz; 17¢ for each additional oz, or fraction of an oz, up to 12 oz. Pieces over 12 oz are subject to priority-mail (heavy pieces) rates. Single postcards, 14¢; double postcards, 28¢ (14¢ for each half). The post office sells prestamped single and double postal cards. Consult your postmaster for information on business-reply mail and presort rates.

The weight limit for first-class mail is 70 lb.

Weight	Rates
First oz	$ .22
Over 1 oz, but not over 2	.39
Over 2 oz, but not over 3	.56
Over 3 oz, but not over 4	.73
Over 4 oz, but not over 5	.90
Over 5 oz, but not over 6	1.07
Over 6 oz, but not over 7	1.24
Over 7 oz, but not over 8	1.41
Over 8 oz, but not over 9	1.58
Over 9 oz, but not over 10	1.75
Over 10 oz, but not over 11	1.92
Over 11 oz, but not over 12	2.09
Over 12 oz, *see* Priority Mail	

Priority Mail (over 12 oz to 70 lb)

The zone rate applies to mailable matter over 12 oz of any class carried by air. Your local post office will supply free official zone tables appropriate to your location.

Airmail

First-class and priority mail receive airmail service.

Express Mail

Express Mail Service is available for any mailable article up to 70 lb in weight and 108 in. in combined length and girth. Flat rates: up to 2 lb, $10.75; over 2 lb and up to 5 lb, $12.85; 6 to 70 pound rates vary by weight and distance (zones).

Articles received by 5 p.m. at a postal facility offering Express Mail Service will be delivered by 3 p.m. the next day or, if you prefer, your shipment can be picked up as early as 10 a.m. the next business day. Rates include Insurance, Shipment Receipt, and Record of Delivery at the destination post office.

Consult Postmaster for other Express Mail Services and rates.

The Postal Service will refund, upon application to originating office, the postage for any Express Mail shipments not meeting the service standard except for those delayed by strike or work stoppage.

Second Class

Second-class mail is used primarily by newspapers, magazines, and other periodicals with second-class mailing privileges. For copies mailed by the public, the rate is the applicable single piece third- or fourth-class rate.

Third Class (under 16 oz)

Third-class mail is used for circulars, books, printed matter, merchandise, seeds, cuttings, bulbs, roots, scions, and plants, and all other mailable matter not in first or second class. There are two rate structures for this class, a single-piece and a bulk rate.

Many community organizations, as well as businesses, find it economical to use this service. Because of the number of categories of third-class mail, you should consult your postmaster for the one best suited to your needs.

Third-Class, Single-Piece Rates

Weight	Rates	Weight	Rates
0 to 1 oz	$ .22	Over 8 to 10 oz	$ 1.08
Over 1 to 2 oz	.39	Over 10 to 12 oz	1.18
Over 2 to 3 oz	.56	Over 12 to 14 oz	1.28
Over 3 to 4 oz	.73	Over 14 but less than 16 oz	1.38
Over 4 to 6 oz	.88		
Over 6 to 8 oz	.98		

Fourth Class (Parcel Post— 16 oz and over)

Fourth-class mail is used for merchandise, books, printed matter, and all other mailable matter not in first, second, or third class. Special fourth-class rates apply to books, library books, publications or records for the blind, and certain controlled-circulation publications.

Packages should be taken to your local post office, where the postage will be determined according to the weight of the package and the distance it is being sent. Information on weight and size limits for fourth-class mail may be obtained there.

Special Services

Registered Mail. When you use registered mail service, you are buying security—the safest way to send valuables. The full value of your mailing must be declared when mailed. You receive a receipt and the movement of your mail is controlled throughout the postal system. For an additional fee, a return receipt showing to whom, when, and where delivered may be obtained.

Fees for articles (in addition to postage)

Value			with Insurance	without Insurance
0.00	to	$ 100	$3.60	$3.55
100.01	to	500	3.90	3.80
500.01	to	1,000	4.25	4.15

For higher values, consult your postmaster.

Certified Mail. Certified mail service provides for a receipt to the sender and a record of delivery at the post office of address. No record is kept at the post office where mailed. It is handled in the ordinary mails and no insurance coverage is provided.
Fee in addition to postage, 75¢.

Return Receipts. Requested at time of mailing:

Showing to whom and date delivered	$ .70
Showing to whom, date, and address where delivered	.90
Requested after mailing:	
Showing to whom and date delivered	4.50

C.O.D. Mail. Consult your postmaster for fees and conditions of mailing.

Insured Mail. Fees, in addition to postage, for coverage against loss or damage:

Liability	Fees
$ .01 to $25	$ .50
$ 25.01 to $50	1.10
$ 50.01 to $100	1.40
$ 100.01 to $150	1.80
$ 150.01 to $200	2.10
$ 200.01 to $300	3.00
$ 300.01 to $400	3.70
$ 400.01 to 500	4.40

Special Delivery. The payment of the special-delivery fee entitles mail to the most expeditious transportation and delivery. The fee is in addition to the regular postage.

	Weight/Fees		
Class of mail	Not more than 2 lb	More than 2 lb but not more than 10 lb	More than 10 lb
First-class	$2.95	$3.15	$4.00
All other classes	3.10	3.60	4.50

Special Handling. Payment of the special-handling fee entitles third- and fourth-class matter to the most expeditious handling and transportation, but not special delivery. The fee is in addition to the regular postage.

Weight	Fees
Not more than 10 lb	$1.10
More than 10 lb	1.60

Money Orders. Money orders are used for the safe transmission of money.

Amount of money order			Fees
$ .01	to	$25	$ .75
$ 25.01	to	$700	1.00

Minimum Mail Sizes

All mail must be at least 0.007 in. thick and mail that is 1/4 in. or less in thickness must be at least 3 1/2 in. in height, at least 5 in. long, and rectangular in shape (except keys and identification devices). NOTE: Pieces greater than 1/4 in. thick can be mailed even if they measure less than 3 1/2 by 5 inches.

Adhesive Stamps Available

Purpose	Form	Denomination and prices
Ordinary postage	Single or sheet	1, 2, 3, 4, 5, 7, 10, 12[1], 13[1], 14, 15[1], 17, 18[1], 19[1], 20[1], 22, 25, 28[1], 29[1], 30, 35[1], 37, 39, 40, and 50¢, $1, $2[1], and $5.
	Books	20 at 22 cents ($4.40), 5 at 22 cents ($1.10), 10 at 22 cents ($2.20), 3 at $10.75 ($32.25), and 3 at $12.85 ($38.55).
	Coil of 100	17, 20[1], and 22¢ (dispenser and stamp affixer for use with these coils are also available).
	Coil of 500	1, 2, 3, 4, 5, 6, 10, 12, 13[1], 14, 15[1], 17, 18, 20[1], 22¢, and $1.
	Coil of 3000	1, 2, 3, 4, 5, 6, 10, 12, 13[1], 14, 15[1], 17, 18, 20[1], 22, and 25¢.
International airmail postage	Single or sheet	33, 39, and 44¢

1. Will be discontinued when stock is exhausted.

Non-Standard Mail

All first-class mail weighing one ounce or less and all single-piece rate third-class mail weighing one ounce or less is nonstandard (and subject to a 10¢ surcharge in addition to the applicable postage and fees) if any of the following dimensions are exceeded: length—11 1/2 inches; height—6 1/8 inches; thickness—1/4 inch, or the piece has a height to length (aspect) ratio which does not fall between 1 to 1.3 and 1 to 2.5 inclusive. (The aspect ratio is found by dividing the length by the height. If the answer is between 1.3 and 2.5 inclusive, the piece has a standard aspect ratio).

International Mail Service

Letters and Letter Packages

Items of mail containing personal handwritten or typewritten communications having the character of current correspondence must be sent as letters or letter packages. Unless prohibited by the country of destination, dutiable merchandise may be transmitted in packages prepaid at the letter rate of postage. Weight limit for all countries, 4 pounds. For rates, consult your local post office.

International Airmail

Destination	Letters and letter packages[1]	Post-cards[2]	Aero-gramme[3]
Central America Colombia, Venezuela, Caribbean Islands, Bahamas, Bermuda, St. Pierre and Miquelon	39¢ per half oz through 2 oz; 33¢ each additional half oz or fraction	33¢	36¢
All other countries except Canada and Mexico	44¢ per half oz through 2 oz; 39¢ each additional half oz through 32 oz; 39¢ each additional oz through 64 oz.	33¢	33¢

1. Weight limit, 4 lb. 2. 14¢ each for Canada and Mexico. 3. Aerogrammes, which can be folded into the form of an envelope and sent by air to all countries, are available at all post offices for 36¢. No enclosures are permitted.

For Canada and Mexico, *see* Surface Rates.

Canada and Mexico—Surface Rates

Letters and Letter Packages

Weight not over Lb	Oz	Rate	Weight not over Lb	Oz	Rate
0	1	$0.22	0	11	$2.02
0	2	0.40	0	12	2.20
0	3	0.58	1	0	2.84
0	4	0.76	1	8	3.38
0	5	0.94	2	0	3.92
0	6	1.12	2	8	4.46
0	7	1.30	3	0	5.00
0	8	1.48	3	8	5.54
0	9	1.66	4	0	6.08
0	10	1.84			

Weight limit—4 pounds. NOTE: Letter class mail to Canada and Mexico receives First Class service in the United States and airmail service in Canada and Mexico.

Countries Other Than Canada and Mexico—Surface Rates

Letters and Letter Packages

Weight not over Lb	Oz	Rate	Weight not over Lb	Oz	Rate
0	1	$0.37	0	11	$3.40
0	2	0.57	0	12	3.40
0	3	0.77	1	0	3.40
0	4	0.97	1	8	4.66
0	5	1.17	2	0	5.92
0	6	1.37	2	8	6.84
0	7	1.57	3	0	7.76
0	8	1.77	3	8	8.68
0	9	3.40	4	0	9.60
0	10	3.40			

Weight limit—4 pounds.

International Surface Parcel Post

Other Than Canada

Weight through lb	Mexico, Central America, Caribbean Islands, Bahamas, Bermuda, St. Pierre and Miquelon	All other countries
2	$ 3.70	$ 3.90
3	4.90	5.20
	$1.20 each additional lb or fraction	$1.30 each additional lb or fraction

Consult your postmaster for weight/size limits of individual countries.

For other international services and rates consult your local postmaster.

Canada Surface Parcel Post

Up to 2lb $3.35, $1.05 for each additional lb up to the maximum weight of 66lb. Minimum weight is 1 lb.

International Money Order Fees

This service available only to certain countries. Consult post office.

United Nations Stamps

United Nations stamps are issued in three different currencies, namely, U.S. dollars, Swiss francs, and Austrian schillings. Stamps in all three currencies are available at face value at each of the U.N. Postal Administration offices in New York, Geneva, and Vienna. They may be purchased over the counter, by mail, or by opening a Customer Deposit Account.

Mail orders for mint (unused) stamps and postal stationery may be sent to the U.N. Postal Administration in New York, Geneva, and Vienna. Write to: United Nations Postal Administration, P.O. Box 5900, Grand Central Station, New York, N.Y. 10017.

Authorized 2-Letter State Abbreviations

When the Post Office instituted the ZIP Code for mail in 1963, it also drew up a list of two-letter abbreviations for the states which would gradually replace the traditional ones in use. Following is the official list, including the District of Columbia, Guam, Puerto Rico, and the Virgin Islands (note that only capital letters are used):

Alabama	AL	Kentucky	KY	Ohio	OH
Alaska	AK	Louisiana	LA	Oklahoma	OK
Arizona	AZ	Maine	ME	Oregon	OR
Arkansas	AR	Maryland	MD	Pennsylvania	PA
California	CA	Massachusetts	MA	Puerto Rico	PR
Colorado	CO	Michigan	MI	Rhode Island	RI
Connecticut	CT	Minnesota	MN	South Carolina	SC
Delaware	DE	Mississippi	MS	South Dakota	SD
Dist. of Columbia	DC	Missouri	MO	Tennessee	TN
Florida	FL	Montana	MT	Texas	TX
Georgia	GA	Nebraska	NE	Utah	UT
Guam	GU	Nevada	NV	Vermont	VT
Hawaii	HI	New Hampshire	NH	Virginia	VA
Idaho	ID	New Jersey	NJ	Virgin Islands	VI
Illinois	IL	New Mexico	NM	Washington	WA
Indiana	IN	New York	NY	West Virginia	WV
Iowa	IA	North Carolina	NC	Wisconsin	WI
Kansas	KS	North Dakota	ND	Wyoming	WY

The Mail Order Merchandise Rule

The mail order rule adopted by the Federal Trade Commission in October 1975 provides that when you order by mail:

You must receive the merchandise when the seller says you will.

If you are not promised delivery within a certain time period, the seller must ship the merchandise to you no later than 30 days after your order comes in.

If you don't receive it shortly after that 30-day period, you can cancel your order and get your money back.

How the Rule Works

The seller must notify you if the promised delivery date (or the 30-day limit) cannot be met. The seller must also tell you what the new shipping date will be and give you the option to cancel the order and receive a full refund or agree to the new shipping date. The seller must also give you a free way to send back your answer, such as a stamped envelope or a postage-paid postcard. *If you don't answer, it means that you agree to the shipping delay.*

The seller must tell you if the shipping delay is going to be more than 30 days. You then can agree to the delay or, if you do not agree, the seller must return your money by the end of the first 30 days of the delay.

If you cancel a prepaid order, the seller must mail you the refund within seven business days. Where there is a credit sale, the seller must adjust your account within one billing cycle.

It would be impossible, however, for one rule to apply uniformly to such a varied field as mail order merchandising. For example, the rule does not apply to mail order photo finishing, magazine subscriptions, and other serial deliveries (except for the initial shipment); to mail order seeds and growing plants; to COD orders; or to credit orders where the buyer's account is not charged prior to shipment of the merchandise.

How to Complain About a Postal Problem

When you have a problem with your mail service, complete a Consumer Service Card which is available from letter carriers and at post offices. This will help your postmaster respond to your problem. If you wish to telephone a complaint, a postal employee will fill out the card for you.

The Consumer Advocate represents consumers at the top management level in the Postal Service. If your postal problems cannot be solved by your local post office, then write to the Consumer Advocate. His staff stands ready to serve you. Write to: The Consumer Advocate, U.S. Postal Service, Washington, D.C. 20260-6320. Or phone: 1-202-245-4514.

Pornography

You can stop the mailing of unsolicited sexually oriented advertisements to you by filling out a Form 2201, *Application for Listing Pursuant to 39 USC 3010*, at your local post office. Thirty days after your name has been added to the Postal Service reference listing, any mailer who sends you sexually oriented advertisements is subject to legal action by the United States Government.

You may also stop the mailing of any further advertisements to you which you consider "erotically arousing or sexually provocative." Fill out Form 2150, *Notice for Prohibitory Order Against Sender of Pandering Advertisement in the Mail*, at your post office for this purpose.

New C.O.D. Rules

Under new Postal Service rules, people who receive C.O.D. parcels can pay with a check made out to the mailer. This enables consumers who have problems with the merchandise to stop payment on the check before it is cashed. Under the old regulations, payment had to be made in cash or by check made out to the Postal Service.

STRUCTURES

The Seven Wonders of the World

(Not all classical writers list the same items as the Seven Wonders, but most of them agree on the following.)

The Pyramids of Egypt. A group of three pyramids, *Khufu, Khafra,* and *Menkaura* at Giza, outside modern Cairo, is often called the first wonder of the world. The largest pyramid, built by Khufu (Cheops), a king of the fourth Dynasty, had an original estimated height of 482 ft (now approximately 450 ft). The base has sides 755 ft long. It contains 2,300,000 blocks; the average weight of each is 2.5 tons. Estimated date of construction is 2800 B.C. Of all the Seven Wonders, the pyramids alone survive.

Hanging Gardens of Babylon. Often listed as the second wonder, these gardens were supposedly built by Nebuchadnezzar about 600 B.C. to please his queen, Amuhia. They are also associated with the mythical Assyrian Queen, Semiramis. Archeologists surmise that the gardens were laid out atop a vaulted building, with provisions for raising water. The terraces were said to rise from 75 to 300 ft.

The Walls of Babylon, also built by Nebuchadnezzar, are sometimes referred to as the second (or the seventh) wonder instead of the Hanging Gardens.

Statue of Zeus (Jupiter) at Olympia. The work of Phidias (5th century B.C.), this colossal figure in gold and ivory was reputedly 40 ft high. All trace of it is lost, except for reproductions on coins.

Temple of Artemis (Diana) at Ephesus. A beautiful structure, begun about 350 B.C. in honor of a non-Hellenic goddess who later became identified with the Greek goddess of the same name. The temple, with Ionic columns 60 ft high, was destroyed by invading Goths in A.D. 262.

Mausoleum at Halicarnassus. This famous monument was erected by Queen Artemisia in memory of her husband, King Mausolus of Caria in Asia Minor, who died in 353 B.C. Some remains of the structure are in the British Museum. This shrine is the source of the modern word "mausoleum."

Colossus at Rhodes. This bronze statue of Helios (Apollo), about 105 ft high, was the work of the sculptor Chares, who reputedly labored for 12 years before completing it in 280 B.C. It was destroyed during an earthquake in 224 B.C.

Pharos of Alexandria. The seventh wonder was the Pharos (lighthouse) of Alexandria, built by Sostratus of Cnidus during the 3rd century B.C. on the island of Pharos off the coast of Egypt. It was destroyed by an earthquake in the 13th century.

Famous Structures

Ancient

The *Great Sphinx of Egypt,* one of the wonders of ancient Egyptian architecture, adjoins the pyramids of Giza and has a length of 240 ft. It was built in the 4th dynasty.

Other Egyptian buildings of note include the *Temples of Karnak* and *Edfu* and the *Tombs at Beni Hassan.*

The *Parthenon of Greece,* built on the Acropolis in Athens, was the chief temple to the goddess Athena. It was believed to have been completed by 438 B.C. The present temple remained intact until the 5th century A.D. Today, though the Parthenon is in ruins, its majestic proportions are still discernible.

Other great structures of ancient Greece were the *Temples at Paestum* (about 540 and 420 B.C.); the *Temple of Poseidon* (about 460 B.C.); the *Temple of Apollo* at Corinth (about 540 B.C.); the *Temple of Apollo* at Bassae (about 450–420 B.C.); the famous *Erechtheum* atop the Acropolis (about 421–405 B.C.); the *Temple of Athena Niké* at Athens (about 426 B.C.); the *Olympieum* at Athens (174 B.C.–A.D. 131); the *Athenian Treasury* at Delphi (about 515 B.C.); the *Propylaea* of the Acropolis at Athens (437–432 B.C.); the *Theater of Dionysus* at Athens (about 350–325 B.C.); the *House of Cleopatra* at Delos (138 B.C.) and the *Theater* at Epidaurus (about 325 B.C.).

The *Colosseum (Flavian Amphitheater) of Rome,* the largest and most famous of the Roman amphitheaters, was opened for use A.D. 80. Elliptical in shape, it consisted of three stories and an upper gallery, rebuilt in stone in its present form in the third century A.D. Its seats rise in tiers, which in turn are buttressed by concrete vaults and stone piers. It could seat between 40,000 and 50,000 spectators. It was principally used for gladiatorial combat.

The *Pantheon* at Rome, begun by Agrippa in 27 B.C. as a temple, was rebuilt in its present circular form by Hadrian (A.D. 110–25). Literally the Pantheon was intended as a temple of "all the gods." It is remarkable for its perfect preservation today, and it has served continuously for 20 centuries as a place of worship.

Famous Roman arches include the *Arch of Constantine* (about A.D. 315) and the *Arch of Titus* (about A.D. 80).

Later European

St. Mark's Cathedral in Venice (1063–67), one of the great examples of Byzantine architecture, was begun in the 9th century. Partly destroyed by fire in 976, it was later rebuilt as a Byzantine edifice.

Other famous Byzantine examples of architecture are *St. Sophia* in Istanbul (A.D. 532–37); *San Vitale* in Ravenna (542); *St. Paul's Outside the Walls,* Rome (5th century); the *Kremlin* baptism and marriage church, Moscow (begun in 1397); and *St. Lorenzo Outside the Walls*, Rome, begun in 588.

The *Cathedral Group* at Pisa (1067–1173), one of the most celebrated groups of structures built in Romanesque-style, consists of the cathedral, the cathedral's baptistery, and the *Leaning Tower.* This trio forms a group by itself in the northwest corner of the city. The cathedral and baptistery are built in varicolored marble. The campanile *(Leaning Tower)* is 179 ft. high and leans more than 16 ft out of the perpendicular. There is little reason to believe that the architects intended to have the tower lean.

Other examples of Romanesque architecture include the *Vézelay Abbey* in France (1130); the *Church of Notre-Dame-du-Port* at Clermont-Ferrand in France (1100); the *Church of San Zeno* (begun in 1138) at Verona, and *Durham Cathedral* in England.

The *Alhambra* (1248–1354), located in Granada, Spain, is universally esteemed as one of the greatest masterpieces of Moslem architecture. Designed as a palace and fortress for the Moorish monarchs of Granada, it is surrounded by a heavily fortified wall more than a mile in perimeter. The location of the Alhambra in the Sierra Nevada provides a magnificent setting for this jewel of Moorish Spain.

The *Tower of London* is a group of buildings and towers covering 13 acres along the north bank of the Thames. The central *White Tower,* begun in 1078 during the reign of William the Conqueror, was originally a fortress and royal residence, but was later used as a prison. The *Bloody Tower* is associated with Anne Boleyn and other notables.

Westminster Abbey, in London, was begun in 1045 and completed in 1065. It was rebuilt and enlarged in 1245–50.

Notre-Dame de Paris (begun in 1163), one of the great examples of Gothic architecture, is a twin-towered church with a steeple over the crossing and immense flying buttresses supporting the masonry at the rear of the church.

Other famous Gothic structures are *Chartres Cathedral* (12th century); *Sainte Chapelle,* Paris (1246–48); *Laon Cathedral,* France (1160–1205); *Reims Cathedral* (about 1210–50; rebuilt after its almost complete destruction in World War I); *Rouen Cathedral* (13th–16th centuries); *Amiens Cathedral* (1218–69); *Beauvais Cathedral* (begun 1247); *Salisbury Cathedral* (1220–60); *York Minster* or the *Cathedral of St. Peter* (begun in the 7th century); *Milan Cathedral* (begun 1386); and *Cologne Cathedral* (13th–19th centuries); badly damaged in World War II.

The Duomo (cathedral) in Florence was founded in 1298, completed by Brunelleschi and consecrated in 1436. The oval-shaped dome dominates the entire structure.

The *Vatican* is a group of buildings in Rome comprising the official residence of the Pope. The *Basilica of St. Peter,* the largest church in the Christian world, was begun in 1450. The *Sistine Chapel,* begun in 1473, is noted for the art masterpieces of Michelangelo, Botticelli, and others. The *Basilica of the Savior* (known as *St. John Lateran*) is the first-ranking Catholic Church in the world, for it is the cathedral of the Pope.

Other examples of Renaissance architecture are the *Palazzo Riccardi,* the *Palazzo Pitti* and the *Palazzo Strozzi* in Florence; the *Farnese Palace* in Rome; *Palazzo Grimani* (completed about 1550) in Venice; the *Escorial* (1563–93) near Madrid; the *Town Hall* of Seville (1527–32); the *Louvre,* Paris; the *Château* at Blois, France; *St. Paul's Cathedral,* London (1675–1710; badly damaged in World War II); the *École Militaire,* Paris (1752); the *Pazzi Chapel,* Florence, designed by Brunelleschi (1429); the Palace of *Fontainebleau* and the *Château de Chambord* in France.

The *Palace of Versailles,* containing the famous Hall of Mirrors, was built during the reign of Louis XIV and served as the royal palace until 1793.

Outstanding European buildings of the 18th and 19th centuries are the *Superga* at Turin, the *Hôtel-Dieu* in Lyons, the *Belvedere Palace* at Vienna, the *Royal Palace* of Stockholm, the *Opera House* of Paris (1863–75); the *Bank of England,* the *British Museum,* the *University of London,* and the *Houses of Parliament,* all in London; the *Panthéon,* the *Church of the Madeleine,* the *Bourse,* and the *Palais de Justice* in Paris.

The *Eiffel Tower,* in Paris, was built for the Exposition of 1889 by Alexandre Eiffel. It is 984 ft high.[1]

1. 1,056 ft, including the television tower.

Asiatic and African

The *Taj Mahal* (1632–50), at Agra, India, built by Shah Jahan as a tomb for his wife, is considered by some as the most perfect example of the Mogul style and by others as the most beautiful building in the world. Four slim white minarets flank the building, which is topped by a white dome; the entire structure is of marble.

Other examples of Indian architecture are the temples at Benares and Tanjore.

Among famed Moslem edifices are the *Dome of the Rock* or *Mosque of Omar,* Jerusalem (A.D. 691); the *Citadel* (1166), and the *Tombs of the Mamelukes* (15th century), in Cairo; the *Tomb of Humayun* in Delhi; the *Blue Mosque* (1468) at Tabriz, and the *Tamerlane Mausoleum* at Samarkand.

Angkor Wat, outside the city of Angkor Thom, Cambodia, is one of the most beautiful examples of Cambodian or Khmer architecture. The sanctuary was built during the 12th century.

Great Wall of China (228 B.C.?), designed specifically as a defense against nomadic tribes, has large watch towers which could be called buildings. It was erected by Emperor Ch'in Shih Huang Ti and is 1,400 miles long. Built mainly of earth and stone, it varies in height between 18 and 30 ft.

Typical of Chinese architecture are the pagodas or temple towers. Among some of the better-known pagodas are the *Great Pagoda of the Wild Geese* at Sian (founded in 652); *Nan t'a* (11th century) at Fang Shan; the *Pagoda of Sung Yueh Ssu* (A.D. 523) at Sung Shan, Honan.

Other well-known Chinese buildings are the *Drum Tower* (1273), the *Three Great Halls* in the Purple Forbidden City (1627), *Buddha's Perfume Tower* (19th century), the *Porcelain Pagoda,* and the *Summer Palace,* all at Peking.

United States

Rockefeller Center, in New York City, extends from 5th Ave. to the Avenue of the Americas between 48th and 52nd Sts. (and halfway to 7th Ave. between 47th and 51st Sts.). It occupies more than 22 acres and has 19 buildings.

The Cathedral of St. John the Divine, at 112th St. and Amsterdam Ave. in New York City, was begun in 1892 and is now in the final stages of completion. When completed, it will be the largest cathedral in the world: 601 ft long, 146 ft wide at the nave, 320 ft wide at the transept. The east end is designed in Romanesque-Byzantine style, and the nave and west end are Gothic.

St. Patrick's Cathedral, at Fifth Ave. and 50th St. in New York City, has a seating capacity of 2,500. The nave was opened in 1877, and the cathedral was dedicated in 1879.

Louisiana Superdome, in New Orleans, is the largest arena in the history of mankind. The main area can accommodate up to 95,000 people. It is the world's largest steel-constructed room. Unobstructed by posts, it covers 13 acres and reaches 27 stories at its peak.

World Trade Center, in New York City, was dedicated in 1973. Its twin towers are 110 stories high (1,350 ft), and the complex contains over 9 million sq ft of office space. A restaurant is on the 107th floor of the North Tower.

World's Highest Dams

Name	River, Country or State	Structural height		Gross reservoir capacity		Year completed
		feet	meters	thousands of acre feet	millions of cubic meters	
Rogun	Vakhsh, U.S.S.R.	1066	325	9,404	11,600	1985
Nurek	Vakhsh, U.S.S.R.	984	300	8,512	10,500	1980
Grande Dixence	Dixence, Switzerland	935	285	324	400	1962
Inguri	Inguri, U.S.S.R.	892	272	801	1,100	1984
Chicoasén	Grijalva, Mexico	869	265	1,346	1,660	1981
Vaiont	Vaiont, Italy	869	265	137	169	1961
Tehri	Bhagirathi, India	856	261	2,869	3,540	UC
Kinshau	Tons, India	830	253	1,946	2,400	1985
Guavio	Orinoco, Colombia	820	250	811	1,000	UC
Mica	Columbia, Canada	794	242	20,000	24,670	1972
Sayano-Shushensk	Yenisei, U.S.S.R.	794	242	25,353	31,300	1980
Mihoesti	Aries, Romania	794	242	5	6	1983
Chivor	Batá, Colombia	778	237	661	815	1975
Mauvoisin	Drance de Bagnes, Switzerland	777	237	146	180	1957
Oroville	Feather, California	770	235	3,538	4,299	1968
Chirkey	Sulak, U.S.S.R.	764	233	2,252	2,780	1977
Bhakra	Sutlej, India	741	226	8,002	9,870	1963
El Cajón	Humuya, Honduras	741	226	4,580	5,650	1984
Hoover	Colorado, Arizona/Nevada	726	221	28,500	35,154	1936
Contra	Verzasca, Switzerland	722	220	70	86	1965
Dabaklamm	Dorferbach, Austria	722	220	191	235	UC
Mratinje	Piva, Yugoslavia	722	220	713	880	1973
Dworshak	N. Fk. Clearwater, Idaho	717	219	3,453	4,259	1974
Glen Canyon	Colorado, Arizona	710	216	27,000	33,304	1964
Toktogul	Naryn, U.S.S.R.	705	215	15,800	19,500	1978
Daniel Johnson	Manicouagan, Canada	703	214	115,000	141,852	1968
San Rogue	Agno, Philippines	689	210	803	990	UC
Luzzone	Brenno di Luzzone, Switzerland	682	208	71	87	1963
Keban	Firat, Turkey	679	207	25,110	31,000	1974
Dez	Dez, Abi, Iran	666	203	2,707	3,340	1963
Almendra	Tormes, Spain	662	202	2,148	2,649	1970
Kölnbrein	Malta, Austria	656	200	166	205	1977
Kārūn	Karun, Iran	656	200	2,351	2,900	1976
Altinkaya	Kizil Irmak, Turkey	640	195	4,672	5,763	1986
New Bullards Bar	No. Yuba, California	637	194	960	1,184	1968
Lakhwar	Yamuna, India	630	192	470	580	1985
New Melones	Stanislaus, California	625	191	2,400	2,960	1979
Itaipu	Paraná, Brazil/Paraguay	623	190	23,510	29,000	1982
Kurobe 4	Kurobe, Japan	610	186	162	199	1964
Swift	Lewis, Washington	610	186	756	932	1958
Mossyrock	Cowlitz, Washington	607	185	1,300	1,603	1968
Oymopinar	Manavgat, Turkey	607	185	251	310	1983
Atatürk	Firat, Turkey	604	184	39,482	48,700	1986
Shasta	Sacramento, California	602	183	4,550	5,612	1945
Bennett WAC	Peace, Canada	600	183	57,006	70,309	1967
Karakaya	Firat, Turkey	591	180	7,767	9,580	UC
Tignes	Isère, France	591	180	186	230	1952
Amir Kabir (Karad)	Karadj, Iran	591	180	166	205	1962
Tachien	Tachia, Taiwan	591	180	188	232	1974
Dartmouth	Mitta-Mitta, Australia	591	180	3,243	4,000	1978
Özköy	Gediz, Turkey	591	180	762	940	1983
Emosson	Barberine, Switzerland	590	180	184	225	1974
Zillergrūndl	Ziller, Austria	590	180	73	90	1986
Los Leones	Los Leones, Chile	587	179	86	106	1986
New Don Pedro	Tuolumne, California	585	178	2,030	2,504	1971
Alpa-Gera	Cormor, Italy	584	178	53	65	1965

Name	River, country, or state	Structural height		Gross reservoir capacity		Year completed
		feet	meters	Thousands of acre feet	millions of cubic meters	
Kopperston Tailings 3	Jones Branch, West Virginia	580	177	—	—	1963
Takase	Takase, Japan	577	176	62	76	1979
Nader Shah	Marun, Iran	574	175	1,313	1,620	1978
Hasan Ugurlu	Yesil Irmak, Turkey	574	175	874	1,078	1980
Pauti-Mazar	Mazar, Ecuador	540	165	405	500	1984
Hungry Horse	S.Fk., Flathead, Montana	564	172	3,470	4,280	1953
Longyangxia	Huanghe, China	564	172	20,025	24,700	1983
Cabora Bassa	Zambezi, Mozambique	561	171	51,075	63,000	1974
Maqarin	Yarmuk, Jordan	561	171	259	320	UC
Amaluza	Paute, Ecuador	558	170	81	100	1982
Idikki	Periyar, India	554	169	1,618	1,996	1974
Charvak	Chirchik, U.S.S.R.	552	168	1,620	2,000	1970
Gura Apelor Retezat	Riul Mare, Romania	552	168	182	225	1980
Grand Coulee	Columbia, Washington	550	168	9,390	11,582	1942
Boruca	Terraba, Costa Rica	548	167	12,128	14,960	UC
Vidraru	Arges, Romania	545	166	380	465	1965
Kremasta (King Paul)	Achelöus, Greece	541	165	3,850	4,750	1965

NOTE: UC = under construction. *Source:* Department of the Interior, Bureau of Reclamation and *International Water Power and Dam Construction.*

World's Largest Dams

Dam	Location	Volume (thousands)		Year completed
		Cubic meters	Cubic yards	
New Cornelia Tailings	Arizona	209,500	274,015	1973
Pati (Chapetón)	Argentina	200,000	261,590	UC
Tarbela	Pakistan	121,720	159,203	1976
Fort Peck	Montana	96,049	125,628	1940
Atatürk	Turkey	84,500	110,522	UC
Yacyretá-Apipe	Paraguay/Argentina	81,000	105,944	UC
Guri (Raul Leoni)	Venezuela	78,000	102,014	1986
Rogun	U.S.S.R.	75,500	98,750	1985
Oahe	South Dakota	70,339	92,000	1963
Mangla	Pakistan	65,651	85,872	1967
Gardiner	Canada	65,440	85,592	1968
Afsluitdijk	Netherlands	63,400	82,927	1932
Oroville	California	59,639	78,008	1968
San Luis	California	59,405	77,700	1967
Nurek	U.S.S.R.	58,000	75,861	1980
Garrison	North Dakota	50,843	66,500	1956
Cochiti	New Mexico	48,052	62,850	1975
Tabka (Thawra)	Syria	46,000	60,168	1976
Bennett W.A.C.	Canada	43,733	57,201	1967
Tucuruí	Brazil	43,000	56,242	1984
Boruca	Costa Rica	43,000	56,242	UC
High Aswan (Sadd-el-Aali)	Egypt	43,000	56,242	1970
San Rogue	Philippines	43,000	56,242	UC
Kiev	U.S.S.R.	42,841	56,034	1964
Dantiwada Left Embankment	India	41,040	53,680	1965
Saratov	U.S.S.R.	40,400	52,843	1967
Mission Tailings 2	Arizona	40,088	52,435	1973
Fort Randall	South Dakota	38,227	50,000	1953
Kanev	U.S.S.R.	37,860	49,520	1976
Mosul	Iraq	36,000	47,086	1982
Kakhovka	U.S.S.R.	35,640	46,617	1955
Itumbiara	Brazil	35,600	46,563	1980
Lauwerszee	Netherlands	35,575	46,532	1969
Beas	India	35,418	46,325	1974
Oosterschelde	Netherlands	35,000	45,778	1986

NOTE: UC = under construction. *Source:* Department of the Interior, Bureau of Reclamation and *International Water Power and Dam Construction.*

World's Largest Hydroelectric Plants

Name of dam	Location	Rated capacity (MW) Present	Ultimate	Year of initial operation
Itaipu	Brazil/Paraguay	1,400	12,600	1984
Grand Coulee	Washington	6,480	10,080	1942
Guri (Raul Leoni)	Venezuela	2,800	10,060	1968
Tucuruí	Brazil	—	7,500	1985
Sayano-Shushensk	U.S.S.R.	—	6,400	1980
Krasnoyarsk	U.S.S.R.	6,096	6,096	1968
Corpus-Posadas	Argentina/Paraguay	—	6,000	UC
LaGrande 2	Canada	5,328	5,328	1982
Churchill Falls	Canada	5,225	5,225	1971
Bratsk	U.S.S.R.	4,100	4,600	1964
Ust'—Ilimsk	U.S.S.R.	3,675	4,500	1974
Cabora Bassa	Mozambique	2,075	4,150	1974
Yacyretá-Apipe	Argentina/Paraguay	—	4,050	UC
Rogun	U.S.S.R.	—	3,600	1985
Paulo Afonso	Brazil	3,409	3,409	1954
Salto Santiago	Brazil	1,332	3,333	1980
Pati (Chapetón)	Argentina	—	3,300	UÇ
Brumley Gap	Virginia	3,200	3,200	1973
Ilha Solteira	Brazil	3,200	3,200	1973
Inga I	Zaire	360	2,820	1974
Gezhouba	China	965	2,715	1981
John Day	Oregon/Washington	2,160	2,700	1969
Nurek	U.S.S.R.	900	2,700	1976
Revelstoke	Canada	900	2,700	1984
Sáo Simao	Brazil	2,680	2,680	1979
LaGrande 4	Canada	2,637	2,637	1984
Mica	Canada	1,736	2,610	1976
Volgograd—22nd Congress	U.S.S.R.	2,560	2,560	1958
Fos do Areia	Brazil	2,511	2,511	1983
Itaparica	Brazil	—	2,500	1985
Bennett W.A.C.	Canada	2,116	2,416	1969
Chicoasén	Mexico	—	2,400	1980
Atatürk	Turkey	—	2,400	UC
LaGrande 3	Canada	2,310	2,310	1982
Volga—V.I. Lenin	U.S.S.R.	2,300	2,300	1955
Iron Gates I	Romania/Yugoslavia	2,300	2,300	1970
Iron Gates II	Romania/Yugoslavia	270	2,160	1983
Bath County	Virginia	—	2,100	1985
High Aswan (Saad-el-Aali)	Egypt	2,100	2,100	1967
Tarbela	Pakistan	1,400	2,100	1977
Piedra del Aquila	Argentina	—	2,100	UC
Itumbiara	Brazil	2,080	2,080	1980
Chief Joseph	Washington	2,069	2,069	1956
McNary	Oregon	980	2,030	1954
Green River	North Carolina	—	2,000	1980
Tehri	India	—	2,000	UC
Cornwall	New York	—	2,000	1978
Ludington	Michigan	1,979	1,979	1973
Robert Moses—Niagara	New York	1,950	1,950	1961
Salto Grande	Argentina/Uruguay	—	1,890	1979

Note: MW = Megawatts, UC = under construction. *Source:* Department of the Interior, Bureau of Reclamation and *International Water Power and Dam Construction.*

The First Skyscraper

A ten-story building isn't anyone's idea of a skyscraper today, but it was in fact the first skyscraper. It was not its height that gave it that distinction but its construction. It was the first building in the world to employ steel skeleton construction and thus became the prototype for the skyscraper.

Designed by William Le Baron Jenny for the Home Insurance Company of New York, it was erected at the corner of La Salle and Adams streets in Chicago. Construction began on May 1, 1884, and was completed in the fall of 1885. It was built of marble and flanked by four columns of polished granite supporting a marble balcony. A steel frame supported the weight of the walls, rather than the walls themselves bearing the weight. Two additional stories were added later.

Four years after completion of the Home Insurance Company Building, the steel-framed skyscraper had totally evolved in Chicago earning it the distinction of being its birth place.

Notable U.S. Skyscrapers

City	Building	Stories	Height ft	Height m	City	Building	Stories	Height ft	Height m
Chicago	Sears Tower	110	1,454	443	Boston	John Hancock Tower	60	790	241
New York	World Trade Center	110	1,377	419	San Francisco	Bank of America	52	779	237
New York	Empire State	102	1,250	381	Minneapolis	IDS Tower	57	775	236
Chicago	Standard Oil (Indiana)	80	1,136	346	New York	One Liberty Plaza	54	775	236
Chicago	John Hancock Center	100	1,127	343	New York	One Penn Plaza	57	774	236
New York	Chrysler	77	1,046	319	Atlanta	Peachtree Plaza	73	754	230
Houston	Texas	75	1,002	305	New York	Exxon	54	750	229
Houston	Allied Bank	71	985	300	Boston	Prudential Tower	52	750	229
New York	American International	66	952	290	Detroit	Detroit Plaza Hotel	73	747	228
New York	Citicorp Center	59	915	279	Dallas	First International	55	744	227
New York	40 Wall Tower	71	900	274	Los Angeles	Security Pacific Plaza	55	743	226
Chicago	Water Tower Place	74	859	262	New York	One Astor Plaza	54	730	222
Los Angeles	United California Bank	62	858	261	Houston	Gulf Tower	52	725	221
San Francisco	Transamerica Pyramid	61	853	260	New York	Marine Midland	52	724	221
Chicago	First National Bank	60	851	259	Houston	One Shell Plaza	50	714	218
New York	RCA	70	850	259	Dallas	First International	56	710	216
Pittsburgh	U.S. Steel Headquarters	64	841	256	Cleveland	Terminal Tower	52	708	216
New York	Chase Manhattan	60	813	248	New York	Union Carbide	52	707	215
New York	Pan Am	59	808	246	New York	General Motors	50	705	215
New York	Woolworth	55	792	241	New York	Metropolitan Life	50	700	213

NOTE: Height does not include TV towers and antennas. *Source: Information Please* questionnaires to building managements.

Notable Tunnels

Name	Location	Length mi.	Length km	Year completed
Railroad, excluding subways				
Seikan	Tsugara Strait, Japan	33.1	53.3	1983
Simplon (I and II)	Alps, Switzerland-Italy	12.3	19.8	1906 & 1922
Apennine	Genoa, Italy	11.5	18.5	1934
St. Gotthard	Swiss Alps	9.3	14.9	1881
Lötschberg	Swiss Alps	9.1	14.6	1911
Mont Cénis	French Alps	8.5[1]	13.7	1871
New Cascade	Cascade Mountains, Washington	7.8	12.6	1929
Vosges	Vosges, France	7.0	11.3	1940
Arlberg	Austrian Alps	6.3	10.1	1884
Moffat	Rocky Mountains, Colorado	6.2	9.9	1928
Shimuzu	Shimuzu, Japan	6.1	9.8	1931
Rimutaka	Wairarapa, New Zealand	5.5	8.9	1955
Vehicular				
St. Gotthard	Alps, Switzerland	10.2	16.4	1980
Mt. Blanc	Alps, France-Italy	7.5	12.1	1965
Mt. Ena	Japan Alps, Japan	5.3	8.5	1976[2]
Great St. Bernard	Alps, Switzerland-Italy	3.4	5.5	1964
Mount Royal	Montreal, Canada	3.2	5.1	1918
Lincoln	Hudson River, New York-New Jersey	2.5	4.0	1937
Queensway Road	Mersey River, Liverpool, England	2.2	3.5	1934
Brooklyn-Battery	East River, New York City	2.1	3.4	1950
Holland	Hudson River, New York-New Jersey	1.7	2.7	1927
Hampton Roads	Norfolk, Virginia	1.4	2.3	1957
Queens-Midtown	East River, New York City	1.3	2.1	1940
Liberty Tubes	Pittsburgh, Pennsylvania	1.2	1.9	1923
Baltimore Harbor	Baltimore, Maryland	1.2	1.9	1957
Allegheny Tunnels	Pennsylvania Turnpike	1.2	1.9	1940[3]

1. Lengthened to its present 8.5 miles in 1881. 2. Parallel tunnel begun in 1976. 3. Parallel tunnel built in 1965, twin tunnel in 1966. NOTE: UC = under construction. *Source:* American Society of Civil Engineers and International Bridge, Tunnel & Turnpike Association.

Notable Modern Bridges

Name	Location	Length of main span, ft	Length of main span, m	Year completed
Suspension				
Humber	Hull, Britain	4,626	1,410	1981
Verrazano-Narrows	Lower New York Bay	4,260	1,298	1964
Golden Gate	San Francisco Bay	4,200	1,280	1937
Mackinac Straits	Michigan	3,800	1,158	1957
Bosporus	Istanbul	3,524	1,074	1973
George Washington	Hudson River at New York City	3,500	1,067	1931
Ponte 25 de Abril	Tagus River at Lisbon	3,323	1,013	1966
Forth Road	Queensferry, Scotland	3,300	1,006	1964
Severn	Severn River at Beachley, England	3,240	988	1966
Tacoma Narrows	Puget Sound at Tacoma, Wash.	2,800	853	1950
Kanmon Strait	Kyushu-Honshu, Japan	2,336	712	1973
Angostura	Orinoco River at Ciudad Bolivar, Venezuela	2,336	712	1967
Transbay (twin spans)	San Francisco Bay	2,310	704	1936
Bronx-Whitestone	East River, New York City	2,300	701	1939
Pierre Laporte	St. Lawrence River at Quebec, Canada	2,190	668	1970
Delaware Memorial (twin bridges)	Delaware River near Wilmington, Del.	2,150	655	1951, 1968
Seaway Skyway	St. Lawrence River at Ogdensburg, N.Y.	2,150	655	1960
Gas Pipe Line	Atchafalaya River, Louisiana	2,000	610	1951
Walt Whitman	Delaware River at Philadelphia	2,000	610	1957
Tancarville	Seine River at Tancarville, France	1,995	608	1959
Lillebaelt	Lillebaelt Strait, Denmark	1,969	600	1970
Ambassador International	Detroit River at Detroit	1,850	564	1929
Throgs Neck	East River, New York City	1,800	549	1961
Benjamin Franklin	Delaware River at Philadelphia	1,750	533	1926
Skjomen	Narvik, Norway	1,722	525	1972
Kvalsund	Hammerfest, Norway	1,722	525	1977
Kleve-Emmerich	Rhine River at Emmerich, West Germany	1,640	500	1965
Bear Mountain	Hudson River at Peekskill, N.Y.	1,632	497	1924
Wm. Preston Lane, Jr., Memorial (twin bridges)	Near Annapolis, Md.	1,600	488	1952, 1973
Williamsburg	East River, New York City	1,600	488	1903
Newport	Narragansett Bay at Newport, R.I.	1,600	488	1969
Brooklyn	East River, New York City	1,595	486	1883
Cantilever				
Quebec Railway	St. Lawrence River at Quebec, Canada	1,800	549	1917
Forth Railway (twin spans)	Queensferry, Scotland	1,710	521	1890
Minato Ohashi	Osaka, Japan	1,673	510	1974
Commodore John Barry	Chester, Pa.	1,644	501	1974
Greater New Orleans	Mississippi River, Louisiana	1,576	480	1958
Howrah	Hooghly River at Calcutta	1,500	457	1943
Transbay Bridge	San Francisco Bay	1,400	427	1936
Baton Rouge	Mississippi River, Louisiana	1,235	376	1968
Tappan Zee	Hudson River at Tarrytown, N.Y.	1,212	369	1955
Longview	Columbia River at Longview, Wash.	1,200	366	1930
Patapsco River	Baltimore Outer Harbor Crossing	1,200	366	1976
Queensboro	East River, New York City	1,182	360	1909
Steel Arch				
New River Gorge	Fayetteville, W. Va.	1,700	518	1977
Bayonne	Kill Van Kull at Bayonne, N.J.	1,675	510	1931
Sydney Harbor	Sydney, Australia	1,670	509	1932
Fremont	Portland, Ore.	1,255	383	1973
Zdákov	Vltava River, Czechoslovakia	1,244	380	1967
Port Mann	Fraser River at Vancouver, British Columbia	1,200	366	1964
Thatcher Ferry	Panama Canal, Panama	1,128	344	1962
Laviolette	St. Lawrence River, Trois Rivieres, Quebec	1,100	335	1967
Runcorn-Widnes	Mersey River, England	1,082	330	1961
Birchenough	Sabi River at Fort Victoria, Rhodesia	1,080	329	1935

Name	Location	Length of main span, ft	m	Year completed
Cable-Stayed				
Annacis	Vancouver, B.C., Canada	1525	465	1986
Yokohama-ko-odan	Kanagawa, Japan	1509	460	UC
Second Hooghly	Calcutta, India	1500	457	UC
Chao Phya	Thailand	1476	450	1986
Barrios de Luna	Spain	1444	440	1983
Iwaguroshima	Kagawa, Japan	1378	420	UC
Shizakuishishima	Kagawa, Japan	1378	420	UC
Meiko Nishi	Aichi, Japan	1329	405	1985
St. Nazaire	Loire River, St. Nazaire, France	1325	404	1975
Rande	Rande, Spain	1312	400	1977
Dame Point	Jacksonville, Florida, U.S.A.	1300	396	UC
Hale Boggs Memorial	Luling, Louisiana, U.S.A.	1222	373	1983
Dusseldorf Flehe	West Germany	1207	368	1979
Tjörn	Sweden	1200	366	1981
Sunshine Skyway	Tampa, Florida, U.S.A.	1200	366	1987
Continuous Truss				
Astoria	Columbia River at Astoria, Oregon	1,232	376	1966
Oshima	Oshima Island, Japan	1,066	325	1976
Croton Reservoir	Croton, N.Y.	1,052	321	1970
Tenmon	Kumamoto, Japan	984	300	1966
Kuronoseto	Nagashima-Kyushu, Japan	984	300	1974
Ravenswood	Ohio River, Ravenswood, W. Va.	902	275	1981
Dubuque	Mississippi River at Dubuque, Iowa	845	258	1943
Braga Memorial	Taunton River at Somerset, Mass.	840	256	1966
Graf Spee	Germany	839	256	1936
Concrete Arch				
Jesse H. Jones Memorial	Houston Ship Channel, Texas	1,500	455	1982
KRK	Zagreb, Yugoslavia	1,280	390	1979
Gladesville	Parramatta River at Sydney, Australia	1,000	305	1964
Amizade	Paraná River at Foz do Iguassu, Brazil	951	290	1964
Arrábida	Porto, Portugal	886	270	1963
Sandö	Angerman River at Kramfors, Sweden	866	264	1943
Shibenik	Krka River, Yugoslavia	808	246	1966
Fiumarella	Catanzaro, Italy	758	231	1961
Zaporozhe	Old Dnepr River, U.S.S.R.	748	228	1952
Novi Sad	Danube River, Yugoslavia	692	211	1961

1. Concrete bridge. NOTE: UC = under construction. *Source: Encyclopaedia Britannica,* American Society of Civil Engineers, and Bridge Division, Federal Highway Administration.

Famous Ship Canals

Name	Location	Length (miles)[1]	Width (feet)	Depth (feet)	Locks	Year opened
Albert	Belgium	80.0	53.0	16.5	6	1939
Amsterdam-Rhine	Netherlands	45.0	164.0	41.0	3	1952
Beaumont-Port Arthur	United States	40.0	200.0	34.0	—	1916
Chesapeake and Delaware	United States	19.0	250.0	27.0	—	1927
Houston	United States	43.0	300.0	34.0	—	1914
Kiel (Nord-Ostsee Kanal)	Germany	61.3	144.0	36.0	4	1895
Panama	Canal Zone	50.7	110.0	41.0	12	1914
St. Lawrence Seaway	U.S. and Canada	2,400.0 [2]	(3)	—	—	1959
Montreal to Prescott	U.S. and Canada	11.5	80.0	30.0	7	1959
Welland	Canada	27.5	80.0	27.0	8	1931
Sault Ste. Marie	Canada	1.2	60.0	16.8	1	1895
Sault Ste. Marie	United States	1.6	80.0	25.0	4	1915
Suez	Egypt	100.6 [4]	197.0	36.0	—	1869

1. Statute miles. 2. From Montreal to Duluth. 3. 442–550 feet; there are 11.5 miles of locks, 80 feet wide and 30 feet deep. 4. From Port Said lighthouse to entrance channel in Suez roads. *Source:* American Society of Civil Engineers.

THE DECLARATION OF INDEPENDENCE

In Congress, July 4, 1776

The unanimous Declaration of the thirteen united States of America.

When in the Course of human events it becomes necessary for one people to dissolve the political bands which have connected them with another, and to assume among the powers of the earth, the separate and equal station to which the Laws of Nature and of Nature's God entitle them, a decent respect to the opinions of mankind requires that they should declare the causes which impel them to the separation.

We hold these truths to be self-evident, that all men are created equal, that they are endowed by their Creator with certain unalienable Rights, that among these are Life, Liberty and the pursuit of Happiness.—That to secure these rights, Governments are instituted among Men, deriving their just powers from the consent of the governed,—That whenever any Form of Government becomes destructive of these ends, it is the Right of the People to alter or to abolish it, and to institute new Government, laying its foundation on such principles and organizing its powers in such form, as to them shall seem most likely to effect their Safety and Happiness. Prudence, indeed, will dictate that Governments long established should not be changed for light and transient causes; and accordingly all experience hath shewn that mankind are more disposed to suffer, while evils are sufferable, than to right themselves by abolishing the forms to which they are accustomed. But when a long train of abuses and usurpations, pursuing invariably the same Object evinces a design to reduce them under absolute Despotism, it is their right, it is their duty, to throw off such Government, and to provide new Guards for their future security.—Such has been the patient sufferance of these Colonies; and such is now the necessity which constrains them to alter their former Systems of Government. The history of the present King of Great Britain is a history of repeated injuries and usurpations, all having in direct object the establishment of an absolute Tyranny over these States. To prove this, let Facts be submitted to a candid world.

He has refused his Assent to Laws, the most wholesome and necessary for the public good.

He has forbidden his Governors to pass Laws of immediate and pressing importance, unless suspended in their operation till his Assent should be obtained; and when so suspended, he has utterly neglected to attend to them.

He has refused to pass other Laws for the accommodation of large districts of people, unless those people would relinquish the right of Representation in the Legislature, a right inestimable to them and formidable to tyrants only.

He has called together legislative bodies at places unusual, uncomfortable, and distant from the depository of their Public Records, for the sole purpose of fatiguing them into compliance with his measures.

He has dissolved Representative Houses repeatedly, for opposing with manly firmness his invasions on the rights of the people.

He has refused for a long time, after such dissolutions, to cause others to be elected; whereby the Legislative Powers, incapable of Annihilation, have returned to the People at large for their exercise; the State remaining in the mean time exposed to all the dangers of invasion from without, and convulsions within.

He has endeavoured to prevent the population of these States; for that purpose obstructing the Laws for Naturalization of Foreigners; refusing to pass others to encourage their migrations hither, and raising the conditions of new Appropriations of Lands.

He has obstructed the Administration of Justice, by refusing his Assent to Laws for establishing Judiciary Powers.

He has made Judges dependent on his Will alone, for the tenure of their offices, and the amount and payment of their salaries.

He has erected a multitude of New Offices, and sent hither swarms of Officers to harass our people, and eat out their substance.

He has kept among us, in times of peace, Standing Armies without the Consent of our legislatures.

He has affected to render the Military independent of and superior to the Civil Power.

He has combined with others to subject us to a jurisdiction foreign to our constitution, and unacknowledged by our laws; giving his Assent to their Acts of pretended Legislation:

For quartering large bodies of armed troops among us:

For protecting them, by a mock Trial, from punishment for any Murders which they should commit on the Inhabitants of these States:

For cutting off our Trade with all parts of the

NOTE: On April 12, 1776, the legislature of North Carolina authorized its delegates to the Continental Congress to join with others in a declaration of separation from Great Britain; the first colony to instruct its delegates to take the actual initiative was Virginia on May 15. On June 7, 1776, Richard Henry Lee of Virginia offered a resolution to the Congress to the effect "that these United Colonies are, and of right ought to be, free and independent States. . . ." A committee, consisting of Thomas Jefferson, John Adams, Benjamin Franklin, Robert R. Livingston, and Roger Sherman was organized to "prepare a declaration to the effect of the said first resolution." The Declaration of Independence was adopted on July 4, 1776.

Most delegates signed the Declaration August 2, but George Wythe (Va.) signed August 27; Richard Henry Lee (Va.), Elbridge Gerry (Mass.), and Oliver Wolcott (Conn.) in September; Matthew Thornton (N.H.), not a delegate until September, in November; and Thomas McKean (Del.), although present on July 4, not until 1781 by special permission, having served in the army in the interim.

world:

For imposing Taxes on us without our Consent:

For depriving us in many cases, of the benefits of Trial by Jury:

For transporting us beyond Seas to be tried for pretended offences:

For abolishing the free System of English Laws in a neighbouring Province, establishing therein an Arbitrary government, and enlarging its Boundaries so as to render it at once an example and fit instrument for introducing the same absolute rule into these Colonies:

For taking away our Charters, abolishing our most valuable Laws and altering fundamentally the Forms of our Governments:

For suspending our own Legislatures, and declaring themselves invested with power to legislate for us in all cases whatsoever.

He has abdicated Government here, by declaring us out of his Protection and waging War against us.

He has plundered our seas, ravaged our Coasts, burnt our towns, and destroyed the lives of our people.

He is at this time transporting large Armies of foreign Mercenaries to compleat the works of death, desolation, and tyranny, already begun with circumstances of Cruelty & Perfidy scarcely paralleled in the most barbarous ages, and totally unworthy the Head of a civilized nation.

He has constrained our fellow Citizens taken Captive on the high Seas to bear Arms against their Country, to become the executioners of their friends and Brethren, or to fall themselves by their Hands.

He has excited domestic insurrections amongst us, and has endeavoured to bring on the inhabitants of our frontiers, the merciless Indian Savages, whose known rule of warfare, is an undistinguished destruction of all ages, sexes and conditions.

In every stage of these Oppressions We have Petitioned for Redress in the most humble terms: Our repeated Petitions have been answered only by repeated injury. A Prince, whose character is thus marked by every act which may define a Tyrant, is unfit to be the ruler of a free people.

Nor have We been wanting in attentions to our Brittish brethren. We have warned them from time to time of attempts by their legislature to extend an unwarrantable jurisdiction over us. We have reminded them of the circumstances of our emigration and settlement here. We have appealed to their native justice and magnanimity, and we have conjured them by the ties of our common kindred to disavow these usurpations, which would inevitably interrupt our connections and correspondence. They too have been deaf to the voice of justice and of consanguinity. We must, therefore, acquiesce in the necessity, which denounces our Separation, and hold them, as we hold the rest of mankind, Enemies in War, in Peace Friends.

We, therefore, the Representatives of the United States of America, in General Congress, Assembled, appealing to the Supreme Judge of the world for the rectitude of our intentions, do, in the Name, and by Authority of the good People of these Colonies, solemnly publish and declare, That these United Colonies are, and of Right ought to be Free and Independent States; that they are Absolved from all Allegiance to the British Crown, and that all political connection between them and the State of Great Britain, is and ought to be totally dissolved; and that as Free and Independent States, they have full Power to levy War, conclude Peace, contract Alliances, establish Commerce, and to do all other Acts and Things which Independent States may of right do.—And for the support of this Declaration, with a firm reliance on the protection of Divine Providence, we mutually pledge to each other our Lives, our Fortunes and our sacred Honor.

—John Hancock

New Hampshire
Josiah Bartlett
Wm. Whipple
Matthew Thornton

Rhode Island
Step. Hopkins
William Ellery

Connecticut
Roger Sherman
Sam'el Huntington
Wm. Williams
Oliver Wolcott

New York
Wm. Floyd
Phil. Livingston
Frans. Lewis
Lewis Morris

New Jersey
Richd. Stockton
Jno. Witherspoon
Fras. Hopkinson
John Hart
Abra. Clark

Pennsylvania
Robt. Morris
Benjamin Rush
Benj. Franklin
John Morton
Geo. Clymer
Jas. Smith
Geo. Taylor
James Wilson
Geo. Ross

Massachusetts-Bay
Saml. Adams
John Adams
Robt. Treat Paine
Elbridge Gerry

Delaware
Caesar Rodney
Geo. Read
Tho. M'Kean

Maryland
Samuel Chase
Wm. Paca
Thos. Stone
Charles Carroll of Carrollton

Virginia
George Wythe
Richard Henry Lee
Th. Jefferson
Benj. Harrison
Ths. Nelson, Jr.
Francis Lightfoot Lee
Carter Braxton

North Carolina
Wm. Hooper
Joseph Hewes
John Penn

South Carolina
Edward Rutledge
Thos. Heyward, Junr.
Thomas Lynch, Junr.
Arthur Middleton

Georgia
Button Gwinnett
Lyman Hall
Geo. Walton

Constitution of the United States of America

(Historical text has been edited to conform to contemporary American usage. The bracketed words are designations for your convenience; they are not part of the Constitution.)

The oldest federal constitution in existence was framed by a convention of delegates from twelve of the thirteen original states in Philadelphia in May, 1787, Rhode Island failing to send a delegate. George Washington presided over the session, which lasted until September 17, 1787. The draft (originally a preamble and seven Articles) was submitted to all thirteen states and was to become effective when ratified by nine states. It went into effect on the first Wednesday in March, 1789, having been ratified by New Hampshire, the ninth state to approve, on June 21, 1788. The states ratified the Constitution in the following order:

Delaware	December 7, 1787	South Carolina	May 23, 1788
Pennsylvania	December 12, 1787	New Hampshire	June 21, 1788
New Jersey	December 18, 1787	Virginia	June 25, 1788
Georgia	January 2, 1788	New York	July 26, 1788
Connecticut	January 9, 1788	North Carolina	November 21, 1789
Massachusetts	February 6, 1788	Rhode Island	May 29, 1790
Maryland	April 28, 1788		

[Preamble]

We the people of the United States, in order to form a more perfect Union, establish justice, insure domestic tranquility, provide for the common defence, promote the general welfare, and secure the blessings of liberty to ourselves and our posterity, do ordain and establish this Constitution for the United States of America.

Article I

Section 1

[Legislative powers vested in Congress.] All legislative powers herein granted shall be vested in a Congress of the United States, which shall consist of a Senate and House of Representatives.

Section 2

[Composition of the House of Representatives.—1.] The House of Representatives shall be composed of members chosen every second year by the people of the several States, and the electors in each State shall have the qualifications requisite for electors of the most numerous branch of the State Legislature.

[Qualifications of Representatives.—2.] No Person shall be a Representative who shall not have attained to the age of twenty-five years, and been seven years a citizen of the United States, and who shall not, when elected, be an inhabitant of that State in which he shall be chosen.

[Apportionment of Representatives and direct taxes—census.[1]—3.] (Representatives and direct taxes shall be apportioned among the several States which may be included within this Union, according to their respective numbers, which shall be determined by adding to the whole number of free persons, including those bound to service for a term of years, and excluding Indians not taxed, three fifths of all other persons.) The actual enumeration shall be made within three years after the first meeting of the Congress of the United States, and within every subsequent term of ten years, in such manner as they shall by law direct. The number of Representatives shall not exceed one for every thirty thousand, but each State shall have at least one Representative; and until such enumeration shall be made, the State of New Hampshire shall be entitled to choose three, Massachusetts eight, Rhode-Island and Providence Plantations one, Connecticut five, New York six, New Jersey four, Pennsylvania eight, Delaware one, Maryland six, Virginia ten, North Carolina five, South Carolina five, and Georgia three.

[Filling of vacancies in representation.—4.] When vacancies happen in the representation from any State, the Executive Authority thereof shall issue writs of election to fill such vacancies.

[Selection of officers; power of impeachment.—5.] The House of Representatives shall choose their Speaker and other officers; and shall have the sole power of impeachment.

Section 3[2]

[The Senate.—1.] The Senate of the United States shall be composed of two Senators from each State, chosen by the Legislature thereof, for six years; and each Senator shall have one vote.

[Classification of Senators; filling of vacancies.—2.] Immediately after they shall be assembled in consequence of the first election, they shall be divided as equally as may be into three classes. The seats of the Senators of the first class shall be vacated at the expiration of the second year, of the second class at the expiration of the fourth year, and of the third class at the expiration of the sixth year, so that one-third may be chosen every second year; and if vacancies happen by resignation, or otherwise, during the recess of the Legislature of any State, the Executive thereof may make temporary appointments (until the next meeting of the Legislature, which shall then fill such vacancies).

[Qualification of Senators.—3.] No person shall be a Senator who shall not have attained to the age of thirty years, and been nine years a citizen of the United States, and who shall not, when elected, be an inhabitant of that State for which he shall be chosen.

[Vice President to be President of Senate.—4.] The Vice President of the United States shall be President of the Senate, but shall have no vote, unless they be equally divided.

[Selection of Senate officers; President pro tempore.—5.] The Senate shall choose their other officers, and also a President pro tempore, in the absence of the Vice President, or when he shall exercise the office of President of the United States.

[Senate to try impeachments.—6.] The Senate

shall have the sole power to try all impeachments. When sitting for that purpose, they shall be on oath or affirmation. When the President of the United States is tried, the Chief Justice shall preside: and no person shall be convicted without the concurrence of two thirds of the members present.

[Judgment in cases of Impeachment.—7.] Judgment in cases of impeachment shall not extend further than to removal from office, and disqualification to hold and enjoy any office of honor, trust, or profit under the United States: but the party convicted shall nevertheless be liable and subject to indictment, trial, judgment and punishment, according to Law.

Section 4

[Control of congressional elections.—1.] The times, places, and manner of holding elections for Senators and Representatives, shall be prescribed in each State by the Legislature thereof; but the Congress may at any time by law make or alter such regulations, except as to the places of choosing Senators.

[Time for assembling of Congress.[3]—2.] The Congress shall assemble at least once in every year, and such meeting shall be on the first Monday in December, unless they shall by law appoint a different day.

Section 5

[Each house to be the judge of the election and qualifications of its members; regulations as to quorum.—1.] Each House shall be the judge of the elections, returns, and qualifications of its own members, and a majority of each shall constitute a quorum to do business; but a smaller number may adjourn from day to day, and may be authorized to compel the attendance of absent members, in such manner, and under such penalties as each House may provide.

[Each house to determine its own rules.—2.] Each House may determine the rules of its proceedings, punish its members for disorderly behavior, and, with the concurrence of two thirds, expel a member.

[Journals and yeas and nays.—3.] Each House shall keep a journal of its proceedings, and from time to time publish the same, excepting such parts as may in their judgment require secrecy; and the yeas and nays of the members of either House on any question shall, at the desire of one fifth of those present, be entered on the journal.

[Adjournment.—4.] Neither House, during the session of Congress, shall, without the consent of the other, adjourn for more than three days, nor to any other place than that in which the two Houses shall be sitting.

Section 6

[Compensation and privileges of members of Congress.—1.] The Senators and Representatives shall receive a compensation for their services, to be ascertained by law, and paid out of the Treasury of the United States. They shall in all cases, except treason, felony, and breach of the peace, be privileged from arrest during their attendance at the session of their respective Houses, and in going to and returning from the same; and for any speech or debate in either House, they shall not be questioned in any other place.

[Incompatible offices; exclusions.—2.] No Senator or Representative shall, during the time for which he was elected, be appointed to any civil office under the authority of the United States, which shall have been created, or the emoluments whereof shall have been increased during such time; and no person holding any office under the United States shall be a member of either House during his continuance in office.

Section 7

[Revenue bills to originate in House.—1.] All bills for raising revenue shall originate in the House of Representatives; but the Senate may propose or concur with amendments as on other bills.

[Manner of passing bills; veto power of President.—2.] Every bill which shall have passed the House of Representatives and the Senate, shall, before it becomes a law, be presented to the President of the United States; if he approve he shall sign it, but if not he shall return it, with his objections to that House in which it shall have originated, who shall enter the objections at large on their journal, and proceed to reconsider it. If after such reconsideration two thirds of that House shall agree to pass the bill, it shall be sent, together with the objections, to the other House, by which it shall likewise be reconsidered, and if approved by two thirds of that House, it shall become a law. But in all such cases the votes of both Houses shall be determined by yeas and nays, and the names of the persons voting for and against the bill shall be entered on the journal of each house, respectively. If any bill shall not be returned by the President within ten days (Sundays excepted) after it shall have been presented to him, the same shall be a law, in like manner as if he had signed it, unless the Congress by their adjournment prevent its return, in which case it shall not be a law.

[Concurrent orders or resolutions, to be passed by President.—3.] Every order, resolution, or vote to which the concurrence of the Senate and House of Representatives may be necessary (except on a question of adjournment) shall be presented to the President of the United States; and before the same shall take effect, shall be approved by him, or being disapproved by him, shall be repassed by two thirds of the Senate and House of Representatives, according to the rules and limitations prescribed in the case of a bill.

Section 8

[General powers of Congress.[4]]

[Taxes, duties, imposts, and excises.—1.] The Congress shall have power to lay and collect taxes, duties, imposts and excises, to pay the debts and provide for the common defense and general welfare of the United States; but all duties, imposts and excises shall be uniform throughout the United States;

[Borrowing of money.—2.] To borrow money on the credit of the United States;

[Regulation of commerce.—3.] To regulate commerce with foreign nations, and among the several States, and with the Indian tribes;

[Naturalization and bankruptcy.—4.] To establish a uniform rule of naturalization, and uniform laws on the subject of bankruptcies throughout the United States;

[Money, weights and measures.—5.] To coin money, regulate the value thereof, and of foreign coin, and fix the standard of weights and measures;

[Counterfeiting.—6.] To provide for the punishment of counterfeiting the securities and current coin of the United States;

[Post offices.—7.] To establish post offices and post roads;

[Patents and copyrights.—8.] To promote the

progress of science and useful arts, by securing for limited times to authors and inventors the exclusive right to their respective writings and discoveries;

[**Inferior courts.—9.**] To constitute tribunals inferior to the Supreme Court;

[**Piracies and felonies.—10.**] To define and punish piracies and felonies committed on the high seas, and offences against the law of nations;

[**War; marque and reprisal.—11.**] To declare war, grant letters of marque and reprisal, and make rules concerning captures on land and water;

[**Armies.—12.**] To raise and support armies, but no appropriation of money to that use shall be for a longer term than two years;

[**Navy.—13.**] To provide and maintain a navy;

[**Land and naval forces.—14.**] To make rules for the government and regulation of the land and naval forces;

[**Calling out militia.—15.**] To provide for calling forth the militia to execute the laws of the Union, suppress insurrections, and repel invasions.

[**Organizing, arming, and disciplining militia.—16.**] To provide for organizing, arming, and disciplining, the militia, and for governing such part of them as may be employed in the service of the United States, reserving to the States, respectively, the appointment of the officers, and the authority of training the militia according to the discipline prescribed by Congress;

[**Exclusive legislation over District of Columbia.—17.**] To exercise exclusive legislation in all cases whatsoever, over such district (not exceeding ten miles square) as may, by cession of particular States, and the acceptance of Congress, become the seat of the Government of the United States, and to exercise like authority over all places purchased by the consent of the Legislature of the State in which the same shall be, for the erection of forts, magazines, arsenals, dock-yards, and other needful buildings;—And

[**To enact laws necessary to enforce Constitution.—18.**] To make all laws which shall be necessary and proper for carrying into execution the foregoing powers, and all other powers vested by this Constitution in the Government of the United States, or in any department or officer thereof.

Section 9

[**Migration or importation of certain persons not to be prohibited before 1808.—1.**] The migration or importation of such persons as any of the States now existing shall think proper to admit, shall not be prohibited by the Congress prior to the year one thousand eight hundred and eight, but a tax or duty may be imposed on such importation, not exceeding ten dollars for each person.

[**Writ of habeas corpus not to be suspended; exception.—2.**] The privilege of the writ of habeas corpus shall not be suspended, unless when in cases of rebellion or invasion the public safety may require it.

[**Bills of attainder and ex post facto laws prohibited.—3.**] No bill of attainder or ex post facto law shall be passed.

[**Capitation and other direct taxes.—4.**] No capitation, or other direct, tax shall be laid, unless in proportion to the census or enumeration herein before directed to be taken.[5]

[**Exports not to be taxed.—5.**] No tax or duty shall be laid on articles exported from any State.

[**No preference to be given to ports of any States; interstate shipping.—6.**] No preference shall be given by any regulation of commerce or revenue to the ports of one State over those of another: nor shall vessels bound to, or from, one State, be obliged to enter, clear, or pay duties in another.

[**Money, how drawn from treasury; financial statements to be published.—7.**] No money shall be drawn from the Treasury, but in consequence of appropriations made by law; and a regular statement and account of the receipts and expenditures of all public money shall be published from time to time.

[**Titles of nobility not to be granted; acceptance by government officers of favors from foreign powers.—8.**] No title of nobility shall be granted by the United States: and no person holding any office of profit or trust under them, shall, without the consent of the Congress, accept of any present, emolument, office, or title, of any kind whatever, from any king, prince, or foreign state.

Section 10

[**Limitations of the powers of the several States.—1.**] No State shall enter into any treaty, alliance, or confederation; grant letters of marque and reprisal; coin money; emit bills of credit; make any thing but gold and silver coin a tender in payment of debts; pass any bill of attainder, ex post facto law, or law impairing the obligation of contracts, or grant any title of nobility.

[**State imposts and duties.—2.**] No State shall, without the consent of the Congress, lay any imposts or duties on imports or exports, except what may be absolutely necessary for executing its inspection laws; and the net produce of all duties and imposts, laid by any State on imports or exports, shall be for the use of the Treasury of the United States; and all such laws shall be subject to the revision and control of the Congress.

[**Further restrictions on powers of States.—3.**] No State shall, without the consent of Congress, lay any duty of tonnage, keep troops, or ships of war in time of peace, enter into any agreement or compact with another state, or with a foreign power, or engage in war, unless actually invaded, or in such imminent danger as will not admit of delay.

Article II

Section 1

[**The President; the executive power.—1.**] The executive power shall be vested in a President of the United States of America. He shall hold his office during the term of four years, and, together with the Vice President, chosen for the same term, be elected, as follows

[**Appointment and qualifications of presidential electors.—2.**] Each State shall appoint, in such manner as the Legislature thereof may direct, a number of electors, equal to the whole number of Senators and Representatives to which the State may be entitled in the Congress: but no Senator or Representative, or person holding an office of trust or profit under the United States, shall be appointed an elector.

[**Original method of electing the President and Vice President.**[6]] (The electors shall meet in their respective States, and vote by ballot for two persons, of whom one at least shall not be an inhabitant of the same State with themselves. And they shall make a list of all the persons voted for, and of the number of votes for each; which list they shall sign and certify, and transmit sealed to the seat of the Government of the United States, directed to the

President of the Senate. The President of the Senate shall, in the presence of the Senate and House of Representatives, open all the certificates, and the votes shall then be counted. The person having the greatest number of votes shall be the President, if such number be a majority of the whole number of electors appointed; and if there be more than one who have such majority, and have an equal number of votes, then the House of Representatives shall immediately choose by ballot one of them for President; and if no person have a majority, then from the five highest on the list the said House shall in like manner choose the President. But in choosing the President, the votes shall be taken by States, the representation from each State having one vote; A quorum for this purpose shall consist of a member or members from two thirds of the States, and a majority of all the states shall be necessary to a choice. In every case, after the choice of the President, the person having the greatest number of votes of the electors shall be the Vice President. But if there should remain two or more who have equal votes, the Senate should choose from them by ballot the Vice President.)

[Congress may determine time of choosing electors and day for casting their votes.—3.] The Congress may determine the time of choosing the electors, and the day on which they shall give their votes; which day shall be the same throughout the United States.

[Qualifications for the office of President.[7]—4.] No person except a natural born citizen, or a citizen of the United States, at the time of the adoption of this Constitution, shall be eligible to the office of President; neither shall any person be eligible to that office who shall not have attained to the age of thirty-five years, and been fourteen years a resident within the United States.

[Filling vacancy in the office of President.[8]—5.] In case of the removal of the President from office, or of his death, resignation, or inability to discharge the powers and duties of the said office, the same shall devolve on the Vice President, and the Congress may by law provide for the case of removal, death, resignation or inability, both of the President and Vice President, declaring what officer shall then act as President, and such officer shall act accordingly, until the disability be removed, or a President shall be elected.

[Compensation of the President.—6.] The President shall, at stated times, receive for his services, a compensation, which shall neither be increased nor diminished during the period for which he shall have been elected, and he shall not receive within that period any other emolument from the United States, or any of them.

[Oath to be taken by the President.—7.] Before he enter on the execution of his office, he shall take the following oath or affirmation:—"I do solemnly swear (or affirm) that I will faithfully execute the office of President of the United States, and will to the best of my ability, preserve, protect, and defend the Constitution of the United States."

Section 2

[The President to be commander in chief of army and navy and head of executive departments; may grant reprieves and pardons.—1.] The President shall be Commander in Chief of the Army and Navy of the United States, and of the militia of the several States, when called into the actual service of the United States; he may require the opinion, in writing, of the principal officer in each of the executive departments, upon any subject relating to the duties of their respective offices, and he shall have power to grant reprieves and pardons for offences against the United States, except in cases of impeachment.

[President may, with concurrence of Senate, make treaties, appoint ambassadors, etc.; appointment of inferior officers, authority of Congress over.—2.] He shall have power, by and with the advice and consent of the Senate, to make treaties, provided two thirds of the Senators present concur; and he shall nominate, and by and with the advice and consent of the Senate, shall appoint ambassadors, other public ministers and consuls, judges of the Supreme Court, and all other officers of the United States, whose appointments are not herein otherwise provided for, and which shall be established by law: but the Congress may by law vest the appointment of such inferior officers, as they think proper, in the President alone, in the courts of law, or in the heads of departments.

[President may fill vacancies in office during recess of Senate.—3.] The President shall have power to fill up all vacancies that may happen during the recess of the Senate, by granting commissions which shall expire at the end of their session.

Section 3

[President to give advice to Congress; may convene or adjourn it on certain occasions; to receive ambassadors, etc.; have laws executed and commission all officers.] He shall from time to time give to the Congress information of the state of the Union, and recommend to their consideration such measures as he shall judge necessary and expedient; he may, on extraordinary occasions, convene both Houses, or either of them, and in case of disagreement between them, with respect to the time of adjournment, he may adjourn them to such time as he shall think proper; he shall receive ambassadors and other public ministers: he shall take care that the laws be faithfully executed, and shall commission all the officers of the United States.

Section 4

[All civil officers removable by impeachment.] The President, Vice President, and all civil officers of the United States shall be removed from office on impeachment for, and conviction of, treason, bribery, or other high crimes and misdemeanors.

Article III

Section 1

[Judicial powers; how vested; term of office and compensation of judges.] The judicial Power of the United States, shall be vested in one Supreme Court, and in such inferior courts as the Congress may from time to time ordain and establish. The judges, both of the supreme and inferior courts, shall hold their offices during good behavior, and shall, at stated times, receive for their services, a compensation, which shall not be diminished during their continuance in office.

Section 2

[Jurisdiction of Federal courts.[9]—1.] The judicial power shall extend to all cases, in law and equity, arising under this Constitution, the laws of the United States, and treaties made, or which shall be made, under their authority; to all cases affecting ambassadors, other public ministers and consuls; to all cases of admiralty and maritime jurisdiction; to controversies to which the United States, shall be a party; to controversies between two or more States; between a State and citizens of another State; between citizens of different States; between citizens of the same State claiming lands under grants of different states, and between a State, or the citizens thereof, and foreign states, citizens, or subjects.

[Original and appellate jurisdiction of Supreme Court.—2.] In all cases affecting ambassadors, other public ministers and consuls, and those in which a State shall be party, the Supreme Court shall have original jurisdiction. In all the other cases before mentioned, the Supreme Court shall have appellate jurisdiction, both as to law and fact, with such exceptions, and under such regulations, as the Congress shall make.

[Trial of all crimes, except impeachment, to be by jury.—3.] The trial of all crimes, except in cases of impeachment, shall be by jury; and such trial shall be held in the State where the said crimes shall have been committed; but when not committed within any State, the trial shall be at such place or places as the Congress may by law have directed.

Section 3

[Treason defined; conviction of.—1.] Treason against the United States, shall consist only in levying war against them, or, in adhering to their enemies, giving them aid and comfort. No person shall be convicted of treason unless on the testimony of two witnesses to the same overt act, or on confession in open court.

[Congress to declare punishment for treason; proviso.—2.] The Congress shall have power to declare the punishment of treason, but no attainder of treason shall work corruption of blood, or forfeiture except during the life of the person attained.

Article IV

Section 1

[Each State to give full faith and credit to the public acts and records of other States.] Full faith and credit shall be given in each State to the public acts, records, and judicial proceedings of every other State. And the Congress may by general laws prescribe the manner in which such acts, records, and proceedings shall be proved, and the effect thereof.

Section 2

[Privileges of citizens.—1.] The citizens of each State shall be entitled to all privileges and immunities of citizens in the several States.

[Extradition between the several States.—2.] A person charged in any State with treason, felony, or other crime, who shall flee from justice, and be found in another State, shall on demand of the Executive authority of the State from which he fled, be delivered up, to be removed to the State having jurisdiction of the crime.

[Persons held to labor or service in one State, fleeing to another, to be returned.—3.] No person held to service or labor in one State, under the laws thereof, escaping into another, shall, in consequence of any law or regulation therein, be discharged from such service or labor, but shall be delivered up on claim of the party to whom such service or labor may be due.

Section 3

[New States.—1.] New States may be admitted by the Congress into this Union; but no new State shall be formed or erected within the jurisdiction of any other State; nor any State be formed by the junction of two or more States, or parts of States, without the consent of the Legislatures of the States concerned as well as of the Congress.

[Regulations concerning territory.—2.] The Congress shall have power to dispose of and make all needful rules and regulations respecting the territory or other property belonging to the United States; and nothing in this Constitution shall be so construed as to prejudice any claims of the United States, or of any particular State.

Section 4

[Republican form of government and protection guaranteed the several States.] The United States shall guarantee to every State in this Union a Republican form of government, and shall protect each of them against invasion; and on application of the Legislature, or of the Executive (when the Legislature cannot be convened) against domestic violence.

Article V

[Ways in which the Constitution can be amended.] The Congress, whenever two thirds of both Houses shall deem it necessary, shall propose amendments to this Constitution, or, on the application of the Legislatures of two thirds of the several States shall call a convention for proposing amendments, which, in either case, shall be valid to all intents and purposes, as part of this Constitution, when ratified by the Legislatures of three fourths of the several States, or by conventions in three fourths thereof, as the one or the other mode of ratification may be proposed by the Congress; provided that no amendment which may be made prior to the year one thousand eight hundred and eight shall in any manner affect the first and fourth clauses in the ninth Section of the first Article; and that no State, without its consent, shall be deprived of its equal suffrage in the Senate.

Article VI

[Debts contracted under the confederation secured.—1.] All debts contracted and engagements entered into, before the adoption of this Constitution, shall be as valid against the United States under this Constitution, as under the Confederation.

[Constitution, laws, and treaties of the United States to be supreme.—2.] This Constitution, and the laws of the United States which shall be made in pursuance thereof; and all treaties made, or which shall be made, under the authority of the United States, shall be the supreme law of the land; and the judges in every State shall be bound thereby, any thing in the Constitution or laws of

1. The clause included in parentheses is amended by the 14th Amendment, Section 2. 2. The first paragraph of this section and the part of the second paragraph included in parentheses are amended by the 17th Amendment. 3. Amended by the 20th Amendment, Section 2. 4. By the 16th Amendment, Congress is given the power to lay and collect taxes on income. 5. See the 16th Amendment. 6. This clause has been superseded by the 12th Amendment. 7. For qualifications of the Vice President, see 12th Amendment. 8. Amended by the 20th Amendment, Sections 3 and 4. 9. This section is abridged by the 11th Amendment. 10. See the 13th Amendment.

any State to the contrary notwithstanding.

[Who shall take constitutional oath; no religious test as to official qualification.—3.] The Senators and Representatives before mentioned, and the members of the several State Legislatures, and all executive and judicial officers, both of the United States and of the several States, shall be bound by oath or affirmation, to support this Constitution; but no religious test shall ever be required as a qualification to any office or public trust under the United States.

Article VII

[Constitution to be considered adopted when ratified by nine States.] The ratification of the conventions of nine States shall be sufficient for the establishment of this Constitution between the States so ratifying the same.

Done in convention by the unanimous consent of the States present the seventeenth day of September in the year of our Lord one thousand seven hundred and eighty seven and of the independence of the United States of America the Twelfth. In witness whereof we have hereunto subscribed our names.

GEORGE WASHINGTON
President and Deputy from Virginia

NEW HAMPSHIRE
John Langdon — Nicholas Gilman

MASSACHUSETTS
Nathaniel Gorham — Rufus King

CONNECTICUT
Wm. Saml. Johnson — Roger Sherman

NEW YORK
Alexander Hamilton

NEW JERSEY
Wil. Livingston — Wm. Paterson
David Brearley — Jona. Dayton

PENNSYLVANIA
B. Franklin — Thomas Mifflin
Robt. Morris — Geo. Clymer
Thos. FitzSimons — Jared Ingersoll
James Wilson — Gouv. Morris

DELAWARE
Geo. Read — Gunning Bedford Jun.
John Dickinson — Richard Bassett
Jaco. Broom

MARYLAND
James McHenry — Dan. of St. Thos. Jenifer
Danl. Carroll

VIRGINIA
John Blair — James Madison, Jr.

NORTH CAROLINA
Wm. Blount — Richd Dobbs Spaight
Hu. Williamson

SOUTH CAROLINA
J. Rutledge — Charles Cotesworth Pinckney
Charles Pinckney — Pierce Butler

GEORGIA
William Few — Abr. Baldwin
Attest: William Jackson, Secretary

Amendments to the Constitution of the United States

(Amendments I to X inclusive, popularly known as the Bill of Rights, were proposed and sent to the states by the first session of the First Congress. They were ratified Dec. 15, 1791.)

Article I

[Freedom of religion, speech, of the press, and right of petition.] Congress shall make no law respecting an establishment of religion, or prohibiting the free exercise thereof; or abridging the freedom of speech, or of the press; or the right of the people peaceably to assemble, and to petition the Government for a redress of grievances.

Article II

[Right of people to bear arms not to be infringed.] A well regulated militia, being necessary to the security of a free State, the right of the people to keep and bear arms, shall not be infringed.

Article III

[Quartering of troops.] No soldier shall, in time of peace be quartered in any house, without the consent of the owner, nor in time of war, but in a manner to be prescribed by law.

Article IV

[Persons and houses to be secure from unreasonable searches and seizures.] The right of the people to be secure in their persons, houses, papers, and effects, against unreasonable searches and seizures, shall not be violated, and no warrants shall issue, but upon probable cause, supported by oath or affirmation, and particularly describing the place to be searched, and the persons or things to be seized.

Article V

[Trials for crimes; just compensation for private property taken for public use.] No person shall be held to answer for a capital, or otherwise infamous crime, unless on a presentment or indictment of a Grand Jury, except in cases arising in the land or naval forces, or in the militia, when in actual service in time of war or public danger; nor shall any person be subject for the same offence to be twice put in jeopardy of life or limb; nor shall be compelled in any criminal case to be a witness, against himself, nor be deprived of life, liberty, or property, without due process of law; nor shall private property be taken for public use, without just compensation.

Article VI

[Civil rights in trials for crimes enumerated.] In all criminal prosecutions, the accused shall enjoy the right to a speedy and public trial, by an impartial jury of the State and district wherein the crime shall have been committed, which district shall have been previously ascertained by law, and to be informed of the nature and cause of the accusation; to be confronted with the witnesses against him; to have compulsory process for obtaining witnesses in his favor, and to have the assistance of counsel for his defense.

Article VII

[Civil rights in civil suits.] In suits at common law, where the value in controversy shall exceed twenty dollars, the right of trial by jury shall be preserved, and no fact tried by a jury, shall be otherwise re-examined in any court of the United States, than according to the rules of the common law.

Article VIII

[Excessive bail, fines, and punishments prohibited.] Excessive bail shall not be required, nor excessive fines imposed, nor cruel and unusual punishments inflicted.

Article IX

[Reserved rights of people.] The enumeration in the Constitution, of certain rights, shall not be construed to deny or disparage others retained by the people.

Article X

[Powers not delegated, reserved to states and people respectively.] The powers not delegated to the United States by the Constitution, nor prohibited by it to the States, are reserved to the States, respectively, or to the people.

Article XI

(The proposed amendment was sent to the states Mar. 5, 1794, by the Third Congress. It was ratified Feb. 7, 1795.)

[Judicial power of United States not to extend to suits against a State.] The judicial power of the United States shall not be construed to extend to any suit in law or equity, commenced or prosecuted against one of the United States by citizens of another State, or by citizens or subjects of any foreign state.

Article XII

(The proposed amendment was sent to the states Dec. 12, 1803, by the Eighth Congress. It was ratified July 27, 1804.)

[Present mode of electing President and Vice-President by electors.[1]] The electors shall meet in their respective states, and vote by ballot for President and Vice President, one of whom, at least, shall not be an inhabitant of the same state with themselves; they shall name in their ballots the person voted for as President, and in distinct ballots the person voted for as Vice President, and they shall make distinct lists of all persons voted for as President, and of all persons voted for as Vice President, and of the number of votes for each, which lists they shall sign and certify, and transmit sealed to the seat of the government of the United States, directed to the President of the Senate; the President of the Senate shall, in the presence of the Senate and House of Representatives, open all the certificates and the votes shall then be counted; the person having the greatest number of votes for President, shall be the President, if such number be a majority of the whole number of electors appointed; and if no person have such majority, then from the persons having the highest numbers not exceeding three on the list of those voted for as President, the House of Representatives shall choose immediately, by ballot, the President. But in choosing the President, the votes shall be taken by states, the representation from each State having one vote; a quorum for this purpose shall consist of a member or members from two thirds of the states, and a majority of all the states shall be necessary to a choice. And if the House of Representatives shall not choose a President whenever the right of choice shall devolve upon them, before the fourth day of March next following, then the Vice President shall act as President, as in the case of the death or other constitutional disability of the President. The person having the greatest number of votes as Vice President, shall be the Vice President, if such number be a majority of the whole number of electors appointed, and if no person have a majority, then from the two highest numbers on the list, the Senate shall choose the Vice President; a quorum for the purpose shall consist of two thirds of the whole number of Senators, and a majority of the whole number shall be necessary to a choice. But no person constitutionally ineligible to the office of President shall be eligible to that of Vice President of the United States.

Article XIII

(The proposed amendment was sent to the states Feb. 1, 1865, by the Thirty-eighth Congress. It was ratified Dec. 6, 1865.)

Section 1

[Slavery prohibited.] Neither slavery nor involuntary servitude, except as a punishment for crime whereof the party shall have been duly convicted, shall exist within the United States, or any place subject to their jurisdiction.

Section 2

[Congress given power to enforce this article.] Congress shall have power to enforce this article by appropriate legislation.

Article XIV

(The proposed amendment was sent to the states June 16, 1866, by the Thirty-ninth Congress. It was ratified July 9, 1868.)

Section 1

[Citizenship defined; privileges of citizens.] All persons born or naturalized in the United States, and subject to the jurisdiction thereof, are citizens of the United States and of the State wherein they reside. No State shall make or enforce any law which shall abridge the privileges or immunities of citizens of the United States; nor shall any State deprive any person of life, liberty, or property, without due process of law; nor deny to any person within its jurisdiction the equal protection of the laws.

Section 2

[Apportionment of Representatives.] Representatives shall be apportioned among the several States according to their respective numbers, counting the whole number of persons in each State, excluding Indians not taxed. But when the right to vote at any election for the choice of electors for President and Vice President of the United States, Representatives in Congress, the executive and judicial officers of a State, or the members of the Legislature thereof, is denied to any of the male inhabitants of such State, being twenty-one years of age, and citizens of the United States, or in any way abridged, except for participation in rebellion, or other crime, the basis of representation therein shall be reduced in the proportion which the number of such male citizens shall bear to the whole number of male citizens twenty-one years of age in such State.

Section 3

[Disqualification for office; removal of disability.] No person shall be a Senator or Representative in Congress, or elector of President and Vice President, or hold any office, civil or military, under the United States, or under any State, who, having previously taken an oath, as a member of Congress, or as an officer of the United States, or as a member of any State Legislature, or as an executive or judicial officer of any State, to support the Constitution of the United States, shall have engaged in insurrection or rebellion against the same, or given aid or comfort to the enemies thereof. But Congress may be a vote of two thirds of each House, remove such disability.

Section 4

[Public debt not to be questioned; payment of debts and claims incurred in aid of rebellion forbidden.] The validity of the public debt of the United States, authorized by law, including debts incurred for payment of pensions and bounties for services in suppressing insurrection or rebellion, shall not be questioned. But neither the United States nor any State shall assume or pay any debt or obligation incurred in aid of insurrection or rebellion against the United States, or any claim for the loss or emancipation of any slave; but all such debts, obligations, and claims shall be held illegal and void.

Section 5

[Congress given power to enforce this article.] The Congress shall have power to enforce, by appropriate legislation, the provisions of this article.

Article XV

(The proposed amendment was sent to the states Feb. 27, 1869, by the Fortieth Congress. It was ratified Feb. 3, 1870.)

Section 1

[Right of certain citizens to vote established.] The right of citizens of the United States to vote shall not be denied or abridged by the United States or by any State on account of race, color, or previous condition of servitude.

Section 2

[Congress given power to enforce this article.] The Congress shall have power to enforce this article by appropriate legislation.

Article XVI

(The proposed amendment was sent to the states July 12, 1909, by the Sixty-first Congress. It was ratified Feb. 3, 1913.)

[Taxes on income; Congress given power to lay and collect.] The Congress shall have power to lay and collect taxes on incomes, from whatever source derived, without apportionment among the several States, and without regard to any census or enumeration.

Article XVII

(The proposed amendment was sent to the states May 16, 1912, by the Sixty-second Congress. It was ratified April 8, 1913.)

[Election of United States Senators; filling of vacancies; qualifications of electors.]

The Senate of the United States shall be composed of two Senators from each State, elected by the people thereof, for six years; and each Senator shall have one vote. The electors in each State shall have the qualifications requisite for electors of the most numerous branch of the State Legislatures.

When vacancies happen in the representation of any State in the Senate, the executive authority of such State shall issue writs of election to fill such vacancies: Provided, that the legislature of any State may empower the executive thereof to make temporary appointment until the people fill the vacancies by election as the legislature may direct.

This amendment shall not be so construed as to affect the election or term of any Senator chosen before it becomes valid as part of the Constitution.

Article XVIII[2]

(The proposed amendment was sent to the states Dec. 18, 1917, by the Sixty-fifth Congress. It was ratified by three quarters of the states by Jan. 16, 1919, and became effective Jan. 16, 1920.)

Section 1

[Manufacture, sale, or transportation of intoxicating liquors, for beverage purposes, prohibited.] After one year from the ratification of this article the manufacture, sale, or transportation of intoxicating liquors within, the importation thereof into, or the exportation thereof from the United States and all territory subject to the jurisdiction thereof for beverage purposes is hereby prohibited.

Section 2

[Congress and the several States given concurrent power to pass appropriate legislation to enforce this article.] The Congress and the several States shall have concurrent power to enforce this article by appropriate legislation.

Section 3

[Provisions of article to become operative, when adopted by three fourths of the States.] This article shall be inoperative unless it shall have been ratified as an amendment to the Constitution by the legislatures of the several States, as provided in the Constitution, within seven years from the date of the submission hereof to the States by Congress.

Article XIX

(The proposed amendment was sent to the states June 4, 1919, by the Sixty-sixth Congress. It was ratified Aug. 18, 1920.)

[The right of citizens to vote shall not be denied because of sex.] The right of citizens of the United States to vote shall not be denied or abridged by the United States or by any State on account of sex.

[Congress given power to enforce this article.] Congress shall have power to enforce this article by appropriate legislation.

Article XX

(The proposed amendment, sometimes called the "Lame Duck Amendment," was sent to the states Mar. 3, 1932, by the Seventy-second Congress. It was ratified Jan. 23, 1933; but, in accordance with Section 5, Sections 1 and 2 did not go into effect until Oct. 15, 1933.)

Section 1

[Terms of President, Vice President, Senators, and Representatives.] The terms of the President and Vice President shall end at noon on the twentieth day of January, and the terms of Senators and Representatives at noon on the third day of January, of the years in which such terms would have ended if this article had not been ratified; and the terms of their successors shall then begin.

Section 2

[Time of assembling Congress.] The Congress shall assemble at least once in every year, and such meeting shall begin at noon on the third day of January, unless they shall by law appoint a different day.

Section 3

[Filling vacancy in office of President.] If, at the time fixed for the beginning of the term of the President, the President-elect shall have died, the Vice President-elect shall become President. If a President shall not have been chosen before the time fixed for the beginning of his term, or if the President-elect shall have failed to qualify, then the Vice President shall have qualified; and the Congress may by law provide for the case wherein neither a President-elect nor a Vice President-elect shall have qualified, declaring who shall then act as President, or the manner in which one who is to act shall be selected, and such person shall act accordingly until a President or Vice President shall have qualified.

Section 4

[Power of Congress in Presidential succession.] The Congress may by law provide for the case of the death of any of the persons from whom the House of Representatives may choose a President whenever the right of choice shall have devolved upon them, and for the case of the death of any of the persons from whom the Senate may choose a Vice President whenever the right of choice shall have devolved upon them.

Section 5

[Time of taking effect.] Sections 1 and 2 shall take effect on the 15th day of October following the ratification of this article.

Section 6

[Ratification.] This article shall be inoperative unless it shall have been ratified as an amendment to the Constitution by the legislatures of three fourths of the several States within seven years from the date of its submission.

Article XXI

(The proposed amendment was sent to the states Feb. 20, 1933, by the Seventy-second Congress. It was ratified Dec. 5, 1933.)

Section 1

[Repeal of Prohibition Amendment.] The eighteenth article of amendment to the Constitution of the United States is hereby repealed.

Section 2

[Transportation of intoxicating liquors.] The transportation or importation into any State, territory, or possession of the United States for delivery or use therein of intoxicating liquors, in violation of the laws thereof, is hereby prohibited.

Section 3

[Ratification.] This article shall be inoperative unless it shall have been ratified as an amendment to the Constitution by convention in the several States, as provided in the Constitution, within seven years from the date of the submission thereof to the States by the Congress.

Article XXII

(The proposed amendment was sent to the states Mar. 21, 1947, by the Eightieth Congress. It was ratified Feb. 27, 1951.)

Section 1

[Limit to number of terms a President may serve.] No person shall be elected to the office of the President more than twice, and no person who has held the office of President, or acted as President, for more than two years of a term to which some other person was elected President shall be elected to the office of the President more than once. But this article shall not apply to any person holding the office of President when this article was proposed by the Congress, and shall not prevent any person who may be holding the office of President, or acting as President, during the term within which this article becomes operative from holding the office of President or acting as President during the remainder of such term.

Section 2

[Ratification.] This article shall be inoperative unless it shall have been ratified as an amendment to the Constitution by the legislatures of three fourths of the several States within seven years from the date of its submission to the States by the Congress.

Article XXIII

(The proposed amendment was sent to the states June 16, 1960, by the Eighty-sixth Congress. It was ratified March 29, 1961.)

Section 1

[Electors for the District of Columbia.] The District constituting the seat of Government of the United States shall appoint in such manner as the Congress may direct:

A number of electors of President and Vice President equal to the whole number of Senators and Representatives in Congress to which the District would be entitled if it were a State, but in no event more than the least populous State; they shall be in addition to those appointed by the States, but they shall be considered, for the purposes of the election of President and Vice President, to be electors appointed by a State; and they shall meet in the District and perform such duties as provided by the twelfth article of amendment.

Section 2

[Congress given power to enforce this article.] The Congress shall have the power to enforce this article by appropriate legislation.

Article XXIV

(The proposed amendment was sent to the states Aug. 27, 1962, by the Eighty-seventh Congress. It was ratified Jan. 23, 1964.)

Section 1

[Payment of poll tax or other taxes not to be prerequisite for voting in federal elections.] The right of citizens of the United States to vote in any primary or other election for President or Vice President, for electors for President or Vice President, or for Senator or Representative in Congress, shall not be denied or abridged by the United States or any State by reasons of failure to pay any poll tax or other tax.

Section 2

[Congress given power to enforce this article.] The Congress shall have the power to enforce this article by appropriate legislation.

Article XXV

(The proposed amendment was sent to the states July 6, 1965, by the Eighty-ninth Congress. It was ratified Feb. 10, 1967.)

Section 1

[Succession of Vice President to Presidency.] In case of the removal of the President from office or of his death or resignation, the Vice President shall become President.

Section 2

[Vacancy in office of Vice President.] Whenever there is a vacancy in the office of the Vice President, the President shall nominate a Vice President who shall take office upon confirmation by a majority vote of both Houses of Congress.

Section 3

[Vice President as Acting President.] Whenever the President transmits to the President pro tempore of the Senate and the Speaker of the House of Representatives his written declaration that he is unable to discharge the powers and duties of his office, and until he transmits to them a written declaration to the contrary, such powers and duties shall be discharged by the Vice President as Acting President.

Section 4

[Vice President as Acting President.] Whenever the Vice President and a majority of either the principal officers of the executive departments or of such other body as Congress may by law provide, transmit to the President pro tempore of the Senate and the Speaker of the House of Representatives their written declaration that the President is unable to discharge the powers and duties of his office, the Vice President shall immediately assume the powers and duties of the office as Acting President.

Thereafter, when the President transmits to the President pro tempore of the Senate and the Speaker of the House of Representatives his written declaration that no inability exists, he shall resume the powers and duties of his office unless the Vice President and a majority of either the principal officers of the executive department or of such other body as Congress may by law provide, transmit within four days to the President pro tempore of the Senate and the Speaker of the House of Representatives their written declaration that the President is unable to discharge the powers and duties of his office. Thereupon Congress shall decide the issue, assembling within forty-eight hours for that purpose if not in session. If the Congress, within twenty-one days after receipt of the latter written declaration, or, if Congress is not in session, within twenty-one days after Congress is required to assemble, determines by two thirds vote of both Houses that the President is unable to discharge the powers and duties of his office, the Vice President shall continue to discharge the same as Acting President; otherwise, the President shall resume the powers and duties of his office.

Article XXVI

(The proposed amendment was sent to the states Mar. 23, 1971, by the Ninety-second Congress. It was ratified July 1, 1971.)

Section 1

[Voting for 18-year-olds.] The right of citizens of the United States, who are 18 years of age or older, to vote shall not be denied or abridged by the United States or by any state on account of age.

Section 2

[Congress given power to enforce this article.] The Congress shall have power to enforce this article by appropriate legislation.

1. Amended by the 20th Amendment, Sections 3 and 4. 2. Repealed by the 21st Amendment.

The White House

Source: Department of the Interior, U.S. National Park Service.

The White House, the official residence of the President, is at 1600 Pennsylvania Avenue in Washington, D.C. The site, covering about 18 acres, was selected by President Washington and Pierre Charles L'Enfant, and the architect was James Hoban. The design of the residence is said to have been suggested by the Duke of Leinster's house in Ireland. The cornerstone was laid Oct. 13, 1792, and the first residents were President and Mrs. John Adams in November 1800. The building was fired by the British in 1814.

From December 1948 to March 1952, the interior of the White House was rebuilt, and the outer walls were strengthened.

The rooms for public functions are on the first floor; the second and third floors are used as the residence of the President and First Family. The most celebrated public room is the East Room, where formal receptions take place. Other public rooms are the Red Room, the Green Room, and the Blue Room. The State Dining Room is used for formal dinners. There are 132 rooms.

The Mayflower Compact

On Sept. 6, 1620, the *Mayflower*, a sailing vessel of about 180 tons, started her memorable voyage from Plymouth, England, with about 100[1] pilgrims aboard, bound for Virginia to establish a private permanent colony in North America. Arriving at what is now Provincetown, Mass., on Nov. 11 (Nov. 21, new style calendar), 41 of the passengers signed the famous "Mayflower Compact" as the boat lay at anchor in that Cape Cod harbor. A small detail of the pilgrims, led by William Bradford, assigned to select a place for permanent settlement landed at what is now Plymouth, Mass., on Dec. 21 (n.s.).

The text of the compact follows:

> In the name of God, Amen. We, whose names are underwritten, the Loyal Subjects of our dread Sovereign Lord, King *James*, by the Grace of God, of *Great Britain, France and Ireland*, King, *Defender of the Faith, &*
>
> Having undertaken for the Glory of God, and Advancement of the Christian Faith, and the Honour of our King and Country, a voyage to plant the first colony in the northern Parts of Virginia; do by these Presents, solemnly and mutually in the Presence of God and one of another, covenant and combine ourselves together into a civil Body Politick, for our better Ordering and Preservation, and Furtherance of the Ends aforesaid; And by Virtue hereof to enact, constitute, and frame, such just and equal Laws, Ordinances, Acts, Constitutions and Offices, from time to time, as shall be thought most meet and convenient for the General good of the Colony; unto which we promise all due Submission and Obedience.
>
> In Witness whereof we have hereunto subscribed our names at *Cape Cod* the eleventh of *November*, in the Reign of our Sovereign Lord, King *James* of *England, France* and *Ireland*, the eighteenth, and of *Scotland* the fifty-fourth. *Anno Domini*, 1620

John Carver
Digery Priest
William Brewster
Edmund Margesson
John Alden
George Soule
James Chilton
Francis Cooke
Moses Fletcher
John Ridgate
Christopher Martin
William Mullins
Thomas English
John Howland
Stephen Hopkins
Edward Winslow
Gilbert Winslow
Miles Standish
Richard Bitteridge
Francis Eaton
John Tilly
John Billington
Thomas Tinker
Samuel Fuller
Richard Clark
John Allerton
Richard Warren
Edward Liester
William Bradford
Thomas Williams
Isaac Allerton
Peter Brown
John Turner
Edward Tilly
John Craxton
Thomas Rogers
John Goodman
Edward Fuller
Richard Gardiner
William White
Edward Doten

1. Historians differ as to whether 100, 101, or 102 passengers were aboard.

The Monroe Doctrine

The Monroe Doctrine was announced in President James Monroe's message to Congress, during his second term on Dec. 2, 1823, in part as follows:

"In the discussions to which this interest has given rise, and in the arrangements by which they may terminate, the occasion has been deemed proper for asserting as a principle in which rights and interests of the United States are involved, that the American continents, by the free and independent condition which they have assumed and maintain, are henceforth not to be considered as subjects for future colonization by any European power. . . . We owe it, therefore, to candor and to the amicable relations existing between the United States and those powers to declare that we should consider any attempt on their part to extend their system to any portion of this hemisphere as dangerous to our peace and safety. With the existing colonies or dependencies of any European power we have not interfered and shall not interfere. But with the governments who have declared their independence and maintain it, and whose independence we have, on great consideration and on just principles, acknowledged, we could not view any interposition for the purpose of oppressing them or controlling in any other manner their destiny by any European power in any other light than as the manifestation of an unfriendly disposition toward the United States."

Order of Presidential Succession

1. The Vice President
2. Speaker of the House
3. President pro tempore of the Senate
4. Secretary of State
5. Secretary of the Treasury
6. Secretary of Defense
7. Attorney General
8. Secretary of the Interior
9. Secretary of Agriculture
10. Secretary of Commerce
11. Secretary of Labor
12. Secretary of Health and Human Services
13. Secretary of Housing and Urban Development
14. Secretary of Transportation
15. Secretary of Energy
16. Secretary of Education

NOTE: An official cannot succeed to the Presidency unless that person meets the Constitutional requirements.

The Star-Spangled Banner

Francis Scott Key, 1814

O say, can you see, by the dawn's early light,
What so proudly we hail'd at the twilight's last gleaming?
Whose broad stripes and bright stars, thro' the perilous fight,
O'er the ramparts we watch'd, were so gallantly streaming?
And the rockets' red glare, the bombs bursting in air,
Gave proof thro' the night that our flag was still there.
O say, does that star-spangled banner yet wave
O'er the land of the free and the home of the brave?

On the shore dimly seen thro' the mists of the deep,
Where the foe's haughty host in dread silence reposes,
What is that which the breeze, o'er the towering steep,
As it fitfully blows, half conceals, half discloses?
Now it catches the gleam of the morning's first beam,
In full glory reflected, now shines on the stream:
'T is the star-spangled banner: O, long may it wave
O'er the land of the free and the home of the brave!

And where is that band who so vauntingly swore
That the havoc of war and the battle's confusion,
A home and a country should leave us no more?
Their blood has wash'd out their foul footsteps' pollution.
No refuge could save the hireling and slave
From the terror of flight or the gloom of the grave:
And the star-spangled banner in triumph doth wave
O'er the land of the free and the home of the brave.

O thus be it ever when free-men shall stand
Between their lov'd home and the war's desolation;
Blest with vict'ry and peace, may the heav'n-rescued land
Praise the Pow'r that hath made and preserv'd us a nation!
Then conquer we must, when our cause it is just,
And this be our motto: "In God is our trust!"
And the star-spangled banner in triumph shall wave
O'er the land of the free and the home of the brave!

On Sept. 13, 1814, Francis Scott Key visited the British fleet in Chesapeake Bay to secure the release of Dr. William Beanes, who had been captured after the burning of Washington, D.C. The release was secured, but Key was detained on ship overnight during the shelling of Fort McHenry, one of the forts defending Baltimore. In the morning, he was so delighted to see the American flag still flying over the fort that he began a poem to commemorate the occasion. First published under the title "Defense of Fort M'Henry," and later as "The Star-Spangled Banner," the poem soon attained wide popularity as sung to the tune "To Anacreon in Heaven." The origin of this tune is obscure, but it may have been written by John Stafford Smith, a British composer born in 1750. "The Star-Spangled Banner" was officially made the National Anthem by Congress in 1931, although it had been already adopted as such by the Army and the Navy.

The Emancipation Proclamation

January 1, 1863

By the President of the United
States of America:

A Proclamation.

Whereas on the 22d day of September, A.D. 1862, a proclamation was issued by the President of the United States, containing, among other things, the following, to wit:

"That on the 1st day of January, A.D. 1863, all persons held as slaves within any State or designated part of a State the people whereof shall then be in rebellion against the United States shall be then, thenceforward, and forever free; and the executive government of the United States, including the military and naval authority thereof, will recognize and maintain the freedom of such persons and will do not act or acts to repress such persons, or any of them, in any efforts they may make for their actual freedom.

"That the executive will on the 1st day of January aforesaid, by proclamation, designate the States and parts of States, if any, in which the people thereof, respectively, shall then be in rebellion against the United States; and the fact that any State or the people thereof shall on that day be in good faith represented in the Congress of the United States by members chosen thereto at elections wherein a majority of the qualified voters of such States shall have participated shall, in the absence of strong countervailing testimony, be deemed conclusive evidence that such State and the people thereof are not then in rebellion against the United States."

Now, therefore, I, Abraham Lincoln, President

of the United States, by virtue of the power in me vested as Commander-in-Chief of the Army and Navy of the United States in time of actual armed rebellion against the authority and government of the United States, and as a fit and necessary war measure for suppressing said rebellion, do, on this 1st day of January, A.D. 1863, and in accordance with my purpose so to do, publicly proclaimed for the full period of one hundred days from the first day above mentioned, order and designate as the States and parts of States wherein the people thereof, respectively, are this day in rebellion against the United States the following, to wit:

Arkansas, Texas, Louisiana (except the parishes of St. Bernard, Plaquemines, Jefferson, St. John, St. Charles, St. James, Ascension, Assumption, Terrebonne, Lafourche, St. Mary, St. Martin, and Orleans, including the city of New Orleans), Mississippi, Alabama, Florida, Georgia, South Carolina, North Carolina, and Virginia (except the forty-eight counties designated as West Virginia, and also the counties of Berkeley, Accomac, Northhampton, Elizabeth City, York, Princess Anne, and Norfolk, including the cities of Norfolk and Portsmouth), and which excepted parts are for the present left precisely as if this proclamation were not issued.

And by virtue of the power and for the purpose aforesaid, I do order and declare that all persons held as slaves within said designated States and parts of States are, and henceforward shall be, free; and that the Executive Government of the United States, including the military and naval authorities thereof, will recognize and maintain the freedom of said persons.

And I hereby enjoin upon the people so declared to be free to abstain from all violence, unless in necessary self-defense; and I recommend to them that, in all cases when allowed, they labor faithfully for reasonable wages.

And I further declare and make known that such persons of suitable condition will be received into the armed service of the United States to garrison forts, positions, stations, and other places, and to man vessels of all sorts in said service.

And upon this act, sincerely believed to be an act of justice, warranted by the Constitution upon military necessity, I invoke the considerate judgment of mankind and the gracious favor of Almighty God.

The Confederate States of America

State	Seceded from Union	Readmitted to Union[1]
1. South Carolina	Dec. 20, 1860	July 9, 1868
2. Mississippi	Jan. 9, 1861	Feb. 23, 1870
3. Florida	Jan. 10, 1861	June 25, 1868
4. Alabama	Jan. 11, 1861	July 13, 1868
5. Georgia	Jan. 19, 1861	July 15, 1870[2]
6. Louisiana	Jan. 26, 1861	July 9, 1868
7. Texas	March 2, 1861	March 30, 1870
8. Virginia	April 17, 1861	Jan. 26, 1870
9. Arkansas	May 6, 1861	June 22, 1868
10. North Carolina	May 20, 1861	July 4, 1868
11. Tennessee	June 8, 1861	July 24, 1866

1. Date of readmission to representation in U.S. House of Representatives. 2. Second readmission date. First date was July 21, 1868, but the representatives were unseated March 5, 1869. NOTE: Four other slave states—Delaware, Kentucky, Maryland, and Missouri—remained in the Union.

Lincoln's Gettysburg Address

The Battle of Gettysburg, one of the most noted battles of the Civil War, was fought on July 1, 2, and 3, 1863. On Nov. 19, 1863, the field was dedicated as a national cemetery by President Lincoln in a two-minute speech that was to become immortal. At the time of its delivery the speech was relegated to the inside pages of the papers, while a two-hour address by Edward Everett, the leading orator of the time, caught the headlines.

The following is the text of the address revised by President Lincoln from his own notes:

Fourscore and seven years ago our fathers brought forth on this continent a new nation conceived in liberty and dedicated to the proposition that all men are created equal. Now we are engaged in a great civil war testing whether that nation, or any nation so conceived and so dedicated, can long endure. We are met on a great battlefield of that war. We have come to dedicate a portion of that field as a final resting-place for those who here gave their lives that that nation might live. It is altogether fitting and proper that we should do this. But, in a larger sense, we cannot dedicate, we cannot consecrate, we cannot hallow this ground. The brave men, living and dead, who struggled here have consecrated it far above our poor power to add or detract. The world will little note nor long remember what we say here, but it can never forget what they did here. It is for us the living rather to be dedicated here to the unfinished work which they who fought here have thus far so nobly advanced. It is rather for us to be here dedicated to the great task remaining before us—that from these honored dead we take increased devotion to that cause for which they gave the last full measure of devotion—that we here highly resolve that these dead shall not have died in vain, that this nation under God shall have a new birth of freedom, and that government of the people, by the people, for the people shall not perish from the earth.

The Early Congresses

At the urging of Massachusetts and Virginia, the First Continental Congress met in Philadelphia on Sept. 5, 1774, and was attended by representatives of all the colonies except Georgia. Patrick Henry of Virginia declared: "The distinctions between Pennsylvanians, New Yorkers and New Englanders are no more. I am not a Virginian but an American." This Congress, which adjourned Oct. 26, 1774, passed intercolonial resolutions calling for extensive boycott by the colonies against British trade.

The following year, most of the delegates from the colonies were chosen by popular election to attend the Second Continental Congress, which assembled in Philadelphia on May 10. As war had already begun between the colonies and England, the chief problems before the Congress were the procuring of military supplies, the establishment of an army and proper defenses, the issuing of continental bills of credit, etc. On June 15, 1775, George Washington was elected to command the Continental army. Congress adjourned Dec. 12, 1776.

Other Continental Congresses were held in Baltimore (1776–77), Philadelphia (1777), Lancaster, Pa. (1777), York, Pa. (1777–78), and Philadelphia (1778–81).

In 1781, the Articles of Confederation, although establishing a league of the thirteen states rather than a strong central government, provided for the continuance of Congress. Known thereafter as the Congress of the Confederation, it held sessions in Philadelphia (1781–83), Princeton, N.J. (1783), Annapolis, Md. (1783–84), and Trenton, N.J. (1784). Five sessions were held in New York City between the years 1785 and 1789.

The Congress of the United States, established by the ratification of the Constitution, held its first meeting on March 4, 1789, in New York City. Several sessions of Congress were held in Philadelphia, and the first meeting in Washington, D.C., was on Nov. 17, 1800.

Presidents of the Continental Congresses

Name	Elected	Birth and Death Dates	Name	Elected	Birth and Death Dates
Peyton Randolph, Va.	9/5/1774	c.1721-1775	John Hanson, Md.	11/5/1781	1715-1783
Henry Middleton, S.C.	10/22/1774	1717-1784	Elias Boudinot, N.J.	11/4/1782	1740-1821
Peyton Randolph, Va.	5/10/1775	c.1721-1775	Thomas Mifflin, Pa.	11/3/1783	1744-1800
John Hancock, Mass.	5/24/1775	1737-1793	Richard Henry Lee, Va.	11/30/1784	1732-1794
Henry Laurens, S.C.	11/1/1777	1724-1792	John Hancock, Mass.[1]	11/23/1785	1737-1793
John Jay, N.Y.	12/10/1778	1745-1829	Nathaniel Gorham, Mass.	6/6/1786	1738-1796
Samuel Huntington, Conn.	9/28/1779	1731-1796	Arthur St. Clair, Pa.	2/2/1787	1734-1818
Thomas McKean, Del.	7/10/1781	1734-1817	Cyrus Griffin, Va.	1/22/1788	1748-1810

1. Resigned May 29, 1786, never having served, because of continued illness.

The Great Seal of the U.S.

On July 4, 1776, the Continental Congress appointed a committee consisting of Benjamin Franklin, John Adams, and Thomas Jefferson "to bring in a device for a seal of the United States of America." After many delays, a verbal description of a design by William Barton was finally approved by Congress on June 20, 1782. The seal shows an American bald eagle with a ribbon in its mouth bearing the device *E pluribus unum* (One out of many). In its talons are the arrows of war and an olive branch of peace. On the reverse side it shows an unfinished pyramid with an eye (the eye of Providence) above it. Although this description was adopted in 1782, the first drawing was not made until four years later, and no die has ever been cut.

The American's Creed

William Tyler Page

"I believe in the United States of America as a government of the people, by the people, for the people; whose just powers are derived from the consent of the governed; a democracy in a republic; a sovereign Nation of many sovereign States; a perfect union, one and inseparable; established upon those principles of freedom, equality, justice, and humanity for which American patriots sacrificed their lives and fortunes.

"I therefore believe it is my duty to my country to love it, to support its Constitution, to obey its laws, to respect its flag, and to defend it against all enemies."

NOTE: William Tyler Page, Clerk of the U.S. House of Representatives, wrote "The American's Creed" in 1917. It was accepted by the House on behalf of the American people on April 3, 1918.

U.S. Capitol

When the French architect and engineer Maj. Pierre L'Enfant first began to lay out the plans for a new Federal city (now Washington, D.C.), he noted that Jenkins' Hill, overlooking the area, seemed to be "a pedestal waiting for a monument." It was here that the U.S. Capitol would be built. The basic structure as we know it today evolved over a period of more than 150 years. In 1792 a competition was held for the design of a capitol building. Dr. William Thornton, a physician and amateur architect, submitted the winning plan, a simple, low-lying structure of classical proportions with a shallow dome. Later, internal modifications were made by Benjamin Henry Latrobe. After the building was burned by the British in 1814, Latrobe and architect Charles Bulfinch were responsible for its reconstruction. Finally, under Thomas Walter, who was Architect of the Capitol from 1851 to 1865, the House and Senate wings and the imposing cast iron dome topped with the Statue of Freedom were added, and the Capitol assumed the form we see today. It was in the old Senate chamber that Daniel Webster cried out, "Liberty and Union, now and forever, one and inseparable!" In Statuary Hall, which used to be the old House chamber, a small disk on the floor marks the spot where John Quincy Adams was fatally stricken after more than 50 years of service to his country. A whisper from one side of this room can be heard across the vast space of the hall. Visitors can see the original Supreme Court chamber a floor below the Rotunda.

In addition to its historical association, the Capitol Building is also a vast artistic treasure house. The works of such famous artists as Gilbert Stuart, Rembrandt Peale, and John Trumbull are displayed on the walls. The Great Rotunda, with its 180-foot- (54.9-m-) high dome, is decorated with a massive fresco by Constantino Brumidi, which extends some 300 feet (90 m) in circumference. Throughout the building are many paintings of events in U.S. history and sculptures of outstanding Americans. The Capitol itself is situated on a 68-acre (27.5-ha) park designed by the 19th-century landscape architect Frederick Law Olmsted. There are free guided tours of the Capitol, which include admission to the House and Senate galleries. Those who wish to visit the visitors' gallery in either wing without taking the tour may obtain passes from their Senators or Congressmen. Visitors may ride on the monorail subway that joins the House and Senate wings of the Capitol with the Congressional office buildings.

Washington Monument

Construction of this magnificent Washington, D.C., monument, which draws some two million visitors a year, took nearly a century of planning, building, and controversy. Provision for a large equestrian statue of George Washington was made in the original city plan, but the project was soon dropped. After Washington's death it was taken up again, and a number of false starts and changes of design were made. Finally, in 1848, work was begun on the monument that stands today. The design, by architect Robert Mills, then featured an ornate base. In 1854, however, political squabbling and a lack of money brought construction to a halt. Work was resumed in 1880, and the monument was completed in 1884 and opened to the public in 1888. The tapered shaft, faced with white marble and rising from walls 15 feet thick (4.6 m) at the base was modeled after the obelisks of ancient Egypt. The monument, one of the tallest masonry constructions in the world, stands just over 555 feet (169 m). Memorial stones from the 50 States, foreign countries, and organizations line the interior walls. The top, reached only by elevator, commands a panoramic view of the city.

The Liberty Bell

The Liberty Bell was cast in England in 1752 for the Pennsylvania Statehouse (now named Independence Hall) in Philadelphia. It was recast in Philadelphia in 1753. It is inscribed with the words, "Proclaim liberty throughout all the land unto all the inhabitants thereof" (Lev. 25:10). The bell was rung on July 8, 1776, for the first public reading of the Declaration of Independence. Hidden in Allentown during the British occupation of Philadelphia, it was replaced in Independence Hall in 1778. The bell cracked on July 8, 1835, while tolling the death of Chief Justice John Marshall. In 1976 the Liberty Bell was moved to a special exhibition building near Independence Hall.

Arlington National Cemetery

Arlington National Cemetery occupies 612 acres in Virginia on the Potomac River, directly opposite Washington. This land was part of the estate of John Parke Custis, Martha Washington's son. His son, George Washington Parke Custis, built the mansion which later became the home of Robert E. Lee. In 1864, Arlington became a military cemetery. More than 200,000 servicemembers and their dependents are buried there. Expansion of the cemetery began in 1966, using a 180-acre tract of land directly east of the present site.

In 1921, an Unknown American Soldier of World War I was buried in the cemetery; the monument at the Tomb was opened to the public without ceremony in 1932. Two additional Unknowns, one from World War II and one from the Korean War, were buried May 30, 1958. The Unknown Serviceman of Vietnam was buried on May 28, 1984. The inscription carved on the Tomb of the Unknowns reads:

HERE RESTS IN
HONORED GLORY
AN AMERICAN
SOLDIER
KNOWN BUT TO GOD

History of the Flag

Source: Encyclopaedia Britannica.

The first official American flag, the Continental or Grand Union flag, was displayed on Prospect Hill, Jan. 1, 1776, in the American lines besieging Boston. It had 13 alternate red and white stripes, with the British Union Jack in the upper left corner.

On June 14, 1777, the Continental Congress adopted the design for a new flag, which actually was the Continental flag with the red cross of St. George and the white cross of St. Andrew replaced on the blue field by 13 stars, one for each state. No rule was made as to the arrangement of the stars, and while they were usually shown in a circle, there were various other designs. It is uncertain when the new flag was first flown, but its first official announcement is believed to have been on Sept. 3, 1777.

The first public assertion that Betsy Ross made the first Stars and Stripes appeared in a paper read before the Historical Society of Pennsylvania on March 14, 1870, by William J. Canby, a grandson. However, Mr. Canby on later investigation found no official documents of any action by Congress on the flag before June 14, 1777. Betsy Ross's own story, according to her daughter, was that Washington, Robert Morris, and George Ross, as representatives of Congress, visited her in Philadelphia in June 1776, showing her a rough draft of the flag and asking her if she could make one. However, the only actual record of the manufacture of flags by Betsy Ross is a voucher in Harrisburg, Pa., for 14 pounds and some shillings for flags for the Pennsylvania navy.

On Jan. 13, 1794, Congress voted to add two stars and two stripes to the flag in recognition of the admission of Vermont and Kentucky to the Union. By 1818, there were 20 states in the Union, and as it was obvious that the flag would soon become unwieldly, Congress voted April 18 to return to the original 13 stripes and to indicate the admission of a new state simply by the addition of a star the following July 4. The 49th star, for Alaska, was added July 4, 1959; and the 50th star, for Hawaii, was added July 4, 1960.

The first Confederate flag, adopted in 1861 by the Confederate convention in Montgomery, Ala., was called the Stars and Bars; but because of its similarity in colors to the American flag, there was much confusion in the Battle of Bull Run. To remedy this situation, Gen. G. T. Beauregard suggested a battle flag, which was used by the Southern armies throughout the war. The flag consisted of a red field on which was placed a blue cross of St. Andrew separated from the field by a white fillet and adorned with 13[1] white stars for the Confederate states. In May 1863, at Richmond, an official flag was adopted by the Confederate Congress. This flag was white and twice as long as wide; the union, two-thirds the width of the flag, contained the battle flag designed for Gen. Beauregard. A broad transverse stripe of red was added Feb. 4, 1865, so that the flag might not be mistaken for a signal of truce.

1. 11 states formally seceded, and unofficial groups in Kentucky and Missouri adopted ordinances of secession. On this basis, these two states were admitted to the Confederacy, although the official state governments remained in the Union.

The Pledge of Allegiance[1] to the Flag

"I pledge allegiance to the Flag of the United States of America, and to the Republic for which it stands, one Nation under God,[2] indivisible, with liberty and justice for all."

1. The original pledge was published in the Sept. 8, 1892, issue of *The Youth's Companion* in Boston. For years, the authorship was in dispute between James B. Upham and Francis Bellamy of the magazine's staff. In 1939, after a study of the controversy, the United States Flag Association decided that authorship be credited to Bellamy. 2. The phrase "under God" was added to the pledge on June 14, 1954.

The Statue of Liberty

The Statue of Liberty ("Liberty Enlightening the World") is a 225-ton, steel-reinforced copper female figure, 152 ft in height, facing the ocean from Liberty[1] Island in New York Harbor. The right hand holds aloft a torch, and the left hand carries a tablet upon which is inscribed: "July IV MDCCLXXVI."

The statue was designed by Frederic Auguste Bartholdi of Alsace as a gift to the United States from the people of France to memorialize the alliance of the two countries in the American Revolution and their abiding friendship. The French people contributed the $250,000 cost.

The 150-foot pedestal was designed by Richard M. Hunt and built by Gen. Charles P. Stone, both Americans. It contains steel underpinnings designed by Alexander Eiffel of France to support the statue. The $270,000 cost was borne by popular subscription in this country. President Grover Cleveland accepted the statue for the United States on Oct. 28, 1886.

On Sept. 26, 1972, President Richard M. Nixon dedicated the American Museum of Immigration, housed in structural additions to the base of the statue. In 1984 scaffolding went up for a major restoration and the torch was extinguished on July 4. It was relit with much ceremony July 4, 1986 to mark its centennial.

On a tablet inside the pedestal is engraved the following sonnet, written by Emma Lazarus (1849–1887):

The New Colossus

Not like the brazen giant of Greek fame.
With conquering limbs astride from land to land;
Here at our sea-washed, sunset gates shall stand
A mighty woman with a torch, whose flame
Is the imprisoned lightning, and her name
Mother of Exiles. From her beacon-hand
Glows world-wide welcome; her mild eyes command
The air-bridged harbor that twin cities frame.
"Keep, ancient lands, your storied pomp!" cries she
With silent lips. "Give me your tired, your poor,
Your huddled masses yearning to breathe free,
The wretched refuse of your teeming shore.
Send these, the homeless, tempest-tost to me,
I lift my lamp beside the golden door!"

1. Called Bedloe's Island prior to 1956.

Presidents

Name and (party)[1]	Term	State of birth	Born	Died	Religion	Age at inaug.	Age at death
1. Washington (F)[2]	1789–1797	Va.	2/22/1732	12/14/1799	Episcopalian	57	67
2. J. Adams (F)	1797–1801	Mass.	10/30/1735	7/4/1826	Unitarian	61	90
3. Jefferson (DR)	1801–1809	Va.	4/13/1743	7/4/1826	Deist	57	83
4. Madison (DR)	1809–1817	Va.	3/16/1751	6/28/1836	Episcopalian	57	85
5. Monroe (DR)	1817–1825	Va.	4/28/1758	7/4/1831	Episcopalian	58	73
6. J. Q. Adams (DR)	1825–1829	Mass.	7/11/1767	2/23/1848	Unitarian	57	80
7. Jackson (D)	1829–1837	S.C.	3/15/1767	6/8/1845	Presbyterian	61	78
8. Van Buren (D)	1837–1841	N.Y.	12/5/1782	7/24/1862	Reformed Dutch	54	79
9. W. H. Harrison (W)[3]	1841	Va.	2/9/1773	4/4/1841	Episcopalian	68	68
10. Tyler (W)	1841–1845	Va.	3/29/1790	1/18/1862	Episcopalian	51	71
11. Polk (D)	1845–1849	N.C.	11/2/1795	6/15/1849	Methodist	49	53
12. Taylor (W)[3]	1849–1850	Va.	11/24/1784	7/9/1850	Episcopalian	64	65
13. Fillmore (W)	1850–1853	N.Y.	1/7/1800	3/8/1874	Unitarian	50	74
14. Pierce (D)	1853–1857	N.H.	11/23/1804	10/8/1869	Episcopalian	48	64
15. Buchanan (D)	1857–1861	Pa.	4/23/1791	6/1/1868	Presbyterian	65	77
16. Lincoln (R)[4]	1861–1865	Ky.	2/12/1809	4/15/1865	Liberal	52	56
17. A. Johnson (U)[5]	1865–1869	N.C.	12/29/1808	7/31/1875	([6])	56	66
18. Grant (R)	1869–1877	Ohio	4/27/1822	7/23/1885	Methodist	46	63
19. Hayes (R)	1877–1881	Ohio	10/4/1822	1/17/1893	Methodist	54	70
20. Garfield (R)[4]	1881	Ohio	11/19/1831	9/19/1881	Disciples of Christ	49	49
21. Arthur (R)	1881–1885	Vt.	10/5/1830	11/18/1886	Episcopalian	50	56
22. Cleveland (D)	1885–1889	N.J.	3/18/1837	6/24/1908	Presbyterian	47	71
23. B. Harrison (R)	1889–1893	Ohio	8/20/1833	3/13/1901	Presbyterian	55	67
24. Cleveland (D)[7]	1893–1897	—	—	—	—	55	—
25. McKinley (R)[4]	1897–1901	Ohio	1/29/1843	9/14/1901	Methodist	54	58
26. T. Roosevelt (R)	1901–1909	N.Y.	10/27/1858	1/6/1919	Reformed Dutch	42	60
27. Taft (R)	1909–1913	Ohio	9/15/1857	3/8/1930	Unitarian	51	72
28. Wilson (D)	1913–1921	Va.	12/28/1856	2/3/1924	Presbyterian	56	67
29. Harding (R)[3]	1921–1923	Ohio	11/2/1865	8/2/1923	Baptist	55	57
30. Coolidge (R)	1923–1929	Vt.	7/4/1872	1/5/1933	Congregationalist	51	60
31. Hoover (R)	1929–1933	Iowa	8/10/1874	10/20/1964	Quaker	54	90
32. F. D. Roosevelt (D)[3]	1933–1945	N.Y.	1/30/1882	4/12/1945	Episcopalian	51	63
33. Truman (D)	1945–1953	Mo.	5/8/1884	12/26/1972	Baptist	60	88
34. Eisenhower (R)	1953–1961	Tex.	10/14/1890	3/28/1969	Presbyterian	62	78
35. Kennedy (D)[4]	1961–1963	Mass.	5/29/1917	11/22/1963	Roman Catholic	43	46
36. L. B. Johnson (D)	1963–1969	Tex.	8/27/1908	1/22/1973	Disciples of Christ	55	64
37. Nixon (R)[8]	1969–1974	Calif.	1/9/1913	—	Quaker	56	—
38. Ford (R)	1974–1977	Neb.	7/14/1913	—	Episcopalian	61	—
39. Carter (D)	1977–1981	Ga.	10/1/1924	—	Southern Baptist	52	—
40. Reagan (R)	1981–	Ill.	2/6/1911	—	Disciples of Christ	69	—

1. F—Federalist; DR—Democratic-Republican; D—Democratic; W—Whig; R—Republican; U—Union. 2. No party for first election. The party system in the U.S. made its appearance during Washington's first term. 3. Died in office. 4. Assassinated in office. 5. The Republican National Convention of 1864 adopted the name Union Party. It renominated Lincoln for President; for Vice President it nominated Johnson, a War Democrat. Although frequently listed as a Republican Vice President and President, Johnson undoubtedly considered himself strictly a member of the Union Party. When that party broke apart after 1868, he returned to the Democratic Party. 6. Johnson was not a professed church member; however, he admired the Baptist principles of church government. 7. Second nonconsecutive term. 8. Resigned Aug. 9, 1974.

Vice Presidents

Name and (party)[1]	Term	State of birth	Birth and death dates	President served under
1. John Adams (F)[2]	1789–1797	Massachusetts	1735–1826	Washington
2. Thomas Jefferson (DR)	1797–1801	Virginia	1743–1826	J. Adams
3. Aaron Burr (DR)	1801–1805	New Jersey	1756–1836	Jefferson
4. George Clinton (DR)[3]	1805–1812	New York	1739–1812	Jefferson and Madison
5. Elbridge Gerry (DR)[3]	1813–1814	Massachusetts	1744–1814	Madison
6. Daniel D. Tompkins (DR)	1817–1825	New York	1774–1825	Monroe
7. John C. Calhoun[4]	1825–1832	South Carolina	1782–1850	J. Q. Adams and Jackson
8. Martin Van Buren (D)	1833–1837	New York	1782–1862	Jackson
9. Richard M. Johnson (D)	1837–1841	Kentucky	1780–1850	Van Buren
10. John Tyler (W)[5]	1841	Virginia	1790–1862	W. H. Harrison
11. George M. Dallas (D)	1845–1849	Pennsylvania	1792–1864	Polk
12. Millard Fillmore (W)[5]	1849–1850	New York	1800–1874	Taylor
13. William R. King (D)[3]	1853	North Carolina	1786–1853	Pierce
14. John C. Breckinridge (D)	1857–1861	Kentucky	1821–1875	Buchanan

Name and (party)[1]	Term	State of birth	Birth and death dates	President served under
15. Hannibal Hamlin (R)	1861–1865	Maine	1809–1891	Lincoln
16. Andrew Johnson (U)[5]	1865	North Carolina	1808–1875	Lincoln
17. Schuyler Colfax (R)	1869–1873	New York	1823–1885	Grant
18. Henry Wilson (R)[3]	1873–1875	New Hampshire	1812–1875	Grant
19. William A. Wheeler (R)	1877–1881	New York	1819–1887	Hayes
20. Chester A. Arthur (R)[5]	1881	Vermont	1830–1886	Garfield
21. Thomas A. Hendricks (D)[3]	1885	Ohio	1819–1885	Cleveland
22. Levi P. Morton (R)	1889–1893	Vermont	1824–1920	B. Harrison
23. Adlai E. Stevenson (D)	1893–1897	Kentucky	1835–1914	Cleveland
24. Garrett A. Hobart (R)[3]	1897–1899	New Jersey	1844–1899	McKinley
25. Theodore Roosevelt (R)[5]	1901	New York	1858–1919	McKinley
26. Charles W. Fairbanks (R)	1905–1909	Ohio	1852–1918	T. Roosevelt
27. James S. Sherman (R)[3]	1909–1912	New York	1855–1912	Taft
28. Thomas R. Marshall (D)	1913–1921	Indiana	1854–1925	Wilson
29. Calvin Coolidge (R)[5]	1921–1923	Vermont	1872–1933	Harding
30. Charles G. Dawes (R)	1925–1929	Ohio	1865–1951	Coolidge
31. Charles Curtis (R)	1929–1933	Kansas	1860–1936	Hoover
32. John N. Garner (D)	1933–1941	Texas	1868–1967	F. D. Roosevelt
33. Henry A. Wallace (D)	1941–1945	Iowa	1888–1965	F. D. Roosevelt
34. Harry S. Truman (D)[5]	1945	Missouri	1884–1972	F. D. Roosevelt
35. Alben W. Barkley (D)	1949–1953	Kentucky	1877–1956	Truman
36. Richard M. Nixon (R)	1953–1961	California	1913–	Eisenhower
37. Lyndon B. Johnson (D)[5]	1961–1963	Texas	1908–1973	Kennedy
38. Hubert H. Humphrey (D)	1965–1969	South Dakota	1911–1978	Johnson
39. Spiro T. Agnew (R)[6]	1969–1973	Maryland	1918–	Nixon
40. Gerald R. Ford (R)[7]	1973–1974	Nebraska	1913–	Nixon
41. Nelson A. Rockefeller (R)[8]	1974–1977	Maine	1908–1979	Ford
42. Walter F. Mondale (D)	1977–1981	Minnesota	1928–	Carter
43. George Bush (R)	1981–	Massachusetts	1924–	Reagan

1. F—Federalist; DR—Democratic-Republican; D—Democratic; W—Whig; R—Republican; U—Union. 2. No party for first election. The party system in the U.S. made its appearance during Washington's first term as President. 3. Died in office. 4. Democratic-Republican with J. Q. Adams; Democratic with Jackson. Calhoun resigned in 1832 to become a U.S. Senator. 5. Succeeded to presidency on death of President. 6. Resigned Oct. 10, 1973, after pleading no contest to Federal income tax evasion charges. 7. Nominated by Nixon on Oct. 12, 1973, under provisions of 25th Amendment. Confirmed by Congress on Dec. 6, 1973, and was sworn in same day. He became President Aug. 9, 1974, upon Nixon's resignation. 8. Nominated by Ford Aug. 20, 1974; confirmed by Congress on Dec. 19, 1974, and was sworn in same day.

Burial Places of the Presidents

President	Burial place	President	Burial place
Washington	Mt. Vernon, Va.	Grant	New York City
J. Adams	Quincy, Mass.	Hayes	Fremont, Ohio
Jefferson	Charlottesville, Va.	Garfield	Cleveland, Ohio
Madison	Montpelier Station, Va.	Arthur	Albany, N.Y.
Monroe	Richmond, Va.	Cleveland	Princeton, N.J.
J. Q. Adams	Quincy, Mass.	B. Harrison	Indianapolis
Jackson	The Hermitage, nr. Nashville, Tenn.	McKinley	Canton, Ohio
		T. Roosevelt	Oyster Bay, N.Y.
Van Buren	Kinderhook, N.Y.	Taft	Arlington National Cemetery
W. H. Harrison	North Bend, Ohio	Wilson	Washington National Cathedral
Tyler	Richmond, Va.	Harding	Marion, Ohio
Polk	Nashville, Tenn.	Coolidge	Plymouth, Vt.
Taylor	Louisville, Ky.	Hoover	West Branch, Iowa
Fillmore	Buffalo, N.Y.	F. D. Roosevelt	Hyde Park, N.Y.
Pierce	Concord, N.H.	Truman	Independence, Mo.
Buchanan	Lancaster, Pa.	Eisenhower	Abilene, Kan.
Lincoln	Springfield, Ill.	Kennedy	Arlington National Cemetery
A. Johnson	Greeneville, Tenn.	L. B. Johnson	Stonewall, Tex.

"In God We Trust"

"In God We Trust" first appeared on U.S. coins after April 22, 1864, when Congress passed an act authorizing the coinage of a 2-cent piece bearing this motto. Thereafter, Congress extended its use to other coins. On July 30, 1956, it became the national motto.

Wives and Children of the Presidents

President	Wife's name	Year and place of wife's birth	Married	Wife died	Children of President[1] Sons	Daughters
Washington	Mrs. Martha Dandridge Custis	1732, Va.	1759	1802	—	—
John Adams	Abigail Smith	1744, Mass.	1764	1818	3	2
Jefferson	Mrs. Martha Wayles Skelton	1748, Va.	1772	1782	1	5
Madison	Mrs. Dorothy "Dolley" Payne Todd	1768, N.C.	1794	1849	—	—
Monroe	Elizabeth "Eliza" Kortright	1768, N.Y.	1786	1830	—	2
J. Q. Adams	Louisa Catherine Johnson	1775, England	1797	1852	3	1
Jackson	Mrs. Rachel Donelson Robards	1767, Va.	1791	1828	—	—
Van Buren	Hannah Hoes	1788, N.Y.	1807	1819	4	—
W. H. Harrison	Anna Symmes	1775, N.J.	1795	1864	6	4
Tyler	Letitia Christian	1790, Va.	1813	1842	3	4
	Julia Gardiner	1820, N.Y.	1844	1889	5	2
Polk	Sarah Childress	1803, Tenn.	1824	1891	—	—
Taylor	Margaret Smith	1788, Md.	1810	1852	1	5
Fillmore	Abigail Powers	1798, N.Y.	1826	1853	1	1
	Mrs. Caroline Carmichael McIntosh	1813, N.J.	1858	1881	—	—
Pierce	Jane Means Appleton	1806, N.H.	1834	1863	3	—
Buchanan	(Unmarried)	—	—	—	—	—
Lincoln	Mary Todd	1818, Ky.	1842	1882	4	—
A. Johnson	Eliza McCardle	1810, Tenn.	1827	1876	3	2
Grant	Julia Dent	1826, Mo.	1848	1902	3	1
Hayes	Lucy Ware Webb	1831, Ohio	1852	1889	7	1
Garfield	Lucretia Rudolph	1832, Ohio	1858	1918	5	2
Arthur	Ellen Lewis Herndon	1837, Va.	1859	1880	2	1
Cleveland	Frances Folsom	1864, N.Y.	1886	1947	2	3
B. Harrison	Caroline Lavinia Scott	1832, Ohio	1853	1892	1	1
	Mrs. Mary Scott Lord Dimmick	1858, Pa.	1896	1948	—	1
McKinley	Ida Saxton	1847, Ohio	1871	1907	—	2
T. Roosevelt	Alice Hathaway Lee	1861, Mass.	1880	1884	—	1
	Edith Kermit Carow	1861, Conn.	1886	1948	4	1
Taft	Helen Herron	1861, Ohio	1886	1943	2	1
Wilson	Ellen Louise Axson	1860, Ga.	1885	1914	—	3
	Mrs. Edith Bolling Galt	1872, Va.	1915	1961	—	—
Harding	Mrs. Florence Kling DeWolfe	1860, Ohio	1891	1924	—	—
Coolidge	Grace Anna Goodhue	1879, Vt.	1905	1957	2	—
Hoover	Lou Henry	1875, Iowa	1899	1944	2	—
F. D. Roosevelt	Anna Eleanor Roosevelt	1884, N.Y.	1905	1962	5	1
Truman	Bess Wallace	1885, Mo.	1919	1982	—	1
Eisenhower	Mamie Geneva Doud	1896, Iowa	1916	1979	2	—
Kennedy	Jacqueline Lee Bouvier	1929, N.Y.	1953	—	2	1
L. B. Johnson	Claudia Alta "Lady Bird" Taylor	1912, Tex.	1934	—	—	2
Nixon	Thelma Catherine "Pat" Ryan	1912, Nev.	1940	—	—	2
Ford	Mrs. Elizabeth "Betty" Bloomer Warren	1918, Ill.	1948	—	3	1
Carter	Rosalynn Smith	1928, Ga.	1946	—	3	1
Reagan	Jane Wyman	1914, Mo.	1940[2]	—	1[3]	1
	Nancy Davis	1923, N.Y.	1952	—	1	1

1. Includes children who died in infancy. 2. Divorced in 1948. 3. Adopted.

Elections

How a President Is Nominated and Elected

The National Conventions of both major parties are held during the summer of a presidential-election year. Earlier, each party selects delegates by primaries, conventions, committees, etc.

For their 1988 National Convention, the Republicans allow each state a base of 6 delegates at large; the District of Columbia, 14; Puerto Rico, 14; Guam and the Virgin Islands, 4 each. In addition, each state receives 3 district delegates for each representative it has in the House of Representatives, regardless of political affiliation. This did not apply to the District of Columbia, Puerto Rico, Guam and the Virgin Islands.

Each state is awarded additional delegates at large on the basis of having supported the Republican candidate for President in 1984 and electing Republican candidates for Senator, Governor, and U.S. Representative between 1984 and 1987 inclusive.

The number of delegates at the 1988 convention, to be held in New Orleans starting August 15, will be 2,277.[1]

Following was the apportionment of delegates:

Alabama	38	Florida	82	Kentucky	38	Montana	20	Ohio	88	Texas	111
Alaska	19	Georgia	48	Louisiana	41	Nebraska	25	Oklahoma	36	Utah	26
Arizona	33	Guam	4	Maine	22	Nevada	20	Oregon	32	Vermont	17
Arkansas	27	Hawaii	20	Maryland	41	N.H.	23	Pa.	96	V.I.	4
California	175	Idaho	22	Mass.	52	N. Jersey	64	P.R.	14	Virginia	50
Colorado	36	Illinois	92	Michigan	77	New Mexico	26	R.I.	21	Washington	41
Connecticut	35	Indiana	51	Minnesota	31	New York	136	S.C.	37	W. Va.	28
Delaware	17	Iowa	37	Mississippi	31	N.C.	54	S.D.	18	Wisconsin	47
D.C.	14	Kansas	34	Missouri	47	N.D.	16	Tennessee	45	Wyoming	18

1. As of March 11, 1987.

The Democrats base the number of delegates on a state's showing in the 1984 and 1986 elections. At the 1988 convention, to be held in Atlanta starting July 18, there will be 3,517[1] [2]delegates casting votes. Following is the apportionment by states:

Alabama	56	Florida	136	Kentucky	55	Montana	19	Ohio	159	Texas	183
Alaska	12	Georgia	77	Louisiana	63	Nebraska	25	Oklahoma	46	Utah	23
Arizona	36	Guam	3	Maine	23	Nevada	16	Oregon	45	Vermont	14
Arkansas	38	Hawaii	20	Maryland	67	N. H.	18	Pa.	178	V.I.	3
California	314	Idaho	18	Mass.	98	New Jersey	109	P.R.	51	Virginia	75
Colorado	45	Illinois	173	Michigan	138	New Mexico	24	R.I.	22	Washington	65
Connecticut	52	Indiana	79	Minnesota	78	New York	255	S.C.	44	W. Va.	37
Delaware	15	Iowa	52	Mississippi	40	N.C.	82	S.D.	15	Wisconsin	81
D. C.	16	Kansas	39	Missouri	77	N.D.	15	Tennessee	70	Wyoming	13

1. Includes 7 delegates for Democrats Abroad and 3 for American Samoa. 2. As of June 16, 1987.

The Conventions

At each convention, a temporary chairman is chosen. After a credentials committee seats the delegates, a permanent chairman is elected. The convention then votes on a platform, drawn up by the platform committee.

By the third or fourth day, presidential nominations begin. The chairman calls the roll of states alphabetically. A state may place a candidate in nomination or yield to another state.

Voting, again alphabetically by roll call of states, begins after all nominations have been made and seconded. A simple majority is required in each party, although this may require many ballots.

Finally, the vice-presidential candidate is selected. Although there is no law saying that the candidates *must* come from different states, it is, practically, necessary for this to be the case. Otherwise, according to the Constitution (*see* Amendment XII), electors from that state could vote for only one of the candidates and would have to cast their other vote for some person of another state. This could result in a presidential candidate's receiving a majority electoral vote and his running mate's failing to.

The Electoral College

The next step in the process is the nomination of electors in each state, according to its laws. These electors must not be Federal office holders. In the November election, the voters cast their votes for electors, not for President. In some states, the ballots include only the names of the presidential and vice-presidential candidates; in others, they include only names of the electors. Nowadays, it is rare for electors to be split between parties. The last such occurrence was in North Carolina in 1968[1]; the last before that, in Tennessee in 1948. On three occasions (1824, 1876, and 1888), the presidential candidate with the largest popular vote failed to obtain an electoral-vote majority.

Each state has as many electors as it has Senators and Representatives. For the 1984 election, the total electors were 538, based on 100 Senators, 435 Representatives, plus 3 electoral votes from the District of Columbia as a result of the 23rd Amendment to the Constitution.

On the first Monday after the second Wednesday in December, the electors cast their votes in their respective state capitols. Constitutionally they may vote for someone other than the party candidate but usually they do not since they are pledged to one party and its candidate on the ballot. Should the presidential or vice-presidential candidate die between the November election and the December meetings, the electors pledged to vote for him could vote for whomever they pleased. However, it seems certain that the national committee would attempt to get an agreement among the state party leaders for a replacement candidate.

The votes of the electors, certified by the states, are sent to Congress, where the president of the Senate opens the certificates and has them counted in the presence of both Houses on January 6. The new President is inaugurated at noon on January 20.

Should no candidate receive a majority of the electoral vote for President, the House of Representatives chooses a President from among the three highest candidates, voting, not as individuals, but as states, with a majority (now 26) needed to elect. Should no vice-presidential candidate obtain the majority, the Senate, voting as individuals, chooses from the highest two.

1. In 1956, 1 of Alabama's 11 electoral votes was cast for Walter B. Jones. In 1960, 6 of Alabama's 11 electoral votes and 1 of Oklahoma's 8 electoral votes were cast for Harry Flood Byrd. (Byrd also received all 8 of Mississippi's electoral votes.)

National Political Conventions Since 1856

Opening date	Party	Where held	Opening date	Party	Where held
June 17, 1856	Republican	Philadelphia	June 10, 1924	Republican	Cleveland
June 2, 1856	Democratic	Cincinnati	June 24, 1924[2]	Democratic	New York City
May 16, 1860	Republican	Chicago	June 12, 1928	Republican	Kansas City
April 23, 1860	Democratic	Charleston and Baltimore	June 26, 1928	Democratic	Houston
			June 14, 1932	Republican	Chicago
June 7, 1864	Republican[1]	Baltimore	June 27, 1932	Democratic	Chicago
Aug. 29, 1864	Democratic	Chicago	June 9, 1936	Republican	Cleveland
May 20, 1868	Republican	Chicago	June 23, 1936	Democratic	Philadelphia
July 4, 1868	Democratic	New York City	June 24, 1940	Republican	Philadelphia
June 5, 1872	Republican	Philadelphia	July 15, 1940	Democratic	Chicago
June 9, 1872	Democratic	Baltimore	June 26, 1944	Republican	Chicago
June 14, 1876	Republican	Cincinnati	July 19, 1944	Democratic	Chicago
June 28, 1876	Democratic	St. Louis	June 21, 1948	Republican	Philadelphia
June 2, 1880	Republican	Chicago	July 12, 1948	Democratic	Philadelphia
June 23, 1880	Democratic	Cincinnati	July 17, 1948	(3)	Birmingham
June 3, 1884	Republican	Chicago	July 22, 1948	Progressive	Philadelphia
July 11, 1884	Democratic	Chicago	July 7, 1952	Republican	Chicago
June 19, 1888	Republican	Chicago	July 21, 1952	Democratic	Chicago
June 6, 1888	Democratic	St. Louis	Aug. 20, 1956	Republican	San Francisco
June 7, 1892	Republican	Minneapolis	Aug. 13, 1956	Democratic	Chicago
June 21, 1892	Democratic	Chicago	July 25, 1960	Republican	Chicago
June 16, 1896	Republican	St. Louis	July 11, 1960	Democratic	Los Angeles
July 7, 1896	Democratic	Chicago	July 13, 1964	Republican	San Francisco
June 19, 1900	Republican	Philadelphia	Aug. 24, 1964	Democratic	Atlantic City
July 4, 1900	Democratic	Kansas City	Aug. 5, 1968	Republican	Miami Beach
June 21, 1904	Republican	Chicago	Aug. 26, 1968	Democratic	Chicago
July 6, 1904	Democratic	St. Louis	July 10, 1972	Democratic	Miami Beach
June 16, 1908	Republican	Chicago	Aug. 21, 1972	Republican	Miami Beach
July 7, 1908	Democratic	Denver	July 12, 1976	Democratic	New York City
June 18, 1912	Republican	Chicago	Aug. 16, 1976	Republican	Kansas City, Mo.
June 25, 1912	Democratic	Baltimore	Aug. 11, 1980	Democratic	New York City
June 7, 1916	Republican	Chicago	July 14, 1980	Republican	Detroit
June 14, 1916	Democratic	St. Louis	Aug. 20, 1984	Republican	Dallas
June 8, 1920	Republican	Chicago	July 16, 1984	Democratic	San Francisco
June 28, 1920	Democratic	San Francisco	July 18, 1988	Democratic	Atlanta
			Aug. 15, 1988	Republican	New Orleans

1. The Convention adopted name Union party to attract War Democrats and others favoring prosecution of war. 2. In session until July 10, 1924. 3. States' Rights delegates from 13 Southern states.

National Committee Chairmen Since 1944

Chairman and (state)	Term	Chairman and (state)	Term
REPUBLICAN		**DEMOCRATIC**	
Herbert Brownell, Jr. (N.Y.)	1944–46	Robert E. Hannegan (Mo.)	1944–47
Carroll Reece (Tenn.)	1946–48	J. Howard McGrath (R.I.)	1947–49
Hugh D. Scott, Jr. (Pa.)	1948–49	William M. Boyle, Jr. (Mo.)	1949–51
Guy G. Gabrielson (N.J.)	1949–52	Frank E. McKinney (Ind.)	1951–52
Arthur E. Summerfield (Mich.)	1952–53	Stephen A. Mitchell (Ill.)	1952–54
Wesley Roberts (Kan.)	1953–	Paul M. Butler (Ind.)	1955–60
Leonard W. Hall (N.Y.)	1953–57	Henry M. Jackson (Wash.)	1960–61
Meade Alcorn (Conn.)	1957–59	John M. Bailey (Conn.)	1961–68
Thruston B. Morton (Ky.)	1959–61	Lawrence F. O'Brien (Mass.)	1968–69
William E. Miller (N.Y.)	1961–64	Fred R. Harris (Okla.)	1969–70
Dean Burch (Ariz.)	1964–65	Lawrence F. O'Brien (Mass.)	1970–72
Ray C. Bliss (Ohio)	1965–69	Jean Westwood (Utah)	1972
Rogers C. B. Morton (Md.)	1969–71	Robert S. Strauss (Tex.)	1972–77
Robert Dole (Kan.)	1971–73	Kenneth M. Curtis (Me.)	1977
George H. Bush (Tex.)	1973–74	John C. White (Tex.)	1977–81
Mary Louise Smith (Iowa)	1974–77	Charles T. Manatt (Calif.)	1981–85
William E. Brock III (Tenn.)	1977–81	Paul G. Kirk, Jr. (Mass.)	1985–
Richard Richards (Utah)	1981–83		
Frank J. Fahrenkopf, Jr. (Nevada)	1983—		

Republican National Committee: 310 First St., S.E., Washington, D. C. 20003.
Democratic National Committee: 430 South Capitol St., S.E., Washington, D.C. 20003.

Presidential Elections, 1789 to 1984

For the original method of electing the President and the Vice President (elections of 1789, 1792, 1796, and 1800), see Article II, Section 1, of the Constitution. The election of 1804 was the first one in which the electors voted for President and Vice President on separate ballots. (See Amendment XII to the Constitution.)

Year	Presidential candidates	Party	Electoral vote
1789[1]	George Washington	(no party)	69
	John Adams	(no party)	34
	Scattering	(no party)	35
	Votes not cast		8
1792	George Washington	Federalist	132
	John Adams	Federalist	77
	George Clinton	Anti-Federalist	50
	Thomas Jefferson	Anti-Federalist	4
	Aaron Burr	Anti-Federalist	1
	Votes not cast		6
1796	John Adams	Federalist	71
	Thomas Jefferson	Dem.-Rep.	68
	Thomas Pinckney	Federalist	59
	Aaron Burr	Dem.-Rep.	30
	Scattering		48
1800[2]	Thomas Jefferson	Dem.-Rep.	73
	Aaron Burr	Dem.-Rep.	73
	John Adams	Federalist	65
	Charles C. Pinckney	Federalist	64
	John Jay	Federalist	1

Year	Presidential candidates	Party	Electoral vote	Vice-presidential candidates	Party	Electoral vote
1804	Thomas Jefferson	Dem.-Rep.	162	George Clinton	Dem.-Rep.	162
	Charles C. Pinckney	Federalist	14	Rufus King	Federalist	14
1808	James Madison	Dem.-Rep.	122	George Clinton	Dem.-Rep.	113
	Charles C. Pinckney	Federalist	47	Rufus King	Federalist	47
	George Clinton	Dem.-Rep.	6	John Langdon	Ind. (no party)	9
	Votes not cast		1	James Madison	Dem.-Rep.	3
				James Monroe	Dem.-Rep.	3
				Votes not cast		1
1812	James Madison	Dem.-Rep.	128	Elbridge Gerry	Dem.-Rep.	131
	De Witt Clinton	Federalist	89	Jared Ingersoll	Federalist	86
	Votes not cast		1	Votes not cast		1
1816	James Monroe	Dem.-Rep.	183	Daniel D. Tompkins	Dem.-Rep.	183
	Rufus King	Federalist	34	John E. Howard	Federalist	22
	Votes not cast		4	James Ross	Ind. (no party)	5
				John Marshall	Federalist	4
				Robert G. Harper	Ind. (no party)	3
				Votes not cast		4
1820	James Monroe	Dem-Rep	231	Daniel D. Tompkins	Dem.-Rep.	218
	John Quincy Adams	Ind. (no party)	1	Richard Stockton	Ind. (no party)	8
	Votes not cast		3	Daniel Rodney	Ind. (no party)	4
				Richard Rush	Ind. (no party)	1
				Robert G. Harper	Ind. (no party)	1
				Votes not cast		3
1824[3]	John Quincy Adams	(no party)	84	John C. Calhoun	(no party)	182
	Andrew Jackson	(no party)	99	Nathan Sanford	(no party)	30
	William H. Crawford	(no party)	41	Nathaniel Macon	(no party)	24
	Henry Clay	(no party)	37	Andrew Jackson	(no party)	13
				Martin Van Buren	(no party)	9
				Henry Clay	(no party)	2
				Votes not cast		1
1828	Andrew Jackson	Democratic	178	John C. Calhoun	Democratic	171
	John Quincy Adams	Natl. Rep.	83	Richard Rush	Natl. Rep.	83
				William Smith	Democratic	7
1832	Andrew Jackson	Democratic	219	Martin Van Buren	Democratic	189
	Henry Clay	Natl. Rep.	49	John Sergeant	Natl. Rep.	49
	John Floyd	Ind. (no party)	11	Henry Lee	Ind. (no party)	11
	William Wirt	Antimasonic[4]	7	Amos Ellmaker	Antimasonic	7
	Votes not cast		2	William Wilkins	Ind. (no party)	30
				Votes not cast		2

Year	Presidential candidates	Party	Electoral vote	Vice-presidential candidates	Party	Electoral vote
1836	Martin Van Buren	Democratic	170	Richard M. Johnson[5]	Democratic	147
	William H. Harrison	Whig	73	Francis Granger	Whig	77
	Hugh L. White	Whig	26	John Tyler	Whig	47
	Daniel Webster	Whig	14	William Smith	Ind. (no party)	23
	W. P. Mangum	Ind. (no party)	11			
1840	William H. Harrison[6]	Whig	234	John Tyler	Whig	234
	Martin Van Buren	Democratic	60	Richard M. Johnson	Democratic	48
				L. W. Tazewell	Ind. (no party)	11
				James K. Polk	Democratic	1
1844	James K. Polk	Democratic	170	George M. Dallas	Democratic	170
	Henry Clay	Whig	105	Theo. Frelinghuysen	Whig	105
1848	Zachary Taylor[7]	Whig	163	Millard Fillmore	Whig	163
	Lewis Cass	Democratic	127	William O. Butler	Democratic	127
1852	Franklin Pierce	Democratic	254	William R. King	Democratic	254
	Winfield Scott	Whig	42	William A. Graham	Whig	42
1856	James Buchanan	Democratic	174	John C. Breckinridge	Democratic	174
	John C. Fremont	Republican	114	William L. Dayton	Republican	114
	Millard Fillmore	American[8]	8	A. J. Donelson	American[8]	8
1860	Abraham Lincoln	Republican	180	Hannibal Hamlin	Republican	180
	John C. Breckinridge	Democratic	72	Joseph Lane	Democratic	72
	John Bell	Const. Union	39	Edward Everett	Const. Union	39
	Stephen A. Douglas	Democratic	12	H. V. Johnson	Democratic	12
1864	Abraham Lincoln[9]	Union[10]	212	Andrew Johnson	Union[15]	212
	George B. McClellan	Democratic	21	G. H. Pendleton	Democratic	21
1868	Ulysses S. Grant	Republican	214	Schuyler Colfax	Republican	214
	Horatio Seymour	Democratic	80	Francis P. Blair, Jr.	Democratic	80
	Votes not counted[11]		23	Votes not counted[11]		23

Year	Presidential candidates	Party	Electoral vote	Popular vote	Vice-presidential candidates and party
1872	Ulysses S. Grant	Republican	286	3,597,132	Henry Wilson—R
	Horace Greeley	Dem., Liberal Rep.	([12])	2,834,125	B. Gratz Brown—D, LR—(47)
	Thomas A. Hendricks	Democratic	42		Scattering—(19)
	B. Gratz Brown	Dem., Liberal Rep.	18		Votes not counted—(14)
	Charles J. Jenkins	Democratic	2		
	David Davis	Democratic	1		
	Votes not counted		17		
1876[13]	Rutherford B. Hayes	Republican	185	4,033,768	William A. Wheeler—R
	Samuel J. Tilden	Democratic	184	4,285,992	Thomas A. Hendricks—D
	Peter Cooper	Greenback	0	81,737	Samuel F. Cary—G
1880	James A. Garfield[14]	Republican	214	4,449,053	Chester A. Arthur—R
	Winfield S. Hancock	Democratic	155	4,442,035	William H. English—D
	James B. Weaver	Greenback	0	308,578	B. J. Chambers—G
1884	Grover Cleveland	Democratic	219	4,911,017	Thomas A. Hendricks—D
	James G. Blaine	Republican	182	4,848,334	John A. Logan—R
	Benjamin F. Butler	Greenback	0	175,370	A. M. West—G
	John P. St. John	Prohibition	0	150,369	William Daniel—P
1888	Benjamin Harrison	Republican	233	5,440,216	Levi P. Morton—R
	Grover Cleveland	Democratic	168	5,538,233	A. G. Thurman—D
	Clinton B. Fisk	Prohibition	0	249,506	John A. Brooks—P
	Alson J. Streeter	Union Labor	0	146,935	Charles E. Cunningham—UL
1892	Grover Cleveland	Democratic	277	5,556,918	Adlai E. Stevenson—D
	Benjamin Harrison	Republican	145	5,176,108	Whitelaw Reid—R
	James B. Weaver	People's[15]	22	1,041,028	James G. Field—Peo
	John Bidwell	Prohibition	0	264,133	James B. Cranfill—P

Year	Presidential candidates	Party	Electoral vote	Popular vote	Vice-presidential candidates and party
1896	William McKinley	Republican	271	7,035,638	Garret A. Hobart—R
	William J. Bryan	Dem., People's[15]	176	6,467,946	Arthur Sewall—D—(149)
					Thomas E. Watson—Peo—(27)
	John M. Palmer	Natl. Dem.	0	133,148	Simon B. Buckner—ND
	Joshua Levering	Prohibition	0	132,007	Hale Johnson—P
1900	William McKinley[16]	Republican	292	7,219,530	Theodore Roosevelt—R
	William J. Bryan	Dem., People's[15]	155	6,358,071	Adlai E. Stevenson—D, Peo
	Eugene V. Debs	Social Democratic	0	94,768	Job Harriman—SD
1904	Theodore Roosevelt	Republican	336	7,628,834	Charles W. Fairbanks—R
	Alton B. Parker	Democratic	140	5,084,491	Henry G. Davis—D
	Eugene V. Debs	Socialist	0	402,400	Benjamin Hanford—S
1908	William H. Taft	Republican	321	7,679,006	James S. Sherman—R
	William J. Bryan	Democratic	162	6,409,106	John W. Kern—D
	Eugene V. Debs	Socialist	0	402,820	Benjamin Hanford—S
1912	Woodrow Wilson	Democratic	435	6,286,214	Thomas R. Marshall—D
	Theodore Roosevelt	Progressive	88	4,126,020	Hiram Johnson—Prog
	William H. Taft	Republican	8	3,483,922	Nicholas M. Butler—R[17]
	Eugene V. Debs	Socialist	0	897,011	Emil Seidel—S
1916	Woodrow Wilson	Democratic	277	9,129,606	Thomas R. Marshall—D
	Charles E. Hughes	Republican	254	8,538,221	Charles W. Fairbanks—R
	A. L. Benson	Socialist	0	585,113	G. R. Kirkpatrick—S
1920	Warren G. Harding[18]	Republican	404	16,152,200	Calvin Coolidge—R
	James M. Cox	Democratic	127	9,147,353	Franklin D. Roosevelt—D
	Eugene V. Debs	Socialist	0	917,799	Seymour Stedman—S
1924	Calvin Coolidge	Republican	382	15,725,016	Charles G. Dawes—R
	John W. Davis	Democratic	136	8,385,586	Charles W. Bryan—D
	Robert M. LaFollette	Progressive, Socialist	13	4,822,856	Burton K. Wheeler—Prog S
1928	Herbert Hoover	Republican	444	21,392,190	Charles Curtis—R
	Alfred E. Smith	Democratic	87	15,016,443	Joseph T. Robinson—D
	Norman Thomas	Socialist	0	267,420	James H. Maurer—S
1932	Franklin D. Roosevelt	Democratic	472	22,821,857	John N. Garner—D
	Herbert Hoover	Republican	59	15,761,841	Charles Curtis—R
	Norman Thomas	Socialist	0	884,781	James H. Maurer—S
1936	Franklin D. Roosevelt	Democratic	523	27,751,597	John N. Garner—D
	Alfred M. Landon	Republican	8	16,679,583	Frank Knox—R
	Norman Thomas	Socialist	0	187,720	George Nelson—S
1940	Franklin D. Roosevelt	Democratic	449	27,244,160	Henry A. Wallace—D
	Wendell L. Willkie	Republican	82	22,305,198	Charles L. McNary—R
	Norman Thomas	Socialist	0	99,557	Maynard C. Krueger—S
1944	Franklin D. Roosevelt[19]	Democratic	432	25,602,504	Harry S. Truman—D
	Thomas E. Dewey	Republican	99	22,006,285	John W. Bricker—R
	Norman Thomas	Socialist	0	80,518	Darlington Hoopes—S
1948	Harry S. Truman	Democratic	303	24,179,345	Alben W. Barkley—D
	Thomas E. Dewey	Republican	189	21,991,291	Earl Warren—R
	J. Strom Thurmond	States' Rights Dem.	39	1,176,125	Fielding L. Wright—SR
	Henry A. Wallace	Progressive	0	1,157,326	Glen Taylor—Prog
	Norman Thomas	Socialist	0	139,572	Tucker P. Smith—S
1952	Dwight D. Eisenhower	Republican	442	33,936,234	Richard M. Nixon—R
	Adlai E. Stevenson	Democratic	89	27,314,992	John J. Sparkman—D
1956	Dwight D. Eisenhower	Republican	457	35,590,472	Richard M. Nixon—R
	Adlai E. Stevenson	Democratic	73[20]	26,022,752	Estes Kefauver—D
1960	John F. Kennedy[22]	Democratic	303	34,226,731	Lyndon B. Johnson—D
	Richard M. Nixon	Republican	219[21]	34,108,157	Henry Cabot Lodge—R

Year	Presidential candidates	Party	Electoral vote	Popular vote	Vice-presidential candidates and party
1964	Lyndon B. Johnson	Democratic	486	43,129,484	Hubert H. Humphrey—D
	Barry M. Goldwater	Republican	52	27,178,188	William E. Miller—R
1968	Richard M. Nixon	Republican	301	31,785,480	Spiro T. Agnew—R
	Hubert H. Humphrey	Democratic	191	31,275,166	Edmund S. Muskie—D
	George C. Wallace	American Independent	46	9,906,473	Curtis F. LeMay—AI
1972	Richard M. Nixon[23]	Republican	520[24]	47,169,911	Spiro T. Agnew—R
	George McGovern	Democratic	17	29,170,383	Sargent Shriver—D
	John G. Schmitz	American	0	1,099,482	Thomas J. Anderson—A
1976	Jimmy Carter	Democratic	297	40,830,763	Walter F. Mondale—D
	Gerald R. Ford	Republican	240[25]	39,147,973	Robert J. Dole—R
	Eugene J. McCarthy	Independent	0	756,631	None
1980	Ronald Reagan	Republican	489	43,899,248	George Bush—R
	Jimmy Carter	Democratic	49	36,481,435	Walter F. Mondale—D
	John B. Anderson	Independent	0	5,719,437	Patrick J. Lucey—I
1984	Ronald Reagan	Republican	525	54,455,075	George Bush—R
	Walter F. Mondale	Democratic	13	37,577,185	Geraldine A. Ferraro—D

1. Only 10 states participated in the election. The New York legislature chose no electors, and North Carolina and Rhode Island had not yet ratified the Constitution. 2. As Jefferson and Burr were tied, the House of Representatives chose the President. In a vote by states, 10 votes were cast for Jefferson, 4 for Burr; 2 votes were not cast. 3. As no candidate had an electoral-vote majority, the House of Representatives chose the President from the first three. In a vote by states, 13 votes were cast for Adams, 7 for Jackson, and 4 for Crawford. 4. The Antimasonic Party on Sept. 26, 1831, was the first party to hold a nominating convention to choose candidates for President and Vice-President. 5. As Johnson did not have an electoral-vote majority, the Senate chose him 33–14 over Granger, the others being legally out of the race. 6. Harrison died April 4, 1841, and Tyler succeeded him April 6. 7. Taylor died July 9, 1850, and Fillmore succeeded him July 10. 8. Also known as the Know-Nothing Party. 9. Lincoln died April 15, 1865, and Johnson succeeded him the same day. 10. Name adopted by the Republican National Convention of 1864. Johnson was a War Democrat. 11. 23 Southern electoral votes were excluded. 12. See Election of 1872 in *Unusual Voting Results* under Elections, Presidential, in Index. 13. See Election of 1876 in *Unusual Voting Results* under Elections, Presidential, in Index. 14. Garfield died Sept. 19, 1881, and Arthur succeeded him Sept. 20. 15. Members of People's Party were called Populists. 16. McKinley died Sept. 14, 1901, and Roosevelt succeeded him the same day. 17. James S. Sherman, Republican candidate for Vice President, died Oct. 30, 1912, and the Republican electoral votes were cast for Butler. 18. Harding died Aug. 2, 1923, and Coolidge succeeded him Aug. 3. 19. Roosevelt died April 12, 1945, and Truman succeeded him the same day. 20. One electoral vote from Alabama was cast for Walter B. Jones. 21. Sen. Harry F. Byrd received 15 electoral votes. 22. Kennedy died Nov. 22, 1963, and Johnson succeeded him the same day. 23. Nixon resigned Aug. 9, 1974, and Gerald R. Ford succeeded him the same day. 24. One electoral vote from Virginia was cast for John Hospers, Libertarian Party. 25. One electoral vote from Washington was cast for Ronald Reagan.

Characteristics of Voters in 1984 Presidential Election

(in thousands)

Characteristic	Persons of voting age	Persons reporting they voted		Persons reporting they did not vote
		Total	Percent	
Male	80,327	47,354	59.0	32,973
Female	89,636	54,524	60.8	35,112
White	146,761	90,152	61.4	56,610
Black	18,432	10,293	55.8	8,139
Spanish origin[1]	9,471	3,092	32.6	6,379
Age: 18-20	11,249	4,131	36.7	7,118
21-24	16,727	7,276	43.5	9,451
25-34	40,292	21,978	54.5	18,313
35-44	30,731	19,514	63.5	11,217
45-54	22,257	15,035	67.5	7,222
55-64	22,050	15,889	72.1	6,160
65-74	16,382	11,761	71.8	4,621
75 and over	10,276	6,294	61.2	3,982
North and West	112,376	69,223	61.6	43,153
South	57,587	32,709	56.8	24,878
Education				
8 years or less	20,580	8,828	42.9	11,752
9-11 years	22,068	9,798	44.4	12,270
12 years	67,807	39,802	58.7	28,005
13-15 years	30,915	20,867	67.5	10,048
16 or more	28,593	22,617	79.1	5,976
Employed	104,173	64,170	61.6	40,003
Unemployed	7,389	3,251	44.0	4,138
Not in labor force	58,401	34,398	58.9	24,003
Total	**169,963**	**101,878**	**59.9**	**68,085**

NOTE: Persons of Spanish origin may be of any race. *Source:* Department of Commerce, Bureau of the Census.

Qualifications for Voting

The Supreme Court decision of March 21, 1972, declared lengthy requirements for voting in state and local elections unconstitutional and suggested that 30 days was an ample period. Most of the states have changed or eliminated their durational residency requirements to comply with the ruling, as shown.

NO DURATIONAL RESIDENCY REQUIREMENT

Alabama,[6] Arkansas, Connecticut,[13] Delaware,[12] District of Columbia,[16] Florida,[5] Georgia,[2] Hawaii,[2] Iowa,[6] Maine, Maryland, Massachusetts,[3] Missouri,[4] Nebraska,[9] New Hampshire,[17] New Mexico,[7] North Carolina, Oklahoma, South Carolina,[2] South Dakota,[10] Tennessee, Texas, Virginia, West Virginia,[2] Wyoming[2]

30-DAY RESIDENCY REQUIREMENT

Alaska,[18] Arizona,[11] Idaho, Illinois, Indiana, Kentucky,[2] Louisiana,[8] Michigan, Mississippi,[2] Montana, Nevada, New Jersey, New York, North Dakota,[3] Ohio, Pennsylvania, Rhode Island, Utah, Washington

OTHER

California,[19] Colorado,[1] Kansas, Minnesota[15] and Oregon, 20 days; Vermont, 17 days;[14] Wisconsin, 10 days

1. 29 days for voters residing overseas, 32 days for all other voters. 2. 30-day registration requirement. 3. No residency required to register to vote. Persons who miss the closing date for registration are ineligible to vote and must wait for the next registration period. 4. Must be registered 28 days prior to vote. 5. 30-day registration requirement for national elections; 30-day for state elections. 6. 10-day registration requirement. 7. Must register 28 days before election. 8. 30 days prior to any primary election. 24 days prior to any general election. 9. Registration requirement, 2nd Friday prior to elections. 10. 15-day registration requirement. 11. Residency in the state 50 days next preceding the election except 30 days for presidential election. 12. Must reside in Delaware and register by the last day that the books are open for registration. 13. Registration deadline 21st day before election; registration and party enrollment deadline the day before primary. 14. Administrative cut-off date for processing applications. 15. Permits registration and voting on election day with approved ID. 16. D.C. must process within 18 days. Registration stops 30 days before any election and until 15 days after. Voters must inform Board of Elections of change of address within 30 days of moving. 17. Registration requirement, 10 days prior to elections. 18. If otherwise qualified but has not been a resident of the election district for at least 30 days preceding the date of a presidential election, is entitled to register and vote for presidential and vice-presidential candidates. 19. 29 days before an election. *Source: Information Please* questionnaires to the states.

Unusual Voting Results

Election of 1872

The presidential and vice-presidential candidates of the Liberal Republicans and the northern Democrats in 1872 were Horace Greeley and B. Gratz Brown. Greeley died Nov. 29, 1872, before his 66 electors voted. In the electoral balloting for President, 63 of Greeley's votes were scattered among four other men, including Brown.

Election of 1876

In the election of 1876 Samuel J. Tilden, the Democratic candidate, received a popular majority but lacked one undisputed electoral vote to carry a clear majority of the electoral college. The crux of the problem was in the 22 electoral votes which were in dispute because Florida, Louisiana, South Carolina, and Oregon each sent in two sets of election returns. In the three southern states, Republican election boards threw out enough Democratic votes to certify the Republican candidate, Hayes. In Oregon, the Democratic governor disqualified a Republican elector, replacing him with a Democrat. Since the Senate was Republican and the House of Representatives Democratic, it seemed useless to refer the disputed returns to the two houses for solution. Instead Congress appointed an Electoral Commission with five representatives each from the Senate, the House, and the Supreme Court. All but one Justice was named, giving the Commission seven Republican and seven Democratic members. The naming of the fifth Justice was left to the other four. He was a Republican who first favored Tilden but, under pressure from his party, switched to Hayes, ensuring his election by the Commission voting 8 to 7 on party lines.

Minority Presidents

Fifteen candidates have become President of the United States with a popular vote less than 50% of the total cast. It should be noted, however, that in elections before 1872, presidential electors were not chosen by popular vote in all states. Adams' election in 1824 was by the House of Representatives, which chose him over Jackson, who had a plurality of both electoral and popular votes, but not a majority in the electoral college.

Besides Jackson in 1824, only two other candidates receiving the largest popular vote have failed to gain a majority in the electoral college—Samuel J. Tilden (D) in 1876 and Grover Cleveland (D) in 1888.

The "minority" Presidents follow:

Vote Received by Minority Presidents

Year	President	Electoral Percent	Popular vote Percent
1824	John Q. Adams	31.8	29.8
1844	James K. Polk (D)	61.8	49.3
1848	Zachary Taylor (W)	56.2	47.3
1856	James Buchanan (D)	58.7	45.3
1860	Abraham Lincoln (R)	59.4	39.9
1876	Rutherford B. Hayes (R)	50.1	47.9
1880	James A. Garfield (R)	57.9	48.3
1884	Grover Cleveland (D)	54.6	48.8
1888	Benjamin Harrison (R)	58.1	47.8
1892	Grover Cleveland (D)	62.4	46.0
1912	Woodrow Wilson (D)	81.9	41.8
1916	Woodrow Wilson (D)	52.1	49.3
1948	Harry S. Truman (D)	57.1	49.5
1960	John F. Kennedy (D)	56.4	49.7
1968	Richard M. Nixon (R)	56.1	43.4

Government Officials

Cabinet Members With Dates of Appointment

Although the Constitution made no provision for a President's advisory group, the heads of the three executive departments (State, Treasury, and War) and the Attorney General were organized by Washington into such a group; and by about 1793, the name "Cabinet" was applied to it. With the exception of the Attorney General up to 1870 and the Postmaster General from 1829 to 1872, Cabinet members have been heads of executive departments.

A Cabinet member is appointed by the President, subject to the confirmation of the Senate; and as his term is not fixed, he may be replaced at any time by the President. At a change in Administration, it is customary for him to tender his resignation, but he remains in office until a successor is appointed.

The table of Cabinet members lists only those members who actually served after being duly commissioned.

The dates shown are those of appointment. "Cont." indicates that the term continued from the previous Administration for a substantial amount of time.

With the creation of the Department of Transportation in 1966, the Cabinet consisted of 12 members. This figure was reduced to 11 when the Post Office Department became an independent agency in 1970 but, with the establishment in 1977 of a Department of Energy, became 12 again. Creation of the Department of Education in 1980 raised the number to 13.

WASHINGTON

Secretary of State	Thomas Jefferson 1789
	Edmund Randolph 1794
	Timothy Pickering 1795
Secretary of the Treasury	Alexander Hamilton 1789
	Oliver Wolcott, Jr. 1795
Secretary of War	Henry Knox 1789
	Timothy Pickering 1795
	James McHenry 1796
Attorney General	Edmund Randolph 1789
	William Bradford 1794
	Charles Lee 1795

J. ADAMS

Secretary of State	Timothy Pickering (Cont.)
	John Marshall 1800
Secretary of the Treasury	Oliver Wolcott, Jr. (Cont.)
	Samuel Dexter 1801
Secretary of War	James McHenry (Cont.)
	Samuel Dexter 1800
Attorney General	Charles Lee (Cont.)
Secretary of the Navy	Benjamin Stoddert 1798

JEFFERSON

Secretary of State	James Madison 1801
Secretary of the Treasury	Samuel Dexter (Cont.)
	Albert Gallatin 1801
Secretary of War	Henry Dearborn 1801
Attorney General	Levi Lincoln 1801
	Robert Smith 1805
	John Breckinridge 1805
	Caesar A. Rodney 1807
Secretary of the Navy	Benjamin Stoddert (Cont.)
	Robert Smith 1801

MADISON

Secretary of State	Robert Smith 1809
	James Monroe 1811
Secretary of the Treasury	Albert Gallatin (Cont.)
	George W. Campbell 1814
	Alexander J. Dallas 1814
	William H. Crawford 1816
Secretary of War	William Eustis 1809
	John Armstrong 1813
	James Monroe 1814
	William H. Crawford 1815
Attorney General	Caesar A. Rodney (Cont.)
	William Pinckney 1811
	Richard Rush 1814
Secretary of the Navy	Paul Hamilton 1809
	William Jones 1813
	B. W. Crowninshield 1814

MONROE

Secretary of State	John Quincy Adams 1817
Secretary of the Treasury	William H. Crawford (Cont.)
Secretary of War	John C. Calhoun 1817
Attorney General	Richard Rush (Cont.)
	William Wirt 1817
Secretary of the Navy	B. W. Crowninshield (Cont.)
	Smith Thompson 1818
	Samuel L. Southard 1823

J. Q. ADAMS

Secretary of State	Henry Clay 1825
Secretary of the Treasury	Richard Rush 1825
Secretary of War	James Barbour 1825
	Peter B. Porter 1828
Attorney General	William Wirt (Cont.)
Secretary of the Navy	Samuel L. Southard (Cont.)

JACKSON

Secretary of State	Martin Van Buren 1829
	Edward Livingston 1831
	Louis McLane 1833
	John Forsyth 1834
Secretary of the Treasury	Samuel D. Ingham 1829
	Louis McLane 1831
	William J. Duane 1833
	Roger B. Taney[3] 1833
	Levi Woodbury 1834
Secretary of War	John H. Eaton 1829
	Lewis Cass 1831
Attorney General	John M. Berrien 1829
	Roger B. Taney 1831
	Benjamin F. Butler 1833
Postmaster General[4]	William T. Barry 1829
	Amos Kendall 1835
Secretary of the Navy	John Branch 1829
	Levi Woodbury 1831
	Mahlon Dickerson 1834

VAN BUREN

Secretary of State	John Forsyth (Cont.)
Secretary of the Treasury	Levi Woodbury (Cont.)
Secretary of War	Joel R. Poinsett 1837
Attorney General	Benjamin F. Butler (Cont.)
	Felix Grundy 1838
	Henry D. Gilpin 1840
Postmaster General	Amos Kendall (Cont.)
	John M. Niles 1840
Secretary of the Navy	Mahlon Dickerson (Cont.)
	James K. Paulding 1838

W. H. HARRISON

Secretary of State	Daniel Webster 1841
Secretary of the Treasury	Thomas Ewing 1841
Secretary of War	John Bell 1841
Attorney General	John J. Crittenden 1841
Postmaster General	Francis Granger 1841
Secretary of the Navy	George E. Badger 1841

TYLER

Secretary of State	Daniel Webster (Cont.)
	Abel P. Upshur 1843
	John C. Calhoun 1844
Secretary of the Treasury	Thomas Ewing (Cont.)

	Walter Forward 1841
	John C. Spencer[3] 1843
	George M. Bibb 1844
Secretary of War	John Bell (Cont.)
	John C. Spencer 1841
	James M. Porter[3] 1843
	William Wilkins 1844
Attorney General	John J. Crittenden (Cont.)
	Hugh S. Legaré 1841
	John Nelson 1843
Postmaster General	Francis Granger (Cont.)
	Charles A. Wickliffe 1841
Secretary of the Navy	George E. Badger (Cont.)
	Abel P. Upshur 1841
	David Henshaw[3] 1843
	Thomas W. Gilmer 1844
	John Y. Mason 1844

POLK

Secretary of State	James Buchanan 1845
Secretary of the Treasury	Robert J. Walker 1845
Secretary of War	William L. Marcy 1845
Attorney General	John Y. Mason 1845
	Nathan Clifford 1846
	Isaac Toucey 1848
Postmaster General	Cave Johnson 1845
Secretary of the Navy	George Bancroft 1845
	John Y. Mason 1846

TAYLOR

Secretary of State	John M. Clayton 1849
Secretary of the Treasury	William M. Meredith 1849
Secretary of War	George W. Crawford 1849
Attorney General	Reverdy Johnson 1849
Postmaster General	Jacob Collamer 1849
Secretary of the Navy	William B. Preston 1849
Secretary of the Interior	Thomas Ewing 1849

FILLMORE

Secretary of State	Daniel Webster 1850
	Edward Everett 1852
Secretary of the Treasury	Thomas Corwin 1850
Secretary of War	Charles M. Conrad 1850
Attorney General	John J. Crittenden 1850
Postmaster General	Nathan K. Hall 1850
	Samuel D. Hubbard 1852
Secretary of the Navy	William A. Graham 1850
	John P. Kennedy 1852
Secretary of the Interior	Thos. M. T. McKennan 1850
	Alex. H. H. Stuart 1850

PIERCE

Secretary of State	William L. Marcy 1853
Secretary of the Treasury	James Guthrie 1853
Secretary of War	Jefferson Davis 1853
Attorney General	Caleb Cushing 1853
Postmaster General	James Campbell 1853
Secretary of the Navy	James C. Dobbin 1853
Secretary of the Interior	Robert McClelland 1853

BUCHANAN

Secretary of State	Lewis Cass 1857
	Jeremiah S. Black 1860
Secretary of the Treasury	Howell Cobb 1857
	Philip F. Thomas 1860
	John A. Dix 1861
Secretary of War	John B. Floyd 1857
	Joseph Holt 1861
Attorney General	Jeremiah S. Black 1857
	Edwin M. Stanton 1860
Postmaster General	Aaron V. Brown 1857
	Joseph Holt 1859
	Horatio King 1861
Secretary of the Navy	Isaac Toucey 1857
Secretary of the Interior	Jacob Thompson 1857

LINCOLN

Secretary of State	William H. Seward 1861
Secretary of the Treasury	Salmon P. Chase 1861
	William P. Fessenden 1864
	Hugh McCulloch 1865
Secretary of War	Simon Cameron 1861
	Edwin M. Stanton 1862
Attorney General	Edward Bates 1861
	James Speed 1864
Postmaster General	Montgomery Blair 1861
	William Dennison 1864
Secretary of the Navy	Gideon Welles 1861
Secretary of the Interior	Caleb B. Smith 1861
	John P. Usher 1863

A. JOHNSON

Secretary of State	William H. Seward (Cont.)
Secretary of the Treasury	Hugh McCulloch (Cont.)
Secretary of War	Edwin M. Stanton (Cont.)
	John M. Schofield 1868
Attorney General	James Speed (Cont.)
	Henry Stanbery 1866
	William M. Evarts 1868
Postmaster General	William Dennison (Cont.)
	Alexander W. Randall 1866
Secretary of the Navy	Gideon Welles (Cont.)
Secretary of the Interior	John P. Usher (Cont.)
	James Harlan 1865
	Orville H. Browning 1866

GRANT

Secretary of State	Elihu B. Washburne 1869
	Hamilton Fish 1869
Secretary of the Treasury	George S. Boutwell 1869
	William A. Richardson 1873
	Benjamin H. Bristow 1874
	Lot M. Morrill 1876
Secretary of War	John A. Rawlins 1869
	William W. Belknap 1869
	Alphonso Taft 1876
	James D. Cameron 1876
Attorney General	Ebenezer R. Hoar 1869
	Amos T. Akerman 1870
	George H. Williams 1871
	Edwards Pierrepont 1875
	Alphonso Taft 1876
Postmaster General	John A. J. Creswell 1869
	Marshall Jewell 1874
	James N. Tyner 1876
Secretary of the Navy	Adolph E. Borie 1869
	George M. Robeson 1869
Secretary of the Interior	Jacob D. Cox 1869
	Columbus Delano 1870
	Zachariah Chandler 1875

HAYES

Secretary of State	William M. Evarts 1877
Secretary of the Treasury	John Sherman 1877
Secretary of War	George W. McCrary 1877
	Alexander Ramsey 1879
Attorney General	Charles Devens 1877
Postmaster General	David M. Key 1877
	Horace Maynard 1880
Secretary of the Navy	Richard W. Thompson 1877
	Nathan Goff, Jr. 1881
Secretary of the Interior	Carl Schurz 1877

GARFIELD

Secretary of State	James G. Blaine 1881
Secretary of the Treasury	William Windom 1881
Secretary of War	Robert T. Lincoln 1881
Attorney General	Wayne MacVeagh 1881
Postmaster General	Thomas L. James 1881
Secretary of the Navy	William H. Hunt 1881
Secretary of the Interior	Samuel J. Kirkwood 1881

ARTHUR

Secretary of State	James G. Blaine (Cont.)
	F. T. Frelinghuysen 1881
Secretary of the Treasury	William Windom (Cont.)
	Charles J. Folger 1881
	Walter Q. Gresham 1884
	Hugh McCulloch 1884
Secretary of War	Robert T. Lincoln (Cont.)
Attorney General	Wayne MacVeagh (Cont.)
	Benjamin H. Brewster 1881
Postmaster General	Thomas L. James (Cont.)
	Timothy O. Howe 1881
	Walter Q. Gresham 1883
	Frank Hatton 1884
Secretary of the Navy	William H. Hunt (Cont.)

	William E. Chandler 1882
Secretary of the Interior	Samuel J. Kirkwood (Cont.)
	Henry M. Teller 1882

CLEVELAND

Secretary of State	Thomas F. Bayard 1885
Secretary of the Treasury	Daniel Manning 1885
	Charles S. Fairchild 1887
Secretary of War	William C. Endicott 1885
Attorney General	Augustus H. Garland 1885
Postmaster General	William F. Vilas 1885
	Don M. Dickinson 1888
Secretary of the Navy	William C. Whitney 1885
Secretary of the Interior	Lucius Q. C. Lamar 1885
	William F. Vilas 1888
Secretary of Agriculture	Norman J. Colman 1889

B. HARRISON

Secretary of State	James G. Blaine 1889
	John W. Foster 1892
Secretary of the Treasury	William Windom 1889
	Charles Foster 1891
Secretary of War	Redfield Proctor 1889
	Stephen B. Elkins 1891
Attorney General	William H. H. Miller 1889
Postmaster General	John Wanamaker 1889
Secretary of the Navy	Benjamin F. Tracy 1889
Secretary of the Interior	John W. Noble 1889
Secretary of Agriculture	Jeremiah M. Rusk 1889

CLEVELAND

Secretary of State	Walter Q. Gresham 1893
	Richard Olney 1895
Secretary of the Treasury	John G. Carlisle 1893
Secretary of War	Daniel S. Lamont 1893
Attorney General	Richard Olney 1893
	Judson Harmon 1895
Postmaster General	Wilson S. Bissell 1893
	William L. Wilson 1895
Secretary of the Navy	Hilary A. Herbert 1893
Secretary of the Interior	Hoke Smith 1893
	David R. Francis 1896
Secretary of Agriculture	Julius Sterling Morton 1893

McKINLEY

Secretary of State	John Sherman 1897
	William R. Day 1898
	John Hay 1898
Secretary of the Treasury	Lyman J. Gage 1897
Secretary of War	Russell A. Alger 1897
	Elihu Root 1899
Attorney General	Joseph McKenna 1897
	John W. Griggs 1898
	Philander C. Knox 1901
Postmaster General	James A. Gary 1897
	Charles E. Smith 1898
Secretary of the Navy	John D. Long 1897
Secretary of the Interior	Cornelius N. Bliss 1897
	Ethan A. Hitchcock 1898
Secretary of Agriculture	James Wilson 1897

T. ROOSEVELT

Secretary of State	John Hay (Cont.)
	Elihu Root 1905
	Robert Bacon 1909
Secretary of the Treasury	Lyman J. Gage (Cont.)
	Leslie M. Shaw 1902
	George B. Cortelyou 1907
Secretary of War	Elihu Root (Cont.)
	William H. Taft 1904
	Luke E. Wright 1908
Attorney General	Philander C. Knox (Cont.)
	William H. Moody 1904
	Charles J. Bonaparte 1906
Postmaster General	Charles E. Smith (Cont.)
	Henry C. Payne 1902
	Robert J. Wynne 1904
	George B. Cortelyou 1905
	George von L. Meyer 1907
Secretary of the Navy	John D. Long (Cont.)
	William H. Moody 1902
	Paul Morton 1904
	Charles J. Bonaparte 1905
	Victor H. Metcalf 1906
	Truman H. Newberry 1908
Secretary of the Interior	Ethan A. Hitchcock (Cont.)
	James R. Garfield 1907
Secretary of Agriculture	James Wilson (Cont.)
Secretary of Commerce and Labor	George B. Cortelyou 1903
	Victor H. Metcalf 1904
	Oscar S. Straus 1906

TAFT

Secretary of State	Philander C. Knox 1909
Secretary of the Treasury	Franklin MacVeagh 1909
Secretary of War	Jacob M. Dickinson 1909
	Henry L. Stimson 1911
Attorney General	George W. Wickersham 1909
Postmaster General	Frank H. Hitchcock 1909
Secretary of the Navy	George von L. Meyer 1909
Secretary of the Interior	Richard A. Ballinger 1909
	Walter L. Fisher 1911
Secretary of Agriculture	James Wilson (Cont.)
Secretary of Commerce and Labor	Charles Nagel 1909

WILSON

Secretary of State	William J. Bryan 1913
	Robert Lansing 1915
	Bainbridge Colby 1920
Secretary of the Treasury	William G. McAdoo 1913
	Carter Glass 1918
	David F. Houston 1920
Secretary of War	Lindley M. Garrison 1913
	Newton D. Baker 1916
Attorney General	James C. McReynolds 1913
	Thomas W. Gregory 1914
	A. Mitchell Palmer 1919
Postmaster General	Albert S. Burleson 1913
Secretary of the Navy	Josephus Daniels 1913
Secretary of the Interior	Franklin K. Lane 1913
	John B. Payne 1920
Secretary of Agriculture	David F. Houston 1913
	Edwin T. Meredith 1920
Secretary of Commerce	William C. Redfield 1913
	Joshua W. Alexander 1919
Secretary of Labor	William B. Wilson 1913

HARDING

Secretary of State	Charles E. Hughes 1921
Secretary of the Treasury	Andrew W. Mellon 1921
Secretary of War	John W. Weeks 1921
Attorney General	Harry M. Daugherty 1921
Postmaster General	Will H. Hays 1921
	Hubert Work 1922
	Harry S. New 1923
Secretary of the Navy	Edwin Denby 1921
Secretary of the Interior	Albert B. Fall 1921
	Hubert Work 1923
Secretary of Agriculture	Henry C. Wallace 1921
Secretary of Commerce	Herbert Hoover 1921
Secretary of Labor	James J. Davis 1921

COOLIDGE

Secretary of State	Charles E. Hughes (Cont.)
	Frank B. Kellogg 1925
Secretary of the Treasury	Andrew W. Mellon (Cont.)
Secretary of War	John W. Weeks (Cont.)
	Dwight F. Davis 1925
Attorney General	Harry M. Daughtery (Cont.)
	Harlan F. Stone 1924
	John G. Sargent 1925
Postmaster General	Harry S. New (Cont.)
Secretary of the Navy	Edwin Denby (Cont.)
	Curtis D. Wilbur 1924
Secretary of the Interior	Hubert Work (Cont.)
	Roy O. West 1928
Secretary of Agriculture	Henry C. Wallace (Cont.)
	Howard M. Gore 1924
	William M. Jardine 1925
Secretary of Commerce	Herbert Hoover (Cont.)
	William F. Whiting 1928
Secretary of Labor	James J. Davis (Cont.)

HOOVER

Secretary of State	Frank B. Kellogg (Cont.)

	Henry L. Stimson 1929
Secretary of the Treasury	Andrew W. Mellon (Cont.)
	Ogden L. Mills 1932
Secretary of War	James W. Good 1929
	Patrick J. Hurley 1929
Attorney General	William D. Mitchell 1929
Postmaster General	Walter F. Brown 1929
Secretary of the Navy	Charles F. Adams 1929
Secretary of the Interior	Ray Lyman Wilbur 1929
Secretary of Agriculture	Arthur M. Hyde 1929
Secretary of Commerce	Robert P. Lamont 1929
	Roy D. Chapin 1932
Secretary of Labor	James J. Davis (Cont.)
	William N. Doak 1930

F. D. ROOSEVELT

Secretary of State	Cordell Hull 1933
	E. R. Stettinius, Jr. 1944
Secretary of the Treasury	William H. Woodin 1933
	Henry Morgenthau, Jr. 1934
Secretary of War	George H. Dern 1933
	Harry H. Woodring 1936
	Henry L. Stimson 1940
Attorney General	Homer S. Cummings 1933
	Frank Murphy 1939
	Robert H. Jackson 1940
	Francis Biddle 1941
Postmaster General	James A. Farley 1933
	Frank C. Walker 1940
Secretary of the Navy	Claude A. Swanson 1933
	Charles Edison 1940
	Frank Knox 1940
	James Forrestal 1944
Secretary of the Interior	Harold L. Ickes 1933
Secretary of Agriculture	Henry A. Wallace 1933
	Claude R. Wickard 1940
Secretary of Commerce	Daniel C. Roper 1933
	Harry L. Hopkins 1938
	Jesse H. Jones 1940
	Henry A. Wallace 1945
Secretary of Labor	Frances Perkins 1933

TRUMAN

Secretary of State	E. R. Stettinius, Jr. (Cont.)
	James F. Byrnes 1945
	George C. Marshall 1947
	Dean Acheson 1949
Secretary of the Treasury	Henry Morgenthau, Jr. (Cont.)
	Frederick M. Vinson 1945
	John W. Snyder 1946
Secretary of Defense	James Forrestal 1947
	Louis A. Johnson 1949
	George C. Marshall 1950
	Robert A. Lovett 1951
Attorney General	Francis Biddle (Cont.)
	Tom C. Clark 1945
	J. Howard McGrath 1949
	James P. McGranery 1952
Postmaster General	Frank C. Walker (Cont.)
	Robert E. Hannegan 1945
	Jesse M. Donaldson 1947
Secretary of the Interior	Harold L. Ickes (Cont.)
	Julius A. Krug 1946
	Oscar L. Chapman 1949
Secretary of Agriculture	Claude R. Wickard (Cont.)
	Clinton P. Anderson 1945
	Charles F. Brannan 1948
Secretary of Commerce	Henry A. Wallace (Cont.)
	W. Averell Harriman 1946
	Charles Sawyer 1948
Secretary of Labor	Frances Perkins (Cont.)
	Lewis B. Schwellenbach 1945
	Maurice J. Tobin 1948
Secretary of War[2]	Henry L. Stimson (Cont.)
	Robert P. Patterson 1945
	Kenneth C. Royall 1947
Secretary of the Navy[2]	James Forrestal (Cont.)

EISENHOWER

Secretary of State	John Foster Dulles 1953
	Christian A. Herter 1959
Secretary of the Treasury	George M. Humphrey 1953
	Robert B. Anderson 1957
Secretary of Defense	Charles E. Wilson 1953
	Neil H. McElroy 1957
	Thomas S. Gates, Jr. 1959
Attorney General	Herbert Brownell, Jr. 1953
	William P. Rogers 1958
Postmaster General	Arthur E. Summerfield 1953
Secretary of the Interior	Douglas McKay 1953
	Frederick A. Seaton 1956
Secretary of Agriculture	Ezra Taft Benson 1953
Secretary of Commerce	Sinclair Weeks 1953
	Lewis L. Strauss[3] 1958
	Frederick H. Mueller 1959
Secretary of Labor	Martin P. Durkin 1953
	James P. Mitchell 1953
Secretary of Health, Education, and Welfare	Oveta Culp Hobby 1953
	Marion B. Folsom 1955
	Arthur S. Flemming 1958

KENNEDY

Secretary of State	Dean Rusk 1961
Secretary of the Treasury	C. Douglas Dillon 1961
Secretary of Defense	Robert S. McNamara 1961
Attorney General	Robert F. Kennedy 1961
Postmaster General	J. Edward Day 1961
	John A. Gronouski 1963
Secretary of the Interior	Stewart L. Udall 1961
Secretary of Agriculture	Orville L. Freeman 1961
Secretary of Commerce	Luther H. Hodges 1961
Secretary of Labor	Arthur J. Goldberg 1961
	W. Willard Wirtz 1962
Secretary of Health, Education, and Welfare	Abraham A. Ribicoff 1961
	Anthony J. Celebrezze 1962

L. B. JOHNSON

Secretary of State	Dean Rusk (Cont.)
Secretary of the Treasury	C. Douglas Dillon (Cont.)
	Henry H. Fowler 1965
	Joseph W. Barr[4] 1968
Secretary of Defense	Robert S. McNamara (Cont.)
	Clark M. Clifford 1968
Attorney General	Robert F. Kennedy (Cont.)
	N. de B. Katzenbach 1965
	Ramsey Clark 1967
Postmaster General	John A. Gronouski (Cont.)
	Lawrence F. O'Brien 1965
	W. Marvin Watson 1968
Secretary of the Interior	Stewart L. Udall (Cont.)
Secretary of Agriculture	Orville L. Freeman (Cont.)
Secretary of Commerce	Luther H. Hodges (Cont.)
	John T. Connor 1964
	A. B. Trowbridge 1967
	C. R. Smith 1968
Secretary of Labor	W. Willard Wirtz (Cont.)
Secretary of Health, Education, and Welfare	Anthony J. Celebrezze (Cont.)
	John W. Gardner 1965
	Wilbur J. Cohen 1968
Secretary of Housing and Urban Development	Robert C. Weaver 1966
	Robert C. Wood[4] 1969
Secretary of Transportation	Alan S. Boyd 1966

NIXON

Secretary of State	William P. Rogers 1969
	Henry A. Kissinger 1973
Secretary of the Treasury	David M. Kennedy 1969
	John B. Connally 1971
	George P. Shultz 1972
	William E. Simon 1974
Secretary of Defense	Melvin R. Laird 1969
	Elliot L. Richardson 1973
	James R. Schlesinger 1973
Attorney General	John N. Mitchell 1969
	Richard G. Kleindienst 1972
	Elliot L. Richardson 1973
	William B. Saxbe 1974
Postmaster General[5]	William M. Blount 1969
Secretary of the Interior	Walter J. Hickel 1969
	Rogers C. B. Morton 1971
Secretary of Agriculture	Clifford M. Hardin 1969
	Earl L. Butz 1971
Secretary of Commerce	Maurice H. Stans 1969
	Peter G. Peterson 1972

	Frederick B. Dent 1973
Secretary of Labor	George P. Shultz 1969
	James D. Hodgson 1970
	Peter J. Brennan 1973
Secretary of Health, Education, and Welfare	Robert H. Finch 1969
	Elliot L. Richardson 1970
	Caspar W. Weinberger 1973
Secretary of Housing and Urban Development	George Romney 1969
	James T. Lynn 1973
Secretary of Transportation	John A. Volpe 1969
	Claude S. Brinegar 1973

FORD

Secretary of State	Henry A. Kissinger (Cont.)
Secretary of the Treasury	William E. Simon (Cont.)
Secretary of Defense	James R. Schlesinger (Cont.)
	Donald H. Rumsfeld 1975
Attorney General	William B. Saxbe (Cont.)
	Edward H. Levi 1975
Secretary of the Interior	Rogers C. B. Morton (Cont.)
	Stanley K. Hathaway 1975
	Thomas S. Kleppe 1975
Secretary of Agriculture	Earl L. Butz (Cont.)
	John Knebel 1976
Secretary of Commerce	Frederick B. Dent (Cont.)
	Rogers C. B. Morton 1975
	Elliot L. Richardson 1976
Secretary of Labor	Peter J. Brennan (Cont.)
	John T. Dunlop 1975
	William J. Usery, Jr. 1976
Secretary of Health, Education, and Welfare	Caspar W. Weinberger (Cont.)
	F. David Mathews 1975
Secretary of Housing and Urban Development	James T. Lynn (Cont.)
	Carla A. Hills 1975
Secretary of Transportation	Claude S. Brinegar (Cont.)
	William T. Coleman, Jr. 1975

CARTER

Secretary of State	Cyrus R. Vance 1977
	Edmund S. Muskie 1980
Secretary of the Treasury	W. Michael Blumenthal 1977
	G. William Miller 1979
Secretary of Defense	Harold Brown 1977
Attorney General	Griffin B. Bell 1977
	Benjamin R. Civiletti 1979
Secretary of the Interior	Cecil D. Andrus 1977
Secretary of Agriculture	Bob S. Bergland 1977
Secretary of Commerce	Juanita M. Kreps 1977
	Philip M. Klutznick 1979
Secretary of Labor	F. Ray Marshall 1977
Secretary of Health and Human Services[6]	Joseph A. Califano, Jr. 1977
	Patricia Roberts Harris 1979
Secretary of Housing and Urban Development	Patricia Roberts Harris 1977
	Moon Landrieu 1979
Secretary of Transportation	Brock Adams 1977
	Neil E. Goldschmidt 1979
Secretary of Energy	James R. Schlesinger 1977
	Charles W. Duncan, Jr. 1979
Secretary of Education	Shirley Mount Hufstedler 1979

REAGAN

Secretary of State	Alexander M. Haig, Jr. 1981
	George P. Shultz 1982
Secretary of the Treasury	Donald T. Regan 1981
	James A. Baker 3rd 1985
Secretary of Defense	Caspar W. Weinberger 1981
Attorney General	William French Smith 1981
	Edwin Meese 3rd 1985
Secretary of the Interior	James G. Watt 1981
	William P. Clark 1983
	Donald P. Hodel 1985
Secretary of Agriculture	John R. Block 1981
Secretary of Commerce	C. William Verity, Jr. 1987[7]
Secretary of Labor	Raymond J. Donovan 1981
	William E. Brock 1985
Secretary of Health and Human Services	Richard S. Schweiker 1981
	Margaret M. Heckler 1983
	Otis R. Bowen 1985
Secretary of Housing and Urban Development	Samuel R. Pierce, Jr. 1981
Secretary of Transportation	Andrew L. Lewis, Jr. 1981
	Elizabeth H. Dole 1983
Secretary of Energy	James B. Edwards 1981
	Donald P. Hodel 1983
	John S. Herrington 1985
Secretary of Education	T. H. Bell 1981
	William J. Bennett 1985

1. The Postmaster General did not become a Cabinet member until 1829. Earlier Postmasters General were: Samuel Osgood (1789), Timothy Pickering (1791), Joseph Habersham (1795), Gideon Granger (1801), Return J. Meigs, Jr. (1814), and John McLean (1823). 2. On July 26, 1947, the Departments of War and of the Navy were incorporated into the Department of Defense. 3. Not confirmed by the Senate. 4. Recess appointment. 5. The Postmaster General is no longer a Cabinet member. 6. Known as Department of Health, Education, and Welfare until May 1980. 7. Subject to Senate confirmation.

How a Bill Becomes a Law

When a Senator or a Representative introduces a bill, he sends it to the clerk of his house, who gives it a number and title. This is the *first reading,* and the bill is referred to the proper committee.

The committee may decide the bill is unwise or unnecessary and *table* it, thus killing it at once. Or it may decide the bill is worthwhile and hold hearings to listen to facts and opinions presented by experts and other interested persons. After members of the committee have debated the bill and perhaps offered amendments, a vote is taken; and if the vote is favorable, the bill is sent back to the floor of the house.

The clerk reads the bill sentence by sentence to the house, and this is known as the *second reading.* Members may then debate the bill and offer amendments. In the House of Representatives, the time for debate is limited by a *cloture rule,* but there is no such restriction in the Senate for cloture, where 60 votes are required. This makes possible a *filibuster,* in which one or more opponents hold the floor to defeat the bill.

The *third reading* is by title only, and the bill is put to a vote, which may be by voice or roll call, depending on the circumstances and parliamentary rules. Members who must be absent at the time but who wish to record their vote may be paired if each negative vote has a balancing affirmative one.

The bill then goes to the other house of Congress, where it may be defeated, or passed with or without amendments. If the bill is defeated, it dies. If it is passed with amendments, a joint Congressional committee must be appointed by both houses to iron out the differences.

After its final passage by both houses, the bill is sent to the President. If he approves, he signs it, and the bill becomes a law. However, if he disapproves, he *vetoes* the bill by refusing to sign it and sending it back to the house of origin with his reasons for the veto. The objections are read and debated, and a roll-call vote is taken. If the bill receives less than a two-thirds vote, it is defeated and goes no farther. But if it receives a two-thirds vote or greater, it is sent to the other house for a vote.

If that house also passes it by a two-thirds vote, the President's veto is *overridden,* and the bill becomes a law.

Should the President desire neither to sign nor to veto the bill, he may retain it for ten days, Sundays excepted, after which time it automatically becomes a law without signature. However, if Congress has adjourned within those ten days, the bill is automatically killed, that process of indirect rejection being known as a *pocket veto.*

Figures and Legends in American Folklore

Appleseed, Johnny (John Chapman, 1774–1847): Massachusetts-born nurseryman; reputed to have spread seeds and seedlings from which rose orchards of the Midwest.

Billy the Kid (William H. Bonney, 1859–1881): New York-born desperado; killed his first man before he reached his teens; after short life of crime in Wild West, was gunned down by Sheriff Pat Garrett; symbol of lawless West.

Boone, Daniel (1734–1820): Frontiersman and Indian fighter, about whom legends of early America have been built; figured in Byron's *Don Juan.*

Brodie, Steve (1863–1901): Reputed to have dived off Brooklyn Bridge on July 23, 1886. (Whether he actually did so has never been proved.)

Buffalo Bill (William F. Cody, 1846–1917): Buffalo hunter and Indian scout; much of legend about him and Wild West stems from his own Wild West show, which he operated in late 19th century.

Bunyan, Paul: Mythical lumberjack; subject of tall tales throughout timber country (that he dug Grand Canyon, for example).

Crockett, David (1786–1836): Frontiersman and member of U.S. Congress, about whom legends have been built of heroic feats; died in defense of Alamo.

Fritchie (or Frietchie), Barbara: Symbol of patriotism; in ballad by John Greenleaf Whittier, 90-year-old Barbara Fritchie defiantly waves Stars and Stripes as "Stonewall" Jackson's Confederate troops march through Frederick, Md.

James, Jesse (1847–1882): Bank and train robber; folklore has given him quality of American Robin Hood.

Jones, Casey (John Luther Jones, 1863–1900): Example of heroic locomotive engineer given to feats of prowess; died in wreck with his hand on brake lever when his Illinois Central "Cannonball" express hit freight train at Vaughan, Miss.

Ross, Betsy (1752–1836): Member of Philadelphia flag-making family; reported to have designed and sewn first American flag. (Report is without confirmation.)

Uncle Sam: Personification of United States and its people; origin uncertain; may be based on inspector of government supplies in Revolutionary War and War of 1812.

Assassinations and Attempts in U. S. Since 1865

Cermak, Anton J. (Mayor of Chicago): Shot Feb. 15, 1933, in Miami by Giuseppe Zangara, who attempted to assassinate Franklin D. Roosevelt; Cermak died March 6.

Ford, Gerald R. (President of U.S.): Escaped assassination attempt Sept. 5, 1975, in Sacramento, Calif., by Lynette Alice (Squeaky) Fromm, who pointed but did not fire .45-caliber pistol. Escaped assassination attempt in San Francisco, Calif., Sept. 22, 1975, by Sara Jane Moore, who fired one shot from a .38-caliber pistol that was deflected.

Garfield, James A. (President of U.S.): Shot July 2, 1881, in Washington, D.C., by Charles J. Guiteau; died Sept. 19.

Jordan, Vernon E., Jr. (civil rights leader): Shot and critically wounded in assassination attempt May 29, 1980, in Fort Wayne, Ind.

Kennedy, John F. (President of U.S.): Shot Nov. 22, 1963, in Dallas, Tex., allegedly by Lee Harvey Oswald; died same day. Injured was Gov. John B. Connally of Texas. Oswald was shot and killed two days later by Jack Ruby.

Kennedy, Robert F. (U.S. Senator from New York): Shot June 5, 1968, in Los Angeles by Sirhan Bishara Sirhan; died June 6.

King, Martin Luther, Jr. (civil rights leader): Shot April 4, 1968, in Memphis by James Earl Ray; died same day.

Lincoln, Abraham (President of U.S.): Shot April 14, 1865, in Washington, D.C., by John Wilkes Booth; died April 15.

Long, Huey P. (U.S. Senator from Louisiana): Shot Sept. 8, 1935, in Baton Rouge by Dr. Carl A. Weiss; died Sept. 10.

McKinley, William (President of U.S.): Shot Sept. 6, 1901, in Buffalo by Leon Czolgosz; died Sept. 14.

Reagan, Ronald (President of U.S.): Shot in left lung in Washington by John W. Hinckley, Jr., on March 30, 1981; three others also wounded.

Roosevelt, Franklin D. (President-elect of U.S.): Escaped assassination unhurt Feb. 15, 1933, in Miami. *See* Cermak.

Roosevelt, Theodore (ex-President of U.S.): Escaped assassination (though shot) Oct. 14, 1912, in Milwaukee while campaigning for President.

Seward, William H. (Secretary of State): Escaped assassination (though injured) April 14, 1865, in Washington, D.C., by Lewis Powell (or Paine), accomplice of John Wilkes Booth.

Truman, Harry S. (President of U.S.): Escaped assassination unhurt Nov. 1, 1950, in Washington, D.C., as 2 Puerto Rican nationalists attempted to shoot their way into Blair House.

Wallace, George C. (Governor of Alabama): Shot and critically wounded in assassination attempt May 15, 1972, at Laurel, Md., by Arthur Herman Bremer. Wallace paralyzed from waist down.

Members of the Supreme Court of the United States

Name; apptd. from	Service Term	Service Yrs	Birth Place	Birth Date	Died	Religion
CHIEF JUSTICES						
John Jay, N.Y.	1789-1795	5	N.Y.	1745	1829	Episcopal
John Rutledge, S.C.	1795	0	S.C.	1739	1800	Church of England
Oliver Ellsworth, Conn.	1796-1800	4	Conn.	1745	1807	Congregational
John Marshall, Va.	1801-1835	34	Va.	1755	1835	Episcopal
Roger B. Taney, Md.	1836-1864	28	Md.	1777	1864	Roman Catholic
Salmon P. Chase, Ohio	1864-1873	8	N.H.	1808	1873	Episcopal
Morrison R. Waite, Ohio	1874-1888	14	Conn.	1816	1888	Episcopal
Melville W. Fuller, Ill.	1888-1910	21	Me.	1833	1910	Episcopal
Edward D. White, La.	1910-1921	10	La.	1845	1921	Roman Catholic
William H. Taft, Conn.	1921-1930	8	Ohio	1857	1930	Unitarian
Charles E. Hughes, N.Y.	1930-1941	11	N.Y.	1862	1948	Baptist
Harlan F. Stone, N.Y.	1941-1946	4	N.H.	1872	1946	Episcopal
Frederick M. Vinson, Ky.	1946-1953	7	Ky.	1890	1953	Methodist
Earl Warren, Calif.	1953-1969	15	Calif.	1891	1974	Protestant
Warren E. Burger, Va.	1969-1986	17	Minn.	1907	—	Presbyterian
William H. Rehnquist, Ariz.	1986-		Wis.	1924	—	Lutheran
ASSOCIATE JUSTICES						
James Wilson, Pa.	1789-1798	8	Scotland	1742	1798	Episcopal
John Rutledge, S.C.	1790-1791	1	S.C.	1739	1800	Church of England
William Cushing, Mass.	1790-1810	20	Mass.	1732	1810	Unitarian
John Blair, Va.	1790-1796	5	Va.	1732	1800	Presbyterian
James Iredell, N.C.	1790-1799	9	England	1751	1799	Episcopal
Thomas Johnson, Md.	1792-1793	0	Md.	1732	1819	Episcopal
William Paterson, N.J.	1793-1806	13	Ireland	1745	1806	Protestant
Samuel Chase, Md.	1796-1811	15	Md.	1741	1811	Episcopal
Bushrod Washington, Va.	1799-1829	30	Va.	1762	1829	Episcopal
Alfred Moore, N.C.	1800-1804	3	N.C.	1755	1810	Episcopal
William Johnson, S.C.	1804-1834	30	S.C.	1771	1834	Presbyterian
Brockholst Livingston, N.Y.	1807-1823	16	N.Y.	1757	1823	Presbyterian
Thomas Todd, Ky.	1807-1826	18	Va.	1765	1826	Presbyterian
Gabriel Duval, Md.	1811-1835	23	Md.	1752	1844	French Protestant
Joseph Story, Mass.	1812-1845	33	Mass.	1779	1845	Unitarian
Smith Thompson, N.Y.	1823-1843	20	N.Y.	1768	1843	Presbyterian
Robert Trimble, Ky.	1826-1828	2	Va.	1777	1828	Protestant
John McLean, Ohio	1830-1861	31	N.J.	1785	1861	Methodist-Epis.
Henry Baldwin, Pa.	1830-1844	14	Conn.	1780	1844	Trinity Church
James M. Wayne, Ga.	1835-1867	32	Ga.	1790	1867	Protestant
Philip P. Barbour, Va.	1836-1841	4	Va.	1783	1841	Episcopal
John Catron, Tenn.	1837-1865	28	Pa.	1786	1865	Presbyterian
John McKinley, Ala.	1837-1852	14	Va.	1780	1852	Protestant
Peter V. Daniel, Va.	1841-1860	18	Va.	1784	1860	Episcopal
Samuel Nelson, N.Y.	1845-1872	27	N.Y.	1792	1873	Protestant
Levi Woodbury, N.H.	1845-1851	5	N.H.	1789	1851	Protestant
Robert C. Grier, Pa.	1846-1870	23	Pa.	1794	1870	Presbyterian
Benjamin R. Curtis, Mass.	1851-1857	5	Mass.	1809	1874	([2])
John A. Campbell, Ala.	1853-1861	8	Ga.	1811	1889	Episcopal
Nathan Clifford, Maine	1858-1881	23	N.H.	1803	1881	([1])
Noah H. Swayne, Ohio	1862-1881	18	Va.	1804	1884	Quaker
Samuel F. Miller, Iowa	1862-1890	28	Ky.	1816	1890	Unitarian
David Davis, Ill.	1862-1877	14	Md.	1815	1886	([4])
Stephen J. Field, Calif.	1863-1897	34	Conn.	1816	1899	Episcopal
William Strong, Pa.	1870-1880	10	Conn.	1808	1895	Presbyterian
Joseph P. Bradley, N.J.	1870-1892	21	N.Y.	1813	1892	Presbyterian
Ward Hunt, N.Y.	1872-1882	9	N.Y.	1810	1886	Episcopal
John M. Harlan, Ky.	1877-1911	33	Ky.	1833	1911	Presbyterian
William B. Woods, Ga.	1880-1887	6	Ohio	1824	1887	Protestant
Stanley Matthews, Ohio	1881-1889	7	Ohio	1824	1889	Presbyterian
Horace Gray, Mass.	1882-1902	20	Mass.	1828	1902	([3])
Samuel Blatchford, N.Y.	1882-1893	11	N.Y.	1820	1893	Presbyterian
Lucius Q. C. Lamar, Miss.	1888-1893	5	Ga.	1825	1893	Methodist
David J. Brewer, Kan.	1889-1910	20	Asia Minor	1837	1910	Protestant
Henry B. Brown, Mich.	1890-1906	15	Mass.	1836	1913	Protestant
George Shiras, Jr., Pa.	1892-1903	10	Pa.	1832	1924	Presbyterian
Howell E. Jackson, Tenn.	1893-1895	2	Tenn.	1832	1895	Baptist
Edward D. White, La.	1894-1910	16	La.	1845	1921	Roman Catholic
Rufus W. Peckham, N.Y.	1895-1909	13	N.Y.	1838	1909	Episcopal
Joseph McKenna, Calif.	1898-1925	26	Pa.	1843	1926	Roman Catholic

	Service		Birth			
Name; apptd. from	**Term**	**Yrs**	**Place**	**Date**	**Died**	**Religion**
Oliver W. Holmes, Mass.	1902-1932	29	Mass.	1841	1935	Unitarian
William R. Day, Ohio	1903-1922	19	Ohio	1849	1923	Protestant
William H. Moody, Mass.	1906-1910	3	Mass.	1853	1917	Episcopal
Horace H. Lurton, Tenn.	1909-1914	4	Ky.	1844	1914	Episcopal
Charles E. Hughes, N.Y.	1910-1916	5	N.Y.	1862	1948	Baptist
Willis Van Devanter, Wyo.	1910-1937	26	Ind.	1859	1941	Episcopal
Joseph R. Lamar, Ga.	1910-1916	4	Ga.	1857	1916	Ch. of Disciples
Mahlon Pitney, N.J.	1912-1922	10	N.J.	1858	1924	Presbyterian
James C. McReynolds, Tenn.	1914-1941	26	Ky.	1862	1946	Disciples of Christ
Louis D. Brandeis, Mass.	1916-1939	22	Ky.	1856	1941	Jewish
John H. Clarke, Ohio	1916-1922	5	Ohio	1857	1945	Protestant
George Sutherland, Utah	1922-1938	15	England	1862	1942	Episcopal
Pierce Butler, Minn.	1923-1939	16	Minn.	1866	1939	Roman Catholic
Edward T. Sanford, Tenn.	1923-1930	7	Tenn.	1865	1930	Episcopal
Harlan F. Stone, N.Y.	1925-1941	16	N.H.	1872	1946	Episcopal
Owen J. Roberts, Pa.	1930-1945	15	Pa.	1875	1955	Episcopal
Benjamin N. Cardozo, N.Y.	1932-1938	6	N.Y.	1870	1938	Jewish
Hugo L. Black, Ala.	1937-1971	34	Ala.	1886	1971	Baptist
Stanley F. Reed, Ky.	1938-1957	19	Ky.	1884	1980	Protestant
Felix Frankfurter, Mass.	1939-1962	23	Austria	1882	1965	Jewish
William O. Douglas, Conn.	1939-1975	36	Minn.	1898	1980	Presbyterian
Frank Murphy, Mich.	1940-1949	9	Mich.	1890	1949	Roman Catholic
James F. Byrnes, S.C.	1941-1942	1	S.C.	1879	1972	Episcopal
Robert H. Jackson, Pa.	1941-1954	13	N.Y.	1892	1954	Episcopal
Wiley B. Rutledge, Iowa	1943-1949	6	Ky.	1894	1949	Unitarian
Harold H. Burton, Ohio	1945-1958	13	Mass.	1888	1964	Unitarian
Tom C. Clark, Tex.	1949-1967	17	Tex.	1899	1977	Presbyterian
Sherman Minton, Ind.	1949-1956	7	Ind.	1890	1965	Roman Catholic
John M. Harlan, N.Y.	1955-1971	16	Ill.	1899	1971	Presbyterian
William J. Brennan, Jr., N.J.	1956-	—	N.J.	1906	—	Roman Catholic
Charles E. Whittaker, Mo.	1957-1962	5	Kan.	1901	1973	Methodist
Potter Stewart, Ohio	1958-1981	23	Mich.	1915	1985	Episcopal
Byron R. White, Colo.	1962-	—	Colo.	1917	—	Episcopal
Arthur J. Goldberg, Ill.	1962-1965	2	Ill.	1908	—	Jewish
Abe Fortas, Tenn.	1965-1969	3	Tenn.	1910	1982	Jewish
Thurgood Marshall, N.Y.	1967-	—	Md.	1908	—	Episcopalian
Harry A. Blackmun, Minn.	1970-	—	Ill.	1908	—	Methodist
Lewis F. Powell, Jr., Va.	1972-1987	15	Va.	1907	—	Presbyterian
William H. Rehnquist, Ariz.	1972-1986	14	Wis.	1924	—	Lutheran
John Paul Stevens, Ill.	1975-	—	Ill.	1920	—	Protestant
Sandra Day O'Connor, Ariz.	1981-	—	Tex.	1930	—	Episcopal
Antonin Scalia, D.C.	1986-	—	N.J.	1936	—	Roman Catholic

1. Congregational; later Unitarian. 2. Unitarian; then Episcopal. 3. Unitarian or Congregational. 4. Not a member of any church.

Impeachments of Federal Officials

Source: Congressional Directory

The procedure for the impeachment of Federal officials is detailed in Article I, Section 3, of the Constitution. See Index.

The Senate has sat as a court of impeachment in the following cases:

William Blount, Senator from Tennessee; charges dismissed for want of jurisdiction, January 14, 1799.

John Pickering, Judge of the U.S. District Court for New Hampshire; removed from office March 12, 1804.

Samuel Chase, Associate Justice of the Supreme Court; acquitted March 1, 1805.

James H. Peck, Judge of the U.S. District Court for Missouri; acquitted Jan. 31, 1831.

West H. Humphreys, Judge of the U.S. District Court for the middle, eastern, and western districts of Tennessee; removed from office June 26, 1862.

Andrew Johnson, President of the United States; acquitted May 26, 1868.

William W. Belknap, Secretary of War; acquitted Aug. 1, 1876.

Charles Swayne, Judge of the U.S. District Court for the northern district of Florida; acquitted Feb. 27, 1905.

Robert W. Archbald, Associate Judge, U.S. Commerce Court; removed Jan. 13, 1913.

George W. English, Judge of the U.S. District Court for eastern district of Illinois; resigned Nov. 4, 1926; proceedings dismissed.

Harold Louderback, Judge of the U.S. District Court for the northern district of California; acquitted May 24, 1933.

Halsted L. Ritter, Judge of the U.S. District Court for the southern district of Florida; removed from office April 17, 1936.

Harry E. Claiborne, Judge of the U.S. District Court for the district of Nevada; removed from office October 9, 1986.

Executive Departments and Agencies

Source: U.S. Government Manual, 1987—1988.

Unless otherwise indicated, addresses shown are in Washington, D.C.

CENTRAL INTELLIGENCE AGENCY (CIA)
Washington, D.C. (20505).
Established: 1947.
Director: William H. Webster.

COUNCIL OF ECONOMIC ADVISERS (CEA)
Executive Office Bldg. (20500).
Members: 3.
Established: Feb. 20, 1946.
Chairman: Beryl Sprinkel.

COUNCIL ON ENVIRONMENTAL QUALITY
722 Jackson Pl., N.W. (20006).
Members: 3.
Established: 1969.
Chairman: A. Alan Hill.

NATIONAL SECURITY COUNCIL (NSC)
Old Executive Office Bldg. (20506).
Members: 4.
Established: July 26, 1947.
Chairman: The President.
Other members: Vice President; Secretary of State; Secretary of Defense.

OFFICE OF ADMINISTRATION
Old Executive Office Bldg. (20500).
Established: Dec. 12, 1977.
Director: Johnathan S. Miller

OFFICE OF MANAGEMENT AND BUDGET
Executive Office Bldg. (20503).
Established: July 1, 1970.
Director: James C. Miller 3rd.

OFFICE OF SCIENCE AND TECHNOLOGY POLICY
Old Executive Office Building (20506).
Established: May 11, 1976
Director: William R. Graham

OFFICE OF THE UNITED STATES TRADE REPRESENTATIVE
600 17th St., N.W. (20506).
Established: Jan. 15, 1963.
Trade Representative: Clayton Yeutter

OFFICE OF POLICY DEVELOPMENT
1600 Pennsylvania Ave., N.W. (20500).
Established: Jan. 21, 1981.
Director: Gary L. Bauer.

Executive Departments

DEPARTMENT OF STATE
2201 C St., N.W. (20520).
Established: 1781 as Department of Foreign Affairs; reconstituted, 1789, following adoption of Constitution; name changed to Department of State Sept. 15, 1789.
Secretary: George P. Shultz.
Deputy Secretary: John C. Whitehead.
Chief Delegate to U.N.: Vernon A. Walters.

DEPARTMENT OF THE TREASURY
15th St. & Pennsylvania Ave., N.W. (20220).
Established: Sept. 2, 1789.
Secretary: James A. Baker, 3rd.
Deputy Secretary: Richard G. Darman.
Treasurer of the U.S.: Katherine D. Ortega.
Comptroller of the Currency: Robert L. Clarke.

DEPARTMENT OF DEFENSE
The Pentagon (20301).
Established: July 26, 1947, as National Department Establishment; name changed to Department of Defense on Aug. 10, 1949. Subordinate to Secretary of Defense are Secretaries of Army, Navy, Air Force.
Secretary: Caspar W. Weinberger.
Deputy Secretary: William Howard Taft, 4th.
Secretary of Army: John O. Marsh, Jr.
Secretary of Navy: James H. Webb.
Secretary of Air Force: E. C. Aldridge, Jr.
Commandant of Marine Corps: Gen. Alfred M. Gray.
Joint Chiefs of Staff: Adm. William J. Crowe, Jr. Chairman; Adm. Carlisle A. H. Trost, Navy; Gen. Larry D. Welch, Air Force: Gen. Carl E. Vuono, Army; Gen. Alfred M. Gray, Marine Corps.

DEPARTMENT OF JUSTICE
Constitution Ave. between 9th & 10th Sts., N.W. (20530).
Established: Office of Attorney General was created Sept. 24, 1789. Although he was one of original Cabinet members, he was not executive department head until June 22, 1870, when Department of Justice was established.
Attorney General: Edwin Meese, 3rd.
Deputy Attorney General: Arnold I. Burns.
Solicitor General: Charles Fried.
Director of FBI: William Steele Sessions.

DEPARTMENT OF THE INTERIOR
C St. between 18th & 19th Sts., N.W. (20240).
Established: March 3, 1849.
Secretary: Donald P. Hodel.
Under Secretary: Ann Dore McLaughlin.

DEPARTMENT OF AGRICULTURE
Independence Ave. between 12th & 14th Sts., S.W. (20250).
Established: May 15, 1862. Administered by Commissioner of Agriculture until 1889, when it was made executive department.
Secretary: Richard E. Lyng
Deputy Secretary: Peter C. Meyers

DEPARTMENT OF COMMERCE
14th St. between Constitution Ave. & E St., N.W. (20230).
Established: Department of Commerce and Labor was created Feb. 14, 1903. On March 4, 1913, all labor activities were transferred out of Department of Commerce and Labor and it was renamed Department of Commerce.
Secretary: C. William Verity, Jr.
Deputy Secretary: Clarence J. Brown.

DEPARTMENT OF LABOR
200 Constitution Ave., N.W. (20210).
Established: Bureau of Labor was created in 1884 under Department of the Interior; later became independent department without executive rank. Returned to bureau status in Department of Commerce and Labor, but on March 4, 1913, became independent executive department under its present name.
Secretary: William E. Brock 3rd.
Deputy Secretary: Dennis E. Whitfield.

DEPARTMENT OF HEALTH AND HUMAN SERVICES[1]
200 Independence Ave., S.W. (20201).
Established: April 11, 1953, replacing Federal Security Agency created in 1939.
Secretary: Otis R. Bowen
Surgeon General: Dr. C. Everett Koop.

1. Originally Department of Health, Education and Welfare. Name changed in May 1980 when Department of Education was activated.

DEPARTMENT OF HOUSING AND URBAN DEVELOPMENT
451 7th St., S.W. (20410).
Established: 1965, replacing Housing and Home Finance Agency created in 1947.
Secretary: Samuel R. Pierce, Jr.
Under Secretary: Carl D. Covitz.

DEPARTMENT OF TRANSPORTATION
400 7th St., S.W. (20590).
Established: Oct. 15, 1966, as result of Department of Transportation Act, which became effective April 1, 1967.
Secretary: Elizabeth Hanford Dole.
Deputy Secretary: James H. Burnley, 4th.

DEPARTMENT OF ENERGY
1000 Independence Ave., S.W. (20585).
Established: Aug. 1977.
Secretary: John S. Herrington.
Deputy Secretary: William F. Martin.

DEPARTMENT OF EDUCATION
400 Maryland Avenue, S.W. (20202).
Established: Oct. 17, 1979.
Secretary: William J. Bennett.
Under Secretary: Vacant.

Major Independent Agencies

ACTION
806 Connecticut Ave., N.W. (20525).
Established: July 1, 1971.
Director: Donna M. Alvarado.

CONSUMER PRODUCT SAFETY COMMISSION
5401 Westbard Ave., Bethesda, Md. (20207).
Members: 5.
Established: Oct. 27, 1972.
Chairman: Terrence M. Scanlon.

ENVIRONMENTAL PROTECTION AGENCY (EPA)
401 M St., S.W. (20460).
Established: Dec. 2, 1970.
Administrator: Lee M. Thomas.

EQUAL EMPLOYMENT OPPORTUNITY COMMISSION (EEOC)
2401 E St., N.W. (20506).
Members: 5.
Established: July 2, 1965.
Chairman: Clarence Thomas.

FARM CREDIT ADMINISTRATION (FCA)
1501 Farm Credit Dr., McLean, Va. (22102).
Members: 13.
Established: July 17, 1916.
Chairman of Federal Farm Credit Board: Frank W. Naylor, Jr.

FEDERAL COMMUNICATIONS COMMISSION (FCC)
1919 M St., N.W. (20554).
Members: 7.
Established: 1934.
Chairman: Dennis R. Patrick.

FEDERAL DEPOSIT INSURANCE CORPORATION (FDIC)
550 17th St., N.W. (20429).
Members: 3.
Established: June 16, 1933.
Chairman: L. William Seidman.

FEDERAL ELECTION COMMISSION (FEC)
999 E St., N.W. (20463).
Members: 6.
Established: 1974.
Chairman: Scott E. Thomas

FEDERAL MARITIME COMMISSION
1100 L St., N.W. (20573).
Members: 5.
Established: Aug. 12, 1961.
Chairman: Edward V. Hickey, Jr.

FEDERAL MEDIATION AND CONCILIATION SERVICE (FMCS)
2100 K St., N.W. (20427).
Established: 1947.
Director: Kay McMurray.

FEDERAL RESERVE SYSTEM (FRS), BOARD OF GOVERNORS OF
20th St. & Constitution Ave., N.W. (20551).
Members: 7.
Established: Dec. 23, 1913.
Chairman: Alan Greenspan.

FEDERAL TRADE COMMISSION (FTC)
Pennsylvania Ave. at 6th St., N.W. (20580).
Members: 5.
Established: Sept. 26, 1914.
Chairman: Daniel Oliver

GENERAL SERVICES ADMINISTRATION (GSA)
18th and F Sts., N.W. (20405).
Established: July 1, 1949.
Administrator: Terence C. Golden

INTERSTATE COMMERCE COMMISSION (ICC)
12th St. & Constitution Ave., N.W. (20423).
Members: 7.
Established: Feb. 4, 1887.
Chairman: Heather J. Gradison.

NATIONAL AERONAUTICS AND SPACE ADMINISTRATION (NASA)
400 Maryland Ave., S.W. (20546).
Established: 1958.
Administrator: James Fletcher

NATIONAL FOUNDATION ON THE ARTS AND THE HUMANITIES
1100 Pennsylvania Ave., N.W., (20506).
Established: 1965.
Chairmen: National Endowment for the Arts, Francis S. M. Hodsoll; National Endowment for the Humanities, Lynne V. Cheney

NATIONAL LABOR RELATIONS BOARD (NLRB)
1717 Pennsylvania Ave., N.W. (20570).
Members: 5.
Established: July 5, 1935.
Chairman: Donald L. Dotson.

NATIONAL MEDIATION BOARD
1425 K St., N.W. (20572).
Members: 3
Established: June 21, 1934.
Chairman: Charles L. Woods

NATIONAL SCIENCE FOUNDATION (NSF)
1800 G St., N.W. (20550).
Established: 1950.
Director: Erich Bloch

NATIONAL TRANSPORTATION SAFETY BOARD
800 Independence Ave., S.W. (20594).
Members: 5
Established: April 1, 1975.
Chairman: James E. Burnett.

NUCLEAR REGULATORY COMMISSION (NRC)
1717 H St., N.W. (20555).
Members: 5.
Established: Jan. 19, 1975.
Chairman: Lando W. Zech, Jr.

OFFICE OF PERSONNEL MANAGEMENT (OPM)
1900 E St., N.W. (20415).
Members: 3
Established: Jan. 1, 1979.
Director: Constance Horner.

SECURITIES AND EXCHANGE COMMISSION (SEC)
450 5th St., N.W. (20549).

Members: 5.
Established: July 2, 1934
Chairman: David S. Ruder.

SELECTIVE SERVICE SYSTEM (SSS)
National Headquarters (20435).
Established: Sept. 16, 1940.
Director: Wilfred L. Ebel (acting).

SMALL BUSINESS ADMINISTRATION (SBA)
1441 L St., N.W. (20416).
Established: July 30, 1953.
Administrator: James Abdnor.

TENNESSEE VALLEY AUTHORITY (TVA)
400 West Summit Hill Drive, Knoxville, Tenn. (37902).
Washington office: Capitol Hill Office Bldg., 412 First St., S.E. (20444).
Members of Board of Directors: 3.
Established: May 18, 1933.
Chairman: C. H. Dean, Jr.

U.S. AGENCY FOR INTERNATIONAL DEVELOPMENT
320 21st St., N.W. (20523).
Established: Oct. 1, 1979.
Acting Director: M. Peter McPherson.

U.S. ARMS CONTROL AND DISARMAMENT AGENCY
320 21st St., N.W., (20451).
Established: Sept. 26, 1961.
Director: Kenneth L. Adelman.

U.S. COMMISSION ON CIVIL RIGHTS
1121 Vermont Avenue, N.W. (20425).
Members: 8.
Established: 1957.
Chairman: Clarence M. Pendleton, Jr.

U.S. INFORMATION AGENCY
301 Fourth St., S.W. (20547).
Established: April 1, 1978.
Director: Charles Z. Wick.

U.S. INTERNATIONAL TRADE COMMISSION
701 E St., N.W. (20436).
Members: 6.
Established: Sept. 8, 1916.
Chairman: Susan Liebeler

U.S. POSTAL SERVICE
475 L'Enfant Plaza West, S.W. (20260).
Postmaster General: Preston R. Tisch
Deputy Postmaster General: Michael S. Coughlin.
Established: Office of Postmaster General and temporary post office system created in 1789. Act of Feb. 20, 1792, made detailed provisions for Post Office Department. Postmaster General became Cabinet member in 1829, and Department received executive status in 1872. In 1970 became independent agency headed by 11-member board of governors. Postmaster General, no longer Cabinet member, is chosen by nine governors, who, with Postmaster General, choose Deputy Postmaster General.

VETERANS ADMINISTRATION (VA)
810 Vermont Ave., N.W. (20420).
Established: July 21, 1930.
Administrator: Thomas K. Turnage.

Other Independent Agencies

Administrative Conference of the United States—2120 L St., N.W. (20037).
American Battle Monuments Commission—5127 Pulaski Bldg. 20 Massachusetts Ave. (20314).
Appalachian Regional Commission—1666 Connecticut Ave., N.W. (20235).
Board for International Broadcasting—Suite 400, 1201 Connecticut Ave., N.W. (20036).
Commission of Fine Arts—708 Jackson Place, N.W. (20006).
Commodity Futures Trading Commission—2033 K St., N.W. (20581).
Export-Import Bank of the United States—811 Vermont Ave., N.W. (20571).
Federal Emergency Management Agency—500 C St., S.W. (20472).
Federal Home Loan Bank Board—1700 G St., N.W. (20552).
Federal Labor Relations Authority—500 C St., S.W. (20424).
Inter-American Foundation—1515 Wilson Blvd., Arlington, Va. (22209).
Merit Systems Protection Board—1120 Vermont Ave., N.W. (20419).
National Commission on Libraries and Information Science—7th & D Sts., S.W. (20024).
National Credit Union Administration—1776 G St., N.W. (20456).
Occupational Safety and Health Review Commission—1825 K St., N.W. (20006).
Panama Canal Commission—2000 L St., N.W. (20036).
Peace Corps—806 Connecticut Ave., N.W. (20526).
Pension Benefit Guaranty Corporation—2020 K St., N.W. (20006).
Postal Rate Commission—1333 H St., N.W. (20268).
President's Committee on Employment of the Handicapped—1111 20th St., N.W. (20036).
President's Council on Physical Fitness and Sports—450 5th St., S.W. (20001).
Railroad Retirement Board (RRB)—844 Rush St., Chicago, Ill. (60611); Washington Liaison Office: Suite 558, 2000 L St. (20036).
U.S. Parole Commission—5550 Friendship Blvd., Chevy Chase, Md. (20815).

Legislative Department

Architect of the Capitol—U.S. Capitol Building (20515)
General Accounting Office (GAO)—441 G St., N.W. (20548)
Government Printing Office (GPO)—North Capitol & H Sts., N.W. (20401)
Library of Congress—10 First St. S.E. (20540)
Office of Technology Assessment—600 Pennsylvania Ave., S.E. (20510)
United States Botanic Garden—Office of Director, 245 First St., S.W. (20024)

Quasi-Official Agencies

American National Red Cross—430 17th St., N.W. (20006).
Legal Services Corporation—400 Virginia Ave. S.W. (20024).
National Academy of Sciences, National Academy of Engineering, National Research Council, Institute of Medicine—2101 Constitution Ave., N.W. (20418).
National Railroad Passenger Corporation (Amtrak)—400 N. Capitol St., N.W. (20001).
Smithsonian Institution—1000 Jefferson Dr., S.W. (20560).
U.S. Railway Association—955 L'Enfant Plaza North, S.W. (20595).

Biographies of the Presidents

GEORGE WASHINGTON was born on Feb. 22, 1732 (Feb. 11, 1731/2, old style) in Westmoreland County, Va. While in his teens, he trained as a surveyor, and at the age of 20 he was appointed adjutant in the Virginia militia. For the next three years, he fought in the wars against the French and Indians, serving as Gen. Edward Braddock's aide in the disastrous campaign against Fort Duquesne. In 1759, he resigned from the militia, married Martha Dandridge Custis, a widow, and settled down as a gentleman farmer at Mount Vernon, Va.

As a militiaman, Washington had been exposed to the arrogance of the British officers, and his experience as a planter with British commercial restrictions increased his anti-British sentiment. He opposed the Stamp Act of 1765 and after 1770 became increasingly prominent in organizing resistance. A delegate to the Continental Congress, Washington was selected as commander in chief of the Continental Army and took command at Cambridge, Mass., on July 3, 1775.

Inadequately supported and sometimes covertly sabotaged by the Congress, in charge of troops who were inexperienced, badly equipped, and impatient of discipline, Washington conducted the war on the policy of avoiding major engagements with the British and wearing them down by harrassing tactics. His able generalship, along with the French alliance and the growing weariness within Britain, brought the war to a conclusion with the surrender of Cornwallis at Yorktown, Va., on Oct. 19, 1781.

The chaotic years under the Articles of Confederation led Washington to return to public life in the hope of promoting the formation of a strong central government. He presided over the Constitutional Convention and yielded to the universal demand that he serve as first President. He was inaugurated on April 30, 1789, in New York, the first national capital. In office, he sought to unite the nation and establish the authority of the new government at home and abroad. Greatly distressed by the emergence of the Hamilton-Jefferson rivalry, Washington worked to maintain neutrality but actually sympathized more with Hamilton. Following his unanimous re-election in 1792, his second term was dominated by the Federalists. His Farewell Address on Sept. 17, 1796 (published but never delivered) rebuked party spirit and warned against "permanent alliances" with foreign powers.

He died at Mount Vernon on Dec. 14, 1799.

JOHN ADAMS was born on Oct. 30 (Oct. 19, old style), 1735, at Braintree (now Quincy), Mass. A Harvard graduate, he considered teaching and the ministry but finally turned to law and was admitted to the bar in 1758. Six years later, he married Abigail Smith. He opposed the Stamp Act, served as lawyer for patriots indicted by the British, and by the time of the Continental Congresses, was in the vanguard of the movement for independence. In 1778, he went to France as commissioner. Subsequently he helped negotiate the peace treaty with Britain, and in 1785 became envoy to London. Resigning in 1788, he was elected Vice President under Washington and was re-elected in 1792.

Though a Federalist, Adams did not get along with Hamilton, who sought to prevent his election to the presidency in 1796 and thereafter intrigued against his administration. In 1798, Adam's independent policy averted a war with France but completed the break with Hamilton and the right-wing Federalists; at the same time, the enactment of the Alien and Sedition Acts, directed against foreigners and against critics of the government, exasperated the Jeffersonian opposition. The split between Adams and Hamilton resulted in Jefferson's becoming the next President. Adams retired to his home in Quincy. He and Jefferson died on the same day, July 4, 1826, the 50th anniversary of the signing of the Declaration of Independence.

His *Defence of the Constitutions of Government of the United States* (1787) contains original and striking, if conservative, political ideas.

THOMAS JEFFERSON was born on April 13 (April 2, old style), 1743, at Shadwell in Goochland (now Albemarle) County, Va. A William and Mary graduate, he studied law, but from the start showed an interest in science and philosophy. His literary skill and political clarity brought him to the forefront of the revolutionary movement in Virginia. As delegate to the Continental Congress, he drafted the Declaration of Independence. In 1776, he entered the Virginia House of Delegates and initiated a comprehensive reform program for the abolition of feudal survivals in land tenure and the separation of church and state.

In 1779, he became governor, but constitutional limitations on his power, combined with his own lack of executive energy, caused an unsatisfactory administration, culminating in Jefferson's virtual abdication when the British invaded Virginia in 1781. He retired to his beautiful home at Monticello, Va., to his family. His wife, Martha Wayles Skelton, whom he married in 1772, died in 1782.

Jefferson's *Notes on Virginia* (1784–85) illustrate his many-faceted interests, his limitless intellectual curiosity, his deep faith in agrarian democracy. Sent to Congress in 1783, he helped lay down the decimal system and drafted basic reports on the organization of the western lands. In 1785 he was appointed minister to France, where the Anglo-Saxon liberalism he had drawn from John Locke, the British philosopher, was stimulated by contact with the thought that would soon ferment in the French Revolution. In 1789, Washington appointed him Secretary of State. While favoring the Constitution and a strengthened central government, Jefferson came to believe that Hamilton contemplated the establishment of a monarchy. Growing differences resulted in Jefferson's resignation on Dec. 31, 1793.

Elected vice president in 1796, Jefferson continued to serve as spiritual leader of the opposition to Federalism, particularly to the repressive Alien and Sedition Acts. He was elected President in 1801 by the House of Representatives as a result of Hamilton's decision to throw the Federalist votes to him rather than to Aaron Burr, who had tied him in electoral votes. He was the first President to be inaugurated in Washington, which he had helped to design.

The purchase of Louisiana from France in 1803, though in violation of Jefferson's earlier constitutional scruples, was the most notable act of his administration. Re-elected in 1804, with the Federalist Charles C. Pinckney opposing him, Jefferson tried desperately to keep the United States out of the Napoleonic Wars in Europe, employing to this end the unpopular embargo policy.

After his retirement to Monticello in 1809, he developed his interest in education, founding the University of Virginia and watching its development with never-flagging interest. He died at Monticello on July 4, 1826. Jefferson had an enormous variety of interests and skills, ranging from education and science to architecture and music.

JAMES MADISON was born in Port Conway, Va., on March 16, 1751 (March 5, 1750/1, old style). A Princeton graduate, he joined the struggle for independence on his return to Virginia in 1771. In the 1770s and 1780s he was active in state politics, where he championed the Jefferson reform program, and in the Continental Congress. Madison was influential in the Constitutional Convention as leader of the group favoring a strong central government and as recorder of the debates; and he subsequently wrote, in collaboration with Alexander Hamilton and John Jay, the *Federalist* papers to aid the campaign for the adoption of the Constitution.

Serving in the new Congress, Madison soon emerged as the leader in the House of the men who opposed Hamilton's financial program and his pro-British leanings in foreign policy. Retiring from Congress in 1797, he continued to be active in Virginia and drafted the Virginia Resolution protesting the Alien and Sedition Acts. His intimacy with Jefferson made him the natural choice for Secretary of State in 1801.

In 1809, Madison succeeded Jefferson as President, defeating Charles C. Pinckney. His attractive wife, Dolley Payne Todd, whom he married in 1794, brought a new social sparkle to the executive mansion. In the meantime, increasing tension with Britain culminated in the War of 1812—a war for which the United States was unprepared and for which Madison lacked the executive talent to clear out incompetence and mobilize the nation's energies. Madison was re-elected in 1812, running against the Federalist De Witt Clinton. In 1814, the British actually captured Washington and forced Madison to flee to Virginia.

Madison's domestic program capitulated to the Hamiltonian policies that he had resisted 20 years before and he now signed bills to establish a United States Bank and a higher tariff.

After his presidency, he remained in retirement in Virginia until his death on June 28, 1836.

JAMES MONROE was born on April 28, 1758, in Westmoreland County, Va. A William and Mary graduate, he served in the army during the first years of the Revolution and was wounded at Trenton. He then entered Virginia politics and later national politics under the sponsorship of Jefferson. In 1786, he married Elizabeth (Eliza) Kortright.

Fearing centralization, Monroe opposed the adoption of the Constitution and, as senator from Virginia, was highly critical of the Hamiltonian program. In 1794, he was appointed minister to France, where his ardent sympathies with the Revolution exceeded the wishes of the State Department. His troubled diplomatic career ended with his recall in 1796. From 1799 to 1802, he was governor of Virginia. In 1803, Jefferson sent him to France to help negotiate the Louisiana Purchase and for the next few years he was active in various negotiations on the Continent.

In 1808, Monroe flirted with the radical wing of the Republican Party, which opposed Madison's candicacy; but the presidential boom came to naught and, after a brief term as governor of Virginia in 1811, Monroe accepted Madison's offer to become Secretary of State. During the War of 1812, he vainly sought a field command and instead served as Secretary of War from September 1814 to March 1815.

Elected President in 1816 over the Federalist Rufus King, and re-elected without opposition in 1820, Monroe, the last of the Virginia dynasty, pursued the course of systematic tranquilization that won for his administrations the name "the era of good feeling." He continued Madison's surrender to the Hamiltonian domestic program, signed the Missouri Compromise, acquired Florida, and with the able assistance of his Secretary of State, John Quincy Adams, promulgated the Monroe Doctrine in 1823, declaring against foreign colonization or intervention in the Americas. He died in New York City on July 4, 1831, the third president to die on the anniversary of Independence.

JOHN QUINCY ADAMS was born on July 11, 1767, at Braintree (now Quincy), Mass., the son of John Adams, the second President. He spent his early years in Europe with his father, graduated from Harvard, and entered law practice. His anti-Jeffersonian newspaper articles won him political attention. In 1794, he became minister to the Netherlands, the first of several diplomatic posts that occupied him until his return to Boston in 1801. In 1797, he married Louisa Catherine Johnson.

In 1803, Adams was elected to the Senate, nominally as a Federalist, but his repeated displays of independence on such issues as the Louisiana Purchase and the embargo caused his party to demand his resignation and ostracize him socially. In 1809, Madison rewarded him for his support of Jefferson by appointing him minister to St. Petersburg. He helped negotiate the Treaty of Ghent in 1814, and in 1815 became minister to London. In 1817 Monroe appointed him Secretary of State where he served with great distinction, gaining Florida from Spain without hostilities and playing an equal part with Monroe in formulating the Monroe Doctrine.

When no presidential candidate received a majority of electoral votes in 1824, Adams, with the support of Henry Clay, was elected by the House in 1825 over Andrew Jackson, who had the original plurality. Adams had ambitious plans of government activity to foster internal improvements and promote the arts and sciences, but congressional obstructionism, combined with his own unwillingness or inability to play the role of a politician, resulted in little being accomplished. After being defeated for re-elected by Jackson in 1828, he successfully ran for the House of Representatives in 1830. There though nominally a Whig, he pursued as ever an independent course. He led the fight to force Congress to receive antislavery petitions and fathered the Smithsonian Institution.

Stricken on the floor of the House, he died on Feb. 23, 1848. His long and detailed *Diary* gives a unique picture of the personalities and politics of the times.

ANDREW JACKSON was born on March 15, 1767, in what is now generally agreed to be Waxhaw, S.C. After a turbulent boyhood as an orphan and a British prisoner, he moved west to Tennessee, where he soon qualified for law practice but found time for such frontier pleasures as horse racing, cockfighting, and dueling. His marriage to Rachel Donelson Robards in 1791 was complicated by subsequent legal uncertainties about the status of her divorce. During the 1790s, Jackson served in the Tennessee Constitutional Convention, the United States House of Representatives and Senate, and on the Tennessee Supreme Court.

After some years as a country gentleman, living at the Hermitage near Nashville, Jackson in 1812 was given command of Tennessee troops sent against the Creeks. He defeated the Indians at Horseshoe Bend in 1814; subsequently he became a major general and won the Battle of New Orleans over veteran British troops, though after the treaty of peace had been signed at Ghent. In 1818, Jackson invaded Florida, captured Pensacola, and hanged two Englishmen named Arbuthnot and Ambrister, creating an international incident. A presidential boom began for him in 1821, and to foster it, he returned to the Senate (1823–25). Though he won a plurality of electoral votes in 1824, he lost in the House when Clay threw his strength to Adams. Four years later, he easily defeated Adams.

As President, Jackson greatly expanded the power and prestige of the presidential office and carried through an unprecedented program of domestic reform, vetoing the bill to extend the United States Bank, moving toward a hard-money currency policy, and checking the program of federal internal improvements. He also vindicated federal authority against South Carolina with its doctrine of nullification and against France on the question of debts. The support given his policies by the workingmen of the East as well as by the farmers of the East, West, and South resulted in his triumphant re-election in 1832 over Clay.

After watching the inauguration of his handpicked successor, Martin Van Buren, Jackson retired to the Hermitage, where he maintained a lively interest in national affairs until his death on June 8, 1845.

MARTIN VAN BUREN was born on Dec. 5, 1782, at Kinderhook, N.Y. After graduating from the village school, he became a law clerk, entered practice in 1803, and soon became active in state politics as state senator and attorney general. In 1820, he was elected to the United States Senate. He threw the support of his efficient political organization, known as the Albany Regency, to William H. Crawford in 1824 and to Jackson in 1828. After leading the opposition to Adams's administration in the Senate, he served briefly as governor of New York (1828–29) and resigned to become Jackson's Secretary of State. He was soon on close personal terms with Jackson and played an important part in the Jacksonian program.

In 1832, Van Buren became vice president; in 1836, President. The Panic of 1837 overshadowed his term. He attributed it to the overexpansion of the credit and favored the establishment of an independent treasury as repository for the federal funds. In 1840, he established a 10-hour day on public works. Defeated by Harrison in 1840, he was the leading contender for the Democratic nomination in 1844 until he publicly opposed immediate annexation of Texas, and was subsequently beaten by the Southern delegations at the Baltimore convention. This incident increased his growing misgivings about the slave power.

After working behind the scenes among the antislavery Democrats, Van Buren joined in the movement that led to the Free-Soil Party and became its candidate for President in 1848. He subsequently returned to the Democratic Party while continuing to object to its pro-Southern policy. He died in Kinderhook on July 24, 1862. His *Autobiography* throws valuable sidelights on the political history of the times.

His wife, Hannah Hoes, whom he married in 1807, died in 1819.

WILLIAM HENRY HARRISON was born in Charles City County, Va., on Feb. 9, 1773. Joining the army in 1791, he was active in Indian fighting in the Northwest, became secretary of the Northwest Territory in 1798 and governor of Indiana in 1800. He married Anna Symmes in 1795. Growing discontent over white encroachments on Indian lands led to the formation of an Indian alliance under Tecumseh to resist further aggressions. In 1811, Harrison won a nominal victory over the Indians at Tippecanoe and in 1813 a more decisive one at the Battle of the Thames, where Tecumseh was killed.

After resigning from the army in 1814, Harrison had an obscure career in politics and diplomacy, ending up 20 years later as a county recorder in Ohio. Nominated for President in 1835 as a military hero whom the conservative politicians hoped to be able to control, he ran surprisingly well against Van Buren in 1836. Four years later, he defeated Van Buren but caught penumonia and died in Washington on April 4, 1841, a month after his inauguration. Harrison was the first president to die in office.

JOHN TYLER was born in Charles City County, Va., on March 29, 1790. A William and Mary graduate, he entered law practice and politics, serving in the House of Representatives (1817–21), as governor of Virginia (1825–27), and as senator (1827–36). A strict constructionist, he supported Crawford in 1824 and Jackson in 1828, but broke with Jackson over his United States Bank policy and became a member of the Southern state-rights group that cooperated with the Whigs. In 1836, he resigned from the Senate rather than follow instructions from the Virginia legislature to vote for a resolution expunging censure of Jackson from the Senate record.

Elected vice president on the Whig ticket in 1840, Tyler succeeded to the presidency on Harrison's death. His strict-constructionist views soon caused a split with the Henry Clay wing of the Whig party and a stalemate on domestic questions. Tyler's more considerable achievements were his support of the Webster-Ashburton Treaty with Britain and his success in bringing about the annexation of Texas.

After his presidency he lived in retirement in Virginia until the outbreak of the Civil War, when he emerged briefly as chairman of a peace convention and then as delegate to the provisional Congress of the Confederacy. He died on Jan. 18, 1862. He married Letitia Christian in 1813 and, two years after her death in 1842, Julia Gardiner.

JAMES KNOX POLK was born in Mecklenburg County, N.C., on Nov. 2, 1795. A graduate of the University of North Carolina, he moved west to Tennessee, was admitted to the bar, and soon became prominent in state politics. In 1825, he was elected to the House of Representatives, where he opposed Adams and, after 1829, became Jackson's floor leader in the fight against the Bank. In 1835, he became Speaker of the House. Four years later, he was elected governor of Tennessee, but was beaten in tries for re-election in 1841 and 1843.

The supporters of Van Buren for the Democratic

nomination in 1844 counted on Polk as his running mate; but, when Van Buren's stand on Texas alienated Southern support, the convention swung to Polk on the ninth ballot. He was elected over Henry Clay, the Whig candidate. Rapidly disillusioning those who thought that he would not run his own administration, Polk proceeded steadily and precisely to achieve four major objectives—the acquisition of California, the settlement of the Oregon question, the reduction of the tariff, and the establishment of the independent treasury. He also enlarged the Monroe Doctrine to exclude all non-American intervention in American affairs, whether forcible or not, and he forced Mexico into a war that he waged to a successful conclusion.

His wife, Sarah Childress, whom he married in 1824, was a woman of charm and ability. Polk died in Nashville, Tenn., on June 15, 1849.

ZACHARY TAYLOR was born at Montebello, Orange County, Va., on Nov. 24, 1784. Embarking on a military career in 1808, Taylor fought in the War of 1812, the Black Hawk War, and the Seminole War, meanwhile holding garrison jobs on the frontier or desk jobs in Washington. A brigadier general as a result of his victory over the Seminoles at Lake Okeechobee (1837), Taylor held a succession of Southwestern commands and in 1846 established a base on the Rio Grande, where his forces engaged in hostilities that precipitated the war with Mexico. He captured Monterrey in September 1846 and, disregarding Polk's orders to stay on the defensive, defeated Santa Anna at Buena Vista in February 1847, ending the war in the northern provinces.

Though Taylor had never cast a vote for president, his party affiliations were Whiggish and his availability was increased by his difficulties with Polk. He was elected president over the Democrat Lewis Cass. During the revival of the slavery controversy, which was to result in the Compromise of 1850, Taylor began to take an increasingly firm stand against appeasing the South; but he died in Washington on July 9, 1850, during the fight over the Compromise. He married Margaret Mackall Smith in 1810. His bluff and simple soldierly qualities won him the name Old Rough and Ready.

MILLARD FILLMORE was born at Locke, Cayuga County, N.Y., on Jan. 7, 1800. A lawyer, he entered politics with the Anti-Masonic Party under the sponsorship of Thurlow Weed, editor and party boss, and subsequently followed Weed into the Whig Party. He served in the House of Representatives (1833–35 and 1837–43) and played a leading role in writing the tariff of 1842. Defeated for governor of New York in 1844, he became State comptroller in 1848, was put on the Whig ticket with Taylor as a concession to the Clay wing of the party, and became president upon Taylor's death in 1850.

As president, Fillmore broke with Weed and William H. Seward and associated himself with the pro-Southern Whigs, supporting the Compromise of 1850. Defeated for the Whig nomination in 1852, he ran for president in 1856 as candidate of the American, or Know-Nothing Party, which sought to unite the country against foreigners in the alleged hope of diverting it from the explosive slavery issue. Fillmore opposed Lincoln during the Civil War. He died in Buffalo on March 8, 1874.

He was married in 1826 to Abigail Powers, who died in 1853, and in 1858 to Caroline Carmichael McIntosh.

FRANKLIN PIERCE was born at Hillsboro, N.H., on Nov. 23, 1804. A Bowdoin graduate, lawyer, and Jacksonian Democrate, he won rapid political advancement in the party, in part because of the prestige of his father, Gov. Benjamin Pierce. By 1831 he was Speaker of the New Hampshire House of Representatives; from 1833 to 1837, he served in the federal House and from 1837 to 1842 in the Senate. His wife, Jane Means Appleton, whom he married in 1834, disliked Washington and the somewhat dissipated life led by Pierce; in 1842 Pierce resigned from the Senate and began a successful law practice in Concord, N.H. During the Mexican War, he was a brigadier general.

Thereafter Pierce continued to oppose antislavery tendencies within the Democratic Party. As a result, he was the Southern choice to break the deadlock at the Democratic convention of 1852 and was nominated on the 49th ballot. In the election, Pierce overwhelmed Gen. Winfield Scott, the Whig candidate.

As president, Pierce followed a course of appeasing the South at home and of playing with schemes of territorial expansion abroad. The failure of his foreign and domestic policies prevented his renomination; and he died in Concord on Oct. 8, 1869, in relative obscurity.

JAMES BUCHANAN was born near Mercersburg, Pa., on April 23, 1791. A Dickinson graduate and a lawyer, he entered Pennsylvania politics as a Federalist. With the disappearance of the Federalist Party, he became a Jacksonian Democrat. He served with ability in the House (1821–31), as minister to St. Petersburg (1832–33), and in the Senate (1834–45), and in 1845 became Polk's Secretary of State. In 1853, Pierce appointed Buchanan minister to Britain, where he participated with other American diplomats in Europe in drafting the expansionist Ostend Manifesto.

He was elected president in 1856, defeating John C. Frémont, the Republican candidate, and former President Millard Fillmore of the American Party. The growing crisis over slavery presented Buchanan with problems he lacked the will to tackle. His appeasement of the South alienated the Stephen Douglas wing of the Democratic Party without reducing Southern militancy on slavery issues. While denying the right of secession, Buchanan also denied that the federal government could do anything about it. He supported the administration during the Civil War and died in Lancaster, Pa., on June 1, 1868.

The only president to remain a bachelor throughout his term, Buchanan used his charming niece, Harriet Lane, as White House hostess.

ABRAHAM LINCOLN was born in Hardin (now Larue) County, Ky., on Feb. 12, 1809. His family moved to Indiana and then to Illinois, and Lincoln gained what education he could along the way. While reading law, he worked in a store, managed a mill, surveyed, and split rails. In 1834, he went to the Illinois legislature as a Whig and became the party's floor leader. For the next 20 years he practiced law in Springfield, except for a single term (1847–49) in Congress, where he denounced the Mexican War. In 1855, he was a candidate for senator annd the next year he joined the new Republican Party.

A leading but unsuccessful candidate for the vice-presidential nomination with Frémont, Lincoln gained national attention in 1858 when, as

Republican candidate for senator from Illinois, he engaged in a series of debates with Stephen A. Douglas, the Democratic candidate. He lost the election, but continued to prepare the way for the 1860 Republican convention and was rewarded with the presidential nomination on the third ballot. He won the election over three opponents.

From the start, Lincoln made clear that, unlike Buchanan, he believed the national government had the power to crush the rebellion. Not an abolitionist, he held the slavery issue subordinate to that of preserving the Union, but soon perceived that the war could not be brought to a successful conclusion without freeing the slaves. His administration was hampered by the incompetence of many Union generals, the inexperience of the troops, and the harassing political tactics both of the Republican Radicals, who favored a hard policy toward the South, and the Democratic Copperheads, who desired a negotiated peace. The Gettysburg Address of Nov. 19, 1863, marks the high point in the record of American eloquence. Lincoln's long search for a winning combination finally brought Generals Ulysses S. Grant and William T. Sherman on the top; and their series of victories in 1864 dispelled the mutterings from both Radicals and Peace Democrats that at one time seemed to threaten Lincoln's re-election. He was re-elected in 1864, defeating Gen. George B. McClellan, the Democratic candidate. His inaugural address urged leniency toward the South: "With malice toward none, with charity for all . . . let us strive on to finish the work we are in; to bind up the nation's wounds . . ." This policy aroused growing opposition on the part of the Republican Radicals, but before the matter could be put to the test, Lincoln was shot by the actor John Wilkes Booth at Ford's Theater, Washington, on April 14, 1865. He died the next morning.

Lincoln's marriage to Mary Todd in 1842 was often unhappy and turbulent, in part because of his wife's pronounced instability.

ANDREW JOHNSON was born at Raleigh, N.C., on Dec. 29, 1808. Self-educated, he became a tailor in Greeneville, Tenn., but soon went into politics, where he rose steadily. He served in the House of Representatives (1843–54), as governor of Tennessee (1853–57), and as a senator (1857–62). Politically he was a Jacksonian Democrat and his specialty was the fight for a more equitable land policy. Alone among the Southern Senators, he stood by the Union during the Civil War. In 1862, he became war governor of Tennessee and carried out a thankless and difficult job with great courage. Johnson became Lincoln's running mate in 1864 as a result of an attempt to give the ticket a nonpartisan and nonsectional character. Succeeding to the presidency on Lincoln's death, Johnson sought to carry out Lincoln's policy, but without his political skill. The result was a hopeless conflict with the Radical Republicans who dominated Congress, passed measures over Johnson's vetoes, and attempted to limit the power of the executive concerning appointments and removals. The conflict culminated with Johnson's impeachment for attempting to remove his disloyal Secretary of War in defiance of the Tenure of Office Act which required senatorial concurrence for such dismissals. The opposition failed by one vote to get the two thirds necessary for conviction.

After his presidency, Johnson maintained an interest in politics and in 1875 was again elected to the Senate. He died near Carter Station, Tenn., on July 31, 1875. He married Eliza McCardle in 1827.

ULYSSES SIMPSON GRANT was born (as Hiram Ulysses Grant) at Point Pleasant, Ohio, on April 27, 1822. He graduated from West Point in 1843 and served without particular distinction in the Mexican War. In 1848 he married Julia Dent. He resigned from the army in 1854, after warnings from his commanding officer about his drinking habits, and for the next six years held a wide variety of jobs in the Middle West. With the outbreak of the Civil War, he sought a command and soon, to his surprise, was made a brigadier general. His continuing successes in the western theaters, culminating in the capture of Vicksburg, Miss., in 1863, brought him national fame and soon the command of all the Union armies. Grant's dogged, implacable policy of concentrating on dividing and destroying the Confederate armies brought the war to an end in 1865. The next year, he was made full general.

In 1868, as Republican candidate for president, Grant was elected over the Democrat, Horatio Seymour. From the start, Grant showed his unfitness for the office. His Cabinet was weak, his domestic policy was confused, many of his intimate associates were corrupt. The notable achievement in foreign affairs was the settlement of controversies with Great Britain in the Treaty of London (1871), negotiated by his able Secretary of State, Hamilton Fish.

Running for re-election in 1872, he defeated Horace Greeley, the Democratic and Liberal Republican candidate. The Panic of 1873 graft scandals close to the presidency created difficulties for his second term.

After retiring from office, Grant toured Europe for two years and returned in time to accede to a third-term boom, but was beaten in the convention of 1880. Illness and bad business judgment darkened his last years, but he worked steadily at the *Personal Memoirs,* which were to be so successful when published after his death at Mount McGregor, near Saratoga, N.Y., on July 23, 1885.

RUTHERFORD BIRCHARD HAYES was born in Delaware, Ohio, on Oct. 4, 1822. A graduate of Kenyon College and the Harvard Law School, he practiced law in Lower Sandusky (now Fremont) and then in Cincinnati. In 1852 he married Lucy Webb. A Whig, he joined the Republican party in 1855. During the Civil War he rose to major general. He served in the House of Representatives from 1865 to 1867 and then confirmed a reputation for honesty and efficiency in two terms as Governor of Ohio (1868–72). His election to a third term in 1875 made him the logical candidate for those Republicans who wished to stop James G. Blaine in 1876, and he was nominated.

The result of the election was in doubt for some time and hinged upon disputed returns from South Carolina, Louisiana, Florida, and Oregon. Samuel J. Tilden, the Democrat, had the larger popular vote but was adjudged by the strictly partisan decisions of the Electoral Commission to have one fewer electoral vote, 185 to 184. The national acceptance of this result was due in part to the general understanding that Hayes would pursue a conciliatory policy toward the South. He withdrew the troops from the South, took a conservative position on financial and labor issues, and urged civil service reform.

Hayes served only one term by his own wish and

spent the rest of his life in various humanitarian endeavors. He died in Fremont on Jan. 17, 1893.

JAMES ABRAM GARFIELD, the last president to be born in a log cabin, was born in Cuyahoga County, Ohio, on Nov. 19, 1831. A Williams graduate, he taught school for a time and entered Republican politics in Ohio. In 1858, he married Lucretia Rudolph. During the Civil War, he had a promising career, rising to major general of volunteers; but he resigned in 1863, having been elected to the House of Representatives, where he served until 1880. His oratorical and parliamentary abilities soon made him the leading Republican in the House, though his record was marred by his unorthodox acceptance of a fee in the DeGolyer paving contract case and by suspicions of his complicity in the Crédit Mobilier scandal.

In 1880, Garfield was elected to the Senate, but instead became the presidential candidate on the 36th ballot as a result of a deadlock in the Republican convention. In the election, he defeated Gen. Winfield Scott Hancock, the Democratic candidate. Garfield's administration was barely under way when he was shot by Charles J. Guiteau, a disappointed office seeker, in Washington on July 2, 1881. He died in Elberton, N.J., on Sept. 19.

CHESTER ALAN ARTHUR was born at Fairfield, Vt., on Oct. 5, 1830. A graduate of Union College, he became a successful New York lawyer. In 1859, he married Ellen Herndon. During the Civil War, he held administrative jobs in the Republican state administration and in 1871 was appointed collector of the Port of New York by Grant. This post gave him control over considerable patronage. Though not personally corrupt, Arthur managed his power in the interests of the New York machine so openly that President Hayes in 1877 called for an investigation and the next year Arthur was suspended.

In 1880 Arthur was nominated for vice president in the hope of conciliating the followers of Grant and the powerful New York machine. As president upon Garfield's death, Arthur, stepping out of his familiar role as spoilsman, backed civil service reform, reorganized the Cabinet, and prosecuted political associates accused of post office graft. Losing machine support and failing to gain the reformers, he was not nominated for a full term in 1884. He died in New York City on Nov. 18, 1886.

STEPHEN GROVER CLEVELAND was born at Caldwell, N.J., on March 18, 1837. He was admitted to the bar in Buffalo, N.Y., in 1859 and lived there as a lawyer, with occasional incursions into Democratic politics, for more than 20 years. He did not participate in the Civil War. As mayor of Buffalo in 1881, he carried through a reform program so ably that the Democrats ran him successfully for governor in 1882. In 1884 he won the Democratic nomination for President. The campaign contrasted Cleveland's spotless public career with the uncertain record of James G. Blaine, the Republican candidate, and Cleveland received enough Mugwump (independent Republican) support to win.

As president, Cleveland pushed civil service reform, opposed the pension grab and attacked the high tariff rates. While in the White House, he married Frances Folsom in 1886. Renominated in 1888, Cleveland was defeated by Benjamin Harrison, polling more popular but fewer electoral votes. In 1892, he was elected over Harrison. When the Panic of 1893 burst upon the country, Cleveland's attempts to solve it by sound-money measures alienated the free-silver wing of the party, while his tariff policy alienated the protectionists. In 1894, he sent troops to break the Pullman strike. In foreign affairs, his firmness caused Great Britain to back down in the Venezuela border dispute.

In his last years Cleveland was an active and much-respected public figure. He died in Princeton, N.J., on June 24, 1908.

BENJAMIN HARRISON was born in North Bend, Ohio, on Aug. 20, 1833, the grandson of William Henry Harrison, the ninth president. A graduate of Miami University in Ohio, he took up the law in Indiana and became active in Republican politics. In 1853, he married Caroline Lavinia Scott. During the Civil War, he rose to brigadier general. A sound-money Republican, he was elected senator from Indiana in 1880. In 1888, he received the Republican nomination for President on the eighth ballot. Though behind on the popular vote, he won over Grover Cleveland in the electoral college by 233 to 168.

As President, Harrison failed to please either the bosses or the reform element in the party. In foreign affairs he backed Secretary of State Blaine, whose policy foreshadowed later American imperialism. Harrison was renominated in 1892 but lost to Cleveland. His wife died in the White House in 1892 and Harrison married her niece, Mary Scott (Lord) Dimmick, in 1896. After his presidency, he resumed law practice. He died in Indianapolis on March 13, 1901.

WILLIAM McKINLEY was born in Niles, Ohio, on Jan. 29, 1843. He taught school, then served in the Civil War, rising from the ranks to become a major. Subsequently he opened a law office in Canton, Ohio, and in 1871 married Ida Saxton. Elected to Congress in 1876, he served there until 1891, except for 1883–85. His faithful advocacy of business interests culminated in the passage of the highly protective McKinley Tariff of 1890. With the support of Mark Hanna, a shrewd Cleveland businessman interested in safeguarding tariff protection, McKinley became governor of Ohio in 1892 and Republican presidential candidate in 1896. The business community, alarmed by the progressivism of William Jennings Bryan, the Democratic candidate, spent considerable money to assure McKinley's victory.

The chief event of McKinley's administration was the war with Spain, which resulted in our acquisition of the Philippines and other islands. With imperialism an issue, McKinley defeated Bryan again in 1900. On Sept. 6, 1901, he was shot at Buffalo, N.Y., by Leon F. Czolgosz, an anarchist, and he died there eight days later.

THEODORE ROOSEVELT was born in New York City on Oct. 27, 1858. A Harvard graduate, he was early interested in ranching, in politics, and in writing picturesque historical narratives. He was a Republican member of the New York Assembly in 1882–84, an unsuccessful candidate for mayor of New York in 1886, a U.S. Civil Service Commissioner under Benjamin Harrison, Police Commissioner of New York City in 1895, and Assistant Secretary of the Navy under McKinley in 1897. He resigned in 1898 to help organize a volunteer regiment, the Rough Riders, and take a more direct part in the war with Spain. He was elected governor of New York in 1898 and vice president in 1900, in spite of lack of enthusiasm on the part of the bosses.

Assuming the presidency of the assassinated McKinley in 1901, Roosevelt embarked on a wide-ranging program of government reform and conservation of natural resources. He ordered antitrust suits against several large corporations, threatened to intervene in the anthracite coal strike of 1902, which prompted the operators to accept arbitration, and, in general, championed the rights of the "little man" and fought the "malefactors of great wealth." He was also responsible for such progressive legislation as the Elkins Act of 1901, which outlawed freight rebates by railroads; the bill establishing the Department of Commerce and Labor; the Hepburn Act, which gave the I.C.C. greater control over the railroads; the Meat Inspection Act; and the Pure Food and Drug Act.

In foreign affairs, Roosevelt pursued a strong policy, permitting the instigation of a revolt in Panama to dispose of Colombian objections to the Panama Canal and helping to maintain the balance of power in the East by bringing the Russo-Japanese War to an end, for which he won the Nobel Peace Prize, the first American to achieve a Nobel prize in any category. In 1904, he decisively defeated Alton B. Parker, his conservative Democratic opponent.

Roosevelt's increasing coldness toward his successor, William Howard Taft, led him to overlook his earlier disclaimer of third-term ambitions and to re-enter politics. Defeated by the machine in the Republican convention of 1912, he organized the Progressive Party (Bull Moose) and polled more votes than Taft, though the split brought about the election of Woodrow Wilson. From 1915 on, Roosevelt strongly favored intervention in the European war. He became deeply embittered at Wilson's refusal to allow him to raise a volunteer division. He died in Oyster Bay, N.Y., on Jan. 6, 1919. He was married twice: in 1880 to Alice Hathaway Lee, who died in 1884, and in 1886 to Edith Kermit Carow.

WILLIAM HOWARD TAFT was born in Cincinnati on Sept. 15, 1857. A Yale graduate, he entered Ohio Republican politics in the 1880s. In 1886 he married Helen Herron. From 1887 to 1890, he served on the Ohio Superior Court; 1890–92, as solicitor general of the United States; 1892–1900, on the federal circuit court. In 1900 McKinley appointed him president of the Philippine Commission and in 1901 governor general. Taft had great success in pacifying the Filipinos, solving the problem of the church lands, improving economic conditions, and establishing limited self-government. His period as Secretary of War (1904–08) further demonstrated his capacity as administrator and conciliator, and he was Roosevelt's hand-picked successor in 1908. In the election, he polled 321 electoral votes to 162 for William Jennings Bryan, who was running for the presidency for the third time.

Though he carried on many of Roosevelt's policies, Taft got into increasing trouble with the progressive wing of the party and displayed mounting irritability and indecision. After his defeat in 1912, he became professor of constitutional law at Yale. In 1921 he was appointed Chief Justice of the United States. He died in Washington on March 8, 1930.

THOMAS WOODROW WILSON was born in Staunton, Va., on Dec. 28, 1856. A Princeton graduate, he turned from law practice to post-graduate work in political science at Johns Hopkins University, receiving his Ph.D. in 1886. He taught at Bryn Mawr, Wesleyan, and Princeton, and in 1902 was made president of Princeton. After an unsuccessful attempt to democratize the social life of the university, he welcomed an invitation in 1910 to be the Democratic gubernatorial candidate in New Jersey, and was elected. His success in fighting the machine and putting through a reform program attracted national attention.

In 1912, at the Democratic convention in Baltimore, Wilson won the nomination on the 46th ballot and went on to defeat Roosevelt and Taft in the election. Wilson proceeded under the standard of the New Freedom to enact a program of domestic reform, including the Federal Reserve Act, the Clayton Antitrust Act, the establishment of the Federal Trade Commission, and other measures designed to restore competition in the face of the great monopolies. In foreign affairs, while privately sympathetic with the Allies, he strove to maintain neutrality in the European war and warned both sides against encroachments on American interests.

Re-elected in 1916 as a peace candidate, he tried to mediate between the warring nations; but when the Germans resumed unrestricted submarine warfare in 1917, Wilson brought the United States into what he now believed was a war to make the world safe for democracy. He supplied the classic formulations of Allied war aims and the armistice of Nov. 11, 1918 was negotiated on the basis of Wilson's Fourteen Points. In 1919 he strove at Versailles to lay the foundations for enduring peace. He accepted the imperfections of the Versailles Treaty in the expectation that they could be remedied by action within the League of Nations. He probably could have secured ratification of the treaty by the Senate if he had adopted a more conciliatory attitude toward the mild reservationists; but his insistence on all or nothing eventually caused the diehard isolationists and diehard Wilsonites to unite in rejecting a compromise.

In September 1919 Wilson suffered a paralytic stroke that limited his activity. After leaving the presidency he lived on in retirement in Washington, dying on Feb. 3, 1924. He was married twice—in 1885 to Ellen Louise Axson, who died in 1914, and in 1915 to Edith Bolling Galt.

WARREN GAMALIEL HARDING was born in Morrow County, Ohio, on Nov. 2, 1865. After attending Ohio Central College, Harding became interested in journalism and in 1884 bought the *Marion* (Ohio) *Star.* In 1891 he married a wealthy widow, Florence Kling De Wolfe. As his paper prospered, he entered Republican politics, serving as state senator (1899–1903) and as lieutenant governor (1904–06). In 1910, he was defeated for governor, but in 1914 was elected to the Senate. His reputation as an orator made him the keynoter at the 1916 Republican convention.

When the 1920 convention was deadlocked between Leonard Wood and Frank O. Lowden, Harding became the dark-horse nominee on his solemn affirmation that there was no reason in his past that he should not be. Straddling the League question, Harding was easily elected over James M. Cox, his Democratic opponent. His Cabinet contained some able men, but also some manifestly unfit for public office. Harding's own intimates were mediocre when they were not corrupt. The impending disclosure of the Teapot Dome scandal in the Interior Department and illegal practices in the Justice Department and Veterans' Bureau, as well as political setbacks, profoundly worried him. On his return from Alaska in 1923, he died unexpectedly in San Francisco on Aug. 2.

JOHN CALVIN COOLIDGE was born in Plymouth, Vt., on July 4, 1872. An Amherst graduate, he went into law practice at Northampton, Mass., in 1897. He married Grace Anna Goodhue in 1905. He entered Republican state politics, becoming successively mayor of Northampton, state senator, lieutenant governor and, in 1919, governor. His use of the state militia to end the Boston police strike in 1919 won him a somewhat undeserved reputation for decisive action and brought him the Republican vice-presidential nomination in 1920. After Harding's death Coolidge handled the Washington scandals with care and finally managed to save the Republican Party from public blame for the widespread corruption.

In 1924, Coolidge was elected without difficulty, defeating the Democrat, John W. Davis, and Robert M. La Follette running on the Progressive ticket. His second term, like his first, was characterized by a general satisfaction with the existing economic order. He stated that he did not choose to run in 1928.

After his presidency, Coolidge lived quietly in Northampton, writing an unilluminating *Autobiography* and conducting a syndicated column. He died there on Jan. 5, 1933.

HERBERT CLARK HOOVER was born at West Branch, Iowa, on Aug. 10, 1874, the first president to be born west of the Mississippi. A Stanford graduate, he worked from 1895 to 1913 as a mining engineer and consultant throughout the world. In 1899, he married Lou Henry. During World War I, he served with distinction as chairman of the American Relief Committee in London, as chairman of the Commission for Relief in Belgium, and as U.S. Food Administrator. His political affiliations were still too indeterminate for him to be mentioned as a possibility for either the Republican or Democratic nomination in 1920, but after the election he served Harding and Coolidge as Secretary of Commerce.

In the election of 1928, Hoover overwhelmed Gov. Alfred E. Smith of New York, the Democratic candidate and the first Roman Catholic to run for the presidency. He soon faced the worst depression in the nation's history, but his attacks upon it were hampered by his devotion to the theory that the forces that brought the crisis would soon bring the revival and then by his belief that there were too many areas in which the federal government had no power to act. In a succession of vetoes, he struck down measures proposing a national employment system or national relief, he reduced income tax rates, and only at the end of his term did he yield to popular pressure and set up agencies such as the Reconstruction Finance Corporation to make emergency loans to assist business.

After his 1932 defeat, Hoover returned to private business. In 1946, President Truman charged him with various world food missions; and from 1947 to 1949 and 1953 to 1955, he was head of the Commission on Organization of the Executive Branch of the Government. He died in New York City on Oct. 20, 1964.

FRANKLIN DELANO ROOSEVELT was born in Hyde Park, N.Y., on Jan. 30, 1882. A Harvard graduate, he attended Columbia Law School and was admitted to the New York bar. In 1910, he was elected to the New York State Senate as a Democrat. Reelected in 1912, he was appointed Assistant Secretary of the Navy by Woodrow Wilson the next year. In 1920, his radiant personality and his war service resulted in his nomination for vice president as James M. Cox's running mate. After his defeat, he returned to law practice in New York. In August 1921, Roosevelt was stricken with infantile paralysis while on vacation at Campobello, New Brunswick. After a long and gallant fight, he recovered partial use of his legs. In 1924 and 1928, he led the fight at the Democratic national conventions for the nomination of Gov. Alfred E. Smith of New York, and in 1928 Roosevelt was himself induced to run for governor of New York. He was elected, and was re-elected in 1930.

In 1932, Roosevelt received the Democratic nomination for president and immediately launched a campaign that brought new spirit to a weary and discouraged nation. He defeated Hoover by a wide margin. His first term was characterized by an unfolding of the New Deal program, with greater benefits for labor, the farmers, and the unemployed, and the progressive estrangement of most of the business community.

At an early stage, Roosevelt became aware of the menace to world peace posed by totalitarian fascism, and from 1937 on he tried to focus public attention on the trend of events in Europe and Asia. As a result, he was widely denounced as a warmonger. He was re-elected in 1936 over Gov. Alfred M. Landon of Kansas by the overwhelming electoral margin of 523 to 8, and the gathering international crisis prompted him to run for an unprecedented third term in 1940. He defeated Wendell L. Willkie.

Roosevelt's program to bring maximum aid to Britain and, after June 1941, to Russia was opposed, until the Japanese attack on Pearl Harbor restored national unity. During the war, Roosevelt shelved the New Deal in the interests of conciliating the business community, both in order to get full production during the war and to prepare the way for a united acceptance of the peace settlements after the war. A series of conferences with Winston Churchill and Joseph Stalin laid down the bases for the postwar world. In 1944 he was elected to a fourth term, running against Gov. Thomas E. Dewey of New York.

On April 12, 1945, Roosevelt died of a cerebral hemorrhage at Warm Springs, Ga., shortly after his return from the Yalta Conference. His wife, Anna Eleanor Roosevelt, whom he married in 1905, was a woman of great ability who made significant contributions to her husband's policies.

HARRY S. TRUMAN was born on a farm near Lamar, Mo., on May 8, 1884. During World War I, he served in France as a captain with the 129th Field Artillery. He married Bess Wallace in 1919. After engaging briefly and unsuccessfully in the haberdashery business in Kansas City, Mo., Truman entered local politics. Under the sponsorship of Thomas Pendergast, Democratic boss of Missouri, he held a number of local offices, preserving his personal honesty in the midst of a notoriously corrupt political machine. In 1934, he was elected to the Senate and was re-elected in 1940. During his first term he was a loyal but quiet supporter of the New Deal, but in his second term, an appointment as head of a Senate committee to investigate war production brought out his special qualities of honesty, common sense, and hard work, and he won widespread respect.

Elected vice president in 1944, Truman became president upon Roosevelt's sudden death in April 1945 and was immediately faced with the problems of winding down the war against the Axis and preparing the nation for postwar adjustment.

The years 1947–48 were distinguished by civil-rights proposals, the Truman Doctrine to contain the spread of Communism, and the Marshall Plan to aid in the economic reconstruction of war-ravaged nations. Truman's general record, highlighted by a vigorous Fair Deal campaign, brought about his unexpected election in 1948 over the heavily favored Thomas E. Dewey.

Truman's second term was primarily concerned with the Cold War with the Soviet Union, the implementing of the North Atlantic Pact, the United Nations police action in Korea, and the vast rearmament program with its accompanying problems of economic stabilization.

On March 29, 1952, Truman announced that he would not run again for the presidency. After leaving the White House, he returned to his home in Independence, Mo., to write his memoirs. He further busied himself with the Harry S. Truman Library there. He died in Kansas City, Mo., on Dec. 26, 1972.

DWIGHT DAVID EISENHOWER was born in Denison, Tex., on Oct. 14, 1890. His ancestors lived in Germany and emigrated to America, settling in Pennsylvania, early in the 18th century. His father, David, had a general store in Hope, Kan., which failed. After a brief time in Texas, the family moved to Abilene, Kan.

After graduating from Abilene High School in 1909, Eisenhower did odd jobs for almost two years. He won an appointment to the Naval Academy at Annapolis, but was too old for admittance. Then he received an appointment in 1910 to West Point, from which he graduated as a second lieutenant in 1915.

He did not see service in World War I, having been stationed at Fort Sam Houston, Tex. There he met Mamie Geneva Doud, whom he married in Denver on July 1, 1916, and by whom he had two sons: Doud Dwight (died in infancy),and John Sheldon Doud.

Eisenhower served in the Philippines from 1935 to 1939 with Gen. Douglas MacArthur. Afterward, Gen. George C. Marshall, the Army Chief of Staff, brought him into the War Department's General Staff and in 1942 placed him in command of the invasion of North Africa. In 1944, he was made Supreme Allied Commander for the invasion of Europe.

After the war, Eisenhower served as Army Chief of Staff from November 1945 until February 1948, when he was appointed president of Columbia University.

In December 1950, President Truman recalled Eisenhower to active duty to command the North Atlantic Treaty Organization forces in Europe. He held his post until the end of May 1952.

At the Republican convention of 1952 in Chicago, Eisenhower won the presidential nomination on the first ballot in a close race with Senator Robert A. Taft of Ohio. In the election, he defeated Gov. Adlai E. Stevenson of Illinois.

Through two terms, Eisenhower hewed to moderate domestic policies. He sought peace through Free World strength in an era of new nationalisms, nuclear missiles, and space exploration. He fostered alliances pledging the United States to resist Red aggression in Europe, Asia, and Latin America. The Eisenhower Doctrine of 1957 extended commitments to the Middle East.

At home, the popular president lacked Republican Congressional majorities after 1954, but he was re-elected in 1956 by 457 electoral votes to 73 for Stevenson.

While retaining most Fair Deal programs, he stressed "fiscal responsibility" in domestic affairs. A moderate in civil rights, he sent troops to Little Rock, Ark., to enforce court-ordered school integration.

With his wartime rank restored by Congress, Eisenhower returned to private life and the role of elder statesman, with his vigor hardly impaired by a heart attack, an ileitis operation, and a mild stroke suffered while in office. He died in Washington on March 28, 1969.

JOHN FITZGERALD KENNEDY was born in Brookline, Mass., on May 29, 1917. His father, Joseph P. Kennedy, was Ambassador to Great Britain from 1937 to 1940.

Kennedy was graduated from Harvard University in 1940 and joined the Navy the next year. He became skipper of a PT boat that was sunk in the Pacific by a Japanese destroyer. Although given up for lost, he swam to a safe island, towing an injured enlisted man.

After recovering from a war-aggravated spinal injury, Kennedy entered politics in 1946 and was elected to Congress. In 1952, he ran against Senator Henry Cabot Lodge, Jr., of Massachusetts, and won.

Kennedy was married on Sept. 12, 1953, to Jacqueline Lee Bouvier, by whom he had three children: Caroline, John Fitzgerald, Jr., and Patrick Bouvier (died in infancy).

In 1957 Kennedy won the Pulitzer Prize for a book he had written earlier, *Profiles in Courage.*

After strenuous primary battles, Kennedy won the Democratic presidential nomination on the first ballot at the 1960 Los Angeles convention. With a plurality of only 118,574 votes, he carried the election over Vice President Richard M. Nixon and became the first Roman Catholic president.

Kennedy brought to the White House the dynamic idea of a "New Frontier" approach in dealing with problems at home, abroad, and in the dimensions of space. Out of his leadership in his first few months in office came the 10-year Alliance for Progress to aid Latin America, the Peace Corps, and accelerated programs that brought the first Americans into orbit in the race in space.

Failure of the U.S.-supported Cuban invasion in April 1961 led to the entrenchment of the Communist-backed Castro regime, only 90 miles from United States soil. When it became known that Soviet offensive missiles were being installed in Cuba in 1962, Kennedy ordered a naval "quarantine" of the island and moved troops into position to eliminate this threat to U.S. security. The world seemed on the brink of a nuclear war until Soviet Premier Khrushchev ordered the removal of the missiles.

A sudden "thaw," or the appearance of one, in the cold war came with the agreement with the Soviet Union on a limited test-ban treaty signed in Moscow on Aug. 6, 1963.

In his domestic policies, Kennedy's proposals for medical care for the aged, expanded area redevelopment, and aid to education were defeated, but on minimum wage, trade legislation, and other measures he won important victories.

Widespread racial disorders and demonstrations led to Kennedy's proposing sweeping civil rights legislation. As his third year in office drew to a close, he also recommended an $11-billion tax cut to bolster the economy. Both measures were pending in Congress when Kennedy, looking forward to a second term, journeyed to Texas for a series of speeches.

While riding in a procession in Dallas on Nov. 22, 1963, he was shot to death by an assassin firing from an upper floor of a building. The alleged assassin, Lee Harvey Oswald, was killed two days later in the Dallas city jail by Jack Ruby, owner of a striptease place.

At 46 years of age, Kennedy became the fourth president to be assassinated and the eighth to die in office.

LYNDON BAINES JOHNSON was born in Stonewall, Tex., on Aug. 27, 1908. On both sides of his family he had a political heritage mingled with a Baptist background of preachers and teachers. Both his father and his paternal grandfather served in the Texas House of Representatives.

After his graduation from Southwest Texas State Teachers College, Johnson taught school for two years. He went to Washington in 1932 as secretary to Rep. Richard M. Kleberg. During this time, he married Claudia Alta Taylor, known as "Lady Bird." They had two children: Lynda Bird and Luci Baines.

In 1935, Johnson became Texas administrator for the National Youth Administration. Two years later, he was elected to Congress as an all-out supporter of Franklin D. Roosevelt, and served until 1949. He was the first member of Congress to enlist in the armed forces after the attack on Pearl Harbor. He served in the Navy in the Pacific and won a Silver Star.

Johnson was elected to the Senate in 1948 after he had captured the Democratic nomination by only 87 votes. He was 40 years old. He became the Senate Democratic leader in 1953. A heart attack in 1955 threatened to end his political career, but he recovered fully and resumed his duties.

At the height of his power as Senate leader, Johnson sought the Democratic nomination for president in 1960. When he lost to John F. Kennedy, he surprised even some of his closest associates by accepting second place on the ticket.

Johnson was riding in another car in the motorcade when Kennedy was assassinated in Dallas on Nov. 22, 1963. He took the oath of office in the presidential jet on the Dallas airfield.

With Johnson's insistent backing, Congress finally adopted a far-reaching civil-rights bill, a voting-rights bill, a Medicare program for the aged, and measures to improve education and conservation. Congress also began what Johnson described as "an all-out war" on poverty.

Amassing a record-breaking majority of nearly 16 million votes, Johnson was elected president in his own right in 1964, defeating Senator Barry Goldwater of Arizona.

The double tragedy of a war in Southeast Asia and urban riots at home marked Johnson's last two years in office. Faced with disunity in the nation and challenges within his own party, Johnson surprised the country on March 31, 1968, with the announcement that he would not be a candidate for re-election. He died of a heart attack suffered at his LBJ Ranch on Jan. 22, 1973.

RICHARD MILHOUS NIXON was born in Yorba Linda, Calif., on Jan. 9, 1913, to Midwestern-bred parents, Francis A. and Hannah Milhous Nixon, who raised their five sons as Quakers.

Nixon was a high school debater and was undergraduate president at Whittier College in California, where he was graduated in 1934. As a scholarship student at Duke University Law School in North Carolina, he graduated third in his class in 1937.

After five years as a lawyer, Nixon joined the Navy in August 1942. He was an air transport officer in the South Pacific and a legal officer stateside before his discharge in 1946 as a lieutenant commander.

Running for Congress in California as a Republican in 1946, Nixon defeated Rep. Jerry Voorhis. As a member of the House Un-American Activities Committee, he made a name as an investigator of Alger Hiss, a former high State Department official, who was later jailed for perjury. In 1950, Nixon defeated Rep. Helen Gahagan Douglas, a Democrat, for the Senate. He was criticized for portraying her as a Communist dupe.

Nixon's anti-Communism, his Western base, and his youth figured in his selection in 1952 to run for vice president on the ticket headed by Dwight D. Eisenhower. Demands for Nixon's withdrawal followed disclosure that California businessmen had paid some of his Senate office expenses. He televised rebuttal, known as "the Checkers speech" (named for a cocker spaniel given to the Nixons), brought him support from the public and from Eisenhower. The ticket won easily in 1952 and again in 1956.

Eisenhower gave Nixon substantive assignments, including missions to 56 countries. In Moscow in 1959, Nixon won acclaim for his defense of U.S. interests in an impromptu "kitchen debate" with Soviet Premier Nikita S. Khrushchev.

Nixon lost the 1960 race for the presidency to John F. Kennedy.

In 1962, Nixon failed in a bid for California's governorship and seemed to be finished as a national candidate. He became a Wall Street lawyer, but kept his old party ties and developed new ones through constant travels to speak for Republicans.

Nixon won the 1968 Republican presidential nomination after a shrewd primary campaign, then made Gov. Spiro T. Agnew of Maryland his surprise choice for vice president. In the election, they edged out the Democratic ticket headed by Vice President Hubert H. Humphrey by 510,314 votes out of 73,212,065 cast.

Committed to wind down the U.S. role in the Vietnamese War, Nixon pursued "Vietnamization"—training and equipping South Vietnamese to do their own fighting. American ground combat forces in Vietnam fell steadily from 540,000 when Nixon took office to none in 1973 when the military draft was ended. But there was heavy continuing use of U.S. air power.

Nixon improved relations with Moscow and reopened the long-closed door to mainland China with a good-will trip there in February 1972. In May of that year, he visited Moscow and signed agreements on arms limitation and trade expansion and approved plans for a joint U.S.-Soviet space mission in 1975.

Inflation was a campaign issue for Nixon, but he failed to master it as president. On Aug. 15, 1971, with unemployment edging up, Nixon abruptly announced a new economic policy: a 90-day wage-price freeze, stimulative tax cuts, a temporary 10% tariff, and spending cuts. A second phase, imposing guidelines on wage, price and rent boosts, was announced October 7.

The economy responded in time for the 1972 campaign, in which Nixon played up his foreign-policy achievements. Played down was the burglary on June 17, 1972, of Democratic national headquarters in the Watergate apartment complex in Washington. The Nixon-Agnew re-election campaign cost a record $60 million and swamped the Democratic ticket headed by Senator George McGovern of South Dakota with a plurality of 17,999,528 out of 77,718,554 votes. Only Massachusetts, with 14 electoral votes, and the District of Columbia, with 3, went for McGovern.

In January 1973, hints of a cover-up emerged at the trial of six men found guilty of the Wtergate burglary. With a Senate investigation under way, Nixon announced on April 30 the resignations of his top aides, H. R. Haldeman and John D. Ehrlichman, and the dismissal of White House counsel John Dean III. Dean was the star witness at televised Senate hearings that exposed both a White House cover-up of Watergate and massive illegalities in Republican fund-raising in 1972.

The hearings also disclosed that Nixon had routinely tape-recorded his office meetings and telephone conversations.

On Oct. 10, 1973, Agnew resigned as vice president, then pleaded no-contest to a negotiated federal charge of evading income taxes on alleged bribes. Two days later, Nixon nominated the House minority leader, Rep. Gerald R. Ford of Michigan, as the new vice president. Congress confirmed Ford on Dec. 6, 1973.

In June 1974, Nixon visited Israel and four Arab nations. Then he met in Moscow with Soviet leader Leonid I. Brezhnev and reached preliminary nuclear arms limitation agreements.

But, in the month after his return, Watergate ended the Nixon regime. On July 24 the Supreme Court ordered Nixon to surrender subpoenaed tapes. On July 30, the Judiciary Committee referred three impeachment articles to the full membership. On August 5, Nixon bowed to the Supreme Court and released tapes showing he halted an FBI probe of the Watergate burglary six days after it occurred. It was in effect an admission of obstruction of justice, and impeachment appeared inevitable.

Nixon resigned on Aug. 9, 1974, the first president ever to do so. A month later, President Ford issued an unconditional pardon for any offenses Nixon might have committed as president, thus forestalling possible prosecution.

In 1940, Nixon married Thelma Catherine (Pat) Ryan. They had two daughters, Patricia (Tricia) Cox and Julie, who married Dwight David Eisenhower II, grandson of the former president.

GERALD RUDOLPH FORD was born in Omaha, Neb., on July 14, 1913, the only child of Leslie and Dorothy Gardner King. His parents were divorced in 1915. His mother moved to Grand Rapids, Mich., and married Gerald R. Ford. The boy was renamed for his stepfather.

Ford captained his high school football team in Grand Rapids, and a football scholarship took him to the University of Michigan, where he starred as varsity center before his graduation in 1935. A job as assistant football coach at Yale gave him an opportunity to attend Yale Law School, from which he graduated in the top third of his class in 1941.

He returned to Grand Rapids to practice law, but entered the Navy in April 1942. He saw wartime service in the Pacific on the light aircraft carrier *Monterey* and was a lieutenant commander when he returned to Grand Rapids early in 1946 to resume law practice and dabble in politics.

Ford was elected to Congress in 1948 for the first of his 13 terms in the House. He was soon assigned to the influential Appropriations Committee and rose to become the ranking Republican on the subcommittee on Defense Department appropriations and an expert in the field.

As a legislator, Ford described himself as "a moderate on domestic issues, a conservative in fiscal affairs, and a dyed-in-the-wool internationalist." He carried the ball for Pentagon appropriations, was a hawk on the war in Vietnam, and kept a low profile on civil-rights issues.

He was also dependable and hard-working and popular with his colleagues. In 1963, he was elected chairman of the House Republican Conference. He served in 1963–64 as a member of the Warren Commission that investigated the assassination of John F. Kennedy. A revolt by dissatisfied younger Republicans in 1965 made him minority leader.

Ford shelved his hopes for the Speakership on Oct. 12, 1973, when Nixon nominated him to fill the vice presidency left vacant by Agnew's resignation under fire. It was the first use of the procedures for filling vacancies in the vice presidency laid down in the 25th Amendment to the Constitution, which Ford had helped enact.

Congress confirmed Ford as vice president on Dec. 6, 1973. Once in office, he said he did not believe Nixon had been involved in the Watergate scandals, but criticized his stubborn court battle against releasing tape recordings of Watergate-related conversations for use as evidence.

The scandals led to Nixon's unprecedented resignation on Aug. 9, 1974, and Ford was sworn in immediately as the 38th president, the first to enter the White House without winning a national election.

Ford assured the nation when he took office that "our long national nightmare is over" and pledged "openness and candor" in all his actions. He won a warm response from the Democratic 93rd Congress when he said he wanted "a good marriage" rather than a honeymoon with his former colleagues. In December 1974 Congressional majorities backed his choice of former New York Gov. Nelson A. Rockefeller as his successor in the again-vacant vice presidency.

The cordiality was chilled by Ford's announcement on Sept. 8, 1974, that he had granted an unconditional pardon to Nixon for any crimes he might have committed as president. Although no formal charges were pending, Ford said he feared "ugly passions" would be aroused if Nixon were brought to trial. The pardon was widely criticized.

To fight inflation, the new president first proposed fiscal restraints and spending curbs and a 5% tax surcharge that got nowhere in the Senate and House. Congress again rebuffed Ford in the spring of 1975 when he appealed for emergency military aid to help the governments of South Vietnam and Cambodia resist massive Communist offensives.

In November 1974, Ford visited Japan, South Korea, and the Soviet Union, where he and Soviet leader Leonid I. Brezhnev conferred in Vladivostok and reached a tentative agreement to limit the number of strategic offensive nuclear weapons. It was Ford's first meeting as president with Brezhnev, who planned a return visit to Washington in the fall of 1975.

Politically, Ford's fortunes improved steadily in the first half of 1975. Badly divided Democrats in Congress were unable to muster votes to override his vetoes of spending bills that exceeded his budget. He faced some right-wing opposition in his own party, but moved to pre-empt it with an early announcement—on July 8, 1975—of his intention to be a candidate in 1976.

Early state primaries in 1976 suggested an easy victory for Ford despite Ronald Reagan's bitter attacks on administration foreign policy and defense programs. But later Reagan primary successes threatened the President's lead. At the Kansas City convention, Ford was nominated by the narrow margin of 1,187 to 1,070. But Reagan had moved the party to the right, and Ford himself was regarded as a caretaker president lacking in strength and vision. He was defeated in November by Jimmy Carter.

In 1948, Ford married Elizabeth Anne (Betty) Bloomer. They had four children, Michael Gerald, John Gardner, Steven Meigs, and Susan Elizabeth.

JAMES EARL CARTER, JR., was born in the tiny village of Plains, Ga., Oct. 1, 1924, and grew up on the family farm at nearby Archery. Both parents were fifth-generation Georgians. His father, James Earl Carter, was known as a segregationist, but treated his black and white workers equally. Carter's mother, Lillian Gordy, was a matriarchal presence in home and community and opposed the then-prevailing code of racial inequality. The future President was baptized in 1935 in the conservative Southern Baptist Church and spoke often of being a "born again" Christian, although committed to the separation of church and state.

Carter married Rosalynn Smith, a neighbor, in 1946. Their first child, John William, was born a year later in Portsmouth, Va. Their other children are James Earl III, born in Honolulu in 1950; Donnel Jeffrey, born in New London, Conn., in 1952, and Amy Lynn, born in Plains in 1967.

In 1946 Carter was graduated from the U.S. Naval Academy at Annapolis and served in the nuclear-submarine program under Adm. Hyman G. Rickover. In 1954, after his father's death, he resigned from the Navy to take over the family's flourishing warehouse and cotton gin, with several thousand acres for growing seed peanuts.

Carter was elected to the Georgia Senate in 1962. In 1966 he lost the race for Governor, but was elected in 1970. His term brought a state government reorganization, sharply reduced agencies, increased economy and efficiency, and new social programs, all with no general tax increase. In 1972 the peanut farmer-politician set his sights on the Presidency and in 1974 built a base for himself as he criss-crossed the country as chairman of the Democratic Campaign Committee, appealing for revival and reform. In 1975 his image as a typical Southern white was erased when he won support of most of the old Southern civil-rights coalition after endorsement by Rep. Andrew Young, black Democrat from Atlanta, who had been the closest aide to the Rev. Martin Luther King, Jr. At Carter's 1971 inauguration as Governor he had called for an end to all forms of racial discrimination.

In the 1976 spring primaries, he won 19 out of 31 with a broad appeal to conservatives and liberals, black and white, poor and well-to-do. Throughout his campaigning Carter set forth his policies in his soft Southern voice, and with his electric-blue stare faced down skeptics who joked about "Jimmy Who?" His toothy smile became his trademark. He was nominated on the first roll-call vote of the 1976 Bicentennial Democratic National Convention in New York, and defeated Gerald R. Ford in November. Likewise, in 1980 he was renominated on the first ballot after vanquishing Senator Edward M. Kennedy of Massachusetts in the primaries. At the convention he defeated the Kennedy forces in their attempt to block a party rule that bound a large majority of pledged delegates to vote for Carter. In the election campaign, Carter attacked his rivals, Ronald Reagan and John B. Anderson, independent, with the warning that a Reagan Republican victory would heighten the risk of war and impede civil rights and economic opportunity. In November Carter lost to Reagan, who won 489 Electoral College votes and 51% of the popular tally, to 49 electoral votes and 41% for Carter.

In his one term, Carter fought hard for his programs against resistance from an independent-minded Democratic Congress that frustrated many pet projects although it overrode only two vetoes. Many of his difficulties were traced to his aides' brusqueness in dealing with Capitol Hill and insensitivity to Congressional feelings and tradition. Observers generally viewed public dissatisfaction with the "stagflation" economy as a principal factor in his defeat. Others included his jittery performance in the debate Oct. 28 with Reagan and the final uncertainties in the negotiations for freeing the Iranians' hostages, along with earlier staff problems, friction with Congress, long gasoline lines, and the months-long Iranian crisis, including the abortive sally in April 1980 to free the hostages. The President, however, did deflect criticism resulting from the activities of his brother, Billy. Yet, assessments of his record noted many positive elements. There was, for one thing, peace throughout his term, with no American combat deaths and with a brake on the advocates of force. Regarded as perhaps his greatest personal achievements were the Camp David accords between Israel and Egypt and the resulting treaty—the first between Israel and an Arab neighbor. The treaty with China and the Panama Canal treaties were also major achievements. Carter worked for nuclear-arms control. His concern for international human rights was credited with saving lives and reducing torture, and he supported the British policy that ended internecine warfare in Rhodesia, now Zimbabwe. Domestically, his environmental record was a major accomplishment. His judicial appointments won acclaim; the Southerner who had forsworn racism made 265 choices for the Federal bench that included minority members and women. On energy, he ended by price decontrols the practice of holding U.S. petroleum prices far below world levels. —*A.P.R., Jr.*

RONALD REAGAN rode to the presidency in 1980 on a tide of resurgent right-wing sentiment among an electorate battered by winds of unwanted change, longing for a distant, simpler era. For most of his first six years in office, he retained the public's favor and used his political power to achieve his fiscal and policy goals.

But in 1986 the Iran-Contra scandal broke, shortly after the Democrats gained control of the Senate. Observers agreed that Reagan's presidency had been weakened by the two unrelated events, and his standing with the public plummeted. Then, the weeks-long Congressional hearings in the summer of 1987 heard an array of Administration present and former officials tell their tales of a White House riven by deceit and undercover maneuvering. Yet no breath of illegality touched the President's personal reputation; on Aug. 12, 1987, he told the nation that he had not known of questionable activities but agreed that he was "ultimately accountable."

Hopes of repairing his tarnished image rested on the brightening prospect of an arms-control agreement with the Soviet Union.

Ronald Reagan, actor turned politician, New Dealer turned conservative, came to the films and politics from a thoroughly Middle-American background—middle class, Middle West and small town. He was born in Tampico, Ill., Feb. 6, 1911, the second son of John Edward Reagan and Nelle Wilson Reagan, and the family later moved to Dixon, Ill. The father, of Irish descent, was a shop clerk and merchant with Democratic sympathies. It was an impoverished family; young Ronald sold homemade popcorn at high school games and worked as a lifeguard to earn money for his college tuition. When the father got a New Deal WPA job, the future President became an ardent Roosevelt Democrat.

Reagan won a B.A. degree in 1932 from Eureka (Ill.) College, where a photographic memory aided in his studies and in debating and college theatricals. In a Depression year, he was making $100 a week as a sports announcer for radio station WHO in Des Moines, Iowa, from 1932 to 1937. His career as a film and TV actor stretched from 1937 to 1966, and his salary climbed to $3,500 a week. As a World War II captain in Army film studios, Reagan recoiled from what he saw as the laziness of Civil Service workers, and moved to the Right. As president of the Screen Actors Guild, he resisted what he considered a Communist plot to subvert the film industry. With advancing age, Reagan left leading-man roles and became a television spokesman for the General Electric Company at $150, 000.

With oratorical skill his trademark, Reagan became an active Republican, and in 1964 made a dramatic speech supporting Senator Barry Goldwater, who became the party's presidential nominee. At the behest of a small group of conservative Southern California businessmen, he ran for governor with a pledge to cut spending, and was elected by almost a million votes over the political veteran, Democratic Gov. Edmund G. Brown, father of the later governor.

In the 1980 election battle against Jimmy Carter, Reagan broadened his appeal by espousing moderate policies, gaining much of his support from disaffected Democrats and blue-collar workers. The incoming Administration immediately set out to "turn the government around" with a new economic program. Over strenuous Congressional opposition, Reagan triumphed on his "supply side" theory to stimulate production and control inflation through tax cuts and sharp reductions in government spending. Through adroit maneuvering and use of personal charm on Congress and the public, he achieved the largest budget and tax cuts in recent U.S. history.

The President won high acclaim for his nomination of Sandra Day O'Connor as the first woman on the Supreme Court. His later nominations met increasing opposition but did much to tilt the Court's orientation to the Right.

In 1982, the President's popularity had slipped as the economy declined into the worst recession in 40 years, with persistent high unemployment and interest rates. Initial support for "supply side" economics faded but the President won crucial battles in Congress.

Internationally, Reagan confronted numerous critical problems in his first term. The successful invasion of Grenada accomplished much diplomatically. But the intervention in Lebanon and the withdrawal of Marines after a disastrous terrorist attack were regarded as military failures. The President also had to cope with Israel's invasion of Lebanon, the Argentine invasion of the Falklands and the precipitate resignation of Secretary of State Alexander M. Haig Jr.

The popular President won reelection in the 1984 landslide, with the economy improving and inflation under control. Domestically, a tax reform bill that Reagan backed became law. But the constantly growing budget deficit remained a constant irritant, with the President and Congress persistently at odds over priorities in spending for defense and domestic programs. His foreign policy met stiffening opposition, with Congress increasingly reluctant to increase spending for the Nicaraguan "Contras" and the Pentagon and to expand the development of the MX missile. But even severe critics praised Reagan's restrained but decisive handling of the crisis following the hijacking of an American plane in Beirut by Moslem extremists. The attack on Libya in April 1986 galvanized the nation, although it drew scathing disapproval from the NATO alliance.

The Iran-Contra crisis burst in late 1986 and for months in 1987 dominated the news, shaking the foundations of the Reagan presidency and straining the Allies' confidence in U.S. credibility.

However, as the year drew on, the prospects improved for an historic agreement with the Soviet Union to abolish intermediate-range atomic weapons. The "Star Wars" issue, on which the Reykjavik summit conference had foundered, still dogged talks on control of long-range weapons.

Barely three months into his first term, Reagan was the target of an assassin's bullet; his courageous comeback won public admiration. In 1985 and in early 1986 the President underwent abdominal surgery for removal of intestinal polyps, which proved to be benign, or cancerous but not dangerous. In 1985, 1986 and 1987, surgeons removed skin cancer cells from Reagan's nose.

Reagan is devoted to his wife, Nancy, whom he married after his divorce from the screen actress Jane Wyman. The Reagans spend much time together at the White House and Camp David and at their California home and ranch when Presidential duties permit. Reagan enjoys horseback riding and is a connoisseur of fine wines. The children of the first marriage are Maureen, his daughter by Miss Wyman, and Michael, an adopted son. In the present marriage the children are Patricia and Ron.

—A.P.R. Jr.

George Bush

Vice President

As a busy surrogate for the President, George Bush faithfully carried out his duties as two-term Vice President. And, with them, he pursued his quest for the Presidential nomination in 1988 as Republican candidate to succeed Ronald Reagan.

In 1987 he was a leading contender in that quest, his supporters in control of several state G.O.P. machines and with Reagan's tacit endorsement. Without direct involvement in the Iran-Contra scandal, he refrained, unlike his rivals, from attacking the President's leadership. He thus avoided implications of disloyalty. Yet his public demeanor caused some critics to fear that he displayed a lack of leadership as well as decisiveness.

In his subdued way, Bush has been influential in White House decisions, particularly in foreign affairs. He was a key supporter of the 1986 Reagan raid on Libya in reprisal for terrorist attacks, and had had a role in the decision to withdraw American forces from Lebanon after its government collapsed in early 1984.

For a few hours in July 1985 Bush emerged as the nation's leader while President Reagan underwent major surgery. And Bush himself had an operation in May 1986 for the removal of a small facial skin cancer.

Bush traveled as the President's representative on important diplomatic missions. Among these were an inspection of African drought areas and attendance at a Geneva conference on famine relief. He led the U.S. delegation to the Chernenko funeral in Moscow, and at Brazil's inauguration of a civilian President. He visited China to show American support for China's economic reforms.

Politically, public-opinion polls gave him strong support despite intense opposition from right-wing front-runners in the Republican sweepstakes.

The 1984 election had been his fifth, and second successful, bid for the Vice-Presidency. By then, despite his reputation as a relative liberal, he had earned acclaim for devotion to Reagan's conservative policies. And right-wingers could relish his record as a two-term Texas Congressman and his background as a former Director of Central Intelligence and a World War II Navy pilot who had won the Distinguished Flying Cross.

George Bush was born June 12, 1924, in Milton, Mass., to Prescott and Dorothy Bush. The family later moved to Connecticut. Bush attended Phillips Academy at Andover, Mass., and served in the Navy from 1942 to 1945. After the war he earned an economics degree and Phi Beta Kappa key at Yale in 2 1/2 years.

In 1945 he married Barbara Pierce of Rye, N.Y., daughter of a magazine publisher, and in 1948 they left Connecticut for a Texas business career. In 1980 he reported an estimated wealth of some $1.4 million. After Bush's second unsuccessful Senate race, President Nixon appointed him U.S. delegate to the United Nations with the rank of Ambassador, and later he became Republican National Chairman. He headed the U.S. liaison office in Peking before becoming Director of Central Intelligence.

The Bushes have lived in 17 cities and 28 homes and have traveled in 26 countries. In her husband's frequent absences, Mrs. Bush has been the "matriarch" of a family of four boys and a girl.

Despite Republican emphasis on his Texas connection, Bush sold his Houston home several years ago and now lives at the Vice President's quarters in Washington and the family estate at Kennebunkport, Me. *—A.P.R., Jr.*

Glossary of Political Terms

Balanced Ticket—A party ticket listing candidates chosen to win support from regional, ethnic, minority, and other elements of the population.

Beauty Contest—The preferential primary in which voters indicate their preference for a candidate in a nonbinding ballot.

Bloc—Group of legislators, usually of both major parties, who vote together for some particular interest.

Brokered Convention—Decisions on candidates and major issues made by party leaders rather than by rank-and-file delegates.

Bullet Vote—Balloting in which the electorate concentrates on single candidates or issues to the neglect of the rest of the slate.

Confirmation—Senate action to validate an appointment, treaty, or other action by the President.

Dark Horse—An entrant into a political contest not previously mentioned. A person unexpectedly nominated, especially at a party convention.

Direct Primary—A party primary in which its members nominate the candidates by direct vote. Also used to choose convention delegates and party leaders. Primaries can be open to members of all parties, making a "crossover" vote possible, or restricted to members of the one party.

Equal Time—The legal right to equivalent time on radio or television to reply to charges in a political campaign made on the same medium.

Favorite Son—A state political leader to whom the party organization pledges its Presidential nominating delegates to avoid early pressure from declared candidates and to increase the state's delegation's bargaining power at the nominating convention.

Gerrymander—The division of a state, county, or other political unit into election districts so as to give one political party a majority in many districts and to concentrate the other party's voting strength into as few districts as possible. In brief, boundary manipulation for political advantage.

Machine Politics—The control of party decisions by the organized group of persons who conduct or direct the activities of a political party or similar organization.

Protest Vote—A vote expressing broad disapproval of an official or party policy, stressing negative reaction.

Slush Fund—A Congressman's office account—contributions are unlimited—the money is used to help run his office, mailings, etc.

Stalking Horse—A candidate used to conceal the candidacy of a more important candidate or to draw votes from a rival.

GREAT DISASTERS

This list is not all-inclusive due to space limitations. Only disasters involving great loss of life and/or property, historical interest, or unusual circumstances are listed. For later disasters see *Current Events* of 1987.

Earthquakes and Volcanic Eruptions

A.D. 79 **Aug. 24, Italy:** eruption of Mt. Vesuvius buried cities of Pompeii and Herculaneum, killing thousands.

1556 **Jan. 24, Shaanxi (Shensi) Province, China:** most deadly earthquake in history; 830,000 killed.

1755 **Nov. 1, Portugal:** one of the most severe of recorded earthquakes leveled Lisbon and was felt as far away as southern France and North Africa; 10,000–20,000 killed in Lisbon.

1883 **Aug. 26–28, Netherlands Indies:** eruption of Krakatau; violent explosions destroyed two thirds of island. Sea waves occurred as far away as Cape Horn, and possibly England. Estimated 36,000 dead.

1902 **May 8, Martinique, West Indies:** Mt. Pelée erupted and wiped out city of St. Pierre; 40,000 dead.

1908 **Dec. 28, Messina, Sicily:** about 85,000 killed and city totally destroyed.

1915 **Jan. 13, Avezzano, Italy:** earthquake left 29,980 dead.

1920 **Dec. 16, Gansu (Kansu) Province, China:** earthquake killed 200,000.

1923 **Sept. 1, Japan:** earthquake destroyed third of Tokyo and most of Yokohama; more than 140,000 killed.

1933 **March 10, Long Beach, Calif.:** 117 left dead by earthquake.

1935 **May 31, India:** earthquake at Quetta killed an estimated 50,000.

1939 **Jan. 24, Chile:** earthquake razed 50,000 sq mi.; about 30,000 killed.

Dec. 27, Northern Turkey: severe quakes destroyed city of Erzingan; about 100,000 casualties.

1950 **Aug. 15, India:** earthquake affected 30,000 sq mi. in Assam; 20,000–30,000 believed killed.

1963 **July 26, Skoplje, Yugoslavia:** four fifths of city destroyed; 1,011 dead, 3,350 injured.

1964 **March 27, Alaska:** strongest earthquake ever to strike North America hit 80 miles east of Anchorage; followed by seismic wave 50 feet high that traveled 8,445 miles at 450 miles per hour; 117 killed.

1970 **May 31, Peru:** earthquake left 50,000 dead, 17,000 missing.

1972 **April 10, Iran:** 5,000 killed in earthquake 600 miles south of Teheran.

Dec. 22, Managua, Nicaragua: earthquake devastated city, leaving up to 6,000 dead.

Worst United States Disasters

Aircraft

1979 **May 25, Chicago:** American Airlines DC-10 lost left engine upon take-off and crashed seconds later, killing all 272 persons aboard and three on the ground in worst U.S. air disaster.

Dam

1928 **March 12, Santa Paula, Calif.:** collapse of St. Francis Dam left 450 dead.

Earthquake

1906 **April 18, San Francisco:** earthquake accompanied by fire razed more than 4 sq mi.; more than 500 dead or missing.

Explosion

1947 **April 16-18, Texas City, Tex.:** most of city destroyed, 561 dead following explosion on ship.

Fire

1871 **Oct. 8, Peshtigo, Wis.:** over 1,200 lives lost and 2 billion trees burned in forest fire.

Flood

1889 **May 31, Johnstown, Pa.:** more than 2,200 died in flood.

Hurricane

1900 **Aug. 27-Sept. 15, Galveston, Tex.:** over 6,000 died from devastation due to both winds and tidal wave.

Marine

1865 **April 27, *Sultana*:** boiler explosion on Mississippi River steamboat near Memphis, 1,547 killed.

Mine

1907 **Dec. 6, Monongha, W. Va.:** coal mine explosion killed 361.

Railroad

1918 **July 9, Nashville, Tenn.:** 101 killed in a two-train collision near Nashville.

Submarine

1963 **April 10, *Thresher*:** atomic-powered submarine sank in North Atlantic: 129 dead.

Tornado

1925 **March 18, Great Tri-State Tornado:** Missouri, Illinois, and Indiana; 695 deaths. Eight additional tornadoes in Kentucky, Tennessee, and Alabama raised day's toll to 792 dead.

1976 **Feb. 4, Guatemala:** earthquake left over 23,000 dead.

July 28, Tangshan, China: earthquake devastated 20-sq-mi. area of city leaving estimated 242,000 dead.

Aug. 17, Mindanao, Philippines: earthquake and tidal wave left up to 8,000 dead or missing.

1977 **March 4, Bucharest:** earthquake razed most of downtown Bucharest; 1,541 reported dead, over 11,000 injured.

1978 **Sept. 16, Tabas, Iran:** earthquake destroyed city in eastern Iran, leaving 25,000 dead.

1980 **Nov. 23, Naples, Italy:** 2,735 killed when earthquake struck southern Italy.

1982 **Dec. 13, Yemen:** 2,800 reported dead in earthquake.

1985 **Sept. 19–20, Mexico:** earthquake registering 8.1 on Richter scale struck central and southwestern regions, devastating part of Mexico City and three coastal states. An estimated 25,000 killed.

Nov. 14–16, Colombia: eruption of Nevada del Ruiz, 85 miles northwest of Bogatá, caused mud slides which buried most of the town of Armero and devastated Chinchiná. An estimated 25,000 were killed.

Floods, Avalanches, and Tidal Waves

1228 **Holland:** 100,000 persons reputedly drowned by sea flood in Friesland.

1642 **China:** rebels destroyed Kaifeng seawall; 300,000 drowned.

1896 **June 15, Sanriku, Japan:** earthquake and tidal wave killed 27,000.

1953 **Northwest Europe:** storm followed by floods devastated North Sea coastal areas. Netherlands was hardest hit with 1,794 dead.

1959 **Dec. 2, Frejus, France:** flood caused by collapse of Malpasset Dam left 412 dead.

1960 **Agadir, Morocco:** 10,000–12,000 dead as earthquake set off tidal wave and fire, destroying most of city.

1962 **Jan. 10, Peru:** avalanche down Huascaran, extinct Andean volcano, killed more than 3,000 persons.

1963 **Oct. 9, Italy:** landslide into the Vaiont Dam; flood killed about 2,000.

1966 **Oct. 21, Aberfan, Wales:** avalanche of coal, waste, mud, and rocks killed 144 persons, including 116 children in school.

1969 **Jan. 18–26, Southern California:** floods and mudslides from heavy rains caused widespread property damage; at least 100 dead. Another downpour (Feb. 23–26) caused further floods and mudslides; at least 18 dead.

1970 **Nov. 13, East Pakistan:** 200,000 killed by cyclone-driven tidal wave from Bay of Bengal. Over 100,000 missing.

1971 **Sept. 29, Orissa State, India:** cyclone and tidal wave off Bay of Bengal killed as many as 10,000.

1972 **Feb. 26, Man, W. Va.:** more than 118 died when slag-pile dam collapsed under pressure of torrential rains and flooded 17-mile valley.

June 9–10, Rapid City, S.D.: flash flood caused 237 deaths and $160 million in damage.

June 20, Eastern Seaboard: tropical storm Agnes, in 10-day rampage, caused widespread flash floods. Death toll was 129, 115,000 were left homeless, and damage estimated at $3.5 billion.

1976 **Aug. 1, Loveland, Colo.:** Flash flood along Route 34 in Big Thompson Canyon left 139 dead.

1977 **Nov. 19, Andhra Pradesh State, India:** cyclone and flood from Bay of Bengal left 7,000–10,000 dead.

Storms and Weather

(For U.S. tornadoes and hurricanes, see Index)

1864 **Oct. 5, India:** most of Calcutta denuded by cyclone; 70,000 killed.

1930 **Sept. 3. Santo Domingo:** hurricane killed about 2,000 and injured 6,000.

1934 **Sept. 21, Japan:** hurricane killed more than 4,000 on Honshu.

1942 **Oct. 16, India:** cyclone devastated Bengal; about 40,000 lives lost.

1963 **May 28–29, East Pakistan:** cyclone killed about 22,000 along coast.

Oct. 2–7, Caribbean: Hurricane Flora killed up to 7,000 in Haiti and Cuba.

1965 **May 11–12 and June 1–2, East Pakistan:** cyclones killed about 47,000.

Dec. 15, Karachi, Pakistan: cyclone killed about 10,000.

1974 **Sept. 20, Honduras:** Hurricane Fifi struck northern section of country, leaving 8,000 dead, 100,000 homeless.

Dec. 25, Darwin, Australia: cyclone destroyed nearly the entire city, causing mass evacuation.

1977 **Nov. 19, India:** cyclone struck state of Andhra Pradesh, killing 10,000.

Fires and Explosions

1666 **Sept. 2, England:** "Great Fire of London" destroyed St. Paul's Church, etc. Damage £10 million.

1835 **Dec. 16, New York City:** 530 buildings destroyed by fire.

1871 **Oct. 8, Chicago:** the "Chicago Fire" burned 17,450 buildings, killed 250 persons; $196 million damage.

1872 **Nov. 9, Boston:** fire destroyed 800 buildings; $75-million damage.

1876 **Dec. 5, New York City:** fire in Brooklyn Theater killed more than 300.

1881 **Dec. 8, Vienna:** at least 620 died in fire at Ring Theatre.

1894 **Sept. 1, Minnesota:** forest fire over 480-square-mile area destroyed six towns and killed 480 people.

1900 **May 1, Scofield, Utah:** explosion of blasting powder in coal mine killed 200.

June 30, Hoboken, N.J.: piers of North German Lloyd Steamship line burned; 326 dead.

1903 **Dec. 30, Chicago:** Iroquois Theatre fire killed 602.

1906 **March 10, France:** explosion in coal mine in Courrières killed 1,060.

1907 **Dec. 19, Jacobs Creek, Pa.:** explosion in coal mine left 239 dead.

1909 **Nov. 13, Cherry, Ill.:** explosion in coal mine killed 259.

1911 **March 25, New York City:** fire in Triangle Shirtwaist Factory fatal to 145.

1913 **Oct. 22, Dawson, N.M.:** coal mine explosion left 263 dead.

1917 **April 10, Eddystone, Pa.:** explosion in munitions plant killed 133.

Dec. 6, Canada: explosion and fire at Halifax when ammunition ship collided with a vessel; 1,500 dead.

Nuclear Power Plant Accidents

1952 **Dec. 12, Chalk River, near Ottawa, Canada:** A partial meltdown of the reactor's uranium fuel core resulted after the accidental removal of four control rods. Although millions of gallons of radioactive water accumulated inside the reactor, there were no injuries.

1957 **Oct. 7, Windscale Pile No. 1, north of Liverpool, England:** Fire in a graphite-cooled reactor spewed radiation over the countryside, contaminating a 200 sq mi area.

1979 **March 28, Three Mile Island, near Harrisburg, Pa.:** One of two reactors lost its coolant, which caused the radioactive fuel to overheat and caused a partial meltdown. Some radioactive material was released.

1986 **April 16, Chernobyl, near Kiev, U.S.S.R.:** Explosion and fire in the graphite core of one of four reactors released radioactive material which spread over part of the Soviet Union, Eastern Europe, Scandinavia, and later Western Europe, in the worst such accident to date.

1930 **April 21, Columbus, Ohio:** fire in Ohio State Penitentiary killed 320 convicts.

1937 **March 18, New London, Tex.:** explosion destroyed schoolhouse; 294 killed.

1942 **April 26, Manchuria:** explosion in Honkeiko Colliery killed 1,549.

Nov. 28, Boston: Cocoanut Grove nightclub fire killed 491.

1944 **July 6, Hartford, Conn.:** fire and ensuing stampede in main tent of Ringling Brothers Circus killed 168, injured 487.

July 17, Port Chicago, Calif.: 322 killed as ammunition ships explode.

Oct. 20, Cleveland: liquid-gas tanks exploded, killing 130.

1946 **Dec. 7, Atlanta:** fire in Winecoff Hotel killed 119.

1949 **Sept. 2, China:** fire on Chongqing (Chungking) waterfront killed 1,700.

1954 **May 26, off Quonset Point, R.I.:** explosion and fire aboard aircraft carrier *Bennington* killed 103 crewmen.

1956 **Aug. 7, Colombia:** about 1,100 reported killed when seven army ammunition trucks exploded at Cali.

Aug. 8, Belgium: 262 died in coal mine fire at Marcinelle.

1960 **Jan. 21, Coalbrook, South Africa:** coal mine explosion killed 437.

Nov. 13, Syria: 152 children killed in moviehouse fire.

1961 **Dec. 17, Niteroi, Brazil:** circus fire fatal to 323.

1962 **Feb. 7, Saarland, West Germany:** coal mine gas explosion killed 298.

1963 **Nov. 9, Japan:** explosion in coal mine at Omuta killed 447.

1965 **May 28, India:** coal mine fire in state of Bihar killed 375.

June 1, near Fukuoka, Japan: coal mine explosion killed 236.

1967 **May 22, Brussels:** fire in L'Innovation, major department store, left 322 dead.

July 29, off North Vietnam: fire on U.S. carrier *Forrestal* killed 134.

1969 **Jan. 14, Pearl Harbor, Hawaii:** nuclear aircraft carrier *Enterprise* ripped by explosions; 27 dead, 82 injured.

1970 **Nov. 1, Saint-Laurent-du-Pont, France:** fire in dance hall killed 146 young people.

1972 **May 13, Osaka, Japan:** 118 people died in fire in nightclub on top floor of Sennichi department store.

June 6, Wankie, Rhodesia: explosion in coal mine killed 427.

1973 **Nov. 29, Kumamoto, Japan:** fire in Taiyo department store killed 101.

1974 **Feb. 1, Sao Paulo, Brazil:** fire in upper stories of bank building killed 189 persons, many of whom leaped to death.

1975 **Dec. 27, Dhanbad, India:** explosion in coal mine followed by flooding from nearby reservoir left 372 dead.

1977 **May 28, Southgate, Ky.:** fire in Beverly Hills Supper Club; 167 dead.

1978 **July 11, Tarragona, Spain:** 140 killed at coastal campsite when tank truck carrying liquid gas overturned and exploded.

Aug. 20, Abadan, Iran: nearly 400 killed when arsonists set fire to crowded theater.

1982 **Dec. 18–21, Caracas, Venezuela:** power-plant fire leaves 128 dead.

1986 **Dec. 31, San Juan, P. R.:** arson fire in Dupont Plaza Hotel set by three hotel employees kills 96.

Shipwrecks

1833 **May 11, *Lady of the Lake:*** bound from England to Quebec, struck iceberg; 215 perished.

1853 **Sept. 29 *Annie Jane:*** emigrant vessel off coast of Scotland; 348 died.

1898 **Nov. 26, *City of Portland:*** Loss of 157 off Cape Cod.

1904 **June 15, *General Slocum:*** excursion steamer burned in East River, New York; 1,021 perished.

1912 **March 5, *Principe de Asturias:*** Spanish steamer struck rock off Sebastien Point; 500 drowned.

April 15, *Titanic:* sank after colliding with iceberg; 1,513 died.

1914 **May 29, *Empress of Ireland:*** sank after collision in St. Lawrence River; 1,024 perished.

1915 **July 24, *Eastland:*** Great Lakes excursion steamer overturned in Chicago River; 812 died.

1928 **Nov. 12, *Vestris:*** British steamer sank in gale off Virginia; 110 died.

1931 **June 14:** French excursion steamer overturned in gale off St. Nazaire; approximately 450 died.

1934 **Sept. 8, *Morro Castle:*** 134 killed in fire off Asbury Park, N.J.

1939 **May 23, *Squalus:*** submarine with 59 men sank off Hampton Beach, N.H.; 33 saved.

June 1, Submarine *Thetis:* sank in Liverpool Bay, England; 99 perished.

1942 **Oct. 2, *Queen Mary:*** rammed and sank a British cruiser; 338 aboard the cruiser died.

1945 **April 9:** U.S. ship, loaded with aerial bombs, exploded at Bari, Italy; at least 360 killed.

1948 **Dec. 3, *Kiangya:*** Chinese refugee ship wrecked in explosion; about 1,000 believed dead.

1949 **Sept. 17, *Noronic:*** Canadian Great Lakes cruise

Space Accidents

1967 **Jan. 27, Apollo 1:** A fire aboard the space capsule on the ground at Cape Kennedy, Fla. killed astronauts Virgil L. Grissom, Edward H. White, and Roger Chaffee.

April 23-24, Soyuz 1: Vladimir M. Komarov was killed when his craft crashed after its parachute lines released at 23,000 feet for re-entry, became snarled.

1971 **June 6-30, Soyuz 11:** Three cosmonauts, Georgi T. Dolrovolsky, Vladislav N. Volkov, and Viktor I. Patsayev, found dead in the craft after its automatic landing. Apparently the cause of death was loss of pressurization in the space craft during re-entry into the earth's atmosphere.

1986 **Jan 28, Challenger Space Shuttle:** Exploded 73 seconds after lift off, killing all seven crew members. They were: Christa McAuliffe, Francis R. Scobee, Michael J. Smith, Judith A. Resnick, Ronald E. McNair, Ellison S. Onizuka, and Gregory B. Jarvis. A booster leak ignited the fuel, causing the explosion.

ship burned at Toronto dock; about 130 died.

1952 **April 26, *Hobson:*** minesweeper collided with aircraft carrier *Wasp* and sank during night maneuvers in mid-Atlantic; 176 persons lost.

1953 **Jan. 9, *Chang Tyong-Ho:*** South Korean ferry foundered off Pusan; 249 reported dead.

Jan. 31, *Princess Victoria:* British ferry sank in Irish Sea; 133 lost.

1956 **July 25, *Andrea Doria:*** Italian liner collided with Swedish liner *Stockholm* off Nantucket Island, Mass., sinking next day; 52, mostly passengers on Italian ship, dead or unaccounted for; over 1,600 rescued.

1962 **April 8, *Dara,*** British liner, exploded and sank in Persian Gulf; 236 persons dead. Caused by time bomb.

1963 **May 4:** U.A.R. ferry capsized and sank in upper Nile; over 200 died.

1968 **Late May, *Scorpion:*** nuclear submarine sank in Atlantic 400 miles S.W. of Azores; 99 dead. (Located Oct. 31.)

1970 **Dec. 15:** ferry in Korean Strait capsized; 261 lost.

1976 **Oct. 20, Luling, La.:** ***George Prince,*** Mississippi River ferry, rammed by Norwegian tanker *Frosta;* 77 dead.

1983 **May 25, *10th of Ramadan,*** Nile steamer, caught fire and sank in Lake Nasser, near Aswan, Egypt; 272 dead and 75 missing.

1987 **March 9, Belgium:** British ferry capsizes after leaving Belgian port of Zeebrugge with 500 abroad; 134 drowned. Water rushing through open bow is believed to be probable cause.

Aircraft Accidents

1921 **Aug. 24, England:** *AR-2* British dirigible, broke in two on trial trip near Hull; 62 died.

1925 **Sept. 3, Caldwell, Ohio:** U.S. dirigible *Shenandoah* broke apart; 14 dead.

1930 **Oct. 5, Beauvais, France:** British dirigible R 101 crashed, killing 47.

1933 **April 4, New Jersey Coast:** U.S. dirigible *Akron* crashed; 73 died.

1937 **May 6, Lakehurst, N.J.:** German zeppelin *Hindenburg* destroyed by fire at tower mooring; 36 killed.

1945 **July 28, New York City:** U.S. Army bomber crashed into Empire State Building; 13 dead.

1952 **Jan. 22, Elizabeth, N.J.:** 29 killed, including former Secretary of War Robert P. Patterson, when airliner hit apartments; seven of dead were on ground.

1953 **June 18, near Tokyo:** crash of U.S. Air Force "Globemaster" killed 129 servicemen.

1960 **Feb. 25, Rio de Janeiro:** U.S. Navy plane, flying Navy musicians to perform at dinner given by visiting President Eisenhower, collided with Brazilian airliner, killing 61.

Dec. 16, New York City: United and Trans World planes collided in fog, crashed in two boroughs, killing 134 in air and on ground.

1961 **Feb. 15, near Brussels:** 72 on board and farmer on ground killed in crash of Sabena plane; U.S. figure skating team wiped out.

1966 **March 5, Japan:** British airliner caught fire and crashed into Mt. Fuji; 124 dead.

Dec. 24, Binh Thai, South Vietnam: crash of military-chartered plane into village killed 129.

1970 **Nov. 14, Huntington, W. Va.:** chartered plane carrying 43 players and coaches of Marshall University football team crashed; 75 dead.

1971 **July 30, Morioka, Japan:** Japanese Boeing 727 and F-86 fighter collided in mid-air; toll was 162.

Sept. 4, near Juneau, Alaska: Alaska Airlines Boeing 727 crashed into Chilkoot Mountains; 111 killed.

1972 **Aug. 14, East Berlin, East Germany:** Soviet-built East German Ilyushin plane crashed, killing 156.

Dec. 3, Santa Cruz de Tenerife, Canary Islands: Spanish charter jet carrying West German tourists crashed on take-off; all 155 aboard killed.

Dec. 30, Miami, Fla.: Eastern Airlines Lockheed 1011 TriStar Jumbo jet crashed into Everglades; 101 killed, 75 survived.

1973 **Jan. 22, Kano, Nigeria:** 171 Nigerian Moslems returning from Mecca and five crewmen died in crash.

April 10, Hochwald, Switzerland: British airliner carrying tourists to Swiss fair crashed in blizzard; 106 dead.

July 11, Paris: Boeing 707 of Varig Airlines, en route to Rio de Janeiro, crashed near airport, killing 122 of 134 passengers.

1974 **March 3, Paris:** Turkish DC-10 jumbo jet crashed in forest shortly after take-off; all 346 passengers and crew killed.

Dec. 4, Colombo, Sri Lanka: Dutch DC-8 carrying Moslems to Mecca crashed on landing approach, killing all 191 persons aboard.

1975 **April 4, near Saigon, Vietnam:** Air Force Galaxy C-5A crashed after take-off, killing 172, mostly Vietnamese children.

Aug. 3, Agadir, Morocco: Chartered Boeing 707, returning Moroccan workers home after vacation in France, plunged into mountainside;

all 188 aboard killed.
1976 **Sept. 10, Zagreb, Yugoslavia:** midair collision between British Airways Trident and Yugoslav charter DC-9 fatal to all 176 persons aboard; worst mid-air collision on record.
1977 **March 27, Santa Cruz de Tenerife, Canary Islands:** Pan American and KLM Boeing 747s collided on runway. All 249 on KLM plane and 333 of 394 aboard Pan Am jet killed. Total of 582 is highest for any type of aviation disaster.
1978 **Jan. 1, Bombay:** Air India 747 with 213 aboard exploded and plunged into sea minutes after takeoff.
Sept. 25, San Diego, Calif.: Pacific Southwest plane collided in midair with Cessna. All 135 on airliner, 2 in Cessna, and 7 on ground killed for total of 144.
Nov. 15, Colombo, Sri Lanka: Chartered Icelandic Airlines DC-8, carrying 249 Moslem pilgrims from Mecca, crashed in thunderstorm during landing approach; 183 killed.
1979 **Nov. 26, Jidda, Saudi Arabia:** Pakistan International Airlines 707 carrying pilgrims returning from Mecca crashed on take-off; all 156 aboard killed.
Nov. 28, Mt. Erebus, Antarctica: Air New Zealand DC-10 crashed on sightseeing flight; 257 killed.
1980 **March 14, Warsaw:** LOT Polish Airlines Ilyushin 62 crashed while attempting landing; 22 boxers and officials of a U.S. amateur boxing team killed along with 65 others.
April 25, Santa Cruz de Tenerife, Canary Islands: Chartered Boeing 727 carrying 138 British vacationers and crew of 8 crashed into mountain while approaching for landing; all killed.
Aug. 19, Riyadh, Saudi Arabia: all 301 aboard Saudi Arabian jet killed when burning plane made safe landing but passengers were unable to escape.
1981 **Dec. 1, Ajaccio, Corsica:** Yugoslav DC-9 Super 80 carrying tourists crashed into mountain on landing approach, killing all 178 aboard.
1983 **June 28**, near Cuenca, Ecuador, Ecuadorean jetliner crashed in mountains, killing 119.
Aug. 30, near island of Sakhalin off Siberia, South Korean civlian jetliner shot shown by Soviet fighter after it strayed off course into Soviet airspace. All 269 people aboard killed.
1985 **June 23:** Air-India Boeing 727 exploded over the Atlantic off the coast of Ireland, all 329 aboard killed.
Aug. 12, Japan Air Lines Boeing 747 crashed into a mountain, killing 520 of the 524 aboard.
Dec. 12, A chartered Arrow Air DC-8, bringing American soldiers home for Christmas, crashed on takeoff from Gander, Newfoundland. All 256 aboard died.

Railroad Accidents

1904 **Aug. 7, Eden, Colo.:** Train derailed on bridge during flash flood; 96 killed.
1910 **March 1, Wellington, Wash.:** two trains swept into canyon by avalanche; 96 dead.
1915 **May 22, Gretna, Scotland:** two passenger trains and troop train collided; 227 killed.
1917 **Dec. 12, Modane, France:** nearly 550 killed in derailment of troop train near mouth of Mt. Cenis tunnel.
1918 **Nov. 1, New York City:** derailment of subway train in Malbone St. tunnel in Brooklyn left 92 dead.
1939 **Dec. 22, near Magdeburg, Germany:** more than 125 killed in collision; 99 killed in another wreck near Friedrichshafen.
1943 **Dec. 16, near Rennert, N.C.:** 72 killed in derailment and collision of two Atlantic Coast Line trains.
1944 **March 2, near Salerno, Italy:** 521 suffocated when Italian train stalled in tunnel.
1949 **Oct. 22, near Nowy Dwor, Poland:** more than 200 reported killed in derailment of Danzig-Warsaw express.
1950 **Nov. 22, Richmond Hill, N.Y.:** 79 died when one Long Island Rail Road commuter train crashed into rear of another.
1951 **Feb. 6, Woodbridge, N.J.:** 85 died when Pennsylvania Railroad commuter train plunged through temporary overpass.
1952 **Oct. 8, Harrow-Wealdstone, England:** two express trains crashed into commuter train; 112 dead.
1953 **Dec. 24, near Sakvice, Czechoslovakia:** two trains crashed; over 100 dead.
1957 **Sept. 1, near Kendal, Jamaica:** about 175 killed when train plunged into ravine.
Sept. 29, near Montgomery, West Pakistan: express train crashed into standing oil train; nearly 300 killed.
Dec. 4, St. John's, England: 92 killed, 187 injured as one commuter train crashed into another in fog.
1960 **Nov. 14, Pardubice, Czechoslovakia:** two trains collided; 110 dead, 106 injured.
1962 **May 3, near Tokyo:** 163 killed and 400 injured when train crashed into wreckage of collision between inbound freight train and outbound commuter train.
1963 **Nov. 9, near Yokohama, Japan:** two passenger trains crashed into derailed freight, killing 162.
1964 **July 26, Custoias, Portugal:** passenger train derailed; 94 dead.
1970 **Feb. 4, near Buenos Aires:**236 killed when express train crashed into standing commuter train.
1972 **July 21, Seville, Spain:** head-on crash of two passenger trains killed 76.
Oct. 6, near Saltillo, Mexico: train carrying religious pilgrims derailed and caught fire, killing 204 and injuring over 1,000.
Oct. 30, Chicago: two Illinois Central commuter trains collided during morning rush hour; 45 dead and over 200 injured.
1974 **Aug. 30, Zagreb, Yugoslavia:** train entering station derailed, killing 153 and injuring over 60.
1977 **Feb. 4, Chicago:** 11 killed and over 180 injured when elevated train hit rear of another, sending two cars to street.
1982 **Jan. 26, Algeria:** Derailment on Algiers—Oran line leaves up to 120 dead.
1982 **July 11, Tepic, Mexico:** Nogales-Guadalajara train plunges down mountain gorge killing 120.

Miscellaneous

1980 **Jan. 20, Sincelejo, Colombia:** Bleachers at a bullring collapsed, leaving 222 dead.
March 30, Stavanger, Norway: Floating hotel in North Sea collapsed, killing 123 oil workers.
1981 **July 18, Kansas City, Mo.:** suspended walkway in Hyatt Regency Hotel collapses; 113 dead, 186 injured.
1984 **Dec. 3, Bhopal, India:** Toxic gas, methyl isocyanate, seeped from Union Carbide insecticide plant, killing more than 2,000; injuring about 150,000.

Weather, Climate, and You

By H.E. Landsberg

The notion that human health and disease are closely linked with daily and seasonal weather probably predates written history. But it was nailed down in writing by the Greek physician Hippocrates (about 400 B. C.). In his book "On Airs, Waters and Places" he records different reactions of human beings to hot and cold winds. He also relates epidemics to seasonal weather changes. Very little was added to Hippocrates' discerning observations for over two thousand years.

Careful scientific investigations have been made only over the past few decades. These have begun to unravel some intricate interactions. One of the great difficulties in these studies is the fact that no two human beings are exactly alike. We do not come uniformly and well calibrated from a factory. We have different genes, different statures, different states of nutrition. And above all we change with age. Quite in contrast, our information on the atmospheric environment is precise. Temperature, humidity, pressure, and wind are all measured with precision and so are their changes from day to day or season to season. You can readily see that it first confuses and then exasperates the research worker in the field if, say, a sudden drop in temperature causes aches and pains in ten percent of a sample population, seems not to affect eighty percent at all, and exhilarates the other ten percent. However, the same people react almost invariably the same way to various weather stimuli.

None of us is immune to the atmospheric environment. Man is physically adapted to a narrow range of temperature. The "naked ape" is a creature of the intertropical regions. Our metabolic mechanism is in best harmony with air temperatures around 25° C (77° F). There is a limited range above and below this temperature where survival is possible. At lower temperatures greater muscular activity will raise metabolic heat. This can include involuntary shivering. At higher temperatures another mechanism can restore thermal equilibrium, and that is sweating. Evaporation of the sweat will use extra heat energy taken from the body. But this process will only work well when humidities are low. At high humidities the evaporative cooling will not work. Overheating occurs and heat stroke can result. Thus combinations of temperatures of 45° C (113° F) and 10% relative humidity; 35° C (95° F) and 40%; 30° C (86° F) and 60%; 27° C (81° F) and 100% define a danger limit. If exceeded, heat prostration, heat stroke, and heat death may occur. Infants, whose heat regulatory mechanism is not yet fully developed, and old people, with impaired circulatory systems, are most likely to suffer.

On the cold end of the scale, wind becomes an important influence. It blows away a thin protective air layer near the skin. We try to keep this insulation intact by progressively thicker clothing as exposure to cold increases. Various combinations of air temperature and wind speed have been combined into a wind chill index, expressed in form of an equivalent temperature reflecting the cold sensation with calm air. Thus 10° C (50° F) and 4.5 meters per second (10 miles per hour) gives a wind chill equivalent of 4.5° (40° F) in calm air. Other combinations are: 0° C (32° F) and 8.9m sec^{-1} (20 mph) equivalent −14° C (7° F), −18° C (0° F) and 2.2m sec^{-1} (5 mph) equivalent −25.2° C (−13° F).

Between the dangerous limits of heat and wind chill, there are sensations of comfort and discomfort. These, again, are widely differentiated, often governed by the state of nutrition. Thus, obese persons suffer more from heat; malnourished individuals are very sensitive to cold.

Many of the weather-related ailments are transmitted via the skin. This integument separates the body from the external world. The skin senses and transmits to the body and the brain many of the changes taking place in the atmosphere. As long as the skin is unimpaired the system works well. But when the skin becomes scarred it may flash a pain signal. Temperature and moisture changes and possibly electrical conditions induce a tension between the healthy skin and the scar tissue. Deformed skin, such as corns, acts the same way.

Let's go back nearly a hundred years. It was the time after the Civil War. Many soldiers had suffered grievous wounds and amputations. They felt the weather changes. The first systematic study of these pains—often called phantom pains, because the brain imagined they came from the missing limb—was undertaken by S. Weir Mitchell, M. D., a distinguished Philadelphia physician, a member of the National Academy of Sciences. He wrote in the April 1877 issue of the prestigious *American Journal of Medical Sciences* an article: "The Relations of Pain to Weather, being a study of the natural history of a case of Traumatic Neuralgia." In this paper he related the case of Union Captain Catlin, whose foot was smashed in August 1864 by an artillery projectile. His leg was amputated below the knee and he made a rapid recovery—except for neuralgic pains. Catlin kept a detailed diary of onset and duration of his pains. Dr. Mitchell interpreted these pains in terms of the coincident weather conditions. He reached the conclusion that an approaching storm with the following combination of conditions: falling barometric pressure, rising temperature and humidity, followed by rain, was most frequently giving his patient pains. It was an astute deduction—unfortunately only too accurate for the many who followed Captain Catlin as victims of hostilities.

Enter now Claus Thurkow, a German soldier who lost his right arm in 1945 at the end of World War II because of multiple shrapnel wounds, and Otto Hoflich, a Ph.D. candidate in meteorology at the University of Hamburg. The scenario is the same in this case: Thurkow kept records of his pains for five years and Hoflich looked at the meteorol-

---

The late Dr. Helmut Landsberg has been called "the father of modern climatology" and was the chief architect of the Nation's modern-day climatological service. He was a former Director of the Environmental Data Service, and Professor Emeritus, Department of Meteorology, University of Maryland. The article is excerpted and reprinted with permission from *NOAA Magazine*.

ogy. Unlike Mitchell a century ago, Hoflich had access to a computer and used sophisticated statistical methods to correlate the pain intervals with the meteorological conditions. The end result, now established beyond reasonable doubt by tests of significance, is almost identical to Mitchell's discerning analysis: falling pressure, reaching a minimum in 24 hours, and high probability of rain—the typical symptoms of a warm front—caused pain. But there were also pain reactions with cold fronts, shower rains, and [clearly moist adiabatic] vertical temperature structure, as well as possible relations to atmospheric electric phenomena.

Very similar meteorological conditions, which have been termed *biotropic*, affect arthritics, an experience which has found folklore expression in the old English ditty:

"Hark how the chairs and tables crack,
Old Betty's bones are on the rack."

With regard to the cold and other virus diseases, we know very little about virus transport by atmospheric currents and their survival times in relation to weather. In this respect we are much better informed about airborne allergens. The best known of these are various plant pollen. Turbulent winds carry these. On sunny days during the warm season the atmosphere is thermally unstable. Strong vertical currents are common. These often exceed the fall velocity of pollen. Hence the pollen stay afloat and may be carried long distances. Those sensitive to them will get their so-called hay fever miseries or even asthmatic attacks.

Our changing weather, so welcome in many respects, also plays a definite role in affecting physiological and pathological conditions. Rapid changes seem to initiate responses in the body. These phenomena have been analyzed by classifying them according to weather phases. These follow the common sequences of weather in the realm of the westerlies. All told, six phases represent fairly well the complex totality of weather. Starting with cool, high pressure, with a few clouds and moderate winds (1); followed by perfectly clear, dry, high pressure and little wind (2); we get into considerable warming, steady or slightly falling pressure, some high clouds (3); then warm, moist air gets into the lower layers, pressure falls, clouds thicken, precipitation is common, winds pick up (4); then an abrupt change takes place, showery precipitation is accompanied by cold, gusty winds and rapidly rising pressure and falling humidity (5); finally with further rising pressure and diminishing clouds, temperatures reach low levels and humidities also drop (6).

Of course, these phases are not equally long either in one sequence or in the course of the year. In winter all of these phases may follow each other in less than three days. Some phases may be so short that it looks as if they had been omitted but they are usually there, even if in vestigial form. In summer it may take two weeks for a weather sequence to pass.

These weather phases have been very successfully correlated with the joys and tragedies of human life. In order to do that one has to rely essentially on hospital records. There everything is charted hour by hour and some of the weather phases may last only a few hours. But the reward of using this or a similar categorization of weather in human biometeorology is great.

You need little imagination to speculate that the quiescent weather phases 1 and 2, the "beautiful weather," stimulate the body very little. They generally make few demands on us and most of these can be met by proper clothing and adequate housing. Quite in contrast, weather phases 4 and 5 are often turbulent and violent. Somehow or other, they stir us up. Let's look at some of the statistics. You probably wouldn't believe that the precise date and hour of your birth was determined by the weather. The end of human pregnancy is uncertain by about plus or minus 10 days of the anticipated birth date. If we distribute the large numbers of cases of births among the weather phases it shows that in far more cases than statistical accident would permit, labor starts in days with weather phase 3, often followed by birth in phase 4.

These same phases seem to follow us toward the termination of life. Coronary thrombosis, the so-called heart attack, also shows a peak in weather phases 3 and 4. It shows a minimum in phases 1 and 6. Bleeding ulcers show their ugly tendency in phase 4. So do migraine attacks. Spasmodic diseases seem to be more prevalent in phases 4 to 6 than during the other weather conditions.

Weather does not only affect health and disease, birth and death, it rules our moods and behavior. This is generally far more difficult to establish than precise events, such as birth and death. Unfortunately, moods sometimes lead to the latter event: suicide. Here again, weather phase 3 shows a clear jump in number over the others. It also leads in cases of behavior problems among school-children, according to a few available statistics. Comfort and discomfort play a role here. When it is hot and sticky children do not learn well. This has been conclusively shown by comparison between air conditioned and non-air conditioned classrooms. Uncomfortable atmospheric conditions also are more conducive to riots than comfortable weather.

It is clearly impossible to give more than a few examples of how the weather affects our bodies. We must also admit that only in a few instances have we unravelled the complete chain of events. Statistical correlations tell us nothing about causal linkages. They only alert us to the possible existence of a relationship that suggests cause and effect. Much painstaking research needs yet to be done to make the information useful for maintenance of health and for management of disease. □

Lightning Caused by Cosmic Rays

Cosmic rays from space probably provide the extra potential that triggers a lightning stroke, according to a report made by Johns Hopkins scientists in the late seventies. Such rays, very high-energy particles moving at almost the speed of light, hit the upper atmosphere as an "air shower." When such a shower passes through a thunderhead, it releases electrons from oxygen and nitrogen atoms through ionization of the air. The free electrons are accelerated by the electric field already existing within the cloud, concentrating enough negative charge at the bottom of the cloud to generate a lightning stroke. The first stroke generated is a preliminary "leader stroke" of low luminosity. It travels the zigzag path of least electrical resistance to the ground. When the leader stroke is about 50 yards above the ground, an electric charge leaps up to meet it. These strokes complete the circuit between the cloud and the ground, clearing the way for the powerful return stroke, usually the first lightning seen. Often other strokes follow so quickly that they may seem to be one single stroke.

Climate of 100 Selected U.S. Cities

City	Average Monthly Temperature (°F)[1] Jan.	April	July	Oct.	Precipitation Average (in.)[1]	Precipitation annual (days)[2]	Snowfall Average annual (in.)[2]	Years[2]
Albany, N.Y.	21.1	46.6	71.4	50.5	35.74	134	65.5	38
Albuquerque, N.M.	34.8	55.1	78.8	57.4	8.12	59	10.6	45
Anchorage, Alaska	13.0	35.4	58.1	34.6	15.20	115	69.2	41[3]
Asheville, N.C.	36.8	55.7	73.2	56.0	47.71	124	17.5	20
Atlanta, Ga.	41.9	61.8	78.6	62.2	48.61	115	1.9	50
Atlantic City, N.J.	31.8	51.0	74.4	55.5	41.93	112	16.4	40[3]
Austin, Texas	49.1	68.7	84.7	69.8	31.50	83	0.9	43
Baltimore, Md.	32.7	54.0	76.8	56.9	41.84	113	21.8	34
Baton Rouge, La.	50.8	68.4	82.1	68.2	55.77	108	0.1	34[3]
Billings, Mont.	20.9	44.6	72.3	49.3	15.09	96	57.2	50
Birmingham, Ala.	42.9	62.8	80.1	62.6	54.52	117	1.3	41
Bismark, N.D.	6.7	42.5	70.4	46.1	15.36	96	40.3	45
Boise, Idaho	29.9	48.6	74.6	51.9	11.71	92	21.4	45
Boston, Mass.	29.6	48.7	73.5	54.8	43.81	127	41.8	49[3]
Bridgeport, Conn.	29.5	48.6	74.0	56.0	41.56	117	26.0	36
Buffalo, N.Y.	23.5	45.4	70.7	51.5	37.52	169	92.2	41
Burlington, Vt.	16.6	42.7	69.6	47.9	33.69	153	78.2	41
Caribou, Maine	10.7	37.3	65.1	43.1	36.59	160	113.3	45
Casper, Wyom.	22.2	42.1	70.9	47.1	11.43	95	80.5	34
Charleston, S.C.	47.9	64.3	80.5	65.8	51.59	113	0.6	42
Charleston, W.Va.	32.9	55.3	74.5	55.9	42.43	151	31.5	37
Charlotte, N.C.	40.5	60.3	78.5	60.7	43.16	111	6.1	45
Cheyenne, Wyom.	26.1	41.8	68.9	47.5	13.31	98	54.1	49
Chicago, Ill.	21.4	48.8	73.0	53.5	33.34	127	40.3	26
Cleveland, Ohio	25.5	48.1	71.6	53.2	35.40	156	53.6	43
Columbia, S.C.	44.7	63.8	81.0	63.4	49.12	109	1.9	37
Columbus, Ohio	27.1	51.4	73.8	53.9	36.97	137	28.3	37[3]
Concord, N.H.	19.9	44.1	69.5	48.3	36.53	125	64.5	43
Dallas–Ft. Worth, Texas	44.0	65.9	86.3	67.9	29.46	78	3.1	31
Denver, Colo.	29.5	47.4	73.4	51.9	15.31	88	59.8	50
Des Moines, Iowa	18.6	50.5	76.3	54.2	30.83	107	34.7	45
Detroit, Mich.	23.4	47.3	71.9	51.9	30.97	133	40.4	26
Dodge City, Kan.	29.5	54.3	80.0	57.7	20.66	78	19.5	42
Duluth, Minn.	6.3	38.3	65.4	44.2	29.68	135	77.4	41[3]
El Paso, Texas	44.2	63.6	82.5	63.6	7.82	47	5.2	45
Fairbanks, Alaska	−12.7	30.2	61.5	25.1	10.37	106	67.5	33
Fargo, N.D.	4.3	42.1	70.6	46.3	19.59	100	35.9	42
Grand Junction, Colo.	25.5	51.7	78.9	54.9	8.00	72	26.1	38
Grand Rapids, Mich.	22.0	46.3	71.4	50.9	34.35	143	72.4	21
Hartford, Conn.	25.2	48.8	73.4	52.4	44.39	127	50.0	30
Helena, Mont.	18.1	42.3	67.9	45.1	11.37	96	47.9	44
Honolulu, Hawaii	72.6	75.7	80.1	79.5	23.47	100	0.0	38[3]
Houston, Texas	51.4	68.7	83.1	69.7	44.76	105	0.4	50
Indianapolis, Ind.	26.0	52.4	75.1	54.8	39.12	125	23.1	53[3]
Jackson, Miss.	45.7	65.1	81.9	65.0	52.82	109	1.2	21
Jacksonville, Fla.	53.2	67.7	81.3	69.5	52.76	116	T	43
Juneau, Alaska	21.8	39.1	55.7	41.8	53.15	220	102.8	41
Kansas City, Mo.	28.4	56.9	80.9	59.6	29.27	98	20.0	43
Knoxville, Tenn.	38.2	59.6	77.6	59.5	47.29	127	12.3	42
Las Vegas, Nev.	44.5	63.5	90.2	67.5	4.19	26	1.4	36
Lexington, Ky.	31.5	55.1	75.9	56.8	45.68	131	16.3	40
Little Rock, Ark.	39.9	62.4	82.1	63.1	49.20	104	5.4	42
Long Beach, Calif.	55.2	60.9	72.8	67.5	11.54	32	T	41[3]
Los Angeles, Calif.	56.0	59.5	69.0	66.3	12.08	36	T	49
Louisville, Ky.	32.5	56.6	77.6	57.7	43.56	125	17.5	37
Madison, Wisc.	15.6	45.8	70.6	49.5	30.84	118	40.8	36
Memphis, Tenn.	39.6	62.6	82.1	62.9	51.57	107	5.5	34
Miami, Fla.	67.1	75.3	82.5	77.9	57.55	129	0.0	42
Milwaukee, Wisc.	18.7	44.6	70.5	50.9	30.94	125	47.0	44
Minneapolis-St. Paul, Minn.	11.2	46.0	73.1	49.6	26.36	115	48.9	46
Mobile, Ala.	50.8	68.0	82.2	68.5	64.64	123	0.3	43
Montgomery, Ala.	46.7	65.2	81.7	65.3	49.16	108	0.3	40
Mt. Washington, N.H.	5.1	22.4	48.7	30.5	89.92	209	246.8	52
Nashville, Tenn.	37.1	59.7	79.4	60.2	48.49	119	11.1	43
Newark, N.J.	31.2	52.1	76.8	57.2	42.34	122	28.2	43
New Orleans, La.	52.4	68.7	82.1	69.2	59.74	114	0.2	38[3]
New York, N.Y.	31.8	51.9	76.4	57.5	42.82	119	26.1	40[3]
Norfolk, Va.	39.9	58.2	78.4	61.3	45.22	115	7.9	36
Oklahoma City, Okla.	35.9	60.2	82.1	62.3	30.89	82	9.0	45

City	Average Monthly Temperature (°F)[1] Jan.	April	July	Oct.	Precipitation Average (in.)[1]	Precipitation annual (days)[2]	Snowfall Average annual (in.)[2]	Years[2]
Olympia, Wash.	37.2	47.3	63.0	50.1	50.96	164	18.0	43
Omaha, Neb.	20.2	52.2	77.7	54.5	30.34	98	31.1	49[3]
Philadelphia, Pa.	31.2	52.9	76.5	56.5	41.42	117	21.9	42[3]
Phoenix, Ariz.	52.3	68.1	92.3	73.4	7.11	36	T	47[3]
Pittsburgh, Pa.	26.7	50.1	72.0	52.5	36.30	154	44.6	32
Portland, Maine	21.5	42.8	68.1	48.5	43.52	128	72.4	44
Portland, Ore.	38.9	50.4	67.7	54.3	37.39	154	6.8	44
Providence, R.I.	28.2	47.9	72.5	53.2	45.32	124	37.1	31
Raleigh, N.C.	39.6	59.4	77.7	59.7	41.76	112	7.7	40
Reno, Nev.	32.2	46.4	69.5	50.3	7.49	51	25.3	42
Richmond, Va.	36.6	57.9	77.8	58.6	44.07	113	14.6	47
Roswell, N.M.	41.4	61.9	81.4	61.7	9.70	52	11.4	37[3]
Sacramento, Calif.	45.3	58.2	75.6	63.9	17.10	58	0.1	36[3]
Salt Lake City, Utah	28.6	49.2	77.5	53.0	15.31	90	59.1	56
San Antonio, Texas	50.4	69.6	84.6	70.2	29.13	81	0.4	42
San Diego, Calif.	56.8	61.2	70.3	67.5	9.32	43	T	44
San Francisco, Calif.	48.5	54.8	62.2	60.6	19.71	63	T	57
Savannah, Ga.	49.1	66.0	81.2	66.9	49.70	111	0.3	34
Seattle-Tacoma, Wash.	39.1	48.7	64.8	52.4	38.60	158	12.8	40
Sioux Falls, S.D.	12.4	46.4	74.0	49.4	24.12	96	39.9	39
Spokane, Wash.	25.7	45.8	69.7	47.5	16.71	114	51.5	37
Springfield, Ill.	24.6	53.3	76.5	56.0	33.78	114	24.5	37
St. Louis, Mo.	28.8	56.1	78.9	57.9	33.91	111	19.8	48[3]
Tampa, Fla.	59.8	71.5	82.1	74.4	46.73	107	T	38
Toledo, Ohio	23.1	47.8	71.8	51.7	31.78	137	38.3	29
Tucson, Ariz.	51.1	64.9	86.2	70.4	11.14	52	1.2	44
Tulsa, Okla.	35.2	61.0	83.2	62.6	38.77	89	9.0	46
Vero Beach, Fla.	61.9	71.7	81.1	75.2	51.41	n.a.	n.a.	0
Washington, D.C.	35.2	56.7	78.9	59.3	39.00	112	17.0	41[3]
Wilmington, Del.	31.2	52.4	76.0	56.3	41.38	117	20.9	37
Wichita, Kan.	29.6	56.3	81.4	59.1	28.61	85	16.4	31

1. Based on 30 year period 1951–80. Data latest available. 2. Data through 1984 based on number of years as indicated in Years column. 3. For snowfall data where number of years differ from that for precipitation data. T = trace. n.a. = not available. *Source:* National Oceanic and Atmospheric Administration.

Wind Chill Factors

Wind speed (mph)	Thermometer reading (degrees Fahrenheit) 35	30	25	20	15	10	5	0	−5	−10	−15	−20	−25	−30	−35	−40	−45
5	33	27	21	19	12	7	0	−5	−10	−15	−21	−26	−31	−36	−42	−47	−52
10	22	16	10	3	−3	−9	−15	−22	−27	−34	−40	−46	−52	−58	−64	−71	−77
15	16	9	2	−5	−11	−18	−25	−31	−38	−45	−51	−58	−65	−72	−78	−85	−92
20	12	4	−3	−10	−17	−24	−31	−39	−46	−53	−60	−67	−74	−81	−88	−95	−103
25	8	1	−7	−15	−22	−29	−36	−44	−51	−59	−66	−74	−81	−88	−96	−103	−110
30	6	−2	−10	−18	−25	−33	−41	−49	−56	−64	−71	−79	−86	−93	−101	−109	−116
35	4	−4	−12	−20	−27	−35	−43	−52	−58	−67	−74	−82	−89	−97	−105	−113	−120
40	3	−5	−13	−21	−29	−37	−45	−53	−60	−69	−76	−84	−92	−100	−107	−115	−123
45	2	−6	−14	−22	−30	−38	−46	−54	−62	−70	−78	−85	−93	−102	−109	−117	−125

NOTES: This chart gives equivalent temperatures for combinations of wind speed and temperatures. For example, the combination of a temperature of 10° Fahrenheit and a wind blowing at 10 mph has a cooling power equal to −9° F. Wind speeds of higher than 45 mph have little additional cooling effect.

Other Recorded Extremes

Highest average annual mean temperature (World): Dallol, Ethiopia (Oct. 1960-Dec. 1966), 94° F (35° C). **(U.S.):** Key West, Fla. (30-year normal), 78.2° F (25.7° C).

Lowest average annual mean temperature (Antarctica): Plateau Station −70° F (−57° C). **(U.S.):** Barrow, Alaska (30-year normal), 9.3° F (−13° C).

Greatest average yearly rainfall (U.S.): Mt. Waialeale, Kauai, Hawaii (32-year avg), 460 in. (1,168 cm). **(India):** Cherrapunji (74-year avg), 450 in. (1,143 cm).

Minimum average yearly rainfall (Chile): Arica (59-year avg), 0.03 in. (0.08 cm) (no rainfall for 14 consecutive years). **(U.S.):** Death Valley, Calif. (42-year avg), 1.63 in. (4.14 cm). Bagdad, Calif., holds the U.S. record for the longest period with no measurable rain, 767 days, from Oct. 3, 1912 to Nov. 8, 1914).

Hottest summer avg in Western Hemisphere (U.S.): Death Valley, Calif., 98° F (36.7° C).

Longest hot spell (W. Australia): Marble Bar, 100° F (38° C) (or above) for 162 consecutive days, Oct. 30, 1923-Apr. 7, 1924.

Largest hailstone (U.S.): Coffeyville, KS, 17.5 in. (44.5 cm), Sept. 3, 1979.

World and U.S. Extremes of Climate

Highest recorded temperature

	Place	Date	Degree Fahrenheit	Degree Centigrade
World (Africa)	El Azizia, Libya	Sept. 13, 1922	136	58
North America (U.S.)	Death Valley, Calif.	July 10, 1913	134	57
Asia	Tirat Tsvi, Israel	June 21, 1942	129	54
Australia	Cloncurry, Queensland	Jan. 16, 1889	128	53
Europe	Seville, Spain	Aug. 4, 1881	122	50
South America	Rivadavia, Argentina	Dec. 11, 1905	120	49
Canada	Midale and Yellow Grass, Saskatchewan	July 5, 1937	113	45
Persian Gulf (sea-surface)		August 5, 1924	96	36
South Pole		Dec. 27, 1978	7.5	−14
Antarctica	Vanda Station	Jan. 5, 1974	59	15

Lowest recorded temperature

	Place	Date	Degree Fahrenheit	Degree Centigrade
World (Antarctica)	Vostok	July 21, 1983	−129	−89
Asia	Verkhoyansk/Oimekon	Feb. 6, 1933	−90	−68
Greenland	Northice	Jan. 9, 1954	−87	−66
North America (excl. Greenland)	Snag, Yukon, Canada	Feb. 3, 1947	−81	−63
Alaska	Prospect Creek, Endicott Mts.	Jan. 23, 1971	−80	−62
U.S., excluding Alaska	Rogers Pass, Mont.	Jan. 20, 1954	−70	−56.5
Europe	Ust 'Shchugor, U.S.S.R.	n.a.	−67	−55
South America	Sarmiento, Argentina	Jan. 1, 1907	−27	−33
Africa	Ifrane, Morocco	Feb. 11, 1935	−11	−24
Australia	Charlotte Pass, N.S.W.	July 22, 1947	−8	−22
United States	Prospect Creek, Alaska	Jan. 23, 1971	−80	−62

Greatest rainfalls

	Place	Date	Inches	Centimeters
1 minute (World)	Unionville, Md.	July 4, 1956	1.23	3.1
20 minutes (World)	Curtea-de-Arges, Romania	July 7, 1889	8.1	20.5
42 minutes (World)	Holt, Mo.	June 22, 1947	12	30.5
12 hours (World)	Belouve, La Réunion	Feb. 28-29, 1964	53	135
24 hours (World)	Cilaos, La Réunion	March 15-16, 1952	74	188
24 hours (N. Hemisphere)	Paishih, Taiwan	Sept. 10-11, 1963	49	125
24 hours (Australia)	Bellenden Ker, Queensland	Jan. 4, 1979	44	114
24 hours (U.S.)	Alvin, Texas	July 25-26, 1979	43	109
24 hours (Canada)	Ucluelet Brynnor Mines, British Columbia	Oct. 6, 1967	19	49
5 days (World)	Cilaos, La Réunion	March 13-18, 1952	152	386
1 month (World)	Cherrapunji, India	July 1861	366	930
12 months (World)	Cherrapunji, India	Aug. 1860-Aug. 1861	1,042	2,647
12 months (U.S.)	Kukui, Maui, Hawaii	Dec. 1981-Dec. 1982	739	1878

Greatest snowfalls

	Place	Date	Inches	Centimeters
1 month (U.S.)	Tamarack, Calif.	Jan. 1911	390	991
24 hours (N. America)	Silver Lake, Colo.	April 14–15, 1921	76	192.5
24 hours (Alaska)	Thompson Pass	Dec. 29, 1955	62	157.5
19 hours (France)	Bessans	April 5-6, 1969	68	173
1 storm (N. America)	Mt. Shasta Ski Bowl, Calif.	Feb. 13-19, 1959	189	480
1 storm (Alaska)	Thompson Pass	Dec. 26-31, 1955	175	445.5
1 season (N. America)	Paradise Ranger Sta., Wash.	1971-1972	1,122	2,850
1 season (Alaska)	Thompson Pass	1952-1953	974.5	2,475
1 season (Canada)	Revelstoke Mt. Copeland, British Columbia	1971-1972	964	2,446.5

Source: U.S. Army Corps of Engineers, Engineer Topographic Laboratories.

Devastating North Atlantic Hurricanes of the 20th Century

The following is a selected list of North Atlantic hurricanes based on casualties, damage, and general public interest. Facts about each storm are taken from Weather records, although in some cases only estimates of wind speed are available. Data given in this list pertain only to U.S. land areas except where indicated otherwise.

Date	Areas hardest hit	Land stations with highest wind speed	Deaths (U.S. only)	Est. damage (millions)	Remarks
1900, Aug. 27–Sept. 15	Galveston, Tex.	Galveston, Tex. (120[1] mph)	6,000	$30	Damage due to both winds and storm wave. Galveston Is. inundated.
1909, Sept. 10–21	Louisiana and Mississippi	New Orleans, La. (53 mph)	350	5	Winds 50–75 mi. W of New Orleans, where deaths occurred, were stronger than 68 mph.
1915, Aug. 5–23	East Texas and Louisiana	Galveston, Tex. (120 mph)	275	50	Water 5–6 ft deep in Galveston business district. 90% of homes demolished. Warnings issued well ahead of time.
1915, Sept. 22–Oct. 1	Mid-Gulf Coast	Burrwood, La. (140 mph)	275	13	Many casualties due to persons insisting on staying in low-lying areas despite warnings.
1919, Sept. 2–15	Florida, Louisiana, and Texas	Sand Key, Fla. (84[1] mph)	287	22	488 persons drowned at sea.
1926, Sept. 11–22	Florida and Alabama	Miami, Fla. (138 mph)	243	112	Most deaths were in Miami area. Said to have been one of most destructive storms of century.
1928, Sept. 6–20	Southern Florida	Lake Okeechobee, Fla. (75[1] mph)	1,836	25	1,870 injured. Nearly all deaths were in Lake Okeechobee area. Winds estimated as high as 160 mph caused Lake to overflow into populated areas.
1935, Aug. 29–Sept. 10	Southern Florida	Tampa, Fla. (86 mph)	408	6	Sustained winds over Florida Keys est. 150–200 mph. Remembered as "Labor Day Storm."
1938, Sept. 10–22	Long Island and Southern New England	Blue Hills Obs., Mass. (183 mph)	600	306	Unusually destructive. Storm center moved as fast as 56 mph at times. 1,754 injured.
1944, Sept. 9–16	North Carolina to New England	Cape Henry, Va. (150[1] mph)	46	100	344 deaths at sea. Shipping lanes were crowded with war-time activity.
1944, Oct. 12–23	Florida	Dry Tortugas Is. (120 mph)	18	100	About 300 were killed in Cuba area before storm reached U.S. Evacuation of thousands from threatened areas in Fla. prevented higher toll.
1947, Sept. 4–21	Florida and Mid-Gulf Coast	Hillsboro Light, Fla. (155 mph)	51	110	Wind damage especially heavy along Gulf Coast and Florida east coast.
1954, Aug. 25–31	North Carolina to New England	Block Island, R.I. (135 mph)	60	461	"CAROL"—more damage than any other single storm to this date. Water and high waves flooded low-lying areas; 1,000 injuries in Long Island—New England area.
1954, Sept. 2–14	New Jersey to New England	Block Island, R.I. (87 mph)	21	40	"EDNA"—New England again heavily hit. Gusts of 120 mph at Martha's Vineyard, Mass.
1954, Oct. 5–18	South Carolina to New York	New York, N.Y. (113 mph) (See Remarks)	95	252	"HAZEL"—several N.C. localities had winds of 130–150 mph with unusually heavy wave damage resulting. Est. 400–1,000 casualties in Haiti. In Canada there were 78 deaths, mostly due to flooding.
1955, Aug. 7–21	North Carolina to New England	Wilmington, N.C. (83 mph)	184	832	"DIANE"—worst floods in history in Southern New England. 16 in. of rain in Hartford area.
1957, June 25–28	Texas to Alabama	Sabine/Pass, Tex. (100 mph)	390	150	"AUDREY"—gave an early start to the hurricane season and wiped out Cameron, La. Two weeks later "BERTHA" struck same area.

Date	Areas hardest hit	Land stations with highest wind speed	Deaths (U.S. only)	Est. damage (millions)	Remarks
1960, Aug. 29–Sept. 13	Florida to New England	Ft. Myers, Fla. (92 mph) Block Island, R.I. (130 mph) (See Remarks)	50	500	"DONNA"—hurricane winds from a single storm swept the entire Atlantic seaboard from Florida to New England for the first time in a 75-year record. Winds estimated near 140 mph with gusts 175–180 mph on Central Keys and lower southwest Florida coast. 115 deaths in Antilles, most from flash floods in Puerto Rico.
1961, Sept. 3–15	Texas coast	Port Lavaca, Tex. (145 mph)	46	408	"CARLA"—devastated Texas Gulf Coast Cities with 15-foot tides and 15-inch rains. Gusts to 175 mph at Port Lavaca.
1964, Aug. 20–Sept. 5	Southern Florida, Eastern Virginia	Miami, Fla. (110 mph)	3	129	"CLEO"—first hurricane in Miami area since 1950. Killed 214 in Caribbean Islands.
1964, Aug. 28–Sept. 16	Northeastern Florida, Southern Georgia	St. Augustine, Fla. (125 mph)	5	250	"DORA"—first storm of full hurricane force on record to move inland from east over northeastern Florida.
1965, Aug. 27–Sept. 12	Southern Florida and Louisiana	Port Sulphur, La. (136 mph)	75	1,420	"BETSY"—Damage in Louisiana, $1.2 billion. 27,000 homes destroyed, 17,500 injured or ill, 300,000 evacuated. Gusts of 165 mph at Pine Key, Fla.
1967, Sept. 5–22	Southern Texas	Brownsville, Texas (109 mph gust)	15	200	"BEULAH"—main damage was caused by torrential rains.
1969, Aug. 14–22	Mississippi, Louisiana, Alabama, Virginia, W. Virginia	Oil drilling rig east of Boothville, La. (172 mph)	256	1,420	"CAMILLE"—68 additional persons missing. One of most destructive killer storms ever to hit U.S.
1970, July 23–Aug. 5	Texas coast	Corpus Christi, Tex. (130 mph)	11	453.8	"CELIA"—Gusts of 161 mph recorded.
1972, June 14–23	Florida to New York	Key West, Fla. (43 mph)	117	2,100	"AGNES"—Devastating floods with many record-breaking river crests. Pa. hardest hit, with 50 deaths.
1975, Sept. 13–24	Florida and Southern Alabama	Ozark, Ala. (104 mph)	21	490	"ELOISE"—Structures destroyed from Panama City Beach, Fla., to Ft. Walton Beach, Fla. Major flooding from rainfall.
1976, Aug. 6–10	New York, New Jersey, and Southern New England	Bridgeport, Conn. (77 mph gust)	5	100	"BELLE"—Crop damage in the Northeast. Considerable Inland stream and road flooding.
1979, Aug. 25–Sept. 7	Florida to New England	Fort Pierce, Fla. (95 mph gust)	5	320	"DAVID"—1200 deaths in the Dominican Republic. Homes 80 percent destroyed in Dominica.
1979, Aug. 29–Sept. 14	Alabama and Mississippi	Dauphin Island, Alabama (145 mph gust)	5	2300	"FREDERIC"—highest dollar damage ever in the United States.
1980, Aug. 3–10	Caribbean Islands to Texas Gulf Coast	Port Mansfield, Texas (120 mph gust.)	28	300	"ALLEN"—Highest tides in 61 years. Over 200 killed in Caribbean Islands. Extensive crop damage in Caribbean.
1983, Aug. 15–21	Texas Coast	Hobby Airport (94 mph)	21	2000	"ALICIA"—Extensive damage in Galveston/Houston area.
1985 Aug. 28–Sept. 4	Florida to Mississippi	Dauphin Island, Ala. (96 mph)	4	1,000	"ELENA"—one million persons evacuated.
1985, Sept. 16—27	North Carolina Outer Banks and Long Island, N.Y.	Chesapeake Bay Bridge (92 mph)	8	1,000	"GLORIA"—downed trees and power outages across southern New England.
1985, Oct. 26–Nov. 1	Louisiana	Pensacola, Fla. (63 mph gust)	12	1,500	"JUAN"—Serious damage to offshore oil rigs. Sustained flooding over SE Louisiana.

1. Wind-measuring equipment disabled at speed indicated. NOTE: Additional hurricanes may be listed in *Current Events*.
Source: Department of Commerce, National Oceanic and Atmospheric Administration.

Record Highest Temperatures by State

State	Temp, °F	Date	Station	Elevation, feet
Alabama	112	Sept. 5, 1925	Centerville	345
Alaska	100	June 27, 1915	Fort Yukon	est. 420
Arizona	127	July 7, 1905*	Parker	345
Arkansas	120	Aug. 10, 1936	Ozark	396
California	134	July 10, 1913	Greenland Ranch	−178
Colorado	118	July 11, 1888	Bennett	5,484
Connecticut	105	July 22, 1926	Waterbury	400
Delaware	110	July 21, 1930	Millsboro	20
Florida	109	June 29, 1931	Monticello	207
Georgia	113	May 27, 1978	Greenville	860
Hawaii	100	Apr. 27, 1931	Pahala	850
Idaho	118	July 28, 1934	Orofino	1,027
Illinois	117	July 14, 1954	E. St. Louis	410
Indiana	116	July 14, 1936	Collegeville	672
Iowa	118	July 20, 1934	Keokuk	614
Kansas	121	July 24, 1936*	Alton (near)	1,651
Kentucky	114	July 28, 1930	Greensburg	581
Louisiana	114	Aug. 10, 1936	Plain Dealing	268
Maine	105	July 10, 1911*	North Bridgton	450
Maryland	109	July 10, 1936*	Cumberland & Frederick	623;325
Massachusetts	107	Aug. 2, 1975	New Bedford & Chester	120;640
Michigan	112	July 13, 1936	Mio	963
Minnesota	114	July 6, 1936*	Moorhead	904
Mississippi	115	July 29, 1930	Holly Springs	600
Missouri	118	July 14, 1954*	Warsaw & Union	687;560
Montana	117	July 5, 1937	Medicine Lake	1,950
Nebraska	118	July 24, 1936*	Minden	2,169
Nevada	122	June 23, 1954*	Overton	1,240
New Hampshire	106	July 4, 1911	Nashua	125
New Jersey	110	July 10, 1936	Runyon	18
New Mexico	116	July 14, 1934*	Orogrande	4,171
New York	108	July 22, 1926	Troy	35
North Carolina	109	Sept. 7, 1954*	Weldon	81
North Dakota	121	July 6, 1936	Steele	1,857
Ohio	113	July 21, 1934*	Gallipolis (near)	673
Oklahoma	120	July 26, 1943*	Tishomingo	670
Oregon	119	Aug. 10, 1898	Pendleton	1,074
Pennsylvania	111	July 10, 1936*	Phoenixville	100
Rhode Island	104	Aug. 2, 1975	Providence	51
South Carolina	111	June 28, 1954*	Camden	170
South Dakota	120	July 5, 1936	Gannvalley	1,750
Tennessee	113	Aug. 9, 1930*	Perryville	377
Texas	120	Aug. 12, 1936	Seymour	1,291
Utah	116	June 28, 1892	Saint George	2,880
Vermont	105	July 4, 1911	Vernon	310
Virginia	110	July 15, 1954	Balcony Falls	725
Washington	118	Aug. 5, 1961*	Ice Harbor Dam	475
West Virginia	112	July 10, 1936*	Martinsburg	435
Wisconsin	114	July 13, 1936	Wisconsin Dells	900
Wyoming	114	July 12, 1900	Basin	3,500

*Also on earlier dates at the same or other places. *Source:* National Oceanic and Atmospheric Administration, Environmental Data and Information Service, National Climatic Center, Asheville, N.C. NOTE: Records as of 1983.

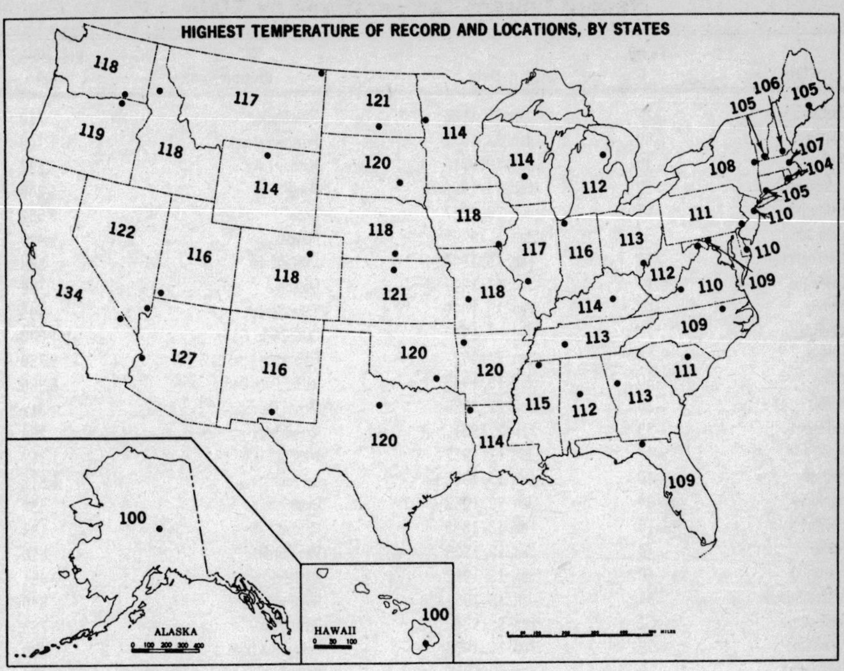

HIGHEST TEMPERATURE OF RECORD AND LOCATIONS, BY STATES

Source: National Oceanic and Atmospheric Administration.

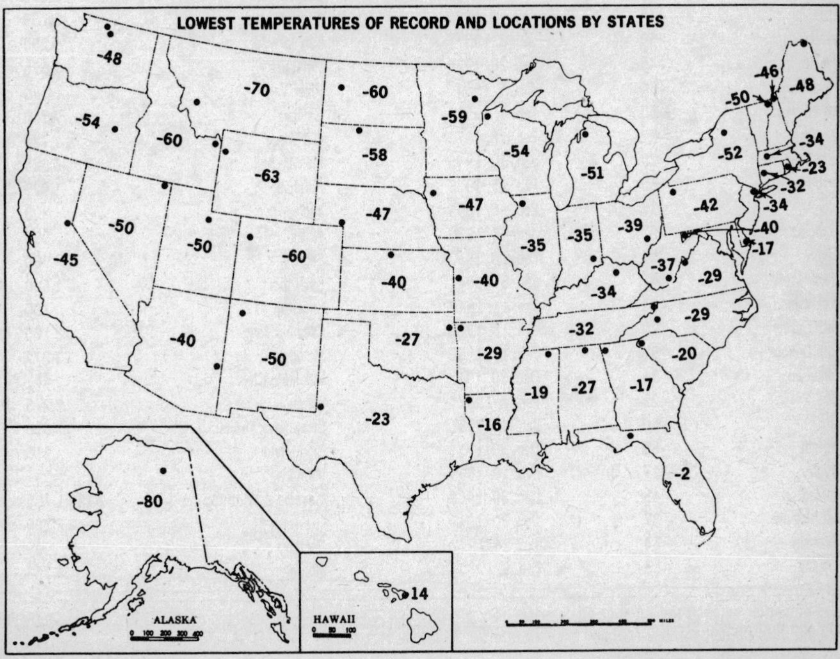

LOWEST TEMPERATURES OF RECORD AND LOCATIONS BY STATES

Record Lowest Temperatures by State

State	Temp, °F	Date	Station	Elevation, feet
Alabama	−27	Jan. 30, 1966	New Market	760
Alaska	−80	Jan. 23, 1971	Prospect Creek	1,100
Arizona	−40	Jan. 7, 1971	Hawley Lake	8,180
Arkansas	−29	Feb. 13, 1905	Pond	1,250
California	−45	Jan. 20, 1937	Boca	5,532
Colorado	−60	Jan. 1, 1979*	Maybell	5,920
Connecticut	−32	Feb. 16, 1943	Falls Village	585
Delaware	−17	Jan. 17, 1893	Millsboro	20
Florida	−2	Feb. 13, 1899	Tallahassee	193
Georgia	−17	Jan. 27, 1940	CCC Camp F-16	est. 1,000
Hawaii	14	Jan. 2, 1961	Haleakala, Maui Is	9,750
Idaho	−60	Jan. 18, 1943	Island Park Dam	6,285
Illinois	−35	Jan. 22, 1930	Mount Carroll	817
Indiana	−35	Feb. 2, 1951	Greensburg	954
Iowa	−47	Jan. 12, 1912	Washta	1,157
Kansas	−40	Feb. 13, 1905	Lebanon	1,812
Kentucky	−34	Jan. 28, 1963	Cynthiana	684
Louisiana	−16	Feb. 13, 1899	Minden	194
Maine	−48	Jan. 19, 1925	Van Buren	510
Maryland	−40	Jan. 13, 1912	Oakland	2,461
Massachusetts	−34	Jan. 18, 1957	Birch Hill Dam	840
Michigan	−51	Feb. 9, 1934	Vanderbilt	785
Minnesota	−59	Feb. 16, 1903*	Pokegama Dam	1,280
Mississippi	−19	Jan. 30, 1966	Corinth	420
Missouri	−40	Feb. 13, 1905	Warsaw	700
Montana	−70	Jan. 20, 1954	Rogers Pass	5,470
Nebraska	−47	Feb. 12, 1899	Camp Clarke	3,700
Nevada	−50	Jan. 8, 1937	San Jacinto	5,200
New Hampshire	−46	Jan. 28, 1925	Pittsburg	1,575
New Jersey	−34	Jan. 5, 1904	River Vale	70
New Mexico	−50	Feb. 1, 1951	Gavilan	7,350
New York	−52	Feb. 18, 1979*	Old Forge	1,720
North Carolina	−29	Jan. 30, 1966	Mt. Mitchell	6,525
North Dakota	−60	Feb. 15, 1936	Parshall	1,929
Ohio	−39	Feb. 10, 1899	Milligan	800
Oklahoma	−27	Jan. 18, 1930	Watts	958
Oregon	−54	Feb. 10, 1933*	Seneca	4,700
Pennsylvania	−42	Jan. 5, 1904	Smethport	est. 1,500
Rhode Island	−23	Jan. 11, 1942	Kingston	100
South Carolina	−20	Jan. 18, 1977	Caesars Head	3,100
South Dakota	−58	Feb. 17, 1936	McIntosh	2,277
Tennessee	−32	Dec. 30, 1917	Mountain City	2,471
Texas	−23	Feb. 8, 1933*	Seminole	3,275
Utah	−50	Jan. 5, 1913*	Strawberry Tunnel	7,650
Vermont	−50	Dec. 30, 1933	Bloomfield	915
Virginia	−29	Feb. 10, 1899	Monterey	—
Washington	−48	Dec. 30, 1968	Mazama & Winthrop	2,120;1,765
West Virginia	−37	Dec. 30, 1917	Lewisburg	2,200
Wisconsin	−54	Jan. 24, 1922	Danbury	908
Wyoming	−63	Feb. 9, 1933	Moran	6,770

*Also on earlier dates at the same or other places. *Source:* National Oceanic and Atmospheric Administration, Environmental Data and Information Service, National Climatic Center, Asheville, N.C. NOTE: Records as of 1983.

Tropical Storms and Hurricanes, 1886–1986

	Jan.–April	May	June	July	Aug.	Sept.	Oct.	Nov.	Dec.	Total
Number of tropical storms (incl. hurricanes)	3	14	55	63	200	286	178	40	6	845
Number of tropical storms that reached hurricane intensity	1	3	23	33	143	181	88	21	3	496

Tornadoes That Caused Outstanding Damage

Date	Number of tornadoes	Deaths	Property losses	States in which storms occurred
1884, Feb. 19	60	800	(1)	Mississippi, Alabama, North and South Carolina, Tennessee, Kentucky, Indiana
1917, May 26–27	(1)	249	$5,555,000	Illinois, Indiana, Arkansas, Kentucky, Tennessee, Alabama, Mississippi
1920, April 20	6	220	3,525,000	Mississippi, Alabama, Tennessee
1924, April 29–30	22	115	4,372,300	Oklahoma, Arkansas, Alabama, Georgia, Louisiana, North and South Carolina, Virginia
1924, June 28	4	96	13,050,000	Ohio and Pennsylvania
1925, March 18	8	792	17,872,000	Missouri, Illinois, Indiana, Kentucky, Tennessee, Alabama
1927, May 8–9	36	227	7,877,000	Texas, Louisiana, Missouri, Nebraska, Indiana, Michigan
1932, March 21	27	321	5,514,000	Alabama, Mississippi, Georgia, Tennessee
1936, April 5–6	22	498	21,800,000	Arkansas, Alabama, Tennessee, Georgia, South Carolina
1944, June 23	4	153	5,160,000	Pennsylvania, West Virginia, Maryland
1947, April 9–10	8	167	10,030,750	Texas, Oklahoma, Kansas
1952, March 21–22	31	343	15,327,100	Arkansas, Tennessee, Missouri, Mississippi, Alabama, Kentucky
1953, June 7–9	12	234	93,230,840	Michigan, Ohio, and New England states
1953, May 11	1	114	39,500,000	Texas
1955, May 25	13	102	11,747,500	Oklahoma and Kansas
1965, April 11–12	47	257	200,000,000	Iowa, Illinois, Wisconsin, Michigan, Indiana, Ohio
1968, May 15	7	63	65,000,000	Arkansas, Iowa, Illinois
1970, May 11	1	26	135,000,000	Texas
1971, Feb. 21	(1)	117	17,000,000	Louisiana, Mississippi
1973, March 31	2	9	115,000,000	Georgia, South Carolina
1973, May 26–28	96	22	(1)	Hawaii and 18 states in South, Southwest, Midwest, and East
1974, April 3–4	144	307	500,000,000 +	13 states in East, South, and Midwest
1975, May 6	3	3	400,000,000 +	Nebraska
1977, April 4	7	22	15,000,000	Alabama
1978, Dec. 3	13	4	100,000,000 +	Louisiana and Arkansas
1979, April 10	10	54	(1)	Texas and Oklahoma
1979, Oct. 3	1	3	200,000,000	Connecticut
1980, May 13	1	5	40,000,000	Michigan
1980, Aug. 9–11	29	0	50,000,000 +	Texas
1981, April 4	1	3	12,900,000	Wisconsin
1983, July 3	22	0	11,000,000 +	Wisconsin
1984, April 26–27	47	16	n.a.	Iowa, Illinois, Kansas, Louisiana, Michigan, Minnesota, Missouri, Oklahoma, South Dakota, Wisconsin
1985, May 31	30	76	102,500,000 +	Ohio, Pennsylvania, New York
1986[2], Feb. 5	1	2	50,000,000	Texas

1. Not definitely known; believed to be large. 2. Preliminary. NOTE: Additional storms may be listed in the *Current Events* section. n.a. = not available. *Source:* Department of Commerce, National Oceanic and Atmospheric Administration and for 1986, *Weatherwise*, February 1987 issue from an article by Edward W. Ferguson, Frederick P. Ostby and Preston W. Leftwich, Jr.

Weather Glossary

blizzard: storm characterized by strong winds, low temperatures, and large amounts of snow.
cyclone: circulation of winds rotating counterclockwise in the northern hemisphere and clockwise in the southern hemisphere. Hurricanes and tornadoes are both examples of cyclones.
flash flood: dangerous rapid rise of water levels in streams, rivers, or over land area.
hurricane: devastating cyclonic storm; winds over 74 mph near storm center; usually tropical in origin; called cyclone in Indian Ocean, typhoon in the Pacific.
tidal waves: series of ocean waves caused by earthquakes; can reach speeds of 600 mph; they grow in height as they reach shore and can crest as high as 100 feet.
tornado: dangerous whirlwind associated with the cumulonimbus clouds of severe thunderstorms; winds up to 300 mph.
tsunami: *see* tidal waves.

Temperature Extremes in The United States

Source: National Oceanic and Atmospheric Administration, Environmental Data and Information Service, and National Center Climatic Center

The Highest Temperature Extremes

Greenland Ranch, California, with 134° F (56.67° C) on July 10, 1913, holds the record for the highest temperature ever officially observed in the United States. This station was located in barren Death Valley, 178 feet below sea level. Death Valley is about 140 miles long, four to six miles wide, and oriented north to south in southwestern California. Much of the valley is below sea level and is flanked by towering mountain ranges with Mt. Whitney, the highest landmark in the 48 conterminous states, rising to 14,495 feet above sea level, less than 100 miles to the west. Death Valley has the hottest summers in the Western Hemisphere, and is the only known place in the United States where nightime temperatures sometimes remain above 100° F (37.78° C).

The highest annual normal (1941-70 mean) temperature in the United States, 78.2° F (25.67° C), and the highest summer (June-August) normal temperature, 92.8° F (33.78° C), are for Death Valley, California. The highest winter (December-February) normal temperature is 72.8° F (22.67° C) for Honolulu, Hawaii.

Amazing temperature rises of 40° to 50° F (4.44 to 10° C) in a few minutes occasionally may be brought about by chinook winds.[1]

Some Outstanding Temperature Rises

In 12 hours: 83° F (46.11° C), Granville, N.D., Feb. 21, 1918, from −33° F to 50° F (−36.11 to 10° C) from early morning to late afternoon.

In 15 minutes: 42° F (23.34° C), Fort Assiniboine, Mont., Jan. 19, 1892, from −5° F to 37° F (−20.56 to 2.78° C).

In seven minutes: 34° F (1.11° C), Kipp, Mont., Dec. 1, 1896. The observer also reported that a total rise of 80° F (26.67° C) occurred in a few hours and that 30 inches of snow disappeared in one-half day.

In two minutes: 49° F (27.22° C), Spearfish, S.D., Jan. 22, 1943 from −4° F (20° C) at 7:30 a.m. to 45° F (7.22° C) at 7:32 a.m.

The Lowest Temperature Extremes

The lowest temperature on record in the United States, −79.8° F (−62.1° C), was observed at Prospect Creek Camp in the Endicott Mountains of northern Alaska (latitude 66° 48′N, longitude 150° 40′W) on Jan. 23, 1971. The lowest ever recorded in the conterminous 48 states, −69.7° F (−56.5° C), occurred at Rogers Pass, in Lewis and Clark County, Mont., on Jan. 20, 1954. Rogers Pass is in mountainous and heavily forested terrain about one-half mile east of and 140 feet below the summit of the Continental Divide.

The lowest annual normal (1941-70 mean) temperature in the United States is 9.3° F (−12.68° C) for Barrow, Alaska, which lies on the Arctic coast. Barrow also has the coolest summers (June-August) with a normal temperature of 36.4° F (2.44° C). The lowest winter (December-February) normal temperature, is −15.7° F (−26.5° C) for Barter Island on the arctic coast of northeast Alaska.

In the 48 conterminous states, Mt. Washington, N.H. (elevation 6,262 feet) has the lowest annual normal temperature 26.9° F (−2.72° C) and the lowest normal summer temperature, 46.8° F (8.22° C). A few stations in the northeastern United States and in the upper Rocky Mountains have normal annual temperatures in the 30s; summer normal temperatures at these stations are in the low 50s. Winter normal temperatures are lowest in northeastern North Dakota, 5.6° F (−14.23° C) for Langdon Experiment Farm, and in northwestern Minnesota, 5.3° F (−14.83° C) for Hallock.

Some Outstanding Temperature Falls

In 24 hours: 100° F (55.57° C), Browing, Mont., Jan. 23-24, 1916, from 44° to −56° F (6.67° to −48.9° C).

In 12 hours: 84° F (46.67° C), Fairfield, Mont., Dec. 24, 1924, from 63° (17.22° C) at noon to −21° F (−29.45° C) at midnight.

In 2 hours: 62° F (34.45° C), Rapid City, S.D., Jan. 12, 1911, from 49° F (9.45° C) at 6:00 a.m. to −13° F (−25° C) at 8:00 a.m.

In 27 minutes: 58° F (32.22° C), Spearfish, S.D., Jan. 22, 1943, from 54° F (12.22° C) at 9:00 a.m. to −4° F (−20° C) at 9:27 a.m.

In 15 minutes: 63° F (26.11° C), Rapid City, S.D., Jan. 10, 1911, from 55° F (12.78° C) at 7:00 a.m. to 8° F (−13.33° C). at 7:15 a.m.

1. A warm, dry wind that descends from the eastern slopes of the Rocky Mountains, causing a rapid rise in temperature.

Winter Indoor Comfort and Relative Humidity

Compared to summer when the moisture content of the air (relative humidity) is an important factor of body discomfort, air moisture has a lesser effect on the human body during outdoor winter activities. But it is a big factor for winter indoor comfort because it has a direct bearing on health and energy consumption.

The colder the outdoor temperature, the more heat must be added indoors for body comfort. However, the heat that is added will cause a drying effect and lower the indoor relative humidity, unless an indoor moisture source is present.

While a room temperature between 71° and 77° F may be comfortable for short periods of time under very dry conditions, prolonged exposure to dry air has varying effects on the human body and usually causes discomfort. The moisture content of the air is important, and by increasing the rela-

Average Indoor Relative Humidity, %, for January

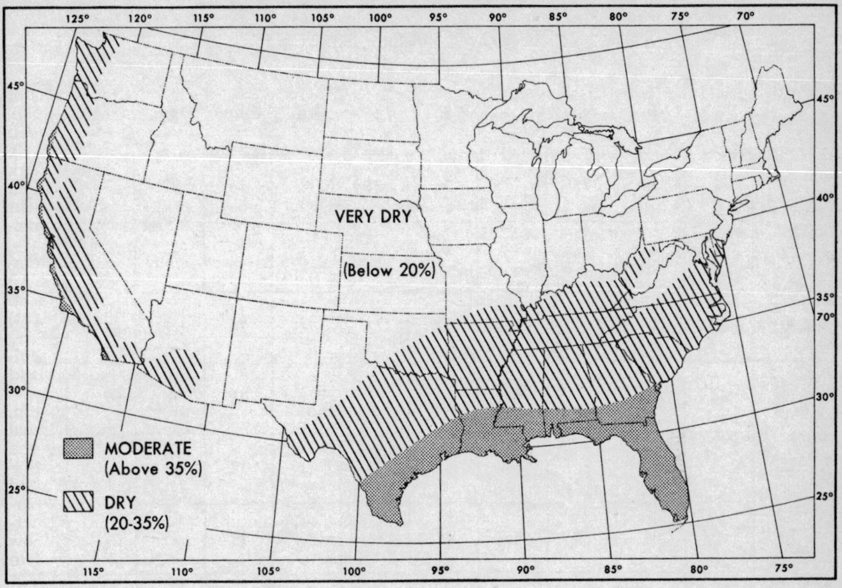

Source: National Oceanic and Atmospheric Administration, Environmental Data and Information Service, National Climatic Center.

tive humidity to above 50% within the above temperature range, 80% or more of all average dressed persons would feel comfortable.

Effects of Dry Air on the Body

Studies have shown that dry air has four main effects on the human body:

1. Breathing dry air is a potential health hazard which can cause such respiratory ailments as asthma, bronchitis, sinusitis, and nosebleeds, or general dehydration since body fluids are depleted during respiration.

2. Skin moisture evaporation can cause skin irritations and eye itching.

3. Irritative effects, such as static electricity which causes mild shocks when metal is touched, are common when the air moisture is low.

4. The "apparent temperature" of the air is lower than what the thermometer indicates, and the body "feels" colder.

These problems can be reduced by simply increasing the indoor relative humidity. This can be done through use of humidifiers, vaporizers, steam generators, sources such as large pans, or water containers made of porous ceramics. Even wet towels or water in a bathtub will be of some help. The lower the room temperature the easier the relative humidity can be brought to its desired level. A relative humidity indicator (hygrometer) may be of assistance in determining the humidity in the house.

Referring to item 4, a more detailed discussion is necessary. While the indoor temperature as read from a thermometer may be 75° F, the apparent temperature (what it feels like) may be warmer or colder depending on the moisture content of the air. Apparent temperature can vary as much as 8° F within a relative humidity range of 10 to 80 percent (these limits are generally possible in a closed room). Because of evaporation the human body cools when exposed to dry air, and the sense of coldness increases as the humidity decreases. With a room temperature of 70° F, for example, a person will feel colder in a dry room than in a moist room; this is especially noticeable when entering a dry room after bathing.

The table on the following page gives apparent temperatures for various combinations of room temperature and relative humidity. As an example of how to read the table, a room temperature of 70° F combined with a relative humidity of 10% feels like 64° F, but at 80% it feels like 71° F.

Although degrees of comfort vary with age, health, activity, clothing, and body characteristics, the table can be used as a general guideline when raising the apparent temperature and the level of comfort through an increase in room moisture, rather than by an addition of heat to the room. This method of changing the apparent temperature can give the direct benefit of reducing heating costs because comfort can be maintained with a lower thermostat setting if moisture is added. For example, an apparent comfortable temperature can be maintained with a thermostat setting of 75° F with 20% relative humidity or with a 70° F setting with 80 percent humidity. A relative humidity of 20 percent is common for homes without a humidifier during winter in the northern United States.

Apparent Temperature for Values of Room Temperature and Relative Humidity

ROOM TEMPERATURE (°F) \ RELATIVE HUMIDITY (%)	0	10	20	30	40	50	60	70	80	90	100
75	68	69	71	72	74	75	76	76	77	78	79
74	66	68	69	71	72	73	74	75	76	77	78
73	65	67	68	70	71	72	73	74	75	76	77
72	64	65	67	68	70	71	72	73	74	75	76
71	63	64	66	67	68	70	71	72	73	74	75
70	63	64	65	66	67	68	69	70	71	72	73
69	62	63	64	65	66	67	68	69	70	71	72
68	61	62	63	64	65	66	67	68	69	70	71
67	60	61	62	63	64	65	66	67	68	68	69
66	59	60	61	62	63	64	65	66	67	67	68
65	59	60	61	61	62	63	64	65	65	66	67
64	58	59	60	60	61	62	63	64	64	65	66
63	57	58	59	59	60	61	62	62	63	64	64
62	56	57	58	58	59	60	61	61	62	63	63
61	56	57	57	58	59	59	60	60	61	61	62
60	55	56	56	57	58	58	59	59	60	60	61

Source: National Oceanic and Atmospheric Administration, Environmental Data and Information Service and National Climatic Center.

PEOPLE

Many public figures not listed here may be found elsewhere in the *Information Please Almanac.*

48 Governors
607 Presidents
609 Presidents' Wives
41 Senators
851 Sports Personalities
623 Supreme Court Justices
607 Vice Presidents

A name in parentheses is the original name or form of name. Localities are places of birth. Country name in parenthesis is the present-day name. Dates of birth appear as month/day/year. **Boldface** years in parentheses are dates of **(birth-death).**

Information has been gathered from many sources, including the individuals themselves. However, the *Information Please Almanac* cannot guarantee the accuracy of every individual item.

A

Aalto, Alvar (architect); Kuortane, Finland **(1898-1976)**
Abbott, Bud (William) (comedian); Asbury Park, N.J. **(1898-1974)**
Abbott, George (stage producer); Forestville, N.Y., 6/25/1887
Abel, Walter (actor); St. Paul **(1898-1987)**
Abelard, Peter (theologian); nr. Nantes, France **(1079-1142)**
Abernathy, Ralph (civil rights leader); Linden, Ala., 3/11/1926
Acheson, Dean (statesman); Middletown, Conn. **(1893-1971)**
Acuff, Roy Claxton (musician); nr. Maynardsville, Tenn. 9/15/1903
Adams, Charles Francis (diplomat); Boston **(1807-1886)**
Adams, Don (actor); New York City, 4/19/1927
Adams, Edie (Edie Enke) (actress); Kingston, Pa., 4/16/1929
Adams, Franklin Pierce (columnist and author); Chicago **(1881-1960)**
Adams, Henry Brooks (historian); Boston **(1838-1918)**
Adams, Joey (comedian); New York City, 1/6/1911
Adams, Maude (Maude Kiskadden) (actress); Salt Lake City, **(1872-1953)**
Adams, Samuel (American Revolutionary patriot); Boston **(1722-1803)**
Adamson, Joy (naturalist); Troppau, Silesia **(1910-1980)**
Addams, Charles (cartoonist); Westfield, N.J., 1/7/1912
Addams, Jane (social worker); Cedarville, Ill. **(1860-1935)**
Adderley, Julian "Cannonball" (jazz saxophonist); Tampa, Fla. **(1928-1975)**
Ade, George (humorist); Kentland, Ind. **(1866-1944)**
Adenauer, Konrad (statesman); Cologne, Germany **(1876-1967)**
Adler, Alfred (psychoanalyst); Vienna **(1870-1937)**
Adler, Larry (musician); Baltimore, 2/10/1914
Adler, Richard (songwriter); New York City, 8/3/1921
Adoree, Renée (Renée La Fonte) (actress); Lille, France **(1898-1933)**
Aeschylus (dramatist); Eleusis (Greece) **(525-456 B.C.)**
Aesop (fabulist); birthplace unknown **(lived c. 600 B.C.)**
Aherne, Brian (actor); King's Norton, England **(1902-1986)**
Aiken, Conrad (poet); Savannah, Ga. **(1889-1973)**
Ailey, Alvin (choreographer); Rogers, Tex., 1/5/1931
Albanese, Licia (operatic soprano); Bari, Italy, 7/22/1913
Albee, Edward (playwright); Washington, D.C., 3/12/1928
Albers, Josef (painter); Bottrop, Germany **(1888-1976)**
Albert, Eddie (Edward Albert Heimberger) (actor); Rock Island, Ill., 4/22/1908
Albertson, Jack (actor); Malden, Mass. **(1910?-1981)**
Albright, Lola (actress); Akron, Ohio, 7/20/1925
Alcott, Louisa May (novelist); Germantown, Pa. **(1832-1888)**
Alda, Alan (actor); New York City, 1/28/1936
Alda, Robert (Alphonso d'Abruzzo) (actor); New York City **(1914-1986)**
Alden, John (American Pilgrim); England **(1599?-1687)**
Alexander the Great (monarch and conqueror); Pella, Macedonia (Greece) **(356-323 B.C.)**
Alger, Horatio (author); Revere, Mass. **(1834-1899)**
Algren, Nelson (novelist); Detroit **(1909-1981)**
Allen, Ethan (American Revolutionary soldier); Litchfield, Conn. **(1738-1789)**
Allen, Fred (John Florence Sullivan) (comedian); Cambridge, Mass. **(1894-1956)**
Allen, Gracie (Grace Ethel Cecile Rosalie Allen) (comedienne); San Francisco **(1906-1964)**
Allen, Mel (Melvin Israel) (sportscaster); Birmingham, Ala., 2/14/1913
Allen, Steve (TV entertainer); New York City, 12/26/1921
Allen, Woody (Allen Stewart Konigsberg) (actor, writer, and director); Brooklyn, N.Y., 12/1/1935
Allison, Fran (actress); LaPorte City, Iowa, 1924(?)
Allman, Gregg (singer); Nashville, Tenn., 12/8/1947
Allyson, June (Jan Allyson) (actress); New York City, 10/7/1923
Alonso, Alicia (ballerina); Havana, 12/21/1921(?)
Alpert, Herb (band leader); Los Angeles, 3/31/1935(?)
Alsop, Joseph W., Jr. (journalist); Avon, Conn., 10/11/1910
Alsop, Stewart (journalist); Avon, Conn. **(1914-1974)**
Altman, Robert (film director); Kansas City, Mo., 2/20/1925
Amati, Nicola (violin maker); Cremona, Italy **(1596-1684)**
Ambler, Eric (suspense writer); London, 6/28/1909
Ameche, Don (Dominic Amici) (actor); Kenosha, Wis., 5/31/1908
Amis, Kingsley (novelist); London, 4/16/1922
Amory, Cleveland (writer and conservationist); Nahant, Mass., 9/2/1917
Amos (Freeman F. Gosden) (radio comedian); Richmond, Va., **(1899-1982)**
Amsterdam, Morey (actor); Chicago, 12/14/1914
Andersen, Hans Christian (author of fairy-tales); Odense, Denmark **(1805-1875)**
Anderson, Eddie. *See* Rochester
Anderson, Ib (ballet dancer); Copenhagen, 12/14/1954
Anderson, Jack (journalist); Long Beach, Calif., 10/19/1922
Anderson, Dame Judith (actress); Adelaide, Australia, 2/10/1898
Anderson, Lindsay (Gordon) (director); Bangalore, India, 4/17/1923
Anderson, Lynn (singer); Grand Forks, N.D., 9/26/1947
Anderson, Marian (contralto); Philadelphia, 2/17/1902
Anderson, Maxwell (dramatist); Atlantic, Pa. **(1888-1959)**
Anderson, Robert (playwright); New York City, 4/28/1917
Andersson, Bibi (actress); Stockholm, 11/11/1935
Andress, Ursula (actress); Switzerland, 3/19/1938
Andrews, Dana (actor); Collins, Miss., 1/1/1909
Andrews, Julie (Julia Wells) (actress and singer); Walton-on-Thames, England, 10/1/1935
Andrews, La Verne (singer); Minneapolis **(1916-1967)**
Andrews, Maxene (singer); Minneapolis, 1/3/1918
Andrews, Patti (singer); Minneapolis, 2/16/1920
Andy (Charles J. Correll) (radio comedian); Peoria, Ill. **(1890-1972)**
Angeles, Victoria de los (Victoria Gamez Cima) (operatic soprano); Barcelona, 11/1/1924
Anka, Paul (singer and composer); Ottawa, 7/30/1941
Ann-Margret (Ann-Margret Olsson) (actress); Valsjobyn, Sweden, 4/28/1941
Annabella (actress); Paris, 1912
Anouilh, Jean (playwright); Bordeaux, France, 6/23/1910
Anthony, Susan Brownell (woman suffragist); Adams, Mass. **(1820-1906)**
Antonioni, Michelangelo (director); Ferrara, Italy, 9/29/1912
Antony, Mark (Marcus Antonius) (statesman); Rome **(83?-30 B.C.)**
Anuszkiewicz, Richard (painter); Erie, Pa., 5/23/1930
Aquinas, St. Thomas (philosopher); nr. Aquino (Italy) **(1225?-1274)**
Arbuckle, Roscoe "Fatty" (actor and director); San Jose, Calif. **(1887-1933)**
Archimedes (physicist and mathematician); Syracuse, Sicily **(287?-212 B.C.)**
Archipenko, Alexandre (sculptor); Kiev, Russia **(1887-1964)**
Arden, Elizabeth (Florence Nightingale Graham) (cosmetics executive); Woodbridge, Canada **(1891-1966)**
Arden, Eve (Eunice Quedens) (actress); Mill Valley, Calif., 4/30/1912
Arendt, Hannah (historian); Hannover, Germany **(1906-1975)**
Aristophanes (dramatist); Athens **448?-380 B.C.)**
Aristotle (philosopher); Stagirus, Macedonia **(384-322 B.C.)**
Arkin, Alan (actor and director); New York City, 3/26/1934
Arledge, Roone (TV executive); Forest Hills, N.Y., 7/8/1931
Arlen, Harold (Hyman Arluck) (composer); Buffalo, N.Y. **(1905-1986)**
Arlen, Richard (actor); Charlottesville, Va. **(1900-1976)**
Arliss, George (actor); London **(1868-1946)**
Armstrong, Louis ("Satchmo") (musician); New Orleans **(1900-1971)**
Armstrong-Jones, Anthony. *See* Snowdon, Earl of
Arnaz, Desi (Desiderio) (actor and producer); Santiago, Cuba **(1917-1986)**

Arness, James (James Aurness) (TV actor); Minneapolis, 5/26/1923
Arno, Peter (cartoonist); New York City **(1904-1968)**
Arnold, Benedict (American Revolutionary War general, charged with treason); Norwich, Conn. **(1741-1801)**
Arnold, Eddy (singer); Henderson, Tenn., 5/15/1918
Arnold, Edward (actor); New York City **(1890-1956)**
Arnold, Matthew (poet and critic); Laleham, England **(1822-1888)**
Arp, Jean (sculptor and painter); Strasbourg (France) **(1887-1966)**
Arquette, Cliff ("Charley Weaver") (actor); Toledo, Ohio **(1905-1974)**
Arrau, Claudio (pianist); Chillán, Chile, 2/6/1903
Arroyo, Martina (soprano); New York City, 2/2/1940
Arthur, Bea (Bernice Frankel) (actress); New York City, 5/13/1926(?)
Arthur, Jean (Gladys Greene) (actress); New York City, 10/17/1905
Asch, Sholem (novelist); Kutno, Poland **(1880-1957)**
Ashkenazy, Vladimir (concert pianist); Gorki, U.S.S.R., 7/6/1937
Ashley, Elizabeth (actress); Ocala, Fla., 8/30/1939
Ashton, Sir Frederick William Mallandaine (choreographer); Guayaquil, Ecuador, 9/17/1904
Asimov, Isaac (author); Petrovichi, Russia, 1/2/1920
Asner, Edward (actor); Kansas City, Mo., 11/15/1929
Astaire, Fred (Frederick Austerlitz) (dancer and actor); Omaha, Neb **(1899-1987)**
Astor, John Jacob (financier); Waldorf (Germany) **(1763-1848)**
Astor, Mary (Lucile Langhanke) (actress); Quincy, Ill., 5/3/1906
Atkins, Chet (guitarist); nr. Luttrell, Tenn., 6/20/1924
Atkinson, Brooks (drama critic); Melrose, Mass. **(1894-1984)**
Attenborough, Richard (actor-director) Cambridge, England, 8/29/1923
Attila (King of Huns, called "Scourge of God") **(406?-453)**
Attlee, Clement Richard (statesman); London **(1883-1967)**
Auchincloss, Louis (author); Lawrence, N.Y., 9/27/1917
Auden, W(ystan) H(ugh) (poet); York, England **(1907-1973)**
Audubon, John James (naturalist and painter); Haiti **(1785-1851)**
Auer, Leopold (violinist and teacher); Veszprém, Hungary **(1845-1930)**
Auer, Mischa (actor); St. Petersburg, Russia **(1905-1967)**
Augustine, Saint (Aurelius Augustinus) (theologian); Tagaste, Numidia (Algeria) **(354-430)**
Augustus (Gaius Octavius) (Roman emperor); Rome **(63 B.C.-A.D. 14)**
Aumont, Jean-Pierre (actor); Paris, 1/5/1913
Austen, Jane (novelist); Steventon, England **(1775-1817)**
Autry, Gene (singer and actor); Tioga, Tex., 9/29/1907
Avalon, Frankie (singer); Philadelphia, 9/18/1940
Avedon, Richard (photographer); New York City, 5/15/1923
Avery, Milton (painter); Altmar, N.Y. **(1893-1965)**
Ax, Emanuel (pianist); Lvov, U.S.S.R., 6/8/1949
Axelrod, George (playwright); New York City, 6/9/1922
Ayckbourn, Alan (playwright); London, 4/12/1939
Ayckroyd, Dan (actor); Ottawa, Ont., Canada, 7/1/1952
Ayres, Lew (actor); Minneapolis, 12/28/1908

B

Bacall, Lauren (Betty Joan Perske) (actress); New York City, 9/16/1924
Bach, Johann Sebastian (composer); Eisenach (East Germany) **(1685-1750)**
Bach, Karl Phillipp Emanuel (composer); Weimar (East Germany) **(1714-1788)**
Bacharach, Burt (songwriter); Kansas City, Mo., 5/12/1929
Backus, Jim (actor); Cleveland, 2/25/1913
Bacon, Francis (painter); Dublin, 1910
Bacon, Francis (philosopher and essayist); London **(1561-1626)**
Bacon, Roger (philosopher and scientist); Ilchester, England **(1214?-1294)**
Baedeker, Karl (travel-guidebook publisher); Essen (Germany) **(1801-1859)**
Baez, Joan (folk singer); Staten Island, N.Y., 1/9/1941
Bagnold, Enid (novelist); Rochester, England **(1889-1981)**
Bailey, F. Lee (lawyer); Waltham, Mass., 6/10/1933
Bailey, Pearl (singer); Newport News, Va., 3/29/1918
Bainter, Fay (actress); Los Angeles **(1891-1968)**
Baird, Bil (William B.) (puppeteer); Grand Island, Neb **(1904-1987)**
Baker, Carroll (actress); Johnstown, Pa., 5/28/1931
Baker, Josephine (singer and dancer); St. Louis **(1906-1975)**
Baker, Russell (columnist); Loudoun County, Va., 8/14/1925
Balanchine, George (choreographer); St. Petersburg, Russia **(1904-1983)**
Balboa, Vasco Nuñez de (explorer); Jerez de los Caballeros (Spain) **(1475-1517)**
Baldwin, Faith (novelist); New Rochelle, N.Y. **(1893-1978)**
Baldwin, James (novelist); New York City, 8/2/1924
Balenciaga, Cristóbal (fashion designer); Guetaria, Spain **(1895-1972)**
Ball, Lucille (Dianne Belmont) (actress and producer); Celoron (nr. Jamestown), N.Y., 8/6/1911
Ballard, Kaye (Catherine Gloria Balotta) (actress); Cleveland, 11/20/1926
Balmain, Pierre (fashion designer); St.-Jean-de-Maurienne, France **(1914-1982)**
Balsam, Martin (actor); New York City, 11/4/1919
Balzac, Honoré de (novelist); Tours, France **(1799-1850)**
Bancroft, Anne (Annemarie Italiano) (actress); New York City, 9/17/1931
Bancroft, George (actor); Philadelphia **(1882-1956)**
Bankhead, Tallulah (actress); Huntsville, Ala. **(1903-1963)**
Banneker, Benjamin (almanacker and mathematician-astronomer on District of Columbia site survey); Ellicott, Md. **(1731-1806)**
Banting, Fredrick Grant (physiologist); Alliston, Ont., Canada **(1891-1941)**
Bara, Theda (Theodosia Goodman) (actress); Cincinnati **(1890-1955)**
Barber, Red (Walter Lanier) (sportscaster); Columbus, Miss., 2/17/1908
Barber, Samuel (composer); West Chester, Pa. **(1910-1981)**
Barca, Pedro Calderón del al (dramatist); Madrid **(1600-1681)**
Bardot, Brigitte (actress); Paris, 1935
Barenboim, Daniel (concert pianist and conductor); Buenos Aires, 11/15/1942
Barnard, Christiaan N. (heart surgeon); Beauford West, South Africa, 1923
Barnum, Phineas Taylor (showman); Bethel, Conn. **(1810-1891)**
Barrie, Sir James Matthew (author); Kirriemuir, Scotland **(1860-1937)**
Barrie, Wendy (actress); Hong Kong **(1913-1978)**
Barry, Gene (Eugene Klass) (actor); New York City, 6/4/1922
Barry, John (naval officer); County Wexford, Ireland **(1745-1803)**
Barrymore, Diana (actress); New York City **(1921-1960)**
Barrymore, Ethel (Ethel Blythe) (actress); Philadelphia **(1879-1959)**
Barrymore, Georgiana Drew (actress); Philadelphia **(1856-1893)**
Barrymore, John (John Blythe) (actor); Philadelphia **(1882-1942)**
Barrymore, Lionel (Lionel Blythe) (actor); Philadelphia **(1878-1954)**
Barrymore, Maurice (Herbert Blythe) (actor and playwright); Agra, India **(1847-1905)**
Bartheime, Donald (novelist); Philadelphia, 4/7/1931
Barthelmess, Richard (actor); New York City **(1897-1963)**
Bartholomew, Freddie (actor); London, 3/28/1924
Bartók, Béla (composer); Nagyszentmiklos (Romania) **(1881-1945)**
Barton, Clara (founder of American Red Cross); Oxford, Mass. **(1821-1912)**
Baruch, Bernard Mannes (statesman), Camden, S.C. **(1870-1965)**
Baryshnikov, Mikhail Nikolayevich (ballet dancer and artistic director); Riga, Latvia, 1/27/1948
Basehart, Richard (actor); Zanesville, Ohio **(1914-1984)**
Basie, Count (William) (band leader); Red Bank, N.J. **(1904-1984)**
Bassey, Shirley (singer); Cardiff, Wales, 1/8/1937
Batchelor, Clarence Daniel (political cartoonist); Osage City, Kan. **(1888-1977)**
Bates, Alan (actor); Allestree, England, 2/17/1934
Battle, Kathleen (soprano); Portsmouth, Ohio, 8/13/48
Baudelaire, Charles Pierre (poet); Paris **(1821-1867)**
Baudouin (King); Palace of Laeken, Belgium, 9/7/1930
Baxter, Anne (actress); Michigan City, Ind. **(1923-1985)**
Baxter, Warner (actor); Columbus, Ohio **(1891-1951)**
Bean, Orson (Dallas Frederick Burrows) (actor); Burlington, Vt., 7/22/1928
Beardsley, Aubrey Vincent (illustrator); Brighton, England **(1872-1898)**
Beaton, Cecil (photographer and designer); London **(1904-1980)**
Beatty, Warren (actor and producer); Richmond, Va., 3/30/1937
Beaumont, Francis (dramatist); Grace-Dieu, England **(1584-1616)**
Becket, Thomas à (Archbishop of Canterbury); London **(1118?-1170)**
Beckett, Samuel (playwright); Dublin, 4/13/1906
Beckmann, Max (painter); Leipzig, Germany **(1884-1950)**
Bede, Saint ("The Venerable Bede") (scholar); Monkwearmouth, England **(673-735)**
Beecham, Sir Thomas (conductor); St. Helens, England **(1879-1961)**
Beecher, Henry Ward (clergyman); Litchfield, Conn. **(1813-1887)**
Beerbohm, Sir Max (author); London **(1872-1956)**
Beery, Noah, Jr. (actor); New York City, 8/10/1916
Beery, Wallace (actor); Kansas City, Mo. **(1886-1949)**
Beethoven, Ludwig van (composer); Bonn (Germany) **(1770-1827)**
Begley, Ed (actor); Hartford, Conn. **(1901-1970)**
Belafonte, Harry (singer and actor); New York City, 3/1/1927
Belasco, David (dramatist and producer); San Francisco **(1854-1931)**
Bell, Alexander Graham (inventor); Edinburgh, Scotland **(1847-1922)**
Bellamy, Edward (author); Chicopee Falls, Mass. **(1850-1898)**
Bellamy, Ralph (actor); Chicago, 6/17/1904
Bellini, Giovanni (painter); Venice **(c.1430-1516)**
Bellow, Saul (novelist); Lachine, Quebec, Canada, 7/10/1915

Bellows, George Wesley (painter and lithographer); Columbus, Ohio **(1882-1925)**
Belmondo, Jean-Paul (actor); Neuilly-sur-Seine, France, 4/9/1933
Belushi, John (comedian, actor); Chicago **(1949-1982)**
Benchley, Peter Bradford (novelist); New York City, 5/8/1940
Benchley, Robert Charles (humorist); Worcester, Mass. **(1889-1945)**
Bendix, William (actor); New York City **(1906-1964)**
Benes, Eduard (statesman); Kozlany (Czechoslovakia) **(1884-1948)**
Benét, Stephen Vincent (poet and story writer); Bethlehem, Pa. **(1898-1943)**
Benét, William Rose (poet and novelist); Ft. Hamilton, Brooklyn, N.Y. **(1886-1950)**
Ben-Gurion, David (David Green) (statesman); Plónsk (Poland) **(1886-1973)**
Benjamin, Richard (actor); New York City, 5/22/1938
Bennett, Constance (actress); New York City **(1905-1965)**
Bennett, Enoch Arnold (novelist and dramatist); Hanley, England **(1867-1931)**
Bennett, James Gordon (editor); Keith, Scotland **(1795-1872)**
Bennett, Joan (actress); Palisades, N.J., 2/27/1910
Bennett, Robert Russell (composer); Kansas City, Mo., **(1894-1981)**
Bennett, Tony (Anthony Benedetto) (singer); Astoria, Queens, N.Y., 8/3/1926
Benny, Jack (Benjamin Kubelsky) (comedian); Chicago **(1894-1974)**
Bentham, Jeremy Heinrich (economist); London **(1748-1832)**
Benton, Thomas Hart (painter); Neosho, Mo. **(1889-1975)**
Berg, Alban (composer); Vienna **(1885-1935)**
Berg, Gertrude (writer and actress); New York City **(1899-1966)**
Bergen, Candice (actress); Beverly Hills, Calif., 5/9/1946
Bergen, Edgar (ventriloquist); Chicago, **(1903-1978)**
Bergen, Polly (actress and singer); Knoxville, Tenn., 7/14/1930
Bergerac, Cyrano de (poet); Paris **(1619-1655)**
Bergman, Ingmar (film director); Uppsala, Sweden, 7/14/1918
Bergman, Ingrid (actress); Stockholm **(1918-1982)**
Bergson, Henri (philosopher); Paris **(1859-1941)**
Berle, Milton (Milton Berlinger) (comedian); New York City, 7/12/1908
Berlin, Irving (Israel Baline) (songwriter); Temum, Russia, 5/11/1888
Berlioz, Louis Hector (composer); La Côte-Saint-André, France **(1803-1869)**
Berman, Lazar (concert pianist); Leningrad, 1930.
Berman, Shelley (Sheldon) (comedian); Chicago, 2/3/1926
Bernardi, Herschel (actor); New York City **(1922-1986)**
Bernhardt, Sarah (Rosine Bernard) (actress); Paris **(1844-1923)**
Bernini, Gian Lorenzo (sculptor and painter); Naples (Italy) **(1598-1680)**
Bernoulli, Jacques (scientist); Basel, Switzerland **(1654-1705)**
Bernstein, Leonard (conductor); Lawrence, Mass., 8/25/1918
Berry, Chuck (Charles Edward Berry) (singer); San Jose, Calif., 1/15/1926
Betjeman, Sir John (Poet Laureate); London **(1906-1984)**
Bickford, Charles (actor); Cambridge, Mass. **(1889-1967)**
Bierce, Ambrose Gwinnett (journalist); Meigs County, Ohio **(1842-1914?)**
Bikel, Theodore (actor and folk singer); Vienna, 5/2/1924
Bing, Sir Rudolf (opera manager); Vienna, 1/9/1902
Bingham, George Caleb (painter); Augusta Co., Va. **(1811-1879)**
Bishop, Joey (Joseph Gottlieb) (comedian); New York City, 2/3/1919
Bismarck-Schönhausen, Prince Otto Eduard Leopold von (statesman); Schönhausen (East Germany) **(1815-1898)**
Bisset, Jacqueline (actress); Weybridge, England, 9/13/1944
Bixby, Bill (actor); San Francisco, 1/22/1934
Bizet, Georges (Alexandre César Léopold Bizet) (composer); Paris **(1838-1875)**
Black, Cilla (singer and actress); Liverpool, England, 5/27/1943
Black, Karen (actress); Park Ridge, Ill., 7/1/1942
Black, Shirley Temple (former actress); Santa Monica, Calif., 4/23/1928
Blackmer, Sidney (actor); Salisbury, N.C. **(1898-1973)**
Blackstone, Sir William (jurist); London **(1723-1780)**
Blaine, Vivian (actress and singer); Newark, N.J., 11/21/1924
Blair, Janet (actress); Altoona, Pa., 4/23/1921
Blake, Amanda (Beverly Louise Neill) (actress); Buffalo, N.Y., 1931
Blake, Eubie (James Hubert) (pianist); Baltimore, **(1883-1983)**
Blake, Robert (Michael Gubitosi) (actor); Nutley, N.J., 9/18/1933
Blake, William (poet and artist); London **(1757-1827)**
Blanc, Mel(vin Jerome) (actor and voice specialist); San Francisco, 5/30/1908
Blass, Bill (fashion designer); Fort Wayne, Ind., 6/22/1922
Bloch, Ernest (composer); Geneva **(1880-1959)**
Blondell, Joan (actress); New York City **(1909-1979)**
Bloom, Claire (actress); London, 2/15/1931
Bloomgarden, Kermit (producer); Brooklyn, N.Y. **(1904-1976)**
Blue, Monte (actor); Indianapolis **(1890-1963)**
Blyth, Ann (actress); New York City, 8/16/1928
Boccaccio, Giovanni (author); Paris **(1313-1375)**
Boccherini, Luigi (Rodolfo) (composer); Lucca, Italy **(1743-1805)**
Boccioni, Umberto (painter and sculptor); Reggio di Calabria, Italy **(1882-1916)**
Bock, Jerry (composer); New Haven, Conn., 11/23/1928
Bogarde, Dirk (Derek Van den Bogaerde) (film actor and director); London, 3/28/1921
Bogart, Humphrey DeForest (actor); New York City **(1899-1957)**
Bogdanovich, Peter (producer and director); Kingston, N.Y., 7/30/1939
Bohlen, Charles E. (diplomat); Clayton, N.Y. **(1904-1974)**
Bohr, Niels (atomic physicist); Copenhagen **(1885-1962)**
Bolger, Ray (dancer and actor); Dorchester, Mass **(1904-1987)**
Bolivar, Simón (South American liberator); Caracas, Venezuela **(1783-1830)**
Bologna, Giovanni da (sculptor); Douai (France) **(1529-1608)**
Bombeck, Erma (author, columnist); Dayton, Ohio 2/21/1927
Bonaparte, Napoleon (Emperor of the French); Ajaccio, Corsica (France) **(1769-1821)**
Bond, Julian (Georgia legislator); Nashville, Tenn., 1/14/1940
Bondi, Beulah (actress); Chicago **(1883-1981)**
Bonnard, Pierre (painter); Fontenayaux-Roses, France **(1867-1947)**
Bono, Sonny (Salvatore) (singer); Detroit, 2/16/1935
Boone, Daniel (frontiersman); nr. Reading, Pa. **(1734-1820)**
Boone, Pat (Charles) (singer); Jacksonville, Fla., 6/1/1934
Boone, Richard (actor); Los Angeles **(1917-1981)**
Booth, Edwin Thomas (actor); Bel Air, Md. **(1833-1893)**
Booth, Evangeline Cory (religious leader); London **(1865-1950)**
Booth, John Wilkes (actor; assassin of Lincoln); Harford County, Md. **(1838-1865)**
Booth, Shirley (Thelma Booth Ford) (actress); New York City, 8/30/1907
Bordoni, Irene (actress); Ajaccio (France) **(1895-1953)**
Borge, Victor (pianist and comedian); Copenhagen, 1/3/1909
Borgia, Cesare (nobleman and soldier); Rome **(1475?-1507)**
Borgia, Lucrezia (Duchess of Ferrara); Rome **(1480-1519)**
Borgnine, Ernest (actor); Hamden, Conn., 1/24/1917
Borromini, Francesco (architect); Bissone (Italy) **(1599-1667)**
Bosch, Hieronymus (Hieronymus van Aeken) (painter); Hertogenbosch (Netherlands) **(c.1450-1516)**
Bosley, Tom (actor); Chicago, 10/1/1927
Boswell, Connee (singer); New Orleans **(1907-1976)**
Boswell, James (diarist and biographer); Edinburgh, Scotland **(1740-1795)**
Botticelli, Sandro (Alessandro di Mariano dei Filipepi) (painter); Florence (Italy) **(1444?-1510)**
Boulez, Pierre (conductor); Montbrison, France, 3/26/1925
Bourke-White, Margaret (photographer); New York City **(1906-1971)**
Bow, Clara (actress); Brooklyn, N.Y. **(1905-1965)**
Bowen, Catherine Drinker (biographer); Haverford, Pa. **(1897-1973)**
Bowie, David (David Robert Jones) (actor and musician); London, 1/8/1947(?)
Bowie, James (soldier); Burke County, Ga. **(1799-1836)**
Bowles, Chester (diplomat); Springfield, Mass. **(1901-1986)**
Boyce, William (composer); London? **(1710-1779)**
Boyd, Bill (William) ("Hopalong Cassidy") (actor); Cambridge, Ohio **(1898-1972)**
Boyd, Stephen (Stephen Millar) (actor); Belfast, Northern Ireland **(1928-1977)**
Boyer, Charles (actor); Figeac, France **(1899-1978)**
Boy George (George Alan O'Dowd) (singer); London, 1961
Boyle, Robert (scientist); Lismore Castle, Munster, Ireland **(1627-1691)**
Bracken, Eddie (actor); Astoria, Queens, N.Y., 2/7/1920
Bradbury, Ray Douglas (science-fiction writer); Waukegan, Ill., 8/22/1920
Bradlee, Benjamin C. (editor); Boston, 8/26/1921
Bradley, Omar N. (5-star general); Clark, Mo. **(1893-1981)**
Brady, Scott (actor); Brooklyn, N.Y., **(1924-1985)**
Brahe, Tycho (astronomer); Knudstrup, Denmark **(1546-1601)**
Brahms, Johannes (composer); Hamburg **(1833-1897)**
Braille, Louis (teacher of blind); Coupvray, France **(1809-1862)**
Brailowsky, Alexander (pianist); Kiev, Russia **(1896-1976)**
Bramante, Donato D'Agnolo (architect); Monte Asdrualdo (now Fermignano, Italy) **(1444-1514)**
Brancusi, Constantin (sculptor); Pestisansi, Romania **(1876-1957)**
Brando, Marlon (actor); Omaha, Neb., 4/3/1924
Brandt, Willy (Herbert Frahm) (ex-Chancellor); Lübeck, Germany, 12/18/1913
Braque, Georges (painter); Argenteuil, France **(1882-1963)**
Brazzi, Rossano (actor); Bologna, Italy, 9/18/1916
Brecht, Bertolt (dramatist and poet); Augsburg, Bavaria **(1898-1956)**
Brel, Jacques (singer and composer); Brussels, **(1929-1978)**
Brennan, Walter (actor); Lynn, Mass. **(1894-1974)**
Brent, George (actor); Dublin **(1904-1979)**
Breslin, Jimmy (journalist): Jamaica, Queens, N.Y., 10/17/1930
Breuer, Marcel (architect and designer); Pécs, Hungary **(1902-1981)**

Brewer, Teresa (singer); Toledo, Ohio, 5/7/1931
Brewster, Kingman, Jr. (ex-president of Yale); Longmeadow, Mass., 6/17/1919
Brezhnev, Leonid I. (Communist Party Secretary); Dneprodzerzhinsk, Ukraine **(1906-1982)**
Brice, Fanny (Fannie Borach) (comedienne); New York City **(1892-1951)**
Bridges, Beau (actor); Los Angeles, 12/9/1941
Bridges, Lloyd (actor); San Leandro, Calif. 1/15/1913
Brinkley, David (TV newscaster); Wilmington, N.C., 7/10/1920
Britt, May (Maybritt Wilkins) (actress); Sweden, 3/22/1936
Britten, Benjamin (composer); Lowestoft, England **(1913-1976)**
Britton, Barbara (actress); Long Beach, Calif. **(1920-1980)**
Bromfield, Louis (novelist); Mansfield, Ohio **(1896-1956)**
Bronson, Charles (Charles Buchinsky) (actor); Ehrenfield, Pa., 11/3/1922(?)
Brontë, Charlotte (novelist); Thornton, England **(1816-1855)**
Brontë, Emily Jane (novelist); Thornton, England **(1818-1848)**
Bronzino, Agnolo (painter); Monticelli (Italy) **(1503-1572)**
Brook, Peter (director); London, 3/21/1925
Brooke, Rupert (poet); Rugby, England **(1887-1915)**
Brooks, Geraldine (Geraldine Stroock) (actress); New York City **(1925-1977)**
Brooks, Gwendolyn (poet); Topeka, Kan., 6/7/1917
Brooks, Mel (Melvin Kaminsky) (writer and film director); Brooklyn, N.Y., 1926(?)
Brothers, Joyce (Bauer) (psychologist, author, radio-TV personality); New York City, 1927(?)
Broun, Matthew Heywood Campbell (journalist); Brooklyn, N.Y. **(1888-1939)**
Brown, Helen Gurley (author); Green Forest, Ark., 2/18/1922
Brown, James (singer); Augusta, Ga., 5/3/1934
Brown, Joe E. (comedian); Holgate, Ohio **(1892-1973)**
Brown, John (abolitionist); Torrington, Conn. **(1800-1859)**
Brown, John Mason (critic); Louisville, Ky. **(1900-1969)**
Brown, Les (band leader); Reinerton, Pa., 1912
Brown, Pamela (actress); London **(1918-1975)**
Brown, Vanessa (Smylla Brind) (actress); Vienna, 3/24/1928
Browne, Jackson (singer and guitarist); Heidelberg, Germany, 10/9/late 1940s
Browning, Elizabeth Barrett (poet); Durham, England **(1806-1861)**
Browning, Robert (poet); London **(1812-1889)**
Brubeck, Dave (musician); Concord, Calif., 12/6/1920
Bruce, Lenny (comedian); Long Island, N.Y. **(1926-1966)**
Brueghel, Pieter (painter); nr. Breda, Flanders (Netherlands) **(1520?-1569)**
Bruhn, Erik (Belton Evers) (ballet dancer); Copenhagen **(1928-1986)**
Brunelleschi, Filippo (architect); Florence (Italy) **(1377-1446)**
Bruno, Giordano (philosopher); Nola, Italy **(1548-1600)**
Brutus, Marcus Junius (Roman politician); **(85?-42 B.C.)**
Bryan, William Jennings (orator and politician); Salem, Ill. **(1860-1925)**
Bryant, Anita (singer); Barnsdall, Okla., 3/25/1940
Bryant, William Cullen (poet and editor); Cummington, Mass. **(1794-1878)**
Brynner, Yul (Taidje Khan) (actor); Sakhalin Island, Russia **(1920-1985)**
Brzezinski, Zbigniew (ex-presidential adviser); Warsaw, 3/28/1928
Buber, Martin (philosopher and theologian); Vienna **(1878-1965)**
Buchanan, Edgar (actor); Humansville, Mo., **(1903-1979)**
Buchholz, Horst (actor); Berlin, 12/4/1933
Buchwald, Art (Arthur) (columnist); Mount Vernon, N.Y., 10/20/1925
Buck, Pearl S(ydenstricker) (author); Hillsboro, W. Va. **(1892-1973)**
Buckley, William F., Jr. (journalist); New York City, 11/24/1925
Buddha. *See* Gautama Buddha
Buffalo Bill (William Frederick Cody) (scout); Scott County, Iowa **(1846-1917)**
Bujold, Genevieve (actress); Montreal, 7/1/1942
Bujones, Fernando (ballet dancer); Miami, Fla., 3/9/1955
Bullins, Ed (playwright); Philadelphia, 7/2/1935
Bumbry, Grace (mezzo-soprano); St. Louis, 1/4/1937
Bunche, Ralph J. (statesman); Detroit **(1904-1971)**
Bundy, McGeorge (educator); Boston, 3/30/1919
Bundy, William Putnam (editor); Washington, D.C., 9/24/1917
Buñuel, Luis (film director); Calanda, Spain, **(1900-1983)**
Bunyan, John (preacher and author); Elstow, England **(1628-1688)**
Burbank, Luther (horticulturist); Lancaster, Mass. **(1849-1926)**
Burke, Adm. Arleigh A. (ex-Chief of Naval Operations); Boulder, Colo., 10/19/1901
Burke, Billie (comedienne); Washington, D.C. **(1885-1970)**
Burke, Edmund (statesman); Dublin **(1729-1797)**
Burne-Jones, Edward Coley (painter); Birmingham, England **(1833-1898)**
Burnett, Carol (comedienne); San Antonio, 4/26/1936
Burney, Fanny (Frances) (writer); King's Lynn, England **(1752-1840)**
Burns, George (Nathan Birnbaum) (comedian); New York City, 1/20/1896
Burns, Robert (poet); Alloway, Scotland **(1759-1796)**
Burr, Aaron (political leader); Newark, N.J. **(1756-1836)**
Burr, Raymond (William Stacey Burr) (actor); New Westminster, British Columbia, Canada, 5/21/1917
Burroughs, Edgar Rice (novelist); Chicago **(1875-1950)**
Burrows, Abe (playwright and director); New York City, **(1910-1985)**
Burstyn, Ellen (Edna Rae Gillooly) (actress); Detroit, 12/7/1932
Burton, Richard (Richard Jenkins) (actor); Pontrhydfen, Wales **(1925-1984)**
Bush, Vannevar (scientist); Everett, Mass. **(1890-1974)**
Bushman, Francis X. (actor); Baltimore **(1883-1966)**
Butler, Samuel (author); Langar, England **(1835-1902)**
Buttons, Red (Aaron Chwatt) (actor); New York City, 2/5/1919
Buzzi, Ruth (comedienne); Wequetequock, Conn., 7/24/1936
Byrd, Richard Evelyn (polar explorer); Winchester, Va. **(1888-1957)**
Byron, George Gordon (6th Baron Byron) (poet); London **(1788-1824)**

C

Caan, James (actor); The Bronx, N.Y., 3/26/1939
Cabot, John (Giovanni Caboto) (navigator); Genoa (?) **(1450-1498)**
Cabot, Sebastian (navigator); Venice **(1476?-1557)**
Cadmus, Paul (painter and etcher); New York City, 12/17/1904
Caesar, Gaius Julius (statesman); Rome (100?-44 B.C.)
Caesar, Sid (comedian); Yonkers, N.Y., 9/8/1922
Cagney, James (actor); New York City **(1899-1986)**
Cahn, Sammy (songwriter); New York City, 6/18/1913
Caine, Michael (Maurice J. Micklewhite) (actor); London, 3/14/1933
Calder, Alexander (sculptor); Lawnton, Pa. **(1898-1976)**
Caldwell, Erskine (novelist); White Oak, Ga **(1903-1987)**
Caldwell, Sarah (opera director and conductor); Maryville, Mo., 1928
Caldwell, Taylor (novelist); Manchester, England **(1900-1985)**
Caldwell, Zoe (actress); Hawthorn, Australia, 9/14/1933
Calhern, Louis (Carl Henry Vogt) (actor); Brooklyn, N.Y. **(1895-1956)**
Calhoun, John Caldwell (statesman); nr. Calhoun Mills, S.C. **(1782-1850)**
Calisher, Hortense (novelist); New York City, 12/20/1911
Callas, Maria (Maria Calogeropoulos) (dramatic soprano); New York City **(1923-1977)**
Calloway, Cab (Cabell) (band leader); Rochester, N.Y., 12/25/1907
Calvet, Corinne (actress); Paris, 4/30/1926
Calvin, John (Jean Chauvin) (religious reformer); Noyon, Picardy **(1509-1564)**
Cambridge, Godfrey (comedian); New York City **(1933-1976)**
Cameron, Rod (Rod Cox) (actor); Calgary, Alberta, Canada, **(1912-1983)**
Campbell, Glen (singer); nr. Delight, Ark., 4/22/1938
Camus, Albert (author); Mondovi, Algeria **(1913-1960)**
Canaletto, (Giovanni Antonio Canale); (painter) Venice **(1697-1768)**
Caniff, Milton (cartoonist); Hillsboro, Ohio, 2/28/1907
Cannon, Dyan (actress); Tacoma, Wash., 1/4/1937
Canova, Judy (comedienne); Jacksonville, Fla., **(1916-1983)**
Cantinflas (Mario Moreno) (comedian); Mexico City, 8/12/1911
Cantor, Eddie (Edward Iskowitz) (actor); New York City **(1892-1964)**
Cantrell, Lana (singer); Sydney, Australia, 1944
Capote, Truman (novelist); New Orleans **(1924-1984)**
Capp, Al (Alfred Gerald Caplin) (cartoonist); New Haven, Conn. **(1909-1979)**
Capra, Frank (film producer, director); Palermo, Italy, 5/18/1897
Caravaggio, Michelangelo Merisi da (painter); Caravaggio (Italy) **(1573-1610)**
Cardin, Pierre (fashion designer); nr. Venice, 7/7/1922
Cardinale, Claudia (actress); Tunis, Tunisia, 1939
Carey, Harry (actor); New York City **(1878-1947)**
Carey, Macdonald (actor); Sioux City, Iowa, 3/15/1913
Carlisle, Kitty (singer and actress); New Orleans, 9/3/1915
Carlson, Richard (actor); Albert Lea, Minn., **(1912-1977)**
Carlyle, Thomas (essayist and historian); Ecclefechan, Scotland **(1795-1881)**
Carmichael, Hoagy (Hoagland Howard) (songwriter); Bloomington, Ind. **(1899-1981)**
Carne, Judy (Joyce Botterill) (singer); Northampton, England, 1939
Carnegie, Andrew (industrialist); Dunfermline, Scotland **(1835-1919)**
Carney, Art (actor); Mt. Vernon, N.Y., 11/4/1918
Carnovsky, Morris (actor); St. Louis, 9/5/1897
Caron, Leslie (actress); Paris, 7/1/1931
Carr, Vikki (singer); El Paso, 7/19/1942
Carracci, Annibale (painter); Bologna (Italy) **(1560-1609)**
Carracci, Lodovico (painter); Bologna (Italy) **(1555-1619)**
Carradine, David (actor); Hollywood, Calif., 12/8/1936
Carradine, John (actor); New York City, 2/5/1906

Carreras, José (tenor); Barcelona, Spain, 12/5/1946
Carrillo, Leo (actor); Los Angeles **(1881-1961)**
Carroll, Diahann (Carol Diahann Johnson) (singer and actress); Bronx, N.Y., 7/17/1935
Carroll, Leo G. (actor); Weedon, England **(1892-1972)**
Carroll, Lewis (Charles Lutwidge Dodgson) (author and mathematician); Daresbury, England **(1832-1898)**
Carroll, Madeleine (actress); West Bromwich, England, 2/26/1909
Carroll, Pat (comedienne); Shreveport, La., 5/5/1927
Carson, Johnny (TV entertainer); Corning, Iowa, 10/23/1925
Carson, Kit (Christopher) (scout); Madison County, Ky. **(1809-1868)**
Carson, Rachel (biologist and author); Springdale, Pa. **(1907-1964)**
Carter, Jack (comedian); New York City, 1923
Cartier, Jacques (explorer); Saint-Malo, Brittany (France) **(1491-1557)**
Cartier-Brisson, Henri (photographer); Chanteloup, France, 8/22/1908
Cartland, Barbara (author); England, 7/9/1901
Caruso, Enrico (Errico) (tenor); Naples, Italy **(1873-1921)**
Carver, George Washington (botanist); Missouri **(1864-1943)**
Cary, Arthur Joyce Lunel (novelist); Londonderry, Ireland **(1888-1957)**
Casals, Pablo (cellist); Vendrell, Spain **(1876-1973)**
Casanova de Seingalt, Giovanni Jacopo (adventurer); Venice **(1725-1798)**
Cash, Johnny (singer); nr. Kingsland, Ark., 2/26/1932
Cass, Peggy (comedienne); Boston, 5/21/1924
Cassatt, Mary (painter); Allegheny, Pa. **(1844-1926)**
Cassavetes, John (actor and director); New York City, 12/9/1929
Cassidy, David (singer); New York City, 4/12/1950
Cassidy, Jack (actor); Richmond Hill, Queens, N.Y. **(1927-1976)**
Cassini, Oleg (Oleg Lolewski-Cassini) (fashion designer); Paris, 4/11/1913
Castagno, Andrea del (painter); San Martino a Corella (Italy) **(c.1421-1457)**
Castellano, Richard (actor); New York City, 9/2/1934
Castle, Irene (Irene Foote) (actress and dancer); New Rochelle, N.Y. **(1893-1969)**
Castle, Vernon Blythe (dancer and aviator); Norwich, England **(1887-1918)**
Castro Ruz, Fidel (Premier); Mayari, Oriente, Cuba, 8/13/1926
Cather, Willa Sibert (novelist); Winchester, Va. **(1876-1947)**
Cato, Marcus Porcius (called Cato the Elder) (statesman); Tusculum (Italy) (234-149 B.C.)
Catt, Carrie Chapman Lane (woman suffragist); Ripon, Wis. **(1859-1947)**
Catton, Bruce (historian); Petoskey, Mich. **(1899-1978)**
Cavaliaro, Carmen (band leader); New York City, 1913
Cavett, Dick (Richard) (TV entertainer); Gibbon, Neb., 11/19/1936
Cellini, Benvenuto (goldsmith and sculptor); Florence (Italy) **(1500-1571)**
Cervantes Saavedra, Miguel de (novelist); Alcalá de Henares, Spain **(1547-1616)**
Cézanne, Paul (painter); Aix-en-Provence, France **(1839-1906)**
Chagall, Marc (painter); Vitebsk, Russia, **(1887-1985)**
Chaliapin, Feodor Ivanovitch (operatic basso); Kazan, Russia **(1873-1938)**
Chamberlain, Arthur Neville (statesman); Edgbaston, England **(1869-1940)**
Chamberlain, Richard (actor); Los Angeles, 3/31/1935(?)
Champion, Gower (choreographer); Geneva, Ill. **(1921-1980)**
Champion, Marge (actress and dancer); Los Angeles, 9/2/1923
Champlain, Samuel de (explorer); nr. Rochefort, France **(1567?-1635)**
Chancellor, John (TV commentator); Chicago, 7/14/1927
Chandler, Raymond (writer); Chicago **(1883-1959)**
Chanel, "Coco" (Gabriel Bonheur) (fashion designer); Issoire, France **(1883-1971)**
Chaney, Lon (actor); Colorado Springs, Colo. **(1883-1930)**
Channing, Carol (actress); Seattle, 1/31/1923
Chaplin, Geraldine (actress); Santa Monica, Calif., 7/31/1944
Chaplin, Sir Charles (actor); London **(1889-1977)**
Charisse, Cyd (Tula Finklea) (dancer and actress); Amarillo, Tex., 3/8/1923
Charlemagne (Holy Roman Emperor); birthplace unknown **(742-814)**
Charles, Ray (Ray Charles Robinson) (pianist, singer, and songwriter); Albany Ga., 9/23/1930
Chase, Chevy (Cornelius Crane Chase) (comedian); New York City, 10/8/1943
Chase, Ilka (author and actress); New York City **(1905-1978)**
Chase, Lucia (founder Ballet Theatre [now American Ballet Theatre]); Waterbury, Conn. **(1907-1986)**
Chatterton, Ruth (actress); New York City **(1893-1961)**
Chaucer, Geoffrey (poet); London **(1340?-1400)**
Chávez, Carlos (composer); nr. Mexico City **(1899-1978)**
Chavez, Cesar (labor leader); nr. Yuma, Ariz., 3/31/1927
Chayefsky, Paddy (Sidney) (playwright); New York City, **(1923-1981)**
Checker, Chubby (Ernest Evans) (performer); Philadelphia, 10/3/1941
Cheever, John (novelist); Quincy, Mass. **(1912-1982)**
Chekhov, Anton Pavlovich (dramatist and short-story writer); Taganrog, Russia **(1860-1904)**
Cher (Cherilyn LaPiere) (singer); El Centro, Calif., 5/20/1946
Cherubini, Luigi (composer); Florence **(1760-1842)**
Chesterton, Gilbert Keith (author); Kensington, England **(1874-1936)**
Chevalier, Maurice (entertainer); Paris **(1888-1972)**
Chiang Kai-shek (Chief of State); Feng-hwa, China **(1887-1975)**
Child, Julia (food expert); Pasadena, Calif., 8/15/1912
Chippendale, Thomas (cabinet-maker); Otley, England **(1718?-1779)**
Chirico, Giorgio de (painter); Vólos, Greece, **(1888-1978)**
Chopin, Frédéric François (composer); nr. Warsaw **(1810-1849)**
Chou En-lai. *See* Zhou Enlai
Christian, Linda (Blanca Rosa Welter) (actress); Tampico, Mexico, 11/13/1924
Christie, Agatha (mystery writer); Torquay, England, **(1890-1976)**
Christie, Julie (actress); Chukua, India, 4/14/1941
Christopher, Jordon (actor and musician); Youngstown, Ohio, 1941
Christy, June (singer); Springfield, Ill., 1925
Churchill, Sir Winston Leonard Spencer (statesman); Blenheim Palace, Oxfordshire, England **(1874-1965)**
Cicero, Marcus Tullius (orator and statesman); Arpinum (Italy) **(106-43 B.C.)**
Cid, El (Rodrigo (or Ruy) Díez de Bivar) (Spanish national hero); nr. Burgos, Spain **(1040?-1099)**
Cilento, Diane (actress); Queensland, Australia, 10/5/1933
Cimabue, Giovanni (painter); Florence (Italy) **(c.1240-c.1302)**
Cimino, Michael (film director); New York City, 1943(?)
Clair, René (René Chomette) (film director); Paris **(1898-1981)**
Claire, Ina (Ina Fagan) (actress); Washington, D.C., **(1895-1985)**
Clapton, Eric (singer and guitarist); Ripley, England, 3/30/1945
Clark, Dane (Barney Zanville) (actor); New York City, 2/18/1915
Clark, Dick (TV personality); Mt. Vernon, N.Y., 11/30/1929
Clark, Mark W. (general); Madison Barracks, N.Y. **(1896-1984)**
Clark, Petula (singer); Epsom, England, 11/15/1934
Clark, Roy (country music artist); Meherrin, Va., 4/15/1933
Clark, William (explorer); Caroline County, Va. **(1770-1838)**
Clarke, Arthur C. (science fiction writer); Minehead, England, 12/16/1917
Claude Lorrain (Claude Gellée) (painter); Champagne, France **(1600-1682)**
Clausewitz, Karl von (military strategist); Burg (East Germany) **(1780-1831)**
Clay, Henry (statesman); Hanover County, Va. **(1777-1852)**
Clay, Lucius D. (banker, ex-general); Marietta, Ga. **(1897-1978)**
Clayburgh, Jill (actress); New York City, 4/30/1944
Clemenceau, Georges (statesman); Mouilleron-en-Pareds, Vondée, France **(1841-1929)**
Clemens, Samuel L. *See* Mark Twain
Cleopatra (Queen of Egypt); Alexandria, Egypt **(69-30 B.C.)**
Cliburn, Van (Harvey Lavan Cliburn, Jr.) (concert pianist); Shreveport, La., 7/12/1934
Clifford, Clark M. (ex-Secretary of Defense); Ft. Scott, Kan., 12/25/1906
Clift, Montgomery (actor); Omaha, Neb. **(1920-1966)**
Clooney, Rosemary (singer); Maysville, Ky., 5/23/1928
Close, Glenn (actress); Greenwich, Conn., 3/19/1947
Clurman, Harold (stage producer); New York City **(1901-1980)**
Cobb, Irvin Shrewsbury (humorist); Paducah, Ky. **(1876-1944)**
Cobb, Lee J. (Leo Jacob) (actor); New York City **(1911-1976)**
Coburn, Charles Douville (actor); Savannah, Ga. **(1877-1961)**
Coburn, James (actor); Laurel, Neb., 8/31/1928
Coca, Imogene (comedienne); Philadelphia, 11/18/1908
Cocker, Joe (John Robert Cocker) (singer); Sheffield, England, 5/20/1944
Coco, James (actor); New York City **(1929-1987)**
Cocteau, Jean (author); Maison-Lafitte, France **(1891-1963)**
Cody, W. F. *See* Buffalo Bill
Cohan, George Michael (actor and dramatist); Providence, R.I. **(1878-1942)**
Colbert, Claudette (Lily Chauchoin) (actress); Paris, 9/13/1903
Colby, William E. (ex-Director of CIA); St. Paul, 1/4/1920
Cole, Nat "King" (singer); Montgomery, Ala. **(1919-1965)**
Cole, Natalie (singer); Los Angeles, 2/6/1950
Cole, Thomas (painter); Lancashire, England **(1801-1848)**
Coleridge, Samuel Taylor (poet); Ottery St. Mary, England **(1772-1834)**
Colette (Sidonie-Gabrielle Colette) (novelist); St.-Sauveur, France **(c. 1873-1954)**
Collingwood, Charles (TV commentator); Three Rivers, Mich. **(1917-1985)**
Collins, Dorothy (Marjorie Chandler) (singer); Windsor, Ontario, Canada, 11/18/1926

Collins, Joan (actress); London 5/23/1933
Collins, Judy (singer); Seattle, 5/1/1939
Colman, Ronald (actor); Richmond, England **(1891-1958)**
Colonna, Jerry (comedian); Boston **(1905-1986)**
Columbus, Christopher (Cristoforo Colombo) (discoverer of America); Genoa (Italy) **(1451-1506)**
Comden, Betty (writer); New York City, 5/3/1919
Comenius, Johann Amos (educational reformer) Nivnice, Moravia (Czechoslovakia) **(1592-1670)**
Commager, Henry Steele (historian); Pittsburgh, 10/25/1902
Como, Perry (Pierino) (singer); Canonsburg, Pa., 5/18/1913
Compton, Karl Taylor (physicist); Wooster, Ohio **(1887-1954)**
Comte, Auguste (philosopher); Montpellier, France **(1798-1857)**
Conant, James B. (educator and statesman); Dorchester, Mass. **(1893-1978)**
Condon, Eddie (jazz musician); Goodland, Ind. **(1905-1973)**
Confucius (K'ung Fu-tzu) (philosopher); Shantung province, China **(c. 551-479 B.C.)**
Congreve, William (dramatist); nr. Leeds, England **(1670-1729)**
Connelly, Marc (playwright); McKeesport, Pa. **(1890-1980)**
Connery, Sean (actor); Edinburgh, Scotland, 8/25/1930
Conniff, Ray (band leader); Attleboro, Mass., 11/6/1916
Connors, Chuck (actor); Brooklyn, N.Y., 4/10/1921
Connors, Mike (Krekor Ohanian) (actor); Fresno, Calif., 8/15/1925
Conrad, Joseph (Teodor Jozef Konrad Korzeniowski) (novelist); Berdichev, Ukraine **(1857-1924)**
Conrad, Robert (Conrad Robert Falk) (actor); Chicago, 3/1/1935
Conrad, William (actor); Louisville, Ky., 9/27/1920
Conried, Hans (Frank Foster) (actor); Baltimore **(1915-1982)**
Constable, John (painter); East Bergholt, Suffolk, England **(1776-1837)**
Constantine II (ex-king); Athens, 6/2/1940
Conte, Richard (actor); New York City **(1916-1975)**
Conti, Tom (actor); Paisley, Scotland, 11/22/1941
Converse, Frank (actor); St. Louis, 1938
Conway, Tim (comedian); Chagrin Falls, Ohio, 12/15/1933
Coogan, Jackie (actor); Los Angeles **(1914-1984)**
Cooke, Alistair (Alfred Alistair); (TV narrator and journalist); Manchester, England, 11/20/1908
Cooley, Denton A(rthur) (heart surgeon); Houston, Tex., 8/22/1920
Coolidge, Rita (singer); Nashville, Tenn., 1944
Cooper, Alice (Vincent Furnier) (rock musician); Detroit, 2/4/1948
Cooper, Gary (Frank James Cooper) (actor); Helena, Mont. **(1901-1961)**
Cooper, Jackie (actor and director); Los Angeles, 9/15/1922
Cooper, James Fenimore (novelist); Burlington, N.J. **(1789-1851)**
Cooper, Peter (industrialist and philanthropist); New York City **(1791-1883)**
Copernicus, Nicolaus (Mikolaj Kopernik) (astronomer); Thorn, Poland **(1473-1543)**
Copland, Aaron (composer); Brooklyn, N.Y., 11/14/1900
Copley, John Singleton (painter); Boston, Mass. **(1738-1815)**
Coppolla, Francis Ford (film director); Detroit, 4/7/1939
Corelli, Arcangelo (composer); Fusignano, Italy **(1653-1713)**
Corelli, Franco (operatic tenor); Ancona, Italy, 4/8/1923
Corneille, Pierre (dramatist); Rouen, France **(1606-1684)**
Cornell, Katharine (actress); Berlin **(1893-1974)**
Coret, Jean Baptiste Camille (painter); Paris **(1796-1875)**
Correggio, Antonio Allegri da (painter); Correggio (Italy) **(1494-1534)**
Corsaro, Frank (opera director); New York harbor, 12/22/1924
Cortés (or Cortez), Hernando (explorer); Medellin, Spain **(1485-1547)**
Cosby, Bill (actor); Philadelphia, 7/12/1937
Cosell, Howard (Howard Cohen) (sportscaster); Winston-Salem, N.C., 3/25/1920
Costa-Gavras, Henri (Kostantinos Gavras) (film director); Athens, 1933
Costello, Elvis (Declan Patrick McManus) (singer-musician-songwriter); London, 1954
Costello, Lou (comedian); Paterson, N.J. **(1908-1959)**
Cotten, Joseph (actor); Petersburg, Va., 5/15/1905
Couperin, François (composer); Paris **(1668-1733)**
Courbet, Gustave (painter); Ornans, France **(1819-1877)**
Courrèges, André (fashion designer); Pau, France, 3/9/1923
Courtenay, Tom (actor); Hull, England, 2/25/1937
Cousins, Norman (publisher); Union Hill, N.J., 6/24/1915
Cousteau, Jacques-Yves (marine explorer); St. André-de-Cubzac, France, 6/11/1910
Coward, Sir Noel (playwright and actor); Teddington, England **(1899-1973)**
Cowles, Gardner, Jr. (newspaper publisher); Algona, Iowa, **(1903-1985)**
Cowper, William (poet); Great Berkhamstead, England **(1731-1800)**
Cozzens, James Gould (novelist); Chicago **(1903-1978)**
Crabbe, Buster (Clarence) (actor); Oakland, Calif. **(1908-1983)**
Crain, Jeanne (actress); Barstow, Calif., 5/25/1925
Cranach, Lucas, the elder (painter); Kronach (Germany) **(1472-1553)**
Crane, Hart (poet); Garrettsville, Ohio **(1899-1932)**
Crane, Stephen (novelist and poet); Newark, N.J. **(1871-1900)**
Cranmer, Thomas (churchman); Aslacton, England **(1489-1556)**
Crawford, Broderick (actor); Philadelphia **(1911-1986)**
Crawford, Cheryl (stage producer); Akron, Ohio **(1902-1986)**
Crawford, Joan (Lucille LeSueur) (actress and business executive); San Antonio **(1908-1977)**
Crenna, Richard (actor); Los Angeles, 11/30/1927
Crespin, Régine (operatic soprano); Marseilles, France, 2/23/1929
Crichton, (John) Michael (novelist); Chicago, 10/23/1942
Crisp, Donald (actor); London **(1880-1974)**
Croce, Benedetto (philosopher); Peseasseroli, Aquila, Italy **(1866-1952)**
Croce, Jim (singer); Philadelphia **(1942-1973)**
Crockett, Davy (David) (frontiersman); Greene County, Tenn. **(1786-1836)**
Cromwell, Oliver (statesman); Huntingdon, England **(1599-1658)**
Cronin, A. J. (Archibald J. Cronin) (novelist); Cardross, Scotland **(1896-1981)**
Cronkite, Walter (TV newscaster); St. Joseph, Mo., 11/4/1916
Cronyn, Hume (actor); London, Ontario, Canada, 7/18/1911
Crosby, Bing (Harry Lillis) (singer, actor); Tacoma, Wash. **(1904-1977)**
Crosby, Bob (musician); Spokane, Wash., 8/23/1913
Cross, Ben (Bernard) (actor); Paddington, England, 12/16/1947
Cross, Milton (opera commentator); New York City **(1897-1975)**
Crouse, Russel (playwright); Findlay, Ohio **(1893-1966)**
Cugat, Xavier (band leader); Barcelona, Spain, 1/1/1900
Cukor, George (film director); New York City **(1899-1983)**
Cullen, Bill (William Lawrence Cullen) (radio and TV entertainer); Pittsburgh, 2/18/1920
Culp, Robert (actor); Berkeley, Calif., 8/16/1930
Cummings, E. E. (Edward Estlin Cummings) (poet); Cambridge, Mass. **(1894-1962)**
Cummings, Robert (actor); Joplin, Mo., 6/9/1910
Curie, Marie (Marja Sklodowska) (physical chemist); Warsaw **(1867-1934)**
Curie, Pierre (physicist); Paris **(1859-1906)**
Curtin, Phyllis (soprano); Clarksburg, W.Va., 12/3/1927
Curtis, Tony (Bernard Schwartz) (actor); Bronx, N.Y., 6/3/1925
Curzon, Clifford (concert pianist); London **(1907-1982)**
Custer, George Armstrong (army officer); New Rumley, Ohio **(1839-1876)**

D

da Gama, Vasco (explorer); Sines, Portugal **(1460-1524)**
Daguerre, Louis (photographic pioneer); nr. Paris **(1787-1851)**
Dahl, Arlene (actress); Minneapolis, 8/11/1928
Dailey, Dan (actor and dancer); New York City, **(1917-1978)**
Daley, Richard J. (Mayor of Chicago); Chicago **(1902-1976)**
Dali, Salvador (painter); Figueras, Spain, 5/11/1904
Dalton, John (chemist); nr. Cockermouth, England **(1766-1844)**
Daly, James (actor); Wisconsin Rapids, Wis. **(1918-1978)**
Daly, John (radio and TV news analyst); Johannesburg, South Africa, 2/20/1914
d'Amboise, Jacques (ballet dancer); Dedham, Mass., 7/28/1934
Damone, Vic (Vito Farinola) (singer); Brooklyn, N.Y., 6/12/1928
Damrosch, Walter Johannes (orchestra conductor); Breslau (Poland) **(1862-1950)**
Dana, Charles Anderson (editor); Hinsdale, N.H. **(1819-1897)**
Dandridge, Dorothy (actress); Cleveland **(1923-1965)**
Dangerfield, Rodney (comedian); Babylon, L.I., N.Y., 1921
Daniels, Bebe (Virginia Daniels) (actress); Dallas **(1901-1971)**
Danilova, Alexandra (ballerina); Peterhof, Russia, 1/20/1904
Dannay, Frederic (novelist, pseudonym Ellery Queen); Brooklyn, N.Y. **(1905-1982)**
Danner, Blythe (actress); Philadelphia, 1944(?)
D'Annunzio, Gabriele (soldier and author); Francaville at Mare, Pescara, Italy **(1863-1938)**
Dante (or Durante) Alighieri (poet); Florence (Italy) **(1265-1321)**
Danton, Georges Jacques (French Revolutionary leader); Arcis-sur-Aube, France **(1759-1794)**
Darnell, Linda (actress); Dallas **(1921-1965)**
Darren, James (actor); Philadelphia, 6/8/1936
Darrieux, Danielle (actress); Bordeaux, France, 5/1/1917
Darrow, Clarence Seward (lawyer); Kinsman, Ohio **(1857-1938)**
Darwin, Charles Robert (naturalist); Shrewsbury, England **(1809-1882)**
daSilva, Howard (actor); Cleveland **(1909-1986)**
Dassin, Jules (film director); Middletown, Conn., 12/18/1911
Daumier, Honoré (caricaturist); Marseilles, France **(1808-1879)**

Dauphin, Claude (actor); Corbeil, France **(1903-1978)**
David, Jacques-Louis (painter); Paris **(1748-1825)**
David (King of Israel and Judah) **(died c. 973 B.C.)**
Davidson, John (singer and actor); Pittsburgh, 12/13/1941
Davies, Marion (Marion Douras) (actress); New York City **(1898?-1961)**
da Vinci, Leonardo (painter and scientist); Vinci, Tuscany (Italy) **(1452-1519)**
Davis, Bette (actress); Lowell, Mass., 4/5/1908
Davis, Elmer Holmes (radio commentator); Aurora, Ind. **(1890-1958)**
Davis, Jefferson (President of the Confederacy); Christian (now Todd) County, Ky. **(1808-1889)**
Davis, Mac (singer); Lubbock, Tex., 1/21/1942
Davis, Miles (jazz trumpeter); Alton, Ill., 5/25/1926
Davis, Ossie (actor and writer); Cogdell, Ga., 12/18/1917
Davis, Sammy, Jr. (actor and singer); New York City, 12/8/1925
Davis, Skeeter (Mary Francis Penick) (singer); Dry Ridge, Ky., 12/30/1931
Davis, Stuart (painter); Philadelphia **(1894-1964)**
Day, Dennis (singer); New York City, 5/21/1917
Day, Doris (Doris von Kappelhoff) (singer and actress); Cincinnati, 4/3/1924
Day, Laraine (La Raine Johnson) (actress); Roosevelt, Utah, 10/13/1920
Dayan, Moshe (ex-Defense Minister of Israel); Dagania, Palestine **(1915-1981)**
Dean, James (actor); Marion, Ind. **(1931-1955)**
Dean, Jimmy (singer); Seth Ward, nr. Plainview, Tex., 8/10/1928
De Bakey, Michael E. (heart surgeon); Lake Charles, La., 9/7/1908
de Beauvoir, Simone (novelist and philosopher); Paris **(1908-1986)**
Debs, Eugene Victor (Socialist leader); Terre Haute, Ind. **(1855-1926)**
Debussy, Claude Achille (composer); St. Germain-en-Laye, France **(1862-1918)**
De Carlo, Yvonne (Peggy Yvonne Middleton) (actress); Vancouver, B.C., Canada, 9/1/1924
de Chirico, Giorgio (painter); Volos, Greece, **(1888-1978)**
Dee, Ruby (Ruby Ann Wallace) (actress); Cleveland, 10/27/1924(?)
Dee, Sandra (Alexandra Zuck) (actress); Bayonne, N.J., 4/23/1942
Defoe, Daniel (novelist); London **(1659?-1731)**
Degas, Hilaire Germain Edgar (painter); Paris **(1834-1917)**
de Gaulle, Charles André Joseph Marie (soldier and statesman); Lille, France **(1890-1970)**
DeHaven, Gloria (actress); Los Angeles, 7/23/1925
de Havilland, Olivia (actress); Tokyo, 7/1/1916
Dekker, Albert (actor); Brooklyn, N.Y. **(1904-1968)**
de Kooning, Willem (painter); Rotterdam, 4/24/1904
Delacroix, Eugène (painter); Charenton-St. Maurice, France **(1798-1863)**
de la Renta, Oscar (fashion designer); Santo Domingo, Dominican Republic, 7/22/1932
Delaunay, Robert (painter); Paris **(1885-1941)**
De Laurentiis, Dino (film producer); Torre Annunziata, Bay of Naples, Italy, 8/8/1919
della Robbia, Andrea (sculptor) Florence **(1435-1525)**
della Robbia, Luca (sculptor); Florence **(1400-1482)**
Delon, Alain (actor); Sceaux, France, 11/8/1935
Del Rio, Dolores (Dolores Ansunsolo) (actress); Durango, Mexico **(1905-1983)**
DeLuise, Dom (comedian); Brooklyn, N.Y., 8/1/1933
Demarest, William (actor); St. Paul **(1892-1983)**
de Mille, Agnes (choreographer); New York City 9/18/1905
De Mille, Cecil Blount (film director); Ashfield, Mass. **(1881-1959)**
Demosthenes (orator); Athens **(385?-322 B.C.)**
Deneuve, Catherine (actress); Paris, 10/22/1943
De Niro, Robert (actor); New York City, 8/17/1943
Dennis, Sandy (actress); Hastings, Neb., 4/27/1937
Denver, John (Henry John Deutschendorf, Jr.) (singer); Roswell, N.M., 12/31/1943
Derain, André (painter); Chatou, Seine-et-Oise, France **(1880-1954)**
Dern, Bruce (actor); Chicago, 6/4/1936
Descartes, René (philosopher and mathematician); La Haye, France **(1596-1650)**
De Seversky, Alexander P. (aviator); Tiflis, Russia **(1894-1974)**
De Sica, Vittorio (film director); Sora, Italy **(1901-1974)**
Desmond, Johnny (composer); Detroit **(1921-1985)**
Desmond, William (actor); Dublin **(1878-1949)**
De Soto, Hernando (explorer); Barcarrota, Spain **(1500?-1542)**
De Valera, Eamon (ex-President of Ireland); New York City **(1882-1975)**
Devine, Andy (actor); Flagstaff, Ariz. **(1905-1977)**
De Vries, Peter (novelist); Chicago, 2/27/1910
Dewey, George (admiral); Montpelier, Vt. **(1837-1917)**
Dewey, John (philosopher and educator); Burlington, Vt. **(1859-1952)**
Dewey, Thomas E. (politician); Owosso, Mich. **(1902-1971)**
Dewhurst, Colleen (actress); Montreal, 1926(?)
Diamond, Neil (singer); Brooklyn, N.Y., 1/24/1941
Diana (Diana Frances Spencer) (Princess of Wales); Sandringham, England, 7/1/61
Dichter, Misha (pianist); Shanghai, 9/27/1945
Dickens, Charles John Huffam (novelist); Portsea, England **(1812-1870)**
Dickey, James (poet); Atlanta, 2/2/1923
Dickinson, Angie (Angeline Brown) (actress); Kulm, N.D., 9/30/1932
Dickinson, Emily Elizabeth (poet); Amherst, Mass. **(1830-1886)**
Diddley, Bo (Elias McDaniel) (guitarist); McComb, Miss., 12/30/1928
Diderot, Denis (encyclopedist); Langres, France **(1713-1784)**
Diefenbaker, John G. (ex-Prime Minister); Grey County, Ontario, Canada **(1895-1979)**
Dietrich, Marlene (Maria Magdalena von Losch) (actress); Berlin, 12/27/1901
Diggs, Dudley (actor); Dublin **(1879-1947)**
Diller, Phyllis (Phyllis Driver) (comedienne); Lima, Ohio, 7/17/1917
Dillman, Bradford (actor); San Francisco, 4/14/1930
Dine, Jim (painter); Cincinnati, 6/16/1935
Diogenes (philosopher); Sinope (Turkey) **(412?-323 B.C.)**
Dion (Dion DiMucci) (singer); Bronx, N.Y., 7/18/1939
Dior, Christian (fashion designer); Granville, France **(1905-1957)**
Disney, Walt(er) Elias (film animator and producer); Chicago **(1901-1966)**
Disraeli, Benjamin (Earl of Beaconsfield) (statesman); London **(1804-1881)**
Dix, Dorothea (civil rights reformer); Hampden, Me. **(1802-1887)**
Dix, Richard (Ernest Carlton Brimmer) (actor); St. Paul **(1894-1949)**
Dixon, Jeane (Jeane Pinckert) (seer); Medford, Wis., 1918
Dobbs, Mattiwilda (soprano); Atlanta, Ga., 7/11/1925
Doctorow, E(dgar) L(aurence) (novelist); New York City, 1/6/1931
Dodgson, C. L. *See* Carroll, Lewis.
Dolin, Anton (dancer); Slinfold, England **(1904-1983)**
Domingo, Placido (tenor); Madrid, 1/21/1941
Domino, Fats (Antoine) (musician); New Orleans, 2/26/1928
Donahue, Phil (television personality); Cleveland, 12/21/1935
Donahue, Troy (Merle Johnson) (actor); New York City, 1/27/1938
Donat, Robert (actor); Withington, England **(1905-1958)**
Donatello (Donato Niccolò di Betto Bardi) (sculptor); Florence **(c. 1386-1466)**
Donne, John (poet); London **(1573-1631)**
Donovan (Donovan Leitch) (singer and songwriter); Glasgow, Scotland, 2/10/1946
Doolittle, James H. (ex-Air Force general); Alameda, Calif., 12/14/1896
Dorati, Antal (orchestra conductor); Budapest, 4/9/1906
Dorsey, Jimmy (band leader); Shenandoah, Pa. **(1904-1957)**
Dorsey, Tommy (band leader); Mahonoy Plains, Pa. **(1905-1956)**
Dos Passos, John (author); Chicago **(1896-1970)**
Dostoevski, Fyodor Mikhailovich (novelist); Moscow **(1821-1881)**
Douglas, Helen Gahagan (ex-Representative); Boonton, N.J. **(1900-1980)**
Douglas, Kirk (Issur Danielovitch) (actor); Amsterdam, N.Y., 12/9/1916
Douglas, Melvyn (Melvyn Hesselberg) (actor); Macon, Ga., **(1901-1981)**
Douglas, Mike (Michael D. Dowd, Jr.) (TV personality); Chicago, 8/11/1925
Douglas, Paul (actor); Philadelphia **(1907-1959)**
Douglas, Stephen Arnold (politician); Brandon, Vt. **(1813-1861)**
Dowling, Eddie (Edward Goucher) (actor and stage producer); Woonsocket, R.I., **(1894-1976)**
Downs, Hugh (TV entertainer); Akron, Ohio, 2/14/1921
Doyle, Sir Arthur Conan (novelist and spiritualist); Edinburgh, Scotland **(1859-1930)**
Drake, Alfred (singer and actor); New York City, 10/7/1914
Drake, Sir Francis (navigator); Tavistock, England **(1545-1596)**
Dreiser, Theodore (writer); Terre Haute, Ind. **(1871-1945)**
Dressler, Marie (Leila Koeber) (actress); Cobourg, Ontario, Canada **(1869-1934)**
Dreyfus, Alfred (French army officer); Mulhouse (France) **(1859-1935)**
Dreyfuss, Richard (actor); Brooklyn, N.Y., 10/29/1947
Drury, Allen (novelist); Houston, 9/2/1918
Dryden, John (poet); Northamptonshire, England **(1631-1700)**
Dubček, Alexander (ex-President of Czechoslovakia); Uhroved (Czechoslovakia), 11/27/1921
Dubinsky, David (David Dobnievski) (labor leader); Brest-Litovsk (U.S.S.R.) **(1892-1982)**
Duchamp, Marcel (painter); Blainville, France **(1887-1968)**
Duchin, Peter (pianist and band leader); New York City, 7/28/1937
Dufay, Guillaume (composer); Cambrai, France **(c. 1400-1474)**
Duff, Howard (actor); Bremerton, Wash., 11/24/1917
Dufy, Raoul (painter); Le Havre, France **(1877-1953)**
Duke, James B. (industrialist); nr. Durham, N.C. **(1856-1925)**
Duke, Patty (Anna Marie Duke) (actress); New York City, 12/14/1946

Dullea, Keir (actor); Cleveland, 5/30/1936(?)
Dulles, Allen Welsh (ex-Director of CIA); Watertown, N.Y. **(1893-1969)**
Dulles, John Foster (statesman); Washington, D.C. **(1888-1959)**
Dumas, Alexandre (called Dumas fils) (novelist); Paris **(1824-1895)**
Dumas, Alexandre (called Dumas père) (novelist); Villers-Cotterets, France **(1802-1870)**
Du Maurier, Daphine (novelist); London, 5/13/1907
Du Maurier, George Louis Palmella Busson (novelist); Paris **(1834-1896)**
Dumont, Margaret (actress); **(1889-1965)**
Dunaway, Faye (actress); Bascom, Fla., 1/14/1941
Duncan, Isadora (dancer); San Francisco **(1878-1927)**
Duncan, Sandy (actress); Henderson, Tex., 2/20/1946
Dunn, James (actor); Santa Monica, Calif. **(1905-1967)**
Dunne, Irene (actress); Louisville, Ky., 12/20/1904
Dunnock, Mildred (actress); Baltimore, 1/25/1906
Duns Scotus, John (theologian); Duns, Scotland **(1265-1303)**
Du Pont, Pierre S. (economist); Paris **(1739-1817)**
Durante, Jimmy (comedian); New York City **(1893-1980)**
Durbin, Deanna (Edna Mae) (actress); Winnipeg, Canada, 12/4/1922
Dürer, Albrecht (painter and engraver); Nūrnberg (Germany) **(1471-1528)**
Durrell, Lawrence George (novelist); Julundur, India, 2/27/1912
Duse, Eleonora (actress); Chioggia, Italy **(1859-1924)**
Duvalier, Jean-Claude (ex-President; son of "Papa Doc"); Port-au-Prince, Haiti, 7/3/1951
Duvall, Robert (actor); San Diego, Calif., 1931
Dvořák, Antonin (composer); Nelahozeves (Czechoslovakia) **(1841-1904)**
Dylan, Bob (Robert Zimmerman) (folk singer and composer); Duluth, Minn., 5/24/1941

E

Eagels, Joanne (actress); Kansas City, Mo. **(1894-1929)**
Eakins, Thomas (painter and sculptor); Philadelphia, **(1844-1916)**
Earhart, Amelia (aviator); Atchison, Kan. **(1898-1937)**
Eastman, George (inventor); Waterville, N.Y. **(1854-1932)**
Eastwood, Clint (actor); San Francisco, 5/31/1931(?)
Ebsen, Buddy (Christian Ebsen, Jr.) (actor); Belleville, Ill., 4/2/1908
Eckstine, Billy (singer); Pittsburgh, 7/8/1914
Eddy, Mary Baker (founder of Christian Science Church); Bow, N.H. **(1821-1910)**
Eddy, Nelson (baritone and actor); Providence, R.I. **(1901-1967)**
Eden, Sir Anthony (Earl of Avon) (ex-Prime Minister); Durham, England **(1897-1977)**
Edison, Thomas Alva (inventor); Milan, Ohio **(1847-1931)**
Edwards, Blake (film writer-producer); Tulsa, Okla. 7/26/1922
Edwards, Jonathan (theologian); East Windsor, Conn. **(1703-1758)**
Edwards, Ralph (TV and radio producer); Tulsa, Okla. 7/26/1922
Edwards, Vincent (actor); Brooklyn, N.Y., 7/7/1928
Egan, Richard (actor); San Francisco, **(1923-1987)**
Eggar, Samantha (actress); London, 5/3/1939
Eglevsky, André (ballet dancer); Moscow **(1917-1977)**
Ehrlich, Paul (bacteriologist); Strzelin (Poland) **(1854-1915)**
Einstein, Albert (physicist); Ulm, Germany **(1879-1955)**
Eisenhower, Milton S. (educator); Abilene, Kan., **(1899-1985)**
Eisenstaedt, Alfred (photographer and photojournalist); Dirschau (Poland), 12/6/1898
Ekberg, Anita (actress); Malmō, Sweden, 9/29/1931
Eldridge, Florence (Florence McKechnie) (actress); Brooklyn, N.Y., 9/5/1901
Elgar, Sir Edward (composer); Worcester, England **(1857-1934)**
Elgart, Larry (band leader); New London, Conn., 3/20/1922
El Greco (Domenicos Theotocopoulos) (painter); Candia, Crete (Greece) **(c.1541-1614)**
Eliot, George (Mary Ann Evans) (novelist); Chilvers Coton, England **(1819-1880)**
Eliot, Thomas Stearns (poet); St. Louis **(1888-1965)**
Ellington, Duke (Edward Kennedy) (jazz musician); Washington, D.C. **(1899-1974)**
Elliot, "Mama" Cass (Ellen Naomi Cohen) (singer); Baltimore **(1941-1974)**
Elman, Mischa (violinist); Stalnoye, Ukraine **(1891-1967)**
Emerson, Ralph Waldo (philosopher and poet); Boston **(1803-1882)**
Enesco, Georges (composer); Dorohoi, Romania **(1881-1955)**
Engels, Friedrich (Socialist writer); Barmen (Germany) **(1820-1895)**
Entremont, Philippe (concert pianist); Rheims, France, 6/7/1934
Epicurus (philosopher); Samos (Greece) **(341-270 B.C.)**
Epstein, Sir Jacob (sculptor); New York City **(1880-1959)**
Erasmus, Desiderius (Gerhard Gerhards) (scholar); Rotterdam **(1466?-1536)**
Erhard, Ludwig (ex-Chancellor); Furth, Germany **(1897-1977)**
Erickson, Leif (actor); Alameda, Calif. **(1911-1986)**
Ericson, Leif (navigator); **(c. 10th century A.D.)**
Erikson, Erik H. (psychoanalyst); Frankfurt, Germany, 6/15/1902
Ernst, Max (painter); Bruhl, Germany **(1891-1976)**
Euclid (mathematician); Megara (Greece) **(c. 300 B.C.)**
Euler, Leonhard (mathematician); Basel, Switzerland **(1707-1783)**
Euripides (dramatist); Salamis (Greece) **(c.484-407 B.C.)**
Evans, Dale (Frances Butts) (actress and singer); Uvalde, Tex., 10/31/1912
Evans, Dame Edith (actress); London **(1888-1976)**
Evans, Linda (actress), Hartford, Conn., 11/18/1942
Evans, Maurice (actor); Dorchester, England, 6/3/1901
Everett, Chad (actor); (Raymon Lee Cramton) South Bend, Ind., 6/11/1936
Evers, Charles (civil rights leader); Decatur, Miss., 9/14/1923(?)
Evers, Medgar (civil rights leader); Decatur, Miss. **(1925-1963)**
Ewell, Tom (Yewell Tompkins) (actor); Owensboro, Ky., 4/29/1909

F

Fabian (Fabian Anthony Forte) (singer); Philadelphia, 2/6/1943
Fabray, Nanette (Nanette Fabarés) (actress); San Diego, Calif., 10/27/1922
Fadiman, Clifton (literary critic); Brooklyn, N.Y., 5/15/1904
Fahrenheit, Gabriel (German physicist); Danzig (Poland); **(1686-1736)**
Fairbanks, Douglas (Douglas Ulman) (actor); Denver **(1883-1939)**
Fairbanks, Douglas, Jr. (actor); New York City, 12/9/1909
Faith, Percy (conductor); Toronto **(1908-1976)**
Falk, Peter (actor); New York City, 9/16/1927
Falla, Manuel de (composer); Cadiz, Spain **(1876-1946)**
Faraday, Michael (physicist); Newington, England **(1791-1867)**
Farber, Barry (radio-TV broadcaster); Baltimore, Md., 1930
Farentino, James (actor); Brooklyn, N.Y., 2/24/1938
Farmer, James (civil rights leader); Marshall, Tex., 1/12/1920
Farnum, William (actor); Boston **(1876-1953)**
Farrell, Charles (actor); Onset Bay, Mass., 1901
Farrell, Eileen (operatic soprano); Willimantic, Conn., 2/13/1920
Farrell, Glenda (actress); Enid, Okla. **(1904-1971)**
Farrell, James T. (novelist); Chicago **(1904-1979)**
Farrell, Suzanne (Roberta Sue Ficker) (ballerina); Cincinnati, 8/16/1945
Farrow, Mia (actress); Los Angeles, 2/9/1946
Fasanella, Ralph (painter); New York City, 9/2/1914
Fassbinder, Rainer Werner (film and stage director); Bad Wořishofen, West Germany **(1946-1982)**
Fast, Howard (novelist); New York City, 11/11/1914
Faulkner, William (novelist); New Albany, Miss. **(1897-1962)**
Fauré, Gabriel Urbain (composer); Pamiers, France **(1845-1924)**
Fawcett, Farrah (actress); Corpus Christi, Tex., 2/2/1947(?)
Faye, Alice (Ann Leppert) (actress); New York City, 5/5/1915
Feiffer, Jules (cartoonist); New York City, 1/26/1929
Feininger, Lyonel (painter); New York City **(1871-1956)**
Feldon, Barbara (actress); Pittsburgh, 3/12/1941
Feliciano, José (singer); Larez, Puerto Rico, 9/10/1945
Felker, Clay S. (editor and publisher); St. Louis, 10/2/1925(?)
Fellini, Federico (film director); Rimini, Italy, 1/20/1920
Fender, Freddie (Baldemar Huerta) (singer); San Benito, Tex., 1937
Ferber, Edna (novelist); Kalamazoo, Mich. **(1885-1968)**
Ferguson, Maynard (jazz trumpeter); Verdun, Quebec, Canada, 5/4/1928
Fermi, Enrico (atomic physicist); Rome **(1901-1954)**
Fernandel (Fernand Joseph Desire Contandin) (actor); Marseilles, France **(1903-1971)**
Ferrer, José (actor and director); Santurce, Puerto Rico, 1/8/1912
Ferrer, Mel (actor); Elberon, N.J., 8/25/1917
Fetchit, Stepin (Lincoln Theodore Perry) (comedian); Key West, Fla. **(1902-1985)**
Fiedler, Arthur (conductor); Boston **(1894-1979)**
Field, Eugene (poet); St. Louis **(1850-1895)**
Field, Marshall (merchant); nr. Conway, Mass. **(1834-1906)**
Field, Sally (actress); Pasadena, Calif., 11/6/1946
Fielding, Henry (novelist); nr. Glastonbury, England **(1707-1754)**
Fields, Gracie (comedienne); Rochdale, England **(1898-1979)**
Fields, Totie (comedienne); Hartford, Conn. **(1931-1978)**
Fields, W. C. (William Claude Dukenfield) (comedian); Philadelphia **(1880-1946)**
Fierstein, Harvey (Forbes) (playwright and actor); Brooklyn, 6/6/1954
Filene, Edward A. (merchant); **(1860-1937)**
Finch, Peter (actor); Kensington, England **(1916-1977)**
Finney, Albert (actor); Salford, England, 5/9/1936
Firkusny, Rudolf (pianist); Napajedia (Czechoslovakia), 2/11/1912

Fischer-Dieskau, Dietrich (baritone); Berlin, 5/28/1925
Fisher, Eddie (Edwin) (singer); Philadelphia, 8/10/1928
Fitzgerald, Barry (William Joseph Shields) (actor); Dublin **(1888-1961)**
Fitzgerald, Edward (radio broadcaster); Troy, N.Y. **(1898(?)-1982)**
Fitzgerald, Ella (singer); Newport News, Va., 4/25/1918
Fitzgerald, F. Scott (Francis Scott Key) (novelist); St. Paul, Minn. **(1896-1940)**
Fitzgerald, Geraldine (actress); Dublin, 11/24/1914
Fitzgerald, Pegeen (radio broadcaster); Norcatur, Kan., 1910
Flack, Roberta (singer); Black Mountain, N.C., 2/10/1940
Flagstad, Kirsten (Wagnerian soprano); Hamar, Norway **(1895-1962)**
Flatt, Lester Raymond (bluegrass musician); Overton County, Tenn. **(1914-1979)**
Flaubert, Gustave (novelist); Rouen, France **(1821-1880)**
Fleming, Sir Alexander (bacteriologist); Lochfield, Scotland **(1881-1955)**
Fleming, Rhonda (Marilyn Louis) (actress); Los Angeles, 8/10/1923
Fletcher, John (dramatist); Rye? England **(1579-1625)**
Flynn, Errol (actor); Hobart, Tasmania **(1909-1959)**
Foch, Nina (actress); Leyden, Netherlands, 4/20/1924
Fodor, Eugene (violinist); Turkey Creek, Colo., 3/5/1950
Fonda, Henry (actor); Grand Island, Neb. **(1905-1982)**
Fonda, Jane (actress); New York City, 12/21/1937
Fonda, Peter (actor); New York City, 2/23/1939
Fontaine, Frank (singer and comedian); Cambridge, Mass. **(1920-1979)**
Fontaine, Joan (Joan de Havilland) (actress); Tokyo, 10/22/1917
Fontanne, Lynn (actress); London, **(1887-1983)**
Fonteyn, Dame Margot (Margaret Hookham) (ballerina); Reigate, England, 5/18/1919
Forbes, Malcolm S(tevenson) (publisher and sportsman); Brooklyn, N.Y., 8/19/1919
Ford, Glenn (Gwyllyn Ford) (actor); Quebec, 5/1/1916
Ford, Harrison (actor); Chicago, 7/13/1942
Ford, Henry (industrialist); Greenfield, Mich. **(1863-1947)**
Ford, Henry, II (auto maker); Detroit, 9/4/1917
Ford, John (film director); Cape Elizabeth, Me. **(1895-1973)**
Ford, Paul (actor); Baltimore **(1901-1976)**
Ford, Tennessee Ernie (Ernie Jennings Ford) (singer); Bristol, Tenn., 2/13/1919
Forrester, Maureen (contralto); Montreal, 7/25/1930
Forsythe, John (actor); Carney's Point, N.J., 1/29/1918
Fosdick, Harry Emerson (clergyman); Buffalo, N.Y. **(1878-1968)**
Fosse, Bob (Robert Louis) (choreographer and director); Chicago, 6/23/1927
Foster, Jodie (Alicia Christian Foster) (actress); Los Angeles, 11/?/1962
Foster, Stephen Collins (composer); nr. Pittsburgh **(1826-1864)**
Foxx, Redd (John Elroy Sanford) (actor and comedian); St. Louis, 12/9/1922
Foy, Eddie, Jr. (dancer and actor); New Rochelle, N.Y. **(1905-1983)**
Fra Angelico (Giovanni da Fiesole) (painter); Vicchio in the Mugello, Tuscany (Italy) **(c.1387-1455)**
Fracci, Carla (ballerina); Milan, Italy, 8/20/1936
Fragonard, Jean Honoré (painter); Grasse, France **(1732-1806)**
Frampton, Peter (rock musician); Beckenham, England, 4/20/1950
France, Anatole (Jacques Anatole François Thibault) (author); Paris **(1844-1924)**
Francescatti, Zino (violinist); Marseilles, France, 8/9/1905
Franciosa, Anthony (Anthony Papaleo) (actor); New York City, 10/25/1928
Francis, Arlene (Arlene Francis Kazanjian) (actress); Boston, 10/20/1908
Francis, Connie (Concetta Franconero) (singer); Newark, N.J., 12/12/1938
Francis, Kay (Katherine Edwina Gibbs) (actress); Oklahoma City **(1903-1968)**
Franciscus, James (actor); Clayton, Mo., 1/31/1934
Francis of Assisi, Saint (Giovanni Francesco Barnardone) (founder of Franciscans); Assisi, Italy **(1182-1226)**
Franck, César Auguste (composer); Liège (Belgium) **(1822-1890)**
Franco Bahamonde, Francisco (Chief of State); El Ferrol, Spain **(1892-1975)**
Franklin, Aretha (singer); Memphis, Tenn., 3/25/1942
Franklin, Benjamin (statesman and scientist); Boston **(1706-1790)**
Frazer, Sir James George (anthropologist); Glasgow, Scotland **(1854-1941)**
Freud, Sigmund (psychoanalyst); Moravia (Czechoslovakia) **(1856-1939)**
Friedan, Betty (Betty Naomi Goldstein) (feminist); Peoria, Ill., 2/4/1921
Fromm, Erich (psychoanalyst); Frankfurt-am-Main, Germany **(1900-1980)**
Frost, David (TV entertainer); Tenterden, England, 4/7/1939
Frost, Robert Lee (poet); San Francisco **(1874-1963)**
Fry, Christopher (playwright); Bristol, England, 12/18/1907
Frye, David (impressionist); Brooklyn, N.Y., 1934
Fuller, R(ichard) Buckminster (Jr.) (architect and educator); Milton, Mass. **(1895-1983)**
Fulton, Robert (inventor); Lancaster County, Pa. **(1765-1815)**
Funt, Allen (TV producer); Brooklyn, N.Y., 9/16/1914
Furness, Betty (Elizabeth) (ex-actress and consumer advocate); New York City, 1/3/1916

G

Gabel, Martin (actor and producer); Philadelphia **(1912-1986)**
Gabin, Jean (actor); Paris **(1904-1976)**
Gable, (William) Clark (actor); Cadiz, Ohio **(1901-1960)**
Gabo, Naum (sculptor); Briansk, Russia **(1890-1977)**
Gabor, Eva (actress); Budapest, 2/11/1926(?)
Gabor, Zsa Zsa (Sari) (actress); Budapest, 2/6/1923
Gabrieli, Giovanni (composer); Venice **(c.1557-1612)**
Gainsborough, Thomas (painter); Sudbury, Suffolk, England **(1727-1788)**
Galbraith, John Kenneth (economist); Iona Station, Ontario, Canada, 10/15/1908
Galilei, Galileo (astronomer and physicist); Pisa (Italy) **(1564-1642)**
Gallico, Paul (novelist); New York City **(1897-1976)**
Gallup, George H. (poll taker); Jefferson, Iowa **(1901-1984)**
Galsworthy, John (novelist and dramatist); Coombe, England **(1867-1933)**
Galway, James (flutist); Belfast, Northern Ireland, 12/8/1939
Gambling, John A. (radio broadcaster); New York City, 1930
Gandhi, Indira (Indira Nehru) (Prime Minister); Allahabad, India **(1917-1984)**
Gandhi, Mohandas Karamchand (called Mahatma Gandhi) (Hindu leader); Porbandar, India **(1869-1948)**
Gannett, Frank E. (editor and publisher); **(1876-1957)**
Garagiola, Joe (Joseph Henry) (sportscaster); St. Louis, 2/12/1926
Garbo, Greta (Greta Gustafsson) (actress); Stockholm, 9/18/1905
Garcia Lorca, Frederico (author); Fuente Vaqueros, Spain **(1898-1936)**
Gardner, Ava (actress); Smithfield, N.C., 12/24/1922
Gardner, Erle Stanley (novelist); Malden, Mass. **(1889-1970)**
Garfield, John (Jules Garfinkle) (actor); New York City **(1913-1952)**
Garfunkel, Art (Arthur) (singer); Newark, N.J., 11/5/1941
Gargan, William (actor); Brooklyn, N.Y., **(1905-1979)**
Garibaldi, Giuseppe (Italian nationalist leader); Nice, France **(1807-1882)**
Garland, Judy (Frances Gumm) (actress and singer); Grand Rapids, Minn. **(1922-1969)**
Garner, Erroll (jazz pianist); Pittsburgh **(1921-1977)**
Garner, James (James Bumgarner) (actor); Norman, Okla., 4/7/1928
Garrett, Betty (actress); St. Joseph, Mo., 5/23/1919
Garrick, David (actor); Hereford, England **(1717-1779)**
Garrison, William Lloyd (abolitionist); Newburyport, Mass. **(1805-1879)**
Garroway, Dave (TV host); Schenectady, N.Y. **(1913-1982)**
Garson, Greer (actress); County Down, Northern Ireland, 9/29/1912(?)
Gary, John (singer); Watertown, N.Y., 11/29/1932
Gassman, Vittorio (film actor and director); Genoa, Italy, 9/1/1922
Gaudí, Antonio (architect); Reus, Spain **(1852-1926)**
Gauguin, Eugne Henri Paul (painter); Paris **(1848-1903)**
Gautama Buddha (Prince Siddhartha) (philosopher); Kapilavastu (India) **(563?-?483 B.C.)**
Gavin, John (actor, diplomat); Los Angeles, 4/8/1935
Gayle, Crystal (Brenda Gayle Webb) (singer); Paintsville, Ky., 1/9/51
Gaynor, Janet (actress); Philadelphia **(1906-1984)**
Gaynor, Mitzi (Francesca Mitzi Marlene de Czanyi von Gerber) (actress); Chicago, 9/4/1931
Gazzara, Ben (Biago Anthony Gazzara) (actor); New York City, 8/28/1930
Gebel-Williams, Gunther (animal trainer); Schweidnitz (Poland), 1934
Geddes, Barbara Bel (actress); New York City, 10/31/1922
Genet, Jean (playwright); Paris **(1910-1986)**
Genghis Khan (Temujin) (conqueror); nr. Lake Baikal, Russia **(1162-1227)**
Gentry, Bobbie (Roberta Streeter) (singer); Chickasaw Co., Miss., 7/27/1944
George, David Lloyd (statesman); Manchester, England **(1863-1945)**
Gere, Richard (actor); Philadelphia, 1950
Gericault, Jean Louis (painter); Rouen, France **(1791-1824)**
Geronimo (Goyathlay) (Apache chieftain); Arizona **(1829-1909)**
Gershwin, George (composer); Brooklyn, N.Y. **(1898-1937)**
Gershwin, Ira (lyricist); New York City, **(1896-1983)**
Getty, J. Paul (oil executive); Minneapolis **(1892-1976)**
Getz, Stan (saxophonist); Philadelphia, 2/2/1927

Ghiberti, Lorenzo (goldsmith and sculptor); Florence **(1378-1455)**
Giacometti, Alberto (sculptor); Switzerland **(1901-1966)**
Giannini, Giancarlo (actor); La Spezia, Italy, 8/1/1942
Gibbon, Edward (historian); Putney, England **(1737-1794)**
Gibson, Charles Dana (illustrator); Roxbury, Mass. **(1867-1944)**
Gibson, Hoot (Edward) (actor); Tememah, Neb. **(1892-1962)**
Gide, André (author); Paris **(1869-1951)**
Gielgud, Sir John (actor); London, 4/14/1904
Gilbert, John (movie actor); Logan, Utah **(1897-1936)**
Gilbert, Sir William Schwenck (librettist); London **(1836-1911)**
Gilels, Emil (concert pianist); Odessa, Ukraine **(1916-1985)**
Gillespie, Dizzy (John Birks Gillespie) (jazz trumpeter); Cheraw, S.C., 10/21/1917
Gimbel, Bernard F. (merchant); Vincennes, Ind. **(1885-1966)**
Gingold, Hermione (actress and comedienne); London **(1897-1987)**
Ginsberg, Allen (poet); Newark, N.J., 6/3/1926
Giordano, Luca (painter); Naples, Italy **(1632-1705)**
Giorgione (painter); Castelfranco, (Italy) **(c.1477-1510)**
Giotto di Bondone (painter); Vespignamo (Italy) **(c.1266-1337)**
Giovanni, Nikki (poet); Knoxville, Tenn., 6/7/1943
Giroud, Françoise (French government official); Geneva, 9/21/1916
Gish, Dorothy (actress); Massillon, Ohio **(1898-1968)**
Gish, Lillian (Lillian de Guiche) (actress); Springfield, Ohio, 10/14/1896(?)
Givenchy, Hubert (fashion designer); Beauvais, France, 2/21/1927
Gladstone, William Ewart (statesman); Liverpool, England **(1809-1898)**
Glass, Philip (composer); Baltimore, 1/31/1937
Gleason, Jackie (comedian); Brooklyn, N.Y. **(1916-1987)**
Gleason, James (actor); New York City **(1886-1959)**
Gluck, Christoph Willibald (composer); Erasbach (Germany) **(1714-1787)**
Gobel, George (comedian); Chicago, 5/20/1920
Godard, Jean Luc (film director); Paris, 12/3/1930
Goddard, Robert Hutchings (father of modern rocketry); Worcester, Mass. **(1882-1945)**
Goddard, Paulette (Marion Levy) (actress); Great Neck, N.Y., 6/3/1911
Godfrey, Arthur (entertainer); New York City **(1903-1983)**
Godunov, Alexander (ballet dancer); Sakhalin, U.S.S.R. 11/28/1949
Goebbels, Joseph Paul (Nazi leader); Rheydt, Germany **(1897-1945)**
Goering, Hermann (Nazi leader); Rosenheim, Germany **(1893-1946)**
Goethals, George Washington (engineer); Brooklyn, N.Y. **(1858-1928)**
Goethe, Johann Wolfgang von (poet); Frankfurt-am-Main, Germany **(1749-1832)**
Gogol, Nikolai Vasilievich (novelist); nr. Mirgorod, Ukraine **(1809-1852)**
Goldberg, Rube (cartoonist); San Francisco **(1883-1970)**
Goldberg, Whoopi (actress); New York City, 1949 (?)
Golden, Harry (Harry Goldhurst) (author); New York City **(1902-1981)**
Goldsmith, Oliver (dramatist and poet); County Longford, Ireland **(1728-1774)**
Goldwyn, Samuel (Samuel Goldfish) (film producer); Warsaw **(1882-1974)**
Golenpaul, Dan (creator of Information Please radio show and editor of almanac of same name); New York City **(1900-1974)**
Gompers, Samuel (labor leader); London **(1850-1924)**
Goodall, Jane (Baroness van Lawick-Goodall) (ethologist); London, 4/3/1934
Goodman, Benny (clarinetist); Chicago **(1909-1986)**
Goodyear, Charles (inventor); New Haven, Conn. **(1800-1860)**
Gorbachev, Mikhail Sergeyevich (Soviet leader); Privolnoye, U.S.S.R., 3/2/1931
Gordimer, Nadine (novelist and short-story writer); Springs, South Africa, 12/20/1923
Gordon, Max (stage producer); New York City; **(1892-1978)**
Gordon, Ruth (actress); Wollaston, Mass. **(1896-1985)**
Gordy, Berry, Jr. (record company executive); Detroit, 11/28/1929
Gore, Lesley (singer); Tenafly, N.J., 1946
Goren, Charles H. (bridge expert); Philadelphia, 3/4/1901
Gorki, Maxim (Alexei Maximovich Peshkov) (author); Nizhni Novgorod, Russia **(1868-1936)**
Gorky, Arshile (painter); Armenia **(1904-1948)**
Gormé, Eydie (singer); Bronx, N.Y., 8/16/1932
Gorshin, Frank (actor); Pittsburgh, 4/5/1934
Gosden, Freeman F. *See* Amos
Gould, Chester (cartoonist); Pawnee, Okla. **(1900-1985)**
Gould, Elliott (Elliott Goldstein) (actor); Brooklyn, N.Y., 8/29/1938
Gould, Glenn (concert pianist); Toronto, **(1932-1982)**
Gould, Morton (composer); Richmond Hill, Queens, N.Y., 12/10/1913
Goulet, Robert (singer); Lawrence, Mass., 11/26/1933
Gounod, Charles François (composer); Paris **(1818-1893)**
Goya y Lucientes, Francisco José de (painter); Fuendetodos, Spain **(1746-1828)**
Grable, Betty (actress); St. Louis **(1916-1973)**
Grace, Princess of Monaco (Grace Kelly) (ex-actress); Philadelphia **(1929-1982)**
Graham, Bill (Wolfgang Grajonca) (rock impresario); Berlin, 1931
Graham, Billy (William F.) (evangelist); Charlotte, N.C., 11/7/1918
Graham, Katharine Meyer (newspaper publisher); New York City, 6/16/1917
Graham, Martha (choreographer); Pittsburgh, 5/11/1894(?)
Grahame, Gloria (Gloria Hallwood) (actress); Los Angeles **(1929-1981)**
Grainger, Percy Aldridge (pianist and composer); Melbourne, Australia **(1882-1961)**
Gramm, Donald (Grambach) (bass-baritone); Milwaukee **(1927-1983)**
Granger, Farley (actor); San Jose, Calif., 7/1/1925
Granger, Stewart (James Stewart) (actor); London, 5/6/1913
Grant, Cary (Alexander Archibald Leach) (actor); Bristol, England **(1904-1986)**
Grant, Lee (Lyova Haskell Rosenthal) (actress); New York City, 10/31/1930
Granville, Bonita (actress and producer); New York City, 1923
Grass, Günter (novelist); Danzig (Poland), 10/16/1927
Grauer, Ben (radio and TV announcer); New York City **(1908-1977)**
Graves, Peter (Peter Arness) (actor); Minneapolis, 3/18/1926
Graves, Robert (writer); London **(1895-1985)**
Gray, Barry (Bernard Yaroslaw) (radio interviewer); Atlantic City, N.J., 7/2/1916
Gray, Dolores (singer and actress); Chicago, 6/7/1930
Gray, Thomas (poet); London **(1716-1771)**
Grayson, Kathryn (Zelma Hednick) (singer and actress); Winston-Salem, N.C., 2/9/1923
Greco, Buddy (singer); Philadelphia, 8/14/1926
Greco, José (dancer); Montorio nei Frentani, Italy, 12/23/1918
Greeley, Horace (journalist and politician); Amherst, N.H. **(1811-1872)**
Green, Adolph (actor and lyricist); New York City, 12/2/1915
Green, Al (singer); Forrest City, Ark., 4/13/1946
Greene, Graham (novelist); Berkhamsted, England, 10/2/1904
Greene, Lorne (actor); Ottawa, 2/12/1915
Greene, Martyn (actor); London **(1899-1975)**
Greenstreet, Sydney (actor); Sandwich, England **(1879-1954)**
Greenwood, Joan (actress and director); London **(1921-1987)**
Greer, Germaine (feminist); Melbourne, 1/29/1939
Gregory, Cynthia (ballerina); Los Angeles, 7/8/1946
Gregory, Dick (comedian); St. Louis, 1932
Greuze, Jean-Baptiste (painter); Tournus, France **(1725-1805)**
Grey, Joel (Joel Katz) (actor); Cleveland, 4/11/1932
Grey, Zane (author); Zanesville, Ohio **(1875-1939)**
Grieg, Edvard Hagerup (composer); Bergen, Norway **(1843-1907)**
Grier, Roosevelt (entertainer and former athlete); Cuthbert, Ga., 7/14/1932
Griffin, Merv (TV entertainer); San Mateo, Calif., 7/6/1925
Griffith, Andy (actor); Mount Airy, N.C., 6/1/1926
Griffith, David Lewelyn Wark (film producer); La Grange, Ky. **(1875-1948)**
Grigorovich, Yuri (choreographer); Leningrad, 1/1/1927
Grimes, Tammy (actress); Lynn, Mass., 1/30/1934
Grimm, Jacob (author of fairy tales); Hanau (Germany) **(1785-1863)**
Grimm, Wilhelm (author of fairy tales); Hanau (Germany) **(1786-1859)**
Gris, Juan (José Victoriano González) (painter); Madrid **(1887-1927)**
Grizzard, George (actor); Roanoke Rapids, N.C., 4/1/1928
Gromyko, Andrei A. (diplomat); Starye Gromyki, Russia, 7/5/1909
Gropius, Walter (architect); Berlin **(1883-1969)**
Gropper, William (painter, illustrator); New York City **(1897-1977)**
Grosz, George (painter); Germany **(1893-1959)**
Guardino, Harry (actor); New York City, 12/23/1925
Guggenheim, Meyer (capitalist); Langnau, Switzerland **(1828-1905)**
Guinness, Sir Alec (actor); London, 4/2/1914
Guitry, Sacha (Alexandre) (actor and film director); St. Petersburg, Russia **(1885-1957)**
Gumbel, Bryant Charles (TV newscaster); New Orleans, 9/29/1948
Gunther, John (author); Chicago **(1901-1970)**
Gutenberg, Johann (printer); Mainz (Germany) **(1400?-?1468)**
Guthrie, Arlo (singer); New York City, 7/10/1947
Guthrie, Woody (folk singer and composer); Okemah, Okla. **(1912-1967)**
Gwenn, Edmund (actor); London **(1875-1959)**

H

Hackett, Bobby (trumpeter); Providence, R.I. **(1915-1976)**
Hackett, Buddy (Leonard Hacker) (comedian and actor); Brooklyn,

N.Y., 8/31/1924
Hackman, Gene (actor); San Bernardino, Calif., 1/30/1931
Hagen, Uta (actress); Göttingen, Germany, 6/12/1919
Haggard, Merle (songwriter); Bakersfield, Calif., 4/6/1937
Hagman, Larry (actor); Weatherford, Tex., 1931
Haig, Alexander Meigs, Jr. (ex-Secretary of State and ex-general); Bala-Cynwyd, Pa., 12/2/1924
Haile Selassie (Ras Tafari Makonnen) (ex-Emperor); Ethiopia **(1892-1975)**
Hailey, Arthur (novelist); Luton, England, 4/5/1920
Halberstam, David (journalist); New York City, 4/10/1934
Hale, Edward Everett (clergyman and author); Boston **(1822-1909)**
Hale, Nathan (American Revolutionary officer); Coventry, Conn. **(1755-1776)**
Halevi, Judah (Jewish poet); Toledo, Spain **(1085-1140)**
Haley, Alex (writer); Ithaca, N.Y., 8/11/1921
Hall, Donald (Andrew, Jr.) (poet) New Haven, Conn., 9/20/1928
Hall, Monty (TV personality); Winnipeg, Canada, 1923
Halley, Edmund (astronomer); London **(1656-1742)**
Hals, Frans (painter); Antwerp (Netherlands) **(1580?-1666)**
Halsey, William Frederick, Jr. (naval officer); Elizabeth, N.J. **(1882-1959)**
Hamill, Pete (journalist); Brooklyn, N.Y., 6/24/1935
Hamilton, Alexander (statesman); Nevis, British West Indies **(1757?-1804)**
Hamilton, George (actor); Memphis, Tenn., 8/12/1939
Hamilton, Margaret (actress); Cleveland **(1902-1985)**
Hamlisch, Marvin (composer and pianist); New York City, 6/2/1944
Hammarskjöld, Dag (U.N. Secretary-General); Jönköping, Sweden **(1905-1961)**
Hammerstein, Oscar, II (librettist and stage producer); New York City **(1895-1960)**
Hampden, Walter (Walter Hampden Dougherty) (actor); Brooklyn, N.Y. **(1879-1955)**
Hampton, Lionel (vibraharpist and band leader); Birmingham, Ala., 4/12/1913
Hamsun, Knut (Knut Pedersen) (novelist); Lom, Norway **(1859-1952)**
Hancock, John (statesman); Braintree, Mass. **(1737-1793)**
Hand, Learned (jurist); Albany, N.Y. **(1872-1961)**
Handel, George Frederick (Georg Friedrich Händel) (composer); Halle (East Germany) **(1685-1759)**
Handy, William Christopher (blues composer); Florence, Ala. **(1873-1958)**
Hannibal (Carthaginian general); North Africa **(247-182 B.C.)**
Hanson, Howard (conductor); Wahoo, Neb., **(1896-1981)**
Harburg, E. Y. "Yip" (songwriter); New York City **(1896-1981)**
Harding, Ann (actress); San Antonio, Tex. **(1902-1981)**
Hardwicke, Sir Cedric (actor); Stourbridge, England **(1893-1964)**
Hardy, Oliver (comedian); Atlanta **(1892-1957)**
Hardy, Thomas (novelist); Dorsetshire, England **(1840-1928)**
Harkness, Edward S. (capitalist); Cleveland **(1874-1940)**
Harlow, Jean (Harlean Carpentier) (actress); Kansas City, Mo. **(1911-1937)**
Harnick, Sheldon (lyricist); Chicago, 4/30/1924
Harper, Valerie (actress); Suffern, N.Y., 8/22/1940(?)
Harrell, Lynn (cellist); New York City, 1/30/1944
Harriman, W. (William) Averell (ex-Governor of New York); New York City **(1891-1986)**
Harris, Barbara (actress); Evanston, Ill., 1935
Harris, Emmylou (singer); Birmingham, Ala., 1949
Harris, Julie (actress); Grosse Pointe Park, Mich., 12/2/1925
Harris, Phil (actor and band leader); Linton, Ind., 6/24/1906
Harris, Richard (actor); Limerick, Ireland, 10/1/1933
Harris, Rosemary (actress); Ashby, England, 9/19/1930
Harris, Roy (composer); Lincoln County, Okla. **(1898-1979)**
Harrison, George (singer and songwriter); Liverpool, England, 2/25/1943
Harrison, Noel (singer and actor); London, 1/29/1936
Harrison, Rex (Reginald Carey) (actor); Huyton, England, 3/5/1908
Hart, Lorenz (lyricist); New York **(1895-1943)**
Hart, Moss (playwright); New York City **(1904-1961)**
Hart, William S. (actor); Newburgh, N.Y. **(1862-1946)**
Harte, Bret (Francis Brett Harte) (author); Albany, N.Y. **(1836-1902)**
Hartford, Huntington (George Huntington Hartford II) (A.&P. heir); New York City, 4/18/1911
Hartford, John (singer and banjoist); New York City, 12/30/1937
Hartman, David Downs (TV newscaster); Pawtucket, R.I., 5/19/1935
Hartman, Elizabeth (actress); Youngstown, Ohio **(1941-1987)**
Harvey, Laurence (Larushka Skikne) (actor); Joniskis, Lithuania **(1928-1973)**
Harvey, William (physician); Folkestone, England **(1578-1657)**
Hasso, Signe (actress); Stockholm, 8/15/1915
Havoc, June (June Hovick) (actress); Seattle, 1916
Haver, June (actress); Rock Island, Ill., 6/10/1926
Hawkins, Jack (actor); London **(1910-1973)**
Hawn, Goldie (actress); Washington, D.C., 11/21/1945
Haworth, Jill (actress); Sussex, England, 1945
Hawthorne, Nathaniel (novelist); Salem, Mass. **(1804-1864)**
Hay, John Milton (statesman); Salem, Ind. **(1838-1905)**
Hayakawa, Sessue (actor); Honshu, Japan **(1890-1973)**
Hayden, Melissa (ballerina); Toronto, 4/25/1923
Hayden, Sterling (Sterling Relyea Walter) (actor and writer); Montclair, N.J. **(1916-1986)**
Haydn, Franz Joseph (composer); Rohrau (Austria) **(1732-1809)**
Hayes, Helen (Helen Hayes Brown) (actress); Washington, D.C., 10/10/1900
Hayes, Isaac (composer); Covington, Tenn., 8/20/1942
Hayward, Louis (actor); Johannesburg, South Africa **(1909-1985)**
Hayward, Susan (Edythe Marrener) (actress); Brooklyn, N.Y. **(1919?-1975)**
Hayworth, Rita (Margarita Cansino) (actress); New York City **(1918-1987)**
Head, Edith (costume designer); Los Angeles **(1907-1981)**
Hearst, William Randolph (publisher); San Francisco **(1863-1951)**
Hearst, William Randolph, Jr. (publisher); New York City, 1/27/1908
Heath, Edward (ex-Prime Minister); Broadstairs, England, 7/9/1916
Heatherton, Joey (actress); Rockville Centre, N.Y., 9/14/1944
Hecht, Ben (author); New York City **(1894-1964)**
Heckart, Eileen (actress); Columbus, Ohio, 3/29/1919
Heflin, Van (Emmet Evan Heflin) (actor); Walters, Okla. **(1910-1971)**
Hefner, Hugh (publisher); Chicago, 4/9/1926
Hegel, Georg Wilhelm Friedrich (philosopher); Stuttgart (Germany) **(1770-1831)**
Heifetz, Jascha (concert violinist); Vilna, Russia, 2/2/1901
Heine, Heinrich (Harry) (poet); Düsseldorf (Germany) **(1797-1856)**
Heinemann, Gustav (ex-President of Germany); Schweim, Germany **(1899-1976)**
Heisenberg, Werner Karl (physicist); Würzburg, Germany **(1901-1976)**
Heller, Joseph (novelist); Brooklyn, N.Y., 5/1/1923
Hellman, Lillian (playwright); New Orleans **(1905-1984)**
Hemingway, Ernest Miller (novelist); Oak Park, Ill. **(1899-1961)**
Hemmings, David (actor); Guilford, England, 11/2/1941
Henderson, Florence (actress); Dale, Ind., 2/14/1934
Henderson, Skitch (Lyle Russell Cedric) (conductor and pianist); Birmingham, England(?), 1/27/1918
Hendrix, Jimi (James Marshall Hendrix) (guitarist); Seattle **(1942-1970)**
Henley, Beth (playwright-actress); Jackson, Miss., 5/8/1952
Henning, Doug (magician and actor); Winnipeg, Canada, 1947(?)
Henreid, Paul (actor); Trieste, 1/10/1908
Henri, Robert (painter); Cincinnati **(1865-1926)**
Henry, O. (William Sydney Porter) (story writer); Greensboro, N.C. **(1862-1910)**
Henry, Patrick (statesman); Hanover County, Va. **(1736-1799)**
Henson, Jim (puppeteer); Greenville, Miss., 9/24/1936
Hepburn, Audrey (actress); Brussels, Belgium, 5/4/1929
Hepburn, Katharine (actress); Hartford, Conn., 11/8/1909
Hepplewhite, George (furniture designer); England **(?-1786)**
Hepworth, Barbara (sculptor); Wakefield, England **(1903-1975)**
Herachel, William (Frederich Wilhelm) (astronomer); Hanover, Germany **(1738-1822)**
Herbert, George (poet); Montgomery Castle, Wales **(1593-1633)**
Herbert, Victor (composer); Dublin **(1859-1924)**
Herblock (Herbert L. Block) (political cartoonist); Chicago, 10/13/1909
Herman, Woody (Woodrow Charles) (band leader); Milwaukee, 5/16/1913
Herod (Herodes) (called Herod the Great) (King of Judea) **(73?-4 B.C.)**
Herodotus (historian); Halicarnassus, Asia Minor (Turkey) **(c. 484-425 B.C.)**
Herrick, Robert (poet); London? **(1591-1674)**
Hershfield, Harry (humorist and raconteur); Cedar Rapids, Iowa **(1885-1974)**
Hersholt, Jean (actor); Copenhagen **(1886-1956)**
Hesburgh, Theodore M. (educator); Syracuse, N.Y., 5/2/1917
Heston, Charlton (actor); Evanston, Ill., 10/4/1924
Heyerdahl, Thor (ethnologist and explorer); Larvik, Norway, 10/6/1914
Hildegarde (Hildegarde Loretta Sell) (singer); Adell, Wis., 2/1/1906
Hill, Arthur (actor); Melfort, Canada, 8/1/1922
Hillary, Sir Edmund (mountain climber); New Zealand, 7/20/1919
Hiller, Wendy (actress); Bramhall, England, 8/15/1912
Hilliard, Harriet. *See* Nelson, Harriet
Hindemith, Paul (composer); Hanau, Germany **(1895-1963)**
Hines, Earl "Fatha" (jazz pianist); Duquesne, Pa. **(1905-1983)**
Hines, Jerome (Jerome Heinz) (basso); Los Angeles, 11/8/1921
Hingle, Pat (actor); Denver, 7/19/1924
Hippocrates (physician); Cos, Greece **(c. 460-c. 377 B.C.)**
Hirohito (Emperor); Tokyo, 4/29/1901
Hiroshige, Ando (painter); Edo? (Tokyo) **(1797-1858)**

Hirsch, Judd (actor); New York City, 3/15/1935
Hirschfeld, Al (Albert) (cartoonist); St. Louis, 6/21/1903
Hirschhorn, Joseph Herman (financier, speculator, and art collector); Mitau, Latvia **(1899-1981)**
Hirt, Al (trumpeter); New Orleans, 11/7/1922
Hitchcock, Alfred J. (film director); London **(1899-1980)**
Hitler, Adolf (German dictator); Braunau, Austria **(1889-1945)**
Hitzig, William Maxwell (physician); Austria, 12/15/1904
Hobbes, Thomas (philosopher); Westport, England **(1588-1679)**
Hobson, Laura Z. (Laura K. Zametkin) (novelist); New York City **(1900-1986)**
Hodges, Eddie (actor); Hattiesburg, Miss., 3/5/1947
Hoffa, James R(iddle) (labor leader); Brazil, Ind., 2/14/1913 (presumed dead, 1977)
Hoffman, Dustin (film actor and director); Los Angeles, 8/8/1937
Hofmann, Hans (painter); Germany **(1880-1966)**
Hogarth, William (painter and engraver); London **(1697-1764)**
Hokusai, Katauhika (artist); Yedo, Japan **(1760-1849)**
Holbein, Hans (the Elder) (painter); Augsburg (Germany) **(1465?-1524)**
Holbein, Hans (the Younger) (painter); Augsburg (Germany) **(1497?-1543)**
Holbrook, Hal (actor); Cleveland, 2/17/1925
Holden, William (William Franklin Beedle, Jr.) (actor); O'Fallon, Ill. **(1918-1981)**
Holder, Geoffrey (dancer); Port-of-Spain, Trinidad, 8/1/1930
Holiday, Billie (Eleanora Fagan) (jazz-blues singer); Baltimore **(1915-1959)**
Holliday, Judy (Judith Tuvim) (comedienne); New York City **(1922-1965)**
Holloway, Stanley (actor); London **(1890-1982)**
Holloway, Sterling (actor); Cedartown, Ga., 1905
Holm, Celeste (actress); New York City, 4/29/1919
Holmes, Oliver Wendell (jurist); Boston **(1841-1935)**
Holt, Jack (actor); Winchester, Va. **(1888-1951)**
Holtz, Lou (comedian); San Francisco **(1898-1980)**
Home, Lord (Alexander Frederick Douglas-Home) (diplomat); London, 7/2/1903
Homeier, Skip (George Vincent Homeier) (actor); Chicago, 10/5/1930
Homer, Winslow (painter); Boston, Mass. **(1836-1910)**
Homer (Greek poet) **(c.850 B.C.?)**
Homolka, Oscar (actor); Vienna **(1898-1978)**
Honegger, Arthur (composer); Le Havre, France **(1892-1955)**
Hook, Sidney (philosopher); New York City, 12/20/1902
Hoover, J. Edgar (FBI director); Washington, D.C. **(1895-1972)**
Hope, Bob (Leslie Townes Hope) (comedian); London, 5/29/1903
Hopkins, Anthony (actor); Port Talbot, Wales, 12/31/1937
Hopkins, Gerald Manley (poet); Stratford, England **(1844-1899)**
Hopkins, Johns (financier); Anne Arundel County, Md. **(1795-1873)**
Hopkins, Miriam (actress); Bainbridge, Ga. **(1902-1972)**
Hopper, Dennis (actor); Dodge City, Kan., 5/17/1936
Hopper, Edward (painter); Nyack, N.Y. **(1882-1967)**
Horace (Quintus Horatius Flaccus) (poet); Venosa (Italy) **(65-8 B.C.)**
Horne, Lena (singer); Brooklyn, N.Y., 6/30/1917
Horne, Marilyn (mezzo-soprano); Bradford, Pa., 1/16/1934
Horowitz, Vladimir (pianist); Kiev, Russia, 10/1/1904
Horton, Edward Everett (comedian); Brooklyn, N.Y. **(1887-1970)**
Houdini, Harry (Ehrich Weiss) (magician); Appleton, Wis. **(1874-1926)**
Houseman, John (Jacques Haussmann) (producer, director, and actor); Bucharest; 9/22/1902
Housman, A(lfred) E(dward) (poet); Fockburg, England **(1859-1936)**
Houston, Samuel (political leader); Rockbridge County, Va. **(1793-1863)**
Howard, Leslie (Leslie Stainer) (actor); London **(1893-1943)**
Howard, Ron (actor-director); Duncan, Okla., 3/1/1954
Howard, Trevor (actor); Kent, England, 9/29/1916
Howe, Elias (inventor); Spencer, Mass. **(1819-1867)**
Howe, Irving (literary critic); New York City, 6/11/1920
Howe, Julia Ward (poet and reformer); New York City **(1819-1910)**
Howes, Sally Ann (actress); London, 7/20/1934
Hudson, Henry (English navigator) **(?-1611)**
Hudson, Rock (born Roy Scherer, Jr.; took Roy Fitzgerald as legal name) (actor); Winnetka, Ill., **(1925-1985)**
Hughes, Charles Evans (jurist); Glens Falls, N.Y. **(1862-1948)**
Hughes, Howard (industrialist and film producer); Houston **(1905-1976)**
Hughes, Langston (poet); Joplin, Mo. **(1902-1967)**
Hugo, Victor Marie (author); Besançon, France **(1802-1885)**
Hume, David (philosopher); Edinburgh, Scotland **(1711-1776)**
Humperdinck, Engelbert (Arnold Dorsey) (singer); Madras, India, 5/2/1936
Humperdinck, Engelbert (composer); Siegburg (Germany) **(1854-1921)**
Hunt, H. L. (industrialist); nr. Vandalia, Ill. **(1889-1974)**
Hunt, Marsha (actress); Chicago, 10/17/1917
Hunter, Kim (Janet Cole) (actress); Detroit, 11/12/1922
Hunter, Tab (Arthur Andrew Gelien) (actor); New York City, 7/11/1931
Huntley, Chet (TV newscaster); Cardwell, Mont. **(1911-1974)**
Hurok, Sol (Solomon) (impresario); Pogar, Russia **(1884-1974)**
Hurst, Fannie (novelist); Hamilton, Ohio **(1889-1968)**
Hurt, John (actor); Shirebrook, England, 1/22/1940
Hus, Jan (Bohemian religious reformer); Husinetz, nr. Budweis (Czechoslovakia) **(c.1369-1415)**
Hussein I (King); Jordan, 11/14/1935
Huston, John (film director and writer); Nevada, Mo., 8/5/1906
Huston, Walter (Walter Houghston) (actor); Toronto **(1884-1950)**
Hutchins, Robert M. (educator); Brooklyn, N.Y. **(1899-1977)**
Hutton, Barbara (Woolworth heiress); New York City **(1912-1979)**
Hutton, Betty (Betty Thornburg) (actress); Battle Creek, Mich., 2/26/1921
Hutton, Lauren (model and actress); Charleston, S.C., 1944
Hutton, Timothy (actor); Los Angeles, 8/16/1960
Huxley, Aldous (author); Godalming, England **(1894-1963)**
Huxley, Sir Julian S. (biologist and author); London **(1887-1975)**
Huxley, Thomas Henry (biologist); Ealing, England **(1825-1895)**

I

Ian, Janis (singer); New York City, 5/7/1951
Ibsen, Henrik (dramatist); Skien, Norway **(1828-1906)**
Inge, William (playwright); Independence, Kan. **(1913-1973)**
Ingres, Jean Auguste Dominique (painter); Montauban, France **(1780-1867)**
Inness, George (painter); nr. Newburgh, N.Y. **(1825-1894)**
Ionesco, Eugene (playwright); Slatina, Romania, 11/26/1912
Ireland, John (actor); Vancouver, B.C., Canada, 1/30/1915
Irons, Jeremy (actor); Cowes, Isle of Wight, England, 9/19/1948
Irving, John (Winslow) (writer), Exeter, N.H., 3/2/1942
Irving, Washington (author); New York City **(1783-1859)**
Isherwood, Christopher (novelist and playwright); nr. Dilsey and High Lane, England **(1904-1986)**
Iturbi, José (concert pianist); Valencia, Spain **(1895-1980)**
Ives, Burl (Icle Ivanhoe) (singer); Hunt, Ill., 6/14/1909
Ives, Charles E(dward) (composer); Danbury, Conn. **(1874-1954)**

J

Jackson, Anne (actress); Millvale, Pa., 9/3/1926
Jackson, Glenda (actress); Hoylake, England, 1937(?)
Jackson, Rev. Jesse (civil rights leader); Greenville, S.C., 10/8/1941
Jackson, Kate (actress); Birmingham, Ala., 10/29/1949
Jackson, Mahalia (gospel singer); New Orleans **(1912-1972)**
Jackson, Michael (singer); Gary, Ind., 8/19/1958
Jackson, Thomas Jonathan ("Stonewall") (general); Clarksburg, Va. (now W. Va.) **(1824-1863)**
Jacobi, Lou (actor); Toronto, 12/28/1913
Jacobs, Jane (urbanologist); Scranton, Pa., 5/1/1916
Jaffe, Sam (actor); New York City **(1891-1984)**
Jagger, Dean (actor); Lima, Ohio, 11/7/1903
Jagger, Mick (Michael Phillip) (singer); Dartford, England, 7/26/1944
James, Harry (trumpeter); Albany, Ga. **(1916-1983)**
James, Henry (novelist); New York City **(1843-1916)**
James, Jesse Woodson (outlaw); Clay County, Mo. **(1847-1882)**
James, William (psychologist); New York City **(1842-1910)**
Jameson, (Margaret) Storm (novelist); Whitby, England **(1897-1986)**
Janis, Byron (pianist); McKeesport, Pa., 3/24/1928
Jannings, Emil (actor); Brooklyn, N.Y. **(1886-1950)**
Janssen, David (David Meyer) (actor); Naponee, Neb. **(1930-1980)**
Jay, John (statesman and jurist); New York City **(1745-1829)**
Jeanmaire, Renée (dancer); Paris, 4/29/1924
Jenner, Edward (physician); Berkeley, England **(1749-1823)**
Jennings, Waylon (singer); Littlefield, Tex., 1937
Jessel, George (entertainer); New York City **(1898-1981)**
Jessup, Philip C. (diplomat); New York City, 1/5/1897
Jiang Qing (political leader); Chucheng, China, 1913 (?)
Joan of Arc (Jeanne d'Arc) (saint and patriot); Domremy-la-Pucelle, France **(1412-1431)**
Joel, Billy (singer); New York City, 5/9/1949
Joffrey, Robert (Abdullah Jaffa Bey Khan) (choreographer); Seattle, 12/24/1930
John, Elton (Reginald Kenneth Dwight) (singer and pianist); Pinner, England, 3/25/1947
Johns, Glynis (actress); Pretoria, South Africa, 10/5/1923
Johns, Jasper (painter and sculptor); Augusta, Ga., 5/15/1930
Johnson, James Weldon (author and educator); Jacksonville, Fla.

(1871-1938)
Johnson, Philip Cortalyou (architect); Cleveland, Ohio, 7/8/1906
Johnson, Samuel (lexicographer and author); Lichfield, England **(1709-1784)**
Johnson, Van (actor); Newport, R.I., 8/20/1916
Joliot-Curie, Frédéric (physicist); Paris **(1900-1958)**
Joliot-Curie, Irène (Irène Curie) (physicist); France **(1897-1956)**
Jolliet (or Joliet), Louis (explorer); Beaupré, Canada **(1645-1700)**
Jolson, Al (Asa Yoelson) (actor and singer); St. Petersburg, Russia **(1886-1950)**
Jones, Carolyn (singer and actress); Amarillo, Tex., **(1933-1983)**
Jones, Dean (actor); Morgan County, Ala., 1/25/1935
Jones, George (singer); Saratoga, Tex., 9/12/1931
Jones, Inigo (architect); London **(1573-1652)**
Jones, James (novelist); Robinson, Ill. **(1921-1977)**
Jones, James Earl (actor); Arkabutla, Miss., 1/17/1931
Jones, Jennifer (Phyllis Isley) (actress); Tulsa, Okla., 3/2/1919
Jones, John Paul (John Paul) (naval officer); Scotland **(1747-1792)**
Jones, Quincy (composer); Chicago, 3/14/1933
Jones, Shirley (singer and actress); Smithtown, Pa., 3/31/1934
Jones, Tom (Thomas Jones Woodward) (singer); Pontypridd, Wales, 6/7/1940
Jong, Erica (writer); New York City, 3/26/1942
Jonson, Ben (Benjamin) (poet and dramatist); Westminster, England **(1572-1637)**
Joplin, Janis (singer); Port Arthur, Tex. **(1943-1970)**
Jory, Victor (actor); Dawson City, Yukon, Canada **(1902-1982)**
Josquin des Prés (usually known as Josquin) (composer); Conde-sur-L'Escaut?, Hainaut (France or Belgium) **(c.1445-1521)**
Jourdan, Louis (Louis Gendre) (actor); Marseilles, France, 6/19/1920
Joyce, James (novelist); Dublin **(1882-1941)**
Juárez, Benito Pablo (statesman); Guelatao, Mexico **(1806-1872)**
Julia, Raul (Raúl Rafael Carlos Julia y Arcelay) (actor); San Juan, Puerto Rico, 3/9/1940
Juliana (Queen); The Hague, Netherlands, 4/30/1909
Jung, Carl Gustav (psychoanalyst); Basel, Switzerland **(1875-1961)**
Jurado, Katy (actress); Guadalajara, Mexico, 1927

K

Kabalevsky, Dmitri (composer); St. Petersburg, Russia **(1904-1987)**
Kafka, Franz (author); Prague **(1883-1924)**
Kádár, János (Communist Party leader); Hungary, 1912
Kahn, Gus (songwriter); Coblenz, Germany **(1886-1941)**
Kahn, Louis I. (architect); Oesel Island, Estonia **(1901-1974)**
Kahn, Madeline (actress); Boston, 9/29/1942
Kaminska, Ida (actress); Odessa, Russia **(1899-1980)**
Kandinsky, Wassily (painter); Moscow **(1866-1944)**
Kanin, Garson (playwright); Rochester, N.Y., 11/24/1912
Kant, Immanuel (philosopher); Königsberg (Kaliningrad, U.S.S.R.) **(1724-1804)**
Kantor, MacKinlay (novelist); Webster City, Iowa **(1904-1977)**
Kaplan, Gabe (Gabriel) (actor); Brooklyn, N.Y., 3/31/1945
Karloff, Boris (William Henry Pratt) (actor); London **(1887-1969)**
Kaufman, George S. (playwright); Pittsburgh **(1889-1961)**
Kaye, Danny (David Daniel Kominski) (comedian); Brooklyn, N.Y. **(1913-1987)**
Kaye, Sammy (band leader); Cleveland **(1910-1987)**
Kazan, Elia (director); Constantinople, Turkey, 9/7/1909
Kazan, Lainie (Levine) (singer); New York City, 5/15/1940
Keach, Stacy (actor); Savannah, Ga., 6/2/1941
Keaton, Buster (Joseph Frank Keaton) (comedian); Piqua, Kan. **(1896-1966)**
Keaton, Diane (actress); Los Angeles, 1/5/1946
Keats, John (poet); London **(1795-1821)**
Keel, Howard (singer and actor); Gillespie, Ill., 4/13/1919
Keeler, Ruby (Lehy Keeler) (actress and dancer); Halifax, Nova Scotia, Canada, 8/25/1910
Kefauver, Estes (legislator); Madisonville, Tenn. **(1903-1963)**
Keith, Brian (actor); Bayonne, N.J., 11/14/1921
Keller, Helen Adams (author and educator); Tuscumbia, Ala. **(1880-1968)**
Kellerman, Sally (actress); Long Beach, Calif., 6/2/1938
Kelly, Emmett (clown); Sedan, Kan., **(1898-1979)**
Kelly, Gene (dancer and actor); Pittsburgh, 8/23/1912
Kelly, Patsy (actress and comedienne); Brooklyn, N.Y. **(1910-1981)**
Kelly, Walt (cartoonist); Philadelphia **(1913-1973)**
Kemal Ataturk (Mustafa Kemal) (Turkish soldier and statesman); Salonika (Greece) **(1881-1938)**
Kempis, Thomas a (mystic); Kempis, Prussia (Germany) **(1380-1471)**
Kennan, George F. (diplomat); Milwaukee, 2/16/1904
Kennedy, Arthur (actor); Worcester, Mass., 2/17/1914
Kennedy, George (actor); New York City, 2/18/1925
Kennedy, Jacqueline. *See* Onassis, Jacqueline
Kennedy, Joseph P. (financier); Boston **(1888-1969)**
Kennedy, Robert Francis (legislator); Brookline, Mass. **(1925-1968)**
Kennedy, Rose Fitzgerald (President's mother); Boston, 7/22/1890
Kent, Rockwell (painter); Tarrytown Heights, N.Y. **(1882-1971)**
Kenton, Stan (Stanley Newcomb) (jazz musician); Wichita, Kan. **(1912-1979)**
Kepler, Johannes (astronomer); Weil (Germany) **(1571-1630)**
Kerensky, Alexander Fedorovich (statesman); Simbirks, Russia **(1881-1970)**
Kern, Jerome David (composer); New York City **(1885-1945)**
Kerr, Deborah (actress); Helensburgh, Scotland, 9/30/1921
Kesey, Ken (novelist); La Junta, Colo., 9/17/1935
Kettering, Charles F. (engineer and inventor); nr. Loudonville, Ohio **(1876-1958)**
Key, Francis Scott (lawyer and author of national anthem); Frederick (now Carroll) County, Md. **(1779-1843)**
Keyes, Frances Parkinson (novelist); Charlottesville, Va. **(1885-1970)**
Keynes (1st Baron of Tilton) (John Maynard Keynes) (economist); Cambridge, England **(1883-1946)**
Khachaturian, Aram (composer); Tiflis, Russia **(1903-1978)**
Khrushchev, Nikita S. (Soviet leader); Kalinovka, nr. Kursk, Ukraine **(1894-1971)**
Kibbee, Guy (actor); El Paso **(1886-1956)**
Kidd, Michael (choreographer); Brooklyn, N.Y., 1917
Kidd, William (called Captain Kidd) (pirate); Greenock, Scotland **(1645?-1701)**
Kieran, John (writer); New York City **(1892-1981)**
Kierkegaard, Sören Aalys (philosopher); Copenhagen **(1813-1855)**
Kiesinger, Kurt Georg (diplomat); Ebingen, Germany, 4/6/1904
Kiley, Richard (actor and singer); Chicago, 3/31/1922
Kilmer, Alfred Joyce (poet); New Brunswick, N.J. **(1886-1918)**
King, Alan (Irwin Alan Kniberg) (entertainer); Brooklyn, N.Y., 12/26/1927
King, B.B. (Riley King) (guitarist); Itta Bena, Miss., 9/16/1925
King, Carole (singer and songwriter); Brooklyn, N.Y., 2/9/1941
King, Coretta Scott (civil rights leader); Marion, Ala., 4/27/1927
King, Martin Luther, Jr. (civil rights leader); Atlanta **(1929-1968)**
King, Pee Wee (Frank) (singer); Abrams, Wis., 2/18/1914
King, Stephen (writer); Portland, Maine, 9/21/1947
Kingsley, Ben (Krishna Bhanji) (actor); Snainton, England, 12/31/1943
Kingsley, Sidney (Sidney Kirschner) (playwright); New York City, 10/18/1906
Kinski, Nastassja (Nastassja Nakszynski) (actress); West Berlin, 1/24/1961
Kipling, Rudyard (author); Bombay **(1865-1936)**
Kipnis, Alexander (basso); Ukraine, **(1891-1978)**
Kirby, George (comedian); Chicago, **1923(?)**
Kirk, Grayson (educator); Jeffersonville, Ohio, 10/12/1903
Kirk, Lisa (actress and singer); Charleroi, Pa., 1925
Kirk, Phyllis (actress); Plainfield, N.J., 9/18/1930
Kirkland, Gelsey (ballerina); Bethlehem, Pa., 12/29/1952
Kirkpatrick, Jeane Jordan (educator-public affairs); Duncan, Okla., 11/19/1926
Kirkpatrick, Ralph (harpsichordist); Leominster, Mass. **(1911-1984)**
Kirkwood, James (actor); Grand Rapids, Mich. **(1883-1963)**
Kirsten, Dorothy (soprano); Montclair, N.J., 7/6/1919
Kissinger, Henry (Heinz Alfred Kissinger) (ex-Secretary of State); Furth, Germany, 5/27/1923
Kitt, Eartha (singer); North, S.C., 1/26/1928
Klee, Paul (painter); Münchenbuchsee, nr. Bern, Switzerland **(1879-1940)**
Klein, Calvin (fashion designer); Bronx, N.Y., 11/19/1942
Klein, Robert (comedian); New York City, 2/8/1942
Kleist, Henrich von (poet); Frankfurt an der Oder (East Germany) **(1777-1811)**
Klemperer, Otto (conductor); Breslau (Poland) **(1885-1973)**
Klemperer, Werner (actor); Cologne, Germany, 3/22/1920
Klugman, Jack (actor); Philadelphia, 4/27/1922
Knievel, Evel (Robert Craig) (daredevil motorcyclist); Butte, Mont., 10/17/1938
Knight, Gladys (singer); Atlanta, 5/28/1944
Knight, Ted (Tadeus Wladyslaw Konopka) (actor); Terryville, Conn., **(1923-1986)**
Knight, John S. (publisher); Bluefield, W. Va. **(1894-1981)**
Knopf, Alfred A. (publisher); New York City, **(1892-1984)**
Knotts, Don (actor); Morgantown, W.Va., 7/21/1924
Knox, John (religious reformer); Haddington, East Lothian, Scotland **(1505-1572)**
Koch, Robert (physician); Klausthal (Germany) **(1843-1910)**
Koestler, Arthur (novelist); Budapest **(1905-1983)**
Kokoschka, Oskar (painter); Póchlarn Austria **(1886-1980)**
Kooper, Al (singer and pianist); Brooklyn, N.Y., 2/5/1944
Korman, Harvey (actor); Chicago, 2/15/1927
Kosciusko, Thaddeus (Tadeusz Andrzej Bonawentura Kosciuszko)

(military officer); Grand Duchy of Lithuania **(1746-1817)**
Kossuth, Lajos (patriot); Monok, Hungary **(1802-1894)**
Kostelanetz, André (orchestra conductor); St. Petersburg, Russia **(1901-1980)**
Kosygin, Aleksei N. (Premier); St. Petersburg, Russia **(1904-1980)**
Koussevitzky, Serge (Sergei) Alexandrovitch (orchestra conductor); Vishni Volochek, Tver, Russia **(1874-1951)**
Kovacs, Ernie (comedian); Trenton, N.J. **(1919-1962)**
Kramer, Stanley E. (film producer and director); New York City, 9/29/1913
Kràus, Lili (pianist); Budapest **(1905-1986)**
Kreisler, Fritz (violinist and composer); Vienna **(1875-1962)**
Kresge, S. S. (merchant); Bald Mount, Pa. **(1867-1966)**
Krips, Josef (orchestra conductor); Vienna **(1902-1974)**
Kristofferson, Kris (singer); Brownsville, Tex., 6/22/1936
Kruger, Otto (actor); Toledo, Ohio **(1885-1974)**
Krupa, Gene (drummer); Chicago **(1909-1973)**
Krupp, Alfred (munitions magnate); Essen, Germany **(1812-1887)**
Kubelik, Rafael (conductor); Bychory (Czechoslovakia), 6/29/1914
Kublai Khan (Mongol conqueror) **(1216-1294)**
Kubrick, Stanley (producer and director); New York City, 7/26/1928
Kuralt, Charles (TV journalist); Wilmington, N.C., 9/10/1934
Kurosawa, Akira (film director); Tokyo, 3/23/1910
Kurtz, Efrem (conductor); St. Petersburg, Russia, 11/7/1900
Ky, Nguyen Cao (ex-Vice President of South Vietnam); Son Tay (Vietnam), 9/8/1930

L

Ladd, Alan (actor); Hot Springs, Ark. **(1913-1964)**
Ladd, Cheryl (Cheryl Stoppelmoor) (actress); Huron, S.D., 7/12/1951
Lafayette, Marquis de (Marie Joseph Paul Yves Roch Gilbert du Motier) (military officer); Auvergne, France **(1757-1834)**
Lafitte, Jean (pirate); Bayonne? France **(1780-1826)**
La Follette, Robert Marin (politician); Primrose, Wis. **(1855-1925)**
La Guardia, Fiorello Henry (Mayor of New York); New York City **(1882-1947)**
Lahr, Bert (Irving Lahrheim) (comedian); New York City **(1895-1967)**
Laine, Frankie (Frank Paul LoVecchio) (singer); Chicago, 3/30/1913
Laird, Melvin (ex-Secretary of Defense); Omaha, Neb., 9/1/1922
Lamarck, Chevalier de (Jean Baptiste Pierre Antoine de Monet) (naturalist); Bazantin, France **(1744-1829)**
Lamarr, Hedy (Hedwig Kiesler) (actress); Vienna, 1915
Lamas, Fernando (actor); Buenos Aires, **(1915-1982)**
Lamb, Charles (Elia) (essayist); London **(1775-1834)**
Lamour, Dorothy (Dorothy Kaumeyer) (actress); New Orleans, 10/10/1914
Lancaster, Burt (actor); New York City, 11/2/1913
Lanchester, Elsa (Elsa Sullivan) (actress); London **(1902-1986)**
Landau, Martin (actor); Brooklyn, N.Y. 1934
Landers, Ann (columnist); Sioux City, Iowa, 7/4/1918
Landon, Michael (Eugene Maurice Orowitz) (actor); Forest Hills, Queens, N.Y., 10/31/1936(?)
Lane, Abbe (singer); New York City, 1933
Lang, Fritz (film director); Vienna **(1890-1976)**
Lang, Paul Henry (music critic); Budapest, 8/28/1901
Lange, Hope (actress); Redding Ridge, Conn., 11/28/1933
Langella, Frank (actor); Bayonne, N.J., 1/1/1940
Langford, Frances (singer); Lakeland, Fla., 4/4/1913
Langmuir, Irving (chemist); Brooklyn, N.Y. **(1881-1957)**
Langtry, Lillie (Emily Le Breton) (actress); Island of Jersey **(1852-1929)**
Lansbury, Angela (actress); London, 10/16/1925
Lansing, Robert (Robert Howell Brown) (actor); San Diego, Calif., 6/5/1928
Lanza, Mario (Alfred Arnold Cocozza) (singer and actor); Philadelphia **(1925-1959)**
Lao-Tzu (or Lao-Tse) (Li Erh) (philosopher); Honan Province, China (c. 604-531 B.C.)
Lardner, Ring (Ringgold Wilmar Lardner) (story writer); Niles, Mich. **(1885-1933)**
La Rouchefoucauld, Francois duc de (author); Paris **(1613-1680)**
La Salle, Sieur de (Robert Cavelier) (explorer); Rouen, France **(1643-1687)**
Lasser, Louise (actress); New York City, 1940(?)
Lauder, Sir Harry (Harry MacLennan) (singer); Portobello, Scotland **(1870-1950)**
Laughton, Charles (actor); Scarborough, England **(1899-1962)**
Lauper, Cyndi (singer); New York City, 6/20/53
Laurel, Stan (Arthur Jefferson) (comedian); Ulverston, England **(1890-1965)**
Laurents, Arthur (playwright); New York City, 7/14/1918
Laurie, Piper (Rosetta Jacobs) (actress); Detroit, 1/22/1932
Lavoisier, Antoine-Laurent (chemist); Paris **(1743-1794)**
Lawford, Peter (actor); London **(1923-1984)**
Lawrence, Carol (Carol Maria Laraia) (dancer and actress); Melrose Park, Ill., 9/5/1932
Lawrence, David Herbert (novelist); Nottingham, England **(1885-1930)**
Lawrence, Gertrude (Gertrud Klasen) (actress); London **(1900-1952)**
Lawrence, Marjorie (singer); Deans Marsh, Australia **(1908-1979)**
Lawrence, Steve (Sidney Leibowitz) (singer); Brooklyn, N.Y., 7/8/1935
Lawrence, Vicki (Ann) (actress); Inglewood, Calif., 3/26/1949
Lawrence of Arabia (Thomas Edward Lawrence, later changed to Shaw) (author and soldier); Tremadoc, Wales **(1888-1935)**
Leachman, Cloris (actress); Des Moines, Iowa, 4/30/1926(?)
Lean, David (film director); Croydon, England, 3/25/1908
Lear, Edward (nonsense poet); London **(1812-1888)**
le Carré, John (David John Moore Cornwell) (novelist); Poole, England, 10/19/1931
Le Corbusier (Charles Edouard Jeanneret) (architect); La Chaux-de-Fonds, Switzerland **(1887-1965)**
Lederer, Francis (actor); Prague, 11/6/1906
Lee, Christopher (actor); London, 5/27/1922
Lee, Gypsy Rose (Rose Louise Hovick) (entertainer); Seattle **(1919-1970)**
Lee, Manfred B. (novelist, pseudonym Ellery Queen); Brooklyn, N.Y. **(1905-1971)**
Lee, Peggy (Norma Engstrom) (singer); Jamestown, N.D., 5/26/1920
Lee, Robert Edward (Confederate general); Stratford Estate, Va. **(1807-1870)**
Leeuwenhoek, Anton van (zoologist); Delft (Netherlands) **(1632-1723)**
Le Gallienne, Eva (actress); London, 1/11/1899
Lehár, Franz (composer); Komárom (Czechoslovakia) **(1870-1948)**
Lehman, Herbert H. (Governor and Senator); New York City **(1878-1963)**
Lehmann, Lotte (soprano); Perleberg (Germany) **(1888-1976)**
Leibniz, Gottfried W. von (scientist); Leipzig (East Germany) **(1646-1716)**
Leigh, Janet (Jeanetta Morrison) (actress); Merced, Calif., 7/6/1927
Leigh, Vivien (Vivien Mary Hartley) (actress); Darjeeling, India **(1913-1967)**
Leighton, Margaret (actress); nr. Birmingham, England **(1922-1976)**
Leinsdorf, Erich (conductor); Vienna, 2/4/1912
Lemmon, Jack (actor); Boston, 2/8/1925
Lenin, N. (Vladimir Ilich Ulyanov) (Soviet leader); Simbirsk, Russia **(1870-1924)**
Lennon, John (singer and songwriter); Liverpool, England **(1940-1980)**
Lenya, Lotte (Karoline Blamauer) (singer and actress); Vienna, Austria **(1898-1981)**
Leonard, Sheldon (actor and director); New York City, 2/22/1907
Lerner, Alan Jay (lyricist); New York City **(1918-1986)**
Lerner, Max (columnist); Minsk, Russia, 12/20/1902
Le Roy, Mervyn (film producer); San Francisco, 10/15/1900
Leslie, Joan (actress); Detroit, 1/26/1925
Lessing, Doris (novelist); Kermanshah, Iran, 10/22/1919
Lester, Mark (actor); Richmond, England, 1958
Letterman, David (TV personality); Indianapolis, 1944
Levant, Oscar (pianist); Pittsburgh **(1906-1972)**
Levene, Sam (actor); New York City **(1905-1980)**
Levenson, Sam (humorist); New York City **(1911-1980)**
Levi, Carlo (novelist); Turin, Italy **(1902-1975)**
Levine, James (music director, Metropolitan Opera); Cincinnati, 6/23/1943
Levine, Joseph E. (film producer); Boston **(1905-1987)**
Lewis, Jerry (Joseph Levitch) (comedian and film director); Newark, N.J., 3/16/1926
Lewis, Jerry Lee (singer); Ferriday, La., 9/29/1935
Lewis, John Llewellyn (labor leader); Lucas, Iowa **(1880-1969)**
Lewis, Meriwether (explorer); Albemarle Co., Va. **(1774-1809)**
Lewis, Shari (Shari Hurwitz) (puppeteer); New York City, 1/17/1934
Lewis, Sinclair (novelist); Sauk Centre, Minn. **(1885-1951)**
Lewis, Ted (entertainer); Circleville, Ohio **(1891-1971)**
Ley, Willy (science writer); Berlin **(1906-1969)**
Liberace (Wladziu Liberace) (pianist); West Allis, Wis. **(1919-1987)**
Lichtenstein, Roy (painter); New York City, 10/27/1923
Lie, Trygve Halvdan (first U.N. Secretary-General); Oslo **(1896-1968)**
Lightfoot, Gordon (singer and songwriter); Orillia, Ontario, Canada, 11/17/1938
Lillie, Beatrice (Lady Peel) (actress and comedienne); Toronto, 5/29/1898
Lin Yutang (author); Changchow, China **(1895-1976)**
Lind, Jenny (Johanna Maria Lind) (soprano); Stockholm **(1820-1887)**
Lindbergh, Anne Morrow (author); Englewood, N.J., 6/22/1906
Lindbergh, Charles A. (aviator); Detroit **(1902-1974)**
Linden, Hal (Harold Lipshitz) (actor); New York City, 3/20/1931
Lindsay, Howard (playwright); Waterford, N.Y. **(1889-1968)**

Lindsay, John Vliet (ex-Mayor of New York City); New York City, 11/24/1921
Lindstrom, Pia (TV newscaster); Stockholm, 11/?/1938
Linkletter, Art (radio-TV personality); Moose Jaw, Saskatchewan, Canada, 7/17/1912
Linnaeus, Carolus (Carl von Linné) (botanist); Råshult, Sweden **(1707-1778)**
Lipchitz, Jacques (sculptor); Druskieniki, Latvia **(1891-1973)**
Lippi, Fra Filippo (painter); Florence **(1406-1469)**
Lippmann, Walter (columnist, author, and political analyst); New York City **(1889-1974)**
Lister, (1st Baron of Lyme Regis) (Joseph Lister) (surgeon); Upton, England **(1827-1912)**
Liszt, Franz (composer and pianist); Raiding (Hungary) **(1811-1886)**
Little, Cleavon (actor and comedian); Chickasha, Okla., 6/1/1939
Little, Rich (impressionist); Ottawa, 11/26/1938
Livesey, Roger (actor); Barry, Wales **(1906-1976)**
Livingstone, David (missionary and explorer); Lanarkshire, Scotland **(1813-1873)**
Livingstone, Mary (Sadye Marks) (comedienne); Seattle **(1909-1983)**
Llewellyn, Richard (novelist); St. David's, Wales **(1906-1983)**
Lloyd, Harold (comedian); Burchard, Neb. **(1894-1971)**
Lloyd George, David (Earl of Dwyfor) (statesman); Manchester, England **(1863-1945)**
Locke, John (philosopher); Somersetshire, England **(1632-1704)**
Lockhart, Gene (actor); London, Ontario, Canada **(1891-1957)**
Lockhart, June (actress); New York City, 6/25/1925
Lockwood, Margaret (actress); Karachi (Pakistan), 9/15/1916
Lodge, Henry Cabot (legislator); Boston **(1850-1924)**
Lodge, Henry Cabot, Jr. (diplomat); Nahant, Mass. **(1902-1985)**
Loesser, Frank (composer); New York City **(1910-1969)**
Loewe, Frederick (composer); Vienna, 6/10/1904
Logan, Joshua (director and producer); Texarkana, Tex., 10/5/1908
Lollobrigida, Gina (actress); Subiaco, Italy, 1928
Lombard, Carole (Carol Jane Peters) (actress); Ft. Wayne, Ind. **(1908-1942)**
Lombardo, Guy (band leader); London, Ontario, Canada **(1902-1977)**
London, George (baritone); Montreal **(1920-1985)**
London, Jack (John Griffith London) (novelist); San Francisco **(1876-1916)**
London, Julie (Julie Peck) (singer and actress); Santa Rosa, Calif., 9/26/1926
Long, Huey Pierce (politician); Winnfield, La. **(1893-1935)**
Longfellow, Henry Wadsworth (poet); Portland, Me. **(1807-1882)**
Longworth, Alice Roosevelt (social figure); New York City **(1884-1980)**
Loos, Anita (novelist); Sissons, Calif., **(1888-1981)**
Lopez, Trini (Trinidad Lopez III) (singer); Dallas, 5/15/1937
Lopez, Vincent (band leader); Brooklyn, N.Y. **(1895-1975)**
Lord, Jack (John Joseph Ryan) (actor); New York City, 12/30/1930
Loren, Sophia (Sofia Scicolone) (actress); Rome, 9/20/1934
Lorre, Peter (Laszlo Löewenstein) (actor); Rosenberg (Czechoslovakia) **(1904-1964)**
Loudon. Dorothy (actress, singer); Boston, 9/17/1933
Louise, Tina (actress); New York City, 2/11/1937
Lowell, Amy (poet); Brookline, Mass. **(1874-1925)**
Lowell, James Russell (poet); Cambridge, Mass. **(1819-1891)**
Lowell, Robert (poet); Boston **(1917-1977)**
Loy, Myrna (Myrna Williams) (actress); nr. Helena, Mont., 8/2/1905
Loyola, St. Ignatius of (Iñigo de Oñez y Loyola) (founder of Jesuits); Gúipuzcoa Province, Spain **(1491-1556)**
Lubitsch, Ernst (film director); Berlin **(1892-1947)**
Luce, Clare Boothe (playwright and former Ambassador); New York City, 4/10/1903
Luce, Henry Robinson (editor and publisher); Tengchow, China **(1898-1967)**
Ludlum, Robert (author); New York City, 5/25/1927
Lugosi, Bela (Bela Lugosi Blasko) (actor); Logos, Hungary **(1888-1956)**
Lukas, Paul (actor); Budapest **(1895-1971)**
Lully, Jean Baptiste (French composer); Florence **(1639-1687)**
Lumet, Sidney (film and TV director); Philadelphia, 6/25/1924
Lunt, Alfred (actor); Milwaukee **(1892-1977)**
Lupino, Ida (actress and director); London, 2/4/1918
Luther, Martin (religious reformer); Eisleben (East Germany) **(1483-1546)**
Lynde, Paul (comedian); Mt. Vernon, Ohio **(1926-1982)**
Lynley, Carol (actress); New York City, 2/13/1942
Lynn, Jeffrey (actor); Auburn, Mass., 1909
Lynn, Loretta (singer); Butcher's Hollow, Ky., 4/14/1935

M

Ma, Yo-Yo (cellist); Paris, 10/7/1955
Maazel, Lorin (conductor); Neuilly, France, 3/5/1930
MacArthur, Charles (playwright); Scranton, Pa. **(1895-1956)**
MacArthur, Douglas (five-star general); Little Rock Barracks, Ark. **(1880-1964)**
MacArthur, James (actor); Los Angeles, 12/8/1937
Macaulay, Thomas Babington (author); Rothley Temple, England **(1800-1859)**
MacDermot, Galt (composer); Montreal, 12/19/1928
MacDonald, James Ramsay (statesman); Lossiemouth, Scotland **(1866-1937)**
MacDonald, Jeanette (actress and soprano); Philadelphia **(1907-1965)**
Macdonald, Ross (Kenneth Millar) (mystery writer); Los Gatos, Calif. **(1915-1983)**
MacDowell, Edward Alexander (composer); New York City **(1861-1908)**
Macfadden, Bernarr (physical culturist); nr. Mill Spring, Mo. **(1868-1955)**
MacGraw, Ali (actress); New York City, 4/1/1939
Machaut, Guillaume de (composer); Marchault, France **(1300-1377)**
Machiavelli, Niccolò (political philosopher); Florence (Italy) **(1469-1527)**
Mack, Ted (TV personality); Greeley, Colo. **(1904-1976)**
MacKenzie, Gisele (Marie Marguerite Louise Gisele LaFleche) (singer and actress); Winnipeg, Manitoba, Canada, 1/10/1927
MacLaine, Shirley (Shirley MacLean Beatty) (actress); Richmond, Va., 4/24/1934
MacLeish, Archibald (poet); Glencoe, Ill. **(1892-1982)**
Macmillan, Harold (ex-Prime Minister); London **(1894-1986)**
MacMurray, Fred (actor); Kankakee, Ill., 8/30/1908
MacNeil, Cornell (baritone); Minneapolis, 1925
MacRae, Gordon (singer); East Orange, N.J. **(1921-1986)**
Madison, Guy (Robert Moseley) (actor); Bakersfield, Calif., 1/19/1922
Madonna (Madonna Louise Ciccone) (singer); Bay City, Mich. 1960
Maeterlinck, Count Maurice (author); Ghent, Belgium **(1862-1949)**
Magellan, Ferdinand (Fernando de Magalhaes) (navigator); Sabrosa, Portugal **(1480?-1521)**
Magnani, Anna (actress); Rome **(1908-1973)**
Magritte, René (painter); Belgium **(1898-1967)**
Magsaysay, Ramón (statesman); Iba, Luzon, Philippines **(1907-1957)**
Mahan, Alfred Thayer (naval historian); West Point, N.Y. **(1840-1914)**
Mahler, Gustav (composer and conductor); Kalischt (Czechoslovakia) **(1860-1911)**
Mailer, Norman (novelist); Long Branch, N.J., 1/31/1923
Mailloi, Aristide (sculptor); Banyuls-sur-Mer, Rousillion, France **(1861-1944)**
Maimonides, Moses (Jewish philosopher); Cordoba, Spain **(1135-1204)**
Main, Marjorie (Mary Tomlinson Krebs) (actress); Acton, Ind. **(1890-1975)**
Mainbocher (Main Rousseau Bocher) (fashion designer); Chicago **(1891-1976)**
Majors, Lee (actor); Wyandotte, Mich., 4/23/1940
Makarova, Natalia (ballerina); Leningrad, 11/21/1940
Makeba, Miriam (singer); Johannesburg, South Africa, 3/4/1932
Malamud, Bernard (novelist); Brooklyn, N.Y., **(1914-1986)**
Malden, Karl (Miaden Sekulovich) (actor); Chicago, 3/22/1913
Malone, Dorothy (actress); Chicago, 1/30/1925
Malraux, André (author); Paris **(1901-1976)**
Malthus, Thomas Robert (economist); nr. Dorking, England **(1766-1834)**
Mamet, David (playwright); Chicago, 11/30/1947
Manchester, Melissa (singer); Bronx, N.Y., 2/15/1951
Manchester, William (writer); Attleboro, Mass., 4/1/1922
Mancini, Henry (composer and conductor); Cleveland, 4/16/1924
Mandela, Winnie (Nomzamo) (South African political activist), Pondoland district of the Transkei, 1936(?)
Mandrell, Barbara (singer); Houston, 12/25/1948
Manet, Edouard (painter); Paris **(1832-1883)**
Mangano, Silvana (actress); Rome, 4/21/1930
Mangione, Chuck (hornist, pianist, and composer); Rochester, N.Y., 11/29/1940
Manilow, Barry (singer); Brooklyn, N.Y., 6/17/1946
Mankiewicz, Frank F. (columnist); New York City, 5/16/1924
Mankiewicz, Joseph L. (film writer and director); Wilkes-Barre, Pa., 2/11/1909
Mann, Horace (educator); Franklin, Mass. **(1796-1859)**
Mann, Thomas (novelist); Lübeck, Germany **(1875-1955)**
Mannes, Marya (writer); New York City, 11/14/1904
Mansfield, Jayne (Jayne Palmer) (actress); Bryn Mawr, Pa. **(1932-1967)**
Mansfield, Katherine (story writer); Wellington, New Zealand **(1888-1923)**
Mantovani, Annunzio (conductor); Venice **(1905-1980)**
Mao Zedong (Tse-tung) (Chinese leader); Shao Shan, China **(1893-**

1976)
Marat, Jean Paul (French revolutionist); Boudry, Neuchâtei, Switzerland **(1743-1793)**
Marceau, Marcel (mime); Strasbourg, France, 3/22/1923
March, Fredric (Frederick Bickel) (actor); Racine, Wis. **(1897-1975)**
Marconi, Guglielmo (inventor); Bologna, Italy **(1874-1937)**
Marcus Aurelius (Marcus Annius Verus) (Roman emperor); Rome **(121-180)**
Marcuse, Herbert (philosopher); Berlin, **(1898-1979)**
Margaret Rose (Princess); Glamis Castle, Angus, Scotland, 8/21/1930
Margrethe II (Queen); Copenhagen, 4/16/1940
Marie Antoinette (Josephe Jeanne Marie Antoinette) (Queen of France); Vienna **(1755-1793)**
Marisol (sculptor); Venezuela, 1930
Markham, Edwin (poet); Oregon City, Ore. **(1852-1940)**
Markova, Dame Alicia (Lilian Alice Marks) (ballerina); London, 12/1/1910
Marley, Bob (reggae singer and songwriter); Kingston, Jamaica **(1945-1981)**
Marlowe, Christopher (dramatist); Canterbury, England **(1564-1593)**
Marlowe, Julia (Sarah Frances Frost) (actress); Cumberlandshire, England **(1866-1950)**
Marquand, J(ohn) P(hillips) (novelist); Wilmington, Del. **(1893-1960)**
Marquette, Jacques (missionary and explorer); Laon, France **(1637-1675)**
Marriner, Neville (conductor); Lincoln, England, 4/15/1924
Marsh, Jean (actress); Stoke Newington, England, 7/1/1934
Marshall, E.G. (actor); Owatonna, Minn., 6/18/1910
Marshall, George Catlett (general); Uniontown, Pa. **(1880-1959)**
Marshall, Herbert (actor); London **(1890-1968)**
Marshall, John (jurist); nr. Germantown, Va. **(1755-1835)**
Marshall, Penny (actress); New York City, 10/15/1942
Martin, Dean (Dino Crocetti) (singer and actor); Steubenville, Ohio, 6/17/1917
Martin, Mary (singer and actress); Weatherford, Tex., 12/1/1913
Martin, Steve (comedian); Waco, Tex., 1945(?)
Martin, Tony (Alvin Morris) (singer); San Francisco, 12/25/1913
Martinelli, Giovanni (tenor); Montagnana, Italy **(1885-1969)**
Martins, Peter (dancer-choreographer); Copenhagen, 10/27/1945
Marvell, Andrew (poet); Winestead, England **(1621-1678)**
Marvin, Lee (actor); New York City, 2/19/1924
Marx, Chico (Leonard) (comedian); New York City **(1891-1961)**
Marx, Groucho (Julius) (comedian); New York City **(1890-1977)**
Marx, Harpo (Arthur) (comedian); New York City **(1893-1964)**
Marx, Karl (Socialist writer); Treves (Germany) **(1818-1883)**
Marx, Zeppo (Herbert) (comedian); New York City **(1901-1979)**
Mary Stuart (Queen of Scotland); Linlithgow, Scotland **(1542-1587)**
Masaryk, Jan Garrigue (statesman); Prague (Czechoslovakia) **(1886-1948)**
Masaryk, Thomas Garrigue (statesman); Hodonin (Czechoslovakia) **(1850-1937)**
Masefield, John (poet); Ledbury, England **(1878-1967)**
Masekela, Hugh (trumpeter); Wilbank, South Africa, 4/4/1939
Mason, James (actor); Huddersfield, England **(1909-1984)**
Massenet, Jules Emile Frédéric (composer); Montaud, France **(1842-1912)**
Massey, Raymond (actor); Toronto, **(1896-1983)**
Massine, Léonide (choreographer); Moscow, **(1895-1979)**
Masters, Edgar Lee (poet); Garnett, Kan. **(1869-1950)**
Mastroianni, Marcello (actor); Fontana Liri, Italy, 9/28/1924
Mather, Cotton (clergyman); Boston **(1663-1728)**
Mathis, Johnny (singer); San Francisco, 9/30/1935
Matisse, Henri (painter); Le Cateau, France **(1869-1954)**
Matthau, Walter (Walter Matuschanskayasky) (actor); New York City, 10/1/1920
Mature, Victor (actor); Louisville, Ky., 1/19/1916
Maugham, W(illiam) Somerset (author); Paris **(1874-1965)**
Mauldin, Bill (political cartoonist); Mountain Park, N.M., 10/29/1921
Maupassant, Henri René Albert Guy de (story writer); Normandy, France **(1850-1893)**
Maurois, André (Emile Herzog) (author); Elbauf, France **(1885-1967)**
Maximilian (Ferdinand Maximilian Joseph) (Emperor of Mexico); Vienna **(1832-1867)**
Maxwell, James Clerk (physicist); Edinburgh, Scotland **(1831-1879)**
May, Elaine (Elaine Berlin) (entertainer-writer); Philadelphia, 4/21/1932
May, Rollo (psychologist); Ada, Ohio, 4/21/1909
Mayall, John (singer and songwriter); Manchester, England, 11/29/1933
Mayo, Charles H. (surgeon); Rochester, Minn. **(1865-1939)**
Mayo, Charles W. (surgeon); Rochester, Minn. **(1898-1968)**
Mayo, Virginia (Jones) (actress); St. Louis, 1920
Mayo, William J. (surgeon); Le Sueur, Minn. **(1861-1939)**
Mazzini, Giuseppe (patriot); Genoa **(1805-1872)**
McBride, Mary Margaret (radio personality); Paris, Mo. **(1899-1976)**
McBride, Patricia (ballerina); Teaneck, N.J., 8/23/1942
McCallum, David (actor); Glasgow, Scotland, 9/19/1933
McCambridge, Mercedes (actress); Joliet, Ill., 3/17/1918
McCarthy, Eugene J. (ex-Senator); Watkins, Minn., 3/29/1916
McCarthy, Joseph Raymond (Senator); Grand Chute, Wis. **(1908-1957)**
McCarthy, Kevin (actor); Seattle, 2/15/1914
McCarthy, Mary (novelist); Seattle, 6/21/1912
McCartney, Paul (singer and songwriter); Liverpool, England, 6/18/1942
McClellan, George Brinton (general); Philadelphia **(1826-1885)**
McClintock, Barbara (geneticist); Hartford, Conn., 6/16/1902
McCloy, John J. (lawyer and banker); Philadelphia, 3/31/1895
McClure, Doug (actor); Glendale, Calif., 5/11/1938
McCormack, John (tenor); Athlone, Ireland **(1884-1945)**
McCormack, John W. (ex-Speaker of House); Boston **(1891-1980)**
McCormack, Patty (actress); New York City, 8/21/1945
McCormick, Cyrus Hall (inventor); Rockbridge County, Va. **(1809-1884)**
McCoy, Col. Tim (actor); Saginaw, Mich. **(1891-1978)**
McCracken, James (dramatic tenor); Gary, Ind., 12/16/1926
McCrea, Joel (actor); Los Angeles, 11/5/1905
McCullers, Carson (novelist); Columbus, Ga. **(1917-1967)**
McDowall, Roddy (actor); London, 9/17/1928
McDowell, Malcolm (actor); Leeds, England, 6/19/1943
McGavin, Darren (actor); San Joaquin, Calif., 5/7/1922
McGinley, Phyllis (poet and writer); Ontario, Ore. **(1905-1978)**
McGoohan, Patrick (actor); Astoria, Queens, N.Y., 1928
McGuire, Dorothy (actress); Omaha, Neb. 6/14/1919
McKellen, Ian (actor); Burnley, England, 5/25/1939
McKenna, Siobhan (actress); Belfast, Northern Ireland **(1923-1986)**
McKuen, Rod (singer and composer); Oakland, Calif., 4/29/1933
McLaglen, Victor (actor); Tunbridge Wells, Kent, England **(1886-1959)**
McLaughlin, John (guitarist); Yorkshire, England, 1942
McLean, Don (singer and songwriter); New Rochelle, N.Y., 10/2/1945
McLuhan, Marshall (Herbert Marshall) (communications writer); Edmonton, Canada **(1911-1980)**
McMahon, Ed (TV personality); Detroit, 3/6/1923
McNamara, Robert S. (former president of World Bank); San Francisco, 6/9/1916
McQueen, Steve (Terence Stephen McQueen) (actor); Indianapolis **(1930-1980)**
Mead, Margaret (anthropologist); Philadelphia, **(1901-1978)**
Meadows, Audrey (actress); Wu Chang, China, 1922(?)
Meadows, Jayne (actress); Wu Chang, China 9/27/1926
Meany, George (labor leader); New York City **(1894-1980)**
Meara, Anne (actress); New York City, 1929
Medici, Lorenzo de' (called Lorenzo the Magnificent) (Florentine ruler); Florence (Italy) **(1449-1492)**
Meeker, Ralph (Ralph Rathgeber) (actor); Minneapolis, 11/21/1920
Mehta, Zubin (conductor); Bombay, 4/29/1936
Meir, Golda (Golda Myerson, nee Mabovitz) (ex-Premier of Israel); Kiev, Russia **(1898-1978)**
Melanie (Melanie Safka) (singer and songwriter); New York City, 2/3/1947
Melba, Dame Nellie (Helen Porter Mitchell) (soprano); nr. Melbourne **(1861-1931)**
Melchior, Lauritz (Lebrecht Hommel) (heroic tenor); Copenhagen **(1890-1973)**
Mellon, Andrew William (financier); Pittsburgh **(1855-1937)**
Melville, Herman (novelist); New York City **(1819-1891)**
Mencken, Henry Louis (writer); Baltimore **(1880-1956)**
Mendel, Gregor Johann (geneticist); Heinzendorf, Austrian Silesia **(1822-1884)**
Mendeleyev, Dmitri Ivanovich (chemist); Tobolsk, Russia **(1834-1907)**
Mendelssohn-Bartholdy, Jakob Ludwig Felix (composer); Hamburg **(1809-1847)**
Mendès-France, Pierre (ex-Premier); Paris **(1905-1982)**
Menjou, Adolphe (actor); Pittsburgh **(1890-1963)**
Mennin, Peter (Peter Mennini) (composer); Erie, Pa. **(1923-1983)**
Menninger, William C. (psychiatrist); Topeka, Kan. **(1899-1966)**
Menotti, Gian Carlo (composer); Cadegliano, Italy, 7/7/1911
Menuhin, Yehudi (violinist and conductor); New York City, 4/22/1916
Menzies, Robert Gordon (ex-Prime Minister); Jeparit, Australia **(1894-1978)**
Mercer, Johnny (songwriter); Savannah, Ga. **(1909-1976)**
Mercer, Mabel (singer); Burton-on-Trent, England **(1900-1984)**
Mercouri, Melina (actress); Athens, 10/18/1925
Meredith, Burgess (actor); Cleveland, 11/16/1908
Merkel, Una (actress); Covington, Ky. **(1903-1986)**
Merman, Ethel (Ethel Zimmerman) (singer and actress); Astoria, Queens, N.Y. **(1909-1984)**
Merrick, David (David Margulois) (stage producer); St. Louis, 11/27/1912

Merrill, Dina (actress); New York City, 12/9/1925
Merrill, Gary (actor); Hartford, Conn., 8/2/1914
Merrill, Robert (baritone); Brooklyn, N.Y., 6/4/1919
Merton, Thomas (clergyman and writer); France **(1915-1968)**
Mesmer, Franz Anton (physician); Itzmang, nr. Constance (Germany) **(1733-1815)**
Mesta, Perle (social figure); Sturgis, Mich. **(1889-1975)**
Metternich, Prince Klemens Wenzel Nepomuk Lothar von (statesman); Coblenz (Germany) **(1773-1859)**
Michelangelo Buonarreti (painter, sculptor, and architect); Caprese (Italy) **(1475-1564)**
Michener, James A. (novelist); New York City, 2/3/1907
Mickiewicz, Adam (Polish poet); Zozie, Belorussia (U.S.S.R.) **(1798-1855)**
Midler, Bette (singer); Honolulu, 1945
Mielziner, Jo (stage designer); Paris **(1901-1976)**
Mies van der Rohe, Ludwig (architect and designer); Aachen, Germany **(1886-1969)**
Mikoyan, Anastas I. (diplomat); Sanain, Armenia, **(1895-1978)**
Miles, Sarah (actress); Essex, England, 12/31/1943
Miles, Sylvia (actress); New York City, 9/9/1932
Miles, Vera (Vera Ralston) (actress); nr. Boise City, Okla., 8/23/1930
Milhaud, Darius (composer); Aix-en-Provence, France **(1892-1974)**
Mill, John Stuart (philosopher); London, **(1806-1873)**
Milland, Ray (Reginald Truscott-Jones) (actor); Neath, Wales **(1907-1986)**
Millay, Edna St. Vincent (poet); Rockland, Me. **(1892-1950)**
Miller, Ann (Lucille Ann Collier) (dancer and actress); Cherino, Tex., 4/12/1923
Miller, Arthur (playwright); New York City, 10/17/1915
Miller, Glenn (band leader); Clarinda, Iowa **(1904-1944)**
Miller, Henry (novelist); New York City **(1891-1980)**
Miller, Jason (John Miller) (playwright); New York City, 1939(?)
Miller, Mitch (Mitchell) (musician); Rochester, N.Y., 7/4/1911
Miller, Roger (singer); Fort Worth, 1/2/1936
Millet, Jean François (painter); Gruchy, France **(1814-1875)**
Millett, Kate (feminist); St. Paul, 9/14/1934
Millikan, Robert A. (physicist); Morrison, Ill. **(1869-1953)**
Mills, Hayley (actress); London, 4/18/1946
Mills, John (actor); Felixstowe, England, 2/22/1908
Milne, A(lan) A(lexander) (author); London **(1882-1956)**
Milstein, Nathan (concert violinist); Odessa, Russia, 12/31/1904
Milton, John (poet); London **(1608-1674)**
Mimieux, Yvette (actress); Hollywood, Calif., 1/8/1941
Mineo, Sal (actor); New York City **(1939-1976)**
Minnelli, Liza (singer and actress); Hollywood, Calif., 3/12/1946
Minnelli, Vincente (film director); Chicago **(1913-1986)**
Minuit, Peter (Governor of New Amsterdam); Wesel (Germany) **(1580-1638)**
Miranda, Carmen (Maria do Carmo da Cunha) (singer and dancer); Lisbon **(1913-1955)**
Miró, Joan (painter); Barcelona **(1893-1983)**
Mitchell, Cameron (actor); Dallastown, Pa., 4/11/1918
Mitchell, Guy (actor); Detroit, 2/27/1927
Mitchell, John N. (former Attorney General); Detroit, 9/15/1913
Mitchell, Joni (Roberta Joan Anderson) (singer and songwriter); Ft. Macleod, Canada, 11/7/1943
Mitchell, Margaret (novelist); Atlanta **(1900-1949)**
Mitchum, Robert (actor); Bridgeport, Conn., 8/6/1917
Mitropoulos, Dimitri (orchestra conductor); Athens **(1896-1960)**
Mix, Tom (actor); Mix Run, Pa. **(1880-1940)**
Modigliani, Amedeo (painter); Leghorn, Italy **(1884-1920)**
Moffo, Anna (soprano); Wayne, Pa., 6/27/1934
Mohammed (prophet); Mecca (Saudi Arabia) **(570-632)**
Molière (Jean Baptiste Poquelin) (dramatist); Paris **(1622-1673)**
Molnar, Ferenc (dramatist); Budapest **(1878-1952)**
Molotov, Vyacheslav M. (V. M. Skryabin) (diplomat); Kukarka, Russia **(1890-1986)**
Mondrian, Piet (painter); Amersfoort, Netherlands **(1872-1944)**
Monet, Claude (painter); Paris **(1840-1926)**
Monk, Meredith (choreographer-composer-performing artist); Lima, Peru, 11/20/1942
Monk, Thelonious (pianist); Rocky Mount, N.C. **(1918-1982)**
Monroe, Marilyn (Norma Jean Mortenson or Baker) (actress); Los Angeles **(1926-1962)**
Monroe, Vaughn (Wilton) (band leader); Akron, Ohio **(1912-1973)**
Monsarrat, Nicholas (novelist); Liverpool, England, **(1910-1979)**
Montaigne, Michel Eyquem de (essayist); nr. Bordeaux, France **(1533-1592)**
Montalban, Ricardo (actor); Mexico City, 11/25/1920
Montand, Yves (Yvo Montand Livi) (actor and singer); Monsummano, Italy, 10/13/1921
Montesquieu, Charles-Louis de Secondat, baron de La Brède and de, (philosopher) nr. Borleaux, France **(1689-1755)**
Monteverdi, Claudio (composer); Cremona? Italy **(1567-1643)**
Montez, Maria (actress); Dominican Republican **(1918-1951)**
Montezuma II (Aztec emperor); Mexico **(1480?-1520)**
Montgomery, Elizabeth (actress); Hollywood, Calif., 4/15/1933
Montgomery, George (George Montgomery Letz) (actor); Brady, Mont., 8/29/1916
Montgomery, Robert (Henry, Jr.) (actor); Beacon, N.Y. **(1904-1981)**
Montgomery of Alamein, 1st Viscount of Hindhead (Sir Bernard Law Montgomery) (military leader); London **(1887-1976)**
Montoya, Carlos (guitarist); Madrid, 12/13/1903
Moore, Clement Clarke (author); New York City **(1779-1863)**
Moore, Dudley (actor-writer-musician); Dagenham, England, 4/19/1935
Moore, Garry (Thomas Garrison Morfit) (TV personality); Baltimore, 1/31/1915
Moore, Grace (soprano); Jellico, Tenn. **(1901-1947)**
Moore, Henry (sculptor); Castleford, England **(1898-1986)**
Moore, Marianne (poet); Kirkwood, Mo. **(1887-1972)**
Moore, Mary Tyler (actress); Brooklyn, N.Y., 12/29/1937
Moore, Melba (Beatrice) (singer and actress); New York City, 10/27/1945
Moore, Roger (actor); London, 10/14/1927(?)
Moore, Thomas (poet); Dublin **(1779-1852)**
Moore, Victor (actor); Hammonton, N.J. **(1876-1962)**
Moorehead, Agnes (actress); Clinton, Mass. **(1906-1974)**
More, Henry (philosopher); Grantham, England **(1614-1687)**
More, Sir Thomas (statesman and author); London **(1478-1535)**
Moreau, Jeanne (actress); Paris, 1/23/1928
Moreno, Rita (Rosita Dolores Alverio) (actress); Humacao, Puerto Rico, 12/11/1931
Morgan, Dennis (actor); Prentice, Wis., 12/10/1920
Morgan, Harry (actor); Detroit, 4/10/1915
Morgan, Helen (singer); Danville, Ohio **(1900?-1941)**
Morgan, Henry (comedian); New York City, 3/31/1915
Morgan, Jane (Florence Currier) (singer); Boston, 1920
Morgan, John Pierpont (financier); Hartford, Conn. **(1837-1913)**
Moriarty, Michael (actor); Detroit, 4/5/1941
Morini, Erica (concert violinist); Vienna, 1/5/1910
Morison, Samuel Eliot (historian); Boston **(1887-1976)**
Morley, Christopher Darlington (novelist); Haverford, Pa. **(1890-1957)**
Morley, Robert (actor); Semley, England, 5/26/1908
Morrison, Jim (James Douglas Morrison) (singer and songwriter); Melbourne, Fla. **(1943-1971)**
Morse, Marston (mathematician); Waterville, Me. **(1892-1977)**
Morse, Robert (actor); Newton, Mass., 5/18/1931
Morse, Samuel Finley Breese (painter and inventor); Charlestown, Mass. **(1791-1872)**
Moses, Grandma (Mrs. Anna Mary Robertson Moses) (painter); Greenwich, N.Y. **(1860-1961)**
Moses, Robert (urban planner); New Haven, Conn., **(1888-1981)**
Mostel, Zero (Samuel Joel Mostel) (actor); Brooklyn, N.Y. **(1915-1977)**
Moussorgsky, Modest Petrovich (composer); Karev, Russia **(1839-1881)**
Moyers, Bill D. (Billy Don) (journalist); Hugo, Okla., 6/5/1934
Moynihan, Daniel Patrick (New York Senator); Tulsa, Okla., 3/16/1927
Mozart, Wolfgang Amadeus (Johannes Chrysostomus Wolfgangus Theophilus Mozart) (composer); Salzburg (Austria) **(1756-1791)**
Mudd, Roger (TV newscaster); Washington, D.C., 2/9/1928
Muggeridge, Malcolm (Thomas) (writer); Croydon, England, 3/24/1903
Muhammad, Elijah (Elijah Poole) (religious leader); Sandersville, Ga. **(1897-1975)**
Mulgrew, Kate (actress); Dubuque, Iowa, 4/?/1929
Mulhare, Edward (actor); Ireland, 1923
Mumford, Lewis (cultural historian and city planner); Flushing, Queens, N.Y., 10/19/1895
Munch, Edvard (painter); Löten, Norway **(1863-1944)**
Munchhausen, Karl Friedrick Hieronymus, baron von (anecdotist); Hanover, Germany **(1720-1797)**
Muni, Paul (Muni Weisenfreund) (actor); Lemburg (Ukraine) **(1895-1967)**
Munsel, Patrice (soprano); Spokane, Wash., 5/14/1925
Murdoch, Iris (novelist); Dublin, 7/15/1919
Murdoch, Rupert (publisher); Melbourne, 3/11/1931
Murillo, Bartolomé Esteban (painter); Seville, Spain **(1617-1682)**
Murphy, Audie (actor and war hero); Kingston, Tex. **(1924-1971)**
Murphy, Eddie (actor-comedian); Brooklyn, N.Y. 4/3/61
Murphy, George (actor, dancer, and ex-Senator); New Haven, Conn., 7/4/1902
Murray, Arthur (dance teacher); New York City, 4/4/1895
Murray, Bill (actor-comedian); Wilmette, Ill. 9/21/1950
Murray, Kathryn (dance teacher); Jersey City, N.J., 1906
Murray, Ken (Don Court) (producer); New York City, 7/14/1903
Murray, Mae (Marie Adrienne Koenig) (actress); Portsmouth, Va. **(1890-1965)**

Murrow, Edward R. (commentator and government official); Greensboro, N.C. **(1908-1965)**
Mussolini, Benito (Italian dictator); Dovia, Forli, Italy **(1883-1945)**
Myerson, Bess (consumer advocate); Bronx, N.Y., 1924
Myrdal, Gunnar (sociologist and economist); Gustaf Parish, Sweden **(1898-1987)**

N

Nabokov, Vladimir (novelist); St. Petersburg, Russia **(1899-1977)**
Nabors, Jim (actor and singer); Sylacauga, Ala., 6/12/1932
Nader, Ralph (consumer advocate); Winsted, Conn., 2/27/1934
Nagel, Conrad (actor); Keokuk, Iowa **(1897-1970)**
Naish, J. Carrol (actor); New York City **(1900-1973)**
Naldi, Nita (Anita Donna Dooley) (actress); New York City **(1899-1961)**
Napoleon Bonaparte. *See* Bonaparte, Napoleon
Nash, Graham (singer); Blackpool, England, 1942
Nash, Ogden (poet); Rye, N.Y. **(1902-1971)**
Nasser, Gamal Abdel (statesman); Beni Mor, Egypt **(1918-1970)**
Nast, Thomas (cartoonist); Landau (Germany) **(1840-1902)**
Nation, Carry Amelia (temperance leader); Garrard County, Ky. **(1846-1911)**
Natwick, Mildred (actress); Baltimore, 6/19/1908
Nazimova, Alla (actress); Yalta, Crimea, Russia **(1879-1945)**
Neagle, Anna (Marjorie Robertson) (actress); London **(1908-1986)**
Neal, Patricia (actress); Packard, Ky., 1/20/1926
Neff, Hildegarde (actress); Ulm, Germany, 12/28/1925
Negri, Pola (Apolina Mathias-Chalupec) (actress); Bromberg (Poland) **(1899-1987)**
Nehru, Jawaharlal (first Prime Minister of India); Allahabad, India **(1889-1964)**
Nelson, Barry (Neilsen) (actor); San Francisco, 1920
Nelson, David (actor); New York City, 10/24/1936
Nelson, Harriet Hilliard (Peggy Lou Snyder) (actress); Des Moines, Iowa, 1914
Nelson, Ozzie (Oswald) (actor); Jersey City, N.J. **(1907-1975)**
Nelson, Ricky (Eric) (singer and actor); Teaneck, N.J. **(1940-1985)**
Nelson, Viscount Horatio (naval officer); Burnham Thorpe, England **(1758-1805)**
Nelson, Willie (singer); Waco, Texas, 4/30/1933
Nenni, Pietro (Socialist leader); Faenza, Italy **(1891-1980)**
Nero (Nero Claudius Caesar Drusus Germanicus) (Roman emperor); Antium (Italy) **(37-68)**
Nero, Peter (pianist); New York City, 5/22/1934
Nesbitt, Cathleen (actress); Cheshire, England **(1889-1982)**
Nevelson, Louise (sculptor); Kiev, Russia, 9/23/1900
Newhart, Bob (entertainer); Chicago, 9/5/1929
Newhouse, Samuel I. (publisher); New York City **(1895-1979)**
Newley, Anthony (actor and song writer); London, 9/24/1931
Newman, Edwin (news commentator); New York City, 1/25/1919
Newman, John Henry (prelate); London **(1801-1890)**
Newman, Paul (actor and director); Cleveland, 1/26/1925
Newman, Randy (singer); Los Angeles, 11/28/1943
Newton, Huey (black activist); New Orleans, 2/17/1942
Newton, Sir Isaac (mathematician and scientist); nr. Grantham, England **(1642-1727)**
Newton, Wayne (singer); Norfolk, Va., 4/3/1942
Newton-John, Olivia (singer); Cambridge, England, 9/26/1948
Nichols, Mike (Michael Peschkowsky) (stage and film director); Berlin, 11/6/1931
Nicholson, Jack (actor); Neptune, N.J., 4/22/1937
Nietzsche, Friedrich Wilhelm (philosopher); nr. Lützen Saxony (East Germany) **(1844-1900)**
Nightingale, Florence (nurse); Florence (Italy) **(1820-1910)**
Nijinsky, Vaslav (ballet dancer); Warsaw **(1890-1950)**
Nilsson, Birgit (soprano); West Karup, Sweden, 5/17/1923
Nilsson, Harry (singer and songwriter); Brooklyn, N.Y., 6/15/1941
Nimitz, Chester W. (naval officer); Fredericksburg, Tex. **(1885-1966)**
Nimoy, Leonard (actor); Boston, 3/26/1931
Nin, Anais (author and diarist); Neuilly, France **(1903-1977)**
Niven, David (actor); Kirriemuir, Scotland, **(1910-1983)**
Nizer, Louis (lawyer and author); London, 2/6/1902
Nobel, Alfred Bernhard (industrialist); Stockholm **(1833-1896)**
Noguchi, Isamu (sculptor); Los Angeles, 11/7/1904
Nolan, Lloyd (actor); San Francisco **(1902-1985)**
Nolte, Nick (actor); Omaha, Neb., 1942
Norell, Norman (Norman Levinson) (fashion designer); Noblesville, Ind. **(1900-1972)**
Norman, Marsha (Marsha Williams) (playwright); Louisville, Ky., 9/21/1947
Norstad, Gen. Lauris (ex-commander of NATO forces); Minneapolis, 3/24/1907
North, John Ringling (circus director); Baraboo, Wis. **(1903-1985)**
North, Sheree (actress); Los Angeles, 1/17/1933
Norton, Eleanor Holmes (New York City government official, lawyer); Washington, D.C., 6/13/1937
Nostradamus (Michel de Notredame) (astrologer); St. Rémy, France **(1503-1566)**
Novaes, Guiomar (pianist); São João de Boa Vista, Brazil **(1895-1979)**
Novak, Kim (Marilyn Novak) (actress); Chicago, 2/13/1933
Novarro, Ramon (Ramon Samaniegoes) (actor); Durango, Mexico **(1899-1968)**
Nugent, Elliott (actor and director); Dover, Ohio, **(1899-1980)**
Nureyev, Rudolf (ballet dancer); U.S.S.R., 3/17/1938
Nuyen, France (actress); Marseilles, France, 7/31/1939
Nyro, Laura (singer and songwriter); Bronx, N.Y., 1947

O

Oakie, Jack (actor); Sedalia, Mo. **(1903-1978)**
Oates, Joyce Carol (novelist); Lockport, N.Y., 6/16/1938
Oberon, Merle (Estelle Merle O'Brien Thompson) (actress); Tasmania **(1911-1979)**
O'Brian, Hugh (Hugh J. Krampe) (actor); Rochester, N.Y., 4/19/1930
O'Brien, Edmond (actor); New York City **(1915-1985)**
O'Brien, Margaret (Angela Maxine O'Brien) (actress); San Diego, Calif., 1/15/1937
O'Brien, Pat (William Joseph O'Brien, Jr.) (actor); Milwaukee, **(1899-1983)**
O'Casey, Sean (playwright); Dublin **(1881-1964)**
Ochs, Adolph Simon (publisher); Cincinnati **(1858-1935)**
O'Connor, Carroll (actor); New York City, 8/2/1924
O'Connor, Donald (actor); Chicago, 8/28/1925
Odets, Clifford (playwright); Philadelphia **(1906-1963)**
Odetta (Odetta Holmes) (folk singer and actress); Birmingham, Ala., 12/31/1930
Offenbach, Jacques (composer); Cologne, Germany **(1819-1880)**
O'Hara, John (novelist); Pottsville, Pa. **(1905-1970)**
O'Hara, Maureen (Maureen FitzSimons) (actress); Dublin, 8/17/1921
Ohlsson, Garrick (pianist); Bronxville, N.Y., 4/3/1948
Ohrbach, Jerry (actor-singer); Bronx, N.Y., 10/20/1935
Olstrakh, David (concert violinist); Odessa, Russia **(1908-1974)**
O'Keeffe, Georgia (painter); Sun Prairie, Wis. **(1887-1986)**
Oland, Warner (actor); Umea, Sweden **(1880-1938)**
Olav V (King of Norway); Sandringham, England, 7/2/1903
Oldenburg, Claes (painter); Stockholm, Sweden, 1/28/1929
Olivier, Lord (Laurence) (actor); Dorking, England, 5/22/1907
Olmsted, Frederick Law (landscape architect); Hartford, Conn. **(1822-1903)**
Olsen, Ole (John Sigvard Olsen) (comedian); Peru, Ind. **(1892-1963)**
Omar Khayyam (poet and astronomer); Nishapur (Iran) **(died c. 1123)**
Onassis, Aristotle (shipping executive); Smyrna, Turkey **(1906-1975)**
Onassis, Christina (shipping executive); New York City, 12/11/1950
Onassis, Jacqueline Kennedy (Jacqueline Bouvier) (President's widow); Southampton, N.Y., 7/28/1929
O'Neal, Ryan (Patrick) (actor); Los Angeles, 4/20/1941
O'Neal, Tatum (actress); Los Angeles, Calif., 11/5/1963
O'Neill, Eugene Gladstone (playwright); New York City **(1888-1953)**
O'Neill, Jennifer (actress); Rio de Janeiro, 2/20/1949
Oppenheimer, J. Robert (nuclear physicist); New York City **(1904-1967)**
Orff, Carl (composer); Munich, Germany **(1895-1982)**
Orlando, Tony (Michael Anthony Orlando Cassavitis) (singer); New York City, 4/3/1944
Ormandy, Eugene (conductor); Budapest **(1899-1985)**
Orozco, José Clemente (painter); Zapotlán, Jalisco, Mexico **(1883-1949)**
Orwell, George (Eric Arthur Blair) (British author); Motihari, India **(1903-1950)**
Osborn, Paul (playwright); Evansville, Ind., 9/4/1901
Osborne, John (playwright); London, 12/12/1929
Osler, Sir William (physician); Bondhead, Ontario, Canada **(1849-1919)**
Osmond, Donny (singer); Ogden, Utah, 12/9/1957
Osmond, Marie (singer); Ogden, Utah, 1959
O'Sullivan, Maureen (actress); County Roscommon, Ireland, 5/17/1911
Otis, Elisha (inventor); Halifax, Vt. **(1811-1861)**
O'Toole, Peter (actor); Connemara, Ireland, 8/2/1933
Ovid (Publius Ovidius Naso) (poet); Sulmona (Italy) **(43 B.C.-?A.D. 17)**
Owens, Buck (Alvis Edgar Owens) (singer); Sherman, Tex., 8/12/1929

P

Paar, Jack (TV personality); Canton, Ohio, 5/1/1918
Pacino, Al (Alfred) (actor); New York City, 4/25/1940
Packard, Vance (author); Granville Summit, Pa., 5/22/1914
Paderewski, Ignace Jan (pianist and statesman); Kurylowka, Russian Podolia **(1860-1941)**
Paganini, Nicolò (violinist); Genoa (Italy) **(1782-1840)**
Page, Geraldine (actress); Kirksville, Mo. **(1924-1987)**
Page, Patti (Clara Ann Fowler) (singer and entertainer); Claremore, Okla., 11/8/1927
Paige, Janis (actress); Tacoma, Wash., 9/16/1922
Paine, Thomas (political philosopher); Thetford, England **(1737-1809)**
Palance, Jack (Walter Palanuik) (actor); Lattimer, Pa., 2/18/1920
Palestrina, Giovanni Pierluigi da (composer); Palestrina, Italy **(1526-1594)**
Paley, William S. (broadcasting executive); Chicago, 9/28/1901
Palladio, Andrea (architect); Padua or Vicenza (Italy) **(1508-1580)**
Palmer, Betsy (actress); East Chicago, Ind., 1929
Palmer, Lilli (Lilli Peiser) (actress); Posen (Germany) **(1914-1986)**
Palmerston, Henry John Templeton (3rd Viscount) (statesman); Broadlands, England **(1784-1865)**
Papanicolaou, George N. (physician); Coumi, Greece **(1883-1962)**
Papas, Irene (actress); Chiliomodion, Greece, 1929
Papp, Joseph (Joseph Papirofsky) (stage producer and director); Brooklyn, N.Y., 6/22/1921
Paracelaus, Philippus (Aureolus Theophrastus Bombastus von Hohenheim) (physican); Einsiedeln, Switzerland **(1493-1541)**
Park, Chung Hee (President of South Korea); Sangmo-ri, Korea **(1917-1979)**
Parker, Dorothy (Dorothy Rothschild) (author); West End, N.J. **(1893-1967)**
Parker, Eleanor (actress); Cedarville, Ohio, 6/26/1922
Parker, Fess (actor); Fort Worth, Tex., 1925
Parker, Suzy (model and actress); San Antonio, 10/28/1933
Parkinson, C(yril) Northcote (historian); Durham, England, 7/30/1909
Parks, Bert (Bert Jacobson) (entertainer); Atlanta, 12/30/1914
Parks, Gordon (film director); Ft. Scott, Kan., 11/30/1912
Parnell, Charles Stewart (statesman); Avondale, Ireland **(1846-1891)**
Parnis, Mollie (Mollie Parnis Livingston) (fashion designer); New York City, 3/18/1905
Parsons, Estelle (actress); Marblehead, Mass., 11/20/1927
Parton, Dolly (singer); Locust Ridge, Tenn. 1/19/1946
Pascal, Blaise (philosopher); Clermont, France **(1623-1662)**
Pasternak, Boris Leonidovich (author); Moscow **(1890-1960)**
Pasternak, Joseph (film producer); Silagy-Somlyo, Romania, 9/19/1901
Pasteur, Louis (chemist); Dôle, France **(1822-1895)**
Paton, Alan (author): Pietermaritzburg, South Africa, 1/11/1903
Patton, George Smith, Jr. (general); San Gabriel, Calif., **(1885-1945)**
Paul, Les (Lester William Polfus) (guitarist); Waukesha, Wis., 6/9/1915
Paul VI (Giovanni Battista Montini) (Pope); Concesio, nr. Brescia, Italy **(1897-1978)**
Pauley, Jane (TV newscaster); Indianapolis, 10/31/1950
Pauling, Linus Carl (chemist); Portland, Ore., 2/28/1901
Pavarotti, Luciano (tenor); Modena, Italy, 10/12/1935
Pavlov, Ivan Petrovich (physiologist); Ryazan district, Russia **(1849-1936)**
Pavlova, Anna (ballerina); St. Petersburg, Russia **(1885-1931)**
Payne, John (actor); Roanoke, Va., 1912
Peale, Norman Vincent (clergyman); Bowersville, Ohio, 5/31/1898
Pearl, Minnie (Sarah Ophelia Colley Cannon) (comedienne and singer); Centerville, Tenn., 10/25/1912
Pears, Peter (tenor); Farnham, England **(1910-1986)**
Pearson, Drew (Andrew Russel Pearson) (columnist); Evanston, Ill. **(1897-1969)**
Pearson, Lester B. (statesman); Toronto **(1897-1972)**
Peary, Robert Edwin (explorer); Cresson, Pa. **(1856-1920)**
Peck, Gregory (actor); La Jolla, Calif., 4/5/1916
Peckinpah, Sam (film director); Fresno, Calif. **(1925-1984)**
Peerce, Jan (tenor); New York City **(1904-1984)**
Pegler, (James) Westbrook (columnist); Minneapolis, **(1894-1969)**
Pei, I(eoh) M(ing) (architect); Canton, China, 4/26/1917
Penn, Arthur (stage and film director); Philadelphia, 9/27/1922
Penn, William (American colonist); London **(1644-1718)**
Penney, James C. (merchant); Hamilton, Mo. **(1875-1971)**
Peppard, George (actor); Detroit, 10/1/1928
Pepys, Samuel (diarist); Bampton, England **(1633-1703)**
Perelman, S(idney) J(oseph) (writer); Brooklyn, N.Y. **(1904-1979)**
Pergolesi, Giovanni Battista (composer); Jesi, Italy **(1710-1736)**
Pericles (statesman); Athens **(died 429 B.C.)**
Perkins, Osgood (actor); West Newton, Mass. **(1892-1937)**
Perkins, Tony (Anthony) (actor); New York City, 4/14/1932
Perlman, Itzhak (violinist); Tel Aviv, Israel, 8/31/1945
Perón, Isabel (María Estela Martínez Cartas) (former chief of state); La Rioja, Argentina, 2/4/1931
Perón, Juan D. (statesman); nr. Lobos, Argentina **(1895-1974)**
Perón, Maria Eva Duarte de (political leader); Los Toldos, Argentina **(1919-1952)**
Perrine, Valerie (actress and dancer); Galveston, Tex., 9/3/1943
Pershing, John Joseph (general); Linn County, Mo. **(1860-1948)**
Pestalozzi, Johann (educator); Zurich, Switzerland **(1746-1827)**
Peters, Bernadette (Bernadette Lazzara) (actress); New York City, 2/28/1944
Peters, Brock (actor-singer); New York City, 7/2/1927
Peters, Jean (actress); Canton, Ohio, 10/15/1926
Peters, Roberta (Roberta Peterman) (soprano); New York City, 5/4/1930
Petit, Roland (choreographer and dancer); Villemombe, France, 1924
Petrarch (Francesco Petrarca) (poet); Arezzo (Italy) **(1304-1374)**
Philip (Philip Mountbatten) (Duke of Edinburgh); Corfu, Greece, 6/10/1921
Piaf, Edith (Edith Gassion) (chanteuse); Paris **(1916-1963)**
Piatigorsky, Gregor (cellist); Ekaterinoslav, Russia **(1903-1976)**
Piazza, Ben (actor); Little Rock, Ark., 7/30/1934
Piazza, Marguerite (soprano); New Orleans, 5/6/1926
Picasso, Pablo (painter and sculptor); Málaga, Spain **(1881-1973)**
Pickford, Jack (Jack Smith) (actor); Toronto **(1896-1933)**
Pickford, Mary (Gladys Mary Smith) (actress); Toronto **(1893-1979)**
Picon, Molly (actress); New York City, 6/1/1898
Pidgeon, Walter (actor); East St. John, New Brunswick, Canada **(1898-1984)**
Pinter, Harold (playwright); London, 10/10/1930
Pinza, Ezio (basso); Rome **(1892-1957)**
Pirandello, Luigi (dramatist and novelist); nr. Girgenti, Italy **(1867-1936)**
Piranesi, Giambattista (artist); Mestre, Italy **(1720-1778)**
Pissaro, Camille Jacob (painter); St. Thomas (U.S. Virgin Islands) **(1830-1903)**
Piston, Walter (composer); Rockland, Me. **(1894-1976)**
Pitman, Sir (Isaac) James (educator and publisher); Bath, England, 8/14/1901
Pitt, William ("Younger Pitt") (statesman); nr. Bromley, England **(1759-1806)**
Pitts, ZaSu (actress); Parsons, Kan. **(1898-1963)**
Pius XII (Eugenio Pacelli) (Pope); Rome **(1876-1958)**
Pizarro, Francisco (explorer); Trujillo, Spain **(1470?-1541)**
Planck, Max (physicist); Kiel, Germany **(1858-1947)**
Plato (Aristocles) (philosopher); Athens (?) **(427?-347 B.C.)**
Pleasence, Donald (actor); Worksop, England, 10/5/1919
Pleshette, Suzanne (actress); New York City, 1/31/1937
Plimpton, George (author); New York City, 3/18/1927
Plisetskaya, Maya (ballerina); Moscow, 11/20/1925
Plowright, Joan (actress); Brigg, England, 10/28/1929
Plummer, Christopher (actor); Toronto, 12/13/1929
Plutarch (biographer); Chaeronea (Greece) **(46?-?120)**
Pocahontas (Matoaka) (American Indian princess); Virginia (?) **(1595?-1617)**
Podhoretz, Norman (author); Brooklyn, N.Y., 1/16/1930
Poe, Edgar Allan (poet and story writer); Boston, Mass. **(1809-1849)**
Poitier, Sidney (film actor and director); Miami, Fla., 2/20/1927
Polanski, Roman (film director); Paris, 8/18/1933
Pollard, Michael J. (actor); Passaic, N.J., 5/30/1939
Pollock, Jackson (painter); Cody, Wyo. **(1912-1956)**
Polo, Marco (traveler); Venice **(1254?-?1324)**
Pompadour, Mme. de (Jeanne Antoinette Poisson) (courtesan); Versailles **(1721-1764)**
Pompey (Gnaeus Pompeius Magnus) (general); Rome (?) **(106-48 B.C.)**
Ponce de León, Juan (explorer); Servas, Spain **(1460?-1521)**
Pons, Lily (coloratura soprano); Cannes, France **(1904-1976)**
Ponti, Carlo (director); Milan, Italy, 12/11/1913
Pope, Alexander (poet); London **(1688-1744)**
Porter, Cole (songwriter); Peru, Ind. **(1892?-1964)**
Porter, Katherine Anne (novelist); Indian Creek, Tex. **(1891-1980)**
Post, Wiley (aviator); Grand Plain, Tex. **(1900-1935)**
Poston, Tom (actor); Columbus, Ohio, 10/17/1927
Potëmkin, Grigori Aleksandrovich, Prince (statesman); Khizovo (Khizov, Belorussia, U.S.S.R.) **(1739-1791)**
Potok, Chaim (author); New York City, 2/17/1929
Poulenc, Francis (composer); Paris **(1899-1963)**
Pound, Ezra (poet); Hailey, Idaho **(1885-1972)**
Poussin, Nicolas (painter); Villers, France **(1594-1665)**
Powell, Adam Clayton, Jr. (Congressman); New Haven, Conn. **(1908-1972)**
Powell, Dick (actor); Mt. View, Ark. **(1904-1963)**

Powell, Eleanor (actress and tap dancer); Springfield, Mass. **(1912-1982)**
Powell, Jane (Suzanne Burce) (actress and singer); Portland, Ore., 4/1/1929
Powell, William (actor); Pittsburgh, **(1892-1984)**
Power, Tyrone (actor); Cincinnati, Ohio **(1914-1958)**
Powers, Stephanie (Taffy Paul) (actress); Hollywood, Calif., 11/12/1942
Praxiteles (sculptor); Athens **(c.370-c.330 B.C.)**
Preminger, Otto (film director and producer); Vienna **(1906-1986)**
Prentiss, Paula (Paula Ragusa) (actress); San Antonio, 1939
Presley, Elvis (singer and actor); Tupelo, Miss. **(1935-1977)**
Preston, Robert (Robert Preston Meservey) (actor); Newton Highlands, Mass **(1918-1987)**
Previn, André (conductor); Berlin, 4/6/1929
Previn, Dory (singer); Rahway, N.J., 10/22/1929(?)
Price, Leontyne (Mary) (soprano); Laurel, Miss., 2/10/1927
Price, Ray (country music artist); Perryville, Tex., 1/12/1926
Price, Vincent (actor); St. Louis, 5/27/1911
Pride, Charley (singer); Sledge, Miss., 3/18/1938(?)
Priestley, J. B. (John B.) (author); Bradford, England **(1894-1984)**
Priestley, Joseph (chemist); nr. Leeds, England **(1733-1804)**
Primrose, William (violist); Glasgow, Scotland **(1904-1982)**
Prince (Prince Roger Nelson) (singer); Minneapolis, 6/7/58
Prince, Harold (stage producer); New York City, 1/30/1928
Prinze, Freddie (actor); New York City **(1954-1977)**
Pritchett, V(ictor) S(awdon) (literary critic); Ipswich, England, 12/16/1900
Procter, William (scientist); Cincinnati **(1872-1951)**
Prokofiev, Sergei Sergeevich (composer); St. Petersburg, Russia **(1891-1953)**
Proust, Marcel (novelist); Paris **(1871-1922)**
Provine, Dorothy (actress); Deadwood, S. Dak., 1/20/1937
Prowse, Juliet (actress); Bombay, 9/25/1936
Pryor, Richard (comedian); Peoria, Ill., 12/1/1940
Ptolemy (Claudius Ptolemaeus) (astronomer and geographer); Ptolemais Hermii (Egypt) **(2nd century A.D.)**
Pucci, Emilio (Marchese di Barsento) (fashion designer); Naples, Italy, 11/20/1914
Puccini, Giacomo (composer); Lucca, Italy **(1858-1924)**
Puente, Tito (band leader); New York City, 4/20/1923
Pulaski, Casimir (military officer); Podolia, Poland **(1748-1779)**
Pulitzer, Joseph (publisher); Makó (Hungary) **(1847-1911)**
Pullman, George (inventor); Brockton, N.Y. **(1831-1897)**
Purcell, Henry (composer); London **(1658-1695)**
Pusey, Nathan M. (educator); Council Bluffs, Iowa, 4/4/1907
Pushkin, Alexander Sergeevich (poet and dramatist); Moscow **(1799-1837)**
Puzo, Mario (novelist); New York City, 10/15/1921
Pyle, Ernest Taylor (journalist); Dana, Ind. **(1900-1945)**
Pythagoras (mathematician and philosopher); Samos (Greece) **(6th century B.C.)**

Q

Quayle, Anthony (actor); Ainsdale, England, 9/7/1913
Queen, Ellery: pen name of the late Frederic Dannay and the late Manfred B. Lee
Queler, Eve (conductor); New York City, 1/1/1936
Quennell, Peter Courtney (biographer); Bromley, England, 3/9/1905
Quinn, Anthony (actor); Chihuahua, Mexico, 4/21/1916

R

Rabe, David (playwright); Dubuque, Iowa, 3/10/1940
Rabelais, François (satirist); nr. Chinon, France **(1494?-1553)**
Rabi, I(sidor) I(saac) (physicist); Rymanow (Poland), 7/29/1898
Rachmaninoff, Sergei Wassilievitch (pianist and composer); Oneg Estate, Novgorod, Russia **(1873-1943)**
Racine, Jean Baptiste (dramatist); La Ferté-Milon, France **(1639-1699)**
Radner, Gilda (comedienne); Detroit, 6/28/1946
Raft, George (actor); New York City **(1895-1980)**
Rainer, Luise (actress); Vienna, 1912
Raines, Ella (actress); Snoqualmie Falls, Wash., 8/6/1921
Rainier III (Prince); Monaco, 5/31/1923
Rains, Claude (actor); London **(1889-1967)**
Raitt, Bonnie (singer); Burbank, Calif., 11/8/1949
Raleigh, Sir Walter (courtier and navigator); London **(1552?-1618)**
Rameau, Jean-Philippe (composer); Dijon? France **(1683-1764)**
Randall, Tony (Leonard Rosenberg) (actor); Tulsa, Okla., 2/26/1920
Randolph, A(sa) Philip (labor leader); Crescent City, Fla. **(1889-1979)**
Raphael (Raffaello Santi) (painter and architect); Urbino (Italy) **(1483-1520)**
Rasputin, Grigori Efimovich (monk); Tobolsk Province, Russia **(1871?-1916)**
Rathbone, Basil (actor); Johannesburg, South Africa **(1892-1967)**
Rather, Dan (TV newscaster); Wharton, Tex., 10/31/1931
Ratoff, Gregory (film director); St. Petersburg, Russia **(1897-1960)**
Rattigan, Terence (playwright); London **(1911-1977)**
Rauschenberg, Robert (painter); Port Arthur, Tex., 10/22/1925
Ravel, Maurice Joseph (composer); Ciboure, France **(1875-1937)**
Rawls, Lou (singer); Chicago, 12/1/1935
Ray, Man (painter); Philadelphia **(1890-1976)**
Ray, Satyajat (film director); Calcutta, 5/2/1922
Rayburn, Gene (TV personality); Christopher, Ill., 12/22/1917
Raye, Martha (Margie Yvonne Reed) (comedienne and actress); Butte, Mont., 8/27/1916
Raymond, Gene (actor); New York City, 8/13/1908
Reasoner, Harry (TV commentator); Dakota City, Iowa, 4/17/1923
Redding, Otis (singer); Dawson, Ga. **(1941-1967)**
Reddy, Helen (singer); Melbourne, 10/25/1941
Redford, Robert (Charles Robert Redford, Jr.) (actor); Santa Monica, Calif., 8/18/1937
Redgrave, Lynn (actress); London, 3/8/1943
Redgrave, Sir Michael (actor); Bristol, England **(1908-1985)**
Redgrave, Vanessa (actress); London, 1/30/1937
Reed, Donna (actress); Denison, Iowa **(1921-1986)**
Reed, Rex (critic); Ft. Worth, 10/2/1940
Reed, Walter (army surgeon); Belroi, Va. **(1851-1902)**
Reese, Della (Deloreese Patricia Early) (singer); Detroit, 7/6/1932
Reeves, Jim (singer); Panola County, Tex. **(1923-1964)**
Reich, Steve (composer): New York City, 10/3/1936
Reid, Wallace (actor); St. Louis **(1891-1923)**
Reiner, Carl (actor); New York City, 3/20/1922
Reiner, Fritz (conductor); Budapest **(1888-1963)**
Reiner, Robert (actor); Bronx, N.Y., 1945
Reinhardt, Max (Max Goldmann) (theater producer); nr. Vienna **(1873-1943)**
Remarque, Erich Maria (novelist); Osnabrük, Germany **(1898-1970)**
Rembrandt (Rembrandt Harmensz van Rijn) (painter); Leyden (Netherlands) **(1605-1669)**
Remick, Lee (Ann) (actress); Boston, 12/14/1935
Rennert, Günther (opera director and producer); Essen, Germany, 4/1/1911
Rennie, Michael (actor); Bradford, England **(1909-1971)**
Renoir, Jean (film director and writer); Paris, **(1894-1979)**
Renoir, Pierre Auguste (painter); Limoges, France **(1841-1919)**
Resnais, Alain (film director); Vannes, France, 6/3/1922
Resnik, Regina (mezzo-soprano); New York City, 8/30/1922
Respighi, Ottorino (composer); Bologna, Italy **(1879-1936)**
Reston, James (journalist); Clydebank, Scotland, 11/3/1909
Reuther, Walter (labor leader); Wheeling, W. Va. **(1907-1970)**
Revere, Paul (silversmith and hero of famous ride); Boston **(1735-1818)**
Revson, Charles (business executive); Boston **(1906-1975)**
Reynolds, Burt (actor); Waycross, Ga., 2/11/1936
Renolds, Debbie (Marie Frances Reynolds) (actress); El Paso, 4/1/1932
Reynolds, Sir Joshua (painter); nr. Plymouth, England **(1723-1792)**
Rhodes, Cecil John (South African statesman); Bishop Stortford, England **(1853-1902)**
Rice, Elmer (playwright); New York City **(1892-1967)**
Rice, Grantland (sports writer); Murfreesboro, Tenn. **(1880-1954)**
Rich, Buddy (Bernard) (drummer); Brooklyn, N.Y. **(1917-1987)**
Rich, Charlie (singer); Colt, Ark., 12/14/1932
Richardson, Elliot L. (ex-Cabinet member); Boston, 7/20/1920
Richardson, Sir Ralph (actor); Cheltenham, England **(1902-1983)**
Richardson, Tony (director); Shipley, England, 6/5/1928
Richelieu, Duc de (Armand Jean du Plessis) (cardinal); Paris **(1585-1642)**
Richie, Lionel (singer-songwriter); Tuskegee, Ala., 1949 (?)
Richter, Charles Francis (seismologist); Hamilton, Canada **(1900-1985)**
Richter, Sviatosiav (pianist); Zhitomir, Ukraine, 3/20/1914
Rickenbacker, Edward V. (aviator); Columbus, Ohio **(1890-1973)**
Rickles, Don (comedian); New York City, 5/8/1926
Rickover, Vice Admiral Hyman G. (atomic energy expert); Russia **(1900-1986)**
Riddle, Nelson (composer); Hackensack, N.J. **(1921-1985)**
Ride, Sally K(risten) (astronaut, astrophysicist); Encino, Calif., 5/26/1951
Ridgway, General Matthew B. (ex-Army Chief of Staff); Ft. Monroe, Va., 3/3/1895
Rigg, Diana (actress); Doncaster, England, 7/20/1938
Riley, James Whitcomb (poet); Greenfield, Ind. **(1849-1916)**
Rimsky-Korsakov, Nikolai Andreevich (composer); Tikhvin, Russia **(1844-1908)**
Rinehart, Mary (née Roberts) (novelist); Pittsburgh **(1876-1958)**

Ritchard, Cyril (actor and director); Sydney, Australia **(1898-1977)**
Ritter, John (Jonathan) (actor); Burbank, Calif., 9/17/1948
Ritter, Tex (Woodward Maurice Ritter) (singer); Panola County, Tex., **(1905-1973)**
Rivera, Chita (Dolores Conchita Figuero del Rivero) (dancer-actress-singer); Washington, D.C. 1/23/1933
Rivera, Diego (painter); Guanajuato, Mexico **(1886-1957)**
Rivera, Geraldo (Miguel) (TV newscaster); New York City, 7/3/1943
Rivers, Joan (comedienne); Brooklyn, N.Y., 6/8/1933
Rivers, Larry (Yitzroch Loiza Grossberg) (painter); New York City, 8/17/1923
Robards, Jason, Jr. (actor); Chicago, 7/26/1922
Robards, Jason, Sr. (actor); Hillsdale, Mich. **(1892-1963)**
Robbins, Harold (Harold Rubin) (novelist); New York City, 5/21/1916
Robbins, Jerome (Jerome Rabinowitz) (choreographer); New York City, 10/11/1918
Robbins, Marty (singer); Glendale, Ariz., **(1925-1982)**
Roberts, (Granville) Oral (evangelist and publisher); nr. Ada, Okla., 1/24/1918
Robertson, Cliff (actor); La Jolla, Calif., 9/9/1925
Robertson, Dale (Dayle) (actor); Oklahoma City, 7/14/1923
Robeson, Paul (singer and actor); Princeton, N.J., **(1898-1976)**
Robespierre, Maximilien François Marie Isidore de (French Revolutionist); Arras, France **(1758-1794)**
Robinson, Bill "Bojangles" (Luther) (dancer); Richmond, Va. **(1878-1949)**
Robinson, Edward G. (Emanuel Goldenberg) (actor); Bucharest **(1893-1973)**
Robinson, Edwin Arlington (poet); Head Tide, Me. **(1869-1935)**
Robson, Dame Flora (actress); South Shields, England **(1902-1984)**
Rochester (Eddie Anderson) (actor); Oakland, Calif. **(1905-1977)**
Rockefeller, David (banker); New York City, 6/12/1915
Rockefeller, John Davison (capitalist); Richford, N.Y. **(1839-1937)**
Rockefeller, John Davison, Jr. (industrialist); Cleveland **(1874-1960)**
Rockefeller, John D., 3rd (philanthropist); New York City **(1906-1978)**
Rockefeller, Laurance S. (conservationist); New York City, 5/26/1910
Rockwell, Norman (painter and illustrator); New York City, **(1894-1978)**
Rodgers, Jimmie (singer); Meridian, Miss. **(1897-1933)**
Rodgers, Richard (composer); New York City **(1902-1979)**
Rodin, François Auguste René (sculptor); Paris **(1840-1917)**
Roentgen, Wilhelm Konrad (physicist); Lennep, Prussia **(1845-1923)**
Rogers, Buddy (Charles) (actor); Olathe, Kan., 8/13/1904
Rogers, Ginger (Virginia McMath) (dancer and actress); Independence, Mo., 7/16/1911
Rogers, Kenny (singer); Houston, 1939(?)
Rogers, Roy (Leonard Slye) (actor); Cincinnati, 11/5/1912
Rogers, Will (William Penn Adair Rogers) (humorist); Oologah, Okla. **(1879-1935)**
Rogers, Will, Jr. (actor); New York City, 10/20/1911
Rogers, William P. (ex-Secretary of State); Norfolk, N.Y., 6/23/1913
Roland, Gilbert (actor); Juarez, Mexico, 12/11/1905
Rolland, Romain (author); Clamecy, France **(1866-1944)**
Rollins, Sonny (saxophonist); New York City, 9/7/1930
Romberg, Sigmund (composer); Szeged (Hungary) **(1887-1951)**
Rome, Harold (composer); Hartford, Conn., 5/27/1908
Romero, Cesar (actor); New York City, 2/15/1907
Romney, George W. (ex-Secretary of HUD); Chihuahua, Mexico, 7/8/1907
Romulo, Carlos P. (diplomat and educator); Manila **(1899-1985)**
Ronsard, Pierre de (poet); La Possonnière nr. Couture (Couture-sur-Loir, France) **(1524-1585)**
Ronstadt, Linda (singer); Tucson, Ariz., 7/30/1946
Rooney, Andy (TV personality); Albany, N.Y., 1/14/1919
Rooney, Mickey (Joe Yule, Jr.) (actor); Brooklyn, N.Y., 9/23/1920
Roosevelt, Anna Eleanor (reformer and humanitarian); New York City **(1884-1962)**
Rorem, Ned (composer); Richmond, Ind., 10/23/23
Rose, Billy (showman); New York City **(1899-1966)**
Rose, Leonard (concert cellist); Washington, D.C. **(1918-1984)**
Ross, Betsy (Betsey Griscom) (flagmaker); Philadelphia **(1752-1836)**
Ross, Diana (singer); Detroit, 3/26/1944
Ross, Katharine (actress); Hollywood, Calif., 1/29/1943
Rossellini, Roberto (film director); Rome **(1906-1977)**
Rossetti, Dante Gabriel (painter and poet); London **(1828-1882)**
Rossini, Gioacchino Antonio (composer); Pesaro (Italy) **(1792-1868)**
Rostand, Edmond (dramatist); Marseilles, France **(1868-1918)**
Rostow, Walt Whitman (economist); New York City, 10/7/1916
Rostropovich, Mstislav (cellist and conductor); Baku, U.S.S.R., 3/12/1927
Roth, Lillian (singer); Boston **(1910-1980)**
Roth, Philip (novelist); Newark, N.J., 3/19/1933
Rothko, Mark (Marcus Rothkovich) (painter); Russia **(1903-1970)**
Rouault, Georges (painter); Paris **(1871-1958)**
Roundtree, Richard (actor); New Rochelle, N.Y., 9/7/1942
Rousseau, Henri (painter); Laval, France **(1844-1910)**
Rousseau, Jean Jacques (philosopher); Geneva **(1712-1778)**
Rovere, Richard H. (journalist); Jersey City, N.J., 5/5/1915
Rowan, Dan (comedian); Beggs, Okla., 7/2/1922
Rowlands, Gena (actress); Cambria, Wis., 6/19/1936(?)
Rubens, Sir Peter Paul (painter); Siegen (Germany) **(1577-1640)**
Rubinstein, Arthur (concert pianist); Lódz (Poland) **(1887-1982)**
Rubinstein, Helena (cosmetics executive); Krakow (Poland) **(1882?-1965)**
Rudel, Julius (conductor); Vienna, 3/6/1921
Ruggles, Charles (actor); Los Angeles **(1892-1970)**
Rule, Janice (actress); Norwood, Ohio, 8/15/1931
Runcie, Robert (Alexander Kennedy) (Archbishop of Canterbury); Liverpool, England, 10/2/1921
Runyon, (Alfred) Damon (journalist); Manhattan, Kan. **(1884-1945)**
Rusk, Dean (ex-Sec. of State); Cherokee County, Ga., 2/9/1909
Ruskin, John (art critic); London **(1819-1900)**
Russell, Lord Bertrand (Arthur William) (mathematician and philosopher); Trelleck, Wales **(1872-1970)**
Russell, Jane (actress); Bemidji, Minn., 6/21/1921
Russell, Leon (pianist and singer); Lawton, Okla., 4/2/1941
Russell, Lillian (Helen Louise Leonard) (soprano); Clinton, Iowa **(1861-1922)**
Russell, Nipsy (comedian); Atlanta, 1924(?)
Russell, Rosalind (actress); Waterbury, Conn. **(1912-1976)**
Rustin, Bayard (civil rights leader); West Chester, Pa. **(1910-1987)**
Rutherford, Dame Margaret (actress); London **(1892-1972)**
Ryan, Robert (actor); Chicago **(1909-1973)**
Rydell, Bobby (singer); Philadelphia, 1942
Rysanek, Leonie (dramatic soprano); Vienna, 11/14/1928

S

Saarinen, Eero (architect); Finland **(1910-1961)**
Sabin, Albert B. (polio researcher); Bialystok (Poland), 8/26/1906
Sadat, Anwar el- (President); Egypt **(1918-1981)**
Sade, Marquis de (Donatien Alphonse Francois, Comte de Sade) (libertine and writer); Paris **(1740-1814)**
Safer, Morley (TV newscaster); Toronto, 11/8/1931
Sagan, Carl (Edward) (astronomer, astrophysicist); New York City, 11/9/1934
Sagan, Françoise (novelist); Cajarc, France, 6/21/1935
Sahl, Mort (Morton Lyon Sahl) (comedian); Montreal, 5/11/1927
Saint, Eva Marie (actress); Newark, N.J., 7/4/1924
Saint-Gaudens, Augustus (sculptor); Dublin **(1848-1907)**
St. James, Susan (Susan Miller) (actress); Los Angeles, 8/14/1946
St. John, Jill (actress); Los Angeles, 8/19/1940
St. Johns, Adela Rogers (journalist and author); Los Angeles, 5/20/1894
Saint-Laurent, Yves (Henri Donat Mathieu) (fashion designer); Oran, Algeria, 8/1/1936
Saint-Saens, Charles Camille (composer); Paris **(1835-1921)**
Sainte-Marie, Buffy (Beverly) (folk singer); Craven, Saskatchewan, Canada, 2/20/1942(?)
Salinger, J(erome) D(avid) (novelist); New York City, 1/1/1919
Salisbury, Harrison E. (journalist); Minneapolis, 11/14/1908
Salk, Jonas (polio researcher); New York City, 10/28/1914
Salk, Leo (psychologist); New York City, 1926
Salomon, Haym (American Revolution financier); Leszno, Poland **(1740-1785)**
Sand, George (Amandine Lucille Aurore Dudevant, née Dupin) (novelist); Paris **(1804-1876)**
Sandburg, Carl (poet and biographer); Galesburg, Ill. **(1878-1967)**
Sanders, George (actor); St. Petersburg, Russia **(1906-1972)**
Sands, Tommy (singer); Chicago, 8/27/1937
Sanger, Margaret (birth control leader); Corning, N.Y. **(1883-1966)**
Santayana, George (philosopher); Madrid **(1863-1952)**
Sappho (poet); Lesbos (Greece) (lived c. 600 B.C.)
Sargent, John Singer (painter); Florence, Italy **(1856-1925)**
Sarnoff, David (radio executive); Minsk, Russia **(1891-1971)**
Saroyan, William (novelist); Fresno, Calif. **(1908-1981)**
Sarrazin, Michael (actor); Quebec, 5/22/1940
Sarto, Andrea del (Andrea Domenico d'Agnolo di Francesco) (painter); Florence (Italy) **(1486-1531)**
Sartre, Jean-Paul (existentialist writer); Paris **(1905-1980)**
Sassoon, Vidal (hair stylist); London, 1/(?)/1928
Saul (King of Israel) **(11th century B.C.)**
Savalas, Telly (Aristoteles) (actor); Garden City, N.Y., 1/21/1924(?)
Savonarola, Girolamo (religious reformer); Ferrara, Italy **(1452-1498)**
Sayão, Bidú (soprano); Rio de Janeiro, 5/11/1902
Scaasi, Arnold (Arnold Isaacs) (fashion designer); Montreal
Scarlatti, Alessandro (composer); Palermo, Italy **(1659-1725)**

Scarlatti, Domenico (composer); Naples, Italy **(1685-1757)**
Scavullo, Francesco (photographer); Staten Island, N.Y. 1/16/1929
Schary, Dore (producer and writer); Newark, N.J. **(1905-1980)**
Schell, Maria (actress); Vienna, 1/15/1926
Schell, Maximilian (actor); Vienna, 12/8/1930
Schiaparelli, Elsa (fashion designer); Rome **(1890?-1973)**
Schiff, Dorothy (newspaper publisher); New York City, 3/11/1903
Schildkraut, Joseph (actor); Vienna **(1896-1964)**
Schiller, Johann Christoph Friedrich von (dramatist and poet); Marbach (Germany) **(1759-1805)**
Schippers, Thomas (conductor); Kalamazoo, Mich. **(1930-1977)**
Schlegel, Friedrich von (philosopher); Hanover? Germany **(1772-1829)**
Schlesinger, Arthur M., Jr. (historian); Columbus, Ohio, 10/15/1917
Schneider, Romy (Rose-Marie Albach) (actress); Vienna **(1938-1982)**
Schoenberg, Arnold (composer); Vienna **(1874-1951)**
Schopenhauer, Arthur (philosopher); Danzig (Poland) **(1788-1860)**
Schubert, Franz Peter (composer); Vienna **(1797-1828)**
Schulberg, Budd (novelist); New York City, 3/27/1914
Schulz, Charles M. (cartoonist); Minneapolis, 11/26/1922
Schuman, Robert (statesman); Luxembourg **(1886-1963)**
Schuman, William (composer); New York City, 8/4/1910
Schumann, Robert Alexander (composer); Zwickau (East Germany) **(1810-1856)**
Schwartz, Arthur (song writer); Brooklyn, N.Y. **(1900-1984)**
Schwarzkopf, Elisabeth (soprano); Jarotschin, Poznán (Poland), 12/9/1915
Schweitzer, Albert (humanitarian); Kaysersburg, Upper Alsace **(1875-1965)**
Scofield, Paul (actor); Hurstpierpoint, England, 1/21/1922
Scorsese, Martin (film director); Flushing, N.Y., 11/17/1942
Scott, George C. (actor); Wise, Va., 10/18/1927
Scott, Lizabeth (Emma Matso) (actress); Scranton, Pa., 1923
Scott, Martha (actress); Jamesport, Mo., 9/22/1914
Scott, Randolph (Randolph Crane) (actor); Orange County, Va **(1898-1987)**
Scott, Robert Falcon (explorer); Devonport, England **(1868-1912)**
Scott, Sir Walter (novelist); Edinburgh, Scotland **(1771-1832)**
Scott, Zachary (actor); Austin, Tex. **(1914-1965)**
Scotto, Renata (operatic soprano); Savona, Italy, 2/?/1936?
Scruggs, Earl Eugene (bluegrass musician); Cleveland County, N.C., 1/6/1924
Sebastian, John (composer); New York City, 3/17/1944
Seberg, Jean (actress); Marshalltown, Iowa **(1938-1979)**
Sedaka, Neil (singer); Brooklyn, N.Y., 3/13/1939
Seeger, Pete (folk singer); New York City, 5/3/1919
Segal, Erich (novelist); Brooklyn, N.Y., 6/16/1937
Segal, George (actor); New York City, 2/13/1936
Segovia, Andrés (guitarist); Linares, Spain **(1893-1987)**
Selleck, Tom (actor); Detroit, 1/29/1945
Sellars, Peter (theater director): Pittsburgh, Pa., 1958 (?)
Sellers, Peter (actor); Southsea, England **(1925-1980)**
Selznick, David O. (film producer); Pittsburgh **(1902-1965)**
Sendak, Maurice (Bernard) (children's book author and illustrator); Brooklyn, N.Y., 6/10/1928
Sennett, Mack (Michael Sinnott) (film producer); Richmond, Quebec, Canada **(1880-1960)**
Serkin, Peter (pianist): New York City, 7/24/1947
Serkin, Rudolf (pianist); Eger (Hungary), 3/28/1903
Serling, Rod (story writer); Syracuse, N.Y. **(1924-1975)**
Sessions, Roger (composer); Brooklyn, N.Y. **(1896-1985)**
Seurat, Georges (painter); Paris **(1859-1891)**
Seuss, Dr. (Theodor Seuss Geisel) (author and illustrator); Springfield, Mass., 3/2/1904
Sevareid, Eric (TV commentator); Velva, N.D., 11/26/1912
Severinsen, Doc (Carl) (band leader); Arlington, Ore., 7/7/1927
Sexton, Anne (poet); Newton, Mass. **(1928-1974)**
Shahn, Ben(jamin) (painter); Kaunas, Lithuania **(1898-1969)**
Shakespeare, William (dramatist); Stratford on Avon, England **(1564-1616)**
Shankar, Ravi (sitar player); Benares, India, 4/7/1920
Shanker, Albert (labor leader); New York City, 9/14/1928
Sharif, Omar (Michael Shalhoub) (actor); Alexandria, Egypt, 4/10/1932
Shatner, William (actor); Montreal, 3/22/1931
Shaw, Artie (Arthur Arshawsky) (band leader); New York City, 5/23/1910
Shaw, George Bernard (dramatist); Dublin, **(1856-1950)**
Shaw, Irwin (novelist); Brooklyn, N.Y., **(1913-1984)**
Shaw, Robert (actor); Lancashire, England **(1927-1978)**
Shaw, Robert (chorale conductor); Red Bluff, Calif., 4/30/1916
Shearer, Moira (ballerina); Dunfermline, Scotland, 1/17/1926
Shearer, Norma (actress); Montreal, **(1902?-1983)**
Shearing, George (pianist); London, 8/13/1920
Sheen, Fulton J. (Peter Sheen) (Roman Catholic bishop); El Paso, Ill. **(1895-1979)**
Sheen, Martin (Ramon Estevez) (actor); Dayton, Ohio, 8/3/1940
Shelley, Percy Bysshe (poet); nr. Horsham, England **(1792-1822)**
Shepard, Sam (playwright); Ft. Sheridan, Ill. 11/5/1943
Sheraton, Thomas (furniture designer); Stockton-on-Tees, England **(1751-1806)**
Sheridan, Ann (actress); Denton, Tex. **(1915-1967)**
Sheridan, Philip (army officer); Albany, N.Y. **(1831-1888)**
Sheridan, Richard Brinsley (dramatist); Dublin, **(1751-1816)**
Sherman, William Tecumseh (army officer); Lancaster, Ohio **(1820-1891)**
Sherwood, Robert Emmet (playwright); New Rochelle, N.Y. **(1896-1955)**
Shevardnadze, Eduard Amvrosiyevich (Minister of Foreign Affairs, U.S.S.R.); Mamati, Georgia, U.S.S.R. 1/25/1928
Shields, Brooke (actress); New York City, 5/31/1965
Shirer, William L. (journalist and historian); Chicago, 2/23/1904
Sholokhov, Mikhail (novelist); Veshenskaya, Russia **(1905-1984)**
Shore, Dinah (Frances Rose Shore) (singer); Winchester, Tenn., 3/1/1917(?)
Short, Bobby (Robert Waltrip Short) (singer and pianist); Danville, Ill., 9/15/1924
Shostakovich, Dmitri (composer); St. Petersburg, Russia **(1906-1975)**
Shriver, Sargent (Robert Sargent Shriver, Jr.) (business executive); Westminster, Md., 11/9/1915
Shulman, Max (novelist); St. Paul, 3/14/1919
Sibelius, Jean (Johann Julius Christian Sibelius) (composer); Tavastehus (Finland) **(1865-1957)**
Sidney, Sylvia (actress); New York City, 8/8/1910
Siepi, Cesare (basso); Milan, Italy, 2/10/1923
Signoret, Simone (Simone Kaminker) (actress); Wiesbaden, Germany **(1921-1985)**
Sikorsky, Igor I. (inventor); Kiev, Russia **(1889-1972)**
Sills, Beverly (Belle Silverman) (soprano, opera director); Brooklyn, N.Y., 5/25/1929
Silone, Ignazio (Secondo Tranquilli) (novelist); Pescina del Marsi, Italy **(1900-1978)**
Silverman, Fred (broadcasting executive); New York City, 9/13/1937
Silvers, Phil (Philip Silversmith) (comedian); Brooklyn, N.Y. **(1912-1985)**
Sim, Alastair (actor); Edinburgh, Scotland **(1900-1976)**
Simenon, Georges (Georges Sim) (mystery writer); Liège, Belgium, 2/13/1903
Simmons, Jean (actress); Crouch Hill, London, 1/31/1929
Simon, Carly (singer and songwriter); New York City, 6/25/1945
Simon, Neil (playwright); Bronx, N.Y., 7/4/1927
Simon, Norton (business executive); Portland, Ore., 2/5/1907
Simon, Paul (singer and songwriter); Newark, N.J., 11/5/1942
Simon, Simone (actress); Marseilles, France, 4/23/1914
Simone, Nina (Eunice Kathleen Waymoa) (singer and pianist); Tryon, N.C., 2/21/1933
Sinatra, Frank (Francis Albert) (singer and actor); Hoboken, N.J., 12/12/1915
Sinclair, Upton Beall (novelist); Baltimore **(1878-1968)**
Singer, Isaac Bashevis (novelist); Radzymin (Poland), 7/14/1904
Siqueiros, David (painter); Chihuahua, Mexico **(1896-1974)**
Sisley, Alfred (painter); Paris **(1839-1899)**
Sitting Bull (Prairie Sioux Indian Chief); on Grand River, S.D. **(c. 1835-1890)**
Skelton, Red (Richard) (comedian); Vincennes, Ind., 7/18/1913
Skinner, B(urrhus) F(rederic) (psychologist); Susquehanna, Pa., 3/20/1904
Skinner, Cornelia Otis (writer and actress); Chicago, **(1901-1979)**
Skinner, Otis (actor); Cambridge, Mass. **(1858-1942)**
Slatkin, Leonard (conductor): Los Angeles, 9/1/1944
Slezak, Walter (actor); Vienna **(1902-1983)**
Sloan, Alfred P., Jr. (industrialist); New Haven, Conn. **(1875-1965)**
Sloan, John (painter); Lock Haven, Pa. **(1871-1951)**
Smetana, Bedrich (composer); Litomysl (Czechoslovakia) **(1824-1884)**
Smith, Adam (economist); Kirkaldy, Scotland **(1723-1790)**
Smith, Alexis (actress); Penticon, Canada, 6/8/1921
Smith, Alfred Emanuel (politician); New York City **(1873-1944)**
Smith, David (sculptor); Decatur, Ind. **(1906-1965)**
Smith, H. Allen (humorist); McLeansboro, Ill. **(1907-1976)**
Smith, Howard K. (TV commentator); Ferriday, La., 5/12/1914
Smith, John (American colonist); Willoughby, Lincolnshire, England **(1580-1631)**
Smith, Joseph (religious leader); Sharon, Vt. **(1805-1844)**
Smith, Kate (Kathryn) (singer); Greenville, Va. **(1909-1986)**
Smith, Maggie (actress); Ilford, England, 12/28/1934
Smith, Red (Walter) (sports columnist); Green Bay, Wis. **(1905-1982)**
Smollet, Tobias (novelist); Dalquhurn, Scotland **(1721-1771)**
Smothers, Dick (Richard) (comedian); Governors Island, New York City, 11/20/1939
Smothers, Tom (Thomas) (comedian); Governors Island, New York

City, 2/2/1937
Snow, Lord (Charles Percy) (author); Leicester, England **(1905-1980)**
Snowdon, Earl of (Anthony Armstrong-Jones) (photographer); London, 3/7/1930
Snyder, Tom (TV personality); Milwaukee, 5/12/1936
Socrates (philosopher); Athens **(469-399 B.C.)**
Solomon (King of Israel); Jerusalem (?) **(died c. 933 B.C.)**
Solon (lawgiver); Salamis (Greece) **(638?-559 B.C.)**
Solti, Sir Georg (conductor); Budapest, 10/21/1912
Solzhenitsyn, Aleksandr (novelist); Kislovodsk, Russia, 12/11/1918
Somers, Suzanne (Suzanne Mahoney) (actress); San Bruno, Calif., 10/16/1946
Sommer, Elke (Elke Schletz) (actress); Berlin, 11/5/1942
Sondheim, Stephen (composer); New York City, 3/22/1930
Sontag, Susan (author and film director); New York City, 1/28/1933
Sophocles (dramatist); nr. Athens **(496?-406 B.C.)**
Sothern, Ann (Harriette Lake) (actress); Valley City, N.D., 1/22/1912
Soul, David (David Solberg) (actor); Chicago, 8/28/(?)
Sousa, John Philip (composer); Washington, D.C. **(1854-1932)**
Soyer, Raphael (painter); Borisoglebsk, Russia, 12/25/1899
Spaak, Paul-Henri (statesman); Brussels **(1899-1972)**
Spacek, Sissy (Mary Elizabeth) (actress); Quitman, Tex., 12/25/1949
Spark, Muriel (novelist); Edinburgh, Scotland, 2/1/1918
Spector, Phil (rock producer); Bronx, N.Y., 12/25/1940
Spencer, Herbert (philosopher); Derby, England **(1820-1903)**
Spender, Stephen (poet); nr. London, 2/28/1909
Spengler, Oswald (philosopher); Blankenburg, (East Germany) **(1880-1936)**
Spenser, Edmund (poet); London **(1552?-1599)**
Spewack, Bella (playwright); Hungary, 3/25/1899
Spiegel, Sam (producer); Jaroslaw (Poland) **(1901-1985)**
Spielberg, Steven (film director); Cincinnati, 12/18/1947
Spillane, Mickey (Frank Spillane) (mystery writer); Brooklyn, N.Y., 3/9/1918
Spinoza, Baruch (philosopher); Amsterdam (Netherlands) **(1632-1677)**
Spivak, Lawrence (TV producer); Brooklyn, N.Y., 1900
Spock, Benjamin (pediatrician); New Haven, Conn., 5/2/1903
Springsteen, Bruce (singer and songwriter); Freehold, N.J., 9/23/1949
Sproul, Robert G. (educator); San Francisco **(1891-1975)**
Stack, Robert (actor); Los Angeles, 1/13/1919
Stafford, Jo (singer); Coalinga, Calif., 1918
Stalin, Joseph Vissarionovich (Iosif V. Dzhugashvili) (Soviet leader); nr. Tiflis, Russia **(1879-1953)**
Stalina, Svetlana Alliluyeva (Stalin's daughter); Moscow, 2/28/1926
Stallone, Sylvester (actor and writer); New York City, 7/6/1946
Stamp, Terrence (actor); London, 1938
Stang, Arnold (comedian); Chelsea, Mass., 1925
Stanislavski (Konstantin Sergeevich Alekseev) (stage producer); Moscow **(1863-1938)**
Stanley, Sir Henry Morton (John Rowlands) (explorer); Denbigh, Wales **(1841-1904)**
Stanley, Kim (Patricia Reid) (actress); Tularosa, N.M., 2/11/1925
Stans, Maurice H. (ex-Secretary of Commerce); Shakope, Minn., 3/22/1908
Stanton, Frank (broadcasting executive); Muskegon, Mich., 3/20/1908
Stanwyck, Barbara (Ruby Stevens) (actress); Brooklyn, N.Y., 7/16/1907
Stapleton, Jean (Jeanne Murray) (actress); New York City, 1/19/1923
Stapleton, Maureen (actress); Troy, N.Y., 6/21/1925
Starker, Janós (cellist); Budapest 7/5/1926
Starr, Kay (Starks) (singer); Dougherty, Okla., 7/21/1922
Starr, Ringo (Richard Starkey) (singer and songwriter); Liverpool, England, 7/7/1940
Stassen, Harold E. (ex-government official); West St. Paul, Minn., 4/13/1907
Steegmuller, Francis (biographer); New Haven, Conn., 7/3/1906
Steele, Tommy (singer); London, 12/17/1936
Stegner, Wallace (Earle) (novelist and critic); Lake Mills, Iowa, 2/18/1909
Steichen, Edward Jean (photographer, artist); Luxembourg **(1879-1973)**
Steiger, Rod (Rodney) (actor); Westhampton, N.Y., 4/14/1925
Stieglitz, Alfred (photographer); Hoboken, N.J. **(1864-1946)**
Stein, Gertrude (author); Allegheny, Pa. **(1874-1946)**
Steinbeck, John Ernst (novelist); Salinas, Calif. **(1902-1968)**
Steinberg, David (comedian); Winnipeg, Manitoba, Canada, 8/19/1942
Steinberg, William (conductor); Cologne, Germany **(1899-1978)**
Steinem, Gloria (feminist); Toledo, Ohio, 3/25/1935(?)
Steinmetz, Charles (electrical engineer); Breslau (Poland) **(1865-1923)**
Stendhal (Marie Henri Beyle) (novelist); Grenoble, France **(1783-1842)**
Sterling, Jan (actress); New York City, 4/3/1923
Stern, Isaac (concert violinist); Kreminlecz, Russia, 7/21/1920
Sterne, Laurence (novelist); Clonmel, Ireland **(1713-1768)**
Stevens, Cat (Steven Georgiou) (singer and songwriter); London, 7/?/1947
Stevens, Connie (Concetta Ingolia) (singer); Brooklyn, N.Y., 8/8/1938
Stevens, George (film director); Oakland, Calif. **(1905-1975)**
Stevens, Risë (mezzo-soprano); New York City, 6/11/1913
Stevens, Stella (actress); Yazoo City, Miss., 10/1/1936
Stevenson, Adlai Ewing (statesman); Los Angeles **(1900-1965)**
Stevenson, McLean (actor); Bloomington, Ind., 11/14/1929(?)
Stevenson, Robert Louis Balfour (novelist and poet); Edinburgh, Scotland **(1850-1894)**
Stewart, James (actor); Indiana, Pa., 5/20/1908
Stewart, Rod (Roderick David) (singer); London, 1/10/1945
Stickney, Dorothy (actress); Dickinson, N.D. 6/21/1903
Stills, Stephen (singer and songwriter); Dallas, 1/3/1945
Sting (Gordon Matthew Sumner) (singer and composer): Wallsend, England, 10/2/1951
Stokes, Carl (TV newscaster); Cleveland, 6/21/1927
Stokowski, Leopold (conductor); London **(1882-1977)**
Stone, Edward Durell (architect); Fayetteville, Ark. **(1902-1978)**
Stone, Ezra (actor and producer); New Bedford, Mass., 12/2/1917
Stone, I(sidor) F(einstein) (journalist); Philadelphia, 12/24/1907
Stone, Irving (Irving Tennenbaum) (novelist); San Francisco, 7/14/1903
Stone, Lewis (actor); Worcester, Mass. **(1879-1953)**
Stone, Lucy (woman suffragist); nr. West Brookfield, Mass. **(1818-1893)**
Stone, Sly (Sylvester) (rock musician); 1944
Storm, Gale (actress); Bloomington, Tex., 1922
Stout, Rex (mystery writer); Noblesville, Ind. **(1886-1975)**
Stowe, Harriet Elizabeth Beecher (novelist); Litchfield, Conn. **(1811-1896)**
Stradivari, Antonio (violinmaker); Cremona (Italy) **(1644-1737)**
Strasberg, Lee (stage director); Budanov, Austria **(1901-1982)**
Strasberg, Susan (actress); New York City, 5/22/1938
Straus, Oskar (composer); Vienna **(1870-1954)**
Strauss, Johann (composer); Vienna **(1825-1899)**
Strauss, Lewis L. (naval officer and scientist); Charleston, W. Va. **(1896-1974)**
Strauss, Richard (composer); Munich, Germany **(1864-1949)**
Stravinsky, Igor (composer); Orlenbaum, Russia **(1882-1971)**
Streep, Meryl (Mary Louise) (actress); Summit, N.J., 6/22/1949
Streisand, Barbra (singer and actress); Brooklyn, N.Y., 4/24/1942
Stritch, Elaine (actress); Detroit, 2/2/1928
Struthers, Sally Ann (actress); Portland, Ore., 7/28/1948
Stuart, Gilbert Charles (painter); Rhode Island **(1755-1828)**
Stuart, James Ewell Brown (known as Jeb) (Confederate army officer); Patrick County, Va. **(1833-1864)**
Stuyvesant, Peter (Governor of New Amsterdam); West Friesland (Netherlands) **(1592-1672)**
Styne, Jule (Julius Kerwin Stein) (songwriter); London, 12/31/1905
Styron, William (William Clark Styron, Jr.) (novelist); Newport News, Va., 6/11/1925
Sullavan, Margaret Brooke (actress); Norfolk, Va. **(1911-1960)**
Sullivan, Sir Arthur Seymour (composer); London **(1842-1900)**
Sullivan, Barry (Patrick Barry) (actor); New York City, 8/29/1912
Sullivan, Ed (columnist and TV personality); New York City **(1901-1974)**
Sullivan, Francis Loftus (actor); London **(1903-1956)**
Sullivan, Frank (Francis John) (humorist); Saratoga Springs, N.Y. **(1892-1976)**
Sullivan, Louis Henry (architect); Boston, Mass. **(1856-1924)**
Sutzberger, Arthur Ochs (newspaper publisher); New York City, 2/5/1926
Sumac, Yma (singer); Ichocan, Peru, 9/10/1927
Summer, Donna (La Donna Andrea Gaines) (singer); Boston, 12/31/1948
Sun Yat-sen (statesman); nr. Macao **(1866-1925)**
Susann, Jacqueline (novelist); Philadelphia **(1926?-1974)**
Susskind, David (TV producer); New York City **(1920-1987)**
Sutherland, Joan (soprano); Sydney, Australia, 11/7/1926
Suzuki, Pat (actress); Cressey, Calif., 1931
Swados, Elizabeth (composer, playwright); Buffalo, N.Y., 2/5/1951
Swanson, Gloria (Gloria May Josephine Svensson) (actress); Chicago, **(1899-1983)**
Swarthout, Gladys (soprano); Deepwater, Mo. **(1904-1969)**
Swayze, John Cameron (news commentator); Wichita, Kan., 4/4/1906
Swendenborg, Emanuel (scientist, philosopher, mystic); Stockholm **(1688-1772)**
Swift, Jonathan (satirist); Dublin **(1667-1745)**
Swinburne, Algernon Charles (poet); London **(1837-1909)**

Swope, Herbert Bayard (journalist); St. Louis **(1882-1958)**
Sydow, von, Max (Carl Adolf von Sydow) (actor); Lund, Sweden, 4/10/1929
Synge, John Millington (dramatist); nr. Dublin **(1871-1909)**
Szilard, Leo (physicist); Budapest **(1898-1964)**

T

Taft, Robert Alphonso (legislator); Cincinnati **(1889-1953)**
Tagore, Sir Rabindranath (poet); Calcutta **(1861-1941)**
Tallchief, Maria (ballerina); Fairfax, Okla., 1/24/1925
Talleyrand-Périgord, Charles Maurice de (statesman); Paris **(1754-1838)**
Talmadge, Norma (actress); Niagara Falls, N.Y. **(1897-1957)**
Talvela, Martti (basso); Hiitola, Finalnd, 2/4/1935
Tamerlane (Timur) (Mongol conqueror); nr. Samarkand (U.S.S.R.) **(1336?-1405)**
Tandy, Jessica (actress); London, 6/7/1909
Tarkington, (Newton) Booth (novelist); Indianapolis **(1869-1946)**
Tate, Allen (John Orley) (poet and critic); Winchester, Ky., **(1899-1979)**
Tate, Sharon (actress); Dallas **(1943-1969)**
Tati, Jacques (Jacques Tatischeff) (actor); Pecq, France **(1908-1982)**
Taylor, Elizabeth (actress); London, 2/27/1932
Taylor, Estelle (actress); Wilmington, Del. **(1899-1958)**
Taylor, Harold (educator); Toronto, 9/28/1914
Taylor, James (singer and songwriter); Boston, 3/12/1948
Taylor, (Joseph) Deems (composer); New York City **(1885-1966)**
Taylor, Laurette (Laurette Cooney) (actress); New York City **(1884-1946)**
Taylor, Gen. Maxwell D. (former Army Chief of Staff); Keytesville, Mo **(1901-1987)**
Taylor, Robert (Spangler Arlington Brugh) (actor); Filley, Neb. **(1911-1969)**
Taylor, Rod (actor); Sydney, Australia, 1/11/1930
Tchaikovsky, Peter (Pëtr) Ilich (composer); Votkinsk, Russia **(1840-1893)**
Teasdale, Sara (poet); St. Louis **(1884-1933)**
Tebaldi, Renata (lyric soprano); Pesaro, Italy, 1/2/1922
Tecumseh (Shawnee Indian chief); nr. Springfield, Ohio **(1768?-1813)**
Telemann, Georg Philipp (composer); Magdeburg (East Germany) **(1681-1767)**
Teller, Edward (atomic physicist); Budapest, 1/15/1908
Temple, Shirley. *See* Black, Shirley Temple
Tennyson, Alfred (1st Baron Tennyson) (poet); Somersby, England **(1809-1892)**
Terhune, Albert Payson (novelist and journalist); Newark, N.J. **(1872-1942)**
Terkel, Studs (writer-interviewer); New York City, 5/16/1912
Terry, Ellen Alicia (actress); Coventry, England **(1848-1928)**
Terry-Thomas (Thomas Terry Hoar Stevens) (actor); London, 7/14/1911
Tesla, Nikola (electrical engineer and inventor); Smiljan (Yugoslavia) **(1856-1943)**
Thackeray, William Makepeace (novelist); Calcutta **(1811-1863)**
Thant, U (U.N. statesman); Pantanaw (Burma) **(1909-1974)**
Tharp, Twyla (dancer and choreographer); Portland, Ind., 7/1/1941(?)
Thatcher, Margaret (Prime Minister); Grantham, England, 10/13/1925
Thaxter, Phyllis (actress); Portland, Me., 1921
Thebom, Blanche (mezzo-soprano); Monessen, Pa., 9/19/1919
Theodorakis, Mikis (composer); Chios, Greece, 7/29/1925
Thieu, Nguyen Van (ex-President of South Vietnam); Trithuy (Vietnam) 4/5/1923
Thomas, Danny (Amos Jacobs) (entertainer and TV producer); Deerfield, Mich., 1/6/1914
Thomas, Dylan Marials (poet); Carmarthenshire, Wales **(1914-1953)**
Thomas, Lowell (explorer, commentator); Woodington, Ohio **(1892-1981)**
Thomas, Marlo (actress); Detroit, 11/21/1943
Thomas, Michael Tilson (conductor); Hollywood, Calif., 12/21/1944
Thomas, Norman Mattoon (Socialist leader): Marion, Ohio **(1884-1968)**
Thomas, Richard (actor); New York City, 6/13/1951
Thompson, Dorothy (writer); Lancaster, N.Y. **(1894-1961)**
Thompson, Hunter (Stockton) (writer); Louisville, Ky. 7/18/1939
Thoreau, Henry David (naturalist and author); Concord, Mass. **(1817-1862)**
Thorndike, Dame Sybil (actress); Gainsborough, England **(1882-1976)**
Thurber, James Grover (author and cartoonist); Columbus, Ohio **(1894-1961)**
Tibbett, Lawrence (baritone); Bakersfield, Calif. **(1896-1960)**
Tierney, Gene (actress); Brooklyn, N.Y., 11/20/1920
Tiffin, Pamela (actress); Oklahoma City, 10/13/1942
Tillstrom, Burr (puppeteer); Chicago **(1917-1985)**
Tintoretto, Il (Jacopo Robusti) (painter); Venice **(1518-1594)**
Tiny Tim (Herbert Khaury) (entertainer); New York City, 1923(?)
Tiomkin, Dmitri (composer); St. Petersburg, Russia **(1894-1979)**
Titian (Tiziano Vecelli) (painter); Pieve di Cadore (Italy) **(1477-1576)**
Tito (Josip Broz or Brozovich) (President of Yugoslavia); Croatia (Yugoslavia) **(1892-1980)**
Tocqueville, Alexis de (writer); Verneuil, France **(1805-1859)**
Todd, Thelma (actress); Lawrence, Mass. **(1905-1935)**
Tolstoi, Count Leo (Lev) Nikolaevich (novelist); Tula Province, Russia **(1828-1910)**
Tomlin, Lily (comedienne); Detroit, 1939(?)
Tone, Franchot (actor); Niagara Falls, N.Y. **(1905-1968)**
Tormé, Mel (Melvin) (singer); Chicago, 9/13/1925
Torn, Rip (Elmore Torn, Jr.) (actor and director); Temple, Tex., 2/6/1931
Torquamada, Tomás de (Spanish Inquisitor); Valladolid, Spain **(1420-1498)**
Toscanini, Arturo (orchestra conductor); Parma, Italy **(1867-1957)**
Toulouse-Lautrec (Henri Marie Raymond de Toulouse-Lautrec Monfa) (painter); Albi, France **(1864-1901)**
Toynbee, Arnold J. (historian); London **(1889-1975)**
Tracy, Spencer (actor); Milwaukee **(1900-1967)**
Traubel, Helen (Wagnerian soprano); St. Louis **(1903-1972)**
Travolta, John (actor); Englewood, N.J., 2/18/1954
Treacher, Arthur (actor); Brighton, England **(1894-1975)**
Trevor, Claire (actress); New York City, 1911
Trigère, (Pauline (fashion designer); Paris, 11/4/1912
Trilling, Lionel (author and educator); New York City **(1905-1975)**
Trotsky, Leon (Lev Davidovich Bronstein) (statesman); Elisavetgrad, Russia **(1879-1940)**
Trudeau, Garry (cartoonist); New York City, 1948
Trudeau, Pierre Elliott (former Prime Minister); Montreal, 10/18/1919
Truffaut, François (film director); Paris **(1932-1984)**
Trujillo y Molina, Rafael Leonidas (Dominican Republic dictator); San Cristóbal, Dominican Republic **(1891-1961)**
Truman, Margaret (author); Independence, Mo., 2/17/1924
Tryon, Thomas (actor and novelist); Hartford, Conn., 1/14/1926
Tsiolkovsky, Konstantin E. (father of cosmonautics); Izhevskoye, Russia **(1857-1935)**
Tucker, Forrest (actor); Plainfield, Ind. **(1919-1986)**
Tucker, Richard (tenor); New York City **(1914-1975)**
Tucker, Sophie (Sophie Abuza) (singer); Europe **(1884?-1966)**
Tudor, Antony (choreographer); London **(1909-1987)**
Tune, Tommy (dancer-choreographer); Wichita Falls, Tex., 2/28/1939
Turgenev, Ivan Sergeevich (novelist); Orel, Russia **(1818-1883)**
Turner, Joseph M.W. (painter); London **(1775-1851)**
Turner, Kathleen (actress); Springfield, Mo., 1956 (?)
Turner, Lana (Julia Jean Mildred Frances Turner) (actress); Wallace, Idaho, 2/8/1920
Turner, Nat (civil rights leader); Southampton County, Va. **(1800-1831)**
Turner, Tina (Annie Mae Bullock) (singer); Brownsville, Tex., 1939
Turpin, Ben (comedian); New Orleans **(1874-1940)**
Tushingham, Rita (actress); Liverpool, England, 3/14/1942
Twain, Mark (Samuel Langhorne Clemens) (author); Florida, Mo. **(1835-1910)**
Tweed, William Marcy (politician); New York City **(1823-1878)**
Twiggy (Leslie Hornby) (model); London, 9/19/1949
Twining, Gen. Nathan F. (former Air Force Chief of Staff); Monroe, Wis. **(1897-1982)**
Twitty, Conway (Harold Lloyd Jenkins) (singer and guitarist); Friars Point, Miss., 9/1/1933
Tyson, Cicely (actress); New York City, 12/19/1939(?)

U

Udall, Stewart L. (ex-Secretary of the Interior); St. Johns, Ariz., 1/31/1920
Uggams, Leslie (singer and actress); New York City, 5/25/1943
Ulanova, Galina (ballerina); St. Petersburg, Russia, 1/10/1910
Ullmann, Liv (actress); Tokyo, 12/16/1939
Ulric, Lenore (actress); New Ulm, Minn. **(1894-1970)**
Untermeyer, Louis (anthologist and poet); New York City **(1885-1977)**
Updike, John (novelist); Shillington, Pa., 3/18/1932
Urey, Harold C. (physicist); Walkerton, Ind. **(1893-1981)**
Uris, Leon (novelist); Baltimore, 8/3/1924
Ustinov, Peter (actor and producer); London, 4/16/1921
Utrillo, Maurice (painter); Paris **(1883-1955)**

V

Vaccaro, Brenda (actress); Brooklyn, N.Y., 11/18/1939
Vadim, Roger (Roger Vadim Plemiannikov) (film director); Paris, 1/26/1928
Valentine, Karen (actress); Santa Rosa, Calif., 1947
Valentino, Rudolph (Rodolpho d'Antonguolla) (actor); Castellaneta, Italy **(1895-1926)**
Valentino (Valentino Garavani) (fashion designer); nr. Milan, Italy, 5/11/1932
Vallee, Rudy (Hubert Prior Rudy Vallée) (band leader and singer); Island Pond, Vt. **(1901-1986)**
Valli, Frankie (Frank Castellaccio) (singer); Newark, N.J., 5/3/1937
Van Allen, James Alfred (space physicist); Mt. Pleasant, Iowa, 9/7/1914
Van Buren, Abigail (Mrs. Morton Phillips) (columnist); Sioux City, Iowa, 7/4/1918
Vance, Vivian (actress); Cherryvale, Kan. **(1912-1979)**
Vanderbilt, Alfred G. (sportsman); London, 9/22/1912
Vanderbilt, Cornelius (financier); Port Richmond, N.Y. **(1794-1877)**
Vanderbilt, Gloria (fashion designer) New York City, 2/20/1924
Van Doren, Carl (writer and educator); Hope, Ill. **(1885-1950)**
Van Doren, Mamie (actress); Rowena, S.D., 2/6/1933
Van Dyke, Dick (actor); West Plains, Mo., 12/13/1925
Vandyke (or Van Dyck), Sir Anthony (painter); Antwerp (Belgium) **(1599-1641)**
Van Eyck, Jan (painter); Maeseyck (Belgium) **(c.1390-1441)**
van Gogh, Vincent (painter); Groot Zundert, Brabant **(1853-1890)**
van Hamel, Martine (ballerina); Brussels, 11/16/1945
Van Heusen, Jimmy (Edward Chester Babcock) (songwriter); Syracuse, N.Y., 1/26/1913
Van Peebles, Melvin (playwright); Chicago, 9/21/1932
Vaughan, Sarah (singer); Newark, N.J., 3/27/1924
Vaughan Williams, Ralph (composer); Down Ampney, England **(1872-1958)**
Vaughn, Robert (actor); New York City, 11/22/1932
Velázquez, Diego Rodriguez de Silva y (painter); Seville, Spain **(1599-1660)**
Velez, Lupe (Guadelupe Velez de Villalobos) (actress); San Luis Potosi, Mexico **(1908-1944)**
Venturi, Robert (Charles) (architect); Philadelphia, 6/25/1925
Verdi, Giuseppe (composer); Roncole (Italy) **(1813-1901)**
Verdon, Gwen (actress); Culver City, Calif., 1/13/1925
Vereen, Ben (actor and singer); Miami, Fla., 10/10/1946
Vermeer, Jan (or Jan van der Meer van Delft) (painter); Delft (Netherlands) **(1632-1675)**
Verne, Jules (author); Nantes, France **(1828-1905)**
Veronese, Paolo (Paolo Cagliari) (painter); Verona **(1528-1588)**
Verrazano, Giovanni da (navigator); Florence (Italy) **(1485?-1528)**
Verrett, Shirley (mezzo-soprano); New Orleans, 5/31/1933
Vesalius, Andreas (anatomist); Brussels, Belgium **(1515-1564)**
Vespucci, Amerigo (navigator); Florence (Italy) **(1454-1512)**
Vickers, Jon (tenor); Prince Albert, Sask, Canada, 10/29/1926
Vico, Giovanni Battista (philosopher); Naples, Italy **(1668-1744)**
Vidal, Gore (novelist); West Point, N.Y., 10/3/1925
Vidor, King (film director and producer); Galveston, Tex. **(1895-1982)**
Villa, Pancho (Doroteo Arango) (bandit); Rio Grande, Mexico **(1877-1923)**
Villella, Edward (ballet dancer); Bayside, Queens, N.Y., 10/1/1936
Villon, François (François de Montcorbier) (poet); Paris **(1431-1463)**
Vinton, Bobby (singer); Canonsburg, Pa., 4/16/1935(?)
Virgil (or Vergil) (Publius Vergilius Maro) (poet); nr. Mantua (Italy) **(70-19 B.C.)**
Vishnevskaya, Galina (soprano); Leningrad, 10/25/1926
Vivaldi, Antonio (composer); Venice **(1678-1741)**
Vlaminck, Maurice de (painter); Paris **(1876-1958)**
Voight, Jon (actor); Yonkers, N.Y., 12/29/1938
Volta, Alessandro (scientist); Como, Italy **(1745-1827)**
Voltaire (François Marie Arouet) (author); Paris **(1694-1778)**
von Braun, Wernher (rocket scientist); Wirsitz, Germany **(1912-1977)**
von Aroldingen, Karin (Karin Awny Hannelore Reinbold von Aroedingen and Eltzinger) (ballet dancer); Greiz (East Germany) 7/9/1941
von Furstenberg, Betsy (Elizabeth Caroline Maria Agatha Felicitas Therese von Furstenberg-Hedringen) (actress); Nelheim-Heusen, Germany, 8/16/1935
von Fürstenberg, Diane (Diane Simone Michelle Halfin) (fashion designer); Brussels, 12/31/1946
von Hindenburg, Paul (statesman): Posen (Poland) **(1847-1934)**
von Karajan, Herbert (conductor); Salzburg (Austria), 4/5/1908
Vonnegut, Kurt, Jr. (novelist); Indianapolis, 11/11/1922
Von Stroheim, Erich Oswald Hans Carl Maria von Nordenwall (film actor and director); Vienna **(1885-1957)**
Vreeland, Diana (Diana Dalziel) (fashion journalist and museum consultant); Paris, 1903(?)

W

Wagner, Lindsay (actress); Los Angeles, 6/22/1949
Wagner, Robert (actor); Detroit, 2/10/1930
Wagner, Robert F. (ex-Mayor of New York City); New York City, 4/20/1910
Wagner, Wilhelm Richard (composer); Leipzig (East Germany) **(1813-1883)**
Waldheim, Kurt (U.N. Secretary-General); St. Andrae-Wörden, Austria, 12/21/1918
Walker, Clint (actor); Hartford, Ill., 5/30/1927
Walker, Nancy (Ann Myrtle Swoyer); (actress and comedienne); Philadelphia, 5/10/1922
Wallace, DeWitt (publisher); St. Paul **(1889-1981)**
Wallace, Irving (novelist); Chicago, 3/19/1916
Wallace, Mike (Myron Wallace) (TV interviewer and commentator); Brookline, Mass., 5/9/1918
Wallach, Eli (actor); Brooklyn, N.Y., 12/7/1915
Waller, Thomas "Fats" (pianist); New York City **(1904-1943)**
Wallis, Hal (film producer); Chicago **(1899-1986)**
Walpole, Horace (statesman and novelist); London **(1717-1797)**
Waltari, Mika (novelist); Helsinki, Finland, **(1903-1979)**
Walter, Bruno (Bruno Walter Schlesinger) (orchestra conductor); Berlin **(1876-1962)**
Walters, Barbara (TV commentator); Boston, 9/25/1931
Walton, Izaak (author); Stafford, England **(1593-1683)**
Wambaugh, Joseph (author and screenwriter); East Pittsburgh, Pa., 1/22/1937
Wanamaker, John (merchant); Philadelphia **(1838-1922)**
Ward, Barbara (economist); York, England **(1914-1981)**
Warhol, Andy (artist and producer); Pennsylvania **(1928(?)-1987)**
Waring, Fred (band leader); Tyrone, Pa., **(1900-1984)**
Warner, H. B. (Henry Bryan Warner Lickford) (actor); London **(1876-1958)**
Warren, Robert Penn (novelist); Guthrie, Ky., 4/24/1905
Warwick, Dionne (singer); East Orange, N.J., 1941
Washington, Booker Taliaferro (educator); Franklin County, Va. **(1856-1915)**
Waters, Ethel (actress and singer); Chester, Pa. **(1896-1977)**
Waters, Muddy (McKinley Morganfield) (singer and guitarist); Rolling Fork, Miss. **(1915-1983)**
Watson, Thomas John (industrialist); Campbell, N.Y. **(1874-1956)**
Watt, James (inventor); Greenock, Scotland **(1736-1819)**
Watteau, Jean-Antoine (painter); Valanciennes, France **(1684-1721)**
Watts, André (concert pianist); Nuremberg, Germany, 6/20/1946
Waugh, Alec (Alexander Raban Waugh) (novelist); London **(1898-1981)**
Waugh, Evelyn (satirist); London **(1903-1966)**
Wayne, Anthony (military officer); Waynesboro (family farm), nr. Paoli, Pa. **(1745-1796)**
Wayne, David (David McMeekan); (actor); Traverse City, Mich., 1/30/1914
Wayne, John (Marion Michael Morrison) (actor); Winterset, Iowa, **(1907-1979)**
Weaver, Dennis (actor); Joplin, Mo., 6/4/1925
Weaver, Fritz (actor); Pittsburgh, 1/19/1926
Webb, Clifton (Webb Parmelee Hollenbeck) (actor); Indianapolis **(1893-1966)**
Webb, Jack (film actor and producer); Santa Monica, Calif. **(1920-1982)**
Weber, Karl Maria Friedrich Ernst von (composer); nr. Lübeck (Germany) **(1786-1826)**
Webster, Daniel (statesman); Salisbury, N.H. **(1782-1852)**
Webster, Noah (lexicographer); West Hartford, Conn. **(1758-1843)**
Weill, Kurt (composer); Dessau, (East Germany) **(1900-1950)**
Weir, Peter (film director); Sydney, Australia, 8/21/1944
Weizmann, Chaim (statesman); Grodno Province, Russia **(1874-1952)**
Welch, Raquel (Raquel Tejada) (actress); Chicago, 9/5/1942
Weld, Tuesday (Susan) (actress); New York City, 8/27/1943
Welk, Lawrence (band leader); Strasburg, N.D., 3/11/1903
Welles, Orson (actor and producer); Kenosha, Wis. **(1915-1985)**
Wellington, Duke of (Arthur Wellesley) (statesman); Ireland **(1769-1852)**
Wells, H(erbert) G(eorge) (author); Bromley, England **(1866-1946)**
Welty, Eudora (novelist); Jackson, Miss., 4/13/1909
Werfel, Franz (novelist); Prague **(1890-1945)**
Werner, Oskar (Josef Schliessmayer) (film actor and director); Vienna **(1922-1984)**
Wertmuller, Lina (film director); Rome, 1926(?)
Wesley, John (religious leader); Epworth Rectory, Lincolnshire, England **(1703-1791)**
West, Dame Rebecca (Cicily Fairfield); (novelist); County Kerry, Ireland **(1892-1983)**
West, Jessamyn (novelist); nr. North Vernon, Ind. **(1902-1984)**
West, Mae (actress); Brooklyn, N.Y. **(1893-1980)**

West, Nathanael (Nathan Weinstein) (novelist); New York City **(1902-1940)**
Westinghouse, George (inventor); Central Bridge, N.Y. **(1846-1914)**
Westmoreland, William Childs (ex-Army Chief of Staff); Saxon, S.C., 3/26/1914
Wharton, Edith Newbold (née Jones) (novelist); New York City **(1862-1937)**
Wheeler, Bert (Albert Jerome Wheeler) (comedian); Paterson, N.J. **(1895-1968)**
Whistler, James Abbott McNeill (painter and etcher); Lowell, Mass. (1834-1903)
White, E(lwyn) B(rooks) (author); Mt. Vernon, N.Y. **(1899-1985)**
White, Stanford (architect); New York City **(1853-1906)**
White, Theodore H. (historian); Boston **(1915-1986)**
White, William Allen (journalist); Emporia, Kan. **(1868-1944)**
Whitehead, Alfred North (mathematician and philosopher); Isle of Thanet, England **(1861-1947)**
Whiteman, Paul (band leader); Denver **(1891-1967)**
Whitman, Walt (Walter) (poet); West Hills, N.Y. **(1819-1892)**
Whitmore, James (actor); White Plains, N.Y., 10/1/1921
Whitney, Cornelius Vanderbilt (sportsman); New York City, 2/20/1899
Whitney, Eli (inventor); Westboro, Mass. **(1765-1825)**
Whitney, John Hay (publisher); Ellsworth, Me. **(1904-1982)**
Whittier, John Greenleaf (poet); Haverhill, Mass. **(1807-1892)**
Widmark, Richard (actor); Sunrise, Minn., 12/26/1914
Wiesel, Elie (Eliezer) (author); Signet, Romania, 9/30/1928
Wilbur, Richard (poet); New York City, 3/1/1921
Wilde, Cornel (film actor and producer); New York City, 10/13/1918
Wilde, Oscar Fingal O'Flahertie Wills (author); Dublin **(1854-1900)**
Wilder, Billy (film producer and director); Vienna, 6/22/1906
Wilder, Gene (Jerome Silberman) (actor); Milwaukee, 6/11/1935(?)
Wilder, Thornton (author); Madison, Wis. **(1897-1975)**
Wilding, Michael (actor); Westcliff, England **(1912-1979)**
Wilkins, Roy (civil rights leader); St. Louis **(1901-1981)**
Williams, Andy (singer); Wall Lake, Iowa, 12/3/1930
Williams, Billy Dee (actor); New York City, 4/6/1937
Williams, Cindy (actress); Van Nuys, Calif., 8/22/(?)
Williams, Edward Bennett (lawyer); Hartford, Conn., 5/31/1920
Williams, Emlyn (actor and playwright); Mostyn, Wales, 11/26/1905
Williams, Esther (actress); Los Angeles, 8/8/1923
Williams, Gluyas (cartoonist); San Francisco **(1888-1982)**
Williams, Hank, Sr. (Hiram King Williams) (singer); Georgiana, Ala. **(1923-1953)**
Williams, Joe (singer); Cordele, Ga., 12/12/1918
Williams, Paul (singer, composer, actor); Omaha, Neb., 9/19/1940
Williams, Robin (comedian); Chicago, 7/?/1952
Williams, Roger (clergyman); London **(1603?-1683)**
Williams, Tennessee (Thomas L. Williams) (playwright); Columbus, Miss. **(1911-1983)**
Williams, William Carlos (physician and poet); Rutherford, N.J. **(1883-1963)**
Willkie, Wendell Lewis (lawyer); Elwood, Ind. **(1892-1944)**
Willson, Meredith (composer); Mason City, Iowa **(1902-1984)**
Wilson, Don (radio and TV announcer); Lincoln, Neb. **(1900-1982)**
Wilson, Edmund (literary critic and author); Red Bank, N.J. **(1895-1972)**
Wilson, Flip (Clerow) (comedian); Jersey City, N.J., 12/8/1933
Wilson, Harold (ex-Prime Minister); Huddersfield, England, 3/11/1916
Wilson, Nancy (singer); Chillicothe, Ohio, 2/20/1937
Wilson, Sloan (novelist); Norwalk, Conn., 5/8/1920
Winchell, Walter (columnist); New York City **(1897-1972)**
Windsor, Duchess of (Bessie Wallis Warfield); Blue Ridge Summit, Pa. **(1896-1986)**
Windsor, Duke of (formerly King Edward VIII of England); Richmond Park, England **(1894-1972)**
Winkler, Henry (actor); New York City, 10/30/1945
Winter, Johnny (guitarist); Leland, Miss., 2/23/1944
Winters, Jonathan (comedian); Dayton, Ohio, 11/11/1925
Winters, Shelley (Shirley Schrift) (actress); East St. Louis, Ill., 8/18/1922
Winthrop, John (first Governor, Massachusetts Bay Colony); Suffolk, England **(1588-1649)**
Wise, Stephen Samuel (rabbi); Budapest **(1874-1949)**
Withers, Jane (actress); Atlanta, 1927
Wittgenstein, Ludwig (Josef Johann) (philosopher); Vienna **(1889-1951)**
Wodehouse, P(elham) G(renville) (novelist); Guildford, England **(1881-1975)**
Wolfe, Thomas Clayton (novelist); Asheville, N.C. **(1900-1938)**
Wolfe, Tom (journalist); Richmond, Va., 3/2/1931
Wolsey, Thomas (prelate and statesman); Ipswich, England **(1475?-1530)**
Wonder, Stevie (Steveland Judkins, later Steveland Morris) (singer and songwriter); Saginaw, Mich., 5/13/1950
Wong, Anna May (Lu Tsong Wong) (actress); Los Angeles **(1907-1961)**
Wood, Grant (painter); Anamosa, Iowa **(1892-1942)**
Wood, Natalie (Natasha Gurdin) (film actress); San Francisco **(1938-1981)**
Woodhouse, Barbara (Blackburn) (dog trainer, author, TV personality): Rathfarnham, Ireland, 5/9/1910
Woodward, Joanne (film actress); Thomasville, Ga., 2/27/1930
Woolf, Adeline Virginia (née Stephens) (novelist); London **(1882-1941)**
Woollcott, Alexander (author-critic); Phalanx, N.J. **(1887-1943)**
Woolley, Monty (Edgar Montillion Woolley) (actor); New York City **(1888-1963)**
Woolworth, Frank (merchant); Rodman, N.Y. **(1852-1919)**
Wordsworth, William (poet); Cockermouth, England **(1770-1850)**
Worley, Jo Anne (actress and singer); Lowell, Ind., 9/6/1937
Wouk, Herman (novelist); New York City, 5/27/1915
Wray, Fay (actress); Alberta, Canada, 1907
Wren, Sir Christopher (architect); East Knoyle, England **(1632-1723)**
Wright, Frank Lloyd (architect); Richland Center, Wis. **(1869-1959)**
Wright, Orville (inventor); Dayton, Ohio **(1871-1948)**
Wright, Richard (novelist); nr. Natchez, Miss. **(1908-1960)**
Wright, Teresa (actress); New York City, 10/27/1918
Wright, Wilbur (inventor); Millville, Ind. **(1867-1912)**
Wyatt, Jane (film actress); Campgaw, N.J., 8/12/1912
Wycliffe, John (church reformer); Hipswell, England **(1320-1384)**
Wyeth, Andrew (painter); Chadds Ford, Pa., 7/12/1917
Wyler, William (film director); Mulhouse (France), **(1902-1981)**
Wyman, Jane (Sarah Jane Fulks) (actress); St. Joseph, Mo., 1/4/1914
Wynette, Tammy (Wynette Pugh) (singer); Tupelo, Miss. 5/5/1942
Wynn, Ed (Isaiah Edwin Leopold) (comedian); Philadelphia **(1886-1966)**
Wynn, Keenan (actor); New York City **(1916-1986)**
Wynter, Dana (actress); London, 6/8/1930

X

Xavier, St. Francis (Jesuit missionary); Pamplona, Navarre (Spain) **(1506-1552)**
Xenophon (soldier, historian and essayist): Athens, Greece, **(434(?)-355(?) B.C.)**
Xerxes, the Great (king): Persian Empire, **(519(?)-465 B.C.)**

Y

Yeats, William Butler (poet); nr. Dublin **(1865-1939)**
Yevtushenko, Yevgeny (poet); Zima, U.S.S.R., 7/18/1933
York, Alvin Cullun (Sergeant York, World War I hero): Tennessee **(1887-1964)**
York, Michael (actor); Fulmer, England, 3/27/1942
York, Susannah (Fletcher) (actress); London, 1/9/1942
Yorty, Samuel W. (ex-Mayor of Los Angeles); Lincoln, Neb., 10/1/1909
Young, Alan (actor); North Shield, England, 11/19/1919
Young, Brigham (religious leader); Whitingham, Vt. **(1801-1877)**
Young, Gig (Byron Barr) (actor); St. Cloud, Minn. **(1917-1978)**
Young, Loretta (Gretchen Young) (actress); Salt Lake City, Utah, 1/6/1913
Young, Neil (singer and songwriter); Toronto, 11/12/1945
Young, Robert (actor); Chicago, 2/22/1907
Youngman, Henny (comedian); Liverpool, England, 1/12/1906

Z

Zanuck, Darryl F. (film producer); Wahoo, Neb. **(1902-1979)**
Zappa, Frank (Francis Vincent Zappa, Jr.) (singer and songwriter); Baltimore, 12/21/1940
Zeffirelli, Franco (director); Florence, Italy, 2/12/1923
Zenger, John Peter (printer and journalist): Germany, **(1697-1746)**
Zhou Enlai (Premier); Hualyin, China **(1898-1976)**
Ziegfeld, Florenz (theatrical producer); Chicago **(1869-1932)**
Zimbalist, Efrem (concert violinist); Rostov-on-Don, Russia **(1889-1985)**
Zimbalist, Efrem, Jr. (actor); New York City, 11/30/1923
Zola, Emile (novelist); Paris **(1840-1902)**
Zoroaster (religious leader); Persian Empire **(c. 6th century B.C.)**
Zukerman, Pinchas (violinist); Tel Aviv, Israel 7/16/1948
Zweig, Stefan (author); Vienna **(1881-1942)**
Zwingli, Huldrych (humanist); Wildaus, Switzerland **(1484-1531)**

Nobel Prizes

The Nobel prizes are awarded under the will of Alfred Bernhard Nobel, Swedish chemist and engineer, who died in 1896. The interest of the fund is divided annually among the persons who have made the most outstanding contributions in the fields of physics, chemistry, and physiology or medicine, who have produced the most distinguished literary work of an idealist tendency, and who have contributed most toward world peace.

In 1968, a Nobel Prize of economic sciences was established by Riksbank, the Swedish bank, in celebration of its 300th anniversary. The prize was awarded for the first time in 1969.

The prizes for physics and chemistry are awarded by the Swedish Academy of Science in Stockholm, the one for physiology or medicine by the Caroline Medical Institute in Stockholm, that for literature by the academy in Stockholm, and that for peace by a committee of five elected by the Norwegian Storting. The distribution of prizes was begun on December 10, 1901, the anniversary of Nobel's death. The amount of each prize varies with the income from the fund and currently is about $190,000. No Nobel prizes were awarded for 1940, 1941, and 1942; prizes for Literature were not awarded for 1914, 1918, and 1943.

PEACE

1901 Henri Dunant (Switzerland); Frederick Passy (France)
1902 Elie Ducommun and Albert Gobat (Switzerland)
1903 Sir William R. Cremer (England)
1904 Institut de Droit International (Belgium)
1905 Bertha von Suttner (Austria)
1906 Theodore Roosevelt (U.S.)
1907 Ernesto T. Moneta (Italy) and Louis Renault (France)
1908 Klas P. Arnoldson (Sweden) and Frederik Bajer (Denmark)
1909 Auguste M. F. Beernaert (Belgium) and Baron Paul H. B. B. d'Estournelles de Constant de Rebecque (France)
1910 Bureau International Permanent de la Paix (Switzerland)
1911 Tobias M. C. Asser (Holland) and Alfred H. Fried (Austria)
1912 Elihu Root (U.S.)
1913 Henri La Fontaine (Belgium)
1915 No award
1916 No award
1917 International Red Cross
1919 Woodrow Wilson (U.S.)
1920 Léon Bourgeois (France)
1921 Karl H. Branting (Sweden) and Christian L. Lange (Norway)
1922 Fridtjof Nansen (Norway)
1923 No award
1924 No award
1925 Sir Austen Chamberlain (England) and Charles G. Dawes (U.S.)
1926 Aristide Briand (France) and Gustav Stresemann (Germany)
1927 Ferdinand Buisson (France) and Ludwig Quidde (Germany)
1928 No award
1929 Frank B. Kellogg (U.S.)
1930 Lars O. J. Söderblom (Sweden)
1931 Jane Addams and Nicholas M. Butler (U.S.)
1932 No award
1933 Sir Norman Angell (England)
1934 Arthur Henderson (England)
1935 Karl von Ossietzky (Germany)
1936 Carlos de S. Lamas (Argentina)
1937 Lord Cecil of Chelwood (England)
1938 Office International Nansen pour les Réfugiés (Switzerland)
1939 No award
1944 International Red Cross
1945 Cordell Hull (U.S.)
1946 Emily G. Balch and John R. Mott (U.S.)
1947 American Friends Service Committee (U.S.) and British Society of Friends' Service Council (England)
1948 No award
1949 Lord John Boyd Orr (Scotland)
1950 Ralph J. Bunche (U.S.)
1951 Léon Jouhaux (France)
1952 Albert Schweitzer (French Equatorial Africa)
1953 George C. Marshall (U.S.)
1954 Office of U.N. High Commissioner for Refugees
1955 No award
1956 No award
1957 Lester B. Pearson (Canada)
1958 Rev. Dominique Georges Henri Pire (Belgium)
1959 Philip John Noel-Baker (England)
1960 Albert John Luthuli (South Africa)
1961 Dag Hammarskjöld (Sweden)
1962 Linus Pauling (U.S.)
1963 Intl. Comm. of Red Cross; League of Red Cross Societies (both Geneva)
1964 Rev. Dr. Martin Luther King, Jr. (U.S.)
1965 UNICEF (United Nations Children's Fund)
1966 No award
1967 No award
1968 René Cassin (France)
1969 International Labour Organization
1970 Norman E. Borlaug (U.S.)
1971 Willy Brandt (West Germany)
1972 No award
1973 Henry A. Kissinger (U.S.); Le Duc Tho (North Vietnam)[1]
1974 Eisaku Sato (Japan); Sean MacBride (Ireland)
1975 Andrei D. Sakharov (U.S.S.R.)
1976 Mairead Corrigan and Betty Williams (both Northern Ireland)
1977 Amnesty International
1978 Menachem Begin (Israel) and Anwar el-Sadat (Egypt)
1979 Mother Teresa of Calcutta (India)
1980 Adolfo Pérez Esquivel (Argentina)
1981 Office of the United Nations High Commissioner for Refugees
1982 Alva Myrdal (Sweden) and Alfonso García Robles (Mexico)
1983 Lech Walesa (Poland)
1984 Bishop Desmond Tutu (South Africa)
1985 International Physicians for the Prevention of Nuclear War
1986 Elie Wiesel (U.S.)

1. Le Duc Tho refused prize, charging that peace had not yet been really established in South Vietnam.

LITERATURE

1901 René F. A. Sully Prudhomme (France)
1902 Theodor Mommsen (Germany)
1903 Björnstjerne Björnson (Norway)
1904 Frédéric Mistral (France) and José Echegaray (Spain)
1905 Henryk Sienkiewicz (Poland)
1906 Giosuè Carducci (Italy)
1907 Rudyard Kipling (England)
1908 Rudolf Eucken (Germany)
1909 Selma Lagerlöf (Sweden)
1910 Paul von Heyse (Germany)
1911 Maurice Maeterlinck (Belgium)
1912 Gerhart Hauptmann (Germany)
1913 Rabindranath Tagore (India)
1915 Romain Rolland (France)
1916 Verner von Heidenstam (Sweden)
1917 Karl Gjellerup (Denmark) and Henrik Pontoppidan (Denmark)
1919 Carl Spitteler (Switzerland)
1920 Knut Hamsun (Norway)
1921 Anatole France (France)
1922 Jacinto Benavente (Spain)
1923 William B. Yeats (Ireland)
1924 Wladyslaw Reymont (Poland)
1925 George Bernard Shaw (England)
1926 Grazia Deledda (Italy)
1927 Henri Bergson (France)
1928 Sigrid Undset (Norway)
1929 Thomas Mann (Germany)
1930 Sinclair Lewis (U.S.)
1931 Erik A. Karlfeldt (Sweden)
1932 John Galsworthy (England)
1933 Ivan G. Bunin (Russia)
1934 Luigi Pirandello (Italy)
1935 No award
1936 Eugene O'Neill (U.S.)
1937 Roger Martin du Gard (France)
1938 Pearl S. Buck (U.S.)
1939 Frans Eemil Sillanpää (Finland)
1944 Johannes V. Jensen (Denmark)
1945 Gabriela Mistral (Chile)
1946 Hermann Hesse (Switzerland)
1947 André Gide (France)
1948 Thomas Stearns Eliot (England)
1949 William Faulkner (U.S.)
1950 Bertrand Russell (England)
1951 Pär Lagerkvist (Sweden)
1952 François Mauriac (France)
1953 Sir Winston Churchill (England)
1954 Ernest Hemingway (U.S.)
1955 Halldór Kiljan Laxness (Iceland)
1956 Juan Ramón Jiménez (Spain)
1957 Albert Camus (France)
1958 Boris Pasternak (U.S.S.R.) (declined)
1959 Salvatore Quasimodo (Italy)
1960 St-John Perse (Alexis St.-Léger Léger) (France)
1961 Ivo Andric (Yugoslavia)
1962 John Steinbeck (U.S.)
1963 Giorgios Seferis (Seferiades) (Greece)
1964 Jean-Paul Sartre (France) (declined)
1965 Mikhail Sholokhov (U.S.S.R.)
1966 Shmuel Yosef Agnon (Israel) and Nelly Sachs (Sweden)
1967 Miguel Angel Asturias (Guatemala)
1968 Yasunari Kawabata (Japan)
1969 Samuel Beckett (France)
1970 Aleksandr Solzhenitsyn (U.S.S.R.)
1971 Pablo Neruda (Chile)
1972 Heinrich Böll (Germany)
1973 Patrick White (Australia)
1974 Eyvind Johnson and Harry Martinson (both Sweden)
1975 Eugenio Montale (Italy)
1976 Saul Bellow (U.S.)
1977 Vicente Aleixandre (Spain)
1978 Isaac Bashevis Singer (U.S.)
1979 Odysseus Elytis (Greece)
1980 Czeslaw Milosz (U.S.)
1981 Elias Canetti (Bulgaria)
1982 Gabriel García Márquez (Colombia)
1983 William Golding (England)
1984 Jaroslav Seifert (Czechoslovakia)
1985 Claude Simon (France)
1986 Wole Soyinka (Nigeria)

PHYSICS

1901 Wilhelm K. Roentgen (Germany), for discovery of Roentgen rays
1902 Hendrik A. Lorentz and Pieter Zeeman (Netherlands), for work on influence of magnetism upon radiation
1903 A. Henri Becquerel (France), for work on spontaneous radioactivity; and Pierre and Marie Curie (France), for study of radiation
1904 John Strutt (Lord Rayleigh) (England), for discovery of argon in investigating gas density
1905 Philipp Lenard (Germany), for work with cathode rays
1906 Sir Joseph Thomson (England), for investigations on passage of electricity through gases
1907 Albert A. Michelson (U.S.), for spectroscopic and metrologic investigations
1908 Gabriel Lippmann (France), for method of reproducing colors by photography
1909 Guglielmo Marconi (Italy) and Ferdinand Braun (Germany), for development of wireless
1910 Johannes D. van der Waals (Netherlands), for work with the equation of state for gases and liquids
1911 Wilhelm Wien (Germany), for his laws governing the radiation of heat
1912 Gustaf Dalén (Sweden), for discovery of automatic regulators used in lighting lighthouses and light buoys
1913 Heike Kamerlingh-Onnes (Netherlands), for work leading to production of liquid helium
1914 Max von Laue (Germany), for discovery of diffraction of Roentgen rays passing through crystals
1915 Sir William Bragg and William L. Bragg (England), for analysis of crystal structure by X rays
1916 No award
1917 Charles G. Barkla (England), for discovery of Roentgen radiation of the elements
1918 Max Planck (Germany), discoveries in connection with quantum theory
1919 Johannes Stark (Germany), discovery of Doppler effect in Canal rays and decomposition of spectrum lines by electric fields
1920 Charles E. Guillaume (Switzerland), for discoveries of anomalies in nickel steel alloys
1921 Albert Einstein (Germany), for discovery of the law of the photoelectric effect
1922 Niels Bohr (Denmark), for investigation of structure of atoms and radiations emanating from them
1923 Robert A. Millikan (U.S.), for work on elementary charge of electricity and photoelectric phenomena
1924 Karl M. G. Siegbahn (Sweden), for investigations in X-ray spectroscopy
1925 James Franck and Gustav Hertz (Germany), for discovery of laws governing impact of electrons upon atoms
1926 Jean B. Perrin (France), for work on disconti-

nous structure of matter and discovery of the equilibrium of sedimentation

1927 Arthur H. Compton (U.S.), for discovery of Compton phenomenon; and Charles T. R. Wilson (England), for method of perceiving paths taken by electrically charged particles

1928 In 1929, the 1928 prize was awarded to Sir Owen Richardson (England), for work on the phenomenon of thermionics and discovery of the Richardson Law

1929 Prince Louis Victor de Broglie (France), for discovery of the wave character of electrons

1930 Sir Chandrasekhara Raman (India), for work on diffusion of light and discovery of the Raman effect

1931 No award

1932 In 1933, the prize for 1932 was awarded to Werner Heisenberg (Germany), for creation of the quantum mechanics

1933 Erwin Schrödinger (Austria) and Paul A. M. Dirac (England), for discovery of new fertile forms of the atomic theory

1934 No award

1935 James Chadwick (England), for discovery of the neutron

1936 Victor F. Hess (Austria), for discovery of cosmic radiation; and Carl D. Anderson (U.S.), for discovery of the positron

1937 Clinton J. Davisson (U.S.) and George P. Thomson (England), for discovery of diffraction of electrons by crystals

1938 Enrico Fermi (Italy), for identification of new radioactivity elements and discovery of nuclear reactions effected by slow neutrons

1939 Ernest Orlando Lawrence (U.S.), for development of the cyclotron

1943 Otto Stern (U.S.), for detection of magnetic momentum of protons

1944 Isidor Isaac Rabi (U.S.), for work on magnetic movements of atomic particles

1945 Wolfgang Pauli (Austria), for work on atomic fissions

1946 Percy Williams Bridgman (U.S.), for studies and inventions in high-pressure physics

1947 Sir Edward Appleton (England), for discovery of layer which reflects radio short waves in the ionosphere

1948 Patrick M. S. Blackett (England), for improvement on Wilson chamber and discoveries in cosmic radiation

1949 Hideki Yukawa (Japan), for mathematical prediction, in 1935, of the meson

1950 Cecil Frank Powell (England), for method of photographic study of atom nucleus, and for discoveries about mesons

1951 Sir John Douglas Cockcroft (England) and Ernest T. S. Walton (Ireland), for work in 1932 on transmutation of atomic nuclei

1952 Edward Mills Purcell and Felix Bloch (U.S.), for work in measurement of magnetic fields in atomic nuclei

1953 Fritz Zernike (Netherlands), for development of "phase contrast" microscope

1954 Max Born (England), for work in quantum mechanics; and Walther Bothe (Germany), for work in cosmic radiation

1955 Polykarp Kusch and Willis E. Lamb, Jr. (U.S.), for atomic measurements

1956 William Shockley, Walter H. Brattain, and John Bardeen (U.S.), for developing electronic transistor

1957 Tsung Dao Lee and Chen Ning Yang (China), for disproving principle of conservation of parity

1958 Pavel A. Cherenkov, Ilya M. Frank, and Igor E. Tamm (U.S.S.R.), for work resulting in development of cosmic-ray counter

1959 Emilio Segre and Owen Chamberlain (U.S.), for demonstrating the existence of the anti-proton

1960 Donald A. Glaser (U.S.), for invention of "bubble chamber" to study subatomic particles

1961 Robert Hofstadter (U.S.), for determination of shape and size of atomic nucleus; Rudolf Mössbauer (Germany), for method of producing and measuring recoil-free gamma rays

1962 Lev D. Landau (U.S.S.R.), for his theories about condensed matter

1963 Eugene Paul Wigner, Maria Goeppert Mayer (both U.S.), and J. Hans D. Jensen (Germany), for research on structure of atom and its nucleus

1964 Charles Hard Townes (U.S.), Nikolai G. Basov, and Aleksandr M. Prochorov (both U.S.S.R.), for developing maser and laser principle of producing high-intensity radiation

1965 Richard P. Feynman, Julian S. Schwinger (both U.S.), and Shinichiro Tomonaga (Japan), for research in quantum electrodynamics

1966 Alfred Kastler (France), for work on energy levels inside atom

1967 Hans A. Bethe (U.S.), for work on energy production of stars

1968 Luis Walter Alvarez (U.S.), for study of subatomic particles

1969 Murray Gell-Mann (U.S.), for study of subatomic particles

1970 Hannes Alfvén (Sweden), for theories in plasma physics; and Louis Néel (France), for discoveries in antiferromagnetism and ferrimagnetism

1971 Dennis Gabor (England), for invention of holographic method of three-dimensional imagery

1972 John Bardeen, Leon N. Cooper, and John Robert Schrieffer (all U.S.), for theory of superconductivity, where electrical resistance in certain metals vanishes above absolute zero temperature

1973 Ivar Giaever (U.S.), Leo Esaki (Japan), and Brian D. Josephson (U.K.), for theories that have advanced and expanded the field of miniature electronics

1974 Antony Hewish (England), for discovery of pulsars; Martin Ryle (England), for using radiotelescopes to probe outer space with high degree of precision

1975 James Rainwater (U.S.) and Ben Mottelson and Aage N. Bohr (both Denmark), for showing that the atomic nucleus is asymmetrical

1976 Burton Richter and Samuel C. C. Ting (both U.S.), for discovery of subatomic particles known as J and psi

1977 Philip W. Anderson and John H. Van Vleck (both U.S.), and Nevill F. Mott (U.K.), for work underlying computer memories and electronic devices

1978 Arno A. Penzias and Robert W. Wilson (both U.S.), for work in cosmic microwave radiation; Piotr L. Kapitsa (U.S.S.R.), for basic inventions and discoveries in low-temperature physics

1979 Steven Weinberg and Sheldon L. Glashow (both U.S.) and Abdus Salam (Pakistan), for developing theory that electromagnetism and the "weak" force, which causes radioactive decay in some atomic nuclei, are facets of the same phenomenon

1980 James W. Cronin and Val L. Fitch (both U.S.), for work concerning the assymetry of subatomic particles

1981 Nicolaas Bloembergen and Arthur L. Schawlow

(both U.S.) and Kai M. Siegbahn (Sweden), for developing technologies with lasers and other devices to probe the secrets of complex forms of matter

1982 Kenneth G. Wilson (U.S.), for analysis of changes in matter under pressure and temperature

1983 Subrahmanyam Chandrasekhar and William A. Fowler (both U.S.) for complementary research on processes involved in the evolution of stars

1984 Carlo Rubbia (Italy) and Simon van der Meer (Netherlands), for their role in discovering three subatomic particles, a step toward developing a single theory to account for all natural forces

1985 Klaus von Klitzing (Germany), for developing an exact way of measuring electrical conductivity

1986 Ernst Ruska, Gerd Binnig (both Germany) and Heinrich Rohrer (Switzerland) for work on microscopes

CHEMISTRY

1901 Jacobus H. van't Hoff (Netherlands), for laws of chemical dynamics and osmotic pressure in solutions

1902 Emil Fischer (Germany), for experiments in sugar and purin groups of substances

1903 Svante A. Arrhenius (Sweden), for his electrolytic theory of dissociation

1904 Sir William Ramsay (England), for discovery and determination of place of inert gaseous elements in air

1905 Adolf von Baeyer (Germany), for work on organic dyes and hydroaromatic combinations

1906 Henri Moissan (France), for isolation of fluorine, and introduction of electric furnace

1907 Eduard Buchner (Germany), discovery of cell-less fermentation and investigations in biological chemistry

1908 Sir Ernest Rutherford (England), for investigations into disintegration of elements

1909 Wilhelm Ostwald (Germany), for work on catalysis and investigations into chemical equilibrium and reaction rates

1910 Otto Wallach (Germany), for work in the field of alicyclic compounds

1911 Marie Curie (France), for discovery of elements radium and polonium

1912 Victor Grignard (France), for reagent discovered by him; and Paul Sabatier (France), for methods of hydrogenating organic compounds

1913 Alfred Werner (Switzerland), for linking up atoms within the molecule

1914 Theodore W. Richards (U.S.), for determining atomic weight of many chemical elements

1915 Richard Willstätter (Germany), for research into coloring matter of plants, especially chlorophyll

1916 No award

1917 No award

1918 Fritz Haber (Germany), for synthetic production of ammonia

1919 No award

1920 Walther Nernst (Germany), for work in thermochemistry

1921 Frederick Soddy (England), for investigations into origin and nature of isotopes

1922 Francis W. Aston (England), for discovery of isotopes in nonradioactive elements and for discovery of the whole number rule

1923 Fritz Pregl (Austria), for method of microanalysis of organic substances discovered by him

1924 No award

1925 In 1926, the 1925 prize was awarded to Richard Zsigmondy (Germany), for work on the heterogeneous nature of colloid solutions

1926 Theodor Svedberg (Sweden), for work on disperse systems

1927 In 1928, the 1927 prize was awarded to Heinrich Wieland (Germany), for investigations of bile acids and kindred substances

1928 Adolf Windaus (Germany), for investigations on constitution of the sterols and their connection with vitamins

1929 Sir Arthur Harden (England) and Hans K. A. S. von Euler-Chelpin (Sweden), for research of fermentation of sugars

1930 Hans Fischer (Germany), for work on coloring matter of blood and leaves and for his synthesis of hemin

1931 Karl Bosch and Friedrich Bergius (Germany), for invention and development of chemical high-pressure methods

1932 Irving Langmuir (U.S.), for work in realm of surface chemistry

1933 No award

1934 Harold C. Urey (U.S.), for discovery of heavy hydrogen

1935 Frédéric and Irène Joliot-Curie (France), for synthesis of new radioactive elements

1936 Peter J. W. Debye (Netherlands), for investigations on dipole moments and diffraction of X rays and electrons in gases

1937 Walter N. Haworth (England), for research on carbohydrates and Vitamin C; and Paul Karrer (Switzerland), for work on carotenoids, flavins, and Vitamins A and B

1938 Richard Kuhn (Germany), for carotinoid study and vitamin research (declined)

1939 Adolf Butenandt (Germany), for work on sexual hormones (declined the prize); and Leopold Ruzicka (Switzerland), for work with polymethylenes

1943 Georg Hevesy De Heves (Hungary), for work on use of isotopes as indicators

1944 Otto Hahn (Germany), for work on atomic fission

1945 Artturi Illmari Virtanen (Finland), for research in the field of conservation of fodder

1946 James B. Sumner (U.S.), for crystallizing enzymes; John H. Northrop and Wendell M. Stanley (U.S.), for preparing enzymes and virus proteins in pure form

1947 Sir Robert Robinson (England), for research in plant substances

1948 Arne Tiselius (Sweden), for biochemical discoveries and isolation of mouse paralysis virus

1949 William Francis Giauque (U.S.), for research in thermodynamics, especially effects of low temperature

1950 Otto Diels and Kurt Alder (Germany), for discovery of diene synthesis enabling scientists to study structure of organic matter

1951 Glenn T. Seaborg and Edwin H. McMillan (U.S.), for discovery of plutonium

1952 Archer John Porter Martin and Richard Laurence Millington Synge (England), for development of partition chromatography

1953 Hermann Staudinger (Germany), for research in giant molecules

1954 Linus C. Pauling (U.S.), for study of forces holding together protein and other molecules

1955 Vincent du Vigneaud (U.S.), for work on pituitary hormones
1956 Sir Cyril Hinshelwood (England) and Nikolai N. Semenov (U.S.S.R.), for parallel research on chemical reaction kinetics
1957 Sir Alexander Todd (England), for research with chemical compounds that are factors in heredity
1958 Frederick Sanger (England), for determining molecular structure of insulin
1959 Jaroslav Heyrovsky (Czechoslovakia), for development of polarography, an electrochemical method of analysis
1960 Willard F. Libby (U.S.), for "atomic time clock" to measure age of objects by measuring their radioactivity
1961 Melvin Calvin (U.S.), for establishing chemical steps during photosynthesis
1962 Max F. Perutz and John C. Kendrew (England), for mapping protein molecules with X-rays
1963 Carl Ziegler (Germany) and Giulio Natta (Italy), for work in uniting simple hydrocarbons into large molecule substances
1964 Dorothy Mary Crowfoot Hodgkin (England), for determining structure of compounds needed in combating pernicious anemia
1965 Robert B. Woodward (U.S.), for work in synthesizing complicated organic compounds
1966 Robert Sanderson Mulliken (U.S.), for research on bond holding atoms together in molecule
1967 Manfred Eigen (Germany), Ronald G. W. Norrish, and George Porter (both England), for work in high-speed chemical reactions
1968 Lars Onsager (U.S.), for development of system of equations in thermodynamics
1969 Derek H. R. Barton (England) and Odd Hassel (Norway), for study of organic molecules
1970 Luis F. Leloir (Argentina), for discovery of sugar nucleotides and their role in biosynthesis of carbohydrates
1971 Gerhard Herzberg (Canada), for contributions to knowledge of electronic structure and geometry of molecules, particularly free radicals
1972 Christian Boehmer Anfinsen, Stanford Moore, and William Howard Stein (all U.S.), for pioneering studies in enzymes
1973 Ernst Otto Fischer (W. Germany) and Geoffrey Wilkinson (U.K.), for work that could solve problem of automobile exhaust pollution
1974 Paul J. Flory (U.S.), for developing analytic methods to study properties and molecular structure of long-chain molecules
1975 John W. Cornforth (Australia) and Vladimir Prelog (Switzerland), for research on structure of biological molecules such as antibiotics and cholesterol
1976 William N. Lipscomb, Jr. (U.S.), for work on the structure and bonding mechanisms of boranes
1977 Ilya Prigogine (Belgium), for contributions to nonequilibrium thermodynamics, particularly the theory of dissipative structures
1978 Peter Mitchell (U.K.), for contributions to the understanding of biological energy transfer
1979 Herbert C. Brown (U.S.) and Georg Wittig (West Germany), for developing a group of substances that facilitate very difficult chemical reactions
1980 Paul Berg and Walter Gilbert (both U.S.) and Frederick Sanger (England), for developing methods to map the structure and function of DNA, the substance that controls the activity of the cell
1981 Roald Hoffmann (U.S.) and Kenichi Fukui (Japan), for applying quantum-mechanics theories to predict the course of chemical reactions
1982 Aaron Klug (U.K.), for research in the detailed structures of viruses and components of life
1983 Henry Taube (U.S.), for research on how electrons transfer between molecules in chemical reactions
1984 R. Bruce Merrifield (U.S.) for research that revolutionized the study of proteins
1985 Herbert A. Hauptman and Jerome Karle (both U.S.) for their outstanding achievements in the development of direct methods for the determination of crystal structures
1986 Dudley R. Herschback, Yuan T. Lee (both U.S.), and John C. Polanyi (Canada) for their work on "reaction dynamics"

PHYSIOLOGY OR MEDICINE

1901 Emil A. von Behring (Germany), for work on serum therapy against diptheria
1902 Sir Ronald Ross (England), for work on malaria
1903 Niels R. Finsen (Denmark), for his treatment of lupus vulgaris with concentrated light rays
1904 Ivan P. Pavlov (U.S.S.R.), for work on the physiology of digestion
1905 Robert Koch (Germany), for work on tuberculosis
1906 Camillo Golgi (Italy) and Santiago Ramón y Cajal (Spain), for work on structure of the nervous system
1907 Charles L. A. Laveran (France), for work with protozoa in the generation of disease
1908 Paul Ehrlich (Germany), and Elie Metchnikoff (U.S.S.R.), for work on immunity
1909 Theodor Kocher (Switzerland), for work on the thyroid gland
1910 Albrecht Kossel (Germany), for achievements in the chemistry of the cell
1911 Allvar Gullstrand (Sweden), for work on the dioptrics of the eye
1912 Alexis Carrel (France), for work on vascular ligature and grafting of blood vessels and organs
1913 Charles Richet (France), for work on anaphylaxy
1914 Robert Bárány (Austria), for work on physiology and pathology of the vestibular system
1915-1918 No award
1919 Jules Bordet (Belgium), for discoveries in connection with immunity
1920 August Krogh (Denmark), for discovery of regulation of capillaries' motor mechanism
1921 No award
1922 In 1923, the 1922 prize was shared by Archibald V. Hill (England), for discovery relating to heat-production in muscles; and Otto Meyerhof (Germany), for correlation between consumption of oxygen and production of lactic acid in muscles
1923 Sir Frederick Banting (Canada) and John J. R. Macleod (Scotland), for discovery of insulin
1924 Willem Einthoven (Netherlands), for discovery of the mechanism of the electrocardiogram
1925 No award
1926 Johannes Fibiger (Denmark), for discovery of the Spiroptera carcinoma
1927 Julius Wagner-Jauregg (Austria), for use of malaria inoculation in treatment of dementia paralytica
1928 Charles Nicolle (France), for work on typhus exanthematicus

1929 Christiaan Eijkman (Netherlands), for discovery of the antineuritic vitamins; and Sir Frederick Hopkins (England), for discovery of growth-promoting vitamins
1930 Karl Landsteiner (U.S.), for discovery of human blood groups
1931 Otto H. Warburg (Germany), for discovery of the character and mode of action of the respiratory ferment
1932 Sir Charles Sherrington (England) and Edgar D. Adrian (U.S.), for discoveries of the function of the neuron
1933 Thomas H. Morgan (U.S.), for discoveries on hereditary function of the chromosomes
1934 George H. Whipple, George R. Minot, and William P. Murphy (U.S.), for discovery of liver therapy against anemias
1935 Hans Spemann (Germany), for discovery of the organizer-effect in embryonic development
1936 Sir Henry Dale (England) and Otto Loewi (Germany), for discoveries on chemical transmission of nerve impulses
1937 Albert Szent-Györgyi von Nagyrapolt (Hungary), for discoveries on biological combustion
1938 Corneille Heymans (Belgium), for determining importance of sinus and aorta mechanisms in the regulation of respiration
1939 Gerhard Domagk (Germany), for antibacterial effect of prontocilate
1943 Henrik Dam (Denmark) and Edward A. Doisy (U.S.), for analysis of Vitamin K
1944 Joseph Erlanger and Herbert Spencer Gasser (U.S.), for work on functions of the nerve threads
1945 Sir Alexander Fleming, Ernst Boris Chain, and Sir Howard Florey (England), for discovery of penicillin
1946 Herman J. Muller (U.S.), for hereditary effects of X-rays on genes
1947 Carl F. and Gerty T. Cori (U.S.), for work on animal starch metabolism; Bernardo A. Houssay (Argentina), for study of pituitary
1948 Paul Mueller (Switzerland), for discovery of insect-killing properties of DDT
1949 Walter Rudolf Hess (Switzerland), for research on brain control of body; and Antonio Caetano de Abreu Freire Egas Moniz (Portugal), for development of brain operation
1950 Philip S. Hench, Edward C. Kendall (both U.S.), and Tadeus Reichstein (Switzerland), for discoveries about hormones of adrenal cortex
1951 Max Theiler (South Africa), for development of anti-yellow-fever vaccine
1952 Selman A. Waksman (U.S.), for co-discovery of streptomycin
1953 Fritz A. Lipmann (Germany-U.S.) and Hans Adolph Krebs (Germany-England), for studies of living cells
1954 John F. Enders, Thomas H. Weller, and Frederick C. Robbins (U.S.), for work with cultivation of polio virus
1955 Hugo Theorell (Sweden), for work on oxidation enzymes
1956 Dickinson W. Richards, Jr., André F. Cournand (both U.S.), and Werner Forssmann (Germany), for new techniques in treating heart disease
1957 Daniel Bovet (Italy), for development of drugs to relieve allergies and relax muscles during surgery
1958 Joshua Lederberg (U.S.), for work with genetic mechanisms; George W. Beadie and Edward L. Tatum (U.S.), for discovering how genes transmit hereditary characteristics
1959 Severo Ochoa and Arthur Kornberg (U.S.), for discoveries related to compounds within chromosomes, which play a vital role in heredity
1960 Sir Macfarlane Burnet (Australia) and Peter Brian Medawar (England), for discovery of acquired immunological tolerance
1961 Georg von Bekesy (U.S.), for discoveries about physical mechanisms of stimulation within cochlea
1962 James D. Watson (U.S.), Maurice H. F. Wilkins, and Francis H. C. Crick (England), for determining structure of deoxyribonucleic acid (DNA)
1963 Alan Lloyd Hodgkin, Andrew Fielding Huxley (both England), and Sir John Carew Eccles (Australia), for research on nerve cells
1964 Konrad E. Bloch (U.S.) and Feodor Lynen (Germany), for research on mechanism and regulation of cholesterol and fatty acid metabolism
1965 François Jacob, André Lwolff, and Jacques Monod (France), for study of regulatory activities in body cells
1966 Charles Brenton Huggins (U.S.), for studies in hormone treatment of cancer of prostate; Francis Peyton Rous (U.S.), for discovery of tumor-producing viruses
1967 Haldan K. Hartline, George Wald, and Ragnar Granit (U.S.), for work on human eye
1968 Robert W. Holley, Har Gobind Khorana, and Marshall W. Nirenberg (U.S.), for studies of genetic code
1969 Max Delbruck, Alfred D. Hershey, and Salvador E. Luria (U.S.), for study of mechanism of virus infection in living cells
1970 Julius Axelrod (U.S.), Ulf S. von Euler (Sweden), and Sir Bernard Katz (England), for studies of how nerve impulses are transmitted within the body
1971 Earl W. Sutherland, Jr. (U.S.), for research on how hormones work
1972 Gerald M. Edelman (U.S.), and Rodney R. Porter (U.K.), for research on the chemical structure and nature of antibodies
1973 Karl von Frisch and Konrad Lorenz (Austria), and Nikolaas Tinbergen (Netherlands), for their studies of individual and social behavior patterns
1974 George E. Palade and Christian de Duve (both U.S.) and Albert Claude (Belgium), for contributions to understanding inner workings of living cells
1975 David Baltimore, Howard M. Temin, and Renato Dulbecco (all U.S.), for work in interaction between tumor viruses and genetic material of the cell
1976 Baruch S. Blumberg and D. Carleton Gajdusek (U.S.), for discoveries concerning new mechanisms for the origin and dissemination of infectious diseases
1977 Rosalyn S. Yalow, Roger C. L. Guillemin, and Andrew V. Schally (all U.S.), for research in role of hormones in chemistry of the body
1978 Daniel Nathans and Hamilton Smith (both U.S.) and Werner Arber (Switzerland), for discovery of restriction enzymes and their application to problems of molecular genetics
1979 Allan McLeod Cormack (U.S.) and Godfrey Newbold Hounsfield (England), for developing computed axial tomography (CAT scan) X-ray technique

1980 Baruj Benacerraf and George D. Snell (both U.S.) and Jean Dausset (France), for discoveries that explain how the structure of cells relates to organ transplants and diseases

1981 Roger W. Sperry and David H. Hubel (both U.S.) and Torsten N. Wiesel (Sweden), for studies vital to understanding the organization and functioning of the brain

1982 Sune Bergstrom and Bengt Samuelsson (Sweden) and John R. Vane (U.K.), for research in prostaglandins, a hormonelike substance involved in a wide range of illnesses

1983 Barbara McClintock (U.S.), for her discovery of mobile genes in the chromosomes of a plant that change the future generations of plants they produce

1984 Cesar Milstein (U.K./Argentina) Georges J.F. Kohler (West Germany), and Niels K. Jerne (U.K./Denmark) for their work in immunology

1985 Michael S. Brown and Joseph L. Goldstein (both U.S.) for their work which has drastically widened our understanding of the cholesterol metabolism and increased our possibilities to prevent and treat atherosclerosis and heart attacks

1986 Rita Levi-Montalcini (dual U.S./Italy) and Stanley Cohen (U.S.) for their contributions to the understanding of substances that influence cell growth

ECONOMIC SCIENCE

1969 Ragnar Frisch (Norway) and Jan Tinbergen (Netherlands), for work in econometrics (application of mathematics and statistical methods to economic theories and problems)

1970 Paul A. Samuelson (U.S.), for efforts to raise the level of scientific analysis in economic theory

1971 Simon Kuznets (U.S.), for developing concept of using a country's gross national product to determine its economic growth

1972 Kenneth J. Arrow (U.S.) and Sir John R. Hicks (U.K.), for theories that help to assess business risk and government economic and welfare policies

1973 Wassily Leontief (U.S.), for devising the input-output technique to determine how different sectors of an economy interact

1974 Gunnar Myrdal (Sweden) and Friedrich A. von Hayek (U.K.), for pioneering analysis of the interdependence of economic, social and institutional phenomena

1975 Leonid V. Kantorovich (U.S.S.R.) and Tjalling C. Koopmans (U.S.), for work on the theory of optimum allocation of resources

1976 Milton Friedman (U.S.), for work in consumption analysis and monetary history and theory, and for demonstration of complexity of stabilization policy

1977 Bertil Ohlin (Sweden) and James E. Meade (U.K.), for contributions to theory of international trade and international capital movements

1978 Herbert A. Simon (U.S.), for research into the decision-making process within economic organizations

1979 Sir Arthur Lewis (England) and Theodore Schultz (U.S.), for work on economic problems of developing nations

1980 Lawrence R. Klein (U.S.), for developing models for forecasting economic trends and shaping policies to deal with them

1981 James Tobin (U.S.), for analyses of financial markets and their influence on spending and saving by families and businesses

1982 George J. Stigler (U.S.), for work on government regulation in the economy and the functioning of industry

1983 Gerard Debreu (U.S.), in recognition of his work on the basic economic problem of how prices operate to balance what producers supply with what buyers want.

1984 Sir Richard Stone (U.K.), for his work to develop the systems widely used to measure the performance of national economics

1985 Franco Modigliani (U.S.) for his pioneering work in analyzing the behavior of household savers and the functioning of financial markets

1986 James M. Buchanan (U.S.) for his development of new methods for analyzing economic and political decision-making

Enrico Fermi Award

Named in honor of Enrico Fermi, the atomic pioneer, the $100,000 award is given in recognition of "exceptional and altogether outstanding" scientific and technical achievement in atomic energy.

1954 Enrico Fermi
1956 John von Neumann
1957 Ernest O. Lawrence
1958 Eugene P. Wigner
1959 Glenn T. Seaborg
1961 Hans A. Bethe
1962 Edward Teller
1963 J. Robert Oppenheimer
1964 Hyman G. Rickover
1966 Otto Hahn, Lise Meitner, and Fritz Strassman
1968 John A. Wheeler
1969 Walter H. Zinn
1970 Norris E. Bradbury
1971 Shields Warren and Stafford L. Warren
1972 Manson Benedict
1976 William L. Russell
1978 Harold M. Agnew and Wolfgang K.H. Panofsky
1980 Alvin M. Weinberg and Rudolf E. Peirls
1981 W. Bennett Lewis
1982 Herbert Anderson and Seth Neddermeyer
1983 Alexander Hollaender and John Lawrence
1984 Robert R. Wilson and Georges Vendryès
1985 Norman C. Rasmussen and Marshall N. Rosenblath
1986 Ernest D. Courant and M. Stanley Livingston

Poets Laureate of the United States

The post was established in 1985. Appointment is for a one-year term, but is renewable.

Robert Penn Warren	1986-1987
Richard Wilbur	1987

Motion Picture Academy Awards (Oscars)

1928

Picture: *Wings,* Paramount
Director: Frank Borzage, *Seventh Heaven;* Lewis Milestone, *Two Arabian Nights*
Actress: Janet Gaynor, *Seventh Heaven, Street Angel, Sunrise*
Actor: Emil Jannings, *The Way of All Flesh, The Last Command*

1929

Picture: *The Broadway Melody,* M-G-M
Director: Frank Lloyd, *The Divine Lady*
Actress: Mary Pickford, *Coquette*
Actor: Warner Baxter, *In Old Arizona*

1930

Picture: *All Quiet on the Western Front,* Universal
Director: Lewis Milestone, *All Quiet on the Western Front*
Actress: Norma Shearer, *The Divorcee*
Actor: George Arliss, *Disraeli*

1931

Picture: *Cimarron:* RKO Radio
Director: Norman Taurog, *Skippy*
Actress: Marie Dressler, *Min and Bill*
Actor: Lionel Barrymore, *A Free Soul*

1932

Picture: *Grand Hotel,* M-G-M
Director: Frank Borzage, *Bad Girl*
Actress: Helen Hayes, *The Sin of Madelon Claudet*
Actor: Fredric March, *Dr. Jekyll and Mr. Hyde,* and Wallace Beery, *The Champ*

1933

Picture: *Cavalcade,* Fox
Director: Frank Lloyd, *Cavalcade*
Actress: Katharine Hepburn, *Morning Glory*
Actor: Charles Laughton, *The Private Life of Henry VIII*

1934

Picture: *It Happened One Night,* Columbia
Director: Frank Capra, *It Happened One Night*
Actress: Claudette Colbert, *It Happened One Night*
Actor: Clark Gable, *It Happened One Night*

1935

Picture: *Mutiny on the Bounty,* M-G-M
Director: John Ford, *The Informer*
Actress: Bette Davis, *Dangerous*
Actor: Victor McLaglen, *The Informer*

1936

Picture: *The Great Ziegfeld,* M-G-M
Director: Frank Capra, *Mr. Deeds Goes to Town*
Actress: Luise Rainer, *The Great Ziegfeld*
Actor: Paul Muni, *The Story of Louis Pasteur*
Supporting Actress: Gale Sondergaard, *Anthony Adverse*
Supporting Actor: Walter Brennan, *Come and Get It*

1937

Picture: *The Life of Emile Zola,* Warner Bros.
Director: Leo McCarey, *The Awful Truth*
Actress: Luise Rainer, *The Good Earth*
Actor: Spencer Tracy, *Captains Courageous*
Supporting Actress: Alice Brady, *In Old Chicago*
Supporting Actor: Joseph Schildkraut, *The Life of Emile Zola*

1938

Picture: *You Can't Take It with You,* Columbia
Director: Frank Capra, *You Can't Take It with You*
Actress: Bette Davis, *Jezebel*
Actor: Spencer Tracy, *Boys Town*
Supporting Actress: Fay Bainter, *Jezebel*
Supporting Actor: Walter Brennan, *Kentucky*

1939

Picture: *Gone with the Wind,* Selznick-M-G-M
Director: Victor Fleming, *Gone with the Wind*
Actress: Vivien Leigh, *Gone with the Wind*
Actor: Robert Donat, *Goodbye, Mr. Chips*
Supporting Actress: Hattie McDaniel, *Gone with the Wind*
Supporting Actor: Thomas Mitchell, *Stagecoach*

1940

Picture: *Rebecca,* Selznick-UA
Director: John Ford, *The Grapes of Wrath*
Actress: Ginger Rogers, *Kitty Foyle*
Actor: James Stewart, *The Philadelphia Story*
Supporting Actress: Jane Darwell, *The Grapes of Wrath*
Supporting Actor: Walter Brennan, *The Westerner*

1941

Picture: *How Green Was My Valley,* 20th Century-Fox
Director: John Ford, *How Green Was My Valley*
Actress: Joan Fontaine, *Suspicion*
Actor: Gary Cooper, *Sergeant York*
Supporting Actress: Mary Astor, *The Great Lie*
Supporting Actor: Donald Crisp, *How Green Was My Valley*

1942

Picture: *Mrs. Miniver,* M-G-M
Director: William Wyler, *Mrs. Miniver*
Actress: Greer Garson, *Mrs. Miniver*
Actor: James Cagney, *Yankee Doodle Dandy*
Supporting Actress: Teresa Wright, *Mrs. Miniver*
Supporting Actor: Van Heflin, *Johnny Eager*

1943

Picture: *Casablanca,* Warner Bros.
Director: Michael Curtiz, *Casablanca*
Actress: Jennifer Jones, *The Song of Bernadette*
Actor: Paul Lukas, *Watch on the Rhine*
Supporting Actress: Katina Paxinou, *For Whom the Bell Tolls*
Supporting Actor: Charles Coburn, *The More the Merrier*

1944

Picture: *Going My Way,* Paramount
Director: Leo McCarey, *Going My Way*
Actress: Ingrid Bergman, *Gaslight*
Actor: Bing Crosby, *Going My Way*
Supporting Actress: Ethel Barrymore, *None But the Lonely Heart*
Supporting Actor: Barry Fitzgerald, *Going My Way*

1945

Picture: *The Lost Weekend,* Paramount
Director: Billy Wilder, *The Lost Weekend*
Actress: Joan Crawford, *Mildred Pierce*
Actor: Ray Milland, *The Lost Weekend*
Supporting Actress: Anne Revere, *National Velvet*
Supporting Actor: James Dunn, *A Tree Grows in Brooklyn*

1946

Picture: *The Best Years of Our Lives,* Goldwyn-RKO Radio
Director: William Wyler, *The Best Years of Our Lives*
Actress: Olivia de Havilland, *To Each His Own*
Actor: Fredric March, *The Best Years of Our Lives*
Supporting Actress: Anne Baxter, *The Razor's Edge*
Supporting Actor: Harold Russell, *The Best Years of Our Lives*

1947

Picture: *Gentleman's Agreement,* 20th Century-Fox
Director: Elia Kazan, *Gentleman's Agreement*
Actress: Loretta Young, *The Farmer's Daughter*
Actor: Ronald Colman, *A Double Life*
Supporting Actress: Celeste Holm, *Gentleman's Agreement*
Supporting Actor: Edmund Gwenn, *Miracle on 34th Street*

1948

Picture: *Hamlet,* Rank-Two Cities-U-I
Director: John Huston, *Treasure of Sierra Madre*
Actress: Jane Wyman, *Johnny Belinda*
Actor: Laurence Olivier, *Hamlet*
Supporting Actress: Claire Trevor, *Key Largo*
Supporting Actor: Walter Huston, *Treasure of Sierra Madre*

1949

Picture: *All the King's Men,* Rossen-Columbia
Director: Joseph L. Mankiewicz, *A Letter to Three Wives*
Actress: Olivia de Havilland, *The Heiress*
Actor: Broderick Crawford, *All the King's Men*
Supporting Actress: Mercedes McCambridge, *All the King's Men*
Supporting Actor: Dean Jagger, *Twelve O'Clock High*

1950

Picture: *All About Eve,* 20th Century-Fox
Director: Joseph L. Mankiewicz, *All About Eve*
Actress: Judy Holliday, *Born Yesterday*
Actor: José Ferrer, *Cyrano de Bergerac*
Supporting Actress: Josephine Hull, *Harvey*
Supporting Actor: George Sanders, *All About Eve*

1951

Picture: *An American in Paris,* M-G-M
Director: George Stevens, *A Place in the Sun*
Actress: Vivien Leigh, *A Streetcar Named Desire*
Actor: Humphrey Bogart, *The African Queen*
Supporting Actress: Kim Hunter, *A Streetcar Named Desire*
Supporting Actor: Karl Malden, *A Streetcar Named Desire*

1952

Picture: *The Greatest Show on Earth,* DeMille-Paramount
Director: John Ford, *The Quiet Man*
Actress: Shirley Booth, *Come Back, Little Sheba*
Actor: Gary Cooper, *High Noon*
Supporting Actress: Gloria Grahame, *The Bad and the Beautiful*
Supporting Actor: Anthony Quinn, *Viva Zapata!*

1953

Picture: *From Here to Eternity,* Columbia
Director: Fred Zinnemann, *From Here to Eternity*
Actress: Audrey Hepburn, *Roman Holiday*
Actor: William Holden, *Stalag 17*
Supporting Actress: Donna Reed, *From Here to Eternity*
Supporting Actor: Frank Sinatra, *From Here to Eternity*

1954

Picture: *On the Waterfront,* Horizon-American Corp., Columbia
Director: Elia Kazan, *On the Waterfront*
Actress: Grace Kelly, *The Country Girl*
Actor: Marlon Brando, *On the Waterfront*
Supporting Actress: Eva Marie Saint, *On the Waterfront*
Supporting Actor: Edmond O'Brien, *The Barefoot Contessa*

1955

Picture: *Marty,* Hecht and Lancaster, United Artists
Director: Delbert Mann, *Marty*
Actress: Anna Magnani, *The Rose Tattoo*
Actor: Ernest Borgnine, *Marty*
Supporting Actress: Jo Van Fleet, *East of Eden*
Supporting Actor: Jack Lemmon, *Mister Roberts*

1956

Picture: *Around the World in 80 Days,* Michael Todd Co., Inc.-U.A.
Director: George Stevens, *Giant*
Actress: Ingrid Bergman, *Anastasia*
Actor: Yul Brynner, *The King and I*
Supporting Actress: Dorothy Malone, *Written on the Wind*
Supporting Actor: Anthony Quinn, *Lust for Life*

1957

Picture: *The Bridge on the River Kwai,* Horizon Picture, Columbia
Director: David Lean, *The Bridge on the River Kwai*
Actress: Joanne Woodward, *The Three Faces of Eve*
Actor: Alec Guinness, *The Bridge on the River Kwai*
Supporting Actress: Miyoshi Umeki, *Sayonara*
Supporting Actor: Red Buttons, *Sayonara*

1958

Picture: *Gigi,* Arthur Freed Productions, Inc., M-G-M
Director: Vincente Minnelli, *Gigi*
Actress: Susan Hayward, *I Want to Live!*
Actor: David Niven, *Separate Tables*
Supporting Actress: Wendy Hiller, *Separate Tables*
Supporting Actor: Burl Ives, *The Big Country*

1959

Picture: *Ben-Hur,* M-G-M
Director: William Wyler, *Ben-Hur*
Actress: Simone Signoret, *Room at the Top*
Actor: Charlton Heston, *Ben-Hur*
Supporting Actress: Shelley Winters, *The Diary of Anne Frank*
Supporting Actor: Hugh Griffith, *Ben-Hur*

1960

Picture: *The Apartment,* Mirisch Co., Inc., United Artists
Director: Billy Wilder, *The Apartment*
Actress: Elizabeth Taylor, *Butterfield 8*
Actor: Burt Lancaster, *Elmer Gantry*
Supporting Actress: Shirley Jones, *Elmer Gantry*
Supporting Actor: Peter Ustinov, *Spartacus*

1961

Picture: *West Side Story,* Mirisch Pictures, Inc., and B and P Enterprises, Inc., United Artists

Director: Robert Wise and Jerome Robbins, *West Side Story*
Actress: Sophia Loren, *Two Women*
Actor: Maximillian Schell, *Judgment at Nuremberg*
Supporting Actress: Rita Moreno, *West Side Story*
Supporting Actor: George Chakiris, *West Side Story*

1962

Picture: *Lawrence of Arabia,* Horizon Pictures, Ltd.-Columbia
Director: David Lean, *Lawrence of Arabia*
Actress: Anne Bancroft, *The Miracle Worker*
Actor: Gregory Peck, *To Kill a Mockingbird*
Supporting Actress: Patty Duke, *The Miracle Worker*
Supporting Actor: Ed Begley, *Sweet Bird of Youth*

1963

Picture: *Tom Jones,* A Woodfall Production, UA-Lopert Pictures
Director: Tony Richardson, *Tom Jones*
Actress: Patricia Neal, *Hud*
Actor: Sidney Poitier, *Lilies of the Field*
Supporting Actress: Margaret Rutherford, *The V.I.P.s*
Supporting Actor: Melvyn Douglas, *Hud*

1964

Picture: *My Fair Lady,* Warner Bros.
Director: George Cukor, *My Fair Lady*
Actress: Julie Andrews, *Mary Poppins*
Actor: Rex Harrison, *My Fair Lady*
Supporting Actress: Lila Kedrova, *Zorba the Greek*
Supporting Actor: Peter Ustinov, *Topkapi*

1965

Picture: *The Sound of Music,* Argyle Enterprises Production, 20th Century-Fox
Director: Robert Wise, *The Sound of Music*
Actress: Julie Christie, *Darling*
Actor: Lee Marvin, *Cat Ballou*
Supporting Actress: Shelley Winters, *A Patch of Blue*
Supporting Actor: Martin Balsam, *A Thousand Clowns*

1966

Picture: *A Man for All Seasons,* Highland Films, Ltd., Production, Columbia
Director: Fred Zinnemann, *A Man for All Seasons*
Actress: Elizabeth Taylor, *Who's Afraid of Virginia Woolf?*
Actor: Paul Scofield, *A Man for All Seasons*
Supporting Actress: Sandy Dennis, *Who's Afraid of Virginia Woolf?*
Supporting Actor: Walter Matthau, *The Fortune Cookie*

1967

Picture: *In the Heat of the Night,* Mirisch Corp. Productions, United Artists
Director: Mike Nichols, *The Graduate*
Actress: Katharine Hepburn, *Guess Who's Coming to Dinner*
Actor: Rod Steiger, *In the Heat of the Night*
Supporting Actress: Estelle Parsons, *Bonnie and Clyde*
Supporting Actor: George Kennedy, *Cool Hand Luke*

1968

Picture: *Oliver!,* Columbia Pictures
Director: Sir Carol Reed, *Oliver!*
Actress: Katharine Hepburn, *The Lion in Winter* and Barbara Streisand, *Funny Girl*
Actor: Cliff Robertson, *Charly*
Supporting Actress: Ruth Gordon, *Rosemary's Baby*
Supporting Actor: Jack Albertson, *The Subject Was Roses*

1969

Picture: *Midnight Cowboy,* Jerome Hellman-John Schlesinger Production, United Artists
Director: John Schlesinger, *Midnight Cowboy*
Actress: Maggie Smith, *The Prime of Miss Jean Brodie*
Actor: John Wayne, *True Grit*
Supporting Actress: Goldie Hawn, *Cactus Flower*
Supporting Actor: Gig Young, *They Shoot Horses Don't They?*

1970

Picture: *Patton,* Frank McCarthy-Franklin J. Schaffner Production, 20th Century Fox
Director: Franklin J. Schaffner, *Patton*
Actress: Glenda Jackson, *Women in Love*
Actor: George C. Scott, *Patton*
Supporting Actress: Helen Hayes, *Airport*
Supporting Actor: John Mills, *Ryan's Daughter*

1971

Picture: *The French Connection,* D'Antoni Productions, 20th Century-Fox
Director: William Friedkin, *The French Connection*
Actress: Jane Fonda, *Klute*
Actor: Gene Hackman, *The French Connection*
Supporting Actress: Cloris Leachman, *The Last Picture Show*
Supporting Actor: Ben Johnson, *The Last Picture Show*

1972

Picture: *The Godfather,* Albert S. Ruddy Production, Paramount
Director: Bob Fosse, *Cabaret*
Actress: Liza Minnelli, *Cabaret*
Actor: Marlon Brando, *The Godfather*
Supporting Actress: Eileen Heckart, *Butterflies Are Free*
Supporting Actor: Joel Gray, *Cabaret*

1973

Picture: *The Sting,* Universal-Bill-Phillips-George Roy Hill Production, Universal
Director: George Roy Hill, *The Sting*
Actress: Glenda Jackson, *A Touch of Class*
Actor: Jack Lemmon, *Save the Tiger*
Supporting Actress: Tatum O'Neal, *Paper Moon*
Supporting Actor: John Houseman, *The Paper Chase*

1974

Picture: *The Godfather, Part II,* Coppola Co. Production, Paramount
Director: Francis Ford Coppola, *The Godfather, Part II*
Actress: Ellen Burstyn, *Alice Doesn't Live Here Anymore*
Actor: Art Carney, *Harry and Tonto*
Supporting Actress: Ingrid Bergman, *Murder on the Orient Express*
Supporting Actor: Robert De Niro, *The Godfather, Part II*

1975

Picture: *One Flew Over the Cuckoo's Nest,* Fantasy Films Production, United Artists
Director: Milos Forman, *One Flew Over the Cuckoo's Nest*
Actress: Louise Fletcher, *One Flew Over the Cuckoo's Nest*

Actor: Jack Nicholson, *One Flew Over the Cuckoo's Nest*
Supporting Actress: Lee Grant, *Shampoo*
Supporting Actor: George Burns, *The Sunshine Boys*

1976

Picture: *Rocky,* Robert Chartoff-Irwin Winkler Production, United Artists
Director: John G. Avildsen, *Rocky*
Actress: Faye Dunaway, *Network*
Actor: Peter Finch, *Network*
Supporting Actress: Beatrice Straight, *Network*
Supporting Actor: Jason Robards, *All the President's Men*

1977

Picture: *Annie Hall,* Jack Rollins-Charles H. Joffe Production, United Artists
Director: Woody Allen, *Annie Hall*
Actress: Diane Keaton, *Annie Hall*
Actor: Richard Dreyfuss, *The Goodbye Girl*
Supporting Actress: Vanessa Redgrave, *Julia*
Supporting Actor: Jason Robards, *Julia*

1978

Picture: *The Deer Hunter,* Michael Cimino Film Production, Universal
Director: Michael Cimino, *The Deer Hunter*
Actress: Jane Fonda, *Coming Home*
Actor: Jon Voight, *Coming Home*
Supporting Actress: Maggie Smith, *California Suite*
Supporting Actor: Christopher Walken, *The Deer Hunter*

1979

Picture: *Kramer vs. Kramer,* Stanley Jaffe Production, Columbia Pictures
Director: Robert Benton, *Kramer vs. Kramer*
Actress: Sally Field, *Norma Rae*
Actor: Dustin Hoffman, *Kramer vs. Kramer*
Supporting Actress: Meryl Streep, *Kramer vs. Kramer*
Supporting Actor: Melvyn Douglas, *Being There*

1980

Picture: *Ordinary People,* Wildwood Enterprises Production, Paramount
Director: Robert Redford, *Ordinary People*
Actress: Sissy Spacek, *Coal Miner's Daughter*
Actor: Robert De Niro, *Raging Bull*
Supporting Actress: Mary Steenburgen, *Melvin and Howard*
Supporting Actor: Timothy Hutton, *Ordinary People*

1981

Picture: *Chariots of Fire,* Enigma Productions, Ladd Company/Warner Bros.
Director: Warren Beatty, *Reds*
Actress: Katharine Hepburn, *On Golden Pond*
Actor: Henry Fonda, *On Golden Pond*
Supporting Actress: Maureen Stapleton, *Reds*
Supporting Actor: John Gielgud, *Arthur*

1982

Picture: *Gandhi,* Indo-British Films Production/Columbia
Director: Richard Attenborough, *Gandhi*
Actress: Meryl Streep, *Sophie's Choice*
Actor: Ben Kingsley, *Gandhi*
Supporting Actress: Jessica Lange, *Tootsie*
Supporting Actor: Louis Gossett, Jr., *An Officer and a Gentleman*

1983

Picture: *Terms of Endearment,* Paramount
Director: James L. Brooks, *Terms of Endearment*
Actress: Shirley MacLaine, *Terms of Endearment*
Actor: Robert Duvall, *Tender Mercies*
Supporting Actress: Linda Hunt, *The Year of Living Dangerously*
Supporting Actor: Jack Nicholson, *Terms of Endearment*

1984

Picture: *Amadeus,* Orion Pictures
Director: Milos Forman, *Amadeus*
Actress: Sally Field, *Places in the Heart*
Actor: F. Murray Abraham, *Amadeus*
Supporting Actress: Dame Peggy Ashcroft, *A Passage to India*
Supporting Actor: Haing S. Ngor, *The Killing Fields*

1985

Picture: *Out of Africa,* Universal
Director: Sydney Pollack, *Out of Africa*
Actress: Geraldine Page, *The Trip to Bountiful*
Actor: William Hurt, *Kiss of the Spider Woman*
Supporting Actress: Anjelica Huston, *Prizzi's Honor*
Supporting Actor: Don Ameche, *Cocoon*

1986

Picture: *Platoon,* Orion Pictures
Director: Oliver Stone, *Platoon*
Actress: Marlee Martin, *Children of a Lesser God*
Actor: Paul Newman, *The Color of Money*
Supporting Actress: Dianne Wiest, *Hannah and Her Sisters*
Supporting Actor: Michael Caine, *Hannah and Her Sisters*

Other Academy Awards for 1986

Art direction: *A Room With a View,* Gianni Quaranta and Brian Ackland-Snow
Cinematography: Chris Menges, *The Mission*
Costume design: Jenny Beavan and John Bright, *A Room With a View*
Documentary (feature): Tie. *Artie Shaw: Time is All You've Got* and *Down and Out in America;* **short subject:** *Women—For America, For the World*
Editing: Claire Simpson, *Platoon*
Foreign-language film: *The Assault,* The Netherlands
Makeup: Chris Walas and Stephan Dupuis, *The Fly*
Music (original score): Herbie Hancock, *Round Midnight*
Screenplay (original): Woody Allen,*Hannah and Her Sisters;* **adaptation:** Ruth Prawer Jhabvala, *A Room With a View*
Short subject (live-action): *Precious Images;* **(animated):** *A Greek Tragedy*
Song: "Take My Breath Away," Giorgio Moroder and Tom Whitlock from *Top Gun*
Sound: John (Doc) Wilkinson, Richard Rogers, Charles (Bud) Grenzbach, and Simon Kaye, *Platoon*
Sound-effects editing: Don Sharpe, *Aliens*
Visual effects: Robert Skotak, Stan Winston, John Richardson, and Suzanne Benson, *Aliens*
Irving Thalberg Award: Steven Spielberg
Honorary Award: Ralph Bellamy

National Society of Film Critics Awards, 1986

Best Film: *Blue Velvet,* David Lynch
Best Documentary: *Marlene,* Maximilian Schell
Best Actress: Chloe Webb, *Sid and Nancy*
Best Actor: Bob Hoskins, *Mona Lisa*
Best Supporting Actress: Dianne Wiest, *Hannah and Her Sisters*
Best Supporting Actor: Dennis Hopper, *Blue Velvet*
Best Director: David Lynch, *Blue Velvet*
Best Screenplay: *My Beautiful Laundrette,* Hanif Kureishi
Best Cinematography: Frederick Elmes, *Blue Velvet*

Poets Laureate of England

Edmund Spenser	1591–1599	Laurence Eusden	1718-1730	Alfred Lord Tennyson	1850-1892
Samuel Daniel	1599–1619	Colley Cibber	1730-1757	Alfred Austin	1896-1913
Ben Jonson	1619–1637	William Whitehead	1757-1785	Robert Bridges	1913-1930
William Davenant	1638–1668	Thomas Warton	1785-1790	John Masefield	1930-1967
John Dryden[1]	1670–1689	Henry James Pye	1790-1813	C. Day Lewis	1967-1972
Thomas Shadwell	1689–1692	Robert Southey	1813-1843	Sir John Betjeman	1972-1984
Nahum Tate	1692–1715	William Wordsworth	1843-1850	Ted Hughes	1984-
Nicholas Rowe	1715-1718				

1. First to bear the title officially. *Source: Encyclopaedia Britannica.*

George Foster Peabody Awards for Broadcasting, 1986

Radio

NBC Radio News, for the radio coverage of the attack on Tripoli, Libya.
Canadian Broadcasting Corporation radio network: *Paris: From Oscar Wilde to Jim Morrison*
Connecticut Public Radio: *One on One*
CBS News: *Newsmark: Where in the World Are We?*
WHAS, Louisville, Ky.: *A Disaster Called Schizophrenia*
Fine Arts Society of Indianapolis, for pioneering classical music on radio in the city and for promoting the understanding and appreciation of the fine arts and performing arts since 1969.

Television

WTMJ, Milwaukee: *Who's Behind the Wheel?*
WFAA, Dallas: *S.M.U. Investigation*
KPIX, San Francisco: *AIDS Lifeline*
CBS News: *Sunday Morning: Vladimir Horowitz*
MacNeil/Lehrer Productions and the **BBC:** *The Story of English*
WOED/Pittsburgh: *Anne of Green Gables*
Churchill Films and **ABC Entertainment:** *The Mouse and the Motorcycle*
Thames Television International and **D.L. Taffner, Ltd.:** *Unknown Chaplin*
WOED/Pittsburgh and **The National Geographic Society:** *The National Geographic Specials*
CBS News: *CBS Reports: The Vanishing Family—Crisis in Black America*
John F. Kennedy Center for the Performing Arts and **CBS Entertainment:** *1986 Kennedy Center Honors: A Celebration of the Performing Arts*
Thames Television International and WGBH, Boston: *Paradise Postponed*
NBC Entertainment: *The Cosby Show*
CBS Entertainment and **Garner-Duchow Productions:** *Promise*
Jim Henson and **The Muppets,** for 30 years of good, clean fun and outstanding television entertainment.
WSB, Atlanta: *The Boy King*
WCCO, Minneapolis: *Project Lifesaver*
WCVB, Boston: *A World of Difference*
ABC News: *This Week with David Brinkley*
Mrs. Dorothy Stimson Bullitt of King Broadcasting, Seattle, a personal award in appreciation for the continuation of her exemplary family-owned broadcast enterprise.

Awards of the Society of Professional Journalists, 1986

(Sigma Delta Chi)

General reporting: Thomas J. Maier and Rex Smith, *Newsday* (circulation more than 100,000); Kent Steward, *The Hays* (Kan.) *Daily News* (circulation less than 100,000)
Editorial writing: Richard Doak, *The Des Moines Register*
Washington correspondence: Alfonso Chardy, *The Miami Herald*
Foreign correspondence: Juan O. Tamayo, *The Miami Herald*
News photography: Kim Komenich, *San Francisco Examiner*
Editorial cartooning: Michael Keefe, *The Denver Post*
Public service in newspaper journalism: *The Seattle Times* (circulation more than 100,000); Wilkes-Barre *Times Leader* (circulation less than 100,000)
Magazine reporting: Ken Case, *Third Coast,* magazine in Austin, Texas
Public service in magazine journalism: *Money* magazine
Radio spot-news reporting: Frederick J. Kennedy and Philip John Till, NBC Radio News
Public service in radio journalism: NBC Radio News
Editorializing on radio: Steve Smith, KNX-AM, Los Angeles
Television spot-news reporting: *The CBS Evening News*
Public service in television journalism: WCCO-TV, Minneapolis (stations in the top 50 markets); WBRZ-TV, Baton Rouge (stations in all other markets)
Editorializing on television: Michael Tuck, KGTV, San Diego
Research about journalism: David H. Weaver and G. Cleveland Wilhoit, Indiana University

Pulitzer Prize Awards

(For years not listed, no award was made.)

Source: Columbia University.

Pulitzer Prizes in Journalism

MERITORIOUS PUBLIC SERVICE

1918 *New York Times;* also special award to Minna Lewinson and Henry Beetle Hough
1919 *Milwaukee Journal*
1921 *Boston Post*
1922 *New York World*
1923 *Memphis Commercial Appeal*
1924 *New York World*
1926 *Columbus* (Ga.) *Enquirer Sun*
1927 *Canton* (Ohio) *Daily News*
1928 *Indianapolis Times*
1929 *New York Evening World*
1931 *Atlanta Constitution*
1932 *Indianapolis News*
1933 *New York World-Telegram*
1934 *Medford* (Ore.) *Mail Tribune*
1935 *Sacramento Bee*
1936 *Cedar Rapids* (Iowa) *Gazette*
1937 *St. Louis Post-Dispatch*
1938 *Bismarck* (N.D.) *Tribune*
1939 *Miami Daily News*
1940 *Waterbury* (Conn.) *Republican* and *American*
1941 *St. Louis Post-Dispatch*
1942 *Los Angeles Times*
1943 *Omaha World-Herald*
1944 *New York Times*
1945 *Detroit Free Press*
1946 *Scranton* (Pa.) *Times*
1947 *Baltimore Sun*
1948 *St. Louis Post-Dispatch*
1949 (Lincoln) *Nebraska State Journal*
1950 *Chicago Daily News;* and *St. Louis Post-Dispatch*
1951 *Miami Herald;* and *Brooklyn Eagle*
1952 *St. Louis Post-Dispatch*
1953 *Whiteville* (N.C.) *News Reporter;* and *Tabor City* (N.C.) *Tribune*
1954 *Newsday* (Garden City, L.I.)
1955 *Columbus* (Ga.) *Ledger* and *Sunday Ledger-Enquirer*
1956 *Watsonville* (Calif.) *Register-Pajaronian*
1957 *Chicago Daily News*
1958 (Little Rock) *Arkansas Gazette*
1959 *Utica* (N.Y.) *Observer Dispatch* and *Utica Daily Press*
1960 *Los Angeles Times*
1961 *Amarillo* (Tex.) *Globe-Times*
1962 *Panama City* (Fla.) *News-Herald*
1963 *Chicago Daily News*
1964 *St. Petersburg* (Fla.) *Times*
1965 *Hutchinson* (Kan.) *News*
1966 *Boston Globe*
1967 *Louisville Courier-Journal* and *Milwaukee Journal*
1968 *Riverside* (Calif.) *Press-Enterprise*
1969 *Los Angeles Times*
1970 *Newsday* (Garden City, L.I.)
1971 *Winston-Salem* (N.C.) *Journal and Sentinel*
1972 *New York Times*
1973 *Washington Post*
1974 *Newsday* (Garden City, L.I.)
1975 *Boston Globe*
1976 *Anchorage* (Alaska) *Daily News*
1977 *Lufkin* (Tex.) *News*
1978 *Philadelphia Inquirer*
1979 *Point Reyes* (Calif.) *Light*
1980 Gannett News Service
1981 *Charlotte* (N.C.) *Observer*
1982 *Detroit News*
1983 *Jackson* (Miss.) *Clarion-Ledger*
1984 *Los Angeles Times*
1985 *The Fort Worth Star-Telegram*
1986 *Denver Post*
1987 Andrew Schneider and Matthew Brelis, *Pittsburgh Press*

EDITORIAL

1917 *New York Tribune*
1918 *Louisville Courier-Journal*
1920 Harvey E. Newbranch *(Omaha Evening World-Herald)*
1922 Frank M. O'Brien *(New York Herald)*
1923 William Allen White *(Emporia* [Kan.] *Gazette)*
1924 *Boston Herald* (Frank Buxton); special prize: Frank I. Cobb *(New York World)*
1925 *Charleston* (S.C.) *News and Courier*
1926 *New York Times* (Edward M. Kingsbury)
1927 *Boston Herald* (F. Lauriston Bullard)
1928 Grover Cleveland Hall *(Montgomery* [Ala.] *Advertiser)*
1929 Louis Isaac Jaffe *(Norfolk Virginian-Pilot)*
1931 Charles S. Ryckman *(Fremont* [Neb.] *Tribune)*
1933 *Kansas City* (Mo.) *Star*
1934 E. P. Chase *(Atlantic* [Iowa] *News Telegraph)*
1936 Felix Morley *(Washington Post);* George B. Parker (Scripps-Howard Newspapers)
1937 John W. Owens *(Baltimore Sun)*
1938 W. W. Waymack *(Des Moines Register and Tribune)*
1939 Ronald G. Callvert *(Portland Oregonian)*
1940 Bart Howard *(St. Louis Post-Dispatch)*
1941 Reuben Maury *(New York Daily News)*
1942 Geoffrey Parsons *(New York Herald Tribune)*
1943 Forrest W. Seymour *(Des Moines Register and Tribune)*
1944 *Kansas City* (Mo.) *Star* (Henry J. Haskell)
1945 George W. Potter *(Providence* [R.I.] *Journal-Bulletin)*
1946 Hodding Carter ([Greenville, Miss.] *Delta Democrat-Times*)
1947 William H. Grimes *(Wall Street Journal)*
1948 Virginius Dabney *(Richmond Times-Dispatch)*
1949 John H. Crider *(Boston Herald);* Herbert Elliston *(Washington Post)*
1950 Carl M. Saunders *(Jackson* [Mich.] *Citizen Patriot)*
1951 William H. Fitzpatrick *(New Orleans States)*
1952 Louis LaCoss *(St. Louis Globe-Democrat)*
1953 Vermont C. Royster *(Wall Street Journal)*
1954 *Boston Herald* (Don Murray)
1955 *Detroit Free Press* (Royce Howes)
1956 Lauren K. Soth *(Des Moines Register and Tribune)*
1957 Buford Boone *(Tuscaloosa* [Ala.] *News)*
1958 Harry S. Ashmore *(Arkansas Gazette)*
1959 Ralph McGill *(Atlanta Constitution)*
1960 Lenoir Chambers *(Virginian-Pilot)*
1961 William J. Dorvillier *(San Juan* [P.R.] *Star)*
1962 Thomas M. Storke *(Santa Barbara* [Calif.] *News-Press)*

1963 Ira B. Harkey, Jr. *(Pascagoula* [Miss.] *Chronicle)*
1964 Hazel Brannon Smith *(Lexington* [Miss.] *Advertiser)*
1965 John R. Harrison *(Gainesville* [Fla.] *Daily Sun)*
1966 Robert Lasch *(St. Louis Post-Dispatch)*
1967 Eugene Patterson *(Atlanta Constitution)*
1968 John S. Knight (Knight Newspapers)
1969 Paul Greenberg *(Pine Bluff* [Ark.] *Commercial)*
1970 Phillip L. Geyelin *(Washington Post)*
1971 Horance G. Davis, Jr. *(Gainesville* [Fla.] *Sun)*
1972 John Strohmeyer *(Bethlehem* [Pa.] *Globe Times)*
1973 Roger Bourne Linscott *(Berkshire Eagle* [Pittsfield, Mass.])
1974 F. Gilman Spencer *(Trenton* [N.J.] *Trentonian)*
1975 John Daniell Maurice *(Charleston* [W. Va.] *Daily Mail)*
1976 Philip P. Kerby *(Los Angeles Times)*
1977 Warren L. Lerude, Foster Church and Norman F. Cardoza *(Reno* [Nev.] *Gazette* and *Nevada State Journal)*
1978 Meg Greenfield *(Washington Post)*
1979 Edwin M. Yoder, Jr. *(Washington Star)*
1980 Robert L. Bartley *(Wall Street Journal)*
1981 Not awarded
1982 Jack Rosenthal *(New York Times)*
1983 *Miami Herald*
1984 Albert Scardino *(Georgia Gazette)*
1985 Richard Aregood (*Philadelphia Daily News*)
1986 Jack Fuller *(Chicago Tribune)*
1987 Jonathan Freedman *(San Diego Tribune)*

CORRESPONDENCE

1929 Paul Scott Mowrer *(Chicago Daily News)*
1930 Leland Stowe *(New York Herald Tribune)*
1931 H. R. Knickerbocker *(Philadelphia Public Ledger* and *New York Evening Post)*
1932 Walter Duranty *(New York Times);* Charles G. Ross *(St. Louis Post-Dispatch)*
1933 Edgar Ansel Mowrer *(Chicago Daily News)*
1934 Frederick T. Birchall *(New York Times)*
1935 Arthur Krock *(New York Times)*
1936 Wilfred C. Barber *(Chicago Tribune)*
1937 Anne O'Hare McCormick *(New York Times)*
1938 Arthur Krock *(New York Times)*
1939 Louis P. Lochner (Associated Press)
1940 Otto D. Tolischus *(New York Times)*
1941 Group award[1]
1942 Carlos P. Romulo *(Philippines Herald)*
1943 Hanson W. Baldwin *(New York Times)*
1944 Ernie Pyle (Scripps-Howard Newspaper Alliance)
1945 Harold V. (Hal) Boyle (Associated Press)
1946 Arnaldo Cortesi *(New York Times)*
1947 Brooks Atkinson *(New York Times)*
1948 Discontinued

EDITORIAL CARTOONING

1922 Rollin Kirby *(New York World)*
1924 Jay Norwood Darling *(New York Tribune)*
1925 Rollin Kirby *(New York World)*
1926 D. R. Fitzpatrick *(St. Louis Post-Dispatch)*
1927 Nelson Harding *(Brooklyn Eagle)*
1928 Nelson Harding *(Brooklyn Eagle)*
1929 Rollin Kirby *(New York World)*
1930 Charles R. Macauley *(Brooklyn Eagle)*
1931 Edmund Duffy *(Baltimore Sun)*
1932 John T. McCutcheon *(Chicago Tribune)*
1933 H. M. Talburt *(Washington Daily News)*
1934 Edmund Duffy *(Baltimore Sun)*
1935 Ross A. Lewis *(Milwaukee Journal)*
1937 C. D. Batchelor *(New York Daily News)*
1938 Vaughn Shoemaker *(Chicago Daily News)*
1939 Charles G. Werner *(Daily Oklahoman* [Oklahoma City])
1940 Edmund Duffy *(Baltimore Sun)*
1941 Jacob Burck *(Chicago Times)*
1942 Herbert L. Block (NEA Service)
1943 Jay Norwood Darling *(New York Herald Tribune)*
1944 Clifford K. Berryman *(Washington Evening Star)*
1945 Bill Mauldin (United Features Syndicate)
1946 Bruce Alexander Russell *(Los Angeles Times)*
1947 Vaughn Shoemaker *(Chicago Daily News)*
1948 Reuben L. Goldberg *(New York Sun)*
1949 Lute Pease *(Newark Evening News)*
1950 James T. Berryman *(Washington Evening Star)*
1951 Reg (Reginald W.) Manning (*Arizona Republic* [Phoenix])
1952 Fred L. Packer *(New York Mirror)*
1953 Edward D. Kuekes *(Cleveland Plain Dealer)*
1954 Herbert L. Block *(Washington Post* and *Times-Herald)*
1955 Daniel R. Fitzpatrick *(St. Louis Post-Dispatch)*
1956 Robert York *(Louisville Times)*
1957 Tom Little *(Nashville Tennessean)*
1958 Bruce M. Shanks *(Buffalo Evening News)*
1959 Bill Mauldin *(St. Louis Post-Dispatch)*
1961 Carey Orr *(Chicago Tribune)*
1962 Edmund S. Valtman *(Hartford Times)*
1963 Frank Miller *(Des Moines Register)*
1964 Paul Conrad (formerly of *Denver Post,* later on *Los Angeles Times*)
1966 Don Wright *(Miami News)*
1967 Patrick B. Oliphant *(Denver Post)*
1968 Eugene Gray Payne *(Charlotte* [N.C.] *Observer)*
1969 John Fischetti *(Chicago Daily News)*
1970 Thomas F. Darcy (*Newsday* [Garden City, L.I.])
1971 Paul Conrad *(Los Angeles Times)*
1972 Jeffrey K. MacNelly *(Richmond* [Va.] *News Leader)*
1974 Paul Szep *(Boston Globe)*
1975 Garry Trudeau (Universal Press Syndicate)
1976 Tony Auth *(Philadelphia Inquirer)*
1977 Paul Szep *(Boston Globe)*
1978 Jeffrey K. MacNelly *(Richmond* [Va.] *News Leader)*
1979 Herbert L. Block *(Washington Post)*
1980 Don Wright *(Miami News)*
1981 Mike Peters *(Dayton* [Ohio] *Daily News)*
1982 Ben Sargent *(Austin* [Tex.] *American-Statesman)*
1983 Richard Locher *(Chicago Tribune)*
1984 Paul Conrad *(Los Angeles Times)*
1985 Jeff MacNelly (*Chicago Tribune*)
1986 Jules Feiffer *(Village Voice)*
1987 Berke Breathed (*Washington Post* Writers Group)

NEWS PHOTOGRAPHY

1942 Milton Brooks *(Detroit News)*
1943 Frank Noel (Associated Press)
1944 Frank Filan (Associated Press); Earle L. Bunker *(Omaha World-Herald)*
1945 Joe Rosenthal (Associated Press)
1947 Arnold Hardy
1948 Frank Cushing *(Boston Traveler)*
1949 Nat Fein *(New York Herald Tribune)*
1950 Bill Crouch *(Oakland Tribune)*
1951 Max Desfor (Associated Press)
1952 John Robinson and Don Ultang *(Des Moines Register & Tribune)*

1. For the public services and the individual achievements of American news reporters in the war zones.

1953 William M. Gallagher *(Flint* [Mich.] *Journal)*
1954 Mrs. Walter M. Schau
1955 John L. Gaunt, Jr. *(Los Angeles Times)*
1956 *New York Daily News*
1957 Harry A. Trask *(Boston Traveler)*
1958 William C. Beall *(Washington Daily News)*
1959 William Seaman *(Minneapolis Star)*
1960 Andrew Lopez (United Press International)
1961 Yasushi Nagao (Mainichi Newspapers, Tokyo)
1962 Paul Vathis (Harrisburg [Pa.] bureau of Associated Press)
1963 Hector Rondon (*La Republica,* Caracas, Venezuela)
1964 Robert H. Jackson *(Dallas Times Herald)*
1965 Horst Faas (Associated Press)
1966 Kyoichi Sawada (United Press International)
1967 Jack R. Thornell (Associated Press)
1968 News: Rocco Morabito *(Jacksonville* [Fla.] *Journal);* features: Toshio Sakai (United Press International)
1969 Spot news: Edward T. Adams (Associated Press); features: Moneta Sleet, Jr.
1970 Spot news: Steve Starr (Associated Press); features: Dallas Kinney *(Palm Beach Post)*
1971 Spot news: John Paul Filo (*Valley Daily News and Daily Dispatch* [Tarentum and New Kensington, Pa.]); features: Jack Dykinga *(Chicago Sun-Times)*
1972 Spot news: Horst Faas and Michel Laurent (Associated Press); features: Dave Kennerly (United Press International)
1973 Spot news: Huynh Cong Ut *(Associated Press);* features: Brian Lanker *(Topeka Capital-Journal)*
1974 Spot news: Anthony K. Roberts (Associated Press); features: Slava Veder (Associated Press)
1975 Spot news: Gerald H. Gay *(Seattle Times);* features: Matthew Lewis *(Washington Post)*
1976 Spot news: Stanley J. Forman *(Boston Herald-American);* features: photographic staff of *Louisville Courier-Journal* and *Times*
1977 Spot news: Neal Ulevich (Associated Press) and Stanley J. Forman *(Boston Herald-American);* features: Robin Hood *(Chattanooga News-Free Press)*
1978 Spot news: John Blair, freelance, Evansville, Ind.; features: J. Ross Baughman (Associated Press)
1979 Spot news: Thomas J. Kelly, 3rd *(Pottstown* [Pa.] *Mercury);* features: photographic staff of *Boston Herald-American*
1980 Features: Erwin H. Hagler *(Dallas Times Herald)*
1981 Spot news: Larry C. Price *(Fort Worth Star-Telegram);* features: Taro M. Yamasaki *(Detroit Free Press)*
1982 Spot news: Ron Edmonds (Associated Press); features: John H. White *(Chicago Sun-Times)*
1983 Spot news: Bill Foley (Associated Press); features: James B. Dickman *(Dallas Times Herald)*
1984 Spot news: Stan Grossfeld *(Boston Globe);* features: Anthony Suau *(Denver Post)*
1985 Spot news: photographic staff of *Register,* Santa Ana, Calif.; features: Stan Grossfeld (*Boston Globe*)
1986 Spot news: Michel duCille and Carol Guzy *(Miami Herald);* features: Tom Gralish *(Philadelphia Inquirer)*
1987 Spot news: Kim Komenich *(San Francisco Examiner);* features: David Peterson *(Des Moines Register)*

NATIONAL TELEGRAPHIC REPORTING

1942 Louis Stark *(New York Times)*
1944 Dewey L. Fleming *(Baltimore Sun)*
1945 James Reston *(New York Times)*
1946 Edward A. Harris *(St. Louis Post-Dispatch)*
1947 Edward T. Folliard *(Washington Post)*

NATIONAL REPORTING

1948 Bert Andrews *(New York Herald Tribune);* Nat S. Finney *(Minneapolis Tribune)*
1949 C. P. Trussel *(New York Times)*
1950 Edwin O. Guthman *(Seattle Times)*
1952 Anthony Leviero *(New York Times)*
1953 Don Whitehead (Associated Press)
1954 Richard Wilson (Cowles Newspapers)
1955 Anthony Lewis *(Washington Daily News)*
1956 Charles L. Bartlett *(Chattanooga Times)*
1957 James Reston *(New York Times)*
1958 Relman Morin (Associated Press) and Clark Mollenhoff *(Des Moines Register & Tribune)*
1959 Howard Van Smith *(Miami News)*
1960 Vance Trimble (Scripps-Howard Newspaper Alliance)
1961 Edward R. Cony *(Wall Street Journal)*
1962 Nathan G. Caldwell and Gene S. Graham *(Nashville Tennessean)*
1963 Anthony Lewis *(New York Times)*
1964 Merriman Smith (United Press International)
1965 Louis M. Kohlmeier *(Wall Street Journal)*
1966 Haynes Johnson *(Washington Evening Star)*
1967 Stanley Penn and Monroe Karmin *(Wall Street Journal)*
1968 Howard James *(Christian Science Monitor);* Nathan K. (Nick) Kotz *(Des Moines Register* and *Minneapolis Tribune)*
1969 Robert Cahn *(Christian Science Monitor)*
1970 William J. Eaton *(Chicago Daily News)*
1971 Lucinda Franks and Thomas Powers (United Press International)
1972 Jack Anderson *(United Feature Syndicate)*
1973 Robert Boyd and Clark Hoyt *(Knight Newspapers)*
1974 Jack White *(Providence* [R.I.] *Journal-Bulletin);* and James R. Polk *(Washington Star-News)*
1975 Donald L. Barlett and James B. Steele *(Philadelphia Inquirer)*
1976 James Risser *(Des Moines Register)*
1977 Walter Mears (Associated Press)
1978 Gaylord D. Shaw *(Los Angeles Times)*
1979 James Risser *(Des Moines Register)*
1980 Bette Swenson Orsini and Charles Stafford *(St. Petersburg Times)*
1981 John M. Crewdson *(New York Times)*
1982 Rick Atkinson *(Kansas City* [Mo.] *Times)*
1983 *Boston Globe*
1984 John N. Wilford *(New York Times)*
1985 Thomas J. Knudson (*Des Moines Register*)
1986 Craig Flournoy and George Rodrigue *(Dallas Morning News)* and Arthur Howe *(Philadelphia Inquirer)*
1987 *Miami Herald,* staff; *New York Times,* staff

INTERNATIONAL TELEGRAPHIC REPORTING

1942 Laurence Edmund Allen (Associated Press)
1943 Ira Wolfert (North American Newspaper Alliance, Inc.)
1944 Daniel De Luce (Associated Press)
1945 Mark S. Watson *(Baltimore Sun)*
1946 Homer W. Bigart *(New York Herald Tribune)*

1947 Eddy Gilmore (Associated Press)

INTERNATIONAL REPORTING

1948 Paul W. Ward *(Baltimore Sun)*
1949 Price Day *(Baltimore Sun)*
1950 Edmund Stevens *(Christian Science Monitor)*
1951 Keyes Beech and Fred Sparks *(Chicago Daily News);* Homer Bigart and Marguerite Higgins *(New York Herald Tribune);* Relman Morin and Don Whitehead (Associated Press)
1952 John M. Hightower (Associated Press)
1953 Austin C. Wehrwein *(Milwaukee Journal)*
1954 Jim G. Lucas (Scripps-Howard Newspapers)
1955 Harrison E. Salisbury *(New York Times)*
1956 William Randolph Hearst, Jr. and Frank Conniff (Hearst Newspapers) and Kingsbury Smith (INS)
1957 Russell Jones (United Press)
1958 *New York Times*
1959 Joseph Martin and Philip Santora *(New York Daily News)*
1960 A. M. Rosenthal *(New York Times)*
1961 Lynn Heinzerling (Associated Press)
1962 Walter Lippmann (New York Herald Tribune Syndicate)
1963 Hal Hendrix *(Miami News)*
1964 Malcolm W. Browne (Associated Press) and David Halberstam *(New York Times)*
1965 J. A. Livingston *(Philadelphia Bulletin)*
1966 Peter Arnett (Associated Press)
1967 R. John Hughes *(Christian Science Monitor)*
1968 Alfred Friendly *(Washington Post)*
1969 William Tuohy *(Los Angeles Times)*
1970 Seymour M. Hersh (Dispatch News Service)
1971 Jimmie Lee Hoagland *(Washington Post)*
1972 Peter R. Kann *(Wall Street Journal)*
1973 Max Frankel *(New York Times)*
1974 Hedrick Smith *(New York Times)*
1975 William Mullen and Ovie Carter *(Chicago Tribune)*
1976 Sydney H. Schanberg *(New York Times)*
1978 Henry Kamm *(New York Times)*
1979 Richard Ben Cramer *(Philadelphia Inquirer)*
1980 Joel Brinkley and Jay Mather *(Louisville Courier-Journal)*
1981 Shirley Christian *(Miami Herald)*
1982 John Darnton *(New York Times)*
1983 Thomas L. Friedman *(New York Times)*
1984 Karen E. House *(Wall Street Journal)*
1985 Josh Friedman, Dennis Bell, and Ozier Muhammad *(Newsday)*
1986 Lewis M. Simons, Pete Carey, and Katherine Ellison *(San Jose Mercury News)*
1987 Michael Parks *(Los Angeles Times)*

REPORTING

1917 Herbert B. Swope *(New York World)*
1918 Harold A. Littledale *(New York Evening Post)*
1920 John J. Leary, Jr. *(New York World)*
1921 Louis Seibold *(New York World)*
1922 Kirke L. Simpson (Associated Press)
1923 Alva Johnston *(New York Times)*
1924 Magner White *(San Diego Sun)*
1925 James W. Mulroy and Alvin H. Goldstein *(Chicago Daily News)*
1926 William Burke Miller *(Louisville Courier-Journal)*
1927 John T. Rogers *(St. Louis Post-Dispatch)*
1929 Paul Y. Anderson *(St. Louis Post-Dispatch)*
1930 Russell D. Owen *(New York Times);* special award: W. O. Dapping *(Auburn* [N.Y.] *Citizen)*
1931 A. B. MacDonald *(Kansas City* [Mo.] *Star)*
1932 W. C. Richards, D. D. Martin, J. S. Pooler, F. D. Webb, J. N. W. Sloan (all of *Detroit Free Press)*
1933 Francis A. Jamieson (Associated Press)
1934 Royce Brier *(San Francisco Chronicle)*
1935 William H. Taylor *(New York Herald Tribune)*
1936 Lauren D. Lyman *(New York Times)*
1937 John J. O'Neill *(New York Herald Tribune);* William Leonard Laurence *(New York Times);* Howard W. Blakeslee (Associated Press); Gobind Behari Lal (Universal Service); David Dietz (Scripps-Howard Newspapers)
1938 Raymond Sprigle *(Pittsburg Post-Gazette)*
1939 Thomas L. Stokes *(New York World-Telegram)*
1940 S. Burton Heath *(New York World-Telegram)*
1941 Westbrook Pegler *(New York World-Telegram)*
1942 Stanton Delaplane *(San Francisco Chronicle)*
1943 George Weller *(Chicago Daily News)*
1944 Paul Schoenstein and associates *(New York Journal-American)*
1945 Jack S. McDowell *(San Francisco Call-Bulletin)*
1946 William Leonard Laurence *(New York Times)*
1947 Frederick Woltman *(New York World-Telegram)*
1948 George E. Goodwin *(Atlanta Journal)*
1949 Malcolm Johnson *(New York Sun)*
1950 Meyer Berger *(New York Times)*
1951 Edward S. Montgomery *(San Francisco Examiner)*
1952 George de Carvalho *(San Francisco Chronicle)*
1953 Editorial staff *(Providence Journal and Evening Bulletin);*[1] Edward J. Mowery *(New York World-Telegram and Sun)*[2]
1954 *Vicksburg* (Miss.) *Sunday Post-Herald;*[1] Alvin Scott McCoy *(Kansas City* [Mo.] *Star)*[2]
1955 Mrs. Caro Brown *(Alice* [Tex.] *Daily Echo);*[1] Roland Kenneth Towery *(Cuero* [Tex.] *Record)*[2]
1956 Lee Hills *(Detroit Free Press);*[1] Arthur Daley *(New York Times)*[2]
1957 *Salt Lake Tribune;*[1] Wallace Turner and William Lambert *(Portland Oregonian)*[2]
1958 *Fargo* [N.D.] *Forum;*[1] George Beveridge *(Washington* [D.C.] *Evening Star)*[2]
1959 Mary Lou Werner *(Washington* [D.C.] *Evening Star);*[1] John Harold Brislin *(Scranton* [Pa.] *Tribune & Scrantonian)*[2]
1960 Jack Nelson *(Atlanta Constitution);*[1] Miriam Ottenberg *(Washington Evening Star)*[2]
1961 Sanche de Gramont *(New York Herald Tribune);*[1] Edgar May *(Buffalo Evening News)*[2]
1962 Robert D. Mullins (*Deseret News,* Salt Lake City);[1] George Bliss *(Chicago Tribune)*[2]
1963 Sylvan Fox, Anthony Shannon, and William Longgood *(New York World-Telegram and Sun);*[1] Oscar Griffin, Jr. (former editor of *Pecos* [Tex.] *Independent and Enterprise,* now on staff of *Houston Chronicle*)[2]

GENERAL LOCAL REPORTING

1964 Norman C. Miller *(Wall Street Journal)*
1965 Melvin H. Ruder (*Hungry Horse News,* Columbia Falls, Mont.)
1966 Staff of *Los Angeles Times*
1967 Robert V. Cox *(Chambersburg* [Pa.] *Public Opinion)*
1968 Staff of *Detroit Free Press*
1969 John Fetterman *(Louisville Times* and *Courier-Journal)*
1970 Thomas Fitzpatrick *(Chicago Sun-Times)*
1971 Staff of *Akron* (Ohio) *Beacon*

1. Reporting under pressure of edition deadlines. 2. Reporting not under pressure of edition deadlines.

1972 Richard Cooper and John Machacek *(Rochester* [N.Y.] *Times-Union)*
1973 *Chicago Tribune*
1974 Arthur M. Petacque and Hugh F. Hough *(Chicago Sun-Times)*
1975 *Xenia* (Ohio) *Daily Gazette*
1976 Gene Miller *(Miami Herald)*
1977 Margo Huston *(Milwaukee Journal)*
1978 Richard Whitt *(Louisville Courier-Journal)*
1979 Staff of *San Diego* (Calif.) *Evening Tribune*
1980 Staff of *Philadelphia Inquirer*
1981 *Longview* (Wash.) *Daily News*
1982 *Kansas City* (Mo.) *Star* and *Kansas City* (Mo.) *Times*
1983 *Fort Wayne* (Ind.) *News-Sentinel*
1984 *Newsday*

GENERAL NEWS REPORTING

1985 Thomas Turcol (*Virginian-Pilot and Ledger-Star*)
1986 Edna Buchanan *(Miami Herald)*
1987 *Akron Beacon Journal,* staff

SPECIAL LOCAL REPORTING

1964 James V. Magee, Albert V. Gaudiosi, and Frederick A. Meyer (*Philadelphia Bulletin*)
1965 Gene Goltz (*Houston Post*)
1966 John A. Frasca *(Tampa Tribune)*
1967 Gene Miller *(Miami Herald)*
1968 J. Anthony Lukas *(New York Times)*
1969 Albert L. Delugach and Denny Walsh *(St. Louis Globe-Democrat)*
1970 Harold Eugene Martin *(Montgomery Advertiser)*
1971 William Hugh Jones *(Chicago Tribune)*
1972 Timothy Leland, Gerard N. O'Neill, Stephen A. Kurkjian, and Ann DeSantis *(Boston Globe)*
1973 Sun Newspapers of Omaha, Neb.
1974 William Sherman *(New York Daily News)*
1975 *Indianapolis Star*
1976 *Chicago Tribune*
1977 Acel Moore and Wendell Rawls, Jr. *(Philadelphia Inquirer)*
1978 Anthony R. Dolan *(Stamford* [Conn.] *Advocate)*
1979 Gilbert M. Gaul and Elliot G. Jaspin *(Pottsville* [Pa.] *Republican)*
1980 Nils J. Bruzelius, Alexander B. Hawes, Jr., Stephen A. Kurkjian, and Joan Vennochi *(Boston Globe)*
1981 Clark Hallas and Robert B. Lowe (*Arizona Daily Star,* Tucson)
1982 Paul Henderson *(Seattle Times)*
1983 Loretta Tofani *(Washington Post)*
1984 *Boston Globe*

INVESTIGATIVE REPORTING

1985 Lucy Morgan and Jack Reed (*St. Petersburg* [Fla.] *Times*) and William K. Marimow (*Philadelphia Inquirer*)
1986 Jeffrey A. Marx and Michael M. York *(Lexington* [Ky.] *Herald Leader)*
1987 Daniel R. Biddle, H.G. Bissinger, and Fredric N. Tulsky *(Philadelphia Inquirer)*

FEATURE WRITING

1979 Jon D. Franklin *(Baltimore Evening Sun)*
1980 Madeleine Blais *(Miami Herald)*
1981 Teresa Carpenter (*Village Voice,* New York)
1982 Saul Pett (Associated Press)
1983 Nan Robertson *(New York Times)*
1984 Peter M. Rinearson *(Seattle Times)*
1985 Alice Steinbach (*Baltimore Sun*)
1986 John Camp *(St. Paul Pioneer Press and Dispatch)*
1987 Steve Twomey *(Philadelphia Inquirer)*

COMMENTARY

1970 Marquis W. Childs *(St. Louis Post-Dispatch)*
1971 William A. Caldwell (*Record* [Hackensack, N.J.])
1972 Mike Royko *(Chicago Daily News)*
1973 David S. Broder *(Washington Post)*
1974 Edwin A. Roberts, Jr. *(National Observer)*
1975 Mary McGrory *(Washington Star)*
1976 Walter W. (Red) Smith *(New York Times)*
1977 George F. Will (*Washington Post* Writers Group)
1978 William Safire *(New York Times)*
1979 Russell Baker *(New York Times)*
1980 Ellen H. Goodman *(Boston Globe)*
1981 Dave Anderson *(New York Times)*
1982 Art Buchwald (*Los Angeles Times* Syndicate)
1983 Claude Sitton *(Raleigh* [N.C.] *News & Observer)*
1984 Vermont Royster *(Wall Street Journal)*
1985 Murray Kempton (*Newsday*)
1986 Jimmy Breslin *(New York Daily News)*
1987 Charles Krauthammer (*Washington Post* Writers Group)

CRITICISM

1970 Ada Louise Huxtable *(New York Times)*
1971 Harold C. Schonberg *(New York Times)*
1972 Frank Peters, Jr. *(St. Louis Post-Dispatch)*
1973 Ronald Powers *(Chicago Sun-Times)*
1974 Emily Genauer (Newsday Syndicate)
1975 Roger Ebert *(Chicago Sun-Times)*
1976 Alan M. Kriegsman *(Washington Post)*
1977 William McPherson *(Washington Post)*
1978 Walter Kerr *(New York Times)*
1979 Paul Gapp *(Chicago Tribune)*
1980 William A. Henry, 3rd *(Boston Globe)*
1981 Jonathan Yardley *(Washington Star)*
1982 Martin Bernheimer *(Los Angeles Times)*
1983 Manuela Hoelterhoff *(Wall Street Journal)*
1984 Paul Goldberger *(New York Times)*
1985 Howard Rosenberg (*Los Angeles Times*)
1986 Donal Henahan *(New York Times)*
1987 Richard Eder *(Los Angeles Times)*

EXPLANATORY JOURNALISM

1985 Jon Franklin (*Baltimore Evening Sun*)
1986 *New York Times*
1987 Jeff Lyon and Peter Gorner *(Chicago Tribune)*

SPECIALIZED REPORTING

1985 Randall Savage and Jackie Crosby (*Macon* [Ga.] *Telegraph and News*)
1986 Andrew Schneider and Mary Pat Flaherty *(Pittsburgh Press)*
1987 Alex S. Jones *(New York Times)*

SPECIAL CITATIONS

1938 *Edmonton* (Alberta) *Journal,* special bronze plaque for editorial leadership in defense of freedom of press in Province of Alberta.
1941 *New York Times* for the public educational value of its foreign news report.
1944 Byron Price, Director of the Office of Censorship, for the creation and administration of the newspaper and radio codes. Mrs. William Allen

White, for her husband's interest and services during the past seven years as a member of the Advisory Board of the Graduate School of Journalism, Columbia University. Richard Rodgers and Oscar Hammerstein II for their musical *Oklahoma!*

1945 The cartographers of the American press for their war maps.

1947 (Pulitzer centennial year.) Columbia University and the Graduate School of Journalism for their efforts to maintain and advance the high standards governing the Pulitzer Prize awards. The *St. Louis Post-Dispatch* for its unswerving adherence to the public and professional ideals of its founder and its leadership in American journalism.

1948 Dr. Frank D. Fackenthal for his interest and service.

1951 Cyrus L. Sulzberger *(New York Times)* for his exclusive interview with Archbishop Stepinac in a Yugoslav prison.

1952 *Kansas City Star* for coverage of 1951 floods; Max Kase *(New York Journal-American)* for exposures of bribery in college basketball.

1953 *New York Times* for its 17-year publication of "News of the Week in Review"; and Lester Markel, its founder.

1957 Kenneth Roberts for his historical novels.

1958 Walter Lippmann *(New York Herald Tribune)* for his "wisdom, perception and high sense of responsibility" in his commentary on national and international affairs.

1960 Garrett Mattingly, for *The Armada.*

1961 *American Heritage Picture History of the Civil War,* as distinguished example of American book publishing.

1964 Gannett Newspapers, Rochester, N.Y.

1973 James Thomas Flexner for his biography *George Washington.*

1974 Roger Sessions for his "life's work in music."

1976 John Hohenberg for "services for 22 years as administrator of the Pulitzer Prizes"; Scott Joplin for his contributions to American music.

1977 Alex Haley for his novel, *Roots.*

1978 E.B. White of *New Yorker* magazine and Richard L. Strout of *Christian Science Monitor.*

1982 Milton Babbitt, "for his life's work as a distinguished and seminal American composer."

1984 Theodor Seuss Geisel (Dr. Seuss) for "books full of playful rhymes, nonsense words and strange illustrations."

1985 William H. Schuman for "more than a half century of contribution to American music as a composer and educational leader."

1987 Joseph Pulitzer Jr., "for extraordinary services to American journalism and letters during his 31 years as chairman of the Pulitzer Prize Board and for his accomplishments as an editor and publisher."

Pulitzer Prizes in Letters

FICTION[1]

1918 *His Family.* Ernest Poole
1919 *The Magnificent Ambersons.* Booth Tarkington
1921 *The Age of Innocence.* Edith Wharton
1922 *Alice Adams.* Booth Tarkington
1923 *One of Ours.* Willa Cather
1924 *The Able McLaughlins.* Margaret Wilson
1925 *So Big.* Edna Ferber
1926 *Arrowsmith.* Sinclair Lewis
1927 *Early Autumn.* Louis Bromfield
1928 *The Bridge of San Luis Rey.* Thornton Wilder
1929 *Scarlet Sister Mary.* Julia Peterkin
1930 *Laughing Boy.* Oliver La Farge
1931 *Years of Grace.* Margaret Ayer Barnes
1932 *The Good Earth.* Pearl S. Buck
1933 *The Store.* T. S. Stribling
1934 *Lamb in His Bosom.* Caroline Miller
1935 *Now in November.* Josephine Winslow Johnson
1936 *Honey in the Horn.* Harold L. Davis
1937 *Gone With the Wind.* Margaret Mitchell
1938 *The Late George Apley.* John Phillips Marquand
1939 *The Yearling.* Marjorie Kinnan Rawlings
1940 *The Grapes of Wrath.* John Steinbeck
1942 *In This Our Life.* Ellen Glasgow
1943 *Dragon's Teeth.* Upton Sinclair
1944 *Journey in the Dark.* Martin Flavin
1945 *A Bell for Adano.* John Hersey
1947 *All the King's Men.* Robert Penn Warren
1948 *Tales of the South Pacific.* James A. Michener
1949 *Guard of Honor.* James Gould Cozzens
1950 *The Way West.* A. B. Guthrie, Jr.
1951 *The Town.* Conrad Richter
1952 *The Caine Mutiny.* Herman Wouk
1953 *The Old Man and the Sea.* Ernest Hemingway
1955 *A Fable.* William Faulkner
1956 *Andersonville.* MacKinlay Kantor
1958 *A Death in the Family.* James Agee
1959 *The Travels of Jaimie McPheeters.* Robert Lewis Taylor
1960 *Advise and Consent.* Allen Drury
1961 *To Kill a Mockingbird.* Harper Lee
1962 *The Edge of Sadness.* Edwin O'Connor
1963 *The Reivers.* William Faulkner
1965 *The Keepers of the House.* Shirley Ann Grau
1966 *Collected Stories of Katherine Anne Porter.* Katherine Anne Porter
1967 *The Fixer.* Bernard Malamud
1968 *The Confessions of Nat Turner.* William Styron
1969 *House Made of Dawn.* N. Scott Momaday
1970 *Collected Stories.* Jean Stafford
1972 *Angle of Repose.* Wallace Stegner
1973 *The Optimist's Daughter.* Eudora Welty
1975 *The Killer Angels.* Michael Shaara
1976 *Humboldt's Gift.* Saul Bellow
1978 *Elbow Room.* James Alan McPherson
1979 *The Stories of John Cheever.* John Cheever
1980 *The Executioner's Song.* Norman Mailer
1981 *A Confederacy of Dunces.* John Kennedy Toole
1982 *Rabbit Is Rich.* John Updike
1983 *The Color Purple.* Alice Walker
1984 *Ironweed.* William Kennedy
1985 *Foreign Affairs,* Alison Lurie
1986 *Lonesome Dove,* Larry McMurtry
1987 *A Summons to Memphis,* Peter Taylor

1. Before 1948, award was for novels only.

DRAMA

1918 *Why Marry?* Jesse Lynch Williams
1920 *Beyond the Horizon.* Eugene O'Neill
1921 *Miss Lulu Bett.* Zona Gale
1922 *Anna Christie.* Eugene O'Neill
1923 *Icebound.* Owen Davis
1924 *Hell-Bent Fer Heaven.* Hatcher Hughes
1925 *They Knew What They Wanted.* Sidney Howard

1926 *Craig's Wife.* George Kelly
1927 *In Abraham's Bosom.* Paul Green
1928 *Strange Interlude.* Eugene O'Neill
1929 *Street Scene.* Elmer L. Rice
1930 *The Green Pastures.* Marc Connelly
1931 *Alison's House.* Susan Glaspell
1932 *Of Thee I Sing.* George S. Kaufman, Morrie Ryskind, and Ira Gershwin
1933 *Both Your Houses.* Maxwell Anderson
1934 *Men in White.* Sidney Kingsley
1935 *The Old Maid.* Zöe Akins
1936 *Idiot's Delight.* Robert E. Sherwood
1937 *You Can't Take It With You.* Moss Hart and George S. Kaufman
1938 *Our Town.* Thornton Wilder
1939 *Abe Lincoln in Illinois.* Robert E. Sherwood
1940 *The Time of Your Life.* William Saroyan
1941 *There Shall Be No Night.* Robert E. Sherwood
1943 *The Skin of Our Teeth.* Thornton Wilder
1945 *Harvey.* Mary Chase
1946 *State of the Union.* Russel Crouse and Howard Lindsay
1948 *A Streetcar Named Desire.* Tennessee Williams
1949 *Death of a Salesman.* Arthur Miller
1950 *South Pacific.* Richard Rodgers, Oscar Hammerstein II, and Joshua Logan
1952 *The Shrike.* Joseph Kramm
1953 *Picnic.* William Inge
1954 *The Teahouse of the August Moon.* John Patrick
1955 *Cat on a Hot Tin Roof.* Tennessee Williams
1956 *The Diary of Anne Frank.* Frances Goodrich and Albert Hackett
1957 *Long Day's Journey Into Night.* Eugene O'Neill
1958 *Look Homeward, Angel.* Ketti Frings
1959 *J.B.* Archibald MacLeish
1960 *Fiorello!* George Abbott, Jerome Weidman, Jerry Bock, and Sheldon Harnick
1961 *All the Way Home.* Tad Mosel
1962 *How to Succeed in Business Without Really Trying.* Frank Loesser and Abe Burrows
1965 *The Subject Was Roses.* Frank D. Gilroy
1967 *A Delicate Balance.* Edward Albee
1969 *The Great White Hope.* Howard Sackler
1970 *No Place to Be Somebody.* Charles Gordone
1971 *The Effect of Gamma Rays on Man-in-the-Moon Marigolds.* Paul Zindel
1973 *That Championship Season.* Jason Miller
1975 *Seascape.* Edward Albee
1976 *A Chorus Line.* Conceived by Michael Bennett
1977 *The Shadow Box.* Michael Cristofer
1978 *The Gin Game.* Donald L. Coburn
1979 *Buried Child.* Sam Shepard
1980 *Talley's Folly.* Lanford Wilson
1981 *Crimes of the Heart.* Beth Henley
1982 *A Soldier's Play.* Charles Fuller
1983 *'Night, Mother.* Marsha Norman
1984 *Glengarry Glen Ross.* David Mamet
1985 *Sunday in the Park with George.* Stephen Sondheim and James Lapine
1987 *Fences.* August Wilson

HISTORY OF UNITED STATES

1917 *With Americans of Past and Present Days.* J. J. Jusserand, Ambassador of France to United States
1918 *A History of the Civil War, 1861–1865.* James Ford Rhodes
1920 *The War With Mexico.* Justin H. Smith
1921 *The Victory at Sea.* William Sowden Sims in collaboration with Burton J. Hendrick
1922 *The Founding of New England.* James Truslow Adams
1923 *The Supreme Court in United States History.* Charles Warren
1924 *The American Revolution—A Constitutional Interpretation.* Charles Howard McIlwain
1925 *A History of the American Frontier.* Frederic L. Paxson
1926 *The History of the United States.* Edward Channing
1927 *Pinckney's Treaty.* Samuel Flagg Bemis
1928 *Main Currents in American Thought.* Vernon Louis Parrington
1929 *The Organization and Administration of the Union Army, 1861–1865.* Fred Albert Shannon
1930 *The War of Independence.* Claude H. Van Tyne
1931 *The Coming of the War: 1914.* Bernadotte E. Schmitt
1932 *My Experiences in the World War.* John J. Pershing
1933 *The Significance of Sections in American History.* Frederick J. Turner
1934 *The People's Choice.* Herbert Agar
1935 *The Colonial Period of American History.* Charles McLean Andrews
1936 *The Constitutional History of the United States.* Andrew C. McLaughlin
1937 *The Flowering of New England.* Van Wyck Brooks
1938 *The Road to Reunion, 1865–1900.* Paul Herman Buck
1939 *A History of American Magazines.* Frank Luther Mott
1940 *Abraham Lincoln: The War Years.* Carl Sandburg
1941 *The Atlantic Migration, 1607–1860.* Marcus Lee Hansen
1942 *Reveille in Washington.* Margaret Leech
1943 *Paul Revere and the World He Lived In.* Esther Forbes
1944 *The Growth of American Thought.* Merle Curti
1945 *Unfinished Business.* Stephen Bonsal
1946 *The Age of Jackson.* Arthur M. Schlesinger, Jr.
1947 *Scientists Against Time.* James Phinney Baxter, 3rd
1948 *Across the Wide Missouri.* Bernard DeVoto
1949 *The Disruption of American Democracy.* Roy Franklin Nichols
1950 *Art and Life in America.* Oliver W. Larkin
1951 *The Old Northwest, Pioneer Period 1815–1840.* R. Carlyle Buley
1952 *The Uprooted.* Oscar Handlin
1953 *The Era of Good Feelings.* George Dangerfield
1954 *A Stillness at Appomattox.* Bruce Catton
1955 *Great River: The Rio Grande in North American History.* Paul Horgan
1956 *The Age of Reform.* Richard Hofstadter
1957 *Russia Leaves the War: Soviet-American Relations, 1917–1920.* George F. Kennan
1958 *Banks and Politics in America: From the Revolution to the Civil War.* Bray Hammond
1959 *The Republican Era: 1869–1901.* Leonard D. White, assisted by Jean Schneider
1960 *In the Days of McKinley.* Margaret Leech
1961 *Between War and Peace: The Potsdam Conference.* Herbert Feis
1962 *The Triumphant Empire, Thunder-Clouds Gather in the West.* Lawrence H. Gipson
1963 *Washington, Village and Capital, 1800–1878.* Constance McLaughlin Green
1964 *Puritan Village: The Formation of a New England Town.* Sumner Chilton Powell
1965 *The Greenback Era.* Irwin Unger

1966 *Life of the Mind in America.* Perry Miller
1967 *Exploration and Empire: The Explorer and Scientist in the Winning of the American West.* William H. Goetzmann
1968 *The Ideological Origins of the American Revolution.* Bernard Bailyn
1969 *Origins of the Fifth Amendment.* Leonard W. Levy
1970 *Present at the Creation: My Years in the State Department.* Dean Acheson
1971 *Roosevelt: The Soldier of Freedom.* James McGregor Burns
1972 *Neither Black Nor White. Slavery and Race Relations in Brazil and the United States.* Carl N. Degler
1973 *People of Paradox: An Inquiry Concerning the Origin of American Civilization.* Michael Kammen
1974 *The Americans: The Democratic Experience, Vol. 3.* Daniel J. Boorstin
1975 *Jefferson and His Time.* Dumas Malone
1976 *Lamy of Santa Fe.* Paul Horgan
1977 *The Impending Crisis: 1841–1861.* David M. Potter (posth)
1978 *The Invisible Hand: The Managerial Revolution in American Business.* Alfred D. Chandler, Jr.
1979 *The Dred Scott Case: Its Significance in Law and Politics.* Don E. Fehrenbacher
1980 *Been in the Storm So Long.* Leon F. Litwack
1981 *American Education: The National Experience; 1783–1876.* Lawrence A. Cremin
1982 *Mary Chestnut's Civil War.* C. Vann Woodward, editor
1983 *The Transformation of Virginia, 1740–1790.* Rhys L. Isaac
1985 *The Prophets of Regulation.* Thomas K. McCraw
1986 *. . . the Heavens and the Earth: A Political History of the Space Age.* Walter A. McDougall
1987 *Voyagers to the West: A Passage in the Peopling of America on the Eve of the Revolution.* Bernard Bailyn

BIOGRAPHY OR AUTOBIOGRAPHY

1917 *Julia Ward Howe.* Laura E. Richards and Maude Howe Elliott, assisted by Florence Howe Hall
1918 *Benjamin Franklin, Self-Revealed.* William Cabell Bruce
1919 *The Education of Henry Adams.* Henry Adams
1920 *The Life of John Marshall.* Albert J. Beveridge
1921 *The Americanization of Edward Bok.* Edward Bok
1922 *A Daughter of the Middle Border.* Hamlin Garland
1923 *The Life and Letters of Walter H. Page,* Burton J. Hendrick
1924 *From Immigrant to Inventor.* Michael Idvorsky Pupin
1925 *Barrett Wendell and His Letters.* M. A. DeWolfe Howe
1926 *The Life of Sir William Osler.* Harvey Cushing
1927 *Whitman.* Emory Holloway
1928 *The American Orchestra and Theodore Thomas.* Charles Edward Russell
1929 *The Training of an American. The Earlier Life and Letters of Walter H. Page.* Burton J. Hendrick
1930 *The Raven.* Marquis James
1931 *Charles W. Eliot.* Henry James
1932 *Theodore Roosevelt.* Henry F. Pringle
1933 *Grover Cleveland.* Allan Nevins
1934 *John Hay.* Tyler Dennett
1935 *R. E. Lee.* Douglas S. Freeman
1936 *The Thought and Character of William James.* Ralph Barton Perry
1937 *Hamilton Fish.* Allan Nevins
1938 *Pedlar's Progress.* Odell Shepard; *Andrew Jackson.* Marquis James
1939 *Benjamin Franklin.* Carl Van Doren
1940 *Woodrow Wilson. Life and Letters,* Vols. VII and VIII. Ray Stannard Baker
1941 *Jonathan Edwards.* Ola E. Winslow
1942 *Crusader in Crinoline.* Forrest Wilson
1943 *Admiral of the Ocean Sea.* Samuel Eliot Morison
1944 *The American Leonardo: The Life of Samuel F. B. Morse.* Carleton Mabee
1945 *George Bancroft: Brahmin Rebel.* Russel Blaine Nye
1946 *Son of the Wilderness.* Linnie Marsh Wolfe
1947 *The Autobiography of William Allen White*
1948 *Forgotten First Citizen: John Bigelow.* Margaret Clapp
1949 *Roosevelt and Hopkins.* Robert E. Sherwood
1950 *John Quincy Adams and the Foundations of American Foreign Policy.* Samuel Flagg Bemis
1951 *John C. Calhoun: American Portrait.* Margaret Louise Coit
1952 *Charles Evans Hughes.* Merlo J. Pusey
1953 *Edmund Pendleton, 1721–1803.* David J. Mays
1954 *The Spirit of St. Louis.* Charles A. Lindbergh
1955 *The Taft Story.* William S. White
1956 *Benjamin Henry Latrobe.* Talbot F. Hamlin
1957 *Profiles in Courage.* John F. Kennedy
1958 *George Washington.* Douglas Southall Freeman (Vols. 1–6) and John Alexander Carroll and Mary Wells Ashworth (Vol. 7)
1959 *Woodrow Wilson, American Prophet.* Arthur Walworth
1960 *John Paul Jones.* Samuel Eliot Morison
1961 *Charles Sumner and the Coming of the Civil War.* David Donald
1963 *Henry James: Vol. II, The Conquest of London, 1870–1881; Vol. III, The Middle Years, 1881–1895.* Leon Edel
1964 *John Keats.* Walter Jackson Bate
1965 *Henry Adams* (3 Vols.). Ernest Samuels
1966 *A Thousand Days.* Arthur M. Schlesinger, Jr.
1967 *Mr. Clemens and Mark Twain.* Justin Kaplan
1968 *Memoirs, 1925–1950.* George F. Kennan
1969 *The Man From New York.* B. L. Reid
1970 *Huey Long.* T. Harry Williams
1971 *Robert Frost: The Years of Triumph, 1915–1938.* Lawrence Thompson
1972 *Eleanor and Franklin: The Story of Their Relationship Based on Eleanor Roosevelt's Private Papers.* Joseph P. Lash
1973 *Luce and His Empire.* W. A. Swanberg
1974 *O'Neill, Son and Artist.* Louis Sheaffer
1975 *The Power Broker: Robert Moses and the Fall of New York.* Robert A. Caro
1976 *Edith Wharton: A Biography.* Richard W. B. Lewis
1977 *A Prince of Our Disorder.* John E. Mack
1978 *Samuel Johnson.* Walter Jackson Bate
1979 *Days of Sorrow and Pain: Leo Baeck and the Berlin Jews.* Leonard Baker
1980 *The Rise of Theodore Roosevelt.* Edmund Morris
1981 *Peter the Great.* Robert K. Massie
1982 *Grant: A Biography.* William S. McFeely
1983 *Growing Up.* Russell Baker
1984 *Booker T. Washington.* Louis R. Harlan

1985 *The Life and Times of Cotton Mather,* Kenneth Silverman
1986 *Louise Bogan: A Portrait,* Elizabeth Frank
1987 *Bearing the Cross: Martin Luther King Jr. and the Southern Christian Leadership Conference,* David J. Garrow

POETRY[1]

1918 *Love Songs.* Sara Teasdale
1919 *Old Road to Paradise.* Margaret Widdemer; *Corn Huskers.* Carl Sandburg
1922 *Collected Poems.* Edwin Arlington Robinson
1923 *The Ballad of the Harp-Weaver; A Few Figs from Thistles;* eight sonnets in *American Poetry, 1922, A Miscellany.* Edna St. Vincent Millay
1924 *New Hampshire: A Poem With Notes and Grace Notes.* Robert Frost
1925 *The Man Who Died Twice.* Edwin Arlington Robinson
1926 *What's O'Clock.* Amy Lowell
1927 *Fiddler's Farewell.* Leonora Speyer
1928 *Tristram.* Edwin Arlington Robinson
1929 *John Brown's Body.* Stephen Vincent Benét
1930 *Selected Poems.* Conrad Aiken
1931 *Collected Poems.* Robert Frost
1932 *The Flowering Stone.* George Dillon
1933 *Conquistador.* Archibald MacLeish
1934 *Collected Verse.* Robert Hillyer
1935 *Bright Ambush.* Audrey Wurdemann
1936 *Strange Holiness.* Robert P. T. Coffin
1937 *A Further Range.* Robert Frost
1938 *Cold Morning Sky.* Marya Zaturenska
1939 *Selected Poems.* John Gould Fletcher
1940 *Collected Poems.* Mark Van Doren
1941 *Sunderland Capture.* Leonard Bacon
1942 *The Dust Which Is God.* William Rose Benét
1943 *A Witness Tree.* Robert Frost
1944 *Western Star.* Stephen Vincent Benét
1945 *V-Letter and Other Poems.* Karl Shapiro
1947 *Lord Weary's Castle.* Robert Lowell
1948 *The Age of Anxiety.* W. H. Auden
1949 *Terror and Decorum.* Peter Viereck
1950 *Annie Allen.* Gwendolyn Brooks
1951 *Complete Poems.* Carl Sandburg
1952 *Collected Poems.* Marianne Moore
1953 *Collected Poems, 1917–1952.* Archibald MacLeish
1954 *The Waking.* Theodore Roethke
1955 *Collected Poems.* Wallace Stevens
1956 *Poems—North & South.* Elizabeth Bishop
1957 *Things of This World.* Richard Wilbur
1958 *Promises: Poems, 1954–1956.* Robert Penn Warren
1959 *Selected Poems, 1928–1958.* Stanley Kunitz
1960 *Heart's Needle.* William Snodgrass
1961 *Times Three: Selected Verse From Three Decades.* Phyllis McGinley
1962 *Poems.* Alan Dugan
1963 *Pictures From Breughel.* William Carlos Williams
1964 *At the End of the Open Road.* Louis Simpson
1965 *77 Dream Songs.* John Berryman
1966 *Selected Poems.* Richard Eberhart
1967 *Live or Die.* Anne Sexton
1968 *The Hard Hours.* Anthony Hecht
1969 *Of Being Numerous.* George Oppen
1970 *Untitled Subjects.* Richard Howard
1971 *The Carrier of Ladders.* William S. Merwin

1. This prize was established in 1922. The 1918 and 1919 awards were made from gifts provided by the Poetry Society.

1972 *Collected Poems.* James Wright
1973 *Up Country.* Maxine Winokur Kumin
1974 *The Dolphin.* Robert Lowell
1975 *Turtle Island.* Gary Snyder
1976 *Self-Portrait in a Convex Mirror.* John Ashbery
1977 *Divine Comedies.* James Merrill
1978 *Collected Poems.* Howard Nemerov: *Poems, 1976–1978.*
1979 *Now and Then.* Robert Penn Warren.
1980 *Selected Poems.* Donald Rodney Justice
1981 *The Morning of the Poem.* James Schuyler
1982 *The Collected Poems.* Sylvia Plath
1983 *Selected Poems.* Galway Kinnell
1984 *American Primitive.* Mary Oliver
1985 *Yin,* Carolyn Kizer
1986 *The Flying Change,* Henry Taylor
1987 *Thomas and Beulah,* Rita Dove

GENERAL NONFICTION

1962 *The Making of the President, 1960.* Theodore H. White
1963 *The Guns of August.* Barbara W. Tuchman
1964 *Anti-Intellectualism in American Life.* Richard Hofstadter
1965 *O Strange New World.* Howard Mumford Jones
1966 *Wandering Through Winter.* Edwin Way Teale
1967 *The Problem of Slavery in Western Culture.* David Brion Davis
1968 *Rousseau and Revolution.* Will and Ariel Durant
1969 *So Human an Animal.* Rene Jules Dubos; *The Armies of the Night.* Norman Mailer
1970 *Gandhi's Truth.* Erik H. Erikson
1971 *The Rising Sun.* John Toland
1972 *Stilwell and the American Experience in China, 1911–1945.* Barbara W. Tuchman
1973 *Fire in the Lake: The Vietnamese and the Americans in Vietnam.* Frances FitzGerald; and *Children of Crisis* (Vols. 1 and 2). Robert M. Coles
1974 *The Denial of Death.* Ernest Becker
1975 *Pilgrim at Tinker Creek.* Annie Dillard
1976 *Why Survive? Being Old in America.* Robert N. Butler
1977 *Beautiful Swimmers: Watermen, Crabs and the Chesapeake Bay.* William W. Warner
1978 *The Dragons of Eden.* Carl Sagan
1979 *On Human Nature.* Edward O. Wilson
1980 *Gödel, Escher, Bach: An Eternal Golden Braid.* Douglas R. Hofstadter
1981 *Fin-de-Siecle Vienna: Politics and Culture.* Carl E. Schorske
1982 *The Soul of a New Machine.* Tracy Kidder
1983 *Is There No Place on Earth for Me?* Susan Sheehan
1984 *Social Transformation of American Medicine.* Paul Starr
1985 *The Good War: An Oral History of World War II,* Studs Terkel
1986 *Move Your Shadow: South Africa, Black and White,* Joseph Lelyveld; *Common Ground: A Turbulent Decade in the Lives of Three American Families,* J. Anthony Lukas
1987 *Arab and Jew: Wounded Spirits in a Promised Land,* David K. Shipler

PULITZER PRIZES IN MUSIC

1943 *Secular Cantata No. 2, A Free Song.* William Schuman
1944 *Symphony No. 4* (Op. 34). Howard Hanson
1945 *Appalachian Spring.* Aaron Copland
1946 *The Canticle of the Sun.* Leo Sowerby
1947 *Symphony No. 3.* Charles Ives
1948 *Symphony No. 3.* Walter Piston

1949 *Louisiana Story* music. Virgil Thomson
1950 *The Consul.* Gian Carlo Menotti
1951 Music for opera *Giants in the Earth.* Douglas Stuart Moore
1952 *Symphony Concertante.* Gail Kubik
1954 *Concerto for Two Pianos and Orchestra.* Quincy Porter
1955 *The Saint of Bleecker Street.* Gian Carlo Menotti
1956 *Symphony No. 3.* Ernst Toch
1957 *Meditations on Ecclesiastes.* Norman Dello Joio
1958 *Vanessa.* Samuel Barber
1959 *Concerto for Piano and Orchestra.* John La Montaine
1960 *Second String Quartet.* Elliott Carter
1961 *Symphony No. 7.* Walter Piston
1962 *The Crucible.* Robert Ward
1963 *Piano Concerto No. 1.* Samuel Barber
1966 *Variations for Orchestra.* Leslie Bassett
1967 *Quartet No. 3.* Leon Kirchner
1968 *Echoes of Time and the River.* George Crumb
1969 *String Quartet No. 3.* Karel Husa
1970 *Time's Encomium.* Charles Wuorinen
1971 *Synchronisms No. 6 for Piano and Electronic Sound.* Mario Davidowsky
1972 *Windows.* Jacob Druckman
1973 *String Quartet No. 3.* Elliott Carter
1974 *Notturno.* Donald Martino
1975 *From the Diary of Virginia Woolf.* Dominick Argento
1976 *Air Music.* Ned Rorem
1977 *Visions of Terror and Wonder.* Richard Wernick
1978 *Déjà Vu for Percussion Quartet and Orchestra.* Michael Colgrass
1979 *Aftertones of Infinity.* Joseph Schwantner
1980 *In Memory of a Summer Day.* David Del Tredici
1981 Not awarded
1982 *Concerto for Orchestra.* Roger Sessions
1983 *Three Movements for Orchestra.* Ellen T. Zwilich
1984 *Canti del Sole.* Bernard Rands
1985 *Symphony RiverRun,* Stephen Albert
1986 *Wind Quintet IV,* George Perle
1987 *The Flight Into Egypt,* John Harbison

New York Drama Critics' Circle Awards

1935–36
Winterset, Maxwell Anderson
1936–37
High Tor, Maxwell Anderson
1937–38
Of Mice and Men, John Steinbeck
Shadow and Substance, Paul Vincent Carroll[1]
1938–39
(No award) *The White Steed,* Paul Vincent Carroll[1]
1939–40
The Time of Your Life, William Saroyan
1940–41
Watch on the Rhine, Lillian Hellman
The Corn Is Green, Emlyn Williams[1]
1941–42
(No award) *Blithe Spirit,* Noel Coward[1]
1942–43
The Patriots, Sidney Kingsley
1943–44
(No award) *Jacobowsky and the Colonel.* Franz Werfel and S. N. Behrman[1]
1944–45
The Glass Menagerie, Tennessee Williams
1945–46
(No award) *Carousel,* Richard Rodgers and Oscar Hammerstein II[2]
1946–47
All My Sons, Arthur Miller
No Exit, Jean-Paul Sartre[1]
Brigadoon, Alan Jay Lerner and Frederick Loewe[2]
1947–48
A Streetcar Named Desire, Tennessee Williams
The Winslow Boy, Terence Rattigan[1]
1948–49
Death of a Salesman, Arthur Miller
The Madwoman of Chaillot, Jean Giraudoux and Maurice Valency[1]
South Pacific, Richard Rodgers, Oscar Hammerstein II, and Joshua Logan[2]
1949–50
The Member of the Wedding, Carson McCullers
The Cocktail Party, T. S. Eliot[1]
The Consul, Gian Carlo Menotti[2]
1950–51
Darkness at Noon, Sidney Kingsley[3]
The Lady's Not for Burning, Christopher Fry[1]
Guys and Dolls, Abe Burrows, Jo Swerling, and Frank Loesser[2]
1951–52
I Am a Camera, John Van Druten[4]
Venus Observed, Christopher Fry[1]
Pal Joey, Richard Rodgers, Lorenz Hart, and John O'Hara[2]
Don Juan in Hell, George B. Shaw[5]
1952–53
Picnic, William Inge
The Love of Four Colonels, by Peter Ustinov[1]
Wonderful Town, Joseph Fields, Jerome Chodorov, Betty Comden, Adolph Green, and Leonard Bernstein[2]
1953–54
The Teahouse of the August Moon, John Patrick
Ondine, Jean Giraudoux[1]
The Golden Apple, John Latouche and Jerome Moross[2]
1954–55
Cat on a Hot Tin Roof, Tennessee Williams
Witness for the Prosecution, Agatha Christie[1]
The Saint of Bleecker Street, Gian Carlo Menotti[2]
1955–56
The Diary of Anne Frank, Frances Goodrich and Albert Hackett
Tiger at the Gates, Jean Giraudoux and Christopher Fry[1]
My Fair Lady, Frederick Loewe and Alan Jay Lerner[2]
1956–57
Long Day's Journey Into Night, Eugene O'Neill
Waltz of the Toreadors, Jean Anouilh[1]
The Most Happy Fella, Frank Loesser[2 6]
1957–58
Look Homeward, Angel, Ketti Frings[7]
Look Back in Anger, John Osborne[1]
The Music Man, Meredith Willson[2]
1958–59
A Raisin in the Sun, Lorraine Hansberry
The Visit, Friedrich Duerrenmatt-Maurice Valency[1]

La Plume de ma Tante, Robert Dhery and Gerard Calvi[2]
1959–60
Toys in the Attic, Lillian Hellman
Five Finger Exercise, Peter Shaffer[1]
Fiorello!, Jerome Weidman, George Abbott, Jerry Bock, and Sheldon Harnick[2]
1960–61
All the Way Home, Tad Mosel[3]
A Taste of Honey, Shelagh Delaney[1]
Carnival, Michael Stewart[2]
1961–62
The Night of the Iguana, Tennessee Williams
A Man for All Seasons, Robert Bolt[1]
How to Succeed in Business Without Really Trying, Abe Burrows, Jack Weinstock, Willie Gilbert, and Frank Loesser[2, 9]
1962–63
Who's Afraid of Virginia Woolf?, Edward Albee
Beyond the Fringe, Alan Bennett, Peter Cook, Jonathan Miller, and Dudley Moore[10]
1963–64
Luther, John Osborne
Hello, Dolly!, Michael Stewart and Jerry Herman[2, 11]
The Trojan Women, Euripides[10, 12]
1964–65
The Subject Was Roses, Frank D. Gilroy
Fiddler on the Roof, Joseph Stein, Jerry Bock, and Sheldon Harnick[2, 13]
1965–66
The Persecution and Assassination of Marat as Performed by the Inmates of the Asylum of Charenton Under the Direction of the Marquis de Sade, Peter Weiss
The Man of La Mancha, Dale Wasserman, Mitch Leigh, and Joe Darion
1966–67
The Homecoming, Harold Pinter
Cabaret, Joe Masteroff, John Kander, and Fred Ebb[2, 14]
1967–68
Rosencrantz and Guildenstern Are Dead, Tom Stoppard
Your Own Thing, Donald Driver, Hal Hester, and Danny Apolinar[2]
1968–69
The Great White Hope, Howard Sackler
1776, Sherman Edwards and Peter Stone[2]
1969–70
Borstal Boy, Frank McMahon[15]
The Effect of Gamma Rays on Man-in-the-Moon Marigolds, Paul Zindel[16]
Company, George Furth and Stephen Sondheim[2]
1970–71
Home, David Storey
The House of Blue Leaves, John Guare[16]
Follies, James Goldman and Stephen Sondheim[2]
1971–72
That Championship Season, Jason Miller
Two Gentlemen of Verona, adapted by John Guare and Mel Shapiro[2]
The Screens, Jean Genet[1]
1972–73
The Changing Room, David Storey
The Hot l Baltimore, by Lanford Wilson[16]
A Little Night Music, Hugh Wheeler and Stephen Sondheim[2]
1973–74
The Contractors, David Storey
Short Eyes, Miguel Piñero[16]
Candide, Leonard Bernstein, Hugh Wheeler, and Richard Wilbur[2]
1974–75
Equus, Peter Shaffer
The Taking of Miss Janie, Ed Bullins[16]
A Chorus Line, James Kirkwood and Nicholas Dante[2]
1975–76
Travesties, Tom Stoppard
Streamers, David Rabe[16]
Pacific Overtures, Stephen Sondheim, John Weidman, and Hugh Wheeler[2]
1976–77
Otherwise Engaged, Simon Gray
American Buffalo, David Marmet[16]
Annie, Thomas Meehan, Charles Strouse, and Martin Charnin[2]
1977–78
Da, Hugh Leonard
Ain't Misbehavin', conceived by Richard Maltby, Jr.[2]
1978–79
The Elephant Man, Bernard Pomerance
Sweeney Todd, Hugh Wheeler and Stephen Sondheim[2]
1979–80
Talley's Folly, Lanford Wilson
Evita,[2] Andrew Lloyd Webber and Tim Rice
Betrayal, Harold Pinter[1]
1980–81
A Lesson From Aloes, Athol Fugard
Crimes of the Heart, Beth Henley[16]
1981–82
The Life and Adventures of Nicholas Nickleby, adapted by David Edgar
A Soldier's Play, Charles Fuller[16]
1982–83
Brighton Beach Memoirs, Neil Simon
Plenty, David Hare[1]
Little Shop of Horrors, Alan Menken and Howard Ashman[2, 17]
1983–84
The Real Thing, Tom Stoppard
Glengarry Glen Ross, David Mamet[16]
Sunday in the Park with George, Stephen W Sondheim and James Lapine[2]
1984-85
Ma Rainey's Black Bottom, August Wilson
(No award for best musical or foreign play)
1985–86
Lie of the Mind, Sam Shepard
Benefactors, Michael Frayn[1]
The Search for Signs of Intelligent Life in the Universe, Lily Tomlin and Jane Wagner[18]
(No award for best musical)
1986-87
Fences, August Wilson
Les Liaisons Dangereuses, Christopher Hampton[1]
Les Miserables, Claude-Michel Schonberg and Alain Boublil[2]

1. Citation for best foreign play. 2. Citation for best musical. 3. Based on a novel by Arthur Koestler. 4. Based on Christopher Isherwood's *Berlin Stories.* 5. For "distinguished and original contribution to the theater." 6. Based on Sidney Howard's *They Knew What They Wanted.* 7. Based on a novel by Thomas Wolfe. 8. Based on James Agee's *A Death in the Family.* 9. Based on a book by Shepherd Mead. 10. Special citation. 11. Based on Thornton Wilder's *The Matchmaker.* 12. Translated by Edith Hamilton. 13. Based on Sholem Aleichem's Tevye stories, translated by Arnold Perl. 14. Based on John Van Druten's *I Am a Camera,* which won the award for the best play in 1951–52. 15. Based on Brendan Behan's autobiography. 16. Citation for best American play. 17. Based on a story by Roger Corman. 18. Special citation.

Antoinette Perry (Tony) Awards, 1987

Dramatic Play: *Fences,* August Wilson
Musical: *Les Misérables*
Actor (play): James Earl Jones, *Fences*
Actress (play): Linda Lavin, *Broadway Bound*
Actor, featured (play): John Randolph, *Broadway Bound*
Actress, featured (play): Mary Alice, *Fences*
Actor (musical): Robert Lindsay, *Me and My Girl*
Actress (musical): Maryann Plunkett, *Me and My Girl*
Actor, featured (musical): Michael Maguire, *Les Misérables*
Actress, featured (musical): Frances Ruffelle, *Les Misérables*
Director (play): Lloyd Richards, *Fences*
Directors (musical): Trevor Nunn and John Caird, *Les Misérables*
Score: Claude-Michel Schönberg, Herbert Kretzmer, and Alain Boublil, *Les Misérables*
Musical book: Alain Boublil and Claude-Michel Schönberg, *Les Misérables*
Scenic design: John Napier, *Les Misérables*
Costume design: John Napier, *Starlight Express*
Lighting: David Hersey, *Les Misérables*
Choreography: Gillian Gregory, *Me and My Girl*
Reproduction of a play or musical: *All My Sons*

1986-87 Obie Award Winners

Best New American Play: Richard Foreman, *The Cure* and *Film Is Evil, Radio Is Good*
Sustained Achievement: Charles Ludlam and the Ridiculous Theatrical Company
Sustained Excellence of Performance: Philip Bosco, Blackeyed-Susan, Andrew Jackness
Performance: Morgan Freeman, *Driving Miss Daisy;* Dana Ivey, *Driving Miss Daisy;* John Kelly, *Pass The Blutwurst, Bitte (The Egon Schiele Story);* Laura Hicks, *On the Verge;* Robin Bartlett, *The Early Girl;* Rob Besserer, *The Hunger Artist;* Anthony Holland, *The Hunger Artist;* Clarice Taylor, *Moms;* Bill Raymond, *Cold Harbor;* Gcina Mhlope, *Born In The RSA*
Sustained Excellence of Direction: Carole Rothman
Direction: Garland Wright, *On The Verge*
Sustained Excellence of Lighting Design: James F. Ingalls
Lighting Design: Paul Gallo, *The Hunger Artist*
Set and Costume Design: Robert Israel, *The Hunger Artist*
Other Awards: Judith Malina, *The Living Theatre Retrospectacle;* The Woza Afrika Foundation; Dario Fo and Franca Rame; The Non-Traditional Casting Project; The La Mama Great Jones Repertory Company for its revival of *Fragments Of A Greek Trilogy*
Cash Grants: The Irish Arts Center, Brooklyn Arts and Cultural Association (BACA), The New Theatre of Brooklyn

Recipients of Kennedy Center Honors

The Kennedy Center for the Performing Arts in Washington, D.C., created its Honors awards in 1978 to recognize the achievements of five distinguished contributors to the performing arts. Following are the recipients:

1978: Marian Anderson (contralto), Fred Astaire (dancer-actor), Richard Rodgers (Broadway composer), Arthur Rubinstein (pianist), George Balanchine (choreographer).

1979: Ella Fitzgerald (jazz singer), Henry Fonda (actor), Martha Graham (dancer-choreographer), Tennessee Williams (playwright), Aaron Copland (composer).

1980: James Cagney (actor), Leonard Bernstein (composer-conductor), Agnes de Mille (choreographer), Lynn Fontanne (actress), Leontyne Price (soprano).

1981: Count Basie (jazz composer-pianist), Cary Grant (actor), Helen Hayes (actress), Jerome Robbins (choreographer), Rudolf Serkin (pianist).

1982: George Abbott (Broadway producer), Lillian Gish (actress), Benny Goodman (jazz clarinetist), Gene Kelly (dancer-actor), Eugene Ormandy (conductor).

1983: Katherine Dunham (dancer-choreographer), Elia Kazan (director-author), James Stewart (actor), Virgil Thomson (music critic-composer), Frank Sinatra (singer).

1984: Lena Horne (singer), Danny Kaye (comedian-actor), Gian Carlo Menotti (composer), Arthur Miller (playwright), Isaac Stern (violinist).

1985: Merce Cunningham (dancer-choreographer), Irene Dunne (actress), Bob Hope (comedian), Alan Jay Lerner (lyricist-playwright), Frederick Loewe (composer), Beverly Sills (soprano and opera administrator).

1986: Lucille Ball (comedienne), Ray Charles (musician), Yehudi Menuhin (violinist), Antony Tudor (choreographer), Hume Cronyn and Jessica Tandy (husband-and-wife acting team).

1987 National Medal of Arts

Romare Bearden, painter
Ella Fitzgerald, singer
Howard Nemerov, poet
Alwin Nikolais, choreographer
Isamu Noguchi, sculptor
Robert Penn Warren, novelist and poet
Patrons: J.W. Fisher, founder of the Gramma Fisher Foundation which supports American opera; **Armand Hammer,** philanthropist; **Sydney** and **Frances Lewis** of Richmond for support of artists and art museums.

Major Grammy Awards for Recording in 1986

Source: National Academy of Recording Arts and Sciences.

Record: "Higher Love," Steve Winwood (Island)
Album: "Graceland," Paul Simon (Warner Bros.)
Song: "That's What Friends Are For," Burt Bacharach and Carole Bayer Sager (Arista)
New Artist: Bruce Hornsby and the Range
Pop Vocalists: Barbra Streisand, "The Broadway Album" (Columbia/CBS); Steve Winwood, "Higher Love" (Island)
Pop Group: Dionne and Friends featuring Elton John, Gladys Knight and Stevie Wonder, "That's What Friends Are For" (Arista)
Pop Instrumentalist: Harold Faltermeyer and Steve Stevens, "Top Gun Anthem," original motion picture soundtrack (Columbia/CBS)
Rock Vocalists: Tina Turner, "Back Where You Started" (Capitol); Robert Palmer, "Addicted To Love" (Island)
Rock Group: Eurythmics, "Missionary Man" (RCA)
Rock Instrumentalist: The Art of Noise featuring Duane Eddy, "Peter Gunn" (China/Chrysalis)
Rhythm and Blues Vocalists: Anita Baker, "Rapture" (Elektra); James Brown, "Living in America" (Scotti Brothers/CBS)
Rhythm and Blues Group: Prince and The Revolution, "Kiss" (Paisley Park)
Rhythm and Blues Instrumentalist: Yellowjackets, "And You Know That" (MCA)
Rhythm and Blues Song: "Sweet Love," Anita Baker, Louis A. Johnson, and Gary Bias (Elektra)
Traditional Blues: "Showdown!" Albert Collins, Robert Cray, and Johnny Copeland (Alligator)
Country Vocalists: Reba McEntire, "Whoever's In New England" (MCA); Ronnie Milsap, "Lost In the Fifties Tonight" (RCA)
Country Group: The Judds (Wynonna and Naomi), "Grandpa (Tell Me 'Bout the Good Old Days)" (RCA)
Country Instrumentalists: Ricky Skaggs, "Raisin' the Dickens" (track from "Love's Gonna Get Ya") (Epic/CBS)
Country Song: "Grandpa (Tell Me 'Bout the Good Old Days)," Jamie O'Hara (RCA)
Jazz Vocalists: Diane Schuur, "Timeless" (GRP); Bobby McFerrin, "Round Midnight" (track from "Soundtrack Round Midnight") (Columbia/CBS)
Jazz Instrumentalists: Soloist, Miles Davis, "Tutu" (Warner Bros.); group, Wynton Marsalis, "J Mood" (Columbia/CBS)
Jazz, Big Band: The Tonight Show Band with Doc Severinsen, "The Tonight Show Band with Doc Severinsen" (Amherst)
Jazz Fusion: Bob James and David Sanborn, "Double Vision" (Warner Bros.)
Gospel Vocalists: Sandi Patti, "Morning Like This" (Word); Philip Bailey, "Triumph" (Myrrh/Word)
Gospel Group: Sandi Patti and Deniece Williams, "They Say" (track from "So Glad I Know") (Sparrow)
Soul Gospel Vocalists: Deniece Williams, "I Surrender All" (track from "So Glad I Know") (Sparrow); Al Green, "Going Away" (A&M)
Soul Gospel Group: The Winans, "Let My People Go" (Qwest)
Traditional Folk: "Riding the Midnight Train," Doc Watson (Sugar Hill)
Reggae: "Babylon the Bandit," Steel Pulse (Elektra)
Latin Pop: "Lelolai" (track from "Te Amare"), Jose Feliciano (RCA)
Tropical Latin: "Escenas," Ruben Blades (Elektra)
Mexican/American: "Ay Te Dejo en San Antonio," Flaco Jimenez (Arhoolie)
For Children: "The Alphabet" (The Sesame Street Muppets), Kathryn King and Geri Van Rees (Golden Books)
Comedy: "Those of You With or Without Children, You'll Understand," Bill Cosby (Geffen)
Spoken Word: "Interviews From the Class of '55—Recording Sessions," Carl Perkins, Jerry Lee Lewis, Roy Orbison, Johnny Cash, Sam Phillips, Rick Nelson and Chips Moman (America Record Corp.)
Instrumental Composition: John Barry, "Out of Africa" (music from the motion picture soundtrack) (MCA)
Instrumental Arrangement: Patrick Williams, "Suite Memories" (track from "Someplace Else") (Soundwings)
Cast Show Album: "Follies in Concert," Thomas Z. Shepard, Album Producer (RCA)
Video-Short Form: "Dire Straits Brothers in Arms," Dire Straits (Warner Reprise Video)
Video-Long Form: "Bring on the Night," Sting (Karl-Lorimar Home Video)
Historical Album: "Atlantic Rhythm and Blues 1947–1974 Vols. 1–7," Bob Porter and Aziz Goksel, Album Producers (Atlantic)
Classical Album: "Horowitz: The Studio Recordings, New York 1985," Vladimir Horowitz. Thomas Frost, Album Producer (Deutsche Grammophon)
Classical Orchestral Recording: "Liszt: A Faust Symphony," Sir Georg Solti, conductor, Chicago Symphony. Michael Haas, Album Producer (London)
Classical Soloist with or without Orchestra: "Horowitz: The Studio Recordings, New York 1985," Vladimir Horowitz (Deutsche Grammophon)
Chamber Music: "Beethoven: Cello & Piano Sonata No. 4 in C/ and Variations," Yo-Yo Ma and Emanuel Ax (CBS Masterworks)
Classical Vocal Soloist: Kathleen Battle, "Mozart: Kathleen Battle Sings Mozart" (Angel)
Classical, Choral: "Orff: Carmina Burana," James Levine, conductor, Chicago Symphony Chorus and Orchestra; Margaret Hillis, Choral Director (Deutsche Grammophon)
Opera: "Bernstein: Candide," John Mauceri, conductor New York City Opera Chorus and Orchestra (New World)
Contemporary Composition: "Lutoslawski: Symphony No. 3," Witold Lutoslawski (CBS Masterworks)
Producers: Non-Classical, Jimmy Jam and Terry Lewis; Classical, Thomas Frost

National Book Critics Circle Awards, 1987

Fiction: *Kate Vaiden,* by Reynolds Price (Atheneum)
General nonfiction: *War Without Mercy: Race and Power in the Pacific War,* by John W. Dower (Pantheon)
Poetry: *Wild Gratitude,* by Edward Hirsch (Alfred A. Knopf)
Criticism: *Less Than One: Selected Essays,* by Joseph Brodsky (Farrar, Straus & Giroux)
Biography/autobiography: *Tombee: Portrait of a Cotton Planter,* by Theodore Rosengarten (William Morrow)

Winners of Bollingen Prize in Poetry

($5,000 award is given biennially. It is administered by Yale University and the Bollingen Foundation.)

1949	Ezra Pound
1950	Wallace Stevens
1951	John Crowe Ransom
1952	Marianne Moore
1953	Archibald MacLeish and William Carlos Williams
1954	W. H. Auden
1955	Léonie Adams and Louise Bogan
1956	Conrad Aiken
1957	Allen Tate
1958	E.E. Cummings
1959	Theodore Roethke
1960	Delmore Schwartz
1961	Yvor Winters
1962	John Hall Wheelock and Richard Eberhart
1963	Robert Frost
1965	Horace Gregory
1967	Robert Penn Warren
1969	John Berryman and Karl Shapiro
1971	Richard Wilbur and Mona Van Duyn
1973	James Merrill
1975	Archie Randolph Ammons
1977	David Ignatow
1979	W. S. Merwin
1981	Howard Nemerov and May Swenson
1983	Anthony Hecht and John Hollander
1985	John Ashbery and Fred Chappell
1987	Stanley Kunitz

American Library Association Awards for Children's Books, 1986

John Newbery Medal for best book: *The Whipping Boy,* Sid Fleischman (Greenwillow)

Newbery Honor Books: *A Fine White Dust,* Cynthia Rylant (Bradbury); *Volcano,* Patricia Lauber (Bradbury); *On My Honor,* Marion Dane Bauer (Clarion)

Randolph Caldecott Medal for best picture book: *Hey, Al,* illustrated by Richard Egielski, written by Arthur Yorinks (Farrar, Straus & Giroux)

Caldecott Honor Books: *Rumpelstiltskin,* retold and illustrated by Paul O. Zelinsky (Dutton); *The Village of Round and Square Houses,* written and illustrated by Ann Grifalconi (Little, Brown); *Alphabatics,* a first picture book by Suse MacDonald (Bradbury)

American Book Awards, 1986

Established by Association of American Publishers

Fiction: *World's Fair* by E. L. Doctorow (Random House)

Nonfiction: *Arctic Dreams* by Barry Lopez (Charles Scribner's Sons)

1987 Christopher Awards

Adult Books

Arctic Dreams: Imagination and Desire in a Northern Landscape, by Barry Lopez (Scribner's)

Beyond Survival, by Theresa Saldana (Bantam Books)

Decision in Philadelphia: The Constitutional Convention of 1787, by Christopher Collier and James Lincoln Collier (Random House)

Faith of a People: The Life of a Basic Christian Community in El Salvador, by Pablo Galdamez, translated by Robert R. Barr (Orbis Books)

Kaffir Boy: The True Story of a Black Youth's Coming of Age in Apartheid South Africa, by Mark Mathabane (Macmillan)

A Loss for Words: The Story of Deafness in a Family, by Lou Ann Walker (Harper & Row)

A Testament of Hope: The Essential Writings of Martin Luther King, Jr., edited by James M. Washington (Harper & Row)

Through the Gospel with Dom Helder Camara, translated by Alan Neame (Orbis Books)

When All You've Ever Wanted Isn't Enough: The Search for a Life That Matters, by Harold S. Kushner (Summit Books)

Young People's Books

Duncan and Dolores, by Barbara Samuels (Bradbury Press)

The Purple Coat, by Amy Hest, pictures by Amy Schwartz (Four Winds Press)

Borrowed Summer, by Marion Walker Doren (Harper & Row)

Class Dismissed II, by Mel Glenn, photographs by Michael J. Berstein (Clarion Books)

Television Specials

Anne of Green Gables (PBS/WQED)

At a Loss for Words . . . Illiterate in America: ABC News Closeup

The George McKenna Story (CBS)

The Girl Who Spelled Freedom (ABC)

The Indomitable Teddy Roosevelt (ABC)

The Muppets—A Celebration of 30 Years (CBS)

Nobody's Child (CBS)

Promise (CBS)

Shadowlands (BBC/PBS)

The Statue of Liberty (PBS/WNET)

The Ted Kennedy, Jr. Story (NBC)

A Winner Never Quits (ABC)

Films

The Mission (Warner Bros.)

Mother Teresa (Petrie Productions)

Special Award

Elie Wiesel

Trevor Ferrell, First Christopher Youth Award

Presidential Medal of Freedom

The nation's highest civilian award, the Presidential Medal of Freedom, was established in 1963 by President John F. Kennedy to continue and expand Presidential recognition of meritorious service which, since 1945, had been granted as the Medal of Freedom. Kennedy selected the first recipients, but was assassinated before he could make the presentations. They were made by President Johnson. NOTE: An asterisk following a year denotes a posthumous award.

SELECTED BY PRESIDENT KENNEDY

Marian Anderson (contralto)	1963
Ralph J. Bunche (statesman)	1963
Ellsworth Bunker (diplomat)	1963
Pablo Casals (cellist)	1963
Genevieve Caulfield (educator)	1963
James B. Conant (educator)	1963
John F. Enders (bacteriologist)	1963
Felix Frankfurter (jurist)	1963
Karl Horton (youth authority)	1963
Robert J. Kiphuth (athletic director)	1963
Edwin H. Land (inventor)	1963
Herbert H. Lehman (statesman)	1963*
Robert A. Lovett (statesman)	1963
J. Clifford MacDonald (educator)	1963*
John J. McCloy (banker and statesman)	1963
George Meany (labor leader)	1963
Alexander Meiklejohn (philosopher)	1963
Ludwig Mies van der Rohe (architect)	1963
Jean Monnet (European statesman)	1963
Luis Muñoz-Marin (Governor of Puerto Rico)	1963
Clarence B. Randall (industrialist)	1963
Rudolf Serkin (pianist)	1963
Edward Steichen (photographer)	1963
George W. Taylor (educator)	1963
Alan T. Waterman (scientist)	1963
Mark S. Watson (journalist)	1963
Annie D. Wauneka (public health worker)	1963
E. B. White (author)	1963
Thornton N. Wilder (author)	1963
Edmund Wilson (author and critic)	1963
Andrew Wyeth (artist)	1963

AWARDED BY PRESIDENT JOHNSON

Dean G. Acheson (statesman)	1964
Eugene R. Black (banker)	1969
Detlev W. Bronk (neurophysiologist)	1964
McGeorge Bundy (government service)	1969
Ellsworth Bunker (diplomat)	1968
Clark Clifford (statesman)	1969
Aaron Copland (composer)	1964
Michael E. DeBakey (surgeon)	1969
Willem de Kooning (artist)	1964
Walt Disney (cartoon film producer)	1964
J. Frank Dobie (author)	1964
David Dubinsky (labor leader)	1969
Lena F. Edwards (physician and humanitarian)	1964
Thomas Stearns Eliot (poet)	1964
Ralph Ellison (author)	1969
Lynn Fontanne (actress)	1964
Henry Ford II (industrialist)	1969
John W. Gardner (educator)	1964
W. Averell Harriman (statesman)	1969
Rev. Theodore M. Hesburgh (educator)	1964
Bob Hope (comedian)	1969
John XXIII (Pope)	1963*
Clarence L. Johnson (aircraft engineer)	1964
Edgar F. Kaiser (industrialist)	1969
Frederick R. Kappel (telecommunications executive)	1964
Helen A. Keller (educator)	1964
John Fitzgerald Kennedy (U.S. President)	1963*
Robert W. Komer (government service)	1968
Mary Lasker (philanthropist)	1969
John L. Lewis (labor leader)	1964
Walter Lippmann (journalist)	1964
Eugene M. Locke (diplomat)	1968
Alfred Lunt (actor)	1964
John W. Macy, Jr. (government service)	1969
Ralph McGill (journalist)	1964
Robert S. McNamara (government service)	1968
Samuel Eliot Morison (historian)	1964
Lewis Mumford (urban planner and critic)	1964
Edward R. Murrow (radio-TV commentator)	1964
Reinhold Niebuhr (theologian)	1964
Gregory Peck (actor)	1969
Leontyne Price (soprano)	1964
A. Philip Randolph (labor leader)	1964
Laurance S. Rockefeller (conservationist)	1969
Walt Whitman Rostow (government service)	1969
Dean Rusk (statesman)	1969
Carl Sandburg (poet and biographer)	1964
Merriman Smith (journalist)	1969
John Steinbeck (author)	1964
Helen B. Taussig (pediatrician)	1964
Cyrus R. Vance (government service)	1969
Carl Vinson (legislator)	1964
Thomas J. Watson, Jr. (industrialist)	1964
James E. Webb (NASA administrator)	1968
Paul Dudley White (physician)	1964
William S. White (journalist)	1969
Roy Wilkins (social welfare executive)	1969
Whitney M. Young, Jr. (social welfare executive)	1969

AWARDED BY PRESIDENT NIXON

Edwin E. Aldrin (astronaut)	1969
Apollo 13 Mission Operations Team	1970
Neil A. Armstrong (astronaut)	1969
Earl Charles Behrens (journalist)	1970
Manlio Brosio (NATO secretary general)	1971
Michael Collins (astronaut)	1969
Edward K. (Duke) Ellington (musician)	1969
Edward T. Folliard (journalist)	1970
John Ford (film director)	1973
Samuel Goldwyn (film producer)	1971
Fred Wallace Haise, Jr. (astronaut)	1970
William M. Henry (journalist)	1970*
Paul G. Hoffman (statesman)	1974
William J. Hopkins (White House service)	1971
Arthur Krock (journalist)	1970
Melvin R. Laird (government service)	1974
David Lawrence (journalist)	1970
George Gould Lincoln (journalist)	1970
James A. Lovell, Jr. (astronaut)	1970
Dr. Charles L. Lowman (orthopedist)	1974
Raymond Moley (journalist)	1970
Eugene Ormandy (conductor)	1970
William P. Rogers (diplomat)	1973
Adela Rogers St. Johns (journalist)	1970
John Leonard Swigert, Jr. (astronaut)	1970
John Paul Vann (adviser, Vietnam war)	1972*
DeWitt and Lila Wallace (founders, *Reader's Digest*)	1972

AWARDED BY PRESIDENT FORD

I. W. Abel (labor leader)	1977
John Bardeen (physicist)	1977
Irving Berlin (composer)	1977
Norman Borlaug (agricultural scientist)	1977
Gen. Omar N. Bradley (soldier)	1977
David K. E. Bruce (diplomat)	1976
Arleigh Burke (national security)	1977
Alexander Calder (sculptor)	1977
Bruce Catton (historian)	1977

Joseph P. DiMaggio (baseball star)	1977
Ariel Durant (author)	1977
Will Durant (author)	1977
Arthur Fiedler (conductor)	1977
Henry J. Friendly (jurist)	1977
Martha Graham (dancer-choreographer)	1976
Claudia "Lady Bird" Johnson (service to U.S. scenic beauty)	1977
Henry A. Kissinger (statesman)	1977
Archibald MacLeish (poet)	1977
James A. Michener (author)	1977
Georgia O'Keeffe (artist)	1977
Jesse Owens (track champion)	1976
Nelson A. Rockefeller (government service)	1977
Norman Rockwell (illustrator)	1977
Arthur Rubinstein (pianist)	1976
Donald H. Rumsfeld (government service)	1977
Katherine Filene Shouse (service to the performing arts)	1977
Lowell Thomas (radio-TV commentator)	1977
James D. Watson (biochemist)	1977

AWARDED BY PRESIDENT CARTER

Ansel Adams (photographer)	1980
Horace M. Albright (government service)	1980
Roger Baldwin (civil libertarian)	1981
Harold Brown (government service)	1981
Zbigniew Brzezinski (government service)	1981
Rachel Carson (author)	1980*
Lucia Chase (ballet director)	1980
Warren M. Christopher (government service)	1981
Walter Cronkite (TV newscaster)	1981
Kirk Douglas (actor)	1981
Arthur J. Goldberg (government service)	1978
Hubert H. Humphrey (government service)	1980*
Archbishop Iakovos (churchman)	1980
Lyndon B. Johnson (U.S. President)	1980*
Rev. Dr. Martin Luther King, Jr. (civil rights leader)	1977*
Margaret Craig McNamara (educator)	1981
Margaret Mead (anthropologist)	1979*
Karl Menninger (psychiatrist)	1981
Clarence Mitchell, Jr. (civil rights leader)	1980
Edmund S. Muskie (government service)	1981
Esther Peterson (government service)	1981
Roger Tory Peterson (ornithologist)	1980
Adm. Hyman Rickover (national security)	1980
Jonas Salk (medical research)	1977
Beverly Sills (opera singer)	1980
Gerard C. Smith (government service)	1981
Robert S. Strauss (government service)	1981
Elbert Parr Tuttle (government service)	1981
Earl Warren (government service)	1981*
Robert Penn Warren (author and poet)	1980
John Wayne (actor)	1980*
Eudora Welty (author)	1980
Tennessee Williams (playwright)	1980
Andrew M. Young (government service)	1981

AWARDED BY PRESIDENT REAGAN

Walter H. Annenberg (publisher and diplomat)	1986
Anne L. Armstrong (diplomat)	1986
Howard H. Baker, Jr. (government service)	1984
George Balanchine (choreographer)	1983
Count Basie (jazz pianist)	1985*
Earl (Red) Blaik (football coach)	1986
James H. (Eubie) Blake (composer-pianist)	1981
Paul W. (Bear) Bryant (football coach)	1983*
James Burnham (editor-historian)	1983
James Francis Cagney (actor)	1984
Whittaker Chambers (public servant)	1984*
James Cheek (educator)	1983
Leo Cherne (economist-humanitarian)	1984
Terence Cardinal Cooke, His Eminence (theologian)	1984*
Denton Arthur Cooley, M.D. (heart surgeon)	1984
Jacques-Yves Cousteau (marine explorer)	1985
Justin W. Dart Sr. (businessman)	1986*
Tennessee Ernie Ford (singer)	1984
R. Buckminster Fuller (architect-geometrician)	1983
Hector P. Garcia, M.D. (humanitarian)	1984
Barry Goldwater (government service)	1986
Gen. Andrew J. Goodpaster (soldier-diplomat)	1984
Rev. Billy Graham (evangelist)	1983
Ella T. Grasso (Connecticut governor)	1981*
Philip C. Habib (diplomat)	1982
Bryce N. Harlow (government service)	1981
Helen Hayes (actress)	1986
Eric Hoffer (philosopher-longshoreman)	1983
Jerome Holland (educator and ambassador)	1985*
Sidney Hook (philosopher-educator)	1985
Vladimir Horowitz (pianist)	1985
Jacob K. Javits (government service)	1983
Walter H. Judd (government service)	1981
Danny Kaye (actor)	1986*
Jeane J. Kirkpatrick (government service)	1985
Lincoln Kirstein (ballet director)	1984
Louis L'Amour (author)	1984
Morris I. Leibman (lawyer)	1981
Gen. Lyman L. Lemnitzer (soldier)	1986
George M. Low (educator and administrator NASA)	1985*
Clare Booth Luce (author-diplomat)	1983
Joseph M.A.H. Luns (diplomat-NATO)	1984
Dumas Malone (historian)	1983
John A. McCone (government service)	1986
Mabel Mercer (jazz singer)	1983
Paul Nitz (government service)	1985
Frederick Patterson (educator)	1986
Norman Vincent Peale (theologian)	1984
Nathan Perlmutter (public service)	1986
Simon Ramo (industrialist)	1983
Frank Reynolds (TV anchor)	1985*
Gen. Matthew B. Ridgway (soldier)	1986
S. Dillon Ripley (cultural and public service)	1985
Jack Roosevelt Robinson (baseball player)	1984*
Gen. Carlos P. Romulo (Philippino statesman)	1984
Mstislav Rostropovich (cellist-conductor)	1986
Vermont Royster (journalist)	1986
Albert B. Sabin (medical research)	1986
Mohamed Anwar el-Sadat (statesman)	1984*
Eunice Kennedy Shriver (humanitarian)	1984
Frank Sinatra (entertainer)	1985
Kate Smith (singer)	1982
James Stewart (actor)	1985
Mother Teresa (humanitarian)	1985
Charles B. Thornton (industrialist)	1981
William B. Walsh (humanitarian)	1986
Gen. Albert Coady Wedemeyer (national security)	1985
Meredith Willson (composer)	1986*
Albert and Roberta Wohlstetter (government service)	1985
Charles E. Yeager (public service)	1985

1987 Bancroft Prizes in American History

A Vigorous Spirit of Enterprise: Merchants and Economic Development in Revolutionary Philadelphia, by Thomas M. Doerflinger (University of North Carolina Press)

Roots of Violence in Black Philadelphia, 1860–1900, by Roger Lane (Harvard University Press)

1987 MacArthur Foundation Awards

The MacArthur Foundation Fellowships, which range from $150,000 to $375,000 given over a five-year period, are designed to free the recipients from economic pressures, enabling them to devote themselves to research, scholarship, or creative artistic pursuits. There are no strings attached. The awards are now subject to Federal taxes and have been increased to account for the tax burden.

Walter Abish, Austrian-born avant-garde writer
Robert Axelrod, political scientist, author, Arthur W. Bromage Professor of Political Science at the University of Michigan
Robert F. Coleman, mathematician and associate professor at the University of California–Berkeley
Douglas Crase, poet
Daniel H. Friedan, physicist and professor at the University of Chicago
David Gross, theoretical physicist and professor at Princeton University
Ira Herskowitz, scientist working in the fields of genetics, biochemistry, and biophysics, professor at the University of California–San Francisco
Irving Howe, literary critic, author, editor
Wesley Charles Jacobs, Jr., a rural planner, Oglala Sioux, working on project for economic development in tribal areas
Peter Jeffery, musicologist and assistant professor at the University of Delaware
Horace Freeland Judson, science writer and Henry R. Luce Professor of Science and Writing at Johns Hopkins University
Stuart Kauffman, biologist and former surgeon and professor of biochemistry at the University of Pennsylvania Medical School
Richard Kenney, poet
Eric Steven Lander, mathematician
Michael C. Malin, geophysicist and assistant professor at Arizona State University
Deborah W. Meier, educator and founder of East Harlem schools
Arnaldo Dante Momigliano, Italian-born historian
David Mumford, mathematician and professor at Harvard University
Tina Rosenberg, journalist
David Rumelhart, psychologist and computer scientist and professor at Stanford University
Robert Morris Sapolsky, endrocrinologist and assistant professor at Stanford University
Meyer Schapiro, art historian
John Schwarz, theoretical physicist and professor at California Institute of Technology
Jon Seger, biologist and mathematician and professor at the University of Utah
Stephen Shenker, theoretical physicist and professor at the University of Chicago
David Shulman, philologist and professor of Indian studies and comparative literature at the Hebrew University
Muriel Sutherland Snowden, community organizer and cofounder of Freedom House in Roxbury, Mass.
Mark Strand, poet, art critic, and professor at the University of Utah
May Swenson, poet
Huynh Sanh Thong, Vietnamese-born translator and editor; director of Yale Southeast Asian Refugee Project in New Haven
William Julius Wilson, sociologist, author, and chairman of sociology department at the University of Chicago
Richard Walter Wrangham, primate ethologist and associate professor at the University of Michigan

Humanitas Prize 1986–87

The Humanitas Prize is given to writers of television programs that "probe the meaning of human life" or supply "enriching human values."

Long-form: *Promise,* story by Kenneth Blackwell, Tennyson Flowers, and Richard Friedenberg, with teleplay by Mr. Friedenberg
Hour episode: *Family Ties,* written by Alan Uger and Gary David Goldberg
Half-hour episode: *Kate and Allie,* written by Bob Randall
Children's animation: *Smurfs,* episode, written by John Loy and Alan Burnett
Children's live-action: *The Day They Came to Arrest the Book,* written by Melvin Van Peebles

1987 United Nations Population Award

The Award seeks "to promote the solution of population questions through encouraging the efforts of people in population-related activities and increasing the awareness of population questions." It was established by the General Assembly in 1981 and is presented annually to an individual, to individuals or to an institution for the most outstanding contribution to increasing the awareness of population questions or to their solutions.

Winners to date are:

1983 Indira Gandhi, Prime Minister of India
Qian Xinzhong, Minister in Charge of the State Family Planning Commission and Deputy for the National People's Congress of China
1984 Carmen Miro of Panama, former Director of the Latin American Demographic Center
Sheldon Segal of the United States, Director of the Population Division of The Rockefeller Foundation
1985 International Planned Parenthood Federation, with headquarters in London, England, a federation of national family planning associations in 121 countries
1986 National Population Council of Mexico, an interministerial body responsible for coordinating population planning in Mexico in the context of socio-economic development
1987 Hussain Muhammad Ershad, President of Bangladesh
National Office for the Family and Population of Tunisia

ENTERTAINMENT & CULTURE

Notable Books, 1986

This list has been compiled by the Notable Books Council, Reference and Adult Services, a division of the American Library Association for use by the general reader and by librarians who work with adult readers. The titles were selected for their significant contribution to the expansion of knowledge or for the pleasure they can provide to adult readers. Criteria include wide general appeal and literary merit.

Atwood, Margaret, **The Handmaid's Tale,** Houghton
Baker, Will, **Mountain Blood,** University of Georgia
Beschloss, Michael R., **MAYDAY: Eisenhower, Khrushchev, and the U-2 Affair,** Harper
Carillo, Charles, **Shepherd Avenue,** Atlantic Monthly Press
Carter, Angela, **Saints and Strangers,** Viking
Charyn, Jerome, **Metropolis: New York as Myth, Market-place, and Magical Land,** Putnam
Critchfield, Richard, **Those Days: An American Album,** Doubleday/Anchor
Denby, Edwin, **The Complete Poems,** Random
Dubus, Andre, **The Last Worthless Evening,** Godine
Duras, Marguerite, **The War: A Memoir,** translated by Barbara Bray, Pantheon
Erdrich, Louise, **The Beet Queen,** Holt
Goldberg, Vicki, **Margaret Bourke-White: A Biography,** Harper
Grooms, Red, **Red Grooms: A Retrospective, 1956–1984,** Abrams/Pennsylvania Academy of Fine Arts
Henley, Patricia, **Friday Night at Silver Stars: Stories,** Graywolf
Hersh, Seymour M., **"The Target Is Destroyed": What Really Happened to Flight 007 and What America Knew About It,** Random
Hochschild, Adam, **Half the Way Home: A Memoir of Father and Son,** Viking
Hugo, Richard, **The Real West Marginal Way: A Poet's Autobiography,** Norton
Ishiguro, Kazuo, **An Artist of the Floating World,** Putnam
Jhabvala, Ruth Prawer, **Out of India,** Morrow
Lopez, Barry, **Arctic Dreams: Imagination and Desire in a Northern Landscape,** Scribner
McFadden, Cyra, **Rain or Shine: A Family Memoir,** Knopf
Malone, Michael, **Handling Sin,** Little, Brown
Maslow, Jonathan Evan, **Bird of Life, Bird of Death: A Naturalist's Journey Through a Land of Political Turmoil,** Simon & Schuster
Matthiessen, Peter, **Men's Lives: The Surfmen and Baymen of the South Fork,** Random
Mehta, Ved, **Sound-shadows of the New World,** Norton
Parfit, Michael, **South Light: A Journey to the Last Continent,** Macmillan
Pratt, Charles W., **In the Orchard,** Tidal Press
Price, Reynolds, **Kate Vaiden,** Atheneum
Rivabella, Omar, **Requiem for a Woman's Soul,** translated by Paul Riviera and Omar Rivabella, Random
Rosengarten, Theodore, **Tombee: Portrait of a Cotton Planter; With the Journal of Thomas B. Chaplin (1822–1890),** Morrow
Roszak, Theodore, **The Cult of Information: The Folklore of Computers and the True Art of Thinking,** Pantheon
Rush, Norman, **Whites,** Knopf
Shipler, David K., **Arab and Jew: Wounded Spirits in a Promised Land,** Times Books
Sperber, A.M., **Murrow: His Life and Times,** Freundlich
Stone, Robert, **Children of Light,** Knopf
Szulc, Tad, **Fidel: A Critical Portrait,** Morrow
Taylor, Peter, **A Summons to Memphis,** Knopf

Source: Reprinted by permission of the American Library Association. Issued as a pamphlet by ALA, 50 E. Huron St., Chicago, Ill. 60611, annually in the spring for the preceding year. © American Library Association 1987.

Major U.S. Symphony Orchestras and Their Music Directors

Source: American Symphony Orchestra League.

Atlanta Symphony: Robert Shaw
Baltimore Symphony: David Zinman
Boston Symphony: Seiji Ozawa
Buffalo Philharmonic: Semyon Bychkov
Chicago Symphony: Sir Georg Solti
Cincinnati Symphony: Jesus Lopez-Cobos
Cleveland Orchestra: Christoph von Dohnanyi
Dallas Symphony: Eduardo Mata
Denver Symphony: Philippe Entremont[1]
Detroit Symphony: Gunther Herbig
Houston Symphony: Sergiu Comissiona
Indianapolis Symphony: Raymond Nelson
Los Angeles Philharmonic: André Previn
Milwaukee Symphony: Zdenek Macal
Minnesota Orchestra: Edo de Waart
National Symphony: (D.C.): Mstislav Rostropovich
New Orleans Symphony Orchestra: Maxim Shostakovich
New York Philharmonic: Zubin Mehta
Oregon Symphony: James DePreist
Philadelphia Orchestra: Riccardo Muti
Phoenix Symphony Orchestra: Theo Alcantara
Pittsburgh Symphony: Lorin Maazel[2]
Rochester Philharmonic: Jerzy Semkow[3,1]
Saint Louis Symphony: Leonard Slatkin
Saint Paul Chamber Orchestra: Stanislaw Skrowaczewski[3]
San Antonio Symphony: Sixten Ehrling[4]
San Diego Symphony: Position not filled
San Francisco Symphony: Herbert Blomstedt
Seattle Symphony: Gerard Schwarz
Syracuse Symphony: Kazuyoshi Akiyama
Utah Symphony: Joseph Silverstein

1. Principal Conductor. 2. Music Director effective Sept. 1, 1988. Currently Principal Guest Conductor and Music Advisor. 3. Music Advisor. 4. Artistic Advisor.

Major Public Libraries

City (branches)	Volumes	Circulation	Budget (in millions)
Akron-Summit County, Ohio (18)	1,075,942	2,472,143	$9.7
Albuquerque, N.M. (8)	526,926	1,963,495	4.6
Annapolis, Md. (13)	1,752,937	3,855,042	8.1
Atlanta (26)	1,381,231	2,421,433	11.4
Austin, Tex. (16)	881,195	2,362,210	8.8
Baltimore (31)	1,908,202	1,541,547	12.8
Baton Rouge, La. (9)	547,106	1,636,567	7.3
Birmingham, Ala. (19)	1,100,000	2,264,594	7.5
Boston (25)	5,568,008	1,685,926	17.5
Buffalo-Erie County, N.Y. (58)	3,522,174	5,939,394	14.2
Charleston-Kanawha County, W.Va. (10)	558,513	1,040,911	2.8
Charlotte, N.C. (19)	936,000	2,951,586	7.4
Chicago (87)	4,764,673	8,134,798	47.2
Cincinnati (40)	3,413,334	6,937,878	20.2
Cleveland (31)	2,647,648	3,848,033	19.5
Columbus-Franklin County, Ohio (20)	1,459,745	4,970,272	23.8
Dallas (19)	1,877,855	4,025,672	15.1
Dayton-Montgomery County Ohio (19)	1,450,213	5,084,823	10.3
Denver (21)	1,976,188	2,785,565	11.8
Des Moines, Iowa (5)	979,559	1,250,816	2.9
Detroit (24)	2,617,973	1,752,280	21.4
D.C. (26)	1,439,957	1,825,677	15.0
El Paso (9)	1,100,000	1,250,000	4.0
Erie, Pa. (6)	420,355	1,466,536	2.1
Evansville-Vanderburgh County, Ind. (7)	614,998	1,932,055	3.2
Fort Wayne-Allen County, Ind. (12)	1,774,745	2,795,335	6.8
Fort Worth (8)	1,668,589	2,840,743	5.7
Grand Rapids, Mich. (5)	634,680	889,615	3.0
Greenville City-County S.C. (11)	741,350	1,220,584	3.7
Honolulu (49)[1]*	n.a.	n.a.	n.a.
Houston (33)	3,400,437	6,779,755	16.8
Independence, Mo. (26)	1,400,000	3,500,000	9.0
Indianapolis-Marion County (23)	1,588,773	4,599,612	12.9
Jackson, Miss. (12)	500,000	788,600	2.1
Jacksonville, Fla. (11)	1,600,157	2,130,627	7.1
Kansas City, Mo. (14)	2,059,452	847,689	5.4
Knoxville, Tenn. (19)	623,916	1,595,847	3.4
Lincoln, Neb. (7)	456,623	1,341,966	2.7
Long Beach, Calif. (11)	870,300	2,638,501	10.5
Los Angeles (County) (102)	4,302,441	11,796,385	45.0

City (branches)	Volumes	Circulation	Budget (in millions)
Louisville, Ky. (14)	881,928	3,048,620	$6.8
Madison, Wis. (7)	556,738	1,853,188	4.5
Memphis, Tenn. (22)	3,331,704	222,273	9.3
Miami-Dade County, Fla. (28)	2,269,302	4,631,004	21.9
Milwaukee (12)	2,047,609	3,456,067	12.6
Minneapolis (14)	1,768,114	2,715,377	11.6
Nashville-Davidson County, Tenn. (15)	601,047	1,908,974	5.7
Newark, N.J. (11)	1,350,000	1,500,000	6.4
New Orleans (11)	898,563	1,064,302	5.6
New York City:			
†The New York Public Library Branches (81)	3,252,844	8,329,234	60.1
Research	8,793,426	—	42.2
Brooklyn (60)	4,450,548	9,024,458	29.1
Queens (60)	5,357,378	10,937,592	34.1
Norfolk, Va. (11)	803,323	888,800	4.0
Oklahoma City-County (10)	811,147	2,860,000	8.7
Omaha, Neb. (9)	560,002	1,812,732	4.3
Philadelphia (52)	4,510,329	5,464,676	34.8
Phoenix, Ariz. (9)	1,349,000	4,819,900	10.8
Pittsburgh (20)	1,813,738	2,944,117	10.9
Portland-Multnomah County, Ore. (14)	1,194,750	3,734,742	7.8
Providence, R.I. (8)	1,103,421	901,053	3.5
Richmond, Va. (10)	706,374	918,160	2.9
Rochester, N.Y. (11)	1,344,144	1,486,658	8.5
Sacramento, Calif. (26)	1,375,121	4,354,634	12.8
St. Louis (14)	1,056,240	1,175,538	5.8
St. Paul (12)	747,123	2,233,525	5.1
St. Petersburg, Fla. (4)*	434,000	1,231,396	1.9
Salt Lake City-County, Utah (14)	1,100,000	3,363,000	8.0
San Antonio (15)	1,566,375	3,004,609	7.4
San Diego, Calif. (31)	1,558,175	4,281,332	12.4
San Francisco (26)	1,974,896	3,221,351	15.5
San Jose, Calif. (18)	1,200,200	3,524,700	14.0
Seattle (22)	1,668,855	4,404,504	14.0
Springfield, Mass. (8)	650,000	1,204,000	4.5
Tampa, Fla. (16)	1,411,028	2,300,000	8.5
Tucson, Ariz. (15)	747,000	4,132,000	8.6
Tulsa City-County, Okla. (20)	785,163	2,342,807	7.4
Wichita, Kan. (11)	877,637	1,303,552	3.1
Winston-Salem-Forsyth County, N.C. (8)	350,000	1,850,000	4.0
Worcester, Mass. (6)	638,844	672,671	2.7
Youngstown-Mahoning County, Ohio (22)	767,140	1,484,502	4.8

1. State-wide system. † Includes Manhattan, Bronx, and Staten Island. * Did not reply to questionnaire.

Glossary of Art Movements

Abstract Expressionism. American art movement of the 1940s that emphasized form and color within a nonrepresentational framework. Jackson Pollock initiated the revolutionary technique of splattering the paint directly on canvas to achieve the subconscious interpretation of the artist's inner vision of reality.

Art Deco. A 1920s style characterized by setbacks, zigzag forms, and the use of chrome and plastic ornamentation. New York's Chrysler Building is an architectural example of the style.

Art Nouveau. An 1890s style in architecture, graphic arts, and interior decoration characterized by writhing forms, curving lines, and asymmetrical organization. Some critics regard the style as the first stage of modern architecture.

Ashcan School. A group of New York realist artists, formed in 1908, who abandoned decorous subject matter and portrayed the more common as well as the sordid aspects of city life.

Assemblage (Collage). Forms of modern sculpture and painting utilizing readymades, found objects, and pasted fragments to form an abstract composition. Louise Nevelson's boxlike enclosures, each with its own composition of assembled objects, illustrate the style in sculpture. Pablo Picasso developed the technique of cutting and pasting natural or manufactured materials to a painted or unpainted surface.

Barbizon School (Landscape Painting). A group of painters who, around the middle of the 19th century, reacted against classical landscape and advocated a direct study of nature. They were influenced by English and Dutch landscape masters. Theodore Rousseau, one of the principal figures of the group, led the fight for outdoor painting. In this respect, the school was a forerunner of Impressionism.

Baroque. European art and architecture of the 17th and 18th centuries. Giovanni Bernini, a major exponent of the style, believed in the union of the arts of architecture, painting, and sculpture to overwhelm the spectator with ornate and highly dramatized themes. Although the style originated in Rome as the instrument of the Church, it spread throughout Europe in such monumental creations as the Palace of Versailles.

Beaux Arts. Elaborate and formal architectural style characterized by symmetry and an abundance of sculptured ornamentation. New York's old Custom House at Bowling Green is an example of the style.

Black or Afro-American Art. The work of American artists of African descent produced in various styles characterized by a mood of protest and a search for identity and historical roots.

Classicism. A form of art derived from the study of Greek and Roman styles characterized by harmony, balance, and serenity. In contrast, the Romantic Movement gave free rein to the artist's imagination and to the love of the exotic.

Constructivism. A form of sculpture using wood, metal, glass, and modern industrial materials expressing the technological society. The mobiles of Alexander Calder are examples of the movement.

Cubism. Early 20th-century French movement marked by a revolutionary departure from representational art. Pablo Picasso and Georges Bracque penetrated the surface of objects, stressing basic abstract geometric forms that presented the object from many angles simultaneously.

Dada. A product of the turbulent and cynical post-World War I period, this anti-art movement extolled the irrational, the absurd, the nihilistic, and the nonsensical. The reproduction of Mona Lisa adorned with a mustache is a famous example. The movement is regarded as a precursor of Surrealism. Some critics regard HAPPENINGS as a recent development of Dada. This movement incorporates environment and spectators as active and important ingredients in the production of random events.

Expressionism. A 20th-century European art movement that stresses the expression of emotion and the inner vision of the artist rather than the exact representation of nature. Distorted lines and shapes and exaggerated colors are used for emotional impact. Vincent Van Gogh is regarded as the precursor of this movement.

Fauvism. The name "wild beasts" was given to the group of early 20th-century French painters because their work was characterized by distortion and violent colors. Henri Matisse and Georges Roualt were leaders of this group.

Futurism. This early 20th-century movement originating in Italy glorified the machine age and attempted to represent machines and figures in motion. The aesthetics of Futurism affirmed the beauty of technological society.

Genre. This French word meaning "type" now refers to paintings that depict scenes of everyday life without any attempt at idealization. Genre paintings can be found in all ages, but the Dutch productions of peasant and tavern scenes are typical.

Impressionism. Late 19th-century French school dedicated to defining transitory visual impressions painted directly from nature, with light and color of primary importance. If the atmosphere changed, a totally different picture would emerge. It was not the object or event that counted but the visual impression as caught at a certain time of day under a certain light. Claude Monet and Camille Pissarro were leaders of the movement.

Mannerism. A mid-16th century movement, Italian in origin, although El Greco was a major practitioner of the style. The human figure, distorted and elongated, was the most frequent subject.

Neoclassicism. An 18th-century reaction to the excesses of Baroque and Rococo, this European art movement tried to recreate the art of Greece and Rome by imitating the ancient classics both in style and subject matter.

Neoimpressionism. A school of painting associated with George Seurat and his followers in late 19th-century France that sought to make Impressionism more precise and formal. They employed a technique of juxtaposing dots of primary colors to achieve brighter secondary colors, with the mixture left to the eye to complete (pointillism).

Op Art. The 1960s movement known as Optical Painting is characterized by geometrical forms that create an optical illusion in which the eye is required to blend the colors at a certain distance.

Pop Art. In this return to representational art, the artist returns to the world of tangible objects in a reaction against abstraction. Materials are drawn from the everyday world of popular culture—comic strips, canned goods, and science fiction.

Realism. A development in mid-19th-century France lead by Gustave Courbet. Its aim was to depict the customs, ideas, and appearances of the time using scenes from everyday life.

Rococo. A French style of interior decoration developed during the reign of Louis XV consisting mainly of asymmetrical arrangements of curves in paneling, porcelain, and gold and silver objects. The characteristics of ornate curves, prettiness, and gaiety can also be found in the painting and sculpture of the period.

Surrealism. A further development of Collage, Cubism, and Dada, this 20th-century movement stresses the weird, the fantastic, and the dreamworld of the subconscious.

Symbolism. As part of a general European movement in the latter part of the 19th century, it was closely allied with Symbolism in literature. It marked a turning away from painting by observation to transforming fact into a symbol of inner experience. Gauguin was an early practitioner.

Top 10 Videocassettes Sales, 1986

1. **Jane Fonda's New Workout** (Karl Lorimar Home Video)
2. **Jane Fonda's Workout** (Karl Lorimar Home Video)
3. **Pinocchio** (Walt Disney Home Video)
4. **Beverly Hills Cop** (Paramount Home Video)
5. **The Sound of Music** (CBS-Fox Video)
6. **Jane Fonda's Prime Time Workout** (Karl Lorimar Home Video)
7. **Casablanca** (CBS-Fox Video)
8. **Gone with the Wind** (MGM/UA Home Video)
9. **The Wizard of Oz** (MGM/UA Home Video)
10. **The Best of John Belushi** (Warner Home Video)

Source: Billboard © 1986 by Billboard Publications, Inc. Compiled by the Billboard Research Department and reprinted with permission.

Top 10 Videocassettes Rentals, 1986

1. **Back to the Future** (MCA Dist. Corp.)
2. **Beverly Hills Cop** (Paramount Home Video)
3. **Prizzi's Honor** (Vestron)
4. **Witness** (Paramount Home Video)
5. **Ghostbusters** (RCA/Columbia Pictures Home Video)
6. **Rambo: First Blood Part II** (HBO/Cannon Video)
7. **Return of the Jedi** (CBS-Fox Video)
8. **Cocoon** (CBS-Fox Video)
9. **Mask** (MCA Dist. Corp.)
10. **Gremlins** (Warner Home Video)

Source: Billboard. © 1986 Billboard Publications, Inc. Compiled by the Billboard Research Department and reprinted with permission.

Top 10 Music Videocassettes, 1986

1. **The Virgin Tour-Madonna Live** (Warner Music Video)
2. **Motown 25: Yesterday, Today, Forever** (MGM/UA Home Video)
3. **No Jacket Required** (Atlantic Video)
4. **The #1 Video Hits** (MusicVision)
5. **John Lennon Live in New York** (Sony Video Software)
6. **The Beatles Live-Ready Steady Go!** (Sony Video Software)
7. **Wham! The Video** (CBS-Fox Video)
8. **Prince and The Revolution Live** (Warner Music Video)
9. **I Can't Wait** (MusicVision)
10. **Dick Clark's Best of Bandstand** (Vestron Music Video)

Source: Billboard. © 1986 by Billboard Publications, Inc. Compiled by the Billboard Research Department and reprinted with permission.

VCR & TV Sales to Retailers, 1986

Television	
Color	18,204,000
Monochrome	3,959,000
Total TV[1]	22,163,000
Projection TV	304,000
Home VCR	13,174,000
Color Video Cameras and Camcorders	1,282,000

1. Excludes projection television.
Source: Electronic Industries Association Consumer Electronics Group.

10 Top-grossing Concerts

(Dec. 7, 1985–Nov. 29, 1986)

1. **Neil Diamond,** $2,927,835, Madison Square Garden, New York, N.Y., July 24–31, 1986.
2. **Bill Cosby,** $2,833,690, Radio City Music Hall, New York, N.Y., Jan. 31–Feb. 2, Feb. 7–9, March 7–9, 1986.
3. **Neil Diamond,** $2,374,884, Greek Theatre, Los Angeles, Calif., Aug. 14–20, 22–28, 1986.
4. **Liberace & The Rockettes, Dancing Waters with Eric Hamelin,** $2,365,033, Radio City Music Hall, New York, N.Y., Oct. 16–Nov. 2, 1986.
5. **The Grateful Dead, Bob Dylan, Tom Petty & The Heartbreakers,** $2,132,700, Robert F. Kennedy Stadium, Washington, D.C., July 6–7, 1986.
6. **Genesis,** $1,898,937, Madison Square Garden, New York, N.Y., Sept. 29–Oct. 3, 1986.
7. **Genesis,** $1,784,772, Rosemont Horizon, Rosemont, Ill., Oct. 5–10, 1986.
8. **Amnesty International "A Conspiracy of Hope,"** $1,757,245, Giants Stadium, East Rutherford, N.J., June 15, 1986.
9. **Genesis,** $1,440,421, The Forum, Inglewood, Calif., Oct. 13–17, 1986.
10. **Texxas World Music Festival: Van Halen, Loverboy, Dio, Krokus, Keel, Bachman-Turner Overdrive,** $1,400,560, Cotton Bowl, Dallas, Texas, July 19, 1986.

Source: Copyright 1986 by Amusement Business. Reprinted by permission.

Top 10 Classical Compact Discs, 1986

1. **Amadeus Soundtrack,** Neville Marriner (Fantasy)
2. **Tchaikovsky: 1812 Overture,** Cincinnati Pops (Kunzel) (Telarc)
3. **Time Warp,** Cincinnati Pops (Kunzel) (Telarc)
4. **Bachbusters,** Don Dorsey (Telarc)
5. **Bernstein: West Side Story,** Te Kanawa, Carreras (Bernstein) (DG)
6. **Star Tracks,** Cincinnati Pops (Kunzel) (Telarc)
7. **Blue Skies,** Kiri Te Kanawa (Riddle) (London)
8. **Horowitz: The Last Romantic,** Vladimir Horowitz (DG)
9. **Telarc Sampler #1,** Various Artists (Telarc)
10. **Swing, Swing, Swing,** Boston Pops (Williams) (Philips)

Source: Billboard. © 1986 by Billboard Publications, Inc. Compiled by the Billboard Research Department and reprinted with permission.

Top 10 Pop Compact Discs, 1986

1. **Brothers in Arms,** Dire Straits (Warner Bros.)
2. **Whitney Houston,** Whitney Houston (Arista)
3. **No Jacket Required,** Phil Collins (Atlantic)
4. **Scarecrow,** John Cougar Mellencamp (Riva)
5. **Dark Side of the Moon,** Pink Floyd (Harvest)
6. **Promise,** Sade (Portrait)
7. **So,** Peter Gabriel (Geffen)
8. **Heart,** Heart (Capitol)
9. **Born in the U.S.A.,** Bruce Springsteen (Columbia)
10. **The Broadway Album,** Barbra Streisand (Columbia)

Source: Billboard. © 1986 by Billboard Publications, Inc. Compiled by the Billboard Research Department and reprinted with permission.

Top 10 Classical Albums, 1986

1. **Horowitz: The Last Romantic,** Vladimir Horowitz (DG)
2. **Amadeus Soundtrack,** Neville Marriner (Fantasy)
3. **Gershwin: Rhapsody in Blue,** Los Angeles Philharmonic (Thomas) (CBS)
4. **Pleasures of Their Company,** Kathleen Battle, Christopher Parkening (Angel)
5. **Webber: Requiem,** Domingo, Brightman (Maazel) (Angel)
6. **Tomas/Jolivet:** Trumpet Concertos, Wynton Marsalis (CBS)
7. **Music of Wolfgang Amadeus Mozart,** Various Artists (Angel)
8. **Romances for Saxophone,** Branford Marsalis (CBS)
9. **The Desert Music,** Steve Reich (Nonesuch)
10. **Glass: Satyagraha,** Philip Glass (CBS)

Source: Billboard © 1986 by Billboard Publications, Inc. Compiled by the Billboard Research Department and reprinted by permission.

Artists of the Year, 1986

Based on combined singles and albums chart performance—through sales and radio play—during the year.

Single of the Year: That's What Friends Are For, Dionne & Friends
Album of the Year: Whitney Houston, Whitney Houston
Female Artist of the Year: Whitney Houston
Male Artist of the Year: John Cougar Mellencamp
Group of the Year: ZZ Top
New Artist of the Year: Miami Sound Machine
Country Artist of the Year: George Strait
Black Artist of the Year: Janet Jackson
Adult Contemporary Artist of the Year: Billy Ocean
Jazz Artist of the Year: Stanley Jordan
Classical Artist of the Year: Neville Marriner
Soundtrack of the Year: Top Gun

Source: Billboard. © 1986 by Billboard Publications, Inc. Compiled by the Billboard Research Department and reprinted with permission.

Top 10 Black Single Recordings, 1986

1. **On My Own,** Patti LaBelle & Michael McDonald (MCA)
2. **Do Me Baby,** Meli'sa Morgan (Capitol)
3. **Secret Lovers,** Atlantic Starr (A&M)
4. **That's What Friends Are For,** Dionne & Friends (Arista)
5. **Nasty,** Janet Jackson (A&M)
6. **Kiss,** Prince & The Revolution (Paisley Park)
7. **Rumors,** Timex Social Club (Jay)
8. **There'll Be Sad Songs (To Make You Cry),** Billy Ocean (Jive)
9. **I Have Learned To Respect the Power of Love,** Stephanie Mills (MCA)
10. **I Can't Wait,** Nu Shooz (Atlantic)

Source: Billboard. © 1986 by Billboard Publications, Inc. Compiled by the Billboard Research Department and reprinted with permission.

Manufacturers' Dollar[1] Shipments of Recordings

(in millions)

	1983	1984	1985	1986
Singles	269	299	281	228
LP's/EP's	1,689	1,549	1,281	983
CD's	17	103	390	930
Cassettes	1,811	2,384	2,412	2,500
8-Tracks	30	36	25	11

1. List price value. *Source:* Recording Industry Association of America, Inc.

Top 10 Country Single Recordings, 1986

1. **Never Be You,** Rosanne Cash (Columbia)
2. **Too Much On My Heart,** The Statler Brothers (Mercury)
3. **I Don't Mind the Thorns (If You're the Rose),** Lee Greenwood (MCA)
4. **Have Mercy,** The Judds (RCA/Curb)
5. **I'll Never Stop Loving You,** Gary Morris (Warner Bros.)
6. **Morning Desire,** Kenny Rogers (RCA)
7. **You Can Dream of Me,** Steve Wariner (MCA)
8. **Whoever's in New England,** Reba McEntire (MCA)
9. **Until I Met You,** Judy Rodman (MTM)
10. **On the Other Hand,** Randy Travis (Warner Bros.)

Source: Billboard. © 1986 by Billboard Publications, Inc. Compiled by the Billboard Research Department and reprinted by permission.

Top 10 Pop Single Recordings, 1986

1. **That's What Friends Are For,** Dionne & Friends (Arista)
2. **Say You, Say Me (Title Song from White Nights),** Lionel Richie (Motown)
3. **I Miss You,** Klymaxx (MCA/Constellation)
4. **On My Own,** Patti LaBelle & Michael McDonald (MCA)
5. **Broken Wings,** Mr. Mister (RCA)
6. **How Will I Know,** Whitney Houston (Arista)
7. **Party All the Time,** Eddie Murphy (Columbia)
8. **Burning Heart,** Survivor (Scotti Bros.)
9. **Kyrie,** Mr. Mister (RCA)
10. **Addicted to Love,** Robert Palmer (Island)

Source: Billboard. © 1986 by Billboard Publications, Inc. Compiled by the Billboard Research Department and reprinted with permission.

Top 10 Pop Albums, 1986

1. **Whitney Houston,** Whitney Houston (Arista)
2. **Heart,** Heart (Capitol)
3. **Scarecrow,** John Cougar Mellencamp (Riva)
4. **Afterburn,** ZZ Top (Warner Bros.)
5. **Brothers in Arms,** Dire Straits (Warner Bros.)
6. **Control,** Janet Jackson (A&M)
7. **Welcome to the Real World,** Mr. Mister (RCA)
8. **Promise,** Sade (Portrait)
9. **No Jacket Required,** Phil Collins (Atlantic)
10. **Primitive Love,** Miami Sound Machine (Epic)

Source: Billboard. © 1986 by Billboard Publications, Inc. Compiled by the Billboard Research Department and reprinted by permission.

Top 15 Regularly Scheduled Network Programs, Dec. 1986[1]

Rank	Program name (network)	Total percent of TV households
1.	Bill Cosby Show (NBC)	34.0
2.	Family Ties (NBC)	31.8
3.	Cheers (NBC)	26.7
4.	Night Court (NBC)	25.3
5.	Golden Girls (NBC)	24.2
6.	Murder, She Wrote (CBS)	23.5
7.	60 Minutes (CBS)	23.4
8.	Who's the Boss? (ABC)	21.3
8.	Dallas (CBS)	21.3
10.	Moonlighting	21.2
10.	Growing Pains	21.2
12.	Newhart	20.2
13.	NFL Monday Night Football (ABC)	19.4
13.	Amen	19.4
15.	NBC Monday Night Movies	18.9
	Total U.S. TV households	**85,900,000**

1. Nov. 24, 1986 through Dec. 21, 1986. NOTE: Percentages are calculated from average audience viewings, 15 minutes or longer and 2 or more telecasts. *Source:* A. C. Nielsen, 1987 Nielsen Report on Television.

Top Evening News Shows 1986–87[1]*

Rank	Program name (network)	Rating (% of TV households)
1.	CBS Evening News	12.0
	NBC Nightly News	12.0
3.	World News Tonight (ABC)	10.6

1. Sept. 22, 1986, through April 19, 1987.

Top Morning News Shows 1986–87[1]*

Rank	Program name (network)	Rating (% of TV households)
1.	Today (NBC)	5.3
2.	Good Morning America (ABC)	4.5
3.	The Morning Program[2]	2.7

1. Sept. 22, 1986, through April 19, 1987. 2. Premiered Jan. 12, 1987.

Top Miniseries 1986–87[1 2]*

Rank	Program name (network)	Rating (% of TV households)
1.	I'll Take Manhattan (CBS)	22.9
2.	Amerika (ABC)	18.8
3.	A Year in the Life (NBC)	16.9
4.	Jesus of Nazareth[3] (NBC)	15.7
5.	Fresno (CBS)	15.5

1. Sept. 22, 1986, through May 30, 1987. 2. Three or more parts. 3. Repeat.

Top 15 Syndicated TV Programs Feb. 1987

Rank	Program	Rating (% U.S.)[1]
1.	Wheel of Fortune	20.1
2.	Jeopardy	13.3
3.	Oprah Winfrey	10.7
4.	PM Magazine	10.2
5.	M.A.S.H.	8.8
6.	People's Court	8.6
7.	New Newlywed Game	8.5
8.	Hollywood Squares	8.2
8.	Three's Company	8.2
10.	Metro Bkbl.	8.1
11.	ACC Bkbl.	8.0
12.	Phil Donahue	7.9
12.	WAC Bkbl.	7.9
14.	Entertainment Tonight	7.6
14.	Shaza Zulu	7.6

1. During February 1987. Ranked on the basis of average 15-minute audience ratings. *Source:* A.C. Nielsen Cassandra Report.

Top Sports Shows 1986–87[1]*

Rank	Program name (network)	Rating (% of TV households)
1.	Super Bowl XXI (CBS)	45.8
2.	1986 World Series, Game 7 (NBC)	38.9
3.	1986 World Series, Game 6 (NBC)	30.3
4.	1986 World Series, Game 5 (NBC)	29.8
5.	NFC Championship Game (CBS)	27.5

1. Sept. 22, 1986, through May 30, 1987.

Top Specials 1986–87[1]*

Rank	Program name (network)	Rating (% of TV households)
1.	59th Annual Academy Awards Presentation (ABC)	27.5
2.	Barbara Walters Special with Bette Davis, Elizabeth Taylor, and Debra Winger (ABC)	23.3
3.	1987 Miss USA Pageant (CBS)	22.7
4.	Barbara Walters Special with Lionel Richie, Betty White, and Richard Pryor (ABC)	22.2
	American Music Awards (ABC)	22.2

1. Sept. 22, 1986, through May 30, 1987.

Top Soap Operas 1986–87[1]*

Rank	Program name (network)	Rating (% of TV households)
1.	General Hospital (ABC)	8.3
2.	The Young and the Restless (CBS)	8.0
3.	One Life to Live (ABC)	7.2
4.	Days of Our Lives (NBC)	7.0
	All My Children (ABC)	7.0
	As the World Turns (CBS)	7.0

1. Sept. 22, 1986, through April 19, 1987.

Weekly TV Viewing by Age

(in hours and minutes)

	Time per week	
	Dec. 1986	Nov. 1985
Women 18–34 years old	29 h 32 min	32 h 21 min
Women 35–54	32 h 34 min	33 h 59 min
Women 55 and over	43 h 58 min	42 h 15 min
Men 18–34	23 h 54 min	26 h 03 min
Men 35–54	28 h 26 min	28 h 53 min
Men 55 and over	39 h 14 min	38 h 01 min
Female Teens	20 h 33 min	23 h 23 min
Male Teens	22 h 38 min	23 h 43 min
Children 6–11	23 h 19 min	27 h 22 min
Children 2–5	28 h 06 min	28 h 15 min
Total Persons	**30 h 20 min**	**31 h 28 min**

NOTE: All figures are estimates based on Nielsen Television Index NAD Report. *Source:* A.C. Nielsen, Nielsen Report on Television.

Television Network Addresses

American Broadcasting Companies (ABC)
1330 Avenue of the Americas
New York, N.Y. 10019
Canadian Broadcasting Corporation (CBC)
1500 Bronson Avenue
Ottawa, Ontario, Canada K1G 3J5
Columbia Broadcasting System (CBS)
51 W. 52nd Street
New York, N.Y. 10019
Fox Television (WNYW)
205 E. 67th Street
New York, N.Y. 10021
National Broadcasting Company (NBC)
30 Rockefeller Plaza
New York, N.Y. 10020
Public Broadcasting Service (PBS)
475 L'Enfant Plaza West, S.W.
Washington, D.C. 20024
Westinghouse Broadcasting (Group W)
90 Park Avenue
New York, N.Y. 10016

Persons Viewing Prime Time[1]

(in millions)

	Total persons[2]
Monday	95.2
Tuesday	94.8
Wednesday	91.7
Thursday	97.7
Friday	92.4
Saturday	88.4
Sunday	103.8
Total average	**94.9**

1. Average minute audiences. 2. Based on National Demographics Report (November 1985). NOTE: Prime time is 8–11 p.m. (EST) except Sun. 7-11 pm (excluding unusual days). *Source:* A. C. Nielsen, 1987 Nielsen Report on Television.

Average Hours of Household TV Usage

(in hours and minutes per day)

	Yearly average	February	July
1970–71	6 h 01 min	6 h 53 min	5 h 08 min
1975–76	6 h 11 min	6 h 49 min	5 h 33 min
1980–81	6 h 44 min	7 h 23 min	6 h 00 min
1981–82	6 h 48 min	7 h 22 min	6 h 09 min
1982–83	6 h 55 min	7 h 33 min	6 h 23 min
1983–84	7 h 08 min	7 h 38 min	6 h 26 min
1984–85	7 h 07 min	7 h 49 min	6 h 34 min
1985–86	7 h 10 min	7 h 48 min	6 h 37 min

NOTE: Estimates are based on total U.S. TV households, excluding unusual days. *Source:* A. C. Nielsen Company, Nielsen Report on Television.

Audience Composition by Selected Program Type[1]

(Average Minute Audience)
(in millions)

	General drama	Suspense and mystery drama	Situation comedy	Adventure	Feature films	All regular network programs 7–11 p.m.
Women (18 and over)	12,810,000	10,350,000	14,220,000	8,150,000	10,510,000	11,330,000
Men (18 and over)	7,060,000	8,070,000	8,990,000	6,600,000	7,730,000	8,260,000
Teens (12–17)	1,240,000	1,490,000	2,770,000	1,670,000	1,710,000	1,710,000
Children (2–11)	1,340,000	1,550,000	3,720,000	1,770,000	2,150,000	2,030,000
Total	**22,450,000**	**21,460,000**	**29,700,000**	**18,190,000**	**22,100,000**	**23,330,000**

1. All figures are estimated for the period Dec. 1986. *Source:* A. C. Nielsen Company, 1987 Nielsen Report on Television.

Hours of TV Usage Per Week by Household Income

	Under $15,000	$15,000–$19,000	$20,000–$29,000	$30,000–39,999	$40,000+
Nov. 1980	46 h 03 min	52 h 38 min	53 h 40 min	n.a.	n.a.
Dec. 1986	55 h 19 min	50 h 29 min	51 h 05 min	50 h 40 min	50 h 59 min

Source: A. C. Nielsen, Nielsen Report on Television. NOTE: n.a. = not available.

Source of Household Viewing—Prime Time

Pay Cable, Basic Cable, and Non-Cable Households

	Nov. 1986			Nov. 1985			Nov. 1984		
	Pay cable	Basic cable	Non-cable	Pay cable	Basic cable	Non-cable	Pay cable	Basic cable	Non-cable
% TV Usage[1]	68.7	65.6	59.2	71.2	68.4	61.0	67.8	63.2	58.6
Pay Cable	10.8	—	—	12.0	—	—	13.0	—	—
Cable-originated programming	7.9	8.8	—	7.5	7.8	—	7.3	6.3	—
Other-on-air stations	12.3	15.0	13.6	12.7	13.6	12.4	12.2	12.8	12.4
Network affiliated stations	46.4	47.4	49.8	46.7	50.6	52.8	43.6	46.9	49.8
Network share[2]	(67)	(72)	(84)	(66)	(74)	(87)	(64)	(74)	(85)

1. May be less than sum of reception sources because of simultaneous viewing. 2. Percent Network/Sum of Sources. *Source:* A. C. Nielsen, Nielsen Report on Television.

Major U.S. Fairs and Expositions

1853 Crystal Palace Exposition, New York City: modeled on similar fair held in London.

1876 Centennial Exposition, Philadelphia: celebrating 100th year of independence.

1893 World's Columbian Exposition, Chicago: commemorating 400th anniversary of Columbus' voyage to America.

1894 Midwinter International Exposition, San Francisco: promoting business revival after Depression of 1893.

1898 Trans-Mississippi and International Exposition, Omaha, Neb.: exhibiting products, resources, industries, and civilization of states and territories west of the Mississippi River.

1901 Pan-American Exposition, Buffalo, N.Y.: promoting social and commercial interest of Western Hemisphere nations.

1904 Louisiana Purchase Exposition, St. Louis: marking 100th anniversary of major land acquisition from France and opening up of the West.

1905 Lewis and Clark Centennial Exposition, Portland, Ore.: commemorating 100th anniversary of exploration of a land route to the Pacific.

1907 Jamestown Ter Centennial Exposition, Hampton Roads, Va.: marking 300th anniversary of first permanent English settlement in America.

1909 Alaska-Yukon-Pacific Exposition, Seattle: celebrating growth of the Puget Sound area.

1915–16 Panama-Pacific International Exposition, San Francisco: celebrating opening of the Panama Canal.

1915–16 Panama-California Exposition, San Diego: promoting resources and opportunities for development and commerce of the Western states.

1926 Sesquicentennial Exposition, Philadelphia: marking 150th year of independence.

1933–34 Century of Progress International Exposition, Chicago: celebrating 100th anniversary of incorporation of Chicago as a city.

1935 California Pacific International Exposition, San Diego: marking 400 years of progress since the first Spaniard landed on the West Coast.

1939–40 New York World's Fair, New York City: "The World of Tomorrow," symbolized by Trylon and Perisphere. Officially commemorating 150th anniversary of inauguration of George Washington as President in New York.

1939–40 Golden Gate International Exposition, Treasure Island, San Francisco: celebrating new Golden Gate Bridge and Oakland Bay Bridge.

1962 The Century 21 Exposition, Seattle: "Man in the Space Age," symbolized by 600-foot steel space needle.

1964–65 New York World's Fair, New York City: "Peace Through Understanding."

1974 Expo '74, Spokane: "Tomorrow's Fresh, New Environment."

1982 World's Fair, Knoxville, Tenn.: "Energy Turns the World," symbolized by the bronze-globed Sunsphere.

1984 Louisiana World Exposition, New Orleans: "The World of Rivers."

Longest Broadway Runs[1]

1. A Chorus Line (M) (1974–)	4,968	14. Pippin (M) (1971–77)	1,994
2. Oh, Calcutta (M) (1976–) (revival)	4,852	15. Cats (M) (1982–)	1,990
3. Grease (M) (1972–80)	3,388	16. South Pacific (M) (1949–54)	1,925
4. Fiddler on the Roof (1964–72)	3,242	17. Magic Show (M) (1974–78)	1,920
5. Life with Father (1939–47)	3,224	18. Deathtrap (1978–82)	1,792
6. Tobacco Road (1933–41)	3,182	19. Gemini (1977–81)	1,788
7. Hello, Dolly! (M) (1964–71)	2,844	20. Harvey (1944–49)	1,775
8. My Fair Lady (M) (1956–62)	2,717	21. Dancin' (M) (1978–82)	1,774
9. 42nd Street (M) (1980–)	2,453	22. Hair (M) (1968–72)	1,750
10. Annie (M) (1977–83)	2,377	23. The Wiz (M) (1975–79)	1,672
11. Oklahoma (M) (1943–48)	2,377	24. Born Yesterday (1946–49)	1,642
12. Man of La Mancha (M) (1965–71)	2,328	25. Cage aux Folles (M) (1983–)	1,625
13. Abie's Irish Rose	2,327		

1. As of July 12, 1987. M = musical. Years are those of opening and closing.

Motion Picture Revenues

Top Money Makers[1]

1.	E.T. The Extra-Terrestrial (Universal 1982)	$228,379,346
2.	Star Wars (20th Century-Fox, 1977)	193,500,000
3.	Return of the Jedi (20th Century-Fox, 1983)	168,002,414
4.	The Empire Strikes Back (20th Century-Fox, 1980)	141,600,000
5.	Jaws (Universal, 1975)	129,961,081
6.	Ghostbusters (Columbia, 1984)	128,264,005
7.	Raiders of the Lost Ark (Paramount, 1981)	115,598,000
8.	Indiana Jones and the Temple of Doom (Paramount, 1984)	109,000,000
9.	Beverly Hills Cop (Paramount, 1984)	108,000,000
10.	Back to the Future (Universal, 1985)	101,955,795
11.	Grease (Paramount, 1978)	96,300,000
12.	Tootsie (Columbia, 1982)	95,268,806
13.	The Exorcist (Warner Brothers, 1973)	89,000,000
14.	The Godfather (Paramount, 1972)	86,275,000
15.	Superman (Warner Brothers, 1978)	82,800,000
16.	Close Encounters Of the Third Kind (Columbia, 1977/80)	82,750,000
17.	Top Gun (Paramount, 1986)	82,000,000
18.	Rambo: First Blood Part II (Tri-Star, 1985)	80,000,000
19.	The Sound of Music (20th Century-Fox, 1965)	79,748,000
20.	Gremlins (Warner Brothers, 1984)	79,500,000
21.	The Sting (Universal, 1973)	78,198,608
22.	Gone With the Wind (MGM/United Artists, 1939)	76,700,000
23.	Rocky IV (MGM/United Artists, 1985)	75,782,000
24.	Saturday Night Fever (Paramount, 1977)	74,100,000
25.	National Lampoon's Animal House (Universal, 1978)	70,778,176

Top Rentals 1986[2]

1.	Top Gun (Paramount)	$82,000,000
2.	The Karate Kid Part II (Columbia)	56,936,752
3.	Crocodile Dundee (Paramount)	51,000,000
4.	Star Trek IV: The Voyage Home (Paramount)	45,000,000
5.	Aliens (20th Century-Fox)	42,500,000
6.	The Color Purple (Warner Brothers)	41,900,000
7.	Back To School (Orion)	41,748,000
8.	The Golden Child (Paramount)	33,000,000
9.	Ruthless People (Buena Vista)	31,000,000
10.	Out of Africa (Universal)	30,051,817
11.	Ferris Bueller's Day Off (Paramount)	28,600,000
12.	Down and Out in Beverly Hills (Buena Vista)	28,100,000
13.	Cobra (Warner Brothers)	27,900,000
14.	Legal Eagles (Universal)	26,500,131
15.	An American Tail (Universal)	22,000,000
16.	Heartbreak Ridge (Warner Brothers)	21,000,000
17.	Stand By Me (Columbia)	21,000,000
18.	The Color of Money (Buena Vista)	20,800,000
19.	Police Academy 3: Back In Training (Warner Brothers)	20,700,000
20.	Poltergeist II (MGM/United Artists)	20,377,000
21.	Three Amigos (Orion)	18,000,000
22.	The Fly (20th Century-Fox)	17,500,000
23.	Short Circuit (Tri-Star)	17,000,000
24.	Pretty In Pink (Paramount)	16,600,000
25.	Hannah and Her Sisters (Orion)	16,587,000

NOTE: United States and Canada only. 1. Figures are not be confused with gross box-office receipts from sale of tickets. 2. Figures are total rentals collected by film distributors as of Dec. 31, 1986. *Source: Variety.*

Miss America Winners

1921 Margaret Gorman, Washington, D.C.
1922-23 Mary Campbell, Columbus, Ohio
1924 Ruth Malcolmson, Philadelphia, Pa.
1925 Fay Lamphier, Oakland, Calif.
1926 Norma Smallwood, Tulsa, Okla.
1927 Lois Delaner, Joliet, Ill.
1933 Marion Bergeron, West Haven, Conn.
1935 Henrietta Leaver, Pittsburgh, Pa.
1936 Rose Coyle, Philadelphia, Pa.
1937 Bette Cooper, Bertrand Island, N.J.
1938 Marilyn Meseke, Marion, Ohio
1939 Patricia Donnelly, Detroit, Mich.
1940 Frances Marie Burke, Philadelphia, Pa.
1941 Rosemary LaPlanche, Los Angeles, Calif.
1942 Jo-Caroll Dennison, Tyler, Texas
1943 Jean Bartel, Los Angeles, Calif.
1944 Venus Ramey, Washington, D.C.
1945 Bess Myerson, New York, N.Y.
1946 Marilyn Buferd, Los Angeles, Calif.
1947 Barbara Walker, Memphis, Tenn.
1948 BeBe Shopp, Hopkins, Minn.
1949 Jacque Mercer, Litchfield, Ariz.
1951 Yolande Betbeze, Mobile, Ala.
1952 Coleen Kay Hutchins, Salt Lake City, Utah
1953 Neva Jane Langley, Macon, Ga.
1954 Evelyn Margaret Ay, Ephrata, Pa.
1955 Lee Meriwether, San Francisco, Calif.
1956 Sharon Ritchie, Denver, Colo.
1957 Marian McKnight, Manning, S.C.
1958 Marilyn Van Derbur, Denver, Colo.
1959 Mary Ann Mobley, Brandon, Miss.
1960 Lynda Lee Mead, Natchez, Miss.
1961 Nancy Fleming, Montague, Mich.
1962 Maria Fletcher, Asheville, N.C.
1963 Jacquelyn Mayer, Sandusky, Ohio
1964 Donna Axum, El Dorado, Ark.
1965 Vonda Kay Van Dyke, Phoenix, Ariz.
1966 Deborah Irene Bryant, Overland Park, Kan.
1967 Jane Anne Jayroe, Laverne, Okla.
1968 Debra Dene Barnes, Moran, Kan.
1969 Judith Anne Ford, Belvidere, Ill.
1970 Pamela Anne Eldred, Birmingham, Mich.
1971 Phyllis Ann George, Denton, Texas
1972 Laurie Lea Schaefer, Columbus, Ohio
1973 Terry Anne Meeuwsen, DePere, Wis.
1974 Rebecca Ann King, Denver, Colo.
1975 Shirley Cothran, Fort Worth, Texas
1976 Tawney Elaine Godin, Yonkers, N.Y.
1977 Dorothy Kathleen Benham, Edina, Minn.
1978 Susan Perkins, Columbus, Ohio
1979 Kylene Baker, Galax, Va.
1980 Cheryl Prewitt, Ackerman, Miss.
1981 Susan Powell, Elk City, Okla.
1982 Elizabeth Ward, Russellville, Ark.
1983 Debra Maffett, Anaheim, Calif.
1984 Vanessa Williams, Milwood, N.Y.[1]
Suzette Charles, Mays Landing, N.J.
1985 Sharlene Wells, Salt Lake City, Utah
1986 Susan Akin, Meridian, Miss.
1987 Kellye Cash, Memphis, Tenn.
1988 (*See* Current Events)

1. Resigned July 23, 1984.

U.S. STATES & CITIES

States and Territories

State flower, bird, etc., are official unless otherwise indicated; dates in parentheses are those of adoption. Largest cities include incorporated places only. For secession and readmission dates of the former Confederate states, *see* Index. For lists of Governors, Senators, and Representatives, *see* Index. For additional state information, *see* the sections on "Business and the Economy," "Elections," "Taxes," and "U.S. Statistics." Source for 1985 est. population, percent population below age 15, age 65 and over, serious crimes, and immigrants from abroad, courtesy of Population Reference Bureau, Inc., Washington, D.C.

ALABAMA

Capital: Montgomery
Governor: Guy Hunt, R (to Jan. 1991)
Lieut. Governor: Jim E. Folsom, Jr., D (to Jan. 1991)
Secy. of State: Glen Browder, D (to Jan. 1991)
Comptroller: (Vacant as of April 7, 1987)
Atty. General: Don Siegelman, D (to Jan. 1991)
Organized as territory: March 3, 1817
Entered Union & (rank): Dec. 14, 1819 (22)
Present constitution adopted: 1901
Motto: *Audemus jura nostra defendere* (We dare defend our rights)
State flower: Camellia (1959)
State bird: Yellowhammer (1927)
State song: "Alabama" (1931)
State tree: Southern pine (longleaf) (1949)
Nickname: Yellowhammer State
Origin of name: May come from Choctaw meaning "thicket-clearers" or "vegetation-gatherers"
1980 population (1980 census) & (rank): 3,893,888 (22)
1985 est. population (July 1) & (rank): 4,021,000 (22)
1984 land area & (rank): 50,767 sq mi. (131,487 sq km) (28)
Geographic center: In Chilton Co., 12 mi. SW of Clanton
Number of counties: 67
Largest cities (1980 census): Birmingham, 284,413; Mobile, 200,452; Montgomery, 178,157; Huntsville, 142,513; Tuscaloosa, 75,143; Gadsden, 47,565
State forests: 8 (14,248.58 ac.)
State parks: 22 (45,614 ac.)
1985 percent pop. below age 15: 23
1985 percent pop. age 65 and over: 12
1985 serious crimes per 100,000 pop.: 3,942
1984 (fiscal year) immigrants: 1,696

Spanish explorers are believed to have arrived at Mobile Bay in 1519, and the territory was visited in 1540 by the explorer Hernando de Soto. The first permanent European settlement in Alabama was founded by the French at Fort Louis in 1702. The British gained control of the area in 1763 by the Treaty of Paris, but had to cede almost all the Alabama region to the U.S. after the American Revolution. The Confederacy was founded at Montgomery in February 1861 and, for a time, the city was the Confederate capital.

During the last part of the 19th century, the economy of the state slowly improved. At Tuskegee Institute, founded in 1881 by Booker T. Washington, Dr. George Washington Carver carried out his famous agricultural research.

In the 1950s and '60s, Alabama was the site of such landmark civil-rights actions as the bus boycott in Montgomery (1955–56) and the "Freedom March" from Selma to Birmingham (1965).

Today, Alabama is the leading heavy-industry state in the South. Textiles, iron, and steel lead its manufacturing, which centers around Birmingham, the "Pittsburgh of the South." Industry is growing rapidly in other areas, including the Tennessee River Valley, with its great Muscle Shoals power plant. Manufacturing also includes cement, feed, fertilizer, chemical, rubber, and aluminum products. The state ranks high in the output of poultry, cotton, cattle, hogs, corn, potatoes, peanuts, and fruit.

Points of interest include the George C. Marshall Space Flight Center at Huntsville, Russell Cave National Monument near Bridgeport, and the White House of the Confederacy in Montgomery.

ALASKA

Capital: Juneau
Governor: Steve Cowper, D (to Dec. 1990)
Lieut. Governor: Stephen McAlpine, D (to Dec. 1990)
Commissioner of Administration: Garrey Peska, D (to Dec. 1990)
Atty. General: Grace Berg Schaible, D (to Dec. 1990)
Organized as territory: 1912
Entered Union & (rank): Jan. 3, 1959 (49)
Constitution ratified: April 24, 1956
Motto: North to the Future
State flower: Forget-me-not
State tree: Sitka spruce
State bird: Willow ptarmigan
State fish: King salmon
State song: "Alaska's Flag"
Nickname: The state is commonly called "The Last Frontier" or "Land of the Midnight Sun"
Origin of name: Corruption of Aleut word meaning "great land" or "that which the sea breaks against"
1980 population (1980 census) & (rank): 401,851 (50)
1985 est. population (July 1) & (rank): 521,000 (49)
1984 land area & (rank): 570,833 sq mi. (1,478,458 sq km) (1)
Geographic center: 60 mi. NW of Mt. McKinley
Number of boroughs: 10
Largest cities (1984 est.): Anchorage, 227,070; Fairbanks, 26,629; Juneau, 25,964; Ketchikan, 12,712; Sitka, 8,194; Kodiak, 6,030; Bethel, 3,869
State forests: None
State parks: 5; 59 waysides and areas (3.3 million ac.)
1985 percent pop. below age 15: 28
1985 percent pop. age 65 and over: 3
1985 serious crimes per 100,000 pop.: 5,877
1984 (fiscal year) immigrants: 970

Vitus Bering, a Dane working for the Russians, and Alexei Chirikov discovered the Alaskan mainland and the Aleutian Islands in 1741. The tremendous land mass of Alaska—equal to one fifth of the continental U.S.—was unexplored in 1867 when Secretary of State William Seward arranged for its purchase from the Russians for $7,200,000. The transfer of the territory took place on Oct. 18, 1867. Despite a price of about two cents an acre, the purchase was widely ridiculed as "Seward's Folly." The first official census (1880) reported a total of 33,426 Alaskans, all but 430 being of aboriginal stock. The Gold Rush of 1898 resulted in a mass influx of more than 30,000 people. Since then, Alaska has returned billions of dollars' worth of products to the U.S.

In 1968, a large oil and gas reservoir near Prudhoe Bay on the Arctic Coast was found. The Prudhoe Bay reservoir, with an estimated recoverable 10 billion barrels of oil and 27 trillion cubic feet of gas, is twice as large as any other oil field in North America. The Trans-Alaska pipeline was completed in 1977 at a cost of $7.7 billion. On June 20, oil started flowing through the 800-mile-long pipeline from Prudhoe Bay to the port of Valdez.

Other industries important to Alaska's economy are fisheries, wood and wood products, and furs.

Denali National Park and Mendenhall Glacier in North Tongass National Forest are of interest, as is the large totem pole collection at Sitka National Historical Park. The Katmai National Park includes the "Valley of Ten Thousand Smokes," an area of active volcanoes.

ARIZONA

Capital: Phoenix
Governor: Evan Mecham, R (to Jan. 1991)
Secy. of State: Rose Mofford, D (to Jan. 1991)
Atty. General: Bob Corbin, R (to Jan. 1991)
State Treasurer: Ray Rottas, R (to Jan. 1991)
Organized as territory: Feb. 24, 1863
Entered Union & (rank): Feb. 14, 1912 (48)
Present constitution adopted: 1911
Motto: *Ditat Deus* (God enriches)
State flower: Flower of saguaro cactus (1931)
State bird: Cactus wren (1931)
State colors: Blue and old gold (1915)
State song: "Arizona," a march song (1919)
State tree: Paloverde (1957)
Nickname: Grand Canyon State
Origin of name: From the Indian "Arizonac," meaning "little spring"
1980 population (1980 census) & (rank): 2,718,425 (29)
1985 est. population (July 1) & (rank): 3,187,000 (27)
1984 land area & (rank): 113,508 sq mi. (293,986 sq km) (6)
Geographic center: In Yavapai Co., 55 mi. ESE of Prescott
Number of counties: 15
Largest cities (1980 census): Phoenix, 789,704; Tucson, 330,537; Mesa, 152,453; Tempe, 106,743; Glendale, 97,172; Scottsdale, 86,622; Yuma, 42,481
State forests: None
State parks: 16
1985 percent pop. below age 15: 23
1985 percent pop. age 65 and over: 12
1985 serious crimes per 100,000 pop.: 7,116
1984 (fiscal year) immigrants: 5,289

Marcos de Niza, a Spanish Franciscan friar, was the first European to explore Arizona. He entered the area in 1539 in search of the mythical Seven Cities of Gold. Although he was followed a year later by another gold seeker, Francisco Vásquez de Coronado, most of the early settlement was for missionary purposes. In 1776 the Spanish established Fort Tucson. In 1848, after the Mexican War, most of the Arizona territory became part of the U.S., and the southern portion of the territory was added by the Gadsden Purchase in 1853.

In 1973 the world's biggest dam, the New Cornelia Tailings, was completed near Ajo.

Arizona history is rich in legends of America's Old West. It was here that the great Indian chiefs Geronimo and Cochise led their people against the frontiersmen. Tombstone, Ariz., was the site of the West's most famous shoot-out—the gunfight at the O.K. Corral. Today, Arizona has the largest U.S. Indian population; more than 14 tribes are represented on 19 reservations.

Manufacturing has become Arizona's most important industry. Principal products include electrical, communications, and aeronautical items. The state produces over half the country's copper. Agriculture is also important to the state's economy.

State attractions include such famous scenery as the Grand Canyon, the Petrified Forest, and the Painted Desert. Hoover Dam, Lake Mead, Fort Apache, and the reconstructed London Bridge at Lake Havasu City are of particular interest.

ARKANSAS

Capital: Little Rock
Governor: Bill Clinton, D (to Jan. 1990)
Lieut. Governor: Winston Bryant, D (to Jan. 1990)
Secy. of State: W. J. McCuen, D (to Jan. 1990)
Atty. General: Steve Clark (to Jan. 1990)
Auditor of State: Julia Hughes Jones, D (to Jan. 1990)
Treasurer of State: Jimmie Lou Fisher, D (to Jan. 1990)
Land Commissioner: Charles Daniels, D (to Jan. 1990)
Organized as territory: March 2, 1819
Entered Union & (rank): June 15, 1836 (25)
Present constitution adopted: 1874
Motto: *Regnat populus* (The people rule)
State flower: Apple Blossom (1901)
State tree: Pine (1939)
State bird: Mockingbird (1929)
State insect: Honeybee
State song: "Arkansas" (1963)
Nickname: Land of Opportunity
Origin of name: From the Quapaw Indians
1980 population (1980 census) & (rank): 2,286,435 (33)
1985 est. population (July 1) & (rank): 2,359,000 (33)
1984 land area & (rank): 52,078 sq mi. (134,883 sq km) (27)
Geographic center: In Pulaski Co., 12 mi. NW of Little Rock
Number of counties: 75
Largest cities (1980 census): Little Rock, 158,461; Fort Smith, 71,626; North Little Rock, 64,288; Pine Bluff, 56,636; Fayetteville, 36,608; Hot Springs, 35,781
State forests: None
State parks: 44
1985 percent pop. below age 15: 23
1985 percent pop. age 65 and over: 14
1985 serious crimes per 100,000 pop.: 3,585
1984 (fiscal year) immigrants: 1,104

Hernando de Soto, in 1541, was among the early European explorers to visit the territory. It was a Frenchman, Henri de Tonty, who in 1686 founded the first permanent white settlement—the Arkansas Post. In 1803 the area was acquired by the U.S. as part of the Louisiana Purchase.

Food products are the state's largest employing sector, with lumber and wood products a close second. Arkansas is also a leader in the production of cotton, rice, and soybeans. The state produces 97% of the nation's high-grade domestic bauxite ore—the source of aluminum. It also has the country's only active diamond mine; located near Murfreesboro, it is operated as a tourist attraction.

Hot Springs National Park is a major state attraction.

Blanchard Springs Caverns, the Arkansas Territorial Capitol Restoration at Little Rock, and Dogpatch U.S.A. near Harrison are of interest.

CALIFORNIA

Capital: Sacramento
Governor: George Deukmejian, R (to Jan. 1991)
Lieut. Governor: Leo McCarthy, D (to Jan. 1991)
Secy. of State: March Fong Eu, D (to Jan. 1991)
Controller: Gray Davis, D (to Jan. 1991)
Atty. General: John Van de Kamp, D (to Jan. 1991)
Treasurer: Jesse M. Unruh, D (to Jan. 1991)
Entered Union & (rank): Sept. 9, 1850 (31)
Present constitution adopted: 1879
Motto: *Eureka* (I have found it)
State flower: Golden poppy (1903)
State tree: California redwoods *(Sequoia sempervirens & Sequoia gigantea)* (1937 & 1953)
State bird: California valley quail (1931)
State animal: California grizzly bear (1953)
State fish: California golden trout (1947)
State colors: Blue and gold (1951)
State song: "I Love You, California" (1951)
Nickname: Golden State
Origin of name: From a book, *Las Sergas de Esplandián,* by Garcia Ordóñez de Montalvo, c. 1500
1980 population (1980 census) & (rank): 23,667,565 (1)
1985 est. population (July 1) & (rank): 26,365,000 (1)
1984 land area & (rank): 156,299 sq mi. (404,815 sq km) (3)
Geographic center: In Madera Co., 35 mi. NE of Madera
Number of counties: 58
Largest cities (1980 census): Los Angeles, 2,966,850; San Diego, 875,538; San Francisco, 678,974; San Jose, 629,442; Long Beach, 361,334; Oakland, 339,337
State forests: 8 (70,283 ac.)
State parks and beaches: 180 (723,000 ac.)
1985 percent pop. below age 15: 22
1985 percent pop. age 65 and over: 10
1985 serious crimes per 100,000 pop.: 6,518
1984 (fiscal year) immigrants: 140,289

Although California was sighted by Spanish navigator Juan Rodríguez Cabrillo in 1542, its first Spanish mission (at San Diego) was not established until 1769. California became a U.S. Territory in 1847 when Mexico surrendered it to John C. Frémont. On Jan. 24, 1848, James W. Marshall discovered gold at Sutter's Mill, starting the California Gold Rush and bringing settlers to the state in large numbers.

In 1964, the U.S. Census Bureau estimated that California had become the most populous state, surpassing New York. California also leads the country in personal income and consumer expenditures.

Leading industries include manufacturing (transportation equipment, machinery, and electronic equipment), agriculture, and tourism. Principal natural resources include petroleum, cement, and natural gas.

The Bank of America National Trust and Savings Association, founded by the Giannini family, ranks first or second in the world.

Death Valley, in the southeast, is 282 feet below sea level, the lowest point in the nation; and Mt. Whitney (14,495 ft) is the highest point in the contiguous 48 states. Lassen Peak is one of two active U.S. volcanos outside of Alaska and Hawaii; its last eruptions were recorded in 1917. The General Sherman Tree in Sequoia National Park is estimated to be about 3,500 years old and a stand of bristlecone pine trees in the White Mountains may be over 4,000 years old.

Other points of interest include Yosemite National Park, Disneyland, Hollywood, the Golden Gate bridge, San Simeon State Park, and Point Reyes National Seashore.

COLORADO

Capital: Denver
Governor: Roy Romer, D (to Jan. 1991)
Lieut. Governor: Michael Callihan, D (to Jan. 1991)
Secy. of State: Natalie Meyer, R (to Jan 1991)
Treasurer: Gail Schoettler, D (to Jan. 1991)
Controller: James A. Stroup
Atty. General: Duane Woodard, R (to Jan. 1991)
Organized as territory: Feb. 28, 1861
Entered Union & (rank): Aug. 1, 1876 (38)
Present constitution adopted: 1876
Motto: *Nil sine Numine* (Nothing without Providence)
State flower: Rocky Mountain columbine (1899)
State tree: Colorado blue spruce (1939)
State bird: Lark bunting (1931)
State animal: Rocky Mountain bighorn sheep
State colors: Blue and white (1911)
State song: "Where the Columbines Grow" (1915)
Nickname: Centennial State
Origin of name: From the Spanish, "ruddy" or "red"
1980 population (1980 census) & (rank): 2,889,735 (28)
1985 est. population (July 1) & rank: 3,231,000 (26)
1984 land area & (rank): 103,595 sq mi. (268,311 sq km) (8)
Geographic center: In Park Co., 30 mi. NW of Pikes Peak
Number of counties: 63
Largest cities (1980 census): Denver, 492,365; Colorado Springs, 214,821; Aurora, 158,588; Lakewood, 113,808; Pueblo, 101,686; Arvada, 84,576; Boulder, 76,685
State forests: 1 (71,000 ac.)
1985 percent pop. below age 15: 22
1985 percent pop. age 65 and over: 9
1985 serious crimes per 100,000 pop.: 6,919
1984 (fiscal year) immigrants: 4,656

First visited by Spanish explorers in the 1500s, the territory was claimed for Spain by Juan de Ulibarri in 1706. The U.S. obtained eastern Colorado as part of the Louisiana Purchase in 1803, the central portion in 1845 with the admission of Texas as a state, and the western part in 1848 as a result of the Mexican War.

Colorado has the highest mean elevation of any state, with more than 1,000 Rocky Mountain peaks over 10,000 feet high and 54 towering above 14, 000 feet. Pikes Peak, the most famous of these mountains, was discovered by U.S. Army Lieut. Zebulon M. Pike in 1806.

Gold was first discovered near present-day Denver in 1858 and at Cripple Creek in 1891. Rich silver deposits were also found in 1875.

Once primarily a mining and agricultural state, today Colorado draws the largest segment of its income from manufacturing. Denver is a leader in electronics and space-age industry. Pueblo, the "Pittsburgh of the West," makes iron, steel, brick, tile, and foundry products.

Rich in natural resources, Colorado now produces most of the world's molybdenum. Uranium, vanadium, gold, silver, lead, tin, zinc, and other minerals are also mined. Colorado's highly developed irrigation system promotes farming of wheat, hay, beans, sugar beets, corn, potatoes, barley, and truck vegetables. Cattle and sheep raising is also important.

Tourism has developed into a major industry largely because of Colorado's magnificent scenery. Among the major attractions are Rocky Mountain National Park, Garden of the Gods, Great Sand Dunes and Dinosaur National Monuments, Pikes Peak and Mt. Evans Highway, and Mesa Verde National Park (prehistoric cliff dwellings).

Colorado Springs, with the nearby U.S. Air Force Academy, is probably the most popular tourist center in the Rocky Mountains, while Aspen and Vail have become leading ski resorts.

CONNECTICUT

Capital: Hartford
Governor: William A. O'Neill, D (to Jan. 1991)
Lieut. Governor: Joseph J. Fauliso, D (to Jan. 1991)
Secy. of State: Julia H. Tashjian, D (to Jan. 1991)
Comptroller: J. Edward Caldwell, D (to Jan. 1991)
Treasurer: Francisco L. Borges, D (to Jan. 1991)
Atty. General: Joseph I. Lieberman, D (to Jan. 1991)
Entered Union & (rank): Jan. 9, 1788 (5)
Present constitution adopted: Dec. 30, 1965
Motto: *Qui transtulit sustinet* (He who transplanted still sustains)
State flower: Mountain laurel (1907)
State tree: White Oak (1947)
State animal: Sperm whale (1975)
State bird: American robin (1943)
State Hero: Nathan Hale (1985)
State insect: Praying mantis (1977)
State mineral: Garnet (1977)
State song: "Yankee Doodle" (1978)
State ship: USS Nautilus (SSN571) (1983)
Official designation: *Constitution State* (1959)
Nickname: Nutmeg State
Origin of name: From an Indian word (Quinnehtukqut) meaning "beside the long tidal river"
1980 population (1980 census) & (rank): 3,107,576 (25)
1985 est. population (July 1) & (rank): 3,174,000 (28)
1984 land area & (rank): 4,872 sq mi. (12,618 km) (48)
Geographic center: In Hartford Co., at East Berlin
Number of counties: 8
Largest cities (1980 census): Bridgeport, 142,546; Hartford, 136,392; New Haven, 126,109; Waterbury, 103,266; Stamford, 102,453; Norwalk, 77,767
State forests: 30 (138,682 ac.)
State parks: 91 (29,856 ac.)
1985 percent pop. below age 15: 19
1985 percent pop. age 65 and over: 13
1985 serious crimes per 100,000 pop.: 4,705
1984 (fiscal year) immigrants: 7,069

The Dutch navigator, Adriaen Block, was the first European of record to explore the area, sailing up the Connecticut River in 1614. In 1633, Dutch colonists built a fort and trading post near present-day Hartford, but soon lost control to English Puritans migrating south from the Massachusetts Bay Colony.

English settlements, established in the 1630s at Windsor, Wethersfield, and Hartford, united in 1639 to form the Connecticut Colony and adopted the *Fundamental Orders,* considered the world's first written constitution.

The colony's royal charter of 1662 was exceptionally liberal. When Gov. Edmund Andros tried to seize it in 1687, it was hidden in the Hartford Oak, commemorated in Charter Oak Place.

Connecticut played a prominent role in the Revolutionary War, serving as the Continental Army's major supplier. Sometimes called the "Arsenal of the Nation," the state became one of the most industrialized in the nation.

Today, Connecticut factories produce weapons, sewing machines, jet engines, helicopters, motors, hardware and tools, cutlery, clocks, locks, ball bearings, silverware, and submarines. Hartford, which has the oldest U.S. newspaper still being published—the *Courant,* established 1764—is the insurance capital of the nation.

Poultry, fruit, and dairy products account for the largest portion of farm income, and Connecticut shade-grown tobacco is acknowledged to be the nation's most valuable crop, per acre.

Connecticut is a popular resort area with its 250-mile Long Island Sound shoreline and many inland lakes. Among the major points of interest are the American Shakespeare Theatre in Stratford, Yale University's Gallery of Fine Arts and Peabody Museum. Other famous museums include the P.T. Barnum, Winchester Gun, and American Clock and Watch. The town of Mystic features a recreated 19th-century New England seaport and the Mystic Marinelife Aquarium.

DELAWARE

Capital: Dover
Governor: Michael N. Castle, R (to Jan. 1989)
Lieut. Governor: S. B. Woo, D (to Jan. 1989)
Secy. of State: Michael Harkins, R (Pleasure of Governor)
State Treasurer: Janet C. Rzewnicki, R (to Jan. 1991)
Atty. General: Charles M. Oberly III, D (to Jan. 1991)
Entered Union & (rank): Dec. 7, 1787 (1)
Present constitution adopted: 1897
Motto: Liberty and independence
State colors: Colonial blue and buff
State flower: Peach blossom
State tree: American holly
State bird: Blue Hen chicken
State insect: Ladybug
State song: "Our Delaware"
Nicknames: Diamond State; First State
Origin of name: From Delaware River and Bay; named in turn for Sir Thomas West, Lord De La Warr
1980 population (1980 census) & (rank): 594,317 (47)
1985 est. population (July 1) & (rank): 622,000 (47)
1984 land area & (rank): 1,932 sq mi. (5,005 sq km) (49)
Geographic center: In Kent Co., 11 mi. S of Dover
Number of counties: 3
Largest cities (1980 census): Wilmington, 70,195; Newark, 25,247; Dover, 23,512; Elsmere, 6,493; Milford, 5,356; Seaford, 5,256; New Castle, 4,709; Lewes, 2,197
State forests: 3 (6,149 ac.)
State parks: 10
1985 percent pop. below age 15: 21
1985 percent pop. age 65 and over: 11
1985 serious crimes per 100,000 pop.: 4,961
1984 (fiscal year) immigrants: 592

Henry Hudson, sailing under the Dutch flag, is credited with Delaware's discovery in 1609. The following year, Capt. Samuel Argall of Virginia named Delaware for his colony's governor, Thomas West, Baron De La Warr. An attempted Dutch settlement failed in 1631. Swedish colonization began at Fort Christina (now Wilmington) in 1638, but New Sweden fell to Dutch forces led by New Netherlands' Gov. Peter Stuyvesant in 1655.

England took over the area in 1664 and it was transferred to William Penn as the southern Three Counties in 1682. Semiautonomous after 1704, Delaware fought as a separate state in the American Revolution and became the first state to ratify the constitution in 1787.

During the Civil War, although a slave state, Delaware did not secede from the Union.

In 1802, Éleuthère Irénée du Pont established a gunpowder mill near Wilmington that laid the foundation for Delaware's huge chemical industry. Delaware's manufactured products now also include vulcanized fiber, glazed kid and morocco leathers, textiles, paper, dental supplies, metal products, machinery, machine tools, and automobiles.

Delaware also grows a great variety of fruits and vegetables and is a U.S. pioneer in the food-canning industry. Corn, soybeans, potatoes, and hay are important crops. Delaware's broiler chicken farms supply the big Eastern markets, and fishing is another major industry.

Points of interest include the Fort Christina Monument, Hagley Museum, Holy Trinity Church (erected in 1698, the oldest Protestant church in the United States still in use), and Winterthur Museum, in and near Wilmington; central New Castle, an almost unchanged late 18th-century capital; and the Delaware Museum of Natural History.

Popular recreation areas include Cape Henlopen, Delaware Seashore, Trapp Pond State Park, and Rehoboth Beach.

DISTRICT OF COLUMBIA

See listing at end of *50 Largest Cities of the United States.*

FLORIDA

Capital: Tallahassee
Governor: Bob Martinez, R (to Jan. 1991)
Lieut. Governor: Bobby Brantley, R (to Jan. 1991)
Secy. of State: George Firestone, D (to Jan. 1991)
Comptroller: Gerald Lewis, D (to Jan. 1991)
Commissioner of Agriculture: Doyle Connor, D (to Jan. 1991)
Atty. General: Bob Butterworth, D (to Jan. 1991)
Organized as territory: March 30, 1822
Entered Union & (rank): March 3, 1845 (27)
Present constitution adopted: 1969
Motto: In God we trust (1868)
State flower: Orange blossom (1909)
State bird: Mockingbird (1927)
State song: "Suwannee River" (1935)
Nickname: Sunshine State (1970)
Origin of name: From the Spanish, meaning "feast of flowers" (Easter)
1980 population (1980 census) & (rank): 9,746,342 (7)
1985 est. population (July 1) & (rank): 11,366,000 (6)
1984 land area & (rank): 54,153 sq mi. (140,256 sq km) (26)
Geographic center: In Hernando Co., 12 mi. NNW of Brooksville
Number of counties: 67
Largest cities (1984 est.): Jacksonville, 571,421; Miami, 383,027; Tampa, 275,512; St. Petersburg, 242,115; Fort Lauderdale, 152,053; Hialeah, 157,137
State forests: 4 (306,881 ac.)
State parks: 130 (215,820 ac.)
1985 percent pop. below age 15: 18
1985 percent pop. age 65 and over: 18
1985 serious crimes per 100,000 pop.: 7,574
1984 (fiscal year) immigrants: 32,364

In 1513, Ponce De Leon, seeking the mythical "Fountain of Youth," discovered and named Florida, claiming it for Spain. Later, Florida would be held at different times by Spain and England until Spain finally sold it to the United States in 1819. (Incidentally, France established a colony named Fort Caroline in 1564 in the state that was to become Florida.)

Florida's early 19th-century history as a U.S. territory was marked by wars with the Seminole Indians that did not end until 1842, although a treaty was actually never signed.

One of the nation's fastest-growing states, Florida's population has gone from 2.8 million in 1950 to more than 11.3 million in 1985.

Florida's economy rests on a solid base of tourism, (the state entertained more than 30.1 million American visitors in 1985) manufacturing, and agriculture.

In recent years, oranges and grapefruit lead Florida's crop list, followed by vegetables, potatoes, melons, strawberries, sugar cane, dairy products, cattle and calves, and forest products.

Major tourist attractions are Miami Beach, Palm Beach, St. Augustine (founded in 1565, thus the oldest permanent city in the U.S.), Daytona Beach, and Fort Lauderdale on the East Coast. West Coast resorts include Sarasota, Tampa, Key West and St. Petersburg. Disney World, located on a 27,000-acre site near Orlando, is a popular attraction.

Also drawing many visitors are the NASA Kennedy Space Center's Spaceport USA, located in the town of Kennedy Space Center, and Everglades National Park.

GEORGIA

Capital: Atlanta
Governor: Joe Frank Harris, D (to Jan. 1991)
Lieut. Governor: Zell Miller, D (to Jan. 1991)
Secy. of State: Max Cleland, D (to Jan. 1991)
Insurance Commissioner: Warren Evans, D (to Jan. 1991)
Atty. General: Michael J. Bowers, D (to Jan. 1991)
Entered Union & (rank): Jan. 2, 1788 (4)
Present constitution adopted: 1977
Motto: Wisdom, justice, and moderation
State flower: Cherokee rose (1916)
State tree: Live oak (1937)
State bird: Brown thrasher (1935)
State song: "Georgia on my Mind" (1922)
Nicknames: Peach State, Empire State of the South
Origin of name: In honor of George II of England
1980 population (1980 census) & (rank): 5,463,105 (13)
1985 est. population (July 1) & (rank): 5,976,000 (11)
1984 land area & (rank): 58,056 sq mi. (150,365 sq km) (21)
Geographic center: In Twiggs Co., 18 mi. SE of Macon
Number of counties: 159
Largest cities (1980 census): Atlanta, 425,022; Columbus, 169,441; Savannah, 141,634; Macon, 116,860; Albany, 74,550; Augusta, 47,532; Athens, 42,549; Warner Robins, 39,893
State forests: 25,258,000 ac. (67% of total state area)
State parks: 53 (42,600 ac.)
1985 percent pop. below age 15: 23
1985 percent pop. age 65 and over: 10
1985 serious crimes per 100,000 pop.: 5,110
1984 (fiscal year) immigrants: 4,690

Hernando de Soto, the Spanish explorer, first traveled parts of Georgia in 1540. British claims later conflicted with those of Spain. After obtaining a royal charter, Gen. James Oglethorpe established the first permanent settlement in Georgia in 1733 as a refuge for English debtors. In 1742, Oglethorpe defeated Spanish invaders in the Battle of Bloody Marsh.

A Confederate stronghold, Georgia was the scene of extensive military action during the Civil War. Union General William T. Sherman burned Atlanta and destroyed a 60-mile wide path to the coast where he captured Savannah in 1864.

The largest state east of the Mississippi, Georgia is typical of the changing South with an ever-increasing industrial development. Atlanta, largest city in the state, is the communications and transportation center for the Southeast and the area's chief distributor of goods.

Georgia leads the nation in the production of paper and board, tufted textile products, and processed chicken. Other major manufactured products are transportation equipment, food products, apparel, and chemicals.

Important agricultural products are corn, cotton, tobacco, soybeans, eggs, and peaches. Georgia produces twice as many peanuts as the next leading state. From its vast stands of pine come more than half the world's resins and turpentine and 74.4% of the U.S. supply. Georgia is also a leader in the production of marble, kaolin, barite, and bauxite.

Principal tourist attractions in Georgia include the Okefenokee National Wildlife Refuge, Andersonville Prison Park and National Cemetery, Chickamauga and Chattanooga National Military Park, the Little White House at Warm Springs where Pres. Franklin D. Roosevelt died in 1945, Sea Island, the enormous Confederate Memorial at Stone Mountain, Kennesaw Mountain National Battlefield Park, and Cumberland Island National Seashore.

HAWAII

Capital: Honolulu (on Oahu)
Governor: John Waihee, D (to Dec. 1990)
Lieut. Governor: Ben Cayetano, D (to Dec. 1990)
Comptroller: Russel S. Nagata, D (to Dec. 1990)
Atty. General: Warren Price, D (to Dec. 1990)
Organized as territory: 1900
Entered Union & (rank): Aug. 21, 1959 (50)
Motto: *Ua Mau Ke Ea O Ka Aina I Ka Pono* (The life of the land is perpetuated in righteousness)
State flower: Hibiscus
State song: "Hawaii Ponoi"
State bird: Nene (Hawaiian goose)
Nickname: Aloha State
Origin of name: Uncertain. The islands may have been named by Hawaii Loa, their traditional discoverer. Or they may have been named after Hawaii or Hawaiki, the traditional home of the Polynesians.
1980 population (1980 census) & (rank): 964,691 (39)
1985 est. population (July 1) & (rank): 1,054,000 (39)
1984 land area & (rank): 6,425 sq mi. (16,641 sq km) (47)
Geographic center: Between islands of Hawaii and Maui
Number of counties: 4 plus one non-functioning county (Kalawao)
Largest cities (1980 census): Honolulu, 365,048; Pearl City, 42,575; Kailua, 35,812; Hilo, 35,269[1]
State parks and historic sites: 74
1985 percent pop. below age 15: 23
1985 percent pop. age 65 and over: 9
1985 serious crimes per 100,000 pop.: 5,201
1984 (fiscal year) immigrants: 8,981

1. There are no political boundaries to Honolulu or any other place, but statistical boundaries are assigned under state law.

First settled by Polynesians sailing from other Pacific islands in the 6th century, Hawaii was visited in 1778 by British Captain James Cook who called the group the Sandwich Islands.

Hawaii was a native kingdom throughout most of the 19th century when the expansion of the vital sugar industry (pineapple came after 1898) meant increasing U.S. business and political involvement. In 1893, Queen Liliuokalani was deposed and a year later the Republic of Hawaii was established with Sanford B. Dole as president. Then, following its annexation in 1898, Hawaii became a U.S. Territory in 1900.

The Japanese attack on the naval base at Pearl Harbor on Dec. 7, 1941, was directly responsible for U.S. entry into World War II.

Hawaii, 2,397 miles west-southwest of San Francisco, is a 1,523-mile chain of islets and eight main islands—Hawaii, Kahoolawe, Maui, Lanai, Molokai, Oahu, Kauai, and Niihau. The Northwestern Hawaiian Islands, other than Midway, are administratively part of Hawaii.

The temperature is mild and Hawaii's soil is fertile for tropical fruits and vegetables. Cane sugar and pineapple are the chief products. Hawaii also grows coffee, bananas and nuts. The tourist business is Hawaii's largest source of outside income.

Hawaii's highest peak is Mauna Kea (13,796 ft.). Mauna Loa (13,679 ft.) is the largest volcanic mountain in the world in cubic content.

Among the major points of interest are Hawaii Volcanoes National Park (Hawaii), Haleakala National Park (Maui), Puuhonua o Honaunau National Historical Park (Hawaii), Polynesian Cultural Center (Oahu), the U.S.S. *Arizona* Memorial at Pearl Harbor, and Iolani Palace (the only royal palace in the U.S.), Bishop Museum, and Waikiki Beach (all in Honolulu).

IDAHO

Capital: Boise
Governor: Cecil D. Andrus, D (to Jan. 1991)
Lieut. Governor: C. L. "Butch" Otter, R (to Jan. 1991)
Secy. of State: Pete T. Cenarrusa, R (to Jan. 1991)
State Auditor: Joe R. Williams, D (to Jan. 1991)
Atty. General: James Jones, R (to Jan. 1991)
Treasurer: Lydia Justice Edwards, R (to Jan. 1991)
Organized as territory: March 3, 1863
Entered Union & (rank): July 3, 1890 (43)
Present constitution adopted: 1890
Motto: *Esto perpetua* (May you last forever)
State flower: Syringa (1931)
State tree: White pine (1935)
State bird: Mountain bluebird (1931)
State horse: Appaloosa (1975)
State gem: Star garnet (1967)
State song: "Here We Have Idaho"
Nicknames: Gem State; Spud State; Panhandle State
Origin of name: Means "Gem of the Mountains"
1980 population (1980 census) & (rank): 944,038 (41)
1985 est. population (July 1) & (rank): 1,005,000 (40)
1984 land area & (rank): 82,413 sq mi. (213,449 sq km) (11)
Geographic center: In Custer Co., at Custer, SW of Challis
Number of counties: 44, plus small part of Yellowstone National Park
Largest cities (1980 census): Boise, 102,160; Pocatello, 46,340; Idaho Falls, 39,590; Lewiston, 27,986; Twin Falls, 26,209; Nampa, 25,112; Coeur d'Alene, 20,054
State forests: 881,000 ac.
State parks: 21 (38,487) ac.
1985 percent pop. below age 15: 27
1985 percent pop. age 65 and over: 11

1985 serious crimes per 100,000 pop.: 3,908
1984 (fiscal year) immigrants: 741

After its acquisition by the U.S. as part of the Louisiana Purchase in 1803, the region was explored by Meriwether Lewis and William Clark in 1805–06. Northwest boundary disputes with Great Britain were settled by the Oregon Treaty in 1846 and the first permanent U.S. settlement in Idaho was established by the Mormons at Franklin in 1860.

After gold was discovered on Orofino Creek in 1860, prospectors swarmed into the territory, but left little more than a number of ghost towns.

In the 1870s, growing white occupation of Indian lands led to a series of battles between U.S. forces and the Nez Percé, Bannock, and Sheepeater tribes.

Mining, lumbering, and irrigation farming have been important for years. Idaho produces more than one third of all the silver mined in the U.S. It also ranks high among the states in antimony, lead, cobalt, garnet, phosphate rock, vanadium, zinc, and mercury.

Idaho's most impressive growth began when World War II military needs made processing agricultural products a big industry, particularly the dehydrating and freezing of potatoes. The state produces about one fourth of the nation's potato crop, as well as wheat, apples, corn, barley, sugar beets, and hops. More money is made from livestock in the state than from all agricultural products.

With the growth of winter sports, tourism now outranks mining in dollar revenue. Idaho's many streams and lakes provide fishing, camping, and boating sites. The nation's largest elk herds draw hunters from all over the world and the famed Sun Valley resort attracts thousands of visitors to its swimming and skiing facilities.

Other points of interest are the Craters of the Moon National Monument; Nez Percé National Historic Park, which includes many sites visited by Lewis and Clark; and the State Historical Museum in Boise.

ILLINOIS

Capital: Springfield
Governor: James R. Thompson, R (to Jan. 1991)
Lieut. Governor: George H. Ryan, R (to Jan. 1991)
Secy. of State: Jim Edgar, R (to Jan. 1991)
Comptroller: Roland J. Burris, D (to Jan. 1991)
Atty. General: Neil F. Hartigan, D (to Jan. 1991)
Treasurer: Jerry Cosentino, D (to Jan. 1991)
Organized as territory: Feb. 3, 1809
Entered Union & (rank): Dec. 3, 1818 (21)
Present constitution adopted: 1970
Motto: State sovereignty, national union
State flower: Violet (1908)
State tree: White oak (1973)
State bird: Cardinal (1929)
State insect: Monarch butterfly
State song: "Illinois" (1925)
State mineral: Fluorite (1965)
Nickname: Prairie State
Origin of name: From an Indian word and French suffix meaning "tribe of superior men"
1980 population (1980 census) & (rank): 11,426,596 (5)
1985 est. population (July 1) & (rank): 11,535,000 (5)
1984 land area & (rank): 55,645 sq mi. (144,120 sq km) (24)
Geographic center: In Logan County 28 mi. NE of Springfield
Number of counties: 102
Largest cities (1984 census): Chicago, 2,992,472; Rockford, 136,531; Peoria, 117,113; Springfield, 101,-570; Decatur, 91,851; Aurora, 85,735
Public use areas: 187 (275,000 ac.), incl. state parks, memorials, forests and conservation areas
1985 percent pop. below age 15: 22
1985 percent pop. age 65 and over: 12
1985 serious crimes per 100,000 pop.: 5,300
1984 (fiscal year) immigrants: 26,617

French explorers Marquette and Joliet, in 1673, were the first Europeans of record to visit the region. In 1699 French settlers established the first permanent settlement at Cahokia, near present-day East St. Louis.

Great Britain obtained the region at the end of the French and Indian War in 1763. The area figured prominently in frontier struggles during the Revolutionary War and in Indian wars during the early 19th century.

Significant episodes in the state's early history include the growing migration of Eastern settlers following the opening of the Erie Canal in 1825; the Black Hawk War, which virtually ended the Indian troubles in the area; and the rise of Abraham Lincoln from farm laborer to President-elect.

Today, Illinois stands high in manufacturing, coal mining, agriculture, and oil production. The sprawling Chicago district (including a slice of Indiana) is a great iron and steel producer, meat packer, grain exchange, and railroad center. Chicago is also famous as a busy long-flight airport city and Great Lakes port.

Illinois ranks first in the nation in export of agricultural products and second in hog production. An important dairying state, Illinois is also a leader in corn, oats, wheat, barley, rye, truck vegetables, and the nursery products.

The state manufactures a great variety of industrial and consumer products: railroad cars, clothing, furniture, tractors, liquor, watches, and farm implements are just some of the items made in its factories and plants.

Central Illinois is noted for shrines and memorials associated with the life of Abraham Lincoln. In Springfield are the Lincoln Home, the Lincoln Tomb, and the restored Old State Capitol. Other points of interest are the home of Mormon leader Joseph Smith in Nauvoo and, in Chicago: the Art Institute, Field Museum, Museum of Science and Industry, Shedd Aquarium, Adler Planetarium, Merchandise Mart, and Chicago Portage National Historic Site.

INDIANA

Capital: Indianapolis
Governor: Robert D. Orr, R (to Jan. 1989)
Lieut. Governor: John M. Mutz, R (to Jan. 1989)
Secy. of State: B. Evan Bayh, D (to Dec. 1990)
Treasurer: Majorie H. O'Laughlin, R (to Dec. 1990)
Atty. General: Linley E. Pearson, R (to Jan. 1989)
Auditor: Ann G. Devore, R (to Dec. 1990)
Organized as territory: May 7, 1800
Entered Union & (rank): Dec. 11, 1816 (19)
Present constitution adopted: 1851
Motto: The Crossroads of America
State flower: Peony (1957)

State tree: Tulip tree (1931)
State bird: Cardinal (1933)
State song: "On the Banks of the Wabash, Far Away" (1913)
Nickname: Hoosier State
Origin of name: Meaning "land of Indians"
1980 population (1980 census) & (rank): 5,490,260 (12)
1985 est. population (July 1) & (rank): 5,499,000 (14)
1984 land area & (rank): 35,932 sq mi. (93,064 sq km) (38)
Geographic center: In Boone Co., 14 mi. NNW of Indianapolis
Number of Counties: 92
Largest cities (1980 census): Indianapolis, 700,807; Fort Wayne, 172,028; Gary, 151,953; Evansville, 130,496; South Bend, 109,727; Hammond, 93,714; Muncie, 77,216
State parks: 19 (54,126 ac.)
State memorials: 16 (941.977 ac.)
1985 percent pop. below age 15: 23
1985 percent pop. age 65 and over: 12
1985 serious crimes per 100,000 pop.: 3,914
1984 (fiscal year) immigrants: 2,398

First explored for France by La Salle in 1679–80, the region figured importantly in the Franco-British struggle for North America that culminated with British victory in 1763.

George Rogers Clark led American forces against the British in the area during the Revolutionary War and, prior to becoming a state, Indiana was the scene of frequent Indian uprisings until the victory of Gen. William Henry Harrison at Tippecanoe in 1811.

Indiana's 41-mile Lake Michigan waterfront—one of the world's great industrial centers—turns out iron, steel, and oil products. Products include automobile parts and accessories, mobile homes and recreational vehicles, truck and bus bodies, aircraft engines, farm machinery, and fabricated structural steel. Phonograph records, wood office furniture, and pharmaceuticals are also manufactured.

The state is a leader in agriculture with corn the principal crop. Hogs, soybeans, wheat, oats, rye, tomatoes, onions, and poultry also contribute heavily to Indiana's agricultural output. Much of the building limestone used in the U.S. is quarried in Indiana which is also a large producer of coal.

Wyandotte Cave, one of the largest in the U.S., is located in Crawford County in southern Indiana and West Baden and French Lick are well known for their mineral springs. Other attractions include Indiana Dunes National Lakeshore, Indianapolis Motor Speedway, Lincoln Boyhood National Memorial, and the George Rogers Clark National Historical Park.

IOWA

Capital: Des Moines
Governor: Terry E. Branstad, R (to Jan. 1991)
Lieut. Governor: Joan Zimmerman, D (to Jan. 1991)
Secy. of State: Elaine Baxter, D (to Jan. 1991)
Treasurer: Michael L. Fitzgerald, D (to Jan. 1991)
Atty. General: Tom Miller, D (to Jan. 1991)
Organized as territory: June 12, 1838
Entered Union & (rank): Dec. 28, 1846 (29)
Present constitution adopted: 1857
Motto: Our liberties we prize and our rights we will maintain
State flower: Wild rose (1897)
State bird: Eastern goldfinch (1933)
State colors: Red, white, and blue (in state flag)
State song: "Song of Iowa"
Nickname: Hawkeye State
Origin of name: Probably from an Indian word meaning "I-o-w-a, this is the place," or "The Beautiful Land"
1980 population (1980 census) & (rank): 2,913,808 (27)
1985 est. population (July 1) & (rank): 2,884,000 (29)
1984 land area & (rank): 55,965 sq mi. (144,950 sq km) (23)
Geographic center: In Story Co., 5 mi. NE of Ames
Number of counties: 99
Largest cities (1980 census): Des Moines, 191,003; Cedar Rapids, 110,243; Davenport, 103,264; Sioux City, 82,003; Waterloo, 75,985; Dubuque, 62,321; Council Bluffs, 56,449; Iowa City, 50,508; Ames, 45,775
State forests: 5 (28,000 ac.)
State parks: 95 (49,237)
1985 percent pop. below age 15: 22
1985 percent pop. age 65 and over: 14
1985 serious crimes per 100,000 pop.: 3,943
1984 (fiscal year) immigrants: 1,564

The first Europeans to visit the area were the French explorers, Father Jacques Marquette and Louis Jolliet in 1673. The U.S. obtained control of the area in 1803 as part of the Louisiana Purchase.

During the first half of the 19th century, there was heavy fighting between white settlers and Indians. Lands were taken from the Indians after the Black Hawk War in 1832 and again in 1836 and 1837.

When Iowa became a state in 1846, its capital was Iowa City; the more centrally located Des Moines became the new capital in 1857. At that time, the state's present boundaries were also drawn.

Although Iowa produces a tenth of the nation's food supply, the value of Iowa's manufactured products is three times that of its agriculture. Major industries are food and associated products, non-electrical machinery, electrical equipment, printing and publishing, and fabricated products.

Iowa stands in a class by itself as an agricultural state. Its farms sell over $9 billion worth of crops and livestock annually. Iowa leads the nation in all livestock and hog marketings, with about 27% of the pork supply and 9% of the grain-fed cattle. Iowa's forests produce hardwood lumber, particularly walnut, and its mineral products include cement, limestone, sand, gravel, gypsum, and coal.

Tourist attractions include the Herbert Hoover birthplace and library near West Branch; the Amana Colonies; Fort Dodge Historical Museum, Fort, and Stockade; the Iowa State Fair at Des Moines in August; and the Effigy Mounds National Monument at Marquette, a prehistoric Indian burial site.

KANSAS

Capital: Topeka
Governor: Mike Hayden, R (to Jan. 1991)
Lieut. Governor: Jack D. Walker, R (to Jan. 1991)
Secy. of State: Bill Graves, R (to Jan. 1991)
Treasurer: Joan Finney, D (to Jan. 1991)
Atty. General: Robert T. Stephan, R (to Jan. 1991)
Organized as territory: May 30, 1854
Entered Union & (rank): Jan. 29, 1861 (34)
Present constitution adopted: 1859
Motto: *Ad astra per aspera* (To the stars through difficulties)
State flower: Sunflower (1903)
State tree: Cottonwood (1937)
State bird: Western meadow lark (1937)
State animal: Buffalo (1955)

State song: "Home on the Range" (1947)
Nicknames: Sunflower State; Jayhawk State
Origin of name: From a Siouan word meaning "people of the south wind"
1980 population (1980 census) & (rank): 2,364,236 (32)
1985 est. population (July 1) & (rank): 2,450,000 (32)
1984 land area & (rank): 81,781 sq mi. (211,814 sq km) (13)
Geographic center: In Barton Co., 15 mi. NE of Great Bend
Number of counties: 105
Largest cities (1980 census): Wichita, 279,835; Kansas City, 161,148; Topeka, 115,266; Overland Park, 81,784; Lawrence, 52,738; Salina, 41,843; Hutchinson, 40,284
State parks: 22 (14,394 ac.)
1985 percent pop. below age 15: 23
1985 percent pop. age 65 and over: 13
1985 serious crimes per 100,000 pop.: 4,375
1984 (fiscal year) immigrants: 2,609

Spanish explorer Francisco de Coronado, in 1541, is considered the first European to have traveled this region. La Salle's extensive land claims for France (1682) included present-day Kansas. Ceded to Spain by France in 1763, the territory reverted back to France in 1800 and was sold to the U.S. as part of the Louisiana Purchase in 1803.

Lewis and Clark, Zebulon Pike, and Stephen H. Long explored the region between 1803 and 1819. The first permanent settlements in Kansas were outposts—Fort Leavenworth (1827), Fort Scott (1842), and Fort Riley (1853)—established to protect travelers along the Santa Fe and Oregon Trails.

Just before the Civil War, the conflict between the pro- and anti-slavery forces earned the region the grim title "Bleeding Kansas."

Today, wheat fields, oil well derricks, herds of cattle, and grain storage elevators are chief features of the Kansas landscape. A leading wheat-growing state, Kansas also raises corn, sorghums, oats, barley, soy beans, and potatoes. Kansas stands high in petroleum production and mines zinc, coal, salt, and lead. It is also the nation's leading producer of helium.

Wichita is one of the nation's leading aircraft manufacturing centers, ranking first in production of private aircraft. Kansas City is an important transportation, milling, and meat-packing center.

Points of interest include the new Kansas Museum of History at Topeka, the Eisenhower boyhood home and the new Eisenhower Memorial Museum and Presidential Library at Abilene, John Brown's cabin at Osawatomie, recreated Front Street in Dodge City, Fort Larned (once the most important military post on the Santa Fe Trail), and Fort Leavenworth and Fort Riley.

KENTUCKY

Capital: Frankfort
Governor: Martha Layne Collins, D (to Dec. 1987)
Lieut. Governor: Steven L. Beshear, D (to Dec. 1987)
Secy. of State: Drexell R. Davis, D (to Jan. 1988)
State Treasurer: Frances Jones Mills, D (to Jan. 1988)
State Auditor: Mary Ann Tobin, D (to Jan. 1988)
Atty. General: David Armstrong, D (to Jan. 1988)
Entered Union & (rank): June 1, 1792 (15)
Present constitution adopted: 1891
Motto: United we stand, divided we fall
State tree: Coffeetree
State flower: Goldenrod
State bird: Kentucky cardinal
State song: "My Old Kentucky Home"
Nickname: Bluegrass State
Origin of name: From an Iroquoian word "Ken-tah-ten" meaning "land of tomorrow"
1980 population (1980 census) & (rank): 3,660,777 (23)
1985 est. population (July 1) & (rank): 3,726,000 (23)
1984 land area & (rank): 39,669 sq mi. (102,743 sq km) (37)
Geographic center: In Marion Co., 3 mi. NNW of Lebanon
Number of counties: 120
Largest cities (1985 proj.): Louisville, 293,834; Lexington, 214,072; Owensboro, 56,419; Covington, 47,725; Bowling Green, 45,549; Paducah, 29,699; Hopkinsville, 30,406
State forests: 9 (44,173 ac.)
State parks: 43 (40,574 ac.)
1985 percent pop. below age 15: 23
1985 percent pop. age 65 and over: 12
1985 serious crimes per 100,000 pop.: 2,947
1984 (fiscal year) immigrants: 1,073

Kentucky was the first region west of the Allegheny Mountains settled by American pioneers. James Harrod established the first permanent settlement at Harrodsburg in 1774; the following year Daniel Boone, who had explored the area in 1767, blazed the Wilderness Trail and founded Boonesboro.

Politically, the Kentucky region was originally part of Virginia, but early statehood was gained in 1792.

During the Civil War, as a slaveholding state with a considerable abolitionist population, Kentucky was caught in the middle of the conflict, supplying both Union and Confederate forces with thousands of troops.

In recent years, manufacturing has shown important gains, but agriculture and mining are still vital to Kentucky's economy. Kentucky prides itself on producing some of the nation's best tobacco, horses, and whiskey. Corn, soybeans, wheat, fruit, hogs, cattle, and dairy farming are also important.

Among the manufactured items produced in the state are furniture, aluminum ware, brooms, shoes, lumber products, machinery, textiles, and iron and steel products. Kentucky also produces significant amounts of petroleum, natural gas, fluorspar, clay, and stone. However, coal accounts for 90% of the total mineral income.

Louisville, the largest city, famed for the Kentucky Derby at Churchill Downs, is also the location of a large state university, whiskey distilleries, and cigarette factories. The Bluegrass country around Lexington is the home of some of the world's finest race horses. Other attractions are Mammoth Cave, the George S. Patton, Jr., Military Museum at Fort Knox, and Old Fort Harrod State Park.

LOUISIANA

Capital: Baton Rouge
Governor: Edwin W. Edwards, R (to March 1988)
Lieut. Governor: Robert L. Freeman, D (to March 1988)
Secy. of State: James H. Brown, Jr., D (to March 1988)
Treasurer: Thomas D. Burbank, D (to March 1988)
Atty. General: William J. Guste, Jr., D (to March 1988)
Organized as territory: March 26, 1804
Entered Union & (rank): April 30, 1812 (18)
Present constitution adopted: 1974
Motto: Union, justice, and confidence
State flower: Magnolia (1900)
State tree: Bald cypress
State bird: Pelican

State song: "Give Me Louisiana," and "You Are My Sunshine"
Nicknames: Pelican State; Sportsman's Paradise; Creole State; Sugar State
Origin of name: In honor of Louis XIV of France
1980 population (1980 census) & (rank): 4,206,312 (19)
1985 est. population (July 1) & (rank): 4,481,000 (18)
1984 land area & (rank): 44,521 sq mi. (115,310 sq km) (33)
Geographic center: In Avoyelles Parish, 3 mi. SE of Marksville
Number of parishes (counties): 64
Largest cities (1980 census): New Orleans, 557,927; Baton Rouge, 219,419; Shreveport, 205,820; Lafayette, 81,961; Lake Charles, 75,226; Monroe, 57,597; Alexandria, 51,565
State forests: 1 (8,000 ac.)
State parks: 30 (13,932 ac.)
1985 percent pop. below age 15: 25
1985 percent pop. age 65 and over: 10
1985 serious crimes per 100,000 pop.: 5,564
1984 (fiscal year) immigrants: 5,403

Louisiana has a rich, colorful historical background. Early Spanish explorers were Piñeda, 1519; Cabeza de Vaca, 1528; and de Soto in 1541. La Salle reached the mouth of the Mississippi and claimed all the land drained by it and its tributaries for Louis XIV of France in 1682.

Louisiana became a French crown colony in 1731, was ceded to Spain in 1763, returned to France in 1800, and sold by Napoleon to the U.S. as part of the Louisiana Purchase (with large territories to the north and northwest) in 1803.

In 1815, Gen. Andrew Jackson's troops defeated a larger British army in the Battle of New Orleans, neither side aware that the treaty ending the War of 1812 had been signed.

As to total value of its mineral output, Louisiana is a leader in natural gas, salt, petroleum, and sulfur production. Much of the oil and sulfur comes from offshore deposits. The state also produces large crops of sweet potatoes, rice, sugarcane, pecans, soybeans, corn, and cotton.

Leading manufactures include chemicals, processed food, petroleum and coal products, paper, lumber and wood products, transportation equipment, and apparel.

Louisiana marshes supply most of the nation's muskrat fur as well as that of opossum, raccoon, mink, and otter, and large numbers of game birds.

Major points of interest include New Orleans with its French Quarter and Superdome, plantation homes near Natchitoches and New Iberia, Cajun country in the Mississippi delta region, Chalmette National Historical Park, and the state capital at Baton Rouge.

MAINE

Capital: Augusta
Governor: John R. McKernan, Jr., R (to Jan. 1991)
Secy. of State: Rodney F. Quinn, D (to Jan. 1989)
Controller: David A. Bourne, R (term indefinite)
Atty. General: James Tierney, D (to Jan. 1991)
Entered Union & (rank): March 15, 1820 (23)
Present constitution adopted: 1820
Motto: *Dirigo* (I direct)
State flower: White pine cone and tassel (1895)
State tree: White pine tree (1945)
State bird: Chickadee (1927)
State fish: Landlocked salmon (1969)
State mineral: Tourmaline (1971)
State song: "State of Maine Song" (1937)
Nickname: Pine Tree State
Origin of name: First used to distinguish the mainland from the offshore islands. It has been considered a compliment to Henrietta Maria, Queen of Charles I of England. She was said to have owned the province of Mayne in France.
1980 population (1980 census) & (rank): 1,125,027 (38)
1985 est. population (July 1) & (rank): 1,164,000 (38)
1984 land area & (rank): 30,995 sq mi. (80,277 sq km) (39)
Geographic center: In Piscataquis Co., 18 mi. N of Dover-Foxcroft
Number of counties: 16
Largest cities (1980 census): Portland, 61,572; Lewiston, 40,481; Bangor, 31,643; Auburn, 23,128; South Portland, 22,712; Augusta, 21,819; Biddeford, 19,638
State forests: 1 (21,000 ac.)
State parks: 26 (247,627 ac.)
State historic sites: 18 (403 ac.)
1985 percent pop. below age 15: 21
1985 percent pop. age 65 and over: 13
1985 serious crimes per 100,000 pop.: 3,672
1984 (fiscal year) immigrants: 798

John Cabot and his son, Sebastian, are believed to have visited the Maine coast in 1498. However, the first permanent English settlements were not established until more than a century later, in 1623.

The first naval action of the Revolutionary War occurred in 1775 when colonials captured the British sloop *Margaretta* off Machias on the Maine coast. In that same year, the British burned Falmouth (now Portland).

Long governed by Massachusetts, Maine became the 23rd state as part of the Missouri Compromise in 1820.

Maine produces 95% of the nation's low-bush blueberries. Farm income is also derived from apples, sweet corn, peas, and beans, with poultry and eggs the largest items.

The state is one of the world's largest pulp-paper producers. It ranks fifth in boot-and-shoe manufacturing. With more than 90% of its area forested, Maine turns out wood products from boats to toothpicks.

Maine leads the world in the production of the familiar flat tins of sardines, producing more than 100 million of them annually. Lobstermen normally catch 80–90% of the nation's true total of lobsters.

A scenic seacoast, beaches, lakes, mountains, and resorts make Maine a popular vacationland. There are more than 2,500 lakes and 5,000 streams, plus 26 state parks, to attract hunters, fishermen, skiers, and campers.

Major points of interest are: Bar Harbor, Allagash National Wilderness Waterway, the Wadsworth-Longfellow House in Portland, Roosevelt Campobello International Park, and the St. Croix Island National Monument.

MARYLAND

Capital: Annapolis
Governor: William Donald Schaefer, D (to Jan. 1991)
Lieut. Gov.: Melvin A. Steinberg, D (to Jan. 1991)
Secy. of State: Winfield M. Kelly, Jr., D (appointed by governor)

Comptroller of the Treasury: Louis L. Goldstein, D (to Jan. 1991)
Treasurer: Lucille Maurer, D (to Jan. 1991)
Atty. General: J. Joseph Curran, Jr., D (to Jan. 1991)
Entered Union & (rank): April 28, 1788 (7)
Present constitution adopted: 1867
Motto: *Fatti maschii, parole femine* (Manly deeds, womanly words)
State flower: Black-eyed susan (1918)
State tree: White oak (1941)
State bird: Baltimore oriole (1947)
State dog: Chesapeake Bay retriever (1964)
State fish: Rockfish (1965)
State insect: Baltimore checkerspot butterfly (1973)
State sport: Jousting (1962)
State song: "Maryland! My Maryland!" (1939)
Nicknames: Free State; Old Line State
Origin of name: In honor of Henrietta Maria (Queen of Charles I of England)
1980 population (1980 census) & (rank): 4,216,975 (18)
1985–86 est. population (July 1) & (rank): 4,392,000 (20)
1984 land area & (rank): 9,837 sq mi. (25,477 sq km) (42)
Geographic center: In Prince Georges Co., 4 1/2 mi. NW of Davidsonville
Number of counties: 23, and 1 independent city
Largest cities (1980 census): Baltimore, 786,775; Rockville, 43,811; Hagerstown, 34,132; Bowie, 33,695; Annapolis, 31,740; Frederick, 28,086; Gaithersburg, 26,424
State forests: 10 (120,921 ac.)
State parks: 42 (70,302 ac.)
1985 percent pop. below age 15: 20
1985 percent pop. age 65 and over: 10
1985 serious crimes per 100,000 pop.: 5,373
1984 (fiscal year) immigrants: 9,749

In 1608, Chesapeake Bay was explored by Capt. John Smith. Charles I granted a royal charter to Cecil Calvert, Lord Baltimore, in 1632 and English Roman Catholics landed on St. Clement's (now Blakistone Island) in 1634. Religious freedom, granted all Christians in the Toleration act passed by the Maryland assembly in 1649, was ended by a Puritan revolt, 1654–58.

In 1814, when the British unsuccessfully tried to capture Baltimore, the bombardment of Fort McHenry inspired Francis Scott Key to write *The Star Spangled Banner.*

Maryland is almost cut in two by the Chesapeake Bay, and the many estuaries and rivers create one of the longest waterfronts of any state. The Bay produces more seafood—oysters, crabs, clams, fin fish—than any comparable body of water. Important agricultural products, in order of cash value, are chickens, dairy products, corn, cattle, tobacco, and vegetables. Maryland is a leader in vegetable canning. Sand, gravel, lime and cement, stone, coal, and clay are the chief mineral products.

Manufacturing industries produce missiles, airplanes, steel, clothing, and chemicals. Baltimore, home of The Johns Hopkins University and Hospital, ranks as the nation's second port in foreign tonnage. Annapolis, site of the U.S. Naval Academy, has one of the earliest state houses (1772–79) still in regular use by a State government.

Among the popular attractions in Maryland are the Fort McHenry National Monument, Harpers Ferry and Chesapeake and Ohio Canal National Historical Parks, St. Marys City restoration near Leonardtown, USS *Constellation* at Baltimore, U.S. Naval Academy in Annapolis, Assateague Island National Seashore, and Catoctin Mountain and Piscataway parks.

MASSACHUSETTS

Capital: Boston
Governor: Michael S. Dukakis, D (to Jan. 1991)
Lieut. Governor: Evelyn F. Murphy, D (to Jan. 1991)
Secy. of the Commonwealth: Michael Joseph Connolly, D (to Jan. 1991)
Treasurer & Receiver-General: Robert Q. Crane, D (to Jan. 1991)
Auditor of the Commonwealth: A. Joseph DeNucci, D (to Jan. 1991)
Atty. General: James M. Shannon, D (to Jan. 1991)
Entered Union & (rank): Feb. 6, 1788 (6)
Motto: *Ense petit placidam sub libertate quietem* (By the sword we seek peace, but peace only under liberty)
State flower: Mayflower (1918)
State tree: American elm (1941)
State bird: Chickadee (1941)
State colors: Blue and gold
State song: "All Hail to Massachusetts" (1966)
State beverage: Cranberry juice (1970)
State insect: Ladybug (1974)
Nicknames: Bay State; Old Colony State
Origin of name: From two Indian words meaning "Great mountain place"
1985 est. population (July 1) & (rank): 5,822,000 (12)
1984 land area & (rank): 7,824 sq mi. (20,265 sq km) (45)
Geographic center: In Worcester Co., in S part of city of Worcester
Number of counties: 14
Largest cities (1980 census): Boston, 562,994; Worcester, 161,799; Springfield, 152,319; New Bedford, 98,478; Cambridge, 95,322; Brockton, 95,172; Fall River, 94,574
State forests and parks: 129 (242,000 ac.)[1]
1985 percent pop. below age 15: 19
1985 percent pop. age 65 and over: 13
1985 serious crimes per 100,000 pop.: 4,758
1984 (fiscal year) immigrants: 13,418

1. The Metropolitan District Commission, an agency of the Commonwealth serving municipalities in the Boston area, has about 14,000 acres of parkways and reservations under its jurisdiction.

Massachusetts has played a significant role in American history since the Pilgrims, seeking religious freedom, founded Plymouth Colony in 1620.

As one of the most important of the 13 colonies, Massachusetts became a leader in resisting British oppression. In 1773, the Boston Tea Party protested unjust taxation. The Minutemen started the American Revolution by battling British troops at Lexington and Concord on April 19, 1775.

During the 19th century, Massachusetts was famous for the vigorous intellectual activity of famous writers and educators and for its expanding commercial fishing, shipping, and manufacturing interests.

Massachusetts pioneered in the manufacture of textiles and shoes. Today, these industries have been replaced in importance by activity in the electronics and communications equipment fields.

The state's cranberry crop is the nation's largest. Also important are dairy and poultry products, nursery and greenhouse produce, vegetables, and fruit.

Tourism has become an important factor in the economy of the state because of its numerous recreational areas and historical landmarks.

Cape Cod has summer theaters, water sports, and an artists' colony at Provincetown. Tanglewood, in the Berkshires, features the summer concerts of the Boston Symphony.

Among the many other points of interest are Old Sturbridge Village, Minute Man National Historical Park between Lexington and Concord, and, in Boston: Old North Church, Old State House, Faneuil Hall, the USS *Constitution* and the John F. Kennedy Library.

MICHIGAN

Capital: Lansing
Governor: James J. Blanchard, D (to Jan. 1991)
Lieut. Governor: Martha W. Griffiths, D (to Jan. 1991)
Secy. of State: Richard H. Austin, D (to Jan. 1991)
Atty. General: Frank J. Kelley, D (to Jan. 1991)
Organized as territory: Jan. 11, 1805
Entered Union & (rank): Jan. 26, 1837 (26)
Present constitution adopted: April 1, 1963, (effective Jan. 1, 1964)
Motto: *Si quaeris peninsulam amoenam circumspice* (If you seek a pleasant peninsula, look around you)
State flower: Apple blossom (1897)
State bird: Robin
State fish: Brook trout (1965)
State gem: Isle Royal Greenstone (Chlorastrolite) (1972)
State stone: Petoskey stone (1965)
Nickname: Wolverine State
Origin of name: From two Indian words meaning "great lake"
1980 population (1980 census) & (rank): 9,262,078 (8)
1985 est. population (July 1) & (rank): 9,088,000 (8)
1984 land area & (rank): 56,954 sq mi. (147,511 sq km) (22)
Geographic center: In Wexford Co., 5 mi. NNW of Cadillac
Number of counties: 83
Largest cities (1980 census): Detroit, 1,203,339; Grand Rapids, 181,843; Warren, 161,134; Flint, 159,611; Lansing, 130,414; Sterling Heights, 108,999; Ann Arbor, 107,966
State forests: 33 (3,762,184 ac.)
State parks and recreation areas: 92 (216,857 ac.)
1985 percent pop. below age 15: 22
1985 percent pop. age 65 and over: 11
1985 serious crimes per 100,000 pop.: 6,366
1984 (fiscal year) immigrants: 8,065

Indian tribes were living in the Michigan region when the first European, Étienne Brulé of France, arrived in 1618. Other French explorers, including Marquette, Jolliet, and La Salle, followed, and the first permanent settlement was established in 1668 at Sault Ste. Marie. France was ousted from the territory by Great Britain in 1763, following the French and Indian War.

After the Revolutionary War, the U.S. acquired most of the region, which remained the scene of constant conflict between the British and U.S. forces and their respective Indian allies through the War of 1812.

Bordering on four of the five Great Lakes, Michigan is divided into Upper and Lower Peninsulas by the Straits of Mackinac, which link Lakes Michigan and Huron. The two parts of the state are connected by the Mackinac Bridge, one of the world's longest suspension bridges. To the north, connecting Lakes Superior and Huron are the busy Sault Ste. Marie Canals.

While Michigan ranks first among the states in production of motor vehicles and parts, it is also a leader in many other manufacturing and processing lines including prepared cereals, machine tools, airplane parts, refrigerators, hardware, steel springs, and furniture.

The state produces important amounts of iron, copper, iodine, gypsum, bromine, salt, lime, gravel, and cement. Michigan's farms grow apples, cherries, pears, grapes, potatoes, and sugar beets and the annual value of its forest products is estimated at $2 billion. With over 36,000 miles of streams, some 11,000 lakes, and a 2,000 mile shoreline, Michigan is a prime area for both commercial and sport fishing.

Points of interest are the automobile plants in Dearborn, Detroit, Flint, Lansing, and Pontiac; Mackinac Island; Pictured Rocks and Sleeping Bear Dunes National Lakeshores, Greenfield Village near Dearborn; and the many summer resorts along both the inland and Great Lakes.

MINNESOTA

Capital: St. Paul
Governor: Rudy Perpich, D (to Jan. 1991)
Lieut. Governor: Marlene Johnson, D (to Jan. 1991)
Secy. of State: Joan Growe (to Jan. 1991)
State Auditor: Arne Carlson, R (to Jan. 1991)
Atty. General: Hubert H. Humphrey III, D (to Jan. 1991)
State Treasurer: Michael McGrath, D (to Jan. 1987)
Organized as territory: March 3, 1849
Entered Union & (rank): May 11, 1858 (32)
Present constitution adopted: 1858
Motto: L'Etoile du Nord (The North Star)
State flower: Showy lady slipper (1902)
State tree: Red (or Norway) pine
State bird: Common loon (also called Great Northern Diver)
State song: "Hail Minnesota"
Nicknames: North Star State; Gopher State; Land of 10,000 Lakes
Origin of name: From a Dakota Indian word meaning "sky-tinted water"
1980 population (1980 census) & (rank): 4,075,970 (21)
1985 est. population (July 1) & (rank): 4,193,000 (21)
1984 land area & (rank): 79,548 sq mi. (206,030 sq km) (14)
Geographic center: In Crow Wing Co., 10 mi. SW of Brainerd
Number of counties: 87
Largest cities (1980 census): Minneapolis, 370,951; St. Paul, 270,230; Duluth, 92,811; Bloomington, 81,831; Rochester, 57,890; Edina, 46,073
State forests: 55 (2,984,000 ac.)
State parks: 92 (202,205 ac.)
1985 percent pop. below age 15: 22
1985 percent pop. age 65 and over: 12
1985 serious crimes per 100,000 pop.: 4,134
1984 (fiscal year) immigrants: 5,243

Following the visits of several French explorers, fur traders, and missionaries, including Marquette and Jolliet and La Salle, the region was claimed for Louis XIV by Daniel Greysolon, Sieur Duluth, in 1679.

The U.S. acquired eastern Minnesota from Great Britain after the Revolutionary War and 20 years later bought the western part from France in the Louisiana Purchase of 1803. Much of the region was explored by U.S. Army Lt. Zebulon M. Pike before cession of the northern strip of Minnesota bordering Canada by Britain in 1818.

The state is rich in natural resources. A few square miles of land in the north in the Mesabi, Cuyuna, and Vermillion ranges, produce more than 60% of the nation's iron ore. The state's farms rank high in yields of corn, wheat, rye, alfalfa, and sugar beets. Other leading farm products include butter, eggs, milk, potatoes, green peas, barley, and livestock.

Minnesota's factory production includes nonelectrical machinery, fabricated metals, flour-mill products, plastics, electronic computers, scientific instruments, and processed foods.

Minneapolis is the trade center of the Northwest; St. Paul is the nation's biggest publisher of calendars and law books. These "twin cities" are the nation's third largest trucking center. Duluth has the nation's largest inland harbor and now handles a significant amount of foreign trade. Rochester is the home of the Mayo Clinic, an internationally famous medical center.

Today, tourism is a major revenue producer in Minnesota, with fishing, hunting, water sports, and winter sports bringing in millions of visitors each year.

Among the most popular attractions are the St. Paul Winter Carnival; the Tyrone Guthrie Theatre, the Institute of Arts, Walker Art Center, and Minnehaha Park, in Minneapolis; Voyageurs National Park; North Shore Drive; and the Minnesota Zoological Gardens.

MISSISSIPPI

Capital: Jackson
Governor: William A. Allain, D (to Jan. 1988)
Lieut. Governor: Brad Dye, D (to Jan. 1988)
Secy. of State: Dick Molpus, D (to Jan. 1988)
Treasurer: Bill Cole, D (to Jan. 1988)
Atty. General: Edwin Lloyd Pittman, D (to Jan. 1988)
Organized as Territory: April 7, 1798
Entered Union & (rank): Dec. 10, 1817 (20)
Present constitution adopted: 1890
Motto: *Virtute et armis* (By valor and arms)
State flower: Flower or bloom of the magnolia or evergreen magnolia (1952)
State tree: Magnolia (1938)
State bird: Mockingbird (1944)
State song: "Go, Mississippi" (1962)
Nickname: Magnolia State
Origin of name: From an Indian word meaning "Father of Waters"
1980 population (1980 census) & (rank): 2,520,638 (31)
1985 est. population (July 1) & (rank): 2,613,000 (31)
1984 land area & (rank): 47,233 sq mi. (122,333 sq km) (31)
Geographic center: In Leake Co., 9 mi. WNW of Carthage
Number of counties: 82
Largest cities (1980 census): Jackson, 202,895; Biloxi, 49,311; Hattiesburg, 40,829; Greenville, 40,613; Gulfport, 39,676; Pascagoula, 29,318
State forests: 1 (1,760 ac.)
State parks: 27 (16,763 ac.)
1985 percent pop. below age 15: 25
1985 percent pop. age 65 and over: 12
1985 serious crimes per 100,000 pop.: 3,266
1984 (fiscal year) immigrants: 786

First explored for Spain by Hernando de Soto who discovered the Mississippi River in 1540, the region was later claimed by France. In 1699, a French group under Sieur d'Iberville established the first permanent settlement near present-day Biloxi.

Great Britain took over the area in 1763 after the French and Indian War, ceding it to the U.S. in 1783 after the Revolution. Spain did not relinquish its claims until 1798, and in 1810 the U.S. annexed West Florida from Spain, including what is now southern Mississippi.

Mississippi, the stronghold of the Old South, has until the past decade been one of the least industrialized states, with more than half its population making a living from the soil. However, a recent industrialization program has attracted manufacturing industries such as lumber, furniture, paper, food processing, apparel, chemicals, transportation equipment, and machinery.

Cotton, nevertheless, is still king with the state ranking second to Texas in cotton production, though soybeans have become Mississippi's largest crop. Other important farm products are corn, peanuts, pecans, rice, sugarcane, sweet potatoes, and hay. Poultry and eggs are also important.

The state abounds in historical landmarks and is the home of the Vicksburg National Military Park where visitors may see the remains of forts, trenches, and other military relics used in the 1863 Union-army siege of the city. Other National Park Service areas are Brices Cross Roads National Battlefield Site, Tupelo National Battlefield, and part of Natchez Trace National Parkway. Pre-Civil War mansions are the special pride of Natchez, Oxford, Hattiesburg, and Jackson.

MISSOURI

Capital: Jefferson City
Governor: John D. Ashcroft, R (to Jan. 1989)
Lieut. Governor: Harriett Woods, D (to Jan. 1989)
Secy. of State: Roy D. Blunt, R (to Jan. 1989)
Auditor: Margaret Kelly, R (to Jan. 1991)
Treasurer: Wendell Bailey, R (to Jan. 1989)
Atty. General: William L. Webster, R (to Jan. 1989)
Organized as territory: June 4, 1812
Entered Union & (rank): Aug. 10, 1821 (24)
Present constitution adopted: 1945
Motto: *Salus populi suprema lex esto* (The welfare of the people shall be the supreme law)
State flower: Hawthorn (1923)
State bird: Bluebird (1927)
State colors: Red, white, and blue (1913)
State song: "Missouri Waltz" (1949)
State rock: Mozarkite (1967)
State mineral: Galena (1967)
Nickname: Show-me State
Origin of name: Named after a tribe called Missouri Indians. "Missouri" means "town of the large canoes."
1980 population (1980 census) & (rank): 4,916,759 (15)
1985 est. population (July 1) & (rank): 5,029,000 (15)
1984 land area & (rank): 68,945 sq mi. (178,568 sq km) (18)
Geographic center: In Miller Co., 20 mi. SW of Jefferson City
Number of counties: 114, plus 1 independent city
Largest cities (1980 census): St. Louis, 453,085; Kansas City, 448,159; Springfield, 133,116; Independence, 111,806; Columbia, 62,061; Florissant, 55,372
State forests and Tower sites: 93 (265,000 ac.)
State parks: 71 (97,314 ac.)[1]
1985 percent pop. below age 15: 22
1985 percent pop. age 65 and over: 14
1985 serious crimes per 100,000 pop.: 4,366
1984 (fiscal year) immigrants: 3,186

1. Includes 24 historic sites and 1 archaeological site.

De Soto visited the Missouri area in 1541. France's claim to the entire region was based on La Salle's travels in 1682. French fur traders established Ste. Genevieve in 1735 and St. Louis was first settled in 1764.

The U.S. gained Missouri from France as part of the Louisiana Purchase in 1803, and the territory was admitted as a state following the Missouri Compromise of 1820. Throughout the pre-Civil War period and during the war, Missourians were sharply divided in their opinions about slavery and in their allegiances, supplying both Union and Confederate forces with troops. However, the state itself remained in the Union.

Historically, Missouri played a leading role as a gateway to the West, St. Joseph being the eastern starting point of the Pony Express, while the much-traveled Santa Fe and Oregon Trails began in Independence. Now a popular vacationland, Missouri has 11 major lakes and numerous fishing streams, springs, and caves. Bagnell Dam, across the Osage River in the Ozarks, completed in 1931, created one of the largest man-made lakes in the world, covering 65,000 acres of surface area.

Manufacturing, paced by the aerospace industry, provides more income and jobs than any other segment of the economy. Missouri is also a leading producer of transportation equipment, shoes, lead, and beer. Among the major crops are corn, soybeans, wheat, oats, barley, potatoes, tobacco, and cotton.

Points of interest include Mark Twain's boyhood home and Mark Twain Cave (Hannibal), the Harry S. Truman Library and Museum (Independence), the house where Jesse James was killed in St. Joseph, Jefferson National Expansion Memorial (St. Louis), and the Ozark National Scenic Riverway.

MONTANA

Capital: Helena
Governor: Ted Schwinden, D (to Jan. 1989)
Lieut. Governor: George Turman, D (to Jan. 1989)
Secy. of State: Jim Waltermire, R (to Jan. 1989)
Auditor: Andrea "Andy" Bennett, R (to Jan. 1989)
Atty. General: Michael Greely, D (to Jan. 1989)
Organized as territory: May 26, 1864
Entered Union & (rank): Nov. 8, 1889 (41)
Present constitution adopted: 1972
Motto: *Oro y plata* (Gold and silver)
State flower: Bitterroot (1895)
State tree: Ponderosa pine (1949)
State stones: Sapphire and agate (1969)
State bird: Western meadow lark (1931)
State song: "Montana" (1945)
Nickname: Treasure State
Origin of name: Chosen from Latin dictionary by J. M. Ashley. It is a Latinized Spanish word.
1985 est. population (July 1) & (rank): 826,000 (44)
1984 land area & (rank): 145,392 sq mi. (376,564 sq km) (4)
Geographic center: In Fergus Co., 12 mi. W of Lewistown
Number of counties: 56, plus small part of Yellowstone National Park
Largest cities (1980 census): Billings, 66,824; Great Falls, 56,725; Butte-Silver Bow, 37,205; Missoula, 33,388; Helena, 23,938; Bozeman, 21,645; Havre, 10,891
State forests: 7 (214,000 ac.)
State parks and recreation areas: 110 (18,273 ac.)
1985 percent pop. below age 15: 24
1985 percent pop. age 65 and over: 12
1985 serious crimes per 100,000 pop.: 4,549
1984 (fiscal year) immigrants: 333

First explored for France by François and Louis-Joseph Verendrye in the early 1740s, much of the region was acquired by the U.S. from France as part of the Louisiana Purchase in 1803. Before western Montana was obtained from Great Britain in the Oregon Treaty of 1846, American trading posts and forts had been established in the territory.

The major Indian wars (1867–1877) included the famous 1876 Battle of the Little Big Horn, better known as "Custer's Last Stand," in which Cheyennes and Sioux killed George A. Custer and more than 200 of his men in southeastern Montana.

Much of Montana's early history was concerned with mining with copper, lead, zinc, silver, coal, and oil as principal products.

Butte, sitting on the "richest hill in the world," is the center of the area that once supplied half of the U.S. copper.

Fields of grain cover much of Montana's plains; it ranks high among the states in wheat and barley, with rye, oats, flaxseed, sugar beets, and potatoes other important crops. Sheep and cattle raising make significant contributions to the state's economy.

Tourist attractions include hunting, fishing, skiing, and dude ranching. Glacier National Park, on the Continental Divide, is a scenic and vacation wonderland with 60 glaciers, 200 lakes, and many streams with good trout fishing.

Other major points of interest include the Custer Battlefield National Monument, Virginia City, Yellowstone National Park, Museum of the Plains Indians at Browning, and the Fort Union Trading Post and Grant-Kohr's Ranch National Historic Sites.

NEBRASKA

Capital: Lincoln
Governor: Kay A. Orr, R (to Jan. 1991)
Lieut. Governor: Wm. Nichol, R (to Jan. 1991)
Secy. of State: Allen J. Beerman, R (to Jan. 1991)
Atty. General: Robert Spire, R (to Jan. 1991)
Auditor: Ray A. C. Johnson, R (to Jan. 1991)
Treasurer: Frank Marsh, R (to Jan. 1991)
Organized as territory: May 30, 1854
Entered Union & (rank): March 1, 1867 (37)
Present constitution adopted: Nov. 1, 1875 (extensively amended 1919–20)
Motto: Equality before the law
State flower: Goldenrod (1895)
State tree: Cottonwood (1972)
State bird: Western meadow lark (1929)
State insect: Honey Bee (1975)
State gem stone: Blue agate (1967)
State rock: Prairie agate (1967)
State fossil: Mammoth (1967)
State song: "Beautiful Nebraska" (1967)
Nicknames: Cornhusker State; Beef State; Tree Planters State
Origin of name: From an Oto Indian word meaning "flat water"
1980 population (1980 census) & (rank): 1,570,006 (35)
1985 est. population (July 1) & (rank): 1,606,000 (35)
1984 land area & (rank): 77,727 sq mi. (198,508 sq km) (15)
Geographic center: In Custer Co., 10 mi. NW of Broken Bow
Number of counties: 93
Largest cities (1980 census): Omaha, 313,911; Lincoln, 171,932; Grand Island, 33,180; North Platte, 24,479; Fremont, 23,979; Hastings, 23,045; Bellevue, 21,813
State forests: None
State parks: 93 areas, 4 categories, 5 major areas
1985 percent pop. below age 15: 23
1985 percent pop. age 65 and over: 14

1985 serious crimes per 100,000 pop.: 3,695
1984 (fiscal year) immigrants: 984

French fur traders first visited Nebraska in the early 1700s. Part of the Louisiana Purchase in 1803, Nebraska was explored by Lewis and Clark in 1804–06.

Robert Stuart pioneered the Oregon Trail across Nebraska in 1812–13 and the first permanent settlement was established at Bellevue in 1823. Western Nebraska was acquired by treaty following the Mexican War in 1848. The Union Pacific began its transcontinental railroad at Omaha in 1865. In 1937, Nebraska became the only state in the Union to have a unicameral (one-house) legislature. Members are elected to it without party designation.

Nebraska is a leading grain-producer with bumper crops of rye, corn, and wheat. More varieties of grass, valuable for forage, grow in this state than in any other in the nation.

The state's sizable cattle and hog industries make Omaha with its surrounding area the nation's largest meat-packing center and the second-largest cattle market in the world.

Manufacturing has become diversified in Nebraska, strengthening the state's economic base. Firms making electronic components, auto accessories, pharmaceuticals, and mobile homes have joined such older industries as clothing, farm machinery, chemicals, and transportation equipment. Oil was discovered in 1939 and natural gas in 1949.

Among the principal attractions are Agate Fossil Beds, Homestead, and Scotts Bluff National Monuments; Chimney Rock National Historic Site; a recreated pioneer village at Minden; the Union stockyards in Omaha; the Stuhr Museum of the Prairie Pioneer with 57 original 19th-century buildings near Grand Island; and the Sheldon Memorial Art Gallery at the University of Nebraska in Lincoln.

NEVADA

Capital: Carson City
Governor: Richard H. Bryan, D (to Jan. 1991)
Lieut. Governor: Robert J. Miller, D (to Jan. 1991)
Secy. of State: Frankie Sue Del Papa, D (to Jan. 1991)
State Treasurer: Ken Santor, R (to Jan. 1991)
Controller: Darrel R. Daines, R (to Jan. 1991)
Atty. General: Brian McKay, R (to Jan. 1991)
Organized as territory: March 2, 1861
Entered Union & (rank): Oct. 31, 1864 (36)
Present constitution adopted: 1864
Motto: All for Our Country
State flower: Sagebrush (1967)
State tree: Single-leaf pinon (1953)
State bird: Mountain bluebird (1967)
State animal: Desert bighorn sheep (1973)
State colors: Silver and blue (unofficial)
State song: "Home Means Nevada" (1933)
Nicknames: Sagebrush State; Silver State; Battle-born State
Origin of name: Spanish: "snowcapped"
1980 population (1980 census) & (rank): 800,493 (43)
1985 est. population (July 1) & (rank): 936,000 (43)
1984 land area & (rank): 109,893 sq mi. (284,624 sq km) (7)
Geographic center: In Lander Co., 26 mi. SE of Austin
Number of counties: 16, plus 1 independent city
Largest cities (est. as of July 1, 1985): Las Vegas, 193,052; Reno, 115,464; North Las Vegas, 45,920; Sparks, 49,612; Carson City, 35,400; Henderson, 37,046; Boulder City, 11,425
State forests: None
State parks: 20 (150,000 ac., including leased lands)
1985 percent pop. below age 15: 20
1985 percent pop. age 65 and over: 10
1985 serious crimes per 100,000 pop.: 6,575
1984 (fiscal year) immigrants: 2,130

Trappers and traders, including Jedediah Smith, and Peter Skene Ogden, entered the Nevada area in the 1820s. In 1843–45, John C. Fremont and Kit Carson explored the Great Basin and Sierra Nevada.

In 1848 following the Mexican War, the U.S. obtained the region and the first permanent settlement was a Mormon trading post near present-day Genoa.

The driest state in the nation with an average annual rainfall of only 3.73 inches, much of Nevada is uninhabited, sagebrush-covered desert.

Nevada was made famous by the discovery of the fabulous Comstock Lode in 1859 and its mines have produced large quantities of gold, silver, copper, lead, zinc, mercury, barite, and tungsten. Oil was discovered in 1954. Copper now far exceeds all other minerals in value of production.

In 1931, the state created two industries, divorce and gambling. For many years, Reno and Las Vegas were the "divorce capitals of the nation." More liberal divorce laws in many states have ended this distinction, but Nevada is the gambling and entertainment capital of the U.S. State gambling taxes account for 45% of tax revenues. Although Nevada leads the nation in per capita gambling revenue, it ranks only fourth in total gambling revenue.

Near Las Vegas, on the Colorado River, stands Hoover Dam, which impounds the waters of Lake Mead, one of the world's largest artificial lakes.

The state's agricultural crop consists mainly of hay, alfalfa seed, barley, and wheat.

Nevada manufactures gaming devices, chemicals, forest products, suntan lotion, and stone-clay-glass products.

Major resort areas flourish in Lake Tahoe, Reno, and Las Vegas. Recreation areas include those at Pyramid Lake, Lake Tahoe, and Lake Mead and Lake Mohave, both in Lake Mead National Recreation Area. Among the other attractions are Hoover Dam, Virginia City, and Lehman Caves National Monument.

NEW HAMPSHIRE

Capital: Concord
Governor: John H. Sununu, R (to Jan. 1989)
Secy. of State: William M. Gardner, D (to Dec. 1986)
Commissioner: Stephen M. Kennedy, R
Atty. General: Stephen E. Merrill (to July 1989)
Entered Union & (rank): June 21, 1788 (9)
Present constitution adopted: 1784
Motto: Live free or die
State flower: Purple lilac (1919)
State tree: White birch (1947)
State bird: Purple finch (1957)
State songs: "Old New Hampshire" (1949) and "New Hampshire, My New Hampshire" (1963)
Nickname: Granite State
Origin of name: From the English county of Hampshire
1980 population (1980 census) & (rank): 920,610 (42)
1985 est. population (July 1) & (rank): 998,000 (41)
1984 land area & (rank): 8,993 sq mi. (23,292 sq km) (44)

Geographic center: In Belknap Co., 3 mi. E of Ashland
Number of counties: 10
Largest cities (1980 census): Manchester, 90,936; Nashua, 67,865; Concord, 30,400; Portsmouth, 26,254; Dover, 22,377; Rochester, 21,560; Keene, 21,449
State forests & parks: 175 (96,975 ac.)
1985 percent pop. below age 15: 21
1985 percent pop. age 65 and over: 12
1985 serious crimes per 100,000: 3,252
1984 (fiscal year) immigrants: 772

Under an English land grant, Capt. John Smith sent settlers to establish a fishing colony at the mouth of the Piscataqua River, near present-day Rye and Dover, in 1623. Capt. John Mason, who participated in the founding of Portsmouth in 1630, gave New Hampshire its name.

After a 38-year period of union with Massachusetts, New Hampshire was made a separate royal colony in 1679. As leaders in the revolutionary cause, New Hampshire delegates received the honor of being the first to vote for the Declaration of Independence on July 4, 1776. New Hampshire is the only state that ever played host at the formal conclusion of a foreign war when, in 1905, Portsmouth was the scene of the treaty ending the Russo-Japanese War.

Abundant water power early turned New Hampshire into an industrial state and manufacturing is the principal source of income in the state. The most important industrial products are leather goods, electrical and other machinery, textiles, and pulp and paper products.

Dairy and poultry farming and growing fruit, truck vegetables, corn, potatoes, and hay are the major agricultural pursuits.

Tourism, because of New Hampshire's scenic and recreational resources, now brings over $400 million into the state annually.

Vacation attractions include Lake Winnipesaukee, largest of 1,300 lakes and ponds; the 724,000-acre White Mountain National Forest; Daniel Webster's birthplace near Franklin; Strawberry Banke, restored building of the original settlement at Portsmouth; and the famous "Old Man of the Mountain" granite head profile, the state's official emblem, at Franconia.

NEW JERSEY

Capital: Trenton
Governor: Thomas H. Kean, R (to Jan. 1990)
Secy. of State: Feather O'Connor, R (to Jan. 1990)
Treasurer: W. Cary Edwards, R (to Jan. 1990)
Atty. General: Irwin I. Kimmelman, R (to Jan. 1990)
Entered Union & (rank): Dec. 18, 1787 (3)
Present constitution adopted: 1947
Motto: Liberty and prosperity
State flower: Purple violet (1913)
State bird: Eastern goldfinch (1935)
State insect: Honeybee (1974)
State tree: Red oak (1950)
State animal: Horse (1977)
State colors: Buff and blue (1965)
Nickname: Garden State
Origin of name: From the Channel Isle of Jersey
1980 population (1980 census) & (rank): 7,364,823 (9)
1985 est. population (July 1) & (rank): 7,562,000 (9)
1984 land area & (rank): 7,468 sq mi. (19,342 sq km) (46)
Geographic center: In Mercer Co., 5 mi. SE of Trenton
Number of counties: 21
Largest cities (1980 census): Newark, 329,248; Jersey City, 223,532; Paterson, 137,970; Elizabeth, 106,201; Trenton, 92,124; Camden, 84,910; Clifton, 77,690
State forests: 11
State parks: 35 (67,111 ac.)
1985 percent pop. below age 15: 20
1985 percent pop. age 65 and over: 13
1985 serious crimes per 100,000 pop.: 5,094
1984 (fiscal year) immigrants: 27,148

New Jersey's early colonial history was involved with that of New York (New Netherlands), of which it was a part. One year after the Dutch surrender to England in 1664, New Jersey was organized as an English colony under Gov. Philip Carteret.

In the late 1600s the colony was divided between Carteret and William Penn; later it would be administered by the royal governor of New York. Finally, in 1738, New Jersey was separated from New York under its own royal governor, Lewis Morris.

Because of its key location between New York City and Philadelphia, New Jersey saw much fighting during the American Revolution.

Today, New Jersey, an area of wide industrial diversification, is known as the Crossroads of the East. Products from over 15,000 factories can be delivered overnight to almost 60 million people, representing 12 states and the District of Columbia. The greatest single industry is chemicals and New Jersey is one of the foremost research centers in the world. Many large oil refineries are located in northern New Jersey and other important manufactures are pharmaceuticals, instruments, machinery, electrical goods, and apparel.

Of the total land area, 43% is forested and about 24% is devoted to agriculture. The state ranks high in production of almost all garden vegetables. Tomatoes, asparagus, corn, and blueberries are important crops, and poultry farming and dairying make significant contributions to the state's economy.

Tourism is the second largest industry in New Jersey. The state has numerous resort areas on 127 miles of Atlantic coastline. In 1977, New Jersey voters approved legislation allowing legalized casino gambling in Atlantic City. Points of interest include the Walt Whitman House in Camden, the Delaware Water Gap, the Edison National Historic Site in West Orange, and Princeton University.

NEW MEXICO

Capital: Santa Fe
Governor: Garrey E. Carruthers, R (to Jan. 1990)
Lieut. Governor: Jack Stahl, R (to Jan. 1990)
Secy. of State: Rebecca Vigil-Giron, D (to Jan. 1990)
Atty. General: Hal Stratton, R (to Jan. 1990)
State Auditor: Harroll H. Adams, D (to Jan. 1990)
State Treasurer: James B. Lewis, D (to Jan. 1990)
Commissioner of Public Lands: William R. Humphries, R (to Jan. 1990)
Organized as territory: Sept. 9, 1850
Entered Union & (rank): Jan. 6, 1912 (47)
Present constitution adopted: 1911
Motto: *Crescit eundo* (It grows as it goes)
State flower: Yucca (1927)
State tree: Pinon (1949)
State animal: Black bear (1963)
State bird: Roadrunner (1949)
State fish: Cutthroat trout (1955)
State vegetables: Chile and frijol (1965)
State gem: Turquoise (1967)
State colors: Red and yellow of old Spain (1925)

State song: "O Fair New Mexico" (1917)
Spanish language state song: "Asi Es Nuevo Mejico" (1971)
Nicknames: Land of Enchantment; Sunshine State
Origin of name: From the country of Mexico
1980 population (1980 census) & (rank): 1,302,981 (37)
1985 est. population (July 1) & (rank): 1,450,000 (37)
1984 land area & (rank): 121,335 sq mi. (314,258 sq km) (5)
Geographic center: In Torrance Co., 12 mi. SSW of Willard
Number of counties: 33
Largest cities (July 1, 1984 est.): Albuquerque, 350,575; Santa Fe, 52,274; Las Cruces, 50,275; Roswell, 45,702; Farmington, 37,332; Hobbs, 35,029
State-owned forested land: 933,000 ac.
State parks: 29 (105,012 ac.)
1985 percent pop. below age 15: 26
1985 percent pop. age 65 and over: 10
1985 serious crimes per 100,000 pop.: 6,486
1984 (fiscal year) immigrants: 2,258

Francisco Vásquez de Coronado, Spanish explorer searching for gold, traveled the region that became New Mexico in 1540–42. In 1598 the first Spanish settlement was established on the Rio Grande River by Juan de Onate and in 1610 Santa Fe was founded and made the capital of New Mexico.

The U.S. acquired most of New Mexico in 1848, as a result of the Mexican War, and the remainder in the 1853 Gadsden Purchase. Union troops captured the territory from the Confederates during the Civil War. With the surrender of Geronimo in 1886, the Apache Wars and most of the Indian troubles in the area were ended.

Since 1945, New Mexico has been a leader in energy research and development with extensive experiments conducted at Los Alamos Scientific Laboratory and Sandia Laboratories in the nuclear, solar, and geothermal areas.

Minerals are the state's richest natural resource and New Mexico leads the U.S. in output of uranium and potassium salts. Petroleum, natural gas, copper, gold, silver, zinc, lead, and molybdenum also contribute heavily to the state's income.

The principal manufacturing industries include food products, chemicals, transportation equipment, lumber, electrical machinery, and stone-clay-glass products. More than two thirds of New Mexico's farm income comes from livestock products, especially sheep. Cotton, pecans, and sorghum are the most important field crops. Corn, peanuts, beans, onions, and lettuce are also grown.

Tourist attractions in New Mexico include the Carlsbad Caverns National Park, Inscription Rock at El Morro National Monument, the ruins at Fort Union, Billy the Kid mementos at Lincoln, and the White Sands and Gila Cliff Dwellings National Monuments.

NEW YORK

Capital: Albany
Governor: Mario M. Cuomo, D (to Jan. 1991)
Lieut. Governor: Stan Lundine, D (to Jan. 1991)
Secy. of State: Gail S. Shaffer, D (to Jan. 1991)
Comptroller: Edward V. Regan, R (to Jan. 1991)
Atty. General: Robert Abrams, D (to Jan. 1991)
Entered Union & (rank): July 26, 1788 (11)
Present constitution adopted: 1777 (last revised 1938)
Motto: *Excelsior* (Ever upward)
State animal: Beaver (1975)
State fish: Brook trout (1975)
State gem: Garnet (1969)
State flower: Rose (1955)
State tree: Sugar maple (1956)
State bird: Bluebird
State song: "I Love New York" (1980)
Nickname: Empire State
Origin of name: In honor of the English Duke of York
1980 population (1980 census) & (rank): 17,558,165 (2)
1985 est. population (July 1) & (rank): 17,783,000 (2)
1984 land area & (rank): 47,377 sq mi. (122,707 sq km) (30)
Geographic center: In Madison Co., 12 mi. S of Oneida and 26 mi. SW of Utica
Number of counties: 62
Largest cities (1984 est.): New York, 7,164,742; Buffalo, 338,982; Rochester, 242,562; Yonkers, 191,234; Syracuse, 164,219; Albany, 99,451; Utica, 72,935
State forest preserves: Adirondacks, 2,500,000 ac., Catskills, 250,000 ac.
State parks: 150 (250,000 ac.)
1985 percent pop. below age 15: 20
1985 percent pop. age 65 and over: 13
1985 serious crimes per 100,000 pop.: 5,589
1984 (fiscal year) immigrants: 107,056

Giovanni da Verrazano, Italian-born navigator sailing for France, discovered New York Bay in 1524. Henry Hudson, an Englishman employed by the Dutch, reached the bay and sailed up the river now bearing his name in 1609, the same year that northern New York was explored and claimed for France by Samuel de Champlain.

In 1624 the first permanent Dutch settlement was established at Fort Orange (now Albany); one year later Peter Minuit is said to have purchased Manhattan Island from the Indians for trinkets worth about $24 and founded the Dutch colony of New Amsterdam (now New York City), which was surrendered to the English in 1664.

For a short time, New York City was the U.S. capital and George Washington was inaugurated there as first President on April 30, 1789.

New York's extremely rapid commercial growth may be partly attributed to Governor De Witt Clinton, who pushed through the construction of the Erie Canal (Buffalo to Albany), which was opened in 1825. Today, the 559-mile Governor Thomas E. Dewey Thruway connects New York City with Buffalo and with Connecticut, Massachusetts, and Pennsylvania express highways. Two toll-free superhighways, the Adirondack Northway (linking Albany with the Canadian border) and the North-South-Expressway (crossing central New York from the Pennsylvania border to the Thousand Islands) have been opened.

New York, with the great metropolis of New York City, is the spectacular nerve center of the nation. It is a leader in manufacturing, foreign trade, commercial and financial transactions, book and magazine publishing, and theatrical production.

New York City is not only a national but an international leader. A leading seaport, its John F. Kennedy International Airport is one of the busiest airports in the world. The largest manufacturing center in the country, in 1982 its manufacturing establishments employed 529,000 persons. The apparel industry is the city's largest manufacturing employer, with printing and publishing second.

Nearly all the rest of the state's manufacturing is done on Long Island, along the Hudson River north to Albany and through the Mohawk Valley, Central New York, and Southern Tier regions to

Buffalo. The St. Lawrence seaway and power projects have opened the North Country to industrial expansion and have given the state a second seacoast.

The state ranks second in the nation in manufacturing with 1,383,300 employees in 1983. The principal industries are machinery, printing and publishing, instruments, apparel, and chemicals.

The convention and tourist business is one of the state's most important sources of income.

New York farms are famous for raising cattle and calves, producing corn for grain, poultry, and the raising of vegetables and fruits. The state is a leading wine producer.

Among the major points of interest are Castle Clinton, Fort Stanwix, and Statue of Liberty National Monuments; Niagara Falls; U.S. Military Academy at West Point; National Historic Sites that include homes of Franklin D. Roosevelt at Hyde Park and Theodore Roosevelt in Oyster Bay and New York City; National Memorials, including Grant's Tomb and Federal Hall in New York City; Fort Ticonderoga; the Baseball Hall of Fame in Cooperstown; and the United Nations, skyscrapers, museums, theaters, and parks in New York City.

NORTH CAROLINA

Capital: Raleigh
Governor: James G. Martin, R (to Jan. 1989)
Lieut. Governor: Robert B. Jordan III, D (to Jan. 1989)
Secy. of State: Thad Eure, D (to Jan. 1989)
Treasurer: Harlan E. Boyles (to Jan. 1989)
Auditor: Edward Renfrow, D (to Jan. 1989)
Atty. General: Lacey H. Thornburg, D (to Jan. 1989)
Entered Union & (rank): Nov. 21, 1789 (12)
Present constitution adopted: 1971
Motto: *Esse quam videri* (To be rather than to seem)
State flower: Dogwood (1941)
State tree: Pine (1963)
State bird: Cardinal (1943)
State mammal: Gray Squirrel (1969)
State insect: Honeybee (1973)
State Reptile: Turtle (1979)
State gem stone: Emerald (1973)
State shell: Scotch bonnet (1965)
State song: "The Old North State" (1927)
State colors: Red and blue (1945)
Nickname: Tar Heel State
Origin of name: In honor of Charles I of England
1980 population (1980 census) & (rank): 5,881,766 (10)
1985 est. population (July 1) & (rank): 6,255,000 (10)
1984 land area & (rank): 48,843 sq mi. (126,504 sq km) (29)
Geographic center: In Chatham Co., 10 mi. NW of Sanford
Number of counties: 100
Largest cities (est. as of July 1, 1984): Charlotte, 338,107; Raleigh, 180,559; Greensboro, 159,744; Winston-Salem, 146,886; Durham, 106,115; High Point, 66,380
State forests: 1
State parks: 28 (120,000 ac.)
1985 percent pop. below age 15: 21
1985 percent pop. age 65 and over: 11
1985 serious crimes per 100,000 pop.: 4,121
1984 (fiscal year) immigrants: 3,207

English colonists, sent by Sir Walter Raleigh, unsuccessfully attempted to settle Roanoke Island in 1585 and 1587. Virginia Dare, born there in 1587, was the first child of English parentage born in America.

In 1653 the first permanent settlements were established by English colonists from Virginia near the Roanoke and Chowan Rivers.

The region was established as an English proprietary colony in 1663–65 and its early history was the scene of Culpepper's Rebellion (1677), the Quaker-led Cary Rebellion of 1708, the Tuscarora Indian War in 1711–13, and many pirate raids.

During the American Revolution, there was relatively little fighting within the state, but many North Carolinians saw action elsewhere. Despite considerable pro-Union, anti-slavery sentiment, North Carolina joined the Confederacy.

North Carolina is the nation's largest furniture, tobacco, brick, and textile producer. It holds second place in the Southeast in population and first place in the value of its industrial and agricultural production. This production is highly diversified, with metalworking, chemicals, and paper constituting enormous industries. Tobacco, corn, cotton, hay, peanuts, and truck and vegetable crops are of major importance. It is the country's leading producer of mica and lithium.

Tourism is also important, with travelers and vacationers spending more than $1 billion annually in North Carolina. Sports include year-round golfing, skiing at mountain resorts, both fresh and salt water fishing, and hunting.

Among the major attractions are the Great Smoky Mountains, the Blue Ridge National Parkway, the Cape Hatteras and Cape Lookout National Seashores, the Wright Brothers National Memorial at Kitty Hawk, Guilford Courthouse and Moores Creek National Military Parks, Carl Sandburg's home near Hendersonville, and the Old Salem Restoration in Winston-Salem.

NORTH DAKOTA

Capital: Bismarck
Governor: George A. Sinner, D (to Jan. 1989)
Lieut. Governor: Ruth Meiers, D (to Jan. 1989)
Secy. of State: Ben Meier, R (to Jan. 1989)
Auditor: Robert W. Peterson, R (to Jan. 1989)
State Treasurer: Robert Hanson, D (to Jan. 1989)
Atty. General: Nicholas Spaeth, D (to Jan. 1989)
Organized as territory: March 2, 1861
Entered Union & (rank): Nov. 2, 1889 (39)
Present constitution adopted: 1889
Motto: Liberty and union, now and forever: one and inseparable
State tree: American Elm (1947)
State bird: Western meadow lark (1947)
State song: "North Dakota Hymn" (1947)
Nickname: Sioux State; Flickertail State
Origin of name: From the Dakotah tribe, meaning "allies"
1980 population (1980 census) & (rank): 652,717 (46)
1985 est. population (July 1) & (rank): 685,000 (46)
1984 land area & (rank): 70,665 sq mi (183,113 sq km) (17)
Geographic center: In Sheridan Co., 5 mi. SW of McClusky
Number of counties: 53
Largest cities (1980 census): Fargo, 61,383; Bismarck, 44,485; Grand Forks, 43,765; Minot, 32,843; Jamestown, 16,280; Dickinson, 15,924; Mandan, 15,513
State forests: None
State parks: 14 (14,922.6 ac.)
1985 percent pop. below age 15: 24
1985 percent pop. age 65 and over: 13
1985 serious crimes per 100,000 pop.: 2,679
1984 (fiscal year) immigrants: 385

North Dakota was explored in 1738–40 by French Canadians led by Vérendrye. In 1803, the

U.S. acquired most of North Dakota from France in the Louisiana Purchase. Lewis and Clark explored the region in 1804–06 and the first settlements were made at Pembina in 1812 by Scottish and Irish families while this area was still in dispute between the U.S. and Great Britain.

In 1818, the U.S. obtained the northeastern part of North Dakota by treaty with Great Britain and took possession of Pembina in 1823.

North Dakota is the most rural of all the states, with farms covering more than 90% of the land. Only Kansas produces more wheat, and the state's coal and oil reserves are plentiful.

Other agricultural products include barley, rye, oats, and flaxseed, sugar beets, and hay; beef cattle, sheep, and hogs are also important to the state's economy.

Recently, manufacturing industries have grown, especially food processing and farm equipment. The state also produces natural gas, lignite, salt, clay, sand, and gravel.

The Garrison Dam on the Missouri River provides extensive irrigation and produces 400,000 kilowatts of electricity for the Missouri Basin areas.

Known for its waterfowl, grouse, and deer hunting and bass, trout, and northern pike fishing, North Dakota has 20 state parks and recreation areas. Points of interest include the International Peace Garden near Dunseith, Fort Union Trading Post National Historic Site, the State Capitol at Bismarck, the Badlands, and Fort Lincoln, now a state park, from which Gen. George Custer set out on his last campaign in 1876.

OHIO

Capital: Columbus
Governor: Richard F. Celeste, D (to Jan. 1991)
Lieut. Governor: Paul Leonard, D (to Jan. 1991)
Secy. of State: Sherrod Brown, D (to Jan. 1991)
Auditor: Thomas E. Ferguson, D (to Jan. 1991)
Treasurer: Mary Ellen Withrow, D (to Jan. 1991)
Atty. General: Anthony J. Celebrezze, Jr., D (to Jan. 1991)
Entered Union & (rank): March 1, 1803 (17)
Present constitution adopted: 1851
Motto: With God, all things are possible
State flower: Scarlet carnation (1904)
State tree: Buckeye (1953)
State bird: Cardinal (1933)
State insect: Ladybug (1975)
State gem stone: Flint (1965)
State song: "Beautiful Ohio"
State drink: Tomato juice (1965)
Nickname: Buckeye State
Origin of name: From an Iroquoian word meaning "great river"
1980 population (1980 census) & (rank): 10,797,624 (6)
1985 est. population (July 1) & (rank): 10,744,000 (7)
1984 land area & (rank): 41,004 sq mi. (106,201 sq km) (35)
Geographic center: In Delaware Co., 25 mi. NNE of Columbus
Number of counties: 88
Largest cities (1980 census): Cleveland, 573,822; Columbus, 565,032; Cincinnati, 385,457; Toledo, 354,635; Akron, 237,177; Dayton, 203,371; Youngstown, 115,436
State forests: 19 (172,744 ac.)
State parks: 71 (198,027 ac.)
1985 percent pop. below age 15: 22
1985 percent pop. age 65 and over: 12
1985 serious crimes per 100,000 pop.: 4,187
1984 (fiscal year) immigrants: 6,254

First explored for France by La Salle in 1669, the Ohio region became British property after the French and Indian War. Ohio was acquired by the U.S. after the Revolutionary War in 1783 and, in 1788, the first permanent settlement was established at Marietta, capital of the Northwest Territory.

The 1790s saw severe fighting with the Indians in Ohio; a major battle was won by Maj. Gen. Anthony Wayne at Fallen Timbers in 1794. In the War of 1812, Commodore Oliver H. Perry defeated the British in the Battle of Lake Erie on Sept. 10, 1813.

Ohio is one of the nation's industrial leaders, ranking third in the value of manufactured products. Important manufacturing centers are located in or near Ohio's major cities. Akron is known for rubber; Canton for roller bearings; Cincinnati for jet engines and machine tools; Cleveland for auto assembly and parts, refining, and steel; Dayton for office machines, refrigeration, and heating and auto equipment; Youngstown and Steubenville for steel; and Toledo for glass and auto parts.

The state's thousands of factories almost overshadow its importance in agriculture and mining. Its fertile soil produces soybeans, corn, oats, grapes, and clover. More than half of Ohio's farm receipts come from dairying and sheep and hog raising. Ohio is the top state in lime production and among the leaders in coal, clay, salt, sand, and gravel. Petroleum, gypsum, cement, and natural gas are also important.

Tourism is a valuable revenue producer, bringing in over $3 billion annually. Attractions include the Indian burial grounds at Mound City Group National Monument, Perry's Victory International Peace Memorial, the Pro Football Hall of Fame at Canton, and the homes of Presidents Grant, Taft, Hayes, Harding, and Garfield.

OKLAHOMA

Capital: Oklahoma City
Governor: Henry Bellmon, R (to Jan. 1991)
Lieut. Governor: Robert S. Kerr, III, D (to Jan. 1991)
Secy. of State: Jeannette Edmondson, D (to Jan. 1991)
Treasurer: Ellis Edwards, D (to Jan. 1991)
Atty. General: Robert Henry, D (to Jan. 1991)
Organized as territory: May 2, 1890
Entered Union & (rank): Nov. 16, 1907 (46)
Present constitution adopted: 1907
Motto: *Labor omnia vincit* (Labor conquers all things)
State flower: Mistletoe (1893)
State tree: Redbud (1937)
State bird: Scissor-tailed flycatcher (1951)
State animal: Bison (1972)
State reptile: Mountain boomer lizard (1969)
State stone: Rose Rock (barite rose) (1968)
State colors: Green and white (1915)
State song: "Oklahoma" (1953)
Nickname: Sooner State
Origin of name: From two Choctaw Indian words meaning "red people"
1980 population (1980 census) & (rank): 3,025,290 (26)
1985 est. population (July 1) & (rank): 3,301,000 (25)
1984 land area & (rank): 68,655 sq mi. (177,817 sq km) (19)
Geographic center: In Oklahoma Co., 8 mi. N of Oklahoma City
Number of counties: 77
Largest cities (1980 census): Oklahoma City, 403,213; Tulsa, 360,919; Lawton, 80,054; Norman, 68,020; Enid, 50,363; Midwest City, 49,559; Muskogee, 40,011

State forests: None
State parks: 36 (57,487 ac.)
1985 percent pop. below age 15: 24
1985 percent pop. age 65 and over: 12
1985 serious crimes per 100,000 pop.: 5,425
1984 (fiscal year) immigrants: 4,915

Francisco Vásquez de Coronado first explored the region for Spain in 1541. The U.S. acquired most of Oklahoma in 1803 in the Louisiana Purchase from France; the Western Panhandle region became U.S. territory with the annexation of Texas in 1845.

Set aside as Indian Territory in 1834, the region was divided into Indian Territory and Oklahoma Territory on May 2, 1890. The two were combined to make a new state, Oklahoma, on Nov. 16, 1907.

On April 22, 1899, the first day homesteading was permitted, 50,000 people swarmed into the area. Those who tried to beat the noon starting gun were called "Sooners." Hence the state's nickname.

Oil has made Oklahoma a rich state and Tulsa one of the world's wealthiest cities per capita. Oil refining, meat packing, food processing, and machinery manufacturing (especially construction and oil equipment) are important industries.

Other minerals produced in Oklahoma include natural gas, helium, gypsum, zinc, cement, coal, copper, and silver.

Oklahoma's rich plains produce bumper yields of wheat, as well as large crops of sorghum, corn, cotton, and peanuts. Its beef cattle herd is among the largest in the nation; more than half of Oklahoma's annual farm receipts are contributed by livestock products.

Tourist attractions include the National Cowboy Hall of Fame in Oklahoma City, the Will Rogers Memorial in Claremore, the Cherokee Cultural Center with a restored Cherokee village, the restored Fort Gibson Stockade near Muskogee, and the Lake Texoma recreation area.

OREGON

Capital: Salem
Governor: Neil Goldschmidt, D (to Jan. 1991)
Secy. of State: Barbara Roberts, R (to Jan. 1989)
Treasurer: Bill Rutherford, R (to Jan. 1989)
Atty. General: David B. Frohnmayer, R (to Jan. 1989)
Organized as territory: Aug. 14, 1848
Entered Union & (rank): Feb. 14, 1859 (33)
Present constitution adopted: 1859
Motto: "Alis volat Propriis" ("She flies with her own wings") (1987)
State flower: Oregon grape (1899)
State tree: Douglas fir (1939)
State animal: Beaver (1969)
State bird: Western meadow lark (1927)
State fish: Chinook salmon (1961)
State rock: Thunderegg (1965)
State colors: Navy blue and gold (1959)
State song: "Oregon, My Oregon" (1927)
Nickname: Beaver State
Poet Laureate: William E. Stafford (1974)
Origin of name: Unknown. However, it is generally accepted that the name, first used by Jonathan Carver in 1778, was taken from the writings of Maj. Robert Rogers, an English army officer.
1980 population (1980 census) & (rank): 2,633,105 (30)
1985 est. population (July 1) & (rank): 2,687,000 (30)
1984 land area & (rank): 96,184 sq mi. (249,117 sq km) (10)
Geographic center: In Crook Co., 25 mi. SSE of Prineville
Number of counties: 36
Largest cities (est. as of July 1, 1985): Portland, 379,000; Eugene, 106,100; Salem, 94,600; Medford, 41,975; Springfield, 40,690
State forests: 820,000 ac.
State parks: 240 (93,330 ac.)
1985 percent pop. below age 15: 22
1985 percent pop. age 65 and over: 13
1985 serious crimes per 100,000 pop.: 6,730
1984 (fiscal year) immigrants: 4,342

Spanish and English sailors are believed to have sighted the Oregon coast in the 1500s and 1600s. Capt. James Cook, seeking the Northwest Passage, charted some of the coastline in 1778. In 1792, Capt. Robert Gray, in the *Columbia,* discovered the river named after his ship and claimed the area for the U.S.

In 1805 the Lewis and Clark expedition explored the area and John Jacob Astor's fur depot, Astoria, was founded in 1811. Disputes for control of Oregon between American settlers and the Hudson Bay Company were finally resolved in the 1846 Oregon Treaty in which Great Britain gave up claims to the region.

Oregon has a five-billion-dollar wood processing industry. Its salmon-fishing industry is one of the world's largest.

In agriculture, the state leads in growing peppermint, winter pears, fresh plums, prunes, blackberries, boysenberries, filberts, Blue Lake beans, and cover seed crops, and also raises strawberries, hops, wheat and other grains, sugar beets, potatoes, green peas, fiber flax, dairy products, livestock and poultry, apples, pears, and cherries. Oregon is the source of all the nickel produced in the U.S.

With the low-cost electric power provided by Bonneville Dam, McNary Dam, and other dams in the Pacific Northwest, Oregon has developed steadily as a manufacturing state. Leading manufactures are lumber and plywood, metalwork, machinery, aluminum, chemicals, paper, food packing, and electronic equipment.

Crater Lake National Park, Mount Hood, and Bonneville Dam on the Columbia are major tourist attractions. Oregon Dunes National Recreation Area has been established near Florence. Other points of interest include the Oregon Caves National Monument, Cape Perpetua in Siuslaw National Forest, Columbia River Gorge between The Dalles and Troutdale, and Hells Canyon.

PENNSYLVANIA

Capital: Harrisburg
Governor: Robert P. Casey, D (to Jan. 1991)
Lieut. Governor: Mark S. Singel, D (to Jan. 1991)
Secy. of the Commonwealth: James J. Haggerty, D (at the pleasure of the Governor)
Auditor General: Don Bailey, D (to Jan. 1989)
Atty. General: Leroy S. Zimmerman, R (to Jan. 1989)
Entered Union & (rank): Dec. 12, 1787 (2)
Present constitution adopted: 1874
Motto: Virtue, liberty, and independence
State flower: Mountain laurel (1933)
State tree: Hemlock (1931)
State bird: Ruffed grouse (1931)
State dog: Great Dane (1965)
State colors: Blue and gold
State song: None
Nickname: Keystone State

Origin of name: In honor of Adm. Sir. William Penn, father of William Penn. It means "Penn's Woodland."
1980 population (1980 census) & (rank): 11,863,895 (4)
1985 est. population (July 1) & (rank): 11,853,000 (4)
1984 land area & (rank): 44,888 sq mi. (116,260 sq km) (32)
Geographic center: In Centre Co., 2 1/2 mi. SW of Bellefonte
Number of counties: 67
Largest cities (1980 census): Philadelphia, 1,688,210; Pittsburgh, 423,959; Erie, 119,123; Allentown, 103, 758; Scranton, 88,117; Reading, 78,686; Bethlehem, 70,419
State forests: 1,930,108 ac.
State parks: 120 (297,438 ac.)
1985 percent pop. below age 15: 20
1985 percent pop. age 65 and over: 14
1985 serious crimes per 100,000 pop.: 3,037
1984 (fiscal year) immigrants: 9,801

Rich in historic lore, Pennsylvania territory was disputed in the early 1600s among the Dutch, the Swedes, and the English. England acquired the region in 1664 with the capture of New York and in 1681 Pennsylvania was granted to William Penn, a Quaker, by King Charles II.

Philadelphia was the seat of the federal government almost continuously from 1776 to 1800; there the Declaration of Independence was signed in 1776 and the U.S. Constitution drawn up in 1787. Valley Forge, of Revolutionary War fame, and Gettysburg, the turning-point of the Civil War, are both in Pennsylvania. The Liberty Bell is located in a glass pavilion across from Independence Hall in Philadelphia.

Approximately 23% of all American pig iron steel is made in Pennsylvania, which ranks first among the states in steel wire and structural metal production. Other manufactures include machinery, chemicals, storage batteries, motor vehicles and trailers, computers, textiles and apparel, shoes, plastics, and explosives. Pennsylvania produces almost all the nation's anthracite coal. Also important are bituminous coal, cement, stone, petroleum, natural gas, lime, clays, zinc, and iron.

Prosperous farms brought in total receipts of more than $1.3 billion in 1973. The state ranked high in milk cows, chickens, and turkeys. Agricultural products include apples, peaches, potatoes, corn, wheat, barley, buckwheat, and mushrooms.

Tourists now spend approximately $6 billion in Pennsylvania annually. Among the chief attractions: the Gettysburg National Military Park, Valley Forge National Historical Park, Independence National Historical Park in Philadelphia, the Pennsylvania Dutch region, the Eisenhower farm near Gettysburg, and the Delaware Water Gap National Recreation Area.

RHODE ISLAND

Capital: Providence
Governor: Edward D. DiPrete, R (to Jan. 1989)
Lieut. Governor: Richard A. Licht, D (to Jan. 1989)
Secy. of State: Kathleen S. Connell, D (to Jan. 1989)
Controller: Edward Casper (civil service)
Atty. General: James E. O'Neil, D (to Jan. 1989)
Entered Union & (rank): May 29, 1790 (13)
Present constitution adopted: 1843
Motto: Hope
State flower: Violet (unofficial)
State tree: Red maple (official)
State bird: Rhode Island Red (official)
State colors: Blue, white, and gold (in state flag)
State song: "Rhode Island" (1946)
Nickname: The Ocean State
Origin of name: From the Greek Island of Rhodes
1980 population (1980 census) & (rank): 947,154 (40)
1985 est. population (July 1) & (rank): 968,000 (42)
1984 land area & (rank): 1,055 sq mi. (2,732 sq km) (50)
Geographic center: In Kent Co., 1 mi. SSW of Crompton
Number of counties: 5
Largest cities (1980 census): Providence, 156,804; Warwick, 87,123; Cranston, 71,992; Pawtucket, 71,204; East Providence, 50,980; Woonsocket, 45,914
State forests: 11 (20,900 ac.)
State parks: 17 (8,200 ac.)
1985 percent pop. below age 15: 19
1985 percent pop. age 65 and over: 14
1985 serious crimes per 100,000 pop.: 4,724
1984 (fiscal year) immigrants: 2,666

From its beginnings, Rhode Island has been distinguished by its support for freedom of conscience and action, started by Roger Williams, who was exiled by the Massachusetts Bay Colony Puritans in 1636, and was the founder of the present state capital, Providence. Williams was followed by other religious exiles who founded Pocasset, now Portsmouth, in 1638 and Newport in 1639.

The first Baptist church in the U.S. was established in Providence in 1638 and Rhode Island provided a haven for Quakers in 1657 and for Jews from Holland in 1659.

Rhode Island's rebellious, authority-defying nature was further demonstrated by the burnings of the British revenue cutters *Liberty* and *Gaspee* prior to the Revolution, by its early declaration of independence from Great Britain in May 1776, its refusal to participate actively in the War of 1812, and by Dorr's Rebellion of 1842, which protested property requirements for voting.

Rhode Island, smallest of the 50 states, is densely populated and highly industrialized. The state pioneered in the manufacture of jewelry and silverware and still retains first place in the U.S. Other leading industries are primary metal processing, metal products, machinery, rubber and plastics, food processing, chemicals, transportation equipment and electronic equipment.

With more than eight tenths of the population living in urban areas, adjacent areas of the state are involved in dairying and poultry and truck farming. Nursery and greenhouse products, potatoes, corn, apples, oats, and hay lead the crop list.

Newport became famous as the summer capital of society in the mid-19th century. Touro Synagogue (1763) is the oldest in the U.S. Other points of interest include the Roger Williams National Memorial in Providence, Samuel Slater's Mill in Pawtucket, the General Nathaniel Greene Homestead in Coventry and Block Island.

SOUTH CAROLINA

Capital: Columbia
Governor: Carroll Campbell, R (to Jan. 1991)
Lieut. Governor: Nick Theodore, D (to Jan. 1991)
Secy. of State: John T. Campbell, D (to Jan. 1991)
Comptroller General: Earl E. Morris, Jr. (to Jan. 1991)
Atty. General: T. Travis Medlock, D (to Jan. 1991)
Entered Union & (rank): May 23, 1788 (8).
Present constitution adopted: 1895
Mottoes: *Animis opibusque parati* (Prepared in mind and

resources) and *Dum spiro spero* (While I breathe, I hope)
State flower: Carolina yellow jessamine (1924)
State tree: Palmetto tree (1939)
State bird: Carolina wren (1948)
State song: "Carolina" (1911)
Nickname: Palmetto State
Origin of name: In honor of Charles I of England
1980 population (1980 census) & (rank): 3,121,833 (24)
1985 est. population (July 1) & (rank): 3,347,000 (24)
1984 land area & (rank): 30,203 sq mi. (78,227 sq km) (40)
Geographic center: In Richland Co., 13 mi. SE of Columbia
Number of counties: 46
Largest cities (1980 census): Columbia, 100,385; Charleston, 69,510; North Charleston, 62,534; Greenville, 58,242; Spartanburg, 43,826; Rock Hill, 35,344
State forests: 4 (124,052 ac.)
State parks: 50 (61,726 ac.)
1985 percent pop. below age 15: 23
1985 percent pop. age 65 and over: 10
1985 serious crimes per 100,000 pop.: 4,841
1984 (fiscal year) immigrants: 1,677

Following exploration of the coast in 1521 by De Gordillo, the Spanish tried unsuccessfully to establish a colony near present-day Georgetown in 1526 and the French also failed to colonize Parris Island near Fort Royal in 1562.

The first English settlement was made in 1670 at Albemarle Point on the Ashley River, but poor conditions drove the settlers to the site of Charleston (originally called Charles Town). South Carolina, officially separated from North Carolina in 1729, was the scene of extensive military action during the Revolution and again during the Civil War. The Civil War began in 1861 as South Carolina troops fired on federal Fort Sumter in Charleston Harbor and the state was the first to secede from the Union.

Once primarily agricultural, South Carolina has built so many large textile and other mills that today its factories produce eight times the output of its farms in cash value. Charleston makes asbestos, wood, pulp, and steel products; chemicals, machinery, and apparel are also important.

Farms have become fewer but larger in recent years. South Carolina grows more peaches than any other state except California; it ranks fourth in tobacco. Other farm products include cotton, peanuts, sweet potatoes, soybeans, corn, and oats. Poultry and dairy products are also important revenue producers.

Points of interest include Fort Sumter National Monument, Fort Moultrie, Fort Johnson, and aircraft carrier USS *Yorktown* in Charleston Harbor; the Middleton, Magnolia, and Cypress Gardens in Charleston; Cowpens National Battlefield; and the Hilton Head resorts.

SOUTH DAKOTA

Capital: Pierre
Governor: George S. Mickelson, R (to Jan. 1991)
Lieut. Governor: Walter Dale Miller, R (to Jan. 1991)
Atty. General: Roger Tellinghuisen, R (to Jan. 1991)
Secy. of State: Joyce Hazeltine, R (to Jan. 1991)
State Auditor: Vern Larson, R (to Jan. 1991)
State Treasurer: David L. Volk, R (to Jan. 1991)
Organized as territory: March 2, 1861
Entered Union & (rank): Nov. 2, 1889 (40)
Present constitution adopted: 1889
Motto: Under God the people rule
State flower: American pasqueflower (1903)
State grass: Western wheat grass (1970)
State tree: Black Hills spruce (1947)
State bird: Ring-necked pheasant (1943)
State insect: Honeybee (1978)
State animal: Coyote (1949)
State mineral stone: Rose quartz (1966)
State gem stone: Fairburn agate (1966)
State colors: Blue and gold (in state flag)
State song: "Hail! South Dakota" (1943)
State fish: Walleye (1982)
Nicknames: Sunshine State; Coyote State
Origin of name: Same as for North Dakota
1980 population (1980 census) & (rank): 690,768 (45)
1985 est. population (July 1) & (rank): 708,000 (45)
1984 land area & (rank): 75,952 sq mi. (196,715 sq km) (16)
Geographic center: In Hughes Co., 8 mi. NE of Pierre
Number of counties: 67 (64 county governments)
Largest cities (1980 census): Sioux Falls, 81,343; Rapid City, 46,492; Aberdeen, 25,851; Watertown, 15,649; Brookings, 14,951; Mitchell, 13,916; Huron, 13,000
State forests: None[1]
State parks: 13 plus 39 recreational areas (87,269 ac.)[2]
1985 percent pop. below age 15: 25
1985 percent pop. age 65 and over: 14
1985 serious crimes per 100,000 pop.: 2,641
1984 (fiscal year) immigrants: 293

1. No designated state forests; about 13,000 ac. of state land is forestland. 2. Acreage includes 39 recreation areas and 80 roadside parks, in addition to 12 state parks.

Exploration of this area began in 1743 when Louis-Joseph and François Verendrye came from France in search of a route to the Pacific.

The U.S. acquired the region as part of the Louisiana Purchase in 1803 and it was explored by Lewis and Clark in 1804–06. Fort Pierre, the first permanent settlement, was established in 1817 and, in 1831, the first Missouri River steamboat reached the fort.

Settlement of South Dakota did not begin in earnest until the arrival of the railroad in 1873 and the discovery of gold in the Black Hills the following year.

Agriculture is South Dakota's basic industry. In 1986, South Dakota ranked first in the U.S. in rye production. It also ranked among the top five states in oats, flaxseed, sunflower seed, alfalfa hay, all other hay, lamb crop, spring wheat, beef cows, and sheep and lambs. In 1986, the state boasted 3,600,000 cattle, 605,000 sheep, and 1,520,000 hogs.

South Dakota is the nation's second leading producer of gold (Nevada ranks first) and the Homestake Mine is the richest in the U.S. Other minerals produced include berylium, bentonite, granite, silver, petroleum, and uranium.

Processing of foods produced by farms and ranches is the largest South Dakota manufacturing industry, followed by lumber, wood products, and machinery, including farm equipment.

The Black Hills are the highest mountains east of the Rockies. Mt. Rushmore, in this group, is famous for the likenesses of Washington, Jefferson, Lincoln, and Theodore Roosevelt, which were carved in granite by Gutzon Borglum. The Badlands offer scenic masses of bare rock and clay unrelieved by any vegetation. Other points of interest are Deadwood, where Wild Bill Hickok was killed in 1876; the Crazy Horse Memorial near Custer; and the Corn Palace in Mitchell.

TENNESSEE

Capital: Nashville
Governor: Ned Ray McWherther, D (to Jan. 1991)
Lieut. Governor: John S. Wilder, D (to Jan. 1989)
Secy. of State: Gentry Crowell, D (to Jan. 1989)
Atty. General: W. J. Michael Cody, D (to 1993)
State Treasurer: Steve Adams, D (to Jan. 1989)
Entered Union & (rank): June 1, 1796 (16)
Present constitution adopted: 1870; amended 1953, 1960, 1966, 1972, 1978
Motto: "Tennessee—America at its best!" (1965)
State flower: Iris (1933)
State tree: Tulip poplar (1947)
State bird: Mockingbird (1933)
State horse: Tennessee walking horse
State animal: Raccoon
State wild flower: Passion flower
State song: "Tennessee Waltz" (1965)
Nickname: Volunteer State
Origin of name: Of Cherokee origin; the exact meaning is unknown
1980 population (1980 census) & (rank): 4,591,120 (17)
1985 est. population (July 1) & (rank): 4,762,000 (17)
1984 land area & (rank): 41,155 sq mi. (106,591 sq km) (34)
Geographic center: In Rutherford Co., 5 mi. NE of Murfreesboro
Number of counties: 95
Largest cities (1980 census): Memphis, 646,174; Nashville, 455,651; Knoxville, 175,045; Chattanooga, 169,558; Clarksville, 54,777; Jackson, 49,131
State forests: 14 (155,752 ac.)
State parks: 21 (130,000 ac.)
1985 percent pop. below age 15: 21
1985 percent pop. age 65 and over: 12
1985 serious crimes per 100,000 pop.: 4,167
1984 (fiscal year) immigrants: 2,065

First visited by the Spanish explorer de Soto in 1541, the Tennessee area would later be claimed by both France and England as a result of the 1670s and 1680s explorations of Marquette and Joliet, La Salle, and the Englishmen James Needham and Gabriel Arthur.

Great Britain obtained the region following the French and Indian War in 1763 and it was rapidly occupied by settlers moving in from Virginia and the Carolinas.

During 1784–87, the settlers formed the "state" of Franklin, which was disbanded when the region was allowed to send representatives to the North Carolina legislature. In 1790 Congress organized the territory south of the Ohio River and Tennessee joined the Union in 1796.

Although Tennessee joined the Confederacy during the Civil War, there was much pro-Union sentiment in the state, which was the scene of extensive military action.

The state is now predominantly industrial; in 1970, 58.8% of its population lived in urban areas. Among the most important products are chemicals, textiles, apparel, electrical machinery, furniture, and leather goods. Other lines include food processing, lumber, primary metals, and metal products. The state is known as the U.S. hardwood-flooring center and ranks first in the production of marble, zinc, pyrite, and ball clay.

Tennessee is one of the leading tobacco-producing states in the nation and its farming income is also derived from livestock and dairy products as well as corn, cotton, and soybeans.

With six other states, Tennessee shares the extensive federal reservoir developments on the Tennessee and Cumberland River systems. The Tennessee Valley Authority operates a number of dams and reservoirs in the state.

Among the major points of interest: the Andrew Johnson National Historic Site at Greenville, American Museum of Atomic Energy at Oak Ridge, Great Smoky Mountains National Park, The Hermitage (home of Andrew Jackson near Nashville), Rock City Gardens near Chattanooga, and three National Military Parks.

TEXAS

Capital: Austin
Governor: William P. Clements, R (to Jan. 1991)
Lieut. Governor: William P. Hobby, D (to Jan. 1991)
Secy. of State: Jack Rains, R (to Jan. 1991)
Comptroller: Bob Bullock, D (to Jan. 1991)
Atty. General: Jim Mattox, D (to Jan. 1991)
Entered Union & (rank): Dec. 29, 1845 (28)
Present constitution adopted: 1876
Motto: Friendship
State flower: Bluebonnet (1901)
State tree: Pecan (1919)
State bird: Mockingbird (1927)
State song: "Texas, Our Texas" (1930)
Nickname: Lone Star State
Origin of name: From an Indian word meaning "friends"
1980 population (1980 census) & (rank): 14,229,288 (3)
1985 est. population (July 1) & (rank): 16,370,000 (3)
1984 land area & (rank): 262,017 sq mi. (678,623 sq km) (2)
Geographic center: In McCulloch Co., 15 mi. NE of Brady
Number of counties: 254
Largest cities (1980 census): Houston, 1,595,138; Dallas, 904,078; San Antonio, 785,023; El Paso, 425,259; Fort Worth, 385,164; Austin, 345,496
State forests: 4 (6,306 ac.)
State parks: 83 (64 developed)
1985 percent pop. below age 15: 25
1985 percent pop. age 65 and over: 9
1985 serious crimes per 100,000 pop.: 6,569
1984 (fiscal year) immigrants: 42,180

Spanish explorers, including Cabeza de Vaca and Coronado, were the first to visit the region in the 16th and 17th centuries, settling at Ysleta near present-day El Paso in 1682. In 1685, La Salle established a short-lived French colony at Matagorda Bay.

Americans, led by Stephen F. Austin, began to settle along the Brazos River in 1821 when Texas was controlled by Mexico, recently independent from Spain. In 1836, following a brief war between the American settlers in Texas and the Mexican government, and famous for the battles of the Alamo and San Jacinto, the Independent Republic of Texas was proclaimed with Sam Houston as president.

After Texas became the 28th U.S. state in 1845, border disputes led to the Mexican War of 1846–48.

Today, Texas, second only to Alaska in land area, leads all other states in such categories as oil, cattle, sheep, and cotton. Possessing enormous natural resources, Texas is a major agricultural state and an industrial giant.

Sulfur, salt, helium, asphalt, graphite, bromine, natural gas, cement, and clays give Texas first place in mineral production—nearly $8 billion in 1973. Chemicals, oil refining, food processing, machinery, and transportation equipment are among the major Texas manufacturing industries.

Texas ranches and farms produce beef cattle, poultry, rice, pecans, peanuts, sorghum, and an extensive variety of fruits and vegetables.

Millions of tourists spend well over $2 billion annually visiting more than 70 state parks, recreation areas, and points of interest such as the Gulf Coast resort area, the Lyndon B. Johnson Space Center in Houston, the Alamo in San Antonio, the state capital in Austin, and the Big Bend and Guadalupe Mountains National Parks.

UTAH

Capital: Salt Lake City
Governor: Norman H. Bangerter, R (to Jan. 1989)
Lieut. Governor: W. Val Oveson, R (to Jan. 1989)
Atty. General: David Wilkinson, R (to Jan. 1989)
Organized as territory: Sept. 9, 1850
Entered Union & (rank): Jan. 4, 1896 (45)
Present constitution adopted: 1896
Motto: Industry
State flower: Sego lily (1911)
State tree: Blue spruce (1933)
State bird: Seagull (1955)
State emblem: Beehive
State song: "Utah, We Love Thee"
Nickname: Beehive State
Origin of name: From the Ute tribe, meaning "people of the mountains"
1970 population & (rank): 1,059,273 (36)
1980 population (1980 census) & (rank): 1,461,037 (36)
1985 est. population (July 1) & (rank): 1,645,000 (36)
1984 land area & (rank): 82,073 sq mi. (212,569 sq km) (12)
Geographic center: In Sanpete Co., 3 mi. N. of Manti
Number of counties: 29
Largest cities (1980 census): Salt Lake City, 163,697; Provo, 52,210; Ogden, 64,407; Orem, 52,399; Sandy City, 52,210; Bountiful, 32,877; West Jordan, 27,192; Logan, 26,844; Murray, 25,750
State forests: None
State parks: 44 (64,097 ac.)
1985 percent pop. below age 15: 33
1985 percent pop. age 65 and over: 8
1985 serious crimes per 100,000 pop.: 5,317
1984 (fiscal year) immigrants: 2,746

The region was first explored for Spain by Franciscan friars, Escalante and Dominguez in 1776. In 1824 the famous American frontiersman Jim Bridger discovered the Great Salt Lake.

Fleeing the religious persecution encountered in eastern and middle-western states, the Mormons reached the Great Salt Lake in 1847 and began to build Salt Lake City. The U.S. acquired the Utah region in the treaty ending the Mexican War in 1848 and the first transcontinental railroad was completed with the driving of a golden spike at Promontory Point in 1869.

Mormon difficulties with the federal government about polygamy did not end until the Mormon Church renounced the practice in 1890, six years before Utah became a state.

In recent years, manufacturing has become Utah's most important industry, ahead of mining, agriculture, and tourism. The state's factories produce transportation equipment, food products, machinery, metal products, and electrical equipment. Utah has also become an important aerospace research and production center and is a leading warehousing and distribution point for much of the western U.S.

Rich in natural resources, Utah has long been a leading producer of copper, gold, silver, lead, zinc, and molybdenum. Oil has also become a major product; with Colorado and Wyoming, Utah shares what have been called the world's richest oil shale deposits.

Ranked eighth among the states in number of sheep in 1973, Utah also produces large crops of apricots and cherries as well as sugar beets, potatoes, onions, alfalfa, winter wheat, and beans. Utah's farmlands and crops require extensive irrigation.

Utah is a great vacationland with 11,000 miles of fishing streams and 147,000 acres of lakes and reservoirs. Among the many tourist attractions are Arches, Bryce Canyon, Canyonlands, Capitol Reef, and Zion National Parks; Dinosaur, Natural Bridges, and Rainbow Bridge National Monuments; the Mormon Tabernacle in Salt Lake City; and Monument Valley.

VERMONT

Capital: Montpelier
Governor: Madeleine M. Kunin, D (to Jan. 1989)
Lieut. Governor: Howard B. Dean, D (to Jan. 1989)
Secy. of State: James H. Douglas, R (to Jan. 1989)
Treasurer: Emory A. Hebard, R (to Jan. 1989)
Auditor of Accounts: Alexander V. Acebo, R (to Jan. 1989)
Atty. General: Jeffrey L. Amestoy, R (to Jan. 1989)
Entered Union & (rank): March 4, 1791 (14)
Present constitution adopted: 1793
Motto: Vermont, Freedom, and Unity
State flower: Red clover (1894)
State tree: Sugar maple (1949)
State bird: Hermit thrush (1941)
State animal: Morgan horse (1961)
State insect: Honeybee (1978)
State song: "Hail, Vermont!" (1938)
Nickname: Green Mountain State
Origin of name: From the French "vert mont," meaning "green mountain"
1980 population (1980 census) & (rank): 511,456 (48)
1985 est. population (July 1) & (rank): 535,000 (48)
1984 land area & (rank): 9,273 sq mi. (24,017 sq km) (43)
Geographic center: In Washington Co., 3 mi. E of Roxbury
Number of counties: 14
Largest cities (1980 census): Burlington, 37,712; Rutland, 18,436; South Burlington, 10,679; Barre, 9,824; Montpelier, 8,241; St. Albans, 7,308; Winooski, 6,318
State forests: 34 (113,953 ac.)
State parks: 45 (31,325 ac.)
1985 percent pop. below age 15: 21
1985 percent pop. age 65 and over: 12
1985 serious crimes per 100,000 pop.: 3,888
1984 (fiscal year) immigrants: 406

The Vermont region was explored and claimed for France by Samuel de Champlain in 1609 and the first French settlement was established at Fort Ste. Anne in 1666. The first English settlers moved into the area in 1724 and built Fort Drummer on the site of present-day Brattleboro. England gained control of the area in 1763 after the French and Indian War.

First organized to drive settlers from New York out of Vermont, the Green Mountain Boys, led by Ethan Allen, won fame by capturing Fort Ticonderoga from the British on May 10, 1775, in the early days of the Revolution.

In 1777 Vermont adopted its first constitution abolishing slavery and providing for universal male suffrage without property qualifications. In 1791 Vermont became the first state after the original 13 to join the Union.

Vermont leads the nation in the production of monument granite, marble, and maple syrup. It is also a leader in the production of asbestos and talc.

In ratio to population, Vermont keeps more dairy cows than any other state. Vermont's soil is devoted to dairying, truck farming, and fruit growing because the rugged, rocky terrain discourages extensive farming.

Principal manufactured goods are machine tools, computer components, stone and clay products, lumber, furniture, and paper.

Tourism is a major industry in Vermont. Vermont's many famous ski areas include Stowe, Killington, Mt. Snow, Bromley, Jay Peak, and Sugarbush. Hunting and fishing also attract many visitors to Vermont each year. Among the many points of interest are the Green Mountain National Forest, Bennington Battle Monument, the Calvin Coolidge Homestead at Plymouth, and the Marble Exhibit in Proctor.

VIRGINIA

Capital: Richmond
Governor: Gerald L. Baliles, D (to Jan. 1990)
Lieut. Governor: L. Douglas Wilder, D (to Jan. 1990)
Secy. of the Commonwealth: Sandra D. Bowen (apptd. by governor)
Comptroller: Edward J. Mazur (apptd. by governor)
Atty. General: Mary Sue Terry, D (to Jan. 1990)
Entered Union & (rank): June 25, 1788 (10)
Present constitution adopted: 1970
Motto: *Sic semper tyrannis* (Thus always to tyrants)
State flower: American dogwood (1918)
State bird: Cardinal (1950)
State dog: American foxhound (1966)
State shell: Oyster shell
State song: "Carry Me Back to Old Virginia" (1940)
Nicknames: The Old Dominion; Mother of Presidents
Origin of name: In honor of Elizabeth "Virgin Queen" of England
1980 population (1980 census) & (rank): 5,346,818 (14)
1985 est. population (July 1) & (rank): 5,706,000 (13)
1984 land area & (rank): 39,703 sq mi. (102,832 sq km) (36)
Geographic center: In Buckingham Co., 5 mi. SW of Buckingham
Number of counties: 95, plus 41 independent cities
Largest cities (1980 census): Norfolk, 266,979; Virginia Beach, 262,199; Richmond, 219,214; Newport News, 144,903; Hampton, 122,617; Chesapeake, 114,486
State forests: 8 (49,566 ac.)
State parks and recreational parks: 22, plus 3 in process of acquisition and/or development (42,722 ac.)[1]
1985 percent pop. below age 15: 21
1985 percent pop. age 65 and over: 10
1985 serious crimes per 100,000 pop.: 3,779
1984 (fiscal year) immigrants: 9,528

1. Does not include portion of Breaks Interstate Park (Va.-Ky., 1,200 ac.) which lies in Virginia.

The history of America is closely tied to that of Virginia, particularly in the Colonial period. Jamestown, founded in 1607, was the first permanent English settlement in North America and slavery was introduced there in 1619. The surrenders ending both the American Revolution (Yorktown) and the Civil War (Appomattox) occurred in Virginia. The state is called the "Mother of Presidents" because eight chief executives of the United States were born there.

Today, Virginia has a large number of diversified manufacturing industries including chemicals, textiles, food products, and clothing. Other important lines are lumber, paper, furniture, cigarettes, electrical machinery, transportation equipment, and stone-glass-clay products.

Agriculture remains an important sector in the Virginia economy and the state ranks among the leaders in the U.S. in tobacco, peanuts, apples, and sweet potatoes. Other crops include corn, vegetables, barley, and peaches. Famous for its turkeys and Smithfield hams, Virginia also has a large dairy industry.

Coal mining accounts for roughly 70% of Virginia's mineral output, and lime, zinc, and stone are also mined.

Points of interest include Mt. Vernon and other places associated with George Washington; Monticello, home of Thomas Jefferson; Stratford, home of the Lees; Richmond, capital of the Confederacy and of Virginia; and Williamsburg, the restored Colonial capital.

The Chesapeake Bay Bridge-Tunnel spans the mouth of Chesapeake Bay, connecting Cape Charles with Norfolk. Consisting of a series of low trestles, two bridges and two mile-long tunnels, the complex is 18 miles (29 km) long. It was opened in 1964.

Other attractions are the Shenandoah National Park, Fredericksburg and Spotsylvania National Military Park, the Booker T. Washington birthplace near Roanoke, Arlington House (the Robert E. Lee Memorial), the Skyline Drive, and the Blue Ridge National Parkway.

WASHINGTON

Capital: Olympia
Governor: Booth Gardner, D (to 1989)
Lieut. Governor: John A. Cherberg, D (to 1989)
Secy. of State: Ralph Munro (to 1989)
State Treasurer: Robert S. O'Brien (to 1989)
Atty. General: Kenneth O. Eikenberry (to 1989)
Organized as territory: March 2, 1853
Entered Union & (rank): Nov. 11, 1889 (42)
Present constitution adopted: 1889
Motto: *Al-Ki* (Indian word meaning "by and by")
State flower: Rhododendron (1949)
State tree: Western hemlock (1947)
State bird: Willow goldfinch (1951)
State fish: Steelhead trout (1969)
State gem: Petrified wood (1975)
State colors: Green and gold (1925)
State song: "Washington, My Home" (1959)
State dance: Square dance (1979)
Nicknames: Evergreen State; Chinook State
Origin of name: In honor of George Washington
1980 population (1980 census) & (rank): 4,132,180 (20)
1985 est. population (July 1) & (rank): 4,409,000 (19)
1984 land area & (rank): 66,511 sq mi (172,264 sq km) (20)
Geographic center: In Chelan Co., 10 mi. WSW of Wenatchee
Number of counties: 39
Largest cities (1980 census): Seattle, 493,846; Spokane, 171,300; Tacoma, 158,501; Bellevue, 73,903; Everett, 54,413; Yakima, 49,826; Bellingham, 45,794
State forest lands: 1,922,880 ac.
State parks: 202 (171,700 ac.)[1]
1985 percent pop. below age 15: 22
1985 percent pop. age 65 and over: 11

1985 serious crimes per 100,000 pop.: 6,529
1984 (fiscal year) immigrants: 9,234

1. Parks and undeveloped areas administered by Parks and Recreation Dept. Game Dept. administers wildlife and recreation areas totaling 762,895 acres.

As part of the vast Oregon Country, Washington territory was visited by Spanish, American, and British explorers—Bruno Heceta for Spain in 1775, the American Capt. Robert Gray in 1792, and Capt. George Vancouver for Britain in 1792–94. Lewis and Clark explored the Columbia River region and coastal areas for the U.S. in 1805–06.

Rival American and British settlers and conflicting territorial claims threatened war in the early 1840s. However, in 1846 the Oregon Treaty set the boundary at the 49th parallel and war was averted.

Washington is a leading lumber producer. Its rugged surface is rich in stands of Douglas fir, hemlock, ponderosa and white pine, spruce, larch, and cedar. The state holds first place in apples, blueberries, hops, and red raspberries and it ranks high in potatoes, winter wheat, pears, grapes, apricots, and strawberries. Livestock and livestock products make important contributions to total farm revenue and the commercial fishing catch of salmon, halibut, and bottomfish makes a significant contribution to the state's economy.

Manufacturing industries in Washington include aircraft and missiles, shipbuilding and other transportation equipment, lumber, food processing, metals and metal products, chemicals, and machinery.

The Columbia River contains one third of the potential water power in the U.S., harnessed by such dams as the Grand Coulee, one of the greatest power producers in the world. Washington has 90 dams throughout the state built for irrigation, power, flood control, and water storage. Its abundance of electrical power makes Washington the nation's largest producer of refined aluminum.

Among the major points of interest: Mt. Rainier, Olympic, and North Cascades. In 1980, Mount St. Helens, a peak in the Cascade Range in Southwestern Washington erupted on May 18th. Also of interest are National Parks; Whitman Mission and Fort Vancouver National Historic Sites; and the Pacific Science Center and Space Needle in Seattle.

WEST VIRGINIA

Capital: Charleston
Governor: Arch A. Moore, Jr., R (to Jan. 1989)
Secy. of State: Ken Heckler, D (to Jan. 1989)
State Auditor: Glen Gainer (to Jan. 1989)
Atty. General: Charlie Brown, D (to Jan. 1989)
Entered Union & (rank): June 20, 1863 (35)
Present constitution adopted: 1872
Motto: *Montani semper liberi* (Mountaineers are always free)
State flower: Rhododendron (1903)
State tree: Sugar maple (1949)
State bird: Cardinal (1949)
State animal: Black bear
State colors: Blue and gold (unofficial)
State songs: "West Virginia, My Home Sweet Home," "The West Virginia Hills," and "This Is My West Virginia" (adopted by Legislature in 1947, 1961 and 1963 as official state songs)
Nickname: Mountain State
Origin of name: Same as for Virginia
1980 population (1980 census) & (rank): 1,950,279 (34)
1985 est. population (July 1) & (rank): 1,936,000 (34)
1984 land area & (rank): 24,119 sq mi. (62,468 sq km) (41)
Geographic center: In Braxton Co., 4 mi. E of Sutton
Number of counties: 55
Largest cities (1980 census): Charleston, 63,968; Huntington, 63,684; Wheeling, 43,070; Parkersburg, 39,967; Morgantown, 27,605; Weirton, 25,371
State forests: 9 (77,000 ac.)
State parks: 34 (65,861 ac.)
1985 percent pop. below age 15: 22
1985 percent pop. age 65 and over: 13
1985 serious crimes per 100,000 pop.: 2,253
1984 (fiscal year) immigrants: 628

West Virginia's early history from 1609 until 1863 is largely shared with Virginia, of which it was a part until Virginia seceded from the Union in 1861. Then the delegates of 40 western counties formed their own government, which was granted statehood in 1863.

First permanent settlement dates from 1731 when Morgan Morgan founded Mill Creek. In 1742 coal was discovered on the Coal River, an event that would be of great significance in determining West Virginia's future.

The state usually ranks 3rd in bituminous coal production with about 15% of the U.S. total. It also is a leader in steel, glass, aluminum, and chemical manufactures; natural gas, oil, quarry products, and hardwood lumber.

Poultry, dairy products, cattle, and sheep account for the major portion of farm receipts. Apples, peaches, wheat, corn, and hay are profitable crops. More than 75% of West Virginia is covered with forests.

Tourism is increasingly popular in mountainous West Virginia and visitors spend over $1.4 billion annually. More than a million acres have been set aside in 34 state parks and recreation areas and in 9 state forests.

Major points of interest include Harpers Ferry and New River Gorge National River, The Greenbrier and Berkeley Springs resorts, the scenic railroad at Cass, and the historic homes at Charles Town.

WISCONSIN

Capital: Madison
Governor: Tommy G. Thompson, R (to Jan. 1991)
Lieut. Governor: Scott McCallum, R (to Jan. 1991)
Secy. of State: Douglas J. La Follette, D (to Jan. 1991)
State Treasurer: Charles P. Smith, D (to Jan. 1991)
Atty. General: Donald J. Hanaway, R (to Jan. 1991)
Superintendent of Public Instruction: Herbert J. Grover, Nonpartisan (to July 1989)
Organized as territory: July 4, 1836
Entered Union & (rank): May 29, 1848 (30)
Present constitution adopted: 1848
Motto: Forward
State flower: Wood violet
State tree: Sugar maple
State bird: Robin
State animal: Badger; "wild life" animal: white-tailed deer; "domestic" animal: dairy cow
State insect: Honeybee (1977)
State fish: Musky (Muskellunge)
State song: "On Wisconsin"
State mineral: Galena (1971)
State rock: Red Granite (1971)
Nickname: Badger State

Origin of name: French corruption of an Indian word whose meaning is disputed
1980 population (1980 census) & (rank): 4,705,521 (16)
1985 est. population (July 1) & (rank): 4,775,000 (16)
1984 land area & (rank): 54,426 sq mi. (140,964 sq km) (25)
Geographic center: In Wood Co., 9 mi. SE of Marshfield
Number of counties: 72
Largest cities (1980 census): Milwaukee, 636,236; Madison, 170,616; Green Bay, 87,899; Racine, 85,725; Kenosha, 77,685; West Allis, 63,982; Appleton, 58,913
State forests: 9 (476,004 ac.)
State parks & scenic trails: 48 parks, 9 trails (66,185 ac.)
1985 percent pop. below age 15: 22
1985 percent pop. age 65 and over: 13
1985 serious crimes per 100,000 pop.: 4,017
1984 (fiscal year) immigrants: 2,469

The Wisconsin region was first explored for France by Jean Nicolet, who landed at Green Bay in 1634. In 1660 a French trading post and Roman Catholic mission were established near present-day Ashland.

Great Britain obtained the region in settlement of the French and Indian War in 1763; the U.S. acquried it in 1783 after the Revolutionary War. However, Great Britain retained actual control until after the War of 1812. The region was successively governed as part of the territories of Indiana, Illinois, and Michigan between 1800 and 1836, when it became a separate territory.

Wisconsin leads the nation in milk and cheese production. In 1984 the state ranked first in the number of milk cows (1,828,000) and produced 17% of the nation's total output of milk. Other important farm products are peas, beets, corn, potatoes, cabbage, maple sugar, and cranberries.

The chief industrial products of the state are automobiles, machinery, furniture, paper, beer, and processed foods. Wisconsin ranks second among the 47 paper-producing states.

Wisconsin pioneered in social legislation, providing pensions for the blind (1907), aid to dependent children (1913), and old-age assistance (1925). In labor legislation, the state was the first to enact an unemployment compensation law (1932) and the first in which a workman's compensation law actually took effect. Wisconsin had the first state-wide primary-election law and the first successful income-tax law. In April 1984, Wisconsin became the first state to adopt the Uniform Marital Property Act. The act took effect on January 1, 1986.

The state has over 8,500 lakes, of which Winnebago is the largest. Water sports, ice-boating, and fishing are popular, as are skiing and hunting. Public parks and forests take up one seventh of the land, with 48 state parks, 9 state forests, 9 state trails, 3 recreational areas, and 2 national forests.

Among the many points of interest are the Apostle Islands National Lakeshore; Ice Age National Scientific Reserve; the Circus World Museum at Baraboo; the Wolf, St. Croix, and Lower St. Croix national scenic riverways; and the Wisconsin Dells.

WYOMING

Capital: Cheyenne
Governor: Michael J. Sullivan, D (to Jan. 1991)
Secy. of State: Kathy Karpan, D (to Jan. 1991)
Auditor: Jack Sidi, R (to Jan. 1991)
Treasurer: Stanford S. Smith, R (to Jan. 1991)
Atty. General: Joseph B. Meyer, D (apptd. by Governor)
Organized as territory: May 19, 1869
Entered Union & (rank): July 10, 1890 (44)
Present constitution adopted: 1890
Motto: Equal rights (1955)
State flower: Indian paintbrush (1917)
State tree: Cottonwood (1947)
State bird: Meadow lark (1927)
State gemstone: Jade (1967)
State insignia: Bucking horse (unofficial)
State song: "Wyoming" (1955)
Nickname: Equality State
Origin of name: From the Delaware Indian word, meaning "mountains and valleys alternating"; the same as the Wyoming Valley in Pennsylvania
1980 population (1980 census) & (rank): 469,557 (49)
1985 est. population (July 1) & (rank): 509,000 (50)
1984 land area & (rank): 96,989 sq mi. (251,201 sq km) (9)
Geographic center: In Fremont Co., 58 mi. ENE of Lander
Number of counties: 23, plus Yellowstone National Park
Largest cities (1980 census): Casper, 51,016; Cheyenne, 47,283; Laramie, 24,410; Rock Springs, 19,458; Sheridan, 15,146; Green River, 12,807; Gillette, 12,134
State forests: None
State parks: 9 (44,732 ac.)
1985 percent pop. below age 15: 27
1985 percent pop. age 65 and over: 8
1985 serious crimes per 100,000 pop. 4,015
1984 (fiscal year) immigrants: 271

The U.S. acquired the territory from France as part of the Louisiana Purchase in 1803. John Colter, a fur-trapper, is the first white man known to have entered present Wyoming. In 1807 he explored the Yellowstone area and brought back news of its geysers and hot springs.

Robert Stuart pioneered the Oregon Trail across Wyoming in 1812–13 and, in 1834, Fort Laramie, the first permanent trading post in Wyoming, was built. Western Wyoming was obtained by the U.S. in the 1846 Oregon Treaty with Great Britain and as a result of the treaty ending the Mexican War in 1848.

When the Wyoming Territory was organized in 1869 Wyoming women became the first in the nation to obtain the right to vote. In 1925 Mrs. Nellie Tayloe Ross was elected first woman governor in the United States.

Wyoming's towering mountains and vast plains provide spectacular scenery, grazing lands for sheep and cattle, and rich mineral deposits.

Mining, particularly oil and natural gas, is the most important industry. In January 1981, Wyoming led the nation in sodium carbonate (natrona) and bentonite production, and was second in uranium.

Wyoming ranks second among the states in wool production. In January 1981, its sheep numbered 1,110,000, exceeded only by Texas and California; it also had 1,350,000 cattle. Principal crops include wheat, oats, sugar beets, corn, potatoes, barley, and alfalfa.

Second in mean elevation to Colorado, Wyoming has many attractions for the tourist trade, notably Yellowstone National Park. Cheyenne is famous for its annual "Frontier Days" celebration. Flaming Gorge, the Fort Laramie National Historic Site, and Devils Tower and Fossil Butte National Monuments are other National points of interest.

Self-Governing Areas

PUERTO RICO

Capital: San Juan
Governor: Rafael Hernández-Colón, Popular Democratic Party
Song: "La Borinqueña"
1970 population: 2,712,033
1980 population: 3,196,520
Largest cities (1980 census): San Juan, 424,600; Bayamón, 185,087; Ponce, 161,739; Carolina, 147,835, Caguas, 87,214; Mayagüez, 82,968

Puerto Rico is an island about 100 miles long and 35 miles wide at the northeastern end of the Caribbean Sea. It is a self-governing Commonwealth freely and voluntarily associated with the U.S. Under its Constitution, a Governor and a Legislative Assembly are elected by direct vote for a four-year period. The judiciary is vested in a Supreme Court and lower courts established by law. The people elect a Resident Commissioner to the U.S. House of Representatives, where he has a voice but no vote. The island was formerly an unincorporated territory of the U.S. after being ceded by Spain as a result of the Spanish-American War.

The Commonwealth, established in 1952, has one of the highest standards of living in Latin America. Featuring Puerto Rican economic development is Operation Bootstrap. There are now over 1,600 manufacturing plants which have been created by this program. It has also greatly increased transportation and communications facilities, electric power, housing, and other industries.

The island's chief exports are chemicals, apparel, fish products and electronic products.

Columbus discovered the island on his second voyage to America in 1493.

GUAM

Capital: Agaña
Governor: Joseph F. Ada
1950 population: 59,498
1960 population: 67,044
1970 population: 84,996
1980 population: 105,979
1980 land area: 209 sq mi. (541 sq km)

Guam, the largest of the Mariana Islands, is independent of the trusteeship assigned to the U.S. in 1947. It was acquired by the U.S. from Spain in 1898 (occupied 1899) and was placed under the Navy Department.

In World War II, Guam was seized by the Japanese on Dec. 11, 1941; but on July 21, 1944, it was once more in U.S. hands.

On Aug. 1, 1950, President Truman signed a bill which granted U.S. citizenship to the people of Guam and established self-government. However, the people do not vote in national elections. In 1972 Guam elected its first delegate to the U.S. Congress. The Executive Branch of the Guam government is under the general supervision of the U.S. Secretary of the Interior. In November 1970, Guam elected its first Governor.

Military installations and tourism are important factors in Guam's economy.

Non-Self-Governing Territories

AMERICAN SAMOA

Capital: Pago Pago
Governor: A.P. Lutali
Lieut. Governor: Eni F. Hunkin
1960 population: 20,051
1970 population: 27,159
1986 population: 36,260
1980 land area: 77 sq mi (199 sq km)

American Samoa, a group of five volcanic islands and two coral atolls located some 2,600 miles south of Hawaii in the South Pacific Ocean, is an unincorporated, unorganized territory of the U.S., administered by the Department of the Interior.

By the Treaty of Berlin, signed Dec. 2, 1899, and ratified Feb. 16, 1900, the U.S. was internationally acknowledged to have rights extending over all the islands of the Samoa group east of longitude 171° west of Greenwich. On April 17, 1900, the chiefs of Tutuila and Aunu'u ceded those islands to the U.S. In 1904, the King and chiefs of Manu'a ceded the islands of Ofu, Olosega and Tau (composing the Manu'a group) to the U.S. Swains Island, some 214 miles north of Samoa, was included as part of the territory by Act of Congress March 4, 1925; and on Feb. 20, 1929, Congress formally accepted sovereignty over the entire group and placed the responsibility for administration in the hands of the President. From 1900 to 1951, by Presidential direction, the Department of the Navy governed the territory. On July 1, 1951, administration was transferred to the Department of the Interior. The first Constitution for the territory was signed on April 27, 1960, and became effective on Oct. 17, 1960. It was revised in 1967.

Congress has provided for a non-voting delegate to sit in the House of Representatives in 1981.

The principal products are canned tuna, pet food, fish meal, mats, and handicrafts.

BAKER, HOWLAND, AND JARVIS ISLANDS

These Pacific islands were not to play a role in the extraterritorial plans of the U.S. until May 13, 1936. President F. D. Roosevelt, at that time, placed them under the control and jurisdiction of the Secretary of the Interior for administration purposes.

Baker Island is a saucer-shaped atoll with an area of approximately one square mile. It is about 1,650 miles from Hawaii.

Howland Island, 36 miles to the northeast, is approximately one and a half miles long and half a mile wide.

Jarvis Island is several hundred miles to the east and is approximately two miles long by one and an eighth miles wide.

Baker, Howland, and Jarvis have been uninhabited since 1942. In 1974, these islands became part of the National Wildlife Refuge System, administered by the U.S. Fish & Wildlife Service, Department of the Interior.

CANTON AND ENDERBURY ISLANDS

Canton and Enderbury islands, the largest of the Phoenix group, are jointly administered by the U.S. and Great Britain after an agreement signed April 6, 1939. The status of Canton and Enderbury was the subject of negotiations between the U.S., U.K., and Gilbert Islands Governments in 1979. The negotiations resulted in the signing on September 20, 1979, of a Treaty of Friendship between the U.S. and the Republic of Kiribati. The Republic of Kiribati declared its independence on July 12, 1979.

Canton is triangular in shape and the largest of the eight islands of this group. It lies about 1,600 miles southwest of Hawaii and was discovered at the turn of the 18th century by U.S. whalers. After World War II it served as an aviation support facility, and later as a missile tracking station.

Enderbury is rectangular in shape and is 3.5 miles long by 1.5 miles wide. It is unpopulated and lies about 32 miles southeast of Canton.

JOHNSTON ATOLL

Johnston is a coral atoll about 700 miles southwest of Hawaii. It consists of four small islands—Johnston Island, Sand Island, Hikina Island, and Akau Island—which lie on a reef about 9 miles long in a northeast-southwest direction.

The atoll was discovered by Capt. Charles James Johnston of *H.M.S. Cornwallis* in 1807. In 1858 it was claimed by Hawaii, and later became a U.S. possession.

Johnston Atoll is a Naval Defense Sea Area and Airspace Reservation and is closed to the public. The administration of Johnston Atoll is under the jurisdiction of the Defense Nuclear Agency, Commander, Johnston Atoll (FCDNA), APO San Francisco, CA 96305.

KINGMAN REEF

Kingman Reef, located about 1,000 miles south of Hawaii, was discovered by Capt. E. Fanning in 1798, but named for Capt. W. E. Kingman, who rediscovered it in 1853. The reef, drying only on its northeast, east and southeast edges, is of atoll character. The reef is triangular in shape, with its apex northward; it is about 9.5 miles long, east and west, and 5 miles wide, north and south, within the 100-fathom curve.

A United States possession, Kingman Reef is a Naval Defense Sea Area and Airspace Reservation, and is closed to the public. The Airspace Entry Control has been suspended, but is subject to immediate reinstatement without notice. No vessel, except those authorized by the Secretary of the Navy, shall be navigated in the area within the 3-mile limit.

MIDWAY ISLANDS

Midway Islands, lying about 1,150 miles west-northwest of Hawaii, were discovered by Captain N. C. Brooks of the Hawaiian bark *Gambia* on July 5, 1859, in the name of the United States. The atoll was formally declared a U.S. possession in 1867, and in 1903 Theodore Roosevelt made it a naval reservation.

Midway Islands consist of a circular atoll, 6 miles in diameter, and enclosing two islands. Eastern Island, on its southeast side, is triangular in shape, and about 1.2 miles long. Sand Island on its south side, is about 2 miles long in a northeast-southwest direction.

The Midway Islands are within a Naval Defense Sea Area. The Navy Department maintains an installation and has jurisdiction over the atoll. Permission to enter the Naval Defense Sea Area must be obtained in advance from the Commander Third Fleet (N31), Pearl Harbor, HI 96860.

U.S. VIRGIN ISLANDS

Capital: Charlotte Amalie (on St. Thomas)
Governor: Alexander A. Farrelly
1970 population: 62,468
1985 population: 110,800 (St. Croix, 55,300; St. Thomas, 52,660; St. John, 2,840)
1980 land area: 132 sq mi (342 sq km): St. Croix, 84 sq. mi. (207 sq km), St. Thomas, 32 sq mi (83 sq km), St. John, 20 sq mi. (52 sq km)

The Virgin Islands, consisting of nine main islands and some 75 islets, were discovered by Columbus in 1493. Since 1666, England has held six of the main islands; the other three (St. Croix, St. Thomas, and St. John), as well as about 50 of the islets, were eventually acquired by Denmark, which named them the Danish West Indies. In 1917, these islands were purchased by the U.S. from Denmark for $25 million.

Congress granted U.S. citizenship to Virgin Islanders in 1927; and, in 1931, administration was transferred from the Navy to the Department of the Interior. Universal suffrage was given in 1936 to all persons who could read and write the English language. The Governor was elected by popular vote for the first time in 1970; previously he had been appointed by the President of the U.S. A unicameral 15-man legislature serves the Virgin Islands, and Congressional legislation gave the islands a non-voting Representative in Congress.

The "Constitution" of the Virgin Islands is the Revised Organic Act of 1954 in which the U.S. Congress defines the three branches of the territorial government, i.e., the Executive Branch, the Legislative Branch, and the Judicial Branch. Residents of the islands substantially enjoy the same rights as those enjoyed by mainlanders with one important exception: citizens of the U.S. who are residents may not vote in presidential elections.

About 80% of the population is black, and there is limited farming, fishing, and cattle raising. Industrial products include rum, watches, costume jewelry, alumina, pharmaceuticals, and petroleum products. Tourism is the principal industry.

WAKE ISLAND

Wake Island, about halfway between Midway and Guam, is an atoll comprising the three islets of Wilkes, Peale, and Wake. They were discovered by the British in 1796 and annexed by the U.S. in 1899. The entire area comprises 3 square miles and has no native population. In 1938, Pan American Airways established a seaplane base and Wake Island has been used as a commercial base since then. On Dec. 8, 1941, it was attacked by the Japanese, who finally took possession on Dec. 23. It was surrendered by the Japanese on Sept. 4, 1945.

The President, acting pursuant to the Hawaii Omnibus Act, assigned responsibility for Wake to the Secretary of the Interior in 1962. The Department of Transportation exercised civil administration of Wake through an agreement with the Department of the Interior until June 1972, at which time the Department of the Air Force assumed responsibility for the Territory.

Trust Territory of the Pacific Islands (Micronesia)

In 1885, Germany assumed a protectorate over the Marshall Islands; and, in 1899, she purchased the Northern Mariana and Caroline Islands from Spain. These islands were occupied by the Japanese in 1914 and were mandated to Japan by the League of Nations in 1919. On April 2, 1947, the U. N. Security Council approved a trusteeship agreement proposed by the U.S. under which the Northern Mariana, Caroline, and Marshall Islands became a Strategic Trust Territory under the administration of the U.S. The measure was approved by the President, with the agreement of Congress, on July 18, 1947. Administration was transferred from the Navy to the Department of the Interior on July 1, 1951. However, during 1953, administration of the islands of the Northern Marianas, except Rota, was transferred back to the Navy. The Department of the Interior again took over administration of these islands in July, 1962. The 1980 population of the Northern Marianas was 16,780.

In February 1975 a covenant was signed by the U.S. and the Marianas Political Status Commission that would make the 14 islands in the Northern Marianas a commonwealth under American sovereignty. The covenant was overwhelmingly ratified by the people of the islands and was approved by President Ford on March 24, 1976.

On April 9, 1978, in Hilo, Hawaii, the heads of the three Micronesian political status commissions and the U.S. negotiator signed a statement of agreed principles which is intended to form the basis of a free association relationship between the U.S. and Micronesia. Compact of Free Association was signed by the U.S. and the Micronesian commissions in 1982. The terms of the Compact of Free Association between the United States and the Federated States of Micronesia became effective as of November 3, 1986.

The entire group with a 1980 population of 116, 149 comprises more than 2,000 islands, but the total land area is only 533 sq mi. (1,381 sq km), many of the islands being only tiny coral reefs.

The Micronesians are the main ethnic group; however, the inhabitants of two outlying islands, Kapingamarangi and Nukuoro, are Polynesian. The population of the Trust Territory in 1980 was estimated to be 116,974.

CAROLINE ISLANDS

The Caroline Islands, east of the Philippines and south of the Marianas, include the Yap, Truk, and the Palau groups and the islands of Ponape and Kosrae, as well as many coral atolls.

The islands are composed chiefly of volcanic rock, and their peaks rise 2,000 to 3,000 feet above sea level. Chief exports of the islands are copra, fish products, and handicrafts.

MARIANA ISLANDS

The Mariana Islands, east of the Philippines and south of Japan, include the islands of Guam, Rota, Saipan, Tinian, Pagan, Guguan, Agrihan, and Aguijan. Guam, the largest, is independent of the trusteeship, having been acquired by the U.S. from Spain in 1898. (For more information, *see* the entry on Guam in this section.) The remaining islands, referred to as the Commonwealth of the Northern Mariana Islands became part of the Unites States pursuant to P.L. 94-241 as of November 3, 1986.

Chief crops are copra and fresh fruits and vegetables.

MARSHALL ISLANDS

The Government of the United States and the Republic of the Marshall Islands signed a Compact of Free Association on October 15, 1986, which became effective as of October 21, 1986. The termination of the Trusteeship Agreement became effective on November 3, 1986.

The Marshall Islands, east of the Carolines, are divided into two chains: the western or Ralik group, including the atolls Jaluit, Kwajalein, Wotho, Bikini, and Enewetak; and the eastern or Ratak group, including the atolls Mili, Majuro, Maloelap, Wotje, and Likiep.

The islands are of the coral-reef type and rise only a few feet above sea level. The chief crop is coconuts; exports include copra, tortoise shell, mother-of-pearl, etc.

Bikini and Enewetak were the scene of several atom-bomb tests after World War II. In April 1977, some 55 original inhabitants, the forerunner of 450 returnees, were resettled after an absence of 30 years.

Tabulated Data on State Governments

State	Governor		Legislature[1]					Highest Court[2]		
	Term, years	Annual salary	Membership U[3]	Membership L[4]	Term, yrs. U[3]	Term, yrs. L[4]	Salaries of members[5]	Members	Term, years	Annual salary[6]
Alabama	4[10]	70,223[16]	35	105	4	4	95 per diem[22]	9	6	$77,420[6]
Alaska	4	81,648	20	40	4	2	22,140 per annum	5	([8])	85,278
Arizona	4	62,500	30	60	2	2	15,000 per annum	5	6	67,500
Arkansas	2	35,000	35	100	4	2	7,500 per annum[25]	7	8	71,870
California[30]	4	85,000	40	80	4	2	37,105[30] per annum	7	12	99,489[25]

State	Governor: Term, years	Governor: Annual salary	Legislature[1]: Membership U[3]	Membership L[4]	Term, yrs. U[3]	Term, yrs. L[4]	Salaries of members[5]		Highest Court[2]: Members	Term, years	Annual salary[6]
Colorado	4	70,000	35	65	4	2	17,500	per annum[26]	7	10	63,000
Connecticut	4	78,000	36	151	2	2	30,400	per biennium	6	8	73,603
Delaware	4[9]	70,000	21	41	4	2	20,900	per annum	5	12	82,600
Florida	4[10]	90,570	40	120	4	2	18,900	per annum	7	6	81,967
Georgia	4[9]	69,356	56	180	2	2	10,000	per annum	7	6	73,762
Hawaii	4	80,000	25	51	4	2	15,600	per year	5	10	78,500
Idaho	4	55,000	42	84	2	2	8,000	per annum	5	6	59,750
Illinois	4	93,266	59	118	4-2	2	35,661	per annum	7	10	93,266
Indiana	4[10]	66,000	50	100	4	2	11,600	per annum	5	([24])	60,000
Iowa	4	64,000	50	100	4	2	14,600	per annum	9	8	60,900
Kansas	4	65,000	40	125	4	2	99	per diem[22]	7	6	59,143[31]
Kentucky	4[7]	65,483	38	100	4	2	100	per diem[22]	7	8	62,506
Louisiana	4	73,440	39	105	4	4	16,800	per annum	7	10	66,566
Maine	4	70,000[16]	33	151	2	2	11,500	per biennium[16]	7	7	61,698
Maryland	4[10]	85,000	47	141	4	4	22,000	per annum	7	10	78,500
Massachusetts	4	85,000	40	160	2	2	39,040	per annum	7	Life	65,000
Michigan	4	92,664[16]	38	110	4	2	38,163	per annum[16]	7	8	94,000
Minnesota	4	91,460	67	134	4	2	22,244	per annum[16]	9	6	73,981[6]
Mississippi	4	63,000	52	122	4	4	10,000	per session[5]	9	8	59,000
Missouri	4[10]	81,000	34	163	4	2	19,530	per annum[5]	7	12	78,300
Montana	4	50,452	50	100	4	2	59.12	per diem[16]	6	8	50,452[6]
Nebraska	4[10]	58,000	49[11]	—	4[11]	—	4,800	per annum	7	6	49,764
Nevada	4	77,500	21	42	4	2	7,800	per biennium	5	6	73,500
New Hampshire	2	66,024	24	([12])	2	2	200	per biennium	5	([13])	66,641
New Jersey	4[10]	85,000	40	80	4[14]	2	25,000	per annum	7	7[15]	93,000
New Mexico	4[7]	63,000	42	70	4	2	75	per diem	5	8	60,375
New York	4	130,000	61	150	2	2	43,000	per annum	7	14	95,500[6]
North Carolina	4[9]	100,000[16]	50	120	2	2	10,140	per annum[16]	7	8	72,600[6]
North Dakota	4	65,000[16]	53	106	4	2	90	per diem[16] [23]	5	10	59,140[6]
Ohio	4	65,000	33	99	4	2	31,659	per annum	7	6	73,000
Oklahoma	4	70,000	48	101	4	2	20,000[16]	per annum	([19])	6	68,006
Oregon	4[10]	72,000	30	60	4	2	901[32]	per annum	7	6	71,292[6]
Pennsylvania	4[10]	85,000	50	203	4	2	35,000	per annum	7	10	76,500
Rhode Island	2	49,500	50	100	2	2	5	per diem[17]	5	([18])	71,093
South Carolina	4[7]	67,500	46	124	4	2	10,000	per annum	5	10	47,000
South Dakota	4[10]	57,325	35	70	2	2	6,000	per biennium	5	3[28]	56,975
Tennessee	4	85,000[27]	33	99	4	2	12,500	per annum	5	8	30,000
Texas	4	91,600	31	150	4	2	7,220[5]	per annum	([20])	9	68,850
Utah	4	60,000	29	75	4	2	65	per diem[16]	5	10	58,000
Vermont	2	63,600	30	150	2	2	340	per week[21]	5	6	51,700[6]
Virginia	4[7]	85,000	40	100	4	2	11,000	per annum	7	12	78,463[6]
Washington	4	68,800	49	98	4	2	15,000	per annum	9	6	64,000
West Virginia	4[10]	72,000	34	100	4	2	7,200	per annum	5	12	55,000
Wisconsin	4	86,149	33	99	4	2	29,992	per annum	7	10	73,903
Wyoming	4	70,000	30	62	4	2	64	per diem[16]	5	8	63,500

1. General Assembly in Ark., Colo., Conn., Del., Ga., Ind., Ky., Md., Mo., N.C., Ohio, Pa., R.I., S.C., Tenn., Vt., Va., Legislative Assembly in N.D., Ore.; General Court in Mass., N.H.; Legislature in other states. Meets biennially in Calif., Ky., Me., Mont., Nev., N.H., N.J., N.C., N.D., Ore., Pa., Texas, Wash. and Wyo.; meets annually in other states. 2. Court of Appeals in Md., N.Y., Supreme Court of Virginia in Va., Supreme Judicial Court in Me., Mass.; Supreme Court in other states. 3. Upper house: Senate in all states. 4. Lower house: Assembly in Calif., Nev., N.Y., Wis.; House of Delegates in Md., Va., W.Va.; General Assembly in N.J.; House of Representatives in other states. 5. Does not include additional payments for expenses, mileage, special sessions, etc., or additional per diem payments beyond salary shown. 6. In some states, Chief Justice receives a higher salary. 7. Cannot succeed himself. 8. Appointed for 3 years; thereafter subject to approval or rejection on a nonpartisan ballot for 10-year term. 9. May serve only 2 terms, consecutive or otherwise. 10. May not serve 3rd consecutive term. 11. Unicameral legislature. 12. Constitutional number: 375–400. 13. Until 70 years old. 14. When term begins in Jan. of 2nd year following U.S. census, term shall be 2 years. 15. 2nd term receive tenure, mandatory retirement at 70. 16. Plus additional expenses. 17. For 60 days only. 18. Term of good behavior. 19. 9 members in Supreme Court, highest in civil cases; 3 in Court of Criminal Appeals. 20. 9 members in Supreme Court, highest in civil cases; 9 in Court of Criminal Appeals. 21. To limit of $11,000 per biennium; $2,000 for special session. 22. When in session. 23. Plus $180 per month when not in session. 24. Appointed for 2 years; thereafter elected popularly for 10-year term. 25. To receive cost of living increase not to exceed 10% in the two year period. 26. Plus $2,500 per month when performing official duties. 27. Adjusted annually according to increase in Consumer Price Index. 28. Subsequent terms, 8 years. 29. Plus $600 per month whether legislature is in session or not. 30. As of July 1, 1986. 31. Plus $600 per month when not in session. 32. Plus $400 monthly when not in session and per diem allowance when in session. NOTE: An asterisk (*) indicates that up-to-date information has not been provided. *Source: Information Please* questionnaires to the states.

50 Largest Cities of the United States

(According to population estimates, July 1984)

Data supplied by Bureau of the Census and by the cities in response to *Information Please* questionnaires.

ALBUQUERQUE, N.M.

Incorporated as city: 1891
Mayor: Ken Schultz (to Dec. 1989)
1980 population (1980 census) & (rank): 331,767 (44)
1985 est. population: 370,584
1984 est. population & rank: 350,575 (44)
1984 land area: 95.3 sq mi. (247 sq km)
Altitude: 4,958 ft.
Location: Central part of state on Rio Grande River
County: Bernalillo
Churches: 211
City-owned parks: 135
Radio stations: 30
Television stations: 7
Assessed valuation (1984): $1,553,000,000
City tax rate (1984): $21.223 per $1,000
Bonded debt (1984): $115,605,000
Revenue (Fiscal 1985): $278,839,594 (est.)
Expenditures (Fiscal 1985): $270,490,645 (est.)
Chamber of Commerce: Greater Albuquerque Chamber of Commerce, 401 2nd St., N.W., Albuquerque, N.M. 87102. Albuquerque Hispano Chamber of Commerce, 1520 Central Ave., S.E., Albuquerque, N.M. 87106

ATLANTA, GA.

Incorporated as city: 1847
Mayor: Andrew Young (to Jan. 1990)
1980 population (1980 census) & (rank): 425,022 (30)
1984 est. population & (rank): 426,090 (31)
1985 city land area: 136 sq mi. (352.2 sq km)
Altitude: Highest, 1,050 ft; lowest, 940
Location: In northwest central part of state, near Chattahoochee River
Counties: Fulton and De Kalb
Churches (18-county area): 1,500+
City-owned parks: 277 (3,178 ac.)
Radio stations (18-county area): AM, 24; FM, 17
Television stations (18-county area): 7 commercial; 2 PBS
Gross assessed valuation (1986): $6,143,253,464
City tax rate (1986): $37.09 per $1,000
Total bonded debt (1986): $149,585,000
Revenue (General Fund only) (1985): $246,243,531
Expenditures (1986): $250,765,631
Chamber of Commerce: Atlanta Chamber of Commerce, 235 International Blvd., Atlanta, Ga. 30301 Information is gathered on 2 geographic areas:
City of Atlanta, and 18 county MSA

AUSTIN, TEX.

Incorporated as city: 1839
Mayor: Frank Cooksey (to 1987)
1980 population (1980 census) & (rank): 345,496 (42)
1984 est. population & rank: 397,001 (34)
1987 est. population: 485,000
1984 land area: 116.0 sq mi. (300 sq km)
Altitude: From 425 ft. to over 1000 ft. elevation
Location: In south central part of state, on the Colorado River
County: Seat of Travis Co.
Churches: 353 churches, representing 45 denominations
City-owned parks and playgrounds: 160 (10,000 ac.)
Radio stations: AM, 6; FM, 12
Television stations: 3 commercial; 1 PBS; 1 independent
Assessed valuation (1985): $23,798,000,000
Tax rate (1985): $1.40 per $100
Bonded debt (1985): $308,268,020
Revenue (1986): $126,807,534
Expenditures (1986): $199,050,622
Chamber of Commerce: Austin Chamber of Commerce, P.O. Box 1967, Austin, Tex. 78764

BALTIMORE, MD.

Incorporated as city: 1797
Mayor: Clarence H. Burns (to Dec. 1987)
1980 population (1980 census) & (rank): 786,775 (10)
1984 est. population & (rank): 763,570 (12)
1984 land area: 80.3 sq mi. (208 sq km)
Altitude: Highest, 490 ft; lowest, sea level
Location: On Patapsco River, about 12 mi. from Chesapeake Bay
County: Independent city
Churches: Roman Catholic, 72; Jewish, 50; Protestant and others, 344
City-owned parks: 347 park areas and tracts (6,314 ac.)
Radio stations: AM, 11; FM, 9
Television stations: 5
Assessed valuation (est. 1986): $5,366,659,000
City tax rate (1985): $6.00 per $100.00
Net bonded debt (July 1985): $249,551,610
Revenue (est. 1986): $1,337,942,106
Expenditures (1986): $1,337,942,106
Chamber of Commerce: Greater Baltimore Committee, 2 Hopkins Plaza, Baltimore, Md. 21201

BATON ROUGE, LA.

Incorporated as a city: 1817
Mayor: Pat Screen (to Dec. 1988)
1980 population (1980 Census) & (rank:) 220,394, Rank (43)
1984 est. population & (rank): 368,571 (39)
1985 est. population: 244,352
1985 Land Area: 74.7 sq mi.
Altitude: Highest, 190 ft; lowest, 15 ft
Location: In southeastern part of state, on Mississippi River
County: Seat of East Baton Rouge Parish
Churches: 454
City Owned Parks: 127 parks, (3,381 ac.)
Radio Stations: AM 7; FM 6
Television Stations: 4
Assessed Valuation (1986): $855,067,680
City Tax Rate (1986): 8.46 ml per $1,000.
Bonded Debt (1986): $64,032,736.
Revenue (1986): $131,732,711.
Expenditures (1986): $131,077,366.
Chamber of Commerce: Greater Baton Rouge Chamber of Commerce, P.O. Box 3217, Baton Rouge, La. 70821

BOSTON, MASS.

Incorporated as city: 1822
Mayor: Raymond L. Flynn (to Jan. 1988)
1980 population (1980 census) & (rank): 562,994 (21)
1984 est. population & (rank): 570,719 (20)
1985 land area: 47.2 sq mi. (122 sq km)
Altitude: Highest, 330 ft; lowest, sea level
Location: On Massachusetts Bay, at mouths of Charles and Mystic Rivers
County: Seat of Suffolk Co.
Churches: Protestant, 187; Roman Catholic, 73; Jewish, 28; others, 100
City-owned parks, playgrounds, etc.: 2,276.36 ac.
Radio stations: AM, 9; FM, 8
Television stations: 7
Assessed valuation (est. Fiscal 1986): $19,000,000,000
City tax rate (1987): $12.02 residential, $23.55 commercial, per $1000
Gross direct bonded debt (July 1, 1986): $493,000,000
Revenue (est. 1988): $1,195,661,953
Expenditures (est. 1988): $1,195,834,000
Chamber of Commerce: Boston Chamber of Commerce, 125 High St., Boston, Mass. 02110

BUFFALO, N.Y.

Incorporated as city: 1832
Mayor: James Griffin (to Dec. 1989)
1980 population (1980 census) & (rank): 357,870 (39)
1984 est. population & (rank): 338,982 (46)
1984 land area: 42.67 sq mi. (109 sq km)
Altitude: Highest, 698 ft; lowest, 571
Location: At east end of Lake Erie, on Niagara River
County: Seat of Erie Co.
Churches: 60 denominations, with over 1,100 churches
County-owned parks: 9 public parks (3,000 ac.)
Radio stations: AM, 10; FM, 13
Television stations: 5 (plus reception from 4 Canadian stations)
Assessed valuation (1986–87): $1,020,563,187
City tax rate (1986–87): $89.89 per $1,000
Total funded debt (long-term, June 30, 1986): $112,650,000
Revenue (general fund, 1986): $394,839,000
Expenditures (Fiscal 1986): $375,530,000
Chamber of Commerce: Greater Buffalo Chamber of Commerce, 107 Delaware Ave., Buffalo, N.Y. 14202

CHARLOTTE, N.C.

Incorporated as city: 1768
Mayor: Harvey Gantt (to Nov. 1987)
1980 population (1980 census) & (rank): 314,447 (47)
1986 est. population: 353,448
1984 est. population & rank: 330,838 (48)
1986 land area: 149 sq mi. (372 sq km)
Altitude: 765 ft
Location: In the southern part of state near the border of South Carolina
County: Seat of Mecklenburg Co.
Churches: Protestant, over 400; Roman Catholic, 8; Jewish, 3; Greek Orthodox, 1
City-owned parks and parkways: 87
Radio stations: AM, 8; FM, 4
Television stations: 4 commercial; 2 PBS
Assessed valuation (1985): $13,491,002,719
City tax rate (includes county 1986): $1.3425 per $100
Bonded debt (April 30, 1986): $292,010,000
Revenue (Fiscal 1985): $235,620,224
Expenditures (Fiscal 1985): $210,456,631
Chamber of Commerce: Charlotte Chamber, P.O. Box 32785, Charlotte, N.C., 28232

CHICAGO, ILL.

Incorporated as city: 1837
Mayor: Harold Washington (to April 1991)
1980 population (1980 census) & (rank): 3,007,603 (3)
1984 est. population & (rank): 2,992,472 (3)
1986 land area: 228.1 sq mi. (591 sq km)
Altitude: Highest, 672 ft; lowest, 578.5
Location: On lower west shore of Lake Michigan
County: Seat of Cook Co.
Churches: Protestant, 850; Roman Catholic, 263; Jewish, 51
City-owned parks: 563
Radio stations: AM, 18, FM, 19
Television stations: 9
Assessed valuation (1985): $15,604,112,127
Total Chicago tax rate (1985): $9.719 per $100
Total gross bonded debt (5/87): $919,357,782
Revenue (est. 1986): $2,386,852,882
Expenditures (est. 1986): $2,384,497,711
Chamber of Commerce: Chicago Association of Commerce & Industry, 200 N. LaSalle, Chicago, Ill. 60602

CINCINNATI, OHIO

Incorporated as city: 1819
Mayor: Charles Luken (to Nov. 1987)
City Manager: Scott Johnson
1980 population (1980 census) & (rank): 385,457 (33)
1986 est. population: 370,000
1984 est. population & (rank): 370,481 (38)
1986 land area: 78.1 sq mi. (202 sq km)
Altitude: Highest, 960 ft; lowest, 441
Location: In southwestern corner of state on Ohio River
County: Seat of Hamilton Co.
Churches: 850
City-owned parks: 96 (4,345 ac.)
Radio stations: AM, 9; FM, 15 (Greater Cincinnati)
Television stations: 6
Assessed valuation (1987): $3,059,633,652
City tax rate (1987): $11.46 per $1,000
Bonded debt (1987): $162,793,000
Revenue (general fund, 1987): $157,660,000
Expenditures (general fund, 1987): $169,260,000
Chamber of Commerce: Cincinnati Chamber of Commerce, 120 W Fifth St., Cincinnati, Ohio 45202

CLEVELAND, OHIO

Incorporated as city: 1836
Mayor: George V. Voinovich (to Dec. 1989)
1980 population (1980 census) & (rank): 573,822 (18)
1984 est. population & (rank): 546,543 (23)
1984 land area: 79.0 sq mi. (205 sq km)
Altitude: Highest, 1048 ft.; lowest, 573
Location: On Lake Erie at mouth of Cuyahoga River
County: Seat of Cuyahoga Co.
Churches: [1] Protestant, 980; Roman Catholic, 187; Jewish, 31; Eastern Orthodox, 22
City-owned parks: 41 (1,930 ac.)
Radio stations: AM, 15; FM, 17
Television stations: 7
Assessed valuation (1987): $3,838,126,426

City tax rate (Dec. 31, 1986): $77.5 per $1,000
Bonded debt (Dec. 31, 1986): $506,675,000
Revenue (est. 1987): $261,961,000
Expenditures (est. 1987): $267,618,000
Chamber of Commerce: Greater Cleveland Growth Association, 690 Union Commerce Building, Cleveland, Ohio 44115

1. 100-mile area.

COLUMBUS, OHIO

Incorporated as city: 1834
Mayor: Dana G. Rinehart (to Jan. 1988)
1980 population (1980 census) & (rank): 565,032 (20)
1987 est. population: 591,262
1984 est. population & (rank): 566,114 (21)
1986 land area: 189.272 sq mi. (490 sq km)
Altitude: Highest, 902 ft; lowest, 702
Location: In central part of state, on Scioto River
County: Seat of Franklin Co.
Churches: Protestant, 436; Roman Catholic, 62; Jewish, 5; Other, 8
City-owned parks: 217 (11,719 ac.)
Radio stations: AM, 7; FM, 11
Television stations: 5 commercial, 1 PBS
Assessed valuation (1987): $5,578,745,214
City tax rate (1986): $57.00 per $1,000
Bonded debt (Dec. 31, 1986): $1,092,787,000
Revenue (1987 est.): $532,286,000
Expenditures (1987 est.): $478,899,000
Chamber of Commerce: Columbus Area Chamber of Commerce, P.O. Box 1527, Columbus, Ohio 43216

DALLAS, TEX.

Incorporated as city: 1856
Mayor: Annette Strauss (to April 1989)
City Manager: Richard Knight, Jr. (apptd. Oct. 1986)
1980 population (1980 census) & (rank): 904,078 (7)
1984 est. population & (rank): 974,234 (7)
1986 est. population: 941,700
1986 land area: 378 sq mi. (979 sq km)
Altitude: Highest, 750 ft; lowest, 375
Location: In northeastern part of state, on Trinity River
County: Seat of Dallas Co.
Churches: 1,974 (in Dallas Co.)
City-owned parks: 296 (47,025 ac.)
Radio stations: AM, 19; FM, 30
Television stations: 10 commercial, 1 PBS
Assessed valuation (1986–87): $51,162,924,000
City tax rate (1986–87): $.503 per $100
Bonded debt (Sept. 30, 1986): $1,391,185,594
Revenue (1986–87): $459,399,499
Expenditures (1986–87): $459,434,070
Chamber of Commerce: Dallas Chamber of Commerce. 1507 Pacific, Dallas, Tex. 75201

DENVER, COLO.

Incorporated as city: 1861
Mayor: Federico Pena (to July 1991)
1980 population (1980 census) & (rank): 492,365 (24)
1985 est. population: 505,100
1984 est. rank (24)
1984 land area: 110.6 sq mi. (287 sq km)
Altitude: Highest, 5,470 ft; lowest, 5,130
Location: In northeast central part of state, on South Platte River
County: Coextensive with Denver Co.
Churches:[1] Protestant, 815; Roman Catholic, 63; Jewish, 13
City-owned parks: 155 (3,600 ac.)
City-owned mountain parks: 40 (13,448 ac.)
Radio stations: AM, 18; FM, 13[1]
Television stations: 5
Assessed valuation (1985): $2,878,477,400
City tax rate (1984): $28.11 per $1,000[2]
Bonded debt (1984): $290,858,000[2]
Revenue (1984): $724,713,800[2]
Expenditures (1984): $671,650,800[2]
Chamber of Commerce: Denver Chamber of Commerce, 1301 Welton, Denver, Colo. 80204

1. Metropolitan area. 2. Excluding school district.

DETROIT, MICH.

Incorporated as city: 1815
Mayor: Coleman A. Young (to Jan. 1990)
1980 population (1980 census) & (rank): 1,203,339 (6)
1986 est. population: 1,089,000
1984 est. population & rank: 1,088,973 (6)
1984 land area: 143 sq mi. (370 sq km)
Altitude: Highest, 685 ft; lowest, 574
Location: In southeastern part of state, on Detroit River
County: Seat of Wayne Co.
Churches: [1]Protestant, 2,204; Roman Catholic, 333; Jewish, 40
City-owned parks: 52 parks (3,843 ac.); 350 sites (5,838 ac.)
Radio stations: AM, 26; FM, 30 (7-county area)
Television stations: 11 (incl. Windsor, Ontario, Canada)[1]
Assessed valuation (1986): $5,240,363,510
City tax rate (1986–87): $31.353 per $1,000
Net bonded debt (May 1987): General obligations, (net): $605,214,200
Revenue (1986–87): $1,693,647,992[2]
Expenditures (1985–86): $1,693,647,992[2]
Chamber of Commerce: Greater Detroit Chamber of Commerce, 622 W. Lafayette, Detroit, Mich. 48226

1. Six-county metropolitan area. 2. Excludes utilities.

EL PASO, TEX.

Incorporated as city: 1873
Mayor: Jonathan Rogers (to April 1989)
1980 population (1980 census) & (rank): 425,259 (29)
1986 est. population: 496,548
1984 est. population & rank: 463,809 (26)
1984 land area: 240.56 sq mi. (621 sq km)
Altitude: 4,000 ft
Location: In far western part of state, on Rio Grande
County: Seat of El Paso Co.
Churches: Protestant, 293; Roman Catholic, 39; Jewish, 3; others, 15
City-owned parks: 114[1] (1,650 ac.)
Radio Stations: AM, 17; FM, 17
Television stations: 6
Assessed valuation (1986): $9,717,001,175
City tax rate (1986): $4.59 per $1,000, city; $6.74, El Paso Independent School District; $7.69, Ysleta Independent School District
Bonded debt (1986): $45,215,000
Revenue (1986): $127,835,194
Expenditures (1986): $119,932,388
Chamber of Commerce: El Paso Chamber of Commerce, 10 Civic Center Plaza, El Paso, Tex. 79944

1. Includes 107 developed and 7 undeveloped parks.

FORT WORTH, TEX.

Incorporated as city: 1873
Mayor: Bob Bolen (to April 1989)
City Manager: Douglas Harman
1980 population (1980 census) & (rank): 385,164 (34)
1984 est. population & (rank): 414,562 (32)
1984 land area: 240.1 sq mi. (622 sq km)
Altitude: Highest, 780 ft; lowest, 520
Location: In north central part of state, on Trinity River
County: Seat of Tarrant Co.
Churches: Protestant, 392; Roman Catholic, 16; Jewish, 2
City-owned parks: 136 (8,189 ac.; 3,500 ac. in Nature Center)
Radio stations: AM, 6; FM, 8
Television stations: 6 (2 local)
Assessed valuation (1984–85): $12,355,737,899
City tax rate (1986–87): $.7390 per $100
Bonded debt (1986–87): $378,760,273
Revenue (1986–87): $322,862,770
Expenditures (1986–87): $322,862,770
Chamber of Commerce: Fort Worth Chamber of Commerce, 700 Throckmorton, Fort Worth, Tex. 76102

HONOLULU, HAWAII

Incorporated as city and county: 1907
Mayor: Frank F. Fasi (to Jan. 1989)
1980 population (1980 census) & (rank): 365,048 (36)
1984 est. population & (rank): 805,000[1] (11)
1984 land area: 617 sq. mi (1,600 sq km)[1]
Altitude: Highest, 4,025 ft; lowest, sea level
Location: The city and county government's jurisdiction includes the entire island of Oahu
Churches: Roman Catholic, 33; Buddhist, 32; Jewish, 2; Protestant and others, 328
City-owned parks: 5,279 ac.
Radio stations: AM, 19; FM, 10
Television stations: 8
Assessed valuation (1985): $31,600,000,000 (100% of market value.)
City and county tax rate (1985): $6.75 per $1,000 (residential); $9.00 per $1,000 (commercial); $10.00 per $1,000 (hotel/resort)
Bonded debt (June 1986): $408,281,000
Net revenue (1985–86): $492,401,700
Net expenditures (1985–86): $460,000,984
Chamber of Commerce: Chamber of Commerce of Hawaii, 735 Bishop St., Honolulu, Hawaii 96813

1. City and county area.

HOUSTON, TEX.

Incorporated as city: 1837
Mayor: Kathryn J. Whitmire (to Dec. 1987)
1980 population (1980 census) & (rank): 1,595,138 (5)
1984 est. population & (rank): 1,705,697 (4)
1984 land area: 579.58 sq mi. (1501.12 sq km)
Altitude: Highest, 120 ft; lowest, sea level
Location: In southeastern part of state, near Gulf of Mexico
County: Seat of Harris Co.
Churches: 1,750[2]
City-owned parks: 306 (32,500 ac.)
Radio stations: AM, 21; FM, 24[1]
Television stations: 8 commercial, 1 PBS
Assessed valuation (1985): $76,940,000,000
City tax rate (1985): $.495 per $100
Bonded debt (June 30, 1986): $2,115,499,000
Revenue (1985–86): $709,770,240
Expenditures (1985–86): $720,709,097
Chamber of Commerce: Houston Chamber of Commerce, 1100 Milam Building, Houston, Tex. 77002

1. Includes annexations since 1970. 2. Harris County.

INDIANAPOLIS, IND.

Incorporated as city: 1832 (reincorporated 1838)
Mayor: William H. Hudnut III (to Jan. 1988)
1980 population (1980 census) & (rank): 700,807 (12)
1984 est. population & (rank): 710,280 (14)
1984 land area: 352.0 sq mi. (912 sq km)
Altitude: Highest, 840 ft; lowest, 700
Location: In central part of the state, on West Fork of White River
County: Seat of Marion Co.
Churches: 1,200[1]
City-owned parks: 134 (10,753 ac.)
Radio stations: AM, 9; FM, 18
Television stations: 7[1]
Assessed valuation (1985): (consolidated city), $3,917, 669,600; (Marion County) $4,187,012,150
City tax rate (Center Township, 1986 payable 1987): $127.30 per $1,000
Gross debt (consolidated city, Dec. 31, 1986): $282,540, 000
Revenue (1986): $304,172,148
Expenditures (1986): $326,447,079
Chamber of Commerce: Indianapolis Chamber of Commerce, 320 N Meridian St., Indianapolis, Ind. 46202

1. Marion County.

JACKSONVILLE, FLA.

Incorporated as city: 1822
Mayor: Jake M. Godbold (to July 1, 1987)
1980 population (1980 census) & (rank): 540,920 (22)
1986 est. population: 651,884
1984 est. population & rank: 577,971 (19)
1987 land area: 759.6 sq mi. (1,967 sq km)
Altitude: Highest, 71 ft; lowest, sea level
Location: On St. Johns River, 20 miles from Atlantic Ocean
County: Duval
Churches: Protestant, 628; Roman Catholic, 19; Jewish, 4; others, 18
City-owned parks and playgrounds: 138 (1,522 ac.)
Radio stations: AM, 13; FM, 10
Television stations: 6 commercial, 1 PBS
Assessed valuation (1985): $11,260,000,000
City tax rate (1986–87): $11.53 per $1,000 (old county area); $11.86 per $1,000 (old city area)
Bonded debt (1986): $346,356,351
Revenue (1983–84): $524,555,492
Expenditures (1983–84): $524,555,492
Chamber of Commerce: Jacksonville Area Chamber of Commerce, Jacksonville, Fla. 32202

KANSAS CITY, MO.

Incorporated as city: 1850
Mayor: Richard L. Berkley (April 10, 1987)
City Manager: David H. Olson (apptd. Nov. 1984)
1980 population (1980 census) & (rank): 448,159 (28)
1984 est. population & (rank): 443,075 (29)
1987 land area: 316.3 sq mi. (819 sq km)
Altitude: Highest, 1,014 ft; lowest, 722
Location: In western part of state, at juncture of Missouri and Kansas Rivers

County: Located in Jackson, Clay, and Platte Co.
Churches: 1,100 churches of all denominations
City-owned parks and playgrounds: 174 (7,600 ac.)
Radio stations: AM, 14; FM, 13[1]
Television stations: 6[1]
Assessed valuation (Jan. 1, 1987): $2,116,572,850
City tax rate (1984–85): $9.86 per $1,000
Bonded debt (1985–86): $42,320,000
Revenue (1985–86): $458,572,801
Expenditures (1987–88): $462,175,855
Budget (gross total, 1987–88): $462,175,855
Chamber of Commerce: Chamber of Commerce of Greater Kansas City, 920 Main St., Kansas City, Mo. 64105

1. Metropolitan area.

LONG BEACH, CALIF.

Incorporated as city: 1892
Mayor: Ernie Kell (to July 1988)
City Manager: James C. Hankla (apptd. March 1, 1987)
1980 population (1980 census) & (rank): 361,334 (37)
1987 est. population: 406,000
1984 est. population & rank: 378,752 (35)
1985 land area: 49.8 sq mi. (129 sq km)
Altitude: Highest, 170 ft; lowest, sea level
Location: On San Pedro Bay, south of Los Angeles
County: In Los Angeles Co.
Churches: 236
City-owned parks: 42 (1,182 ac.)
Radio stations: AM, 2; FM, 2
Television stations: 1 (cable)
Assessed valuation (1987): $14,983,918,442
City tax rate (1986–87): $0.0027 per $1,000
Bonded debt (1985–86): $378,305,000
Revenue (1986–87): $984,010,484
Expenditures (1986–87): $972,229,578
Chamber of Commerce: Long Beach Area Chamber of Commerce, 50 Ocean Gate Plaza, Long Beach, Calif. 90802

LOS ANGELES, CALIF.

Incorporated as city: 1850
Mayor: Tom Bradley (to June 1989)
1980 population (1980 census) & (rank): 2,966,850 (3)
1987 est. population: 3,311,544
1984 est. population & rank: 3,096,721 (2)
1987 land area: 467.2 sq mi. (1,210 sq km)
Altitude: Highest, 5,081 ft; lowest, sea level
Location: In southwestern part of state, on Pacific Ocean
County: Seat of Los Angeles Co.
Churches: 1,963 of all denominations
City-owned parks: 354 (14,997 ac.)
Radio stations: AM, 32; FM, 40
Television stations: 18
Assessed valuation (1986–87): $113,841,822,000
City tax rate (1986–87): $0.0055 per $1,000
Gross debt (June 30, 1987): general obligation bonds, $25,502,000; revenue bonds, $2,900,657,000
Revenue (1985–86): $2,077,107,652
Expenditures (1985–86): $1,916,494,046
Chamber of Commerce: Los Angeles Chamber of Commerce, 404 S Bixel St., Los Angeles, Calif. 90017

MEMPHIS, TENN.

Incorporated as city: 1826
Mayor: Richard C. Hackett (to Dec. 1987)
1980 population (1980 census) & (rank): 646,356 (15)
1984 est. population & (rank): 648,399 (16)
1986 land area: 290 sq mi. (751.30 sq km)
Altitude: Highest, 331 ft
Location: In southwestern corner of state, on Mississippi River
County: Seat of Shelby Co.
Churches: 800
Parks and playgrounds: 214 (5,572 ac.)
Radio stations: AM, 12; FM, 8
Television stations: 6
Assessed valuation (1986): $3,258,912,195
City tax rate (1983): $31.30 per $1,000
Bonded debt (June 30, 1986): $467,390,000
Revenue (1986): $811,795,969
Expenditures (1986): $740,716,835[1]
Chamber of Commerce: Memphis Area Chamber of Commerce, P.O. Box 224, Memphis, Tenn. 38101

1. Includes all Governmental Fund types and Expendable Trust Funds.

MIAMI, FLA.

Incorporated as city: 1896
Mayor: Xavier L. Suarez (to Nov. 1987)
City manager: Cesar Odio (apptd. Dec. 1985)
1980 population (1980 census) & (rank): 371,975 (41)
1986 est. population: 380,446
1984 est. population & rank: 372,634 (37)
1986 land area: 34.3 sq mi. (89 sq km)
Altitude: Average, 12 ft
Location: In southeastern part of state, on Biscayne Bay
County: Seat of Dade Co.
Churches: Protestant, 592; Roman Catholic, 53; Jewish, 48
City-owned parks: 105
Radio stations: AM, 18; FM, 20
Television stations: 8 commercial, 2 PBS
Assessed valuation (1985–86): $10,184,933,000
City tax rate (1985–86): $9.8571 per $1,000
Bonded debt (1983–84): $190,697,000
Revenue (1985–86): $187,756,889
Expenditures (1985–86): $187,756,889
Chamber of Commerce: Greater Miami Chamber of Commerce, 1601 Biscayne Blvd., Miami, Fla. 33132

MILWAUKEE, WIS.

Incorporated as city: 1846
Mayor: Henry W. Maier (to April 1988)
1980 population (1980 census) & (rank): 636,236 (17)
1984 est. population & (rank): 620,811 (18)
1984 land area: 95.8 sq mi. (248 sq km)
Altitude: 580.60 ft
Location: In southeastern part of state, on Lake Michigan
County: Seat of Milwaukee Co.
Churches: 411
County-owned parks: 14,061 ac.
Radio stations: AM, 9; FM, 14
Television stations: 9
Assessed valuation (1986): $11,140,002,650
City tax rate (1986): $34.27 per $1,000
Gross debt (1986): $298,916,912
Revenue (1986): $605,198,929
Expenditures (1986): $617,908,146
Chamber of Commerce: Metropolitan Milwaukee Association of Commerce, 828 N. Broadway, Milwaukee, Wis. 53202

MINNEAPOLIS, MINN.

Incorporated as city: 1867
Mayor: Donald M. Fraser (to Jan. 1990)
1980 population (1980 census) & (rank): 370,951 (35)
1984 est. population & (rank): 358,335 (42)
1984 land area: 55.1 sq mi. (143 sq km)
Altitude: Highest, 945 ft; lowest, 695
Location: In southeast central part of state, on Mississippi River
County: Seat of Hennepin Co.
Churches: 419
City-owned parks: 153
Radio stations: AM, 17; FM, 15 (metro area)
Television stations: 6 (metro area)
Assessed valuation (1986): $2,888,632,388
City tax rate (1986): $35.066 per $1,000
Net debt (Dec. 31, 1986): $72,770,000
Revenue (1986): $364,213,583
Expenditures (1986): $359,807,316
Chamber of Commerce: Greater Minneapolis Chamber of Commerce, 15 S Fifth Street, Minneapolis, Minn. 55402

1. Assessed valuations on majority of properties now range from 18% (homesteads) to 43% (commercial, industrial) of actual market value.

NASHVILLE, TENN.

Incorporated as city: 1806
Mayor: Richard H. Fulton (to Sept. 1987)
1980 population (1980 census) & (rank): 455,651 (25)
1984 est. population & (rank): 462,450 (27)
1986 est. population: 504,900
1986 land area: 533 sq mi. (1,380 sq km)
Altitude: Highest, 1,100 ft; lowest, approx. 400 ft
Location: In north central part of state, on Cumberland River
County: Davidson
Churches: Protestant, 739; Roman Catholic, 15; Jewish, 3
City-owned parks: 72 (6,650 ac.)
Radio stations: AM, 11; FM, 8
Television stations: 7
Assessed valuation (1986): $4,943,979,000
City tax rate (1986): $39.20 per $1,000
Bonded debt (June 1986): $434,466,000
Revenue (1986): $473,645,000
Expenditures (1986): $445,886,000
Chamber of Commerce: Nashville Area Chamber of Commerce, 161 Fourth Ave. North, Nashville, Tenn. 37219

NEWARK, N.J.

Incorporated as city: 1836
Mayor: Sharpe James (to June 1990)
1980 population (1980 census) & (rank): 329,248 (47)
1984 est. population & (rank): 314,387 (49)
1984 land area: 24.1 sq mi. (62 sq km)
Altitude: Highest, 273.4 ft; lowest, sea level
Location: In northeastern part of state, on Passaic River and Newark Bay
County: Seat of Essex Co.
Churches: Roman Catholic, 32; Jewish, 4; Protestant and others, 250
City-owned parks: 40 (and 20 mini parks); (39.3 ac.)
County-governed parks in city: 7 (743.97 ac.)
Radio stations: AM, 2; FM, 4
Television stations: 2
Assessed valuation (1986): $1,004,730,400
City tax rate (1986): $12.83 per $100
Net bonded debt (1986): $55,255,980.19
Revenue (est. 1986): $297,032,530.70 (actual)
Expenditures (est. 1986): $287,058,441.03 (actual)
Chamber of Commerce: Greater Newark Chamber of Commerce, 40 Clinton St., Newark, N.J. 07102

NEW ORLEANS, LA.

Incorporated as city: 1805
Mayor: Sidney J. Barthelemy (to May 1990)
1980 population (1980 census) & (rank): 557,927 (22)
1986 est. population: 563,811
1984 est. population & rank: 559,101 (22)
1984 land area: 199.4 sq mi. (516 sq km)
Altitude: Highest, 15 ft; lowest, –4
Location: In southeastern part of state, between Mississippi River and Lake Ponchartrain
Parish: Seat of Orleans Parish
Churches: 644
City-owned parks: 250 (4,460 ac.)
Radio stations: AM, 12; FM, 10
Television stations: 7
Assessed valuation (1985): $1,615,447,954
City tax rate (1986): $114.07 per $1,000
Bonded debt (Dec. 31, 1986): $320,159,000
Revenue (est. 1986): $284,660,000
Expenditures (est. 1986): $284,660,000
Chamber of Commerce: New Orleans and the River Region Chamber of Commerce, 301 Camp Street, New Orleans, La. 70130

NEW YORK, N.Y.

Chartered as "Greater New York": 1898
Mayor: Edward Koch (to Dec. 31, 1989)
Borough Presidents: Bronx, Fernando Ferrer; Brooklyn, Howard Golden; Manhattan, Andrew Stein; Queens, Claire Shulman; Staten Island, Ralph J. Lamperti
1980 population (1980 census) & (rank): 7,071,639 (1)[1]
1984 est. population & (rank): 7,164,742 (1)[1]
1984 land area: 303.7 sq mi. (786 sq km) (Queens, 109; Brooklyn, 72; Staten Island, 55; Bronx, 42.5; Manhattan, 23.0)
Altitude: Highest, 410 ft; lowest, sea level
Location: In south of state, at mouth of Hudson River (also known as the North River as it passes Manhattan)
Counties: Consists of 5 counties: Bronx, Kings (Brooklyn), New York (Manhattan), Queens, Richmond (Staten Island)
Churches: Protestant, 1,766; Jewish, 1,256; Roman Catholic, 437; Orthodox, 66
City-owned parks: 1,588 (26,148 ac.)
Radio stations: AM and FM, 7; AM only, 10; FM only, 12
Television stations: 6 commercial, 1 PBS
Assessed valuation (1986–87): $55,089,444,700
City tax rate (1985–86): $9.323 commercial, $.0910 residential, per $100
Revenues (1985–86): $20,019,777
Expenditures (1985–86): $18,577,602
Chamber of Commerce: New York Chamber of Commerce and Industry, 65 Liberty St., New York, N.Y. 10005

1. For population of boroughs, *see* Index.

OAKLAND, CALIF.

Incorporated as city: 1854
Mayor: Lionel J. Wilson (to June 30, 1989)
City Manager: Henry L. Gardner (apptd. June 1981)
1980 population (1980 census) & (rank): 339,337 (44)
1985 est. population: 354,197
1984 est. population & rank: 351,898(43)

1984 land area: 53.9 sq mi.
Altitude: Highest, 1,700 ft; lowest, sea level
Location: In west central part of state, on east side of San Francisco Bay
County: Seat of Alameda Co.
Churches: 374, representing over 78 denominations in the City; over 500 churches in Alameda County
City-owned parks: 2,196 ac.
Radio stations: AM, 3; FM, 2
Television stations: 9 commercial; 3 PBS
Assessed valuation (1985–86): $10,395,146,864
City tax rate (1986–87): $.1575%[1]
Bonded debt (est. June 1985): $1,375,600
Revenue (1984–85 est.): $215,536,000
Expenditures (1984–85): $227,348,000
Chamber of Commerce: Oakland Chamber of Commerce, 1939 Harrison St., Suite 400, Oakland, Calif. 94612

1. Code area 17001.

OKLAHOMA CITY, OKLA.

Incorporated as city: 1890
Mayor: Ron Norick
City Manager: Terry Childers
1980 population (1980 census) & (rank): 403,213 (32)
1984 est. population & (rank): 443,172 (28)
1986 land area: 648.3 sq mi. (1,679.1 sq km)
Altitude: Highest, 1,320 ft; lowest, 1,140
Location: In central part of state, on North Canadian River
County: Seat of Oklahoma Co.
Churches: Roman Catholic, 15; Jewish, 2; Protestant and others, 741
City-owned parks: 138 (3,944 ac.)
Television stations: 8
Radio stations: AM, 10; FM, 14
Assessed valuation (1985–86): $1,788,077,649
City tax rate (1985–86): $13.56 per $1,000
Bonded debt (1986–87): $134,530,670
Revenue (general fund, 1985–86): $176,971,336
Expenditures (general fund, 1985–86): $169,688,238
Chamber of Commerce: Oklahoma City Chamber of Commerce, 1 Santa Fe Plaza, Oklahoma City, Okla. 73102

OMAHA, NEB.

Incorporated as city: 1857
Mayor: Bernie Simon (to June 1989)
1980 population (1980 census) & (rank): 313,911 (48)
1986 est. population: 345,786
1984 est. population & rank: 332,237 (47)
1984 land area: 90.9 sq mi. (235 sq km)
Altitude: Highest, 1,270 ft
Location: In eastern part of state, on Missouri River
County: Seat of Douglas Co.
Churches: Protestant, 246; Roman Catholic, 44; Jewish, 4
City-owned parks: 99 (3,671.6 ac.)
Radio stations: AM, 7; FM, 6
Television stations: 4
Assessed valuation (1987): $8,599,541,155
City tax rate (1987): $0.6192 per $100
Bonded debt (1986): $117,367,000
Revenue (1986): $228,165,982
Expenditures (1986): $225,588,604
Chamber of Commerce: Omaha Chamber of Commerce, 1301 Harway St., Omaha, Neb. 68102

PHILADELPHIA, PA.

First charter as city: 1701
Mayor: W. Wilson Goode (to Jan. 1988)
1980 population (1980 census) & (rank): 1,688,210 (4)
1984 est. population & (rank): 1,646,713 (5)
1984 land area: 136.0 sq mi. (352 sq km)
Altitude: Highest, 440 ft; lowest, sea level
Location: In southeastern part of state, at junction of Schuylkill and Delaware Rivers
County: Seat of Philadelphia Co. (coterminous)
Churches: Roman Catholic, 133; Jewish, 55; Protestant and others, 830
City-owned parks: 630 (10,252 ac.)
Radio stations: AM, 10; FM, 22
Television stations: 8
Assessed valuation (1987): $7,178,803,475
City and school district tax rate (1985): $74.75 per $1,000
Net bonded debt (June 30, 1986): $930,359,000 (incl. revenue bonds of $693,506,000 for water and sewer; $407,363,000 for gas works; $161,922,000 for aviation)
Revenue (1986): $1,651,657,000
Expenditures (1986): $1,661,299,000
Chamber of Commerce: Philadelphia Chamber of Commerce, 1346 Chestnut St., Suite 800, Philadelphia, Pa. 19107

PHOENIX, ARIZ.

Incorporated as city: 1881
Mayor: Terry Goddard (to Jan. 1988)
City Manager: Marvin A. Andrews (appt. Oct. 1976)
1980 population (1980 census) & (rank): 789,704 (9)
1984 est. population & (rank): 853,266 (9)
1986 land area: 375.3 sq mi. (971 sq km)
Altitude: Highest, 2,740 ft.; lowest, 1,017
Location: In center of state, on Salt River
County: Seat of Maricopa Co.
City-owned parks: 132 (29,128 ac.)
Radio stations: AM, 20; FM, 19
Television stations: 9 commercial; 1 PBS
Assessed valuation (1986–87): $4,568,111,003
City tax rate (1986–87): $16.30 per $1,000 A.V.
Bonded debt (April 1987): $1,183,494,000
Revenues (est. 1986–87): $852,425,000
Expenditures (est. 1986–87): $779,604,000
Chamber of Commerce: Phoenix Chamber of Commerce, 805 N Second St., Phoenix, Ariz. 85004

PITTSBURGH, PA.

Incorporated as city: 1816
Mayor: Richard S. Caliguiri (to Jan. 1990)
1980 population (1980 census) & (rank): 423,959 (31)
1984 est. population & (rank): 402,583 (33)
1987 land area: 55.5 sq mi. (144 sq km)
Altitude: Highest, 1,240 ft; lowest, 715
Location: In southwestern part of state, at beginning of Ohio River
County: Seat of Allegheny Co.
Churches: Protestant, 348; Roman Catholic, 86; Jewish, 28; Orthodox, 26
City-owned parks and playgrounds: 295 (2,572 ac.)
Radio stations: AM, 18; FM, 9
Television stations: 8
Assessed valuation (1987): land, $576,153,260; buildings, $2,194,431,656
City tax rate (1985): $27 per $1,000 buildings; $151.50 per $1,000 land

Net direct debt (July 1986): $354,818,398
Revenue (1987 est.): $278,911,053
Expenditures (1987 est.): $278,911,053
Chamber of Commerce: The Chamber of Commerce of Greater Pittsburgh, 3 Gateway Center, Pittsburgh, Pa. 15222

PORTLAND, ORE.

Incorporated as city: 1851
Mayor: John (Bud) Clark (to Dec. 1988)
1980 population (1980 census) & (rank): 366,383 (35)
1986 est. population: 341,415
1984 est. population & rank: 365,861 (40)
1986 land area: 125 sq mi. (524 sq km)
Altitude: Highest, 1,073 ft; lowest, sea level
Location: In northwestern part of state, on Willamette River
County: Seat of Multnomah Co.
Churches: Protestant, 332; Roman Catholic, 39; Jewish, 4; Buddhist, 4; Vedanta Society, 1
City-owned parks: 175 (8,000 ac.)
Radio stations: AM, 14; FM, 12
Television stations: 5 commercial, 1 PBS
Assessed valuation (1985–86): $13,494,651,000 (at 100% of cash value)
City tax rate (1985–86): $13.30 per $1,000
Bonded debt (July 1, 1986): $114,000,000
Revenue (est. 1986–87): $736,200,000
Expenditures (est. 1986–87): $736,200,000
Chamber of Commerce: Portland Chamber of Commerce, 221 NW 2nd Ave., Portland, Ore. 97209

ST. LOUIS, MO.

Incorporated as city: 1822
Mayor: Vincent Schoemehl, Jr. (to April 1989)
1980 population (1980 census) & (rank): 453,085 (27)
1987 est. population: 435,900
1984 est. population & rank: 429,296 (30)
1987 land area: 61.4 sq mi. (159 sq km)
Altitude: Highest, 616 ft; lowest, 413
Location: In east central part of state, on Mississippi River
County: Independent city
Churches: 900[1]
City-owned parks: 89 (2,639 ac.)
Radio stations: AM, 18; FM, 20[1]
Television stations: 6 commercial; 1 PBS
Assessed valuation (1985): $1,852,378,900
City tax rate (1985): $6.112 per $100
Bonded debt (1986): $47,475,000
Revenue (1986): $269,599,232
Expenditures (1986): $264,964,113
Chamber of Commerce: St. Louis Regional Commerce and Growth Association, 10 Broadway, St. Louis, Mo. 63102

1. Metropolitan area.

SAN ANTONIO, TEX.

Incorporated as city: 1837
Mayor: Henry Cisneros (to May 1989)
City Manager: Louis J. Fox (apptd. Jan. 1982)
1980 population (1980 census) & (rank): 786,023 (11)
1984 est. population & (rank): 842,779 (10)
1984 land area: 269.10 sq mi. (697 sq km)
Altitude: 700 ft
Location: In south central part of state, on San Antonio River
County: Seat of Bexar Co.
City-owned parks: Approximately 5,881 ac.
Radio stations: AM, 13; FM, 12
Television stations: 5
Assessed valuation (1985): $17,057,304,959
City tax rate (1985): $.4141 per $100
Net funded debt (Sept. 1985): $263,063,203
Revenue (Fiscal 1984–85): $256,183,614
Expenditures (Fiscal 1984–85): $242,724,031
Chamber of Commerce: Greater San Antonio Chamber of Commerce, P.O. Box 1628, 602 E Commerce, San Antonio, Tex. 78296

SAN DIEGO, CALIF.

Incorporated as city: 1850
Mayor: Maureen O'Connor (to Dec. 1988)
City Manager: John Lockwood (apptd. Sept. 1986)
1980 population (1980 census) & (rank): 875,538 (8)
1986 est. population: 1,013,400
1984 est. population & rank: 960,452 (8)
1986 land area: 403.4 sq mi. (1,045 sq km)
Altitude: Highest, 1,591 ft; lowest, sea level
Location: In southwesternmost part of state, on San Diego Bay
County: Seat of San Diego Co.
Churches: Roman Catholic, 80; Jewish, 8; Protestant 334; Eastern Orthodox, 7; other, 6
City park and recreation facilities: 328 (29,393 ac.)
Radio stations: AM, 13; FM, 20
Television stations: 7
Assessed valuation (1987): $38,313,937,198
City tax rate (1987): $2.19 per $1,000
Bonded debt (1987): $14,790,000
Revenue (est. 1988): $704,590,715
Expenditures (est. 1988): $704,590,715
Chamber of Commerce: San Diego Chamber of Commerce, 110 W. C St., Suite 1600, San Diego, Calif. 92101

SAN FRANCISCO, CALIF.

Incorporated as city: 1850
Mayor: Dianne Feinstein (to Jan. 1988)
1980 population (1980 census) & (rank): 678,974 (13)
1984 est. population & (rank): 712,753 (13)
1986 est. popoulation: 741,568
1986 land area: 46.1 sq mi. (120 sq km)
Altitude: Highest, 925 ft; lowest, sea level
Location: In northern part of state between Pacific Ocean and San Francisco Bay
County: Coextensive with San Francisco Co.
Churches: 540 of all denominations
City-owned parks and squares: 217
Radio stations: 22
Television stations: 7
Assessed valuation (1986–87): $33,631,432,000 (100% of valuation)
City and county tax rate (1986–87): $1.14 per $100
Bonded debt (1986–87): $1,000,545,000
Revenue (1986–87): $1,096,636,000
Expenditures (1986–87): $961,448,000
Chamber of Commerce: Greater San Francisco Chamber of Commerce, 465 California St., San Francisco, Calif. 94104

SAN JOSE, CALIF.

Incorporated as city: 1850
Mayor: Thomas McEnery (to Dec. 31, 1990)
City Manager: Gerald E. Newfarmer (apptd. July 1983)
1980 population (1980 census) & (rank): 629,546 (17)

1987 est. population: 719,466
1984 est. population & rank: 686,178 (15)
1987 land area: 171.2 sq. mi (443 sq km)
Altitude: Highest, 4,372 ft.; lowest, sea level
Location: In northern part of state, on south San Francisco Bay, 50 miles from San Francisco
County: Seat of Santa Clara County
Churches: 403
City-owned parks and playgrounds: 151 (3,136 ac.)
Radio stations: 14
Television stations: 4
Assessed valuation (1986–87): $28,857,932,819 (100% of valuation)
City tax rate (1986–87): $1.55 per $1,000
Bonded debt (June 1986): $12,968,000
Revenue (1986–87): $1,025,695,000
Expenditures (1986–87): $1,025,695,000
Chamber of Commerce: San Jose Chamber of Commerce, One Paseo de San Antonio, San Jose, Calif. 95113

SEATTLE, WASH.

Incorporated as city: 1869
Mayor: Charles Royer (to Jan. 1989)
1980 population (1980 census) & (rank): 493,846 (23)
1984 est. population & (rank): 488,474 (25)
1984 land area: 144.6 sq mi. (375 sq km)
Altitude: Highest, 540 ft; lowest, sea level
Location: In west central part of state, on Puget Sound
County: Seat of King Co.
Churches: Roman Catholic, 36; Jewish, 13; Protestant and others, 535
City-owned parks, playgrounds, etc.: 278 (4,773.4 ac.)
Radio stations: AM, 22; FM, 26
Television stations: 3 commercial; 1 educational
Assessed valuation (1985): $22,344,255,000
City B & O tax rate (1985): $3.60 per $1,000
Bonded debt (1985): $210,505,000
Revenue (1985): $882,014,041
Expenditures (1985): $853,559,659
Chamber of Commerce: Seattle Chamber of Commerce, 1200 One Union Square, Seattle, Wash. 98101

TOLEDO, OHIO

Incorporated as city: 1837
Mayor: Donna Owens (to Dec. 1987)
City Manager: Phillip Hawkey
1980 population (1980 census) & (rank): 354,635 (40)
1984 est. population & (rank): 343,939 (45)
1984 land area: 84.2 sq mi. (218 sq km)
Altitude: 630 ft
Location: In northwestern part of state, on Maumee River at Lake Erie
County: Seat of Lucas Co.
Churches: Protestant, 301; Roman Catholic, 55; Jewish, 4; others, 98
City-owned parks and playgrounds: 134 (2,650.90 ac.)
Radio stations: AM, 8; FM, 8
Television stations: 5
Assessed valuation (Jan. 1, 1987): $2,773,893,086
City tax rate (Jan. 1, 1987): $66.45 per $1,000
Bonded debt (Jan. 1, 1987): $172,962,613
Revenue (est. 1987): $291,308,363
Expenditures (est. 1987): $262,852,343
Chamber of Commerce: Toledo Area Chamber of Commerce, 218 Huron St., Toledo, Ohio 43604

TUCSON, ARIZ.

Incorporated as city: 1877
Mayor: Lewis C. Murphy (to Dec. 1987)
1980 population (1980 census) & (rank): 330,537 (45)
1987 est. population: 391,120
1984 est. rank (41)
1986 land area: 130 sq mi. (336.7 sq km)
Altitude: 2,500 ft
Location: In southeastern part of state, on the Santa Cruz River
County: Seat of Pima Co.
Churches: Protestant, 325; Roman Catholic, 40; other, 74
City-owned parks and parkways: (24,182 ac.)
Radio stations: AM, 14; FM, 7
Television stations: 3 commercial; 1 educational; 3 other
Assessed valuation (1986): $1,489,174,604 secondary, $1,343,109,299 primary
City tax rate (1986): $.6874 per $100 secondary, $.2698 per $100 primary
Net bonded debt (1985–86): $112,587,609
Revenue (1985–86): $249,285,298
Expenditures (1985–86): $283,490,154
Chamber of Commerce: Tucson Metropolitan Chamber of Commerce, P.O. Box 991, Tucson, Ariz. 85702

TULSA, OKLA.

Incorporated as city: 1898
Mayor: Dick Crawford (to May 1988)
1980 population (1980 census) & (rank): 360,919 (38)
1986 est. population: 377,900
1984 est. population & rank: 374,535 (36)
1985 land area: 187.5 sq mi. (486 sq km)
Altitude: 674 ft
Location: In northeastern part of state, on Arkansas River
County: Seat of Tulsa Co.
Churches: Protestant, 593; Roman Catholic, 32; Jewish, 2; others, 4
City parks and playgrounds: 113 (5,050 ac.)
Radio stations: AM, 7; FM, 10
Television stations: 5 commercial; 1 PBS; 1 cable
Assessed valuation (1986–87): $1,615,599,122
City tax rate (1986–87): $82.73 per $1,000
Bonded debt (July 1986): $133,899,852
Revenue (1985–86): $295,022,000
Expenditures (1985–86): $299,861,000
Chamber of Commerce: Metropolitan Tulsa Chamber of Commerce, 616 S Boston, Tulsa, Okla. 74119

VIRGINIA BEACH, VA.

Incorporated as city: 1963
Mayor: Robert Jones (to June 30, 1988)
1980 population (1980 census) & (rank): 262,199 (57)
1987 est. population: 362,000
1984 est. population & rank: 308,664 (50)
1986 land area: 258.7 sq mi. (670 sq km)
Altitude: 12 ft
Location: Southeastern most portion of state, on Atlantic coastline
County: None
Churches: Protestant, 159; Catholic, 8; Jewish, 4
City-owned parks: 108 (1,406 ac.)
Radio stations: AM 18, FM 22
Television stations: 4 commercial, 1 PBS, 1 cable
City tax rate (1985–1986): $.8 per $100
Bonded debt (1985–1986): $321,410,000
Revenue (1985–86): $368,642,012
Expenditures (1985–86): $375,447,761
Chamber of Commerce: Hampton Roads Chamber of Commerce, 4512 Virginia Beach Blvd., Virginia Beach, Va., 23456

WASHINGTON, D.C.

Land ceded to Congress: 1788 by Maryland; 1789 by Virginia (retroceded to Virginia Sept. 7, 1846)
Seat of government transferred to D. C.: Dec. 1, 1800
Created municipal corporation: Feb. 21, 1871
Mayor: Marion Barry, Jr. (to Jan. 1990)
Motto: *Justitia omnibus* (Justice to all)
Flower: American beauty rose
Tree: Scarlet oak
Origin of name: In honor of Columbus
1980 population (1980 census) & (rank): 638,432 (15)
1984 est. population & (rank): 622,823 (17)
1984 land area: 68.25 sq mi. (176.12 sq km)
Geographic center: Near corner of Fourth and L Sts., NW
Altitude: Highest, 420 ft; lowest, sea level
Location: Between Virginia and Maryland, on Potomac River
Churches: Protestant, 446; Roman Catholic, 23; Jewish, 10; others, 23
City parks: 753 (7,725 ac.)
Radio stations: AM, 15; FM, 16
Television stations: 6 (including 2 UHF stations)
Assessed valuation (1986): $24,887,897,678[1]
City tax rate (1984–85): $20.30 per $1,000 (hotels); $18.20 per $1,000 (commercial)
Bonded debt: (Fiscal 1986): $2,059,489,000
Revenue (Fiscal 1987, est.): $2,931,793,000
Expenditures (Fiscal 1987, est.): $2,931,793,000
Chamber of Commerce: D.C. Chamber of Commerce, 1319 F St., NW, Washington, D.C. 20004

1. On taxable property only. More than 50% of all land in District of Columbia is owned by the Federal government and tax-exempt organizations, and therefore is nontaxable.

The District of Columbia—identical with the City of Washington—is the capital of the United States and the first carefully planned capital in the world.

D.C. history began in 1790 when Congress directed selection of a new capital site, 10 miles square, along the Potomac. When the site was determined, it included 30.75 square miles on the Virginia side of the river. In 1846, however, Congress returned that area to Virginia.

The city was planned and partly laid out by Major Pierre Charles L. 'Enfant, a French engineer. This work was perfected and completed by Major Andrew Ellicott. In 1814, during the War of 1812, a British force fired the capital, and it was from the white paint applied to cover fire damage that the President's home was called the White House.

Until Nov. 3, 1967, the District of Columbia was administered by three commissioners appointed by the President. On that day, a government consisting of a mayor-commissioner and a 9-member Council, all appointed by the President with the approval of the Senate, took office. On May 7, 1974, the citizens of the District of Columbia approved the Home Rule Charter, giving them their first form of elected government in over 100 years. The District also has one non-voting member in the House of Representatives.

On Aug. 22, 1978, the Senate passed a proposed constitutional amendment to give Washington, D.C., voting representation in the Congress. The House had approved the legislation in the spring. The amendment had to be ratified by at least 28 state legislatures within seven years to become effective. As of 1985 it died.

Population of 50 Largest U.S. Cities by Rank

(Population estimates for July 1, 1984)

City	Population	1984 Rank	1980 Rank
New York, NY	7,164,742	1	1
Los Angeles, CA	3,096,721	2	3
Chicago, IL	2,992,472	3	2
Houston, TX	1,705,697	4	5
Philadelphia, PA	1,646,713	5	4
Detroit, MI	1,088,973	6	6
Dallas, TX	974,234	7	7
San Diego, CA	960,452	8	8
Phoenix, AZ[1]	853,266	9	9
San Antonio, TX	842,779	10	11
Honolulu, HI[2]	805,266	11	12
Baltimore, MD	763,570	12	10
San Francisco, CA	712,753	13	14
Indianapolis, IN	710,280	14	13
San Jose, CA	686,178	15	18
Memphis, TN	648,399	16	15
Washington, DC	622,823	17	16
Milwaukee, WI	620,811	18	17
Jacksonville, FL	577,971	19	23
Boston, MA	570,719	20	21
Columbus, OH	566,114	21	20
New Orleans, LA	559,101	22	22
Cleveland, OH	546,543	23	19
Denver, CO	504,588	24	25
Seattle, WA	488,474	25	24
El Paso, TX	463,809	26	29
Nashville–Davidson, TN	462,450	27	26
Oklahoma City, OK	443,172	28	32
Kansas City, MO	443,075	29	28
St. Louis, MO	429,296	30	27
Atlanta, GA	426,090	31	30
Fort Worth, TX	414,562	32	34
Pittsburgh, PA	402,583	33	31
Austin, TX	397,001	34	42
Long Beach, CA	378,752	35	37
Tulsa, OK	374,535	36	38
Miami, FL	372,634	37	41
Cincinnati, OH	370,481	38	33
Baton Rouge, LA[3]	368,571	39	43
Portland, OR	365,861	40	36
Tucson, AZ[1]	365,422	41	45
Minneapolis, MN	358,335	42	35
Oakland, CA	351,898	43	44
Albuquerque, NM	350,575	44	46
Toledo, OH	343,939	45	40
Buffalo, NY	338,982	46	39
Omaha, NE[1]	332,237	47	48
Charlotte, NC	330,838	48	49
Newark, NJ	314,387	49	47
Virginia Beach, VA	308,664	50	57

1. The 1980 count includes population annexed since January 1, 1980. 2. The city of Honolulu, coextensive with Honolulu County, is a Federal funding area not recognized as a city for census purposes. Honolulu census-designated place in 1980 had a population of 365,048. 3. The figure refers to the area as defined for Federal funding purposes rather within corporate limits. *Source:* U.S. Department of Commerce, Bureau of the Census.

Tabulated Data on City Governments

City	Mayor: Term, years	Mayor: Salary[1]	City manager's salary[2]	Council or Commission: Name	Members	Term, years	Salary[3]
Albuquerque, N.M.	4	$52,600	52,500[4]	Council	9	4	$5,260
Atlanta	4	50,000	—	Council	19	4	12,500
Austin, Tex.	3	26,000	100,000	Council	6	3	30,000
Baltimore*	4	53,000	—	Council	19	4	23,000
Baton Rouge, La.	4	67,000	—	Council	12	4	3,600
Boston	4	100,000	—	Council	13	2	45,000
Buffalo, N.Y.	4	59,000	—	Council	13	2[5]	29,000
Charlotte, N.C.*	2	12,000	75,000	Council	11	2	6,000
Chicago	4	80,000	—	Council	50	4	40,000
Cincinnati	2	35,667	86,625	Council	9	2	32,167
Cleveland	4	62,956	—	Council	21	4	26,664
Columbus, Ohio	4	75,000	—	Council	7	4	15,000
Dallas*	2	50[6]	—	Council	11	2	50[6]
Denver*	4	59,879	—	Council	13	4	21,890[22]
Detroit	4	115,000	—	Council	9	4	53,000
El Paso	2	25,000	—	Council	7[7]	2	15,000
Fort Worth	2	10[8]	100,000	Council	9	2	10[8]
Honolulu	4	75,000	70,305[9]	Council	9	4	26,400[3]
Houston*	2	115,192	—	Council	14	2	30,718
Indianapolis	4	73,650	—	Council	29	4	7,938[10]
Jacksonville, Fla.	4	40,000	—	Council	19	4	18,666
Kansas City, Mo.	4	45,000	94,500	Council	13[7]	4	18,480
Long Beach, Calif.*	2	1,000[12]	—	Council	9[13]	4	1,000[12]
Los Angeles	4	88,778	—	Council	15	4	53,266
Memphis, Tenn.	4	60,000	59,500[5]	Council	13	4	6,000
Miami, Fla.	2	5,000[14]	92,000	Commission	5[7]	4	5,000
Milwaukee	4	74,393	—	Council	16	4	31,391
Minneapolis	4	59,000	71,161	Council	13	4	43,500
Nashville, Tenn.*	4	50,000	—	Council	41	4	5,400
Newark, N.J.	4	63,814	70,000[16]	Council	9	4	29,780[24]
New Orleans	4	75,905	76,404	Council	7	4	42,500
New York	4	110,000	97,500[15]	Council	35	4	47,500
Oakland, Calif.	4	15,000	90,000	Council	9[7]	4	([17])
Oklahoma City	4	2,000	75,000	Council	8	4	20[18]
Omaha, Neb.	4	55,000	—	Council	7	4	14,700[3]
Philadelphia	4	70,000	62,500[19]	Council	17	4	40,000
Phoenix, Ariz.	2	37,500	115,000	Council	9[7]	2	18,000
Pittsburgh	4	59,280	—	Council	9	4	33,800
Portland, Ore.*	4	60,656	—	Commission	4	4	48,630
St. Louis	4	71,266	—	Board of Aldermen	29	4	18,500
San Antonio*	2	3,000[20]	100,000	Council	11[7]	2	20[21]
San Diego, Calif.	4	50,000	105,000	Council	8	4	45,000
San Francisco*	4	107,348	106,146	Board of Supervisors	11	4	23,928
San Jose, Calif.	4	40,400	107,700	Council	10	4	31,100
Seattle*	4	80,762	—	Council	9	4	54,005
Toledo, Ohio	2	36,900	80,000	Council	9[13]	2	7,800
Tucson, Ariz.	4	24,000	72,000	Council	7	4	12,000
Tulsa, Okla.	2	50,000	—	Commission	4	2	38,500
Virginia Beach, Va.	2	17,000	90,000[25]	Council	11	4	15,000
Washington, D.C.	4	81,830	72,300	Council	13	4	47,475[23]

1. Annual salary unless otherwise indicated. 2. Annual salary. City Manager's term is indefinite and at will of Council (or Mayor). 3. Annual salary unless otherwise indicated. In some cities, President of Council receives a higher salary. 4. City Administrative Officer appointed by Mayor, approved by Council. 5. For 9 District Councilmen; 4 years for 3 Councilmen-at-Large. 6. Per Council meeting; not over $2,600 per year. 7. Including Mayor. 8. Per week and per Council meeting. 9. Managing Director appointed by Mayor; no Council approval required. 10. Plus $40 per meeting for three meetings a month. 11. Chief Administrative Officer appointed by Mayor; not subject to Council confirmation. 12. Per month. 13. Including Mayor and Vice-Mayor. 14. Plus $2,500 expense account. 15. No City Manager; salary is for Deputy Mayor. 16. Business Administrator, appointed by Mayor and confirmed by Council. 17. Flat $500 per month, or $6,000 annually. 18. Per Council meeting; not to exceed 5 meetings a month. 19. Appointed by Mayor, with title of Managing Director. 20. Plus Council pay. 21. Per Council meeting; not over $1,040 per year. 22. Council President receives $28,992. 23. Council Chairman receives $57,475. 24. Annual allowance in lieu of expenses: Council members $13,000; Council President $15,000. 25. Plus $4,000 in travel expenses. NOTE: An asterisk (*) indicates up-to-date information not provided. *Source: Information Please* questionnaires to the cities.

Where Have All Our Records Gone?

By Emma Cobb

The disappearing record: A few years after the last American troops left Vietnam in 1973, the Pentagon turned over a big batch of microfilm, more than one hundred rolls, to the National Archives. The film carried every enemy document captured by U.S. forces during the war—a spectacular trove of information for some future historian, and most of it not existing in any other form. But no historian now would dare approach that file, because the automated, coded index to the three million random images cannot be read by any instrument known to still exist today.

Strangely, the machine that could have done the job was widely available a mere twenty years ago. But following a classic pattern, it enjoyed a brief popularity and then was suddenly obsolete. The Army's equipment was apparently left in Saigon and probably destroyed. So government archivists are now trying to coax another machine (related to the original) into translating the index code.

Franklin D. Roosevelt once praised the keeping of records by "modern processes like the microfilm," which he called the "only form of insurance that will stand the test of time." It wasn't until after Vietnam, the first war to be fought in the age of both the copying machine and the computer, that a difficult truth began to emerge: The technologies that generate the rich record of the past can also obscure it.

A two-hundred-page report issued last year by the Committee on the Records of Government makes this point resoundingly clear; the committee found that "the United States is in danger of losing its memory." Technological obsolescence is largely to blame, along with the sheer uncontrolled volume of paper records, which has made some of them impossible to catalog and ever retrieve.

After the typewriter became truly practical in the 1870s, the annual accumulation of paper records grew each year, and when photocopying and xerography took hold, the stash swelled to huge proportions. In 1968 alone, U.S. government records increased by 4,500,000 cubic feet. Then computer tapes began to hold a fair portion of the total government record. By 1983 the combined agencies had about twelve million tapes, and three-quarters of all federal information was being electronically stored.

Some of these records—if they haven't simply deteriorated beyond repair—may require equipment long gone. The dangers inherent in electronic record-keeping are superbly illustrated by the saga of the U.S. Census Bureau, a pioneer in the use of electronic tabulating devices. The bureau used the very first one for the 1890 census, a year after the invention was patented by an American, Herman Hollerith. Census information was recorded on cards as a punched code, which was then "read" by Hollerith's machine as it kept a tally of individual responses.

The success of the method carried the punch-card system, with improvements, well into this century. The cards themselves, though, tended to pile up. So in 1936 the National Archives dumped its collection of eight million punch cards from the 1930 census. And after the next two censuses, cards were again routinely destroyed.

It was simply that no one had thought of a coded card as an actual record. It meant little to the naked eye, and the most important statistical information was securely down on paper. But the only way to make new tabulations is to run the punch cards through again—and now that's no longer possible.

In a poignant reversal the Census Bureau eventually found itself with plenty of compact records but no way of getting at them. For the 1960 census, punch cards were abandoned in favor of magnetic tape—five thousand reels of it were processed on the agency's nine-year-old UNIVAC 1 computer. But by 1975 not one bit of information could be retrieved from any of the tapes.

Of two UNIVACs left in the world that could read the data, one was in Japan, and the other—the one used for the census—had already been dismantled at the Smithsonian Institution. The tape had been wound on metal reels that no later UNIVAC computers would accept. And even if you could get the reels into a more current machine, it wouldn't be able to read the antiquated code that the census data had been entered in.

Though the original schedules were on microfilm, the idea of recoding some 180 million individual responses was unthinkable. Instead the National Archives took a device that was part of the original coding process and, around 1970, whacked it into shape as a reading instrument. From 642 tapes that were deemed to be of permanent value, 99 percent of the data was recovered and transferred to standard magnetic tape in an updated code.

But it was a Herculean task; the jury-rigged mechanism couldn't get through a single reel without breaking down. And the cost was tremendous, but funds were provided because the census was so important.

In the meantime, more chaos is generated every day by the U.S. government, whose agencies have at least nineteen thousand large computers and more than two hundred thousand personal computers all over the world. It's anybody's guess as to how many of these use incompatible or outdated equipment and codes, but there are sure to be problems when people start trying to look back at the record.

Emma Cobb is Senior Editor of *American Heritage of Invention and Technology* in which this article first appeared.

The picture isn't entirely grim though. Charles Dollar, the former head of the machine-readable records division at the Library of Congress, says that a standardized coding system is just around the corner, and once it takes effect in federal offices, it will spread elsewhere. Meanwhile all we can do is keep transferring the records to newer media when possible.

At this point the problems start to come less from technology and more from its users. David Allison, a historian for the Department of Energy who used to work at the Navy Research Lab in Bethesda, remembers that the crucial index to a decade of electronically recorded Navy correspondence was lost when the file was moved from a personal computer to a database system—no one bothered to make a hard copy and code it into the new system.

That sort of thing happens all the time, says Allison, because "technical people who work with automated equipment have zero interest in the past. None of them say: Where are the records going to be five years from now? The tough issues are not technical. In fact, if the technical problems were harder, there would probably be more interest in them."

As standards for electronic records take effect, something resembling serenity may return. True, there will be some gaps in the historical record, but Thomas Brown, an archivist at the National Archives, remains sanguine. "The United States isn't really losing its memory," he says. "It's only suffering from temporary amnesia." □

Social Security Is the Major Source of Retirement Income

In 1935, the Social Security Act established a national system that would collect a share of workers' earnings and pay them benefits in old age. The social insurance features of the program, later expanded to provide other benefits, including disability income and health insurance, have transformed the economic status of older Americans. The number of Social Security beneficiaries has grown from less than 1 percent of the aged population in 1940 to over 90 percent today, and Social Security payments are now the largest single component of the income of the aged.

Social Security accounted for 38 percent of aggregate income of the aged in 1984, compared with 31 percent in 1962. Because much of the aggregate income of the elderly is received by a relatively small minority, Social Security payments play an even more important part for many beneficiaries. In 1984, it provided the majority of the income received by 62 percent of them. Social Security is the only source of income for 1 beneficiary in 7, and accounts for almost all the income (90 percent or more) for about 1 in 4.

Nearly half (46 percent) of all aged persons and couples receive only Social Security, and their median annual incomes of $6,270 are comparatively low. Only the very small group (4 percent) with neither work, pensions, nor Social Security have an even smaller median income. About one-third of the aged (couples and single persons) also have no earnings but receive a higher cash income from an employer pension instead of Social Security ($11,430) or in addition to Social Security ($14,400).

Very few aged couples and single persons (about 2 percent overall) have only earnings and no retirement benefits. However, this small group, which despite its age has not yet retired, reports a relatively high median income of $25,560. Work is sometime referred to as "the poor man's pension" and this is borne out by the relatively low cash incomes of persons with only Social Security benefits who are still working. Their median income of $14,850 is almost exactly the same as the $14,400 median income of the elderly who have employer pensions to supplement Social Security and who do not work.

The proportion of married couples and single beneficiaries relying on Social Security for the majority of their income has decreased only slightly over the years (from 47 percent and 59 percent in 1941-42 to 42 percent and 57 percent in 1982), but a much smaller proportion now relies entirely on the program. The completely dependent group has fallen from 13 percent to 3 percent among the married couples and from 23 percent to 11 percent of single retirees over this period.

Household Size Declining in U.S.

The average number of people per household in the United States plunged to 2.67 in 1986, the least ever recorded, according to the Census Bureau.

The aging of the population and the fact that there were fewer children per family, more one-parent families, and more people living alone accounted for the decline. The new figure was down from 2.69 in 1985, 2.76 in 1980, and 3.14 in 1970.

Although the total population and the adult population continue to grow, the number of people under 18 years old has declined slightly since 1980. While the total population grew by 6.4%, from 226.5 million to 241.1 million, the population 18 and over grew 9.2%, from 162.8 million to 177.8 million, but the population under 18 declined from 63.8 million to 63.3 million.

Reflecting the new demographics, the lower household size was accompanied by a 10.5% increase in the number of households. There were 88.8 million households on July 1, 1986, up from 80.4 million in the 1980 census. The number of households grew faster than the population in every state except California, where they grew by the same 14% proportion.

From 1980 to 1986, the number of households grew most rapidly in Alaska, up 36%; Arizona, 26%; Nevada, 25%; Florida, 24%; and Texas, 20%.

Iowa, West Virginia, Michigan, and Ohio lost population since 1980 but showed small increases in the number of households.

Generally, the number of households grew fastest where the population was growing most rapidly. The South and the West showed the largest concentrations in growth. These regions accounted for 91% of the nation's population increase and 74% of the increase in the number of households. In the South, the number of households grew by 14.8%, while the population rose 10.1%. In the West, the number of households increased 14.6%, and the population grew 12.9%.

The Census Bureau projects that the average number of people per household will continue to go down, to 2.48 in the year 2000, from the current 2.67.

Population

Colonial Population Estimates (in round numbers)

Year	Population	Year	Population	Year	Population	Year	Population
1610	350	1660	75,100	1710	331,700	1760	1,593,600
1620	2,300	1670	111,900	1720	466,200	1770	2,148,100
1630	4,600	1680	151,500	1730	629,400	1780	2,780,400
1640	26,600	1690	210,400	1740	905,600		
1650	50,400	1700	250,900	1750	1,170,800		

National Censuses[1]

Year	Resident population[2]	Land area, sq mi.	Pop. per sq mi.	Year	Resident population[2]	Land area, sq mi.	Pop. per sq mi.
1790	3,929,214	864,746	4.5	1890	62,947,714	2,969,640	21.2
1800	5,308,483	864,746	6.1	1900	75,994,575	2,969,834	25.6
1810	7,239,881	1,681,828	4.3	1910	91,972,266	2,969,565	31.0
1820	9,638,453	1,749,462	5.5	1920	105,710,620	2,969,451	35.6
1830	12,866,020	1,749,462	7.4	1930	122,775,046	2,977,128	41.2
1840	17,069,453	1,749,462	9.8	1940	131,669,275	2,977,128	44.2
1850	23,191,876	2,940,042	7.9	1950	150,697,361	2,974,726	50.7
1860	31,443,321	2,969,640	10.6	1960	179,323,175	3,540,911	50.6
1870	39,818,449	2,969,640	13.4	1970	203,302,031	3,540,023	57.4
1880	50,155,783	2,969,640	16.9	1980	226,545,805	3,618,770	62.6

1. Beginning with 1960, figures include Alaska and Hawaii. 2. Excludes armed forces overseas. NOTE: n.a. = not available. *Source:* Department of Commerce, Bureau of the Census.

Population Distribution by Age, Race, Nativity, and Sex

							Race and nativity				
	Age						White[1]				
Year	Total	Under 5	5–19	20–44	45–62	65 and over	Total	Native born	Foreign born	Black	Other races[1]
PERCENT DISTRIBUTION											
1860[2]	100.0	15.4	35.8	35.7	10.4	2.7	85.6	72.6	13.0	14.1	0.3
1870[2]	100.0	14.3	35.4	35.4	11.9	3.0	87.1	72.9	14.2	12.7	0.2
1880[2]	100.0	13.8	34.3	35.9	12.6	3.4	86.5	73.4	13.1	13.1	0.3
1890[3]	100.0	12.2	33.9	36.9	13.1	3.9	87.5	73.0	14.5	11.9	0.3
1900	100.0	12.1	32.3	37.7	13.7	4.1	87.9	74.5	13.4	11.6	0.5
1910	100.0	11.6	30.4	39.0	14.6	4.3	88.9	74.4	14.5	10.7	0.4
1920	100.0	10.9	29.8	38.4	16.1	4.7	89.7	76.7	13.0	9.9	0.4
1930	100.0	9.3	29.5	38.3	17.4	5.4	89.8	78.4	11.4	9.7	0.5
1940	100.0	8.0	26.4	38.9	19.8	6.8	89.8	81.1	8.7	9.8	0.4
1950	100.0	10.7	23.2	37.6	20.3	8.1	89.5	82.8	6.7	10.0	0.5
1960	100.0	11.3	27.1	32.2	20.1	9.2	88.6	83.4	5.2	10.5	0.9
1970[2]	100.0	8.4	29.5	31.7	20.6	9.8	87.6	83.4	4.3	11.1	1.4
1980	100.0	7.2	24.8	37.1	19.6	11.3	83.1	n.a.	n.a.	11.7	5.2
MALES PER 100 FEMALES											
1860[2]	104.7	102.4	101.2	107.9	111.5	98.3	105.3	103.7	115.1	99.6	260.8
1870[2]	102.2	102.9	101.2	99.2	114.5	100.5	102.8	100.6	115.3	96.2	400.7
1880[2]	103.6	103.0	101.3	104.0	110.2	101.4	104.0	102.1	115.9	97.8	362.2
1890[3]	105.0	103.6	101.4	107.3	108.3	104.2	105.4	102.9	118.7	99.5	165.2
1900	104.4	102.1	100.9	105.8	110.7	102.0	104.9	102.8	117.4	98.6	185.2
1910	106.0	102.5	101.3	108.1	114.4	101.1	106.6	102.7	129.2	98.9	185.6
1920	104.0	102.5	100.8	102.8	115.2	101.3	104.4	101.7	121.7	99.2	156.6
1930	102.5	103.0	101.4	100.5	109.1	100.5	102.9	101.1	115.8	97.0	150.6
1940	100.7	103.2	102.0	98.1	105.2	95.5	101.2	100.1	111.1	95.0	140.5

Year	Age						Race and nativity				
							White[1]				
	Total	Under 5	5–19	20–44	45–62	65 and over	Total	Native born	Foreign born	Black	Other races[1]
1950	98.6	103.9	102.5	96.2	100.1	89.6	99.0	98.8	102.0	93.7	129.7
1960	97.1	103.4	102.7	95.6	95.7	82.8	97.4	97.6	94.2	93.3	109.7
1970[2]	94.8	104.0	103.3	95.1	91.6	72.1	95.3	95.9	83.8	90.8	100.2
1980	94.5	104.7	104.0	98.1	90.7	67.6	94.8	n.a.	n.a.	89.6	100.3

1. The 1980 census data for white and other races categories are not directly comparable to those shown for the preceding years because of the changes in the way some persons reported their race, as well as changes in 1980 procedures relating to racial classification. 2. Excludes persons for whom age is not available. 3. Excludes persons enumerated in the Indian Territory and on Indian reservations. NOTES: Data exclude Armed Forces overseas. Beginning in 1960, includes Alaska and Hawaii, n.a. = not available. *Source:* Department of Commerce, Bureau of the Census.

Population and Rank of Large Metropolitan Areas, 1980–1985

(over 150,000)

Standard metropolitan statistical area	1985 Est.		1980 Census		Change 1980–85	
	Number	Rank	Number	Rank	Number	%
Akron, Ohio	646,200	—	660,328	—	−14,100	−2.1
Albany–Schenectady–Troy, N.Y.	841,400	47	835,880	46	5,500	0.7
Albuquerque, N.M.	464,300	76	420,262	79	44,000	10.5
Allentown–Bethlehem, Pa.–N.J.	650,000	56	635,481	54	14,500	2.3
Amarillo, Texas	192,800	155	173,699	157	19,100	11.0
Anaheim–Santa Ana, Calif.	2,122,700	—	1,932,921	—	189,800	9.8
Anchorage, Alaska	235,900	137	174,431	156	61,500	35.3
Ann Arbor, Mich.	262,600	—	264,740	—	−2,200	−0.8
Appleton–Oshkosh–Neenah, Wis.	303,700	113	291,369	107	12,400	4.2
Asheville, N.C.	168,000	172	160,934	171	7,100	4.4
Atlanta	2,471,700	13	2,138,143	16	333,500	15.6
Atlantic City, N.J.	292,600	114	276,385	113	16,200	5.9
Augusta, Ga.–S.C.	380,500	91	345,923	95	34,500	10.0
Aurora–Elgin, Ill.	335,800	—	315,607	—	20,200	6.4
Austin, Texas	695,500	54	536,688	63	158,800	29.6
Bakersfield, Calif.	480,900	74	403,089	84	77,800	19.3
Baltimore	2,252,800	17	2,199,497	15	53,300	2.4
Baton Rouge, La.	544,000	68	494,151	69	49,900	10.1
Beaumont–Port Arthur, Texas	381,400	90	375,497	88	5,900	1.6
Beaver County, Pa.	194,700	—	204,441	—	−9,700	−4.8
Benton Harbor, Mich.	162,800	175	171,276	161	−8,400	−4.9
Bergen–Passaic, N.J.	1,301,000	—	1,292,970	—	8,100	0.6
Biloxi–Gulfport, Miss.	198,900	152	182,161	153	16,800	9.2
Binghamton, N.Y.	262,800	123	263,460	123	−600	−0.2
Birmingham, Ala.	903,800	44	884,014	42	19,800	2.2
Boise City, Idaho	191,500	156	173,125	158	18,400	10.6
Boston	2,831,700	—	2,805,911	—	25,800	0.9
Brandenton, Fla.	173,100	166	148,445	181	24,600	16.6
Brazoria, Texas	188,200	—	169,587	—	18,600	11.0
Bremerton, Wash.	169,300	169	147,152	182	22,100	15.0
Bridgeport–Milford, Conn.	444,100	—	438,557	—	5,500	1.3
Brockton, Mass.	186,900	—	182,891	—	4,000	2.2
Brownsville–Harlingen, Texas	249,800	130	209,727	138	40,100	19.1
Buffalo, N.Y.	971,400	—	1,015,472	—	−44,100	−4.3
Canton, Ohio	401,200	86	404,421	83	−3,300	−0.8
Cedar Rapids, Iowa	167,600	173	169,775	163	−2,200	−1.3
Champaign–Urbana–Rantoul, Ill.	168,900	170	168,392	164	500	0.3
Charleston, S.C.	481,700	73	430,346	76	51,400	11.9
Charleston, W. Va.	269,000	121	269,595	118	−600	−0.2
Charlotte–Gastonia–Rock Hill, N.C.-S.C.	1,049,000	35	971,447	36	77,500	8.0
Chattanooga, Tenn.–Ga.	425,600	81	426,540	77	−900	−0.2
Chicago	6,176,900	3	6,060,401	3	116,500	1.9
Chico, Calif.	163,300	174	143,851	184	19,400	13.5
Cincinnati, Ohio–Ky.–Ind.	1,412,000	—	1,401,471	—	10,500	0.7
Clarksville–Hopkinsville, Tenn.–Ky.	153,100	183	150,220	179	2,800	1.9
Cleveland	1,860,000	—	1,898,825	—	−38,800	−2.0
Colorado Springs, Colo.	365,900	95	309,424	105	56,500	18.3
Columbia, S.C.	439,400	78	409,955	82	29,500	7.2
Columbus, Ga.–Ala.	248,500	131	239,196	131	9,300	3.9
Columbus, Ohio	1,287,600	29	1,243,827	28	43,800	3.5

Standard metropolitan statistical area	1985 Est.		1980 Census		Change, 1980–85	
	Number	Rank	Number	Rank	Number	%
Corpus Christi, Texas	358,800	97	326,228	99	32,600	10.0
Dallas–Fort Worth	3,511,600	9	2,930,539	10	581,100	19.8
Danbury, Conn.	183,200	—	170,369	—	12,900	7.5
Davenport–Rock Island–Moline, Iowa–Ill.	377,200	92	384,749	86	−7,500	−2.0
Dayton–Springfield, Ohio	931,100	42	942,083	39	−10,900	−1.2
Daytona Beach, Fla.	310,600	111	258,762	124	51,800	15.0
Denver–Boulder, Colo.	1,827,100	22	1,618,461	21	208,600	12.9
Des Moines, Iowa	372,100	93	367,561	89	4,500	1.2
Detroit, Mich.	4,318,600	—	4,488,024	—	−169,400	−3.8
Duluth, Minn.–Wis.	247,800	132	266,650	119	−18,800	−7.1
El Paso, Texas	545,000	67	479,899	70	65,100	13.6
Erie, Pa.	280,600	118	279,780	111	800	0.3
Eugene–Springfield, Ore.	261,300	124	275,226	115	−13,900	−5.1
Evansville, Ind.–Ky.	281,800	116	276,252	114	5,500	2.0
Fall River, Mass.–R.I.	156,900	—	157,222	—	−300	−0.2
Fayetteville, N.C.	258,000	127	247,160	127	10,900	4.4
Flint, Mich.	433,900	80	450,449	73	−16,500	−3.7
Fort Collins–Loveland, Colo.	170,500	167	149,184	180	21,300	14.3
Fort Lauderdale–Hollywood–Pompano Beach, Fla.	1,125,200	—	1,018,257	—	106,900	10.5
Fort Myers–Cape Coral, Fla.	267,200	122	205,266	140	61,900	30.2
Fort Pierce, Fla.	198,700	153	151,196	178	47,500	31.4
Fort Smith, Ark.–Okla.	173,200	165	162,813	169	10,400	6.4
Fort Wayne, Ind.	350,900	100	354,156	93	−3,300	−0.9
Fresno, Calif.	580,000	64	514,621	67	65,300	12.7
Gainsville, Fla.	196,700	154	171,392	160	25,300	14.8
Galveston–Texas City, Texas	213,400	—	195,738	—	17,700	9.0
Gary–Hammond, Ind.	621,500	—	642,733	—	−21,200	−3.3
Grand Rapids, Mich.	634,900	57	601,680	56	33,300	5.5
Green Bay, Wis.	184,700	159	175,280	155	9,500	5.4
Greensboro–Winston-Salem–High Point, N.C.	892,500	45	851,444	44	41,100	4.8
Greenville–Spartanburg, S.C.	599,600	61	570,211	59	29,400	5.2
Hamilton–Middletown, Ohio	267,900	—	258,787	—	9,100	3.5
Harrisburg–Lebanon–Carlisle, Pa.	572,900	65	556,242	62	16,600	3.0
Hartford, Conn.	732,100	—	715,923	—	16,200	2.3
Hickory, N.C.	215,000	146	202,711	142	12,300	6.1
Honolulu	814,600	49	762,565	47	52,100	6.8
Houma–Thibodaux, La.	190,100	157	176,876	154	13,200	7.5
Houston, Texas	3,221,700	—	2,734,617	—	487,100	17.8
Huntington–Ashland, W.Va.–Ky.–Ohio	331,800	105	336,410	97	−4,600	−1.4
Huntsville, Ala.	219,300	142	196,966	144	22,300	11.3
Indianapolis	1,203,100	32	1,166,575	30	36,600	3.1
Jackson, Miss.	384,700	89	362,038	92	22,700	6.3
Jacksonville, Fla.	823,500	48	722,252	50	101,200	14.0
Jersey City, N.J.	558,500	—	556,972	—	1,500	0.3
Johnson City–Kingsport–Bristol, Tenn.–Va.	442,700	77	433,638	75	9,000	2.1
Johnstown, Pa.	256,300	128	264,506	121	−8,200	−3.1
Joliet, Ill.	365,000	—	355,042	—	9,900	2.8
Kalamazoo, Mich.	215,500	145	212,378	136	3,100	1.5
Kansas City, Mo.–Kan.	1,493,900	25	1,433,464	25	60,500	4.2
Killeen–Temple, Texas	228,000	138	214,587	135	13,500	6.3
Knoxville, Tenn.	592,700	62	565,970	60	26,700	4.7
Lafayette, La.	217,200	144	190,231	150	27,000	14.2
Lake Charles, La.	174,300	163	167,223	165	7,100	4.2
Lake County, Ill.	465,300	—	440,387	—	24,900	5.7
Lakeland–Winter Haven, Fla.	368,500	94	321,652	101	46,900	14.6
Lancaster, Pa.	386,600	88	362,346	91	24,300	6.7
Lansing–East Lansing, Mich.	418,500	82	419,750	80	−1,300	−0.3
Las Vegas, Nev.	556,700	66	463,087	72	93,600	20.2
Lawrence–Haverhill, Mass.–N.H.	362,700	—	339,090	—	23,600	7.0
Lexington–Fayette, Ky.	329,400	107	317,548	103	11,800	3.7
Lima, Ohio	152,400	184	154,795	175	−2,400	−1.6
Lincoln, Neb.	205,400	150	192,884	147	12,600	6.5
Little Rock–North Little Rock, Ark.	498,500	72	474,464	71	24,100	5.1
Longview–Marshall, Texas	170,200	168	151,760	176	18,400	12.1
Lorain–Elyria, Ohio	270,100	—	274,909	—	−4,800	−1.7
Los Angeles–Long Beach, Calif.	8,108,700	2	7,477,422	2	631,300	8.4
Louisville, Ky.–Ind.	964,300	40	956,486	38	7,900	0.8
Lowell, Mass.–N.H.	252,500	—	243,142	—	9,400	3.9
Lubbock, Texas	222,800	140	211,651	137	11,100	5.2
Macon–Warner Robins, Ga.	280,200	119	263,591	122	16,600	6.3
Madison, Wis.	341,900	103	323,545	100	18,400	5.7

Standard metropolitan statistical area	1985 Est.		1980 Census		Change, 1980–85	
	Number	Rank	Number	Rank	Number	%
McAllen–Edinburg–Mission, Texas	352,200	99	283,323	110	68,900	24.3
Melbourne–Titusville–Palm Bay, Fla.	345,700	102	272,959	116	72,700	26.6
Memphis, Tenn.-Ark.-Miss.	944,700	41	913,472	40	31,200	3.4
Merced, Calif.	158,700	178	134,557	197	24,100	17.9
Miami–Hialeah, Fla.	1,753,100	—	1,625,611	—	127,500	7.8
Middlesex–Somerset–Hunterdon, N.J.	930,400	—	886,383	—	44,000	5.0
Milwaukee, Wis.	1,378,600	—	1,397,020	—	−18,400	−1.3
Minneapolis–St. Paul, Minn.-Wis.	2,262,400	16	2,137,133	17	125,200	5.9
Mobile, Ala.	469,100	75	443,536	74	25,600	5.8
Modesto, Calif.	305,800	112	265,900	120	39,900	15.0
Monmouth–Ocean, N.J.	918,000	—	849,211	—	68,800	8.1
Montgomery, Ala.	288,700	115	272,687	117	16,000	5.9
Muskegon, Mich.	156,700	181	157,589	173	−900	−0.6
Nashua, N.H.	157,700	—	142,527	—	15,100	10.6
Nashville, Tenn.	909,700	43	850,505	45	59,200	7.0
Nassau–Suffolk, N.Y.	2,644,700	—	2,605,813	—	38,900	1.5
Newark, N.J.	1,882,200	—	1,879,147	—	3,000	0.2
New Bedford, Mass.	168,500	171	166,699	166	1,800	1.1
New Haven–Meriden, Conn.	510,100	71	500,462	68	9,600	1.9
New London–Norwich, Conn.-R.I.	258,800	125	250,839	125	7,900	3.2
New Orleans	1,324,400	27	1,256,668	27	67,800	5.4
New York, N.Y.	8,465,800	1	8,274,961	1	190,900	2.3
Niagara Falls, N.Y.	216,500	—	227,354	—	−10,900	−4.8
Norfolk–Virginia Beach–Newport News, Va.	1,289,500	28	1,160,311	31	129,200	11.1
Ocala, Fla.	162,100	176	122,488	212	39,600	32.3
Oklahoma City, Okla.	975,900	39	860,969	43	114,900	13.3
Omaha, Neb.-Iowa	611,600	59	585,122	57	26,500	4.5
Orange County, N.Y.	277,600	—	259,603	—	18,000	6.9
Orlando, Fla.	866,400	46	699,906	51	166,500	23.8
Oxnard–Ventura, Calif.	600,000	—	529,174	—	70,800	13.4
Parkersburg–Marietta, W.Va.-Ohio	157,800	179	157,889	172	−100	−0.1
Pawtucket–Woonsocket–Attleboro, R.I.-Mass.	313,600	—	307,403	—	6,100	2.0
Pensacola, Fla.	328,500	108	289,782	109	38,700	13.4
Peoria, Ill.	347,700	101	365,864	90	−18,200	−5.0
Philadelphia, Pa.-N.J.	4,784,200	—	4,716,559	—	67,600	1.4
Phoenix, Ariz.	1,846,600	21	1,509,262	24	337,400	22.4
Pittsburgh	2,142,700	—	2,218,870	—	−76,200	−3.4
Portland, Maine	203,900	151	193,831	145	10,100	5.2
Portland, Ore.	1,146,600	—	1,105,750	—	40,800	3.7
Portsmouth–Dover–Rochester, N.H.-Maine	208,800	149	190,938	148	17,800	9.3
Poughkeepsie, N.Y.	255,100	129	245,055	129	10,100	4.1
Providence, R.I.	630,400	—	618,514	—	11,900	1.9
Provo–Orem, Utah	237,600	135	218,106	134	19,500	8.9
Racine, Wis.	171,700	—	173,132	—	−1,400	−0.8
Raleigh–Durham, N.C.	632,000	58	560,774	61	71,300	12.7
Reading, Pa.	318,100	109	312,509	104	5,500	1.8
Reno, Nev.	217,300	143	193,623	146	23,700	12.3
Richmond–Petersburg, Va.	800,700	50	761,311	48	39,400	5.2
Riverside–San Bernardino, Calif.	1,906,700	—	1,558,215	—	348,500	22.4
Roanoke, Va.	223,300	139	220,393	133	2,900	1.3
Rochester, N.Y.	982,300	38	971,230	37	11,000	1.1
Rockford, Ill.	279,900	120	279,514	112	400	0.1
Sacramento, Calif.	1,258,200	30	1,099,814	32	158,400	14.4
Saginaw–Bay City–Midland, Mich.	407,400	84	421,518	78	−14,100	−3.3
St. Cloud, Minn.	173,400	164	163,256	168	10,200	6.2
St. Louis, Mo.-Ill.	2,412,400	14	2,376,971	14	35,500	1.5
Salem–Gloucester, Mass.	260,000	—	258,231	—	1,800	0.7
Salem, Ore.	258,800	126	249,895	126	8,900	3.6
Salinas–Seaside–Monterey, Calif.	329,900	106	290,444	108	39,500	13.6
Salt Lake City–Ogden, Utah	1,024,800	37	910,222	41	114,600	12.6
San Antonio, Texas	1,235,700	31	1,072,125	34	163,600	15.3
San Diego, Calif.	2,132,700	19	1,861,846	19	270,900	14.5
San Francisco–Oakland, Calif.	3,483,800	—	3,250,605	—	233,200	9.3
San Jose, Calif.	1,398,500	—	1,295,071	—	103,400	8.0
Santa Barbara–Santa Maria–Lompoc, Calif.	332,000	104	298,694	106	33,300	11.1
Santa Cruz, Calif.	213,800	—	188,141	—	25,600	13.6
Santa Rosa–Petaluma, Calif.	334,500	—	299,681	—	34,800	11.6
Sarasota, Fla.	242,500	133	202,251	143	40,300	19.9
Savannah, Ga.	236,000	136	220,553	132	15,400	7.0
Scranton–Wilkes-Barre, Pa.	723,400	52	728,796	49	−5,400	−0.7
Seattle, Wash.	1,724,000	—	1,607,618	—	116,300	7.2

Standard metropolitan statistical area	1985 Est.		1980 Census		Change, 1980–85	
	Number	Rank	Number	Rank	Number	%
Shreveport, La.	362,400	96	333,158	98	29,300	8.8
South Bend–Mishawaka, Ind.	241,000	134	241,617	130	–600	–0.2
Spokane, Wash.	356,300	98	341,835	96	14,500	4.2
Springfield, Ill.	189,600	158	187,770	151	1,900	1.0
Springfield, Mass.	517,100	69	515,259	66	1,900	0.4
Springfield, Mo.	221,600	141	207,704	139	13,800	6.7
Stamford, Conn.	197,300	—	198,854	—	–1,600	–0.8
Steubenville–Weirton, Ohio–W.Va.	155,900	182	163,734	167	–7,800	–4.8
Stockton, Calif.	418,300	83	347,342	94	71,000	20.4
Syracuse, N.Y.	651,200	55	642,971	53	8,200	1.3
Tacoma, Wash.	523,500	—	485,667	—	37,800	7.8
Tallahassee, Fla.	214,000	147	190,329	149	23,700	12.4
Tampa–St. Petersburg–Clearwater, Fla.	1,868,700	20	1,613,621	22	255,100	15.8
Toledo, Ohio	608,100	60	616,864	55	–8,800	–1.4
Topeka, Kan.	159,100	177	154,916	174	4,200	2.7
Trenton, N.J.	314,900	—	307,863	—	7,100	2.3
Tucson, Ariz.	585,900	63	531,443	64	54,500	10.2
Tulsa, Okla.	733,100	51	657,173	52	76,000	11.6
Tyler, Texas	150,100	185	128,366	206	21,700	16.9
Utica–Rome, N.Y.	317,700	110	320,180	102	–2,500	–0.8
Vallejo–Fairfield–Napa, Calif.	378,800	—	334,402	—	44,400	13.3
Vancouver, Wash.	207,300	—	192,227	—	15,100	7.8
Visalia–Tulare–Porterville, Calif.	281,100	117	245,738	128	35,300	14.4
Waco, Texas	184,100	160	170,755	162	13,300	7.8
Washington, D.C.–Md.–Va.	3,489,500	10	3,250,921	8	238,600	7.3
Waterbury, Conn.	209,700	148	204,968	141	4,700	2.3
Waterloo–Cedar Falls, Iowa	157,500	180	162,781	170	–5,300	–3.2
West Palm Beach–Boca Raton–Delray Beach, Fla.	723,100	53	576,754	58	146,400	25.4
Wheeling, W.Va.–Ohio	179,700	162	185,566	152	–5,900	–3.2
Wichita, Kan.	435,400	79	411,870	81	23,600	5.7
Wilmington, Del.–N.J.–Md.	544,000	—	523,221	—	20,700	4.0
Worcester, Mass.	405,000	85	402,918	85	2,100	0.5
Yakima, Wash.	182,100	161	172,508	159	9,500	5.5
York, Pa.	393,700	87	381,255	87	12,500	3.3
Youngstown–Warren, Ohio	512,800	70	531,350	65	–18,500	–3.5

NOTE: The general concept of a standard metropolitan statistical area (SMSA) is one of a large population nucleus together with adjacent communities that have a high degree of economic and social integration with that nucleus. — Source does not list rank separately. It is given for the Consolidated Metropolitan Statistical Area of which this area is a part. *Source:* Department of Commerce, Bureau of the Census.

Resident Population by Age, Sex, Race, and Spanish Origin, 1986

(in thousands)

Age	White		Black		Spanish origin		Other races		All persons	
	Male	Female	Male	Female	Male	Female	Male	Female	Male	Female
Under 5	7,527	7,148	1,380	1,341	1,019	981	367	365	9,274	8,854
5-9	7,172	6,804	1,354	1,319	946	907	326	317	8,851	8,440
10-14	6,849	6,492	1,314	1,277	878	845	324	308	8,487	8,077
15-19	7,758	7,449	1,401	1,383	846	816	324	296	9,483	9,128
20-24	8,533	8,413	1,358	1,455	1,011	927	341	317	10,232	10,185
25-29	9,347	9,150	1,325	1,470	1,052	942	353	364	11,026	10,984
30-34	8,846	8,703	1,163	1,328	854	801	358	377	10,367	10,407
35-39	8,029	8,031	931	1,105	649	651	296	331	9,256	9,467
40-44	6,143	6,266	662	801	475	499	224	249	7,030	7,316
45-49	5,061	5,213	575	707	375	401	181	190	5,817	6,110
50-54	4,603	4,826	517	639	314	342	140	162	5,260	5,627
55-59	4,742	5,159	504	604	276	309	113	146	5,359	5,909
60-64	4,549	5,190	447	550	222	254	100	125	5,097	5,865
65-69	3,928	4,707	370	481	145	181	79	97	4,377	5,285
70-74	2,946	3,947	262	377	101	143	59	72	3,268	4,396
75-79	1,980	3,105	175	277	n.a.	n.a.	42	50	2,197	3,432
80-84	1,083	2,053	86	153	n.a.	n.a.	20	28	1,189	2,233
85 and over	712	1,837	67	146	n.a.	n.a.	14	21	792	2,004
All ages	99,808	104,493	13,892	15,414	9,294	9,202	3,661	3,811	117,360	123,718
15 and over	78,260	84,049	9,844	14,361	6,452	6,469	2,644	3,060	90,748	97,347
20 and over	70,502	76,601	8,443	10,094	5,605	5,652	2,320	2,525	81,265	89,220
65 and over	10,648	15,649	961	1,434	379	526	213	267	11,823	17,350
75 and over	3,775	6,995	328	578	132	201	76	97	4,178	7,669
Median age	31.5	33.9	25.5	28.4	24.7	25.7	27.1	29.2	30.6	33.0

NOTE: n.a. = not available. Source: Department of Commerce, Bureau of the Census

Population by State

State	1980	Percent change, 1970–80	Pop. per sq. mi., 1980	Pop. rank, 1980	1970	1950	1900	1790
Alabama	3,893,888	+13.1	76.7	22	3,444,354	3,061,743	1,828,697	—
Alaska	401,851	+32.8	0.7	50	302,583	128,643	63,592	—
Arizona	2,718,425	+53.1	23.9	29	1,775,399	749,587	122,931	—
Arkansas	2,286,435	+18.9	43.9	33	1,923,322	1,909,511	1,311,564	—
California	23,667,565	+18.5	151.4	1	19,971,069	10,586,223	1,485,053	—
Colorado	2,889,735	+30.8	27.9	28	2,209,596	1,325,089	539,700	—
Connecticut	3,107,576	+ 2.5	637.8	25	3,032,217	2,007,280	908,420	237,946
Delaware	594,317	+ 8.4	307.6	47	548,104	318,085	184,735	59,096
D.C.	638,432	−15.6	—	—	756,668	802,178	278,718	—
Florida	9,746,324	+43.5	180.0	7	6,791,418	2,771,305	528,542	—
Georgia	5,463,105	+19.1	94.1	13	4,587,930	3,444,578	2,216,331	82,548
Hawaii	964,691	+25.3	150.1	39	769,913	499,794	154,001	—
Idaho	944,038	+32.4	11.5	41	713,015	588,637	161,772	—
Illinois	11,426,518	+ 2.8	205.3	5	11,110,285	8,712,176	4,821,550	—
Indiana	5,490,260	+ 5.7	152.8	12	5,195,392	3,934,224	2,516,462	—
Iowa	2,913,808	+ 3.1	52.1	27	2,825,368	2,621,073	2,231,853	—
Kansas	2,364,236	+ 5.1	28.9	32	2,249,071	1,905,299	1,470,495	—
Kentucky	3,660,257	+13.7	92.3	23	3,220,711	2,944,806	2,147,174	73,677
Louisiana	4,206,312	+15.4	94.5	19	3,644,637	2,683,516	1,381,625	—
Maine	1,125,027	+13.2	36.3	38	993,722	913,774	694,466	96,540
Maryland	4,216,975	+ 7.5	428.7	18	3,923,897	2,343,001	1,188,044	319,728
Massachusetts	5,737,037	+ 0.8	733.3	11	5,689,170	4,690,514	2,805,346	378,787
Michigan	9,262,078	+ 4.3	162.6	8	8,881,826	6,371,766	2,420,982	—
Minnesota	4,075,970	+ 7.1	51.2	21	3,806,103	2,982,483	1,751,394	—
Mississippi	2,520,638	+13.7	53.4	31	2,216,994	2,178,914	1,551,270	—
Missouri	4,916,759	+ 5.1	71.3	15	4,677,623	3,954,653	3,106,665	—
Montana	786,690	+13.3	5.4	44	694,409	591,024	243,329	—
Nebraska	1,569,825	+ 5.7	20.5	35	1,485,333	1,325,510	1,066,300	—
Nevada	800,493	+63.8	7.3	43	488,738	160,083	42,335	—
New Hampshire	920,610	+24.8	102.4	42	737,681	533,242	411,588	141,885
New Jersey	7,364,823	+ 2.7	986.2	9	7,171,112	4,835,329	1,883,669	184,139
New Mexico	1,302,981	+28.1	10.7	37	1,017,055	681,187	195,310	—
New York	17,558,072	− 3.7	370.6	2	18,241,391	14,830,192	7,268,894	340,120
North Carolina	5,881,813	+15.7	120.4	10	5,084,411	4,061,929	1,893,810	393,751
North Dakota	652,717	+ 5.7	9.4	46	617,792	619,636	319,146	—
Ohio	10,797,624	+ 1.3	263.3	6	10,657,423	7,946,627	4,157,545	—
Oklahoma	3,025,290	+18.2	44.1	26	2,559,463	2,233,351	790,391[1]	—
Oregon	2,633,149	+25.9	27.4	30	2,091,533	1,521,341	413,536	—
Pennsylvania	11,863,895	+ 0.5	264.3	4	11,800,766	10,498,012	6,302,115	434,373
Rhode Island	947,154	− 0.3	897.8	40	949,723	791,896	428,556	68,825
South Carolina	3,121,833	+20.5	103.4	24	2,590,713	2,117,027	1,340,316	249,073
South Dakota	690,768	+ 3.7	9.1	45	666,257	652,740	401,570	—
Tennessee	4,591,120	+16.9	111.6	17	3,926,018	3,291,718	2,020,616	35,691
Texas	14,229,288	+27.1	54.3	3	11,198,655	7,711,194	3,048,710	—
Utah	1,461,037	+37.9	17.8	36	1,059,273	688,862	276,749	—
Vermont	511,456	+15.0	55.2	48	444,732	377,747	343,641	85,425
Virginia	5,346,818	+14.9	134.7	14	4,651,448	3,318,680	1,854,184	747,610[2]
Washington	4,132,180	+21.1	62.1	20	3,413,244	2,378,963	518,103	—
West Virginia	1,950,279	+11.8	80.8	34	1,744,237	2,005,552	958,800	—
Wisconsin	4,705,521	+ 6.5	86.5	16	4,417,821	3,434,575	2,069,042	—
Wyoming	469,557	+41.3	4.8	49	332,416	290,529	92,531	—
Total U.S.	**226,545,805**	**+11.4**	**62.6**	—	**203,302,031**	**151,325,798**	**76,212,168**	**3,929,214**

1. Includes population of Indian Territory: 1900, 392,960. 2. Until 1863, Virginia included what is now West Virginia. *Source:* Department of Commerce, Bureau of the Census.

Immigrants Changing Ethnic Makeup of U.S.

As immigrants from Europe continue to decline and those from Asia and Latin America continue to increase, the ethnic makeup of the United States is undergoing significant change. If the present trends continue, in a hundred years non-Hispanic whites of European origin will no longer be in the majority.

From 1981–1985 immigration from Europe dropped to 11% of the total legal immigration. Asia provided 48% and Latin America 35% of legal immigrants during the same five-year period. At the same time illegal immigrants grew by up to 500, 000 a year with an estimated three-quarters of them coming from Latin America.

The Census Bureau estimated that immigration now accounts for 28% of U.S. population growth. By 2030 immigration will account for all growth, if the current low rate of 1.8 births per woman continues.

Incorporated Places Over 25,000 Population

Asterisk denotes more than one ZIP code for a city and refers to Postmaster. To find the ZIP code for a particular address, consult the ZIP code directory available in every post office. For latest population figures of many cities, see listing for individual states in the United States section.

City and major ZIP code	1980 census	1970 census
Aberdeen, SD (57401)	25,851	26,476
Abilene, TX (79604*)	98,315	89,653
Addison, IL (60101)	29,759	24,482
Akron, OH (44309*)	237,177	275,425
Alameda, CA (94501)	63,852	70,968
Albany, GA (31706*)	74,550	72,623
Albany, NY (12212*)	101,727	115,781
Albany, OR (97321)	26,678	18,181
Albuquerque, NM (87101*)	331,767	244,501
Alexandria, LA (71301*)	51,565	41,811
Alexandria, VA (22313*)	103,217	110,927
Alhambra, CA (91802*)	64,615	62,125
Allen Park, MI (48101)	34,196	40,747
Allentown, PA (18101*)	103,758	109,871
Alton, IL (62002)	34,171	39,700
Altoona, PA (16603*)	57,078	63,115
Amarillo, TX (79120*)	149,230	127,010
Ames, IA (50010)	45,775	39,505
Anaheim, CA (92803*)	219,311	166,408
Anchorage, AK (99502*)	174,431	48,081
Anderson, IN (46018*)	64,695	70,787
Anderson, SC (29621*)	27,965	27,556
Annapolis, MD (21401*)	31,740	30,095
Ann Arbor, MI (48106*)	107,966	100,035
Anniston, AL (36201*)	29,523	31,533
Antioch, CA (94509)	42,683	28,060
Appleton, WI (54911*)	58,913	56,377
Arcadia, CA (91006)	45,994	45,138
Arlington, TX (76010*)	160,113	90,229
Arlington Heights, IL (60004*)	66,116	65,058
Arvada, CO (80001*)	84,576	49,844
Asheville, NC (28810*)	53,583	57,820
Ashland, KY (41101)	27,064	29,245
Athens, GA (30601*)	42,549	44,342
Atlanta, GA (30304*)	425,022	495,039
Atlantic City, NJ (08401*)	40,199	47,859
Attleboro, MA (02703)	34,196	32,907
Auburn, AL (36830)	28,471	22,767
Auburn, NY (13021)	32,548	34,599
Auburn, WA (98002*)	26,417	21,653
Augusta, GA (30901*)	47,532	59,864
Aurora, CO (80010*)	158,588	74,974
Aurora, IL (60507*)	81,293	74,389
Austin, TX (78710*)	345,496	253,539
Azusa, CA (91702)	29,380	25,217
Bakersfield, CA (93302*)	105,735	69,515
Baldwin Park, CA (91706)	50,554	47,285
Baltimore, MD (21233*)	786,775	905,787
Bangor, ME (04401)	31,643	33,168
Barberton, OH (44203)	29,751	33,052
Bartlesville, OK (74003*)	34,568	29,683
Baton Rouge, LA (70821*)	219,419	165,921
Battle Creek, MI (49016*)	35,724	38,931
Bay City, MI (48706)	41,593	49,449
Bayonne, NJ (07002)	65,047	72,743
Baytown, TX (77520*)	56,923	43,980
Beaumont, TX (77704*)	118,102	117,548
Beavercreek, OH (45401)	31,589	—
Beaverton, OR (97005*)	30,582	18,577
Bell, CA (90201)	25,450	21,836
Belleville, IL (62220*)	41,580	41,223
Belleville, NJ (07109)	35,367	37,629
Bellevue, WA (98009*)	73,903	61,196
Bellflower, CA (90706)	53,441	52,334
Bell Gardens, CA (90201)	34,117	29,308
Bellingham, WA (98225*)	45,794	39,375
Beloit, WI (53511)	35,207	35,729
Bergenfield, NJ (07621)	25,568	29,000
Berkeley, CA (94704*)	103,328	114,091
Berwyn, IL (60402)	46,840	52,502
Bessemer, AL (35020*)	31,729	33,428
Bethel Park, PA (15102)	34,755	34,758
Bethlehem, PA (18016*)	70,419	72,686
Bettendorf, IA (52722)	27,381	22,126
Beverly, MA (01915)	37,655	38,348
Beverly Hills, CA (90213*)	32,367	33,416
Billings, MT (59101*)	66,842	61,581
Biloxi, MS (39530*)	49,311	48,486
Binghamton, NY (13902*)	55,860	64,123
Birmingham, AL (35203*)	284,413	300,910
Bismarck, ND (58501)	44,485	34,703
Blacksburg, VA (24060)	30,638	9,384
Blaine, MN (55433)	28,558	20,573
Bloomfield, NJ (07003)	47,792	52,029
Bloomington, IL (61701)	44,189	39,992
Bloomington, IN (47401)	52,044	43,262
Bloomington, MN (55420*)	81,831	81,970
Blue Springs, MO (64015)	25,927	6,779
Boca Raton, FL (33432*)	49,505	28,506
Boise, ID (83708*)	102,160	74,990
Bolingbrook, IL (60439)	37,261	7,651
Bossier City, LA (71111*)	50,817	43,769
Boston, MA (02205*)	562,994	641,071
Boulder, CO (80302*)	76,685	66,870
Bountiful, UT (84010)	32,877	27,751
Bowie, MD (20715*)	33,695	35,028
Bowling Green, KY (42101)	40,450	36,705
Bowling Green, OH (43402)	25,728	14,656
Boynton Beach, FL (33435*)	35,624	18,115
Bradenton, FL (33506*)	30,170	21,040
Brea, CA (92621)	27,913	18,447
Bremerton, WA (98310*)	36,208	35,307
Bridgeport, CT (06602*)	142,546	156,542
Bristol, CT (06010)	57,370	55,487
Brockton, MA (02403*)	95,172	89,040
Broken Arrow, OK (74012*)	35,761	11,018
Brookfield, WI (53005)	34,035	31,761
Brooklyn Center, MN (55429*)	31,230	35,173
Brooklyn Park, MN (55007)	43,332	26,230
Brook Park, OH (44142)	26,195	30,774
Brownsville, TX (78520*)	84,997	52,522
Brunswick, OH (44212)	28,104	15,852
Bryan, TX (77801*)	44,337	33,719
Buena Park, CA (90622*)	64,165	63,646
Buffalo, NY (14240*)	357,870	462,768
Burbank, CA (91505*)	84,625	88,871
Burbank, IL (60459)	28,462	—
Burlingame, CA (94010)	26,173	27,320
Burlington, IA (52601)	29,529	32,366
Burlington, NC (27215)	37,266	35,930
Burlington, VT (05401)	37,712	38,633
Burnsville, MN (55337)	35,674	19,940
Burton, MI (48502)	29,976	—
Butte, MT (59701)	37,205	23,368
Calumet City, IL (60409)	39,697	33,107
Camarillo, CA (93010)	37,797	19,219
Cambridge, MA (02140)	95,322	100,361
Camden, NJ (08101*)	84,910	102,551

City and major ZIP code	1980 census	1970 census
Campbell, CA (95008)	27,067	23,797
Canton, OH (44711*)	93,077	110,053
Cape Coral, FL (33910)	32,103	—
Cape Girardeau, MO (63701)	34,361	31,282
Carbondale, IL (62901)	26,414	22,816
Carlsbad, CA (92008)	35,490	14,944
Carlsbad, NM (88220)	25,496	21,297
Carrollton, TX (75006*)	40,595	13,855
Carson, CA (90749)	81,221	71,150
Carson City, NV (89701)	32,022	15,468
Casper, WY (82601*)	51,016	39,361
Cedar Falls, IA (50613)	36,322	29,597
Cedar Rapids, IA (52401*)	110,243	110,642
Cerritos, CA (90701)	53,020	15,856
Champaign, IL (61820*)	58,133	56,837
Chandler, AZ (85224)	29,673	13,763
Chapel Hill, NC (27514)	32,421	26,199
Charleston, SC (29423*)	69,510	66,945
Charleston, WV (25301*)	63,968	71,505
Charlotte, NC (28228*)	314,447	241,420
Charlottesville, VA (22906*)	39,916	38,880
Chattanooga, TN (37401*)	169,558	119,923
Chelsea, MA (02150)	25,431	30,625
Chesapeake, VA (23320*)	114,486	89,580
Chester, PA (19013*)	45,794	56,331
Cheyenne, WY (82001*)	47,283	41,254
Chicago, IL (60607*)	3,005,072	3,369,357
Chicago Heights, IL (60411)	37,026	40,900
Chico, CA (95926)	26,603	19,580
Chicopee, MA (01021*)	55,112	66,676
Chino, CA (91710)	40,165	20,411
Chula Vista, CA (92010*)	83,927	67,901
Cicero, IL (60650)	61,232	67,058
Cincinnati, OH (45234*)	385,457	453,514
Claremont, CA (91711)	30,950	24,776
Clarksville, TN (37041*)	54,777	31,719
Clearwater, FL (33575*)	85,528	52,074
Cleveland, OH (44101*)	573,822	750,879
Cleveland, TN (37311)	26,415	21,446
Cleveland Heights, OH (44118)	56,438	60,767
Clifton, NJ (07015*)	74,388	82,437
Clinton, IA (52732)	32,828	34,719
Clovis, CA (93612)	33,021	13,856
Clovis, NM (88101)	31,194	28,495
College Station, TX (77840)	37,272	17,676
Colorado Springs, CO (80901*)	214,821	135,517
Columbia, MO (65201*)	62,061	58,812
Columbia, SC (29201*)	100,385	113,542
Columbia, TN (38401)	26,571	21,471
Columbus, GA (31908*)	169,441	155,028
Columbus, IN (47201*)	30,614	26,457
Columbus, MS (39701*)	27,383	25,795
Columbus, OH (43216*)	565,032	540,025
Compton, CA (90220*)	81,286	78,547
Concord, CA (94520*)	103,255	85,164
Concord, NH (03301*)	30,400	30,022
Coon Rapids, MN (55433)	35,826	30,505
Coral Gables, FL (33114)	43,241	42,494
Coral Springs, FL (33065)	37,349	1,489
Corona, CA (91720)	37,791	27,519
Corpus Christi, TX (78408*)	231,999	204,525
Corvallis, OR (97333*)	40,960	35,056
Costa Mesa, CA (92626*)	82,562	72,660
Council Bluffs, IA (51501)	56,449	60,348
Covina, CA (91722*)	33,751	30,395
Covington, KY (41011*)	49,563	52,535
Cranston, RI (02910*)	71,992	74,287
Crystal, MN (55428*)	25,543	30,925
Culver City, CA (90230)	38,139	34,451
Cumberland, MD (21502*)	25,933	29,724
Cupertino, CA (95014)	34,015	17,895

City and major ZIP code	1980 census	1970 census
Cuyahoga Falls, OH (44222*)	43,890	49,815
Cypress, CA (90630)	40,391	31,569
Dallas, TX (75260*)	904,078	844,401
Daly City, CA (94015*)	78,519	66,922
Danbury, CT (06810*)	60,470	50,781
Danville, IL (61832)	38,985	42,570
Danville, VA (24541*)	45,642	46,391
Davenport, IA (52802*)	103,264	98,469
Davis, CA (95616)	36,640	23,488
Dayton, OH (45401*)	193,444	243,023
Daytona Beach, FL (32015*)	54,176	45,327
Dearborn, MI (48120*)	90,660	104,199
Dearborn Heights, MI (48127)	67,706	80,069
Decatur, AL (35602*)	42,002	38,044
Decatur, IL (62521*)	94,081	90,397
Deerfield Beach, FL (33441)	39,193	16,662
De Kalb, IL (60115)	33,099	32,949
Del City, OK (73155*)	28,424	27,133
Delray Beach, FL (33444*)	34,325	19,915
Del Rio, TX (78840)	30,034	21,330
Denton, TX (76201*)	48,063	39,874
Denver, CO (80202*)	492,365	514,678
Des Moines, IA (50318*)	191,003	201,404
Des Plaines, IL (60018*)	53,568	57,239
Detroit, MI (48233*)	1,203,339	1,514,063
Dothan, AL (36303*)	48,750	36,733
Downers Grove, IL (60515*)	42,572	32,544
Downey, CA (90241*)	82,602	88,573
Dubuque, IA (52001)	62,321	62,309
Duluth, MN (55806*)	92,811	100,578
Duncanville, TX (75138*)	27,781	14,105
Dunedin, FL (33528)	30,203	17,639
Durham, NC (27701*)	100,538	95,438
East Chicago, IN (46312)	39,786	49,982
East Cleveland, OH (44112)	36,957	39,660
East Detroit, MI (48021)	38,280	45,920
East Lansing, MI (48823)	51,392	47,540
Easton, PA (18042)	26,027	29,450
East Orange, NJ (07019*)	77,690	75,471
East Point, GA (30364)	37,486	39,315
East Providence, RI (02914)	50,980	48,207
East St. Louis, IL (62201*)	55,200	70,169
Eau Claire, WI (54701*)	51,509	44,619
Edina, MN (55424*)	46,073	44,046
Edmond, OK (73034)	34,637	16,633
Edmonds, WA (98020)	27,679	23,684
El Cajon, CA (92020*)	73,892	52,273
El Dorado, AR (71730)	25,270	25,283
Elgin, IL (60120)	63,798	55,691
Elizabeth, NJ (07207*)	106,201	112,654
Elk Grove, IL (60007)	28,907	20,346
Elkhart, IN (46515*)	41,305	43,152
Elmhurst, IL (60126)	44,276	46,392
Elmira, NY (14901*)	35,327	39,945
El Monte, CA (91734*)	79,494	69,892
El Paso, TX (79910*)	425,259	322,261
Elyria, OH (44035*)	57,538	53,427
Emporia, KS (66801)	25,287	23,327
Englewood, CO (80110*)	30,021	33,695
Enid, OK (73701)	50,363	44,986
Erie, PA (16515*)	119,123	129,265
Escondido, CA (92025*)	64,355	36,792
Euclid, OH (44117)	59,999	71,552
Eugene, OR (97401*)	105,624	79,028
Evanston, IL (60204*)	73,706	80,113
Evansville, IN (47708*)	130,496	138,764
Everett, MA (02149)	37,195	42,485
Everett, WA (98201*)	54,413	53,622
Fairborn, OH (45324)	29,702	32,267
Fairfield, CA (94533)	58,099	44,146
Fairfield, OH (45014)	30,777	14,680

City and major ZIP code	1980 census	1970 census
Fair Lawn, NJ (07410)	32,229	38,040
Fall River, MA (02722*)	92,574	96,898
Fargo, ND (58102*)	61,383	53,365
Farmington, NM (87401)	31,222	21,979
Farmington Hills, MI (48024)	58,056	—
Fayetteville, AR (72701)	36,608	30,729
Fayetteville, NC (28302*)	59,507	53,510
Ferndale, MI (48220)	26,227	30,850
Findlay, OH (45840)	35,594	35,800
Fitchburg, MA (01420)	39,580	43,343
Flagstaff, AZ (86001)	34,743	26,117
Flint, MI (48502*)	159,611	193,317
Florence, AL (35631*)	37,029	34,031
Florence, SC (29501)	29,176	25,997
Florissant, MO (63033*)	55,372	65,908
Fond du Lac, WI (54935)	35,863	35,515
Fontana, CA (92335)	37,107	20,673
Fort Collins, CO (80521*)	65,092	43,337
Fort Dodge, IA (50501)	29,423	31,263
Fort Lauderdale, FL (33310*)	153,279	139,590
Fort Lee, NJ (07024)	32,449	30,631
Fort Myers, FL (33906*)	36,638	27,351
Fort Pierce, FL (33450*)	33,802	29,721
Fort Smith, AR (72901*)	71,626	62,802
Fort Wayne, IN (46802*)	172,028	178,269
Fort Worth, TX (76101*)	385,164	393,455
Fountain Valley, CA (92728)	55,080	31,886
Frankfort, KY (40601)	25,973	21,902
Frederick, MD (21701)	28,086	23,641
Freeport, IL (61032)	26,266	27,736
Freeport, NY (11520)	38,272	40,374
Fremont, CA (94538*)	131,945	100,869
Fresno, CA (93706*)	218,202	165,655
Fridley, MN (55432)	30,228	29,233
Fullerton, CA (92631*)	102,034	85,987
Gadsden, AL (35901*)	47,565	53,928
Gainesville, FL (32602*)	81,371	64,510
Gaithersburg, MD (20877*)	26,424	8,344
Galesburg, IL (61401)	35,305	36,290
Galveston, TX (77553*)	61,902	61,809
Gardena, CA (90247*)	45,165	41,021
Garden City, MI (48135)	35,640	41,864
Garden Grove, CA (92640*)	123,307	121,155
Garfield, NJ (07026)	26,803	30,797
Garfield Heights, OH (44125)	34,938	41,417
Garland, TX (75040*)	138,857	81,437
Gary, IN (46401*)	151,953	175,415
Gastonia, NC (28052)	47,333	47,322
Glendale, AZ (85301*)	97,172	36,228
Glendale, CA (91209*)	139,060	132,664
Glendora, CA (91740)	38,500	32,143
Glenview, IL (60025)	32,060	24,880
Gloucester, MA (01930)	27,768	27,941
Goldsboro, NC (27530)	31,871	26,960
Grand Forks, ND (58201)	43,765	39,008
Grand Island, NE (68801)	33,180	32,358
Grand Junction, CO (81501*)	27,956	20,170
Grand Prairie, TX (75051*)	71,462	50,904
Grand Rapids, MI (49501*)	181,843	197,649
Granite City, IL (62040)	36,815	40,685
Great Falls, MT (59403*)	56,725	60,091
Greeley, CO (80631*)	53,006	38,902
Green Bay, WI (54301*)	87,899	87,809
Greenfield, WI (53220)	31,467	24,424
Greensboro, NC (27420*)	155,642	144,076
Greenville, MS (38701*)	40,613	39,648
Greenville, NC (27834)	35,740	29,063
Greenville, SC (29602*)	58,242	61,436
Gresham, OR (97030)	33,005	10,030
Gulfport, MS (39503*)	39,676	40,791

City and major ZIP code	1980 census	1970 census
Hackensack, NJ (07602*)	36,039	36,008
Hagerstown, MD (21740)	34,132	35,862
Hallandale, FL (33009)	36,517	23,849
Haltom City, TX (76117)	29,014	28,127
Hamilton, OH (45012*)	63,189	67,865
Hammond, IN (46320*)	93,714	107,983
Hampton, VA (23670*)	122,617	120,779
Hanover Park, IL (60103)	28,850	11,735
Harlingen, TX (78551*)	43,543	33,503
Harrisburg, PA (17105*)	53,264	68,061
Hartford, CT (06101*)	136,392	158,017
Harvey, IL (60426)	35,810	34,636
Hattiesburg, MS (39401)	40,829	38,277
Haverhill, MA (01830)	46,865	46,120
Hawthorne, CA (90250)	56,447	53,304
Hayward, CA (94544*)	94,342	93,058
Hazleton, PA (18201)	27,318	30,426
Hempstead, NY (11551*)	40,404	39,411
Hendersonville, TN (37075)	26,561	412
Hialeah, FL (33010*)	145,254	102,452
Highland, IN (46322)	25,935	24,947
Highland Park, IL (60035)	30,611	32,263
Highland Park, MI (48203)	27,909	35,444
High Point, NC (27260*)	63,808	63,229
Hillsboro, OR (97123*)	27,664	14,675
Hilo, HI (96720)	35,269	26,353
Hobbs, NM (88240)	29,153	26,025
Hoboken, NJ (07030)	42,460	45,380
Hoffman Estates, IL (60195)	37,272	22,238
Holland, MI (49423)	26,281	26,479
Hollywood, FL (33022*)	121,323	106,873
Holyoke, MA (01040)	44,678	50,112
Honolulu, HI (96820*)	365,048	324,871
Hopkinsville, KY (42240)	27,318	21,395
Hot Springs, AR (71901*)	35,781	35,631
Houma, LA (70360)	32,602	30,922
Houston, TX (77201*)	1,595,138	1,233,535
Huber Heights, OH (45424)	35,480	—
Huntington, WV (25704*)	63,684	74,315
Huntington Beach, CA (92647*)	170,505	115,960
Huntington Park, CA (90255)	46,223	33,744
Huntsville, AL (35813*)	142,513	139,282
Hurst, TX (76053)	31,420	27,215
Hutchinson, KS (67501)	40,284	36,885
Idaho Falls, ID (83401*)	39,590	35,776
Independence, MO (64051*)	111,806	111,630
Indianapolis, IN (46206*)	700,807	736,856
Inglewood, CA (90311*)	94,245	89,985
Inkster, MI (48141)	35,190	38,595
Iowa City, IA (52240*)	50,508	46,850
Irvine, CA (92713)	62,134	—
Irving, TX (75061*)	109,943	97,260
Irvington, NJ (07111)	61,493	59,743
Ithaca, NY (14850)	28,732	26,226
Jackson, MI (49201*)	39,739	45,484
Jackson, MS (39205*)	202,895	153,968
Jackson, TN (38301*)	49,131	39,996
Jacksonville, AR (72076)	27,589	19,832
Jacksonville, FL (32203*)	540,920	504,265
Jamestown, NY (14701)	35,775	39,795
Janesville, WI (53545*)	51,071	46,426
Jefferson City, MO (65101)	33,619	32,407
Jersey City, NJ (07303*)	223,532	260,350
Johnson City, TN (37601)	39,753	33,770
Johnstown, PA (15901*)	35,496	42,476
Joliet, IL (60436*)	77,956	78,827
Jonesboro, AR (72401)	31,530	27,050
Joplin, MO (64801)	39,023	39,256
Kalamazoo, MI (49001*)	79,722	85,555
Kankakee, IL (60901)	30,141	30,944

City and major ZIP code	1980 census	1970 census
Kansas City, KS (66110*)	161,148	168,213
Kansas City, MO (64108*)	448,159	507,330
Kearny, NJ (07032)	35,735	37,585
Kenner, LA (70062*)	66,382	29,858
Kennewick, WA (99336)	34,397	15,212
Kenosha, WI (53141*)	77,685	78,805
Kent, OH (44240)	26,164	28,183
Kentwood, MI (49508)	30,438	20,310
Kettering, OH (45429)	61,186	71,864
Killeen, TX (76541*)	46,296	35,507
Kingsport, TN (37662*)	32,027	31,938
Kingsville, TX (78363)	28,808	28,915
Kinston, NC (28501)	25,234	23,020
Kirkwood, MO (63122)	27,987	31,679
Knoxville, TN (37901*)	175,045	174,587
Kokomo, IN (46902*)	47,808	44,042
La Crosse, WI (54601*)	48,347	50,286
Lafayette, IN (47901*)	43,011	44,955
Lafayette, LA (70501*)	81,961	68,908
La Habra, CA (90631)	45,232	41,350
Lake Charles, LA (70601*)	75,226	77,998
Lakeland, FL (33802*)	47,406	42,803
Lakewood, CA (90714*)	74,654	83,025
Lakewood, CO (80215)	113,808	92,743
Lakewood, OH (44107)	61,963	70,173
Lake Worth, FL (33461*)	27,048	23,714
La Mesa, CA (92041)	50,308	39,178
La Mirada, CA (90638)	40,986	30,808
Lancaster, CA (93534*)	48,027	—
Lancaster, OH (43130)	34,953	32,911
Lancaster, PA (17604*)	54,725	57,690
Lansing, IL (60438)	29,039	25,805
Lansing, MI (48924*)	130,414	131,403
La Puente, CA (91747*)	30,882	31,092
Laredo, TX (78041*)	91,449	69,024
Largo, FL (33540*)	58,977	24,230
Las Cruces, NM (88001*)	45,086	37,857
Las Vegas, NV (89114*)	164,674	125,787
Lauderdale Lakes, FL (33313)	25,426	10,577
Lauderhill, FL (33313)	37,271	8,465
Lawrence, IN (46226)	25,591	16,353
Lawrence, KS (66044)	52,738	45,698
Lawrence, MA (01842*)	63,175	66,915
Lawton, OK (73501*)	80,054	74,470
Leavenworth, KS (66048)	33,656	25,147
Lebanon, PA (17042)	25,711	28,572
Lee's Summit, MO (64063)	28,741	16,230
Leominster, MA (01453)	34,508	32,939
Lewiston, ID (83501)	27,986	26,068
Lewiston, ME (04240)	40,481	41,779
Lexington, KY (40511*)	204,165	108,137
Lima, OH (45802*)	47,381	53,734
Lincoln, NE (68501*)	171,932	149,518
Lincoln Park, MI (48146)	45,105	52,984
Linden, NJ (07036)	37,836	41,409
Lindenhurst, NY (11757)	26,919	28,359
Little Rock, AR (72231*)	158,461	132,483
Littleton, CO (80120*)	28,631	26,466
Livermore, CA (94550)	48,349	37,703
Livonia, MI (48150*)	104,814	110,109
Lodi, CA (95240)	35,221	28,691
Logan, UT (84321)	26,844	22,333
Lombard, IL (60148)	37,295	34,043
Lompoc, CA (93436)	26,267	25,284
Long Beach, CA (90809*)	361,334	358,879
Long Beach, NY (11561)	34,073	33,127
Long Branch, NJ (07740)	29,819	31,774
Longmont, CO (80501)	42,942	23,209
Longview, TX (75602*)	62,762	45,547
Longview, WA (98632)	31,052	28,373
Lorain, OH (44052*)	75,416	78,185

City and major ZIP code	1980 census	1970 census
Los Altos, CA (94022)	25,769	25,062
Los Angeles, CA (90052*)	2,966,850	2,811,801
Los Gatos, CA (95030)	26,906	22,613
Louisville, KY (40231*)	298,840	361,706
Loveland, CO (80537)	30,244	16,220
Lowell, MA (01853*)	92,418	94,239
Lubbock, TX (79408*)	173,979	149,101
Lufkin, TX (75901)	28,562	23,049
Lynchburg, VA (24506*)	66,743	54,083
Lynn, MA (01901*)	78,471	90,294
Lynwood, CA (90262)	48,548	43,354
Macon, GA (31213*)	116,896	122,423
Madisón, WI (53707*)	170,616	171,809
Madison Heights, MI (48071)	35,375	38,599
Malden, MA (02148)	53,386	56,127
Manchester, NH (03103*)	90,936	87,754
Manhattan, KS (66502)	32,644	27,575
Manhattan Beach, CA (90266)	31,542	35,352
Manitowoc, WI (54220)	32,547	33,430
Mankato, MN (56001)	28,651	30,895
Mansfield, OH (44901*)	53,927	55,047
Maple Heights, OH (44137)	29,735	34,093
Maplewood, MN (55109)	26,990	25,186
Margate, FL (33063*)	35,900	8,867
Marietta, GA (30060*)	30,829	27,216
Marion, IN (46952*)	35,874	39,607
Marion, OH (43302)	37,040	38,646
Marlborough, MA (01752)	30,617	27,936
Marshalltown, IA (50158)	26,938	26,219
Mason City, IA (50401)	30,144	30,279
Massillon, OH (44646)	30,557	32,539
Maywood, IL (60153)	27,998	29,019
McAllen, TX (78501)	66,281	37,636
McKeesport, PA (15134*)	31,012	37,977
Medford, MA (02155)	58,076	64,397
Medford, OR (97501)	39,603	28,973
Melbourne, FL (32901*)	46,536	40,236
Melrose, MA (02176)	30,055	33,180
Memphis, TN (38101*)	646,174	623,988
Menlo Park, CA (94025)	26,369	26,826
Menomonee Falls, WI (53051)	27,845	31,697
Mentor, OH (44060)	42,065	36,912
Merced, CA (95340)	36,499	22,670
Meriden, CT (06450)	57,118	55,959
Meridian, MS (39301)	46,577	45,083
Merrillville, IN (46410)	27,677	—
Mesa, AZ (85201*)	152,453	63,049
Mesquite, TX (75149*)	67,053	55,131
Miami, FL (33152*)	346,865	334,859
Miami Beach, FL (33139)	96,298	87,072
Michigan City, IN (46360)	36,850	39,369
Middletown, CT (06457)	39,040	36,924
Middletown, OH (45042)	43,719	48,767
Midland, MI (48640)	37,250	35,176
Midland, TX (79702*)	70,525	59,463
Midwest City, OK (73140*)	49,559	48,212
Milford, CT (06460)	49,101	50,858
Milpitas, CA (95035)	37,820	26,561
Milwaukee, WI (53201*)	636,236	717,372
Minneapolis, MN (55401*)	370,951	434,400
Minnetonka, MN (55343)	38,683	35,776
Minot, ND (58701)	32,843	32,290
Miramar, FL (33023)	32,813	23,997
Mishawaka, IN (46544*)	40,201	36,060
Missoula, MT (59806*)	33,388	29,497
Mobile, AL (36601*)	200,452	190,026
Modesto, CA (95350*)	106,602	61,712
Moline, IL (61265)	45,709	46,237
Monroe, LA (71203*)	57,597	56,374
Monroeville, PA (15146)	30,977	29,011
Monrovia, CA (91016)	30,531	30,562

City and major ZIP code	1980 census	1970 census
Montclair, NJ (07042*)	38,321	44,043
Montebello, CA (90640)	52,929	42,807
Monterey, CA (93940)	27,558	26,302
Monterey Park, CA (91754)	54,338	49,166
Montgomery, AL (36119*)	177,857	133,386
Moore, OK (73153*)	35,063	18,761
Moorhead, MN (56560)	29,998	29,687
Morgantown, WV (26505)	27,605	29,431
Mountain View, CA (94042*)	58,655	54,132
Mount Prospect, IL (60056)	52,634	34,995
Mount Vernon, NY (10551*)	66,713	72,778
Muncie, IN (47302*)	77,216	69,082
Murfreesboro, TN (37130)	32,845	26,360
Murray, UT (84107)	25,750	21,206
Muskegon, MI (49440*)	40,823	44,631
Muskogee, OK (74401)	40,011	37,331
Nacogdoches, TX (75961)	27,149	22,544
Nampa, ID (83651)	25,112	20,768
Napa, CA (94558*)	50,879	36,103
Naperville, IL (60566*)	42,330	22,794
Nashua, NH (03061*)	67,865	55,820
Nashville, TN (37202*)	455,651	426,029
National City, CA (92050)	48,772	43,184
Naugatuck, CT (06770)	26,456	23,034
New Albany, IN (47150)	37,103	38,402
Newark, CA (94560)	32,126	27,153
Newark, DE (19711*)	25,247	21,298
Newark, NJ (07102*)	329,248	381,930
Newark, OH (43055)	41,200	41,836
New Bedford, MA (02741*)	98,478	101,777
New Berlin, WI (53151)	30,529	26,910
New Britain, CT (06050*)	73,840	83,441
New Brunswick, NJ (08901*)	41,442	41,885
New Castle, PA (16101*)	33,621	38,559
New Haven, CT (06511*)	126,109	137,707
New Iberia, LA (70560)	32,766	30,147
New London, CT (06320)	28,842	31,630
New Orleans, LA (70113*)	557,927	593,471
Newport, RI (02840)	29,259	34,562
Newport Beach, CA (92660*)	62,556	49,582
Newport News, VA (23607*)	144,903	138,177
New Rochelle, NY (10802*)	70,794	75,385
Newton, MA (02158)	83,622	91,263
New York, NY (10001*)	7,071,639	7,895,563
Bronx borough (10451*)	1,168,972	1,471,701
Brooklyn borough (11201*)	2,230,936	2,602,012
Manhattan borough (10001*)	1,428,285	1,539,233
Queens borough[1]	1,891,325	1,987,174
Staten Island borough (10314*)	352,121	295,443
Niagara Falls, NY (14302*)	71,384	85,615
Niles, IL (60648)	30,363	31,432
Norfolk, VA (23501*)	266,979	307,951
Normal, IL (61761)	35,672	26,396
Norman, OK (73070*)	68,020	52,117
Norristown, PA (19401*)	34,684	38,169
Northampton, MA (01060)	29,286	29,664
Northbrook, IL (60062)	30,778	25,422
North Charleston, SC (29406)	62,534	—
North Chicago, IL (60064)	38,774	47,275
Northglenn, CO (80233)	29,847	27,785
North Las Vegas, NV (89030)	42,739	46,067
North Little Rock, AR (72114*)	64,288	60,040
North Miami, FL (33161)	42,566	34,767
North Miami Beach, FL (33160)	36,553	30,544
North Olmsted, OH (44070)	36,486	34,861
North Richland Hills, TX (76118)	30,592	16,514
North Tonawanda, NY (14120)	35,760	36,012
Norwalk, CA (90650)	85,286	90,164
Norwalk, CT (06856*)	77,767	79,288
Norwich, CT (06360)	38,074	41,739
Norwood, OH (45212*)	26,342	30,420
Novato, CA (94947)	43,916	31,006
Nutley, NJ (07110)	28,998	31,913
Oak Forest, IL (60452)	26,096	19,271
Oakland, CA (94615*)	339,337	361,561
Oak Lawn, IL (60454*)	60,590	60,305
Oak Park, IL (60301*)	54,887	62,511
Oak Park, MI (48237)	31,537	36,762
Oak Ridge, TN (37830)	27,662	28,319
Ocala, FL (32678*)	37,170	22,583
Oceanside, CA (92054*)	76,698	40,494
Odessa, TX (79760*)	90,027	78,380
Ogden, UT (84401*)	64,407	69,478
Oklahoma City, OK (73125*)	403,136	368,164
Olathe, KS (66061*)	37,258	17,917
Olympia, WA (98501*)	27,447	23,296
Omaha, NE (68108*)	313,911	346,929
Ontario, CA (91761*)	88,820	64,118
Orange, CA (92667*)	91,788	77,365
Orange, NJ (07051*)	31,136	32,566
Orem, UT (84057*)	52,399	25,729
Orlando, FL (32802*)	128,291	99,006
Oshkosh, WI (54901)	49,620	53,082
Ottumwa, IA (52501)	27,381	29,610
Overland Park, KS (66204)	81,784	77,934
Owensboro, KY (43201)	54,450	50,329
Oxnard, CA (93030*)	108,195	71,225
Pacifica, CA (94044)	36,866	36,020
Paducah, KY (42001)	29,315	31,627
Palatine, IL (60067*)	32,166	26,050
Palm Springs, CA (92263*)	32,366	20,936
Palo Alto, CA (94303*)	55,225	56,040
Panama City, FL (32401*)	33,346	32,096
Paramount, CA (90723)	36,407	34,734
Paramus, NJ (07652)	26,474	28,381
Paris, TX (75460)	25,498	23,441
Parkersburg, WV (26101*)	39,967	44,208
Park Forest, IL (60466)	26,222	30,638
Park Ridge, IL (60068)	38,704	42,614
Parma, OH (44129)	92,548	100,216
Pasadena, CA (91109*)	118,550	112,951
Pasadena, TX (77501*)	112,560	89,957
Pascagoula, MS (39567)	29,318	27,264
Passaic, NJ (07055)	52,463	55,124
Paterson, NJ (07510*)	137,970	144,824
Pawtucket, RI (02860*)	71,204	76,984
Peabody, MA (01960)	45,976	48,080
Pembroke Pines, FL (33024)	35,776	15,496
Pensacola, FL (32501*)	57,619	59,507
Peoria, IL (61601*)	124,160	126,963
Perth Amboy, NJ (08861*)	38,951	38,798
Petaluma, CA (94952)	33,834	24,870
Petersburg, VA (23804*)	41,055	36,103
Phenix City, AL (36867)	26,928	25,281
Philadelphia, PA (19104*)	1,688,210	1,949,996
Phoenix, AZ (85026*)	789,704	584,303
Pico Rivera, CA (90660)	53,387	54,170
Pine Bluff, AR (71601*)	56,636	57,389
Pinellas Park, FL (33565)	32,811	22,287
Pittsburg, CA (94565)	33,034	21,423
Pittsburgh, PA (15219*)	423,959	520,089
Pittsfield, MA (01201)	51,974	57,020
Placentia, CA (92670)	35,041	21,948
Plainfield, NJ (07061*)	45,555	46,862
Plano, TX (75074*)	72,331	17,872
Plantation, FL (33318)	48,653	23,523
Pleasant Hill, CA (94523)	25,124	24,610
Pleasanton, CA (94566)	35,160	18,328
Plum, PA (15239)	25,390	21,932

City and major ZIP code	1980 census	1970 census
Plymouth, MN (55447*)	31,615	18,077
Pocatello, ID (83201)	46,340	40,036
Pomona, CA (91766*)	92,742	87,384
Pompano Beach, FL (33060*)	52,618	38,587
Ponca City, OK (74601*)	26,238	25,940
Pontiac, MI (48056*)	76,715	85,279
Portage, IN (46368)	27,409	19,127
Portage, MI (49081)	38,157	33,590
Port Arthur, TX (77640)	61,251	57,371
Port Huron, MI (48060)	33,981	35,794
Portland, ME (04101*)	61,572	65,116
Portland, OR (97208*)	366,383	379,967
Portsmouth, NH (03801)	26,254	25,717
Portsmouth, OH (45662)	25,943	27,633
Portsmouth, VA (23705*)	104,577	110,963
Poughkeepsie, NY (12601*)	29,757	32,029
Prichard, AL (36610*)	39,541	41,578
Providence, RI (02940*)	156,804	179,116
Provo, UT (84603*)	74,108	53,131
Pueblo, CO (81003*)	101,686	97,774
Quincy, IL (62301)	42,554	45,288
Quincy, MA (02269)	84,743	87,966
Racine, WI (53401*)	85,725	95,162
Rahway, NJ (07065*)	26,723	29,114
Raleigh, NC (27611*)	150,255	122,830
Rancho Cucamonga, CA (91730)	55,250	—
Rancho Palos Verdes, CA (90274)	36,577	—
Rapid City, SD (57701)	46,492	43,836
Raytown, MO (64133*)	31,759	33,306
Reading, PA (19603*)	78,686	87,643
Redding, CA (96001*)	41,995	16,659
Redlands, CA (92373)	43,619	36,355
Redondo Beach, CA (90277*)	57,102	57,451
Redwood City, CA (94064*)	54,951	55,686
Reno, NV (89510*)	100,756	72,863
Renton, WA (98057*)	30,612	25,878
Revere, MA (02151)	42,423	43,159
Rialto, CA (92376)	37,474	28,370
Richardson, TX (75080*)	72,496	48,405
Richfield, MN (55423)	37,851	47,231
Richland, WA (99352)	33,578	26,290
Richmond, CA (94802*)	74,676	79,043
Richmond, IN (47374)	41,349	43,999
Richmond, VA (23232*)	219,214	249,332
Ridgewood, NJ (07451*)	25,208	27,547
Riverside, CA (92507*)	170,591	140,089
Riviera Beach, FL (33404)	26,489	21,401
Roanoke, VA (24022*)	100,220	92,115
Rochester, MN (55901*)	57,890	53,766
Rochester, NY (14692*)	241,741	295,011
Rockford, IL (61125*)	139,712	147,370
Rock Hill, SC (29730)	35,344	33,846
Rock Island, IL (61201)	47,036	50,166
Rockville, MD (20850*)	43,811	42,739
Rockville Centre, NY (11570)	25,412	27,444
Rocky Mount, NC (27801)	41,283	34,284
Rome, GA (30161)	29,654	30,759
Rome, NY (13440)	43,826	50,148
Rosemead, CA (91770)	42,604	40,972
Roseville, MI (48066)	54,311	60,529
Roseville, MN (55113*)	35,820	34,438
Roswell, NM (88201)	39,676	33,908
Royal Oak, MI (48068*)	70,893	86,238
Sacramento, CA (95813*)	275,741	257,105
Saginaw, MI (48065*)	77,508	91,849
St. Charles, MO (63301)	36,087	31,834
St. Clair Shores, MI (48080*)	76,210	88,093
St. Cloud, MN (56301)	42,566	39,691
St. Joseph, MO (64501*)	76,691	72,748
St. Louis, MO (63155*)	453,085	622,236
St. Louis Park, MN (55426*)	42,931	48,883
St. Paul, MN (55101*)	270,230	309,866
St. Petersburg, FL (33730*)	238,647	216,159
Salem, MA (01970)	38,220	40,556
Salem, OR (97301*)	89,233	68,725
Salina, KS (67401)	41,843	37,714
Salinas, CA (93907*)	80,479	58,896
Salt Lake City, UT (84119*)	163,697	175,885
San Angelo, TX (76902*)	73,240	63,884
San Antonio, TX (78284*)	786,023	654,153
San Bernardino, CA (92403*)	118,794	106,869
San Bruno, CA (94066)	35,417	36,254
San Buenaventura (Ventura), CA (93002*)	74,393	57,964
San Clemente, CA (92672)	27,325	17,063
San Diego, CA (92199*)	875,538	697,471
Sandusky, OH (44870)	31,360	32,674
Sandy City, UT (84070*)	52,210	6,438
San Francisco, CA (94188*)	678,974	715,674
San Gabriel, CA (91776*)	30,072	29,336
San Jose, CA (95101*)	629,546	459,913
San Leandro, CA (94577*)	63,952	68,698
San Luis Obispo, CA (93401)	34,252	28,036
San Mateo, CA (94402*)	77,561	78,991
San Rafael, CA (94901*)	44,700	38,977
Santa Ana, CA (92711*)	204,023	155,710
Santa Barbara, CA (93102*)	74,414	70,215
Santa Clara, CA (95050*)	87,746	86,118
Santa Cruz, CA (95060*)	41,483	32,076
Santa Fe, NM (87501*)	48,953	41,167
Santa Maria, CA (93456*)	39,685	32,749
Santa Monica, CA (90406*)	88,314	88,289
Santa Rosa, CA (95402*)	83,320	50,006
Sarasota, FL (33578*)	48,868	40,237
Saratoga, CA (95070)	29,261	26,810
Savannah, GA (31401*)	141,390	118,349
Sayreville, NJ (08872)	29,969	32,508
Schaumburg, IL (60194)	53,305	18,531
Schenectady, NY (12301*)	67,972	77,958
Scottsdale, AZ (85251*)	88,622	67,823
Scranton, PA (18505*)	88,117	102,696
Seal Beach, CA (90740)	25,975	24,441
Seaside, CA (93955)	36,567	36,883
Seattle, WA (98109*)	493,846	530,831
Selma, AL (36701)	26,684	27,379
Shaker Heights, OH (44120)	32,487	36,306
Shawnee, KS (66202*)	29,653	20,946
Shawnee, OK (74801)	26,506	25,075
Sheboygan, WI (53081)	48,085	48,484
Shelton, CT (06484)	31,314	27,165
Sherman, TX (75090)	30,413	29,061
Shreveport, LA (71102*)	205,820	182,064
Simi Valley, CA (93065*)	77,500	59,832
Sioux City, IA (51101*)	82,003	85,925
Sioux Falls, SD (57101*)	81,343	72,488
Skokie, IL (60076*)	60,278	68,322
Slidell, LA (70458)	26,718	16,101
Somerville, MA (02143)	77,372	88,779
Somerville, NJ (08876)	29,969	32,508
South Bend, IN (46624*)	109,727	125,580
South Euclid, OH (44121)	25,713	29,579
Southfield, MI (48037*)	75,568	69,285
South Gate, CA (90280)	66,784	56,909
Southgate, MI (48195)	32,058	33,909
South San Francisco, CA (94080)	49,393	46,646
Sparks, NV (89431)	40,780	24,187
Spartanburg, SC (29301*)	43,826	44,546
Spokane, WA (99210*)	171,300	170,516
Springfield, IL (62703*)	100,054	91,753
Springfield, MA (01101*)	152,319	163,905
Springfield, MO (65801*)	133,116	120,096
Springfield, OH (45501*)	72,563	81,941

City and major ZIP code	1980 census	1970 census
Springfield, OR (97477*)	41,621	26,874
Stamford, CT (06904*)	102,453	108,798
State College, PA (16801*)	36,130	32,833
Sterling Heights, MI (48077)	108,999	61,365
Steubenville, OH (43952)	26,400	30,771
Stillwater, OK (74074*)	38,268	31,126
Stockton, CA (95208*)	149,779	109,963
Stow, OH (44224)	25,303	20,061
Strongsville, OH (44136)	28,577	15,182
Suffolk, VA (23434*)	47,621	9,858
Sunnyvale, CA (94086*)	106,618	95,976
Sunrise, FL (33338)	39,681	7,403
Superior, WI (54880)	29,571	32,237
Syracuse, NY (13220*)	170,105	197,297
Tacoma, WA (98413*)	158,501	154,407
Tallahassee, FL (32301*)	81,548	72,624
Tamarac, FL (33320)	29,376	5,193
Tampa, FL (33630*)	271,523	277,714
Taunton, MA (02780)	45,001	43,756
Taylor, MI (48180)	77,568	70,020
Tempe, AZ (85282*)	106,743	63,550
Temple, TX (76501*)	42,354	33,431
Temple City, CA (91780)	28,972	31,034
Terre Haute, IN (47808*)	61,125	70,335
Texarkana, TX (75501*)	31,271	30,497
Texas City, TX (77590*)	41,403	38,908
Thornton, CO (80229)	40,343	13,326
Thousand Oaks, CA (91360*)	77,072	35,873
Tinley Park, IL (60477)	26,171	12,572
Titusville, FL (32780)	31,910	30,515
Toledo, OH (43601*)	354,635	383,062
Topeka, KS (66603*)	115,266	125,011
Torrance, CA (90510*)	129,881	134,968
Torrington, CT (06790)	30,987	31,952
Trenton, NJ (08650*)	92,124	104,786
Troy, MI (48099*)	67,102	39,419
Troy, NY (12180*)	56,638	62,918
Tucson, AZ (85726*)	330,537	262,933
Tulsa, OK (74101*)	360,919	330,350
Turlock, CA (95380)	26,287	13,992
Tuscaloosa, AL (35403*)	75,211	65,773
Tustin, CA (92680)	32,317	22,313
Twin Falls, ID (83301)	26,209	21,914
Tyler, TX (75712*)	70,508	57,770
Union City, CA (94587)	39,406	14,724
Union City, NJ (07087)	55,593	57,305
University City, MO (63130)	42,738	47,527
Upland, CA (91786)	47,647	32,551
Upper Arlington, OH (43221)	35,648	38,727
Urbana, IL (61801)	35,978	33,976
Utica, NY (13504*)	75,632	91,373
Vacaville, CA (95688)	43,367	21,690
Valdosta, GA (31601)	37,596	32,303
Vallejo, CA (94590*)	80,303	71,710
Valley Stream, NY (11580*)	35,769	40,413
Vancouver, WA (98661*)	42,834	41,859
Vicksburg, MS (39180)	25,434	25,478
Victoria, TX (77901*)	50,695	41,349
Vineland, NJ (08360)	53,753	47,399
Virginia Beach, VA (23450*)	262,199	172,106
Visalia, CA (93277*)	49,729	27,130
Vista, CA (92083)	35,834	24,688
Waco, TX (76701*)	101,261	95,326
Walla Walla, WA (99362)	25,618	23,619
Walnut Creek, CA (94596*)	53,643	39,844
Waltham, MA (02154)	58,200	61,582
Warner Robins, GA (31093)	39,893	33,491
Warren, MI (48089*)	161,134	179,260
Warren, OH (44481*)	56,629	63,494
Warwick, RI (02887*)	87,123	83,694
Washington, DC (20013*)	638,432	756,668
Waterbury, CT (06701*)	103,266	108,033
Waterloo, IA (50701*)	75,985	75,533
Watertown, NY (13601)	27,861	30,787
Waukegan, IL (60085*)	67,653	65,134
Waukesha, WI (53186)	50,365	39,695
Wausau, WI (54401)	32,426	32,806
Wauwatosa, WI (53213)	51,308	58,676
Weirton, WV (26062)	25,371	27,131
West Allis, WI (53213)	63,982	71,649
West Covina, CA (91793*)	80,291	68,034
Westfield, MA (01085)	36,465	31,433
Westfield, NJ (07091*)	30,447	33,720
West Haven, CT (06516)	53,184	52,851
West Jordan, UT (84084)	27,192	4,221
Westland, MI (48185)	84,603	86,749
West Memphis, AR (72301)	28,138	26,070
West Mifflin, PA (15122)	26,279	28,070
Westminster, CA (92683)	71,133	60,076
Westminster, CO (80030*)	50,211	19,512
West New York, NJ (07093)	39,194	40,627
West Orange, NJ (07052)	39,510	43,715
West Palm Beach, FL (33401*)	63,305	57,375
Wheaton, IL (60187)	43,043	31,138
Wheat Ridge, CO (80033)	30,293	29,778
Wheeling, WV (26003)	43,070	48,188
White Plains, NY (10602*)	46,999	50,346
Whittier, CA (90605*)	69,717	72,863
Wichita, KS (67276*)	279,835	276,554
Wichita Falls, TX (76307*)	94,201	96,265
Wilkes-Barre, PA (18701*)	51,551	58,856
Williamsport, PA (17701)	33,401	37,918
Wilmette, IL (60091)	28,229	32,134
Wilmington, DE (19850*)	70,195	80,386
Wilmington, NC (28402*)	44,000	46,169
Wilson, NC (27893)	34,424	29,347
Winona, MN (55987)	25,075	26,438
Winston-Salem, NC (27102*)	131,885	133,683
Woburn, MA (01801)	36,626	37,406
Woodland, CA (95695)	30,235	20,677
Woonsocket, RI (02895)	45,914	46,820
Worcester, MA (01613*)	161,799	176,572
Wyandotte, MI (48192)	34,006	41,061
Wyoming, MI (49509)	59,616	56,560
Yakima, WA (98903*)	49,826	45,588
Yonkers, NY (10701*)	195,351	204,297
Yorba Linda, CA (92686)	28,254	11,856
York, PA (17405*)	44,619	50,335
Youngstown, OH (44501*)	115,436	140,909
Yuma, AZ (85364*)	42,481	29,007
Zanesville, OH (43701)	28,655	33,045

1. Queens has four major ZIP codes: 11690*—Far Rockaway; 11351*—Flushing; 11431*—Jamaica; 11101*—Long Island City. *Sources:* Department of Commerce, Bureau of the Census; *National ZIP Code & Post Office Directory.*

U.S. Growth Rate Continues To Decline

The average annual growth rate between April 1980 and January 1, 1987, was 9.9 per 1,000 population. This fell below the 10.5 per 1,000 rate during the 1970s and is well below the 12.6 rate of the 1960s and the 17.1 rate for the 1950s which marked the peak of the baby-boom period.

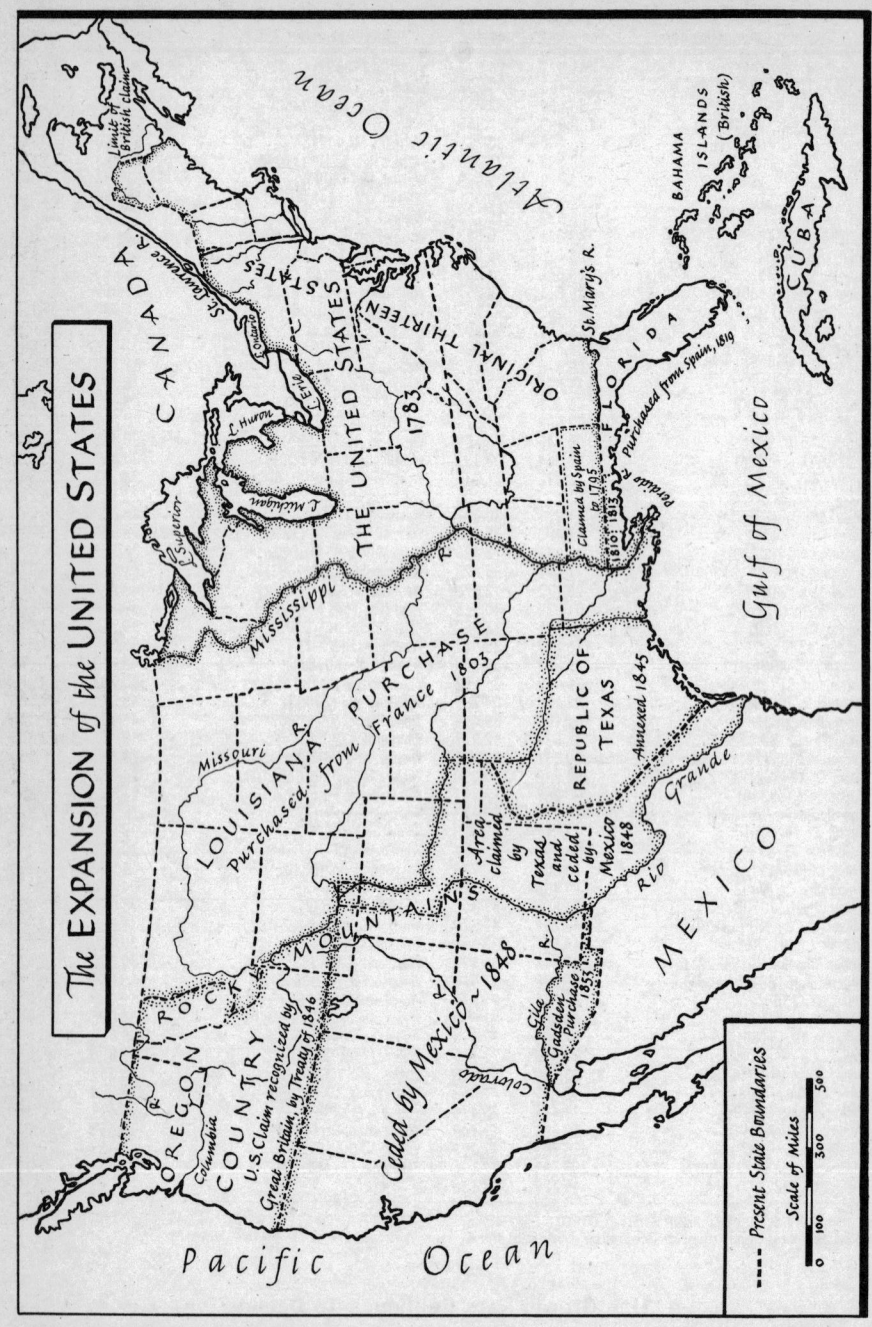

The EXPANSION of the UNITED STATES
Atlantic Ocean
Pacific Ocean
Gulf of Mexico
CANADA
Limit of British claim
St. Lawrence R.
L. Ontario
L. Erie
L. Huron
L. Michigan
L. Superior
THE UNITED STATES
ORIGINAL THIRTEEN STATES
1783
St. Mary's R.
FLORIDA
Purchased from Spain, 1819
Perdido R.
Claimed by Spain to 1795
1810
1813
BAHAMA ISLANDS (British)
CUBA
Mississippi R.
Missouri R.
LOUISIANA PURCHASE
Purchased from France 1803
REPUBLIC OF TEXAS
Annexed 1845
Rio Grande
Area claimed by Texas and ceded by Mexico 1848
ROCKY MOUNTAINS
Ceded by Mexico ~ 1848
Gila R.
Gadsden Purchase 1853
Colorado
MEXICO
OREGON COUNTRY
U.S. Claim recognized by Great Britain, by Treaty of 1846
Columbia R.
Present State Boundaries
Scale of Miles
0
100
300
500

Territorial Expansion

Accession	Date	Area[1]
United States	—	3,618,770
Territory in 1790	—	891,364
Louisiana Purchase	1803	831,321
Florida	1819	69,866
Texas	1845	384,958
Oregon	1846	283,439
Mexican Cession	1848	530,706
Gadsden Purchase	1853	29,640
Alaska	1867	591,004
Hawaii	1898	6,471
Other territory	—	4,664
Philippines	1898	115,600[2]
Puerto Rico	1899	3,515
Guam	1899	209
American Samoa	1900	77
Canal Zone[3]	1904	553
Virgin Islands of U.S.	1917	132
Trust Territory of Pacific Islands	1947	717[4]
All other	—	14
Total, 1980	—	**3,623,434**

1. Total land and water area in square miles. 2. Became independent in 1946. 3. Reverted to Panama. 4. Land area only; includes Northern Mariana Islands. *Source:* Department of Commerce, Bureau of the Census.

Total Population

Area	1960	1970	1980
50 states of U.S.	179,323,175	203,302,031	226,545,805
48 coterminous	178,464,236	202,229,535	225,179,263
Alaska	226,167	302,583	401,851
Hawaii	632,772	769,913	964,691
American Samoa	20,051	27,159	32,297
Canal Zone	42,122	44,198	(1)
Canton Island	320	n.a.	—
Corn Islands	1,872	(2)	—
Guam	67,044	84,996	105,979
Johnston Atoll	156	1,007	327
Midway	2,356	2,220	453
Puerto Rico	2,349,544	2,712,033	3,196,520
Swan Islands	28	22	n.a.
Trust Ter. of Pac. Is.	70,724	90,940	132,929[3]
Virgin Is. of U.S.	32,099	62,468	96,569
Wake Island	1,097	1,647	302
Population abroad	1,374,421	1,737,836	995,546
Armed forces	609,720	1,057,776	515,408
Other[4]	n.a.	n.a.	n.a.
Total	**183,285,009**	**208,066,557**	**231,106,727**

1. Granted independence on Oct. 1, 1979. 2. Returned to Nicaragua April 25, 1971. 3. Includes Northern Mariana Islands. 4. Includes Baker Island, Enderbury Island, Howland Island, and Jarvis Island, all uninhabited. NOTE: n.a. = unavailable. *Source:* Department of Commerce, Bureau of the Census.

Population by Race, 1980 Census

State	White	Black	Spanish origin	Other
Ala.	2,869,688	995,623	33,100	24,750
Alaska	308,455	13,619	9,497	78,407
Ariz.	2,240,033	75,034	440,915	402,799
Ark.	1,890,002	373,192	17,873	22,319
Calif.	18,031,689	1,819,282	4,543,770	3,817,591
Colo.	2,570,596	101,702	339,300	216,517
Conn.	2,799,420	217,433	124,499	90,723
Del.	488,543	95,971	9,671	10,711
D.C.	171,796	488,229	17,652	17,626
Fla.	8,178,387	1,342,478	857,898	219,127
Ga.	3,948,007	1,465,457	61,261	50,801
Hawaii	318,608	17,352	71,479	629,040
Idaho	901,641	2,716	36,615	39,578
Ill.	9,225,575	1,675,229	635,525	517,657
Ind.	5,004,567	414,732	87,020	70,880
Iowa	2,838,805	41,700	25,536	32,882
Kan.	2,167,752	126,127	63,333	69,329
Ky.	3,379,648	259,490	27,403	22,295
La.	2,911,243	1,237,263	99,105	55,466
Me.	1,109,850	3,128	5,005	11,682
Md.	3,158,412	958,050	64,740	99,984
Mass.	5,362,836	221,279	141,043	152,922
Mich.	7,868,956	1,198,710	162,388	190,678
Minn.	3,936,948	53,342	32,124	86,858
Miss.	1,615,190	887,206	24,731	18,242
Mo.	4,346,267	514,274	51,667	56,903
Mont.	740,148	1,786	9,974	44,756
Neb.	1,490,569	48,389	28,020	31,048
Nev.	699,377	50,791	53,786	49,016
N.H.	910,099	3,990	5,587	6,521
N.J.	6,127,090	924,786	491,867	312,282
N.M.	976,465	24,042	476,089	299,461
N.Y.	13,961,106	2,401,842	1,659,245	1,194,340
N.C.	4,453,010	1,316,050	56,607	105,369
N.D.	625,536	2,568	3,903	24,591
Ohio	9,597,266	1,076,734	119,880	123,419
Okla.	2,597,783	204,658	57,413	222,825
Ore.	2,490,192	37,059	65,833	105,412
Pa.	10,654,325	1,047,609	154,004	164,794
R.I.	896,692	27,584	19,707	22,878
S.C.	2,145,122	948,146	33,414	25,940
S.D.	638,955	2,144	4,028	49,079
Tenn.	3,835,078	725,949	34,081	29,723
Tex.	11,197,663	1,710,250	2,985,643	1,320,470
Utah	1,382,550	9,225	60,302	69,262
Vt.	506,736	1,135	3,304	3,585
Va.	4,229,734	1,008,311	79,873	108,234
Wash.	3,777,296	105,544	119,986	247,323
W. Va.	1,874,751	65,051	12,707	9,842
Wis.	4,442,598	182,593	62,981	80,144
Wyo.	447,716	3,364	24,499	19,736
Total	**188,340,790**	**26,488,218**	**14,605,883**	**11,675,817**

Source: Department of Commerce, Bureau of the Census.

Women Are Postponing Marriage

Today's women are marrying later than at any time since the Census Bureau began keeping that data in 1890. The median age of American women marrying for the first time is 23.3 years as opposed to the record low of 20.1 in 1956. This trend has developed as children of the post-World War II generation have opted for education and career over early marriage and children.

Immigration to U.S. by Country of Origin

(Figures are totals, not annual averages, and were tabulated as follows: 1820–67, alien passengers arrived; 1868–91 and 1895–97, immigrant aliens arrived; 1892–94 and 1898 to present, immigrant aliens admitted. Data before 1906 relate to country whence alien came; 1906-80, to country of last permanent residence; 1981 to present data based on country of birth.

Countries	1986	1820–1986	1971-80	1961–70	1951–60	1941–50	1931–40	1820–1930
Europe: Albania[1]	53	2,797	329	98	59	85	2,040	—
Austria[2]	463	4,320,941	9,478	20,621	67,106	24,860	3,563	3,658,978
Belgium	620	206,749	5,329	9,192	18,575	12,189	4,817	153,388
Bulgaria[3]	221	69,369	1,188	619	104	375	938	64,918
Czechoslovakia[1]	1,118	144,831	6,023	3,273	918	8,347	14,393	105,620
Denmark	554	368,068	4,439	9,201	10,984	5,393	2,559	332,466
Estonia[1]	6	1,234	91	163	185	212	506	—
Finland[1]	322	35,931	2,868	4,192	4,925	2,503	2,146	17,447
France	2,518	767,874	25,069	45,237	51,121	38,809	12,623	582,375
Germany[2]	7,127	7,033,204	74,414	190,796	477,765	226,578	114,058	5,907,893
Great Britain: England	13,657	5,036,807	137,374	174,452	156,171	112,252	21,756	2,619,435
Scotland	—	—	—	29,849	32,854	16,131	6,887	726,887
Wales	—	—	—	2,052	2,589	3,209	735	85,659
Not specified[4]	—	—	—	3,675	3,884	—	—	793,741
Greece	2,512	684,313	92,369	85,969	47,608	8,973	9,119	421,489
Hungary[2]	1,006	—	6,550	5,401	36,637	3,469	7,861	473,373
Ireland	1,839	4,699,365	11,490	37,461	57,332	26,967	13,167	4,578,941
Italy	3,089	5,326,818	129,368	214,111	185,491	57,661	68,028	4,651,195
Latvia[1]	26	2,825	207	510	352	361	1,192	—
Lithuania[1]	49	4,204	248	562	242	683	2,201	—
Luxembourg[1]	24	3,065	307	556	684	820	565	—
Netherlands	1,261	368,918	10,492	30,606	52,277	14,860	7,150	246,609
Norway[5]	354	859,487	3,941	15,484	22,935	10,100	4,740	800,115
Poland[6]	8,481	567,810	37,234	53,539	9,985	7,571	17,026	397,729
Portugal	3,766	484,946	101,710	76,065	19,588	7,423	3,329	252,715
Romania[7]	5,198	196,015	12,393	2,531	1,039	1,076	3,871	153,074
Spain	1,591	273,916	34,141	44,659	7,894	2,898	3,258	166,865
Sweden[5]	1,098	1,279,181	6,531	17,116	21,697	10,665	3,960	1,213,488
Switzerland	677	354,523	8,235	18,453	17,675	10,547	5,512	290,168
U.S.S.R.[8]	2,588	3,427,872	38,961	2,336	584	548	1,356	3,341,991
Yugoslavia[3]	2,011	127,599	30,540	20,381	8,225	1,576	5,835	50,952
Other Europe	283	57,748	4,049	4,203	8,155	3,983	2,361	33,699
Total Europe	62,512	36,722,338	800,368	1,123,363	1,325,640	621,124	347,552	32,121,210
Asia: China[9]	25,106	773,520	124,326	34,764	9,657	16,709	4,928	377,245
India	26,227	350,858	164,154	27,189	1,973	1,761	496	9,377
Japan[10]	3,959	439,138	49,775	39,988	46,250	1,555	1,948	275,643
Turkey	1,753	402,224	13,399	10,142	3,519	798	1,065	360,171
Other Asia	211,203	2,951,634	1,236,544	315,688	88,707	11,537	7,644	35,895
Total Asia[11]	268,248	4,917,374	1,588,178	427,771	150,106	32,360	16,081	1,058,331
America: Canada and Newfoundland[12]	11,039	4,205,229	169,939	413,310	377,952	171,718	108,527	2,897,201
Central America	28,380	503,046	134,640	101,330	44,751	21,665	5,861	43,293
Mexico[13]	66,533	2,634,506	640,294	453,937	299,811	60,589	22,319	755,936
South America	41,874	1,014,296	295,741	257,954	91,628	21,831	7,803	113,499
West Indies	101,632	2,304,590	741,126	470,213	123,091	49,725	15,502	431,469
Other America[13]	130	110,026	789	19,630	59,711	29,276	25	31
Total America	249,588	10,771,393	1,982,529	1,716,374	996,944	354,804	160,037	4,241,429
Africa	17,463	251,799	80,779	28,954	14,092	7,367	1,750	24,310
Australia and New Zealand	1,964	134,936	23,788	19,562	11,506	13,805	2,231	52,301
Pacific Islands[14]	141	25,602	1,806	1,769	4,698	5,437	780	10,365
Countries not specified[15]	1,792	298,624	15,866	3,884	12,493	142	—	254,066
Total all countries	**601,708**	**53,122,066**	**4,493,314**	**3,321,677**	**2,515,479**	**1,035,039**	**528,431**	**37,762,012**

1. Countries established since beginning of World War I are included with countries to which they belonged. 2. Data for Austria-Hungary not reported until 1861. Austria and Hungary recorded separately after 1905, Austria included with Germany 1938–45. 3. Bulgaria, Serbia, Montenegro first reported in 1899. Bulgaria reported separately since 1920. In 1920, separate enumeration for Kingdom of Serbs, Croats, Slovenes; since 1922, recorded as Yugoslavia. 4. United Kingdom not specified; for 1901–51, included in "Other Europe." 5. Norway included with Sweden 1820–68. 6. Included with Austria-Hungary, Germany, and Russia 1899–1919. 7. No record of immigration until 1880. 8. From 1931–63, the U.S.S.R. was broken down into European U.S.S.R. and Asian U.S.S.R. Since 1964, total U.S.S.R. has been reported in Europe. 9. Beginning in 1957, China includes Taiwan. 10. No record of immigration until 1861. 11. From 1952, Asia included Philippines. From 1934–51, Philippines were included in Pacific Islands; before 1934, recorded in separate tables as insular travel. 12. Includes all British North American possessions, 1820–98. 13. No record of immigration, 1886–93. 14. Included with "Countries not specified" prior to 1925. 15. Includes 32,897 persons returning in 1906 to their homes in U.S. *Source:* Department of Justice, Immigration and Naturalization Service. NOTE: Data are latest available.

Immigrant and Nonimmigrant Aliens Admitted to U.S.

Period[1]	Immigrants	Non-immigrants	Total	Period[1]	Immigrants	Non-immigrants	Total
1901–10	8,795,386	1,007,909	9,803,295	1979[2]	460,348	7,060,082	7,520,430
1911–20	5,735,811	1,376,271	7,112,082	1980	530,639	n.a.	—
1921–30	4,107,209	1,774,896	5,882,090	1981	596,600	11,756,903	12,353,503
1931–40	528,431	1,574,071	2,102,502	1982	594,131	11,779,359	12,373,490
1941–50	1,035,039	2,461,359	3,496,398	1983[3]	559,763	9,849,458	10,409,221
1951–60	2,515,479	7,113,023	9,628,502	1984	543,903	9,426,759	9,970,662
1961–70	3,321,677	24,107,224	27,428,901	1985	570,009	9,675,650	10,245,659
1971–77	2,797,209	45,236,597	48,033,806	1986	601,708	n.a.	—

1. Fiscal year ending June 30 prior to 1977. After 1977 for fiscal year ending Sept. 30, except as noted. 2. Figures for October 1978–June 1979. 3. Figures for calendar year 1983. Nonimmigrant aliens include visitors for business or pleasure, students, foreign government officials, and others temporarily in the U.S. NOTE: n.a. = not available. *Source:* Department of Justice, Immigration and Naturalization Service.

Persons Naturalized Since 1907

Period[1]	Civilian	Military	Total	Period[1]	Civilian	Military	Total
1907–30	2,713,389	300,506	3,013,895	1981	162,227	4,090	166,317
1931–40	1,498,573	19,891	1,518,464	1982	170,071	3,617	173,688
1941–50	1,837,229	149,799	1,987,028	1983	175,752	3,196	178,948
1951–60	1,148,241	41,705	1,189,946	1984	192,113	2,965	197,023[2]
1961–70	1,084,195	36,068	1,120,263	1985	238,394	3,266	244,717[3]
1971–80	1,397,846	66,926	1,464,772	1907–85	10,618,039	632,029	11,255,061[4]

1. Fiscal year ending June 30. Starting 1977, Fiscal year ending Sept. 30. 2. Including 1,945 unidentified. 3. Including 3,057 unidentified. 4. Including 5,002 unidentified. *Source:* Department of Justice, Immigration and Naturalization Service. NOTE: Data are latest available.

Population of Largest Indian Reservations, 1987

Navajo (Ariz., N.M., Utah)	173,018	Rosebud (S.D.)	11,685[1]	Zuni (N.M.)	8,135
Cherokee (Okla.)	58,232	Gila River (Ariz.)	10,688	Pawnee (Okla.)	7,657
Creek (Okla.)	54,606	Papago-Sells (Ariz.)	10,138	Northern Pueblos (N.M.)	7,651
Choctaw (Okla.)	21,858	Turtle Mountain (N.D.)	9,889	Shawnee (Okla. Texas)	7,263
Pine Ridge (S.D.)	19,246	Hopi (Ariz.)	9,040	Blackfeet (Mont.)	7,193
Southern Pueblos (N.M.)	17,079	Standing Rock (N.D., S.D.)	8,612	Yakima (Wash.)	6,846
Chicksaw (Okla.)	11,780	Fort Apache (Ariz.)	8,421	Wind River (Wyo.)	5,124

NOTE: The Bureau of Indian Affairs lists 861,500 Indians residing on or near Federal reservations as of January 1987. The total Indian population of the United States, according to the 1980 updated census, is 1,534,000, including Aleuts and Eskimos. *Source:* Department of the Interior, Bureau of Indian Affairs. 1. 1984 data.

Persons Below Poverty Level by Age, Region, Race, and Spanish Origin, 1985

Age and region	Number below poverty level (1,000)				Percent below poverty level			
	All races[2]	White	Black	Spanish origin[1]	All races[2]	White	Black	Spanish origin[1]
Under 16 years	11,761	7,472	3,764	2,344	21.2	16.6	44.4	40.4
16 to 21	3,788	2,557	1,076	686	17.1	14.0	33.8	33.0
22 to 44	9,823	7,018	2,381	1,578	11.3	9.5	23.6	23.0
45 to 64	4,236	3,114	988	408	9.5	8.0	22.2	16.8
65 and older	3,456	2,698	717	219	12.6	11.0	31.5	23.9
Northeast	5,751	4,245	1,411	1,241	11.6	9.8	28.0	39.2
Midwest	8,191	5,960	1,980	362	13.9	11.4	35.3	27.4
South	12,921	7,634	5,050	1,588	16.0	11.9	32.7	27.7
West	6,201	5,020	486	2,045	13.0	12.1	20.1	26.0
Total	**33,064**	**22,859**	**8,926**	**5,236**	**14.0**	**11.4**	**31.3**	**29.0**

1. Persons of Spanish origin may be any race. 2. Includes races not shown separately. *Source:* U.S. Bureau of the Census.

Population Projections to 2080[1]

(in millions)

Sex, race, age group	2000	2050	2075	2080
MALE, WHITE	108.8	115.1	112.7	112.2
Up to 19 years	30.5	27.7	26.7	26.5
20 to 39 years	31.2	29.3	28.2	27.9
40 to 59 years	30.5	28.9	28.1	27.8
60 to 79 years	13.8	22.2	22.0	22.2
80 and over	2.8	7.0	7.6	7.6
FEMALE, WHITE	114.0	123.0	119.9	119.4
Up to 19 years	29.0	26.3	25.3	25.2
20 to 39 years	30.2	28.3	27.2	26.9
40 to 59 years	31.1	28.7	27.9	27.6
60 to 79 years	17.4	25.4	24.8	24.9
80 and over	6.3	14.3	14.5	14.5
MALE, BLACK	17.1	25.0	26.5	26.6
Up to 19 years	6.4	6.8	6.6	6.5
20 to 39 years	5.4	7.0	6.9	6.8
40 to 59 years	3.8	6.2	6.7	6.7
60 to 79 years	1.3	4.0	4.8	5.0
80 and over	0.2	1.0	1.4	1.4
FEMALE, BLACK	18.7	27.2	28.8	29.0
Up to 19 years	6.2	6.7	6.5	6.4
20 to 39 years	5.5	7.0	6.8	6.7
40 to 59 years	4.4	6.5	6.9	6.9
60 to 79 years	2.0	4.9	5.7	5.9
80 and over	0.6	2.2	2.9	3.0
TOTALS[2]	268.0	308.8	310.6	310.7
Up to 19 years	74.9	72.1	70.6	70.3
20 to 39 years	75.2	76.3	74.9	74.4
40 to 59 years	72.4	74.9	75.3	74.8
60 to 79 years	35.4	59.8	61.7	62.5
80 and over	10.1	15.7	28.2	28.5
Males	130.4	148.8	149.9	149.9
Females	137.6	160.1	160.7	160.8
White	222.8	238.1	232.6	231.6
Black	35.7	52.1	55.3	55.6
Median age	36.3	41.6	42.6	42.8

1. Based on average of 1.9 lifetime births per woman. 2. Includes all races. NOTE: Zero population growth is expected to be reached by 2050. Details may not add because of rounding. *Source:* Department of Commerce, Bureau of the Census.

Marriage and Divorce

Marriages and Divorces

Year	Marriage Number	Marriage Rate[2]	Divorce[1] Number	Divorce[1] Rate[2]
1900	709,000	9.3	55,751	.7
1905	842,000	10.0	67,976	.8
1910	948,166	10.3	83,045	.9
1915	1,007,595	10.0	104,298	1.0
1920	1,274,476	12.0	170,505	1.6
1925	1,188,334	10.3	175,449	1.5
1930	1,126,856	9.2	195,961	1.6
1935	1,327,000	10.4	218,000	1.7
1940	1,595,879	12.1	264,000	2.0
1945	1,612,992	12.2	485,000	3.5
1949	1,579,798	10.6	397,000	2.7
1950	1,667,231	11.1	385,144	2.6
1951	1,594,694	10.4	381,000	2.5
1952	1,539,318	9.9	392,000	2.5
1953	1,546,000	9.8	390,000	2.5
1954	1,490,000	9.2	379,000	2.4
1955	1,531,000	9.3	377,000	2.3
1956	1,585,000	9.5	382,000	2.3
1957	1,518,000	8.9	381,000	2.2
1958	1,451,000	8.4	368,000	2.1
1959	1,494,000	8.5	395,000	2.2
1960	1,523,000	8.5	393,000	2.2
1961	1,548,000	8.5	414,000	2.3
1962	1,577,000	8.5	413,000	2.2
1963	1,654,000	8.8	428,000	2.3
1964	1,725,000	9.0	450,000	2.4
1965	1,800,000	9.3	479,000	2.5
1966	1,857,000	9.5	499,000	2.5
1967	1,927,000	9.7	523,000	2.6
1968	2,069,258	10.4	584,000	2.9
1969	2,145,438	10.6	639,000	3.2
1970	2,158,802	10.6	708,000	3.5
1971	2,190,481	10.6	773,000	3.7
1972	2,282,154	11.0	845,000	4.1
1973	2,284,108	10.9	915,000	4.4
1974	2,229,667	10.5	977,000	4.6
1975	2,152,662	10.1	1,036,000	4.9
1976	2,154,807	10.0	1,083,000	5.0
1977	2,178,367	10.1	1,091,000	5.0
1978	2,282,272	10.5	1,130,000	5.2
1979	2,341,799	10.6	1,181,000	5.4
1980	2,406,708	10.6	1,182,000	5.2
1981	2,438,000	10.6	1,219,000	5.3
1982	2,495,000	10.8	1,180,000	5.1
1983	2,444,000	10.5	1,179,000	5.0
1984	2,487,000	10.5	1,155,000	4.9
1985	2,425,000	10.2	1,187,000	5.0
1986[3]	2,400,000	10.0	1,159,000	4.8

1. Includes annulments. 2. Per 1,000 population. Divorce rates for 1941–46 are based on population including armed forces overseas. Marriage rates are based on population excluding armed forces overseas. 3. Provisional. NOTE: Marriage and divorce figures for most years include some estimated data. Alaska is included beginning 1959, Hawaii beginning 1960. *Source:* Department of Health and Human Services, National Center for Health Statistics.

Percent of Population Ever Married

Age group, years[1]	1986	1980	1970	1960	1950	1940	1930	1920	1910	1900
Males: 15 to 19	1.7	2.7	2.6	3.3	2.9	1.5	1.5	1.8	1.0	0.9
20 to 24	24.5	31.2	45.3	46.9	41.0	27.8	29.0	29.1	24.7	22.2
25 to 29	58.6	67.0	80.9	79.2	76.2	64.0	63.2	60.5	57.1	54.1
30 to 34	77.8	84.1	90.6	88.1	86.8	79.3	78.8	75.8	73.9	72.3
35 to 44	90.0	92.5	93.3	91.9	90.4	86.0	85.7	83.8	83.3	83.0
45 to 54	94.1	93.9	92.5	92.6	91.5	88.9	88.6	88.0	88.8	89.7
Females: 15 to 19	5.8	8.8	9.7	13.5	14.4	10.0	10.9	10.8	9.8	9.4
20 to 24	42.1	49.8	64.2	71.6	67.7	52.8	53.9	54.4	51.5	48.4
25 to 29	71.9	79.1	89.5	89.5	86.7	77.2	78.3	76.9	75.0	72.4
30 to 34	85.8	90.5	93.8	93.1	90.7	85.3	86.8	85.1	83.8	83.4
35 to 44	92.9	94.5	94.8	93.9	91.7	89.6	90.0	88.6	88.6	88.9
45 to 54	95.3	95.3	95.1	93.0	92.2	91.3	90.9	90.4	91.4	92.2

1. Prior to 1980 data are for persons 14 years and older. *Source:* Department of Commerce, Bureau of the Census.

Persons Living Alone, by Sex and Age

(numbers in thousands)

	1986		1980		1975		1970		1960	
Sex and age[1]	Number	Percent	Number	Percent	Number	Percent	Number	Percent	Number	Percent
BOTH SEXES										
15 to 24 years	1,388	6.6	1,726	9.4	1,111	8.0	556	5.1	234	3.3
25 to 44 years	6,523	30.8	4,729	25.8	2,744	19.7	1,604	14.8	1,212	17.2
45 to 64 years	4,949	23.4	4,514	24.7	4,076	29.2	3,622	33.4	2,720	38.5
65 years and over	8,318	39.3	7,328	40.1	6,008	43.1	5,071	46.7	2,898	41.0
Total, 15 years and over	**21,178**	**100.0**	**18,296**	**100.0**	**13,939**	**100.0**	**10,851**	**100.0**	**7,063**	**100.0**
MALE										
15 to 24 years	735	8.9	947	13.6	610	4.4	274	2.5	124	1.8
25 to 44 years	3,952	47.7	2,920	41.9	1,689	12.1	933	8.6	686	9.7
45 to 64 years	1,918	23.2	1,613	23.2	1,329	9.5	1,152	10.6	965	13.7
65 years and over	1,681	20.3	1,486	21.3	1,290	9.3	1,174	10.8	853	12.1
Total, 15 years and over	**8,285**	**100.0**	**6,966**	**100.0**	**4,918**	**35.3**	**3,532**	**32.5**	**2,628**	**37.2**
FEMALE										
15 to 24 years	654	5.1	779	6.9	501	3.6	282	2.6	110	1.6
25 to 44 years	2,571	19.9	1,809	16.0	1,055	7.6	671	6.2	526	7.4
45 to 64 years	3,031	23.5	2,901	25.6	2,747	19.7	2,470	22.8	1,755	24.8
65 years and over	6,636	51.5	5,842	51.6	4,718	33.8	3,897	35.9	2,045	29.0
Total, 15 years and over	**12,893**	**100.0**	**11,330**	**100.0**	**9,021**	**64.7**	**7,319**	**67.5**	**4,436**	**62.8**

1. Prior to 1980, data are for persons 14 years and older. *Source:* Department of Commerce, Bureau of the Census.

Characteristics of Unmarried-Couple Households, 1986

(number in thousands)

Characteristics	Number	Percent
Unmarried-couple households	2,220	100.0
Age of Householders:		
Under 25 years	489	22.0
25–44 years	1,344	60.5
45–64 years	277	12.5
65 years and over	110	5.0

Characteristics	Number	Percent
Presence of children:		
No children under 15 years	1,558	70.2
Some children under 15 years	662	29.8
Sex of householders:		
Male	1,361	61.3
Female	860	38.7

Source: U.S. Bureau of the Census.

Households, Families, and Married Couples

Date	Households: Number	Households: Average population per household	Families: Number	Families: Average population per family	Married couples: Number
June 1890	12,690,000	4.93	—	—	—
April 1930	29,905,000	4.11	—	—	25,174,000
April 1940	34,949,000	3.67	32,166,000	3.76	28,517,000
April 1950	43,554,000	3.37	39,303,000	3.54	36,091,000
April 1955	47,874,000	3.33	41,951,000	3.59	37,556,000
March 1960[1]	52,799,000	3.33	45,111,000	3.67	40,200,000
March 1965	57,436,000	3.29	47,956,000	3.70	42,478,000
March 1970	63,401,000	3.14	51,586,000	3.58	45,373,000
March 1975	71,120,000	2.94	55,712,000	3.42	47,547,000
March 1980	80,776,000	2.76	59,550,000	3.29	49,714,000
March 1983	83,918,000	2.73	61,393,000	3.26	50,666,000
March 1984	85,407,000	2.71	61,997,000	3.24	50,864,000
March 1985	86,789,000	2.69	62,706,000	3.23	51,114,000
March 1986	88,458,000	2.67	63,558,000	3.21	51,704,000

1. First year in which figures for Alaska and Hawaii are included. *Source:* Department of Commerce, Bureau of the Census.

Families Maintained by Women, With No Husband Present

(numbers in thousands)

	1986		1980		1975		1970		1960	
	Number	Percent	Number	Percent	Number	Percent	Number	Percent	Number	Percent
Age of women:										
Under 35 years	3,379	33.1	3,015	34.6	2,356	32.5	1,364	24.4	796	17.7
35 to 44 years	2,641	25.9	1,916	22.0	1,510	20.9	1,074	19.2	940	20.9
45 to 64 years	2,751	26.9	2,514	28.9	2,266	31.3	2,021	36.1	1,731	38.5
65 years and over	1,440	14.1	1,260	14.5	1,108	15.3	1,131	20.2	1,027	22.9
Median age	41.1	—	41.7	—	43.4	—	48.5	—	50.1	—
Presence of children:										
No own children under 18 years	4,106	40.2	3,260	37.4	2,838	39.2	2,665	47.7	2,397	53.3
With own children under 18 years	6,105	59.8	5,445	62.6	4,404	60.8	2,926	52.3	2,097	46.7
Total own children under 18 years	10,840	—	10,204	—	9,227	—	6,694	—	4,674	—
Average per family	1.06	—	1.17	—	1.27	—	1.20	—	1.04	—
Average per family with children	1.78	—	1.87	—	2.10	—	2.29	—	2.24	—
Race:										
White	7,111	69.6	6,052	69.5	5,212	72.0	4,165	74.5	3,547	78.9
Black[1]	2,874	28.1	2,495	28.7	1,940	26.8	1,382	24.7	947	21.1
Other	226	2.2	158	1.8	90	1.2	44	0.8	n.a.	n.a.
Marital status:										
Married, husband absent	1,792	17.5	1,769	20.3	1,647	22.7	1,326	23.7	1,099	24.5
Widowed	2,631	25.8	2,570	29.5	2,559	35.3	2,396	42.9	2,325	51.7
Divorced	3,824	37.4	3,008	34.6	2,110	29.1	1,259	22.5	694	15.4
Single	1,963	19.2	1,359	15.6	926	12.8	610	10.9	376	8.4
Total families maintained by women	**10,211**	**100.0**	**8,705**	**100.0**	**7,242**	**100.0**	**5,591**	**100.0**	**4,494**	**100.0**

1. Includes other races in 1960. NOTE: n.a. = not available. (—) as shown in this table, means "not applicable." *Source:* Department of Commerce, Bureau of the Census.

Median Age at First Marriage

Year	Males	Females	Year	Males	Females	Year	Males	Females	Year	Males	Females
1900	25.9	21.9	1930	24.3	21.3	1960	22.8	20.3	1984	25.4	23.0
1910	25.1	21.6	1940	24.3	21.5	1970	23.2	20.8	1985	25.5	23.3
1920	24.6	21.2	1950	22.8	20.3	1980	24.7	22.0	1986	25.7	23.1

Source: Department of Commerce, Bureau of the Census.

Selected Family Characteristics

Characteristics[1]	1985 Number (thousands)	1985 Median income
ALL RACES		
All families	63,558	27,735
Type of residence		
Nonfarm	61,996	27,881
Farm	1,562	21,853
Location of residence		
Inside metropolitan areas	48,746	30,045
1,000,000 or more	26,417	31,919
Inside central cities	10,405	25,158
Outside central cities	16,012	36,211
Under 1,000,000	22,329	27,934
Inside central cities	8,595	25,528
Outside central cities	13,734	29,490
Outside metropolitan areas	14,812	21,956
Region		
Northeast	13,175	30,544
North Central	15,771	27,930
South	22,183	25,077
West	12,429	29,778
Type of family		
Married-couple family	50,933	31,100
Wife in paid labor force	27,489	36,431
Wife not in paid labor force	23,445	24,556
Male householder, no wife present	2,414	22,622
Female householder, no husband present	10,211	13,660
Number of earners[2]	62,636	27,843
No earners	9,162	12,073
1 earner	18,217	21,190
2 earners	26,350	33,411
3 earners	6,338	41,805
4 earners	2,568	51,229
Size of family		
2 persons	25,472	23,132
3 persons	15,400	29,265
4 persons	13,355	32,777
5 persons	6,106	31,794
6 persons	2,044	30,819
7 persons or more	1,181	27,473
Occupation group of longest[4] job of householder	48,335	31,966
Executives, administrators and managerial	6,807	46,448
Professional specialty	5,910	44,207
Technical and related support	1,305	36,659
Sales	5,367	34,793
Administrative support, including clerical	4,282	28,695
Precision production, craft and repair	9,270	31,077
Machine operators, assemblers and inspectors	3,901	27,009
Transportation and material moving	3,020	28,499
Handlers, equipment cleaners, helpers, laborers	1,880	22,716
Service workers		
Private household	185	9,418
Other	4,472	21,723
Farming, forestry and fishing	1,900	17,749

Characteristics	1985 Number (thousands)	1985 Median income
Tenure status		
Owner occupied	45,489	32,199
Renter occupied	17,146	17,796
Occupier paid no cash rent	923	17,031
Educational attainment of householder		
Elementary	8,066	15,370
High school	29,156	25,419
College		
1 to 3 years	10,217	32,177
4 years or more	12,944	46,423
4 years	7,075	43,187
5 years or more	5,869	50,525
Total, 25 years and over	60,384	28,672
WHITE		
All families	54,991	29,152
Type of residence		
Nonfarm	53,457	29,359
Farm	1,534	21,903
Location of residence		
Inside metropolitan areas	41,538	31,575
1,000,000 or more	21,706	34,229
Inside central cities	7,160	28,777
Outside central cities	14,546	36,739
Under 1,000,000	19,832	29,160
Inside central cities	7,001	27,385
Outside central cities	12,832	30,056
Outside metropolitan areas	13,453	22,839
Region		
Northeast	11,654	31,491
North Central	14,200	28,964
South	18,211	27,104
West	10,897	30,239
Type of family		
Married-couple families	45,924	31,602
Wife in paid labor force	24,305	36,992
Wife not in paid labor force	21,618	25,307
Male householder, no wife present	1,956	24,190
Female householder, no husband present	7,111	15,825
Number of earners[2]	54,267	29,253
No earners	7,704	13,682
1 earner	15,468	22,884
2 earners	23,304	34,084
3 earners	5,564	42,821
4 earners or more	2,227	52,382
BLACK		
All families	6,921	16,786
Type of residence		
Nonfarm	6,901	16,805
Farm	20	(B)
Location of residence		
Inside metropolitan areas	5,803	17,772
1,000,000 or more	3,747	19,286
Inside central cities	2,743	16,835
Outside central cities	1,004	26,667
Under 1,000,000	2,056	15,683
Inside central cities	1,399	14,999
Outside central cities	658	17,057

Characteristics[1]	1985 Number (thousands)	1985 Median income
Outside metropolitan areas	1,118	12,357
Region		
Northeast	1,252	18,085
North Central	1,368	15,956
South	3,710	15,816
West	591	24,453
Type of family		
Married-couple families	3,680	24,570
Wife in paid labor force	2,359	30,502
Wife not in paid labor force	1,320	15,129
Male householder, no wife present	368	16,416
Female householder, no husband present	2,874	9,305
Number of earners[2]	6,767	16,665
No earners	1,299	5,733
1 earner	2,304	12,624
2 earners	2,345	26,963
3 earners	577	34,010
4 earners or more	241	39,229
SPANISH ORIGIN OF HOUSEHOLDER[3]		
All families	4,206	19,027
Type of residence		
Nonfarm	4,188	19,065
Farm	18	(B)

Characteristics	1985 Number (thousands)	1985 Median income
Location of residence		
Inside metropolitan areas	3,849	19,349
1,000,000 or more	2,704	19,661
Inside central cities	1,652	16,721
Outside central cities	1,052	25,266
Under 1,000,000	1,145	18,097
Inside central cities	681	16,658
Outside central cities	465	20,635
Outside metropolitan areas	357	15,827
Region		
Northeast	803	15,309
North Central	291	22,306
South	1,376	19,139
West	1,737	19,998
Type of family		
Married-couple families	2,962	22,269
Wife in paid labor force	1,453	28,132
Wife not in paid labor force	1,509	17,116
Male householder, no wife present	264	19,773
Female householder, no husband present	980	8,792
Number of earners[2]	4,164	19,081
No earners	602	6,167
1 earner	1,408	14,939
2 earners	1,592	24,596
3 earners	378	32,449
4 earners or more	184	42,140

1. Family data are as of March 1986. 2. Excludes families with members in the Armed Forces. 3. Persons of Spanish origin may be of any race. 4. Includes persons whose longest job was in the Armed Forces. (B) Base less than 75,000. Statistics not given because of unreliability. *Source:* Department of Commerce, Bureau of the Census. NOTE: Data are the latest available.

Births

Live Births and Birth Rates

Year	Births[1]	Rate[2]	Year	Births[1]	Rate[2]	Year	Births[1]	Rate[2]
1910	2,777,000	30.1	1953[3]	3,965,000	25.1	1970[3]	3,731,386	18.4
1915	2,965,000	29.5	1954[3]	4,078,000	25.3	1971[3]	3,555,970	17.2
1920	2,950,000	27.7	1955	4,104,000	25.0	1972	3,258,411	15.6
1925	2,909,000	25.1	1956[3]	4,218,000	25.2	1973	3,136,965	14.9
1930	2,618,000	21.3	1957[3]	4,308,000	25.3	1974	3,159,958	14.9
1935	2,377,000	18.7	1958[3]	4,255,000	24.5	1975	3,144,198	14.8
1940	2,559,000	19.4	1959[3]	4,295,000	24.3	1976	3,167,788	14.8
1943	3,104,000	22.7	1960[3]	4,257,850	23.7	1977	3,326,632	15.4
1944	2,939,000	21.2	1961[3]	4,268,326	23.3	1978	3,333,279	15.3
1945	2,858,000	20.4	1962[3]	4,167,362	22.4	1979	3,494,398	15.9
1946	3,411,000	24.1	1963[3]	4,098,020	21.7	1980	3,612,258	15.9
1947	3,817,000	26.6	1964[3]	4,027,490	21.0	1982	3,680,537	15.9
1948	3,637,000	24.9	1965[3]	3,760,358	19.4	1983	3,638,933	15.5
1949	3,649,000	24.5	1966[3]	3,606,274	18.4	1984	3,669,141	15.5
1950	3,632,000	24.1	1967[4]	3,520,959	17.8	1985	3,749,000	15.7
1951[3]	3,823,000	24.9	1968[3]	3,501,564	17.5	1986	3,731,000	15.5
1952[3]	3,913,000	25.1	1969[3]	3,600,206	17.8			

1. Figures through 1959 include adjustment for underregistration; beginning 1960, figures represent number registered. For comparison, the 1959 registered count was 4,245,000. 2. Rates are per 1,000 population estimated as of July 1 for each year except 1940, 1950, 1960, 1970, and 1980, which are as of April 1, the census date; for 1942–46 based on population including armed forces overseas. 3. Based on 50% sample of births. 4. Based on a 20 to 50% sample of births. 5. Provisional. NOTE: Alaska is included beginning 1959; Hawaii beginning 1960. Since 1972, based on 100% of births in selected states and on 50% sample in all other states. *Sources:* Department of Health and Human Services, National Center for Health Statistics.

Live Births by Age of Mother

Year[1] and race	Total	Age of mother: Under 15 yr	15–19 yr	20–24 yr	25–29 yr	30–34 yr	35–39 yr	40–44 yr	45 yr and over
1940	2,558,647	3,865	332,667	799,537	693,268	431,468	222,015	68,269	7,558
1945	2,858,449	4,028	298,868	832,746	785,299	554,906	296,852	78,853	6,897
1950	3,631,512	5,413	432,911	1,155,167	1,041,360	610,816	302,780	77,743	5,322
1955	4,014,112	6,181	493,770	1,290,939	1,133,155	732,540	352,320	89,777	5,430
1960	4,257,850	6,780	586,966	1,426,912	1,092,816	687,722	359,908	91,564	5,182
1965	3,760,358	7,768	590,894	1,337,350	925,732	529,376	282,908	81,716	4,614
1970	3,731,386	11,752	644,708	1,418,874	994,904	427,806	180,244	49,952	3,146
1975	3,144,198	12,642	582,238	1,093,676	936,786	375,500	115,409	26,319	1,628
1980	3,612,258	10,169	552,161	1,226,200	1,108,291	550,354	140,793	23,090	1,200
1981	3,629,238	9,632	527,392	1,212,000	1,128,188	581,454	146,056	23,326	1,190
1982	3,680,537	9,773	513,758	1,205,979	1,151,934	605,273	167,920	24,664	1,236
1983	3,638,933	9,752	489,286	1,160,274	1,147,720	624,516	180,353	25,882	1,150
1984	3,669,141	9,965	469,682	1,141,578	1,165,711	658,496	195,755	26,846	1,108
White	2,923,502	3,959	320,953	898,919	969,061	549,595	159,246	20,974	795
Black	592,745	5,720	134,392	203,562	147,111	73,858	24,028	3,906	168
Other	152,894	286	14,337	39,097	49,539	35,043	12,481	1,966	145

1. Data for 1940–55 are adjusted for underregistration. Beginning 1960, registered births only are shown. Data for 1960–70 based on a 50% sample of births. Since 1972, based on 100% of births in selected states and on 50% sample in all other states. Beginning 1960, including Alaska and Hawaii. NOTE: Data refer only to births occurring within the U.S. Figures are shown to the last digit as computed for convenience in summation. They are not assumed to be accurate to the last digit. Figures for age of mother not stated are distributed. *Sources:* Department of Commerce, Bureau of the Census; and Department of Health and Human Services, National Center for Health Statistics. NOTE: Data are latest available.

Births to Unmarried Women

(in thousands, except as indicated)

Age and race	1984	1980	1975	1970	1965	1960	1955	1950	1940
By age of mother:									
Under 15 years	9.0	9.0	11.0	9.5	6.1	4.6	3.9	3.2	2.1
15–19 years	261.1	262.8	222.5	190.4	123.1	87.1	68.9	56.0	40.5
20–24 years	279.2	237.3	134.0	126.7	90.7	68.0	55.7	43.1	27.2
25–29 years	137.0	99.6	50.2	40.6	36.8	32.1	28.0	20.9	10.5
30–34 years	59.3	41.0	19.8	19.1	19.6	18.9	16.1	10.8	5.2
35–39 years	20.9	13.2	8.1	9.4	11.4	10.6	8.3	6.0	3.0
40 years and over	3.8	2.9	2.3	3.0	3.7	3.0	2.4	1.7	1.0
By race:									
White	391.9	320.1	186.4	175.1	123.7	82.5	64.2	53.5	40.3
Black and other	378.4	345.7	261.6	223.6	167.5	141.8	119.2	88.1	49.2
Total of above births	**770.3**	**665.8**	**447.9**	**398.7**	**291.2**	**224.3**	**183.4**	**141.6**	**89.5**
Percent of all births[1]	21.0	18.4	14.2	10.7	7.7	5.3	4.5	3.9	3.5
Rate[2]	31.0	29.4	24.8	26.4	23.4	21.8	19.3	14.1	7.1

1. Through 1955, based on data adjusted for underregistration; thereafter, registered births. 2. Rate per 1,000 unmarried (never married, widowed, and divorced) women, 15–44 years old. *Sources:* Department of Health and Human Services, National Center for Health Statistics. NOTE: Data are latest available.

Baby-Boomers Come of Age

The social stigma of living out-of-wedlock has become a thing of the past. The social acceptance and increasing popularity of cohabitation can be seen in a recent survey. The Census Bureau reports that the number of unwed couples has risen from 523, 000 in 1970 to 2,220,000 in 1986.

Most of these couples are young (65% under 34) and have never been married (52%), but many have been divorced (34%). They tend to be more educated than the general population and put education and career before marriage and family. Some will later marry, but in the meantime, they all enjoy the emotional security the arrangement provides, without the legal or economic restrictions of marriage.

These figures reflect a change here but they are low by European standards. In Sweden, for example, cohabitation is four times as popular as it is in the U.S.

Live Births and Birth Rates

State	1985[1] number	1985[1] rate	1984[1] number	1984[1] rate	State	1985[1] number	1985[1] rate	1984[1] number	1984[1] rate
Alabama	58,807	14.6	58,604	14.7	Montana	13,236	16.0	13,846	16.8
Alaska	12,570	24.1	12,247	24.5	Nebraska	25,688	16.0	26,483	16.5
Arizona	58,829	18.5	54,821	18.0	Nevada	15,357	16.4	15,276	16.8
Arkansas	35,079	14.9	33,440	14.2	New Hampshire	15,724	15.8	12,656	13.0
California	470,733	17.9	455,075	17.8	New Jersey	103,308	13.7	97,488	13.0
Colorado	55,319	17.1	54,471	17.1	New Mexico	28,904	19.9	26,285	18.5
Connecticut	36,878	11.6	39,237	12.4	New York	256,049	14.4	251,062	14.2
Delaware	9,843	15.8	9,487	15.5	North Carolina	89,859	14.4	86,705	14.1
D.C.	20,541	32.8	19,123	30.7	North Dakota	12,717	18.6	12,738	18.6
Florida	163,560	14.4	155,236	14.1	Ohio	160,898	15.0	159,939	14.9
Georgia	99,792	16.7	91,761	15.7	Oklahoma	51,910	15.7	53,425	16.2
Hawaii	18,228	17.3	18,658	18.0	Oregon	40,448	15.1	39,536	14.8
Idaho	17,492	17.4	17,072	17.1	Pennsylvania	162,286	13.7	159,911	13.4
Illinois	177,803	15.4	175,907	15.3	Rhode Island	13,517	14.0	13,219	13.7
Indiana	80,774	14.7	79,134	14.4	South Carolina	49,300	14.7	48,215	14.6
Iowa	42,084	14.6	42,611	14.6	South Dakota	12,253	17.3	12,383	17.5
Kansas	38,957	15.9	38,570	15.8	Tennessee	70,547	14.8	70,407	14.9
Kentucky	51,710	13.9	51,964	14.0	Texas	314,981	19.2	306,192	19.2
Louisiana	81,136	18.1	83,195	18.6	Utah	38,431	23.4	39,677	24.0
Maine	16,211	13.9	16,513	14.3	Vermont	7,925	14.8	7,419	14.0
Maryland	60,019	13.7	58,790	13.5	Virginia	83,184	14.6	79,342	14.1
Massachusetts	82,872	14.2	79,386	13.7	Washington	76,205	17.3	73,605	16.9
Michigan	134,090	14.8	134,517	14.8	West Virginia	25,589	13.2	25,059	12.8
Minnesota	66,270	15.8	65,788	15.8	Wisconsin	73,085	15.3	73,088	15.3
Mississippi	42,385	16.2	42,695	16.4	Wyoming	8,838	17.4	9,026	17.7
Missouri	77,186	15.3	78,517	15.7	**Total**	**3,759,407**	**15.8**	**3,697,000**	**15.7**

1. Provisional. NOTE: Based on 100% of births in selected states and 50% sample in others. Rates are per 1,000 population. *Source:* Department of Health and Human Services, National Center for Health Statistics.

Live Births by Race or National Origin

Race	1984	1983	Race	1984	1983
White	2,923,502	2,904,250	Chinese	16,186	14,354
Black	592,745	586,027	Filipino	19,864	17,676
American Indian[1]	41,451	41,571	Other[2]	63,828	66,383
Japanese	9,350	8,672	**Total[3]**	**3,669,141**	**3,638,933**

1. Includes Eskimos and Aleuts. 2. Hawaiian and other Asian or Pacific Islander. 3. Includes births of other races not shown separately. Data are latest available. *Source:* Department of Health and Human Services, National Center for Health Statistics.

Live Births by Sex and Sex Ratio[1]

Year	Total[2]			White			Black		
	Male	Female	Males per 1,000 females	Male	Female	Males per 1,000 females	Male	Female	Males per 1,000 females
1970[3]	1,915,378	1,816,008	1,055	1,590,140	1,501,124	1,059	290,508	281,854	1,031
1976[4]	1,624,436	1,543,352	1,053	1,319,717	1,247,897	1,058	260,661	253,818	1,027
1977[4]	1,705,916	1,620,716	1,053	1,383,440	1,307,630	1,058	275,556	268,665	1,026
1978[4]	1,709,394	1,623,885	1,053	1,378,222	1,302,894	1,058	279,598	271,942	1,028
1979[4]	1,791,267	1,703,131	1,052	1,442,981	1,365,439	1,057	293,013	284,842	1,029
1980[4]	1,852,616	1,759,642	1,053	1,490,140	1,408,592	1,058	299,033	290,583	1,029
1981[4]	1,860,272	1,768,966	1,052	1,494,451	1,414,232	1,057	297,864	289,923	1,027
1982[4]	1,885,676	1,794,861	1,051	1,509,704	1,432,350	1,054	301,121	291,520	1,033
1983[4]	1,865,553	1,773,380	1,052	1,492,385	1,411,865	1,057	297,011	289,016	1,028
1984[4]	1,879,490	1,789,651	1,050	1,500,326	1,423,176	1,054	300,951	291,794	1,031

1. Excludes births to nonresidents of U.S. 2. Includes races other than white and black. 3. Based on 50% sample of births. 4. Based on 100% of births for selected states and 50% sample in all others. *Source:* Department of Health and Human Services, National Center for Health Statistics. NOTE: Data are latest available.

Mortality

Death Rates for Selected Causes

Cause of death	Death rates per 100,000							
	1985[1]	1984	1980	1950	1945–49	1940–44	1920–24	1900–04
Typhoid fever	n.a.	—	0.0	0.1	0.2	0.6	7.3	26.7
Communicable diseases of childhood	n.a.	n.a.	0.0	1.3	2.3	4.6	33.8	65.2
Measles	—	—	0.0	0.3	0.6	1.1	7.3	10.0
Scarlet fever	n.a.	0.0	0.0	0.2	0.1	0.4	4.0	11.8
Whooping cough	—	—	0.0	0.7	1.0	2.2	8.9	10.7
Diphtheria	n.a.	—	0.0	0.3	0.7	1.0	13.7	32.7
Pneumonia and influenza	27.9	25.0	23.3	31.3	41.3	63.7	140.3	184.3
Influenza	0.8	0.6	1.1	4.4	5.0	13.0	34.8	22.8
Pneumonia	27.1	24.4	22.0	26.9	37.2	50.7	105.5	161.5
Tuberculosis	0.7	0.8	0.8	22.5	33.3	43.4	96.7	184.7
Cancer	191.7	191.6	182.5	139.8	134.0	123.1	86.9	67.7
Diabetes mellitus	16.2	15.6	15.0	16.2	24.1	26.2	17.1	12.2
Major cardiovascular diseases	410.7	412.9	434.5	510.8	493.1	490.4	369.9	359.5
Diseases of the heart	325.0	324.4	335.2	356.8	325.1	303.2	169.8	153.0
Cerebrovascular diseases	64.0	65.6	74.6	104.0	93.8	91.7	93.5	106.3
Nephritis and nephrosis	9.4	8.5	7.6	16.4	48.4	72.1	81.5	84.3
Syphilis	0.0	0.0	0.1	5.0	8.4	12.7	17.6	12.9
Appendicitis	0.2	0.2	0.3	2.0	3.5	7.2	14.0	9.4
Accidents, all forms	38.6	40.1	46.0	60.6	67.6	73.0	70.8	79.2
Motor vehicle accidents	18.8	19.6	23.0	23.1	22.3	22.7	12.9	n.a.
Infant mortality[2]	10.6	10.7	12.5	29.2	33.3	42.4	76.7	n.a.
Neonatal mortality[2]	n.a.	7.0	8.4	20.5	22.9	26.2	39.7	n.a.
Fetal mortality[2]	n.a.	8.2	n.a.	22.9	24.3	28.5	39.2[3]	n.a.
Maternal mortality[2]	n.a.	0.0	0.1	0.8	1.4	2.8	6.9	n.a.
All causes	**874.8**	**866.8**	**874.2**	**963.8**	**1,003.3**	**1,062.0**	**1,196.6**	**1,621.6**

1. Based on a 10% sample of deaths. 2. Rates per 1,000 live births. 3. 1922–24. NOTE: Includes only deaths occurring within the registration areas. Beginning with 1940, area includes the entire United States; beginning with 1960, Alaska and Hawaii are included. Rates per 100,000 population residing in areas, enumerated as of April 1 for 1940, 1950 and 1980 and estimated as of July 1 for all other years. Due to changes in statistical methods, death rates are not strictly comparable. n.a. = not available. *Source:* Department of Health and Human Services, National Center for Health Statistics.

Accident Rates, 1985

Class of accident		One every	Class of accident		One every
All accidents	Deaths	6 minutes	Workers off-job	Deaths	15 minutes
	Injuries	4 seconds		Injuries	12 seconds
Motor-vehicle	Deaths	12 minutes	Home	Deaths	26 minutes
	Injuries	19 seconds		Injuries	10 seconds
Work	Deaths	45 minutes	Public non-motor-vehicle	Deaths	28 minutes
	Injuries	16 seconds		Injuries	13 seconds

NOTE: Data are latest available. *Source:* National Safety Council.

Improper Driving as Factor in Accidents, 1985

Kind of improper driving	Fatal accidents			Injury accidents			All accidents[1]		
	Total	Urban	Rural	Total	Urban	Rural	Total	Urban	Rural
Improper driving	**55.2**	**53.8**	**55.6**	**61.5**	**64.3**	**57.5**	**56.4**	**57.3**	**54.9**
Speed too fast[2]	23.1	22.3	23.5	19.3	18.0	21.3	15.5	13.5	19.6
Right of way	12.2	15.9	10.3	23.9	26.0	21.0	22.2	25.3	15.5
Drove left of center	9.9	5.5	12.1	3.3	2.0	5.0	2.8	1.9	4.8
Improper overtaking	1.9	1.3	2.1	1.9	1.9	1.9	1.8	1.8	2.1
Made improper turn	1.4	2.9	0.7	2.3	2.3	2.3	3.5	3.9	2.8
Followed too closely	0.6	0.5	0.5	5.3	6.4	3.6	5.7	6.7	3.8
Other improper driving	6.1	5.4	6.4	5.5	7.7	2.4	4.9	4.2	6.3
No improper driving	**44.8**	**46.2**	**44.4**	**38.5**	**35.7**	**42.5**	**43.6**	**42.7**	**45.1**
Total	100.0%	100.0%	100.0%	100.0%	100.0%	100.0%	100.0%	100.0%	100.0%

1. Principally property-damage accidents, but also includes fatal and injury accidents. 2. Includes "speed too fast for conditions." *Source:* Urban and rural reports from eight state traffic authorities to National Safety Council. NOTE: Figures are latest available.

Motor-Vehicle Deaths by Type of Accident

Year	Deaths from collisions with— Pedestrians	Other motor vehicles	Railroad trains	Street cars	Pedalcycles	Animal-drawn vehicle or animal	Fixed objects	Deaths from non-collision accidents	Total deaths[1]
1965	8,900	20,800	1,556	5	680	120	2,200	14,900	49,161
1970	9,900	23,200	1,459	3	780	100	3,800	15,400	54,633
1975	8,400	19,550	979	1	1,000	100	3,130	12,700	45,853
1980	9,700	22,000	800	—	1,200	100	4,400	15,100	53,300
1983	8,000	19,300	600	—	1,100	100	3,000	12,500	44,600
1984	8,200	20,300	700	—	1,000	100	3,200	12,700	46,200
1985	8,400	20,200	500	—	1,000	100	2,600	12,800	45,600

1. Totals do not equal sums of various types because totals are estimated; these have been made to nearest 10 deaths for some types and to nearest 50 deaths for others. NOTE: Figures are latest available. *Source:* National Safety Council.

Accidental Deaths by Principal Types

Year	Motor vehicle	Falls	Drowning	Fire burns	Ingestion of food or object	Firearms	Poison (solid, liquid)	Poison by gas
1975	45,853	14,896	8,000	6,071	3,106	2,380	4,694	1,577
1980	53,300	12,600	7,100	5,600	2,900	1,800	3,000	1,300
1981	51,500	12,000	6,100	5,100	2,900	1,900	2,800	1,400
1982	46,000	11,600	6,200	5,000	2,900	1,900	3,000	1,400
1983	44,600	11,700	6,600	4,600	3,200	1,900	3,000	1,300
1984	46,200	11,600	5,700	4,800	3,100	1,800	3,900	1,300
1985	45,600	11,300	5,700	4,900	3,200	1,600	3,800	1,200

NOTE: Figures are latest available. *Source:* National Safety Council.

Deaths and Death Rates

State	Total deaths[1] 1985 rate	Total deaths[1] 1984 rate	Motor vehicle traffic deaths[2] 1985 rate	1984 rate	1983 rate
Alabama	9.3	9.4	2.7	2.9	3.2
Alaska	3.9	4.0	3.3	3.7	3.2
Arizona	8.0	8.0	3.1	4.2	2.6
Arkansas	10.2	10.0	3.2	3.2	3.2
California	7.7	7.6	2.5	2.5	2.6
Colorado	6.4	6.6	2.3	2.5	2.6
Connecticut	8.9	8.8	2.1	2.2	2.1
Delaware	8.8	8.3	2.0	2.5	2.3
D.C.	13.0	13.3	1.8	2.0	1.8
Florida	10.8	10.6	3.2	3.3	3.3
Georgia	8.0	8.1	2.9	2.8	3.1
Hawaii	5.8	5.7	2.1	1.9	2.2
Idaho	6.8	6.6	3.4	3.1	3.2
Illinois	8.6	8.5	2.1	2.2	2.3
Indiana	8.8	8.6	2.3	2.3	2.5
Iowa	9.4	9.0	2.3	2.0	2.5
Kansas	8.8	8.9	2.6	2.7	2.2
Kentucky	9.2	9.0	2.7	2.7	3.0
Louisiana	8.3	8.2	2.8	3.0	4.3
Maine	9.8	9.3	2.1	2.5	2.8
Maryland	8.2	8.0	2.4	2.1	2.1
Massachusetts	9.4	10.2	1.9	1.7	1.7
Michigan	8.5	8.3	2.3	2.5	2.1
Minnesota	8.3	8.1	1.9	1.8	1.8
Mississippi	9.2	8.6	3.4	3.7	4.1
Missouri	10.8	10.4	2.4	2.6	2.5
Montana	8.0	8.1	3.1	3.2	4.0
Nebraska	9.3	9.3	1.9	2.4	2.1
Nevada	8.2	8.0	3.5	3.4	3.8
New Hamshire	8.3	7.9	2.5	2.6	2.6
New Jersey	9.3	8.8	1.9	1.8	1.7
New Mexico	6.6	6.9	4.1	4.0	4.3
New York	9.6	9.5	2.2	2.4	2.5
North Carolina	8.5	8.4	3.0	3.0	2.8
North Dakota	8.7	8.6	1.6	1.9	2.1
Ohio	9.2	9.0	2.2	2.2	2.1
Oklahoma	8.8	8.9	2.4	2.6	2.7
Oregon	8.9	8.7	2.7	2.7	2.7
Pennsylvania	10.5	10.3	2.4	2.4	2.6
Rhode Island	10.2	10.0	2.1	1.6	1.6
South Carolina	7.7	7.7	3.5	3.5	3.4
South Dakota	9.3	9.1	1.9	2.2	2.6
Tennessee	9.6	9.7	3.1	3.0	2.9
Texas	7.4	7.5	2.6	2.8	3.0
Utah	5.7	5.6	2.7	2.7	2.5
Vermont	9.0	8.4	2.6	2.6	2.3
Virginia	7.8	7.8	2.1	2.3	2.1
Washington	8.1	8.1	2.3	2.2	2.2
West Virginia	10.2	9.8	3.3	3.5	4.4
Wisconsin	8.7	8.7	2.1	2.4	2.2
Wyoming	6.1	5.9	3.1	3.1	3.2
Total U.S.	**8.6**	**8.7**	**2.6**	**2.7**	**2.7**

1. Provisional rates per 1,000 population, by place of occurrence. 2. Per 100 million vehicle-miles. *Sources:* Department of Health and Human Services, National Center for Health Statistics; National Safety Council.

Annual Death Rates

Year	Rate	Year	Rate	Year	Deaths	Rate
1900	17.2	1940	10.8	1964	1,798,051	9.4
1905	15.9	1941	10.5	1965	1,828,136	9.4
1910	14.7	1942	10.3	1966	1,863,149	9.5
1915	13.2	1943	10.9	1967	1,851,323	9.4
1918	18.1[1]	1944	10.6	1968	1,930,082	9.7
1920	13.0	1945	10.6	1969	1,921,990	9.5
1923	12.1	1946	10.0	1970[2]	1,921,031	9.5
1924	11.6	1947	10.1	1971	1,927,542	9.3
1925	11.7	1948	9.9	1972	1,963,944	9.4
1926	12.1	1949	9.7	1973	1,973,003	9.3
1927	11.3	1950	9.6	1974	1,934,388	9.1
1928	12.0	1951	9.7	1975	1,892,879	8.8
1929	11.9	1952	9.6	1976	1,909,440	8.8
1930	11.3	1953	9.6	1977	1,899,597	8.6
1931	11.1	1954	9.2	1978	1,927,788	8.7
1932	10.9	1955	9.3	1979	1,913,841	8.5
1933	10.7	1956	9.4	1980	1,989,841	8.7
1934	11.1	1957	9.6	1982	1,974,797	8.5
1935	10.9	1958	9.5	1983	2,019,201	8.6
1936	11.6	1959	9.4	1984	2,039,369	8.6
1937	11.3	1960	9.5	1985[3]	2,084,000	8.7
1938	10.6	1962	9.5	1986[3]	2,099,000	8.7
1939	10.6	1963	9.6			

1. Year of influenza epidemic. 2. First year for which deaths of nonresidents are excluded. 3. Provisional. NOTE: Includes only deaths occurring within the registration area. Beginning with 1933, area includes entire U.S.; with 1959 includes Alaska, and with 1960 includes Hawaii. Excludes fetal deaths. Rates per 1,000 population residing in area, as of April 1 for 1940, 1950, 1960, 1970, and 1980, and estimated as of July 1 for all other years. *Sources:* Department of Health and Human Services, National Center for Health Statistics.

Death Rates by Age, Race, and Sex

Age	1985[1]	1984[2]	1980[2]	1975[2]	1970	1960	1985[1]	1984[2]	1980[2]	1975[2]	1970[2]	1960
	White males						White females					
Under 1 year	10.5	10.4	12.3	15.9	21.1	26.9	8.1	8.2	9.6	12.2	16.1	20.1
1–4	0.5	0.5	0.7	0.7	0.8	1.0	0.4	0.4	0.5	0.6	0.8	0.9
5–14	0.3	0.3	0.4	0.4	0.5	0.5	0.2	0.2	0.2	0.3	0.3	0.3
15–24	1.3	1.4	1.7	1.7	1.7	1.4	0.5	0.5	0.6	0.6	0.6	0.5
25–34	1.6	1.5	1.7	1.7	1.8	1.6	0.6	0.6	0.7	0.7	0.8	0.9
35–44	2.5	2.4	2.6	3.0	3.4	3.3	1.2	1.2	1.2	1.6	1.9	1.9
45–54	6.1	6.2	7.0	7.9	8.8	9.3	3.5	3.4	3.7	4.1	4.6	4.6
55–64	16.4	16.0	17.3	19.5	22.0	22.3	8.7	8.6	8.8	9.4	10.1	10.8
65–74	38.3	37.5	40.4	43.6	48.1	48.5	20.7	20.3	20.7	21.5	24.7	27.8
75–84	91.0	84.6	88.3	96.1	101.0	103.0	54.3	51.4	54.0	60.3	67.0	77.0
85 and over	186.4	185.5	191.0	182.6	185.5	217.5	146.8	143.2	149.8	144.9	159.8	194.8
	All other males						All other females					
Under 1 year	17.6	19.1	23.5	30.0	40.2	51.9	14.3	16.1	19.4	25.2	31.7	40.7
1–4	0.7	0.8	1.0	1.1	1.4	2.1	0.7	0.7	0.8	0.9	1.2	1.7
5–14	0.4	0.4	0.4	0.6	0.6	0.8	0.3	0.3	0.3	0.3	0.4	0.5
15–24	1.7	1.6	2.0	2.4	3.0	2.1	0.5	0.6	0.7	0.9	1.1	1.1
25–34	3.0	2.9	3.6	4.5	5.0	3.9	1.1	1.2	1.4	1.6	2.2	2.6
35–44	5.5	5.1	5.9	7.4	8.7	7.3	2.3	2.5	2.9	3.6	4.9	5.5
45–54	11.0	11.0	13.1	14.2	16.5	15.5	5.8	5.8	6.9	7.8	9.8	11.4
55–64	23.5	23.7	26.1	28.1	30.5	31.5	13.8	13.3	14.2	16.4	18.9	24.1
65–74	45.0	44.3	47.5	49.7	54.7	56.6	27.0	26.5	28.6	31.7	36.8	39.8
75–84	91.5	83.2	86.9	86.0	89.8	86.6	59.2	56.9	58.6	59.8	63.9	67.1
85 and over	144.6	141.3	157.7	116.9	114.1	152.4	111.9	111.0	119.2	91.8	102.9	128.7

1. Provisional. Based on a 10% sample of deaths. 2. Excludes deaths of nonresidents of U.S. NOTE: Excludes fetal deaths. Rates are per 1,000 population in each group, enumerated as of April 1 for 1960, 1970, and 1980, and estimated as of July 1 for all other years. NOTE: Data are latest available. *Sources:* Department of Health and Human Services, National Center for Health Statistics.

Expectation of Life

Expectation of Life in the United States

	Age								
Calendar period	0	10	20	30	40	50	60	70	80
WHITE MALES									
1850[1]	38.3	48.0	40.1	34.0	27.9	21.6	15.6	10.2	5.9
1890[1]	42.50	48.45	40.66	34.05	27.37	20.72	14.73	9.35	5.40
1900-1902[2]	48.23	50.59	42.19	34.88	27.74	20.76	14.35	9.03	5.10
1909-1911[2]	50.23	51.32	42.71	34.87	27.43	20.39	13.98	8.83	5.09
1919-1921[3]	56.34	54.15	45.60	37.65	29.86	22.22	15.25	9.51	5.47
1929-1931	59.12	54.96	46.02	37.54	29.22	21.51	14.72	9.20	5.26
1939-1941	62.81	57.03	47.76	38.80	30.03	21.96	15.05	9.42	5.38
1949-1951	66.31	58.98	49.52	40.29	31.17	22.83	15.76	10.07	5.88
1959-1961	67.55	59.78	50.25	40.98	31.73	23.22	16.01	10.29	5.89
1969-1971	67.94	59.69	50.22	41.07	31.87	23.34	16.07	10.38	6.18
1979-1981	70.82	61.98	52.45	43.31	34.04	25.26	17.56	11.35	6.76
1982	71.5	62.6	53.0	43.8	34.5	25.6	17.9	11.6	7.0
1983	71.1	62.7	53.1	43.9	34.6	25.7	17.9	11.5	6.9
1984	71.8	62.8	53.3	44.0	34.7	25.8	18.0	11.6	6.9
WHITE FEMALES									
1850[1]	40.5	47.2	40.2	35.4	29.8	23.5	17.0	11.3	6.4
1890[1]	44.46	49.62	42.03	35.36	28.76	22.09	15.70	10.15	5.75
1900-1902[2]	51.08	52.15	43.77	36.42	29.17	21.89	15.23	9.59	5.50
1909-1911[2]	53.62	53.57	44.88	36.96	29.26	21.74	14.92	9.38	5.35
1919-1921[3]	58.53	55.17	46.46	38.72	30.94	23.12	15.93	9.94	5.70
1929-1931	62.67	57.65	48.52	39.99	31.52	23.41	16.05	9.98	5.63
1939-1941	67.29	60.85	51.38	42.21	33.25	24.72	17.00	10.50	5.88
1949-1951	72.03	64.26	54.56	45.00	35.64	26.76	18.64	11.68	6.59
1959-1961	74.19	66.05	56.29	46.63	37.13	28.08	19.69	12.38	6.67
1969-1971	75.49	66.97	57.24	47.60	38.12	29.11	20.79	13.37	7.59
1979-1981	78.22	69.21	59.44	49.76	40.16	30.96	22.45	14.89	8.65
1982	78.8	69.7	59.9	50.2	40.6	31.3	22.8	15.3	9.0
1983	78.7	69.6	59.8	50.1	40.4	31.2	22.6	15.1	8.8
1984	78.7	69.6	59.8	50.1	40.5	31.2	22.6	15.1	8.9
ALL OTHER MALES[4]									
1900-1902[2]	32.54	41.90	35.11	29.25	23.12	17.34	12.62	8.33	5.12
1909-1911[2]	34.05	40.65	33.46	27.33	21.57	16.21	11.67	8.00	5.53
1919-1921[3]	47.14	45.99	38.36	32.51	26.53	20.47	14.74	9.58	5.83
1929-1931	47.55	44.27	35.95	29.45	23.36	17.92	13.15	8.78	5.42
1939-1941	52.33	48.54	39.74	32.25	25.23	19.18	14.38	10.06	6.46
1949-1951	58.91	52.96	43.73	35.31	27.29	20.25	14.91	10.74	7.07
1959-1961	61.48	55.19	45.78	37.05	28.72	21.28	15.29	10.81	6.87
1969-1971	60.98	53.67	44.37	36.20	28.29	21.24	15.35	10.68	7.57
1979-1981	65.63	57.40	47.87	39.13	30.64	22.92	16.54	11.36	7.22
1982	66.8	58.4	48.8	39.9	31.3	23.4	16.8	11.7	7.5
1983	67.2	58.8	49.1	40.2	31.5	23.5	16.8	11.5	7.4
1984	67.4	58.9	49.3	40.3	31.6	23.7	16.9	11.5	7.2
ALL OTHER FEMALES[4]									
1900-1902[2]	35.04	43.02	36.89	30.70	24.37	18.67	13.60	9.62	6.48
1909-1911[2]	37.67	42.84	36.14	29.61	23.34	17.65	12.78	9.22	6.05
1919-1921[3]	46.92	44.54	37.15	31.48	25.60	19.76	14.69	10.25	6.58
1929-1931	49.51	45.33	37.22	30.67	24.30	18.60	14.22	10.38	6.90
1939-1941	55.51	50.83	42.14	34.52	27.31	21.04	16.14	11.81	8.00
1949-1951	62.70	56.17	46.77	38.02	29.82	22.67	16.95	12.29	8.15
1959-1961	66.47	59.72	50.07	40.83	32.16	24.31	17.83	12.46	7.66
1969-1971	69.05	61.49	51.85	42.61	33.87	25.97	19.02	13.30	9.01
1979-1981[5]	74.00	65.64	55.88	46.39	37.16	28.59	20.49	14.44	9.17
1982[5]	75.0	66.5	56.8	47.2	37.9	29.2	21.5	15.0	9.5
1983	74.9	66.4	56.6	47.0	37.7	29.0	21.3	14.6	9.3
1984	75.0	66.5	56.7	47.1	37.8	29.1	21.3	14.6	9.1

1. Massachusetts only; white and nonwhite combined, the latter being about 1% of the total. 2. Original Death Registration States. 3. Death Registration States of 1920. 4. Data for periods 1900–1902 to 1929–1931 relate to blacks only. *Sources:* Department of Health and Human Services, National Center for Health Statistics. NOTE: Data are latest available.

Expectation of Life and Mortality Probabilities, 1984

Age	Expectation of life in years					Mortality probability per 1,000				
	Total persons	White		All other		Total persons	White		All other	
		Male	Female	Male	Female		Male	Female	Male	Female
0	74.7	71.8	78.7	67.4	75.0	10.8	10.5	8.3	17.3	14.8
1	74.6	71.6	78.4	67.5	75.2	.7	.7	.6	1.0	.9
2	73.6	70.7	77.4	66.6	74.2	.5	.5	.4	.8	.7
3	72.7	69.7	76.5	65.7	73.3	.4	.4	.3	.7	.6
4	71.7	68.7	75.5	64.7	72.3	.4	.4	.3	.6	.5
5	70.7	67.8	74.5	63.7	71.4	.3	.3	.2	.5	.4
6	69.7	66.8	73.5	62.8	70.4	.3	.3	.2	.4	.3
7	68.8	65.8	72.6	61.8	69.4	.2	.3	.2	.4	.2
8	67.8	64.8	71.6	60.8	68.4	.2	.2	.2	.3	.2
9	66.8	63.8	70.6	59.9	67.4	.2	.2	.2	.3	.2
10	65.8	62.8	69.6	58.9	66.5	.2	.2	.1	.3	.2
11	64.8	61.9	68.6	57.9	65.5	.2	.2	.2	.3	.2
12	63.8	60.9	67.6	56.9	64.5	.2	.3	.2	.3	.2
13	62.8	59.9	66.6	55.9	63.5	.3	.4	.2	.4	.3
14	61.9	58.9	65.6	54.9	62.5	.4	.6	.3	.6	.3
15	60.9	57.9	64.7	54.0	61.5	.6	.8	.4	.7	.3
16	59.9	57.0	63.7	53.0	60.6	.7	1.0	.4	.9	.4
17	59.0	56.0	62.7	52.1	59.6	.8	1.2	.5	1.1	.4
18	58.0	55.1	61.7	51.1	58.6	.9	1.3	.5	1.3	.5
19	57.1	54.2	60.8	50.2	57.6	1.0	1.4	.5	1.5	.5
20	56.1	53.3	59.8	49.3	56.7	1.0	1.5	.5	1.7	.6
21	55.2	52.3	58.8	48.3	55.7	1.1	1.6	.5	1.9	.7
22	54.2	51.4	57.9	47.4	54.7	1.1	1.6	.5	2.1	.7
23	53.3	50.5	56.9	46.5	53.8	1.1	1.6	.5	2.2	.8
24	52.4	49.6	55.9	45.6	52.8	1.1	1.6	.5	2.3	.8
25	51.4	48.7	55.0	44.7	51.9	1.1	1.5	.5	2.4	.9
26	50.5	47.7	54.0	43.8	50.9	1.1	1.5	.5	2.4	.9
27	49.5	46.8	53.0	42.9	50.0	1.1	1.5	.5	2.5	1.0
28	48.6	45.9	52.0	42.1	49.0	1.1	1.5	.5	2.6	1.0
29	47.6	44.9	51.1	41.2	48.1	1.2	1.5	.6	2.8	1.1
30	46.7	44.0	50.1	40.3	47.1	1.2	1.5	.6	2.9	1.2
31	45.7	43.1	49.1	39.4	46.2	1.2	1.6	.6	3.1	1.3
32	44.8	42.1	48.2	38.5	45.2	1.3	1.6	.7	3.2	1.4
33	43.9	41.2	47.2	37.6	44.3	1.3	1.6	.7	3.4	1.4
34	42.9	40.3	46.2	36.8	43.3	1.4	1.7	.8	3.6	1.5
35	42.0	39.3	45.2	35.9	42.4	1.7	1.7	.8	3.9	1.6
36	41.0	38.4	44.3	35.0	41.5	1.5	1.8	.9	4.1	1.7
37	40.1	37.5	43.3	34.2	40.5	1.7	1.9	1.0	4.4	2.0
38	39.2	36.5	42.4	33.3	39.6	1.8	2.0	1.1	4.6	2.1
39	38.2	35.6	41.4	32.5	38.7	1.9	2.2	1.2	4.9	2.3
40	37.3	34.7	40.5	31.6	37.8	2.1	2.4	1.3	5.3	2.6
41	36.4	33.8	39.5	30.8	36.9	2.3	2.6	1.4	5.6	2.9
42	35.5	32.9	38.6	30.0	36.0	2.5	2.9	1.6	6.0	3.2
43	34.6	32.0	37.6	29.2	35.1	2.7	3.1	1.7	6.5	3.4
44	33.7	31.1	36.7	28.3	34.2	3.0	3.4	1.9	7.0	3.7
45	32.8	30.2	35.8	27.5	33.4	3.3	3.7	2.1	7.6	4.0
46	31.9	29.3	34.8	26.7	32.5	3.6	4.1	2.3	8.2	4.3
47	31.0	28.4	33.9	26.0	31.6	3.9	4.5	2.5	8.8	4.6
48	30.1	27.5	33.0	25.2	30.8	4.3	5.0	2.8	9.5	5.0
49	29.2	26.7	32.1	24.4	29.9	4.8	5.6	3.1	10.3	5.4
50	28.4	25.8	31.2	23.7	29.1	5.3	6.2	3.5	11.2	5.8
51	27.5	25.0	30.3	22.9	28.2	5.8	7.0	3.8	12.1	6.3
52	26.7	24.1	29.4	22.2	27.4	6.4	7.7	4.2	13.1	6.8
53	25.8	23.3	28.5	21.5	26.6	7.0	8.5	4.6	14.2	7.5
54	25.0	22.5	27.7	20.8	25.8	7.7	9.4	5.1	15.3	8.3
55	24.2	21.7	26.8	20.1	25.0	8.5	10.4	5.6	16.5	9.1
56	23.4	21.0	25.9	19.5	24.2	9.3	11.5	6.1	17.8	9.9
57	22.6	20.2	25.1	18.8	23.5	10.1	12.6	6.7	19.2	10.8
58	21.8	19.4	24.3	18.2	22.7	11.1	13.9	7.3	20.8	11.7
59	21.1	18.7	23.4	17.5	22.0	12.1	15.2	8.0	22.7	12.8
60	20.3	18.0	22.6	16.9	21.3	12.2	16.6	8.8	24.7	13.9
61	19.6	17.3	21.8	16.3	20.6	14.4	18.1	9.6	26.8	15.1
62	18.9	16.6	21.0	15.8	19.9	15.6	19.7	10.5	28.6	16.1
63	18.2	15.9	20.3	15.2	19.2	16.8	21.5	11.4	30.1	17.0
64	17.5	15.3	19.5	14.7	18.5	18.1	23.3	12.4	31.3	17.8
65	16.8	14.6	18.7	14.1	17.8	19.5	25.3	13.5	32.4	18.5

Age	Expectation of life in years: Total persons	White: Male	White: Female	All other: Male	All other: Female	Mortality probability per 1,000: Total persons	White: Male	White: Female	All other: Male	All other: Female
66	16.1	14.0	18.0	13.6	17.2	21.0	27.4	14.7	33.7	19.3
67	15.5	13.4	17.2	13.1	16.5	22.7	29.7	16.0	35.5	20.6
68	14.8	12.8	16.5	12.5	15.8	24.7	32.5	17.4	38.3	22.6
69	14.2	12.2	15.8	12.0	15.2	27.0	35.5	19.1	41.9	25.0
70	13.5	11.6	15.1	11.5	14.6	29.4	38.8	20.8	46.1	27.9
71	12.9	11.0	14.4	11.0	14.0	32.0	42.2	22.8	50.4	30.8
72	12.3	10.5	13.7	10.6	13.4	34.7	46.0	24.9	54.3	33.4
73	11.8	10.0	13.1	10.2	12.8	37.6	50.0	27.3	57.2	35.4
74	11.2	9.5	12.4	9.8	12.3	40.6	54.4	29.9	59.2	37.0
75	10.7	9.0	11.8	9.4	11.7	43.9	59.1	32.8	61.0	38.6
76	10.1	8.5	11.2	8.9	11.2	47.4	64.1	36.0	63.3	40.7
77	9.6	8.1	10.6	8.5	10.6	51.4	69.6	39.6	66.5	43.6
78	9.1	7.7	10.0	8.1	10.1	55.9	75.5	43.6	71.2	47.6
79	8.6	7.2	9.4	7.6	9.6	60.9	82.0	48.1	77.5	52.7
80	8.1	6.9	8.9	7.2	9.1	66.5	88.9	53.3	85.4	59.0
81	7.7	6.5	8.3	6.9	8.6	72.9	96.4	59.2	95.2	66.7
82	7.3	6.1	7.8	6.6	8.2	80.1	104.5	66.1	106.7	75.7
83	6.8	5.8	7.3	6.3	7.9	88.3	113.1	74.2	120.0	86.2
84	6.5	5.4	6.9	6.1	7.6	97.8	122.1	84.0	135.0	98.6
85	6.1	5.1	6.5	6.0	7.4	—	—	—	—	—

Source: Department of Health and Human Services, National Center for Health Statistics. NOTE: Data are latest available.

Law Enforcement and Crime

Full-Time Law Enforcement Employees, 1986

City	Officers	Civilians	Total	1985 Total
Atlanta	1,326	305	1,631	1,567
Baltimore	2,976	517	3,493	3,485
Birmingham, Ala.	666	197	863	803
Boston	1,946	595	2,541	2,202
Buffalo, N.Y.	1,032	116	1,148	1,106
Chicago	12,264	1,764	14,028	13,786
Cincinnati	875	175	1,050	1,051
Cleveland	1,701	151	1,852	1,928
Columbus, Ohio	1,224	330	1,554	1,542
Dallas	2,290	562	2,852	2,681
Denver	1,310	327	1,637	1,659
Detroit	5,062	650	5,712	5,285
El Paso	711	210	921	900
Fort Worth	853	273	1,126	1,007
Honolulu	1,605	355	1,960	1,983
Houston	4,618	1,184	5,802	5,708
Indianapolis	952	332	1,284	1,289
Jacksonville, Fla.	963	667	1,630	1,617
Kansas City, Mo.	1,097	558	1,655	1,631
Long Beach, Calif.	659	308	967	1,028
Los Angeles	6,951	2,407	9,358	9,635
Louisville, Ky.	648	186	834	835
Memphis, Tenn.	1,139	433	1,572	1,563
Miami, Fla.	1,038	396	1,434	1,431
Milwaukee	1,978	369	2,347	2,388
Minneapolis	697	92	789	768
New Orleans	1,305	221	1,526	1,764
New York	27,425	6,428	33,853	32,328
Newark, N.J.	1,045	146	1,191	1,280
Norfolk, Va.	624	68	692	682
Oakland, Calif.	635	309	944	915
Oklahoma City	737	180	917	919
Omaha, Neb.	581	169	750	738
Philadelphia	6,868	785	7,653	7,764
Phoenix, Ariz.	1,725	665	2,390	2,360
Pittsburgh	1,128	127	1,255	1,379
Portland, Ore.	745	287	1,032	949
Rochester, N.Y.	605	133	738	701
St. Louis	1,563	544	2,107	2,140
St. Paul	513	126	639	642
San Antonio	1,637	345	1,982	1,559
San Diego, Calif.	1,629	628	2,257	1,951
San Francisco	1,899	640	2,539	2,753
San Jose, Calif.	1,005	284	1,289	1,246
Seattle	1,063	389	1,452	1,414
Tampa, Fla.	717	205	922	896
Toledo, Ohio	754	56	810	810
Tucson, Ariz.	682	212	894	854
Tulsa, Okla.	696	142	838	857
Washington, D.C.	3,877	537	4,414	4,341

NOTE: As of Oct. 31, 1986. *Source:* Department of Justice, Federal Bureau of Investigation, *Uniform Crime Reports for the United States, 1987.*

Estimated Arrests, 1986[1]

Murder and non-negligent manslaughter	19,190	Weapons—carrying, possession, etc.	190,500
Forcible rape	37,140	Prostitution and commercial vice	112,600
Robbery	145,800	Sex offenses, except forcible rape and prostitution	100,600
Aggravated assault	351,770	Drug abuse violations	824,100
Burglary	450,600	Gambling	30,500
Larceny—theft	1,400,200	Offenses against family and children	58,400
Motor vehicle theft	153,600	Driving under the influence	1,793,300
Arson	18,700	Liquor laws	600,200
Total violent crime	553,900	Drunkenness	933,900
Total property crime	2,023,200	Disorderly conduct	676,400
Other assaults	711,000	Vagrancy	38,700
Forgery and counterfeiting	92,200	All other offenses, except traffic	2,730,500
Fraud	349,300	Curfew and loitering law violations	86,200
Embezzlement	12,600	Runaways	165,200
Stolen property—buying, receiving, possessing	135,800	**Total**	**12,487,500**
Vandalism	259,600		

1. Arrest totals based on all reporting agencies and estimates for unreported areas. 2. Because of rounding, items may not add to totals. *Source:* Department of Justice, Federal Bureau of Investigation, *Uniform Crime Reports for the United States,* 1987.

Number of Arrests by Sex and Age

	Male				Female			
	Total		Under 18		Total		Under 18	
Offense	1986	1985	1986	1985	1986	1985	1986	1985
Serious crimes	1,709,919	1,540,744	516,494	482,653	457,152	416,585	124,911	117,719
Murder[1]	14,083	12,904	1,303	1,124	1,983	1,815	93	115
Forcible rape	30,780	28,865	4,709	4,316	348	303	89	80
Robbery	114,495	105,401	26,049	26,758	9,750	8,639	1,938	1,951
Aggravated assault	255,176	211,228	31,734	28,330	38,776	32,926	5,794	5,202
Burglary—breaking or entering	345,886	326,959	124,652	124,388	29,658	26,753	10,171	9,764
Larceny—theft	819,754	744,423	277,561	255,810	362,345	334,053	100,722	95,379
Motor vehicle theft	116,348	97,835	44,840	36,256	12,166	10,093	5,479	4,619
Arson	13,397	13,129	5,646	5,671	2,126	2,003	625	609
All other								
Other assaults	503,732	416,735	66,371	57,218	90,170	75,937	19,534	17,259
Forgery and counterfeiting	50,612	46,286	4,875	4,962	25,934	23,181	2,359	2,302
Fraud	161,523	151,773	13,357	13,350	123,267	111,825	4,370	3,812
Embezzlement	6,678	5,624	414	451	3,822	3,184	282	195
Stolen property—buying, receiving, possessing	101,069	89,619	26,090	23,032	13,036	11,890	2,649	2,386
Vandalism	199,882	181,600	86,826	81,987	23,349	20,192	8,653	7,730
Weapons—carrying, possessing, etc.	148,372	134,210	23,556	22,421	11,832	10,970	1,614	1,628
Prostitution and commercialized vice	33,553	29,584	750	708	63,329	67,592	1,442	1,638
Sex offenses, except forcible rape and prostitution	77,278	74,602	12,760	12,599	6,656	6,108	993	1,107
Drug abuse violations	591,806	562,754	58,490	63,255	100,076	90,038	9,861	10,932
Gambling	21,390	21,995	570	666	4,449	3,879	40	33
Offenses against family and children	40,250	35,553	1,569	1,444	7,077	5,086	952	804
Driving under the influence	1,290,900	1,208,416	19,731	16,089	167,631	157,131	3,018	2,420
Liquor laws	407,942	350,942	98,295	76,322	82,494	67,823	34,040	27,483
Drunkenness	708,317	726,214	22,539	19,112	69,549	70,573	4,050	3,697
Disorderly conduct	461,975	435,198	67,526	59,944	102,907	99,252	15,460	14,291
Vagrancy	29,052	24,592	2,097	2,016	3,940	3,001	453	447
All other offenses, except traffic	1,923,173	1,671,002	219,762	206,878	349,416	307,269	57,114	53,649
Curfew and loitering law violations	54,087	49,258	54,087	49,258	18,540	15,985	18,540	15,985
Runaways	58,601	53,808	58,601	53,808	79,985	72,473	79,985	72,473
Total	**8,586,328**	**7,810,509**	**1,356,804**	**1,248,235**	**1,805,849**	**1,639,974**	**390,871**	**357,990**

1. Includes non-negligent manslaughter. NOTE: 10,743 agencies reporting; 1986 estimated population 198,488,000. *Source:* Department of Justice, Federal Bureau of Investigation, *Uniform Crime Reports for the United States, 1987.*

Arrests by Race, 1986
(in thousands)

Offense	White	Black	Other[1]	Total
Serious crimes				
Murder[2]	8,028	7,659	266	15,953
Forcible rape	16,012	14,357	408	30,777
Robbery	45,746	76,678	1,225	123,649
Aggravated assault	172,220	116,700	4,201	293,121
Burglary	258,326	110,482	5,273	374,081
Larceny-theft	799,908	354,489	25,085	1,179,482
Motor vehicle theft	81,196	44,317	2,236	127,749
Arson	11,651	3,640	149	15,440
All other				
Other assaults	388,404	193,386	9,582	591,372
Forgery and counterfeiting	50,731	24,906	805	76,442
Fraud	188,700	93,968	2,235	284,903
Embezzlement	7,356	3,023	116	10,495
Stolen property—buying, receiving, possessing	69,838	42,423	1,169	113,430
Vandalism	174,663	44,330	3,622	222,615
Weapons—carrying, possession, etc.	102,744	54,767	1,880	159,391
Prostitution and commercial vice	57,836	37,440	1,288	96,564
Sex offenses, except forcible rape and prostitution	65,368	17,095	1,273	83,736
Drug abuse violation[5]	463,457	219,159	6,199	688,815
Gambling	12,879	11,701	805	25,385
Offenses against family and children	30,455	14,892	724	46,071
Driving under the influence	1,277,912	139,596	23,354	1,440,862
Liquor laws	427,626	47,798	12,506	487,930
Drunkenness	616,200	137,043	19,618	772,861
Disorderly conduct	380,682	172,301	7,905	560,888
Vagrancy	22,048	9,700	1,226	32,974
All other offenses except traffic	1,463,752	761,114	38,097	2,262,963
Suspicion	5,663	1,706	75	7,444
Curfew and loitering law violations	54,717	15,769	1,602	72,088
Runaways	116,659	18,495	3,307	138,461
Total	**7,370,777**	**2,788,934**	**176,231**	**10,335,942**

1. Includes American Indian, Alaskan Native, and Asian or Pacific Islander. 2. Includes non-negligent manslaughter. NOTE: Figures represent arrests reported by 10,699 agencies serving a total 1986 population of 197,663,000 as estimated by FBI. *Source:* Department of Justice, Federal Bureau of Investigation, *Uniform Crime Reports for the United States, 1987.*

Total Arrests, by Age Groups, 1986

Age	Arrests	Age	Arrests	Age	Arrests	Age	Arrests	Age	Arrests
Under 15	536,609	18	494,197	22	472,524	30–34	1,285,311	50–54	206,910
15	333,648	19	492,884	23	459,699	35–39	837,662	55 and over	335,053
16	416,663	20	481,996	24	441,062	40–44	485,647		
17	460,755	21	482,724	25–29	1,863,945	45–49	304,888	**Total**	**10,392,177**

NOTE: Based on reports furnished to the FBI by 10,743 agencies covering a 1986 estimated population of 198,488,000. *Source:* Department of Justice, Federal Bureau of Investigation, *Uniform Crime Reports for the United States, 1987.*

Federal Prosecutions of Public Corruption: 1976 to 1985

(Prosecution of persons who have corrupted public office in violation of Federal Criminal Statutes. As of Dec. 31, 1985)

Prosecution status	1985	1984	1983	1982	1981	1980	1979	1978	1977	1976
Total:[1] Indicted	1,182	936	1,073	729	878	721	687	557	507	563
Convicted	997	934	972	671	730	552	555	409	440	380
Awaiting trial	256	269	222	186	231	213	187	205	210	199
Federal officials: Indicted	563	408	460	158	198	123	128	133	129	111
Convicted	470	429	424	147	159	131	115	91	94	101
Awaiting trial	90	77	58	38	23	16	21	42	32	1
State officials: Indicted	79	58	81	49	87	72	58	55	50	59
Convicted	66	52	65	43	66	51	32	56	38	35
Awaiting trial	20	21	26	18	36	28	30	20	33	30
Local officials: Indicted	248	203	270	257	244	247	212	171	157	194
Convicted	221	196	226	232	211	168	156	127	164	100
Awaiting trial	49	74	61	58	102	82	67	72	62	98

1. Includes individuals who are neither public officials nor employees, but who were involved with public officials or employees in violating the law, now shown separately. *Source:* U.S. Department of Justice, *Federal Prosecutions of Corrupt Public Officials, 1970–1980,* and *Report to Congress on the Activities and Operations of the Public Integrity Section,* annual.

Crime Rates for Population Groups and Selected Cities, 1985

(offenses known to the police per 100,000 population, as of July 1)

	Violent crime					Property crime				
Group and city	Murder	Forcible rape	Robbery	Aggravated assault	Total	Burglary—breaking or entering	Larceny—theft	Motor vehicle theft	Total	Total all crimes
Cities over 250,000	19.0	78	684	563	1,344	2,156	4,339	1,111	7,606	8,951
100,000–249,999	10.2	52	298	441	802	1,949	4,471	582	7,002	7,804
50,000–99,999	5.9	36	186	307	536	1,456	3,521	522	5,499	6,035
25,000–49,999	4.7	28	124	263	420	1,265	3,480	385	5,130	5,550
10,000–24,999	3.7	20	70	214	307	1,000	2,965	283	4,247	4,554
Under 10,000	3.5	17	41	211	272	881	2,850	215	3,946	4,218
Total, 8,413 cities	**9.2**	**43**	**289**	**359**	**700**	**1,524**	**3,671**	**589**	**5,784**	**6,484**
Suburbs	4.7	25	88	223	341	1,063	2,506	315	3,883	4,224
Rural areas	5.6	19	15	138	177	668	967	108	1,744	1,921
Selected cities:										
Baltimore	27.6	77	1,008	898	2,010	1,799	3,985	781	6,565	8,575
Chicago	22.2	60	897	970	1,949	1,756	4,044	1,497	7,297	9,246
Dallas	30.2	115	607	688	1,440	3,154	7,359	1,030	11,542	12,982
Detroit	58.2	144	1,538	635	2,375	3,703	4,219	3,452	11,375	13,750
Indianapolis	12.5	73	381	514	980	1,740	2,953	613	5,307	6,287
Los Angeles	24.4	73	877	684	1,658	2,007	3,953	1,621	7,581	9,239
Memphis	18.6	138	766	565	1,488	2,427	3,452	1,794	7,673	9,160
New York	19.3	54	1,107	701	1,881	1,738	3,648	1,106	6,491	8,372
Philadelphia	16.6	62	572	337	988	1,159	2,184	770	4,113	5,101
Phoenix	10.0	71	272	491	844	2,621	5,248	552	8,420	9,264
San Antonio	20.9	95	311	198	625	2,843	5,350	870	9,062	9,687
San Diego	9.7	34	310	279	632	1,656	3,564	1,018	6,237	6,870
San Francisco	11.6	70	697	517	1,296	1,603	4,281	809	6,693	7,988
Washington, D.C.	23.5	54	835	712	1,625	1,598	3,973	803	6,374	7,999

Source: U.S. Federal Bureau of Investigation, *Crime in the United States,* annual.

Percent of Firearms Usage in Selected Crimes, by Region: 1983–1985

	Murder[1]			Aggravated assault			Robbery		
Region	1985	1984	1983	1985	1984	1983	1985	1984	1983
Northeast	50.9	51.1	50.5	13.5	13.6	14.1	28.3	29.7	30.6
Midwest	60.7	60.5	59.0	22.2	21.8	22.2	37.2	36.8	34.7
South	63.1	63.2	63.8	25.4	25.3	24.9	41.7	42.1	44.3
West	54.3	54.9	53.6	19.9	20.5	20.4	35.1	35.7	37.2
U.S. Total	**58.7**	**58.8**	**58.3**	**21.3**	**21.1**	**21.2**	**35.3**	**35.8**	**36.7**

1. Murder includes non-negligent manslaughter. *Source:* U.S. Federal Bureau of Investigation, *Crime in the United States,* annual.

Reported Child Neglect and Abuse Cases: 1982 to 1984

		Total number of reports (1,000)			Reports per 1,000 population		
Division	Percent change 1983-84	1984	1983	1982	1984	1983	1982
New England	+25.3	73.3	58.5	49.9	5.8	4.7	4.0
Middle Atlantic	+44.2	145.6	101.0	105.5	3.9	2.7	4.0
North Central	+22.0	290.6	235.4	222.8	5.3	8.8	8.6
South Atlantic	−22.1	178.1	228.5	182.1	4.5	5.9	4.8
South Central	+19.4	188.4	165.3	171.2	4.6	8.2	8.9
Mountain	+20.2	59.5	49.5	41.5	4.7	4.0	3.6
Pacific	+19.9	195.8	163.3	151.0	5.7	4.9	4.6
U.S. Total	**+13.0**	**1,131.3**	**1,001.4**	**924.1**	**4.8**	**4.3**	**4.0**

Source: American Humane Association, *National Analysis of Official Child Neglect and Abuse Reporting,* annual.

Prisoners Under Sentence of Death

Characteristic	1985	1984	1983	Characteristic	1985	1984	1983
White	903	804	690	Marital status:			
Black and other	688	601	512	Never married	655	570	484
Under 20 years	13	11	12	Married	487	443	368
20–24 years	212	215	217	Divorced or separated[1]	449	392	350
25–34 years	804	702	597	Time elapsed since sentencing:			
35–54 years	531	453	359	Less than 12 months	273	279	251
55 years and over	31	24	17	12–47 months	739	694	622
				48–71 months	303	228	186
Schooling completed:				72 months and over	276	204	143
7 years or less	147	121	99	Legal status at arrest:			
8 years	159	137	123	Not under sentence	861	739	605
9–11 years	483	401	358	On parole or probation	350	279	225
12 years	440	385	319	In prison or escaped	81	66	58
More than 12 years	127	110	88	Unknown	299	321	314
Unknown	235	251	215	**Total**	**1,591**	**1,405**	**1,202**

1. Includes widows, widowers, and unknown. NOTE: As of Dec. 31. Excludes prisoners under sentence of death confined in local correctional systems pending appeal or who had not been committed to prison. *Source:* U.S. Bureau of Justice Statistics, *Capital Punishment,* annual.

Methods of Execution[1]

State	Method	State	Method
Alabama[2]	Electrocution	Nevada[2]	Lethal injection
Alaska	No death penalty	New Hampshire[2]	Hanging
Arizona[2]	Lethal gas	New Jersey	Lethal injection
Arkansas[2]	Lethal injection	New Mexico	Lethal injection
California*	Lethal gas	New York	No death penalty
Colorado[2]	Lethal gas	North Carolina[2]	Lethal gas or injection
Connecticut[2]	Electrocution	North Dakota	No death penalty
Delaware	Hanging	Ohio[2]	Electrocution
D.C.	No death penalty	Oklahoma	Lethal injection
Florida	Electrocution	Oregon[5]	Lethal injection
Georgia[2]	Electrocution	Pennsylvania[2]	Electrocution
Hawaii	No death penalty	Rhode Island	No death penalty([3])
Idaho[2]	Lethal injection or firing squad	South Carolina[2]	Electrocution
		South Dakota	Lethal injection
Illinois	Lethal injection	Tennessee[2]	Electrocution
Indiana[2]	Electrocution	Texas[2]	Lethal injection
Iowa	No death penalty	Utah[2]	Firing squad or lethal injection
Kansas	No death penalty	Vermont	Electrocution[7]
Kentucky[2]	Electrocution	Virginia	Electrocution
Louisiana[2]	Electrocution	Washington[2]	Hanging or lethal injection
Maine	No death penalty	West Virginia	No death penalty
Maryland[2]	Lethal gas	Wisconsin	No death penalty
Massachusetts[5]	No death penalty	Wyoming	Lethal injection
Michigan	No death penalty	U.S. (Fed. Govt.)*	([4])
Minnesota	No death penalty	American Samoa	No death penalty
Mississippi[2]	Lethal injection	Guam	No death penalty
Missouri	Lethal gas	Puerto Rico	No death penalty
Montana[2]	Hanging, or lethal injection[6]	Virgin Islands	No death penalty
Nebraska[2]	Electrocution		

1. On July 1, 1976, by a 7-2 decision, the U.S. Supreme Court upheld the death penalty as not being "cruel or unusual." However, in another ruling the same day, the Court, by a 5-4 vote, stated that states may not impose "mandatory" capital punishment on every person convicted of murder. These decisions left uncertain the fate of condemned persons throughout the U.S. On Oct. 4, the Court refused to reconsider its July ruling, which allows some states to proceed with executions of condemned prisoners. The first execution in this country since 1967 was in Utah on Jan. 17, 1977. Gary Mark Gilmore was executed by shooting. 2. Voted to restore death penalty after June 29, 1972, Supreme Court decision ruling capital punishment unconstitutional. 3. Person shall be executed by gas if he commits murder while serving a prison term. 4. Method shall be that used by state in which sentence is imposed. If state does not have death penalty, federal judge shall prescribe method for carrying out sentence. 5. Death penalty has been passed, but not been used. 6. Defendant may choose between hanging and a lethal injection. *Source: Information Please* questionnaires to the states. 7. Last execution in 1954. NOTE: An asterisk after the name of the state indicates non-reply.

Motor Vehicle Laws, 1986

State	Age for license: Motor-cycle	Age for license: Moped	Age for driver's license[1]: Regular	Age for driver's license[1]: Learner's	Age for driver's license[1]: Restrictive	Driver's license duration	Fee	Annual safety inspection required
Alabama	14	14	16	15[5]	14[11]	4 yrs.	$15.00	no[18]
Alaska	16	14	16	14	14[11]	5	5.00	no[18]
Arizona	16	16	18	15 7 mo.[6,8]	16[6]	3 or 4	5.25/7	no[19]
Arkansas	16	10	16	([5])	14[6]	2 or 4	7/13.00	yes
California	18	15 1/2	18	15[4,7]	16[4]	4	10.00	no[18]
Colorado	16	16	21	15 1/2[5]	16[6]	4	6.50	no[20]
Connecticut	18	16	18		16[4]	2 or 4	24.75/38	yes[21,22]
Delaware	18	16	18	([5])	16[4,6]	4	12.50	yes
D. C.	16	16	18	([5])	16[6]	4	15.00	yes
Florida	15	15	16	([5])	15[6]	4	15.00	no
Georgia	16	15	21	15	16[6]	4	4.50	no[20]
Hawaii	15	15	18	([5])	15[6]	4[14]	3-12.00	yes[23]
Idaho	16	16	16	([5])	14[4]	3	12.00	no
Illinois	18	16	18	([5])	16[4,6]	3 or 4	10.00	no[24]
Indiana	16	15[13]	18	15[8]	16 1 mo.[4,6]	4[15]	6.00	no
Iowa	18	14	18	14	16[4]	6[16]	20.00	([25])
Kansas	14	14	16	([5])	14	4	13.00	([18])
Kentucky	16	16	18	([5])	16[6]	4	8.00	no
Louisiana	15	15	17		15[2,17]	5	12.50	yes
Maine	17	16	17	([5])	15[4]	4	16.00	yes
Maryland	18	16	18	([5])	16[4,6]	4	20.00	no[26]
Massachusetts	17	16	18	([5])	16 1/2[4,6]	4	25.00	yes[22]
Michigan	18	15	18		16[4,6]	2 or 4	3.75/7.50	no[18]
Minnesota	18	15	19	15[8]	16[4]	4	10.00	no[18]
Mississippi	15[13]	15	15	([5])		4	13.00	yes
Missouri	16	16	16		15[4]	3	7.50	yes
Montana	16	16	18	([5])	15[4,6]	4	12.00	no
Nebraska	16	14	16	15[5]	14	4	10.00	no
Nevada	16	16	16	15 1/2[5]	14[6,10]	4	10.00[17]	no
New Hampshire	18	16	16[4]		16[4]	4	20.00	6 mos.
New Jersey	17	15	17		16	4	16–17.50	2 yrs.
New Mexico	16	13	16	15	14[12]	4	10.00	no
New York	16	16	17[3]		16[6]	4	17.50	yes
North Carolina	18	16	18		15[4,6]	4	10.00	yes
North Dakota	16	14	16	([5])	14[4,6]	4	.8.00	no[18]
Ohio	18	14	18	16[5,6]	14[3]	4	9.00	no[18]
Oklahoma	14		16		15 1/2[4]	2	9.00	yes
Oregon	16	16	16	15[5]	14	4	25.00	no[18]
Pennsylvania	16	13	18[3]	16[8]	16[6]	4	21.50	yes
Rhode Island	18	16	18	([5])	16[4]	5	20.00	yes
South Carolina	15	13[13]	16	15[9]	15	4	10.00	yes
South Dakota	14	14	16	([5])	14	4	6.00	no
Tennessee	16	14	16	([5])	15	4	13.00	no
Texas	18	15	16[4]	15[7]	15[3]	4	16.00	yes
Utah	16	16	16[4]	([5])		4	10.00	yes
Vermont	18	16	18	15[9]	16[7]	2 or 4	10/16	yes
Virginia	18	16[13]	18	15 8 mo.[5,6]	16[4,6]	5	12.00	yes
Washington	18	16	18	15[8]	16[4]	4	14.00	no[18]
West Virginia	16	16	18	([5])	16[6]	4	10.00	yes
Wisconsin	18	16	18	([5])	16[4]	4	9.00	no
Wyoming	16	16	16	15[6,7]	14[6,7]	4	5–10.00	no

1. Full driving privileges at age given in "Regular" column. A license restricted or qualified in some manner may be obtained at age given in "Restricted" column. 2. 70 or older. 3. Upon proof of hardship. 4. Must have completed approved driver education course. 5. Learner's permit required. 6. Guardian's or parental consent required. 7. Driver with learner's permit must be accompanied by locally licensed operator 18 years or older. 8. Must be enrolled in driver education course. 9. Driver with learner's permit must be accompanied by locally licensed operator 21 years or older. 10. To and from school or transporting handicapped. 11. Restricted to mopeds. 12. For use while enrolled in driver education course. Must be accompanied by instructor. 13. No license required. 14. 2 years if 15-24 or over 65. 15. 3 years if over 75. 16. 2 years if under 18 or over 65. 17. 70 and older, $5.00. 18. State troopers are authorized to inspect at their discretion. 19. Arizona emission inspection fee $5. 20. Annual emissions test in some counties. 21. Used motor vehicles being registered in Connecticut from out-of-state are required to be inspected and approved and Connecticut cars 10 years old and older must be inspected upon being sold or transferred. 22. Annual emissions test. 23. If car is 10 years or older, every 6 months. 24. Trucks and buses only. 25. Prior to first registration and transfers. 26. All used vehicles upon resale or transfer. NOTES: A driver's license is required in every state. The national speed limit is 55 miles per hour. All states have an *implied consent* Chemical Test Law for alcohol. *Source:* American Automobile Association.

Law Enforcement Officers Killed or Assaulted: 1975 to 1985

(Covers officers killed feloniously and accidentally in line of duty; includes federal officers.)

	1985	1984	1983	1982	1981	1980	1979	1977	1976	1975
Northeast	19	21	20	17	17	31	21	14	19	28
Midwest	23	22	26	41	29	23	28	26	30	40
South	64	69	64	75	80	72	77	65	69	71
West	29	32	34	27	27	32	32	18	17	36
Puerto Rico	10	3	6	3	3	6	4	1	4	8
Total killed	**148**[8]	**147**	**152**[7]	**164**[6]	**157**[5]	**165**[3]	**164**[4]	**125**[3]	**140**[2]	**185**[1]
Assaults:										
Population (1,000)[9]	198,935	195,794	198,341	176,563	177,836	182,288	182,027	168,868	156,085	151,927
Number of—										
Agencies	9,906	10,002	9,908	8,829	9,019	9,235	9,638	8,742	7,665	7,435
Police officers	389,808	372,268	377,620	319,101	332,856	345,554	340,764	322,205	291,610	290,638
Firearm	2,793	2,654	3,067	2,642	3,330	3,295	3,237	2,809	2,768	3,282
Knife or cutting instrument	1,715	1,662	1,829	1,452	1,733	1,653	1,720	1,481	1,402	1,287
Other dangerous weapon	5,263	5,148	5,527	4,879	4,800	5,415	5,543	4,626	4,676	4,516
Hands, fists, feet, etc.	51,953	50,689	51,901	46,802	47,253	47,484	48,531	40,240	40,233	35,782
Total assaulted	**61,724**	**60,153**	**62,324**	**55,775**	**57,116**	**57,847**	**59,031**	**49,156**	**49,079**	**44,867**

1. Includes one officer each in Virgin Islands and Guam. 2. Includes one officer in Colombia. 3. Includes one officer in Virgin Islands. 4. Includes 2 officers in Guam. 5. Includes one officer in American Samoa. 6. Includes one officer in Mariana Islands. 7. Includes one officer each in Guam and Mariana Islands. 8. Includes one officer in Guam and 2 in foreign locations. 9. Represents the number of persons covered by agencies shown. *Source: Statistical Abstract of the United States, 1987.*

Minimum Legal Age for Purchase of Liquor, Wine, and Beer

State	Liquor	Wine	Beer	State	Liquor	Wine	Beer
Alabama	21	21	21	Montana	21	21	21
Alaska	21	21	21	Nebraska	21	21	21
Arizona	21	21	21	Nevada	21	21	21
Arkansas	21	21	21	New Hampshire	21	21	21
California	21	21	21	New Jersey	21	21	21
Colorado	21	21	21[1]	New Mexico	21	21	21
Connecticut	21	21	21	New York	21	21	21
Delaware	21	21	21	North Carolina	21	21	21
D.C.	21	21	21	North Dakota	21	21	21
Florida[2]	21	21	21	Ohio	21	21	19
Georgia	21	21	21	Oklahoma	21	21	21
Hawaii	21	21	21	Oregon	21	21	21
Idaho	21	21	21	Pennsylvania	21	21	21
Illinois	21	21	21	Rhode Island	21	21	21
Indiana	21	21	21	South Carolina	21	21	21
Iowa[3]	21	21	21	South Dakota	21	21	21
Kansas	21	21	21	Tennessee[4]	21	21	21
Kentucky	21	21	21	Texas	21	21	21[4]
Louisiana	21	21	21	Utah	21	21	21
Maine	21	21	21	Vermont	21	21	21
Maryland	21	21	21	Virginia	21	21	21
Massachusetts	21	21	21	Washington	21	21	21
Michigan	21	21	21	West Virginia	21	21	21
Minnesota	21	21	21	Wisconsin[3]	21	21	21[3]
Mississippi	21	21	21	Wyoming	19	19	19
Missouri	21	21	21				

1. 3.2 beer: 18. 2. Exempts military personnel: 18. 3. Exempts those 19 or older on effective date. 4. Except off-base military personnel, persons consuming alcohol in a religious service, or accompanied by parent or guardian. *Source:* Distilled Spirits Council of the United States.

Women Behind Bars

The number of women in prison has been steadily increasing. The female percentage of our prison population went from 4.2% to 4.9% during the five-year period 1981-1986. And in 1986, the number of female prisoners increased at a rate of 15.1%, almost twice that of men (8.3%). Still, men are 21 times more likely to be jailed than women.

California has the largest number of female inmates (3,564) and showed an increase of 22.6% from 1985 to 1986. Oklahoma showed an increase of 33.9% over that time period, and has the largest percentage of female inmates in the country (7.1%).

U.S. District Courts—Criminal Cases Commenced and Defendants Disposed of, by Nature of Offense: 1984 and 1985

[For years ending June 30]

Nature of offense	1985 cases commenced[1]	Disposition of defendants, 1985: Not convicted, Total	Not convicted, Acquitted	Convicted, Total	Convicted, Guilty plea	Convicted, Court or jury	Sentenced, Imprisonment	Sentenced, Probation	Sentenced, Fine and other	1984: Cases commenced[1]	1984: Defendants disposed of
General offenses:											
Homicide	160	40	15	130	86	44	91	16	23	156	164
Robbery	1,235	140	20	1,247	1,041	206	1,136	106	5	1,329	1,383
Assault	553	128	26	427	335	92	248	150	29	525	572
Burglary	158	39	2	126	114	12	95	30	1	155	199
Larceny-theft	3,575	740	101	3,368	3,064	304	1,396	1,705	267	3,400	4,138
Embezzlement and fraud	7,917	1,494	217	7,550	6,792	758	2,769	4,533	248	7,646	9,108
Auto theft	299	73	11	388	339	49	273	106	9	286	419
Forgery, counterfeiting	2,115	306	35	2,066	1,919	147	1,016	1,031	19	1,966	2,426
Sex offenses	266	37	9	163	126	37	125	37	1	163	124
DAPCA[3]	6,693	1,968	367	9,209	7,500	1,709	6,786	2,185	238	5,611	9,191
Misc. general offenses	15,575	3,865	543	13,856	12,507	1,349	4,744	4,505	4,607	14,674	16,777
Total[2]	**38,546**	**8,830**	**1,346**	**38,530**	**33,823**	**4,707**	**18,679**	**14,404**	**5,447**	**35,911**	**44,501**

1. Excludes transfers. 2. Includes items not shown separately. 3. All marijuana, narcotics, and controlled substances under the Drug, Abuse, Prevention and Control Act. *Source: Statistical Abstract of the United States,* 1987.

Murder Victims by Weapons Used

Year	Murder victims, total	Guns: Total	Guns: Percent	Cutting or stabbing	Blunt object[1]	Strangulation and hands, fists, feet	Arson[3]	All other[2]
1965	8,773	5,015	57.2	2,021	505	894	226	112
1968	12,503	8,105	64.8	2,317	713	936	294	138
1969	13,575	8,876	65.4	2,534	613	1,039	322	191
1970	13,649	9,039	66.2	2,424	604	1,031	353	198
1971	16,183	10,712	66.2	3,017	645	1,295	314	200
1972	15,832	10,379	65.6	2,974	672	1,291	331	185
1973	17,123	11,249	65.7	2,985	848	1,445	173	423
1974	18,632	12,474	66.9	3,228	976	1,417	153	384
1975	18,642	12,061	64.7	3,245	1,001	1,646	193	496
1977	18,033	11,274	62.5	3,440	849	1,431	252	787
1978	18,714	11,910	63.6	3,526	896	1,422	255	705
1979	20,591	13,040	63.3	3,954	997	1,557	276	767
1980	21,860	13,650	62.0	4,212	1,094	1,666	291	947
1981	20,053	12,523	62.4	3,886	1,038	1,469	258	658
1982	19,485	11,721	60.2	4,065	957	1,657	279	630
1983	18,673	10,895	58.0	4,075	1,062	1,656	216	769
1984	16,689	9,819	58.8	3,540	973	1,407	192	758
1985	17,545	10,296	58.7	3,694	972	1,491	243	849
1986	19,257	11,381	59.1	3,957	1,099	1,651	230	939

1. Refers to club, hammer, etc. 2. Includes poison, explosives, unknown, drowning, and not stated. 3. Before 1973, includes drowning. *Source:* Department of Justice, Federal Bureau of Investigation, *Uniform Crime Reports for the United States, 1986.*

Recidivism of Young Parolees

A study of a group of young parolees, 17 to 22, who were released from prison in 1978 reported that approximately 69% of them were rearrested for a serious crime within six years of their release.

Recidivism rates were highest in the first two years after the offender's release from prison. Within one year 32% had been rearrested; within two years 47% had been rearrested.

The rate was higher among men, blacks, and persons who had not completed high school than among women, whites, and high school graduates.

Firsts in America

This selection is based on our editorial judgment. Other sources may list different firsts.

Admiral in U.S. Navy: David Glasgow Farragut, 1866.

Air-mail route, first transcontinental: Between New York City and San Francisco, 1920.

Assembly, representative: House of Burgesses, founded in Virginia, 1619.

Bank established: Bank of North America, Philadelphia, 1781.

Birth in America to English parents: Virginia Dare, born Roanoke Island, N.C., 1587.

Botanic garden: Established by John Bartram in Philadelphia, 1728 and is still in existence in its original location.

Cartoon, colored: "The Yellow Kid," by Richard Outcault, in *New York World,* 1895.

College: Harvard, founded 1636.

College to confer degrees on women: Oberlin (Ohio) College, 1841.

College to establish coeducation: Oberlin (Ohio) College, 1833.

Electrocution of a criminal: William Kemmler in Auburn Prison, Auburn, N.Y., Aug. 6, 1890.

Five and Ten Cents Store: Founded by Frank Woolworth, Utica, N.Y., 1879 (moved to Lancaster, Pa., same year).

Fraternity: Phi Beta Kappa; founded Dec. 5, 1776; at College of William and Mary.

Law to be declared unconstitutional by U.S. Supreme Court: Judiciary Act of 1789. Case: *Marbury* v. *Madison,* 1803.

Library, circulating: Philadelphia, 1731.

Newspaper, illustrated daily: *New York Daily Graphic,* 1873.

Newspaper published daily: *Pennsylvania Packet and General Advertiser,* Philadelphia, Sept., 1784.

Newspaper published over a continuous period: *The Boston News-Letter,* April, 1704.

Newsreel: Pathé Frères of Paris, in 1910, circulated a weekly issue of their *Pathé Journal.*

Oil well, commercial: Titusville, Pa., 1859.

Panel quiz show on radio: *Information Please,* May 17, 1938.

Postage stamps issued: 1847.

Public School: Boston Latin School, Boston, 1635.

Railroad, transcontinental: Central Pacific and Union Pacific railroads, joined at Promontory, Utah, May 10, 1869.

Savings bank: The Provident Institute for Savings, Boston, 1816.

Science museum: Founded by Charleston (S.C.) Library Society, 1773.

Skyscraper: Home Insurance Co., Chicago, 1885 (10 floors, 2 added later).

Slaves brought into America: At Jamestown, Va., 1619, from a Dutch ship.

Sorority: Kappa Alpha Theta, at De Pauw University, 1870.

State to abolish capital punishment: Michigan, 1847.

State to enter Union after original 13: Vermont, 1791.

Steam-heated building: Eastern Hotel, Boston, 1845.

Steam railroad (carried passengers and freight): Baltimore & Ohio, 1830.

Strike on record by union: Journeymen Printers, New York City, 1776.

Subway: Opened in Boston, 1897.

"Tabloid" picture newspaper: *The Illustrated Daily News* (now *The Daily News*), New York City, 1919.

Vaudeville theater: Gaiety Museum, Boston, 1883.

Woman astronaut to ride in space: Dr. Sally K. Ride, 1983.

Woman astronaut to walk in space: Dr. Kathryn D. Sullivan, 1984.

Woman cabinet member: Frances Perkins, Secretary of Labor, 1933.

Woman candidate for President: Victoria Claflin Woodhull, nominated by National Woman's Suffrage Assn. on ticket of Nation Radical Reformers, 1872.

Woman candidate for Vice-President: Geraldine A. Ferraro, nominated by a major party on ticket of the Democratic Party, 1984.

Woman doctor of medicine: Elizabeth Blackwell; M.D. from Geneva Medical College of Western New York, 1849.

Woman elected governor of a state: Mrs. Nellie Tayloe Ross, Wyoming, 1925.

Woman elected to U.S. Senate: Mrs. Hattie Caraway, Arkansas; elected Nov., 1932.

Woman graduate of law school: Mrs. Ada H. Kepley, Union College of Law, Chicago, 1870.

Woman member of U.S. House of Representatives: Jeannette Rankin; elected Nov., 1916.

Woman member of U.S. Senate: Mrs. Rebecca Latimer Felton of Georgia; appointed Oct. 3, 1922.

Woman member of U.S. Supreme Court: Mrs. Sandra Day O'Connor; appointed July 1981.

Woman suffrage granted: Wyoming Territory, 1869.

Written constitution: *Fundamental Orders of Connecticut,* 1639.

U.S. SOCIETIES & ASSOCIATIONS

ource: Information Please questionnaires to organizations. Names are listed alphabetically according to key word in title; gure in parentheses is year of founding; other figure is membership. An asterisk (*) before a name indicates that up-to-date information has not been provided.

The following is a partial list selected for general eadership interest. A comprehensive listing of ap-roximately 20,000 national and international or-anizations can be found in the "**Encyclopedia of ssociations,**" 20th Ed., 1986, Vol. I, Parts 1-3 Katherine Gruber, Editor; Iris Cloyd, Research ditor), published by Gale Research Company, ook Tower, Detroit, Mich. 48226, available in ost public libraries.

bortion Federation, National (1977): 900 Pennsylvania Ave. S.E., Washington, D.C., 20003. 285. Phone: (202) 546-9060.

bortion Rights Action League, National (1969): 1101 14th St. N.W., Washington, D.C. 20005. 145,000. Phone: (202) 371-0779.

ccountants, American Institute of Certified Public (1887): 1211 Avenue of the Americas, New York, N.Y. 10036. 250,000. Phone: (212) 575-6200.

ccountants, National Association of (1919): 10 Paragon Dr., P.O. Box 433, Montvale, N.J., 07645. 90,000. Phone: (201) 573-6222.

CME, Inc.—The association of management consulting firms (1929): 230 Park Ave., New York, N.Y. 10169. 60 firms. Phone: (212) 697-9693.

coustical Society of America (1929): 500 Sunnyside Blvd., Woodbury, N.Y. 11797. 5,700. Phone: (516) 349-7800.

ctors' Equity Association (1913): 165 W. 46th St., New York, N.Y. 10036. Phone: (212) 869-8530.

ctuaries, Society of (1949): 500 Park Blvd., Itasca, Ill. 60143. 10,500. Phone: (312) 773-3010.

dirondack Mountain Club (1922): 172 Ridge St., Glen Falls, N.Y. 12801. 12,000. Phone: (518) 793-7737.

eronautic Association, National (1905): 1400 Eye St. N.W., Washington, D.C. 20005. 200,000. Phone: (202) 898-1313.

eronautics and Astronautics, American Institute of (1932): 1633 Broadway, New York, N.Y. 10019. 38,000. Phone: (212) 581-4300.

erospace Industries Association of America (1919): 1725 De Sales St. N.W., Washington, D.C. 20036. 50 companies. Phone: (202) 429-4600.

erospace Medical Association (1929): Washington National Airport, Washington, D.C. 20001-4977. 4,200. Phone: (703) 892-2240.

frican-American Institute, The (1953): 833 United Nations Plaza, New York, N.Y. 10017. Phone: (212) 949-5666.

Afro-American Life and History, Association for the Study of (1915): 1401 14th St. N.W., Washington, D.C. 20005. 2,000. Phone: (202) 667-2822.

FS International/Intercultural Programs (1947): 313 E. 43rd St., New York, N.Y. 10017. 100,000. Phone: (202) 949-4242.

ging Association, American (1970): Univ. of Nebraska Medical Center, 42nd and Dewey Ave., Omaha, Neb. 68105. 500. Phone: (402) 559-4416.

gricultural Engineers, American Society of (1907): 2950 Niles Rd., St. Joseph, Mich. 49085. 12,000. Phone: (616) 429-0300.

Agricultural History Society (1919): 1301 New York Ave. N.W., Washington, D.C. 20005. 1,400. Phone: (202) 786-1896.

Agronomy, American Society of (1907): 677 S. Segoe Rd., Madison, Wis. 53711-1086. 13,000. Phone: (608) 273-8080.

Aircraft Association, Experimental (1953): Wittman Field, Oshkosh, Wis. 54903-3086. 110,000. Phone: (414) 426-4800.

Aircraft Owners and Pilots Association (1939): 421 Aviation Way, Frederick, Md. 21701. 265,000. Phone: (301) 695-2000.

Air Force Association (1946): 1501 Lee Highway, Arlington, Va., 22209. 231,000. Phone: (703) 247-5800.

Air Line Pilots Association (1931): 1625 Massachusetts Ave. N.W., Washington, D.C. 20036 and 535 Herndon Pkwy., Herndon, Va. 22070. 39,000. Phone: (703) 689-2270.

Air Pollution Control Association (1907): P.O. Box 2861, Pittsburgh, Pa. 15230. 8,000. Phone: (412) 232-3444.

Air Transport Association of America (1936): 1709 New York Ave. N.W., Washington, D.C. 20006. 27 airlines. Phone: (202) 626-4000.

Al-Anon Family Group Headquarters, Inc. (1951): P.O. Box 862, Midtown Station, New York, N.Y. 10018-0862. 27,000 groups worldwide. Phone: (800) 356-9996 and (212) 245-3151.

Alcoholics Anonymous (1935): P.O. Box 459, Grand Central Station, New York, N.Y. 10163. 1,000,000. Address communications to General Service Office. Phone: (212) 686-1100.

Alcoholism, National Council on (1944): 12 W. 21st St., New York, N.Y. 10010. 190 affiliates. Phone: (212) 206-6770.

Alcohol Problems, American Council on (1900): 3426 Bridgeland Dr., Bridgeton, Mo. 63044. 3,500. Phone: (314) 739-5944.

Alexander Graham Bell Association for the Deaf (1890): 3417 Volta Place N.W., Washington, D.C. 20007. 6,000. Phone: (202) 337-5220.

Allergy and Immunology, American Academy of (1943): 611 E. Wells St., Milwaukee, Wis. 53202. 3,962. Phone: (414) 272-6071.

Alzheimer's Disease and Related Disorders Association, Inc., The (ADRDA) (1980): 70 E. Lake St., Chicago, Ill. 60601-5997. 164 Chapters and Affiliates, over 1000 Support Groups. Toll-free information: 1-800-621-0379.

America-Mideast Educational and Training Services (AMIDEAST) (1951): 1100 17th St. N.W., Washington, D.C. 20036. 200. Phone: (202) 785-0022.

American Federation of Labor and Congress of Industrial Organizations (AFL-CIO) (1955): 815 16th St. N.W., Washington, D.C. 20006. 13,100,000. Phone: (202) 637-5010.

American Friends Service Committee (1917): 1501 Cherry St., Philadelphia, Pa. 19102. Phone: (215) 241-7060.

***American Indian Affairs, Association on** (1923):

95 Madison Ave., New York, N.Y. 10016. 50,000. Phone: (212) 689-8720.

American Legion, The (1919): P.O. Box 1055, Indianapolis, Ind. 46206. 2,800,000. Phone: (317) 635-8411.

American Legion Auxiliary (1919): 777 N. Meridian St., Indianapolis, Ind. 46204. 950,000. Phone: (317) 635-6291.

American Mensa, Ltd. (1945): 2626 E. 14th St., Brooklyn, N.Y. 11235-3992. Phone: (718) 934-3700.

American Montessori Society (1960): 150 Fifth Ave., New York, N.Y. 10011. 10,000. Phone: (212) 924-3209.

American Planning Association (1978): 1776 Massachusetts Ave. N.W., Washington, D.C. 20036. 21,000. Phone: (202) 872-0611.

Americans for Democratic Action, Inc. (1947): 815 15th St. N.W., Washington, D.C. 20005. 75,000. Phone: (202) 638-6447.

American Society for Public Administration (ASPA) (1939): 1120 G St. N.W., Washington, D.C. 20005. 18,000. Phone: (202) 393-7878.

American States, Organization of (1948): General Secretariat, Washington, D.C. 20006. 32 countries. Phone: (202) 789-3841.

American Universities, Association of (1900): One Dupont Circle N.W., Suite 730, Washington, D.C. 20036. Phone: (202) 466-5030.

Amnesty International/USA (1961): 322 Eighth Ave., New York, N.Y. 10001. 150,000. Phone: (212) 807-8400.

***AMVETS (American Veterans of World War II, Korea, and Vietnam)** (1944): 4647 Forbes Blvd., Lanham, Md. 20706. 200,000. Phone: (301) 459-9600.

***AMVETS Auxiliary National Department** (1946): 4647 Forbes Blvd., Lanham, Md. 20706. 75,000. Phone: (301) 459-9600.

Animal Protection Institute of America (1968): 6130 Freeport Blvd., Suite 100, Sacramento, Calif. 95822. Phone: (916) 422-1921.

Animals, Fund For (1967): 200 W. 57th St., New York, N.Y. 10019. 175,000. Phone: (212) 246-2096.

Animals, The American Society for the Prevention of Cruelty to (ASPCA) (1866): 441 E. 92nd St., New York, N.Y. 10128. 260,000. Phone: (212) 876-7700..

Animal Welfare Institute (1951): P.O. Box 3650, Washington, D.C. 20007. 8,600. Phone: (202) 337-2332.

Anthropological Association, American (1902): 1703 New Hampshire Ave. N.W., Washington, D.C. 20009. 10,294. Phone: (202) 232-8800.

Anti-Defamation League of B'nai B'rith (1913): 823 United Nations Plaza, New York, N.Y. 10017. Phone: (212) 490-2525.

Antiquarian Society, American (1812): 185 Salisbury St., Worcester, Mass. 01609. 483. Phone: (617) 755-5221.

Anti-Vivisection Society, The American (1883): Suite 204, Noble Plaza, 801 Old York Rd., Jenkintown, Pa. 19046. 15,000. Phone: (215) 887-0816.

Appraisers, American Society of (1936): P.O. Box 17265, Washington, D.C. 20041. 5,500. Phone: (703) 478-2228.

Arbitration Association, American (1926): 140 W. 51st St., New York, N.Y. 10020. 4,825. Phone: (212) 484-4000.

Arboriculture, International Society of (1924): 5 Lincoln Square, Urbana, Ill. 61801. 5,200. Phone: (217) 328-2032.

***Archaeological Institute of America** (1879): P.O. Box 1901, Kenmore Station, Boston, Mass 02215. 9,000. Phone: (617) 353-9361.

Archaeology, Institute of Nautical (1973): Texas A&M University, Drawer AU, College Station, Tex 77840. 750. Phone: (409) 845-6694.

Architects, American Institute of (1857): 1735 New York Ave. N.W., Washington, D.C. 20006 52,000. Phone: (202) 626-7300.

Architectural Historians, Society of (1940): 1232 Pine St., Philadelphia, Pa. 19107. 4,200. Phone (215) 735-0224.

Army, Association of the United States (1950) 2425 Wilson Blvd., Arlington, Va. 22201. 160 000. Phone: (703) 841-4300.

***Arthritis Foundation** (1948): 1314 Spring St. N.W., Atlanta, Ga. 30309. 72 loca chapters/divisions. Phone: (404) 872-7100.

Arts, National Endowment for the (1965): 1100 Pennsylvania Ave. N.W., Washington, D.C. 20506 Phone: (202) 682-5414.

***Arts, The American Federation of** (1909): 41 E 65th St., New York, N.Y. 10021. 1,400. Phone (212) 988-7700.

Arts and Letters, American Academy and Institute of (1898): 633 W. 155th St., New York, N.Y 10032. 250. Phone: (212) 368-5900.

ASM International (1920): Metals Park, Ohic 44073. 52,000. Phone: (216) 338-5151.

Astronomical Society, American (1899): Louisiana State University, Box BK, LSU Observatory, Baton Rouge, La. 70803. 4,000. Phone: (504) 388-8276.

Atheists, American (1963): P.O. Box 2117, Austin Tex. 78768. 40,000. Phone: (512) 458-1244.

Auctioneers Association, National (1949): 8880 Ballentine, Overland Park, Kan. 66214. 6,000 Phone: (913) 541-8084.

Audubon Society, National (1905): 950 Third Ave. New York, N.Y. 10022. 510,000. Phone: (212) 832-3200.

Authors League of America (1912): 234 W. 44th St., New York, N.Y. 10036. 14,000. Phone: (212) 391-9198.

Autism, National Society for Children and Adults With (1965): 1234 Massachusetts Ave. N.W. Washington, D.C. 20005. 7,000. Phone: (202) 783-0125.

Automobile Association, American (1902): 8111 Gatehouse Rd., Falls Church, Va. 22047. 28,000 000. Phone: (703) 222-6000.

Automobile Club, National (1924): One Market Plaza, San Francisco, Calif. 94105. 427,780 Phone: (415) 777-4000.

Automobile Dealers Association, National (1917) 8400 Westpark Dr., McLean, Va. 22102. 20 000. Phone: (703) 821-7100.

Automotive Engineers, Inc., Society of (1905) 400 Commonwealth Dr., Warrendale, Pa. 15096 48,000. Phone: (412) 776-4841.

Automotive Hall of Fame (1939): P.O. Box 1727 Midland, Mich. 48641-1727. Phone: (517) 631-5760.

Bar Association, American (1878): 750 N. Lake Shore Dr., Chicago, Ill. 60611. 330,000. Phone (312) 988-5000.

***Bar Association, Federal** (1920): 1815 H St N.W., Washington, D.C. 20006. 14,000. Phone (202) 638-0252.

Barber Shop Quartet Singing in America, Society for the Preservation and Encouragement of (1938): 6315 Third Ave., Kenosha, Wis., 53140-5199. 38,000. Phone: (414) 654-9111.

Bible Society, American (1816): 1865 Broadway

New York, N.Y. 10023. 600,000. Phone: (212) 581-7400.

Biblical Literature, Society of (1880): P.O. Box 1608, Decatur, Ga. 30031-1608. 6,000. Phone: (404) 636-4744.

Bibliographical Society of America (1904): P.O. Box 397, Grand Central Station, New York, N.Y. 10163. 1,400. Phone: (718) 638-7957.

Bide-A-Wee Home Association (1903): 410 E. 38th St., New York, N.Y. 10016. 8,600. Phone: (212) 532-6395.

Big Brothers/Big Sisters of America (1977): 230 N. 13th St., Philadelphia, Pa. 19107. Phone: (215) 567-7000.

Biological Chemists, American Society of (1906): 9650 Rockville Pike, Bethesda, Md. 20814. 7, 000. Phone: (301) 530-7145.

Biological Sciences, American Institute of (1947): 730 11th St. N.W., Washington, D.C. 20001-4584. 12,500. Phone: (202) 628-1500.

Blind, American Council of the (1961): 1010 Vermont Ave. N.W., Suite 1100, Washington, D.C. 20005. 20,000. Phone: (202) 393-3666.

Blind, National Federation of the (1940): 1800 Johnson St., Baltimore, Md. 21230. 50,000. Phone: (301) 659-9314.

Blindness, National Society to Prevent (1908): 500 E. Remington Rd., Schaumburg, Ill. 60173-4557. 26 affiliates. Phone: (312) 843-2020.

Blindness, Research to Prevent (1960): 598 Madison Ave., New York, N.Y. 10022. 3,300. Phone: (212) 752-4333.

Blue Cross and Blue Shield Association (1946 and 1948): 676 St. Clair St., Chicago, Ill. 60611. 75 Plans. Phone: (312) 440-5569.

B'nai B'rith International (1843): 1640 Rhode Island Ave. N.W., Washington, D.C. 20036. 500, 000. Phone: (202) 857-6500.

Booksellers Association, American (1900): 137 W. 25th St., New York, N.Y. 10001. 5,557. Phone: (212) 867-9060.

Botanical Gardens & Arboreta, American Association of (1971): P.O. Box 206, Swarthmore, Pa. 19081. 1,100. Phone: (215) 328-9145.

Boys Clubs of America (1906): 771 First Ave., New York, N.Y. 10017. 1,285,000. Phone: (212) 351-5900.

Boy Scouts of America (1910): 1325 Walnut Hill Lane, Irving, Tex. 75038-3096. 4,754,479. Phone: (214) 580-2000.

Bridge, Tunnel, and Turnpike Association, International (1932): 2120 L St. N.W., Suite 305, Washington, D.C. 20037. 215 agencies. Phone: (202) 659-4620.

Broadcasters, National Association of (1922): 1771 N St. N.W., Washington, D.C. 20036. 5,700. Phone: (202) 429-5300.

Brookings Institution, The (1927): 1775 Massachusetts Ave. N.W., Washington, D.C. 20036. Phone: (202) 797-6000.

Brooks Bird Club, Inc., The (1932): 707 Warwood Ave., Wheeling, W. Va. 26003. 1,000. Phone: (304) 547-5253.

Business Bureaus, Council of Better (1970): 1515 Wilson Blvd., Arlington, Va. 22209. Phone: (703) 276-0100.

Business Clubs, National Association of American (1922): 3315 No. Main St., High Point, N.C. 27260. 6,800. Phone: (919) 869-2166.

***Business Education Association, National** (1946): 1914 Association Dr., Reston, Va. 22091. 18,000. Phone: (703) 860-8300.

Business Law Association, American (1923): Dept. of Insurance, Legal Studies, and Real Estate, Univ. of Georgia, Athens, Ga. 30602. 1,200. Phone: (404) 542-3795.

Business Women's Association, American (1949): 9100 Ward Parkway, P.O. Box 8728, Kansas City, Mo. 64114. 112,000. Phone: (816) 361-6621.

Campers & Hikers Association, National (1949): 4804 Transit Rd., Bldg. 2, Depew, N.Y. 14043-4704. 28,000 families. Phone: (716) 668-6242.

Camp Fire, Inc. (1910): 4601 Madison Ave., Kansas City, Mo. 64112. 400,000. Phone: (816) 756-1950.

Camping Association, The American (1910): Bradford Woods, Martinsville, Ind. 46151. 6,000. Phone: (317) 342-8456.

Cancer Council, Inc., United (1959): 650 E. Carmel Dr., Suite 340, Carmel, Ind. 46032. 39 agencies. Phone: (317) 844-6627.

Cancer Society, American (1913): 90 Park Ave., New York, N.Y. 10016. 2,443,842 volunteers. Phone: (212) 736-3030.

CARE, Inc. (1945): 660 First Ave., New York, N.Y. 10016. 23 agencies plus 19 public members. Phone: (212) 686-3110.

Carnegie Endowment for International Peace (1910): 11 Du Pont Circle N.W., Washington, D.C. 20036. Phone: (202) 797-6400.

Cartoonists Society, National (1946): 9 Ebony Court, Brooklyn, N.Y. 11229. 450. Phone: (718) 743-6510.

Catholic Bishops, National Conference of (1966): 1312 Massachusetts Ave. N.W., Washington, D.C. 20005. Phone: (202) 659-6774.

Catholic Charities USA (1910): 1319 F St. N.W., Washington, D.C. 20004. 3,300 individuals, 850 agencies and institutions. Phone: (202) 639-8400.

Catholic Conference, United States (1966): 1312 Massachusetts Ave. N.W., Washington, D.C. 20005. Phone: (202) 659-6600.

Catholic Daughters of the Americas (1903): 10 W. 71st St., New York, N.Y. 10023. 160,000. Phone: (212) 877-3041.

Catholic Historical Society, American (1884): 263 S. Fourth St., Philadelphia, Pa. 19106. 950. Phone: (215) 925-5752.

Catholic War Veterans of the U.S.A. Inc. (1935): 419 N. Lee St., Alexandria, Va. 22314. 35,000. Phone: (703) 549-3622.

Ceramic Society, Inc., The American (1899): 757 Brooksedge Plaza Dr., Westerville, Ohio 43081-2821. Phone: (614) 268-8645.

***Cerebral Palsy Associations, United** (1949): 66 E. 34th St., New York, N.Y. 10016. 250 affiliates. Phone: (212) 481-6300.

***Chamber of Commerce of the U.S.** (1912): 1615 H St. N.W., Washington, D.C. 20062. 220,486. Phone: (202) 659-6000.

***Chartered Life Underwriters, American Society of** (1929): 270 Bryn Mawr Ave., Bryn Mawr, Pa. 19010. 32,000. Phone: (215) 896-4300.

Chemical Engineers, American Institute of (1908): 345 E. 47th St., New York, N.Y. 10017. 60,000. Phone: (212) 705-7338.

Chemical Manufacturers Association, Inc. (1872): 2501 M St. N.W., Washington, D.C. 20037. 200 companies. Phone: (202) 887-1108.

Chemical Society, American (1876): 1155 16th St. N.W., Washington, D.C. 20036. 135,000. Phone: (202) 872-4600.

Chemists, American Institute of (1923): 7315 Wisconsin Ave., Bethesda, Md. 20814. 7,000. Phone: (301) 652-2447.

***Chemists, American Society of Biological** (1906): 9650 Rockville Pike, Bethesda, Md. 20814.

6,600. Phone: (301) 530-7145.

Chemists and Chemical Engineers, Association of Consulting (1928): 50 E. 41st St., New York, N.Y. 10017. 130. Phone: (212) 684-6255.

Chess Federation, United States (1939): 186 Rt. 9W, New Windsor, N.Y. 12550. 60,000. Phone: (914) 562-8350.

***Child Labor Committee, National** (1904): 1501 Broadway, Rm. 1111, New York, N.Y. 10036. Phone: (212) 840-1801.

Children's Aid Society, The (1853): 105 E. 22nd St., New York, N.Y. 10010. 1,207. Phone: (212) 949-4800.

Children's Book Council (1945): 67 Irving Place, New York, N.Y. 10003. 65 publishing houses. Phone: (212) 254-2666.

Children Under Six, Southern Association on (1948): Box 5403, Brady Station, Little Rock, Ark. 72215. 14,000. Phone: (501) 227-6404.

Child Welfare League of America (1920): 440 First St. N.W., Suite 310, Washington, D.C. 20001. Phone: (202) 638-2952.

***Chiropractic Association, American** (1963): 1701 Clarendon Blvd., Arlington, Va. 22209. 21, 300. Phone: (703) 276-8800.

Christians and Jews, National Conference of (1928): 71 Fifth Ave., New York, N.Y. 10003. 200,000. Phone: (212) 206-0006.

Churches of Christ in the USA, National Council of the (1950): 475 Riverside Drive, New York, N.Y. 10115. 32 Protestant and Orthodox communions. Phone: (212) 870-2200.

Cities, National League of (1924): 1301 Pennsylvania Ave. N.W., Washington, D.C. 20004. 15, 000 cities. Phone: (202) 626-3000.

Civil Air Patrol (1941): Maxwell AFB, Ala. 36112-5572. 66,000. Phone: (205) 293-6019.

Civil Engineers, American Society of (1852): 345 E. 47th St., New York, N.Y. 10017. 102,345. Phone: (212) 705-7496.

Civil Liberties Union, American (1920): 132 W. 43rd St., New York, N.Y. 10036. 200,000. Phone: (212) 944-9800.

Clinical Chemistry, Inc., American Association for (1948): 1725 K St., N.W., Suite 1010, Washington, D.C. 20006. 7,600. Phone: (202) 857-0717.

Clinical Pathologists, American Society of (1922): 2100 W. Harrison St., Chicago, Ill. 60612. 34, 000. Phone: (312) 738-1336.

Collectors Association, American (1939): Box 35106, Minneapolis, Minn. 55435. Over 3,300. Phone: (612) 926-6547.

College Board, The (1900): 45 Columbus Ave., New York, N.Y. 10023. 2,550 institutions. Phone: (212) 713-8000.

College Placement Council (1956): 62 E. Highland Ave., Bethlehem, Pa. 18017. 2,500. Phone: (215) 868-1421.

Colleges, Association of American (1915): 1818 R St. N.W., Washington, D.C. 20009. 580 institutions. Phone: (202) 745-0880.

Colored Women's Clubs, National Association of (1896): 5808 16th St. N.W., Washington, D.C. 20011. 40,000. Phone: (202) 726-2044.

Common Cause (1970): 2030 M St. N.W., Washington, D.C. 20036. 280,000. Phone: (202) 833-1200.

Community and Junior Colleges, American Association of (1920): One Dupont Circle N.W., Suite 410, Washington, D.C. 20036-1176. 1,221 institutions. Phone: (202) 293-7050.

Community Cultural Center Association, American (1978): 19 Foothills Dr., Pompton Plains, N.J. 07444. Phone: (201) 835-2661.

Composers, Authors, and Publishers, American Society of (ASCAP) (1914): One Lincoln Plaza, New York, N.Y. 10023. 40,000. Phone: (212) 595-3050.

Composers/USA, National Association of (1932): P.O. Box 49652, Barrington Station, Los Angeles, Calif. 90049. 550. Phone: (213) 541-8213.

Concerned Scientists, Union of (1969): 26 Church St., Cambridge, Mass. 02238. Phone: (617) 547-5552.

Congress of Racial Equality (CORE) (1942): 1457 Flatbush Ave., Brooklyn, N.Y. 11210. Nationwide network of chapters. Phone: (718) 434-3580.

Conscientious Objectors, Central Committee for (1948): 2208 South St., Philadelphia, Pa. 19146. Phone: (215) 545-4626.

Conservation Engineers, Association of (1961): Alabama Dept. of Cons. & Natural Resources, Engineering Section, 64 N. Union St., Montgomery, Ala 36130. Phone: (205) 261-3476.

Consumer Federation of America (1968): 1424 16th St. N.W., Washington, D.C. 20036. 220 member organizations. Phone: (202) 387-6121.

Consumer Interests, American Council on (1953): 240 Stanley Hall, Univ. of Missouri, Columbia, Mo. 65211. 1,800. Phone: (314) 882-3817.

Consumers League, National (1899): 815 15th St. N.W., Suite 516, Washington, D.C. 20005. Phone: (202) 639-8140.

Consumers Union (1936): 256 Washington St., Mt. Vernon, N.Y. 10553. 3,500,000 subscribers to *Consumer Reports.* Phone: (914) 667-9400.

Contract Bridge League, American (1927): P.O. Box 161192, Memphis, Tenn. 38186. 200,000. Phone: (901) 332-5586.

Cooperative Business Association, National (formerly Cooperative League of the U.S.A) (1916): 1401 New York Ave. N.W., Suite 1100, Washington, D.C. 20005. Phone: (202) 638-6222.

Counselors and Family Therapists, National Academy of (1972): 225 Jericho Turnpike, Suite 4, Floral Park, N.Y. 11001. 900. Phone: (516) 352-1188.

***Country Music Association** (1958): Box 22299, Nashville, Tenn. 37202. 8,000. Phone: (615) 244-2840.

Credit Association, International (1912): P.O. Box 27357, St. Louis, Mo. 63141. 15,000. Phone: (314) 991-3030.

Credit Management, National Association of (1896): 520 Eighth Ave., New York, N.Y. 10018. 42,000. Phone: (212) 947-5070.

Credit Union National Association (1934): P.O. Box 431, Madison, Wis. 53701. 52 state leagues representing 18,000 credit unions. Phone: (608) 231-4000.

Crime and Delinquency, National Council on (1907): 77 Maiden Lane, San Francisco, Calif. 94108. Nationwide membership. Phone: (415) 956-5651.

Criminal Investigators Association, International (ICIA) (1982): P.O. Box 15350, Chevy Chase, Md. 20815. 1,000. Phone: (202) 293-9088.

Dairy Council, National (1915): 6300 N. River Rd., Rosement, Ill. 60018. Phone: (312) 696-1020.

Daughters of the American Revolution, National Society (1890): 1776 D St. N.W., Washington, D.C. 20006. 210,000. Phone: (202) 628-1776.

Daughters of the Confederacy, United (1894): 328 N. Boulevard, Richmond, Va. 23220. 27,000. Phone: (804) 355-1636.

Deaf, National Association of the (1880): 814 Thayer Ave., Silver Spring, Md. 20910. Phone:

(301) 587-1788.

Defenders of Wildlife (1947): 1244 19th St. N.W., Washington, D.C. 20036. 80,000. Phone: (202) 659-9510.

Defense Preparedness Association, American (1919): Rosslyn Center, Suite 900, 1700 N. Moore St., Arlington, Va. 22209. 45,000. Phone: (703) 522-1820.

***Democratic Club, National** (1834): The 60 East Club, 60 E. 42nd St., New York, N.Y. 10165. Phone: (212) 689-1313.

Dental Association, American (1859): 211 E. Chicago Ave., Chicago, Ill. 60611. 145,000. Phone: (312) 440-7450.

Diabetes Association, American (1940): 1660 Duke St., Alexandria, Va. 22314. Phone: (703) 549-1500.

Dietetic Association, The American (1917): 430 N. Michigan Ave., Chicago, Ill. 60611. 55,000. Phone: (312) 280-5000.

Dignity (1969): 1500 Massachusetts Ave. N.W., Suite 11, Washington, D.C. 20005. 5,000. Phone: (202) 861-0017.

Disabled American Veterans (1920): 807 Maine Ave. S.W., Washington, D.C. 20024. Phone: (202) 554-3501.

Dowsers, Inc., The American Society of (1961): Danville, Vt. 05828. 3,500. Phone: (802) 684-3417.

Drug, Chemical, and Allied Trades Association (1890): 42-40 Bell Blvd., Suite 604, Bayside, N.Y. 11361. 504. Phone: (718) 229-8891.

Ducks Unlimited (1937): One Waterfowl Way, Long Grove, Ill. 60047. 610,000. Phone: (312) 438-4300.

Earthwatch (1970): 680 Mt. Auburn St., Box 403, Watertown, Mass. 02272. 34,000. Phone: (617) 926-8200.

Eastern Star, Order of, (1876): 1618 New Hampshire Ave. N.W., Washington, D.C. 20009. 2,500, 000. Phone: (202) 667-4737.

Easter Seal Society, The National (1921): 2023 W. Ogden Ave., Chicago, Ill. 60612. 48 affiliated state societies and Puerto Rico. Phone: (312) 243-8400.

Economic Association, American (1885): 1313 21st Ave. So., Nashville, Tenn. 37212. 20,000 members, 5,500 inst. subscribers. Phone: (615) 322-2595.

Economic Development, Committee for (1942): 477 Madison Ave., New York, N.Y. 10022. 225. Phone: (212) 688-2063.

Edison Electric Institute (1933): 1111 19th St. N.W., Washington, D.C. 20036-3691. 200. Phone: (202) 778-6400.

Education, American Council on (1918): One Dupont Circle N.W., Washington, D.C. 20036. 1,600 (organizational members). Phone: (202) 939-9300.

***Education, Council for Advancement and Support of** (1974): 11 Dupont Circle N.W., Washington, D.C. 20036. 12,000. Phone: (202) 328-5900.

Educational Exchange, International, Council on (1947): 205 E. 42nd St., New York, N.Y. 10017. 179. Phone: (212) 661-1414.

Educational Film Library Association (1943): 45 John St., Suite #301, New York, N.Y. 10038. 1, 600. Phone: (212) 227-5599.

***Educational Research Association, American** (1906): 1230 17th St. N.W., Washington, D.C. 20036. 14,000. Phone: (202) 223-9485.

Education Association, National (1857): 1201 16th St. N.W., Washington, D.C. 20036. 1,801, 936. Phone: (202) 833-4000.

Electrochemical Society, The (1902): 10 S. Main St., Pennington, N.J. 08534. 6,274. Phone: (609) 737-1902.

Electronic Industries Association (1924): 2001 Eye St. N.W., Washington, D.C. 20006. 1,000 member companies. Phone: (202) 457-4900.

Electroplaters and Surface Finishers Society, American (1909): 12644 Research Pkwy., Orlando, Fla. 32826. 10,000. Phone: (305) 281-6441.

Elks of the U.S.A., Benevolent and Protective Order of the (1868): 2750 Lake View Ave., Chicago, Ill. 60614. 1,600,000. Phone: (312) 477-2750.

Energy Engineers, Association of (1978): 4025 Pleasantdale Rd., Suite 420, Atlanta, Ga. 30340. 6,000. Phone: (404) 447-5083.

***English-Speaking Union of the United States** (1920): 16 E. 69th St., New York, N.Y. 10021. 32,000. Phone: (212) 879-6800.

Entomological Society of America (1889): 4603 Calvert Rd., College Park, Md. 20740. 9,000. Phone: (301) 864-1334.

***Exceptional Children, The Council for** (1922): 1920 Association Dr., Reston, Va. 22091. 49, 000. Phone: (703) 620-3660.

***Experimental Test Pilots, The Society of** (1956): 44814 Elm St., Lancaster, Calif. 93534. 1,781. Phone: (805) 942-9574.

Exploration Geophysicists, Society of (1930): P.O. Box 702740, Tulsa, Okla. 74170. 19,000. Phone: (918) 493-3516.

Family Physicians, American Academy of (1947): 1740 W. 92nd St., Kansas City, Mo. 64114. 59, 500. Phone: (816) 333-9700.

Family Relations, National Council on (1938): 1910 W. County Rd. B, Suite 147, St. Paul, Minn. 55113. 4,000. Phone: (612) 633-6933.

Family Service America (1911): 11700 W. Lake Park Dr., Park Place, Milwaukee, Wis. 53224. Approx. 300 member agencies. Phone: (414) 359-2111.

Farm Bureau Federation, American (1919): 225 Touhy Ave., Park Ridge, Ill. 60068. 3.3 million member families. Phone: (312) 399-5700.

***Farmer Cooperatives, National Council of** (1929): 50 F St. N.W., Washington, D.C. 20001. 165. Phone: (202) 659-1525.

Federal Employees, National Federation of (1917): 1016 16th St. N.W., Washington, D.C. 10036. Rep. 150,000. Phone: (202) 862-4400.

Feline and Canine Friends, Inc. (1973): 505 N. Bush St., Anaheim, Calif. 92805. 1,000. Phone: (714) 635-7975.

Fellowship of Reconciliation (1915): Box 271, Nyack, N.Y. 10960. 35,000. Phone: (914) 358-4601.

Female Executives, National Association for (1972): 1041 Third Ave., New York, N.Y. 10021. 175,000. Phone: (212) 371-0740.

Financial Analysts Federation (1947): 1633 Broadway, Suite 1402, New York, N.Y. 10019. 15,500. Phone: (212) 957-2860.

Fire Protection Association, National (1896): Batterymarch Park, Quincy, Mass. 02269. 37,000. Phone: (617) 770-3000.

Fleet Reserve Association (1924): 1303 New Hampshire Ave. N.W., Washington, D.C. 20036. 167,000. Phone: (202) 785-2768.

Flight Test Engineers, Society of (1968): P.O. Box 4047, Lancaster, Calif. 93539. 1,100. Phone: (805) 948-3067.

Flying Saucer Clubs of America, Amalgamated (1959): P.O. Box 39, Yucca Valley, Calif. 92286. 5,600. Phone: (619) 365-1141.

Foreign Policy Association (1918): 729 Seventh Ave., New York, N.Y. 10019. Phone: (212) 481-8450.

Foreign Relations, Council on (1921): 58 E. 68th St., New York, N.Y. 10021. 2,400. Phone: (212) 734-0400.

Foreign Student Affairs, National Association for (1948): 1860 19th St. N.W., Washington, D.C. 20009. 5,600. Phone: (202) 462-4811.

Foreign Study, American Institute for (1965): 102 Greenwich Ave., Greenwich, Conn. 06830. 300, 000. Phone: (203) 869-9090.

Foreign Trade Council, Inc., National (1914): 100 E. 42nd St., New York, N.Y. 10017. Over 550 companies. Phone: (212) 867-5630.

Forensic Sciences, American Academy of (1948): 225 S. Academy Blvd., Colorado Springs, Colo. 80910. 3,000. Phone: (303) 596-6006.

Forest Council, American (1932): 1250 Connecticut Ave. N.W., Suite 320, Washington, D.C. 20036. 100. Phone: (202) 463-2455.

Foresters, Society of American (1900): 5400 Grosvenor Lane, Bethesda, Md. 20814. 20,000. Phone: (301) 897-8720.

Forestry Association, American (1875): 1319 18th St. N.W., Washington, D.C. 20036. 40,000. Phone: (202) 467-5810.

Fortean Organization, International (1965): P.O. Box 367, Arlington, Va. 22210-0367. 800. Phone: (703) 522-9232.

Foster Parents Plan International (1937). Box 804, East Greenwich, R.I. 02818. Phone: (401) 826-2500.

Foundrymen's Society, American (1896): Golf & Wolf Rds., Des Plaines, Ill. 60016-2277. 14,000. Phone: (312) 824-0181.

4-H Program (early 1900s): Room 3860-S, U.S. Department of Agriculture, Washington, D.C. 20250. 4,300,000. Phone: (202) 447-5853.

Freedom of Information Center (1958): Box 858, Univ. of Missouri-Columbia, Columbia, Mo. 65205. Phone: (314) 882-4856.

***French-American Chamber of Commerce in the U.S.** (1896): 509 Madison Ave., Suite 1900, New York, N.Y. 10022. Trade Association. Phone: (212) 581-4554.

French Institute/Alliance Française (1911): 22 E. 60th St., New York, N.Y. 10022. 8,500. Phone: (212) 355-6100.

Friends of Animals (1957): One Pine St., Neptune, N.J. 07753. 125,000. Phone: (201) 922-2600.

Friends of the Earth (1969): 530 Seventh St. S.E., Washington, D.C. 20003. 18,000. Phone: (202) 543-4312.

Future Farmers of America (1928): 5632 Mt. Vernon Hgwy., Alexandria, Va. 22309. 430,000. Phone: (703) 360-3600.

Future Homemakers of America, Inc. (1945): 1910 Association Dr., Reston, Va. 22091. 300, 000. Phone: (703) 476-4900.

Gamblers Anonymous: Box 17173, Los Angeles, Calif. 90017. Phone: (213) 386-8789.

Genealogical Society, National (1903): 4527 17th St. N., Arlington, Va. 22207. 8,000. Phone: (703) 525-0050.

Genetic Association, American (1903): 818 18th St. N.W., Washington, D.C. 20006. 1,600. Phone: (202) 659-2096.

Geographers, Association of American (1904): 1710 16th St. N.W., Washington, D.C. 20009. 5, 800. Phone: (202) 234-1450.

Geographical Society, The American (1851): 156 Fifth Ave., Suite 600, New York, N.Y. 10010. 763. Phone: (212) 242-0214.

Geographic Education, National Council for (1915): Western Illinois University, Macomb, Ill. 61455. 3,200. Phone: (309) 298-2470.

Geographic Society, National (1888): 17th and M Sts. N.W., Washington, D.C. 20036. 10,500,000. Phone: (202) 857-7000.

Geological Institute, American (1948): 4220 King St., Alexandria, Va. 22302. 18 member societies representing 70,000 geoscientists. Phone: (703) 379-2480.

Geological Society of America, Inc. (1888): 3300 Penrose Pl., P.O. Box 9140, Boulder, Colo. 80301. 17,200. Phone: (303) 447-2020.

Geriatrics Society, American (1942): 770 Lexington Ave., Suite 400, New York, N.Y. 10021. 5, 500. Phone: (212) 308-1414.

Gideons International, The (1889): 2900 Lebanon Rd., Nashville, Tenn. 37214. 90,000. Phone: (615) 883-8533.

Gifted, The Association for the (1958): The Council for Exceptional Children, 1920 Association Dr., Reston, Va. 22091. 2,100. Phone: (703) 620-3660.

Girls Clubs of America (1945): 205 Lexington Ave., New York, N.Y. 10016. 250,000. Phone: (212) 689-3700.

Girl Scouts of the U.S.A. (1912): 830 Third Ave., New York, N.Y. 10022. 2,900,000. Phone: (212) 940-7500.

Graphic Artists, Society of American (1916): 32 Union Square, Rm. 1214, New York, N.Y. 10003. Phone: (212) 260-5706.

Graphoanalysis Society, International (1929): 111 N. Canal St., Chicago, Ill. 60606. 10,000. Phone: (312) 930-9446.

Gray Panthers, The National (1970): 311 S. Juniper St., Suite 601, Philadelphia, Pa. 19107. Over 100 chapters. Phone: (215) 545-6555.

Greenpeace U.S.A. (1979): 2007 R St. N.W., Washington, D.C. 20009. 550,000. Phone: (202) 462-1177.

Group Psychotherapy Association, American (1942): 25 E. 21st St., 6th Floor, New York, N.Y. 10010. 3,200 Phone: (212) 477-2677.

Guide Dog Foundation for the Blind, Inc. (1946): 371 E. Jericho Turnpike, Smithtown, N.Y. 11787. 710. Phone: (516) 265-2121.

***Hadassah, The Women's Zionist Organization of America** (1912): 50 W. 58th St., New York, N.Y. 10019. 385,000. Phone: (212) 355-7900.

Handgun Control, Inc. (1974): 1400 K St. N.W., Washington, D.C. 20005. 150,000. Phone: (202) 898-0792.

Health, Physical Education, Recreation, and Dance, American Alliance for (1885): 1900 Association Dr., Reston, Va. 22091. 35,000. Phone: (703) 476-3400.

Hearing and Speech Action, National Association for (1910): 10801 Rockville Pike, Rockville, Md. 20852. 1500. Phone: (800) 638-8255.

Heart Association, American (1924): 7320 Greenville Ave., Dallas, Tex. 75231. 200,000 members, 2,000,000 volunteers. Phone: (214) 373-6300.

Heating, Refrigerating, and Air-Conditioning Engineers, Inc., American Society of (1894): 1791 Tullie Circle N.E., Atlanta, Ga. 30329. 50,000. Phone: (404) 636-8400.

Helicopter Association, International (1948): 1619 Duke St., Alexandria, Va. 22314-3406. 1, 200. Phone: (703) 683-4646.

Hemispheric Affairs, Council on (1975): 1612 20th St. N.W., Washington, D.C. 20009. Phone: (202) 745-7000.

Historians, The Organization of American (1907): Indiana Univ., 112 N. Bryan St., Bloomington, Ind. 47401. 8,500. Phone: (812) 335-7311.
Historical Association, American (1884): 400 A St. S.E., Washington, D.C. 20003. 15,000. Phone: (202) 544-2422.
Historic Preservation, National Trust for (1949): 1785 Massachusetts Ave. N.W., Washington, D.C. 20036. 200,000. Phone: (202) 673-4000.
Home Economics Association, American (1909): 2010 Massachusetts Ave. N.W., Washington, D.C. 20036. 25,000. Phone: (202) 862-8300.
Horse Council, Inc., American (1969): 1700 K St. N.W., Washington, D.C. 20006. More than 150 organizations and 2 million individuals. Phone: (202) 296-4031.
Horse Shows Association, Inc., American (1917): 220 E. 42nd St., New York, N.Y. 10017-5806. 47,000. Phone: (212) 972-2472.
Horticultural Association, National Junior (1935): 441 E. Pine, Freemont, Mich. 49412. 12,500. Phone: (616) 652-3270.
Horticultural Society, American (1922): Box 0105, Mt. Vernon, Va. 22121. 45,000. Phone: (703) 768-5700.
Hospital Association, American (1898): 840 N. Lake Shore Dr., Chicago, Ill. 60611. 6,184 institutions. Phone: (312) 280-6622.
Humane Association, American (1877): 9725 E. Hampden, Denver, Colo. 80231. Phone: (303) 695-0811.
Humane Society of the United States (1954): 2100 L St. N.W., Washington, D.C. 20037. 585, 000. Phone: (202) 452-1100.
Humanities, National Endowment for the (1965): 1100 Pennsylvania Ave. N.W., Washington, D.C. 20506. Phone: (202) 786-0438.
***Hydrogen Energy, International Association for** (1975): P.O. Box 248266, Coral Gables, Fla. 33124. 2,500. Phone: (305) 284-4666.
Illustrators, Society of (1901): 128 E. 63rd St., New York, N.Y. 10021. 975. Phone: (212) 838-2560.
***Indian Rights Association** (1882): 1505 Race St., Philadelphia, Pa. 19102. 1,000. Phone: (215) 563-8349.
Industrial Engineers, Institute of (1948): 25 Technology Park/Atlanta, Norcross, Ga. 30092. 43, 000. Phone: (404) 449-0460.
Interfraternity Conference, National (1909): 3901 W. 86th St., Suite 280, Indianapolis, Ind. 46268. 59. Phone: (317) 872-1112.
***Iron and Steel Institute, American** (1908): 1000 16th St. N.W., Washington, D.C. 20036. 1,500. Phone: (202) 452-7100.
Izaak Walton League of America (1922): 1701 N. Ft. Myer Dr., Suite 1100, Arlington, Va. 22209. 50,000. Phone: (703) 528-1818.
***Jaycees, The United States** (1920): P.O. Box 7, Tulsa, Okla. 74121. 272,000. Phone: (918) 584-2481.
Jewish Appeal, United (1939): 99 Park Ave., New York, N.Y. 10016. Phone: (212) 818-9100.
***Jewish Committee, American** (1906): 165 E. 56th St., New York, N.Y. 10022. 50,000. Phone: (212) 751-4000.
Jewish Community Centers, World Confederation of (1946): 12 Hess St., Jerusalem, Israel 94185. Phone: (02) 247-767.
Jewish Congress, American (1918): 15 E. 84th St., New York, N.Y. 10028. 50,000. Phone: (212) 879-4500.
Jewish Historical Society, American (1892): 2 Thornton Rd., Waltham, Mass. 02154. 3,750. Phone: (617) 891-8110.
Jewish War Veterans of the U.S.A. (1896): 1811 R St. N.W., Washington, D.C. 20009. Phone: (202) 265-6280.
Jewish Women, National Council of (1893): 15 E. 26th St., New York, N.Y. 10010. 100,000. Phone: (212) 532-1740.
John Birch Society (1958): 395 Concord Ave., Belmont, Mass. 02178. Under 100,000. Phone: (617) 489-0600.
Journalists, Society of Professional, Sigma Delta Chi (1909): 53 W. Jackson Blvd., Suite 731, Chicago, Ill. 60604-3610. 22,000. Phone: (312) 922-7424.
Journalists and Authors, American Society of (1948): 1501 Broadway, Suite 1907, New York, N.Y. 10036. 750. Phone: (212) 997-0947.
Judaism, American Council for (1943): 298 Fifth Ave., New York, N.Y. 10001. 10,000. Phone: (212) 947-8878.
Junior Achievement (1919): 45 Clubhouse Dr., Colorado Springs, Colo. 80906. 8,184,565. Phone: (303) 540-8000.
Junior Leagues, Inc., Association of (1921): 660 First Ave., New York, N.Y. 10016. 269 Leagues, 163,000 members. Phone: (212) 355-4380.
Junior Statesmen of America (1934): 650 Bair Island Rd., Suite 201, Redwood City, Calif. 94063. 10,000. Phone: (415) 366-2700.
JWB (1917): 15 E. 26th St., New York, N.Y. 10010-1579. 275 affiliated community centers, YM-YWHAs, and camps. Phone: (212) 532-4949.
Kennel Club, American (1884): 51 Madison Ave., New York, N.Y. 10010. 446 member clubs. Phone: (212) 696-8234.
Kiwanis International (1915): 3636 Woodview Trace, Indianapolis, Ind. 46268. 305,000. Phone: (317) 875-8755.
***Knights of Columbus** (1882): One Columbus Plaza, New Haven, Conn. 06507. 1,425,265. Phone: (203) 772-2130.
Knights of Pythias, Supreme Lodge (1864): 2785 E. Desert Inn Rd. #150, Las Vegas, Nev. 89121. 104,736. Phone: (702) 735-3302.
Knights Templar, Grand Encampment of (1816): 14 E. Jackson Blvd., Suite 1700, Chicago, Ill. 60604. 340,000. Phone: (312) 427-5670.
La Leche League International (1956): 9616 Minneapolis Ave., Franklin Park, Ill. 60131. 40,000. Phone: (312) 455-7730.
Law, American Society of International (1906): 2223 Massachusetts Ave. N.W., Washington, D.C. 20008. 4,500. Phone: (202) 265-4313.
League of Women Voters of the U.S. (1920): 1730 M St. N.W., Washington, D.C. 20036. 114,000. Phone: (202) 429-1965.
Legal Aid and Defender Association, National (1911): 1625 K St. N.W., Suite 800, Washington, D.C. 20006. 5,000. Phone: (202) 452-0620.
Legal Secretaries, National Association of (1950): 2250 E. 73rd St., Suite 550, Tulsa, Okla. 74136. 18,000. Phone: (918) 493-3540.
Leukemia Society of America (1949): 733 Third Ave., New York, N.Y. 10017. Phone: (212) 573-8484.
Library Association, American (1876): 50 E. Huron St., Chicago, Ill. 60611. 43,500. Phone: (312) 944-6780.
Life Insurance, American Council of (1976): 1001 Pennsylvania Ave. N.W., Washington, D.C. 20004-2599. 630. Phone: (202) 624-2000.
***Life Underwriters, American Society of Chartered** (1928): 270 Bryn Mawr Ave., Bryn Mawr, Pa. 19010. 32,000. Phone: (215) 896-4300.

Life Underwriters, National Association of (1890): 1922 F St. N.W., Washington, D.C. 20006. Phone: (202) 331-6001.

Lions Clubs International (1917): 300 22nd St., Oak Brook, Ill. 60570. 1,348,142. Phone: (312) 571-5466.

Lung Association, American (1904): 1740 Broadway, New York, N.Y. 10019-4374. 138 constituent and affiliate associations. Phone: (212) 315-8700.

Magazine Editors, American Society of (1963): 575 Lexington Ave., New York, N.Y. 10022. 550. Phone: (212) 752-0055.

Magazine Publishers Association (1919): 575 Lexington Ave., New York, N.Y. 10022. 251 publishing companies rep. 1,200 magazines. Phone: (212) 752-0055.

Management Association, American (1923): 135 W. 50th St., New York, N.Y. 10020. 80,000. Phone: (212) 586-8100.

Management Consultants, Institute of (1968): 19 W. 44th St., Suite 810, New York, N.Y. 10036. 1,800. Phone: (212) 921-2885.

Manufacturers, National Association of (1895): 1331 Pennsylvania Ave. N.W., Suite 1500–North Lobby, Washington, D.C. 20004-1703. 13,500. Phone: (202) 637-3065.

Manufacturers' Agents National Association (MANA) (1947): 23016 Mill Creek Rd., P.O. Box 3467, Laguna Hills, Calif. 92654. 9,000. Phone: (714) 859-4040.

March of Dimes Birth Defects Foundation (1938): 1275 Mamaroneck Ave., White Plains, N.Y. 10605. 243 chapters. Phone: (914) 428-7100.

Marine Corps Association (1913): Box 1775 Marine Corps Base, Quantico, Va. 22134. Phone: (703) 640-6161.

Marine Corps League (1923): 956 N. Monroe St., P.O. Box 11100, Arlington, Va. 22210-2101. 30,000. Phone: (703) 524-1137.

Marine Technology Society (1963): 2000 Florida Ave., Suite 500, Washington, D.C. 20009. 2,500. Phone: (202) 462-7557.

Masons, Ancient and Accepted Scottish Rite, Northern Masonic Jurisdiction, Supreme Council 33 (1867): 33 Marrett Rd., Lexington, Mass. 02173. 456,580. Phone: (617) 862-4410.

Masons, Ancient and Accepted Scottish Rite, Southern Jurisdiction, Supreme Council (1801): 1733 16th St. N.W., Washington, D.C. 20009. 621,069. Phone: (202) 232-3579.

Masons, Royal Arch, General Grand Chapter International (1797): 1084 New Circle Rd. N.E., Lexington, Ky. 40505. 360,000. Phone: (606) 252-4618.

Massachusetts Audubon Society (1896): South Great Rd., Lincoln, Mass. 01773. 37,000 member households. Phone: (617) 259-9500.

Mathematical Association of America (1915): 1529 18th St. N.W., Washington, D.C. 20036. Phone: (202) 387-5200.

Mathematical Society, American (1888): P.O. Box 6248, Providence, R.I. 02940. 22,030. Phone: (401) 272-9500.

Mathematical Statistics, Institute of (1935): 3401 Investment Blvd. #7, Hayward, Calif. 94545. 3,400. Phone: (415) 783-8141.

Mayflower Descendants, General Society of (1897): 4 Winslow St., P.O. Box 3297, Plymouth, Mass. 02361. 21,000. Phone: (617) 746-3188.

***Mayors, U.S. Conference of** (1932): 1620 Eye St. N.W., Washington, D.C. 20006. 7 standing committees. Phone: (202) 293-7330.

***Mechanical Engineers, American Society of** (1880): 345 E. 47th St., New York, N.Y. 10017. 115,000. Phone: (212) 705-7722.

Mechanics, American Academy of (1969): Dept. of Civil Engineering, Northwestern Univ., Evanston, Ill. 60201. 1,200. Phone: (312) 491-4046.

Medical Association, American (1847): 535 N. Dearborn St., Chicago, Ill. 60610-4377. Phone: (312) 645-5000.

Medical Library Association (1898): 919 N. Michigan Ave., Chicago, Ill. 60611. 5,000. Phone: (312) 266-2456.

Mental Health Association, National (1909): 1021 Prince St., Alexandria, Va., 22314-2971. 1,000,000. Phone: (703) 684-7722.

Meteorological Society, American (1919): 45 Beacon St., Boston, Mass. 02108. 10,000. Phone: (617) 227-2425.

Military Chaplains Association of the U.S.A. (1925): P.O. Box 645, Riverdale, Md. 20737. 1,625. Phone: (301) 699-3505.

Mining, Metallurgical and Petroleum Engineers, American Institute of (1871): 345 E. 47th St., New York, N.Y. 10017. 4 Member Societies: Society of Mining Engineers, The Metallurgical Society, Iron & Steel Society, Society of Petroleum Engineers. Phone: (212) 705-7695.

Mining and Metallurgical Society of America (1910): 275 Madison Ave., Suite 2301, New York, N.Y. 10016. 300. Phone: (212) 684-4150.

Model Aeronautics, Academy of (1936): 1810 Samuel Morse Dr., Reston, Va. 22090. 125,000. Phone: (703) 435-0750.

Modern Language Association of America (1883): 10 Astor Place, New York, N.Y. 10003. 27,024. Phone: (212) 475-9500.

***Modern Woodmen of America** (1883): Mississippi River at 17th St., Rock Island, Ill. 61201. 550,000. Phone: (309) 786-6481.

Moose, Loyal Order of (1888): Mooseheart, Ill. 60539. 1,767,101. Phone: (312) 859-2000.

Mothers Against Drunk Driving (MADD) (1980): 669 Airport Fwy., Suite 310, Hurst, Tex. 76053. 600,000. Phone: (817) 268-6233.

Motion Picture & Television Engineers, Society of (1916): 595 W. Hartsdale Ave., White Plains, N.Y. 10607. 9,000. Phone: (914) 761-1100.

Motion Picture Arts & Sciences, Academy of (1927): 8949 Wilshire Blvd., Beverly Hills, Calif. 90211. Phone: (213) 278-8990.

Multiple Sclerosis Society, National (1946): 205 E. 42nd St., New York, N.Y. 10017. Phone: (212) 986-3240.

Muscular Dystrophy Association (1950): 810 Seventh Ave., New York, N.Y. 10019. 2,300,000 volunteers. Phone: (212) 586-0808.

Museum of Natural History, American (1869): Central Park West at 79th St., New York, N.Y. 10024. 500,000. Phone: (212) 769-5000.

***Museums, American Association of** (1906): 1055 Thomas Jefferson St. N.W., Washington, D.C. 20007. 9,000. Phone: (202) 338-5300.

***Music Council, National** (1940): 570 Seventh Ave., 20th floor, New York, N.Y. 10018. 65 National Music Organizations. Phone: (212) 302-2369.

Musicians, American Federation of (1896): 1501 Broadway, Suite 600 Paramount Bldg., New York, N.Y. 10036. 230,000. Phone: (212) 869-1330.

Music Publishers Association, Inc., National (1917): 205 E. 42nd St., New York, N.Y. 10017. Trade Organization/Harry Fox Agency-Licensing Organization. Phone: (212) 370-5330.

Muzzle Loading Rifle Association, National

(1933): P.O. Box 67, Friendship, Ind. 47021. 30,000. Phone: (812) 667-5131.

Narcolepsy and Cataplexy Foundation of America (1975): 1410 York Ave., Suite 2D, Mail Box 22, New York, N.Y. 10021. 3,964. Phone: (212) 628-6315.

National Association for the Advancement of Colored People (1909): 4805 Mt. Hope Dr., Baltimore, Md. 21215. 450,000. Phone: (301) 358-8900.

National Grange, The (1867): 1616 H St. N.W., Washington, D.C. 20006. 400,000. Phone: (202) 628-3507.

***National PTA (National Congress of Parents and Teachers)** (1897): 700 N. Rush St., Chicago, Ill. 60611. 5,840,000. Phone: (312) 787-0977.

***Natural Science for Youth Foundation** (1961): 11 Wildwood Valley, Atlanta, Ga. 30338. 350. Phone: (203) 966-5643.

***Nature Conservancy, The** (1951): 1800 N. Kent St., Arlington, Va. 22209. 275,000. Phone: (703) 841-5300.

Naval Architects and Marine Engineers, The Society of (1893): 601 Pavonia Ave., Jersey City, N.J. 07306. 12,200. Phone: (201) 798-4800.

Naval Engineers, American Society of (1888): 1452 Duke St., Alexandria, Va. 22314. 8,000. Phone: (703) 836-6727.

Naval Institute, United States (1873): Annapolis, Md. 21402. 97,000. Phone: (301) 268-6110.

Navigation, The Institute of (1945): 815 15th St. N.W., Suite 832, Washington, D.C. 20005. 3,000. Phone: (202) 783-4121.

Navy League of the United States (1902): 2300 Wilson Blvd., Arlington, Va. 22201. 54,328; William G. Sizemore, Executive Director.

Neurofibromatosis Foundation, The National (1978): 141 Fifth Ave., Suite 7S, New York, N.Y. 10010. 15,000. Phone: (212) 460-8980.

Newspaper Editors, American Society of (1922): P.O. Box 17004, Washington, D.C. 20041. 985. Phone: (703) 620-6087.

Newspaper Publishers Association, American (1887): The Newspaper Center, P.O. Box 17407, Dulles International Airport, Washington, D.C. 20041. 1,395. Phone: (703) 648-1000.

Nuclear Society, American (1954): 555 N. Kensington Ave., La Grange Park, Ill. 60525. 15,000. Phone: (312) 352-6611.

Numismatic Association, American (1891): 818 N. Cascade Ave., Colorado Springs, Colo. 80903. 37,000. Phone: (303) 632-2646.

Nurses' Association, American (1896): 1101 14th St. N.W. Washington, D.C. 20005. 188,000. Phone: (202) 789-1800.

Nutrition, American Institute of (1930): 9650 Rockville Pike, Bethesda, Md. 20814. 2,400. Phone: (301) 530-7050.

Odd Fellows, Sovereign Grand Lodge, Independent Order of (1819): 422 Trade St., Winston-Salem, N.C. 27101. 700,000. Phone: (919) 725-5955.

Olympic Committee, United States (1921): 1750 East Boulder St., Colorado Springs, Colo. 80909. Phone: (303) 632-5551.

Optical Society of America (1916): 1816 Jefferson Place N.W., Washington, D.C. 20036. 9,500. Phone: (202) 223-8130.

Optometric Association, American (1898): 243 N. Lindbergh Blvd., St. Louis, Mo. 63141. 25,000. Phone: (314) 991-4100.

Organization of American States, General Secretariat (1890): 1889 F St. N.W., Washington, D.C. 20006. 32 member nations. Phone: (202) 458-3000.

Ornithologists' Union, American (1883): c/o National Museum of Natural History, Smithsonian Institution, Washington, D.C. 20560. 4,000. Phone: (202) 357-1970.

ORT Federation, American (1922): 817 Broadway, New York, N.Y. 10003. 160,000. Phone: (212) 677-4400.

Osteopathic Association, American (1897): 212 E. Ohio St., Chicago, Ill. 60611-3269. 30,000. Phone: (312) 280-5800.

Overeaters Anonymous (1960): P.O. Box 92870, Los Angeles, Calif. 90009. 100,000. Phone: (213) 542-8363.

Parents Without Partners (1957): 8807 Colesville Rd., Silver Spring, Md. 20910. 209,729. Phone: (301) 588-9354.

Parks & Conservation Association, National (1919): 1015 31st St. N.W., Washington, D.C. 20007. 55,000. Phone: (202) 944-8530.

Pathologists, American Association of (1976): 9650 Rockville Pike, Bethesda, Md. 20814. 2,500. Phone: (301) 530-7130.

People for the American Way (1980): 1424 16th St. N.W., Suite 601, Washington, D.C. 20036. 250,000. Phone: (202) 462-4777.

Petroleum Geologists, American Association of (1917): P.O. Box 979, Tulsa, Okla. 74101-0979. 43,000. Phone: (918) 584-2555.

Pharmaceutical Association, American (1852): 2215 Constitution Ave. N.W., Washington, D.C. 20037. 50,000. Phone: (202) 628-4410.

Philatelic Society, American (1886): P.O. Box 8000, State College, Pa. 16803. 55,000. Phone: (814) 237-3803.

Philosophical Society, American (1743): 104 S. 5th St., Philadelphia, Pa. 19106-3387. 600. Phone: (215) 627-0706.

Photogrammetry and Remote Sensing, American Society for (1934): 210 Little Falls St., Falls Church, Va. 22046. 8,000. Phone: (703) 534-6617.

Photographic Society of America (1934): 2005 Walnut St., Philadelphia, Pa. 19103. 14,000. Phone: (215) 563-1663.

Photography, International Center of (1974): 1130 Fifth Ave., New York, N.Y. 10128. Phone: (212) 860-1777.

Physical Society, American (1899): 335 E. 45th St., New York, N.Y. 10017. 39,000. Phone: (212) 682-7341.

Physical Therapy Association, American (APTA) (1921): 1111 N. Fairfax St., Alexandria, Va. 22314. 44,000. Phone: (703) 684-2782.

Physics, American Institute of (1931): 335 E. 45th St., New York, N.Y. 10017. 100,000. Phone: (212) 661-9404.

Planetary Society, The (1979): 65 N. Catalina Ave., Pasadena, Calif. 91106. 110,000. Phone: (818) 793-5100.

Planned Parenthood Federation of America Inc., (1916): 810 Seventh Ave., New York, N.Y. 10019. 187 affiliates. Phone: (212) 603-4662.

Plastics Engineers, Society of (1942): 14 Fairfield Dr., Brookfield Center, Conn. 06805. 25,000. Phone: (203) 775-0471.

Police, American Federation of (1966): Records Center, 1100 N.E. 125th St., North Miami, Fla. 33161. 55,000. Phone: (305) 891-1700.

Police, International Association of Chiefs of (1893): 13 Firstfield Rd., Gaithersburg, Md. 20878. 13,000. Phone: (301) 948-0922.

Police Hall of Fame, American (1960): 14600 S. Tamiami Trail, North Port, Fla. 33596. 55,000. Phone: (305) 891-1700.

Police Organizations, National Association of (1979): c/o R. Scully, Detroit Police Officers Association, 2990 W. Grand Blvd., Detroit, Mich. 48202. 200,000. Phone: (313) 224-4266.

Political and Social Science, American Academy of (1889): 3937 Chestnut St., Philadelphia, Pa. 19104. Phone: (215) 386-4594.

Political Science, Academy of (1880): 2852 Broadway, New York, N.Y. 10025. 11,000. Phone: (212) 866-6752.

Powder Metallurgy Institute, American (1958): 105 College Rd. East, Princeton, N.J. 08540. 2, 400. Phone: (609) 452-7700.

Practical Nurse Education and Service, National Association for (1941): 10801 Peartree Lane, Suite 151, St. Ann, Mo. 63074. Phone: (314) 426-2662.

***Press Club, National** (1908): National Press Bldg., 529 14th St. N.W., Rm. 1386, Washington, D.C. 20045. 4,500. Phone: (202) 662-7500.

Professional Engineers, National Society of (1934): 1420 King St., Alexandria, Va. 22314. 75,000. Phone: (703) 684-2800.

Professional Photographers of America, Inc. (1880): 1090 Executive Way, Des Plaines, Ill. 60018. 14,000. Phone: (312) 299-8161.

Psychiatric Association, American (1844): 1400 K St. N.W., Washington, D.C. 20005. 33,293. Phone: (202) 682-6000.

Psychoanalytic Association, The American (1911): 309 E. 49th St., New York, N.Y. 10017. 3,000 analysts. Phone: (212) 752-0450.

Psychological Association, American (1892): 1200 17th St. N.W., Washington, D.C. 20036. 67,000. Phone: (202) 955-7660.

Public Health Association, American (1872): 1015 15th St. N.W., Washington, D.C. 20005. 31,802. Phone: (202) 789-5600.

Puppeteers of America (1937): 5 Cricklewood Path, Pasadena, Calif. 91107. Phone: (818) 797-5748.

Quality Control, The American Society for (1946): 310 W. Wisconsin Ave., Milwaukee, Wis. 53203. 53,000. Phone: (414) 272-8575.

Railroads, Association of American (1934): 50 F St. N.W., Washington, D.C. 20001. Phone: (202) 639-2100.

Recording Arts and Sciences, National Academy of (1958): 303 N. Glenoaks Blvd., Suite M-140, Burbank, Calif. 91502. 7,300. Phone: (213) 849-8233.

Red Cross, American (1881): 17th and D Sts. N.W., Washington, D.C. 20006. Over 2,900 chapters. Phone: (202) 639-3292.

***Rehabilitation Association, National** (1925): 633 S. Washington St., Alexandria, Va. 22314. 17, 000. Phone: (703) 836-0850.

Research and Enlightenment, Association for (1931): 67th St. & Atlantic Ave. (P.O. Box 595), Virginia Beach, Va. 23451. 70,000. Phone: (804) 428-3588.

Reserve Officers Association of the United States (1922): 1 Constitution Ave. N.E., Washington, D.C. 20002. 125,000. Phone: (202) 479-2200.

Retarded Citizens, Association for (1950): 2501 Avenue J, Arlington, Tex. 76006. 1,300 units. Phone: (817) 640-0204.

Retired Federal Employees, National Association of (1921): 1533 New Hampshire Ave. N.W., Washington, D.C. 20036. 495,000. Phone: (202) 234-0832.

Retired Persons, American Association of (1958): 1909 K St. N.W., Washington, D.C. 20049. 25, 000,000. Phone: (202) 728-4308.

Reye's Syndrome Foundation, National (1974): 426 N. Lewis St., Bryan, Ohio 43506. Phone: (800) 233-7393.

RID-USA (Remove Intoxicated Drivers) (1978): Box 520, Schenectady, N.Y. 12301. Over 130 chapters. Phone: (518) 372-0034.

***Rifle Association of America, National** (1871): 1600 Rhode Island Ave. N.W., Washington, D.C. 20036. 3,000,000. Phone: (202) 828-6000.

Right to Life, National Committee (1973): 419 7th St. N.W., Washington, D.C. 20004. Phone: (202) 626-8800.

Rotary International (1905): 1600 Ridge Ave., Evanston, Ill. 60201. 1,030,000. Phone: (312) 328-0100.

Safety Council, National (1913): 444 N. Michigan Ave., Chicago, Ill. 60611. Phone: (312) 527-4800.

Salvation Army, The (1865): 799 Bloomfield Ave., Verona, N.J. 07044. 427,825. Phone: (201) 239-0606.

SANE, Committee for a SANE Nuclear Policy (1957): 711 G St. S.E., Washington, D.C. 20003. 155,000. Phone: (202) 546-7100.

***Save Our Shores, Inc.** (1969): P.O. Box 103, North Quincy, Mass. 02171. 50,000. Phone: (617) 328-1121.

Save-the-Redwoods League (1918): 114 Sansome St., San Francisco, Calif. 94104. 40,000. Phone: (415) 362-2352.

***Savings Institutions, National Council of** (1920): 1101 15th St. N.W., Suite 400, Washington, D.C. 20005. Phone: (202) 331-0270.

Science, American Association for the Advancement of (1848): 1333 H St. N.W., Washington, D.C. 20005. 133,000. Phone: (202) 326-6440.

***Science Fiction Society, World** (1939): c/o Southern California Institute for Fan Interests, P.O. Box 8442, Van Nuys, Calif. 91409. 5,000. Phone: (213) 938-9436.

Science Writers, Inc., National Association of (1934): P.O. Box 294, Greenlawn, N.Y. 11740. 1,290. Phone: (516) 757-5664.

Scientists, Federation of American (FAS) (1945): 307 Massachusetts Ave. N.E., Washington, D.C. 20002. 5,000. Phone: (202) 546-3300.

SCRABBLE® Crossword Game Players (1972): P.O. Box 700, Front Street Garden, Greenport, N.Y. 11944. 7,000. Phone: (516) 477-0033.

Screen Actors Guild (1933): 7065 Hollywood Blvd., Hollywood, Calif. 90028. Phone: (213) 465-4600.

Sculpture Society, National (1893): 15 E. 26th St., New York, N.Y. 10010. 350. Phone: (212) 889-6960.

***Seeing Eye** (1929): Washington Valley Rd., Morristown, N.J. 07960. Phone: (201) 539-4425.

Senior Citizens, National Alliance of (1974): 2525 Wilson Blvd., Arlington, Va. 22201. 2.2 million. Phone: (703) 528-4380.

Separationists, Society of (1963): P.O. Box 2117, Austin, Tex. 78768-2117. 30,000. Phone: (512) 458-1244.

Shrine of North America (Shriners Hospitals) (1872): Box 25356, Tampa, Fla. 33622. 900, 000. Phone: (813) 885-2575.

Sierra Club (1892): 730 Polk St., San Francisco, Calif. 94109. 407,000. Phone: (415) 776-2211.

SIETAR—The International Society for Intercultural Education, Training, and Research (1974): 1505 22nd St. N.W., Washington, D.C. 20037. 1, 500. Phone: (202) 296-4710.

Simon Wiesenthal Center (1978): 9760 W. Pico

Blvd., Los Angeles, Calif. 90035. 265,000. Phone: (213) 553-9036.

Small Business United, National (1937): 1155 15th St. N.W., Washington, D.C. 20005. 40,000. Phone: (202) 293-8830.

Social Welfare, National Conference on (1873): 1015 18th St. N.W., Suite 601, Washington, D.C. 20036. 4,000. Phone: (202) 785-0817.

Social Work Education, Council on (1919): 1744 R St. N.W., Washington, D.C. 20009. 5,000. Phone: (202) 667-2300.

Social Workers, National Association of (1955): 7981 Eastern Ave., Silver Spring, Md. 20910. Phone: (301) 565-0333.

Sociological Association, American (1905): 1722 N St. N.W., Washington, D.C. 20036. 12,000. Phone: (202) 833-3410.

Soil Conservation Society of America (1945): 7515 N.E. Ankeny Rd., Ankeny, Iowa 50021. 14, 000. Phone: (515) 289-2331.

Songwriters Guild of America, The (1931): 276 Fifth Ave., New York, N.Y. 10001. 4,200. Phone: (212) 686-6820.

Sons of Italy in America, Order (1905): 219 E St. N.E., Washington, D.C. 20002. 100,000. Phone: (202) 547-2900.

Sons of the American Revolution, National Society of the (1889): 1000 S. 4th St., Louisville, Ky. 40203. 24,900. Phone: (502) 589-1776.

Soroptimist International of the Americas (1921): 1616 Walnut St., Philadelphia, Pa. 19103. 30, 000. Phone: (215) 732-0512.

***Southern Christian Leadership Conference** (1957): 334 Auburn Ave. N.E., Atlanta, Ga. 30303. 1,000,000; 350 chapters, 260 affiliated organizations. Phone: (404) 522-1420.

Space Education Association, U.S. (1973): 746 Turnpike Rd., Elizabethtown, Pa. 17022-1161. 1, 000. Phone: (717) 367-3265.

Space Society, National (1974): 922 Pennsylvania Ave. S.E., Washington, D.C. 20003. 20,000. Phone: (202) 543-1900.

Special Olympics (1968): 1350 New York Ave. N.W., Suite 500, Washington, D.C., 20005. 1, 000,000. Phone: (202) 628-3630.

Speech-Language-Hearing Association, American (1925): 10801 Rockville Pike, Rockville, Md. 20852. 46,000. Phone: (301) 897-5700.

Sports Car Club of America (1944): 9033 E. Easter Place, Englewood, Colo. 80112. 42,000. Phone: (303) 694-7222.

State Garden Clubs, Inc., National Council of (1929): 4401 Magnolia Ave., St. Louis, Mo. 63110. 308,623. Phone: (314) 776-7574.

State Governments, The Council of (1933): P.O. Box 11910, Iron Works Pike, Lexington, Ky. 40578. All state officials, all 50 states. Phone: (606) 252-2291.

Statistical Association, American (1839): 1429 Duke St., Alexandria, Va. 22314. 15,200.

Student Association, United States (1978): 1012 14th St. N.W., Washington, D.C. 20005. Phone: (202) 775-8943.

***Students Against Drunken Driving (SADD)** (1981): 10812 Ashfield Rd., Adelphi, Md., 20783. 175 local groups. Phone: (301) 937-7936.

Surgeons, American College of (1913): 55 E. Erie, St., Chicago, Ill. 60611. 49,000. Phone: (312) 664-4050.

Surveying and Mapping, American Congress on (1941): 210 Little Falls St., Falls Church, Va. 22046. 10,700. Phone: (703) 241-2446.

Symphony Orchestra League, American (1942): 633 E St. N.W., Washington, D.C. 20004. 4,732. Phone: (202) 628-0099.

TASH: The Association for Persons with Severe Handicaps (1973): 7010 Roosevelt Way, N.E., Seattle, Wash. 98115. 6,700. Phone: (206) 523-8446.

Tax Foundation, Inc. (1937): One Thomas Circle N.W., Suite 500, Washington, D.C. 20005. 1,000. Phone: (202) 822-9050.

Teachers, American Federation of (1916): 555 New Jersey Ave. N.W., Washington, D.C., 20001. 630,000. Phone: (202) 879-4440.

***Television Arts and Sciences, National Academy of** (1948): 110 W. 57th St., New York, N.Y., 10019. 15,000. Phone: (212) 586-8424.

Testing & Materials, American Society for (1898): 1916 Race St., Philadelphia, Pa. 19103. 30,000. Phone: (215) 299-5400.

***Theatre Guild** (1919): 226 W. 47th St., New York, N.Y. 10036. 105,000. Phone: (212) 869-5470.

Theosophical Society in America, The (1875): P.O. Box 270, Wheaton, Ill. 60189-0270. 4,900. Phone: (312) 668-1571.

Toastmasters International (1924): P.O. Box 10400, 2200 N. Grand Ave., Santa Ana, Calif., 92711. 130,000. Phone: (714) 542-6793.

Toughlove (1977): P.O. Box 1069, Doylestown, Pa. 18901. 2,000 groups internationally. Phone: (215) 348-7090.

TransAfrica Forum (1982): 545 Eighth St. S.E., Suite 200, Washington, D.C. 20003. Phone: (202) 547-2550.

Travel Agents, American Society of (ASTA) (1931): 1101 King St., Alexandria, Va. 22314-2980. 22,000. Phone: (703) 793-2782.

Travelers Aid Services (1905/1982); 2 Lafayette St., New York, N.Y. 10007. Lucy N. Friedman, Executive Director. (Result of merger of Travelers Aid Society of New York and Victim Services Agency in 1982). Phone: (212) 577-7700.

UFOs, National Investigations Committee on (1967): 14617 Victory Blvd., Suite 4, Van Nuys, Calif. 91411. Phone: (818) 989-5942.

***UNICEF, U.S. Committee for** (1947): 331 E. 38th St., New York, N.Y. 10016. 2,500,000 volunteers. Phone: (212) 686-5522.

United Negro College Fund Inc. (1944): 500 E. 62nd St., New York, N.Y. 10021. Phone: (212) 326-1100.

United Way of America (1918): 701 N. Fairfax St., Alexandria, Va. 22314. 2200 local groups. Phone: (703) 836-7100.

University Foundation, International (1973): 1301 S. Noland Rd., Independence, Mo. 64055. 12, 000. Phone: (816) 461-3633.

University Women, American Association of (1881): 2401 Virginia Ave. N.W., Washington, D.C. 20037. 175,000. Phone: (202) 785-7700.

***Urban League, National** (1910): 500 E. 62nd St., New York, N.Y. 10021. 116. Phone: (212) 310-9000.

USO (United Service Organizations) (1941): 601 Indiana Ave. N.W., Washington, D.C. 20036. Phone: (202) 783-8121.

Variety Clubs International (1927): 1560 Broadway, Suite 1209, New York, N.Y. 10036. 15,000. Phone: (212) 704-9872.

Veterans Committee, American (AVC) (1944): 1717 Massachusetts Ave. N.W., Suite 203, Washington, D.C. 20036. 25,000. Phone: (202) 667-0090.

Veterans of Foreign Wars of the U.S. (1899): V.F.W. Bldg., 34th and Broadway, Kansas City, Mo. 64111. V.F.W. and Auxiliary, 2,850,000.

Phone: (816) 756-3390.

Veterinary Medical Association, American (1863): 930 N. Meacham Rd., Schaumburg, Ill. 60196. 44,000. Phone: (312) 885-8070.

Visually Handicapped, Division for the (1952): The Council for Exceptional Children, 1920 Association Dr., Reston, Va. 22091. 1,000. Phone: (703) 620-3660.

Volunteers of America (1896): 3813 N. Causeway Blvd., Metairie, La. 70002. 4 regional, 100 local groups. Phone: (504) 837-2652.

***War Resisters League** (1923): 339 Lafayette St., New York, N.Y. 10012. 18,000. Phone: (212) 228-0450.

Washington Legal Foundation (1976): 1705 N St. N.W., Washington, D.C. 20036. 200,000. Phone: (202) 857-0240.

Water Quality Association (1974): 4151 Naperville Rd., Lisle, Ill. 60532. Phone: (312) 369-1600.

Water Resources Association, American (1964): 5410 Grosvenor Lane, Suite 220, Bethesda, Md. 20814. 3,500. Phone: (301) 493-8600.

Welding Society, American (1919): 550 N.W. LeJeune Rd., Miami, Fla. 33126. 32,000. Phone: (305) 443-9353.

Whale Protection Fund (1976): 1725 De Sales St. N.W., Suite 500, Washington, D.C. 20036. 450, 000. Phone: (202) 429-5609.

Wildlife Federation, National (1936): 1412 16th St. N.W., Washington, D.C. 20036. 4,600,000. Phone: (202) 797-6800.

***Wildlife Fund, World** (1961): 1255 23rd St. N.W., Washington, D.C. 20037. 220,000. Phone: (202) 387-0800.

Woman's Christian Temperance Union, National (1874): 1730 Chicago Ave., Evanston, Ill. 60201. 200,000. Phone: (312) 864-1396.

Women, National Organization for (NOW) (1966): 1401 New York Ave. N.W., Suite 800, Washington, D.C. 20005-2102. 150,000. Phone: (202) 347-2279.

Women's American ORT (1927): 315 Park Ave. South, New York, N.Y. 10010. 145,000. Phone: (212) 505-7700.

Women's Clubs, General Federation of (1890): 1734 N St., N.W., Washington, D.C. 20036. 500, 000. Phone: (202) 347-3168.

Women's Educational and Industrial Union (1877): 356 Boylston St., Boston, Mass. 02116. 2,200. Phone: (617) 536-5651.

***Women's International League for Peace and Freedom** (1915): 1213 Race St., Philadelphia, Pa. 19107. 15,000. Phone: (215) 563-7110.

Women Strike for Peace (1961): 145 S. 13th St., Philadelphia, Pa. 19107. 9,000. Phone: (215) 923-0861.

World Future Society (1966): 4916 St. Elmo Ave., Bethesda, Md. 75231. 25,000. Phone: (301) 656-8274.

***World Health, American Association for** (1951): 525 23rd St. N.W., Washington, D.C. 20037. 500. Phone: (202) 861-4322.

World Peace, International Association of Educators for (1969): P.O. Box 3282, Mastin Lake Station, Huntsville, Ala. 35810. 20,000. Phone: (205) 534-5501.

World Peace Foundation (1910): 22 Batterymarch St., Boston, Mass. 02109. Phone: (617) 482-3875.

Writers Union, National (1983): 13 Astor Pl., 7th Fl., New York, NY 10003. 2,500. Phone: (212) 254-0279.

YMCA of the USA (1844): 101 N. Wacker Dr., Chicago, Ill. 60606. 13,500,000. Phone: (312) 977-0031.

Young Men's and Young Women's Hebrew Association (1874): 1395 Lexington Ave., New York, N.Y. 10018. 9,000. Phone: (212) 427-6000.

Young Women's Christian Association of the U.S.A. (1858 in U.S.A., 1855 in England): 726 Broadway, New York, N.Y. 10003. 2,030,922. Phone: (212) 614-2846.

Youth Development Foundation, National (1971): 3460 Hollenberg, Suite A, Bridgeton, Mo. 63044. Phone: (314) 928-0838.

Youth Hostels, Inc., American (1934): P.O. Box 37613, Washington, D.C. 20013-7613. 100, 000. Phone: (202) 783-6161.

Zero Population Growth (1968): 1601 Connecticut Ave. N.W., Washington, D.C. 20009. 15,000. Phone: (202) 332-2000.

***Zionist Organization of America** (1897): ZOA House, 4 E. 34th St., New York, N.Y. 10016. 135, 000. Phone: (212) 481-1500.

Zoological Parks and Aquariums, American Association of (1924): Oglebay Park, Wheeling, W. Va. 26003. 5,000. Phone: (304) 242-2160.

Zoologists, American Society of (1890): Box 2739, California Lutheran Univ., Thousand Oaks, Calif. 91360. 4,300. Phone: (805) 492-3585.

National Nonprofit Associations, 1970–1985

Type	1985	1980	1975	1970
Trade, business, commercial	3,719	3,118	2,837	2,895
Agriculture	882	677	612	508
Legal, governmental, public administration, military	658	529	450	346
Scientific, engineering, technical	1,270	1,039	874	548
Educational and cultural	2,822	2,376	2,132	1,383
Social welfare	1,450	994	777	475
Health, medical	1,886	1,413	1,138	830
Public affairs	1,935	1,068	835	498
Fraternal, foreign interest, nationality, ethnic	492	435	460	610
Religious	953	797	736	806
Veteran, hereditary, patriotic	281	208	213	198
Hobby, avocational	1,311	910	681	444
Athletic sports	737	504	449	336
Labor unions	252	235	234	226
Chambers of Commerce[1]	142	105	112	110
Greek letter societies	331	318	326	334
Total	**19,121**	**14,726**	**12,866**	**10,734[2]**

1. National and binational. 2. Includes associations not shown separately. *Source:* Gale Research Co., Detroit, Mich. Compiled from *Encyclopedia of Associations,* annual. (Copyright). From: *Statistical Abstract of the United States 1987.*

Why Johnny Can't Think

By Norman Lear

When it comes to science education, my personal experience—and, now, my worries for the future—may be typical of my generation.

I'm a man in my sixties. I learned a little about science in school, several decades before the era of spaceflight, computers, and genetic engineering. During World War II, I had the opportunity to study applied aerodynamics as a radio operator/gunner in the Air Force. For the past three decades, I've been a television writer and producer and have learned something about the daily miracle of TV production and broadcasting.

In other words, when it comes to science, like most people of my generation, I might charitably be classified as marginally literate.

Here's what worries me: The generation of Americans that's growing up now will need to cope with a world much more technologically advanced than the one I entered. But they're even more ill-prepared than I was. And I fear that the inadequacies of the science education that they've received are typical of their schooling in other important subjects as well.

Recently, I've had the opportunity to learn about the state of science education—and education in general. Through my work in People for the American Way, I came to learn about how textbooks and curricula have deteriorated, largely as a result of pressure by the religious right and other groups to avoid mention of controversial subjects.

It came as a little bit of a surprise to me that more than six decades after the Scopes trial, the teaching of evolution is still on trial. For a scientific theory to be banished from the textbooks and banned from classrooms—not because it has been disproved but because it offends some people—is an alarming indication of the state of science education.

Many educators have told me that alarm *is* warranted. Our textbook reviews have discovered that the censorship of evolution is typical of the declining quality of science textbooks. Instead of serving as intellectually stimulating classroom materials that encourage students to learn by themselves about the natural world, science texts have degenerated into pedagogical pabulum that encourages memorization and rote learning.

These facts explain why we may be in the process of producing a generation of scientific illiterates. Consider these recent news stories:

- In a survey conducted for the National Science Foundation, only one third of the public understood what a molecule is, fewer than one third understood radiation, and only one sixth understood DNA.

- The same study found Americans suspicious of science and embracing pseudoscience and even superstition. Fifty-three percent declared scientists are dangerous because they know too much, 46 percent rejected the theory of evolution, 43 percent believed UFOs carry visitors from outer space, and a significant number expressed a belief in astrology.

- During 1986, Japan—a country half our size—graduated twice as many science Ph.D's as the United States did.

Not only science, but also hundreds of controversial subjects have been downplayed—or eliminated entirely. Censorship by organized pressure groups—and self-censoring by textbook publishers—affect treatment of such tragic chapters of history as slavery, the Holocaust, the Great Depression, and even such literary classics as *Romeo and Juliet.*

Curiously enough, there's one issue on which I find myself agreeing with Jerry Falwell and Pat Robertson: Textbooks and curricula *do* shortchange the subject of religion. This view was confirmed by a review of high-school textbooks conducted by a panel of historians and educators for People for the American Way; they found history texts minimize the important role religious people, religious values, religious leaders, and religious institutions have played—and continue to play—in American life.

What's lacking in science curricula is lacking in education in other subjects as well—not only specific information but respect for the spirit of free inquiry, which is at the heart of the scientific method and any education worthy of the name.

For anyone to be denied an education is a personal tragedy, but if this generation grows up uneducated, it will be a national tragedy as well. Today's high-school students will inherit awesome responsibilities: to revive our stagnant industrial base and develop new industries; to find a way that the world's nations can live in peace at a time when a growing number of countries have the capacity to destroy the world; and to preserve and expand our democracy at a time when an anxious people may be vulnerable to demagogues preaching a politics of scapegoating and simple solutions. These challenges will certainly overwhelm a generation cheated of the oportunity to study modern science, to read the classics, or even to think for themselves.

Thirty years ago, when the Soviet *Sputnik* launch started American thinking about the failures of our educational system, there was a popular book called *Why Johnny Can't Read.* Three decades later, a similar book might be entitled *Why Johnny and Janey Can't Think.* □

Norman Lear, writer, film and television producer, is best known for the TV series "All in the Family." He is a cofounder of People for the American Way. This article is reprinted from the February 1987 issue of OMNI with permission from People for the American Way.

School Enrollment, October 1986

(in thousands)

Age	White		Black		Spanish origin[1]		All races	
	Enrolled	Percent	Enrolled	Percent	Enrolled	Percent	Enrolled	Percent
3 and 4 years	2,296	39.1	411	38.2	231	28.7	2,813	38.9
5 and 6 years	5,524	95.3	1,100	95.2	761	93.7	6,617	95.3
7 to 9 years	8,162	99.3	1,548	99.8	1,051	99.4	10,056	99.3
10 to 13 years	10,417	99.2	2,016	99.0	1,427	99.3	12,931	99.1
14 and 15 years	5,677	97.8	1,079	96.6	636	96.3	7,007	97.6
16 and 17 years	5,587	92.0	1,015	93.2	581	83.8	6,861	92.3
18 and 19 years	3,192	54.8	518	49.4	278	45.3	3,872	54.6
20 and 21 years	2,042	33.5	268	25.7	160	21.1	2,430	33.0
22 to 24 years	1,759	17.4	261	16.6	145	12.8	2,154	17.9
25 to 29 years	1,589	8.8	197	7.5	168	8.6	1,882	8.8
30 to 34 years	1,021	5.9	143	5.9	74	4.6	1,230	6.0
Total	**47,267**	**47.4**	**8,556**	**51.1**	**5,513**	**47.8**	**58,153**	**48.2**

1. Persons of Spanish origin may be of any race. NOTE: Figures include persons enrolled in nursery school, kindergarten, elementary school, high school, and college. *Source:* Department of Commerce, Bureau of the Census.

Persons Not Enrolled in School, October 1986

(in thousands)

Age	Population	Total not enrolled		High school graduate		Not high school graduate (dropouts)[1]	
		Number	Percent	Number	Percent	Number	Percent
14 and 15 years	7,182	176	2.4	—	—	176	2.4
16 and 17 years	7,433	572	7.7	117	1.6	455	6.1
18 and 19 years	7,095	3,223	45.4	2,351	33.1	872	12.3
20 and 21 years	7,358	4,928	67.0	3,838	52.2	1,089	14.8
22 to 24 years	12,059	9,905	82.1	8,180	67.8	1,726	14.3

1. Persons who are not enrolled in school and who are not high school graduates are considered dropouts. *Source:* Department of Commerce, Bureau of the Census.

School Enrollment by Grade, Control, and Race

(in thousands)

Grade level and type of control	White			Black			All races[1]		
	Oct. 1986[3]	Oct. 1980[4]	Oct. 1970	Oct. 1986[3]	Oct. 1980[4]	Oct. 1970	Oct. 1986[3]	Oct. 1980[4]	Oct. 1970
Nursery school: Public	601	432	198	200	180	129	835	633	333
Private	1,543	1,205	695	115	115	49	1,719	1,354	763
Kindergarten: Public	2,589	2,172	2,233	600	440	374	3,328	2,690	2,674
Private	572	423	473	47	50	53	633	486	536
Grades 1–8: Public	19,090	19,743	24,923	4,134	4,058	4,668	24,163	24,398	30,001
Private	2,671	2,768	3,715	193	202	200	2,958	3,051	3,949
Grades 9–12: Public	10,229	12,056[2]	11,599	2,040	2,200[2]	1,794	12,746	14,556[2]	13,545
Private	1,030	—	1,124	91	—	41	1,166	—	1,170
College: Public	6,821	8,875[2]	5,168	896	1,007[2]	422	8,153	10,180[2]	5,699
Private	2,122	—	1,591	242	—	100	2,452	—	1,714
Total: Public	39,329	—	44,121	7,869	—	7,387	49,225	—	52,225
Private	7,937	—	7,598	687	—	443	8,929	—	8,132
Grand Total	**47,266**	**47,673**	**51,719**	**8,556**	**8,251**	**7,830**	**58,154**	**57,348**	**60,357**

1. Includes persons of Spanish origin. 2. Total public and private. Breakdown not available. 3. Estimates controlled to 1980 census base. 4. Estimates controlled to 1970 census base. *Source:* Department of Commerce, Bureau of the Census.

State Compulsory School Attendance Laws

State	Enactment[1]	Age limits	State	Enactment[1]	Age limits
Alabama	1915	7-16	Montana	1883	7-16
Alaska	1929	7-16	Nebraska	1887	7-16[2]
Arizona	1899	8-16	Nevada	1873	7-17
Arkansas	1909	7-17	New Hampshire	1871	6-16
California	1874	6-16	New Jersey	1875	6-16
Colorado	1889	7-16	New Mexico	1891	6-18
Connecticut	1872	7-16	New York	1874	6-16
Delaware	1907	5-16	North Carolina	1907	7-16
D. C.	1864	7-17	North Dakota	1883	7-16
Florida	1915	6-16	Ohio	1877	6-18
Georgia	1916	7-16	Oklahoma	1907	7-18
Hawaii	1896	6-18	Oregon	1889	7-18
Idaho	1887	7-16	Pennsylvania	1895	8-17
Illinois	1883	7-16	Rhode Island	1883	7-16
Indiana	1897	7-16	South Carolina	1915	5-17
Iowa	1902	7-16	South Dakota	1883	7-16[2]
Kansas	1874	7-16	Tennessee	1905	7-17
Kentucky	1896	6-18	Texas	1915[3]	7-16[4]
Louisiana	1910	7-16	Utah	1890	6-18
Maine	1875	7-17	Vermont	1867	7-16
Maryland	1902	6-16	Virginia	1908	5-17
Massachusetts	1852	6-16	Washington	1871	8-18
Michigan	1871	6-16	West Virginia	1897	6-16
Minnesota	1885	7-16	Wisconsin	1879	6-18
Mississippi	1918	6-14	Wyoming	1876	7-16
Missouri	1905	7-16			

1. Date of enactment of first compulsory attendance law. 2. May leave anytime after completing 8th grade. 3. A compulsory school attendance law was contained in a law of 1873 establishing free public schools. However, the provision was omitted in superseding legislation passed in 1876. 4. Must complete academic year in which 16th birthday occurs. *Source:* Department of Education, National Center for Educational Statistics.

High School and College Graduates

Year of graduation	High School			College[1]		
	Men	Women	Total	Men	Women	Total
1900	38,075	56,808	94,883	22,173	5,237	27,410
1910	63,676	92,753	156,429	28,762	8,437	37,199
1920	123,684	187,582	311,266	31,980	16,642	48,622
1929-30	300,376	366,528	666,904	73,615	48,869	122,484
1939-40	578,718	642,757	1,221,475	109,546	76,954	186,500
1949-50	570,700	629,000	1,199,700	328,841	103,217	432,058
1959-60	898,000	966,000	1,864,000	254,063	138,377	392,440
1964-65	1,314,000	1,351,000	2,665,000	316,286	213,717	530,003
1967-68	1,341,000	1,361,000	2,702,000	390,507	276,203	666,710
1968-69	1,402,000	1,427,000	2,829,000	444,380	319,805	764,185
1969-70	1,433,000	1,463,000	2,896,000	484,174	343,060	827,234
1970-71	1,456,000	1,487,000	2,943,000	511,138	366,538	877,676
1971-72	1,490,000	1,518,000	3,008,000	541,313	389,371	930,684
1972-73	1,501,000	1,536,000	3,037,000	564,680	407,700	972,380
1973-74	1,515,000	1,565,000	3,080,000	575,843	423,749	999,592
1974-75	1,541,000	1,599,000	3,140,000	533,797	425,052	978,849
1975-76	1,554,000	1,601,000	3,155,000	557,817	430,578	988,395
1976-77	1,548,000	1,606,000	3,154,000	547,919	435,989	983,908
1977-78	1,535,000	1,599,000	3,134,000	487,000	434,000	921,000
1978-79	1,531,800	1,602,400	3,134,200	529,996	460,242	990,238
1979-80	1,500,000	1,558,000	3,058,000	526,327	473,221	999,548
1980-81	1,483,000	1,537,000	3,020,000	470,000	465,000	935,000
1981-82	1,474,000	1,527,000	3,001,000	473,000	480,000	953,000
1982-83	1,437,000	1,451,000	2,888,000	479,140	490,370	969,510
1983-84	n.a.	n.a.	2,773,000	482,319	491,990	974,309
1984-85	n.a.	n.a.	2,683,000	482,528	496,949	979,477

1. Includes bachelor's and first-professional degrees for years 1900–1960. 2. n.a. = not available. NOTE: Includes graduates from public and private schools. Beginning in 1959–60, figures include Alaska and Hawaii. Because of rounding, details may not add to totals. Most recent data available. *Source:* Department of Education, Center for Education Statistics.

Federal Funds for Some Major Programs for Education, Fiscal Year 1988[1]

Program	Amount in thousands	Program	Amount in thousands
Elementary–secondary		Higher education facilities	22,500
Educationally disadvantaged	$ 4,144,163	Aid for institutional development	60,526
Special programs	784,337	**Vocational education**	7,148
Bilingual education	143,095	**Adult basic and secondary education**	130,000
School assistance in federally affected areas	548,000	**Education for the handicapped**	
Higher education		State grant program	1,259,381
Program development	12,500	Preschool grants	85,500
Student assistance		Special populations	45,100
Pell grants	3,208,000	Training and information	57,900
Work study/grants	—	All other	40,300
Direct loans to students	696,000	**Indian education**	64,234
Special programs for the disadvantaged	82,370	**Education research and improvement**	70,231
		Total	**$11,461,285**

1. Estimated outlay for fiscal year 1988. *Source: Budget of the United States Government,* Fiscal Year 1988.

Funding for Public Elementary and Secondary Education, 1977–78 to 1984–85

(In thousands except percent)

School year	Total	Federal	State	Local	% Federal	% State	% Local[1]
1977–78	81,443,160	7,694,194	35,013,266	38,735,700	9.4	43.0	47.6
1978–79	87,994,143	8,600,116	40,132,136	39,261,891	9.8	45.6	44.6
1979–80	96,881,165	9,503,537	45,348,814	42,028,813	9.8	46.8	43.4
1980–81	105,949,087	9,768,262	50,182,659	45,998,166	9.2	47.4	43.4
1981–82	110,191,257	8,186,466	52,436,435	49,568,356	7.4	47.6	45.0
1982–83	117,497,502	8,339,990	56,282,157	52,875,354	7.1	47.9	45.0
1983–84	126,055,419	8,576,547	60,232,981	57,245,892	6.8	47.8	45.4
1984–85[2]	137,350,722	8,952,358	66,983,340	61,415,023	6.5	48.8	44.7

1. Includes a relatively small amount from nongovernmental sources (gifts and tuition and transportation fees from patrons). 2. Preliminary data. *Source:* U.S. Department of Education, National Center for Education Statistics.

Major U.S. College and University Libraries

(Top 50 based on number of volumes in library)

Institution	Volumes	Microforms[1]	Institution	Volumes	Microforms[1]
Harvard	11,136,662	4,154,154	Pennsylvania State	2,808,553	2,687,484
Yale	8,236,679	2,395,015	U of Iowa	2,754,851	2,724,049
U of Illinois	7,000,170	2,894,312	U of Pittsburgh	2,661,196	2,021,116
U of California–Berkeley	6,845,732	3,385,553	Johns Hopkins	2,621,732	1,477,129
U of Michigan	5,920,576	3,090,623	U of Kansas	2,571,998	1,750,968
U of Texas	5,579,326	3,672,370	U of Florida	2,539,417	2,358,980
Columbia	5,551,739	3,388,230	Rochester	2,512,828	2,172,768
U of California—Los Angeles	5,486,955	3,835,492	U of Georgia	2,510,730	3,375,262
Stanford	5,447,869	3,036,169	U of Southern California	2,497,483	1,761,485
Cornell	4,870,570	3,989,843	U of Oklahoma	2,492,364	3,116,897
U of Chicago	4,756,076	1,474,116	SUNY–Buffalo	2,371,181	3,088,337
U of Wisconsin	4,607,542	1,156,515	U of Missouri	2,318,012	3,776,024
U of Washington	4,549,114	4,558,183	Rutgers	2,300,292	2,288,283
U of Minnesota	4,286,431	2,642,377	Louisiana State	2,210,758	1,117,553
Ohio State	4,077,575	2,552,137	U of South Carolina	2,175,766	2,252,284
Princeton	3,856,638	1,991,432	Syracuse	2,158,536	3,091,703
Indiana	3,786,962	1,256,323	U of Massachusetts	2,129,588	1,385,671
Duke	3,510,645	1,332,419	Wayne State	2,129,392	1,730,818
U of Pennsylvania	3,376,901	1,972,178	Arizona State	2,108,370	2,285,508
North Carolina	3,301,751	2,622,754	U of Colorado	2,096,954	980,582
Northwestern	3,206,698	1,669,565	U of Hawaii	2,089,176	2,333,732
U of Arizona	3,139,481	3,149,171	U of California–Davis	2,082,128	2,361,350
Michigan State	3,129,802	2,192,757	Washington U–St. Louis	2,069,700	1,441,660
New York	2,932,055	2,097,678	MIT	2,029,455	1,494,660
U of Virginia	2,812,167	3,578,749	Brown	2,015,469	971,022

1. Includes reels of microfilm and number of microcards, microprint sheets, and microfiches. *Source:* Association of Research Libraries.

College and University Endowments, 1985–86

(top 75 in millions of dollars)

Institution	Endowment (market value)	Voluntary support[1]	Expenditures[2]
Harvard U	$3,865.7	$146.2	$n.a.
Princeton U	1,900.0	87.5	188.5
Yale U	1,750.7	110.2	423.4
Columbia U	1,282.8	94.5	559.3
Texas A&M U	1,195.3	62.2	n.a.
Stanford U	1,183.9	179.3	626.0
Washington U	972.5	146.1	342.5
Massachusetts Inst. of Tech.	971.3	71.5	467.6
U of Chicago	800.7	59.0	300.8
Rice U	795.8	17.3	82.4
Northwestern U	738.5	49.3	331.8
Emory U	731.8	30.1	n.a.
U of Minnesota	730.6	93.7	277.6
Cornell U	711.7	114.2	640.6
U of Rochester	583.2	23.9	230.4
U of Pennsylvania	540.1	79.5	575.2
New York U	521.3	48.4	507.6
Dartmouth C	520.6	40.5	137.4
Johns Hopkins U	491.5	60.1	431.2
Rockefeller U	475.7	21.5	76.9
Vanderbilt U	446.5	44.6	189.5
U of Notre Dame	388.1	48.3	86.0
U of Southern California	361.8	72.1	447.9
California Inst. of Tech.	349.0	77.6	124.0
U of Virginia	340.0	36.3	238.4
Duke U	338.7	64.1	260.8
Brown U	315.4	29.5	136.3
Case Western Reserve U	307.3	26.4	165.1
U of Michigan	291.7	57.1	633.5
Princeton Theol. Sem.	284.2	2.4	14.5
Southern Methodist U	282.1	29.9	103.9
Smith C	272.7	17.6	42.8
Wellesley C	265.0	15.1	43.4
Williams C	247.8	11.5	35.4
U of Texas—Austin	244.6	56.8	485.5
Wesleyan U	244.0	7.7	46.8
Loyola U of Chicago	240.0	33.8	110.0
Loyola U–New Orleans	$235.0	$2.5	$36.0
U of Delaware	232.2	10.8	152.9
Swarthmore C	230.0	9.7	31.4
Carnegie—Mellon U	228.8	34.3	164.7
Amherst C	224.5	10.3	33.2
George Washington U	209.2	15.0	192.9
Grinnell C	207.6	6.0	20.6
Ohio State U	207.1	50.4	578.7
U of Richmond	204.5	9.8	29.7
Vassar C	204.3	20.3	33.3
Baylor U	203.0	25.0	75.7
Pomona C	199.3	33.0	25.9
Oberlin C	197.3	10.5	n.a.
Berea C	193.7	8.2	13.9
Wake Forest U	186.0	20.1	134.5
Texas Christian U	183.4	20.2	51.3
Tulane U	182.1	24.4	137.0
U of Pittsburgh	177.7	15.6	358.6
Rensselaer Poly. Inst.	177.4	20.4	106.2
Georgetown U	174.0	27.0	184.3
Lehigh U	169.6	17.8	90.4
Middlebury C	167.8	7.6	30.3
Thomas Jefferson U	153.5	9.4	100.6
Lafayette C	149.1	7.9	27.7
Boston U	139.2	23.4	344.5
U of Kansas	138.4	13.4	163.3
SUNY–Buffalo	131.7	8.1	285.4
U of Nebraska	130.3	28.4	303.4
Mount Holyoke C	130.2	9.3	32.3
U of Washington	127.4	64.5	491.1
Syracuse U	124.7	17.7	165.9
U of Illinois	123.9	82.9	884.2
Carleton C	123.9	8.8	25.9
U of Cincinnati	123.7	18.7	263.4
St. Louis U	120.5	13.5	114.6
Brandeis U	120.0	24.8	82.4
Bowdoin C	118.0	7.8	24.4
U of Wisconsin–Madison	117.1	72.9	596.7

1. Gifts from business, alumni, religious denominations, and others. 2. Figure represents about 80% of typical operating budget. Does not include auxiliary enterprises and capital outlays. NOTE: C = College; U = University; n.a. = not available. *Source:* Council for Financial Aid to Education.

Institutions of Higher Education—Average Salaries and Fringe Benefits for Faculty Members, 1970-1986[1]

(in thousands of dollars)

Control and Academic Rank	1986	1985	1984	1983	1982	1981	1980	1979	1978	1975	1970
Average Salaries											
Public: All ranks	33.4	31.2	29.4	28.6	26.2	23.9	22.1	20.5	19.3	16.6	13.1
Professor	42.3	39.6	37.1	36.0	33.7	31.0	28.8	26.8	25.4	21.7	17.3
Associate professor	32.2	30.2	28.4	27.5	25.7	23.4	21.9	20.5	19.5	16.7	13.2
Assistant professor	26.7	25.0	23.5	22.6	21.2	19.2	18.0	16.8	16.0	13.7	10.9
Instructor	20.9	19.5	19.1	17.7	16.7	15.1	14.8	13.9	13.1	11.2	9.1
Private: All ranks	35.4	33.0	31.1	29.2	26.8	24.4	22.1	21.2	19.4	16.6	13.1
Professor	47.0	44.1	41.5	38.8	35.8	32.7	30.1	28.1	26.2	22.4	17.8
Associate professor	32.9	30.9	29.4	27.5	25.4	23.1	21.0	19.8	18.7	16.0	12.6
Assistant professor	26.8	25.0	23.7	22.1	20.4	18.4	17.0	16.0	15.1	13.0	10.3
Instructor	19.8	19.0	18.4	17.6	15.9	14.4	13.3	13.2	12.1	10.9	8.6
Average Fringe Benefits—All Ranks Combined											
Public	7.3	7.0	6.0	5.4	5.1	4.7	3.9	3.4	3.0	2.5	1.9
Private	8.0	7.2	6.4	5.7	5.4	4.9	4.1	3.6	3.3	2.8	2.2

1. Figures are for 9 months teaching for full-time faculty members in four-year colleges and universities. *Source:* U.S. Bureau of the Census, *Statistical Abstract of the United States: 1987*.

Accredited U.S. Senior Colleges and Universities

Source: The Guidance Information System™, a product of Houghton Mifflin Company, Educational Software Division.

Schools listed are those that offer at least a Bachelor's degree, and are fully accredited by one of the institutional and professional accrediting associations. Included are accredited colleges outside the U.S.

Tuition, room, and board listed are average annual figures (including fees) subject to fluctuation, usually covering two semesters, two out of three trimesters, or three out of four quarters, depending on school calendar.

For further information, write to the Registrar of the school concerned.

NOTE: n.a. = information not available. — = does not apply. Enrollment figures are approximate. (C) = Coeducational, (M) = primarily for men, (W) = primarily for women.

Abbreviations used for controls:

AB	American Baptist
AC	Advent Christian
AG	Assemblies of God
AL	American Lutheran
AME	African Methodist Episcopal
B	Baptist
BC	Brethren in Christ
Br	Brethren
CB	Church of Brethren
CC	Church of Christ
CE	Christian Evangelical
CG	Church of God
ChC	Christian Church
CMA	Christian & Missionary Alliance
CME	Christian Methodist Episcopal
CP	Cumberland Presbyterian
CR	Christian Reformed
DC	Disciples of Christ
E	Episcopal
EC	Evangelical Covenant
EFC	Evangelical Free Church
EL	Evangelical Lutheran
F	Friends
FG	Foursquare Gospel
FM	Free Methodist
FWB	Free Will Baptist
GGF	Grace Gospel Fellowship
ID	Interdenominational
Ind	Independent
L	Lutheran
LCA	Lutheran Church of America
LDS	Latter Day Saints
MB	Mennonite Brethren
MC	Missionary Church
Men	Mennonite
Mor	Moravian
Naz	Nazarene
ND	Non-denominational
OBS	Open Bible Standard
P	Private
PH	Pentecostal Holiness
Pub	Public
PUS	Presbyterian, U.S.
RC	Roman Catholic
RCA	Reformed Church in America
RP	Reformed Presbyterian
SB	Southern Baptist
SDA	Seventh Day Adventist
UCC	United Church of Christ
UM	United Methodist
UP	United Presbyterian
W	Wesleyan
WM	Wesleyan Methodist

Institution and location	Enrollment	Control	Tuition ($) Res.	Tuition ($) Nonres.	Rm/Bd ($)
Abilene Christian University; Abilene, Tex. 79699	3,830 (C)	P/CC	3,900	3,900	2,230
Academy of Art College; San Francisco, Calif. 94108	2,100 (C)	P/Ind	3,960	3,960	4,000
Adams State College; Alamosa, Colo. 81102	1,670 (C)	Pub	1,166	2,910	2,560
Adelphi University; Garden City, N.Y. 11530	5,759 (C)	P	6,880	6,880	3,140
Adrian College; Adrian, Mich. 49221	1,186 (C)	P/UM	7,036	7,036	2,224
Agnes Scott College; Decatur, Ga. 30030	518 (W)	P	8,440	8,440	3,310
Akron, University of; Akron, Ohio 44325	22,342 (C)	Pub	1,890	4,130	2,700
Alabama A&M University; Normal, Ala. 35762	2,934 (C)	Pub	980	1,872	1,920
Alabama State University; Montgomery, Ala. 36195	3,199 (C)	Pub	960	1,920	1,620
Alabama, University of; University, Ala. 35486	13,326 (C)	Pub	1,500	3,280	3,070
Alabama, University of–Birmingham; Birmingham, Ala. 35294	9,970 (C)	Pub	1,476	2,862	2,898
Alabama, University of–Huntsville; Huntsville, Ala. 35899	6,116 (C)	Pub	1,395	2,790	2,990
Alaska, University of–Anchorage; Anchorage, Alas. 99508	4,091 (C)	Pub	918	2,358	3,200
Alaska, University of–Fairbanks; Fairbanks, Alas. 99701	4,646 (C)	Pub	1,280	2,840	2,450
Alaska, University of–Juneau; Juneau, Alas. 99801	2,057 (C)	Pub	960	2,400	1,600
Alaska Bible College; Glennallen, Alas. 99588	74 (C)	P/ID	2,060	2,060	3,000
Alaska Pacific University; Anchorage, Alas. 99508	701 (C)	P/UM	4,600	5,000	3,700
Albany College of Pharmacy; Albany, N.Y. 12208	630 (C)	P	5,450	5,450	3,300
Albany State College; Albany, Ga. 31705	1,902 (C)	Pub	1,326	2,508	2,004
Albertus Magnus College· New Haven, Conn. 06511	400 (W)	P/RC	7,520	7,520	4,155
Albion College; Albion, Mich. 49224	1,618 (C)	P/UM	7,758	7,758	3,384
Albright College; Reading, Pa. 19603	1,347 (C)	P/UM	8,970	8,970	2,880
Alcorn State University; Lorman, Miss. 39096	2,515 (C)	Pub	1,550	2,732	1,650
Alderson-Broaddus College; Philippi, W. Va. 26416	755 (C)	P/AB	6,178	6,178	2,250
Alfred University; Alfred, N.Y. 14802	2,147 (C)	P	9,971	9,971	3,424
Alice Lloyd College; Pippa Passes, Ky. 41844	598 (C)	P	2,600	2,600	2,030
Allegheny College; Meadville, Pa. 16335	1,870 (C)	P	9,575	9,575	2,925
Allentown College of St. Francis de Sales; Center Valley, Pa. 18034	825 (C)	P/RC	5,600	5,600	3,170

Institution and location	Enrollment	Control	Tuition ($) Res.	Tuition ($) Nonres.	Rm/Bd ($)
Alliance College; Cambridge Springs, Pa. 16403	255 (C)	P	3,300	3,300	2,350
Alma College; Alma, Mich. 48801	989 (C)	P	8,026	8,026	2,982
Alvernia College; Reading, Pa. 19607	787 (C)	P/RC	3,690	3,690	2,770
Alverno College; Milwaukee, Wis. 53215	1,832 (W)	P	4,920	4,920	2,100
Amber University; Garland, Tex. 75041	310 (C)	P	3,600	3,600	n.a.
American Baptist College; Nashville, Tenn. 37207	163 (C)	P/B	1,500	1,500	1,100
American College in Paris; Paris, France 75007	900 (C)	P	8,345	8,345	n.a.
American College of Switzerland; 1854 Leysin (HM), Switzerland	331 (C)	P	11,056	11,056	2,304
American International College; Springfield, Mass. 01109	1,391 (C)	P	5,250	5,250	2,581
American Technological University; Killeen, Tex. 76540	288 (C)	P	2,720	2,720	2,380
American University; Washington, D.C. 20016	5,200 (C)	P	8,934	8,934	4,250
American University in Cairo; New York, N.Y. 10017	2,169 (C)	P	1,504	6,100	3,820
Americas, University of the–Puebla; Puebla, Mexico 72820	4,250 (C)	P	1,800	1,800	900
Amherst College; Amherst, Mass. 01002	1,564 (C)	P	12,160	12,160	3,600
Anderson College; Anderson, Ind. 46012	2,000 (C)	P/CG	5,280	5,280	2,070
Andrews University; Berrien Springs, Mich. 49104	1,912 (C)	P/SDA	6,300	6,300	3,150
Angelo State University; San Angelo, Tex. 76909	5,428 (C)	Pub	870	3,990	3,200
Anna Maria College for Men and Women; Paxton, Mass. 01612	550 (C)	P	5,560	5,560	3,200
Antillian College; Mayaguez, P.R. 00709	728 (C)	P/SDA	2,250	2,250	1,440
Antioch College; Yellow Springs, Ohio 45387	473 (C)	P	8,420	8,420	2,930
Antioch Los Angeles; Venice, Calif. 90291	187	P	5,400	5,400	n.a.
Antioch San Francisco; San Francisco, Calif. 94108	104	P	5,400	5,400	n.a.
Antioch Santa Barbara; Santa Barbara, Calif. 93101	35	P	5,400	5,400	n.a.
Antioch Seattle; Seattle, Wash. 98109	81	P	5,500	5,500	n.a.
Antioch University–Philadelphia; Philadelphia, Pa. 19130	444 (C)	P	3,850	3,850	n.a.
Appalachian Bible College; Bradley, W. Va. 25818	188 (C)	P/Ind	2,945	2,945	2,450
Appalachian State University; Boone, N.C. 28608	8,771 (C)	Pub	835	3,680	1,650
Aquinas College; Grand Rapids, Mich. 49506	2,800 (C)	P/RC	5,992	5,992	2,952
Arizona, University of; Tucson, Ariz. 85721	23,945 (C)	Pub	1,196	4,628	2,712
Arizona College of the Bible; Phoenix, Ariz. 85021	209 (C)	P/ID	3,450	3,450	2,750
Arizona State University; Tempe, Ariz. 85287	31,085 (C)	Pub	1,196	4,628	2,500
Arkansas, Univ. of, at Fayetteville; Fayetteville, Ark. 72701	15,000 (C)	Pub	1,000	1,512	2,295
Arkansas, Univ. of, at Little Rock; Little Rock, Ark. 72204	9,050 (C)	Pub	1,000	2,520	n.a.
Arkansas, Univ. of, at Monticello; Monticello, Ark. 71655	1,825 (C)	Pub	850	1,850	1,720
Arkansas, Univ. of, at Pine Bluff; Pine Bluff, Ark. 71601	2,917 (C)	Pub	890	2,150	1,670
Arkansas Baptist College; Little Rock, Ark. 72202	233	P	1,350	1,350	1,938
Arkansas College; Batesville, Ark. 72501	729 (C)	P/PUS	4,500	4,500	2,460
Arkansas State University; State University, Ark. 72467	8,526 (C)	Pub	872	2,072	1,920
Arkansas Tech. University; Russellville, Ark. 72801	3,600 (C)	Pub	920	1,800	1,900
Arlington Baptist College; Arlington, Tex. 76012	209 (C)	P	1,800	1,800	2,000
Armstrong State College; Savannah, Ga. 31419	2,750 (C)	Pub	1,696	4,632	2,505
Armstrong University; Berkeley, Calif. 94704	240 (C)	P	2,808	2,808	n.a.
Arnold & Marie Schwartz College of Pharmacy & Health Sciences. *See* Long Island University Center, Brooklyn Center					
Art Center College of Design; Pasadena, Calif. 91103	1,167 (C)	P	6,935	6,935	n.a.
Art Institute of Chicago, School of the; Chicago, Ill. 60603	1,120 (C)	P	7,200	7,200	n.a.
Asbury College; Wilmore, Ky. 40390	951 (C)	P	5,157	5,157	2,049
Ashland College; Ashland, Ohio 44805	1,880 (C)	P/Br	7,367	7,367	3,085
Assumption College; Worcester, Mass. 01609	1,660 (C)	P/RC	6,950	6,950	3,750
Athens State College; Athens, Ala. 35611	1,392 (C)	Pub	1,200	2,400	2,674
Atlanta Christian College; East Point, Ga. 30344	147 (C)	P	2,376	2,376	2,150
Atlanta College of Art; Atlanta, Ga. 30309	268 (C)	P	5,800	5,800	3,400
Atlantic, College of the; Bar Harbor, Maine 04609	137 (C)	P	7,775	7,775	2,800
Atlantic Christian College; Wilson, N.C. 27893	1,303 (C)	P/DC	4,300	4,300	2,000
Atlantic Union College; South Lancaster, Mass. 01561	610 (C)	P/SDA	6,859	6,859	2,800
Auburn University; Auburn University, Ala. 36849	17,093 (C)	Pub	1,323	3,969	2,700
Auburn University at Montgomery; Montgomery, Ala. 36193	5,142 (C)	Pub	1,095	3,285	2,600
Augsburg College; Minneapolis, Minn. 55454	1,700 (C)	P/AL	6,190	6,190	2,500
Augusta College; Augusta, Ga. 30910	3,457 (C)	Pub	1,191	3,273	n.a.
Augustana College; Rock Island, Ill. 61201	2,100 (C)	P/LCA	6,690	6,690	2,700
Augustana College; Sioux Falls, S.D. 57197	1,805 (C)	P/AL	6,890	6,890	2,225
Aurora College; Aurora, Ill. 60506	1,482 (C)	P/AC	6,270	6,270	2,976
Austin College; Sherman, Tex. 75090	1,152 (C)	P/PUS	5,995	5,995	2,952
Austin Peay State University; Clarksville, Tenn. 37040	4,632 (C)	Pub	1,029	3,177	2,500
Averett College; Danville, Va. 24541	1,000 (C)	P/SB	4,550	4,550	3,150
Avila College; Kansas City, Mo. 64145	1,400 (C)	P/RC	5,180	5,180	2,600
Azusa Pacific University; Azusa, Calif. 91702	1,377 (C)	P/Ind	5,700	5,700	3,000
Babson College; Wellesley, Mass. 02157	1,552 (C)	P	10,316	10,316	5,052
Baker University; Baldwin City, Kan. 66006	776 (C)	P/UM	4,900	4,900	2,650
Baldwin-Wallace College; Berea, Ohio 44017	3,440 (C)	P/UM	7,254	7,254	3,142
Ball State University; Muncie, Ind. 47306	15,567 (C)	Pub	1,662	3,825	2,187
Baltimore, University of; Baltimore, Md. 21201	2,675 (C)	Pub	1,670	2,958	n.a.
Baltimore Hebrew College; Baltimore, Md. 21215	500 (C)	P	2,130	2,130	n.a.

Institution and location	Enrollment	Control	Tuition ($) Res.	Tuition ($) Nonres.	Rm/Bd ($)
Baptist Bible College; Springfield, Mo. 65803	1,300 (C)	P/B	1,550	1,550	1,970
Baptist Bible College of Pennsylvania; Clarks Summit, Pa. 18411	646 (C)	P	4,480	4,480	2,319
Baptist Bible Institute; Graceville, Fla. 32440	357 (C)	P/SB	1,089	1,089	2,300
Baptist Christian College; Shreveport, La. 71108	350	P	3,200	3,200	n.a.
Baptist College at Charleston; Charleston, S.C. 29411	1,794 (C)	P/SB	5,290	5,290	2,764
Barat College; Lake Forest, Ill. 60045	612 (C)	P	5,665	5,665	2,700
Barber-Scotia College; Concord, N.C. 28025	370 (C)	P/UP	3,110	3,110	2,286
Bard College; Annandale-on-Hudson, N.Y. 12504	836 (C)	P	12,190	12,190	4,010
Barnard College of Columbia University; New York, N.Y. 10027	2,200 (W)	P	12,104	12,104	5,192
Barry University; Miami Shores, Fla. 33161	3,069 (C)	P	5,995	5,995	3,500
Bartlesville Wesleyan College; Bartlesville, Okla. 74003	491 (C)	P/W	4,200	4,200	2,200
Bassist College; Portland, Ore. 97201	230	P	4,750	4,750	n.a.
Bates College; Lewiston, Maine 04240	1,450 (C)	P	12,820	12,820	2,815
Baylor College of Medicine; Houston, Tex. 77025	42 (C)	P	3,750	3,750	n.a.
Baylor University; Waco, Tex. 76706	10,184 (C)	P/SB	4,050	4,050	3,336
Beaver College; Glenside, Pa. 19038	1,225 (C)	P	7,600	7,600	3,400
Behrend College. *See* Pennsylvania State University					
Belhaven College; Jackson, Miss. 39202	609 (C)	P/PUS	4,890	4,890	1,940
Bellarmine College; Louisville, Ky. 40205	2,076 (C)	P/RC	4,500	4,500	2,110
Bellevue College; Bellevue, Neb. 68005	2,675 (C)	P	1,770	1,770	n.a.
Belmont Abbey College; Belmont, N.C. 28012	890 (C)	P/RC	3,817	4,767	3,770
Belmont College; Nashville, Tenn. 37203	2,314 (C)	P/SB	3,750	3,750	2,640
Beloit College; Beloit, Wis. 53511	1,075 (C)	P	9,198	9,198	2,688
Bemidji State University; Bemidji, Minn. 56601	3,932 (C)	Pub	1,691	2,581	1,785
Benedict College; Columbia, S.C. 29204	1,469 (C)	P/Ind	3,655	3,655	1,800
Benedictine College; Atchison, Kan. 66002	898 (C)	P/RC	4,875	4,875	2,485
Benjamin Franklin University; Washington, D.C. 20036	316 (C)	P	3,700	3,700	n.a.
Bennett College; Greensboro, N.C. 27401	576 (W)	P/UM	4,000	4,000	2,000
Bennington College; Bennington, Vt. 05201	561 (C)	P	14,850	14,850	3,140
Bentley College; Waltham, Mass. 02254	3,875 (C)	P	8,020	8,020	3,672
Berea College; Berea, Ky. 40404	1,587 (C)	P	141	141	2,034
Berklee College of Music; Boston, Mass. 02215	2,500 (C)	P	5,400	5,400	4,000
Bernard M. Baruch Coll. *See* New York, City Univ. of					
Berry College; Mount Berry, Ga. 30149	1,339 (C)	P	4,680	4,680	2,316
Bethany Bible College; Santa Cruz, Calif. 95066	538 (C)	P/AG	3,550	3,550	960
Bethany College; Bethany, W. Va. 26032	786 (C)	P/DC	8,470	8,470	2,920
Bethany College; Lindsborg, Kan. 67456	724 (C)	P/LCA	4,980	4,980	2,687
Bethel College; McKenzie, Tenn. 38201	469 (C)	P/CP	2,850	2,850	1,815
Bethel College; Mishawaka, Ind. 46545	483 (C)	P/MC	4,836	4,836	2,160
Bethel College; North Newton, Kan. 67117	643 (C)	P/Men	5,031	5,031	2,598
Bethel College; St. Paul, Minn. 55112	1,722 (C)	P/B	7,100	7,100	2,900
Bethune-Cookman College; Daytona Beach, Fla. 32015	1,815 (C)	P	3,775	3,775	2,383
Biola University; La Mirada, Calif. 90639	2,024 (C)	P/Ind	5,732	5,732	3,018
Birmingham-Southern College; Birmingham, Ala. 35254	1,575 (C)	P/UM	5,600	5,600	2,500
Blackburn College; Carlinville, Ill. 62626	500 (C)	P	5,700	5,700	2,800
Black Hills State College; Spearfish, S.D. 57783	2,135 (C)	Pub	1,450	2,566	1,860
Bloomfield College; Bloomfield, N.J. 07003	1,180 (C)	P	5,700	5,700	2,850
Bloomsburg State Coll. *See* Bloomsburg Univ. of Pennsylvania					
Bloomsburg University of Pennsylvania; Bloomsburg, Pa. 17815	6,052 (C)	Pub	3,884	5,134	900
Bluefield College; Bluefield, Va. 24605	356 (C)	P/SB	3,880	3,880	2,770
Bluefield State College; Bluefield, W. Va. 24701	2,600 (C)	Pub	890	2,400	n.a.
Blue Mountain College; Blue Mountain, Miss. 38610	345 (C)	P/SB	2,784	2,784	1,850
Bluffton College; Bluffton, Ohio 45817	596 (C)	P/Men	5,985	5,985	2,466
Boca Raton, College of; Boca Raton, FL 33431	900	P	7,300	7,300	3,400
Boise State University; Boise, Idaho 83725	9,913 (C)	Pub	1,058	2,958	2,415
Boricua College; New York, N.Y. 10032	1,000 (C)	P	4,100	4,100	n.a.
Borromeo College of Ohio; Wickliffe, Ohio 44092	71 (M)	P/RC	3,800	3,800	2,000
Boston College; Chestnut Hill, Mass. 02167	10,231 (C)	P/RC	10,205	10,205	4,876
Boston Conservatory; Boston, Mass. 02215	355 (C)	P	6,950	6,950	4,150
Boston University; Boston, Mass. 02215	13,886 (C)	P	11,950	11,950	4,900
Bowdoin College; Brunswick, Maine 04011	1,350 (C)	P	11,615	11,615	4,060
Bowie State College; Bowie, Md. 20715	1,847 (C)	Pub	1,678	3,023	2,817
Bowling Green State University; Bowling Green, Ohio 43403	15,203 (C)	Pub	2,028	4,170	2,104
Bradford College; Bradford, Mass. 01830	500 (C)	P	7,495	7,495	3,845
Bradley University; Peoria, Ill. 61625	4,274 (C)	P	7,080	7,080	3,250
Brandeis University; Waltham, Mass. 02254	2,808 (C)	P	12,100	12,100	5,150
Brenau: The Women's College; Gainesville, Ga. 30501	542 (W)	P	4,641	4,641	3,859
Brescia College; Owensboro, Ky. 42301	709 (C)	P/RC	4,200	4,200	2,060
Briar Cliff College; Sioux City, Iowa 51104	1,200 (C)	P/RC	5,040	5,040	2,142
Bridgeport, University of; Bridgeport, Conn. 06601	3,447 (C)	P	7,810	7,810	3,980
Bridgeport Engineering Institute; Bridgeport, Conn. 06606	830 (C)	P	2,810	2,810	n.a.
Bridgewater College; Bridgewater, Va. 22812	800 (C)	P	6,000	6,000	2,985
Bridgewater State College; Bridgewater, Mass. 02324	5,400 (C)	Pub	1,336	3,532	2,222

Institution and location	Enrollment	Control	Tuition ($) Res.	Tuition ($) Nonres.	Rm/Bd ($)
Brigham Young University; Provo, Utah 84602	25,412 (C)	P/LDS	1,620	1,620	2,500
Brigham Young University–Hawaii; Laie, Oahu, Hawaii 96762	1,984 (C)	P/LDS	1,250	1,876	2,000
Brooklyn Center. *See* Long Island University Center					
Brooklyn College. *See* New York, City University of					
Brooks Institute of Photography; Santa Barbara, Calif. 93108	596 (C)	P	3,900	3,900	n.a.
Brown University; Providence, R.I. 02912	5,900 (C)	P	12,790	12,790	4,075
Bryan College; Dayton, Tenn. 37321	442 (C)	P	4,650	4,650	3,200
Bryant College; Smithfield, R.I. 02917	3,071 (C)	P	6,650	6,650	4,605
Bryn Mawr College; Bryn Mawr, Pa. 19010	1,101 (W)	P	11,000	11,000	4,650
Bucknell University; Lewisburg, Pa. 17837	3,232 (C)	P	11,480	11,480	3,135
Buena Vista College; Storm Lake, Iowa 50588	950 (C)	P	7,275	7,275	2,395
Burlington College; Burlington, Vt. 05401	204 (C)	P	4,650	4,650	n.a.
Butler University; Indianapolis, Ind. 46208	2,405 (C)	P	6,864	6,864	2,820
Cabrini College; Radnor, Pa. 19087	970 (W)	P/RC	5,618	5,618	4,028
Caldwell College; Caldwell, N.J. 07006	765 (W)	P	6,000	6,000	3,500
California, University of; Berkeley, Calif. 94720					
UC, Berkeley; Berkeley, Calif. 94720	22,321 (C)	Pub	1,450	5,536	7,648
UC, Davis; Davis, Calif. 95616	14,362 (C)	Pub	1,355	5,438	3,220
UC, Irvine; Irvine, Calif. 92717	11,880 (C)	Pub	1,517	5,807	4,367
UC, Los Angeles; Los Angeles, Calif. 90024	22,901 (C)	Pub	1,406	5,492	2,950
UC, Riverside; Riverside, Calif. 92521	4,253 (C)	Pub	1,440	5,730	3,804
UC, San Diego; La Jolla, Calif. 92093	13,094 (C)	Pub	1,554	5,814	4,416
UC, Santa Barbara; Santa Barbara, Calif. 93106	15,277 (C)	Pub	1,319	4,086	5,853
UC, Santa Cruz; Santa Cruz, Calif. 95064	7,867 (C)	Pub	1,394	5,480	4,065
California Baptist College; Riverside, Calif. 92504	617 (C)	P/SB	4,844	4,844	2,682
California College of Arts and Crafts; Oakland, Calif. 94618	1,035 (C)	P	6,900	6,900	3,295
California Institute of Technology; Pasadena, Calif. 91125	833 (C)	P	11,000	11,000	4,400
California Institute of the Arts; Valencia, Calif. 91355	625 (C)	P	7,800	7,800	3,600
California Lutheran University; Thousand Oaks, Calif. 91360	1,459 (C)	P/AL	7,640	7,640	2,900
California Maritime Academy; Vallejo, Calif. 94590	400 (C)	Pub	988	3,208	3,753
California Polytechnic State University; San Luis Obispo, Calif. 93407	15,000 (C)	Pub	875	4,655	3,115
California State Coll. (Pa.). *See* California Univ. of Pennsylvania					
California State College–Bakersfield; Bakersfield, Calif. 93311	2,691 (C)	Pub	648	4,878	3,026
California State Polytechnic University–Pomona; Pomona, Calif. 91768	16,039 (C)	Pub	645	3,689	3,570
California State University–Chico; Chico, Calif. 95929	13,024 (C)	Pub	710	4,220	2,434
California St. Univ.–Dominguez Hills; Carson, Calif. 90747	5,159 (C)	Pub	652	4,308	2,752
California State Univ.–Fresno; Fresno, Calif. 93740	14,613 (C)	Pub	786	5,196	3,000
California State Univ.–Fullerton; Fullerton, Calif. 92634	20,086 (C)	Pub	674	3,301	n.a.
California State Univ.–Hayward; Hayward, Calif. 94542	9,176 (C)	Pub	720	4,248	n.a.
California State Univ.–Long Beach; Long Beach, Calif. 90840	27,006 (C)	Pub	656	4,436	3,500
California State Univ.–Los Angeles; Los Angeles, Calif. 90032	15,670 (C)	Pub	924	4,176	2,000
California State Univ.–Northridge; Northridge, Calif. 91330	23,507 (C)	Pub	700	4,520	3,180
California State Univ.–Sacramento; Sacramento, Calif. 95819	18,200 (C)	Pub	651	4,881	3,046
California State Univ.–San Bernardino; San Bernardino, Calif. 92407	5,196 (C)	Pub	800	4,800	3,350
California State Univ.–Stanislaus; Turlock, Calif. 95380	3,423 (C)	Pub	736	4,485	3,100
California Univ. of Pennsylvania; California, Pa. 15419	4,681 (C)	Pub	1,894	3,170	1,950
Calumet College of St. Joseph; Whiting, Ind. 46394	935 (C)	P/RC	2,760	2,760	n.a.
Calvary Bible College; Kansas City, Mo. 64147	356 (C)	P/Ind	2,852	2,852	2,160
Calvin College; Grand Rapids, Mich. 49506	4,037 (C)	P/CR	5,650	5,650	2,480
Cameron University; Lawton, Okla. 73505	5,309 (C)	Pub	500	1,406	1,700
Campbellsville College; Campbellsville, Ky. 42718	613 (C)	P/SB	3,750	3,750	2,580
Campbell University; Buie's Creek, N.C. 27506	2,631 (C)	P/SB	5,202	5,257	2,500
Canisius College; Buffalo, N.Y. 14208	2,884 (C)	P	6,100	6,100	3,170
Capital University; Columbus, Ohio 43209	1,807 (C)	P/AL	7,980	7,980	3,095
Capitol College; Laurel, Md. 20708	1,020 (C)	P	5,112	5,112	n.a.
Cardinal Glennon College; St. Louis, Mo. 63119	64	P/RC	5,000	5,000	1,250
Cardinal Stritch College; Milwaukee, Wis. 53217	1,236 (C)	P/RC	5,360	5,360	2,650
Carleton College; Northfield, Minn. 55057	1,853 (C)	P	11,015	11,015	2,625
Carlow College; Pittsburgh, Pa. 15213	1,073 (W)	P/RC	6,576	6,576	3,720
Carnegie–Mellon University; Pittsburgh, Pa. 15213	4,280 (C)	P	11,160	11,160	3,890
Carroll College; Helena, Mont. 59625	1,406 (C)	P/RC	4,470	4,470	2,605
Carroll College; Waukesha, Wis. 53186	1,231 (C)	P/UP	7,670	7,670	2,580
Carson–Newman College; Jefferson City, Tenn. 37760	1,681 (C)	P/SB	4,776	4,776	2,070
Carthage College; Kenosha, Wis. 53140	834 (C)	P/LCA	6,260	6,260	2,500
Case Western Reserve University; Cleveland, Ohio 44106	3,206 (C)	P	10,000	10,000	4,000
Castleton State College; Castleton, Vt. 05735	1,325 (C)	Pub	2,167	4,548	3,042
Catawba College; Salisbury, N.C. 28144	900 (C)	P/UCC	5,600	5,600	2,400
Cathedral College of the Immaculate Conception; Douglaston, N.Y. 11362	71 (M)	P/RC	4,400	4,400	2,000
Catholic University of America; Washington, D.C. 20064	2,500 (C)	P	7,900	7,900	3,500

Institution and location	Enrollment	Control	Tuition ($) Res.	Tuition ($) Nonres.	Rm/Bd ($)
Catholic University of Puerto Rico; Ponce, P.R. 00732	10,660 (C)	P/RC	1,965	1,965	2,200
Cayey University College. *See* Puerto Rico, University of					
Cedar Crest College; Allentown, Pa. 18104	529 (W)	P	8,370	8,370	3,580
Cedarville College; Cedarville, Ohio 45314	1,821 (C)	P/B	4,124	4,124	2,610
Centenary College; Hackettstown, N.J. 07840	525 (W)	P	6,500	6,500	3,850
Centenary College of Louisiana; Shreveport, La. 71104	738 (C)	P/UM	4,340	4,340	2,530
Center for Creative Studies, College of Art and Design; Detroit, Mich. 48202	951 (C)	P	6,500	6,500	3,070
Central Arkansas, University of; Conway, Ark. 72032	5,689 (C)	Pub	900	1,670	1,870
Central Baptist College; Conway, Ark. 72032	232 (C)	P/B	1,000	1,000	1,280
Central Bible College; Springfield, Mo. 65803	757 (C)	P/AG	2,280	2,280	2,400
Central Christian College of the Bible; Moberly, Mo. 65270	75 (C)	P/ChC	1,700	1,700	1,750
Central College; Pella, Iowa 50219	1,527 (C)	P/RCA	6,852	6,852	2,690
Central Connecticut State University; New Britain, Conn. 06050	10,718 (C)	Pub	1,372	3,512	2,817
Central Florida, University of; Orlando, Fla. 32816	12,616 (C)	Pub	1,049	3,537	2,585
Central Methodist College; Fayette, Mo. 65248	660 (C)	P/UM	5,090	5,090	2,560
Central Michigan University; Mt. Pleasant, Mich. 48858	14,450 (C)	Pub	1,470	3,750	2,616
Central Missouri State University; Warrensburg, Mo. 64093	7,688 (C)	Pub	1,254	2,342	2,070
Central New England College of Technology; Worcester, Mass. 01610	2,674 (C)	P	6,000	6,000	n.a.
Central State University; Edmond, Okla. 73034	9,745 (C)	Pub	498	1,377	1,666
Central State University; Wilberforce, Ohio 45384	2,674 (C)	Pub	1,269	3,231	2,955
Central Washington University; Ellensburg, Wash. 98926	6,384 (C)	Pub	1,272	4,425	2,821
Central Wesleyan College; Central, S.C. 29630	450 (C)	P/WM	4,990	4,990	2,490
Centre College; Danville, Ky. 40422	804 (C)	P	7,550	7,550	3,015
Chadron State College; Chadron, Neb. 69337	2,240 (C)	Pub	1,086	1,701	1,836
Chaminade University of Honolulu; Honolulu, Hawaii 96816	2,606 (C)	P/RC	4,210	4,210	3,000
Chapman College; Orange, Calif. 92666	1,578 (C)	P	8,900	8,900	3,400
Charleston, College of; Charleston, S.C. 29424	5,145 (C)	Pub	1,760	3,160	2,390
Charleston, University of; Charleston, W. Va. 25304	1,400 (C)	P	5,300	5,300	3,100
Charter Oak College; Hartford, Conn. 06106	900 (C)	Pub	150	190	n.a.
Chatham College; Pittsburgh, Pa. 15232	600 (W)	P	7,364	7,364	3,586
Chestnut Hill College; Philadelphia, Pa. 19118	733 (W)	P/RC	5,550	5,550	3,150
Cheyney University of Pennsylvania; Cheyney, Pa. 19319	1,351 (C)	Pub	1,775	3,043	2,260
Chicago, University of—The College; Chicago, Ill. 60637	3,000 (C)	P	11,350	11,350	4,529
Chicago State University; Chicago, Ill. 60628	7,327 (C)	Pub	1,758	3,218	n.a.
Christ College–Irvine; Irvine, Calif. 92715	500 (C)	P/L	4,800	4,800	1,650
Christian Brothers College; Memphis, Tenn. 38104	1,642 (C)	P/RC	5,200	5,200	2,850
Christian Heritage College; El Cajon, Calif. 92021	436	P/Ind	4,430	4,430	2,450
Christopher Newport College; Newport News, Va. 23606	4,089 (C)	Pub	1,770	2,820	n.a.
Church College of Hawaii. *See* Brigham Young University—Hawaii Campus					
Cincinnati Bible College; Cincinnati, Ohio 45204	540 (C)	P/ChC	2,526	2,526	2,410
Cincinnati, University of; Cincinnati, Ohio 45221	28,507 (C)	Pub	2,046	4,944	3,060
Circleville Bible College; Circleville, Ohio 43113	186 (C)	P/CC	2,995	2,995	2,150
Citadel–The Military College of South Carolina; Charleston, S.C. 29409	2,000 (M)	Pub	4,431	6,529	1,725
City College (NYC). *See* New York, City University of					
City University; Bellevue, Wash. 98008	3,000 (C)	P	3,720	3,720	n.a.
Claflin College; Orangeburg, S.C. 29115	756 (C)	P/UM	3,002	3,002	1,755
Claremont Colleges:					
Claremont McKenna College; Claremont, Calif. 91711	840 (C)	P	10,800	10,800	4,300
Claremont Men's College. *See* Claremont McKenna College					
Harvey Mudd College; Claremont, Calif. 91711	522 (C)	P	10,800	10,800	4,625
Pitzer College; Claremont, Calif. 91711	740 (C)	P	10,728	10,728	3,418
Pomona College; Claremont, Calif. 91711	1,325 (C)	P	10,000	10,000	4,100
Scripps College; Claremont, Calif. 91711	600 (W)	P	10,074	10,074	4,626
Clarion State College. *See* Clarion University of Pennsylvania					
Clarion University of Pennsylvania; Clarion, Pa. 16214	5,374 (C)	Pub	1,795	3,070	2,010
Clark College; Atlanta, Ga. 30314	1,883 (C)	P	4,460	4,460	2,080
Clark University; Worcester, Mass. 01610	2,236 (C)	P	11,663	11,663	3,595
Clarke College; Dubuque, Iowa 52001	744 (W)	P/RC	6,230	6,230	2,465
Clarkson College of Technology. *See* Clarkson University					
Clarkson University; Potsdam, N.Y. 13676	3,600 (C)	P	9,500	9,500	3,930
Clearwater Christian College; Clearwater, Fla. 33519	250	P	3,000	3,000	2,500
Cleary College; Ypsilanti, Mich. 48197	881 (C)	P	3,510	3,510	n.a.
Clemson University; Clemson, S.C. 29634	10,360 (C)	Pub	1,682	3,910	2,150
Cleveland College of Jewish Studies; Beachwood, Ohio 44122	325	P	1,000	1,000	n.a.
Cleveland Institute of Art; Cleveland, Ohio 44106	503 (C)	P	5,450	5,450	3,200
Cleveland Institute of Music; Cleveland, Ohio 44106	133 (C)	P	7,996	7,996	3,700
Cleveland State University; Cleveland, Ohio 44115	13,000 (C)	Pub	1,911	3,822	2,350
Clinch Valley College. *See* Virginia, University of					
Coe College; Cedar Rapids, Iowa 52402	1,133 (C)	P/UP	7,290	7,290	2,600

Institution and location	Enrollment	Control	Tuition ($) Res.	Tuition ($) Nonres.	Rm/Bd ($)
Cogswell College; Cupertino, Calif. 95014	200 (C)	P	5,760	6,500	n.a.
Coker College; Hartsville, S.C. 29550	369 (C)	P	5,660	5,660	2,855
Colby College; Waterville, Me. 04901	1,769 (C)	P	11,160	11,160	4,250
Colby-Sawyer College; New London, N.H. 03257	450 (W)	P	9,100	9,100	3,800
Coleman College; La Mesa, Calif. 92041	950 (C)	P	6,375	6,375	n.a.
Colgate University; Hamilton, N.Y. 13346	2,660 (C)	P	11,290	11,290	4,000
College Misericordia; Dallas, Pa. 18612	1,025 (W)	P/RC	4,788	4,788	2,850
College for Human Services; New York, N.Y. 10014. *See* Human Services, College for					
College of Great Falls; Great Falls, Mont. 59405. *See* Great Falls, College of					
Colorado, University of; Boulder, Colo. 80309:					
U. of Colorado at Boulder; Boulder, Colo. 80309	18,927 (C)	Pub	1,600	6,400	2,962
U. of Colorado at Colorado Springs; Colorado Springs, Colo. 80933	3,914 (C)	Pub	1,196	4,290	n.a.
U. of Colorado at Denver; Denver, Colo. 80202	2,979 (C)	Pub	1,040	4,534	n.a.
Colorado Christian College; Lakewood, Colo. 80226	355 (C)	P	4,615	4,615	1,750
Colorado College; Colorado Springs, Colo. 80903	1,880 (C)	P	8,840	8,840	2,775
Colorado School of Mines; Golden, Colo. 80401	1,731 (C)	Pub	2,884	7,996	3,150
Colorado State University; Fort Collins, Colo. 80523	15,333 (C)	Pub	1,699	4,941	2,870
Colorado Technical College; Colorado Springs, Colo. 80907	650 (C)	P	5,100	5,100	n.a.
Colorado Women's College. *See* Denver, Univ. of					
Columbia Bible College; Columbia, S.C. 29230	514 (C)	P	3,669	3,669	2,307
Columbia Christian College; Portland, Ore. 97216	243 (C)	P	4,293	4,293	2,576
Columbia College; Chicago, Ill. 60605	5,298 (C)	P	4,348	4,348	n.a.
Columbia College; Columbia, Mo. 65216	660 (C)	P	5,070	5,070	2,535
Columbia College; Columbia, S.C. 29203	1,100 (W)	P/UM	6,200	6,200	2,640
Columbia Union College; Takoma Park, Md. 20912	1,015 (C)	P/SDA	5,733	5,733	1,990
Columbia University–Columbia College; New York, N.Y. 10027	2,900 (M)	P	11,750	11,750	4,830
Columbus College; Columbus, Ga. 31993	3,267 (C)	Pub	1,272	3,474	n.a.
Columbus College of Art and Design; Columbus, Ohio 43215	1,000 (C)	P	5,890	5,890	3,300
Combs College of Music; Philadelphia, Pa. 19118	46 (C)	P	5,225	5,225	3,720
Conception Seminary College; Conception, Mo. 64433	114	P/RC	3,860	3,860	2,520
Concord College; Athens, W. Va. 24712	2,356 (C)	Pub	908	2,418	2,463
Concordia College; Ann Arbor, Mich. 48105	422 (C)	P/L	4,964	4,964	2,920
Concordia College; Bronxville, N.Y. 10708	560 (C)	P/L	5,680	5,680	3,360
Concordia College; Moorhead, Minn. 56560	2,525 (C)	P/AL	6,755	6,755	2,145
Concordia College; Portland, Ore. 97211	450 (C)	P	5,950	5,950	3,250
Concordia College; River Forest, Ill. 60305	953 (C)	P/L	5,040	5,040	2,844
Concordia College; St. Paul, Minn. 55104	946 (C)	P/L	5,610	5,610	2,295
Concordia College–Wisconsin; Mequon, Wis. 53092	861 (C)	P/L	5,200	5,200	3,000
Concordia Lutheran College; Austin, Tex. 78705	464 (C)	P/L	4,200	4,200	2,900
Concordia Teachers College; Seward, Neb. 68434	753 (C)	P/L	5,200	5,200	2,100
Connecticut, University of; Storrs, Conn. 06268	16,239 (C)	Pub	1,937	5,501	2,536
Connecticut College; New London, Conn. 06320	1,634 (C)	P	11,950	11,950	3,500
Conservatory of Music of Puerto Rico; Hato Rey, P.R. 00918	236 (C)	Pub	210	210	n.a.
Converse College; Spartanburg, S.C. 29301	802 (W)	P	6,900	6,900	3,000
Cooper Union; New York, N.Y. 10003	985 (C)	P	300	300	n.a.
Coppin State College; Baltimore, Md. 21216	2,300 (C)	Pub	1,451	2,707	n.a.
Corcoran School of Art; Washington, D.C. 20006	193 (C)	P	5,885	5,885	4,450
Cornell College; Mt. Vernon, Iowa 52314	1,161 (C)	P	8,286	8,286	2,914
Cornell University; Ithaca, N.Y. 14853	12,714 (C)	P	12,300	12,300	4,020
Cornish College of the Arts; Seattle, Wash. 98102	429 (C)	P	5,508	5,508	n.a.
Corpus Christi State Univ.; Corpus Christi, Tex. 78412	1,970 (C)	Pub	840	3,960	1,850
Covenant College; Lookout Mountain, Tenn. 37350	485 (C)	P/RP	5,400	5,400	2,970
Creighton University; Omaha, Neb. 68178	3,984 (C)	P	6,126	6,126	2,936
Culver-Stockton College; Canton, Mo. 63435	843 (C)	P	5,190	5,190	2,040
Cumberland College; Williamsburg, Ky. 40769	1,832 (C)	P/SB	3,480	3,480	1,976
Cumberland University of Tennessee; Lebanon, Tenn. 37087	707 (C)	P	3,300	3,300	2,480
Curry College; Milton, Mass. 02186	1,234 (C)	P	8,450	8,450	4,200
C. W. Post Center. *See* Long Island Univ. Center					
Daemen College; Amherst, N.Y. 14226	1,500 (C)	P	5,930	5,930	2,980
Dakota State College; Madison, S.D. 57042	940 (C)	Pub	1,587	1,587	1,850
Dakota Wesleyan University; Mitchell, S.D. 57301	692 (C)	P/UM	3,890	3,890	2,300
Dallas, University of; Irving, Tex. 75062	1,042 (C)	P/RC	6,020	6,020	3,040
Dallas Baptist University; Dallas, Tex. 75211	1,627 (C)	P/SB	3,850	3,850	2,400
Dallas Christian College; Dallas, Tex. 75234	135 (C)	P/ChC	1,888	1,888	2,160
Dana College; Blair, Neb. 68008	396 (C)	P/AL	5,660	5,660	2,350
Daniel Webster College; Nashua, N.H. 03063	396 (C)	P	7,900	7,900	3,514
Dartmouth College; Hanover, N.H. 03755	4,263 (C)	P	12,474	12,474	4,600
David Lipscomb College; Nashville, Tenn. 37203	2,132 (C)	P/CC	3,485	3,485	2,310
Davidson College; Davidson, N.C. 28036	1,389 (C)	P/PUS	9,405	9,405	2,985
Davis and Elkins College; Elkins, W. Va. 26241	828 (C)	P/PUS	5,875	5,875	3,121
Dayton, University of; Dayton, Ohio 45469	6,311 (C)	P/RC	6,290	6,290	3,050

			Tuition ($)		
Institution and location	Enrollment	Control	Res.	Nonres.	Rm/Bd ($)
Defiance College; Defiance, Ohio 43512	992 (C)	P/UCC	5,270	5,270	2,515
Delaware, University of; Newark, Del. 19716	13,839 (C)	P	2,100	4,800	2,400
Delaware State College; Dover, Del. 19901	2,058 (C)	Pub	906	2,082	2,000
Delaware Valley College of Science and Agriculture; Doylestown, Pa. 18901	1,100 (C)	P	6,000	6,000	2,800
DeLourdes College; Des Plaines, Ill. 60016	137	P/RC	2,430	2,430	n.a.
Delta State University; Cleveland, Miss. 38732	3,378 (C)	Pub	1,350	2,532	1,440
Denison University; Granville, Ohio 43023	2,118 (C)	P	10,440	10,440	2,960
Denver, University of; Denver, Colo. 80208	3,408 (C)	P	8,892	8,892	3,525
Colorado Women's College; Denver, Colo. 80220	453 (W)	P	5,760	5,760	2,840
DePaul University; Chicago, Ill. 60604	7,976 (C)	P	5,850	5,850	3,325
DePauw University; Greencastle, Ind. 46135	2,368 (C)	P/UM	8,850	8,850	3,375
Deree College–Division of the American College of Greece; Athens, Greece GR-153 42	2,525 (C)	P	2,190	2,300	n.a.
Detroit, University of; Detroit, Mich. 48221	3,687 (C)	P/RC	6,360	6,360	2,688
Detroit Bible College. *See* William Tyndale College					
Detroit College of Business; Dearborn, Mich. 48126	3,739 (C)	P	3,645	3,645	n.a.
DeVry Institute of Technology; Decatur, Ga. 30341	3,023 (C)	P	3,990	3,990	n.a.
DeVry Institute of Technology; Chicago, Ill. 60618	3,531 (C)	P	3,990	3,990	n.a.
DeVry Institute of Technology; City of Industry, Calif. 91744	2,479	P	3,990	3,990	n.a.
DeVry Institute of Technology; Columbus, Ohio 43209	2,934 (C)	P	3,846	3,846	n.a.
DeVry Institute of Technology; Irving, Tex. 75038	2,327 (C)	P	3,990	3,990	n.a.
DeVry Institute of Technology; Kansas City, Mo. 64131	1,632 (C)	P	3,990	3,990	n.a.
DeVry Institute of Technology; Lombard, Ill. 60148	3,211	P	3,846	3,846	n.a.
DeVry Institute of Technology; Phoenix, Ariz. 85021	3,106 (C)	P	3,990	3,990	n.a.
DeVry Technical Institute; Woodbridge, N.J. 07095	2,861	P	3,990	3,990	n.a.
Dickinson College; Carlisle, Pa. 17013	1,888 (C)	P/UM	11,250	11,250	3,400
Dickinson State College; Dickinson, N.D. 58601	1,249 (C)	Pub	1,143	2,119	1,630
Dillard University; New Orleans, La. 70122	1,200 (C)	P	4,200	4,200	2,700
District of Columbia, Univ. of the; Washington, D.C. 20008	12,780 (C)	Pub	634	2,434	n.a.
Divine Word College; Epworth, Iowa 52045	72 (M)	P/RC	3,800	3,800	1,200
Doane College; Crete, Neb. 68333	611 (C)	P/UCC	6,020	6,020	2,180
Dr. Martin Luther College; New Ulm, Minn. 56073	484 (C)	P/EL	2,055	2,055	1,730
Dominican College of Blauvelt; Orangeburg, N.Y. 10962	1,562 (C)	P	3,970	3,970	3,300
Dominican College of San Rafael; San Rafael, Calif. 94901	468 (C)	P/RC	7,200	7,200	4,150
Dominican School of Philosophy and Theology; Berkeley, Calif. 94709	10 (M)	P/RC	4,000	4,000	n.a.
Don Bosco College; Newton, N.J. 07860	50 (M)	P/RC	2,860	2,860	1,925
Dordt College; Sioux Center, Iowa 51250	971 (C)	P/CR	5,690	5,690	1,900
Dowling College; Oakdale, N.Y. 11769	2,523 (C)	P	4,700	4,700	3,200
Drake University; Des Moines, Iowa 50311	3,724 (C)	P	7,530	7,530	3,130
Drew University–College of Liberal Arts; Madison, N.J. 07940	1,486 (C)	P/UM	11,116	11,116	3,450
Drexel University; Philadelphia, Pa. 19104	7,365 (C)	P	6,819	6,819	3,517
Drury College; Springfield, Mo. 65802	956 (C)	P/UCC	5,075	5,075	2,204
Dubuque, Univ. of–Coll. of Liberal Arts; Dubuque, Iowa 52001	986 (C)	P/UP	5,675	5,675	2,250
Duke University; Durham, N.C. 27706	6,027 (C)	P	10,320	10,320	3,87
Duquesne University; Pittsburgh, Pa. 15282	4,208 (C)	P/RC	6,270	6,270	3,048
Dyke College; Cleveland, Ohio 44115	1,380 (C)	P	3,350	3,350	n.a.
D'Youville College; Buffalo, N.Y. 14201	1,100 (C)	P	5,940	5,940	2,880
Earlham College; Richmond, Ind. 47374	1,062 (C)	P/F	9,696	9,696	3,015
East Carolina University; Greenville, N.C. 27834	11,833 (C)	Pub	764	3,610	2,070
East Central University; Ada, Okla. 74820	3,427 (C)	Pub	800	1,700	2,100
Eastern College; St. Davids, Pa. 19087	899 (C)	P/AB	6,980	6,980	2,620
Eastern Connecticut State Univ.; Willimantic, Conn. 06226	3,873 (C)	Pub	1,382	3,532	2,720
Eastern Illinois University; Charleston, Ill. 61920	9,982 (C)	Pub	1,493	3,653	2,212
Eastern Kentucky University; Richmond, Ky. 40475	12,422 (C)	Pub	1,090	3,090	2,150
Eastern Mennonite College; Harrisonburg, Va. 22801	774 (C)	P/Men	5,828	5,828	2,422
Eastern Michigan University; Ypsilanti, Mich. 48197	16,282 (C)	Pub	1,514	3,592	2,736
Eastern Montana College; Billings, Mont. 59101	3,920 (C)	Pub	1,125	2,583	3,375
Eastern Nazarene College; Quincy, Mass. 02170	719 (C)	P/Naz	4,966	4,966	2,675
Eastern New Mexico University; Portales, N.M. 88130	3,017 (C)	Pub	802	2,506	1,796
Eastern Oregon State College; La Grande, Ore. 97850	1,489 (C)	Pub	1,422	1,422	2,505
Eastern Washington University; Cheney, Wash. 99004	7,619 (C)	Pub	1,224	4,206	2,452
Eastman School of Music; Rochester, N.Y. 14604	433	P	10,775	10,775	3,936
East Stroudsburg University of Pennsylvania; East Stroudsburg, Pa. 18301	3,895 (C)	Pub	1,570	2,748	2,000
East Tennessee State University; Johnson City, Tenn. 37614	8,260 (C)	Pub	948	3,096	1,940
East Texas Baptist University; Marshall, Tex. 75670	699 (C)	P/SB	3,150	3,150	2,363
East Texas State University; Commerce, Tex. 75428	2,807 (C)	Pub	870	3,990	2,596
East-West University; Chicago, Ill. 60605	600	P	3,993	3,993	n.a.

Institution and location	Enrollment	Control	Tuition ($) Res.	Tuition ($) Nonres.	Rm/Bd ($)
Eckerd College; St. Petersburg, Fla. 33733	1,202 (C)	P/PUS	8,865	8,865	3,030
Edgewood College; Madison, Wis. 53711	800 (C)	P/RC	5,100	5,100	2,420
Edinboro University of Pennsylvania; Edinboro, Pa. 16444	5,491 (C)	Pub	1,890	3,286	2,060
Edward Waters College; Jacksonville, Fla. 32209	686	P/AME	2,815	2,815	3,440
Elizabeth City State University; Elizabeth City, N.C. 27909	1,600 (C)	Pub	930	3,774	1,934
Elizabethtown College; Elizabethtown, Pa. 17022	1,428 (C)	P/CB	8,050	8,050	3,150
Elmhurst College; Elmhurst, Ill. 60126	1,795 (C)	P/UCC	5,550	5,550	2,630
Elmira College; Elmira, N.Y. 14901	1,612 (C)	P	7,500	7,500	3,000
Elms College; Chicopee, Mass. 01013-2839	600	P	7,050	7,050	3,200
Elon College; Elon College, N.C. 27244	3,129 (C)	P/UCC	4,200	4,200	2,460
Embry-Riddle Aeronautical Univ.; Daytona Beach, Fla. 32014	4,884 (C)	P	4,230	4,230	2,550
Prescott Campus; Prescott, Ariz. 86301	1,225 (C)	P	4,230	4,230	2,550
Emerson College; Boston, Mass. 02116	2,089 (C)	P	8,270	8,270	5,250
Emmanuel College; Boston, Mass. 02115	960 (W)	P/RC	7,500	7,500	4,070
Emmanuel College School of Christian Ministries; Franklin Springs, Ga. 30639	30 (C)	P/PH	2,430	2,430	1,935
Emory and Henry College; Emory, Va. 24327	769 (C)	P/UM	5,544	5,544	3,015
Emory University; Atlanta, Ga. 30322	4,802 (C)	P	10,190	10,190	3,612
Emporia State University; Emporia, Kan. 66801	3,769 (C)	Pub	1,136	2,386	2,140
Erskine College; Due West, S.C. 29639	457 (C)	P/RP	6,700	6,700	2,675
Esther Boyer College of Music, Temple University; Philadelphia, Pa. 19122	50 (C)	P	3,300	5,796	3,370
Eugene Bible College; Eugene, Ore. 97405	153 (C)	P/OBS	2,915	2,915	2,130
Eureka College; Eureka, Ill. 61530	460 (C)	P/DC	6,175	6,175	2,800
Evangel College; Springfield, Mo. 65802	1,600 (C)	P/AG	3,460	3,460	2,400
Evansville, University of; Evansville, Ind. 47714	3,239 (C)	P/UM	7,042	7,042	2,970
Evergreen State College; Olympia, Wash. 98505	2,830 (C)	Pub	1,212	4,206	2,790
Fairfield University; Fairfield, Conn. 06430	2,911 (C)	P/RC	8,300	8,300	4,250
Fairhaven College–Western Washington University; Bellingham, Wash. 98225	228 (C)	Pub	1,200	4,194	2,275
Fairleigh Dickinson Univ.–Madison; Madison, N.J. 07940	2,458 (C)	P	6,291	6,291	3,955
Fairleigh Dickinson Univ.–Rutherford; Rutherford, N.J. 07070	1,511 (C)	P	6,291	6,291	3,955
Fairleigh Dickinson Univ.–Teaneck; Teaneck, N.J. 07666	3,545 (C)	P	6,291	6,291	3,955
Fairmont State College; Fairmont, W. Va. 26554	5,239 (C)	Pub	856	2,316	2,400
Faith Baptist Bible College; Ankeny, Iowa 50021	297 (C)	P/B	3,320	3,320	2,398
Faulkner University; Montgomery, Ala. 36193	1,600 (C)	P	3,360	3,360	2,500
Fayetteville State University; Fayetteville, N.C. 28301	2,479 (C)	Pub	914	4,162	1,820
Felician College; Lodi, N.J. 07644	600 (W)	P/RC	4,400	4,400	n.a.
Ferris State College; Big Rapids, Mich. 49307	10,762 (C)	Pub	1,671	3,381	2,454
Ferrum College; Ferrum, Va. 24088	1,272 (C)	P/UM	5,700	5,700	2,800
Findlay College; Findlay, Ohio 45840	1,588 (C)	P/CG	6,345	6,345	2,900
Fisk University; Nashville, Tenn. 37203	520 (C)	P	4,314	4,314	2,085
Fitchburg State College; Fitchburg, Mass. 01420	4,785 (C)	Pub	1,244	3,440	2,200
Flagler College; St. Augustine, Fla. 32085	1,081 (C)	P	3,700	3,700	2,300
Flaming Rainbow University; Stilwell, Okla. 74960	221	P	3,630	3,630	n.a.
Florida, University of; Gainesville, Fla. 32611	28,226 (C)	Pub	970	2,969	3,240
Florida A&M University; Tallahassee, Fla. 32307	5,103 (C)	Pub	1,020	3,067	2,060
Florida Atlantic University; Boca Raton, Fla. 33431	10,256 (C)	Pub	1,200	3,600	2,800
Florida Christian College; Kissimmee, Fla. 32742	130	P	2,295	2,295	2,145
Florida Institute of Technology; Melbourne, Fla. 32901	2,963 (C)	P	6,439	6,439	2,907
Florida International University; Miami, Fla. 33199	16,438 (C)	Pub	925	2,964	3,500
Florida Memorial College; Miami, Fla. 33054	1,750 (C)	P/AB	3,125	3,125	2,400
Florida Southern College; Lakeland, Fla. 33801	1,859 (C)	P/UM	4,800	4,800	3,200
Florida State University; Tallahassee, Fla. 32306	16,722 (C)	Pub	984	3,033	2,714
Fontbonne College; St. Louis, Mo. 63105	860 (W)	P/RC	5,850	5,850	3,900
Fordham University–Lincoln Center; New York, N.Y. 10023	2,192 (C)	P	6,390	6,390	n.a.
Fordham Univ.–Rose Hill Campus; New York, N.Y. 10458	5,056 (C)	P	7,670	7,670	4,500
Forsyth School for Dental Hygienists; Boston, Mass. 02115	120 (C)	P	6,500	6,500	4,500
Fort Hays State University; Hays, Kan. 67601	3,930 (C)	Pub	1,247	2,737	2,163
Fort Lauderdale College; Fort Lauderdale, Fla. 33301	500 (C)	P	4,400	4,400	n.a.
Fort Lewis College; Durango, Colo. 81301	3,606 (C)	Pub	1,088	3,858	2,908
Fort Valley State College; Fort Valley, Ga. 31030	1,811 (C)	Pub	1,326	3,408	1,980
Fort Wayne Bible College; Fort Wayne, Ind. 46807	351 (C)	P/MC	4,374	4,374	2,570
Framingham State College; Framingham, Mass. 01701	3,211 (C)	Pub	1,398	3,594	2,070
Francis Marion College; Florence, S.C. 29501	3,349 (C)	Pub	1,100	2,200	2,700
Franklin College; Sorengo, Switzerland	200	P	9,400	9,400	5,400
Franklin and Marshall College; Lancaster, Pa. 17604	2,001 (C)	P/UCC	11,400	11,400	3,400
Franklin College; Franklin, Ind. 46131	706 (C)	P/AB	6,830	6,830	2,580
Franklin Pierce College; Rindge, N.H. 03461	1,037 (C)	P	7,985	7,985	3,450
Franklin University; Columbus, Ohio 43215	4,239 (C)	P	2,858	2,858	n.a.
Freed-Hardeman College; Henderson, Tenn. 38340	1,083 (C)	P/CC	3,550	3,550	2,450
Free Will Baptist Bible College; Nashville, Tenn. 37205	332 (C)	P/FWB	2,600	2,600	2,340
Fresno Pacific College; Fresno, Calif. 93702	450 (C)	P/MB	5,390	5,390	2,600

Institution and location	Enrollment	Control	Tuition ($) Res.	Tuition ($) Nonres.	Rm/Bd ($)
Friends Bible College; Haviland, Kan. 67059	85 (C)	P/F	4,340	4,340	2,100
Friends University; Wichita, Kan. 67213	1,094 (C)	P/F	4,725	4,725	2,150
Friends World College; Huntington, N.Y. 11743	450	P	5,700	5,700	3,900
Frostburg State College; Frostburg, Md. 21532	3,250 (C)	Pub	1,684	3,082	3,002
Furman University; Greenville, S.C. 29613	2,423 (C)	P/SB	7,314	7,314	3,328
Gallaudet College; Washington, D.C. 20002	1,406 (C)	P	2,504	2,504	3,096
Gannon University; Erie, Pa. 16541	3,959 (C)	P/RC	4,800	4,800	2,300
Gardner-Webb College; Boiling Springs, N.C. 28017	1,588 (C)	P/SB	4,930	4,930	2,780
General Motors Institute. *See* GMI Engineering and Management Institute					
Geneva College; Beaver Falls, Pa. 15010	996 (C)	P/RP	5,710	5,710	2,880
George Fox College; Newberg, Ore. 97132	548 (C)	P/F	6,370	6,370	2,860
George Mason University; Fairfax, Va. 22030	12,392 (C)	Pub	1,824	3,648	3,908
Georgetown College; Georgetown, Ky. 40324	985 (C)	P/SB	4,262	4,262	2,788
Georgetown University; Washington, D.C. 20057	5,462 (C)	P/RC	10,950	10,950	4,530
George Washington University; Washington, D.C. 20052	6,141 (C)	P	9,006	9,006	4,840
Georgia, University of; Athens, Ga. 30602	19,219 (C)	Pub	1,662	4,422	2,370
Georgia College; Milledgeville, Ga. 31061	3,168 (C)	Pub	1,128	3,048	1,710
Georgia Institute of Technology; Atlanta, Ga. 30332	8,940 (C)	Pub	1,806	5,367	3,390
Georgian Court College; Lakewood, N.J. 08701	1,234 (W)	P/RC	4,930	4,930	3,000
Georgia Southern College; Statesboro, Ga. 30458	6,723 (C)	Pub	1,341	3,423	2,115
Georgia Southwestern College; Americus, Ga. 31709	1,930 (C)	Pub	1,320	3,300	2,000
Georgia State University; Atlanta, Ga. 30303	15,178 (C)	Pub	1,320	4,383	n.a.
Gettysburg College; Gettysburg, Pa. 17325	1,850 (C)	P/L	10,840	10,840	3,040
Glassboro State College; Glassboro, N.J. 08028	5,500 (C)	Pub	1,450	2,168	3,250
Glenville State College; Glenville, W. Va. 26351	2,063 (C)	Pub	850	2,300	2,450
GMI Engineering & Management Institute; Flint, Mich. 48502	3,092 (C)	P	5,872	5,872	2,258
Goddard College; Plainfield, Vt. 05667	275 (C)	P	7,706	7,706	2,702
God's Bible School and College; Cincinnati, Ohio 45210	235	P	2,173	2,173	2,050
Golden Gate University; San Francisco, Calif. 94105	2,289 (C)	P	3,618	3,618	n.a.
Goldey Beacom College; Wilmington, Del. 19808	1,768 (C)	P	3,900	3,900	2,950
Gonzaga University; Spokane, Wash. 99258	2,356 (C)	P	7,300	7,300	3,100
Gordon College; Wenham, Mass. 01984	1,258 (C)	P	7,722	7,722	2,850
Goshen College; Goshen, Ind. 46526	1,068 (C)	P/Men	5,720	5,720	2,530
Goucher College; Baltimore, Md. 21204	812 (W)	P	9,350	9,350	4,530
Governors State University; University Park, Ill. 60466	2,555 (C)	Pub	1,168	3,424	n.a.
Grace Bible College; Grand Rapids, Mich. 49509	118 (C)	P/GGF	2,650	2,650	2,200
Grace College; Winona Lake, Ind. 46590	734 (C)	P	4,333	4,333	2,460
Grace College of the Bible; Omaha, Neb. 68108	250 (C)	P/Ind	2,940	2,940	2,100
Graceland College; Lamoni, Iowa 50140	953 (C)	P	5,760	5,760	2,190
Grambling State University; Grambling, La. 71245	4,829 (C)	Pub	1,094	1,774	2,062
Grand Canyon College; Phoenix, Ariz. 85017	1,572 (C)	P/SB	3,468	3,468	2,240
Grand Rapids Baptist College; Grand Rapids, Mich. 49505	698 (C)	P/B	4,045	4,045	2,810
Grand Valley State College; Allendale, Mich. 49401	6,667 (C)	Pub	1,566	3,668	2,750
Grand View College; Des Moines, Iowa 50316	1,288 (C)	P/LCA	4,840	4,840	2,120
Gratz College; Philadelphia, Pa. 19141	144 (C)	P	810	810	n.a.
Great Falls, College of; Great Falls, Mont. 59405	1,092 (C)	P/RC	3,518	3,518	2,600
Great Lakes Bible College; Lansing, Mich. 48901	154 (C)	P/CC	2,663	2,663	2,313
Green Mountain College; Poultney, Vt. 05764	450 (C)	P	6,080	6,080	3,620
Greensboro College; Greensboro, N.C. 27401	575 (C)	P/UM	4,750	4,750	2,446
Greenville College; Greenville, Ill. 62246	634 (C)	P/FM	6,148	6,148	2,854
Griffin College; Seattle, Wash. 98121	1,000 (C)	P	5,000	5,000	n.a.
Grinnell College; Grinnell, Iowa 50112	1,250 (C)	P	9,157	9,157	2,772
Grove City College; Grove City, Pa. 16127	2,133 (C)	P	3,600	3,600	2,020
Guam, University of; Mangilao, Guam 96913	2,280 (C)	Pub	731	1,211	2,200
Guilford College; Greensboro, N.C. 27410	1,234 (C)	P/F	6,808	6,808	3,062
Gustavus Adolphus College; St. Peter, Minn. 56082	2,152 (C)	P/LCA	8,425	8,425	2,375
Gwynedd-Mercy College; Gwynedd Valley, Pa. 19437	1,913 (W)	P/RC	5,500	5,500	3,000
Hahnemann University of Allied Health Professions; Philadelphia, Pa. 19102	759 (C)	P	5,400	5,400	3,500
Hamilton College; Clinton, N.Y. 13323	1,600 (C)	P	11,700	11,700	3,650
Hamline University; St. Paul, Minn. 55104	1,177 (C)	P/UM	7,475	7,475	2,815
Hampden-Sydney College; Hampden-Sydney, Va. 23943	824 (M)	P/PUS	8,950	8,950	2,750
Hampshire College; Amherst, Mass. 01002	1,005 (C)	P	12,630	12,630	3,345
Hampton University; Hampton, Va. 23668	5,000 (C)	P	4,400	4,400	2,064
Hannibal-LaGrange College; Hannibal, Mo. 63401	764 (C)	P/SB	3,264	3,264	1,794
Hanover College; Hanover, Ind. 47243	1,064 (C)	P/UP	4,980	4,980	2,220
Harding University; Searcy, Ark. 72143	2,625 (C)	P/CC	3,561	3,561	2,508
Hardin-Simmons University; Abilene, Tex. 79698	1,804 (C)	P	3,828	3,828	2,390
Harris-Stowe State College; St. Louis, Mo. 63103	1,340 (C)	Pub	1,098	2,152	n.a.
Hartford, University of; West Hartford, Conn. 06117	5,379 (C)	P	9,175	9,175	4,295
Hartwick College; Oneonta, N.Y. 13820	1,416 (C)	P	9,350	9,350	3,250

Institution and location	Enrollment	Control	Tuition ($) Res.	Tuition ($) Nonres.	Rm/Bd ($)
Harvard and Radcliffe Colleges; Cambridge, Mass. 02138	6,620	P	12,015	12,015	5,085
Harvey Mudd College. *See* Claremont Colleges					
Hastings College; Hastings, Neb. 68901	830 (C)	P/UP	5,550	5,550	2,220
Haverford College; Haverford, Pa. 19041	1,100 (C)	P	11,600	11,600	4,225
Hawaii, University of, at Hilo; Hilo, Hawaii 96720	1,158 (C)	Pub	255	1,730	3,094
Hawaii, University of, at Manoa; Honolulu, Hawaii 96822	13,341 (C)	Pub	1,096	3,746	2,835
Hawaii, University of-West Oahu College; Pearl City, Hawaii 96782	443 (C)	Pub	680	2,340	n.a.
Hawaii Loa College; Kaneohe, Hawaii 96744	402 (C)	P	6,800	6,800	3,700
Hawaii Pacific College; Honolulu, Hawaii 96813	3,952 (C)	P	3,730	3,730	n.a.
Hawthorne College; Antrim, N.H. 03440	350 (C)	P	6,670	6,670	3,270
Health Sciences, University of-School of Related Health Sciences; North Chicago, Ill. 60064	70 (C)	P	5,578	5,578	n.a.
Hebrew College; Brookline, Mass. 02146	70 (C)	P	2,810	2,810	n.a.
Heidelberg College; Tiffin, Ohio 44883	1,087 (C)	P	8,670	8,670	2,830
Hellenic College; Brookline, Mass. 02146	71	P	4,310	4,310	2,750
Henderson State University; Arkadelphia, Ark. 71923	2,933 (C)	Pub	872	1,744	1,680
Hendrix College; Conway, Ark. 72023	1,007 (C)	P/UM	5,000	5,000	2,235
Herbert H. Lehman College. *See* New York, City University of					
Heritage College; Toppenish, Wash. 98948	282	P	2,640	2,640	n.a.
High Point College; High Point, N.C. 27261	1,392 (C)	P/UM	4,900	4,900	2,380
Hillsdale College; Hillsdale, Mich. 49242	1,000 (C)	P	6,870	6,870	3,030
Hiram College; Hiram, Ohio 44234	1,100 (C)	P	8,404	8,404	2,634
Hobart and William Smith Colleges; Geneva, N.Y. 14456	1,900 (C)	P	11,250	11,250	4,005
Hofstra University; Hempstead, N.Y. 11550	8,323 (C)	P	6,770	6,770	3,500
Hollins College; Hollins College, Va. 24020	850 (W)	P	8,250	8,250	3,650
Holy Apostles College and Seminary; Cromwell, Conn. 06416	85 (M)	P/RC	2,750	2,750	2,870
Holy Cross, College of the; Worcester, Mass. 01610	2,673 (C)	P/RC	10,100	10,100	4,400
Holy Family College; Philadelphia, Pa. 19114	715 (C)	P	4,400	4,400	4,900
Holy Names College; Oakland, Calif. 94619	400 (C)	P/RC	6,970	6,970	3,500
Hong Kong Baptist College; Kowloon, Hong Kong	2,200	Pub	550	550	n.a.
Hood College; Frederick, Md. 21701	1,100 (W)	P	9,010	9,010	4,575
Hope College; Holland, Mich. 49423	2,442 (C)	P/RCA	7,280	7,280	3,034
Hotel and Restaurant Management, School of, of Widener University; Wilmington, Del. 19803	460 (C)	P	5,700	5,700	3,760
Houghton College; Houghton, N.Y. 14744	1,151 (C)	P/W	6,000	6,000	2,595
Houghton College–Buffalo Suburban Campus; West Seneca, N.Y. 14225	130 (C)	P	5,115	5,115	2,300
Houston, Univ. of—Clear Lake; Houston, Tex. 77058	3,168 (C)	Pub	758	3,254	n.a.
Houston, Univ. of—Downtown; Houston, Tex. 77002	7,213 (C)	Pub	328	2,880	2,714
Houston, Univ. of—University Park; Houston, Tex. 77004	18,587 (C)	Pub	744	3,240	3,200
Houston Baptist University; Houston, Tex. 77074	2,818 (C)	P	3,960	3,960	2,163
Howard Payne University; Brownwood, Tex. 76801	1,000 (C)	P/SB	2,490	2,490	2,160
Howard University; Washington, D.C. 20059	8,874 (C)	P	3,915	3,915	2,860
Human Services, College for; New York, N.Y. 10014	728 (C)	P	6,525	6,525	n.a.
Humboldt State University; Arcata, Calif. 95521	6,221 (C)	Pub	760	4,230	3,100
Hunter College. *See* New York, City University of					
Huntingdon College; Montgomery, Ala. 36194	755 (C)	P/UM	4,250	4,250	2,810
Huntington College; Huntington, Ind. 46750	433 (C)	P/BC	5,500	5,500	2,295
Huron College; Huron, S.D. 57350	400 (C)	P	4,240	4,240	2,375
Husson College; Bangor, Me. 04401	1,769 (C)	P	5,900	5,900	3,100
Huston-Tillotson College; Austin, Tex. 78702	524 (C)	P	3,300	3,300	2,416
Idaho, College of; Caldwell, Idaho 83605	670 (C)	P	5,800	5,800	2,556
Idaho, University of; Moscow, Idaho 83843	6,092 (C)	Pub	1,042	3,042	2,224
Idaho State University; Pocatello, Idaho 83209	6,500 (C)	Pub	1,800	2,900	2,144
Illinois, Univ. of, at Chicago; Chicago, Ill. 60680	16,197 (C)	Pub	2,139	4,953	3,561
Illinois, Univ. of, at Urbana–Champaign; Urbana, Ill. 61801	27,199 (C)	Pub	1,960	4,772	3,370
Illinois Benedictine College; Lisle, Ill. 60532	1,504 (C)	P/RC	5,800	5,800	2,800
Illinois College; Jacksonville, Ill. 62650	745 (C)	P	4,250	4,250	2,400
Illinois Institute of Technology; Chicago, Ill. 60616	2,925 (C)	P	8,700	8,700	3,650
Illinois State University; Normal, Ill. 61761	18,253 (C)	Pub	1,429	3,421	2,289
Illinois Wesleyan University; Bloomington, Ill. 61702	1,650 (C)	P	7,290	7,290	2,880
Immaculata College; Immaculata, Pa. 19345	1,800 (W)	P/RC	5,000	5,000	3,450
Incarnate Word College; San Antonio, Tex. 78209	1,600 (C)	P/RC	4,700	4,700	2,328
Indiana Central University; Indianapolis, Ind. 46227	2,581 (C)	P/UM	6,440	6,440	2,550
Indiana Institute of Technology; Fort Wayne, Ind. 46803	800 (C)	P	4,650	4,650	2,580
Indiana State University; Terre Haute, Ind. 47809	9,519 (C)	Pub	1,650	3,886	2,312
Indiana University–Bloomington; Bloomington, Ind. 47405	23,000 (C)	Pub	1,680	4,650	2,425
Indiana University–East; Richmond, Ind. 47374	1,354 (C)	Pub	1,433	3,518	n.a.
Indiana University–Kokomo; Kokomo, Ind. 46902	2,857 (C)	Pub	1,433	3,518	n.a.
Indiana University–Northwest; Gary, Ind. 46408	4,516 (C)	Pub	1,386	3,351	n.a.
Indiana University of Pennsylvania; Indiana, Pa. 15705	10,969 (C)	Pub	1,904	3,300	2,214

Institution and location	Enrollment	Control	Tuition ($) Res.	Tuition ($) Nonres.	Rm/Bd ($)
Indiana University–Purdue University at Fort Wayne; Fort Wayne, Ind. 46805	9,147 (C)	Pub	1,478	3,600	n.a.
Indiana University–Purdue University at Indianapolis; Indianapolis, Ind. 46202	15,118 (C)	Pub	1,290	3,432	2,420
Indiana University–South Bend; South Bend, Ind. 46634	4,324 (C)	Pub	1,520	3,600	n.a.
Indiana University–Southeast; New Albany, Ind. 47150	3,833 (C)	Pub	1,192	2,814	n.a.
Insurance, College of; New York, N.Y. 10007	940 (C)	P	4,860	4,860	5,562
Inter American University–Arecibo Regional College; Arecibo, P.R. 00612	3,715 (C)	P	1,760	1,760	n.a.
International Bible College; Florence, Ala. 35630	156	P	1,964	1,964	750
International Institute of the Americas of World University; Hato Rey, P.R. 00917	4,600 (C)	P	2,280	2,280	n.a.
International Training, School for; Brattleboro, Vt. 05301	70 (C)	P	6,300	6,300	2,700
Iona College; New Rochelle, N.Y. 10801	3,536 (C)	P	5,650	5,650	3,700
Iowa, University of; Iowa City, Iowa 52242	21,339 (C)	Pub	1,564	4,900	2,366
Iowa State University; Ames, Iowa 50011	22,388 (C)	Pub	1,564	4,900	2,242
Iowa Wesleyan College; Mount Pleasant, Iowa 52641	652 (C)	P/UM	5,600	5,600	2,370
Ithaca College; Ithaca, N.Y. 14850	5,237 (C)	P	7,646	7,646	3,506
ITT Technical Institute; West Covina, Calif. 91790-2767	700 (C)	P	5,800	5,800	n.a.
Jackson College for Women. *See* Tufts University					
Jackson State University; Jackson, Miss. 39217	6,500 (C)	Pub	1,172	1,186	2,132
Jacksonville State University; Jacksonville, Ala. 36265	6,241 (C)	Pub	800	1,050	1,600
Jacksonville University; Jacksonville, Fla. 32211	1,927 (C)	P	6,170	6,170	3,010
James Madison University; Harrisonburg, Va. 22807	8,496 (C)	Pub	2,392	4,222	2,828
Jamestown College; Jamestown, N.D. 58401	545 (C)	P/UP	5,620	5,620	1,995
Jarvis Christian College; Hawkins, Tex. 75765	560 (C)	P	3,000	3,000	2,585
Jersey City State College; Jersey City, N.J. 07305	5,224 (C)	Pub	1,575	2,175	3,210
Jewish Theological Seminary of America; New York, N.Y. 10027	127	P	4,504	4,504	4,800
John Brown University; Siloam Springs, Ark. 72761	849 (C)	P	3,780	3,780	2,625
John Carroll University; University Heights, Ohio 44118	2,946 (C)	P/RC	6,304	6,304	3,650
John F. Kennedy University–Evenings; Orinda, Calif. 94563	306 (C)	P	3,351	3,351	n.a.
John Jay Coll. of Criminal Justice. *See* New York, City Univ. of					
Johns Hopkins University; Baltimore, Md. 21218	2,564 (C)	P	11,000	11,000	5,000
Johnson and Wales College; Providence, R.I. 02903	5,400 (C)	P	6,285	6,285	3,200
Johnson Bible College; Knoxville, Tenn. 37998	392 (C)	P/ChC	2,350	2,350	2,730
Johnson C. Smith University; Charlotte, N.C. 28216	1,130 (C)	P	3,717	3,717	1,910
Johnson State College; Johnson, Vt. 05656	1,130 (C)	Pub	2,287	4,735	3,210
Johnston College, Calif. *See* Redlands, University of					
John Wesley College; High Point, N.C. 27260	62 (C)	P/ID	2,060	2,060	2,400
Jones College–Jacksonville; Jacksonville, Fla. 32211	1,700 (C)	P	2,147	2,147	n.a.
Judson College; Elgin, Ill. 60120	498 (C)	P/B	6,160	6,160	3,120
Judson College; Marion, Ala. 36756	411 (W)	P/SB	3,475	3,475	3,365
Juilliard School; New York, N.Y. 10023	511 (C)	P	7,250	7,250	n.a.
Juniata College; Huntingdon, Pa. 16652	1,117 (C)	P	8,750	8,750	2,900
Kalamazoo College; Kalamazoo, Mich. 49007	1,102 (C)	P/AB	8,988	8,988	3,189
Kansas, University of; Lawrence, Kan. 66045	19,073 (C)	Pub	1,320	3,490	2,136
Kansas, University of–College of Health Sciences; Kansas City, Kan. 66103	551 (C)	Pub	1,080	2,990	n.a.
Kansas City Art Institute; Kansas City, Mo. 64111	450 (C)	P	7,800	7,800	2,670
Kansas City College and Bible School; Overland Park, Kan. 66204	100	P	1,420	1,420	1,950
Kansas Newman College; Wichita, Kan. 67213	901 (C)	P	3,528	3,528	2,170
Kansas State University; Manhattan, Kan. 66506	13,218 (C)	Pub	1,332	3,502	2,286
Kansas Wesleyan University; Salina, Kan. 67401	666 (C)	P/UM	4,300	4,300	2,600
Kean College of New Jersey; Union, N.J. 07083	13,000 (C)	Pub	1,417	2,017	2,658
Kearney State College; Kearney, Neb. 68849	6,614 (C)	Pub	1,150	1,750	1,800
Keene State College; Keene, N.H. 03431	2,815 (C)	Pub	1,878	4,278	2,254
Kendall College; Evanston, Ill. 60201	346 (C)	P	5,175	5,175	3,276
Kendall School of Design; Grand Rapids, Mich. 49503	738 (C)	P	5,000	5,000	n.a.
Kennesaw College; Marietta, Ga. 30061	7,294 (C)	Pub	1,075	3,225	n.a.
Kent State University; Kent, Ohio 44242	16,336 (C)	Pub	2,104	3,704	2,492
Kentucky, University of; Lexington, Ky. 40506	16,247 (C)	Pub	1,412	4,052	2,600
Kentucky Christian College; Grayson, Ky. 41143	455 (C)	P/ChC	2,616	2,616	2,320
Kentucky State University; Frankfort, Ky. 40601	2,116 (C)	Pub	1,052	2,932	2,068
Kentucky Wesleyan College; Owensboro, Ky. 42301	812 (C)	P/UM	4,300	4,300	2,500
Kenyon College; Gambier, Ohio 43022	1,509 (C)	P	11,017	11,017	2,925
Keuka College; Keuka Park, N.Y. 14478	450 (W)	P	6,300	6,300	2,580
King College; Bristol, Tenn. 37620	585 (C)	P/PUS	4,050	4,050	2,700
King's College; Briarcliff Manor, N.Y. 10510	647 (C)	P/ND	5,780	5,780	2,485
King's College; Wilkes-Barre, Pa. 18711	2,299 (C)	P/RC	5,940	5,940	3,100
Knox College; Galesburg, Ill. 61401	967 (C)	P	9,120	9,120	2,850
Knoxville College; Knoxville, Tenn. 37921	500 (C)	P	3,267	3,267	2,034
Kutztown Univ. of Pennsylvania; Kutztown, Pa. 19530	5,724 (C)	Pub	1,738	3,006	1,840

Institution and location	Enrollment	Control	Tuition ($) Res.	Tuition ($) Nonres.	Rm/Bd ($)
Laboratory Institute of Merchandising; New York, N.Y. 10022	278	P	6,520	6,520	5,000
Lafayette College; Easton, Pa. 18042	2,032 (C)	P	10,850	10,850	3,800
LaGrange College; LaGrange, Ga. 30240	925 (C)	P/UM	3,090	3,090	2,010
Lake Erie College; Painesville, Ohio 44077	1,000 (W)	P	6,400	6,400	3,000
Lake Forest College; Lake Forest, Ill. 60045	1,142 (C)	P	10,745	10,745	2,630
Lakeland College; Sheboygan, Wis. 53082	407 (C)	P/UCC	6,200	6,200	2,830
Lake Superior State College; Sault Ste. Marie, Mich. 49783	2,571 (C)	Pub	1,527	2,832	2,642
Lamar University; Beaumont, Tex. 77710	14,230 (C)	Pub	1,285	4,405	2,450
Lambuth College; Jackson, Tenn. 38301	650 (C)	P/UM	4,182	4,182	2,284
Lancaster Bible College; Lancaster, Pa. 17601	360 (C)	P	4,720	4,720	2,450
Lander College; Greenwood, S.C. 29646	2,290 (C)	Pub	1,470	2,070	1,940
Lane College; Jackson, Tenn. 38301	555 (C)	P/CME	3,000	3,000	1,850
Langston University; Langston, Okla. 73050	2,026 (C)	Pub	936	2,438	2,375
Laredo State University; Laredo, Tex. 78040	398 (C)	Pub	648	3,930	2,500
La Roche College; Pittsburgh, Pa. 15237	1,575 (C)	P	4,760	4,760	2,750
La Salle University; Philadelphia, Pa. 19141	3,013 (C)	P/RC	6,150	6,150	3,170
La Verne, University of; La Verne, Calif. 91750	1,147 (C)	P/Ind	7,765	7,765	3,704
Lawrence Institute of Technology; Southfield, Mich. 48075	6,142 (C)	P	1,934	1,934	1,944
Lawrence University; Appleton, Wis. 54912	1,072 (C)	P	9,900	9,900	2,730
Lebanon Valley College; Annville, Pa. 17003	764 (C)	P/UM	8,150	8,150	3,250
Lee College; Cleveland, Tenn. 37311	1,212 (C)	P	3,228	3,228	2,320
Lee College of the University of Judaism; Los Angeles, Calif. 90077	111	P	4,650	4,650	3,350
Lehigh University; Bethlehem, Pa. 18015	4,453 (C)	P	11,400	11,400	3,680
Le Moyne College; Syracuse, N.Y. 13214	1,800 (C)	P	6,420	6,420	2,860
LeMoyne-Owen College; Memphis, Tenn. 38126	955 (C)	P	5,070	5,070	n.a.
Lenoir-Rhyne College; Hickory, N.C. 28603	1,431 (C)	P/LCA	4,831	4,831	1,850
Lesley College; Cambridge, Mass. 02238	500 (C)	P	7,800	7,800	4,250
LeTourneau College; Longview, Tex. 75607	774 (C)	P	5,354	5,354	3,110
Lewis and Clark College; Portland, Ore. 97219	1,651 (C)	P	9,348	9,348	3,790
Lewis-Clark State College; Lewiston, Idaho 83501	2,048 (C)	Pub	1,008	2,908	2,250
Lewis University; Romeoville, Ill. 60441	2,393 (C)	P/RC	5,668	5,668	2,690
Liberty University; Lynchburg, Va. 24506	5,515 (C)	P/B	3,210	3,210	3,030
L.I.F.E. Bible College; Los Angeles, Calif. 90026	456 (C)	P/FG	2,412	2,412	2,025
Limestone College; Gaffney, S.C. 29340	1,500 (C)	P	5,460	5,460	2,440
Lincoln Christian College; Lincoln, Ill. 62656	286 (C)	P/CC	3,040	3,040	2,020
Lincoln Memorial University; Harrogate, Tenn. 37752	1,283 (C)	P	3,400	3,400	2,200
Lincoln University; Jefferson City, Mo. 65101	2,322 (C)	Pub	927	1,854	2,629
Lincoln University; Lincoln University, Pa. 19352	1,050 (C)	Pub	1,930	2,930	2,300
Lincoln University; San Francisco, Calif. 94118	178	P	2,850	2,850	n.a.
Lindenwood College; St. Charles, Mo. 63301	1,167 (C)	P	5,200	5,200	3,200
Linfield College; McMinnville, Ore. 97128	1,107 (C)	P	7,480	7,480	2,514
Livingstone College; Salisbury, N.C. 28144	618 (C)	P/AME	3,140	3,140	2,160
Livingston University; Livingston, Ala. 35470	1,264 (C)	Pub	1,188	1,188	1,773
Lock Haven University; Lock Haven, Pa. 17745	2,600 (C)	Pub	1,600	2,868	1,864
Loma Linda University; Loma Linda, Calif. 92350	3,115 (C)	P/SDA	6,450	6,450	2,733
Loma Linda University-La Sierra; Riverside, Calif. 92515	1,592 (C)	P/SDA	6,840	6,840	2,808
Long Island University; Greenvale, N.Y. 11548:					
Brooklyn Center; Brooklyn, N.Y. 11201	3,997 (C)	P	6,000	6,000	3,320
C.W. Post Campus; Greenvale; N.Y. 11548	5,807 (C)	P	6,920	6,920	3,556
Southampton Campus; Southampton, N.Y. 11968	1,149 (C)	P	7,590	7,590	4,410
Longwood College; Farmville, Va. 23901	2,693 (C)	Pub	2,638	3,976	2,884
Loras College; Dubuque, Iowa 52001	2,000 (C)	P	5,800	5,800	2,300
Loretto Heights College; Denver, Colo. 80236	715 (C)	P	6,740	6,740	3,360
Louisiana College; Pineville, La. 71359	1,266 (C)	P/SB	2,292	2,292	2,088
Louisiana State Univ. and A&M Coll.; Baton Rouge, La. 70803	23,224 (C)	Pub	1,727	4,527	2,014
LSU-Shreveport; Shreveport, La. 71115	3,723 (C)	Pub	980	2,210	n.a.
Louisiana Tech University; Ruston, La. 71272	9,411 (C)	Pub	1,415	2,360	2,025
Louisville, University of; Louisville, Ky. 40292	15,788 (C)	Pub	1,340	3,820	2,200
Lourdes College; Sylvania, Ohio 43560	860 (C)	P/RC	3,050	3,050	n.a.
Lowell, University of; Lowell, Mass. 01854	8,298 (C)	Pub	1,430	3,986	2,791
Loyola College; Baltimore, Md. 21210	3,007 (C)	P/RC	7,200	7,200	3,535
Loyola Marymount University; Los Angeles, Calif. 90045	4,025 (C)	P/RC	7,289	7,289	3,400
Loyola University; New Orleans, La. 70118	3,580 (C)	P/RC	4,828	4,828	3,466
Loyola University of Chicago; Chicago, Ill. 60011	8,823 (C)	P	6,065	6,065	3,300
Lubbock Christian Univ.; Lubbock, Tex. 79407	1,041 (C)	P/CC	4,260	4,260	2,120
Lutheran Bible Institute; Issaquah, Wash. 98027	175 (C)	P/L	3,450	3,450	2,537
Luther College; Decorah, Iowa 52101	2,109 (C)	P/AL	7,330	7,330	2,420
Lycoming College; Williamsport, Pa. 17701	1,250 (C)	P	7,680	7,680	3,000
Lynchburg College; Lynchburg, Va. 24501	1,700 (C)	P	6,625	6,625	3,400
Lyndon State College; Lyndonville, Vt. 05851	900 (C)	Pub	2,322	4,772	3,210

Institution and location	Enrollment	Control	Tuition ($) Res.	Tuition ($) Nonres.	Rm/Bd ($)
Macalester College; St. Paul, Minn. 55105	1,768 (C)	P	9,730	9,730	3,050
MacMurray College; Jacksonville, Ill. 62650	650 (C)	P/UM	6,400	6,400	2,730
Madonna College; Livonia, Mich. 48150	3,718 (C)	P	2,840	2,840	2,460
Magdalen College; Bedford, N.H. 03102	50	P	4,000	4,000	2,500
Maharishi International University; Fairfield, Iowa 52556	344 (C)	P	6,060	6,060	2,112
Maine, Univ. of–Farmington; Farmington, Me. 04938	2,261 (C)	Pub	1,413	3,630	2,850
Maine, Univ. of–Fort Kent; Fort Kent, Me. 04743	750 (C)	Pub	1,413	3,630	2,743
Maine, Univ. of–Machias; Machias, Me. 04654	886 (C)	Pub	4,348	6,565	2,875
Maine, Univ. of–Orono; Orono, Me. 04469	9,635 (C)	Pub	1,509	4,560	3,094
Maine, Univ. of–Presque Isle; Presque Isle, Me. 04769	1,351 (C)	Pub	1,413	3,630	2,692
Maine Maritime Academy; Castine, Me. 04420	550 (C)	Pub	2,390	4,510	3,150
Mallinckrodt College; Wilmette, Ill. 60091	260 (C)	P/RC	2,730	2,730	n.a.
Malone College; Canton, Ohio 44709	1,039 (C)	P/F	5,370	5,370	2,610
Manchester College; North Manchester, Ind. 46962	931 (C)	P/CB	6,330	6,330	2,420
Manhattan Christian College; Manhattan, Kan. 66502	190 (C)	P/CC	1,920	1,920	2,060
Manhattan College; Riverdale, Bronx, N.Y. 10471	4,000 (C)	P	6,300	6,300	4,000
Manhattan School of Music; New York, N.Y. 10027	435 (C)	P	6,500	6,500	n.a.
Manhattanville College; Purchase, N.Y. 10577	1,050 (C)	P	8,900	8,900	4,450
Mankato State University; Mankato, Minn. 56001	13,100 (C)	Pub	1,628	2,452	1,712
Mannes College of Music; New York, N.Y. 10024	120 (C)	P	6,100	6,100	2,500
Mansfield University; Mansfield, Pa. 16933	2,701 (C)	Pub	1,600	2,818	1,988
Marian College; Indianapolis, Ind. 46222	1,100 (C)	P/RC	4,900	4,900	2,350
Marian College of Fond du Lac; Fond du Lac, Wis. 54935	411 (C)	P/RC	5,550	5,550	2,250
Marietta College; Marietta, Ohio 45750	1,147 (C)	P	8,700	8,700	2,650
Marion College; Marion, Ind. 46953	1,050 (C)	P/WM	5,336	5,336	2,490
Marist College; Poughkeepsie, N.Y. 12601	2,800 (C)	P	5,904	5,904	3,560
Marlboro College; Marlboro, Vt. 05344	200 (C)	P	10,417	10,417	3,910
Marquette University; Milwaukee, Wis. 53233	8,819 (C)	P	6,476	6,476	3,225
Marshall University; Huntington, W. Va. 25705	8,600 (C)	Pub	1,042	2,772	2,932
Mars Hill College; Mars Hill, N.C. 28754	1,419 (C)	P/SB	4,490	4,490	1,860
Martin Center College; Indianapolis, Ind. 42605	200	P	2,250	2,250	n.a.
Mary, University of; Bismarck, N.D. 58501	1,100	P	4,200	4,200	2,050
Mary Baldwin College; Staunton, Va. 24401	804 (W)	P/PUS	7,150	7,150	4,850
Marycrest College; Davenport, Iowa 52804	1,500 (C)	P/RC	5,670	5,670	2,050
Marygrove College; Detroit, Mich. 48221	1,022 (C)	P/RC	4,485	4,485	3,228
Mary Hardin–Baylor, University of; Belton, Tex. 76513	1,307 (C)	P/SB	3,450	3,450	2,290
Maryland, Univ. of–Baltimore County; Catonsville, Md. 21228	8,541 (C)	Pub	1,800	4,906	3,035
Maryland, Univ. of–College Park; College Park, Md. 20742	30,362 (C)	Pub	1,740	4,846	3,641
Maryland, Univ. of–Eastern Shore; Princess Anne, Md. 21853	1,281 (C)	Pub	1,502	4,198	2,980
Maryland, Univ. of, University College; College Park, Md. 20742	11,200 (C)	Pub	2,460	2,460	n.a.
Maryland Institute–College of Art; Baltimore, Md. 21217	800 (C)	P	7,400	7,400	3,100
Marylhurst Coll. for Lifelong Learning; Marylhurst, Ore. 97036	1,420 (C)	P	5,400	5,400	n.a.
Marymount College; Tarrytown, N.Y. 10591	1,256	P	6,710	6,710	4,130
Marymount College of Kansas; Salina, Kan. 67401	506 (C)	P/RC	4,400	4,400	2,500
Marymount Univ.; Arlington, Va. 22207	1,481 (W)	P	5,940	5,940	3,530
Marymount Manhattan College; New York, N.Y. 10021	1,550 (C)	P	5,900	5,900	n.a.
Maryville College; Maryville, Tenn. 37801	523 (C)	P	5,265	5,265	2,825
Maryville College; St. Louis, Mo. 63141	2,043 (C)	P	5,500	5,500	2,850
Mary Washington College; Fredericksburg, Va. 22401	2,880 (C)	Pub	2,122	4,130	3,320
Marywood College; Scranton, Pa. 18509	2,116 (W)	P/RC	5,000	5,000	2,700
Massachusetts, Univ. of–Amherst; Amherst, Mass. 01003	19,445 (C)	Pub	2,000	5,000	3,000
Massachusetts, Univ. of–Boston; Boston, Mass. 02125	11,406 (C)	Pub	1,296	4,120	n.a.
Massachusetts College of Art; Boston, Mass. 02115	1,199 (C)	Pub	960	3,216	n.a.
Massachusetts College of Pharmacy and Allied Health Sciences; Boston, Mass. 02115	785 (C)	P	6,600	6,600	4,360
Massachusetts Institute of Technology; Cambridge, Mass. 02139	4,353 (C)	P	11,800	11,800	4,350
Massachusetts Maritime Academy; Buzzards Bay, Mass. 02532	800 (C)	Pub	3,658	3,658	2,750
Master's College, The; Newhall, Calif. 91322	555	P/B	4,580	4,580	2,990
Mayville State College; Mayville, N.D. 58257	730 (C)	Pub	1,137	2,205	1,713
McKendree College; Lebanon, Ill. 62258	1,200 (C)	P/UM	4,600	4,600	2,600
McMurry College; Abilene, Tex. 79697	1,657 (C)	P/UM	3,840	3,840	2,080
McNeese State University; Lake Charles, La. 70609	6,650 (C)	Pub	992	1,872	1,650
McPherson College; McPherson, Kan. 67460	475 (C)	P/CB	4,650	4,650	2,490
Medaille College; Buffalo, N.Y. 14214	967 (C)	P	4,530	4,530	n.a.
Medical College of Georgia; Augusta, Ga. 30912	707 (C)	Pub	1,443	3,987	2,873
Medical University of South Carolina; Charleston, S.C. 29425	707 (C)	Pub	1,500	3,000	3,100
Memphis College of Art; Memphis, Tenn. 38112	250 (C)	P	5,700	5,700	2,500
Memphis State University; Memphis, Tenn. 38152	16,005 (C)	Pub	1,220	3,650	2,456
Menlo College; Atherton, Calif. 94025	630 (C)	P	7,670	7,670	4,320
Mercer University; Macon, Ga. 31207	2,100 (C)	P/SB	6,282[1]	6,282	2,937
Mercer University–Atlanta; Atlanta, Ga. 30341	1,466 (C)	P/SB	4,568	4,568	n.a.
Mercy College; Dobbs Ferry, N.Y. 10522	8,800 (C)	P	4,200	4,200	n.a.
Mercy College of Detroit; Detroit, Mich. 48219	1,914 (C)	P/RC	5,008	5,008	1,920

Institution and location	Enrollment	Control	Tuition ($) Res.	Nonres.	Rm/Bd ($)
Mercyhurst College; Erie, Pa. 16546	1,761 (C)	P/RC	6,555	6,555	2,490
Meredith College; Raleigh, N.C. 27607	1,507 (C)	P	4,200	4,200	1,850
Merrimack College; North Andover, Mass. 01845	2,300 (C)	P/RC	7,400	7,400	4,000
Mesa College; Grand Junction, Colo. 81502	4,000 (C)	Pub	1,274	3,220	2,448
Messiah College; Grantham, Pa. 17027	1,916 (C)	P	6,100	6,100	3,060
Methodist College; Fayetteville, N.C. 28301	1,360 (C)	P	5,700	5,700	2,650
Metropolitan State College; Denver, Colo. 80204	14,557 (C)	Pub	1,186	5,162	n.a.
Metropolitan State University; St. Paul, Minn. 55101	4,332 (C)	Pub	1,371	2,220	n.a.
Miami, University of; Coral Gables, Fla. 33124	8,501 (C)	P	9,787	9,787	4,080
Miami Christian College; Miami, Fla. 33167	197 (C)	P/ID	3,985	3,985	2,610
Miami University; Oxford, Ohio 45056	13,681 (C)	Pub	2,584	5,460	2,426
Michigan, Univ. of–Ann Arbor; Ann Arbor, Mich. 48109	22,000 (C)	Pub	2,222	7,268	2,900
Michigan, Univ. of–Dearborn; Dearborn, Mich. 48128	6,398 (C)	Pub	1,770	5,434	n.a.
Michigan, Univ. of–Flint; Flint, Mich. 48502	6,047 (C)	Pub	1,536	4,972	n.a.
Michigan State University; East Lansing, Mich. 48824	33,914 (C)	Pub	2,025	5,332	2,538
Michigan Technological University; Houghton, Mich. 49931	5,913 (C)	Pub	1,869	4,221	2,608
Mid-America Bible College; Oklahoma City, Okla. 73170	231	P/CG	3,382	3,382	2,076
Mid-America Nazarene College; Olathe, Kan. 66061	1,040 (C)	P	3,863	3,863	2,566
Middlebury College; Middlebury, Vt. 05753	1,900 (C)	P	15,500	15,500	—
Midland Lutheran College; Fremont, Neb. 68025	845 (C)	P/L	5,500	5,500	2,230
Middle Tennessee State Univ.; Murfreesboro, Tenn. 37132	11,408 (C)	Pub	1,036	3,466	1,682
Mid-South Bible College; Memphis, Tenn. 38182	254 (C)	P	2,880	2,880	2,200
Midwestern State University; Wichita Falls, Tex. 76308	3,791 (C)	Pub	870	3,990	2,152
Miles College; Birmingham, Ala. 35208	465 (C)	P/CME	3,500	3,500	2,100
Millersville University of Pennsylvania; Millersville, Pa. 17551	6,493 (C)	Pub	1,680	3,076	2,280
Milligan College; Milligan College, Tenn. 37682	600 (C)	P	4,456	4,456	2,372
Millikin University; Decatur, Ill. 62522	1,562 (C)	P	6,471	6,471	2,850
Millsaps College; Jackson, Miss. 39210	1,228 (C)	P/UM	6,035	6,035	2,600
Mills College; Oakland, Calif. 94613	770 (C)	P	9,200	9,200	4,300
Milwaukee School of Engineering; Milwaukee, Wis. 53202	1,710 (C)	P	6,750	6,750	2,535
Minneapolis Coll. of Art and Design; Minneapolis, Minn. 55404	622 (C)	P	6,900	6,900	2,700
Minnesota, Univ. of–Duluth; Duluth, Minn. 55812	7,350 (C)	Pub	1,685	4,280	2,600
Minnesota, Univ. of–Morris; Morris, Minn. 56267	1,774 (C)	Pub	1,909	4,770	1,599
Minnesota, Univ. of–Twin Cities; Minneapolis, Minn. 55455	31,301 (C)	Pub	1,975	4,525	2,571
Minnesota Bible College; Rochester, Minn. 55902	79 (C)	P/CC	2,400	2,400	3,800
Minot State College; Minot, N.D. 58701	2,950 (C)	Pub	1,098	2,166	1,560
Mississippi, University of; University, Miss. 38677	7,373 (C)	Pub	1,727	2,909	2,475
Mississippi, Univ. of, Medical Center; Jackson, Miss. 39216	544 (C)	Pub	1,595	2,777	2,324
Mississippi College; Clinton, Miss. 39058	1,880 (C)	P	3,556	3,556	2,400
Mississippi State University; Mississippi State, Miss. 39762	9,979 (C)	Pub	1,777	2,959	2,440
Mississippi University for Women; Columbus, Miss. 39701	1,982 (W)	Pub	1,075	2,257	1,760
Mississippi Valley State University; Itta Bena, Miss. 38941	2,344 (C)	Pub	1,500	2,682	1,575
Missouri, Univ. of–Columbia; Columbia, Mo. 65211	16,907 (C)	Pub	1,383	4,161	2,280
Missouri, Univ. of–Kansas City; Kansas City, Mo. 64110	7,141 (C)	Pub	1,669	4,645	5,046
Missouri, Univ. of–Rolla; Rolla, Mo. 65401	5,092 (C)	Pub	1,718	4,988	2,815
Missouri, Univ. of–St. Louis; St. Louis, Mo. 63121	9,473 (C)	Pub	1,468	4,268	n.a.
Missouri Baptist College; St. Louis, Mo. 63141	530 (C)	P/SB	3,800	3,800	2,000
Missouri Southern State College; Joplin, Mo. 64801	4,610 (C)	Pub	990	1,830	1,756
Missouri Valley College; Marshall, Mo. 65340	564 (C)	P	5,000	5,000	3,100
Missouri Western State College; St. Joseph, Mo. 64507	3,936 (C)	Pub	975	1,835	1,750
Mobile College; Mobile, Ala. 36613	789 (C)	P/SB	3,750	3,750	2,500
Molloy College; Rockville Centre, N.Y. 11570	1,472 (C)	P/RC	5,200	5,200	n.a.
Monmouth College; Monmouth, Ill. 61462	700 (C)	P/UP	8,620	8,620	2,840
Monmouth College; West Long Branch, N.J. 07764	3,873 (C)	P	7,368	7,368	3,396
Montana, University of; Missoula, Mont. 59812	6,963 (C)	Pub	1,330	3,147	2,502
Montana College of Mineral Science and Technology; Butte, Mont. 59701	1,850 (C)	Pub	1,069	2,887	2,700
Montana State University; Bozeman, Mont. 59717	9,369 (C)	Pub	1,295	3,113	2,721
Monterey Institute of Intl. Studies; Monterey, Calif. 93940	68 (C)	P	6,850	6,850	n.a.
Montclair State College; Upper Montclair, N.J. 07043	10,224 (C)	Pub	1,280	1,920	3,300
Montevallo, University of; Montevallo, Ala. 35115	2,250 (C)	Pub	1,254	2,150	2,274
Moody Bible Institute; Chicago, Ill. 60610	1,398 (C)	P/ID	460	460	3,300
Moore College of Art; Philadelphia, Pa. 19103	656 (W)	P	6,870	6,870	3,700
Moorhead State University; Moorhead, Minn. 56560	7,367 (C)	Pub	1,592	2,769	1,830
Moravian College; Bethlehem, Pa. 18018	1,190 (C)	P/Mor	8,155	8,155	2,780
Morehead State University; Morehead, Ky. 40351	4,454 (C)	Pub	1,130	3,130	2,170
Morehouse College; Atlanta, Ga. 30314	2,005 (M)	P	4,190	4,190	2,890
Morgan State University; Baltimore, Md. 21239	3,180 (C)	Pub	1,538	3,073	3,220
Morningside College; Sioux City, Iowa 51106	1,380 (C)	P/UM	6,486	6,486	2,230
Morris Brown College; Atlanta, Ga. 30314	1,400 (C)	P/AME	3,700	3,700	2,200
Morris College; Sumter, S.C. 29150	700 (C)	P	2,904	2,904	2,004
Mount Angel Seminary; St. Benedict, Ore. 97373	34	P/RC	2,730	2,730	2,600
Mount Holyoke College; South Hadley, Mass. 01075	1,906 (W)	P	12,000	12,000	3,475

Institution and location	Enrollment	Control	Tuition ($) Res.	Nonres.	Rm/Bd ($)
Mount Marty College; Yankton, S.D. 57078	503 (C)	P/RC	4,570	4,570	2,120
Mount Mary College; Milwaukee, Wis. 53222	1,292 (W)	P/RC	5,200	5,200	2,390
Mount Mercy College; Cedar Rapids, Iowa 52402	1,334 (C)	P	5,580	5,580	2,275
Mount Olive College; Mount Olive, N.C. 28365	420 (C)	P	4,000	4,000	2,550
Mount Saint Mary College; Newburgh, N.Y. 12550	1,130 (C)	P	4,800	4,800	2,750
Mount St. Joseph on the Ohio, College of; Mount St. Joseph, Ohio 45051	2,040 (W)	P/RC	5,704	5,704	3,046
Mount Saint Mary's College; Emmitsburg, Md. 21727	1,500 (C)	P/RC	6,500	6,500	3,000
Mount St. Mary's College; Los Angeles, Calif. 90049	798 (W)	P/RC	6,660	6,660	3,848
Mount Saint Vincent, College of; Riverdale, N.Y. 10471	1,050 (C)	P	6,150	6,150	3,750
Mount Senario College; Ladysmith, Wis. 54848	760 (C)	P	4,200	4,200	2,200
Mount Union College; Alliance, Ohio 44601	1,000 (C)	P	8,130	8,130	2,470
Mount Vernon College; Washington, D.C. 20007	474 (W)	P	7,992	7,992	4,644
Mount Vernon Nazarene College; Mount Vernon, Ohio 43050	1,030 (C)	P	4,384	4,384	2,420
Muhlenberg College; Allentown, Pa. 18104	1,534 (C)	P/L	9,980	9,980	2,880
Multnomah School of the Bible; Portland, Ore. 97220	545 (C)	P	4,070	4,070	2,320
Mundelein College; Chicago, Ill. 60660	1,041 (W)	P/RC	5,970	5,970	2,775
Murray State University; Murray, Ky. 42071	5,868 (C)	Pub	100	2,820	1,880
Museum Art School, Portland. *See* Pacific Northwest Coll. of Art					
Muskingum College; New Concord, Ohio 43762	1,022 (C)	P/UP	8,655	8,655	2,795
NAES College; Chicago, Ill. 60659	45	P	3,375	3,375	n.a.
Naropa Institute; Boulder, Colo. 80302	115	P	6,750	6,750	n.a.
Nathaniel Hawthorne College. *See* Hawthorne College					
National College; Rapid City, S.D. 57709	1,054	P	4,800	4,800	2,790
National College–Albuquerque; Albuquerque, N.M. 87108	375	P	4,080	4,080	n.a.
National College, Colorado Springs Branch; Colorado Springs, Colo. 80932	375	P	3,600	3,600	n.a.
National College of Chiropractic; Lombard, Ill. 60148	886 (C)	P	8,280	8,280	4,500
National College of Education; Evanston, Ill. 60201	420 (C)	P	5,200	5,200	4,100
National University; San Diego, Calif. 92108	7,058 (C)	P	5,580	5,580	n.a.
Nazareth College in Kalamazoo; Nazareth, Mich. 49001-1282	746 (C)	P	6,125	6,125	2,820
Nazareth College of Rochester; Rochester, N.Y. 14610	1,478 (C)	P	5,700	5,700	3,200
Nebraska, University of–Lincoln; Lincoln, Neb. 68508	19,720 (C)	Pub	1,513	3,770	2,170
Nebraska, University of–Omaha; Omaha, Neb. 68182	11,640 (C)	Pub	1,421	3,679	n.a.
Nebraska Christian College; Norfolk, Neb. 68701	140	P	1,577	1,577	1,863
Nebraska Wesleyan University; Lincoln, Neb. 68504	1,347 (C)	P/UM	5,786	5,786	2,300
Neumann College; Aston, Pa. 19014	1,041 (C)	P	4,720	4,720	n.a.
Nevada, University of–Las Vegas; Las Vegas, Nev. 89154	8,672 (C)	Pub	1,080	3,280	2,400
Nevada, University of–Reno; Reno, Nev. 89557	6,870 (C)	Pub	1,152	3,352	2,400
Newberry College; Newberry, S.C. 29108	606 (C)	P/LCA	5,900	5,900	2,500
New Church College, Academy of the; Bryn Athyn, Pa. 19009	123 (C)	P	2,436	2,436	2,304
New College of California; San Francisco, Calif. 94110	400 (C)	P	3,600	3,600	n.a.
New College of the University of South Florida; Sarasota, Fla. 33580	420 (C)	Pub	1,098	3,026	3,030
New England, University of; Biddeford, Me. 04005	630 (C)	P	6,950	6,950	3,350
New England Baptist Bible College; South Portland, Me. 04106	41	P	1,750	1,750	n.a.
New England College; Henniker, N.H. 03242	1,087 (C)	P	8,300	8,300	3,600
New England College–Arundel Campus; Sussex BN18 ODA, England	250	P	7,550	7,550	3,350
New England Conservatory of Music; Boston, Mass. 02115	407 (C)	P	8,850	8,850	4,400
New England Institute of Technology; Providence, R.I. 02907	1,900 (C)	P	4,950	4,950	2,700
New Hampshire, University of; Durham, N.H. 03824	9,046 (C)	Pub	2,629	6,799	2,700
New Hampshire College; Manchester, N.H. 03104	1,600 (C)	P	7,272	7,272	4,036
New Haven, University of; West Haven, Conn. 06516	1,834 (C)	P	6,820	6,820	3,600
New Jersey Institute of Technology; Newark, N.J. 07102	4,902 (C)	Pub	2,712	4,844	3,195
New Mexico, University of; Albuquerque, N.M. 87131	19,748 (C)	Pub	1,152	4,374	3,068
New Mexico Highlands University; Las Vegas, N.M. 87701	1,664 (C)	Pub	750	2,904	1,850
New Mexico Inst. of Mining & Technology; Socorro, N.M. 87801	948 (C)	Pub	1,047	4,215	2,450
New Mexico State University; Las Cruces, N.M. 88003	13,718 (C)	Pub	1,026	3,652	2,210
New Orleans, University of; New Orleans, La. 70148	16,083 (C)	Pub	1,524	3,900	2,418
New Rochelle, College of-School of Arts & Sciences and School of Nursing; New Rochelle, N.Y. 10801	676 (C)	P	7,200	7,200	3,550
New School of Social Research; New York, N.Y. 10011	250 (C)	P	7,500	7,500	4,500
New York, City University of; New York, N.Y. 10021:					
Bernard M. Baruch College; New York, N.Y. 10010	12,268 (C)	Pub	1,284	2,584	n.a.
Brooklyn College; Brooklyn, N.Y. 11210	11,000 (C)	Pub	1,250	2,550	n.a.
City College; New York, N.Y. 10031	10,500 (C)	Pub	1,321	2,621	n.a.
College of Staten Island; Staten Island, N.Y. 10301	8,600 (C)	Pub	1,328	2,629	n.a.
Hunter College; New York, N.Y. 10021	15,494 (C)	Pub	1,250	2,550	2,135
Herbert H. Lehman College; Bronx, N.Y. 10468	10,000 (C)	Pub	1,275	2,375	n.a.
John Jay College of Criminal Justice; New York, N.Y. 10019	6,234 (C)	Pub	1,316	2,616	n.a.
Queens College; Flushing, N.Y. 11367	16,000 (C)	Pub	1,250	2,500	n.a.
York College; Jamaica, N.Y. 11451	4,300 (C)	Pub	1,250	2,550	n.a.

Institution and location	Enrollment	Control	Tuition ($)		Rm/Bd ($)
			Res.	Nonres.	
New York, State University of; Albany, N.Y. 12246:					
SUNY–Albany; Albany, N.Y. 12222	11,645 (C)	Pub	1,478	3,328	2,892
SUNY–Buffalo; Buffalo, N.Y. 14214	18,388 (C)	Pub	1,619	3,469	3,080
SUNY–Purchase; Purchase, N.Y. 10577	3,864 (C)	Pub	1,350	3,200	2,760
SUNY–Stony Brook; Stony Brook, N.Y. 11794	11,279 (C)	Pub	1,495	3,345	3,110
SUNY–College at Brockport; Brockport, N.Y. 14420	5,810 (C)	Pub	1,475	3,325	2,950
SUNY–College at Buffalo; Buffalo, N.Y. 14222	10,050 (C)	Pub	1,457	3,307	2,850
SUNY–College at Cortland; Cortland, N.Y. 13045	5,225 (C)	Pub	1,375	3,225	2,910
SUNY–College at Fredonia; Fredonia, N.Y. 14063	4,510 (C)	Pub	1,450	3,350	2,800
SUNY–College at Geneseo; Geneseo, N.Y. 14454	4,550 (C)	Pub	1,350	3,200	2,500
SUNY–College at New Paltz; New Paltz, N.Y. 12561	4,228 (C)	Pub	1,350	3,200	3,360
SUNY–College at Old Westbury; Old Westbury, N.Y. 11568	3,755 (C)	Pub	1,350	3,200	3,000
SUNY–College at Oneonta; Oneonta, N.Y. 13820	5,390 (C)	Pub	1,545	3,400	2,800
SUNY–College at Oswego; Oswego, N.Y. 13126	7,211 (C)	Pub	1,350	3,200	2,716
SUNY–College at Plattsburgh; Plattsburgh, N.Y. 12901	5,692 (C)	Pub	1,468	3,318	2,964
SUNY–College at Potsdam; Potsdam, N.Y. 13676	3,848 (C)	Pub	1,500	3,325	2,870
College of Agriculture and Life Sciences at Cornell; Ithaca, N.Y. 14853	3,047 (C)	Pub	4,882	8,668	4,020
SUNY–College of Ceramics at Alfred University; Alfred, N.Y. 14802	696 (C)	Pub	2,975	4,300	3,230
SUNY–College of Environmental Science and Forestry; Syracuse, N.Y. 13210	1,000 (C)	Pub	1,350	3,250	3,810
SUNY–College of Human Ecology at Cornell; Ithaca, N.Y. 14853	1,240 (C)	Pub	4,882	8,668	4,020
SUNY–College of Technology; Utica, N.Y. 13504	2,341 (C)	Pub	1,485	3,335	n.a.
SUNY–Empire State College; Saratoga Springs, N.Y. 12866	5,200 (C)	Pub	2,081	4,856	n.a.
SUNY–Fashion Institute of Technology; New York, N.Y. 10001	3,967 (C)	Pub	1,500	2,850	3,500
SUNY–Health Science Center at Syracuse; Syracuse, N.Y. 13210	123 (C)	Pub	2,880	3,700	3,305
SUNY–Maritime College; Fort Schuyler, Bronx, N.Y. 10465	730 (C)	Pub	1,425	3,250	3,014
SUNY–School of Industrial and Labor Relations of Cornell; Ithaca, N.Y. 14853	630 (C)	Pub	4,650	8,100	3,825
SUNY–University Center at Binghamton; Binghamton, N.Y. 13901	9,352 (C)	Pub	1,503	3,353	3,440
New York, University of the State of, Regents College Degrees; Albany, N.Y. 12230	15,000 (C)	Pub	225	225	n.a.
New York City Technical Coll. *See* New York, City Univ. of					
New York Institute of Technology; Central Islip, N.Y. 11722	1,616 (C)	P	5,370	5,370	3,600
New York Institute of Technology; Old Westbury, N.Y. 11568	6,429 (C)	P	5,370	5,370	n.a.
New York Institute of Technology; Metropolitan Center; New York, N.Y. 10023	2,841 (C)	P	5,370	5,370	n.a.
New York University; New York, N.Y. 10003	15,000 (C)	P	9,850	9,850	5,050
Niagara University; Niagara University, N.Y. 14109	2,675 (C)	P	6,000	6,000	3,130
Nicholls State University; Thibodaux, La. 70310	6,185 (C)	Pub	1,228	2,578	1,820
Nichols College; Dudley, Mass. 01570	813 (C)	P	5,666	5,666	3,264
Norfolk State University; Norfolk, Va. 23504	6,808 (C)	Pub	1,308	2,420	2,280
North Adams State College; North Adams, Mass. 01247	2,100 (C)	Pub	1,306	3,502	2,475
North Alabama, University of; Florence, Ala. 35632	4,456 (C)	Pub	1,050	1,450	2,048
North Carolina, Univ. of–Asheville; Asheville, N.C. 28804	2,686 (C)	Pub	760	3,262	2,100
North Carolina, Univ. of–Chapel Hill; Chapel Hill, N.C. 27514	14,294 (C)	Pub	819	4,159	3,055
North Carolina, Univ. of–Charlotte; Charlotte, N.C. 28223	9,916 (C)	Pub	716	3,562	2,218
North Carolina, Univ. of–Greensboro; Greensboro, N.C. 27412	7,649 (C)	Pub	888	3,808	2,340
North Carolina, Univ. of–Wilmington; Wilmington, N.C. 28403	5,672 (C)	Pub	866	4,114	2,260
North Carolina Agricultural and Technical State University; Greensboro, N.C. 27411	5,146 (C)	Pub	938	4,186	1,882
North Carolina Central University; Durham, N.C. 27707	3,532 (C)	Pub	966	4,115	2,045
North Carolina School of the Arts; Winston-Salem, N.C. 27117	468 (C)	Pub	1,239	4,203	2,470
North Carolina State University–Raleigh; Raleigh, N.C. 27695	20,714 (C)	Pub	839	3,759	2,576
North Carolina Wesleyan College; Rocky Mount, N.C. 27801	1,322 (C)	P/UM	5,240	5,240	2,500
North Central Bible College; Minneapolis, Minn. 55404	1,095 (C)	P	3,520	3,520	2,466
North Central College; Naperville, Ill. 60566	1,997 (C)	P	6,966	6,966	2,943
North Dakota, University of; Grand Forks, N.D. 58202	9,376 (C)	Pub	1,266	2,460	1,962
North Dakota State University; Fargo, N.D. 58105	9,292 (C)	Pub	1,194	2,388	1,878
Northeastern Bible College; Essex Fells, N.J. 07021	228 (C)	P	4,000	4,000	2,500
Northeastern Illinois University; Chicago, Ill. 60625	7,881 (C)	Pub	1,320	3,480	n.a.
Northeastern State Univ.; Tahlequah, Okla. 74464	6,500 (C)	Pub	650	1,748	1,768
Northeastern University; Boston, Mass. 02115	15,512 (C)	P	8,498	8,498	5,265
Northeast Louisiana University; Monroe, La. 71209	9,213 (C)	Pub	1,250	2,400	2,200
Northeast Missouri State University; Kirksville, Mo. 63501	6,542 (C)	Pub	1,270	2,400	1,950
Northern Arizona University; Flagstaff, Ariz. 86011	10,526 (C)	Pub	1,196	4,086	2,259
Northern Colorado, University of; Greeley, Colo. 80639	7,688 (C)	Pub	1,187	3,585	2,677
Northern Illinois University; DeKalb, Ill. 60115	18,434 (C)	Pub	1,630	3,862	2,376
Northern Iowa, University of; Cedar Falls, Iowa 50614	10,482 (C)	Pub	1,548	3,880	2,018
Northern Kentucky University; Highland Heights, Ky. 41076	7,656 (C)	Pub	1,080	3,080	2,600
Northern Michigan University; Marquette, Mich. 49855	6,933 (C)	Pub	1,536	3,536	2,636
Northern Montana College; Havre, Mont. 59501	1,600 (C)	Pub	1,312	3,246	2,591

Institution and location	Enrollment	Control	Tuition ($) Res.	Tuition ($) Nonres.	Rm/Bd ($)
Northern State College; Aberdeen, S.D. 57401	2,560 (C)	Pub	1,262	2,305	1,550
North Florida, University of; Jacksonville, Fla. 32216	4,902 (C)	Pub	977	2,907	1,600
North Georgia College; Dahlonega, Ga. 30591	1,752 (C)	Pub	1,305	2,406	1,875
Northland College; Ashland, Wis. 54806	566 (C)	P	6,035	6,035	3,020
North Park College; Chicago, Ill. 60625	1,203 (C)	P/EC	6,500	6,500	2,900
Northrop University; Los Angeles, Calif. 90045	1,391 (C)	P	6,120	6,120	4,088
North Texas State University; Denton, Tex. 76203	15,404 (C)	Pub	896	4,016	2,942
Northwest Bible College; Minot, N.D. 58701	103 (C)	P/CG	2,670	2,670	1,900
Northwest Christian College; Eugene, Ore. 97401	232 (C)	P/DC	4,945	4,945	3,836
Northwest College; Kirkland, Wash. 98083	580 (C)	P	3,930	3,930	2,097
Northwestern College; Orange City, Iowa 51041	841 (C)	P/RCA	6,000	6,000	2,200
Northwestern College; Roseville, Minn. 55113	967 (C)	P/ID	6,525	6,525	2,295
Northwestern Oklahoma State University; Alva, Okla. 73717	1,926 (C)	Pub	675	1,850	1,536
Northwestern State Univ. of Louisiana; Natchitoches, La. 71497	2,773 (C)	Pub	1,402	2,482	1,880
Northwestern University; Evanston, Ill. 60201	7,200 (C)	P	11,637	11,637	3,999
Northwest Missouri State University; Maryville, Mo. 64468	3,813 (C)	Pub	1,080	1,980	2,080
Northwest Nazarene College; Nampa, Idaho 83651	1,075 (C)	P/Naz	4,776	4,776	2,295
Northwood Institute of Florida; West Palm Beach, Fla. 33409	300	P	5,200	5,200	3,600
Northwood Institute of Michigan; Midland, Mich. 48640	1,950 (C)	P	5,400	5,400	2,850
Northwood Institute of Texas; Cedar Hill, Tex. 75104	200	P	5,400	5,400	2,942
Norwich University; Northfield, Vt. 05663	1,844 (C)	P	9,200	9,200	3,600
Notre Dame, College of; Belmont, Calif. 94002	581 (C)	P/RC	6,500	6,500	3,900
Notre Dame, University of; Notre Dame, Ind. 46556	7,500 (C)	P	7,985	7,985	2,545
Notre Dame College; Manchester, N.H. 03104	585 (W)	P/RC	5,200	5,200	3,375
Notre Dame College of Ohio; Cleveland, Ohio 44121	802 (W)	P/RC	4,680	4,680	2,656
Notre Dame of Maryland, College of; Baltimore, Md. 21210	510 (W)	P/RC	6,700	6,700	3,600
Nova University; Ft. Lauderdale, Fla. 33314	1,800 (C)	P	4,650	4,650	4,400
Nyack College; Nyack, N.Y. 10960	511 (C)	P/CMA	5,180	5,180	2,772
Oakland City College; Oakland City, Ind. 47660	625 (C)	P/B	5,200	5,200	2,288
Oakland University; Rochester, Mich. 48063	10,329 (C)	Pub	1,585	3,957	2,755
Oakwood College; Huntsville, Ala. 35896	993 (C)	P/SDA	4,815	4,815	2,790
Oberlin College; Oberlin, Ohio 44074	2,757 (C)	P	11,015	11,015	3,755
Oblate College; Washington, D.C. 20017	43 (M)	P/RC	3,050	3,050	n.a.
Occidental College; Los Angeles, Calif. 90041	1,586 (C)	P	10,219	10,219	3,965
Oglethorpe University; Atlanta, Ga. 30319	950 (C)	P	6,700	6,700	3,350
Ohio Dominican College; Columbus, Ohio 43219	1,182 (C)	P/RC	5,250	5,250	2,960
Ohio Institute of Technology, Columbus. *See* DeVry Institute of Technology, Columbus					
Ohio Northern University; Ada, Ohio 45810	1,964 (C)	P/UM	6,540	6,540	2,550
Ohio State University; Columbus, Ohio 43210	40,828 (C)	Pub	1,704	4,416	2,814
Ohio University; Athens, Ohio 45701	13,000 (C)	Pub	2,060	4,170	2,877
Ohio University–Zanesville; Zanesville, Ohio 43701	1,250 (C)	Pub	1,768	3,768	n.a.
Ohio Wesleyan University; Delaware, Ohio 43015	1,446 (C)	P/UM	9,207	9,207	3,661
Oklahoma, University of–Health Sciences Center; Oklahoma City, Okla. 73190	938 (C)	Pub	883	2,552	n.a.
Oklahoma, University of–Norman; Norman, Okla. 73019	15,914 (C)	Pub	867	2,523	2,396
Oklahoma Baptist University; Shawnee, Okla. 74801	1,638 (C)	P/B	3,360	3,360	2,160
Oklahoma Christian College; Oklahoma City, Okla. 73111	1,476 (C)	P/CC	3,200	3,200	2,200
Oklahoma City University; Oklahoma City, Okla. 73106	1,193 (C)	P/UM	3,960	3,960	2,696
Oklahoma State University; Stillwater, Okla. 74078	16,873 (C)	Pub	840	2,496	2,374
Old Dominion University; Norfolk, Va. 23508	11,301 (C)	Pub	2,222	4,070	3,606
Olivet College; Olivet, Mich. 49076	733 (C)	P/UCC	5,480	5,480	2,350
Olivet Nazarene Univ.; Kankakee, Ill. 60901	1,536 (C)	P/NAZ	4,300	4,300	2,400
Oral Roberts University; Tulsa, Okla. 74171	3,917 (C)	P	4,880	4,880	2,780
Oregon, University of; Eugene, Ore. 97403	13,357 (C)	Pub	1,487	4,190	2,277
Oregon Coll. of Education. *See* Western Oregon State Coll.					
Oregon Health Science University; Portland, Ore. 97201	400 (C)	Pub	4,724	9,554	2,924
Oregon Institute of Technology; Klamath Falls, Ore. 97601	2,996 (C)	Pub	1,535	4,320	2,560
Oregon State University; Corvallis, Ore. 97331	12,463 (C)	Pub	1,461	4,164	2,445
Orlando College; Orlando, Fla. 32810	750 (C)	P	3,795	3,795	n.a.
Otis Art Institute of Parsons School of Design; Los Angeles, Calif. 90057	705 (C)	P	7,170	7,170	3,218
Ottawa University; Ottawa, Kan. 66067	470 (C)	P/AB	5,066	5,066	2,504
Ottawa University–Phoenix Center; Phoenix, Ariz. 85021	250	P	2,280	2,280	n.a.
Otterbein College; Westerville, Ohio 43081	1,975 (C)	P/UM	7,656	7,656	3,036
Ouachita Baptist University; Arkadelphia, Ark. 71923	1,403 (C)	P/B	3,400	3,400	1,800
Our Lady of Angels College. *See* Neumann College					
Our Lady of Holy Cross College; New Orleans, La. 70114	606 (C)	P/RC	4,270	4,270	n.a.
Our Lady of the Lake–University of San Antonio; San Antonio, Tex. 78285	1,779 (C)	P/RC	4,680	4,680	2,400
Ozarks, College of the; Clarksville, Ark. 72830	670 (C)	P/UP	2,110	2,110	1,750
Ozarks, School of the; Point Lookout, Mo. 65726	1,241 (C)	P	4,120	4,120	3,216

Institution and location	Enrollment	Control	Tuition ($) Res.	Tuition ($) Nonres.	Rm/Bd ($)
Pace University; New York, N.Y. 10038	9,026 (C)	P	5,968	5,968	3,606
Pace University–College of White Plains; White Plains, N.Y. 10603	1,835 (C)	P	5,968	5,968	3,606
Pace University–Pleasantville–Briarcliff; Pleasantville, N.Y. 10570	4,343 (C)	P	5,968	5,968	3,606
Pacific, University of the; Stockton, Calif. 95211	3,148 (C)	P	11,042	11,042	4,196
Pacific Christian College; Fullerton, Calif. 92631	500 (C)	P/ChC	5,000	5,000	3,000
Pacific Lutheran University; Tacoma, Wash. 98447	3,082 (C)	P	7,155	7,155	3,210
Pacific Northwest College of Art; Portland, Ore. 97205	170 (C)	P	4,650	4,650	n.a.
Pacific Oaks College; Pasadena, Calif. 91103	50 (C)	P	6,300	6,300	n.a.
Pacific Union College; Angwin, Calif. 94508	1,476 (C)	P/SDA	6,885	6,885	2,505
Pacific University; Forest Grove, Ore. 97116	768 (C)	P/UCC	7,300	7,300	2,700
Paier College of Art, Inc.; Hamden, Conn. 06511	338 (C)	P	7,615	7,615	n.a.
Paine College; Augusta, Ga. 30910	752 (C)	P/UM	3,500	3,500	1,950
Palm Beach Atlantic College; West Palm Beach, Fla. 33401	1,143 (C)	P/SB	4,800	4,800	2,300
Pan American University; Edinburg, Tex. 78539	9,000 (C)	Pub	780	3,900	2,080
Panhandle State University; Goodwell, Okla. 73939	1,276 (C)	Pub	645	1,766	1,620
Park College; Parkville, Mo. 64152	471 (C)	P/LDS	5,160	5,160	2,480
Parks College of St. Louis University; Cahokia, Ill. 62206	1,100 (C)	P/RC	4,250	4,250	2,770
Parsons School of Design; New York, N.Y. 10011	1,780 (C)	P	8,540	8,540	4,300
Patten College; Oakland, Calif. 94601	199 (C)	P/CE	2,800	2,800	2,850
Paul Quinn College; Waco, Tex. 76704	500 (C)	P	2,100	2,100	2,550
Peabody Conservatory of Music; Baltimore, Md. 21202	256 (C)	P	7,850	7,850	3,300
Pembroke State University; Pembroke, N.C. 28372	1,955 (C)	Pub	650	3,152	1,530
Pennsylvania, University of; Philadelphia, Pa. 19104	9,200 (C)	P	11,976	11,976	6,085
Pennsylvania State University; University Park, Pa. 16802	29,531 (C)	Pub	2,996	6,018	2,960
Pennsylvania State University–Behrend; Erie, Pa. 16563	2,400 (C)	Pub	2,996	6,018	2,110
Pennsylvania State University–Berks; Reading, Pa. 19608	220 (C)	Pub	2,494	5,544	n.a.
Pennsylvania State University at Harrisburg–The Capital College; Middletown, Pa. 17057	1,733 (C)	Pub	2,562	5,146	3,460
Pepperdine University; Los Angeles, Calif. 90034	600 (C)	P/CC	9,600	9,600	n.a.
Pepperdine University–Seaver College; Malibu, Calif. 90265	2,529 (C)	P	11,148	11,148	4,535
Peru State College; Peru, Neb. 68421	1,474 (C)	Pub	915	1,530	2,090
Pfeiffer College; Misenheimer, N.C. 28109	811 (C)	P/UM	3,575	4,525	2,300
Pharmacy, School of (Ga.). *See* Mercer Univ.					
Philadelphia College of the Arts; Philadelphia, Pa. 19102	1,327 (C)	P	8,100	8,100	3,700
Philadelphia College of Bible; Langhorne, Pa. 19047	546 (C)	P	4,650	4,650	2,820
Philadelphia College of Pharmacy and Science; Philadelphia, Pa. 19104	1,280 (C)	P	6,200	6,200	2,950
Philadelphia College of Textiles and Science; Philadelphia, Pa. 19144	1,645 (C)	P	5,900	5,900	3,150
Philander Smith College; Little Rock, Ark. 72202	572 (C)	P/UM	1,628	1,628	2,000
Phillips University; Enid, Okla. 73702	660 (C)	P	4,248	4,248	2,170
Phoenix, University of; Phoenix, Ariz. 85040	5,000 (C)	P	4,500	4,500	n.a.
Piedmont Bible College; Winston-Salem, N.C. 27101	268 (C)	P	2,800	2,800	2,100
Piedmont College; Demorest, Ga. 30535	443 (C)	P/Ind	1,565	2,440	2,400
Pikeville College; Pikeville, Ky. 41501	753 (C)	P/UP	3,420	3,420	2,250
Pillsbury Baptist Bible College; Owatonna, Minn. 55060	400	P	2,824	2,824	2,246
Pine Manor College; Chestnut Hill, Mass. 02167	535 (W)	P	9,500	9,500	5,200
Pittsburgh, University of; Pittsburgh, Pa. 15260	18,826 (C)	P	3,220	6,320	2,930
Pittsburgh, University of–Bradford; Bradford, Pa. 16701	979 (C)	P	3,100	6,200	2,870
Pittsburgh, University of,–Johnstown; Johnstown, Pa. 15904	3,215 (C)	P	2,970	5,860	2,572
Pittsburgh State University; Pittsburg, Kan. 66762	4,295 (C)	Pub	1,102	2,352	2,238
Pitzer College. *See* Claremont Colleges					
Plymouth State College; Plymouth, N.H. 03264	3,200 (C)	Pub	1,761	4,311	2,300
Point Loma Nazarene College; San Diego, Calif. 92106	1,609 (C)	P/Naz	5,472	5,472	2,805
Point Park College; Pittsburgh, Pa. 15222	2,861 (C)	P	5,420	5,420	2,680
Polytechnic Univ.; Brooklyn, N.Y. 11201	2,402 (C)	P	9,200	9,200	4,250
Pomona College. *See* Claremont Colleges					
Pontifical College Josephinum; Columbus, Ohio 43085	105	P/RC	2,585	2,585	2,055
Portland, University of; Portland, Ore. 97203	1,965 (C)	P	5,940	5,940	2,690
Portland School of Art; Portland, Me. 04101	226 (C)	P	5,850	5,850	3,100
Portland State University; Portland, Ore. 97207	12,252 (C)	Pub	1,566	4,269	2,323
Post College; Waterbury, Conn. 06708	1,642 (C)	P	6,050	6,050	3,410
Potsdam Coll. of Arts & Science. *See* New York, State Univ. of					
Prairie View A&M University; Prairie View, Tex. 77446	3,884	Pub	866	3,986	2,778
Pratt Institute; Brooklyn, N.Y. 11205	2,717 (C)	P	7,800	7,800	3,700
Presbyterian College; Clinton, S.C. 29325	1,043 (C)	P	5,588	5,588	2,342
Prescott College; Prescott, Ariz. 86301	243 (C)	P	4,600	4,600	n.a.
Princeton University; Princeton, N.J. 08544	4,600 (C)	P	11,780	11,780	4,200
Principia College; Elsah, Ill. 62028	660 (C)	P	8,748	8,748	3,870
Providence College; Providence, R.I. 02918	3,674 (C)	P	7,770	7,770	3,700
Puerto Rico, Polytechnic University of; Hato Rey, San Juan, P.R. 00918	1,835	P	7,500	7,500	n.a.
Puerto Rico, University of–Cayey University College; Cayey, P.R. 00633	3,412 (C)	Pub	662	2,000	n.a.

Institution and location	Enrollment	Control	Tuition ($) Res.	Tuition ($) Nonres.	Rm/Bd ($)
Puerto Rico, University of–Humacao University College; Humacao, P.R. 00661	3,545 (C)	Pub	600	2,095	n.a.
Puerto Rico, University of–Mayaguez Campus; Mayaguez, P.R. 00708	9,700 (C)	Pub	665	2,625	n.a.
Puerto Rico, University of–Medical Science; San Juan, P.R. 00936	535 (C)	Pub	[3]	[4]	n.a.
Puget Sound, University of; Tacoma, Wash. 98416	2,760 (C)	P	8,310	8,310	3,300
Puget Sound Christian College; Edmonds, Wash. 98020	105 (C)	P	2,700	2,700	2,250
Purdue University; West Lafayette, Ind. 47907	26,923 (C)	Pub	1,726	5,126	2,830
Purdue University–Calumet; Hammond, Ind. 46323	6,398 (C)	Pub	1,531	3,782	n.a.
Queens College; Charlotte, N.C. 28274	650 (W)	P/PUS	6,150	6,150	3,325
Queens College (NYC). *See* New York, City University of					
Quincy College; Quincy, Ill. 62301	1,443 (C)	P/RC	5,720	5,720	2,560
Quinnipiac College; Hamden, Conn. 06518	1,932 (C)	P	7,350	7,350	4,000
Radcliffe College. *See* Harvard and Radcliffe Colleges					
Rabbinical College of America; Morristown, N.J. 07960	230 (M)	P	3,500	3,500	3,000
Radford University; Radford, Va. 24142	6,410 (C)	Pub	1,920	2,754	3,212
Ramapo College of New Jersey; Mahwah, N.J. 07430	3,858 (C)	Pub	1,450	2,050	3,500
Randolph-Macon College; Ashland, Va. 23005	1,013 (C)	P	7,140	7,140	3,300
Randolph-Macon Woman's College; Lynchburg, Va. 24503	750 (W)	P/UM	8,700	8,700	4,000
Redlands, University of; Redlands, Calif. 92374	1,200 (C)	P	9,050	9,050	3,140
Reed College; Portland, Ore. 97202	1,172 (C)	P	10,600	10,600	3,350
Reformed Bible College; Grand Rapids, Mich. 49506	166 (C)	P	3,650	3,650	2,300
Regis College; Denver, Colo. 80221	1,050 (C)	P/RC	7,358	7,358	3,750
Regis College; Weston, Mass. 02193	1,059 (W)	P/RC	7,560	7,560	3,850
Reno Business College; Reno, Nev. 89503	300 (C)	P	4,000	4,000	n.a.
Rensselaer Polytechnic Institute; Troy, N.Y. 12180	4,700 (C)	P	11,500	11,500	3,850
Research College of Nursing; Kansas City, Mo. 64132	238	P	5,340	5,340	2,375
Rhode Island, University of; Kingston, R.I. 02881	9,428 (C)	Pub	2,235	6,042	3,716
Rhode Island College; Providence, R.I. 02908	6,429 (C)	Pub	1,380	3,880	3,300
Rhode Island School of Design; Providence, R.I. 02903	1,780 (C)	P	10,430	10,430	4,440
Rhodes College; Memphis, Tenn. 38112	1,226	P/PUS	8,580	8,580	3,255
Rice University; Houston, Tex. 77251	2,600 (C)	P	4,900	4,900	4,050
Richmond, University of; Richmond, Va. 23173	2,777 (C)	P/B	8,335	8,335	2,590
Richmond College, The American International College of London; London, England TW10 6JP	950 (C)	P	6,330	6,330	2,565
Rider College; Lawrenceville, N.J. 08648	3,100 (C)	P	6,850	6,850	3,210
Ringling School of Art and Design; Sarasota, Fla. 33580	400 (C)	P	5,600	5,600	3,500
Rio Grande College; Rio Grande, Ohio 45674	1,621 (C)	P	1,170	4,170	2,700
Ripon College; Ripon, Wis. 54971	850 (C)	P	9,623	9,623	2,373
Rivier College; Nashua, N.H. 03060	650 (W)	P/RC	5,790	5,790	3,200
Roanoke Bible College; Elizabeth City, N.C. 27909	136 (C)	P	1,832	1,832	1,746
Roanoke College; Salem, Va. 24153	1,268 (C)	P/LCA	7,700	7,700	3,100
Robert Morris College; Coraopolis, Pa. 15108	5,106 (C)	P	3,720	3,720	2,600
Roberts Wesleyan College; Rochester, N.Y. 14624	680 (C)	P/FM	5,814	5,814	2,508
Rochester, University of; Rochester, N.Y. 14627	4,602 (C)	P	11,456	11,456	4,598
Rochester Institute of Technology; Rochester, N.Y. 14623	11,500 (C)	P	8,421	8,421	3,903
Rockford College; Rockford, Ill. 61108	1,200 (C)	P	6,990	6,990	2,700
Rockhurst College; Kansas City, Mo. 64110	2,132 (C)	P/RC	5,530	5,530	2,925
Rocky Mountain College; Billings, Mont. 59102	500 (C)	P	4,350	4,350	2,565
Roger Williams College; Bristol, R.I. 02809	2,300 (C)	P	6,608	6,608	3,626
Rollins College; Winter Park, Fla. 32789	1,350 (C)	P	9,754	9,754	3,690
Roosevelt University; Chicago, Ill. 60605	4,007 (C)	P	5,472	5,472	3,390
Rosary College; River Forest, Ill. 60305	900 (C)	P/RC	6,400	6,400	3,080
Rose-Hulman Institute of Technology; Terre Haute, Ind. 47803	1,300 (M)	P	7,980	7,980	2,850
Rosemont College; Rosemont, Pa. 19010	600 (W)	P/RC	6,500	6,500	4,225
Rush University; Chicago, Ill. 60612	212 (C)	P	5,730	5,730	3,255
Russell Sage College; Troy, N.Y. 12180	1,362 (W)	P	7,500	7,500	3,130
Rust College; Holly Springs, Miss. 38635	900 (C)	P	3,102	3,102	1,398
Rutgers University–Camden College of Arts and Sciences; Camden, N.J. 08102	2,866 (C)	Pub	2,455	4,585	3,128
Rutgers University–College of Engineering; New Brunswick, N.J. 08903	2,623 (C)	Pub	2,769	5,133	2,984
Rutgers University–College of Nursing–Newark; Newark, N.J. 07102	512 (C)	Pub	2,431	4,561	3,054
Rutgers University–College of Pharmacy; New Brunswick, N.J. 08903	737 (C)	Pub	2,653	4,901	2,984
Rutgers University–Cook College; New Brunswick, N.J. 08903	3,088 (C)	Pub	2,667	4,915	2,984
Rutgers University–Douglass College; New Brunswick, N.J. 08903	3,506 (C)	Pub	2,548	4,678	2,984
Rutgers University–Livingston College; New Brunswick, N.J. 08903	3,407 (C)	Pub	2,579	4,709	2,984
Rutgers University–Mason Gross School of the Arts; New Brunswick, N.J. 08903	415 (C)	Pub	2,535	4,665	2,984

Institution and location	Enrollment	Control	Tuition ($) Res.	Tuition ($) Nonres.	Rm/Bd ($)
Rutgers University–Newark College of Arts and Sciences; Newark, N.J. 07102	3,802 (C)	Pub	2,436	4,566	n.a.
Rutgers University–Rutgers College; New Brunswick, N.J. 08903	9,116 (C)	Pub	2,562	4,692	2,984
Rutgers University—University College–Camden; Camden, N.J. 08102	986 (C)	Pub	([5])	([6])	n.a.
Rutgers University—University College–Newark; Newark, N.J. 07102	1,877 (C)	Pub	([5])	([6])	n.a.
Rutgers University—University College–New Brunswick; New Brunswick, N.J. 08903	3,128 (C)	Pub	([5])	([6])	n.a.
Sacred Heart, Univ. of the; Santurce, P.R. 00924	7,998 (C)	P/RC	2,760	2,760	3,550
Sacred Heart College; Belmont, N.C. 28012	360 (W)	P/RC	2,910	3,910	2,570
Sacred Heart Seminary; Detroit, Mich. 48206	265	P/RC	2,600	2,600	1,850
Sacred Heart University; Bridgeport, Conn. 06606	3,975 (C)	P	4,816	4,816	n.a.
Saginaw Valley State College; University Center, Mich. 48710	4,271 (C)	Pub	1,628	3,317	2,530
St. Alphonsus College; Suffield, Conn. 06078	43	P/RC	4,500	4,500	2,900
St. Ambrose College; Davenport, Iowa 52803	2,197 (C)	P/RC	6,330	6,330	2,650
St. Andrews Presbyterian College; Laurinburg, N.C. 28352	747 (C)	P/PUS	5,575	6,575	3,075
St. Anselm College; Manchester, N.H. 03102	1,761 (C)	P	7,250	7,250	3,750
St. Augustine's College; Raleigh, N.C. 27611	1,716 (C)	P/E	3,500	3,500	2,450
St. Benedict, College of; St. Joseph, Minn. 56374	1,765 (W)	P/RC	6,670	6,670	2,635
St. Bonaventure University; St. Bonaventure, N.Y. 14778	2,350 (C)	P	5,950	5,950	3,315
St. Catherine, College of; St. Paul, Minn. 55105	2,305 (W)	P/RC	6,940	6,940	2,590
St. Cloud State University; St. Cloud, Minn. 56301	11,263 (C)	Pub	1,678	2,568	1,845
St. Edward's University; Austin, Tex. 78704	2,224 (C)	P/RC	4,960	4,960	2,800
St. Elizabeth, College of; Convent Station, N.J. 07961	991 (C)	P	6,000	6,000	3,000
St. Francis, College of; Joliet, Ill. 60435	1,100 (C)	P/RC	5,490	5,490	2,810
St. Francis College; Brooklyn Heights, N.Y. 11201	2,436 (C)	P	4,410	4,410	n.a.
St. Francis College; Fort Wayne, Ind. 46808	897 (C)	P/RC	4,448	4,448	2,650
St. Francis College; Loretto, Pa. 15940	1,485 (C)	P/RC	5,376	5,376	3,000
St. Hyacinth College and Seminary; Granby, Mass. 01033	61 (M)	P/RC	3,000	3,000	3,000
St. John Fisher College; Rochester, N.Y. 14618	1,600 (C)	P	5,750	5,750	3,060
St. John's College; Annapolis, Md. 21404	391 (C)	P	10,200	10,200	3,475
St. John's Seminary College; Camarillo, Calif. 93010	91 (M)	P/RC	2,900	2,900	2,900
St. John's College; Santa Fe, N.M. 87501	301 (C)	P	9,720	9,720	3,300
St. John's Seminary College of Liberal Arts; Brighton, Mass. 02135	75	P/RC	2,700	2,700	2,300
St. John's University; Collegeville, Minn. 56321	1,803 (M)	P/RC	6,670	6,670	2,900
St. John's University; Jamaica, N.Y. 11439	14,413 (C)	P/RC	4,730	4,730	n.a.
St. John Vianney College Seminary; Miami, Fla. 33165	56 (M)	P/RC	2,375	2,375	2,875
St. Joseph, College of; Rutland, Vt. 05701	378 (C)	P/RC	4,900	4,900	2,800
St. Joseph College; West Hartford, Conn. 06117	760 (W)	P/RC	7,500	7,500	3,750
St. Joseph's College; Brooklyn, N.Y. 11205	873 (C)	P	4,200	4,200	n.a.
St. Joseph's College; North Windham, Me. 04062	583 (C)	P/RC	5,675	5,675	3,250
St. Joseph's College; Rensselaer, Ind. 47978	850 (C)	P/RC	6,210	6,210	2,670
St. Joseph's College–Suffolk; Patchogue, N.Y. 11772	1,445 (C)	P	4,130	4,130	n.a.
St. Joseph Seminary College; St. Benedict, La. 70457	80 (M)	P	3,850	3,850	3,000
St. Joseph's University; Philadelphia, Pa. 19131	2,559 (C)	P/RC	5,800	5,800	3,700
St. Lawrence University; Canton, N.Y. 13617	2,285 (C)	P	11,350	11,350	3,715
St. Leo College; St. Leo, Fla. 33574	1,093 (C)	P/RC	5,620	5,620	2,680
St. Louis Christian College; Florissant, Mo. 63033	160 (C)	P	2,080	2,080	1,600
St. Louis College of Pharmacy; St. Louis, Mo. 63110	721 (C)	P	3,950	3,950	2,800
St. Louis University; St. Louis, Mo. 63103	6,563 (C)	P	6,120	6,120	3,210
St. Martin's College; Lacey, Wash. 98503	440 (C)	P	6,960	6,960	3,194
St. Mary, College of; Omaha, Neb. 68124	1,276 (W)	P/RC	4,920	4,920	2,400
St. Mary College; Leavenworth, Kan. 66048	1,008 (W)	P	4,840	4,840	2,760
St. Mary of the Plains College; Dodge City, Kan. 67801	686 (C)	P/RC	4,250	4,250	2,225
St. Mary-of-the-Woods Coll.; St. Mary-of-the-Woods, Ind. 47876	850 (W)	P/RC	6,480	6,480	2,805
St. Mary's College; Notre Dame, Ind. 46556	1,792 (W)	P/RC	7,490	7,490	3,217
St. Mary's College; Orchard Lake, Mich. 48033	280 (C)	P	3,050	3,050	2,450
St. Mary's College; Winona, Minn. 55987	1,200 (C)	P	6,710	6,710	2,650
St. Mary's College of California; Moraga, Calif. 94575	2,000 (C)	P/RC	7,150	7,150	3,646
St. Mary's College of Maryland; St. Mary's City, Md. 20686	1,396 (C)	Pub	2,270	3,770	3,600
St. Mary's University of San Antonio; San Antonio, Tex. 78284	2,310 (C)	P/RC	5,626	5,626	2,570
St. Meinrad College; St. Meinrad, Ind. 47577	169 (M)	P/RC	3,058	3,058	3,492
St. Michael's College; Winooski, Vt. 05404	1,667 (C)	P/RC	7,720	7,720	3,280
St. Norbert College; De Pere, Wis. 54115	1,735 (C)	P/RC	6,915	6,915	2,720
St. Olaf College; Northfield, Minn. 55057	3,094 (C)	P/AL	8,215	8,215	2,535
St. Paul Bible College; Bible College, Minn. 55375	551 (C)	P/CMA	4,400	4,400	2,700
St. Paul's College; Lawrenceville, Va. 23868	736 (C)	P	3,690	3,690	2,605
St. Peter's College; Jersey City, N.J. 07306	2,200 (C)	P/RC	5,904	5,904	4,935
St. Rose, The College of; Albany, N.Y. 12203	2,265 (C)	P	5,670	5,670	3,210
St. Scholastica, College of; Duluth, Minn. 55811	1,535 (C)	P/RC	6,594	6,594	2,634
St. Teresa, College of; Winona, Minn. 55987	342 (W)	P	6,200	6,200	2,300

Institution and location	Enrollment	Control	Tuition ($) Res.	Nonres.	Rm/Bd ($)
St. Thomas, College of; St. Paul, Minn. 55105	4,600 (C)	P	6,352	6,352	2,438
St. Thomas, University of; Houston, Tex. 77006	1,108 (C)	P/RC	3,500	3,500	3,140
St. Thomas Aquinas College; Sparkill, N.Y. 10968	1,827 (C)	P	4,500	4,500	2,800
Saint Thomas University; Miami, Fla. 33054	2,100 (C)	P/RC	5,250	5,250	3,150
Saint Vincent College; Latrobe, Pa. 15650	1,247 (C)	P/RC	5,940	5,940	2,750
St. Xavier College; Chicago, Ill. 60655	2,154 (C)	P/RC	6,160	6,160	3,362
Salem College; Salem, W. Va. 26426	669 (C)	P	5,390	5,390	2,910
Salem College; Winston-Salem, N.C. 27108	717 (W)	P	5,790	5,790	6,100
Salem State College; Salem, Mass. 01970	5,331 (C)	Pub	1,212	3,408	2,244
Salisbury State College; Salisbury, Md. 21801	4,299 (C)	Pub	1,996	3,394	3,160
Salve Regina—The Newport College; Newport, R.I. 02840-4192	1,628 (C)	P	7,600	7,600	4,360
Samford University; Birmingham, Ala. 35229	2,960 (C)	P/SB	4,576	4,576	2,522
Sam Houston State University; Huntsville, Tex. 77341	8,902 (C)	Pub	880	4,000	2,330
San Diego, University of; San Diego, Calif. 92110	3,400 (C)	P/RC	7,340	7,340	4,160
San Diego State University; San Diego, Calif. 92182	29,589 (C)	Pub	630	3,756	3,104
Imperial Valley Campus; Calexico, Calif. 92231	200 (C)	Pub	718	4,227	n.a.
San Francisco, University of; San Francisco, Calif. 94117	2,826 (C)	P/RC	7,740	7,740	3,900
San Francisco Art Institute; San Francisco, Calif. 94133	514 (C)	P	7,680	7,680	n.a.
San Francisco Conservatory of Music, The; San Francisco, Calif. 94122	138 (C)	P	6,695	6,695	n.a.
San Francisco State Univ.; San Francisco, Calif. 94132	19,588 (C)	Pub	750	5,160	3,198
Sangamon State University; Springfield, Ill. 62708	1,889 (C)	Pub	1,074	3,042	2,210
San Jose Bible College; San Jose, Calif. 95108	175 (C)	P/ChC	3,840	3,840	2,100
San Jose State University; San Jose, Calif. 95192	21,044 (C)	Pub	800	5,210	5,250
Santa Clara, University of; Santa Clara, Calif. 95053	3,555 (C)	P/RC	8,133	8,133	4,104
Santa Fe, College of; Santa Fe, N.M. 87501	1,463 (C)	P/RC	5,340	5,340	2,400
Sarah Lawrence College; Bronxville, N.Y. 10708	850 (C)	P	12,375	12,375	5,065
Savannah College of Art and Design; Savannah, Ga. 31401	1,070 (C)	P	5,250	5,250	2,250
Savannah State College; Savannah, Ga. 31404	2,300 (C)	Pub	1,350	5,100	4,000
Schiller International University; 6900 Heidelberg, W. Ger.	1,361	P	6,100	6,100	4,400
Schreiner College; Kerrville, Tex. 78028	518 (C)	P	4,775	4,775	3,240
Science and Arts, University of, of Oklahoma; Chickasha, Okla. 73018	1,325 (C)	Pub	656	1,920	1,600
Scranton, University of; Scranton, Pa. 18510	3,425 (C)	P/RC	5,920	5,920	3,060
Scripps College. *See* Claremont Colleges					
Seattle Pacific University; Seattle, Wash. 98119	2,300 (C)	P/FM	6,405	6,405	3,153
Seattle University; Seattle, Wash. 98122	3,149 (C)	P/RC	7,470	7,470	3,408
Seaver College. *See* Pepperdine University					
Seton Hall University; South Orange, N.J. 07079	4,494 (C)	P/RC	6,200	6,200	3,720
Seton Hall College; Greensburg, Pa. 15601	865 (W)	P	6,470	6,470	2,950
Shaw University; Raleigh, N.C. 27611	1,500 (C)	P	2,140	2,140	910
Sheldon Jackson College; Sitka, Alaska 99835	203 (C)	P/UP	3,976	3,976	3,600
Shenandoah College and Conservatory; Winchester, Va. 22601	814 (C)	P	6,600	6,600	2,800
Shepherd College; Shepherdstown, W. Va. 25443	3,853 (C)	Pub	890	2,400	2,550
Shimer College; Waukegan, Ill. 60085	100 (C)	P	7,200	7,200	1,400
Shippensburg University; Shippensburg, Pa. 17257	5,193 (C)	Pub	1,916	3,076	1,990
Shorter College; Rome, Ga. 30161	800 (C)	P	3,970	3,970	2,450
Siena College; Loudonville, N.Y. 12211	2,700 (C)	P	6,005	6,005	3,450
Siena Heights College; Adrian, Mich. 49221	1,454 (C)	P	5,190	5,190	2,950
Sierra Nevada College; Incline Village, Nev. 89450	225 (C)	P	2,800	2,800	3,200
Silver Lake College; Manitowoc, Wis. 54220	530 (C)	P/RC	5,100	5,100	n.a.
Simmons College; Boston, Mass. 02115	1,843 (W)	P	10,044	10,044	4,500
Simon's Rock of Bard College; Great Barrington, Mass. 01230	300 (C)	P	11,170	11,170	3,650
Simpson College; Indianola, Iowa 50125	1,395 (C)	P	6,995	6,995	2,468
Simpson College; San Francisco, Calif. 94134	195 (C)	P/CMA	4,470	4,470	2,600
Sioux Falls College; Sioux Falls, S.D. 57105	870 (C)	P/B	4,950	4,950	2,300
Skidmore College; Saratoga Springs, N.Y. 12866	2,227 (C)	P	9,877	9,877	3,780
Slippery Rock State College. *See* Slippery Rock University of Pennsylvania					
Slippery Rock Univ. of Pennsylvania; Slippery Rock, Pa. 16057	5,831 (C)	Pub	1,922	3,318	2,032
Smith College; Northampton, Mass. 01063	2,588 (W)	P	11,260	11,260	4,390
Sojourner-Douglass College; Baltimore, Md. 21205	500 (C)	P	4,125	4,125	n.a.
Sonoma State University; Rohnert Park, Calif. 94928	4,034 (C)	Pub	707	4,937	3,200
South, University of the; Sewanee, Tenn. 37375	1,020 (C)	P/E	9,285	9,285	2,410
South Alabama, University of; Mobile, Ala. 36688	8,440 (C)	Pub	1,581	2,081	2,430
Southampton College. *See* Long Island Univ. Center					
South Carolina, University of; Columbia, S.C. 29208	14,551 (C)	Pub	2,028	4,148	2,500
South Carolina, Univ. of-Aiken; Aiken, S.C. 29801	2,069 (C)	Pub	1,400	2,940	n.a.
South Carolina, Univ. of-Coastal Carolina; Conway, S.C. 29526	3,176 (C)	Pub	1,400	2,540	3,300
South Carolina, Univ. of-Spartanburg; Spartanburg, S.C. 29303	2,952 (C)	Pub	1,400	2,940	2,660
South Carolina State College; Orangeburg, S.C. 29117	3,359 (C)	Pub	1,200	2,400	2,196
South Dakota, University of; Vermillion, S.D. 57069	4,167 (C)	Pub	1,512	2,832	1,902

Institution and location	Enrollment	Control	Tuition ($) Res.	Nonres.	Rm/Bd ($)
South Dakota School of Mines and Technology; Rapid City, S.D. 57701	2,020 (C)	Pub	1,790	3,264	1,940
South Dakota State University; Brookings, S.D. 57007	6,020 (C)	Pub	1,628	3,036	1,572
Southeastern Baptist College; Laurel, Miss. 39440	80	P	1,800	1,800	1,400
Southeastern Bible College; Birmingham, Ala. 35256	231 (C)	P/ID	3,400	3,400	2,400
Southeastern College of the Assemblies of God; Lakeland, Fla. 33801	1,096 (C)	P/AG	2,250	2,250	1,600
Southeastern Louisiana University; Hammond, La. 70402	7,260 (C)	Pub	1,330	2,680	2,070
Southeastern Massachusetts University; North Dartmouth, Mass. 02747	5,500 (C)	Pub	1,080	3,636	3,350
Southeastern Oklahoma State Univ.; Durant, Okla. 74701	3,616 (C)	Pub	720	2,000	1,980
Southeastern University; Washington, D.C. 20024	559 (C)	P	4,500	4,500	n.a.
Southeast Missouri State Univ.; Cape Girardeau, Mo. 63701	8,500 (C)	Pub	1,000	2,000	1,875
Southern Arkansas University; Magnolia, Ark. 71753	2,013 (C)	Pub	870	1,430	1,738
Southern California, Univ. of; Los Angeles, Calif. 90089	16,528 (C)	P	9,626	9,626	3,750
Southern California College; Costa Mesa, Calif. 92626	886 (C)	P/AG	4,888	4,888	2,900
Southern College of Seventh-Day Adventists; Collegedale, Tenn. 37315	1,327 (C)	P/SDA	5,500	5,500	2,496
Southern Colorado, University of; Pueblo, Colo. 81001	3,496 (C)	Pub	1,302	4,506	3,458
Southern Connecticut State Univ.; New Haven, Conn. 06515	5,716 (C)	Pub	1,250	3,390	2,900
Southern Illinois Univ.–Carbondale; Carbondale, Ill. 62901	19,137 (C)	Pub	1,660	3,882	2,636
Southern Illinois Univ.–Edwardsville; Edwardsville, Ill. 62026	8,363 (C)	Pub	1,353	3,445	2,650
Southern Indiana, University of; Evansville, Ind. 47714	4,026	Pub	1,333	3,286	2,390
Southern Maine, University of; Gorham, Me. 04038	9,424 (C)	Pub	1,509	4,560	3,090
Southern Methodist University; Dallas, Tex. 75275	5,749 (C)	P/UM	8,392	8,392	3,868
Southern Missionary College. *See* Southern College of Seventh-Day Adventists					
Southern Mississippi, Univ. of; Hattiesburg, Miss. 39406	11,129 (C)	Pub	1,391	2,573	2,060
Southern Nazarene Univ.; Bethany, Okla. 73008	1,200 (C)	P	3,390	3,390	2,388
Southern Oregon State College; Ashland, Ore. 97520	4,015 (C)	Pub	1,488	3,801	2,550
Southern Technical Institute; Marietta, Ga. 30060	3,756 (C)	Pub	1,212	3,234	2,675
Southern University–Baton Rouge; Baton Rouge, La. 70813	9,488 (C)	Pub	1,124	2,646	2,164
Southern University–New Orleans; New Orleans, La. 70126	3,200 (C)	Pub	1,318	2,876	n.a.
Southern Utah State College; Cedar City, Utah 84720	3,000 (C)	Pub	1,059	2,797	2,059
Southern Vermont College; Bennington, Vt. 05201	600 (C)	P	3,900	3,900	2,880
South Florida, University of; Tampa, Fla. 33620	19,965 (C)	Pub	1,025	3,075	2,520
Southwest, College of the; Hobbs, N.M. 88240	184 (C)	P	2,060	2,060	1,530
Southwest Baptist University; Bolivar, Mo. 65613	2,150 (C)	P	3,950	3,950	1,645
Southwestern Adventist College; Keene, Tex. 76059	795 (C)	P	4,321	4,321	2,910
Southwestern Assemblies of God College; Waxahachie, Tex. 75165	701 (C)	P	2,420	2,420	2,500
Southwestern College; Winfield, Kan. 67156	585 (C)	P/UM	3,070	3,070	2,397
Southwestern Conservative Baptist Bible College; Phoenix, Ariz. 85032	134 (C)	P/B	3,300	3,300	2,400
Southwestern Louisiana, University of; Lafayette, La. 70504	14,092 (C)	Pub	1,449	3,069	2,210
Southwestern Oklahoma State Univ.; Weatherford, Okla. 73096	4,300 (C)	Pub	664	1,900	1,250
Southwestern University; Georgetown, Tex. 78626	1,119 (C)	P/UM	6,400	6,400	3,410
Southwest Missouri State Univ.; Springfield, Mo. 65804	14,000 (C)	Pub	1,200	2,400	2,080
Southwest State University; Marshall, Minn. 56258	2,285 (C)	Pub	1,728	2,600	1,900
Southwest Texas State Univ.; San Marcos, Tex. 78666	19,775 (C)	Pub	778	4,018	2,294
Spalding University; Louisville, Ky. 40203	771 (C)	P/RC	4,272	4,272	2,460
Spelman College; Atlanta, Ga. 30314	1,781 (W)	P	4,737	4,737	3,480
Spertus College of Judaica; Chicago, Ill. 60605	100 (C)	P	2,880	2,880	n.a.
Spring Arbor College; Spring Arbor, Mich. 49283	746 (C)	P	6,290	6,290	2,383
Springfield College; Springfield, Mass. 01109	2,063 (C)	P	6,800	6,800	3,090
Spring Garden College; Philadelphia, Pa. 19119	1,200 (C)	P	6,200	6,200	3,800
Spring Hill College; Mobile, Ala. 36608	924 (C)	P/RC	6,600	6,600	3,230
Stanford University; Stanford, Calif. 94305	6,572 (C)	P	11,880	11,880	4,955
Staten Island, Coll. of (NYC). *See* New York, City Univ. of					
Stephen F. Austin State Univ.; Nacogdoches, Tex. 75962	11,000 (C)	Pub	870	4,000	2,700
Stephens College; Columbia, Mo. 65215	978 (W)	P	8,400	8,400	3,100
Sterling College; Sterling, Kan. 67579	530 (C)	P/PUS	4,500	4,500	2,400
Stetson University; Deland, Fla. 32720	2,096 (C)	P	6,730	6,730	2,600
Steubenville, University of; Steubenville, Ohio 43952	957 (C)	P/RC	5,220	5,220	2,900
Stevens Institute of Technology; Hoboken, N.J. 07030	1,400 (C)	P	10,450	10,450	3,750
Stillman College; Tuscaloosa, Ala. 35403	791 (C)	P/PUS	2,700	2,700	2,100
Stockton State College; Pomona, N.J. 08240	3,977 (C)	Pub	1,616	2,256	3,200
Stonehill College; North Easton, Mass. 02357	1,805 (C)	P/RC	6,900	6,900	3,660
Strayer College; Washington, D.C. 20005	1,185 (C)	P	3,240	3,240	n.a.
Suffolk University; Boston, Mass. 02108	3,133 (C)	P	6,300	6,300	n.a.
Sul Ross State University; Alpine, Tex. 79832	1,580 (C)	Pub	748	3,244	2,606
Sul Ross State Univ.–Uvalde Study Center; Uvalde, Tex. 78801	23 (C)	Pub	752	3,204	n.a.
Susquehanna University; Selinsgrove, Pa. 17870	1,465 (C)	P/L	7,600	7,600	3,000
Swain School of Design; New Bedford, Mass. 02740	146 (C)	P	6,100	6,100	3,000
Swarthmore College; Swarthmore, Pa. 19081	1,300 (C)	P	12,150	12,150	4,600

Institution and location	Enrollment	Control	Tuition ($) Res.	Nonres.	Rm/Bd ($)
Sweet Briar College; Sweet Briar, Va. 24595	663 (W)	P	9,000	9,000	3,080
Syracuse University; Syracuse, N.Y. 13210	14,415 (C)	P	8,710	8,710	4,430
Tabor College; Hillsboro, Kan. 67063	360 (C)	P/MB	4,550	4,550	2,430
Talladega College; Talladega, Ala. 35160	576 (C)	P	3,367	3,367	2,030
Tampa, University of; Tampa, Fla. 33606	2,096 (C)	P	7,522	7,522	3,142
Tampa College; Tampa, Fla. 33614	1,500 (C)	P	3,508	3,508	n.a.
Tarkio College; Tarkio, Mo. 64491	700 (C)	P/UP	5,070	5,070	3,100
Tarleton State University; Stephenville, Tex. 76402	4,000 (C)	Pub	786	4,026	2,224
Taylor University; Upland, Ind. 46989	1,424 (C)	P/ID	6,230	6,230	2,590
Temple University; Philadelphia, Pa. 19122	16,046 (C)	Pub	3,300	5,796	3,494
Temple University–Ambler; Ambler, Pa. 19002	3,883 (C)	Pub	3,300	5,796	3,494
Tennessee, Univ. of–Chattanooga; Chattanooga, Tenn. 37402	6,134 (C)	Pub	1,010	3,156	1,730
Tennessee, Univ. of–Knoxville; Knoxville, Tenn. 37996	19,255 (C)	Pub	1,323	3,756	2,601
Tennessee, Univ. of–Martin; Martin, Tenn. 38238	5,064 (C)	Pub	1,173	3,606	2,370
Tennessee, Univ. of–Memphis, Health Science Center; Memphis, Tenn. 38163	406 (C)	Pub	1,359	3,789	2,567
Tennessee State University; Nashville, Tenn. 37203	5,826 (C)	Pub	954	3,102	2,832
Tennessee Technological Univ.; Cookeville, Tenn. 38505	6,614 (C)	Pub	951	2,148	2,001
Tennessee Temple University; Chattanooga, Tenn. 37404	1,712 (C)	P/B	2,980	2,980	2,400
Tennessee Wesleyan College; Athens, Tenn. 37303	546 (C)	P/UM	3,986	3,986	2,655
Texas, University of–Arlington; Arlington, Tex. 76019	19,796 (C)	Pub	874	3,994	3,500
Texas, University of–Austin; Austin, Tex. 78712	35,007 (C)	Pub	830	3,730	3,200
Texas, University of–Dallas; Richardson, Tex. 75083	3,954 (C)	Pub	870	3,990	n.a.
Texas, University of–El Paso; El Paso, Tex. 79968	11,656 (C)	Pub	900	3,960	2,600
Texas, University of–Health Science Center at Dallas; Dallas, Tex. 75235	304 (C)	Pub	700	3,510	n.a.
Texas, University of–Health Science Center at San Antonio; San Antonio, Tex. 78284	700 (C)	Pub	2,550	9,750	n.a.
Texas, University of, Medical Branch–Galveston; Galveston, Tex. 77550	615 (C)	Pub	3,837	14,637	2,500
Texas, University of–Permian Basin; Odessa, Tex. 79762	1,503 (C)	Pub	855	3,975	2,900
Texas, University of–San Antonio; San Antonio, Tex. 78285	10,948 (C)	Pub	840	3,234	3,420
Texas, University of–Tyler; Tyler, Tex. 75701	2,152 (C)	Pub	850	3,600	n.a.
Texas A&I University–Kingsville; Kingsville, Tex. 78363	3,995 (C)	Pub	840	4,000	2,200
Texas A&M University; College Station, Tex. 77843	29,701 (C)	Pub	870	3,600	3,990
Texas A&M University at Galveston; Galveston, Tex. 77553	524 (C)	Pub	695	3,815	2,950
Texas Christian University; Fort Worth, Tex. 76129	5,768 (C)	P/DC	5,400	5,400	2,600
Texas College; Tyler, Tex. 75702	600 (C)	P/CME	4,980	4,980	2,150
Texas Lutheran College; Seguin, Tex. 78155	1,011 (C)	P	3,950	3,950	2,325
Texas Southern University; Houston, Tex. 77004	7,200 (C)	Pub	384	2,880	2,600
Texas Tech University; Lubbock, Tex. 79409	23,479 (C)	Pub	1,150	4,300	2,600
Texas Wesleyan College; Fort Worth, Tex. 76105	1,495 (C)	P/UM	4,250	4,250	3,350
Texas Woman's University; Denton, Tex. 76204	3,751 (W)	Pub	926	4,254	2,615
Thiel College; Greenville, Pa. 16125	916 (C)	P/LCA	7,200	7,200	3,290
Thomas A. Edison State College; Trenton, N.J. 08625	5,300 (C)	Pub	200	300	n.a.
Thomas Aquinas College; Santa Paula, Calif. 93060	126 (C)	P/RC	7,500	7,500	3,400
Thomas College; Waterville, Me. 04901	421 (C)	P	6,330	6,330	3,400
Thomas Jefferson University; Philadelphia, Pa. 19107	984 (C)	P	7,800	7,800	3,400
Thomas More College; Crestview Hills, Ky. 41017	1,120 (C)	P	4,470	4,470	2,750
Tiffin University; Tiffin, Ohio 44883	704 (C)	P	4,060	4,060	2,550
Tift College; Forsyth, Ga. 31029	500 (W)	P/B	3,372	3,372	2,928
Toccoa Falls College; Toccoa Falls, Ga. 30598	670 (C)	P	3,510	3,510	2,310
Toledo, University of; Toledo, Ohio 43606	18,237 (C)	Pub	1,669	3,784	2,300
Tougaloo College; Tougaloo, Miss. 39174	782 (C)	P	3,355	3,355	1,500
Touro College; New York, N.Y. 10036	4,298 (C)	P	4,620	4,620	3,500
Towson State University; Towson, Md. 21204	14,200 (C)	Pub	1,683	3,081	3,714
Transylvania University; Lexington, Ky. 40508	816 (C)	P/DC	6,725	6,725	2,898
Trenton State College; Ewing Township, N.J. 08625	6,861 (C)	Pub	1,760	2,400	3,475
Trevecca Nazarene College; Nashville, Tenn. 37203	847 (C)	P	3,963	3,963	2,250
Trinity Bible College; Ellendale, N.D. 58436	492 (C)	P	2,796	2,796	2,344
Trinity Christian College; Palos Heights, Ill. 60463	477 (C)	P/CR	5,690	5,690	2,505
Trinity College; Burlington, Vt. 05401	950 (W)	P/RC	5,490	5,490	3,050
Trinity College; Deerfield, Ill. 60015	650 (C)	P/EFC	5,900	5,900	2,830
Trinity College; Hartford, Conn. 06106	1,754 (C)	P	11,700	11,700	3,720
Trinity College; Washington, D.C. 20017	750 (W)	P/RC	8,055	8,055	4,998
Trinity University; San Antonio, Tex. 78284	2,417 (C)	P	7,560	7,560	3,320
Tri-State University; Angola, Ind. 46703	1,043 (C)	P	5,665	5,665	2,685
Troy State University; Troy, Ala. 36082	4,063 (C)	Pub	1,171	1,714	1,890
Troy State University–Montgomery; Montgomery, Ala. 36195	1,526 (C)	Pub	1,080	1,080	n.a.
Troy State University–Dothan/Ft. Rucker; Dothan, Ala. 36301	1,029 (C)	Pub	1,035	1,275	n.a.
Tufts University; Medford, Mass. 02155	4,432 (C)	P	11,750	11,750	4,940
Tulane University; New Orleans, La. 70118	6,635 (C)	P	11,280	11,280	4,670
Tulsa, University of; Tulsa, Okla. 74104	3,273 (C)	P	6,240	6,240	2,850
Tusculum College; Greeneville, Tenn. 37743	698 (C)	P/UP	4,509	4,509	2,800

Institution and location	Enrollment	Control	Tuition ($) Res.	Tuition ($) Nonres.	Rm/Bd ($)
Tuskegee University; Tuskegee, Ala. 36088	3,300 (C)	P	4,200	4,200	2,150
Union College; Barbourville, Ky. 40906	807 (C)	P	4,290	4,290	2,050
Union College; Lincoln, Neb. 68506	631 (C)	P/SDA	6,380	6,380	2,190
Union College; Schenectady, N.Y. 12308	2,020 (C)	P	10,338	10,388	3,525
Union for Experimenting Colleges and Universities; Cincinnati, Ohio 45201	200	P	5,800	5,800	n.a.
Union University; Jackson, Tenn. 38305	1,546 (C)	P/SB	3,240	3,240	2,190
U.S. Air Force Academy; Colorado Springs, Colo. 80840	4,542 (C)	Pub	1,000	1,000	—
U.S. Coast Guard Academy; New London, Conn. 06320	775 (C)	Pub	1,000	1,000	—
U.S. International University; San Diego, Calif. 92131	1,500 (C)	P	7,470	7,470	3,585
U.S. Merchant Marine Academy; Kings Point, N.Y. 11024	959 (C)	Pub	805	805	—
U.S. Military Academy; West Point, N.Y. 10996	4,500 (C)	Pub	1,000	1,000	—
U.S. Naval Academy; Annapolis, Md. 21402	4,500 (C)	Pub	1,500	1,500	—
United Wesleyan College; Allentown, Pa. 18103	186 (C)	P	3,700	3,700	2,300
Unity College; Unity, Me. 04988	283 (C)	P	4,857	5,936	3,209
Upper Iowa University; Fayette, Iowa 52142	1,299 (C)	P	6,035	6,035	2,460
Upsala College; East Orange, N.J. 07019	1,290 (C)	P	6,800	6,800	3,170
Urbana Univ.; Urbana, Ohio 43078	710 (C)	P	4,860	4,860	2,550
Ursinus College; Collegeville, Pa. 19426	1,170 (C)	P	7,250	7,250	3,300
Ursuline College; Pepper Pike, Ohio 44124	1,427 (W)	P/RC	4,200	4,200	2,450
Utah, University of; Salt Lake City, Utah 84112	20,386 (C)	Pub	1,128	3,186	3,270
Utah State University; Logan, Utah 84322	11,690 (C)	Pub	1,101	2,967	3,750
Utica College of Syracuse University; Utica, N.Y. 13502	1,359 (C)	P	6,975	6,975	2,920
Valdosta State College; Valdosta, Ga. 31698	5,257 (C)	Pub	1,377	3,579	1,836
Valley City State College; Valley City, N.D. 58072	1,075 (C)	Pub	1,128	2,196	1,797
Valley Forge Christian College; Phoenixville, Pa. 19460	535 (C)	P/AG	2,540	2,540	2,200
Valparaiso University; Valparaiso, Ind. 46383	3,200 (C)	P/L	7,092	7,092	2,450
Vanderbilt University; Nashville, Tenn. 37212	5,322 (C)	P	10,500	10,500	3,960
VanderCook College of Music; Chicago, Ill. 60616	102 (C)	P	5,358	5,358	3,418
Vassar College; Poughkeepsie, N.Y. 12601	2,250 (C)	P	11,100	11,100	4,100
Vennard College; University Park, Iowa 52595	184 (C)	P	3,099	3,099	1,886
Vermont, University of; Burlington, Vt. 05401	1,851 (C)	Pub	3,432	9,300	3,646
Villa Julie College; Stevenson, Md. 21153	1,141	P	4,260	4,260	n.a.
Villa Maria College; Erie, Pa. 16505	505 (W)	P	4,950	4,950	2,600
Villanova University; Villanova, Pa. 19085	6,300 (C)	P	7,300	7,300	4,100
Virginia, University of; Charlottesville, Va. 22906	11,000 (C)	Pub	2,250	5,470	2,950
Virginia, University of–Clinch Valley College; Wise, Va. 24293	1,354 (C)	Pub	1,472	2,336	2,532
Virginia Commonwealth University; Richmond, Va. 23284	14,286 (C)	Pub	2,110	4,730	3,160
Virginia Intermont College; Bristol, Va. 24201	393 (C)	P/B	4,925	4,925	2,950
Virginia Military Institute; Lexington, Va. 24450	1,300 (M)	Pub	4,055	7,055	2,635
Virginia Polytechnic Institute and State University; Blacksburg, Va. 24061	18,310 (C)	Pub	2,187	4,407	1,875
Virginia State University; Petersburg, Va. 23803	3,402 (C)	Pub	1,800	3,100	2,200
Virginia Union University; Richmond, Va. 23220	1,112 (C)	P/B	4,159	4,159	2,350
Virginia Wesleyan College; Norfolk, Va. 23502	1,116 (C)	P/UM	6,200	6,200	3,550
Virgin Islands, Univ. of the; St. Thomas, V.I. 00802	2,321 (C)	Pub	690	1,890	2,492
Visual Arts, School of; New York, N.Y. 10010	2,300 (C)	P	6,200	6,200	3,500
Viterbo College; La Crosse, Wis. 54601	992 (C)	P/RC	5,180	5,180	2,426
Voorhees College; Denmark, S.C. 29042	574 (C)	P/E	2,740	2,740	2,244
Wabash College; Crawfordsville, Ind. 47933	800 (M)	P	7,425	7,425	2,985
Wadhams Hall Seminary College; Ogdensburg, N.Y. 13669	50 (M)	P	2,995	2,995	3,000
Wagner College; Staten Island, N.Y. 10301	1,600 (C)	P/L	7,210	7,210	4,050
Wake Forest University; Winston-Salem, N.C. 27109	3,418 (C)	P/B	7,250	7,250	2,700
Walla Walla College; College Place, Wash. 99324	1,456 (C)	P/SDA	6,789	6,789	2,400
Walsh College; Canton, Ohio 44720	1,203 (C)	P/RC	4,656	4,656	2,550
Walsh College of Accountancy and Business Administration; Troy, Mich. 48007	1,589 (C)	P	2,258	2,258	n.a.
Warner Pacific College; Portland, Ore. 97215	390 (C)	P/CG	5,900	5,900	2,523
Warner Southern College; Lake Wales, Fla. 33853	294 (C)	P/CG	4,245	4,245	2,245
Warren Wilson College; Swannanoa, N.C. 28778	455 (C)	P	6,250	6,250	—
Wartburg College; Waverly, Iowa 50677	1,329 (C)	P/AL	6,930	6,930	2,580
Washburn University of Topeka; Topeka, Kan. 66621	6,009 (C)	Pub	1,794	2,634	2,430
Washington, University of; Seattle, Wash. 98195	25,084 (C)	Pub	1,731	4,809	2,590
Washington and Jefferson College; Washington, Pa. 15301	1,135 (C)	P	8,720	8,720	2,690
Washington and Lee University; Lexington, Va. 24450	1,450 (M)	P	8,300	8,300	3,308
Washington Bible College; Lanham, Md. 20706	313 (C)	P	2,005	2,005	2,900
Washington College; Chestertown, Md. 21620	800 (C)	P	8,710	8,710	3,540
Washington State University; Pullman, Wash. 99164	14,370 (C)	Pub	1,732	4,810	2,766
Washington University; St. Louis, Mo. 63130	4,443 (C)	P	11,512	11,512	4,168
Wayland Baptist University; Plainview, Tex. 79072	1,676 (C)	P	3,180	3,180	2,460
Waynesburg College; Waynesburg, Pa. 15370	803 (C)	P	5,790	5,790	2,530

Institution and location	Enrollment	Control	Tuition ($) Res.	Tuition ($) Nonres.	Rm/Bd ($)
Wayne State College; Wayne, Neb. 68787	2,386 (C)	Pub	1,052	1,637	1,854
Wayne State University; Detroit, Mich. 48202	19,217 (C)	Pub	1,760	3,860	3,100
Webber College; Babson Park, Fla. 33827	301 (C)	P	4,450	4,450	2,330
Webb Institute of Naval Architecture; Glen Cove, N.Y. 11542	87 (C)	P	—	—	3,150
Weber State College; Ogden, Utah 84408	11,215 (C)	Pub	950	2,574	2,280
Webster University; St. Louis, Mo. 63119	1,300 (C)	P	5,100	5,100	2,600
Wellesley College; Wellesley, Mass. 02181	2,200 (W)	P	11,420	11,420	4,300
Wells College; Aurora, N.Y. 13026	500 (W)	P	9,230	9,230	3,320
Wentworth Institute of Technology; Boston, Mass. 02115	4,020 (C)	P	6,040	6,040	4,384
Wesleyan College; Macon, Ga. 31297	444 (W)	P/UM	5,785	5,785	3,165
Wesleyan University; Middletown, Conn. 06457	2,673 (C)	P	12,350	12,350	4,345
Wesley College; Florence, Miss. 39073	70 (C)	P/M	1,600	1,600	1,850
West Chester Univ. of Pennsylvania; West Chester, Pa. 19383	8,967 (C)	Pub	1,811	3,207	2,168
West Coast Christian College; Fresno, Calif. 93710	274 (C)	P/CG	2,530	2,530	2,400
West Coast University; Los Angeles, Calif. 90020	850 (C)	P	6,240	6,240	n.a.
West Coast University; Orange, Calif. 92668	260	P	5,022	5,022	n.a.
Western Baptist College; Salem, Ore. 97301	270 (C)	P/B	4,908	4,908	2,580
Western Carolina University; Cullowhee, N.C. 28723	4,782 (C)	Pub	894	4,142	1,870
Western Connecticut State University; Danbury, Conn. 06810	6,025 (C)	Pub	1,265	3,025	2,500
Western Illinois University; Macomb, Ill. 61455	9,824 (C)	Pub	1,415	3,455	2,170
Western International University; Phoenix, Ariz. 85021	500	P	3,420	3,420	n.a.
Western Kentucky University; Bowling Green, Ky. 42101	10,276 (C)	Pub	1,090	3,090	2,150
Western Maryland College; Westminster, Md. 21157	1,136 (C)	P	8,750	8,750	3,220
Western Michigan University; Kalamazoo, Mich. 49008	15,958 (C)	Pub	1,496	3,626	2,588
Western Montana College; Dillon, Mont. 59725	926 (C)	Pub	919	2,350	2,460
Western New England College; Springfield, Mass. 01119	2,694 (C)	P	5,952	5,952	3,850
Western New Mexico University; Silver City, N.M. 88061	1,314 (C)	Pub	600	2,156	2,030
Western Oregon State College; Monmouth, Ore. 97361	2,897 (C)	Pub	1,428	3,741	2,307
Western State College of Colorado; Gunnison, Colo. 81230	2,000 (C)	Pub	1,638	3,702	2,314
Western Washington University; Bellingham, Wash. 98225	8,375 (C)	Pub	1,236	4,224	2,450
Westfield State College; Westfield, Mass. 01085	3,000 (C)	Pub	935	3,000	2,263
West Florida, University of; Pensacola, Fla. 32514	4,029 (C)	Pub	1,099	3,400	2,769
West Georgia College; Carrollton, Ga. 30118	4,937 (C)	Pub	1,317	3,399	1,770
West Liberty State College; West Liberty, W. Va. 26074	2,558 (C)	Pub	840	2,300	2,414
West Los Angeles, Univ. of; Los Angeles, Calif. 90066	260 (C)	P	2,550	2,550	n.a.
Westmar College; LeMars, Iowa 51031	530 (C)	P/UM	5,602	5,602	2,520
Westminster Choir College; Princeton, N.J. 08540	243 (C)	P	6,774	6,774	3,240
Westminster College; Fulton, Mo. 65251	650 (M)	P	6,100	6,100	2,800
Westminster College; New Wilmington, Pa. 16142	1,150 (C)	P/UP	7,090	7,090	2,330
Westminster Coll. of Salt Lake City; Salt Lake City, Utah 84105	1,423 (C)	P	4,930	4,930	2,950
Westmont College; Santa Barbara, Calif. 93108	1,169 (C)	P	7,470	7,470	3,710
West Oahu College. *See* Hawaii, University of.					
West Texas State University; Canyon, Tex. 79016	4,956 (C)	Pub	862	3,982	2,480
West Virginia Institute of Technology; Montgomery, W. Va. 25136	2,798 (C)	Pub	940	2,500	2,941
West Virginia State College; Institute, W. Va. 25112	4,465 (C)	Pub	840	2,300	2,271
West Virginia University; Morgantown, W. Va. 26506	13,915 (C)	Pub	1,260	3,240	2,800
West Virginia Wesleyan College; Buckhannon, W. Va. 26201	1,258 (C)	P/UM	6,100	6,100	3,060
Wheaton College; Norton, Mass. 02766	1,050 (W)	P	11,549	11,549	4,080
Wheaton College; Wheaton, Ill. 60187	2,236 (C)	P	7,256	7,256	2,952
Wheeling College; Wheeling, W. Va. 26003	664 (C)	P	6,600	6,600	3,250
Wheelock College; Boston, Mass. 02215	543 (W)	P	10,224	10,224	3,990
White Plains, Coll. of, of Pace Univ. *See* Pace Univ.					
Whitman College; Walla Walla, Wash. 99362	1,195 (C)	P	7,960	7,960	3,330
Whittier College; Whittier, Calif. 90608	1,200 (C)	P	8,625	8,625	3,430
Whitworth College; Spokane, Wash. 99251	1,268 (C)	P/UP	7,700	7,700	2,940
Wichita State University; Wichita, Kan. 67208	13,500 (C)	Pub	1,285	3,090	2,260
Widener University; Chester, Pa. 19013	2,100 (C)	P	7,200	7,200	3,550
Wilberforce University; Wilberforce, Ohio 45384	797 (C)	P/AME	4,370	4,370	2,402
Wiley College; Marshall, Tex. 75670	557 (C)	P	2,932	2,932	2,050
Wilkes College; Wilkes-Barre, Pa. 18766	1,730 (C)	P	6,150	6,150	3,140
Willamette University; Salem, Ore. 97301	1,379 (C)	P	7,560	7,560	3,100
William and Mary, College of; Williamsburg, Va. 23185	4,986 (C)	Pub	2,750	7,234	3,274
William Carey College; Hattiesburg, Miss. 39401	1,546 (C)	P	3,168	3,168	2,000
William Jewell College; Liberty, Mo. 64068	1,450 (C)	P/B	5,530	5,530	2,420
William Paterson College; Wayne, N.J. 07470	7,740 (C)	Pub	1,386	1,986	3,316
William Penn College; Oskaloosa, Iowa 52577	500 (C)	P/F	6,170	6,170	2,180
Williams College; Williamstown, Mass. 01267	2,025 (C)	P	11,700	11,700	3,830
William Smith College. *See* Hobart and William Smith Colleges					
William Tyndale College; Farmington Hills, Mich. 48018	335 (C)	P	2,656	2,656	2,590
William Woods College; Fulton, Mo. 65251	750 (W)	P	6,130	6,130	2,370
Wilmington College; New Castle, Del. 19720	1,300 (C)	P	3,700	3,700	2,830
Wilmington College of Ohio; Wilmington, Ohio 45177	779 (C)	P/F	6,540	6,540	2,620

Institution and location	Enrollment	Control	Tuition ($) Res.	Nonres.	Rm/Bd ($)
Wilson College; Chambersburg, Pa. 17201	444 (W)	P/UP	7,410	7,410	3,290
Wingate College; Wingate, N.C. 28174	1,623 (C)	P/SB	3,870	3,870	2,400
Winona State University; Winona, Minn. 55987	5,000 (C)	Pub	1,650	2,550	1,800
Winston-Salem State University; Winston-Salem, N.C. 27110	2,400 (C)	Pub	845	3,095	1,925
Winthrop College; Rock Hill, S.C. 29733	4,309 (C)	Pub	2,078	3,682	2,124
Wisconsin, University of-Eau Claire; Eau Claire, Wis. 54701	10,627 (C)	Pub	1,500	4,400	2,040
Wisconsin, University of-Green Bay; Green Bay, Wis. 54302	4,530 (C)	Pub	1,370	4,170	2,385
Wisconsin, University of-La Crosse; La Crosse, Wis. 54601	9,118 (C)	Pub	1,400	4,250	1,620
Wisconsin, University of-Madison; Madison, Wis. 53706	30,673 (C)	Pub	1,820	5,580	2,900
Wisconsin, University of-Milwaukee; Milwaukee, Wis. 53201	21,721 (C)	Pub	1,626	4,970	2,711
Wisconsin, University-Oshkosh; Oshkosh, Wis. 54901	9,007 (C)	Pub	1,550	4,700	2,150
Wisconsin, University of-Parkside; Kenosha, Wis. 53141	5,500 (C)	Pub	1,387	4,190	1,808
Wisconsin, University of-Platteville; Platteville, Wis. 53818	5,193 (C)	Pub	1,616	4,450	1,810
Wisconsin, University of-River Falls; River Falls, Wis. 54022	5,500 (C)	Pub	1,437	4,239	2,000
Wisconsin, University of-Stevens Point; Stevens Point, Wis. 54481	8,883 (C)	Pub	1,480	4,280	2,090
Wisconsin, University of-Stout; Menomonie, Wis. 54751	7,169 (C)	Pub	1,477	4,480	1,892
Wisconsin, University of-Superior; Superior, Wis. 54880	1,800 (C)	Pub	1,395	4,197	1,935
Wisconsin, University of-Whitewater; Whitewater, Wis. 53190	9,687 (C)	Pub	1,300	4,000	1,800
Wisconsin Lutheran College; Milwaukee, Wis. 53226	162	P	4,990	4,990	2,700
Wittenberg University; Springfield, Ohio 45501	2,150 (C)	P	9,100	9,100	2,980
Wofford College; Spartanburg, S.C. 29301	1,103 (C)	P/UM	5,675	5,675	3,010
Woodbury University; Burbank, Calif. 91504-1099	725 (C)	P	7,230	7,230	n.a.
Wooster, College of; Wooster, Ohio 44691	1,711 (C)	P	9,220	9,220	2,910
Worcester Polytechnic Institute; Worcester, Mass. 01609	2,775 (C)	P	10,800	10,800	3,915
Worcester State College; Worcester, Mass. 01602	3,500 (C)	Pub	1,173	2,269	2,125
World College West; Petaluma, Calif. 94952	110 (C)	P	6,200	6,200	3,000
Wright State University; Dayton, Ohio 45435	13,232 (C)	Pub	1,752	3,504	2,840
Wyoming, University of; Laramie, Wyo. 82071	8,073 (C)	Pub	778	2,442	2,670
Xavier University; Cincinnati, Ohio 45207	3,973 (C)	P	5,900	5,900	2,900
Xavier University of Louisiana; New Orleans, La. 70125	1,772 (C)	P	4,100	4,100	2,650
Yale University; New Haven, Conn. 06520	5,129 (C)	P	11,340	11,340	4,700
Yeshiva University; New York, N.Y. 10033	1,642 (C)	P	7,450	7,450	3,520
York College (NYC). *See* New York, City University of					
York College of Pennsylvania; York, Pa. 17405	2,448 (C)	P	3,576	3,576	2,308
Youngstown State Univ.; Youngstown, Ohio 44555	13,889 (C)	Pub	1,500	2,550	2,460

1. In-city, $4,185. 2. Out-of-state, $6,016. 3. $15 per credit. 4. $50 per credit. 5. $70 per credit. 6. $140 per credit.

The Ivy League

The Ivy League consists of a group of colleges and universities in the northeastern United States widely regarded as high in academic and social prestige. It includes Harvard (established in 1636), Yale (1701), Pennsylvania (1740), Princeton (1746), Columbia (1754), Brown (1764), Dartmouth (1769), and Cornell (1853). Although competition between the colleges dates back to football meetings in the 1870s, the Ivy League was not formally organized as an athletic conference until 1956.

Trends in College Enrollment

According to the Center for Education Statistics, from 1970 to 1980 college enrollment increased by more than 40 percent. Since 1980 enrollment has grown at a slower pace. Between 1980 and 1985 it increased only about one percent, from 12.1 million to 12.2 million and all of this growth was in part-time enrollment. During this same period the number of men enrolled fell by one percent while the number of women rose by three percent.

There has also been a marked shift in the age of students. The number of older students has been growing more rapidly than the number of younger students. Between 1970 and 1985, the enrollment of students under age 25 increased by 15 percent. However, during this same period, enrollment of persons 25 and over rose by 114 percent. From 1980 to 1985 enrollment of students under 25 decreased by five percent, while the enrollment of persons 25 and over increased by 12 percent.

The proportion of minority students in the college population rose between 1976 and 1984. In 1976 minorities made up 15.4 percent of college students, whereas by 1984 they represented 17.0 percent of the student body. However, much of this change is attributable to the sharply rising number of Asians attending college. The picture for black students is one of regression. In 1976 the proportion of black students within the college community was 9.4 percent. By 1984 it had fallen to 8.8 percent. This drop reflects the declining enrollment of black males.

As to the kinds of colleges students are attending, the Center noted that contrary to trends in the 1970s, enrollment in the 1980s has grown faster at private institutions than at public ones. Also, despite the sizable number of small colleges, most students attend the larger colleges. In fall 1985, 38 percent of higher education institutions had fewer than 1,000 students. However, these small colleges accounted for less than five percent of the total college enrollment. Although only 10 percent of the colleges enrolled more than 10,000 students, they accounted for 50 percent of total enrollment.

As to the future, enrollment in colleges and universities will be affected by a continuing decline in the population of 18- to 24-year olds. Their number peaked in 1981 and then began a decline that is expected to continue throughout the next 10 years.

Selected Degree Abbreviations

A.B. Bachelor of Arts
AeEng. Aeronautical Engineer
A.M.T. Master of Arts in Teaching
B.A. Bachelor of Arts
B.A.E. Bachelor of Arts in Education, or Bachelor of Art Education, Aeronautical Engineering, Agricultural Engineering, or Architectural Engineering
B.Ag. Bachelor of Agriculture
B.A.M. Bachelor of Applied Mathematics
B.Arch. Bachelor of Architecture
B.B.A. Bachelor of Business Administration
B.C.E. Bachelor of Civil Engineering
B.Ch.E. Bachelor of Chemical Engineering
B.C.L. Bachelor of Canon Law
B.D. Bachelor of Divinity
B.E. Bachelor of Education or Bachelor of Engineering
B.E.E. Bachelor of Electrical Engineering
B.F. Bachelor of Forestry
B.F.A. Bachelor of Fine Arts
B.J. Bachelor of Journalism
B.L.S. Bachelor of Liberal Studies or Bachelor of Library Science
B.Litt. Bachelor of Literature
B.M. Bachelor of Medicine or Bachelor of Music
B.M.S. Bachelor of Marine Science
B.N. Bachelor of Nursing
B.Pharm. Bachelor of Pharmacy
B.R.E. Bachelor of Religious Education
B.S. Bachelor of Science
B.S.Ed. Bachelor of Science in Education
C.E. Civil Engineer
Ch.E. Chemical Engineer
D.B.A. Doctor of Business Administration
D.C. Doctor of Chiropractic
D.D. Doctor of Divinity[1]
D.D.S. Doctor of Dental Surgery or Doctor of Dental Science
D.L.S. Doctor of Library Science
D.M.D. Doctor of Dental Medicine
D.O. Doctor of Osteopathy
D.M.S. Doctor of Medical Science
D.P.A. Doctor of Public Administration[2]
D.P.H. Doctor of Public Health
D.R.E. Doctor of Religious Education
D.S.W. Doctor of Social Welfare or Doctor of Social Work
D.Sc. Doctor of Science[3]
D.V.M. Doctor of Veterinary Medicine
Ed.D. Doctor of Education[2]
Ed.S. Education Specialist
E.E. Electrical Engineer
E.M. Engineer of Mines
E.Met. Engineer of Metallurgy
I.E. Industrial Engineer or Industrial Engineering
J.D. Doctor of Laws[2]
J.S.D. Doctor of Juristic Science
L.H.D. Doctor of Humane Letters[3]
Litt.B. Bachelor of Letters
Litt.M. Master of Letters[4]
LL.B. Bachelor of Laws
LL.D. Doctor of Laws[3]
LL.M. Master of Laws
M.A. Master of Arts
M.Aero.E. Master of Aeronautical Engineering
M.B.A. Master of Business Administration
M.C.E. Master of Christian Education or Master of Civil Engineering
M.C.S. Master of Computer Science
M.D. Doctor of Medicine
M.Div. Master of Divinity
M.E. Master of Engineering
M.Ed. Master of Education
M.Eng. Master of Engineering
M.F.A. Master of Fine Arts
M.H.A. Master of Hospital Administration
M.L.S. Master of Library Science
M.M. Master of Music
M.M.E. Master of Mechanical Engineering or Master of Music Education
M.Mus. Master of Music
M.N. Master of Nursing
M.R.E. Master of Religious Education
M.S. Master of Science
M.S.W. Master of Social Work
M.Th. Master of Theology
Nuc.E. Nuclear Engineer
O.D. Doctor of Optometry
Pharm.D. Doctor of Pharmacy[2]
Ph.B. Bachelor of Philosophy
Ph.D. Doctor of Philosophy
S.B. Bachelor of Science
Sc.D. Doctor of Science[3]
S.J.D. Doctor of Juridical Science or Doctor of the Science of Law
S.Sc.D Doctor of Social Science
S.T.B. Bachelor of Sacred Theology
S.T.D. Doctor of Sacred Theology
S.T.M. Master of Sacred Theology
Th.B. Bachelor of Theology
Th.D. Doctor of Theology
Th.M. Master of Theology

1. Honorary. 2. Earned and honorary. 3. Usually honorary. 4. Sometimes honorary.

Academic Costume: Colors Associated With Fields

Field	Color	Field	Color
Agriculture	Maize	Medicine	Green
Arts, Letters, Humanities	White	Music	Pink
Commerce, Accountancy, Business	Drab	Nursing	Apricot
Dentistry	Lilac	Oratory (Speech)	Silver gray
Economics	Copper	Pharmacy	Olive Green
Education	Light Blue	Philosophy	Dark blue
Engineering	Orange	Physical Education	Sage Green
Fine Arts, Architecture	Brown	Public Admin. including Foreign Service	Peacock blue
Forestry	Russet	Public Health	Salmon pink
Journalism	Crimson	Science	Golden yellow
Law	Purple	Social Work	Citron
Library Science	Lemon	Theology	Scarlet
		Veterinary Science	Gray

SPORTS

Major Sports Contents

For sports not listed, see index listing under "Sports"

Sports Personalities

A name in parentheses is the original name or form of name. Localities are places of birth. Dates of birth appear as month/day/year. **Boldface** years in parentheses are dates of **(birth-death).**
Information has been gathered from many sources, including the individuals themselves. However, the *Information Please Almanac* cannot guarantee the accuracy of every individual item.

Aaron, Hank (Henry) (baseball); Mobile, Ala., 2/5/1934
Aaron, Tommie (baseball); Mobile, Ala. **(1939–1984)**
Abdul-Jabbar, Kareem (Lewis Ferdinand Alcindor, Jr.) (basketball); New York City, 4/16/1947
Adderly, Herbert A. (football); Philadelphia, 6/8/1939
Affleck, Francis (auto racing) **(1951-1985)**
Alcindor, Lew. *See* Abdul-Jabbar
Ali, Muhammad (Cassius Clay) (boxing); Louisville, Ky., 1/18/1942
Allen, Dick (Richard Anthony) (baseball); Wampum, Pa., 3/8/1942
Allison, Bobby (Robert Arthur) (auto racing); Hueytown, Ala., 12/3/1937
Alston, Walter (baseball); Venice, Ohio **(1911-1984)**
Alworth, Lance (football); Houston, 8/3/1940
Anderson, Donny (Gary Donny) (football); Brooklyn, N.Y., 4/3/1949
Anderson, Ken (football); Batavia, Ill., 2/15/1949
Anderson, Sparky (George) (baseball); Bridgewater, S.D., 2/22/1934
Andretti, Mario (auto racing); Montona, Trieste, Italy, 2/28/1940
Anthony, Earl (bowling); Kent, Wash., 4/27/1938
Appling, Luke (baseball); High Point, N.C., 4/2/1907
Arcaro, Eddie (George Edward) (jockey); Cincinnati, 2/19/1916
Ashe, Arthur (tennis); Richmond, Va., 7/10/1943
Austin, Tracy (tennis); Rolling Hills, Calif., 12/2/1962
Averill, Earl (baseball); Everett, Wash. **(1915–1983)**
Babashoff, Shirley (swimming); Whittier, Calif., 1/31/1957
Baer, Max (boxing); Omaha, Neb. **(1909-1959)**
Bakken, Jim (James Leroy) (football); Madison, Wis., 11/2/1940
Banks, Ernie (baseball); Dallas, 1/31/1931
Bannister, Roger (runner); Harrow, England, 3/24/1929
Barry, Rick (Richard) (basketball); Elizabeth, N.J., 3/28/1944
Bauer, Hank (Henry) (baseball); East St. Louis, Ill., 7/31/1922
Baugh, Sammy (football); Temple, Tex., 3/17/1914
Bayi, Filbert (runner); Karratu, Tanganyika, 6/23/1953
Baylor, Elgin (basketball); Washington, D.C., 9/16/1934
Beamon, Bob (long jumper); New York City, 8/2/1946
Becker, Boris (tennis); Leiman, W. Germany, 11/22/1967
Bee, Clair (basketball); Cleveland, Ohio **(1896–1983)**
Beliveau, Jean (hockey); Three Rivers, Quebec, Canada, 8/31/1931
Bell, Rickey (football); Inglewood, Calif. **(1949-1984)**
Beman, Deane (golf); Washington, D.C., 4/22/1938
Bench, Johnny (Johnny Lee) (baseball); Oklahoma City, 12/7/1947
Berg, Patty (Patricia Jane) (golf); Minneapolis, 2/13/1918
Berning, Susie Maxwell (golf); Pasadena, Calif., 7/22/1941
Berra, Yogi (Lawrence) (baseball); St. Louis, 5/12/1925
Biletnikoff, Frederick (football); Erie, Pa., 2/23/1943
Bird, Larry (basketball); French Lick, Ind., 12/7/1956
Blaik, Earl H. (football); Detroit, 2/15/1897
Blanda, George Frederick (football); Youngwood, Pa., 9/17/1927
Blue, Vida (baseball); Mansfield, La., 7/28/1949
Borg, Björn (tennis); Stockholm, 6/6/1956
Boros, Julius (golf); Fairfield, Conn., 3/3/1920
Bossy, Mike (hockey); Montreal, 1/22/1957
Boston, Ralph (long jumper); Laurel, Miss., 5/9/1939
Bradley, Bill (William Warren) (basketball); Crystal City, Mo., 7/28/1943
Bradshaw, Terry (football); Shreveport, La., 9/2/1948
Brathwaite, Chris (track); Eugene, Ore. **(1949-1984)**
Breedlove, Craig (Norman) (speed driving); Los Angeles, 3/23/1938
Brett, George (baseball); Glendale, W. Va., 5/15/1953
Brock, Louis Clark (baseball); El Dorado, Ark., 6/18/1939
Brown, Jimmy (football); St. Simon Island, Ga., 2/17/1936
Brown, Larry (football); Clairton, Pa., 9/19/1947
Brumel, Valeri (high jumper); Tolbuzino, Siberia, 4/14/1942
Bryant, Paul "Bear" (football); Tuscaloosa, Ala. **(1913–1983)**
Bryant, Rosalyn Evette (track); Chicago, 1/7/1956
Burton, Michael (swimming); Des Moines, Iowa, 7/3/1947
Butkus, Dick (Richard Marvin) (football); Chicago, 12/9/1942
Campanella, Roy (baseball); Homestead, Pa., 11/19/1921
Campbell, Earl (football); Tyler, Tex., 3/29/1955
Caponi, Donna Maria (golf); Detroit, 1/29/1945
Cappelletti, Gino (football); Keewatin, Minn., 3/26/1934
Carew, Rod (Rodney Cline) (baseball); Gatun, Panama, 10/1/1945
Carlos, John (sprinter); New York City, 6/5/1945
Carlton, Steven Norman (baseball); Miami, Fla., 12/22/1944
Carner, Joanne Gunderson (Mrs. Don) (golf); Kirkland, Wash., 3/4/1939
Casals, Rosemary (tennis); San Francisco, 9/16/1948
Casper, Billy (golf); San Diego, Calif., 6/24/1931
Caulkins, Tracy (swimming); Wimona, Minn., 1/11/63
Cauthen, Steve (jockey); Covington, Ky., 5/1/1960
Chamberlain, Wilt (Wilton) (basketball); Philadelphia, 8/21/1936
Chapot, Frank (equestrian); Camden, N.J., 2/24/1934

Chinaglia, Giorgio (soccer); Carrara, Italy, 1/24/1947
Clarke, Bobby (Robert Earle) (hockey); Flin Flon, Manitoba, Canada, 8/13/1949
Clay, Cassius. *See* Ali, Muhammad
Clemente, Roberto Walker (baseball); Carolina, Puerto Rico **(1934-1972)**
Cobb, Tyrus Raymond (Ty) (baseball); Narrows, Ga. **(1886-1961)**
Cochran, Barbara Ann (skiing); Claremont, N.H., 1/4/1951
Cochran, Marilyn (skiing); Burlington, Vt., 2/7/1950
Cochran, Robert (skiing); Claremont, N.H., 12/11/1951
Coe, Sebastian Newbold (track); London, England, 9/29/1956
Colavito, Rocky (Rocco Domenico) (baseball); New York City, 8/10/1933
Comaneci, Nadia (gymnast); Onesti, Romania, 11/12/1961
Connors, Jimmy (James Scott) (tennis); East St. Louis, Ill., 9/2/1952
Cordero, Angel (jockey); Santurce, Puerto Rico, 5/8/1942
Cournoyer, Yvan Serge (hockey); Drummondville, Quebec, Canada, 11/22/1943
Court, Margaret Smith (tennis); Albury, New South Wales, Australia, 7/16/1942
Cousy, Bob (basketball); New York City, 8/9/1928
Crabbe, Buster (swimming); Scottsdale, Ariz. **(1908–1983)**
Crenshaw, Ben (golf); Austin, Tex., 1/11/1952
Cronin, Joe (baseball); San Francisco, **(1906–1984)**
Cruyff, Johan (soccer); Amsterdam, Netherlands, 4/25/47
Csonka, Larry (Lawrence Richard) (football); Stow, Ohio, 12/25/1946
Dancer, Stanley (harness racing); New Egypt, N.J., 7/25/1927
Dark, Alvin (baseball); Comanche, Okla., 1/7/1922
Davenport, Willie (track); Troy, Ala., 6/6/1943
Dawson, Leonard Ray (football); Alliance, Ohio, 6/20/1935
Dean, Dizzy (Jay Hanna) (baseball); Lucas, Ark. **(1911-1974)**
DeBusschere, Dave (basketball); Detroit, 10/16/1940
Delvecchio, Alex Peter (hockey); Fort William, Ontario, Canada, 12/4/1931
Demaret, Jim (golf); Houston **(1910-1983)**
Dempsey, Jack (William H.) (boxing); Manassa, Colo. **(1895-1983)**
DeVicenzo, Roberto (golf); Buenos Aires, 4/14/1923
Dibbs, Edward George (tennis); Brooklyn, New York, 2/23/1951
Dietz, James W. (rowing); New York, N.Y., 1/12/1949
DiMaggio, Joe (baseball); Martinez, Calif., 11/25/1914
Dionne, Marcel (hockey); Drummondville, Quebec, Canada, 8/3/1951
Dominguín, Luis Miguel (matador); Madrid, 12/9/1926
Dorsett, Tony (football); Rochester, Pa., 4/7/1954
Dryden, Kenneth (hockey); Hamilton, Ontario, Canada, 8/4/1947
Drysdale, Don (baseball); Van Nuys, Calif., 7/23/1936
Duran, Roberto (boxing); Panama City, 6/16/1951
Durocher, Leo (baseball); West Springfield, Mass., 7/27/1906
Durr, François (tennis); Algiers, Algeria, 12/25/1942
El Cordobés, (Manuel Benítez Pérez) (matador); Palma del Río, Córdoba, Spain, 5/4/1936(?)
Elder, Lee (golf); Dallas, 7/14/1934
Emerson, Roy (tennis); Kingsway, Australia, 11/3/1936
Ender, Kornelia (swimming); Plauen, East Germany, 10/25/1958
Erving, Julius (Dr. J) (basketball); Roosevelt, N.Y., 2/22/1950
Esposito, Phil (Philip Anthony) (hockey); Sault Ste. Marie, Ontario, Canada, 2/20/1942
Evans, Lee (runner); Mandena, Calif., 2/25/1947
Ewbank, Weeb (football); Richmond, Ind., 5/6/1907
Feller, Robert (Bobby) (baseball); Van Meter, Iowa, 11/3/1918
Feuerbach, Allan Dean (track); Preston, Iowa, 1/12/1948
Finley, Charles O. (sportsman); Ensley, Ala., 2/22/1918
Fischer, Bobby (chess); Chicago, 3/9/1943
Fitzsimmons, Bob (Robert Prometheus) (boxing); Cornwall, England **(1862-1917)**
Fleming, Peggy Gale (ice skating); San Jose, Calif., 7/27/1948
Ford, Whitey (Edward) (baseball); New York City, 10/21/1928
Foreman, George (boxing); Marshall, Tex., 1/10/1949
Fosbury, Richard (high jumper); Portland, Ore., 3/6/1947
Fox, Nellie (Jacob Nelson) (baseball); St. Thomas, Pa. **(1927-1975)**
Foxx, James Emory (baseball); Sudlersville, Md., **(1907-1967)**
Foyt, A. J. (auto racing); Houston, 1/16/1935
Francis, Emile (hockey); North Battleford, Sask., 9/13/1926
Fratianne, Linda (figure skating); Los Angeles, 8/2/1960
Frazier, Joe (boxing); Beauford, S.C., 1/17/1944
Frazier, Walt (basketball); Atlanta, 3/29/1945
Frick, Ford C. (baseball); Wawaka, Ind., **(1894-1978)**
Furniss, Bruce (swimming); Fresno, Calif., 5/27/1957
Gable, Dan (wrestling); Waterloo, Iowa, 10/25/1945
Gabriel, Roman (football); Wilmington, N.C., 8/5/1940
Gallagher, Michael Donald (skiing); Yonkers, N.Y., 10/3/1941
Garms, Debs (baseball); Glen Rose, Tex. **(1908-1984)**
Garvey, Steve (baseball); Tampa, Fla., 12/22/1948
Gehrig, Lou (Henry Louis) (baseball); New York City **(1903-1941)**
Gehringer, Charlie (baseball); Fowlerville, Mich., 5/11/1903
Geoffrion, Bernie (Boom Boom) (hockey); Montreal, 2/14/1931
Gerulaitis, Vitas (tennis); Brooklyn, N.Y., 7/26/1954
Giacomin, Ed (hockey); Sudbury, Ontario, Canada, 6/6/1939
Gibson, Bob (baseball); Omaha, Neb., 11/9/1935
Gifford, Frank (football); Santa Monica, Calif., 8/16/1930
Gilbert, Rod (Rodrique) (hockey); Montreal, 7/1/1941
Giles, Warren (baseball executive); Tiskilwa, Ill. **(1896–1979)**
Gilmore, Artis (basketball); Chipley, Fla., 9/21/1949
Glance, Harvey (track); Phenix City, Ala., 3/28/1957
Gonzalez, Pancho (tennis); Los Angeles, 5/9/1928
Goodell, Brian Stuart (swimming); Stockton, Calif., 4/2/1959
Goodrich, Gail (basketball); Los Angeles, 4/23/1943
Goolagong Cawley, Evonne (tennis); Griffith, Australia, 7/31/1951
Gossage, Rich (Goose) (baseball); Colorado Springs, Colo., 4/5/1951
Gottfried, Brian (tennis); Baltimore, Md., 1/27/1952
Graham, David (golf); Windson, Australia, 5/23/1946
Graham, Otto Everett (football); Waukegan, Ill., 12/6/1921
Grange, Red (Harold) (football); Forksville, Pa., 6/13/1904
Green, Hubert (golf); Birmingham, Ala., 12/28/1946
Greene, Charles E. (sprinter); Pine Bluff, Ark., 3/21/1945
Gretzky, Wayne (hockey); Brantford, Ont., 1/26/1961
Griese, Bob (Robert Allen) (football); Evansville, Ind., 2/3/1945
Grove, Lefty (Robert Moses) (baseball); Lonaconing, Md., **(1900-1975)**
Groza, Lou (football); Martins Ferry, Ohio, 1/25/1924
Guidry, Ronald Ames (baseball); Lafayette, La., 8/28/1950
Gunter, Nancy Richey (tennis); San Angelo, Tex., 8/23/1942
Halas, George (football); Chicago **(1895-1983)**
Hall, Gary (swimming); Fayetteville, N.C., 8/7/1951
Hamill, Dorothy (figure skating); Chicago, 1956(?)
Hammond, Kathy (runner); Sacramento, Calif., 11/2/1951
Harris, Franco (football); Ft. Dix, N.J., 3/7/1950
Hartack, William, Jr. (jockey); Colver, Pa., 12/9/1932
Haughton, William (harness racing); Gloversville, N.Y. **(1923-1986)**
Havlicek, John (basketball); Martins Ferry, Ohio, 4/8/1940
Hayes, Elvin (basketball); Rayville, La., 11/17/1945
Hayes, Woody (football) Upper Arlington, Ohio **(1913-1987)**
Haynie, Sandra (golf); Fort Worth, 6/4/1943
Heiden, Eric (speed skating); Madison, Wis., 6/14/1958
Hencken, John (swimming); Culver City, Calif., 5/29/1954
Henderson, Rickey (baseball); Chicago, 12/25/1958
Henie, Sonja (ice skater); Oslo **(1912-1969)**
Hernandez, Keith (baseball); San Francisco, 10/20/1953
Hickcox, Charles (swimming); Phoenix, Ariz., 2/6/1947
Hines, James (sprinter); Dumas, Ark., 9/10/1946
Hodges, Gil (baseball); Princeton, Ind. **(1924-1972)**
Hogan, Ben (golf); Dublin, Tex., 8/13/1912
Holmes, Larry (boxing); Cuthert, Ga., 11/3/1949
Hornsby, Rogers (baseball); Winters, Tex. **(1896-1963)**
Hornung, Paul (football); Louisville, Ky., 12/23/1935
Houk, Ralph (baseball); Lawrence, Kan., 8/9/1919
Howard, Elston (baseball); St. Louis **(1929-1980)**
Howe, Gordon (hockey); Floral, Sask., Canada, 3/31/1928
Howell, Jim Lee (football); Lonoke, Ark., 9/27/1914
Howsen, Dick (baseball) Miami, Fla. **(1937-1987)**
Hubbell, Carl (baseball); Carthage, Mo., 6/22/1903
Huff, Sam (Robert Lee) (football); Morgantown, W. Va., 10/4/1934
Hull, Bobby (hockey); Point Anne, Ontario, Canada, 1/3/1939
Hunter, Jim (Catfish) (baseball); Hertford, N.C., 4/8/1946
Huntley, Joni (track); McMinnville, Ore., 8/4/1956
Hutson, Donald (football); Pine Bluff, Ark., 1/31/1913
Insko, Del (harness racing); Amboy, Minn., 7/10/1931
Irwin, Hale (golf); Joplin, Mo., 6/3/1945
Jackson, Reggie (baseball); Wyncote, Pa., 5/18/1946
Jeffries, James J. (boxing); Carroll, Ohio **(1875-1953)**
Jenkins, Ferguson Arthur (baseball); Chatham, Ontario, Canada, 12/13/1943
Jenner, (W.) Bruce (track); Mt. Kisco, N.Y., 10/28/1949
Jezek, Linda (swimming); Palo Alto, Calif., 3/10/1960
Johnson, Earvin (Magic) (basketball); E. Lansing, Mich., 8/14/1959
Johnson, Anthony (rowing); Washington, D.C., 11/16/1940
Johnson, Jack (John Arthur) (boxing); Galveston, Tex. **(1876-1946)**
Johnson, Rafer (decathlon); Hillsboro, Tex., 8/18/1935
Jones, Deacon (David) (football); Eatonville, Fla., 12/9/1938
Juantoreno, Alberto (track); Santiago, Cuba, 12/3/1951
Jurgensen, Sonny (football); Wilmington, N.C., 8/23/1934
Kaat, Jim (baseball); Zeeland, Mich., 11/7/1938
Kaline, Al (Albert) (baseball); Baltimore, 12/19/1934
Keino, Kipchoge (runner); Kapchemoiymo, Kenya, 1/?/1940
Kelly, Leroy (football); Philadelphia, 5/20/1942
Kelly, Red (Leonard Patrick) (hockey); Simcoe, Ontario, Canada, 7/9/1927
Killebrew, Harmon (baseball); Payette, Idaho, 6/29/1936
Killy, Jean-Claude (skiing); Saint-Cloud, France, 8/30/1943
Kilmer, Bill (William Orland) (football); Topeka, Kan., 9/5/1939
King, Billie Jean (Billie Jean Moffitt) (tennis); Long Beach, Calif., 11/22/1943

Kinsella, John (swimming); Oak Park, Ill., 8/26/1952
Kodes, Jan (tennis); Prague, 3/1/1946
Kolb, Claudia (swimming); Hayward, Calif., 12/19/1949
Koosman, Jerry Martin (baseball); Appleton, Minn., 12/23/1942
Korbut, Olga (gymnast); Grodno, Byelorussia, U.S.S.R., 5/16/1955
Koufax, Sandy (Sanford) (baseball); Brooklyn, N.Y., 12/30/1935
Kramer, Jack (tennis); Las Vegas, Nev., 8/1/1921
Kramer, Jerry (football); Jordan, Mont., 1/23/1936
Kuhn, Bowie Kent (baseball); Takoma Park, Md., 10/28/1926
Kwalik, Ted (Thaddeus John) (football); McKees Rocks, Pa., 4/15/1947
Lafleur, Guy Damien (hockey); Thurson, Quebec, Canada, 8/20/1951
Laird, Ronald (walker); Louisville, Ky., 5/31/1935
Lamonica, Daryle (football); Fresno, Calif., 7/17/1941
Landis, Kenesaw Mountain (1st baseball commissioner); Millville, Ohio **(1866-1944)**
Landry, Tom (football); Mission, Tex., 9/11/1924
Landy, John (runner); Australia, 4/4/1930
Larrieu, Francie (track); Palo Alto, Calif., 11/28/1952
Lasorda, Tom (baseball); Norristown, Pa., 9/22/1927
Laver, Rod (tennis); Rockhampton, Australia, 8/9/1938
Layne, Bobby (football) Lubbock, Texas **(1927-1986)**
Lendl, Ivan (tennis); Prague, 3/7/1960
Leonard, Benny (Benjamin Leiner) (boxing); New York City **(1896-1947)**
Leonard, Sugar Ray (boxing); Wilmington, N.C., 5/17/1956
Lewis, Carl (track); Willingboro, N.J., 7/1/1961
Linehan, Kim (swimming); Bronxville, N.Y., 12/11/1962
Liquori, Marty (runner); Montclair, N.J., 9/11/1949
Little, Floyd Douglas (football); New Haven, Conn., 7/4/1942
Little, Lou (football); Leominster, Mass., **(1893-1979)**
Littler, Gene (golf); La Jolla, Calif., 7/21/1930
Lloyd, Chris Evert (Christine Marie) (tennis); Fort Lauderdale, Fla., 12/21/1954
Lombardi, Vince (football); Brooklyn, N.Y. **(1913-1970)**
Longden, Johnny (horse racing); Wakefield, England, 2/14/1907
Lopez, Al (baseball); Tampa, Fla., 8/20/1908
Lopez, Nancy (golf); Torrance, Calif., 1/6/1957
Louis, Joe (Joe Louis Barrow) (boxing); Lafayette, Ala. **(1914-1981)**
Lynn, Frederic Michael (baseball); Chicago, Ill., 2/3/1952
Lynn, Janet (figure skating); Rockford, Ill., 4/6/1953
Mack, Connie (Cornelius Alexander McGillicuddy) (baseball executive); East Brookfield, Mass. **(1862-1956)**
Mackey, John (football); New York City, 9/24/1941
Mahovlich, Frank (Francis William) (hockey); Timmins, Ontario, Canada, 1/10/1938
Mahre, Phil (skiing); White Pass, Wash., 5/10/1957
Mandlikova, Hana (tennis); Prague, Czechoslovakia, 2/1962
Mann, Carol (golf); Buffalo, N.Y., 2/3/1941
Manning, Madeline (runner); Cleveland, 1/11/1948
Mantle, Mickey Charles (baseball); Spavinaw, Okla., 10/20/1931
Marciano, Rocky (boxing); Brockton, Mass. **(1923-1969)**
Marichal, Juan (baseball); Laguna Verde, Montecristi, Dominican Republic, 10/20/1937
Maris, Roger (baseball); Hibbing, Minn. **(1934-1985)**
Martin, Billy (Alfred Manuel) (baseball); Berkeley, Calif., 5/16/1928
Martin, Rick (Richard Lionel) (hockey); Verdun, Quebec, Canada, 7/26/1951
Mathews, Ed (Edwin) (baseball); Texarkana, Tex., 10/13/1931
Matson, Randy (shot putter); Kilgore, Tex., 3/5/1945
Mays, Willie (baseball); Westfield, Ala., 5/6/1931
McAdoo, Bob (basketball); Greensboro, N.C., 9/25/1951
McCarthy, Joe (Joseph Vincent) (baseball); Philadelphia **(1887-1978)**
McCovey, Willie Lee (baseball); Mobile, Ala., 1/10/1938
McEnroe, John Patrick, Jr. (tennis); Wiesbaden, Germany, 2/16/1959
McGraw, John Joseph (baseball); Truxton, N.Y. **(1873-1934)**
McLain, Dennis (baseball); Chicago, 3/24/1944
McMillan, Kathy Laverne (track); Raeford, N.C., 11/7/1957
Merrill, Janice (track); New London, Conn., 6/18/1962
Meyer, Deborah (swimming); Haddonfield, N.J., 8/14/1952
Middlecoff, Cary (golf); Halls, Tenn., 1/6/1921
Mikita, Stan (hockey); Sokolce, Czechoslovakia, 5/20/1940
Milburn, Rodney, Jr. (hurdler); Opelousas, La., 5/18/1950
Miller, Johnny (golf); San Francisco, 4/29/1947
Montgomery, Jim (swimming); Madison, Wis., 1/24/1955
Moore, Archie (boxing); Benoit, Miss., 12/13/1916
Morgan, Joe Leonard (baseball); Bonham, Tex., 9/19/1943
Morrall, Earl (football); Muskegon, Mich., 5/17/1934
Morton, Craig L. (football); Flint, Mich., 2/5/1943
Mosconi, Willie (pocket billiards); Philadelphia, 6/27/1913
Moser, Annemarie. *See* Proell, Annemarie
Moses, Edward Corley (track); Dayton, Ohio, 8/31/1958
Mungo, Van Lingo (baseball); Pageland, S.C. **(1911-1985)**
Munson, Thurman (baseball); Akron, Ohio, **(1947-1979)**
Murphy, Calvin (basketball), Norwalk, Conn., 5/9/1948
Musial, Stan (baseball); Donora, Pa., 11/21/1920
Myers, Linda (archery); York, Pa., 6/19/1947
Naber, John (swimming); Evanston, Ill., 1/20/1956
Namath, Joe (Joseph William) (football); Beaver Falls, Pa., 5/31/1943
Nastase, Ilie (tennis); Bucharest, 7/19/1946
Navratilova, Martina (tennis); Prague, 10/18/1956
Nehemiah, Renaldo (track); Newark, N.J., 3/24/1959
Nelson, Cindy (skiing); Lutsen, Minn., 8/19/1955
Newcombe, John (tennis); Sydney, Australia, 5/23/1943
Niekro, Phil (baseball); Lansing, Ohio, 4/1/1939
Nicklaus, Jack (golf); Columbus, Ohio, 1/21/1940
North, Lowell (yachting); Springfield, Mo., 12/2/1929
Oerter, Al (discus thrower); New York City, 9/19/1936
Okker, Tom (tennis); Amsterdam, 2/22/1944
Oldfield, Barney (racing driver); Fulton County, Ohio **(1878-1946)**
Oliva, Tony (Pedro) (baseball); Pinar Del Rio, Cuba, 7/20/1940
Olsen, Merlin Jay (football); Logan, Utah, 9/15/1940
O'Malley, Walter (baseball executive); New York City **(1903–1979)**
Orantes, Manuel (tennis); Granada, Spain, 2/6/1949
Orr, Bobby (hockey); Parry Sound, Ontario, Canada, 3/20/1948
Ovett, Steve (track); Brighton, England, 10/9/1955
Owens, Jesse (track); Decatur, Ala. **(1914-1980)**
Pace, Darrell (archery); Cincinnati, 10/23/1956
Paige, Satchel (Leroy) (baseball); Mobile, Ala., **(1906-1982)**
Palmer, Arnold (golf); Latrobe, Pa., 9/10/1929
Palmer, James Alvin (baseball); New York City, 10/15/1945
Parent, Bernard Marcel (hockey); Montreal, 4/3/1945
Park, Brad (Douglas Bradford) (hockey); Toronto, Ontario, Canada, 7/6/1948
Parseghian, Ara (football); Akron, Ohio, 5/21/1923
Pasarell, Charles (tennis); San Juan, Puerto Rico, 2/12/1944
Patterson, Floyd (boxing); Waco, N.C., 1/4/1935
Peete, Calvin (golf); Detroit, Mich., 7/18/1943
Pelé (Edson Arantes do Nascimento) (soccer); Tres Coracoes, Brazil, 10/23/1940
Perry, Gaylord (baseball); Williamston, N.C., 9/15/1938
Perry, Jim (baseball); Williamston, N.C., 9/15/1938
Pettit, Bob (basketball); Baton Rouge, La., 12/12/1932
Petty, Richard Lee (auto racing); Randleman, N.C., 7/2/1937
Pincay, Laffit, Jr. (jockey); Panama City, Panama, 12/29/1946
Plante, Jacques (hockey); Shawinigan Falls, Quebec, Canada, 1/17/1929
Player, Gary (golf); Johannesburg, South Africa, 11/1/1935
Plunkett, Jim (football); San Jose, Calif., 12/5/1947
Potvin, Denis Charles (hockey); Hull, Quebec, Canada, 10/29/1953
Powell, Boog (John) (baseball); Lakeland, Fla., 8/17/1941
Prefontaine, Steve Roland (runner); Coos Bay, Ore. **(1951-1975)**
Prince, Bob (baseball announcer); Pittsburgh **(1917-1985)**
Proell, Annemarie Moser (Alpine skier); Kleinarl, Austria, 3/27/1953
Ralston, Dennis (tennis); Bakersfield, Calif., 7/27/1942
Rankin, Judy Torluemke (golf); St. Louis, Mo., 2/18/1945
Ratelle, Jean (Joseph Gilbert Yvon Jean) (hockey); St. Jean, Quebec, Canada, 10/29/1953
Rawls, Betsy (Elizabeth Earle) (golf); Spartanburg, S.C., 5/4/1928
Reed, Willis (basketball); Hico, La., 6/25/1942
Reese, Pee Wee (Harold) (baseball); Ekron, Ky., 7/23/1919
Resch, Glenn "Chico" (hockey); Moose Jaw, Saskatchewan, Canada, 7/10/1948
Richard, Maurice (hockey); Montreal, 8/14/1924
Riessen, Martin (tennis); Hinsdale, Ill., 12/4/1941
Rigney, William (baseball); Alameda, Calif., 1/29/1918
Rizzuto, Phil (baseball); New York City, 9/25/1918
Roark, Helen Wills Moody (tennis); Centerville, Calif., 10/6/1906
Robertson, Oscar (basketball); Charlotte, Tenn., 11/24/1938
Robinson, Arnie (track); San Diego, Calif., 4/7/1948
Robinson, Brooks (baseball); Little Rock, Ark., 5/18/1937
Robinson, Frank (baseball); Beaumont, Tex., 8/31/1935
Robinson, Jackie (baseball); Cairo, Ga. **(1919-1972)**
Robinson, Larry Clark (hockey); Marvelville, Ontario, Canada, 6/2/1951
Robinson, (Sugar) Ray (boxing); Detroit, 5/3/1920
Rockne, Knute Kenneth (football); Voss, Norway **(1888-1931)**
Rockwell, Martha (skiing); Providence, R.I., 4/26/1944
Rono, Harry (track); Kiptaragon, Kenya, 2/12/1952
Rose, Pete (Peter Edward) (baseball); Cincinnati, 4/14/1942
Rosenbloom, Maxie (boxing); New York City **(1904-1976)**
Rosewall, Ken (tennis); Sydney, Australia, 11/2/1934
Rote, Kyle (football); San Antonio, 10/27/1928
Rozelle, Pete (Alvin Ray) (commissioner of National Football League); South Gate, Calif., 3/1/1926
Rudolph, Wilma Glodean (sprinter); St. Bethlehem, Tenn., 6/23/1940
Russell, Bill (basketball); Monroe, La., 2/12/1934
Ruth, Babe (George Herman Ruth) (baseball); Baltimore **(1895-1948)**
Rutherford, Johnny (auto racing); Fort Worth, 3/12/1938

Ryan, Nolan (Lynn Nolan, Jr.) (baseball); Refugio, Tex., 1/31/1947
Ryon, Luann (archery); Long Beach, Calif., 1/13/1953
Ryun, Jim (runner); Wichita, Kan., 4/29/1947
Salazar, Alberto (track); Havana, 8/7/1958
Samuels, Howard (horse racing, soccer); New York City **(1920-1984)**
Santana, Manuel (Manuel Santana Martinez) (tennis); Chamartin, Spain, 5/10/1938
Sayers, Gale (football); Wichita, Kan., 5/30/1943
Schmidt, Mike (baseball); Dayton, Ohio, 9/27/1949
Schoendienst, Al (Albert) (baseball); Germantown, Ill., 2/2/1923
Schollander, Donald (swimming); Charlotte, N.C., 4/30/1946
Seagren, Bob (Robert Lloyd) (pole vaulter); Pomona, Calif., 10/17/1946
Seaver, Tom (baseball); Fresno, Calif., 11/17/1944
Seidler, Maren (track); Brooklyn, N.Y., 6/11/1962
Selke, Frank (ice hockey); Canada **(1893-1985)**
Shepherd, Lee (auto racing) **(1945-1985)**
Shoemaker, Willie (jockey); Fabens, Tex., 8/19/1931
Shore, Eddie (ice hockey); Saskatchewan, Canada **(1902-1985)**
Shorter, Frank (runner); Munich, Germany, 10/31/1947
Shriver, Pam (tennis); Baltimore, 7/4/1962
Shula, Don (Donald Francis) (football); Grand River, Ohio, 1/4/1930
Silvester, Jay (discus thrower); Tremonton, Utah, 2/27/1937
Simpson, O. J. (Orenthal James) (football); San Francisco, 7/9/1947
Sims, Billy (football); St. Louis, 9/18/1955
Smith, Bubba (Charles Aaron) (football); Orange, Tex., 2/28/1945
Smith, Ronnie Ray (sprinter); Los Angeles, 3/28/1949
Smith, Stanley Roger (tennis); Pasadena, Calif., 12/14/1946
Smith, Tommie (sprinter); Clarksville, Tex., 6/5/1944
Smoke, Marcia Jones (canoeing); Oklahoma City, 7/18/1941
Snead, Sam (golf); Hot Springs, Va., 5/27/1912
Sneva, Tom (auto racing); Spokane, Wash., 6/1/1948
Snider, Duke (Edwin) (baseball); Los Angeles, 9/19/1926
Solomon, Harold (tennis); Washington, D.C., 9/17/1952
Spahn, Warren (baseball); Buffalo, N.Y., 4/23/1921
Speaker, Tristram (baseball); Hubbard City, Tex. **(1888-1958)**
Spinks, Leon (boxing); St. Louis, 7/11/1953
Spitz, Mark (swimming); Modesto, Calif., 2/10/1950
Stabler, Kenneth (football); Foley, Ala., 12/25/1945
Stagg, Amos Alonzo (football); West Orange, N.J. **(1862-1965)**
Stargell, Willie (Wilver Dornell) (baseball); Earlsboro, Okla., 3/6/1941
Starr, Bart (football); Montgomery, Ala., 1/9/1934
Staub, Daniel (Rusty) (baseball); New Orleans, 4/4/1944
Staubach, Roger (football); Cincinnati, 2/5/1942
Steinkraus, William C. (equestrian); Cleveland, 10/12/1925
Stenerud, Jan (football); Fetsund, Norway, 11/26/1942
Stengel, Casey (Charles Dillon) (baseball); Kansas City, Mo. **(1891-1975)**
Stenmark, Ingemar (Alpine skier); Tarnaby, Sweden, 3/18/1956
Stockton, Richard LaClede (tennis); New York City, 2/18/1951
Stones, Dwight Edwin (track); Los Angeles, 12/6/1953
Strawberry, Darryl (baseball); Los Angeles, 3/12/1962
Sullivan, John Lawrence (boxing); Boston **(1858-1918)**
Sutton, Don (Donald Howard) (baseball); Clio, Ala., 4/2/1945
Swann, Lynn (football); Alcoa, Tenn., 3/7/1952
Tanner, Leonard Roscoe III (tennis); Chattanooga, Tenn., 10/15/1951
Tarkenton, Fran (Francis) (football); Richmond, Va., 2/3/1940
Tebbetts, Birdie (George R.) (baseball); Nashua, N.H., 11/10/1914
Thoeni, Gustavo (Alpine skier); Trafoi, Italy, 2/28/1951
Thompson, David (basketball); Shelby, N.C., 7/13/1954
Thorpe, Jim (James Francis) (all-around athlete); nr. Prague, Okla. **(1888-1953)**
Tilden, William Tatem II (tennis); Philadelphia **(1893-1953)**
Tittle, Y. A. (Yelberton Abraham) (football); Marshall, Tex., 10/24/1926
Toomey, William (decathlon); Philadelphia, 1/10/1939
Trevino, Lee (golf); Dallas, 12/1/1939
Tunney, Gene (James J.) (boxing); New York City **(1898-1978)**
Tyus, Wyomia (runner); Griffin, Ga., 8/29/1945
Ueberroth, Peter (baseball); Evanston, Ill., 9/2/1937
Unitas, John (football); Pittsburgh, 5/7/1933
Unser, Al (auto racing); Albuquerque, N. Mex., 5/29/1939
Unser, Bobby (auto racing); Albuquerque N. Mex., 2/20/1934
Valenzuela, Fernando (baseball); Sonora, Mexico, 11/1/1960
Van Brocklin, Norm (football); Eagle Butte, S. Dak. **(1926-1983)**
Vilas, Guillermo (tennis); Mar del Plata, Argentina, 8/17/1952
Viren, Lasse (track); Myrskyla, Finland, 7/12/1949
Wade, Virginia (tennis); Bournemouth, England, 7/10/1945
Wagner, Honus (John Peter Honus) (baseball); Carnegie, Pa. **(1867-1955)**
Wakefield, Dick (baseball); Chicago **(1921-1985)**
Walcott, Jersey Joe (Arnold Cream) (boxing); Merchantville, N.J., 1/31/1914
Walsh, Adam (football) **(1902-1985)**
Walton, Bill (basketball); La Mesa, Calif., 11/5/1952
Waterfield, Bob (football); Burbank, Calif. **(1921–1983)**
Watson, Martha Rae (track); Long Beach, Calif., 8/19/1946
Watson, Tom (golf); Kansas City, Mo., 9/4/1949
Weaver, Earl (baseball); St. Louis, 8/14/1930
Webster, Alex (football); Kearny, N.J., 4/19/1931
Weiskopf, Tom (golf); Massillon, Ohio, 11/9/1942
Weiss, George (baseball executive); New Haven, Conn. **(1895-1972)**
Weissmuller, Johnny (swimmer and actor); Windber, Pa. **(1904-1984)**
Weld, Philip (sailing); Cambridge, Mass. **(1915-1984)**
West, Jerry (basketball); Cheylan, W. Va., 5/28/1938
White, Willye B. (long jumper); Money, Miss., 1/1/1936
Whitworth, Kathy (golf); Monahans, Tex., 9/27/1939
Widing, Juha (ice hockey); Vancouver, Canada **(1948-1985)**
Wilkens, Mac Maurice (track); Eugene, Ore., 11/15/1950
Wilkins, Lennie (basketball); 11/25/1937
Wilkinson, Bud (football); Minneapolis, 4/23/1916
Williams, Del (football); New Orleans **(1945-1984)**
Williams, Dick (baseball); St. Louis, 5/7/1929
Williams, Ted (baseball); San Diego, Calif., 8/30/1918
Wills, Maury (baseball); Washington, D.C., 10/2/1932
Winfield, Dave (baseball); St. Paul, Minn., 10/3/1951
Wohlhuter, Richard C. (runner); Geneva, Ill. 12/23/1945
Wood, Joseph (Smokey) (baseball); Kansas City, Mo. **(1890-1985)**
Woodhead, Cynthia (swimming); Riverside, Calif., 2/7/1964
Wottle, David James (runner); Canton, Ohio, 8/7/1950
Wright, Mickey (Mary Kathryn) (golf); San Diego, Calif., 2/14/1935
Yarborough, Cale (William Caleb) (auto racing); Timmonsville, S.C., 3/27/1939
Yarbrough, Leeroy (auto racing); Jacksonville, Fla. **(1938-1984)**
Yastrzemski, Carl (baseball); Southampton, N.Y., 8/22/1939
Young, Cy (Denton True) (baseball); Gilmore, Ohio **(1867-1955)**
Young, Sheila (speed skater, bicycle racer); Detroit, 10/14/1950

JIM THORPE'S OLYMPIC MEDALS RETURNED

More than 70 years after he won the pentathlon and decathlon at Stockholm, Sweden, Jim Thorpe's Olympic gold medals were returned posthumously to him by the International Olympic Committee. Thorpe, an Oklahoma Sac and Fox Indian, became one of the greatest all-around athletes ever produced in America. He was an all-American football player at the Carlisle Institute, an Indian trade school in Pennsylvania, and starred in baseball and track and field. After winning the medals in the 1912 Olympics, he was forced to give them up when he admitted he had played two seasons for money as a semipro baseball player in 1909 and 1910. Under the rules, he had lost his amateur status by taking money and thus was theoretically ineligible for the Olympics. In October of 1982, after many years of vigorous efforts by his family and other officials in athletics, the I.O.C. reinstated Thorpe in its archives as a co-winner of the two events. At ceremonies in Los Angeles in January 1983, Antonio Samaranch, president of the I.O.C. presented Thorpe's children with gold medals to replace those he had turned back. Thorpe, who later in his career played major-league baseball and pro football, died at the age of 65 in 1953.

THE OLYMPIC GAMES

(W)—Site of Winter Games. (S)—Site of Summer Games

1896	Athens
1900	Paris
1904	St. Louis
1906	Athens
1908	London
1912	Stockholm
1920	Antwerp
1924	Chamonix (W)
1924	Paris (S)
1928	St. Moritz (W)
1928	Amsterdam (S)
1932	Lake Placid (W)
1932	Los Angeles (S)
1936	Garmisch-Partenkirchen (W)
1936	Berlin (S)
1948	St. Moritz (W)
1948	London (S)
1952	Oslo (W)
1952	Helsinki (S)
1956	Cortina d'Ampezzo, Italy (W)
1956	Melbourne (S)
1960	Squaw Valley, Calif. (W)
1960	Rome (S)
1964	Innsbruck, Austria (W)
1964	Tokyo (S)
1968	Grenoble, France (W)
1968	Mexico City (S)
1972	Sapporo, Japan (W)
1972	Munich (S)
1976	Innsbruck, Austria (W)
1976	Montreal (S)
1980	Lake Placid (W)
1980	Moscow (S)
1984	Sarajevo, Yugoslavia (W)
1984	Los Angeles (S)
1988	Calgary, Alberta (W)
1988	Seoul, South Korea (S)

The first Olympic Games of which there is record were held in 776 B.C., and consisted of one event, a great foot race of about 200 yards held on a plain by the River Alpheus (now the Ruphia) just outside the little town of Olympia in Greece. It was from that date that the Greeks began to keep their calendar by "Olympiads," the four-year spans between the celebrations of the famous games.

The modern Olympic Games, which started in Athens in 1896, are the result of the devotion of a French educator, Baron Pierre de Coubertin, to the idea that, since young people and athletics have gone together through the ages, education and athletics might go hand-in-hand toward a better international understanding.

The principal organization responsible for the staging of the Games every four years is the International Olympic Committee (IOC). Other important roles are played by the National Olympic Committees in each participating country, international sports federations, and the organizing committee of the host city.

The headquarters of the 89-member International Olympic Committee are in Lausanne, Switzerland. The president of the IOC is Juan Antonio Samaranch of Spain.

The Olympic motto is "Citius, Altius, Fortius,"—"Faster, Higher, Stronger." The Olympic symbol is five interlocking circles colored blue, yellow, black, green, and red, on a white background, representing the five continents. At least one of those colors appears in the national flag of every country.

The ideal of peaceful international athletic competition has been severely tested the past four Olympiads, dating back to the 1972 raid by Arab terrorists on the Olympic village in Munich, Germany. Eleven Israelis, five terrorists, and a German police officer were all killed in the seige.

In 1976, political problems kept one-quarter of the IOC-member nations from competing. The most pressing was the conflict over recognition of Taiwan or Mainland China as the correct representative of that country. An additional 31 nations withdrew over the failure to bar New Zealand, which had a soccer team touring apartheid South Africa.

A total of 66 nations, including the United States, did not participate in 1980, over the Soviet Union's invasion of Afghanistan. Those Summer Games were scheduled for Moscow.

Considering this action, it was almost inevitable that the Soviet Union would take some similar action for the 1984 games, held in Los Angeles. Officially, the Soviet Union, and nearly the entire Soviet-communist bloc, withdrew over dissatisfaction with security measures in Los Angeles.

The 1988 games are scheduled for Seoul, South Korea, and there has been talk of a boycott my several Communist nations if North Korea is not included as a co-sponsor.

Summer Games

(EVENTS LISTED ARE THOSE CURRENTLY HELD)

TRACK AND FIELD—MEN

100-Meter Dash

1896	Thomas Burke, United States	12s
1900	Francis W. Jarvis, United States	10.8s
1904	Archie Hahn, United States	11s
1906	Archie Hahn, United States	11.2s
1908	Reginald Walker, South Africa	10.8s
1912	Ralph Craig, United States	10.8s
1920	Charles Paddock, United States	10.8s
1924	Harold Abrahams, Great Britain	10.6s
1928	Percy Williams, Canada	10.8s
1932	Eddie Tolan, United States	10.3s
1936	Jesse Owens, United States	10.3s[1]
1948	Harrison Dillard, United States	10.3s
1952	Lindy Remigino, United States	10.4s
1956	Bobby Morrow, United States	10.5s
1960	Armin Hary, Germany	10.2s
1964	Robert Hayes, United States	10s
1968	James Hines, United States	9.9s
1972	Valery Borzov, U.S.S.R.	10.14s
1976	Hasely Crawford, Trinidad and Tobago	10.06s
1980	Allan Wells, Britain	10.25s
1984	Carl Lewis, United States	9.99s

1. Wind assisted.

200-Meter Dash

1900	John Tewksbury, United States	22.2s
1904	Archie Hahn, United States	21.6s
1908	Robert Kerr, Canada	22.6s
1912	Ralph Craig, United States	21.7s

1920	Allan Woodring, United States	22s
1924	Jackson Scholz, United States	21.6s
1928	Percy Williams, Canada	21.8s
1932	Eddie Tolan, United States	21.2s
1936	Jesse Owens, United States	20.7s
1948	Melvin E. Patton, United States	21.1s
1952	Andrew Stanfield, United States	20.7s
1956	Bobby Morrow, United States	20.6s
1960	Livio Berruti, Italy	20.5s
1964	Henry Carr, United States	20.3s
1968	Tommie Smith, United States	19.8s
1972	Valery Borzov, U.S.S.R.	20s
1976	Don Quarrie, Jamaica	20.23s
1980	Pietro Mennea, Italy	20.19s
1984	Carl Lewis, United States	19.80s

400-Meter Dash

1896	Thomas Burke, United States	54.2s
1900	Maxwell Long, United States	49.4s
1904	Harry Hillman, United States	49.2s
1906	Paul Pilgrim, United States	53.2s
1908	Wyndham Halswelle, Great Britain (walkover)	50s
1912	Charles Reidpath, United States	48.2s
1920	Bevil Rudd, South Africa	49.6s
1924	Eric Liddell, Great Britain	47.6s
1928	Ray Barbuti, United States	47.8s
1932	William Carr, United States	46.2s
1936	Archie Williams, United States	46.5s
1948	Arthur Wint, Jamaica, B.W.I.	46.2s
1952	George Rhoden, Jamaica, B.W.I.	45.9s
1956	Charles Jenkins, United States	46.7s
1960	Otis Davis, United States	44.9s
1964	Mike Larrabee, United States	45.1s
1968	Lee Evans, United States	43.8s
1972	Vincent Matthews, United States	44.66s
1976	Alberto Juantorena, Cuba	44.26s
1980	Viktor Markin, U.S.S.R.	44.60s
1984	Alonzo Babers, United States	44.27s

800-Meter Run

1896	Edwin Flack, Australia	2m11s
1900	Alfred Tysoe, Great Britain	2m1.4s
1904	James Lightbody, United States	1m56s
1906	Paul Pilgrim, United States	2m1.2s
1908	Mel Sheppard, United States	1m52.8s
1912	Ted Meredith, United States	1m51.9s
1920	Albert Hill, Great Britain	1m53.4s
1924	Douglas Lowe, Great Britain	1m52.4s
1928	Douglas Lowe, Great Britain	1m51.8s
1932	Thomas Hampson, Great Britain	1m49.8s
1936	John Woodruff, United States	1m52.9s
1948	Malvin Whitfield, United States	1m49.2s
1952	Malvin Whitfield, United States	1m49.2s
1956	Tom Courtney, United States	1m47.7s
1960	Peter Snell, New Zealand	1m46.3s
1964	Peter Snell, New Zealand	1m45.1s
1968	Ralph Doubell, Australia	1m44.3s
1972	David Wottle, United States	1m45.9s
1976	Alberto Juantorena, Cuba	1m43.5s
1980	Steve Ovett, Britain	1m45.4s
1984	Joaquin Cruz, Brazil	1m43.0s

1,500-Meter Run

1896	Edwin Flack, Australia	4m33.2s
1900	Charles Bennett, Great Britain	4m6s
1904	James Lightbody, United States	4m5.4s
1906	James Lightbody, United States	4m12s
1908	Mel Sheppard, United States	4m3.4s
1912	Arnold Jackson, Great Britain	3m56.8s
1920	Albert Hill, Great Britain	4m1.8s
1924	Paavo Nurmi, Finland	3m53.6s
1928	Harry Larva, Finland	3m53.2s
1932	Luigi Beccali, Italy	3m51.2s
1936	Jack Lovelock, New Zealand	3m47.8s
1948	Henri Eriksson, Sweden	3m49.8s
1952	Joseph Barthel, Luxembourg	3m45.2s
1956	Ron Delany, Ireland	3m41.2s
1960	Herb Elliott, Australia	3m35.6s
1964	Peter Snell, New Zealand	3m38.1s
1968	Kipchoge Keino, Kenya	3m34.9s
1972	Pekka Vasala, Finland	3m36.3s
1976	John Walker, New Zealand	3m39.17s
1980	Sebastian Coe, Britain	3m38.4s
1984	Sebastian Coe, Britain	3m32.53s

5,000-Meter Run

1912	Hannes Kolehmainen, Finland	14m36.6s
1920	Joseph Guillemot, France	14m55.6s
1924	Paavo Nurmi, Finland	14m31.2s
1928	Willie Ritola, Finland	14m38s
1932	Lauri Lehtinen, Finland	14m30s
1936	Gunnar Hockert, Finland	14m22.2s
1948	Gaston Reiff, Belgium	14m17.6s
1952	Emil Zatopek, Czechoslovakia	14m6.6s
1956	Vladimir Kuts, U.S.S.R.	13m39.6s
1960	Murray Halberg, New Zealand	13m43.4s
1964	Bob Schul, United States	13m48.8s
1968	Mohamed Gammoudi, Tunisia	14m.05s
1972	Lasse Viren, Finland	13m26.4s
1976	Lasse Viren, Finland	13m24.76s
1980	Miruts Yifter, Ethiopia	13m21s
1984	Savd Advita, Morocco	13m5.59s

10,000-Meter Run

1912	Hannes Kolehmainen, Finland	31m20.8s
1920	Paavo Nurmi, Finland	31m45.8s
1924	Willie Ritola, Finland	30m23.2s
1928	Paavo Nurmi, Finland	30m18.8s
1932	Janusz Kusocinski, Poland	30m11.4s
1936	Ilmari Salminen, Finland	30m15.4s
1948	Emil Zatopek, Czechoslovakia	29m59.6s
1952	Emil Zatopek, Czechoslovakia	29m17s
1956	Vladimir Kuts, U.S.S.R.	28m45.6s
1960	Peter Bolotnikov, U.S.S.R.	28m32.2s
1964	Billy Mills, United States	28m24.4s
1968	Naftali Temu, Kenya	29m27.4s
1972	Lasse Viren, Finland	27m38.4s
1976	Lasse Viren, Finland	27m40.38s
1980	Miruts Yifter, Ethiopia	27m42.7s
1984	Alberto Cova, Italy	27m47.5s

Marathon

1896	Spiridon Loues, Greece	2h58m50s
1900	Michel Teato, France	2h59m45s
1904	Thomas Hicks, United States	3h28m53s
1906	William J. Sherring, Canada	2h51m23.65s
1908	John J. Hayes, United States	2h55m18.4s
1912	Kenneth McArthur, South Africa	2h36m54.8s
1920	Hannes Kolehmainen, Finland	2h32m35.8s
1924	Albin Stenroos, Finland	2h41m22.6s
1928	A. B. El Quafi, France	2h32m57s
1932	Juan Zabala, Argentina	2h31m36s
1936	Kitei Son, Japan	2h29m19.2s
1948	Delfo Cabrera, Argentina	2h34m51.6s
1952	Emil Zatopek, Czechoslovakia	2h23m3.2s
1956	Alain Mimoun, France	2h25m
1960	Abebe Bikila, Ethiopia	2h15m16.2s
1964	Abebe Bikila, Ethiopia	2h12m11.2s
1968	Mamo Wold, Ethiopia	2h20m26.4s
1972	Frank Shorter, United States	2h12m19.8s
1976	Walter Cierpinski, East Germany	2h09m55s
1980	Walter Cierpinski, East Germany	2h11m3s
1984	Carlos Lopes, Portugal	2hr9m.55s

110-Meter Hurdles

1896	Thomas Curtis, United States	17.6s
1900	Alvin Kraenzlein, United States	15.4s
1904	Frederick Schule, United States	16s
1906	R. G. Leavitt, United States	16.2s
1908	Forrest Smithson, United States	15s
1912	Frederick Kelly, United States	15.1s
1920	Earl Thomson, Canada	14.8s
1924	Daniel Kinsey, United States	15s
1928	Sydney Atkinson, South Africa	14.8s
1932	George Saling, United States	14.6s
1936	Forrest Towns, United States	14.2s
1948	William Porter, United States	13.9s
1952	Harrison Dillard, United States	13.7s
1956	Lee Calhoun, United States	13.5s
1960	Lee Calhoun, United States	13.8s
1964	Hayes Jones, United States	13.6s
1968	Willie Davenport, United States	13.3s
1972	Rodney Milburn, United States	13.24s
1976	Guy Drut, France	13.30s
1980	Thomas Munkett, East Germany	13.39s
1984	Roger Kingdom, United States	13.20s

200-Meter Hurdles

1900	Alvin Kraenzlein, United States	25.4s
1904	Harry Hillman, United States	24.6s

400-Meter Hurdles

1900	John Tewksbury, United States	57.6s
1904	Harry Hillman, United States	53s
1908	Charles Bacon, United States	55s
1920	Frank Loomis, United States	54s
1924	F. Morgan Taylor, United States	52.6s
1928	Lord David Burghley, Great Britain	53.4s
1932	Robert Tisdall, Ireland	51.8s[1]
1936	Glenn Hardin, United States	52.4s
1948	Roy Cochran, United States	51.1s
1952	Charles Moore, United States	50.8s
1956	Glenn Davis, United States	50.1s
1960	Glenn Davis, United States	49.3s
1964	Rex Cawley, United States	49.6s
1968	David Hemery, Great Britain	48.1s
1972	John Akii-Bua, Uganda	47.8s
1976	Edwin Moses, United States	47.64s
1980	Volker Beck, East Germany	48.70s
1984	Edwin Moses, United States	47.75s

1. Record not allowed.

2,500-Meter Steeplechase

1900	George Orton, United States	7m34s
1904	James Lightbody, United States	7m39.6s

3,000-Meter Steeplechase

1920	Percy Hodge, Great Britain	10m0.4s
1924	Willie Ritola, Finland	9m33.6s
1928	Toivo Loukola, Finland	9m21.8s
1932	Volmari Iso-Hollo, Finland	10m33.4s[1]
1936	Volmari Iso-Hollo, Finland	9m3.8s
1948	Thure Sjoestrand, Sweden	9m4.6s
1952	Horace Ashenfelter, United States	8m45.4s
1956	Chris Brasher, Great Britain	8m41.2s
1960	Zdzislaw Krzyskowiak, Poland	8m34.2s
1964	Gaston Roelants, Belgium	8m30.8s
1968	Amos Biwott, Kenya	8m51s
1972	Kipchoge Keino, Kenya	8m23.6s
1976	Anders Gardervd, Sweden	8m08.02s
1980	Bronislaw Malinowski, Poland	8m9.7s
1984	Julius Korir, Kenya	8m11.80s

1. About 3,450 meters—extra lap by error.

10,000-Meter Walk

1912	George Goulding, Canada	46m28.4s
1920	Ugo Frigerio, Italy	48m6.2s
1924	Ugo Frigerio, Italy	47m49s
1948	John Mikaelsson, Sweden	45m13.2s
1952	John Mikaelsson, Sweden	45m2.8s

20,000-Meter Walk

1956	Leonid Spirin, U.S.S.R.	1h31m27.4s
1960	Vladimir Golubnichy, U.S.S.R.	1h34m7.2s
1964	Ken Mathews, Great Britain	1h29m34s
1968	Vladimir Golubnichy, U.S.S.R.	1h33m58.4s
1972	Peter Frenkel, East Germany	1h26m42.4s
1976	Daniel Bautista, Mexico	1h24m40.6s
1980	Maurizio Damiliano, Italy	1h23m35.5s
1984	Ernesto Conto, Mexico	1m23.13s

50,000-Meter Walk

1932	Thomas W. Green, Great Britain	4h50m10s
1936	Harold Whitlock, Great Britain	4h30m41.1s
1948	John Ljunggren, Sweden	4h41m52s
1952	Giuseppe Dordoni, Italy	4h28m7.8s
1956	Norman Read, New Zealand	4h30m42.8s
1960	Donald Thompson, Great Britain	4h25m30s
1964	Abdon Pamich, Italy	4h11m12.4s
1968	Christoph Hohne, East Germany	4h20m13.6s
1972	Bern Kannernberg, West Germany	3h56m11.6s
1980	Hartwig Gauder, East Germany	3h49m24s
1984	Raul Gonzalez, Mexico	3hr47m26s

400-Meter Relay (4 × 100)

1912	Great Britain	42.4s
1920	United States	42.2s
1924	United States	41s
1928	United States	41s
1932	United States	40s
1936	United States	39.8s
1948	United States	40.6s
1952	United States	40.1s
1956	United States	39.5s
1960	Germany	39.5s
1964	United States	39s
1968	United States	38.2s
1972	United States	38.19s
1976	United States	38.33s
1980	U.S.S.R.	38.26s
1984	United States	37.83s

1,600-Meter Relay (4 × 400)

1912	United States	3m16.6s
1920	Great Britain	3m22.2s
1924	United States	3m16s
1928	United States	3m14.2s
1932	United States	3m8.2s
1936	Great Britain	3m9s
1948	United States	3m10.4s
1952	Jamaica, B.W.I.	3m3.9s
1956	United States	3m4.8s
1960	United States	3m2.2s
1964	United States	3m0.7s
1968	United States	2m56.1s
1972	Kenya	2m59.8s
1976	United States	2m58.65s
1980	U.S.S.R.	3m01.1s
1984	United States	2m57.91s

Team Race

		Pts
1900	Great Britain (5,000 meters)	26
1904	United States (4 miles)	27
1908	Great Britain (3 miles)	6
1912	United States (3,000 meters)	9

1920	United States (3,000 meters)	10
1924	Finland (3,000 meters)	9

Standing High Jump

1900	Ray Ewry, United States	5 ft 5 in.
1904	Ray Ewry, United States	4 ft 11 in.
1906	Ray Ewry, United States	5 ft 1 5/8 in.
1908	Ray Ewry, United States	5 ft 2 in.
1912	Platt Adams, United States	5 ft 4 1/8 in.

Running High Jump

1896	Ellery Clark, United States	5 ft 11 1/4 in.
1900	Irving Baxter, United States	6 ft 2 3/4 in.
1904	Samuel Jones, United States	5 ft 11 in.
1906	Con Leahy, Ireland	5 ft 9 7/8 in.
1908	Harry Porter, United States	6 ft 3 in.
1912	Alma Richards, United States	6 ft 4 in.
1920	Richmond Landon, United States	6 ft 4 1/4 in.
1924	Harold Osborn, United States	6 ft 5 15/16 in.
1928	Robert W. King, United States	6 ft 4 3/8 in.
1932	Duncan McNaughton, Canada	6 ft 5 5/8 in.
1936	Cornelius Johnson, United States	6 ft 7 15/16 in.
1948	John Winter, Australia	6 ft 6 in.
1952	Walter Davis, United States	6 ft 8 5/16 in.
1956	Charles Dumas, United States	6 ft 11 1/4 in.
1960	Robert Shavlakadze, U.S.S.R.	7 ft 1 in.
1964	Valeri Brumel, U.S.S.R.	7 ft 1 3/4 in.
1968	Dick Fosbury, United States	7 ft 4 1/4 in.
1972	Yuri Tarmak, U.S.S.R.	7 ft 3 3/4 in.
1976	Jacek Wszola, Poland	(2.25m) 7 ft 4 1/2 in.
1980	Gerd Wessig, East Germany	7 ft 8 3/4 in.
1984	Dietmar Mogenburg, West Germany	7 ft 8 1/2 in.

Long Jump

1896	Ellery Clark, United States	20 ft 9 3/4 in.
1900	Alvin Kraenzlein, United States	23 ft 6 7/8 in.
1904	Myer Prinstein, United States	24 ft 1 in.
1906	Myer Prinstein, United States	23 ft 7 1/2 in.
1908	Frank Irons, United States	24 ft 6 1/2 in.
1912	Albert Gutterson, United States	24 ft 11 1/4 in.
1920	William Petterssen, Sweden	23 ft 5 1/2 in.
1924	DeHart Hubbard, United States	24 ft 5 1/8 in.
1928	Edward B. Hamm, United States	25 ft 4 3/4 in.
1932	Edward Gordon, United States	25 ft 3/4 in.
1936	Jesse Owens, United States	26 ft. 5 5/16 in.
1948	Willie Steele, United States	25 ft 8 in.
1952	Jerome Biffle, United States	24 ft 10 in.
1956	Gregory Bell, United States	25 ft 8 1/4 in.
1960	Ralph Boston, United States	26 ft 7 3/4 in.
1964	Lynn Davies, Great Britain	26 ft 5 3/4 in.
1968	Bob Beamon, United States	29 ft 2 1/2 in.
1972	Randy Williams, United States	27 ft 1/2 in.
1976	Arnie Robinson, United States	(8.35m) 24 ft 7 3/4 in.
1980	Lutz Dombrowski, E. Germany	28 ft 1/4 in.
1984	Carl Lewis, United States	28 ft 1/4 in.

Triple Jump

1896	James B. Connolly, United States	45 ft
1900	Myer Prinstein, United States	47 ft 4 1/4 in.
1904	Myer Prinstein, United States	47 ft
1906	P. G. O'Connor, Ireland	46 ft 2 in.
1908	Timothy Ahearne, Great Britain	48 ft 11 1/4 in.
1912	Gustaf Lindblom, Sweden	48 ft 5 1/8 in.
1920	Vilho Tuulos, Finland	47 ft 6 7/8 in.
1924	Archie Winter, Australia	50 ft 11 1/8 in.
1928	Mikio Oda, Japan	49 ft 10 13/16 in.
1932	Chuhei Nambu, Japan	51 ft 7 in.
1936	Naoto Tajima, Japan	52 ft 5 7/8 in.
1948	Arne Ahman, Sweden	50 ft 6 1/4 in.
1952	Adhemar da Silva, Brazil	53 ft 2 1/2 in.
1956	Adhemar da Silva, Brazil	53 ft 7 1/2 in.
1960	Jozef Schmidt, Poland	55 ft 1 3/4 in.
1964	Jozef Schmidt, Poland	55 ft 3 1/4 in.
1968	Viktor Saneyev, U.S.S.R.	57 ft 3/4 in.
1972	Viktor Saneyev, U.S.S.R.	56 ft 11 in.
1976	Viktor Saneyev, U.S.S.R.	(17.29m) 56 ft 8 3/4 in.
1980	Jaak Uudmae, U.S.S.R.	56 ft 11 1/8 in.
1984	Al Joyner, United States	56 ft 7 1/2 in.

Pole Vault

1896	William Hoyt, United States	10 ft 9 3/4 in.
1900	Irving Baxter, United States	10 ft 9 7/8 in.
1904	Charles Dvorak, United States	11 ft 6 in.
1906	Fernand Gouder, France	11 ft 6 in.
1908	Alfred Gilbert, United States, and Edward Cook, United States (tie)	12 ft 2 in.
1912	Harry Babcock, United States	12 ft 11 1/2 in.
1920	Frank Foss, United States	13 ft 5 9/16 in.
1924	Lee Barnes, United States	12 ft 11 1/2 in.
1928	Sabin W. Carr, United States	13 ft 9 3/8 in.
1932	William Miller, United States	14 ft 1 7/8 in.
1936	Earle Meadows, United States	14 ft 3 1/4 in.
1948	Guinn Smith, United States	14 ft 1 1/4 in.
1952	Robert Richards, United States	14 ft 11 1/8 in.
1956	Robert Richards, United States	14 ft 11 1/2 in.
1960	Don Bragg, United States	15 ft 5 1/8 in.
1964	Fred Hansen, United States	16 ft 8 3/4 in.
1968	Bob Seagren, United States	17 ft 8 1/2 in.
1972	Wolfgang Nordwig, East Germany	18 ft 1/2 in.
1976	Tadeusz Slusarski, Poland	(5.50m) 18 ft 1/2 in.
1980	Wladyslaw Kozakiewicz, Poland	18 ft 11 1/2 in.
1984	Pierre Quinon, France	18 ft 10 1/4 in.

16-lb Shot-Put

1896	Robert Garrett, United States	36 ft 9 3/4 in.
1900	Richard Sheldon, United States	46 ft 3 1/8 in.
1904	Ralph Rose, United States	48 ft 7 in.
1906	Martin Sheridan, United States	40 ft 4 4/5 in.
1908	Ralph Rose, United States	46 ft 7 1/2 in.
1912	Pat McDonald, United States	50 ft 4 in.
1920	Ville Porhola, Finland	48 ft 7 1/8 in.
1924	Clarence Houser, United States	49 ft 2 1/2 in.
1928	John Kuck, United States	52 ft 11 11/16 in.
1932	Leo Sexton, United States	52 ft 6 3/16 in.
1936	Hans Woellke, Germany	53 ft 1 3/4 in.
1948	Wilbur Thompson, United States	56 ft 2 in.
1952	Parry O'Brien, United States	57 ft 1 1/2 in.
1956	Parry O'Brien, United States	60 ft 11 in.
1960	Bill Nieder, United States	64 ft 6 3/4 in.
1964	Dallas Long, United States	66 ft 8 1/4 in.
1968	Randy Matson, United States	67 ft 4 3/4 in.
1972	Wladyslaw Komar, Poland	69 ft 6 in.
1976	Udo Beyer, East Germany	(21.05m) 69 ft 3/4 in.
1980	Vladimir Kiselyov, U.S.S.R.	70 ft 1/2 in.
1984	Alessandro Andrei, Italy	69 ft 9 in.

Discus Throw

1896	Robert Garrett, United States	95 ft 7 1/2 in.
1900	Rudolf Bauer, Hungary	118 ft 2 7/8 in.
1904	Martin Sheridan, United States	128 ft 10 1/2 in.
1906	Martin Sheridan, United States	136 ft 1/3 in.
1908	Martin Sheridan, United States	134 ft 2 in.
1912	Armas Taipale, Finland	145 ft 9/16 in.
1920	Elmer Niklander, Finland	146 ft 7 in.
1924	Clarence Houser, United States	151 ft 5 1/4 in.
1928	Clarence Houser, United States	155 ft 2 4/5 in.
1932	John Anderson, United States	162 ft 4 7/8 in.
1936	Ken Carpenter, United States	165 ft 7 3/8 in.
1948	Adolfo Consolini, Italy	173 ft 2 in.
1952	Simeon Iness, United States	180 ft 6 1/2 in.
1956	Al Oerter, United States	184 ft 10 1/2 in.
1960	Al Oerter, United States	194 ft 2 in.
1964	Al Oerter, United States	200 ft 1 1/2 in.
1968	Al Oerter, United States	212 ft 6 in.
1972	Ludvik Danek, Czechoslovakia	211 ft 3 in.

1976	Mac Wilkins, United States	(67.5m) 221 ft 5 in.
1980	Viktor Rashchupkin, U.S.S.R.	218 ft 8 in.
1984	Rolf Dannenberg, West Germany	218 ft 6 in.

Javelin Throw

1906	Eric Lemming, Sweden	175 ft 6 in.
1908	Eric Lemming, Sweden	179 ft 10 1/2 in.
1912	Eric Lemming, Sweden	198 ft 11 1/4 in.
1920	Jonni Myyra, Finland	215 ft 9 3/4 in.
1924	Jonni Myyra, Finland	206 ft 6 3/4 in.
1928	Eric Lundquist, Sweden	218 ft 6 1/8 in.
1932	Matti Jarvinen, Finland	238 ft 7 in.
1936	Gerhard Stoeck, Germany	235 ft 8 5/16 in.
1948	Kaj Rautavaara, Finland	228 ft 10 1/2 in.
1952	Cy Young, United States	242 ft 3/4 in.
1956	Egil Danielsen, Norway	281 ft 2 1/4 in.
1960	Viktor Tsibulenko, U.S.S.R.	277 ft 8 3/8 in.
1964	Pauli Nevala, Finland	271 ft 2 1/4 in.
1968	Janis Lusis, U.S.S.R.	295 ft 7 in.
1972	Klaus Wolfermann, West Germany	296 ft 10 in.
1976	Miklos Nemeth, Hungary	(94.58m) 310 ft 4 in.
1980	Dainis Kula, U.S.S.R.	299 ft 2 3/8 in.
1984	Arto Haerkoenen, Finland	284 ft 8 in.

16-lb Hammer Throw

1900	John Flanagan, United States	167 ft 4 in.
1904	John Flanagan, United States	168 ft 1 in.
1908	John Flanagan, United States	170 ft 4 1/4 in.
1912	Matt McGrath, United States	179 ft 7 1/8 in.
1920	Pat Ryan, United States	173 ft 5 5/8 in.
1924	Fred Tootell, United States	174 ft 10 1/4 in.
1928	Patrick O'Callaghan, Ireland	168 ft 7 1/2 in.
1932	Patrick O'Callaghan, Ireland	176 ft 11 1/8 in.
1936	Karl Hein, Germany	185 ft 4 in.
1948	Imre Nemeth, Hungary	183 ft 11 1/2 in.
1952	Jozsef Csermak, Hungary	197 ft 11 9/16 in.
1956	Harold Connolly, United States	207 ft 2 3/4 in.
1960	Vasily Rudenkov, U.S.S.R.	220 ft 1 5/8 in.
1964	Romuald Klim, U.S.S.R.	228 ft 9 1/2 in.
1968	Gyula Zsivotzky, Hungary	240 ft 8 in.
1972	Anatoly Bondarchuk, U.S.S.R.	247 ft 8 1/2 in.
1976	Yuri Sedykh, U.S.S.R.	(77.52m) 254 ft 4 in.
1980	Yuri Sedykh, U.S.S.R.	(81.80m) 268 ft 4 1/2 in.
1984	Juha Tiainen, Finland	256 ft 2 in.

Decathlon

1912	Jim Thorpe, United States	—
	Hugo Wieslander, Sweden	—
1920	Helge Lovland, Norway	6,804.35 pts.
1924	Harold Osborn, United States	7,710.775 pts.
1928	Paavo Yrjola, Finland	8,053.29 pts.
1932	James Bausch, United States	8,462.23 pts.
1936	Glenn Morris, United States	7,900 pts.[1]
1948	Robert B. Mathias, United States	7,139 pts.
1952	Robert B. Mathias, United States	7,887 pts.
1956	Milton Campbell, United States	7,937 pts.
1960	Rafer Johnson, United States	8,392 pts.
1964	Willi Holdorf, Germany	7,887 pts.[1]
1968	Bill Toomey, United States	8,193 pts.
1972	Nikolai Avilov, U.S.S.R.	8,454 pts.
1976	Bruce Jenner, United States	8,618 pts.
1980	Daley Thompson, Britain	8,495 pts.
1984	Daley Thompson, Britain	8,797 pts.

1. Point system revised.

TRACK AND FIELD—WOMEN

100-Meter Dash

1928	Elizabeth Robinson, United States	12.2s
1932	Stella Walsh, Poland	11.9s
1936	Helen Stephens, United States	11.5s
1948	Fanny Blankers-Koen, Netherlands	11.9s
1952	Marjorie Jackson, Australia	11.5s
1956	Betty Cuthbert, Australia	11.5s
1960	Wilma Rudolph, United States	11s
1964	Wyomia Tyus, United States	11.4s
1968	Wyomia Tyus, United States	11s
1972	Renate Stecher, East Germany	11.07s
1976	Annegret Richter, West Germany	11.08s
1980	Lyudmila Kondratyeva, U.S.S.R.	11.06s

200-Meter Dash

1948	Fanny Blankers-Koen, Netherlands	24.4s
1952	Marjorie Jackson, Australia	23.7s
1956	Betty Cuthbert, Australia	23.4s
1960	Wilma Rudolph, United States	24s
1964	Edith McGuire, United States	23s
1968	Irena Szewinska, Poland	22.5s
1972	Renate Stecher, East Germany	22.4s
1976	Baerbel Eckert, East Germany	22.37s
1980	Barbara Wockel, East Germany	22.03s
1984	Valerie Brisco-Hooks, United States	21.81s

400-Meter Dash

1964	Betty Cuthbert, Australia	52s
1968	Colette Besson, France	52s
1972	Monika Zehrt, East Germany	51.08s
1976	Irena Szewinska, Poland	49.29s
1980	Marita Koch, East Germany	48.88s
1984	Valerie Brisco-Hooks, United States	48.83s

800-Meter Run

1928	Lina Radke, Germany	2m16.8s
1960	Ljudmila Shevcova, U.S.S.R.	2m4.3s
1964	Ann Packer, Great Britain	2m1.1s
1968	Madeline Manning, United States	2m0.9s
1972	Hildegard Falck, West Germany	1m58.6s
1976	Tatiana Kazankina, U.S.S.R.	1m54.94s
1980	Nadezhda Olizarenko, U.S.S.R.	1m53.5s
1984	Doina Melinte, Romania	1m57.60s

1,500-Meter Run

1972	Ludmila Bragina, U.S.S.R.	4m01.4s
1976	Tatiana Kazankina, U.S.S.R.	4m05.48s

3,000-Meter Run

1984	Maricica Puica, Romania	8m35.96s

80-Meter Hurdles

1932	Mildred Didrikson, United States	11.7s
1936	Trebisonda Valla, Italy	11.7s
1948	Fanny Blankers-Koen, Netherlands	11.2s
1952	Shirley S. de la Hunty, Australia	10.9s
1956	Shirley S. de la Hunty, Australia	10.7s
1960	Irina Press, U.S.S.R.	10.8s
1964	Karin Balzer, Germany	10.5s[1]
1968	Maureen Caird, Australia	10.3s

1. Wind assisted.

100-Meter Hurdles

1972	Annelie Ehrhardt, East Germany	12.59s
1976	Johanna Schaller, East Germany	12.77s
1980	Vera Komisova, U.S.S.R.	12.56s
1984	Benita Fitzgerald-Brown, United States	12.84s

400-Meter Hurdle

1984	Nawai El Moutawakel, Morocco	54.61s

400-Meter Relay

1928	Canada	48.4s
1932	United States	47s
1936	United States	46.9s
1948	Netherlands	47.5s
1952	United States	45.9s
1956	Australia	44.5s
1960	United States	44.5s
1964	Poland	43.6s
1968	United States	42.8s
1972	West Germany	42.81s
1976	East Germany	42.55s
1980	East Germany	41.60s
1984	United States	41.65s

1,600-Meter Relay

1972	East Germany	3m23s
1976	East Germany	3m19.23s
1980	U.S.S.R.	3m20.2s
1984	United States	3m18.29s

Marathon

1984	Joan Benoit, United States	2 hr 24 m 52s

Running High Jump

1928	Ethel Catherwood, Canada	5 ft 3 in.
1932	Jean Shiley, United States	5 ft 5 1/4 in.
1936	Ibolya Csak, Hungary	5 ft 3 in.
1948	Alice Coachman, United States	5 ft 6 1/8 in.
1952	Ester Brand, South Africa	5 ft 5 3/4 in.
1956	Mildred McDaniel, United States	5 ft 9 1/4 in.
1960	Iolanda Balas, Romania	6 ft 3/4 in.
1964	Iolanda Balas, U.S.S.R.	6 ft 2 3/4 in.
1968	Miloslava Rezkova, Czechoslovakia	5 ft 11 3/4 in.
1972	Ulrike Meyfarth, West Germany	6 ft 3 5/8 in.
1976	Rosemarie Ackerman, E. Germany	(1.93m) 6 ft 4 in.
1980	Sara Simeoni, Italy	6 ft 5 1/2 in.
1984	Ulrike Meyfarth, West Germany	6 ft 7 1/2 in.

Long Jump

1948	Olga Gyarmati, Hungary	18 ft 8 1/4 in.
1952	Yvette Williams, New Zealand	20 ft 5 3/4 in.
1956	Elzbieta Krzesinska, Poland	20 ft 9 3/4 in.
1960	Vera Krepkina, U.S.S.R.	20 ft 10 3/4 in.
1964	Mary Rand, Great Britain	22 ft 2 in.
1968	Viorica Ciscopoleanu, Romania	22 ft 4 1/2 in.
1972	Heidemarie Rosendahl, West Germany	22 ft 3 in.
1976	Angela Voigt, East Germany	(6.72m) 22 ft 1/2 in.
1980	Tatiana Kolpakova, U.S.S.R.	23 ft 2 in.
1984	Anisoara Stanciu, Romania	22 ft 10 in.

Shot-Put

1948	Micheline Ostermeyer, France	45 ft 1 1/2 in.
1952	Galina Zybina, U.S.S.R.	50 ft 1 1/2 in.
1956	Tamara Tishkyevich, U.S.S.R.	54 ft 5 in.
1960	Tamara Press, U.S.S.R.	56 ft 9 7/8 in.
1964	Tamara Press, U.S.S.R.	59 ft 6 in.
1968	Margitta Gummel, East Germany	64 ft 4 in.
1972	Nadezhda Chizhova, U.S.S.R.	69 ft
1976	Ivanka Christova, Bulgaria	(21.16m) 69 ft 5 in.
1980	Ilona Sluplanek, East Germany	73 ft 6 in.
1984	Claudia Losch, West Germany	67 ft 2 1/4 in.

Discus Throw

1928	Helena Konopacka, Poland	129 ft 11 7/8 in.
1932	Lillian Copeland, United States	133 ft 2 in.
1936	Gisela Mauermayer, Germany	156 ft 3 3/16 in.
1948	Micheline Ostermeyer, France	137 ft 6 1/2 in.
1952	Nina Romaschkova, U.S.S.R.	168 ft 8 7/16 in.
1956	Olga Fikotova, Czechoslovakia	176 ft 1 1/2 in.
1960	Nina Ponomareva, U.S.S.R.	180 ft 8 1/4 in.
1964	Tamara Press, U.S.S.R.	187 ft 10 3/4 in.
1968	Lia Manoliu, Romania	191 ft 2 1/2 in.
1972	Faina Melnik, U.S.S.R.	218 ft 7 in.
1976	Evelin Schlaak, East Germany	(69.0m) 226 ft 4 in.
1980	Evelin Jahl, East Germany	229 ft 6 1/2 in.
1984	Ria Stalman, Netherlands	214 ft 5 in.

Javelin Throw

1932	Mildred Didrikson, United States	143 ft 4 in.
1936	Tilly Fleischer, Germany	148 ft 2 3/4 in.
1948	Herma Bauma, Austria	149 ft 6 in.
1952	Dana Zatopek, Czechoslovakia	165 ft 7 in.
1956	Inessa Janzeme, U.S.S.R.	176 ft 8 in.
1960	Elvira Ozolina, U.S.S.R.	183 ft 8 in.
1964	Mihaela Penes, Romania	198 ft 7 1/2 in.
1968	Angela Nemeth, Hungary	198 ft 0 in.
1972	Ruth Fuchs, East Germany	209 ft 7 in.
1976	Ruth Fuchs, East Germany	(65.94m) 216 ft 4 in.
1980	Maria Colon, Cuba	224 ft 5 in.
1984	Tessa Sanderson, Britain	228 ft 2 in.

Pentathlon

1964	Irina Press, U.S.S.R.	5,246 pts.
1968	Ingrid Becker, West Germany	5,098 pts.
1972	Mary Peters, Britain	4,801 pts.
1976	Siegrun Siegl, East Germany	4,745 pts.
1980	Nadyezhda Tkachenko, U.S.S.R.	5,083 pts.
1984	Daniele Masala, Italy	5,469 pts.

SWIMMING—MEN

100 Meters Freestyle

1896	Alfred Hajos, Hungary	1m22.2s
1904	Zoltan de Halmay, Hungary	1m2.8s[1]
1906	Charles Daniels, United States	1m13s
1908	Charles Daniels, United States	1m5.6s
1912	Duke P. Kahanamoku, United States	1m3.4s
1920	Duke P. Kahanamoku, United States	1m1.4s
1924	John Weissmuller, United States	59s
1928	John Weissmuller, United States	58.6s
1932	Yasuji Miyazaki, Japan	58.2s
1936	Ferenc Csik, Hungary	57.6s
1948	Walter Ris, United States	57.3s
1952	Clarke Scholes, United States	57.4s
1956	Jon Henricks, Australia	55.4s
1960	John Devitt, Australia	55.2s
1964	Don Schollander, United States	53.4s
1968	Michael Wenden, Australia	52.2s
1972	Mark Spitz, United States	51.22s
1976	Jim Montgomery, United States	49.99s
1980	Jorg Woithe, East Germany	50.40s
1984	Rowdy Gaines, United States	49.80s

1. 100 yards.

200-Meter Freestyle

1900	Frederick Lane, Australia	2m25.2s
1904	Charles Daniels, United States	2m44.2s[1]
1968	Michael Wenden, Australia	1m55.2s
1972	Mark Spitz, United States	1m52.78s
1976	Bruce Furniss, United States	1m50.29s
1980	Sergei Kopliakov, U.S.S.R.	1m49.81s
1984	Michael Gross, West Germany	1m47.44s

1. 220 yards

400-Meter Freestyle

1896	Paul Neumann, Austria	8m12.6s[1]
1904	Charles Daniels, United States	6m16.2s[2]
1906	Otto Sheff, Austria	6m23.8s
1908	Henry Taylor, Great Britain	5m36.8s

1912	George Hodgson, Canada	5m24.4s
1920	Norman Ross, United States	5m26.8s
1926	Jonn Weissmuller, United States	5m4.2s
1928	Albert Zorilla, Argentina	5m1.6s
1932	Clarence Crabbe, United States	4m48.4s
1936	Jack Medica, United States	4m44.5s
1948	William Smith, United States	4m41s
1952	Jean Boiteux, France	4m30.7s
1956	Murray Rose, Australia	4m27.3s
1960	Murray Rose, Australia	4m18.3s
1964	Don Schollander, United States	4m12.2s
1968	Mike Burton, United States	4m9s
1972	Bradford Cooper, Australia	4m00.27s[3]
1976	Brian Goodell, United States	3m51.93s
1980	Vladimir Salnikov, U.S.S.R.	3m51.31s
1984	George DiCarlo, United States	3m51.23s

1. 500 meters. 2. 440 yards. 3. Rick DeMont, United States, won but was disqualified following day for medical reasons.

1,500 Meter Freestyle

1904	Emil Rausch, Germany	27m18.2s[1]
1906	Henry Taylor, Great Britain	28m28s[2]
1908	Henry Taylor, Great Britain	22m48.4s
1912	George Hodgson, Canada	22m
1920	Norman Ross, United States	22m23.2s
1924	Andrew Charlton, Australia	20m6.6s
1928	Arne Borg, Sweden	19m51.8s
1932	Kusuo Kitamura, Japan	19m12.4s
1936	Noboru Terada, Japan	19m13.7s
1948	James McLane, United States	19m18.5s
1952	Ford Konno, United States	18m30s
1956	Murray Rose, Australia	17m58.9s
1960	Jon Konrads, Australia	17m19.6s
1964	Robert Windle, Australia	17m1.7s
1968	Michael Burton, United States	16m38.9s
1972	Michael Burton, United States	15m52.58s
1976	Brian Goodell, United States	15m02.4s
1980	Vladimir Salnikov, U.S.S.R.	14m58.27s
1984	Michael O'Brien, United States	15m05.2s

1. One mile. 2. 1,600 meters

100-Meter Backstroke

1904	Walter Brack, Germany	1m16.8s[1]
1908	Arno Bieberstein, Germany	1m24.6s
1912	Harry Hebner, United States	1m21.2s
1920	Warren Kealoha, United States	1m15.2s
1924	Warren Kealoha, United States	1m13.2s
1928	George Kojac, United States	1m8.2s
1932	Masaji Kiyokawa, Japan	1m8.6s
1936	Adolph Kiefer, United States	1m5.9s
1948	Allen Stack, United States	1m6.4s
1952	Yoshinobu Oyakawa, United States	1m5.4s
1956	David Thiele, Australia	1m2.2s
1960	David Thiele, Australia	1m1.9s
1968	Roland Matthes, East Germany	58.7s
1972	Roland Matthes, East Germany	56.58s
1976	John Naber, United States	55.49s
1980	Bengt Baron, Sweden	56.53s
1984	Rick Carey, United States	55.79s

1. 100 yards

200-Meter Backstroke

1900	Ernst Hoppenberg, Germany	2m47s
1964	Jed Graef, United States	2m10.3s
1968	Roland Matthes, East Germany	2m9.6s
1972	Roland Matthes, East Germany	2m2.82s
1976	John Naber, United States	1m59.19s
1980	Sandor Wladar, Hungary	2:01.93s
1984	Rick Carey, United States	2m00.23s

100-Meter Breaststroke

1968	Donald McKenzie, United States	1m7.7s
1972	Nobutaka Taguchi, Japan	1m4.94s
1976	John Hencken, United States	1m03.11s
1980	Duncan Goodhew, Britain	1m03.34s
1984	Steve Lindquist, United States	1m01.65s

200-Meter Breaststroke

1908	Frederick Holman, Great Britain	3m9.2s
1912	Walter Bathe, Germany	3m1.8s
1920	Haken Malmroth, Sweden	3m4.4s
1924	Robert Skelton, United States	2m56.6s
1928	Yoshiyuki Tsuruta, Japan	2m48.8s
1932	Yoshiyuki Tsuruta, Japan	2m45.4s
1936	Tetsuo Hamuro, Japan	2m41.5s
1948	Joseph Verdeur, United States	2m39.3s
1952	John Davies, Australia	2m34.4s
1956	Masura Furukawa, Japan	2m34.7s
1960	Bill Mulliken, United States	2m37.4s
1964	Ian O'Brien, Australia	2m27.8s
1968	Felipe Munoz, Mexico	2m28.7s
1972	John Hencken, United States	2m21.55s
1976	David Willkie, Britain	2m15.11s
1980	Robertas Zulpa, U.S.S.R.	2m15.85s
1984	Victor Davis, Canada	2m13.34s

100-Meter Butterfly

1968	Douglas Russell, United States	55.9s
1972	Mark Spitz, United States	54.27s
1976	Matt Vogel, United States	54.35s
1980	Par Arvidsson, Sweden	54.92s
1984	Michael Gross, West Germany	53.08s

200-Meter Butterfly

1956	Bill Yorzyk, United States	2m19.3s
1960	Mike Troy, United States	2m12.8s
1964	Kevin Berry, Australia	2m6.6s
1968	Carl Robie, United States	2m8.7s
1972	Mark Spitz, United States	2m00.7s
1976	Mike Bruner, United States	1m59.23s
1980	Sergei Fesenko, U.S.S.R.	1m59.76s
1984	Jon Sieben, Australia	1m57.0s

200-Meter Individual Medley

1968	Charles Hickcox, United States	2m12s
1972	Gunnar Larsson, Sweden	2m7.17s

400-Meter Individual Medley

1964	Dick Roth, United States	4m45.4s
1968	Charles Hickcox, United States	4m48.4s
1972	Gunnar Larsson, Sweden	4m31.98s
1976	Rod Strachan, United States	4m23.68s
1980	Aleksandr Sidorenko, U.S.S.R.	4m22.8s
1984	Alex Baumann, Canada	4m17.41s

400-Meter Freestyle Relay

1964	United States	3m32.2s
1968	United States	3m31.7s
1972	United States	3m26.42s

800-Meter Freestyle Relay

1908	Great Britain	10m55.6s
1912	Australia	10m11.2s
1920	United States	10m4.4s
1924	United States	9m53.4s
1928	United States	9m36.2s
1932	Japan	8m58.4s
1936	Japan	8m51.5s
1948	United States	8m46s
1952	United States	8m31.1s
1956	Australia	8m23.6s
1960	United States	8m10.2s
1964	United States	7m52.1s

1968	United States	7m52.3s
1972	United States	7m35.78s
1976	United States	7m23.22s
1980	U.S.S.R.	7m23.50s
1984	United States	7m16.59s

400-Meter Medley Relay

1960	United States	4m5.4s
1964	United States	3m58.4s
1968	United States	3m54.9s
1972	United States	3m48.16s
1976	United States	3m42.22s
1980	Australia	3m45.70s
1984	United States	3m39.30s

Springboard Dive

		Points
1908	Albert Zuerner, Germany	85.5
1912	Paul Guenther, Germany	79.23
1920	Louis Kuehn, United States	675
1924	Albert White, United States	696.4
1928	Pete Desjardins, United States	185.04
1932	Michael Galitzen, United States	161.38
1936	Richard Degener, United States	163.57
1948	Bruce Harlan, United States	163.64
1952	David Browning, United States	205.59
1956	Robert Clotworthy, United States	159.56
1960	Gary Tobian, United States	170.00
1964	Ken Sitzberger, United States	159.90
1968	Bernard Wrightson, United States	170.15
1972	Vladimir Vasin, U.S.S.R.	594.09
1976	Phil Boggs, United States	619.05
1980	Alexsandr Portnov, U.S.S.R.	905.02
1984	Greg Louganis, United States	754.41

Platform Dive

		Points
1904	G. E. Sheldon, United States	12.75
1906	Gottlob Walz, Germany	156
1908	Hialmar Johansson, Sweden	83.75
1912	Erik Adlerz, Sweden	73.94
1920	Clarence Pinkston, United States	100.67
1924	Albert White, United States	487.3
1928	Pete Desjardins, United States	98.74
1932	Harold Smith, United States	124.80
1936	Marshall Wayne, United States	113.58
1948	Samuel Lee, United States	130.05
1952	Samuel Lee, United States	156.28
1956	Joaquin Capilla, Mexico	152.44
1960	Bob Webster, United States	165.56
1964	Bob Webster, United States	148.58
1968	Klaus Dibiasi, Italy	164.18
1972	Klaus Dibiasi, Italy	504.12
1976	Klaus Dibiasi, Italy	600.51
1980	Falk Hoffman, E. Germany	835.65
1984	Greg Louganis, United States	710.91

SWIMMING—WOMEN

100-Meter Freestyle

1912	Fanny Durack, Australia	1m22.2s
1920	Ethelda Bleibtrey, United States	1m13.6s
1924	Ethel Lackie, United States	1m12.4s
1928	Albina Osipowich, United States	1m11s
1932	Helene Madison, United States	1m6.8s
1936	Hendrika Mastenbroek, Netherlands	1m5.9s
1948	Greta Andersen, Denmark	1m6.3s
1952	Katalin Szoke, Hungary	1m6.8s
1956	Dawn Fraser, Australia	1m2s
1960	Dawn Fraser, Australia	1m1.2s
1964	Dawn Fraser, Australia	59.5s
1968	Marge Jan Henne, United States	1m
1972	Sandra Neilson, United States	58.59s
1976	Kornelia Ender, East Germany	55.65s
1980	Barbara Krause, East Germany	54.79s
1984	Carrie Steinseifer, United States	55.92s

200-Meter Freestyle

1968	Debbie Meyer, United States	2m10.5s
1972	Shane Gould, Australia	2m3.56s
1976	Kornelia Ender, East Germany	1m59.26s
1980	Barbara Krause, East Germany	1m58.33s
1984	Mary Wayle, United States	1m59.23s

400-Meter Freestyle

1920	Ethelda Bleibtrey, United States	4m34s[1]
1924	Martha Norelius, United States	6m2.2s
1928	Martha Norelius, United States	5m42.8s
1932	Helene Madison, United States	5m28.5s
1936	Hendrika Mastenbroek, Netherlands	5m26.4s
1948	Ann Curtis, United States	5m17.8s
1952	Valerie Gyenge, Hungary	5m12.1s
1956	Lorraine Crapp, Australia	4m54.6s
1960	Chris von Saltza, United States	4m50.6s
1964	Ginny Duenkel, United States	4m43.3s
1968	Debbie Meyer, United States	4m31.8s
1972	Shane Gould, Australia	4m19.04s
1976	Petra Thumer, East Germany	4m09.89s
1980	Ines Diers, East Germany	4m08.76s
1984	Tiffany Cohen, United States	4m07.10s

1. 300 meters.

800-Meter Freestyle

1968	Debbie Meyer, United States	9m24s
1972	Keena Rothhammer, United States	8m53.68s
1976	Petra Thumer, East Germany	8m37.14s
1980	Michelle Ford, Australia	8m28.90s
1984	Tiffany Cohen, United States	8m24.95s

100-Meter Backstroke

1924	Sybil Bauer, United States	1m23.2s
1928	Marie Braun, Netherlands	1m22s
1932	Eleanor Holm, United States	1m19.4s
1936	Dina Senff, Netherlands	1m18.9s
1948	Karen Harup, Denmark	1m14.4s
1952	Joan Harrison, South Africa	1m14.3s
1956	Judy Grinham, Great Britain	1m12.9s
1960	Lynn Burke, United States	1m9.3s
1964	Cathy Ferguson, United States	1m7.7s
1968	Kaye Hall, United States	1m6.2s
1972	Melissa Belote, United States	1m5.78s
1976	Ulrike Richter, East Germany	1m01.83s
1980	Rica Reinisch, East Germany	1m00.86s
1984	Theresa Andrews, United States	1m02.55s

200-Meter Backstroke

1968	Pokey Watson, United States	2m24.8s
1972	Melissa Belote, United States	2m19.19s
1976	Ulrike Richter, East Germany	2m13.43s
1980	Rica Reinisch, East Germany	2m11.77s
1984	Jolanda DeRover, Netherlands	2m12.38s

100-Meter Breaststroke

1968	Djurdjica Bjedov, Yugoslavia	1m15.8s
1972	Catherine Carr, United States	1m13.58s
1976	Hannelore Anke, East Germany	1m11.16s
1980	Ute Geweniger, East Germany	1m10.22s
1984	Petra Van Staveren, Netherlands	1m09.88s

200-Meter Breaststroke

1924	Lucy Morton, Great Britain	3m33.2s
1928	Hilde Schrader, Germany	3m12.6s
1932	Clare Dennis, Australia	3m6.3s
1936	Hideko Maehata, Japan	3m3.6s

1948	Nel van Vliet, Netherlands	2m57.2s
1952	Eva Szekely, Hungary	2m51.7s
1956	Ursala Happe, Germany	2m53.1s
1960	Anita Lonsbrough, Great Britain	2m49.5s
1964	Galina Prozumenschikova, U.S.S.R.	2m46.4s
1968	Sharon Wichman, United States	2m44.4s
1972	Beverly Whitfield, Australia	2m41.71s
1976	Marina Koshevaia, U.S.S.R.	2m33.35s
1980	Lina Kachushite, U.S.S.R.	2m29.54s
1984	Anne Ottenbrite, Canada	2m30.38s

100-Meter Butterfly

1956	Shelley Mann, United States	1m11s
1960	Carolyn Schuler, United States	1m9.5s
1964	Sharon Stouder, United States	1m4.7s
1968	Lynn McClements, Australia	1m5.5s
1972	Mayumi Aoki, Japan	1m3.34s
1976	Kornelia Ender, East Germany	1m00.13s
1980	Caren Metschuck, East Germany	1m00.42s
1984	Mary Meagher, United States	59.26s

200-Meter Butterfly

1968	Ada Kok, Netherlands	2m24.7s
1972	Karen Moe, United States	2m15.57s
1976	Andrea Pollack, East Germany	2m11.41s
1980	Ines Geissler, East Germany	2m10.44s
1984	Mary Meagher, United States	2m06.90s

200-Meter Individual Medley

1968	Claudia Kolb, United States	2m24.7s
1972	Shane Gould, Australia	2m23.07s
1984	Tracy Caulkins, United States	1m12.64s

400-Meter Individual Medley

1964	Donna de Varona, United States	5m18.7s
1968	Claudia Kolb, United States	5m8.5s
1972	Gail Neall, Australia	5m2.97s
1976	Ulrike Tauber, East Germany	4m42.77s
1980	Petra Schneider, East Germany	4m36.29s
1984	Tracy Caulkins, United States	4m39.21s

400-Meter Freestyle Relay

1912	Great Britain	5m52.8s
1920	United States	5m11.6s
1924	United States	4m58.8s
1928	United States	4m47.6s
1932	United States	4m38s
1936	Netherlands	4m36s
1948	United States	4m29.2s
1952	Hungary	4m24.4s
1956	Australia	4m17.1s
1960	United States	4m8.9s
1964	United States	4m3.8s
1968	United States	4m2.5s
1972	United States	3m55.19s
1976	United States	3m44.82s
1980	East Germany	3m42.71s
1984	United States	3m44.43s

400-Meter Medley Relay

1960	United States	4m41.1s
1964	United States	4m33.9s
1968	United States	4m28.3s
1972	United States	4m20.75s
1976	East Germany	4m07.95s
1980	East Germany	4m06.67s
1984	United States	4m08.34s

Springboard Dive

		Points
1920	Aileen Riggin, United States	539.90
1924	Elizabeth Becker, United States	474.5
1928	Helen Meany, United States	78.62
1932	Georgia Coleman, United States	87.52
1936	Marjorie Gestring, United States	89.27
1948	Victoria M. Draves, United States	108.74
1952	Patricia McCormick, United States	147.30
1956	Patricia McCormick, United States	142.36
1960	Ingrid Kramer, Germany	155.81
1964	Ingrid Kramer Engel, Germany	145.00
1968	Sue Gossick, United States	150.77
1972	Micki King, United States	450.03
1976	Jennifer Chandler, United States	506.19
1980	Irina Kalinina, U.S.S.R.	725.91
1984	Sylvie Bernier, Canada	530.70

Platform Dive

		Points
1912	Greta Johansson, Sweden	39.9
1920	Stefani Fryland, Denmark	34.60

DISTRIBUTION OF MEDALS 1984 SUMMER GAMES

Country	Gold	Silver	Bronze	Total
United States	83	61	30	174
West Germany	17	19	23	59
Rumania	20	16	17	53
Canada	10	18	16	44
Britain	5	10	22	37
China	15	8	9	32
Italy	14	6	12	32
Japan	10	8	14	32
France	5	7	15	27
Australia	4	8	12	24
South Korea	6	6	7	19
Sweden	2	11	6	19
Yugoslavia	7	4	7	18
Netherlands	5	2	6	13
Finland	4	3	6	13
New Zealand	8	1	2	11
Brazil	1	5	2	8
Switzerland	0	4	4	8
Mexico	2	3	1	6
Denmark	0	3	3	6
Spain	1	2	2	5
Belgium	1	1	2	4
Austria	1	1	1	3
Portugal	1	0	2	3
Jamaica	0	1	2	3
Norway	0	1	2	3
Turkey	0	0	3	3
Venezuela	0	0	3	3
Morocco	2	0	0	2
Kenya	1	0	1	2
Greece	0	1	1	2
Nigeria	0	1	1	2
Puerto Rico	0	1	1	2
Algeria	0	0	2	2
Pakistan	1	0	0	1
Colombia	0	1	0	1
Egypt	0	1	0	1
Ireland	0	1	0	1
Ivory Coast	0	1	0	1
Peru	0	1	0	1
Syria	0	1	0	1
Thailand	0	1	0	1
Cameroon	0	0	1	1
Dominican Republic	0	0	1	1
Iceland	0	0	1	1
Taiwan	0	0	1	1
Zambia	0	0	1	1

1924	Caroline Smith, United States	166
1928	Elizabeth B. Pinkston, United States	31.60
1932	Dorothy Poynton, United States	40.26
1936	Dorothy Poynton Hill, United States	33.92
1948	Victoria M. Draves, United States	68.87
1952	Patricia McCormick, United States	79.37
1956	Patricia McCormick, United States	84.85
1960	Ingrid Kramer, Germany	91.28
1964	Lesley Bush, United States	99.80
1968	Milena Duchkova, Czechoslovakia	109.59
1972	Ulrika Knape, Sweden	390.00
1976	Elena Vaytsekhovskaia, U.S.S.R.	406.59
1980	Martina Jaschke, East Germany	596.25
1984	Zhou Jihong, China	435.51

BASKETBALL—MEN

1904	United States	1964	United States
1936	United States	1968	United States
1948	United States	1972	U.S.S.R.
1952	United States	1976	United States
1956	United States	1980	Yugoslavia
1960	United States	1984	United States

BASKETBALL—WOMEN

1976 U.S.S.R.
1980 U.S.S.R.
1984 United States

BOXING

(U.S. winners only)

(U.S. boycotted Olympics in 1980)

Flyweight—112 pounds (51 kilograms)

1904	George V. Finnegan	1952	Nate Brooks
1920	Frank De Genaro	1976	Leo Randolph
1924	Fidel La Barba	1984	Steve McCrory

Bantamweight—119 (54 kg)

1904 O.L. Kirk

Featherweight—126 pounds (57 kg)

1904	O.L. Kirk	1984	Meldrick Taylor
1924	Jackie Fields		

Lightweight—132 pounds (60 kg)

1904	H.J. Spanger	1976	Howard Davis
1920	Samuel Mosberg	1984	Pernell Whitaker
1968	Ronnie Harris		

Light Welterweight—140 pounds (63.5 kg)

1952	Charles Adkins	1976	Ray Leonard
1972	Ray Seales	1984	Jerry Page

Welterweight—148 pounds (67 kg)

1904	Al Young	1984	Mark Breland
1932	Edward Flynn		

Light Middleweight—157 pounds (71 kg)

1960	Wilbert McClure	1984	Frank Tate

Middleweight—165 pounds (75 kg)

1904	Charles Mayer	1960	Eddie Cook
1932	Carmen Barth	1976	Michael Spinks
1952	Floyd Patterson		

Light Heavyweight—179 pounds (81 kg)

1920	Edward Eagan	1960	Cassius Clay
1952	Norvel Lee	1976	Leon Spinks
1956	James Boyd		

Heavyweight—201 pounds

1904	Sam Berger	1964	Joe Frazier
1952	Edward Sanders	1968	George Foreman
1956	Pete Rademacher	1984	Henry Tillman

Super Heavyweight (unlimited)

1984 Tyrell Biggs

Winter Games

FIGURE SKATING—MEN

1908 Ulrich Salchow, Sweden
1920 Gillis Grafstrom, Sweden
1924 Gillis Grafstrom, Sweden
1928 Gillis Grafstrom, Sweden
1932 Karl Schaefer, Austria
1936 Karl Schaefer, Austria
1948 Richard Button, United States
1952 Richard Button, United States
1956 Hayes Alan Jenkins, United States
1960 David Jenkins, United States
1964 Manfred Schnelldorfer, Germany
1968 Wolfgang Schwartz, Austria
1972 Ondrej Nepela, Czechoslovakia
1976 John Curry, Great Britain
1980 Robin Cousins, Great Britain
1984 Scott Hamilton, United States

FIGURE SKATING—WOMEN

1908 Madge Syers, Britain
1920 Magda Julin-Maurey, Sweden
1924 Herma Szabo-Planck, Austria
1928 Sonja Henie, Norway
1932 Sonja Henie, Norway
1936 Sonja Henie, Norway
1948 Barbara Ann Scott, Canada
1952 Jeannette Altwegg, Great Britain
1956 Tenley Albright, United States
1960 Carol Heiss, United States
1964 Sjoukje Dijkstra, Netherlands
1968 Peggy Fleming, United States
1972 Beatrix Schuba, Austria
1976 Dorothy Hamill, United States
1980 Anett Poetzsch, East Germany
1984 Katarina Witt, East Germany

SPEED SKATING—MEN

(U.S. winners only)

500 Meters

1924	Charles Jewtraw	44.0
1932	John A. Shea	43.4
1952	Kenneth Henry	43.2

1964	Terrence McDermott	40.1
1980	Eric Heiden	38.03

1,000 Meters

1976	Peter Mueller	1:19.32
1980	Eric Heiden	1:15.18

1,500 Meters

1932	John A. Shea	2:57.5
1980	Eric Heiden	1:55.44

5,000 Meters

1932	Irving Jaffee	9:40.8
1980	Eric Heiden	7:02.29

10,000 Meters

1932	Irving Jaffee	19:13.6
1980	Eric Heiden	14:28.13

SPEED SKATING—WOMEN

500 Meters

1972	Anne Henning	43.33
1976	Sheila Young	42.76

1,500 Meters

1972	Dianne Holum	2:20.85

SKIING, ALPINE—MEN

Downhill

1948	Henri Oreiller, France	2m55.0s
1952	Zeno Colo, Italy	2m30.8s
1956	Anton Sailer, Austria	2m52.2s
1960	Jean Vuarnet, France	2m06.2s
1964	Egon Zimmermann, Austria	2m18.16s
1968	Jean-Claude Killy, France	1m59.85s
1972	Bernhard Russi, Switzerland	1m51.43s
1976	Franz Klammer, Austria	1m45.72s
1980	Leonhard Stock, Austria	1m45.50s
1984	Bill Johnson, United States	1m45.59s

Slalom

1948	Edi Reinalter, Switzerland	2m10.3s
1952	Othmar Schneider, Austria	2m00.0s
1956	Anton Sailer, Austria	194.7 pts.
1960	Ernst Hinterseer, Austria	2m08.9s
1964	Josef Stiegler, Austria	2m10.13
1968	Jean-Claude Killy, France	1m39.73s
1972	Francisco Fernandez Ochoa, Spain	1m49.27s
1976	Piero Gros, Italy	2m03.29s
1980	Ingemar Stenmark, Sweden	1m44.26s
1984	Phil Mahre, United States	1m39.41s

Giant Slalom

1952	Stein Eriksen, Norway	2m25.0s
1956	Anton Sailer, Austria	3m00.1s
1960	Roger Staub, Switzerland	1m48.3s
1964	François Bonlieu, France	1m46.71s
1968	Jean-Claude Killy, France	3m29.28s
1972	Gustavo Thoeni, Italy	3m09.52s
1976	Heini Hemmi, Switzerland	3m26.97s
1980	Ingemar Stenmark, Sweden	2m40.74s
1984	Max Julen, Switzerland	1m20.54s

DISTRIBUTION OF MEDALS 1984 WINTER GAMES

(Sarajevo, Yugoslavia)

	Gold	Silver	Bronze	Total
Soviet Union	6	10	9	25
East Germany	9	9	6	24
Finland	4	3	6	13
Norway	3	2	4	9
United States	4	4	0	8
Sweden	4	2	2	8
Czechoslovakia	0	2	4	6
Switzerland	2	2	1	5
Canada	2	1	1	4
West Germany	2	1	1	4
France	0	1	2	3
Italy	2	0	0	2
Liechtenstein	0	0	2	2
Britain	1	0	0	1
Yugoslavia	0	1	0	1
Austria	0	0	1	1

SKIING, ALPINE—WOMEN

Downhill

1948	Hedi Schlunegger, Switzerland	2m28.3s
1952	Trude Jochum-Beiser, Austria	1m47.1s
1956	Madeleine Berthod, Switzerland	1m40.1s
1960	Heidi Biebl, Germany	1m37.6s
1964	Christl Haas, Austria	1m55.39s
1968	Olga Pall, Austria	1m40.87s
1972	Marie-Therese Nadig, Switzerland	1m36.68s
1976	Rosi Mittermeier, West Germany	1m46.16s
1980	Annemarie Proell Moser, Austria	1m37.52s
1984	Michela Figini, Switzerland	1m13.36s

Slalom

1948	Gretchen Fraser, United States	1m57.2s
1952	Andrea Mead Lawrence, United States	2m10.6s
1956	Renee Colliard, Switzerland	112.3 pts.
1960	Anne Heggtveigt, Canada	1m49.6s
1964	Christine Goitschel, France	1m29.86s
1968	Marielle Goitschel, France	1m25.86s
1972	Barbara Cochran, United States	1m31.24s
1976	Rosi Mittermeier, West Germany	1m30.54s
1980	Hanni Wenzel, Liechtenstein	1m25.09s
1984	Paoletta Magoni, Italy	1m36.47s

Giant Slalom

1952	Andrea M. Lawrence, United States	2m06.8s
1956	Ossi Reichert, Germany	1m56.5s
1960	Yvonne Ruegg, Switzerland	1m39.9s
1964	Marielle Goitschel, France	1m52.24s
1968	Nancy Greene, Canada	1m51.97s
1972	Marie-Therese Nadig, Switzerland	1m29.90s
1976	Kathy Kreiner, Canada	1m29.13s
1980	Hanni Wenzel, Liechtenstein	2m41.66s
1984	Debbie Armstrong, United States	2m20.98s

ICE HOCKEY

1920	Canada	1960	United States
1924	Canada	1964	U.S.S.R.
1928	Canada	1968	U.S.S.R.
1932	Canada	1972	U.S.S.R.
1936	Great Britain	1976	U.S.S.R.
1948	Canada	1980	United States
1952	Canada	1984	U.S.S.R.
1956	U.S.S.R.		

SKIING, NORDIC, JUMPING

90-Meter Hill

		Points
1924	Jacob T. Thams, Norway	227.5
1928	Alfred Andersen, Norway	230.5
1932	Birger Ruud, Norway	228.0
1936	Birger Ruud, Norway	232.0
1948	Peter Hugsted, Norway	228.1
1952	A. Bergmann, Norway	226.0
1956	Antti Hyvarinen, Finland	227.0
1960	Helmut Recknagel, Germany	227.2
1964	Toralf Engan, Norway	230.7
1968	Vladimir Beloussov, U.S.S.R.	231.3
1972	Wojciech Fortuna, Poland	219.9
1976	Karl Schnabl, Austria	234.8
1980	Jouko Tormanen, Finland	271.0
1984	Matti Nykaenen, Finland	231.2

Small Hill (70 meters)

1964	Veikko Kankkonen, Finland	229.9
1968	Jiri Raska, Czechoslovakia	216.5
1972	Yukio Kasaya, Japan	244.2
1976	Hans-Georg Aschenbach, East Germany	252.0
1980	Anton Innauer, Austria	266.3
1984	Jens Weissflog, East Germany	215.2

FINAL OVER-ALL 1984 OLYMPIC HOCKEY STANDINGS

GROUP A

	W	L	T	Pts	GF	GA
Soviet Union	7	0	0	14	48	5
West Germany	4	1	0	9	34	21
Sweden	4	2	1	9	33	16
Italy	1	4	0	2	15	31
Yugoslavia	1	4	0	2	8	37
Poland	1	5	0	2	20	44

GROUP B

	W	L	T	Pts	GF	GA
Czechoslovakia	6	1	0	12	40	9
Canada	4	3	0	8	24	16
United States	2	2	2	6	23	21
Finland	2	3	1	5	31	26
Austria	1	4	0	2	13	37
Norway	0	4	1	1	15	43

Seventh Place
United States 7, Poland 4

Third place
Sweden 2, Canada 0

Fifth Place
West Germany 7, Finland 4

Championship
Soviet Union 2, Czechoslovakia 0

Medal Round
Czechoslovakia 2, Sweden 0
Soviet Union 4, Canada 0

Other 1984 Olympic Games Champions

SUMMER

Archery
Men—Darrell Pace, United States
Women—Hyang-Soun Seo, South Korea

Boxing
106 lb—Paul Gonzalez, United States
112 lb—Steve McCrory, United States
119 lb—Maurizio Stecca, Italy
126 lb—Meldrick Taylor, United States
132 lb—Pernell Whitaker, United States
139 lb—Jerry Page, United States
148 lb—Mark Breland, United States
157 lb—Frank Tate, United States
165 lb—Joun-Sup Shin, South Korea
179 lb—Anton Josipovic, Yugoslavia
201 lb—Henry Tillman, United States
Over 201—Tyrell Biggs, United States

Canoeing
500 m—Larry Cain, Canada
1,000 m—Ulrich Eiche, West Germany
500-m pairs—Yugoslavia (Matija Ljubekt and Mirko Nisovic)
1,000-m pairs—Romania (Ivan Potzaichin and Toma Simionov)

Kayak—Men
500 m—Ian Ferguson, New Zealand
1,000 m—Alan Thompson, New Zealand
500-m pairs—New Zealand (Ian Ferguson and Paul MacDonald)
1,000-m pairs—Canada (Hugh Fisher and Alwyn Moris)
1,000-m fours—New Zealand (Grant Bramwell, Ian Ferguson, Paul MacDonald, Alan Thompson)

Kayak—Women
500 m—Agneta Andersson, Sweden
500-m pairs—Sweden (Agneta Andersson and Anna Olsson)
500-m fours—Romania (Agafia Constantin, Nastasia Ionescu, Tecia Marinescu, Maria Stefan)

Cycling—Men
4,000-m Individual pursuit—Steve Hegg, United States
Individual road race—Alexi Grewal, United States
1,000-m Time trials—Fredy Schmidtke, West Germany
4,000-m Team pursuit—Australia
Sprint—Mark Gorski, United States
Points race—Roger Ilegems, Belgium
100-km road team trials—Italy

Cycling—Women
Individual road race—Connie Carpenter, United States

Equestrian
Dressage—Dr. Reiner Klimke, West Germany
Dressage team—West Germany
Jumping—Joe Fargia, United States
Jumping, team—United States
Three-day event—Mark Todd, New Zealand
Team three-day event—United States

Fencing
Foil—Mauro Numa, Italy
Team foil—Italy
Epee—Philippe Boisse, France
Team epee—West Germany
Sabre—Jean-Francois Lamour, France
Team sabre—Italy
Women's foil—Luan Jujie, China
Women's team foil—West Germany

Gymnastics—Men
All-around—Koji Gushiken, Japan
Floor exercises—Li Ning, China
Horizontal bar—Shinji Morisue, Japan
Parallel bars—Bart Conner, United States
Pommel horse—Li Ning, China and Peter Vidmar, United States
Rings—Koji Gushiken, Japan and Li Ning, China
Vault—Lou Yun, China
Team—United States

Gymnastics—Women
All-around—Mary Lou Retton, United States
Balance beam—Simona Pauca, Romania, and Ecaterina Szabo, Romania
Floor exercises—Ecaterina Szabo, Romania
Uneven bars—Ma Yanhonjg, China
Vault—Evaterina Szabo, Romania
Team—Romania

Judo
Lightweight—Byeong-Keun Ahn, South Korea
Extra lightweight—Shinji Hosokawa, Japan
Half lightweight—Yoshiyuki Matsuoka, Japan
Half middleweight—Frank Wieneke, West Germany
Middleweight—Peter Seisenbacher, Austria
Half heavyweight—Hyoung-Za Ha, South Korea
Heavyweight—Hitoshi Saito, Japan

Modern Pentathlon
Individual—Daniele Masala, Italy
Team—Italy

Rowing—Men
Singles—Pertti Karppinen, Finland
Doubles—United States (Bradley Lewis and Paul Enquist)
Quadruples—West Germany (Albert Hedderich, Raimond Hormann, Dieter Wiedenmann, Michael Dursch)
Pairs—Romania (Petru Iosub, Valer Toma)
Pairs with coxswain—Italy (Carmine Abbaginale, Giuseppe Abbaginale)
Fours—New Zealand (Leslie O'Connell, Conrad Robertson, Shane O'Brien, Keith Trask)
Fours with coxswain—Britain (Martin Cross, Richard Budgett, Andrew Holmes, Steve Redgrave)
Eights—Canada (Pat Turner, Kevin Neufield, Mark Evans, Grant Main, Paul Steele, Mike Evans, Dean Crawford, Blair Horm, Brian McMahon)

Rowing—Women
Singles—Valeria Racila, Romania
Doubles—Romania
Pairs—Romania
Pairs with coxswain—Romania
Fours with coxswain—Romania
Quadruple sculls—Romania
Eights—United States

Shooting—Men
Free pistol—Xu Haifeng, China
Rapid-fire pistol—Takeo Kamachi, Japan
Small-bore rifle—Ed Etzel, United States
Small-bore rifle, 3 positions—Malcolm Cooper, Britain
Rifle running game target—Li Yuwei, China
Trap—Luciano Giovanetti, Italy
Skeet—Matthew Dryke, United States
Air rifle—Philippe Heberle, France

Shooting—Women
Air rifle—Pat Spurgin, United States
Small-bore rifle, 3 positions—Wu Xiaoxuan, China
Sport pistol—Linda Thom, Canada

Synchronized Swimming
Solo—Tracie Ruiz, United States
Duet—United States (Candy Costie and Tracie Ruiz)

Weight Lifting
115 lb—Zeng Guoqiang, China
123 lb—Wu Shude, China
132 lb—Chen Weiqang, China
149 lb—Yao Jingyuang, China
165 lb—Karl Heinz Radschinsky, West Germany
182 lb—Petre Becheru, Romania
198 lb—Nicu Vlad, Romania
220 lb—Rolf Miller, West Germany
242 lb—Noberto Oberburger, Italy
Over 242—Dinko Lukim, Australia

Wrestling—Freestyle
106 lb—Bobby Weaver, United States
114.5 lb—Saban Trstena, Yugoslavia
125.5 lb—Hideaki Tomiyama, Japan
136.5 lb—Randy Lewis, United States
149.5 lb—In-Tak You, South Korea
163 lb—David Schultz, United States
181 lb—Mark Schultz, United States
198.5 lb—Ed Banach, United States
220 lb—Lou Banach, United States
Over 220—Bruce Baumgartner, United States

Wrestling—Greco-Roman
106 lb—Vincenzo Maenza, Italy
114.5 lb—Atsuji Miyahara, Japan
125.5 lb—Pasquale Passarelli, West Germany
136.5 lb—Weon Kee Kim, South Korea
150 lb—Viado Lisjak, Yugoslavia
163 lb—Jouko Salomaki, Finland
181 lb—Ion Draica, Romania
198.5 lb—Steven Fraser, United States
220 lb—Vasile Andrei, Romania
Over 220—Jeff Blatnick, United States

Yachting
Windglider—Stephan Van Den Berg, Netherlands
Finn—Russell Coutts, New Zealand
Flying Dutchmen—United States (Jonathan McKee, Bill Buchan)
470 Class—Spain
Soling—United States (Robert Haines Jr., Ed Trevelyan, Rod Davis)
Star—United States (William Buchan, Steve Erickson)
Tornado—New Zealand

Team Champions
Field hockey, men—Pakistan
Field hockey, women—Netherlands
Handball, men—Yugoslavia
Handball, women—Yugoslavia
Soccer—France
Volleyball, men—United States
Volleyball, women—China
Water polo—Yugoslavia

WINTER

Biathlon
Individual—Eirik Kvalfoss, Norway (10 km); P. Angerer, West Germany (20 km)
Relay—Soviet Union (Dmitry Vassiliev, Youry Kachkarov, Algulmantas Shalna, Serguey Bouliguin)

Bobsledding
2-man—East Germany (Wolfgang Hoppe, captain)
4-man—East Germany (Wolfgang Hoppe, Roland Wetzig, Dietmar Schauerhanmer, Andreas Kirchner)

Figure Skating
Men—Scott Hamilton, United States
Women—Katarina Witt, East Germany
Pairs—Elena Valova and Oleg Vasiliev, Soviet Union
Dance—Jayne Torvill and Christopher Dean, Britain

Speed Skating—Men
500 m—Sergei Fokicheu, Soviet Union
1,000 m—Gaetan Boucher, Canada
1,500 m—Gaetan Boucher, Canada
5,000 m—Tomas Gustafson, Sweden
10,000 m—Igor Malkov, Soviet Union

Speed Skating—Women
500 m—Christina Rothernberger, East Germany
1,000 m—Karin Enke, East Germany
1,500 m—Karin Enke, East Germany
3,000 m—Andrea Schoene, East Germany

Hockey
Team—Soviet Union

Luge
Men—Paul Hildgartner, Italy
Doubles—Hans Stangassinger and Franz Wembacher, West Germany
Women—Steffi Martin, East Germany

Skiing, Nordic—Men
Combined—Tom Sandberg, Norway
70-m jump—Jens Weissflog, East Germany
90-m jump—Matti Nykaenen, Finland

Cross-Country Skiing—Men
15 km—Gunde Svan, Sweden
30 km—Nikolai Zimiatov, Soviet Union
50 km—Thomas Wassberg, Sweden
40-km relay—Sweden (Thomas Wassberg, Benny Kohlberg, Jan Ottoson, Gunde Svan)

Cross-Country Skiing—Women
5 km—Marja-Liisa Hamalainen, Finland
10 km—Marja-Liisa Hamalainen, Finland
20 km—Marja-Liisa Hamalainen, Finland
20-km relay—Norway (Inger Helene Nybraaten, Anne Jahra, Brit Petersen, Berit Aunli)

FOOTBALL

The pastime of kicking around a ball goes back beyond the limits of recorded history. Ancient savage tribes played football of a primitive kind. There was a ball-kicking game played by Athenians, Spartans, and Corinthians 2500 years ago, which the Greeks called *Episkuros.* The Romans had a somewhat similar game called *Harpastum* and are supposed to have carried the game with them when they invaded the British Isles in the First Century, B.C.

Undoubtedly the game known in the United States as Football traces directly to the English game of Rugby, though the modifications have been many. Informal football was played on college lawns well over a century ago, and an annual Freshman-Sophomore series of "scrimmages" began at Yale in 1840. The first formal intercollegiate football game was the Princeton-Rutgers contest at New Brunswick, N.J., on Nov. 6, 1869, with Rutgers winning by 6 goals to 4.

In those days, games were played with 25, 20, 15, or 11 men on a side. In 1880, there was a convention at which Walter Camp of Yale persuaded the delegates to agree to a rule calling for 11 players on a side. The game grew so rough that it was attacked as brutal, and some colleges abandoned the sport. Conditions were so bad in 1906 that President Theodore Roosevelt called a meeting of Yale, Harvard, and Princeton representatives at the White House in the hope of reforming and improving the game. The outcome was that the game, with the forward pass introduced and some other modifications of the rules inserted, became faster and cleaner.

The first professional game was played in 1895 at Latrobe, Pa. The National Football League was founded in 1921. The All-American Conference went into action in 1946. At the end of the 1949 season the two circuits merged, retaining the name of the older league. In 1960, the American Football League began operations. In 1970, the leagues merged. The United States Football League played its first season in 1983, from March to July. It suspended spring operation after the 1985 season, and planned a 1986 move to fall, but suspended operations again. It did not function as a league through 1987.

College Football

NATIONAL COLLEGE FOOTBALL CHAMPIONS

The "National Collegiate A. A. Football Guide" recognizes as unofficial national champion the team selected each year by press association polls. Where The Associated Press poll (of writers) does not agree with the United Press International poll (of coaches), the guide lists both teams selected.

1937	Pittsburgh
1938	Texas Christian
1939	Texas A & M
1940	Minnesota
1941	Minnesota
1942	Ohio State
1943	Notre Dame
1944	Army
1945	Army
1946	Notre Dame
1947	Notre Dame
1948	Michigan
1949	Notre Dame
1950	Oklahoma
1951	Tennessee
1952	Michigan State
1953	Maryland
1954	Ohio State and U.C.L.A.
1955	Oklahoma
1956	Oklahoma
1957	Auburn and Ohio State
1958	Louisiana State
1959	Syracuse
1960	Minnesota
1961	Alabama
1962	So. California
1963	Texas
1964	Alabama
1965	Alabama and Michigan State
1966	Notre Dame
1967	So. California
1968	Ohio State
1969	Texas
1970	Texas and Nebraska
1971	Nebraska
1972	So. California
1973	Notre Dame
1974	Oklahoma and So. California
1975	Oklahoma
1976	Pittsburgh
1977	Notre Dame
1978	Alabama and So. California
1979	Alabama
1980	Georgia
1981	Clemson
1982	Penn State
1983	Miami
1984	Brigham Young
1985	Oklahoma
1986	Penn State

RECORD OF ANNUAL MAJOR BOWL COLLEGE FOOTBALL GAMES

Rose Bowl
(At Pasadena, Calif.)

1902	Michigan 49, Stanford 0
1916	Washington State 14, Brown 0
1917	Oregon 14, Pennsylvania 0
1918	Mare Island Marines 19, Camp Lewis 7
1919	Great Lakes 17, Mare Island Marines 0
1920	Harvard 7, Oregon 6
1921	California 28, Ohio State 0
1922	Washington and Jefferson 0, California 0
1923	So. California 14, Penn State 3
1924	Navy 14, Washington 14
1925	Notre Dame 27, Stanford 10
1926	Alabama 20, Washington 19
1927	Alabama 7, Stanford 7
1928	Stanford 7, Pittsburgh 6
1929	Georgia Tech 8, California 7
1930	So. California 47, Pittsburgh 14
1931	Alabama 24, Washington State 0
1932	So. California 21, Tulane 12
1933	So. California 35, Pittsburgh 0
1934	Columbia 7, Stanford 0
1935	Alabama 29, Stanford 13
1936	Stanford 7, So. Methodist 0
1937	Pittsburgh 21, Washington 0
1938	California 13, Alabama 0
1939	So. California 7, Duke 3
1940	So. California 14, Tennessee 0
1941	Stanford 21, Nebraska 13
1942	Oregon State 20, Duke 16[1]
1943	Georgia 9, U.C.L.A. 0
1944	So. California 29, Washington 0
1945	So. California 25, Tennessee 0
1946	Alabama 34, So. California 14
1947	Illinois 45, U.C.L.A. 14
1948	Michigan 49, So. California 0
1949	Northwestern 20, California 14
1950	Ohio State 17, California 14
1951	Michigan 14, California 6
1952	Illinois 40, Stanford 7
1953	So. California 7, Wisconsin 0
1954	Michigan State 28, U.C.L.A. 20
1955	Ohio State 20, So. California 7
1956	Michigan State 17, U.C.L.A. 14
1957	Iowa 35, Oregon State 19
1958	Ohio State 10, Oregon 7
1959	Iowa 38, California 12
1960	Washington 44, Wisconsin 8
1961	Washington 17, Minnesota 7
1962	Minnesota 21, U.C.L.A. 3
1963	So. California 42, Wisconsin 37
1964	Illinois 17, Washington 7
1965	Michigan 34, Oregon State 7
1966	U.C.L.A. 14, Michigan State 12
1967	Purdue 14, So. California 13
1968	So. California 14, Indiana 3

1969	Ohio State 27, So. California 16
1970	So. California 10, Michigan 3
1971	Stanford 27, Ohio State 17
1972	Stanford 13, Michigan 12
1973	So. California 42, Ohio State 17
1974	Ohio State 42, So. California 21
1975	So. California 18, Ohio State 17
1976	U.C.L.A. 23, Ohio State 10
1977	So. California 14, Michigan 6
1978	Washington 27, Michigan 20
1979	So. California 17, Michigan 10
1980	So. California 17, Ohio State 16
1981	Michigan 23, Washington 6
1982	Washington 28, Iowa 0
1983	U.C.L.A. 24, Michigan 14
1984	U.C.L.A. 45, Illinois 9
1985	USC 20, Ohio St. 17
1986	U.C.L.A. 45, Iowa 28
1987	Arizona State 22, Michigan 15

1. Played at Durham, N.C.

Orange Bowl

(At Miami)

1933	Miami (Fla.) 7, Manhattan 0
1934	Duquesne 33, Miami (Fla.) 7
1935	Bucknell 26, Miami (Fla.) 0
1936	Catholic 20, Mississippi 19
1937	Duquesne 13, Mississippi State 12
1938	Auburn 6, Michigan State 0
1939	Tennessee 17, Oklahoma 0
1940	Georgia Tech 21, Missouri 7
1941	Mississippi State 14, Georgetown 7
1942	Georgia 40, Texas Christian 26
1943	Alabama 37, Boston College 21
1944	Louisiana State 19, Texas A&M 14
1945	Tulsa 26, Georgia Tech 12
1946	Miami (Fla.) 13, Holy Cross 6
1947	Rice 8, Tennessee 0
1948	Georgia Tech 20, Kansas 14
1949	Texas 41, Georgia 28
1950	Santa Clara 21, Kentucky 13
1951	Clemson 15, Miami (Fla.) 14
1952	Georgia Tech 17, Baylor 14
1953	Alabama 61, Syracuse 6
1954	Oklahoma 7, Maryland 0
1955	Duke 34, Nebraska 7
1956	Oklahoma 20, Maryland 6
1957	Colorado 27, Clemson 21
1958	Oklahoma 48, Duke 21
1959	Oklahoma 21, Syracuse 6
1960	Georgia 14, Missouri 0
1961	Missouri 21, Navy 14
1962	Louisiana State 25, Colorado 7
1963	Alabama 17, Oklahoma 0
1964	Nebraska 13, Auburn 7
1965	Texas 21, Alabama 17
1966	Alabama 39, Nebraska 28
1967	Florida 27, Georgia Tech 12
1968	Oklahoma 26, Tennessee 24
1969	Penn State 15, Kansas 14
1970	Penn State 10, Missouri 3
1971	Nebraska 17, Louisiana State 12
1972	Nebraska 38, Alabama 6
1973	Nebraska 40, Notre Dame 6
1974	Penn State 16, Louisiana State 9
1975	Notre Dame 13, Alabama 11
1976	Oklahoma 14, Michigan 6
1977	Ohio State 27, Colorado 10
1978	Arkansas 31, Oklahoma 6
1979	Oklahoma 31, Nebraska 24
1980	Oklahoma 24, Florida State 7
1981	Oklahoma 18, Florida State 17
1982	Clemson 22, Nebraska 15
1983	Nebraska 21, Louisiana State 20
1984	Miami 31, Nebraska 30
1985	Washington 28, Oklahoma 17
1986	Oklahoma 25, Penn St. 10
1987	Oklahoma 42, Arkansas 8

Sugar Bowl

(At New Orleans)

1935	Tulane 20, Temple 14
1936	Texas Christian 3, Louisiana State 2
1937	Santa Clara 21, Louisiana State 14
1938	Santa Clara 6, Louisiana State 0
1939	Texas Christian 15, Carnegie Tech 7
1940	Texas A & M 14, Tulane 13
1941	Boston College 19, Tennessee 13
1942	Fordham 2, Missouri 0
1943	Tennessee 14, Tulsa 7
1944	Georgia Tech 20, Tulsa 18
1945	Duke 29, Alabama 26
1946	Oklahoma A & M 33, St. Mary's (Calif.) 13
1947	Georgia 20, North Carolina 10
1948	Texas 27, Alabama 7
1949	Oklahoma 14, North Carolina 6
1950	Oklahoma 35, Louisiana State 0
1951	Kentucky 13, Oklahoma 7
1952	Maryland 28, Tennessee 13
1953	Georgia Tech 24, Mississippi 7
1954	Georgia Tech 42, West Virginia 19
1955	Navy 21, Mississippi 0
1956	Georgia Tech 7, Pittsburgh 0
1957	Baylor 13, Tennessee 7
1958	Mississippi 39, Texas 7
1959	Louisiana State 7, Clemson 0
1960	Mississippi 21, Louisiana State 0
1961	Mississippi 14, Rice 6
1962	Alabama 10, Arkansas 3
1963	Mississippi 17, Arkansas 13
1964	Alabama 12, Mississippi 7
1965	Louisiana State 13, Syracuse 10
1966	Missouri 20, Florida 18
1967	Alabama 34, Nebraska 7
1968	Louisiana State 20, Wyoming 13
1969	Arkansas 16, Georgia 2
1970	Mississippi 27, Arkansas 22
1971	Tennessee 34, Air Force Academy 13
1972	Oklahoma 40, Auburn 22
1973	Oklahoma 14, Penn State 0
1974	Notre Dame 24, Alabama 23
1975	Nebraska 13, Florida 10
1976	Alabama 13, Penn State 6
1977	Pittsburgh 27, Georgia 3
1978	Alabama 35, Ohio State 6
1979	Alabama 14, Penn State 7
1980	Alabama 24, Arkansas 9
1981	Georgia 17, Notre Dame 10
1982	Pittsburgh 24, Georgia 20
1983	Penn State 27, Georgia 23
1984	Auburn 9, Michigan 7
1985	Nebraska 28, LSU 10
1986	Tennessee 35, Miami, Fla. 7
1987	Nebraska 30, Louisiana State 15

Cotton Bowl

(At Dallas)

1937	Texas Christian 16, Marquette 6
1938	Rice 28, Colorado 14
1939	St. Mary's (Calif.) 20, Texas Tech. 13
1940	Clemson 6, Boston College 3
1941	Texas A & M 13, Fordham 12
1942	Alabama 29, Texas A & M 21
1943	Texas 14, Georgia Tech 7
1944	Randolph Field 7, Texas 7
1945	Oklahoma A & M 34, Texas Christian 0
1946	Texas 40, Missouri 27
1947	Louisiana State 0, Arkansas 0
1948	So. Methodist 13, Penn State 13
1949	So. Methodist 21, Oregon 13
1950	Rice 27, North Carolina 13
1951	Tennessee 20, Texas 14
1952	Kentucky 20, Texas Christian 7
1953	Texas 16, Tennessee 0
1954	Rice 28, Alabama 6
1955	Georgia Tech 14, Arkansas 6
1956	Mississippi 14, Texas Christian 13
1957	Texas Christian 28, Syracuse 27
1958	Navy 20, Rice 7
1959	Air Force 0, Texas Christian 0
1960	Syracuse 23, Texas 14
1961	Duke 7, Arkansas 6
1962	Texas 12, Mississippi 7
1963	Louisiana State 13, Texas 0
1964	Texas 28, Navy 6
1965	Arkansas 10, Nebraska 7
1966	Louisiana State 14, Arkansas 7
1967	Georgia 24, So. Methodist 9
1968	Texas A & M 20, Alabama 16
1969	Texas 36, Tennessee 13
1970	Texas 21, Notre Dame 17
1971	Notre Dame 24, Texas 11
1972	Penn State 30, Texas 6
1973	Texas 17, Alabama 13
1974	Nebraska 19, Texas 3
1975	Penn State 41, Baylor 20
1976	Arkansas 31, Georgia 10
1977	Houston 30, Maryland 21
1978	Notre Dame 38, Texas 10
1979	Notre Dame 35, Houston 34
1980	Houston 17, Nebraska 14
1981	Alabama 30, Baylor 2
1982	Texas 14, Alabama 12
1983	Southern Methodist 7, Pittsburgh 3
1984	Georgia 10, Texas 9
1985	Boston College 45, Houston 28
1986	Texas A & M 36, Auburn 16
1987	Ohio State 28, Texas A & M 12

Gator Bowl

(At Jacksonville, Fla. Played on Saturday nearest New Year's Day of year indicated)

1953	Florida 14, Tulsa 13
1954	Texas Tech 35, Auburn 13
1955	Auburn 33, Baylor 13
1956	Vanderbilt 25, Auburn 13
1957	Georgia Tech 21, Pittsburgh 14
1958	Tennessee 3, Texas A & M 0
1959	Mississippi 7, Florida 3
1960	Arkansas 14, Georgia Tech 7
1961	Florida 13, Baylor 12
1962	Penn State 30, Georgia Tech 15
1963	Florida 17, Penn State 7
1964	No. Carolina 35, Air Force 0
1965	Florida State 36, Oklahoma 19
1966	Georgia Tech 31, Texas Tech 21
1967	Tennessee 18, Syracuse 12
1968	Penn State 17, Florida State 17
1969	Missouri 35, Alabama 10
1970	Florida 14, Tennessee 13
1971	Auburn 35, Mississippi 28
1972	Georgia 7, North Carolina 3
1973	Auburn 24, Colorado 3
1974	Texas Tech 28, Tennessee 19
1975	Auburn 27, Texas 3

1976	Maryland 13, Florida 0	1980	North Carolina 17, Michigan 15	1984	Florida 14, Iowa 6
1977	Notre Dame 20, Penn State 9	1981	Pittsburgh 37, South Carolina 9	1985	Oklahoma St. 21, South Carolina 14
1978	Pittsburgh 34, Clemson 3	1982	North Carolina 31, Arkansas 27	1986	Florida State 34, Oklahoma St. 23
1979	Clemson 17, Ohio State 15	1983	Florida State 31, West Virginia 12	1987	Clemson 27, Stanford 21

RESULTS OF OTHER 1986 SEASON BOWL GAMES

All-American (Birmingham, Ala., Dec. 31)—Florida State 27, Indiana 13
Aloha (Honolulu, Dec. 27)—Arizona 30, North Carolina 21
Bluebonnet (Houston, Dec. 31)—Baylor 21, Colorado 9
California (Fresno, Dec. 13)—San Jose State 37, Miami, Ohio 7
Fiesta (Tempe, Ariz., Jan 2)—Penn State 14, Miami 10
Florida Citrus (Orlando, Jan. 1)—Auburn 16, Southern Cal 7
Freedom (Anaheim, Calif., Dec. 30)—UCLA 31, Brigham Young 10
Hall of Fame (Tampa, Fla., Dec. 23)—Boston College 27, Georgia 24
Holiday (San Diego, Dec. 30)—Iowa 39, San Diego State 38
Independence (Shreveport, La., Dec. 20)—Mississippi 20, Texas Tech 17
Liberty (Memphis, Dec. 29)—Tennessee 21, Minnesota 14
Peach (Atlanta, Dec. 31)—Virginia Tech 25, North Carolina State 24
Sun (El Paso, Tex., Dec. 25)—Alabama 28, Washington 6

HEISMAN MEMORIAL TROPHY WINNERS

The Heisman Memorial Trophy is presented annually by the Downtown Athletic Club of New York City to the nation's outstanding college football player, as determined by a poll of sportswriters and sportscasters.

1935	Jay Berwanger, Chicago	1952	Billy Vessels, Oklahoma	1969	Steve Owens, Oklahoma
1936	Larry Kelley, Yale	1953	Johnny Lattner, Notre Dame	1970	Jim Plunkett, Stanford
1937	Clinton Frank, Yale	1954	Alan Ameche, Wisconsin	1971	Pat Sullivan, Auburn
1938	Davey O'Brien, Texas Christian	1955	Howard Cassady, Ohio State	1972	Johnny Rodgers, Nebraska
1939	Nile Kinnick, Iowa	1956	Paul Hornung, Notre Dame	1973	John Cappelletti, Penn State
1940	Tom Harmon, Michigan	1957	John Crow, Texas A & M	1974-75	Archie Griffin, Ohio State
1941	Bruce Smith, Minnesota	1958	Pete Dawkins, Army	1976	Tony Dorsett, Pittsburgh
1942	Frank Sinkwich, Georgia	1959	Billy Cannon, Louisiana State	1977	Earl Campbell, Texas
1943	Angelo Bertelli, Notre Dame	1960	Joe Bellino, Navy	1978	Billy Sims, Oklahoma
1944	Leslie Horvath, Ohio State	1961	Ernie Davis, Syracuse	1979	Charles White, Southern California
1945	Felix Blanchard, Army	1962	Terry Baker, Oregon State	1980	George Rogers, South Carolina
1946	Glenn Davis, Army	1963	Roger Staubach, Navy	1981	Marcus Allen, Southern California
1947	Johnny Lujack, Notre Dame	1964	John Huarte, Notre Dame	1982	Hershel Walker, Georgia
1948	Doak Walker, So. Methodist	1965	Mike Garrett, Southern California	1983	Mike Rozier, Nebraska
1949	Leon Hart, Notre Dame	1966	Steve Spurrier, Florida	1984	Doug Flutie, Boston College
1950	Vic Janowicz, Ohio State	1967	Gary Beban, U.C.L.A.	1985	Bo Jackson, Auburn
1951	Dick Kazmaier, Princeton	1968	O. J. Simpson, Southern California	1986	Vinnie Testeverde, Miami

COLLEGE FOOTBALL HALL OF FAME

(Kings Island, Interstate 71, Kings Mills, Ohio)

(Date given is player's last year of competition)

Players

Abell, Earl—Colgate, 1915
Agase, Alex—Purdue/Illinois, 1946
Agganis, Harry—Boston Univ., 1952
Albert, Frank—Stanford, 1941
Aldrich, Chas. (Ki)—T.C.U., 1938
Aldrich, Malcolm—Yale, 1921
Alexander, John—Syracuse, 1920
Alworth, Lance—Arkansas, 1961
Ameche, Alan (Horse)—Wisconsin, 1954
Amling, Warren—Ohio State, 1946
Anderson, H. (Hunk)—Notre Dame, 1921
Atkins, Doug—Tennessee, 1952
Bacon, C. Everett—Wesleyan, 1912
Bagnell, Francis (Reds)—Penn, 1950
Baker, Hobart (Hobey)—Princeton, 1913
Baker, John—So. Calif., 1931
Baker, Terry—Oregon State, 1962
Ballin, Harold—Princeton, 1914
Banker, Bill—Tulane, 1929
Banonis, Vince—Detroit, 1941
Barnes, Stanley—S. California, 1921
Barrett, Charles—Cornell, 1915
Baston, Bert—Minnesota, 1916
Battles, Cliff—W. Va. Wesleyan, 1931
Baugh, Sammy—Texas Christian U., 1936
Bausch, James—Kansas, 1930
Beagle, Ron—Navy, 1955
Beckett, John—Oregon, 1913
Bednarik, Chuck—Pennsylvania, 1948
Bellino, Joe—Navy, 1960
Benbrook, A.—Michigan, 1911
Bertelli, A.—Notre Dame, 1943
Berry, Charlie—Lafayette, 1924
Berwanger, John (Jay)—Chicago, 1935
Bettencourt, Larry—St. Mary's, 1927
Blanchard, Felix (Doc)—Army, 1946
Bock, Ed—Iowa State, 1938
Bomar, Lynn—Vanderbilt, 1924
Bomeisler, Doug (Bo)—Yale, 1913
Booth, Albie—Yale, 1931
Borries, Fred—Navy, 1934
Bosely, Bruce—West Virginia, 1955
Bottari, Vic—California, 1939
Boynton, Ben—Williams, 1920
Bozis, Al—Georgetown, 1941
Brewer, Charles—Harvard, 1895
Bright, John—Drake, 1951
Brodie, John—Stanford, 1956
Brooke, George—Pennsylvania, 1895
Brown, George—Navy, San Diego St., 1947
Brown, Gordon—Yale, 1900
Brown, John, Jr.—Navy, 1913
Brown, Johnny Mack—Alabama, 1925
Brown, Raymond (Tay)—So. California, 1932
Bunker, Paul—Army, 1902
Butkus, Dick—Illinois, 1964
Butler, Robert—Wisconsin, 1912
Cafego, George—Tennessee, 1939
Cagle, Chris—SW La./Army, 1929
Cain, John—Alabama, 1932
Cameron, Eddie—Wash. & Lee, 1924
Campbell, David C.—Harvard, 1901
Cannon, Billy—L.S.U., 1959
Cannon, Jack—Notre Dame, 1929
Carideo, Frank—Notre Dame, 1930
Caroline, J.C.—Illinois, 1954
Carney, Charles—Illinois, 1921
Carpenter, Bill—Army, 1959
Carpenter, C. Hunter—VPI, 1905
Carroll, Charles—Washington, 1928
Casey, Edward L.—Harvard, 1919
Cassady, Howard—Ohio State, 1955
Chamberlain, Guy—Nebraska, 1915
Chapman, Sam—Cal.-Berkeley, 1938
Christman, Paul—Missouri, 1940
Clark, Earl (Dutch)—Colo. College, 1929
Clevenger, Zora—Indiana, 1903
Cochran, Gary—Princeton, 1895
Cody, Josh—Vanderbilt, 1920
Coleman, Don—Mich. State, 1951
Conerly, Chuck—Mississippi, 1947
Connor, George—Notre Dame, 1947
Corbin, W.—Yale, 1888
Corbus, William—Stanford, 1933
Cowan, Hector—Princeton, 1889
Coy, Edward H. (Tad)—Yale, 1909
Crawford, Fred—Duke, 1933

Crow, John D.—Texas A&M, 1957
Crowley, James—Notre Dame, 1924
Cutter, Slade—Navy, 1934
Czarobski, Ziggie—Notre Dame, 1947
Dale, Carroll—Virginia Tech, 1959
Dalrymple, Gerald—Tulane, 1931
Daniell, James—Ohio State, 1941
Dawkins, Pete—Army, 1958
Dalton, John—Navy, 1912
Daly, Charles—Harvard/Army, 1902
Daniell, Averell—Pittsburgh, 1936
Davies, Tom—Pittsburgh, 1921
Davis, Ernest—Syracuse, 1961
Davis, Glenn—Army, 1946
Davis, Robert T.—Georgia Tech, 1947
De Rogatis, Al—Duke, 1940
DesJardien, Paul—Chicago, 1914
Devino, Aubrey—Iowa, 1921
DeWitt, John—Princeton, 1903
Ditka, Mike—Pittsburgh 1960
Dobbs, Glenn—Tulsa, 1942
Dodd, Bobby—Tennessee, 1930
Donan, Holland—Princeton, 1950
Donchess, Joseph—Pittsburgh, 1929
Dougherty, Nathan—Tennessee, 1909
Drahos, Nick—Cornell, 1940
Driscoll, Paddy—Northwestern, 1917
Drury, Morley—So. California, 1927
Dudley, William (Bill)—Virginia, 1941
Eckersall, Walter—Chicago, 1906
Edwards, Turk—Washington State, 1931
Edwards, William—Princeton, 1900
Eichenlaub, R.—Notre Dame, 1913
Evans, Ray—Kansas, 1947
Exendine, Albert—Carlisle, 1908
Falaschi, Nello—Santa Clara, 1937
Fears, Tom—Santa Clara/UCLA, 1947
Feathers, Beattie—Tennessee, 1933
Fenimore, Robert—Oklahoma State, 1947
Fenton, G.E. (Doc)—La. State U., 1910
Ferraro, John—So. California, 1944
Fesler, Wesley—Ohio State, 1930
Fincher, Bill—Georgia Tech, 1920
Fischer, Bill—Notre Dame, 1948
Fish, Hamilton—Harvard, 1909
Fisher, Robert—Harvard, 1911
Flowers, Abe—Georgia Tech, 1920
Fortmann, Daniel—Colgate, 1935
Francis, Sam—Nebraska, 1936
Franco, Edmund (Ed)—Fordham, 1937
Frank, Clint—Yale, 1937
Franz, Rodney—California, 1949
Friedman, Benny—Michigan, 1926
Gain, Bob—Kentucky, 1950
Galiffa, Arnold—Army, 1949
Gallarneau, Hugh—Stanford, 1941
Garbisch, Edgar—Army, 1924
Garrett, Mike—USC, 1965
Gelbert, Charles—Pennsylvania, 1896
Geyer, Forest—Oklahoma, 1915
Giel, Paul—Minnesota, 1953
Gifford, Frank—So. California, 1951
Gilbert, Walter—Auburn, 1936
Gipp, George—Notre Dame, 1920
Gladchuk, Chet—Boston College, 1940
Glass, Bill—Baylor, 1956
Goldberg, Marshall—Pittsburgh, 1938
Goodreault, Gene—Boston College, 1940
Gordon, Walter—California, 1918
Governale, Paul—Columbia, 1942
Graham, Otto—Northwestern, 1943
Grange, Harold (Red)—Illinois, 1925
Grayson, Robert—Stanford, 1935
Green, Joe—North Texas State, 1968
Griese, Bob—Purdue, 1966
Griffin, Archie—Ohio State, 1975
Gulick, Merel—Hobart, 1929
Guyon, Joe—Georgia Tech, 1919
Hale, Edwin—Mississippi Col, 1921
Hamilton, Robert (Bones)—Stanford, 1935
Hamilton, Tom—Navy, 1925
Hanson, Vic—Syracuse, 1926
Hardwick, H. (Tack)—Harvard, 1914
Hare, T. Truxton—Pennsylvania, 1900
Harley, Chick—Ohio State, 1919
Harmon, Tom—Michigan, 1940
Harpster, Howard—Carnegie Tech, 1928
Hart, Edward J.—Princeton, 1911
Hart, Leon—Notre Dame, 1949
Hartman, Bill—Georgia, 1937
Hazel, Homer—Rutgers, 1924
Healey, Ed—Dartmouth, 1916
Heffelfinger, W. (Pudge)—Yale, 1891
Hein, Mel—Washington State, 1930
Heinrich, Don—Washington, 1952
Hendricks, Ted—Miami, 1968
Henry, Wilber—Wash. & Jefferson, 1919
Herschberger, Clarence—Chicago, 1899
Herwig, Robert—California, 1937
Heston, Willie—Michigan, 1904
Hickman, Herman—Tennessee, 1931
Hickok, William—Yale, 1895
Hill, Dan—Duke, 1938
Hillebrand, A.R. (Doc)—Princeton, 1900
Hinkey, Frank—Yale, 1894
Hinkle, Carl—Vanderbilt, 1937
Hinkle, Clark—Bucknell, 1932
Hirsch, Elroy—Wis./Mich., 1943
Hitchcock, James—Auburn, 1932
Hoffman, Frank—Notre Dame, 1931
Hogan, James J.—Yale, 1904
Holland, Jerome (Brud)—Cornell, 1938
Holleder, Don—Army, 1955
Hollenbeck, William—Penn., 1908
Holovak, Michael—Boston College, 1942
Holub, E.J.—Texas Tech, 1960
Hornung, Paul—Notre Dame, 1956
Horrell, Edwin—California, 1924
Horvath, Les—Ohio State, 1944
Howe, Arthur—Yale, 1911
Howell, Millard (Dixie)—Alabama, 1934
Hubbard, Cal—Centenary, 1926
Hubbard, John—Amherst, 1906
Hubert, Allison—Alabama, 1925
Huff, Robert Lee (Sam)—W. Va., 1955
Humble, Weldon G.—Rice, 1946
Hunt, Joel—Texas A&M, 1927
Huntington, Ellery—Colgate, 1914
Hutson, Don—Alabama, 1934
Ingram, James—Navy, 1906
Isbell, Cecil—Purdue, 1937
Jablonsky, Harvey—Wash. U./Army, 1933
Janowicz, Vic—Ohio State, 1951
Jenkins, Darold—Missouri, 1941
Jensen, Jack—Cal-Berkeley, 1948
Joesting, Herbert—Minnesota, 1927
Johnson, James—Carlisle, 1903
Jones, Calvin—Iowa, 1955
Jones, Gomer—Ohio State, 1935
Jordan, Lee Roy—Alabama, 1962
Juhan, Frank—Univ. of South, 1910
Justice, Charlie—North Carolina, 1949
Kaer, Mort—So. California, 1926
Kavanaugh, Kenneth—La. State U., 1939
Kaw, Edgar—Cornell, 1922
Kazmaier, Richard—Princeton, 1951
Keck, James—Princeton, 1921
Kelley, Larry—Yale, 1936
Kelly, William—Montana, 1926
Kenna, Ed—Syracuse, 1966
Kern, George—Boston College, 1941
Ketcham, Henry—Yale, 1913
Killinger, William—Penn State, 1922
Kimbrough, John—Texas A&M, 1940
Kinard, Frank—Mississippi, 1937
King, Phillip—Princeton, 1893
Kinnick, Nile—Iowa, 1939
Kipke, Harry—Michigan, 1923
Kirkpatrick, John Reed—Yale, 1910
Kitzmiller, John—Oregon, 1929
Koch, Barton—Baylor, 1931
Kitner, Malcolm—Texas, 1942
Kramer, Ron—Michigan, 1956
Krueger, Charlie—Texas A&M, 1957
Lach, Steve—Duke, 1941
Lane, Myles—Dartmouth, 1927
Lattner, Joseph J.—Notre Dame, 1953
Lauricella, Hank—Tennessee, 1952
Lautenschlaeger—Tulane, 1925
Layden, Elmer—Notre Dame, 1924
Layne, Bobby—Texas, 1947
Lea, Langdon—Princeton, 1895
LeBaron, Eddie—Univ. of Pacific, 1949
Leech, James—Va. Mil. Inst., 1920
Lilly, Bob—Texas Christian, 1960
Little, Floyd—Syracuse, 1966
Lio, Augie—Georgetown, 1940
Locke, Gordon—Iowa, 1922
Lourie, Don—Princeton, 1921
Lucas, Richard—Penn State, 1959
Luckman, Sid—Columbia, 1938
Lujack, John—Notre Dame, 1947
Lund, J.L. (Pug)—Minnesota, 1934
Macomber, Bart—Illinois, 1915
MacLeod, Robert—Dartmouth, 1938
Maegle, Dick—Rice, 1954
Mahan, Edward W.—Harvard, 1915
Majors, John—Tennessee, 1956
Mallory, William—Yale, 1893
Mann, Gerald—So. Methodist, 1927
Markov, Vic—Washington, 1937
Marshall, Robert—Minnesota, 1907
Matson, Ollie—San Fran. U., 1952
Matthews, Ray—Texas Christ. U., 1928
Maulbetsch, John—Michigan, 1914
Mauthe, J.L. (Pete)—Penn State, 1912
Maxwell, Robert—Chi./Swarthmore, 1906
McAfee, George—Duke, 1939
McColl, William F.—Stanford, 1951
McCormick, James B.—Princeton, 1907
McDonald, Tom—Oklahoma, 1956
McDowall, Jack—No. Car. State, 1927
McElhenny, Hugh—Washington, 1951
McEver, Gene—Tennessee, 1931
McEwan, John—Minn./Army, 1916
McFadden, J.B.—Clemson, 1939
McFadin, Bud—Texas, 1950
McClung, Thomas L.—Yale, 1891
McGinley, Edward—Pennsylvania, 1924
McGovern, J.—Minnesota, 1910
McGraw, Thurman—Colorado State, 1949
McKeever, Mike—USC, 1960
McLaren, George—Pittsburgh, 1918
McMillan, Dan—U.S.C./Calif., 1922
McMillin, A.N. (Bo)—Centre, 1921
McWhorter, Robert—Georgia, 1913
Mercer, Leroy—Pennsylvania, 1912
Meredith, Don—Southern Methodist, 1959
Metzger, Bert—Notre Dame, 1930
Mickal, Abe—La. State U., 1935
Miller, Creighton—Notre Dame, 1943
Miller, Don—Notre Dame, 1925
Miller, Edgar (Rip)—Notre Dame, 1924
Miller, Eugene—Penn State, 1913
Miller, Fred—Notre Dame, 1928
Milstead, Century—Wabash, Yale, 1923
Minds, John—Pennsylvania, 1897
Minisi, Anthony—Navy, Pennsylvania, 1947
Moffatt, Alex—Princeton, 1884
Montgomery, Cliff—Columbia, 1933
Moomaw, Donn—U.C.L.A., 1952
Morley, William—Columbia, 1903
Morris, George—Georgia Tech, 1952
Morton, William—Dartmouth, 1931
Moscrip, Monk—Stanford, 1935
Muller, Harold (Brick)—Calif., 1922
Nagurski, Bronko—Minnesota, 1929
Nevers, Ernie—Stanford, 1925
Newell, Marshall—Harvard, 1893
Newman, Harry—Michigan, 1932
Nobis, Tommy—Texas, 1965
Nomellini, Leo—Minnesota, 1949
Oberlander, Andrew—Dartmouth, 1925
O'Brien, Davey—Texas Christ. U., 1938
O'Dea, Pat—Wisconsin, 1899
O'Hearn, J.—Cornell, 1915
Olds, Robin—Army, 1942
Oliphant, Elmer—Purdue/Army, 1917
Olsen, Merlin—Utah State, 1961
Oosterbaan, Ben—Michigan, 1927
O'Rourke, Charles—Boston College, 1940
Orsi, John—Colgate, 1931
Osgood, W.D.—Cornell/Penn, 1895
Osmanski, William—Holy Cross, 1938
Owen, George—Harvard, 1922
Owens, Jim—Oklahoma, 1949
Pardee, Jack—Texas A & M, 1956
Parilli, Vito (Babe)—Kentucky, 1951

Parker, Clarence (Ace)—Duke, 1936
Parker, Jackie—Miss. State, 1953
Parker, James—Ohio State, 1956
Pazzetti, V.J.—Wes./Lehigh, 1912
Peabody, Endicott—Harvard, 1941
Peck, Robert—Pittsburgh, 1916
Pennock, Stanley B.—Harvard, 1914
Pfann, George—Cornell, 1923
Phillips, H.D.—U. of South, 1904
Pingel, John—Michigan State, 1938
Pihos, Pete—Indiana, 1945
Pinckert, Ernie—So. California, 1931
Poe, Arthur—Princeton, 1899
Pollard, Fritz—Brown, 1916
Poole, Barney—Miss./Army, 1947
Pregulman, Merv—Michigan, 1943
Price, Eddie—Tulane, 1949
Pund, Henry—Georgia Tech, 1928
Ramsey, Gerrard—Wm. & Mary, 1942
Reeds, Claude—Oklahoma, 1913
Reid, Mike—Penn St. 1970
Reid, Steve—Northwestern, 1936
Reid, William—Harvard, 1900
Renfro, Mel—Oregon, 1963
Rentner, Ernest—Northwestern, 1932
Reynolds, Robert—Nebraska, 1952
Reynolds, Robert—Stanford, 1935
Richter, Les—California, 1951
Rinehart, Charles—Lafayette, 1897
Rodgers, Ira—West Virginia, 1919
Rogers, Edward L.—Minnesota, 1903
Romig, Joe—Colorado, 1961
Rosenberg, Aaron—So. California, 1934
Rote, Kyle—So. Methodist, 1950
Routt, Joe—Texas A&M, 1937
Salmon, Louis—Notre Dame, 1904
Sauer, George—Nebraska, 1933
Sayers, Gale—Kansas, 1964
Scarbath, Jack—Maryland, 1952
Scarlett, Hunter—Pennsylvania, 1909
Schoonover, Wear—Arkansas, 1929
Schreiner, Dave—Wisconsin, 1942
Schultz, Adolf (Germany)—Mich., 1908
Schwab, Frank—Lafayette, 1922
Schwartz, Marchmont—Notre Dame, 1931
Schwegler, Paul—Washington, 1931
Scott, Clyde—Arkansas, 1949
Scott, Richard—Navy 1947
Scott, Tom—Virginia, 1953
Seibels, Henry—Sewanee, 1899
Shakespeare, Bill—Notre Dame, 1935
Shelton, Murray—Cornell, 1915
Shevlin, Tom—Yale, 1905
Shively, Bernie—Illinois, 1926
Simons, Claude—Tulane, 1934
Simpson, O.J.—So. Calif., 1968
Sington, Fred—Alabama, 1930
Sinkwich, Frank—Georgia, 1942
Sitko, Emil—Notre Dame, 1949
Skladany, Joe—Pittsburgh, 1933
Slater, F.F. (Duke)—Iowa, 1921
Smith, Bruce—Minnesota, 1941
Smith, Ernie—So. California, 1932
Smith, Harry—So. California, 1939
Smith, Jim Ray—Baylor, 1954
Smith, John (Clipper)—Notre Dame, 1927
Smith, Riley—Alabama, 1935
Smith, Vernon—Georgia, 1931
Snow, Neil—Michigan, 1901
Sparlis, Al—U.C.L.A., 1945
Spears, Clarence W.—Dartmouth, 1915
Spears, W.D.—Vanderbilt, 1927
Sprackling, William—Brown, 1911
Sprague, M. (Bud)—Texas/Army, 1928
Spurrier, Steve—Florida, 1966
Stafford, Harrison—Texas, 1932
Stagg, Amos Alonzo—Yale, 1889
Staubach, Roger—Navy, 1963
Steffen, Walter—Chicago, 1908
Steffy, Joe—Army, 1947
Stein, Herbert—Pittsburgh, 1921
Steuber, Robert—Missouri, 1943
Stevens, Mal—Yale, 1923
Stinchcomb, Gaylord—Ohio State, 1920
Stevenson, Vincent—Pennsylvania, 1905
Strom, Brock—Air Force, 1959
Strong, Ken—New York Univ., 1928
Strupper, George—Georgia Tech, 1917
Stuhldreher, Harry—Notre Dame, 1924
Stydahar, Joe—West Virginia, 1935
Suffridge, Robert—Tennessee, 1940
Suhey, Steve—Pennsylvania State, 1947
Sundstrom, Frank—Cornell, 1923
Swanson, Clarence—Nebraska, 1921
Swiacki, Bill—Holy Cross/Colombia, 1947
Swink, Jim—Texas Christian, 1956
Taliafarro, George—Indiana, 1948
Tarkenton, Fran—Georgia, 1960
Taylor, Charles—Stanford, 1942
Thompson, Joe—Pittsburgh, 1907
Thorne, Samuel B.—Yale, 1906
Thorpe, Jim—Carlisle, 1912
Ticknor, Ben—Harvard, 1930
Tigert, John—Vanderbilt, 1904
Tinsley, Gaynell—La. State U., 1936
Tipton, Eric—Duke, 1938
Tonnemaker, Clayton—Minnesota, 1949
Torrey, Robert—Pennsylvania, 1906
Travis, Ed Tarkio—Missouri, 1920
Trippi, Charles—Georgia, 1946
Tryon, J. Edward—Colgate, 1925
Utay, Joe—Texas A&M, 1907
Van Brocklin, Norm—Oregon, 1948
Van Sickel, Dale—Florida, 1929
Van Surdam, Henderson—Wesleyan, 1905
Very, Dexter—Penn State, 1912
Vessels, Billy—Oklahoma, 1931
Vick, Ernie—Michigan, 1921
Wagner, Huber—Pittsburgh, 1913
Walker, Doak—So. Methodist, 1949
Wallace, Bill—Rice, 1935
Walsh, Adam—Notre Dame, 1924
Warburton, I. (Cotton)—So. Calif., 1934
Ward, Robert (Bob)—Maryland, 1951
Warner, William—Cornell, 1903
Washington, Ken—U.C.L.A., 1939
Webster, George—Michigan St. 1966
Wedemeyer, Herman J.—St. Mary's, 1947
Weekes, Harold—Columbia, 1902
Weir, Ed—Nebraska, 1925
Welch, Gus—Carlisle, 1914
Weller, John—Princeton, 1935
Wendell, Percy—Harvard, 1913
West, D. Belford—Colgate, 1919
Westfall, Bob—Michigan, 1941
Weyand, Alex—Army, 1915
Wharton, Charles—Pennsylvania, 1896
Wheeler, Arthur—Princeton, 1894
White, Byron (Whizzer)—Colorado, 1937
Whitmire, Don—Alabama/Navy, 1944
Wickhorst, Frank—Navy, 1926
Widseth, Ed—Minnesota, 1936
Wildung, Richard—Minnesota, 1942
Williams, James—Rice, 1949
Willis, William—Ohio State, 1945
Wilson, George—Washington, 1925
Wilson, Harry—Penn State/Army, 1923
Wistert, Albert A.—Michigan, 1942
Wistert, Al—Michigan, 1949
Wistert, Frank (Whitey)—Mich., 1933
Wood, Barry—Harvard, 1931
Wojciechowicz, Alex—Fordham, 1936
Wyant, Andrew—Bucknell/Chicago, 1894
Wyatt, Bowden—Tennessee, 1938
Wyckoff, Clint—Cornell, 1896
Yarr, Tom—Notre Dame, 1931
Yary, Ron—USC, 1968
Yoder, Lloyd—Carnegie Tech, 1926
Young, Claude (Buddy)—Illinois, 1946
Young, Harry—Wash. & Lee, 1916
Young, Walter—Oklahoma, 1938
Zarnas, Gus—Ohio State, 1937

Coaches

Bill Alexander
Dr. Ed Anderson
Ike Armstrong
Matty Bell
Hugo Bezdek
Dana X. Bible
Bernie Bierman
Bob Blackman
Earl (Red) Blaik
Frank Broyles
Paul "Bear" Bryant
Charles W. Caldwell
Walter Camp
Len Casanova
Frank Cavanaugh
Fritz Crisler
Duffy Daugherty
Bob Devaney
Dan Devine
Gil Dobie
Michael Donohue
Gus Dorais
Bill Edwards
Charles (Rip) Engle
Don Faurot
Jake Gaither
Ernest Godfrey
Andy Gustafson
Jack Harding
Edward K. Hall
Richard Harlow
Jesse Harper
Percy Haughton
Woody Hayes
John W. Heisman
R. A. (Bob) Higgins
Orin E. Hollingberry
William Ingram
Morley Jennings
Howard Jones
L. (Biff) Jones
Thomas (Tad) Jones
Ralph (Shug) Jordan
Andy Kerr
Frank Leahy
George E. Little
Lou Little
El (Slip) Madigan
Charley McClendon
Herbert McCracken
Daniel McGugin
DeOrmond (Tuss) McLaughry
L. R. (Dutch) Meyer
Bernie Moore
Scrappy Moore
Ray Morrison
George A. Munger
Clarence Munn
Frank Murray
William Murray
Ed (Hooks) Mylin
Earle (Greasy) Neale
Jess Neely
David Nelson
Robert Neyland
Homer Norton
Frank (Buck) O'Neill
Bennie Owen
Ara Parseghian
James Phalea
E. N. Robinson
Knute Rockne
E. L. (Dick) Romney
William W. Roper
Darrell Royal
George F. Sanford
Francis A. Schmidt
Floyd (Ben) Schwartzwalder
Clark Shaughnessy
Buck Shaw
Andrew L. Smith
Carl Snavely
Amos A. Stagg
Jock Sutherland
James Tatum
Frank W. Thomas
Thad Vann
John H. Vaught
Wallace Wade
Lynn Waldorf
Glenn (Pop) Warner
E. E. (Tad) Wieman
John W. Wilce
Bud Wilkinson
Henry L. Williams
George W. Woodruff
Fielding H. Yost
Robert Zuppke

1986 N.C.A.A. CHAMPIONSHIP PLAYOFFS

DIVISION 1-AA

Quarterfinals

Arkansas State 55, Delaware 14
Eastern Kentucky 24, Eastern Illinois 22
Georgia Southern 55, Nicholls State 31
Nevada–Reno 33, Tennessee State 6

Semifinals

Arkansas State 24, Eastern Kentucky 10
Georgia Southern 48, Nevada–Reno 38

Championship

Georgia Southern 48, Arkansas State 21

DIVISION II

Quarterfinals

North Dakota State 50, Ashland 0
Central Ohio State 31, Towson State 0
Troy State 31, Virginia State 7
South Dakota 26, California–Davis 23

Semifinals

North Dakota State 35, Central Ohio State 12
South Dakota 42, Troy State 28

Championship

North Dakota State 27, South Dakota 7

DIVISION III

Quarterfinals

Ithaca 29, Montclair State 15
Salisbury State 31, Susquehanna 17
Augustana (Ill.) 16, Mount Union 7
Concordia–Moorhead 17, Central (Iowa) 14

Semifinals

Salisbury State 44, Ithaca 40
Augustana 41, Concordia–Moorhead 7

Championship

Augustana 31, Salisbury 3

NATIONAL ASSOCIATION OF INTERCOLLEGIATE ATHLETICS 1986 CHAMPIONSHIPS

DIVISION I

Quarterfinals

Pittsburg (Kansas) State 58, Washburn (Kansas) 24
Cameron (Oklahoma) 35, Central Arkansas 34
Hillsdale (Michigan) 27, Mesa (Colorado) 17
Carson–Newman (Tennessee) 30, Shepard (W. Virginia) 10

Semifinals

Cameron 17, Pittsburg State 6
Carson–Newman 19, Hillsdale 16 (OT)

Championship

Carson–Newman 17, Cameron 0

DIVISION II

Quarterfinals

Wisconsin–LaCrosse 35, Hanover (Indiana) 33
Baker (Kansas) 49, Huron (South Dakota) 20
Linfield (Oregon) 27, Pacific Lutheran (Washington) 21 (OT)
Carroll (Montana) 21, Dickinson State (North Dakota) 16

Semifinals

Baker 16, Wisconsin–LaCrosse 14
Linfield 53, Carroll 7

Championship

Linfield 17, Baker 0

Professional Football

NATIONAL FOOTBALL LEAGUE FINAL STANDING 1986

AMERICAN CONFERENCE

Eastern Division

	W	L	T	Pct	Pts	Op
New England	11	5	0	.688	412	307
New York Jets[1]	10	6	0	.625	364	386
Miami	8	8	0	.500	430	405
Buffalo	4	12	0	.250	287	348
Indianapolis	3	13	0	.188	229	400

Central Division

	W	L	T	Pct	Pts	Op
Cleveland	12	4	0	.750	391	310
Cincinnati	10	6	0	.625	409	394
Pittsburgh	6	10	0	.375	307	336
Houston	5	11	0	.313	274	329

Western Division

	W	L	T	Pct	Pts	Op
Denver	11	5	0	.688	378	327
Kansas City[1]	10	6	0	.625	358	326
Seattle	10	6	0	.625	366	293
Los Angeles Raiders	8	8	0	.500	323	346
San Diego	4	12	0	.250	335	396

1. Wild card qualifier for playoffs.

Playoffs: Jets 35, Kansas City 15; Cleveland 23, Jets 20 (OT); Denver 22, New England 17.
Conference championship: Denver 23, Cleveland 20 (OT).

NATIONAL CONFERENCE

Eastern Division

	W	L	T	Pct	Pts	Op
New York Giants	14	2	0	.875	371	236
Washington[1]	12	4	0	.750	368	296
Dallas	7	9	0	.438	346	337
Philadelphia	5	10	1	.344	256	312
St. Louis	4	11	1	.281	218	351

Central Division

	W	L	T	Pct	Pts	Op
Chicago	14	2	0	.875	352	187
Minnesota	9	7	0	.563	398	273
Detroit	5	11	0	.313	277	326
Green Bay	4	12	0	.250	254	418
Tampa Bay	2	14	0	.125	239	473

Western Division

	W	L	T	Pct	Pts	Op
San Francisco	10	5	1	.656	374	247
Los Angeles Rams[1]	10	6	0	.625	309	267
Atlanta	7	8	1	.469	280	280
New Orleans	7	9	0	.438	288	287

1. Wild card qualifier for playoffs.

Playoffs: Washington 19, Rams 7; Washington 27, Chicago 13; Giants 49, San Francisco 3.
Conference championship: Giants 17, Washington 0.

LEAGUE CHAMPIONSHIP—SUPER BOWL XXI

(Jan. 25, 1987, at The Rose Bowl, Pasadena, Calif. Attendance: 101,063)

Scoring

	1st Q	2nd Q	3rd Q	4th Q	Final
Denver (AFC)	10	0	0	10	20
New York Giants (NFC)	7	2	17	13	39

Scoring—Giants: Touchdowns: Mowatt, 6-yard pass from Simms; Bavaro, 13-yard pass from Simms; McConkey, 44-yard pass from Simms; McConkey, 6-yard pass from Simms; Anderson, 2-yard run. Field goals: Allegre, 21. Safety: Martin. Denver: Touchdowns: Elway, 4-yard run; Johnson, 47-yard pass from Elway. Field goals: Karlis, 48, 28.

Statistics of the Game

	New York	Denver
First downs	24	23
Yards gained rushing	136	52
Yards gained passing	263	320
Passes completed	22	26
Passes attempted	25	41
Passes intercepted by	1	0
Punts	3-46	2-41
Fumbles lost	0	0
Yards penalized	48	28
Time of possession	34:39	25:21

SUPER BOWLS I–XX

Game	Date	Winner	Loser	Site	Attendance
XXI	Jan. 25, 1987	Giants (NFC) 39	Denver (AFC) 20	Rose Bowl, Pasadena, Calif.	101,063
XX	Jan. 26, 1986	Chicago (NFC) 46	New England (AFC) 10	Superdome, New Orleans	73,818
XIX	Jan. 20, 1985	San Francisco (NFC) 38	Miami (AFC) 16	Stanford Stadium, Palo Alto, Calif.	84,059
XVIII	Jan. 22, 1984	Los Angeles Raiders (AFC) 38	Washington (NFC) 9	Tampa Stadium, Tampa, Fla	72,920
XVII	Jan. 30, 1983	Washington (NFC) 27	Miami (AFC) 17	Rose Bowl, Pasadena, Calif.	103,667
XVI	Jan. 24, 1982	San Francisco (NFC) 26	Cincinnati (AFC) 21	Silverdome, Pontiac, Mich.	81,270
XV	Jan. 25, 1981	Oakland (AFC) 27	Philadelphia (NFC) 10	Superdome, New Orleans	75,500
XIV	Jan. 20, 1980	Pittsburgh (AFC) 31	Los Angeles (NFC) 19	Rose Bowl, Pasadena	103,985
XIII	Jan. 21, 1979	Pittsburgh (AFC) 35	Dallas (NFC) 31	Orange Bowl, Miami	79,484
XII	Jan. 15, 1978	Dallas (NFC) 27	Denver (AFC) 10	Superdome, New Orleans	75,583
XI	Jan. 9, 1977	Oakland (AFC) 32	Minnesota (NFC) 14	Rose Bowl, Pasadena	103,424
X	Jan. 18, 1976	Pittsburgh (AFC) 21	Dallas (NFC) 17	Orange Bowl, Miami	80,187
IX	Jan. 12, 1975	Pittsburgh (AFC) 16	Minnesota (NFC) 6	Tulane Stadium, New Orleans	80,997
VIII	Jan. 13, 1974	Miami (AFC) 24	Minnesota (NFC) 7	Rice Stadium, Houston	71,882
VII	Jan. 14, 1973	Miami (AFC) 14	Washington (NFC) 7	Memorial Coliseum, Los Angeles	90,182
VI	Jan. 16, 1972	Dallas (NFC) 24	Miami (AFC) 3	Tulane Stadium, New Orleans	81,591
V	Jan. 17, 1971	Baltimore (AFC) 16	Dallas (NFC) 13	Orange Bowl, Miami	79,204
IV	Jan. 11, 1970	Kansas City (AFL) 23	Minnesota (NFL) 7	Tulane Stadium, New Orleans	80,562
III	Jan. 12, 1969	New York (AFL) 16	Baltimore (NFL) 7	Orange Bowl, Miami	75,389
II	Jan. 14, 1968	Green Bay (NFL) 33	Oakland (AFL) 14	Orange Bowl, Miami	75,546
I	Jan. 15, 1967	Green Bay (NFL) 35	Kansas City (AFL) 10	Memorial Coliseum, Los Angeles	61,946

1. Super Bowls I to IV were played before the American Football League and National Football League merged into the NFL, which was divided into two conferences, the NFC and AFC.

NATIONAL LEAGUE CHAMPIONS

Year	Champion (W-L-T)
1921	Chicago Bears (Staley's) (10–1–1)
1922	Canton Bulldogs (10–0–2)
1923	Canton Bulldogs (11–0–1)
1924	Cleveland Indians (7–1–1)
1925	Chicago Cardinals (11–2–1)
1926	Frankford Yellow Jackets (14–1–1)
1927	New York Giants (11–1–1)
1928	Providence Steamrollers (8–1–2)
1929	Green Bay Packers (12–0–1)
1930	Green Bay Packers (10–3–1)
1931	Green Bay Packers (12–2–0)
1932	Chicago Bears (7–1–6)

Year	Eastern Conference winners (W-L-T)	Western Conference winners (W-L-T)	League champion playoff results
1933	New York Giants (11–3–0)	Chicago Bears (10–2–1)	Chicago Bears 23, New York 21
1934	New York Giants (8–5–0)	Chicago Bears (13–0–0)	New York 30, Chicago Bears 13
1935	New York Giants (9–3–0)	Detroit Lions (7–3–2)	Detroit 26, New York 7
1936	Boston Redskins (7–5–0)	Green Bay Packers (10–1–1)	Green Bay 21, Boston 6
1937	Washington Redskins (8–3–0)	Chicago Bears (9–1–1)	Washington 28, Chicago Bears 21
1938	New York Giants (8–2–1)	Green Bay Packers (8–3–0)	New York 23, Green Bay 17
1939	New York Giants (9–1–1)	Green Bay Packers (9–2–0)	Green Bay 27, New York 0
1940	Washington Redskins (9–2–0)	Chicago Bears (8–3–0)	Chicago Bears 73, Washington 0
1941	New York Giants (8–3–0)	Chicago Bears (10–1–1)[2]	Chicago Bears 37, New York 9
1942	Washington Redskins (10–1–1)	Chicago Bears (11–0–0)	Washington 14, Chicago Bears 6
1943	Washington Redskins (6–3–1)[2]	Chicago Bears (8–1–1)	Chicago Bears 41, Washington 21
1944	New York Giants (8–1–1)	Green Bay Packers (8–2–0)	Green Bay 14, New York 7
1945	Washington Redskins (8–2–0)	Cleveland Rams (9–1–0)	Cleveland 15, Washington 14
1946	New York Giants (7–3–1)	Chicago Bears (8–2–1)	Chicago Bears 24, New York 14
1947	Philadelphia Eagles (8–4–0)[2]	Chicago Cardinals (9–3–0)	Chicago Cardinals 28, Philadelphia 21
1948	Philadelphia Eagles (9–2–1)	Chicago Cardinals (11–1–0)	Philadelphia 7, Chicago Cardinals 0
1949	Philadelphia Eagles (11–1–0)	Los Angeles Rams (8–2–2)	Philadelphia 14, Los Angeles 0
1950[1]	Cleveland Browns (10–2–0)[2]	Los Angeles Rams (9–3–0)[2]	Cleveland 30, Los Angeles 28
1951[1]	Cleveland Browns (11–1–0)	Los Angeles Rams (8–4–0)	Los Angeles 24, Cleveland 17
1952[1]	Cleveland Browns (8–4–0)	Detroit Lions (9–3–0)[2]	Detroit 17, Cleveland 7
1953	Cleveland Browns (11–1–0)	Detroit Lions (10–2–0)	Detroit 17, Cleveland 16

1954	Cleveland Browns (9–3–0)	Detroit Lions (9–2–1)	Cleveland 56, Detroit 10
1955	Cleveland Browns (9–2–1)	Los Angeles Rams (8–3–1)	Cleveland 38, Los Angeles 14
1956	New York Giants (8–3–1)	Chicago Bears (9–2–1)	New York 47, Chicago Bears 7
1957	Cleveland Browns (9–2–1)	Detroit Lions (8–4–0)[3]	Detroit 59, Cleveland 14
1958	New York Giants (9–3–0)[2]	Baltimore Colts (9–3–0)	Baltimore 23, New York 17[3]
1959	New York Giants (10–2–0)	Baltimore Colts (9–3–0)	Baltimore 31, New York 16
1960	Philadelphia Eagles (10–2–0)	Green Bay Packers (8–4–0)	Philadelphia 17, Green Bay 13
1961	New York Giants (10–3–1)	Green Bay Packers (11–3–0)	Green Bay 37, New York 0
1962	New York Giants (12–2–0)	Green Bay Packers (13–1–0)	Green Bay 16, New York 7
1963	New York Giants (11–3–0)	Chicago Bears (11–1–2)	Chicago 14, New York 10
1964	Cleveland Browns (10–3–1)	Baltimore Colts (12–2–0)	Cleveland 27, Baltimore 0
1965	Cleveland Browns (11–3–0)	Green Bay Packers (11–3–1)[2]	Green Bay 23, Cleveland 12
1966	Dallas Cowboys (10–3–1)	Green Bay Packers (12–2–0)	Green Bay 34, Dallas 27
1967	Dallas Cowboys (9–5–0)[2]	Green Bay Packers (9–4–1)[2]	Green Bay 21, Dallas 17
1968	Cleveland Browns (10–4–0)[2]	Baltimore Colts (13–1–0)[2]	Baltimore 34, Cleveland 0
1969	Cleveland Browns (10–3–1)[2]	Minnesota Vikings (12–2–0)[2]	Minnesota 27, Cleveland 7

1. League was divided into American and National Conferences, 1950–52 and again in 1970, when leagues merged. 2. Won divisional playoff. 3. Won at 8:15 of sudden death overtime period.

NATIONAL CONFERENCE CHAMPIONS

Year	Eastern Division	Central Division	Western Division	Champion
1970	Dallas Cowboys (10–4–0)	Minnesota Vikings (12–2–0)	San Francisco 49ers (10–3–1)	Dallas
1971	Dallas Cowboys (11–3–0)	Minnesota Vikings (11–3–0)	San Francisco 49ers (9–5–0)	Dallas
1972	Washington Redskins (11–3–0)	Green Bay Packers (10–4–0)	San Francisco 49ers (8–5–1)	Washington
1973	Dallas Cowboys (10–4–0)	Minnesota Vikings (12–2–0)	Los Angeles Rams (12–2–0)	Minnesota
1974	St. Louis Cardinals (10–4–0)	Minnesota Vikings (10–4–0)	Los Angeles Rams (10–4–0)	Minnesota
1975	St. Louis Cardinals (11–3–0)	Minnesota Vikings (12–2–0)	Los Angeles Rams (10–4–0)	Dallas
1976	Dallas Cowboys (11–3–0)	Minnesota Vikings (11–2–1)	Los Angeles Rams (10–3–1)	Minnesota
1977	Dallas Cowboys (12–2–0)	Minnesota Vikings (9–5–0)	Los Angeles Rams (10–4–0)	Dallas
1978	Dallas Cowboys (12–4–0)	Minnesota Vikings (8–7–1)	Los Angeles Rams (12–4–0)	Dallas
1979	Dallas Cowboys (11–5–0)	Tampa Bay Buccaneers (10–6–0)	Los Angeles Rams (9–7–0)	Los Angeles
1980	Philadelphia Eagles (12–4–0)	Minnesota Vikings (9–7–0)	Atlanta Falcons (12–4–0)	Philadelphia
1981	Dallas Cowboys (12–4–0)	Tampa Bay Buccaneers (9–7–0)	San Francisco 49ers (13–3–0)	San Francisco
1982*	Washington Redskins won conference title and also had best regular-season record (8–1–0)			
1983	Washington Redskins (14–2–0)	Detroit Lions (8–8–0)	San Francisco 49ers (10–6–0)	Washington
1984	Washington Redskins (11–5–0)	Chicago Bears (10–6–0)	San Francisco 49ers (15–1)	San Francisco
1985	Dallas Cowboys (10-6-0)	Chicago Bears (15-1-0)	Los Angeles Rams (11-5-0)	Chicago
1986	New York Giants (14–2–0)	Chicago Bears (14–2–0)	San Francisco 49ers (10–5–1)	New York

*Schedule reduced to 9 games from usual 16, with no standings kept in Eastern, Central, and Western Divisions, because of 57-day player strike.

AMERICAN CONFERENCE CHAMPIONS

Year	Eastern Division	Central Division	Western Division	Champion
1970	Baltimore Colts (11–2–1)	Cincinnati Bengals (8–6–0)	Oakland Raiders (8–4–2)	Baltimore
1971	Miami Dolphins (10–3–1)	Cleveland Browns (9–5–0)	Kansas City Chiefs (10–3–1)	Miami
1972	Miami Dolphins (14–0–0)	Pittsburgh Steelers (11–3–0)	Oakland Raiders (10–3–1)	Miami
1973	Miami Dolphins (12–2–0)	Cincinnati Bengals (10–4–0)	Oakland Raiders (9–4–1)	Miami
1974	Miami Dolphins (11–3–0)	Pittsburgh Steelers (10–3–1)	Oakland Raiders (12–2–0)	Pittsburgh
1975	Baltimore Colts (10–4–0)	Pittsburgh Steelers (12–2–0)	Oakland Raiders (12–2–0)	Pittsburgh
1976	Baltimore Colts (11–3–0)	Pittsburgh Steelers (10–4–0)	Oakland Raiders (13–1–0)	Oakland
1977	Baltimore Colts (10–4–0)	Pittsburgh Steelers (9–5–0)	Denver Broncos (12–2–0)	Denver
1978	New England Patriots (11–5–0)	Pittsburgh Steelers (14–2–0)	Denver Broncos (10–6–0)	Pittsburgh
1979	Miami Dolphins (10–6–0)	Pittsburgh Steelers (12–4–0)	San Diego Chargers (12–4–0)	Pittsburgh
1980	Buffalo Bills (11–5–0)	Cleveland Browns (11–5–0)	San Diego Chargers (11–5–0)	Oakland
1981	Miami Dolphins (11–4–1)	Cincinnati Bengals (12–4–0)	San Diego Chargers (10–6–0)	Cincinnati
1982*	Miami Dolphins won the conference title, but the Los Angeles Raiders had best regular-season record (8–1–0).			
1983	Miami (12–4–0)	Pittsburgh (10–6–0)	Los Angeles Raiders (12–4–0)	Los Angeles Raiders
1984	Miami (14–2–0)	Pittsburgh (9–7–0)	Denver (13–3–0)	Miami
1985	Miami (12-4-0)	Cleveland (8-8)	Los Angeles Raiders (12-4-0)	New England
1986	New England (11–5–0)	Cleveland (12–4–0)	Denver (11–5–0)	Denver

*Schedule reduced to 9 games from usual 16, with no standings kept in Eastern, Central, and Western Divisions, because of 57-day player strike.

AMERICAN LEAGUE CHAMPIONS

Year	Eastern Division (W-L-T)	Western Division (W-L-T)	League champion, playoffs results
1960	Houston Oilers (10-4-0)	Los Angeles Chargers (10-4-0)	Houston 24, Los Angeles 16
1961	Houston Oilers (10-3-1)	San Diego Chargers (12-2-0)	Houston 10, San Diego 3
1962	Houston Oilers (11-3-0)	Dallas Texans (11-3-0)	Dallas 20, Houston 17[1]
1963	Boston Patriots (8-6-1)[2]	San Diego Chargers (11-3-0)	San Diego 51, Boston 10
1964	Buffalo Bills (12-2-0)	San Diego Chargers (8-5-1)	Buffalo 20, San Diego 7
1965	Buffalo Bills (10-3-1)	San Diego Chargers (9-2-3)	Buffalo 23, San Diego 0

1966	Buffalo Bills (9-4-1)	Kansas City Chiefs (11-2-1)	Kansas City 31, Buffalo 7
1967	Houston Oilers (9-4-1)	Oakland Raiders (13-1-0)	Oakland 40, Houston 7
1968	New York Jets (11-3-0)	Oakland Raiders (12-2-0)[2]	New York 27, Oakland 23
1969	New York Jets (10-4-0)	Oakland Raiders (12-1-1)	Kansas City 17, Oakland 7[3]

1. Won at 2:45 of second sudden death overtime period. 2. Won divisional playoff. 3. Kansas City defeated New York, 13–6, and Oakland defeated Houston, 56–7, in interdivisional playoffs.

NATIONAL FOOTBALL LEAGUE GOVERNMENT

Commissioner's Office: Pete Rozelle, commissioner; Don Weiss, executive director; Tom Sullivan, treasurer; John Schoemer, comptroller; Jay Moyer, executive vice-president/legal counsel; Jan Van Duser, director of operations; Jim Heffernan, director of public relations; Joe Browne, director of communications; Warren Welsh, director of security; Charles R. Jackson, assistant director of security; Joel Bussert, director of player personnel; Art McNally, supervisor of officials; Joe Rhein, director of administration; Mel Blount, director of player relations; Jim Steeg, director of special events.

American Conference: Lamar Hunt, president; Al Ward, assistant to the president; Pete Abitante, director of information.

National Conference: Wellington Mara, president; Bill Granholm, assistant to the president; Dick Maxwell, director of information.

PRO FOOTBALL HALL OF FAME

(National Football Museum, Canton, Ohio)

Teams named are those with which player is best identified; figures in parentheses indicate number of playing seasons.

Adderley, Herb, defensive back, Packers, Cowboys (12)	1961–72
Alworth, Lance, wide receiver, Chargers, Cowboys (11)	1962–72
Atkins, Doug, defensive end, Browns, Bears, Saints (17)	1953–69
Badgro, Morris, end, N.Y. Yankees, Giants, Bklyn. Dodgers (8)	1927, 1930–36
Battles, Cliff, back, Redskins (6)	1932–37
Baugh, Sammy, quarterback, Redskins (16)	1937–52
Bednarik, Chuck, center-lineback, Eagles (14)	1949–62
Bell, Bert, N.F.L. founder, owner Eagles and Steelers, N.F.L. Commissioner	1946–59
Bell, Bobby, linebacker, Chiefs (12)	1963–74
Berry, Raymond, end, Colts (13)	1955–67
Bidwell, Charles W., owner Chicago Cardinals	1933–47
Blanda, George, quarterback-kicker, Bears, Oilers, Raiders (27)	1949–75
Brown, Jim, fullback, Browns (9)	1957–65
Brown, Paul E., coach, Browns (1946–62), Bengals (1968–75)	1946–75
Brown, Roosevelt, tackle, Giants (13)	1953–65
Brown, Willie, cornerback, Broncos, Raiders (16)	1963–78
Butkus, Dick, linebacker, Bears (9)	1965–73
Canadeo, Tony, back, Packers (11)	1941–52
Carr, Joe, president N.F.L. (18)	1921–39
Chamberlin, Guy, end 4 teams (9)	1919–27
Christiansen, Jack, defensive back, Lions (8)	1951–58
Clark, Earl (Dutch), Qback, Spartans, Lions (7)	1931–38
Connor, George, tackle, linebacker, Bears (8)	1948–55
Conzelman, Jimmy, Qback 5 teams (10), owner	1921–48
Csonka, Larry, back, Dolphins, Giants (11)	1968–79
Davis, Willie, defensive end, Packers (10)	1960–69
Dawson, Len, quarterback, Steelers, Browns, Texans, Chiefs (19)	1957–75
Donovan, Art, defensive tackle, Colts (12)	1950–61
Driscoll, John (Paddy), Qback, Cards, Bears (11)	1919–29
Dudley, Bill, back, Steelers, Lions, Redskins (9)	1942–53
Edwards, Albert Glen (Turk), tackle, Redskins (9)	1932–40
Ewbank, Weeb, coach Colts, Jets (20)	1954–73
Fears, Tom, end, Rams (9); coach, Saints	1948–56
Flaherty, Ray, end, Yankees, Giants (9); coach, Redskins, Yankees (14)	1928–49
Ford, Len, end, def. end, Browns, Packers (11)	1948–58
Fortmann, Daniel J., guard, Bears (8)	1936–43
Gatski, Frank, offensive lineman, Browns (12)	1946–57
George, Bill, linebacker, Bears, Rams (15)	1952–66
Gifford, Frank, back, Giants (12)	1952–64
Gillman, Sid, coach, Rams, Chargers, Oilers (18)	1955–70, 73–74
Graham, Otto, quarterback, Browns (10)	1946–55
Grange, Harold (Red), back, Bears, Yankees (9)	1925–34
Greene, Joe, defensive tackle, Steelers (13)	1968–1981
Gregg, Forrest, tackle, Packers (15)	1956–71
Groza, Lou, place-kicker, tackle, Browns (21)	1946–67
Guyon, Joe, back, 6 teams (8)	1919–27
Halas, George, N.F.L. founder, owner and coach, Staleys and Bears, end (11)	1919–67
Healey, Ed, tackle, Bears (8)	1920–27
Hein, Mel, center, Giants (15)	1931–45
Henry, Wilbur (Pete), tackle, Bulldogs, Giants (8)	1920–28
Herber, Arnie, Qback, Packers, Giants (13)	1930–45
Hewitt, Bill, end, Bears, Eagles (9)	1932–43
Hinkle, Clarke, fullback, Packers (10)	1932–41
Hirsch, Elroy (Crazy Legs), back, end, Rams (12)	1946–57
Hornung, Paul, running back, Packers (9)	1957–62 1964–66
Houston, Ken def. back, Oilers, Redskins (14)	1967–80
Hubbard, R. (Cal), tackle, Giants, Packers (9)	1927–36
Huff, Sam, linebacker, Giants, Redskins (13)	1956–67, 1969
Hunt, Lamar, Founder A.F.L., owner Texans, Chiefs	1959–
Hutson, Don, end, Packers (11)	1935–45
Johnson, John Henry, back, 49ers, Lions, Steelers, Oilers (13)	1954–66
Jones, David (Deacon), defensive end, Rams, Chargers, Redskins (14)	1961–74
Jurgensen, Sonny, quarterback, Eagles, Redskins (18)	1957–74
Kiesling, Walt, guard 6 teams (13)	1926–38
Kinard, Frank (Bruiser), tackle, Dodgers (9)	1938–47
Lambeau, Earl (Curly), N.F.L. founder, coach, end, back, Packers (11)	1919–53
Lane, Richard (Night Train), defensive back, Rams, Cardinals, Lions (14)	1952–65
Langer, Jim, center, Dolphins, Vikings (12)	1970–81
Lanier, Willie, linebacker, Chiefs (11)	1967–77
Lary, Yale, defensive back, punter, Lions (11)	1952–64
Laveill, Dante, end, Browns (11)	1946–56
Layne, Bobby, Qback, Bears, Lions, Steelers (15)	1948–62
Leemans, Alphonse (Tuffy), back, Giants (8)	1936–43
Lilly, Bob, defensive tackle, Cowboys (14)	1961–74
Lombardi, Vince, coach, Packers, Redskins (11)	1959–70
Luckman, Sid, quarterback, Bears (12)	1939–50
Lyman, Roy (Link), tackle, Bulldogs, Bears (11)	1922–34
Mara, Tim, N.F.L. founder, owner Giants	1925–59
Marchetti, Gino, defensive end, Colts (14)	1952–66
Marshall, George P., N.F.L. founder, owner Redskins	1932–65
Matson, Ollie, back, Cardinals, Rams, Lions, Eagles (14)	1952–66
Maynard, Don, receiver, Giants, Jets, Cardinals (15)	1958–73
McAfee, George, back, Bears (8)	1940–50
McCormack, Mike, tackle, N.Y. Yankees, Cleveland Browns (10)	1951–1962
McElhenny, Hugh, back, 49ers, Vikings, Giants (13)	1952–64

McNally, John (Blood), back, 7 teams (15)	1925–39
Michalske, August, guard, Yankees, Packers (11)	1926–37
Millner, Wayne, end, Redskins (7)	1936–45
Mitchell, Bobby, wide receiver, Browns, Redskins (11)	1958–68
Mix, Ron, tackle, Chargers (11)	1960–71
Moore, Lenny, back, Colts (12)	1956–67
Motley, Marion, fullback, Browns, Steelers (9)	1946–55
Musso, George, guard-tackle, Bears (12)	1933–44
Nagurski, Bronko, fullback, Bears (9)	1930–43
Namath, Joe, quarterback, Jets, Rams (13)	1965–77
Neale, Earle (Greasy), coach, Eagles	1941–50
Nevers, Ernie, fullback, Chicago Cardinals (5)	1926–31
Nitschke, Ray, linebacker, Packers (15)	1958–72
Nomellini, Leo, defensive tackle, 49ers (14)	1950–63
Olsen, Merlin, defensive tackle, Rams (15)	1962–76
Otto, Jim, center, Raiders (15)	1960–74
Owen, Steve, tackle, Giants (9), coach, Giants (13)	1924–53
Parker, Clarence (Ace), quarterback, Dodgers (7)	1937–46
Parker, Jim, guard, tackle, Colts (11)	1957–67
Perry, Joe, fullback, 49ers, Colts (16)	1948–63
Pihos, Pete, end, Eagles (9)	1947–55
Ray, Hugh, Shorty, N.F.L. advisor	1938–52
Reeves, Dan, owner Rams	1941–71
Ringo, Jim, center, Packers (15)	1953–67
Robustelli, Andy, def. end, Rams, Giants (14)	1951–64
Rooney, Art, N.F.L. founder, owner Steelers	1933–
Rozelle, Pete, commissioner, NFL,	1960–present
Sayers, Gale, back, Bears (7)	1965–71
Schmidt, Joe, linebacker, Lions (13)	1953–65
Simpson, O.J., back, Bills, 49ers (11)	1969–79
Starr, Bart, quarterback, coach, Packers (16)	1956–71
Staubach, Roger, quarterback, Cowboys (11)	1969–79
Stautner, Ernie, defensive tackle, Steelers (14)	1950–63
Strong, Ken, back, Giants, Yankees (14)	1929–47
Stydahar, Joe, tackle, Bears (9); coach, Rams, Cardinals (5)	1936–54
Tarkenton, Fran, quarterback, Vikings, Giants (18)	1961–78
Taylor, Charlie, wide receiver, Redskins (14)	1964–77
Taylor, Jim, fullback, Packers, Saints (10)	1958–67
Thorpe, Jim, back, 7 teams (12)	1915–28
Tittle, Y. A., Qback, Colts, 49ers, Giants (17)	1948–64
Trafton, George, center, Bears (13)	1920–32
Trippi, Charley, back, Chicago Cardinals (9)	1947–55
Tunnell, Emlen, def. back, Giants, Packers (14)	1948–61
Turner, Clyde (Bulldog), center, Bears (13)	1940–52
Unitas, John, quarterback, Colts (18)	1956–73
Upshaw, Gene, guard, Raiders (15)	1967–81
Van Brocklin, Norm, Qback, Rams, Eagles (12)	1949–60
Van Buren, Steve, back, Eagles (8)	1944–51
Walker, Doak, running back, def. back, kicker, Lions (6)	1950–55
Warfield, Paul, wide receiver, Browns, Dolphins (13)	1964–74, 76–77
Waterfield, Bob, quarterback, Rams (8)	1945–52
Weinmeister, Arnie, tackle, N.Y. Yankees, Giants (6)	1948–53
Willis, Bill, Guard, Browns (8)	1946–53
Wilson, Larry, defensive back, Cardinals (13)	1960–72
Wojciechowicz, Alex, center, Lions, Eagles (13)	1938–50

N.F.L. INDIVIDUAL LIFETIME, SEASON, AND GAME RECORDS

(American Football League records were incorporated into N.F.L. records after merger of the leagues)

All-Time Leading Touchdown Scorers

	Yrs	Rush	Pass rec	Returns	TD
Jim Brown	9	106	20	0	126
Walter Payton[1]	12	106	14	0	120
John Riggins	14	104	12	0	116
Lenny Moore	12	63	48	2	113
Don Hutson	11	3	99	3	105
Franco Harris	12	91	9	0	100
Jim Taylor	10	83	10	0	93
Bobby Mitchell	11	18	65	8	91
Leroy Kelly	10	74	13	3	90
Charley Taylor	13	11	79	0	90

1. Still active.

All-Time Leading Receivers

	Yrs	Pass rec	Yds	Avg
Charley Joiner[1]	18	750	12,146	16.2
Steve Largent[1]	11	694	11,129	16.0
Charley Taylor	13	649	9,110	14.0
Don Maynard	15	633	11,834	18.7
Raymond Berry	13	631	9,275	14.7
Harold Carmichael	14	590	8,985	15.2
Fred Biletnikoff	14	589	8,974	15.2
Harold Jackson	16	579	10,372	17.9
Lionel Taylor	10	567	7,195	12.7
Lance Alworth	11	542	10,226	18.9
Bobby Mitchell	11	521	7,954	15.3

1. Still active in National Football League.

All-Time Leading Passers

Rank		Player	Yrs.	Att.	Comp.	Yds.	TD	Int.	Rating pts.
1	(—)	Dan Marino[1]	4	2050	1249	16,177	142	67	95.2
2	(1)	Joe Montana[1]	8	2878	1818	21,498	141	76	91.2
3	(2)	Otto Graham	10	2626	1464	23,584	174	135	86.6
4	(—)	Dave Krieg[1]	7	1822	1046	13,677	107	73	84.1
5	(3)	Roger Staubach	11	2958	1685	22,700	153	109	83.4
6	(7)	Danny White[1]	11	2546	1517	19,068	142	112	83.2
7	(4)	Sonny Jurgensen	18	4262	2433	32,224	255	189	82.625
8	(5)	Len Dawson	19	3741	2136	28,711	239	183	82.555
9	(8)	Ken Anderson[1]	16	4475	2654	32,838	197	160	81.9
10	(9)	Dan Fouts[1]	14	5240	3091	40,523	244	227	80.9
11	(6)	Neil Lomax[1]	6	2247	1287	15,989	92	67	80.7
12	(10)	Bart Starr	16	3149	1808	24,718	152	138	80.5
13	(11)	Fran Tarkenton	18	6467	3686	47,003	342	266	80.4
14T	(13T)	Bert Jones	10	2551	1430	18,190	124	101	78.2
14T	(13T)	Johnny Unitas	18	5186	2830	40,239	290	253	78.2
16	(15)	Frank Ryan	13	2133	1090	16,042	149	111	77.6
17	(12)	Bill Kenney[1]	8	2043	1118	14,621	90	72	77.5
18	(16)	Joe Theismann	12	3602	2044	25,206	160	138	77.4
19	(17)	Bob Griese	14	3429	1926	25,092	192	172	77.1
20	(19)	Gary Danielson[1]	11	1847	1049	13,159	77	77	75.6

1. Still active in N.F.L.

All-Time Leading Scorers

	Yrs	TD	FG	PAT	Pts
George Blanda	26	9	335	943	2,002
Jan Stenerud	19	0	373	580	1,699
Lou Groza	21	1	264	810	1,608
Jim Turner	16	1	304	521	1,439
Mark Moseley[1]	16	0	300	482	1,382
Jim Bakken	17	0	282	534	1,380
Fred Cox	15	0	282	519	1,365
Gino Cappelletti	11	42	176	350	1,130
Don Cockroft	13	0	216	432	1,080
Garo Yepremian	14	0	210	444	1,074

1. Still active in N.F.L.

All-Time Leading Rushers

	Yrs	Att	Yds	Avg
Walter Payton[1]	12	3,692	16,193	4.4
Jim Brown	9	2,359	12,312	5.2
Franco Harris	13	2,949	12,120	4.1
Tony Dorsett	10	2,625	,11,580	4.4
John Riggins	14	2,916	11,352	3.9
O.J. Simpson	11	2,404	11,236	4.7
Joe Perry	16	1,929	9,723	5.0
Earl Campbell	8	2,187	9,407	4.3
Jim Taylor	10	1,941	8,597	4.4
Larry Csonka	11	1,891	8,081	4.3

1. Still active in National Football League.

Scoring

Most points scored, lifetime—2,002, George Blanda, Chicago Bears, 1949–58; Baltimore, 1950; Houston, 1960–66; Oakland, 1967–75 (9tds, 943 pat, 335 fgs).

Most points, season—176, Paul Hornung, Green Bay, 1960 (15 td, 41 pat, 15 fg).

Most points, game—40, Ernie Nevers, Chicago Cardinals, 1929 (6 td, 4 pat).

Most points, per quarter—29, Don Hutson, Green Bay, 1945 (4 td, 5 pat).

Most touchdowns, lifetime—126, Jim Brown, Cleveland, 1957–65.

Most touchdowns, season—24, John Riggins, Washington, 1983.

Most touchdowns, game—6, Ernie Nevers, Chicago Cardinals, 1929; William Jones, Cleveland, 1951; Gale Sayers, Chicago Bears, 1965.

Most points after touchdown, lifetime—943, George Blanda, Chicago Bears, 1949–58; Baltimore, 1950; Houston, 1960–66; Oakland, 1967–75.

Most points after touchdown, game—9, Pat Harder, Chicago Cardinals, 1948; Bob Waterfield, Los Angeles, 1950; Charlie Gogolak, Washington, 1966.

Most consecutive points after touchdown—234, Tommy Davis, San Francisco, 1959–65.

Most points after touchdown, no misses, season—56, Danny Villanueva, Dallas, 1966.

Most field goals, lifetime—373, Jan Stenerud, Kansas City Chiefs, 1967–79; Green Bay Packers, 1980–84; Minnesota Vikings, 1985.

Most field goals, season—35, Ali Haji-Sheikh, N.Y. Giants, 1983.

Most field goals, game—7, Jim Bakken, St. Louis, 1967.

Longest field goal—63 yards, Tom Dempsey, New Orleans, 1970.

Rushing

Most yards gained, lifetime—16,193, Walter Payton, Chicago Bears, 1975–still active.

Most yards gained, season—2,105, Eric Dickerson, Los Angeles, 1983-still active.

Most yards gained, game—275, Walter Payton, Chicago, 1977.

Most touchdowns, lifetime—106, Jim Brown, Cleveland, 1957–65.

Most touchdowns, season—24, John Riggins, Washington, 1983.

Most touchdowns, game—6, Ernie Nevers, Chicago Cardinals, 1929.

Longest run from scrimmage—99 yards, Tony Dorsett, Dallas, 1982 (touchdown).

Most yards gained, game—554, Norm Van Brocklin, Los Angeles, 1951.

Most touchdown passes, lifetime—342, Fran Tarkenton, Minnesota, 1961–66, 72–78; New York Giants, 1967–71.

Most touchdown passes, season—48, Dan Marino, Miami, 1984.

Most touchdown passes, game—7, Sid Luckman, Chicago Bears, 1943; Adrian Burk, Philadelphia, 1954; George Blanda, Houston 1961; Y.A. Tittle, New York Giants, 1963; Joe Kapp, Minnesota, 1969.

Most consecutive games, touchdown passes—47, John Unitas, Baltimore.

Most consecutive passes attempted, none intercepted—294, Bart Starr, Green Bay, 1964–65.

Longest pass completion—99 yards, Frank Filchock (to Andy Farkas), Washington, 1939; George Izo (to Bob Mitchell), Washington, 1963; Karl Sweetan (to Pat Studstill), Detroit, 1966; Sonny Jurgensen (to Gerry Allen), Washington, 1968, (all for touchdowns).

Most pass receptions, lifetime—750, Charlie Joiner, Houston Oilers, 1969–72, Cincinnati Bengals, 1972–75, San Diego Chargers, 1976–85.

Most pass receptions, season—106, Art Monk, Washington, 1984.

Most pass receptions, game—18, Tom Fears, Los Angeles, 1950.

Most consecutive games, pass receptions—139, Steve Largent, 1977–current.

Most yards gained, pass receptions, lifetime—12,146, Charlie Joiner, Houston 1964–79, Cincinnati 1972–75, San Diego 1976–86.

Most yards gained receptions, season—1,746, Charley Hennigan, Houston, 1961.

Most yards gained receptions, game—309, Stephone Paige, Kansas City, 1985.

Most touchdown pass receptions, lifetime—99, Don Hutson, Green Bay, 1935–45.

Most touchdown pass receptions, season—18, Mark Clayton, Miami, 1984.

Most touchdown pass receptions, game—5, Bob Shaw, Chicago Cards, 1950.

Most consecutive games, touchdown pass receptions—11, Elroy Hirsch, Los Angeles, 1950–51; Buddy Dial, Pittsburgh, 1959–60.

Most pass interceptions, lifetime—81, Paul Krause, Washington, 1964–67; Minnesota, 1968–79.

Most pass interceptions, season–14, Richard (Night Train) Lane, Los Angeles, 1952.

Most pass interceptions, game—4, by 15 players.

Longest pass interception return—102 yards, Bob Smith, Chicago Bears, 1949; Erich Barnes, New York Giants, 1961; Gary Barbaro, Kansas City, 1977; Louis Breeden, Cincinnati, 1981.

Kicking

Longest punt—98 yards, Steve O'Neal, New York Jets, 1969.

Highest average punting, lifetime—45.16 yards, Rohn Stark, Indianapolis, 1982–current.

Longest punt return—98 yards, Gil LeFebvre, Cincinnati Reds, 1933; Charlie West, Minnesota, 1968; Dennis Morgan, Dallas, 1974.

Longest kick-off return—106 yards, Roy Green, St. Louis, 1979; Al Carmichael, Green Bay, 1956; Noland Smith, Kansas City, 1967.

Passing

Most passes completed, lifetime—3,686, Fran Tarkenton, Minnesota, 1961–66, 72–78; New York Giants, 1967–71.

Most passes completed, season—378, Dan Marino, 1986.

Most passes completed, game—42, Richard Todd, New York Jets, 1980.

Most consecutive passes completed—20, Ken Anderson, Cincinnati, 1983.

Most yards gained, lifetime—47,003, Fran Tarkenton, Minnesota, 1961–66, 72–78; New York Giants, 1967–71.

Most yards gained, season—5,084, Dan Marino, Miami, 1984.

TEAM NICKNAMES AND HOME FIELD CAPACITIES

AMERICAN CONFERENCE
Eastern Division

Buffalo Bills	Rich Stadium (AT)	80,020
Indianapolis Colts[1]	Hoosier Dome (AT)	61,500
Miami Dolphins	Orange Bowl (G)	75,059
New England Patriots	Sullivan Stadium (ST)	61,297
New York Jets[2]	Giants Stadium (AT)	76,891

Central Division

Cincinnati Bengals	Riverfront Stadium (AT)	59,754
Cleveland Browns	Municipal Stadium (G)	80,322
Houston Oilers	Astrodome (AT)	50,496
Pittsburgh Steelers	Three Rivers Stadium (AT)	59,000

Western Division

Denver Broncos	Mile High Stadium (G)	75,103
Kansas City Chiefs	Arrowhead Stadium (TT)	78,067
Los Angeles Raiders[3]	Memorial Coliseum (G)	92,498
San Diego Chargers	Jack Murphy Stadium (G)	53,675
Seattle Seahawks	Kingdome (AT)	64,757

1. Moved franchise from Baltimore prior to 1984 season. 2. Moved to Giants Stadium; East Rutherford, N.J. prior to 1984 season. 3. Moved franchise to Los Angeles for 1982 season. Shift is still being argued in courts, as city of Oakland tries to regain franchise.

NATIONAL CONFERENCE
Eastern Division

Dallas Cowboys	Texas Stadium (TT)	65,101
New York Giants	Giants Stadium (AT)[1]	76,891
Philadelphia Eagles	Veterans Stadium (AT)	72,204
St. Louis Cardinals	Busch Memorial Stadium (AT)	51,392
Washington Redskins	R.F. Kennedy Stadium (G)	55,045

Central Division

Chicago Bears	Soldier Field (AT)	65,793
Detroit Lions	Pontiac Silverdome (AT)	80,638
Green Bay Packers	Lambeau Field (G)	56,189
	Milwaukee Stadium (G)	55,958
Minnesota Vikings	Hubert Humphrey Metrodome (ST)	62,212
Tampa Bay Buccaneers	Tampa Stadium	72,812

Western Division

Atlanta Falcons	Atlanta-Fulton Stadium	60,748
Los Angeles Rams	Anaheim Stadium	69,007
New Orleans Saints	Louisiana Superdome	71,330
San Francisco 49ers	Candlestick Park	61,185

1. At East Rutherford, N.J. NOTE: Stadium playing surfaces in parentheses: (AT) Astro Turf; (G) Grass; (ST) Super Turf; (TT) Tartan Turf.

UNITED STATES FOOTBALL LEAGUE

The United States Football League, which was scheduled to change from a spring-summer league to a fall league in 1986, suspended operations instead and, though not officially disbanded, did not function as a league through 1987. A revival in the future was unlikely.

The final demise of the United States Football League was a legal decision in late spring of 1986. The USFL had filed a much-publicized antitrust suit against the older established National Football League, in the hopes of winning a huge cash settlement that would have kept the league going.

The USFL technically won the decision, but turned out to be the big loser when the jury awarded the struggling league just $1 in damages. The decision was unsuccessfully appealed, and the league voted itself out of operation.

Thus ended the most recent attempt to establish a viable alternative to the National Football League. Of the several attempts, only the old American Football League, which won merger with the NFL in the late 1960s, achieved any measure of success. Indeed, many of the same owners who had been part of the defunct World Football League, which tried to buck the NFL in the early 1970s, were behind the original USFL franchises that played their first season in the spring and summer of 1983.

The 12-team USFL was financed at the start by two two-year television contracts—one for $9 million a year from ABC and one for $6 million a year from the ESPN cable sports network. Ironically, three years later, it was the inability of the USFL to land a major network television package that was the central focus of the league's suit against the NFL.

Initial TV ratings in 1983 were much higher than expected, but the ratings fell as the season wore on. The quality of play was uneven, and critics pointed to the large number of NFL castoffs on USFL rosters.

The league did establish some measure of credibility by signing several outstanding college players—most notably Georgia running back Herschel Walker and Boston College quarterback Doug Flutie by real estate baron Donald Trump's New Jersey Generals, University of Nebraska running back Mike Rozier by the Pittsburgh Maulers, and Brigham Young quarterback Steve Young by the Los Angeles Express. All but Young were Heisman Trophy winners, symbolic of the best player in college football.

But the credibility such players brought did not come cheap. In fact, the multi-million dollar contracts required to land these players, along with established NFL stars like Buffalo Bills running back Joe Cribbs, Cleveland Browns quarterback Brian Sipe, and Tampa Bay quarterback Doug Williams, eventually spelled the league's demise.

The Michigan Panthers defeated the Philadelphia Stars, 24-22, in the 12-team USFL's first championship game on July 17, 1983, in Denver. In 1984, with 18 teams now operating—most at severe financial losses—the Stars beat the Arizona Wranglers, 22-3, for the league title on July 15. The following year, in the final USFL championship game, the Stars, now playing in Baltimore, defeated the Oakland Invaders, 28-24, on July 14 at Giants Stadium in East Rutherford, N.J.

The USFL owners, spurred on by Trump, chose to go into direct competition with the NFL, and planned to skip the 1986 spring season and resume play in September 1986 with nine or 10 teams. But the court decision changed those plans for good.

BASKETBALL

Basketball may be the one sport whose exact origin is definitely known. In the winter of 1891–92, Dr. James Naismith, an instructor in the Y.M.C.A. Training College (now Springfield College) at Springfield, Mass., deliberately invented the game of basketball in order to provide indoor exercise and competition for the students between the closing of the football season and the opening of the baseball season. He affixed peach baskets overhead on the walls at opposite ends of the gymnasium and organized teams to play his new game in which the purpose was to toss an association (soccer) ball into one basket and prevent the opponents from tossing the ball into the other basket. The game is fundamentally the same today, though there have been improvements in equipment and some changes in rules.

Because Dr. Naismith had eighteen available players when he invented the game, the first rule was; "There shall be nine players on each side." Later the number of players became optional, depending upon the size of the available court, but the five-player standard was adopted when the game spread over the country. United States soldiers brought basketball to Europe in World War I, and it soon became a world-wide sport.

College Basketball

NATIONAL COLLEGIATE A.A. CHAMPIONS

1939	Oregon	1950	C.C.N.Y.	1961	Cincinnati	1978	Kentucky
1940	Indiana	1951	Kentucky	1962	Cincinnati	1979	Michigan State
1941	Wisconsin	1952	Kansas	1963	Loyola (Chicago)	1980	Louisville
1942	Stanford	1953	Indiana	1964	U.C.L.A.	1981	Indiana
1943	Wyoming	1954	La Salle	1965	U.C.L.A.	1982	North Carolina
1944	Utah	1955	San Francisco	1966	Texas Western	1983	North Carolina State
1945	Oklahoma A & M	1956	San Francisco	1967–73	U.C.L.A.	1984	Georgetown
1946	Oklahoma A & M	1957	North Carolina	1974	No. Carolina State	1985	Villanova
1947	Holy Cross	1958	Kentucky	1975	U.C.L.A.	1986	Louisville
1948	Kentucky	1959	California	1976	Indiana	1987	Indiana
1949	Kentucky	1960	Ohio State	1977	Marquette		

NATIONAL INVITATION TOURNAMENT (NIT) CHAMPIONS

1939	Long Island U.	1952	La Salle	1964	Bradley	1976	Kentucky
1940	Colorado	1953	Seton Hall	1965	St. John's (N.Y.C.)	1977	St. Bonaventure
1941	Long Island U.	1954	Holy Cross	1966	Brigham Young	1978	Texas
1942	West Virginia	1955	Duquesne	1967	So. Illinois	1979	Indiana
1943–44	St. John's (N.Y.C.)	1956	Louisville	1968	Dayton	1980	Virginia
1945	DePaul	1957	Bradley	1969	Temple	1981	Tulsa
1946	Kentucky	1958	Xavier (Cincinnati)	1970	Marquette	1982	Bradley
1947	Utah	1959	St. John's (N.Y.C.)	1971	North Carolina	1983	Fresno State
1948	St. Louis	1960	Bradley	1972	Maryland	1984	Michigan
1949	San Francisco	1961	Providence	1973	Virginia Tech	1985	U.C.L.A.
1950	C.C.N.Y.	1962	Dayton	1974	Purdue	1986	Ohio State
1951	Brigham Young	1963	Providence	1975	Princeton	1987	Southern Mississippi

N.C.A.A. MAJOR COLLEGE INDIVIDUAL SCORING RECORDS

Single Season Averages

Player, Team	Year	G	FG	FT	Pts	Avg
Pete Maravich, Louisiana State	1969–70	31	522 [1]	337	1381 [1]	44.5 [1]
Pete Maravich	1968–69	26	433	282	1148	44.2
Pete Maravich	1967–68	26	432	274	1138	43.8
Frank Selvy, Furman	1953–54	29	427	355 [1]	1209	41.7
Johnny Neumann, Mississippi	1970–71	23	366	191	923	40.1
Freeman Williams, Portland State	1976–77	26	417	176	1010	38.8
Billy McGill, Utah	1961–62	26	394	221	1009	38.8
Calvin Murphy, Niagara	1967–68	24	337	242	916	38.2
Austin Carr, Notre Dame	1969–70	29	444	218	1106	38.1

1. Record.

N.C.A.A. CAREER SCORING TOTALS

Division I

Player, Team	Last year	G	FG	FT	Pts	Avg
Pete Maravich, Louisiana State	1970	83	1387[1]	893[1]	3667[1]	44.2[1]
Austin Carr, Notre Dame	1971	74	1017	526	2560	34.6
Oscar Robertson, Cincinnati	1960	88	1052	869	2973	33.8
Calvin Murphy, Niagara	1970	77	947	654	2548	33.1
Dwight Lamar[2]	1973	57	768	326	1862	32.7
Frank Selvy, Furman	1954	78	922	694	2538	32.5
Rick Mount, Purdue	1970	72	910	503	2323	32.3
Darrel Floyd, Furman	1956	71	868	545	2281	32.1
Nick Werkman, Seton Hall	1964	71	812	649	2273	32.0

1. Record. 2. Also played two seasons in college division.

Division II

Player, Team	Last year	G	FG	FT	Pts	Avg
Travis Grant, Kentucky State	1972	121	1760[1]	525	4045[1]	33.4[1]
John Rinka, Kenyon	1970	99	1261	729	3251	32.8
Florindo Vieira, Quinnipiac	1957	69	761	741	2263	32.8
Willie Shaw, Lane	1964	76	960	459	2379	31.3
Mike Davis, Virginia Union	1969	89	1014	730	2758	31.0
Henry Logan, Western Carolina	1968	107	1263	764	3290	30.7
Willie Scott, Alabama State	1969	103	1277	601	3155	30.6
Gregg Northington, Alabama State	1972	75	894	403	2191	29.2
Bob Hopkins, Grambling	1956	126	1403	953	3759	29.8

1. Record.

TOP SINGLE-GAME SCORING MARKS

Player, Team (Opponent)	Yr	Pts	Player, Team (Opponent)	Yr	Pts
Selvy, Furman (Newberry)	1954	100[1]	Floyd, Furman (Morehead)	1955	67
Williams, Portland State (Rocky Mtn.)	1978	81	Maravich, LSU (Tulane)	1969	66
Mlkvy, Temple (Wilkes)	1951	73	Handlan, W & L (Furman)	1951	66
Williams, Portland State (So. Oregon)	1977	71	Roberts, Oral Roberts (N.C. A&T)	1977	66
Maravich, LSU (Alabama)	1970	69	Williams, Portland State (Geo. Fox Coll.)	1978	66
Murphy, Niagara (Syracuse)	1969	68	Roberts, Oral Roberts (Oregon)	1977	65

1. Record.

MEN'S N.C.A.A. BASKETBALL CHAMPIONSHIPS—1987

DIVISION I

First Round—East

Texas Christian 76, Marshall 60
Notre Dame 84, Middle Tennessee State 71
Michigan 97, Navy 82
North Carolina 113, Pennsylvania 82
Purdue 104, Northeastern 95
Florida 82, North Carolina State 70
Western Kentucky 64, West Virginia 62
Syracuse 79, Georgia Southern 73

First Round—Southeast

New Orleans 83, Brigham Young 79
Alabama 88, North Carolina A&T 71
Austin Peay 68, Illinois 67
Providence 90, Alabama-Birmingham 68
Southwest Missouri State 65, Clemson 60
Kansas 66, Houston 55
Georgetown 75, Bucknell 53
Ohio State 91, Kentucky 77

First Round—Midwest

Xavier 70, Missouri 69
Duke 58, Texas A&M 51
Auburn 62, San Diego 61
Indiana 92, Fairfield 58
Temple 75, Southern 56
Louisiana State 85, Georgia Tech 79
St. John's 57, Wichita State 55
DePaul 76, Louisiana Tech 62

First Round—West

Kansas State 82, Georgia 79 OT
UNLV 95, Idaho State 70
UCLA 92, Central Michigan 73
Wyoming 64, Virginia 60
Iowa 99, Santa Clara 76
Texas El Paso 98, Arizona 91 OT
Pittsburgh 93, Marist 68
Oklahoma 74, Tulsa 69

Second Round—East

Notre Dame 58, Texas Christian 57
North Carolina 109, Michigan 97
Florida 85, Purdue 66
Syracuse 104, Western Kentucky 84

Second Round—Southeast

Providence 90, Austin Peay 87 OT
Alabama 101, New Orleans 76
Georgetown 82, Ohio State 79
Kansas 67, Southwest Missouri State 63

Second Round—Midwest

Indiana 107, Auburn 90
Duke 65, Xavier 60
Louisiana State 72, Temple 62
DePaul 83, St. John's 75 OT

Second Round—West

UNLV 80, Kansas State 61
Wyoming 78, UCLA 68
Oklahoma 96, Pittsburgh 93
Iowa 84 Texas–El Paso 82

Third Round—East

Syracuse 87, Florida 81
North Carolina 74, Notre Dame 68

Third Round—Southeast

Providence 103, Alabama 82
Georgetown 70, Kansas 57

Third Round—Midwest

Louisiana State 63, DePaul 58
Indiana 88, Duke 82

Third Round—West

Iowa 93, Oklahoma 91 OT
UNLV 92, Wyoming 78

Regional Finals

East—Syracuse 79, North Carolina 75
Southeast—Providence 88, Georgetown 73
Midwest—Indiana 77, Louisiana State 76
West—UNLV 84, Iowa 81

National Semifinals

(Saturday, March 28, 1987 at New Orleans, La.)

Syracuse 77, Providence 63
Indiana 97, UNLV 93

National Final

(Monday, March 30, 1987 at New Orleans, La.)

Indiana 74, Syracuse 73

DIVISION II
Semifinals

Kentucky Wesleyan 98, Delta State (Miss.) 75
Gannon (Pa.) 61, Eastern Montana 55

Championship

Kentucky Wesleyan 92, Gannon 74

DIVISION III
Championship

North Park 106, Clark 100

WOMEN'S N.C.A.A. BASKETBALL CHAMPIONSHIPS—1987

DIVISION I
First Round—East

St. Joseph's 67, South Alabama 56
Duke 70, Manhattan 55

First Round—Mideast

Illinois 80, Bowling Green 64
Tennessee Tech 78, Southern Mississippi 66

First Round—Midwest

Northwestern 62, Kansas State 61 OT
Kansas 78, Northeastern Louisiana 72

First Round—West

Washington 86, New Mexico State 73
Oregon 75, Eastern Washington 56

Second Round—East

Rutgers 78, Duke 64
North Carolina State 68, Villanova 67
Texas 86, St. Joseph's 56
James Madison 68, Vanderbilt 60

Second Round—Mideast

Old Dominion 76, North Carolina 58
Auburn 92, Illinois 58
Virginia 76, Memphis State 75
Tennessee 95, Tennessee Tech 59

Second Round—Midwest

Louisiana Tech 82, Northwestern 60
Georgia 82, Kansas 51
Iowa 68, New Orleans 46
Southern Illinois 70, Louisiana State 56

Second Round—West

Mississippi 80, Penn State 75
Long Beach State 72, Washington 57
Ohio State 76, Oregon 62
Southern California 81, Western Kentucky 69

Third Round—East

Texas 91, James Madison 57
Rutgers 75, North Carolina State 60

Third Round—Mideast

Auburn 77, Old Dominion 61
Tennessee 66, Virginia 58

Third Round—Midwest

Iowa 62, Georgia 60
Louisiana Tech 66, Southern Illinois 53

Third Round—West

Ohio State 74, Southern California 63
Long Beach State 94, Mississippi 55

Regional Finals

East—Texas 85, Rutgers 77
Mideast—Tennessee 77, Auburn 61
Midwest—Louisiana Tech 66, Iowa 65
West—Long Beach State 102, Ohio State 82

National Semifinals

(Friday March 27, at Austin, Texas)

Tennessee 74, Long Beach State 64
Louisiana Tech 79, Texas 75

National Championship

(Sunday, March 29, at Austin, Texas)

Tennessee 67, Louisiana Tech 44

DIVISION II
Semifinals

New Haven (CT) 77, Northern Kentucky 74 (OT)
Cal-Poly Pomona 72, Pittsburgh-Johnstown 70

Championship

New Haven 77, Cal-Poly Pomona 75

DIVISION III
Semifinals

Concordia (MN) 74, Kean (NJ) 69
Wisconsin-Stevens Point 74, Scranton (PA) 59

Championship

Wisconsin-Stevens Point 81, Concordia 74

LEADING N.C.A.A. SCORERS—1986–1987

Division I

	FG	3-PT FG	FT	Pts	Avg
1. Kevin Houston, Army	311	63	268	953	32.9
2. Dennis Hopson, Ohio State	338	67	215	958	29.0
3. David Robinson, Navy	350	1	202	903	28.2
4. Terrance Bailey, Wagner	284	42	178	788	28.1
5. Hersey Hawkins, Bradley	294	31	169	788	27.2
6. Darrin Fitzgerald, Butler	250	158	76	734	26.2
7. Gay Elmore, VMI	266	23	158	713	25.5

8. Frank Ross, American	235	86	127	683	25.3
9. Daren Queenan, Lehigh	260	9	191	720	24.8
10. Byron Larkin, Xavier	278	32	204	792	24.7
11. Eric Riggins, Rutgers	245	2	200	692	24.7
12. Clarence Grier, Campbell	287	7	158	739	24.6
13. Tony White, Tennessee	259	28	165	711	24.5
14. Derrick Chievous, Missouri	282	13	244	821	24.1
15. Danny Manning, Kansas	347	1	165	860	23.9
16. Scott Brooks, UC-Irvine	206	111	142	665	23.8
17. Tilman Bevely, Youngstown St.	257	61	87	662	23.6
18. Reggie Williams, Georgetown	284	78	156	802	23.6
19. Reggie Lewis, Northeastern	248	30	150	676	23.3
20. Ron Simpson, Rider	236	98	57	627	23.2
21. Armon Gilliam, UNLV	359	0	185	903	23.2
22. Bernard Jackson, Loyola, Ill.	242	37	141	662	22.8
23. Ledell Eackles, New Orleans	239	70	84	632	22.6
24. Ben Hinson, Baptist	260	64	93	677	22.6
25. Jeff Grayer, Iowa St.	228	7	142	605	22.4

NATIONAL ASSOCIATION OF INTERCOLLEGIATE ATHLETICS—1987

MEN'S TOURNAMENT

Round of 16

Central Washington 84, St. Thomas Aquinas (NY) 83
Georgetown (KY) 67, Oklahoma City 64
Auburn–Montgomery 76, St. Joseph's (ME) 66
Trevecca Nazarene (TN) 73, St. Mary's (TX) 68
Hawaii–Hilo 65, College of Charleston (SC) 57
West Virginia State 92, Oregon Tech 90 (OT)
Washburn (KA) 74, Taylor (IN) 44
Waynesburg (PA) 86, Valley City State (ND) 84

Quarterfinals

Central Washington 92, Hawaii–Hilo 75
Georgetown 81, Trevecca Nazarene 66
Washburn 69, Auburn–Montgomery 61
West Virginia State 73, Waynesburg 67

Semifinals

West Virginia State 74, Georgetown 67
Washburn 65, Central Washington 63

Championship

Washburn 79, West Virginia State 77

WOMEN'S TOURNAMENT

Round of 16

North Georgia 86, Ind.–Purdue–Indianapolis 70
Saginaw Valley State 87, Bluefield State 70
Wisconsin–Green Bay 87, Auburn Montgomery 61
Wingate (NC) 66, Fresno Pacific 52
Arkansas Tech 69, Bemidji State (MN) 68
Southwest Oklahoma 74, Kearney State (NE) 69 (OT)
Wayland Baptist (TX) 95, St. Joseph's (ME) 61
St. Ambrose (IOWA) 90, Western Oregon 80

Quarterfinals

North Georgia 82, Wingate 51
Arkansas Tech 58, Saginaw Valley State 56
Wisconsin–Green Bay 74, Wayland Baptist 73
Southwest Oklahoma 78, St. Ambrose 63

Semifinals

Southwest Oklahoma 70, Arkansas Tech 68
North Georgia 85, Wisconsin–Green Bay 78

Championship

Southwest Oklahoma 60, North Georgia 58

NATIONAL INVITATION TOURNAMENT (N.I.T.)—1987

(March 24, 1987 at Madison Square Garden, N.Y.)

Semifinals

LaSalle 92, Arkansas–Little Rock 73
Southern Mississippi 82, Nebraska 75

Third Place

Nebraska 76, Arkansas–Little Rock 67 (OT)

Championship

(March 26, 1987, at Madison Square Garden, N.Y.)

Southern Mississippi 84, LaSalle 80

N.C.A.A. LEADING REBOUNDERS—1986-1987

	Games	No.	Avg
1. Jerome Lane, Pittsburgh	33	444	13.5
2. Chris Dudley, Yale	24	320	13.3
3. Andre Moore, Loyola, Ill.	29	360	12.4
4. David Robinson, Navy	32	378	11.8
5. Brian Rowsom, NC–Wilmington	30	345	11.5
6. Largest Agbejemisin, Wagner	29	333	11.5
7. Bob McCann, Morehead St.	28	317	11.3
8. Melvin Stewart, Texas Southern	29	316	10.9
9. Gerry Beaselink, Connecticut	28	300	10.7
10. Greg Anderson, Houston	30	318	10.6
11. Harry Willis, Weber St.	29	303	10.4
12. Lester Fonville, Jackson St.	29	300	10.3
13. Carl Curry, Mississippi Valley	28	288	10.3
14. Bruon Kongawoin, Houston Baptist	29	297	10.2
15. Booker James, Western Michigan	27	274	10.1
16. Dyron Nix, Tennessee	29	294	10.1
17. Randy Anderson, Stetson	31	311	10.0
18. Derek Robinson, Maryland–Eastern	25	249	10.0
19. Harvey Grant, Oklahoma	34	338	9.9
20. James Gully, Lamar	29	288	9.9
21. Fred West, Texas Southern,	29	287	9.9
22. David Holloway, Prairie View	28	277	9.9
23. Ken Norman, Illinois	31	303	9.8
24. Lionel Simmons, LaSalle	33	322	9.8
25. Ronnie Grandison, New Orleans	30	292	9.7

Professional Basketball

NATIONAL BASKETBALL ASSOCIATION CHAMPIONS

Source: Matt Winick, Director of Media Information, National Basketball Association.

The National Basketball Association was originally the Basketball Association of America. It took its current name in 1949 when it merged with the National Basketball League.

Season	Eastern Conference (W-L)	Western Conference (W-L)	Playoff Champions[1]
1946–47	Washington Capitols (49–11)	Chicago Stags (39–22)	Philadelphia Warriors
1947–48	Philadelphia Warriors (27–21)	St. Louis Bombers (29–19)	Baltimore Bullets
1948–49	Washington Capitols (38–22)	Rochester Royals (45–15)	Minneapolis Lakers
1949–50	Syracuse Nationals (51–13)	Indianapolis Olympians (39–25)	Minneapolis Lakers
1950–51	Philadelphia Warriors (40–26)	Minneapolis Lakers (44–24)	Rochester Royals
1951–52	Syracuse Nationals (40–26)	Rochester Royals (41–25)	Minneapolis Lakers
1952–53	New York Knickerbockers (47–23)	Minneapolis Lakers (48–22)	Minneapolis Lakers
1953–54	New York Knickerbockers (44–28)	Minneapolis Lakers (46–26)	Minneapolis Lakers
1954–55	Syracuse Nationals (43–29)	Ft. Wayne Pistons (43–29)	Syracuse Nationals
1955–56	Philadelphia Warriors (45–27)	Ft. Wayne Pistons (37–35)	Philadelphia Warriors

Season	Eastern Conference (W-L)	Western Conference (W-L)	Playoff Champions[1]
1956-57	Boston Celtics (44-28)	St. Louis Hawks (38-34)	Boston Celtics
1957-58	Boston Celtics (48-23)	St. Louis Hawks (41-31)	St. Louis Hawks
1958-59	Boston Celtics (52-20)	St. Louis Hawks (49-23)	Boston Celtics
1959-60	Boston Celtics (59-16)	St. Louis Hawks (46-29)	Boston Celtics
1960-61	Boston Celtics (57-22)	St. Louis Hawks (51-28)	Boston Celtics
1961-62	Boston Celtics (60-20)	Los Angeles Lakers (54-26)	Boston Celtics
1962-63	Boston Celtics (58-22)	Los Angeles Lakers (53-27)	Boston Celtics
1963-64	Boston Celtics (59-21)	San Francisco Warriors (48-32)	Boston Celtics
1964-65	Boston Celtics (62-18)	Los Angeles Lakers (49-31)	Boston Celtics
1965-66	Philadelphia 76ers (55-25)	Los Angeles Lakers (45-35)	Boston Celtics
1966-67	Philadelphia 76ers (68-13)	San Francisco Warriors (44-37)	Philadelphia 76ers
1967-68	Philadelphia 76ers (62-20)	St. Louis Hawks (56-26)	Boston Celtics
1968-69	Baltimore Bullets (57-25)	Los Angeles Lakers (55-27)	Boston Celtics
1969-70	New York Knickerbockers (60-22)	Atlanta Hawks (48-34)	New York Knicks
1970-71	Baltimore Bullets (42-40)	Milwaukee Bucks (66-16)	Milwaukee Bucks
1971-72	New York Knickerbockers (48-34)	Los Angeles Lakers (69-13)	Los Angeles Lakers
1972-73	New York Knickerbockers (57-25)	Los Angeles Lakers (69-22)	New York Knicks
1973-74	Boston Celtics (56-26)	Milwaukee Bucks (59-23)	Boston Celtics
1974-75	Washington Bullets (60-22)	Golden State Warriors (48-34)	Golden State Warriors
1975-76	Boston Celtics (54-28)	Phoenix Suns (42-40)	Boston Celtics
1976-77	Philadelphia 76ers (50-32)	Portland Trail Blazers (49-33)	Portland Trail Blazers
1977-78	Washington Bullets (44-38)	Seattle Super Sonics (47-35)	Washington Bullets
1978-79	Washington Bullets (54-28)	Seattle Super Sonics (52-30)	Seattle Super Sonics
1979-80	Philadelphia 76ers (59-23)	Los Angeles Lakers (60-22)	Los Angeles Lakers
1980-81	Boston Celtics (62-20)	Phoenix Suns (57-25)	Boston Celtics
1981-82	Boston Celtics (63-19)	Los Angeles Lakers (57-25)	Los Angeles Lakers
1982-83	Philadelphia 76ers (65-17)	Los Angeles Lakers (58-24)	Philadelphia 76ers
1983-84	Boston Celtics (56-26)	Los Angeles Lakers (58-24)	Boston Celtics
1984-85	Boston Celtics (63-19)	Los Angeles Lakers (62-20)	Los Angeles Lakers
1985-86	Boston Celtics (67-15)	Houston Rockets (51-31)	Boston Celtics
1986-87	Boston Celtics (59-23)	Los Angeles Lakers (65-17)	Los Angeles Lakers

1. Playoffs may involve teams other than conference winners.

INDIVIDUAL N.B.A. SCORING CHAMPIONS

Season	Player, Team	G	FG	FT	Pts	Avg
1953-54	Neil Johnston, Philadelphia Warriors	72	591	577	1759	24.4
1954-55	Neil Johnston, Philadelphia Warriors	72	521	589	1631	22.7
1955-56	Bob Pettit, St. Louis Hawks	72	646	557	1849	25.7
1956-57	Paul Arizin, Philadelphia Warriors	71	613	591	1817	25.6
1957-58	George Yardley, Detroit Pistons	72	673	655	2001	27.8
1958-59	Bob Pettit, St. Louis Hawks	72	719	667	2105	29.2
1959-60	Wilt Chamberlain, Philadelphia Warriors	72	1065	577	2707	37.6
1960-61	Wilt Chamberlain, Philadelphia Warriors	79	1251	531	3033	38.4
1961-62	Wilt Chamberlain, Philadelphia Warriors	80	1597	835	4029	50.4
1962-63	Wilt Chamberlain, San Francisco Warriors	80	1463	660	3586	44.8
1963-64	Wilt Chamberlain, San Francisco Warriors	80	1204	540	2948	36.9
1964-65	Wilt Chamberlain, San Francisco Warriors-Phila. 76ers	73	1063	408	2534	34.7
1965-66	Wilt Chamberlain, Philadelphia 76ers	79	1074	501	2649	33.5
1966-67	Rick Barry, San Francisco Warriors	78	1011	753	2775	35.6
1967-68	Dave Bing, Detroit Pistons	79	835	472	2142	27.1
1968-69	Elvin Hayes, San Diego Rockets	82	930	467	2327	28.4
1969-70	Jerry West, Los Angeles Lakers	74	831	647	2309	31.2
1970-71	Lew Alcindor,[1] Milwaukee Bucks	82	1063	470	2596	31.7
1971-72	Kareem Abdul-Jabbar, Milwaukee Bucks	81	1159	504	2822	34.8
1972-73	Nate Archibald, Kansas City-Omaha Kings	80	1028	663	2719	34.0
1973-74	Bob McAdoo, Buffalo Braves	74	901	459	2261	30.8
1974-75	Bob McAdoo, Buffalo Braves	82	1095	641	2831	34.5
1975-76	Bob McAdoo, Buffalo Braves	78	934	559	2427	31.1
1976-77	Pete Maravich, New Orleans Jazz	73	886	501	2273	31.1
1977-78	George Gervin, San Antonio Spurs	82	864	504	2232	27.2
1978-79	George Gervin, San Antonio	80	947	471	2365	29.6
1979-80	George Gervin, San Antonio	78	1024	505	2585	33.1
1980-81	Adrian Dantley, Utah Jazz	80	909	632	2452	30.7
1981-82	George Gervin, San Antonio	79	993	555	2551	32.3
1982-83	Alex English, Denver Nuggets	82	959	406	2326	28.4
1983-84	Adrian Dantley, Utah Jazz	79	802	813	2418	30.6
1984-85	Bernard King, New York Knicks	55	691	426	1809	32.9
1985-86	Dominique Wilkins, Atlanta Hawks	78	888	527	2366	30.3
1986-87	Michael Jordan, Chicago Bulls	82	1098	833	3041	37.1[2]

1. (Kareem Abdul-Jabbar). 2. Also had 12 3-point field goals.

N.B.A. LIFETIME LEADERS

(Through 1986–1987 season)

Scoring

	Yrs	FG	FT	Pts
(a) Kareem Abdul Jabbar	18	15,044	6,385	36,474
Wilt Chamberlain	14	12,681	6,057	31,419
Julius Erving*	16	11,818	6,256	30,026
Dan Issel*	15	10,421	6,591	27,482
Elvin Hayes	16	10,976	5,356	27,313
Oscar Robertson	14	9,508	7,694	26,710
George Gervin*	14	11,362	2,737	26,595
John Havlicek	16	10,513	5,369	26,395
Rick Barry*	14	9,695	5,713	25,279
Jerry West	14	9,016	7,160	25,192
Elgin Baylor	14	8,693	5,763	23,149
(a) Moses Malone*	13	7,843	6,310	22,267
Hal Greer	15	8,504	4,578	21,586
Walt Bellamy	14	7,914	5,113	20,941
Bob Petit	11	7,349	6,182	20,880

(a) active player. *Includes statistics compiled in the American Basketball Association.

Scoring Average

(400 games or 10,000 points minimum)

	Games	Pts	Avg
Wilt Chamberlain	1,045	31,419	30.1
Elgin Baylor	846	23,148	27.4
Jerry West	932	25,192	27.0
Bob Petit	792	20,880	26.4
(a) Adrian Dantley	758	19,678	26.0
(a) Kareem Abdul-Jabbar	1,406	36,474	25.9
Oscar Robertson	1,040	26,710	25.7
George Gervin*	1,060	26,595	25.1
Rick Barry*	1,020	25,279	24.8
(a) Larry Bird	635	15,726	24.8
Julius Erving*	1,243	30,026	24.2
Pete Maravich	658	15,948	24.2
(a) Moses Malone	967	22,267	23.1

(a) active player. *Includes statistics compiled in the American Basketball Association.

Rebounds

Wilt Chamberlain	23,924
Bill Russell	21,620
(a) Kareem Abdul Jabbar	16,628
Elvin Hayes	16,279
(a) Artis Gilmore*	16,119
Nate Thurmond	14,464
Walt Bellamy	14,241
Wes Unseld	13,769
(a) Moses Malone*	13,453
Jerry Lucas	12,942

(a) active player. * includes statistyics compiled in the American Basketball Association.

Free-Throw Percentage

(1,200 free throws made, minimum)

	FTA	FTM	Pct
Rick Barry	4,243	3,818	.900
Calvin Murphy	3,864	3,445	.892
Bill Sharmin	3,557	3,143	.884
(a) Larry Bird	3,311	2,895	.874
Mike Newlin	3,456	3,008	.870
(a) Kiki Vanderweghe	3,244	2,819	.868
Fred Brown	2,211	1,896	.858
Larry Siegfried	1,945	1,662	.854
James Silas	1,690	1,440	.852
Flynn Robinson	1,881	1,597	.849

(a) Active player.

Field-Goal Percentage

(2,000 field goals minimum)

	FGA	FGM	Pct
(a) Artis Gilmore	9,389	5,633	.600
(a) Darryl Dawkins	6,051	3,466	.573
(a) Larry Nance	5,489	3,098	.564
(a) Kevin McHale	6,836	3,846	.563
(a) Kareem Abdul-Jabbar	26,745	15,044	.562
(a) Bill Cartwright	5,277	2,920	.553
(a) Buck Williams	5,700	3,142	.551
Bobby Jones	6,199	3,412	.550
(a) Adrian Dantley	12,770	7,005	.549
(a) Cedric Maxwell	5,934	3,250	.547

Assists

Oscar Robertson	9,887
Lenny Wilkens	7,211
Bob Cousy	6,955
Guy Rodgers	6,917
Nate Archibald	6,476
Jerry West	6,238
John Havlicek	6,114
Norm Nixon	6,047
Dave Bing	5,397
Kevin Porter	5,314

N.B.A. MOST VALUABLE PLAYERS

1956	Bob Pettit
1957	Bob Cousy
1958	Bill Russell
1959	Bob Pettit
1960	Wilt Chamberlain
1961–63	Bill Russell
1964	Oscar Robertson
1965	Bill Russell
1966–68	Wilt Chamberlain
1969	Wes Unseld
1970	Willis Reed
1971–72	Lew Alcindor (Kareem Abdul-Jabbar)
1973	Dave Cowens
1974	Kareem Abdul-Jabbar, Milwaukee
1975	Bob McAdoo, Buffalo
1976–77	Kareem Abdul-Jabbar, Los Angeles
1978	Bill Walton, Portland
1979	Moses Malone, Houston
1980	Kareem Abdul-Jabbar, Los Angeles
1981	Julius Erving, Philadelphia
1982	Moses Malone, Houston
1983	Moses Malone, Philadelphia
1984	Larry Bird, Boston
1985	Larry Bird, Boston
1986	Larry Bird, Boston
1987	Ervin Johnson, Los Angeles

N.B.A. TEAM RECORDS

Most points, game—186, Detroit vs. Denver, 3 overtimes, 1983
Most points, quarter—58, Buffalo vs. Boston, 1968
Most points, half—97, Atlanta vs. San Diego, 1970
Most points, overtime period—22, Detroit vs. Cleveland, 1973
Most field goals, game—74, Detroit, 1983
Most field goals, quarter—23, Boston, 1959; Buffalo, 1972
Most field goals, half—40, Boston, 1959; Syracuse, 1963; Atlanta, 1979
Most assists, game—53, Milwaukee, 1978
Most rebounds, game—109, Boston 1960
Most points, both teams, game—370 (Detroit 186, Denver 184) 3 overtimes, Denver, December 13, 1983
Most points, both teams, quarter—96 (Boston 52, Minneapolis 44), 1959; (Detroit 53, Cincinnati 43), 1972
Most points, both teams, half—170 (Philadelphia 90, Cincinnati 80), Philadelphia, 1971
Longest winning streak—33, Los Angeles, 1971–72
Longest losing streak—20, Philadelphia, 1973
Longest winning streak at home—36, Philadelphia, 1966–67
Most games won, season—69, Los Angeles, 1971–72
Most games lost, season—73, Philadelphia, 1972–73
Highest average points per game—126.5, Denver, 1981–82

N.B.A. INDIVIDUAL RECORDS

Most points, game—100, Wilt Chamberlain, Philadelphia vs. New York at Hershey, Pa., 1962
Most points, quarter—33, George Gervin, San Antonio, 1978
Most points, half—59, Wilt Chamberlain, Philadelphia, 1962
Most free throws, game—28, Wilt Chamberlain, Philadelphia, vs. New York at Hershey, Pa. 1962; 28, Adrian Dantley, Utah, vs. Houston, 1984
Most free throws, quarter—14, Rick Barry, San Francisco, 1966
Most free throws, half—19, Oscar Robertson, Cincinnati, 1964
Most field goals, game—36, Wilt Chamberlain, Philadelphia, 1962
Most consecutive field goals, game—18, Wilt Chamberlain, San Francisco, 1963; Wilt Chamberlain, Philadelphia, 1967
Most assists, game—29, Kevin Porter, New Jersey Nets, 1978
Most rebounds, game—55, Wilt Chamberlain, Philadelphia, 1963

NATIONAL BASKETBALL ASSOCIATION FINAL STANDINGS OF THE CLUBS—1986–1987

EASTERN CONFERENCE

Atlantic Division

	W	L	Pct	Games behind
Boston Celtics	59	23	.720	—
Philadelphia 76ers	45	37	.549	14
Washington Bullets	42	40	.512	17
New Jersey Nets	24	58	.293	35
New York Knicks	24	58	.293	35

Central Division

	W	L	Pct	Games behind
Atlanta Hawks	57	25	.695	—
Detroit Pistons	52	30	.634	5
Milwaukee Bucks	50	32	.610	7
Indiana Pacers	41	41	.500	16
Chicago Bulls	40	42	.488	17
Cleveland Cavaliers	31	51	.378	26

WESTERN CONFERENCE

Midwest Division

	W	L	Pct	Games behind
Dallas Mavericks	55	27	.671	—
Utah Jazz	44	38	.537	11
Houston Rockets	42	40	.512	13
Denver Nuggets	37	45	.451	18
Sacramento Kings	29	53	.354	26
San Antonio Spurs	28	54	.341	27

Pacific Division

	W	L	Pct	Games behind
Los Angeles Lakers	65	17	.793	—
Portland Trail Blazers	49	33	.598	16
Golden State Warriors	42	40	.512	23
Seattle SuperSonics	39	43	.476	26
Phoenix Suns	36	46	.439	29
Los Angeles Clippers	12	70	.146	53

N.B.A. PLAYOFFS—1987

EASTERN CONFERENCE

First Round

Boston defeated Chicago, 3 games to 0
Detroit defeated Washington, 3 games to 0
Atlanta defeated Indiana, 3 games to 1
Milwaukee defeated Philadelphia, 3 games to 2

Semifinal Round

Boston defeated Milwaukee, 4 games to 3
Detroit defeated Atlanta, 4 games to 1

Conference Finals

Boston defeated Detroit, 4 games to 3
May 19—Boston 104, Detroit 91
May 21—Boston 110, Detroit 101
May 23—Detroit 122, Boston 104
May 24—Detroit 145, Boston 119
May 26—Boston 108, Detroit 107
May 28—Detroit 113, Boston 105
May 30—Boston 117, Detroit 114

WESTERN CONFERENCE

First Round

Los Angeles Lakers defeated Denver, 3 games to 0
Seattle defeated Dallas, 3 games to 1
Houston defeated Portland, 3 games to 1
Golden State defeated Utah, 3 games to 2

Semifinal Round

Seattle defeated Houston, 4 games to 2
Los Angeles Lakers defeated Golden State, 4 games to 1

Conference Finals

Los Angeles Lakers defeated Seattle, 4 games to 0
May 16—Los Angeles 92, Seattle 87
May 19—Los Angeles 112, Seattle 104
May 23—Los Angeles 122, Seattle 121
May 25—Los Angeles 133, Seattle 102

CHAMPIONSHIP

Los Angeles defeated Boston, 4 games to 2
June 2—Los Angeles Lakers 126, Boston 113

June 4—Los Angeles Lakers 141, Boston 122
June 7—Boston 109, Los Angeles Lakers 103
June 9—Los Angeles Lakers 107, Boston 106
June 11—Boston 123, Los Angeles Lakers 108
June 14—Los Angeles Lakers 106, Boston 93

FIELD-GOAL LEADERS—1986–1987

(Minimum 300 FG made)

	FG	Att	Pct
Kevin McHale, Boston	790	1,307	.604
Artis Gilmore, San Antonio	346	580	.597
Charles Barkley, Philadelphia	557	937	.594
James Lee Donaldson, Dallas	311	531	.586
Kareem Abdul-Jabbar, L.A. Lakers	560	993	.564
Buck Williams, New Jersey	521	936	.557
Robert Parish, Boston	588	1,057	.556
Ken Johnson, Portland	494	889	.556
Rodney McCray, Houston	432	783	.552
Larry Nance, Phoenix	585	1,062	.551

FREE-THROW LEADERS—1986–1987

(Minimum 125 FT made)

	FT	Att	Pct
Larry Bird, Boston	414	455	.910
Danny Ainge, Boston	148	165	.897
Bill Laimbeer, Detroit	245	274	.894
Byron Scott, L.A. Lakers	224	251	.892
Craig Hodges, Milwaukee	131	147	.891
John Long, Indiana	219	246	.890
Kiki Vandeweghe, Portland	467	527	.886
Rolando Blackman, Dallas	419	474	.884
Ricky Pierce, Milwaukee	387	440	.880

REBOUND LEADERS—1986–1987

(Minimum 70 games or 800 rebounds)

	G	Off	Def	Total	Avg
Charles Barkley, Philadelphia	68	390	604	994	14.6
Charles Oakley, Chicago	82	299	775	1,074	13.1
Buck Williams, New Jersey	82	322	701	1,023	12.5
James Donaldson, Dallas	82	295	678	973	11.9
Bill Laimbeer, Detroit	82	243	712	955	11.6
Michael Cage, L.A. Clippers	80	354	568	922	11.5
Larry Smith, Golden State	80	366	551	917	11.5
Akeem Olajuwon, Houston	75	315	543	858	11.4
Moses Malone, Washington	73	340	484	824	11.3
Robert Parish, Boston	80	254	597	851	10.6

3-POINT FIELD-GOAL LEADERS—1986–1987

(Minimum 25 made)

	FG	Att	Pct
Kiki Vandeweghe, Portland	39	81	.481
Detlef Schrempf, Dallas	33	69	.478
Danny Ainge, Boston	85	192	.443
Byron Scott, L.A. Lakers	65	149	.436
Trent Tucker, New York	68	161	.422
Kevin McKenna, New Jersey	52	124	.419
Larry Bird, Boston	90	225	.400
Michael Cooper, L.A. Lakers	89	231	.385
Eric Floyd, Golden State	73	190	.384
Michael McGee, Atlanta	86	229	.376

LEADING SCORERS—1986–1987

	G	FG	FT	Pts	Avg
Michael Jordan, Chicago	82	1,098	833	3041	37.1
Dominique Wilkins, Atlanta	79	828	607	2294	29.0
Alex English, Denver	82	965	411	2345	28.6
Larry Bird, Boston	74	786	414	2076	28.1
Kiki Vandeweghe, Portland	79	808	467	2122	26.9
Kevin McHale, Boston	77	790	428	2008	26.1
Mark Aguirre, Dallas	80	787	429	2056	25.7
Dale Ellis, Seattle	82	785	385	2041	24.9
Moses Malone, Washington	73	595	570	1760	24.1
Ervin Johnson, L.A. Lakers	80	683	535	1909	23.9
Walter Davis, Phoenix	79	779	288	1887	23.6
Akeem Olajuwon, Houston	75	677	400	1755	23.4
Tom Chambers, Seattle	82	660	535	1909	23.3
Xavier McDaniel, Seattle	82	806	275	1890	23.0
Charles Barkley, Philadelphia	68	557	429	1564	23.0
Ron Harper, Cleveland	82	734	386	1874	22.9
Larry Nance, Phoenix	69	585	381	1552	22.5
Jeff Malone, Washington	80	689	376	1758	22.0
Clyde Drexler, Portland	82	707	357	1782	21.7
Karl Malone, Utah	82	728	323	1779	21.7

STEALS LEADERS—1986–1987

(Minimum 70 games or 125 steals)

	G	Stl	Avg
Alvin Robertson, San Antonio	81	260	3.21
Michael Jordan, Chicago	82	236	2.88
Maurice Cheeks, Philadelphia	68	180	2.65
Ron Harper, Cleveland	82	209	2.55
Clyde Drexler, Portland	82	204	2.49
Lafayette Lever, Denver	82	201	2.45
Derek Harper, Dallas	77	167	2.17
John Stockton, Utah	82	177	2.16
Glenn Rivers, Atlanta	82	171	2.09
Terry Porter, Portland	80	159	1.99

ASSISTS LEADERS—1986–1987

(Minimum 70 games or 400 assists)

	G	No.	Avg
Ervin Johnson, L.A. Lakers	80	977	12.2
Eric Floyd, Golden State	82	848	10.3
Isiah Thomas, Detroit	81	813	10.0
Glenn Rivers, Atlanta	82	823	10.0
Terry Porter, Portland	80	715	8.9
Reggie Theus, Sacramento	79	692	8.8
Nate McMillan, Seattle	71	583	8.2
John Stockton, Utah	82	670	8.2
Lafayette Lever, Denver	82	654	8.0
Maurice Cheeks, Philadelphia	68	538	7.9

BLOCKED-SHOTS LEADERS—1986–1987

(Minimum 70 games or 100 blocked shots)

	G	No.	Avg
Mark Eaton, Utah	79	321	4.06
Manute Bol, Washington	82	302	3.68
Akeem Olajuwon, Houston	75	254	3.39
Benoit Benjamin, L.A. Clippers	72	187	2.60
Alton Lister, Seattle	75	180	2.40
Patrick Ewing, New York	63	147	2.33
Kevin McHale, Boston	77	172	2.23
Larry Nance, Phoenix	69	148	2.14
Roy Hinson, Philadelphia	76	161	2.12
Caldwell Jones, Washington	79	165	2.09

HOCKEY

Ice hockey, by birth and upbringing a Canadian game, is an offshoot of field hockey. Some historians say that the first ice hockey game was played in Montreal in December 1879 between two teams composed almost exclusively of McGill University students, but others assert that earlier hockey games took place in Kingston, Ontario, or Halifax, Nova Scotia. In the Montreal game of 1879, there were fifteen players on a side, who used an assortment of crude sticks to keep the puck in motion. Early rules allowed nine men on a side, but the number was reduced to seven in 1886 and later to six.

The first governing body of the sport was the Amateur Hockey Association of Canada, organized in 1887. In the winter of 1894–95, a group of college students from the United States visited Canada and saw hockey played. They became enthused over the game and introduced it as a winter sport when they returned home. The first professional league was the International Hockey League, which operated in northern Michigan in 1904–06.

Until 1910, professionals and amateurs were allowed to play together on "mixed teams," but this arrangement ended with the formation of the first "big league," the National Hockey Association, in eastern Canada in 1910. The Pacific Coast League was organized in 1911 for western Canadian hockey. The league included Seattle and later other American cities. The National Hockey League replaced the National Hockey Association in 1917. Boston, in 1924, was the first American city to join that circuit. The league expanded to include western cities in 1967. The Stanley Cup was competed for by "mixed teams" from 1894 to 1910, thereafter by professionals. It was awarded to the winner of the N.H.L. playoffs from 1926–67 and now to the league champion. The World Hockey Association was organized in October 1972 and was dissolved after the 1978–79 season when the N.H.L. absorbed four of the teams.

STANLEY CUP WINNERS

Emblematic of World Professional Championship; N.H.L. Championship after 1967

1894	Montreal A.A.A.
1895	Montreal Victorias
1896	Winnipeg Victorias
1897–99	Montreal Victorias
1900	Montreal Shamrocks
1901	Winnipeg Victorias
1902	Montreal A.A.A.
1903–05	Ottawa Silver Seven
1906	Montreal Wanderers
1907	Kenora Thistles[1]
1907	Mont. Wanderers[2]
1908	Montreal Wanderers
1909	Ottawa Senators
1910	Montreal Wanderers
1911	Ottawa Senators
1912–13	Quebec Bulldogs
1914	Toronto
1915	Vancouver Millionaires
1916	Montreal Canadiens
1917	Seattle Metropolitans
1918	Toronto Arenas
1919	No champion
1920–21	Ottawa Senators
1922	Toronto St. Patricks
1923	Ottawa Senators
1924	Montreal Canadiens
1925	Victoria Cougars
1926	Montreal Maroons
1927	Ottawa Senators
1928	N.Y. Rangers
1929	Boston Bruins
1930–31	Montreal Canadiens
1932	Toronto Maple Leafs
1933	N.Y. Rangers
1934	Chicago Black Hawks
1935	Montreal Maroons
1936–37	Detroit Red Wings
1938	Chicago Black Hawks
1939	Boston Bruins
1940	N.Y. Rangers
1941	Boston Bruins
1942	Toronto Maple Leafs
1943	Detroit Red Wings
1944	Montreal Canadiens
1945	Toronto Maple Leafs
1946	Montreal Canadiens
1947–49	Toronto Maple Leafs
1950	Detroit Red Wings
1951	Toronto Maple Leafs
1952	Detroit Red Wings
1953	Montreal Canadiens
1954–55	Detroit Red Wings
1956–60	Montreal Canadiens
1961	Chicago Black Hawks
1962–64	Toronto Maple Leafs
1965–66	Montreal Canadiens
1967	Toronto Maple Leafs
1968–69	Montreal Canadiens
1970	Boston Bruins
1971	Montreal Canadiens
1972	Boston Bruins
1973	Montreal Canadiens
1974–75	Philadelphia Flyers
1976–79	Montreal Canadiens
1980–83	New York Islanders
1984	Edmonton Oilers
1985	Edmonton Oilers
1986	Montreal Canadiens
1987	Edmonton Oilers

1. January. 2. March.

NATIONAL HOCKEY LEAGUE YEARLY TROPHY WINNERS

The Hart Trophy—Most Valuable Player

1924	Frank Nighbor, Ottawa
1925	Billy Burch, Hamilton
1926	Nels Stewart, Montreal Maroons
1927	Herb Gardiner, Montreal Canadiens
1928	Howie Morenz, Montreal Canadiens
1929	Roy Worters, New York Americans
1930	Nels Stewart, Montreal Maroons
1931–32	Howie Morenz, Montreal Canadiens
1933	Eddie Shore, Boston
1934	Aurel Joliat, Montreal Canadiens
1935–36	Eddie Shore, Boston
1937	Babe Siebert, Montreal Canadiens
1938	Eddie Shore, Boston
1939	Toe Blake, Montreal Canadiens
1940	Ebbie Goodfellow, Detroit
1941	Bill Cowley, Boston
1942	Tom Anderson, New York Americans
1943	Bill Cowley, Boston
1944	Babe Pratt, Toronto
1945	Elmer Lach, Montreal Canadiens
1946	Max Bentley, Chicago
1947	Maurice Richard, Montreal Canadiens
1948	Buddy O'Connor, New York Rangers
1949	Sid Abel, Detroit
1950	Chuck Rayner, New York Rangers
1951	Milt Schmidt, Boston
1952–53	Gordon Howe, Detroit
1954	Al Rollins, Chicago
1955	Ted Kennedy, Toronto
1956	Jean Belveau, Montreal Canadiens
1957–58	Gordon Howe, Detroit
1959	Andy Bathgate, New York Rangers

1960	Gordon Howe, Detroit
1961	Bernie Geoffrion, Montreal Canadiens
1962	Jacques Plante, Montreal Canadiens
1963	Gordon Howe, Detroit
1964	Jean Beliveau, Montreal Canadiens
1965–66	Bobby Hull, Chicago
1967–68	Stan Mikita, Chicago
1969	Phil Esposito, Boston
1970–72	Bobby Orr, Boston
1973	Bobby Clarke, Philadelphia
1974	Phil Esposito, Boston
1975–76	Bobby Clarke, Philadelphia
1977–78	Guy Lafleur, Montreal
1979	Bryan Trottier, N.Y. Islanders
1980	Wayne Gretzky, Edmonton
1981	Wayne Gretzky, Edmonton
1982	Wayne Gretzky, Edmonton
1983	Wayne Gretzky, Edmonton
1984	Wayne Gretzky, Edmonton
1985	Wayne Gretzky, Edmonton
1986	Wayne Gretzky, Edmonton
1987	Wayne Gretzky, Edmonton

Vezina Trophy—Leading Goalkeeper

1956–60	Jacques Plante, Montreal
1961	Johnny Bower, Toronto
1962	Jacques Plante, Montreal
1963	Glenn Hall, Chicago
1964	Charlie Hodge, Montreal
1965	Terry Sawchuk—Johnny Bower, Toronto
1966	Lorne Worsley—Charlie Hodge, Montreal
1967	Glenn Hall—Denis DeJordy, Chicago
1968	Lorne Worsley—Rogatien Vachon, Montreal
1969	Glenn Hall—Jacques Plante, St. Louis
1970	Tony Esposito, Chicago
1971	Ed Giacomin—Gilles Villemure, New York
1972	Tony Esposito—Gary Smith, Chicago
1973	Ken Dryden, Montreal
1974	Bernie Parent, Philadelphia, and Tony Esposito, Chicago
1975	Bernie Parent, Philadelphia
1976	Ken Dryden, Montreal
1977–79	Ken Dryden—Michel Larocque, Montreal
1980	Bob Sauve—Don Edwards, Buffalo
1981	Richard Sevigny, Denis Herron and Michel Larocque, Montreal
1982	Billy Smith, New York Islanders
1983	Pete Peeters, Boston
1984	Tom Barrasso, Buffalo
1985	Pelle Lindbergh, Philadelphia
1986	John Vanbiesbrouck, New York Rangers
1987	Ron Hextall, Philadelphia

James Norris Trophy—Defenseman

1954	Red Kelly, Detroit
1955–58	Doug Harvey, Montreal
1959	Tom Johnson, Montreal
1960–62	Doug Harvey, Montreal, New York (62)
1963–65	Pierre Pilote, Chicago
1966	Jacques Laperriere, Montreal
1967	Harry Howell, New York
1968–75	Bobby Orr, Boston
1976	Denis Potvin, N.Y. Islanders
1977	Larry Robinson, Montreal
1978	Denis Potvin, N.Y. Islanders
1980	Larry Robinson, Montreal
1981	Randy Carlyle, Pittsburgh
1982	Doug Wilson, Chicago
1983–84	Rod Langway, Washington
1985	Paul Coffey, Edmonton
1986	Paul Coffey, Edmonton
1987	Ray Bourque, Boston

Lady Byng Trophy—Sportsmanship

1960	Don McKenney, Boston
1961	Red Kelly, Detroit
1962–63	Dave Keon, Toronto
1964	Ken Wharram, Chicago
1965	Bobby Hull, Chicago
1966	Alex Delvecchio, Detroit
1967–68	Stan Mikita, Chicago
1969	Alex Delvecchio, Detroit
1970	Phil Goyette, St. Louis
1971	John Bucyk, Boston
1972	Jean Ratelle, New York
1973	Gil Perreault, Buffalo
1974	John Buyck, Boston
1975	Marcel Dionne, Detroit
1976	Jean Ratelle, N.Y. Rangers–Boston
1977	Marcel Dionne, Los Angeles
1978	Butch Goring, Los Angeles
1979	Bob MacMillan, Atlanta
1980	Wayne Gretzky, Edmonton
1981	Rick Kehoe, Pittsburgh
1982	Rick Middleton, Boston
1983–84	Mike Bossy, N.Y. Islanders
1985	Jari Kurri, Edmonton
1986	Mike Bossy, N.Y. Islanders
1987	Joe Mullen, Calgary

Calder Trophy—Rookie

1962	Bobby Rousseau, Montreal
1963	Kent Douglas, Toronto
1964	Jacques Laperriere, Montreal
1965	Roger Crozier, Detroit
1966	Brit Selby, Toronto
1967	Bobby Orr, Boston
1968	Derek Sanderson, Boston
1969	Danny Grant, Minnesota
1970	Tony Esposito, Chicago
1971	Gilbert Perreault, Buffalo
1972	Ken Dryden, Montreal
1973	Steve Vickers, New York Rangers
1974	Denis Potvin, N.Y. Islanders
1975	Eric Vail, Atlanta
1976	Bryan Trottier, N.Y. Islanders
1977	Willi Plett, Atlanta
1978	Mike Bossy, N.Y. Islanders
1979	Bobby Smith, Minnesota
1980	Ray Bourque, Boston
1981	Peter Stastny, Quebec
1982	Dale Hawerchuk, Winnipeg
1983	Steve Larmer, Chicago
1984	Tom Barrasso, Buffalo
1985	Mario Lemieux, Pittsburgh
1986	Gary Suter, Calgary
1987	Luc Robitaille, Los Angeles

Art Ross Trophy—Leading scorer

1955	Bernie Geoffrion, Montreal
1956	Jean Beliveau, Montreal
1957	Gordie Howe, Detroit
1958–59	Dickie Moore, Montreal
1960	Bobby Hull, Chicago
1961	Bernie Geoffrion, Montreal
1962	Bobby Hull, Chicago
1963	Gordie Howe, Detroit
1964–65	Stan Mikita, Chicago
1966	Bobby Hull, Chicago
1967–68	Stan Mikita, Chicago
1969	Phil Esposito, Boston
1970	Bobby Orr, Boston
1971–74	Phil Esposito, Boston
1975	Bobby Orr, Boston
1976–78	Guy Lafleur, Montreal

1979	Bryan Trottier, N.Y. Islanders
1980	Marcel Dionne, Los Angeles
1981–87	Wayne Gretzky, Edmonton

N.H.L. CHAMPIONS
Prince of Wales Trophy

1939	Boston	1956	Montreal
1940	Boston	1957	Detroit
1941	Boston	1958–62	Montreal
1942	New York	1963	Toronto
1943	Detroit	1964	Montreal
1944–47	Montreal	1965	Detroit
1948	Toronto	1966	Montreal
1948–55	Detroit	1967	Chicago

Eastern Division

1968–69	Montreal	1972	Boston
1970	Chicago	1973	Montreal
1971	Boston	1974	Boston

Prince of Wales Conference

1975	Buffalo
1976–79	Montreal
1980	Buffalo
1981	Montreal
1982	New York Islanders
1983	New York Islanders
1984	New York Islanders
1985	Philadelphia
1986	Montreal
1987	Philadelphia

CAMPBELL BOWL
Western Division

1968	Philadelphia	1971–73	Chicago
1969	St. Louis	1974	Philadelphia
1970	St. Louis		

Clarence Campbell Conference

1975	Philadelphia
1976–77	Philadelphia
1978–79	N.Y. Islanders
1980	Philadelphia
1981	New York Islanders
1982	Edmonton
1983	Edmonton
1984	Edmonton
1985	Edmonton
1986	Calgary
1987	Edmonton

NATIONAL HOCKEY LEAGUE
Final Standing of the Clubs—1986–87

PRINCE OF WALES CONFERENCE
Patrick Division

	W	L	T	GF	GA	Pts
Philadelphia Flyers	46	26	8	310	245	100
Washington Capitals	38	32	10	285	278	86
New York Islanders	35	33	12	279	281	82
New York Rangers	34	38	8	307	323	76
Pittsburgh Penguins	30	38	12	297	290	72
New Jersey Devils	29	45	6	293	368	64

Adams Division

	W	L	T	GF	GA	Pts
Hartford Whalers	43	30	7	287	270	93
Montreal Canadiens	41	29	10	277	241	90
Boston Bruins	39	34	7	301	276	85
Quebec Nordiques	31	39	10	267	276	72
Buffalo Sabres	28	44	8	280	308	64

CLARENCE CAMPBELL CONFERENCE
Norris Division

	W	L	T	GF	GA	Pts
St. Louis Blues	32	33	15	281	293	79
Detroit Red Wings	34	36	10	260	274	78
Chicago Black Hawks	29	37	14	290	310	72
Toronto Maple Leafs	32	42	6	286	319	70
Minnesota North Stars	30	40	10	296	314	70

Smythe Division

	W	L	T	GF	GA	Pts
Edmonton Oilers	50	24	6	372	284	106
Calgary Flames	46	31	3	318	289	95
Winnipeg Jets	40	32	8	279	271	88
Los Angeles Kings	31	41	8	318	341	70
Vancouver Canucks	29	43	8	282	314	66

Stanley Cup Playoffs—1987

Preliminary Round

Philadelphia Flyers defeated New York Rangers, 4 games to 2
New York Islanders defeated Washington Capitals, 4 games to 3
Quebec Nordiques defeated Hartford Whalers, 4 games to 2
Montreal Canadiens defeated Boston Bruins, 4 games to 0
Toronto Maple Leafs defeated St. Louis Blues, 4 games to 2
Detroit Red Wings defeated Chicago Black Hawks, 4 games to 0
Edmonton Oilers defeated Los Angeles Kings, 4 games to 1
Winnipeg Jets defeated Calgary Flames, 4 games to 2

Quarterfinal Round

Philadelphia Flyers defeated New York Islanders, 4 games to 3
Montreal Canadiens defeated Quebec Nordiques, 4 games to 3
Detroit Red Wings defeated Toronto Maple Leafs, 4 games to 3
Edmonton Oilers defeated Winnipeg Jets, 4 games to 0

Semifinal Round

Philadelphia Flyers defeated Montreal Canadiens, 4 games to 2
May 4—Philadelphia 4, Montreal 3 (OT)[1]
May 6—Montreal 5, Philadelphia 2[1]
May 8—Philadelphia 4, Montreal 3
May 10—Philadelphia 6, Montreal 3
May 12—Montreal 5, Philadelphia 2[1]
May 14—Philadelphia 4, Montreal 3

1. At Philadelphia.

Edmonton Oilers defeated Detroit Red Wings, 4 games to 1
May 5—Detroit 3, Edmonton 1[1]
May 7—Edmonton 4, Detroit 1[1]
May 9—Edmonton 2, Detroit 1
May 11—Edmonton 3, Detroit 2

May 13—Edmonton 6, Detroit 3[1]

1. At Edmonton.

Championship

Edmonton Oliers defeated Philadelphia Flyers, 4 games to 3
May 17—Edmonton 4, Philadelphia 2[1]
May 20—Edmonton 3, Philadelphia 2 (OT)[1]
May 22—Philadelphia 5, Edmonton 3
May 24—Edmonton 4, Philadelphia 1
May 26—Philadelphia 4, Edmonton 3[1]
May 28—Philadelphia 3, Edmonton 2
May 31—Edmonton 3, Philadelphia 1[1]

1. At Edmonton.

N.H.L. LEADING GOALTENDERS—1986–87

(Minimum 1,400 minutes)

	G	Min	GA	Avg
Brian Hayward, Montreal	37	2178	102	2.81
Patrick Roy, Montreal	46	2686	131	2.93
Ron Hextall, Philadelphia	66	3799	190	3.00
Daniel Berthiaume, Winnipeg	31	1758	93	3.17
Glen Hanlon, Detroit	36	1963	104	3.18
Mario Gosselin, Quebec	30	1625	86	3.18
Pete Peeters, Washington	37	2002	107	3.21
Mike Liut, Hartford	59	3476	187	3.23
Eldon Reddick, Winnipeg	48	2762	149	3.24
Bob Mason, Washington	45	2536	137	3.24
Rejean Lemelin, Calgary	34	1735	94	3.25
Kelly Hrudey, N.Y. Islanders	46	2634	145	3.30
Bill Ranford, Boston	41	2234	124	3.33
Doug Keans, Boston	36	1942	108	3.34
Clint Malarchuk, Quebec	54	3092	175	3.40
Pat Riggin, Boston-Pittsburgh	27	1501	83	3.36
Gilles Meloche, Pittsburgh	43	2343	134	3.43
Grant Fuhr, Edmonton	44	2388	137	3.44
Kari Takko, Minnesota	38	2075	119	3.44
Greg Stefan, Detroit	43	2351	135	3.45
Andy Moog, Edmonton	46	2461	144	3.51
Billy Smith, N.Y. Islanders	40	2252	132	3.52
Greg Millen, St. Louis	42	2482	146	3.53
Rick Wamsley, St. Louis	41	2410	142	3.54

OTHER N.H.L. AWARDS—1987

Smythe (Most valuable in playoffs)—Ron Hextall, Philadelphia

N.H.L. LEADING SCORERS—1986–87

	GP	G	A	Pts
Wayne Gretzky, Edmonton	79	62	121	183
Jari Kuri, Edmonton	79	54	54	108
Mario Lemieux, Pittsburgh	63	54	53	107
Mark Messier, Edmonton	77	37	70	107
Doug Gilmour, St. Louis	80	42	63	105
Dino Ciccarelli, Minnesota	80	52	51	103
Dale Hawerchuk, Winnipeg	80	47	53	100
Michel Goulet, Quebec	75	49	47	96
Tim Kerr, Philadelphia	75	58	37	95
Ray Bourque, Boston	78	23	72	95
Ron Francis, Hartford	75	30	63	93
Denis Savard, Chicago	70	40	50	90
Steve Yzerman, Detroit	80	31	59	90
Joe Mullen, Calgary	79	47	40	87
Walt Poddubney, N.Y. Rangers	75	40	47	87
Bryan Trottier, N.Y. Islanders	80	23	64	87
Luc Robitalle, Los Angeles	79	45	39	84
Steve Larmer, Chicago	80	28	56	84
Marcel Dionne, N.Y. Rangers–L.A	81	28	56	84
Bernie Nicholls, Los Angeles	80	33	48	81
Larry Murphy, Washington	80	23	58	81
Dan Quinn, Calgary–Pittsburgh	80	31	49	80
Mats Naslund, Montreal	79	25	55	80

N.H.L. CAREER SCORING LEADERS

(Listed in order of total points scored; figures in parentheses indicate the top 10 in goals scored)

	Yrs	Games	G	A	Pts
Gordie Howe (1)	26	1,767	801	1,049	1,850
Marcel Dionne (3)[1]	16	1,244	693	990	1,683
Phil Esposito (2)	18	1,282	717	873	1,590
Wayne Gretzky (6)[1]	8	632	543	977	1,520
Stan Mikita (7)	22	1,394	541	926	1,467
John Bucyk (5)	23	1,540	556	813	1,369
Gil Perreault	16	1,171	503	807	1,310
Alex Delvecchio	24	1,549	456	825	1,281
Jean Ratelle	21	1,281	491	776	1,267
Guy Lafleur (9)	14	961	518	728	1,246
Norm Ullman	20	1,410	490	739	1,229
Jean Beliveau (10)	20	1,215	507	712	1,219
Bobby Clarke	15	1,144	358	852	1,210
Bobby Hull (4)	16	1,063	610	560	1,170
Darryl Sittler	15	1,096	484	637	1,121
Frank Mahovlich (8)	18	1,181	533	570	1,103
Henri Richard	20	1,256	358	688	1,046
Rod Gilbert	18	1,065	406	615	1,021

1. Still active in the N.H.L.

BOWLING

AMERICAN BOWLING CONGRESS CHAMPIONS

Year	Singles	All-events	Year	Singles	All-events
1959	Ed Lubanski	Ed Lubanski	1974	Gene Krause	Bob Hart
1960	Paul Kulbaga	Vince Lucci	1975	Jim Setser	Bobby Meadows
1961	Lyle Spooner	Luke Karen	1976	Mike Putzer	Jim Lindquist
1962	Andy Renaldo	Billy Young	1977	Frank Gadaleto	Bud Debenham
1963	Fred Delello	Bus Owalt	1978	Rich Mersek	Chris Cobus
1964	Jim Stefanich	Les Zikes, Jr.	1979	Rick Peters	Bob Basacchi
1965	Ken Roeth	Tom Hathaway	1980	Mike Eaton	Steve Fehr
1966	Don Chapman	John Wilcox	1981	Rob Vital	Rod Toft
1967	Frank Perry	Gary Lewis	1982	Bruce Bohm	Rich Wonders
1968	Wayne Kowalski	Vince Mazzanti	1983	Rick Kendrick	Tony Cariello
1969	Greg Campbell	Eddie Jackson	1984	Bob Antczak and Neal Young (tie)	Bob Goike
1970	Jake Yoder	Mike Berlin			
1971	Al Cohn	Al Cohn	1985	Glen Harbison	Barry Asher
1972	Bill Pointer	Mac Lowry	1986	Jess Mackey	Ed Marazka
1973	Ed Thompson	Ron Woolet	1987	Terry Taylor	Ryan Schafer

PROFESSIONAL BOWLERS ASSOCIATION

National Championship Tournament

1960	Don Carter	1967	Dave Davis	1974	Earl Anthony	1981	Earl Anthony
1961	Dave Soutar	1968	Wayne Zahn	1975	Earl Anthony	1982	Earl Anthony
1962	Carmen Salvino	1969	Mike McGrath	1976	Paul Colwell	1983	Earl Anthony
1963	Billy Hardwick	1970	Mike McGrath	1977	Tommy Hudson	1984	Bob Chamberlain
1964	Bob Strampe	1971	Mike Lemongello	1978	Warren Nelson	1985	Mike Aulby
1965	Dave Davis	1972	Johnny Guenther	1979	Mike Aulby	1986	Tom Crites
1966	Wayne Zahn	1973	Earl Anthony	1980	Johnny Petraglia	1987	Randy Pedersen

BOWLING PROPRIETORS' ASSOCIATION OF AMERICA—MEN

United States Open[1]

1971	Mike Lemongello	1976	Paul Moser	1981	Marshall Holman	1986	Steve Cook
1972	Don Johnson	1977	Johnny Petraglia	1982	Dave Husted	1987	Del Ballard
1973	Mike McGrath	1978	Nelson Burton, Jr.	1983	Gary Dickinson		
1974	Larry Laub	1979	Joe Berardi	1984	Mark Roth		
1975	Steve Neff	1980	Steve Martin	1985	Marshall Holman		

1. Replaced All-Star tournament and is rolled as part of B.P.A. tour.

WOMEN'S INTERNATIONAL BOWLING CONGRESS CHAMPIONS

Year	Singles	All-events	Year	Singles	All-events
1959	Mae Bolt	Pat McBride	1974	Shirley Garms	Judy C. Soutar
1960	Marge McDaniels	Judy Roberts	1975	Barbara Leicht	Virginia Norton
1961	Elaine Newton	Evelyn Teal	1976	Bev Shonk	Betty Morris
1962	Martha Hoffman	Flossie Argent	1977	Akiko Yamaga	Akiko Yamaga
1963	Dot Wilkinson	Helen Shablis	1978	Mae Bolt	Annese Kelly
1964	Jean Havlish	Jean Havlish	1979	Betty Morris	Betty Morris
1965	Doris Rudell	Donna Zimmerman	1980	Betty Morris	Cheryl Robinson
1966	Gloria Bouvia	Kate Helbig	1981	Virginia Norton	Virginia Norton
1967	Gloria Paeth	Carol Miller	1982	Gracie Freeman	Aleta Rzepecki
1968	Norma Parks	Susie Reichley	1983	Aleta Rzepecki	Virginia Norton
1969	Joan Bender	Helen Duval	1984	Freida Gates	Shinobu Saitoh
1970	Dorothy Fothergill	Dorothy Fothergill	1985	Polly Schwarzel	Aleta Sill
1971	Mary Scruggs	Lorrie Nichols	1986	Dana Stewart	Robin Romeo
1972	D. D. Jacobson	Mildred Martorella			Maria Lewis (tie)
1973	Bobby Buffaloe	Toni Calvery	1987	Regi Junak	Leanne Barrette

WIBC QUEENS TOURNAMENT CHAMPIONS

1961	Janet Harman	1968	Phyllis Massey	1975	Cindy Powell	1982	Katsuko Sugimoto
1962	Dorothy Wilkinson	1969	Ann Feigel	1976	Pamela Buckner	1983	Aleta Rzepecki
1963	Irene Monterosso	1970	Mildred Martorella	1977	Dana Stewart	1984	Kazue Inahashi
1964	D.D. Jacobson	1971	Mildred Martorella	1978	Loa Boxberger	1985	Aleta Sill
1965	Betty Kuczynski	1972	Dorothy Fothergill	1979	Donna Adamek	1986	Cora Fiebig
1966	Judy Lee	1973	Dorothy Fothergill	1980	Donna Adamek	1987	Cathy Almeida
1967	Mildred Martorella	1974	Judy Soutar	1981	Katsuko Sugimoto		

BOWLING PROPRIETORS' ASSOCIATION OF AMERICA—WOMEN

United States Open

1971	Paula Carter	1976	Patty Costello (Pa.)	1981	Donna Adamek	1986	Wendy MacPherson
1972	Lorrie Nichols	1977	Betty Morris	1982	Shinobu Saitoh	1987	Carol Nurman
1973	Mildred Martorella	1978	Donna Adamek	1983	Dana Miller		
1974	Pat Costello (Calif.)	1979	Diana Silva	1984	Karen Ellingsworth		
1975	Paula Carter	1980	Pat Costello (Calif.)	1985	Pat Mercatanti		

AMERICAN BOWLING CONGRESS TOURNAMENT—1987

(Niagara Falls, N.Y., Feb. 14-May 25, 1987)

Regular Division

Singles—Terry Taylor, Nashville, Tenn.	749
Doubles—Ray Betchkal and Dennis Schlichting, Rachinew, Wis.	1380
All Events—Ryan Shafer, Elmira, N.Y.	2044
Team—Sound Track, Salamanca, N.Y.	3197
Team All-Events—Murdock Machine, Detroit	9185

Booster Division

Team—De Fazio's Stadium Grill, Niagara Falls, N.Y.	2794

PROFESSIONAL BOWLERS ASSOCIATION CHAMPIONSHIP—1987

(Toledo, Ohio, March 22-28, 1987)

Winner—Randy Pedersen, Santa Maria, Calif. (defeated Amleto Monacelli, Venezuela, 233-222)
Third place—Marshall Holman, Medford, Or.
Fourth Place—David Ozio, Vidor, Texas
Fifth place—Pete Weber, St. Louis, Mo.

WIBC QUEENS TOURNAMENT—1987

(Hartford, Conn., May 12-16, 1987)

Winner—Cathy Almeida, Blackwood, N.J. (defeated Lorrie Nichols, Algonquin, Ill., 850-817 in four-game final)
Third place—Cheryl Daniels, Detroit, Mich.
Fourth place—Kim Kinyon, Lockport, N.Y.
Fifth place—Donna Adamek, Duarte, Calif.

WOMEN'S INTERNATIONAL BOWLING CONGRESS TOURNAMENT—1987

(Hartford, Conn., April 2-June 3, 1987)

Open Division

Singles—Regi Jonak, St. Peter's, Mo.	728
Doubles—Laura Grant, Norwalk, Conn. and Robin Romeo, Van Nuys, Calif.	1328
All Events—Leanne Barrette, Oklahoma City, Okla.	1972
Team—Tool Warehouse, Hollywood, Fla.	3033

Division I

Singles—Kathleen Lovett, Arthurdale, W.Va., and Schanda Plank, Grand Rapids, Mich. (tie)	656
Doubles—Gloria Penn and Ruth Jensen, Plainfield, N.J., and Bound Brook, N.J.	1232
All-Events—Arlene Army, Millbury, Mass.	1767
Team—Classy Ladies, Hartford, Conn.	2754

Division II

Singles—Luann Stavola, Atlantic Highlands, N.J.	608
Doubles—Ann Wilson, Ashdown, Ark., and Francis Scarborough, Texarcana, Ark.	1130
All-Events—Kathy Burley, Bethlehem, Pa.	1610
Team—Eller's Chihuahuas, Plain City, Ohio	2621

SKIING

ALPINE WORLD CUP OVERALL WINNERS

Year	Men	Women	Team
1967	Jean-Claude Killy, France	Nancy Greene, Canada	France
1968	Jean-Claude Killy, France	Nancy Greene, Canada	France
1969	Karl Schranz, Austria	Gertrude Gabl, Austria	Austria
1970	Karl Schranz, Austria	Michel Jacot, France	France
1971	Gustavo Thoeni, Italy	Annemarie Proell, Austria	France
1972	Gustavo Thoeni, Italy	Annemarie Proell, Austria	France
1973	Gustavo Thoeni, Italy	Annemarie Proell Moser, Austria	Austria
1974	Piero Gros, Italy	Annemarie Proell Moser, Austria	Austria
1975	Gustavo Thoeni, Italy	Annemarie Proell Moser, Austria	Austria
1976	Ingemar Stenmark, Sweden	Rosi Mittermaier, West Germany	Austria
1977	Ingemar Stenmark, Sweden	Lise-Marie Morerod, Switzerland	Austria
1978	Ingemar Stenmark, Sweden	Hanni Wenzel, Liechtenstein	Austria
1979	Peter Luescher, Switzerland	Annemarie Proell Moser, Austria	Austria
1980	Andreas Wenzel, Liechtenstein	Hanni Wenzel, Liechtenstein	Liechtenstein
1981	Phil Mahre, United States	Marie-Theres Nadig, Switzerland	Switzerland
1982	Phil Mahre, United States	Erika Hess, Switzerland	Austria
1983	Phil Mahre, United States	Tamara McKinney, United States	
1984	Pirman Zurbriggen, Switzerland	Erika Hess, Switzerland	
1985	Marc Girardelli, Luxembourg	Michela Figini, Switzerland	
1986	Marc Girardelli, Luxembourg	Maria Walliser, Switzerland	Switzerland
1987	Pirmin Zubriggen, Switzerland	Maria Walliser, Switzerland	Switzerland

UNITED STATES CHAMPIONSHIPS—1987

ALPINE

Men's Events

Downhill—Douglas Lewis	1:23.80
Slalom—Bob Ormsby	1:37.77
Giant Slalom—Felix McGrath	2:05.19

Women's Events

Downhill—Pam Fletcher	1:22.32
Slalom—Tamara McKinney	1:35.04
Giant Slalom—Debbie Armstrong	2:15.41

NORDIC
Men's Cross Country

15 kilometers—Todd Boonstra	:45:39.4
30 kilometers—Dan Simoneau	1:38:15.6
50 kilometers—Bill Spencer	2:24:43.3 [1]

1. Actual winning time was 2:23:28.3 by Kristian Naiss, but only U.S. citizens are eligible for national championship, so Spencer, who finished third, was declared champion.

Women's Cross Country

5 kilometers—Nancy Fiddler	:17:49.8
10 kilometers—Leslie Kritchko	:33:14.3
25 kilometers—Lessie Thompson	1:19:25.0

NORDIC WORLD CUP—1987

Overall—Men Cross Country

1. Torgny Mogren, Sweden	115
2. Thomas Wassberg, Sweden	98
3. Gunde Svan, Sweden	83
4. Vegard Ulvang, Norway	74
5. Vladimir Smirnov, Soviet Union	64
Best American finish—none	

Overall Women Cross Country

1. Marjo Matikainsen, Finland	127
2. Anfisa Reztsova, Soviet Union	97
3. Mariannew Dahlmo, Norway	95
4. Marie Helene Westin, Sweden	85
5. Brit Petterson, Norway	75
Best American finish—none	

Nordic Men's Combined

1. Torbjoern Loekken, Norway	146
2. Hermann Weinbuch, West Germany	100
3. Hyppolyt Kempf, Switzerland	90
4. Hubert Schwartz, West Germany	89
5. Thomas Mueller, West Germany	86
Best American finish—Kerry Lynch	20 (19th place)

ALPINE WORLD CUP—1987

Overall—Men

Pirmin Zurbriggen, Switzerland	339
Marc Girardelli, Luxemburg	190
Markus Wasmeier, West Germany	174
Joel Gaspoz, Switzerland	153
Richard Pramotton, Italy	139
Best American finish—Doug Lewis	17 (53rd place)

Overall—Women

Maria Walliser, Switzerland	269
Vreni Schneider, Switzerland	262
Brigitte Ortli, Switzerland	206
Erika Hess, Switzerland	169
Michela Figini, Switzerland	162
Best American Finish—Tamara McKinney	127 (6th place)

Event Leaders—Men

Downhill—Pirmin Zurbriggen, Switzerland	125
2. Peter Mueller, Switzerland	105
3. Franz Heinzer, Switzerland	90
Best American finish—Doug Lewis	17 (19th place)
Slalom—Bojan Krizaj	105
2. Ingemar Stenmarl, Sweden	96
3. Armin Bittner, West Germany	78
Best American finish—Felix McGrath	7 (31st place)
Giant Slalom—Pirmin Zurbriggen, Switzerland	102
Joel Gaspoz, Switzerland	102
2. Richard Pramotton, Italy	95
Best American finish—Felix McGrath	2 (34th place)
Combined—Pirmin Zurbriggen, Switzerland	50
2. Andreas Wenzel, Liechtenstein	20
Best American finish—none	

Event Leaders—Women

Downhill—Michela Figini, Switzerland	93
2. Maria Walliser, Switzerland	90
3. Laurie Graham, Canada	86
Best American finish—Debbie Armstrong	26 (12th place)
Slalom—Corrine Schmidhauser, Switzerland	110
2. Tamara McKinney, United States	99
3. Erika Hess, Switzerland	96
Giant Slalom—Maria Walliser, Switzerland	120
Vreni Schneider, Switzerland	120
2. Blanca Ochoa-Fernandez, Spain	78
Best American finish—Tamara McKinney	30 (10th)
Combined—Brigitte Ortli, Switzerland	25
2. Vreni Schneider, Switzerland	20
3. Erika Hess, Switzerland	15
Best American finish—none	

WORLD UNIVERSITY GAMES—1987

Men's Alpine Events

Downhill—Peter Jurko, Czechoslovakia
Slalom—Peter Propangelov, Bulgaria
Giant slalom—Peter Jurko, Czechoslovakia
Combined—Peter Jurko, Czechoslovakia

Women's Alpine Events

Downhill—Ludmila Milanova, Czechoslovakia
Slalom—Ivan Valesova, Czechoslovakia
Giant slalom—Ludmila Milanova, Czechoslovakia
Combined—Ludmila Milanova, Czechoslovakia

Men's Nordic Events

15 kilometer—Vladimir Nikitin, Soviet Union
30 kilometer—Vladimir Nikitin, Soviet Union
70-meter jump—Peter Ciz, Czechoslovakia
90-meter jump—Jiri Malec, Czechoslovakia
Nordic combined—Frantisek Repka, Czechoslovakia
4 × 10 kilometer relay—Soviet Union

Women's Events

5 kilometer—Tamara Tikhonova, Soviet Union
10 kilometer—Alzbeta Havrancikova, Czechoslovakia
3 × 5 kilometer relay—Czechoslovakia

N.C.A.A RESULTS—1987

Men

Slalom—John Skajem, Colorado	1:25.27
Giant slalom—John Skajem, Colorado	2:11.48
Cross Country—Asmund Drivenes, Utah	36:17.6
Cross country relay—Utah	1:15:56.0

Women

Slalom—Eva Pfosi, Dartmouth	1:31.98
Giant slalom—Vibeke Hoff, Utah	2:13.18
Cross country—Cristen Petty, Colorado	29:26.3
Cross country relay—Vermont	47:05.6

Team (men & women)

1. Utah	710
2. Vermont	627
3. Colorado	593

FISHING

SELECTED WORLD ALL-TACKLE FISHING RECORDS

Caught with Rod and Reel in Fresh Water (as of Aug 1, 1987)

Source: International Game Fish Association.

Species	lb-oz	Where caught	Year	Angler
Bass, Largemouth	22-4	Montgomery Lake, Ga.	1932	George W. Perry
Bass, Peacock	26-8	Mataveni River, Columbia	1982	Rod Neubert
Bass, Redeye	8-3	Flint River, Ga.	1977	David A. Hubbard
Bass, Rock	3-0	York River, Ontario	1974	Peter Gulgin
Bass, Smallmouth	11-15	Dale Hollow Lake, Ky.	1955	David L. Hayes
Bass, Spotted	9-4	Parris Lake, Calif.	1987	Steven West[1] & Gilbert Rowe
Bass, Striped	78-8	Atlantic City, N.J.	1982	Albert McReynolds
Bass, Striped (landlocked)	59-12	Colorado River, Ariz.	1977	Frank W. Smith
Bass, White	5-14	Kerr Lake, N.C.	1986	Jim King
Bass, Whiterock	22-6	Augusta, Ga.	1986	Jerry Adams
Bass, Yellow	2-4	Lake Monroe, Ind.	1977	Donald L. Stalker
Bluegill	4-12	Ketona Lake, Ala.	1950	T.S. Hudson
Bowfin	21-8	Florence, S.C.	1980	Robert L. Harmon
Buffalo, Bigmouth	70-5	Bussey Brake, Bastrop, La.	1980	Delbert Sisk
Buffalo, Smallmouth	68-8	Lake Hamilton, Ark.	1984	Jerry L. Dolezal
Bullhead, Black	8-0	Lake Waccabuc, N.Y.	1951	Kani Evans
Bullhead, Brown	5-8	Veal Pond, Ga.	1975	Jimmy Andrews
Burbot	18-4	Pickford, Mich.	1980	Tom Courtemanche
Carp	57-13	Potomac River, Wash., D.C.	1983	David Nikolow
Catfish, Blue	97-0	Missouri River, S.D.	1959	Edward B. Elliott
Catfish, Channel	58-0	Santee–Cooper Res., S.C.	1964	W.B. Whaley
Catfish, Flathead	98-0	Lewisville, Tex.	1986	William Stevens
Char, Arctic	32-9	Tree River, Canada	1985	Peter Goulding
Crappie, Black	4-8	Kerr Lake, Va.	1981	L. Carl Herring, Jr.
Crappie, White	5-3	Enid Dam, Mississippi	1957	Fred L. Bright
Dolly Varden	8-1	Nakwasina River, Alaska	1985	Loyal Johnson
Drum, Freshwater	54-8	Nickajack Lake, Tenn.	1972	Benny E. Hull
Gar, Alligator	279	Rio Grande River, Tex.	1951	Bill Valverde
Gar, Longnose	50-5	Trinity River, Texas	1954	Townsend Miller
Gar, Shortnose	5-0	Vian, Okla.	1985	Buddy Croslin
Inconnu	38-2	Kobuk River, Alaska	1982	Mark L. Feldman
Muskellunge	69-15	St. Lawrence River, N.Y.	1957	Arthur Lawton
Muskellunge, Tiger	51-3	Lac-Vieux-Desert, Wisc.-Mich.	1919	John A. Knobla
Perch, White	4-12	Messalonskee Lake, Maine	1949	Mrs. Earl Small
Perch, Yellow	4-3	Bordentown, N.J.	1865	Dr. C.C. Abbot
Pickerel, Eastern Chain	9-6	Homerville, Ga.	1961	Baxley McQuaig, Jr.
Redhorse, Northern	3-11	Missouri River, S.D.	1977	Phillip Laumeyer
Redhorse, Silver	11-7	Plum Creek, Wisconsin	1985	Neal D.G. Long
Salmon, Atlantic	79-2	Tana River, Norway	1928	Henrik Henriksen
Salmon, Chinook	97-4	Kenai River, Alaska	1985	Les Anderson
Salmon, Chum	27-3	Raymond Cove, Alaska	1977	Robert A. Jahnke
Salmon, Coho	31-0	Cowichan Bay, B.C., Canada	1947	Mrs. Lee Hallberg
Salmon, Landlocked	22-8	Sebago Lake, Maine	1907	Edward Blakely
Salmon, Pink	12-9	Moose & Kenai Rivers, Alaska	1974	Steven Alan Lee
Salmon, Sockeye	12-8	Situk River, Yakutat, Alaska	1983	Mike Boswell
Shad, American	11-1	Delaware River, N.J.	1984	Charles J. Mower
Sturgeon	468-0	Benicia, Calif.	1983	Joey Pallotta III
Sturgeon, White	380-0	Snake River, Idaho	1973	Del Canty
Sunfish, Green	2-2	Stockton Lake, Missouri	1971	Paul M. Dilley
Sunfish, Redbreast	1-12	Suwannee River, Fla.	1984	Alvin Buchanan
Sunfish, Redear	4-10	Mill Pond, Fla.	1985	C.L. Windham
Tigerfish	61-11	Lake Tanganyika, Zambia	1984	Don Hunter
Trout, Brook	14-8	Nipigon River, Ontario	1916	Dr. W.J. Cook
Trout, Brown	35-15	Nahuel Huapi, Argentina	1952	Eugenio Cavaglia
Trout, Bull	32-0	Lake Pend Orielle, Idaho	1949	N.L. Higgins
Trout, Cutthroat	41-0	Pyramid Lake, Nev.	1925	John Skimmerhorn
Trout, Golden	11-0	Cook's Lake, Wyoming	1948	Charles S. Reed
Trout, Lake	65-0	Great Bear Lake, N.W.T., Canada	1970	Larry Daunis
Trout, Rainbow	42-2	Bell Island, Alaska	1970	David Robert White
Trout, Tiger	20-13	Lake Michigan, Wisc.	1978	Peter M. Friedland
Walleye	25-0	Old Hickory Lake, Tenn.	1960	Mabry Harper
Whitefish, Lake	14-6	Meaford, Ontario, Canada	1984	Dennis M. Laycock
Whitefish, Mountain	5-0	Athabasca River, Alberta, Canada	1963	Orville Welch
Whitefish, Round	6-0	Putahow River, Manitoba, Canada	1984	Allan J. Ristori

1. West and Rowe caught same size record spotted bass in 1987 in same location, Parris Lake, Calif. 3 months apart—West in Feb. and Rowe in April.

Caught With Rod and Reel in Salt Water (as of Aug. 1, 1987)

Source: International Game Fish Association.

Species	lb-oz	Where caught	Year	Angler
Albacore	88-2	Canary Islands	1977	Siegfried Dickemann
Amberjack	155-10	Challenger Bank, Bermuda	1981	Joseph Dawson
Barracuda	83	Lagos, Nigeria	1952	K. J. W. Hackett
Bass, Black Sea	9-8	Virginia Beach, Va.	1987	Joe Mizelle, Jr.
Bass, Giant Sea	563-8	Anacapa Island, Calif.	1968	J. D. McAdam, Jr.
Bass, Striped	78-8	Atlantic City, N.J.	1982	Albert J. McReynolds
Blackfish (Tautog)	21-8	Wachapreague, Virginia	1984	Tommy Wood
Bluefish	31-12	North Carolina	1972	James M. Hussey
Bonefish	19	Zululand, S. Africa	1962	Brian W. Batchelor
Bonito, Atlantic	18-4	Fayal Island, Azores	1984	D. Gama Higgs
Bonito, Pacific	23-8	Victoria, Mahe	1975	Mrs. Anne Cochain
Cobia	135-9	Shark Bay, Australia	1985	Peter Goulding
Cod, Atlantic	98-12	Isle of Shoals, N.H.	1969	Alphonse Bielevich
Cod, Pacific	30-0	Andrew Bay, Alaska	1984	Donald R. Vaughn
Conger	102-8	Plymouth, Devon, England	1983	Raymond Ewart Street
Dolphin	87	Papagallo Gulf, Costa Rica	1976	Manual Salazar
Drum, Black	113-1	Lewes, Del.	1975	G. M. Townsend
Drum, Red	94-2	Avon, North Carolina	1984	David G. Deuel
Flounder, Summer	22-7	Montauk, N.Y.	1975	Charles Nappi
Halibut, Atlantic	250	Gloucester, Mass.	1981	Louis P. Sirard
Halibut, California	45	Santa Cruz Island, Calif.	1982	Jack C. Meserve
Hailbut, Pacific	350	Homer, Alaska	1982	Vern S. Foster
Jack, Crevalle	54-7	Port Michel, Gabon	1982	Thomas F. Gibson, Jr.
Jack, Horse-eye	24-8	Miami, Fla.	1982	Tito Schnau
Jack, Pacific Crevalle	24-0	Cabo San Lucas, Mexico	1987	Sharon Swanson
Jewfish	680	Fernandina Beach, Fla.	1961	Lynn Joyner
Lingcod	61-0	San Juan Island, Wash.	1986	Tom Nelson
Mackerel, King	90	Key West, Florida	1976	Norton I. Thomton
Mackerel, Spanish	12-0	Ft. Pierce, Florida	1984	John F. Colligan
Marlin, Atlantic Blue	1282	St. Thomas, Virgin Islands	1977	Larry Martin
Marlin, Black	1560	Cabo Blanco, Peru	1953	A. C. Glassel, Jr.
Marlin, Pacific Blue	1376	Kaaiwi Point, Kona, Hawaii	1982	Jay Wm. deBeaubien
Marlin, Striped	494	Tutukaka, New Zealand	1986	Bill Boniface
Marlin, White	181-14	Victoria, Brazil	1979	Evandro Luiz Coser
Permit	51-8	Lake Worth, Fla.	1978	William M. Kenney
Pollack	26-7	Salcombe, England	1984	Robert Perry
Pollack (virens)	46-7	Brielle, N.J.	1975	John T. Holton
Pompano, African	41-8	Fort Lauderdale, Fla.	1979	Wayne Sommers
Sailfish, Atlantic	128-1	Luanda, Angola, Africa	1974	Harm Steyn
Sailfish, Pacific	221	Santa Cruz Is., Galapagos Is.	1947	C. W. Stewart
Seabass, White	83-12	San Felipe, Mexico	1953	L. C. Baumgardner
Shark, Blue	437	Catherine Bay, Australia	1976	Peter Hyde
Shark, Hammerhead	991	Sarasota, Fla.	1982	Allen Ogle
Shark, Mako	1080	Montauk, N.Y.	1979	James L. Melanson
Shark, Porbeagle	465	Padstow, Cornwall, England	1976	Jorge Potier
Shark, Thresher	802	Tutukaka, New Zealand	1981	Dianne North
Shark, Tiger	1780	Cherry Grove, S.C.	1964	Walter Maxwell
Shark, White	2664	South Australia	1959	Alfred Dean
Snapper, Cubera	121-8	Cameron, La.	1982	Mike Hebert
Snook	53-10	Costa Rica	1978	Gilbert Ponzi
Spearfish	90-13	Madeira Island, Portugal	1980	Joseph Larkin
Swordfish	1182	Iquique, Chile	1953	L. E. Marron
Tanguigue	99	Scottburgh, Natal, South Africa	1982	Michael John Wilkinson
Tarpon	283	Lake Maracalbo, Venezuela	1956	M. Salazar
Trevally, Bigeye	15-0	Isla Coiba, Panama	1984	Sally S. Timms
Trevally, Giant	137-9	McKenzie State Park, Hawaii	1983	Roy K. Gushiken
Tuna, Atlantic Bigeye	375-8	Ocean City, Md.	1977	Cecil Browne
Tuna, Blackfin	42	Bermuda	1978	Alan J. Card
Tuna, Bluefin	1496	Nova Scotia, Canada	1979	Ken Fraser
Tuna, Dog-tooth	194	Kwan-Tall Island, Korea	1980	Kim Chul
Tuna, Longtail	79-2	Montague Island, Australia	1982	Tim Simpson
Tuna, Pacific Big-Eyed	435	Cobo Blanco, Peru	1957	R.V. A. Lee
Tuna, Skipjack	41-12	Black River, Mauritius	1982	Bruno de Ravel
Tuna, Southern Bluefin	348-5	Whakatane, New Zealand	1981	Rex Wood
Tuna, Yellowfin	388-12	Mexico	1977	Curt Wiesenmutter
Wahoo	149	Cat Cay, Bahamas	1962	John Pirovano
Weakfish	19-2	Jones Beach Inlet, N.Y.	1984	Dennis Roger Rooney
Yellowtail, California	71-15	Alijos Rocks, Mexico	1979	Michael Carpenter
Yellowtail, Southern	114-10	Tauranga, New Zealand	1984	Mike Godfrey

SPEED SKATING

U.S. OUTDOOR CHAMPIONS

Men

1959–60	Ken Bartholomew
1961	Ed Rudolph
1962	Floyd Bedbury
1963	Tom Gray
1964	Neil Blatchford
1965–66	Rich Wurster
1967	Mike Passarella
1968–70	Peter Cefalu
1971	Jack Walters
1972	Barth Levy
1973	Mike Woods
1974	Leigh Barczewski, Mike Passarella
1975	Rich Wurster
1976	John Wurster
1977	Jim Chapin
1978	Bill Heinkel
1979	Erik Henriksen
1980	Greg Oly
1981	Tom Grannes
1982	Greg Oly
1983	Michael Ralston
1984	Michael Ralston
1985	Andy Gabel
1986	Eric Klein
1987	Dave Paulicic

Women

1960	Mary Novak
1961	Jean Ashworth
1962	Jean Omelenchuk
1963	Jean Ashworth
1964	Diane White
1965	Jean Omelenchuk
1966	Diane White
1967	Jean Ashworth
1968	Helen Lutsch
1969	Sally Blatchford
1970–71	Sheila Young
1972	Ruth Moore, Nancy Thorne
1973	Nancy Class
1974	Kris Garbe
1975	Nancy Swider
1976	Connie Carpenter
1977	Liz Crowe
1978	Paula Class, Betsy Davis
1979	Gretchen Byrnes
1980	Shari Miller
1981	Lisa Merrifield
1982	Lisa Merrifield
1983	Janet Hainstock
1984	Janet Hainstock
1985	Betsy Davis
1986	Deb Perkins
1987	Laura Zuckerman

WORLD SPEED SKATING RECORDS

Men

Distance	Time	Skater	Place	Year
500 m	0:36.55	Nick Thometz, United States	Heerenveen, The Netherlands	1987
1000 m	1:12.58	Pavel Pegov, Soviet Union	Medeo, U.S.S.R.	1983
1500 m	1:52.70	Nikolai Gulyaev, Soviet Union	Heerenveen, The Netherlands	1987
3000 m	3:59.27	Leo Visser, Netherlands	Heerenveen, The Netherlands	1987
5000 m	6:47.01	Leo Visser, Netherlands	Heerenveen, The Netherlands	1987
10,000 m	14:03.92	Geir Karlstad, Norway	Heerenveen, The Netherlands	1987
All-around	160.807	Victor Shasherin, Soviet Union	Medeo, U.S.S.R	1984

Women

Distance	Time	Skater	Place	Year
500 m	0:39.43	Bonnie Blair, United States	Heerenveen, The Netherlands	1987
1,000 m	1:19.31	Natalya Petruseva, U.S.S.R.	Medeo	1983
1,500 m	2:03.34	Andrea Schone, E. Germany	Medeo	1984
3,000 m	4:20.91	Andrea Schone, E. Germany	Medeo	1984
5,000 m	7:32.82	Andrea Schone, E. Germany	Sarajevo, Yugoslavia	1985
All-around	171.760	Andrea Schone, E. Germany	Medeo	1984

U.S. INDOOR CHAMPIONS—1987

Men—Brian Arseneau, Arlington Heights, Ill.
Women—Maura D'Andrea, Saratoga Springs, N.Y.
Intermediate men—Mark Greenwald, Park Ridge, Ill.
Intermediate women—Wendy Goelz, Buffalo, N.Y.
Junior boys—Justin Brown, Saratoga Springs, N.Y.
Junior girls—Amy Peterson, St. Paul, Minn.

WORLD SPRINT CHAMPIONSHIPS—1987

(Saint Foy, Quebec, Canada, Jan. 31-Feb. 1, 1987)

Men

500 m—Akira Kuroiwa, Japan	:37.9
1000 m—Nick Thometz, Minnetonka, Minn.	1:19.58
Overall champion—Akira Kuroiwa, Japan	154.955 pts

Women

500 m—Bonnie Blair, Champaign, Ill.	:40.5
1000 m—Karin Enke-Kania, East Germany	1:22.25
Overall champion—Karin Enke-Kania, East Germany	166.685 pts

U.S. OUTDOOR CHAMPIONS—1987

Men—Dave Pavlicic, Florissant, Mo.
Women—Laura Zuckerman, Whitefish Bay, Wisc.
Intermediate men—John Coyle, West Bloomfield, Mich.
Intermediate women—Jody Franzen, Menomonee Falls, Wis.
Junior boys—Ryan Vanderboom, New Berlin, Wis.
Junior girls—Heather Haster, White Bear Lake, Minn.

WORLD CHAMPIONSHIPS—1987

Men

(Feb. 14-15, Heerenveen, The Netherlands)

Overall champion—Nikolai Gulyaev, Soviet Union	159.356 pts
500 m—Sergei Fokichev, Soviet Union	0:37.48
1500 m—Nikolai Gulyaev, Soviet Union[1]	1:52.70
5000 m—Leo Visser, Holland[1]	6:47.01
10,000 m—Geir Karlstad, Norway	14:03.92

1. World record.

Women

(Feb. 7-8, West Allis, Wis.)

Overall champion—Karin Enke-Kania, East Germany	176.721 pts
500 m—Karin Enke-Kania, East Germany	:41.38
1,500 m—Karin Enke-Kania, East Germany	2:08.90
3,000 m—Andrea Ehrig, East Germany	4:30.10
5,000 m—Andrea Ehrig, East Germany	7:46.96

SPORTS ORGANIZATIONS AND BUREAUS

(Note: Addresses are subject to change)

Amateur Athletic Union of the U.S. 3400 West 86th St., P.O. Box 68207, Indianapolis, Ind. 46268

Amateur Basketball Association. 1750 East Boulder St., Colorado Springs, Colo. 80909

Amateur Hockey Association of the U.S. 2997 Broadmoor Valley Road, Colorado Springs, Colo. 80906

Amateur Softball Association. 2801 N.E. 50th St., Oklahoma City, Okla. 73111

American Amateur Racketball Association. 815 North Weber St., Suite 101, Colorado Springs, Colo. 80903

American Association of Professional Baseball Clubs. P.O. Box 1353, 1200 Niagara St., Buffalo, N.Y. 14240

American Bowling Congress. 5301 South 76th St., Greendale, Wis. 53129-0500

American Hockey League. 218 Memorial Ave., West Springfield, Mass. 01089

American Horse Shows Association. 220 E. 42nd St., New York, N.Y. 10017-5806

American Kennel Club Inc. 51 Madison Ave., New York, N.Y. 10010

American League (baseball). 350 Park Ave., New York, N.Y. 10022

Athletics Congress/USA, The. P.O. Box 120, Indianapolis, Ind. 46206

Baseball Hall of Fame. Cooperstown, N.Y. 13326

Football Hall of Fame (college). Kings Island, Ohio 45034

Intercollegiate (Big Ten) Conference (1896). 1111 Plaza Dr., Suite 600, Schaumburg, Ill. 60173-4990

International Game Fish Association. 3000 East Las Olas Blvd., Fort Lauderdale, Fla. 33316

International League (baseball). Box 608, Grove City, Ohio 43123

International Olympic Committee. Chateau de Vidy, 1007 Lausanne, Switzerland

International Tennis Hall of Fame. 194 Bellevue Ave., Newport, R.I. 02840

Ladies Professional Golf Association. 4675 Sweetwater Blvd., Sugar Land, Texas, 77479

Little League Baseball. P.O. Box 3485 Williamsport, Pa. 17701

National Archery Association. 1750 E. Boulder St., Colorado Springs, Colo. 80909

National Association for Stock Car Auto Racing. P.O. Box K, Daytona Beach, Fla. 32015—9947

National Association of Intercollegiate Athletics. 1221 Baltimore St., Kansas City, Mo. 64105

National Baseball Congress. P.O. Box 1420, Wichita, Kan. 67201

National Collegiate Athletic Association. P.O. Box 1906, Mission, Kan. 66201

National Duckpin Bowling Congress. Fairview Ave., Baltimore-Linthicum, Md. 21090

National Field Archery Association. Rt. 2, Box 514, Redlands, Calif. 92373

National Football Foundation. 1865 Palmer Ave., Larchmont, N.Y. 10538. *See also:* Football Hall of Fame (college)

National Football League. 410 Park Ave., New York, N.Y. 10022

National Hockey League. 1155 Metcalfe St., Suite 960, Montreal, Que., Canada H3B 2W2

National Horseshoe Pitchers Association. Box 278, Munroe Falls, Ohio 44262

National Hot Rod Association. P.O. Box 5555, Glendora, Calif. 91740

National Junior College Athletic Association. P.O. Box 7305, Colorado Springs, Colo. 80933—7305

National Rifle Association of America. 1600 Rhode Island Ave., N.W., Washington, D.C. 20036

National Skeet Shooting Association. P.O. Box 680007, San Antonio, Tex. 78268-0007

New York Racing Association. P.O. Box 90, Jamaica, N.Y. 11417

National Shuffleboard Association. Box 5441, Trailer Estates, Bradenton, Fla. 34281-5441

New York State Athletic Commission (boxing and wrestling). 270 Broadway, New York, N.Y. 10007

North American Yacht Racing Union. *See* United States Yacht Racing Union

North American Soccer League. 1841 Broadway, Suite 411, New York, N.Y. 10023

PGA TOUR, Inc., 112 TPC Blvd., Sawgrass, Ponte Vedra, Fla. 32082

Pro Football Hall of Fame. Canton, Ohio 44708

Roller Skating Rink Operators Association. P.O. Box 81846, Lincoln, Neb. 68501

Thoroughbred Racing Assns. of N. America. 3000 Marcus Ave., Lake Success, N.Y. 11042

USA Amateur Boxing Federation. 1750 East Boulder St., Colorado Springs, Colo. 80909

United States Amateur Confederation of Roller Skating. P.O. Box 83067, Lincoln, Neb. 68501

United States Auto Club. 4910 West 16th St., Speedway, Ind. 46224

United States-International Professional Shuffleboard, Inc. 1901 S.W. 87th Terrace, Fort Lauderdale, Fla. 33324

U.S. Baseball Federation. 2160 Greenwood Ave., Trenton, N.J. 08609

U.S. Chess Federation. 186 Route 9W, New Windsor, N.Y. 12550

U.S. Cycling Federation. 1750 East Boulder St., Colorado Springs, Colo. 80909

U.S. Fencing Assn. 1750 E. Boulder St., Colorado Springs, Colo. 80909

U.S. Figure Skating Association. 20 First Street, Colorado Springs, Colo. 80906

U.S. Football League. 52 Vanderbilt Ave., New York, N.Y. 10017

U.S. Golf Association. Golf House, Liberty Corner Road, Far Hills, N.J. 07931

United States Gymnastics Federation. 1099 N. Meridian St., Indianapolis, Ind. 46204

U.S. Handball Association. 930 N. Benton Ave., Tucson, Ariz. 85711

U.S. Olympic Committee. 1750 East Boulder Street, Colorado Springs, Colo. 80909

U.S. Polo Association. 1301 W. 22nd St., Oak Brook, Ill. 60521

U.S. Rowing Assn. 251 N. Illinois St., Suite 980, Indianapolis, Ind. 46204

U.S. Soccer Federation. 1750 East Boulder St., Colorado Springs, Colo. 80909—5791

U.S. Tennis Association. 1212 Avenue of the Americas, New York, N.Y. 10036

U.S. Trotting Association. 750 Michigan Ave., Columbus, Ohio 43215

U.S. Yacht Racing Union. P.O. Box 209, Goat Island, Newport, R.I. 02840

Women's International Bowling Congress. 5301 S. 76th St., Greendale, Wis. 53129

FIGURE SKATING

WORLD CHAMPIONS

Men

1960	Alain Giletti, France
1961	No competition
1962	Donald Jackson, Canada
1963	Don McPherson, Canada
1964	Manfred Schnelldorfer, West Germany
1965	Alain Calmat, France
1966-68	Emmerich Danzer, Austria
1969-70	Tim Wood, United States
1971-73	Ondrej Nepela, Czechoslovakia
1974	Jan Hoffman, East Germany
1975	Sergei Yolkov, U.S.S.R.
1976	John Curry, Britain
1977	Vladimir Kovalev, U.S.S.R.
1978	Charles Tickner, United States
1979	Vladimir Kovalev, U.S.S.R.
1980	Jan Hoffman, East Germany
1981	Scott Hamilton, United States
1982	Scott Hamilton, United States
1983	Scott Hamilton, United States
1984	Scott Hamilton, United States
1985	Alexandr Fadeev, U.S.S.R.
1986	Brian Boitano, United States

Women

1956-60	Carol Heiss, United States
1961	No competition
1962-64	Sjoukje Dijkstra, Netherlands
1965	Petra Burka, Canada
1966-68	Peggy Fleming, United States
1969-70	Gabriele Seyfert, East Germany
1971-72	Beatrix Schuba, Austria
1973	Karen Magnusson, Canada
1974	Christine Errath, East Germany
1975	Dianne de Leeuw, Netherlands
1976	Dorothy Hamill, United States
1977	Linda Fratianne, United States
1978	Anett Poetzsch, East Germany
1979	Linda Fratianne, United States
1980	Anett Poetzsch, East Germany
1981	Denise Beillmann, Switzerland
1982	Elaine Zayak, United States
1983	Rosalynn Sumners, United States
1984	Katarina Witt, East Germany
1985	Katarina Witt, East Germany
1986	Debi Thomas, United States
1987	Katarina Witt, East Germany

U.S. CHAMPIONS

Men

1946-52	Richard Button
1953-56	Hayes Jenkins
1957-60	David Jenkins
1961	Bradley Lord
1962	Monty Hoyt
1963	Tommy Liz
1964	Scott Allen
1965	Gary Visconti
1966	Scott Allen
1967	Gary Visconti
1968-70	Tim Wood
1971	John M. Petkevich
1972	Ken Shelley
1973-75	Gordon McKellen
1976	Terry Kubicka
1977-80	Charles Tickner
1981	Scott Hamilton
1982	Scott Hamilton
1983	Scott Hamilton
1984	Scott Hamilton
1985	Brian Boitano
1986	Brian Boitano
1987	Brian Boitano

Women

1943-48	Gretchen Merrill
1949-50	Yvonne Sherman
1951	Sonya Klopfer
1952-56	Tenley Albright
1957-60	Carol Heiss
1961	Laurence Owen
1962	Barbara Roles Pursley
1963	Lorraine Hanlon
1964-68	Peggy Fleming
1969-73	Janet Lynn
1974-76	Dorothy Hamill
1977-80	Linda Fratianne
1981	Elaine Zayak
1982	Rosalynn Sumners
1983	Rosalynn Sumners
1984	Rosalynn Sumners
1985	Tiffany Chin
1986	Debi Thomas
1987	Jill Trenary

UNITED STATES CHAMPIONS—1987

(Tacoma, Wash., Feb. 1-8, 1987)

Men's singles—Brian Boitano, Sunnyvale, Calif.
Women's singles—Jill Trenary, Minnetonka, Minn.
Pairs—Jill Watson and Peter Oppegard, Bloomfield, Mich.
Dance—Suzanne Semanick, Bridgeville, Pa. and Scott Gregory, Skaneateles, N.Y.
Junior men's singles—Todd Eldredge, South Chatham, Mass.
Junior women's singles—Jeri Campbell, Garden City, Mich.
Junior pairs—Kellie Lynn Creel, Orange, Calif. and David McGovern, Long Beach, Calif.
Junior dance—Jennifer Benz and Jeffrey Benz, Export, Pa.

WORLD CHAMPIONS—1987

(Cincinnati, Ohio, March 9-14, 1987)

Men's singles—Brian Orser, Canada
Women's singles—Katarina Witt, East Germany
Pairs—Ekaterina Gordeva and Sergei Grinkov, Soviet Union
Dance—Natalia Bestemianova and Andrei Bukin, Soviet Union

VOLLEYBALL

U.S. VOLLEYBALL ASSOCIATION CHAMPIONSHIPS—1987

National Champions

Men—Molten, Torrance, Calif.; Runnerup: Reebock, Westwood, Calif.
Women—Chrysler Californians, Pleasanton, Calif.; Runnerup: Reebock, Westwood, Calif., and Merrill Lynch, Albuquerque, N. Mex.
Senior men—Billaver Chiropractic/Norfleet, Pacific Palisades, Calif.; Runnerup: Nick's Fish Market Chuck's Steak House/San Diego, Calif.
Senior women—Hawaiian Airlines, Honolulu; Runnerup: Viking Volleyball Club/Newburgh Body & Paint, Portland, Ore.
Golden Masters—I Dig Sportswear/Legends, Long Beach, Calif.; Runnerup: Old Guys Golf & Skiing Society, Albuquerque, N. Mex.
Men's Club—Norfleet, Pacific Palisades, Calif; Runnerup: Raymond Construction, Huntington Beach, Calif.

N.C.A.A. CHAMPIONSHIPS

Men

(May 1-2, 1987, University of California at Los Angeles, Los Angeles, Calif.)

Final—UCLA, Los Angeles, Calif., defeated Southern California, Los Angeles, Calif., 15-11, 15-2, 16-14.

Women

DIVISION I—University of the Pacific, Stockton, Calif., champion
DIVISION II—University of California, Riverside, champion
DIVISION III—University of California, San Diego, La Jolla, Calif., champion

NAIA CHAMPIONSHIPS

Brigham Young University of Hawaii defeated Lewis & Clark College, Oregon, 5-15, 15-10, 15-13 in final match
Third place—University of Puget Sound, Washington
Fourth place—Texas Wesleyan College, Fort Worth, Texas

SWIMMING

WORLD RECORDS—MEN

(Through Aug. 23, 1986)
Approved by the International Swimming Federation (F.I.N.A.)
(F.I.N.A. discontinued acceptance of records in yards in 1968)
Source: United States Swim Team.

Distance	Record	Holder	Country	Date
Freestyle				
50 meters	0:22.32	Tom Jager	United States	Aug. 13, 1987
100 meters	0:48.74	Matt Biondi	United States	June 24, 1986
200 meters	1:47.44	Michael Gross	West Germany	July 29, 1984
400 meters	3:47.80	Michael Gross	West Germany	June 27, 1985
800 meters	7:50.64	Vladimir Salnikov	Soviet Union	July 4, 1986
1,500 meters	14:54.76	Vladimir Salnikov	Soviet Union	Feb. 22, 1983
Backstroke				
100 meters	0:55.19	Rick Carey	United States	Aug. 21, 1983
200 meters	1:58.14	Igor Poliansky	Soviet Union	March 1, 1985
Breaststroke				
100 meters	1:01.65	Steve Lundquist	United States	July 29, 1984
200 meters	2:13.34	Victor Davis	Canada	Aug. 2, 1984
Butterfly				
100 meters	0:52.84	Pablo Morales	United States	June 23, 1986
200 meters	1:56.65	Michael Gross	West Germany	Aug. 10, 1985
Individual Medley				
200-meter individual medley	2:00.56	Tamas Darnyi	Hungary	Aug. 23, 1987
400-meter individual medley	4:15.42	Tamas Darnyi	Hungary	Aug. 19, 1987
Freestyle Relay				
400 meters	3:17.08	United States	National Team	Aug. 10, 1985
800-meters	7:13.10	West Germany	National Team	Aug. 19, 1987
Medley Relay				
400 meters	3:38.28	United States	National Team	Aug. 10, 1985

WORLD RECORDS—WOMEN

Distance	Record	Holder	Country	Date
Freestyle				
50 Meters	0:25.28	Tamara Costache	Romania	Aug. 23, 1986
100 Meters	0:54.73	Kristin Otto	East Germany	Aug. 19, 1986
200 Meters	1:57.75	Kristin Otto	East Germany	May 23, 1984
400 Meters	4:06.28	Tracy Wickham	Australia	Aug. 24, 1978
800 Meters	8:19.53	Anke Mohring	East Germany	Aug. 22, 1987
1,500 Meters	16:00.73	Janet Evans	United States	July 31, 1987
Backstroke				
100 Meters	1:00.59	Ina Kleber	East Germany	Aug. 24, 1984
200 Meters	2:09.91	Cornelia Sirch	East Germany	Aug. 7, 1982
Breaststroke				
100 Meters	1:07.91	Silke Hoerner	East Germany	Aug. 21, 1987
200 Meters	2:27.40	Silke Hoerner	East Germany	Aug. 18, 1986
Butterfly				
100 Meters	0:57.93	Mary T. Meagher	United States	Aug. 16, 1982
200 Meters	2:05.96	Mary T. Meagher	United States	Aug. 13, 1982
Individual Medley				
200 Meters	2:11.73	Ute Geweniger	East Germany	July 4, 1981
400 Meters	4:36.10	Petra Schneider	East Germany	Aug. 1, 1982

Freestyle

400 Meters	3:40.57	East German National Team	East Germany	Aug. 19, 1986
800 Meters	7:55.47	East German National Team	East Germany	Aug. 18, 1987

Medley Relay

400 Meters	4:03.69	East German National Team	East Germany	Aug. 24, 1984

U.S. SHORT-COURSE SWIMMING RECORDS

Source: United States Swimming Team.

MEN

Freestyle

50 yards—Matt Biondi, 1987	0:19.15
100 yards—Matt Biondi, 1987	0:41.80
200 yards—Matt Biondi, 1987	1:33.03
500 yards—Mike O'Brien, 1985	4:13.06
1,000 yards—Mike O'Brien, 1985	8:47.38
1,650 yards—Jeff Kostoff, 1986	14:37.87

Backstroke

100 yards—Jay Mortensen, 1987	0:47.94
200 yards—Rick Carey, 1983	1:44.43

Breaststroke

100 yards—Steve Lundquist, 1983	0:52.48
200 yards—Steve Lundquist, 1981	1:55.01

Butterfly

100 yards—Pablo Morales, 1986	0:46.26
200 yards—Pablo Morales, 1987	1:42.60

Individual Medley

200 yards—Bill Barrett, 1982	1:45.00
400 yards—Jeff Kostoff, 1985	3:46.54

Relays

200-yard freestyle—Mission Viejo, 1981	1:18.55
400-yard freestyle—California, 1986	2:53.02
800-yard freestyle—Florida Aquatic Club, 1979	6:25.42
400-yard medley—S.M.U., 1983	3:12.63

WOMEN

Freestyle

50 yards—Tammy Thomas, 1983	0:22.13
100 yards—Tammy Thomas, 1983	0:48.40
200 yards—Cynthia Woodhead, 1979	1:44.10
500 yards—Tracy Caulkins, 1979	4:36.25
1000 yards—Tiffany Cohen, 1985	9:28.32
1,650 yards—Tiffany Cohen, 1983	15:46.54

Backstroke

100 yards—Betsy Mitchell, 1987	0:53.98
200 yards—Betsy Mitchell, 1987	1:55.16

Breaststroke

100 yards—Tracy Caulkins, 1981	1:01.13
200 yards—Tracy Caulkins, 1980	2:11.46

Butterfly

100 yards—Mary T. Meagher, 1987	0:52.42
200 yards—Mary T. Meagher, 1981	1:52.99

Individual Medley

200 yards—Tracy Caulkins, 1984	1:57.06
400 yards—Tracy Caulkins, 1981	4:04.63

Relays

200-yard freestyle—Stanford, 1981	1:31.12
400-yard freestyle—Stanford, 1987	3:17.69
800-yard freestyle—Florida, 1984	7:06.98
200-yard medley—Stanford, 1986	1:40.22
400-yard medley—Stanford, 1987	3:38.17

U.S. SHORT COURSE CHAMPIONSHIPS

(Boca Raton, Fla., August, 1987)

Men's Events

50-yard freestyle—Tom Jager	0:19.52
100-yard freestyle—Tom Jager	0:43.44
200-yard freestyle—Marius Podkoscielny	1:37.71
500-yard freestyle—Marius Podkoscielny	4:16.60
1,000-yard freestyle—Marius Podkoscielny	8:54.93
1,650-yard freestyle—Lars Jorgensen	14:57.26
100-yard backstroke—Mark Rhodenbaugh	0:48.66
200-yard backstroke—Thomas Darney	1:45.51
100-yard breaststroke—Richard May	0:54.49
200-yard breaststroke—Mike Barrowman	1:58.36
100-yard butterfly—Chris O'Neil	0:47.45
200-yard butterfly—Melvin Stewart	1:44.32
200-yard individual medley—Darny Thomas	1:46.06
400-yard individual medley—Darny Thomas	3:43.04
400-yard freestyle relay—Curl Swim Club	2:57.46
800-yard freestyle relay—Mission Viejo	6:31.80
400-yard medley relay—Longhorn Aquatic	3:18.67
Team champions—1. Mission Viejo	473
2. Mission Bay	367
3. San Jose	246

Women's Events

50-yard freestyle—Dara Torres	0:22.71
100-yard freestyle—Laura Walker	0:49.58
200-yard freestyle—Mitzi Kremer	1:46.01
500-yard freestyle—Whitney Hedgepeth	4:41.03
1,000-yard freestyle—Janet Evans	9:32.59
1,650-yard freestyle—Janet Evans	15:56.53
100-yard backstroke—Anne Mahoney	0:55.25
200-yard backstroke—Anne Mahoney	1:58.68
100-yard breaststroke—Hiroko Nagasaki	1:02.22
200-yard breaststroke—Hiroko Nagasaki	2:09.74
100-yard butterfly—Janel Jorgensen	0:53.87
200-yard butterfly—Julia Gorman	1:58.16
200-yard individual medley—Katy Arris	2:00.86
400-yard individual medley—Janet Evans	4:12.32
400-yard freestyle relay—Mission Bay "A"	3:19.72
800-yard freestyle relay—Mission Viejo "A"	7:16.57
400-yard medley relay—Mission Bay "A"	3:43.14
Team champions—1. Mission Bay	632
2. Mission Viejo	486
3. Pine Crest	188

U.S. LONG-COURSE CHAMPIONSHIPS

(Clovis, Calif., July 27-31, 1987)

Men's Events

50-m freestyle—Matt Biondi	0:22.33
100-m freestyle—Matt Biondi	0:49.34
200-m freestyle—Richard Oppel	1:48.88
400-m freestyle—Matt Cetlinski	3:49.69
800-m freestyle—Sean Killion	7:52.45
1,500-m freestyle—Daniel Jorgensen	15:17.04
100-m backstroke—Jay Mortenson	0:56.58
200-m backstroke—Scott Johnson	2:01.68
100-m breaststroke—Richard Schroeder	1:03.40
200-m breaststroke—Steve Bentley	2:15.30
100-m butterfly—Pablo Morales	0:53.74
200-m butterfly—Melvin Stewart	1:58.13
200-m individual medley—Dave Wharton	2:02.76
400-m individual medley—Dave Wharton	4:17.81
400-m medley relay—Concord-Pleasant Hill	3:45.31
400-m freestyle relay—San Jose	3:24.19
800-m freestyle relay—San Jose	7:26.53
All-events team champion—1. Concord-Pleasant Hill	456
2. Mission Bay	294
3. Foxcatcher	257

Women's Events

50-m freestyle—Lisa Dorman	0:25.94
100-m freestyle—Dara Torres	0:56.14
200-m freestyle—Francie O'Leary	2:01.27
400-m freestyle—Janet Evans	4:08.89
800-m freestyle—Janet Evans	8:22:44
1,500-m freestyle—Janet Evans	16:00.73
100-m backstroke—Betsy Mitchell	1:02.30
200-m backstroke—Andrea Hayes	2:12.37
100-m breaststroke—Susan Johnson	1:11.40
200-m breaststroke—Amy Shaw	2:29.78
100-m butterfly—LaDonnis Loury	1:00.99
200-m butterfly—Melanie Buddemeyer	2:12.27
200-m individual medley—Katy Arris	2:17.52
400-m individual medley—Janet Evans	4:41.74
400-m medley relay—Concord-Pleasant Hill	4:16.27
400-m freestyle relay—Concord-Pleasant Hill	3:48.98
800-m freestyle relay—Pine Crest	8:11.19
All-events team champion—1. Mission Bay	416
2. Fullerton	252
3. Concord-Pleasant Hill	248

NATIONAL COLLEGIATE ATHLETIC ASSOCIATION MEN'S CHAMPIONSHIP—1987

(Austin, Texas, April 2-4, 1987)

Division I

50-yard freestyle—Matt Biondi, California	0:19.15
100-yard freestyle—Matt Biondi, California	0:41.80
200-yard freestyle—Matt Biondi, California	1:33.03
500-yard freestyle—Daniel Jorgensen, USC	4:16.25
1,650-yard freestyler—Jeff Kostoff, Stanford	14:47.75
100-yard backstroke—David Berkoff, Harvard	0:48.41
200-yard backstroke—Doug Gjertson, Texas	1:45.12
100-yard breaststroke—Todd Torres, LSU	0:53.96
200-yard breaststroke—John Van Sant, Army	1:57.65
100-yard butterfly—Pablo Morales, Stanford	0:46.47
200-yard butterfly—Pablo Morales, Stanford	1:42.60
200-yard individual medley—Pablo Morales, Stanford	1:45.42
400-yard individual medley—Jeff Kostoff, Stanford	3:47.40
400-yard medley relay—Stanford	3:12.05
400-yard freestyle relay—California	2:53.52
800-yard freestyle relay—Florida	6:22.22
1-meter diving—Jose Rocha, Auburn	549.20 points
3-meter diving—Michael Weantuck, Ohio State	641.45 points
Team championship—1. Stanford	374
2. USC	296
3. Florida	293

NATIONAL COLLEGIATE ATHLETIC ASSOCIATION WOMEN'S CHAMPIONSHIPS—1987

(Indianapolis, Ind., March 19-21, 1987)

Division I

50-yard freestyle—Jenna Johnson, Stanford	0:22.57
100-yard freestyle—Jenna Johnson, Stanford	0:48.82
200-yard freestyle—Mitzi Kremer, Clemson	1:45.99
500-yard freestyle—Mitzi Kremer, Clemson	4:41.13
1,650-yard freestyle—Tami Bruce, Florida	16:02.15
100-yard backstroke—Betsy Mitchell, Texas	0:54.18
200-yard backstroke—Betsy Mitchell, Texas	1:55.16
100-yard breaststroke—Tracey McFarlane, Texas	1:00.68
200-yard breaststroke—Susan Rapp, Stanford	2:11.93
100-yard butterfly—Mary T. Meagher, California	0:52.42
200-yard butterfly—Mary T. Meagher, California	1:55.54
200-yard individual medley—Betsy Mitchell, Texas	1:59.66
400-yard individual medley—Janelle Bosse, Ohio State	4:14.63
200-yard freestyle relay—Texas	1:31.01
400-yard freestyle relay—Stanford	3:17.69
800-yard freestyle relay—Texas	7:10.61
1-meter diving—Karen LaFace, Ohio State	478.00
3-meter diving—Kim Fuggett, Ohio State	550.70
Team champion—1. Texas	648 1/2
2. Stanford	631 1/2
3. Florida	315

U.S. DIVING CHAMPIONSHIPS—1987

INDOOR

(Baton Rouge, La., April 14-16, 1987)

Men's Events

1-meter—Doug Shaffer, Mission Bay	589.92
3-meter—Kent Ferguson, Mission Bay	660.84
10-meter—Matt Scoggin, Longhorn	615.72
Team—Mission Bay	181

Women's Events

1-meter—Kim Fugett, McDonald's	449.61
3-meter—Megan Neyer, Mission Bay	660.84
10-meter—Michele Mitchell, Mission Bay	419.31
Team—Mission Bay	193

OUTDOOR

(Bartlesville, Okla. July 28-Aug. 1, 1987)

Men's Events

1-meter—Doug Shaffer, Mission Bay	587.40
3-meter—Greg Louganis, Mission Bay	714.69
10-meter—Greg Louganis, Mission Bay	657.12

Women's Events

1-meter—Megan Neyer, Mission Bay	438.84
3-meter—Kelly McCormick, McDonald's	552.39
10-meter—Mary Ellen Clark, McDonald's	396.09

BOXING

Whether it be called pugilism, prize fighting or boxing, there is no tracing "the Sweet Science" to any definite source. Tales of rivals exchanging blows for fun, fame or money go back to earliest recorded history and classical legend. There was a mixture of boxing and wrestling called the "pancratium" in the ancient Olympic Games and in such contests the rivals belabored one another with hands fortified with heavy leather wrappings that were sometimes studded with metal. More than one Olympic competitor lost his life at this brutal exercise.

There was little law or order in pugilism until Jack Broughton, one of the early champions of England, drew up a set of rules for the game in 1743. Broughton, called "the father of English boxing," also is credited with having invented boxing gloves. However, these gloves—or "mufflers" as they were called—were used only in teaching "the manly art of self-defense" or in training bouts. All professional championship fights were contested with "bare knuckles" until 1892, when John L. Sullivan lost the heavyweight championship of the world to James J. Corbett in New Orleans in a bout in which both contestants wore regulation gloves.

The Broughton rules were superseded by the London Prize Ring Rules of 1838. The 8th Marquis of Queensberry, with the help of John G. Chambers, put forward the "Queensberry Rules" in 1866, a code that called for gloved contests. Amateurs took quickly to the Queensberry Rules, the professionals slowly.

HISTORY OF WORLD HEAVYWEIGHT CHAMPIONSHIP FIGHTS

(Bouts in which a new champion was crowned)

Source: Nat Fleischer's Ring *Boxing Encyclopedia and Record Book*, published and copyrighted by The Ring Book Shop, Inc., 120 West 31st St., New York, N.Y. 10001.

Date	Where held	Winner, weight, age	Loser, weight, age	Rounds	Referee
Sept. 7, 1892	New Orleans, La.	James J. Corbett, 178 (26)	John L. Sullivan, 212 (33)	21	Prof. John Duffy
March 17, 1897	Carson City, Nev.	Bob Fitzsimmons, 167 (34)	James J. Corbett, 183 (30)	KO 14	George Siler
June 9, 1899	Coney Island, N.Y.	James J. Jeffries, 206 (24)[1]	Bob Fitzsimmons, 167 (37)	KO 11	George Siler
Feb. 23, 1906	Los Angeles	Tommy Burns, 180 (24)[2]	Marvin Hart, 188 (29)	20	James J. Jeffries
Dec. 26, 1908	Sydney, N.S.W.	Jack Johnson, 196 (30)	Tommy Burns, 176 (27)	KO 14	Hugh McIntosh
April 5, 1915	Havana, Cuba	Jess Willard, 230 (33)	Jack Johnson, 205 1/2 (37)	KO 26	Jack Welch
July 4, 1919	Toledo, Ohio	Jack Dempsey, 187 (24)	Jess Willard, 245 (37)	KO 3	Ollie Pecord
Sept. 23, 1926	Philadelphia	Gene Tunney, 189 (28)[3]	Jack Dempsey, 190 (31)	10	Pop Reilly
June 12, 1930	New York	Max Schmeling, 188 (24)	Jack Sharkey, 197 (27)	WF 4	Jim Crowley
June 21, 1932	Long Island City	Jack Sharkey, 205 (29)	Max Schmeling, 188 (26)	15	Gunboat Smith
June 29, 1933	Long Island City	Primo Carnera, 260 1/2 (26)	Jack Sharkey, 201 (30)	KO 6	Arthur Donovan
June 14, 1934	Long Island City	Max Baer, 209 1/2 (25)	Primo Carnera, 263 1/4 (27)	KO 11	Arthur Donovan
June 13, 1935	Long Island City	Jim Braddock, 193 3/4 (29)	Max Baer, 209 1/2 (26)	15	Jack McAvoy
June 22, 1937	Chicago	Joe Louis, 197 1/4 (23)	Jim Braddock, 197 (31)	KO 8	Tommy Thomas
June 22, 1949	Chicago	Ezzard Charles, 181 3/4 (27)[4]	Joe Walcott, 195 1/2 (35)	15	Davey Miller
Sept. 27, 1950	New York	Ezzard Charles, 184 1/2 (29)[5]	Joe Louis, 218 (36)	15	Mark Conn
July 18, 1951	Pittsburgh	Joe Walcott, 194 (37)	Ezzard Charles, 182 (30)	KO 7	Buck McTiernan
Sept. 23, 1952	Philadelphia	Rocky Marciano, 184 (29)[6]	Joe Walcott, 196 (38)	KO 13	Charley Daggert
Nov. 30, 1956	Chicago	Floyd Patterson, 182 1/4 (21)	Archie Moore, 187 3/4 (42)	KO 5	Frank Sikora
June 26, 1959	New York	Ingemar Johansson, 196 (26)	Floyd Patterson, 182 (24)	KO 3	Ruby Goldstein
June 20, 1960	New York	Floyd Patterson, 190 (25)	Ingemar Johansson, 194 3/4 (27)	KO 5	Arthur Mercante
Sept. 25, 1962	Chicago	Sonny Liston, 214 (28)	Floyd Patterson, 189 (27)	KO 1	Frank Sikora
Feb. 25, 1964	Miami Beach, Fla.	Cassius Clay, 210 (22)[7]	Sonny Liston, 218 (30)	KO 7	Barney Felix
March 4, 1968	New York	Joe Frazier, 204 1/2 (24)[8]	Buster Mathis, 243 1/2 (23)	KO 11	Arthur Mercante
April 27, 1968	Oakland, Calif.	Jimmy Ellis, 197 (28)[9]	Jerry Quarry, 195 (22)	15	Elmer Costa
Feb. 16, 1970	New York	Joe Frazier, 205 (26)[10]	Jimmy Ellis, 201 (29)	KO 5	Tony Perez
Jan. 22, 1973	Kingston, Jamaica	George Foreman, 217 1/2 (24)	Joe Frazier, 214 (29)	KO 2	Arthur Mercante
Oct. 30, 1974	Kinshasa, Zaire	Muhammad Ali, 216 1/2 (32)	George Foreman, 220 (26)	KO 8	Zack Clayton
Feb. 15, 1978	Las Vegas, Nev.	Leon Spinks, 197 (25)	Muhammad Ali, 224 1/2 (36)	15	Howard Buck
June 9, 1978	Las Vegas, Nev.	Larry Holmes, 212 (28)[11]	Ken Norton, 220 (32)	15	Mills Lans
Sept. 15, 1978	New Orleans	Muhammad Ali, 221 (36)[12]	Leon Spinks, 201 (25)	15	Lucien Joubert
Oct. 20, 1979	Pretoria, S. Africa	John Tate, 240 (24)[13]	Gerrie Coetzee, 222 (24)	15	Carlos Berrocal
March 31, 1980	Knoxville, Tenn.	Mike Weaver, 207 1/2 (27)	John Tate, 232 (25)	KO 15	Ernesto Magana Ansorena
Dec. 10, 1982	Las Vegas, Nev.	Michael Dokes, 216 (24)	Mike Weaver, 209 1/2 (30)	KO 1	Joey Curtis
Sept. 23, 1983	Richfield, Ohio	Gerrie Coetzee, 215 (28)	Michael Dokes, 217 (25)	KO 10	Tony Perez
March 9, 1984	Las Vegas, Nev.	Tim Witherspoon, 220 1/2 (26)[14]	Greg Page, 239 1/2 (25)	12	Mills Lane
August 31, 1984	Las Vegas, Nev.	Pinklon Thomas, 216 (26)	Tim Witherspoon, 217 (26)	12	Richard Steele
Nov. 9, 1984	Las Vegas, Nev.	Larry Holmes, 221 1/2 (35)[15]	James Smith 227 (31)	KO 12	Dave Pearl
Dec. 1, 1984	Sun City, S. Africa	Greg Page, 236 (25)[16]	Gerry Coetzee, 217 (29)	KO 8	unavailable
April 29, 1985	Buffalo, N.Y.	Tony Tubbs, 229 (26)[16]	Greg Page, 239 1/2 (26)	15	unavailable.
Sept. 21,1985	Las Vegas, Nev.	Michael Spinks, 200 (29)	Larry Holmes, 221 (35)	15	Carlos Padilla
Jan. 17, 1986	Atlanta, Ga.	Tim Witherspoon, 227 (28)	Tony Tubbs, 229 (27)	15	unavailable
Nov. 23, 1986	Las Vegas, Nev.	Mike Tyson, 217 (20)[17]	Trevor Berbick, 220 (29)	KO2	unavailable
Dec. 12, 1986	New York, N.Y.	James Smith, 230 (33)[16]	Tim Witherspoon, 218 (29)	KO1	unavailable
March 7, 1987	Las Vegas, Nev.	Mike Tyson, 217 (20)[16]	James Smith, 230 (33)	12	unavailable

1. Jeffries retired as champion in March 1905. He named Marvin Hart and Jack Root as leading contenders and agreed to referee their fight in Reno, Nev., on July 3, 1905, with the stipulation that he would term the winner the champion. Hart, 190 (28), knocked out Root, 171 (29), in the 12th round. 2. Burns claimed the title after defeating Hart. 3. Tunney retired as champion after defeating Tom Heeney on July 26, 1928. 4. After Louis announced his retirement as champion on March 1, 1949, Charles won recognition from the National Boxing Association as champion by defeating Walcott. 5. Charles gained undisputed recognition as champion by defeating Louis, who came out of retirement. 6. Retired as Champion April 27, 1956. 7. The World Boxing Association later withdrew its recognition of Clay as champion and declared the winner of a bout between Ernie Terrell and Eddie Machen would gain its version of the title. Terrell, 199 (25), won a 15-round decision from Machen, 192 (32), in Chicago on March 5, 1965. Clay, 212 1/4 (25) and Terrell, 212 1/2 (27) met in Houston on Feb. 6, 1967, Clay winning a 15-round decision. 8. Winner recognized by New York, Massachusetts, Maine, Illinois, Texas and Pennsylvania to fill vacated title when Clay was stripped of championship for failing to accept U. S. Induction. 9. Bout was final of eight-man tournament to fill Clay's place and is recognized by World Boxing Association. 10. Bout settled controversy over title. 11. Holmes won World Boxing Council title after WBC had withdrawn recognition of Spinks, March 18, 1978, and awarded its title to Norton, WBC, said Spinks had reneged on agreement to fight Norton 12. Ali regained World Boxing Association championship. 13. Tate won WBA title after Ali retired and left it vacant. 14. Tim Witherspoon and Greg Page fought for the WBC heavyweight title vacated by Larry Holmes, who could not come to agreement on a deal to fight Page, the No. 1 contender. Holmes declared he would fight under the banner of the International Boxing Federation. Several dates were set and postponed for fights between Holmes and Gerry Coetzee, the WBA champ, the latest being Nov. 16, 1984.15. First fight under banner of International Boxing Federation. 16. New W.B.A. champion. 17. New W.B.C. champion.

OTHER WORLD BOXING TITLEHOLDERS

(Through Aug. 20, 1984)

Light Heavyweight

1903	Jack Root, George Gardner
1903–05	Bob Fitzsimmons
1905–12	Philadelphia Jack O'Brien[1]
1912–16	Jack Dillon
1916–20	Battling Levinsky
1920–22	Georges Carpentier
1923	Battling Siki
1923–25	Mike McTigue
1925–26	Paul Berlenbach
1926–27	Jack Delaney[2]
1927	Mike McTigue
1927–29	Tommy Loughran
1930	Jimmy Slattery
1930–34	Maxie Rosenbloom
1934–35	Bob Olin
1935–39	John Henry Lewis
1939	Melio Bettina
1939–41	Billy Conn[2]
1941	Anton Christoforidis (NBA)
1941–48	Gus Lesnevich
1948–50	Freddie Mills
1950–52	Joey Maxim
1952–61	Archie Moore[3]
1961–63	Harold Johnson
1963–65	Willie Pastrano
1965–66	José Torres
1966–67	Dick Tiger
1968	Dick Tiger, Bob Foster
1969–70	Bob Foster
1971	Vicente Rondon (WBA), Bob Foster (WBC)
1972–73	Bob Foster (WBA, WBC)
1974	John Conteh (WBA), Bob Foster (WBC)[14]
1975–76	Victor Galindez (WBA), John Conteh (WBC)
1977	Victor Galindez (WBA), John Conteh (WBC)[4], Miguel Cuello (WBC)
1978	Victor Galindez (WBA), Mike Rossman (WBA), Miguel Cuello (WBC), Mate Parlov (WBC), Marvin Johnson (WBC)
1979	Mike Rossman (WBA), Vict Galindez (WBA), Marvin Johnson (WBC), Matthew (Franklin) Saad Muhammad (WBC)
1980	Matthew Saad Muhammad (WBC), Marvin Johnson (WBA), Eddie (Gregory) Mustafa Muhammad (WBA)
1981	Matthew Saad Muhammad (WBC), Eddie Mustafa Muhammad (WBA), Michael Spinks (WBA), Dwight Braxton (WBC)
1982	Dwight Braxton (WBC), Michael Spinks (WBA)
1983	Michael Spinks (undisputed)
1984	Michael Spinks (undisputed)
1985	Michael Spinks (undisputed)[5]
1986	Marvin Johnson (WBA) Dennis Andries (WBC)
1987	Thomas Hearns (WBC) Virgil Hill (WBA) Bobby Czyz (IBF)

1. Retired. 2. Abandoned title. 3. NBA withdrew recognition in 1961, New York Commission in 1962; recognized thereafter only by California and Europe. 4. WBC withdrew recognition. 5. Spinks relinquished title in 1985 to fight for heavyweight title.

Middleweight

1867–72	Tom Chandler
1872–81	George Rooke
1881–82	Mike Donovan[1]
1884–91	Jack (Nonpareil) Dempsey
1891–97	Bob Fitzsimmons[2]
1908	Stanley Ketchel, Billy Papke
1908–10	Stanley Ketchel[3]
1913	Frank Klaus
1913–14	George Chip
1914–17	Al McCoy
1917–20	Mike O'Dowd
1920–23	Johnny Wilson
1923–26	Harry Greb
1926	Tiger Flowers
1926–31	Mickey Walker[2]
1931–41	Gorilla Jones, Ben Jeby, Marcel Thil, Lou Brouillard, Vince Dundee, Teddy Yarosz, Babe Risko, Freddy Steele, Al Hostak, Solly Kreiger, Fred Apostoli, Ceferino Garcia, Ken Overlin, Billy Soose, Tony Zale[4]
1941–47	Tony Zale
1947–48	Rocky Graziano
1948	Tony Zale
1948–49	Marcel Cerdan
1949–51	Jake LaMotta
1952	Ray Robinson, Randy Turpin
1951–52	Ray Robinson[1]
1953–55	Carl Olson
1955–57	Ray Robinson[5]
1957	Gene Fullmer, Ray Robinson
1957–58	Carmen Basilio
1958–60	Ray Robinson[6]
1960–61	Paul Pender[7]
1959–62	Gene Fullmer (NBA)
1961–62	Terry Downes[1]
1962	Paul Pender[1]
1962–63	Dick Tiger
1963–65	Joey Giardello
1965–66	Dick Tiger
1966	Emile Griffith
1967	Nino Benvenuti, Emile Griffith
1968	Emile Griffith, Nino Benvenuti
1969	Nino Benvenuti
1970	Nino Benvenuti, Carlos Monzon
1971–73	Carlos Monzon
1974–75	Carlos Monzon (WBA), Rodrigo Valdez (WBC)
1976	Carlos Monzon (WBA, WBC), Rodrigo Valdez (WBC)
1977	Carlos Monzon (WBA, WBC)[1], Rodrigo Valdez (WBA, WBC)
1978	Rodrigo Valdez, Hugo Corro
1979	Hugo Corro, Vito Antuofermo
1980	Vito Antuofermo, Alan Minter, Marvin Hagler
1981	Marvin Hagler
1982–86	Marvelous Marvin Hagler (undisputed)
1987	Marvin Hagler (undisputed) Sugar Ray Leonard (undisputed)

1. Retired. 2. Abandoned title. 3. Died. 4. National Boxing Association and New York Commission disagreed on champions. Those listed were accepted by one or the other until Zale gained world-wide recognition. 5. Ended retirement in 1954. 6. NBA withdrew recognition. 7. Recognized by New York, Massachusetts, and Europe.

Welterweight

1892–94	Mysterious Billy Smith
1894–96	Tommy Ryan
1896	Kid McCoy[2]
1896–1900	Mysterious Billy Smith
1900	Rube Ferns
1900–01	Matty Matthews
1901	Ruby Ferns
1901–04	Joe Walcott
1904	Dixie Kid[2]
1904–06	Joe Walcott
1906–07	Honey Mellody
1907	Mike (Twin) Sullivan[2]
1915–19	Ted Lewis
1919–22	Jack Britton
1922–26	Mickey Walker
1926–27	Pete Latzo
1927–29	Joe Dundee
1929–30	Jackie Fields
1930	Young Jack Thompson
1930–31	Tommy Freeman
1931	Young Jack Thompson
1931–32	Lou Brouillard
1932–33	Jackie Fields
1933	Young Corbett 3rd
1933–34	Jimmy McLarnin, Barney Ross
1934–35	Jimmy McLarnin
1935–38	Barney Ross
1938–40	Henry Armstrong
1940–41	Fritzie Zivic
1941–46	Freddie Cochrane
1946	Marty Servo[1]
1946–51	Ray Robinson[2]
1951	Johnny Bratton (NBA)
1951–54	Kid Gavilan
1954–55	Johnny Saxton
1955	Tony DeMarco
1955–56	Carmen Basilio
1956	Johnny Saxton
1956–57	Carmen Basilio[2]
1958	Virgil Akins
1959–60	Don Jordan
1960–61	Benny (Kid) Paret
1961	Emile Griffith
1961–62	Benny (Kid) Paret
1962–63	Emile Griffith, Luis Rodriguez
1963–66	Emile Griffith[2]
1966–69	Curtis Cokes
1969	Curtis Cokes, José Napoles
1970	José Napoles, Billy Backus
1971	Billy Backus, José Napoles
1972–74	José Napoles
1975	José Napoles (WBA, WBC)[3], Angel Espada (WBA), John Stracey (WBC)
1976	Angel Espada (WBA), José Cuevas (WBA), John Stracey (WBC), Carlos Palomino
1977–78	José Cuevas (WBA), Carlos Palomino (WBC)
1979	José Cuevas (WBA), Carlos Palomino (WBC), Wilfredo Benitez (WBC)
1980	José Cuevas (WBA), Ray Leonard (WBC), Roberto Duran (WBC), Thomas Hearns (WBA)
1981	Ray Leonard (WBC), Thomas Hearns (WBA), Ray Leonard (WBC,WBA)
1982	Ray Leonard
1983–85	Donald Curry (WBA)
1983–85	Milton McCrory (WBC)
1985–86	Donald Curry (undisputed)
1987	Mark Breland (WBA) Marlon Starling (WBA) Lloyd Honeychan (IBF)

1. Retired. 2. Abandoned title. 3. WBA withdrew recognition.

Lightweight

1869–99	Kid Lavigne
1899–1902	Frank Erne
1902–08	Joe Gans
1908–10	Battling Nelson
1910–12	Ad Wolgast
1912–14	Willie Ritchie
1914–17	Freddy Welsh
1917–25	Benny Leonard[1]
1925	Jimmy Goodrich
1925–26	Rocky Kansas
1926–30	Sammy Mandell
1930	Al Singer
1930–33	Tony Canzoneri
1933–35	Barney Ross[2]
1935–36	Tony Canzoneri
1936–38	Lou Ambers
1938–39	Henry Armstrong
1939–40	Lou Ambers
1940–41	Lew Jenkins
1941–42	Sammy Angott[1]
1943–47	Beau Jack (N.Y.), Bob Montgomery (N.Y.), Sammy Angott (NBA), Juan Zurita (NBA), Ike Williams (NBA)
1947–51	Ike Williams
1951–52	James Carter
1952	Lauro Salas
1952–54	James Carter
1954	Paddy DeMarco
1954–55	James Carter
1955–56	Wallace Smith
1956–62	Joe Brown
1962–65	Carlos Ortiz
1965	Ismael Laguna
1965–68	Carlos Ortiz
1968	Teo Cruz
1969	Teo Cruz, Mando Ramos
1970	Mando Ramos, Ismael Laguna, Ken Buchanan
1971	Ken Buchanan (WBA), Mando Ramos (WBC), Pedro Carrasco (WBC)
1972	Ken Buchanan (WBA), Roberto Duran (WBA), Pedro Carrasco (WBC), Mando Ramos (WBC), Chango Carmona (WBC), Rodolfo Gonzalez (WBC)
1973	Roberto Duran (WBA), Rodolfo Gonzalez (WBC))
1974	Roberto Duran (WBA), Rodolfo Gonzalez (WBC), Guts Ishimatsu (WBC)
1975	Roberto Duran (WBA), Guts Ishimatsu (WBC)
1976	Roberto Duran (WBA), Guts Ishimatsu (WBC), Esteban De Jesus (WBC)
1977	Roberto Duran (WBA), Esteban De Jesus (WBC)
1978	Roberto Duran (WBA, WBC)
1979	Roberto Duran[2], Jim Watt (WBC), Ernesto Espana (WBA)
1980	Ernesto Espana (WBA), Hilmer Kenty (WBA), Jim Watt (WBC)
1981	Hilmer Kenty (WBA), Sean O'Grady (WBA), James Watt (WBC), Alexis Arguello (WBC), Arturo Frias (WBA)
1982	Arturo Frias (WBA), Ray Mancini (WBA), Alexis Arguello (WBC)
1983	Edwin Rosario (WBC), Ray Mancini (WBA)
1984	Edwin Rosario (WBC), Livingstone Bramble (WBA)
1985	Jose Luis Ramirez (WBC) Hector Camacho (WBC) Livingstone Bramble (WBA)
1986	Hector Camacho (WBC) Livingstone Bramble (WBA) Jim Paul (IBF)
1987	Edwin Rosario (WBA) Jose Luis Ramirez (WBC) Greg Haugen (IBF)

1. Retired. 2. Abandoned title.

Featherweight

1889	Dal Hawkins[1]
1890	Billy Murphy
1892–1900	George Dixon
1900–01	Terry McGovern
1901	Young Corbett[1]
1901–12	Abe Attell
1912–23	Johnny Kilbane
1923	Eugene Criqui
1923–25	Johnny Dundee[1]
1925–27	Louis (Kid) Kaplan[1]
1927–28	Benny Bass
1928	Tony Canzoneri
1928–29	Andre Routis
1929–32	Battling Battalino[1]
1932	Tommy Paul (NBA), Kid Chocolate (N.Y.)
1933–36	Freddie Miller
1936–37	Petey Sarron
1937–38	Henry Armstrong[1]
1938–40	Joey Archibald
1940–41	Harry Jefra, Joey Archibald
1941–42	Chalky Wright
1942–48	Willie Pep
1948–49	Sandy Saddler[2]
1949–50	Willie Pep
1950-57	Sandy Saddler

1957–59	Kid Bassey
1959–63	Davey Moore
1963–64	Sugar Ramos
1964–67	Vicente Saldivar[2]
1968	Howard Winstone, José Legra,[3] Paul Rojas (WBA), Sho Saijo (WBA)
1969	Sho Saijo (WBA), Johnny Famechon[3]
1970	Sho Saijo (WBA), Johnny Famechon,[3] Vicente Salvidar,[3] Kuniaki Shibata[3]
1971	Sho Saijo (WBA), Antonio Gomez (WBA), Kuniaki Shibata (WBC)
1972	Antonio Gomez (WBA), Ernesto Marcel (WBA), Kuniaki Shibata (WBC), Clemente Sanchez (WBC), José Legra (WBC)
1973	Ernesto Marcel (WBA), José Legra (WBC), Eder Jofre (WBC)
1974	Ernesto Marcel (WBA)[2], Ruben Olivares (WBA), Alexis Arguello (WBA), Eder Jofre (WBC), Bobby Chacon (WBC)
1975	Alexis Arguello (WBA), Bobby Chacon (WBC), Ruben Olivares (WBC), David Kotey (WBC)
1976	Alexis Arguello (WBA),[2] David Kotey (WBC), Danny Lopez (WBC)
1977	Rafael Ortega (WBA), Danny Lopez (WBC)
1978	Rafael Ortega (WBA), Cecilio Lastra (WBA), Eusebio Pedroza (WBA), Danny Lopez (WBC)
1979	Eusebio Pedroza (WBA), Danny Lopez (WBC)
1980	Eusebio Pedroza (WBA), Danny Lopez (WBC), Salvador Sanchez (WBC)
1981	Eusebio Pedroza (WBA), Salvador Sanchez (WBC)
1982	Eusebio Pedroza (WBA), Salvador Sanchez (WBC)[4]
1983	Juan Laporte (WBC), Eusebio Pedroza (WBA)
1984	Wilfred Gomez (WBC), Eusebio Pedroza (WBA)
1985	Eusebio Pedroza (WBA) Barry McGuigan (WBA) Azumah Nelson (WBC)
1986	Barry McGuigan (WBA) Stevie Cruz (WBA) Azumah Nelson (WBC)
1987	Azumah Nelson (WBC) Antonio Esparragoza (WBA)

1. Abandoned title. 2. Retired. 3. Recognized in Europe, Mexico, and Orient. 4. Killed in auto accident.

Bantamweight

1890–92	George Dixon[1]
1894–99	Jimmy Barry[2]
1899–1900	Terry McGovern[1]
1901	Harry Harris[1]
1902–03	Harry Forbes
1903–04	Frankie Neil
1904	Joe Bowker[1]
1905–07	Jimmy Walsh[1]
1910–14	Johnny Coulon
1914–17	Kid Williams
1917–20	Pete Herman
1920	Joe Lynch
1920–21	Joe Lynch, Pete Herman, Johnny Buff
1922	Johnny Buff, Joe Lynch
1923	Joe Lynch
1924	Joe Lynch, Abe Goldstein
1924	Abe Goldstein, Eddie (Cannonball) Martin
1925	Eddie (Cannonball) Martin, Charlie (Phil) Rosenberg[3]
1927–28	Bud Taylor (NBA)[1]
1929–34	Al Brown
1935	Al Brown, Baltazar Sangchili
1936	Baltazar Sangchili, Tony Marino, Sixto Escobar
1937	Sixto Escobar, Harry Jeffra
1938	Harry Jeffra, Sixto Escobar
1939–40	Sixto Escobar[2]
1940–42	Lou Salica
1942–46	Manuel Ortiz
1947	Manuel Ortiz, Harold Dade
1948–50	Manuel Ortiz
1950–52	Vic Toweel
1952–54	Jimmy Carruthers[2]
1954–55	Robert Cohen
1956	Robert Cohen, Mario D'Agata, Raul Macias (NBA)
1957	Mario D'Agata, Alphonse Halimi
1958–59	Alphonse Halimi
1959–60	Jose Becerra[2]
1960–61	Alphonse Halimi[4]
1961–62	Johnny Caldwell[4]
1961–65	Eder Jofre
1965–68	Masahika (Fighting) Harada
1968	Masahika (Fighting) Harada, Lionel Rose
1969	Lionel Rose, Ruben Olivares
1970	Ruben Olivares, Chucho Castillo
1971	Chucho Castillo, Ruben Olivares
1972	Ruben Olivares, Rafael Herrera, Enrique Pinder
1973	Enrique Pinder (WBA), Romeo Anaya (WBA), Arnold Taylor (WBA), Rodolfo Martinez (WBC), Rafael Herrera
1974	Arnold Taylor (WBA), Soo Hwan Hong (WBA), Rafael Herrera (WBC), Rodolfo Martinez (WBC)
1975	Soo Hwan Hong (WBA), Alfonso Zamora (WBA), Rodolfo Martinez (WBC)
1976	Alfonso Zamora (WBA), Rodolfo Martinez (WBC), Carlos Zarate (WBC)
1977	Alfonso Zamora (WBA), Jorge Lujan (WBA), Carlos Zarate (WBC)
1978	Jorge Lujan (WBA), Carlos Zarate (WBC)
1979	Jorge Lujan (WBA), Carlos Zarate (WBC), Lupe Pinto (WBC)
1980	Jorge Lujan (WBA), Lupe Pintor (WBC), Julian Solis (WBA), Jeff Chandler (WBA)
1981	Lupe Pintor (WBC), Jeff Chandler (WBA)
1982	Lupe Pintor (WBC), Jeff Chandler (WBA)
1983	Jeff Chandler (WBA), Albert Dauila (WBC)
1984	Richie Sandqual (WBA), Albert Dauila (WBC)
1985	Richard Sandoval (WBA) Daniel Zaragoza (WBC) Miguel Lora (WBC)
1986	Richard Sandoval (WBA) Bernardo Pinango (WBA) Jeff Fenech (IBF)
1987	Bernardo Pinango (WBA) Takuya Muguruma (WBA) Miguel Lora (WBC)

1. Abandoned title. 2. Retired. 3. Deprived of title for failing to make weight. 4. Recognized in Europe.

Flyweight

1916–23	Jimmy Wilde
1923–25	Pancho Villa[1]
1925	Frankie Genaro
1925–27	Fidel La Barba[2]
1927–31	Corporal Izzy Schwartz, Frankie Genaro, Emile (Spider) Pladner, Midget Wolgast, Young Perez[3]
1932–35	Jackie Brown
1935–38	Bennie Lynch[4]
1939	Peter Kane[4]
1943–47	Jackie Paterson[1]
1947–50	Rinty Monaghan[2]
1950	Terry Allen
1950–52	Dado Marino
1952–54	Yoshio Shirai
1954–60	Pascual Perez
1960–62	Pone Kingpetch
1962–63	Masahika (Fighting) Harada
1963–64	Hiroyuki Ebihara
1964–65	Pone Kingpetch
1965–66	Salvatore Burrini
1966	Walter McGown, Chartchai Chionoi

1966–68	Charchai Chionoi
1969	Bernabe Villacampa, Efran Torres (WBA)
1970	Bernabe Villacampa, Chartchai Chionoi, Erbito Salavarria, Berkrerk Chartvanchai (WBA), Masao Ohba (WBA)
1971	Masao Ohba (WBA), Erbito Salavarria (WBC)
1972	Masao Ohba (WBA), Erbito Salavarria (WBC), Betulio Gonzalez (WBC), Venice Borkorsor (WBC)
1973	Masao Ohba (WBA), Chartchai Chionoi (WBA), Venice Borkorsor (WBC), Betulio Gonzalez (WBC)
1974	Chartchai Chionoi (WBA), Susumu Hanagata (WBA), Betulio Gonzalez (WBC), Shoji Oguma (WBC)
1975	Susumu Hanagata (WBA), Erbito Salavarria (WBA), Shoji Oguma (WBC), Miguel Canto (WBC)
1976	Erbito Salavarria (WBA), Alfonso Lopez (WBA), Guty Espadas (WBA), Miguel Canto (WBC)
1977	Guty Espadas (WBA), Miguel Canto (WBC)
1978	Guty Espadas (WBA), Betulio Gonzalez (WBA), Miguel Canto (WBC)
1979	Betulio Gonzalez (WBA), Miguel Canto (WBC), Park Chan-Hee (WBC)
1980	Luis Ibarra (WBA), Kim Tae Shik (WBA), Park Chan-Hee (WBC), Shoji Oguma (WBC)
1983	Frank Cedeno (WBC), Santos Lacia (WBA)
1984	Koji Kobayashy (WBA), Gabriel Bernal (WBC), Santos Laciar (WBA)
1985	Sot Chitalasa (WBC) Santos Laciar (WBA)
1986	Hilario Zapata (WBA) Julio Cesar-Chevez (WBC)
1987	Shin Hi Sop (IBF) Chang Ho Choi (IBF) Sot Hitalada (WBC)

1. Died. 2. Retired. 3. Claimants to NBA and New York Commission titles. 4. Abandoned title.

BOXING—AMATEUR

NATIONAL GOLDEN GLOVES CHAMPIONSHIPS—1987

(April 15–19, Knoxville, Tenn.)

106 lb—Eric Griffin, Baton Rouge, La.
112 lb—Carl Daniels, St. Louis, Mo.
119 lb—Fernando Rodriguez, Philadelphia, Pa.
125 lb—Donald Stokes, Baton Rouge, La.
132 lb—Skipper Kelp, Magna, Utah
139 lb—Todd Foster, Magna, Utah
147 lb—Roger Turner, Grand Rapids, Mich.
156 lb—Roy Jones, Knoxville, Tenn.
165 lb—Fabian Williams, Grand Rapids, Mich.
178 lb—Terry McGroom, Chicago, Ill.
201 lb—Dave Sherbrooke, Minneapolis, Minn.
Over 201 lb—Nathaniel Fitch, Knoxville, Tenn.

UNITED STATES CHAMPIONSHIPS—1987

(March 31–April 4, 1987, Buffalo, N.Y.)

106 lb—Brian Lonon, Fort Hood, Tex.
112 lb—Arthur Johnson, St. Louis, Mo.
119 lb—Michael Collins, LaPorte, Tex.
125 lb—Kelcie Banks, Chicago, Ill.
132 lb—Charles Murray, Rochester, N.Y.
139 lb—Nick Kakouris, St. Louis, Mo.
147 lb—Kenneth Gould, Rockford, Ill.
156 lb—Gerald McClellan, Milwaukee, Wis.
165 lb—Anthony Hembrick, U.S. Army/Fort Bragg, N.C.
178 lb—Andrew Maynard, U.S. Army/Fort Carson, Colo.
201 lb—Michael Bent, Cambria Heights, N.Y.
Over 201 lb—Charlton Hollis, Fort Lauderdale, Fla.

WORLD AMATEUR CHAMPIONSHIPS—1986

(May 12-18, 1986, at Reno, Nev.)

106 lb—Juan Torres, Cuba
112 lb—Pedro Reyes, Cuba
119 lb—Moon Sung-Kil, Korea
125 lb—Kelcie Banks, United States
132 lb—Adolfo Horta, Cuba
139 lb—Vasill Shishov, Soviet Union
147 lb—Kenneth Gould, United States
156 lb—Angel Espinosa, Cuba
165 lb—Darin Allen, United States
178 lb—Pablo Romero, Cuba
201—Felix Savon, Cuba
Over 201 lb—Biagio Chianese, Italy

FENCING

WORLD CHAMPIONS—1987

Men's foil—Mathias Gey, West Germany
Men's epee—Volker Fischer, West Germany
Men's sabre—Jean-Francois Lamour, France
Women's foil—Elisabeta Tufan, Romania
Men's foil team—West Germany
Men's epee team—Soviet Union
Men's sabre team—Soviet Union
Women's foil team—Hungary

UNITED STATES CHAMPIONS—1987
U.S. Fencing Association

(winner, club, region)

Men's foil—Michael Marx, Salle Auriol Fencing Club, Oregon
Men's epee—Timothy C. Glass, Bayou City Blades, Illinois
Men's sabre—Steve Mormando, New York Fencers Club, New York City
Women's foil—Caitlin Billodeau, New York Fencers Club, New York City
Women's epee—Donna Lee Stone, South Santelli, New Jersey
Men's foil team—New York Fencers Club
Men's sabre team—New York Fencers Club
Men's epee team—New York Athletic Club
Women's foil team—Tanner City Fencers Club, New England division

HORSE RACING

Ancient drawings on stone and bone prove that horse racing is at least 3000 years old, but Thoroughbred Racing is a modern development. Practically every thoroughbred in training today traces its registered ancestry back to one or more of three sires that arrived in England about 1728 from the Near East and became known, from the names of their owners, as the Byerly Turk, the Darley Arabian, and the Godolphin Arabian. The Jockey Club (English) was founded at Newmarket in 1750 or 1751 and became the custodian of the Stud Book as well as the court of last resort in deciding turf affairs.

Horse racing took place in this country before the Revolution, but the great lift to the breeding industry came with the importation in 1798, by Col. John Hoomes of Virginia, of Diomed, winner of the Epsom Derby of 1780. Diomed's lineal descendants included such famous stars of the American turf as American Eclipse and Lexington. From 1800 to the time of the Civil War there were race courses and breeding establishments plentifully scattered through Virginia, North Carolina, South Carolina, Tennessee, Kentucky, and Louisiana.

The oldest stake event in North America is the Queen's Plate, a Canadian fixture that was first run in the Province of Quebec in 1836. The oldest stake event in the United States is The Travers, which was first run at Saratoga in 1864. The gambling that goes with horse racing and trickery by jockeys, trainers, owners, and track officials caused attacks on the sport by reformers and a demand among horse racing enthusiasts for an honest and effective control of some kind, but nothing of lasting value to racing came of this until the formation in 1894 of The Jockey Club.

"TRIPLE CROWN" WINNERS IN THE UNITED STATES[1]

(Kentucky Derby, Preakness and Belmont Stakes)

Year	Horse	Owner	Year	Horse	Owner
1919	Sir Barton	J. K. L. Ross	1946	Assault	Robert J. Kleberg
1930	Gallant Fox	William Woodward	1948	Citation	Warren Wright
1935	Omaha	William Woodward	1973	Secretariat	Meadow Stable
1937	War Admiral	Samuel D. Riddle	1977	Seattle Slew	Karen Taylor
1941	Whirlaway	Warren Wright	1978	Affirmed	Louis Wolfson
1943	Count Fleet	Mrs. John Hertz			

1. Statistics relative to thoroughbred racing in this publication are reproduced from the *American Racing Manual*, by special permission of the copyright owners. TRIANGLE PUBLICATIONS, INC. Reproduction prohibited.

KENTUCKY DERBY

Churchill Downs; 3-year-olds; 1 1/4 miles.

Year	Winner	Jockey	Wt.	Win val.	Year	Winner	Jockey	Wt.	Win val.
1875	Aristides	O. Lewis	100	$2,850	1909	Wintergreen	V. Powers	117	$4,850
1876	Vagrant	R. Swim	97	2,950	1910	Donau	F. Herbert	117	4,850
1877	Baden Baden	W. Walker	100	3,300	1911	Meridian	G. Archibald	117	4,850
1878	Day Star	J. Carter	100	4,050	1912	Worth	C. H. Shilling	117	4,850
1879	Lord Murphy	C. Schauer	100	3,550	1913	Donerail	R. Goose	117	5,475
1880	Fonso	G. Lewis	105	3,800	1914	Old Rosebud	J. McCabe	114	9,125
1881	Hindoo	J. McLaughlin	105	4,410	1915	Regret	J. Notler	112	11,450
1882	Apollo	B. Hurd	102	4,560	1916	George Smith	J. Loftus	117	9,750
1883	Leonatus	W. Donohue	105	3,760	1917	Omar Khayyam	C. Borel	117	16,600
1884	Buchanan	I. Murphy	110	3,990	1918	Exterminator	W. Knapp	114	14,700
1885	Joe Cotton	E. Henderson	110	4,630	1919	Sir Barton	J. Loftus	112 1/2	20,825
1886	Ben Ali	P. Duffy	118	4,890	1920	Paul Jones	T. Rice	126	30,375
1887	Montrose	I. Lewis	118	4,200	1921	Behave Yourself	C. Thompson	126	38,450
1888	Macbeth II	G. Covington	115	4,740	1922	Morvich	A. Johnson	126	46,775
1889	Spokane	T. Kiley	118	4,970	1923	Zev	E. Sande	126	53,600
1890	Riley	I. Murphy	118	5,460	1924	Black Gold	J. D. Mooney	126	52,775
1891	Kingman	I. Murphy	122	4,680	1925	Flying Ebony	E. Sande	126	52,950
1892	Azra	A. Clayton	122	4,230	1926	Bubbling Over	A. Johnson	126	50,075
1893	Lookout	E. Kunze	122	4,090	1927	Whiskery	L. McAtee	126	51,000
1894	Chant	F. Goodale	122	4,020	1928	Reigh Count	C. Lang	126	55,375
1895	Halma	J. Perkins	122	2,970	1929	Clyde Van Dusen	L. McAtee	126	53,950
1896	Ben Brush	W. Simms	117	4,850	1930	Gallant Fox	E. Sande	126	50,725
1897	Typhoon H	F. Garner	117	4,850	1931	Twenty Grand	C. Kurtsinger	126	48,725
1898	Plaudit	W. Simms	117	4,850	1932	Burgoo King	E. James	126	52,350
1899	Manuel	F. Taral	117	4,850	1933	Brokers Tip	D. Meade	126	48,925
1900	Lieut. Gibson	J. Boland	117	4,850	1934	Cavalcade	M. Garner	126	28,175
1901	His Eminence	J. Winkfield	117	4,850	1935	Omaha	W. Saunders	126	39,525
1902	Alan-a-Dale	J. Winkfield	117	4,850	1936	Bold Venture	I. Hanford	126	37,725
1903	Judge Himes	H. Booker	117	4,850	1937	War Admiral	C. Kurtsinger	126	52,050
1904	Elwood	F. Prior	117	4,850	1938	Lawrin	E. Arcaro	126	47,050
1905	Agile	J. Martin	122	4,850	1939	Johnstown	J. Stout	126	46,350
1906	Sir Huon	R. Troxler	117	4,850	1940	Gallahadion	C. Bierman	126	60,150
1907	Pink Star	A. Minder	117	4,850	1941	Whirlaway	E. Arcaro	126	61,275
1908	Stone Street	A. Pickens	117	4,850	1942	Shut Out	W. D. Wright	126	64,225

Year	Winner	Jockey	Wt.	Win val.	Year	Winner	Jockey	Wt.	Win val.
1943	Count Fleet	J. Longden	126	$ 60,725	1965	Lucky Debonair	W. Shoemaker	126	$112,000
1944	Pensive	C. McCreary	126	64,675	1966	Kauai King	D. Brumfield	126	120,500
1945	Hoop Jr.	E. Arcaro	126	64,850	1967	Proud Clarion	R. Ussery	126	119,700
1946	Assault	W. Mehrtens	126	96,400	1968	Forward Pass[1]	I. Valenzuela	126	122,600
1947	Jet Pilot	E. Guerin	126	92,160	1969	Majestic Prince	W. Hartack	126	113,200
1948	Citation	E. Arcaro	126	83,400	1970	Dust Commander	M. Manganello	126	127,800
1949	Ponde	S. Brooks	126	91,600	1971	Canonero II	G. Avila	126	145,500
1950	Middleground	W. Boland	126	92,650	1972	Riva Ridge	R. Turcotte	126	140,300
1951	Count Turf	C. McCreary	126	98,050	1973	Secretariat	R. Turcotte	126	155,050
1952	Hill Gail	E. Arcaro	126	96,300	1974	Cannonade	A. Cordero, Jr.	126	274,000
1953	Dark Star	H. Moreno	126	90,050	1975	Foolish Pleasure	J. Vasquez	126	209,600
1954	Determine	R. York	126	102,050	1976	Bold Forbes	A. Cordero, Jr.	126	165,200
1955	Swaps	W. Shoemaker	126	108,400	1977	Seattle Slew	J. Cruguet	126	214,700
1956	Needles	D. Erb	126	123,450	1978	Affirmed	S. Cauthen	126	186,900
1957	Iron Liege	W. Hartack	126	107,950	1979	Spectacular Bid	R. Franklin	126	228,650
1958	Tim Tam	I. Valenzuela	126	116,400	1980	Genuine Risk	J. Vasquez	126	250,550
1959	Tomy Lee	W. Shoemaker	126	119,650	1981	Pleasant Colony	J. Velasquez	126	317,200
1960	Venetian Way	W. Hartack	126	114,850	1982	Gato del Sol	E. Delahoussaye	126	417,600
1961	Carry Back	J. Sellers	126	120,500	1983	Sunny's Halo	E. Delahoussaye	126	426,000
1962	Decidedly	W. Hartack	126	119,650	1984	Swale	L. Pincay, Jr.	126	537,400
1963	Chateauguay	B. Baeza	126	108,900	1985	Spend a Buck	A. Cordero, Jr.	126	406,800
1964	Northern Dancer	W. Hartack	126	114,300	1986	Ferdinand	W. Shoemaker	126	609,400
					1987	Alysheba	C. McCarron	126	618,600

1. Dancer's Image finished first but was disqualified after traces of drug were found in system.

PREAKNESS STAKES

Pimlico; 3-year-olds; 1 3/16 miles; first race 1873.

Year	Winner	Jockey	Wt.	Win Val.	Year	Winner	Jockey	Wt.	Win val.
1919	Sir Barton	J. Loftus	126	$24,500	1958	Tim Tam	I. Valenzuela	126	$97,900
1930	Gallant Fox	E. Sande	126	51,925	1959	Royal Orbit	W. Harmatz	126	136,200
1931	Mate	G. Ellis	126	48,225	1960	Bally Ache	R. Ussery	126	121,000
1932	Burgoo King	E. James	126	50,375	1961	Carry Back	J. Sellers	126	126,200
1933	Head Play	C. Kurtsinger	126	26,850	1962	Greek Money	J. Rotz	126	135,800
1934	High Quest	R. Jones	126	25,175	1963	Candy Spots	W. Shoemaker	126	127,500
1935	Omaha	W. Saunders	126	25,325	1964	Northern Dancer	W. Hartack	126	124,200
1936	Bold Venture	G. Woolf	126	27,325	1965	Tom Rolfe	R. Turcotte	126	128,100
1937	War Admiral	C. Kurtsinger	126	45,600	1966	Kauai King	D. Brumfield	126	129,000
1938	Dauber	M. Peters	126	51,875	1967	Damascus	W. Shoemaker	126	141,500
1939	Challedon	G. Seabo	126	53,710	1968	Forward Pass	I. Valenzuela	126	142,700
1940	Bimelech	F.A. Smith	126	53,230	1969	Majestic Prince	W. Hartack	126	129,500
1941	Whirlaway	E. Arcaro	126	49,365	1970	Personality	E. Belmonte	126	151,300
1942	Alsab	B. James	126	58,175	1971	Canonero II	G. Avila	126	137,400
1943	Count Fleet	J. Longden	126	43,190	1972	Bee Bee Bee	E. Nelson	126	135,300
1944	Pensive	C. McCreary	126	60,075	1973	Secretariat	R. Turcotte	126	129,900
1945	Polynesian	W.D. Wright	126	66,170	1974	Little Current	M. Rivera	126	156,000
1946	Assault	W. Mehrtens	126	96,620	1975	Master Derby	D. McHargue	126	158,100
1947	Faultless	D. Dodson	126	98,005	1976	Elocutionist	J. Lively	126	129,700
1948	Citation	E. Arcaro	126	91,870	1977	Seattle Slew	J. Cruguet	126	138,600
1949	Capot	T. Atkinson	126	79,985	1978	Affirmed	S. Cauthen	126	136,200
1950	Hill Prince	E. Arcaro	126	56,115	1979	Spectacular Bid	R. Franklin	126	165,300
1951	Bold	E. Arcaro	126	83,110	1980	Codex	A. Cordero	126	180,600
1952	Blue Man	C. McCreary	126	86,135	1981	Pleasant Colony	J. Velasquez	126	270,800
1953	Native Dancer	E. Guerin	126	65,200	1982	Aloma's Ruler	J. Kaenel	126	209,900
1954	Hasty Road	J. Adams	126	91,600	1983	Deputed Testimony	D. Miller	126	251,200
1955	Nashua	E. Arcaro	126	67,550	1984	Gate Dancer	A. Cordero	126	243,600
1956	Fabius	W. Hartack	126	84,250	1985	Tank's Prospect	Pat Day	126	423,200
1957	Bold Ruler	E. Arcaro	126	65,250	1986	Snow Chief	A. Solis	126	411,900
					1987	Alysheba	C. McCarron	126	421,100

BELMONT STAKES

Belmont Park; 3-year-olds; 1 1/2 miles.

Run at Jerome Park 1867 to 1890; at Morris Park 1890–94; at Belmont Park 1905–62; at Aqueduct 1963–67. Distance 1 5/8 miles prior to 1874; reduced to 1 1/2 miles, 1874; reduced to 1 1/4 miles, 1890; reduced to 1 1/8 miles, 1893; increased to 1 1/4 miles, 1895; increased to 1 3/8 miles, 1896; reduced to 1 1/4 miles in 1904; increased to 1 1/2 miles, 1926.

Year	Winner	Jockey	Wt.	Win val.	Year	Winner	Jockey	Wt.	Win val.
1919	Sir Barton	J. Loftus	126	$11,950	1936	Granville	J. Stout	126	$29,800
1930	Gallant Fox	E. Sande	126	66,040	1937	War Admiral	C. Kurtsinger	126	38,020
1931	Twenty Grand	C. Kurtsinger	126	58,770	1938	Pasteurized	J. Stout	126	34,530
1932	Faireno	T. Malley	126	55,120	1939	Johnstown	J. Stout	126	37,020
1933	Hurryoff	M. Garner	126	49,490	1940	Bimelech	F.A. Smith	126	35,030
1934	Peace Chance	W.D. Wright	126	43,410	1941	Whirlaway	E. Arcaro	126	39,77-
1935	Omaha	W. Saunders	126	35,480	1942	Shut Out	E. Arcaro	126	44,520

Year	Winner	Jockey	Wt.	Win val.
1943	Count Fleet	J. Longden	126	$35,340
1944	Bounding Home	G.L. Smith	126	55,000
1945	Pavot	E. Arcaro	126	56,675
1946	Assault	W. Mehrtens	126	75,400
1947	Phalanx	R. Donoso	126	78,900
1948	Citation	E. Arcaro	126	77,700
1949	Capot	T. Atkinson	126	60,900
1950	Middleground	W. Boland	126	61,350
1951	Counterpoint	D. Gorman	126	82,000
1952	One Count	E. Arcaro	126	82,400
1953	Native Dancer	E. Guerin	126	82,500
1954	High Gun	E. Guerin	126	89,000
1955	Nashua	E. Arcaro	126	83,700
1956	Needles	D. Erb	126	83,600
1957	Gallant Man	W. Shoemaker	126	77,300
1958	Cavan	P. Anderson	126	73,440
1959	Sword Dancer	W. Shoemaker	126	93,525
1960	Celtic Ash	W. Hartack	126	96,785
1961	Sherluck	B. Baeza	126	104,900
1962	Jaipur	W. Shoemaker	126	109,550
1963	Chateauguay	B. Baeza	126	101,700
1964	Quadrangle	M. Ycaza	126	110,850
1965	Hail to All	J. Sellers	126	$104,150
1966	Amberoid	W. Boland	126	117,700
1967	Damascus	W. Shoemaker	126	104,950
1968	Stage Door Johnny	H. Gustines	126	117,700
1969	Arts and Letters	B. Baeza	126	104,050
1970	High Echelon	J. Rotz	126	115,000
1971	Pass Catcher	R. Blum	126	97,710
1972	Riva Ridge	R. Turcotte	126	93,540
1973	Secretariat	R. Turcotte	126	90,120
1974	Little Current	M. Rivera	126	101,970
1975	Avatar	W. Shoemaker	126	116,160
1976	Bold Forbes	A. Cordero, Jr.	126	117,000
1977	Seattle Slew	J. Cruguet	126	109,080
1978	Affirmed	S. Cauthen	126	110,580
1979	Coastal	R. Hernandez	126	161,400
1980	Temperence Hill	E. Maple	126	176,220
1981	Summing	G. Martens	126	170,580
1982	Conquistador Cielo	L. Pincay, Jr.	126	159,720
1983	Caveat	L. Pincay, Jr.	126	215,100
1984	Swale	L. Pincay, Jr.	126	310,020
1985	Creme Fraiche	Eddie Maple	126	307,740
1986	Danzig Connection	C. McCarron	126	338,640
1987	Bet Twice	C. Perret	126	329,160

TRIPLE CROWN RACES—1987

Kentucky Derby (Churchill Downs, Louisville, Ky., May 2, 1987). Gross purse: $793,600 (record). Distance: 1 1/4 miles. Order of finish: 1. Alysheba (McCarron), mutuel return: $18.80, $6.00, $6.20. 2. Bet Twice (Perret), $10.00, $7.20. 3. Avies Copy (Solomone), $6.80. 4. Cryptoclearance (Santos). 5. Templar Hill (Hutton). 6. Gulch (Shoemaker). 7. Leo Castelli (Vasquez). 8. Candi's Gold (Hawley). 9. Conquistarose (Bailey). 10. On the Line (Stevens). 11. Shawkit Won (Migliore). 12. Mas'ful Advocate (Pincay). 13. War (McCauley). 14. Momentus (Brumfield). 15. No More Flowers (Guerra). 16. Capote (Cordero). 17. Demons Begone (Day). Winner's purse: $618,600. Margin of victory: three quarters of a length. Attendance: 130,532. Time of race: 2:03 2/5.

Preakness Stakes (Pimlico, Md., May 16, 1987). Gross purse: $543, 600. Distance: 1 3/16 miles. Order of finish: 1. Alysheba (McCarron), mutuel return: $6.00, $4.60, $3.40. 2. Bet Twice (Perret), $4.60, $3.60. 3. Cryptoclearance (Santos), $3.00. 4. Gulch (Cordero). 5. Avies Copy (Solomone). 6. Phantom Jet (Allen). 7. Lookinforthebigone (Stevens). 8. No More Flowers (Guerra). 9. Harriman (Bracciale). Winner's purse: $421,100. Margin of victory: half a length. Attendance: 87,945 (record). Time of race: 1:55 4/5.

Belmont Stakes (Elmont, N.Y., June 6, 1987). Gross purse: $548, 600. Distance: 1 1/2 miles. Order of finish: 1. Bet Twice (Perret). mutuel return: $18.00, $5.00, $3.80. 2. Cryptoclearance (Pincay), $4.80, $3.80. 3. Gulch (Day), $4.40. 4. Alysheba (McCarron). 5. Shawklit Won (Cordero). 6. Gone West (Maple). 7. Avies Copy (Solomone). 8. Manassa Jack (Delgado). 9. Leo Castelli (Santos). Winner's purse: $329,160. Margin of victory: 14 lengths. Attendance: 64,772. Time of race: 2:28 1/5.

ECLIPSE AWARDS—1987

The Eclipse Awards in thoroughbred racing are given on the basis of voting by three groups: The Daily Racing Form, the National Turf Writers Association, and the racing secretaries at tracks who are members of the Thoroughbred Racing Association.

Horse of the Year	Snow Chief
Two-year-old colt	Capote
Two-year-old filly	Brave Raj
Three-year-old colt	Snow Chief
Three-year-old filly	Tiffany Lass
Older colt or gelding	Turkoman
Older filly or mare	Lady's Secret
Male turf horse	Manila
Female turf horse	Estrapade
Sprinter	Smile
Steeplechase	Flatterer
Owner	Eugene V. and Joyce Klein
Trainer	D. Wayne Lukas
Jockey	Pat Day
Breeder	Paul Mellon
Apprentice jockey	Allen Stacy

When Is a Horse a Horse?

Terms by which a horse is known in racing, as explained by John I. Day of the Thoroughbred Racing Associations: a *foal* is a young horse of either sex and while unweaned is known as a *suckling.* When separated from his *dam,* or maternal parent, he is a *weanling* until Jan. 1 following his birth, when he becomes a *yearling.* He may be a *colt,* if male, and remain so (unless he becomes a *gelding,* or unsexed) until he is 5 years old; or, if female, a *filly* until 5. From 5 on, they are *horses* or *mares* and when they become parents, *sires* or *dams.*

Origin of Individual Racing Silks

The practice of using individual racing silks to distinguish horses is over 200 years old. They were first introduced in October 1762 at Newmarket, England, when a group of sportsmen conceived the unique idea. In the quaint phraseology of the time, "for the greater convenience of distinguishing horses in the running, as also for the prevention of disputes arising from not knowing the colours worn by riders, seventeen gentlemen came to the decision to register their colours," and the stewards of the Newmarket meeting "hoped" in the name of the Jockey Club that the gentlemen "would take care that their riders be provided with dresses accordingly." Lord Grosvenor, the Lord Derby of that day, chose orange as his color.

TRACK AND FIELD

Running, jumping, hurdling and throwing weights—track and field sports, in other words—are as natural to young people as eating, drinking and breathing. Unorganized competition in this form of sport goes back beyond the Cave Man era. Organized competition begins with the first recorded Olympic Games in Greece, 776 B.C., when Coroebus of Elis won the only event on the program, a race of approximately 200 yards. The Olympic Games, with an ever-widening program of events, continued until "the glory that was Greece" had faded and "the grandeur that was Rome" was tarnished, and finally were abolished by decree of Emperor Theodosius I of Rome in A.D. 394. The Tailteann Games of Ireland are supposed to have antedated the first Olympic Games by some centuries, but we have no records of the specific events and winners thereof.

Professional contests of speed and strength were popular at all times and in many lands, but the widespread competition of amateur athletes in track and field sports is a comparatively modern development. The first organized amateur athletic meet of record was sponsored by the Royal Military Academy at Woolwich, England, in 1849. Oxford and Cambridge track and field rivalry began in 1864, and the English amateur championships were established in 1866. In the United States such organizations as the New York Athletic Club and the Olympic Club of San Francisco conducted track and field meets in the 1870s, and a few colleges joined to sponsor a meet in 1874. The success of the college meet led to the formation of the Intercollegiate Association of Amateur Athletes of America and the holding of an annual set of championship games beginning in 1876. The Amateur Athletic Union, organized in 1888, has been the ruling body in American amateur athletics since that time. In 1980, The Athletics Congress of the U.S.A. took over the governing of track and field from the A.A.U.

WORLD RECORDS—MEN

(Through Sept. 1, 1987)

Recognized by the International Athletic Federation.

The I.A.A.F. decided late in 1976 not to recognize records in yards except for the one-mile run.

The I.A.A.F. also requires automatic timing for all records for races of 400 meters or less.

Event	Record	Holder	Home Country	Where Made	Date
Running					
100 m	0:09.83	Ben Johnson	Canada	Rome	August 30, 1987
200 m	0:19.72	Pietro Mennea	Italy	Mexico City	Sept. 17, 1979
400 m	0:43.86	Lee Evans	U.S.	Mexico City	Oct. 18, 1968
800 m	1:41.8	Sebastian Coe	England	Florence, Italy	June 10, 1981
1,000 m	2:12.40	Sebastian Coe	England	Oslo, Norway	July 11, 1981
1,500 m	3:29.45	Said Aouita	Morocco	Berlin	August 23, 1985
1 mile	3:46.31	Steve Cram	Great Britain	Oslo	July 27, 1985
2,000 m	4:50.81	Said Aouita	Morocco	Paris	July 16, 1987
3,000 m	7:32.1	Henry Rono	Kenya	Oslo	June 27, 1978
3,000-m steeplechase	8:05.1	Henry Rono	Kenya	Seattle, Wash.	May 13, 1978
5,000 m	12:58.39	Said Aouita	Morocco	Rome	July 22, 1987
10,000 m	27:13.81	Fernando Mamede	Portugal	Stockholm, Swe.	July 2, 1984
25,000 m	1:13:55.8	Toshihiko Seko	Japan	Christchurch, N.Z.	March 22, 1981
30,000 m	1:29:18.8	Toshihiko Seko	Japan	Christchurch, N.Z.	March 22, 1981
20,000 m	57:24.2	Jos Hermans	Netherlands	Papandal, Neth.	May 1, 1976
1 hour	13 mi. 24 yd	Jos Hermans	Netherlands	Papandal, Neth.	May 1, 1976
Marathon	2:07:11.0	Carlos Lopes	Portugal	Rotterdam	April 20, 1985
Walking					
20,000 m	1:18:39.9	Ernesto Canto	Mexico	Fana, Norway	May 5, 1984
2 hours	17 mi. 1,092 yd	Ralph Kowalsky	East Germany	East Berlin	March 28, 1982
30,000 m	2:06:27.0	Maurizio Damilano	Italy	Milanese, Italy	May 5, 1985
50,000 m	3:41.39	Raul Gonzales	Mexico	Bergen, Norway	May 25, 1979
Hurdles					
110 m	0:12.93	Renaldo Nehemiah	U.S.	Zurich, Switzerland	Aug. 19, 1981
400 m	0:47.02	Edwin Moses	U.S.	Koblenz, W. Ger.	Aug. 31, 1983
Relay Races					
400 m (4×100)	0:37.83	Olympic Team	U.S.	Los Angeles, Ca.	Aug. 11, 1984
800 m (4×200)	1:20.26	So. California (Joel Andrews, James Sanford, Billy Mullins, Clancy Edwards)	U.S.	Tempe, Ariz.	May 27, 1978
1,600 m (4×400)	2:56.16	National Team (Vince Matthews, Ron Freeman, Larry James, Lee Evans)	U.S.	Mexico City	Oct. 20, 1968
3,200 m (4×800)	7:03.89	National Team (Peter Elliot, Garry Cook, Steve Cram, Sebastian Coe)	Britain	London	Aug. 30, 1982

Field Events

High Jump	7 ft 11 1/4 in.	Patrik Sjoberg	Sweden	Stockholm	June 30, 1987
Long jump	29 ft 2 1/2 in.	Bob Beamon	U.S.	Mexico City	Oct. 18, 1968
Triple Jump	58 ft 11 1/2 in.	Willie Banks	Los Angeles, Calif.	Indianapolis	June 16, 1985
Pole vault	19 ft 9 1/4 in.	Sergey Bubka	U.S.S.R.	Prague	June 23, 1987
Shot-put	75 ft 2 in.	Alessandro Andrei	Italy	Italy	August 12, 1987
Discus throw	243 ft 0 in.	Juergen Schult	East Germany	Neubrandenburg	June 6, 1986
Hammer throw	284 ft 7 in.	Yuriy Syedikh	U.S.S.R.	Stuttgart	Aug. 28, 1986
Javelin throw	343 ft 10 in.	Uwe Hohn	E. Germany	Oslo, Norway	July 20, 1984
Decathlon	8,798pts.	Jurgen Hingsen	W. Germany	Mannheim, W. Ger.	June 8-9, 1984

WORLD RECORDS—WOMEN

(Through Sept. 1, 1987)

Event	Record	Holder	Home Country	Where Made	Date
Running					
100 m	0:10.76	Evelyn Ashford	U.S.	Zurich, Switz.	Aug. 22, 1984
200 m	0:21.71	Heike Drechsler	East Germany	Stuttgart	Aug. 28, 1986
400 m	0:47.99	Jarmila Kratochvilova	Czechoslovakia	Helsinki, Fin.	Aug. 10, 1983
800 m	1:53.28	Jarmila Kratochvilova	Czechoslovakia	Munich, W. Ger.	July 26, 1983
1,500 m	3:52.47	Tatyana Kazankina	U.S.S.R.	Zurich, Switz.	Aug. 13, 1980
1 mile	4:16.71	Mary Decker Slaney	U.S.A.	Zurich	Aug. 21, 1985
3,000 m	8:22.62	Tatyana Kazankina	U.S.S.R.	Moscow	Aug. 26, 1984
5,000 m	14:37.33	Ingrid Kristiansen	Norway	Stockholm	Aug. 5, 1986
10,000 m	30:13.74	Ingrid Kristiansen	Norway	Oslo	July 5, 1986
Marathon	2:21:06.0	Ingrid Kristiansen	Norway	London	April 21, 1985
Hurdles					
100-m hurdles	0:12.25	Ginka Zagorcheva	Bulgaria	Greece	August 8, 1987
400 m	0:53.33	Maria Stepanova	U.S.S.R.	Stuttgart	Aug. 28, 1986
Relay Races					
400 m (4×100)	0:41.53	East Germany	E. Germany	Berlin, E. Ger.	July 31, 1983
800 m (4×200)	1:28.15	East Germany	E. Germany	Jena, E. Ger.	Aug. 9, 1980
1,600 m (4×400)	3:15.92	East Germany	E. Germany	Erfurt, E. Ger.	June 3, 1984
3,200 m (4×800)	7:52.3	U.S.S.R.	U.S.S.R.	Podolsk, U.S.S.R.	Aug. 16, 1976
Field Events					
High jump	6 ft 10 1/4 in.	Stefka Kostadinova	Bulgaria	Rome	August 30, 1987
Long jump	24 ft 5 1/4 in.	Jackie Joyner-Kersee	USA	Indianapolis	August 13, 1987
Triple jump	45 ft 5 1/4 in.	Sheila Hudson	USA	San Jose	June 26, 1987
Shot-put	74 ft 3 in.	Natalya Lisovskaya	U.S.S.R.	Moscow	June 7, 1987
Discus throw	254 ft 1 in.	Fatima Whitbread	East Germany	Stuttgart	Aug. 28, 1986
Javelin throw	258 ft 10 in.	Petra Felke	East Germany	Leipzig	July 30, 1987
Heptathlon	7,161 pts	Jackie Joyner	United States	Houston, Tex.	Aug 1–2, 1986

AMERICAN RECORDS—MEN

(Through Sept. 1, 1987)
Officially approved by The Athletics Congress.

Event	Record	Holder	Where Made	Date
Running				
100 m	0:09.93	Calvin Smith	Colorado Springs, Colo.	July 3, 1983
200 m	0:19.75	Carl Lewis	Indianapolis, Ind.	June 19, 1983
400 m	0:43.86	Lee Evans	Mexico City	Oct. 16, 1968
800 m	1:42.69	Johnny Gray	Koblenz, W. Ger.	Aug. 29, 1985
1,000 m	2:13.9	Richard Wohlhuter	Oslo, Norway	July 30, 1974
1,500 m	3:29.77	Sydney Maree	Cologne, W. Ger.	Aug. 25, 1985
1 mile	3:47.69	Steve Scott	Oslo, Norway	July 7, 1982
2,000 m	4:54.71	Steve Scott	Ingelhelm, W. Ger.	Aug. 31, 1982
3,000 m	7:35.84	Doug Padilla	Oslo, Norway	July 9, 1983
5,000 m	13:01.15	Sydney Maree	Oslo, Norway	July 27, 1985
10,000 m	27:20.56	Mark Nenow	Brussels	Sept. 5, 1986
20,000 m	58:15.0	Bill Rodgers	Boston, Mass.	Aug. 9, 1977
25,000 m	1:14:11.8	Bill Rodgers	Saratoga, Cal.	Feb. 21, 1979
30,000 m	1:31.49	Bill Rodgers	Saratoga, Cal.	Feb. 21, 1979
1 hour	12 mi., 1351 yds	Bill Rodgers	Boston, Mass.	Aug. 9, 1977
3,000-m steeplechase	8:09.17	Henry Marsh	Koblenz, W. Ger.	Aug. 29, 1985

Hurdles				
110 m	0:12.93	Renaldo Nehemiah	Zurich, Switz.	Aug. 19, 1981
400 m	0:47.02	Edwin Moses	Koblenz, W. Ger.	Aug. 31, 1983
Relay Races				
400 m (4×100)	0:37.83	U.S. Olympic Team	Los Angeles, Cal.	Aug. 11, 1984
800 m (4×200)	1:20.26	Southern California	Tempe, Ariz.	May 27, 1978
1,600 m (4×400)	2:56.16	U.S. Olympic Team	Mexico City	Oct. 20, 1968
3,200 m (4×800)	7:06.50	Santa Monica Track Club	Walnut	Apr. 26, 1986
Field Events				
High jump	7 ft 8 3/4 in.	Jimmy Howard	Rehlingen	June 8, 1987
Long jump	29 ft 2 1/2 in.	Bob Beamon	Mexico City	Oct. 18, 1968
Triple jump	58 ft 11 1/2 in.	Willie Banks	Indianapolis, Ind.	June 16, 1985
Pole vault	19 ft 6 1/4 in.	Joe Dial	Norman	June 18, 1987
Shot-put	73 ft 10 3/4 in.	John Brenner	Walnut	April 26, 1987
Discus throw	237 ft 4 in.	Ben Plucknett	Stockholm, Swe.	July 7, 1981
Javelin throw	327 ft 2 in.	Tom Petranoff	Los Angeles, Cal.	May 15, 1983
Hammer throw	265 ft 4 in.	Jud Logan	Walnut	April 27, 1986
Decathlon	8,617 pts	Bruce Jenner	Montreal, Can.	July 29–30, 1976

AMERICAN RECORDS—WOMEN

(Through Sept. 1, 1987)

Event	Record	Holder	Where Made	Date
Running				
100 m	0:10.76	Evelyn Ashford	Zurich, Switz.	Aug. 22, 1984
200 m	0:21.81	Valerie Brisco-Hooks	Los Angeles, Cal.	Aug. 9, 1984
400 m	0:48.83	Valerie Brisco-Hooks	Los Angeles, Cal.	Aug. 6, 1984
800 m	1:56.90	Mary Decker Slaney	Bern	Aug. 16, 1985
1,500 m	3:57.12	Mary Decker Slaney	Stockholm, Swe.	July 26, 1983
1000 m	2:34.8	Mary Decker Slaney	Eugene, Ore.	July 4, 1985
1 mile	4:16.71	Mary Decker Slaney	Zurich	Aug. 21, 1985
3,000 m	8:29.69	Mary Decker Slaney	Cologne	Aug. 25, 1985
5,000 m	15:06.53	Mary Decker Slaney	Eugene, Ore.	June 1, 1985
10,000 m	31:35.3	Mary Decker Slaney	Eugene, Ore.	July 16, 1982
Hurdles				
100 m	12.79	Stephanie Hightower	Karl-Marx-Stadt, E. Ger.	July 10, 1982
400 m hurdle	0:54.23	Judy Brown King	Indianapolis	August 12, 1987
Relay Races				
400 m (4×100)	0:41.61	U.S. National Team	Colorado Springs, Col.	July 3, 1983
800 m (4×200)	1:32.6	U.S. National Team	Bourges, France	June 24, 1979
1,600 m (4×400)	3:18.29	U.S. Olympic Team	Los Angeles, Cal.	Aug. 11, 1984
Field Events				
High jump	6 ft 7 in.	Louise Ritter	Rome, Italy	Sept. 1, 1983
Long jump	24 ft. 5 1/4 in.	Jackie Joyner-Kersee	Indianapolis	August 12, 1987
Triple jump	45 ft. 5 1/4 in.	Sheila Hudson	San Jose	June 26, 1987
Shot-put	62 ft. 10 3/4 in.	Ramona Pagel	London	July 10, 1987
Discus throw	216 ft 10 in.	Carol Cady	San Jose, Calif.	May 31, 1986
Javelin throw	227 ft 5 in.	Kate Schmidt	Furth, W. Ger.	Sept. 10, 1977
Heptathlon	7,161 pts	Jackie Joyner	Moscow	July 6–7, 1986

HISTORY OF THE RECORD FOR THE MILE RUN

Time	Athlete	Country	Year	Location
4:36.5	Richard Webster	England	1865	England
4:29.0	William Chinnery	England	1868	England
4:28.8	Walter Gibbs	England	1868	England
4:26.0	Walter Slade	England	1874	England
4:24.5	Walter Slade	England	1875	London

4:23.2	Walter George	England	1880	London
4:21.4	Walter George	England	1882	London
4:18.4	Walter George	England	1884	Birmingham, England
4:18.2	Fred Bacon	Scotland	1894	Edinburgh, Scotland
4:17.0	Fred Bacon	Scotland	1895	London
4:15.6	Thomas Conneff	United States	1895	Travers Island, N.Y.
4:15.4	John Paul Jones	United States	1911	Cambridge, Mass.
4:14.4	John Paul Jones	United States	1913	Cambridge, Mass.
4:12.6	Norman Taber	United States	1915	Cambridge, Mass.
4:10.4	Paavo Nurmi	Finland	1923	Stockholm
4:09.2	Jules Ladoumegue	France	1931	Paris
4:07.6	Jack Lovelock	New Zealand	1933	Princeton, N.J.
4:06.8	Glenn Cunningham	United States	1934	Princeton, N.J.
4:06.4	Sydney Wooderson	England	1937	London
4:06.2	Gundar Hägg	Sweden	1942	Göteborg, Sweden
4:06.2	Arne Andersson	Sweden	1942	Stockholm
4:04.6	Gunder Hägg	Sweden	1942	Stockholm
4:02.6	Arne Andersson	Sweden	1943	Göteborg, Sweden
4:01.6	Arne Andersson	Sweden	1944	Malmö, Sweden
4:01.4	Gunder Hägg	Sweden	1945	Malmö, Sweden
3:59.4	Roger Bannister	England	1954	Oxford, England
3:58.0	John Landy	Australia	1954	Turku, Finland
3:57.2	Derek Ibbotson	England	1957	London
3:54.5	Herb Elliott	Australia	1958	Dublin
3:54.4	Peter Snell	New Zealand	1962	Wanganui, N.Z.
3:54.1	Peter Snell	New Zealand	1964	Auckland, N.Z.
3:53.6	Michel Jazy	France	1965	Rennes, France
3:51.3	Jim Ryun	United States	1966	Berkeley, Calif.
3:51.1	Jim Ryun	United States	1967	Bakersfield, Calif.
3:51.0	Filbert Bayi	Tanzania	1975	Kingston, Jamaica
3:49.4	John Walker	New Zealand	1975	Göteborg, Sweden
3:49.0	Sebastian Coe	England	1979	Oslo
3:48.8	Steve Ovett	England	1980	Oslo
3:48.53	Sebastian Coe	England	1981	Zurich, Switzerland
3:48.40	Steve Ovett	England	1981	Koblenz, W. Ger.
3:47.33	Sebastian Coe	England	1981	Brussels
3:46.31	Steve Cram	England	1985	Oslo

TOP TEN WORLD'S FASTEST INDOOR MILES

Time	Athlete	Country	Date	Location
3:49.78	Eamonn Coghlan	Ireland	Feb. 27, 1983	East Rutherford, N.J.
3:50.6	Eamonn Coghlan	Ireland	Feb. 20, 1981	San Diego
3:51.2	Ray Flynn[1]	Ireland	Feb. 27, 1983	East Rutherford, N.J.
3:51.8	Steve Scott[1]	United States	Feb. 20, 1981	San Diego
3:52.28	Steve Scott[2]	United States	Feb. 27, 1983	East Rutherford, N.J.
3:52:30	Frank O'Mara	Ireland	Feb. , 1986	New York
3:52.37	Eamonn Coughlan	Ireland	Feb. 9, 1985	East Rutherford, N.J.
3:52.40	Sydney Maree	United States	Feb. 9, 1985	East Rutherford, N.J.
3:52.56	Jose Abascal[3]	Spain	Feb. 27, 1983	East Rutherford, N.J.
3:52.6	Eamonn Coghlan	Ireland	Feb. 16, 1979	San Diego
3:52.8	John Walker[2]	New Zealand	Feb. 20, 1981	San Diego

1. Finished second. 2. Finished third. 3. Finished fourth. 4. Finished fifth.

TOP TEN WORLD'S FASTEST OUTDOOR MILES

Time	Athlete	Country	Date	Location
3:46.31	Steve Cram	England	July 27, 1985	Oslo
3:47.33	Sebastian Coe	England	Aug. 28, 1981	Brussels
3:47.69	Steve Scott	United States	July 7, 1982	Oslo
3:47.79	Jose Gonzalez	Spain	July 27, 1985	Oslo
3:48.40	Steve Ovett	England	Aug. 26, 1981	Koblenz, W. Ger.
3:48.53	Sebastian Coe	England	Aug. 19, 1981	Zurich
3:48.53	Steve Scott	United States	June 26, 1982	Oslo
3:48.8	Steve Ovett	England	July 1, 1980	Oslo
3:48.83	Sydney Maree	United States	Sept. 9, 1981	Rieti, Italy
3:48.85	Sydney Maree[1]	United States	June 26, 1982	Oslo

1. Finished second. NOTE: Professional marks not included.

TOP TEN POLE VAULT DISTANCES

(Some of early dates are the winning heights of A.A.U. champion for that year, used to show progression from one foot level to the next. Figures from A.A.U. records and *Track & Field News*.)

Fiberglas Poles

1987	Sergey Bubka	19 ft, 9 1/4"
1986	Sergey Bubka	19 ft 8 1/2 in.
1985	Sergey Bubka	19 ft 8 1/4 in.
1984	Sergey Bubka	19 ft 5 3/4 in.
1984	Thierry Vigneron	19 ft 4 3/4 in.
1984	Sergey Bubka	19 ft 4 1/4 in.
1984	Sergey Bubka	19 ft 3 1/2 in.
1984	Sergey Bubka	19 ft 2 1/4 in.
1984	Sergey Bubka	19 ft 1 1/2 in.
1983	Thierry Vigneron	19 ft 1 1/2 in.

THE ATHLETICS CONGRESS NATIONAL CHAMPIONSHIPS INDOOR

(Madison Square Garden, New York, Feb. 27, 1987)

Men's Events

(Running events in meters)

55 m—Lee McRae, Pittsburgh	0:06.14
400 m—Antonio McKay, Atlanta	0:47.00
500 m—Ian Morris, Trinidad	1:01.55
800 m—Stanley Redwine, Athletics West	1:48.13
Mile—Eamonn Coughlan, New York	3:59.25
3000 m—Doug Padilla, Athletics West	7:51.03
55m Hurdles—Greg Foster, World Clas A.C.	0:06.99
5000-m walk—Tim Lewis, Reebok-Eastside	19:30.70
Mile relay—Atlantic Coast Club	3:20.04
High jump—Igor Paklin, U.S.S.R.	7 ft 7 3/4 in.
Pole vault—Earl Bell, Pacific Coast Club	18 ft 9 1/4 in.
Long jump—Brian Cooper, McNeese State	26 ft 11 1/4 in.
Triple jump—Michael Conley, Tyson International	58 ft 3 1/4 in.
Shot-put—Ulf Timmermann, East Germany	70 ft 11 3/4 in.
35-pound weight throw—Lance Deal, New York A.C.	74 ft 5 in.
Team—New York Athletic Club	27 points
Outstanding athlete—Mike Conley, Tyson International	

Women's Events

(Running events in meters)

55 m—Anelia Nuneva, Bulgaria	0:06.64
200 m—Grace Jackson, Atoms Track Club	0:23.51
400 m—Diane Dixon, Atoms Track Club	0:52.20
800 m—Christine Wachtel, East Germany	2:03.51
Mile—Donna Melinte, Romania	4:30.29
3000 m—Matricica Puica, Romania	8:43.49
55-m hurdles—Cornelia Oschkenat, East Germany	0:07.37
3000-m walk—Maryanne Torrellas, Abraxas T.C.	13:05.41
Mile relay—Atoms Track Club	3:41.54
High jump—Tamara Bykova, Soviet Union	6 ft 3 1/2 in.
Long jump—Heike Drechsler, East Germany	24 ft 0 1/4 in.
Shot-put—Ilona Briesenick, East Germany	66 ft 4 1/2 in.
Team—Atom Track Club	15 points
Outstanding athlete—Heike Drechsler, East Germany	

THE ATHLETICS CONGRESS NATIONAL CHAMPIONSHIPS OUTDOOR—1987

(San Jose, Calif., June 23-27, 1987)

Men's Events

(Running events in meters)

100 m—Mark Witherspoon, Santa Monica T.C.	0:10.04
200 m—Carl Lewis, Santa Monica T.C.	0:20.12
400 m—Harry Reynolds, Ohio State	0:44.46
800 m—Johnny Gray, Santa Monica T.C.	1:45.15
1500 m—Jim Spivey, Athletics West	3:43.66
3000m steeplechase—Henry Marsh, Athletics West	8:20.26
5000m—Sydney Maree, Puma Track Club	13:51.45
10,000m—Gerard Donakowski, Athletics West	28:25.10
110 m hurdles—Greg Foster, World Class A.C.	0:13.29
400 m hurdles—Edwin Moses, Team Adidas	0:47.99
20 k walk—Tim Lewis, Reebok	1:24.12
High jump—Jerome Carter, unattached	7 ft 7 in.
Pole vault—Joe Dial, Athletics West	19 ft 0 1/4 in.
Long jump—Carl Lewis, Santa Monica T.C.	28 ft 4 1/2 in.
Triple jump—Mike Conley, Tyson International	58 ft 7 1/2 in.
Shot-put—John Brenner, Mazda T.C.	69 ft 9 in.
Discus—John Powell, Mazda T.C.	217 ft 3 in.
Hammer throw—Jud Logan, New York Atletic Club	259 ft 4 in.
Javelin throw—Duncan Atwood, unattached	271 ft 5 in.
Decathlon—Tim Bright, Athletics West	8.340 pointts
Team—Athletics West	127 points

Women's Events

(Running Events in meters)

100 m—Diane Williams, Puma T.C.	0:10.90
200 m—Pam Marshall, Mazda Track Club	0:21.06
400 m—Lillie Leatherwood-King, Reebok	0:49.95
800 m—Essie Washington, Santa Monica T.C.	1:59.07
1500 m—Regina Jacobs, Los Angeles T.C.	4:03.70
3000 m—Mary Knisely, Team New Balance	8:57.60
5000 m—Nan Davis, Athletics West	15:57.46
10,000 m—Lynn Jennings, Athletics West	32:19.15
100-m hurdles—LaVonna Martin, Coast Athletics	0:12.80
400-m hurdles—Judi Brown King, Athletics West	0:54.45
10,000-m walk—Maryanne Torrellas, Reebok	47:23.80
High jump—Coleen Sommer, Mazda Track Club	6 ft 5 in.
Long jump—Jackie Joyner-Kersee, World Class AC	23 ft 4 1/4 in.
Triple jump—Sheila Hudson, Team Adidas	45 ft 5 1/4 in.
Shot-put—Ramona Pagel, Mazda T.C.	62 ft 3 in.
Discus—Connie Price, Coast Athletics	212 ft 5 in.
Javelin throw—Karin Smith, Coast Athletics	203 ft 8 in.
Heptathlon—Jackie Joyner Kersee, World Class AC	6,979 points
Team—Mazda Track Club	79 points

N.C.A.A. CHAMPIONSHIPS—1987

INDOOR

(Oklahoma City, Okla., March 13-14, 1987)

Men's Events

55 m—Lee McRae, Pittsburgh	0:06.13
55 m hurdles—Keith Tally, Alabama	0:07.13
500 m—Roddie Haley, Arkansas	0:59.89
1000 m—Robin Van Helden, LSU	2:20.51
3000 m—Joe Falcon, Arkansas	7:56.79
Mile—Michael Stahr, Georgetown	4:02.33
1600-m relay—Southern Methodist	3:07.63
3200-m relay—Arkansas	7:18.67
High jump—James Lott, Texas	7 ft 6 in.
Long jump—Andre Ester, NE Louisiana	26 ft 8 1/4 in.
Triple jump—Frank Rutherford, Houston	56 ft 1 in.
Pole vault—Doug Fraley, Fresno St.	18 ft 2 3/4 in.
Shot-put—Lars Nilsen, Southern Methodist	66 ft 5 in.
35-pound weight throw—Fred Schumacher, San Jose	66 ft 10 in.
Team—Arkansas	39 points
Southern Methodist	31 points
Division II champion—St. Augustine, Raleigh, N.C.	
Division III champion—Wisconsin-LaCrosse	

Women's Events

55 m—Gwen Torrence, Georgia	0:06.56
55 m hurdles—LaVonna Martin, Tennessee	0:07.57
500 m—Linetta Wilson, Nebraska	1:08.89
1000 m—Trena Hull, Nevada-Las Vegas	2:41.08
3000 m—Vicki Huber, Villanova	9:06.45
Mile—Suzy Favor, Wisconsin	4:41.68
1600 m relay—LSU	3:35.49
3200 m relay—Villanova	8:24.72
High jump—Lisa Bernhagen, Stanford	6 ft 3 1/4 in.
Long jump—Sheila Echols, LSU	21 ft 6 in.
Triple jump—Yvette Bates, USC	45 ft 3 in.
Shot-put—Pam Dukes, Stanford	57 ft 1 in.
Team—Louisiana State	49 points
Tennessee	30 points
Division II champion—St. Augustine, Raleigh, N.C.	
Division III champion—Massachusetts-Boston	

OUTDOOR

(Baton Rouge, La., June 3-6, 1987)

Men's Events

100 m—Raymond Stewart, Texas Christian	0:10.14
200 m—Floyd Heard, Texas	0:20.03
400 m—Harry Reynolds, Ohio State	0:44.12
800 m—Tracy Baskin, Seton Hall	1:46.58
1500 m—Abdi Bile, George Mason	3:35.79
3000 m-steeplechase—Dan Nelson, Oregon	8:35.37
5000 m—Dean Crowe, Boston U.	13:43.40
10,000 m—Joe Falcon, Arkansas	29:10.66
110-m hurdles—Eric Reid, LSU	0:13.51
400-m hurdles—Kevin Ypoung, UCLA	0:48.90
High jump—Tom Smith, Illinois St.	7 ft 5 in.
Triple jump—Frank Rutherford, Houston	56 ft 1 in.
Discus—Clifford Felkins, Abilene Christian	200 ft 1 in.
Shot-put—Gary Frank, Mississippi St.	65 ft 3 in.
Javelin—Dag Wennlund, Texas-Austin	252 ft 10 in.
Hammer throw—Stefan Jonsson, Washington State	224 ft 8 in.
Team—UCLA	81 points
Texas	28 points

Women's Events

100 m—Gwen Torrence, Georgia	0:11.25
200 m—Gwen Torrence, Georgia	0:22.37
400 m—Lillie Leatherwood-King, Alabama	0:50.90
800 m—Julie Jenkins, Brigham Young	2:02.57
1500 m—Suzy Favor, Wisconsin	4:09.85
3000 m—Vicki Huber, Villanova	8:54.41
5000 m—Annie Schweitzer, Texas	15:46.00
100-m hurdles—Lavona Martin, Tennessee	0:13.05
400-m hurdles—Linetta Wilson, Nebraska	0:55.63
1600-m relay—USC	3:28.93
High jump—Mazel Thomas, Abilene Christian	6 ft 2 in.
Triple jump—Sheila Hudson, California	45 ft 2 in.
Long jump—Sheila Echols, LSU	22 ft 9 3/4 in.
Shot-put—Regina Cavanaugh, Rice	56 ft 10 3/4 in.
Team—Louisiana State	62 points
Alabama	53 points

UNITED STATES CROSS COUNTRY CHAMPIONSHIPS—1986

(San Francisco, Calif., November 29, 1986)

Men (10,350 meters)

1. Pat Porter, Athletics West	30:36
2. Steve Jones, Reebok	30:46
3. Keith Hanson, unattached	30:47
4. Richard O'Flynn, New Balance T.C.	30:55
5. Art Boileau, Oregon T.C.	30:59
6. Chris Fox, Athletics West	31:00
7. Paul Donovan, Reebok	31:02
8. Marcus O'Sullivan, New Balance T.C.	31:06
9. Thom Hunt, Team Nike	31:09
10. John Treacy, New Balance T.C.	31:11
Team—Athletics West	

Women (5,175 meters)

1. Lesley Welch, Puma T. C.	16:51
2. Suzanne Girard-Eberle, unattached	17:09
3. Lynn Jennings, Athletics West	17:17
4. Leslie Seymour, Club Sota	17:18
5. Sabrina Dornhoefer, Athletics West	17:22
6. Sylvia Mosqueda, East L.A. T.C.	17:23
7. Margaret Thomas, Athletics West	17:25
8. Caroline Mullen, Western Michigan	17:33
9. Sue Addison, Reebok	17:42
10. Kathy Pfeifer, Reebok	17:45
Team—Athletics West	

POWERBOAT RACING

WORLD CUP OFFSHORE CHAMPIONSHIPS—1986

(November 9, 1986, Key West, Fla.)

Superboat Class—Al Copeland, Sr.
Open Class—Bob Kaiser, Grosse Point, Mich.
Modified Class—John D'Elia, Greenwich, Conn.
Pro Stock—Nick Cutro, Lake George, N.Y.
Stock A World Cup—Bill Erickson, Minnetonka, Minn.
Stock B World Cup—Ken Kalibat, Island Park, N.Y.

STANDARD MEASUREMENTS IN SPORTS

BASEBALL

Home plate to pitcher's box: 60 feet 6 inches.
Plate to second base: 127 feet 3 3/8 inches.
Distance from base to base (home plate included): 90 feet.
Size of bases: 15 inches by 15 inches.
Pitcher's plate: 24 inches by 6 inches.
Batter's box: 4 feet by 6 feet.
Home plate: 17 inches by 12 inches by 12 inches, cut to a point at rear.
Home plate to backstop: Not less than 60 feet (recommended).
Weight of ball: Not less than 5 ounces nor more than 5 1/4 ounces.
Circumference of ball: Not less than 9 inches nor more than 9 1/4 inches.
Bat: Must be round, not over 2 3/4 inches in diameter at thickest part, nor more than 42 inches in length, and of solid wood in one piece or laminated wood.

BASKETBALL

(National Collegiate A.A. Men's Rules)

Playing court: College: 94 feet long by 50 feet wide (ideal dimensions). High School: 84 feet long by 50 feet wide (ideal inside dimensions).
Baskets: Rings 18 inches in inside diameter, with white cord 12-mesh nets, 15 to 18 inches in length. Each ring is made of metal, is not more than 5/8 of an inch in diameter, and is bright orange in color.
Height of basket: 10 feet (upper edge).
Weight of ball: Not less than 20 ounces nor more than 22.
Circumference of ball: No greater than 30 inches and not less than 29 1/2.
Free-throw line: 15 feet from the face of the backboard, 2 inches wide.

BOWLING

Lane dimensions: Overall length 62 feet 10 3/16 inches, measuring from foul line to pit (not including tail plank), with 1/2 inch tolerance permitted. Foul line to center of No. 1 pinspot 60 feet, with 1/2 inch tolerance permitted. Lane width, 41 1/2 inches with a tolerance of 1/2 inch permitted. Approach, not less than 15 feet. Gutters, 9 5/16 inches wide with 3/16 plus or 5/16 minus tolerances permitted.
Ball: Circumference, not more than 27 inches. Weight, 16 pounds maximum.

BOXING

Ring: Professional matches take place in an area not less than 18 nor more than 24 feet square including apron. It is enclosed by four covered ropes, each not less than one inch in diameter. The floor has a 2-inch padding of Ensolite (or equivalent) underneath ring cover that extends at least 6 inches beyond the roped area in the case of elevated rings. For U.S.A./A.B.F. or amateur boxing, not less than 16 nor more than 20 feet square within the ropes. The floor must extend beyond the ring ropes not less than 2 feet. The ring posts shall be connected to the three ring ropes with the extension not shorter than 18 inches and must be properly padded.
Gloves: In professional fights, not less than 8-ounce gloves generally are used. U.S.A./A.B.F., 10 ounces for 106 pounds through 156 pounds; 12-ounce for 165 pounds through +201 pounds; for international competition, 8 ounces for lighter classes, 10 ounces for heavier divisions.
Headguards: Mandatory in amateur boxing.

FOOTBALL

(N.C.A.A.)

Length of field: 120 yards. (including 10 yards of end zone at each end).
Width of field: 53 1/3 yards (160 feet).
Height of goal posts: At least 30 feet.
Height of crossbar: 10 feet.
Width of goal posts (above crossbar): 23 feet 4 inches, inside to inside, and not more than 24 feet, outside to outside.
Length of ball: 10 7/8 to 11 7/16 inches (long axis).
Circumference of ball: 20 3/4 to 21 1/4 inches (middle); 27 3/4 to 28 1/2 inches (long axis).

GOLF

The ball, specifications: Broadened to require that the ball be designed to perform as if it were spherically symmetrical. The weight of the ball shall not be greater than 1.620 ounces avoirdupois, and the size shall not be less than 1.680 inches in diameter.
Velocity of ball: Not greater than 250 feet per second when tested on U.S.G.A. apparatus, with 2 percent tolerance.
Hole: 4 1/4 inches in diameter and at least 4 inches deep.
Clubs: 14 is the maximum number permitted.
Overall distance standard: A brand of ball shall not exceed a distance of 280 yards plus 6% when tested on USGA apparatus under specified conditions, on an outdoor range at USGA Headquarters.

HOCKEY

Size of rink: 200 feet long by 85 feet wide surrounded by a wooden wall not less than 40 inches and not more than 48 inches above level of ice.
Size of goal: 6 feet wide by 4 feet in height.
Puck: 1 inch thick and 3 inches in diameter, made of vulcanized rubber; weight 5 1/2 to 6 ounces.
Length of stick: Not more than 60 inches from heel to end of shaft nor 12 1/2 inches from heel to end of blade. Blade should not be more than 3 inches in width but not less than 2 inches, except goal keeper's stick, which shall not exceed 3 1/2 inches in width except at the heel, where it must not exceed 4 1/2 inches.

TENNIS

Size of court: Rectangle 78 feet long and 27 feet wide (singles); 78 feet long and 36 feet wide (doubles).
Height of net: 3 feet in center, gradually rising to reach 3-foot 6-inch posts at a point 3 feet outside each side of court.
Ball: Shall be more than 2 1/2 inches and less than 2 5/8 inches in diameter and weigh more than 2 ounces and less than 2 1/16 ounces.
Service line: 21 feet from net.

COLLEGE SOCCER

(1986 N.C.A.A. Division I Playoffs)

MEN

Quarterfinals

Harvard 2, Hartwick 0
Duke 2, Loyola (Md.) 1
Akron 2, Penn State 1 (OT)
Fresno State 1, Southern Methodist 0

Semifinals

Duke 3, Harvard 1
Akron 1, Fresno State 0

Championship

(at Tacoma, Wash., Dec. 13, 1986)

Duke 1, Akron 0

WOMEN

Quarterfinals

Colorado College 1, California 0
Massachusetts 1, Connecticut 0
North Carolina 8, California–Santa Barbara 0
George Mason 2, North Carolina State 1 (2 OT)

Semifinals

North Carolina 3, George Mason 2
Colorado College 1, Massachusetts 0

Championship

(At Fairfax, Va., Nov. 23, 1986)

North Carolina 2, Colorado College 0

TENNIS

Lawn tennis is a comparatively modern modification of the ancient game of court tennis. Major Walter Clopton Wingfield thought that something like court tennis might be played outdoors on lawns, and in December, 1873, at Nantclwyd, Wales, he introduced his new game under the name of *Sphairistike* at a lawn party. The game was a success and spread rapidly, but the name was a total failure and almost immediately disappeared when all the players and spectators began to refer to the new game as "lawn tennis." In the early part of 1874, a young lady named Mary Ewing Outerbridge returned from Bermuda to New York, bringing with her the implements and necessary equipment of the new game, which she had obtained from a British Army supply store in Bermuda. Miss Outerbridge and friends played the first game of lawn tennis in the United States on the grounds of the Staten Island Cricket and Baseball Club in the spring of 1874.

For a few years, the new game went along in haphazard fashion until about 1880, when standard measurements for the court and standard equipment within definite limits became the rule. In 1881, the U.S. Lawn Tennis Association (whose name was changed in 1975 to U.S. Tennis Association) was formed and conducted the first national championship at Newport, R.I. The international matches for the Davis Cup began with a series between the British and United States players on the courts of the Longwood Cricket Club, Chestnut Hill, Mass., in 1900, with the home players winning.

Professional tennis, which got its start in 1926 when the French star Suzanne Lenglen was paid $50,000 for a tour, received full recognition in 1968. Staid old Wimbledon, the London home of what are considered the world championships, let the pros compete. This decision ended a long controversy over open tennis and changed the format of the competition. The United States championships were also opened to the pros and the site of the event, long held at Forest Hills, N.Y., was shifted to the National Tennis Center in Flushing Meadows, N.Y., in 1978. Pro tours for men and women became worldwide in play that continued throughout the year.

DAVIS CUP CHAMPIONSHIPS

No matches in 1901, 1910, 1915–18, and 1940–45.

1900	United States 3, British Isles 0
1902	United States 3, British Isles 2
1903	British Isles 4, United States 1
1904	British Isles 5, Belgium 0
1905	British Isles 5, United States 0
1906	British Isles 5, United States 0
1907	Australasia 3, British Isles 2
1908	Australasia 3, United States 2
1909	Australasia 5, United States 0
1911	Australasia 5, United States 0
1912	British Isles 3, Australasia 2
1913	United States 3, British Isles 2
1914	Australasia 3, United States 2
1919	Australasia 4, British Isles 1
1920	United States 5, Australasia 0
1921	United States 5, Japan 0
1922	United States 4, Australasia 1
1923	United States 4, Australasia 1
1924	United States 5, Australasia 0
1925	United States 5, France 0
1926	United States 4, France 1
1927	France 3, United States 2
1928	France 4, United States 1
1929	France 3, United States 2
1930	France 4, United States 1
1931	France 3, Great Britain 2
1932	France 3, United States 2
1933	Great Britain 3, France 2
1934	Great Britain 4, United States 1
1935	Great Britain 5, United States 0
1936	Great Britain 3, Australia 2
1937	United States 4, Great Britain 1
1938	United States 3, Australia 2
1939	Australia 3, United States 2
1946	United States 5, Australia 0
1947	United States 4, Australia 1
1948	United States 5, Australia 0
1949	United States 4, Australia 1
1950	Australia 4, United States 1
1951	Australia 3, United States 2
1952	Australia 4, United States 1
1953	Australia 3, United States 2
1954	United States 3, Australia 2
1955	Australia 5, United States 0
1956	Australia 5, United States 0
1957	Australia 3, United States 2
1958	United States 3, Australia 2
1959	Australia 3, United States 2
1960	Australia 4, Italy 1
1961	Australia 5, Italy 0
1962	Australia 5, Mexico 0
1963	United States 3, Australia 2
1964	Australia 3, United States 2
1965	Australia 4, Spain 1
1966	Australia 4, India 1
1967	Australia 4, Spain 1
1968	United States 4, Australia 1
1969	United States 5, Romania 0
1970	United States 5, West Germany 0
1971	United States 3, Romania 2
1972	United States 3, Romania 2
1973	Australia 5, United States 0
1974	South Africa (Default by India)
1975	Sweden 3, Czechoslovakia 2
1976	Italy 4, Chile 1
1977	Australia 3, Italy 1
1978	United States 4, Britain 1
1979	United States 5, Italy 0
1980	Czechoslovakia 3, Italy 2
1981	United States 3, Argentina 1
1982	United States 3, France 0
1983	Australia 3, Sweden 2
1984	Sweden 4, United States 1
1985	Sweden 3, West Germany 2
1986	Australia 3, Sweden 2

FEDERATION CUP CHAMPIONSHIPS

World team competition for women conducted by International Lawn Tennis Federation.

1963	United States 2, Australia 1
1964	Australia 2, United States 1
1965	Australia 2, United States 1
1966	United States 3, West Germany 0
1967	United States 2, Britain 0
1968	Australia 3, Netherlands 0
1969	United States 2, Australia 1
1970	Australia 3, West Germany 0
1971	Australia 3, Britain 0
1972	South Africa 2, Britain 1
1973	Australia 3, South Africa 0
1974	Australia 2, United States 1
1975	Czechoslovakia 3, Australia 0
1976	United States 2, Australia 1
1977	United States 2, Australia 1
1978	United States 2, Australia 1
1979	United States 3, Australia 0
1980	United States 3, Australia 0
1981	United States 3, Britain 0
1982	United States 3, West Germany 0
1983	Czechoslovakia 2, West Germany 1
1984	Czechoslovakia 2, Australia 1
1985	Czechoslovakia 2, United States 1
1986	United States 3, Czechoslovakia 0
1987	West Germany 2, United States 1

U.S. CHAMPIONS

Singles—Men

NATIONAL

Year	Champion
1881–87	Richard D. Sears
1888–89	Henry Slocum, Jr.
1890–92	Oliver S. Campbell
1893–94	Robert D. Wrenn
1895	Fred H. Hovey
1896–97	Robert D. Wrenn
1898–1900	Malcolm Whitman
1901–02	William A. Larned
1903	Hugh L. Doherty
1904	Holcombe Ward
1905	Beals C. Wright
1906	William J. Clothier
1907–11	William A. Larned
1912–13	Maurice McLoughlin
1914	R. N. Williams II
1915	William Johnston
1916	R. N. William II
1917–18	R. Lindley Murray[2]
1919	William Johnston
1920–25	Bill Tilden
1926–27	Jean Rene Lacoste
1928	Henri Cochet
1929	Bill Tilden
1930	John H. Doeg
1931–32	Ellsworth Vines
1933–34	Fred J. Perry
1935	Wilmer L. Allison
1936	Fred J. Perry
1937–38	Don Budge
1939	Robert L. Riggs
1940	Donald McNeill
1941	Robert L. Riggs
1942	Fred Schroeder
1943	Joseph Hunt
1944–45	Frank Parker
1946–47	Jack Kramer
1948–49	Richard Gonzales
1950	Arthur Larsen
1951–52	Frank Sedgman
1953	Tony Trabert
1954	Vic Seixas
1955	Tony Trabert
1956	Ken Rosewall
1957	Mal Anderson
1958	Ashley Cooper
1959–60	Neale Fraser
1961	Roy Emerson
1962	Rod Laver
1963	Rafael Osuna
1964	Roy Emerson
1965	Manuel Santana
1966	Fred Stolle
1967	John Newcombe
1968	Arthur Ashe
1969	Rod Laver

OPEN

Year	Champion
1968	Arthur Ashe
1969	Rod Laver
1970	Ken Rosewall
1971	Stan Smith
1972	Ilie Nastase
1973	John Newcombe
1974	Jimmy Connors
1975	Manuel Orantes
1976	Jimmy Connors
1977	Guillermo Vilas
1978	Jimmy Connors
1979	John McEnroe
1980–81	John McEnroe
1982	Jimmy Connors
1983	Jimmy Connors
1984	John McEnroe
1985–87	Ivan Lendl

Singles—Women

NATIONAL

Year	Champion
1887	Ellen F. Hansel
1888–89	Bertha Townsend
1890	Ellen C. Roosevelt
1891–92	Mabel E. Cahill
1893	Aline M. Terry
1894	Helen R. Helwig
1895	Juliette P. Atkinson
1896	Elisabeth H. Moore
1897–98	Juliette P. Atkinson
1899	Marion Jones
1900	Myrtle McAteer
1901	Elisabeth H. Moore
1902	Marion Jones
1903	Elisabeth H. Moore
1904	May Sutton
1905	Elisabeth H. Moore
1906	Helen Homans
1907	Evelyn Sears
1908	Maud Bargar-Wallach
1909–11	Hazel V. Hotchkiss
1912–14	Mary K. Browne
1915–18	Molla Bjurstedt
1919	Hazel Hotchkiss Wightman
1920–22	Molla Bjurstedt Mallory
1923–25	Helen N. Wills
1926	Molla B. Mallory
1927–29	Helen N. Wills
1930	Betty Nuthall
1931	Helen Wills Moody
1932–35	Helen Jacobs
1936	Alice Marble
1937	Anita Lizana
1938–40	Alice Marble
1941	Sarah Palfrey Cooke
1942–44	Pauline Betz
1945	Sarah Cooke
1946	Pauline Betz
1947	Louise Brough
1948–50	Margaret Osborne duPont
1951–53	Maureen Connolly
1954–55	Doris Hart
1956	Shirley Fry
1957–58	Althea Gibson
1959	Maria Bueno
1960–61	Darlene Hard
1962	Margaret Smith
1963–64	Maria Bueno
1965	Margaret Smith
1966	Maria Bueno
1967	Billie Jean King
1968–69	Margaret Smith Court[3]

OPEN

Year	Champion
1968	Virginia Wade
1969–70	Margaret Court
1971–72	Billie Jean King
1973	Margaret Court
1974	Billie Jean King
1975–78	Chris Evert
1979	Tracy Austin
1980	Chris Evert-Lloyd
1981	Tracy Austin
1982	Chris Evert-Lloyd
1983–84	Martina Navratilova
1985	Hana Mandlikova
1986–87	Martina Navratilova

Doubles—Men

NATIONAL

Year	Champions
1920	Bill Johnston–C. J. Griffin
1921–22	Bill Tilden–Vincent Richards
1923	Bill Tilden–B. I. C. Norton
1924	H. O. Kinsey—R. G. Kinsey
1925–26	Vincent Richards—R. N. Williams II
1927	Bill Tilden—Frank Hunter
1928	G. M. Lott, Jr.-V. Hennessy
1929–30	G. M. Lott, Jr.-J. H. Doeg
1931	W. L. Allison–John Van Ryn
1932	E. H. Vines, Jr.–Keith Gledh
1933–34	G. M. Lott, Jr.–L. R. Stoefen
1935	W. L. Allison–John Van Ryn
1936	Don Budge—Gene Mako
1937	G. von Cramm–H. Henkel
1938	Don Budge–Gene Mako
1939	A. K. Quist–J. E. Bromwich
1940–41	Jack Kramer–F. R. Schroeder
1942	Gardnar Mulloy–Bill Talbert
1943	Jack Kramer—Frank Parker
1944	Don McNeill—Bob Falkenburg
1945	Gardnar Mulloy–Bill Talbert
1946	Gardnar Mulloy–Bill Talbert
1947	Jack Kramer–Fred Schroeder
1948	Gardnar Mulloy–Bill Talbert
1949	John Bromwich–William Sidwell
1950	John Bromwich–Frank Sedgman
1951	Frank Sedgman–Ken McGregor
1952	Vic Seixas-Mervyn Rose
1953	Mervyn Rose–Rex Hartwig
1954	Vic Seixas–Tony Trabert
1955	Kosei Kamo–Atsushi Miyagi
1956	Lewis Hoad–Ken Rosewall
1957	Ashley Cooper–Neale Fraser
1958	Ham Richardson–Alex Olmedo
1959–60	Neale Fraser–Roy Emerson
1961	Chuck McKinley–Dennis Ralston
1962	Rafael Osuna–Antonio Palafox
1963–64	Chuck McKinley–Dennis Ralston
1965–66	Fred Stolle–Roy Emerson
1967	John Newcombe–Tony Roche
1968	Stan Smith–Bob Lutz[3]
1969	Richard Crealy–Allan Stone[3]

OPEN

1968	Stan Smith–Bob Lutz
1969	Fred Stolle–Ken Rosewall
1970	Nikki Pilic–Fred Barthes
1971	John Newcombe–Roger Taylor
1972	Cliff Drysdale–Roger Taylor
1973	John Newcombe–Owen Davidson
1974	Bob Lutz–Stan Smith
1975	Jimmy Connors–Ilie Nastase
1976	Marty Riessen–Tom Okker
1977	Frew McMillan–Bob Hewitt
1978	Bob Lutz–Stan Smith
1979	John McEnroe–Peter Fleming
1980	Stan Smith–Bob Lutz
1981	John McEnroe–Peter Fleming
1982	Kevin Curren–Steve Denton
1983	John McEnroe–Peter Fleming
1984	John Fitzgerald–Tomas Smid
1985	Ken Flach–Robert Seguso
1986	Andres Gomez–Slobodan Zivojinovic
1987	Stefan Edberg–Anders Jarryd

1. Challenge round abandoned in 1912. 2. Patriotic Tournament in 1917. 3. With the inaugural of the Open Tournament in 1968, the United States Lawn Tennis Association held a national championship at Longwood, Chestnut Hill, Mass. which barred contract professionals in 1968 and 1969.

Doubles—Women

NATIONAL

1924	G. W. Wightman–Helen Wills
1925	Mary K. Browne–Helen Wills
1926	Elizabeth Ryan–Eleanor Goss
1927	L. A. Godfree–Ermyntrude Harvey
1928	Hazel Hotchkiss Wightman–Helen Wills
1929	Phoebe Watson–L. R. C. Michell
1930	Betty Nuthall–Sarah Palfrey
1931	Betty Nuthall–E. B. Wittingstall
1932	Helen Jacobs–Sarah Palfrey
1933	Betty Nuthall–Freda James
1934	Helen Jacobs–Sarah Palfrey
1935	Helen Jacobs–Sarah Palfrey Fabyan
1936	Marjorie G. Van Ryn–Carolin Babcock
1937–40	Sarah Palfrey Fabyan–Alice Marble
1941	Sarah Palfrey Cooke–Margaret Osborne
1942–47	A. Louise Brough–Margaret Osborne
1948–50	A. Louise Brough–Margaret O. duPont
1951–54	Doris Hart–Shirley Fry
1955–57	A. Louise Brough–Margaret O. duPont
1958–59	Darlene Hard–Jeanne Arth
1960	Darlene Hard–Maria Bueno
1961	Darlene Hard–Lesley Turner
1962	Darlene Hard–Maria Bueno
1963	Margaret Smith–Robyn Ebbern
1964	Karen Hantze Susman–Billie Jean Moffitt
1965	Nancy Richey–Carole Caldwell Graebner
1966	Nancy Richey–Maria Bueno
1967	Billie Jean King–Rosemary Casals
1968	Margaret Court–Maria Bueno[3]
1969	Margaret Court–Virginia Wade[3]

OPEN

1968	Maria Bueno–Margaret Court
1969	Darlene Hard–Francoise Durr
1970	Margaret Court–Judy Dalton
1971	Rosemary Casals–Judy Dalton
1972	Francoise Durr–Betty Stove
1973	Margaret Court–Virginia Wade
1974	Billie Jean King–Rosemary Casals
1975	Margaret Court–Virginia Wade
1976	Linky Boshoff–Ilana Kloss
1977	Martina Navratilova–Betty Stove
1978	Billie Jean King–Martina Navratilova
1979	Betty Stove–Wendy Turnbull
1980	Billie Jean King–Martina Navratilova
1981	Kathy Jordan–Anne Smith
1982	Rosemary Casals–Wendy Turnbull
1983–84	Martina Navratilova–Pam Shriver
1985	Claudia Khode-Kilsch–Helena Sukova
1986–87	Martina Navratilova–Pam Shriver

1. Challenge round abandoned in 1912. 2. Patriotic Tournament in 1917. 3. With the inaugural of the Open Tournament in 1968, the United States Lawn Tennis Association held a national championship at Longwood, Chestnut Hill, Mass. which barred contract professionals in 1968 and 1969.

U.S. INDOOR CHAMPIONS

Singles—Men

1964	Charles McKinley
1965	Erik Lundquist
1966	Charles Pasarell
1967	Charles Pasarell
1968	Cliff Richey
1969	Stan Smith
1970	Ilie Nastase
1971	Clark Graebner
1972	Stan Smith
1973–75	Jimmy Connors
1976	Ilie Nastase
1977	Bjorn Borg
1978–79	Jimmy Connors
1980	John McEnroe
1981	Gene Mayer
1982	Johan Kriek
1983–84	Jimmy Connors
1985	Stefan Edberg
1986	Brad Gilbert
1987	Stefan Edberg

Singles—Women

1964	Mary Ann Eisel
1965	Nancy Richey
1966	Billie Jean King
1967	Billie Jean King
1968	Billie Jean King
1969	Mary Ann Eisel
1970	Mary Ann Curtis
1971	Billie Jean King
1972	Not held
1973	Evonne Goolagong
1974	Billie Jean King
1975	Martina Navratilova
1976	Virginia Wade
1977	Chris Evert
1978	Chris Evert
1979	Evonne Goolagong
1980	Tracy Austin
1981	Martina Navratilova
1982	Barbara Potter
1983	Kim Shaefer
1984	Martina Navratilova
1985	Hana Mandlikova
1986	Martina Navratilova
1987	Helena Sukova

Doubles—Men

1967	Arthur Ashe–Charles Pasarell
1968	Thomas Koch–Tom Okker
1969	Stan Smith–Bob Lutz
1970	Arthur Ashe–Stan Smith
1971	Manuel Orantes–Juan Gisbert
1972	Manuel Orantes–Andres Gimeno
1973	Juan Gisbert–Jurgen Fassbender
1974	Jimmy Connors–Frew McMillan
1975	Jimmy Connors–Ilie Nastase
1976–77	Sherwood Stewart–Fred McNair
1978	Brian Gottfried–Raul Ramirez
1979	Wojtek Fibak–Tom Okker
1980	John McEnroe–Brian Gottfried
1981	Gene Mayer–Sandy Mayer
1982	Kevin Curren–Steve Denton
1983	Peter McNamara–Paul McNamee
1984	Fritz Bushning–Peter Fleming
1985	Pavel Slozil–Tomas Smid
1986	Ken Flach–Robert Seguso
1987	Anders Jarryd-Jonas Svensson

Doubles—Women

1967	Carol Aucamp–Mary Ann Eisel
1968	Rosemary Casals–Billie Jean King
1969	Mary Ann Eisel–Valerie Ziegenfuss

1970	Peaches Bartkowicz–Nancy Richey
1971	Billie Jean King–Rosemary Casals
1972	Not held
1973	Olga Morozova–Marina Kroshina
1974	Not held
1975	Billie Jean King–Rosemary Casals
1976	Rosemary Casals–Francoise Durr
1977	Martina Navratilova–Betty Stove
1978	Kerry Reid–Wendy Turnbull
1979	Billie Jean King–Martina Navratilova
1980	Ann Kiyomora–Candy Reynolds
1981	Martina Navratilova–Pam Shriver
1982	Rosemary Casals–Wendy Turnbull
1983	Billie Jean King–Sharon Walsh
1984–85	Martina Navratilova–Pam Shriver
1986	Kathy Jordan–Elizabeth Smylie
1987	Gigi Fernandez–Lori McNeil

BRITISH (WIMBLEDON) CHAMPIONS

(Amateur from inception in 1877 through 1967)

Singles—Men

1908–09	Arthur Gore
1910–13	A. F. Wilding
1914	N. E. Brookes
1919	G. L. Patterson
1920–21	Bill Tilden
1922	G. L. Patterson
1923	William Johnston
1924	Jean Borotra
1925	Rene Lacoste
1926	Jean Borotra
1927	Henri Cochet
1928	Rene Lacoste
1929	Jean Cochet
1930	Bill Tilden
1931	S. B. Wood
1932	Ellsworth Vines
1933	J. H. Crawford
1934–36	Fred Perry
1937–38	Don Budge
1939	Robert L. Riggs
1946	Yvon Petra
1947	Jack Kramer
1948	R. Falkenburg
1949	Fred Schroeder
1950	Budge Patty
1951	Richard Savitt
1952	Frank Sedgman
1953	Vic Siexas
1954	Jaroslav Drobny
1955	Tony Trabert
1956–57	Lewis Hoad
1958	Ashley Cooper
1959	Alex Olmedo
1960	Neale Fraser
1961–62	Rod Laver
1963	Chuck McKinley
1964–65	Roy Emerson
1966	Manuel Santana
1967	John Newcombe
1968–69	Rod Laver
1970–71	John Newcombe
1972	Stan Smith
1973	Jan Kodes
1974	Jimmy Connors
1975	Arthur Ashe
1976–80	Bjorn Borg
1981	John McEnroe
1982	Jimmy Connors
1983–84	John McEnroe
1985–86	Boris Becker
1987	Pat Cash

Singles—Women

1919–23	Lenglen
1924	Kathleen McKane
1925	Lenglen
1926	Godfree
1927–29	Helen Wills
1930	Helen Wills Moody
1931	Frl. C. Aussen
1932–33	Helen Wills Moody
1934	D. E. Round
1935	Helen Wills Moody
1936	Helen Jacobs
1937	D. E. Round
1938	Helen Wills Moody
1939	Alice Marble
1946	Pauline M. Betz
1947	Margaret Osborne
1948–50	A. Louise Brough
1951	Doris Hart
1952–54	Maureen Connolly
1955	A. Louise Brough
1956	Shirley Fry
1957–58	Althea Gibson
1959–60	Maria Bueno
1961	Angela Mortimer
1962	Karen Susman
1963	Margaret Smith
1964	Maria Bueno
1965	Margaret Smith
1966–67	Billie Jean King
1968	Billie Jean King
1969	Ann Jones
1970	Margaret Court
1971	Evonne Goolagong
1972–73	Billie Jean King
1974	Chris Evert
1975	Billie Jean King
1976	Chris Evert
1977	Virginia Wade
1978–79	Martina Navratilova
1980	Evonne Goolagong Cawley
1981	Chris Evert-Lloyd
1982–87	Martina Navratilova

Doubles—Men

1953	K. Rosewall–L. Hoad
1954	R. Hartwig–M. Rose
1955	R. Hartwig–L. Hoad
1956	L. Hoad–K. Rosewall
1957	Gardnar Mulloy–Budge Patty
1958	Sven Davidson–Ulf Schmidt
1959	Roy Emerson–Neale Fraser
1960	Dennis Ralston–Rafael Osuna
1961	Roy Emerson–Neale Fraser
1962	Fred Stolle–Bob Hewitt
1963	Rafael Osuna–Antonio Palafox
1964	Fred Stolle–Bob Hewitt
1965	John Newcombe–Tony Roche
1966	John Newcombe–Ken Fletcher
1967	Bob Hewitt–Frew McMillan
1968–70	John Newcombe–Tony Roche
1971	Rod Laver–Roy Emerson
1972	Bob Hewitt–Frew McMillan
1973	Jimmy Connors–Ilie Nastase
1974	John Newcombe–Tony Roche
1975	Vitas Gerulaitis–Sandy Mayer
1976	Brian Gottfried–Raul Ramirez
1977	Ross Case–Geoff Masters
1978	Fred McMillan–Bob Hewitt
1979	Peter Fleming–John McEnroe
1980	Peter McNamara–Paul McNamee
1981	John McEnroe–Peter Fleming
1982	Paul McNamee–Peter McNamara
1983–84	John McEnroe–Peter Fleming
1985	Heinz Gunthardt–Balazs Taroczy
1986	Joakim Nystrom–Mats Wilander
1987	Ken Flach–Robert Seguso

Doubles–Women

1956	Althea Gibson–Angela Buxton
1957	Althea Gibson–Darlene Hard
1958	Althea Gibson–Maria Bueno
1959	Darlene Hard–Jeanne Arth
1960	Darlene Hard–Maria Bueno
1961	Karen Hantze–Billie Jean Moffitt
1962	Karen Hantze Susman–Billie Jean Moffitt
1963	Darlene Hard–Maria Bueno
1964	Margaret Smith–Les Turnerley
1965	Billie Jean Moffitt–Maria Bueno
1966	Nancy Richey–Maria Bueno
1967–68	Billie Jean King–Rosemary Casals
1969	Margaret Court–Judy Tegart
1970–71	Billie Jean King–Rosemary Casals
1972	Billie Jean King–Betty Stove
1973	Billie Jean King–Rosemary Casals
1974	Evonne Goolagong–Peggy Michel
1975	Ann Kiyomura–Kazuko Sawamatsu
1976	Chris Evert–Martina Navratilova
1977	Helen Cawley–JoAnne Russell
1978	Wendy Turnbull–Kerry Reid
1979	Billie Jean King–Martina Navratilova
1980	Kathy Jordan–Anne Smith
1981	Martina Navratilova–Pam Shriver
1982–84	Pam Shriver–Martina Navratilova
1985	Kathy Jordan–Elizabeth Smylie
1986	Pam Shriver–Martina Navratilova
1987	Claudia Khode-Kilsch–Helena Sukova

UNITED STATES CHAMPIONS—1987

U.S. Open

(Flushing Meadow, Aug. 31-Sept. 14, 1987)

Men's singles—Final: Ivan Lendl, Czechoslovakia, defeated Mats Wilander, Sweden, 6-7 (7-9), 6-0, 7-6 (7-4), 6-4.

Semifinals—Wilander defeated Stefan Edberg, Sweden, 6-4, 3-6, 6-3, 6-4; Lendl defeated Jimmy Connors, Sanibel Harbour, Fla., 6-4, 6-2, 6-2.

Women's singles—Final: Martina Navratilova, Fort Worth, Texas, defeated Steffi Graf, West Germany, 7-6 (7-4), 6-1.

Semifinals—Navratilova defeated Helena Sukova, Czechoslovakia, 6-2, 6-2; Graf defeated Lori McNeil, Houston, Texas, 4-6, 6-2, 6-4.

Men's doubles—Finals: Stefan Edberg and Anders Jarryd, Sweden, defeated Ken Flach and Robert Seguso, Sebring, Fla., 7-6 (7-1), 6-2, 4-6, 5-7, 7-6 (7-2).

Women's doubles—Finals: Martina Navratilova, Forth Worth Texas and Pam Shriver, Lutherville, Md., defeated Elizabeth Smylie, Australia, and Kathy Jordan, King of Prussia, Pa., 5-7, 6-4, 6-2.

Mixed doubles—Final: Martina Navratilova, Fort Worth, Texas, and Emilio Sanchez, Spain, defeated Betsy Nagelsen, Kapalua, Hawaii and Paul Annacone, Bridgehampton, N.Y., 6-4, 6-7 (6-8), 7-6 (14-12).

U.S. Clay Court

(Indianapolis, Ind., July 13-19, 1987)

Men's singles—Mats Wilander, Sweden, defeated Kent Carlsson, Sweden, 7-5, 6-3.

Men's doubles—Laurie Warder, Australia, and Blaine Wilenborg, Miami Shores, Fla. defeated Joakim Nystrom and Mats Wilander, Sweden, 6-4, 7-5.

International Players Championships

(Key Biscayne, Fla., March 2-8, 1987)

Men's singles—Miloslav Mecir, Czechoslovakia, defeated Ivan Lendl, Czechoslovakia, 7-5, 6-2, 7-5.

Women's singles—Steffi Graff, West Germany, defeated Chris Evert, Boca Raton, Fla., 6-1, 6-2

Men's doubles—Paul Annacone, Bridgehampton, N.Y., and Christo Van Rensburg, South Africa, defeated Ken Flach and Robert Seguso, Prairie Oaks, Fla., 6-2, 6-4, 6-4.

Women's doubles—Martina Navratilova, Forth Worth, Texas, and Pam Shriver, Lutherville, Md. defeated Steffi Graf, West Germany and Gabriela Sabatini, Argentina, 6-4, 6-0.

Mixed doubles—Miiloslav Mecir and Jana Novotna, Czechoslovakia, defeated Christo Van Rensburg and Monica Reinach, South Africa, 6-3, 3-6, 6-3.

Tournament of Champions

(Forest Hills, N.Y., May 4-10, 1987)

Singles final—Andres Gomez, Ecuador, defeated Yannick Noah, France, 6-4, 7-6, 7-6.

Doubles final—Guy Forget and Yannick Noah, France, defeated Peter Fleming, Glen Cove, N.Y., and Gary Donnelly, Scotsdale, Ariz., 4-6, 6-4, 6-1.

U.S. National Indoor

(Memphis, Tenn. Feb. 9-15, 1987)

Singles final—Stefan Edberg, Sweden, defeated Jimmy Connors, Sanibel Island, Fla., 6-3, 2-1, injury default.

Doubles final—Anders Jarryd and Jonas Svensson, Sweden, defeated Sergio Casal and Emilio Sanchez, Spain, 6-4, 6-2.

U.S. Pro Indoor

(Philadelphia, Pa., Feb. 2-8, 1987)

Singles final—Tim Mayotte, Bradenton, Fla., defeated John McEnroe, Cove Neck, N.Y., 3-6, 6-1, 6-3, 6-1.

Doubles final—Sergio Casal and Emilio Sanchez, Spain, defeated Christo Steyn and Danie Visser, South Africa, 3-6, 6-1, 7-6.

U.S. Pro

(Brookline, Mass., July 6-12, 1987)

Singles final—Mats Wilander, Sweden, defeated Kent Carlsson, Sweden, 7-6, 6-1.

Doubles final—Hans Gildemeister, Chile, and Anders Gomez, Ecuador, defeated Mats Wilander and Joakim Nystrom, 7-6, 3-6, 6-1.

OTHER 1987 CHAMPIONS

Wimbledon Open

Men's singles—Pat Cash, Australia, defeated Ivan Lendl, Czechoslovakia, 7-6, 6-2, 7-5.

Women's singles—Martina Navratilova, United States, defeated Steffi Graf, West Germany, 7-5, 6-3.

Men's doubles—Ken Flach and Robert Seguso, United States, defeated Sergio Casal and Emilio Sanchez, Spain, 3-6, 6-7, 7-6, 6-1, 6-4.

Women's doubles—Claudia Khode-Kilsch, West Germany, and Helena Sukova, Czechoslovakia, defeated Betsy Nagelsen, United States, and Elizabeth Smylie, Australia, 7-5, 7-5.

Mixed doubles—Jeremy Bates and Jo Durie, Great Britain, defeated Darren Cahill and Nicole Provis, Australia, 7-6, 6-3.

French Open

Men's singles—Ivan Lendl, Czechoslovakia, defeated Mats Wilander, Sweden, 7-5, 6-2, 3-6, 7-6.

Women's singles—Steffi Graf, West Germany, defeated Martina Navratilova, United States, 6-4, 4-6, 8-6.

Men's doubles—Andres Jarryd, Sweden and Robert Seguso, United States, defeated Guy Forget and Yannick Noah, France, 6-7, 6-7, 6-3, 6-4, 6-2.

Women's doubles—Martina Navratilova and Pam Shriver, United States, defeated Steffi Graf, West Germany and Gabriela Sabatini, Argentina, 6-2, 6-1.

Mixed doubles—Pam Shriver, United States, and Emilio Sanchez, Spain, defeated Lori McNeil and Sherwood Stewart, United States, 6-3, 7-6.

Australian Open

Men's singles—Stefan Edberg, Sweden, defeated Pat Cash, Australia, 6-3, 6-4, 3-6, 5-7, 6-3.

Women's singles—Hana Mandlikova, Czechoslovakia, defeated Martina Navratilova, United States, 7-5, 7-6.

Men's doubles—Stefan Edberg and Anders Jarryd, Sweden, defeated Peter Doonan and Laurie Warder, Australia, 6-4, 6-4, 7-6

Women's doubles—Martina Navratilova and Pam Shriver, United States, defeated Zina Garrison and Lori McNeil, United States, 6-1, 6-0.

Mixed doubles—Zina Garrison and Sherwood Stewart, United States, defeated Andrew Castle and Anne Hobbs, Great Britain, 3-6, 7-6, 6-3.

DAVIS CUP RESULTS—1987

Finals

Australia 3, Sweden 2 (at Melbourne, Australia)

Singles—Pat Cash, Australia, defeated Stefan Edberg, Sweden, 13-11, 13-11, 6-4; Mikael Pernfors, Sweden, defeated Paul McNamee, Australia, 6-3, 6-1, 6-3; Pat Cash, Australia, defeated Mikael Pernfors, Sweden, 2-6, 4-6, 6-3, 6-4, 6-3; Stefan Edberg, Sweden, defeated Paul McNamee, Australia, 10-8, 6-4.

Doubles—Pat Cash and John Fitzgerald, Australia, defeated Stefan Edberg and Anders Jarryd, Sweden, 6-3, 6-4, 4-6, 6-1.

MEN'S FINAL TENNIS EARNINGS—1986

Player and amount: Ivan Lendl, $1,987,537; Boris Becker $1,434, 324; Stefan Edberg, $972,906; Joakim Nystrom, $817,342; Mats Wilander, $643,652; Anders Gomez, $579,121; Yannick Noah, $553,015; Guy Forget, $478,820; Henri Leconte, $437,422; Anders Jarryd, $402,036.

WOMEN'S FINAL EARNINGS—1986

Player and amount: Martina Navratilova, $1,905,841; Chris Evert $833,755; Helena Sukova $695,846; Steffi Graf, $612,118; Pam Shriver, $566,163; Hana Mandlikova $421,145; Claudia Khode-Kilsch, $367,906.

ROWING

Rowing goes back so far in history that there is no possibility of tracing it to any particular aboriginal source. The oldest rowing race still on the calendar is the "Doggett's Coat and Badge" contest among professional watermen of the Thames (England) that began in 1715. The first Oxford-Cambridge race was held at Henley in 1829. Competitive rowing in the United States began with matches between boats rowed by professional oarsmen of the New York water front. They were oarsmen who rowed the small boats that plied as ferries from Manhattan Island to Brooklyn and return, or who rowed salesmen down the harbor to meet ships arriving from Europe. Since the first salesman to meet an incoming ship had some advantage over his rivals, there was keen competition in the bidding for fast boats and the best oarsmen. This gave rise to match races.

Amateur boat clubs sprang up in the United States between 1820 and 1830 and seven students of Yale joined together to purchase a four-oared lap-streak gig in 1843. The first Harvard-Yale race was held Aug. 3, 1852, on Lake Winnepesaukee, N.H. The first time an American college crew went abroad was in 1869 when Harvard challenged Oxford and was defeated on the Thames. There were early college rowing races on Lake Quinsigamond, near Worcester, Mass., and on Saratoga Lake, N.Y., but the Intercollegiate Rowing Association in 1895 settled on the Hudson, at Poughkeepsie, as the setting for the annual "Poughkeepsie Regatta." In 1950 the I.R.A. shifted its classic to Marietta, Ohio, and in 1952 it was moved to Syracuse, N.Y. The National Association of Amateur Oarsmen, organized in 1872, has conducted annual championship regattas since that time.

INTERCOLLEGIATE ROWING ASSOCIATION REGATTA

(Varsity Eight-Oared Shells)

Rowed at 4 miles, Poughkeepsie, N.Y., 1895–97, 1899–1916, 1925–32, 1934–41. Rowed at 3 miles, Saratoga, N.Y., 1898; Poughkeepsie, 1921–24, 1947–49; Syracuse, N.Y., 1952–1963, 1965–67. Rowed at 2,000 meters, Syracuse, N.Y., 1964 and from 1968 on. Rowed at 2 miles, Ithaca, N.Y., 1920; Marietta, Ohio, 1950–51. Suspended 1917–19, 1933, 1942–46.

Year	Time	First	Second
1895	21:25	Columbia	Cornell
1896	19:59	Cornell	Harvard
1897	20:47 4/5	Cornell	Columbia
1898	15:51 1/2	Pennsylvania	Cornell
1899	20:04	Pennsylvania	Wisconsin
1900	19:44 3/5	Pennsylvania	Wisconsin
1901	18:53 1/5	Cornell	Columbia
1902	19:03 3/5	Cornell	Wisconsin
1903	18:57	Cornell	Georgetown
1904	20:22 3/5	Syracuse	Cornell
1905	20:29	Cornell	Syracuse
1906	19:36 4/5	Cornell	Pennsylvania
1907	20:02 2/5	Cornell	Columbia
1908	19:24 1/5	Syracuse	Columbia
1909	19:02	Cornell	Columbia
1910	20:42 1/5	Cornell	Pennsylvania
1911	20:10 4/5	Cornell	Columbia
1912	19:31 2/5	Cornell	Wisconsin
1913	19:28 3/5	Syracuse	Cornell
1914	19:37 4/5	Columbia	Pennsylvania
1915	19:36 3/5	Cornell	Stanford
1916	20:15 2/5	Syracuse	Cornell
1920	11:02 3/5	Syracuse	Cornell
1921	14:07	Navy	California
1922	13:33 3/5	Navy	Washington
1923	14:03 1/5	Washington	Navy
1924	15:02	Washington	Wisconsin
1925	19:24 4/5	Navy	Washington
1926	19:28 3/5	Washington	Navy
1927	20:57	Columbia	Washington
1928	18:35 4/5	California	Columbia
1929	22:58	Columbia	Washington
1930	21:42	Cornell	Syracuse
1931	18:54 1/5	Navy	Cornell
1932	19:55	California	Cornell
1934	19:44	California	Washington
1935	18:52	California	Cornell
1936	19:09 3/5	Washington	California
1937	18:33 3/5	Washington	Navy
1938	18:19	Navy	California
1939	18:12 3/5	California	Washington
1940	22:42	Washington	Cornell
1941	18:53 3/10	Washington	California
1947	13:59 1/5	Navy	Cornell
1948	14:06 2/5	Washington	California
1949	14:42 3/5	California	Washington
1950	8:07.5	Washington	California
1951	7:50.5	Wisconsin	Washington
1952	15:08.1	Navy	Princeton
1953	15:29.6	Navy	Cornell
1954	16:04.4	Navy[1]	Cornell
1955	15:49.9	Cornell	Pennsylvania
1956	16:22.4	Cornell	Navy
1957	15:26.6	Cornell	Pennsylvania
1958	17:12.1	Cornell	Navy
1959	18:01.7	Wisconsin	Syracuse
1960	15:57	California	Navy
1961	16:49.2	California	Cornell
1962	17:02.9	Cornell	Washington
1963	17:24	Cornell	Navy
1964	6:31.1	California	Washington
1965	16:51.3	Navy	Cornell
1966	16:03.4	Wisconsin	Navy
1967	16:13.9	Pennsylvania	Wisconsin
1968	6:15.6	Pennsylvania	Washington
1969	6:30.4	Pennsylvania	Dartmouth
1970	6:39.3	Washington	Wisconsin
1971	6:06	Cornell	Washington
1972	6:22.6	Pennsylvania	Brown
1973	6:21	Wisconsin	Brown
1974	6:33	Wisconsin	Mass. Inst. of Technology
1975	6:08.2	Wisconsin	M.I.T.
1976	6:31	California	Princeton
1977	6:32.4	Cornell	Pennsylvania
1978	6:39.5	Syracuse	Brown
1979	6:26.4	Brown	Wisconsin
1980	6:46	Navy	Northeastern
1981	5:57.3	Cornell	Navy
1982	5:57.5	Cornell	Princeton
1983	6:14.4	Brown	Navy
1984	5:54.7	Navy	Pennsylvania
1985	5:49.9	Princeton	Brown
1986	5:50.2	Brown	Pennsylvania
1987	6:02.9	Brown	Wisconsin

1. Disqualified.

HARNESS RACING

Oliver Wendell Holmes, the famous Autocrat of the Breakfast Table, wrote that the running horse was a gambling toy but the trotting horse was useful and, furthermore, "horse-racing is not a republican institution; horse-trotting is." Oliver Wendell Holmes was a born-and-bred New Englander, and New England was the nursery of the harness racing sport in America. Pacers and trotters were matters of local pride and prejudice in Colonial New England, and, shortly after the Revolution, the Messenger and Justin Morgan strains produced many winners in harness racing "matches" along the turnpikes of New York, Connecticut, Rhode Island, Massachusetts, Vermont, and New Hampshire.

There was English thoroughbred blood in Messenger and Justin Morgan, and, many years later, it was blended in Rysdyk's Hambletonian, foaled in 1849. Hambletonian was not particularly fast under harness but his descendants have had almost a monopoly of prizes, titles, and records in the harness racing game. Hambletonian was purchased as a foal with its dam for a total of $124 by William Rysdyk of Goshen, N.Y., and made a modest fortune for the purchaser.

Trotters and pacers often were raced under saddle in the old days, and, in fact, the custom still survives in some places in Europe. Dexter, the great trotter that lowered the mile record from 2:19 3/4 to 2:17 1/4 in 1867, was said to handle just as well under saddle as when pulling a sulky. But as sulkies were lightened in weight and improved in design, trotting under saddle became less common and finally faded out in this country.

WORLD RECORDS

Established in a Race or Against Time at One Mile

Source: Research Specialist, United States Trotting Association

	Record	Holder	Driver	Where Made	Year
Trotting on Mile Track					
All Age	1:52 1/5	Mack Lobell	John Campbell	Springfield, Ill.	1987
	1:53 2/5	Prakas	Bill O'Donnell	DuQuoin, IIll.	1985
	1:54*	Arndon	Del Miller	Lexington, Ky.	1982
	1:54 4/5[1]	Lindy's Crown	Howard Beissinger	Du Quoin, Ill.	1980
2-year-old	1:56[1]	TV Yankee	Tom Haughton	Lexington, Ky.	1982
	1:55 4/5*	Fancy Crown	George Sholte	Lexington, Ky.	1983
3-year-old	1:52 1/5	Mack Lobell	John Campbell	Springfield, Ill.	1987
	1:53 2/5	Praka	Bill O'Donnell	DuQuoin, Ill.	1985
	1:53 4/5	Fancy Crown	Bill O'Donnell	Springfield, Ill.	1984
	1:54*	Arndon	Del Miller	Lexington, Ky.	1982
	1:55[1]	Speedy Somolli	Howard Beissinger	Du Quoin, Ill.	1978
	1:55[1]	Florida Pro	George Sholty	Du Quoin, Ill.	1978
	1:55[1]	Jazz Cosmos	Mickey McNichol	Lexington, Ky.	1982
4-year-old	1:54 3/5	Premium Lobell	Dan Shetter	DuQuoin, Ill.	1984
	1:54 4/5[1]	Lindy's Crown	Howard Beissinger	DuQuoin, Ill.	1980
	1:54 4/5*	Nevele Pride	Stanely Dancer	Indianapolis	1969
Trotting on Five-Eights Mile Track					
All Age	1:57 1/5[1]	Lindy's Crown	Howard Beissinger	Wilmington, Del.	1980
2-year-old	1:58 2/5[1]	Mr. Drew	Jan Nordin	Wilmington, Del.	1982
3-year-old	1:57 2	Baltic Speed	Jan Nordin	Pompano Beach, Fla.	1984
	1:57 2/5[1]	Arndon	Del Miller	Montreal, Quebec	1982
4-year-old	1:57 1/5[1]	Lindy's Crown	Howard Beissinger	Wilmington, Del.	1980
Trotting on Half-Mile Track					
All Age	1:56 4/5[1]	Nevele Pride	Stanley Dancer	Saratoga Springs, N.Y.	1969
2-year-old	2:00[1]	Incredible Nevele	Glen Garnsey	Delaware, Ohio	1981
3-year-old	1:57.1	Fancy Crown	Bill O'Donnell	Delaware, Ohio	1984
4-year-old	1:56 4/5[1]	Nevele Pride	Stanley Dancer	Saratoga Springs, N.Y.	1969
Pacing on Mile Track					
All Age	1:49 3/5[1]	Nihilator	Bill O'Donnell	East Rutherford, N.J.	1985
	1:49 1/5*	Niatross	Clint Galbraith	Lexington, Ky.	1980
2-year-old	1:52.4	Nihilator	Bill O'Donnell	East Rutherford, N.J.	1984
3-year-old	1:51 3/5[1]	Trenton	Tommy Haughton	Springfield, Ill.	1982
	1:49 1/5*	Niatross	Clint Galbraith	Lexington, Ky.	1980
	1:49.3	Nihilator	Bill O'Donnell	East Rutherford, N.J.	1985
4-year-old	1:50 4/5*	Fan Hanover	Glen Garnsey	Lexington, Ky.	1982
	1:51 4/5[1]	It's Fritz	Martin Allen	Lexington, Ky.	1983
	1:51.4	On the Road Again	William Gilmour	East Rutherford, N.J.	1985
	1:51.4	Save Fuel	John Campbell	East Rutherford, N.J.	1985
Pacing on Five-Eighths Mile Track					
All Age	1:52 1/5[1]	It's Fritz	Martin Allen	Meadow Lands, Pa.	1983
2-year-old	1:54.1	Dragon's Lair	Jeff Mallet	Meadowlands, Lands, Pa.	1984
3-year-old	1:52.1	Marauder	Dick Richardson, Jr.	Meadow Lands, Pa.	1985
4-year-old	1:52 1/5[1]	It's Fritz	Martin Allen	Meadow Lands, Pa.	1983
Pacing on Half-Mile Track					
All Age	1:53 3/5[1]	It's Fritz	Martin Allen	Louisville, Ky.	1983
2-year-old	1:56.0	Cervantes Osborne	Donald Irvine, Jr.	Delaware, Ohio	1984
	1:56 1/5[1]	Signed N. Sealed	Bill O'Donnell	Louisville, Ky.	1983
3-year-old	1:53.3	Legal Notice	John Hayes, Jr.	Delaware, Ohio	1984
4-year-old	1:53 3/5[1]	It's Fritz	Martin Allen	Louisville, Ky.	1983

1. Record set in race. *Record set in time trial.

HARNESS RACING RECORDS FOR THE MILE

Trotters

Time	Trotter, age, driver	Year
2:00	Lou Dillon, 5, Millard Sanders	1903
1:58 1/2	Lou Dillon, 5, Millard Sanders	1903
1:58	Uhlan, 8, Charles Tanner	1912
1:58	Peter Manning, 5, T. W. Murphy	1921
1:57 3/4	Peter Manning, 5, T. W. Murphy	1921
1:57	Peter Manning, 6, T. W. Murphy	1922
1:56 3/4	Peter Manning, 6, T. W. Murphy	1922
1:56 3/4	Greyhound, 5, Sep Palin	1937
1:56	Greyhound, 5, Sep Palin	1937
1:55 1/4	Greyhound, 6, Sep Palin	1938
1:54 4/5	Nevele Pride, 4, Stanley Dancer	1969
1:54 4/5	Lindy's Crown, 4, Howard Beissinger	1980
1:54	Arndon, 3, Del Miller	1982
1:52 1/5	Mack Lobell, 3, John Campbell	1987

Pacers

Time	Pacer, age, driver	Year
2:00 1/2	John R. Gentry, 7, W.J. Andrews	1896
1:59 1/4	Star Pointer, 8, D. McClary	1897
1:59	Dan Patch, 7, M. E. McHenry	1903
1:56 1/4	Dan Patch, 7, M. E. McHenry	1903
1:56	Dan Patch, 8, H. C. Hersey	1904
1:55	Billy Direct, 4, Vic Fleming	1938
1:55	Adios Harry, 4, Luther Lyons	1955
1:54 3/5	Adios Butler, 4, Paige West	1960
1:54	Bret Hanover, 4, Frank Ervin	1966
1:53 3/5	Bret Hanover, 4, Frank Ervin	1966
1:52	Steady Star, 4, Joe O'Brien	1971
1:49 1/5	Niatross, 3, Clint Galbraith	1980

HISTORY OF TRADITIONAL HARNESS RACING STAKES

The Hambletonian

Three-year-old trotters. One mile. Guy McKinney won first race at Syracuse in 1926; held at Goshen, N.Y., 1930–1942, 1944–1956; at Yonkers, N.Y., 1943; at Du Quoin, Ill., 1957–1980. Since 1981, the race has been held at The Meadowland in East Rutherford, N.J.

Year	Winner	Driver	Best time	Total purse
1967	Speedy Streak	Del Cameron	2:00	$ 122,650
1968	Nevele Pride	Stanley Dancer	1:59 2/5	116,190
1969	Lindy's Pride	Howard Beissinger	1:57 3/5	124,910
1970	Timothy T.	John Simpson, Jr.	1:58 2/5[1]	143,630
1971	Speedy Crown	Howard Beissinger	1:57 2/5	129,770
1972	Super Bowl	Stanley Dancer	1:56 2/5	119,090
1973	Flirth	Ralph Baldwin	1:57 1/5	144,710
1974	Christopher T	Billy Haughton	1:58 3/5	160,150
1975	Bonefish	Stanely Dancer	1:59[2]	232,192
1976	Steve Lobell	Billy Haughton	1:56 2/5	263,524
1977	Green Speed	Billy Haughton	1:55 3/5	284,131
1978	Speedy Somolli	Howard Beissinger	1:55[3]	241,280
1979	Legend Hanover	George Sholty	1:56 1/5	300,000
1980	Burgomeister	Billy Haughton	1:56 3/5	293,570
1981	Shiaway St. Pat	Ray Remmen	2:01 1/5[4]	838,000
1982	Speed Bowl	Tommy Haughton	1:56 4/5	875,750
1983	Duenna	Stanley Dancer	1:57 2/5	1,000,000
1984	Historic Free	Ben Webster	1:56 2/5	1,219,000
1985	Prakas	Bill O'Donnell	1:54 3/5	1,272,000
1986	Nuclear Kosmos	Ulf Thoresen	1:56	1,172,082
1987	Mack Lobell	John Campbell	1:53 3/5	1,046,300

1. By Formal Notice. 2. By Yankee Bambino. 3. By Speedy Somolli and Florida Pro. 4. By Super Juan.

Little Brown Jug

Three-year-old pacers. One Mile. Raced at Delaware County Fair Grounds, Delaware, Ohio.

1967	Best of All	Jim Hackett	1:59[1]	$ 84,778
1968	Rum Customer	Billy Haughton	1:59 3/5	104,226
1969	Laverne Hanover	Billy Haughton	2:00 2/5	109,731
1970	Most Happy Fella	Stanley Dancer	1:57 1/5	100,110
1971	Nansemond	Herve Filion	1:57 2/5	102,994
1972	Strike Out	Keith Waples	1:56 3/5	104,916
1973	Melvin's Woe	Joe O'Brien	1:57 3/5	120,000
1974	Ambro Omaha	Billy Haughton	1:57	132,630
1975	Seatrain	Ben Webster	1:57[2]	147,813
1976	Keystone Ore	Stanley Dancer	1:56 4/5[3]	153,799
1977	Governor Skipper	John Chapman	1:56 1/5	150,000
1978	Happy Escort	William Popfinger	1:55 2/5[4]	186,760
1979	Hot Hitter	Herve Filion	1:55 3/5	226,455
1980	Niatross	Clint Galbraith	1:54 4/5	207,361
1981	Fan Hanover	Glen Garnsey	1:56[5]	243,799
1982	Merger	John Campbell	1:56 3/5	328,900
1983	Ralph Hanover	Ron Waples	1:55 3/5	358,800
1984	Colt 46	Norman Boring	1:53 3/5	366,717
1985	Nihilator	Bill O'Donnell	1:52 1/5	350,730
1986	Barberry Spur	Bill O'Donnell	1:52 4/5	407,684
1987	Jaguar Spur	Richard Stillings	1:55 3/5	412,330

1. By Nardin's Byrd. 2. By Armbro Ranger. 3. By Falcon Almahurst. 4. By Falcon Almahurst. 5. By Seahawk Hanover.

HARNESS HORSE OF THE YEAR

Chosen in poll conducted by United States Trotting Association in conjunction with the U.S. Harness Writers Assn.

1959	Bye Bye Byrd, Pacer	1968	Nevele Pride, Trotter	1977	Green Speed, Trotter
1960	Adios Butler, Pacer	1969	Nevele Pride, Trotter	1978	Abercrombie, Pacer
1961	Adios Butler, Pacer	1970	Fresh Yankee, Trotter	1979	Niatross, Pacer
1962	Su Mac Lad, Trotter	1971	Albatross, Pacer	1980	Niatross, Pacer
1963	Speedy Scot, Trotter	1972	Albatross, Pacer	1981	Fan Hanover, Pacer
1964	Bret Hanover, Pacer	1973	Sir Dalrae, Pacer	1982	Cam Fella, Pacer
1965	Bret Hanover, Pacer	1974	Delmonica Hanover, Trotter	1983	Cam Fella, Pacer
1966	Bret Hanover, Pacer	1975	Savoir, Trotter	1984	Fancy Crown, Trotter
1967	Nevele Pride, Trotter	1976	Keystone Ore, Pacer	1985	Nihilator, Trotter
				1986	Forrest Skipper

WEIGHTLIFTING

U.S. WEIGHTLIFTING FEDERATION MEN'S NATIONAL CHAMPIONSHIPS

(Detroit, Mich., May 2-3, 1987)

	Snatch	C&J[1]	Total[2]
52 kg—Ken Nishihara, Torrance, Calif.	80	107.5	187.5
56 kg—Gene Gilsdorf, Onaga, Kan.	85	117.5	202.5
60 kg—Brian Miuyamoto, Waimanolo, Ha.	105	127.5	232.5
67.5 kg—Carl Schake, Butler, Pa.	127.5	147.5	275.0
75 kg—Roberto Urrutia, Hollywood, Fla.	135.0	165.0	300.0
82.5 kg—Derrick Crass, Belleville, Ill.	140	170	310.0
90 kg—Tommy Calandro, Baton Rouge, La.	150	185	335.0
100 kg—Ken Clark, Pacifica, Calif.	150	187.5	337.5
110 kg—Rick Schutz, Mount Prospect, Ill.	155	190	345.0
Over 110 kg—Matio Martinez, San Francisco	177.5	215	392.5

1. Clean and jerk. 2. All results in kilograms.

WOMEN'S NATIONAL CHAMPIONSHIPS

(Houston, Tex., April 11-12, 1987)

	Snatch	C&J[1]	Total[2]
44 kg—Sibby Harris, Atlanta, Ga.	47.5	57.5	105
48 kg—Kathie Nichol, Cedarhurst, N.Y.	35	40	75
52 kg—Rachel Silverman, San Francisco	52.5	72.5	125
56 kg—Maro Bohakjran, Marietta, Ga.	52.5	72.5	125
60 kg—Giselle Sheptatin, San Francisco	72.5	82.5	155
67.5 kg—Arlys Kovach, Los Angeles	85	97.5	182.5
75 kg—Glenda Ford, Los Angeles	72.5	95	167.5
82.5 kg—Karyn Tarter, Pelham, N.Y.	90	110	200
Over 82.5 kg—Becky Levi, Tucson, Ariz.	85	110	195

1. Clean and jerk. 2. All results in kilograms.

WRESTLING

U.S.A. NATIONAL CHAMPIONSHIPS—1987

Freestyle

(Las Vegas, Nev., April 16–18, 1987)

105.5 lb (48 kg)—Takashi Irie, Japan
114.5 lb (52 kg)—Mitsuru Sato, Japan
125.5 lb (57 kg)—Barry Davis, Hawkeye Wrestling Club
136.5 lb (62 kg)—Takum Adach, Japan
149.5 lb (68 kg)—Andre Metzger, Foxcatcher Wrestling Club
163.5 lb (74 kg)—Dave Schultz, Foxcatcher Wrestling Club
180.5 lb (82 kg)—Mark Schultz, Foxcatcher Wrestling Club
198.5 lb (90 kg)—Jim Scherr, Wildcat Wrestling Club
220.0 lb (100 kg)—Bill Scherr, Sunkist Kids
Unlimited—Bruce Baumgartner, New York Athletic Club

Greco-Roman

(Schenectady, N.Y., May 1, 1987)

105.5 lb (48 kg)—Eric Wetzel, U.S. Marine Corps
114.5 lb (52 kg)—Shawn Sheldon, Adirondack Wrestling Club
125.5 lb (57 kg)—Eric Seward, U.S. Marine Corps
136.5 lb (62 kg)—Frank Famiano, Adirondack Wrestling Club
149.5 lb (68 kg)—James Martinez, Minnesota Wrestling Club
163.5 lb (74 kg)—David Butler, Navy
180.5 lb (82 kg)—Chris Catalfo, Adirondack Wrestling Club
198.5 lb (90 kg)—Derrick Waldroup, Army
220.0 lb (100 kg)—Dennis Koslowski, Minnesota Wrestling Club
Unlimited—Duane Koslowski, Minnesota Wrestling Club

N.C.A.A. CHAMPIONSHIPS—1987

(College Park, Md., March 19–21, 1987)

118 lb—Ricky Bonomo, Bloomsburg
126 lb—Bill Kelly, Iowa State
134 lb—John Smith, Oklahoma State
142 lb—Pete Yozzo, Lehigh
150 lb—Tim Krieger, Iowa State
158 lb—Stewart Carter, Iowa State
167 lb—Royce Alger, Iowa
177 lb—Rico Chiapparelli, Iowa
190 lb—Eric Voelker, Iowa State
Heavyweight—Carlton Haselrig, Pittsburgh-Johnstown
Team—Iowa State, 133; 2. Iowa, 108; 3. Penn State, 97 1/4

WORLD CUP—1986[1]

(Toledo, Ohio, April, 1986)

105.5 lb (48 kg)—Sergey Karamachakov, Soviet Union
114.5 lb (52 kg)—Vladimir Togouzov, Soviet Union
125.5 lb (57 kg)—Sergey Beloglazov, Soviet Union
136.5 lb (62 kg)—Avirmediin Enkee, Mongolia
149.5 lb (68 kg)—Arsen Fadzaev, Soviet Union
163.0 lb (74 kg)—Nate Carr, United States
180.5 lb (82 kg)—Jim Scherr, United States
198.0 lb (90 kg)—Makharbek Khadartsev, Soviet Union
220.0 lb (100 kg)—Dan Severn, United States
Heavyweight—Bruce Baumgartner, United States

1. World Cup 1987 was scheduled for late November after Information Please went to press.

GOLF

It may be that golf originated in Holland—historians believe it did—but certainly Scotland fostered the game and is famous for it. In fact, in 1457 the Scottish Parliament, disturbed because football and golf had lured young Scots from the more soldierly exercise of archery, passed an ordinance that "futeball and golf be utterly cryit doun and nocht usit." James I and Charles I of the royal line of Stuarts were golf enthusiasts, whereby the game came to be known as "the royal and ancient game of golf."

The golf balls used in the early games were leather-covered and stuffed with feathers. Clubs of all kinds were fashioned by hand to suit individual players. The great step in spreading the game came with the change from the feather ball to the guttapercha ball about 1850. In 1860, formal competition began with the establishment of an annual tournament for the British Open championship. There are records of "golf clubs" in the United States as far back as colonial days but no proof of actual play before John Reid and some friends laid out six holes on the Reid lawn in Yonkers, N.Y., in 1888 and played there with golf balls and clubs brought over from Scotland by Robert Lockhart. This group then formed the St. Andrews Golf Club of Yonkers, and golf was established in this country.

However, it remained a rather sedate and almost aristocratic pastime until a 20-year-old ex-caddy, Francis Ouimet of Boston, defeated two great British professionals, Harry Vardon and Ted Ray, in the United States Open championship at Brookline, Mass., in 1913. This feat put the game and Francis Ouimet on the front pages of the newspapers and stirred a wave of enthusiasm for the sport. The greatest feat so far in golf history is that of Robert Tyre Jones, Jr., of Atlanta, who won the British Open, the British Amateur, the U.S. Open, and the U.S. Amateur titles in one year, 1930.

THE MASTERS TOURNAMENT WINNERS

Augusta National Golf Club, Augusta, Ga.

Year	Winner	Score	Year	Winner	Score	Year	Winner	Score
1934	Horton Smith	284	1954	Sam Snead[1]	289	1972	Jack Nicklaus	286
1935	Gene Sarazen[1]	282	1955	Cary Middlecoff	279	1973	Tommy Aaron	283
1936	Horton Smith	285	1956	Jack Burke	289	1974	Gary Player	278
1937	Byron Nelson	283	1957	Doug Ford	283	1975	Jack Nicklaus	276
1938	Henry Picard	285	1958	Arnold Palmer	284	1976	Ray Floyd	271
1939	Ralph Guldahl	279	1959	Art Wall, Jr.	284	1977	Tom Watson	276
1940	Jimmy Demaret	280	1960	Arnold Palmer	282	1978	Gary Player	277
1941	Craig Wood	280	1961	Gary Player	280	1979	Fuzzy Zoeller[1]	280
1942	Byron Nelson[1]	280	1962	Arnold Palmer[1]	280	1980	Severiano Ballesteros	275
1943–45	No Tournaments		1963	Jack Nicklaus	286	1981	Tom Watson	280
1946	Herman Keiser	282	1964	Arnold Palmer	276	1982	Craig Stadler[1]	284
1947	Jimmy Demaret	281	1965	Jack Nicklaus	271	1983	Severiano Ballesteros	280
1948	Claude Harmon	279	1966	Jack Nicklaus[1]	288	1984	Ben Crenshaw	277
1949	Sam Snead	282	1967	Gay Brewer, Jr.	280	1985	Bernhard Langer	282
1950	Jimmy Demaret	283	1968	Bob Goalby	277	1986	Jack Nicklaus	279
1951	Ben Hogan	280	1969	George Archer	281	1987	Larry Mize[1]	285
1952	Sam Snead	286	1970	Billy Casper[1]	279			
1953	Ben Hogan	274	1971	Charles Coody	279			

1. Winner in playoff.

U.S. OPEN CHAMPIONS

Year	Winner	Score	Where played	Year	Winner	Score	Where played
1895	Horace Rawlins	173	Newport	1919	Walter Hagen[2]	301	Brae Burn
1896	James Foulis	152	Shinnecock Hills	1920	Edward Ray	295	Inverness
1897	Joe Lloyd	162	Chicago	1921	Jim Barnes	289	Columbia
1898[3]	Fred Herd	328	Myopia	1922	Gene Sarazen	288	Skokie
1899	Willie Smith	315	Baltimore	1923	R. T. Jones, Jr.[1 2]	296	Inwood
1900	Harry Vardon	313	Chicago	1924	Cyril Walker	297	Oakland Hills
1901	Willie Anderson[1]	331	Myopia	1925	Willie Macfarlane[1]	291	Worcester
1902	Laurie Auchterlonie	307	Garden City	1926	R. T. Jones, Jr.[2]	293	Scioto
1903	Willie Anderson[1]	307	Baltusrol	1927	Tommy Armour[1]	301	Oakmont
1904	Willie Anderson	303	Glen View	1928	Johnny Farrell[1]	294	Olympia Fields
1905	Willie Anderson	314	Myopia	1929	R. T. Jones, Jr.[1 2]	294	Winged Foot
1906	Alex Smith	295	Onwentsia	1930	R. T. Jones, Jr.[2]	287	Interlachen
1907	Alex Ross	302	Philadelphia	1931	Billy Burke[1]	292	Inverness
1908	Fred McLeod[1]	322	Myopia	1932	Gene Sarazen	286	Fresh Meadow
1909	George Sargent	290	Englewood	1933	John Goodman[2]	287	North Shore
1910	Alex Smith[1]	298	Philadelphia	1934	Olin Dutra	293	Merion
1911	John McDermott[1]	307	Chicago	1935	Sam Parks, Jr.	299	Oakmont
1912	John McDermott	294	Buffalo	1936	Tony Manero	282	Baltusrol
1913	Francis Ouimet[1 2]	304	Brookline	1937	Ralph Guldahl	281	Oakland Hills
1914	Walter Hagen	290	Midlothian	1938	Ralph Guldahl	284	Cherry Hills
1915	Jerome D. Travers[2]	297	Baltusrol	1939	Byron Nelson[1]	284	Philadelphia
1916	Charles Evans, Jr.[2]	286	Minikahda	1940	Lawson Little[1]	287	Canterbury
1917–18	No tournaments[4]			1941	Craig Wood	284	Colonial

Year	Winner	Score	Where played	Year	Winner	Score	Where played
1942–45	No tournaments[5]			1967	Jack Nicklaus	275	Baltusrol
1946	Lloyd Mangrum[1]	284	Canterbury	1968	Lee Trevino	275	Oak Hill
1947	Lew Worsham[1]	282	St. Louis	1969	Orville Moody	281	Champions G. C.
1948	Ben Hogan	276	Riviera	1970	Tony Jacklin	281	Hazeltine
1949	Cary Middlecoff	286	Medinah	1971	Lee Trevino[1]	280	Merion
1950	Ben Hogan[1]	287	Merion	1972	Jack Nicklaus	290	Pebble Beach
1951	Ben Hogan	287	Oakland Hills	1973	Johnny Miller	279	Oakmont
1952	Julius Boros	281	Northwood	1974	Hale Irwin	287	Winged Foot
1953	Ben Hogan	283	Oakmont	1975	Lou Graham[1]	287	Medinah
1954	Ed Furgol	284	Baltusrol	1976	Jerry Pate	277	Atlanta A.C.
1955	Jack Fleck[1]	287	Olympic	1977	Hubert Green	278	Southern Hills
1956	Cary Middlecoff	281	Oak Hill	1978	Andy North	285	Cherry Hills
1957	Dick Mayer[1]	298	Inverness	1979	Hale Irwin	284	Inverness
1958	Tommy Bolt	283	Southern Hills	1980	Jack Nicklaus	272	Baltusrol
1959	Bill Casper, Jr.	282	Winged Foot	1981	David Graham	273	Merion
1960	Arnold Palmer	280	Cherry Hills	1982	Tom Watson	282	Pebble Beach
1961	Gene Littler	281	Oakland Hills	1983	Larry Nelson	280	Oakmont
1962	Jack Nicklaus[1]	283	Oakmont	1984	Fuzzy Zoeller[1]	276	Winged Foot
1963	Julius Boros[1]	293	Country Club	1985	Andy North	279	Oakland Hills
1964	Ken Venturi	278	Congressional	1986	Ray Floyd	279	Shinnecock Hills
1965	Gary Player[1]	282	Bellerive	1987	Scott Simpson	277	Olympic Golf Club
1966	Bill Casper[1]	278	Olympic				

1. Winner in playoff. 2. Amateur. 3. In 1898, competition was extended to 72 holes. 4. In 1917, Jack Hutchison, with a 292, won an Open Patriotic Tournament for the benefit of the American Red Cross at Whitemarsh Valley Country Club. 5. In 1942, Ben Hogan, with a 271 won a Hale American National Open Tournament for the benefit of the Navy Relief Society and USO at Ridgemoor Country Club.

U.S. AMATEUR CHAMPIONS

1895	Charles B. Macdonald	1922	Jess W. Sweetser	1949	Charles Coe	1970	Lanny Wadkins
1896–97	H. J. Whigham	1923	Max R. Marston	1950	Sam Urzetta	1971	Gary Cowan
1898	Findlay S. Douglas	1924–25	R. T. Jones, Jr.	1951	Billy Maxwell	1972	Vinny Giles 3d
1899	H. M. Harriman	1926	George Von Elm	1952	Jack Westland	1973[3]	Craig Stadler
1900–01	Walter J. Travis	1927–28	R. T. Jones, Jr.	1953	Gene Littler	1974	Jerry Pate
1902	Louis N. James	1929	H. R. Johnston	1954	Arnold Palmer	1975	Fred Ridley
1903	Walter J. Travis	1930	R. T. Jones, Jr.	1955–56	Harvie Ward	1976	Bill Sander
1904–05	H. Chandler Egan	1931	Francis Ouimet	1957	Hillman Robbins	1977	John Fought
1906	Eben M. Byers	1932	Ross Somerville	1958	Charles Coe	1978	John Cook
1907–08	Jerome D. Travers	1933	G. T. Dunlap, Jr.	1959	Jack Nicklaus	1979	Mark O'Meara
1909	Robert A. Gardner	1934–35	Lawson Little	1960	Deane Beman	1980	Hal Sutton
1910	W. C. Fownes, Jr.	1936	John W. Fischer	1961	Jack Nicklaus	1981	Nathaniel Crosby
1911	Harold H. Hilton	1937	John Goodman	1962	Labron Harris, Jr.	1982	Jay Sigel
1912–13	Jerome D. Travers	1938	Willie Turnesa	1963	Deane Beman	1983	Jay Sigel
1914	Francis Ouimet	1939	Marvin H. Ward	1964	Bill Campbell	1984	Scott Verplank
1915	Robert A. Gardner	1940	R. D. Chapman	1965[2]	Robert Murphy, Jr.	1985	Sam Randolph
1916	Charles Evans, Jr.	1941	Marvin H. Ward	1966	Gary Cowan[1]	1986	Buddy Alexander
1919	S. D. Herron	1946	Ted Bishop	1967	Bob Dickson	1987	Bill Mayfair
1920	Charles Evans, Jr.	1947	Robert Riegel	1968	Bruce Fleisher		
1921	Jesse P. Guilford	1948	Willie Turnesa	1968	Steven Melnyk		

1. Winner in playoff. 2. Tourney switched to medal play through 1972. 3. Return to match play.

U.S. P.G.A. CHAMPIONS

1916	Jim Barnes	1940	Byron Nelson	1957	Lionel Hebert	1973	Jack Nicklaus
1919	Jim Barnes	1941	Victor Ghezzi	1958[2]	Dow Finsterwald	1974	Lee Trevino
1920	Jock Hutchison	1942	Sam Snead	1959	Bob Rosburg	1975	Jack Nicklaus
1921	Walter Hagen	1944	Bob Hamilton	1960	Jay Hebert	1976	Dave Stockton
1922–23	Gene Sarazen	1945	Byron Nelson	1961	Jerry Barber[1]	1977	Lanny Wadkins[1]
1924–27	Walter Hagen	1946	Ben Hogan	1962	Gary Player	1978	John Mahaffey
1928–29	Leo Diegel	1947	Jim Ferrier	1963	Jack Nicklaus	1979	David Graham[1]
1930	Tommy Armour	1948	Ben Hogan	1964	Bobby Nichols	1980	Jack Nicklaus
1931	Tom Creavy	1949	Sam Snead	1965	Dave Marr	1981	Larry Nelson
1932	Olin Dutra	1950	Chandler Harper	1966	Al Geiberger	1982	Ray Floyd
1933	Gene Sarazen	1951	Sam Snead	1967	Don January[1]	1983	Hal Sutton
1934	Paul Runyan	1952	Jim Turnesa	1968	Julius Boros	1984	Lee Trevino
1935	Johnny Revolta	1953	Walter Burkemo	1969	Ray Floyd	1985	Hubert Green
1936–37	Denny Shute	1954	Chick Harbert	1970	Dave Stockton	1986	Bob Tway
1938	Paul Runyan	1955	Doug Ford	1971	Jack Nicklaus	1987	Larry Nelson
1939	Henry Picard	1956	Jack Burke, Jr.	1972	Gary Player		

1. Winner in playoff. 2. Switched to medal play.

U.S. WOMEN'S AMATEUR CHAMPIONS

1916	Alexa Stirling	1938	Patty Berg	1959	Barbara McIntire	1974	Cynthia Hill		
1919–20	Alexa Stirling	1939–40	Betty Jameson	1960	JoAnne Gunderson	1975	Beth Daniel		
1921	Marion Hollins	1941	Mrs. Frank Newell	1961	Anne Quast Decker	1976	Donna Horton		
1922	Glenna Collett	1946	Mildred Zaharias	1962	JoAnne Gunderson	1977	Beth Daniel		
1923	Edith Cummings	1947	Louise Suggs	1963	Anne Quast Welts	1978	Cathy Sherk		
1924	Dorothy Campbell Hurd	1948	Grace Lenczyk	1964	Barbara McIntire	1979	Carolyn Hill		
		1949	Mrs. D. G. Porter	1965	Jean Ashley	1980	Juli Inkster		
1925	Glenna Collett	1950	Beverly Hanson	1966	JoAnne Gunderson	1981	Juli Inkster		
1926	Helen Stetson	1951	Dorothy Kirby	1967	Lou Dill	1982	Juli Inkster		
1927	Mrs. M. B. Horn	1952	Jacqueline Pung	1968	JoAnne G. Carner	1983	Joanne Pacillo		
1928–30	Glenna Collett	1953	Mary Lena Faulk	1969	Catherine LaCoste	1984	Deb Richard		
1931	Helen Hicks	1954	Barbara Romack	1970	Martha Wilkinson	1985	Michiko Hattori		
1932–34	Virginia Van Wie	1955	Patricia Lesser	1971	Laura Baugh	1986	Kay Cockerill		
1935	Glenna Collett Vare	1956	Marlene Stewart	1972	Mary Ann Budke	1987	Kay Cockerill		
1936	Pamela Barton	1957	JoAnne Gunderson	1973	Carol Semple				
1937	Mrs. J. A. Page, Jr.	1958	Anne Quast						

U.S. WOMEN'S OPEN CHAMPIONS

Year	Winner	Score	Year	Winner	Score	Year	Winner	Score
1946	Patty Berg (match play)	—	1960	Betsy Rawls	291	1974	Sandra Haynie	295
1947	Betty Jameson	295	1961	Mickey Wright	293	1975	Sandra Palmer	295
1948	Mildred D. Zaharias	300	1962	Murle Lindstrom	301	1976	JoAnne Carner	292
1949	Louise Suggs	291	1963	Mary Mills	289	1977	Hollis Stacy	292
1950	Mildred D. Zaharias	291	1964	Mickey Wright[1]	290	1978	Hollis Stacy	289
1951	Betsy Rawls	293	1965	Carol Mann	290	1979	Jerilyn Britz	284
1952	Louise Suggs	284	1966	Sandra Spuzich	297	1980	Amy Alcott	280
1953	Betsy Rawls[1]	302	1967	Catherine LaCoste	294	1981	Pat Bradley	279
1954	Mildred D. Zaharias	291	1968	Susie Berning	289	1982	Janet Alex	283
1955	Fay Crocker	299	1969	Donna Caponi	294	1983	Jan Stephenson	290
1956	Katherine Cornelius[1]	302	1970	Donna Caponi	287	1984	Hollis Stacy	290
1957	Betsy Rawls	299	1971	JoAnne Carner	288	1985	Kathy Baker	280
1958	Mickey Wright	290	1972	Susie Berning	299	1986	Jane Geddes	287
1959	Mickey Wright	287	1973	Susie Berning	290	1987	Laura Davies	285

1. Winner in playoff. 2. Amateur.

BRITISH OPEN CHAMPIONS

(First tournament, held in 1860, was won by Willie Park, Sr.)

Year	Winner	Score	Year	Winner	Score	Year	Winner	Score
1920	George Duncan	303	1947	Fred Daly	294	1968	Gary Player	289
1921	Jock Hutchison[1]	296	1948	Henry Cotton	283	1969	Tony Jacklin	280
1922	Walter Hagen	300	1949	Bobby Locke[1]	283	1970	Jack Nicklaus[1]	283
1923	A. G. Havers	295	1950	Bobby Locke	279	1971	Lee Trevino	278
1924	Walter Hagen	301	1951	Max Faulkner	285	1972	Lee Trevino	278
1925	Jim Barnes	300	1952	Bobby Locke	287	1973	Tom Weiskopf	276
1926	R. T. Jones, Jr.	291	1953	Ben Hogan	282	1974	Gary Player	282
1927	R. T. Jones, Jr.	285	1954	Peter Thomson	283	1975	Tom Watson[1]	279
1928	Walter Hagen	292	1955	Peter Thomson	281	1976	Johnny Miller	279
1929	Walter Hagen	292	1956	Peter Thomson	286	1977	Tom Watson	268
1930	R. T. Jones, Jr.	291	1957	Bobby Locke	279	1978	Jack Nicklaus	281
1931	Tommy Armour	296	1958	Peter Thomson[1]	278	1979	Severiano Ballesteros	283
1932	Gene Sarazen	283	1959	Gary Player	284	1980	Tom Watson	271
1933	Denny Shute[1]	292	1960	Kel Nagle	278	1981	Bill Rogers	276
1934	Henry Cotton	283	1961	Arnold Palmer	284	1982	Tom Watson	284
1935	A. Perry	283	1962	Arnold Palmer	276	1983	Tom Watson	275
1936	A. H. Padgham	287	1963	Bob Charles[1]	277	1984	Severiano Ballesteros	276
1937	Henry Cotton	290	1964	Tony Lema	279	1985	Sandy Lyle	282
1938	R. A. Whitcombe	295	1965	Peter Thomson	285	1986	Greg Norman	280
1939	R. Burton	290	1966	Jack Nicklaus	282	1987	Nick Faldo	279
1940	Sam Snead	290	1967	Roberto de Vicenzo	278			

1. Winner in playoff.

OTHER 1987 PGA TOUR WINNERS

(Through August 31, 1987)

MONY Tournament of Champions—Mac O'Grady (278)	$90,000
Bob Hope Chrysler Classic—Corey Pavin (342)	162,000
Phoenix Open—Paul Azinger (268)	108,000
AT&T Pebble Beach National Pro-Am—Johnny Miller (278)	108,000
Hawaiian Open—Corey Pavin (270)	108,000
Andy Williams Open—George Burns (266)	90,000
Los Angeles Open—T.C. Chen (275)	108,000
Doral Ryder Open—Lanny Wadkins (277)	180,000
Honda Classic—Mark Calcvcghia (279)	108,000
Bay Hill Classic—Payne Stewart (264)	108,000
USF & G Classic—Ben Crenshaw (268)	90,000
Tournament Players Championship—Sandy Lyle (274)	180,000
Greater Greensboro Open—Scott Simpson (282)	108,000
Heritage Classic—Davis Love III (271)	117,000
Houston Open—Jay Haas (276)	108,000
Las Vegas Invitational—Paul Azinger (271)	225,000
Byron Nelson Classic—Fred Couples (266)	108,000
Colonial Invitational—Keith Clearwater (266)	108,000
Atlanta Classic—Dave Barr (265)	108,000
Memorial Tournament—Dave Pooley (272)	140,000
Kemper Open—Tom Kite (270)	126,000
Westchester Classic—J.C. Snead (276)	108,000
Greater Hartford Open—Paul Azinger (269)	126,000
Canadian Open—Curtis Strange (278)	108,000
Busch Classic—Mark McCumber (267)	110,160
Buick Open—Robert Wrenn (262)	108,000
St. Jude Classic—Curtis Strange (275)	130,328
The International—John Cook (284)	180,000
Western Open—D.A. Weibring (207)	144,000
World Series—Curtis Strange (275)	144,000

OTHER 1987 LPGA TOUR WINNERS

(Through August 31, 1987)

Mazda Classic—Kathy Postlewait (286)	$30,000
Sarasota Classic—Nancy Lopez (281)	30,000
Hawaiian Ladies Open—Cindy Rarick (207)	45,000
Women's Kemper Open—Jan Geddes (276)	45,000
Glendale Federal Classic—Jan Geddes (286)	37,500
Tucson Open—Betsy King (281)	30,000
Turquoise Classic—Pat Bradley (286)	45,000
Nabisco-Dinah Shore—Betsy King (283)	80,000
Kyocera Inamori Classic—Ayako Okamoto (275)	30,000
Santa Barbara Open—Jan Stephenson (215)	45,000
S&H Golf Classic—Cindy Hill (271)	33,750
United Virginia Bank Classic—Jody Rosenthal (209)	37,500
Chrysler-Plymouth Classic—Ayako Okamoto (215)	33,750
Corning Classic—Cindy Rarick (275)	41,250
McDonalds Championship—Betsy King (278)	75,000
Mayflower Classic—Colleen Walker (278)	52,500
Lady Keystone Open—Ayako Okamoto (208)	45,000
Rochester International—Deb Richard (280)	45,000
Jamie Farr Toledo Classic—Jan Geddes (280)	33,750
du Maurier Classic—Jody Rosenthal (272)	60,000
Boston Five Classic—Jan Geddes (277)	45,000
Columbia Savings LPGA Pro-Am—Chris Johnson (277)	37,500
Henredon Classic—Mary Beth Zimmerman (206)	45,000
Mastercard International—Val Skinner (212)	33,750
Atlantic City Classic—Betsy King (207)	33,750
Nestle World Championship—Ayako Okamoto (282)	81,500

JAMES E. SULLIVAN MEMORIAL AWARD WINNERS

(Amateur Athlete of Year Chosen in Amateur Athletic Union Poll)

1930	Robert Tyre Jones, Jr.	Golf
1931	Bernard E. Berlinger	Track and field
1932	James A. Bausch	Track and field
1933	Glenn Cunningham	Track and field
1934	William R. Bonthron	Track and field
1935	W. Lawson Little, Jr.	Golf
1936	Glenn Morris	Track and field
1937	J. Donald Budge	Tennis
1938	Donald R. Lash	Track and field
1939	Joseph W. Burk	Rowing
1940	J. Gregory Rice	Track and field
1941	Leslie MacMitchell	Track and field
1942	Cornelius Warmerdam	Track and field
1943	Gilbert L. Dodds	Track and field
1944	Ann Curtis	Swimming
1945	Felix (Doc) Blanchard	Football
1946	Y. Arnold Tucker	Football
1947	John B. Kelly, Jr.	Rowing
1948	Robert B. Mathias	Track and field
1949	Richard T. Button	Figure skating
1950	Fred Wilt	Track and field
1951	Robert E. Richards	Track and field
1952	Horace Ashenfelter	Track and field
1953	Major Sammy Lee	Diving
1954	Malvin Whitfield	Track and field
1955	Harrison Dillard	Track and field
1956	Patricia McCormick	Diving
1957	Bobby Jo Morrow	Track and Field
1958	Glenn Davis	Track and field
1959	Parry O'Brien	Track and field
1960	Rafer Johnson	Track and field
1961	Wilma Rudolph Ward	Track and field
1962	Jim Beatty	Track and field
1963	John Pennel	Track and field
1964	Don Schollander	Swimming
1965	Bill Bradley	Basketball
1966	Jim Ryun	Track and field
1967	Randy Matson	Track and field
1968	Debbie Meyer	Swimming
1969	Bill Toomey	Decathlon
1970	John Kinsella	Swimming
1971	Mark Spitz	Swimming
1972	Frank Shorter	Marathon
1973	Bill Walton	Basketball
1974	Rick Wohlhuter	Track
1975	Tim Shaw	Swimming
1976	Bruce Jenner	Track and field
1977	John Naber	Swimming
1978	Tracy Caulkins	Swimming
1979	Kurt Thomas	Gymnastics
1980	Eric Heiden	Speed skating
1981	Carl Lewis	Track and field
1982	Mary Decker Tabb	Track and field
1983	Edwin Moses	Track and field
1984	Greg Louganis	Diving
1985	Joan Benoit-Samuelson	Marathon
1986	Jackie Joyner-Kersee	Heptathlon

SOCCER

WORLD CUP

1930 Uruguay	1946 No competition	1962 Brazil	1978 Argentina
1934 Italy	1950 Uruguay	1966 England	1982 Italy
1938 Italy	1954 West Germany	1970 Brazil	1986 Argentina
1942 No competition	1958 Brazil	1974 West Germany	

WORLD CUP—1986

A capacity crowd of 114,500 fans filled Aztec Stadium in Mexico City on Sunday, June 29, and another 500 million were estimated to have watched on television, as Argentina defeated West Germany, 3–2, for the championship of the 13th World Cup Tournament.

Argentina's Diego Maradona was the star of the tournament. His pass to teammate Jorge Burruchaga led to the winning goal, after Argentina had squandered a 2–0 lead. He was the only unanimous selection to the post-tournament all-star team.

More than 140 world nations play soccer. The World Cup, the most popular and best attended sporting event in the world, is a quadrennial event, and will next be played in 1990. Two years of elimination precede the 52-game championship tournament.

Once again, the United States was eliminated from the 1986 tourney during preliminary play. In early action, the American team defeated the Netherlands-Antilles and Trinidad-Tobago, but on May 31, 1985, lost a 1–0 game to Costa Rica and was eliminated.

That marked the ninth consecutive World Cup tournament the United States had failed to qualify for. Not since 1950 has an American squad been part of the world's most prestigious sporting event.

The early elimination of the United States from the 1986 World Cup was a big blow to soccer in America. With the North American Soccer League out of business since the end of the 1984 season because of mounting financial losses, an American appearance in the World Cup had been counted on as a much-needed boost for the sport in this country. It was not to be.

Instead, the lone professional soccer league of significance remaining in the United States in 1986 was the Major Indoor Soccer League, a derivation of the game played indoors on hockey-sized fields. There remained, outdoors, the long-established American Soccer League, but it was a league that existed on a very low budget, low fan appeal basis.

WORLD CUP—1986

SEMIFINALS

1. (at Guadalajara, Mexico, June 25, 1986)

West Germany 2, France 0

2. (at Mexico City, Mexico, June 25, 1986)

Argentina 2, Belgium 0

THIRD PLACE

(at Puebla, Mexico, June 28, 1986)

France 4, Belgium 2 (overtime)

The following are the results of matches played by the four teams which reached the semifinals:

FINALS

(at Mexico City, Mexico, June 29, 1986)

Argentina 3, West Germany 2

Argentina (Group A)
Argentina 3, South Korea 1
Argentina 1, Italy 1
Argentina 2, Bulgaria 0
Argentina 1, Uruguay 0
Argentina 2, England 1

West Germany (Group E)
West Germany 1, Uruguay 1
West Germany 2, Scotland 1
Denmark 2, West Germany 0
West Germany 1, Morocco 0
West Germany 4, Mexico 1

France (Group C)
France 1, Canada 0
France 1, Soviet Union 1
France 3, Hungary 0
France 2, Italy 0*
France 5, Brazil 4

*Italy was defending champion.

Belgium (Group B)
Mexico 2, Belgium 1
Belgium 2, Iraq 1
Belgium 2, Paraguay 2
Belgium 4, Soviet Union 3 (Overtime)
Belgium 6, Spain 5

MAJOR INDOOR SOCCER LEAGUE—1987 FINAL STANDING

EASTERN DIVISION

	W	L	Pct	GB
Cleveland Force	34	18	.654	—
Baltimore Blast	33	19	.635	1
Dallas Sidekicks	28	24	.538	6
Minnesota Strikers	26	26	.500	8
Chicago Sting	23	29	.442	11

WESTERN DIVISION

	W	L	Pct	GB
Tacoma Stars	35	17	.673	—
Kansas City Comets	28	24	.538	7
San Diego Sockers	27	25	.519	8
Wichita Wings	27	25	.519	8
St. Louis Steamers	19	33	.365	16
Los Angeles Lazers	16	36	.308	19

CHAMPIONSHIP PLAYOFFS

Quarterfinals

Cleveland defeated Minnesota, 3 games to 2
Dallas defeated Baltimore, 3 games to 2
San Diego defeated Kansas City, 3 games to 2
Tacoma defeated Wichita, 3 games to 2

Semifinals

Dallas defeated Cleveland, 4 games to 1
Tacoma defeated San Diego, 4 games to 3

Championship

Dallas defeated Tacoma, 4 games to 3

NORTH AMERICAN SOCCER LEAGUE CHAMPIONS

1968—Atlanta Chiefs
1969—Kansas City Stars
1970—Rochester Lancers
1971—Dallas Tornado
1972—New York Cosmos
1973—Philadelphia Atoms
1974—Los Angeles Aztecs
1975—Tampa Bay Rowdies
1976—Toronto Metro-Croatia
1977—New York Cosmos
1978—New York Cosmos
1979—Vancouver Whitecaps
1980—New York Cosmos
1981—Chicago Sting
1982—New York Cosmos
1983—Tulsa Roughnecks
1984—Chicago Sting

YACHTING

AMERICA'S CUP RECORD

First race in 1851 around Isle of Wight, Cowes, England. First defense and all others through 1920 held 30 miles off New York Bay. Races since 1930 held 30 miles off Newport, R.I. Conducted as one race only in 1851 and 1870; best four-of-seven basis, 1871; best two-of-three, 1876–1887; best three-of-five, 1893–1901; best four-of-seven, since 1930. Figures in parentheses indicate number of races won.

Year	Winner and owner	Loser and owner
1851	AMERICA (1), John C. Stevens, U.S.	AURORA, T. Le Marchant, England[1]
1870	MAGIC (1), Franklin Osgood, U.S.	CAMBRIA, James Ashbury, England[2]
1871	COLUMBIA (2), Franklin Osgood, U.S.[3]	LIVONIA (1), James Ashbury, England
	SAPPHO (2), William P. Douglas, U.S.	
1876	MADELEINE (2), John S. Dickerson, U.S.	COUNTESS OF DUFFERIN, Chas. Gifford, Canada
1881	MISCHIEF (2), J. R. Busk, U.S.	ATALANTA, Alexander Cuthbert, Canada
1885	PURITAN (2), J. M. Forbes-Gen. Charles Paine, U.S.	GENESTA, Sir Richard Sutton, England
1886	MAYFLOWER (2), Gen. Charles Paine, U.S.	GALATEA, Lt. William Henn, England
1887	VOLUNTEER (2), Gen. Charles Paine, U.S.	THISTLE, James Bell et al., Scotland
1893	VIGILANT (3), C. Oliver Iselin et al., U.S.	VALKYRIE II, Lord Dunraven, England
1895	DEFENDER (3), C. O. Iselin-W. K. Vanderbilt-E. D. Morgan, U.S.	VALKYRIE III, Lord Dunraven-Lord Lonsdale-Lord Wolverton, England
1899	COLUMBIA (3), J. P. Morgan-C. O. Iselin, U.S.	SHAMROCK I, Sir Thomas Lipton, Ireland
1901	COLUMBIA (3), Edwin D. Morgan, U.S.	SHAMROCK II, Sir Thomas Lipton, Ireland
1903	RELIANCE (3), Cornelius Vanderbilt et al., U.S.	SHAMROCK III, Sir Thomas Lipton, Ireland
1920	RESOLUTE (3), Henry Walters et al., U.S.	SHAMROCK IV (2), Sir Thomas Lipton, Ireland
1930	ENTERPRISE (4), Harold S. Vanderbilt et al., U.S.	SHAMROCK V, Sir Thomas Lipton, Ireland
1934	RAINBOW (4), Harold S. Vanderbilt, U.S.	ENDEAVOUR (2), T. O. M. Sopwith, England
1937	RANGER (4), Harold S. Vanderbilt, U.S.	ENDEAVOUR II, T. O. M. Sopwith, England
1958	COLUMBIA (4), Henry Sears et al., U.S.	SCEPTRE, Hugh Goodson et al., England
1962	WEATHERLY (4), Henry D. Mercer et al., U.S.	GRETEL (1), Sir Frank Packer et al., Australia
1964	CONSTELLATION (4), New York Y.C. Syndicate, U.S.	SOVEREIGN (0), J. Anthony Bowden, England
1967	INTREPID (4), New York Y.C. Syndicate, U.S.	DAME PATTIE (0), Sydney (Aust.) Syndicate
1970	INTREPID (4), New York Y.C. Syndicate, U.S.	GRETEL II (1), Sydney (Aust.) Syndicate
1974	COURAGEOUS (4), New York, N.Y. Syndicate, U.S.	SOUTHERN CROSS (0), Sydney (Aust.) Syndicate
1977	COURAGEOUS (4), New York, N.Y. Syndicate, U.S.	AUSTRALIA (0), Sun City (Aust.) Syndicate
1980	FREEDOM (4), New York, N.Y. Syndicate, U.S.	AUSTRALIA (1), Alan Bond et al, Australia
1983	AUSTRALIA II (4) Alan Bond et al., Australia,	LIBERTY (3) New York, N.Y. Syndicate, U.S.
1987	STARS & STRIPES (4), Dennis Conner et al., United States	KOOKABURRA III (0), Iain Murray et al., Australia

1. Fourteen British yachts started against America; Aurora finished second. 2. Cambria sailed against 23 U.S. yachts and finished tenth. 3. Columbia was disabled in the third race, after winning the first two; Sappho substituted and won the fourth and fifth.

Yanks Sweep America's Cup Back Where It Belongs

For more than a century it had been taken for granted. The United States simply always won the America's Cup yacht race. Most Americans expected that would never change.

Then, in 1983, the 132-year streak ended abruptly, as challenger *Australia II* defeated the American yacht *Liberty*, 4-3.

And so it was in 1987 that Americans, more than ever before, got interested in and followed the exploits of skipper Dennis Conner, as he raced his yacht, *"Stars & Stripes"* against defending Australian yacht *"Kookaburra III"* at Freemantle, Australia. This was the first time the competition had been held outside the United States.

Three years in the planning and four months in the sailing, *Stars & Stripes* did it, recapturing the America's Cup in four straight races.

Stars & Stripes won the four races by time margins of 1:41, 1:10, 1:46, and 1:59.

Conner, a 44-year-old resident of San Diego, Calif., became a national hero, visiting the White House and having a tickertape parade thrown for him and his crew down Fifth Avenue in New York City.

The crew included navigator Peter Isler, 33, of Honolulu; tactician Tom Whidden, 39, of New York; mainstaff trimmer Jon Wright, 38, of Philadelphia; Pitman Jay Brown, 28 of Vero Beach, Fla.; bowman Scott Vogel, 26, of Shoreham, N.Y.; sewerman John Barnitt, 24, of San Diego; grinders Henry Childers, 26, of Warwick, R.I. and Jim Kavle, 26, of Philadelphia; and trimmers Adam Ostenfeld, 31, of New York, Bill Trenkle, 29, of Garden City, N.Y., and Kyle Smith, 31, of New Orleans.

Stars and Stripes made it through a long qualifying series of competitions with a record of 27-7, but was 12-1 through the semifinals and finals.

AUTO RACING

INDIANAPOLIS 500

Year	Winner	Car	Time	mph	Second place
1911	Ray Harroun	Marmon	6:42:08	74.59	Ralph Mulford
1912	Joe Dawson	National	6:21:06	78.72	Teddy Tetzloff
1913	Jules Goux	Peugeot	6:35:05	75.93	Spencer Wishart
1914	René Thomas	Delage	6:03:45	82.47	Arthur Duray
1915	Ralph DePalma	Mercedes	5:33:55.51	89.84	Dario Resta
1916[1]	Dario Resta	Peugeot	3:34:17	84.00	Wilbur D'Alene
1919	Howard Wilcox	Peugeot	5:40:42.87	88.05	Eddie Hearne
1920	Gaston Chevrolet	Monroe	5:38:32	88.62	René Thomas
1921	Tommy Milton	Frontenac	5:34:44.65	89.62	Roscoe Sarles
1922	Jimmy Murphy	Murphy Special	5:17:30.79	94.48	Harry Hartz
1923	Tommy Milton	H. C. S. Special	5:29.50.17	90.95	Harry Hartz
1924	L. L. Corum–Joe Boyer	Dusenberg Special	5:05:23.51	98.23	Earl Cooper
1925	Peter DePaolo	Dusenberg Special	4:56:39.45	101.13	Dave Lewis
1926[2]	Frank Lockhart	Miller Special	4:10:14.95	95.904	Harry Hartz
1927	George Souders	Dusenberg Special	5:07:33.08	97.54	Earl DeVore
1928	Louis Meyer	Miller Special	5:01:33.75	99.48	Lou Moore
1929	Ray Keech	Simplex Special	5:07:25.42	97.58	Louis Meyer
1930	Billy Arnold	Miller–Hartz Special	4:58:39.72	100.448	Shorty Cantlon
1931	Louis Schneider	Bowes Special	5:10:27.93	96.629	Fred Frame
1932	Fred Frame	Miller–Hartz Special	4:48:03.79	104.144	Howard Wilcox
1933	Louis Meyer	Tydol Special	4:48:00.75	104.162	Wilbur Shaw
1934	Bill Cummings	Boyle Products Special	4:46:05.20	104.863	Mauri Rose
1935	Kelly Petillo	Gilmore Special	4:42:22.71	106.240	Wilbur Shaw
1936	Louis Meyer	Ring Free Special	4:35:03.39	109.069	Ted Horn
1937	Wilbur Shaw	Shaw–Gilmore Special	4:24:07.80	113.580	Ralph Hepburn
1938	Floyd Roberts	Burd Piston Ring Special	4:15:58.40	117.200	Wilbur Shaw
1939	Wilbur Shaw	Boyle Special	4:20:47.39	115.035	Jimmy Snyder
1940	Wilbur Shaw	Boyle Special	4:22:31.17	114.277	Rex Mays
1941	Floyd Davis–Mauri Rose	Noc-Out Hose Clamp Special	4:20:36.24	115.117	Rex Mays
1946	George Robson	Thorne Engineering Special	4:21:26.71	114.820	Jimmy Jackson
1947	Mauri Rose	Blue Crown Special	4:17:52.17	116.338	Bill Holland
1948	Mauri Rose	Blue Crown Special	4:10:23.33	119.814	Bill Holland
1949	Bill Holland	Blue Crown Special	4:07:15.97	121.327	Johnny Parsons
1950[3]	Johnnie Parsons	Wynn's Friction Proof Special	2:46:55.97	124.002	Bill Holland
1951	Lee Wallard	Belanger Special	3:57:38.05	126.244	Mike Nazaruk
1952	Troy Ruttman	Agajanian Special	3:52:41.88	128.922	Jim Rathmann
1953	Bill Vukovich	Fuel Injection Special	3:53:01.69	128.740	Art Cross
1954	Bill Vukovich	Fuel Injection Special	3:49:17.27	130.840	Jim Bryan
1955	Bob Sweikert	John Zink Special	3:53:59.13	128.209	Tony Bettenhausen
1956	Pat Flaherty	John Zink Special	3:53:28.84	128.490	Sam Hanks
1957	Sam Hanks	Belond Exhaust Special	3:41:14.25	135.601	Jim Rathmann
1958	Jimmy Bryan	Belond A-P Special	3:44:13.80	133.791	George Amick
1959	Rodger Ward	Leader Card 500 Roadster	3:40:49.20	135.857	Jim Rathmann
1960	Jim Rathmann	Ken-Paul Special	3:36:11.36	138.767	Rodger Ward
1961	A. J. Foyt	Bowes Special	3:35:37.49	139.130	Eddie Sachs
1962	Rodger Ward	Leader Card Special	3:33:50.33	140.293	Len Sutton
1963	Parnelli Jones	Agajanian Special	3:29:35.40	143.137	Jim Clark
1964	A. J. Foyt	Offenhauser Special	3:23:35.83	147.350	Rodger Ward
1965	Jim Clark	Lotus–Ford	3:19:05.34	150.686	Parnelli Jones
1966	Graham Hill	Lola–Ford	3:27:52.53	144.317	Jim Clark
1967[4]	A. J. Foyt	Coyote–Ford	3:18:24.22	151.207	Al Unser
1968	Bobby Unser	Eagle–Offenhauser	3:16:13.76	152.882	Dan Gurney
1969	Mario Andretti	STP Hawk–Ford	3:11:14.71	156.867	Dan Gurney
1970	Al Unser	P. J. Colt–Ford	3:12:37.04	155.749	Mark Donohue
1971	Al Unser	P. J. Colt–Ford	3:10:11.56	157.735	Peter Revson
1972	Mark Donohue	McLaren–Offenhauser	3:04:05.54	162.962	Al Unser
1973[5]	Gordon Johncock	Eagle–Offenhauser	2:05:26.59	159.036	Bill Vukovich
1974	Johnny Rutherford	McLaren–Offenhauser	3:09:10.06	158.589	Bobby Unser
1975[6]	Bobby Unser	Eagle–Offenhauser	2:54:55.08	149.213	Johnny Rutherford
1976[7]	Johnny Rutherford	McLaren–Offenhauser	1:42:52.48	148.725	A. J. Foyt
1977	A. J. Foyt	Coyote–Foyt	3:05:57.16	161.331	Tom Sneva
1978	Al Unser	Lola–Cosworth	3:05:54.99	161.363	Tom Sneva
1979	Rick Mears	Penske–Cosworth	3:08:27.97	158.899	A. J. Foyt
1980	Johnny Rutherford	Chaparral–Cosworth	3:29:59.56	142.862	Tom Sneva
1981[8]	Bobby Unser	Eagle–Offenhauser	3:35:41.78	139.029	Mario Andretti

1982	Gordon Johncock	Wildcat-Cosworth	3:05:09.14	162.029	Rick Mears
1983	Tom Sneva	March-Cosworth	3:05:03.06	162.117	Al Unser
1984	Rick Mears	March-Cosworth	3:03:21.00	162.962	Roberto Guerrero
1985	Danny Sullivan	March-Cosworth	3:16:06.069	152.982	Mario Andretti
1986	Bobby Rahal	March-Cosworth	2:55:43.48	170.722	Kevin Cogan
1987	Al Unser, Sr.	March-Cosworth	3:04:59.147	162.175	Roberto Guerrero

1. 300 miles. 2. Race ended at 400 miles because of rain. 3. Race ended at 345 miles because of rain. 4. Race, postponed after 18 laps because of rain on May 30, was finished on May 31. 5. Race postponed May 28 and 29 was cut to 332.5 miles because of rain, May 30. 6. Race ended at 435 miles because of rain. 7. Race ended at 255 miles because of rain. 8. Andretti was awarded the victory the day after the race after Bobby Unser, whose car finished first, was penalized one lap and dropped from first place to second for passing other cars illegally under a yellow caution flag. Unser appealed the decision to the U.S. Auto Club and was upheld. A panel ruled the penalty was too severe and instead fined Unser $40,000, but restored the victory to him.

U.S. AUTO CLUB NATIONAL CHAMPIONS

1910	Ray Harroun	1926	Harry Hartz	1950	Henry Banks	1970	Al Unser
1911	Ralph Mulford	1927	Peter DePaolo	1951	Tony Bettenhausen	1971–72	Joe Leonard
1912	Ralph DePalma	1928–29	Louis Meyer	1952	Chuck Stevenson	1973	Roger McCluskey
1913	Earl Cooper	1930	Billy Arnold	1953	Sam Hanks	1974	Bobby Unser
1914	Ralph DePalma	1931	Louis Schneider	1954	Jimmy Bryan	1975	A. J. Foyt
1915	Earl Cooper	1932	Bob Carey	1955	Bob Sweikert	1976	Gordon Johncock
1916	Dario Resta	1933	Louis Meyer	1956–57	Jimmy Bryan	1977–78	Tom Sneva
1917	Earl Cooper	1934	Bill Cummings	1958	Tony Bettenhausen	1979	A. J. Foyt
1918	Ralph Mulford	1935	Kelly Petillo	1959	Rodger Ward	1980	Johnny Rutherford
1919	Howard Wilcox	1936	Mauri Rose	1960–61	A. J. Foyt	1981–82	George Snider
1920	Gaston Chevrolet	1937	Wilbur Shaw	1962	Rodger Ward	1983	Tom Sneva
1921	Tommy Milton	1938	Floyd Roberts	1963–64	A. J. Foyt	1984	Rick Mears
1922	James Murphy	1939	Wilbur Shaw	1965–66	Mario Andretti	1985	Danny Sullivan
1923	Eddie Hearne	1940–41	Rex Mays	1967	A. J. Foyt	1986	Bobby Rahal
1924	James Murphy	1946–48	Ted Horn	1968	Bobby Unser		
1925	Peter DePaolo	1949	Johnnie Parsons	1969	Mario Andretti		

NATIONAL ASSOCIATION FOR STOCK CAR AUTO RACING (NASCAR) GRAND NATIONAL CHAMPIONS

1949	Red Byron	1956–57	Buck Baker	1966	David Pearson	1979	Richard Petty
1950	Bill Rexford	1958–59	Lee Petty	1967	Richard Petty	1980	Dale Earnhardt
1951	Herb Thomas	1960	Rex White	1968–69	David Pearson	1981	Darrell Waltrip
1952	Tim Flock	1961	Ned Jarrett	1970	Bobby Isaac	1982	Darrell Waltrip
1953	Herb Thomas	1962–63	Joe Weatherly	1971–72	Richard Petty	1983	Bobby Allison
1954	Lee Petty	1964	Richard Petty	1973	Benny Parsons	1984	Terry Labonte
1955	Tim Flock	1965	Ned Jarrett	1974–75	Richard Petty	1985	Darrell Waltrip
				1976–78	Cale Yarborough	1986	Dale Earnhardt

WORLD GRAND PRIX DRIVER CHAMPIONS

1950	Giuseppe Farina, Italy, Alfa Romeo	1969	Jackie Stewart, Scotland, Matra-Ford
1951	Juan Fangio, Argentina, Alfa Romeo	1970	Jochen Rindt, Austria, Lotus-Ford
1952	Alberto Ascari, Italy, Ferrari	1971	Jackie Stewart, Scotland, Tyrrell-Ford
1953	Alberto Ascari, Italy, Ferrari	1972	Emerson Fittipaldi, Brazil, Lotus-Ford
1955	Juan Fangio, Argentina, Maserati, Mercedes-Benz	1973	Jackie Stewart, Scotland, Tyrrell-Ford
1955	Juan Fangio, Argentina, Mercedes-Benz	1974	Emerson Fittipaldi, Brazil, McLaren-Ford
1956	Juan Fangio, Argentina, Lancia-Ferrari	1975	Niki Lauda, Austria, Ferrari
1957	Juan Fangio, Argentina, Masserati	1976	James Hunt, Britain, McLaren-Ford
1958	Mike Hawthorn, England, Ferrari	1977	Niki Lauda, Austria, Ferrari
1959	Jack Brabham, Australia, Cooper	1978	Mario Andretti, Nazareth, Pa., Lotus
1960	Jack Brabham, Australia, Cooper	1979	Jody Scheckter, South Africa
1961	Phil Hill, United States, Ferrari	1980	Alan Jones, Australia
1962	Graham Hill, England, BRM	1981	Nelson Piquet, Brazil
1963	Jim Clark, Scotland, Lotus-Ford	1982	Kiki Rosberg, Finland
1964	John Surtees, England, Ferrari	1983	Nelson Piquet, Brazil
1965	Jim Clark, Scotland, Lotus-Ford	1984	Nikki Lauda, Austria
1966	Jack Brabham, Australia, Brabham-Repco	1985	Alain Prost, France
1967	Denis Hulme, New Zealand, Brabham-Repco	1986	Alain Prost, France
1968	Graham Hill, England, Lotus-Ford		

U.S. AUTO CLUB

1987 Major Races

Indianapolis 500 (Indianapolis Motor Speedway, May 24, 1987, 500 miles)—1. Al Unser Sr., Albuquerque, N.M.; March-Cosworth; 200 laps; time: 3:04:59.147. Average speed: 162.175 mph; First place prize: $526,763. 2. Roberto Guerrero, Colombia; March-Cosworth; 200 laps; $305,103. 3. Fabrizio Barbaza, Monza, Italy; March-Cosworth; 198 laps; $204,663. 4. Al Unser Jr., Albuquerque, N.M.; March-Cosworth; 196 laps; $142,963. 5. G. Bettenhausen, West Germany; March-Cosworth; 195 laps; $132,213.

Pocono 500 (Long Pond, Pa., Pocono International Raceway, June 14, 1987, 500 miles)—1. Tim Richmond, Asland, Ohio; Chevrolet; 200 laps; time: 4:05.57. Average speed: 122.166 mph. First place prize: $40,325. 2. Bill Elliot, Dawsonville, Ga.; Ford; 200 laps; $30, 600. 3. Kyle Petty, Randleman, N.C.; Ford, 200 laps; $24,575. 4. Cale Yarborough, Sardis, S.C.; Oldsmobile; 200 laps; $11,505. 5. Dale Earnhardt, Kannapolis, N.C.; Chevrolet; 200 laps; $22,400.

1986 NASCAR LEADING MONEY WINNERS

1. Dale Earnhardt	$1,168,100
2. Bill Elliot	887,730
3. Darrell Waltrip	844,345
4. Tim Richmond	772,720
5. Geoff Bodine	696,605
6. Ricky Rudd	561,025
7. Harry Gant	539,450
8. Terry Labonte	487,690

FINAL 1986 WINSTON CUP GRAND NATIONAL POINT LEADERS

Pos.	Driver name	Points
1.	Dale Earnhardt	4468
2.	Darrell Waltrip	4180
3.	Tim Richmond	4174
4.	Bill Elliott	3844
5.	Ricky Rudd	3823
6.	Rusty Wallace	3762
7.	Bobby Allison	3698
8.	Geoff Bodine	3678
9.	Bobby Hillin, Jr.	3546
10.	Kyle Petty	3537
11.	Harry Gant	3498
12.	Terry Labonte	3473
13.	Neil Bonnett	3369
14.	Richard Petty	3314
15.	Joe Ruttman	3295
16.	Ken Schrader	3052
17.	Dave Marcis	2912
18.	Morgan Shepherd	2986
19.	Mike Waltrip	2853
20.	Buddy Arrington	2776
21.	Alan Kulwicki	2705
22.	Jimmy Means	2495
23.	Tommy Ellis	2393
24.	Buddy Baker	1924
25.	Eddie Bierschwale	1860

PADDLE TENNIS

NATIONAL OPEN CHAMPIONS—1987

Men's singles—Scott Freedman, Culver City, Calif.

Women's singles—Kathy May Paben, Los Angeles, Calif.

Men's doubles—Dave Stahl, Culver City, Calif. and Richard Roth, Woodland Hills, Calif.

Women's doubles—Kathy May Paben, Los Angeles, Calif., and Morgan Bowman, Rolling Hills Estates, Calif.

Mixed doubles—Morgan Bowman, Rolling Hills Estates, Calif., and Scott Freedman, Culver City, Calif.

Beach men's doubles—Sol Hauptman, Culver City, Calif., and Jeff Fleitman, Los Angeles, Calif.

Beach women's doubles—Morgan Bowman, Rolling Hills Estates, Calif., and Kathy May Paben, Los Angeles, Calif.

LACROSSE

NATIONAL INTERCOLLEGIATE CHAMPIONS

1946	Navy
1947–48	Johns Hopkins
1949	Johns Hopkins, Navy
1950	Johns Hopkins
1951	Army, Princeton
1952	Virginia, R.P.I.
1953	Princeton
1954	Navy
1955–56	Maryland
1957	Johns Hopkins
1958	Army
1959	Army, Johns Hopkins, Maryland
1960	Navy
1961	Army, Navy
1962–66	Navy
1967	Johns Hopkins, Maryland, Navy
1968	Johns Hopkins
1969	Army, Johns Hopkins
1970	Johns Hopkins, Navy, Virginia
1971[1]	Cornell
1972	Virginia
1973	Maryland
1974	Johns Hopkins
1975	Maryland
1976–77	Cornell
1978–80	Johns Hopkins
1981	North Carolina
1982	North Carolina
1983	Syracuse
1984	Johns Hopkins
1985	Johns Hopkins
1986	North Carolina
1987	Johns Hopkins

1. First year of N.C.A.A. Championship Tournaments.

N.C.A.A. CHAMPIONSHIPS—1987

DIVISION I

Final

(Rutgers University, New Brunswick, N.J., May 25, 1987)

Johns Hopkins 11, Cornell 10

Semifinals

(May 23, 1987)

Johns Hopkins 13, Maryland 8

Cornell 18, Syracuse 15

DIVISION III

(Geneva, N.Y., May 16, 1987)

Hobart 9, Ohio Wesleyan, 5[1]

1. Hobart set NCAA record for consecutive championships in team competition with 8th straight Division III title.

RODEO

PROFESSIONAL RODEO COWBOY ASSOCIATION, ALL AROUND COWBOY

1953	Bill Linderman
1954	Buck Rutherford
1955	Casey Tibbs
1956–59	Jim Shoulders
1960	Harry Tompkins
1961	Benny Reynolds
1962	Tom Nesmith
1963–65	Dean Oliver
1966–70	Larry Mahan
1971–72	Phil Lyne
1973	Larry Mahan
1974	Tom Ferguson
1975	Leo Camarillo and Tom Ferguson
1976–79	Tom Ferguson
1980	Paul Tierney
1981	Jimmie Cooper
1982	Chris Lybbert
1983	Roy Cooper
1984	Dee Pickett
1985	Lewis Field
1986	Lewis Field[1]

1. Next championship scheduled December 1987, in Las Vegas, Nev., after *Information Please Almanac* went to press.

SOFTBALL

Source: Amateur Softball Association.

AMATEUR CHAMPIONS

1959	Aurora (Ill.) Sealmasters
1960	Clearwater (Fla.) Bombers
1961	Aurora (Ill.) Sealmasters
1962–63	Clearwater (Fla.) Bombers
1964	Burch Gage & Tool, Detroit
1965	Aurora (Ill.) Sealmasters
1966	Clearwater (Fla.) Bombers
1967	Aurora (Ill.) Sealmasters
1968	Clearwater (Fla.) Bombers
1969	Raybestos Cardinals, Stratford, Conn.
1971	Welty Way, Cedar Rapids, Iowa
1972	Raybestos Cardinals, Stratford, Conn.
1973	Clearwater (Fla.) Bombers
1974	Santa Rosa (Calif.)
1975	Rising Sun Hotel, Reading, Pa.
1976	Raybestos Cardinals, Stratford, Conn.
1977	Billard Barbell, Reading, Pa.
1978	Reading, Pa.
1979	Midland, Mich.
1980	Peterbilt Western, Seattle
1981	Archer Daniels Midland, Decatur, Ill.
1982	Peterbilt Western, Seattle
1983	Franklin Cardinals, West Haven, Conn.
1984	California Coors Kings, Merced, Calif.
1985	Pay 'n Pak, Bellevue, Washington
1986	Pay 'n Pak, Bellevue, Washington
1987	Pay 'n Pak, Bellevue, Washington

AMATEUR SOFTBALL CHAMPIONS—1987

Men's major fast pitch—Pay 'n Pak, Bellevue, Wash.
Women's major fast pitch—Orange County Majestics, Orange County, Calif.
Men's Class A fast pitch—Jolly Molly, Reading, Calif.
Women's Class A fast pitch—Inland Cities Raiders, Cypress, Calif.
Men's Class B fast pitch—San Antonio Jayhawks, San Antonio, Tex.
Women's Class B fast pitch—Silver Bulletys, Bay City, Mich.
Men's major slow pitch—Starpath Systems, Lexington, Ky.
Women's major slow pitch—Key Ford Mustangs, Pensacola, Fla.
Men's major industrial slow pitch—Sikorsky Aircraft, Shelton, Conn.
Men's major church slow pitch—12th Street Baptist, Gadsden, Ala.
Men's 16 major slow pitch—Sports Station, Blue Island, Ill.
Women's major industrial slow pitch—Provident Vets, Chattanooga, Tenn.
Women's major church slow pitch—N. Cleveland Church of God, Cleveland, Tenn.
Men's Class A slow pitch—Minneapolis Merchants, Minneapolis, Minn.
Women's Class A slow pitch—Stompers, Richmond, Va.
Men's Class A industrial slow pitch—UA Local 1112 Cochran Pontiac, Youngstown, Ohio
Men's Class A church slow pitch—Rehobeth Presbyterian, Tucker, Ga.
Men's 16 Class A slow pitch—Aces, Chicago, Ill.
Men's Super slow pitch—Steele's Sports, Grafton, Ohio.
Men's modified—WTB Broadway, Spokane, Wash.
Women's modified—Talk of the Town, Staten Island, N.Y.
Men's Class A Modified Pitch—LSI-Triangle, Delano, Minn.
Men's Masters slow pitch (35 and over)—Budweiser, Detroit, Mich.
Men's Masters slow pitch (45 and over)—John Hanson Savings & Loan, Beltville, Md.
Men's Masters fast pitch (40 and over)—Tulsa Masters, Tulsa, Okla.
Coed slow pitch—SA Cannan's, San Antonio, Tex.

YOUTH TOURNAMENTS—1987

Boys 18-and-under slow pitch—Bandidos, Miami, Fla.
Boys 15-and-under slow pitch—Roxboro Reds, Roxboro, N.C.
Boys 12-and-under slow pitch—Wranglers, Tifton, Ga.
Boys 18-and-under fast pitch—Prescott Merchants, Prescott, Ariz.
Boys 15-and-under fast pitch—Machesney Park Flyers, Machesney, Il.
Boys 12-and-under fast pitch—Rice Lake Voyagers, Rice Lake, Wis.
Girls 18-and-under slow pitch—Bandits, Jonesboro, Ga.
Girls 15-and-under slow pitch—Pembroke Pine Cardinals, Hollywood, Fla.
Girls 12-and-under slow pitch—South Dade Wildcats, Miami, Fla.
Girls 18-and-under fast pitch—Raiders, Santa Maria, Calif.
Girls 15-and-under fast pitch—Batbusters, Fountain Valley, Calif.
Girls 12-and-under fast pitch—Orcutt Mini Express, Santa Monica, Calif.

HANDBALL

U.S.H.A. NATIONAL FOUR-WALL CHAMPIONS

Singles

1960	Jimmy Jacobs
1961	John Sloan
1962–63	Oscar Obert
1964–65	Jimmy Jacobs
1966–67	Paul Haber
1968	Simon (Stuffy) Singer
1969–71	Paul Haber
1972	Fred Lewis
1973	Terry Muck
1974	Fred Lewis
1975	Jay Bilyeu
1976	Vern Roberts, Jr.
1977	Naty Alvarado
1978	Fred Lewis
1979	Naty Alvarado
1980	Naty Alvarado
1981	Fred Lewis
1982	Naty Alvarado
1983	Naty Alvarado
1984	Naty Alvarado
1985	Naty Alvarado
1986	Naty Alvarado
1987	Naty Alvarado

Doubles

1960	Jimmy Jacobs–Dick Weisman
1961	John Sloan–Vic Hershkowitz
1962–63	Jimmy Jacobs–Marty Decatur
1964	John Sloan–Phil Elbert
1965	Jimmy Jacobs–Marty Decatur
1966	Pete Tyson–Bob Lindsay
1967–68	Jimmy Jacobs–Marty Decatur
1969	Lou Kramberg–Lou Russo
1970	Karl and Ruby Obert
1971	Ray Neveau–Simie Fein
1972	Kent Fusselman–Al Drews
1973–74	Ray Neveau–Simie Fein
1975	Marty Decatur–Steve Lott
1976	Gary Rohrer–Dan O'Connor
1977	Skip McDowell–Matt Kelly
1978	Stuffy Singer–Marty Decatur
1979	Stuffy Singer–Marty Decatur
1980	Skip McDowell–Harry Robertson
1981	Tom Kopatich–Jack Roberts
1982	Naty Alvarado–Vern Roberts
1983	Naty Alvarado–Vern Roberts
1984	Naty Alvarado–Vern Roberts
1985	Naty Alvarado–Vern Roberts
1986–87	Jon Kemdler–Poncho Monreal

1987 PAN AMERICAN GAMES CHAMPIONSHIPS

Archery

Men—Jay Barrs, United States
Women—Denise Parker, United States

Boxing

106 lb—Luis Rolon, Puerto Rico
112 lb—Adalberto Regalado, Cuba
119 lb—Manuel Martinez, Cuba
125 lb—Kelcie Banks, United States
132 lb—Julio Gonzales, Cuba
139 lb—Candelario Duvergel, Cuba
147 lb—Juan Lemus, Cuba
156 lb—Orestes Solano, Cuba
165 lb—Angel Espinosa, Cuba
178 lb—Pablo Romero, Cuba
201 lb—Felix Savon, Cuba
Over 201 lb—Jorge Gonzales, Cuba

Canoe-Kayak—Men

Canoe singles—Bruce Merritt, United States
500m kayak singles—Norman Bellingham, United States
500m canoe singles—Jim Terrell, United States
1,000m kayak doubles—Norman Bellingham and Greg Barton, United States
Two-man kayak—Mike Herbert and Terry Kent, United States
Four-man kayak—United States

Canoe-Kayak—Women

500m kayak singles—Traci Phillips, United States
Two-woman kayak—Shirley Dery-Batlik and Sheira Conover, United States
Four-woman kayak—United States

Cycling—Men

Sprint—Ken Carpenter, United States
Individual pursuit—Gabriel Curuchet, Argentina

Cycling—Women

Sprint—Connie Paraskevin-Young, United States
Individual pursuit—Rebecca Twigg-Whitehead, United States

Diving—Men

3-meter springboard—Greg Louganis, United States
10-meter platform—Greg Louganis, United States

Diving—Women

3-meter springboard—Kelly McCormick, United States
10-meter platform—Michelle Mitchell, United States

Equestrian

Three-day event individual—Mike Huber, United States
Three-day event team—United States
Individual jumping—Ian Miller, Canada
Team jumping—Canada
Individual dressage—Christilot Boyled, Canada
Team dressage—United States

Fencing

Men's foil—Guillermo Betancourt, Cuba
Men's team foil—Cuba
Men's epee—Carlos Pedrosa, Cuba
Men's individual sabre—Jean Pauk Banos, Canada
Men's team sabre—Cuba
Women's foil—Caitlin Bilodeaux, United States
Women's team foil—United States

Gymnastics—Men

All-around—Scott Johnson, United States
Floor exercise—Casimiro Suarez, Cuba
Horizontal bar—Felix Aguilera, Cuba
Parallel bars—Scott Johnson, United States
Pommel horse—Tim Daggett, United States
Still rings—Scott Johnson, United States
Vault—Casimiro Suarez, Cuba
Team—United States

Gymnastics—Women

All-around—Sabrina Mar, United States
Floor exercise—Kristie Phillips, United States
Balance beam—Kelly Garrison-Steves, United States
Uneven bars—Melissa Marlowe, United States
Vault—Laura Rodriguez, Cuba
Team—United States

Roller Skating—Artistic

Men's figure skating—Skip Clinton, United States
Women's figure skating—Patti Jefferson, United States
Free dance—Robert Ferendo and Lori Walsh, United States
Pairs—Ken Benson and Robyn Young, United States

Roller Skating—Men's Racing

5,000m—Jose Luis Lozano, Argentina
10,000m—Jose Luis Lozano, Argentina
20,000m—Jose Luis Lozano, Argentina
10,000m relay—Argentina

Roller Skating—Women's Racing

3,000m—Darlene Kessinger, United States
5,000m—Luz Mery Tristan, Colombia
5,000m relay—United States

Rowing—Men

Singles—Paul Fuchs, United States
Singles petite—Sergio Fernandez, Argentina
Doubles—John Bigelow and Greg Walker, United States
Lightweight doubles—Brian Thorne and John Murphy, Canada
Pairs without coxswain—Ricardo Carvalho and Ronaldo Carvalho, Brazil
Lightweight pairs without coxswain—Pablo Bullgach and Marchello Freije, Argentina
Fours without coxswain—Cuba
Eights—United States

Rowing—Women

Singles—Silken Laumann, Canada
Lightweight singles—Michele Murphy, Canada
Doubles—Peggy Johnston and Susan Cooper, United States
Pairs without coxswain—Kirsten Barnes and Kathleen Heddle, Canada
Lightweight pairs without coxswain—Hildegard Emslander and Cola Parker, United States

Shooting—Men

Rapid-fire pistol—Bernardo Tovar, Colombia
Automatic trap—Dan Carlisle, United States
Air rifle—Guy Lorien, Canada
Small bore rifle-prone—Pat Vamplew, Canada
Skeet—Matt Dryke, United States
Team skeet—United States
Team air pistol—United States
Running game target—Mike English, United States
Pistol-10meters—Don Nygord, United States
Center fire pistol—Berto Renzo, Venezuela
Center fire team—United States

Shooting—Women

Air pistol—Tania Perez, Canada
Three-position small bore rifle—Irma Sanchez, Cuba
Small bore rifle-prone—Deena Wigger, United States

Swimming—Men

50m freestyle—Tom Williams, United States
100m freestyle—Todd Dudley, United States
200m freestyle—John Witchel, United States
400m freestyle—Paul Robinson, United States
1,500m freestyle—Alex Kostich, United States
100m backstroke—Andy Gill, United States
200m backstroke—Mike O'Brien, United States
200m butterfly—Bill Stapleton, United States
100m breaststroke—Richard Kornhammer, United States
200m breaststroke—Jeff Kubiak, United States
200m individual medley—Bill Stapleton, United States
400m individual medley—Jerry Frentsos, United States
400m medley relay—United States
400m freestyle relay—United States
800m freestyle relay—United States

Swimming—Women

50m freestyle—Jennifer Thompson, United States
100m freestyle—Sylvia Poll, Costa Rica
200m freestyle—Sylvia Poll, Costa Rica
400m freestyle—Julie Martin, United States
800m freestyle—Tammy Bruce, United States
100m backstroke—Sylvia Poll, Costa Rica
200m backstroke—Katie Welch, United States
100m butterfly—Janet Jorgensen, United States
200m butterfly—Kara McGrath, United States
100m breaststroke—Keltie Dugan, Canada
200m breaststroke—Dorsey Tierney, United States
200m individual medley—Susan Habermas, United States
400m individual medley—Tammy Bruce, United States
400m medley relay—United States
400m freestyle relay—United States
800m freestyle relay—United States

Table Tennis

Men's singles—Gideon Ng, Canada
Men's doubles—Horatio Pintea and Gideon Ng, Canada
Women's singles—Insook Bhushan, United States
Women's doubles—Diana Gee and Insook Bhushan, United States
Mixed doubles—Khoa Nguyen and Insook Bhushan, United States

Taekwondo

Fin weight—Dae Sung Lee, United States
Flyweight—Carlos Rivas, Venezuela
Lightweight—Steve Capener, United States
Middleweight—Herb Perez, United States
Welterweight—Ernesto Rodriguez, Mexico
Heavyweight—Jimmy Kim, United States

Tennis

Men's singles—Fernando Roese, Brazil
Men's doubles—Pat McEnroe and Luke Jensen, United States
Women's singles—Gisele Miro, Brazil
Women's doubles—Sonia Hahn and Ronni Reis, United States
Mixed doubles—Lucila Becerra and Gilberto Cicero, Mexico

Track and Field—Men

100m—Lee McRae, United States
200m—Floyd Heard, United States
400m—Raymond Pierre, United States
800m—Johnny Gray, United States
1,500m—Joaquim Cruz, Brazil
3,000m—Adauto Domingues, Brazil
5,000m—Arturo Barrios, Mexico
10,000m—Bruce Bickford, United States
Marathon—Ivo Rodrigues, Brazil
110m hurdles—Andrew Parker, Jamaica
400m hurdles—Winthrop Graham, Jamaica
4 × 100 relay—United States
4 × 400 relay—United States
20-k walk—Carlos Mercenario, Mexico
50-k walk—Martin Bermudez, Mexico
Shot-put—Geri Weil, Chile
Javelin—Duncan Atwood, United States
Hammer—Judd Logan, United States
Pole vault—Mike Tully, United States
Discus—Mariano Delis, Cuba
High jump—Javier Sotomayor, Cuba
Long jump—Carl Lewis, United States
Triple jump—Michael Conley, United States
Decathlon—Mike Gonzales, United States

Track and Fielα—Women

100m—Gail Devers, United States
200m—Gwen Torrence, United States
400m—Judith King, United States
800m—Anna Quirot, Cuba
1,500m—Linda Sheskey, United States
3,000m—Mary Knisley, United States
10,000m—Marty Cooksey, United States
Marathon—Maricarmen Cardenas, Mexico
100m hurdles—Lavonna Martin, United States
400m hurdles—Judi Brown-King, United States
4 × 100 relay—United States
4 × 400 relay—United States
10,000m walk—Maria Colin, Mexico
Javelin—Ivonne Leal, Cuba
Shot put—Ramona Pagel, United States
Discus—Maritza Marten, Cuba
Long jump—Jackie Joyner-Kersee, United States
High jump—Coleen Sommer, United States
Heptathlon—Cindy Greiner, United States

Weightlifting

52k—Juan Hernandez, Cuba
56k—Pedro Negrin, Cuba
60k—Julio Loscos, Cuba
67.5k—Raoul Mora, Cuba
75k—Pablo Lara, Cuba
82.5k—Pedro Rodriguez, Cuba
90k—Omar Semanat, Cuba
100k—Denis Garon, Canada
110k—David Bolduc, Canada
Over 110k—Mario Martinez, United States

Wrestling—Freestyle

105.5 lb—Aldo Martinez, Cuba
114.5 lb—Carlos Varela, Cuba
125.5 lb—Alejandro Puerto, Cuba
136.5 lb—John Smith, United States
149.5 lb—Andre Metzger, United States
163 lb—David Schultz, United States
198 lb—Doug Cox, Canada
Unlimited—Bruce Barmgartner, United States

Greco-Roman Wrestling

48 kg—Reinaldo Jimenez, Cuba
52 kg—Pedro Roque, Cuba
57 kg—Amadoris Gonzales, Cuba
62 kg—Nario Olivera, Cuba
68 kg—Alkexis Jiminez, Cuba
74 kg—David Butler, United States
82 kg—Chris Catalfo, United States
90 kg—Guillermo Cruz, Cuba
100 kg—Hector Milan, Cuba
130 kg—Duane Koslowski, United States

Yachting

Laser—United States
Soling—United States
Star—Canada
Lightning—Argentina
Snipe—United States
Sailboard (men)—United States
Sailboard (women)—United States

Team sports

Baseball—Cuba
Basketball, men—Brazil
Basketball, women—United States
Field hockey, men—Canada
Field hockey, women—Argentina
Soccer—Brazil
Softball, men—Canada
Softball, women—United States
Team handball—United States
Volleyball, men—United States
Volleyball, women—Cuba
Water polo—United States

History of Bowling

According to the "Browser's Book of Beginnings," published by Houghton Mifflin Company, the origin of this sport can be traced to items found in the tomb of an Egyptian child who was buried around 5200 B.C. The game was played by setting up nine vertical stone shafts as pins and rolling a round stone ball to topple them. The ball first had to roll under an archway constructed of three pieces of carved marble. A noisy game, and undoubtedly subject to frequent equipment changes because of breaking stones, it nonetheless remained the model for many games that followed.

A later Polynesian version, called *ula maike,* also played with stone balls and pins, introduced the modern lane distance of 60 feet.

In Italy about 2000 years ago, **bocci**, a game still widely played, began in the Alps. Similar to bowling, bocci called for the underhand tossing of stones at a fixed object.

The contemporary idea of bowling at wooden pins originated in Germany, not as a sport but as part of a religious ceremony. In fact Martin Luther, the leader of the Reformation, even posited arguments as to why nine pins was the ideal and only number to be used at the end of the lane.

Bowling at wooden pins in the United States likely arose either from the German custom or from that of early Dutch settlers, who set up what is known today as Bowling Green, at the tip of Manhattan Island in New York City, where the game was played until 1840.

The origin of the tenth pin that now characterizes Western bowling apparently rests with a law prohibiting the game of ninepins because so much betting was associated with it. A tenth pin was added in 1845 to thwart the legal ban.

Source: From *Browser's Book of Beginnings* by Charles Panati, Copyright © 1984 by Charles Carroll Hudson. Reprinted by permission of Houghton Mifflin Company.

BASEBALL

The popular tradition that baseball was invented by Abner Doubleday at Cooperstown, N.Y., in 1839 has been enshrined in the Hall of Fame and National Museum of Baseball erected in that town, but research has proved that a game called "Base Ball" was played in this country and England before 1839. The first team baseball as we know it was played at the Elysian Fields, Hoboken, N.J., on June 19, 1846, between the Knickerbockers and the New York Nine. The next fifty years saw a gradual growth of baseball and an improvement of equipment and playing skill.

Historians have it that the first pitcher to throw a curve was William A. (Candy) Cummings in 1867. The Cincinnati Red Stockings were the first all-professional team, and in 1869 they played 64 games without a loss. The standard ball of the same size and weight, still the rule, was adopted in 1872. The first catcher's mask was worn in 1875. The National League was organized in 1876. The first chest protector was worn in 1885. The three-strike rule was put on the books in 1887, and the four-ball ticket to first base was instituted in 1889. The pitching distance was lengthened to 60 feet 6 inches in 1893, and the rules have been modified only slightly since that time.

The American League, under the vigorous leadership of B. B. Johnson, became a major league in 1901. Judge Kenesaw Mountain Landis, by action of the two major leagues, became Commissioner of Baseball in 1921, and upon his death (1944), Albert B. Chandler, former United States Senator from Kentucky, was elected to that office (1945). Chandler failed to obtain a new contract and was succeeded by Ford C. Frick (1951), the National League president. Frick retired after the 1965 season, and William D. Eckert, a retired Air Force lieutenant general, was named to succeed him. Eckert resigned under pressure in December, 1968. Bowie Kuhn, a New York attorney, became interim commissioner for one year in February. His appointment was made permanent with two seven-year contracts until August 1983. In August 1983, Kuhn's contract was not renewed, and a search begun for his successor. Peter Ueberroth was named new Commissioner and took office Oct. 1, 1984.

MAJOR LEAGUE ALL-STAR GAME

Year	Date	Winning league and manager	Runs	Losing league and manager	Runs	Winning pitcher	Losing pitcher	Site	Paid attendance
1933	July 6	A.L. (Mack)	4	N.L. (McGraw)	2	Gomez	Hallahan	Chicago A.L.	47,595
1934	July 10	A.L. (Cronin)	9	N.L. (Terry)	7	Harder	Mungo	New York N.L.	48,363
1935	July 8	A.L. (Cochrane)	4	N.L. (Frisch)	1	Gomez	Walker	Cleveland A.L.	69,831
1936	July 7	N.L. (Grimm)	4	A.L. (McCarthy)	3	J. Dean	Grove	Boston N.L.	25,556
1937	July 7	A.L. (McCarthy)	8	N.L. (Terry)	3	Gomez	J. Dean	Washington A.L.	31,391
1938	July 6	N.L. (Terry)	4	A.L. (McCarthy)	1	Vander Meer	Gomez	Cincinnati N.L.	27,067
1939	July 11	A.L. (McCarthy)	3	N.L. (Hartnett)	1	Bridges	Lee	New York A.L.	62,892
1940	July 9	N.L. (McKechnie)	4	A.L. (Cronin)	0	Derringer	Ruffing	St. Louis N.L.	32,373
1941	July 8	A.L. (Baker)	7	N.L. (McKechnie)	5	E. Smith	Passeau	Detroit A.L.	54,674
1942	July 6	A.L. (McCarthy)	3	N.L. (Durocher)	1	Chandler	Cooper	New York N.L.	34,178
1943	July 13[1]	A.L. (McCarthy)	5	N.L. (Southworth)	3	Leonard	Cooper	Philadelphia A.L.	31,938
1944	July 11[1]	N.L. (Southworth)	7	A.L. (McCarthy)	1	Raffensberger	Hughson	Pittsburgh N.L.	29,589
1946	July 9	A.L. (O'Neill)	12	N.L. (Grimm)	0	Feller	Passeau	Boston A.L.	34,906
1947	July 8	A.L. (Cronin)	2	N.L. (Dyer)	1	Shea	Sain	Chicago N.L.	41,123
1948	July 13	A.L. (Harris)	5	N.L. (Durocher)	2	Raschi	Schmitz	St. Louis A.L.	34,009
1949	July 12	A.L. (Boudreau)	11	N.L. (Southworth)	7	Trucks	Newcombe	Brooklyn N.L.	32,577
1950	July 11	N.L. (Shotton)	4	A.L. (Stengel)	3[3]	Blackwell	Gray	Chicago A.L.	46,127
1951	July 10	N.L. (Sawyer)	8	A.L. (Stengel)	3	Maglie	Lopat	Detroit A.L.	52,075
1952	July 8	N.L. (Durocher)	3	A.L. (Stengel)	2[4]	Rush	Lemon	Philadelphia N.L.	32,785
1953	July 14	N.L. (Dressen)	5	A.L. (Stengel)	1	Spahn	Reynolds	Cincinnati N.L.	30,846
1954	July 13	A.L. (Stengel)	11	N.L. (Alston)	9	Stone	Conley	Cleveland A.L.	68,751
1955	July 12	N.L. (Durocher)	6	A.L. (Lopez)	5[3]	Conley	Sullivan	Milwaukee N.L.	45,643
1956	July 10	N.L. (Alston)	7	A.L. (Stengel)	3	Friend	Pierce	Washington A.L.	28,843
1957	July 9	A.L. (Stengel)	6	N.L. (Alston)	5	Bunning	Simmons	St. Louis N.L.	30,693
1958	July 8	A.L. (Stengel)	4	N.L. (Haney)	3	Wynn	Friend	Baltimore A.L.	48,829
1959[2]	July 7	N.L. (Haney)	5	A.L. (Stengel)	4	Antonelli	Ford	Pittsburgh N.L.	35,277
	Aug. 3	A.L. (Stengel)	5	N.L. (Haney)	3	Walker	Drysdale	Los Angeles N.L.	55,105
1960[2]	July 11	N.L. (Alston)	5	A.L. (Lopez)	3	Friend	Monbouquette	Kansas City A.L.	30,619
	July 13	N.L. (Alston)	6	A.L. (Lopez)	0	Law	Ford	New York A.L.	38,362
1961[2]	July 11	N.L. (Murtaugh)	5	A.L. (Richards)	4[6]	Miller	Wilhelm	San Francisco N.L.	44,115
	July 31	N.L (Murtaugh)	1	A.L. (Richards)	1[7]	—	—	Boston A.L.	31,851
1962[2]	July 10	N.L. (Hutchinson)	3	A.L. (Houk)	1	Marichal	Pascual	Washington A.L.	45,480
	July 30	A.L. (Houk)	9	N.L. (Hutchinson)	4	Herbert	Mahaffey	Chicago N.L.	38,359
1963	July 9	N.L. (Dark)	5	A.L. (Houk)	3	Jackson	Bunning	Cleveland A.L.	44,160
1964	July 7	N.L. (Alston)	7	A.L. (Lopez)	4	Marichal	Radatz	New York N.L.	50,850
1965	July 13	N.L. (March)	6	A.L. (Lopez)	5	Koufax	McDowell	Minnesota A.L.	46,706
1966	July 12	N.L. (Alston)	2	A.L. (Mele)	1[6]	Perry	Rickert	St. Louis N.L.	49,926
1967	July 11	N.L. (Alston)	2	A.L. (Bauer)	1[8]	Drysdale	Hunter	Anaheim A.L.	46,309
1968	July 9	N.L. (Schoendienst)	1	A.L. (Williams)	0	Drysdale	Tiant	Houston N.L.	48,321
1969	July 23	N.L. (Schoendienst)	9	A.L. (M. Smith)	3	Carlton	Stottlemyre	Washington A.L.	45,259
1970	July 14	N.L. (Hodges)	5	A.L. (Weaver)	4	Osteen	Wright	Cincinnati N.L.	51,838
1971	July 13	A.L. (Weaver)	6	N.L. (Anderson)	4	Blue	Ellis	Detroit A.L.	53,559

1972	July 25	N.L. (Murtaugh)	4	A.L. (Weaver)	3[6]	McGraw	McNally	Atlanta N.L.	53,107
1973	July 24[1]	N.L. (Anderson)	7	A.L. (Williams)	1	Wise	Blyleven	Kansas City A.L.	40,849
1974	July 23[1]	N.L. (Berra)	7	A.L. (Williams)	2	Brett	Tiant	Pittsburgh N.L.	50,706
1975	July 15[1]	N.L. (Alston)	6	A.L. (Dark)	3	Matlack	Hunter	Milwaukee A.L.	51,540
1976	July 13	N.L. (Anderson)	7	A.L. (D. Johnson)	1	R. Jones	Fidrych	Philadelphia N.L.	63,974
1977	July 19[1]	N.L. (Anderson)	7	A.L. (Martin)	5	Sutton	Palmer	New York A.L.	56,683
1978	July 11[1]	N.L. (Lasorda)	7	A.L. (Martin)	3	Sutter	Gossage	San Diego N.L.	51,549
1979	July 17[1]	N.L. (Lasorda)	7	A.L. (Lemon)	6	Sutter	Kern	Seattle A.L.	58,905
1980	July 8[1]	N.L. (Tanner)	4	A.L. (Weaver)	2	Reuss	John	Los Angeles N.L.	56,088
1981	Aug. 9[1]	N.L. (Green)	5	A.L. (Frey)	4	Blue	Fingers	Cleveland* A.L.	72,086
1982	July 13[1]	N.L. (Lasorda)	4	A.L. (Martin)	1	Rogers	Eckersley	Montreal N.L.	59,057
1983	July 6[1]	A.L. (Kuenn)	13	N.L. (Herzog)	3	Steib	Soto	Chicago A.L.	43,801
1984	July 11[1]	N.L. (Owens)	3	A.L. (Altobelli)	1	Leg	Steib	San Francisco, N.L.	57,756
1985	July 16[1]	N.L. (Williams)	6	A.L. (Anderson)	1	Hoyt	Morris	Minneapolis, A.L.	54,960
1986	July 15[1]	A.L. (Howser)	3	N.L. (Herzog)	2	Clemens	Gooden	Houston, N.L.	45,774
1987	July 14[1]	N.L. (Johnson)	2	A.L. (McNamara)	0	Smith	Howell	Oakland, A.L.	49,671

1. Night game. 2. Two games. 3. Fourteen innings. 4. Five innings, rain. 5. Twelve innings. 6. Ten innings. 7. Called because of rain after nine innings. 8. Fifteen innings. NOTE: No game in 1945. *Game was originally scheduled for July 14, but was put off because of players' strike.

NATIONAL BASEBALL HALL OF FAME

Cooperstown, N.Y.

Fielders

Member	Active years
Aaron, Henry (Hank)	1954–1976
Anson, Adrian (Cap)	1876–1897
Aparicio, Luis	1956–1973
Appling, Lucius (Luke)	1930–1950
Averill, H. Earl	1929–1941
Baker, J. Frank (Home Run)	1908–1922
Bancroft, David	1915–1930
Banks, Ernest	1953–1971
Beckley, Jacob	1888–1907
Bell, James (Cool Papa)[1]	1920–1947
Berra, Lawrence (Yogi)	1946–1965
Bottomley, James	1922–1937
Boudreau, Louis	1938–1952
Bresnahan, Roger	1897–1915
Brock, Lou	1961–1980
Brouthers, Dennis	1879–1896
Burkett, Jesse	1890–1905
Campanella, Roy	1948–1957
Carey, Max	1910–1929
Chance, Frank	1898–1914
Charleston, Oscar[1]	1915–1954
Clarke, Fred	1894–1915
Clemente, Roberto	1955–1972
Cobb, Tyrus	1905–1928
Cochrane, Gordon (Mickey)	1925–1937
Collins, Edward	1906–1930
Collins, James	1895–1908
Comiskey, Charles	1882–1894
Combs, Earle	1924–1935
Connor, Roger	1880–1897
Crawford, Samuel	1899–1917
Cronin, Joseph	1926–1945
Cuyler, Hazen (Kiki)	1921–1938
Dandridge, Ray[1]	1933–1953
Delahanty, Edward	1888–1903
Dickey, William	1928–1946
Dihigo, Martin[1]	1923–1945
DiMaggio, Joseph	1936–1951
Doerr, Bobby	1937–1951
Duffy, Hugh	1888–1906
Eyers, John	1902–1919
Ewing, William	1880–1897
Flick, Elmer	1898–1910
Foxx, James	1925–1945
Frisch, Frank	1919–1937
Gehrig, H. Louis (Lou)	1923–1939
Gehringer, Charles	1924–1942
Gibson, Josh[1]	1929–1946
Goslin, Leon (Goose)	1921–1938
Greenberg, Henry (Hank)	1933–1947
Hafey, Charles (Chick)	1924–1937
Hamilton, William	1888–1901
Hartnett, Charles (Gabby)	1922–1941
Heilmann, Harry	1914–1932
Herman, William	1931–1947
Hooper, Harry	1909–1925
Hornsby, Rogers	1915–1937
Irvin, Monford (Monte)[1]	1939–1956
Jackson, Travis	1922–1936
Jennings, Hugh	1891–1918
Johnson, William (Judy)[1]	1921–1937
Kaline, Albert W.	1953–1974
Keeler, William (Wee Willie)	1892–1910
Kell, George	1943–1957
Kelley, Joseph	1891–1908
Kelly, George	1915–1932
Kelly, Michael (King)	1878–1893
Killebrew, Harmon	1954–1975
Kiner, Ralph	1946–1955
Klein, Charles H. (Chuck)	1928–1944
Lajoie, Napoleon	1896–1916
Leonard, Walter (Buck)[1]	1933–1955
Lindstrom, Frederick	1924–1936
Lloyd, John Henry[1]	1905–1931
Lombardi, Ernie	1932–1947
Mantle, Mickey	1951–1968
Manush, Henry (Heinie)	1923–1939
Maranville, Walter (Rabbit)	1912–1935
Mathews, Edwin	1952–1968
Mays, Willie	1951–1973
McCarthy, Thomas	1884–1896
McGraw, John J.	1891–1906
McCovey, Willie	1959–1980
Medwick, Joseph (Ducky)	1932–1948
Mize, John (The Big Cat)	1936–1953
Musial, Stanley	1941–1963
O'Rourke, James	1876–1894
Ott, Melvin	1926–1947
Reese, Harold (Pee Wee)	1940–1958
Rice, Edgar (Sam)	1915–1934
Robinson, Brooks	1955–1977
Robinson, Frank	1956–1976
Robinson, Jack	1947–1956
Robinson, Wilbert	1886–1902
Roush, Edd	1913–1931
Ruth, George (Babe)	1914–1935
Schalk, Raymond	1912–1929
Sewell, Joseph	1920–1933
Simmons, Al	1924–1944
Sisler, George	1915–1930
Slaughter, Enos	1938–1959
Snider, Edwin D. (Duke)	1947–1964
Speaker, Tristram	1907–1928
Terry, William	1923–1936
Thompson, Samuel	1885–1906
Tinker, Joseph	1902–1916
Traynor, Harold (Pie)	1920–1937
Vaughan, Arky	1932–1948
Wagner, John (Honus)	1897–1917
Wallace, Roderick (Bobby)	1894–1918
Waner, Lloyd	1927–1945
Waner, Paul	1926–1945
Ward, John (Monte)	1878–1894
Wheat, Zachariah	1909–1927
Williams, Billy	1959–1976
Williams, Theodore	1939–1960
Wilson, Lewis R. (Hack)	1923–1934
Youngs, Ross (Pep)	1917–1926

1. Negro League player selected by special committee.

Pitchers

Alexander, Grover	1911–1930
Bender, Charles (Chief)	1903–1925
Brown, Mordecai (3-Finger)	1903–1916
Chesbro, John	1899–1909
Clarkson, John	1882–1894
Coveleski, Stanley	1912–1928
Dean, Jerome (Dizzy)	1930–1947

Drysdale, Don	1956–1969
Faber, Urban (Red)	1914–1933
Feller, Robert	1936–1956
Ferrell, Rick	1929–1947
Ford, Edward (Whitey)	1950–1967
Foster, Andrew (Rube)	1897–1926
Galvin, James (Pud)	1876–1892
Gibson, Bob	1959–1975
Gomez, Vernon (Lefty)	1930–1943
Griffith, Clark	1891–1914
Grimes, Burleigh	1916–1934
Grove, Robert (Lefty)	1925–1941
Haines, Jesse	1918–1937
Hoyt, Waite	1918–1938
Hubbell, Carl	1928–1943
Hunter, Jim (Catfish)	1965–1979
Johnson, Walter	1907–1927
Joss, Adrian	1902–1910
Keefe, Timothy	1880–1893
Koufax, Sanford (Sandy)	1955-1966
Lemon, Robert	1946–1958
Lyons, Theodore	1923–1946
Marichal, Juan	1960–1975
Marquard, Richard (Rube)	1908–1924
Mathewson, Christopher	1900–1916
McGinnity, Joseph	1899–1908
Nichols, Charles (Kid)	1890–1906
Paige, Leroy (Satchel)[1]	1926–1965
Pennock, Herbert	1912–1934
Plank, Edward	1901–1917
Radbourn, Charles (Hoss)	1880–1891
Rixey, Eppa	1912–1933
Roberts, Robert (Robin)	1948–1966
Ruffing, Charles (Red)	1924–1947
Rusie, Amos	1889–1901
Spahn, Warren	1942–1965
Vance, Arthur (Dazzy)	1915–1935
Waddell, George	1897–1910
Walsh, Edward	1904–1917
Welch, Michael (Mickey)	1880–1892
Wilhelm, Hoyt	1952–1972
Wynn, Early	1939–1963
Young, Denton (Cy)	1890–1911

Officials and Others

Alston, Walter[2]
Barrow, Edward[2,3]
Bulkeley, Morgan G.[3]
Cartwright, Alexander[3]
Chadwick, Henry[4]
Chandler, A.B.[7]
Conlan, John[3]
Connolly, Thomas[5]
Cummings, William A.[6]
Evans, William G.[5,3]
Frick, Ford C.[7,3]
Giles, Warren C.[3]
Gowdy, Curt[9]
Harridge, William[3]
Harris, Stanley R.[8]
Hubbard, R. Calvin[5]
Higgins, Miller J.[2]
Johnson, B. Bancroft[3]
Klem, William[5]
Landis, Kenesaw M.[7]
Lopez, Alfonso R.[8]
Mack, Connie[2,3]
MacPhail, Leland S.[3]
McCarthy, Joseph V.[2]
McKechnie, William B.[2]
Rickey, W. Branch[2,3]
Smith, Ken[10]
Spalding, Albert G.[5]
Stengel, Charles D.[8]
Weiss, George M.[3]
Wright, George[6]
Wright, Harry[6,2]
Yawkey, Thomas[3]

1. Negro league player selected by special committee. 2. Manager. 3. Executive. 4. Writer-statistician. 5. Umpire. 6. Early player. 7. Commissioner. 8. Player-manager. 9. Broadcaster. 10. Sportswriter.

OTHER LIFETIME BATTING, PITCHING, AND BASE-RUNNING RECORDS

(An asterisk indicates active player)

Sources: Baseball Record Book, published and copyrighted by The Sporting News, St. Louis, Mo. 63166; *The Book of Baseball Records,* published and copyrighted by Seymour Siwoff, New York, N.Y. 10036; and *The Complete Handbook of Baseball,* published and copyrighted by New American Library, New York, N.Y. 10019. All records through 1987 unless noted.

Hits (3,000 or more)

Pete Rose	4,256
Ty Cobb	4,191
Henry Aaron	3,771
Stan Musial	3,630
Tris Speaker	3,515
Honus Wagner	3,430
Carl Yastrzemski	3,419
Eddie Collins	3,311
Willie Mays	3,283
Nap Lajoie	3,251
Paul Waner	3,152
Cap Anson	3,081
Rod Carew	3,053
Lou Brock	3,023
Al Kaline	3,007
Roberto Clemente	3,000

Earned Run Average[1]

Walter Johnson	2.37
Grover Alexander	2.56
Whitey Ford	2.74
Jim Palmer	2.83
Tom Seaver	2.86
Stanley Coveleski	2.88
Juan Marichal	2.89
Wilbur Cooper	2.89
Bob Gibson	2.91
Carl Mays	2.92
Don Drysdale	2.95
Carl Hubbell	2.98
Gaylord Perry	2.99
Bert Blyleven*	3.08
Steve Carlton*	3.04

1. Through 1986 season.

Runs Scored

Ty Cobb	2,245
Henry Aaron	2,174
Babe Ruth	2,174
Pete Rose	2,165
Willie Mays	2,062
Stan Musial	1,949
Lou Gehrig	1,888
Tris Speaker	1,881
Mel Ott	1,859
Frank Robinson	1,829
Eddie Collins	1,816
Carl Yastrzemski	1,816
Ted Williams	1,798
Charlie Gehringer	1,774
Jimmie Foxx	1,751
Honus Wagner	1,740
Willie Keeler	1,720
Cap Anson	1,712
Jesse Burkett	1,708
Billy Hamilton	1,690
Mickey Mantle	1,677
John McPhee	1,674
George Van Haltren	1,650

*Active payer through 1986

Strikeouts, Pitching

Nolan Ryan*	4,547
Steve Carlton*	4,131
Tom Seaver	3,640
Gaylord Perry	3,534
Don Sutton*	3,530
Walter Johnson	3,508
Phil Niekro*	3,342
Ferguson Jenkins	3,192
Bob Gibson	3,117
Jim Bunning	2,855
Mickey Lolich	2,832
Cy Young	2,819
Warren Spahn	2,583
Bob Feller	2,581
Tim Keefe	2,538
Christy Mathewson	2,505

Home Runs (350 or More)

Henry Aaron	755
Babe Ruth	714
Willie Mays	660
Frank Robinson	586
Harmon Killebrew	573
Reggie Jackson	563
Mickey Mantle	536
Jimmie Foxx	534
Mike Schmidt*	530
Ted Williams	521
Willie McCovey	521
Eddie Matthews	512
Ernie Banks	512
Mel Ott	511
Lou Gehrig	493
Stan Musial	475
Willie Stargell	475
Carl Yastrzemski	452
Dave Kingman	442
Billy Williams	426
Duke Snider	406
Al Kaline	399
Johnny Bench	389
Frank Howard	382
Orlando Cepeda	379
Norm Cash	377
Rocky Colavito	374
Tony Perez	371
Gil Hodges	370
Ralph Kiner	369
Joe DiMaggio	361

Lee May	360
Johnny Mize	359
Yogi Berra	358
Dick Allen	351

*Active player through 1986.

Shutouts

Walter Johnson	110
Grover Alexander	90
Christy Mathewson	83
Cy Young	77
Ed Plank	64
Warren Spahn	63
Tom Seaver	60
Ed Walsh	58
Don Sutton*	58
James Galvin	57
Bob Gibson	56
Steve Carlton*	55
Jim Palmer	53
Gaylord Perry	53
Juan Marichal	52

Strikeouts, Batting

Reggie Jackson*	2,459
Willie Stargell	1,912
Tony Perez	1,845
Bobby Bonds	1,757
Lou Brock	1,730
Mickey Mantle	1,710
Harmon Killebrew	1,699
Dick Allen	1,556
Lee May	1,552
Willie McCovey	1,550
Frank Robinson	1,532
Willie Mays	1,526
Eddie Matthews	1,487
Frank Howard	1,460
Jim Wynn	1,427

Bases on Balls

Babe Ruth	2,056
Ted Williams	2,019
Carl Yastrzemski	1,845
Joe Morgan	1,799
Mickey Mantle	1,734
Mel Ott	1,708
Eddie Yost	1,614
Stan Musial	1,599
Harmon Killebrew	1,559
Lou Gehrig	1,508
Willie Mays	1,464
Jimmie Foxx	1,452
Eddie Mathews	1,444
Frank Robinson	1,420
Henry Aaron	1,402

RECORD OF WORLD SERIES GAMES

(Through 1986)

Source: The Book of Baseball Records, published by Seymour Siwoff, New York City.

Figures in parentheses for winning pitchers (WP) and losing pitchers (LP) indicate the game number in the series.

1903—Boston A.L. 5 (Jimmy Collins); Pittsburgh N.L. 3 (Fred Clarke). WP—Bos.: Dinneen (2, 6, 8), Young (5, 7); Pitts.: Phillippe (1, 3, 4). LP—Bos.: Young (1), Hughes (3), Dinneen (4); Pitts.: Leever (2, 6), Kennedy (5), Phillippe (7, 8).

1904—No series.

1905—New York N.L. 4 (John J. McGraw); Philadelphia A.L. 1 (Connie Mack). WP—N.Y.: Mathewson (1, 3, 5); McGinnity (4); Phila.: Bender (2). LP—N.Y.: McGinnity (2); Phila.: Plank (1, 4), Coakley (3), Bender (5).

1906—Chicago A.L. 4 (Fielder Jones); Chicago N.L. 2 (Frank Chance). WP—Chi.: A.L.: Altrock (1), Walsh (3, 5), White (6); Chi.: N.L.: Reulbach (2), Brown (4). LP—Chi. A.L.: White (2), Altrock. (4); Chi.: N.L.: Brown (1, 6), Pfeister (3, 5).

1907—Chicago N.L. 4 (Frank Chance); Detroit A.L. 0 (Hugh Jennings). First game tied 3–3, 12 innings. WP—Pfeister (2), Reulbach (3), Overall (4), Brown (5). LP—Mullin (2, 5), Siever (3), Donovan (4).

1908—Chicago N.L. 4 (Frank Chance); Detroit A.L. 1 (Hugh Jennings). WP—Chi.: Brown (1, 4), Overall (2, 5); Det.: Mullin (3). LP—Chi.: Pfeister (3); Det.: Summers (1, 4), Donovan (2, 5).

1909—Pittsburgh N.L. 4 (Fred Clarke); Detroit A.L. 3 (Hugh Jennings). WP—Pitts.: Adams (1, 5, 7), Maddox (3); Det.: Donovan (2), Mullin (4, 6). LP—Pitts.: Camnitz (2), Leifield (4), Willis (6); Det.: Mullin (1), Summers (3, 5), Donovan (7).

1910—Philadelphia A.L. 4 (Connie Mack); Chicago N.L. 1 (Frank Chance). WP—Phila.: Bender (1), Coombs (2, 3, 5); Chi.: Brown (4). LP—Phila.: Bender (4); Chi.: Overall (1), Brown (2, 5), McIntyre (3).

1911—Philadelphia A.L. 4 (Connie Mack); New York N.L. 2 (John J. McGraw). WP—Phila.: Plank (2), Coombs (3), Bender (4, 6); N.Y.: Mathewson (1), Crandall (5). LP—Phila.: Bender (1), Plank (5); N.Y.: Marquard (2), Mathewson (3, 4), Ames (6).

1912—Boston A.L. 4 (J. Garland Stahl); New York N.L. 3 (John J. McGraw). Second game tied, 6–6, 11 innings. WP—Bos.: Wood (1, 4, 8), Bedient (5); N.Y.: Marquard (3, 6), Tesreau (7). LP—Bos.: O'Brien (3, 6), Wood (7); N.Y.: Tesreau (1, 4), Mathewson (5, 8).

1913—Philadelphia A.L. 4 (Connie Mack); New York N.L. 1 (John J. McGraw). WP—Phila.: Bender (1, 4), Bush (3), Plank (5); N.Y.: Mathewson (2); LP—Phila.: Plank (2); N.Y.: Marquard (1), Tesreau (3), Demaree (4), Mathewson (5).

1914—Boston N.L. 4 (George Stallings); Philadelphia A.L. 0 (Connie Mack). WP—Rudolph (1, 4), James (2, 3). LP—Bender (1), Plank (2), Bush (3), Shawkey (4).

1915—Boston A.L. 4 (Bill Carrigan); Philadelphia N.L. 1 (Pat Moran). WP—Bos.: Foster (2, 5), Leonard (3), Shore (4); Phila.: Alexander (1). LP—Bos.: Shore (1); Phila.: Mayer (2), Alexander (3), Chalmers (4), Rixey (5).

1916—Boston A.L. 4 (Bill Carrigan); Brooklyn N.L. 1 (Wilbert Robinson). WP—Bos.: Shore (1, 5), Ruth (2), Leonard (4); Bklyn.: Coombs (3). LP—Bos.: Mays (3); Bklyn.: Marquard (1, 4), Smith (2), Pfeffer (5).

1917—Chicago A.L. 4 (Clarence Rowland); New York N.L. 2 (John J. McGraw). WP—Chi.: Cicotte (1), Faber (2, 5, 6); N.Y.: Benton (3), Schupp (4), LP—Chi.: Cicotte (3), Faber (4); N.Y.: Sallee (1, 5), Anderson (2), Benton (6).

1918—Boston A.L. 4 (Ed Barrow); Chicago N.L. 2 (Fred Mitchell). WP—Bos.: Ruth (1, 4), Mays (3, 6); Chi.: Tyler (2), Vaughn (5). LP—Bos.: Bush (2), Jones (5); Chi.: Vaughn (1, 3), Douglas (4), Tyler (6).

1919—Cincinnati N.L. 5 (Pat Moran); Chicago A.L. 3 (William Gleason). WP—Cin.: Ruether (1), Sallee (2), Ring (4), Eller (5, 8); Chi.: Kerr (3, 6), Cicotte (7). LP—Cin.: Fisher (3), Ring (6), Sallee (7); Chi.: Cicotte (1, 4), Williams (2, 5, 8).

1920—Cleveland A.L. 5 (Tris Speaker); Brooklyn N.L. 2 (Wilbert Robinson). WP—Cleve.: Coveleski (1, 4, 7), Bagby (5), Mails (6); Bklyn.: Grimes (2), Smith (3). LP—Cleve.: Bagby (2), Caldwell (3). Bklyn.: Marquard (1), Cadore (4), Grimes (5, 7), Smith (6).

1921—New York N.L. 5 (John J. McGraw); New York A.L. 3 (Miller Huggins). WP—N.Y. N.L.: Barnes (3, 6), Douglas (4, 7), Nehf (8); N.Y. A.L.: Mays (1), Hoyt (2, 5). LP—N.Y. N.L.: Nehf (2, 5), Douglas (1). N.Y. A.L.: Quinn (3), Mays (4, 7), Shawkey (6), Hoyt (8).

1922—New York N.L. 4 (John J. McGraw); New York A.L. 0 (Miller Huggins). Second game tied 3–3, 10 innings. WP—Ryan (1), Scott (3), McQuillan (4), Nehf (5); LP—Bush (1, 5), Hoyt (3), Mays (4).

1923—New York A.L. 4 (Miller Huggins); New York N.L. 2 (John J. McGraw). WP—N.Y. A.L.: Pennock (2, 6), Shawkey (4), Bush (5); N.Y. N.L.: Ryan (1), Nehf (3). LP—N.Y. A.L.: Bush (1), Jones (3); N.Y. N.L.: McQuillan (2), Scott (4), Bentley (5), Nehf (6).

1924—Washington A.L. 4 (Bucky Harris); New York N.L. 3 (John J. McGraw). WP—Wash.: Zachary (2, 6), Mogridge (4), Johnson (7); N.Y.: Nehf (1), McQuillan (3), Bentley (5). LP—Wash.: Johnson (1, 5), Marberry (3); N.Y.: Bentley (2, 7), Barnes (4), Nehf (6).

1925—Pittsburgh N.L. 4 (Bill McKechnie); Washington A.L. 3 (Bucky Harris). WP—Pitts.: Aldridge (2, 5), Kremer (6, 7); Wash.: Johnson (1, 4), Ferguson (3). LP—Pitts.: Meadows (1), Kremer (3), Yde (4); Wash.: Coveleski (2, 5), Ferguson (6), Johnson (7).

1926—St. Louis N.L. 4 (Rogers Hornsby); New York A.L. 3 (Miller Huggins). WP—St. L.: Alexander (2, 6), Haines (3, 7); N.Y.: Pennock (1, 5), Hoyt (4). LP—St. L.: Sherdel (1, 5), Reinhart (4); N.Y.: Shocker (2), Ruether (3), Shawkey (6), Hoyt (7).

1927—New York A.L. 4 (Miller Huggins); Pittsburgh N.L. 0 (Donie Bush). WP—Hoyt (1), Pipgras (2), Pennock (3), Moore (4). LP—Kremer (1), Aldridge (2), Meadows (3), Miljus (4).

1928—New York A.L. 4 (Miller Huggins); St. Louis N.L. 0 (Bill McKechnie). WP—Hoyt (1, 4), Pipgras (2), Zachary (3). LP—Sherdel (1, 4), Alexander (2), Haines (3).

1929—Philadelphia A.L. 4 (Connie Mack); Chicago N.L. 1 (Joe McCarthy). WP—Phila.: Ehmke (1), Earnshaw (2), Rommel (4), Walberg (5); Chi.: Bush (3). LP—Phila.: Earnshaw (3) Chi.: Root (1), Malone (2, 5), Blake (4).

1930—Philadelphia A.L. 4 (Connie Mack); St. Louis N.L. 2 (Gabby Street). WP—Phila.: Grove (1, 5), Earnshaw (2, 6); St. L.: Hallahan (3), Haines (4). LP—Phila.: Walberg (3), Grove (4); St. L.: Grimes (1, 5), Rhem (2), Hallahan (6).

1931—St. Louis N.L. 4 (Gabby Street); Philadelphia A.L. 3 (Connie Mack). WP—St. L.: Hallahan (2, 5), Grimes (3, 7); Phila.: Grove (1, 6), Earnshaw (4). LP—St. L.: Derringer (1, 6), Johnson (4); Phila.: Earnshaw (2, 7), Grove (3), Hoyt (5).

1932—New York A.L. (Joe McCarthy); Chicago N.L. 0 (Charles Grimm). WP—Ruffing (1), Gomez (2), Pipgras (3), Moore (4). LP—Bush (1), Warneke (2), Root (3), May (4).

1933—New York N.L. 4 (Bill Terry); Washington A.L. 1 (Joe Cronin.). WP—N.Y.: Hubbell (1, 4), Schumacher (2), Luque (5); Wash.: Whitehill (3). LP—N.Y.: Fitzsimmons (3); Wash.: Stewart (1), Crowder (2), Weaver (4), Russell (5).

1934—St. Louis N.L. 4 (Frank Frisch); Detroit A.L. 3 (Mickey Cochrane). WP—St. L.: J. Dean (1, 7), P. Dean (3, 6); Det.: Rowe (2), Auker (4), Bridges (5). LP—St. L.: W. Walker (2, 4), J. Dean (5); Det.: Crowder (1), Bridges (3), Rowe (6), Auker (7).

1935—Detroit A.L. 4 (Mickey Cochrane); Chicago N.L. 2 (Charles Grimm). WP—Det.: Bridges (2, 6), Rowe (3), Crowder (4); Chi.: Warneke (1, 5); LP—Det.: Rowe (1, 5), Chi.: Root (2), French (3, 6), Carleton (4).

1936—New York A.L. 4 (Joe McCarthy); New York N.L. 2 (Bill Terry). WP—N.Y. A.L.: Gomez (2, 6), Hadley (3), Pearson (4); N.Y. N.L.: Hubbell (1), Schumacher (5); LP—N.Y. A.L.: Ruffing (1), Malone (5); N.Y. N.L.: Schumacher (2), Fitzsimmons (3, 6), Hubbell (4).

1937—New York A.L. 4 (Joe McCarthy); New York N.L. 1 (Bill Terry). WP—N.Y. A.L.: Gomez (1, 5), Ruffing (2), Pearson (3); N.Y. N.L.: Hubbell (4). LP—N.Y. A.L.: Hadley (4); N.Y. N.L.: Hubbell (1), Melton (2, 5), Schumacher (3).

1938—New York A.L. 4 (Joe McCarthy); Chicago N.L. 0 (Gabby Hartnett). WP—Ruffing (1, 4), Gomez (2), Pearson (3) LP—Lee (1, 4), Dean (2), Bryant (3).

1939—New York A.L. 4 (Joe McCarthy); Cincinnati N.L. 0 (Bill McKechnie). WP—Ruffing (1), Pearson (2), Hadley (3), Murphy (4). LP—Derringer (1), Walters (2, 4), Thompson (3).

1940—Cincinnati N.L. 4 (Bill McKechnie); Detroit A.L. 3 (Del Baker). WP—Cin.: Walters (2, 6), Derringer (4, 7); Det.: Newsom (1, 5), Bridges (3). LP—Cin.: Derringer (1), Turner (3), Thompson (5); Det.: Rowe (2, 6), Trout (4), Newsom (7).

1941—New York A.L. 4 (Joe McCarthy); Brooklyn N.L. 1 (Leo Durocher). WP—N.Y.: Ruffing (1), Russo (3), Murphy (4), Bonham (5); Bklyn: Wyatt (2). LP—N.Y.: Chandler (2); Bklyn: Davis (1), Casey (3, 4), Wyatt (5).

1942—St. Louis N.L. 4 (Billy Southworth); New York A.L. 1 (Joe McCarthy). WP—St. L.: Beazley (2, 5), White (3), Lanier (4); N.Y.: Ruffing (1). LP—St. L.: Cooper (1); N.Y.: Bonham (2), Chandler (3), Donald (4), Ruffing (5).

1943—New York A.L. 4 (Joe McCarthy); St. Louis N.L. 1 (Billy Southworth). WP—N.Y.: Chandler (1, 5), Borowy (3), Russo (4); St. L.: Cooper (2). LP—N.Y.: Bonham (2); St. L.: Lanier (1), Brazle (3), Brecheen (4), Cooper (5).

1944—St. Louis N.L. 4 (Billy Southworth); St. Louis A.L. 2 (Luke Sewell). WP—St. L. N.L.: Donnelly (2), Brecheen (4), Cooper (5), Lanier (6); St. L. A.L.: Galehouse (1), Kramer (3). LP—St. L. N.L.: Cooper (1), Wilks (3); St. L. A.L.: Muncrief (2), Jakucki (4), Galehouse (5), Potter (6).

1945—Detroit A.L. 4 (Steve O'Neill); Chicago N.L. 3 (Charles Grimm). WP—Det.: Trucks (2), Trout (4), Newhouser (5, 7); Chi.: Borowy (1, 6), Passeau (3). LP—Det.: Newhouser (1), Overmire (3), Trout (6); Chi.: Wyse (2), Prim (4), Borowy (5, 7).

1946—St. Louis N.L. 4 (Eddie Dyer); Boston A.L. 3 (Joe Cronin). WP—St. L.: Brecheen (2, 6, 7), Munger (4); Bos.: Johnson (1), Ferriss (3), Dobson (5). LP—St. L.: Pollet (1), Dickson (3), Brazle (5); Bos.: Harris (2, 6), Hughson (4), Klinger (7).

1947—New York A.L. 4 (Bucky Harris); Brooklyn N.L. 3 (Burt Shotton). WP—N.Y.: Shea (1, 5), Reynolds (2), Page (7); Bklyn.: Casey (3, 4), Branca (6). LP—N.Y.: Newsom (3), Bevens (4), Page (6); Bklyn.: Branca (1), Lombardi (2), Barney (5), Gregg (7).

1948—Cleveland A.L. 4 (Lou Boudreau); Boston N.L. 2 (Billy Southworth). WP—Cleve.: Lemon (2, 6), Bearden (3), Gromek (4); Bos.: Sain (1), Spahn (5). LP—Cleve.: Feller (1, 5); Bos.: Spahn (2), Bickford (3), Sain (4), Voiselle (6).

1949—New York A.L. 4 (Casey Stengel); Brooklyn N.L. 1 (Burt Shotton). WP—N.Y.: Reynolds (1), Page (3), Lopat (4), Raschi (5); Bklyn.: Roe (2). LP—N.Y.: Raschi (2); Bklyn.: Newcombe (1, 4), Branca (3), Barney (5).

1950—New York A.L. 4 (Casey Stengel); Philadelphia N.L. 0 (Eddie Sawyer). WP—Raschi (1), Reynolds (2), Ferrick (3), Ford (4). LP—Konstanty (1), Roberts (2), Meyer (3), Miller (4).

1951—New York A.L. 4 (Casey Stengel); New York N.L. 2 (Leo Durocher). WP—N.Y. A.L.: Lopat (2, 5), Reynolds (4), Raschi (6); N.Y. N.L.: Koslo (1), Hearn (3). LP—N.Y. A.L.: Reynolds (1), Raschi (3); N.Y. N.L.: Jansen (2, 5), Maglie (4), Koslo (6).

1952—New York A.L. 4 (Casey Stengel); Brooklyn N.L. 3 (Chuck Dressen). WP—N.Y.: Raschi (2, 6), Reynolds (4, 7); Bklyn.: Black (1), Roe (3), Erskine (5). LP—N.Y.: Reynolds (1), Lopat (3), Sain (5); Bklyn.: Erskine (2), Black (4, 7), Loes (6).

1953—New York A.L. 4 (Casey Stengel); Brooklyn N.L. 2 (Chuck Dressen). WP—N.Y.: Sain (1), Lopat (2), McDonald (5), Reynolds (6); Bklyn.: Erskine (3), Loes (4). LP—N.Y.: Raschi (3), Ford (4); Bklyn.: Labine (1, 6), Roe (2), Podres (5).

1954—New York N.L. 4 (Leo Durocher); Cleveland A.L. 0 (Al Lopez). WP—Grissom (1), Antonelli (2), Gomez (3), Liddie (4). LP—Lemon (1, 4), Wynn (2), Garcia (3).

1955—Brooklyn N.L. 4 (Walter Alston); New York A.L. 3 (Casey Stengel). WP—Bklyn.: Podres (3, 7), Labine (4), Craig (5); N.Y.: Ford (1, 6), Byrne (2). LP—Bklyn.: Newcombe (1), Loes (2), Spooner (6); N.Y.: Turley (3), Larsen (4), Grim (5), Byrne (7).

1956—New York A.L. 4 (Casey Stengel); Brooklyn N.L. 3 (Walter Alston). WP—N.Y.: Ford (3), Sturdivant (4), Larsen (5), Kucks (7); Bklyn.: Maglie (1), Bessent (2), Labine (6). LP—N.Y.: Ford (1), Morgan (2), Turley (6); Bklyn.: Craig (3), Erskine (4), Maglie (5), Newcombe (7).

1957—Milwaukee N.L. 4 (Fred Haney); New York A.L. 3 (Casey Stengel). WP—Mil.: Burdette (2, 5, 7), Spahn (4); N.Y.: Ford (1), Larsen (3), Turley (6). LP—Mil.: Spahn (1), Buhl (3), Johnson (6); N.Y.: Shantz (2), Grim (4), Ford (5), Larsen (7).

1958—New York A.L. 4 (Casey Stengel); Milwaukee N.L. 3 (Fred Haney). WP—N.Y.: Larsen (3), Turley (5, 7), Duren (6); Mil.: Spahn (1, 4), Burdette (2). LP—N.Y.: Duren (1), Turley (2), Ford (4); Mil.: Rush (3), Burdette (5, 7), Spahn (6).

1959—Los Angeles N.L. 4 (Walter Alston); Chicago A.L. 2 (Al Lopez). WP—L.A.: Podres (2), Drysdale (3), Sherry (4, 6); Chi.: Wynn (1), Shaw (5). LP—L.A.: Craig (1), Koufax (5); Chi.: Shaw (2), Donovan (3), Staley (4), Wynn (6).

1960—Pittsburgh N.L. 4 (Danny Murtaugh); New York A.L. 3 (Casey Stengel). WP—Pitts.: Law (1, 4), Haddix (5, 7); N.Y.: Turley (2), Ford (3, 6). LP—Pitts.: Friend (2, 6), Mizell (3); N.Y.: Ditmar (1, 5), Terry (4, 7).

1961—New York A.L. 4 (Ralph Houk); Cincinnati N.L. 1 (Fred Hutchinson). WP—N.Y.: Ford (1, 4), Arroyo (3), Daley (5); Cin.: Jay (2). LP—N.Y.: Terry (2); Cin.: O'Toole (1, 4), Purkey (3), Jay (5).

1962—New York A.L. 4 (Ralph Houk); San Francisco N.L. 3 (Al Dark). WP—N.Y.: Ford (1), Stafford (3), Terry (5, 7); S.F. Sanford (2), Larsen (4), Pierce (6). LP—N.Y.: Terry (2), Coates (4), Ford (6); S.F.: O'Dell (1), Pierce (3), Sanford (5, 7).

1963—Los Angeles N.L. 4 (Walter Alston); New York A.L. 0 (Ralph Houk). WP—Koufax (1, 4), Podres (2), Drysdale (3). LP—Ford (1, 4), Downing (2), Bouton (3).

1964—St. Louis N.L. 4 (Johnny Keane); New York A.L. 3 (Yogi Berra). WP—St. L.: Sadecki (1), Craig (4), Gibson (5, 7); N.Y.: Stottlemyre (2), Bouton (3, 6). LP—St. L.: Gibson (2), Schultz (3), Simmons (6); N.Y.: Ford (1), Downing (4), Mikkelsen (5), Stottlemyre (7).

1965—Los Angeles N.L. 4 (Walter Alston); Minnesota A.L. 3 (Sam Mele). WP—L.A.: Osteen (3), Drysdale (4), Koufax (5, 7); Minn.: Grant (1, 6), Kaat (2). LP—L.A.: Drysdale (1), Koufax (2), Osteen (6); Minn.: Pascual (3), Grant (4), Kaat (5, 7).

1966—Baltimore A.L. 4 (Hank Bauer); Los Angeles N.L. 0 (Walter Alston). WP—Drabowsky (1), Palmer (2), Bunker (3), McNally (4). LP—Drysdale (1, 4), Koufax (2), Osteen (3).

1967—St. Louis N.L. 4 (Red Schoendienst); Boston A.L. 3 (Dick Williams). WP—St. L.: Gibson (1, 4, 7), Briles (3); Bos.: Lonborg (2, 5); Wyatt (6). LP—St. L.: Hughes (2), Carlton (5), Lamabe (6); Bos.: Santiago (1, 4), Bell (3), Lonborg (7).

1968—Detroit A.L. 4 (Mayo Smith); St. Louis N.L. 3 (Red Schoendienst). WP—Det.: Lolich (2, 5, 7), McLain (6); St. L.: Gibson (1, 4), Washburn (3), LP—Det.: McLain (1, 4), Wilson (3); St. L.: Briles (2), Hoerner (5), Washburn (6), Gibson (7).

1969—New York N.L. 4 (Gil Hodges); Baltimore A.L. 1 (Earl Weaver). WP—N.Y.: Koosman (2, 5), Gentry (3), Seaver (4); Balt.: Cuellar (1). LP—N.Y.: Seaver (1); Balt.: McNally (2), Palmer (3), Hall (4), Watt (5).

1970—Baltimore A.L. 4 (Earl Weaver); Cincinnati N.L. 1 (Sparky Anderson) 1. WP—Balt.: Palmer (1), Phoebus (2), McNally (3), Cuellar (5); Cin.: Carroll (4). LP—Cin.: Nolan (1), Wilcox (2), Cloninger (3), Merritt (5); Balt.: Watt (4).

1971—Pittsburgh N.L. 4 (Danny Murtaugh); Baltimore A.L. 3 (Earl Weaver). WP—Pitts.: Blass (3, 7), Kison (4), Briles (5); Balt.: McNally (1, 6), Palmer (2). LP—Pitts.: Ellis (1), R. Johnson (2), Miller (6); Balt.: Cuellar (3, 7), Watt (4) McNally (5).

1972—Oakland A.L. 4 (Dick Williams); Cincinnati N.L. (Sparky Anderson) 3. WP—Oakland: Holtzman (1), Hunter (2, 7), Fingers (4); Cincinnati: Billingham (3), Grimsley (5, 6). LP—Oakland: Odom (3), Fingers (5), Blue (6); Cincinnati: Nolan (1), Grimsley (2), Carroll (4), Borbon (7).

1973—Oakland A.L. 4 (Dick Williams): New York N.L. 3 (Yogi Berra). WP—Oakland: Holtzman (1, 7), Lindblad (3), Hunter (6). New York: McGraw (2), Matlack (4), Koosman (5). LP—Oakland: Fingers (2), Holtzman (4), Blue (5). New York: Matlack (1, 7) Parker (3), Seaver (6).

1974—Oakland A.L. 4 (Al Dark); Los Angeles N.L. 1 (Walter Alston). WP—Oakland: Fingers (1), Hunter (3), Holtzman (4), Odom (5). Los Angeles: Sutton (2). LP—Oakland: Blue (2), Los Angeles: Messersmith (1, 4), Downing (3), Marshall (5).

1975—Cincinnati N.L. 4 (Sparky Anderson); Boston A.L. 3 (Darrell Johnson). WP—Cincinnati: Eastwick (2–3), Gullett (5), Carroll (7); Boston: Tiant (1–4), Wise (6). LP—Cincinnati: Gullett (1), Norman (4), Darcy (6); Boston: Drago (2), Willoughby (3), Cleveland (5), Burton (7).

1976—Cincinnati N.L. 4 (Sparky Anderson); New York A.L. 0 (Billy Martin). WP—Gullett (1), Billingham (2), Zachry (3), Nolan (4). LP—Alexander (1), Hunter (2), Ellis (3), Figueroa (4).

1977—New York A.L. 4 (Billy Martin); Los Angeles N.L. 2 (Tom Lasorda). WP—New York: Lyle (1), Torrez (3, 6), Guidry (4); Los Angeles: Hooton (2), Sutton (5). LP—New York: Hunter (2), Gullett (5); Los Angeles: Rhoden (1), John (3), Rau (4), Hooton (6).

1978—New York A.L. 4 (Bob Lemon), Los Angeles N.L. 2 (Tom Lasorda); WP—New York: Guidry (3), Gossage (4); Beattie (5), Hunter (6); Los Angeles: John (1), Hooton (2). LP—New York: Figuero (1), Hunter (2); Los Angeles: Sutton (3–6), Welch (4), Hooton (5).

1979—Pittsburgh N.L. 4 (Chuck Tanner), Baltimore A.L. 3 (Earl Weaver); WP—Pittsburgh: D. Robinson (2), Blyleven (5), Candelaria (6), Jackson (7); Baltimore: Flanagan (1), McGregor (3), Stoddard (4). LP—Pittsburgh: Kison (1), Candelaria (3), Tekulve (4); Baltimore: Stanhouse (2), Flanagan (5), Palmer (6), McGregor (7).

1980—Philadelphia N.L. 4 (Dallas Green), Kansas City A.L. 2 (Jim Frey); WP—Philadelphia: Walk (1), Carlton (2), McGraw (5), Carlton (6); Kansas City: Quisenberry (3), Leonard (4). LP—Philadelphia: McGraw (3), Christenson (4); Kansas City: Leonard (1), Quisenberry (2), Quisenberry (5), Gale (6).

1981—Los Angeles N.L. 4 (Tom Lasorda), New York A.L. 2 (Bob Lemon); WP—Los Angeles: Valenzuela (3), Howe (4), Reuss (5), Hooton (6); New York: Guidry (1), John (2). LP—Los Angeles: Reuss (1), Hooton (2); New York: Frazier (3), Frazier (4), Guidry (5), Frazier (6).

1982—St. Louis N.L. 4 (Whitey Herzog), Milwaukee A.L. (Harvey Kuenn); WP—St. Louis: Sutter (2), Andujar (3), Stuper (6), Andujar (7). Milwaukee: Caldwell (1), Slaton (4), Caldwell (5). LP—St. Louis: Forsch (1), Bair (4), Forsch (5). Milwaukee: McClure (2), Vuckovich (3), Sutton (6), McClure (7).

1983—Baltimore A.L. 4 (Joe Altobelli), Philadelphia N.L. 1 (Paul Owens); WP—Baltimore: Boddicker (2), Palmer (3), Davis (4), McGregor (5). Philadelphia: Denny (1).

1984—Detroit A.L. 4 (Sparky Anderson), San Diego N.L. 1 (Dick Williams); WP—Det.: Morris (1,4), Wilcox (3), Lopez (5), San Diego: Hawkins (2). LP—Det.: Petry (2), San Diego: Thurmond (1), Lollar (3), Show (4), Hawkins (5).

1985—Kansas City A.L. 4 (Dick Howser), St. Louis N.L. 3 (Whitey Herzog); WP—KC: Saberhagen (3,7) Quisenberry (6), Jackson (5). St. Louis: Tudor (1,4) Dayley (2). LP—KC: Jackson (1), Leibrandt (2), Black (4); St. Louis: Andujar (3), Forsch (5), Worrell (6), Tudor (7).

1986—New York N.L. 4 (Dave Johnson); Boston A.L. (John McNamara) 3 WP—N.Y.—Ojeda (3), Darling (4), Aguilera (6), McDowell (7), Bos: Hurst (1), (5), Crawford (2). LP—N.Y. Darling (1), Gooden (2, 5).

BASEBALL HALTED BY PLAYERS STRIKE FOR SECOND TIME IN FOUR YEARS

Major League baseball, after months of haggling, endured a strike by players for the second time since 1981 in August 1985. Unlike the 1981 strike, which lasted seven weeks and canceled 713 games, this one was ended quickly. The players walked on Tuesday, Aug. 6, and were back on the field three days later on Thursday, Aug. 8.

While in 1981 the major issue was over compensation for free agent signings to the club losing players, the 1985 strike was primarily over the pension fund, and how much of the reported $1.1 billion the owners receive through network television agreements would go into the plan.

The players were seeking an increase of $45 million over the $15 million they'd been receiving under the contract signed in 1981. The owners were adamant in refusing such a large increase.

There were other matters at question, including the issue of arbitration. Under the 1981 agreement, a player with two years of major league service who couldn't come to terms with ownership could take his case to binding arbitration. The owners were looking to increase the number of years vested service required to three years, and pointed to substantial operating losses caused, in part, by large salaries granted by arbitrators and the increasing spiral of free agent salaries.

In the end, the players wound up with approximately $35 million for their pension fund, and the owners got their desired three years for arbitration, albeit the rule would not be scheduled to take effect until 1987.

The games canceled by the strike were rescheduled for later in the season, unlike the 1981 affair when far too many games were lost to be made up.

The 1981 strike settlement had been complicated by the decision to play a split season—awarding divisional championships to the teams in first place before the strike began, and starting a new second season to crown four additional champions. Those eight teams played off in a preliminary series. The survivors played for the league title and the right to move on to the World Series.

Former commissioner Bowie Kuhn was much criticized for this plan, as he was for not taking action to prevent or shorten the 1981 strike. That may have been Ueberroth's motivation when he decided he would step in. His initial overtures were lambasted by both sides in the conflict. But in the end, both sides agreed Ueberroth had been helpful in bringing them back to the bargaining table and pressing for a settlement.

WORLD SERIES CLUB STANDING
(Through 1986)

	Series	Won	Lost	Pct.
Oakland (A)	3	3	0	1.000
Pittsburgh (N)	7	5	2	.714
St. Louis (N)	14	9	5	.643
New York (A)	33	22	11	.667
Cleveland (A)	3	2	1	.667
New York (N-Mets)	3	2	1	.667
Philadelphia (A)	8	5	3	.625
Boston (A)	9	5	4	.550
Los Angeles (N)	8	4	4	.500
Milwaukee (N)	2	1	1	.500
Boston (N)	2	1	1	.500
Chicago (A)	4	2	2	.500
Cincinnati (N)	8	4	4	.500
Baltimore (A)	6	3	3	.500
Detroit (A)	9	4	5	.444
New York (N-Giants)	14	5	9	.357
Washington (A)	3	1	2	.333
Philadelphia (N)	4	1	3	.250
Chicago (N)	10	2	8	.200
Brooklyn (N)	9	1	8	.111
St. Louis (A)	1	0	1	.000
San Francisco (N)	1	0	1	.000
Minnesota (A)	1	0	1	.000
Kansas City (A)	2	1	1	.500
Milwaukee (A)	1	0	1	.000
San Diego (N)	1	0	1	.000

Recapitulation

	Won
American League	47
National League	35

SINGLE GAME AND SINGLE SERIES RECORDS
(Through 1986)

Most hits game—5, Paul Molitor, Milwaukee A.L., first game vs. St. Louis, N.L., 1982.

Most 4-hit games, series—2, Robin Yount, Milwaukee A.L., first and fifth games vs. St. Louis N.L., 1982.

Most hits inning—2, held by many players.

Most hits series—13 (7 games) Bobby Richardson, New York A.L., 1964; Lou Brock, St. Louis N.L., 1968; 12 (6 games) Billy Martin, New York A.L., 1953; 12 (8 games) Buck Herzog, New York N.L., 1912; Joe Jackson, Chicago A.L., 1919; 10 (4 games) Babe Ruth, New York A.L., 1928; 9 (5 games) held by 8 players.

Most home runs, series—5 (6 games) Reggie Jackson, New York A.L., 1977; 4 (7 games) Babe Ruth, New York A.L., 1926; Duke Snider, Brooklyn N.L., 1952, 1955; Hank Bauer, New York A.L., 1958; Gene Tenace, Oakland A.L., 1972; 4 (4 games) Lou Gehrig, New York A.L., 1928; 3 (6 games) Babe Ruth, New York A.L., 1923; Ted Kluszewski, Chicago A.L., 1959; 3 (5 games) Donn Clendenon, New York Mets N.L., 1969.

Most home runs, game—3, Babe Ruth, New York A.L., 1926 and 1928; Reggie Jackson, New York A.L., 1977.

Most strikeouts, series—12 (6 games) Willie Wilson, Kansas City A.L., 1980; 11 (7 games) Ed Mathews, Milwaukee N.L., 1958; Wayne Garrett, New York N.L., 1973: 10 (8 games) George Kelly, New York N.L., 1921; 9 (6 games) Jim Bottomley, St. Louis N.L., 1930; 9 (5 games) Carmelo Martinez, San Diego, N.L., 1984; Duke Snider, Brooklyn N.L., 1949; 7 (4 games) Bob Muesel, New York A.L., 1927.

Most stolen bases, game—3, Honus Wagner, Pittsburgh N.L., 1909; Willie Davis, Los Angeles N.L., 1965; Lou Brock, St. Louis N.L., 1967 and 1968.

Most strikeouts by pitcher, game—17, Bob Gibson, St. Louis N.L. 1968.

Most strikeouts by pitcher in succession—6, Horace Eller, Cincinnati N.L., 1919; Moe Drabowsky, Baltimore A.L., 1966.

Most strikeouts by pitcher, series—35 (7 games) Bob Gibson, St. Louis N.L., 1968; 28 (8 games) Bill Dinneen, Boston A.L., 1903; 23 (4 games) Sandy Koufax, Los Angeles, 1963; 20 (6 games) Chief Bender, Philadelphia A.L., 1911; 18 (5 games) Christy Mathewson, New York N.L., 1905.

Most bases on balls, series—11 (7 games) Babe Ruth, New York A.L., 1926; Gene Tenace, Oakland A.L., 1973; 9 (6 games) Willie Randolph, New York A.L., 1981; 7 (5 games) James Sheckard, Chicago N.L., 1910; Mickey Cochrane, Philadelphia A.L., 1929; Joe Gordon, New York A.L., 1941; 7 (4 games) Hank Thompson, New York N.L., 1954.

Most consecutive scoreless innings one series—27, Christy Mathewson, New York N.L., 1905.

LIFETIME WORLD SERIES RECORDS
(Through 1986)

Most hits—71, Yogi Berra, New York A.L., 1947, 1949–53, 1955–58, 1960–63.

Most runs—42, Mickey Mantle, New York A.L., 1951–53, 1955–58, 1960–64.

Most runs batted in—40, Mickey Mantle, New York A.L., 1951–53, 1955–58, 1960–64.

Most home runs—18, Mickey Mantle, New York A.L., 1951–53, 1955–58, 1960–64.

Most bases on balls—43, Mickey Mantle, New York A.L., 1951–53, 1955–58, 1960–64.

Most strikeouts—54, Mickey Mantle, New York A.L., 1951–53, 1955–58, 1960–64.

Most stolen bases—14, Eddie Collins, Philadelphia A.L. 1910–11, 13–14; Chicago A.L., 1917, 1919. Lou Brock, St. Louis N.L., 1964, 67–68.

Most victories, pitcher—10, Whitey Ford, New York A.L., 1950, 1953, 1955–58, 1960–64.

Most times member of winning team—10, Yogi Berra, New York A.L., 1947, 1949–53, 1956, 1958, 1961–62.

Most victories, no defeats—6, Vernon Gomez, New York A.L., 1932, 1936(2), 1937(2), 1938.

Most shutouts—4, Christy Mathewson, New York N.L., 1905 (3), 1913.

Most innings pitched—146, Whitey Ford, New York A.L., 1950, 1953, 1955–58, 1960–1964.

Most consecutive scoreless innings—33 2/3, Whitey Ford, New York A.L., 1960 (18), 1961 (14), 1962 (1 2/3).

Most strikeouts by pitcher—94, Whitey Ford, New York A.L., 1950, 1953, 1955–58, 1960–64.

AMERICAN LEAGUE HOME RUN CHAMPIONS

Year	Player, team	No.
1901	Nap Lajoie, Phila.	13
1902	Ralph Seybold, Phila.	16
1903	Buck Freeman, Bost.	13
1904	Harry Davis, Phila.	10
1905	Harry Davis, Phila.	8
1906	Harry Davis, Phila.	12
1907	Harry Davis, Phila.	8
1908	Sam Crawford, Det.	7
1909	Ty Cobb, Det.	9
1910	J. Garland Stahl, Bost.	10
1911	Franklin Baker, Phila.	9
1912	Franklin Baker, Phila.	10
1913	Franklin Baker, Phila.	12
1914	Franklin Baker, Phila., and Sam Crawford, Det.	8
1915	Robert Roth, Chi.-Cleve.	7
1916	Wally Pipp, N.Y.	12
1917	Wally Pipp, N.Y.	9
1918	Babe Ruth, Bost., and Clarence Walker, Phila.	11
1919	Babe Ruth, Bost.	29
1920	Babe Ruth, N.Y.	54
1921	Babe Ruth, N.Y.	59
1922	Ken Williams, St. L.	39
1923	Babe Ruth, N.Y.	41
1924	Babe Ruth, N.Y.	46
1925	Bob Meusel, N.Y.	33
1926	Babe Ruth, N.Y.	47
1927	Babe Ruth, N.Y.	60
1928	Babe Ruth, N.Y.	54
1929	Babe Ruth, N.Y.	46
1930	Babe Ruth, N.Y.	49
1931	Lou Gehrig, N.Y., and Babe Ruth, N.Y.	46
1932	Jimmy Foxx, Phila.	58
1933	Jimmy Foxx, Phila.	48
1934	Lou Gehrig, N.Y.	49
1935	Jimmy Foxx, Phila., and Hank Greenberg, Det.	36
1936	Lou Gehrig, N.Y.	49
1937	Joe DiMaggio, N.Y.	46
1938	Hank Greenberg, Det.	58
1939	Jimmy Foxx, Bost.	35
1940	Hank Greenberg, Det.	41
1941	Ted Williams, Bost.	37
1942	Ted Williams, Bost.	36
1943	Rudy York, Det.	34
1944	Nick Etten, N.Y.	22
1945	Vern Stephens, St. L.	24
1946	Hank Greenberg, Det.	44
1947	Ted Williams, Bost.	32
1948	Joe DiMaggio, N.Y.	39
1949	Ted Williams, Bost.	43
1950	Al Rosen, Cleve.	37
1951	Gus Zernial, Chi.-Phila.	33
1952	Larry Doby, Cleve.	32
1953	Al Rosen, Cleve.	43
1954	Larry Doby, Cleve.	32
1955	Mickey Mantle, N.Y.	37
1956	Mickey Mantle, N.Y.	52
1957	Roy Sievers, Wash.	42
1958	Mickey Mantle, N.Y.	42
1959	Rocky Colavito, Cleve., and Harmon Killebrew, Wash.	42
1960	Mickey Mantle, N.Y.	40
1961	Roger Maris, N.Y.	61
1962	Harmon Killebrew, Minn.	48
1963	Harmon Killebrew, Minn.	45
1964	Harmon Killebrew, Minn.	49
1965	Tony Conigliaro, Bost.	32
1966	Frank Robinson, Balt.	49
1967	Carl Yastrzemski, Bost., and Harmon Killebrew, Minn.	44
1968	Frank Howard, Wash.	44
1969	Harmon Killebrew, Minn.	49
1970	Frank Howard, Wash.	44
1971	Bill Melton, Chicago	33
1972	Dick Allen, Chicago	37
1973	Reggie Jackson, Oak.	32
1974	Dick Allen, Chicago	32
1975	Reggie Jackson, Oak., and George Scott, Mil.	36
1976	Graig Nettles, N.Y.	32
1977	Jim Rice, Boston	39
1978	Jim Rice, Boston	46
1979	Gorman Thomas, Milwaukee	45
1980	Reggie Jackson, N.Y., and Ben Oglivie, Mil.	41
1981*	Tony Armas, Oak., Dwight Evans, Bost., Bobby Grich, Calif., and Eddie Murray, Balt. (tie)	22
1982	Gorman Thomas, Mil., and Reggie Jackson, Calif.	39
1983	Jim Rice, Boston	39
1984	Tony Armas, Boston	43
1985	Darrell Evans, Detroit	40
1986	Jesse Barfield, Toronto	40
1987	Mark McGwire, Oakland	49

AMERICAN LEAGUE BATTING CHAMPIONS

Year	Player, team	Avg
1901	Nap Lajoie, Phila.	.422
1902	Ed Delahanty, Wash.	.376
1903	Nap Lajoie, Cleve.	.355
1904	Nap Lajoie, Cleve.	.381
1905	Elmer Flick, Cleve.	.306
1906	George Stone, St. L.	.358
1907	Ty Cobb, Det.	.350
1908	Ty Cobb, Det.	.324
1909	Ty Cobb, Det.	.377
1910	Ty Cobb, Det.	.385
1911	Ty Cobb, Det.	.420
1912	Ty Cobb, Det.	.410
1913	Ty Cobb, Det.	.390
1914	Ty Cobb, Det.	.368
1915	Ty Cobb, Det.	.369
1916	Tris Speaker, Cleve.	.386
1917	Ty Cobb, Det.	.383
1918	Ty Cobb, Det.	.382
1919	Ty Cobb, Det.	.384
1920	George Sisler, St. L.	.407
1921	Harry Heilmann, Det.	.394
1922	George Sisler, St. L.	.420
1923	Harry Heilmann, Det.	.403
1924	Babe Ruth, N.Y.	.378
1925	Harry Heilmann, Det.	.393
1926	Heinie Manush, Det.	.378
1927	Harry Heilmann, Det.	.398
1928	Goose Goslin, Wash.	.379
1929	Lew Fonseca, Cleve.	.369
1930	Al Simmons, Phila.	.381
1931	Al Simmons, Phila.	.390
1932	Dale Alexander, Det.-Bost.	.367
1933	Jimmy Foxx, Phila.	.356
1934	Lou Gehrig, N.Y.	.363
1935	Buddy Myer, Wash.	.349
1936	Luke Appling, Chi.	.388
1937	Charley Gehringer, Det.	.371
1938	Jimmy Foxx, Bost.	.349
1939	Joe DiMaggio, N.Y.	.381
1940	Joe DiMaggio, N.Y.	.352
1941	Ted Williams, Bost.	.406
1942	Ted Williams, Bost.	.356
1943	Luke Appling, Chi.	.328
1944	Lou Boudreau, Cleve.	.327
1945	George Sternweiss, N.Y.	.309
1946	Mickey Vernon, Wash.	.353
1947	Ted Williams, Bost.	.343
1948	Ted Williams, Bost.	.369
1949	George Kell, Det.	.343
1950	Billy Goodman, Bost.	.354
1951	Ferris Fain, Phila.	.344
1952	Ferris Fain, Phila.	.327
1953	Mickey Vernon, Wash.	.337
1954	Bobby Avila, Cleve.	.341
1955	Al Kaline, Det.	.340
1956	Mickey Mantle, N.Y.	.353
1957	Ted Williams, Bost.	.388
1958	Ted Williams, Bost.	.328
1959	Harvey Kuenn, Det.	.353
1960	Pete Runnels, Bost.	.320
1961	Norman Cash, Det.	.361
1962	Pete Runnels, Bost.	.326
1963	Carl Yastrzemski, Bost.	.321
1964	Tony Oliva, Minn.	.323
1965	Tony Oliva, Minn.	.321
1966	Frank Robinson, Balt.	.316
1967	Carl Yastrzemski, Bost.	.326
1968	Carl Yastrzemski, Bost.	.301
1969	Rod Carew, Minn.	.332
1970	Alex Johnson, Calif.	.329
1971	Tony Oliva, Minn.	.337
1972	Rod Carew, Minn.	.318
1973	Rod Carew, Minn.	.350
1974	Rod Carew, Minn.	.364
1975	Rod Carew, Minn.	.359
1976	George Brett, Kansas City	.333
1977	Rod Carew, Minn.	.388
1978	Rod Carew, Minn.	.333
1979	Fred Lynn, Boston	.333
1980	George Brett, Kansas City	.390
1981*	Carney Lansford, Bost.	.336
1982	Willie Wilson, Kansas City	.332
1983	Wade Boggs, Boston	.361
1984	Don Mattingly, New York	.343
1985	Wade Boggs, Boston	.368
1986	Wade Boggs, Boston	.357
1987	Wade Boggs, Boston	.363

*Split season because of player strike.

NATIONAL LEAGUE HOME RUN CHAMPIONS

Year	Player, team	No.
1876	George Hall, Phila. Athletics	5
1877	George Shaffer, Louisville	3
1878	Paul Hines, Providence	4
1879	Charles Jones, Bost.	9
1880	James O'Rourke, Bost., and Harry Stovey, Worcester	6
1881	Dan Brouthers, Buffalo	8
1882	George Wood, Det.	7
1883	William Ewing, N.Y.	10
1884	Ed Williamson, Chi.	27
1885	Abner Dalrymple, Chi.	11
1886	Arthur Richardson, Det.	11
1887	Roger Conoor, N.Y., and Wm. O'Brien, Wash.	17
1888	Roger Connor, N.Y.	14
1889	Sam Thompson, Phila.	20
1890	Tom Burns, Bklyn, and Mike Tiernan, N.Y.	13
1891	Harry Stovey, Bost., and Mike Tiernan, N.Y.	16
1892	Jim Holliday, Cin.	13
1893	Ed Delahanty, Phila.	19
1894	Hugh Duffy, Bost., and Robert Lowe, Bost.	18
1895	Bill Joyce, Wash.	17
1896	Ed Delhanty, Phila., and Sam Thompson, Phila.	13
1897	Nap Lajoie, Phila.	10
1898	James Colins, Bost.	14
1899	John Freeman, Wash.	25
1900	Herman Long, Bost.	12
1901	Sam Crawford, Con.	16
1902	Tom Leach, Pitts.	6
1903	James Sheckard, Bklyn.	9
1904	Harry Lumley, Bklyn.	9
1905	Fred Odwell, Cin.	9
1906	Tim Jordan, Bklyn	12
1907	David Brain, Bost.	10
1908	Tim Jordan, Bklyn.	12
1909	John Murray, N.Y.	7
1910	Fred Beck, Bost., and Frank Schulte, Chi.	10
1911	Frank Schulte, Chi.	21
1912	Henry Zimmerman, Chi.	14
1913	Cliff Cravath, Phila.	19
1914	Cliff Cravath, Phila.	19
1915	Cliff Cravath, Phila.	24
1916	Davis Robertson, N.Y., and Fred Williams, Chi.	12
1917	Davis Robertson, N.Y., and Cliff Cravath, Phila.	12
1918	Cliff Cravath, Phila.	8
1919	Cliff Cravath, Phila.	12
1920	Cy Williams, Phila.	15
1921	George Kelly, N.Y.	23
1922	Rogers Hornsby, St. L.	42
1923	Cy Williams, Phila.	41
1924	Jacques Fournier, Bklyn.	27
1925	Rogers Hornsby, St. L.	39
1926	Hack Wilson, Chi.	21
1927	Hack Wilson, Chi., and Cy Williams, Phila.	30
1928	Hack Wilson, Chi., and Jim Bottomley, St. L.	31
1929	Chuck Klein, Phila.	43
1930	Hack Wilson, Chi.	56
1931	Chuck Klein, Phila.	31
1932	Chuck Klein, Phila., and Mel Ott, N.Y.	38
1933	Chuck Klein, Phila.	28
1934	Mel Ott, N.Y., and Rip Collins, St. L.	35
1935	Wally Berger, Bost.	34
1936	Mel Ott, N.Y.	33
1937	Mel Ott, N.Y., and Joe Medwick, St. L.	31
1938	Mel Ott, N.Y.	36
1939	John Mize, St. L.	28
1940	John Mize, St. L.	43
1941	Dolph Camilli, Bklyn.	34
1942	Mel Ott, N.Y.	30
1943	Bill Nicholson, Chi.	29
1944	Bill Nicholson, Chi.	33
1945	Tommy Holmes, Bost.	28
1946	Ralph Kiner, Pitts.	23
1947	Ralph Kiner, Pitts., and John Mize, N.Y.	51
1948	Ralph Kiner, Pitts., and John Mize, N.Y.	40
1949	Ralph Kiner, Pitts.	54
1950	Ralph Kiner, Pitts.	47
1951	Ralph Kiner, Pitts.	42
1952	Ralph Kiner, Pitts., and Hank Sauer, Chi.	37
1953	Ed Mathews, Mil.	47
1954	Ted Kluszewski, Cin.	49
1955	Willie Mays, N.Y.	51
1956	Duke Snider, Bklyn.	43
1957	Henry Aaron, Mil.	44
1958	Ernie Banks, Chi.	47
1959	Ed Mathews, Mil.	46
1960	Ernie Banks, Chi.	41
1961	Orlando Cepeda, San Fran.	46
1962	Willie Mays, San Fran.	49
1963	Henry Aaron, Mil., and Willie McCovey, San Fran.	44
1964	Willie Mays, San Fran.	47
1965	Willie Mays, San Fran.	52
1966	Henry Aaron, Atlanta	44
1967	Henry Aaron, Atlanta	39
1968	Willie McCovey, San Fran.	36
1969	Willie McCovey, San Fran.	45
1970	Johnny Bench, Cin.	45
1971	Willie Stargell, Pitts.	48
1972	Johnny Bench, Cin.	40
1973	Willie Stargell, Pitts.	44
1974	Mike Schmidt, Phila.	36
1975	Mike Schmidt, Phila.	38
1976	Mike Schmidt, Phila.	38
1977	George Foster, Cin.	52
1978	George Foster, Cin.	40
1979	Dave Kingman, Chicago	48
1980	Mike Schmidt, Phila.	48
1981*	Mike Schmidt, Phila.	31
1982	Dave Kingman, N.Y.	37
1983	Mike Schmidt, Phila.	40
1984	Mike Schmidt, Phila. and Dale Murphy, Atlanta	36
1985	Dale Murphy, Atlanta	37
1986	Mike Schmidt, Phila.	37
1987	Andre Dawson, Chicago	49

*Split season because of player strike.

NATIONAL LEAGUE BATTING CHAMPIONS

Year	Player, Team	Avg
1876	Roscoe Barnes, Chicago	.404
1877	Jim White, Boston	.385
1878	Abner Dalrymple, Mil.	.356
1879	Cap Anson, Chicago	.407
1880	George Gore, Chicago	.365
1881	Cap Anson, Chicago	.399
1882	Dan Brouthers, Buffalo	.367
1883	Dan Brouthers, Buffalo	.371
1884	James O'Rourke, Buffalo	.350
1885	Roger Connor, N. Y.	.371
1886	King Kelly, Chicago	.388
1887	Cap Anson, Chicago	.421
1888	Cap Anson, Chicago	.343
1889	Dan Brouthers, Boston	.373
1890	John Glasscock, N. Y.	.336
1891	William Hamilton, Phila.	.338
1892	Dan Brouthers, Bklyn., and Clarence Childs, Cleve.	.335
1893	Hugh Duffy, Boston	.378
1894	Hugh Duffy, Boston	.438
1895	Jesse Burkett, Cleveland	.423
1896	Jesse Burkett, Cleveland	.410
1897	Willie Keeler, Baltimore	.432
1898	Willie Keeler, Baltimore	.379
1899	Ed Delahanty, Phila.	.408
1900	Honus Wagner, Pittsburgh	.381
1901	Jesse Burkett, St. Louis	.382
1902	Clarence Beaumont, Pitts.	.357
1903	Honus Wagner, Pittsburgh	.355
1904	Honus Wagner, Pittsburgh	.349
1905	Cy Seymour, Cincinnati	.377
1906	Honus Wagner, Pittsburgh	.339
1907	Honus Wagner, Pittsburgh	.350
1908	Honus Wagner, Pittsburgh	.354
1909	Honus Wagner, Pittsburgh	.339
1910	Sherwood Magee, Philadelphia	.331
1911	Honus Wagner, Pittsburgh	.334
1912	Henry Zimmerman, Chicago	.372
1913	Jake Daubert, Brooklyn	.350
1914	Jake Daubert, Brooklyn	.329
1915	Larry Doyle, New York	.320
1916	Hal Chase, Cincinnati	.339
1917	Edd Roush, Cincinnati	.341
1918	Jack Wheat, Brooklyn	.335
1919	Edd Roush, Cincinnati	.321
1920	Rogers Hornsby, St. Louis	.370
1921	Rogers Hornsby, St. Louis	.397
1922	Rogers Hornsby, St. Louis	.401
1923	Rogers Hornsby, St. Louis	.384
1924	Rogers Hornsby, St. Louis	.424
1925	Rogers Hornsby, St. Louis	.403
1926	Gene Hargrave, Cincinnati	.353
1927	Paul Waner; Pittsburgh	.380
1928	Rogers Hornsby, Boston	.387
1929	Lefty O'Doul, Phila.	.398
1930	Bill Terry, N.Y.	.401

Year	Player, Team	Avg	Year	Player, Team	Avg	Year	Player, Team	Avg
1931	Chick Hafey, St. Louis	.349	1950	Stan Musial, St. Louis	.346	1969	Pete Rose, Cincinnati	.348
1932	Lefty O'Doul, Brooklyn	.368	1951	Stan Musial, St. Louis	.355	1970	Rico Carty, Atlanta	.366
1933	Chuck Klein, Phila.	.368	1952	Stan Musial, St. Louis	.336	1971	Joe Torre, St. Louis	.363
1934	Paul Waner, Pittsburgh	.362	1953	Carl Furillo, Brooklyn	.344	1972	Billy Williams, Chicago	.333
1935	Arky Vaughan, Pittsburgh	.385	1954	Willie Mays, N. Y.	.345	1973	Pete Rose, Cincinnati	.338
1936	Paul Waner, Pittsburgh	.373	1955	Richie Ashburn, Phila.	.338	1974	Ralph Garr, Atlanta	.353
1937	Joe Medwick, St. Louis	.374	1956	Henry Aaron, Mil.	.328	1975	Bill Madlock, Chicago	.354
1938	Ernie Lombardi, Cin.	.342	1957	Stan Musial, St. Louis	.351	1976	Bill Madlock, Chicago	.339
1939	John Mize, St. Louis	.349	1958	Richie Ashburn, Phila.	.350	1977	Dave Parker, Pittsburgh	.338
1940	Debs Garms, Pittsburgh	.355	1959	Henry Aaron, Mil.	.355	1978	Dave Parker, Pittsburgh	.334
1941	Pete Reiser, Brooklyn	.343	1960	Dick Groat, Pittsburgh	.325	1979	Keith Hernandez, St. Louis	.344
1942	Ernie Lombardi, Boston	.330	1961	Roberto Clemente, Pitts.	.351	1980	Bill Buckner, Chicago	.324
1943	Stan Musial, St. Louis	.357	1962	Tommy Davis, L. A.	.346	1981*	Bill Madlock, Pittsburgh	.341
1944	Dixie Walker, Brooklyn	.357	1963	Tommy Davis, L. A.	.326	1982	Al Oliver, Montreal	.331
1945	Phil Cavarretta, Chicago	.355	1964	Roberto Clemente, Pitts.	.339	1983	Bill Madlock, Pittsburgh	.323
1946	Stan Musial, St. Louis	.365	1965	Roberto Clemente, Pitts.	.329	1984	Tony Gwynn, San Diego	.351
1947	Harry Walker, St. L.-Phila.	.363	1966	Matty Alou, Pittsburgh	.342	1985	Willie McGee, St. Louis	.353
1948	Stan Musial, St. Louis	.376	1967	Roberto Clemente, Pitts.	.357	1986	Tim Raines, Montreal	.334
1949	Jackie Robinson, Brooklyn	.342	1968	Pete Rose, Cincinnati	.335	1987	Tony Gwynn, San Diego	.370

AMERICAN LEAGUE PENNANT WINNERS

Year	Club	Manager	Won	Lost	Pct	Year	Club	Manager	Won	Lost	Pct
1901	Chicago	Clark C. Griffith	83	53	.610	1946	Boston	Joseph E. Cronin	104	50	.675
1902	Philadelphia	Connie Mack	83	53	.610	1947[1]	New York	Stanley R. Harris	97	57	.630
1903[1]	Boston	Jimmy Collins	91	47	.659	1948[1]	Cleveland	Lou Boudreau	97	58	.626
1904[2]	Boston	Jimmy Collins	95	59	.617	1949[1]	New York	Casey Stengel	97	57	.630
1905	Philadelphia	Connie Mack	92	56	.622	1950[1]	New York	Casey Stengel	98	56	.636
1906[1]	Chicago	Fielder A. Jones	93	58	.616	1951[1]	New York	Casey Stengel	98	56	.636
1907	Detroit	Hugh A. Jennings	92	58	.613	1952[1]	New York	Casey Stengel	95	59	.617
1908	Detroit	Hugh A. Jennings	90	63	.588	1953[1]	New York	Casey Stengel	99	52	.656
1909	Detroit	Hugh A. Jennings	98	54	.645	1954	Cleveland	Al Lopez	111	43	.721
1910[1]	Philadelphia	Connie Mack	102	48	.680	1955	New York	Casey Stengel	96	58	.623
1911[1]	Philadelphia	Connie Mack	101	50	.669	1956[1]	New York	Casey Stengel	97	57	.630
1912[1]	Boston	J. Garland Stahl	105	47	.691	1957	New York	Casey Stengel	98	56	.636
1913[1]	Philadelphia	Connie Mack	96	57	.627	1958[1]	New York	Casey Stengel	92	62	.597
1914	Philadelphia	Connie Mack	99	53	.651	1959	Chicago	Al Lopez	94	60	.610
1915[1]	Boston	William F. Carrigan	101	50	.669	1960	New York	Casey Stengel	97	57	.630
1916[1]	Boston	William F. Carrigan	91	63	.591	1961[1]	New York	Ralph Houk	109	53	.673
1917[1]	Chicago	Clarence H. Rowland	100	54	.649	1962[1]	New York	Ralph Houk	96	66	.593
1918[1]	Boston	Ed Barrow	75	51	.595	1963	New York	Ralph Houk	104	57	.646
1919	Chicago	William Gleason	88	52	.629	1964	New York	Yogi Berra	99	63	.611
1920[1]	Cleveland	Tris Speaker	98	56	.636	1965	Minnesota	Sam Mele	102	60	.630
1921	New York	Miller J. Huggins	98	55	.641	1966[1]	Baltimore	Hank Bauer	97	53	.606
1922	New York	Miller J. Huggins	94	60	.610	1967	Boston	Dick Williams	92	70	.568
1923[1]	New York	Miller J. Huggins	98	54	.645	1968[1]	Detroit	Mayo Smith	103	59	.636
1924[1]	Washington	Stanley R. Harris	92	62	.597	1969	Baltimore[3]	Earl Weaver	109	53	.673
1925	Washington	Stanley R. Harris	96	55	.636	1970[1]	Baltimore[3]	Earl Weaver	108	54	.667
1926	New York	Miller J. Huggins	91	63	.591	1971	Baltimore[4]	Earl Weaver	101	57	.639
1927[1]	New York	Miller J. Huggins	110	44	.714	1972[1]	Oakland[5]	Dick Williams	93	62	.600
1928[1]	New York	Miller J. Huggins	101	53	.656	1973[1]	Oakland[6]	Dick Williams	94	68	.580
1929[1]	Philadelphia	Connie Mack	104	46	.693	1974[1]	Oakland[6]	Alvin Dark	90	72	.556
1930[1]	Philadelphia	Connie Mack	102	52	.662	1975	Boston[4]	Darrell Johnson	95	65	.594
1931	Philadelphia	Connie Mack	107	45	.704	1976	New York[7]	Billy Martin	97	62	.610
1932[1]	New York	Joseph V. McCarthy	107	47	.695	1977[1]	New York[7]	Billy Martin	100	62	.617
1933	Washington	Joseph E. Cronin	99	53	.651	1978[1]	New York[7]	Billy Martin and Bob Lemon	100	63	.613
1934	Detroit	Gordon Cochrane	101	53	.656						
1935[1]	Detroit	Gordon Cochrane	93	58	.616	1979	Baltimore[8]	Earl Weaver	102	57	.642
1936[1]	New York	Joseph V. McCarthy	102	51	.667	1980	Kansas City[9]	Jim Frey	97	65	.599
1937[1]	New York	Joseph V. McCarthy	102	52	.662	1981	New York[10]	Gene Michael-Bob Lemon	59	48	.551*
1938[1]	New York	Joseph V. McCarthy	99	53	.651						
1939[1]	New York	Joseph V. McCarthy	106	45	.702	1982	Milwaukee[11]	Harvey Kuenn	95	67	.586
1940	Detroit	Delmar D. Baker	90	64	.584	1983[1]	Baltimore[12]	Joe Altobelli	98	64	.605
1941[1]	New York	Joseph V. McCarthy	101	53	.656	1984[1]	Detroit[13]	Sparky Anderson	104	58	.642
1942	New York	Joseph V. McCarthy	103	51	.669	1985[1]	Kansas City[14]	Dick Howser	91	71	.562
1943[1]	New York	Joseph V. McCarthy	98	56	.636	1986	Boston[11]	John McNamara	95	66	.590
1944	St. Louis	Luke Sewell	89	65	.578	1987	Minnesota[15]	Tom Kelly	85	77	.525
1945[1]	Detroit	Steve O'Neill	88	65	.575						

*Split season because of player strike. 1. World Series winner. 2. No World Series. 3. Defeated Minnesota, Western Division winner, in playoff. 4. Defeated Oakland, Western Division Leader, in playoff. 5. Defeated Detroit, Eastern Division winner, in playoff. 6. Defeated Baltimore, Eastern Division winner, in playoff. 7. Defeated Kansas City, Western Division winner, in playoff. 8. Defeated California, Western Division winner, in playoff. 9. Defeated New York, Eastern Division winner, in playoff. 10. Defeated Oakland, Western Division winner, in playoff. 11. Defeated California, Western Division winner, in playoff. 12. Defeated Chicago, Western Division winner in playoff. 13. Defeated Kansas City, Western Division winner, in playoff. 14. Defeated Toronto, Eastern Division winner, in playoff. 15. Defeated Detroit, Eastern winner, in playoff.

NATIONAL LEAGUE PENNANT WINNERS

Year	Club	Manager	Won	Lost	Pct
1876	Chicago	Albert G. Spalding	52	14	.788
1877	Boston	Harry Wright	31	17	.646
1878	Boston	Harry Wright	41	19	.683
1879	Providence	George Wright	55	23	.705
1880	Chicago	Adrian C. Anson	67	17	.798
1881	Chicago	Adrian C. Anson	56	28	.667
1882	Chicago	Adrian C. Anson	55	29	.655
1883	Boston	John F. Morrill	63	35	.643
1884	Providence	Frank C. Bancroft	84	28	.750
1885	Chicago	Adrian C. Anson	87	25	.777
1886	Chicago	Adrian C. Anson	90	34	.726
1887	Detroit	W. H. Watkins	79	45	.637
1888	New York	James J. Mutrie	84	47	.641
1889	New York	James J. Mutrie	83	43	.659
1890	Brooklyn	William H. McGunnigle	86	43	.667
1891	Boston	Frank G. Selee	87	51	.630
1892	Boston	Frank G. Selee	102	48	.680
1893	Boston	Frank G. Selee	86	44	.662
1894	Baltimore	Edward H. Hanlon	89	39	.695
1895	Baltimore	Edward H. Hanlon	87	43	.669
1896	Baltimore	Edward H. Hanlon	90	39	.698
1897	Boston	Frank G. Selee	93	39	.705
1898	Boston	Frank G. Selee	102	47	.685
1899	Brooklyn	Edward H. Hanlon	88	42	.677
1900	Brooklyn	Edward H. Hanlon	82	54	.603
1901	Pittsburgh	Fred C. Clarke	90	49	.647
1902	Pittsburgh	Fred C. Clarke	103	36	.741
1903	Pittsburgh	Fred C. Clarke	91	49	.650
1904	New York[2]	John J. McGraw	106	47	.693
1905	New York[1]	John J. McGraw	105	48	.686
1906	Chicago	Frank L. Chance	116	36	.763
1907	Chicago[1]	Frank L. Chance	107	45	.704
1908	Chicago[1]	Frank L. Chance	99	55	.643
1909	Pittsburgh[1]	Fred C. Clarke	110	42	.724
1910	Chicago	Frank L. Chance	104	50	.675
1911	New York	John J. McGraw	99	54	.647
1912	New York	John J. McGraw	103	48	.682
1913	New York	John J. McGraw	101	51	.664
1914	Boston[1]	George T. Stallings	94	59	.614
1915	Philadelphia	Patrick J. Moran	90	62	.592
1916	Brooklyn	Wilbert Robinson	94	60	.610
1917	New York	John J. McGraw	98	56	.636
1918	Chicago	Fred L. Mitchell	84	45	.651
1919	Cincinnati[1]	Patrick J. Moran	96	44	.686
1920	Brooklyn	Wilbert Robinson	93	61	.604
1921	New York[1]	John J. McGraw	94	59	.614
1922	New York[1]	John J. McGraw	93	61	.604
1923	New York	John J. McGraw	95	58	.621
1924	New York	John J. McGraw	93	60	.608
1925	Pittsburgh[1]	William B. McKechnie	95	58	.621
1926	St. Louis[1]	Rogers Hornsby	89	65	.578
1927	Pittsburgh	Donie Bush	94	60	.610
1928	St. Louis	William B. McKechnie	95	59	.617
1929	Chicago	Joseph V. McCarthy	98	54	.645
1930	St. Louis	Gabby Street	92	62	.597
1931	St. Louis[1]	Gabby Street	101	53	.656
1932	Chicago	Charles J. Grimm	90	64	.584
1933	New York[1]	William H. Terry	91	61	.599
1934	St. Louis[1]	Frank F. Frisch	95	58	.621
1935	Chicago	Charles J. Grimm	100	54	.649
1936	New York	William H. Terry	92	62	.597
1937	New York	William H. Terry	95	57	.625
1938	Chicago	Gabby Hartnett	89	63	.586
1939	Cincinnati	William B. McKechnie	97	57	.630
1940	Cincinnati[1]	William B. McKechnie	100	53	.654
1941	Brooklyn	Leo E. Durocher	100	54	.649
1942	St. Louis[1]	William H. Southworth	106	48	.688
1943	St. Louis	William H. Southworth	105	49	.682
1944	St. Louis[1]	William H. Southworth	105	49	.682
1945	Chicago	Charles J. Grimm	98	56	.636
1946	St. Louis[1]	Edwin H. Dyer	98	58	.628
1947	Brooklyn	Burton E. Shotton	94	60	.610
1948	Boston	William H. Southworth	91	62	.595
1949	Brooklyn	Burton E. Shotton	97	57	.630
1950	Philadelphia	Edwin M. Sawyer	91	63	.591
1951	New York	Leo E. Durocher	98	59	.624
1952	Brooklyn	Charles W. Dressen	96	57	.630
1953	Brooklyn	Charles W. Dressen	105	49	.682
1954	New York[1]	Leo E. Durocher	97	57	.630
1955	Brooklyn[1]	Walter Alston	98	55	.641
1956	Brooklyn	Walter Alston	93	61	.604
1957	Milwaukee[1]	Fred Haney	95	59	.617
1958	Milwaukee	Fred Haney	92	62	.597
1959	Los Angeles[1]	Walter Alston	88	68	.564
1960	Pittsburgh[1]	Danny Murtaugh	95	59	.617
1961	Cincinnati	Fred Hutchinson	93	61	.604
1962	San Francisco	Alvin Dark	103	62	.624
1963	Los Angeles[1]	Walter Alston	99	63	.611
1964	St. Louis[1]	Johnny Keane	93	69	.574
1965	Los Angeles[1]	Walter Alston	97	65	.599
1966	Los Angeles	Walter Alston	95	67	.586
1967	St. Louis[1]	Red Schoendienst	101	60	.627
1968	St. Louis	Red Schoendienst	97	65	.599
1969	New York[1,3]	Gil Hodges	100	62	.617
1970	Cincinnati[4]	Sparky Anderson	102	60	.630
1971	Pittsburgh[1,5]	Danny Murtaugh	97	65	.599
1972	Cincinnati[4]	Sparky Anderson	95	59	.617
1973	New York[6]	Yogi Berra	82	79	.509
1974	Los Angeles[6]	Walter Alston	102	60	.630
1975	Cincinnati[1,4]	Sparky Anderson	108	54	.667
1976	Cincinnati[7,1]	Sparky Anderson	102	60	.630
1977	Los Angeles[7]	Tom Lasorda	98	64	.605
1978	Los Angeles[7]	Tom Lasorda	95	67	.586
1979[1]	Pittsburgh[6]	Chuck Tanner	98	64	.605
1980[1]	Philadelphia[4]	Dallas Green	91	71	.562
1981	Los Angeles[1,9]	Tom Lasorda	63	47	.573*
1982[1]	St. Louis[10]	Whitey Herzog	92	70	.568
1983	Philadelphia[11]	Paul Owens	90	72	.556
1984	San Diego[12]	Dick Williams	92	70	.568
1985	St. Louis[11]	Whitey Herzog	101	61	.623
1986	New York[8]	Dave Johnson	108	54	.667
1987	St. Louis[13]	Whitey Herzog	95	67	.586

*Split season because of player strike. 1. World Series winner. 2. No World Series. 3. Defeated Atlanta, Western Division winner, in playoff. 4. Defeated Pittsburgh, Eastern Division winner, in playoff. 5. Defeated San Francisco, Western Division winner, in playoff. 6. Defeated Cincinnati, Western Division winner, in playoff. 7. Defeated Philadelphia, Eastern Division winner, in playoff. 8. Defeated Houston, Western Division winner, in playoff. 9. Defeated Montreal, Eastern Division winner, in playoff. 10. Defeated Atlanta, Western Division winner, in playoff. 11. Defeated Los Angeles, Western Division in playoff. 12. Defeated Chicago, Eastern Division champion in playoff. 13. Defeated San Francisco, Western winner, in playoff.

MOST VALUABLE PLAYERS

(Baseball Writers Association selections)

American League

1931 Lefty Grove, Philadelphia
1932–33 Jimmy Foxx, Philadelphia
1934 Mickey Cochrane, Detroit
1935 Hank Greenberg, Detroit
1936 Lou Gehrig, New York
1937 Charlie Gehringer, Detroit
1938 Jimmy Foxx, Boston
1939 Joe DiMaggio; New York
1940 Hank Greenberg, Detroit
1941 Joe DiMaggio, New York
1942 Joe Gordon, New York
1943 Spurgeon Chandler, New York
1944–45 Hal Newhouser, Detroit
1946 Ted Williams, Boston
1947 Joe DiMaggio, New York
1948 Lou Boudreau, Cleveland
1949 Ted Williams, Boston
1950 Phil Rizzuto, New York
1951 Yogi Berra, New York
1952 Bobby Shantz, Philadelphia
1953 Al Rosen, Cleveland
1954–55 Yogi Berra, New York
1956–57 Mickey Mantle, New York
1958 Jackie Jensen, Boston
1959 Nellie Fox, Chicago
1960–61 Roger Maris, New York
1962 Mickey Mantle, New York
1963 Elston Howard, New York
1964 Brooks Robinson, Baltimore
1965 Zoilo Versalles, Minnesota
1966 Frank Robinson, Baltimore
1967 Carl Yastrzemski, Boston
1968 Dennis McLain, Detroit
1969 Harmon Killebrew, Minnesota
1970 John (Boog) Powell, Baltimore
1971 Vida Blue, Oakland
1972 Dick Allen, Chicago
1973 Reggie Jackson, Oakland
1974 Jeff Burroughs, Texas
1975 Fred Lynn, Boston
1976 Thurman Munson, New York
1977 Rod Carew, Minnesota
1978 Jim Rice, Boston
1979 Don Baylor, California
1980 George Brett, Kansas City
1981 Rollie Fingers, Milwaukee
1982 Robin Yount, Milwaukee
1983 Cal RipKen, Jr., Baltimore
1984 Willie Hernandez, Detroit
1985 Don Mattingly, New York
1986 Roger Clemens, Boston

National League

1931 Frank Frisch, St. Louis
1932 Chuck Klein, Philadelphia
1933 Carl Hubbell, New York
1934 Dizzy Dean, St. Louis
1935 Gabby Hartnett, Chicago
1936 Carl Hubbell, New York
1937 Joe Medwick, St. Louis
1938 Ernie Lombardi, Cincinnati
1939 Bucky Walters, Cincinnati
1940 Frank McCormick, Cincinnati
1941 Dolph Camilli, Brooklyn
1942 Mort Cooper, St. Louis
1943 Stan Musial, St. Louis
1944 Marty Marion, St. Louis
1945 Phil Cavarretta, Chicago
1946 Stan Musial, St. Louis
1947 Bob Elliott, Boston
1948 Stan Musial, St. Louis
1949 Jackie Robinson, Brooklyn
1950 Jim Konstanty, Philadelphia
1951 Roy Campanella, Brooklyn
1952 Hank Sauer, Chicago
1953 Roy Campanella, Brooklyn
1954 Willie Mays, New York
1955 Roy Campanella, Brooklyn
1956 Don Newcombe, Brooklyn
1957 Henry Aaron, Milwaukee
1958–59 Ernie Banks, Chicago
1960 Dick Groat, Pittsburgh
1961 Frank Robinson, Cincinnati
1962 Maury Wills, Los Angeles
1963 Sandy Koufax, Los Angeles
1964 Ken Boyer, St. Louis
1965 Willie Mays, San Francisco
1966 Roberto Clemente, Pittsburgh
1967 Orlando Cepeda, St. Louis
1968 Bob Gibson, St. Louis
1969 Willie McCovey, San Francisco
1970 Johnny Bench, Cincinnati
1971 Joe Torre, St. Louis
1972 Johnny Bench, Cincinnati
1973 Pete Rose, Cincinnati
1974 Steve Garvey, Los Angeles
1975–76 Joe Morgan, Cincinnati
1977 George Foster, Cincinnati
1978 Dave Parker, Pittsburgh
1979 Willie Stargell, Pittsburgh
1979 Keith Hernandez, St. Louis
1980 Mike Schmidt, Philadelphia
1981 Mike Schmidt, Philadelphia
1982 Dale Murphy, Atlanta
1983 Dale Murphy, Atlanta
1984 Ryne Sandberg, Chicago
1985 Willie McGee, St. Louis
1986 Mike Schmidt, Philadelphia

CY YOUNG AWARD

1956 Don Newcombe, Brooklyn N.L.
1957 Warren Spahn, Milwaukee N.L.
1958 Bob Turley, New York A.L.
1959 Early Wynn, Chicago A.L.
1960 Vernon Law, Pittsburgh, N.L.
1961 Whitey Ford, New York A.L.
1962 Don Drysdale, Los Angeles N.L.
1963 Sandy Koufax, Los Angeles N.L.
1964 Dean Chance, Los Angeles A.L.
1965 Sandy Koufax, Los Angeles N.L.
1966 Sandy Koufax, Los Angeles N.L.
1967 Jim Lonborg, Boston A.L.; Mike McCormick, San Francisco N.L.
1968 Dennis, McLain, Detroit A.L.; Bob Gibson, St. Louis N.L.
1969 Mike Cuellar, Baltimore, and Dennis McLain, Detroit, tied in A.L.; Tom Seaver, N.Y. N.L.
1970 Jim Perry, Minnesota A.L; Bob Gibson, St. Louis N.L.
1971 Vida Blue, Oakland A.L.; Ferguson Jenkins, Chicago N.L.
1972 Gaylord Perry, Cleveland A.L.; Steve Carlton, Phila. N.L.
1973 Jim Palmer, Baltimore A.L.; Tom Seaver, New York N.L.
1974 Catfish Hunter, Oakland A.L.; Mike Marshall, Los Angeles N.L.
1975 Jim Palmer, Baltimore A.L.; Tom Seaver, New York N.L.
1976 Jim Palmer, Baltimore A.L.; Randy Jones, San Diego N.L.
1977 Sparky Lyle, N.Y., A.L.; Steve Carlton, Philadelphia N.L.
1978 Ron Guidry, N.Y., A.L.; Gaylord Perry, San Diego N.L.
1979 Mike Flanagan, Baltimore, A.L.; Bruce Sutter, Chicago, N.L.
1980 Steve Stone, Baltimore, A.L.; Steve Carlton, Philadelphia, N.L.
1981 Rollie Fingers, Milwaukee, A.L.; Fernando Valenzuela, Los Angeles, N.L.
1982 Pete Vuckovich, Milwaukee, A.L.; Steve Carlton, Philadelphia, N.L.
1983 LaMarr Hoyt, Chicago, A.L.; John Denny, Philadelphia, N.L.
1984 Willie Hernandez, Detroit, A.L.; Rick Sutcliffe, Chicago, N.L.
1985 Bret Saberhagen, A.L.; Dwight Gooden, N.L.
1986 Roger Clemens, A.L.; Mike Scott, N.L.

ROOKIE OF THE YEAR

(Baseball Writers Association selections)

American League

1949 Roy Sievers, St. Louis
1950 Walt Dropo, Boston
1951 Gil McDougald, New York
1952 Harry Byrd, Philadelphia
1953 Harvey Kuenn, Detroit
1954 Bob Grim, New York
1955 Herb Score, Cleveland
1956 Luis Aparicio, Chicago
1957 Tony Kubek, New York
1958 Albie Pearson, Washington
1959 Bob Allison, Washington
1960 Ron Hansen, Baltimore
1961 Don Schwall, Boston
1962 Tom Tresh, New York
1963 Gary Peters, Chicago
1964 Tony Oliva, Minnesota
1965 Curt Blefary, Baltimore
1966 Tommy Agee, Chicago

1967 Rod Carew, Minnesota
1968 Stan Bahnsen, New York
1969 Lou Piniella, Kansas City
1970 Thurman Munson, New York
1971 Chris Chambliss, Cleveland
1972 Carlton Fisk, Boston
1973 Alonzo Bumbry, Baltimore
1974 Mike Hargrove, Texas
1975 Fred Lynn, Boston
1976 Mark Fidrych, Detroit
1977 Eddie Murray, Baltimore
1978 Lou Whitaker, Detroit
1979 Alfredo Griffin, Toronto
1979 John Castino, Minnesota
1980 Joe Charboneau, Cleveland
1981 Dave Righetti, New York
1982 Cal Ripken, Jr., Baltimore
1983 Ron Kittle, Chicago
1984 Alvin Davis, Seattle
1985 Ozzie Guillen, Chicago
1986 Jose Canseco, Oakland

National League

1949 Don Newcombe, Brooklyn
1950 Sam Jethroe, Boston
1951 Willie Mays, New York
1952 Joe Black, Brooklyn
1953 Jim Gilliam, Brooklyn
1954 Wally Moon, St. Louis
1955 Bill Virdon, St. Louis
1956 Frank Robinson, Cincinnati
1957 Jack Sanford, Philadelphia
1958 Orlando Cepeda, San Francisco
1959 Willie McCovey, San Francisco
1960 Frank Howard, Los Angeles
1961 Billy Williams, Chicago
1962 Ken Hubbs, Chicago
1963 Pete Rose, Cincinnati
1964 Richie Allen, Philadelphia
1965 Jim Lefebvre, Los Angeles
1966 Tommy Helms, Cincinnati
1967 Tom Seaver, New York
1968 Johnny Bench, Cincinnati
1969 Ted Sizemore, Los Angeles
1970 Carl Morton, Montreal
1971 Earl Williams, Atlanta
1972 Jon Matlack, New York
1973 Gary Matthews, San Francisco
1974 Bake McBride, St. Louis
1975 John Montefusco, San Francisco
1976 Pat Zachry, Cincinnati
1977 Andre Dawson, Montreal
1978 Bob Horner, Atlanta
1979 Rick Sutcliffe, Los Angeles
1980 Steve Howe, Los Angeles
1981 Fernando Valenzuela, Los Angeles
1982 Steve Sax, Los Angeles
1983 Darryl Strawberry, New York
1984 Dwight Gooden, New York
1985 Vince Coleman, St. Louis
1986 Todd Worrell, St. Louis

BASEBALL'S PERFECTLY PITCHED GAMES[1]

(no opposing runner reached base)

John Richmond—Worcester vs. Cleveland (NL) June 12, 1880	1-0
John M. Ward—Providence vs. Buffalo (NL) June 17, 1880	5-0
Cy Young—Boston vs. Philadelphia (AL) May 5, 1904	3-0
Addie Joss—Cleveland vs. Chicago (AL) Oct. 2, 1908	1-0
Ernest Shore[2]—Boston vs. Washington (AL) June 23, 1917	4-0
Charles Robertson—Chicago vs. Detroit (AL) April 30, 1922	2-0
Don Larsen[3]—New York (AL) vs. Brooklyn (NL) Oct. 8, 1956	2-0
Jim Bunning—Philadelphia vs. New York (NL) June 21, 1964	6-0
Sandy Koufax—Los Angeles vs. Chicago (NL) Sept. 9, 1965	1-0
Jim Hunter—Oakland vs. Minnesota (AL) May 8, 1968	4-0
Len Barker—Cleveland vs. Toronto (AL) May 15, 1981	3-0
Mike Witt—California vs. Texas (AL) Sept. 30, 1984	1-0

1. Harvey Haddix, of Pittsburgh, pitched 12 perfect innings against Milwaukee (NL), May 26, 1959 but lost game in 13th on error and hit. 2. Shore, relief pitcher for Babe Ruth who walked first batter before being ejected by umpire, retired 26 batters who faced him and baserunner was out stealing. 3. World Series.

MAJOR LEAGUE LIFETIME RECORDS

Source: The Book of Baseball Records, published and copyrighted by Seymour Siwoff, New York, N.Y. 10036.

Leading Batters, by Average
(Over 2,000 Hits)

	Years	At Bats	Hits	Avg
Ty Cobb	24	11,429	4,191	.367
Rogers Hornsby	23	8,173	2,930	.358
Dan Brouthers	19	6,725	2,349	.349
Ed Delahanty	16	7,493	2,593	.346
Tris Speaker	22	10,196	3,515	.345
Willie Keeler	19	8,564	2,955	.345
Ted Williams	19	7,706	2,654	.345
Billy Hamilton	14	6,262	2,157	.344
Harry Heilmann	17	7,787	2,660	.342
Babe Ruth	22	8,399	2,873	.342
Jesse Burkett	16	8,389	2,872	.342
Bill Terry	14	6,428	2,193	.341
Lou Gehrig	17	8,001	2,721	.340
George Sisler	15	8,267	2,812	.340
Nap Lajoie	21	9,589	3,251	.339
Cap Anson	22	9,084	3,081	.339
Sam Thompson	15	6,004	2,016	.336
Al Simmons	20	8,761	2,927	.334
Eddie Collins	25	9,949	3,311	.333
Paul Waner	20	9,459	3,152	.333
Stan Musial	22	10,972	3,630	.331
Rod Carew	19	9,214	3,053	.331
Heinie Manush	17	7,653	2,524	.330
Hugh Duffy	17	6,999	2,307	.330
Honus Wagner	21	10,427	3,430	.329
Joe DiMaggio	13	6,821	2,214	.325
Jimmie Foxx	20	8,134	2,646	.325

Leading Pitchers
(Over 250 Victories)

	Years	W	L	Pct
Cy Young	22	511	315	.619
Walter Johnson	21	416	279	.599
Grover Alexander	20	373	208	.642
Christy Mathewson	17	373	188	.665
James Galvin	15	365	309	.542
Warren Spahn	21	363	245	.597
Charles Nichols	15	360	202	.641
Tim Keefe	14	346	225	.606
Steve Carlton*	23	329	243	.575
John Clarkson	12	328	175	.652
Eddie Plank	17	325	190	.631
Don Sutton*	22	321	250	.562
Phil Niekro	24	318	274	.537
Mickey Welch	13	316	214	.596
Gaylord Perry	22	314	265	.542
Tom Seaver	20	311	205	.603

	Years	W	L	Pct
Hoss Radbourne	21	308	191	.617
Lefty Grove	20	300	141	.680
Early Wynn	23	300	244	.551
Robin Roberts	19	286	245	.539
Ferguson Jenkins	19	284	226	.557
Jim Kaat	25	283	236	.545
Tony Mullane	14	282	221	.561
Red Ruffing	22	273	225	.548
Burleigh Grimes	19	270	212	.560
Jim Palmer	18	268	149	.643
Bob Feller	18	266	162	.621
Eppa Rixey	21	266	251	.515
Gus Weyhing	14	265	236	.529
Jim McCormick	10	264	217	.549
Ted Lyons	21	260	230	.531
Red Faber	20	254	212	.545
Carl Hubbell	16	253	154	.622
Bob Gibson	17	251	174	.591

*Active through 1987.

MAJOR LEAGUE ALL-TIME PITCHING RECORDS

(Through 1986)

Most Games Won—511, Cy Young, Cleveland N.L., 1890–98, St. Louis N.L., 1899–1900, Boston A.L., 1901–08, Cleveland A.L., 1909–11, Boston N.L., 1911.

Most Games Won, Season—60, Hoss Radbourne, Providence N.L., 1884. (Since 1900—41, Jack Chesbro, New York A.L., 1904.)

Most Consecutive Games Won—24, Carl Hubbell, New York N.L., 1936 (16) and 1937 (8).

Most Consecutive Games Won, Season—19, Tim Keefe, New York N.L., 1888; Rube Marquard, New York N.L., 1912.

Most Years Won 20 or More Games—16, Cy Young, Cleveland N.L., 1891–98, St. Louis N.L., 1899–1900, Boston A.L., 1901–04, 1907–08.

Most Shutouts—113, Walter Johnson, Wash. A.L., 1907–27.

Most Shutouts, Season—16, Grover Alexander, Philadelphia N.L., 1916.

Most Consecutive Shutouts—6, Don Drysdale, Los Angeles, N.L., 1968.

Most Consecutive Scoreless Innings—58, Don Drysdale, Los Angeles, N.L., 1968.

Most Strikeouts—4,547, Nolan Ryan, New York N.L., California A.L., Houston N.L., 1968–1985 (Still active)

Most Strikeouts, Season—505, Matthew Kilroy, Baltimore A.A., 1886. (Since 1900—383, Nolan Ryan, California, A.L., 1973.)

Most Strikeouts, Game—21, Tom Cheney, Washington A.L., 1962, 16 innings. Nine innings: 20, Roger Clemens, Boston, A.L., 1986; 19, Charles McSweeney, Providence N.L., 1884; Hugh Dailey, Chicago U.A., 1884. (Since 1900—19, Steve Carlton, St. Louis N.L. vs. New York, Sept. 15, 1969; Tom Seaver, New York N.L. vs. San Diego, April 22, 1970; Nolan Ryan, California A.L. vs. Boston, Aug. 12, 1974.)

Most Consecutive Strikeouts—10, Tom Seaver, New York N.L. vs. San Diego, April 22, 1970.

Most Games, Season—106, Mike Marshall, Los Angeles, N.L., 1974.

Most Complete Games, Season—74, William White, Cincinnati N.L., 1879. (Since 1900—48, Jack Chesbro, New York A.L., 1904.)

MAJOR LEAGUE INDIVIDUAL ALL-TIME RECORDS

(Through 1986)

Highest Batting Average—442, James O'Neill, St. Louis, A.A., 1887; .438, Hugh Duffy, Boston, N.L., 1894 (Since 1900—.424, Rogers Hornsby, St. Louis, N.L., 1924; .422, Nap Lajoie, Phil., A.L., 1901)

Most Times at Bat—12,364, Henry Aaron, Milwaukee N.L., 1954–65; Atlanta N.L., 1966–74; Milwaukee A.L., 1975–76.

Most Years Batted .300 or Better—23, Ty Cobb, Detroit A.L., 1906–26, Philadelphia A.L., 1927–28.

Most hits—4,256, Pete Rose, Cincinnati 1963–79, Philadelphia 1980–83, Montreal 1984, Cincinnati 1984 (still active)

Most Hits, Season—257, George Sisler, St. Louis A.L., 1920.

Most Hits, Game (9 innings)—7, Wilbert Robinson, Baltimore N.L., 6 singles, 1 double, 1892. Rennie Stennett, Pittsburgh N.L., 4 singles, 2 doubles, 1 triple, 1975.

Most Hits, Game (extra innings)—9, John Burnett, Cleveland A.L., 18 innings, 7 singles, 2 doubles, 1932.

Most Hits in Succession—12, Mike Higgins, Boston A.L., in four games, 1938; Walt Dropo, Detroit A.L., in three games, 1952.

Most Consecutive Games Batted Safely—56, Joe DiMaggio, New York A.L., 1941.

Most Runs—2,244, Ty Cobb, Detroit A.L., 1905–26, Philadelphia A.L., 1927–28.

Most Runs, Season—196, William Hamilton, Philadelphia N.L., 1894. (Since 1900—177, Babe Ruth, New York A.L., 1921.)

Most Runs, Game—7, Guy Hecker, Louisville A.A., 1886. (Since 1900—6, by Mel Ott, New York N.L., 1934, 1944; Johnny Pesky, Boston A.L., 1946; Frank Torre, Milwaukee N.L., 1957.)

Most Runs Batted in—2,297, Henry Aaron, Milwaukee N.L., 1954–1965; Atlanta N.L., 1966–74; Milwaukee A.L., 1975–76.

Most Runs Batted in, Season—190, Hack Wilson, Chicago N.L., 1930.

Most Runs Batted In, Game—12, Jim Bottomley, St. Louis N.L., 1924.

Most Home Runs—755, Henry Aaron, Milwaukee N.L., 1954–1965; Atlanta N.L., 1966–74; Milwaukee A.L., 1975–76.

Most Home Runs, Season—61, Roger Maris, New York A.L., 1961 (162-game season); 60, Babe Ruth, New York A.L., 1927 (154-game season)

Most Home Runs with Bases Filled—23, Lou Gehrig, New York A.L., 1927–39.

Most 2-Base Hits—793, Tris Speaker, Boston A.L., 1907–15, Cleveland A.L., 1916–26, Washington A.L., 1927, Philadelphia A.L., 1928.

Most 2-Base Hits, Season—67, Earl Webb, Boston A.L., 1931.

Most 2-base Hits, Game—4, by many.

Most 3-Base Hits—312, Sam Crawford, Cincinnati N.L., 1899–1902, Detroit A.L., 1903–17.

Most 3-Base Hits, Season—36, Owen Wilson, Pittsburgh N.L., 1912.

Most 3-Base Hits, Game—4, George Strief, Philadelphia A.A., 1885; William Joyce, New York N.L., 1897. (Since 1900—3, by many.)

Most Games Played—3,298, Henry Aaron, Milwaukee N.L., 1954–1965; Atlanta, N.L., 1966–74; Milwaukee A.L., 1975–76.

Most Consecutive Games Played—2,130, Lou Gehrig, New York A.L., 1925–39.

Most Bases on Balls—2,056, Babe Ruth, Boston A.L., 1914–19; New York A.L., 1920–34, Boston N.L., 1935.

Most Bases on Balls, Season—170, Babe Ruth, New York A.L., 1923.

Most bases on Balls, Game—6, Jimmy Foxx, Boston A.L., 1938.

Most Strikeouts, Season—189, Bobby Bonds, San Francisco N.L., 1970.

Most Strikeouts, Game (9 innings)—5, by many.

Most Strikeouts, Game (extra innings)—6, Carl Weilman, St. Louis A.L., 15 innings, 1913; Don Hoak, Chicago N.L., 17 innings, 1956; Fred Reichardt, California A.L., 17, innings, 1966; Billy Cowan, California A.L., 20, 1971; Cecil Cooper, Boston A.L., 15, 1974.

Most pinch—hits, lifetime—150, Manny Mota, S.F., 1962; Pitt., 1963–68; Montreal, 1969; L.A., 1969–80, N.L.

Most Pinch-hits, season—25, Jose Morales, Montreal N.L., 1976.

Most consecutive pinch-hits—9, Dave Philley, Phil., N.L., 1958 (8), 1959 (1).

Most pinch-hit home runs, lifetime—18, Gerald Lynch, Pitt.-Cin. N.L., 1957–66.

Most pinch-hit home runs, season—6, Johnny Frederick, Brooklyn, N.L., 1932.

Most stolen bases, lifetime (since 1900)—938, Lou Brock, Chicago N.L. 1961–64; St. Louis, N.L. 1964–79.

Most stolen bases, season—156, Harry Stovey, Phil., A.A., 1888. Since 1900: 130, Rickey Henderson, Oak., A.L., 1982; 118, Lou Brock, St. Lou., 1974.

Most stolen bases, game—7, George Gore, Chicago N.L. 1881; William Hamilton, Philadelphia N.L. 1894. (Since 1900—6, Eddie Collins, Philadelphia A.L., 1912.)

Most time stealing home, lifetime—35, Ty Cobb, Detroit-Phil. A.L., 1905–28.

MAJOR LEAGUE ATTENDANCE RECORDS

(Through 1986)

Single game—78,672, San Francisco at Los Angeles (N.L.), April 18, 1958. (At Memorial Coliseum.)

Doubleheader—84,587, New York at Cleveland (A.L.), Sept. 12, 1954.

Night—78,382, Chicago at Cleveland (A.L.), Aug. 20, 1948.

Season, home—3,608,881, Los Angeles (N.L.), 1982.

Season, road—2,461,240, New York (A.L.), 1980.

Season, league—27,278,076, American League, 1987.

Season, both leagues—52,008,918, 1987.

World Series, single game—92,706, Chicago (A.L.) at Los Angeles (N.L.), Oct. 6, 1959.

World Series, all games (6)—420,784, Chicago (A.L.) and Los Angeles (N.L.), 1959.

MOST HOME RUNS IN ONE SEASON

(45 or More)

HR	Player/Team	Year	HR	Player/Team	Year
61	Roger Maris, New York (AL)	1961	48	Jimmy Foxx, Philadelphia (AL)	1933
60	Babe Ruth, New York (AL)	1927	48	Harmon Killebrew, Minnesota (AL)	1962
59	Babe Ruth, New York (AL)	1921	48	Willie Stargell, Pittsburgh (NL)	1971
58	Jimmy Foxx, Philadelphia (AL)	1932	48	Dave Kingman, Chicago (NL)	1979
58	Hank Greenberg, Detroit (AL)	1938	48	Mike Schmidt, Philadelphia (NL)	1980
56	Hack Wilson, Chicago (NL)	1930	47	Babe Ruth, New York (AL)	1926
54	Babe Ruth, New York (AL)	1920	47	Ralph Kiner, Pittsburgh (NL)	1950
54	Babe Ruth, New York (AL)	1928	47	Ed Mathews, Milwaukee (NL)	1953
54	Ralph Kiner, Pittsburgh (NL)	1949	47	Ernie Banks, Chicago (NL)	1958
54	Mickey Mantle, New York (AL)	1961	47	Willie Mays, San Francisco (NL)	1964
52	Mickey Mantle, New York (AL)	1956	47	Henry Aaron, Atlanta (NL)	1971
52	Willie Mays, San Francisco (NL)	1965	47	Reggie Jackson, Oakland (AL)	1969
52	George Foster, Cincinnati (NL)	1977	47	George Bell, Toronto (AL)	1987
51	Ralph Kiner, Pittsburgh (NL)	1947	46	Babe Ruth, New York (AL)	1924
51	John Mize, New York (NL)	1947	46	Babe Ruth, New York, (AL)	1929
51	Willie Mays, New York (NL)	1955	46	Babe Ruth, New York (AL)	1931
50	Jimmy Foxx, Boston (AL)	1938	46	Lou Gehrig, New York (AL)	1931
49	Babe Ruth, New York (AL)	1930	46	Joe DiMaggio, New York (AL)	1937
49	Lou Gehrig, New York (AL)	1934	46	Ed Mathews, Milwaukee (NL)	1959
49	Lou Gehrig, New York (AL)	1936	46	Orlando Cepeda, San Francisco (NL)	1961
49	Ted Kluszewski, Cincinnati (NL)	1954	46	Jim Rice, Boston (AL)	1978
49	Willie Mays, San Francisco (NL)	1962	45	Harmon Killebrew, Minnesota (AL)	1963
49	Harmon Killebrew, Minnesota (AL)	1964	45	Willie McCovey, San Francisco (NL)	1969
49	Frank Robinson, Baltimore (AL)	1966	45	Johnny Bench, Cincinnati (NL)	1970
49	Harmon Killebrew, Minnesota (AL)	1969	45	Gorman Thomas, Milwaukee (AL)	1979
49	Mark McGwire, Oakland (AL)	1987	45	Henry Aaron, Milwaukee (NL)	1962
49	Andre Dawson, Chicago (NL)	1987			

MAJOR LEAGUE BASEBALL EXPANDS PLAYOFFS TO BEST 4-OF-7

After 16 years of five-game league championship playoffs, baseball expanded to a seven-game format in 1985 for the purpose of reaping a reported additional $9 million in network television revenue.

An agreement was reached between management and players to expand the series for 1985. The decision immediately increased baseball's revenue from $20 to $29 million for the playoffs.

The formula for splitting that money was part of the agreement with the players which settled the Aug. 6–8 major league players strike.

The playoffs had been a best 3-of-5 affair since 1969, when divisional play was first initiated. The World Series remained a best 4-of-7 format.

MAJOR LEAGUE BALL PARK STATISTICS*

lf—Left-field foul line; cf—center field; rf—right-field foul line

Club, nickname, and grounds	Distance, feet lf	cf	rf	Seating capacity	Record Attendance[4] Day game	Double-header[3]	Night game
American League							
Baltimore Orioles—Memorial Stadium	309	405	309	53,208	51,956	46,796	51,883
Boston Red Sox—Fenway Park	315	390	302	33,465	36,388	41,995	36,228
California Angels—Anaheim Stadium	333	404	333	67,335	62,020	41,723	61,640
Chicago White Sox—Comiskey Park	341	401	341	43,651	54,215	55,555	53,940
Cleveland Indians—Municipal Stadium	320	400	320	74,208	74,420	84,587	78,382
Detroit Tigers—Tiger Stadium	340	440	325	52,687	57,888	58,369	56,586
Kansas City Royals—Royals Stadium	330	410	330	40,635	41,095	40,525	41,860
Milwaukee Brewers—County Stadium	315	402	315	53,192	55,120	54,630	55,716
Minnesota Twins—Hubert H. Humphrey Metrodome	343	408	327	55,122	46,463	43,419	52,299
New York Yankees—Yankee Stadium[1]	312	417	310	57,545	69,755	81,841	74,747
Oakland A's—Oakland Coliseum	330	397	330	50,219	48,758	48,562	49,300
Seattle Mariners—Kingdome	316	410	316	59,438	47,353	25,344	57,762
Texas Rangers—Arlington Stadium	330	400	330	41,284	40,078	42,163	41,097
Toronto Blue Jays—Exhibition Stadium	330	400	330	43,737	44,649	41,308	39,347
National League							
Atlanta Braves—Atlanta Stadium	330	402	330	52,934	51,275	46,489	53,775
Chicago Cubs—Wrigley Field	355	400	353	37,272	46,572	46,965	No lights
Cincinnati Reds—Riverfront Stadium	330	404	330	52,392	53,390	52,147	53,328
Houston Astros—Astrodome	340	406	340	45,000	49,442	45,115	50,908
Los Angeles Dodgers—Dodger Stadium[2]	330	400	330	56,000	78,672	53,856	72,140
Montreal Expos—Olympic Stadium	325	404	325	58,838	57,592	59,282	57,121
New York Mets—Shea Stadium	338	410	338	55,300	56,738	57,175	56,658
Philadelphia Phillies—Veterans Stadium	330	408	330	66,507	63,283	40,720	63,501
Pittsburgh Pirates—Three Rivers Stadium	335	400	335	54,598	51,695	49,341	48,846
St. Louis Cardinals—Busch Memorial Stadium	330	414	330	50,222	50,548	49,743	50,340
San Diego Padres—Jack Murphy Stadium	330	405	330	51,319	36,750	43,473	50,569
San Francisco Giants—Candlestick Park	335	400	335	58,000	56,197	50,924	55,920

*At end of 1982 season. 1. Distance and capacity after rebuilding; attendance records prior to rebuilding. 2. Played also in Los Angeles Coliseum. 3. Two day games. 4. Through 1982 season.

PETE ROSE BREAKS TY COBB'S ALL-TIME HIT RECORD

Baseball fans in Cincinnati and all over the country waited patiently for the moment throughout the 1985 season. On Sept. 11, 1985, it finally came. Pete Rose singled to left field against San Diego Padres right-hander Eric Show at 8:01 P.M. EDT to break a record most had long thought would stand forever—Ty Cobb's career mark of 4,191 base hits.

Base hit 4,192 came before a crowd of 47,237 at Cincinnati's Riverfront Stadium in the first inning of a game the Reds would win 2–0.

Rose, 44 years old and a 23-year major league veteran, broke the record in the city and playing for the team with which he began his major league career in 1963. Rose played with the Reds through 1978, before signing with the Philadelphia Phillies in 1979 as a free agent. He stayed there until 1984, when he again signed as a free agent—this time with the Montreal Expos.

Rose's stay in Montreal was brief. In August, 1984, he was brought back to Cincinnati to serve as player-manager of a struggling, once-proud franchise. And while he pursued Cobb's record in 1985, he kept a surprising young Reds team in the chase for the National League Western Division championship most of the season.

Rose broke Cobb's record on the 57th anniversary of Cobb's last game—Sept. 11, 1928, against the Yankees at Yankee Stadium while playing for the old Philadelphia Athletics.

Ironically also, Padres first baseman Steve Garvey, second baseman Jerry Royster, and umpire Lee Weyer, who were all in Cincinnati for the historic hit, had all been in Atlanta in 1974 when Hank Aaron had broken another longtime record—Babe Ruth's mark of 714 career home runs.

Rose tied the record in Chicago on Sunday, Sept. 9, against Cubs pitcher Reggie Patterson.

His first major league base hit came on April 13, 1963. It was a triple against Pittsburgh Pirates pitcher Bob Friend. Other historic Rose hits came as follows: 1,000: June 26, 1968, against New York Mets pitcher Dick Selma; 2,000: June 19, 1973, against Ron Bryant, San Francisco Giants; 3,000: May 5, 1978, against Steve Rogers, Montreal Expos; 4,000: April 13, 1984, against Jerry Koosman, Philadelphia Phillies.

Rose also holds major league record for most games played, most at bats, most singles, most hits by a switch hitter, total bases by a switch hitter, most seasons with 200 or more hits, most consecutive seasons with 100 hits or more, most seasons 600 or more at-bats, most seasons 150 or more games played, highest fielding percentage by an outfielder, 1,000 games or more, and only player to play 500 games or more at five positions—first base, second base, third base, left field, and right field.

MAJOR LEAGUE BASEBALL—1987

AMERICAN LEAGUE
(Final Standing—1987)

EASTERN DIVISION

Team	W	L	Pct	GB
Detroit Tigers	98	64	.605	—
Toronto Blue Jays	96	66	.593	2
Milwaukee Brewers	91	71	.562	7
New York Yankees	89	73	.549	9
Boston Red Sox	78	84	.481	20
Baltimore Orioles	67	95	.414	31
Cleveland Indians	61	101	.377	37

WESTERN DIVISION

Team	W	L	Pct	GB
Minnesota Twins	85	77	.525	—
Kansas City Royals	83	79	.512	2
Oakland Athletics	81	81	.500	4
Seattle Mariners	78	84	.481	7
Chicago White Sox	77	85	.475	8
California Angels	75	87	.463	10
Texas Rangers	75	87	.463	10

AMERICAN LEAGUE LEADERS—1987

Batting—Wade Boggs, Boston	.363
Runs—Paul Molitor, Milwaukee	114
Hits—Kirby Puckett, Minnesota and Kevin Seitzer, Kansas City	207
Runs batted in—Georghe Bell, Toronto	134
Triples—Willie Wilson, Kansas City	15
Doubles—Paul Molitor, Milwaukee	41
Home runs—Mark McGuire, Oakland	49
Stolen bases—Harold Reynolds, Seattle	60
Game winning RBIs—Danny Tartabull, Kansas City	21

Pitching

Victories—Roger Clemens, Boston and Dave Stewart, Oakland	20
Earned run average—Jimmy Key, Toronto	2.76
Strikeouts—Mark Langston, Seattle	262
Shutouts—Roger Clemens, Boston	7
Complete games—Roger Clemens, Boston	18
Saves—Tom Henke, Toronto	34

AMERICAN LEAGUE AVERAGES—1987

Batting—Club

	AB	R	H	HR	RBI	Pct
Boston	5587	842	1549	174	801	.277
Milwaukee	5625	862	1552	163	832	.276
Seattle	5509	760	1499	161	716	.272
Detroit	5688	904	1548	230	847	.272
Toronto	5635	845	1514	214	790	.269
Texas	5563	823	1478	194	771	.266
Cleveland	5607	742	1476	187	691	.263
Kansas City	5498	715	1441	167	678	.262
New York	5511	788	1445	196	749	.262
Minnesota	5440	786	1420	196	732	.261
Oakland	5513	806	1429	199	760	.259
Chicago	5538	748	1427	173	704	.258
Baltimore	5604	732	1442	213	704	.257
California	5570	770	1406	172	710	.252

Batting Leaders
(350 or more at bats)

Player/Team	AB	R	H	HR	RBI	Pct
Boggs, Bsn	551	108	200	24	89	.363
Molitor, Mil	465	114	164	16	75	.353
Trammell, Det	597	109	205	28	105	.343
Puckett, Min	624	96	207	28	99	.332
Greenwell, Bsn	412	71	135	19	89	.328
Mattingly, NY	569	93	186	30	115	.327
Seitzer, KC	641	105	207	15	83	.323
T. Fernandez, Tor	578	90	186	5	67	.322
Franco, Cle	495	86	158	8	52	.319
Sheets, Blt	469	74	148	31	94	.316
Yount, Mil	635	99	198	21	103	.312
Tartabull, KC	582	95	180	34	101	.309
G. Bell, Tor	610	111	188	47	134	.308
Tabler, Cle	553	66	170	11	86	.307
Dw. Evans, Bsn	541	109	165	34	123	.305
Randolph NY	449	96	137	7	67	.305
Brantley, Sea	351	52	106	14	54	.302
Jacoby, Cle	540	73	162	32	69	.300
Brock, Mil	532	81	159	13	85	.299
Surhoff, Mil	395	50	118	7	68	.299
P. Bradley, Sea	603	101	179	14	67	.297
A. Davis, Sea	580	86	171	29	100	.295
Butler, Cle	522	91	154	9	41	.295
Baines, Chi	505	59	148	20	93	.293
Barrett, Bsn	559	72	164	3	43	.293

NATIONAL LEAGUE
(Final Standing—1987)

EASTERN DIVISION

Team	W	L	Pct	GB
St. Louis Cardinals	95	67	.586	—
New York Mets	92	70	.568	3
Montreal Expos	91	71	.562	4
Philadelphia Phillies	80	82	.494	15
Pittsburgh Pirates	80	82	.494	15
Chicago Cubs	76	85	.472	18 1/2

WESTERN DIVISION

Team	W	L	Pct	GB
San Francisco Giants	90	72	.556	—
Cincinnati Reds	84	78	.519	6
Houston Astros	76	86	.469	14
Los Angeles Dodgers	73	89	.451	17
Atlanta Braves	69	92	.429	20 1/2
San Diego Padres	65	97	.401	25

NATIONAL LEAGUE LEADERS—1987

Batting—Tony Gwynn, San Diego	.370
Runs—Tim Raines, Montreal	123
Hits—Tony Gwynn, San Diego	218
Runs batted in—Andre Dawson, Chicago	137
Triples—Juan Samuel, Philadelphia	15
Doubles—Tim Wallach, Montreal	42
Home runs—Andre Dawson, Chicago	49
Stolen bases—Vince Coleman, St. Louis	109
Game-winning RBIs—Howard Johnson, New York; Andre Dawson, Chicago; Dave Parker, Cincinnati; and Tim Wallach, Montreal	16

Pitching

Victories—Rick Sutcliffe, Chicago	18
Earned run average—Nolan Ryan, Houston	2.76
Strikeouts—Nolan Ryan, Houston	270
Shutouts—Rick Reuschel, Pittsburgh-San Francisco and Bob Welch, Los Angeles	4
Complete games—Rick Reuschel, Pittsburgh-San Francisco and Fernando Valenzuela, Los Angeles	12
Saves—Steve Bedrosian, Philadelphia	40

Calderon, Chi	542	93	159	28	83	.293
R. Henderson, NY	358	78	104	17	37	.291

Leading Pitchers
(10 or more decisions)

Player/Club	IP	H	BB	SO	W	L	ERA
Plesac, Mil	79	63	23	89	5	6	2.61
Thigpen, Chi	89	86	24	52	7	5	2.73
Key, Tor	261	210	66	161	17	8	2.76
Viola, Min	252	230	66	197	17	10	2.90
Clemens, Bsn	282	248	83	256	20	9	2.97
Henneman, Det	97	86	30	75	11	3	2.98
Mohorcic, Tex	99	88	19	48	7	6	2.99
Eckersley, Oak	116	99	17	113	6	8	3.03
D. Jones, Cle	91	101	24	87	6	5	3.15
Eichhorn, Tor	128	110	52	96	10	6	3.17
M. Williams, Tex	109	63	94	129	8	6	3.23
Saberhagen, KC	257	246	53	163	18	10	3.36
Morris, Det	266	227	93	208	18	11	3.38
Buice, Cal	114	87	40	109	6	7	3.39
Leibrandt, KC	240	235	88	151	16	11	3.41
Righetti, NY	95	95	44	77	8	6	3.51
Clancy, Tor	241	234	80	180	15	11	3.54
Bannister, Chi	229	216	49	124	16	11	3.58
Black, KC	122	126	35	61	8	6	3.60
Hudson, NY	155	137	57	100	11	7	3.61
Crim, Mil	130	133	39	56	6	8	3.67
Guidry, NY	118	111	38	96	5	8	3.67
Stewart, Oak	261	224	105	205	20	13	3.68
Schmidt, Blt	124	128	26	70	10	5	3.77

Pitching—Club

	ERA	H	ER	BB	SO	ShO	SA
Toronto	3.75	1323	606	568	1063	8	43
Kansas City	3.88	1424	614	549	915	11	26
Detroit	4.01	1435	653	569	980	10	32
Chicago	4.29	1436	690	537	792	12	36
New York	4.39	1474	705	542	900	10	47
California	4.39	1480	711	503	940	7	36
Oakland	4.40	1440	707	533	1041	6	40
Seattle	4.53	1499	720	498	917	10	33
Milwaukee	4.62	1548	752	529	1039	6	45
Texas	4.63	1388	743	760	1103	3	27
Minnesota	4.66	1464	739	564	989	4	39
Boston	4.78	1582	763	517	1031	13	16
Baltimore	5.04	1568	811	549	870	6	30
Cleveland	5.29	1565	836	606	849	8	25

NATIONAL LEAGUE AVERAGES—1987

Batting—Club

	AB	R	H	HR	RBI	Pct
New York	5601	823	1499	192	771	.268
Cincinnati	5561	783	1478	191	746	.266
Montreal	5499	737	1459	118	694	.265
Chicago	5573	722	1471	211	684	.264
Pittsburgh	5539	723	1464	131	684	.264
St. Louis	5500	798	1448	94	747	.263
Philadelphia	4383	595	1146	143	562	.261
San Francisco	5572	780	1448	203	727	.260
San Diego	5422	665	1409	112	617	.260
Atlanta	5428	747	1401	152	695	.258
Houston	5484	648	1386	122	602	.253
Los Angeles	5535	634	1390	125	593	.251

Batting Leaders
(350 or more at bats)

Player/Team	AB	R	H	HR	RBI	Pct
Gwynn, SD	589	119	218	7	54	.370
Guerrero, LA	545	89	184	27	88	.338
Daniels, Cin	368	73	123	26	64	.334
Raines, Mon	530	123	175	18	68	.330
Aldrete, SF	357	50	116	9	51	.325
Kruk, SD	447	72	140	20	90	.313
D. James, Atl	495	80	154	10	61	.311
Ready, SD	350	69	108	12	54	.309
W. Clark, SF	529	89	163	35	91	.308
Galarraga, Mon	551	73	168	13	91	.305
O. Smith, StL	600	104	182	0	75	.303
M. Thompson, Phi	527	86	159	7	43	.302
Bonilla, Pit	467	58	140	15	77	.300
Santiago, SD	546	64	164	18	79	.300
M. Wilson, NY	385	58	115	9	34	.299
Wallach, Mon	593	89	177	26	123	.298
Hatcher, Htn	564	96	167	11	63	.296
D. Murphy, Atl	566	115	167	44	105	.295
Marshall, LA	402	45	118	16	72	.294
Sandberg, Chi	523	81	154	16	59	.294
C. James, Phi	358	48	105	17	54	.293
D. Martinez, Chi	458	70	134	8	36	.293
E. Davis, Cin	474	120	139	37	100	.293
Schmidt, Phi	522	87	153	35	113	.293
VanSlyke, Pit	564	93	165	21	82	.293
Maldonado, SF	442	69	129	20	85	.292

Leading Pitchers
(10 or more decisions)

Player/Team	IP	H	BB	SO	W	L	ERA
Franco, Cin	82	76	27	61	8	5	2.52
Dayley, StL	61	52	33	63	9	5	2.66
Worrell, StL	95	87	34	93	8	6	2.66
Ryan, Htn	212	154	87	270	8	16	2.76
J. Robinson, Pit	123	89	54	101	8	9	2.85
Dunne, Pit	163	143	68	72	13	6	3.03
R. Murphy, Cin	101	91	32	99	8	5	3.04
Hershiser, LA	265	247	74	190	16	16	3.06
Tekulve, Phi	105	96	29	59	6	4	3.09
Reuschel, SF	227	207	42	106	13	9	3.09
L. Smith, Chi	84	84	32	96	4	10	3.12
Garrelts, SF	106	70	55	127	11	7	3.13
Gooden, NY	180	162	53	148	15	7	3.21
Welch, LA	252	204	86	195	15	9	3.22
Leach, NY	131	132	29	61	11	1	3.22
Scott, Htn	248	199	79	233	16	13	3.23
Martinez, Mon	145	133	40	84	11	4	3.30
Walk, Pit	117	107	51	78	8	2	3.31
D. Robinson, SF	108	105	40	79	11	7	3.42
Dravecky, SF	191	186	64	139	10	12	3.43
Andersen, Htn	102	94	41	93	9	5	3.45
Hammaker, SF	168	158	57	107	10	10	3.53
Magrane, StL	170	157	60	101	9	7	3.54
Darwin, Htn	196	184	69	134	9	10	3.59
Aguilera, NY	115	124	33	77	11	3	3.60

Pitching—Club

	ERA	H	ER	BB	SO	ShO	SA
San Francisco	3.69	1392	600	538	1033	10	38
Los Angeles	3.75	1423	608	568	1092	8	31
New York	3.84	1407	621	510	1030	7	51
Houston	3.85	1362	616	525	1136	13	32
Montreal	3.90	1417	625	446	1010	8	50
St. Louis	3.95	1484	643	533	872	7	48
Philadelphia	4.18	1171	537	459	660	6	41
Pittsburgh	4.20	1376	675	563	912	13	40
Cincinnati	4.25	1486	686	484	916	6	43
San Diego	4.29	1395	679	600	891	10	33
Chicago	4.55	1517	724	626	1010	6	45
Atlanta	4.65	1529	737	586	831	4	32

MAJOR LEAGUE BASEBALL—1987

AMERICAN LEAGUE PLAYOFFS—1987

1st game, Minneapolis, Minnesota, Oct. 7, 1987

Detroit	001	001	120	—	5	10	0
Minnesota	010	030	04x	—	8	10	0

Alexander, Hennerman, Hernandez, King; Viola, Reardon.
Winner: Reardon. Loser: Alexander. Attendance: 53,269.

2nd game, Minneapolis, Minnesota, Oct. 8, 1987

Detroit	020	000	010	—	3	7	1
Minnesota	030	210	00x	—	6	6	0

Morris; Blyleven, Berenguer.
Winner: Blyleven. Loser: Morris. Attendance: 55,245.

3rd game, Detroit, Michigan, Oct. 10, 1987

Minnesota	000	202	200	—	6	6	1
Detroit	005	000	02x	—	7	7	0

Straker, Schatzeder, Berenguer, Reardon; Terrell, Hennerman.
Winner: Hennerman. Loser: Reardon. Attendance: 49,730.

4th game, Detroit, Michigan, Oct. 11, 1987

Minnesota	001	111	010	—	5	7	1
Detroit	100	011	000	—	3	3	1

Viola, Atherton, Berenguer, Reardon; Tanana, Petry, Thurmond.
Winner: Viola. Loser: Tanana. Attendance: 51,939.

5th game, Detroit, Michigan, Oct. 12, 1987

Minnesota	040	000	113	—	9	15	1
Detroit	000	300	011	—	5	9	1

Blyleven, Schatzeder, Berenguer, Reardon; Alexander, King, Hennerman, Robinson.
Winner: Blyleven. Loser: Alexander. Attendance: 47,448.

Minnesota wins series, 4 games to 1.

NATIONAL LEAGUE PLAYOFFS—1987

1st game, St. Louis, Missouri, Oct. 6, 1987

San Francisco	100	100	010	—	3	7	1
St. Louis	001	103	00x	—	5	5	1

Reuschel, Lefferts, Garrelts; Mathews, Worrell, Dayley.
Winner: Mathews. Loser: Reuschel. Attendance: 55,331.

2nd game, St. Louis, Missouri, Oct. 7, 1987

San Francisco	020	100	020	—	5	10	0
St. Louis	000	000	000	—	0	2	1

Dravecky; Tudor, Forsch.
Winner: Dravecky. Loser: Tudor. Attendance: 55,331.

3rd game, San Francisco, California, Oct. 9, 1987

St. Louis	000	002	400	—	6	11	1
San Francisco	031	000	001	—	5	7	1

Magrane, Forsch, Worrell; Hammaker, Robinson, Lefferts, LaCoss.
Winner: Forsch. Loser: Robinson. Attendance 57,913.

4th game, San Francisco, California, Oct. 10, 1987

St. Louis	020	000	000	—	2	9	0
San Francisco	000	120	01x	—	4	9	2

Cox; Krukow.
Winner: Krukow; Loser: Cox. Attendance: 57,997.

5th game, San Francisco, California, Oct. 11, 1987

St. Louis	101	100	000	—	3	7	0
San Francisco	101	400	00x	—	6	7	1

Mathews, Forsch, Horton, Dayley; Reuschel, Price.
Winner: Price. Loser: Forsch. Attendance: 59,363.

6th game, St. Louis, Missouri, Oct. 13, 1987

San Francisco	000	000	000	—	0	6	0
St. Louis	010	000	00x	—	1	5	0

Reuschel, Robinson; Tudor, Worrell, Dayley.
Winner: Tudor. Loser: Worrell. Attendance: 55,331.

7th game, St. Louis, Missouri, Oct. 14, 1987

San Francisco	000	000	000	—	0	12	1
St. Louis	040	002	00x	—	6	8	0

Hammaker, Price, Downs, Garrelts, LaCoss, Robinson, Cox
Winner: Cox. Loser: Hammaker. Attendance: 55,331

St. Louis wins series, 4 games to 3.

HENDERSON OF A'S SETS STOLEN-BASES RECORD

Rickey Henderson of the Oakland A's broke the major league record for stolen bases in one season on Aug. 27, 1982, at Milwaukee when he stole his 119th base in the third inning. The previous record of 118 was held by Lou Brock of St. Louis and was set in 1974. Henderson had broken the American League stolen-bases mark in 1980 when he surpassed Ty Cobb's record of 96, set in 1915. Henderson finished the 1980 season with 100 stolen bases. In 1982 he completed the season with 130. The major league record for career stolen bases is held by Brock with 938.

NOLAN RYAN BREAKS 4,000 STRIKEOUT MARK

The date was July 11, 1985. The opponent, his original team, the New York Mets. The batter—former teammate Danny Heap. And when Heap swung and missed at an 0-2 curve ball in the top of the sixth inning of a game between the Mets and the Houston Astros, Nolan Ryan had become the first pitcher in the history of major league baseball to strike out 4,000 batters.

At the age of 38, Ryan, who also holds the record for most strikeouts in a season at 383 and who has hurled a record five no-hitters, was pitching in his 19th major league season. His career had included stops in New York with the Mets, California with the Angels, and Houston with the Astros.

When he won his 10th and final game of the 1985 season, bringing his career win total to 241, he had recorded a total of 209 strikeouts for the season and had a career total of 4,083. It also marked the 10th time in his career that he had struck out 200 or more batters.

WORLD SERIES—1987
Minnesota Twins (A) defeated St. Louis (N), 4 games to 3

1st Game—Minneapolis, Oct. 17

ST. LOUIS (N)	AB	R	H	BI	MINNESOTA (A)	AB	R	H	BI
Coleman, lf	4	0	0	0	Gladden, lf	4	1	2	5
Smith, ss	4	0	0	0	Gagne, ss	5	0	0	0
Herr, 2b	4	0	0	0	Puckett, cf	5	0	1	0
Lindeman, 1b	4	1	2	0	Gaetti, 3b	5	1	2	0
McGee, cf	3	0	2	0	Baylor, dh	5	1	1	0
Pena, c	3	0	0	1	Brunansky, rf	3	1	1	0
Lake, c	0	0	0	0	Davidson, ph	0	0	0	0
Oquendo, rf	3	0	0	0	Hrbek, 1b	2	2	1	2
Pagnozzi, dh	3	0	1	0	Larkin, 1b	0	0	0	0
Lawless, 3b	3	0	0	0	Lombardozzi, 2b	3	3	2	2
Magrane, p	0	0	0	0	Laudner, c	3	1	1	1
Forsch, p	0	0	0	0	Viola, p	0	0	0	0
Horton, p	0	0	0	0	Atherton, p	0	0	0	0
Total	**31**	**1**	**5**	**0**	**Total**	**35**	**10**	**11**	**10**
St. Louis					**010 000 000**		**1**	**5**	**1**
Minnesota					**000 720 10x**		**10**	**11**	**0**

Game-winning RBI—Hrbek (1). E—Lawless. DP—St. Louis 1, Minnesota 1. LOB—St. Louis 3, Minnesota 7. SB—Gladden (1).

	IP	H	R	ER	BB	SO
St. Louis						
Magrane, L, 0–1	3	4	5	5	4	1
Forsch	3	4	4	4	2	0
Horton	2	3	1	1	0	1
Minnesota						
Viola, W, 1–0	8	5	1	1	0	5
Atherton	1	0	0	0	0	0

Magrane pitched to 5 batters in the 4th. Time of Game—2:39. Attendance—55,171.

2nd Game—Minneapolis, Oct. 18

ST. LOUIS (N)	AB	R	H	BI	MINNESOTA (A)	AB	R	H	BI
Coleman, lf	4	1	1	0	Gladden, lf	5	0	1	1
Smith, ss	4	0	1	0	Gagne, ss	4	0	1	1
Herr, 2b	4	0	0	0	Puckett, cf	4	1	1	0
Driessen, 1b	4	1	1	1	Hrbek, 1b	3	1	1	0
McGee, cf	4	0	1	1	Gaetti, 3b	3	2	2	1
Pendleton, dh	4	1	1	0	Bush, dh	3	1	1	2
Ford, rf	3	1	2	0	Larkin, ph	1	0	0	0
Oquendo, 3b	4	0	1	0	Brunansky, rf	3	1	0	0
Pena, c	4	0	1	2	Lombardozzi, 2b	3	0	0	0
					Smalley, ph	1	0	1	0
					Newman, 2b	0	0	0	0
					Laudner, c	3	2	2	3
Total	**35**	**4**	**9**	**4**	**Total**	**33**	**8**	**10**	**8**
St. Louis					**000 010 120**		**4**	**9**	**0**
Minnesota					**010 601 00x**		**8**	**10**	**0**

Game-winning RBI—Gaetti (1). LOB—St. Louis 5, Minnesota 5. 2B—Bush, Gagne, Driessen, Smalley. HR—Gaetti (1), Laudner (1). SB—Coleman (1).

	IP	H	R	ER	BB	SO
St. Louis						
Cox, L, 0–1	3 2/3	6	7	7	2	3
Tunnell	2 1/3	3	1	1	1	1
Dayley	1 1/3	0	0	0	0	1
Worrell	2/3	1	0	0	1	0
Minnesota						
Blyleven, W, 1–0	7	6	2	2	1	8
Berenguer	1	3	2	2	0	0
Reardon	1	0	0	0	0	0

Wild pitch—Cox. Time of Game—2:42. Attendance—55,257.

3rd Game—St. Louis, Oct. 20

MINNESOTA (A)	AB	R	H	BI	ST. LOUIS (N)	AB	R	H	BI
Gladden, lf	4	0	1	0	Coleman, lf	4	1	1	2
Gagne, ss	3	1	0	0	Smith, ss	4	0	2	1
Puckett, cf	3	0	1	0	Herr, 2b	4	0	1	0
Gaetti, 3b	4	0	0	0	Driessen, 1b	4	0	0	0
Brunansky, rf	4	0	1	1	Worrell, p	0	0	0	0
Hrbek, 1b	4	0	0	0	McGee, cf	4	0	2	0
Laudner, c	3	0	2	0	Ford, rf	4	0	1	0
Bush, ph	1	0	0	0	Oquendo, 3b	3	1	1	0
Lombardozzi, 2b	3	0	0	0	Pena, c	2	1	1	0
Straker, p	2	0	0	0	Tudor, p	2	0	0	0
Larkin, ph	1	0	0	0	Pendleton, ph	0	0	0	0
Berenguer, p	0	0	0	0	Lindeman, 1b	0	0	0	0
Schatzeder, p	0	0	0	0					
Total	**32**	**1**	**5**	**1**	**Total**	**31**	**3**	**9**	**3**
Minnesota					**000 001 000**		**1**	**5**	**1**
St. Louis					**000 000 30x**		**3**	**9**	**1**

Game-winning RBI—Coleman (1). E—Pena, Gagne. DP—Minnesota 1. LOB—Minnesota 6, St. Louis 7. 2B—McGee, Laudner, Coleman. 3B—Puckett. SB—Coleman 2 (3). S—Pendleton.

	IP	H	R	ER	BB	SO
Minnesota						
Straker	6	4	0	0	2	4
Berenguer, L, 0–1	1/3	4	3	3	0	0
Schatzeder	1 2/3	1	0	0	0	1
St. Louis						
Tudor, W, 1–0	7	4	1	1	2	7
Worrell, S, 1	2	1	0	0	0	1

Balk—Straker. Time of Game—2:45. Attendance— 55,347.

4th Game—St. Louis, Oct. 21

MINNESOTA (A)	AB	R	H	BI	ST. LOUIS (N)	AB	R	H	BI
Gladden, lf	5	0	1	0	Coleman, lf	4	1	1	0
Newman, 2b	3	0	1	0	Smith, ss	4	1	0	0
Baylor, ph	1	0	1	0	Herr, 2b	3	1	2	0
Puckett, cf	4	0	1	1	Lindeman, 1b	4	1	2	2
Gaetti, 3b	3	0	1	0	McGee, cf	4	0	2	2
Brunansky, rf	4	0	0	0	Pena, c	3	1	1	0
Hrbek, 1b	4	0	1	0	Oquendo, rf	4	1	1	0
Laudner, c	3	0	0	0	Lawless, 3b	4	1	1	3
Butera, c	0	0	0	0	Mathews, p	1	0	0	0
Gagne, ss	4	1	1	1	Forsch, p	2	0	0	0
Viola, p	1	0	0	0	Dayley, p	1	0	0	0
Schatzeder, p	0	0	0	0					
Larkin, ph	0	1	0	0					
Niekro, p	0	0	0	0					
Smalley, ph	1	0	0	0					
Frazier, p	0	0	0	0					
Davidson, ph	1	0	0	0					
Total	**34**	**2**	**7**	**2**	**Total**	**34**	**7**	**10**	**7**
Minnesota					**001 010 000**		**2**	**7**	**1**
St. Louis					**001 600 00x**		**7**	**10**	**1**

Game-winning RBI—Lawless (1). E—Puckett, Lindeman. DP—St. Louis 1. LOB—Minnesota 10, St. Louis 9. 2B—McGee, Coleman. HR—Gagne (1), Lawless (1). SB—Gaetti (1), Brunansky (1), Coleman (4).

	IP	H	R	ER	BB	SO
Minnesota						
Viola, L, 1—1	3 1/3	6	5	5	3	4
Schatzeder	2/3	2	2	2	1	1
Niekro	2	1	0	0	1	1
Frazier	2	1	0	0	0	2
St. Louis						
Mathews	3 2/3	2	1	1	2	3
Forsch W, 1—0	2 2/3	4	1	1	1	3
Dayley S, 1	2 2/3	1	0	0	0	2

HBP—Gaetti by Mathews, Lindeman by Niekro, Puckett by Forsch. WP—Mathews. Time of Game—3:11. Attendance— 55,347.

5th Game—St. Louis, Oct. 22

MINNESOTA (A)	AB	R	H	BI	ST. LOUIS (N)	AB	R	H	BI
Gladden, lf	3	1	1	0	Coleman, lf	3	2	1	0
Gagne, ss	4	1	1	0	Smith, ss	4	1	2	1
Baylor, ph	1	0	0	0	Herr, 2b	4	0	0	0
Puckett, cf	4	0	0	0	Driessen, 1b	3	1	1	0
Hrbek, 1b	4	0	1	0	Dayley, p	0	0	0	0
Gaetti, 3b	4	0	1	2	Worrell, p	0	0	0	0
Brunansky, rf	4	0	1	0	McGee, cf	4	0	0	0
Laudner, c	2	0	0	0	Ford, rf	4	0	1	2
Newman, ph	1	0	0	0	Oquendo, 3b	4	0	2	0
Lombardozzi, 2b	2	0	1	0	Pena, c	4	0	3	0
Smalley, ph	0	0	0	0	Johnson, pr	0	0	0	0
Blyleven, p	1	0	0	0	Lake, c	0	0	0	0
Larkin, ph	1	0	0	0	Cox, p	2	0	0	0
Atherton, p	0	0	0	0	Lindeman, 1b	1	0	0	0
Reardon, p	0	0	0	0					
Bush, ph	1	0	0	0					
Total	**32**	**2**	**6**	**2**	**Total**	**33**	**4**	**10**	**3**
Minnesota					**000 000 020**		**2**	**6**	**1**
St. Louis					**000 003 10x**		**4**	**10**	**0**

Game-winning RBI—Ford (1). E—Gagne. DP—Minnesota 1. LOB—Minnesota 9, St. Louis 8. 3B—Gaetti. SB—Gladden (2), Coleman 2 (6), Smith 2 (2), Johnson (1). S—Cox, Blyleven.

	IP	H	R	ER	BB	SO
Minnesota						
Blyleven L, 1—1	6	7	3	2	1	4
Atherton	1/3	0	1	1	1	0
Reardon	1 2/3	3	0	0	0	3
St. Louis						
Cox W, 1—1	7 1/3	5	2	2	3	6
Dayley	1/3	0	0	0	0	0
Worrell S, 2	1 1/3	1	0	0	2	0

Balk—Atherton. Time of Game—3:21. Attendance—55,347.

6th Game—Minneapolis, Oct. 24

ST. LOUIS (N)	AB	R	H	BI	MINNESOTA (A)	AB	R	H	BI
Coleman, lf	5	0	0	0	Gladden, lf	5	1	2	0
Smith, ss	4	1	1	0	Gagne, ss	5	1	1	0
Herr, 2b	5	1	3	1	Puckett, cf	4	4	4	1
Driessen, 1b	2	1	1	0	Gaetti, 3b	5	1	1	1
Pagnozzi, ph	1	0	0	0	Baylor, dh	3	2	2	3
Morris, rf	2	0	0	0	Bush, dh	1	0	0	0
McGee, cf	4	1	2	1	Brunansky, rf	4	1	1	1
Pendleton, dh	3	1	2	1	Hrbek, 1b	4	1	1	4
Ford, rf	1	0	0	0	Laudner, c	5	0	0	0
Lindeman, rf	3	0	0	0	Lombardozzi, 2b	4	0	3	1
Oquendo, 3b	3	0	1	2					
Pena, c	3	0	1	0					
Total	**36**	**5**	**11**	**5**	**Total**	**40**	**11**	**15**	**11**
St. Louis					**110 210 000**		**5**	**11**	**2**
Minnesota					**200 044 01x**		**11**	**15**	**0**

Game-winning RBI—Lombardozzi (1). E—McGee, Lindeman, DP—Minnesota 1. LOB—St. Louis 8, Minnesota 9. 2B—Driessen, Lombardozzi, Gaetti. 3B—Gladden. HR—Herr (1), Baylor (1), Hrbek (1). SB—Puckett (1), Pendleton 2 (2). SF—Oquendo.

	IP	H	R	ER	BB	SO
St. Louis						
Tudor L, 1—1	4	11	6	6	1	1
Horton	1	2	1	1	0	0
Forsch	2/3	0	2	2	2	0
Dayley	1/3	1	1	1	0	0
Tunnell	2	1	1	0	1	0
Minnesota						
Straker	3	5	4	4	1	2
Schatzeder W, 1—0	2	1	1	1	2	1
Berenguer	3	3	0	0	0	1
Reardon	1	2	0	0	0	0

Straker pitched to 3 batters in the 4th, Tudor pitched to 4 batters in the 5th, Horton pitched to 1 batter in the 6th. PB—Pena. Time of Game—3:22. Attendance—55,293.

7th Game—Minneapolis, Oct. 25

ST. LOUIS (N)	AB	R	H	BI	MINNESOTA (A)	AB	R	H	BI
Coleman, lf	4	0	0	0	Gladden, lf	5	0	1	1
Smith, ss	4	0	0	0	Gagne, ss	5	1	2	1
Herr, 2b	4	0	1	0	Puckett, cf	4	0	2	1
Lindeman, 1b	3	1	1	0	Gaetti, 3b	3	0	0	0
Ford, ph	1	0	0	0	Baylor, dh	3	0	1	0
McGee, cf	4	1	1	0	Brunansky, rf	3	2	1	0
Pena, dh	3	0	2	1	Hrbek, 1b	3	0	0	0
Oquendo, rf	3	0	0	0	Laudner, c	3	1	2	0
Lawless, 3b	3	0	0	0	Lombardozzi, 2b	2	0	1	1
Lake, c	3	0	1	1	Smalley, ph	0	0	0	0
					Newman, 2b	1	0	0	0
Total	**32**	**2**	**6**	**2**	**Total**	**32**	**4**	**10**	**4**
St. Louis					**020 000 000**		**2**	**6**	**1**
Minnesota					**010 011 01x**		**4**	**10**	**0**

Game-winning RBI—Gagne (1). E—Lindeman. LOB—St. Louis 3, Minnesota 10. 2B—Puckett, Pena, Gladden. SB—Gaetti (2), Pena (1).

	IP	H	R	ER	BB	SO
St. Louis						
Magrane	4 1/3	5	2	2	1	4
Cox L, 1—2	2/3	2	1	1	3	0
Worrell	3	3	1	1	1	2
Minnesota						
Viola, W, 2—1	8	6	2	2	0	7
Reardon S, 1	1	0	0	0	0	0

HBP—Baylor by Magrane. Time of Game—3:04. Attendance—55,376.

Cheating Becomes an Issue

Three major league baseball players were suspended for cheating incidents during the 1987 season. Minnesota Twins pitcher Joe Niekro and Philadelphia Phillies pitcher Kevin Gross both were issued 10-day suspensions for having an emery board and sandpaper, respectively, which could be used to doctor the baseball. In addition, Houston Astros outfielder Billy Hatcher was suspended for 10 days when a bat he was using broke and revealed illegal cork inside.

While those three were the only players actually caught, cheating was a major league-wide issue in 1987, prompting Commissioner Peter Ueberroth to institute a rule allowing each manager to check one opposing hitter's bat per game.

CHESS

WORLD CHAMPIONS

1894–1921	Emanuel Lasker, Germany
1921–27	Jose R. Capablanca, Cuba
1927–35	Alexander A. Alekhine, U.S.S.R.
1935–37	Dr. Max Euwe, Netherlands
1937–46	Alexander A. Alekhine, U.S.S.R.[1]
1948–57	Mikhail Botvinnik, U.S.S.R.
1957–58	Vassily Smyslov, U.S.S.R.
1958–60	Mikhail Botvinnik, U.S.S.R.
1960–61	Mikhail Tal, U.S.S.R.
1961–63	Mikhail Botvinnik, U.S.S.R.
1963–68	Tigran Petrosian, U.S.S.R.
1969–71	Boris Spassky, U.S.S.R.
1972–74	Bobby Fischer, Los Angeles
1975	Bobby Fischer[2], Anatoly Karpov, U.S.S.R.
1976–85	Anatoly Karpov, U.S.S.R.[3]
1985–	Gary Kasparov, U.S.S.R.[4]

1. Alekhine, a French citizen, died while champion. 2. Relinquished title. 3. In 1978, Karpov defeated Viktor Korchnoi 6 games to 5. 4. Next match was scheduled for late October 1987, after *Information Please* went to press.

UNITED STATES CHAMPIONS

1909–36	Frank J. Marshall, New York
1936–44	Samuel Reshevsky, New York[1]
1944–46	Arnold S. Denker, New York
1946	Samuel Reshevsky, Boston
1948	Herman Steiner, Los Angeles
1951–52	Larry Evan, New York
1954–57	Arthur Bisguier, New York
1958–61	Bobby Fischer, Brooklyn, N.Y.
1962	Larry Evans, New York
1963–67	Bobby Fischer, New York
1968	Larry Evans, New York
1969–71	Samuel Reshevsky, Spring Valley, N.Y.
1972	Robert Byrne, Ossining, N.Y.
1973	Lubomir Kavelek, Washington; John Grefe, San Francisco
1974–77	Walter Browne, Berkeley, Calif.
1978–79	Lubomir Kavalek, New York
1980	Tie, Walter Browne, Berkeley, Calif. Larry Christiansen, Modesto, Calif. Larry Evans, Reno, Nev.
1981–82[2]	Tie, Walter Browne, Berkeley, Calif. Yasser Seirawan, Seattle, Wash.
1983	Tie, Walter Browne, Berkeley, Calif. Larry Christiansen, Los Angeles, Calif., Roman Dzindzichashvili, Corona, N.Y.
1984–85	Lev Alburt, New York City
1986	Yasser Seirawan, Seattle, Wash.[3]

1. In 1942, Isaac I. Kashdan of New York was co-champion for a while because of a tie with Reshevsky in that year's tournament. Reshevsky won the play-off. 2. Championship not contested in 1982. 3. 1987 United States Championship tournament set for November, after *Information Please* went to press.

GYMNASTICS

AMERICAN CUP CHAMPIONSHIPS—1987

(Annandale, Va., March 7-8, 1987)

Men's Events

	Pts
All-around—Brian Ginsberg, United States	58.150
Floor exercise—Brian Ginsberg, United States	9.800
Parallel bars—Vladimir Gogoladze, Soviet Union & Tony Pineda, Mexico (tie)	9.750
Pommel horse—Brian Ginsberg & Scott Johnson, United States (tie)	9.750
Still rings—Brian Ginsberg & Scott Johnson, United States (tie)	9.800
Vault—Vladimir Gogoladze, Soviet Union, Scott Johnson, United States, & Sylvio Kroll, East Germany (tie)	9.550
Horizontal bars—Vladimir Gogoladze, Soviet Union	9.800

Women's Events

All-around—Kristie Phillips, United States	39.275
Floor exercise—Phoebe Mills, United States	9.875
Vault—Olga Strazheva, Soviet Union	9.975
Uneven bars—Olga Strazheva, Soviet Union	9.850
Balance beam—Olga Strazheva, Soviet Union	9.900

WORLD CHAMPIONSHIPS—1985[1]

(Montreal, Canada, Nov. 3-10, 1985)

Men's Events

	Pts
All-around—Yuri Korolev, Soviet Union	117.850
Floor exercise—Tong Fei, China	19.750
High bar—Tong Fei, China	19.850
Still Rings—Li Ning, China, and Yuri Korolev, Soviet Union (tie)	19.750
Pommell horse—Valentin Mogilnyi, Soviet Union	19.750
Parallel bars—Sylvio Kroll, West Germany	19.800
Vault—Yuri Korolev, Soviet Union	19.625
Team—Soviet Union	

Women's Events

	Pts
All-around—Elena Shoushounova, Soviet Union and Oksana Omeliantchik, Soviet Union (tie)	78.663
Floor exercise—Oksana Omeliantchik, Soviet Union	19.900
Balance beam—Daniela Silivas, Romania	19.813
Uneven bars—Gabriele Fahnrich, West Germany	19.938
Vault—Elena Shoushounova, Soviet Union	19.826
Team—Soviet Union	

1. World Gymnastics championships are held every other year. Next were scheduled for October, 1987, after *Information Please* went to press.

CURLING

UNITED STATES CHAMPIONSHIPS—1987

Men (Lake Placid, N.Y., March 1-7, 1987)—Seattle, Wash., Jim Vukich, skip (defeated Madison, Wis., Steve Brown, skip, 10-7 in final).

Women (St. Paul, Minn., Feb. 10-14, 1987)—Seattle, Wash., Sharon Good, skip (defeated St. Paul, Minn., Barb Polski, skip, 7-6 in final).

WORLD CHAMPIONSHIPS—1987

Men (Vancouver, British Columbia, March 30-April 5, 1987)-Canada, Russ Howard, skip (defeated West Germany, Roger Schmidt, skip, 9-5 in final).

Women (Lake Forest, Ill., March 22-28, 1987)—Canada, Pat Sanders, skip (defeated West Germany, Andrea Schopp, skip, 14-2 in final).

CURRENT EVENTS

What Happened in 1986-87

Highlights of the important events of the year from September 1986 to August 1987, organized month by month, in three categories for easy reference. The Countries of the World section (starting on page 149) covers specific international events, country by country.

1986-87

SEPTEMBER 1986

International

Twenty-one Killed in Plane Hijacking (Sept. 6): More than 100 wounded at Karachi, Pakistan, by gunmen who capture New York-bound Pan American jumbo jet Boeing 747 and begin shooting and detonating grenades inside darkened passenger cabin. Four Arabs arrested and questioned on method of evading detection by posing as airport security personnel.

Twenty-one Killed in Istanbul Synagogue (Sept. 6): Jews perish as two Arab terrorists lock doors and attack congregation at Sabbath service with submachine guns and hand grenades. Gunmen found dead with other victims in carnage.

Tutu Installed as Archbishop (Sept. 7): Ceremonies blend Anglican and African tradition at installation of apartheid opponent Desmond M. Tutu in Cape Town as first black to lead Anglican Church in southern Africa.

Pakistani Opposition Leader Freed (Sept. 8): Benazir Bhutto released after arrest in government crackdown on dissidents. Vows to continue campaign to overthrow regime of President Mohammad Zia ul-Haq.

Attack on Pinochet Fails (Sept. 8): Chilean government expands state of siege after ambush of President Augusto Pinochet's motorcade. Socialists and other leaders seized, six opposition magazines shut.

Americans Kidnapped in Beirut (Sept. 9): Gunmen seize Frank Herbert Reed, 53, director of private Lebanese International School in Moslem West Beirut. **(Sept. 12):** Four armed men seize Joseph James Cicippio, 56, chief accountant for American University of Beirut and its hospital.

Seoul Airport Blast Kills Five (Sept. 14): Powerful bomb wounds 19 others outside terminal building at Kimpo International Airport. North Korea unofficially blamed.

Mine Blast Kills 177 in South Africa (Sept. 16): Fire breaks out in gold mine in worst such accident since December 1978. **(Sept. 17):** Toll of injured set at 235 with five missing. Most of victims are black miners. Union charges negligence by owners.

Western Europe Acts Against Pretoria (Sept. 16): Foreign ministers of 12 E.E.C. nations agree to limited economic actions against apartheid.

U.S. Expels 25 Russian Diplomats (Sept. 17): Orders members of Soviet U.N. mission to leave by Oct. 1.

Pact to Ease Europe War Threat (Sept. 21): Negotiators for NATO and Warsaw Pact approve new security package. Two alliances agree to give warning of significant military exercises.

Bombs Kill 10, Wound 162 in Paris (Sept. 25): French police arrest nine in a series of explosions. Committee seeking freedom for Arab prisoners blamed. Prime Minister Chirac **(Sept. 14)** orders visas for many foreigners. Principal explosions: inside main police headquarters **(Sept. 15)**, one dead, 51 wounded; outside crowded department store **(Sept. 17)**, five dead, 50 wounded.

Moscow Frees American Newsman (Sept. 30): Allows Nicholas S. Daniloff, correspondent for *U.S. News & World Report*, charged with espionage, to return to U.S. Under agreement worked out in secret talks, accused Soviet spy, Gennadi F. Zakharov, is allowed to plead no contest in U.S. court and fly back to Russia in exchange for group of Soviet dissidents.

Preliminary Summit Talks Set (Sept. 30): U.S. and Soviet Union announce President Reagan and Communist leader, Gorbachev, will meet in Iceland. Agreement reported key element in arrangements for release of U.S. correspondent and accused Soviet spy.

Reagan Names Black Envoy to South Africa (Sept. 30): Selects Edward J. Perkins, veteran diplomat.

National

Reagans Ask For "National Crusade" on Drugs (Sept. 14): President and wife, Nancy, in rare joint TV address, warn much is to be done against "cancer."

Reagan Orders Federal Drug Testing (Sept. 15): Orders agency heads to establish broad program to detect drug use, and formally proposes $900 million to combat national epidemic.

Rose Made U.S. National Flower (Sept. 23): Congress approves "national floral emblem," ending debate going back into late nineteenth century.

General

Harvard Celebrates 350th Anniversary (Sept. 4): Prince Charles among speakers as ceremonies open. He warns against triumph of technology over man. **(Sept. 6):** On final day of festival, Dr. Derek Bok, university president, deplores professors who stress pursuit of affluence.

Delta and Western Airlines Merge (Sept. 9): Announce $860-million deal to open major new markets to Atlanta-based Delta.

Stock Market Plunges 86.61 Points (Sept. 11): Industrial average falls in record trading session.

Texas Air Moves to Buy People Express (Sept. 15): Corporation to create nation's largest air carrier with $125-million acquisition.

OCTOBER 1986

International

Congress Overrides Reagan, Sanctions Veto (Sept. 29): House, 313-83, rejects President's action. (**Oct. 2**): Senate, 78-21, rejects President's pleas and upholds stiff economic sanctions against South Africa. Law bans new investment by Americans; prohibits imports of such products as steel and coal; cancels U.S. landing rights for South African airlines. Both votes well above two-thirds required.

Dutch Inaugurate $2.4-Billion Dike (Oct. 4): Sea Barrier is most advanced in nine centuries.

Soviet Dissident and Wife Reach U.S. (Oct. 5): Yuri F. Orlov freed from Siberia in arrangement tied to release of U.S. journalist held as spy.

Nicaraguans Down U.S. Cargo Plane (Oct. 5): Two crewmen killed. Reagan Administration says aircraft was operated by private group led by retired U.S. Army major general and was carrying arms from El Salvador for insurgents. Spokesmen deny link to U.S. Government. (**Oct. 9**): Captured American, Eugene Hasenfus, 45, of Wisconsin, says members of C.I.A. in El Salvador directly supervised supply flights to the "contras."

Sunni Clergyman Assassinated (Oct. 7): Sheik Sobie al-Saleh, 60, shot in Beirut. Killing denounced nationwide. Sheik admired by both Moslems and Christians.

San Salvador Quake Kills 976 (Oct. 10): Devastates Salvadoran capital with force of 5.4 on Richter scale. (**Oct. 11**): After-shocks rock city. Poorly equipped rescue workers claw through rubble to recover survivors and bodies of dead. (**Oct. 13**): Strong after-shock frightens El Salvador. (**Oct. 14**): Government appeals for more relief as estimates of damage and homeless rise. President José Napoleón Duarte sets injured toll at 8,176, with thousands homeless. Damage estimates range from $1 billion to $2 billion.

Reykjavik Summit Ends in Stalemate (Oct. 12): President Reagan and Soviet leader, Mikhail S. Gorbachev, fail to reach agreement on arms control in two days of Iceland conference. They reach understanding on most arms issues, but possible accord is blocked as Soviet insists that U.S. abandon "Star Wars" program, which Reagan refuses. (**Oct. 13**): Reagan blames Gorbachev and defends decision not to compromise on space-based defenses. (**Oct. 14**): Gorbachev says Reagan proved lacking in courage to reach accord.

Queen Elizabeth Visits China (Oct. 12): Greeted in Peking as first British monarch to enter country.

Moscow Releases Jewish Scientist (Oct. 16): Allows David Goldfarb, geneticist, and wife, Cecilia, to leave on private plane of industrialist, Armand Hammer, to end long-standing rights case.

Air Crash Kills Mozambique Head (Oct. 19): Samora M. Machel, president since independence from Portugal in 1975, dies in South Africa.

New Israeli Cabinet Sworn (Oct. 20): Yitzhak Shamir, Likud bloc leader, switches jobs with Foreign Minister Shimon Peres, Labor Party leader, under rotation agreement signed in 1984.

Two Corporations Cut South Africa Ties (Oct. 20): G.M., largest company doing business there, to sell operations to local investors. (**Oct. 21**): I.B.M. joins corporations withdrawing, citing deteriorating business and political conditions.

U.S. and Soviet Trade Diplomatic Ousters (Oct. 21): Washington orders expulsion of 55 Soviet diplomats in retaliation for Moscow's dismissal of five Americans. It is latest in series that began Sept. 17 when U.S. ordered expulsion of 25 members of Soviet U.N. mission on grounds that they were intelligence agents. (**Oct. 22**): Moscow ousts five more members of U.S. Embassy and withdraws Embassy's 260 Soviet employees.

Jordanian Convicted in Bombing Plot (Oct. 24): London court sentences Nezar Hindawi, 32, to 45 years in prison for giving his unknowing pregnant lover a device to blow up Israeli airliner. Prosecution charges Syrian intelligence agents supplied bomb.

British Break Relations With Syria (Oct. 24): Find "conclusive evidence" that Syrian diplomats and intelligence agents were involved in attempt to bomb Israeli airliner. Syria responds by breaking relations with Britain and barring her planes and ships.

Red Cross Ousts South African Delegation (Oct. 25): International conference at Geneva protests "evil and inhuman" policy of apartheid. (**Oct. 26**): Pretoria reacts by ordering 25 foreign Red Cross workers out of country. Action might harm apartheid foes.

Saudi Oil Chief Dismissed (Oct. 29): King of Saudi Arabia ousts Sheik Ahmed Zaki Yamani as oil minister. Yamani was chief architect of Arab move to control oil resources. Hisham Nazer, planning minister, serves as acting oil minister.

National

False News Reports Charged (Oct. 2): Reagan Administration denies allegations of "disinformation" about Libya and leader, Col. Muammar el-Quadaffi.

State Department Spokesman Quits (Oct. 8): Bernard Kalb protests "reported disinformation program" by Administration against Libya's Col. Muammar el-Quaddafi.

Congress Votes Anti-Drug Bill (Oct. 17): Measure authorizes $1.7 billion for law enforcement, treatment, and education. Senate accepts compromise to eliminate death penalty, ending deadlock.

Landmark Immigration Bill Voted (Oct. 17): Compromise approved by Congress prohibits hiring of illegal aliens and offers amnesty to millions residing in country.

Budget-Reduction Measure Enacted (Oct. 21): President signs bill for $11.7-billion cut in $576-billion comprehensive appropriations bill for 1987. Law meets $154-billion ceiling set by Congress in move to balance the budget by 1991.

Tax Reform Law in Force (Oct. 22): President Reagan signs most thorough revision of federal income tax code in 40 years. Law lowers top rate for individuals from 50 percent to 28 percent, and for corporations from 46 percent to 34 percent. Law eliminates many deductions and abolishes tax shelters almost completely.

General

Longshoremen End Strike (Oct. 3): Tie-up of ports from Maine to Virginia called off by 30,000 workers of International Longshoremen's Association.

Soviet Nuclear Sub Sinks After Fire (Oct. 6): Crippled craft founders after three days 1,200 miles east of New York. Blast killed three crewmen.

Columbus Landing Site Questioned (Oct. 8): Researchers with computers and new analysis methods conclude he landed at small Bahamas island 65 miles from where historians had thought he did.

Fundamentalists Win Schoolbook Suit (Oct. 24): U.S. Court in Atlanta decides for Christian parents who detected godless influences in certain texts.

NOVEMBER 1986

International

Hostage Freed After 18 Months (Nov. 2): David P. Jacobsen, 55, an American, released in Lebanon by Islamic Holy War, pro-Iranian Fundamentalist group.

Israel Seizes Nuclear Technician (Nov. 9): Arrests Mordechai Vanunu, who had sold British newspaper what he said were secrets of underground Israeli atomic bomb factory. Secret agents track him down for closed trial.

Toxic Chemicals Contaminate Rhine (Nov. 10): More than 1,000 tons, including eight tons of mercury, spilled after fire in storage warehouse at Basel, Switzerland. **(Nov. 12):** Scientists report serious ecological damage over 185 miles. Experts say decades of wildlife restoration have been wiped out.

Leftist Leader Slain in Manila (Nov. 13): Rolando Olalia and driver found dead in midst of tense political situation for President Corazon C. Aquino. Party leaders accuse military, but top officials deny guilt.

Reagan and Thatcher Agree on Arms (Nov. 15): After Camp David talks, British leader says President agreed not to press for abolition of long-range missiles.

Nicaraguan Court Convicts American (Nov. 15): Finds Eugene Hasenfus, 45, flight-cargo handler, guilty of terrorism and crimes against state for part in weapons supply flight to Nicaraguan rebels. He is sentenced to 30 years in prison.

Renault President Assassinated (Nov. 17): Georges Besse, 58, shot near Paris home. Known for checking decline of auto company and other concerns. **(Nov. 18):** Direct Action, leftist extremist group, claims responsibility.

Thousands Flee Island Volcano in Japan (Nov. 21): Rocks and flames spewed out, sending lava toward large town.

Philippine President Acts in Crisis (Nov. 23): Corazon C. Aquino dismisses Defense Minister and gives Communist insurgents seven days to agree to cease-fire. Troops led by Chief of Staff Gen. Fidel V. Ramos block coup by armed forces loyal to Defense Minister Juan Ponce Enrile. **(Nov. 26):** Communists agree to 60-day cease-fire.

Bonn Expels Three Syrian Envoys (Nov. 27): West Germany acts after court implicates officials in bombing.

Argentina Ends Divorce Ban (Nov. 28): Supreme Court rules 98-year-old law is unconstitutional.

Sikh Extremists Kill 23 (Nov. 30): Four hijack bus in Punjab and slay Hindus, wounding others.

National

Mrs. Reagan's Maid Exonerated (Nov. 3): U.S. Court drops munitions smuggling charge against Anita Sanabria Castelo, 45, cleared of illegal intent.

Democrats Triumphant in Elections (Nov. 4): Party adds eight seats in Senate, gaining edge of 55 to 45, and renews majority in House. Democrats make sweeping gains in South and strength in G.O.P. Western states. G.O.P. gains governorships in several states.

U.S. Weapons Sent to Iran (Nov. 6): Intelligence sources in Washington say spare parts were sent in secret operation to gain release of hostages in Lebanon, and that Israel did the same. Operation also said to be way to influence relations with Teheran. **(Nov. 7):** Administration discloses President Reagan approved secret contacts 18 months previously. Officials say U.S., with Israel as intermediary, combined arms shipments with intensified efforts to free Lebanon hostages.

President Retorts to Critics (Nov. 13): Reagan defends "secret diplomatic initiative" to Iran against intense domestic and international criticism of shipments of "small amounts of defensive weapons and spare parts." Denies U.S. sought to exchange weapons for American hostages in Lebanon. **(Nov. 14):** Administration acknowledges C.I.A. was directly involved in secret arms shipments.

Reagan Halts Weapons Sales to Iran (Nov. 19): Takes full responsibility for decision on secret arms shipments and acknowledges differences in White House. Denies exchanging arms for hostages.

Teheran Paid $12 Million for Weapons (Nov. 21): Capitol hearings reveal Iran payment for 2,008 American-made anti-tank missiles, deposited in Swiss bank account. Many arms came from Israeli stockpiles.

Washington in Disarray Over Arms Deals (Nov. 25): President says he had not been in full control over Iran policy and that as a result up to $30 million to pay for arms had been secretly diverted to Nicaraguan contras. Reagan announces two who held responsible posts have left White House: Vice Admiral John M. Poindexter and Marine Lieut. Col. Oliver L. North. President's crisis called most serious of six years. Secretary of State Shultz given control of Iran policy-making.

Reagan Orders Security Council Inquiry (Nov. 26): Names former Senator John G. Tower to head "special review board," with former Secretary of State Edmund S. Muskie and former national security adviser, Brent Scowcroft, as members.

General

British Helicopter Crash Kills 45 (Nov. 6): Civilian twin-rotor Boeing Vertol Chinook carrying 47 from oil rig plunges into icy North Sea off Shetland Islands. Two passengers rescued.

Father and Son Sentenced in Spy Ring (Nov. 6): U.S. judge in Baltimore metes life to John A. Walker, Jr., 49, retired Navy warrant officer, who confessed to one of most damaging operations in U.S. history. Son, Michael L. Walker, 23, gets 25 years. Court recommends two serve sentences without parole.

Italian Wins New York Marathon (Nov. 2): Gianni Poli, 25, outpaces Rob de Castella, 29, Australian. Poli wins 17th marathon with 2 hours 11 minutes 6 seconds. Grete Waitz, 33, of Norway is women's winner for eighth time in nine years with 2. 28.06.

Militants Sink Four Icelandic Whaling Ships (Nov. 9): Charge violation of international whaling moratorium.

Two-hundred Dead in Wreck Off Haiti (Nov. 12): Overloaded coastal ferry sinks in rough seas.

Notre Dame Chooses 16th President (Nov. 14): Names Rev. Edward A. Malloy, 45, specialist in ethics.

Wall Street Speculator Penalized $100 Million (Nov. 14): Ivan F. Boesky assessed by government for illegal insider trading, and barred for life from securities industry. Stock and bond markets shaken as spreading scandal threatens to involve others.

Global Fight on AIDS Begins: (Nov. 20): World Health Organization announces first coordinated effort to combat "health disaster of pandemic proportions."

Three Sentenced in Iran Arms Plot (Nov. 24): Navy veteran and divorced couple sent to prison by San Diego federal judge for conspiracy to smuggle $10 million worth of stolen F-14 plane parts.

DECEMBER 1986

International

Pope Visits Six Nations (Dec. 1): John Paul II pleads for sanctity of marriage in sermon at Seychelles in Indian Ocean after two-week tour.

Ex-Police Chief Guilty in Argentina (Dec. 2): Gen. Ramón Camps convicted on 73 counts of torture in arrest of Jacobo Timerman, newspaper editor, and sentenced to 25 years by six-member tribunal.

Fourteen Doomed in Grenada Killing (Dec. 4): Former Deputy Prime Minister Bernard Coard and 13 others sentenced to death in 1983 slaying of Prime Minister Maurice Bishop during coup.

French Students Win After Disorders (Dec. 5): Violence flares as organized movement confronts government in two-week protest against government plan for university reform. (**Dec. 7**): Paris streets see worst rioting in 18 years. (**Dec. 8**): Prime Minister surrenders and announces government is withdrawing legislation to overhaul country's university system.

Soviet Airliner Crash Kills 69 (Dec. 12): Victims include schoolchildren. Twelve persons rescued as Aeroflot Tu-134 crashes in East German fog.

Fifty-four Die in Pakistan Rioting (Dec. 14): Toll of wounded set at 310 in ethnic battles in Karachi between Pathans and Mohajirs, longtime enemies.

Nicaragua Frees Eugene Hasenfus (Dec. 17): Pardons American cargo-handler captured in October when arms-laden plane aiding contras was shot down.

Ban on Andrei D. Sakharov Lifted (Dec. 19): Soviet allows physicist banished to Gorky for human rights activity to return to Moscow. Wife, Yelena G. Bonner, rights campaigner, pardoned.

Thousands in China Rally for Rights (Dec. 20): Students march on Shanghai streets demanding democracy and press freedom. (**Dec. 21**): More thousands flood Peoples Square as authorities attack demonstrators for disruption. Disorders spread to capital, Beijing, and other major cities. (**Dec. 22**): After three days, Shanghai police ban further rallies without permit.

Sixty-two Dead as Iraqi Airliner Crashes (Dec. 25): Boeing 737 with 107 aboard burns on remote airstrip in Saudi Arabia after being commandeered by gunmen. (**Dec. 26**): Iran denies charges by Iraq and Jordan that she instigated hijacking.

National

Reagan's Approval Rate Plunges (Dec. 1): Public backing falls to 46 percent from 67 percent in previous month as concern over Iran-contra issue grows.

Reagan Announces Special Counsel Plan (Dec. 2): Says illegal acts may have been committed in diversion of funds from Iran arms sales to Nicaraguan rebels. Names Frank C. Carlucci national security adviser.

Poindexter Silent at Hearing (Dec. 3): Vice Adm. John M. Poindexter, former national security adviser, invokes Fifth Amendment at Senate hearing on Iran arms sales and diversion of funds.

Reagan Admits Flaws in Iran Policy (Dec. 6): Shifts from defiant attitude, but continues in radio address to defend secret diplomatic initiatives.

Democrats Pick Congressional Leaders (Dec. 8): Choose Jim Wright of Texas as House Speaker, Rep. Thomas S. Foley of Washington majority leader, and Tony Coelho of California majority whip, third-ranking post. G.O.P. names Robert H. Michel of Illinois as House minority leader, Trent Lott, Mississippi, as whip.

Shultz Charges Secret Link to Envoy (Dec. 8): Secretary of State tells House inquiry White House broke chain of command to deal with Ambassador to Lebanon in negotiations to release hostages.

Primaries Cleared for Independents (Dec. 10): Supreme Court, 5-4, rejects as violation of constitutional rights legal limits on parties' admission of nonmembers to ballots on nominations.

Spy for Soviet Gets Life Sentence (Dec. 16): Ronald W. Pelton, former National Security Agency employee, penalized by federal judge in Baltimore for selling vital military secrets to Russians.

Senate Panel Set Up for Iran Inquiry (Dec. 16): Daniel K. Inouye, Hawaiian Democrat, to head special 11-member group. Warren B. Rudman of New Hampshire designated as ranking Republican member.

House Forms Panel on Iran (Dec. 17): Lee H. Hamilton of Indiana, Democrat, heads 15-member inquiry. Dick Cheney of Wyoming is ranking Republican.

C.I.A. Director Undergoes Surgery (Dec. 18): Tumor removed from left side of William J. Casey's brain. (**Dec. 23**): Lymphoma found to be malignant.

Counsel Named for Iran Inquiry (Dec. 19): Lawrence E. Walsh, former Federal judge, appointed by three-judge federal panel and given wide powers to investigate arms deals and diversion of funds.

Team to Coordinate Iran Strategy (Dec. 26): Reagan sets up special unit to direct Administration's response in arms-contra affair. David E. Abshire, departing delegate to NATO, will head it.

Astronauts' Families Agree on Claims (Dec. 29): Justice Department expects each family to get $750,000 payment for deaths in *Challenger* disaster.

U.S. Raises Duties on Europe Imports (Dec. 30): Reagan acts to retaliate for trade policies said to cost American farms $400 million a year.

Hotel Fire Kills 96 in Puerto Rico (Dec. 31): Blaze rages through packed Dupont Plaza luxury hotel. American tourists among victims. (**Jan. 4**): Federal and Commonwealth investigation blames arson.

General

People's Temple Survivor Convicted in Killing (Dec. 1): Larry Layton, 40, guilty of conspiring to murder U.S. Congressman slain in cult ambush in Guyana in 1978.

G.M. Board Ousts Billionaire (Dec. 1): H. Ross Perot of Texas leaves after months of disagreement over policy. Will sell back stock for $700 million.

Hare Krishna Member Guilty in Killing (Dec. 5): Jury in Virginia convicts Thomas Dresher, 37, of murder in disappearance of man from sect compound.

Muscle Makes Auxiliary Heart for Dog (Dec. 9): Doctors at University of Pennsylvania fashion pump to increase blood circulation. Aid to humans sought.

One of Nation's Biggest Bank Mergers (Dec. 15): Chemical Bank announces agreement to acquire Houston-based Texas Commerce Bank for about $1.19 billion.

Dwight Gooden Reports Beating (Dec. 15): Mets pitching star, 22, says Tampa, Fla., police "harassed and abused" him in fight following traffic violation.

Wayne Newton Wins Defamation Suit (Dec. 17): Federal jury in Las Vegas rules NBC falsely linked entertainer to organized crime in telecasts in 1980 and 1981. Awards $19.2 million in damages.

John Z. DeLorean Acquitted (Dec. 17): Federal jury in Detroit finds him not guilty of embezzling $8.5 million from sports car enterprise.

JANUARY 1987

International

Jetliner Crash Kills 49 in Africa (Jan. 3): Brazilian Varig Airlines Boeing 707 disintegrates in Ivory Coast forest after engine fire.

French Bomb Chad Airfield (Jan. 7): Jets attack Libyan-held base in north in retaliation for air raids.

In Rare Action, K.G.B. Disciplines Aides (Jan. 8): Soviet internal security agency punishes officials in illegal arrest of Soviet reporter who exposed government corruption in mining industry.

China Cracks Down on Dissidents (Jan. 14): Wang Ruowang, Shanghai writer and Marxist theorist, expelled from Communist Party after being linked to pro-democracy student demonstrations. Earlier, Fang Lizhi, astrophysicist, dismissed as vice president of University of Science and Technology in Hefei, denounced as pro-Western and expelled from party. (**Jan. 24**): Party expels Liu Binyan, muckraking reporter who attacked corruption in party ranks.

Bonn Arrests Hijacking Suspect (Jan. 15): Seizes an Arab, Mohammed Ali Hamadei, 22, of Lebanon, believed one of two men who hijacked T.W.A. jet in 1985, forced it to land in Beirut, and held 39 Americans hostage for 17 days after killing an American Navy diver. (**Jan. 27**): Brother of suspect, Abbas Ali Hamadei, 28, arrested in inquiry into West Beirut kidnappings.

Afghan Cease-Fire Reported (Jan. 15): Kabul government announces first let-up in seven-year war involving Soviet troops and Afghan rebels.

Rebellious Troops Seize Ecuador President (Jan. 16): Hold León Febres Cordero and demand release of Air Force general imprisoned after two uprisings. President, 54, released after agreeing to free general.

Chinese Communist Chief Forced Out (Jan. 16): Hu Yaobang resigns as general secretary for "major mistakes," following demonstrations for freedom. Prime Minister Zhao Ziyang temporary replacement.

Soviet Invites Dancer to Return (Jan. 19): Asks Mikhail Baryshnikov, ballet star who defected in 1974, to appear as guest at Bolshoi Theater in Moscow.

American Hostage Reported Killed (Jan. 20): Vice President Bush says William Buckley, believed to be C.I.A. chief in Lebanon, was slain by abductors.

Troops Kill 12 Demonstrators in Manila (Jan. 23): Fire into crowd in first such incident during President Aquino's tenure. At least 94 wounded.

Four Kidnapped in West Beirut (Jan. 24): Gunmen in police disguise abduct three American teachers and Indian professor from Beirut University College.

Helmut Kohl Wins in West Germany (Jan. 25): Chancellor's center-right coalition takes bare 53.4% of popular vote, giving it 266 of 496 seats in Parliament for next four years.

Gorbachev Demands Party Reforms (Jan. 27): In address to leaders, charges Communist Party with stagnation and systematic failures. Calls for secret balloting and a choice of candidates for officials. (**Jan. 28**): Communist Central Committee approves proposals for more flexibility within party.

Shultz Meets African Rebel Leader (Jan. 28): Hears Oliver Tambo, head of African National Congress, press for international economic sanctions.

Nicaragua Frees American Prisoner (Jan. 28): Releases Sam Nesley Hall, arrested on espionage charges at military base. Government reports Hall is psychologically unstable.

U.S. Bars Travel to Lebanon (Jan. 28): Restricts use of passports. Nation builds up naval force in Mediterranean to protect strategic interests.

Marcos Blocked in Coup Attempt (Jan. 29): U.S. foils plan to return to Philippines to rally supporters after dissident soldiers end two-day occupation of television station in apparent coup attempt.

U.S. Confirms Bible for Iran (Jan. 29): Volume with signed inscription by Reagan was carried by American agents for delivery to Iranian leaders.

National

Reagan Undergoes Prostate Surgery (Jan. 4): Four small noncancerous polyps removed from colon at Bethesda Naval Hospital. (**Jan. 5**): Operation removes obstruction from enlarged prostate. President's recovery smooth and uneventful.

Reagan's Budget Goes to Congress (Jan. 5): President reveals plans for spending $1.02 trillion in 1988 fiscal year. Democrats quick to attack.

The 100th Congress Convenes (Jan. 6): Formally installs new leaders and swears in new members. House welcomes Jim Wright of Texas as new Speaker, Robert C. Byrd of West Virginia as new majority leader.

Jobless Rate Lowest Since 1980: (Jan. 9): Unemployment level reported off to 6.6% for December. Level reported at 7% for all 1986.

Court Backs Job Rights in Pregnancy (Jan. 13): Supreme bench rules employers may be required to grant special protection to employees.

Supreme Court Bars Soliciting Curb (Jan. 20): Votes, 6-3, to find free speech violation in Illinois city's restriction on hours and days for door-to-door soliciting.

Reagan's State of the Union Message (Jan. 27): President tells Congress and nation he has "one major regret," failure to free American hostages and establish contacts with Iran. Praises Administration's economic record and offers plans to spur U.S. competitiveness.

Senate Report on Iran Affair (Jan. 29): Intelligence Committee charges Administration officials deceived one another and Congress. Finds funds for contras were controlled by former officials.

General

Hotel Fire Kills 96 in Puerto Rico (Dec. 31): Blaze rages through packed Dupont Plaza luxury hotel. American tourists among victims. (**Jan. 4**): Federal and Commonwealth investigators blame arson. (**Jan. 6**): Investigation focuses on hotel employees who are members of Teamsters Union. (**Jan. 14**): Teamsters officials say inquiry has vindicated them. (**Jan. 29**): Three hotel workers under arrest on charges of murder and arson.

Sixteen Dead in Amtrak Rail Wreck (Jan. 4): Northbound passenger train collides with three Conrail freight engines near Baltimore. Traffic disrupted. (**Jan. 14**): Traces of marijuana found in Conrail engineer and brakeman.

Dow Above 2000 for First Time (Jan. 8): Key industrial average sets stock market record.

Official Kills Himself in Public (Jan. 22): R. Budd Dwyer, 47, Pennsylvania state treasurer convicted of bribery, shoots himself at televised news conference in his state capital office.

Rights Marchers Jeered in Georgia Town (Jan. 24): National Guardsmen separate crowd of 10,000 from members and sympathizers of Ku Klux Klan in all-white town of Cumming.

FEBRUARY 1987

International

Iran Releases American Reporter (Feb. 1): Gerald F. Seib of *Wall Street Journal* detained, accused as Zionist spy. **(Feb. 6):** Seib arrives in Switzerland.

Voters Back President Aquino (Feb. 2): Peaceful plebiscite approves by nearly 80% proposed Philippine Constitution that would keep her in office until 1992. It bans political activities by the military and creates two-house Parliament.

Ex-Chilean Agent Admits Slaying (Feb. 4): Armando Fernández Larios, 37, confesses to involvement in 1937 murder in Washington of former Chilean Ambassador Orlando Letelier.

Soviet Frees 140 Accused of Subversion (Feb. 10): U.S. says number represents 20% of political prisoners.

Contra Leader Resigns in Dispute (Feb. 16): Adolfo Calero, 55, quits triumvirate in move to unify Washington-backed Nicaraguan anti-Sandinista forces.

Irish Prime Minister Defeated (Feb. 18): Garret FitzGerald loses national election to Charles J. Haughey and Fianna Fail party, which lacks majority.

Street Battles Rage in Western Beirut (Feb. 18): Fifty killed, 120 wounded in two days of fighting during factional disputes in Moslem area.

Sanctions Against Poland Lifted (Feb. 19): Reagan terms move a reward for freeing of political prisoners.

Brazil Suspending Interest Payments (Feb. 20): Announces halt in payments to foreign commercial banks to protect diminishing hard-currency reserves.

French Seize Terrorist Suspects (Feb. 22): Report arrest of four leading members of main French underground organization, Direct Action.

Six Nations Reach Accord on Dollar (Feb. 22): U.S. and five allies agree at Paris conference to cooperate closely to stabilize American currency.

Syrians Patrol Beirut (Feb. 23): Troops trade fire with militiamen in effort to stop fighting.

Boris Pasternak Reinstated (Feb. 23): Soviet writers' union posthumously completes rehabilitation of poet, author of "Doctor Zhivago" and Nobel laureate.

Soviet Frees Jewish Rights Activist (Feb. 23): Iosif Z. Begun, 54, welcomed in Moscow after release from prison. Pledges to devote himself to human rights in general, Jewish rights in particular.

Soviet Ends Test Moratorium (Feb. 26): Underground nuclear blast follows 18-month halt. Government regrets U.S. continuation of testing program.

Soviet Offers Arms Control Plan (Feb. 28): Gorbachev says nation is ready to sign "without delay" agreement to eliminate Soviet and American medium-range nuclear missiles in Europe within five years. "Star Wars" link abandoned.

Lebanese Terrorist Gets Life (Feb. 28): French court finds Georges Ibrahim Abdallah guilty in killings of an American and an Israeli diplomat in 1982.

National

Congress Overrides Clean Water Veto (Jan. 30): President Reagan rejects measure for $20-billion outlay for projects throughout nation as "loaded with waste and larded with pork." **(Feb. 3):** House, 401-26, overrides veto. **(Feb. 4):** Senate, 86-14, completes action in major rebuff to Reagan.

Sanitation for Field Hands Ordered (Feb. 6): Federal Appeals Court rules Labor Department must require farmers to provide toilets and drinking water.

Surgeon General Backs TV Condom Ads (Feb. 10): Dr. C. Everett Koop says they offer best protection against infection with deadly AIDS virus.

Reagan Rejects Revised Treaty on Captives (Feb. 15): Decides against ratification of part of Geneva Treaty changes believed to offer legal protection to terrorists.

Cuomo Bars Presidential Race (Feb. 19): New York Governor decides against 1988 bid as "best thing" for family, Democratic party, and the state.

Supreme Court Upholds Racial Quotas (Feb. 25): Vote of 5-4 rejects Administration position and affirms federal court order in Alabama for temporary use of quotas in promotions of state troopers as well as in hiring.

Review Board Criticizes Reagan (Feb. 26): Tower Commission terms President confused and remote and says he failed to understand secret arms deals with Iran, and had to take responsibility for policy that caused "chaos" at home and embarrassment abroad. Report bluntly blames Donald T. Regan, White House chief of staff, and other advisers for giving Reagan poor advice and neglecting legal and political risks.

Donald Regan Removed (Feb. 27): President replaces chief of staff with former Senator Howard H. Baker, Jr. Congress shows favorable response.

General

USX Strike Ends (Feb. 1): Steel company resuming production after six-month tie-up. Four-year contract further erodes wage levels.

U.S. Regains America's Cup (Feb. 4): *Stars & Stripes*, piloted by Dennis Conner, wins Australia yacht race.

London Printers Defeated (Feb. 5): Union ends year-long protest against Rupert Murdoch's modernization program and dismissal of more than 5,500.

Twelve Youths Indicted in Racial Attack (Feb. 6): U.S. grand jury in Queens, N.Y., includes murder charges in report on assault on blacks by group of whites in Howard Beach section that resulted in death of one hit by car. New York black community aroused.

Eastern Airlines to Pay $9.5-Million Fine (Feb. 10): Sum is largest civil penalty against an airline to be assessed by F.A.A. More than 78,000 safety and maintenance violations charged.

Three Wall Street Leaders Arrested (Feb. 12): Charged by U.S. with insider trading that produced millions of dollars in illegal profits. **(Feb. 13):** Martin A. Siegel, 38, a principal architect of takeover strategies, pleads guilty to insider trading after identifying the others accused.

Bar Opposes Tobacco Advertising Ban (Feb. 16): A.B.A. refuses to back federal law as unconstitutional.

Clue to Alzheimer's Disease Reported (Feb. 19): Boston researchers link defective gene to hereditary form of mysterious brain disorder.

Four Skiers Perish in Avalanche (Feb. 19): Crushed while sliding outside Colorado ski slope boundary.

Massive Explosion of Large Star Reported (Feb. 24): Astronomers observe supernova closer to Earth than any since 1604, a rare boon to scientists.

Chicago Mayor Wins Primary (Feb. 24): Harold Washington, city's first black executive, defeats Jane M. Byrne, his challenger on Democratic ballot.

Football Banned at Southern Methodist U. (Feb. 25): National Collegiate Athletic Association metes penalty for next season because of improper payments to team members.

Two Russian Astronauts Launched (Feb. 6): Head toward rendezvous with orbiting space station *Mir.* They are Comdr. Uri Romanenko, a veteran of three space flights, and Aleksandr Lavelkin, civilian flight engineer.

MARCH 1987

International

Syrians Restore Order to Beirut (March 4): More than 7,000 soldiers, backed by tanks, evict militiamen from Moslem sector. Residents move freely after being pinned down by fighting between rival Shiite and Druse militiamen.

Leading Contra Resigns (March 9): Arturo Cruz, Nicaraguan rebel, charges bitter infighting has crippled American-backed opposition to Sandinistas.

Five Czech Jazz Fans Sentenced (March 10): Short jail terms meted advocates of cultural freedom.

Israel Ending Arms for South Africa (March 18): Cabinet decides not to negotiate new sales contracts.

Two Terrorists Slay Italian General (March 20): Licio Giorgieri, senior Air Force officer, slain by pair on motorcycle. Union of Fighting Communists takes blame for self-styled "execution."

Macao Reverting to China (March 23): Enclave on South China coast, gambling haven, to be ceded by Portugal under agreement. Macao had existed for 430 years as a Portuguese colony.

Eighty-Five Dead in Raids on Pakistan (March 24): Afghan planes stage three forays on border villages.

Chad Recaptures Strategic Town (March 27): Drives Libyans from stronghold at Faya-Largeau.

Greeks and Turks Allay Crisis (March 28): Settle dispute over oil-drilling rights in Aegean.

Israeli Spy Recruiter Resigns (March 29): Col. Aviem Sella, who signed Jonathan Jay Pollard, American naval intelligence analyst, gives up recent promotion but will remain in Air Force.

Salvadoran Rebels Kill U.S. Adviser (March 31): Slay Staff Sgt. Gregory A. Fronius, 27, and at least 43 Salvadoran soldiers in attack on Army base.

National

Reagan Withdraws C.I.A. Nomination (March 2): Avoids Senate fight by canceling choice of Robert M. Gates because of link to Iran-contra scandal.

New Nominee to Head C.I.A. (March 3): President chooses William H. Webster, F.B.I. chief, as Director of Central Intelligence in action to move Administration beyond Iran-contra controversy.

U.S. Indicts Israeli Officer (March 31): Federal jury accuses Aviem Sella of Israel Air Force of espionage conspiracy with three other Israelis and Jonathan Jay Pollard to get American secrets.

Spy for Israel Gets Life (March 4): Jonathan Jay Pollard, 32, former civilian Navy intelligence analyst, sentenced by Federal Court. Wife, Anne Henderson Pollard, 26, gets two concurrent five-year terms for role in espionage conspiracy.

Reagan Admits "Mistake" (March 4): In TV address to nation, he accepts "full responsibility" for Iran-contra affair. Says policy toward Iran deteriorated into trade of arms for hostages. But he does not say idea of selling arms to Iran was flawed.

Court Rejects North's Challenge (March 12): Federal judge dismisses two lawsuits brought by Lieut. Col. Oliver L. North and authorizes special prosecutor to continue Iran arms investigation.

Fee for Illegal Aliens (March 15): Administration sets $185 charge for legal status under new law.

Reagan Victorious on Contra Aid (March 18): Senate, 52-48, blocks cutting off of final installment of this year's military aid to Nicaraguan rebels.

Reagan Repudiates Iran Policy (March 19): In nationally broadcast news conference, he says he would not order same actions again. Denies knowledge about diversion of arms sales profits to contras.

Federal Approval for AIDS Drug (March 20): F.D.A. sanctions azidothymidine, AZT, first substance to prolong lives of victims, although not a cure.

High Court Backs Affirmative Action (March 25): In setback to Reagan Administration, Justices rule, 6-3, employers may sometimes favor women and minorities over better-qualified white men in hiring and promoting.

Congress Overrides Reagan Highway Veto (March 27): President rejects $87.9-billion highway and mass transit measure as "budget busting." Bill would also allow 65 m.p.h. speed limit on rural interstate arteries. (**March 31**): House, 350-73, overrides veto. (**April 2**): Senate, 67-33, exactly required two-thirds, also overrides veto. President, in meeting at Capitol, fails to sway 13 Republicans who had voted for measure.

Trade Retaliation Against Japan (March 27): Reagan decides to double import price of wide range of electronic products to combat Tokyo's reported failure to honor semiconductor agreement.

General

Cult Figure Gets Life in Killing (March 2): Larry Layton, 40, former member of People's Temple, sentenced in murder of Representative Leo J. Ryan at jungle airstrip in Guyana in 1978.

Michelangelo Model Reported (March 5): Renaissance scholar says he uncovered eight-inch plaster believed used to make statue of David.

Death Toll 134 as Ferry Capsizes (March 7): British craft with 500 aboard rolls on her side after leaving Belgian port of Zeebrugge. (**March 9**): British Government blames inrush of water through open bow as probable cause.

Vatican Condemns Test-Tube Fertilization (March 10): Urges all governments to limit strictly medical interference in human procreation. Seeks outlawing of surrogate motherhood and experiments on living embryos.

Hundreds Dead in Ecuador Earthquake (March 11): Thousands missing after two temblors and floods devastate remote northeastern region. Main oil pipeline ruptured. (**March 13**): Nation suspends payments on $8.3-billion foreign debt.

British Toads Get Own Tunnel (March 13): Nation's first opened to provide safe transit under dangerous Henley roadway to mating ponds.

Libel Judgment of $2 Million Upset (March 13): U.S. Appeals Court reverses verdict against *Washington Post,* ruling article in 1979 did not libel William P. Tavoulareas, former Mobil Oil president.

Shipwrecked Russians Rescued (March 14): Coast Guard saves 37, including three women and infant, from Soviet freighter stricken in Atlantic gale.

New Superconductor Dazzles Scientists (March 17): Analysis shows ceramic material can be made into magnets far more powerful than any now existing.

Eisenhower Official Admits Tax Fraud (March 26): Robert B. Anderson, 77, once Treasury Secretary, pleads guilty in Federal Court to illegally operating Caribbean bank and evading levies on income.

Van Gogh Painting Sells for Record $39.9 Million (March 30): Crowd at Christie's in London shocked by anonymous telephone bidding duel.

Father Awarded Custody of Baby M (March 31): New Jersey judge upholds surrogate mother agreement in favor of William Stern. Denies visiting rights to biological mother, Mary Beth Whitehead. Case arouses wide controversy across nation.

APRIL 1987

International

South Africa Bars Protests for Detainees (April 11): Tightens state of emergency by outlawing any calls for freedom, including letters to government, petitions, and T-shirt slogans.

Pope Ends Trip to South America (April 13): Returns to Rome after two-week visit to Argentina, Chile, and Uruguay. At Montevideo he labels Chilean government of Augusto Pinochet "dictatorial" and says Roman Catholics must fight for democracy. In final hours in Argentina, John Paul II indicates opposition to era of dictatorial rule.

Statue Honors Raoul Wallenberg (April 14): Budapest erects monument to Swedish diplomat who saved thousands of Hungarian Jews from Nazis.

Sri Lanka Rebels Kill 127 (April 17): Guerrillas ambush three buses and two trucks in jungle and slay men, women, and children. Tamil rebels charge discrimination by ruling Sinhalese.

Argentine Army Blocks Rebellion (April 17): Two-day crisis eases as Army expresses loyalty to government and moves against officers opposed to prosecution of military on human rights charges.

Bus Bombing Injures 18 in Athens (April 24): Sixteen Americans and two Greeks wounded by terrorists on trip to United States air base.

I.R.A. Slays Judge and Wife (April 25): Car bomb kills second most senior jurist in Northern Ireland. Set off on main road from Belfast to Dublin.

Nicaraguan Contras Kill American (April 28): Government reports Benjamin Ernest Linder, 27, volunteer worker, was slain in ambush by rebels.

Accord on Ozone Protection (April 30): Conference of 31 nations agrees to freeze and ultimately reduce production and use of harmful chemicals.

National

Reagan Agrees to Acid Rain Talks (April 6): Says he will consider proposal for U.S.-Canadian negotiations for "bilateral accord" for control.

Supreme Court Rules Against Texaco (April 6): Holds District Court should not have excused $10-billion bond pending appeal of damage award won by Pennzoil in 1985. (**April 12**): Texaco files for bankruptcy pending outcome of feud. Largest company ever to enter a bankruptcy petition.

Joint Space Exploration Resumed (April 15): U.S. and Soviet sign agreement, the only one reached in three-day Moscow visit by Secretary of State Shultz.

Export of Big Rockets Limited (April 16): U.S., Japan, and five allies agree to control trade in large weapons and related technology in move to limit spread of nuclear devices.

Reagan Fights Japanese Imports (April 17): Imposes 100% tariff on computers, televisions, and power tools in retaliation for Japan's alleged violation on exports of semiconductors.

U.S. Deports Nazi Criminal (April 20): Karl Linnas, 67, native of Estonia, under death sentence in Soviet Union for actions as commandant of Nazi concentration camp in World War II.

Justices Uphold Takeover Protection (April 21): Supreme Court, 6-3, affirms state law restricting hostile offers for companies incorporated in that state.

Court Widens Death Penalty Impact (April 21): Justices rule, 5-4, some accomplices in crimes leading to a death may be executed even if they did not kill. (**April 22**): Supreme Court, 5-4, rules state's capital punishment system is constitutional even though killers of whites are sentenced more often.

Physicists Question "Star Wars" (April 22): Panel of leading scientists says decade of intensive research will be needed just to determine feasibility of anti-missile space defense system.

U.S. Bars Kurt Waldheim (April 27): Justice Department puts Austrian President on list of banned, citing evidence of participation in Nazi war crimes.

Justices Back "Political Propaganda" Label (April 28): Supreme Court, 5-3, rejects claim that use of phrase for three Canadian films is violation of free speech right by implying U.S. disapproval.

Fund-Raiser Pleads Guilty in Contra Scandal (April 29): Carl R. Channell admits conspiring to defraud U.S. by raising tax-exempt funds to arm Nicaraguan rebels. Implicates Lieut. Col. Oliver L. North.

General

Dwight Gooden Fails Cocaine Test (April 1): Star pitcher of Mets, 22, placed on disabled list to undergo two months' treatment.

Parkinson Treatment Found Effective (April 1): Team of Mexican doctors reports victims of neurological disease are improved by adrenal gland transplant.

Industrial Stocks Soar to Record (April 3): Dow Jones average up nearly 70 points on relief over interest rates and more stable outlook for dollar.

Jury Acquits Amy Carter (April 15): Jimmy Carter's daughter, Abbie Hoffman, and 13 others cleared in Massachusetts trial of charges in demonstration against campus recruiting by C.I.A.

Play About Blacks Wins Pulitzer (April 16): "Fences" by August Wilson takes prize. Fiction award goes to Peter Taylor for novel "Summons to Memphis."

Drug Raids Staged on Wall Street (April 17): Federal agents arrest 16 brokers and a senior partner on charges of selling cocaine and trading it for stocks and customer information.

Dallas Elects First Woman Mayor (April 19): Annette Strauss, a Democrat and City Councilwoman, won a decisive runoff election for mayor over businessman Fred Meyer, capturing 56% of the vote.

Conviction in Investor Murder Trial (April 22): Joe Hunt, 27, leader of Billionaire Boys Club, guilty in murder and robbery of California man whose body was never found.

Twenty-eight Dead in Building Collapse (April 23): Construction workers trapped in collapse of high-rise apartment building under construction in Bridgeport, Conn. Investigators sift debris.

Twelve Dead in Florida Shooting Spree (April 23): At least 14 wounded as armed man fires on crowds at two shopping centers in Palm Bay.

Boesky Pleads Guilty (April 23): Ivan F. Boesky, speculator at center of Wall Street insider-trading scandal, admits in Federal Court that he had made fraudulent statements.

Gene-Altered Bacteria Tested (April 24): Sprayed on California strawberry plants to prevent frost damage in historic experiment with new organism to aid agriculture.

Ten Neo-Nazis Indicted in Plot (April 24): Leaders and followers of Aryan Nation charged in Federal Court with conspiring to overthrow Government. Three indicted in Denver killing.

Dwight Gooden Back at Shea Stadium (April 30): Mets star pitcher ends four weeks of drug treatment.

Three Lutheran Denominations Merge (April 30): New church with 5.3 million members formed by groups with diverse ethnic and geographic roots.

MAY 1987

International

Jewish-Born Nun Beatified (May 1): John Paul II, on second day of visit to Germany, honors Edith Stein, Carmelite killed at Auschwitz. **(May 4):** Pope ends five-day visit to Europe by celebrating ecumenical service with other Christian leaders, stressing Third Reich lesson for church.

Quebec Accepts Canadian Constitution (May 1): After 20 years, province ends holdout, gaining status as "distinct society" within Canada.

Soviet Ship Attacked in Persian Gulf (May 8): Freighter first Soviet vessel to be victim in Iran-Iraq war. Attacked by Iranians.

Nine Slain in Ulster Battle (May 8): Security forces kill attackers who ram bulldozer into County Armagh police station. Casualties revealed to be Irish Republican Army leaders and bystander.

Polish Jet Crash Kills 183 (May 9): All aboard perish as Soviet-built Ilyushin 62M on charter flight to New York cracks up and burns when pilot fails to bring faltering craft back to Warsaw Airport. Plane carried 22 holders of U.S. passports and 16 Poles living in U.S. **(May 10):** Polish pilot praised for guiding crippled aircraft into uninhabited area.

Thirty-seven Dead in Attack on U.S. Frigate (May 17): The Stark is struck by two missiles from Iraqi warplane in Persian Gulf. **(May 18):** Iraqi President apologizes for "accident". **(May 19):** U.S. commander says frigate's electronic defenses were turned off because officers did not fear an Iraqi missile attack.

Soviet Gives Up Commercial Whaling (May 23): Last hunting fleet is heading home from Antarctic.

Voice of America Jamming Stops (May 25): Soviet ends blocking of radio broadcasting into country for the first time in seven years.

Israel's Leaders Cleared in Spy Case (May 26): Two Government investigations absolve top officials of complicity in Washington espionage operation involving Jonathan Jay Pollard.

West German Pilot Flies Over Moscow (May 29): Matthias Rust, 19, covers 400 miles of heavily defended Soviet territory in tiny plane and buzzes Red Square. **(May 30):** Politburo rebukes Soviet military and relieves Defense Minister Sergei L. Sokolov of duties. Moves seen as assertion of civilian control over the military.

National

Reagan and Nakasone End Talks (May 1): President and Japan's Prime Minister disappointed by failure to resolve problems of Japan's huge trade lead. Earlier, Nakasone had ordered Bank of Japan to lower interest rates.

High Court Rules on Obscenity (May 4): Justices, 5-4, decide judges and juries must apply "reasonable person" standard in assessing social value of sexually explicit material.

Rotary Clubs Must Admit Women (May 4): Supreme Court rules, 7-0, that states may outlaw discrimination. Barriers by private clubs still in doubt.

First Witness in Iran-Contra Hearing (May 5): Maj. Gen. Richard V. Secord testifies government officials, including William J. Casey, then Director of Central Intelligence, helped supply weapons to Nicaraguan rebels.

Thousands of Aliens Seek Legal Status (May 5): Flock to government centers under new immigration law.

Executive Pleads Guilty in Contra Affair (May 6): Richard R. Miller, public relations man, admits conspiracy charges and implicates Lieut. Col. Oliver L. North in illegal fund-raising scheme to buy arms for Nicaraguan rebels.

Gary Hart Quits Presidential Race (May 8): "Angry and defiant" at end of four-year drive. Campaign wrecked by *Miami Herald*'s reporting that he spent part of weekend with woman model.

Reagan Disclaims Aid Appeal to Saudis (May 12): Denies soliciting funds for Nicaraguan rebels in private meetings with King Fahd in 1985.

Reagan Reported Briefed on Contra Aid (May 13): Robert C. McFarlane, former National Security Adviser, tells Congressional hearing he informed President "frequently" on what McFarlane's staff was doing to help Nicaraguans.

Reagan Admits Role in Contra Aid (May 15): Says he was deeply involved in private efforts to help Nicaraguan rebels even during two years when Congress had forbidden government aid.

Air Traffic System Reformed (May 17): F.A.A. adopts new computer system to reduce delays and increase safety, using national single screen.

Pretrial Jailing Upheld (May 26): Supreme Court, 6-3, in important criminal-law decision, rules federal judges may hold criminal defendants before trial if they are deemed threat to public safety.

Reagan Urges Wide AIDS Testing (May 31): In first such stand, calls for wide state and federal programs to detect hidden spread of virus.

General

Engineer Indicted in Fatal Crash (May 4): Ricky L. Gates, 32, charged with manslaughter in deaths of 16 in Maryland collision of Conrail locomotive and Amtrak passenger train on January 4.

AIDS Fatal to Connecticut Congressman (May 7): Rep. Stewart B. McKinney, 56, succumbs to infection said to have been brought on by blood transfusion. Known for achievements as liberal.

Utah Mine Operator Fined (May 11): Federal agency imposes $111,470 penalty against Utah Power and Light Company, former operator of pit where 27 workers died in fire in 1984.

A Three-Way Heart Transplant (May 12): In complex operation in Baltimore, a medical first, healthy organ is taken from one person and transplanted into another. First donor, a cystic fibrosis patient, gets heart and lungs of accident victim.

Soviet Launches Most Powerful Rocket (May 16): Tests "Energia," world's mightiest, able to put 100-ton space shuttle into orbit.

Health Workers Infected With AIDS (May 19): Three acquire virus after skin is briefly exposed to blood of patients with disease. This is first such documented spread of malady.

Texas Tornado Kills 29 (May 22): Saragosa, a poor Hispanic farming community, devastated. Twenty injured. Whole town in mourning.

Donovan Acquitted in Fraud Trial (May 25): Bronx jury clears former Secretary of Labor Raymond J. Donovan and seven other construction executives in state trial. Donovan first sitting Cabinet officer to have been indicted.

Five Acquitted in "Twilight Zone" Trial (May 29): John Landis, movie director, and four associates cleared by Los Angeles jury in death of actor Vic Morrow and two child actors in crash of helicopter during filming.

JUNE 1987

International

Lebanon Prime Minister Assassinated (June 1): Blast in helicopter kills Rashid Karami, 65, Sunni Moslem. Officials and others on craft injured.

Reagan Lifts Part of Japanese Tariff (June 8): At Venice conference, he removes 17% of penalties on electronic goods imposed in protest against "dumping" of semiconductor computer chips.

No Breakthroughs in Venice Talks (June 10): Leaders of major non-Communist nations—Britain, Canada, France, Italy, Japan, U.S., and West Germany—end 13th summit conference with sober appraisal of world economy and generalized proposals to deal with problems of unemployment and protectionism. Political declaration endorses free navigation in Persian Gulf, but Reagan suffers setbacks.

Afghan Rebels Fell Airliner (June 11): Use U.S. missile to shoot down passenger plane, killing 53 of 55.

Margaret Thatcher Wins Rare Third Term (June 11): Conservative Prime Minister gets 100-seat majority in 650-seat House of Commons in general election, slight decline from 1983. Voting shows middle class has emerged as political anchor.

Jean-Bedel Bokassa Doomed (June 12): Former dictator of Central African Republic, 66, sentenced to death for 20 murders of real or imagined opponents during his 14-year reign.

Pope's Visit Stirs Poland (June 14): In week-long stay, John Paul II delights government opposition by extolling aspirations of Solidarity. In challenge to government's reform claims, he refuses to mention Polish or Soviet proposals for nuclear disarmament, and emphasizes human rights.

Two Hanoi Officials Replaced (June 18): National Assembly removes Prime Minister Pham Van Dong and President Truong Chinh, last founders of Vietnam Communist Party, still in power after 50 years.

U.S. Journalist Kidnapped in Lebanon (June 18): Charles Glass, 36, ABC correspondent, abducted in Shiite Moslem Beirut suburb, with two Lebanese, one the son of Defense Minister. The latter are later released.

Pope Receives Kurt Waldheim (June 25): John Paul II praises Austrian President for peace activities but does not mention controversy over World War II service as Nazi officer. Meeting provokes worldwide protests by Jewish organizations.

Soviet Economic Reforms Voted (June 26): Communist Party's Central Committee backs Gorbachev's moves to stimulate stagnant economy. Names three of his supporters as full members of Politburo. Actions give leader stronger hand to pursue his policies of liberalizing nation's policies.

National

Supreme Court Upholds Severance Pay (June 1): Ruling, 5-4, affirms Maine law requiring employers to pay benefits to some laid off in plant closings.

New Federal Reserve Chairman Named (June 2): President Reagan chooses Alan Greenspan, conservative economist, to succeed Paul A. Volcker as policy maker.

U.S. Funds Denied Gary Hart (June 4): Federal Election Commission refuses matching outlay to pay debts in abandoned campaign for Democratic Presidential nomination in 1988.

U.S. Plans Random AIDS Tests (June 5): Will take blood samples from 45,000 around country in national survey on extent of virus infection. (**June 8**): Attorney General says medical condition of inmates with AIDS might be factor in release on parole. Civil libertarians attack proposal.

Marine Freed in Embassy Spying (June 12): U.S. drops case against Cpl. Arnold Bracy, 21, as charges collapse. Bracy had denounced confession as coerced and results of lie-detector test as misused. Aid to Soviet agents had been charged.

Curb on Evolution Theory Upset (June 19): Supreme Court, 7-2, rules states may not require teaching of creationism, in blow to Fundamentalist Christians.

General Dynamics Charges Dropped (June 20): Justice Department deals blow to fraud prosecutions in action on production of Sergeant York weapon. (**June 23**): It reports documents found belatedly show billing procedures were proper.

Reagan Vetoes Fairness Doctrine (June 20): Rejects bill that makes a law of policy requiring broadcasters to present clashing views on controversies.

Justices Back Drinking Age Rise (June 23): Supreme Court, 7-2, upholds federal law aimed at prodding states to set legal age at 21 by withholding highway grants from those that refuse.

Mail Fraud Scope Narrowed (June 24): Supreme Court, 7-2, rejects broad definition of statute under which Federal prosecutors have fought corruption.

Reagan Names AIDS Commission Head (June 25): Appoints Dr. W. Eugene Mayberry of Mayo Clinic as chief of new Presidential advisory panel.

Lie By William J. Casey Indicated (June 26): Transcript reports former C.I.A. head misled Congressional investigators about secret arms sales to Iran and supply operation for contras.

Justice Lewis F. Powell, Jr., Retires (June 26): Moderate had provided key fifth votes in crucial Supreme Court rulings for abortion rights and affirmative action. He cites his age, 75, and health.

General

U.S. Sifts Fraud in Athletes' Payments (June 2): Grand jury investigates whether violation of National Collegiate Athletic Association rules could harm schools. Inquiry involves top college and professional football and basketball players.

Brokerage Firm Settles Charges (June 4): Kidder, Peabody & Co. agrees to pay record $25.3 million to settle U.S. insider trading case.

U.S. Investigates PTL Ministry (June 10): Three agencies examine charges of wire fraud, mail fraud, and misuse of funds by evangelical organization.

Black Named Baseball Assistant (June 11): Dr. Harry Edwards, sports sociologist, chosen as special aide to Commissioner Peter Ueberroth.

PTL Files in Bankrupcty (June 12): Evangelical ministry seeks protection from creditors in face of heavy debt. Relief under federal law would enable television ministry to continue.

"Subway Vigilante" Acquitted (June 16): New York jury clears Bernhard H. Goetz, 39, electrical engineer, of attempted-murder charges in shooting of four black teen-agers on Manhattan subway car in December 1984 during alleged robbery attempt. Goetz found guilty of illegal gun possession. Case stirred international debate on limits on use of force in self-defense.

Five Sentenced in Puerto Rico Murders (June 19): Former police officers get up to 30 years for 1978 slaying of two young advocates of independence.

Former Treasury Head Sentenced (June 25): Robert B. Anderson, 77, gets month in jail, five months' house arrest, and five years' probation for evading income taxes and operating illegal offshore bank.

JULY 1987

International

Sweeping Changes Approved in South Korea (July 1): President Chun Doo Hwan accepts direct Presidential elections. Action follows weeks of street protests and U.S. pressure. Thousands of students had skirmished with riot policemen in Seoul and other major cities.

Crossing Crash Kills 125 in Zaire (July 4): Many injured as trailer-truck crashes into train in worst railway crossing accident in African history.

Klaus Barbie Convicted in France (July 4): Wartime Gestapo chief of Lyons, 73, found guilty of crimes against humanity and gets life sentence.

Bus Raids Kill 72 in India (July 6): Gunmen believed to be militant Sikhs kill 38 Hindus in Punjab state. (July 8): Sikh terrorists kill at least 34 passengers in state of Haryana.

Soviet Diplomats Visit Israel (July 13): Delegation is first since Moscow broke Israeli ties after 1967 war.

Taiwan Ends 38 Years of Martial Law (July 14): National Government sees "new milestone" for democracy.

Six Americans Killed in Salvador (July 16): Die as helicopter crashes on mission to evacuate wounded American military adviser. One wounded in crash.

France Severs Ties With Iran (July 17): Acts following encirclement of Iranian Embassy in hunt for Iranian suspected of involvement in terrorist bomb attacks in France.

Floods Ravage Northern Italy (July 19): At least 14 perish; damage extensive in Alpine villages.

Portugal Gets Majority Government (July 19): Social Democrats swept back into office with first majority government since democracy returned in 1974.

Flood Toll Over 100 in South Korea (July 22): Water and landslides level villages in southern province.

Mine Damages Kuwait Tanker (July 24): Vessel escorted by U.S. naval ships damaged in Persian Gulf.

Jet Crew Seizes Hijacker (July 24): Overpowers Lebanese gunman at Geneva Airport after he kills French passenger and assaults steward. Swiss plan trial.

Coalition Government in Italy (July 28): Giovanni Goria, Christian Democrat, at 44 is youngest Prime Minister to take office in Italy's postwar republic.

India and Sri Lanka Sign Pact (July 29): Move to end four years of ethnic violence. Anti-government riots across Sri Lanka protest accord.

Three Chernobyl Officials Sentenced (July 29): Draw 10 years in labor camp for violating safety regulations in world's worst nuclear power accident.

U.S. Copter Crashes in Persian Gulf (July 30): One killed, three missing from craft serving in naval force escorting Kuwaiti tankers.

National

Bork Nominated for Supreme Court (July 1): Reagan chooses Appeals Court Judge Robert H. Bork, strongly conservative, to replace Justice Lewis F. Powell, Jr. Wide opposition develops.

North Cites Orders From Superiors (July 7-10): Marine Lieut. Col. Oliver L. North tells Congressional Iran-contra inquiry that his secret White House operations were conducted only to obey higher officials. Testifies he assumed but did not know first-hand that President Reagan knew and approved of diversions of arms sale profits to aid Nicaraguan rebels. Says late C.I.A. head, William J. Casey, helped him and that other senior officials had been fully aware of activities. Recalls that Casey sought to use arms sale profits to set up secret extra-official espionage agency. Appearance wins widespread national support. (July 14): Robert C. McFarlane, former National Security adviser, returns to stand to contradict North and testify he himself had not authorized many of secret activities. Committee dismisses North with severe rebuke for part in policy based on a "series of lies."

Poindexter Testifies in Inquiry (July 15-22): Former National Security adviser, Admiral John M. Poindexter, tells Congressional Iran-contra hearing he personally authorized use of Iran arms sale profits to aid Nicaraguan rebels. Testifies he kept information from President to spare him political embarrassment. Senators disagree on whether testimony can be believed. Witness disputes testimony by Lieut. Col. Oliver L. North that he sent admiral five memorandums discussing use of profits for rebels. Congressmen from both parties challenge Poindexter's statement that sensitive foreign initiatives need to be kept secret from Congress and other Government agencies.

Former Reagan Top Aide Indicted (July 17): U.S. jury charges Lyn Nofziger, once President's principal political adviser, with profiting illegally from influence he gained as White House official.

Shultz Charges High-Level Deceit (July 23-24): Secretary of State George P. Shultz tells Congressional Iran-contra inquiry he was deceived repeatedly by top officials who withheld vital information from him and the President to keep Iran arms sales alive. Denies he had kept himself in dark about U.S. policies in Iran and Nicaragua. Says Rear Admiral John M. Poindexter, National Security adviser, and Director of Central Intelligence William J. Casey had repeatedly misled him. Congressmen of both parties praise Shultz as emblem of candor and sanity.

Malcolm Baldrige Killed (July 25): Administration mourns death of Commerce Secretary, killed while practicing for steer-roping competition in California.

Attorney General Testifies in Inquiry (July 28-29): Edwin Meese 3rd tells Congressional Iran-contra panel top National Security Council officials misled him because he had no reason to disbelieve them. Concedes Lieut. Col. Oliver L. North must have lied to him or to committee. Defends himself against charge of sloppy inquiry into Iran arms sales.

Reagan's Ex-Chief Aide Takes Stand (July 30-31): Donald T. Regan, former White House Chief of Staff, tells Iran-contra inquiry he and President were often misled by security officials, and Reagan felt he had been "snookered." Regan says he did not control National Security Council.

Defense Secretary Takes Stand (July 31 and Aug. 3): Caspar W. Weinberger testifies he thought he had stopped Iran arms sales but failed because of official deception and intrigue. Recalls he was excluded from receiving information.

General

Eighteen Aliens Die in Boxcar (July 2): Illegal immigrants, trapped on Texas siding, found dead in 120-degree heat. A 19th escapes by punching hole in floor of locked car to breathe.

Chrysler Fined Over Health Hazards (July 6): Must pay $1.5 million for violations cited by Occupational Safety and Health Administration at plant in Newark, Del.

Texas Bridge Flooded, Six Dead (July 17): Four missing as rain-swollen river sweeps away bus and van carrying teen-agers leaving church camp.

AUGUST 1987

International

Hundreds Die in Mecca Clashes (Aug. 1): Moslems perish in fighting between Iranian Shiite pilgrims and riot police in Islam's holiest site. Iranians in Teheran sack Saudi and Kuwaiti embassies.

Merger of British Parties Voted (Aug. 6): Six-year-old Social Democratic body joins Liberal Party in combined centrist organization.

Peace Accord in Central America (Aug. 7): Presidents of five nations sign agreement that by Nov. 7 each country must end restrictions on dissent, decree political amnesty, end press censorship and agree to elections under international supervision. **(Aug. 25):** Nicaragua's President Ortega names four to reconciliation commission on compliance. Exiled priests welcomed back.

Chad Troops Rout Libyans (Aug. 13): Drive 1,000 of foe from disputed border strip, their last stronghold.

Rudolf Hess a Suicide at 93 (Aug. 17): Once deputy to Adolf Hitler. Parachuted to Scotland early in World War II in self-styled peace bid. Dies in Spandau Prison, Berlin, serving life sentence meted by Nuremberg tribunal. Note indicates he intended to kill himself with electrical cord.

Sri Lanka Leader Escapes in Attack (Aug. 18): President J.R. Jayewardene unhurt by grenade on Parliament floor during debate on ethnic groups' violence. One legislator is killed.

American Journalist Escapes in Beirut (Aug. 18): Charles Glass, longtime correspondent for ABC News, eludes kidnappers in Beirut after two months as hostage. Aid by Syria in freeing him reported.

Pope Conciliatory to Jews (Aug. 19): Letter from John Paul II recognizes suffering in Holocaust in gesture to Jews angered by audience with President Kurt Waldheim of Austria.

South Korean Labor Dispute Ends (Aug. 19): After two days of violent protests by 40,000 employees, Hyundai Group agrees to recognize union. Workers had occupied factory buildings and shipyard.

Bonn Offers to Scrap Missiles (Aug. 26): Will get rid of 72 Pershing 1A missiles if U.S. and Soviet agree to destroy all medium- and shorter-range weapons. Issue had been stumbling block.

Coup Challenges Aquino Government (Aug. 28): Hundreds of dissident Philippine soldiers besiege Presidential palace in Manila and government television station. **(Aug. 29):** Leaders at large after government suppresses uprising. Toll estimated at 40 dead, mostly civilians, hundreds wounded.

Iraq Breaks Truce in War (Aug. 29): After 45-day ceasefire, bombs Iranian offshore oil installations in Persian Gulf. Iranian supertanker set ablaze.

Black Miners End South Africa Strike (Aug. 30): More than 250,000 back in gold and coal production after three weeks. Fail to win improvements in pre-strike increases, but union shows strength. Nine killed, 300 wounded, and 400 arrested.

South Korea Parties Reach Accord (Aug. 31): Main groupings agree on basic outline for new constitution, paving way for first direct elections in 16 years.

National

Iran-Contra Public Hearings End (Aug. 3): House and Senate chairmen of 11-week Congressional investigation term testimony "chilling and depressing."

First New Air Force Rocket Produced (Aug. 3): Marks nation's recovery from two-year launcher crisis.

Congress Votes Banking Law Revision (Aug. 4): Senate, 96-2, completes action on bill Reagan favors to aid weakened savings and loan industry.

F.C.C. Ends Fairness Doctrine (Aug. 4): Unanimously terms it unconstitutional curb on free speech.

Reagan Revises Secret-Operations Policy (Aug. 7): Tells Congress he will inform it within 48 hours of start of most major activities. Move aimed to correct flaws revealed by Iran-Contra inquiry.

New Commerce Secretary Named (Aug. 10): Reagan appoints C. William Verity, Jr., retired chairman of Armco, Inc., to succeed Malcolm Baldrige.

Reagan Says Policy Went "Astray" (Aug. 12): Says he was not told details of Iran arms sales and diversion of arms to Contras, and should have been. Accepts responsibility in nationwide address.

Small Plane Near Reagan Helicopter (Aug. 13): AWOL Army private flies aircraft close to President's near ranch. **(Aug. 14):** F.A.A. revokes license of pilot, Ralph W. Myers, 34.

Reagan Envoy to Central America Quits (Aug. 14): Philip C. Habib reportedly displeased by failure to assign him to new diplomatic peace efforts.

U.S. Trade Deficit Up Sharply (Aug. 15): Possible record set by $15.71-billion gap in June imports.

Swiss Court Clears Confidential Data (Aug. 20): Highest tribunal rejects claims of leading figures in Iran-Contra affair to restrict deposit data.

Marine Guilty of Embassy Spying (Aug. 21): Sgt. Clayton Lonetree, 25, convicted by court-martial on 13 counts as first of corps to be tried for espionage. Criminal acts charged at Moscow and Vienna. **(Aug. 24):** He is sentenced to 30 years in prison.

Religious Objection to Texts Overruled (Aug. 24): U.S. Appeals Court judge reverses Tennessee judge's ruling allowing Fundamentalists to keep children from school because of alleged godless books.

Ban on "Humanistic" Texts Voided (Aug. 26): U.S. Appeals Court in Atlanta reverses judge's edict on 44 books from Alabama schools as godless.

Revamped Shuttle Rocket Passes Test (Aug. 30): Redesigned version of booster that caused *Challenger* disaster succeeds after three aborted firings.

General

Tornadoes Kill 27 in Canadian City (Aug. 1): Two-hundred injured as five twisters strike trailer park and industrial area at Edmonton, Alberta.

Heat Wave Kills Nearly 100 (Aug. 3): Millions swelter in Midwest and East. In some areas, temperatures approach or break 100 degrees for 17 days.

Elvis Presley's Memory Honored (Aug. 12): Ten years after death, Memphis holds nine-day tribute.

Colon Cancer Linked to Gene Defect (Aug. 12): British scientists find clue to common malignancy.

Detroit Air Crash Kills 153 (Aug. 16): Northwest Airlines McDonnell Douglas MD-30 plunges to heavily traveled boulevard. Girl, 4, only survivor. **(Aug. 22):** U.S. Transportation Department adds nine airports to list for tight traffic restrictions.

Jewels Retrieved From Titanic Wreckage (Aug. 20): French expedition raises bag, also holding coins and currency.

Art Scholar Seized in Documents Thefts (Aug. 18): Charles Merrill Mount, historian and portrait painter, accused twice by U.S. of stealing major treasures.

Ex-Nurse's Aide Admits 24 Killings (Aug. 18): Donald Harvey, 35, pleads guilty to charge of murdering patients, mostly elderly, at Cincinnati hospital.

Gunman Kills 14 in English Village (Aug. 19): Mother among victims. Man kills himself after siege.

Forty-seven Lost in South Africa Mine Mishap (Aug. 31): Trapped as elevator plunges to bottom of gold mine shaft. Explosion blamed for accident.

The Iran-Contra Affair

The "Iran-Contra Affair" dominated the headlines and TV news from late 1986 through most of 1987. Nationwide audiences heard and read of revelations of arms sales to Iran that turned into deals to free hostages. They learned of the diversion of profits from those sales to aid the Nicaraguan rebels, the Contras. As investigative findings spewed forth, key officials were nudged out of office, others impugned. A pattern of deceit by Administration officials and the destruction of important documents emerged.

Throughout, President Reagan remained personally untainted. He did take responsibility for what had happened "on my watch." Thus he admitted fostering the over-all policy of the Iran arms sales and the deals to free hostages held in the Middle East. But he disclaimed knowledge of questionable details in the execution of that policy and of the diversion of funds.

The scandal broke early in November 1986 with a report in an obscure Lebanese magazine of American arms sales to Iran. On Nov. 25, Attorney General Edwin L. Meese revealed the fund diversion. Soon Israel and other countries were involved in the drama and mighty and humble actors joined the cast.

A Senate report in January 1987 disclosed that the affair went back as far as 1982, when Israel, later a go-between, shipped non-American arms to Iran, and that Israelis made private deals involving American arms. In the following years there were numerous meetings between American officials with Iranians and intermediaries. On Jan. 17, 1986, President Reagan signed an order authorizing arms shipments to Iran to improve relations and secure the release of hostages. On Oct. 29, 1986, in apparently the final deal, the C.I.A. arranged for the shipment of 500 antitank TOW missiles to Iran. On Nov. 4, the Speaker of the Iranian Parliament, Hojatolislam Hashemi, revealed that Robert C. McFarlane, National Security Adviser, and four other Americans had visited Iran on a secret mission.

One outstanding investigation was that of the Tower Commission, set up by the White House after the scandal broke. The panel, headed by former Senator John G. Tower of Texas, found failures in Reagan's "Hands Off" administrative style, but did not suggest structural changes. The panel did find faults in the original policy and flaws in its execution. In the words of one member, former Secretary of State Edmund S. Muskie, "The Iran initiative was handled almost casually and through informal channels." The third member, Brent Scowcroft, said, "The problem at heart was one of people, not of process."

Three months of later hearings by a joint Senate-House investigating committee uncovered grave abuses in the American system of Government, but no evidence to contradict the President's assertion that he did not know of the covert diversion of arms sales profits to the Contras. Direct U.S. aid had been prohibited during the life of the Boland amendment, part of appropriations measures passed by Congress and signed by Reagan. Meanwhile, a special prosecutor conducted a criminal inquiry.

One Congressional witness, Marine Lieut. Col. Oliver L. North, with be-medalled uniform and boyish manner, became a public folk hero, testifying that his superiors had been aware of his undercover operations. Rear Admiral John M. Poindexter, former National Security Adviser, testified that he had approved the fund diversion without informing the President. Also testifying were Secretary of State George P. Shultz and Defense Secretary Caspar W. Weinberger, who had counseled against the arms deals with Iran.

During the summer of 1987, the Congressional committee heard secret testimony by lesser officials as it worked on its report on foreign policy defects.

Arms Control

Arms control, for years the critical issue in East-West relations, appeared closer to reality as 1987 neared its end. A summit meeting of President Reagan and the Soviet leader, Mikhail Gorbachev, was decided upon as the last act of a long-drawn-out drama, with the announcement in September that the two world leaders were expected to sign an agreement for a world-wide ban on medium- and short-range nuclear missiles.

The basic accord was hammered out in negotiations in Washington between U.S. Secretary of State George P. Shultz and Soviet Foreign Minister Eduard A. Shevardnadze.

Under the Shultz-Shevardnadze accord, all land-based missiles with ranges between 300 and 3,400 miles would be scrapped. The U.S. weapons involved include the ground-based cruiser missiles, with a range of 1,550 miles, deployed in Western Europe, and the Pershing 2, with a 1,120-mile range, stationed in West Germany. In late August, Chancellor Helmut Kohl said Bonn would eliminate their 72 Pershing 1A's if the U.S. and the U.S.S.R. reached an arms agreement. Shultz and Shevardnadze agreed to a compromise by which no mention of the German missiles would be made in the final draft.

On Jan 15 1986, Gorbachev proposed a new treaty to eliminate U.S. and Soviet intermediate-range missiles in Europe, with the first step the reduction in British and French arsenals, which were not mentioned in reports on the September accord. At the Reykjavik Summit conference in October 1986, the two leaders agreed to limit their missiles in Europe, to clamp a lid of 100 medium-range missiles each outside of Europe, and made progress on breaking a deadlock over nuclear testing. But the conference foundered on the issue of abandoning the space-based antimissile system known as "Star Wars," as the Russians demanded.

In July 1987 Gorbachev made his historic offer for the worldwide missile ban. And Bonn's action on the Pershing 1A's immediately brightened the world's hopes.

On limiting long-range strategic weapons, negotiations continued in Geneva with "Star Wars" a key obstacle to agreement. The issue clouded the talks as U.S. and Soviet negotiators strove for a 50 percent reduction. The Soviets offered such a treaty in late July, but the U.S., while finding it "helpful," said the demand for concessions on space-based defense was "unacceptable."

Late Events

Twenty Ships Hit in Persian Gulf (Sept. 3): Toll rises in six days since Iran and Iraq resumed "tanker war." Two seamen killed in attacks.

Soviet Sentences German Pilot (Sept. 4): Mathias Rust, 19, gets four years in labor camp for flying single-engine plane across border to Red Square.

John Paul II Visits North America (Sept. 10): Welcomed at Miami by Reagans and large crowds. **(Sept. 11):** In dialogue with Jewish leaders, Pope defends Pope Pius XII on Nazi-era conduct. **(Sept. 20):** Celebrates mass for Indians in Canada's Far North, then flies home. During tour Pontiff enunciates orthodox church teachings on dissent, birth control, and other divisive issues in U.S.

Transportation Secretary Resigns (Sept. 14): Elizabeth Hanford Dole to work on Presidential campaign of her husband, Republican Senator Robert Dole.

Constitution Celebrates 200th Year (Sept. 17): Ceremonies in Philadelphia mark climax of year-long commemoration of signing of document in 1787.

Summit Meeting on Arms Control (Sept. 18): U.S. and U.S.S.R. announce plans for Reagan and Gorbachev to sign agreement for worldwide ban on medium- and short-range nuclear missiles. Both sides stress differences on "Star Wars" missile defense.

Miss America Receives Crown (Sept. 19): Kaye Lani Rae Rafko, a registered nurse at St. Vincent's Medical Center, Toledo, Ohio, becomes the 1988 title-holder. She is from Monroe, Mich.

Football Players Strike (Sept. 23): National Football League members walk out after talks stall on new contract over issue of "free agency" for four-year players, pensions, and salaries. **(Oct. 15):** Strike ends but without a new contract.

Biden Quits Presidential Race (Sept. 23): Joseph R. Biden, Delaware Democratic Senator, drops out after criticism mounts over plagiarism of speeches.

Columbia Avalanche Kills at Least 120 (Sept. 28): Mud and rock thunder down mountainside onto slum near Medellin. Up to 500 reported missing.

Severe Earthquake Strikes Los Angeles Area (Oct. 1): The quake, measuring 6.1 on the Richter scale (about VIII on the Modified Mercali scale) shook the Los Angeles area at 7:42 a.m., leaving more than 100 injured and six dead. The earthquake was centered between Whittier and Pasadena, 30 miles from the San Andreas Fault. Damage was most serious at Whittier.

Stocks Suffer Record Loss (Oct. 14): Dow Jones Industrial Average plunges 95.46 points to 2,412.70, the largest one-day point loss in history. **(Oct. 16):** Dow drops 108.36 points. The first time it has lost more than 100 points in a single session. **(Oct. 19):** Stocks plunge 508 points giving Wall Street its worse day in history. **(Oct. 20):** Dow climbs 102 points, a record one-day point rise.

Senate Votes Down Bork (Oct. 23): By a vote of 58 to 42, the Senate rejected Robert H. Bork as a Supreme Court Justice.

1987 Nobel Prize Winners

Peace: President Oscar Arias Sánchez (Costa Rican), for his "outstanding contribution to the possible return of stability and peace to a region long torn by strife and civil war."

Medicine: Dr. Susumu Tonegawa (Japanese), a scientist working at the Massachusetts Institute of Technology, for his discoveries of how the body can suddenly marshal its immunological defenses against millions of different disease agents that it has never encountered before.

Physics: Dr. K. Alex Müller (Swiss) an I.B.M. fellow at its Zurich Research Laboratory, and Dr. J. Georg Bednorz (German), also on the staff of the I.B.M. laboratory, for their discovery of high-temperature superconductors.

Chemistry: Dr. Donald J. Cram (American), a professor of chemistry at the University of California in Los Angeles, Dr. Charles J. Pedersen (American); a research chemist for E.I. du Pont de Nemours & Company until his retirement in 1969; and Dr. Jean-Marie Lehn (French), professor of chemistry at the Louis Pasteur University in Strasbourg and the College de France in Paris, for wide-ranging research that has included the creation of artifical molecules that can mimic vital chemical reactions of the processes of life.

Economics: Dr. Robert M. Solow (American), a professor at the Massachusetts Institute of Technology, for seminal contributions to the theory of economic growth.

Literature: Joseph Brodisky (Russian-born, U.S. citizen), a poet and essayist, "for an all-embracing authorship, imbued with clarity of thought and poetic intensity."

Major Emmy Awards for TV, 1987

Drama series: *L.A. Law* (NBC)
- **Actress:** Sharon Gless, *Cagney and Lacey* (CBS)
- **Actor:** Bruce Willis, *Moonlighting* (ABC)
- **Supporting actress:** Bonnie Bartlett, *St. Elsewhere* (NBC)
- **Supporting actor:** John Hillerman, *Magnum, P.I.* (CBS)

Comedy series: *The Golden Girls* (NBC)
- **Actress:** Rue McClanahan, *The Golden Girls* (NBC)
- **Actor:** Michael J. Fox, *Family Ties* (NBC)
- **Supporting actress:** Jackee, *227* (NBC)
- **Supporting actor:** John Larroquette, *Night Court* (NBC)

Variety, music or comedy program: *The 1987 Tony Awards* (CBS)

Limited series or special: *A Year in the Life* (NBC)
- **Actress:** Gena Rowlands, *The Betty Ford Story* (ABC)
- **Actor:** James Woods, *Hallmark Hall of Fame: Promise* (CBS)
- **Supporting actress:** Piper Laurie, *Hallmark Hall of Fame: Promise* (CBS)
- **Supporting actor:** Dabney Coleman, *Sworn To Silence* (ABC)

Drama special: *Hallmark Hall of Fame: Promise* (CBS)

Individual performance in a variety or music program: Robin Williams, *A Carol Burnett Special: Carol, Carl, Whoopie & Robin* (ABC)

Guest performer in a dramatic series: Alfre Woodard, *L.A. Law: Pilot* (NBC)

Guest performer in a comedy series: John Cleese, *Cheers: Simon Says* (NBC)

Animated program: *Cathy* (CBS)

Governor's Award: Grant Tinker

Network totals: NBC 16, CBS 11, ABC 4

Deaths in 1986–1987

(As of September 1, 1987)

Adams, Sherman, 87: chief assistant to President Eisenhower. Resigned under fire after disclosures that he had accepted gifts from a longtime friend who sought governmental favors. Oct. 27, 1986.

Abel, Walter, 88: stage and screen actor in varied roles for more than 50 years. Appeared in earliest plays of Eugene O'Neill. March 26, 1987.

Arnaz, Desi, 69: actor, musician, producer, important in early television. Created situation comedy "I Love Lucy" with wife, Lucille Ball. Dec. 2, 1986.

Astaire, Fred, 88: as national legend, career spanned six performing decades on stage, screen, and television. Astaire became nation's most popular dancer and set standards for motion picture musical comedies. June 22, 1987.

Baird, Bil (sic), 82: puppeteer who enchanted millions across world. Trained generation of other gifted ones, including Jim Henson, Muppet's creator. March 18, 1987.

Baldrige, Malcolm, 64: Reagan's Secretary of Commerce, expert on trade, and key advocate of free trade. Competed in professional rodeos and was killed practicing for steer-roping contest, July 25, 1987.

Bennett, Michael, 44: influential theater director and choreographer, creator of "Chorus Line," Broadway's longest-running show. AIDS victim. July 2, 1987.

Bishop, Jim, 79: former syndicated columnist and author of 21 books, including "The Day Kennedy Was Shot." July 26, 1987.

Bolger, Ray, 83: Broadway and Hollywood song-and-dance man. Was best known as the Scarecrow in "The Wizard of Oz." Jan. 15, 1987.

Brown, Harrison, 69: nuclear chemist, a pioneer in producing plutonium for first atomic bombs. Later tried to prevent use of nuclear weapons. Dec. 8, 1986.

Burns, Arthur F., 83: former chairman of Federal Reserve Board, chairman of Council of Economic Advisers, and Ambassador to West Germany. June 26, 1987.

Caldwell, Erskine, 83: prolific Southern novelist who won fame and notoriety with stories of decadence and poverty in Deep South. April 11, 1987.

Casey, William J., 74: former Director of Central Intelligence, chairman of Securities and Exchange Commission, and Under Secretary of State. May 6, 1987.

Cohen, Wilbur J., 73: Secretary of Health, Education, and Welfare in Johnson Administration, creator of Medicare and other social legislation. May 18, 1987.

Crawford, Cheryl, 84: theatrical producer and cofounder of Group Theater and Actors Studio. Oct. 7, 1986.

Dahlberg, Rev. Dr. Edwin T., 93: confirmed pacifist and former president of National Council of Churches. Advocated admission of China to U.N. Sept. 6, 1986.

Ellman, Richard, 69: Oxford professor whose 1959 biography of James Joyce became definitive work on Irish novelist. May 13, 1987.

Gingold, Hermione, 89: English actress, Broadway and film star. Appeared in "Gigi" and "The Music Man." May 24, 1987.

Gleason, Jackie, 71: comedian, actor, and musician, a leading entertainment star of 1950s and 1960s. TV comedy series, "The Honeymooners," seen by millions as classic in reruns. June 24, 1987.

Grant, Cary, 82: handsome and sophisticated star of Hollywood movies. Films included "Topper," "The Philadelphia Story," "Arsenic and Old Lace," "To Catch a Thief," and "Charade." Nov. 30, 1986.

Greenberg, Hank, 75: Detroit Tigers baseball star with 22-year career in sport as player and executive. Won place in Hall of Fame as batter. Sept. 4, 1986.

Hammond, John, 76: expert on jazz music, critic, talent scout, and record producer who discovered many famous popular stars. July 10, 1987.

Harrison, Lieut. Gen. William K., 91: veteran Army commander, headed United Nations armistice delegation in Korean war. May 25, 1987.

Hayworth, Rita, 68: Hollywood beauty who achieved legendary fame in 1940s and 1950s. Favorite dancing partner of Fred Astaire and pinup girl for servicemen in wartime. Victim of Alzheimer's disease. May 14, 1987.

Heidt, Horace, 85: band leader known for radio talent shows that started careers of such stars as Art Carney and Gordon MacRae. Dec. 1, 1986.

Heller, Walter W., 71: chief economic adviser of Presidents Kennedy and Johnson. Developed theory of revenue sharing of federal taxes. June 15, 1987.

Hemingway, Mary, 78: widow of Ernest Hemingway and foreign correspondent for *Time* and *Life* magazines during World War II. Nov. 26, 1986.

Hess, Rudolf, 93: onetime deputy to Adolf Hitler, sentenced to life at Nuremberg trial. Early in World War II parachuted to Scotland in apparent peace bid. Aug. 17, 1987.

Hill, Abram, 76: leader in development of black theater. Sponsored careers of famous black actors. Oct. 6, 1986.

Huie, William B., 76: author of books about civil rights era in South and "The Execution of Private Slovik." Nov. 22, 1986.

Huston, John, 81: film director, writer and actor known for prize-winning movies, among them "The Maltese Falcon," and "The African Queen." Aug. 28, 1987.

Kabalevsky, Dmitri, 82: prolific Soviet composer, known for suite "The Comedians." (Announced Feb. 17, 1987).

Kaye, Danny, 74: nimble comedian, known for rapid-fire patter, who sang, danced, joked, pantomimed, and mimicked in long career on Broadway and in Hollywood. March 3, 1987.

Kaye, Nora, 67: a leading American ballerina known internationally as a dramatic dancer. Feb. 28, 1987.

Kaye, Sammy, 77: bandleader for 50 years with one of most popular "sweet bands" of swing era. June 2, 1987.

Keyserling, Leon H., 79: Chairman of Council of Economic Advisers under President Truman. Advocate of full employment who drafted major New Deal legislation. Aug. 9, 1987.

Kraus, Lili, 83: Hungarian-born pianist praised by critics for sensitivity in Mozart's music. Nov. 6, 1986.

Lanchester, Elsa, 84: stage and screen actress known for eccentric and comic roles, such as "The Bride of Frankenstein." Widow of actor Charles Laughton. Dec. 26, 1986.

Landsdale, Maj. Gen. Edward G. (ret.), 79: Air Force officer whose theories on counterinsurgency were successful in Philippines after World War II but failed in Vietnam. Feb. 23, 1987.

Lartigue, Jacques-Henri, 92: celebrated French photographer known for "freshness, play, and absurdities of human condition" in his work. Sept. 12, 1986.

Lash, Joseph P., 77: newspaperman and historian, author of biographies of Eleanor Roosevelt and other noted figures. Aug. 22, 1987

Levine, Joseph E., 81: one of most successful film producers and distributors. Bought, imported, and distributed about 500 movies. July 31, 1987.

Liberace, (Wladziu Valentino), 67: flamboyant pianist known for extravagant showmanship, costumes, and giant candelabra. AIDS-related disease blamed for death. Feb. 4, 1987.

Lifar, Serge, 81: internationally known dancer and choreographer, considered creator of modern French ballet. Dec. 15, 1986.

Ludlam, Charles, 44: innovative and prolific artist in theatrical avant-garde is victim of AIDS. May 28, 1987.

MacDonald, John D., 70: novelist whose mysteries sold millions of copies. Dec. 28, 1986.

MacLean, Alistair, 64: one of biggest-selling adventure writers. Author of "The Guns of Navarone." Feb. 2, 1987.

Macmillan, Harold, 92: British Prime Minister from January 1957 to October 1963. As Conservative leader, helped Britain adapt to changing world role. Dec. 29, 1986.

Marvin, Lee, 63: film actor known for "tough guy" roles, winning Academy Award for work in "Cat Ballou." Aug. 29, 1987.

Minsky, Morton, 85: last of four brothers who made burlesque shows a New York institution. March 23, 1987.

Molotov, Vyacheslav M., 96: close Stalin associate who shared power through cruel economic policies and purges. A member of the Soviet leadership from 1921–1957. Nov. 8, 1986.

Moore, Gerald, 87: English pianist famed as accompanist for most of musical artists of his time. March 13, 1987.

Mulliken, Dr. Robert S., 90: Nobel laureate and University of Chicago scientist who led chemistry into atomic age. Created molecular orbital theory. Oct. 31, 1986.

Myrdal, Gunnar, 88: Swedish economist and socialist. Author of "An American Dilemma," which weakened the "separate but equal" racial doctrine. Architect of Swedish welfare state. May 17, 1987.

Nathan, Dr. Otto, 93: economist who was executor and co-trustee of Albert Einstein's estate and developed Einstein archive. Jan. 27, 1987.

Negri, Pola, 88: regarded as most colorful and mysterious of silent screen vamps of 1920s and 1930s. Aug. 1, 1987.

Nixon, Edward Daniel, 87: former N.A.A.C.P. Alabama president, civil rights leader who selected Dr. Martin Luther King, Jr., to lead Montgomery bus boycott. Feb. 25, 1987.

Peller, Mrs. Clara, 86: spoke famous hamburger challenge "Where's the Beef?" in television commercial for fast-food chain. Aug. 11, 1987.

Perlmutter, Nathan, 64: national director of Anti-Defamation League of B'nai B'rith. Known as a chief spokesman for American Jews on many issues. July 12, 1987.

Persichetti, Vincent, 72: prolific American composer with varied works. Also known as educator, theorist, pianist and conductor. Aug. 14, 1987.

Picasso, Jacqueline, 60: second wife of Pablo Picasso, inspiration of later painting, and benefactor of New York's Museum of Modern Art. Oct. 15, 1986.

Poppele, Jacob R., 88: pioneer in development of radio and television. Started WOR, one of first radio stations. Oct. 7, 1986.

Preston, Robert, 68: versatile film actor best known as confidence man in "The Music Man." March 21, 1987.

Rich, Buddy (Bernard), 89: noted jazz drummer who performed in theaters and with big bands. April 2, 1987.

Rubinoff, David, 89: violinist and conductor prominent during Depression. Was regular on Eddie Cantor radio program. Oct. 6, 1986.

Rustin, Bayard, 75: pacifist and black civil rights activist. A chief organizer of 1963 march on Washington. Aug. 24, 1987.

Scott, Randolph, 89: Hollywood leading man who won fame as quiet, fast-drawing hero of Western movies. March 2, 1987.

Segovia, Andrés, 94: guitarist who became one of century's outstanding concert artists. Restored prestige of the classical guitar. June 2, 1987.

Stromgren, Prof. Bengt Georg Daniel, 79: internationally known astronomer, former director of Chicago's Yerkes Observatory. July 4, 1987.

Susskind, David, 66: television producer and one of earliest and best-known talk-show hosts. Feb. 22, 1987.

Sweet, Blanche, 90: early motion picture star who won fame in D.W. Griffith films. Sept. 6, 1986.

Szent-Gyorgi, Dr. Albert, 93: Hungarian-born biologist who won Nobel Prize for isolation of vitamin C. Oct. 22, 1986.

Taylor, Gen. Maxwell D., 85: major factor in U.S. military and diplomatic strategy from World War II through Vietnam war. Pioneer commander of airborne troops. April 19, 1987.

Tudor, Antony, 79: a leading choreographer of century, master of psychological ballet. April 20, 1987.

Unruh, Jesse M., 64: Democratic politician with national influence from base in California Government. Gained prominence as Speaker of California Assembly from 1961 to 1968. Aug. 4, 1987.

von Trapp, Maria Augusta, 82: leader of Austrian singing family portrayed in play and film "The Sound of Music." March 28, 1987.

Wallis, Hal B., 88: producer, co-producer, or supervisor of more than 400 films in half-century career. They included "The Maltese Falcon" and "Casablanca." Oct. 5, 1986.

Warhol, Andy, 58: world-famed artist, founder of Pop Art, known for painting and prints of presidents, movie stars, soup cans, and other artifacts. Feb. 22, 1987.

Wesley, Charles Harris, 95: one of nation's most eminent black scholars. Author of numerous works on black history. Aug. 16, 1987.

Wynn, Keenan, 70: versatile supporting actor in more than 200 films and 250 TV shows. Oct. 15, 1986.

Wyzanski, Judge Charles E., Jr., 80: legal thinker who served on federal bench in Massachusetts for 45 years. Once headed Harvard University's Board of Overseers. Sept. 3, 1986.

Zorinsky, Edward, 58: Nebraska Senator who switched from Republican to Democrat. Key figure on Senate Agriculture, Nutrition, and Forestry Committee and Foreign Relations Committee. March 6, 1987.